C000112356

THE HOLY BIBLE

New International Version

THE

HOLY BIBLE

New International Version

Popular Cross Reference Edition

Hodder & Stoughton

LONDON SYDNEY AUCKLAND

First published in Great Britain 1979
This edition 1992
First impression 1992

The NIV text may be quoted in any form (written, visual, electronic or audio), up to and inclusive of one thousand (1,000) verses without express written permission of the publisher, providing the verses quoted do not amount to a complete book of the Bible nor do the verses quoted account for 50 per cent or more of the total text of the work in which they are quoted.

Notice of copyright must appear on the title or copyright page of the work as follows:

Scripture quotations taken from the HOLY BIBLE,
NEW INTERNATIONAL VERSION.
Copyright © 1973, 1978, 1984 by International Bible Society.
Used by permission.

When quotations from the NIV are used in non-saleable media, such as church bulletins, orders of service, posters, transparencies, or similar media, a complete copyright notice is not required but the initials (NIV) must appear at the end of each quotation.

Permission requests which exceed the above guidelines must be directed to, and approved in writing by Hodder & Stoughton Publishers, 47 Bedford Square, London WC1B 3DP.

INTERNATIONAL BIBLE SOCIETY
PO Box 62970, Colorado Springs, CO 80962-2970

British Library Cataloguing in Publication Data is available for this title.

You will be pleased to know that a portion of
the purchase price of your new NIV Bible has
been allocated to the International Bible
Society to help spread the Gospel of Jesus
Christ around the world.

This publication is not included under licences issued by the Copyright Licensing Agency. Typeset by Auto-Graphics Inc., Pomona, CA 91768 USA. Printed in Great Britain for Hodder & Stoughton Ltd, Mill Road, Dunton Green, Sevenoaks, Kent, by Richard Clay Ltd, St Ives plc.

CONTENTS

The Books of the Old Testament

The Books of the New Testament

TRANSLATORS' PREFACE

to the New International Version

The New International Version is a completely new translation of the Holy Bible made by over a hundred scholars working directly from the best available Hebrew, Aramaic and Greek texts. It had its beginning in 1965 when, after several years of exploratory study by committees from the Christian Reformed Church and the National Association of Evangelicals, a group of scholars met at Palos Heights, Illinois, and concurred in the need for a new translation of the Bible in contemporary English. This group, though not made up of official church representatives, was transdenominational. Its conclusion was endorsed by a large number of leaders from many denominations who met in Chicago in 1966.

Responsibility for the new version was delegated by the Palos Heights group to a self-governing body of fifteen, the Committee on Bible Translation, composed for the most part of biblical scholars from colleges, universities and seminaries. In 1967 the New York Bible Society (now the International Bible Society) generously undertook the financial sponsorship of the project—a sponsorship that made it possible to enlist the help of many distinguished scholars. The fact that participants from the United States, Great Britain, Canada, Australia and New Zealand worked together gave the project its international scope. That they were from many denominations—including Anglican, Assemblies of God, Baptist, Brethren, Christian Reformed, Church of Christ, Evangelical Free, Lutheran, Mennonite, Methodist, Nazarene, Presbyterian, Wesleyan and other churches—helped to safeguard the translation from sectarian bias.

How it was made helps to give the New International Version its distinctiveness. The translation of each book was assigned to a team of scholars. Next, one of the Intermediate Editorial Committees revised the initial translation, with constant reference to the Hebrew, Aramaic or Greek. Their work then went to one of the General Editorial Committees, which checked it in detail and made another thorough revision. This revision in turn was carefully reviewed by the Committee on Bible Translation, which made further changes and then released the final version for publication. In this way the entire Bible underwent three revisions, during each of which the translation was examined for its faithfulness to the original languages and for its English style.

All this involved many thousands of hours of research and discussion regarding the meaning of the texts and the precise way of putting them into English. It may well be that no other translation has been made by a more thorough process of review and revision from committee to committee than this one.

From the beginning of the project, the Committee on Bible Translation held to certain goals for the New International Version: that it would be an accurate translation and one that would have clarity and literary quality and so prove suitable for public and private reading, teaching, preaching, memorising and liturgical use. The Committee also sought to preserve some measure of continuity with the long tradition of translating the Scriptures into English.

In working towards these goals, the translators were united in their commitment to the authority and infallibility of the Bible as God's Word in written form. They believe that it contains the divine answer to the deepest needs of humanity, that it sheds unique light on our path in a dark world, and that it sets forth the way to our eternal well-being.

The first concern of the translators has been the accuracy of the translation and its fidelity to the thought of the biblical writers. They have weighed the significance of the lexical and grammatical details of the Hebrew, Aramaic and Greek texts. At the same time, they have striven for more than a word-for-word translation. Because thought patterns and syntax differ from language to language, faithful communication of the meaning of the writers of the Bible demands frequent modifications in sentence structure and constant regard for the contextual meanings of words.

A sensitive feeling for style does not always accompany scholarship. Accordingly the Committee on Bible Translation submitted the developing version to a number of stylistic consultants. Two of them read every book of both Old and New Testaments twice—once before and once after the last major revision—and made invaluable suggestions. Samples of the translation were tested for clarity and ease of reading by various kinds of people—young and old, highly educated and less well educated, ministers and laymen.

Concern for clear and natural English—that the New International Version should be idiomatic but not idiosyncratic, contemporary but not dated—motivated the translators and consultants. At the same time, they tried to reflect the differing styles of the biblical writers. In view of the international use of English, the translators sought to avoid obvious Americanisms on the one hand and obvious Anglicisms on the other. A British edition reflects the comparatively few differences of significant idiom and of spelling.

As for the traditional pronouns "thou", "thee" and "thine" in reference to the Deity, the translators judged that to use these archaisms (along with old verb forms such as "doest," "wouldest" and "hadst") would violate accuracy in translation. Neither Hebrew, Aramaic nor Greek uses special pronouns for the persons of the Godhead. A present-day translation is not enhanced by forms that in the time of the King James Version were used in everyday speech, whether referring to God or man.

For the Old Testament the standard Hebrew text, the Masoretic Text as published in the latest editions of *Biblia Hebraica*, was used throughout. The Dead Sea Scrolls contain material bearing on an earlier stage of the Hebrew text. They were consulted, as were the Samaritan Pentateuch and the ancient scribal traditions relating to textual changes. Sometimes a variant Hebrew reading in the margin of the Masoretic Text was followed instead of the text itself. Such instances, being variants within the Masoretic tradition, are not specified by footnotes. In rare cases, words in the consonantal text were divided differently from the way they appear in the Masoretic Text. Footnotes indicate this. The translators also consulted the more important early versions—the Septuagint; Aquila, Symmachus and Theodotion; the Vulgate; the Syriac Peshitta; the Targums; and for the Psalms the *Juxta Hebraica* of Jerome. Readings from these versions were occasionally followed where the Masoretic Text seemed doubtful and where accepted principles of textual criticism showed that one or more of these textual witnesses appeared to provide the correct reading. Such instances are footnoted. Sometimes vowel letters and vowel signs did not, in the judgment of the translators, represent the correct vowels for the original consonantal text. Accordingly some words were read with a different set of vowels. These instances are usually not indicated by footnotes.

The Greek text used in translating the New Testament was an eclectic one. No other piece of ancient literature has such an abundance of manuscript witnesses as does the New Testament. Where existing manuscripts differ, the translators made their choice of readings according to accepted principles of New Testament textual criticism. Footnotes call attention to places where there was uncertainty about what the original text was. The best current printed texts of the Greek New Testament were used.

There is a sense in which the work of translation is never wholly finished. This applies to all great literature and uniquely so to the Bible. In 1973 the New Testament in the New International Version was published. Since then, suggestions for corrections and revisions have been received from various sources. The Committee on Bible Translation carefully considered the suggestions and adopted a number of them. These were incorporated in the first printing of the entire Bible in 1978. Additional revisions were made by the Committee on Bible Translation in 1983 and appear in printings after that date.

As in other ancient documents, the precise meaning of the biblical texts is sometimes uncertain. This is more often the case with the Hebrew and Aramaic texts than with the Greek text. Although archaeological and linguistic discoveries in this century aid in understanding difficult passages, some uncertainties remain. The more significant of these have been called to the reader's attention in the footnotes.

In regard to the divine name *YHWH*, commonly referred to as the *Tetragrammaton*, the translators adopted the device used in most English versions of rendering that name as "LORD" in capital letters to distinguish it from *Adonai*, another Hebrew word rendered "Lord", for which small letters are used. Wherever the two names stand together in the Old Testament as a compound name of God, they are rendered "Sovereign LORD".

Because for most readers today the phrases "the LORD of hosts" and "God of hosts" have little meaning, this version renders them "the LORD Almighty" and "God Almighty". These renderings convey the sense of the Hebrew, namely, "he who is sovereign over all the 'hosts' (powers) in heaven and on earth, especially over the 'hosts' (armies) of Israel." For readers unacquainted with Hebrew this does not make clear the distinction between *Sabaoth* ("hosts" or "Almighty") and *Shaddai* (which can also be translated "Almighty"), but the latter occurs infrequently and is always footnoted. When *Adonai* and *YHWH Sabaoth* occur together, they are rendered "the Lord, the LORD Almighty".

As for other proper nouns, the familiar spellings of the Authorised Version are generally retained. Names traditionally spelled with "ch", except where it is final, are usually spelled in this translation with "k" or "c", since the biblical languages do not have the sound that "ch" frequently indicates in English—for example, in *chant*. For well-known names such as Zechariah, however, the traditional spelling has been retained. Variation in the spelling of names in the original languages has usually not been indicated. Where a person or place has two or more different names in the Hebrew, Aramaic or Greek texts, the more familiar one has generally been used, with footnotes where needed.

To achieve clarity the translators sometimes supplied words not in the original texts but required by the context. If there was uncertainty about such material, it is enclosed in brackets. Also for the sake of clarity or style, nouns, including some proper nouns, are sometimes substituted for pronouns, and vice versa. And though the Hebrew writers often shifted back and forth between first, second and third personal pronouns without change of antecedent, this translation often makes them uniform, in accordance with English style and without the use of footnotes.

Poetical passages are printed as poetry, that is, with indentation of lines and with separate stanzas. These are generally designed to reflect the structure of Hebrew poetry. This poetry is normally characterised by parallelism in balanced lines. Most of the poetry in the Bible is in the Old Testament, and scholars differ regarding the scansion of Hebrew lines. The translators determined the stanza divisions for the most part by analysis of the subject matter. The stanzas therefore serve as poetic paragraphs.

As an aid to the reader, italicised sectional headings are inserted in most of the books. They are not to be regarded as part of the NIV text, are not for oral reading, and are not intended to dictate the interpretation of the sections they head.

The footnotes in this version are of several kinds, most of which need no explanation. Those giving alternative translations begin with "Or" and generally introduce the alternative with the last word preceding it in the text, except when it is a single-word alternative; in poetry quoted in a footnote a slant mark indicates a line division. Footnotes introduced by "Or" do not have uniform significance. In some cases two possible translations were considered to have about equal validity. In other cases, though the translators were convinced that the translation in the text was correct, they judged that another interpretation was possible and of sufficient importance to be represented in a footnote.

In the New Testament, footnotes that refer to uncertainty regarding the original text are introduced by "Some manuscripts" or similar expressions. In the Old Testament, evidence for the reading chosen is given first and evidence for the alternative is added after a semicolon (for example: Septuagint; Hebrew *father*). In such notes the term "Hebrew" refers to the Masoretic Text.

It should be noted that minerals, flora and fauna, architectural details, articles of clothing and jewellery, musical instruments and other articles cannot always be identified with precision. Also measures of capacity in the biblical period are particularly uncertain (see the table of weights and measures following the text).

Like all translations of the Bible, made as they are by imperfect man, this one undoubtedly falls short of its goals. Yet we are grateful to God for the extent to which he has enabled us to realise these goals and for the strength he has given us and our colleagues to complete our task. We offer this version of the Bible to him in whose name and for whose glory it has been made. We pray that it will lead many into a better understanding of the Holy Scriptures and a fuller knowledge of Jesus Christ the incarnate Word, of whom the Scriptures so faithfully testify.

The Committee on Bible Translation
June 1978 (Revised August 1983)

Names of the translators and editors may be secured from the International Bible Society, P O Box 62970, Colorado Springs, CO 80962-2970 USA

INTRODUCTION

to the Cross-Reference System

The New International Version has one of the most thorough, accurate and well-organised cross-reference systems available. It began with the vision of one individual more than a decade ago and by the time it was completed involved more than forty people and half a dozen computers.

The cross references link words or phrases in the NIV text with biblical references listed in the centre column. The raised letters indicating these cross references are set in an italic typeface to distinguish them from the NIV footnote letters, which use a bold typeface. When a single word has both a cross reference and a footnote, the NIV footnote comes first, as in Matthew 1:21, "Jesus,[c][q]".

The lists of references are in biblical order with one exception: if reference is made to a verse within the same chapter, that verse (indicated by "ver") is listed first.

In the Old Testament some references are marked with an asterisk (*), meaning that the Old Testament verse or phrase is quoted in the New Testament (see Genesis 1:3). The corresponding information is provided in the New Testament by the NIV footnote (see 2 Corinthians 4:6).

An important feature of this cross-reference system is in its notation of parallel and reference passages. When two or more sections of Scripture are nearly identical or deal with the same event, the "parallel passage" ("pp") is listed at the sectional heading (see Matthew 21:33–46). These parallel passages are especially common in the Gospels and in Samuel, Kings and Chronicles. When the passages are similar but do not deal with the same event, they are listed with "Ref" at the sectional headings (see Matthew 22:2–14).

To conserve space and avoid repetition, parallel passages or references that are noted at sectional headings are not repeated in the centre column.

ABBREVIATIONS

for the Books of the Bible

The Old Testament

Genesis	*Ge*	Ecclesiastes	*Ecc*
Exodus	*Ex*	Song of Songs	*SS*
Leviticus	*Lev*	Isaiah	*Isa*
Numbers	*Nu*	Jeremiah	*Jer*
Deuteronomy	*Dt*	Lamentations	*Lam*
Joshua	*Jos*	Ezekiel	*Eze*
Judges	*Jdg*	Daniel	*Da*
Ruth	*Ru*	Hosea	*Hos*
1 Samuel	*1Sa*	Joel	*Joel*
2 Samuel	*2Sa*	Amos	*Am*
1 Kings	*1Ki*	Obadiah	*Ob*
2 Kings	*2Ki*	Jonah	*Jnh*
1 Chronicles	*1Ch*	Micah	*Mic*
2 Chronicles	*2Ch*	Nahum	*Na*
Ezra	*Ezr*	Habakkuk	*Hab*
Nehemiah	*Ne*	Zephaniah	*Zep*
Esther	*Est*	Haggai	*Hag*
Job	*Job*	Zechariah	*Zec*
Psalms	*Ps*	Malachi	*Mal*
Proverbs	*Pr*		

The New Testament

Matthew	*Mt*	1 Timothy	*1Ti*
Mark	*Mk*	2 Timothy	*2Ti*
Luke	*Lk*	Titus	*Tit*
John	*Jn*	Philemon	*Phm*
Acts	*Ac*	Hebrews	*Heb*
Romans	*Ro*	James	*Jas*
1 Corinthians	*1Co*	1 Peter	*1Pe*
2 Corinthians	*2Co*	2 Peter	*2Pe*
Galatians	*Gal*	1 John	*1Jn*
Ephesians	*Eph*	2 John	*2Jn*
Philippians	*Php*	3 John	*3Jn*
Colossians	*Col*	Jude	*Jude*
1 Thessalonians	*1Th*	Revelation	*Rev*
2 Thessalonians	*2Th*		

THE OLD TESTAMENT

GENESIS

The Beginning

1 In the beginning[a] God created the heavens and the
earth.[b] 2 Now the earth was[a]
formless and empty,[c] darkness was over the surface of
the deep, and the Spirit of
God[d] was hovering over the
waters.

3 And God said,[e] "Let there be
light," and there was light.[f]
4 God saw that the light was
good, and he separated the
light from the darkness. 5 God
called the light "day", and the
darkness he called "night".[g]
And there was evening, and
there was morning—the first
day.
6 And God said, "Let there be an expanse[h] between the waters to
separate water from water."
7 So God made the expanse and
separated the water under the
expanse from the water above
it.[i] And it was so. 8 God called
the expanse "sky". And there
was evening, and there was
morning—the second day.
9 And God said, "Let the water under the sky be gathered to one
place,[j] and let dry ground appear." And it was so. 10 God
called the dry ground "land",
and the gathered waters he
called "seas". And God saw
that it was good.
11 Then God said, "Let the
land produce vegetation:[k]
seed-bearing plants and trees
on the land that bear fruit with
seed in it, according to their
various kinds." And it was so.
12 The land produced vegetation: plants bearing seed according to their kinds and
trees bearing fruit with seed
in it according to their kinds.
And God saw that it was good.
13 And there was evening, and
there was morning—the third
day.
14 And God said, "Let there be
lights[l] in the expanse of the
sky to separate the day from
the night, and let them serve
as signs[m] to mark seasons[n]
and days and years, 15 and let
them be lights in the expanse
of the sky to give light on the
earth." And it was so. 16 God
made two great lights—the
greater light to govern[o] the
day and the lesser light to govern[p] the night. He also made
the stars.[q] 17 God set them in
the expanse of the sky to give
light on the earth, 18 to govern
the day and the night,[r] and to
separate light from darkness.
And God saw that it was good.
19 And there was evening,
and there was morning—the
fourth day.
20 And God said, "Let the water
teem with living creatures,
and let birds fly above the
earth across the expanse of
the sky." 21 So God created the
great creatures of the sea and
every living and moving thing
with which the water teems,[s]
according to their kinds, and
every winged bird according
to its kind. And God saw that it
was good. 22 God blessed them
and said, "Be fruitful and increase in number and fill the
water in the seas, and let the
birds increase on the earth."[t]
23 And there was evening, and
there was morning—the fifth
day.

1:1 *a* Jn 1:1-2 *b* Job 38:4; Ps 90:2; Isa 42:5; Isa 44:24; Isa 45:12,18; Ac 17:24; Heb 11:3; Rev 4:11
1:2 *c* Jer 4:23 *d* Ps 104:30
1:3 *e* Ps 33:6,9; Ps 148:5; Heb 11:3 *f* 2Co 4:6*
1:5 *g* Ps 74:16
1:6 *h* Jer 10:12
1:7 *i* Job 38:8-11, 16; Ps 148:4
1:9 *j* Job 38:8-11; Ps 104:6-9; Pr 8:29; Jer 5:22; 2Pe 3:5
1:11 *k* Ps 65:9-13; Ps 104:14
1:14 *l* Ps 74:16 *m* Jer 10:2 *n* Ps 104:19
1:16 *o* Ps 136:8 *p* Ps 136:9 *q* Job 38:7, 31-32; Ps 8:3; Isa 40:26
1:18 *r* Jer 33:20,25
1:21 *s* Ps 104:25-26
1:22 *t* ver 28; Ge 8:17

a2 Or possibly *became*

24And God said, "Let the land produce living creatures according to their kinds: livestock,
creatures that move along the
ground, and wild animals,
each according to its kind."
And it was so. 25God made the
wild animals[u] according to
their kinds, the livestock according to their kinds, and all
the creatures that move along
the ground according to their
kinds. And God saw that it was
good.
26Then God said, "Let us[v]
make man in our image,[w] in
our likeness, and let them
rule[x] over the fish of the sea
and the birds of the air, over
the livestock, over all the
earth,[b] and over all the creatures that move along the
ground."

27So God created man
in his own image,[y]
in the image of God
he created him;
male and female[z]
he created them.

28God blessed them and said
to them, "Be fruitful and increase in number; fill the
earth[a] and subdue it. Rule
over the fish of the sea and the
birds of the air and over every
living creature that moves on
the ground."
29Then God said, "I give you
every seed-bearing plant on
the face of the whole earth and
every tree that has fruit with
seed in it. They will be yours
for food.[b] 30And to all the
beasts of the earth and all
the birds of the air and all the
creatures that move on the
ground—everything that has
the breath of life in it—I give
every green plant for food.[c]"
And it was so.
31God saw all that he had
made,[d] and it was very good.[e]
And there was evening, and
there was morning—the sixth
day.

2 Thus the heavens and the
earth were completed in all
their vast array.

2By the seventh day God had finished the work he had been doing; so on the seventh day he
rested[a] from all his work.[a]
3And God blessed the seventh
day and made it holy,[b] because on it he rested from all
the work of creating that he
had done.

Adam and Eve

4This is the account of the heavens and the earth when they were
created.

When the LORD God made the
earth and the heavens—5and no
shrub of the field had yet appeared
on the earth[b] and no plant of the
field had yet sprung up,[c] for the
LORD God had not sent rain on
the earth[b][d] and there was no man to
work the ground, 6but streams[c]
came up from the earth and
watered the whole surface of the
ground—7the LORD God formed
the man[d] from the dust[e] of the
ground[f] and breathed into his nostrils the breath[g] of life,[h] and the
man became a living being.[i]
8Now the LORD God had planted a
garden in the east, in Eden;[j] and
there he put the man he had
formed. 9And the LORD God made
all kinds of trees grow out of the
ground—trees that were pleasing
to the eye and good for food. In the
middle of the garden were the tree
of life[k] and the tree of the knowledge of good and evil.[l]
10A river watering the garden
flowed from Eden; from there it

1:25 u Jer 27:5
1:26 v Ps 100:3; w Ge 9:6, Jas 3:9; x Ps 8:6-8
1:27 y 1Co 11:7; z Ge 5:2, Mt 19:4*, Mk 10:6*
1:28 a Ge 9:1,7, Lev 26:9
1:29 b Ps 104:14
1:30 c Ps 104:14,27, Ps 145:15
1:31 d Ps 104:24; e 1Ti 4:4
2:2 a Ex 20:11, Ex 31:17, Heb 4:4*
2:3 b Lev 23:3, Isa 58:13
2:5 c Ge 1:11; d Ps 65:9-10
2:7 e Ge 3:19; f Ps 103:14; g Job 33:4; h Ac 17:25; i 1Co 15:45*
2:8 j Ge 3:23,24, Isa 51:3
2:9 k Ge 3:22,24, Rev 2:7, Rev 22:2,14,19; l Eze 47:12

b26 Hebrew; Syriac *all the wild animals*
a2 Or *ceased*; also in verse 3 b5 Or *land*; also in verse 6 c6 Or *mist* d7 The Hebrew for *man (adam)* sounds like and may be related to the Hebrew for *ground (adamah)*; it is also the name *Adam* (see Gen. 2:20).

was separated into four head-
waters. 11The name of the first is
the Pishon; it winds through the entire land of Havilah, where there is
gold. 12(The gold of that land is
good; aromatic resin[e] and onyx
are also there.) 13The name of the
second river is the Gihon; it winds
through the entire land of Cush.[f]
14The name of the third river is the
Tigris;[m] it runs along the east side
of Asshur. And the fourth river is
the Euphrates.
15The LORD God took the man and
put him in the Garden of Eden to
work it and take care of it. 16And
the LORD God commanded the man,
"You are free to eat from any tree
in the garden; 17but you must not
eat from the tree of the knowledge
of good and evil, for when you eat
of it you will surely die."[n]
18The LORD God said, "It is not
good for the man to be alone. I will
make a helper suitable for him."[o]
19Now the LORD God had formed
out of the ground all the beasts of
the field[p] and all the birds of the
air. He brought them to the man to
see what he would name them; and
whatever the man called each living creature,[q] that was its name.
20So the man gave names to all the
livestock, the birds of the air and
all the beasts of the field.
But for Adam[g] no suitable
helper was found. 21So the LORD
God caused the man to fall into a
deep sleep; and while he was sleeping, he took one of the man's ribs[h]
and closed up the place with flesh.
22Then the LORD God made a
woman from the rib[i][r] he had
taken out of the man, and he
brought her to the man.
23The man said,

"This is now bone of my bones
and flesh of my flesh;[s]
she shall be called 'woman',[j]
for she was taken out of man."

24For this reason a man will leave
his father and mother and be
united[t] to his wife, and they will
become one flesh.[u]
25The man and his wife were both
naked,[v] and they felt no shame.

The Fall of Man

3 Now the serpent[a] was more
crafty than any of the wild animals the LORD God had made. He
said to the woman, "Did God really
say, 'You must not eat from any
tree in the garden'?"
2The woman said to the serpent,
"We may eat fruit from the trees in
the garden, 3but God did say, 'You
must not eat fruit from the tree
that is in the middle of the garden,
and you must not touch it, or you
will die.' "
4"You will not surely die," the
serpent said to the woman.[b] 5"For
God knows that when you eat of it
your eyes will be opened, and you
will be like God,[c] knowing good
and evil."
6When the woman saw that the
fruit of the tree was good for food
and pleasing to the eye, and also desirable[d] for gaining wisdom, she
took some and ate it. She also gave
some to her husband, who was with
her, and he ate it.[e] 7Then the eyes
of both of them were opened, and
they realised that they were naked;
so they sewed fig leaves together
and made coverings for themselves.
8Then the man and his wife heard
the sound of the LORD God as he
was walking[f] in the garden in the
cool of the day, and they hid[g] from
the LORD God among the trees of
the garden. 9But the LORD God
called to the man, "Where are
you?"
10He answered, "I heard you in
the garden, and I was afraid because I was naked; so I hid."

2:14 m Da 10:4
2:17 n Dt 30:15,19; Ro 5:12; Ro 6:23; Jas 1:15
2:18 o 1Co 11:9
2:19 p Ps 8:7; q Ge 1:24
2:22 r 1Co 11:8,9,12
2:23 s Ge 29:14; Eph 5:28-30
2:24 t Mal 2:15; u Mt 19:5*; Mk 10:7-8*; 1Co 6:16*; Eph 5:31*
2:25 v Ge 3:7,10-11
3:1 a 2Co 11:3; Rev 12:9; Rev 20:2
3:4 b Jn 8:44; 2Co 11:3
3:5 c Isa 14:14; Eze 28:2
3:6 d Jas 1:14-15; 1Jn 2:16; e 1Ti 2:14
3:8 f Dt 23:14; g Job 31:33; Ps 139:7-12; Jer 23:24

e 12 Or *good; pearls* f 13 Possibly south-east Mesopotamia g 20 Or *the man* h 21 Or *took part of the man's side* i 22 Or *part* j 23 The Hebrew for *woman* sounds like the Hebrew for *man.*

11And he said, "Who told you that you were naked? Have you eaten from the tree from which I commanded you not to eat?"

12The man said, "The woman you put here with me—she gave me some fruit from the tree, and I ate it."

13Then the LORD God said to the woman, "What is this you have done?"

The woman said, "The serpent deceived me,[h] and I ate."

14So the LORD God said to the serpent, "Because you have done this,

"Cursed[i] are you above all the
 livestock
 and all the wild animals!
You will crawl on your belly
 and you will eat dust[j]
 all the days of your life.
15And I will put enmity
 between you and the woman,
 and between your offspring[a][k]
 and hers;[l]
he will crush[b] your head,[m]
 and you will strike his heel."

16To the woman he said,

"I will greatly increase your
 pains in childbearing;
with pain you will give birth
 to children.
Your desire will be for your
 husband,
 and he will rule over you.[n]"

17To Adam he said, "Because you listened to your wife and ate from the tree about which I commanded you, 'You must not eat of it,'

"Cursed[o] is the ground because
 of you;
through painful toil you will
 eat of it
all the days of your life.[p]
18It will produce thorns and
 thistles for you,
and you will eat the plants of
 the field.[q]
19By the sweat of your brow
 you will eat your food[r]
until you return to the ground,
 since from it you were taken;
for dust you are
 and to dust you will return."[s]

20Adam[c] named his wife Eve,[d] because she would become the mother of all the living.

21The LORD God made garments of skin for Adam and his wife and clothed them. 22And the LORD God said, "The man has now become like one of us, knowing good and evil. He must not be allowed to reach out his hand and take also from the tree of life[t] and eat, and live for ever." 23So the LORD God banished him from the Garden of Eden[u] to work the ground[v] from which he had been taken. 24After he drove the man out, he placed on the east side[e] of the Garden of Eden cherubim[w] and a flaming sword[x] flashing back and forth to guard the way to the tree of life.[y]

Cain and Abel

4 Adam[a] lay with his wife Eve, and she became pregnant and gave birth to Cain.[b] She said, "With the help of the LORD I have brought forth[c] a man." 2Later she gave birth to his brother Abel.[a]

Now Abel kept flocks, and Cain worked the soil. 3In the course of time Cain brought some of the fruits of the soil as an offering to the LORD.[b] 4But Abel brought fat portions[c] from some of the firstborn of his flock.[d] The LORD looked with favour on Abel and his offering,[e] 5but on Cain and his offering he did not look with favour. So Cain was very angry, and his face was downcast.

6Then the LORD said to Cain, "Why are you angry? Why is your face downcast? 7If you do what is right, will you not be accepted? But if you do not do what is right, sin is

[a]15 Or *seed* [b]15 Or *strike* [c]20 Or *The man* [d]20 *Eve* probably means *living.* [e]24 Or *placed in front* [a]1 Or *The man* [b]1 *Cain* sounds like the Hebrew for *brought forth* or *acquired.* [c]1 Or *have acquired*

3:13 *h* 2Co 11:3; 1Ti 2:14
3:14 *i* Dt 28:15-20 *j* Isa 65:25; Mic 7:17
3:15 *k* Jn 8:44; Ac 13:10; 1Jn 3:8 *l* Isa 7:14; Mt 1:23; Rev 12:17 *m* Ro 16:20; Heb 2:14
3:16 *n* 1Co 11:3; Eph 5:22
3:17 *o* Ge 5:29; Ro 8:20-22 *p* Job 5:7; Job 14:1; Ecc 2:23
3:18 *q* Ps 104:14
3:19 *r* 2Th 3:10 *s* Ge 2:7; Ps 90:3; Ps 104:29; Ecc 12:7
3:22 *t* Rev 22:14
3:23 *u* Ge 2:8 *v* Ge 4:2
3:24 *w* Ex 25:18-22 *x* Ps 104:4 *y* Ge 2:9
4:2 *a* Lk 11:51
4:3 *b* Nu 18:12
4:4 *c* Lev 3:16 *d* Ex 13:2,12 *e* Heb 11:4

crouching at your door;[f] it desires
to have you, but you must master
it.[g]"
8Now Cain said to his brother
Abel, "Let's go out to the field."[d]
And while they were in the field,
Cain attacked his brother Abel and
killed him.[h]
9Then the LORD said to Cain,
"Where is your brother Abel?"
"I don't know," he replied. "Am I
my brother's keeper?"
10The LORD said, "What have you
done? Listen! Your brother's blood
cries out to me from the ground.[i]
11Now you are under a curse and
driven from the ground, which
opened its mouth to receive your
brother's blood from your hand.
12When you work the ground, it will
no longer yield its crops for you.
You will be a restless wanderer on
the earth."
13Cain said to the LORD, "My punishment is more than I can bear.
14Today you are driving me from
the land, and I will be hidden from
your presence;[j] I will be a restless
wanderer on the earth, and whoever finds me will kill me."[k]
15But the LORD said to him, "Not
so;[e] if anyone kills Cain[l], he will
suffer vengeance seven times
over.[m]" Then the LORD put a mark
on Cain so that no-one who found
him would kill him. 16So Cain went
out from the LORD's presence and
lived in the land of Nod,[f] east of
Eden.[n]
17Cain lay with his wife, and she
became pregnant and gave birth to
Enoch. Cain was then building a
city, and he named it after his son[o]
Enoch. 18To Enoch was born Irad,
and Irad was the father of Mehujael, and Mehujael was the father
of Methushael, and Methushael
was the father of Lamech.
19Lamech married two women,
one named Adah and the other Zillah. 20Adah gave birth to Jabal; he
was the father of those who live in
tents and raise livestock. 21His
brother's name was Jubal; he was
the father of all who play the harp
and flute. 22Zillah also had a son,
Tubal-Cain, who forged all kinds of
tools out of[g] bronze and iron.
Tubal-Cain's sister was Naamah.
23Lamech said to his wives,

"Adah and Zillah, listen to me;
wives of Lamech, hear my words.
I have killed[h][p] a man for wounding me,
a young man for injuring me.
24If Cain is avenged[q] seven times,[r]
then Lamech seventy-seven times."

25Adam lay with his wife again,
and she gave birth to a son and
named him Seth,[i][s] saying, "God
has granted me another child in
place of Abel, since Cain killed
him."[t] 26Seth also had a son, and he
named him Enosh.
At that time men began to call
on[j] the name of the LORD.[u]

From Adam to Noah

5 This is the written account of
Adam's line.
When God created man, he made
him in the likeness of God.[a] 2He
created them male and female[b]
and blessed them. And when they
were created, he called them
"man".[a]
3When Adam had lived 130 years,
he had a son in his own likeness, in
his own image;[c] and he named him
Seth. 4After Seth was born, Adam
lived 800 years and had other sons
and daughters. 5Altogether, Adam
lived 930 years, and then he died.[d]
6When Seth had lived 105 years,
he became the father[b] of Enosh.

4:7 *f* Nu 32:23 *g* Ro 6:16
4:8 *h* Mt 23:35; 1Jn 3:12
4:10 *i* Ge 9:5; Nu 35:33; Heb 12:24; Rev 6:9-10
4:14 *j* 2Ki 17:18; Ps 51:11; Ps 139:7-12; Jer 7:15; Jer 52:3 *k* Ge 9:6; Nu 35:19,21, 27,33
4:15 *l* Eze 9:4,6 *m* ver 24; Ps 79:12
4:16 *n* Ge 2:8
4:17 *o* Ps 49:11
4:23 *p* Ex 20:13; Lev 19:18
4:24 *q* Dt 32:35 *r* ver 15
4:25 *s* Ge 5:3 *t* ver 8
4:26 *u* Ge 12:8; 1Ki 18:24; Ps 116:17; Joel 2:32; Zep 3:9; Ac 2:21; 1Co 1:2
5:1 *a* Ge 1:27; Eph 4:24; Col 3:10
5:2 *b* Ge 1:27; Mt 19:4; Mk 10:6; Gal 3:28
5:3 *c* Ge 1:26; 1Co 15:49
5:5 *d* Ge 3:19

d8 Samaritan Pentateuch, Septuagint, Vulgate and Syriac; Masoretic Text does not have *"Let's go out to the field."* **e**15 Septuagint, Vulgate and Syriac; Hebrew *Very well* **f**16 *Nod* means *wandering* (see verses 12 and 14). **g**22 Or *who instructed all who work in* **h**23 Or *I will kill* **i**25 *Seth* probably means *granted.* **j**26 Or *to proclaim* **a**2 Hebrew *adam* **b**6 *Father* may mean *ancestor*; also in verses 7–26.

7 And after he became the father of Enosh, Seth lived 807 years and had other sons and daughters. 8 Altogether, Seth lived 912 years, and then he died.

9 When Enosh had lived 90 years, he became the father of Kenan. 10 And after he became the father of Kenan, Enosh lived 815 years and had other sons and daughters. 11 Altogether, Enosh lived 905 years, and then he died.

12 When Kenan had lived 70 years, he became the father of Mahalalel. 13 And after he became the father of Mahalalel, Kenan lived 840 years and had other sons and daughters. 14 Altogether, Kenan lived 910 years, and then he died.

15 When Mahalalel had lived 65 years, he became the father of Jared. 16 And after he became the father of Jared, Mahalalel lived 830 years and had other sons and daughters. 17 Altogether, Mahalalel lived 895 years, and then he died.

18 When Jared had lived 162 years, he became the father of Enoch.[e] 19 And after he became the father of Enoch, Jared lived 800 years and had other sons and daughters. 20 Altogether, Jared lived 962 years, and then he died.

21 When Enoch had lived 65 years, he became the father of Methuselah. 22 And after he became the father of Methuselah, Enoch walked with God[f] 300 years and had other sons and daughters. 23 Altogether, Enoch lived 365 years. 24 Enoch walked with God;[g] then he was no more, because God took him away.[h]

25 When Methuselah had lived 187 years, he became the father of Lamech. 26 And after he became the father of Lamech, Methuselah lived 782 years and had other sons and daughters. 27 Altogether, Methuselah lived 969 years, and then he died.

28 When Lamech had lived 182 years, he had a son. 29 He named him Noah[c] and said, "He will comfort us in the labour and painful toil of our hands caused by the ground the LORD has cursed.[i]" 30 After Noah was born, Lamech lived 595 years and had other sons and daughters. 31 Altogether, Lamech lived 777 years, and then he died.

32 After Noah was 500 years old, he became the father of Shem, Ham and Japheth.

The Flood

6 When men began to increase in number on the earth[a] and daughters were born to them, 2 the sons of God saw that the daughters of men were beautiful, and they married any of them they chose. 3 Then the LORD said, "My Spirit will not contend with[a] man for ever,[b] for he is mortal;[b][c] his days will be a hundred and twenty years."

4 The Nephilim[d] were on the earth in those days—and also afterwards—when the sons of God went to the daughters of men and had children by them. They were the heroes of old, men of renown.

5 The LORD saw how great man's wickedness on the earth had become, and that every inclination of the thoughts of his heart was only evil all the time.[e] 6 The LORD was grieved[f] that he had made man on the earth, and his heart was filled with pain. 7 So the LORD said, "I will wipe mankind, whom I have created, from the face of the earth—men and animals, and creatures that move along the ground, and birds of the air—for I am grieved that I have made them." 8 But Noah found favour in the eyes of the LORD.[g]

9 This is the account of Noah.

Noah was a righteous man, blameless among the people of his

5:18
e Jude 1:14

5:22
f ver 24
Ge 6:9
Ge 17:1
Ge 48:15
Mic 6:8
Mal 2:6

5:24
g ver 22
h 2Ki 2:1,11
Heb 11:5

5:29
i Ge 3:17
Ro 8:20

6:1
a Ge 1:28

6:3
b Isa 57:16
c Ps 78:39

6:4
d Nu 13:33

6:5
e Ge 8:21
Ps 14:1-3

6:6
f 1Sa 15:11,35
Isa 63:10

6:8
g Ge 19:19
Ex 33:12,13,17
Lk 1:30
Ac 7:46

c29 *Noah* sounds like the Hebrew for *comfort.*
a3 Or *My spirit will not remain in*
b3 Or *corrupt*

time,[h] and he walked with God.[i]
10 Noah had three sons: Shem, Ham
and Japheth.[j]
11 Now the earth was corrupt in
God's sight and was full of violence.[k] 12 God saw how corrupt the
earth had become, for all the people on earth had corrupted their
ways.[l] 13 So God said to Noah, "I
am going to put an end to all people,
for the earth is filled with violence
because of them. I am surely going
to destroy both them and the
earth.[m] 14 So make yourself an ark
of cypress[c] wood;[n] make rooms in
it and coat it with pitch[o] inside and
out. 15 This is how you are to build it:
The ark is to be 450 feet long, 75
feet wide and 45 feet high.[d] 16 Make
a roof for it and finish[e] the ark to
within 18 inches[f] of the top. Put a
door in the side of the ark and make
lower, middle and upper decks. 17 I
am going to bring floodwaters on
the earth to destroy all life under
the heavens, every creature that
has the breath of life in it. Everything on earth will perish.[p] 18 But I
will establish my covenant with
you,[q] and you will enter the
ark[r]—you and your sons and your
wife and your sons' wives with you.
19 You are to bring into the ark two
of all living creatures, male and female, to keep them alive with you.
20 Two[s] of every kind of bird, of
every kind of animal and of every
kind of creature that moves along
the ground will come to you to be
kept alive. 21 You are to take every
kind of food that is to be eaten and
store it away as food for you and
for them."
22 Noah did everything just as
God commanded him.[t]

7 The LORD then said to Noah,
"Go into the ark, you and your
whole family,[a] because I have
found you righteous[b] in this generation. 2 Take with you seven[a] of
every kind of clean[c] animal, a
male and its mate, and two of every
kind of unclean animal, a male and
its mate, 3 and also seven of every
kind of bird, male and female, to
keep their various kinds alive
throughout the earth. 4 Seven days
from now I will send rain on the
earth for forty days and forty
nights, and I will wipe from the
face of the earth every living creature I have made."
5 And Noah did all that the LORD
commanded him.[d]
6 Noah was six hundred years old
when the floodwaters came on the
earth. 7 And Noah and his sons and
his wife and his sons' wives entered
the ark to escape the waters of the
flood. 8 Pairs of clean and unclean
animals, of birds and of all creatures that move along the ground,
9 male and female, came to Noah
and entered the ark, as God had
commanded Noah. 10 And after the
seven days the floodwaters came
on the earth.
11 In the six hundredth year of
Noah's life, on the seventeenth day
of the second month—on that day
all the springs of the great deep[e]
burst forth, and the floodgates of
the heavens[f] were opened. 12 And
rain fell on the earth for forty days
and forty nights.[g]
13 On that very day Noah and his
sons, Shem, Ham and Japheth, together with his wife and the wives
of his three sons, entered the ark.
14 They had with them every wild
animal according to its kind, all
livestock according to their kinds,
every creature that moves along
the ground according to its kind
and every bird according to its
kind, everything with wings.
15 Pairs of all creatures that have
the breath of life in them came to
Noah and entered the ark.[h] 16 The
animals going in were male and female of every living thing, as God

6:9 h Ge 7:1; Eze 14:14,20; Heb 11:7; 2Pe 2:5; i Ge 5:22
6:10 j Ge 5:32
6:11 k Eze 7:23; Eze 8:17
6:12 l Ps 14:1-3
6:13 m ver 17; Eze 7:2-3
6:14 n Heb 11:7; 1Pe 3:20; o Ex 2:3
6:17 p Ge 7:4,21-23; 2Pe 2:5
6:18 q Ge 9:9-16; r Ge 7:1,7,13
6:20 s Ge 7:15
6:22 t Ge 7:5,9,16
7:1 a Mt 24:38; Heb 11:7; 1Pe 3:20; 2Pe 2:5; b Ge 6:9; Eze 14:14
7:2 c ver 8; Ge 8:20; Lev 10:10; Lev 11:1-47
7:5 d Ge 6:22
7:11 e Eze 26:19; f Ge 8:2
7:12 g ver 4
7:15 h Ge 6:19

c14 The meaning of the Hebrew for this word is uncertain.
d15 Hebrew *300 cubits long, 50 cubits wide and 30 cubits high* (about 140 metres long, 23 metres wide and 13.5 metres high)
e16 Or *Make an opening for light by finishing*
f16 Hebrew *a cubit* (about 0.5 metre)
a2 Or *seven pairs*; also in verse 3

had commanded Noah. Then the LORD shut him in.

17For forty days[i] the flood kept coming on the earth, and as the waters increased they lifted the ark high above the earth. 18The waters rose and increased greatly on the earth, and the ark floated on the surface of the water. 19They rose greatly on the earth, and all the high mountains under the entire heavens were covered.[j] 20The waters rose and covered the mountains to a depth of more than twenty feet.[b,c] 21Every living thing that moved on the earth perished—birds, livestock, wild animals, all the creatures that swarm over the earth, and all mankind.[k] 22Everything on dry land that had the breath of life[l] in its nostrils died. 23Every living thing on the face of the earth was wiped out; men and animals and the creatures that move along the ground and the birds of the air were wiped from the earth.[m] Only Noah was left, and those with him in the ark.[n]

24The waters flooded the earth for a hundred and fifty days.[o]

8

But God remembered[a] Noah and all the wild animals and the livestock that were with him in the ark, and he sent a wind over the earth,[b] and the waters receded. 2Now the springs of the deep and the floodgates of the heavens[c] had been closed, and the rain had stopped falling from the sky. 3The water receded steadily from the earth. At the end of the hundred and fifty days the water had gone down, 4and on the seventeenth day of the seventh month the ark came to rest on the mountains of Ararat. 5The waters continued to recede until the tenth month, and on the first day of the tenth month the tops of the mountains became visible.

6After forty days Noah opened the window he had made in the ark 7and sent out a raven, and it kept flying back and forth until the water had dried up from the earth. 8Then he sent out a dove to see if the water had receded from the surface of the ground. 9But the dove could find no place to set its feet because there was water over all the surface of the earth; so it returned to Noah in the ark. He reached out his hand and took the dove and brought it back to himself in the ark. 10He waited seven more days and again sent out the dove from the ark. 11When the dove returned to him in the evening, there in its beak was a freshly plucked olive leaf! Then Noah knew that the water had receded from the earth. 12He waited seven more days and sent the dove out again, but this time it did not return to him.

13By the first day of the first month of Noah's six hundred and first year, the water had dried up from the earth. Noah then removed the covering from the ark and saw that the surface of the ground was dry. 14By the twenty-seventh day of the second month the earth was completely dry.

15Then God said to Noah, 16"Come out of the ark, you and your wife and your sons and their wives.[d] 17Bring out every kind of living creature that is with you—the birds, the animals, and all the creatures that move along the ground—so they can multiply on the earth and be fruitful and increase in number upon it."[e]

18So Noah came out, together with his sons and his wife and his sons' wives. 19All the animals and all the creatures that move along the ground and all the birds—everything that moves on the earth—came out of the ark, one kind after another.

20Then Noah built an altar to the LORD[f] and, taking some of all the clean animals and clean[g] birds, he

7:17 i ver 4
7:19 j Ps 104:6
7:21 k Ge 6:7,13
7:22 l Ge 1:30
7:23 m Mt 24:39; Lk 17:27; 1Pe 3:20; 2Pe 2:5 n Heb 11:7
7:24 o Ge 8:3
8:1 a Ge 9:15; Ge 19:29; Ex 2:24; 1Sa 1:11,19 b Ex 14:21
8:2 c Ge 7:11
8:16 d Ge 7:13
8:17 e Ge 1:22
8:20 f Ge 12:7-8; Ge 13:18; Ge 22:9 g Ge 7:8; Lev 11:1-47

b20 Hebrew *fifteen cubits* (about 6.9 metres)
c20 Or *rose more than twenty feet, and the mountains were covered*

sacrificed burnt offerings[h] on it.
21The LORD smelled the pleasing
aroma[i] and said in his heart:
"Never again will I curse the
ground[j] because of man, even
though[a] every inclination of his
heart is evil from childhood.[k] And
never again will I destroy all living
creatures,[l] as I have done.

22"As long as the earth endures,
 seedtime and harvest,
 cold and heat,
 summer and winter,
 day and night
 will never cease."[m]

God's Covenant With Noah

9 Then God blessed Noah and
his sons, saying to them, "Be
fruitful and increase in number
and fill the earth.[a] 2The fear and
dread of you will fall upon all the
beasts of the earth and all the birds
of the air, upon every creature that
moves along the ground, and upon
all the fish of the sea; they are
given into your hands. 3Everything
that lives and moves will be food
for you.[b] Just as I gave you the
green plants, I now give you everything.

4"But you must not eat meat that
has its lifeblood still in it.[c] 5And
for your lifeblood I will surely demand an accounting. I will demand
an accounting from every animal.[d]
And from each man, too, I will demand an accounting for the life of
his fellow man.[e]

6"Whoever sheds the blood of
  man,
 by man shall his blood be
  shed;[f]
for in the image of God[g]
 has God made man.

7As for you, be fruitful and increase in number; multiply on the
earth and increase upon it."[h]

8Then God said to Noah and to his
sons with him: 9"I now establish my
covenant with you[i] and with your
descendants after you 10and with
every living creature that was with
you—the birds, the livestock and
all the wild animals, all those that
came out of the ark with you—
every living creature on earth. 11I
establish my covenant[j] with you:
Never again will all life be cut off
by the waters of a flood; never
again will there be a flood to destroy the earth.[k]"

12And God said, "This is the sign
of the covenant[l] I am making between me and you and every living
creature with you, a covenant for
all generations to come: 13I have set
my rainbow in the clouds, and it
will be the sign of the covenant between me and the earth. 14Whenever I bring clouds over the earth
and the rainbow appears in the
clouds, 15I will remember my covenant[m] between me and you and all
living creatures of every kind.
Never again will the waters become a flood to destroy all life.
16Whenever the rainbow appears in
the clouds, I will see it and remember the everlasting covenant[n] between God and all living creatures
of every kind on the earth."

17So God said to Noah, "This is
the sign of the covenant[o] I have established between me and all life
on the earth."

The Sons of Noah

18The sons of Noah who came out
of the ark were Shem, Ham and Japheth. (Ham was the father of Canaan.)[p] 19These were the three
sons of Noah, and from them came
the people who were scattered over
the earth.[q]

20Noah, a man of the soil,
proceeded[a] to plant a vineyard.
21When he drank some of its wine,
he became drunk and lay uncovered inside his tent. 22Ham, the
father of Canaan, saw his father's
nakedness and told his two
brothers outside. 23But Shem and

8:20 h Ge 22:2,13 Ex 10:25
8:21 i Lev 1:9,13 2Co 2:15 j Ge 3:17 k Ge 6:5 Ps 51:5 Jer 17:9 l Ge 9:11,15 Isa 54:9
8:22 m Ge 1:14 Jer 33:20,25
9:1 a Ge 1:22
9:3 b Ge 1:29
9:4 c Lev 3:17 Lev 17:10-14 Dt 12:16, 23-25 1Sa 14:33
9:5 d Ex 21:28-32 e Ge 4:10
9:6 f Ge 4:14 Ex 21:12,14 Lev 24:17 Mt 26:52 g Ge 1:26
9:7 h Ge 1:22
9:9 i Ge 6:18
9:11 j ver 16 Isa 24:5 k Ge 8:21 Isa 54:9
9:12 l ver 17 Ge 17:11
9:15 m Ex 2:24 Lev 26:42,45 Dt 7:9 Eze 16:60
9:16 n ver 11 Ge 17:7,13,19 2Sa 7:13 2Sa 23:5
9:17 o ver 12 Ge 17:11
9:18 p ver 25-27 Ge 10:6,15
9:19 q Ge 10:32

[a]21 Or *man, for*

[a]20 Or *soil, was the first*

Japheth took a garment and laid it across their shoulders; then they walked in backwards and covered their father's nakedness. Their faces were turned the other way so that they would not see their father's nakedness.

24When Noah awoke from his wine and found out what his youngest son had done to him, 25he said,

> "Cursed be Canaan![r]
> The lowest of slaves
> will he be to his brothers.[s]"

26He also said,

> "Blessed be the LORD, the God
> of Shem!
> May Canaan be the slave of
> Shem.[b]
> 27May God extend the territory of
> Japheth;[c]
> may Japheth live in the tents
> of Shem,
> and may Canaan be his[d]
> slave."

28After the flood Noah lived 350 years. 29Altogether, Noah lived 950 years, and then he died.

The Table of Nations

10 This is the account[a] of Shem, Ham and Japheth, Noah's sons, who themselves had sons after the flood.

The Japhethites

10:2–5pp 1Ch 1:5–7

> 2The sons[a] of Japheth:
> Gomer,[b] Magog,[c] Madai, Javan, Tubal,[d] Meshech and Tiras.
> 3The sons of Gomer:
> Ashkenaz,[e] Riphath and Togarmah.[f]
> 4The sons of Javan:
> Elishah, Tarshish,[g] the Kittim and the Rodanim.[b] 5(From these the maritime peoples spread out into their territories by their clans within their nations, each with its own language.)

9:25
r ver 18
s Ge 25:23; Jos 9:23

10:1
a Ge 2:4

10:2
b Eze 38:6
c Eze 38:2; Rev 20:8
d Isa 66:19

10:3
e Jer 51:27
f Eze 27:14; Eze 38:6

10:4
g Eze 27:12,25; Jnh 1:3

10:6
h ver 15; Ge 9:18

10:10
i Ge 11:9
j Ge 11:2

10:11
k Ps 83:8; Mic 5:6
l Jnh 1:2; Jnh 4:11; Na 1:1

10:14
m Ge 21:32,34; Ge 26:1,8

10:15
n ver 6; Ge 9:18
o Eze 28:21
p Ge 23:3,20

10:16
q 1Ch 11:4

10:18
r Ge 12:6; Ex 13:11

10:19
s Ge 11:31; Ge 13:12; Ge 17:8
t ver 15

The Hamites

10:6–20pp 1Ch 1:8–16

> 6The sons of Ham:
> Cush, Mizraim,[c] Put and Canaan.[h]
> 7The sons of Cush:
> Seba, Havilah, Sabtah, Raamah and Sabteca.
> The sons of Raamah:
> Sheba and Dedan.

8Cush was the father[d] of Nimrod, who grew to be a mighty warrior on the earth. 9He was a mighty hunter before the LORD; that is why it is said, "Like Nimrod, a mighty hunter before the LORD." 10The first centres of his kingdom were Babylon,[i] Erech, Akkad and Calneh, in[e] Shinar.[f][j] 11From that land he went to Assyria,[k] where he built Nineveh,[l] Rehoboth Ir,[g] Calah 12and Resen, which is between Nineveh and Calah; that is the great city.

> 13Mizraim was the father of
> the Ludites, Anamites, Lehabites, Naphtuhites, 14Pathrusites, Casluhites (from whom the Philistines[m] came) and Caphtorites.
> 15Canaan[n] was the father of
> Sidon[o] his firstborn,[h] and of the Hittites,[p] 16Jebusites,[q] Amorites, Girgashites, 17Hivites, Arkites, Sinites, 18Arvadites, Zemarites and Hamathites.

Later the Canaanite[r] clans scattered 19and the borders of Canaan[s] reached from Sidon[t] towards Gerar as far as Gaza, and then

[b]26 Or *be his slave* [c]27 *Japheth* sounds like the Hebrew for *extend.* [d]27 Or *their*
[a]2 *Sons* may mean *descendants* or *successors* or *nations*; also in verses 3, 4, 6, 7, 20–23, 29 and 31. [b]4 Some manuscripts of the Masoretic Text and Samaritan Pentateuch (see also Septuagint and 1 Chron. 1:7); most manuscripts of the Masoretic Text *Dodanim* [c]6 That is, Egypt; also in verse 13 [d]8 *Father* may mean *ancestor* or *predecessor* or *founder*; also in verses 13, 15, 24 and 26. [e]10 Or *Erech and Akkad—all of them in* [f]10 That is, Babylonia [g]11 Or *Nineveh with its city squares* [h]15 Or *of the Sidonians, the foremost*

towards Sodom, Gomorrah, Admah
and Zeboiim, as far as Lasha.
20These are the sons of Ham by
their clans and languages, in their
territories and nations.

The Semites

10:21–31pp Ge 11:10–27; 1Ch 1:17–27

21Sons were also born to Shem,
whose older brother was[i] Japheth; Shem was the ancestor of all
the sons of Eber.[u]

22The sons of Shem:
Elam,[v] Asshur, Arphaxad,[w]
Lud and Aram.
23The sons of Aram:
Uz,[x] Hul, Gether and Meshech.[j]
24Arphaxad was the father of[k]
Shelah,
and Shelah the father of
Eber.[y]
25Two sons were born to Eber:
One was named Peleg,[l] because in his time the earth
was divided; his brother was
named Joktan.
26Joktan was the father of
Almodad, Sheleph, Hazar-
maveth, Jerah, 27Hadoram,
Uzal, Diklah, 28Obal, Abi-
mael, Sheba, 29Ophir, Havilah and Jobab. All these
were sons of Joktan.

30The region where they lived
stretched from Mesha towards
Sephar, in the eastern hill country.
31These are the sons of Shem by
their clans and languages, in their
territories and nations.

32These are the clans of Noah's
sons,[z] according to their lines of
descent, within their nations. From
these the nations spread out over
the earth[a] after the flood.

The Tower of Babel

11 Now the whole world had
one language and a com-
mon speech. 2As men moved eastward,[a] they found a plain in

10:21 *u* ver 24; Nu 24:24
10:22 *v* Jer 49:34 *w* Lk 3:36
10:23 *x* Job 1:1
10:24 *y* ver 21
10:32 *z* ver 1 *a* Ge 9:19
11:2 *a* Ge 10:10
11:3 *b* Ex 1:14 *c* Ge 14:10
11:4 *d* Dt 1:28; Dt 9:1 *e* Ge 6:4 *f* Dt 4:27
11:5 *g* ver 7; Ge 18:21; Ex 3:8; Ex 19:11,18,20
11:7 *h* Ge 1:26 *i* Ge 42:23
11:8 *j* Ge 9:19; Lk 1:51
11:9 *k* Ge 10:10
11:12 *l* Lk 3:35

Shinar[b][a] and settled there.
3They said to each other, "Come,
let's make bricks[b] and bake them
thoroughly." They used brick instead of stone, and bitumen[c] for
mortar. 4Then they said, "Come, let
us build ourselves a city, with a
tower that reaches to the heavens,[d] so that we may make a
name[e] for ourselves and not be
scattered over the face of the
whole earth."[f]
5But the LORD came down[g] to see
the city and the tower that the men
were building. 6The LORD said, "If
as one people speaking the same
language they have begun to do
this, then nothing they plan to do
will be impossible for them. 7Come,
let us[h] go down and confuse their
language so they will not understand each other."[i]
8So the LORD scattered them
from there over all the earth,[j] and
they stopped building the city.
9That is why it was called Babel[c][k]—because there the LORD
confused the language of the whole
world. From there the LORD scattered them over the face of the
whole earth.

From Shem to Abram

11:10–27pp Ge 10:21–31; 1Ch 1:17–27

10This is the account of Shem.

Two years after the flood, when
Shem was 100 years old, he became
the father[d] of Arphaxad. 11And
after he became the father of Arphaxad, Shem lived 500 years and
had other sons and daughters.
12When Arphaxad had lived 35
years, he became the father of Shelah.[l] 13And after he became the

[i]21 Or *Shem, the older brother of* [j]23 See Septuagint and 1 Chron. 1:17; Hebrew *Mash.*
[k]24 Hebrew; Septuagint *father of Cainan, and Cainan was the father of* [l]25 *Peleg* means *division.* [a]2 Or *from the east*; or *in the east*
[b]2 That is, Babylonia [c]9 That is, Babylon; *Babel* sounds like the Hebrew for *confused.*
[d]10 *Father* may mean *ancestor*; also in verses 11–25.

father of Shelah, Arphaxad lived
403 years and had other sons and
daughters.[e]
14 When Shelah had lived 30
years, he became the father of
Eber. 15 And after he became the
father of Eber, Shelah lived 403
years and had other sons and
daughters.
16 When Eber had lived 34 years,
he became the father of Peleg.
17 And after he became the father of
Peleg, Eber lived 430 years and had
other sons and daughters.
18 When Peleg had lived 30 years,
he became the father of Reu. 19 And
after he became the father of Reu,
Peleg lived 209 years and had other
sons and daughters.
20 When Reu had lived 32 years,
he became the father of Serug.[m]
21 And after he became the father of
Serug, Reu lived 207 years and had
other sons and daughters.
22 When Serug had lived 30 years,
he became the father of Nahor.
23 And after he became the father of
Nahor, Serug lived 200 years and
had other sons and daughters.
24 When Nahor had lived 29 years,
he became the father of Terah.[n]
25 And after he became the father of
Terah, Nahor lived 119 years and
had other sons and daughters.
26 After Terah had lived 70 years,
he became the father of Abram,[o]
Nahor[p] and Haran.

27 This is the account of Terah.

Terah became the father of
Abram, Nahor and Haran. And Haran became the father of Lot.[q]
28 While his father Terah was still
alive, Haran died in Ur of the Chaldeans,[r] in the land of his birth.
29 Abram and Nahor both married.
The name of Abram's wife was
Sarai,[s] and the name of Nahor's
wife was Milcah;[t] she was the
daughter of Haran, the father of
both Milcah and Iscah. 30 Now Sarai
was barren; she had no children.[u]
31 Terah took his son Abram, his
grandson Lot son of Haran, and his
daughter-in-law Sarai, the wife of
his son Abram, and together they
set out from Ur of the Chaldeans[v]
to go to Canaan.[w] But when they
came to Haran, they settled there.
32 Terah lived 205 years, and he
died in Haran.

The Call of Abram

12 The LORD had said to
Abram, "Leave your coun-
try, your people and your father's
household and go to the land I will
show you.[a]

2 "I will make you into a great
nation[b]
and I will bless you;[c]
I will make your name great,
and you will be a blessing.
3 I will bless those who bless you,
and whoever curses you I will
curse;[d]
and all peoples on earth
will be blessed through you.[e]"

4 So Abram left, as the LORD had
told him; and Lot went with him.
Abram was seventy-five years old
when he set out from Haran.[f] 5 He
took his wife Sarai, his nephew Lot,
all the possessions they had accumulated and the people[g] they
had acquired in Haran, and they set
out for the land of Canaan, and they
arrived there.
6 Abram travelled through the
land[h] as far as the site of the great
tree of Moreh[i] at Shechem. At that
time the Canaanites[j] were in the
land. 7 The LORD appeared to
Abram[k] and said, "To your offspring[a] I will give this land."[l] So
he built an altar there to the LORD,[m]
who had appeared to him.
8 From there he went on towards
the hills east of Bethel[n] and

11:20 m Lk 3:35
11:24 n Lk 3:34
11:26 o Lk 3:34 p Jos 24:2
11:27 q ver 31 Ge 12:4 Ge 14:12 Ge 19:1 2Pe 2:7
11:28 r ver 31 Ge 15:7
11:29 s Ge 17:15 t Ge 22:20
11:30 u Ge 16:1 Ge 18:11
11:31 v Ge 15:7 Ne 9:7 Ac 7:4 w Ge 10:19
12:1 a Ac 7:3* Heb 11:8
12:2 b Ge 15:5 Ge 17:2,4 Ge 18:18 Ge 22:17 Dt 26:5 c Ge 24:1,35
12:3 d Ge 27:29 Ex 23:22 Nu 24:9 e Ge 18:18 Ge 22:18 Ge 26:4 Ac 3:25 Gal 3:8*
12:4 f Ge 11:31
12:5 g Ge 14:14 Ge 17:23
12:6 h Heb 11:9 i Ge 35:4 Dt 11:30 j Ge 10:18
12:7 k Ge 17:1 Ge 18:1 Ex 6:3 l Ge 13:15,17 Ge 15:18 Ge 17:8 Ps 105:9-11 m Ge 13:4
12:8 n Ge 13:3

e *12,13* Hebrew; Septuagint (see also Luke 3:35, 36 and note at Gen. 10:24) *35 years, he became the father of Cainan.* 13 *And after he became the father of Cainan, Arphaxad lived 430 years and had other sons and daughters, and then he died. When Cainan had lived 130 years, he became the father of Shelah. And after he became the father of Shelah, Cainan lived 330 years and had other sons and daughters* a *7* Or *seed*

pitched his tent, with Bethel on the
west and Ai on the east. There he
built an altar to the LORD and called
on the name of the LORD. 9Then
Abram set out and continued towards the Negev.[o]

Abram in Egypt

12:10–20Ref Ge 20:1–18; 26:1–11

10Now there was a famine in the
land, and Abram went down to
Egypt to live there for a while because the famine was severe. 11As
he was about to enter Egypt, he
said to his wife Sarai, "I know what
a beautiful woman you are. 12When
the Egyptians see you, they will
say, 'This is his wife.' Then they
will kill me but will let you live.
13Say you are my sister,[p] so that I
will be treated well for your sake
and my life will be spared because
of you."
14When Abram came to Egypt,
the Egyptians saw that she was a
very beautiful woman. 15And when
Pharaoh's officials saw her, they
praised her to Pharaoh, and she
was taken into his palace. 16He
treated Abram well for her sake,
and Abram acquired sheep and cattle, male and female donkeys, menservants and maidservants, and
camels.
17But the LORD inflicted serious
diseases on Pharaoh and his household[q] because of Abram's wife
Sarai. 18So Pharaoh summoned
Abram. "What have you done to
me?"[r] he said. "Why didn't you tell
me she was your wife? 19Why did
you say, 'She is my sister,' so that I
took her to be my wife? Now then,
here is your wife. Take her and
go!" 20Then Pharaoh gave orders
about Abram to his men, and they
sent him on his way, with his wife
and everything he had.

Abram and Lot Separate

13 So Abram went up from
Egypt to the Negev,[a] with
his wife and everything he had, and
Lot went with him. 2Abram had
become very wealthy in livestock
and in silver and gold.
3From the Negev he went from
place to place until he came to
Bethel,[b] to the place between
Bethel and Ai where his tent had
been earlier 4and where he had
first built an altar.[c] There Abram
called on the name of the LORD.
5Now Lot, who was moving about
with Abram, also had flocks and
herds and tents. 6But the land could
not support them while they stayed
together, for their possessions
were so great that they were not
able to stay together.[d] 7And quarrelling[e] arose between Abram's
herdsmen and the herdsmen of Lot.
The Canaanites and Perizzites
were also living in the land[f] at that
time.
8So Abram said to Lot, "Let's not
have any quarrelling between you
and me,[g] or between your herdsmen and mine, for we are
brothers.[h] 9Is not the whole land
before you? Let's part company. If
you go to the left, I'll go to the right;
if you go to the right, I'll go to the
left."
10Lot looked up and saw that the
whole plain of the Jordan was well
watered, like the garden of the
LORD,[i] like the land of Egypt, towards Zoar.[j] (This was before the
LORD destroyed Sodom and Gomorrah.)[k] 11So Lot chose for himself
the whole plain of the Jordan and
set out towards the east. The two
men parted company: 12Abram
lived in the land of Canaan, while
Lot lived among the cities of the
plain[l] and pitched his tents near
Sodom.[m] 13Now the men of Sodom
were wicked and were sinning
greatly against the LORD.[n]
14The LORD said to Abram after
Lot had parted from him, "Lift
up your eyes from where you are
and look north and south, east
and west.[o] 15All the land that you
see I will give to you and your

12:9 o Ge 13:1,3
12:13 p Ge 20:2; Ge 26:7
12:17 q 1Ch 16:21
12:18 r Ge 20:9; Ge 26:10
13:1 a Ge 12:9
13:3 b Ge 12:8
13:4 c Ge 12:7
13:6 d Ge 36:7
13:7 e Ge 26:20,21; f Ge 12:6
13:8 g Pr 15:18; Pr 20:3; h Ps 133:1
13:10 i Ge 2:8-10; Isa 51:3; j Ge 19:22,30; k Ge 14:8; Ge 19:17-29
13:12 l Ge 19:17,25, 29; m Ge 14:12
13:13 n Ge 18:20; Eze 16:49-50; 2Pe 2:8
13:14 o Ge 28:14; Dt 3:27

offspring[a] for ever.[p] [16]I will make your offspring like the dust of the earth, so that if anyone could count the dust, then your offspring could be counted. [17]Go, walk through the length and breadth of the land,[q] for I am giving it to you."

[18]So Abram moved his tents and went to live near the great trees of Mamre[r] at Hebron,[s] where he built an altar to the LORD.[t]

Abram Rescues Lot

14 At this time Amraphel king of Shinar,[a][a] Arioch king of Ellasar, Kedorlaomer king of Elam and Tidal king of Goiim [2]went to war against Bera king of Sodom, Birsha king of Gomorrah, Shinab king of Admah, Shemeber king of Zeboiim,[b] and the king of Bela (that is, Zoar).[c] [3]All these latter kings joined forces in the Valley of Siddim (the Salt Sea[b][d]). [4]For twelve years they had been subject to Kedorlaomer, but in the thirteenth year they rebelled.

[5]In the fourteenth year, Kedorlaomer and the kings allied with him went out and defeated the Rephaites[e] in Ashteroth Karnaim, the Zuzites in Ham, the Emites[f] in Shaveh Kiriathaim [6]and the Horites[g] in the hill country of Seir,[h] as far as El Paran[i] near the desert. [7]Then they turned back and went to En Mishpat (that is, Kadesh), and they conquered the whole territory of the Amalekites, as well as the Amorites who were living in Hazezon Tamar.[j]

[8]Then the king of Sodom, the king of Gomorrah,[k] the king of Admah, the king of Zeboiim[l] and the king of Bela (that is, Zoar) marched out and drew up their battle lines in the Valley of Siddim [9]against Kedorlaomer king of Elam, Tidal king of Goiim, Amraphel king of Shinar and Arioch king of Ellasar—four kings against five. [10]Now the Valley of Siddim was full of tar pits, and when the kings of Sodom and Gomorrah fled, some of the men fell into them and the rest fled to the hills.[m] [11]The four kings seized all the goods of Sodom and Gomorrah and all their food; then they went away. [12]They also carried off Abram's nephew Lot and his possessions, since he was living in Sodom.

[13]One who had escaped came and reported this to Abram the Hebrew. Now Abram was living near the great trees of Mamre[n] the Amorite, a brother[c] of Eshcol and Aner, all of whom were allied with Abram. [14]When Abram heard that his relative had been taken captive, he called out the 318 trained men born in his household[o] and went in pursuit as far as Dan.[p] [15]During the night Abram divided his men to attack them and he routed them, pursuing them as far as Hobah, north of Damascus. [16]He recovered all the goods and brought back his relative Lot and his possessions, together with the women and the other people.

[17]After Abram returned from defeating Kedorlaomer and the kings allied with him, the king of Sodom came out to meet him in the Valley of Shaveh (that is, the King's Valley).[q]

[18]Then Melchizedek[r] king of Salem[d][s] brought out bread and wine. He was priest of God Most High, [19]and he blessed Abram,[t] saying,

"Blessed be Abram by God
Most High,
Creator[e] of heaven and
earth.[u]
[20]And blessed be[f] God Most
High,[v]
who delivered your enemies
into your hand."

13:15 p Ge 12:7; Gal 3:16*
13:17 q ver 15; Nu 13:17-25
13:18 r Ge 14:13,24; Ge 18:1; s Ge 35:27; t Ge 8:20
14:1 a Ge 10:10
14:2 b Ge 10:19; c Ge 13:10
14:3 d Nu 34:3,12; Dt 3:17; Jos 3:16; Jos 15:2,5
14:5 e Ge 15:20; Dt 2:11,20; f Dt 2:10
14:6 g Dt 2:12,22; h Dt 2:1,5,22; i Ge 21:21; Nu 10:12
14:7 j 2Ch 20:2
14:8 k Ge 13:10; Ge 19:17-29; l Dt 29:23
14:10 m Ge 19:17,30
14:13 n ver 24; Ge 13:18
14:14 o Ge 15:3; p Dt 34:1; Jdg 18:29
14:17 q 2Sa 18:18
14:18 r Ps 110:4; Heb 5:6; s Ps 76:2; Heb 7:2
14:19 t Heb 7:6; u ver 22
14:20 v Ge 24:27

[a] *15* Or *seed*; also in verse 16 [a] *1* That is, Babylonia; also in verse 9 [b] *3* That is, the Dead Sea [c] *13* Or *a relative*; or *an ally* [d] *18* That is, Jerusalem [e] *19* Or *Possessor*; also in verse 22 [f] *20* Or *And praise be to*

Then Abram gave him a tenth of everything.[w]

21 The king of Sodom said to Abram, "Give me the people and keep the goods for yourself."

22 But Abram said to the king of Sodom, "I have raised my hand[x] to the LORD, God Most High, Creator of heaven and earth,[y] and have taken an oath 23 that I will accept nothing belonging to you,[z] not even a thread or the thong of a sandal, so that you will never be able to say, 'I made Abram rich.' 24 I will accept nothing but what my men have eaten and the share that belongs to the men who went with me—to Aner, Eshcol and Mamre. Let them have their share."

God's Covenant With Abram

15 After this, the word of the LORD came to Abram[a] in a vision:

"Do not be afraid,[b] Abram.
  I am your shield,[a][c]
  your very great reward."[b]

2 But Abram said, "O Sovereign LORD, what can you give me since I remain childless[d] and the one who will inherit[c] my estate is Eliezer of Damascus?" 3 And Abram said, "You have given me no children; so a servant[e] in my household will be my heir."

4 Then the word of the LORD came to him: "This man will not be your heir, but a son coming from your own body will be your heir.[f]" 5 He took him outside and said, "Look up at the heavens and count the stars[g]—if indeed you can count them." Then he said to him, "So shall your offspring be."[h]

6 Abram believed the LORD, and he credited it to him as righteousness.[i]

7 He also said to him, "I am the LORD, who brought you out of Ur of the Chaldeans to give you this land to take possession of it."

8 But Abram said, "O Sovereign LORD, how can I know[j] that I shall gain possession of it?"

9 So the LORD said to him, "Bring me a heifer, a goat and a ram, each three years old, along with a dove and a young pigeon."

10 Abram brought all these to him, cut them in two and arranged the halves opposite each other;[k] the birds, however, he did not cut in half.[l] 11 Then birds of prey came down on the carcasses, but Abram drove them away.

12 As the sun was setting, Abram fell into a deep sleep,[m] and a thick and dreadful darkness came over him. 13 Then the LORD said to him, "Know for certain that your descendants will be strangers in a country not their own, and they will be enslaved[n] and ill-treated four hundred years.[o] 14 But I will punish the nation they serve as slaves, and afterwards they will come out[p] with great possessions.[q] 15 You, however, will go to your fathers in peace and be buried at a good old age.[r] 16 In the fourth generation your descendants will come back here, for the sin of the Amorites[s] has not yet reached its full measure."

17 When the sun had set and darkness had fallen, a smoking brazier with a blazing torch appeared and passed between the pieces.[t] 18 On that day the LORD made a covenant with Abram and said, "To your descendants I give this land,[u] from the river[d] of Egypt[v] to the great river, the Euphrates—19 the land of the Kenites, Kenizzites, Kadmonites, 20 Hittites, Perizzites, Rephaites, 21 Amorites, Canaanites, Girgashites and Jebusites."

14:20 w Ge 28:22; Dt 26:12; Heb 7:4
14:22 x Ex 6:8; Da 12:7; Rev 10:5-6 y ver 19
14:23 z 2Ki 5:16
15:1 a Da 10:1 b Ge 21:17; Ge 26:24; Ge 46:3; 2Ki 6:16; Ps 27:1; Isa 41:10, 13-14 c Dt 33:29; 2Sa 22:3,31; Ps 3:3
15:2 d Ac 7:5
15:3 e Ge 24:2,34
15:4 f Gal 4:28
15:5 g Ps 147:4; Jer 33:22 h Ge 12:2; Ge 22:17; Ex 32:13; Ro 4:18*; Heb 11:12
15:6 i Ps 106:31; Ro 4:3*, 20-24*; Gal 3:6*; Jas 2:23*
15:8 j Lk 1:18
15:10 k ver 17; Jer 34:18 l Lev 1:17
15:12 m Ge 2:21
15:13 n Ex 1:11 o ver 16; Ex 12:40; Ac 7:6,17
15:14 p Ac 7:7* q Ex 12:32-38
15:15 r Ge 25:8
15:16 s 1Ki 21:26
15:17 t ver 10
15:18 u Ge 12:7 v Nu 34:5

a1 Or *sovereign* b1 Or *shield; / your reward will be very great* c2 The meaning of the Hebrew for this phrase is uncertain. d18 Or *Wadi*

Hagar and Ishmael

16 Now Sarai, Abram's wife, had borne him no children.[a] But she had an Egyptian maidservant[b] named Hagar; [2]so she said to Abram, "The LORD has kept me from having children. Go, sleep with my maidservant; perhaps I can build a family through her."[c]

Abram agreed to what Sarai said. [3]So after Abram had been living in Canaan[d] ten years, Sarai his wife took her Egyptian maidservant Hagar and gave her to her husband to be his wife. [4]He slept with Hagar, and she conceived.

When she knew she was pregnant, she began to despise her mistress. [5]Then Sarai said to Abram, "You are responsible for the wrong I am suffering. I put my servant in your arms, and now that she knows she is pregnant, she despises me. May the LORD judge between you and me."[e]

[6]"Your servant is in your hands," Abram said. "Do with her whatever you think best." Then Sarai ill-treated Hagar; so she fled from her.

[7]The angel of the LORD[f] found Hagar near a spring in the desert; it was the spring that is beside the road to Shur.[g] [8]And he said, "Hagar, servant of Sarai, where have you come from, and where are you going?"

"I'm running away from my mistress Sarai," she answered.

[9]Then the angel of the LORD told her, "Go back to your mistress and submit to her." [10]The angel added, "I will so increase your descendants that they will be too numerous to count."[h]

[11]The angel of the LORD also said to her:

"You are now with child
  and you will have a son.
You shall name him Ishmael,[a]
  for the LORD has heard of your
    misery.[i]
[12]He will be a wild donkey of a
    man;
  his hand will be against
    everyone
  and everyone's hand against
    him,
and he will live in hostility
  towards[b] all his brothers.[j]"

[13]She gave this name to the LORD who spoke to her: "You are the God who sees me," for she said, "I have now seen[c] the One who sees me."[k] [14]That is why the well was called Beer Lahai Roi;[d] it is still there, between Kadesh and Bered.

[15]So Hagar bore Abram a son,[l] and Abram gave the name Ishmael to the son she had borne. [16]Abram was eighty-six years old when Hagar bore him Ishmael.

The Covenant of Circumcision

17 When Abram was ninety-nine years old, the LORD appeared to him and said, "I am God Almighty;[a][a] walk before me and be blameless.[b] [2]I will confirm my covenant between me and you[c] and will greatly increase your numbers."

[3]Abram fell face down, and God said to him, [4]"As for me, this is my covenant with you:[d] You will be the father of many nations.[e] [5]No longer will you be called Abram;[b] your name will be Abraham,[c][f] for I have made you a father of many nations.[g] [6]I will make you very fruitful;[h] I will make nations of you, and kings will come from you.[i] [7]I will establish my covenant as an everlasting covenant between me and you and your descendants after you for the generations to come, to be your God[j] and the God of your descendants after you.[k] [8]The whole land of

16:1 *a* Ge 11:30; Gal 4:24-25 *b* Ge 21:9
16:2 *c* Ge 30:3-4, 9-10
16:3 *d* Ge 12:5
16:5 *e* Ge 31:53
16:7 *f* Ge 21:17; Ge 22:11,15; Ge 31:11 *g* Ge 20:1
16:10 *h* Ge 13:16; Ge 17:20
16:11 *i* Ex 2:24; Ex 3:7,9
16:12 *j* Ge 25:18
16:13 *k* Ge 32:30
16:15 *l* Gal 4:22
17:1 *a* Ge 28:3; Ex 6:3 *b* Dt 18:13
17:2 *c* Ge 15:18
17:4 *d* Ge 15:18 *e* ver 16; Ge 12:2; Ge 35:11; Ge 48:19
17:5 *f* ver 15; Ne 9:7 *g* Ro 4:17*
17:6 *h* Ge 35:11 *i* Mt 1:6
17:7 *j* Ex 29:45,46 *k* Ro 9:8; Gal 3:16

a11 *Ishmael* means *God hears.* b12 Or *live to the east / of* c13 Or *seen the back of*
d14 *Beer Lahai Roi* means *well of the Living One who sees me.* a1 Hebrew *El-Shaddai*
b5 *Abram* means *exalted father.* c5 *Abraham* means *father of many.*

Canaan,[l] where you are now an
alien,[m] I will give as an everlasting
possession to you and your descendants after you;[n] and I will be
their God."
9Then God said to Abraham, "As
for you, you must keep my covenant, you and your descendants
after you for the generations to
come. 10This is my covenant with
you and your descendants after
you, the covenant you are to keep:
Every male among you shall be circumcised.[o] 11You are to undergo
circumcision,[p] and it will be the
sign of the covenant[q] between me
and you. 12For the generations to
come every male among you who is
eight days old must be circumcised,[r] including those born in
your household or bought with
money from a foreigner—those
who are not your offspring.
13Whether born in your household
or bought with your money, they
must be circumcised. My covenant
in your flesh is to be an everlasting
covenant. 14Any uncircumcised
male, who has not been circumcised in the flesh, will be cut off
from his people;[s] he has broken
my covenant."
15God also said to Abraham, "As
for Sarai your wife, you are no
longer to call her Sarai; her name
will be Sarah. 16I will bless her and
will surely give you a son by her.[t]
I will bless her so that she will be
the mother of nations;[u] kings of
peoples will come from her."
17Abraham fell face down; he
laughed[v] and said to himself, "Will
a son be born to a man a hundred
years old? Will Sarah bear a child
at the age of ninety?" 18And Abraham said to God, "If only Ishmael
might live under your blessing!"
19Then God said, "Yes, but your
wife Sarah will bear you a son,[w]
and you will call him Isaac.[d] I will
establish my covenant with him[x]
as an everlasting covenant for his
descendants after him. 20And as for
Ishmael, I have heard you: I will
surely bless him; I will make him
fruitful and will greatly increase
his numbers.[y] He will be the
father of twelve rulers,[z] and I will
make him into a great nation.[a]
21But my covenant I will establish
with Isaac, whom Sarah will bear to
you by this time next year."[b]
22When he had finished speaking
with Abraham, God went up from
him.
23On that very day Abraham took
his son Ishmael and all those born
in his household or bought with his
money, every male in his household, and circumcised them, as God
told him. 24Abraham was ninety-
nine years old when he was circumcised,[c] 25and his son Ishmael was
thirteen; 26Abraham and his son
Ishmael were both circumcised on
that same day. 27And every male in
Abraham's household, including
those born in his household or
bought from a foreigner, was circumcised with him.

The Three Visitors

18 The LORD appeared to
Abraham near the great
trees of Mamre[a] while he was sitting at the entrance to his tent in
the heat of the day. 2Abraham
looked up and saw three men[b]
standing nearby. When he saw
them, he hurried from the entrance
of his tent to meet them and bowed
low to the ground.
3He said, "If I have found favour
in your eyes, my lord,[a] do not pass
your servant by. 4Let a little water
be brought, and then you may all
wash your feet[c] and rest under
this tree. 5Let me get you something to eat,[d] so you can be refreshed and then go on your
way—now that you have come to
your servant."
"Very well," they answered, "do
as you say."
6So Abraham hurried into the
tent to Sarah. "Quick," he said, "get

17:8 *l* Ps 105:9,11 *m* Ge 23:4 Ge 28:4 Ex 6:4 *n* Ge 12:7
17:10 *o* ver 23 Ge 21:4 Jn 7:22 Ac 7:8 Ro 4:11
17:11 *p* Ex 12:48 Dt 10:16 *q* Ro 4:11
17:12 *r* Lev 12:3 Lk 2:21
17:14 *s* Ex 4:24-26
17:16 *t* Ge 18:10 *u* Ge 35:11 Gal 4:31
17:17 *v* Ge 18:12 Ge 21:6
17:19 *w* Ge 18:14 Ge 21:2 *x* Ge 26:3
17:20 *y* Ge 16:10 *z* Ge 25:12-16 *a* Ge 21:18
17:21 *b* Ge 21:2
17:24 *c* Ro 4:11
18:1 *a* Ge 13:18 Ge 14:13
18:2 *b* ver 16,22 Ge 32:24 Jos 5:13 Jdg 13:6-11 Heb 13:2
18:4 *c* Ge 19:2 Ge 43:24
18:5 *d* Jdg 13:15

d19 *Isaac* means *he laughs.* **a**3 Or *O Lord*

three seahs[b] of fine flour and knead it and bake some bread."

7Then he ran to the herd and selected a choice, tender calf and gave it to a servant, who hurried to prepare it. 8He then brought some curds and milk and the calf that had been prepared, and set these before them.[e] While they ate, he stood near them under a tree.

9"Where is your wife Sarah?" they asked him.

"There, in the tent," he said.

10Then the LORD[c] said, "I will surely return to you about this time next year, and Sarah your wife will have a son."[f]

Now Sarah was listening at the entrance to the tent, which was behind him. 11Abraham and Sarah were already old and well advanced in years,[g] and Sarah was past the age of childbearing.[h] 12So Sarah laughed[i] to herself as she thought, "After I am worn out and my master[d][j] is old, will I now have this pleasure?"

13Then the LORD said to Abraham, "Why did Sarah laugh and say, 'Will I really have a child, now that I am old?' 14Is anything too hard for the LORD?[k] I will return to you at the appointed time next year and Sarah will have a son."

15Sarah was afraid, so she lied and said, "I did not laugh."

But he said, "Yes, you did laugh."

Abraham Pleads for Sodom

16When the men got up to leave, they looked down towards Sodom, and Abraham walked along with them to see them on their way. 17Then the LORD said, "Shall I hide from Abraham[l] what I am about to do?[m] 18Abraham will surely become a great and powerful nation,[n] and all nations on earth will be blessed through him. 19For I have chosen him, so that he will direct his children[o] and his household after him to keep the way of the LORD[p] by doing what is right and just, so that the LORD will bring about for Abraham what he has promised him."

20Then the LORD said, "The outcry against Sodom and Gomorrah is so great and their sin so grievous 21that I will go down[q] and see if what they have done is as bad as the outcry that has reached me. If not, I will know."

22The men turned away and went towards Sodom,[r] but Abraham remained standing before the LORD.[e] 23Then Abraham approached him and said: "Will you sweep away the righteous with the wicked?[s] 24What if there are fifty righteous people in the city? Will you really sweep it away and not spare[f] the place for the sake of the fifty righteous people in it?[t] 25Far be it from you to do such a thing—to kill the righteous with the wicked, treating the righteous and the wicked alike. Far be it from you! Will not the Judge[g] of all the earth do right?"[u]

26The LORD said, "If I find fifty righteous people in the city of Sodom, I will spare the whole place for their sake.[v]"

27Then Abraham spoke up again: "Now that I have been so bold as to speak to the Lord, though I am nothing but dust and ashes,[w] 28what if the number of the righteous is five less than fifty? Will you destroy the whole city because of five people?"

"If I find forty-five there," he said, "I will not destroy it."

29Once again he spoke to him, "What if only forty are found there?"

He said, "For the sake of forty, I will not do it."

30Then he said, "May the Lord not

18:8 e Ge 19:3
18:10 f Ro 9:9*
18:11 g Ge 17:17 h Ro 4:19
18:12 i Ge 17:17; Ge 21:6 j 1Pe 3:6
18:14 k Jer 32:17,27; Zec 8:6; Mt 19:26; Lk 1:37; Ro 4:21
18:17 l Am 3:7 m Ge 19:24
18:18 n Gal 3:8*
18:19 o Dt 4:9-10; Dt 6:7 p Jos 24:15; Eph 6:4
18:21 q Ge 11:5
18:22 r Ge 19:1
18:23 s Nu 16:22
18:24 t Jer 5:1
18:25 u Job 8:3,20; Ps 58:11; Ps 94:2; Isa 3:10-11; Ro 3:6
18:26 v Jer 5:1
18:27 w Ge 2:7; Ge 3:19; Job 30:19; Job 42:6

[b]6 That is, probably about 39 pints (about 22 litres) [c]*10* Hebrew *Then he*
[d]*12* Or *husband* [e]*22* Masoretic Text; an ancient Hebrew scribal tradition *but the LORD remained standing before Abraham*
[f]*24* Or *forgive*; also in verse 26 [g]*25* Or *Ruler*

be angry, but let me speak. What if
only thirty can be found there?"
He answered, "I will not do it if I
find thirty there."
31 Abraham said, "Now that I have
been so bold as to speak to the Lord,
what if only twenty can be found
there?"
He said, "For the sake of twenty,
I will not destroy it."
32 Then he said, "May the Lord not
be angry, but let me speak just
once more.[x] What if only ten can
be found there?"
He answered, "For the sake of
ten,[y] I will not destroy it."
33 When the LORD had finished
speaking with Abraham, he left,
and Abraham returned home.

Sodom and Gomorrah Destroyed

19 The two angels arrived at
Sodom[a] in the evening,
and Lot was sitting in the gateway
of the city.[b] When he saw them, he
got up to meet them and bowed
down with his face to the ground.
2 "My lords," he said, "please turn
aside to your servant's house. You
can wash your feet[c] and spend the
night and then go on your way early
in the morning."
"No," they answered, "we will
spend the night in the square."
3 But he insisted so strongly that
they did go with him and entered
his house. He prepared a meal for
them, baking bread without yeast,
and they ate.[d] 4 Before they had
gone to bed, all the men from every
part of the city of Sodom—both
young and old—surrounded the
house. 5 They called to Lot, "Where
are the men who came to you tonight? Bring them out to us so that
we can have sex with them."[e]
6 Lot went outside to meet them[f]
and shut the door behind him 7 and
said, "No, my friends. Don't do this
wicked thing. 8 Look, I have two
daughters who have never slept
with a man. Let me bring them out
to you, and you can do what you like
with them. But don't do anything to
these men, for they have come under the protection of my roof."[g]
9 "Get out of our way," they replied. And they said, "This fellow
came here as an alien, and now he
wants to play the judge![h] We'll
treat you worse than them." They
kept bringing pressure on Lot and
moved forward to break down the
door.
10 But the men inside reached out
and pulled Lot back into the house
and shut the door. 11 Then they
struck the men who were at the
door of the house, young and old,
with blindness[i] so that they could
not find the door.
12 The two men said to Lot, "Do
you have anyone else here—sons-
in-law, sons or daughters, or anyone else in the city who belongs to
you?[j] Get them out of here, 13 because we are going to destroy this
place. The outcry to the LORD
against its people is so great that he
has sent us to destroy it."[k]
14 So Lot went out and spoke to his
sons-in-law, who were pledged to
marry[a] his daughters. He said,
"Hurry and get out of this place,
because the LORD is about to destroy the city![l]" But his sons-in-
law thought he was joking.[m]
15 With the coming of dawn, the
angels urged Lot, saying, "Hurry!
Take your wife and your two
daughters who are here, or you will
be swept away[n] when the city is
punished.[o]"
16 When he hesitated, the men
grasped his hand and the hands of
his wife and of his two daughters
and led them safely out of the city,
for the LORD was merciful to them.
17 As soon as they had brought them
out, one of them said, "Flee for
your lives![p] Don't look back,[q] and
don't stop anywhere in the plain!
Flee to the mountains or you will be
swept away!"

18:32
x Jdg 6:39
y Jer 5:1
19:1
a Ge 18:22
b Ge 18:1
19:2
c Ge 18:4
Lk 7:44
19:3
d Ge 18:6
19:5
e Jdg 19:22
Isa 3:9
Ro 1:24-27
19:6
f Jdg 19:23
19:8
g Jdg 19:24
19:9
h Ex 2:14
Ac 7:27
19:11
i Dt 28:28-29
2Ki 6:18
Ac 13:11
19:12
j Ge 7:1
19:13
k 1Ch 21:15
19:14
l Nu 16:21
m Ex 9:21
Lk 17:28
19:15
n Nu 16:26
o Rev 18:4
19:17
p Jer 48:6
q ver 26

a14 Or *were married to*

18But Lot said to them, "No, my lords,[b] please! 19Your[c] servant has found favour in your[c] eyes, and you[c] have shown great kindness to me in sparing my life. But I can't flee to the mountains; this disaster will overtake me, and I'll die. 20Look, here is a town near enough to run to, and it is small. Let me flee to it—it is very small, isn't it? Then my life will be spared."

21He said to him, "Very well, I will grant this request too; I will not overthrow the town you speak of. 22But flee there quickly, because I cannot do anything until you reach it." (That is why the town was called Zoar.[d])

23By the time Lot reached Zoar, the sun had risen over the land. 24Then the LORD rained down burning sulphur on Sodom and Gomorrah[r]—from the LORD out of the heavens.[s] 25Thus he overthrew those cities and the entire plain, including all those living in the cities—and also the vegetation in the land.[t] 26But Lot's wife looked back,[u] and she became a pillar of salt.[v]

27Early the next morning Abraham got up and returned to the place where he had stood before the LORD.[w] 28He looked down towards Sodom and Gomorrah, towards all the land of the plain, and he saw dense smoke rising from the land, like smoke from a furnace.[x]

29So when God destroyed the cities of the plain, he remembered Abraham, and he brought Lot out of the catastrophe[y] that overthrew the cities where Lot had lived.

Lot and His Daughters

30Lot and his two daughters left Zoar and settled in the mountains,[z] for he was afraid to stay in Zoar. He and his two daughters lived in a cave. 31One day the older daughter said to the younger, "Our father is old, and there is no man around here to lie with us, as is the custom all over the earth. 32Let's get our father to drink wine and then lie with him and preserve our family line through our father."

33That night they got their father to drink wine, and the older daughter went in and lay with him. He was not aware of it when she lay down or when she got up.

34The next day the older daughter said to the younger, "Last night I lay with my father. Let's get him to drink wine again tonight, and you go in and lie with him so we can preserve our family line through our father." 35So they got their father to drink wine that night also, and the younger daughter went and lay with him. Again he was not aware of it when she lay down or when she got up.

36So both of Lot's daughters became pregnant by their father. 37The older daughter had a son, and she named him Moab;[e] he is the father of the Moabites[a] of today. 38The younger daughter also had a son, and she named him Ben-Ammi;[f] he is the father of the Ammonites[b] of today.

Abraham and Abimelech

20:1–18Ref Ge 12:10–20; 26:1–11

20 Now Abraham moved on from there[a] into the region of the Negev and lived between Kadesh and Shur. For a while he stayed in Gerar,[b] 2and there Abraham said of his wife Sarah, "She is my sister.[c]" Then Abimelech king of Gerar sent for Sarah and took her.[d]

3But God came to Abimelech in a dream[e] one night and said to him, "You are as good as dead because of the woman you have taken; she is a married woman."[f]

19:24 r Dt 29:23; Isa 1:9; Isa 13:19; s Lk 17:29; 2Pe 2:6; Jude 7
19:25 t Ps 107:34; Eze 16:48
19:26 u ver 17; v Lk 17:32
19:27 w Ge 18:22
19:28 x Rev 9:2; Rev 18:9
19:29 y 2Pe 2:7
19:30 z ver 19
19:37 a Dt 2:9
19:38 b Dt 2:19
20:1 a Ge 18:1; b Ge 26:1,6,17
20:2 c ver 12; Ge 12:13; Ge 26:7; d Ge 12:15
20:3 e Job 33:15; Mt 27:19; f Ps 105:14

b18 Or *No, Lord*; or *No, my lord*
c19 The Hebrew is singular.
d22 *Zoar* means *small.*
e37 *Moab* sounds like the Hebrew for *from father.*
f38 *Ben-Ammi* means *son of my people.*

4Now Abimelech had not gone
near her, so he said, "Lord, will you
destroy an innocent nation?[g] 5Did
he not say to me, 'She is my sister,'
and didn't she also say, 'He is my
brother'? I have done this with a
clear conscience and clean hands."
6Then God said to him in the
dream, "Yes, I know you did this
with a clear conscience, and so I
have kept[h] you from sinning
against me. That is why I did not let
you touch her. 7Now return the
man's wife, for he is a prophet, and
he will pray for you[i] and you will
live. But if you do not return her,
you may be sure that you and all
yours will die."
8Early the next morning Abimelech summoned all his officials,
and when he told them all that had
happened, they were very much
afraid. 9Then Abimelech called
Abraham in and said, "What have
you done to us? How have I
wronged you that you have brought
such great guilt upon me and my
kingdom? You have done things to
me that should not be done.[j]"
10And Abimelech asked Abraham,
"What was your reason for doing
this?"
11Abraham replied, "I said to myself, 'There is surely no fear of
God[k] in this place, and they will
kill me because of my wife.'[l] 12Be-
sides, she really is my sister, the
daughter of my father though not
of my mother; and she became my
wife. 13And when God caused me to
wander from my father's household, I said to her, 'This is how you
can show your love to me: Everywhere we go, say of me, "He is my
brother." ' "
14Then Abimelech brought sheep
and cattle and male and female
slaves and gave them to Abraham,[m] and he returned Sarah
his wife to him. 15And Abimelech
said, "My land is before you; live
wherever you like."[n]
16To Sarah he said, "I am giving
your brother a thousand shekels[a]

20:4 *g* Ge 18:25
20:6 *h* 1Sa 25:26,34
20:7 *i* ver 17; 1Sa 7:5; Job 42:8
20:9 *j* Ge 12:18; Ge 26:10; Ge 34:7
20:11 *k* Ge 42:18; Ps 36:1; *l* Ge 12:12; Ge 26:7
20:14 *m* Ge 12:16
20:15 *n* Ge 13:9
20:17 *o* Job 42:9
20:18 *p* Ge 12:17
21:1 *a* 1Sa 2:21; *b* Ge 8:1; Ge 17:16,21; Gal 4:23
21:2 *c* Ge 17:19; *d* Gal 4:22; Heb 11:11
21:3 *e* Ge 17:19
21:4 *f* Ge 17:10,12; Ac 7:8
21:6 *g* Ge 17:17; Isa 54:1
21:9 *h* Ge 16:15; *i* Gal 4:29
21:10 *j* Gal 4:30*
21:11 *k* Ge 17:18

of silver. This is to cover the
offence against you before all
who are with you; you are completely vindicated."
17Then Abraham prayed to
God,[o] and God healed Abimelech,
his wife and his slave girls so they
could have children again, 18for the
LORD had closed up every womb in
Abimelech's household because of
Abraham's wife Sarah.[p]

The Birth of Isaac

21 Now the LORD was gracious
to Sarah[a] as he had said,
and the LORD did for Sarah what he
had promised.[b] 2Sarah became
pregnant and bore a son[c] to Abraham in his old age,[d] at the very
time God had promised him. 3Abra-
ham gave the name Isaac[a][e] to the
son Sarah bore him. 4When his son
Isaac was eight days old, Abraham
circumcised him,[f] as God commanded him. 5Abraham was a hundred years old when his son Isaac
was born to him.
6Sarah said, "God has brought
me laughter,[g] and everyone who
hears about this will laugh with
me." 7And she added, "Who would
have said to Abraham that Sarah
would nurse children? Yet I have
borne him a son in his old age."

Hagar and Ishmael Sent Away

8The child grew and was weaned,
and on the day Isaac was weaned
Abraham held a great feast. 9But
Sarah saw that the son whom Hagar the Egyptian had borne to
Abraham[h] was mocking,[i] 10and
she said to Abraham, "Get rid of
that slave woman and her son, for
that slave woman's son will never
share in the inheritance with my
son Isaac."[j]
11The matter distressed Abraham greatly because it concerned
his son.[k] 12But God said to him,

[a]16 That is, about 25 pounds (about 11.5 kilograms) [a]3 *Isaac* means *he laughs.*

"Do not be so distressed about the
boy and your maidservant. Listen
to whatever Sarah tells you, because it is through Isaac that your
offspring[b] will be reckoned.[l] 13I
will make the son of the maidservant into a nation[m] also, because he is your offspring."
14Early the next morning Abraham took some food and a skin of
water and gave them to Hagar. He
set them on her shoulders and then
sent her off with the boy. She went
on her way and wandered in the
desert of Beersheba.[n]
15When the water in the skin was
gone, she put the boy under one of
the bushes. 16Then she went off and
sat down nearby, about a bow-shot
away, for she thought, "I cannot
watch the boy die." And as she sat
there nearby, she[c] began to sob.
17God heard the boy crying,[o] and
the angel of God called to Hagar
from heaven and said to her, "What
is the matter, Hagar? Do not be
afraid; God has heard the boy
crying as he lies there. 18Lift the
boy up and take him by the hand,
for I will make him into a great
nation.[p]"
19Then God opened her eyes[q]
and she saw a well of water. So she
went and filled the skin with water
and gave the boy a drink.
20God was with the boy[r] as he
grew up. He lived in the desert and
became an archer. 21While he was
living in the Desert of Paran, his
mother got a wife for him[s] from
Egypt.

The Treaty at Beersheba

22At that time Abimelech and
Phicol the commander of his forces
said to Abraham, "God is with you
in everything you do. 23Now
swear[t] to me here before God that
you will not deal falsely with me or
my children or my descendants.
Show to me and the country where
you are living as an alien the same
kindness I have shown to you."
24Abraham said, "I swear it."
25Then Abraham complained to
Abimelech about a well of water
that Abimelech's servants had
seized.[u] 26But Abimelech said, "I
don't know who has done this. You
did not tell me, and I heard about it
only today."
27So Abraham brought sheep and
cattle and gave them to Abimelech,
and the two men made a treaty.[v]
28Abraham set apart seven ewe
lambs from the flock, 29and Abimelech asked Abraham, "What is the
meaning of these seven ewe lambs
you have set apart by themselves?"
30He replied, "Accept these
seven lambs from my hand as a
witness[w] that I dug this well."
31So that place was called Beersheba,[d][x] because the two men
swore an oath there.
32After the treaty had been made
at Beersheba, Abimelech and Phicol the commander of his forces returned to the land of the Philistines.
33Abraham planted a tamarisk tree
in Beersheba, and there he called
upon the name of the LORD,[y] the
Eternal God.[z] 34And Abraham
stayed in the land of the Philistines
for a long time.

Abraham Tested

22 Some time later God
tested[a] Abraham. He said
to him, "Abraham!"
"Here I am," he replied.
2Then God said, "Take your
son[b], your only son, Isaac, whom
you love, and go to the region of
Moriah.[c] Sacrifice him there as a
burnt offering on one of the mountains I will tell you about."
3Early the next morning Abraham got up and saddled his donkey.
He took with him two of his servants and his son Isaac. When he
had cut enough wood for the burnt
offering, he set out for the place

21:12 *l* Ro 9:7* Heb 11:18*
21:13 *m* ver 18
21:14 *n* ver 31,32
21:17 *o* Ex 3:7
21:18 *p* ver 13
21:19 *q* Nu 22:31
21:20 *r* Ge 26:3,24 Ge 28:15 Ge 39:2,21,23
21:21 *s* Ge 24:4,38
21:23 *t* ver 31 Jos 2:12
21:25 *u* Ge 26:15,18, 20-22
21:27 *v* Ge 26:28,31
21:30 *w* Ge 31:44,47, 48,50,52
21:31 *x* Ge 26:33
21:33 *y* Ge 4:26 *z* Dt 33:27
22:1 *a* Dt 8:2,16 Heb 11:17 Jas 1:12-13
22:2 *b* ver 12,16 Jn 3:16 Heb 11:17 1Jn 4:9 *c* 2Ch 3:1

[b]12 Or *seed* [c]16 Hebrew; Septuagint *the child*
[d]31 *Beersheba* can mean *well of seven* or *well of the oath.*

God had told him about. [4]On the
third day Abraham looked up and
saw the place in the distance. [5]He
said to his servants, "Stay here
with the donkey while I and the boy
go over there. We will worship and
then we will come back to you."
[6]Abraham took the wood for the
burnt offering and placed it on his
son Isaac,[d] and he himself carried
the fire and the knife. As the two
of them went on together, [7]Isaac
spoke up and said to his father
Abraham, "Father?"
"Yes, my son?" Abraham replied.
"The fire and wood are here,"
Isaac said, "but where is the lamb[e]
for the burnt offering?"
[8]Abraham answered, "God himself will provide the lamb for the
burnt offering, my son." And the
two of them went on together.
[9]When they reached the place
God had told him about, Abraham
built an altar there and arranged
the wood on it. He bound his son
Isaac and laid him on the altar,[f] on
top of the wood. [10]Then he reached
out his hand and took the knife to
slay his son. [11]But the angel of the
LORD called out to him from
heaven, "Abraham! Abraham!"
"Here I am," he replied.
[12]"Do not lay a hand on the boy,"
he said. "Do not do anything to him.
Now I know that you fear God,[g] because you have not withheld from
me your son, your only son.[h]"
[13]Abraham looked up and there
in a thicket he saw a ram[a] caught
by its horns. He went over and took
the ram and sacrificed it as a burnt
offering instead of his son.[i] [14]So
Abraham called that place The
LORD Will Provide. And to this day
it is said, "On the mountain of the
LORD it will be provided.[j]"
[15]The angel of the LORD called to
Abraham from heaven a second
time [16]and said, "I swear by myself,[k] declares the LORD, that because you have done this and have
not withheld your son, your only
son, [17]I will surely bless you and
make your descendants[l] as numerous as the stars in the sky[m] and
as the sand on the seashore.[n] Your
descendants will take possession of
the cities of their enemies,[o] [18]and
through your offspring[b] all nations on earth will be blessed,[p] because you have obeyed me."[q]
[19]Then Abraham returned to his
servants, and they set off together
for Beersheba. And Abraham
stayed in Beersheba.

Nahor's Sons

[20]Some time later Abraham was
told, "Milcah is also a mother; she
has borne sons to your brother Nahor:[r] [21]Uz the firstborn, Buz his
brother, Kemuel (the father of
Aram), [22]Kesed, Hazo, Pildash, Jid-
laph and Bethuel." [23]Bethuel became the father of Rebekah.[s]
Milcah bore these eight sons to
Abraham's brother Nahor. [24]His
concubine, whose name was Reu-
mah, also had sons: Tebah, Gaham,
Tahash and Maacah.

The Death of Sarah

23 Sarah lived to be a hundred
and twenty-seven years
old. [2]She died at Kiriath Arba[a]
(that is, Hebron)[b] in the land of Canaan, and Abraham went to mourn
for Sarah and to weep over her.
[3]Then Abraham rose from beside
his dead wife and spoke to the Hittites.[a] He said, [4]"I am an alien and
a stranger[c] among you. Sell me
some property for a burial site here
so that I can bury my dead."
[5]The Hittites replied to Abraham, [6]"Sir, listen to us. You are a
mighty prince[d] among us. Bury
your dead in the choicest of our
tombs. None of us will refuse you
his tomb for burying your dead."
[7]Then Abraham rose and bowed

22:6 d Jn 19:17
22:7 e Lev 1:10
22:9 f Heb 11:17-19; Jas 2:21
22:12 g 1Sa 15:22; Jas 2:21-22; h ver 2; Jn 3:16
22:13 i Ro 8:32
22:14 j ver 8
22:16 k Lk 1:73; Heb 6:13
22:17 l Heb 6:14*; m Ge 15:5; n Ge 26:24; Ge 32:12; o Ge 24:60
22:18 p Ge 12:2,3; Ac 3:25*; Gal 3:8*; q ver 10
22:20 r Ge 11:29
22:23 s Ge 24:15
23:2 a Jos 14:15; b ver 19; Ge 13:18
23:4 c Ge 17:8; 1Ch 29:15; Ps 105:12; Heb 11:9,13
23:6 d Ge 14:14-16; Ge 24:35

[a] *13* Many manuscripts of the Masoretic Text, Samaritan Pentateuch, Septuagint and Syriac; most manuscripts of the Masoretic Text *a ram behind ⌞him⌟* [b] *18* Or *seed* [a] *3* Or *the sons of Heth*; also in verses 5, 7, 10, 16, 18 and 20

down before the people of the land, the Hittites. 8He said to them, "If you are willing to let me bury my dead, then listen to me and intercede with Ephron son of Zohar[e] on my behalf 9so that he will sell me the cave of Machpelah, which belongs to him and is at the end of his field. Ask him to sell it to me for the full price as a burial site among you."

10Ephron the Hittite was sitting among his people and he replied to Abraham in the hearing of all the Hittites who had come to the gate[f] of his city. 11"No, my lord," he said. "Listen to me; I give[b][g] you the field, and I give[b] you the cave that is in it. I give[b] it to you in the presence of my people. Bury your dead."

12Again Abraham bowed down before the people of the land 13and he said to Ephron in their hearing, "Listen to me, if you will. I will pay the price of the field. Accept it from me so that I can bury my dead there."

14Ephron answered Abraham, 15"Listen to me, my lord; the land is worth four hundred shekels[c] of silver,[h] but what is that between me and you? Bury your dead."

16Abraham agreed to Ephron's terms and weighed out for him the price he had named in the hearing of the Hittites: four hundred shekels of silver,[i] according to the weight current among the merchants.

17So Ephron's field in Machpelah near Mamre[j]—both the field and the cave in it, and all the trees within the borders of the field—was legally made over 18to Abraham as his property in the presence of all the Hittites who had come to the gate of the city. 19Afterwards Abraham buried his wife Sarah in the cave in the field of Machpelah near Mamre (which is at Hebron) in the land of Canaan. 20So the field and the cave in it were legally made over[k] to Abraham by the Hittites as a burial site.

Isaac and Rebekah

24 Abraham was now old and well advanced in years, and the LORD had blessed him in every way.[a] 2He said to the chief[a] servant in his household, the one in charge of all that he had,[b] "Put your hand under my thigh.[c] 3I want you to swear by the LORD, the God of heaven and the God of earth,[d] that you will not get a wife for my son[e] from the daughters of the Canaanites,[f] among whom I am living, 4but will go to my country and my own relatives[g] and get a wife for my son Isaac."

5The servant asked him, "What if the woman is unwilling to come back with me to this land? Shall I then take your son back to the country you came from?"

6"Make sure that you do not take my son back there," Abraham said. 7"The LORD, the God of heaven, who brought me out of my father's household and my native land and who spoke to me and promised me on oath, saying, 'To your offspring[b][h] I will give this land'[i]—he will send his angel before you[j] so that you can get a wife for my son from there. 8If the woman is unwilling to come back with you, then you will be released from this oath of mine. Only do not take my son back there." 9So the servant put his hand under the thigh[k] of his master Abraham and swore an oath to him concerning this matter.

10Then the servant took ten of his master's camels and left, taking with him all kinds of good things from his master. He set out for Aram Naharaim[c] and made his way to the town of Nahor. 11He made the camels kneel down near the well[l] outside the town; it was

23:8 *e* Ge 25:9
23:10 *f* Ge 34:20-24; Ru 4:4
23:11 *g* 2Sa 24:23
23:15 *h* Eze 45:12
23:16 *i* Jer 32:9; Zec 11:12
23:17 *j* Ge 25:9; Ge 49:30-32; Ge 50:13; Ac 7:16
23:20 *k* Jer 32:10
24:1 *a* ver 35
24:2 *b* Ge 39:4-6 *c* ver 9; Ge 47:29
24:3 *d* Ge 14:19 *e* Ge 28:1; Dt 7:3 *f* Ge 10:15-19
24:4 *g* Ge 12:1; Ge 28:2
24:7 *h* Gal 3:16* *i* Ge 12:7; Ge 13:15 *j* Ex 23:20,23
24:9 *k* ver 2
24:11 *l* Ex 2:15

b*11* Or *sell* c*15* That is, about 10 pounds (about 4.5 kilograms) a*2* Or *oldest* b*7* Or *seed*
c*10* That is, North-west Mesopotamia

towards evening, the time the women go out to draw water.[m]

12Then he prayed, "O LORD, God of my master Abraham,[n] give me success today, and show kindness to my master Abraham. 13See, I am standing beside this spring, and the daughters of the townspeople are coming out to draw water. 14May it be that when I say to a girl, 'Please let down your jar that I may have a drink,' and she says, 'Drink, and I'll water your camels too'—let her be the one you have chosen for your servant Isaac. By this I will know[o] that you have shown kindness to my master."

15Before he had finished praying,[p] Rebekah[q] came out with her jar on her shoulder. She was the daughter of Bethuel son of Milcah,[r] who was the wife of Abraham's brother Nahor.[s] 16The girl was very beautiful,[t] a virgin; no man had ever lain with her. She went down to the spring, filled her jar and came up again.

17The servant hurried to meet her and said, "Please give me a little water from your jar."

18"Drink,[u] my lord," she said, and quickly lowered the jar to her hands and gave him a drink.

19After she had given him a drink, she said, "I'll draw water for your camels too,[v] until they have finished drinking." 20So she quickly emptied her jar into the trough, ran back to the well to draw more water, and drew enough for all his camels. 21Without saying a word, the man watched her closely to learn whether or not the LORD had made his journey successful.[w]

22When the camels had finished drinking, the man took out a gold nose ring[x] weighing a beka[d] and two gold bracelets weighing ten shekels.[e] 23Then he asked, "Whose daughter are you? Please tell me, is there room in your father's house for us to spend the night?"

24She answered him, "I am the daughter of Bethuel, the son that Milcah bore to Nahor.[y]" 25And she added, "We have plenty of straw and fodder, as well as room for you to spend the night."

26Then the man bowed down and worshipped the LORD,[z] 27saying, "Praise be to the LORD,[a] the God of my master Abraham, who has not abandoned his kindness and faithfulness[b] to my master. As for me, the LORD has led me on the journey[c] to the house of my master's relatives."[d]

28The girl ran and told her mother's household about these things. 29Now Rebekah had a brother named Laban,[e] and he hurried out to the man at the spring. 30As soon as he had seen the nose ring, and the bracelets on his sister's arms, and had heard Rebekah tell what the man said to her, he went out to the man and found him standing by the camels near the spring. 31"Come, you who are blessed by the LORD,"[f] he said. "Why are you standing out here? I have prepared the house and a place for the camels."

32So the man went to the house, and the camels were unloaded. Straw and fodder were brought for the camels, and water for him and his men to wash their feet.[g] 33Then food was set before him, but he said, "I will not eat until I have told you what I have to say."

"Then tell us," ⌞Laban⌟ said.

34So he said, "I am Abraham's servant. 35The LORD has blessed my master abundantly,[h] and he has become wealthy. He has given him sheep and cattle, silver and gold, menservants and maidservants, and camels and donkeys.[i] 36My master's wife Sarah has borne him a son in her[f] old age,[j] and he has given him everything he owns.[k] 37And my master made me swear an oath, and said, 'You must not get

24:11 m ver 13; 1Sa 9:11
24:12 n ver 27,42,48; Ge 26:24; Ex 3:6,15,16
24:14 o Jdg 6:17,37
24:15 p ver 45; q Ge 22:23; r Ge 22:20; s Ge 11:29
24:16 t Ge 26:7
24:18 u ver 14
24:19 v ver 14
24:21 w ver 12
24:22 x ver 47
24:24 y ver 15
24:26 z ver 48,52; Ex 4:31
24:27 a Ex 18:10; Ru 4:14; 1Sa 25:32; b ver 49; Ge 32:10; Ps 98:3; c ver 21; d ver 12,48
24:29 e ver 4; Ge 29:5,12,13
24:31 f Ge 26:29; Ru 3:10; Ps 115:15
24:32 g Ge 43:24; Jdg 19:21
24:35 h ver 1; i Ge 13:2
24:36 j Ge 21:2,10; k Ge 25:5

[d]22 That is, about 1/5 ounce (about 6 grams)
[e]22 That is, about 4 ounces (about 115 grams)
[f]36 Or *his*

a wife for my son from the daughters of the Canaanites, in whose
land I live,[l] 38but go to my father's
family and to my own clan, and get
a wife for my son.'[m]
39"Then I asked my master,
'What if the woman will not come
back with me?'[n]
40"He replied, 'The LORD, before
whom I have walked, will send his
angel with you[o] and make your
journey a success, so that you can
get a wife for my son from my own
clan and from my father's family.
41Then, when you go to my clan,
you will be released from my oath
even if they refuse to give her to
you—you will be released from my
oath.'[p]
42"When I came to the spring today, I said, 'O LORD, God of my
master Abraham, if you will, please
grant success[q] to the journey on
which I have come. 43See, I am
standing beside this spring;[r] if a
maiden comes out to draw water
and I say to her, "Please let me
drink a little water from your
jar,"[s] 44and if she says to me,
"Drink, and I'll draw water for
your camels too," let her be the one
the LORD has chosen for my master's son.'
45"Before I finished praying in
my heart,[t] Rebekah came out,
with her jar on her shoulder.[u] She
went down to the spring and drew
water, and I said to her, 'Please
give me a drink.'[v]
46"She quickly lowered her jar
from her shoulder and said, 'Drink,
and I'll water your camels too.'[w] So
I drank, and she watered the
camels also.
47"I asked her, 'Whose daughter
are you?'[x]
"She said, 'The daughter of Bethuel son of Nahor, whom Milcah
bore to him.'[y]
"Then I put the ring in her nose
and the bracelets on her arms,[z]
48and I bowed down and worshipped the LORD.[a] I praised
the LORD, the God of my master
Abraham, who had led me on the
right road to get the granddaughter
of my master's brother for his son.[b]
49Now if you will show kindness
and faithfulness[c] to my master,
tell me; and if not, tell me, so I may
know which way to turn."
50Laban and Bethuel answered,
"This is from the LORD;[d] we can
say nothing to you one way or the
other.[e] 51Here is Rebekah; take
her and go, and let her become the
wife of your master's son, as the
LORD has directed."
52When Abraham's servant heard
what they said, he bowed down to
the ground before the LORD.[f]
53Then the servant brought out
gold and silver jewellery and articles of clothing and gave them to
Rebekah; he also gave costly
gifts[g] to her brother and to her
mother. 54Then he and the men who
were with him ate and drank and
spent the night there.
When they got up the next morning, he said, "Send me on my way[h]
to my master."
55But her brother and her mother
replied, "Let the girl remain with
us ten days or so; then you[g] may
go."
56But he said to them, "Do not detain me, now that the LORD has
granted success to my journey.
Send me on my way so I may go to
my master."
57Then they said, "Let's call the
girl and ask her about it." 58So they
called Rebekah and asked her,
"Will you go with this man?"
"I will go," she said.
59So they sent their sister Rebekah on her way, along with her
nurse[i] and Abraham's servant and
his men. 60And they blessed Rebekah and said to her,

"Our sister, may you increase
to thousands upon thousands;[j]
may your offspring possess
the gates of their enemies."[k]

24:37 l ver 3
24:38 m ver 4
24:39 n ver 5
24:40 o ver 7
24:41 p ver 8
24:42 q ver 12
24:43 r ver 13; s ver 14
24:45 t 1Sa 1:13; u ver 15; v ver 17
24:46 w ver 18-19
24:47 x ver 23; y ver 24; z Eze 16:11-12
24:48 a ver 26; b ver 27
24:49 c Ge 47:29; Jos 2:14
24:50 d Ps 118:23; e Ge 31:7,24, 29,42
24:52 f ver 26
24:53 g ver 10,22
24:54 h ver 56,59
24:59 i Ge 35:8
24:60 j Ge 17:16; k Ge 22:17

g55 Or *she*

the people: "Anyone who molests[m] this man or his wife shall surely be put to death."

12 Isaac planted crops in that land and the same year reaped a hundredfold, because the LORD blessed him.[n] 13 The man became rich, and his wealth continued to grow until he became very wealthy.[o] 14 He had so many flocks and herds and servants[p] that the Philistines envied him.[q] 15 So all the wells[r] that his father's servants had dug in the time of his father Abraham, the Philistines stopped up,[s] filling them with earth.

16 Then Abimelech said to Isaac, "Move away from us; you have become too powerful for us.[t]"

17 So Isaac moved away from there and encamped in the Valley of Gerar and settled there. 18 Isaac reopened the wells[u] that had been dug in the time of his father Abraham, which the Philistines had stopped up after Abraham died, and he gave them the same names his father had given them.

19 Isaac's servants dug in the valley and discovered a well of fresh water there. 20 But the herdsmen of Gerar quarrelled with Isaac's herdsmen and said, "The water is ours!"[v] So he named the well Esek,[b] because they disputed with him. 21 Then they dug another well, but they quarrelled over that one also; so he named it Sitnah.[c] 22 He moved on from there and dug another well, and no-one quarrelled over it. He named it Rehoboth,[d] saying, "Now the LORD has given us room and we will flourish[w] in the land."

23 From there he went up to Beersheba. 24 That night the LORD appeared to him and said, "I am the God of your father Abraham.[x] Do not be afraid,[y] for I am with you; I will bless you and will increase the number of your descendants[z] for the sake of my servant Abraham."[a]

25 Isaac built an altar[b] there and called on the name of the LORD. There he pitched his tent, and there his servants dug a well.

26 Meanwhile, Abimelech had come to him from Gerar, with Ahuzzath his personal adviser and Phicol the commander of his forces.[c] 27 Isaac asked them, "Why have you come to me, since you were hostile to me and sent me away?[d]"

28 They answered, "We saw clearly that the LORD was with you;[e] so we said, 'There ought to be a sworn agreement between us'—between us and you. Let us make a treaty with you 29 that you will do us no harm, just as we did not molest you but always treated you well and sent you away in peace. And now you are blessed by the LORD."[f]

30 Isaac then made a feast[g] for them, and they ate and drank. 31 Early the next morning the men swore an oath[h] to each other. Then Isaac sent them on their way, and they left him in peace.

32 That day Isaac's servants came and told him about the well they had dug. They said, "We've found water!" 33 He called it Shibah,[e] and to this day the name of the town has been Beersheba.[f][i]

34 When Esau was forty years old,[j] he married Judith daughter of Beeri the Hittite, and also Basemath daughter of Elon the Hittite.[k] 35 They were a source of grief to Isaac and Rebekah.[l]

Jacob Gets Isaac's Blessing

27 When Isaac was old and his eyes were so weak that he could no longer see,[a] he called for Esau his older son[b] and said to him, "My son."

"Here I am," he answered.

[b]20 *Esek* means *dispute.* [c]21 *Sitnah* means *opposition.* [d]22 *Rehoboth* means *room.*
[e]33 *Shibah* can mean *oath* or *seven.*
[f]33 *Beersheba* can mean *well of the oath* or *well of seven.*

26:11 m Ps 105:15
26:12 n ver 3; Job 42:12
26:13 o Pr 10:22
26:14 p Ge 24:36; q Ge 37:11
26:15 r Ge 21:30; s Ge 21:25
26:16 t Ex 1:9
26:18 u Ge 21:30
26:20 v Ge 21:25
26:22 w Ge 17:6; Ex 1:7
26:24 x Ge 24:12; Ex 3:6; y Ge 15:1; z ver 4; a Ge 17:7
26:25 b Ge 12:7,8; Ge 13:4,18; Ps 116:17
26:26 c Ge 21:22
26:27 d ver 16
26:28 e Ge 21:22
26:29 f Ge 24:31; Ps 115:15
26:30 g Ge 19:3
26:31 h Ge 21:31
26:33 i Ge 21:14
26:34 j Ge 25:20; k Ge 28:9; Ge 36:2
26:35 l Ge 27:46
27:1 a Ge 48:10; 1Sa 3:2; b Ge 25:25

2 Isaac said, "I am now an old man
and don't know the day of my
death.[c] 3 Now then, get your weapons—your quiver and bow—and go
out to the open country[d] to hunt
some wild game for me. 4 Prepare
me the kind of tasty food I like and
bring it to me to eat, so that I may
give you my blessing[e] before I
die."

5 Now Rebekah was listening as
Isaac spoke to his son Esau. When
Esau left for the open country to
hunt game and bring it back, 6 Rebekah said to her son Jacob,[f]
"Look, I overheard your father say
to your brother Esau, 7 'Bring me
some game and prepare me some
tasty food to eat, so that I may give
you my blessing in the presence of
the LORD before I die.' 8 Now, my
son, listen carefully and do what I
tell you:[g] 9 Go out to the flock and
bring me two choice young goats,
so that I can prepare some tasty
food for your father, just the way
he likes it. 10 Then take it to your
father to eat, so that he may give
you his blessing before he dies."

11 Jacob said to Rebekah his
mother, "But my brother Esau is a
hairy man,[h] and I'm a man with
smooth skin. 12 What if my father
touches me?[i] I would appear to be
tricking him and would bring down
a curse on myself rather than a
blessing."

13 His mother said to him, "My
son, let the curse fall on me.[j] Just
do what I say;[k] go and get them for
me."

14 So he went and got them and
brought them to his mother, and
she prepared some tasty food, just
the way his father liked it. 15 Then
Rebekah took the best clothes[l] of
Esau her older son, which she had
in the house, and put them on her
younger son Jacob. 16 She also covered his hands and the smooth part
of his neck with the goatskins.
17 Then she handed to her son Jacob
the tasty food and the bread she
had made.

18 He went to his father and said,
"My father."

"Yes, my son," he answered.
"Who is it?"

19 Jacob said to his father, "I am
Esau your firstborn. I have done as
you told me. Please sit up and eat
some of my game so that you may
give me your blessing."[m]

20 Isaac asked his son, "How did
you find it so quickly, my son?"

"The LORD your God gave me
success,[n]" he replied.

21 Then Isaac said to Jacob,
"Come near so I can touch you,[o]
my son, to know whether you really
are my son Esau or not."

22 Jacob went close to his father
Isaac, who touched him and said,
"The voice is the voice of Jacob,
but the hands are the hands of
Esau." 23 He did not recognise him,
for his hands were hairy like those
of his brother Esau;[p] so he blessed
him. 24 "Are you really my son
Esau?" he asked.

"I am," he replied.

25 Then he said, "My son, bring
me some of your game to eat, so
that I may give you my blessing."[q]

Jacob brought it to him and he
ate; and he brought some wine and
he drank. 26 Then his father Isaac
said to him, "Come here, my son,
and kiss me."

27 So he went to him and kissed
him[r]. When Isaac caught the smell
of his clothes,[s] he blessed him and
said,

"Ah, the smell of my son
  is like the smell of a field
  that the LORD has blessed.[t]
28 May God give you of heaven's
    dew[u]
  and of earth's richness[v]—
  an abundance of grain and
    new wine.[w]
29 May nations serve you
  and peoples bow down to
    you.[x]
Be lord over your brothers,
  and may the sons of your
    mother bow down to you.[y]

27:2 c Ge 47:29
27:3 d Ge 25:27
27:4 e ver 10,25,31 Ge 49:28 Dt 33:1 Heb 11:20
27:6 f Ge 25:28
27:8 g ver 13,43
27:11 h Ge 25:25
27:12 i ver 22
27:13 j Mt 27:25 k ver 8
27:15 l ver 27
27:19 m ver 4
27:20 n Ge 24:12
27:21 o ver 12
27:23 p ver 16
27:25 q ver 4
27:27 r Heb 11:20 s SS 4:11 t Ps 65:9-13
27:28 u Dt 33:13 v ver 39 w Ge 45:18 Nu 18:12 Dt 33:28
27:29 x Isa 45:14,23 Isa 49:7,23 y Ge 9:25 Ge 25:23 Ge 37:7

May those who curse you be
cursed
and those who bless you be
blessed.[z]"

30After Isaac finished blessing
him and Jacob had scarcely left his
father's presence, his brother Esau
came in from hunting. 31He too prepared some tasty food and brought
it to his father. Then he said to him,
"My father, sit up and eat some of
my game, so that you may give me
your blessing."[a]

32His father Isaac asked him,
"Who are you?"[b]

"I am your son," he answered,
"your firstborn, Esau."

33Isaac trembled violently and
said, "Who was it, then, that hunted
game and brought it to me? I ate it
just before you came and I blessed
him—and indeed he will be
blessed![c]"

34When Esau heard his father's
words, he burst out with a loud and
bitter cry[d] and said to his father,
"Bless me—me too, my father!"

35But he said, "Your brother
came deceitfully[e] and took your
blessing."

36Esau said, "Isn't he rightly
named Jacob?[a][f] He has deceived
me these two times: He took my
birthright,[g] and now he's taken my
blessing!" Then he asked, "Haven't
you reserved any blessing for me?"

37Isaac answered Esau, "I have
made him lord over you and have
made all his relatives his servants,
and I have sustained him with grain
and new wine.[h] So what can I possibly do for you, my son?"

38Esau said to his father, "Do you
have only one blessing, my father?
Bless me too, my father!" Then
Esau wept aloud.[i]

39His father Isaac answered him,

"Your dwelling will be
away from the earth's
richness,
away from the dew[j] of
heaven above.
40You will live by the sword
and you will serve[k] your
brother.[l]
But when you grow restless,
you will throw his yoke
from off your neck.[m]"

27:29 *z* Ge 12:3; Nu 24:9; Zep 2:8
27:31 *a* ver 4
27:32 *b* ver 18
27:33 *c* ver 29; Ge 28:3,4; Ro 11:29
27:34 *d* Heb 12:17
27:35 *e* Jer 9:4; Jer 12:6
27:36 *f* Ge 25:26; *g* Ge 25:33
27:37 *h* ver 28
27:38 *i* Heb 12:17
27:39 *j* ver 28
27:40 *k* 2Sa 8:14; *l* Ge 25:23; *m* 2Ki 8:20-22
27:41 *n* Ge 37:4; *o* Ge 32:11; *p* Ge 50:4,10; *q* Ob 1:10
27:43 *r* ver 8; *s* Ge 24:29; *t* Ge 11:31
27:44 *u* Ge 31:38,41
27:45 *v* ver 35
27:46 *w* Ge 26:35
28:1 *a* Ge 24:3
28:2 *b* Ge 25:20
28:3 *c* Ge 17:1; *d* Ge 17:6

Jacob Flees to Laban

41Esau held a grudge[n] against
Jacob[o] because of the blessing his
father had given him. He said to
himself, "The days of mourning[p]
for my father are near; then I will
kill my brother Jacob."[q]

42When Rebekah was told what
her older son Esau had said, she
sent for her younger son Jacob and
said to him, "Your brother Esau is
consoling himself with the thought
of killing you. 43Now then, my son,
do what I say:[r] Flee at once to my
brother Laban[s] in Haran.[t] 44Stay
with him for a while[u] until your
brother's fury subsides. 45When
your brother is no longer angry
with you and forgets what you did
to him,[v] I'll send word for you to
come back from there. Why should
I lose both of you in one day?"

46Then Rebekah said to Isaac,
"I'm disgusted with living because
of these Hittite women. If Jacob
takes a wife from among the
women of this land, from Hittite
women like these, my life will not
be worth living."[w]

28 So Isaac called for Jacob
and blessed[a] him and commanded him: "Do not marry a Canaanite woman.[a] 2Go at once to
Paddan Aram,[b] to the house of
your mother's father Bethuel.[b]
Take a wife for yourself there,
from among the daughters of Laban, your mother's brother. 3May
God Almighty[c][c] bless you and
make you fruitful[d] and increase
your numbers until you become a
community of peoples. 4May he
give you and your descendants the

a36 *Jacob* means *he grasps the heel* (figuratively, *he deceives*). a1 Or *greeted* b2 That is, North-west Mesopotamia; also in verses 5, 6 and 7 c3 Hebrew *El-Shaddai*

blessing given to Abraham,[e] so
that you may take possession of the
land where you now live as an
alien,[f] the land God gave to Abraham." 5Then Isaac sent Jacob on
his way, and he went to Paddan
Aram,[g] to Laban son of Bethuel the
Aramean, the brother of Rebekah,[h] who was the mother of
Jacob and Esau.

6Now Esau learned that Isaac had
blessed Jacob and had sent him to
Paddan Aram to take a wife from
there, and that when he blessed
him he commanded him, "Do not
marry a Canaanite woman,"[i] 7and
that Jacob had obeyed his father
and mother and had gone to Paddan
Aram. 8Esau then realised how displeasing the Canaanite women[j]
were to his father Isaac;[k] 9so he
went to Ishmael and married Mahalath, the sister of Nebaioth[l] and
daughter of Ishmael son of Abraham, in addition to the wives he already had.[m]

Jacob's Dream at Bethel

10Jacob left Beersheba and set
out for Haran.[n] 11When he reached
a certain place, he stopped for the
night because the sun had set. Taking one of the stones there, he put
it under his head and lay down to
sleep. 12He had a dream[o] in which
he saw a stairway[d] resting on the
earth, with its top reaching to
heaven, and the angels of God were
ascending and descending on it.[p]
13There above it[e] stood the LORD,[q]
and he said: "I am the LORD, the
God of your father Abraham and
the God of Isaac.[r] I will give you
and your descendants the land[s] on
which you are lying. 14Your descendants will be like the dust of
the earth, and you[t] will spread out
to the west and to the east, to the
north and to the south.[u] All peoples
on earth will be blessed through
you and your offspring.[v] 15I am
with you[w] and will watch over
you[x] wherever you go, and I will
bring you back to this land. I will
not leave you[y] until I have done
what I have promised you."[z]

16When Jacob awoke from his
sleep, he thought, "Surely the LORD
is in this place, and I was not aware
of it." 17He was afraid and said,
"How awesome is this place![a] This
is none other than the house of God;
this is the gate of heaven."

18Early the next morning Jacob
took the stone he had placed under
his head and set it up as a pillar[b]
and poured oil on top of it.[c] 19He
called that place Bethel,[f] though
the city used to be called Luz.[d]

20Then Jacob made a vow,[e] saying, "If God will be with me and will
watch over me[f] on this journey I
am taking and will give me food to
eat and clothes to wear 21so that I
return safely[g] to my father's
house, then the LORD[g] will be my
God[h] 22and[h] this stone that I have
set up as a pillar will be God's
house,[i] and of all that you give me
I will give you a tenth.[j]"

Jacob Arrives in Paddan Aram

29 Then Jacob continued on
his journey and came to
the land of the eastern peoples.[a]
2There he saw a well in the field,
with three flocks of sheep lying
near it because the flocks were
watered from that well. The stone
over the mouth of the well was
large. 3When all the flocks were
gathered there, the shepherds
would roll the stone away from the
well's mouth and water the sheep.
Then they would return the stone
to its place over the mouth of the
well.

4Jacob asked the shepherds, "My
brothers, where are you from?"

"We're from Haran,[b]" they replied.

28:4 e Ge 12:2,3 f Ge 17:8
28:5 g Hos 12:12 h Ge 24:29
28:6 i ver 1
28:8 j Ge 24:3 k Ge 26:35
28:9 l Ge 25:13 m Ge 26:34
28:10 n Ge 11:31
28:12 o Ge 20:3 p Jn 1:51
28:13 q Ge 12:7 Ge 35:7,9 Ge 48:3 r Ge 26:24 s Ge 13:15 Ge 35:12
28:14 t Ge 26:4 u Ge 13:14 v Ge 12:3 Ge 18:18 Ge 22:18 Gal 3:8
28:15 w Ge 26:3 Ge 48:21 x Nu 6:24 Ps 121:5,7-8 y Dt 31:6,8 z Nu 23:19
28:17 a Ex 3:5 Jos 5:15
28:18 b Ge 35:14 c Lev 8:11
28:19 d Jdg 1:23,26
28:20 e Ge 31:13 Jdg 11:30 2Sa 15:8 f ver 15
28:21 g Jdg 11:31 h Dt 26:17
28:22 i Ge 35:7,14 j Ge 14:20 Lev 27:30
29:1 a Jdg 6:3,33
29:4 b Ge 28:10

[d] *12* Or *ladder* [e] *13* Or *There beside him*
[f] *19* *Bethel* means *house of God.*
[g] *20,21* Or *Since God . . . father's house, the LORD*
[h] *21,22* Or *house, and the LORD will be my God,* *22then*

5He said to them, "Do you know
Laban, Nahor's grandson?"
"Yes, we know him," they answered.
6Then Jacob asked them, "Is he
well?"
"Yes, he is," they said, "and here
comes his daughter Rachel with
the sheep."
7"Look," he said, "the sun is still
high; it is not time for the flocks to
be gathered. Water the sheep and
take them back to pasture."
8"We can't," they replied, "until
all the flocks are gathered and the
stone has been rolled away from
the mouth of the well. Then we will
water the sheep."
9While he was still talking with
them, Rachel came with her
father's sheep,[c] for she was a
shepherdess. 10When Jacob saw
Rachel daughter of Laban, his
mother's brother, and Laban's
sheep, he went over and rolled the
stone away from the mouth of the
well and watered his uncle's
sheep.[d] 11Then Jacob kissed Rachel and began to weep aloud.[e]
12He had told Rachel that he was a
relative[f] of her father and a son of
Rebekah. So she ran and told her
father.[g]
13As soon as Laban[h] heard the
news about Jacob, his sister's son,
he hurried to meet him. He embraced him and kissed him and
brought him to his home, and there
Jacob told him all these things.
14Then Laban said to him, "You are
my own flesh and blood."[i]

Jacob Marries Leah and Rachel

After Jacob had stayed with him
for a whole month, 15Laban said to
him, "Just because you are a relative of mine, should you work for
me for nothing? Tell me what your
wages should be."
16Now Laban had two daughters;
the name of the older was Leah, and
the name of the younger was Rachel. 17Leah had weak[a] eyes, but
Rachel was lovely in form, and
beautiful. 18Jacob was in love with
Rachel and said, "I'll work for you
seven years in return for your
younger daughter Rachel."[j]
19Laban said, "It's better that I
give her to you than to some other
man. Stay here with me." 20So
Jacob served seven years to get
Rachel, but they seemed like only
a few days to him because of his
love for her.[k]
21Then Jacob said to Laban,
"Give me my wife. My time is completed, and I want to lie with her.[l]"
22So Laban brought together all
the people of the place and gave a
feast.[m] 23But when evening came,
he took his daughter Leah and gave
her to Jacob, and Jacob lay with
her. 24And Laban gave his servant
girl Zilpah to his daughter as her
maidservant.
25When morning came, there was
Leah! So Jacob said to Laban,
"What is this you have done to
me?[n] I served you for Rachel,
didn't I? Why have you deceived
me?[o]"
26Laban replied, "It is not our
custom here to give the younger
daughter in marriage before the
older one. 27Finish this daughter's
bridal week;[p] then we will give
you the younger one also, in return
for another seven years of work."
28And Jacob did so. He finished
the week with Leah, and then Laban
gave him his daughter Rachel to be
his wife. 29Laban gave his servant
girl Bilhah[q] to his daughter Rachel
as her maidservant.[r] 30Jacob lay
with Rachel also, and he loved Rachel more than Leah.[s] And he
worked for Laban another seven
years.[t]

Jacob's Children

31When the LORD saw that Leah
was not loved,[u] he opened her
womb,[v] but Rachel was barren.

29:9 c Ex 2:16
29:10 d Ex 2:17
29:11 e Ge 33:4
29:12 f Ge 13:8; Ge 14:14,16; g Ge 24:28
29:13 h Ge 24:29
29:14 i Ge 2:23; Jdg 9:2; 2Sa 19:12-13
29:18 j Hos 12:12
29:20 k SS 8:7; Hos 12:12
29:21 l Jdg 15:1
29:22 m Jdg 14:10; Jn 2:1-2
29:25 n Ge 12:18; o Ge 27:36
29:27 p Jdg 14:12
29:29 q Ge 30:3; r Ge 16:1
29:30 s ver 16; t Ge 31:41
29:31 u Dt 21:15-17; v Ge 11:30; Ge 30:1; Ps 127:3

a17 Or *delicate*

32 Leah became pregnant and gave
birth to a son. She named him Reuben,[b] for she said, "It is because
the LORD has seen my misery.[w]
Surely my husband will love me
now."
33 She conceived again, and when
she gave birth to a son she said,
"Because the LORD heard that I am
not loved, he gave me this one too."
So she named him Simeon.[c][x]
34 Again she conceived, and when
she gave birth to a son she said,
"Now at last my husband will become attached to me,[y] because I
have borne him three sons." So he
was named Levi.[d][z]
35 She conceived again, and when
she gave birth to a son she said,
"This time I will praise the LORD."
So she named him Judah.[e][a] Then
she stopped having children.

30 When Rachel saw that she
was not bearing Jacob any
children,[a] she became jealous of
her sister.[b] So she said to Jacob,
"Give me children, or I'll die!"
2 Jacob became angry with her
and said, "Am I in the place of God,
who has kept you from having children?"[c]
3 Then she said, "Here is Bilhah,
my maidservant. Sleep with her so
that she can bear children for me
and that through her I too can build
a family."[d]
4 So she gave him her servant Bilhah as a wife.[e] Jacob slept with
her,[f] 5 and she became pregnant
and bore him a son. 6 Then Rachel
said, "God has vindicated me;[g] he
has listened to my plea and given
me a son." Because of this she
named him Dan.[a][h]
7 Rachel's servant Bilhah conceived again and bore Jacob a
second son. 8 Then Rachel said, "I
have had a great struggle with my
sister, and I have won."[i] So she
named him Naphtali.[b][j]
9 When Leah saw that she had
stopped having children, she took
her maidservant Zilpah and gave
her to Jacob as a wife.[k] 10 Leah's
servant Zilpah bore Jacob a son.
11 Then Leah said, "What good fortune!"[c] So she named him Gad.[d][l]
12 Leah's servant Zilpah bore
Jacob a second son. 13 Then Leah
said, "How happy I am! The women
will call me[m] happy."[n] So she
named him Asher.[e][o]
14 During wheat harvest, Reuben
went out into the fields and found
some mandrake plants,[p] which he
brought to his mother Leah. Rachel
said to Leah, "Please give me some
of your son's mandrakes."
15 But she said to her, "Wasn't it
enough[q] that you took away my
husband? Will you take my son's
mandrakes too?"
"Very well," Rachel said, "he can
sleep with you tonight in return for
your son's mandrakes."
16 So when Jacob came in from
the fields that evening, Leah went
out to meet him. "You must sleep
with me," she said. "I have hired
you with my son's mandrakes." So
he slept with her that night.
17 God listened to Leah,[r] and she
became pregnant and bore Jacob a
fifth son. 18 Then Leah said, "God
has rewarded me for giving my
maidservant to my husband." So
she named him Issachar.[f][s]
19 Leah conceived again and bore
Jacob a sixth son. 20 Then Leah said,
"God has presented me with a precious gift. This time my husband
will treat me with honour, because
I have borne him six sons." So she
named him Zebulun.[g][t]
21 Some time later she gave birth
to a daughter and named her Dinah.
22 Then God remembered Rachel;[u] he listened to her and

29:32 w Ge 16:11; Ge 31:42; Ex 4:31; Dt 26:7; Ps 25:18
29:33 x Ge 34:25; Ge 49:5
29:34 y Ge 30:20; 1Sa 1:2-4; z Ge 49:5-7
29:35 a Ge 49:8; Mt 1:2-3
30:1 a Ge 29:31; 1Sa 1:5-6; b Lev 18:18
30:2 c Ge 16:2; Ge 20:18; Ge 29:31
30:3 d Ge 16:2
30:4 e ver 9,18; f Ge 16:3-4
30:6 g Ps 35:24; Ps 43:1; La 3:59; h Ge 49:16-17
30:8 i Hos 12:3-4; j Ge 49:21
30:9 k ver 4
30:11 l Ge 49:19
30:13 m Ps 127:3; n Pr 31:28; Lk 1:48; o Ge 49:20
30:14 p SS 7:13
30:15 q Nu 16:9,13
30:17 r Ge 25:21
30:18 s Ge 49:14
30:20 t Ge 35:23; Ge 49:13; Mt 4:13
30:22 u Ge 8:1; 1Sa 1:19-20

[b]32 *Reuben* sounds like the Hebrew for *he has seen my misery*; the name means *see, a son.*
[c]33 *Simeon* probably means *one who hears.*
[d]34 *Levi* sounds like and may be derived from the Hebrew for *attached.* [e]35 *Judah* sounds like and may be derived from the Hebrew for *praise.*
[a]6 *Dan* here means *he has vindicated.*
[b]8 *Naphtali* means *my struggle.* [c]11 Or "*A troop is coming!*" [d]11 *Gad* can mean *good fortune* or *a troop.* [e]13 *Asher* means *happy.*
[f]18 *Issachar* sounds like the Hebrew for *reward.*
[g]20 *Zebulun* probably means *honour.*

opened her womb.[v] 23She became
pregnant and gave birth to a son[w]
and said, "God has taken away my
disgrace."[x] 24She named him Joseph,[h][y] and said, "May the LORD
add to me another son."[z]

Jacob's Flocks Increase

25After Rachel gave birth to Joseph, Jacob said to Laban, "Send
me on my way[a] so that I can go
back to my own homeland. 26Give
me my wives and children, for
whom I have served you,[b] and I
will be on my way. You know how
much work I've done for you."

27But Laban said to him, "If I
have found favour in your eyes,
please stay. I have learned by divination that[i] the LORD has blessed
me because of you."[c] 28He added,
"Name your wages,[d] and I will pay
them."

29Jacob said to him, "You know
how I have worked for you[e] and
how your livestock has fared under
my care.[f] 30The little you had before I came has increased greatly,
and the LORD has blessed you wherever I have been. But now, when
may I do something for my own
household?[g]"

31"What shall I give you?" he
asked.

"Don't give me anything," Jacob
replied. "But if you will do this one
thing for me, I will go on tending
your flocks and watching over
them: 32Let me go through all your
flocks today and remove from
them every speckled or spotted
sheep, every dark-coloured lamb
and every spotted or speckled
goat.[h] They will be my wages.
33And my honesty will testify for
me in the future, whenever you
check on the wages you have paid
me. Any goat in my possession that
is not speckled or spotted, or any
lamb that is not dark-coloured, will
be considered stolen."

34"Agreed," said Laban. "Let it be
as you have said." 35That same day

30:22 v Ge 29:31
30:23 w ver 6; x Isa 4:1; Lk 1:25
30:24 y Ge 35:24; Ge 37:2; Ge 39:1; Ge 49:22-26; z Ge 35:17
30:25 a Ge 24:54
30:26 b Ge 29:20,30; Hos 12:12
30:27 c Ge 26:24; Ge 39:3,5
30:28 d Ge 29:15
30:29 e Ge 31:6; f Ge 31:38-40
30:30 g 1Ti 5:8
30:32 h Ge 31:8,12
30:35 i Ge 31:1
30:43 j ver 30; Ge 12:16; Ge 13:2; Ge 24:35; Ge 26:13-14

he removed all the male goats that
were streaked or spotted, and all
the speckled or spotted female
goats (all that had white on them)
and all the dark-coloured lambs,
and he placed them in the care of
his sons.[i] 36Then he put a three-
day journey between himself and
Jacob, while Jacob continued to
tend the rest of Laban's flocks.

37Jacob, however, took fresh-cut
branches from poplar, almond and
plane trees and made white stripes
on them by peeling the bark and ex-
posing the white inner wood of the
branches. 38Then he placed the
peeled branches in all the watering
troughs, so that they would be directly in front of the flocks when
they came to drink. When the
flocks were in heat and came to
drink, 39they mated in front of the
branches. And they bore young
that were streaked or speckled or
spotted. 40Jacob set apart the
young of the flock by themselves,
but made the rest face the streaked
and dark-coloured animals that belonged to Laban. Thus he made separate flocks for himself and did not
put them with Laban's animals.
41Whenever the stronger females
were in heat, Jacob would place the
branches in the troughs in front of
the animals so that they would
mate near the branches, 42but if the
animals were weak, he would not
place them there. So the weak animals went to Laban and the strong
ones to Jacob. 43In this way the man
grew exceedingly prosperous and
came to own large flocks, and
maidservants and menservants,
and camels and donkeys.[j]

Jacob Flees From Laban

31 Jacob heard that Laban's
sons were saying, "Jacob
has taken everything our father
owned and has gained all this
wealth from what belonged to our

[h]24 *Joseph* means *may he add.*
[i]27 Or possibly *have become rich and*

father." 2 And Jacob noticed that Laban's attitude towards him was not what it had been.

3 Then the LORD said to Jacob, "Go back[a] to the land of your fathers and to your relatives, and I will be with you."[b]

4 So Jacob sent word to Rachel and Leah to come out to the fields where his flocks were. 5 He said to them, "I see that your father's attitude towards me is not what it was before, but the God of my father has been with me.[c] 6 You know that I've worked for your father with all my strength,[d] 7 yet your father has cheated me by changing my wages ten times.[e] However, God has not allowed him to harm me.[f] 8 If he said, 'The speckled ones will be your wages,' then all the flocks gave birth to speckled young; and if he said, 'The streaked ones will be your wages,'[g] then all the flocks bore streaked young. 9 So God has taken away your father's livestock and has given them to me.[h]

10 "In the breeding season I once had a dream in which I looked up and saw that the male goats mating with the flock were streaked, speckled or spotted. 11 The angel of God[i] said to me in the dream, 'Jacob.' I answered, 'Here I am.' 12 And he said, 'Look up and see that all the male goats mating with the flock are streaked, speckled or spotted, for I have seen all that Laban has been doing to you.[j] 13 I am the God of Bethel,[k] where you anointed a pillar and where you made a vow to me. Now leave this land at once and go back to your native land.[l]' "

14 Then Rachel and Leah replied, "Do we still have any share in the inheritance of our father's estate? 15 Does he not regard us as foreigners? Not only has he sold us, but he has used up what was paid for us.[m] 16 Surely all the wealth that God took away from our father belongs to us and our children. So do whatever God has told you."

31:3 a ver 13; Ge 32:9 b Ge 21:22; Ge 26:3; Ge 28:15
31:5 c Ge 21:22; Ge 26:3
31:6 d Ge 30:29
31:7 e ver 41; Job 19:3 f ver 52; Ps 37:28; Ps 105:14
31:8 g Ge 30:32
31:9 h ver 1,16; Ge 30:42
31:11 i Ge 16:7; Ge 48:16
31:12 j Ex 3:7
31:13 k Ge 28:10-22 l ver 3; Ge 32:9
31:15 m Ge 29:20
31:18 n Ge 35:27 o Ge 10:19
31:19 p ver 30,32, 34-35; Ge 35:2; Jdg 17:5; 1Sa 19:13; Hos 3:4
31:20 q Ge 27:36 r ver 27
31:21 s Ge 37:25
31:24 t Ge 20:3; Job 33:15 u Ge 24:50
31:26 v Ge 27:36 w 1Sa 30:2-3
31:27 x Ex 15:20 y Ge 4:21
31:28 z ver 55
31:29 a ver 7 b ver 53

17 Then Jacob put his children and his wives on camels, 18 and he drove all his livestock ahead of him, along with all the goods he had accumulated in Paddan Aram,[a] to go to his father Isaac[n] in the land of Canaan.[o]

19 When Laban had gone to shear his sheep, Rachel stole her father's household gods.[p] 20 Moreover, Jacob deceived[q] Laban the Aramean by not telling him he was running away.[r] 21 So he fled with all he had, and crossing the River,[b] he headed for the hill country of Gilead.[s]

Laban Pursues Jacob

22 On the third day Laban was told that Jacob had fled. 23 Taking his relatives with him, he pursued Jacob for seven days and caught up with him in the hill country of Gilead. 24 Then God came to Laban the Aramean in a dream at night and said to him,[t] "Be careful not to say anything to Jacob, either good or bad."[u]

25 Jacob had pitched his tent in the hill country of Gilead when Laban overtook him, and Laban and his relatives camped there too. 26 Then Laban said to Jacob, "What have you done? You've deceived me,[v] and you've carried off my daughters like captives in war.[w] 27 Why did you run off secretly and deceive me? Why didn't you tell me, so that I could send you away with joy and singing to the music of tambourines[x] and harps?[y] 28 You didn't even let me kiss my grandchildren and my daughters goodbye.[z] You have done a foolish thing. 29 I have the power to harm you;[a] but last night the God of your father[b] said to me, 'Be careful not to say anything to Jacob, either good or bad.' 30 Now you have gone off because you longed to return to

[a]18 That is, North-west Mesopotamia
[b]21 That is, the Euphrates

your father's house. But why did
you steal my gods?[c]"
31 Jacob answered Laban, "I was
afraid, because I thought you
would take your daughters away
from me by force. 32 But if you find
anyone who has your gods, he shall
not live.[d] In the presence of our
relatives, see for yourself whether
there is anything of yours here
with me; and if so, take it." Now
Jacob did not know that Rachel had
stolen the gods.
33 So Laban went into Jacob's tent
and into Leah's tent and into the
tent of the two maidservants, but
he found nothing. After he came
out of Leah's tent, he entered Rachel's tent. 34 Now Rachel had taken
the household gods and put them
inside her camel's saddle and was
sitting on them. Laban searched[e]
through everything in the tent but
found nothing.
35 Rachel said to her father,
"Don't be angry, my lord, that I
cannot stand up in your presence;[f]
I'm having my period." So he
searched but could not find the
household gods.
36 Jacob was angry and took Laban to task. "What is my crime?" he
asked Laban. "What sin have I committed that you hunt me down?
37 Now that you have searched
through all my goods, what have
you found that belongs to your
household? Put it here in front of
your relatives[g] and mine, and let
them judge between the two of us.
38 "I have been with you for
twenty years now. Your sheep and
goats have not miscarried, nor
have I eaten rams from your
flocks. 39 I did not bring you animals
torn by wild beasts; I bore the loss
myself. And you demanded payment from me for whatever was
stolen by day or night.[h] 40 This was
my situation: The heat consumed
me in the daytime and the cold at
night, and sleep fled from my eyes.
41 It was like this for the twenty
years I was in your household.
I worked for you fourteen years
for your two daughters[i] and six
years for your flocks, and you
changed my wages ten times.[j] 42 If
the God of my father,[k] the God of
Abraham and the Fear of Isaac,[l]
had not been with me,[m] you would
surely have sent me away empty-
handed. But God has seen my hardship and the toil of my hands,[n]
and last night he rebuked you."
43 Laban answered Jacob, "The
women are my daughters, the children are my children, and the
flocks are my flocks. All you see is
mine. Yet what can I do today about
these daughters of mine, or about
the children they have borne?
44 Come now, let's make a covenant,[o] you and I, and let it serve
as a witness between us."[p]
45 So Jacob took a stone and set it
up as a pillar.[q] 46 He said to his relatives, "Gather some stones." So
they took stones and piled them
in a heap, and they ate there by
the heap. 47 Laban called it Jegar
Sahadutha,[c] and Jacob called it
Galeed.[d]
48 Laban said, "This heap is a witness between you and me today."
That is why it was called Galeed.
49 It was also called Mizpah,[e][r] because he said, "May the LORD keep
watch between you and me when
we are away from each other. 50 If
you ill-treat my daughters or if you
take any wives besides my daughters, even though no-one is with us,
remember that God is a witness[s]
between you and me."
51 Laban also said to Jacob, "Here
is this heap, and here is this pillar[t]
I have set up between you and me.
52 This heap is a witness, and this
pillar is a witness,[u] that I will not
go past this heap to your side to
harm you and that you will not go
past this heap and pillar to my side
to harm me.[v] 53 May the God of

31:30 *c* ver 19; Jdg 18:24
31:32 *d* Ge 44:9
31:34 *e* ver 37; Ge 44:12
31:35 *f* Ex 20:12; Lev 19:3,32
31:37 *g* ver 23
31:39 *h* Ex 22:13
31:41 *i* Ge 29:30 *j* ver 7
31:42 *k* ver 5; Ex 3:15; 1Ch 12:17 *l* ver 53; Isa 8:13 *m* Ps 124:1-2 *n* Ge 29:32
31:44 *o* Ge 21:27; Ge 26:28 *p* Jos 24:27
31:45 *q* Ge 28:18
31:49 *r* Jdg 11:29; 1Sa 7:5-6
31:50 *s* Jer 29:23; Jer 42:5
31:51 *t* Ge 28:18
31:52 *u* Ge 21:30 *v* ver 7; Ge 26:29

c47 The Aramaic *Jegar Sahadutha* means *witness heap.* d47 The Hebrew *Galeed* means *witness heap.* e49 *Mizpah* means *watchtower.*

Abraham[w] and the God of Nahor, the God of their father, judge between us."[x]

So Jacob took an oath[y] in the name of the Fear of his father Isaac.[z] [54]He offered a sacrifice there in the hill country and invited his relatives to a meal. After they had eaten, they spent the night there.

[55]Early the next morning Laban kissed his grandchildren and his daughters[a] and blessed them. Then he left and returned home.[b]

Jacob Prepares to Meet Esau

32 Jacob also went on his way, and the angels of God[a] met him. [2]When Jacob saw them, he said, "This is the camp of God!"[b] So he named that place Mahanaim.[a][c]

[3]Jacob sent messengers ahead of him to his brother Esau[d] in the land of Seir, the country of Edom.[e] [4]He instructed them: "This is what you are to say to my master Esau: 'Your servant Jacob says, I have been staying with Laban and have remained there till now. [5]I have cattle and donkeys, sheep and goats, menservants and maidservants.[f] Now I am sending this message to my lord, that I may find favour in your eyes.[g]' "

[6]When the messengers returned to Jacob, they said, "We went to your brother Esau, and now he is coming to meet you, and four hundred men are with him."[h]

[7]In great fear[i] and distress Jacob divided the people who were with him into two groups,[b] and the flocks and herds and camels as well. [8]He thought, "If Esau comes and attacks one group,[c] the group[c] that is left may escape."

[9]Then Jacob prayed, "O God of my father Abraham, God of my father Isaac,[j] O LORD, who said to me, 'Go back to your country and your relatives, and I will make you prosper,'[k] [10]I am unworthy of all the kindness and faithfulness[l] you have shown your servant. I had only my staff when I crossed this Jordan, but now I have become two groups. [11]Save me, I pray, from the hand of my brother Esau, for I am afraid he will come and attack me,[m] and also the mothers with their children.[n] [12]But you have said, 'I will surely make you prosper and will make your descendants like the sand[o] of the sea, which cannot be counted.[p]' "

[13]He spent the night there, and from what he had with him he selected a gift[q] for his brother Esau: [14]two hundred female goats and twenty male goats, two hundred ewes and twenty rams, [15]thirty female camels with their young, forty cows and ten bulls, and twenty female donkeys and ten male donkeys. [16]He put them in the care of his servants, each herd by itself, and said to his servants, "Go ahead of me, and keep some space between the herds."

[17]He instructed the one in the lead: "When my brother Esau meets you and asks, 'To whom do you belong, and where are you going, and who owns all these animals in front of you?' [18]then you are to say, 'They belong to your servant[r] Jacob. They are a gift sent to my lord Esau, and he is coming behind us.' "

[19]He also instructed the second, the third and all the others who followed the herds: "You are to say the same thing to Esau when you meet him. [20]And be sure to say, 'Your servant Jacob is coming behind us.' " For he thought, "I will pacify him with these gifts I am sending on ahead; later, when I see him, perhaps he will receive me."[s] [21]So Jacob's gifts went on ahead of him, but he himself spent the night in the camp.

31:53 w Ge 28:13 x Ge 16:5 y Ge 21:23,27 z ver 42
31:55 a ver 28 b Ge 18:33 Ge 30:25
32:1 a Ge 16:11 2Ki 6:16-17 Ps 34:7 Ps 91:11 Heb 1:14
32:2 b Ge 28:17 c 2Sa 2:8,29
32:3 d Ge 27:41-42 e Ge 25:30 Ge 36:8,9
32:5 f Ge 12:16 Ge 30:43 g Ge 33:8,10,15
32:6 h Ge 33:1
32:7 i ver 11
32:9 j Ge 28:13 Ge 31:42 k Ge 31:13
32:10 l Ge 24:27
32:11 m Ps 59:2 n Ge 27:41
32:12 o Ge 22:17 p Ge 28:13-15 Hos 1:10 Ro 9:27
32:13 q Ge 43:11,15, 25,26 Pr 18:16
32:18 r Ge 18:3
32:20 s Ge 33:10 Pr 21:14

[a]2 *Mahanaim* means *two camps.* [b]7 Or *camps*; also in verse 10 [c]8 Or *camp*

Jacob Wrestles With God

22That night Jacob got up and
took his two wives, his two maidservants and his eleven sons and
crossed the ford of the Jabbok.[t]
23After he had sent them across the
stream, he sent over all his possessions. 24So Jacob was left alone, and
a man[u] wrestled with him till daybreak. 25When the man saw that
he could not overpower him, he
touched the socket of Jacob's hip[v]
so that his hip was wrenched as he
wrestled with the man. 26Then the
man said, "Let me go, for it is daybreak."

But Jacob replied, "I will not let
you go unless you bless me."[w]

27The man asked him, "What is
your name?"

"Jacob," he answered.

28Then the man said, "Your name
will no longer be Jacob, but Israel,[d][x] because you have struggled with God and with men and
have overcome."

29Jacob said, "Please tell me your
name."[y]

But he replied, "Why do you ask
my name?"[z] Then he blessed[a] him
there.

30So Jacob called the place Peniel,[e] saying, "It is because I saw
God face to face,[b] and yet my life
was spared."

31The sun rose above him as he
passed Peniel,[f] and he was limp-
ing because of his hip. 32Therefore
to this day the Israelites do not eat
the tendon attached to the socket of
the hip, because the socket of
Jacob's hip was touched near the
tendon.

Jacob Meets Esau

33 Jacob looked up and there
was Esau, coming with his
four hundred men;[a] so he divided
the children among Leah, Rachel
and the two maidservants. 2He put
the maidservants and their children in front, Leah and her children next, and Rachel and Joseph
in the rear. 3He himself went on
ahead and bowed down to the
ground[b] seven times as he approached his brother.

4But Esau ran to meet Jacob and
embraced him; he threw his arms
around his neck and kissed him.
And they wept.[c] 5Then Esau
looked up and saw the women and
children. "Who are these with
you?" he asked.

Jacob answered, "They are the
children God has graciously given
your servant.[d]"

6Then the maidservants and
their children approached and
bowed down. 7Next, Leah and her
children came and bowed down.
Last of all came Joseph and Rachel,
and they too bowed down.

8Esau asked, "What do you mean
by all these droves I met?"[e]

"To find favour in your eyes, my
lord,"[f] he said.

9But Esau said, "I already have
plenty, my brother. Keep what you
have for yourself."

10"No, please!" said Jacob. "If I
have found favour in your eyes, accept this gift from me. For to see
your face is like seeing the face of
God,[g] now that you have received
me favourably.[h] 11Please accept
the present[i] that was brought to
you, for God has been gracious
to me[j] and I have all I need." And
because Jacob insisted, Esau
accepted it.

12Then Esau said, "Let us be on
our way; I'll accompany you."

13But Jacob said to him, "My lord
knows that the children are tender
and that I must care for the ewes
and cows that are nursing their
young. If they are driven hard just
one day, all the animals will die.
14So let my lord go on ahead of his
servant, while I move along slowly
at the pace of the droves before me
and that of the children, until I
come to my lord in Seir.[k]"

32:22 [t] Dt 2:37; Dt 3:16; Jos 12:2
32:24 [u] Ge 18:2
32:25 [v] ver 32
32:26 [w] Hos 12:4
32:28 [x] Ge 17:5; Ge 35:10; 1Ki 18:31
32:29 [y] Jdg 13:17 [z] Jdg 13:18 [a] Ge 35:9
32:30 [b] Ge 16:13; Ex 24:11; Nu 12:8; Jdg 6:22; Jdg 13:22
33:1 [a] Ge 32:6
33:3 [b] Ge 18:2; Ge 42:6
33:4 [c] Ge 45:14-15
33:5 [d] Ge 48:9; Ps 127:3; Isa 8:18
33:8 [e] Ge 32:14-16 [f] Ge 24:9; Ge 32:5
33:10 [g] Ge 16:13 [h] Ge 32:20
33:11 [i] 1Sa 25:27 [j] Ge 30:43
33:14 [k] Ge 32:3

[d] 28 *Israel* means *he struggles with God.*
[e] 30 *Peniel* means *face of God.*
[f] 31 Hebrew *Penuel,* a variant of *Peniel*

[15]Esau said, "Then let me leave some of my men with you."

"But why do that?" Jacob asked. "Just let me find favour in the eyes of my lord."[l]

[16]So that day Esau started on his way back to Seir. [17]Jacob, however, went to Succoth,[m] where he built a place for himself and made shelters for his livestock. That is why the place is called Succoth.[a]

[18]After Jacob came from Paddan Aram,[b][n] he arrived safely at the[c] city of Shechem[o] in Canaan and camped within sight of the city. [19]For a hundred pieces of silver,[d] he bought from the sons of Hamor, the father of Shechem,[p] the plot of ground[q] where he pitched his tent. [20]There he set up an altar and called it El Elohe Israel.[e]

Dinah and the Shechemites

34 Now Dinah,[a] the daughter Leah had borne to Jacob, went out to visit the women of the land. [2]When Shechem son of Hamor the Hivite, the ruler of that area, saw her, he took her and raped her. [3]His heart was drawn to Dinah daughter of Jacob, and he loved the girl and spoke tenderly to her. [4]And Shechem said to his father Hamor, "Get me this girl as my wife."

[5]When Jacob heard that his daughter Dinah had been defiled, his sons were in the fields with his livestock; so he kept quiet about it until they came home.

[6]Then Shechem's father Hamor went out to talk with Jacob.[b] [7]Now Jacob's sons had come in from the fields as soon as they heard what had happened. They were filled with grief and fury, because Shechem had done a disgraceful thing in[a] Israel[c] by lying with Jacob's daughter—a thing that should not be done.[d]

[8]But Hamor said to them, "My son Shechem has his heart set on your daughter. Please give her to him as his wife. [9]Intermarry with us; give us your daughters and take our daughters for yourselves. [10]You can settle among us;[e] the land is open to you.[f] Live in it, trade[b] in it,[g] and acquire property in it."

[11]Then Shechem said to Dinah's father and brothers, "Let me find favour in your eyes, and I will give you whatever you ask. [12]Make the price for the bride[h] and the gift I am to bring as great as you like, and I'll pay whatever you ask me. Only give me the girl as my wife."

[13]Because their sister Dinah had been defiled, Jacob's sons replied deceitfully as they spoke to Shechem and his father Hamor. [14]They said to them, "We can't do such a thing; we can't give our sister to a man who is not circumcised.[i] That would be a disgrace to us. [15]We will give our consent to you on one condition only: that you become like us by circumcising all your males.[j] [16]Then we will give you our daughters and take your daughters for ourselves. We'll settle among you and become one people with you. [17]But if you will not agree to be circumcised, we'll take our sister[c] and go."

[18]Their proposal seemed good to Hamor and his son Shechem. [19]The young man, who was the most honoured of all his father's household, lost no time in doing what they said, because he was delighted with Jacob's daughter.[k] [20]So Hamor and his son Shechem went to the gate of their city[l] to speak to their fellow townsmen. [21]"These men are friendly towards us," they said. "Let them live in our land and trade

33:15 *l* Ge 34:11; Ge 47:25; Ru 2:13
33:17 *m* Jos 13:27; Jdg 8:5,6,8, 14,14-16,15, 16; Ps 60:6
33:18 *n* Ge 25:20; Ge 28:2 *o* Jos 24:1; Jdg 9:1
33:19 *p* Jos 24:32 *q* Jn 4:5
34:1 *a* Ge 30:21
34:6 *b* Jdg 14:2-5
34:7 *c* Dt 22:21; Jdg 20:6; 2Sa 13:12 *d* Jos 7:15
34:10 *e* Ge 47:6,27 *f* Ge 13:9; Ge 20:15 *g* Ge 42:34
34:12 *h* Ex 22:16; Dt 22:29; 1Sa 18:25
34:14 *i* Ge 17:14; Jdg 14:3
34:15 *j* Ex 12:48
34:19 *k* ver 3
34:20 *l* Ru 4:1; 2Sa 15:2

[a]17 *Succoth* means *shelters.* [b]18 That is, North-west Mesopotamia [c]18 Or *arrived at Shalem, a* [d]19 Hebrew *hundred kesitahs*; a kesitah was a unit of money of unknown weight and value. [e]20 *El Elohe Israel* can mean *God, the God of Israel* or *mighty is the God of Israel.*
[a]7 Or *against* [b]10 Or *move about freely*; also in verse 21 [c]17 Hebrew *daughter*

in it; the land has plenty of room for them. We can marry their daughters and they can marry ours. 22 But the men will consent to live with us as one people only on the condition that our males be circumcised, as they themselves are. 23 Won't their livestock, their property and all their other animals become ours? So let us give our consent to them, and they will settle among us."

24 All the men who went out of the city gate[m] agreed with Hamor and his son Shechem, and every male in the city was circumcised.

25 Three days later, while all of them were still in pain, two of Jacob's sons, Simeon and Levi, Dinah's brothers, took their swords[n] and attacked the unsuspecting city, killing every male.[o] 26 They put Hamor and his son Shechem to the sword and took Dinah from Shechem's house and left. 27 The sons of Jacob came upon the dead bodies and looted the city where[d] their sister had been defiled. 28 They seized their flocks and herds and donkeys and everything else of theirs in the city and out in the fields. 29 They carried off all their wealth and all their women and children, taking as plunder everything in the houses.

30 Then Jacob said to Simeon and Levi, "You have brought trouble on me by making me a stench[p] to the Canaanites and Perizzites, the people living in this land.[q] We are few in number,[r] and if they join forces against me and attack me, I and my household will be destroyed."

31 But they replied, "Should he have treated our sister like a prostitute?"

Jacob Returns to Bethel

35 Then God said to Jacob, "Go up to Bethel[a] and settle there, and build an altar there to God, who appeared to you when you were fleeing from your brother Esau."[b]

34:24
m Ge 23:10

34:25
n Ge 49:5
o Ge 49:7

34:30
p Ex 5:21
1Sa 13:4
q Ge 13:7
r Ge 46:27
1Ch 16:19
Ps 105:12

35:1
a Ge 28:19
b Ge 27:43

35:2
c Ge 18:19
Jos 24:15
d Ge 31:19
e Ex 19:10,14

35:3
f Ge 32:7
g Ge 28:15, 20-22
Ge 31:3,42

35:4
h Jos 24:25-26

35:5
i Ex 15:16
Ex 23:27
Jos 2:9

35:6
j Ge 28:19
Ge 48:3

35:7
k Ge 28:13

35:8
l Ge 24:59

35:9
m Ge 32:29

35:10
n Ge 17:5

35:11
o Ge 17:1
Ex 6:3
p Ge 28:3
Ge 48:4
q Ge 17:6

35:12
r Ge 13:15
Ge 28:13
s Ge 12:7
Ge 26:3

35:13
t Ge 17:22

2 So Jacob said to his household[c] and to all who were with him, "Get rid of the foreign gods[d] you have with you, and purify yourselves and change your clothes.[e] 3 Then come, let us go up to Bethel, where I will build an altar to God, who answered me in the day of my distress[f] and who has been with me wherever I have gone.[g]" 4 So they gave Jacob all the foreign gods they had and the rings in their ears, and Jacob buried them under the oak at Shechem.[h] 5 Then they set out, and the terror of God[i] fell upon the towns all around them so that no-one pursued them.

6 Jacob and all the people with him came to Luz[j] (that is, Bethel) in the land of Canaan. 7 There he built an altar, and he called the place El Bethel,[a] because it was there that God revealed himself to him[k] when he was fleeing from his brother.

8 Now Deborah, Rebekah's nurse,[l] died and was buried under the oak below Bethel. So it was named Allon Bacuth.[b]

9 After Jacob returned from Paddan Aram,[c] God appeared to him again and blessed him.[m] 10 God said to him, "Your name is Jacob,[d] but you will no longer be called Jacob; your name will be Israel."[e][n] So he named him Israel.

11 And God said to him, "I am God Almighty;[f][o] be fruitful and increase in number. A nation[p] and a community of nations will come from you, and kings will come from your body.[q] 12 The land I gave to Abraham and Isaac I also give to you, and I will give this land to your descendants after you.[r]"[s] 13 Then God went up from him[t] at the place where he had talked with him.

[d] 27 Or *because* [a] 7 *El Bethel* means *God of Bethel.* [b] 8 *Allon Bacuth* means *oak of weeping.* [c] 9 That is, North-west Mesopotamia; also in verse 26 [d] 10 *Jacob* means *he grasps the heel* (figuratively, *he deceives*). [e] 10 *Israel* means *he struggles with God.* [f] 11 Hebrew *El-Shaddai*

[14]Jacob set up a stone pillar at the place where God had talked with him, and he poured out a drink offering on it; he also poured oil on it.[u] [15]Jacob called the place where God had talked with him Bethel.[g][v]

The Deaths of Rachel and Isaac

35:23–26pp 1Ch 2:1–2

[16]Then they moved on from Bethel. While they were still some distance from Ephrath, Rachel began to give birth and had great difficulty. [17]And as she was having great difficulty in childbirth, the midwife said to her, "Don't be afraid, for you have another son."[w] [18]As she breathed her last—for she was dying—she named her son Ben-Oni.[h] But his father named him Benjamin.[i]

[19]So Rachel died and was buried on the way to Ephrath (that is, Bethlehem[x]). [20]Over her tomb Jacob set up a pillar, and to this day that pillar marks Rachel's tomb.[y]

[21]Israel moved on again and pitched his tent beyond Migdal Eder. [22]While Israel was living in that region, Reuben went in and slept with his father's concubine[z] Bilhah,[a] and Israel heard of it.

Jacob had twelve sons:

[23]The sons of Leah:
 Reuben the firstborn[b] of Jacob,
 Simeon, Levi, Judah,[c] Issachar and Zebulun.[d]

[24]The sons of Rachel:
 Joseph[e] and Benjamin.[f]

[25]The sons of Rachel's maidservant Bilhah:
 Dan and Naphtali.[g]

[26]The sons of Leah's maidservant Zilpah:
 Gad[h] and Asher.[i]

These were the sons of Jacob, who were born to him in Paddan Aram.

[27]Jacob came home to his father Isaac in Mamre,[j] near Kiriath Arba[k] (that is, Hebron), where Abraham and Isaac had stayed. [28]Isaac lived a hundred and eighty years.[l] [29]Then he breathed his last and died and was gathered to his people,[m] old and full of years.[n] And his sons Esau and Jacob buried him.[o]

Esau's Descendants

36:10–14pp 1Ch 1:35–37
36:20–28pp 1Ch 1:38–42

36

This is the account of Esau (that is, Edom).[a]

[2]Esau took his wives from the women of Canaan:[b] Adah daughter of Elon the Hittite,[c] and Oholibamah daughter of Anah[d] and granddaughter of Zibeon the Hivite—[3]also Basemath daughter of Ishmael and sister of Nebaioth.

[4]Adah bore Eliphaz to Esau, Basemath bore Reuel,[e] [5]and Oholibamah bore Jeush, Jalam and Korah. These were the sons of Esau, who were born to him in Canaan.

[6]Esau took his wives and sons and daughters and all the members of his household, as well as his livestock and all his other animals and all the goods he had acquired in Canaan,[f] and moved to a land some distance from his brother Jacob. [7]Their possessions were too great for them to remain together; the land where they were staying could not support them both because of their livestock.[g] [8]So Esau[h] (that is, Edom) settled in the hill country of Seir.[i]

[9]This is the account of Esau the father of the Edomites in the hill country of Seir.

[10]These are the names of Esau's sons:
 Eliphaz, the son of Esau's

35:14 *u* Ge 28:18
35:15 *v* Ge 28:19
35:17 *w* Ge 30:24
35:19 *x* Ge 48:7; Ru 1:1,19; Mic 5:2; Mt 2:16
35:20 *y* 1Sa 10:2
35:22 *z* Ge 49:4; 1Ch 5:1 *a* Ge 29:29; Lev 18:8
35:23 *b* Ge 46:8 *c* Ge 29:35 *d* Ge 30:20
35:24 *e* Ge 30:24 *f* ver 18
35:25 *g* Ge 30:8
35:26 *h* Ge 30:11 *i* Ge 30:13
35:27 *j* Ge 13:18; Ge 18:1 *k* Jos 14:15
35:28 *l* Ge 25:7,20
35:29 *m* Ge 25:8; Ge 49:33 *n* Ge 15:15 *o* Ge 25:9
36:1 *a* Ge 25:30
36:2 *b* Ge 28:8-9 *c* Ge 26:34 *d* ver 25
36:4 *e* 1Ch 1:35
36:6 *f* Ge 12:5
36:7 *g* Ge 13:6; Ge 17:8; Ge 28:4
36:8 *h* Dt 2:4 *i* Ge 32:3

[g]15 *Bethel* means *house of God.* [h]18 *Ben-Oni* means *son of my trouble.* [i]18 *Benjamin* means *son of my right hand.*

wife Adah, and Reuel, the son of Esau's wife Basemath.

11 The sons of Eliphaz:[j]
Teman,[k] Omar, Zepho, Gatam and Kenaz.

12 Esau's son Eliphaz also had a concubine named Timna, who bore him Amalek.[l] These were grandsons of Esau's wife Adah.[m]

13 The sons of Reuel:
Nahath, Zerah, Shammah and Mizzah. These were grandsons of Esau's wife Basemath.

14 The sons of Esau's wife Oholibamah daughter of Anah and granddaughter of Zibeon, whom she bore to Esau:
Jeush, Jalam and Korah.

15 These were the chiefs[n] among Esau's descendants:
The sons of Eliphaz the firstborn of Esau:
Chiefs Teman,[o] Omar, Zepho, Kenaz,
16 Korah,[a] Gatam and Amalek. These were the chiefs descended from Eliphaz in Edom; they were grandsons of Adah.[p]

17 The sons of Esau's son Reuel:[q]
Chiefs Nahath, Zerah, Shammah and Mizzah. These were the chiefs descended from Reuel in Edom; they were grandsons of Esau's wife Basemath.

18 The sons of Esau's wife Oholibamah:
Chiefs Jeush, Jalam and Korah. These were the chiefs descended from Esau's wife Oholibamah daughter of Anah.

19 These were the sons of Esau (that is, Edom),[r] and these were their chiefs.

20 These were the sons of Seir the Horite,[s] who were living in the region:
Lotan, Shobal, Zibeon, Anah,
21 Dishon, Ezer and Dishan. These sons of Seir in Edom were Horite chiefs.

22 The sons of Lotan:
Hori and Homam.[b] Timna was Lotan's sister.

23 The sons of Shobal:
Alvan, Manahath, Ebal, Shepho and Onam.

24 The sons of Zibeon:
Aiah and Anah. This is the Anah who discovered the hot springs[c] in the desert while he was grazing the donkeys of his father Zibeon.

25 The children of Anah:
Dishon and Oholibamah daughter of Anah.

26 The sons of Dishon:[d]
Hemdan, Eshban, Ithran and Keran.

27 The sons of Ezer:
Bilhan, Zaavan and Akan.

28 The sons of Dishan:
Uz and Aran.

29 These were the Horite chiefs:
Lotan, Shobal, Zibeon, Anah,
30 Dishon, Ezer and Dishan. These were the Horite chiefs, according to their divisions, in the land of Seir.

The Rulers of Edom

36:31–43pp 1Ch 1:43–54

31 These were the kings who reigned in Edom before any Israelite king[t] reigned:[e]

32 Bela son of Beor became king of Edom. His city was named Dinhabah.

33 When Bela died, Jobab son of Zerah from Bozrah[u] succeeded him as king.

34 When Jobab died, Husham from the land of the

36:11 j ver 15-16; Job 2:11 k Am 1:12; Hab 3:3
36:12 l Ex 17:8,16; Nu 24:20; 1Sa 15:2 m ver 16
36:15 n Ex 15:15 o Job 2:11
36:16 p ver 12
36:17 q 1Ch 1:37
36:19 r Ge 25:30
36:20 s Ge 14:6; Dt 2:12,22; 1Ch 1:38
36:31 t Ge 17:6; 1Ch 1:43
36:33 u Jer 49:13,22

[a] *16* Masoretic Text; Samaritan Pentateuch (see also Gen. 36:11 and 1 Chron. 1:36) does not have *Korah.* [b] *22* Hebrew *Hemam,* a variant of *Homam* (see 1 Chron. 1:39) [c] *24* Vulgate; Syriac *discovered water*; the meaning of the Hebrew for this word is uncertain. [d] *26* Hebrew *Dishan,* a variant of *Dishon* [e] *31* Or *before an Israelite king reigned over them*

Temanites[v] succeeded him
as king.
35When Husham died, Hadad
son of Bedad, who defeated
Midian in the country of
Moab,[w] succeeded him as
king. His city was named
Avith.
36When Hadad died, Samlah
from Masrekah succeeded
him as king.
37When Samlah died, Shaul from
Rehoboth on the river[f] succeeded him as king.
38When Shaul died, Baal-Hanan
son of Acbor succeeded him
as king.
39When Baal-Hanan son of Acbor died, Hadad[g] succeeded
him as king. His city was
named Pau, and his wife's
name was Mehetabel daugh-
ter of Matred, the daughter
of Me-Zahab.

40These were the chiefs descended from Esau, by name, according to their clans and regions:
Timna, Alvah, Jetheth,
41Oholibamah, Elah, Pinon,
42Kenaz, Teman, Mibzar,
43Magdiel and Iram. These
were the chiefs of Edom, according to their settlements
in the land they occupied.

This was Esau the father of the
Edomites.

Joseph's Dreams

37 Jacob lived in the land
where his father had
stayed,[a] the land of Canaan.[b]

2This is the account of Jacob.

Joseph, a young man of seventeen, was tending the flocks[c] with
his brothers, the sons of Bilhah[d]
and the sons of Zilpah,[e] his
father's wives, and he brought
their father a bad report[f] about
them.
3Now Israel loved Joseph more
than any of his other sons,[g]
because he had been born to him
in his old age;[h] and he made a
richly ornamented[a] robe[i] for him.
4When his brothers saw that their
father loved him more than any of
them, they hated him[j] and could
not speak a kind word to him.
5Joseph had a dream,[k] and when
he told it to his brothers, they hated
him all the more. 6He said to them,
"Listen to this dream I had: 7We
were binding sheaves of corn out in
the field when suddenly my sheaf
rose and stood upright, while your
sheaves gathered round mine and
bowed down to it."[l]
8His brothers said to him, "Do
you intend to reign over us? Will
you actually rule us?"[m] And they
hated him all the more because of
his dream and what he had said.
9Then he had another dream, and
he told it to his brothers. "Listen,"
he said, "I had another dream, and
this time the sun and moon and
eleven stars were bowing down to
me."
10When he told his father as well
as his brothers,[n] his father rebuked him and said, "What is this
dream you had? Will your mother
and I and your brothers actually
come and bow down to the ground
before you?"[o] 11His brothers were
jealous of him,[p] but his father kept
the matter in mind.[q]

Joseph Sold by His Brothers

12Now his brothers had gone to
graze their father's flocks near
Shechem, 13and Israel said to Joseph, "As you know, your brothers
are grazing the flocks near Shechem. Come, I am going to send you
to them."
"Very well," he replied.
14So he said to him, "Go and see if
all is well with your brothers and

36:34
v Eze 25:13

36:35
w Ge 19:37; Nu 22:1; Dt 1:5; Ru 1:1,6

37:1
a Ge 17:8
b Ge 10:19

37:2
c Ps 78:71
d Ge 35:25
e Ge 35:26
f 1Sa 2:24

37:3
g Ge 25:28
h Ge 44:20
i 2Sa 13:18-19

37:4
j Ge 27:41; Ge 49:22-23; Ac 7:9

37:5
k Ge 20:3; Ge 28:12

37:7
l Ge 42:6,9; Ge 43:26,28; Ge 44:14; Ge 50:18

37:8
m Ge 49:26

37:10
n ver 5
o ver 7; Ge 27:29

37:11
p Ac 7:9
q Lk 2:19,51

f37 Possibly the Euphrates g39 Many manuscripts of the Masoretic Text, Samaritan Pentateuch and Syriac (see also 1 Chron. 1:50); most manuscripts of the Masoretic Text *Hadar*
a3 The meaning of the Hebrew for *richly ornamented* is uncertain; also in verses 23 and 32.

with the flocks, and bring word
back to me." Then he sent him off
from the Valley of Hebron.[r]
When Joseph arrived at Shechem, [15]a man found him wandering around in the fields and asked
him, "What are you looking for?"
[16]He replied, "I'm looking for my
brothers. Can you tell me where
they are grazing their flocks?"
[17]"They have moved on from
here," the man answered. "I heard
them say, 'Let's go to Dothan.[s]' "
So Joseph went after his brothers
and found them near Dothan. [18]But
they saw him in the distance, and
before he reached them, they plotted to kill him.[t]
[19]"Here comes that dreamer!"
they said to each other. [20]"Come
now, let's kill him and throw him
into one of these cisterns[u] and say
that a ferocious animal devoured
him. Then we'll see what comes of
his dreams."[v]
[21]When Reuben heard this, he
tried to rescue him from their
hands. "Let's not take his life," he
said.[w] [22]"Don't shed any blood.
Throw him into this cistern here in
the desert, but don't lay a hand on
him." Reuben said this to rescue
him from them and take him back
to his father.
[23]So when Joseph came to his
brothers, they stripped him of his
robe—the richly ornamented robe
he was wearing—[24]and they took
him and threw him into the cistern.[x] Now the cistern was empty;
there was no water in it.
[25]As they sat down to eat their
meal, they looked up and saw a
caravan of Ishmaelites coming
from Gilead. Their camels were
loaded with spices, balm and
myrrh,[y] and they were on their
way to take them down to Egypt.[z]
[26]Judah said to his brothers,
"What will we gain if we kill our
brother and cover up his blood?[a]
[27]Come, let's sell him to the Ishmaelites and not lay our hands on him;
after all, he is our brother,[b] our

37:14 r Ge 13:18; Ge 35:27
37:17 s 2Ki 6:13
37:18 t 1Sa 19:1; Mk 14:1; Ac 23:12
37:20 u Jer 38:6,9 v Ge 50:20
37:21 w Ge 42:22
37:24 x Jer 41:7
37:25 y Ge 43:11 z ver 28
37:26 a ver 20; Ge 4:10
37:27 b Ge 42:21
37:28 c Ge 25:2; Jdg 6:1-3 d Ge 45:4-5; Ps 105:17; Ac 7:9
37:29 e ver 34; Ge 44:13; Job 1:20
37:30 f ver 22; Ge 42:13,36
37:31 g ver 3,23
37:33 h ver 20 i Ge 44:20,28
37:34 j ver 29 k 2Sa 3:31 l Ge 50:3,10,11
37:35 m Ge 42:38; Ge 44:22,29, 31
37:36 n Ge 39:1
38:2 a 1Ch 2:3
38:3 b ver 6; Ge 46:12; Nu 26:19

own flesh and blood." His brothers
agreed.
[28]So when the Midianite[c] merchants came by, his brothers pulled
Joseph up out of the cistern and
sold him for twenty shekels[b] of silver to the Ishmaelites, who took
him to Egypt.[d]
[29]When Reuben returned to the
cistern and saw that Joseph was not
there, he tore his clothes.[e] [30]He
went back to his brothers and said,
"The boy isn't there! Where can I
turn now?"[f]
[31]Then they got Joseph's robe,[g]
slaughtered a goat and dipped the
robe in the blood. [32]They took the
ornamented robe back to their
father and said, "We found this. Examine it to see whether it is your
son's robe."
[33]He recognised it and said, "It is
my son's robe! Some ferocious animal[h] has devoured him. Joseph
has surely been torn to pieces."[i]
[34]Then Jacob tore his clothes,[j]
put on sackcloth[k] and mourned for
his son many days.[l] [35]All his sons
and daughters came to comfort
him, but he refused to be comforted. "No," he said, "in mourning
will I go down to the grave[c][m] to my
son." So his father wept for him.
[36]Meanwhile, the Midianites[d]
sold Joseph in Egypt to Potiphar,
one of Pharaoh's officials, the captain of the guard.[n]

Judah and Tamar

38 At that time, Judah left his
brothers and went down to
stay with a man of Adullam named
Hirah. [2]There Judah met the
daughter of a Canaanite man
named Shua.[a] He married her and
lay with her; [3]she became pregnant
and gave birth to a son, who was
named Er.[b] [4]She conceived again
and gave birth to a son and named

[b]*28* That is, about 8 ounces (about 0.2 kilogram)
[c]*35* Hebrew *Sheol* [d]*36* Samaritan Pentateuch, Septuagint, Vulgate and Syriac (see also verse 28); Masoretic Text *Medanites*

him Onan. 5 She gave birth to still another son and named him Shelah. It was at Kezib that she gave birth to him.

6 Judah got a wife for Er, his firstborn, and her name was Tamar. 7 But Er, Judah's firstborn, was wicked in the LORD's sight; so the LORD put him to death.[c]

8 Then Judah said to Onan, "Lie with your brother's wife and fulfil your duty to her as a brother-in-law to produce offspring for your brother."[d] 9 But Onan knew that the offspring would not be his; so whenever he lay with his brother's wife, he spilled his semen on the ground to keep from producing offspring for his brother. 10 What he did was wicked in the LORD's sight; so he put him to death also.[e]

11 Judah then said to his daughter-in-law Tamar, "Live as a widow in your father's house until my son Shelah grows up."[f] For he thought, "He may die too, just like his brothers." So Tamar went to live in her father's house.

12 After a long time Judah's wife, the daughter of Shua, died. When Judah had recovered from his grief, he went up to Timnah,[g] to the men who were shearing his sheep, and his friend Hirah the Adullamite went with him.

13 When Tamar was told, "Your father-in-law is on his way to Timnah to shear his sheep," 14 she took off her widow's clothes, covered herself with a veil to disguise herself, and then sat down at the entrance to Enaim, which is on the road to Timnah. For she saw that, though Shelah[h] had now grown up, she had not been given to him as his wife.

15 When Judah saw her, he thought she was a prostitute, for she had covered her face. 16 Not realising that she was his daughter-in-law,[i] he went over to her by the roadside and said, "Come now, let me sleep with you."

"And what will you give me to sleep with you?" she asked.

17 "I'll send you a young goat[j] from my flock," he said.

"Will you give me something as a pledge[k] until you send it?" she asked.

18 He said, "What pledge should I give you?"

"Your seal[l] and its cord, and the staff in your hand," she answered. So he gave them to her and slept with her, and she became pregnant by him. 19 After she left, she took off her veil and put on her widow's clothes[m] again.

20 Meanwhile Judah sent the young goat by his friend the Adullamite in order to get his pledge back from the woman, but he did not find her. 21 He asked the men who lived there, "Where is the shrine-prostitute[n] who was beside the road at Enaim?"

"There hasn't been any shrine-prostitute here," they said.

22 So he went back to Judah and said, "I didn't find her. Besides, the men who lived there said, 'There hasn't been any shrine-prostitute here.' "

23 Then Judah said, "Let her keep what she has, or we will become a laughing-stock. After all, I did send her this young goat, but you didn't find her."

24 About three months later Judah was told, "Your daughter-in-law Tamar is guilty of prostitution, and as a result she is now pregnant."

Judah said, "Bring her out and have her burned to death!"[o]

25 As she was being brought out, she sent a message to her father-in-law. "I am pregnant by the man who owns these," she said. And she added, "See if you recognise whose seal and cord and staff these are."[p]

26 Judah recognised them and said, "She is more righteous than I,[q] since I wouldn't give her to my son Shelah.[r]" And he did not sleep with her again.

27 When the time came for her to

38:7 c ver 10; Ge 46:12; 1Ch 2:3
38:8 d Dt 25:5-6; Mt 22:24-28
38:10 e Ge 46:12; Dt 25:7-10
38:11 f Ru 1:13
38:12 g ver 14; Jos 15:10,57
38:14 h ver 11
38:16 i Lev 18:15; Lev 20:12
38:17 j Eze 16:33; k ver 20
38:18 l ver 25
38:19 m ver 14
38:21 n Lev 19:29; Hos 4:14
38:24 o Lev 21:9; Dt 22:21,22
38:25 p ver 18
38:26 q 1Sa 24:17; r ver 11

give birth, there were twin boys in her womb.[s] 28As she was giving birth, one of them put out his hand; so the midwife took a scarlet thread and tied it on his wrist and said, "This one came out first." 29But when he drew back his hand, his brother came out, and she said, "So this is how you have broken out!" And he was named Perez.[a][t] 30Then his brother, who had the scarlet thread on his wrist, came out and he was given the name Zerah.[b][u]

Joseph and Potiphar's Wife

39 Now Joseph had been taken down to Egypt. Potiphar, an Egyptian who was one of Pharaoh's officials, the captain of the guard,[a] bought him from the Ishmaelites who had taken him there.[b]

2The LORD was with Joseph[c] and he prospered, and he lived in the house of his Egyptian master. 3When his master saw that the LORD was with him[d] and that the LORD gave him success in everything he did,[e] 4Joseph found favour in his eyes and became his attendant. Potiphar put him in charge of his household, and he entrusted to his care everything he owned.[f] 5From the time he put him in charge of his household and of all that he owned, the LORD blessed the household of the Egyptian because of Joseph.[g] The blessing of the LORD was on everything Potiphar had, both in the house and in the field. 6So he left in Joseph's care everything he had; with Joseph in charge, he did not concern himself with anything except the food he ate.

Now Joseph was well-built and handsome,[h] 7and after a while his master's wife took notice of Joseph and said, "Come to bed with me!"[i]

8But he refused.[j] "With me in charge," he told her, "my master does not concern himself with anything in the house; everything he owns he has entrusted to my care. 9No-one is greater in this house than I am.[k] My master has withheld nothing from me except you, because you are his wife. How then could I do such a wicked thing and sin against God?"[l] 10And though she spoke to Joseph day after day, he refused to go to bed with her or even to be with her.

11One day he went into the house to attend to his duties, and none of the household servants was inside. 12She caught him by his cloak[m] and said, "Come to bed with me!" But he left his cloak in her hand and ran out of the house.

13When she saw that he had left his cloak in her hand and had run out of the house, 14she called her household servants. "Look," she said to them, "this Hebrew has been brought to us to make sport of us! He came in here to sleep with me, but I screamed.[n] 15When he heard me scream for help, he left his cloak beside me and ran out of the house."

16She kept his cloak beside her until his master came home. 17Then she told him this story:[o] "That Hebrew slave you brought us came to me to make sport of me. 18But as soon as I screamed for help, he left his cloak beside me and ran out of the house."

19When his master heard the story his wife told him, saying, "This is how your slave treated me," he burned with anger.[p] 20Joseph's master took him and put him in prison,[q] the place where the king's prisoners were confined.

But while Joseph was there in the prison, 21the LORD was with him; he showed him kindness and granted him favour in the eyes of the prison warder.[r] 22So the warder put Joseph in charge of all those held in the prison, and he was made responsible for all that was done

38:27 s Ge 25:24
38:29 t Ge 46:12; Nu 26:20,21; Ru 4:12,18; 1Ch 2:4; Mt 1:3
38:30 u 1Ch 2:4
39:1 a Ge 37:36 b Ge 37:25; Ps 105:17
39:2 c Ge 21:20,22; Ac 7:9
39:3 d Ge 21:22; Ge 26:28 e Ps 1:3
39:4 f ver 8,22; Ge 24:2
39:5 g Ge 26:24; Ge 30:27
39:6 h 1Sa 16:12
39:7 i 2Sa 13:11; Pr 7:15-18
39:8 j Pr 6:23-24
39:9 k Ge 41:33,40 l Ge 20:6; Ge 42:18; 2Sa 12:13
39:12 m Pr 7:13
39:14 n Dt 22:24,27
39:17 o Ex 23:1,7; Ps 101:5
39:19 p Pr 6:34
39:20 q Ge 40:3; Ps 105:18
39:21 r Ex 3:21

a29 *Perez* means *breaking out.* b30 *Zerah* can mean *scarlet* or *brightness.*

there.[s] [23]The warder paid no attention to anything under Joseph's
care, because the LORD was with
Joseph and gave him success in
whatever he did.[t]

The Cupbearer and the Baker

40 Some time later, the cupbearer[a] and the baker of
the king of Egypt offended their
master, the king of Egypt. [2]Phar-
aoh was angry[b] with his two officials, the chief cupbearer and the
chief baker, [3]and put them in custody in the house of the captain of
the guard,[c] in the same prison
where Joseph was confined. [4]The
captain of the guard assigned them
to Joseph,[d] and he attended them.
After they had been in custody
for some time, [5]each of the two
men—the cupbearer and the baker
of the king of Egypt, who were being held in prison—had a dream the
same night, and each dream had a
meaning of its own.[e]
[6]When Joseph came to them the
next morning, he saw that they
were dejected. [7]So he asked Pharaoh's officials who were in custody
with him in his master's house,
"Why are your faces so sad today?"[f]
[8]"We both had dreams," they answered, "but there is no-one to interpret them."[g]
Then Joseph said to them, "Do
not interpretations belong to
God?[h] Tell me your dreams."
[9]So the chief cupbearer told Joseph his dream. He said to him, "In
my dream I saw a vine in front of
me, [10]and on the vine were three
branches. As soon as it budded, it
blossomed, and its clusters ripened
into grapes. [11]Pharaoh's cup was in
my hand, and I took the grapes,
squeezed them into Pharaoh's cup
and put the cup in his hand."
[12]"This is what it means,[i]" Joseph said to him. "The three
branches are three days. [13]Within
three days Pharaoh will lift up your

39:22 *s* ver 4
39:23 *t* ver 3
40:1 *a* Ne 1:11
40:2 *b* Pr 16:14,15
40:3 *c* Ge 39:20
40:4 *d* Ge 39:4
40:5 *e* Ge 41:11
40:7 *f* Ne 2:2
40:8 *g* Ge 41:8,15 *h* Ge 41:16 Da 2:22,28,47
40:12 *i* Ge 41:12,15, 25 Da 2:36 Da 4:19
40:14 *j* Lk 23:42 *k* Jos 2:12 1Sa 20:14,42 1Ki 2:7
40:15 *l* Ge 37:26-28
40:18 *m* ver 12
40:19 *n* ver 13
40:20 *o* Mt 14:6-10 *p* Mk 6:21
40:21 *q* ver 13
40:22 *r* ver 19 *s* Ps 105:19
40:23 *t* Job 19:14 Ecc 9:15
41:1 *a* Ge 20:3
41:2 *b* ver 26 *c* Isa 19:6

head and restore you to your position, and you will put Pharaoh's cup
in his hand, just as you used to do
when you were his cupbearer.
[14]But when all goes well with you,
remember me[j] and show me kindness;[k] mention me to Pharaoh and
get me out of this prison. [15]For I
was forcibly carried off from the
land of the Hebrews,[l] and even
here I have done nothing to deserve
being put in a dungeon."
[16]When the chief baker saw that
Joseph had given a favourable interpretation, he said to Joseph, "I
too had a dream: On my head were
three baskets of bread.[a] [17]In the
top basket were all kinds of baked
goods for Pharaoh, but the birds
were eating them out of the basket
on my head."
[18]"This is what it means," Joseph
said. "The three baskets are three
days.[m] [19]Within three days Pharaoh will lift off your head[n] and
hang you on a tree.[b] And the birds
will eat away your flesh."
[20]Now the third day was Pharaoh's birthday,[o] and he gave a
feast for all his officials.[p] He lifted
up the heads of the chief cupbearer
and the chief baker in the presence
of his officials: [21]He restored the
chief cupbearer to his position, so
that he once again put the cup into
Pharaoh's hand,[q] [22]but he hanged[c]
the chief baker,[r] just as Joseph
had said to them in his interpretation.[s]
[23]The chief cupbearer, however,
did not remember Joseph; he forgot him.[t]

Pharaoh's Dreams

41 When two full years had
passed, Pharaoh had a
dream:[a] He was standing by the
Nile, [2]when out of the river there
came up seven cows, sleek and
fat,[b] and they grazed among the
reeds.[c] [3]After them, seven other

[a]16 Or *three wicker baskets* [b]19 Or *and impale you on a pole* [c]22 Or *impaled*

cows, ugly and gaunt, came up out of the Nile and stood beside those on the riverbank. 4And the cows that were ugly and gaunt ate up the seven sleek, fat cows. Then Pharaoh woke up.

5He fell asleep again and had a second dream: Seven ears of corn, healthy and good, were growing on a single stalk. 6After them, seven other ears of corn sprouted—thin and scorched by the east wind. 7The thin ears of corn swallowed up the seven healthy, full ears. Then Pharaoh woke up; it had been a dream.

8In the morning his mind was troubled,[d] so he sent for all the magicians[e] and wise men of Egypt. Pharaoh told them his dreams, but no-one could interpret them for him.

9Then the chief cupbearer said to Pharaoh, "Today I am reminded of my shortcomings. 10Pharaoh was once angry with his servants,[f] and he imprisoned me and the chief baker in the house of the captain of the guard.[g] 11Each of us had a dream the same night, and each dream had a meaning of its own.[h] 12Now a young Hebrew was there with us, a servant of the captain of the guard. We told him our dreams, and he interpreted them for us, giving each man the interpretation of his dream.[i] 13And things turned out exactly as he interpreted them to us: I was restored to my position, and the other man was hanged."[a][j]

14So Pharaoh sent for Joseph, and he was quickly brought from the dungeon.[k] When he had shaved and changed his clothes, he came before Pharaoh.

15Pharaoh said to Joseph, "I had a dream, and no-one can interpret it. But I have heard it said of you that when you hear a dream you can interpret it."[l]

16"I cannot do it," Joseph replied to Pharaoh, "but God will give Pharaoh the answer he desires."[m]

17Then Pharaoh said to Joseph, "In my dream I was standing on the bank of the Nile, 18when out of the river there came up seven cows, fat and sleek, and they grazed among the reeds. 19After them, seven other cows came up—scrawny and very ugly and lean. I had never seen such ugly cows in all the land of Egypt. 20The lean, ugly cows ate up the seven fat cows that came up first. 21But even after they ate them, no-one could tell that they had done so; they looked just as ugly as before. Then I woke up.

22"In my dreams I also saw seven ears of corn, full and good, growing on a single stalk. 23After them, seven other ears sprouted—withered and thin and scorched by the east wind. 24The thin ears of corn swallowed up the seven good ears. I told this to the magicians, but none could explain it to me.[n]"

25Then Joseph said to Pharaoh, "The dreams of Pharaoh are one and the same. God has revealed to Pharaoh what he is about to do.[o] 26The seven good cows[p] are seven years, and the seven good ears of corn are seven years; it is one and the same dream. 27The seven lean, ugly cows that came up afterwards are seven years, and so are the seven worthless ears of corn scorched by the east wind: They are seven years of famine.[q]

28"It is just as I said to Pharaoh: God has shown Pharaoh what he is about to do. 29Seven years of great abundance[r] are coming throughout the land of Egypt, 30but seven years of famine[s] will follow them. Then all the abundance in Egypt will be forgotten, and the famine will ravage the land.[t] 31The abundance in the land will not be remembered, because the famine that follows it will be so severe. 32The reason the dream was given to Pharaoh in two forms is that the matter has been firmly decided[u] by God, and God will do it soon.

41:8 d Da 2:1,3; Da 4:5,19 e Ex 7:11,22; Da 1:20; Da 2:2,27; Da 4:7
41:10 f Ge 40:2 g Ge 39:20
41:11 h Ge 40:5
41:12 i Ge 40:12
41:13 j Ge 40:22
41:14 k Ps 105:20; Da 2:25
41:15 l Da 5:16
41:16 m Ge 40:8; Da 2:30; Ac 3:12; 2Co 3:5
41:24 n ver 8
41:25 o Da 2:45
41:26 p ver 2
41:27 q Ge 12:10; 2Ki 8:1
41:29 r ver 47
41:30 s ver 54; Ge 47:13 t ver 56
41:32 u Nu 23:19; Isa 46:10-11

a13 Or *impaled*

33“And now let Pharaoh look for a
discerning and wise man[v] and put
him in charge of the land of Egypt.
34Let Pharaoh appoint commissioners over the land to take a fifth[w] of
the harvest of Egypt during the
seven years of abundance.[x] 35They
should collect all the food of these
good years that are coming and
store up the grain under the authority of Pharaoh, to be kept in the
cities for food.[y] 36This food should
be held in reserve for the country,
to be used during the seven years
of famine that will come upon
Egypt,[z] so that the country may
not be ruined by the famine.”
37The plan seemed good to Pharaoh and to all his officials.[a] 38So
Pharaoh asked them, “Can we find
anyone like this man, one in whom
is the spirit of God?”[b][b]
39Then Pharaoh said to Joseph,
“Since God has made all this known
to you, there is no-one so discerning and wise as you. 40You shall be
in charge of my palace, and all my
people are to submit to your orders.[c] Only with respect to the
throne will I be greater than you.”

Joseph in Charge of Egypt

41So Pharaoh said to Joseph, “I
hereby put you in charge of the
whole land of Egypt.”[d] 42Then
Pharaoh took his signet ring[e] from
his finger and put it on Joseph’s
finger. He dressed him in robes of
fine linen and put a gold chain
around his neck.[f] 43He had him
ride in a chariot as his second-in-
command,[c] and men shouted before him, “Make way!”[d][g] Thus he
put him in charge of the whole land
of Egypt.
44Then Pharaoh said to Joseph, “I
am Pharaoh, but without your word
no-one will lift hand or foot in all
Egypt.”[h] 45Pharaoh gave Joseph
the name Zaphenath-Paneah and
gave him Asenath daughter of Potiphera, priest of On,[e] to be his
wife.[i] And Joseph went throughout the land of Egypt.
46Joseph was thirty years old[j]
when he entered the service[k] of
Pharaoh king of Egypt. And Joseph
went out from Pharaoh’s presence
and travelled throughout Egypt.
47During the seven years of abundance the land produced plenti-
fully. 48Joseph collected all the
food produced in those seven years
of abundance in Egypt and stored it
in the cities. In each city he put the
food grown in the fields surrounding it. 49Joseph stored up huge
quantities of grain, like the sand of
the sea; it was so much that he
stopped keeping records because it
was beyond measure.
50Before the years of famine
came, two sons were born to Joseph
by Asenath daughter of Potiphera,
priest of On.[l] 51Joseph named his
firstborn[m] Manasseh[f] and said,
“It is because God has made me
forget all my trouble and all my
father’s household.” 52The second
son he named Ephraim[g][n] and said,
“It is because God has made me
fruitful[o] in the land of my suffering.”
53The seven years of abundance
in Egypt came to an end, 54and the
seven years of famine began,[p] just
as Joseph had said. There was famine in all the other lands, but in the
whole land of Egypt there was food.
55When all Egypt began to feel the
famine,[q] the people cried to Pharaoh for food. Then Pharaoh told all
the Egyptians, “Go to Joseph and
do what he tells you.”[r]
56When the famine had spread
over the whole country, Joseph
opened the storehouses and sold
grain to the Egyptians, for the famine[s] was severe throughout Egypt.

41:33 [v] ver 39
41:34 [w] 1Sa 8:15 [x] ver 48
41:35 [y] ver 48
41:36 [z] ver 56
41:37 [a] Ge 45:16
41:38 [b] Nu 27:18; Job 32:8; Da 4:8,8-9,18; Da 5:11,14
41:40 [c] Ps 105:21-22; Ac 7:10
41:41 [d] Ge 42:6; Da 6:3
41:42 [e] Est 3:10 [f] Da 5:7,16,29
41:43 [g] Est 6:9
41:44 [h] Ps 105:22
41:45 [i] ver 50; Ge 46:20,27
41:46 [j] Ge 37:2 [k] 1Sa 16:21; Da 1:19
41:50 [l] Ge 46:20; Ge 48:5
41:51 [m] Ge 48:14,18, 20
41:52 [n] Ge 48:1,5; Ge 50:23 [o] Ge 17:6; Ge 28:3; Ge 49:22
41:54 [p] ver 30; Ps 105:11; Ac 7:11
41:55 [q] Dt 32:24 [r] ver 41
41:56 [s] Ge 12:10

[b]38 Or *of the gods* [c]43 Or *in the chariot of his second-in-command*; or *in his second chariot* [d]43 Or *Bow down* [e]45 That is, Heliopolis; also in verse 50 [f]51 *Manasseh* sounds like and may be derived from the Hebrew for *forget.* [g]52 *Ephraim* sounds like the Hebrew for *twice fruitful.*

57And all the countries came to Egypt to buy grain from Joseph,[t] because the famine was severe in all the world.

Joseph's Brothers Go to Egypt

42 When Jacob learned that there was grain in Egypt,[a] he said to his sons, "Why do you just keep looking at each other?" 2He continued, "I have heard that there is grain in Egypt. Go down there and buy some for us, so that we may live and not die."[b]

3Then ten of Joseph's brothers went down to buy grain from Egypt. 4But Jacob did not send Benjamin, Joseph's brother, with the others, because he was afraid that harm might come to him.[c] 5So Israel's sons were among those who went to buy grain,[d] for the famine was in the land of Canaan also.[e]

6Now Joseph was the governor of the land,[f] the one who sold grain to all its people. So when Joseph's brothers arrived, they bowed down to him with their faces to the ground.[g] 7As soon as Joseph saw his brothers, he recognised them, but he pretended to be a stranger and spoke harshly to them.[h] "Where do you come from?" he asked.

"From the land of Canaan," they replied, "to buy food."

8Although Joseph recognised his brothers, they did not recognise him.[i] 9Then he remembered his dreams[j] about them and said to them, "You are spies! You have come to see where our land is unprotected."

10"No, my lord," they answered. "Your servants have come to buy food. 11We are all the sons of one man. Your servants are honest men, not spies."

12"No!" he said to them. "You have come to see where our land is unprotected."

13But they replied, "Your servants were twelve brothers, the sons of one man, who lives in the land of Canaan. The youngest is now with our father, and one is no more."[k]

14Joseph said to them, "It is just as I told you: You are spies! 15And this is how you will be tested: As surely as Pharaoh lives,[l] you will not leave this place unless your youngest brother comes here. 16Send one of your number to get your brother; the rest of you will be kept in prison, so that your words may be tested to see if you are telling the truth.[m] If you are not, then as surely as Pharaoh lives, you are spies!" 17And he put them all in custody[n] for three days.

18On the third day, Joseph said to them, "Do this and you will live, for I fear God:[o] 19If you are honest men, let one of your brothers stay here in prison, while the rest of you go and take grain back for your starving households. 20But you must bring your youngest brother to me,[p] so that your words may be verified and that you may not die." This they proceeded to do.

21They said to one another, "Surely we are being punished because of our brother.[q] We saw how distressed he was when he pleaded with us for his life, but we would not listen; that's why this distress[r] has come upon us."

22Reuben replied, "Didn't I tell you not to sin against the boy?[s] But you wouldn't listen! Now we must give an accounting[t] for his blood."[u] 23They did not realise that Joseph could understand them, since he was using an interpreter.

24He turned away from them and began to weep, but then turned back and spoke to them again. He had Simeon taken from them and bound before their eyes.[v]

25Joseph gave orders to fill their bags with grain,[w] to put each man's silver back in his sack,[x] and to give them provisions for their journey.[y] After this was done for them,

41:57 t Ge 42:5; Ge 47:15
42:1 a Ac 7:12
42:2 b Ge 43:8
42:4 c ver 38
42:5 d Ge 41:57; e Ge 12:10; Ac 7:11
42:6 f Ge 41:41; g Ge 37:7-10
42:7 h ver 30
42:8 i Ge 37:2
42:9 j Ge 37:7
42:13 k Ge 37:30,33; Ge 44:20
42:15 l 1Sa 17:55
42:16 m ver 11
42:17 n Ge 40:4
42:18 o Ge 20:11; Lev 25:43
42:20 p ver 15,34; Ge 43:5; Ge 44:23
42:21 q Ge 37:26-28; r Hos 5:15
42:22 s Ge 37:21-22; t Ge 9:5; u 1Ki 2:32; 2Ch 24:22; Ps 9:12
42:24 v ver 13; Ge 43:14,23; Ge 45:14-15
42:25 w Ge 43:2; x Ge 44:1,8; y Ro 12:17, 20-21

26they loaded their grain on their donkeys and left.

27At the place where they stopped for the night one of them opened his sack to get feed for his donkey, and he saw his silver in the mouth of his sack.[z] 28"My silver has been returned," he said to his brothers. "Here it is in my sack."

Their hearts sank and they turned to each other trembling and said, "What is this that God has done to us?"[a]

29When they came to their father Jacob in the land of Canaan, they told him all that had happened to them. They said, 30"The man who is lord over the land spoke harshly to us[b] and treated us as though we were spying on the land. 31But we said to him, 'We are honest men; we are not spies.[c] 32We were twelve brothers, sons of one father. One is no more, and the youngest is now with our father in Canaan.'

33"Then the man who is lord over the land said to us, 'This is how I will know whether you are honest men: Leave one of your brothers here with me, and take food for your starving households and go.[d] 34But bring your youngest brother to me so I will know that you are not spies but honest men. Then I will give your brother back to you, and you can trade[a] in the land.[e]' "

35As they were emptying their sacks, there in each man's sack was his pouch of silver! When they and their father saw the money pouches, they were frightened.[f] 36Their father Jacob said to them, "You have deprived me of my children. Joseph is no more and Simeon is no more, and now you want to take Benjamin.[g] Everything is against me!"

37Then Reuben said to his father, "You may put both of my sons to death if I do not bring him back to you. Entrust him to my care, and I will bring him back."

38But Jacob said, "My son will not go down there with you; his brother is dead[h] and he is the only one left. If harm comes to him[i] on the journey you are taking, you will bring my grey head down to the grave[b][j] in sorrow.[k]"

The Second Journey to Egypt

43 Now the famine was still severe in the land.[a] 2So when they had eaten all the grain they had brought from Egypt, their father said to them, "Go back and buy us a little more food."

3But Judah said to him, "The man warned us solemnly, 'You will not see my face again unless your brother is with you.'[b] 4If you will send our brother along with us, we will go down and buy food for you. 5But if you will not send him, we will not go down, because the man said to us, 'You will not see my face again unless your brother is with you.[c]' "

6Israel asked, "Why did you bring this trouble on me by telling the man you had another brother?"

7They replied, "The man questioned us closely about ourselves and our family. 'Is your father still living?'[d] he asked us. 'Do you have another brother?'[e] We simply answered his questions. How were we to know he would say, 'Bring your brother down here'?"

8Then Judah said to Israel his father, "Send the boy along with me and we will go at once, so that we and you and our children may live and not die.[f] 9I myself will guarantee his safety; you can hold me personally responsible for him. If I do not bring him back to you and set him here before you, I will bear the blame before you all my life.[g] 10As it is, if we had not delayed, we could have gone and returned twice."

11Then their father Israel said to them, "If it must be, then do this: Put some of the best products of the land in your bags and take them

42:27 z Ge 43:21-22
42:28 a Ge 43:23
42:30 b ver 7
42:31 c ver 11
42:33 d ver 19,20
42:34 e Ge 34:10
42:35 f Ge 43:12,15,18
42:36 g Ge 43:14
42:38 h Ge 37:33 i ver 4 j Ge 37:35 k Ge 44:29,34
43:1 a Ge 12:10 Ge 41:56-57
43:3 b Ge 42:15 Ge 44:23
43:5 c Ge 42:15 2Sa 3:13
43:7 d ver 27 e Ge 42:13
43:8 f Ge 42:2 Ps 33:18-19
43:9 g Ge 42:37 Ge 44:32 Phm 1:18-19

[a]34 Or *move about freely* [b]38 Hebrew *Sheol*

down to the man as a gift[h]—a little
balm[i] and a little honey, some
spices[j] and myrrh, some pistachio
nuts and almonds. 12 Take double
the amount of silver with you, for
you must return the silver that was
put back into the mouths of your
sacks.[k] Perhaps it was a mistake.
13 Take your brother also and go
back to the man at once. 14 And may
God Almighty[a][l] grant you mercy
before the man so that he will let
your other brother and Benjamin
come back with you.[m] As for me, if
I am bereaved, I am bereaved."[n]
15 So the men took the gifts and
double the amount of silver, and
Benjamin also. They hurried[o]
down to Egypt and presented themselves[p] to Joseph. 16 When Joseph
saw Benjamin with them, he said to
the steward of his house,[q] "Take
these men to my house, slaughter
an animal and prepare dinner;[r]
they are to eat with me at noon."
17 The man did as Joseph told him
and took the men to Joseph's house.
18 Now the men were frightened[s]
when they were taken to his house.
They thought, "We were brought
here because of the silver that was
put back into our sacks the first
time. He wants to attack us and
overpower us and seize us as slaves
and take our donkeys."
19 So they went up to Joseph's
steward and spoke to him at the entrance to the house. 20 "Please, sir,"
they said, "we came down here the
first time to buy food.[t] 21 But at the
place where we stopped for the
night we opened our sacks and each
of us found his silver—the exact
weight—in the mouth of his sack.
So we have brought it back with
us.[u] 22 We have also brought additional silver with us to buy food. We
don't know who put our silver in
our sacks."
23 "It's all right," he said. "Don't
be afraid. Your God, the God of
your father, has given you treasure in your sacks;[v] I received your
silver." Then he brought Simeon
out to them.[w]
24 The steward took the men into
Joseph's house,[x] gave them water
to wash their feet[y] and provided
fodder for their donkeys. 25 They
prepared their gifts for Joseph's
arrival at noon, because they had
heard that they were to eat there.
26 When Joseph came home, they
presented to him the gifts[z] they
had brought into the house, and
they bowed down before him to the
ground.[a] 27 He asked them how
they were, and then he said, "How
is your aged father you told me
about? Is he still living?"[b]
28 They replied, "Your servant
our father is still alive and well."
And they bowed low to pay him
honour.[c]
29 As he looked about and saw his
brother Benjamin, his own
mother's son, he asked, "Is this
your youngest brother, the one you
told me about?"[d] And he said, "God
be gracious to you,[e] my son."
30 Deeply moved[f] at the sight of his
brother, Joseph hurried out and
looked for a place to weep. He went
into his private room and wept[g]
there.
31 After he had washed his face,
he came out and, controlling himself,[h] said, "Serve the food."
32 They served him by himself,
the brothers by themselves, and
the Egyptians who ate with him by
themselves, because Egyptians
could not eat with Hebrews,[i] for
that is detestable to Egyptians.[j]
33 The men had been seated before
him in the order of their ages, from
the firstborn to the youngest; and
they looked at each other in astonishment. 34 When portions were
served to them from Joseph's
table, Benjamin's portion was five
times as much as anyone else's.[k]
So they feasted and drank freely
with him.

43:11 h Ge 32:20; Pr 18:16 i Ge 37:25; Jer 8:22 j 1Ki 10:2
43:12 k Ge 42:25
43:14 l Ge 17:1; Ge 28:3; Ge 35:11 m Ge 42:24 n Est 4:16
43:15 o Ge 45:9,13 p Ge 47:2,7
43:16 q Ge 44:1,4,12 r ver 31; Lk 15:23
43:18 s Ge 42:35
43:20 t Ge 42:3
43:21 u ver 15; Ge 42:27,35
43:23 v Ge 42:28 w Ge 42:24
43:24 x ver 16 y Ge 18:4; Ge 24:32
43:26 z Mt 2:11 a Ge 37:7,10
43:27 b ver 7
43:28 c Ge 37:7
43:29 d Ge 42:13 e Nu 6:25; Ps 67:1
43:30 f Jn 11:33,38 g Ge 42:24; Ge 45:2,14,15; Ge 46:29
43:31 h Ge 45:1
43:32 i Gal 2:12 j Ge 46:34; Ex 8:26
43:34 k Ge 37:3; Ge 45:22

a14 Hebrew *El-Shaddai*

A Silver Cup in a Sack

44 Now Joseph gave these instructions to the steward of
his house: "Fill the men's sacks
with as much food as they can
carry, and put each man's silver in
the mouth of his sack.[a] 2Then put
my cup, the silver one, in the mouth
of the youngest one's sack, along
with the silver for his grain." And
he did as Joseph said.
3As morning dawned, the men
were sent on their way with their
donkeys. 4They had not gone far
from the city when Joseph said to
his steward, "Go after those men at
once, and when you catch up with
them, say to them, 'Why have you
repaid good with evil?[b] 5Isn't this
the cup my master drinks from and
also uses for divination?[c] This is a
wicked thing you have done.' "
6When he caught up with them,
he repeated these words to them.
7But they said to him, "Why does
my lord say such things? Far be it
from your servants to do anything
like that! 8We even brought back to
you from the land of Canaan the silver we found inside the mouths of
our sacks.[d] So why would we steal
silver or gold from your master's
house? 9If any of your servants is
found to have it, he will die;[e] and
the rest of us will become my lord's
slaves."
10"Very well, then," he said, "let
it be as you say. Whoever is found
to have it will become my slave; the
rest of you will be free from
blame."
11Each of them quickly lowered
his sack to the ground and opened
it. 12Then the steward proceeded to
search, beginning with the oldest
and ending with the youngest. And
the cup was found in Benjamin's
sack.[f] 13At this, they tore their
clothes.[g] Then they all loaded
their donkeys and returned to the
city.
14Joseph was still in the house
when Judah and his brothers came
in, and they threw themselves to
the ground before him.[h] 15Joseph
said to them, "What is this you have
done? Don't you know that a man
like me can find things out by divination?[i]"
16"What can we say to my lord?"
Judah replied. "What can we say?
How can we prove our innocence?
God has uncovered your servants'
guilt. We are now my lord's
slaves[j]—we ourselves and the one
who was found to have the cup.[k]"
17But Joseph said, "Far be it from
me to do such a thing! Only the man
who was found to have the cup will
become my slave. The rest of you,
go back to your father in peace."
18Then Judah went up to him and
said: "Please, my lord, let your servant speak a word to my lord. Do
not be angry[l] with your servant,
though you are equal to Pharaoh
himself. 19My lord asked his servants, 'Do you have a father or a
brother?'[m] 20And we answered,
'We have an aged father, and there
is a young son born to him in his old
age.[n] His brother is dead,[o] and he
is the only one of his mother's sons
left, and his father loves him.'[p]
21"Then you said to your servants, 'Bring him down to me so I
can see him for myself.'[q] 22And we
said to my lord, 'The boy cannot
leave his father; if he leaves him,
his father will die.'[r] 23But you told
your servants, 'Unless your youngest brother comes down with you,
you will not see my face again.'[s]
24When we went back to your servant my father, we told him what
my lord had said.
25"Then our father said, 'Go back
and buy a little more food.'[t] 26But
we said, 'We cannot go down. Only
if our youngest brother is with us
will we go. We cannot see the man's
face unless our youngest brother is
with us.'
27"Your servant my father said to
us, 'You know that my wife bore me
two sons.[u] 28One of them went
away from me, and I said, "He has

44:1 a Ge 42:25
44:4 b Ps 35:12
44:5 c Ge 30:27; Dt 18:10-14
44:8 d Ge 42:25; Ge 43:21
44:9 e Ge 31:32
44:12 f ver 2
44:13 g Ge 37:29; Nu 14:6; 2Sa 1:11
44:14 h Ge 37:7,10
44:15 i ver 5; Ge 30:27
44:16 j ver 9; Ge 43:18; k ver 2
44:18 l Ge 18:30; Ex 32:22
44:19 m Ge 43:7
44:20 n Ge 37:3; o Ge 37:33; p Ge 42:13
44:21 q Ge 42:15
44:22 r Ge 37:35
44:23 s Ge 43:5
44:25 t Ge 43:2
44:27 u Ge 46:19

surely been torn to pieces."[v] And I have not seen him since. 29If you take this one from me too and harm comes to him, you will bring my grey head down to the grave[a] in misery.'[w]

30"So now, if the boy is not with us when I go back to your servant my father and if my father, whose life is closely bound up with the boy's life,[x] 31sees that the boy isn't there, he will die. Your servants will bring the grey head of our father down to the grave in sorrow. 32Your servant guaranteed the boy's safety to my father. I said, 'If I do not bring him back to you, I will bear the blame before you, my father, all my life!'[y]

33"Now then, please let your servant remain here as my lord's slave[z] in place of the boy,[a] and let the boy return with his brothers. 34How can I go back to my father if the boy is not with me? No! Do not let me see the misery that would come upon my father."[b]

Joseph Makes Himself Known

45 Then Joseph could no longer control himself[a] before all his attendants, and he cried out, "Make everyone leave my presence!" So there was no-one with Joseph when he made himself known to his brothers. 2And he wept[b] so loudly that the Egyptians heard him, and Pharaoh's household heard about it.[c]

3Joseph said to his brothers, "I am Joseph! Is my father still living?"[d] But his brothers were not able to answer him,[e] because they were terrified at his presence.

4Then Joseph said to his brothers, "Come close to me." When they had done so, he said, "I am your brother Joseph, the one you sold into Egypt![f] 5And now, do not be distressed[g] and do not be angry with yourselves for selling me here,[h] because it was to save lives that God sent me ahead of you.[i] 6For two years now there has been famine in the land, and for the next five years there will not be ploughing and reaping. 7But God sent me ahead of you to preserve for you a remnant[j] on earth and to save your lives by a great deliverance.[a][k]

8"So then, it was not you who sent me here, but God. He made me father[l] to Pharaoh, lord of his entire household and ruler of all Egypt.[m] 9Now hurry back to my father and say to him, 'This is what your son Joseph says: God has made me lord of all Egypt. Come down to me; don't delay.[n] 10You shall live in the region of Goshen[o] and be near me—you, your children and grandchildren, your flocks and herds, and all you have. 11I will provide for you there,[p] because five years of famine are still to come. Otherwise you and your household and all who belong to you will become destitute.'

12"You can see for yourselves, and so can my brother Benjamin, that it is really I who am speaking to you. 13Tell my father about all the honour accorded me in Egypt and about everything you have seen. And bring my father down here quickly.[q]"

14Then he threw his arms around his brother Benjamin and wept, and Benjamin embraced him, weeping. 15And he kissed[r] all his brothers and wept over them. Afterwards his brothers talked with him.[s]

16When the news reached Pharaoh's palace that Joseph's brothers had come,[t] Pharaoh and all his officials were pleased. 17Pharaoh said to Joseph, "Tell your brothers, 'Do this: Load your animals and return to the land of Canaan, 18and bring your father and your families back to me. I will give you the best

44:28 v Ge 37:33
44:29 w Ge 42:38
44:30 x 1Sa 18:1
44:32 y Ge 43:9
44:33 z Ge 43:18; a Jn 15:13
44:34 b Est 8:6
45:1 a Ge 43:31
45:2 b Ge 29:11; c ver 16; Ge 46:29
45:3 d Ac 7:13; e ver 15
45:4 f Ge 37:28
45:5 g Ge 42:21; h Ge 42:22; i ver 7-8; Ge 50:20; Ps 105:17
45:7 j 2Ki 19:4,30, 31; Isa 10:20,21; Mic 4:7; Zep 2:7; k Ex 15:2; Est 4:14; Isa 25:9
45:8 l Jdg 17:10; m Ge 41:41
45:9 n Ge 43:10
45:10 o Ge 46:28,34; Ge 47:1
45:11 p Ge 47:12
45:13 q Ac 7:14
45:15 r Lk 15:20; s ver 3
45:16 t Ac 7:13

[a]29 Hebrew *Sheol*; also in verse 31 [a]7 Or *save you as a great band of survivors*

of the land of Egypt[u] and you can
enjoy the fat of the land.'[v]
19"You are also directed to tell
them, 'Do this: Take some carts[w]
from Egypt for your children and
your wives, and get your father and
come. 20Never mind about your belongings, because the best of all
Egypt will be yours.' "
21So the sons of Israel did this. Joseph gave them carts, as Pharaoh
had commanded, and he also gave
them provisions for their journey.[x] 22To each of them he gave
new clothing, but to Benjamin he
gave three hundred shekels[b] of silver and five sets of clothes.[y] 23And
this is what he sent to his father:
ten donkeys loaded with the best
things of Egypt, and ten female
donkeys loaded with grain and
bread and other provisions for his
journey. 24Then he sent his
brothers away, and as they were
leaving he said to them, "Don't
quarrel on the way!"[z]
25So they went up out of Egypt
and came to their father Jacob in
the land of Canaan. 26They told him,
"Joseph is still alive! In fact, he is
ruler of all Egypt." Jacob was
stunned; he did not believe them.[a]
27But when they told him everything Joseph had said to them, and
when he saw the carts[b] Joseph had
sent to carry him back, the spirit of
their father Jacob revived. 28And
Israel said, "I'm convinced! My son
Joseph is still alive. I will go and
see him before I die."

Jacob Goes to Egypt

46 So Israel set out with all
that was his, and when he
reached Beersheba,[a] he offered
sacrifices to the God of his father
Isaac.[b]
2And God spoke to Israel in a
vision at night[c] and said, "Jacob!
Jacob!"
"Here I am,"[d] he replied.
3"I am God, the God of your
father,"[e] he said. "Do not be afraid
to go down to Egypt, for I will make
you into a great nation[f] there.[g] 4I
will go down to Egypt with you, and
I will surely bring you back
again.[h] And Joseph's own hand
will close your eyes.[i]"
5Then Jacob left Beersheba, and
Israel's sons took their father
Jacob and their children and their
wives in the carts[j] that Pharaoh
had sent to transport him. 6They
also took with them their livestock
and the possessions they had acquired in Canaan, and Jacob and all
his offspring went to Egypt.[k] 7He
took with him to Egypt his sons
and grandsons and his daughters
and granddaughters—all his offspring.[l]

8These are the names of the sons
of Israel[m] (Jacob and his descendants) who went to Egypt:

Reuben the firstborn of Jacob.
9The sons of Reuben:[n]
Hanoch, Pallu, Hezron and
Carmi.
10The sons of Simeon:[o]
Jemuel,[p] Jamin, Ohad, Jakin, Zohar and Shaul the son
of a Canaanite woman.
11The sons of Levi:[q]
Gershon, Kohath and Mer-
ari.
12The sons of Judah:[r]
Er, Onan, Shelah, Perez and
Zerah (but Er and Onan had
died in the land of Canaan).
The sons of Perez:[s]
Hezron and Hamul.
13The sons of Issachar:[t]
Tola, Puah,[a][u] Jashub[b] and
Shimron.
14The sons of Zebulun:[v]
Sered, Elon and Jahleel.
15These were the sons Leah bore
to Jacob in Paddan Aram,[c] besides
his daughter Dinah. These sons and

45:18 u Ge 27:28; Ge 46:34; Ge 47:6,11,27; Nu 18:12,29 v Ps 37:19
45:19 w Ge 46:5
45:21 x Ge 42:25
45:22 y Ge 37:3; Ge 43:34
45:24 z Ge 42:21-22
45:26 a Ge 44:28
45:27 b ver 19
46:1 a Ge 21:14; Ge 28:10 b Ge 26:24; Ge 28:13; Ge 31:42
46:2 c Ge 15:1; Job 33:14-15 d Ge 22:1; Ge 31:11
46:3 e Ge 28:13 f Ge 12:2; Dt 26:5 g Ex 1:7
46:4 h Ge 28:15; Ge 48:21; Ex 3:8 i Ge 50:1,24
46:5 j Ge 45:19
46:6 k Dt 26:5; Jos 24:4; Ps 105:23; Isa 52:4; Ac 7:15
46:7 l Ge 45:10
46:8 m Ex 1:1; Nu 26:4
46:9 n 1Ch 5:3
46:10 o Ge 29:33; Nu 26:14 p Ex 6:15
46:11 q Ge 29:34; Nu 3:17
46:12 r Ge 29:35 s 1Ch 2:5; Mt 1:3
46:13 t Ge 30:18 u 1Ch 7:1
46:14 v Ge 30:20

[b]*22* That is, about 7½ pounds (about 3.5 kilograms)
[a]*13* Samaritan Pentateuch and Syriac (see also 1 Chron. 7:1); Masoretic Text *Puvah*
[b]*13* Samaritan Pentateuch and some Septuagint manuscripts (see also Num. 26:24 and 1 Chron. 7:1); Masoretic Text *Job*
[c]*15* That is, North-west Mesopotamia

daughters of his were thirty-three
in all.

16 The sons of Gad:[w]
Zephon,[d][x] Haggi, Shuni, Ez-
bon, Eri, Arodi and Areli.
17 The sons of Asher:[y]
Imnah, Ishvah, Ishvi and
Beriah.
Their sister was Serah.
The sons of Beriah:
Heber and Malkiel.
18 These were the children born to
Jacob by Zilpah,[z] whom Laban had
given to his daughter Leah[a]—six-
teen in all.

19 The sons of Jacob's wife Rachel:
Joseph and Benjamin.[b] 20 In
Egypt, Manasseh[c] and Ephraim[d] were born to Joseph
by Asenath daughter of Potiphera, priest of On.[e]
21 The sons of Benjamin:[e]
Bela, Beker, Ashbel, Gera,
Naaman, Ehi, Rosh, Mup-
pim, Huppim and Ard.
22 These were the sons of Rachel
who were born to Jacob—fourteen
in all.

23 The son of Dan:
Hushim.
24 The sons of Naphtali:
Jahziel, Guni, Jezer and
Shillem.
25 These were the sons born to
Jacob by Bilhah,[f] whom Laban
had given to his daughter Rachel[g]—seven in all.

26 All those who went to Egypt
with Jacob—those who were his direct descendants, not counting his
sons' wives—numbered sixty-six
persons.[h] 27 With the two sons[f]
who had been born to Joseph in
Egypt, the members of Jacob's
family, which went to Egypt, were
seventy[g] in all.[i]

28 Now Jacob sent Judah ahead of
him to Joseph to get directions to
Goshen.[j] When they arrived in the
region of Goshen, 29 Joseph had his

46:16 w Ge 30:11 x Nu 26:15
46:17 y Ge 30:13 1Ch 7:30-31
46:18 z Ge 30:10 a Ge 29:24
46:19 b Ge 44:27
46:20 c Ge 41:51 d Ge 41:52
46:21 e Nu 26:38-41 1Ch 7:6-12 1Ch 8:1
46:25 f Ge 30:8 g Ge 29:29
46:26 h ver 5-7 Ex 1:5 Dt 10:22
46:27 i Ac 7:14
46:28 j Ge 45:10
46:29 k Ge 45:14-15 Lk 15:20
46:31 l Ge 47:1
46:33 m Ge 47:3
46:34 n Ge 45:10 o Ge 43:32 Ex 8:26
47:1 a Ge 46:31
47:3 b Ge 46:33
47:4 c Ge 15:13 Dt 26:5 d Ge 43:1 e Ge 46:34

chariot made ready and went to Goshen to meet his father Israel. As
soon as Joseph appeared before
him, he threw his arms around his
father[h] and wept for a long time.[k]
30 Israel said to Joseph, "Now I
am ready to die, since I have seen
for myself that you are still alive."
31 Then Joseph said to his
brothers and to his father's household, "I will go up and speak to
Pharaoh and will say to him, 'My
brothers and my father's household, who were living in the land of
Canaan, have come to me.[l] 32 The
men are shepherds; they tend livestock, and they have brought along
their flocks and herds and everything they own.' 33 When Pharaoh
calls you in and asks, 'What is your
occupation?'[m] 34 you should answer, 'Your servants have tended
livestock from our boyhood on, just
as our fathers did.' Then you will be
allowed to settle in the region of
Goshen,[n] for all shepherds are detestable to the Egyptians.[o]"

47

Joseph went and told Pharaoh, "My father and
brothers, with their flocks and
herds and everything they own,
have come from the land of Canaan
and are now in Goshen."[a] 2 He
chose five of his brothers and presented them before Pharaoh.
3 Pharaoh asked the brothers,
"What is your occupation?"[b]
"Your servants are shepherds,"
they replied to Pharaoh, "just as
our fathers were." 4 They also said
to him, "We have come to live here
awhile,[c] because the famine is severe in Canaan[d] and your servants' flocks have no pasture. So
now, please let your servants settle
in Goshen."[e]
5 Pharaoh said to Joseph, "Your
father and your brothers have

[d] *16* Samaritan Pentateuch and Septuagint (see also Num. 26:15); Masoretic Text *Ziphion*
[e] *20* That is, Heliopolis [f] *27* Hebrew; Septuagint *the nine children* [g] *27* Hebrew (see also Exodus 1:5 and footnote); Septuagint (see also Acts 7:14) *seventy-five* [h] *29* Hebrew *around him*

come to you, 6and the land of Egypt is before you; settle your father and your brothers in the best part of the land.[f] Let them live in Goshen. And if you know of any among them with special ability,[g] put them in charge of my own livestock."

7Then Joseph brought his father Jacob in and presented him before Pharaoh. After Jacob blessed[a] Pharaoh,[h] 8Pharaoh asked him, "How old are you?"

9And Jacob said to Pharaoh, "The years of my pilgrimage are a hundred and thirty.[i] My years have been few and difficult,[j] and they do not equal the years of the pilgrimage of my fathers.[k]" 10Then Jacob blessed[b] Pharaoh[l] and went out from his presence.

11So Joseph settled his father and his brothers in Egypt and gave them property in the best part of the land, the district of Rameses,[m] as Pharaoh directed. 12Joseph also provided his father and his brothers and all his father's household with food, according to the number of their children.[n]

Joseph and the Famine

13There was no food, however, in the whole region because the famine was severe; both Egypt and Canaan wasted away because of the famine.[o] 14Joseph collected all the money that was to be found in Egypt and Canaan in payment for the grain they were buying, and he brought it to Pharaoh's palace.[p] 15When the money of the people of Egypt and Canaan was gone, all Egypt came to Joseph and said, "Give us food. Why should we die before your eyes?[q] Our money is used up."

16"Then bring your livestock," said Joseph. "I will sell you food in exchange for your livestock, since your money is gone." 17So they brought their livestock to Joseph, and he gave them food in exchange for their horses,[r] their sheep and goats, their cattle and donkeys. And he brought them through that year with food in exchange for all their livestock.

18When that year was over, they came to him the following year and said, "We cannot hide from our lord the fact that since our money is gone and our livestock belongs to you, there is nothing left for our lord except our bodies and our land. 19Why should we perish before your eyes—we and our land as well? Buy us and our land in exchange for food, and we with our land will be in bondage to Pharaoh. Give us seed so that we may live and not die, and that the land may not become desolate."

20So Joseph bought all the land in Egypt for Pharaoh. The Egyptians, one and all, sold their fields, because the famine was too severe for them. The land became Pharaoh's, 21and Joseph reduced the people to servitude,[c] from one end of Egypt to the other. 22However, he did not buy the land of the priests, because they received a regular allotment from Pharaoh and had food enough from the allotment[s] Pharaoh gave them. That is why they did not sell their land.

23Joseph said to the people, "Now that I have bought you and your land today for Pharaoh, here is seed for you so you can plant the ground. 24But when the crop comes in, give a fifth[t] of it to Pharaoh. The other four-fifths you may keep as seed for the fields and as food for yourselves and your households and your children."

25"You have saved our lives," they said. "May we find favour in the eyes of our lord;[u] we will be in bondage to Pharaoh."

26So Joseph established it as a law concerning land in Egypt—still

47:6 f Ge 45:18 g Ex 18:21,25
47:7 h ver 10 2Sa 14:22
47:9 i Ge 25:7 j Heb 11:9,13 k Ge 35:28
47:10 l ver 7
47:11 m Ex 1:11 Ex 12:37
47:12 n Ge 45:11
47:13 o Ge 41:30 Ac 7:11
47:14 p Ge 41:56
47:15 q ver 19 Ex 16:3
47:17 r Ex 14:9
47:22 s Dt 14:28-29 Ezr 7:24
47:24 t Ge 41:34
47:25 u Ge 32:5

a7 Or *greeted* b10 Or *said farewell to*
c21 Samaritan Pentateuch and Septuagint (see also Vulgate); Masoretic Text *and he moved the people into the cities*

in force today—that a fifth of the
produce belongs to Pharaoh. It was
only the land of the priests that did
not become Pharaoh's.[v]
27Now the Israelites settled in
Egypt in the region of Goshen.
They acquired property there and
were fruitful and increased greatly
in number.[w]
28Jacob lived in Egypt[x] seventeen years, and the years of his life
were a hundred and forty-seven.
29When the time drew near for Israel to die,[y] he called for his son
Joseph and said to him, "If I have
found favour in your eyes, put your
hand under my thigh[z] and promise
that you will show me kindness and
faithfulness.[a] Do not bury me in
Egypt, 30but when I rest with my fathers, carry me out of Egypt and
bury me where they are buried."[b]
"I will do as you say," he said.
31"Swear to me,"[c] he said. Then
Joseph swore to him,[d] and Israel
worshipped as he leaned on the top
of his staff.[d][e]

Manasseh and Ephraim

48 Some time later Joseph
was told, "Your father is
ill." So he took his two sons Manasseh and Ephraim[a] along with him.
2When Jacob was told, "Your son
Joseph has come to you," Israel rallied his strength and sat up on the
bed.
3Jacob said to Joseph, "God
Almighty[a] appeared to me at Luz[b]
in the land of Canaan, and there he
blessed me[c] 4and said to me, 'I am
going to make you fruitful and will
increase your numbers.[d] I will
make you a community of peoples,
and I will give this land as an everlasting possession to your descendants after you.'
5"Now then, your two sons born
to you in Egypt[e] before I came to
you here will be reckoned as mine;
Ephraim and Manasseh will be
mine,[f] just as Reuben and Simeon
are mine. 6Any children born to you
after them will be yours; in the territory they inherit they will be
reckoned under the names of their
brothers. 7As I was returning from
Paddan,[b] to my sorrow Rachel
died in the land of Canaan while we
were still on the way, a little distance from Ephrath. So I buried her
there beside the road to Ephrath"
(that is, Bethlehem).[g]
8When Israel saw the sons of Joseph, he asked, "Who are these?"
9"They are the sons God has
given me here,"[h] Joseph said to his
father.
Then Israel said, "Bring them to
me so that I may bless[i] them."
10Now Israel's eyes were failing
because of old age, and he could
hardly see.[j] So Joseph brought his
sons close to him, and his father
kissed them[k] and embraced them.
11Israel said to Joseph, "I never
expected to see your face again,
and now God has allowed me to see
your children too."[l]
12Then Joseph removed them
from Israel's knees and bowed
down with his face to the ground.
13And Joseph took both of them,
Ephraim on his right towards Israel's left hand and Manasseh on
his left towards Israel's right
hand,[m] and brought them close to
him. 14But Israel reached out his
right hand and put it on Ephraim's
head, though he was the younger,
and crossing his arms, he put his
left hand on Manasseh's head, even
though Manasseh was the firstborn.[n]
15Then he blessed[o] Joseph and
said,

"May the God before whom my
fathers
Abraham and Isaac walked,
the God who has been my
shepherd[p]
all my life to this day,

47:26 v ver 22
47:27 w Ge 17:6; Ge 46:3; Ex 1:7
47:28 x Ps 105:23
47:29 y Dt 31:14; z Ge 24:2; a Ge 24:49
47:30 b Ge 49:29-32; Ge 50:5,13; Ac 7:15-16
47:31 c Ge 21:23; d Ge 24:3; e Heb 11:21 fn; 1Ki 1:47
48:1 a Ge 41:52
48:3 b Ge 28:19; c Ge 28:13; Ge 35:9-12
48:4 d Ge 17:6
48:5 e Ge 41:50-52; Ge 46:20; f 1Ch 5:1; Jos 14:4
48:7 g Ge 35:19
48:9 h Ge 33:5; i Ge 27:4
48:10 j Ge 27:1; k Ge 27:27
48:11 l Ge 50:23; Ps 128:6
48:13 m Ps 110:1
48:14 n Ge 41:51
48:15 o Ge 17:1; p Ge 49:24

d31 Or *Israel bowed down at the head of his bed*
a3 Hebrew *El-Shaddai*   b7 That is, North-west Mesopotamia

16 the Angel who has delivered me
   from all harm
 —may he bless these boys.[q]
May they be called by my name
 and the names of my fathers
   Abraham and Isaac,[r]
and may they increase greatly
   upon the earth."

17 When Joseph saw his father
placing his right hand on Ephraim's head[s] he was displeased;
so he took hold of his father's hand
to move it from Ephraim's head to
Manasseh's head. 18 Joseph said to
him, "No, my father, this one is the
firstborn; put your right hand on
his head."

19 But his father refused and said,
"I know, my son, I know. He too will
become a people, and he too will
become great.[t] Nevertheless, his
younger brother will be greater
than he,[u] and his descendants will
become a group of nations." 20 He
blessed them that day and said,

"In your[c] name will Israel
   pronounce this blessing:
'May God make you like
   Ephraim[v] and Manasseh.[w]' "

So he put Ephraim ahead of Manasseh.

21 Then Israel said to Joseph, "I
am about to die, but God will be
with you[d][x] and take you[d] back to
the land of your[d] fathers.[y] 22 And
to you, as one who is over your
brothers,[z] I give the ridge of
land[e][a] I took from the Amorites
with my sword and my bow."

Jacob Blesses His Sons

49:1–28Ref Dt 33:1–29

49 Then Jacob called for his sons and said: "Gather round so that I can tell you what will happen to you in days to come.[a]

2 "Assemble and listen, sons of
   Jacob;
 listen to your father Israel.[b]

3 "Reuben, you are my
   firstborn,[c]
 my might, the first sign of my
   strength,[d]
 excelling in honour, excelling
   in power.
4 Turbulent as the waters,[e] you
   will no longer excel,
 for you went up onto your
   father's bed,
 onto my couch and defiled it.[f]

5 "Simeon and Levi are
   brothers—
 their swords[a] are weapons of
   violence.[g]
6 Let me not enter their council,
 let me not join their
   assembly,[h]
 for they have killed men in
   their anger[i]
 and hamstrung oxen as they
   pleased.
7 Cursed be their anger, so
   fierce,
 and their fury, so cruel!
 I will scatter them in Jacob
 and disperse them in Israel.[j]

8 "Judah,[b] your brothers will
   praise you;
 your hand will be on the neck
   of your enemies;
 your father's sons will bow
   down to you.[k]
9 You are a lion[l]'s cub,
   O Judah;[m]
 you return from the prey, my
   son.
 Like a lion he crouches and lies
   down,
 like a lioness—who dares to
   rouse him?
10 The sceptre will not depart
   from Judah,[n]
 nor the ruler's staff from
   between his feet,

48:16 q Heb 11:21 r Ge 28:13
48:17 s ver 14
48:19 t Ge 17:20 u Ge 25:23
48:20 v Nu 2:18 w Nu 2:20 Ru 4:11
48:21 x Ge 26:3 Ge 46:4 y Ge 28:13 Ge 50:24
48:22 z Ge 37:8 a Jos 24:32 Jn 4:5
49:1 a Nu 24:14 Jer 23:20
49:2 b Ps 34:11
49:3 c Ge 29:32 d Dt 21:17 Ps 78:51
49:4 e Isa 57:20 f Ge 35:22 Dt 27:20
49:5 g Ge 34:25 Pr 4:17
49:6 h Pr 1:15 Eph 5:11 i Ge 34:26
49:7 j Jos 19:1,9 Jos 21:1-42
49:8 k Dt 33:7 1Ch 5:2
49:9 l Nu 24:9 Eze 19:5 Mic 5:8 m Rev 5:5
49:10 n Nu 24:17,19 Ps 60:7

c*20* The Hebrew is singular. d*21* The Hebrew is plural. e*22* Or *And to you I give one portion more than to your brothers—the portion*
a*5* The meaning of the Hebrew for this word is uncertain. b*8* *Judah* sounds like and may be derived from the Hebrew for *praise*.

until he comes to whom it
belongs[c]
and the obedience of the
nations is his.[o]
11 He will tether his donkey to a
vine,
his colt to the choicest branch;
he will wash his garments in
wine,
his robes in the blood of
grapes.
12 His eyes will be darker than
wine,
his teeth whiter than milk.[d]

13 "Zebulun[p] will live by the
seashore
and become a haven for ships;
his border will extend towards
Sidon.

14 "Issachar[q] is a scrawny[e]
donkey
lying down between two
saddlebags.[f]
15 When he sees how good is his
resting place
and how pleasant is his land,
he will bend his shoulder to the
burden
and submit to forced labour.

16 "Dan[g][r] will provide justice for
his people
as one of the tribes of Israel.
17 Dan[s] will be a serpent by the
roadside,
a viper along the path,
that bites the horse's heels
so that its rider tumbles
backwards.

18 "I look for your deliverance,
O LORD.[t]

19 "Gad[h][u] will be attacked by a
band of raiders,
but he will attack them at
their heels.

20 "Asher's[v] food will be rich;
he will provide delicacies fit
for a king.

21 "Naphtali[w] is a doe set free
that bears beautiful fawns.[i]

22 "Joseph[x] is a fruitful vine,
a fruitful vine near a spring,
whose branches climb over a
wall.[j]
23 With bitterness archers
attacked him;
they shot at him with
hostility.[y]
24 But his bow remained steady,
his strong arms[z] stayed[k]
supple,
because of the hand of the
Mighty One of Jacob,[a]
because of the Shepherd, the
Rock of Israel,[b]
25 because of your father's God,[c]
who helps you,
because of the Almighty,[l]
who blesses you
with blessings of the heavens
above,
blessings of the deep that lies
below,[d]
blessings of the breast and
womb.
26 Your father's blessings are
greater
than the blessings of the
ancient mountains,
than[m] the bounty of the
age-old hills.
Let all these rest on the head of
Joseph,
on the brow of the prince
among[n] his brothers.[e]

27 "Benjamin[f] is a ravenous wolf;
in the morning he devours the
prey,
in the evening he divides the
plunder."

28 All these are the twelve tribes
of Israel, and this is what their
father said to them when he

49:10 o Ps 2:9; Isa 42:1,4
49:13 p Ge 30:20; Dt 33:18-19; Jos 19:10-11
49:14 q Ge 30:18
49:16 r Ge 30:6; Dt 33:22; Jdg 18:26-27
49:17 s Jdg 18:27
49:18 t Ps 119:166, 174
49:19 u Ge 30:11; Dt 33:20; 1Ch 5:18
49:20 v Ge 30:13; Dt 33:24
49:21 w Ge 30:8; Dt 33:23
49:22 x Ge 30:24; Dt 33:13-17
49:23 y Ge 37:24
49:24 z Ps 18:34; a Ps 132:2,5; Isa 1:24; Isa 41:10; b Isa 28:16
49:25 c Ge 28:13; d Ge 27:28
49:26 e Dt 33:15-16
49:27 f Ge 35:18; Jdg 20:12-13

[c] 10 Or *until Shiloh comes;* or *until he comes to whom tribute belongs* [d] 12 Or *will be dull from wine, / his teeth white from milk* [e] 14 Or *strong* [f] 14 Or *campfires* [g] 16 *Dan* here means *he provides justice.* [h] 19 *Gad* can mean *attack* and *band of raiders.* [i] 21 Or *free; / he utters beautiful words* [j] 22 Or *Joseph is a wild colt, / a wild colt near a spring, / a wild donkey on a terraced hill* [k] 23,24 Or *archers will attack ... will shoot ... will remain ... will stay* [l] 25 Hebrew *Shaddai* [m] 26 Or *of my progenitors, / as great as* [n] 26 Or *the one separated from*

blessed them, giving each the blessing appropriate to him.

The Death of Jacob

29 Then he gave them these instructions:[g] "I am about to be gathered to my people.[h] Bury me with my fathers[i] in the cave in the field of Ephron the Hittite, 30 the cave in the field of Machpelah,[j] near Mamre in Canaan, which Abraham bought as a burial place from Ephron the Hittite, along with the field.[k] 31 There Abraham[l] and his wife Sarah[m] were buried, there Isaac and his wife Rebekah[n] were buried, and there I buried Leah. 32 The field and the cave in it were bought from the Hittites."[a]

33 When Jacob had finished giving instructions to his sons, he drew his feet up into the bed, breathed his last and was gathered to his people.[o]

50 Joseph threw himself upon his father and wept over him and kissed him.[a] 2 Then Joseph directed the physicians in his service to embalm his father Israel. So the physicians embalmed him,[b] 3 taking a full forty days, for that was the time required for embalming. And the Egyptians mourned for him seventy days.[c]

4 When the days of mourning had passed, Joseph said to Pharaoh's court, "If I have found favour in your eyes, speak to Pharaoh for me. Tell him, 5 'My father made me swear an oath[d] and said, "I am about to die; bury me in the tomb I dug for myself[e] in the land of Canaan."[f] Now let me go up and bury my father; then I will return.' "

6 Pharaoh said, "Go up and bury your father, as he made you swear to do."

7 So Joseph went up to bury his father. All Pharaoh's officials accompanied him—the dignitaries of his court and all the dignitaries of Egypt—8 besides all the members of Joseph's household and his brothers and those belonging to his father's household. Only their children and their flocks and herds were left in Goshen. 9 Chariots and horsemen[a] also went up with him. It was a very large company.

10 When they reached the threshing-floor of Atad, near the Jordan, they lamented loudly and bitterly;[g] and there Joseph observed a seven-day period[h] of mourning for his father. 11 When the Canaanites who lived there saw the mourning at the threshing-floor of Atad, they said, "The Egyptians are holding a solemn ceremony of mourning." That is why that place near the Jordan is called Abel Mizraim.[b]

12 So Jacob's sons did as he had commanded them: 13 They carried him to the land of Canaan and buried him in the cave in the field of Machpelah, near Mamre, which Abraham had bought as a burial place from Ephron the Hittite, along with the field.[i] 14 After burying his father, Joseph returned to Egypt, together with his brothers and all the others who had gone with him to bury his father.

Joseph Reassures His Brothers

15 When Joseph's brothers saw that their father was dead, they said, "What if Joseph holds a grudge against us and pays us back for all the wrongs we did to him?"[j] 16 So they sent word to Joseph, saying, "Your father left these instructions before he died: 17 'This is what you are to say to Joseph: I ask you to forgive your brothers the sins and the wrongs they committed in treating you so badly.' Now please forgive the sins of the servants of the God of your father." When their message came to him, Joseph wept.

18 His brothers then came and threw themselves down before

49:29
g Ge 50:16
h Ge 25:8
i Ge 15:15; Ge 47:30; Ge 50:13

49:30
j Ge 23:9
k Ge 23:20

49:31
l Ge 25:9
m Ge 23:19
n Ge 35:29

49:33
o ver 29; Ge 25:8; Ac 7:15

50:1
a Ge 46:4

50:2
b ver 26; 2Ch 16:14

50:3
c Ge 37:34; Nu 20:29; Dt 34:8

50:5
d Ge 47:31
e 2Ch 16:14; Isa 22:16
f Ge 47:31

50:10
g 2Sa 1:17; Ac 8:2
h 1Sa 31:13; Job 2:13

50:13
i Ge 23:20; Ac 7:16

50:15
j Ge 37:28; Ge 42:21-22

a32 Or *the sons of Heth*
a9 Or *charioteers*
b11 *Abel Mizraim* means *mourning of the Egyptians.*

him.[k] "We are your slaves,"[l] they
said.
19But Joseph said to them, "Don't
be afraid. Am I in the place of
God?[m] 20You intended to harm
me,[n] but God intended[o] it for
good[p] to accomplish what is now
being done, the saving of many
lives.[q] 21So then, don't be afraid. I
will provide for you and your children.[r]" And he reassured them
and spoke kindly to them.

The Death of Joseph

22Joseph stayed in Egypt, along
with all his father's family. He
lived a hundred and ten years[s]
23and saw the third generation[t] of
Ephraim's children. Also the children of Makir[u] son of Manasseh
were placed at birth on Joseph's
knees.[c]
24Then Joseph said to his
brothers, "I am about to die.[v] But
God will surely come to your aid[w]
and take you up out of this land to
the land[x] he promised on oath
to Abraham, Isaac and Jacob."[y]
25And Joseph made the sons of Israel swear an oath and said, "God
will surely come to your aid, and
then you must carry my bones up
from this place."[z]
26So Joseph died at the age of a
hundred and ten. And after they
embalmed him,[a] he was placed in
a coffin in Egypt.

50:18 *k* Ge 37:7 *l* Ge 43:18
50:19 *m* Ro 12:19 Heb 10:30
50:20 *n* Ge 37:20 *o* Mic 4:11-12 *p* Ro 8:28 *q* Ge 45:5
50:21 *r* Ge 45:11 Ge 47:12
50:22 *s* Ge 25:7 Jos 24:29
50:23 *t* Job 42:16 *u* Nu 32:39,40
50:24 *v* Ge 48:21 *w* Ex 3:16-17 *x* Ge 15:14 *y* Ge 12:7 Ge 26:3 Ge 28:13 Ge 35:12
50:25 *z* Ge 47:29-30 Ex 13:19 Jos 24:32 Heb 11:22 **50:26** *a* ver 2

c23 That is, were counted as his

EXODUS

The Israelites Oppressed

1 These are the names of the sons of Israel[a] who went to Egypt with Jacob, each with his family: 2 Reuben, Simeon, Levi and Judah; 3 Issachar, Zebulun and Benjamin; 4 Dan and Naphtali; Gad and Asher. 5 The descendants of Jacob numbered seventy[a] in all;[b] Joseph was already in Egypt.

6 Now Joseph and all his brothers and all that generation died,[c] 7 but the Israelites were fruitful and multiplied greatly and became exceedingly numerous,[d] so that the land was filled with them.

8 Then a new king, who did not know about Joseph, came to power in Egypt. 9 "Look," he said to his people, "the Israelites have become much too numerous[e] for us. 10 Come, we must deal shrewdly[f] with them or they will become even more numerous and, if war breaks out, will join our enemies, fight against us and leave the country."[g]

11 So they put slave masters[h] over them to oppress them with forced labour,[i] and they built Pithom and Rameses[j] as store cities[k] for Pharaoh. 12 But the more they were oppressed, the more they multiplied and spread; so the Egyptians came to dread the Israelites 13 and worked them ruthlessly.[l] 14 They made their lives bitter with hard labour in brick and mortar and with all kinds of work in the fields; in all their hard labour the Egyptians used them ruthlessly.[m]

15 The king of Egypt said to the Hebrew midwives, whose names were Shiphrah and Puah, 16 "When you help the Hebrew women in childbirth and observe them on the delivery stool, if it is a boy, kill him; but if it is a girl, let her live." 17 The midwives, however, feared[n] God and did not do what the king of Egypt had told them to do;[o] they let the boys live. 18 Then the king of Egypt summoned the midwives and asked them, "Why have you done this? Why have you let the boys live?"

19 The midwives answered Pharaoh, "Hebrew women are not like Egyptian women; they are vigorous and give birth before the midwives arrive."[p]

20 So God was kind to the midwives[q] and the people increased and became even more numerous. 21 And because the midwives feared God, he gave them families[r] of their own.

22 Then Pharaoh gave this order to all his people: "Every boy that is born[b] you must throw into the Nile, but let every girl live."[s]

The Birth of Moses

2 Now a man of the house of Levi married a Levite woman,[a] 2 and she became pregnant and gave birth to a son. When she saw that he was a fine child, she hid him for three months.[b] 3 But when she could hide him no longer, she got a papyrus basket for him and coated it with tar and pitch. Then she placed the child in it and put it among the reeds along the bank of the Nile. 4 His sister[c] stood at a distance to see what would happen to him.

5 Then Pharaoh's daughter went down to the Nile to bathe, and her

1:1 a Ge 46:8
1:5 b Ge 46:26
1:6 c Ge 50:26
1:7 d Ge 46:3; Dt 26:5; Ac 7:17
1:9 e Ps 105:24-25
1:10 f Ps 83:3; g Ac 7:17-19
1:11 h Ex 3:7; i Ge 15:13; Ex 2:11; Ex 5:4; Ex 6:6-7; j Ge 47:11; k 1Ki 9:19; 2Ch 8:4
1:13 l Dt 4:20
1:14 m Ex 2:23; Ex 6:9; Nu 20:15; Ps 81:6; Ac 7:19
1:17 n ver 21; Pr 16:6; o Da 3:16-18; Ac 4:18-20; Ac 5:29
1:19 p Jos 2:4-6; 2Sa 17:20
1:20 q ver 12; Pr 11:18; Isa 3:10
1:21 r 1Sa 2:35; 2Sa 7:11, 27-29; 1Ki 11:38
1:22 s Ac 7:19
2:1 a Ex 6:20; Nu 26:59
2:2 b Ac 7:20; Heb 11:23
2:4 c Ex 15:20; Nu 26:59

[a]5 Masoretic Text (see also Gen. 46:27); Dead Sea Scrolls and Septuagint (see also Acts 7:14 and note at Gen. 46:27) *seventy-five*   [b]22 Masoretic Text; Samaritan Pentateuch, Septuagint and Targums *born to the Hebrews*

attendants were walking along the river bank.[d] She saw the basket among the reeds and sent her slave girl to get it. 6She opened it and saw the baby. He was crying, and she felt sorry for him. "This is one of the Hebrew babies," she said.

7Then his sister asked Pharaoh's daughter, "Shall I go and get one of the Hebrew women to nurse the baby for you?"

8"Yes, go," she answered. And the girl went and got the baby's mother. 9Pharaoh's daughter said to her, "Take this baby and nurse him for me, and I will pay you." So the woman took the baby and nursed him. 10When the child grew older, she took him to Pharaoh's daughter and he became her son. She named him Moses,[a] saying, "I drew him out of the water."

Moses Flees to Midian

11One day, after Moses had grown up, he went out to where his own people[e] were and watched them at their hard labour. He saw an Egyptian beating a Hebrew, one of his own people. 12Glancing this way and that and seeing no-one, he killed the Egyptian and hid him in the sand. 13The next day he went out and saw two Hebrews fighting. He asked the one in the wrong, "Why are you hitting your fellow Hebrew?"[f]

14The man said, "Who made you ruler and judge over us?[g] Are you thinking of killing me as you killed the Egyptian?" Then Moses was afraid and thought, "What I did must have become known."

15When Pharaoh heard of this, he tried to kill Moses, but Moses fled from Pharaoh and went to live in Midian,[h] where he sat down by a well. 16Now a priest of Midian[i] had seven daughters, and they came to draw water[j] and fill the troughs to water their father's flock. 17Some shepherds came along and drove them away, but Moses got up and came to their rescue and watered their flock.[k]

18When the girls returned to Reuel[l] their father, he asked them, "Why have you returned so early today?"

19They answered, "An Egyptian rescued us from the shepherds. He even drew water for us and watered the flock."

20"And where is he?" he asked his daughters. "Why did you leave him? Invite him to have something to eat."[m]

21Moses agreed to stay with the man, who gave his daughter Zipporah[n] to Moses in marriage. 22Zipporah gave birth to a son, and Moses named him Gershom,[b] saying, "I have become an alien[o] in a foreign land."

23During that long period,[p] the king of Egypt died. The Israelites groaned in their slavery and cried out, and their cry[q] for help because of their slavery went up to God. 24God heard their groaning and he remembered his covenant[r] with Abraham, with Isaac and with Jacob. 25So God looked on the Israelites and was concerned[s] about them.

Moses and the Burning Bush

3 Now Moses was tending the flock of Jethro[a] his father-in-law, the priest of Midian, and he led the flock to the far side of the desert and came to Horeb,[b] the mountain[c] of God. 2There the angel of the LORD[d] appeared to him in flames of fire from within a bush.[e] Moses saw that though the bush was on fire it did not burn up. 3So Moses thought, "I will go over and see this strange sight—why the bush does not burn up."

4When the LORD saw that he had

2:5 d Ex 7:15; Ex 8:20
2:11 e Ac 7:23; Heb 11:24-26
2:13 f Ac 7:26
2:14 g Ac 7:27*
2:15 h Ac 7:29; Heb 11:27
2:16 i Ex 3:1; j Ge 24:11
2:17 k Ge 29:10
2:18 l Nu 10:29
2:20 m Ge 31:54
2:21 n Ex 18:2
2:22 o Ex 18:3-4; Heb 11:13
2:23 p Ac 7:30; q Ex 3:7,9; Dt 26:7; Jas 5:4
2:24 r Ex 6:5; Ps 105:10,42
2:25 s Ex 3:7; Ex 4:31
3:1 a Ex 2:18; b 1Ki 19:8; c Ex 18:5
3:2 d Ge 16:7; e Dt 33:16; Mk 12:26; Ac 7:30

a10 *Moses* sounds like the Hebrew for *draw out.*
b22 *Gershom* sounds like the Hebrew for *an alien there.*

gone over to look, God called to him from within the bush, "Moses! Moses!"

And Moses said, "Here I am."

5"Do not come any closer," God said. "Take off your sandals, for the place where you are standing is holy ground."[f] 6Then he said, "I am the God of your father, the God of Abraham, the God of Isaac and the God of Jacob."[g] At this, Moses hid his face, because he was afraid to look at God.

7The LORD said, "I have indeed seen the misery of my people in Egypt. I have heard them crying out because of their slave drivers, and I am concerned[h] about their suffering. 8So I have come down[i] to rescue them from the hand of the Egyptians and to bring them up out of that land into a good and spacious land, a land flowing with milk and honey[j]—the home of the Canaanites, Hittites, Amorites, Perizzites, Hivites and Jebusites.[k] 9And now the cry of the Israelites has reached me, and I have seen the way the Egyptians are oppressing[l] them. 10So now, go. I am sending you to Pharaoh to bring my people the Israelites out of Egypt."[m]

11But Moses said to God, "Who am I,[n] that I should go to Pharaoh and bring the Israelites out of Egypt?"

12And God said, "I will be with you.[o] And this will be the sign to you that it is I who have sent you: When you have brought the people out of Egypt, you[a] will worship God on this mountain."

13Moses said to God, "Suppose I go to the Israelites and say to them, 'The God of your fathers has sent me to you,' and they ask me, 'What is his name?' Then what shall I tell them?"

14God said to Moses, "I AM WHO I AM.[b] This is what you are to say to the Israelites: 'I AM[p] has sent me to you.' "

15God also said to Moses, "Say to the Israelites, 'The LORD,[c] the God of your fathers—the God of Abraham, the God of Isaac and the God of Jacob—has sent me to you.' This is my name[q] for ever, the name by which I am to be remembered from generation to generation.

16"Go, assemble the elders[r] of Israel and say to them, 'The LORD, the God of your fathers—the God of Abraham, Isaac and Jacob—appeared to me and said: I have watched over you and have seen what has been done to you in Egypt. 17And I have promised to bring you up out of your misery in Egypt[s] into the land of the Canaanites, Hittites, Amorites, Perizzites, Hivites and Jebusites—a land flowing with milk and honey.'

18"The elders of Israel will listen[t] to you. Then you and the elders are to go to the king of Egypt and say to him, 'The LORD, the God of the Hebrews, has met with us. Let us take a three-day journey into the desert to offer sacrifices[u] to the LORD our God.' 19But I know that the king of Egypt will not let you go unless a mighty hand[v] compels him. 20So I will stretch out my hand[w] and strike the Egyptians with all the wonders[x] that I will perform among them. After that, he will let you go.[y]

21"And I will make the Egyptians favourably disposed[z] towards this people, so that when you leave you will not go empty-handed.[a] 22Every woman is to ask her neighbour and any woman living in her house for articles of silver and gold[b] and for clothing, which you will put on your sons and daughters. And so you will plunder[c] the Egyptians."

3:5 f Ge 28:17; Jos 5:15; Ac 7:33*
3:6 g Ex 4:5; Mt 22:32*; Mk 12:26*; Lk 20:37*; Ac 7:32*
3:7 h Ex 2:25
3:8 i Ge 50:24; j ver 17; Ex 13:5; Dt 1:25; k Ge 15:18-21
3:9 l Ex 1:14; Ex 2:23
3:10 m Mic 6:4
3:11 n Ex 6:12,30; 1Sa 18:18
3:12 o Ge 31:3; Jos 1:5; Ro 8:31
3:14 p Ex 6:2-3; Jn 8:58; Heb 13:8
3:15 q Ps 135:13; Hos 12:5
3:16 r Ex 4:29
3:17 s Ge 15:16; Jos 24:11
3:18 t Ex 4:1,8,31; u Ex 5:1,3
3:19 v Ex 4:21; Ex 5:2
3:20 w Ex 6:1,6; Ex 9:15; x Dt 6:22; Ne 9:10; Ac 7:36; y Ex 12:31-33
3:21 z Ex 12:36; a Ps 105:37
3:22 b Ex 11:2; c Eze 39:10

[a] *12* The Hebrew is plural. [b] *14* Or *I WILL BE WHAT I WILL BE* [c] *15* The Hebrew for *LORD* sounds like and may be derived from the Hebrew for *I AM* in verse 14.

Signs for Moses

4 Moses answered, "What if they do not believe me or listen[a] to me and say, 'The LORD did not appear to you'?"

2Then the LORD said to him, "What is that in your hand?"

"A staff,"[b] he replied.

3The LORD said, "Throw it on the ground."

Moses threw it on the ground and it became a snake, and he ran from it. 4Then the LORD said to him, "Reach out your hand and take it by the tail." So Moses reached out and took hold of the snake and it turned back into a staff in his hand. 5"This," said the LORD, "is so that they may believe[c] that the LORD, the God of their fathers—the God of Abraham, the God of Isaac and the God of Jacob—has appeared to you."

6Then the LORD said, "Put your hand inside your cloak." So Moses put his hand into his cloak, and when he took it out, it was leprous,[a] like snow.[d]

7"Now put it back into your cloak," he said. So Moses put his hand back into his cloak, and when he took it out, it was restored,[e] like the rest of his flesh.

8Then the LORD said, "If they do not believe you or pay attention to the first miraculous sign, they may believe the second. 9But if they do not believe these two signs or listen to you, take some water from the Nile and pour it on the dry ground. The water you take from the river will become blood[f] on the ground."

10Moses said to the LORD, "O Lord, I have never been eloquent, neither in the past nor since you have spoken to your servant. I am slow of speech and tongue."[g]

11The LORD said to him, "Who gave man his mouth? Who makes him deaf or mute? Who gives him sight or makes him blind?[h] Is it not I, the LORD? 12Now go; I will help you speak and will teach you what to say."[i]

13But Moses said, "O Lord, please send someone else to do it."

14Then the LORD's anger burned against Moses and he said, "What about your brother, Aaron the Levite? I know he can speak well. He is already on his way to meet[j] you, and his heart will be glad when he sees you. 15You shall speak to him and put words in his mouth;[k] I will help both of you speak and will teach you what to do. 16He will speak to the people for you, and it will be as if he were your mouth[l] and as if you were God to him. 17But take this staff[m] in your hand so that you can perform miraculous signs[n] with it."

Moses Returns to Egypt

18Then Moses went back to Jethro his father-in-law and said to him, "Let me go back to my own people in Egypt to see if any of them are still alive."

Jethro said, "Go, and I wish you well."

19Now the LORD had said to Moses in Midian, "Go back to Egypt, for all the men who wanted to kill[o] you are dead."[p] 20So Moses took his wife and sons, put them on a donkey and started back to Egypt. And he took the staff[q] of God in his hand.

21The LORD said to Moses, "When you return to Egypt, see that you perform before Pharaoh all the wonders[r] I have given you the power to do. But I will harden his heart[s] so that he will not let the people go. 22Then say to Pharaoh, 'This is what the LORD says: Israel is my firstborn son,[t] 23and I told you, "Let my son go,[u] so that he may worship me." But you refused to let him go; so I will kill your firstborn son.' "[v]

4:1 a Ex 3:18; Ex 6:30
4:2 b ver 17,20
4:5 c Ex 19:9
4:6 d Nu 12:10; 2Ki 5:1,27
4:7 e Nu 12:13-15; Dt 32:39; 2Ki 5:14; Mt 8:3
4:9 f Ex 7:17-21
4:10 g Ex 6:12; Jer 1:6
4:11 h Ps 94:9; Mt 11:5
4:12 i Isa 50:4; Jer 1:9; Mt 10:19-20; Mk 13:11; Lk 12:12; Lk 21:14-15
4:14 j ver 27
4:15 k Nu 23:5,12,16
4:16 l Ex 7:1-2
4:17 m ver 2; n Ex 7:9-21
4:19 o Ex 2:15; p Ex 2:23
4:20 q Ex 17:9; Nu 20:8-9,11
4:21 r Ex 3:19,20; s Ex 7:3,13; Ex 9:12,35; Ex 14:4,8; Dt 2:30; Isa 63:17; Jn 12:40; Ro 9:18
4:22 t Isa 63:16; Isa 64:8; Jer 31:9; Hos 11:1; Ro 9:4
4:23 u Ex 5:1; Ex 7:16; v Ex 11:5; Ex 12:12,29

a6 The Hebrew word was used for various diseases affecting the skin—not necessarily leprosy.

24At a lodging place on the way,
the LORD met ⌞Moses⌟[b] and was
about to kill[w] him. 25But Zipporah
took a flint knife, cut off her son's
foreskin[x] and touched ⌞Moses'⌟ feet
with it.[c] "Surely you are a bridegroom of blood to me," she said.
26So the LORD let him alone. (At that
time she said "bridegroom of
blood", referring to circumcision.)
27The LORD said to Aaron, "Go
into the desert to meet Moses." So
he met Moses at the mountain[y] of
God and kissed[z] him. 28Then
Moses told Aaron everything the
LORD had sent him to say,[a] and also
about all the miraculous signs he
had commanded him to perform.
29Moses and Aaron brought together all the elders[b] of the Israelites, 30and Aaron told them
everything the LORD had said to
Moses. He also performed the
signs before the people, 31and they
believed.[c] And when they heard
that the LORD was concerned[d]
about them and had seen their
misery, they bowed down and
worshipped.

Bricks Without Straw

5 Afterwards Moses and Aaron
went to Pharaoh and said,
"This is what the LORD, the God of
Israel, says: 'Let my people go, so
that they may hold a festival[a] to
me in the desert.' "
2Pharaoh said, "Who is the
LORD,[b] that I should obey him and
let Israel go? I do not know the
LORD and I will not let Israel go."[c]
3Then they said, "The God of the
Hebrews has met with us. Now let
us take a three-day journey into the
desert to offer sacrifices to the
LORD our God, or he may strike us
with plagues[d] or with the sword."
4But the king of Egypt said,
"Moses and Aaron, why are you
taking the people away from their
labour?[e] Get back to your work!"
5Then Pharaoh said, "Look, the people of the land are now numerous,[f]

4:24
w Nu 22:22
4:25
x Ge 17:14
Jos 5:2,3
4:27
y Ex 3:1
z ver 14
4:28
a ver 8-9,16
4:29
b Ex 3:16
4:31
c ver 8
Ex 3:18
d Ex 2:25
5:1
a Ex 3:18
5:2
b 2Ki 18:35
Job 21:15
c Ex 3:19
5:3
d Ex 3:18
5:4
e Ex 1:11
5:5
f Ex 1:7,9
5:14
g Isa 10:24
5:17
h ver 8

and you are stopping them from
working."
6That same day Pharaoh gave
this order to the slave drivers and
foremen in charge of the people:
7"You are no longer to supply the
people with straw for making
bricks; let them go and gather their
own straw. 8But require them to
make the same number of bricks as
before; don't reduce the quota.
They are lazy; that is why they are
crying out, 'Let us go and sacrifice
to our God.' 9Make the work harder
for the men so that they keep working and pay no attention to lies."
10Then the slave drivers and the
foremen went out and said to the
people, "This is what Pharaoh says:
'I will not give you any more straw.
11Go and get your own straw wherever you can find it, but your work
will not be reduced at all.' " 12So the
people scattered all over Egypt to
gather stubble to use for straw.
13The slave drivers kept pressing
them, saying, "Complete the work
required of you for each day, just
as when you had straw." 14The Israelite foremen appointed by Pharaoh's slave drivers were beaten[g]
and were asked, "Why didn't you
meet your quota of bricks yesterday or today, as before?"
15Then the Israelite foremen
went and appealed to Pharaoh:
"Why have you treated your servants this way? 16Your servants are
given no straw, yet we are told,
'Make bricks!' Your servants are
being beaten, but the fault is with
your own people."
17Pharaoh said, "Lazy, that's
what you are—lazy![h] That is why
you keep saying, 'Let us go and sacrifice to the LORD.' 18Now get to
work. You will not be given any
straw, yet you must produce your
full quota of bricks."
19The Israelite foremen realised
they were in trouble when they

[b]24 Or ⌞*Moses' son*⌟; Hebrew *him*
[c]25 Or *and drew near* ⌞*Moses'*⌟ *feet*

were told, "You are not to reduce the number of bricks required of you for each day." 20When they left Pharaoh, they found Moses and Aaron waiting to meet them, 21and they said, "May the LORD look upon you and judge you! You have made us a stench[i] to Pharaoh and his officials and have put a sword in their hand to kill us."[j]

God Promises Deliverance

22Moses returned to the LORD and said, "O Lord, why have you brought trouble upon this people?[k] Is this why you sent me? 23Ever since I went to Pharaoh to speak in your name, he has brought trouble upon this people, and you have not rescued[l] your people at all."

6 Then the LORD said to Moses, "Now you will see what I will do to Pharaoh: Because of my mighty hand[a] he will let them go;[b] because of my mighty hand he will drive them out of his country."[c]

2God also said to Moses, "I am the LORD. 3I appeared to Abraham, to Isaac and to Jacob as God Almighty,[a][d] but by my name[e] the LORD[b][f] I did not make myself known to them.[c] 4I also established my covenant[g] with them to give them the land of Canaan, where they lived as aliens.[h] 5Moreover, I have heard the groaning[i] of the Israelites, whom the Egyptians are enslaving, and I have remembered my covenant.

6"Therefore, say to the Israelites: 'I am the LORD, and I will bring you out from under the yoke of the Egyptians. I will free you from being slaves to them, and I will redeem[j] you with an outstretched arm[k] and with mighty acts of judgment. 7I will take you as my own people, and I will be your God.[l] Then you will know[m] that I am the LORD your God, who brought you out from under the yoke of the Egyptians. 8And I will bring you to the land[n] I swore with uplifted hand[o] to give to Abraham, to Isaac and to Jacob.[p] I will give it to you as a possession. I am the LORD.' "

9Moses reported this to the Israelites, but they did not listen to him because of their discouragement and cruel bondage.

10Then the LORD said to Moses, 11"Go, tell Pharaoh king of Egypt to let the Israelites go out of his country."

12But Moses said to the LORD, "If the Israelites will not listen to me, why would Pharaoh listen to me, since I speak with faltering lips?"[d][q]

Family Record of Moses and Aaron

13Now the LORD spoke to Moses and Aaron about the Israelites and Pharaoh king of Egypt, and he commanded them to bring the Israelites out of Egypt.

14These were the heads of their families:[e][r]

The sons of Reuben the firstborn son of Israel were Hanoch and Pallu, Hezron and Carmi. These were the clans of Reuben.

15The sons of Simeon[s] were Jemuel, Jamin, Ohad, Jakin, Zohar and Shaul the son of a Canaanite woman. These were the clans of Simeon.

16These were the names of the sons of Levi according to their records: Gershon,[t] Kohath and Merari.[u] Levi lived 137 years.

17The sons of Gershon, by clans, were Libni and Shimei.[v]

18The sons of Kohath were Amram, Izhar, Hebron and Uzziel.[w] Kohath lived 133 years.

5:21 *i* Ge 34:30 *j* Ex 14:11
5:22 *k* Nu 11:11
5:23 *l* Jer 4:10
6:1 *a* Ex 3:19 *b* Ex 3:20 *c* Ex 12:31,33, 39
6:3 *d* Ge 17:1 *e* Ps 68:4 Ps 83:18 Isa 52:6 *f* Ex 3:14
6:4 *g* Ge 15:18 *h* Ge 28:4,13
6:5 *i* Ex 2:23
6:6 *j* Dt 7:8 1Ch 17:21 *k* Dt 26:8
6:7 *l* Dt 4:20 2Sa 7:24 *m* Ex 16:12 Isa 41:20
6:8 *n* Ge 15:18 Ge 26:3 *o* Ge 14:22 *p* Ps 136:21-22
6:12 *q* ver 30 Ex 4:10 Jer 1:6
6:14 *r* Ge 46:9
6:15 *s* Ge 46:10 1Ch 4:24
6:16 *t* Ge 46:11 *u* Nu 3:17
6:17 *v* 1Ch 6:17
6:18 *w* 1Ch 6:2,18

[a]3 Hebrew *El-Shaddai* [b]3 See note at Exodus 3:15. [c]3 Or *Almighty, and by my name the LORD did I not let myself be known to them?* [d]12 Hebrew *I am uncircumcised of lips*; also in verse 30 [e]14 The Hebrew for *families* here and in verse 25 refers to units larger than clans.

19The sons of Merari were
Mahli and Mushi.[x]
These were the clans of Levi
according to their records.
20Amram married his
father's sister Jochebed, who
bore him Aaron and Moses.[y]
Amram lived 137 years.
21The sons of Izhar[z] were
Korah, Nepheg and Zicri.
22The sons of Uzziel were Mishael, Elzaphan[a] and Sithri.
23Aaron married Elisheba,
daughter of Amminadab[b] and
sister of Nahshon, and she bore
him Nadab and Abihu,[c] Eleazar[d] and Ithamar.[e]
24The sons of Korah[f] were
Assir, Elkanah and Abiasaph.
These were the Korahite clans.
25Eleazar son of Aaron married one of the daughters of
Putiel, and she bore him
Phinehas.[g]

These were the heads of the
Levite families, clan by clan.

26It was this same Aaron and
Moses to whom the LORD said,
"Bring the Israelites out of Egypt
by their divisions."[h] 27They were
the ones who spoke to Pharaoh king
of Egypt about bringing the Israelites out of Egypt. It was the same
Moses and Aaron.

Aaron to Speak for Moses

28Now when the LORD spoke to
Moses in Egypt, 29he said to him, "I
am the LORD.[i] Tell Pharaoh king of
Egypt everything I tell you."
30But Moses said to the LORD,
"Since I speak with faltering lips,[j]
why would Pharaoh listen to me?"

7 Then the LORD said to Moses,
"See, I have made you like
God[a] to Pharaoh, and your brother
Aaron will be your prophet. 2You
are to say everything I command
you, and your brother Aaron is to
tell Pharaoh to let the Israelites go
out of his country. 3But I will
harden Pharaoh's heart,[b] and
though I multiply my miraculous
signs and wonders in Egypt, 4he
will not listen[c] to you. Then I will
lay my hand on Egypt and with
mighty acts of judgment[d] I will
bring out my divisions, my people
the Israelites. 5And the Egyptians
will know that I am the LORD[e]
when I stretch out my hand[f]
against Egypt and bring the Israelites out of it."
6Moses and Aaron did just as the
LORD commanded[g] them. 7Moses
was eighty years old[h] and Aaron
eighty-three when they spoke to
Pharaoh.

Aaron's Staff Becomes a Snake

8The LORD said to Moses and
Aaron, 9"When Pharaoh says to
you, 'Perform a miracle,'[i] then say
to Aaron, 'Take your staff and
throw it down before Pharaoh,' and
it will become a snake."[j]
10So Moses and Aaron went to
Pharaoh and did just as the LORD
commanded. Aaron threw his staff
down in front of Pharaoh and his officials, and it became a snake.
11Pharaoh then summoned the wise
men and sorcerers, and the Egyptian magicians[k] also did the same
things by their secret arts:[l] 12Each
one threw down his staff and it became a snake. But Aaron's staff
swallowed up their staffs. 13Yet
Pharaoh's heart[m] became hard and
he would not listen to them, just as
the LORD had said.

The Plague of Blood

14Then the LORD said to Moses,
"Pharaoh's heart is unyielding;[n]
he refuses to let the people go. 15Go
to Pharaoh in the morning as he
goes out to the water. Wait on the
bank of the Nile to meet him, and
take in your hand the staff that was
changed into a snake. 16Then say to
him, 'The LORD, the God of the Hebrews, has sent me to say to you:
Let my people go, so that they may
worship[o] me in the desert. But

6:19 x 1Ch 6:19; 1Ch 23:21
6:20 y Ex 2:1-2; Nu 26:59
6:21 z 1Ch 6:38
6:22 a Lev 10:4; Nu 3:30
6:23 b Ru 4:19,20; c Lev 10:1; d Nu 3:2,32; e Nu 26:60
6:24 f Nu 26:11
6:25 g Nu 25:7,11; Jos 24:33; Ps 106:30
6:26 h Ex 7:4; Ex 12:17,41,51
6:29 i ver 11; Ex 7:2
6:30 j ver 12; Ex 4:10
7:1 a Ex 4:16
7:3 b Ex 4:21; Ex 11:9
7:4 c Ex 11:9; d Ex 3:20; Ex 6:6
7:5 e ver 17; Ex 8:19,22; f Ex 3:20
7:6 g ver 2
7:7 h Dt 31:2; Dt 34:7; Ac 7:23,30
7:9 i Isa 7:11; Jn 2:18; j Ex 4:2-5
7:11 k Ge 41:8; 2Ti 3:8; l ver 22; Ex 8:7,18
7:13 m Ex 4:21
7:14 n Ex 8:15,32; Ex 10:1,20,27
7:16 o Ex 3:18; Ex 5:1,3

until now you have not listened.
17This is what the LORD says: By
this you will know that I am the
LORD:[p] With the staff that is in my
hand I will strike the water of the
Nile, and it will be changed into
blood.[q] 18The fish in the Nile will
die, and the river will stink; the
Egyptians will not be able to drink
its water.' "[r]

19The LORD said to Moses, "Tell
Aaron, 'Take your staff and stretch
out your hand[s] over the waters of
Egypt—over the streams and canals, over the ponds and all the reservoirs'—and they will turn to
blood. Blood will be everywhere in
Egypt, even in the wooden buckets
and stone jars."

20Moses and Aaron did just as the
LORD had commanded. He raised
his staff in the presence of Pharaoh
and his officials and struck the
water of the Nile,[t] and all the
water was changed into blood.[u]
21The fish in the Nile died, and the
river smelled so bad that the Egyptians could not drink its water.
Blood was everywhere in Egypt.

22But the Egyptian magicians did
the same things by their secret
arts,[v] and Pharaoh's heart became
hard; he would not listen to Moses
and Aaron, just as the LORD had
said. 23Instead, he turned and went
into his palace, and did not take
even this to heart. 24And all the
Egyptians dug along the Nile to get
drinking water, because they could
not drink the water of the river.

The Plague of Frogs

25Seven days passed after the
8 LORD struck the Nile. 1Then
the LORD said to Moses, "Go to
Pharaoh and say to him, 'This is
what the LORD says: Let my people
go, so that they may worship[a] me.
2If you refuse to let them go, I will
plague your whole country with
frogs. 3The Nile will teem with
frogs. They will come up into your
palace and your bedroom and onto
your bed, into the houses of your
officials and on your people,[b] and
into your ovens and kneading
troughs. 4The frogs will go up on
you and your people and all your
officials.' "

5Then the LORD said to Moses,
"Tell Aaron, 'Stretch out your hand
with your staff[c] over the streams
and canals and ponds, and make
frogs come up on the land of
Egypt.' "

6So Aaron stretched out his hand
over the waters of Egypt, and
the frogs[d] came up and covered the
land. 7But the magicians did the
same things by their secret arts;[e]
they also made frogs come up on
the land of Egypt.

8Pharaoh summoned Moses and
Aaron and said, "Pray[f] to the LORD
to take the frogs away from me and
my people, and I will let your people go to offer sacrifices[g] to the
LORD."

9Moses said to Pharaoh, "I leave
to you the honour of setting the
time for me to pray for you and
your officials and your people that
you and your houses may be rid of
the frogs, except for those that remain in the Nile."

10"Tomorrow," Pharaoh said.

Moses replied, "It will be as you
say, so that you may know there is
no-one like the LORD our God.[h]
11The frogs will leave you and your
houses, your officials and your people; they will remain only in the
Nile."

12After Moses and Aaron left
Pharaoh, Moses cried out to the
LORD about the frogs he had
brought on Pharaoh. 13And the LORD
did what Moses asked. The frogs
died in the houses, in the courtyards and in the fields. 14They were
piled into heaps, and the land reek-
ed of them. 15But when Pharaoh
saw that there was relief, he hardened his heart[i] and would not listen
to Moses and Aaron, just as the
LORD had said.

7:17 p Ex 5:2 q Ex 4:9; Rev 11:6; Rev 16:4
7:18 r ver 21,24
7:19 s Ex 8:5-6,16; Ex 9:22; Ex 10:12,21; Ex 14:21
7:20 t Ex 17:5 u Ps 78:44; Ps 105:29
7:22 v ver 11
8:1 a Ex 3:12,18; Ex 4:23
8:3 b Ex 10:6
8:5 c Ex 7:19
8:6 d Ps 78:45; Ps 105:30
8:7 e Ex 7:11
8:8 f ver 28; Ex 9:28; Ex 10:17 g ver 25
8:10 h Ex 9:14; Dt 4:35; Dt 33:26; 2Sa 7:22; 1Ch 17:20; Ps 86:8; Isa 46:9; Jer 10:6
8:15 i Ex 7:14

The Plague of Gnats

16Then the LORD said to Moses,
"Tell Aaron, 'Stretch out your staff
and strike the dust of the ground,'
and throughout the land of Egypt
the dust will become gnats." 17They
did this, and when Aaron stretched
out his hand with the staff and
struck the dust of the ground,
gnats[j] came upon men and animals. All the dust throughout the
land of Egypt became gnats. 18But
when the magicians[k] tried to produce gnats by their secret arts,[l]
they could not. And the gnats were
on men and animals.
19The magicians said to Pharaoh,
"This is the finger[m] of God." But
Pharaoh's heart was hard and he
would not listen, just as the LORD
had said.

The Plague of Flies

20Then the LORD said to Moses,
"Get up early in the morning[n] and
confront Pharaoh as he goes to the
water and say to him, 'This is what
the LORD says: Let my people go, so
that they may worship[o] me. 21If
you do not let my people go, I will
send swarms of flies on you and
your officials, on your people and
into your houses. The houses of the
Egyptians will be full of flies, and
even the ground where they are.
22" 'But on that day I will deal differently with the land of Goshen,
where my people live;[p] no swarms
of flies will be there, so that you
will know[q] that I, the LORD, am in
this land. 23I will make a distinction[a] between my people and your
people. This miraculous sign will
occur tomorrow.' "
24And the LORD did this. Dense
swarms of flies poured into Pharaoh's palace and into the houses of
his officials, and throughout Egypt
the land was ruined by the flies.[r]
25Then Pharaoh summoned[s]
Moses and Aaron and said, "Go,
sacrifice to your God here in the
land."
26But Moses said, "That would
not be right. The sacrifices we offer the LORD our God would be detestable to the Egyptians.[t] And if
we offer sacrifices that are detestable in their eyes, will they not
stone us? 27We must take a three-
day journey into the desert to offer
sacrifices[u] to the LORD our God, as
he commands us."
28Pharaoh said, "I will let you go
to offer sacrifices to the LORD your
God in the desert, but you must not
go very far. Now pray[v] for me."
29Moses answered, "As soon as I
leave you, I will pray to the LORD,
and tomorrow the flies will leave
Pharaoh and his officials and his
people. Only be sure that Pharaoh
does not act deceitfully[w] again by
not letting the people go to offer
sacrifices to the LORD."
30Then Moses left Pharaoh and
prayed to the LORD,[x] 31and the
LORD did what Moses asked: The
flies left Pharaoh and his officials
and his people; not a fly remained.
32But this time also Pharaoh hardened his heart[y] and would not let
the people go.

The Plague on Livestock

9 Then the LORD said to Moses,
"Go to Pharaoh and say to him,
'This is what the LORD, the God of
the Hebrews, says: "Let my people
go, so that they may worship[a] me."
2If you refuse to let them go and
continue to hold them back, 3the
hand[b] of the LORD will bring a terrible plague on your livestock in
the field—on your horses and donkeys and camels and on your cattle
and sheep and goats. 4But the LORD
will make a distinction between the
livestock of Israel and that of
Egypt,[c] so that no animal belonging to the Israelites will die.' "
5The LORD set a time and said,
"Tomorrow the LORD will do this in
the land." 6And the next day the

[a]23 Septuagint and Vulgate; Hebrew *will put a deliverance*

8:17 j Ps 105:31
8:18 k Ex 9:11; Da 5:8 l Ex 7:11
8:19 m Ex 7:5; Ex 10:7; Ps 8:3; Lk 11:20
8:20 n Ex 7:15; Ex 9:13 o ver 1; Ex 3:18
8:22 p Ex 9:4,6,26; Ex 10:23; Ex 11:7 q Ex 7:5; Ex 9:29
8:24 r Ps 78:45; Ps 105:31
8:25 s ver 8; Ex 9:27
8:26 t Ge 43:32; Ge 46:34
8:27 u Ex 3:18
8:28 v ver 8; Ex 9:28; 1Ki 13:6
8:29 w ver 15
8:30 x ver 12
8:32 y ver 8,15; Ex 4:21
9:1 a Ex 8:1
9:3 b Ex 7:4
9:4 c ver 26; Ex 8:22

LORD did it: All the livestock[d] of the Egyptians died,[e] but not one animal belonging to the Israelites died. 7Pharaoh sent men to investigate and found that not even one of the animals of the Israelites had died. Yet his heart was unyielding and he would not let the people go.[f]

The Plague of Boils

8Then the LORD said to Moses and Aaron, "Take handfuls of soot from a furnace and have Moses toss it into the air in the presence of Pharaoh. 9It will become fine dust over the whole land of Egypt, and festering boils[g] will break out on men and animals throughout the land."

10So they took soot from a furnace and stood before Pharaoh. Moses tossed it into the air, and festering boils broke out on men and animals. 11The magicians[h] could not stand before Moses because of the boils that were on them and on all the Egyptians. 12But the LORD hardened Pharaoh's heart[i] and he would not listen to Moses and Aaron, just as the LORD had said to Moses.

The Plague of Hail

13Then the LORD said to Moses, "Get up early in the morning, confront Pharaoh and say to him, 'This is what the LORD, the God of the Hebrews, says: Let my people go, so that they may worship[j] me, 14or this time I will send the full force of my plagues against you and against your officials and your people, so you may know[k] that there is no-one like[l] me in all the earth. 15For by now I could have stretched out my hand and struck you and your people[m] with a plague that would have wiped you off the earth. 16But I have raised you up[a] for this very purpose,[n] that I might show you my power[o] and that my name might be proclaimed in all the earth. 17You still set yourself against my people and will not let them go. 18Therefore, at this time tomorrow I will send the worst hailstorm[p] that has ever fallen on Egypt, from the day it was founded till now.[q] 19Give an order now to bring your livestock and everything you have in the field to a place of shelter, because the hail will fall on every man and animal that has not been brought in and is still out in the field, and they will die.' "

20Those officials of Pharaoh who feared[r] the word of the LORD hurried to bring their slaves and their livestock inside. 21But those who ignored the word of the LORD left their slaves and livestock in the field.

22Then the LORD said to Moses, "Stretch out your hand towards the sky so that hail will fall all over Egypt—on men and animals and on everything growing in the fields of Egypt." 23When Moses stretched out his staff towards the sky, the LORD sent thunder[s] and hail,[t] and lightning flashed down to the ground. So the LORD rained hail on the land of Egypt; 24hail fell and lightning flashed back and forth. It was the worst storm in all the land of Egypt since it had become a nation. 25Throughout Egypt hail struck everything in the fields—both men and animals; it beat down everything growing in the fields and stripped every tree.[u] 26The only place it did not hail was the land of Goshen,[v] where the Israelites were.[w]

27Then Pharaoh summoned Moses and Aaron. "This time I have sinned,"[x] he said to them. "The LORD is in the right,[y] and I and my people are in the wrong. 28Pray[z] to the LORD, for we have had enough thunder and hail. I will let you go;[a] you don't have to stay any longer."

29Moses replied, "When I have gone out of the city, I will spread

9:6 d ver 19-21 Ex 11:5 e Ps 78:48-50
9:7 f Ex 7:14 Ex 8:32
9:9 g Dt 28:27,35 Rev 16:2
9:11 h Ex 8:18
9:12 i Ex 4:21
9:13 j Ex 8:20
9:14 k Ex 8:10 l 2Sa 7:22 1Ch 17:20 Ps 86:8 Isa 46:9 Jer 10:6
9:15 m Ex 3:20
9:16 n Pr 16:4 o Ro 9:17*
9:18 p ver 23 q ver 24
9:20 r Pr 13:13
9:23 s Ps 18:13 t Jos 10:11 Ps 78:47 Ps 105:32 Isa 30:30 Eze 38:22 Rev 8:7 Rev 16:21
9:25 u Ps 105:32-33
9:26 v ver 4 w Ex 8:22 Ex 10:23 Ex 11:7 Ex 12:13
9:27 x Ex 10:16 y 2Ch 12:6 Ps 129:4 La 1:18
9:28 z Ex 10:17 a Ex 8:8

a16 Or *have spared you*

out my hands[b] in prayer to the LORD. The thunder will stop and there will be no more hail, so you may know that the earth[c] is the LORD's. 30 But I know that you and your officials still do not fear the LORD God."

31 (The flax and barley[d] were destroyed, since the barley was in the ear and the flax was in bloom. 32 The wheat and spelt, however, were not destroyed, because they ripen later.)

33 Then Moses left Pharaoh and went out of the city. He spread out his hands towards the LORD; the thunder and hail stopped, and the rain no longer poured down on the land. 34 When Pharaoh saw that the rain and hail and thunder had stopped, he sinned again: He and his officials hardened their hearts. 35 So Pharaoh's heart[e] was hard and he would not let the Israelites go, just as the LORD had said through Moses.

The Plague of Locusts

10 Then the LORD said to Moses, "Go to Pharaoh, for I have hardened his heart[a] and the hearts of his officials so that I may perform these miraculous signs[b] of mine among them 2 that you may tell your children[c] and grandchildren how I dealt harshly with the Egyptians and how I performed my signs among them, and that you may know that I am the LORD."

3 So Moses and Aaron went to Pharaoh and said to him, "This is what the LORD, the God of the Hebrews, says: 'How long will you refuse to humble[d] yourself before me? Let my people go, so that they may worship me. 4 If you refuse to let them go, I will bring locusts[e] into your country tomorrow. 5 They will cover the face of the ground so that it cannot be seen. They will devour what little you have left[f] after the hail, including every tree that is growing in your fields.

9:29 b 1Ki 8:22,38; Ps 143:6; Isa 1:15; c Ex 19:5; Ps 24:1; 1Co 10:26
9:31 d Ru 1:22; Ru 2:23
9:35 e Ex 4:21
10:1 a Ex 4:21; b Ex 7:3
10:2 c Ex 12:26-27; Ex 13:8,14; Dt 4:9; Ps 44:1; Ps 78:4,5; Joel 1:3
10:3 d 1Ki 21:29; Jas 4:10; 1Pe 5:6
10:4 e Rev 9:3
10:5 f Ex 9:32; Joel 1:4
10:7 g Ex 23:33; Jos 23:7-13; 1Sa 18:21; Ecc 7:26; h Ex 8:19
10:8 i Ex 8:8
10:12 j Ex 7:19
10:13 k Ps 105:34
10:14 l Ps 78:46; Joel 2:1-11, 25
10:15 m ver 5; Ps 105:34-35

6 They will fill your houses and those of all your officials and all the Egyptians—something neither your fathers nor your forefathers have ever seen from the day they settled in this land till now.'" Then Moses turned and left Pharaoh.

7 Pharaoh's officials said to him, "How long will this man be a snare[g] to us? Let the people go, so that they may worship the LORD their God. Do you not yet realise that Egypt is ruined?"[h]

8 Then Moses and Aaron were brought back to Pharaoh. "Go, worship[i] the LORD your God," he said. "But just who will be going?"

9 Moses answered, "We will go with our young and old, with our sons and daughters, and with our flocks and herds, because we are to celebrate a festival to the LORD."

10 Pharaoh said, "The LORD be with you—if I let you go, along with your women and children! Clearly you are bent on evil.[a] 11 No! Let only the men go; and worship the LORD, since that's what you have been asking for." Then Moses and Aaron were driven out of Pharaoh's presence.

12 And the LORD said to Moses, "Stretch out your hand[j] over Egypt so that locusts will swarm over the land and devour everything growing in the fields, everything left by the hail."

13 So Moses stretched out his staff over Egypt, and the LORD made an east wind blow across the land all that day and all that night. By morning the wind had brought the locusts;[k] 14 they invaded all Egypt and settled down in every area of the country in great numbers. Never before had there been such a plague of locusts,[l] nor will there ever be again. 15 They covered all the ground until it was black. They devoured[m] all that was left after the hail—everything growing in the fields and the fruit on the trees.

[a]10 Or *Be careful, trouble is in store for you!*

Nothing green remained on tree or
plant in all the land of Egypt.
16 Pharaoh quickly summoned
Moses and Aaron and said, "I have
sinned[n] against the LORD your God
and against you. 17 Now forgive my
sin once more and pray[o] to the
LORD your God to take this deadly
plague away from me."
18 Moses then left Pharaoh and
prayed to the LORD.[p] 19 And the
LORD changed the wind to a very
strong west wind, which caught up
the locusts and carried them into
the Red Sea.[b] Not a locust was left
anywhere in Egypt. 20 But the LORD
hardened Pharaoh's heart,[q] and he
would not let the Israelites go.

The Plague of Darkness

21 Then the LORD said to Moses,
"Stretch out your hand towards the
sky so that darkness[r] will spread
over Egypt—darkness that can be
felt." 22 So Moses stretched out his
hand towards the sky, and total
darkness[s] covered all Egypt for
three days. 23 No-one could see anyone else or leave his place for three
days. Yet all the Israelites had light
in the places where they lived.[t]
24 Then Pharaoh summoned
Moses and said, "Go, worship the
LORD. Even your women and children[u] may go with you; only leave
your flocks and herds behind."
25 But Moses said, "You must allow us to have sacrifices and burnt
offerings to present to the LORD
our God. 26 Our livestock too must
go with us; not a hoof is to be left
behind. We have to use some of
them in worshipping the LORD
our God, and until we get there we
will not know what we are to use to
worship the LORD."
27 But the LORD hardened Pharaoh's heart,[v] and he was not willing to let them go. 28 Pharaoh said to
Moses, "Get out of my sight! Make
sure you do not appear before me
again! The day you see my face you
will die."

10:16 n Ex 9:27
10:17 o Ex 8:8
10:18 p Ex 8:30
10:20 q Ex 4:21; Ex 11:10
10:21 r Dt 28:29
10:22 s Ps 105:28; Rev 16:10
10:23 t Ex 8:22
10:24 u ver 8-10
10:27 v ver 20; Ex 4:21
10:29 w Heb 11:27
11:2 a Ex 3:21,22
11:3 b Dt 34:11
11:4 c Ex 12:29
11:5 d Ex 4:23; Ps 78:51
11:6 e Ex 12:30
11:7 f Ex 8:22
11:8 g Ex 12:31-33
11:9 h Ex 7:4
11:10 i Ex 4:21; Ex 10:20,27

29 "Just as you say," Moses replied, "I will never appear[w] before
you again."

The Plague on the Firstborn

11 Now the LORD said to
Moses, "I will bring one
more plague on Pharaoh and on
Egypt. After that, he will let you go
from here, and when he does, he
will drive you out completely. 2 Tell
the people that men and women
alike are to ask their neighbours
for articles of silver and gold."[a]
3 (The LORD made the Egyptians
favourably disposed towards the
people, and Moses himself was
highly regarded[b] in Egypt by
Pharaoh's officials and by the
people.)
4 So Moses said, "This is what the
LORD says: 'About midnight[c] I will
go throughout Egypt. 5 Every firstborn[d] son in Egypt will die, from
the firstborn son of Pharaoh, who
sits on the throne, to the firstborn
son of the slave girl, who is at her
hand mill, and all the firstborn of
the cattle as well. 6 There will be
loud wailing[e] throughout Egypt—
worse than there has ever been or
ever will be again. 7 But among the
Israelites not a dog will bark at any
man or animal.' Then you will know
that the LORD makes a distinction[f]
between Egypt and Israel. 8 All
these officials of yours will come to
me, bowing down before me and
saying, 'Go,[g] you and all the people
who follow you!' After that I will
leave." Then Moses, hot with
anger, left Pharaoh.
9 The LORD had said to Moses,
"Pharaoh will refuse to listen[h] to
you—so that my wonders may be
multiplied in Egypt." 10 Moses and
Aaron performed all these wonders before Pharaoh, but the LORD
hardened Pharaoh's heart,[i] and he
would not let the Israelites go out
of his country.

[b] 19 Hebrew *Yam Suph*; that is, Sea of Reeds

The Passover

12:14–20pp Lev 23:4–8; Nu 28:16–25; Dt 16:1–8

12 The LORD said to Moses and Aaron in Egypt, 2“This month is to be for you the first month,[a] the first month of your year. 3Tell the whole community of Israel that on the tenth day of this month each man is to take a lamb[a] for his family, one for each household. 4If any household is too small for a whole lamb, they must share one with their nearest neighbour, having taken into account the number of people there are. You are to determine the amount of lamb needed in accordance with what each person will eat. 5The animals you choose must be year-old males without defect,[b] and you may take them from the sheep or the goats. 6Take care of them until the fourteenth day of the month,[c] when all the people of the community of Israel must slaughter them at twilight.[d] 7Then they are to take some of the blood and put it on the sides and tops of the door-frames of the houses where they eat the lambs. 8That same night[e] they are to eat the meat roasted[f] over the fire, along with bitter herbs,[g] and bread made without yeast.[h] 9Do not eat the meat raw or cooked in water, but roast it over the fire—head, legs and inner parts. 10Do not leave any of it till morning;[i] if some is left till morning, you must burn it. 11This is how you are to eat it: with your cloak tucked into your belt, your sandals on your feet and your staff in your hand. Eat it in haste;[j] it is the LORD's Passover.[k]

12“On that same night I will pass through[l] Egypt and strike down every firstborn—both men and animals—and I will bring judgment on all the gods[m] of Egypt. I am the LORD.[n] 13The blood will be a sign for you on the houses where you are; and when I see the blood, I will pass over you. No destructive plague will touch you when I strike Egypt.

14“This is a day you are to commemorate;[o] for the generations to come you shall celebrate it as a festival to the LORD—a lasting ordinance.[p] 15For seven days you are to eat bread made without yeast.[q] On the first day remove the yeast from your houses, for whoever eats anything with yeast in it from the first day until the seventh must be cut off[r] from Israel. 16On the first day hold a sacred assembly, and another one on the seventh day. Do no work at all on these days, except to prepare food for everyone to eat—that is all you may do.

17“Celebrate the Feast of Unleavened Bread, because it was on this very day that I brought your divisions out of Egypt.[s] Celebrate this day as a lasting ordinance for the generations to come. 18In the first month[t] you are to eat bread made without yeast, from the evening of the fourteenth day until the evening of the twenty-first day. 19For seven days no yeast is to be found in your houses. And whoever eats anything with yeast in it must be cut off from the community of Israel, whether he is an alien or native-born. 20Eat nothing made with yeast. Wherever you live, you must eat unleavened bread.”

21Then Moses summoned all the elders of Israel and said to them, “Go at once and select the animals for your families and slaughter the Passover[u] lamb. 22Take a bunch of hyssop, dip it into the blood in the basin and put some of the blood[v] on the top and on both sides of the door-frame. Not one of you shall go out of the door of his house until morning. 23When the LORD goes through the land to strike down the Egyptians, he will see the blood[w] on the top and sides of the door-frame and will pass over[x] that

12:2 a Ex 13:4; Dt 16:1
12:5 b Lev 22:18-21; Heb 9:14
12:6 c Lev 23:5; Nu 9:1-3,5,11 d Ex 16:12; Dt 16:4,6
12:8 e Ex 34:25; Nu 9:12 f Dt 16:7 g Nu 9:11 h Dt 16:3-4; 1Co 5:8
12:10 i Ex 23:18; Ex 34:25
12:11 j Dt 16:3 k ver 13,21,27, 43; Dt 16:1
12:12 l Ex 11:4; Am 5:17 m Nu 33:4 n Ex 6:2
12:14 o Ex 13:9 p ver 17,24; Ex 13:5,10; 2Ki 23:21
12:15 q Ex 13:6-7; Ex 23:15; Ex 34:18; Lev 23:6; Dt 16:3 r Ge 17:14; Nu 9:13
12:17 s ver 41; Ex 13:3
12:18 t ver 2; Lev 23:5-8; Nu 28:16-25
12:21 u ver 11; Mk 14:12-16
12:22 v ver 7; Heb 11:28
12:23 w Rev 7:3 x ver 13

[a]3 The Hebrew word can mean *lamb* or *kid*; also in verse 4.

doorway, and he will not permit the
destroyer[y] to enter your houses
and strike you down.
24"Obey these instructions as a
lasting ordinance for you and your
descendants. 25When you enter the
land that the LORD will give you as
he promised, observe this ceremony. 26And when your children[z]
ask you, 'What does this ceremony
mean to you?' 27then tell them, 'It is
the Passover[a] sacrifice to the
LORD, who passed over the houses
of the Israelites in Egypt and
spared our homes when he struck
down the Egyptians.' " Then the
people bowed down and worshipped.[b] 28The Israelites did just
what the LORD commanded Moses
and Aaron.
29At midnight[c] the LORD struck
down all the firstborn[d] in Egypt,
from the firstborn of Pharaoh, who
sat on the throne, to the firstborn of
the prisoner, who was in the dungeon, and the firstborn of all the
livestock[e] as well. 30Pharaoh and
all his officials and all the Egyptians got up during the night, and
there was loud wailing[f] in Egypt,
for there was not a house without
someone dead.

The Exodus

31During the night Pharaoh summoned Moses and Aaron and said,
"Up! Leave my people, you and the
Israelites! Go, worship[g] the LORD
as you have requested. 32Take your
flocks and herds,[h] as you have
said, and go. And also bless me."
33The Egyptians urged the people to hurry and leave[i] the country. "For otherwise," they said, "we
will all die!" 34So the people took
their dough before the yeast was
added, and carried it on their shoulders in kneading troughs wrapped
in clothing. 35The Israelites did as
Moses instructed and asked the
Egyptians for articles of silver
and gold[j] and for clothing. 36The
LORD had made the Egyptians
favourably disposed towards the
people, and they gave them what
they asked for; so they plundered[k] the Egyptians.
37The Israelites journeyed from
Rameses to Succoth.[l] There were
about six hundred thousand men[m]
on foot, besides women and children. 38Many other people[n] went
up with them, as well as large
droves of livestock, both flocks and
herds. 39With the dough they had
brought from Egypt, they baked
cakes of unleavened bread. The
dough was without yeast because
they had been driven out[o] of Egypt
and did not have time to prepare
food for themselves.
40Now the length of time the Israelite people lived in Egypt[b] was
430 years.[p] 41At the end of the 430
years, to the very day, all the
LORD's divisions[q] left Egypt.[r]
42Because the LORD kept vigil that
night to bring them out of Egypt, on
this night all the Israelites are to
keep vigil to honour the LORD for
the generations to come.[s]

Passover Restrictions

43The LORD said to Moses and
Aaron, "These are the regulations
for the Passover:[t]
"No foreigner[u] is to eat of it.
44Any slave you have bought may
eat of it after you have circumcised[v] him, 45but a temporary resident and a hired worker[w] may not
eat of it.
46"It must be eaten inside one
house; take none of the meat outside the house. Do not break any of
the bones.[x] 47The whole community of Israel must celebrate it.
48"An alien living among you who
wants to celebrate the LORD's Passover must have all the males in his
household circumcised; then he
may take part like one born in the
land.[y] No uncircumcised male
may eat of it. 49The same law

12:23 y 1Co 10:10; Heb 11:28
12:26 z Ex 10:2; Ex 13:8,14-15; Jos 4:6
12:27 a ver 11; b Ex 4:31
12:29 c Ex 11:4; d Ex 4:23; Ps 78:51; e Ex 9:6
12:30 f Ex 11:6
12:31 g Ex 8:8
12:32 h Ex 10:9,26
12:33 i Ps 105:38
12:35 j Ex 3:22
12:36 k Ex 3:22
12:37 l Nu 33:3-5; m Ex 38:26; Nu 1:46; Nu 11:13,21
12:38 n Nu 11:4
12:39 o ver 31-33; Ex 6:1; Ex 11:1
12:40 p Ge 15:13; Ac 7:6; Gal 3:17
12:41 q ver 17; Ex 6:26; r Ex 3:10
12:42 s Ex 13:10; Dt 16:1,6
12:43 t ver 11; u ver 48; Nu 9:14
12:44 v Ge 17:12-13
12:45 w Lev 22:10
12:46 x Nu 9:12; Jn 19:36*
12:48 y Nu 9:14

b40 Masoretic Text; Samaritan Pentateuch and Septuagint *Egypt and Canaan*

applies to the native-born and to
the alien[z] living among you."
50All the Israelites did just what
the LORD had commanded Moses
and Aaron. 51And on that very day
the LORD brought the Israelites out
of Egypt by their divisions.[a]

Consecration of the Firstborn

13 The LORD said to Moses,
2"Consecrate to me every
firstborn male.[a] The first offspring of every womb among the
Israelites belongs to me, whether
man or animal."
3Then Moses said to the people,
"Commemorate this day, the day
you came out of Egypt, out of the
land of slavery, because the LORD
brought you out of it with a mighty
hand.[b] Eat nothing containing
yeast.[c] 4Today, in the month of
Abib,[d] you are leaving. 5When the
LORD brings you into the land of the
Canaanites, Hittites, Amorites, Hivites and Jebusites[e]—the land he
swore to your forefathers to give
you, a land flowing with milk and
honey—you are to observe this ceremony[f] in this month: 6For seven
days eat bread made without yeast
and on the seventh day hold a festival[g] to the LORD. 7Eat unleavened
bread during those seven days;
nothing with yeast in it is to be seen
among you, nor shall any yeast be
seen anywhere within your borders. 8On that day tell your son,[h] 'I
do this because of what the LORD
did for me when I came out of
Egypt.' 9This observance will be
for you like a sign on your hand and
a reminder on your forehead[i] that
the law of the LORD is to be on your
lips. For the LORD brought you out
of Egypt with his mighty hand.
10You must keep this ordinance[j] at
the appointed time year after year.
11"After the LORD brings you into
the land of the Canaanites and
gives it to you, as he promised on
oath to you and your forefathers,
12you are to give over to the LORD
the first offspring of every womb.
All the firstborn males of your livestock belong to the LORD.[k] 13Re-
deem with a lamb every firstborn
donkey, but if you do not redeem it,
break its neck.[l] Redeem every
firstborn among your sons.[m]
14"In days to come when your
son[n] asks you, 'What does this
mean?' say to him, 'With a mighty
hand the LORD brought us out of
Egypt, out of the land of slavery.[o]
15When Pharaoh stubbornly refused to let us go, the LORD killed
every firstborn in Egypt, both man
and animal. This is why I sacrifice
to the LORD the first male offspring
of every womb and redeem each of
my firstborn sons.'[p] 16And it will
be like a sign on your hand and a
symbol on your forehead[q] that the
LORD brought us out of Egypt with
his mighty hand."

Crossing the Sea

17When Pharaoh let the people
go, God did not lead them on the
road through the Philistine country, though that was shorter. For
God said, "If they face war, they
might change their minds and return to Egypt."[r] 18So God led[s] the
people around by the desert road
towards the Red Sea.[a] The Israelites went up out of Egypt armed for
battle.[t]
19Moses took the bones of Joseph[u] with him because Joseph
had made the sons of Israel swear
an oath. He had said, "God will
surely come to your aid, and then
you must carry my bones up with
you from this place."[b][v]
20After leaving Succoth they
camped at Etham on the edge of the
desert.[w] 21By day the LORD went
ahead of them in a pillar of cloud[x]
to guide them on their way and by
night in a pillar of fire to give them
light, so that they could travel by
day or night. 22Neither the pillar of

[a]*18* Hebrew *Yam Suph*; that is, Sea of Reeds
[b]*19* See Gen. 50:25.

12:49 z Nu 15:15-16, 29; Gal 3:28
12:51 a ver 41; Ex 6:26
13:2 a ver 12,13,15; Ex 22:29; Nu 3:13; Dt 15:19; Lk 2:23*
13:3 b Ex 3:20; Ex 6:1; c Ex 12:19
13:4 d Ex 12:2
13:5 e Ex 3:8; f Ex 12:25-26
13:6 g Ex 12:15-20
13:8 h ver 14; Ex 10:2; Ps 78:5-6
13:9 i ver 16; Dt 6:8; Dt 11:18
13:10 j Ex 12:24-25
13:12 k Lev 27:26; Lk 2:23*
13:13 l Ex 34:20; m Nu 18:15
13:14 n Ex 10:2; Ex 12:26-27; Dt 6:20; o ver 3,9
13:15 p Ex 12:29
13:16 q ver 9
13:17 r Ex 14:11; Nu 14:1-4; Dt 17:16
13:18 s Ps 136:16; t Jos 1:14
13:19 u Jos 24:32; Ac 7:16; v Ge 50:24-25
13:20 w Nu 33:6
13:21 x Ex 14:19,24; Ex 33:9-10; Nu 9:16; Dt 1:33; Ne 9:12,19; Ps 78:14; Ps 99:7; Ps 105:39; Isa 4:5; 1Co 10:1

cloud by day nor the pillar of fire by night left its place in front of the people.

14

Then the LORD said to Moses, 2"Tell the Israelites to turn back and camp near Pi Hahiroth, between Migdol[a] and the sea. They are to camp by the sea, directly opposite Baal Zephon. 3Pharaoh will think, 'The Israelites are wandering around the land in confusion, hemmed in by the desert.' 4And I will harden Pharaoh's heart,[b] and he will pursue them. But I will gain glory[c] for myself through Pharaoh and all his army, and the Egyptians will know that I am the LORD."[d] So the Israelites did this.

5When the king of Egypt was told that the people had fled, Pharaoh and his officials changed their minds about them and said, "What have we done? We have let the Israelites go and have lost their services!" 6So he had his chariot made ready and took his army with him. 7He took six hundred of the best chariots, along with all the other chariots of Egypt, with officers over all of them. 8The LORD hardened the heart[e] of Pharaoh king of Egypt, so that he pursued the Israelites, who were marching out boldly.[f] 9The Egyptians—all Pharaoh's horses and chariots, horsemen[a] and troops—pursued the Israelites and overtook[g] them as they camped by the sea near Pi Hahiroth, opposite Baal Zephon.

10As Pharaoh approached, the Israelites looked up, and there were the Egyptians, marching after them. They were terrified and cried[h] out to the LORD. 11They said to Moses, "Was it because there were no graves in Egypt that you brought us to the desert to die?[i] What have you done to us by bringing us out of Egypt? 12Didn't we say to you in Egypt, 'Leave us alone; let us serve the Egyptians'? It would have been better for us to serve the Egyptians than to die in the desert!"

13Moses answered the people, "Do not be afraid.[j] Stand firm and you will see[k] the deliverance the LORD will bring you today. The Egyptians you see today you will never see[l] again. 14The LORD will fight[m] for you; you need only to be still."[n]

15Then the LORD said to Moses, "Why are you crying out to me? Tell the Israelites to move on. 16Raise your staff[o] and stretch out your hand over the sea to divide the water[p] so that the Israelites can go through the sea on dry ground. 17I will harden the hearts of the Egyptians so that they will go in after them.[q] And I will gain glory through Pharaoh and all his army, through his chariots and his horsemen. 18The Egyptians will know that I am the LORD when I gain glory through Pharaoh, his chariots and his horsemen."

19Then the angel of God, who had been travelling in front of Israel's army, withdrew and went behind them. The pillar of cloud[r] also moved from in front and stood behind them, 20coming between the armies of Egypt and Israel. Throughout the night the cloud brought darkness to the one side and light to the other; so neither went near the other all night long.

21Then Moses stretched out his hand over the sea, and all that night the LORD drove the sea back with a strong east wind[s] and turned it into dry land. The waters were divided,[t] 22and the Israelites went through the sea on dry ground,[u] with a wall of water on their right and on their left.

23The Egyptians pursued them, and all Pharaoh's horses and chariots and horsemen followed them into the sea. 24During the last watch of the night the LORD looked down

14:2 a Nu 33:7; Jer 44:1
14:4 b Ex 4:21 c Ro 9:17,22-23 d Ex 7:5
14:8 e ver 4; Ex 11:10 f Nu 33:3; Ac 13:17
14:9 g Ex 15:9
14:10 h Jos 24:7; Ne 9:9; Ps 34:17
14:11 i Ps 106:7-8
14:13 j Ge 15:1 k 2Ch 20:17; Isa 41:10, 13-14 l ver 30
14:14 m ver 25; Ex 15:3; Dt 1:30; Dt 3:22; 2Ch 20:29 n Ps 37:7; Ps 46:10; Isa 30:15
14:16 o Ex 4:17; Nu 20:8-9,11 p Isa 10:26
14:17 q ver 4
14:19 r Ex 13:21
14:21 s Ex 15:8 t Ps 74:13; Ps 114:5; Isa 63:12
14:22 u Ex 15:19; Ne 9:11; Ps 66:6; Heb 11:29

a9 Or *charioteers*; also in verses 17, 18, 23, 26 and 28

from the pillar of fire and cloud[v] at
the Egyptian army and threw it into
confusion. 25He made the wheels of
their chariots come off[b] so that
they had difficulty driving. And the
Egyptians said, "Let's get away
from the Israelites! The LORD is
fighting[w] for them against Egypt."
26Then the LORD said to Moses,
"Stretch out your hand over the sea
so that the waters may flow back
over the Egyptians and their chariots and horsemen." 27Moses
stretched out his hand over the sea,
and at daybreak the sea went back
to its place.[x] The Egyptians were
fleeing towards[c] it, and the LORD
swept them into the sea.[y] 28The
water flowed back and covered the
chariots and horsemen—the entire
army of Pharaoh that had followed
the Israelites into the sea. Not one
of them survived.
29But the Israelites went through
the sea on dry ground,[z] with a wall
of water on their right and on their
left. 30That day the LORD saved[a] Israel from the hands of the Egyptians, and Israel saw the Egyptians
lying dead on the shore. 31And
when the Israelites saw the great
power the LORD displayed against
the Egyptians, the people feared
the LORD and put their trust[b] in
him and in Moses his servant.

The Song of Moses and Miriam

15 Then Moses and the Israelites sang this song[a] to the
LORD:

"I will sing[b] to the LORD,
for he is highly exalted.
The horse and its rider
he has hurled into the sea.
2The LORD is my strength[c] and
my song;
he has become my salvation.[d]
He is my God,[e] and I will
praise him,
my father's God, and I will
exalt[f] him.
3The LORD is a warrior;[g]
the LORD is his name.[h]
4Pharaoh's chariots and his
army[i]
he has hurled into the sea.
The best of Pharaoh's officers
are drowned in the Red Sea.[a]
5The deep waters have covered
them;
they sank to the depths like a
stone.[j]

6"Your right hand,[k] O LORD,
was majestic in power.
Your right hand, O LORD,
shattered the enemy.
7In the greatness of your
majesty
you threw down those who
opposed you.
You unleashed your burning
anger;[l]
it consumed them like stubble.
8By the blast of your nostrils[m]
the waters piled up.[n]
The surging waters stood firm
like a wall;[o]
the deep waters congealed in
the heart of the sea.

9"The enemy boasted,
'I will pursue,[p] I will overtake
them.
I will divide the spoils;[q]
I will gorge myself on them.
I will draw my sword
and my hand will destroy
them.'
10But you blew with your breath,
and the sea covered them.
They sank like lead
in the mighty waters.[r]

11"Who among the gods is like
you,[s] O LORD?
Who is like you—
majestic in holiness,[t]
awesome in glory,[u]
working wonders?

14:24 v Ex 13:21
14:25 w ver 14
14:27 x Jos 4:18 y Ex 15:1,21 Ps 78:53 Ps 106:11
14:29 z ver 22
14:30 a Ps 106:8,10,21
14:31 b Ps 106:12 Jn 2:11
15:1 a Rev 15:3 b Ps 106:12
15:2 c Ps 59:17 d Ps 18:2,46 Isa 12:2 Hab 3:18 e Ge 28:21 f Ex 3:6,15-16 Isa 25:1
15:3 g Ex 14:14 Ps 24:8 Rev 19:11 h Ex 6:2-3,7-8 Ps 83:18
15:4 i Ex 14:6-7
15:5 j ver 10 Ne 9:11
15:6 k Ps 118:15
15:7 l Ps 78:49-50
15:8 m Ex 14:21 n Ps 78:13 o Ex 14:22
15:9 p Ex 14:5-9 q Jdg 5:30 Isa 53:12
15:10 r ver 5 Ex 14:27-28
15:11 s Ex 8:10 Dt 3:24 Ps 77:13 t Isa 6:3 Rev 4:8 u Ps 8:1

b25 Or *He jammed the wheels of their chariots* (see Samaritan Pentateuch, Septuagint and Syriac)
c27 Or *from*
a4 Hebrew *Yam Suph*; that is, Sea of Reeds; also in verse 22

12 You stretched out your right
hand
and the earth swallowed them.
13 "In your unfailing love you will
lead[v]
the people you have redeemed.
In your strength you will guide
them
to your holy dwelling.[w]
14 The nations will hear and
tremble;[x]
anguish will grip the people of
Philistia.
15 The chiefs[y] of Edom will be
terrified,
the leaders of Moab will be
seized with trembling,[z]
the people[b] of Canaan will
melt[a] away;
16 terror[b] and dread will fall
upon them.
By the power of your arm
they will be as still as a
stone[c]—
until your people pass by,
O LORD,
until the people you bought[c][d]
pass by.
17 You will bring them in and
plant[e] them
on the mountain[f] of your
inheritance—
the place, O LORD, you made for
your dwelling,
the sanctuary, O Lord, your
hands established.
18 The LORD will reign
for ever and ever."

19 When Pharaoh's horses, chariots and horsemen[d] went into the
sea,[g] the LORD brought the waters
of the sea back over them, but the
Israelites walked through the sea
on dry ground.[h] 20 Then Miriam[i]
the prophetess,[j] Aaron's sister,
took a tambourine in her hand, and
all the women followed her, with
tambourines and dancing.[k] 21 Miriam sang to them:

"Sing to the LORD,
for he is highly exalted.
The horse and its rider
he has hurled into the sea."[l]

15:13 v Ne 9:12; Ps 77:20; w Ps 78:54
15:14 x Dt 2:25
15:15 y Ge 36:15; z Nu 22:3; a Jos 5:1
15:16 b Ex 23:27; Jos 2:9; c 1Sa 25:37; d Ps 74:2
15:17 e Ps 44:2; f Ps 78:54,68
15:19 g Ex 14:28; h Ex 14:22
15:20 i Nu 26:59; j Jdg 4:4; k Jdg 11:34; 1Sa 18:6; Ps 30:11; Ps 150:4
15:21 l ver 1; Ex 14:27
15:23 m Nu 33:8
15:24 n Ex 14:12; Ex 16:2
15:25 o Ex 14:10; p Jdg 3:4
15:26 q Dt 7:12; r Dt 28:27, 58-60; s Ex 23:25-26
15:27 t Nu 33:9
16:1 a Nu 33:11,12
16:2 b Ex 14:11; Ex 15:24; 1Co 10:10
16:3 c Ex 17:3; d Nu 11:4,34

The Waters of Marah and Elim

22 Then Moses led Israel from the
Red Sea and they went into the
Desert of Shur. For three days they
travelled in the desert without
finding water. 23 When they came to
Marah, they could not drink its
water because it was bitter. (That
is why the place is called Marah.[e][m]) 24 So the people grumbled[n]
against Moses, saying, "What are
we to drink?"

25 Then Moses cried out[o] to the
LORD, and the LORD showed him a
piece of wood. He threw it into the
water, and the water became
sweet.

There the LORD made a decree
and a law for them, and there he
tested[p] them. 26 He said, "If you listen carefully to the voice of the
LORD your God and do what is right
in his eyes, if you pay attention to
his commands and keep all his decrees,[q] I will not bring on you any
of the diseases[r] I brought on the
Egyptians, for I am the LORD, who
heals[s] you."

27 Then they came to Elim, where
there were twelve springs and seventy palm trees, and they camped[t]
there near the water.

Manna and Quail

16 The whole Israelite community set out from Elim
and came to the Desert of Sin,[a]
which is between Elim and Sinai, on
the fifteenth day of the second
month after they had come out of
Egypt. 2 In the desert the whole
community grumbled[b] against
Moses and Aaron. 3 The Israelites
said to them, "If only we had died
by the LORD's hand in Egypt![c]
There we sat round pots of meat
and ate all the food[d] we wanted,
but you have brought us out into
this desert to starve this entire assembly to death."

[b] 15 Or *rulers* [c] 16 Or *created* [d] 19 Or *charioteers* [e] 23 *Marah* means *bitter*.

4 Then the LORD said to Moses, "I will rain down bread from heaven[e] for you. The people are to go out each day and gather enough for that day. In this way I will test them and see whether they will follow my instructions. 5 On the sixth day they are to prepare what they bring in, and that is to be twice[f] as much as they gather on the other days."

6 So Moses and Aaron said to all the Israelites, "In the evening you will know that it was the LORD who brought you out of Egypt,[g] 7 and in the morning you will see the glory[h] of the LORD, because he has heard your grumbling[i] against him. Who are we, that you should grumble against us?"[j] 8 Moses also said, "You will know that it was the LORD when he gives you meat to eat in the evening and all the bread you want in the morning, because he has heard your grumbling against him. Who are we? You are not grumbling against us, but against the LORD."[k]

9 Then Moses told Aaron, "Say to the entire Israelite community, 'Come before the LORD, for he has heard your grumbling.' "

10 While Aaron was speaking to the whole Israelite community, they looked towards the desert, and there was the glory[l] of the LORD appearing in the cloud.[m]

11 The LORD said to Moses, 12 "I have heard the grumbling[n] of the Israelites. Tell them, 'At twilight you will eat meat, and in the morning you will be filled with bread. Then you will know that I am the LORD your God.' "

13 That evening quail[o] came and covered the camp, and in the morning there was a layer of dew[p] around the camp. 14 When the dew was gone, thin flakes like frost[q] on the ground appeared on the desert floor. 15 When the Israelites saw it, they said to each other, "What is it?" For they did not know what it was.

Moses said to them, "It is the bread[r] the LORD has given you to eat. 16 This is what the LORD has commanded: 'Each one is to gather as much as he needs. Take an omer[a][s] for each person you have in your tent.' "

17 The Israelites did as they were told; some gathered much, some little. 18 And when they measured it by the omer, he who gathered much did not have too much, and he who gathered little did not have too little.[t] Each one gathered as much as he needed.

19 Then Moses said to them, "No-one is to keep any of it until morning."[u]

20 However, some of them paid no attention to Moses; they kept part of it until morning, but it was full of maggots and began to smell. So Moses was angry with them.

21 Each morning everyone gathered as much as he needed, and when the sun grew hot, it melted away. 22 On the sixth day, they gathered twice[v] as much—two omers[b] for each person—and the leaders of the community[w] came and reported this to Moses. 23 He said to them, "This is what the LORD commanded: 'Tomorrow is to be a day of rest, a holy Sabbath[x] to the LORD. So bake what you want to bake and boil what you want to boil. Save whatever is left and keep it until morning.' "

24 So they saved it until morning, as Moses commanded, and it did not stink or get maggots in it. 25 "Eat it today," Moses said, "because today is a Sabbath to the LORD. You will not find any of it on the ground today. 26 Six days you are to gather it, but on the seventh day, the Sabbath,[y] there will not be any."

27 Nevertheless, some of the people went out on the seventh day to gather it, but they found none.

16:4 e Dt 8:3; Jn 6:31*
16:5 f ver 22
16:6 g Ex 6:6
16:7 h ver 10; Isa 35:2; Isa 40:5; i ver 12; Nu 14:2,27,28; j Nu 16:11
16:8 k 1Sa 8:7; Ro 13:2
16:10 l ver 7; Nu 16:19; m Ex 13:21; 1Ki 8:10
16:12 n ver 7
16:13 o Nu 11:31; Ps 78:27-28; Ps 105:40; p Nu 11:9
16:14 q ver 31; Nu 11:7-9; Ps 105:40
16:15 r ver 4; Jn 6:31
16:16 s ver 32,36
16:18 t 2Co 8:15*
16:19 u ver 23; Ex 12:10; Ex 23:18
16:22 v ver 5; w Ex 34:31
16:23 x Ge 2:3; Ex 20:8; Ex 23:12; Lev 23:3
16:26 y Ex 20:9-10

a 16 That is, probably about 4 pints (about 2 litres); also in verses 18, 32, 33 and 36 b 22 That is, probably about 7½ pints (about 4.5 litres)

28 Then the LORD said to Moses,
"How long will you[c] refuse to keep
my commands[z] and my instructions? 29 Bear in mind that the LORD
has given you the Sabbath; that is
why on the sixth day he gives you
bread for two days. Everyone is to
stay where he is on the seventh
day; no-one is to go out." 30 So the
people rested on the seventh day.
31 The people of Israel called the
bread manna.[d][a] It was white like
coriander seed and tasted like
wafers made with honey. 32 Moses
said, "This is what the LORD has
commanded: 'Take an omer of
manna and keep it for the generations to come, so they can see the
bread I gave you to eat in the desert
when I brought you out of Egypt.' "
33 So Moses said to Aaron, "Take a
jar and put an omer of manna[b] in
it. Then place it before the LORD to
be kept for the generations to
come."
34 As the LORD commanded
Moses, Aaron put the manna in
front of the Testimony,[c] that it
might be kept. 35 The Israelites ate
manna[d] for forty years,[e] until
they came to a land that was settled; they ate manna until they
reached the border of Canaan.[f]
36 (An omer is one tenth of an
ephah.)

Water From the Rock

17 The whole Israelite community set out from the
Desert of Sin,[a] travelling from
place to place as the LORD commanded. They camped at Rephidim, but there was no water[b] for
the people to drink. 2 So they quarrelled with Moses and said, "Give
us water[c] to drink."
Moses replied, "Why do you
quarrel with me? Why do you put
the LORD to the test?"[d]
3 But the people were thirsty for
water there, and they grumbled[e]
against Moses. They said, "Why did
you bring us up out of Egypt to
make us and our children and livestock die of thirst?"
4 Then Moses cried out to the
LORD, "What am I to do with these
people? They are almost ready to
stone[f] me."
5 The LORD answered Moses,
"Walk on ahead of the people. Take
with you some of the elders of Israel and take in your hand the staff
with which you struck the Nile,[g]
and go. 6 I will stand there before
you by the rock at Horeb. Strike the
rock, and water[h] will come out of
it for the people to drink." So Moses
did this in the sight of the elders of
Israel. 7 And he called the place
Massah[a] and Meribah[b][i] because
the Israelites quarrelled and because they tested the LORD saying,
"Is the LORD among us or not?"

The Amalekites Defeated

8 The Amalekites[j] came and attacked the Israelites at Rephidim.
9 Moses said to Joshua, "Choose
some of our men and go out to fight
the Amalekites. Tomorrow I will
stand on top of the hill with the
staff[k] of God in my hands."
10 So Joshua fought the Amalekites as Moses had ordered, and
Moses, Aaron and Hur[l] went to the
top of the hill. 11 As long as Moses
held up his hands, the Israelites
were winning,[m] but whenever he
lowered his hands, the Amalekites
were winning. 12 When Moses'
hands grew tired, they took a stone
and put it under him and he sat on
it. Aaron and Hur held his hands
up—one on one side, one on the
other—so that his hands remained
steady till sunset. 13 So Joshua overcame the Amalekite army with the
sword.
14 Then the LORD said to Moses,
"Write[n] this on a scroll as something to be remembered and make
sure that Joshua hears it, because

[c]28 The Hebrew is plural. [d]31 *Manna* means *What is it?* (see verse 15). [a]7 *Massah* means *testing*. [b]7 *Meribah* means *quarrelling*.

16:28 z 2Ki 17:14; Ps 78:10; Ps 106:13
16:31 a Nu 11:7-9
16:33 b Heb 9:4
16:34 c Ex 25:16,21,22; Ex 40:20; Nu 17:4,10
16:35 d Jn 6:31,49; e Ne 9:21; f Jos 5:12
17:1 a Ex 16:1; b Nu 33:14
17:2 c Nu 20:2; d Dt 6:16; Ps 78:18,41; 1Co 10:9
17:3 e Ex 15:24; Ex 16:2-3
17:4 f Nu 14:10; 1Sa 30:6
17:5 g Ex 7:20
17:6 h Nu 20:11; Ps 114:8; 1Co 10:4
17:7 i Nu 20:13,24; Ps 81:7
17:8 j Ge 36:12; Dt 25:17-19
17:9 k Ex 4:17
17:10 l Ex 24:14
17:11 m Jas 5:16
17:14 n Ex 24:4; Ex 34:27; Nu 33:2

I will completely blot out the memory of Amalek[o] from under heaven."

15 Moses built an altar and called it The LORD is my Banner. 16 He said, "For hands were lifted up to the throne of the LORD. The[c] LORD will be at war against the Amalekites from generation to generation."

Jethro Visits Moses

18 Now Jethro, the priest of Midian[a] and father-in-law of Moses, heard of everything God had done for Moses and for his people Israel, and how the LORD had brought Israel out of Egypt.

2 After Moses had sent away his wife Zipporah,[b] his father-in-law Jethro received her 3 and her two sons.[c] One son was named Gershom,[a] for Moses said, "I have become an alien in a foreign land";[d] 4 and the other was named Eliezer,[b][e] for he said, "My father's God was my helper; he saved me from the sword of Pharaoh."

5 Jethro, Moses' father-in-law, together with Moses' sons and wife, came to him in the desert, where he was camped near the mountain[f] of God. 6 Jethro had sent word to him, "I, your father-in-law Jethro, am coming to you with your wife and her two sons."

7 So Moses went out to meet his father-in-law and bowed down[g] and kissed[h] him. They greeted each other and then went into the tent. 8 Moses told his father-in-law about everything the LORD had done to Pharaoh and the Egyptians for Israel's sake and about all the hardships they had met along the way and how the LORD had saved[i] them.

9 Jethro was delighted to hear about all the good things the LORD had done for Israel in rescuing them from the hand of the Egyptians. 10 He said, "Praise be to the LORD,[j] who rescued you from the hand of the Egyptians and of Pharaoh, and who rescued the people from the hand of the Egyptians. 11 Now I know that the LORD is greater than all other gods,[k] for he did this to those who had treated Israel arrogantly."[l] 12 Then Jethro, Moses' father-in-law, brought a burnt offering and other sacrifices to God, and Aaron came with all the elders of Israel to eat bread with Moses' father-in-law in the presence[m] of God.

13 The next day Moses took his seat to serve as judge for the people, and they stood round him from morning till evening. 14 When his father-in-law saw all that Moses was doing for the people, he said, "What is this you are doing for the people? Why do you alone sit as judge, while all these people stand round you from morning till evening?"

15 Moses answered him, "Because the people come to me to seek God's will.[n] 16 Whenever they have a dispute, it is brought to me, and I decide between the parties and inform them of God's decrees and laws."[o]

17 Moses' father-in-law replied, "What you are doing is not good. 18 You and these people who come to you will only wear yourselves out. The work is too heavy for you; you cannot handle it alone.[p] 19 Listen now to me and I will give you some advice, and may God be with you.[q] You must be the people's representative before God and bring their disputes[r] to him. 20 Teach them the decrees and laws,[s] and show them the way to live[t] and the duties they are to perform.[u] 21 But select capable men[v] from all the people—men who fear God, trustworthy men who hate dishonest gain[w]—and appoint them as officials[x] over thousands, hundreds, fifties

17:14 o 1Sa 15:3; 1Sa 30:17-18
18:1 a Ex 2:16; Ex 3:1
18:2 b Ex 2:21; Ex 4:25
18:3 c Ex 4:20; Ac 7:29; d Ex 2:22
18:4 e 1Ch 23:15
18:5 f Ex 3:1
18:7 g Ge 43:28; h Ge 29:13
18:8 i Ex 15:6,16; Ps 81:7
18:10 j Ge 14:20; Ps 68:19-20
18:11 k Ex 12:12; Ex 15:11; 2Ch 2:5; l Lk 1:51
18:12 m Dt 12:7
18:15 n Nu 9:6,8; Dt 17:8-13
18:16 o Lev 24:12
18:18 p Nu 11:11,14, 17
18:19 q Ex 3:12; r Nu 27:5
18:20 s Dt 5:1; t Ps 143:8; u Dt 1:18
18:21 v Ac 6:3; w Dt 16:19; Ps 15:5; Eze 18:8; x Dt 1:13,15; 2Ch 19:5-10

c16 Or "*Because a hand was against the throne of the LORD, the* a3 *Gershom* sounds like the Hebrew for *an alien there.* b4 *Eliezer* means *my God is helper.*

and tens. 22Have them serve as
judges for the people at all times,
but have them bring every difficult
case[y] to you; the simple cases they
can decide themselves. That will
make your load lighter, because
they will share[z] it with you. 23If
you do this and God so commands,
you will be able to stand the strain,
and all these people will go home
satisfied."
24Moses listened to his father-in-
law and did everything he said.
25He chose capable men from all Israel and made them leaders of the
people, officials over thousands,
hundreds, fifties and tens.[a] 26They
served as judges for the people at
all times. The difficult cases they
brought to Moses, but the simple
ones they decided themselves.[b]
27Then Moses sent his father-in-
law on his way, and Jethro returned
to his own country.[c]

At Mount Sinai

19 In the third month after the
Israelites left Egypt—on
the very day—they came to the
Desert of Sinai. 2After they set out
from Rephidim,[a] they entered the
Desert of Sinai, and Israel camped
there in the desert in front of the
mountain.[b]
3Then Moses went up to God, and
the LORD called[c] to him from the
mountain and said, "This is what
you are to say to the house of Jacob
and what you are to tell the people
of Israel: 4'You yourselves have
seen what I did to Egypt,[d] and how
I carried you on eagles' wings[e] and
brought you to myself. 5Now if you
obey me fully[f] and keep my covenant,[g] then out of all nations you
will be my treasured possession.[h]
Although the whole earth[i] is mine,
6you[a] will be for me a kingdom of
priests[j] and a holy nation.'[k] These
are the words you are to speak to
the Israelites."

18:22 y Dt 1:17-18 z Nu 11:17
18:25 a Dt 1:13-15
18:26 b ver 22
18:27 c Nu 10:29-30
19:2 a Ex 17:1 b Ex 3:1
19:3 c Ex 3:4 Ac 7:38
19:4 d Dt 29:2 e Isa 63:9
19:5 f Ex 15:26 g Dt 5:2 h Dt 14:2 Ps 135:4 i Ex 9:29 Dt 10:14
19:6 j 1Pe 2:5 k Dt 7:6 Dt 26:19 Isa 62:12
19:8 l Ex 24:3,7 Dt 5:27
19:9 m ver 16 Ex 24:15-16 n Dt 4:12,36
19:10 o Lev 11:44 Heb 10:22 p Ge 35:2
19:11 q ver 16
19:13 r Heb 12:20*
19:16 s Heb 12:18-19 Rev 4:1 t Heb 12:21

7So Moses went back and summoned the elders of the people and
set before them all the words the
LORD had commanded him to
speak. 8The people all responded
together, "We will do everything
the LORD has said."[l] So Moses
brought their answer back to the
LORD.
9The LORD said to Moses, "I am
going to come to you in a dense
cloud,[m] so that the people will hear
me speaking[n] with you and will always put their trust in you." Then
Moses told the LORD what the people had said.
10And the LORD said to Moses,
"Go to the people and consecrate[o]
them today and tomorrow. Make
them wash their clothes[p] 11and be
ready by the third day,[q] because
on that day the LORD will come
down on Mount Sinai in the sight of
all the people. 12Put limits for the
people around the mountain and
tell them, 'Be careful that you do
not go up the mountain or touch the
foot of it. Whoever touches the
mountain shall surely be put to
death. 13He shall surely be stoned[r]
or shot with arrows; not a hand is to
be laid on him. Whether man or animal, he shall not be permitted to
live.' Only when the ram's horn
sounds a long blast may they go up
to the mountain."
14After Moses had gone down the
mountain to the people, he consecrated them, and they washed their
clothes. 15Then he said to the people, "Prepare yourselves for the
third day. Abstain from sexual
relations."
16On the morning of the third day
there was thunder and lightning,
with a thick cloud over the mountain, and a very loud trumpet
blast.[s] Everyone in the camp
trembled.[t] 17Then Moses led the

[a] 5,6 Or *possession, for the whole earth is mine.* 6*You*

people out of the camp to meet with
God, and they stood at the foot of
the mountain. 18Mount Sinai was
covered with smoke,[u] because the
LORD descended on it in fire.[v] The
smoke billowed up from it like
smoke from a furnace,[w] the whole
mountain[b] trembled[x] violently,
19and the sound of the trumpet
grew louder and louder. Then
Moses spoke and the voice[y] of God
answered[z] him.[c]
20The LORD descended to the top
of Mount Sinai and called Moses to
the top of the mountain. So Moses
went up 21and the LORD said to him,
"Go down and warn the people so
they do not force their way through
to see[a] the LORD and many of them
perish. 22Even the priests, who approach[b] the LORD, must consecrate themselves, or the LORD will
break out against them."[c]
23Moses said to the LORD, "The
people cannot come up Mount
Sinai, because you yourself warned
us, 'Put limits[d] around the mountain and set it apart as holy.' "
24The LORD replied, "Go down
and bring Aaron[e] up with you. But
the priests and the people must not
force their way through to come up
to the LORD, or he will break out
against them."
25So Moses went down to the people and told them.

The Ten Commandments

20:1–17pp Dt 5:6–21

20 And God spoke all these
words:

2"I am the LORD your God,
who brought you out of
Egypt, out of the land of
slavery.[a]
3"You shall have no other gods
before[a] me.[b]
4"You shall not make for yourself an idol[c] in the form
of anything in heaven
above or on the earth be-
neath or in the waters
below. 5You shall not bow
down to them or wor-
ship[d] them; for I, the
LORD your God, am a
jealous God,[e] punishing
the children for the sin of
the fathers to the third
and fourth generation[f]
of those who hate me,
6but showing love to a
thousand[g] ⌞generations⌟
of those who love me and
keep my command-
ments.
7"You shall not misuse the
name of the LORD your
God, for the LORD will not
hold anyone guiltless
who misuses his name.[h]
8"Remember the Sabbath[i]
day by keeping it holy.
9Six days you shall la-
bour and do all your
work,[j] 10but the seventh
day is a Sabbath to the
LORD your God. On it you
shall not do any work,
neither you, nor your son
or daughter, nor your
manservant or maid-
servant, nor your ani-
mals, nor the alien within
your gates. 11For in six
days the LORD made the
heavens and the earth,
the sea, and all that is in
them, but he rested[k] on
the seventh day. There-
fore the LORD blessed the
Sabbath day and made it
holy.
12"Honour your father and
your mother,[l] so that
you may live long in the
land the LORD your God
is giving you.
13"You shall not murder.[m]

19:18 u Ps 104:32 v Ex 3:2; Ex 24:17; Dt 4:11; 2Ch 7:1; Ps 18:8; Heb 12:18 w Ge 19:28 x Jdg 5:5; Ps 68:8; Jer 4:24
19:19 y Ne 9:13 z Ps 81:7
19:21 a Ex 3:5; 1Sa 6:19
19:22 b Lev 10:3 c 2Sa 6:7
19:23 d ver 12
19:24 e Ex 24:1,9
20:2 a Ex 13:3
20:3 b Dt 6:14; Jer 35:15
20:4 c Lev 26:1; Dt 4:15-19,23; Dt 27:15
20:5 d Isa 44:15,17, 19 e Ex 34:14; Dt 4:24 f Nu 14:18; Jer 32:18
20:6 g Dt 7:9
20:7 h Lev 19:12; Mt 5:33
20:8 i Ex 31:13-16; Lev 26:2
20:9 j Ex 34:21; Lk 13:14
20:11 k Ge 2:2
20:12 l Mt 15:4*; Mk 7:10*; Eph 6:2
20:13 m Mt 5:21*; Ro 13:9*

[b]*18* Most Hebrew manuscripts; a few Hebrew manuscripts and Septuagint *all the people*
[c]*19* Or *and God answered him with thunder*
[a]*3* Or *besides*

14“You shall not commit adultery.[n]

15“You shall not steal.[o]

16“You shall not give false testimony against your neighbour.[p]

17“You shall not covet[q] your neighbour’s house. You shall not covet your neighbour’s wife, or his manservant or maidservant, his ox or donkey, or anything that belongs to your neighbour.”

18When the people saw the thunder and lightning and heard the trumpet[r] and saw the mountain in smoke, they trembled with fear. They stayed at a distance 19and said to Moses, “Speak to us yourself and we will listen. But do not have God speak to us or we will die.”[s]

20Moses said to the people, “Do not be afraid. God has come to test you, so that the fear[t] of God will be with you to keep you from sinning.”[u]

21The people remained at a distance, while Moses approached the thick darkness[v] where God was.

Idols and Altars

22Then the LORD said to Moses, “Tell the Israelites this: ‘You have seen for yourselves that I have spoken to you from heaven:[w] 23Do not make any gods to be alongside me;[x] do not make for yourselves gods of silver or gods of gold.[y]

24“ ‘Make an altar of earth for me and sacrifice on it your burnt offerings and fellowship offerings,[b] your sheep and goats and your cattle. Wherever I cause my name[z] to be honoured, I will come to you and bless[a] you. 25If you make an altar of stones for me, do not build it with dressed stones, for you will defile it if you use a tool[b] on it. 26And do not go up to my altar on steps, lest your nakedness be exposed on it.’

20:14 n Mt 19:18*
20:15 o Lev 19:11,13; Mt 19:18*
20:16 p Ex 23:1,7; Mt 19:18*
20:17 q Ro 7:7*; Ro 13:9*; Eph 5:3
20:18 r Ex 19:16-19; Heb 12:18-19
20:19 s Dt 5:5,23-27; Gal 3:19
20:20 t Dt 4:10; Isa 8:13; u Pr 16:6
20:21 v Dt 5:22
20:22 w Ne 9:13
20:23 x ver 3; y Ex 32:4,8,31
20:24 z Dt 12:5; Dt 16:6,11; 2Ch 6:6; a Ge 12:2
20:25 b Dt 27:5-6
21:1 a Dt 4:14
21:2 b Jer 34:8,14
21:5 c Dt 15:16
21:6 d Ex 22:8-9; e Ne 5:5
21:10 f 1Co 7:3-5
21:12 g Ge 9:6; Mt 26:52
21:13 h Nu 35:10-34; Dt 19:2-13; Jos 20:9; 1Sa 24:4,10,18

21 “These are the laws[a] you are to set before them:

Hebrew Servants

21:2-6pp Dt 15:12-18
21:2-11Ref Lev 25:39-55

2“If you buy a Hebrew servant, he is to serve you for six years. But in the seventh year, he shall go free,[b] without paying anything. 3If he comes alone, he is to go free alone; but if he has a wife when he comes, she is to go with him. 4If his master gives him a wife and she bears him sons or daughters, the woman and her children shall belong to her master, and only the man shall go free.

5“But if the servant declares, ‘I love my master and my wife and children and do not want to go free,’[c] 6then his master must take him before the judges.[a][d] He shall take him to the door or the doorpost and pierce his ear with an awl. Then he will be his servant for life.[e]

7“If a man sells his daughter as a servant, she is not to go free as menservants do. 8If she does not please the master who has selected her for himself,[b] he must let her be redeemed. He has no right to sell her to foreigners, because he has broken faith with her. 9If he selects her for his son, he must grant her the rights of a daughter. 10If he marries another woman, he must not deprive the first one of her food, clothing and marital rights.[f] 11If he does not provide her with these three things, she is to go free, without any payment of money.

Personal Injuries

12“Anyone who strikes a man and kills him shall surely be put to death.[g] 13However, if he does not do it intentionally, but God lets it happen, he is to flee to a place[h] I

b24 Traditionally *peace offerings* a6 Or *before God* b8 Or *master so that he does not choose her* will designate. 14But if a man schemes and kills another man deliberately,[i] take him away from my altar and put him to death.[j]

15"Anyone who attacks[c] his father or his mother must be put to death.

16"Anyone who kidnaps another and either sells[k] him or still has him when he is caught must be put to death.[l]

17"Anyone who curses his father or mother must be put to death.[m]

18"If men quarrel and one hits the other with a stone or with his fist[d] and he does not die but is confined to bed, 19the one who struck the blow will not be held responsible if the other gets up and walks around outside with his staff; however, he must pay the injured man for the loss of his time and see that he is completely healed.

20"If a man beats his male or female slave with a rod and the slave dies as a direct result, he must be punished, 21but he is not to be punished if the slave gets up after a day or two, since the slave is his property.[n]

22"If men who are fighting hit a pregnant woman and she gives birth prematurely[e] but there is no serious injury, the offender must be fined whatever the woman's husband demands[o] and the court allows. 23But if there is serious injury, you are to take life for life,[p] 24eye for eye, tooth for tooth,[q] hand for hand, foot for foot, 25burn for burn, wound for wound, bruise for bruise.

26"If a man hits a manservant or maidservant in the eye and destroys it, he must let the servant go free to compensate for the eye. 27And if he knocks out the tooth of a manservant or maidservant, he must let the servant go free to compensate for the tooth.

28"If a bull gores a man or a woman to death, the bull must be stoned to death,[r] and its meat must not be eaten. But the owner of the bull will not be held responsible. 29If, however, the bull has had the habit of goring and the owner has been warned but has not kept it penned up and it kills a man or woman, the bull must be stoned and the owner also must be put to death. 30However, if payment is demanded of him, he may redeem his life by paying whatever is demanded.[s] 31This law also applies if the bull gores a son or a daughter. 32If the bull gores a male or female slave, the owner must pay thirty shekels[f][t] of silver to the master of the slave, and the bull must be stoned.

33"If a man uncovers a pit or digs one and fails to cover it and an ox or a donkey falls into it, 34the owner of the pit must pay for the loss; he must pay its owner, and the dead animal will be his.

35"If a man's bull injures the bull of another and it dies, they are to sell the live one and divide both the money and the dead animal equally. 36However, if it was known that the bull had the habit of goring, yet the owner did not keep it penned up, the owner must pay, animal for animal, and the dead animal will be his.

Protection of Property

22 "If a man steals an ox or a sheep and slaughters it or sells it, he must pay back[a] five head of cattle for the ox and four sheep for the sheep.

2"If a thief is caught breaking in[b] and is struck so that he dies, the defender is not guilty of bloodshed;[c] 3but if it happens[a] after sunrise, he is guilty of bloodshed.

"A thief must certainly make restitution, but if he has nothing, he must be sold[d] to pay for his theft.

4"If the stolen animal is found alive in his possession—whether

21:14 *i* Heb 10:26 *j* Dt 19:11-12; 1Ki 2:28-34
21:16 *k* Ge 37:28 *l* Ex 22:4; Dt 24:7
21:17 *m* Lev 20:9-10; Mt 15:4*; Mk 7:10*
21:21 *n* Lev 25:44-46
21:22 *o* ver 30; Dt 22:18-19
21:23 *p* Lev 24:19; Dt 19:21
21:24 *q* Mt 5:38*
21:28 *r* ver 32; Ge 9:5
21:30 *s* ver 22; Nu 35:31
21:32 *t* Zec 11:12-13; Mt 26:15; Mt 27:3,9
22:1 *a* 2Sa 12:6; Pr 6:31; Lk 19:8
22:2 *b* Mt 6:19-20; Mt 24:43 *c* Nu 35:27
22:3 *d* Ex 21:2; Mt 18:25

[c]15 Or *kills* [d]18 Or *with a tool* [e]22 Or *she has a miscarriage* [f]32 That is, about 12 ounces (about 0.3 kilogram) [a]3 Or *if he strikes him*

ox or donkey or sheep—he must pay back double.[e]

5“If a man grazes his livestock in a field or vineyard and lets them stray and they graze in another man’s field, he must make restitution from the best of his own field or vineyard.

6“If a fire breaks out and spreads into thornbushes so that it burns shocks of grain or standing corn or the whole field, the one who started the fire must make restitution.

7“If a man gives his neighbour silver or goods for safekeeping and they are stolen from the neighbour’s house, the thief, if he is caught, must pay back double.[f] 8But if the thief is not found, the owner of the house must appear before the judges[b][g] to determine whether he has laid his hands on the other man’s property. 9In all cases of illegal possession of an ox, a donkey, a sheep, a garment, or any other lost property about which somebody says, ‘This is mine,’ both parties are to bring their cases before the judges.[h] The one whom the judges declare[c] guilty must pay back double to his neighbour.

10“If a man gives a donkey, an ox, a sheep or any other animal to his neighbour for safekeeping and it dies or is injured or is taken away while no-one is looking, 11the issue between them will be settled by the taking of an oath[i] before the LORD that the neighbour did not lay hands on the other person’s property. The owner is to accept this, and no restitution is required. 12But if the animal was stolen from the neighbour, he must make restitution to the owner. 13If it was torn to pieces by a wild animal, he shall bring in the remains as evidence and he will not be required to pay for the torn animal.[j]

14“If a man borrows an animal from his neighbour and it is injured or dies while the owner is not present, he must make restitution. 15But if the owner is with the animal, the borrower will not have to pay. If the animal was hired, the money paid for the hire covers the loss.

Social Responsibility

16“If a man seduces a virgin[k] who is not pledged to be married and sleeps with her, he must pay the bride-price, and she shall be his wife. 17If her father absolutely refuses to give her to him, he must still pay the bride-price for virgins.

18“Do not allow a sorceress[l] to live.

19“Anyone who has sexual relations with an animal[m] must be put to death.

20“Whoever sacrifices to any god other than the LORD must be destroyed.[d][n]

21“Do not ill-treat an alien[o] or oppress him, for you were aliens[p] in Egypt.

22“Do not take advantage of a widow or an orphan.[q] 23If you do and they cry out[r] to me, I will certainly hear their cry.[s] 24My anger will be aroused, and I will kill you with the sword; your wives will become widows and your children fatherless.[t]

25“If you lend money to one of my people among you who is needy, do not be like a money-lender; charge him no interest.[e][u] 26If you take your neighbour’s cloak as a pledge,[v] return it to him by sunset, 27because his cloak is the only covering he has for his body. What else will he sleep in? When he cries out to me, I will hear, for I am compassionate.[w]

28“Do not blaspheme God[f][x] or curse the ruler of your people.[y]

29“Do not hold back offerings[z]

22:4 e Ge 43:12
22:7 f ver 4
22:8 g Ex 21:6; Dt 17:8-9; Dt 19:17
22:9 h ver 28; Dt 25:1
22:11 i Heb 6:16
22:13 j Ge 31:39
22:16 k Dt 22:28
22:18 l Lev 20:27; Dt 18:11; 1Sa 28:3
22:19 m Lev 18:23; Dt 27:21
22:20 n Dt 17:2-5
22:21 o Lev 19:33; p Dt 10:19
22:22 q Dt 24:6,10, 12,17
22:23 r Lk 18:7; s Dt 15:9; Ps 18:6
22:24 t Ps 69:24; Ps 109:9
22:25 u Lev 25:35-37; Dt 23:20; Ps 15:5
22:26 v Dt 24:6
22:27 w Ex 34:6
22:28 x Lev 24:11,16; y Ecc 10:20; Ac 23:5*
22:29 z Ex 23:15,16, 19

b8 Or *before God*; also in verse 9 c9 Or *whom God declares* d20 The Hebrew term refers to the irrevocable giving over of things or persons to the LORD, often by totally destroying them.
e25 Or *excessive interest* f28 Or *Do not revile the judges*

from your granaries or your vats.[g]
“You must give me the firstborn
of your sons.[a] 30Do the same with
your cattle and your sheep.[b] Let
them stay with their mothers for
seven days, but give them to me on
the eighth day.[c]
31“You are to be my holy people.[d] So do not eat the meat of an
animal torn by wild beasts;[e] throw
it to the dogs.

Laws of Justice and Mercy

23 “Do not spread false reports.[a] Do not help a
wicked man by being a malicious
witness.[b]
2“Do not follow the crowd in doing wrong. When you give testimony in a lawsuit, do not pervert
justice[c] by siding with the crowd,
3and do not show favouritism to a
poor man in his lawsuit.
4“If you come across your enemy's ox or donkey wandering off,
be sure to take it back to him.[d] 5If
you see the donkey[e] of someone
who hates you fallen down under
its load, do not leave it there; be
sure you help him with it.
6“Do not deny justice[f] to your
poor people in their lawsuits.
7Have nothing to do with a false
charge[g] and do not put an innocent
or honest person to death, for I will
not acquit the guilty.
8“Do not accept a bribe,[h] for a
bribe blinds those who see and
twists the words of the righteous.
9“Do not oppress an alien;[i] you
yourselves know how it feels to be
aliens, because you were aliens in
Egypt.

Sabbath Laws

10“For six years you are to sow
your fields and harvest the crops,
11but during the seventh year let
the land lie unploughed and un-
used. Then the poor among your
people may get food from it, and
the wild animals may eat what they

22:29
a Ex 13:2
22:30
b Ex 13:12; Dt 15:19
c Lev 22:27
22:31
d Lev 19:2
e Eze 4:14
23:1
a Ex 20:16; Ps 101:5
b Ps 35:11; Ac 6:11
23:2
c Dt 16:19
23:4
d Dt 22:1-3
23:5
e Dt 22:4
23:6
f ver 2
23:7
g Eph 4:25
23:8
h Dt 10:17; Dt 16:19; Pr 15:27
23:9
i Ex 22:21
23:12
j Ex 20:9
23:13
k 1Ti 4:16
23:14
l Ex 34:23,24
23:15
m Ex 12:17
n Ex 34:20
23:16
o Ex 34:22
p Dt 16:13
23:17
q Dt 16:16
23:18
r Ex 34:25
s Dt 16:4
23:19
t Ex 22:29; Dt 26:2,10
u Dt 14:21
23:20
v Ex 14:19; Ex 32:34

leave. Do the same with your vineyard and your olive grove.
12“Six days do your work,[j] but
on the seventh day do not work, so
that your ox and your donkey may
rest and the slave born in your
household, and the alien as well,
may be refreshed.
13“Be careful[k] to do everything I
have said to you. Do not invoke the
names of other gods; do not let
them be heard on your lips.

The Three Annual Festivals

14“Three times[l] a year you are to
celebrate a festival to me.
15“Celebrate the Feast of Unleavened Bread;[m] for seven days eat
bread made without yeast, as I
commanded you. Do this at the appointed time in the month of Abib,
for in that month you came out of
Egypt.
“No-one is to appear before me
empty-handed.[n]
16“Celebrate the Feast of Harvest with the firstfruits[o] of the
crops you sow in your field.
“Celebrate the Feast of Ingathering at the end of the year, when you
gather in your crops from the
field.[p]
17“Three times[q] a year all the
men are to appear before the Sovereign LORD.
18“Do not offer the blood of a sacrifice to me along with anything
containing yeast.[r]
“The fat of my festival offerings
must not be kept until morning.[s]
19“Bring the best of the firstfruits[t] of your soil to the house of
the LORD your God.
“Do not cook a young goat in its
mother's milk.[u]

God's Angel to Prepare the Way

20“See, I am sending an angel[v]
ahead of you to guard you along the

[g]29 The meaning of the Hebrew for this phrase is uncertain.

way and to bring you to the place I
have prepared.[w] 21 Pay attention to
him and listen[x] to what he says. Do
not rebel against him; he will not
forgive your rebellion,[y] since my
Name is in him. 22 If you listen carefully to what he says and do all that
I say, I will be an enemy[z] to your
enemies and will oppose those who
oppose you. 23 My angel will go
ahead of you and bring you into the
land of the Amorites, Hittites, Perizzites, Canaanites, Hivites and
Jebusites,[a] and I will wipe them
out. 24 Do not bow down before their
gods or worship[b] them or follow
their practices.[c] You must demolish[d] them and break their sacred
stones to pieces. 25 Worship the
LORD your God,[e] and his blessing[f]
will be on your food and water. I
will take away sickness[g] from
among you, 26 and none will miscarry or be barren[h] in your land. I
will give you a full life span.[i]

27 “I will send my terror[j] ahead
of you and throw into confusion[k]
every nation you encounter. I will
make all your enemies turn their
backs and run. 28 I will send the hornet[l] ahead of you to drive the Hivites, Canaanites and Hittites out
of your way. 29 But I will not drive
them out in a single year, because
the land would become desolate
and the wild animals[m] too numerous for you. 30 Little by little I will
drive them out before you, until
you have increased enough to take
possession of the land.

31 “I will establish your borders
from the Red Sea[a] to the Sea of the
Philistines,[b] and from the desert
to the River.[c][n] I will hand over to
you the people who live in the land
and you will drive them out[o] before you. 32 Do not make a covenant[p] with them or with their
gods. 33 Do not let them live in your
land, or they will cause you to sin
against me, because the worship of
their gods will certainly be a
snare[q] to you.”

23:20 w Ex 15:17
23:21 x Nu 14:11; Dt 18:19 y Ps 78:8,40,56
23:22 z Ge 12:3; Dt 30:7
23:23 a ver 20; Jos 24:8,11
23:24 b Ex 20:5 c Dt 12:30-31 d Ex 34:13; Nu 33:52
23:25 e Dt 6:13; Mt 4:10 f Dt 7:12-15; Dt 28:1-14 g Ex 15:26
23:26 h Dt 7:14; Mal 3:11 i Job 5:26
23:27 j Ex 15:14; Dt 2:25 k Dt 7:23
23:28 l Dt 7:20; Jos 24:12
23:29 m Dt 7:22
23:31 n Ge 15:18 o Jos 21:44; Jos 24:12,18
23:32 p Ex 34:12; Dt 7:2
23:33 q Dt 7:16; Ps 106:36
24:1 a Ex 6:23; Lev 10:1-2 b Nu 11:16
24:3 c Ex 19:8; Dt 5:27
24:4 d Dt 31:9 e Ge 28:18
24:6 f Heb 9:18
24:7 g Heb 9:19
24:8 h Heb 9:20*; 1Pe 1:2
24:9 i ver 1
24:10 j Mt 17:2; Jn 1:18; Jn 6:46 k Eze 1:26 l Rev 4:3
24:11 m Ge 32:30; Ex 19:21

The Covenant Confirmed

24 Then he said to Moses,
“Come up to the LORD, you
and Aaron, Nadab and Abihu,[a] and
seventy of the elders[b] of Israel.
You are to worship at a distance,
2 but Moses alone is to approach the
LORD; the others must not come
near. And the people may not come
up with him.”

3 When Moses went and told the
people all the LORD’s words and
laws, they responded with one
voice, “Everything the LORD has
said we will do.”[c] 4 Moses then
wrote[d] down everything the LORD
had said.

He got up early the next morning
and built an altar at the foot of the
mountain and set up twelve stone
pillars[e] representing the twelve
tribes of Israel. 5 Then he sent
young Israelite men, and they offered burnt offerings and sacrificed young bulls as fellowship
offerings[a] to the LORD. 6 Moses
took half of the blood[f] and put it in
bowls, and the other half he sprinkled on the altar. 7 Then he took the
Book of the Covenant[g] and read it
to the people. They responded, “We
will do everything the LORD has
said; we will obey.”

8 Moses then took the blood,
sprinkled it on the people and said,
“This is the blood of the covenant[h]
that the LORD has made with you in
accordance with all these words.”

9 Moses and Aaron, Nadab and
Abihu, and the seventy elders[i] of
Israel went up 10 and saw[j] the God
of Israel. Under his feet was something like a pavement made of sapphire,[b][k] clear as the sky[l] itself.
11 But God did not raise his hand
against these leaders of the Israelites; they saw[m] God, and they ate
and drank.

[a]31 Hebrew *Yam Suph*; that is, Sea of Reeds
[b]31 That is, the Mediterranean [c]31 That is, the Euphrates [a]5 Traditionally *peace offerings*
[b]10 Or *lapis lazuli*

12 The LORD said to Moses, "Come up to me on the mountain and stay here, and I will give you the tablets of stone,[n] with the law and commands I have written for their instruction."

13 Then Moses set out with Joshua[o] his assistant, and Moses went up on the mountain[p] of God. 14 He said to the elders, "Wait here for us until we come back to you. Aaron and Hur are with you, and anyone involved in a dispute can go to them."

15 When Moses went up on the mountain, the cloud[q] covered it, 16 and the glory[r] of the LORD settled on Mount Sinai. For six days the cloud covered the mountain, and on the seventh day the LORD called to Moses from within the cloud.[s] 17 To the Israelites the glory of the LORD looked like a consuming fire[t] on top of the mountain. 18 Then Moses entered the cloud as he went on up the mountain. And he stayed on the mountain forty[u] days and forty nights.[v]

Offerings for the Tabernacle

25:1–7pp Ex 35:4–9

25 The LORD said to Moses, 2 "Tell the Israelites to bring me an offering. You are to receive the offering for me from each man whose heart prompts[a] him to give. 3 These are the offerings you are to receive from them: gold, silver and bronze; 4 blue, purple and scarlet yarn and fine linen; goat hair; 5 ram skins dyed red and hides of sea cows;[a] acacia wood; 6 olive oil[b] for the light; spices for the anointing oil and for the fragrant incense; 7 and onyx stones and other gems to be mounted on the ephod[c] and breastpiece.[d]

8 "Then have them make a sanctuary[e] for me, and I will dwell[f] among them. 9 Make this tabernacle and all its furnishings exactly like the pattern[g] I will show you.

The Ark

25:10–20pp Ex 37:1–9

10 "Have them make a chest[h] of acacia wood—two and a half cubits long, a cubit and a half wide, and a cubit and a half high.[b] 11 Overlay it with pure gold, both inside and out, and make a gold moulding around it. 12 Cast four gold rings for it and fasten them to its four feet, with two rings on one side and two rings on the other. 13 Then make poles of acacia wood and overlay them with gold. 14 Insert the poles into the rings on the sides of the chest to carry it. 15 The poles are to remain in the rings of this ark; they are not to be removed.[i] 16 Then put in the ark the Testimony,[j] which I will give you.

17 "Make an atonement cover[c][k] of pure gold—two and a half cubits long and a cubit and a half wide.[d] 18 And make two cherubim out of hammered gold at the ends of the cover. 19 Make one cherub on one end and the second cherub on the other; make the cherubim of one piece with the cover, at the two ends. 20 The cherubim are to have their wings spread upwards, overshadowing[l] the cover with them. The cherubim are to face each other, looking towards the cover. 21 Place the cover on top of the ark[m] and put in the ark the Testimony,[n] which I will give you. 22 There, above the cover between the two cherubim[o] that are over the ark of the Testimony, I will meet[p] with you and give you all my commands for the Israelites.

The Table

25:23–29pp Ex 37:10–16

23 "Make a table[q] of acacia wood—two cubits long, a cubit

24:12 n Ex 32:15-16
24:13 o Ex 17:9 p Ex 3:1
24:15 q Ex 19:9
24:16 r Ex 16:10 s Ps 99:7
24:17 t Ex 3:2; Dt 4:36; Heb 12:18,29
24:18 u Dt 9:9 v Ex 34:28
25:2 a Ex 35:21; 1Ch 29:5,7,9; Ezr 2:68; 2Co 8:11-12; 2Co 9:7
25:6 b Ex 27:20; Ex 30:22-32
25:7 c Ex 28:4,6-14 d Ex 28:15-30
25:8 e Ex 36:1-5; Heb 9:1-2 f Ex 29:45; 1Ki 6:13; 2Co 6:16; Rev 21:3
25:9 g ver 40; Ac 7:44; Heb 8:5
25:10 h Dt 10:1-5; Heb 9:4
25:15 i 1Ki 8:8
25:16 j Dt 31:26; Heb 9:4
25:17 k Ro 3:25
25:20 l 1Ki 8:7; 1Ch 28:18; Heb 9:5
25:21 m Ex 26:34 n ver 16
25:22 o Nu 7:89; 1Sa 4:4; 2Sa 6:2; 2Ki 19:15; Ps 80:1; Isa 37:16 p Ex 29:42-43
25:23 q Heb 9:2

[a]5 That is, large aquatic mammals [b]10 That is, about 3¾ feet (about 1.1 metres) long and 2¼ feet (about 0.7 metre) wide and high
[c]17 Traditionally *a mercy seat* [d]17 That is, about 3¾ feet (about 1.1 metres) long and 2¼ feet (about 0.7 metre) wide

wide and a cubit and a half high.[e]
24 Overlay it with pure gold and
make a gold moulding around it.
25 Also make around it a rim a handbreadth[f] wide and put a gold
moulding on the rim. 26 Make four
gold rings for the table and fasten
them to the four corners, where the
four legs are. 27 The rings are to be
close to the rim to hold the poles
used in carrying the table. 28 Make
the poles of acacia wood, overlay
them with gold and carry the table
with them. 29 And make its plates
and dishes of pure gold, as well as
its pitchers and bowls for the pouring out of offerings.[r] 30 Put the
bread of the Presence[s] on this
table to be before me at all times.

The Lampstand

25:31–39pp Ex 37:17–24

31 "Make a lampstand[t] of pure
gold and hammer it out, base and
shaft; its flowerlike cups, buds and
blossoms shall be of one piece with
it. 32 Six branches are to extend
from the sides of the lampstand—
three on one side and three on the
other. 33 Three cups shaped like
almond flowers with buds and blossoms are to be on one branch, three
on the next branch, and the same
for all six branches extending from
the lampstand. 34 And on the lampstand there are to be four cups
shaped like almond flowers with
buds and blossoms. 35 One bud shall
be under the first pair of branches
extending from the lampstand, a
second bud under the second pair,
and a third bud under the third
pair—six branches in all. 36 The
buds and branches shall all be of
one piece with the lampstand, hammered out of pure gold.

37 "Then make its seven lamps[u]
and set them up on it so that they
light the space in front of it. 38 Its
wick trimmers and trays are to be
of pure gold. 39 A talent[g] of pure
gold is to be used for the lampstand
and all these accessories. 40 See that

25:29 r Nu 4:7
25:30 s Lev 24:5-9
25:31 t 1Ki 7:49; Zec 4:2; Heb 9:2; Rev 1:12
25:37 u Ex 27:21; Lev 24:3-4; Nu 8:2
25:40 v Ex 26:30; Nu 8:4; Ac 7:44; Heb 8:5*

you make them according to the
pattern[v] shown you on the mountain.

The Tabernacle

26:1–37pp Ex 36:8–38

26 "Make the tabernacle with
ten curtains of finely
twisted linen and blue, purple and
scarlet yarn, with cherubim
worked into them by a skilled
craftsman. 2 All the curtains are to
be the same size—twenty-eight cubits long and four cubits wide.[a]
3 Join five of the curtains together,
and do the same with the other five.
4 Make loops of blue material along
the edge of the end curtain in one
set, and do the same with the end
curtain in the other set. 5 Make fifty
loops on one curtain and fifty loops
on the end curtain of the other set,
with the loops opposite each other.
6 Then make fifty gold clasps and
use them to fasten the curtains together so that the tabernacle is a
unit.

7 "Make curtains of goat hair for
the tent over the tabernacle—
eleven altogether. 8 All eleven curtains are to be the same
size—thirty cubits long and four
cubits wide.[b] 9 Join five of the curtains together into one set and the
other six into another set. Fold the
sixth curtain double at the front of
the tent. 10 Make fifty loops along
the edge of the end curtain in one
set and also along the edge of the
end curtain in the other set. 11 Then
make fifty bronze clasps and put
them in the loops to fasten the tent
together as a unit. 12 As for the additional length of the tent curtains,
the half curtain that is left over is
to hang down at the rear of the

[e] *23* That is, about 3 feet (about 0.9 metre) long and 1½ feet (about 0.5 metre) wide and 2¼ feet (about 0.7 metre) high
[f] *25* That is, about 3 inches (about 8 centimetres)
[g] *39* That is, about 75 pounds (about 34 kilograms)
[a] *2* That is, about 42 feet (about 13 metres) long and 6 feet (about 1.8 metres) wide
[b] *8* That is, about 45 feet (about 13.5 metres) long and 6 feet (about 1.8 metres) wide

tabernacle. 13The tent curtains will
be a cubit[c] longer on both sides;
what is left will hang over the sides
of the tabernacle so as to cover it.
14Make for the tent a covering of
ram skins dyed red, and over that a
covering of hides of sea cows.[d][a]

15"Make upright frames of acacia wood for the tabernacle. 16Each
frame is to be ten cubits long and a
cubit and a half wide,[e] 17with two
projections set parallel to each
other. Make all the frames of the
tabernacle in this way. 18Make
twenty frames for the south side of
the tabernacle 19and make forty silver bases to go under them—two
bases for each frame, one under
each projection. 20For the other
side, the north side of the tabernacle, make twenty frames 21and
forty silver bases—two under each
frame. 22Make six frames for the
far end, that is, the west end of the
tabernacle, 23and make two frames
for the corners at the far end. 24At
these two corners they must be
double from the bottom all the way
to the top, and fitted into a single
ring; both shall be like that. 25So
there will be eight frames and sixteen silver bases—two under each
frame.

26"Also make crossbars of acacia
wood: five for the frames on one
side of the tabernacle, 27five for
those on the other side, and five for
the frames on the west, at the far
end of the tabernacle. 28The centre
crossbar is to extend from end to
end at the middle of the frames.
29Overlay the frames with gold and
make gold rings to hold the crossbars. Also overlay the crossbars
with gold.

30"Set up the tabernacle according to the plan[b] shown you on the
mountain.

31"Make a curtain[c] of blue, purple and scarlet yarn and finely
twisted linen, with cherubim[d]
worked into it by a skilled craftsman. 32Hang it with gold hooks on
four posts of acacia wood overlaid

26:14
a Ex 36:19 Nu 4:25
26:30
b Ex 25:9,40 Ac 7:44 Heb 8:5
26:31
c 2Ch 3:14 Mt 27:51 Heb 9:3
d Ex 36:35
26:33
e Ex 40:3,21 Lev 16:2
f Heb 9:2-3
26:34
g Ex 25:21 Ex 40:20 Heb 9:5
26:35
h Heb 9:2
i Ex 40:22,24
27:1
a Eze 43:13
27:2
b Ps 118:27
27:8
c Ex 25:9,40

with gold and standing on four silver bases. 33Hang the curtain from
the clasps and place the ark of the
Testimony behind the curtain.[e]
The curtain will separate the Holy
Place from the Most Holy Place.[f]
34Put the atonement cover[g] on the
ark of the Testimony in the Most
Holy Place. 35Place the table[h] outside the curtain on the north side of
the tabernacle and put the lampstand[i] opposite it on the south
side.

36"For the entrance to the tent
make a curtain of blue, purple and
scarlet yarn and finely twisted
linen—the work of an embroiderer.
37Make gold hooks for this curtain
and five posts of acacia wood overlaid with gold. And cast five bronze
bases for them.

The Altar of Burnt Offering

27:1–8pp Ex 38:1–7

27 "Build an altar[a] of acacia
wood, three cubits[a] high;
it is to be square, five cubits long
and five cubits wide.[b] 2Make a
horn[b] at each of the four corners,
so that the horns and the altar are
of one piece, and overlay the altar
with bronze. 3Make all its utensils
of bronze—its pots to remove the
ashes, and its shovels, sprinkling
bowls, meat forks and firepans.
4Make a grating for it, a bronze network, and make a bronze ring at
each of the four corners of the network. 5Put it under the ledge of the
altar so that it is halfway up the
altar. 6Make poles of acacia wood
for the altar and overlay them with
bronze. 7The poles are to be inserted into the rings so they will be
on two sides of the altar when it is
carried. 8Make the altar hollow, out
of boards. It is to be made just as
you were shown[c] on the mountain.

[c] *13* That is, about 1½ feet (about 0.5 metre)
[d] *14* That is, large aquatic mammals
[e] *16* That is, about 15 feet (about 4.5 metres) long and 2¼ feet (about 0.7 metre) wide
[a] *1* That is, about 4½ feet (about 1.4 metres)
[b] *1* That is, about 7½ feet (about 2.3 metres) long and wide

The Courtyard

27:9-19pp Ex 38:9-20

9"Make a courtyard for the tabernacle. The south side shall be a hundred cubits[c] long and is to have curtains of finely twisted linen, 10with twenty posts and twenty bronze bases and with silver hooks and bands on the posts. 11The north side shall also be a hundred cubits long and is to have curtains, with twenty posts and twenty bronze bases and with silver hooks and bands on the posts.

12"The west end of the courtyard shall be fifty cubits[d] wide and have curtains, with ten posts and ten bases. 13On the east end, towards the sunrise, the courtyard shall also be fifty cubits wide. 14Curtains fifteen cubits[e] long are to be on one side of the entrance, with three posts and three bases, 15and curtains fifteen cubits long are to be on the other side, with three posts and three bases.

16"For the entrance to the courtyard, provide a curtain twenty cubits[f] long, of blue, purple and scarlet yarn and finely twisted linen—the work of an embroiderer—with four posts and four bases. 17All the posts around the courtyard are to have silver bands and hooks, and bronze bases. 18The courtyard shall be a hundred cubits long and fifty cubits wide,[g] with curtains of finely twisted linen five cubits[h] high, and with bronze bases. 19All the other articles used in the service of the tabernacle, whatever their function, including all the tent pegs for it and those for the courtyard, are to be of bronze.

Oil for the Lampstand

27:20-21pp Lev 24:1-3

20"Command the Israelites to bring you clear oil of pressed olives for the light so that the lamps may be kept burning. 21In the Tent of Meeting,[d] outside the curtain that is in front of the Testimony,[e] Aaron and his sons are to keep the lamps[f] burning before the LORD from evening till morning. This is to be a lasting ordinance[g] among the Israelites for the generations to come.

The Priestly Garments

28 "Have Aaron[a] your brother brought to you from among the Israelites, with his sons Nadab and Abihu, Eleazar and Ithamar, so that they may serve me as priests.[b] 2Make sacred garments[c] for your brother Aaron, to give him dignity and honour. 3Tell all the skilled men[d] to whom I have given wisdom[e] in such matters that they are to make garments for Aaron, for his consecration, so that he may serve me as priest. 4These are the garments they are to make: a breastpiece,[f] an ephod, a robe,[g] a woven tunic,[h] a turban and a sash. They are to make these sacred garments for your brother Aaron and his sons, so that they may serve me as priests. 5Make them use gold, and blue, purple and scarlet yarn, and fine linen.

The Ephod

28:6-14pp Ex 39:2-7

6"Make the ephod of gold, and of blue, purple and scarlet yarn, and of finely twisted linen—the work of a skilled craftsman. 7It is to have two shoulder pieces attached to two of its corners, so that it can be fastened. 8Its skilfully woven waistband is to be like it—of one piece with the ephod and made with gold, and with blue, purple and scarlet yarn, and with finely twisted linen.

9"Take two onyx stones and

27:21
d Ex 28:43
e Ex 26:31,33
f Ex 25:37; Ex 30:8; 1Sa 3:3; 2Ch 13:11
g Ex 29:9; Lev 3:17; Lev 16:34; Nu 18:23; Nu 19:21

28:1
a Heb 5:4
b Nu 18:1-7; Heb 5:1

28:2
c Ex 29:5,29; Ex 31:10; Ex 39:1; Lev 8:7-9,30

28:3
d Ex 31:6; Ex 36:1
e Ex 31:3

28:4
f ver 15-30
g ver 31-35
h ver 39

c*9* That is, about 150 feet (about 46 metres); also in verse 11 d*12* That is, about 75 feet (about 23 metres); also in verse 13 e*14* That is, about 22½ feet (about 6.9 metres); also in verse 15 f*16* That is, about 30 feet (about 9 metres) g*18* That is, about 150 feet (about 46 metres) long and 75 feet (about 23 metres) wide h*18* That is, about 7½ feet (about 2.3 metres)

engrave on them the names of the
sons of Israel 10in the order of their
birth—six names on one stone and
the remaining six on the other.
11Engrave the names of the sons of
Israel on the two stones the way a
gem cutter engraves a seal. Then
mount the stones in gold filigree
settings 12and fasten them on the
shoulder pieces of the ephod as
memorial stones for the sons of Israel. Aaron is to bear the names on
his shoulders as a memorial before
the LORD. 13Make gold filigree settings 14and two braided chains of
pure gold, like a rope, and attach
the chains to the settings.

The Breastpiece

28:15–28pp Ex 39:8–21

15"Fashion a breastpiece for
making decisions—the work of a
skilled craftsman. Make it like the
ephod: of gold, and of blue, purple
and scarlet yarn, and of finely
twisted linen. 16It is to be square—a
span[a] long and a span wide—and
folded double. 17Then mount four
rows of precious stones on it. In the
first row there shall be a ruby, a topaz and a beryl; 18in the second row
a turquoise, a sapphire[b] and an
emerald; 19in the third row a jacinth, an agate and an amethyst;
20in the fourth row a chrysolite, an
onyx and a jasper.[c] Mount them in
gold filigree settings. 21There are
to be twelve stones, one for each of
the names of the sons of Israel,
each engraved like a seal with the
name of one of the twelve tribes.

22"For the breastpiece make
braided chains of pure gold, like a
rope. 23Make two gold rings for it
and fasten them to two corners of
the breastpiece. 24Fasten the two
gold chains to the rings at the corners of the breastpiece, 25and the
other ends of the chains to the two
settings, attaching them to the
shoulder pieces of the ephod at the
front. 26Make two gold rings and attach them to the other two corners
of the breastpiece on the inside
edge next to the ephod. 27Make two
more gold rings and attach them to
the bottom of the shoulder pieces
on the front of the ephod, close to
the seam just above the waistband
of the ephod. 28The rings of the
breastpiece are to be tied to the
rings of the ephod with blue cord,
connecting it to the waistband, so
that the breastpiece will not swing
out from the ephod.

29"Whenever Aaron enters the
Holy Place,[i] he will bear the
names of the sons of Israel over his
heart on the breastpiece of decision as a continuing memorial before the LORD. 30Also put the Urim
and the Thummim[j] in the breastpiece, so they may be over Aaron's
heart whenever he enters the presence of the LORD. Thus Aaron will
always bear the means of making
decisions for the Israelites over his
heart before the LORD.

Other Priestly Garments

28:31–43pp Ex 39:22–31

31"Make the robe of the ephod entirely of blue cloth, 32with an opening for the head in its centre. There
shall be a woven edge like a collar[d]
around this opening, so that it will
not tear. 33Make pomegranates of
blue, purple and scarlet yarn
around the hem of the robe, with
gold bells between them. 34The
gold bells and the pomegranates
are to alternate around the hem of
the robe. 35Aaron must wear it
when he ministers. The sound of
the bells will be heard when he enters the Holy Place before the LORD
and when he comes out, so that he
will not die.

36"Make a plate of pure gold and
engrave on it as on a seal: HOLY TO
THE LORD.[k] 37Fasten a blue cord to

28:29
i ver 12

28:30
j Lev 8:8
Nu 27:21
Dt 33:8
Ezr 2:63
Ne 7:65

28:36
k Zec 14:20

[a] *16* That is, about 9 inches (about 23 centimetres)
[b] *18* Or *lapis lazuli*
[c] *20* The precise identification of some of these precious stones is uncertain.
[d] *32* The meaning of the Hebrew for this word is uncertain.

it to attach it to the turban; it is to be on the front of the turban. 38 It will be on Aaron's forehead, and he will bear the guilt[l] involved in the sacred gifts the Israelites consecrate, whatever their gifts may be. It will be on Aaron's forehead continually so that they will be acceptable to the LORD.

39 "Weave the tunic of fine linen and make the turban of fine linen. The sash is to be the work of an embroiderer. 40 Make tunics, sashes and headbands for Aaron's sons,[m] to give them dignity and honour. 41 After you put these clothes on your brother Aaron and his sons, anoint[n] and ordain them. Consecrate them so they may serve me as priests.[o]

42 "Make linen undergarments[p] as a covering for the body, reaching from the waist to the thigh. 43 Aaron and his sons must wear them whenever they enter the Tent of Meeting[q] or approach the altar to minister in the Holy Place, so that they will not incur guilt and die.[r]

"This is to be a lasting ordinance[s] for Aaron and his descendants.

Consecration of the Priests

29:1-37pp Lev 8:1-36

29 "This is what you are to do to consecrate them, so that they may serve me as priests: Take a young bull and two rams without defect. 2 And from fine wheat flour, without yeast, make bread, and cakes mixed with oil, and wafers spread with oil.[a] 3 Put them in a basket and present them in it—along with the bull and the two rams. 4 Then bring Aaron and his sons to the entrance to the Tent of Meeting and wash them with water.[b] 5 Take the garments[c] and dress Aaron with the tunic, the robe of the ephod, the ephod itself and the breastpiece. Fasten the ephod on him by its skilfully woven waistband.[d] 6 Put the turban on his head and attach the sacred diadem[e] to the turban. 7 Take the anointing oil[f] and anoint him by pouring it on his head. 8 Bring his sons and dress them in tunics 9 and put headbands on them. Then tie sashes on Aaron and his sons.[a][g] The priesthood is theirs by a lasting ordinance.[h] In this way you shall ordain Aaron and his sons.

10 "Bring the bull to the front of the Tent of Meeting, and Aaron and his sons shall lay their hands on its head.[i] 11 Slaughter it in the LORD's presence at the entrance to the Tent of Meeting. 12 Take some of the bull's blood and put it on the horns[j] of the altar with your finger, and pour out the rest of it at the base of the altar. 13 Then take all the fat[k] around the inner parts, the covering of the liver, and both kidneys with the fat on them, and burn them on the altar. 14 But burn the bull's flesh and its hide and its offal outside the camp.[l] It is a sin offering.

15 "Take one of the rams, and Aaron and his sons shall lay their hands on its head. 16 Slaughter it and take the blood and sprinkle it against the altar on all sides. 17 Cut the ram into pieces and wash the inner parts and the legs, putting them with the head and the other pieces. 18 Then burn the entire ram on the altar. It is a burnt offering to the LORD, a pleasing aroma,[m] an offering made to the LORD by fire.

19 "Take the other ram,[n] and Aaron and his sons shall lay their hands on its head. 20 Slaughter it, take some of its blood and put it on the lobes of the right ears of Aaron and his sons, on the thumbs of their right hands, and on the big toes of their right feet. Then sprinkle blood against the altar on all sides. 21 And take some of the blood[o] on the altar and some of the anointing oil[p] and sprinkle it on Aaron and

[a]9 Hebrew; Septuagint *on them*

28:38 *l* Lev 10:17; Lev 22:9,16; Nu 18:1; Heb 9:28; 1Pe 2:24
28:40 *m* ver 4; Ex 39:41
28:41 *n* Ex 29:7; Lev 10:7; *o* Ex 29:7-9; Ex 30:30; Ex 40:15; Lev 8:1-36; Heb 7:28
28:42 *p* Lev 6:10; Lev 16:4,23; Eze 44:18
28:43 *q* Ex 27:21; *r* Ex 20:26; *s* Lev 17:7
29:2 *a* Lev 2:1,4; Lev 6:19-23
29:4 *b* Ex 40:12; Heb 10:22
29:5 *c* Ex 28:2; Lev 8:7; *d* Ex 28:8
29:6 *e* Lev 8:9
29:7 *f* Ex 30:25,30,31; Lev 8:12; Lev 21:10; Nu 35:25; Ps 133:2
29:9 *g* Ex 28:40; *h* Ex 40:15; Nu 3:10; Nu 18:7; Nu 25:13; Dt 18:5
29:10 *i* Lev 1:4
29:12 *j* Ex 27:2
29:13 *k* Lev 3:3,5,9
29:14 *l* Lev 4:11-12,21; Heb 13:11
29:18 *m* Ge 8:21
29:19 *n* ver 3
29:21 *o* Heb 9:22; *p* Ex 30:25,31

his garments and on his sons and their garments. Then he and his sons and their garments will be consecrated.[q]

22 "Take from this ram the fat, the fat tail, the fat around the inner parts, the covering of the liver, both kidneys with the fat on them, and the right thigh. (This is the ram for the ordination.) 23 From the basket of bread made without yeast, which is before the LORD, take a loaf, and a cake made with oil, and a wafer. 24 Put all these in the hands of Aaron and his sons and wave them before the LORD as a wave offering.[r] 25 Then take them from their hands and burn them on the altar along with the burnt offering for a pleasing aroma to the LORD, an offering made to the LORD by fire. 26 After you take the breast of the ram for Aaron's ordination, wave it before the LORD as a wave offering, and it will be your share.[s]

27 "Consecrate those parts of the ordination ram that belong to Aaron and his sons:[t] the breast that was waved and the thigh that was presented. 28 This is always to be the regular share from the Israelites for Aaron and his sons. It is the contribution the Israelites are to make to the LORD from their fellowship offerings.[b][u]

29 "Aaron's sacred garments will belong to his descendants so that they can be anointed and ordained in them.[v] 30 The son[w] who succeeds him as priest and comes to the Tent of Meeting to minister in the Holy Place is to wear them seven days.

31 "Take the ram for the ordination and cook the meat in a sacred place. 32 At the entrance to the Tent of Meeting, Aaron and his sons are to eat the meat of the ram and the bread[x] that is in the basket. 33 They are to eat these offerings by which atonement was made for their ordination and consecration. But no-one else may eat[y] them, because they are sacred. 34 And if any of the meat of the ordination ram or any bread is left over till morning,[z] burn it up. It must not be eaten, because it is sacred.

35 "Do for Aaron and his sons everything I have commanded you, taking seven days to ordain them. 36 Sacrifice a bull each day[a] as a sin offering to make atonement. Purify the altar by making atonement for it, and anoint it to consecrate[b] it. 37 For seven days make atonement for the altar and consecrate it. Then the altar will be most holy, and whatever touches it will be holy.[c]

38 "This is what you are to offer on the altar regularly each day:[d] two lambs a year old. 39 Offer one in the morning and the other at twilight.[e] 40 With the first lamb offer a tenth of an ephah[c] of fine flour mixed with a quarter of a hin[d] of oil from pressed olives, and a quarter of a hin of wine as a drink offering. 41 Sacrifice the other lamb at twilight with the same grain offering and its drink offering as in the morning—a pleasing aroma, an offering made to the LORD by fire.

42 "For the generations to come[f] this burnt offering is to be made regularly at the entrance to the Tent of Meeting before the LORD. There I will meet you and speak to you;[g] 43 there also I will meet with the Israelites, and the place will be consecrated by my glory.[h]

44 "So I will consecrate the Tent of Meeting and the altar and will consecrate Aaron and his sons to serve me as priests.[i] 45 Then I will dwell[j] among the Israelites and be their God.[k] 46 They will know that I am the LORD their God, who brought them out of Egypt so that I might dwell among them. I am the LORD their God.[l]

29:21 q ver 1
29:24 r Lev 7:30
29:26 s Lev 7:31-34
29:27 t Lev 7:31,34; Dt 18:3
29:28 u Lev 10:15
29:29 v Nu 20:26,28
29:30 w Nu 20:28
29:32 x Mt 12:4
29:33 y Lev 10:14; Lev 22:10,13
29:34 z Ex 12:10
29:36 a Heb 10:11; b Ex 40:10
29:37 c Ex 30:28-29; Ex 40:10; Mt 23:19
29:38 d Nu 28:3-8; 1Ch 16:40; Da 12:11
29:39 e Eze 46:13-15
29:42 f Ex 30:8; g Ex 25:22
29:43 h 1Ki 8:11
29:44 i Lev 21:15
29:45 j Ex 25:8; Lev 26:12; Zec 2:10; Jn 14:17; k 2Co 6:16; Rev 21:3
29:46 l Ex 20:2

b28 Traditionally *peace offerings* c40 That is, probably about 4 pints (about 2 litres) d40 That is, probably about 1½ pints (about 1 litre)

The Altar of Incense

30:1–5pp Ex 37:25–28

30 "Make an altar[a] of acacia wood for burning incense.[b] 2It is to be square, a cubit long and a cubit wide, and two cubits high[a]—its horns[c] of one piece with it. 3Overlay the top and all the sides and the horns with pure gold, and make a gold moulding around it. 4Make two gold rings for the altar below the moulding—two on opposite sides—to hold the poles used to carry it. 5Make the poles of acacia wood and overlay them with gold. 6Put the altar in front of the curtain that is before the ark of the Testimony—before the atonement cover[d] that is over the Testimony—where I will meet with you.

7"Aaron must burn fragrant incense[e] on the altar every morning when he tends the lamps. 8He must burn incense again when he lights the lamps at twilight so that incense will burn regularly before the LORD for the generations to come. 9Do not offer on this altar any other incense[f] or any burnt offering or grain offering, and do not pour a drink offering on it. 10Once a year Aaron shall make atonement[g] on its horns. This annual atonement must be made with the blood of the atoning sin offering for the generations to come. It is most holy to the LORD."

Atonement Money

11Then the LORD said to Moses, 12"When you take a census[h] of the Israelites to count them, each one must pay the LORD a ransom[i] for his life at the time he is counted. Then no plague[j] will come on them when you number them. 13Each one who crosses over to those already counted is to give a half shekel,[b] according to the sanctuary shekel,[k] which weighs twenty gerahs. This half shekel is an offering to the LORD. 14All who cross over, those twenty years old or more, are to give an offering to the LORD. 15The rich are not to give more than a half shekel and the poor are not to give less[l] when you make the offering to the LORD to atone for your lives. 16Receive the atonement money from the Israelites and use it for the service of the Tent of Meeting.[m] It will be a memorial for the Israelites before the LORD, making atonement for your lives."

Basin for Washing

17Then the LORD said to Moses, 18"Make a bronze basin,[n] with its bronze stand, for washing. Place it between the Tent of Meeting and the altar, and put water in it. 19Aaron and his sons are to wash their hands and feet[o] with water[p] from it. 20Whenever they enter the Tent of Meeting, they shall wash with water so that they will not die. Also, when they approach the altar to minister by presenting an offering made to the LORD by fire, 21they shall wash their hands and feet so that they will not die. This is to be a lasting ordinance[q] for Aaron and his descendants for the generations to come."

Anointing Oil

22Then the LORD said to Moses, 23"Take the following fine spices: 500 shekels[c] of liquid myrrh,[r] half as much (that is, 250 shekels) of fragrant cinnamon, 250 shekels of fragrant cane, 24500 shekels of cassia[s]—all according to the sanctuary shekel—and a hin[d] of olive oil. 25Make these into a sacred anointing oil, a fragrant blend, the work of a perfumer.[t] It will be the sacred anointing oil.[u] 26Then use it to anoint[v] the Tent of Meeting, the ark of the Testimony, 27the table

30:1 *a* Ex 37:25 *b* Rev 8:3
30:2 *c* Ex 27:2
30:6 *d* Ex 25:22; Ex 26:34
30:7 *e* ver 34-35; Ex 27:21; 1Sa 2:28
30:9 *f* Lev 10:1
30:10 *g* Lev 16:18-19, 30
30:12 *h* Ex 38:25; Nu 1:2,49; 2Sa 24:1 *i* Nu 31:50; Mt 20:28 *j* 2Sa 24:13
30:13 *k* Nu 3:47; Mt 17:24
30:15 *l* Pr 22:2; Eph 6:9
30:16 *m* Ex 38:25-28
30:18 *n* Ex 38:8; Ex 40:7,30
30:19 *o* Ex 40:31-32; Isa 52:11 *p* Ps 26:6
30:21 *q* Ex 27:21; Ex 28:43
30:23 *r* Ge 37:25
30:24 *s* Ps 45:8
30:25 *t* Ex 37:29 *u* Ex 40:9
30:26 *v* Ex 40:9; Lev 8:10; Nu 7:1

[a]*2* That is, about 1½ feet (about 0.5 metre) long and wide and about 3 feet (about 0.9 metre) high
[b]*13* That is, about ⅕ ounce (about 6 grams); also in verse 15
[c]*23* That is, about 12½ pounds (about 6 kilograms)
[d]*24* That is, probably about 6½ pints (about 4 litres)

and all its articles, the lampstand and its accessories, the altar of incense, 28 the altar of burnt offering and all its utensils, and the basin with its stand. 29 You shall consecrate them so they will be most holy, and whatever touches them will be holy.[w]

30 "Anoint Aaron and his sons and consecrate[x] them so they may serve me as priests. 31 Say to the Israelites, 'This is to be my sacred anointing oil for the generations to come. 32 Do not pour it on men's bodies and do not make any oil with the same formula. It is sacred, and you are to consider it sacred.[y] 33 Whoever makes perfume like it and whoever puts it on anyone other than a priest must be cut off[z] from his people.' "

Incense

34 Then the LORD said to Moses, "Take fragrant spices—gum resin, onycha and galbanum—and pure frankincense, all in equal amounts, 35 and make a fragrant blend of incense, the work of a perfumer.[a] It is to be salted and pure and sacred. 36 Grind some of it to powder and place it in front of the Testimony in the Tent of Meeting, where I will meet with you. It shall be most holy[b] to you. 37 Do not make any incense with this formula for yourselves; consider it holy[c] to the LORD. 38 Whoever makes any like it to enjoy its fragrance must be cut off[d] from his people."

Bezalel and Oholiab

31:2-6pp Ex 35:30-35

31 Then the LORD said to Moses, 2 "See I have chosen Bezalel[a] son of Uri, the son of Hur, of the tribe of Judah, 3 and I have filled him with the Spirit of God, with skill, ability and knowledge in all kinds of crafts[b]—4 to make artistic designs for work in gold, silver and bronze, 5 to cut and set stones, to work in wood, and to engage in all kinds of craftsmanship. 6 Moreover, I have appointed Oholiab son of Ahisamach, of the tribe of Dan, to help him. Also I have given skill to all the craftsmen to make everything I have commanded you: 7 the Tent of Meeting,[c] the ark of the Testimony[d] with the atonement cover[e] on it, and all the other furnishings of the tent—8 the table[f] and its articles, the pure gold lampstand[g] and all its accessories, the altar of incense, 9 the altar of burnt offering and all its utensils, the basin with its stand—10 and also the woven garments[h], both the sacred garments for Aaron the priest and the garments for his sons when they serve as priests, 11 and the anointing oil[i] and fragrant incense for the Holy Place. They are to make them just as I commanded you."

The Sabbath

12 Then the LORD said to Moses, 13 "Say to the Israelites, 'You must observe my Sabbaths.[j] This will be a sign[k] between me and you for the generations to come, so that you may know that I am the LORD, who makes you holy.[a][l]

14 " 'Observe the Sabbath, because it is holy to you. Anyone who desecrates it must be put to death;[m] whoever does any work on that day must be cut off from his people. 15 For six days, work[n] is to be done, but the seventh day is a Sabbath of rest,[o] holy to the LORD. Whoever does any work on the Sabbath day must be put to death. 16 The Israelites are to observe the Sabbath, celebrating it for the generations to come as a lasting covenant. 17 It will be a sign[p] between me and the Israelites for ever, for in six days the LORD made the heavens and the earth, and on the seventh day he abstained from work and rested.[q]' "

30:29 *w* Ex 29:37
30:30 *x* Ex 29:7; Lev 8:2,12,30
30:32 *y* ver 25,37
30:33 *z* ver 38; Ge 17:14
30:35 *a* ver 25
30:36 *b* ver 32; Ex 29:37; Lev 2:3
30:37 *c* ver 32
30:38 *d* ver 33
31:2 *a* Ex 36:1,2; 1Ch 2:20
31:3 *b* 1Ki 7:14
31:7 *c* Ex 36:8-38 *d* Ex 37:1-5 *e* Ex 37:6
31:8 *f* Ex 37:10-16 *g* Ex 37:17-24
31:10 *h* Ex 28:2; Ex 39:1,41
31:11 *i* Ex 30:22-32
31:13 *j* Ex 20:8; Lev 19:3,30 *k* Eze 20:12,20 *l* Lev 11:44
31:14 *m* Nu 15:32-36
31:15 *n* Ex 20:8-11 *o* Ge 2:3; Ex 16:23
31:17 *p* ver 13 *q* Ge 2:2-3

a 13 Or *who sanctifies you;* or *who sets you apart as holy*

18When the LORD finished speaking to Moses on Mount Sinai, he gave him the two tablets of the Testimony, the tablets of stone[r] inscribed by the finger of God.[s]

The Golden Calf

32 When the people saw that Moses was so long in coming down from the mountain,[a] they gathered round Aaron and said, "Come, make us gods[a] who will go before us. As for this fellow Moses who brought us up out of Egypt, we don't know what has happened to him."[b]

2Aaron answered them, "Take off the gold ear-rings[c] that your wives, your sons and your daughters are wearing, and bring them to me." 3So all the people took off their ear-rings and brought them to Aaron. 4He took what they handed him and made it into an idol cast in the shape of a calf,[d] fashioning it with a tool. Then they said, "These are your gods,[b] O Israel, who brought you up out of Egypt."

5When Aaron saw this, he built an altar in front of the calf and announced, "Tomorrow there will be a festival[e] to the LORD." 6So the next day the people rose early and sacrificed burnt offerings and presented fellowship offerings.[c][f] Afterwards they sat down to eat and drink and got up to indulge in revelry.[g]

7Then the LORD said to Moses, "Go down, because your people, whom you brought up out of Egypt,[h] have become corrupt.[i] 8They have been quick to turn away from what I commanded them and have made themselves an idol[j] cast in the shape of a calf. They have bowed down to it and sacrificed[k] to it and have said, 'These are your gods, O Israel, who brought you up out of Egypt.'[l]

9"I have seen these people," the LORD said to Moses, "and they are a stiff-necked[m] people. 10Now leave me alone so that my anger may burn against them and that I may destroy them. Then I will make you into a great nation."[n]

11But Moses sought the favour[o] of the LORD his God. "O LORD," he said, "why should your anger burn against your people, whom you brought out of Egypt with great power and a mighty hand?[p] 12Why should the Egyptians say, 'It was with evil intent that he brought them out, to kill them in the mountains and to wipe them off the face of the earth'?[q] Turn from your fierce anger; relent and do not bring disaster on your people. 13Remember[r] your servants Abraham, Isaac and Israel, to whom you swore by your own self:[s] 'I will make your descendants as numerous as the stars[t] in the sky and I will give your descendants all this land[u] I promised them, and it will be their inheritance for ever.'" 14Then the LORD relented[v] and did not bring on his people the disaster he had threatened.

15Moses turned and went down the mountain with the two tablets of the Testimony[w] in his hands.[x] They were inscribed on both sides, front and back. 16The tablets were the work of God; the writing was the writing of God, engraved on the tablets.[y]

17When Joshua heard the noise of the people shouting, he said to Moses, "There is the sound of war in the camp."

18Moses replied:

"It is not the sound of victory,
  it is not the sound of defeat;
  it is the sound of singing that I
    hear."

19When Moses approached the camp and saw the calf[z] and the dancing, his anger burned and he threw the tablets out of his hands,

31:18 r Ex 24:12 s Ex 32:15-16 Ex 34:1,28 Dt 4:13 Dt 5:22
32:1 a Ex 24:18 Dt 9:9-12 b Ac 7:40*
32:2 c Ex 35:22
32:4 d Dt 9:16 Ne 9:18 Ps 106:19 Ac 7:41
32:5 e Lev 23:2,37 2Ki 10:20
32:6 f Nu 25:2 Ac 7:41 g ver 17-19 1Co 10:7*
32:7 h ver 4,11 i Ge 6:11-12 Dt 9:12
32:8 j Ex 20:4 k Ex 22:20 l 1Ki 12:28
32:9 m Ex 33:3,5 Ex 34:9 Isa 48:4 Ac 7:51
32:10 n Nu 14:12 Dt 9:14
32:11 o Dt 9:18 p Dt 9:26
32:12 q Nu 14:13-16 Dt 9:28
32:13 r Ex 2:24 s Ge 22:16 Heb 6:13 t Ge 15:5 Ge 26:4 u Ge 12:7
32:14 v 2Sa 24:16 Ps 106:45
32:15 w Ex 31:18 x Dt 9:15
32:16 y Ex 31:18
32:19 z Dt 9:16

a1 Or *a god*; also in verses 23 and 31
b4 Or *This is your god*; also in verse 8
c6 Traditionally *peace offerings*

breaking them to pieces[a] at the
foot of the mountain. 20And he took
the calf they had made and burned
it in the fire; then he ground it to
powder, scattered it on the water[b]
and made the Israelites drink it.
21He said to Aaron, "What did
these people do to you, that you led
them into such great sin?"
22"Do not be angry, my lord,"
Aaron answered. "You know how
prone these people are to evil.[c]
23They said to me, 'Make us gods
who will go before us. As for this
fellow Moses who brought us up
out of Egypt, we don't know what
has happened to him.'[d] 24So I told
them, 'Whoever has any gold jewellery, take it off.' Then they gave
me the gold, and I threw it into the
fire, and out came this calf!"[e]
25Moses saw that the people were
running wild and that Aaron had let
them get out of control and so become a laughing-stock to their enemies. 26So he stood at the entrance
to the camp and said, "Whoever is
for the LORD, come to me." And all
the Levites rallied to him.
27Then he said to them, "This is
what the LORD, the God of Israel,
says: 'Each man strap a sword to
his side. Go back and forth through
the camp from one end to the other,
each killing his brother and friend
and neighbour.' "[f] 28The Levites
did as Moses commanded, and that
day about three thousand of the
people died. 29Then Moses said,
"You have been set apart to the
LORD today, for you were against
your own sons and brothers, and he
has blessed you this day."
30The next day Moses said to the
people, "You have committed a
great sin.[g] But now I will go up to
the LORD; perhaps I can make
atonement[h] for your sin."
31So Moses went back to the LORD
and said, "Oh, what a great sin
these people have committed![i]
They have made themselves gods
of gold.[j] 32But now, please forgive
their sin—but if not, then blot me[k]
out of the book[l] you have written."
33The LORD replied to Moses,
"Whoever has sinned against me I
will blot out[m] of my book. 34Now go,
lead the people to the place[n] I
spoke of, and my angel[o] will go before you. However, when the time
comes for me to punish,[p] I will
punish them for their sin."
35And the LORD struck the people
with a plague because of what they
did with the calf[q] Aaron had made.

33 Then the LORD said to
Moses, "Leave this place,
you and the people you brought up
out of Egypt, and go up to the land
I promised on oath to Abraham,
Isaac and Jacob, saying, 'I will give
it to your descendants.'[a] 2I will
send an angel[b] before you and
drive out the Canaanites, Amorites,
Hittites, Perizzites, Hivites and
Jebusites.[c] 3Go up to the land flowing with milk and honey.[d] But I
will not go with you, because you
are a stiff-necked[e] people and I
might destroy[f] you on the way."
4When the people heard these
distressing words, they began to
mourn[g] and no-one put on any
ornaments. 5For the LORD had said
to Moses, "Tell the Israelites,
'You are a stiff-necked people. If I
were to go with you even for a moment, I might destroy you. Now take
off your ornaments and I will decide what to do with you.' " 6So
the Israelites stripped off their
ornaments at Mount Horeb.

The Tent of Meeting

7Now Moses used to take a tent
and pitch it outside the camp some
distance away, calling it the "tent
of meeting".[h] Anyone enquiring of
the LORD would go to the tent of
meeting outside the camp. 8And
whenever Moses went out to the
tent, all the people rose and stood at
the entrances to their tents,[i]
watching Moses until he entered
the tent. 9As Moses went into the
tent, the pillar of cloud[j] would

32:19 a Dt 9:17
32:20 b Dt 9:21
32:22 c Dt 9:24
32:23 d ver 1
32:24 e ver 4
32:27 f Nu 25:3,5 Dt 33:9
32:30 g 1Sa 12:20 h Lev 1:4 Nu 25:13
32:31 i Dt 9:18 j Ex 20:23
32:32 k Ro 9:3 l Ps 69:28 Da 12:1 Php 4:3 Rev 3:5 Rev 21:27
32:33 m Dt 29:20 Ps 9:5
32:34 n Ex 3:17 o Ex 23:20 p Dt 32:35 Ps 99:8 Ro 2:5-6
32:35 q ver 4
33:1 a Ge 12:7
33:2 b Ex 32:34 c Ex 23:27-31 Jos 24:11
33:3 d Ex 3:8 e Ex 32:9 f Ex 32:10
33:4 g Nu 14:39
33:7 h Ex 29:42-43
33:8 i Nu 16:27
33:9 j Ex 13:21

come down and stay at the entrance, while the LORD spoke[k] with Moses. 10Whenever the people saw the pillar of cloud standing at the entrance to the tent, they all stood and worshipped, each at the entrance to his tent. 11The LORD would speak to Moses face to face,[l] as a man speaks with his friend. Then Moses would return to the camp, but his young assistant Joshua son of Nun did not leave the tent.

Moses and the Glory of the LORD

12Moses said to the LORD, "You have been telling me, 'Lead these people,'[m] but you have not let me know whom you will send with me. You have said, 'I know you by name[n] and you have found favour with me.' 13If you are pleased with me, teach me your ways[o] so I may know you and continue to find favour with you. Remember that this nation is your people."[p]

14The LORD replied, "My Presence[q] will go with you, and I will give you rest."[r]

15Then Moses said to him, "If your Presence does not go with us, do not send us up from here. 16How will anyone know that you are pleased with me and with your people unless you go with us?[s] What else will distinguish me and your people from all the other people on the face of the earth?"[t]

17And the LORD said to Moses, "I will do the very thing you have asked, because I am pleased with you and I know you by name."

18Then Moses said, "Now show me your glory."

19And the LORD said, "I will cause all my goodness to pass in front of you, and I will proclaim my name, the LORD, in your presence. I will have mercy on whom I will have mercy, and I will have compassion on whom I will have compassion.[u] 20But," he said, "you cannot see my face, for no-one may see[v] me and live."

21Then the LORD said, "There is a place near me where you may stand on a rock. 22When my glory passes by, I will put you in a cleft in the rock and cover you with my hand[w] until I have passed by. 23Then I will remove my hand and you will see my back; but my face must not be seen."

The New Stone Tablets

34 The LORD said to Moses, "Chisel out two stone tablets like the first ones, and I will write on them the words that were on the first tablets,[a] which you broke.[b] 2Be ready in the morning, and then come up on Mount Sinai.[c] Present yourself to me there on top of the mountain. 3No-one is to come with you or be seen anywhere on the mountain;[d] not even the flocks and herds may graze in front of the mountain."

4So Moses chiselled out two stone tablets like the first ones and went up Mount Sinai early in the morning, as the LORD had commanded him; and he carried the two stone tablets in his hands. 5Then the LORD came down in the cloud and stood there with him and proclaimed his name, the LORD.[e] 6And he passed in front of Moses, proclaiming, "The LORD, the LORD, the compassionate[f] and gracious God, slow to anger,[g] abounding in love[h] and faithfulness,[i] 7maintaining love to thousands,[j] and forgiving wickedness, rebellion and sin.[k] Yet he does not leave the guilty unpunished;[l] he punishes the children and their children for the sin of the fathers to the third and fourth generation."

8Moses bowed to the ground at once and worshipped. 9"O Lord, if I have found favour in your eyes," he said, "then let the Lord go with us.[m] Although this is a stiff-necked people, forgive our wickedness and

33:9 k Ex 31:18; Ps 99:7
33:11 l Nu 12:8; Dt 34:10
33:12 m Ex 3:10 n ver 17; Jn 10:14-15; 2Ti 2:19
33:13 o Ps 25:4; Ps 86:11; Ps 119:33 p Ex 34:9; Dt 9:26,29
33:14 q Isa 63:9 r Jos 21:44; Jos 22:4
33:16 s Nu 14:14 t Ex 34:10
33:19 u Ro 9:15*
33:20 v Ge 32:30; Isa 6:5
33:22 w Ps 91:4
34:1 a Dt 10:2,4 b Ex 32:19
34:2 c Ex 19:11
34:3 d Ex 19:12-13, 21
34:5 e Ex 33:19
34:6 f Ps 86:15 g Nu 14:18; Ro 2:4 h Ne 9:17; Ps 103:8; Joel 2:13 i Ps 108:4
34:7 j Ex 20:6 k Ps 103:3; Ps 130:4,8; Da 9:9; 1Jn 1:9 l Job 10:14; Na 1:3
34:9 m Ex 33:15

our sin, and take us as your inheritance."[n]

10 Then the LORD said: "I am making a covenant[o] with you. Before all your people I will do wonders never before done in any nation in all the world.[p] The people you live among will see how awesome is the work that I, the LORD, will do for you. 11 Obey what I command you today. I will drive out before you the Amorites, Canaanites, Hittites, Perizzites, Hivites and Jebusites.[q] 12 Be careful not to make a treaty with those who live in the land where you are going, or they will be a snare[r] among you. 13 Break down their altars, smash their sacred stones and cut down their Asherah poles.[a][s] 14 Do not worship any other god,[t] for the LORD, whose name is Jealous, is a jealous God.[u]

15 "Be careful not to make a treaty with those who live in the land; for when they prostitute[v] themselves to their gods and sacrifice to them, they will invite you and you will eat their sacrifices.[w] 16 And when you choose some of their daughters as wives[x] for your sons and those daughters prostitute themselves to their gods,[y] they will lead your sons to do the same.

17 "Do not make cast idols.[z]

18 "Celebrate the Feast of Unleavened Bread.[a] For seven days eat bread made without yeast,[b] as I commanded you. Do this at the appointed time in the month of Abib,[c] for in that month you came out of Egypt.

19 "The first offspring[d] of every womb belongs to me, including all the firstborn males of your livestock, whether from herd or flock. 20 Redeem the firstborn donkey with a lamb, but if you do not redeem it, break its neck.[e] Redeem all your firstborn sons.

"No-one is to appear before me empty-handed.[f]

21 "Six days you shall labour, but on the seventh day you shall rest;[g] even during the ploughing season and harvest you must rest.

22 "Celebrate the Feast of Weeks with the firstfruits of the wheat harvest, and the Feast of Ingathering[h] at the turn of the year.[b] 23 Three times[i] a year all your men are to appear before the Sovereign LORD, the God of Israel. 24 I will drive out nations[j] before you and enlarge your territory, and no-one will covet your land when you go up three times each year to appear before the LORD your God.

25 "Do not offer the blood of a sacrifice to me along with anything containing yeast,[k] and do not let any of the sacrifice from the Passover Feast remain until morning.[l]

26 "Bring the best of the firstfruits of your soil to the house of the LORD your God.

"Do not cook a young goat in its mother's milk."[m]

27 Then the LORD said to Moses, "Write[n] down these words, for in accordance with these words I have made a covenant with you and with Israel." 28 Moses was there with the LORD forty days and forty nights[o] without eating bread or drinking water. And he wrote on the tablets[p] the words of the covenant—the Ten Commandments.[q]

The Radiant Face of Moses

29 When Moses came down from Mount Sinai with the two tablets of the Testimony in his hands,[r] he was not aware that his face was radiant[s] because he had spoken with the LORD. 30 When Aaron and all the Israelites saw Moses, his face was radiant, and they were afraid to come near him. 31 But Moses called to them; so Aaron and all the leaders of the community came back to him, and he spoke to them. 32 Afterwards all the Israelites came near him, and he gave them

34:9 n Ps 33:12
34:10 o Dt 5:2-3; p Ex 33:16; Dt 4:32
34:11 q Ex 33:2
34:12 r Ex 23:32-33
34:13 s Ex 23:24; Dt 12:3; 2Ki 18:4
34:14 t Ex 20:3; u Ex 20:5; Dt 4:24
34:15 v Jdg 2:17; w Nu 25:2; 1Co 8:4
34:16 x Dt 7:3; y 1Ki 11:4
34:17 z Ex 32:8
34:18 a Ex 12:17; b Ex 12:15; c Ex 12:2
34:19 d Ex 13:2
34:20 e Ex 13:13,15; f Ex 23:15; Dt 16:16
34:21 g Ex 20:9; Lk 13:14
34:22 h Ex 23:16
34:23 i Ex 23:14
34:24 j Ex 23:28; Ex 33:2; Ps 78:55
34:25 k Ex 23:18; l Ex 12:8,10
34:26 m Ex 23:19
34:27 n Ex 17:14; Ex 24:4
34:28 o Ge 7:4; Ex 24:18; Mt 4:2; p ver 1; Ex 31:18; q Dt 4:13; Dt 10:4
34:29 r Ex 32:15; s Ps 34:5; Mt 17:2; 2Co 3:7,13

[a] 13 That is, symbols of the goddess Asherah
[b] 22 That is, in the autumn

all the commands[t] the LORD had given him on Mount Sinai.

33 When Moses finished speaking to them, he put a veil[u] over his face. 34 But whenever he entered the LORD's presence to speak with him, he removed the veil until he came out. And when he came out and told the Israelites what he had been commanded, 35 they saw that his face was radiant. Then Moses would put the veil back over his face until he went in to speak with the LORD.

Sabbath Regulations

35 Moses assembled the whole Israelite community and said to them, "These are the things the LORD has commanded[a] you to do: 2 For six days, work is to be done, but the seventh day shall be your holy day, a Sabbath[b] of rest to the LORD. Whoever does any work on it must be put to death. 3 Do not light a fire in any of your dwellings on the Sabbath day."[c]

Materials for the Tabernacle

35:4–9pp Ex 25:1–7
35:10–19pp Ex 39:32–41

4 Moses said to the whole Israelite community, "This is what the LORD has commanded: 5 From what you have, take an offering for the LORD. Everyone who is willing is to bring to the LORD an offering of gold, silver and bronze; 6 blue, purple and scarlet yarn and fine linen; goat hair; 7 ram skins dyed red and hides of sea cows;[a] acacia wood; 8 olive oil for the light; spices for the anointing oil and for the fragrant incense; 9 and onyx stones and other gems to be mounted on the ephod and breastpiece.

10 "All who are skilled among you are to come and make everything the LORD has commanded:[d] 11 the tabernacle[e] with its tent and its covering, clasps, frames, crossbars, posts and bases; 12 the ark[f] with its poles and the atonement cover and the curtain that shields it; 13 the table[g] with its poles and all its articles and the bread of the Presence; 14 the lampstand[h] that is for light with its accessories, lamps and oil for the light; 15 the altar[i] of incense with its poles, the anointing oil[j] and the fragrant incense;[k] the curtain for the doorway at the entrance to the tabernacle; 16 the altar[l] of burnt offering with its bronze grating, its poles and all its utensils; the bronze basin with its stand; 17 the curtains of the courtyard with its posts and bases, and the curtain for the entrance to the courtyard;[m] 18 the tent pegs for the tabernacle and for the courtyard, and their ropes; 19 the woven garments worn for ministering in the sanctuary—both the sacred garments[n] for Aaron the priest and the garments for his sons when they serve as priests."

20 Then the whole Israelite community withdrew from Moses' presence, 21 and everyone who was willing and whose heart moved him came and brought an offering to the LORD for the work on the Tent of Meeting, for all its service, and for the sacred garments. 22 All who were willing, men and women alike, came and brought gold jewellery of all kinds: brooches, earrings, rings and ornaments. They all presented their gold as a wave offering to the LORD. 23 Everyone who had blue, purple or scarlet yarn[o] or fine linen, or goat hair, ram skins dyed red or hides of sea cows brought them. 24 Those presenting an offering of silver or bronze brought it as an offering to the LORD, and everyone who had acacia wood for any part of the work brought it. 25 Every skilled woman[p] spun with her hands and brought what she had spun—blue, purple or scarlet yarn or fine linen.

34:32 t Ex 24:3
34:33 u 2Co 3:13
35:1 a Ex 34:32
35:2 b Ex 20:9-10; Ex 34:21; Lev 23:3
35:3 c Ex 16:23
35:10 d Ex 31:6
35:11 e Ex 26:1-37
35:12 f Ex 25:10-22
35:13 g Ex 25:23-30; Lev 24:5-6
35:14 h Ex 25:31
35:15 i Ex 30:1-6; j Ex 30:25; k Ex 30:34-38
35:16 l Ex 27:1-8
35:17 m Ex 27:9
35:19 n Ex 28:2; Ex 31:10; Ex 39:1
35:23 o 1Ch 29:8
35:25 p Ex 28:3

a7 That is, large aquatic mammals; also in verse 23

26And all the women who were willing and had the skill spun the goat
hair. 27The leaders[q] brought onyx
stones and other gems to be
mounted on the ephod and breastpiece. 28They also brought spices
and olive oil for the light and for
the anointing oil and for the fragrant incense.[r] 29All the Israelite
men and women who were willing[s]
brought to the LORD freewill offerings[t] for all the work the LORD
through Moses had commanded
them to do.

Bezalel and Oholiab

35:30–35pp Ex 31:2–6

30Then Moses said to the Israelites, "See, the LORD has chosen Bezalel son of Uri, the son of Hur, of
the tribe of Judah, 31and he has
filled him with the Spirit of God,
with skill, ability and knowledge in
all kinds of crafts[u]—32to make artistic designs for work in gold, silver and bronze, 33to cut and set
stones, to work in wood and to engage in all kinds of artistic craftsmanship. 34And he has given both
him and Oholiab[v] son of Ahisamach, of the tribe of Dan, the ability to teach[w] others. 35He has filled
them with skill to do all kinds of
work[x] as craftsmen, designers,
embroiderers in blue, purple and
scarlet yarn and fine linen, and
weavers—all of them master
craftsmen and designers.

36
1So Bezalel, Oholiab and
every skilled person[a] to whom the
LORD has given skill and ability to
know how to carry out all the work
of constructing the sanctuary[b] are
to do the work just as the LORD has
commanded."

2Then Moses summoned Be-
zalel[c] and Oholiab[d] and every
skilled person to whom the LORD
had given ability and who was willing[e] to come and do the work.
3They received from Moses all
the offerings[f] the Israelites had
brought to carry out the work of
constructing the sanctuary. And
the people continued to bring freewill offerings morning after morning. 4So all the skilled craftsmen
who were doing all the work on the
sanctuary left their work 5and said
to Moses, "The people are bringing
more than enough[g] for doing the
work the LORD commanded to be
done."

6Then Moses gave an order and
they sent this word throughout the
camp: "No man or woman is to
make anything else as an offering
for the sanctuary." And so the people were restrained from bringing
more, 7because what they already
had was more[h] than enough to do
all the work.

The Tabernacle

36:8–38pp Ex 26:1–37

8All the skilled men among the
workmen made the tabernacle with
ten curtains of finely twisted linen
and blue, purple and scarlet yarn,
with cherubim worked into them
by a skilled craftsman. 9All the curtains were the same size—twenty-
eight cubits long and four cubits
wide.[a] 10They joined five of the
curtains together and did the same
with the other five. 11Then they
made loops of blue material along
the edge of the end curtain in one
set, and the same was done with the
end curtain in the other set. 12They
also made fifty loops on one curtain
and fifty loops on the end curtain of
the other set, with the loops opposite each other. 13Then they made
fifty gold clasps and used them to
fasten the two sets of curtains together so that the tabernacle was a
unit.[i]

14They made curtains of goat
hair for the tent over the tabernacle—eleven altogether. 15All
eleven curtains were the same
size—thirty cubits long and four

35:27 q 1Ch 29:6; Ezr 2:68
35:28 r Ex 25:6
35:29 s ver 21; 1Ch 29:9; t ver 4-9; Ex 25:1-7; Ex 36:3; 2Ki 12:4
35:31 u ver 35; 2Ch 2:7,14
35:34 v Ex 31:6; w 2Ch 2:14
35:35 x ver 31; Ex 31:3,6; 1Ki 7:14
36:1 a Ex 28:3; b Ex 25:8
36:2 c Ex 31:2; d Ex 31:6; e Ex 25:2; Ex 35:21,26; 1Ch 29:5
36:3 f Ex 35:29
36:5 g 2Ch 24:14; 2Ch 31:10; 2Co 8:2-3
36:7 h 1Ki 7:47
36:13 i ver 18

a9 That is, about 42 feet (about 13 metres) long and 6 feet (about 1.8 metres) wide

cubits wide.[b] 16They joined five of
the curtains into one set and the
other six into another set. 17Then
they made fifty loops along the
edge of the end curtain in one set
and also along the edge of the end
curtain in the other set. 18They
made fifty bronze clasps to fasten
the tent together as a unit.[j] 19Then
they made for the tent a covering
of ram skins dyed red, and over
that a covering of hides of sea
cows.[c]
20They made upright frames of
acacia wood for the tabernacle.
21Each frame was ten cubits long
and a cubit and a half wide,[d] 22with
two projections set parallel to each
other. They made all the frames of
the tabernacle in this way. 23They
made twenty frames for the south
side of the tabernacle 24and made
forty silver bases to go under
them—two bases for each frame,
one under each projection. 25For
the other side, the north side of the
tabernacle, they made twenty
frames 26and forty silver bases—
two under each frame. 27They
made six frames for the far end,
that is, the west end of the tabernacle, 28and two frames were made
for the corners of the tabernacle at
the far end. 29At these two corners
the frames were double from the
bottom all the way to the top and
fitted into a single ring; both were
made alike. 30So there were eight
frames and sixteen silver bases—
two under each frame.
31They also made crossbars of
acacia wood: five for the frames on
one side of the tabernacle, 32five
for those on the other side, and five
for the frames on the west, at the
far end of the tabernacle. 33They
made the centre crossbar so that it
extended from end to end at the
middle of the frames. 34They overlaid the frames with gold and made
gold rings to hold the crossbars.
They also overlaid the crossbars
with gold.
35They made the curtain[k] of
blue, purple and scarlet yarn and
finely twisted linen, with cherubim
worked into it by a skilled craftsman. 36They made four posts of
acacia wood for it and overlaid
them with gold. They made gold
hooks for them and cast their four
silver bases. 37For the entrance to
the tent they made a curtain of
blue, purple and scarlet yarn and
finely twisted linen—the work of
an embroiderer;[l] 38and they made
five posts with hooks for them.
They overlaid the tops of the posts
and their bands with gold and made
their five bases of bronze.

The Ark

37:1–9pp Ex 25:10–20

37 Bezalel[a] made the ark[b] of
acacia wood—two and a
half cubits long, a cubit and a half
wide, and a cubit and a half high.[a]
2He overlaid it with pure gold,[c]
both inside and out, and made a
gold moulding around it. 3He cast
four gold rings for it and fastened
them to its four feet, with two rings
on one side and two rings on the
other. 4Then he made poles of acacia wood and overlaid them with
gold. 5And he inserted the poles
into the rings on the sides of the ark
to carry it.
6He made the atonement cover[d]
of pure gold—two and a half cubits
long and a cubit and a half wide.[b]
7Then he made two cherubim[e] out
of hammered gold at the ends of
the cover. 8He made one cherub on
one end and the second cherub on
the other; at the two ends he made
them of one piece with the cover.
9The cherubim had their wings
spread upwards, overshadowing[f]
the cover with them. The cherubim

36:18 j ver 13
36:35 k Ex 39:38; Mt 27:51; Lk 23:45; Heb 9:3
36:37 l Ex 27:16
37:1 a Ex 31:2; b Ex 30:6; Ex 39:35; Dt 10:3
37:2 c ver 11,26
37:6 d Ex 26:34; Ex 31:7; Heb 9:5
37:7 e Eze 41:18
37:9 f Heb 9:5

[b] *15* That is, about 45 feet (about 13.5 metres) long and 6 feet (about 1.8 metres) wide [c] *19* That is, large aquatic mammals [d] *21* That is, about 15 feet (about 4.5 metres) long and 2¼ feet (about 0.7 metre) wide [a] *1* That is, about 3¾ feet (about 1.1 metres) long and 2¼ feet (about 0.7 metre) wide and high [b] *6* That is, about 3¾ feet (about 1.1 metres) long and 2¼ feet (about 0.7 metre) wide

faced each other, looking towards
the cover.[g]

The Table

37:10–16pp Ex 25:23–29

10They[c] made the table[h] of acacia wood—two cubits long, a cubit
wide, and a cubit and a half high.[d]
11Then they overlaid it with pure
gold[i] and made a gold moulding
around it. 12They also made around
it a rim a handbreadth[e] wide and
put a gold moulding on the rim.
13They cast four gold rings for the
table and fastened them to the four
corners, where the four legs were.
14The rings[j] were put close to the
rim to hold the poles used in carrying the table. 15The poles for carrying the table were made of acacia
wood and were overlaid with gold.
16And they made from pure gold
the articles for the table—its plates
and dishes and bowls and its pitchers for the pouring out of drink offerings.

The Lampstand

37:17–24pp Ex 25:31–39

17They made the lampstand[k] of
pure gold and hammered it out,
base and shaft; its flowerlike cups,
buds and blossoms were of one
piece with it. 18Six branches extended from the sides of the lampstand—three on one side and three
on the other. 19Three cups shaped
like almond flowers with buds and
blossoms were on one branch,
three on the next branch and the
same for all six branches extending from the lampstand. 20And on
the lampstand were four cups
shaped like almond flowers with
buds and blossoms. 21One bud was
under the first pair of branches extending from the lampstand, a
second bud under the second pair,
and a third bud under the third
pair—six branches in all. 22The
buds and the branches were all of
one piece with the lampstand, hammered out of pure gold.[l]
23They made its seven lamps,[m] as
well as its wick trimmers and
trays, of pure gold. 24They made
the lampstand and all its accessories from one talent[f] of pure
gold.

The Altar of Incense

37:25–28pp Ex 30:1–5

25They made the altar of incense[n] out of acacia wood. It was
square, a cubit long and a cubit
wide, and two cubits high[g]—its
horns[o] of one piece with it. 26They
overlaid the top and all the sides
and the horns with pure gold, and
made a gold moulding around it.
27They made two gold rings[p] below
the moulding—two on opposite
sides—to hold the poles used to
carry it. 28They made the poles of
acacia wood and overlaid them
with gold.[q]
29They also made the sacred
anointing oil[r] and the pure, fragrant incense[s]—the work of a perfumer.

The Altar of Burnt Offering

38:1–7pp Ex 27:1–8

38 They[a] built the altar of
burnt offering of acacia
wood, three cubits[b] high; it was
square, five cubits long and five cubits wide.[c] 2They made a horn at
each of the four corners, so that the
horns and the altar were of one
piece, and they overlaid the altar
with bronze.[a] 3They made all its
utensils[b] of bronze—its pots, shovels, sprinkling bowls, meat forks
and firepans. 4They made a grating
for the altar, a bronze network, to
be under its ledge, halfway up the

37:9 g Dt 10:3
37:10 h Heb 9:2
37:11 i ver 2
37:14 j ver 27
37:17 k Heb 9:2; Rev 1:12
37:22 l ver 17; Nu 8:4
37:23 m Ex 40:4,25
37:25 n Ex 30:34-36; Lk 1:11; Heb 9:4; Rev 8:3; o Ex 27:2; Rev 9:13
37:27 p ver 14
37:28 q Ex 25:13
37:29 r Ex 31:11; s Ex 30:1,25; Ex 39:38
38:2 a 2Ch 1:5
38:3 b Ex 31:9

c*10* Or *He*; also in verses 11–29 d*10* That is, about 3 feet (about 0.9 metre) long, 1½ feet (about 0.5 metre) wide, and 2¼ feet (about 0.7 metre) high e*12* That is, about 3 inches (about 8 centimetres) f*24* That is, about 75 pounds (about 34 kilograms) g*25* That is, about 1½ feet (about 0.5 metre) long and wide, and about 3 feet (about 0.9 metre) high a*1* Or *He*; also in verses 2–9 b*1* That is, about 4½ feet (about 1.4 metres) c*1* That is, about 7½ feet (about 2.3 metres) long and wide

altar. 5 They cast bronze rings to hold the poles for the four corners of the bronze grating. 6 They made the poles of acacia wood and overlaid them with bronze. 7 They inserted the poles into the rings so they would be on the sides of the altar for carrying it. They made it hollow, out of boards.

Basin for Washing

8 They made the bronze basin[c] and its bronze stand from the mirrors of the women[d] who served at the entrance to the Tent of Meeting.

The Courtyard

38:9–20pp Ex 27:9–19

9 Next they made the courtyard. The south side was a hundred cubits[d] long and had curtains of finely twisted linen, 10 with twenty posts and twenty bronze bases, and with silver hooks and bands on the posts. 11 The north side was also a hundred cubits long and had twenty posts and twenty bronze bases, with silver hooks and bands on the posts.

12 The west end was fifty cubits[e] wide and had curtains, with ten posts and ten bases, with silver hooks and bands on the posts. 13 The east end, towards the sunrise, was also fifty cubits wide. 14 Curtains fifteen cubits[f] long were on one side of the entrance, with three posts and three bases, 15 and curtains fifteen cubits long were on the other side of the entrance to the courtyard, with three posts and three bases. 16 All the curtains around the courtyard were of finely twisted linen. 17 The bases for the posts were bronze. The hooks and bands on the posts were silver, and their tops were overlaid with silver; so all the posts of the courtyard had silver bands.

18 The curtain for the entrance to the courtyard was of blue, purple and scarlet yarn and finely twisted linen—the work of an embroiderer. It was twenty cubits[g] long and, like the curtains of the courtyard, five cubits[h] high, 19 with four posts and four bronze bases. Their hooks and bands were silver, and their tops were overlaid with silver. 20 All the tent pegs[e] of the tabernacle and of the surrounding courtyard were bronze.

The Materials Used

21 These are the amounts of the materials used for the tabernacle, the tabernacle of the Testimony,[f] which were recorded at Moses' command by the Levites under the direction of Ithamar[g] son of Aaron, the priest. 22 (Bezalel[h] son of Uri, the son of Hur, of the tribe of Judah, made everything the LORD commanded Moses; 23 with him was Oholiab[i] son of Ahisamach, of the tribe of Dan—a craftsman and designer, and an embroiderer in blue, purple and scarlet yarn and fine linen.) 24 The total amount of the gold from the wave offering used for all the work on the sanctuary[j] was 29 talents and 730 shekels,[i] according to the sanctuary shekel.[k]

25 The silver obtained from those of the community who were counted in the census[l] was 100 talents and 1,775 shekels,[j] according to the sanctuary shekel—26 one beka per person,[m] that is, half a shekel,[k] according to the sanctuary shekel,[n] from everyone who had crossed over to those counted, twenty years old or more,[o] a total of 603,550 men.[p] 27 The 100 talents[l] of silver were used to cast the bases[q] for the sanctuary and

38:8 *c* Ex 30:18; Ex 40:7 *d* Dt 23:17; 1Sa 2:22; 1Ki 14:24
38:20 *e* Ex 35:18
38:21 *f* Nu 1:50,53; Nu 8:24; Nu 9:15; Nu 10:11; Nu 17:7; 1Ch 23:32; 2Ch 24:6; Ac 7:44; Rev 15:5 *g* Nu 4:28,33
38:22 *h* Ex 31:2
38:23 *i* Ex 31:6
38:24 *j* Ex 30:16 *k* Ex 30:13; Lev 27:25; Nu 3:47; Nu 18:16
38:25 *l* Ex 30:12
38:26 *m* Ex 30:12 *n* Ex 30:13 *o* Ex 30:14 *p* Ex 12:37; Nu 1:46
38:27 *q* Ex 26:19

d *9* That is, about 150 feet (about 46 metres)
e *12* That is, about 75 feet (about 23 metres)
f *14* That is, about 22½ feet (about 6.9 metres)
g *18* That is, about 30 feet (about 9 meters)
h *18* That is, about 7½ feet (about 2.3 metres)
i *24* The weight of the gold was about one ton (about 1 metric ton). j *25* The weight of the silver was about 3 ⅓ tons (about 3.4 metric tons).
k *26* That is, about ⅕ ounce (about 6 grams)
l *27* That is, about 3 ⅓ tons (about 3.4 metric tons)

for the curtain—100 bases from the 100 talents, one talent for each base. 28They used the 1,775 shekels[m] to make the hooks for the posts, to overlay the tops of the posts, and to make their bands.

29The bronze from the wave offering was 70 talents and 2,400 shekels.[n] 30They used it to make the bases for the entrance to the Tent of Meeting, the bronze altar with its bronze grating and all its utensils, 31the bases for the surrounding courtyard and those for its entrance and all the tent pegs for the tabernacle and those for the surrounding courtyard.

The Priestly Garments

39 From the blue, purple and scarlet yarn[a] they made woven garments for ministering in the sanctuary.[b] They also made sacred garments[c] for Aaron, as the LORD commanded Moses.

The Ephod

39:2–7pp Ex 28:6–14

2They[a] made the ephod of gold, and of blue, purple and scarlet yarn, and of finely twisted linen. 3They hammered out thin sheets of gold and cut strands to be worked into the blue, purple and scarlet yarn and fine linen—the work of a skilled craftsman. 4They made shoulder pieces for the ephod, which were attached to two of its corners, so that it could be fastened. 5Its skilfully woven waistband was like it—of one piece with the ephod and made with gold, and with blue, purple and scarlet yarn, and with finely twisted linen, as the LORD commanded Moses.

6They mounted the onyx stones in gold filigree settings and engraved them like a seal with the names of the sons of Israel. 7Then they fastened them on the shoulder pieces of the ephod as memorial[d] stones for the sons of Israel, as the LORD commanded Moses.

39:1
a Ex 35:23
b Ex 35:19
c ver 41
Ex 28:2

39:7
d Lev 24:7
Jos 4:7

39:8
e Lev 8:8

39:14
f Rev 21:12

The Breastpiece

39:8–21pp Ex 28:15–28

8They fashioned the breastpiece[e]—the work of a skilled craftsman. They made it like the ephod: of gold, and of blue, purple and scarlet yarn, and of finely twisted linen. 9It was square—a span[b] long and a span wide—and folded double. 10Then they mounted four rows of precious stones on it. In the first row there was a ruby, a topaz and a beryl; 11in the second row a turquoise, a sapphire[c] and an emerald; 12in the third row a jacinth, an agate and an amethyst; 13in the fourth row a chrysolite, an onyx and a jasper.[d] They were mounted in gold filigree settings. 14There were twelve stones, one for each of the names of the sons of Israel, each engraved like a seal with the name of one of the twelve tribes.[f]

15For the breastpiece they made braided chains of pure gold, like a rope. 16They made two gold filigree settings and two gold rings, and fastened the rings to two of the corners of the breastpiece. 17They fastened the two gold chains to the rings at the corners of the breastpiece, 18and the other ends of the chains to the two settings, attaching them to the shoulder pieces of the ephod at the front. 19They made two gold rings and attached them to the other two corners of the breastpiece on the inside edge next to the ephod. 20Then they made two more gold rings and attached them to the bottom of the shoulder pieces on the front of the ephod, close to the seam just above the waistband of the ephod. 21They tied the rings of

[m]28 That is, about 45 pounds (about 20 kilograms)
[n]29 The weight of the bronze was about 2⅓ tons (about 2.4 metric tons). [a]2 Or *He*; also in verses 7, 8 and 22 [b]9 That is, about 9 inches (about 23 centimetres) [c]11 Or *lapis lazuli*
[d]13 The precise identification of some of these precious stones is uncertain.

the breastpiece to the rings of the ephod with blue cord, connecting it to the waistband so that the breastpiece would not swing out from the ephod – as the LORD commanded Moses.

Other Priestly Garments

39:22–31pp Ex 28:31–43

22 They made the robe of the ephod entirely of blue cloth – the work of a weaver – 23 with an opening in the centre of the robe like the opening of a collar,[e] and a band around this opening, so that it would not tear. 24 They made pomegranates of blue, purple and scarlet yarn and finely twisted linen around the hem of the robe. 25 And they made bells of pure gold and attached them around the hem between the pomegranates. 26 The bells and pomegranates alternated around the hem of the robe to be worn for ministering, as the LORD commanded Moses.

27 For Aaron and his sons, they made tunics of fine linen[g] – the work of a weaver – 28 and the turban[h] of fine linen, the linen headbands and the undergarments of finely twisted linen. 29 The sash was of finely twisted linen and blue, purple and scarlet yarn – the work of an embroiderer – as the LORD commanded Moses.

30 They made the plate, the sacred diadem, out of pure gold and engraved on it, like an inscription on a seal: HOLY TO THE LORD. 31 Then they fastened a blue cord to it to attach it to the turban, as the LORD commanded Moses.

Moses Inspects the Tabernacle

39:32–41pp Ex 35:10–19

32 So all the work on the tabernacle, the Tent of Meeting, was completed. The Israelites did everything just as the LORD commanded Moses.[i] 33 Then they brought the tabernacle to Moses: the tent and all its furnishings, its clasps, frames, crossbars, posts and bases; 34 the covering of ram skins dyed red, the covering of hides of sea cows[f] and the shielding curtain; 35 the ark of the Testimony[j] with its poles and the atonement cover; 36 the table with all its articles and the bread of the Presence; 37 the pure gold lampstand[k] with its row of lamps and all its accessories, and the oil for the light; 38 the gold altar,[l] the anointing oil, the fragrant incense, and the curtain[m] for the entrance to the tent; 39 the bronze altar with its bronze grating, its poles and all its utensils; the basin with its stand; 40 the curtains of the courtyard with its posts and bases, and the curtain for the entrance to the courtyard;[n] the ropes and tent pegs for the courtyard; all the furnishings for the tabernacle, the Tent of Meeting; 41 and the woven garments worn for ministering in the sanctuary, both the sacred garments for Aaron the priest and the garments for his sons when serving as priests.

42 The Israelites had done all the work just as the LORD had commanded Moses.[o] 43 Moses inspected the work and saw that they had done it just as the LORD had commanded. So Moses blessed[p] them.

Setting Up the Tabernacle

40 Then the LORD said to Moses: 2 "Set up the tabernacle, the Tent of Meeting,[a] on the first day of the first month.[b] 3 Place the ark[c] of the Testimony in it and shield the ark with the curtain. 4 Bring in the table and set out what belongs on it.[d] Then bring in the lampstand[e] and set up its lamps. 5 Place the gold altar[f] of incense in front of the

39:27 g Lev 6:10
39:28 h Ex 28:4
39:32 i ver 42-43 Ex 25:9
39:35 j Ex 30:6
39:37 k Ex 25:31
39:38 l Ex 30:1-10 m Ex 36:35
39:40 n Ex 27:9-19
39:42 o Ex 25:9
39:43 p Lev 9:22,23 Nu 6:23-27 2Sa 6:18 1Ki 8:14,55 2Ch 30:27
40:2 a Nu 1:1 b ver 17 Ex 12:2
40:3 c ver 21 Nu 4:5 Ex 26:33
40:4 d Ex 25:30 e ver 22-25 Ex 26:35
40:5 f ver 26 Ex 30:1

e23 The meaning of the Hebrew for this word is uncertain. f34 That is, large aquatic mammals

ark of the Testimony and put the
curtain at the entrance to the tabernacle.
6“Place the altar of burnt offering in front of the entrance to the
tabernacle, the Tent of Meeting;
7place the basin[g] between the Tent
of Meeting and the altar and put
water in it. 8Set up the courtyard
around it and put the curtain at the
entrance to the courtyard.
9“Take the anointing oil and
anoint[h] the tabernacle and everything in it; consecrate it and all its
furnishings, and it will be holy.
10Then anoint the altar of burnt offering and all its utensils; consecrate[i] the altar, and it will be most
holy. 11Anoint the basin and its
stand and consecrate them.
12“Bring Aaron and his sons to
the entrance to the Tent of Meeting and wash them with water.[j]
13Then dress Aaron in the sacred
garments,[k] anoint him and consecrate[l] him so that he may serve
me as priest. 14Bring his sons and
dress them in tunics. 15Anoint them
just as you anointed their father, so
that they may serve me as priests.
Their anointing will be to a priesthood that will continue for all generations to come.[m]” 16Moses did
everything just as the LORD commanded him.
17So the tabernacle[n] was set up
on the first day of the first month[o]
in the second year. 18When Moses
set up the tabernacle, he put the
bases in place, erected the frames,
inserted the crossbars and set up
the posts. 19Then he spread the tent
over the tabernacle and put the
covering over the tent, as the LORD
commanded him.
20He took the Testimony[p] and
placed it in the ark, attached the
poles to the ark and put the atonement cover over it. 21Then he
brought the ark into the tabernacle
and hung the shielding curtain[q]
and shielded the ark of the

40:7 *g* ver 30; Ex 30:18
40:9 *h* Ex 30:26; Lev 8:10
40:10 *i* Ex 29:36
40:12 *j* Lev 8:1-13
40:13 *k* Ex 28:41 *l* Lev 8:12
40:15 *m* Ex 29:9; Nu 25:13
40:17 *n* Nu 7:1 *o* ver 2
40:20 *p* Ex 16:34; Ex 25:16; Dt 10:5; 1Ki 8:9; Heb 9:4
40:21 *q* Ex 26:33
40:22 *r* Ex 26:35
40:23 *s* ver 4
40:24 *t* Ex 26:35
40:25 *u* ver 4; Ex 25:37
40:26 *v* ver 5; Ex 30:6
40:27 *w* Ex 30:7
40:28 *x* Ex 26:36
40:29 *y* ver 6; Ex 29:38-42
40:30 *z* ver 7
40:32 *a* Ex 30:20
40:33 *b* Ex 27:9 *c* ver 8
40:34 *d* Nu 9:15-23; 1Ki 8:12
40:35 *e* 1Ki 8:11; 2Ch 5:13-14

Testimony, as the LORD commanded him.
22Moses placed the table[r] in the
Tent of Meeting on the north side
of the tabernacle outside the curtain 23and set out the bread[s] on it
before the LORD, as the LORD commanded him.
24He placed the lampstand[t] in
the Tent of Meeting opposite the
table on the south side of the tabernacle 25and set up the lamps[u]
before the LORD, as the LORD
commanded him.
26Moses placed the gold altar[v] in
the Tent of Meeting in front of the
curtain 27and burned fragrant incense on it, as the LORD commanded[w] him. 28Then he put up the
curtain[x] at the entrance to the tabernacle.
29He set the altar of burnt offering near the entrance to the tabernacle, the Tent of Meeting, and
offered on it burnt offerings and
grain offerings,[y] as the LORD commanded him.
30He placed the basin[z] between
the Tent of Meeting and the altar
and put water in it for washing,
31and Moses and Aaron and his sons
used it to wash their hands and
feet. 32They washed whenever they
entered the Tent of Meeting or approached the altar,[a] as the LORD
commanded Moses.
33Then Moses set up the courtyard[b] around the tabernacle and
altar and put up the curtain[c] at the
entrance to the courtyard. And so
Moses finished the work.

The Glory of the LORD

34Then the cloud[d] covered the
Tent of Meeting, and the glory of
the LORD filled the tabernacle.
35Moses could not enter the Tent of
Meeting because the cloud had settled upon it, and the glory of the
LORD filled the tabernacle.[e]
36In all the travels of the Israel-

ites, whenever the cloud lifted
from above the tabernacle, they
would set out;[f] 37but if the cloud
did not lift, they did not set out—
until the day it lifted. 38So the
cloud[g] of the LORD was over the
tabernacle by day, and fire was in
the cloud by night, in the sight of all
the house of Israel during all their
travels.

40:36 f Nu 9:17-23 Nu 10:13 Ne 9:19

40:38 g Ex 13:21 Nu 9:15 1Co 10:1

LEVITICUS

The Burnt Offering

1 The LORD called to Moses[a] and spoke to him from the Tent of Meeting.[b] He said, 2"Speak to the Israelites and say to them: 'When any of you brings an offering to the LORD, bring as your offering an animal from either the herd or the flock.[c]

3" 'If the offering is a burnt offering from the herd, he is to offer a male without defect.[d] He must present it at the entrance to the Tent[e] of Meeting so that it[a] will be acceptable to the LORD. 4He is to lay his hand on the head[f] of the burnt offering, and it will be accepted on his behalf to make atonement[g] for him. 5He is to slaughter[h] the young bull before the LORD, and then Aaron's sons the priests shall bring the blood and sprinkle it against the altar on all sides[i] at the entrance to the Tent of Meeting. 6He is to skin[j] the burnt offering and cut it into pieces. 7The sons of Aaron the priest are to put fire on the altar and arrange wood[k] on the fire. 8Then Aaron's sons the priests shall arrange the pieces, including the head and the fat,[l] on the burning wood that is on the altar. 9He is to wash the inner parts and the legs with water, and the priest is to burn all of it on the altar.[m] It is a burnt offering, an offering made by fire, an aroma pleasing to the LORD.[n]

10" 'If the offering is a burnt offering from the flock, from either the sheep or the goats,[o] he is to offer a male without defect. 11He is to slaughter it at the north side of the altar before the LORD, and Aaron's sons the priests shall sprinkle its blood against the altar on all sides.[p] 12He is to cut it into pieces, and the priest shall arrange them, including the head and the fat, on the burning wood that is on the altar. 13He is to wash the inner parts and the legs with water, and the priest is to bring all of it and burn it on the altar. It is a burnt offering, an offering made by fire, an aroma pleasing to the LORD.

14" 'If the offering to the LORD is a burnt offering of birds, he is to offer a dove or a young pigeon.[q] 15The priest shall bring it to the altar, wring off the head and burn it on the altar; its blood shall be drained out on the side of the altar.[r] 16He is to remove the crop with its contents[b] and throw it to the east side of the altar, where the ashes[s] are. 17He shall tear it open by the wings, not severing it completely,[t] and then the priest shall burn it on the wood[u] that is on the fire on the altar. It is a burnt offering, an offering made by fire, an aroma pleasing to the LORD.

The Grain Offering

2 " 'When someone brings a grain offering[a] to the LORD, his offering is to be of fine flour. He is to pour oil[b] on it, put incense on it 2and take it to Aaron's sons the priests. The priest shall take a handful of the fine flour[c] and oil, together with all the incense,[d] and burn this as a memorial portion[e] on the altar, an offering made by fire, an aroma pleasing to the LORD. 3The rest of the grain offering belongs to Aaron and his sons;[f] it is a most holy part of the offerings made to the LORD by fire.

4" 'If you bring a grain offering baked in an oven, it is to consist of fine flour: cakes made without

1:1 *a* Ex 19:3; Ex 25:22 *b* Nu 7:89
1:2 *c* Lev 22:18-19
1:3 *d* Ex 12:5; Dt 15:21; Heb 9:14; 1Pe 1:19 *e* Lev 17:9
1:4 *f* Ex 29:10,15; Lev 3:2 *g* 2Ch 29:23-24
1:5 *h* Lev 3:2,8 *i* Heb 12:24; 1Pe 1:2
1:6 *j* Lev 7:8
1:7 *k* Lev 6:12
1:8 *l* ver 12
1:9 *m* Ex 29:18 *n* ver 13; Ge 8:21; Nu 15:8-10; Eph 5:2
1:10 *o* ver 3; Ex 12:5
1:11 *p* ver 5
1:14 *q* Ge 15:9; Lev 5:7; Lk 2:24
1:15 *r* Lev 5:9
1:16 *s* Lev 6:10
1:17 *t* Ge 15:10 *u* Lev 5:8
2:1 *a* Lev 6:14-18 *b* Nu 15:4
2:2 *c* Lev 5:11 *d* Lev 6:15; Isa 66:3 *e* ver 9,16; Lev 5:12; Lev 6:15; Lev 24:7; Ac 10:4
2:3 *f* ver 10; Lev 6:16; Lev 10:12,13

a3 Or *he* b16 Or *crop and the feathers*; the meaning of the Hebrew for this word is uncertain.

yeast and mixed with oil, or[a] wafers made without yeast and spread with oil.[g] 5 If your grain offering is prepared on a griddle, it is to be made of fine flour mixed with oil, and without yeast. 6 Crumble it and pour oil on it; it is a grain offering. 7 If your grain offering is cooked in a pan,[h] it is to be made of fine flour and oil. 8 Bring the grain offering made of these things to the LORD; present it to the priest, who shall take it to the altar. 9 He shall take out the memorial portion[i] from the grain offering and burn it on the altar as an offering made by fire, an aroma pleasing to the LORD.[j] 10 The rest of the grain offering belongs to Aaron and his sons;[k] it is a most holy part of the offerings made to the LORD by fire.

11 " 'Every grain offering you bring to the LORD must be made without yeast,[l] for you are not to burn any yeast or honey in an offering made to the LORD by fire. 12 You may bring them to the LORD as an offering of the firstfruits,[m] but they are not to be offered on the altar as a pleasing aroma. 13 Season all your grain offerings with salt. Do not leave the salt of the covenant[n] of your God out of your grain offerings; add salt to all your offerings.

14 " 'If you bring a grain offering of firstfruits[o] to the LORD, offer crushed heads of new grain roasted in the fire. 15 Put oil and incense on it; it is a grain offering. 16 The priest shall burn the memorial portion[p] of the crushed grain and the oil, together with all the incense, as an offering made to the LORD by fire.

The Fellowship Offering

3 " 'If someone's offering is a fellowship offering,[a][a] and he offers an animal from the herd, whether male or female, he is to present before the LORD an animal without defect.[b] 2 He is to lay his hand on the head[c] of his offering and slaughter it[d] at the entrance to the Tent of Meeting. Then Aaron's sons the priests shall sprinkle the blood against the altar on all sides. 3 From the fellowship offering he is to bring a sacrifice made to the LORD by fire: all the fat[e] that covers the inner parts or is connected to them, 4 both kidneys with the fat on them near the loins, and the covering of the liver, which he will remove with the kidneys. 5 Then Aaron's sons[f] are to burn it on the altar on top of the burnt offering[g] that is on the burning wood, as an offering made by fire, an aroma pleasing to the LORD.

6 " 'If he offers an animal from the flock as a fellowship offering[h] to the LORD, he is to offer a male or female without defect. 7 If he offers a lamb, he is to present it before the LORD.[i] 8 He is to lay his hand on the head of his offering and slaughter it[j] in front of the Tent of Meeting. Then Aaron's sons shall sprinkle its blood against the altar on all sides. 9 From the fellowship offering he is to bring a sacrifice made to the LORD by fire: its fat, the entire fat tail cut off close to the backbone, all the fat that covers the inner parts or is connected to them, 10 both kidneys with the fat on them near the loins, and the covering of the liver, which he will remove with the kidneys. 11 The priest shall burn them on the altar[k] as food,[l] an offering made to the LORD by fire.

12 " 'If his offering is a goat, he is to present it before the LORD. 13 He is to lay his hand on its head and slaughter it in front of the Tent of Meeting. Then Aaron's sons shall sprinkle[m] its blood against the altar on all sides. 14 From what he offers he is to make this offering to the LORD by fire: all the fat that covers the inner parts or is connected to them, 15 both kidneys with

[a]4 Or *and* [a]1 Traditionally *peace offering*; also in verses 3, 6 and 9

2:4 g Ex 29:2
2:7 h Lev 7:9
2:9 i ver 2; j Ex 29:18; Lev 6:15
2:10 k ver 3
2:11 l Ex 23:18; Ex 34:25; Lev 6:16
2:12 m Lev 7:13; Lev 23:10
2:13 n Nu 18:19; Eze 43:24
2:14 o Lev 23:10
2:16 p ver 2
3:1 a Lev 7:11-34; b Lev 1:3; Lev 22:21
3:2 c Ex 29:10,15; d Lev 1:5
3:3 e Ex 29:13
3:5 f Lev 7:29-34; g Ex 29:13, 38-42
3:6 h ver 1
3:7 i Lev 17:8-9
3:8 j ver 2; Lev 1:5
3:11 k ver 5; l ver 16; Lev 21:6,17
3:13 m Ex 24:6

the fat on them near the loins, and the covering of the liver, which he will remove with the kidneys. 16 The priest shall burn them on the altar as food, an offering made by fire, a pleasing aroma. All the fat is the LORD's.[n]

17 " 'This is a lasting ordinance for the generations to come,[o] wherever you live: You must not eat any fat or any blood.[p]' "

The Sin Offering

4 The LORD said to Moses, 2 "Say to the Israelites: 'When anyone sins unintentionally[a] and does what is forbidden in any of the LORD's commands—

3 " 'If the anointed priest sins, bringing guilt on the people, he must bring to the LORD a young bull[b] without defect as a sin offering[c] for the sin he has committed. 4 He is to present the bull at the entrance to the Tent of Meeting before the LORD.[d] He is to lay his hand on its head and slaughter it before the LORD. 5 Then the anointed priest shall take some of the bull's blood[e] and carry it into the Tent of Meeting. 6 He is to dip his finger into the blood and sprinkle some of it seven times before the LORD, in front of the curtain of the sanctuary. 7 The priest shall then put some of the blood on the horns of the altar of fragrant incense that is before the LORD in the Tent of Meeting. The rest of the bull's blood he shall pour out at the base of the altar[f] of burnt offering[g] at the entrance to the Tent of Meeting. 8 He shall remove all the fat[h] from the bull of the sin offering—the fat that covers the inner parts or is connected to them, 9 both kidneys with the fat on them near the loins, and the covering of the liver, which he will remove with the kidneys[i]— 10 just as the fat is removed from the ox[a] sacrificed as a fellowship offering.[b] Then the priest shall burn them on the altar of burnt offering. 11 But the hide of the bull and all its flesh, as well as the head and legs, the inner parts and offal[j]— 12 that is, all the rest of the bull—he must take outside the camp[k] to a place ceremonially clean,[l] where the ashes are thrown, and burn it in a wood fire on the ash heap.

13 " 'If the whole Israelite community sins unintentionally[m] and does what is forbidden in any of the LORD's commands, even though the community is unaware of the matter, they are guilty. 14 When they become aware of the sin they committed, the assembly must bring a young bull[n] as a sin offering[o] and present it before the Tent of Meeting. 15 The elders of the community are to lay their hands on the bull's head[p] before the LORD, and the bull shall be slaughtered before the LORD. 16 Then the anointed priest is to take some of the bull's blood[q] into the Tent of Meeting. 17 He shall dip his finger into the blood and sprinkle it before the LORD[r] seven times in front of the curtain. 18 He is to put some of the blood on the horns of the altar that is before the LORD[s] in the Tent of Meeting. The rest of the blood he shall pour out at the base of the altar of burnt offering at the entrance to the Tent of Meeting. 19 He shall remove all the fat[t] from it and burn it on the altar, 20 and do with this bull just as he did with the bull for the sin offering. In this way the priest will make atonement[u] for them, and they will be forgiven.[v] 21 Then he shall take the bull outside the camp and burn it as he burned the first bull. This is the sin offering for the community.[w]

22 " 'When a leader[x] sins unintentionally[y] and does what is forbidden in any of the commands of the

a10 The Hebrew word can include both male and female. b10 Traditionally *peace offering*; also in verses 26, 31 and 35

3:16 n 1Sa 2:16
3:17 o Lev 6:18; Lev 17:7 p Ge 9:4; Lev 7:25-26; Lev 17:10-16; Dt 12:16; Ac 15:20
4:2 a Lev 5:15-18; Ps 19:12; Heb 9:7
4:3 b ver 14; Ps 66:15 c Lev 9:2-22; Heb 9:13-14
4:4 d Lev 1:3
4:5 e Lev 16:14
4:7 f ver 34; Lev 8:15 g ver 18,30; Lev 5:9; Lev 9:9; Lev 16:18
4:8 h Lev 3:3-5
4:9 i Lev 3:4
4:11 j Ex 29:14; Lev 9:11; Nu 19:5
4:12 k Heb 13:11 l Lev 6:11
4:13 m ver 2; Lev 5:2-4,17; Nu 15:24-26
4:14 n ver 3 o ver 23,28
4:15 p Lev 1:4; Lev 8:14,22; Nu 8:10
4:16 q ver 5
4:17 r ver 6
4:18 s ver 7
4:19 t ver 8
4:20 u Heb 10:10-12 v Nu 15:25
4:21 w Lev 16:5,15
4:22 x Nu 31:13 y ver 2

LORD his God, he is guilty. 23When he is made aware of the sin he committed, he must bring as his offering a male goat without defect. 24He is to lay his hand on the goat's head and slaughter it at the place where the burnt offering is slaughtered before the LORD. It is a sin offering. 25Then the priest shall take some of the blood of the sin offering with his finger and put it on the horns of the altar of burnt offering and pour out the rest of the blood at the base of the altar.[z] 26He shall burn all the fat on the altar as he burned the fat of the fellowship offering. In this way the priest will make atonement for the man's sin, and he will be forgiven.[a]

27" 'If a member of the community sins unintentionally[b] and does what is forbidden in any of the LORD's commands, he is guilty. 28When he is made aware of the sin he committed, he must bring as his offering[c] for the sin he committed a female goat[d] without defect. 29He is to lay his hand on the head[e] of the sin offering[f] and slaughter it at the place of the burnt offering. 30Then the priest is to take some of the blood with his finger and put it on the horns of the altar of burnt offering[g] and pour out the rest of the blood at the base of the altar. 31He shall remove all the fat, just as the fat is removed from the fellowship offering, and the priest shall burn it on the altar as an aroma pleasing to the LORD.[h] In this way the priest will make atonement for him, and he will be forgiven.

32" 'If he brings a lamb as his sin offering, he is to bring a female without defect.[i] 33He is to lay his hand on its head and slaughter it for a sin offering at the place where the burnt offering is slaughtered.[j] 34Then the priest shall take some of the blood of the sin offering with his finger and put it on the horns of the altar of burnt offering and pour out the rest of the blood at the base of the altar.[k] 35He shall remove all the fat, just as the fat is removed from the lamb of the fellowship offering, and the priest shall burn it on the altar[l] on top of the offerings made to the LORD by fire. In this way the priest will make atonement for him for the sin he has committed, and he will be forgiven.

5 " 'If a person sins because he does not speak up when he hears a public charge to testify[a] regarding something he has seen or learned about, he will be held responsible.[b]

2" 'Or if a person touches anything ceremonially unclean—whether the carcasses of unclean wild animals or of unclean livestock or of unclean creatures that move along the ground[c]—even though he is unaware of it, he has become unclean and is guilty.

3" 'Or if he touches human uncleanness[d]—anything that would make him unclean—even though he is unaware of it, when he learns of it he will be guilty.

4" 'Or if a person thoughtlessly takes an oath[e] to do anything, whether good or evil—in any matter one might carelessly swear about—even though he is unaware of it, in any case when he learns of it he will be guilty.

5" 'When anyone is guilty in any of these ways, he must confess[f] in what way he has sinned 6and, as a penalty for the sin he has committed, he must bring to the LORD a female lamb or goat from the flock as a sin offering;[g] and the priest shall make atonement for him for his sin.

7" 'If he cannot afford[h] a lamb, he is to bring two doves or two young pigeons to the LORD as a penalty for his sin—one for a sin offering and the other for a burnt offering. 8He is to bring them to the priest, who shall first offer the one for the sin offering. He is to wring its head from its neck,[i] not

4:25 z ver 7,18,30,34 Lev 9:9
4:26 a Lev 5:10
4:27 b ver 2 Nu 15:27
4:28 c ver 23 d ver 3
4:29 e ver 4,24 f Lev 1:4
4:30 g ver 7
4:31 h Ge 8:21
4:32 i ver 28
4:33 j ver 29
4:34 k ver 7
4:35 l ver 26,31
5:1 a Pr 29:24 b ver 17
5:2 c Lev 11:11, 24-40 Dt 14:8
5:3 d Nu 19:11-16
5:4 e Nu 30:6,8
5:5 f Lev 16:21 Lev 26:40 Nu 5:7 Pr 28:13
5:6 g Lev 4:28
5:7 h Lev 12:8 Lev 14:21
5:8 i Lev 1:15

severing it completely,[j] 9and is to sprinkle some of the blood of the sin offering against the side of the altar; the rest of the blood must be drained out at the base of the altar.[k] It is a sin offering. 10The priest shall then offer the other as a burnt offering in the prescribed way[l] and make atonement for him for the sin he has committed, and he will be forgiven.[m]

11" 'If, however, he cannot afford two doves or two young pigeons, he is to bring as an offering for his sin a tenth of an ephah[a] of fine flour[n] for a sin offering. He must not put oil or incense on it, because it is a sin offering. 12He is to bring it to the priest, who shall take a handful of it as a memorial portion and burn it on the altar on top of the offerings made to the LORD by fire. It is a sin offering. 13In this way the priest will make atonement[o] for him for any of these sins he has committed, and he will be forgiven. The rest of the offering will belong to the priest,[p] as in the case of the grain offering.' "

The Guilt Offering

14The LORD said to Moses: 15"When a person commits a violation and sins unintentionally in regard to any of the LORD's holy things, he is to bring to the LORD as a penalty[q] a ram[r] from the flock, one without defect and of the proper value in silver, according to the sanctuary shekel.[b][s] It is a guilt offering. 16He must make restitution[t] for what he has failed to do in regard to the holy things, add a fifth of the value[u] to that and give it all to the priest, who will make atonement for him with the ram as a guilt offering, and he will be forgiven.

17"If a person sins and does what is forbidden in any of the LORD's commands, even though he does not know it,[v] he is guilty and will be held responsible. 18He is to bring to the priest as a guilt offering a ram from the flock, one without defect and of the proper value. In this way the priest will make atonement for him for the wrong he has committed unintentionally, and he will be forgiven.[w] 19It is a guilt offering; he has been guilty of[c] wrongdoing against the LORD."

6 The LORD said to Moses: 2"If anyone sins and is unfaithful to the LORD[a] by deceiving his neighbour[b] about something entrusted to him or left in his care[c] or stolen, or if he cheats him, 3or if he finds lost property and lies about it,[d] or if he swears falsely, or if he commits any such sin that people may do—4when he thus sins and becomes guilty, he must return[e] what he has stolen or taken by extortion, or what was entrusted to him, or the lost property he found, 5or whatever it was he swore falsely about. He must make restitution[f] in full, add a fifth of the value to it and give it all to the owner on the day he presents his guilt offering.[g] 6And as a penalty he must bring to the priest, that is, to the LORD, his guilt offering,[h] a ram from the flock, one without defect and of the proper value. 7In this way the priest will make atonement[i] for him before the LORD, and he will be forgiven for any of these things he did that made him guilty."

The Burnt Offering

8The LORD said to Moses: 9"Give Aaron and his sons this command: 'These are the regulations for the burnt offering: The burnt offering is to remain on the altar hearth throughout the night, till morning, and the fire must be kept burning on the altar. 10The priest shall then put on his linen clothes, with linen undergarments next to his body,[j]

5:8 j Lev 1:17
5:9 k Lev 4:7,18
5:10 l Lev 1:14-17; m Lev 4:26
5:11 n Lev 2:1
5:13 o Lev 4:26; p Lev 2:3
5:15 q Lev 22:14; r Nu 5:8; s Ex 30:13
5:16 t Lev 6:4; u Lev 22:14; Nu 5:7
5:17 v ver 15; Lev 4:2
5:18 w ver 15
6:2 a Nu 5:6; Ac 5:4; Col 3:9; b Pr 24:28; c Ex 22:7
6:3 d Dt 22:1-3
6:4 e Lk 19:8
6:5 f Nu 5:7; g Lev 5:15
6:6 h Lev 5:15
6:7 i Lev 4:26
6:10 j Ex 28:39-42, 43; Ex 39:28

a11 That is, probably about 4 pints (about 2 litres)
b15 That is, about 2/5 ounce (about 11.5 grams)
c19 Or *has made full expiation for his*

and shall remove the ashes of the
burnt offering that the fire has consumed on the altar and place them
beside the altar. 11 Then he is to take
off these clothes and put on others,
and carry the ashes outside the
camp to a place that is ceremonially clean.[k] 12 The fire on the altar
must be kept burning; it must not
go out. Every morning the priest is
to add firewood and arrange the
burnt offering on the fire and burn
the fat of the fellowship offerings[a]
on it. 13 The fire must be kept burning on the altar continuously; it
must not go out.

The Grain Offering

14 " 'These are the regulations for
the grain offering:[l] Aaron's sons
are to bring it before the LORD, in
front of the altar. 15 The priest is to
take a handful of fine flour and oil,
together with all the incense on the
grain offering,[m] and burn the
memorial portion[n] on the altar as
an aroma pleasing to the LORD.
16 Aaron and his sons[o] shall eat the
rest[p] of it, but it is to be eaten without yeast[q] in a holy place;[r] they
are to eat it in the courtyard of the
Tent of Meeting. 17 It must not be
baked with yeast; I have given it as
their share of the offerings made to
me by fire. Like the sin offering
and the guilt offering, it is most
holy.[s] 18 Any male descendant of
Aaron may eat it.[t] It is his regular
share of the offerings made to the
LORD by fire for the generations to
come. Whatever touches it will become holy.' "[b][u]

19 The LORD also said to Moses,
20 "This is the offering Aaron and
his sons are to bring to the LORD on
the day he[c] is anointed: a tenth of
an ephah[d][v] of fine flour as a regular grain offering,[w] half of it in the
morning and half in the evening.
21 Prepare it with oil on a griddle;[x]
bring it well-mixed and present the
grain offering broken[e] in pieces as
an aroma pleasing to the LORD.

6:11 k Lev 4:12
6:14 l Lev 2:1; Lev 15:4
6:15 m Lev 2:9; n Lev 2:2
6:16 o Lev 2:3; p Eze 44:29; q Lev 2:11; r Lev 10:13
6:17 s ver 29; Ex 40:10; Nu 18:9,10
6:18 t ver 29; Nu 18:9-10; u ver 27
6:20 v Ex 16:36; w Ex 29:2
6:21 x Lev 2:5
6:25 y Lev 1:3; z Lev 1:5,11
6:26 a ver 16; b Lev 10:17-18
6:27 c Ex 29:37
6:28 d Lev 11:33; Lev 15:12
6:29 e ver 18; f ver 17
6:30 g Lev 4:18; h Lev 4:12
7:1 a Lev 5:14-6:7
7:3 b Ex 29:13; Lev 3:4,9

22 The son who is to succeed him as
anointed priest shall prepare it. It
is the LORD's regular share and is to
be burned completely. 23 Every
grain offering of a priest shall be
burned completely; it must not be
eaten."

The Sin Offering

24 The LORD said to Moses, 25 "Say
to Aaron and his sons: 'These are
the regulations for the sin offering:
The sin offering is to be slaughtered before the LORD[y] in the
place[z] where the burnt offering is
slaughtered; it is most holy. 26 The
priest who offers it shall eat it; it is
to be eaten in a holy place,[a] in the
courtyard[b] of the Tent of Meeting.
27 Whatever touches any of the
flesh will become holy,[c] and if any
of the blood is spattered on a garment, you must wash it in a holy
place. 28 The clay pot[d] that the
meat is cooked in must be broken;
but if it is cooked in a bronze pot,
the pot is to be scoured and rinsed
with water. 29 Any male in a priest's
family may eat it;[e] it is most
holy.[f] 30 But any sin offering whose
blood is brought into the Tent of
Meeting to make atonement in the
Holy Place[g] must not be eaten; it
must be burned.[h]

The Guilt Offering

7 " 'These are the regulations
for the guilt offering,[a] which
is most holy: 2 The guilt offering is
to be slaughtered in the place
where the burnt offering is slaughtered, and its blood is to be sprinkled against the altar on all sides.
3 All its fat[b] shall be offered: the fat
tail and the fat that covers the inner parts, 4 both kidneys with the
fat on them near the loins, and the
covering of the liver, which is to be

a *12* Traditionally *peace offerings* b *18* Or *Whoever touches them must be holy*; similarly in verse 27 c *20* Or *each* d *20* That is, probably about 4 pints (about 2 litres) e *21* The meaning of the Hebrew for this word is uncertain.

removed with the kidneys. 5 The priest shall burn them on the altar as an offering made to the LORD by fire. It is a guilt offering. 6 Any male in a priest's family may eat it,[c] but it must be eaten in a holy place; it is most holy.[d]

7 " 'The same law applies to both the sin offering and the guilt offering: They belong to the priest[e] who makes atonement with them. 8 The priest who offers a burnt offering for anyone may keep its hide for himself. 9 Every grain offering baked in an oven or cooked in a pan or on a griddle[f] belongs to the priest who offers it, 10 and every grain offering, whether mixed with oil or dry, belongs equally to all the sons of Aaron.

The Fellowship Offering

11 " 'These are the regulations for the fellowship offering[a] a person may present to the LORD:

12 " 'If he offers it as an expression of thankfulness, then along with this thank-offering[g] he is to offer cakes of bread made without yeast and mixed with oil, wafers[h] made without yeast and spread with oil, and cakes of fine flour well-kneaded and mixed with oil. 13 Along with his fellowship offering of thanksgiving he is to present an offering with cakes of bread made with yeast.[i] 14 He is to bring one of each kind as an offering, a contribution to the LORD; it belongs to the priest who sprinkles the blood of the fellowship offerings. 15 The meat of his fellowship offering of thanksgiving must be eaten on the day it is offered; he must leave none of it till morning.[j]

16 " 'If, however, his offering is the result of a vow or is a freewill offering, the sacrifice shall be eaten on the day he offers it, but anything left over may be eaten on the next day.[k] 17 Any meat of the sacrifice left over till the third day must be burned up. 18 If any meat of the fellowship offering is eaten on the third day, it will not be accepted.[l] It will not be credited[m] to the one who offered it, for it is impure; the person who eats any of it will be held responsible.

19 " 'Meat that touches anything ceremonially unclean must not be eaten; it must be burned up. As for other meat, anyone ceremonially clean may eat it. 20 But if anyone who is unclean eats any meat of the fellowship offering belonging to the LORD, that person must be cut off from his people.[n] 21 If anyone touches something unclean[o]—whether human uncleanness or an unclean animal or any unclean, detestable thing—and then eats any of the meat of the fellowship offering belonging to the LORD, that person must be cut off from his people.' "

Eating Fat and Blood Forbidden

22 The LORD said to Moses, 23 "Say to the Israelites: 'Do not eat any of the fat of cattle, sheep or goats.[p] 24 The fat of an animal found dead or torn by wild animals[q] may be used for any other purpose, but you must not eat it. 25 Anyone who eats the fat of an animal from which an offering by fire may be[b] made to the LORD must be cut off from his people. 26 And wherever you live, you must not eat the blood[r] of any bird or animal. 27 If anyone eats blood,[s] that person must be cut off from his people.' "

The Priests' Share

28 The LORD said to Moses, 29 "Say to the Israelites: 'Anyone who brings a fellowship offering to the LORD is to bring part of it as his sacrifice to the LORD. 30 With his own hands he is to bring the offering made to the LORD by fire; he is to bring the fat, together with the

7:6 c Lev 6:18; Nu 18:9-10 d Lev 2:3
7:7 e Lev 6:17,26; 1Co 9:13
7:9 f Lev 2:5
7:12 g ver 13,15 h Lev 2:4; Nu 6:15
7:13 i Lev 23:17; Am 4:5
7:15 j Lev 22:30
7:16 k Lev 19:5-8
7:18 l Lev 19:7 m Nu 18:27
7:20 n Lev 22:3-7
7:21 o Lev 5:2; Lev 11:24,28
7:23 p Lev 3:17; Lev 17:13-14
7:24 q Ex 22:31
7:26 r Ge 9:4
7:27 s Lev 17:10-24; Ac 15:20,29

[a] 11 Traditionally *peace offering*; also in verses 13–37 [b] 25 Or *fire is*

breast, and wave the breast before
the LORD as a wave offering.[t]
31 The priest shall burn the fat on
the altar, but the breast belongs to
Aaron and his sons.[u] 32 You are to
give the right thigh of your fellowship offerings to the priest as a
contribution.[v] 33 The son of Aaron
who offers the blood and the fat
of the fellowship offering shall
have the right thigh as his share.
34 From the fellowship offerings of
the Israelites, I have taken the
breast that is waved and the thigh[w]
that is presented and have given
them to Aaron the priest and his
sons[x] as their regular share from
the Israelites.' "

35 This is the portion of the offerings made to the LORD by fire that
were allotted to Aaron and his sons
on the day they were presented to
serve the LORD as priests. 36 On the
day they were anointed,[y] the LORD
commanded that the Israelites give
this to them as their regular share
for the generations to come.

37 These, then, are the regulations
for the burnt offering,[z] the grain
offering,[a] the sin offering, the
guilt offering, the ordination offering[b] and the fellowship offering,
38 which the LORD gave Moses on
Mount Sinai on the day he commanded the Israelites to bring
their offerings to the LORD,[c] in the
Desert of Sinai.

The Ordination of Aaron and His Sons

8:1-36pp Ex 29:1-37

8 The LORD said to Moses,
2 "Bring Aaron and his sons,
their garments, the anointing oil,[a]
the bull for the sin offering, the two
rams and the basket containing
bread made without yeast,[b] 3 and
gather the entire assembly[c] at the
entrance to the Tent of Meeting."
4 Moses did as the LORD commanded him, and the assembly
gathered at the entrance to the
Tent of Meeting.

5 Moses said to the assembly,
"This is what the LORD has commanded to be done." 6 Then Moses
brought Aaron and his sons forward and washed them with
water.[d] 7 He put the tunic on Aaron,
tied the sash around him, clothed
him with the robe and put the
ephod on him. He also tied the
ephod to him by its skilfully woven
waistband; so it was fastened on
him.[e] 8 He placed the breastpiece
on him and put the Urim and Thummim[f] in the breastpiece. 9 Then he
placed the turban on Aaron's head
and set the gold plate, the sacred
diadem,[g] on the front of it, as the
LORD commanded Moses.

10 Then Moses took the anointing
oil[h] and anointed[i] the tabernacle
and everything in it, and so consecrated them. 11 He sprinkled some
of the oil on the altar seven times,
anointing the altar and all its utensils and the basin with its stand, to
consecrate them.[j] 12 He poured
some of the anointing oil on Aaron's
head and anointed[k] him to consecrate him.[l] 13 Then he brought
Aaron's sons forward, put tunics on
them, tied sashes around them and
put headbands on them, as the
LORD commanded Moses.

14 He then presented the bull[m] for
the sin offering,[n] and Aaron and
his sons laid their hands on its
head. 15 Moses slaughtered the bull
and took some of the blood, and
with his finger he put it on all the
horns of the altar[o] to purify the
altar.[p] He poured out the rest of
the blood at the base of the altar. So
he consecrated it to make atonement for it.[q] 16 Moses also took all
the fat around the inner parts, the
covering of the liver, and both kidneys and their fat, and burned it on
the altar. 17 But the bull with its hide
and its flesh and its offal[r] he
burned up outside the camp,[s] as
the LORD commanded Moses.

18 He then presented the ram[t]
for the burnt offering, and Aaron
and his sons laid their hands on its

7:30 t Ex 29:24; Nu 6:20
7:31 u ver 34
7:32 v ver 34; Lev 9:21; Nu 6:20
7:34 w Lev 10:15; x Ex 29:27; Nu 18:18-19
7:36 y Ex 40:13,15; Lev 8:12,30
7:37 z Lev 6:9; a Lev 6:14; b ver 1,11
7:38 c Lev 1:2
8:2 a Ex 30:23-25, 30; b Ex 29:2-3
8:3 c Nu 8:9
8:6 d Ex 29:4; Ex 30:19; Ps 26:6; Ac 22:16; 1Co 6:11; Eph 5:26
8:7 e Ex 28:4
8:8 f Ex 28:30
8:9 g Ex 28:36
8:10 h ver 2; i Ex 30:26
8:11 j Ex 30:29
8:12 k Lev 21:10,12; l Ex 30:30
8:14 m Lev 4:3; n Ps 66:15; Eze 43:19
8:15 o Lev 4:7; p Heb 9:22; q Eze 43:20
8:17 r Lev 4:11; s Lev 4:12
8:18 t ver 2

head. 19Then Moses slaughtered
the ram and sprinkled the blood
against the altar on all sides. 20He
cut the ram into pieces and burned
the head, the pieces and the fat.
21He washed the inner parts and
the legs with water and burned the
whole ram on the altar as a burnt
offering, a pleasing aroma, an offering made to the LORD by fire, as
the LORD commanded Moses.
22He then presented the other
ram, the ram for the ordination,[t]
and Aaron and his sons laid their
hands on its head. 23Moses slaughtered the ram and took some of its
blood and put it on the lobe of
Aaron's right ear, on the thumb
of his right hand and on the big
toe of his right foot. 24Moses also
brought Aaron's sons forward and
put some of the blood on the lobes
of their right ears, on the thumbs
of their right hands and on the big
toes of their right feet. Then he
sprinkled blood against the altar
on all sides.[u] 25He took the fat, the
fat tail, all the fat around the inner
parts, the covering of the liver,
both kidneys and their fat and the
right thigh. 26Then from the basket
of bread made without yeast, which
was before the LORD, he took a cake
of bread, and one made with oil,
and a wafer; he put these on the fat
portions and on the right thigh.
27He put all these in the hands of
Aaron and his sons and waved them
before the LORD as a wave offering.
28Then Moses took them from their
hands and burned them on the altar
on top of the burnt offering as an
ordination offering, a pleasing
aroma, an offering made to the
LORD by fire. 29He also took the
breast—Moses' share of the ordination ram[v]—and waved it before
the LORD as a wave offering, as the
LORD commanded Moses.
30Then Moses took some of the
anointing oil and some of the blood
from the altar and sprinkled them
on Aaron and his garments[w] and on
his sons and their garments. So he
consecrated[x] Aaron and his garments and his sons and their garments.
31Moses then said to Aaron and
his sons, "Cook the meat at the entrance to the Tent of Meeting and
eat it there with the bread from the
basket of ordination offerings, as I
commanded, saying,[a] 'Aaron and
his sons are to eat it.' 32Then burn
up the rest of the meat and the
bread. 33Do not leave the entrance
to the Tent of Meeting for seven
days, until the days of your ordination are completed, for your ordination will last seven days. 34What
has been done today was commanded by the LORD[y] to make
atonement for you. 35You must stay
at the entrance to the Tent of Meeting day and night for seven days
and do what the LORD requires,[z]
so that you will not die; for that
is what I have been commanded." 36So Aaron and his sons did
everything the LORD commanded
through Moses.

The Priests Begin Their Ministry

9 On the eighth day[a] Moses
summoned Aaron and his sons
and the elders of Israel. 2He said to
Aaron, "Take a bull calf for your
sin offering and a ram for your
burnt offering, both without defect, and present them before the
LORD. 3Then say to the Israelites:
'Take a male goat for a sin offering,
a calf and a lamb—both a year old
and without defect—for a burnt offering, 4and an ox[a] and a ram for a
fellowship offering[b] to sacrifice
before the LORD, together with a
grain offering mixed with oil. For
today the LORD will appear to
you.[b]' "
5They took the things Moses
commanded to the front of the Tent

8:22 t ver 2
8:24 u Heb 9:18-22
8:29 v Lev 7:31-34
8:30 w Ex 28:2; x Nu 3:3
8:34 y Heb 7:16
8:35 z Nu 3:7; Nu 9:19; Dt 11:1; 1Ki 2:3; Eze 48:11
9:1 a Eze 43:27
9:4 b Ex 29:43

a31 Or *I was commanded:* a4 The Hebrew word can include both male and female; also in verses 18 and 19. b4 Traditionally *peace offering*; also in verses 18 and 22

of Meeting, and the entire assembly came near and stood before the
LORD. 6 Then Moses said, "This is
what the LORD has commanded you
to do, so that the glory of the LORD[c]
may appear to you."

7 Moses said to Aaron, "Come to
the altar and sacrifice your sin offering and your burnt offering and
make atonement for yourself and
the people; sacrifice the offering
that is for the people and make
atonement for them, as the LORD
has commanded.[d]"

8 So Aaron came to the altar and
slaughtered the calf as a sin offering[e] for himself. 9 His sons brought
the blood to him,[f] and he dipped
his finger into the blood and put it
on the horns of the altar; the rest of
the blood he poured out at the base
of the altar.[g] 10 On the altar he
burned the fat, the kidneys and the
covering of the liver from the sin
offering, as the LORD commanded
Moses; 11 the flesh and the hide[h] he
burned up outside the camp.[i]

12 Then he slaughtered the burnt
offering. His sons handed him the
blood, and he sprinkled it against
the altar on all sides. 13 They handed
him the burnt offering piece by
piece, including the head, and he
burned them on the altar.[j] 14 He
washed the inner parts and the legs
and burned them on top of the
burnt offering on the altar.

15 Aaron then brought the offering that was for the people.[k] He
took the goat for the people's sin
offering and slaughtered it and
offered it for a sin offering as he
did with the first one.

16 He brought the burnt offering
and offered it in the prescribed
way.[l] 17 He also brought the grain
offering, took a handful of it and
burned it on the altar in addition to
the morning's burnt offering.[m]

18 He slaughtered the ox and the
ram as the fellowship offering for
the people.[n] His sons handed him
the blood, and he sprinkled it
against the altar on all sides. 19 But
the fat portions of the ox and the
ram—the fat tail, the layer of fat,
the kidneys and the covering of
the liver—20 these they laid on the
breasts, and then Aaron burned
the fat on the altar. 21 Aaron waved
the breasts and the right thigh before the LORD as a wave offering,[o]
as Moses commanded.

22 Then Aaron lifted his hands towards the people and blessed
them.[p] And having sacrificed the
sin offering, the burnt offering and
the fellowship offering, he stepped
down.

23 Moses and Aaron then went
into the Tent of Meeting. When
they came out, they blessed the
people; and the glory of the LORD[q]
appeared to all the people. 24 Fire[r]
came out from the presence of the
LORD and consumed the burnt offering and the fat portions on the
altar. And when all the people saw
it, they shouted for joy and fell face
down.[s]

The Death of Nadab and Abihu

10 Aaron's sons Nadab and
Abihu[a] took their censers,
put fire in them[b] and added incense; and they offered unauthorised fire before the LORD, contrary
to his command.[c] 2 So fire came out
from the presence of the LORD and
consumed them,[d] and they died
before the LORD. 3 Moses then said
to Aaron, "This is what the LORD
spoke of when he said:

" 'Among those who approach
me[e]
I will show myself holy;[f]
in the sight of all the people
I will be honoured.[g]' "

Aaron remained silent.

4 Moses summoned Mishael and
Elzaphan,[h] sons of Aaron's uncle
Uzziel,[i] and said to them, "Come
here; carry your cousins outside
the camp,[j] away from the front of
the sanctuary." 5 So they came and
carried them, still in their tunics,[k]

9:6 c ver 23; Ex 24:16
9:7 d Heb 5:1,3; Heb 7:27
9:8 e Lev 4:1-12
9:9 f ver 12,18; g Lev 4:7
9:11 h Lev 4:11; i Lev 4:12; Lev 8:17
9:13 j Lev 1:8
9:15 k Lev 4:27-31
9:16 l Lev 1:1-13
9:17 m Lev 2:1-2; Lev 3:5
9:18 n Lev 3:1-11
9:21 o Ex 29:24,26; Lev 7:30-34
9:22 p Nu 6:23; Dt 21:5; Lk 24:50
9:23 q ver 6
9:24 r Jdg 6:21; 2Ch 7:1; s 1Ki 18:39
10:1 a Ex 24:1; Nu 3:2-4; Nu 26:61; b Lev 16:12; c Ex 30:9
10:2 d Nu 3:4; Nu 16:35; Nu 26:61
10:3 e Ex 19:22; f Ex 30:29; Lev 21:6; Eze 28:22; g Isa 49:3
10:4 h Ex 6:22; i Ex 6:18; j Ac 5:6,9,10
10:5 k Lev 8:13

outside the camp, as Moses ordered.

6 Then Moses said to Aaron and his sons Eleazar and Ithamar, "Do not let your hair become unkempt,[a][c] and do not tear your clothes, or you will die and the LORD will be angry with the whole community.[d] But your relatives, all the house of Israel, may mourn for those the LORD has destroyed by fire. 7 Do not leave the entrance to the Tent of Meeting or you will die, because the LORD's anointing oil[e] is on you." So they did as Moses said.

8 Then the LORD said to Aaron, 9 "You and your sons are not to drink wine[f] or other fermented drink[g] whenever you go into the Tent of Meeting, or you will die. This is a lasting ordinance for the generations to come. 10 You must distinguish between the holy and the common, between the unclean and the clean,[h] 11 and you must teach[i] the Israelites all the decrees the LORD has given them through Moses.[j]"

12 Moses said to Aaron and his remaining sons, Eleazar and Ithamar, "Take the grain offering left over from the offerings made to the LORD by fire and eat it prepared without yeast beside the altar,[k] for it is most holy. 13 Eat it in a holy place, because it is your share and your sons' share of the offerings made to the LORD by fire; for so I have been commanded. 14 But you and your sons and your daughters may eat the breast that was waved and the thigh that was presented. Eat them in a ceremonially clean place;[l] they have been given to you and your children as your share of the Israelites' fellowship offerings.[b] 15 The thigh[m] that was presented and the breast that was waved must be brought with the fat portions of the offerings made by fire, to be waved before the LORD as a wave offering. This will be the regular share for you and your children, as the LORD has commanded."

16 When Moses enquired about the goat of the sin offering[n] and found that it had been burned up, he was angry with Eleazar and Ithamar, Aaron's remaining sons, and asked, 17 "Why didn't you eat the sin offering[o] in the sanctuary area? It is most holy; it was given to you to take away the guilt of the community by making atonement for them before the LORD. 18 Since its blood was not taken into the Holy Place,[p] you should have eaten the goat in the sanctuary area, as I commanded."

19 Aaron replied to Moses, "Today they sacrificed their sin offering and their burnt offering[q] before the LORD, but such things as this have happened to me. Would the LORD have been pleased if I had eaten the sin offering today?" 20 When Moses heard this, he was satisfied.

Clean and Unclean Food

11:1–23pp Dt 14:3–20

11 The LORD said to Moses and Aaron, 2 "Say to the Israelites: 'Of all the animals that live on land, these are the ones you may eat:[a] 3 You may eat any animal that has a split hoof completely divided and that chews the cud.

4 " 'There are some that only chew the cud or only have a split hoof, but you must not eat them. The camel, though it chews the cud, does not have a split hoof; it is ceremonially unclean for you. 5 The coney,[a] though it chews the cud, does not have a split hoof; it is unclean for you. 6 The rabbit, though it chews the cud, does not have a split hoof; it is unclean for you. 7 And the pig,[b] though it has a split hoof completely divided, does not chew the cud; it is unclean for you. 8 You

10:6 c Lev 21:10; d Nu 1:53; Nu 16:22; Jos 7:1; Jos 22:18; 2Sa 24:1
10:7 e Ex 28:41; Lev 21:12
10:9 f Hos 4:11; g Pr 20:1; Isa 28:7; Eze 44:21; Lk 1:15; Eph 5:18; 1Ti 3:3; Tit 1:7
10:10 h Lev 11:47; Lev 20:25; Eze 22:26
10:11 i Mal 2:7; j Dt 24:8
10:12 k Lev 6:14-18; Lev 21:22
10:14 l Ex 29:24, 26-27; Lev 7:31,34; Nu 18:11
10:15 m Lev 7:34
10:16 n Lev 9:3
10:17 o Lev 6:24-30
10:18 p Lev 6:26,30
10:19 q Lev 9:12
11:2 a Ac 10:12-14
11:7 b Isa 65:4; Isa 66:3,17

[a]6 Or *Do not uncover your heads*
[b]14 Traditionally *peace offerings*
[a]5 That is, the hyrax or rock badger

must not eat their meat or touch
their carcasses; they are unclean
for you.[c]
9“ ‘Of all the creatures living in
the water of the seas and the
streams, you may eat any that have
fins and scales. 10But all creatures
in the seas or streams that do not
have fins and scales—whether
among all the swarming things or
among all the other living creatures in the water—you are to detest.[d] 11And since you are to detest
them, you must not eat their meat
and you must detest their carcasses. 12Anything living in the
water that does not have fins and
scales is to be detestable to you.
13“ ‘These are the birds you are to
detest and not eat because they are
detestable: the eagle, the vulture,
the black vulture, 14the red kite,
any kind of black kite, 15any kind
of raven, 16the horned owl, the
screech owl, the gull, any kind of
hawk, 17the little owl, the cormorant, the great owl, 18the white owl,
the desert owl, the osprey, 19the
stork, any kind of heron, the hoopoe
and the bat.[b]
20“ ‘All flying insects that walk on
all fours are to be detestable to
you.[e] 21There are, however, some
winged creatures that walk on all
fours that you may eat: those that
have jointed legs for hopping on
the ground. 22Of these you may eat
any kind of locust,[f] katydid,
cricket or grasshopper. 23But all
other winged creatures that have
four legs you are to detest.
24“ ‘You will make yourselves unclean by these; whoever touches
their carcasses will be unclean till
evening. 25Whoever picks up one of
their carcasses must wash his
clothes,[g] and he will be unclean till
evening.[h]
26“ ‘Every animal that has a split
hoof not completely divided or that
does not chew the cud is unclean
for you; whoever touches ⌊the carcass of⌋ any of them will be unclean.
27Of all the animals that walk on all
fours, those that walk on their paws
are unclean for you; whoever
touches their carcasses will be unclean till evening. 28Anyone who
picks up their carcasses must wash
his clothes, and he will be unclean
till evening. They are unclean for
you.
29“ ‘Of the animals that move
about on the ground, these are unclean for you: the weasel, the rat,[i]
any kind of great lizard, 30the
gecko, the monitor lizard, the wall
lizard, the skink and the cha-
meleon. 31Of all those that move
along the ground, these are unclean
for you. Whoever touches them
when they are dead will be unclean
till evening. 32When one of them
dies and falls on something, that article, whatever its use, will be unclean, whether it is made of wood,
cloth, hide or sackcloth.[j] Put it in
water; it will be unclean till evening, and then it will be clean. 33If
one of them falls into a clay pot,
everything in it will be unclean,
and you must break the pot.[k] 34Any
food that could be eaten but has
water on it from such a pot is unclean, and any liquid that could be
drunk from it is unclean. 35Any-
thing that one of their carcasses
falls on becomes unclean; an oven
or cooking pot must be broken up.
They are unclean, and you are to
regard them as unclean. 36A spring,
however, or a cistern for collecting
water remains clean, but anyone
who touches one of these carcasses
is unclean. 37If a carcass falls on
any seeds that are to be planted,
they remain clean. 38But if water
has been put on the seed and a carcass falls on it, it is unclean for you.
39“ ‘If an animal that you are allowed to eat dies, anyone who
touches the carcass will be unclean
till evening. 40Anyone who eats
some of the carcass must wash his

11:8 c Isa 52:11; Heb 9:10
11:10 d Lev 7:18
11:20 e Ac 10:14
11:22 f Mt 3:4; Mk 1:6
11:25 g Lev 14:8,47; Lev 15:5; h ver 40; Nu 31:24
11:29 i Isa 66:17
11:32 j Lev 15:12
11:33 k Lev 6:28; Lev 15:12

b19 The precise identification of some of the birds, insects and animals in this chapter is uncertain.

clothes, and he will be unclean till evening.[l] Anyone who picks up the carcass must wash his clothes, and he will be unclean till evening.

[41]" 'Every creature that moves about on the ground is detestable; it is not to be eaten. [42]You are not to eat any creature that moves about on the ground, whether it moves on its belly or walks on all fours or on many feet; it is detestable. [43]Do not defile yourselves by any of these creatures.[m] Do not make yourselves unclean by means of them or be made unclean by them. [44]I am the LORD your God;[n] consecrate yourselves[o] and be holy,[p] because I am holy.[q] Do not make yourselves unclean by any creature that moves about on the ground. [45]I am the LORD who brought you up out of Egypt[r] to be your God;[s] therefore be holy, because I am holy.[t]

[46]" 'These are the regulations concerning animals, birds, every living thing that moves in the water and every creature that moves about on the ground. [47]You must distinguish between the unclean and the clean, between living creatures that may be eaten and those that may not be eaten.[u] ' "

Purification After Childbirth

12 The LORD said to Moses, [2]"Say to the Israelites: 'A woman who becomes pregnant and gives birth to a son will be ceremonially unclean for seven days, just as she is unclean during her monthly period.[a] [3]On the eighth day the boy is to be circumcised.[b] [4]Then the woman must wait thirty-three days to be purified from her bleeding. She must not touch anything sacred or go to the sanctuary until the days of her purification are over. [5]If she gives birth to a daughter, for two weeks the woman will be unclean, as during her period. Then she must wait sixty-six days to be purified from her bleeding.

[6]" 'When the days of her purification for a son or daughter are over,[c] she is to bring to the priest at the entrance to the Tent of Meeting a year-old lamb[d] for a burnt offering and a young pigeon or a dove for a sin offering.[e] [7]He shall offer them before the LORD to make atonement for her, and then she will be ceremonially clean from her flow of blood.

" 'These are the regulations for the woman who gives birth to a boy or a girl. [8]If she cannot afford a lamb, she is to bring two doves or two young pigeons,[f] one for a burnt offering and the other for a sin offering.[g] In this way the priest will make atonement for her, and she will be clean.[h] ' "

Regulations About Infectious Skin Diseases

13 The LORD said to Moses and Aaron, [2]"When anyone has a swelling[a] or a rash or a bright spot[b] on his skin that may become an infectious skin disease,[a][c] he must be brought to Aaron the priest[d] or to one of his sons[b] who is a priest. [3]The priest is to examine the sore on his skin, and if the hair in the sore has turned white and the sore appears to be more than skin deep,[c] it is an infectious skin disease. When the priest examines him, he shall pronounce him ceremonially unclean.[e] [4]If the spot[f] on his skin is white but does not appear to be more than skin deep and the hair in it has not turned white, the priest is to put the infected person in isolation for seven days.[g] [5]On the seventh day[h] the priest is to examine him,[i] and if he sees that the sore is unchanged and has not spread in the skin, he is to keep him in isolation another seven

a2 Traditionally *leprosy*; the Hebrew word was used for various diseases affecting the skin—not necessarily leprosy; also elsewhere in this chapter. b2 Or *descendants* c3 Or *be lower than the rest of the skin*; also elsewhere in this chapter

11:40 *l* Lev 17:15; Lev 22:8; Eze 44:31
11:43 *m* Lev 20:25
11:44 *n* Ex 6:2,7; Isa 43:3; Isa 51:15 *o* Lev 20:7 *p* Ex 19:6 *q* Lev 19:2; Ps 99:3; Eph 1:4; 1Th 4:7; 1Pe 1:15,16*
11:45 *r* Lev 25:38,55; Ex 6:7; Ex 20:2 *s* Ge 17:7 *t* Ex 19:6; 1Pe 1:16*
11:47 *u* Lev 10:10
12:2 *a* Lev 15:19; Lev 18:19
12:3 *b* Ge 17:12; Lk 1:59; Lk 2:21
12:6 *c* Lk 2:22 *d* Ex 29:38; Lev 23:12; Nu 6:12,14; Nu 7:15 *e* Lev 5:7
12:8 *f* Ge 15:9; Lev 14:22 *g* Lev 5:7; Lk 2:22-24* *h* Lev 4:26
13:2 *a* ver 10,19,28, 43 *b* ver 4,38,39; Lev 14:56 *c* ver 3,9,15; Ex 4:6; Lev 14:3,32; Nu 5:2; Dt 24:8 *d* Dt 24:8
13:3 *e* ver 8,11,20,30; Lev 21:1; Nu 9:6
13:4 *f* ver 2 *g* ver 5,21,26, 33,46; Lev 14:38; Nu 12:14,15; Dt 24:9
13:5 *h* Lev 14:9 *i* ver 27,32,34, 51

days. 6 On the seventh day the
priest is to examine him again, and
if the sore has faded and has not
spread in the skin, the priest shall
pronounce him clean;[j] it is only a
rash. The man must wash his
clothes,[k] and he will be clean.[l]
7 But if the rash does spread in his
skin after he has shown himself to
the priest to be pronounced clean,
he must appear before the priest
again.[m] 8 The priest is to examine
him, and if the rash has spread in
the skin, he shall pronounce him
unclean; it is an infectious disease.

9 "When anyone has an infectious
skin disease, he must be brought to
the priest. 10 The priest is to examine him, and if there is a white
swelling in the skin that has turned
the hair white and if there is raw
flesh in the swelling, 11 it is a
chronic skin disease[n] and the
priest shall pronounce him unclean. He is not to put him in isolation, because he is already unclean.

12 "If the disease breaks out all
over his skin and, so far as the
priest can see, it covers all the skin
of the infected person from head to
foot, 13 the priest is to examine him,
and if the disease has covered his
whole body, he shall pronounce
that person clean. Since it has all
turned white, he is clean. 14 But
whenever raw flesh appears on
him, he will be unclean. 15 When the
priest sees the raw flesh, he shall
pronounce him unclean. The raw
flesh is unclean; he has an infectious disease.[o] 16 Should the raw
flesh change and turn white, he
must go to the priest. 17 The priest is
to examine him, and if the sores
have turned white, the priest shall
pronounce the infected person
clean;[p] then he will be clean.

18 "When someone has a boil[q] on
his skin and it heals, 19 and in the
place where the boil was, a white
swelling or reddish-white[r] spot[s]
appears, he must present himself
to the priest. 20 The priest is to examine it, and if it appears to be
more than skin deep and the hair in
it has turned white, the priest shall
pronounce him unclean. It is an infectious skin disease[t] that has broken out where the boil was. 21 But if,
when the priest examines it, there
is no white hair in it and it is not
more than skin deep and has faded,
then the priest is to put him in isolation for seven days. 22 If it is spreading in the skin, the priest shall
pronounce him unclean; it is infectious. 23 But if the spot is unchanged
and has not spread, it is only a scar
from the boil, and the priest shall
pronounce him clean.[u]

24 "When someone has a burn on
his skin and a reddish-white or
white spot appears in the raw flesh
of the burn, 25 the priest is to examine the spot, and if the hair in it has
turned white, and it appears to be
more than skin deep, it is an infectious disease that has broken out in
the burn. The priest shall pronounce him unclean; it is an infectious skin disease.[v] 26 But if the
priest examines it and there is no
white hair in the spot and if it is not
more than skin deep and has faded,
then the priest is to put him in isolation for seven days.[w] 27 On the seventh day the priest is to examine
him,[x] and if it is spreading in the
skin, the priest shall pronounce
him unclean; it is an infectious skin
disease. 28 If, however, the spot is
unchanged and has not spread in
the skin but has faded, it is a swelling from the burn, and the priest
shall pronounce him clean; it is
only a scar from the burn.[y]

29 "If a man or woman has a sore
on the head[z] or on the chin, 30 the
priest is to examine the sore, and if
it appears to be more than skin
deep and the hair in it is yellow and
thin, the priest shall pronounce
that person unclean; it is an itch, an
infectious disease of the head or
chin. 31 But if, when the priest examines this kind of sore, it does not
seem to be more than skin deep and
there is no black hair in it, then the

13:6 *j* ver 13,17,23,28,34; Mt 8:3; Lk 5:12-14 *k* Lev 11:25 *l* Lev 11:25; Lev 14:8,9,20,48; Lev 15:8; Nu 8:7
13:7 *m* Lk 5:14
13:11 *n* Ex 4:6; Lev 14:8; Nu 12:10; Mt 8:2
13:15 *o* ver 2
13:17 *p* ver 6
13:18 *q* Ex 9:9
13:19 *r* ver 24,42; Lev 14:37 *s* ver 2
13:20 *t* ver 2
13:23 *u* ver 6
13:25 *v* ver 11
13:26 *w* ver 4
13:27 *x* ver 5
13:28 *y* ver 2
13:29 *z* ver 43,44

priest is to put the infected person in isolation for seven days.[a] 32 On the seventh day the priest is to examine the sore,[b] and if the itch has not spread and there is no yellow hair in it and it does not appear to be more than skin deep, 33 he must be shaved except for the diseased area, and the priest is to keep him in isolation another seven days. 34 On the seventh day the priest is to examine the itch,[c] and if it has not spread in the skin and appears to be no more than skin deep, the priest shall pronounce him clean. He must wash his clothes, and he will be clean.[d] 35 But if the itch does spread in the skin after he is pronounced clean, 36 the priest is to examine him, and if the itch has spread in the skin, the priest does not need to look for yellow hair; the person is unclean.[e] 37 If, however, in his judgment it is unchanged and black hair has grown in it, the itch is healed. He is clean, and the priest shall pronounce him clean.

38 "When a man or woman has white spots on the skin, 39 the priest is to examine them, and if the spots are dull white, it is a harmless rash that has broken out on the skin; that person is clean.

40 "When a man has lost his hair and is bald,[f] he is clean. 41 If he has lost his hair from the front of his scalp and has a bald forehead, he is clean. 42 But if he has a reddish-white sore on his bald head or forehead, it is an infectious disease breaking out on his head or forehead. 43 The priest is to examine him, and if the swollen sore on his head or forehead is reddish-white like an infectious skin disease, 44 the man is diseased and is unclean. The priest shall pronounce him unclean because of the sore on his head.

45 "The person with such an infectious disease must wear torn clothes,[g] let his hair be unkempt,[d] cover the lower part of his face[h] and cry out, 'Unclean! Unclean!'[i] 46 As long as he has the infection he remains unclean. He must live alone; he must live outside the camp.[j]

Regulations About Mildew

47 "If any clothing is contaminated with mildew—any woollen or linen clothing, 48 any woven or knitted material of linen or wool, any leather or anything made of leather—49 and if the contamination in the clothing, or leather, or woven or knitted material, or any leather article, is greenish or reddish, it is a spreading mildew and must be shown to the priest.[k] 50 The priest is to examine the mildew[l] and isolate the affected article for seven days. 51 On the seventh day he is to examine it,[m] and if the mildew has spread in the clothing, or the woven or knitted material, or the leather, whatever its use, it is a destructive mildew; the article is unclean.[n] 52 He must burn up the clothing, or the woven or knitted material of wool or linen, or any leather article that has the contamination in it, because the mildew is destructive; the article must be burned up.[o]

53 "But if, when the priest examines it, the mildew has not spread in the clothing, or the woven or knitted material, or the leather article, 54 he shall order that the contaminated article be washed. Then he is to isolate it for another seven days. 55 After the affected article has been washed, the priest is to examine it, and if the mildew has not changed its appearance, even though it has not spread, it is unclean. Burn it with fire, whether the mildew has affected one side or the other. 56 If, when the priest examines it, the mildew has faded after the article has been washed, he is to tear the contaminated part out of the clothing, or the leather, or the woven or knitted material.

13:31 *a* ver 4
13:32 *b* ver 5
13:34 *c* ver 5 *d* Lev 11:25
13:36 *e* ver 30
13:40 *f* Lev 21:5; 2Ki 2:23; Isa 3:24; Isa 15:2; Isa 22:12; Eze 27:31; Eze 29:18; Am 8:10; Mic 1:16
13:45 *g* Lev 10:6 *h* Eze 24:17,22; Mic 3:7 *i* Lev 5:2; La 4:15; Lk 17:12
13:46 *j* Nu 5:1-4; Nu 12:14; 2Ki 7:3; 2Ki 15:5; Lk 17:12
13:49 *k* Mk 1:44
13:50 *l* Eze 44:23
13:51 *m* ver 5 *n* Lev 14:44
13:52 *o* ver 55,57

[d]45 Or *clothes, uncover his head*

57But if it reappears in the clothing, or in the woven or knitted material, or in the leather article, it is spreading, and whatever has the mildew must be burned with fire. 58The clothing, or the woven or knitted material, or any leather article that has been washed and is rid of the mildew, must be washed again, and it will be clean."

59These are the regulations concerning contamination by mildew in woollen or linen clothing, woven or knitted material, or any leather article, for pronouncing them clean or unclean.

Cleansing From Infectious Skin Diseases

14 The LORD said to Moses, 2"These are the regulations for the diseased person at the time of his ceremonial cleansing, when he is brought to the priest:[a] 3The priest is to go outside the camp and examine him.[b] If the person has been healed of his infectious skin disease,[a] 4the priest shall order that two live clean birds and some cedar wood, scarlet yarn and hyssop be brought for the one to be cleansed.[c] 5Then the priest shall order that one of the birds be killed over fresh water in a clay pot. 6He is then to take the live bird and dip it, together with the cedar wood, the scarlet yarn and the hyssop, into the blood of the bird that was killed over the fresh water.[d] 7Seven times he shall sprinkle[e] the one to be cleansed of the infectious disease and pronounce him clean. Then he is to release the live bird in the open fields.

8"The person to be cleansed must wash his clothes,[f] shave off all his hair and bathe with water;[g] then he will be ceremonially clean.[h] After this he may come into the camp,[i] but he must stay outside his tent for seven days. 9On the seventh day he must shave off all his hair; he must shave his head, his beard, his eyebrows and the rest of his hair. He must wash his clothes and bathe himself with water, and he will be clean.

10"On the eighth day[j] he must bring two male lambs and one ewe lamb a year old, each without defect, along with three-tenths of an ephah[b] of fine flour mixed with oil for a grain offering,[k] and one log[c] of oil.[l] 11The priest who pronounces him clean shall present both the one to be cleansed and his offerings before the LORD at the entrance to the Tent of Meeting.

12"Then the priest is to take one of the male lambs and offer it as a guilt offering,[m] along with the log of oil; he shall wave them before the LORD as a wave offering.[n] 13He is to slaughter the lamb in the holy place[o] where the sin offering and the burnt offering are slaughtered. Like the sin offering, the guilt offering belongs to the priest;[p] it is most holy. 14The priest is to take some of the blood of the guilt offering and put it on the lobe of the right ear of the one to be cleansed, on the thumb of his right hand and on the big toe of his right foot.[q] 15The priest shall then take some of the log of oil, pour it in the palm of his own left hand, 16dip his right forefinger into the oil in his palm, and with his finger sprinkle some of it before the LORD seven times. 17The priest is to put some of the oil remaining in his palm on the lobe of the right ear of the one to be cleansed, on the thumb of his right hand and on the big toe of his right foot, on top of the blood of the guilt offering. 18The rest of the oil in his palm the priest shall put on the

14:2
a Mt 8:2-4; Mk 1:40-44; Lk 5:12-14; Lk 17:14

14:3
b Lev 13:46

14:4
c ver 6,49,51,52; Nu 19:6; Ps 51:7

14:6
d ver 4

14:7
e 2Ki 5:10,14; Isa 52:15; Eze 36:25

14:8
f Lev 11:25; Lev 13:6
g ver 9
h ver 20
i Nu 5:2,3; Nu 12:14,15; 2Ch 26:21

14:10
j Mt 8:4; Mk 1:44; Lk 5:14
k Lev 2:1
l ver 12,15,21, 24

14:12
m Lev 5:18; Lev 6:6-7
n Ex 29:24

14:13
o Ex 29:11
p Lev 6:24-30; Lev 7:7

14:14
q Ex 29:20; Lev 8:23

[a]*3* Traditionally *leprosy*; the Hebrew word was used for various diseases affecting the skin—not necessarily leprosy; also elsewhere in this chapter. [b]*10* That is, probably about 11½ pints (about 6.5 litres) [c]*10* That is, probably about ½ pint (about 0.3 litre); also in verses 12, 15, 21 and 24

head of the one to be cleansed and
make atonement for him before the
LORD.
19 "Then the priest is to sacrifice
the sin offering and make atonement for the one to be cleansed
from his uncleanness. After that,
the priest shall slaughter the burnt
offering 20 and offer it on the altar,
together with the grain offering,
and make atonement for him, and
he will be clean.[r]
21 "If, however, he is poor[s] and
cannot afford these,[t] he must take
one male lamb as a guilt offering to
be waved to make atonement for
him, together with a tenth of an
ephah[d] of fine flour mixed with oil
for a grain offering, a log of oil,
22 and two doves or two young
pigeons,[u] which he can afford, one
for a sin offering and the other for
a burnt offering.
23 "On the eighth day he must
bring them for his cleansing to the
priest at the entrance to the Tent of
Meeting, before the LORD.[v] 24 The
priest is to take the lamb for the
guilt offering,[w] together with the
log of oil,[x] and wave them before
the LORD as a wave offering.[y] 25 He
shall slaughter the lamb for the
guilt offering and take some of its
blood and put it on the lobe of the
right ear of the one to be cleansed,
on the thumb of his right hand and
on the big toe of his right foot.[z]
26 The priest is to pour some of the
oil into the palm of his own left
hand,[a] 27 and with his right forefinger sprinkle some of the oil from
his palm seven times before the
LORD. 28 Some of the oil in his palm
he is to put on the same places he
put the blood of the guilt offering—
on the lobe of the right ear of the
one to be cleansed, on the thumb
of his right hand and on the big
toe of his right foot. 29 The rest of
the oil in his palm the priest shall
put on the head of the one to be
cleansed, to make atonement for
him before the LORD.[b] 30 Then he
shall sacrifice the doves or the
young pigeons, which the person
can afford,[c] 31 one[e] as a sin offering and the other as a burnt offering,[d] together with the grain
offering. In this way the priest
will make atonement before the
LORD on behalf of the one to be
cleansed.[e]"
32 These are the regulations for
anyone who has an infectious skin
disease[f] and who cannot afford
the regular offerings[g] for his
cleansing.

Cleansing From Mildew

33 The LORD said to Moses and
Aaron, 34 "When you enter the land
of Canaan,[h] which I am giving you
as your possession,[i] and I put a
spreading mildew in a house in that
land, 35 the owner of the house must
go and tell the priest, 'I have seen
something that looks like mildew in
my house.' 36 The priest is to order
the house to be emptied before he
goes in to examine the mildew, so
that nothing in the house will be
pronounced unclean. After this the
priest is to go in and inspect the
house. 37 He is to examine the mildew on the walls, and if it has
greenish or reddish[j] depressions
that appear to be deeper than the
surface of the wall, 38 the priest
shall go out of the doorway of the
house and close it up for seven
days.[k] 39 On the seventh day[l] the
priest shall return to inspect the
house. If the mildew has spread on
the walls, 40 he is to order that the
contaminated stones be torn out
and thrown into an unclean place
outside the town.[m] 41 He must have
all the inside walls of the house
scraped and the material that is
scraped off dumped into an unclean place outside the town.

14:20 r ver 8
14:21 s Lev 5:7; Lev 12:8 t ver 22,32
14:22 u Lev 5:7
14:23 v ver 10,11
14:24 w Nu 6:14 x ver 10 y ver 12
14:25 z ver 14; Ex 29:20
14:26 a ver 15
14:29 b ver 18
14:30 c Lev 5:7
14:31 d ver 22; Lev 5:7; Lev 15:15,30 e ver 18,19
14:32 f Lev 13:2 g ver 21
14:34 h Ge 12:5; Ex 6:4; Nu 13:2 i Ge 17:8; Ge 48:4; Nu 27:12; Nu 32:22; Dt 3:27; Dt 7:1; Dt 32:49
14:37 j Lev 13:19
14:38 k Lev 13:4
14:39 l Lev 13:5
14:40 m ver 45

d21 That is, probably about 4 pints (about 2 litres)
e31 Septuagint and Syriac; Hebrew 31 *such as the person can afford, one*

42Then they are to take other stones
to replace these and take new clay
and plaster the house.
43"If the mildew reappears in the
house after the stones have been
torn out and the house scraped and
plastered, 44the priest is to go and
examine it and, if the mildew
has spread in the house, it is
a destructive mildew; the house
is unclean.[n] 45It must be torn
down—its stones, timbers and
all the plaster—and taken out
of the town to an unclean place.
46"Anyone who goes into the
house while it is closed up will be
unclean till evening.[o] 47Anyone
who sleeps or eats in the house
must wash his clothes.[p]
48"But if the priest comes to examine it and the mildew has not
spread after the house has been
plastered, he shall pronounce the
house clean,[q] because the mildew
is gone. 49To purify the house he is
to take two birds and some cedar
wood, scarlet yarn and hyssop.[r]
50He shall kill one of the birds over
fresh water in a clay pot.[s] 51Then
he is to take the cedar wood, the
hyssop,[t] the scarlet yarn and the
live bird, dip them into the blood of
the dead bird and the fresh water,
and sprinkle the house seven
times.[u] 52He shall purify the house
with the bird's blood, the fresh
water, the live bird, the cedar
wood, the hyssop and the scarlet
yarn. 53Then he is to release the
live bird in the open fields[v] outside
the town. In this way he will make
atonement for the house, and it will
be clean.[w]"
54These are the regulations for
any infectious skin disease,[x] for
an itch, 55for mildew[y] in clothing
or in a house, 56and for a swelling,
a rash or a bright spot,[z] 57to determine when something is clean or
unclean.
These are the regulations for
infectious skin diseases and
mildew.[a]

Discharges Causing Uncleanness

15 The LORD said to Moses and
Aaron, 2"Speak to the Is-
raelites and say to them: 'When any
man has a bodily discharge,[a] the
discharge is unclean. 3Whether it
continues flowing from his body or
is blocked, it will make him unclean. This is how his discharge
will bring about uncleanness:
4" 'Any bed the man with a discharge lies on will be unclean, and
anything he sits on will be unclean.
5Anyone who touches his bed must
wash his clothes[b] and bathe with
water,[c] and he will be unclean till
evening.[d] 6Whoever sits on anything that the man with a discharge
sat on must wash his clothes and
bathe with water, and he will be unclean till evening.
7" 'Whoever touches the man[e]
who has a discharge[f] must wash
his clothes and bathe with water,
and he will be unclean till evening.
8" 'If the man with the discharge
spits[g] on someone who is clean,
that person must wash his clothes
and bathe with water, and he will
be unclean till evening.
9" 'Everything the man sits on
when riding will be unclean, 10and
whoever touches any of the things
that were under him will be unclean till evening; whoever picks
up those things[h] must wash his
clothes and bathe with water, and
he will be unclean till evening.
11" 'Anyone the man with a discharge touches without rinsing his
hands with water must wash his
clothes and bathe with water, and
he will be unclean till evening.
12" 'A clay pot[i] that the man
touches must be broken, and any
wooden article[j] is to be rinsed
with water.
13" 'When a man is cleansed from
his discharge, he is to count off
seven days[k] for his ceremonial
cleansing; he must wash his clothes
and bathe himself with fresh

14:44 n Lev 13:51
14:46 o Lev 11:24
14:47 p Lev 11:25
14:48 q Lev 13:6
14:49 r ver 4; 1Ki 4:33
14:50 s ver 5
14:51 t ver 6; Ps 51:7; u ver 4,7
14:53 v ver 7; w ver 20
14:54 x Lev 13:2,30
14:55 y Lev 13:47-52
14:56 z Lev 13:2
14:57 a Lev 10:10
15:2 a ver 16,32; Lev 22:4; Nu 5:2; 2Sa 3:29; Mt 9:20
15:5 b Lev 11:25; c Lev 14:8; d Lev 11:24
15:7 e ver 19; Lev 22:5; f ver 16; Lev 22:4
15:8 g Nu 12:14
15:10 h Nu 19:10
15:12 i Lev 6:28; j Lev 11:32
15:13 k Lev 8:33

water, and he will be clean.[l] 14 On the eighth day he must take two doves or two young pigeons[m] and come before the LORD to the entrance to the Tent of Meeting and give them to the priest. 15 The priest is to sacrifice them, the one for a sin offering[n] and the other for a burnt offering.[o] In this way he will make atonement before the LORD for the man because of his discharge.[p]

16 " 'When a man has an emission of semen,[q] he must bathe his whole body with water, and he will be unclean till evening.[r] 17 Any clothing or leather that has semen on it must be washed with water, and it will be unclean till evening. 18 When a man lies with a woman and there is an emission of semen,[s] both must bathe with water, and they will be unclean till evening.

19 " 'When a woman has her regular flow of blood, the impurity of her monthly period[t] will last seven days, and anyone who touches her will be unclean till evening.

20 " 'Anything she lies on during her period will be unclean, and anything she sits on will be unclean. 21 Whoever touches her bed must wash his clothes and bathe with water, and he will be unclean till evening.[u] 22 Whoever touches anything she sits on must wash his clothes and bathe with water, and he will be unclean till evening. 23 Whether it is the bed or anything she was sitting on, when anyone touches it, he will be unclean till evening.

24 " 'If a man lies with her and her monthly flow[v] touches him, he will be unclean for seven days; any bed he lies on will be unclean.

25 " 'When a woman has a discharge of blood for many days at a time other than her monthly period[w] or has a discharge that continues beyond her period, she will be unclean as long as she has the discharge, just as in the days of her period. 26 Any bed she lies on while her discharge continues will be unclean, as is her bed during her monthly period, and anything she sits on will be unclean, as during her period. 27 Whoever touches them will be unclean; he must wash his clothes and bathe with water, and he will be unclean till evening.

28 " 'When she is cleansed from her discharge, she must count off seven days, and after that she will be ceremonially clean. 29 On the eighth day she must take two doves or two young pigeons[x] and bring them to the priest at the entrance to the Tent of Meeting. 30 The priest is to sacrifice one for a sin offering and the other for a burnt offering. In this way he will make atonement for her before the LORD for the uncleanness of her discharge.[y]

31 " 'You must keep the Israelites separate from things that make them unclean, so they will not die in their uncleanness for defiling my dwelling-place,[a][z] which is among them.' "

32 These are the regulations for a man with a discharge, for anyone made unclean by an emission of semen,[a] 33 for a woman in her monthly period, for a man or a woman with a discharge, and for a man who lies with a woman who is ceremonially unclean.[b]

The Day of Atonement

16:2–34pp Lev 23:26–32; Nu 29:7–11

16 The LORD spoke to Moses after the death of the two sons of Aaron who died when they approached the LORD.[a] 2 The LORD said to Moses: "Tell your brother Aaron not to come whenever he chooses[b] into the Most Holy Place[c] behind the curtain in front of the atonement cover on the ark, or else he will die, because I

15:13 l ver 5
15:14 m Lev 14:22
15:15 n Lev 5:7 o Lev 14:31 p Lev 14:18,19
15:16 q ver 2 Lev 22:4 Dt 23:10 r ver 5 Dt 23:11
15:18 s 1Sa 21:4
15:19 t ver 24 Lev 12:2
15:21 u ver 27
15:24 v ver 19 Lev 12:2 Lev 18:19 Lev 20:18 Eze 18:6
15:25 w Mt 9:20 Mk 5:25 Lk 8:43
15:29 x Lev 14:22
15:30 y Lev 5:10 Lev 14:20,31 Lev 18:19 2Sa 11:4 Mk 5:25 Lk 8:43
15:31 z Lev 20:3 Nu 5:3 Nu 19:13,20 2Sa 15:25 2Ki 21:7 Ps 33:14 Ps 74:7 Ps 76:2 Eze 5:11 Eze 23:38
15:32 a ver 2
15:33 b ver 19,24,25
16:1 a Lev 10:1
16:2 b Ex 30:10 Heb 9:7 c Heb 9:25 Heb 10:19

[a] *31* Or *my tabernacle*

appear[d] in the cloud[e] over the atonement cover.

3"This is how Aaron is to enter the sanctuary area:[f] with a young bull for a sin offering and a ram for a burnt offering. 4He is to put on the sacred linen tunic, with linen undergarments next to his body; he is to tie the linen sash around him and put on the linen turban.[g] These are sacred garments;[h] so he must bathe himself with water[i] before he puts them on. 5From the Israelite community[j] he is to take two male goats[k] for a sin offering and a ram for a burnt offering.

6"Aaron is to offer the bull for his own sin offering to make atonement for himself and his household.[l] 7Then he is to take the two goats and present them before the LORD at the entrance to the Tent of Meeting. 8He is to cast lots for the two goats—one lot for the LORD and the other for the scapegoat.[a] 9Aaron shall bring the goat whose lot falls to the LORD and sacrifice it for a sin offering. 10But the goat chosen by lot as the scapegoat shall be presented alive before the LORD to be used for making atonement[m] by sending it into the desert as a scapegoat.

11"Aaron shall bring the bull for his own sin offering to make atonement for himself and his household,[n] and he is to slaughter the bull for his own sin offering. 12He is to take a censer full of burning coals[o] from the altar before the LORD and two handfuls of finely ground fragrant incense[p] and take them behind the curtain. 13He is to put the incense on the fire before the LORD, and the smoke of the incense will conceal the atonement cover above the Testimony, so that he will not die.[q] 14He is to take some of the bull's blood[r] and with his finger sprinkle it on the front of the atonement cover; then he shall sprinkle some of it with his finger seven times before the atonement cover.[s]

16:2 d Ex 25:22 e Ex 40:34
16:3 f Heb 9:24,25
16:4 g Ex 28:39 h Ex 28:42 i ver 24 Heb 10:22
16:5 j Lev 4:13-21 k 2Ch 29:23
16:6 l Lev 9:7 Heb 5:3 Heb 7:27 Heb 9:7,12
16:10 m Isa 53:4-10 Ro 3:25 1Jn 2:2
16:11 n Heb 7:27 Heb 9:7
16:12 o Lev 10:1 p Ex 30:34-38
16:13 q Ex 28:43 Lev 22:9
16:14 r Lev 4:5 Heb 9:7,13,25 s Lev 4:6
16:15 t Heb 9:7,12 u Heb 9:3
16:16 v Ex 29:36
16:18 w Lev 4:7 x Lev 4:25
16:19 y Eze 43:20
16:21 z Lev 5:5
16:22 a Isa 53:12

15"He shall then slaughter the goat for the sin offering for the people[t] and take its blood behind the curtain[u] and do with it as he did with the bull's blood: He shall sprinkle it on the atonement cover and in front of it. 16In this way he will make atonement[v] for the Most Holy Place because of the uncleanness and rebellion of the Israelites, whatever their sins have been. He is to do the same for the Tent of Meeting, which is among them in the midst of their uncleanness. 17No-one is to be in the Tent of Meeting from the time Aaron goes in to make atonement in the Most Holy Place until he comes out, having made atonement for himself, his household and the whole community of Israel.

18"Then he shall come out to the altar[w] that is before the LORD and make atonement for it. He shall take some of the bull's blood and some of the goat's blood and put it on all the horns of the altar.[x] 19He shall sprinkle some of the blood on it with his finger seven times to cleanse it and consecrate it from the uncleanness of the Israelites.[y]

20"When Aaron has finished making atonement for the Most Holy Place, the Tent of Meeting and the altar, he shall bring forward the live goat. 21He is to lay both hands on the head of the live goat and confess[z] over it all the wickedness and rebellion of the Israelites—all their sins—and put them on the goat's head. He shall send the goat away into the desert in the care of a man appointed for the task. 22The goat will carry on itself all their sins[a] to a solitary place; and the man shall release it in the desert.

23"Then Aaron is to go into the Tent of Meeting and take off the

[a] 8 That is, the goat of removal; Hebrew *azazel*; also in verses 10 and 26

linen garments he put on before he entered the Most Holy Place, and he is to leave them there.[b] 24He shall bathe himself with water in a holy place and put on his regular garments.[c] Then he shall come out and sacrifice the burnt offering for himself and the burnt offering for the people, to make atonement for himself and for the people. 25He shall also burn the fat of the sin offering on the altar.

26"The man who releases the goat as a scapegoat must wash his clothes[d] and bathe himself with water; afterwards he may come into the camp. 27The bull and the goat for the sin offerings, whose blood was brought into the Most Holy Place to make atonement, must be taken outside the camp;[e] their hides, flesh and offal are to be burned up. 28The man who burns them must wash his clothes and bathe himself with water; afterwards he may come into the camp.

29"This is to be a lasting ordinance for you: On the tenth day of the seventh month you must deny yourselves[b][f] and not do any work—whether native-born or an alien living among you—30because on this day atonement will be made for you, to cleanse you. Then, before the LORD, you will be clean from all your sins.[g] 31It is a sabbath of rest, and you must deny yourselves;[h] it is a lasting ordinance. 32The priest who is anointed and ordained to succeed his father as high priest is to make atonement. He is to put on the sacred linen garments[i] 33and make atonement for the Most Holy Place, for the Tent of Meeting and the altar, and for the priests and all the people of the community.[j]

34"This is to be a lasting ordinance for you: Atonement is to be made once a year[k] for all the sins of the Israelites."

And it was done, as the LORD commanded Moses.

16:23 *b* Eze 42:14; Eze 44:19
16:24 *c* ver 3-5
16:26 *d* Lev 11:25
16:27 *e* Lev 4:12,21; Heb 13:11
16:29 *f* Lev 23:27,32; Nu 29:7; Isa 58:3
16:30 *g* Jer 33:8; Eph 5:26
16:31 *h* Isa 58:3,5
16:32 *i* ver 4; Nu 20:26,28
16:33 *j* ver 11,16-18
16:34 *k* Heb 9:7,25
17:4 *a* Dt 12:5-21; *b* Ge 17:14
17:6 *c* Lev 3:2; *d* Nu 18:17
17:7 *e* Ex 22:20; 2Ch 11:15; *f* Ex 32:8; Ex 34:15; Dt 32:17; 1Co 10:20
17:9 *g* ver 4
17:10 *h* Ge 9:4; Lev 3:17; Dt 12:16,23; 1Sa 14:33
17:11 *i* ver 14; Ge 9:4

Eating Blood Forbidden

17 The LORD said to Moses, 2"Speak to Aaron and his sons and to all the Israelites and say to them: 'This is what the LORD has commanded: 3Any Israelite who sacrifices an ox,[a] a lamb or a goat in the camp or outside of it 4instead of bringing it to the entrance to the Tent of Meeting to present it as an offering to the LORD in front of the tabernacle of the LORD[a]—that man shall be considered guilty of bloodshed; he has shed blood and must be cut off from his people.[b] 5This is so that the Israelites will bring to the LORD the sacrifices they are now making in the open fields. They must bring them to the priest, that is, to the LORD, at the entrance to the Tent of Meeting and sacrifice them as fellowship offerings.[b] 6The priest is to sprinkle the blood against the altar of the LORD[c] at the entrance to the Tent of Meeting and burn the fat as an aroma pleasing to the LORD.[d] 7They must no longer offer any of their sacrifices to the goat idols[c][e] to whom they prostitute themselves.[f] This is to be a lasting ordinance for them and for the generations to come.'

8"Say to them: 'Any Israelite or any alien living among them who offers a burnt offering or sacrifice 9and does not bring it to the entrance to the Tent of Meeting[g] to sacrifice it to the LORD—that man must be cut off from his people.

10" 'Any Israelite or any alien living among them who eats any blood—I will set my face against that person who eats blood[h] and will cut him off from his people. 11For the life of a creature is in the blood,[i] and I have given it to you to make atonement for yourselves on the altar; it is the blood that makes

b29 Or *must fast*; also in verse 31
a3 The Hebrew word can include both male and female. b5 Traditionally *peace offerings*
c7 Or *demons*

atonement for one's life.[j] 12 Therefore I say to the Israelites, "None of you may eat blood, nor may an alien living among you eat blood."

13 " 'Any Israelite or any alien living among you who hunts any animal or bird that may be eaten must drain out the blood and cover it with earth,[k] 14 because the life of every creature is its blood. That is why I have said to the Israelites, "You must not eat the blood of any creature, because the life of every creature is its blood; anyone who eats it must be cut off."[l]

15 " 'Anyone, whether native-born or alien, who eats anything found dead or torn by wild animals[m] must wash his clothes and bathe with water, and he will be ceremonially unclean till evening; then he will be clean. 16 But if he does not wash his clothes and bathe himself, he will be held responsible.' "

Unlawful Sexual Relations

18 The LORD said to Moses, 2 "Speak to the Israelites and say to them: 'I am the LORD your God.[a] 3 You must not do as they do in Egypt, where you used to live, and you must not do as they do in the land of Canaan, where I am bringing you. Do not follow their practices.[b] 4 You must obey my laws and be careful to follow my decrees. I am the LORD your God.[c] 5 Keep my decrees and laws, for the man who obeys them will live by them.[d] I am the LORD.

6 " 'No-one is to approach any close relative to have sexual relations. I am the LORD.

7 " 'Do not dishonour your father[e] by having sexual relations with your mother.[f] She is your mother; do not have relations with her.

8 " 'Do not have sexual relations with your father's wife;[g] that would dishonour your father.[h]

9 " 'Do not have sexual relations with your sister,[i] either your father's daughter or your mother's daughter, whether she was born in the same home or elsewhere.

10 " 'Do not have sexual relations with your son's daughter or your daughter's daughter; that would dishonour you.

11 " 'Do not have sexual relations with the daughter of your father's wife, born to your father; she is your sister.

12 " 'Do not have sexual relations with your father's sister;[j] she is your father's close relative.

13 " 'Do not have sexual relations with your mother's sister, because she is your mother's close relative.

14 " 'Do not dishonour your father's brother by approaching his wife to have sexual relations; she is your aunt.[k]

15 " 'Do not have sexual relations with your daughter-in-law.[l] She is your son's wife; do not have relations with her.

16 " 'Do not have sexual relations with your brother's wife;[m] that would dishonour your brother.

17 " 'Do not have sexual relations with both a woman and her daughter.[n] Do not have sexual relations with either her son's daughter or her daughter's daughter; they are her close relatives. That is wickedness.

18 " 'Do not take your wife's sister as a rival wife and have sexual relations with her while your wife is living.

19 " 'Do not approach a woman to have sexual relations during the uncleanness of her monthly period.[o]

20 " 'Do not have sexual relations with your neighbour's wife[p] and defile yourself with her.

21 " 'Do not give any of your children[q] to be sacrificed[a] to Molech,[r] for you must not profane the name of your God.[s] I am the LORD.

22 " 'Do not lie with a man as one

17:11 j Heb 9:22
17:13 k Lev 7:26; Dt 12:16
17:14 l ver 11; Ge 9:4
17:15 m Ex 22:31; Dt 14:21
18:2 a Ex 6:7; Lev 11:44; Eze 20:5
18:3 b ver 24-30; Ex 23:24; Lev 20:23
18:4 c ver 2
18:5 d Eze 20:11; Ro 10:5*; Gal 3:12*
18:7 e Lev 20:11; f Eze 22:10
18:8 g 1Co 5:1; h Lev 20:11
18:9 i Lev 20:17
18:12 j Lev 20:19
18:14 k Lev 20:20
18:15 l Lev 20:12
18:16 m Lev 20:21
18:17 n Lev 20:14
18:19 o Lev 15:24; Lev 20:18
18:20 p Ex 20:14; Lev 20:10; Mt 5:27,28; 1Co 6:9; Heb 13:4
18:21 q Dt 12:31; r Lev 20:2-5; s Lev 19:12; Lev 21:6; Eze 36:20

a21 Or *to be passed through the fire,*

lies with a woman;[t] that is detestable.

23 " 'Do not have sexual relations with an animal and defile yourself with it. A woman must not present herself to an animal to have sexual relations with it; that is a perversion.[u]

24 " 'Do not defile yourselves in any of these ways, because this is how the nations that I am going to drive out before you[v] became defiled.[w] 25 Even the land was defiled; so I punished it for its sin,[x] and the land vomited out its inhabitants.[y] 26 But you must keep my decrees and my laws. The native-born and the aliens living among you must not do any of these detestable things, 27 for all these things were done by the people who lived in the land before you, and the land became defiled. 28 And if you defile the land, it will vomit you out as it vomited out the nations that were before you.

29 " 'Everyone who does any of these detestable things—such persons must be cut off from their people. 30 Keep my requirements[z] and do not follow any of the detestable customs that were practised before you came and do not defile yourselves with them. I am the LORD your God.[a]' "

Various Laws

19 The LORD said to Moses, 2 "Speak to the entire assembly of Israel and say to them: 'Be holy because I, the LORD your God, am holy.[a]

3 " 'Each of you must respect his mother and father,[b] and you must observe my Sabbaths. I am the LORD your God.[c]

4 " 'Do not turn to idols or make gods of cast metal for yourselves.[d] I am the LORD your God.

5 " 'When you sacrifice a fellowship offering[a] to the LORD, sacrifice it in such a way that it will be accepted on your behalf. 6 It shall be eaten on the day you sacrifice it or on the next day; anything left over until the third day must be burned up. 7 If any of it is eaten on the third day, it is impure and will not be accepted. 8 Whoever eats it will be held responsible because he has desecrated what is holy to the LORD; that person must be cut off from his people.

9 " 'When you reap the harvest of your land, do not reap to the very edges of your field or gather the gleanings of your harvest.[e] 10 Do not go over your vineyard a second time or pick up the grapes that have fallen. Leave them for the poor and the alien. I am the LORD your God.

11 " 'Do not steal.[f]

" 'Do not lie.[g]

" 'Do not deceive one another.

12 " 'Do not swear falsely by my name[h] and so profane the name of your God. I am the LORD.

13 " 'Do not defraud your neighbour or rob him.[i]

" 'Do not hold back the wages of a hired man overnight.[j]

14 " 'Do not curse the deaf or put a stumbling-block in front of the blind,[k] but fear your God. I am the LORD.

15 " 'Do not pervert justice;[l] do not show partiality[m] to the poor or favouritism to the great, but judge your neighbour fairly.

16 " 'Do not go about spreading slander[n] among your people.

" 'Do not do anything that endangers your neighbour's life.[o] I am the LORD.

17 " 'Do not hate your brother in your heart.[p] Rebuke your neighbour frankly[q] so that you will not share in his guilt.

18 " 'Do not seek revenge[r] or bear a grudge[s] against one of your people, but love your neighbour as yourself.[t] I am the LORD.

19 " 'Keep my decrees.

18:22 t Lev 20:13; Dt 23:18; Ro 1:27
18:23 u Ex 22:19; Lev 20:15; Dt 27:21
18:24 v ver 3,27,30; w Dt 18:12
18:25 x Lev 20:23; Dt 9:5; Dt 18:12; y ver 28; Lev 20:22
18:30 z Dt 11:1; a ver 2
19:2 a 1Pe 1:16*; Lev 11:44
19:3 b Ex 20:12; c Lev 11:44
19:4 d Ex 20:4,23; Ex 34:17; Lev 26:1; Ps 96:5; Ps 115:4-7
19:9 e Lev 23:10,22; Dt 24:19-22
19:11 f Ex 20:15; g Eph 4:25
19:12 h Ex 20:7; Mt 5:33
19:13 i Ex 22:15, 25-27; j Dt 24:15; Jas 5:4
19:14 k Dt 27:18
19:15 l Ex 23:2,6; m Dt 1:17
19:16 n Ps 15:3; Eze 22:9; o Ex 23:7
19:17 p 1Jn 2:9; 1Jn 3:15; q Mt 18:15; Lk 17:3
19:18 r Ro 12:19; s Ps 103:9; t Mt 5:43*; Mt 19:16*; Mt 22:39*; Mk 12:31*; Lk 10:27*; Jn 13:34; Ro 13:9*; Gal 5:14*; Jas 2:8*

[a] 5 Traditionally *peace offering*

" 'Do not mate different kinds of animals.

" 'Do not plant your field with two kinds of seed.[u]

" 'Do not wear clothing woven of two kinds of material.[v]

20" 'If a man sleeps with a woman who is a slave girl promised to another man but who has not been ransomed or given her freedom, there must be due punishment. Yet they are not to be put to death, because she had not been freed. 21The man, however, must bring a ram to the entrance to the Tent of Meeting for a guilt offering to the LORD.[w] 22With the ram of the guilt offering the priest is to make atonement for him before the LORD for the sin he has committed, and his sin will be forgiven.

23" 'When you enter the land and plant any kind of fruit tree, regard its fruit as forbidden.[b] For three years you are to consider it forbidden;[b] it must not be eaten. 24In the fourth year all its fruit will be holy,[x] an offering of praise to the LORD. 25But in the fifth year you may eat its fruit. In this way your harvest will be increased. I am the LORD your God.

26" 'Do not eat any meat with the blood still in it.[y]

" 'Do not practise divination or sorcery.[z]

27" 'Do not cut the hair at the sides of your head or clip off the edges of your beard.[a]

28" 'Do not cut your bodies for the dead or put tattoo marks on yourselves. I am the LORD.

29" 'Do not degrade your daughter by making her a prostitute,[b] or the land will turn to prostitution and be filled with wickedness.

30" 'Observe my Sabbaths and have reverence for my sanctuary. I am the LORD.[c]

31" 'Do not turn to mediums or seek out spiritists,[d] for you will be defiled by them. I am the LORD your God.

32" 'Rise in the presence of the aged, show respect for the elderly[e] and revere your God. I am the LORD.

33" 'When an alien lives with you in your land, do not ill-treat him. 34The alien living with you must be treated as one of your native-born.[f] Love him as yourself, for you were aliens in Egypt.[g] I am the LORD your God.

35" 'Do not use dishonest standards when measuring length, weight or quantity. 36Use honest scales and honest weights, an honest ephah[c] and an honest hin.[d][h] I am the LORD your God, who brought you out of Egypt.

37" 'Keep all my decrees and all my laws and follow them. I am the LORD.' "

Punishments for Sin

20 The LORD said to Moses, 2"Say to the Israelites: 'Any Israelite or any alien living in Israel who gives[a] any of his children to Molech must be put to death. The people of the community are to stone him. 3I will set my face against that man and I will cut him off from his people; for by giving his children to Molech, he has defiled my sanctuary[a] and profaned my holy name.[b] 4If the people of the community close their eyes when that man gives one of his children to Molech and they fail to put him to death,[c] 5I will set my face against that man and his family and will cut off from their people both him and all who follow him in prostituting themselves to Molech.

6" 'I will set my face against the person who turns to mediums and spiritists to prostitute himself by following them, and I will cut him off from his people.[d]

7" 'Consecrate yourselves and be holy,[e] because I am the LORD your

19:19 u Dt 22:9 v Dt 22:11
19:21 w Lev 5:15
19:24 x Pr 3:9
19:26 y Lev 17:10 z Dt 18:10
19:27 a Lev 21:5
19:29 b Dt 23:18
19:30 c Lev 26:2
19:31 d Lev 20:6 Isa 8:19
19:32 e 1Ti 5:1
19:34 f Ex 12:48 g Dt 10:19
19:36 h Dt 25:13-15
20:3 a Lev 15:31 b Lev 18:21
20:4 c Dt 17:2-5
20:6 d Lev 19:31
20:7 e Eph 1:4 1Pe 1:16*

b*23* Hebrew *uncircumcised* c*36* An ephah was a dry measure. d*36* A hin was a liquid measure. a*2* Or *sacrifices*; also in verses 3 and 4

God. 8Keep my decrees and follow them. I am the LORD, who makes you holy.[b][f]

9" 'If anyone curses his father or mother,[g] he must be put to death.[h] He has cursed his father or his mother, and his blood will be on his own head.[i]

10" 'If a man commits adultery with another man's wife[j]—with the wife of his neighbour—both the adulterer and the adulteress must be put to death.

11" 'If a man sleeps with his father's wife, he has dishonoured his father.[k] Both the man and the woman must be put to death; their blood will be on their own heads.

12" 'If a man sleeps with his daughter-in-law,[l] both of them must be put to death. What they have done is a perversion; their blood will be on their own heads.

13" 'If a man lies with a man as one lies with a woman, both of them have done what is detestable.[m] They must be put to death; their blood will be on their own heads.

14" 'If a man marries both a woman and her mother,[n] it is wicked. Both he and they must be burned in the fire, so that no wickedness will be among you.[o]

15" 'If a man has sexual relations with an animal,[p] he must be put to death, and you must kill the animal.

16" 'If a woman approaches an animal to have sexual relations with it, kill both the woman and the animal. They must be put to death; their blood will be on their own heads.

17" 'If a man marries his sister[q], the daughter of either his father or his mother, and they have sexual relations, it is a disgrace. They must be cut off before the eyes of their people. He has dishonoured his sister and will be held responsible.

18" 'If a man lies with a woman during her monthly period[r] and has sexual relations with her, he has exposed the source of her flow, and she has also uncovered it. Both of them must be cut off from their people.

19" 'Do not have sexual relations with the sister of either your mother or your father,[s] for that would dishonour a close relative; both of you would be held responsible.

20" 'If a man sleeps with his aunt,[t] he has dishonoured his uncle. They will be held responsible; they will die childless.

21" 'If a man marries his brother's wife,[u] it is an act of impurity; he has dishonoured his brother. They will be childless.

22" 'Keep all my decrees and laws and follow them, so that the land[v] where I am bringing you to live may not vomit you out. 23You must not live according to the customs of the nations[w] I am going to drive out before you.[x] Because they did all these things, I abhorred them. 24But I said to you, "You will possess their land; I will give it to you as an inheritance, a land flowing with milk and honey."[y] I am the LORD your God, who has set you apart from the nations.[z]

25" 'You must therefore make a distinction between clean and unclean animals and between unclean and clean birds.[a] Do not defile yourselves by any animal or bird or anything that moves along the ground—those which I have set apart as unclean for you. 26You are to be holy to me[c] because I, the LORD, am holy,[b] and I have set you apart from the nations to be my own.

27" 'A man or woman who is a medium or spiritist among you must be put to death.[c] You are to stone them; their blood will be on their own heads.' "

20:8 f Ex 31:13
20:9 g Dt 27:16 h Ex 21:17 Mt 15:4* Mk 7:10* i ver 11 2Sa 1:16
20:10 j Ex 20:14 Dt 5:18 Dt 22:22
20:11 k Lev 18:7 Dt 27:23
20:12 l Lev 18:15
20:13 m Lev 18:22
20:14 n Lev 18:17 o Dt 27:23
20:15 p Lev 18:23
20:17 q Lev 18:9
20:18 r Lev 15:24 Lev 18:19
20:19 s Lev 18:12-13
20:20 t Lev 18:14
20:21 u Lev 18:16
20:22 v Lev 18:25-28
20:23 w Lev 18:3 x Lev 18:24,27, 30
20:24 y Ex 3:8 Ex 13:5 Ex 33:3 z Ex 33:16
20:25 a Lev 11:1-47 Dt 14:3-21
20:26 b Lev 19:2
20:27 c Lev 19:31

b8 Or *who sanctifies you*; or *who sets you apart as holy* c26 Or *be my holy ones*

Rules for Priests

21 The LORD said to Moses, "Speak to the priests, the sons of Aaron, and say to them: 'A priest must not make himself ceremonially unclean for any of his people who die,[a] 2except for a close relative, such as his mother or father, his son or daughter, his brother, 3or an unmarried sister who is dependent on him since she has no husband—for her he may make himself unclean. 4He must not make himself unclean for people related to him by marriage,[a] and so defile himself.

5" 'Priests must not shave their heads or shave off the edges of their beards[b] or cut their bodies.[c] 6They must be holy to their God and must not profane the name of their God.[d] Because they present the offerings made to the LORD by fire,[e] the food of their God, they are to be holy.

7" 'They must not marry women defiled by prostitution or divorced from their husbands,[f] because priests are holy to their God.[g] 8Regard them as holy,[h] because they offer up the food of your God. Consider them holy, because I the LORD am holy—I who make you holy.[b]

9" 'If a priest's daughter defiles herself by becoming a prostitute, she disgraces her father; she must be burned in the fire.[i]

10" 'The high priest, the one among his brothers who has had the anointing oil poured on his head and who has been ordained to wear the priestly garments,[j] must not let his hair become unkempt[c] or tear his clothes.[k] 11He must not enter a place where there is a dead body.[l] He must not make himself unclean,[m] even for his father or mother, 12nor leave the sanctuary of his God or desecrate it, because he has been dedicated by the anointing oil[n] of his God. I am the LORD.

13" 'The woman he marries must be a virgin.[o] 14He must not marry a widow, a divorced woman, or a woman defiled by prostitution, but only a virgin from his own people, 15so that he will not defile his offspring among his people. I am the LORD, who makes him holy.' "[d]

16The LORD said to Moses, 17"Say to Aaron: 'For the generations to come none of your descendants who has a defect may come near to offer the food of his God.[p] 18No man who has any defect[q] may come near: no man who is blind or lame, disfigured or deformed; 19no man with a crippled foot or hand, 20or who is hunchbacked or dwarfed, or who has any eye defect, or who has festering or running sores or damaged testicles.[r] 21No descendant of Aaron the priest who has any defect is to come near to present the offerings made to the LORD by fire. He has a defect; he must not come near to offer the food of his God. 22He may eat the most holy food of his God,[s] as well as the holy food; 23yet because of his defect, he must not go near the curtain or approach the altar, and so desecrate my sanctuary. I am the LORD, who makes them holy.' "[e]

24So Moses told this to Aaron and his sons and to all the Israelites.

22 The LORD said to Moses, 2"Tell Aaron and his sons to treat with respect the sacred offerings the Israelites consecrate to me, so that they will not profane my holy name. I am the LORD.

3"Say to them: 'For the generations to come, if any of your descendants is ceremonially unclean and yet comes near the sacred

21:1 *a* Eze 44:25
21:5 *b* Eze 44:20 *c* Lev 19:28 Dt 14:1
21:6 *d* Lev 18:21 *e* Lev 3:11
21:7 *f* ver 13,14 *g* Eze 44:22
21:8 *h* ver 6
21:9 *i* Ge 38:24 Lev 19:29
21:10 *j* Lev 16:32 *k* Lev 10:6
21:11 *l* Nu 19:11,13,14 *m* Lev 19:28
21:12 *n* Ex 29:6-7 Lev 10:7
21:13 *o* Eze 44:22
21:17 *p* ver 6
21:18 *q* Lev 22:19-25
21:20 *r* Dt 23:1 Isa 56:3
21:22 *s* 1Co 9:13

a4 Or *unclean as a leader among his people*
b8 Or *who sanctify you*; or *who set you apart as holy* c10 Or *not uncover his head*
d15 Or *who sanctifies him*; or *who sets him apart as holy* e23 Or *who sanctifies them*; or *who sets them apart as holy*

offerings that the Israelites consecrate to the LORD, that person must be cut off from my presence.[a] I am the LORD.

4“ ‘If a descendant of Aaron has an infectious skin disease[a] or a bodily discharge,[b] he may not eat the sacred offerings until he is cleansed. He will also be unclean if he touches something defiled by a corpse[c] or by anyone who has an emission of semen, 5or if he touches any crawling thing[d] that makes him unclean, or any person[e] who makes him unclean, whatever the uncleanness may be. 6The one who touches any such thing will be unclean till evening. He must not eat any of the sacred offerings unless he has bathed himself with water. 7When the sun goes down, he will be clean, and after that he may eat the sacred offerings, for they are his food.[f] 8He must not eat anything found dead[g] or torn by wild animals,[h] and so become unclean[i] through it. I am the LORD.

9“ ‘The priests are to keep my requirements so that they do not become guilty and die[j] for treating them with contempt. I am the LORD, who makes them holy.[b]

10“ ‘No-one outside a priest’s family may eat the sacred offering, nor may the guest of a priest or his hired worker eat it. 11But if a priest buys a slave with money, or if a slave is born in his household, that slave may eat his food.[k] 12If a priest’s daughter marries anyone other than a priest, she may not eat any of the sacred contributions. 13But if a priest’s daughter becomes a widow or is divorced, yet has no children, and she returns to live in her father’s house as in her youth, she may eat of her father’s food. No unauthorised person, however, may eat any of it.

14“ ‘If anyone eats a sacred offering by mistake, he must make restitution to the priest for the offering and add a fifth of the value[l] to it. 15The priests must not desecrate the sacred offerings the Israelites present to the LORD[m] 16by allowing them to eat the sacred offerings and so bring upon them guilt requiring payment.[n] I am the LORD, who makes them holy.’ ”

Unacceptable Sacrifices

17The LORD said to Moses, 18“Speak to Aaron and his sons and to all the Israelites and say to them: ‘If any of you—either an Israelite or an alien living in Israel—presents a gift[o] for a burnt offering to the LORD, either to fulfil a vow or as a freewill offering, 19you must present a male without defect[p] from the cattle, sheep or goats in order that it may be accepted on your behalf. 20Do not bring anything with a defect,[q] because it will not be accepted on your behalf. 21When anyone brings from the herd or flock a fellowship offering[c][r] to the LORD to fulfil a special vow or as a freewill offering, it must be without defect or blemish to be acceptable. 22Do not offer to the LORD the blind, the injured or the maimed, or anything with warts or festering or running sores. Do not place any of these on the altar as an offering made to the LORD by fire. 23You may, however, present as a freewill offering an ox[d] or a sheep that is deformed or stunted, but it will not be accepted in fulfilment of a vow. 24You must not offer to the LORD an animal whose testicles are bruised, crushed, torn or cut.[s] You must not do this in your own land, 25and you must not accept such animals from the hand of a foreigner and offer them as the food of your God.[t] They will not be accepted on your behalf, because they are deformed and have defects.’ ”

22:3 *a* Lev 7:20,21; Nu 19:13
22:4 *b* Lev 14:1-32; Lev 15:2-15 *c* Lev 11:24-28, 39
22:5 *d* Lev 11:24-28, 43 *e* Lev 15:7
22:7 *f* Nu 18:11
22:8 *g* Lev 11:39 *h* Ex 22:31; Lev 17:15 *i* Lev 11:40
22:9 *j* ver 16; Ex 28:43
22:11 *k* Ge 17:13; Ex 12:44
22:14 *l* Lev 5:15
22:15 *m* Nu 18:32
22:16 *n* ver 9
22:18 *o* Lev 1:2
22:19 *p* Lev 1:3
22:20 *q* Dt 15:21; Dt 17:1; Mal 1:8,14; Heb 9:14; 1Pe 1:19
22:21 *r* Lev 3:6; Nu 15:3,8
22:24 *s* Lev 21:20
22:25 *t* Lev 21:6

a4 Traditionally *leprosy*; the Hebrew word was used for various diseases affecting the skin—not necessarily leprosy. b9 Or *who sanctifies them*; or *who sets them apart as holy*; also in verse 16 c21 Traditionally *peace offering* d23 The Hebrew word can include both male and female.

26 The LORD said to Moses,
27 "When a calf, a lamb or a goat is
born, it is to remain with its mother
for seven days.[u] From the eighth
day on, it will be acceptable as an
offering made to the LORD by fire.
28 Do not slaughter a cow or a sheep
and its young on the same day.[v]
29 "When you sacrifice a thank-
offering[w] to the LORD, sacrifice it
in such a way that it will be accepted on your behalf. 30 It must be
eaten that same day; leave none of
it till morning.[x] I am the LORD.
31 "Keep[y] my commands and follow them. I am the LORD. 32 Do not
profane my holy name.[z] I must
be acknowledged as holy by the
Israelites.[a] I am the LORD, who
makes[e] you holy[f] 33 and who
brought you out of Egypt to be your
God.[b] I am the LORD."

23 The LORD said to Moses,
2 "Speak to the Israelites
and say to them: 'These are my appointed feasts,[a] the appointed
feasts of the LORD, which you are to
proclaim as sacred assemblies.[b]

The Sabbath

3 " 'There are six days when you
may work,[c] but the seventh day is
a Sabbath of rest,[d] a day of sacred
assembly. You are not to do any
work; wherever you live, it is a Sabbath to the LORD.

The Passover and Unleavened Bread

23:4-8pp Ex 12:14-20; Nu 28:16-25; Dt 16:1-8

4 " 'These are the LORD's appointed feasts, the sacred assemblies you are to proclaim at their
appointed times: 5 The LORD's Passover begins at twilight on the fourteenth day of the first month.[e] 6 On
the fifteenth day of that month the
LORD's Feast of Unleavened Bread
begins; for seven days you must eat
bread made without yeast. 7 On the
first day hold a sacred assembly[f]
and do no regular work. 8 For seven
days present an offering made to
the LORD by fire. And on the seventh day hold a sacred assembly
and do no regular work.' "

Firstfruits

9 The LORD said to Moses,
10 "Speak to the Israelites and say to
them: 'When you enter the land I
am going to give you and you reap
its harvest, bring to the priest a
sheaf[g] of the first grain you harvest. 11 He is to wave the sheaf before the LORD[h] so it will be
accepted on your behalf; the priest
is to wave it on the day after the
Sabbath. 12 On the day you wave the
sheaf, you must sacrifice as a burnt
offering to the LORD a lamb a year
old without defect, 13 together with
its grain offering[i] of two-tenths of
an ephah[a] of fine flour mixed with
oil—an offering made to the LORD
by fire, a pleasing aroma—and its
drink offering of a quarter of a
hin[b] of wine. 14 You must not eat
any bread, or roasted or new grain,
until the very day you bring this offering to your God.[j] This is to be a
lasting ordinance for the generations to come,[k] wherever you live.

Feast of Weeks

23:15-22pp Nu 28:26-31; Dt 16:9-12

15 " 'From the day after the Sabbath, the day you brought the sheaf
of the wave offering, count off
seven full weeks. 16 Count off fifty
days up to the day after the seventh
Sabbath,[l] and then present an offering of new grain to the LORD.
17 From wherever you live, bring
two loaves made of two-tenths of an
ephah of fine flour, baked with
yeast, as a wave offering of firstfruits[m] to the LORD. 18 Present with
this bread seven male lambs, each
a year old and without defect, one
young bull and two rams. They will

22:27 u Ex 22:30
22:28 v Dt 22:6,7
22:29 w Lev 7:12; Ps 107:22
22:30 x Lev 7:15
22:31 y Dt 4:2,40; Ps 105:45
22:32 z Lev 18:21; a Lev 10:3
22:33 b Lev 11:45
23:2 a ver 4,37,44; Nu 29:39; b ver 21,27
23:3 c Ex 20:9; d Ex 20:10; Ex 31:13-17; Lev 19:3; Dt 5:13; Heb 4:9,10
23:5 e Ex 12:18-19; Nu 28:16-17; Dt 16:1-8
23:7 f ver 3,8
23:10 g Ex 23:16,19; Ex 34:26
23:11 h Ex 29:24
23:13 i Lev 2:14-16; Lev 6:20
23:14 j Ex 34:26; k Nu 15:21
23:16 l Nu 28:26; Ac 2:1
23:17 m Ex 34:22; Lev 2:12

e 32 Or *made* f 32 Or *who sanctifies you*; or *who sets you apart as holy* a 13 That is, probably about 7½ pints (about 4.5 litres); also in verse 17 b 13 That is, probably about 1½ pints (about 1 litre)

be a burnt offering to the LORD, together with their grain offerings and drink offerings—an offering made by fire, an aroma pleasing to the LORD. 19Then sacrifice one male goat for a sin offering and two lambs, each a year old, for a fellowship offering.[c] 20The priest is to wave the two lambs before the LORD as a wave offering, together with the bread of the firstfruits. They are a sacred offering to the LORD for the priest. 21On that same day you are to proclaim a sacred assembly[n] and do no regular work.[o] This is to be a lasting ordinance for the generations to come, wherever you live.

22" 'When you reap the harvest[p] of your land, do not reap to the very edges of your field or gather the gleanings of your harvest.[q] Leave them for the poor and the alien. I am the LORD your God.' "

Feast of Trumpets

23:23–25pp Nu 29:1–6

23The LORD said to Moses, 24"Say to the Israelites: 'On the first day of the seventh month you are to have a day of rest, a sacred assembly commemorated with trumpet blasts.[r] 25Do no regular work,[s] but present an offering made to the LORD by fire.' "

Day of Atonement

23:26–32pp Lev 16:2–34; Nu 29:7–11

26The LORD said to Moses, 27"The tenth day of this seventh month[t] is the Day of Atonement.[u] Hold a sacred assembly[v] and deny yourselves,[d] and present an offering made to the LORD by fire. 28Do no work on that day, because it is the Day of Atonement, when atonement is made for you before the LORD your God. 29Anyone who does not deny himself on that day must be cut off from his people.[w] 30I will destroy from among his people[x] anyone who does any work on that day. 31You shall do no work at all. This is to be a lasting ordinance for the generations to come, wherever you live. 32It is a sabbath of rest for you, and you must deny yourselves. From the evening of the ninth day of the month until the following evening you are to observe your sabbath."

Feast of Tabernacles

23:33–43pp Nu 29:12–39; Dt 16:13–17

33The LORD said to Moses, 34"Say to the Israelites: 'On the fifteenth day of the seventh month the LORD's Feast of Tabernacles[y] begins, and it lasts for seven days. 35The first day is a sacred assembly; do no regular work. 36For seven days present offerings made to the LORD by fire, and on the eighth day hold a sacred assembly[z] and present an offering made to the LORD by fire. It is the closing assembly; do no regular work.

37(" 'These are the LORD's appointed feasts, which you are to proclaim as sacred assemblies for bringing offerings made to the LORD by fire—the burnt offerings and grain offerings, sacrifices and drink offerings[a] required for each day. 38These offerings are in addition to those for the LORD's Sabbaths[b] and[e] in addition to your gifts and whatever you have vowed and all the freewill offerings you give to the LORD.)

39" 'So beginning with the fifteenth day of the seventh month, after you have gathered the crops of the land, celebrate the festival to the LORD for seven days;[c] the first day is a day of rest, and the eighth day also is a day of rest. 40On the first day you are to take choice fruit from the trees, and palm fronds, leafy branches and poplars,[d] and rejoice before the LORD

23:21 n ver 2 o ver 3
23:22 p Lev 19:9 q Lev 19:10; Dt 24:19-21; Ru 2:15
23:24 r Lev 25:9; Nu 10:9,10; Nu 29:1
23:25 s ver 21
23:27 t Lev 16:29 u Ex 30:10 v Nu 29:7
23:29 w Ge 17:14; Nu 5:2
23:30 x Lev 20:3
23:34 y Ex 23:16; Dt 16:13; Ezr 3:4; Ne 8:14; Zec 14:16; Jn 7:2
23:36 z 2Ch 7:9; Ne 8:18; Jn 7:37
23:37 a ver 2,4
23:38 b Eze 45:17
23:39 c Ex 23:16; Dt 16:13
23:40 d Ne 8:14-17

c19 Traditionally *peace offering* d27 Or *and fast*; also in verses 29 and 32 e38 Or *These feasts are in addition to the LORD's Sabbaths, and these offerings are*

your God for seven days. 41Celebrate this as a festival to the LORD for seven days each year. This is to be a lasting ordinance for the generations to come; celebrate it in the seventh month. 42Live in booths[e] for seven days: All native-born Israelites are to live in booths 43so that your descendants will know[f] that I made the Israelites live in booths when I brought them out of Egypt. I am the LORD your God.' "

44So Moses announced to the Israelites the appointed feasts of the LORD.

Oil and Bread Set Before the LORD

24:1-3pp Ex 27:20-21

24 The LORD said to Moses, 2"Command the Israelites to bring you clear oil of pressed olives for the light so that the lamps may be kept burning continually. 3Outside the curtain of the Testimony in the Tent of Meeting, Aaron is to tend the lamps before the LORD from evening till morning, continually. This is to be a lasting ordinance for the generations to come. 4The lamps on the pure gold lampstand[a] before the LORD must be tended continually.

5"Take fine flour and bake twelve loaves of bread,[b] using two-tenths of an ephah[a] for each loaf. 6Set them in two rows, six in each row, on the table of pure gold[c] before the LORD. 7Along each row put some pure incense as a memorial portion[d] to represent the bread and to be an offering made to the LORD by fire. 8This bread is to be set out before the LORD regularly,[e] Sabbath after Sabbath,[f] on behalf of the Israelites, as a lasting covenant. 9It belongs to Aaron and his sons,[g] who are to eat it in a holy place, because it is a most holy part of their regular share of the offerings made to the LORD by fire."

23:42 *e* Ne 8:14-16
23:43 *f* Dt 31:13; Ps 78:5
24:4 *a* Ex 25:31; Ex 31:8
24:5 *b* Ex 25:30
24:6 *c* Ex 25:23-30; 1Ki 7:48
24:7 *d* Lev 2:2
24:8 *e* Nu 4:7; 1Ch 9:32; 2Ch 2:4; *f* Mt 12:5
24:9 *g* Lev 8:31; Mt 12:4; Mk 2:26; Lk 6:4
24:11 *h* Ex 3:15
24:12 *i* Ex 18:16; Nu 15:34
24:14 *j* Lev 20:27; Dt 13:9; Dt 17:5,7; Dt 21:21
24:15 *k* Ex 22:28
24:16 *l* 1Ki 21:10,13; Mt 26:66
24:17 *m* Ge 9:6; Ex 21:12; Nu 35:30-31; Dt 27:24
24:18 *n* ver 21
24:20 *o* Ex 21:24; Mt 5:38*
24:21 *p* ver 17
24:22 *q* Ex 12:49; *r* Nu 9:14; Nu 15:16

A Blasphemer Stoned

10Now the son of an Israelite mother and an Egyptian father went out among the Israelites, and a fight broke out in the camp between him and an Israelite. 11The son of the Israelite woman blasphemed the Name[h] with a curse; so they brought him to Moses. (His mother's name was Shelomith, the daughter of Dibri the Danite.) 12They put him in custody until the will of the LORD should be made clear to them.[i]

13Then the LORD said to Moses: 14"Take the blasphemer outside the camp. All those who heard him are to lay their hands on his head, and the entire assembly is to stone him.[j] 15Say to the Israelites: 'If anyone curses his God,[k] he will be held responsible; 16anyone who blasphemes the name of the LORD must be put to death.[l] The entire assembly must stone him. Whether an alien or native-born, when he blasphemes the Name, he must be put to death.

17" 'If anyone takes the life of a human being, he must be put to death.[m] 18Anyone who takes the life of someone's animal must make restitution[n]—life for life. 19If anyone injures his neighbour, whatever he has done must be done to him: 20fracture for fracture, eye for eye, tooth for tooth.[o] As he has injured the other, so he is to be injured. 21Whoever kills an animal must make restitution, but whoever kills a man must be put to death.[p] 22You are to have the same law for the alien[q] and the native-born.[r] I am the LORD your God.' "

23Then Moses spoke to the Israelites, and they took the blasphemer outside the camp and stoned him. The Israelites did as the LORD commanded Moses.

[a]5 That is, probably about 7½ pints (about 4.5 litres)

The Sabbath Year

25 The LORD said to Moses on Mount Sinai, 2"Speak to the Israelites and say to them: 'When you enter the land I am going to give you, the land itself must observe a sabbath to the LORD. 3For six years sow your fields, and for six years prune your vineyards and gather their crops.[a] 4But in the seventh year the land is to have a sabbath of rest, a sabbath to the LORD. Do not sow your fields or prune your vineyards. 5Do not reap what grows of itself or harvest the grapes of your untended vines. The land is to have a year of rest. 6Whatever the land yields during the sabbath year[b] will be food for you—for yourself, your manservant and maidservant, and the hired worker and temporary resident who live among you, 7as well as for your livestock and the wild animals in your land. Whatever the land produces may be eaten.

The Year of Jubilee

25:8–38Ref Dt 15:1–11
25:39–55Ref Ex 21:2–11; Dt 15:12–18

8" 'Count off seven sabbaths of years—seven times seven years—so that the seven sabbaths of years amount to a period of forty-nine years. 9Then have the trumpet[c] sounded everywhere on the tenth day of the seventh month; on the Day of Atonement sound the trumpet throughout your land. 10Consecrate the fiftieth year and proclaim liberty[d] throughout the land to all its inhabitants. It shall be a jubilee[e] for you; each one of you is to return to his family property and each to his own clan. 11The fiftieth year shall be a jubilee for you; do not sow and do not reap what grows of itself or harvest the untended vines. 12For it is a jubilee and is to be holy for you; eat only what is taken directly from the fields.

13" 'In this Year of Jubilee[f] everyone is to return to his own property.

14" 'If you sell land to one of your countrymen or buy any from him, do not take advantage of each other.[g] 15You are to buy from your countryman on the basis of the number of years[h] since the Jubilee. And he is to sell to you on the basis of the number of years left for harvesting crops. 16When the years are many, you are to increase the price, and when the years are few, you are to decrease the price,[i] because what he is really selling you is the number of crops. 17Do not take advantage of each other,[j] but fear your God.[k] I am the LORD your God.[l]

18" 'Follow my decrees and be careful to obey my laws, and you will live safely in the land.[m] 19Then the land will yield its fruit,[n] and you will eat your fill and live there in safety. 20You may ask, "What will we eat in the seventh year[o] if we do not plant or harvest our crops?" 21I will send you such a blessing[p] in the sixth year that the land will yield enough for three years. 22While you plant during the eighth year, you will eat from the old crop and will continue to eat from it until the harvest of the ninth year comes in.[q]

23" 'The land must not be sold permanently, because the land is mine[r] and you are but aliens[s] and my tenants. 24Throughout the country that you hold as a possession, you must provide for the redemption[t] of the land.

25" 'If one of your countrymen becomes poor and sells some of his property, his nearest relative[u] is to come and redeem[v] what his countryman has sold. 26If, however, a man has no-one to redeem it for him but he himself prospers and acquires sufficient means to redeem it, 27he is to determine the value for the years since he sold it and refund the balance to the man to whom he sold it; he can then go

25:3 *a* Ex 23:10
25:6 *b* ver 20
25:9 *c* Lev 23:24
25:10 *d* Isa 61:1; Jer 34:8,15,17; Lk 4:19 *e* Nu 36:4
25:13 *f* ver 10
25:14 *g* Lev 19:13; 1Sa 12:3,4
25:15 *h* Lev 27:18,23
25:16 *i* ver 27,51,52
25:17 *j* Pr 22:22; Jer 7:5,6; 1Th 4:6 *k* Lev 19:14 *l* Lev 19:32
25:18 *m* Lev 26:4,5; Dt 12:10; Ps 4:8; Jer 23:6
25:19 *n* Lev 26:4
25:20 *o* ver 4
25:21 *p* Dt 28:8,12; Hag 2:19; Mal 3:10
25:22 *q* Lev 26:10
25:23 *r* Ex 19:5 *s* Ge 23:4; 1Ch 29:15; Ps 39:12; Heb 11:13; 1Pe 2:11
25:24 *t* ver 29,48; Ru 4:7
25:25 *u* Ru 2:20; Jer 32:7 *v* Lev 27:13,19,31; Ru 4:4

back to his own property. 28But if he does not acquire the means to repay him, what he sold will remain in the possession of the buyer until the Year of Jubilee. It will be returned in the Jubilee, and he can then go back to his property.[w]

29" 'If a man sells a house in a walled city, he retains the right of redemption a full year after its sale. During that time he may redeem it. 30If it is not redeemed before a full year has passed, the house in the walled city shall belong permanently to the buyer and his descendants. It is not to be returned in the Jubilee. 31But houses in villages without walls round them are to be considered as open country. They can be redeemed, and they are to be returned in the Jubilee.

32" 'The Levites always have the right to redeem their houses in the Levitical towns,[x] which they possess. 33So the property of the Levites is redeemable—that is, a house sold in any town they hold—and is to be returned in the Jubilee, because the houses in the towns of the Levites are their property among the Israelites. 34But the pasture-land belonging to their towns must not be sold; it is their permanent possession.[y]

35" 'If one of your countrymen becomes poor[z] and is unable to support himself among you, help him[a] as you would an alien or a temporary resident, so that he can continue to live among you. 36Do not take interest[b] of any kind[a] from him, but fear your God, so that your countryman may continue to live among you. 37You must not lend him money at interest or sell him food at a profit. 38I am the LORD your God, who brought you out of Egypt to give you the land of Canaan and to be your God.[c]

39" 'If one of your countrymen becomes poor among you and sells himself to you, do not make him work as a slave.[d] 40He is to be treated as a hired worker or a temporary resident among you; he is to work for you until the Year of Jubilee. 41Then he and his children are to be released, and he will go back to his own clan and to the property[e] of his forefathers. 42Because the Israelites are my servants, whom I brought out of Egypt, they must not be sold as slaves. 43Do not rule over them ruthlessly,[f] but fear your God.

44" 'Your male and female slaves are to come from the nations around you; from them you may buy slaves. 45You may also buy some of the temporary residents living among you and members of their clans born in your country, and they will become your property. 46You can will them to your children as inherited property and can make them slaves for life, but you must not rule over your fellow Israelites ruthlessly.

47" 'If an alien or a temporary resident among you becomes rich and one of your countrymen becomes poor and sells himself to the alien living among you or to a member of the alien's clan, 48he retains the right of redemption after he has sold himself. One of his relatives[g] may redeem him: 49An uncle or a cousin or any blood-relative in his clan may redeem him. Or if he prospers,[h] he may redeem himself. 50He and his buyer are to count the time from the year he sold himself up to the Year of Jubilee. The price for his release is to be based on the rate paid to a hired man[i] for that number of years. 51If many years remain, he must pay for his redemption a larger share of the price paid for him. 52If only a few years remain until the Year of Jubilee, he is to compute that and pay for his redemption accordingly. 53He is to be treated as a man hired from year to year; you must

25:28 w ver 10
25:32 x Nu 35:1-8; Jos 21:2
25:34 y Nu 35:2-5
25:35 z Dt 24:14,15 a Dt 15:8; Ps 37:21,26; Lk 6:35
25:36 b Ex 22:25; Dt 23:19-20
25:38 c Ge 17:7; Lev 11:45
25:39 d Ex 21:2; Dt 15:12; 1Ki 9:22
25:41 e ver 28
25:43 f Ex 1:13; Eze 34:4; Col 4:1
25:48 g Ne 5:5
25:49 h ver 26
25:50 i Job 7:1; Isa 16:14; Isa 21:16

a36 Or *take excessive interest*; similarly in verse 37

see to it that his owner does not rule
over him ruthlessly.
54" 'Even if he is not redeemed in
any of these ways, he and his children are to be released in the Year
of Jubilee, 55for the Israelites belong to me as servants. They are
my servants, whom I brought out of
Egypt. I am the LORD your God.

Reward for Obedience

26 " 'Do not make idols[a] or set
up an image or a sacred
stone[b] for yourselves, and do not
place a carved stone[c] in your land
to bow down before it. I am the
LORD your God.
2" 'Observe my Sabbaths and
have reverence for my sanctuary.[d] I am the LORD.
3" 'If you follow my decrees and
are careful to obey[e] my commands, 4I will send you rain[f] in its
season, and the ground will yield its
crops and the trees of the field
their fruit.[g] 5Your threshing will
continue until grape harvest and
the grape harvest will continue
until planting, and you will eat all
the food you want[h] and live in
safety in your land.[i]
6" 'I will grant peace in the land,[j]
and you will lie down[k] and no-one
will make you afraid.[l] I will remove savage beasts[m] from the
land, and the sword will not pass
through your country. 7You will
pursue your enemies, and they will
fall by the sword before you. 8Five
of you will chase a hundred, and a
hundred of you will chase ten thousand, and your enemies will fall by
the sword before you.[n]
9" 'I will look on you with favour
and make you fruitful and increase
your numbers,[o] and I will keep my
covenant[p] with you. 10You will still
be eating last year's harvest when
you will have to move it out to make
room for the new.[q] 11I will put my
dwelling-place[a][r] among you, and
I will not abhor you. 12I will walk[s]
among you and be your God, and
you will be my people.[t] 13I am the
LORD your God, who brought you
out of Egypt so that you would no
longer be slaves to the Egyptians; I
broke the bars of your yoke[u] and
enabled you to walk with heads
held high.

Punishment for Disobedience

14" 'But if you will not listen to me
and carry out all these commands,[v] 15and if you reject my decrees and abhor my laws and fail to
carry out all my commands and so
violate my covenant, 16then I will
do this to you: I will bring upon you
sudden terror, wasting diseases
and fever[w] that will destroy your
sight and drain away your life.[x]
You will plant seed in vain, because
your enemies will eat it.[y] 17I will
set my face[z] against you so that
you will be defeated by your enemies; those who hate you will rule
over you,[a] and you will flee even
when no-one is pursuing you.[b]
18" 'If after all this you will not
listen to me, I will punish you for
your sins seven times over.[c] 19I
will break down your stubborn
pride[d] and make the sky above you
like iron and the ground beneath
you like bronze.[e] 20Your strength
will be spent in vain,[f] because
your soil will not yield its crops,
nor will the trees of the land yield
their fruit.[g]
21" 'If you remain hostile towards
me and refuse to listen to me, I will
multiply your afflictions seven
times over,[h] as your sins deserve.
22I will send wild animals[i] against
you, and they will rob you of your
children, destroy your cattle and
make you so few in number that
your roads will be deserted.
23" 'If in spite of these things you
do not accept my correction[j] but
continue to be hostile towards me,
24I myself will be hostile towards
you and will afflict you for your

26:1 a Ex 20:4; Lev 19:4; Dt 5:8 b Ex 23:24 c Nu 33:52
26:2 d Lev 19:30
26:3 e Dt 7:12; Dt 11:13,22; Dt 28:1,9
26:4 f Dt 11:14 g Ps 67:6
26:5 h Dt 11:15; Joel 2:19,26; Am 9:13 i Lev 25:18
26:6 j Ps 29:11; Ps 85:8; Ps 147:14 k Ps 4:8 l Zep 3:13 m ver 22
26:8 n Dt 32:30; Jos 23:10
26:9 o Ge 17:6; Ne 9:23 p Ge 17:7
26:10 q Lev 25:22
26:11 r Ex 25:8; Ps 76:2; Eze 37:27
26:12 s Ge 3:8 t 2Co 6:16*
26:13 u Eze 34:27
26:14 v Dt 28:15-68; Mal 2:2
26:16 w Dt 28:22,35 x 1Sa 2:33 y Job 31:8
26:17 z Lev 17:10 a Ps 106:41 b ver 36,37; Dt 28:7,25; Ps 53:5
26:18 c ver 21
26:19 d Isa 25:11 e Dt 28:23
26:20 f Ps 127:1; Isa 17:11 g Dt 11:17
26:21 h ver 18
26:22 i Dt 32:24
26:23 j Jer 2:30; Jer 5:3

a11 Or *my tabernacle*

sins seven times over. 25And I will
bring the sword upon you to avenge
the breaking of the covenant. When
you withdraw into your cities, I will
send a plague[k] among you, and you
will be given into enemy hands.
26When I cut off your supply of
bread,[l] ten women will be able to
bake your bread in one oven, and
they will dole out the bread by
weight. You will eat, but you will
not be satisfied.
27" 'If in spite of this you still do
not listen to me but continue to be
hostile towards me, 28then in my
anger I will be hostile towards you,
and I myself will punish you for
your sins seven times over. 29You
will eat the flesh of your sons and
the flesh of your daughters.[m] 30I
will destroy your high places,[n] cut
down your incense altars[o] and pile
your dead bodies on the lifeless
forms of your idols,[p] and I will abhor you. 31I will turn your cities
into ruins and lay waste your sanctuaries,[q] and I will take no delight
in the pleasing aroma of your offerings. 32I will lay waste the land,[r] so
that your enemies who live there
will be appalled. 33I will scatter you
among the nations[s] and will draw
out my sword and pursue you. Your
land will be laid waste, and your
cities will lie in ruins. 34Then the
land will enjoy its sabbath years all
the time that it lies desolate and
you are in the country of your enemies;[t] then the land will rest and
enjoy its sabbaths. 35All the time
that it lies desolate, the land will
have the rest it did not have during
the sabbaths you lived in it.
36" 'As for those of you who are
left, I will make their hearts so
fearful in the lands of their enemies that the sound of a wind-blown
leaf will put them to flight.[u] They
will run as though fleeing from the
sword, and they will fall, even
though no-one is pursuing them.
37They will stumble over one another as though fleeing from the

26:25 k Nu 14:12; Eze 5:17
26:26 l Ps 105:16; Isa 3:1; Mic 6:14
26:29 m Dt 28:53
26:30 n 2Ch 34:3; Eze 6:3 o Eze 6:6 p Eze 6:13
26:31 q Ps 74:3-7
26:32 r Jer 9:11
26:33 s Dt 4:27; Eze 12:15; Eze 20:23; Zec 7:14
26:34 t ver 43; 2Ch 36:21
26:36 u Eze 21:7
26:37 v Jos 7:12
26:38 w Dt 4:26
26:39 x Eze 4:17
26:40 y Jer 3:12-15; Lk 15:18; 1Jn 1:9
26:41 z Eze 44:7,9; Ac 7:51
26:42 a Ge 22:15-18; Ge 28:15 b Ge 26:5
26:44 c Ro 11:2 d Dt 4:31; Jer 30:11 e Jer 33:26
26:45 f Ge 17:7 g Ex 6:8; Lev 25:38
26:46 h Lev 7:38; Lev 27:34
27:2 a Nu 6:2

sword, even though no-one is pursuing them. So you will not be able
to stand before your enemies.[v]
38You will perish among the nations; the land of your enemies will
devour you.[w] 39Those of you who
are left will waste away in the lands
of their enemies because of their
sins; also because of their fathers'
sins they will waste away.[x]
40" 'But if they will confess their
sins and the sins of their fathers[y]—their treachery against
me and their hostility towards me,
41which made me hostile towards
them so that I sent them into the
land of their enemies—then when
their uncircumcised hearts[z] are
humbled and they pay for their sin,
42I will remember my covenant
with Jacob[a] and my covenant with
Isaac[b] and my covenant with
Abraham, and I will remember the
land. 43For the land will be deserted
by them and will enjoy its sabbaths
while it lies desolate without them.
They will pay for their sins because
they rejected my laws and abhorred my decrees. 44Yet in spite of
this, when they are in the land of
their enemies, I will not reject
them or abhor[c] them so as to destroy them completely,[d] breaking
my covenant[e] with them. I am the
LORD their God. 45But for their sake
I will remember[f] the covenant
with their ancestors whom I
brought out of Egypt[g] in the sight
of the nations to be their God. I am
the LORD.' "
46These are the decrees, the laws
and the regulations that the LORD
established on Mount Sinai between himself and the Israelites
through Moses.[h]

Redeeming What Is the LORD's

27 The LORD said to Moses,
2"Speak to the Israelites
and say to them: 'If anyone makes
a special vow[a] to dedicate persons
to the LORD by giving equivalent
values, 3set the value of a male

between the ages of twenty and
sixty at fifty shekels[a] of silver, according to the sanctuary shekel;[b] [b]
4and if it is a female, set her value
at thirty shekels.[c] 5If it is a person
between the ages of five and
twenty, set the value of a male at
twenty shekels[d] and of a female at
ten shekels.[e] 6If it is a person between one month and five years,
set the value of a male at five shekels[f] [c] of silver and that of a female
at three shekels[g] of silver. 7If it is
a person sixty years old or more,
set the value of a male at fifteen
shekels[h] and of a female at ten
shekels. 8If anyone making the vow
is too poor to pay[d] the specified
amount, he is to present the person
to the priest, who will set the value[e] for him according to what the
man making the vow can afford.
9" 'If what he vowed is an animal
that is acceptable as an offering to
the LORD, such an animal given to
the LORD becomes holy. 10He must
not exchange it or substitute a good
one for a bad one, or a bad one for
a good one;[f] if he should substitute
one animal for another, both it and
the substitute become holy. 11If
what he vowed is a ceremonially
unclean animal—one that is not acceptable as an offering to the
LORD—the animal must be presented to the priest, 12who will
judge its quality as good or bad.
Whatever value the priest then
sets, that is what it will be. 13If the
owner wishes to redeem[g] the animal, he must add a fifth to its
value.
14" 'If a man dedicates his house
as something holy to the LORD, the
priest will judge its quality as good
or bad. Whatever value the priest
then sets, so it will remain. 15If the
man who dedicates his house redeems it,[h] he must add a fifth to its
value, and the house will again become his.
16" 'If a man dedicates to the
LORD part of his family land, its
value is to be set according to the
amount of seed required for it—
fifty shekels of silver to a homer[i]
of barley seed. 17If he dedicates his
field during the Year of Jubilee, the
value that has been set remains.
18But if he dedicates his field after
the Jubilee, the priest will determine the value according to the
number of years that remain[i]
until the next Year of Jubilee, and
its set value will be reduced. 19If
the man who dedicates the field
wishes to redeem it, he must add a
fifth to its value, and the field will
again become his. 20If, however, he
does not redeem the field, or if he
has sold it to someone else, it can
never be redeemed. 21When the
field is released in the Jubilee,[j] it
will become holy, like a field devoted to the LORD;[k] it will become
the property of the priests.[j]
22" 'If a man dedicates to the
LORD a field he has bought, which is
not part of his family land, 23the
priest will determine its value up to
the Year of Jubilee, and the man
must pay its value on that day as
something holy to the LORD. 24In
the Year of Jubilee the field will revert to the person from whom he
bought it,[l] the one whose land it
was. 25Every value is to be set according to the sanctuary shekel,[m]
twenty gerahs[n] to the shekel.
26" 'No-one, however, may dedicate the firstborn of an animal,
since the firstborn already belongs
to the LORD;[o] whether an ox[k] or a
sheep, it is the LORD's. 27If it is one
of the unclean animals,[p] he may
buy it back at its set value, adding
a fifth of the value to it. If he does

27:3 *b* Ex 30:13 Nu 3:47 Nu 18:16
27:6 *c* Nu 18:16
27:8 *d* Lev 5:11 *e* ver 12,14
27:10 *f* ver 33
27:13 *g* ver 15,19 Lev 25:25
27:15 *h* ver 13,20
27:18 *i* Lev 25:15
27:21 *j* Lev 25:10 *k* ver 28 Nu 18:14 Eze 44:29
27:24 *l* Lev 25:28
27:25 *m* Ex 30:13 Nu 18:16 *n* Nu 3:47 Eze 45:12
27:26 *o* Ex 13:2,12
27:27 *p* ver 11

a3 That is, about 1¼ pounds (about 0.6 kilogram); also in verse 16 b3 That is, about ⅖ ounce (about 11.5 grams); also in verse 25 c4 That is, about 12 ounces (about 0.3 kilogram) d5 That is, about 8 ounces (about 0.2 kilogram) e5 That is, about 4 ounces (about 115 grams); also in verse 7 f6 That is, about 2 ounces (about 55 grams) g6 That is, about 1¼ ounces (about 35 grams) h7 That is, about 6 ounces (about 170 grams) i16 That is, probably about 6 bushels (about 220 litres) j21 Or *priest*
k26 The Hebrew word can include both male and female.

not redeem it, it is to be sold at its
set value.
28" 'But nothing that a man owns
and devotes[l][q] to the LORD—
whether man or animal or family
land—may be sold or redeemed;
everything so devoted is most holy
to the LORD.
29" 'No person devoted to destruction[m] may be ransomed; he
must be put to death.
30" 'A tithe[r] of everything from
the land, whether grain from the
soil or fruit from the trees, belongs
to the LORD; it is holy to the LORD.
31If a man redeems any of his tithe,
he must add a fifth of the value to
it. 32The entire tithe of the herd and
flock—every tenth animal that
passes under the shepherd's
rod[s]—will be holy to the LORD.
33He must not pick out the good
from the bad or make any substitu-
tion.[t] If he does make a substitu-
tion, both the animal and its
substitute become holy and cannot
be redeemed.' "

34These are the commands the
LORD gave Moses on Mount Sinai
for the Israelites.[u]

27:28 q Nu 18:14; Jos 6:17-19
27:30 r Ge 28:22; 2Ch 31:6; Mal 3:8
27:32 s Jer 33:13; Eze 20:37
27:33 t ver 10
27:34 u Lev 26:46; Dt 4:5

l28 The Hebrew term refers to the irrevocable giving over of things or persons to the LORD.
m29 The Hebrew term refers to the irrevocable giving over of things or persons to the LORD, often by totally destroying them.

NUMBERS

The Census

1 The LORD spoke to Moses in
the Tent of Meeting[a] in the
Desert of Sinai[b] on the first day of
the second month[c] of the second
year after the Israelites came out
of Egypt. He said: 2"Take a census[d] of the whole Israelite community by their clans and families,
listing every man by name, one by
one. 3You and Aaron are to number
by their divisions all the men in Israel twenty years old or more[e]
who are able to serve in the army.
4One man from each tribe, each the
head of his family,[f] is to help
you.[g] 5These are the names of the
men who are to assist you:

from Reuben,[h] Elizur son of Shedeur;
6from Simeon, Shelumiel son of Zurishaddai;
7from Judah,[i] Nahshon son of Amminadab;[j]
8from Issachar,[k] Nethanel son of Zuar;
9from Zebulun,[l] Eliab son of Helon;
10from the sons of Joseph:
from Ephraim,[m] Elishama son of Ammihud;
from Manasseh, Gamaliel son of Pedahzur;
11from Benjamin, Abidan son of Gideoni;
12from Dan,[n] Ahiezer son of Ammishaddai;
13from Asher,[o] Pagiel son of Ocran;
14from Gad, Eliasaph son of Deuel;[p]
15from Naphtali,[q] Ahira son of Enan."

16These were the men appointed
from the community, the leaders[r]
of their ancestral tribes. They
were the heads of the clans of
Israel.[s]
17Moses and Aaron took these
men whose names had been given,
18and they called the whole community together on the first day of the
second month.[t] The people indicated their ancestry[u] by their
clans and families, and the men
twenty years old or more were
listed by name, one by one, 19as the
LORD commanded Moses. And so
he counted them in the Desert of
Sinai:

20From the descendants of Reuben[v] the firstborn son of Israel:
All the men twenty years old or more who were able to serve in the army were listed by name, one by one, according to the records of their clans and families.
21The number from the tribe of Reuben was 46,500.

22From the descendants of Simeon:[w]
All the men twenty years old or more who were able to serve in the army were counted and listed by name, one by one, according to the records of their clans and
families. 23The number from the tribe of Simeon was 59,300.

24From the descendants of Gad:[x]
All the men twenty years old or more who were able to serve in the army were listed by name, according to the records of their clans and families.
25The number from the tribe of Gad was 45,650.

26From the descendants of Judah:[y]
All the men twenty years old

1:1 a Ex 40:2 b Ex 19:1 c Ex 40:17
1:2 d Ex 30:11-16 Nu 26:2
1:3 e Ex 30:14
1:4 f ver 16 g Ex 18:21 Dt 1:15
1:5 h Ge 29:32 Dt 33:6
1:7 i Ge 29:35 Ps 78:68 j Ru 4:20 Lk 3:32
1:8 k Ge 30:18
1:9 l ver 30
1:10 m ver 32
1:12 n ver 38
1:13 o ver 40
1:14 p Nu 2:14
1:15 q ver 42
1:16 r Ex 18:25 s ver 4 Ex 18:21 Nu 7:2
1:18 t ver 1 u Ezr 2:59 Heb 7:3
1:20 v Nu 26:5-11 Rev 7:5
1:22 w Nu 26:12-14 Rev 7:7
1:24 x Ge 30:11 Nu 26:15-18 Rev 7:5
1:26 y Ge 29:35 Nu 26:19-22 Mt 1:2 Rev 7:5

or more who were able to
serve in the army were
listed by name, according to
the records of their clans
and families. 27The number
from the tribe of Judah was
74,600.

28From the descendants of Issachar:[z]
All the men twenty years old
or more who were able to
serve in the army were
listed by name, according to
the records of their clans
and families. 29The number
from the tribe of Issachar
was 54,400.

30From the descendants of Zebulun:[a]
All the men twenty years old
or more who were able to
serve in the army were
listed by name, according to
the records of their clans
and families. 31The number
from the tribe of Zebulun
was 57,400.

32From the sons of Joseph:
From the descendants of Ephraim:[b]
All the men twenty years old
or more who were able to
serve in the army were
listed by name, according to
the records of their clans
and families. 33The number
from the tribe of Ephraim
was 40,500.

34From the descendants of Manasseh:[c]
All the men twenty years old
or more who were able to
serve in the army were
listed by name, according to
the records of their clans
and families. 35The number
from the tribe of Manasseh
was 32,200.

36From the descendants of Benjamin:[d]
All the men twenty years old
or more who were able to
serve in the army were
listed by name, according to
the records of their clans
and families. 37The number
from the tribe of Benjamin
was 35,400.

38From the descendants of Dan:[e]
All the men twenty years old
or more who were able to
serve in the army were
listed by name, according to
the records of their clans
and families. 39The number
from the tribe of Dan was
62,700.

40From the descendants of Asher:[f]
All the men twenty years old
or more who were able to
serve in the army were
listed by name, according to
the records of their clans
and families. 41The number
from the tribe of Asher was
41,500.

42From the descendants of Naphtali:[g]
All the men twenty years old
or more who were able to
serve in the army were
listed by name, according to
the records of their clans
and families. 43The number
from the tribe of Naphtali
was 53,400.

44These were the men counted by
Moses and Aaron[h] and the twelve
leaders of Israel, each one representing his family. 45All the Israelites twenty years old or more who
were able to serve in Israel's army
were counted according to their
families. 46The total number was
603,550.[i]

47The families of the tribe of
Levi,[j] however, were not
counted[k] along with the others.
48The LORD had said to Moses:
49"You must not count the tribe of
Levi or include them in the census
of the other Israelites. 50Instead,
appoint the Levites to be in charge

1:28
z Nu 26:23-25
Rev 7:7

1:30
a Nu 26:26-27
Rev 7:8

1:32
b Nu 26:35-37

1:34
c Nu 26:28-34
Rev 7:6

1:36
d Nu 26:38-41
2Ch 17:17
Rev 7:8

1:38
e Ge 30:6
Nu 26:42-43

1:40
f Nu 26:44-47
Rev 7:6

1:42
g Nu 26:48-50
Rev 7:6

1:44
h Nu 26:64

1:46
i Ex 12:37
Ex 38:26
Nu 2:32
Nu 26:51

1:47
j Nu 2:33
Nu 26:57
k Nu 4:3,49

of the tabernacle of the Testimony[l]—over all its furnishings and everything belonging to it. They are to carry the tabernacle and all its furnishings; they are to take care of it and encamp round it. 51Whenever the tabernacle is to move, the Levites are to take it down, and whenever the tabernacle is to be set up, the Levites shall do it.[m] Anyone else who goes near it shall be put to death. 52The Israelites are to set up their tents by divisions, each man in his own camp under his own standard.[n] 53The Levites, however, are to set up their tents round the tabernacle of the Testimony so that wrath will not fall[o] on the Israelite community. The Levites are to be responsible for the care of the tabernacle of the Testimony.[p]"

54The Israelites did all this just as the LORD commanded Moses.

The Arrangement of the Tribal Camps

2 The LORD said to Moses and Aaron: 2"The Israelites are to camp round the Tent of Meeting some distance from it, each man under his standard[a] with the banners of his family."

> 3On the east, towards the sunrise, the divisions of the camp of Judah are to encamp under their standard. The leader of the people of Judah is Nahshon son of Amminadab.[b] 4His division numbers 74,600.
>
> 5The tribe of Issachar will camp next to them. The leader of the people of Issachar is Nethanel son of Zuar.[c] 6His division numbers 54,400.
>
> 7The tribe of Zebulun will be next. The leader of the people of Zebulun is Eliab son of Helon.[d] 8His division numbers 57,400.
>
> 9All the men assigned to the camp of Judah, according to their divisions, number 186,400. They will set out first.[e]
>
> 10On the south will be the divisions of the camp of Reuben under their standard. The leader of the people of Reuben is Elizur son of Shedeur.[f] 11His division numbers 46,500.
>
> 12The tribe of Simeon will camp next to them. The leader of the people of Simeon is Shelumiel son of Zurishaddai.[g] 13His division numbers 59,300.
>
> 14The tribe of Gad will be next. The leader of the people of Gad is Eliasaph son of Deuel.[a][h] 15His division numbers 45,650.
>
> 16All the men assigned to the camp of Reuben,[i] according to their divisions, number 151,450. They will set out second.
>
> 17Then the Tent of Meeting and the camp of the Levites[j] will set out in the middle of the camps. They will set out in the same order as they encamp, each in his own place under his standard.
>
> 18On the west will be the divisions of the camp of Ephraim[k] under their standard. The leader of the people of Ephraim is Elishama son of Ammihud.[l] 19His division numbers 40,500.
>
> 20The tribe of Manasseh will be next to them. The leader of the people of Manasseh is Gamaliel son of Pedahzur.[m] 21His division numbers 32,200.
>
> 22The tribe of Benjamin will be next. The leader of the people of Benjamin is Abidan son of Gideoni.[n] 23His division numbers 35,400.
>
> 24All the men assigned to the

1:50 *l* Ex 38:21; Ac 7:44
1:51 *m* Nu 3:38; Nu 4:1-33
1:52 *n* Nu 2:2; Ps 20:5
1:53 *o* Lev 10:6; Nu 16:46; Nu 18:5; *p* Nu 18:2-4
2:2 *a* Nu 1:52; Ps 74:4; Isa 31:9
2:3 *b* Nu 10:14; Ru 4:20; 1Ch 2:10
2:5 *c* Nu 1:8
2:7 *d* Nu 1:9
2:9 *e* Nu 10:14
2:10 *f* Nu 1:5
2:12 *g* Nu 1:6
2:14 *h* Nu 1:14
2:16 *i* Nu 10:18
2:17 *j* Nu 1:53; Nu 10:21
2:18 *k* Ge 48:20; Jer 31:18-20; *l* Nu 1:10
2:20 *m* Nu 1:10
2:22 *n* Nu 1:11; Ps 68:27

a*14* Many manuscripts of the Masoretic Text, Samaritan Pentateuch and Vulgate (see also Num. 1:14); most manuscripts of the Masoretic Text *Reuel*

camp of Ephraim,[o] according
to their divisions, number
108,100. They will set out
third.[p]

25On the north will be the divisions of the camp of Dan, under their standard. The leader
of the people of Dan is Ahiezer
son of Ammishaddai.[q] 26His
division numbers 62,700.
27The tribe of Asher will
camp next to them. The leader
of the people of Asher is Pagiel
son of Ocran.[r] 28His division
numbers 41,500.
29The tribe of Naphtali will
be next. The leader of the people of Naphtali is Ahira son of
Enan.[s] 30His division numbers
53,400.
31All the men assigned to the
camp of Dan number 157,600.
They will set out last,[t] under
their standards.

32These are the Israelites,
counted according to their
families. All those in the
camps, by their divisions, number 603,550.[u] 33The Levites,
however, were not counted[v]
along with the other Israelites,
as the LORD commanded
Moses.

34So the Israelites did everything
the LORD commanded Moses; that
is the way they encamped under
their standards, and that is the way
they set out, each with his clan and
family.

The Levites

3 This is the account of the family of Aaron and Moses[a] at the
time the LORD talked with Moses on
Mount Sinai.
2The names of the sons of Aaron
were Nadab the firstborn and
Abihu, Eleazar and Ithamar.[b]
3Those were the names of Aaron's
sons, the anointed priests,[c] who
were ordained to serve as priests.
4Nadab and Abihu, however, fell
dead before the LORD[d] when they
made an offering with unauthorised fire before him in the Desert
of Sinai.[e] They had no sons; so only
Eleazar and Ithamar served as
priests during the lifetime of their
father Aaron.[f]
5The LORD said to Moses, 6"Bring
the tribe of Levi[g] and present
them to Aaron the priest to assist
him.[h] 7They are to perform duties
for him and for the whole community at the Tent of Meeting by doing the work[i] of the tabernacle.
8They are to take care of all the furnishings of the Tent of Meeting,
fulfilling the obligations of the Israelites by doing the work of the
tabernacle. 9Give the Levites to
Aaron and his sons;[j] they are the
Israelites who are to be given
wholly to him.[a] 10Appoint Aaron
and his sons to serve as priests;[k]
anyone else who approaches the
sanctuary must be put to death."[l]
11The LORD also said to Moses,
12"I have taken the Levites[m] from
among the Israelites in place of the
first male offspring[n] of every Israelite woman. The Levites are
mine,[o] 13for all the firstborn are
mine.[p] When I struck down all the
firstborn in Egypt, I set apart for
myself every firstborn in Israel,
whether man or animal. They are to
be mine. I am the LORD."
14The LORD said to Moses in the
Desert of Sinai, 15"Count[q] the Levites by their families and clans.
Count every male a month old or
more."[r] 16So Moses counted them,
as he was commanded by the word
of the LORD.
17These were the names of the
sons of Levi:[s]
Gershon, Kohath and Mer-
ari.[t]
18These were the names of the
Gershonite clans:
Libni and Shimei.[u]

2:24 o Nu 10:22 p Ps 80:2
2:25 q Nu 1:12
2:27 r Nu 1:13
2:29 s Nu 1:15
2:31 t Nu 10:25
2:32 u Ex 38:26 Nu 1:46
2:33 v Nu 1:47 Nu 26:57-62
3:1 a Ex 6:27
3:2 b Ex 6:23 Nu 26:60
3:3 c Ex 28:41
3:4 d Lev 10:2 e Lev 10:1 f 1Ch 24:1
3:6 g Dt 10:8 Dt 31:9 1Ch 15:2 h Nu 8:6-22 Nu 18:1-7 2Ch 29:11
3:7 i Lev 8:35 Nu 1:50
3:9 j Nu 8:19 Nu 18:6
3:10 k Ex 29:9 l Nu 1:51
3:12 m Mal 2:4 n ver 41 Nu 8:16,18 o Ex 13:2
3:13 p Ex 13:12
3:15 q ver 39 r Nu 26:62
3:17 s Ge 46:11 t Ex 6:16
3:18 u Ex 6:17

a9 Most manuscripts of the Masoretic Text; some manuscripts of the Masoretic Text, Samaritan Pentateuch and Septuagint (see also Num. 8:16) *to me*

19 The Kohathite clans:
Amram, Izhar, Hebron and Uzziel.[v]
20 The Merarite clans:[w]
Mahli and Mushi.[x]
These were the Levite clans, according to their families.

21 To Gershon belonged the clans of the Libnites and Shimeites;[y] these were the Gershonite clans.
22 The number of all the males a month old or more who were counted was 7,500.
23 The Gershonite clans were to camp on the west, behind the tabernacle.
24 The leader of the families of the Gershonites was Eliasaph son of Lael.
25 At the Tent of Meeting the Gershonites were responsible for the care of the tabernacle[z] and tent, its coverings,[a] the curtain at the entrance[b] to the Tent of Meeting,
26 the curtains of the courtyard[c], the curtain at the entrance to the courtyard surrounding the tabernacle and altar, and the ropes[d]—and everything related to their use.

27 To Kohath belonged the clans of the Amramites, Izharites, Hebronites and Uzzielites;[e] these were the Kohathite clans.
28 The number of all the males a month old or more was 8,600.[b] The Kohathites were responsible for the care of the sanctuary.
29 The Kohathite clans were to camp on the south side[f] of the tabernacle.
30 The leader of the families of the Kohathite clans was Elizaphan son of Uzziel.
31 They were responsible for the care of the ark,[g] the table,[h] the lampstand,[i] the altars,[j] the articles of the sanctuary used in ministering, the curtain,[k] and everything related to their use.[l]
32 The chief leader of the Levites was Eleazar son of Aaron, the priest. He was appointed over those who were responsible for the care of the sanctuary.

33 To Merari belonged the clans of the Mahlites and the Mushites;[m] these were the Merarite clans.
34 The number of all the males a month old or more who were counted was 6,200.
35 The leader of the families of the Merarite clans was Zuriel son of Abihail; they were to camp on the north side of the tabernacle.[n]
36 The Merarites were appointed[o] to take care of the frames of the tabernacle, its crossbars, posts, bases, all its equipment, and everything related to their use,
37 as well as the posts of the surrounding courtyard with their bases, tent pegs and ropes.

38 Moses and Aaron and his sons were to camp to the east[p] of the tabernacle, towards the sunrise, in front of the Tent of Meeting.[q] They were responsible for the care of the sanctuary[r] on behalf of the Israelites. Anyone else who approached the sanctuary was to be put to death.[s]

39 The total number of Levites counted at the LORD's command by Moses and Aaron according to their clans, including every male a month old or more, was 22,000.[t]

40 The LORD said to Moses, "Count all the firstborn Israelite males who are a month old or more[u] and make a list of their names.
41 Take the Levites for me in place of all the firstborn of the Israelites,[v] and the livestock of the Levites in place of all the firstborn of the livestock of the Israelites. I am the LORD."
42 So Moses counted all the firstborn of the Israelites, as the LORD commanded him.
43 The total number of firstborn males a month old or more, listed by name, was 22,273.[w]
44 The LORD also said to Moses,
45 "Take the Levites in place of all the firstborn of Israel, and the

3:19 v Ex 6:18
3:20 w Ge 46:11; x Ex 6:19
3:21 y Ex 6:17
3:25 z Ex 25:9; a Ex 26:14; b Ex 26:36; Nu 4:25
3:26 c Ex 27:9; d Ex 35:18
3:27 e 1Ch 26:23
3:29 f Nu 1:53
3:31 g Ex 25:10-22; h Ex 25:23; i Ex 25:31; j Ex 27:1; Ex 30:1; k Ex 26:33; l Nu 4:15
3:33 m Ex 6:19
3:35 n Nu 1:53; Nu 2:25
3:36 o Nu 4:32
3:38 p Nu 2:3; q Nu 1:53; r ver 7; Nu 18:5; s ver 10; Nu 1:51
3:39 t Nu 26:62
3:40 u ver 15
3:41 v ver 12
3:43 w ver 39

[b]28 Hebrew; some Septuagint manuscripts *8,300*

livestock of the Levites in place of their livestock. The Levites are to be mine. I am the LORD. 46 To redeem[x] the 273 firstborn Israelites who exceed the number of the Levites, 47 collect five shekels[c][y] for each one, according to the sanctuary shekel,[z] which weighs twenty gerahs.[a] 48 Give the money for the redemption of the additional Israelites to Aaron and his sons."

49 So Moses collected the redemption money from those who exceeded the number redeemed by the Levites. 50 From the firstborn of the Israelites he collected silver weighing 1,365 shekels,[d][b] according to the sanctuary shekel. 51 Moses gave the redemption money to Aaron and his sons, as he was commanded by the word of the LORD.

The Kohathites

4 The LORD said to Moses and Aaron: 2 "Take a census[a] of the Kohathite branch of the Levites by their clans and families. 3 Count all the men from thirty to fifty years of age[b] who come to serve in the work in the Tent of Meeting.

4 "This is the work of the Kohathites in the Tent of Meeting: the care of the most holy things.[c] 5 When the camp is to move, Aaron and his sons are to go in and take down the shielding curtain[d] and cover the ark of the Testimony with it.[e] 6 Then they are to cover this with hides of sea cows,[a] spread a cloth of solid blue over that and put the poles[f] in place.

7 "Over the table of the Presence[g] they are to spread a blue cloth and put on it the plates, dishes and bowls, and the jars for drink offerings; the bread that is continually there[h] is to remain on it. 8 Over these they are to spread a scarlet cloth, cover that with hides of sea cows and put its poles in place.

9 "They are to take a blue cloth and cover the lampstand that is for light, together with its lamps, its wick trimmers and trays,[i] and all its jars for the oil used to supply it. 10 Then they are to wrap it and all its accessories in a covering of hides of sea cows and put it on a carrying frame.

11 "Over the gold altar[j] they are to spread a blue cloth and cover that with hides of sea cows and put its poles in place.

12 "They are to take all the articles used for ministering in the sanctuary, wrap them in a blue cloth, cover that with hides of sea cows and put them on a carrying frame.

13 "They are to remove the ashes from the bronze altar[k] and spread a purple cloth over it. 14 Then they are to place on it all the utensils used for ministering at the altar, including the firepans, meat forks,[l] shovels and sprinkling bowls.[m] Over it they are to spread a covering of hides of sea cows and put its poles[n] in place.

15 "After Aaron and his sons have finished covering the holy furnishings and all the holy articles, and when the camp is ready to move, the Kohathites are to come to do the carrying.[o] But they must not touch the holy things or they will die.[p] The Kohathites are to carry those things that are in the Tent of Meeting.

16 "Eleazar[q] son of Aaron, the priest, is to have charge of the oil for the light,[r] the fragrant incense, the regular grain offering[s] and the anointing oil. He is to be in charge of the entire tabernacle and everything in it, including its holy furnishings and articles."

17 The LORD said to Moses and Aaron, 18 "See that the Kohathite tribal clans are not cut off from the Levites. 19 So that they may live and not die when they come near the most holy things,[t] do this for

3:46 x Ex 13:13; Nu 18:15
3:47 y Lev 27:6; z Ex 30:13; a Lev 27:25
3:50 b ver 46-48
4:2 a Ex 30:12
4:3 b ver 23; Nu 8:25; 1Ch 23:3,24,27; Ezr 3:8
4:4 c ver 19
4:5 d Ex 26:31,33; e Ex 25:10,16
4:6 f Ex 25:13-15; 1Ki 8:7; 2Ch 5:8
4:7 g Ex 25:23,29; Lev 24:6; h Ex 25:30
4:9 i Ex 25:31,37,38
4:11 j Ex 30:1
4:13 k Ex 27:1-8
4:14 l 2Ch 4:16; m Jer 52:18; n Ex 27:6
4:15 o Nu 7:9; p Nu 1:51; 2Sa 6:6,7
4:16 q Lev 10:6; r Ex 25:6; s Ex 29:41; Lev 6:14-23
4:19 t ver 15

c47 That is, about 2 ounces (about 55 grams)
d50 That is, about 35 pounds (about 15.5 kilograms)
a6 That is, large aquatic mammals; also elsewhere in this chapter

them: Aaron and his sons are to go into the sanctuary and assign to each man his work and what he is to carry. 20But the Kohathites must not go in to look[u] at the holy things, even for a moment, or they will die."

The Gershonites

21The LORD said to Moses, 22"Take a census also of the Gershonites by their families and clans. 23Count all the men from thirty to fifty years of age[v] who come to serve in the work at the Tent of Meeting.

24"This is the service of the Gershonite clans as they work and carry burdens: 25They are to carry the curtains of the tabernacle,[w] the Tent of Meeting,[x] its covering[y] and the outer covering of hides of sea cows, the curtains for the entrance to the Tent of Meeting, 26the curtains of the courtyard surrounding the tabernacle and altar, the curtain for the entrance, the ropes and all the equipment used in its service. The Gershonites are to do all that needs to be done with these things. 27All their service, whether carrying or doing other work, is to be done under the direction of Aaron and his sons. You shall assign to them as their responsibility all they are to carry. 28This is the service of the Gershonite clans[z] at the Tent of Meeting. Their duties are to be under the direction of Ithamar son of Aaron, the priest.

The Merarites

29"Count the Merarites by their clans and families.[a] 30Count all the men from thirty to fifty years of age who come to serve in the work at the Tent of Meeting. 31This is their duty as they perform service at the Tent of Meeting: to carry the frames of the tabernacle, its crossbars, posts and bases,[b] 32as well as the posts of the surrounding courtyard with their bases, tent pegs, ropes, all their equipment and everything related to their use. Assign to each man the specific things he is to carry. 33This is the service of the Merarite clans as they work at the Tent of Meeting under the direction of Ithamar son of Aaron, the priest."

The Numbering of the Levite Clans

34Moses, Aaron and the leaders of the community counted the Kohathites[c] by their clans and families. 35All the men from thirty to fifty years of age who came to serve in the work in the Tent of Meeting, 36counted by clans, were 2,750. 37This was the total of all those in the Kohathite clans[d] who served in the Tent of Meeting. Moses and Aaron counted them according to the LORD's command through Moses.

38The Gershonites[e] were counted by their clans and families. 39All the men from thirty to fifty years of age who came to serve in the work at the Tent of Meeting, 40counted by their clans and families, were 2,630. 41This was the total of those in the Gershonite clans who served at the Tent of Meeting. Moses and Aaron counted them according to the LORD's command.

42The Merarites were counted by their clans and families. 43All the men from thirty to fifty years of age who came to serve in the work at the Tent of Meeting, 44counted by their clans, were 3,200. 45This was the total of those in the Merarite clans.[f] Moses and Aaron counted them according to the LORD's command through Moses.

46So Moses, Aaron and the leaders of Israel counted all the Levites by their clans and families. 47All the men from thirty to fifty years of age[g] who came to do the work of serving and carrying the Tent of

4:20
u Ex 19:21 1Sa 6:19

4:23
v ver 3 1Ch 23:3,24, 27

4:25
w Ex 27:10-18 Nu 3:26
x Nu 3:25
y Ex 26:14

4:28
z Nu 7:7

4:29
a Ge 46:11

4:31
b Nu 3:36

4:34
c ver 2

4:37
d Nu 3:27

4:38
e Ge 46:11

4:45
f ver 29

4:47
g ver 3

Meeting 48 numbered 8,580.[h] 49 At the LORD's command through Moses, each was assigned his work and told what to carry.

Thus they were counted,[i] as the LORD commanded Moses.

The Purity of the Camp

5 The LORD said to Moses, 2 "Command the Israelites to send away from the camp anyone who has an infectious skin disease[a][a] or a discharge[b] of any kind, or who is ceremonially unclean[c] because of a dead body. 3 Send away male and female alike; send them outside the camp so that they will not defile their camp, where I dwell among them.[d]" 4 The Israelites did this; they sent them outside the camp. They did just as the LORD had instructed Moses.

Restitution for Wrongs

5 The LORD said to Moses, 6 "Say to the Israelites: 'When a man or woman wrongs another in any way[b] and so is unfaithful[e] to the LORD, that person is guilty[f] 7 and must confess[g] the sin he has committed. He must make full restitution[h] for his wrong, add one fifth to it and give it all to the person he has wronged. 8 But if that person has no close relative to whom restitution can be made for the wrong, the restitution belongs to the LORD and must be given to the priest, along with the ram with which atonement is made for him.[i] 9 All the sacred contributions the Israelites bring to a priest will belong to him.[j] 10 Each man's sacred gifts are his own, but what he gives to the priest will belong to the priest.[k]' "

The Test for an Unfaithful Wife

11 Then the LORD said to Moses, 12 "Speak to the Israelites and say to them: 'If a man's wife goes astray[l] and is unfaithful to him 13 by sleeping with another man,[m] and this is hidden from her husband and her impurity is undetected (since there is no witness against her and she has not been caught in the act), 14 and if feelings of jealousy[n] come over her husband and he suspects his wife and she is impure—or if he is jealous and suspects her even though she is not impure— 15 then he is to take his wife to the priest. He must also take an offering of a tenth of an ephah[c][o] of barley flour[p] on her behalf. He must not pour oil on it or put incense on it, because it is a grain offering for jealousy, a reminder[q] offering to draw attention to guilt.

16 " 'The priest shall bring her and make her stand before the LORD. 17 Then he shall take some holy water in a clay jar and put some dust from the tabernacle floor into the water. 18 After the priest has made the woman stand before the LORD, he shall loosen her hair[r] and place in her hands the reminder offering, the grain offering for jealousy, while he himself holds the bitter water that brings a curse. 19 Then the priest shall put the woman under oath and say to her, "If no other man has slept with you and you have not gone astray[s] and become impure while married to your husband, may this bitter water that brings a curse not harm you. 20 But if you have gone astray[t] while married to your husband and you have defiled yourself by sleeping with a man other than your husband"— 21 here the priest is to put the woman under this curse of the oath[u]—"may the LORD cause your people to curse and denounce you when he causes your thigh to waste away and your abdomen to swell.[d] 22 May this water[v] that brings a

4:48 h Nu 3:39
4:49 i Nu 1:47
5:2 a Lev 13:46 b Lev 15:2 Mt 9:20 c Lev 13:3 Nu 9:6-10
5:3 d Lev 26:12 Nu 35:34 2Co 6:16
5:6 e Lev 6:2 f Lev 5:14-6:7
5:7 g Lev 5:5 Lev 26:40 Jos 7:19 Lk 19:8 h Lev 6:5
5:8 i Lev 6:6,7 Lev 7:7
5:9 j Lev 6:17 Lev 7:6-14
5:10 k Lev 10:13
5:12 l Ex 20:14
5:13 m Lev 18:20 Lev 20:10
5:14 n Pr 6:34 SS 8:6
5:15 o Ex 16:36 p Lev 6:20 q Eze 29:16
5:18 r Lev 10:6 1Co 11:6
5:19 s ver 12,29
5:20 t ver 12
5:21 u Jos 6:26 1Sa 14:24 Ne 10:29
5:22 v Ps 109:18

[a]2 Traditionally *leprosy*; the Hebrew word was used for various diseases affecting the skin—not necessarily leprosy. [b]6 Or *woman commits any wrong common to mankind* [c]15 That is, probably about 4 pints (about 2 litres)
[d]21 Or *causes you to have a miscarrying womb and barrenness*

curse[w] enter your body so that
your abdomen swells and your
thigh wastes away."[e]

" 'Then the woman is to say,
"Amen. So be it.[x]"

23" 'The priest is to write these
curses on a scroll[y] and then wash
them off into the bitter water. 24He
shall make the woman drink the
bitter water that brings a curse,
and this water will enter her and
cause bitter suffering. 25The priest
is to take from her hands the grain
offering for jealousy, wave it before the LORD[z] and bring it to the
altar. 26The priest is then to take a
handful of the grain offering as a
memorial offering and burn it on
the altar; after that, he is to make
the woman drink the water. 27If she
has defiled herself and been unfaithful to her husband, then when
she is made to drink the water that
brings a curse, it will go into her
and cause bitter suffering; her
abdomen will swell and her thigh
waste away,[f] and she will become
accursed[a] among her people. 28If,
however, the woman has not defiled herself and is free from impurity, she will be cleared of guilt and
will be able to have children.

29" 'This, then, is the law of jealousy when a woman goes astray[b]
and defiles herself while married
to her husband, 30or when feelings
of jealousy come over a man because he suspects his wife. The
priest is to make her stand before
the LORD and is to apply this entire
law to her. 31The husband will be
innocent of any wrongdoing, but
the woman will bear the consequences[c] of her sin.' "

The Nazirite

6 The LORD said to Moses,
2"Speak to the Israelites and
say to them: 'If a man or woman
wants to make a special vow[a], a
vow of separation to the LORD as a
Nazirite,[b] 3he must abstain from
wine[c] and other fermented drink
and must not drink vinegar[d] made
from wine or from other fermented
drink. He must not drink grape
juice or eat grapes or raisins. 4As
long as he is a Nazirite, he must not
eat anything that comes from the
grapevine, not even the seeds or
skins.

5" 'During the entire period of his
vow of separation no razor[e] may
be used on his head.[f] He must be
holy until the period of his separation to the LORD is over; he must let
the hair of his head grow long.
6Throughout the period of his separation to the LORD he must not go
near a dead body.[g] 7Even if his own
father or mother or brother or sister dies, he must not make himself
ceremonially unclean[h] on account
of them, because the symbol of his
separation to God is on his head.
8Throughout the period of his separation he is consecrated to the
LORD.

9" 'If someone dies suddenly in
his presence, thus defiling the hair
he has dedicated,[i] he must shave
his head on the day of his cleansing[j]—the seventh day. 10Then on
the eighth day he must bring two
doves or two young pigeons[k] to the
priest at the entrance to the Tent of
Meeting. 11The priest is to offer one
as a sin offering and the other as a
burnt offering[l] to make atonement[m] for him because he sinned
by being in the presence of the
dead body. That same day he is to
consecrate his head. 12He must
dedicate himself to the LORD for
the period of his separation and
must bring a year-old male lamb as
a guilt offering. The previous days
do not count, because he became
defiled during his separation.

13" 'Now this is the law for the
Nazirite when the period of his
separation is over.[n] He is to be
brought to the entrance to the Tent

5:22 w ver 18 x Dt 27:15
5:23 y Jer 45:1
5:25 z Lev 8:27
5:27 a Isa 43:28 Isa 65:15 Jer 26:6 Jer 29:18 Jer 42:18 Jer 44:12,22 Zec 8:13
5:29 b ver 19
5:31 c Lev 5:1 Lev 20:17
6:2 a Ge 28:20 Ac 21:23 b Jdg 13:5 Jdg 16:17 Am 2:11,12
6:3 c Lk 1:15 d Ru 2:14 Ps 69:21 Pr 10:26
6:5 e Ps 52:2 Ps 57:4 Ps 59:7 Isa 7:20 Eze 5:1 f 1Sa 1:11
6:6 g Lev 21:1-3 Nu 19:11-22
6:7 h Nu 9:6
6:9 i ver 18 j Lev 14:9
6:10 k Lev 5:7 Lev 14:22
6:11 l Ge 8:20 m Ex 29:36
6:13 n Ac 21:26

e22 Or *body and cause you to be barren and have a miscarrying womb* f27 Or *suffering; she will have barrenness and a miscarrying womb*

of Meeting. 14 There he is to present
his offerings to the LORD: a year-
old male lamb without defect for a
burnt offering, a year-old ewe lamb
without defect for a sin offering,[o]
a ram without defect for a fellowship offering,[a] 15 together with
their grain offerings and drink offerings,[p] and a basket of bread
made without yeast—cakes made
of fine flour mixed with oil, and
wafers spread with oil.[q]
16 " 'The priest is to present them
before the LORD and make the sin
offering and the burnt offering.
17 He is to present the basket of unleavened bread and is to sacrifice
the ram as a fellowship offering to
the LORD, together with its grain
offering and drink offering.
18 " 'Then at the entrance to the
Tent of Meeting, the Nazirite must
shave off the hair that he dedicated.[r] He is to take the hair and
put it in the fire that is under the
sacrifice of the fellowship offering.
19 " 'After the Nazirite has shaved
off the hair of his dedication, the
priest is to place in his hands a
boiled shoulder of the ram, and a
cake and a wafer from the basket,
both made without yeast. 20 The
priest shall then wave them before
the LORD as a wave offering; they
are holy and belong to the priest,
together with the breast that was
waved and the thigh that was presented. After that, the Nazirite may
drink wine.[s]
21 " 'This is the law of the Nazirite
who vows his offering to the LORD
in accordance with his separation,
in addition to whatever else he can
afford. He must fulfil the vow he
has made, according to the law of
the Nazirite.' "

The Priestly Blessing

22 The LORD said to Moses, 23 "Tell
Aaron and his sons, 'This is how
you are to bless[t] the Israelites.
Say to them:

24 " ' "The LORD bless you[u]
and keep you;[v]
25 the LORD make his face shine
upon you[w]
and be gracious to you;[x]
26 the LORD turn his face[y]
towards you
and give you peace.[z]" '

27 "So they will put my name[a] on
the Israelites, and I will bless
them."

Offerings at the Dedication of the Tabernacle

7 When Moses finished setting
up the tabernacle,[a] he anointed it and consecrated it and
all its furnishings.[b] He also
anointed and consecrated the altar
and all its utensils.[c] 2 Then the
leaders of Israel,[d] the heads of
families who were the tribal leaders in charge of those who were
counted, made offerings. 3 They
brought as their gifts before the
LORD six covered carts and twelve
oxen—an ox from each leader and
a cart from every two. These they
presented before the tabernacle.
4 The LORD said to Moses, 5 "Accept these from them, that they
may be used in the work at the Tent
of Meeting. Give them to the Levites as each man's work requires."
6 So Moses took the carts and
oxen and gave them to the Levites.
7 He gave two carts and four oxen to
the Gershonites,[e] as their work required, 8 and he gave four carts and
eight oxen to the Merarites,[f] as
their work required. They were all
under the direction of Ithamar son
of Aaron, the priest. 9 But Moses did
not give any to the Kohathites, because they were to carry on their
shoulders[g] the holy things, for
which they were responsible.
10 When the altar was anointed,[h]
the leaders brought their offerings
for its dedication[i] and presented

[a]14 Traditionally *peace offering*; also in verses 17 and 18

6:14 o Lev 14:10; Nu 15:27
6:15 p Nu 15:1-7; q Ex 29:2; Lev 2:4
6:18 r ver 9; Ac 21:24
6:20 s Ecc 9:7
6:23 t Dt 21:5; 1Ch 23:13
6:24 u Dt 28:3-6; Ps 28:9; v 1Sa 2:9; Ps 17:8
6:25 w Job 29:24; Ps 31:16; Ps 80:3; Ps 119:135; x Ge 43:29; Ps 25:16; Ps 86:16
6:26 y Ps 4:6; Ps 44:3; z Ps 29:11; Ps 37:11,37; Jn 14:27
6:27 a Dt 28:10; 2Sa 7:23; 2Ch 7:14; Ne 9:10; Jer 25:29
7:1 a Ex 40:17; b Ex 40:9; c ver 84,88; Ex 40:10
7:2 d Nu 1:5-16
7:7 e Nu 4:24-26, 28
7:8 f Nu 4:31-33
7:9 g Nu 4:15
7:10 h ver 1; i 2Ch 7:9

them before the altar. [11]For the
LORD had said to Moses, "Each day
one leader is to bring his offering
for the dedication of the altar."

[12]The one who brought his offering
on the first day was Nahshon son of
Amminadab of the tribe of Judah.
[13]His offering was one silver
plate weighing a hundred and
thirty shekels,[a] and one silver
sprinkling bowl weighing seventy shekels,[b] both according
to the sanctuary shekel,[j] each
filled with fine flour mixed
with oil as a grain offering;[k]
[14]one gold dish weighing ten
shekels,[c] filled with incense;[l]
[15]one young bull,[m] one ram and
one male lamb a year old, for a
burnt offering;[n] [16]one male
goat for a sin offering;[o] [17]and
two oxen, five rams, five male
goats and five male lambs a
year old, to be sacrificed as a
fellowship offering.[d][p] This
was the offering of Nahshon
son of Amminadab.[q]

[18]On the second day Nethanel son
of Zuar,[r] the leader of Issachar,
brought his offering.
[19]The offering he brought was
one silver plate weighing a
hundred and thirty shekels,
and one silver sprinkling bowl
weighing seventy shekels, both
according to the sanctuary
shekel, each filled with fine
flour mixed with oil as a grain
offering; [20]one gold dish[s]
weighing ten shekels, filled
with incense; [21]one young bull,
one ram and one male lamb a
year old, for a burnt offering;
[22]one male goat for a sin offering; [23]and two oxen, five rams,
five male goats and five male
lambs a year old, to be sacrificed as a fellowship offering.
This was the offering of Nethanel son of Zuar.

[24]On the third day, Eliab son of
Helon,[t] the leader of the people of
Zebulun, brought his offering.
[25]His offering was one silver
plate weighing a hundred and
thirty shekels, and one silver
sprinkling bowl weighing seventy shekels, both according to
the sanctuary shekel, each
filled with fine flour mixed
with oil as a grain offering;
[26]one gold dish weighing ten
shekels, filled with incense;
[27]one young bull, one ram and
one male lamb a year old, for a
burnt offering; [28]one male goat
for a sin offering; [29]and two
oxen, five rams, five male
goats and five male lambs a
year old, to be sacrificed as a
fellowship offering. This was
the offering of Eliab son of
Helon.

[30]On the fourth day Elizur son of
Shedeur,[u] the leader of the people
of Reuben, brought his offering.
[31]His offering was one silver
plate weighing a hundred and
thirty shekels, and one silver
sprinkling bowl weighing seventy shekels, both according to
the sanctuary shekel, each
filled with fine flour mixed
with oil as a grain offering;
[32]one gold dish weighing ten
shekels, filled with incense;
[33]one young bull, one ram and
one male lamb a year old, for a
burnt offering; [34]one male goat
for a sin offering; [35]and two
oxen, five rams, five male
goats and five male lambs a
year old, to be sacrificed as a
fellowship offering. This was
the offering of Elizur son of
Shedeur.

[36]On the fifth day Shelumiel son of
Zurishaddai,[v] the leader of the

7:13 *j* Ex 30:13; Nu 3:47 *k* Lev 2:1
7:14 *l* Ex 30:34
7:15 *m* Ex 24:5; Ex 29:3; Nu 28:11 *n* Lev 1:3
7:16 *o* Lev 4:3,23
7:17 *p* Lev 3:1 *q* Nu 1:7
7:18 *r* Nu 1:8
7:20 *s* ver 14
7:24 *t* Nu 1:9
7:30 *u* Nu 1:5
7:36 *v* Nu 1:6

[a] *13* That is, about 3¼ pounds (about 1.5 kilograms); also elsewhere in this chapter [b] *13* That is, about 1¾ pounds (about 0.8 kilogram); also elsewhere in this chapter [c] *14* That is, about 4 ounces (about 115 grams); also elsewhere in this chapter [d] *17* Traditionally *peace offering*; also elsewhere in this chapter

people of Simeon, brought his offering.
37His offering was one silver
plate weighing a hundred and
thirty shekels, and one silver
sprinkling bowl weighing seventy shekels, both according to
the sanctuary shekel, each
filled with fine flour mixed
with oil as a grain offering;
38one gold dish weighing ten
shekels, filled with incense;
39one young bull, one ram and
one male lamb a year old, for a
burnt offering; 40one male goat
for a sin offering; 41and two
oxen, five rams, five male
goats and five male lambs a
year old, to be sacrificed as a
fellowship offering. This was
the offering of Shelumiel son
of Zurishaddai.

42On the sixth day Eliasaph son of
Deuel,[w] the leader of the people of
Gad, brought his offering.
43His offering was one silver
plate weighing a hundred and
thirty shekels, and one silver
sprinkling bowl weighing seventy shekels, both according to
the sanctuary shekel, each
filled with fine flour mixed
with oil as a grain offering;
44one gold dish weighing ten
shekels, filled with incense;
45one young bull, one ram and
one male lamb a year old, for a
burnt offering; 46one male goat
for a sin offering; 47and two
oxen, five rams, five male
goats and five male lambs a
year old, to be sacrificed as a
fellowship offering. This was
the offering of Eliasaph son of
Deuel.

48On the seventh day Elishama son
of Ammihud,[x] the leader of the
people of Ephraim, brought his offering.
49His offering was one silver
plate weighing a hundred and
thirty shekels, and one silver
sprinkling bowl weighing
seventy shekels, both according
to the sanctuary shekel, each
filled with fine flour mixed
with oil as a grain offering;
50one gold dish weighing ten
shekels, filled with incense;
51one young bull, one ram and
one male lamb a year old, for a
burnt offering; 52one male goat
for a sin offering; 53and two
oxen, five rams, five male
goats and five male lambs a
year old, to be sacrificed as a
fellowship offering. This was
the offering of Elishama son of
Ammihud.[y]

54On the eighth day Gamaliel son of
Pedahzur,[z] the leader of the people of Manasseh, brought his offering.
55His offering was one silver
plate weighing a hundred and
thirty shekels, and one silver
sprinkling bowl weighing seventy shekels, both according to
the sanctuary shekel, each
filled with fine flour mixed
with oil as a grain offering;
56one gold dish weighing ten
shekels, filled with incense;
57one young bull, one ram and
one male lamb a year old, for a
burnt offering; 58one male goat
for a sin offering; 59and two
oxen, five rams, five male
goats and five male lambs a
year old, to be sacrificed as a
fellowship offering. This was
the offering of Gamaliel son of
Pedahzur.

60On the ninth day Abidan son of
Gideoni,[a] the leader of the people
of Benjamin, brought his offering.
61His offering was one silver
plate weighing a hundred and
thirty shekels, and one silver
sprinkling bowl weighing seventy shekels, both according to
the sanctuary shekel, each
filled with fine flour mixed
with oil as a grain offering;
62one gold dish weighing ten
shekels, filled with incense;

7:42 w Nu 1:14
7:48 x Nu 1:10
7:53 y Nu 1:10
7:54 z Nu 1:10; Nu 2:20
7:60 a Nu 1:11

63 one young bull, one ram and
one male lamb a year old, for a
burnt offering; 64 one male goat
for a sin offering; 65 and two
oxen, five rams, five male
goats and five male lambs a
year old, to be sacrificed as a
fellowship offering. This was
the offering of Abidan son of
Gideoni.

66 On the tenth day Ahiezer son of
Ammishaddai,[b] the leader of the
people of Dan, brought his offering.
67 His offering was one silver
plate weighing a hundred and
thirty shekels, and one silver
sprinkling bowl weighing seventy shekels, both according to
the sanctuary shekel, each
filled with fine flour mixed
with oil as a grain offering;
68 one gold dish weighing ten
shekels, filled with incense;
69 one young bull, one ram and
one male lamb a year old, for a
burnt offering; 70 one male goat
for a sin offering; 71 and two
oxen, five rams, five male
goats and five male lambs a
year old, to be sacrificed as a
fellowship offering. This was
the offering of Ahiezer son of
Ammishaddai.

72 On the eleventh day Pagiel son of
Ocran,[c] the leader of the people of
Asher, brought his offering.
73 His offering was one silver
plate weighing a hundred and
thirty shekels, and one silver
sprinkling bowl weighing seventy shekels, both according to
the sanctuary shekel, each
filled with fine flour mixed
with oil as a grain offering;
74 one gold dish weighing ten
shekels, filled with incense;
75 one young bull, one ram and
one male lamb a year old, for a
burnt offering; 76 one male goat
for a sin offering; 77 and two
oxen, five rams, five male
goats and five male lambs a
year old, to be sacrificed as a
fellowship offering. This was
the offering of Pagiel son of
Ocran.

78 On the twelfth day Ahira son of
Enan,[d] the leader of the people of
Naphtali, brought his offering.
79 His offering was one silver
plate weighing a hundred and
thirty shekels, and one silver
sprinkling bowl weighing seventy shekels, both according to
the sanctuary shekel, each
filled with fine flour mixed
with oil as a grain offering;
80 one gold dish weighing ten
shekels, filled with incense;
81 one young bull, one ram and
one male lamb a year old, for a
burnt offering; 82 one male goat
for a sin offering; 83 and two
oxen, five rams, five male
goats and five male lambs a
year old, to be sacrificed as a
fellowship offering. This was
the offering of Ahira son of
Enan.

84 These were the offerings of the
Israelite leaders for the dedication
of the altar when it was anointed:[e]
twelve silver plates, twelve silver sprinkling bowls[f] and twelve
gold dishes.[g] 85 Each silver plate
weighed a hundred and thirty shekels, and each sprinkling bowl seventy shekels. Altogether, the silver
dishes weighed two thousand four
hundred shekels,[e] according to
the sanctuary shekel. 86 The twelve
gold dishes filled with incense
weighed ten shekels each, according to the sanctuary shekel. Altogether, the gold dishes weighed a
hundred and twenty shekels.[f]
87 The total number of animals for
the burnt offering came to twelve
young bulls, twelve rams and
twelve male lambs a year old, together with their grain offering.
Twelve male goats were used for

7:66
b Nu 1:12
Nu 2:25

7:72
c Nu 1:13

7:78
d Nu 1:15
Nu 2:29

7:84
e ver 1,10
f Nu 4:14
g ver 14

e85 That is, about 61 pounds (about 28 kilograms)
f86 That is, about 3 pounds (about 1.4 kilograms)

the sin offering. 88The total number of animals for the sacrifice of the fellowship offering came to twenty-four oxen, sixty rams, sixty male goats and sixty male lambs a year old. These were the offerings for the dedication of the altar after it was anointed.[h]

89When Moses entered the Tent of Meeting to speak with the LORD,[i] he heard the voice speaking to him from between the two cherubim above the atonement cover[j] on the ark of the Testimony. And he spoke with him.

Setting Up the Lamps

8 The LORD said to Moses, 2"Speak to Aaron and say to him, 'When you set up the seven lamps, they are to light the area in front of the lampstand.[a]' "

3Aaron did so; he set up the lamps so that they faced forward on the lampstand, just as the LORD commanded Moses. 4This is how the lampstand was made: It was made of hammered gold[b]—from its base to its blossoms. The lampstand was made exactly like the pattern[c] the LORD had shown Moses.

The Setting Apart of the Levites

5The LORD said to Moses: 6"Take the Levites from among the other Israelites and make them ceremonially clean.[d] 7To purify them, do this: Sprinkle the water of cleansing[e] on them; then make them shave their whole bodies[f] and wash their clothes,[g] and so purify themselves. 8Make them take a young bull with its grain offering of fine flour mixed with oil;[h] then you are to take a second young bull for a sin offering. 9Bring the Levites to the front of the Tent of Meeting[i] and assemble the whole Israelite community.[j] 10You are to bring the Levites before the LORD, and the Israelites are to lay their hands on them.[k] 11Aaron is to present the Levites before the LORD as a wave offering[l] from the Israelites, so that they may be ready to do the work of the LORD.

12"After the Levites lay their hands on the heads of the bulls,[m] use the one for a sin offering to the LORD and the other for a burnt offering, to make atonement[n] for the Levites. 13Make the Levites stand in front of Aaron and his sons and then present them as a wave offering to the LORD. 14In this way you are to set the Levites apart from the other Israelites, and the Levites will be mine.[o]

15"After you have purified the Levites and presented them as a wave offering,[p] they are to come to do their work at the Tent of Meeting. 16They are the Israelites who are to be given wholly to me. I have taken them as my own in place of the firstborn, the first male offspring[q] from every Israelite woman. 17Every firstborn male in Israel, whether man or animal,[r] is mine. When I struck down all the firstborn in Egypt, I set them apart for myself.[s] 18And I have taken the Levites in place of all the firstborn sons in Israel.[t] 19Of all the Israelites, I have given the Levites as gifts to Aaron and his sons[u] to do the work at the Tent of Meeting on behalf of the Israelites[v] and to make atonement for them[w] so that no plague will strike the Israelites when they go near the sanctuary."

20Moses, Aaron and the whole Israelite community did with the Levites just as the LORD commanded Moses. 21The Levites purified themselves and washed their clothes.[x] Then Aaron presented them as a wave offering before the LORD and made atonement for them to purify them.[y] 22After that, the Levites came to do their work at the Tent of Meeting under the supervision of Aaron and his sons. They did with the Levites just as the LORD commanded Moses.

23The LORD said to Moses, 24"This

7:88 h ver 1,10
7:89 i Ex 25:21,22; Ex 33:9,11; j Ps 80:1; Ps 99:1
8:2 a Ex 25:37; Lev 24:2,4
8:4 b Ex 25:18,36; c Ex 25:9
8:6 d Lev 22:2; Isa 1:16; Isa 52:11
8:7 e Nu 19:9,17; f Lev 14:9; Dt 21:12; g Lev 14:8
8:8 h Lev 2:1; Nu 15:8-10
8:9 i Ex 40:12; j Lev 8:3
8:10 k Ac 6:6
8:11 l Lev 7:30
8:12 m Ex 29:10; n Ex 29:36
8:14 o Nu 3:12
8:15 p Ex 29:24
8:16 q Nu 3:12
8:17 r Ex 4:23; s Ex 13:2; Lk 2:23
8:18 t Nu 3:12
8:19 u Nu 3:9; v Nu 1:53; w Nu 16:46
8:21 x ver 7; y ver 12

applies to the Levites: Men twenty-
five years old or more[z] shall come
to take part in the work at the Tent
of Meeting,[a] 25but at the age of
fifty, they must retire from their
regular service and work no
longer. 26They may assist their
brothers in performing their duties
at the Tent of Meeting, but they
themselves must not do the work.
This, then, is how you are to assign
the responsibilities of the Levites."

The Passover

9 The LORD spoke to Moses in
the Desert of Sinai in the first
month[a] of the second year after
they came out of Egypt.[b] He said,
2"Make the Israelites celebrate the
Passover at the appointed time.
3Celebrate it at the appointed time,
at twilight on the fourteenth day of
this month, in accordance with all
its rules and regulations.[c]"
4So Moses told the Israelites to
celebrate the Passover, 5and they
did so in the Desert of Sinai at twilight on the fourteenth day of the
first month.[d] The Israelites did
everything just as the LORD commanded Moses.
6But some of them could not
celebrate the Passover on that day
because they were ceremonially
unclean[e] on account of a dead
body. So they came to Moses and
Aaron[f] that same day 7and said to
Moses, "We have become unclean
because of a dead body, but why
should we be kept from presenting
the LORD's offering with the other
Israelites at the appointed time?"
8Moses answered them, "Wait
until I find out what the LORD commands concerning you."[g]
9Then the LORD said to Moses,
10"Tell the Israelites: 'When any of
you or your descendants are unclean because of a dead body or are
away on a journey, they may still
celebrate[h] the LORD's Passover.
11They are to celebrate it on the

8:24
z 1Ch 23:3
a Ex 38:21
Nu 4:3

9:1
a Ex 40:2
b Nu 1:1

9:3
c Ex 12:2-11,
43-49
Lev 23:5-8
Dt 16:1-8

9:5
d Ex 12:1-13
Jos 5:10

9:6
e Lev 5:3
f Ex 18:15
Nu 27:2

9:8
g Ex 18:15
Nu 27:5,21
Ps 85:8

9:10
h 2Ch 30:2

9:11
i Ex 12:8

9:12
j Ex 12:10,43
k Ex 12:46
Jn 19:36*

9:13
l Ge 17:14
Ex 12:15

9:14
m Ex 12:48,49

9:15
n Ex 40:34
o Ex 13:21

9:17
p Ex 40:36-38
Nu 10:11,12
1Co 10:1

fourteenth day of the second month
at twilight. They are to eat the
lamb, together with unleavened
bread and bitter herbs.[i] 12They
must not leave any of it till morning[j] or break any of its bones.[k]
When they celebrate the Passover,
they must follow all the regulations. 13But if a man who is ceremonially clean and not on a journey
fails to celebrate the Passover, that
person must be cut off from his
people[l] because he did not present
the LORD's offering at the appointed time. That man will bear
the consequences of his sin.
14" 'An alien[m] living among you
who wants to celebrate the LORD's
Passover must do so in accordance
with its rules and regulations. You
must have the same regulations for
the alien and the native-born.' "

The Cloud Above the Tabernacle

15On the day the tabernacle, the
Tent of the Testimony, was set up,
the cloud[n] covered it. From evening till morning the cloud above
the tabernacle looked like fire.[o]
16That is how it continued to be; the
cloud covered it, and at night it
looked like fire. 17Whenever the
cloud lifted from above the Tent,
the Israelites set out; wherever the
cloud settled, the Israelites encamped.[p] 18At the LORD's command the Israelites set out, and at
his command they encamped. As
long as the cloud stayed over the
tabernacle, they remained in camp.
19When the cloud remained over
the tabernacle a long time, the Israelites obeyed the LORD's order
and did not set out. 20Sometimes the
cloud was over the tabernacle only
a few days; at the LORD's command
they would encamp, and then at his
command they would set out.
21Sometimes the cloud stayed only
from evening till morning, and
when it lifted in the morning, they

set out. Whether by day or by night, whenever the cloud lifted, they set out. 22Whether the cloud stayed over the tabernacle for two days or a month or a year, the Israelites would remain in camp and not set out; but when it lifted, they would set out. 23At the LORD's command they encamped, and at the LORD's command they set out. They obeyed the LORD's order, in accordance with his command through Moses.

The Silver Trumpets

10 The LORD said to Moses: 2"Make two trumpets[a] of hammered silver, and use them for calling the community[b] together and for having the camps set out. 3When both are sounded, the whole community is to assemble before you at the entrance to the Tent of Meeting. 4If only one is sounded, the leaders[c]—the heads of the clans of Israel—are to assemble before you. 5When a trumpet blast is sounded, the tribes camping on the east are to set out.[d] 6At the sounding of a second blast, the camps on the south are to set out.[e] The blast will be the signal for setting out. 7To gather the assembly, blow the trumpets,[f] but not with the same signal.[g]

8"The sons of Aaron, the priests, are to blow the trumpets. This is to be a lasting ordinance for you and the generations to come.[h] 9When you go into battle in your own land against an enemy who is oppressing you,[i] sound a blast on the trumpets. Then you will be remembered[j] by the LORD your God and rescued from your enemies.[k] 10Also at your times of rejoicing—your appointed feasts and New Moon festivals[l]—you are to sound the trumpets[m] over your burnt offerings and fellowship offerings,[a] and they will be a memorial for you before your God. I am the LORD your God."

10:2 a Ne 12:35; Ps 47:5 b Jer 4:5,19; Jer 6:1; Hos 5:8; Joel 2:1,15; Am 3:6
10:4 c Ex 18:21; Nu 1:16; Nu 7:2
10:5 d ver 14
10:6 e ver 18
10:7 f Eze 33:3; Joel 2:1 g 1Co 14:8
10:8 h Nu 31:6
10:9 i Jdg 2:18; Jdg 6:9; 1Sa 10:18; Ps 106:42 j Ge 8:1 k Ps 106:4
10:10 l Ps 81:3 m Lev 23:24
10:11 n Ex 40:17 o Nu 9:17
10:13 p Dt 1:6
10:14 q Nu 2:3-9 r Nu 1:7
10:17 s Nu 4:21-32
10:18 t Nu 2:10-16
10:21 u Nu 4:20 v ver 17
10:22 w Nu 2:24
10:25 x Nu 2:31; Jos 6:9

The Israelites Leave Sinai

11On the twentieth day of the second month of the second year,[n] the cloud lifted[o] from above the tabernacle of the Testimony. 12Then the Israelites set out from the Desert of Sinai and travelled from place to place until the cloud came to rest in the Desert of Paran. 13They set out, this first time, at the LORD's command through Moses.[p]

14The divisions of the camp of Judah went first, under their standard.[q] Nahshon son of Amminadab[r] was in command. 15Nethanel son of Zuar was over the division of the tribe of Issachar, 16and Eliab son of Helon was over the division of the tribe of Zebulun. 17Then the tabernacle was taken down, and the Gershonites and Merarites, who carried it, set out.[s] 18The divisions of the camp of Reuben went next, under their standard.[t] Elizur son of Shedeur was in command. 19Shelumiel son of Zurishaddai was over the division of the tribe of Simeon, 20and Eliasaph son of Deuel was over the division of the tribe of Gad. 21Then the Kohathites set out, carrying the holy things.[u] The tabernacle was to be set up before they arrived.[v]

22The divisions of the camp of Ephraim[w] went next, under their standard. Elishama son of Ammihud was in command. 23Gamaliel son of Pedahzur was over the division of the tribe of Manasseh, 24and Abidan son of Gideoni was over the division of the tribe of Benjamin.

25Finally, as the rear guard[x] for all the units, the divisions of the camp of Dan set out, under their standard. Ahiezer son of Ammishaddai was in command. 26Pagiel son of Ocran was over the division of the tribe of Asher, 27and Ahira son of Enan was over the division of the tribe of Naphtali. 28This was

a*10* Traditionally *peace offerings*

the order of march for the Israelite
divisions as they set out.
29 Now Moses said to Hobab[y] son
of Reuel[z] the Midianite, Moses'
father-in-law,[a] "We are setting out
for the place about which the LORD
said, 'I will give it to you.'[b] Come
with us and we will treat you well,
for the LORD has promised good
things to Israel."
30 He answered, "No, I will not
go;[c] I am going back to my own
land and my own people."
31 But Moses said, "Please do not
leave us. You know where we
should camp in the desert, and you
can be our eyes.[d] 32 If you come
with us, we will share with you[e]
whatever good things the LORD
gives us.[f]"
33 So they set out[g] from the
mountain of the LORD and travelled
for three days. The ark of the covenant of the LORD[h] went before
them during those three days to
find them a place to rest. 34 The
cloud of the LORD was over them by
day when they set out from the
camp.[i]
35 Whenever the ark set out,
Moses said,

"Rise up, O LORD!
  May your enemies be
    scattered;[j]
  may your foes flee before
    you.[k]"

36 Whenever it came to rest, he
said,

"Return,[l] O LORD,
  to the countless thousands of
    Israel.[m]"

Fire From the LORD

11 Now the people complained about their hard-
ships in the hearing of the LORD,
and when he heard them his anger
was aroused. Then fire from the
LORD burned among them[a] and
consumed some of the outskirts of
the camp. 2 When the people cried
out to Moses, he prayed to the
LORD[b] and the fire died down. 3 So
that place was called Taberah,[a][c]
because fire from the LORD had
burned among them.

Quail From the LORD

4 The rabble with them began to
crave other food,[d] and again the
Israelites started wailing[e] and
said, "If only we had meat to eat!
5 We remember the fish we ate in
Egypt at no cost—also the cucum-
bers, melons, leeks, onions and gar-
lic.[f] 6 But now we have lost our
appetite; we never see anything
but this manna!"
7 The manna was like coriander
seed[g] and looked like resin.[h] 8 The
people went around gathering it,
and then ground it in a hand mill or
crushed it in a mortar. They cooked
it in a pot or made it into cakes. And
it tasted like something made with
olive oil. 9 When the dew[i] settled
on the camp at night, the manna
also came down.
10 Moses heard the people of
every family wailing, each at the
entrance to his tent. The LORD
became exceedingly angry, and
Moses was troubled. 11 He asked the
LORD, "Why have you brought this
trouble on your servant? What
have I done to displease you that
you put the burden of all these
people on me?[j] 12 Did I conceive
all these people? Did I give them
birth? Why do you tell me to carry
them in my arms, as a nurse carries
an infant,[k] to the land you promised on oath to their forefathers?[l]
13 Where can I get meat for all these
people?[m] They keep wailing to me,
'Give us meat to eat!' 14 I cannot
carry all these people by myself;
the burden is too heavy for me.[n]
15 If this is how you are going to
treat me, put me to death[o] right
now[p]—if I have found favour in
your eyes—and do not let me face
my own ruin."

10:29 y Jdg 4:11 z Ex 2:18 a Ex 3:1 b Ge 12:7
10:30 c Mt 21:29
10:31 d Job 29:15
10:32 e Dt 10:18 f Ps 22:27-31 Ps 67:5-7
10:33 g ver 12 Dt 1:33 h Jos 3:3
10:34 i Nu 9:15-23
10:35 j Ps 68:1 k Dt 7:10 Dt 32:41 Ps 68:2 Isa 17:12-14
10:36 l Isa 63:17 m Dt 1:10
11:1 a Lev 10:2
11:2 b Nu 21:7
11:3 c Dt 9:22
11:4 d Ex 12:38 e Ps 78:18 1Co 10:6
11:5 f Ex 16:3
11:7 g Ex 16:31 h Ge 2:12
11:9 i Ex 16:13
11:11 j Ex 5:22
11:12 k Isa 40:11 Isa 49:23 l Ex 13:5
11:13 m Jn 6:5-9
11:14 n Ex 18:18
11:15 o Ex 32:32 p 1Ki 19:4 Jnh 4:3

[a] 3 *Taberah* means *burning*.

16The LORD said to Moses: "Bring me seventy of Israel's elders who are known to you as leaders and officials among the people. Make them come to the Tent of Meeting, that they may stand there with you. 17I will come down and speak with you there, and I will take of the Spirit that is on you and put the Spirit on them.[q] They will help you carry the burden of the people so that you will not have to carry it alone.

18"Tell the people: 'Consecrate yourselves[r] in preparation for tomorrow, when you will eat meat. The LORD heard you when you wailed,[s] "If only we had meat to eat! We were better off in Egypt!"[t] Now the LORD will give you meat, and you will eat it. 19You will not eat it for just one day, or two days, or five, ten or twenty days, 20but for a whole month—until it comes out of your nostrils and you loathe it[u]—because you have rejected the LORD,[v] who is among you, and have wailed before him, saying, "Why did we ever leave Egypt?" ' "

21But Moses said, "Here I am among six hundred thousand men[w] on foot, and you say, 'I will give them meat to eat for a whole month!' 22Would they have enough if flocks and herds were slaughtered for them? Would they have enough if all the fish in the sea were caught for them?"[x]

23The LORD answered Moses, "Is the LORD's arm too short?[y] You will now see whether or not what I say will come true for you."[z]

24So Moses went out and told the people what the LORD had said. He brought together seventy of their elders and made them stand round the Tent. 25Then the LORD came down in the cloud[a] and spoke with him,[b] and he took of the Spirit[c] that was on him and put the Spirit on the seventy elders.[d] When the Spirit rested on them, they prophesied,[e] but they did not do so again.[b]

26However, two men, whose names were Eldad and Medad, had remained in the camp. They were listed among the elders, but did not go out to the Tent. Yet the Spirit also rested on them, and they prophesied in the camp. 27A young man ran and told Moses, "Eldad and Medad are prophesying in the camp."

28Joshua son of Nun, who had been Moses' assistant[f] since youth, spoke up and said, "Moses, my lord, stop them!"[g]

29But Moses replied, "Are you jealous for my sake? I wish that all the LORD's people were prophets[h] and that the LORD would put his Spirit on them!" 30Then Moses and the elders of Israel returned to the camp.

31Now a wind went out from the LORD and drove quail[i] in from the sea. It brought them[c] down all around the camp to about three feet[d] above the ground, as far as a day's walk in any direction. 32All that day and night and all the next day the people went out and gathered quail. No-one gathered less than ten homers.[e] Then they spread them out all around the camp. 33But while the meat was still between their teeth[j] and before it could be consumed, the anger of the LORD burned against the people, and he struck them with a severe plague.[k] 34Therefore the place was named Kibroth Hattaavah,[f][l] because there they buried the people who had craved other food.

35From Kibroth Hattaavah the people travelled to Hazeroth[m] and stayed there.

11:17 *q* ver 25,29; 1Sa 10:6; 2Ki 2:9,15; Joel 2:28
11:18 *r* Ex 19:10 *s* Ex 16:7 *t* ver 5; Ac 7:39
11:20 *u* Ps 78:29; Ps 106:14,15 *v* Jos 24:27; 1Sa 10:19
11:21 *w* Ex 12:37
11:22 *x* Mt 15:33
11:23 *y* Isa 50:2; Isa 59:1 *z* Nu 23:19; Eze 12:25; Eze 24:14
11:25 *a* Nu 12:5 *b* ver 17 *c* 1Sa 10:6 *d* Ac 2:17 *e* 1Sa 10:10
11:28 *f* Ex 33:11; Jos 1:1 *g* Mk 9:38-40
11:29 *h* 1Co 14:5
11:31 *i* Ex 16:13; Ps 78:26-28
11:33 *j* Ps 78:30 *k* Ps 106:15
11:34 *l* Dt 9:22
11:35 *m* Nu 33:17

b25 Or *prophesied and continued to do so*
c31 Or *They flew* d31 Hebrew *two cubits* (about 0.9 metre) e32 That is, probably about 60 bushels (about 2.2 kilolitres) f34 *Kibroth Hattaavah* means *graves of craving.*

Miriam and Aaron Oppose Moses

12 Miriam and Aaron began to talk against Moses because of his Cushite wife,[a] for he had married a Cushite. 2“Has the LORD spoken only through Moses?” they asked. “Hasn’t he also spoken through us?”[b] And the LORD heard this.[c]

3(Now Moses was a very humble man,[d] more humble than anyone else on the face of the earth.)

4At once the LORD said to Moses, Aaron and Miriam, “Come out to the Tent of Meeting, all three of you.” So the three of them came out. 5Then the LORD came down in a pillar of cloud;[e] he stood at the entrance to the Tent and summoned Aaron and Miriam. When both of them stepped forward, 6he said, “Listen to my words:

“When a prophet of the LORD is
among you,
I reveal myself to him in
visions,[f]
I speak to him in dreams.[g]
7But this is not true of my
servant Moses;[h]
he is faithful in all my house.[i]
8With him I speak face to face,
clearly and not in riddles;[j]
he sees the form of the
LORD.[k]
Why then were you not afraid
to speak against my servant
Moses?”

9The anger of the LORD burned against them, and he left them.[l]

10When the cloud lifted from above the Tent, there stood Miriam—leprous,[a] like snow.[m] Aaron turned towards her and saw that she had leprosy;[n] 11and he said to Moses, “Please, my lord, do not hold against us the sin we have so foolishly committed.[o] 12Do not let her be like a stillborn infant coming from its mother’s womb with its flesh half eaten away.”

13So Moses cried out to the LORD, “O God, please heal her![p]”

14The LORD replied to Moses, “If her father had spat in her face,[q] would she not have been in disgrace for seven days? Confine her outside the camp[r] for seven days; after that she can be brought back.” 15So Miriam was confined outside the camp for seven days, and the people did not move on till she was brought back.

16After that, the people left Hazeroth[s] and encamped in the Desert of Paran.

Exploring Canaan

13 The LORD said to Moses, 2“Send some men to explore[a] the land of Canaan, which I am giving to the Israelites. From each ancestral tribe send one of its leaders.”

3So at the LORD’s command Moses sent them out from the Desert of Paran. All of them were leaders of the Israelites. 4These are their names:

from the tribe of Reuben,
Shammua son of Zaccur;
5from the tribe of Simeon,
Shaphat son of Hori;
6from the tribe of Judah,
Caleb son of Jephunneh;[b]
7from the tribe of Issachar,
Igal son of Joseph;
8from the tribe of Ephraim,
Hoshea son of Nun;
9from the tribe of Benjamin,
Palti son of Raphu;
10from the tribe of Zebulun,
Gaddiel son of Sodi;
11from the tribe of Manasseh (a
tribe of Joseph), Gaddi son
of Susi;
12from the tribe of Dan,
Ammiel son of Gemalli;
13from the tribe of Asher,
Sethur son of Michael;

[a]10 The Hebrew word was used for various diseases affecting the skin—not necessarily leprosy.

12:1 a Ex 2:21
12:2 b Nu 16:3; c Nu 11:1
12:3 d Mt 11:29
12:5 e Nu 11:25
12:6 f Ge 15:1; Ge 46:2; g Ge 31:10; 1Ki 3:5; Heb 1:1
12:7 h Jos 1:1-2; Ps 105:26; i Heb 3:2,5
12:8 j Dt 34:10; k Ex 20:4; Ps 17:15
12:9 l Ge 17:22
12:10 m Ex 4:6; Dt 24:9; n 2Ki 5:1,27
12:11 o 2Sa 19:19; 2Sa 24:10
12:13 p Isa 30:26; Jer 17:14
12:14 q Dt 25:9; Job 17:6; Job 30:9-10; Isa 50:6; r Lev 13:46; Nu 5:2-3
12:16 s Nu 11:35
13:2 a Dt 1:22
13:6 b ver 30; Nu 14:6,24; Nu 34:19; Jdg 1:12-15

14 from the tribe of Naphtali,
Nahbi son of Vophsi;
15 from the tribe of Gad, Geuel
son of Maki.

16 These are the names of the men
Moses sent to explore the land.
(Moses gave Hoshea son of Nun[c]
the name Joshua.)[d]
17 When Moses sent them to explore Canaan, he said, "Go up
through the Negev[e] and on into the
hill country.[f] 18 See what the land
is like and whether the people who
live there are strong or weak, few
or many. 19 What kind of land do
they live in? Is it good or bad? What
kind of towns do they live in? Are
they unwalled or fortified? 20 How
is the soil? Is it fertile or poor? Are
there trees on it or not? Do your
best to bring back some of the fruit
of the land.[g]" (It was the season for
the first ripe grapes.)
21 So they went up and explored
the land from the Desert of Zin[h] as
far as Rehob,[i] towards Lebo[a] Hamath.[j] 22 They went up through the
Negev and came to Hebron, where
Ahiman, Sheshai and Talmai,[k] the
descendants of Anak,[l] lived. (Hebron had been built seven years before Zoan in Egypt.)[m] 23 When they
reached the Valley of Eshcol,[b]
they cut off a branch bearing a single cluster of grapes. Two of them
carried it on a pole between them,
along with some pomegranates and
figs. 24 That place was called the
Valley of Eshcol because of the
cluster of grapes the Israelites cut
off there. 25 At the end of forty days
they returned from exploring the
land.

Report on the Exploration

26 They came back to Moses and
Aaron and the whole Israelite community at Kadesh in the Desert of
Paran. There they reported to
them[n] and to the whole assembly
and showed them the fruit of the
land. 27 They gave Moses this account: "We went into the land to
which you sent us, and it does flow
with milk and honey![o] Here is its
fruit.[p] 28 But the people who live
there are powerful, and the cities
are fortified and very large.[q] We
even saw descendants of Anak
there. 29 The Amalekites live in the
Negev; the Hittites, Jebusites and
Amorites live in the hill country;
and the Canaanites live near the
sea and along the Jordan."
30 Then Caleb silenced the people
before Moses and said, "We should
go up and take possession of the
land, for we can certainly do it."
31 But the men who had gone up
with him said, "We can't attack
those people; they are stronger
than we are."[r] 32 And they spread
among the Israelites a bad report[s]
about the land they had explored.
They said, "The land we explored
devours[t] those living in it. All the
people we saw there are of great
size.[u] 33 We saw the Nephilim[v]
there (the descendants of Anak[w]
come from the Nephilim). We
seemed like grasshoppers in our
own eyes, and we looked the same
to them."

The People Rebel

14 That night all the people of
the community raised their
voices and wept aloud. 2 All the Israelites grumbled against Moses
and Aaron, and the whole assembly
said to them, "If only we had died in
Egypt! Or in this desert![a] 3 Why is
the LORD bringing us to this land
only to let us fall by the sword? Our
wives and children will be taken as
plunder. Wouldn't it be better for
us to go back to Egypt?" 4 And they
said to each other, "We should
choose a leader and go back to
Egypt.[b]"
5 Then Moses and Aaron fell face
down[c] in front of the whole Israelite assembly gathered there.
6 Joshua son of Nun and Caleb son

13:16 c ver 8; d Dt 32:44
13:17 e Ge 12:9; f Jdg 1:9
13:20 g Dt 1:25
13:21 h Nu 20:1; Nu 27:14; Nu 33:36; Jos 15:1; i Jos 19:28; j Jos 13:5
13:22 k Jos 15:14; l Jos 15:13; m Ps 78:12,43; Isa 19:11,13
13:26 n Nu 32:8
13:27 o Ex 3:8; p Dt 1:25
13:28 q Dt 1:28; Dt 9:1,2
13:31 r Dt 1:28; Dt 9:1; Jos 14:8
13:32 s Nu 14:36,37; t Eze 36:13,14; u Am 2:9
13:33 v Ge 6:4; w Dt 1:28
14:2 a Nu 11:1
14:4 b Ne 9:17
14:5 c Nu 16:4,22,45

[a] 21 Or *towards the entrance to* [b] 23 *Eshcol* means *cluster*; also in verse 24.

of Jephunneh, who were among
those who had explored the land,
tore their clothes 7and said to the
entire Israelite assembly, "The
land we passed through and explored is exceedingly good.[d] 8If
the LORD is pleased with us,[e] he
will lead us into that land, a land
flowing with milk and honey,[f] and
will give it to us. 9Only do not
rebel[g] against the LORD. And do
not be afraid of the people of the
land,[h] because we will swallow
them up. Their protection is gone,
but the LORD is with us. Do not be
afraid of them."

10But the whole assembly talked
about stoning[i] them. Then the
glory of the LORD[j] appeared at the
Tent of Meeting to all the Israelites. 11The LORD said to Moses,
"How long will these people treat
me with contempt? How long will
they refuse to believe in me,[k] in
spite of all the miraculous signs I
have performed among them? 12I
will strike them down with a plague
and destroy them, but I will make
you into a nation[l] greater and
stronger than they."

13Moses said to the LORD, "Then
the Egyptians will hear about it! By
your power you brought these people up from among them.[m] 14And
they will tell the inhabitants of this
land about it. They have already
heard[n] that you, O LORD, are with
these people and that you, O LORD,
have been seen face to face, that
your cloud stays over them, and
that you go before them in a pillar
of cloud by day and a pillar of fire
by night.[o] 15If you put these people
to death all at one time, the nations
who have heard this report about
you will say, 16'The LORD was not
able to bring these people into the
land he promised them on oath;
so he slaughtered them in the
desert.'[p]

17"Now may the Lord's strength
be displayed, just as you have
declared: 18'The LORD is slow
to anger, abounding in love and

14:7 d Nu 13:27; Dt 1:25
14:8 e Dt 10:15; f Nu 13:27
14:9 g Dt 1:26; Dt 9:7,23,24; h Dt 1:21; Dt 7:18; Dt 20:1
14:10 i Ex 17:4; j Lev 9:23
14:11 k Ps 78:22; Ps 106:24
14:12 l Ex 32:10
14:13 m Ex 32:11-14; Ps 106:23
14:14 n Ex 15:14; o Ex 13:21
14:16 p Jos 7:7
14:18 q Ex 34:6; Ps 145:8; Jnh 4:2; r Ex 20:5
14:19 s Ex 34:9; t Ps 106:45; u Ps 78:38
14:20 v Ps 106:23; Mic 7:18-20
14:21 w Dt 32:40; Isa 49:18; x Ps 72:19; Isa 6:3; Hab 2:14
14:22 y Ex 14:11; Ex 32:1; 1Co 10:5
14:23 z Nu 32:11; a Heb 3:18
14:24 b ver 6-9; Jos 14:8,14; c Nu 32:12
14:25 d Dt 1:40
14:27 e Ex 16:12
14:28 f ver 21
14:29 g Nu 26:65; h Nu 1:45

forgiving sin and rebellion.[q] Yet he
does not leave the guilty unpunished; he punishes the children for
the sin of the fathers to the third
and fourth generation.'[r] 19In accordance with your great love, forgive[s] the sin of these people,[t] just
as you have pardoned them from
the time they left Egypt until
now."[u]

20The LORD replied, "I have forgiven them,[v] as you asked.
21Nevertheless, as surely as I live[w]
and as surely as the glory of the
LORD fills the whole earth,[x] 22not
one of the men who saw my glory
and the miraculous signs I performed in Egypt and in the desert
but who disobeyed me and tested
me ten times[y]—23not one of them
will ever see the land I promised on
oath[z] to their forefathers. No-one
who has treated me with contempt
will ever see it.[a] 24But because my
servant Caleb has a different spirit
and follows me wholeheartedly,[b] I
will bring him into the land he went
to, and his descendants will inherit
it.[c] 25Since the Amalekites and Canaanites are living in the valleys,
turn[d] back tomorrow and set out
towards the desert along the route
to the Red Sea."[a]

26The LORD said to Moses and
Aaron: 27"How long will this
wicked community grumble
against me? I have heard the complaints of these grumbling Israelites.[e] 28So tell them, 'As surely as
I live,[f] declares the LORD, I will
do to you the very things I heard
you say: 29In this desert your bodies will fall[g]—every one of you
twenty years old or more[h] who
was counted in the census and who
has grumbled against me. 30Not one
of you will enter the land I swore
with uplifted hand to make your
home, except Caleb son of Jephunneh and Joshua son of Nun. 31As for
your children that you said would
be taken as plunder, I will bring

[a]25 Hebrew *Yam Suph*; that is, Sea of Reeds

them in to enjoy the land you have rejected.[i] 32But you—your bodies will fall[j] in this desert. 33Your children will be shepherds here for forty years, suffering for your unfaithfulness, until the last of your bodies lies in the desert. 34For forty years—one year for each of the forty days you explored the land[k]—you will suffer for your sins and know what it is like to have me against you.' 35I, the LORD, have spoken, and I will surely do these things[l] to this whole wicked community, which has banded together against me. They will meet their end in this desert; here they will die."

36So the men Moses had sent[m] to explore the land, who returned and made the whole community grumble against him by spreading a bad report[n] about it—37these men responsible for spreading the bad report[o] about the land were struck down and died of a plague[p] before the LORD. 38Of the men who went to explore the land, only Joshua son of Nun and Caleb son of Jephunneh survived.[q]

39When Moses reported this to all the Israelites, they mourned[r] bitterly. 40Early the next morning they went up towards the high hill country. "We have sinned[s]," they said. "We will go up to the place the LORD promised."

41But Moses said, "Why are you disobeying the LORD's command? This will not succeed![t] 42Do not go up, because the LORD is not with you. You will be defeated by your enemies,[u] 43for the Amalekites and Canaanites will face you there. Because you have turned away from the LORD, he will not be with you and you will fall by the sword."

44Nevertheless, in their presumption they went up[v] towards the high hill country, though neither Moses nor the ark of the LORD's covenant moved from the camp.[w] 45Then the Amalekites and Canaanites who lived in that hill country came down and attacked them and beat them down all the way to Hormah.[x]

Supplementary Offerings

15 The LORD said to Moses, 2"Speak to the Israelites and say to them: 'After you enter the land I am giving you[a] as a home 3and you present to the LORD offerings made by fire, from the herd or the flock,[b] as an aroma pleasing to the LORD[c]—whether burnt offerings[d] or sacrifices, for special vows or freewill offerings[e] or festival offerings[f]—4then the one who brings his offering shall present to the LORD a grain offering[g] of a tenth of an ephah[a] of fine flour mixed with a quarter of a hin[b] of oil. 5With each lamb for the burnt offering or the sacrifice, prepare a quarter of a hin of wine[h] as a drink offering.

6" 'With a ram[i] prepare a grain offering[j] of two-tenths of an ephah[c] of fine flour mixed with a third of a hin[d] of oil,[k] 7and a third of a hin of wine as a drink offering. Offer it as an aroma pleasing to the LORD.

8" 'When you prepare a young bull as a burnt offering or sacrifice, for a special vow or a fellowship offering[e][l] to the LORD, 9bring with the bull a grain offering of three-tenths of an ephah[f][m] of fine flour mixed with half a hin[g] of oil. 10Also bring half a hin of wine as a drink offering. It will be an offering made by fire, an aroma pleasing to the LORD. 11Each bull or ram, each lamb or young goat, is to be prepared in this manner. 12Do this for each one, for as many as you prepare.

14:31 i Ps 106:24
14:32 j 1Co 10:5
14:34 k Nu 13:25
14:35 l Nu 23:19
14:36 m Nu 13:4-16; n Nu 13:32
14:37 o 1Co 10:10; p Nu 16:49
14:38 q Jos 14:6
14:39 r Ex 33:4
14:40 s Dt 1:41
14:41 t 2Ch 24:20
14:42 u Dt 1:42
14:44 v Dt 1:43; w Nu 31:6
14:45 x Nu 21:3; Dt 1:44; Jdg 1:17
15:2 a Lev 23:10
15:3 b Lev 1:2; c ver 24; Ge 8:21; Ex 29:18; d Nu 28:19,27; e Lev 22:18,21; Ezr 1:4; f Lev 23:1-44
15:4 g Lev 2:1; Lev 6:14
15:5 h Nu 28:7,14
15:6 i Lev 5:15; j Nu 28:12; k Eze 46:14
15:8 l Lev 1:3; Lev 3:1
15:9 m Lev 14:10

a4 That is, probably about 4 pints (about 2 litres)
b4 That is, probably about 1½ pints (about 1 litre); also in verse 5
c6 That is, probably about 7½ pints (about 4.5 litres)
d6 That is, probably about 2¼ pints (about 1.2 litres); also in verse 7
e8 Traditionally *peace offering*
f9 That is, probably about 11½ pints (about 6.5 litres)
g9 That is, probably about 3 pints (about 2 litres); also in verse 10

13 "'Everyone who is native-born[n] must do these things in this way when he brings an offering made by fire as an aroma pleasing to the LORD. 14 For the generations to come, whenever an alien or anyone else living among you presents an offering made by fire as an aroma pleasing to the LORD, he must do exactly as you do. 15 The community is to have the same rules for you and for the alien living among you; this is a lasting ordinance for the generations to come.[o] You and the alien shall be the same before the LORD: 16 The same laws and regulations will apply both to you and to the alien living among you.[p]' "

17 The LORD said to Moses, 18 "Speak to the Israelites and say to them: 'When you enter the land to which I am taking you 19 and you eat the food of the land,[q] present a portion as an offering to the LORD. 20 Present a cake from the first of your ground meal[r] and present it as an offering from the threshing-floor.[s] 21 Throughout the generations to come you are to give this offering to the LORD from the first of your ground meal.[t]

Offerings for Unintentional Sins

22 "'Now if you unintentionally fail to keep any of these commands the LORD gave Moses[u]—23 any of the LORD's commands to you through him, from the day the LORD gave them and continuing through the generations to come—24 and if this is done unintentionally without the community being aware of it,[v] then the whole community is to offer a young bull for a burnt offering[w] as an aroma pleasing to the LORD, along with its prescribed grain offering and drink offering, and a male goat for a sin offering.[x] 25 The priest is to make atonement for the whole Israelite community, and they will be forgiven,[y] for it was not intentional and they have brought to the LORD for their wrong an offering made by fire and a sin offering. 26 The whole Israelite community and the aliens living among them will be forgiven, because all the people were involved in the unintentional wrong.[z]

27 "'But if just one person sins unintentionally,[a] he must bring a year-old female goat for a sin offering. 28 The priest is to make atonement before the LORD for the one who erred by sinning unintentionally, and when atonement has been made for him, he will be forgiven.[b] 29 One and the same law applies to everyone who sins unintentionally, whether he is a native-born Israelite or an alien.

30 "'But anyone who sins defiantly,[c] whether native-born or alien,[d] blasphemes the LORD, and that person must be cut off from his people. 31 Because he has despised the LORD's word and broken his commands,[e] that person must surely be cut off; his guilt remains on him.[f]' "

The Sabbath-Breaker Put to Death

32 While the Israelites were in the desert, a man was found gathering wood on the Sabbath day.[g] 33 Those who found him gathering wood brought him to Moses and Aaron and the whole assembly, 34 and they kept him in custody, because it was not clear what should be done to him.[h] 35 Then the LORD said to Moses, "The man must die.[i] The whole assembly must stone him outside the camp.[j]" 36 So the assembly took him outside the camp and stoned him to death, as the LORD commanded Moses.

Tassels on Garments

37 The LORD said to Moses, 38 "Speak to the Israelites and say to them: 'Throughout the generations

15:13 n Lev 16:29
15:15 o ver 29; Nu 9:14
15:16 p Nu 9:14
15:19 q Jos 5:11,12
15:20 r Ex 34:26; Lev 23:14; Dt 26:2,10; s Lev 2:14
15:21 t Ro 11:16
15:22 u Lev 4:2
15:24 v Lev 5:15; w Lev 4:14; x Lev 4:3
15:25 y Lev 4:20; Ro 3:25; Heb 2:17
15:26 z ver 24
15:27 a Lev 4:27
15:28 b Lev 4:35
15:30 c Nu 14:40-44; Dt 1:43; Dt 17:13; Ps 19:13; d ver 14
15:31 e 2Sa 12:9; Ps 119:126; Pr 13:13; f Lev 5:1; Eze 18:20
15:32 g Ex 31:14,15; Ex 35:2,3
15:34 h Nu 9:8
15:35 i Ex 31:14,15; Dt 21:21; j Lev 20:2; Lev 24:14; Ac 7:58

to come you are to make tassels on
the corners of your garments,[k]
with a blue cord on each tassel.
39 You will have these tassels to look
at and so you will remember[l] all
the commands of the LORD, that
you may obey them and not prostitute yourselves by going after the
lusts of your own hearts and eyes.
40 Then you will remember to obey
all my commands and will be consecrated to your God.[m] 41 I am the
LORD your God, who brought you
out of Egypt to be your God. I am
the LORD your God.' "

Korah, Dathan and Abiram

16 Korah[a] son of Izhar, the
son of Kohath, the son of
Levi, and certain Reubenites—Dathan and Abiram, sons of Eliab,[b]
and On son of Peleth—became
insolent[a] 2 and rose up against
Moses. With them were 250 Israelite men, well-known community
leaders who had been appointed
members of the council.[c] 3 They
came as a group to oppose Moses
and Aaron[d] and said to them, "You
have gone too far! The whole community is holy,[e] every one of them,
and the LORD is with them.[f] Why
then do you set yourselves above
the LORD's assembly?"[g]
4 When Moses heard this, he fell
face down.[h] 5 Then he said to Korah
and all his followers: "In the morning the LORD will show who belongs
to him and who is holy,[i] and he will
make that person come near him.
The man he chooses[j] he will cause
to come near him. 6 You, Korah, and
all your followers are to do this:
Take censers 7 and tomorrow put
fire and incense in them before the
LORD. The man the LORD chooses
will be the one who is holy. You
Levites have gone too far!"
8 Moses also said to Korah, "Now
listen, you Levites! 9 Isn't it enough
for you that the God of Israel has
separated you from the rest of the
Israelite community and brought
you near himself to do the work at
the LORD's tabernacle and to stand
before the community and minister to them?[k] 10 He has brought you
and all your fellow Levites near
himself, but now you are trying to
get the priesthood too.[l] 11 It is
against the LORD that you and all
your followers have banded together. Who is Aaron that you
should grumble[m] against him?[n]"
12 Then Moses summoned Dathan
and Abiram, the sons of Eliab. But
they said, "We will not come! 13 Isn't
it enough that you have brought us
up out of a land flowing with milk
and honey to kill us in the desert?[o]
And now you also want to lord it
over us?[p] 14 Moreover, you haven't
brought us into a land flowing with
milk and honey[q] or given us an
inheritance of fields and vineyards.[r] Will you gouge out the eyes
of[b] these men?[s] No, we will not
come!"
15 Then Moses became very
angry and said to the LORD, "Do not
accept their offering. I have not
taken so much as a donkey[t] from
them, nor have I wronged any of
them."
16 Moses said to Korah, "You and
all your followers are to appear before the LORD tomorrow—you and
they and Aaron.[u] 17 Each man is to
take his censer and put incense in
it—250 censers in all—and present
it before the LORD. You and Aaron
are to present your censers also."
18 So each man took his censer, put
fire and incense in it, and stood
with Moses and Aaron at the entrance to the Tent of Meeting.
19 When Korah had gathered all his
followers in opposition to them[v]
at the entrance to the Tent of
Meeting, the glory of the LORD[w]
appeared to the entire assembly.
20 The LORD said to Moses and
Aaron, 21 "Separate yourselves

15:38 k Dt 22:12; Mt 23:5
15:39 l Dt 4:23; Dt 6:12; Ps 73:27
15:40 m Lev 11:44; Ro 12:1; Col 1:22; 1Pe 1:15
16:1 a Jude 1:11; b Nu 26:8; Dt 11:6
16:2 c Nu 1:16; Nu 26:9
16:3 d ver 7; Ps 106:16; e Ex 19:6; f Nu 14:14; g Nu 12:2
16:4 h Nu 14:5
16:5 i Lev 10:3; 2Ti 2:19*; j Nu 17:5; Ps 65:4
16:9 k Nu 3:6; Dt 10:8
16:10 l Nu 3:10; Nu 18:7
16:11 m 1Co 10:10; n Ex 16:7
16:13 o Nu 14:2; p Ac 7:27,35
16:14 q Lev 20:24; r Ex 22:5; Ex 23:11; Nu 20:5; s Jdg 16:21; 1Sa 11:2
16:15 t 1Sa 12:3
16:16 u ver 6
16:19 v ver 42; w Ex 16:7; Nu 14:10; Nu 20:6

a1 Or *Peleth—took ⌞men⌟*   b14 Or *you make slaves of*; or *you deceive*

from this assembly so that I can put
an end to them at once."[x]
22 But Moses and Aaron fell face
down[y] and cried out, "O God, God
of the spirits of all mankind,[z] will
you be angry with the entire assembly when only one man sins?"[a]
23 Then the LORD said to Moses,
24 "Say to the assembly, 'Move away
from the tents of Korah, Dathan
and Abiram.' "
25 Moses got up and went to Dathan and Abiram, and the elders of
Israel followed him. 26 He warned
the assembly, "Move back from the
tents of these wicked men![b] Do not
touch anything belonging to them,
or you will be swept away[c] because of all their sins." 27 So they
moved away from the tents of Korah, Dathan and Abiram. Dathan
and Abiram had come out and were
standing with their wives, children
and little ones at the entrances to
their tents.
28 Then Moses said, "This is how
you will know that the LORD has
sent me[d] to do all these things and
that it was not my idea: 29 If these
men die a natural death and experience only what usually happens to
men, then the LORD has not sent
me.[e] 30 But if the LORD brings about
something totally new, and the
earth opens its mouth and swallows
them, with everything that belongs
to them, and they go down alive
into the grave,[c][f] then you will
know that these men have treated
the LORD with contempt."
31 As soon as he finished saying
all this, the ground under them
split apart[g] 32 and the earth opened
its mouth and swallowed them,[h]
with their households and all Korah's men and all their possessions.
33 They went down alive into the
grave, with everything they
owned; the earth closed over them,
and they perished and were gone
from the community. 34 At their
cries, all the Israelites around
them fled, shouting, "The earth is
going to swallow us too!"

16:21 x Ex 32:10
16:22 y Nu 14:5 z Nu 27:16; Job 12:10; Heb 12:9 a Ge 18:23
16:26 b Isa 52:11 c Ge 19:15
16:28 d Ex 3:12; Jn 5:36; Jn 6:38
16:29 e Ecc 3:19
16:30 f ver 33; Ps 55:15
16:31 g Mic 1:3-4
16:32 h Nu 26:11; Dt 11:6; Ps 106:17
16:35 i Nu 11:1-3; Nu 26:10 j Lev 10:2
16:38 k Pr 20:2 l Nu 26:10; Eze 14:8; 2Pe 2:6
16:40 m Ex 30:7-10; Nu 1:51 n 2Ch 26:18 o Nu 3:10
16:42 p ver 19; Nu 20:6
16:46 q Lev 10:6 r Nu 18:5; Nu 25:13; Dt 9:22

35 And fire came out from the
LORD[i] and consumed[j] the 250
men who were offering the incense.
36 The LORD said to Moses, 37 "Tell
Eleazar son of Aaron, the priest, to
take the censers out of the smouldering remains and scatter the
coals some distance away, for the
censers are holy—38 the censers
of the men who sinned at the cost
of their lives.[k] Hammer the censers into sheets to overlay the
altar, for they were presented
before the LORD and have become
holy. Let them be a sign[l] to the Israelites."
39 So Eleazar the priest collected
the bronze censers brought by
those who had been burned up, and
he had them hammered out to overlay the altar, 40 as the LORD directed
him through Moses. This was to remind the Israelites that no-one except a descendant of Aaron should
come to burn incense[m] before the
LORD,[n] or he would become like
Korah and his followers.[o]
41 The next day the whole Israelite community grumbled against
Moses and Aaron. "You have killed
the LORD's people," they said.
42 But when the assembly gathered in opposition[p] to Moses and
Aaron and turned towards the Tent
of Meeting, suddenly the cloud covered it and the glory of the LORD appeared. 43 Then Moses and Aaron
went to the front of the Tent of
Meeting, 44 and the LORD said to
Moses, 45 "Get away from this assembly so that I can put an end to
them at once." And they fell face
down.
46 Then Moses said to Aaron,
"Take your censer and put incense
in it, along with fire from the altar,
and hurry to the assembly[q] to
make atonement[r] for them. Wrath
has come out from the LORD; the

c30 Hebrew *Sheol*; also in verse 33

plague[s] has started." 47So Aaron did as Moses said, and ran into the midst of the assembly. The plague had already started among the people,[t] but Aaron offered the incense and made atonement for them. 48He stood between the living and the dead, and the plague stopped.[u] 49But 14,700 people died from the plague, in addition to those who had died because of Korah.[v] 50Then Aaron returned to Moses at the entrance to the Tent of Meeting, for the plague had stopped.

The Budding of Aaron's Staff

17 The LORD said to Moses, 2"Speak to the Israelites and get twelve staffs from them, one from the leader of each of their ancestral tribes. Write the name of each man on his staff. 3On the staff of Levi write Aaron's name,[a] for there must be one staff for the head of each ancestral tribe. 4Place them in the Tent of Meeting in front of the Testimony,[b] where I meet with you.[c] 5The staff belonging to the man I choose[d] will sprout, and I will rid myself of this constant grumbling against you by the Israelites."

6So Moses spoke to the Israelites, and their leaders gave him twelve staffs, one for the leader of each of their ancestral tribes, and Aaron's staff was among them. 7Moses placed the staffs before the LORD in the Tent of the Testimony.[e]

8The next day Moses entered the Tent of the Testimony and saw that Aaron's staff, which represented the house of Levi, had not only sprouted but had budded, blossomed and produced almonds.[f] 9Then Moses brought out all the staffs from the LORD's presence to all the Israelites. They looked at them, and each man took his own staff.

10The LORD said to Moses, "Put back Aaron's staff in front of the Testimony, to be kept as a sign to the rebellious.[g] This will put an end to their grumbling against me, so that they will not die." 11Moses did just as the LORD commanded him.

12The Israelites said to Moses, "We shall die! We are lost, we are all lost![h] 13Anyone who even comes near the tabernacle of the LORD will die.[i] Are we all going to die?"

Duties of Priests and Levites

18 The LORD said to Aaron, "You, your sons and your father's family are to bear the responsibility for offences against the sanctuary,[a] and you and your sons alone are to bear the responsibility for offences against the priesthood. 2Bring your fellow Levites from your ancestral tribe to join you and assist you when you and your sons minister[b] before the Tent of the Testimony. 3They are to be responsible to you and are to perform all the duties of the Tent,[c] but they must not go near the furnishings of the sanctuary or the altar, or both they and you will die.[d] 4They are to join you and be responsible for the care of the Tent of Meeting—all the work at the Tent—and no-one else may come near where you are.

5"You are to be responsible for the care of the sanctuary and the altar,[e] so that wrath will not fall on the Israelites again. 6I myself have selected your fellow Levites from among the Israelites as a gift to you,[f] dedicated to the LORD to do the work at the Tent of Meeting. 7But only you and your sons may serve as priests in connection with everything at the altar and inside the curtain.[g] I am giving you the service of the priesthood as a gift.[h] Anyone else who comes near the sanctuary must be put to death.[i]"

16:46 s Nu 8:19; Ps 106:29
16:47 t Nu 25:6-8
16:48 u Nu 25:8; Ps 106:30
16:49 v ver 32
17:3 a Nu 1:3
17:4 b ver 7; c Ex 25:22
17:5 d Nu 16:5
17:7 e Ex 38:21; Ac 7:44
17:8 f Eze 17:24; Heb 9:4
17:10 g Dt 9:24
17:12 h Isa 6:5
17:13 i Nu 1:51
18:1 a Ex 28:38
18:2 b Nu 3:10
18:3 c Nu 1:51; d ver 7; Nu 4:15
18:5 e Nu 16:46
18:6 f Nu 3:9
18:7 g Heb 9:3,6; h ver 20; Ex 29:9; i Nu 3:10

Offerings for Priests and Levites

8Then the LORD said to Aaron, "I myself have put you in charge of the offerings presented to me; all the holy offerings the Israelites give me I give to you and your sons as your portion and regular share.[j] 9You are to have the part of the most holy offerings that is kept from the fire. From all the gifts they bring me as most holy offerings, whether grain[k] or sin[l] or guilt offerings,[m] that part belongs to you and your sons. 10Eat it as something most holy; every male shall eat it.[n] You must regard it as holy.

11"This also is yours: whatever is set aside from the gifts of all the wave offerings[o] of the Israelites. I give this to you and your sons and daughters as your regular share. Everyone in your household who is ceremonially clean[p] may eat it.

12"I give you all the finest olive oil and all the finest new wine and grain they give to the LORD as the firstfruits of their harvest.[q] 13All the land's firstfruits that they bring to the LORD will be yours.[r] Everyone in your household who is ceremonially clean may eat it.

14"Everything in Israel that is devoted[a] to the LORD[s] is yours. 15The first offspring of every womb, both man and animal, that is offered to the LORD is yours.[t] But you must redeem[u] every firstborn son and every firstborn male of unclean animals.[v] 16When they are a month old, you must redeem them at the redemption price set at five shekels[b][w] of silver, according to the sanctuary shekel,[x] which weighs twenty gerahs.

17"But you must not redeem the firstborn of an ox, a sheep or a goat; they are holy.[y] Sprinkle their blood[z] on the altar and burn their fat as an offering made by fire, an aroma pleasing to the LORD. 18Their meat is to be yours, just as the breast of the wave offering[a] and the right thigh are yours. 19Whatever is set aside from the holy offerings the Israelites present to the LORD I give to you and your sons and daughters as your regular share. It is an everlasting covenant of salt[b] before the LORD for both you and your offspring."

20The LORD said to Aaron, "You will have no inheritance in their land, nor will you have any share among them;[c] I am your share and your inheritance[d] among the Israelites.

21"I give to the Levites all the tithes[e] in Israel as their inheritance[f] in return for the work they do while serving at the Tent of Meeting. 22From now on the Israelites must not go near the Tent of Meeting, or they will bear the consequences of their sin and will die.[g] 23It is the Levites who are to do the work at the Tent of Meeting and bear the responsibility for offences against it. This is a lasting ordinance for the generations to come. They will receive no inheritance[h] among the Israelites. 24Instead, I give to the Levites as their inheritance the tithes that the Israelites present as an offering to the LORD. That is why I said concerning them: 'They will have no inheritance among the Israelites.' "

25The LORD said to Moses, 26"Speak to the Levites and say to them: 'When you receive from the Israelites the tithe I give you[i] as your inheritance, you must present a tenth of that tithe as the LORD's offering.[j] 27Your offering will be reckoned to you as grain from the threshing-floor or juice from the winepress. 28In this way you also will present an offering to the LORD from all the tithes[k] you receive from the Israelites. From these tithes you must give the LORD's

18:8 j Lev 6:16; Lev 7:6, 31-34,36
18:9 k Lev 2:1; l Lev 6:25; m Lev 5:15; Lev 7:7
18:10 n Lev 6:16
18:11 o Ex 29:26; p Lev 22:1-16
18:12 q Ex 23:19; Ne 10:35
18:13 r Ex 22:29; Ex 23:19
18:14 s Lev 27:28
18:15 t Ex 13:2; u Nu 3:46; v Ex 13:13
18:16 w Lev 27:6; x Ex 30:13
18:17 y Dt 15:19; z Lev 3:2
18:18 a Lev 7:30
18:19 b Lev 2:13; 2Ch 13:5
18:20 c Dt 12:12; d Dt 10:9; Dt 14:27; Dt 18:1-2; Jos 13:33; Eze 44:28
18:21 e Dt 14:22; Mal 3:8; f Lev 27:30-33; Heb 7:5
18:22 g Lev 22:9; Nu 1:51
18:23 h ver 20
18:26 i ver 21; j Ne 10:38
18:28 k Mal 3:8

a *14* The Hebrew term refers to the irrevocable giving over of things or persons to the LORD.
b *16* That is, about 2 ounces (about 55 grams)

portion to Aaron the priest. [29]You must present as the LORD's portion the best and holiest part of everything given to you.'

[30]"Say to the Levites: 'When you present the best part, it will be reckoned to you as the product of the threshing-floor or the winepress.[l] [31]You and your households may eat the rest of it anywhere, for it is your wages for your work at the Tent of Meeting. [32]By presenting the best part[m] of it you will not be guilty in this matter; then you will not defile the holy offerings[n] of the Israelites, and you will not die.' "

The Water of Cleansing

19 The LORD said to Moses and Aaron: [2]"This is a requirement of the law that the LORD has commanded: Tell the Israelites to bring you a red heifer[a] without defect or blemish[b] and that has never been under a yoke.[c] [3]Give it to Eleazar[d] the priest; it is to be taken outside the camp[e] and slaughtered in his presence. [4]Then Eleazar the priest is to take some of its blood on his finger and sprinkle[f] it seven times towards the front of the Tent of Meeting. [5]While he watches, the heifer is to be burned—its hide, flesh, blood and offal.[g] [6]The priest is to take some cedar wood, hyssop[h] and scarlet wool[i] and throw them onto the burning heifer. [7]After that, the priest must wash his clothes and bathe himself with water.[j] He may then come into the camp, but he will be ceremonially unclean till evening. [8]The man who burns it must also wash his clothes and bathe with water, and he too will be unclean till evening.

[9]"A man who is clean shall gather up the ashes of the heifer[k] and put them in a ceremonially clean place outside the camp. They shall be kept by the Israelite community for use in the water of cleansing;[l] it is for purification from sin. [10]The man who gathers up the ashes of the heifer must also wash his clothes, and he too will be unclean till evening. This will be a lasting ordinance both for the Israelites and for the aliens living among them.

[11]"Whoever touches the dead body[m] of anyone will be unclean for seven days.[n] [12]He must purify himself with the water on the third day and on the seventh day;[o] then he will be clean. But if he does not purify himself on the third and seventh days, he will not be clean. [13]Whoever touches the dead body[p] of anyone and fails to purify himself defiles the LORD's tabernacle.[q] That person must be cut off from Israel.[r] Because the water of cleansing has not been sprinkled on him, he is unclean;[s] his uncleanness remains on him.

[14]"This is the law that applies when a person dies in a tent: Anyone who enters the tent and anyone who is in it will be unclean for seven days, [15]and every open container without a lid fastened on it will be unclean.

[16]"Anyone out in the open who touches someone who has been killed with a sword or someone who has died a natural death,[t] or anyone who touches a human bone or a grave,[u] will be unclean for seven days.

[17]"For the unclean person, put some ashes[v] from the burned purification offering into a jar and pour fresh water over them. [18]Then a man who is ceremonially clean is to take some hyssop,[w] dip it in the water and sprinkle the tent and all the furnishings and the people who were there. He must also sprinkle anyone who has touched a human bone or a grave or someone who has been killed or someone who has died a natural death. [19]The man who is clean is to sprinkle the unclean person on the third and seventh days, and on the seventh day

18:30 *l* ver 27
18:32 *m* Lev 22:15 *n* Lev 19:8
19:2 *a* Ge 15:9; Heb 9:13 *b* Lev 22:19-25 *c* Dt 21:3; 1Sa 6:7
19:3 *d* Nu 3:4 *e* Lev 4:12,21; Heb 13:11
19:4 *f* Lev 4:17
19:5 *g* Ex 29:14
19:6 *h* ver 18; Ps 51:7 *i* Lev 14:4
19:7 *j* Lev 11:25; Lev 16:26,28; Lev 22:6
19:9 *k* Heb 9:13 *l* ver 13; Nu 8:7
19:11 *m* Lev 21:1; Nu 5:2 *n* Nu 31:19
19:12 *o* ver 19; Nu 31:19
19:13 *p* Lev 20:3 *q* Lev 15:31; 2Ch 36:14 *r* Lev 7:20; Lev 22:3 *s* Hag 2:13
19:16 *t* Nu 31:19 *u* Mt 23:27
19:17 *v* ver 9
19:18 *w* ver 6

he is to purify him.[x] The person
being cleansed must wash his
clothes and bathe with water, and
that evening he will be clean. 20But
if a person who is unclean does not
purify himself, he must be cut off
from the community, because he
has defiled the sanctuary of the
LORD. The water of cleansing has
not been sprinkled on him, and he is
unclean. 21This is a lasting ordinance for them.
"The man who sprinkles the
water of cleansing must also wash
his clothes, and anyone who
touches the water of cleansing will
be unclean till evening. 22Anything
that an unclean[y] person touches
becomes unclean, and anyone who
touches it becomes unclean till
evening."

Water From the Rock

20 In the first month the
whole Israelite community
arrived at the Desert of Zin,[a] and
they stayed at Kadesh.[b] There
Miriam[c] died and was buried.
2Now there was no water for the
community,[d] and the people gathered in opposition[e] to Moses and
Aaron. 3They quarrelled[f] with
Moses and said, "If only we had
died when our brothers fell dead
before the LORD![g] 4Why did you
bring the LORD's community into
this desert, that we and our livestock should die here?[h] 5Why did
you bring us up out of Egypt to this
terrible place? It has no grain or
figs, grapevines or pomegranates.[i] And there is no water to
drink!"
6Moses and Aaron went from the
assembly to the entrance to the
Tent of Meeting and fell face
down,[j] and the glory of the LORD[k]
appeared to them. 7The LORD said
to Moses, 8"Take the staff,[l] and
you and your brother Aaron gather
the assembly together. Speak to
that rock before their eyes and it
will pour out its water.[m] You will
bring water out of the rock for the
community so that they and their
livestock can drink."
9So Moses took the staff from the
LORD's presence,[n] just as he commanded him. 10He and Aaron gathered the assembly together in front
of the rock and Moses said to them,
"Listen, you rebels, must we bring
you water out of this rock?"[o]
11Then Moses raised his arm and
struck the rock twice with his staff.
Water[p] gushed out, and the community and their livestock drank.
12But the LORD said to Moses and
Aaron, "Because you did not trust
in me enough to honour me as
holy[q] in the sight of the Israelites,
you will not bring this community
into the land I give them."[r]
13These were the waters of Meribah,[a][s] where the Israelites quarrelled[t] with the LORD and where
he showed himself holy among
them.

Edom Denies Israel Passage

14Moses sent messengers from
Kadesh[u] to the king of Edom,[v]
saying:

"This is what your brother
Israel says: You know[w] about
all the hardships that have
come upon us. 15Our fore-
fathers went down into
Egypt,[x] and we lived there
many years.[y] The Egyptians
ill-treated[z] us and our fathers,
16but when we cried out to the
LORD, he heard our cry[a] and
sent an angel[b] and brought us
out of Egypt.
"Now we are here at Kadesh,
a town on the edge of your
territory. 17Please let us pass
through your country. We will
not go through any field or
vineyard, or drink water from
any well. We will travel along
the king's highway and not
turn to the right or to the left

19:19 x Eze 36:25; Heb 10:22
19:22 y Lev 5:2; Hag 2:13,14
20:1 a Nu 13:21; b Nu 33:36; c Ex 15:20
20:2 d Ex 17:1; e Nu 16:19
20:3 f Ex 17:2; g Nu 14:2; Nu 16:31-35
20:4 h Ex 14:11; Ex 17:3; Nu 14:3; Nu 16:13
20:5 i Nu 16:14
20:6 j Nu 14:5; k Nu 16:19
20:8 l Ex 4:17,20; m Ex 17:6; Isa 43:20
20:9 n Nu 17:10
20:10 o Ps 106:32,33
20:11 p Ex 17:6; Dt 8:15; Ps 78:16; Isa 48:2; 1Co 10:4
20:12 q Nu 27:14; r ver 24; Dt 1:37; Dt 3:27
20:13 s Ex 17:7; t Dt 33:8; Ps 95:8; Ps 106:32
20:14 u Jdg 11:16-17; v Dt 2:4; w Jos 2:11; Jos 9:9
20:15 x Ge 46:6; y Ge 15:13; Ex 12:40; z Ex 1:11; Dt 26:6
20:16 a Ex 2:23; Ex 3:7; b Ex 14:19

[a] 13 *Meribah* means *quarrelling*.

until we have passed through
your territory.[c]"

18But Edom answered:

"You may not pass through
here; if you try, we will march
out and attack you with the
sword."

19The Israelites replied:

"We will go along the main
road, and if we or our livestock[d] drink any of your
water, we will pay for it.[e] We
only want to pass through on
foot—nothing else."

20Again they answered:

"You may not pass through."

Then Edom came out against
them with a large and powerful
army. 21Since Edom refused to let
them go through their territory,
Israel turned away from them.[f]

The Death of Aaron

22The whole Israelite community
set out from Kadesh and came to
Mount Hor.[g] 23At Mount Hor, near
the border of Edom,[h] the LORD said
to Moses and Aaron, 24"Aaron will
be gathered to his people.[i] He will
not enter the land I give the Israelites, because both of you rebelled
against my command[j] at the
waters of Meribah. 25Call Aaron
and his son Eleazar and take them
up Mount Hor.[k] 26Remove Aaron's
garments and put them on his son
Eleazar, for Aaron will be gathered
to his people;[l] he will die there."
27Moses did as the LORD commanded: They went up Mount Hor
in the sight of the whole community. 28Moses removed Aaron's garments and put them on his son
Eleazar.[m] And Aaron died there[n]
on top of the mountain. Then Moses
and Eleazar came down from the
mountain, 29and when the whole
community learned that Aaron had
died, the entire house of Israel
mourned for him[o] thirty days.

20:17 c Nu 21:22
20:19 d Ex 12:38 e Dt 2:6,28
20:21 f Dt 2:8 Jdg 11:18
20:22 g Nu 33:37
20:23 h Nu 33:37
20:24 i Ge 25:8 j ver 10
20:25 k Nu 33:38
20:26 l ver 24
20:28 m Ex 29:29 n Nu 33:38 Dt 10:6 Dt 32:50
20:29 o Dt 34:8
21:1 a Nu 33:40 Jos 12:14 b Jdg 1:9,16
21:4 c Nu 20:22 d Dt 2:8 Jdg 11:18
21:5 e Ps 78:19 f Nu 14:2,3 g Nu 11:6
21:6 h Dt 8:15 Jer 8:17 i 1Co 10:9
21:7 j Ps 78:34 Hos 5:15 k Ex 8:8 Ac 8:24 l Nu 11:2
21:8 m Jn 3:14
21:9 n 2Ki 18:4 o Jn 3:14-15
21:10 p Nu 33:43

Arad Destroyed

21 When the Canaanite king of
Arad,[a] who lived in the
Negev,[b] heard that Israel was
coming along the road to Atharim,
he attacked the Israelites and captured some of them. 2Then Israel
made this vow to the LORD: "If you
will deliver these people into our
hands, we will totally destroy[a]
their cities." 3The LORD listened to
Israel's plea and gave the Canaanites over to them. They completely
destroyed them and their towns; so
the place was named Hormah.[b]

The Bronze Snake

4They travelled from Mount
Hor[c] along the route to the Red
Sea,[c] to go round Edom. But the
people grew impatient on the
way;[d] 5they spoke against God[e]
and against Moses, and said, "Why
have you brought us up out of
Egypt to die in the desert?[f] There
is no bread! There is no water! And
we detest this miserable food!"[g]
6Then the LORD sent venomous
snakes[h] among them; they bit the
people and many Israelites died.[i]
7The people came to Moses[j] and
said, "We sinned when we spoke
against the LORD and against you.
Pray that the LORD[k] will take the
snakes away from us." So Moses
prayed[l] for the people.
8The LORD said to Moses, "Make
a snake and put it up on a pole;[m]
anyone who is bitten can look at it
and live." 9So Moses made a bronze
snake[n] and put it up on a pole.
Then when anyone was bitten by a
snake and looked at the bronze
snake, he lived.[o]

The Journey to Moab

10The Israelites moved on and
camped at Oboth.[p] 11Then they set

a2 The Hebrew term refers to the irrevocable giving over of things or persons to the LORD, often by totally destroying them; also in verse 3.
b3 *Hormah* means *destruction.* c4 Hebrew *Yam Suph*; that is, Sea of Reeds

out from Oboth and camped in Iye
Abarim, in the desert that faces
Moab[q] towards the sunrise.
12From there they moved on and
camped in the Zered Valley.[r]
13They set out from there and
camped alongside the Arnon[s],
which is in the desert extending
into Amorite territory. The Arnon
is the border of Moab, between
Moab and the Amorites. 14That is
why the Book of the Wars of the
LORD says:

"... Waheb in Suphah[d] and the
ravines,
the Arnon 15and[e] the slopes of
the ravines
that lead to the site of Ar[t]
and lie along the border of
Moab."

16From there they continued on to
Beer,[u] the well where the LORD
said to Moses, "Gather the people
together and I will give them
water."
17Then Israel sang this song:[v]

"Spring up, O well!
Sing about it,
18about the well that the princes
dug,
that the nobles of the people
sank—
the nobles with sceptres and
staffs."

Then they went from the desert to
Mattanah, 19from Mattanah to Nahaliel, from Nahaliel to Bamoth,
20and from Bamoth to the valley in
Moab where the top of Pisgah overlooks the wasteland.

Defeat of Sihon and Og

21Israel sent messengers to say
to Sihon[w] king of the Amorites:

22"Let us pass through your
country. We will not turn aside
into any field or vineyard, or
drink water from any well. We
will travel along the king's
highway until we have passed
through your territory.[x]"

23But Sihon would not let Israel
pass through his territory.[y] He
mustered his entire army and
marched out into the desert against
Israel. When he reached Jahaz,[z]
he fought with Israel. 24Israel, however, put him to the sword[a] and
took over his land from the Arnon
to the Jabbok, but only as far as the
Ammonites,[b] because their border
was fortified. 25Israel captured all
the cities of the Amorites[c] and occupied them, including Heshbon
and all its surrounding settlements. 26Heshbon was the city of
Sihon[d] king of the Amorites, who
had fought against the former king
of Moab and had taken from him all
his land as far as the Arnon.
27That is why the poets say:

"Come to Heshbon and let it be
rebuilt;
let Sihon's city be restored.

28"Fire went out from Heshbon,
a blaze from the city of
Sihon.[e]
It consumed Ar[f] of Moab,
the citizens of Arnon's
heights.[g]
29Woe to you, O Moab![h]
You are destroyed, O people
of Chemosh![i]
He has given up his sons as
fugitives[j]
and his daughters as
captives[k]
to Sihon king of the Amorites.

30"But we have overthrown them;
Heshbon is destroyed all the
way to Dibon.[l]
We have demolished them as
far as Nophah,
which extends to Medeba."

31So Israel settled in the land of
the Amorites.
32After Moses had sent spies to
Jazer,[m] the Israelites captured its
surrounding settlements and drove
out the Amorites who were there.

21:11 q Nu 33:44
21:12 r Dt 2:13,14
21:13 s Nu 22:36; Jdg 11:13,18
21:15 t ver 28; Dt 2:9,18
21:16 u Jdg 9:21
21:17 v Ex 15:1
21:21 w Dt 1:4; Dt 2:26-27; Jdg 11:19-21
21:22 x Nu 20:17
21:23 y Nu 20:21; z Dt 2:32; Jdg 11:20
21:24 a Dt 2:33; Ps 135:10-11; Am 2:9; b Dt 2:37
21:25 c Nu 13:29; Jdg 10:11; Am 2:10
21:26 d Dt 29:7; Ps 135:11
21:28 e Jer 48:45; f ver 15; g Nu 22:41; Isa 15:2
21:29 h Isa 25:10; Jer 48:46; i Jdg 11:24; 1Ki 11:7,33; 2Ki 23:13; Jer 48:7,46; j Isa 15:5; k Isa 16:2
21:30 l Nu 32:3; Isa 15:2; Jer 48:18,22
21:32 m Nu 32:1,3,35; Jer 48:32

d*14* The meaning of the Hebrew for this phrase is uncertain. e*14,15* Or "*I have been given from Suphah and the ravines / of the Arnon* 15*to*

33Then they turned and went up
along the road towards Bashan[n],[o]
and Og king of Bashan and his
whole army marched out to meet
them in battle at Edrei.[p]
34The LORD said to Moses, "Do
not be afraid of him, for I have
handed him over to you, with his
whole army and his land. Do to him
what you did to Sihon king of the
Amorites, who reigned in Heshbon.[q]"
35So they struck him down, together with his sons and his whole
army, leaving them no survivors.
And they took possession of his
land.

Balak Summons Balaam

22 Then the Israelites travelled to the plains of Moab
and camped along the Jordan
across from Jericho.[a][a]
2Now Balak son of Zippor[b] saw
all that Israel had done to the Amorites, 3and Moab was terrified because there were so many people.
Indeed, Moab was filled with
dread[c] because of the Israelites.
4The Moabites said to the elders
of Midian, "This horde is going to
lick up everything around us, as an
ox licks up the grass of the field."
So Balak son of Zippor, who was
king of Moab at that time, 5sent
messengers to summon Balaam
son of Beor,[d] who was at Pethor,
near the River,[b] in his native land.
Balak said:

"A people has come out of
Egypt; they cover the face of
the land and have settled next
to me. 6Now come and put a
curse[e] on these people, because they are too powerful for
me. Perhaps then I will be able
to defeat them and drive them
out of the country. For I know
that those you bless are
blessed, and those you curse
are cursed."

7The elders of Moab and Midian
left, taking with them the fee for
divination.[f] When they came to
Balaam, they told him what Balak
had said.
8"Spend the night here," Balaam
said to them, "and I will bring you
back the answer the LORD gives
me.[g]" So the Moabite princes
stayed with him.
9God came to Balaam[h] and
asked,[i] "Who are these men with
you?"
10Balaam said to God, "Balak son
of Zippor, king of Moab, sent me
this message: 11'A people that has
come out of Egypt covers the face
of the land. Now come and put a
curse on them for me. Perhaps then
I will be able to fight them and
drive them away.' "
12But God said to Balaam, "Do
not go with them. You must not put
a curse on those people, because
they are blessed.[j]"
13The next morning Balaam got
up and said to Balak's princes, "Go
back to your own country, for the
LORD has refused to let me go with
you."
14So the Moabite princes returned to Balak and said, "Balaam
refused to come with us."
15Then Balak sent other princes,
more numerous and more distinguished than the first. 16They came
to Balaam and said:

"This is what Balak son of
Zippor says: Do not let anything keep you from coming to
me, 17because I will reward
you handsomely[k] and do whatever you say. Come and put a
curse[l] on these people for
me."

18But Balaam answered them,
"Even if Balak gave me his palace
filled with silver and gold, I could
not do anything great or small to go
beyond the command of the LORD

21:33 n Dt 3:3 o Dt 3:4 p Dt 1:4; Dt 3:1,10; Jos 13:12,31
21:34 q Dt 3:2
22:1 a Nu 33:48
22:2 b Jdg 11:25
22:3 c Ex 15:15
22:5 d Dt 23:4; Jos 13:22; Jos 24:9; Ne 13:2; Mic 6:5; 2Pe 2:15
22:6 e ver 12,17; Nu 23:7,11,13
22:7 f Nu 23:23; Nu 24:1
22:8 g ver 19
22:9 h Ge 20:3 i ver 20
22:12 j Ge 12:2; Ge 22:17; Nu 23:20
22:17 k ver 37; Nu 24:11 l ver 6

[a]1 Hebrew *Jordan of Jericho*; possibly an ancient name for the Jordan River [b]5 That is, the Euphrates

my God.[m] 19Now stay here tonight as the others did, and I will find out what else the LORD will tell me.[n]"

20That night God came to Balaam[o] and said, "Since these men have come to summon you, go with them, but do only what I tell you."[p]

Balaam's Donkey

21Balaam got up in the morning, saddled his donkey and went with the princes of Moab. 22But God was very angry[q] when he went, and the angel of the LORD[r] stood in the road to oppose him. Balaam was riding on his donkey, and his two servants were with him. 23When the donkey saw the angel of the LORD standing in the road with a drawn sword[s] in his hand, she turned off the road into a field. Balaam beat her[t] to get her back on the road.

24Then the angel of the LORD stood in a narrow path between two vineyards, with walls on both sides. 25When the donkey saw the angel of the LORD, she pressed close to the wall, crushing Balaam's foot against it. So he beat her again.

26Then the angel of the LORD moved on ahead and stood in a narrow place where there was no room to turn, either to the right or to the left. 27When the donkey saw the angel of the LORD, she lay down under Balaam, and he was angry[u] and beat her with his staff. 28Then the LORD opened the donkey's mouth,[v] and she said to Balaam, "What have I done to you to make you beat me these three times?[w]"

29Balaam answered the donkey, "You have made a fool of me! If I had a sword in my hand, I would kill you right now.[x]"

30The donkey said to Balaam, "Am I not your own donkey, which you have always ridden, to this day? Have I been in the habit of doing this to you?"

"No," he said.

31Then the LORD opened Balaam's eyes,[y] and he saw the angel of the LORD standing in the road with his sword drawn. So he bowed low and fell face down.

32The angel of the LORD asked him, "Why have you beaten your donkey these three times? I have come here to oppose you because your path is a reckless one before me.[c] 33The donkey saw me and turned away from me these three times. If she had not turned away, I would certainly have killed you by now,[z] but I would have spared her."

34Balaam said to the angel of the LORD, "I have sinned.[a] I did not realise you were standing in the road to oppose me. Now if you are displeased, I will go back."

35The angel of the LORD said to Balaam, "Go with the men, but speak only what I tell you." So Balaam went with the princes of Balak.

36When Balak heard that Balaam was coming, he went out to meet him at the Moabite town on the Arnon[b] border, at the edge of his territory. 37Balak said to Balaam, "Did I not send you an urgent summons? Why didn't you come to me? Am I really not able to reward you?"

38"Well, I have come to you now," Balaam replied. "But can I say just anything? I must speak only what God puts in my mouth."[c]

39Then Balaam went with Balak to Kiriath Huzoth. 40Balak sacrificed cattle and sheep,[d] and gave some to Balaam and the princes who were with him. 41The next morning Balak took Balaam up to Bamoth Baal,[e] and from there he saw part of the people.[f]

Balaam's First Oracle

23 Balaam said, "Build me seven altars here, and prepare seven bulls and seven rams[a] for me." 2Balak did as Balaam said,

22:18 m ver 38; Nu 23:12,26; Nu 24:13; 1Ki 22:14; 2Ch 18:13; Jer 42:4
22:19 n ver 8
22:20 o Ge 20:3; p ver 35,38; Nu 23:5,12, 16,26; Nu 24:13; 2Ch 18:13
22:22 q Ex 4:14; r Ge 16:7; Ex 23:20; Jdg 13:3,6,13
22:23 s Jos 5:13; t ver 25,27
22:27 u Nu 11:1; Jas 1:19
22:28 v 2Pe 2:16; w ver 32
22:29 x Dt 25:4; Pr 12:10; Pr 27:23-27; Mt 15:19
22:31 y Ge 21:19
22:33 z ver 29
22:34 a Ge 39:9; Nu 14:40; 1Sa 15:24,30; 2Sa 12:13; 2Sa 24:10; Job 33:27; Ps 51:4
22:36 b Nu 21:13
22:38 c Nu 23:5,16, 26
22:40 d Nu 23:1,14, 29; Eze 45:23
22:41 e Nu 21:28; f Nu 23:13
23:1 a Nu 22:40

c32 The meaning of the Hebrew for this clause is uncertain.

and the two of them offered a bull
and a ram on each altar.[b]
3Then Balaam said to Balak,
"Stay here beside your offering
while I go aside. Perhaps the LORD
will come to meet with me.[c] Whatever he reveals to me I will tell
you." Then he went off to a barren
height.
4God met with him,[d] and Balaam
said, "I have prepared seven altars,
and on each altar I have offered a
bull and a ram."
5The LORD put a message in Balaam's mouth[e] and said, "Go back
to Balak and give him this message."[f]
6So he went back to him and
found him standing beside his
offering, with all the princes of
Moab.[g] 7Then Balaam[h] uttered
his oracle:[i]

"Balak brought me from Aram,
the king of Moab from the
eastern mountains.
'Come,' he said, 'curse Jacob for
me;
come, denounce Israel.'[j]
8How can I curse
those whom God has not
cursed?[k]
How can I denounce
those whom the LORD has not
denounced?
9From the rocky peaks I see
them,
from the heights I view them.
I see people who live apart
and do not consider
themselves one of the
nations.[l]
10Who can count the dust of
Jacob[m]
or number the fourth part of
Israel?
Let me die the death of the
righteous,[n]
and may my end be like
theirs![o]"

11Balak said to Balaam, "What
have you done to me? I brought you
to curse my enemies, but you have
done nothing but bless them!"[p]

23:2 b ver 14,30
23:3 c ver 15
23:4 d ver 16
23:5 e Dt 18:18; Jer 1:9; f Nu 22:20
23:6 g ver 17
23:7 h Nu 22:5; i ver 18; Nu 24:3,21; j Nu 22:6; Dt 23:4
23:8 k Nu 22:12
23:9 l Ex 33:16; Dt 32:8; Dt 33:28
23:10 m Ge 13:16; n Ps 116:15; Isa 57:1; o Ps 37:37
23:11 p Nu 24:10; Ne 13:2
23:12 q Nu 22:20,38
23:14 r ver 2
23:16 s Nu 22:38
23:19 t Isa 55:9; Hos 11:9; u 1Sa 15:29; Mal 3:6; Tit 1:2; Jas 1:17
23:20 v Ge 22:17; Nu 22:12; w Isa 43:13
23:21 x Ps 32:2,5; Ro 4:7-8; y Isa 40:2; Jer 50:20; z Ex 29:45,46; Ps 145:18; a Dt 33:5; Ps 89:15-18
23:22 b Nu 24:8

12He answered, "Must I not speak
what the LORD puts in my
mouth?"[q]

Balaam's Second Oracle

13Then Balak said to him, "Come
with me to another place where you
can see them; you will see only a
part but not all of them. And from
there, curse them for me." 14So he
took him to the field of Zophim on
the top of Pisgah, and there he built
seven altars and offered a bull and
a ram on each altar.[r]
15Balaam said to Balak, "Stay
here beside your offering while I
meet with him over there."
16The LORD met with Balaam and
put a message in his mouth[s] and
said, "Go back to Balak and give
him this message."
17So he went to him and found
him standing beside his offering,
with the princes of Moab. Balak
asked him, "What did the LORD
say?"
18Then he uttered his oracle:

"Arise, Balak, and listen;
hear me, son of Zippor.
19God is not a man,[t] that he
should lie,
nor a son of man, that he
should change his mind.[u]
Does he speak and then not act?
Does he promise and not
fulfil?
20I have received a command to
bless;
he has blessed,[v] and I cannot
change it.[w]
21"No misfortune is seen in
Jacob,[x]
no misery observed in
Israel.[a][y]
The LORD their God is with
them;[z]
the shout of the King[a] is
among them.
22God brought them out of
Egypt;[b]

[a]21 Or *He has not looked on Jacob's offences / or on the wrongs found in Israel.*

they have the strength of a
wild ox.[c]
23There is no sorcery against
Jacob,
no divination[d] against Israel.
It will now be said of Jacob
and of Israel, 'See what God
has done!'
24The people rise like a lioness;[e]
they rouse themselves like a
lion[f]
that does not rest till he
devours his prey
and drinks the blood of his
victims."

25Then Balak said to Balaam,
"Neither curse them at all nor bless
them at all!"
26Balaam answered, "Did I not
tell you I must do whatever the
LORD says?"

Balaam's Third Oracle

27Then Balak said to Balaam,
"Come, let me take you to another
place.[g] Perhaps it will please God
to let you curse them for me from
there." 28And Balak took Balaam to
the top of Peor,[h] overlooking the
wasteland.
29Balaam said, "Build me seven
altars here, and prepare seven
bulls and seven rams for me." 30Ba-
lak did as Balaam had said, and offered a bull and a ram on each altar.

24 Now when Balaam saw that
it pleased the LORD to bless
Israel, he did not resort to sorcery[a] as at other times, but turned
his face towards the desert.[b]
2When Balaam looked out and saw
Israel encamped tribe by tribe, the
Spirit of God came upon him[c] 3and
he uttered his oracle:

"The oracle of Balaam son of
Beor,
the oracle of one whose eye
sees clearly,
4the oracle of one who hears the
words of God,[d]
who sees a vision from the
Almighty,[a][e]
who falls prostrate, and whose
eyes are opened:

5"How beautiful are your tents,
O Jacob,
your dwelling-places, O Israel!
6"Like valleys they spread out,
like gardens beside a river,
like aloes[f] planted by the LORD,
like cedars beside the
waters.[g]
7Water will flow from their
buckets;
their seed will have abundant
water.

"Their king will be greater than
Agag;[h]
their kingdom will be
exalted.[i]
8"God brought them out of
Egypt;
they have the strength of a
wild ox.
They devour hostile nations
and break their bones in
pieces;[j]
with their arrows they pierce
them.[k]
9Like a lion they crouch and lie
down,
like a lioness[l]—who dares to
rouse them?

"May those who bless you be
blessed
and those who curse you be
cursed!"[m]

10Then Balak's anger burned
against Balaam. He struck his
hands together[n] and said to him, "I
summoned you to curse my enemies, but you have blessed them[o]
these three times.[p] 11Now leave at
once and go home! I said I would
reward you handsomely,[q] but the
LORD has kept you from being rewarded."
12Balaam answered Balak, "Did I
not tell the messengers you sent
me,[r] 13'Even if Balak gave me his
palace filled with silver and gold, I

23:22 c Dt 33:17; Job 39:9
23:23 d Nu 24:1; Jos 13:22
23:24 e Na 2:11; f Ge 49:9
23:27 g ver 13
23:28 h Ps 106:28
24:1 a Nu 23:23; b Nu 23:28
24:2 c Nu 11:25,26; 1Sa 10:10; 1Sa 19:20; 2Ch 15:1
24:4 d Nu 22:20; e Ge 15:1
24:6 f Ps 45:8; g Ps 1:3; Ps 104:16
24:7 h 1Sa 15:8; i 2Sa 5:12; 1Ch 14:2; Ps 145:11-13
24:8 j Ps 2:9; Jer 50:17; k Ps 45:5
24:9 l Ge 49:9; Nu 23:24; m Ge 12:3
24:10 n Eze 21:14; o Nu 23:11; p Ne 13:2
24:11 q Nu 22:17
24:12 r Nu 22:18

a4 Hebrew *Shaddai*; also in verse 16

could not do anything of my own
accord, good or bad, to go beyond
the command of the LORD[s]—and I
must say only what the LORD
says'?[t] 14 Now I am going back to
my people, but come, let me warn
you of what this people will do to
your people in days to come."[u]

Balaam's Fourth Oracle

15 Then he uttered his oracle:

"The oracle of Balaam son of
Beor,
the oracle of one whose eye
sees clearly,
16 the oracle of one who hears the
words of God,
who has knowledge from the
Most High,
who sees a vision from the
Almighty,
who falls prostrate, and whose
eyes are opened:

17 "I see him, but not now;
I behold him, but not near.[v]
A star will come out of Jacob;[w]
a sceptre will rise out of
Israel.[x]
He will crush the foreheads of
Moab,[y]
the skulls[b] of[c] all the sons of
Sheth.[d]
18 Edom[z] will be conquered;
Seir, his enemy, will be
conquered,
but Israel will grow strong.
19 A ruler will come out of Jacob[a]
and destroy the survivors of
the city."

Balaam's Final Oracles

20 Then Balaam saw Amalek[b] and
uttered his oracle:

"Amalek was first among the
nations,
but he will come to ruin at
last."

21 Then he saw the Kenites[c] and
uttered his oracle:

"Your dwelling-place is secure,
your nest is set in a rock;
22 yet you Kenites will be
destroyed
when Asshur[d] takes you
captive."

23 Then he uttered his oracle:

"Ah, who can live when God
does this?[e]
24 Ships will come from the
shores of Kittim;[e]
they will subdue Asshur and
Eber,[f]
but they too will come to
ruin.[g]"

25 Then Balaam[h] got up and returned home and Balak went his
own way.

Moab Seduces Israel

25 While Israel was staying in
Shittim,[a] the men began to
indulge in sexual immorality[b] with
Moabite women,[c] 2 who invited
them to the sacrifices[d] to their
gods.[e] The people ate and bowed
down before these gods. 3 So Israel
joined in worshipping the Baal of
Peor.[f] And the LORD's anger
burned against them.

4 The LORD said to Moses, "Take
all the leaders of these people, kill
them and expose them in broad
daylight before the LORD,[g] so that
the LORD's fierce anger[h] may turn
away from Israel."

5 So Moses said to Israel's judges,
"Each of you must put to death[i]
those of your men who have joined
in worshipping the Baal of Peor."

6 Then an Israelite man brought
to his family a Midianite woman
right before the eyes of Moses and
the whole assembly of Israel while
they were weeping at the entrance
to the Tent of Meeting. 7 When Phinehas son of Eleazar, the son of

24:13 s Nu 22:18; t Nu 22:20
24:14 u Ge 49:1; Nu 31:8,16; Da 2:28; Mic 6:5
24:17 v Rev 1:7; w Mt 2:2; x Ge 49:10; y Nu 21:29; Isa 15:1-16:14
24:18 z Am 9:12
24:19 a Ge 49:10; Mic 5:2
24:20 b Ex 17:14
24:21 c Ge 15:19
24:22 d Ge 10:22
24:24 e Ge 10:4; f Ge 10:21; g ver 20
24:25 h Nu 31:8
25:1 a Jos 2:1; Mic 6:5; b 1Co 10:8; Rev 2:14; c Nu 31:16
25:2 d Ex 34:15; e Ex 20:5; Dt 32:38; 1Co 10:20
25:3 f Ps 106:28; Hos 9:10
25:4 g Dt 4:3; h Dt 13:17
25:5 i Ex 32:27

b17 Samaritan Pentateuch (see also Jer. 48:45); the meaning of the word in the Masoretic Text is uncertain. c17 Or possibly *Moab, / batter* d17 Or *all the noisy boasters* e23 Masoretic Text; with a different word division of the Hebrew *A people will gather from the north.*

Aaron, the priest, saw this, he left the assembly, took a spear in his hand 8and followed the Israelite into the tent. He drove the spear through both of them—through the Israelite and into the woman's body. Then the plague against the Israelites was stopped;[j] 9but those who died in the plague[k] numbered 24,000.[l]

10The LORD said to Moses, 11"Phinehas son of Eleazar, the son of Aaron, the priest, has turned my anger away from the Israelites;[m] for he was as zealous as I am for my honour[n] among them, so that in my zeal I did not put an end to them. 12Therefore tell him I am making my covenant of peace[o] with him. 13He and his descendants will have a covenant of a lasting priesthood,[p] because he was zealous for the honour of his God and made atonement[q] for the Israelites."

14The name of the Israelite who was killed with the Midianite woman was Zimri son of Salu, the leader of a Simeonite family. 15And the name of the Midianite woman who was put to death was Cozbi[r] daughter of Zur, a tribal chief of a Midianite family.[s]

16The LORD said to Moses, 17"Treat the Midianites[t] as enemies and kill them, 18because they treated you as enemies when they deceived you in the affair of Peor[u] and their sister Cozbi, the daughter of a Midianite leader, the woman who was killed when the plague came as a result of Peor."

The Second Census

26 After the plague the LORD said to Moses and Eleazar son of Aaron, the priest, 2"Take a census[a] of the whole Israelite community by families—all those twenty years old or more who are able to serve in the army[b] of Israel." 3So on the plains of Moab[c] by the Jordan across from Jericho,[a][d] Moses and Eleazar the priest spoke with them and said, 4"Take a census of men twenty years old or more, as the LORD commanded Moses."

These were the Israelites who came out of Egypt:

5The descendants of Reuben, the firstborn son of Israel, were:

through Hanoch,[e] the Hanochite clan;
through Pallu,[f] the Palluite clan;
6through Hezron, the Hezronite clan;
through Carmi, the Carmite clan.

7These were the clans of Reuben; those numbered were 43,730.

8The son of Pallu was Eliab, 9and the sons of Eliab[g] were Nemuel, Dathan and Abiram. The same Dathan and Abiram were the community[h] officials who rebelled against Moses and Aaron and were among Korah's followers when they rebelled against the LORD.[i] 10The earth opened its mouth and swallowed them along with Korah, whose followers died when the fire devoured the 250 men. And they served as a warning sign.[j] 11The line of Korah,[k] however, did not die out.[l]

12The descendants of Simeon by their clans were:

through Nemuel, the Nemuelite clan;
through Jamin,[m] the Jaminite clan;
through Jakin, the Jakinite clan;
13through Zerah,[n] the Zerahite clan;
through Shaul, the Shaulite clan.

14These were the clans of Simeon; there were 22,200 men.[o]

15The descendants of Gad by their clans were:

25:8 j Nu 16:46-48; Ps 106:30
25:9 k Nu 14:37; 1Co 10:8; l Nu 31:16
25:11 m Ps 106:30; n Ex 20:5; Dt 32:16,21; Ps 78:58
25:12 o Isa 54:10; Eze 34:25; Mal 2:4,5
25:13 p Ex 29:9; q Nu 16:46
25:15 r ver 18; s Nu 31:8; Jos 13:21
25:17 t Nu 31:1-3
25:18 u Nu 31:16
26:2 a Ex 30:11-16; Ex 38:25-26; Nu 1:2; b Nu 1:3
26:3 c Nu 33:48; d Nu 22:1
26:5 e Ge 46:9; f 1Ch 5:3
26:9 g Nu 16:1; h Nu 1:16; i Nu 16:2
26:10 j Nu 16:35,38
26:11 k Ex 6:24; l Nu 16:33; Dt 24:16
26:12 m 1Ch 4:24
26:13 n Ge 46:10
26:14 o Nu 1:23

[a]3 Hebrew *Jordan of Jericho*; possibly an ancient name for the Jordan River; also in verse 63

through Zephon,[p] the Zephonite clan;
through Haggi, the Haggite clan;
through Shuni, the Shunite clan;
16 through Ozni, the Oznite clan;
through Eri, the Erite clan;
17 through Arodi,[b] the Arodite clan;
through Areli, the Arelite clan.
18 These were the clans of Gad;[q] those numbered were 40,500.

19 Er and Onan were sons of Judah, but they died[r] in Canaan.
20 The descendants of Judah by their clans were:
through Shelah,[s] the Shelanite clan;
through Perez, the Perezite clan;
through Zerah, the Zerahite clan.[t]
21 The descendants of Perez were:
through Hezron,[u] the Hezronite clan;
through Hamul, the Hamulite clan.
22 These were the clans of Judah;[v] those numbered were 76,500.

23 The descendants of Issachar by their clans were:
through Tola,[w] the Tolaite clan;
through Puah, the Puite[c] clan;
24 through Jashub,[x] the Jashubite clan;
through Shimron, the Shimronite clan.
25 These were the clans of Issachar;[y] those numbered were 64,300.

26 The descendants of Zebulun by their clans were:
through Sered, the Seredite clan;
through Elon, the Elonite clan;
through Jahleel, the Jahleelite clan.
27 These were the clans of Zebulun;[z] those numbered were 60,500.

26:15 *p* Ge 46:16
26:18 *q* Nu 1:25; Jos 13:24-28
26:19 *r* Ge 38:2-10; Ge 46:12
26:20 *s* 1Ch 2:3 *t* Jos 7:17
26:21 *u* Ru 4:19; 1Ch 2:9
26:22 *v* Nu 1:27
26:23 *w* Ge 46:13; 1Ch 7:1
26:24 *x* Ge 46:13
26:25 *y* Nu 1:29
26:27 *z* Nu 1:31
26:29 *a* Jos 17:1 *b* Jdg 11:1
26:30 *c* Jos 17:2; Jdg 6:11
26:33 *d* Nu 27:1 *e* Nu 36:11
26:34 *f* Nu 1:35
26:37 *g* Nu 1:33

28 The descendants of Joseph by their clans through Manasseh and Ephraim were:
29 The descendants of Manasseh:
through Makir,[a] the Makirite clan (Makir was the father of Gilead[b]);
through Gilead, the Gileadite clan.
30 These were the descendants of Gilead:
through Iezer,[c] the Iezerite clan;
through Helek, the Helekite clan;
31 through Asriel, the Asrielite clan;
through Shechem, the Shechemite clan;
32 through Shemida, the Shemidaite clan;
through Hepher, the Hepherite clan.
33 (Zelophehad[d] son of Hepher had no sons; he had only daughters, whose names were Mahlah, Noah, Hoglah, Milcah and Tirzah.)[e]
34 These were the clans of Manasseh; those numbered were 52,700.[f]

35 These were the descendants of Ephraim by their clans:
through Shuthelah, the Shuthelahite clan;
through Beker, the Bekerite clan;
through Tahan, the Tahanite clan.
36 These were the descendants of Shuthelah:
through Eran, the Eranite clan.
37 These were the clans of Ephraim;[g] those numbered were 32,500.

These were the descendants of Joseph by their clans.

b17 Samaritan Pentateuch and Syriac (see also Gen. 46:16); Masoretic Text *Arod*
c23 Samaritan Pentateuch, Septuagint, Vulgate and Syriac (see also 1 Chron. 7:1); Masoretic Text *through Puvah, the Punite*

38 The descendants of Benjamin[h] by their clans were:
through Bela, the Belaite clan;
through Ashbel, the Ashbelite clan;
through Ahiram, the Ahiramite clan;
39 through Shupham,[d] the Shuphamite clan;
through Hupham, the Huphamite clan.
40 The descendants of Bela through Ard[i] and Naaman were:
through Ard,[e] the Ardite clan;
through Naaman, the Naamite clan.
41 These were the clans of Benjamin;[j] those numbered were 45,600.

42 These were the descendants of Dan by their clans:
through Shuham,[k] the Shuhamite clan.
These were the clans of Dan: 43 All of them were Shuhamite clans; and those numbered were 64,400.

44 The descendants of Asher by their clans were:
through Imnah, the Imnite clan;
through Ishvi, the Ishvite clan;
through Beriah, the Beriite clan;
45 and through the descendants of Beriah:
through Heber, the Heberite clan;
through Malkiel, the Malkielite clan.
46 (Asher had a daughter named Serah.)
47 These were the clans of Asher;[l] those numbered were 53,400.

48 The descendants of Naphtali[m] by their clans were:
through Jahzeel, the Jahzeelite clan;
through Guni, the Gunite clan;
49 through Jezer, the Jezerite clan;
through Shillem, the Shillemite clan.
50 These were the clans of Naphtali;[n] those numbered were 45,400.

51 The total number of the men of Israel was 601,730.[o]

52 The LORD said to Moses, 53 "The land is to be allotted to them as an inheritance based on the number of names.[p] 54 To a larger group give a larger inheritance, and to a smaller group a smaller one; each is to receive its inheritance according to the number[q] of those listed. 55 Be sure that the land is distributed by lot.[r] What each group inherits will be according to the names for its ancestral tribe. 56 Each inheritance is to be distributed by lot among the larger and smaller groups."

57 These were the Levites[s] who were counted by their clans:
through Gershon, the Gershonite clan;
through Kohath, the Kohathite clan;
through Merari, the Merarite clan.
58 These also were Levite clans:
the Libnite clan,
the Hebronite clan,
the Mahlite clan,
the Mushite clan,
the Korahite clan.
(Kohath was the forefather of Amram;[t] 59 the name of Amram's wife was Jochebed,[u] a descendant of Levi, who was born to the Levites[f] in Egypt. To Amram she bore Aaron, Moses[v] and their sister Miriam. 60 Aaron was the father of Nadab and Abihu, Eleazar and

26:38 h Ge 46:21; 1Ch 7:6
26:40 i Ge 46:21; 1Ch 8:3
26:41 j Nu 1:37
26:42 k Ge 46:23
26:47 l Nu 1:41
26:48 m Ge 46:24; 1Ch 7:13
26:50 n Nu 1:43
26:51 o Ex 12:37; Ex 38:26; Nu 1:46; Nu 11:21
26:53 p Jos 11:23; Jos 14:1; Eze 45:8
26:54 q Nu 33:54
26:55 r Nu 34:14
26:57 s Ge 46:11; Ex 6:16-19
26:58 t Ex 6:20
26:59 u Ex 2:1; v Ex 6:20

d 39 A few manuscripts of the Masoretic Text, Samaritan Pentateuch, Vulgate and Syriac (see also Septuagint); most manuscripts of the Masoretic Text *Shephupham*
e 40 Samaritan Pentateuch and Vulgate (see also Septuagint); Masoretic Text does not have *through Ard*.
f 59 Or *Jochebed, a daughter of Levi, who was born to Levi*

Ithamar.[w] 61But Nadab and Abihu[x] died when they made an offering before the LORD with unauthorised fire.)[y]

62All the male Levites a month old or more numbered 23,000.[z] They were not counted[a] along with the other Israelites because they received no inheritance[b] among them.[c]

63These are the ones counted by Moses and Eleazar the priest when they counted the Israelites on the plains of Moab[d] by the Jordan across from Jericho. 64Not one of them was among those counted[e] by Moses and Aaron the priest when they counted the Israelites in the Desert of Sinai. 65For the LORD had told those Israelites they would surely die in the desert,[f] and not one of them was left except Caleb son of Jephunneh and Joshua son of Nun.[g]

Zelophehad's Daughters

27:1–11pp Nu 36:1–12

27 The daughters of Zelophehad[a] son of Hepher,[b] the son of Gilead, the son of Makir,[c] the son of Manasseh, belonged to the clans of Manasseh son of Joseph. The names of the daughters were Mahlah, Noah, Hoglah, Milcah and Tirzah. They approached 2the entrance to the Tent of Meeting and stood before Moses, Eleazar the priest, the leaders and the whole assembly, and said, 3"Our father died in the desert.[d] He was not among Korah's followers, who banded together against the LORD,[e] but he died for his own sin and left no sons.[f] 4Why should our father's name disappear from his clan because he had no son? Give us property among our father's relatives."

5So Moses brought their case[g] before the LORD[h] 6and the LORD said to him, 7"What Zelophehad's daughters are saying is right. You must certainly give them property as an inheritance[i] among their father's relatives and give their father's inheritance over to them.[j]

8"Say to the Israelites, 'If a man dies and leaves no son, give his inheritance over to his daughter. 9If he has no daughter, give his inheritance to his brothers. 10If he has no brothers, give his inheritance to his father's brothers. 11If his father had no brothers, give his inheritance to the nearest relative in his clan, that he may possess it. This is to be a legal requirement[k] for the Israelites, as the LORD commanded Moses.' "

Joshua to Succeed Moses

12Then the LORD said to Moses, "Go up this mountain in the Abarim Range[l] and see the land[m] I have given the Israelites. 13After you have seen it, you too will be gathered to your people,[n] as your brother Aaron[o] was, 14for when the community rebelled at the waters in the Desert of Zin, both of you disobeyed my command to honour me as holy[p] before their eyes." (These were the waters of Meribah[q] Kadesh, in the Desert of Zin.)

15Moses said to the LORD, 16"May the LORD, the God of the spirits of all mankind,[r] appoint a man over this community 17to go out and come in before them, one who will lead them out and bring them in, so that the LORD's people will not be like sheep without a shepherd."[s]

18So the LORD said to Moses, "Take Joshua son of Nun, a man in whom is the spirit,[a][t] and lay your hand on him.[u] 19Make him stand before Eleazar the priest and the entire assembly and commission him[v] in their presence.[w] 20Give him some of your authority so that the whole Israelite community will obey him.[x] 21He is to stand before

[a]18 Or *Spirit*

26:60 w Nu 3:2
26:61 x Lev 10:1-2; y Nu 3:4
26:62 z Nu 3:39; a Nu 1:47; b Nu 18:23; c Nu 2:33; Dt 10:9
26:63 d ver 3
26:64 e Nu 14:29; Dt 2:14-15; Heb 3:17
26:65 f Nu 14:28; 1Co 10:5; g Jos 14:6-10
27:1 a Nu 26:33; b Jos 17:2,3; c Nu 36:1
27:3 d Nu 26:65; e Nu 16:2; f Nu 26:33
27:5 g Ex 18:19; h Nu 9:8
27:7 i Job 42:15; j Jos 17:4
27:11 k Nu 35:29
27:12 l Nu 33:47; Jer 22:20; m Dt 3:23-27; Dt 32:48-52
27:13 n Nu 31:2; o Nu 20:28
27:14 p Nu 20:12; q Ex 17:7; Dt 32:51; Ps 106:32
27:16 r Nu 16:22
27:17 s Dt 31:2; 1Ki 22:17; Eze 34:5; Zec 10:2; Mt 9:36; Mk 6:34
27:18 t Ge 41:38; Nu 11:25-29; u ver 23; Dt 34:9
27:19 v Dt 3:28; Dt 31:14,23; w Dt 31:7
27:20 x Jos 1:16,17

Eleazar the priest, who will obtain
decisions for him by enquiring[y] of
the Urim[z] before the LORD. At his
command he and the entire community of the Israelites will go out,
and at his command they will come
in."
22Moses did as the LORD commanded him. He took Joshua and
made him stand before Eleazar the
priest and the whole assembly.
23Then he laid his hands on him and
commissioned him, as the LORD instructed through Moses.

Daily Offerings

28 The LORD said to Moses,
2"Give this command to the
Israelites and say to them: 'See that
you present to me at the appointed
time the food[a] for my offerings
made by fire, as an aroma pleasing
to me.' 3Say to them: 'This is the offering made by fire that you are
to present to the LORD: two lambs
a year old without defect, as a
regular burnt offering each day.[b]
4Prepare one lamb in the morning
and the other at twilight, 5together
with a grain offering of a tenth of
an ephah[a] of fine flour mixed with
a quarter of a hin[b] of oil[c] from
pressed olives. 6This is the regular
burnt offering instituted at Mount
Sinai[d] as a pleasing aroma, an offering made to the LORD by fire.
7The accompanying drink offering[e] is to be a quarter of a hin of
fermented drink with each lamb.
Pour out the drink offering to the
LORD at the sanctuary.[f] 8Prepare
the second lamb at twilight, along
with the same kind of grain offering and drink offering that you
prepare in the morning. This is an
offering made by fire, an aroma
pleasing to the LORD.[g]

Sabbath Offerings

9" 'On the Sabbath[h] day, make an
offering of two lambs a year old
without defect, together with its
drink offering and a grain offering
of two-tenths of an ephah[c] [i] of fine
flour mixed with oil. 10This is the
burnt offering for every Sabbath,
in addition to the regular burnt offering[j] and its drink offering.

Monthly Offerings

11" 'On the first of every month,[k]
present to the LORD a burnt offering of two young bulls, one ram and
seven male lambs a year old, all
without defect.[l] 12With each bull
there is to be a grain offering[m] of
three-tenths of an ephah[d] [n] of fine
flour mixed with oil; with the ram,
a grain offering of two-tenths of an
ephah of fine flour mixed with oil;
13and with each lamb, a grain offering[o] of a tenth of an ephah of fine
flour mixed with oil. This is for a
burnt offering, a pleasing aroma,
an offering made to the LORD by
fire. 14With each bull there is to be
a drink offering[p] of half a hin[e] of
wine; with the ram, a third of a
hin;[f] and with each lamb, a quarter of a hin. This is the monthly
burnt offering to be made at each
new moon[q] during the year. 15Be-
sides the regular burnt offering[r]
with its drink offering, one male
goat is to be presented to the LORD
as a sin offering.[s]

The Passover

28:16–25pp Ex 12:14–20; Lev 23:4–8; Dt 16:1–8

16" 'On the fourteenth day of the
first month the LORD's Passover[t]
is to be held. 17On the fifteenth day
of this month there is to be a festival; for seven days[u] eat bread
made without yeast.[v] 18On the first
day hold a sacred assembly and do
no regular work.[w] 19Present to the

27:21 y Jos 9:14; z Ex 28:30
28:2 a Lev 3:11
28:3 b Ex 29:38
28:5 c Lev 2:1; Nu 15:4
28:6 d Ex 19:3
28:7 e Ex 29:41; f Lev 3:7
28:8 g Lev 1:9
28:9 h Ex 20:10; i Lev 23:13
28:10 j ver 3
28:11 k Nu 10:10; l Lev 1:3
28:12 m Nu 15:6; n Nu 15:9
28:13 o Lev 6:14
28:14 p Nu 15:7; q Ezr 3:5
28:15 r ver 3,23,24; s Lev 4:3
28:16 t Ex 12:6,18; Lev 23:5; Dt 16:1
28:17 u Ex 12:19; v Ex 23:15; Ex 34:18; Lev 23:6; Dt 16:3-8
28:18 w Ex 12:16; Lev 23:7

a5 That is, probably about 4 pints (about 2 litres); also in verses 13, 21 and 29 b5 That is, probably about 1½ pints (about 1 litre); also in verses 7 and 14 c9 That is, probably about 7½ pints (about 4.5 litres); also in verses 12, 20 and 28 d12 That is, probably about 11½ pints (about 6.5 litres); also in verses 20 and 28
e14 That is, probably about 3 pints (about 2 litres)
f14 That is, probably about 2¼ pints (about 1.2 litres)

LORD an offering made by fire, a
burnt offering of two young bulls,
one ram and seven male lambs a
year old, all without defect. 20With
each bull prepare a grain offering
of three-tenths of an ephah[x] of fine
flour mixed with oil; with the ram,
two-tenths; 21and with each of the
seven lambs, one-tenth. 22Include
one male goat as a sin offering[y] to
make atonement for you.[z] 23Pre-
pare these in addition to the regular morning burnt offering. 24In
this way prepare the food for the
offering made by fire every day for
seven days as an aroma pleasing to
the LORD; it is to be prepared in addition to the regular burnt offering
and its drink offering. 25On the seventh day hold a sacred assembly
and do no regular work.

Feast of Weeks

28:26–31pp Lev 23:15–22; Dt 16:9–12

26" 'On the day of firstfruits,[a]
when you present to the LORD an
offering of new grain during the
Feast of Weeks,[b] hold a sacred assembly and do no regular work.[c]
27Present a burnt offering of two
young bulls, one ram and seven
male lambs a year old as an aroma
pleasing to the LORD. 28With each
bull there is to be a grain offering
of three-tenths of an ephah of fine
flour mixed with oil; with the ram,
two-tenths; 29and with each of the
seven lambs, one-tenth.[d] 30Include
one male goat to make atonement
for you. 31Prepare these together
with their drink offerings, in addition to the regular burnt offering[e]
and its grain offering. Be sure the
animals are without defect.

Feast of Trumpets

29:1–6pp Lev 23:23–25

29 " 'On the first day of the
seventh month hold a sa-
cred assembly and do no regular
work.[a] It is a day for you to sound
the trumpets. 2As an aroma pleasing to the LORD,[b] prepare a burnt
offering of one young bull, one ram
and seven male lambs a year old,
all without defect.[c] 3With the bull
prepare a grain offering of three-
tenths of an ephah[a] of fine flour
mixed with oil; with the ram, two-
tenths;[b] 4and with each of the
seven lambs, one-tenth.[c] 5Include
one male goat[d] as a sin offering to
make atonement for you. 6These
are in addition to the monthly[e] and
daily burnt offerings[f] with their
grain offerings and drink offerings
as specified. They are offerings
made to the LORD by fire—a pleasing aroma.

Day of Atonement

29:7–11pp Lev 16:2–34; 23:26–32

7" 'On the tenth day of this seventh month hold a sacred assembly. You must deny yourselves[d][g]
and do no work.[h] 8Present as an
aroma pleasing to the LORD a burnt
offering of one young bull, one ram
and seven male lambs a year old,
all without defect. 9With the bull
prepare a grain offering[i] of three-
tenths of an ephah of fine flour
mixed with oil; with the ram, two-
tenths; 10and with each of the seven
lambs, one-tenth.[j] 11Include one
male goat as a sin offering, in
addition to the sin offering for
atonement and the regular burnt
offering[k] with its grain offering,
and their drink offerings.

Feast of Tabernacles

29:12–39pp Lev 23:33–43; Dt 16:13–17

12" 'On the fifteenth day of the
seventh[l] month,[m] hold a sacred
assembly and do no regular work.
Celebrate a festival to the LORD for
seven days. 13Present an offering
made by fire as an aroma pleasing
to the LORD, a burnt offering of

28:20 x Lev 14:10
28:22 y Ro 8:3 z Nu 15:28
28:26 a Ex 34:22 b Ex 23:16 c ver 18 Dt 16:10
28:29 d ver 13
28:31 e ver 3,19
29:1 a Lev 23:24
29:2 b Nu 28:2 c Nu 28:3
29:5 d Nu 28:15
29:6 e Nu 28:11 f Nu 28:3
29:7 g Ac 27:9 h Ex 31:15 Lev 16:29 Lev 23:26-32
29:9 i ver 3,18
29:10 j Nu 28:13
29:11 k Lev 16:3 Nu 28:3
29:12 l 1Ki 8:2 m Lev 23:24

[a]3 That is, probably about 11½ pints (about 6.5 litres); also in verses 9 and 14 [b]3 That is, probably about 7½ pints (about 4.5 litres); also in verses 9 and 14 [c]4 That is, probably about 4 pints (about 2 litres); also in verses 10 and 15 [d]7 Or *must fast*

thirteen young bulls, two rams and
fourteen male lambs a year old, all
without defect. 14With each of the
thirteen bulls prepare a grain offering[n] of three-tenths of an ephah
of fine flour mixed with oil; with
each of the two rams, two-tenths;
15and with each of the fourteen
lambs, one-tenth. 16Include one
male goat as a sin offering, in addition to the regular burnt offering
with its grain offering and drink
offering.[o]
17" 'On the second day[p] prepare
twelve young bulls, two rams and
fourteen male lambs a year old, all
without defect.[q] 18With the bulls,
rams and lambs, prepare their
grain offerings[r] and drink offerings[s] according to the number
specified.[t] 19Include one male
goat as a sin offering,[u] in addition
to the regular burnt offering with
its grain offering, and their drink
offerings.
20" 'On the third day prepare
eleven bulls, two rams and fourteen male lambs a year old, all
without defect.[v] 21With the bulls,
rams and lambs, prepare their
grain offerings and drink offerings
according to the number specified.[w] 22Include one male goat as a
sin offering, in addition to the regular burnt offering with its grain
offering and drink offering.
23" 'On the fourth day prepare ten
bulls, two rams and fourteen male
lambs a year old, all without defect.
24With the bulls, rams and lambs,
prepare their grain offerings and
drink offerings according to the
number specified. 25Include one
male goat as a sin offering, in addition to the regular burnt offering
with its grain offering and drink
offering.
26" 'On the fifth day prepare nine
bulls, two rams and fourteen male
lambs a year old, all without defect.
27With the bulls, rams and lambs,
prepare their grain offerings and
drink offerings according to the
number specified. 28Include one
male goat as a sin offering, in addition to the regular burnt offering
with its grain offering and drink
offering.
29" 'On the sixth day prepare
eight bulls, two rams and fourteen
male lambs a year old, all without
defect. 30With the bulls, rams and
lambs, prepare their grain offerings and drink offerings according
to the number specified. 31Include
one male goat as a sin offering, in
addition to the regular burnt offering with its grain offering and
drink offering.
32" 'On the seventh day prepare
seven bulls, two rams and fourteen
male lambs a year old, all without
defect. 33With the bulls, rams and
lambs, prepare their grain offerings and drink offerings according
to the number specified. 34Include
one male goat as a sin offering, in
addition to the regular burnt offering with its grain offering and
drink offering.
35" 'On the eighth day hold an assembly[x] and do no regular work.
36Present an offering made by fire
as an aroma pleasing to the LORD,[y]
a burnt offering of one bull, one
ram and seven male lambs a year
old,[z] all without defect. 37With the
bull, the ram and the lambs, prepare their grain offerings and
drink offerings according to the
number specified. 38Include one
male goat as a sin offering, in addition to the regular burnt offering
with its grain offering and drink
offering.
39" 'In addition to what you vow[a]
and your freewill offerings, prepare these for the LORD at your
appointed feasts:[b] your burnt
offerings,[c] grain offerings, drink
offerings and fellowship offerings.' "[e]
40Moses told the Israelites all
that the LORD commanded him.

29:14 n ver 3
29:16 o ver 6
29:17 p Lev 23:36 q Nu 28:3
29:18 r ver 9 s Nu 28:7 t Nu 15:4-12
29:19 u Nu 28:15
29:20 v ver 17
29:21 w ver 18
29:35 x Lev 23:36
29:36 y Lev 1:9 z ver 2
29:39 a Nu 6:2 b Lev 23:2 c Lev 1:3 1Ch 23:31 2Ch 31:3

e39 Traditionally *peace offerings*

Vows

30 Moses said to the heads of
the tribes of Israel:[a] "This
is what the LORD commands:
2When a man makes a vow to the
LORD or takes an oath to bind himself by a pledge, he must not break
his word but must do everything he
said.[b]
3"When a young woman still living in her father's house makes a
vow to the LORD or binds herself by
a pledge 4and her father hears
about her vow or pledge but says
nothing to her, then all her vows
and every pledge by which she
bound herself will stand.[c] 5But if
her father forbids her when he
hears about it, none of her vows or
the pledges by which she bound
herself will stand; the LORD will release her because her father has
forbidden her.
6"If she marries after she makes
a vow[d] or after her lips utter a rash
promise by which she binds herself
7and her husband hears about it but
says nothing to her, then her vows
or the pledges by which she bound
herself will stand. 8But if her husband[e] forbids her when he hears
about it, he nullifies the vow that
binds her or the rash promise by
which she binds herself, and the
LORD will release her.
9"Any vow or obligation taken by
a widow or divorced woman will be
binding on her.
10"If a woman living with her
husband makes a vow or binds herself by a pledge under oath 11and
her husband hears about it but says
nothing to her and does not forbid
her, then all her vows or the
pledges by which she bound herself will stand. 12But if her husband
nullifies them when he hears about
them, then none of the vows or
pledges that came from her lips
will stand.[f] Her husband has nulli-
fied them, and the LORD will release her. 13Her husband may
confirm or nullify any vow she
makes or any sworn pledge to deny
herself. 14But if her husband says
nothing to her about it from day to
day, then he confirms all her vows
or the pledges binding on her. He
confirms them by saying nothing to
her when he hears about them. 15If,
however, he nullifies them some
time after he hears about them,
then he is responsible for her
guilt."
16These are the regulations the
LORD gave Moses concerning rela-
tionships between a man and his
wife, and between a father and
his young daughter still living in
his house.

Vengeance on the Midianites

31 The LORD said to Moses,
2"Take vengeance on the
Midianites[a] for the Israelites.
After that, you will be gathered to
your people.[b]"
3So Moses said to the people,
"Arm some of your men to go to
war against the Midianites and to
carry out the LORD's vengeance[c]
on them. 4Send into battle a thousand men from each of the tribes of
Israel." 5So twelve thousand men
armed for battle, a thousand from
each tribe, were supplied from the
clans of Israel. 6Moses sent them
into battle, a thousand from each
tribe, along with Phinehas son of
Eleazar, the priest, who took with
him articles from the sanctuary[d]
and the trumpets[e] for signalling.
7They fought against Midian, as
the LORD commanded Moses, and
killed every man.[f] 8Among their
victims were Evi, Rekem, Zur,
Hur and Reba[g]—the five kings of
Midian.[h] They also killed Balaam
son of Beor with the sword.[i] 9The
Israelites captured the Midianite
women and children and took all
the Midianite herds, flocks and
goods as plunder. 10They burned all
the towns where the Midianites had
settled, as well as all their camps.[j]

30:1 a Nu 1:4
30:2 b Dt 23:21-23; Jdg 11:35; Job 22:27; Ps 22:25; Ps 50:14; Ps 116:14; Pr 20:25; Ecc 5:4,5; Jnh 1:16
30:4 c ver 7
30:6 d Lev 5:4
30:8 e Ge 3:16
30:12 f Eph 5:22; Col 3:18
31:2 a Ge 25:2; b Nu 20:26; Nu 27:13
31:3 c Jdg 11:36; 1Sa 24:12; 2Sa 4:8; 2Sa 22:48; Ps 94:1; Ps 149:7
31:6 d Nu 14:44; e Nu 10:9
31:7 f Dt 20:13; Jdg 21:11; 1Ki 11:15,16
31:8 g Jos 13:21; h Nu 25:15; i Jos 13:22
31:10 j Ge 25:16; 1Ch 6:54; Ps 69:25; Eze 25:4

11They took all the plunder and
spoils, including the people and
animals,[k] 12and brought the captives, spoils and plunder to Moses
and Eleazar the priest and the Israelite assembly[l] at their camp on
the plains of Moab, by the Jordan
across from Jericho.[a]
13Moses, Eleazar the priest and
all the leaders of the community
went to meet them outside the
camp. 14Moses was angry with the
officers of the army[m]—the commanders of thousands and commanders of hundreds—who returned
from the battle.
15"Have you allowed all the
women to live?" he asked them.
16"They were the ones who followed Balaam's advice[n] and were
the means of turning the Israelites
away from the LORD in what happened at Peor,[o] so that a plague
struck the LORD's people. 17Now
kill all the boys. And kill every
woman who has slept with a man,[p]
18but save for yourselves every
girl who has never slept with a
man.
19"All of you who have killed anyone or touched anyone who was
killed[q] must stay outside the camp
seven days. On the third and seventh days you must purify yourselves[r] and your captives. 20Purify
every garment[s] as well as everything made of leather, goat hair or
wood."
21Then Eleazar the priest said to
the soldiers who had gone into
battle, "This is the requirement of
the law that the LORD gave Moses:
22Gold, silver, bronze, iron,[t] tin,
lead 23and anything else that can
withstand fire must be put through
the fire,[u] and then it will be clean.
But it must also be purified with
the water of cleansing.[v] And whatever cannot withstand fire must be
put through that water. 24On the
seventh day wash your clothes and
you will be clean.[w] Then you may
come into the camp."

31:11 k Dt 20:14
31:12 l Nu 27:2
31:14 m ver 48; Ex 18:21; Dt 1:15
31:16 n 2Pe 2:15; Rev 2:14 o Nu 25:1-9
31:17 p Dt 7:2; Dt 20:16-18; Jdg 21:11
31:19 q Nu 19:16 r Nu 19:12
31:20 s Nu 19:19
31:22 t Jos 6:19; Jos 22:8
31:23 u 1Co 3:13 v Nu 19:9,17
31:24 w Lev 11:25
31:26 x Nu 1:19
31:27 y Jos 22:8; 1Sa 30:24
31:28 z Nu 18:21
31:30 a Nu 3:7; Nu 18:3
31:37 b ver 38-41
31:41 c Nu 5:9; Nu 18:8

Dividing the Spoils

25The LORD said to Moses, 26"You
and Eleazar the priest and the family heads of the community are to
count all the people[x] and animals
that were captured. 27Divide[y] the
spoils between the soldiers who
took part in the battle and the rest
of the community. 28From the soldiers who fought in the battle, set
apart as tribute for the LORD[z] one
out of every five hundred, whether
persons, cattle, donkeys, sheep or
goats. 29Take this tribute from
their half share and give it to Eleazar the priest as the LORD's part.
30From the Israelites' half, select
one out of every fifty, whether persons, cattle, donkeys, sheep, goats
or other animals. Give them to the
Levites, who are responsible for
the care of the LORD's tabernacle.[a]" 31So Moses and Eleazar the
priest did as the LORD commanded
Moses.
32The plunder remaining from
the spoils that the soldiers took was
675,000 sheep, 3372,000 cattle,
3461,000 donkeys 35and 32,000
women who had never slept with a
man.
36The half share of those who
fought in the battle was:

337,500 sheep, 37of which the tribute for the LORD[b] was 675;
3836,000 cattle, of which the tribute
for the LORD was 72;
3930,500 donkeys, of which the tribute for the LORD was 61;
4016,000 people, of which the tribute for the LORD was 32.

41Moses gave the tribute to Eleazar the priest as the LORD's part,[c]
as the LORD commanded Moses.
42The half belonging to the Israelites, which Moses set apart
from that of the fighting men—
43the community's half—was
337,500 sheep, 4436,000 cattle,
4530,500 donkeys 46and 16,000

[a]12 Hebrew *Jordan of Jericho*; possibly an ancient name for the Jordan River

people. 47From the Israelites' half,
Moses selected one out of every
fifty persons and animals, as the
LORD commanded him, and gave
them to the Levites, who were responsible for the care of the LORD's
tabernacle.
48Then the officers who were
over the units of the army—the
commanders of thousands and
commanders of hundreds—went to
Moses 49and said to him, "Your servants have counted the soldiers
under our command, and not one
is missing.[d] 50So we have brought
as an offering to the LORD the gold
articles each of us acquired—
armlets, bracelets, signet rings,
ear-rings and necklaces—to make
atonement for ourselves[e] before
the LORD."
51Moses and Eleazar the priest
accepted from them the gold—all
the handcrafted articles. 52All the
gold from the commanders of thousands and commanders of hundreds that Moses and Eleazar
presented as a gift to the LORD
weighed 16,750 shekels.[b] 53Each
soldier had taken plunder[f] for
himself. 54Moses and Eleazar the
priest accepted the gold from the
commanders of thousands and commanders of hundreds and brought
it into the Tent of Meeting as a
memorial[g] for the Israelites before
the LORD.

The Transjordan Tribes

32 The Reubenites and Gadites, who had very large
herds and flocks, saw that the lands
of Jazer[a] and Gilead were suitable
for livestock.[b] 2So they came to
Moses and Eleazar the priest and to
the leaders of the community, and
said, 3"Ataroth,[c] Dibon, Jazer,
Nimrah,[d] Heshbon, Elealeh,[e]
Sebam, Nebo and Beon[f]—4the
land the LORD subdued[g] before the
people of Israel—are suitable for
livestock,[h] and your servants have
livestock. 5If we have found favour
in your eyes," they said, "let this
land be given to your servants as
our possession. Do not make us
cross the Jordan."
6Moses said to the Gadites and
Reubenites, "Shall your countrymen go to war while you sit here?
7Why do you discourage the Israelites from going over into the land
the LORD has given them?[i] 8This is
what your fathers did when I sent
them from Kadesh Barnea to look
over the land.[j] 9After they went up
to the Valley of Eshcol[k] and
viewed the land, they discouraged
the Israelites from entering the
land the LORD had given them.
10The LORD's anger was aroused[l]
that day and he swore this oath:
11'Because they have not followed
me wholeheartedly, not one of the
men twenty years old or more[m]
who came up out of Egypt will see
the land I promised on oath[n] to
Abraham, Isaac and Jacob[o]—12not
one except Caleb son of Jephunneh
the Kenizzite and Joshua son of
Nun, for they followed the LORD
wholeheartedly.'[p] 13The LORD's
anger burned against Israel[q] and
he made them wander in the desert
for forty years, until the whole generation of those who had done evil
in his sight was gone.[r]
14"And here you are, a brood of
sinners, standing in the place of
your fathers and making the LORD
even more angry with Israel.[s] 15If
you turn away from following him,
he will again leave all this people in
the desert, and you will be the
cause of their destruction.[t]"
16Then they came up to him and
said, "We would like to build pens
here for our livestock[u] and cities
for our women and children. 17But
we are ready to arm ourselves and
go ahead of the Israelites[v] until we
have brought them to their place.[w]
Meanwhile our women and children will live in fortified cities, for

31:49 d Jer 23:4
31:50 e Ex 30:16
31:53 f Dt 20:14
31:54 g Ex 28:12
32:1 a Nu 21:32 b Ex 12:38
32:3 c ver 34 d ver 36 e ver 37 Isa 15:4 Isa 16:9 Jer 48:34 f ver 38 Jos 13:17 Eze 25:9
32:4 g Nu 21:34 h Ex 12:38
32:7 i Nu 13:27-14:4
32:8 j Nu 13:3,26 Dt 1:19-25
32:9 k Nu 13:23 Dt 1:24
32:10 l Nu 11:1
32:11 m Ex 30:14 n Nu 14:23 o Nu 14:28-30
32:12 p Nu 14:24,30 Dt 1:36 Ps 63:8
32:13 q Ex 4:14 r Nu 14:28-35 Nu 26:64,65
32:14 s ver 10 Dt 1:34 Ps 78:59
32:15 t Dt 30:17-18 2Ch 7:20
32:16 u Ex 12:38 Dt 3:19
32:17 v Jos 4:12,13 w Nu 22:4 Dt 3:20

b52 That is, about 420 pounds (about 190 kilograms)

protection from the inhabitants of the land. 18 We will not return to our homes until every Israelite has received his inheritance.[x] 19 We will not receive any inheritance with them on the other side of the Jordan, because our inheritance has come to us on the east side of the Jordan."[y]

20 Then Moses said to them, "If you will do this—if you will arm yourselves before the LORD for battle,[z] 21 and if all of you will go armed over the Jordan before the LORD until he has driven his enemies out before him—22 then when the land is subdued before the LORD, you may return[a] and be free from your obligation to the LORD and to Israel. And this land will be your possession before the LORD.[b]

23 "But if you fail to do this, you will be sinning against the LORD; and you may be sure that your sin will find you out.[c] 24 Build cities for your women and children, and pens for your flocks,[d] but do what you have promised.[e]"

25 The Gadites and Reubenites said to Moses, "We your servants will do as our lord commands. 26 Our children and wives, our flocks and herds will remain here in the cities of Gilead.[f] 27 But your servants, every man armed for battle, will cross over to fight before the LORD, just as our lord says."

28 Then Moses gave orders about them[g] to Eleazar the priest and Joshua son of Nun and to the family heads of the Israelite tribes. 29 He said to them, "If the Gadites and Reubenites, every man armed for battle, cross over the Jordan with you before the LORD, then when the land is subdued before you, give them the land of Gilead as their possession. 30 But if they do not cross over with you armed, they must accept their possession with you in Canaan."

31 The Gadites and Reubenites answered, "Your servants will do what the LORD has said.[h] 32 We will cross over before the LORD into Canaan armed, but the property we inherit will be on this side of the Jordan."

33 Then Moses gave to the Gadites,[i] the Reubenites and the half-tribe of Manasseh son of Joseph the kingdom of Sihon king of the Amorites[j] and the kingdom of Og king of Bashan—the whole land with its cities and the territory around them.[k]

34 The Gadites built up Dibon, Ataroth, Aroer,[l] 35 Atroth Shophan, Jazer,[m] Jogbehah, 36 Beth Nimrah[n] and Beth Haran as fortified cities, and built pens for their flocks. 37 And the Reubenites rebuilt Heshbon, Elealeh and Kiriathaim, 38 as well as Nebo[o] and Baal Meon (these names were changed) and Sibmah. They gave names to the cities they rebuilt.

39 The descendants of Makir[p] son of Manasseh went to Gilead, captured it and drove out the Amorites who were there. 40 So Moses gave Gilead to the Makirites,[q] the descendants of Manasseh, and they settled there. 41 Jair, a descendant of Manasseh, captured their settlements and called them Havvoth Jair.[a][r] 42 And Nobah captured Kenath and its surrounding settlements and called it Nobah after himself.[s]

Stages in Israel's Journey

33 Here are the stages in the journey of the Israelites when they came out of Egypt[a] by divisions under the leadership of Moses and Aaron.[b] 2 At the LORD's command Moses recorded the stages in their journey. This is their journey by stages:

> 3 The Israelites set out from Rameses on the fifteenth day of the first month, the day after the Passover.[c] They marched

32:18 x Jos 22:1-4
32:19 y Jos 12:1
32:20 z Dt 3:18
32:22 a Jos 22:4; b Dt 3:18-20
32:23 c Ge 4:7; Ge 44:16; Isa 59:12
32:24 d ver 1,16; e Nu 30:2
32:26 f Jos 1:14
32:28 g Dt 3:18-20; Jos 1:13
32:31 h ver 29
32:33 i Jos 13:24-28; 1Sa 13:7; j Dt 2:26; k Nu 21:24; Jos 12:6
32:34 l Dt 2:36; Jdg 11:26
32:35 m ver 3
32:36 n ver 3
32:38 o ver 3; Isa 15:2; Jer 48:1,22
32:39 p Ge 50:23
32:40 q Dt 3:15; Jos 17:1
32:41 r Dt 3:14; Jos 13:30; Jdg 10:4; 1Ch 2:23
32:42 s 2Sa 18:18; Ps 49:11
33:1 a Mic 6:4; b Ps 77:20
33:3 c Ex 13:4

a41 Or *them the settlements of Jair*

out boldly[d] in full view of all
the Egyptians, 4 who were
burying all their firstborn,
whom the LORD had struck
down among them; for the
LORD had brought judgment on
their gods.[e]
5 The Israelites left Rameses
and camped at Succoth.[f]
6 They left Succoth and camped at Etham, on the edge of the
desert.[g]
7 They left Etham, turned
back to Pi Hahiroth, to the east
of Baal Zephon,[h] and camped
near Migdol.[i]
8 They left Pi Hahiroth[a] and
passed through the sea[j] into
the desert, and when they had
travelled for three days in the
Desert of Etham, they camped
at Marah.[k]
9 They left Marah and went to
Elim, where there were twelve
springs and seventy palm trees,
and they camped[l] there.
10 They left Elim and camped
by the Red Sea.[b]
11 They left the Red Sea and
camped in the Desert of Sin.[m]
12 They left the Desert of Sin
and camped at Dophkah.
13 They left Dophkah and
camped at Alush.
14 They left Alush and
camped at Rephidim, where
there was no water for the
people to drink.
15 They left Rephidim[n] and
camped in the Desert of
Sinai.[o]
16 They left the Desert of
Sinai and camped at Kibroth
Hattaavah.[p]
17 They left Kibroth Hattaavah and camped at Hazeroth.[q]
18 They left Hazeroth and
camped at Rithmah.
19 They left Rithmah and
camped at Rimmon Perez.
20 They left Rimmon Perez
and camped at Libnah.[r]
21 They left Libnah and
camped at Rissah.
22 They left Rissah and camped at Kehelathah.
23 They left Kehelathah and
camped at Mount Shepher.
24 They left Mount Shepher
and camped at Haradah.
25 They left Haradah and
camped at Makheloth.
26 They left Makheloth and
camped at Tahath.
27 They left Tahath and camped at Terah.
28 They left Terah and camped at Mithcah.
29 They left Mithcah and
camped at Hashmonah.
30 They left Hashmonah and
camped at Moseroth.[s]
31 They left Moseroth and
camped at Bene Jaakan.
32 They left Bene Jaakan
and camped at Hor Haggid-
gad.
33 They left Hor Haggidgad
and camped at Jotbathah.[t]
34 They left Jotbathah and
camped at Abronah.
35 They left Abronah and
camped at Ezion Geber.[u]
36 They left Ezion Geber and
camped at Kadesh, in the Desert of Zin.[v]
37 They left Kadesh and
camped at Mount Hor,[w] on
the border of Edom.[x] 38 At the
LORD's command Aaron the
priest went up Mount Hor,
where he died[y] on the first day
of the fifth month of the fortieth year after the Israelites
came out of Egypt.[z] 39 Aaron
was a hundred and twenty-
three years old when he died on
Mount Hor.
40 The Canaanite king of
Arad,[a] who lived in the Negev
of Canaan, heard that the Israelites were coming.

33:3 *d* Ex 14:8
33:4 *e* Ex 12:12
33:5 *f* Ex 12:37
33:6 *g* Ex 13:20
33:7 *h* Ex 14:9 *i* Ex 14:2
33:8 *j* Ex 14:22 *k* Ex 15:23
33:9 *l* Ex 15:27
33:11 *m* Ex 16:1
33:15 *n* Ex 17:1 *o* Ex 19:1
33:16 *p* Nu 11:34
33:17 *q* Nu 11:35
33:20 *r* Jos 10:29
33:30 *s* Dt 10:6
33:33 *t* Dt 10:7
33:35 *u* Dt 2:8 1Ki 9:26 1Ki 22:48
33:36 *v* Nu 20:1
33:37 *w* Nu 20:22 *x* Nu 20:16 Nu 21:4
33:38 *y* Dt 10:6 *z* Nu 20:25-28
33:40 *a* Nu 21:1

[a] *8* Many manuscripts of the Masoretic Text, Samaritan Pentateuch and Vulgate; most manuscripts of the Masoretic Text *left from before Hahiroth* [b] *10* Hebrew *Yam Suph*; that is, Sea of Reeds; also in verse 11

41They left Mount Hor and
camped at Zalmonah.
42They left Zalmonah and
camped at Punon.
43They left Punon and camped at Oboth.[b]
44They left Oboth and camped at Iye Abarim, on the
border of Moab.[c]
45They left Iyim[c] and camped at Dibon Gad.
46They left Dibon Gad and
camped at Almon Diblathaim.
47They left Almon Dibla-
thaim and camped in the
mountains of Abarim,[d] near
Nebo.
48They left the mountains
of Abarim and camped on
the plains of Moab by the
Jordan across from Jericho.[d][e]
49There on the plains of Moab
they camped along the Jordan
from Beth Jeshimoth to Abel
Shittim.[f]

50On the plains of Moab by the
Jordan across from Jericho the
LORD said to Moses, 51"Speak to
the Israelites and say to them:
'When you cross the Jordan into Canaan,[g] 52drive out all the inhabitants
of the land before you. Destroy all
their carved images and their cast
idols, and demolish all their high
places.[h] 53Take possession of the
land and settle in it, for I have
given you the land to possess.[i]
54Distribute the land by lot, according to your clans.[j] To a larger
group give a larger inheritance,
and to a smaller group a smaller
one. Whatever falls to them by lot
will be theirs. Distribute it according to your ancestral tribes.
55" 'But if you do not drive out the
inhabitants of the land, those you
allow to remain will become barbs
in your eyes and thorns[k] in your
sides. They will give you trouble in
the land where you will live. 56And
then I will do to you what I plan to
do to them.' "

Boundaries of Canaan

34 The LORD said to Moses,
2"Command the Israelites
and say to them: 'When you enter
Canaan, the land that will be allotted to you as an inheritance[a] will
have these boundaries:[b]

3" 'Your southern side will include some of the Desert of Zin[c]
along the border of Edom. On the
east, your southern boundary will
start from the end of the Salt
Sea,[a][d] 4cross south of Scorpion[b]
Pass,[e] continue on to Zin and go
south of Kadesh Barnea.[f] Then it
will go to Hazar Addar and over to
Azmon, 5where it will turn, join the
Wadi of Egypt[g] and end at the
Sea.[c]
6" 'Your western boundary will
be the coast of the Great Sea. This
will be your boundary on the west.
7" 'For your northern boundary,[h] run a line from the Great Sea
to Mount Hor 8and from Mount
Hor to Lebo[d] Hamath.[i] Then the
boundary will go to Zedad, 9con-
tinue to Ziphron and end at Hazar
Enan. This will be your boundary
on the north.
10" 'For your eastern boundary,
run a line from Hazar Enan to Shepham. 11The boundary will go down
from Shepham to Riblah[j] on the
east side of Ain and continue along
the slopes east of the Sea of Kinnereth.[e][k] 12Then the boundary will
go down along the Jordan and end
at the Salt Sea.
" 'This will be your land, with its
boundaries on every side.' "
13Moses commanded the Israelites: "Assign this land by lot as an
inheritance.[l] The LORD has ordered that it be given to the nine
and a half tribes, 14because the
families of the tribe of Reuben, the

33:43 b Nu 21:10
33:44 c Nu 21:11
33:47 d Nu 27:12
33:48 e Nu 22:1
33:49 f Nu 25:1
33:51 g Jos 3:17
33:52 h Ex 23:24; Ex 34:13; Lev 26:1; Dt 7:2,5; Dt 12:3; Jos 11:12; Ps 106:34-36
33:53 i Dt 11:31; Jos 21:43
33:54 j Nu 26:54
33:55 k Jos 23:13; Jdg 2:3; Ps 106:36
34:2 a Ge 17:8; Dt 1:7-8; Ps 78:54-55; b Eze 47:15
34:3 c Jos 15:1-3; d Ge 14:3
34:4 e Jos 15:3; f Nu 32:8
34:5 g Ge 15:18; Jos 15:4
34:7 h Eze 47:15-17
34:8 i Nu 13:21; Jos 13:5
34:11 j 2Ki 23:33; Jer 39:5; k Dt 3:17; Jos 11:2; Jos 13:27
34:13 l Jos 14:1-5

c45 That is, Iye Abarim d48 Hebrew *Jordan of Jericho*; possibly an ancient name for the Jordan River; also in verse 50 a3 That is, the Dead Sea; also in verse 12 b4 Hebrew *Akrabbim* c5 That is, the Mediterranean; also in verses 6 and 7 d8 Or *to the entrance to* e11 That is, Galilee

tribe of Gad and the half-tribe of
Manasseh have received their inheritance.[m] 15These two and a half
tribes have received their inheritance on the east side of the Jordan
of Jericho,[f] towards the sunrise."
16The LORD said to Moses,
17"These are the names of the men
who are to assign the land for you
as an inheritance: Eleazar the
priest and Joshua[n] son of Nun.
18And appoint one leader from each
tribe to help[o] assign the land.
19These are their names:

Caleb[p] son of Jephunneh,
from the tribe of Judah;[q]
20Shemuel son of Ammihud,
from the tribe of Simeon;[r]
21Elidad son of Kislon,
from the tribe of Benja-
min;[s]
22Bukki son of Jogli,
the leader from the tribe
of Dan;
23Hanniel son of Ephod,
the leader from the tribe of
Manasseh son of Joseph;
24Kemuel son of Shiphtan,
the leader from the tribe of
Ephraim son of Joseph;
25Elizaphan son of Parnach,
the leader from the tribe
of Zebulun;
26Paltiel son of Azzan,
the leader from the tribe of
Issachar;
27Ahihud son of Shelomi,
the leader from the tribe
of Asher;[t]
28Pedahel son of Ammihud,
the leader from the tribe of
Naphtali."

29These are the men the LORD
commanded to assign the inheritance to the Israelites in the land of
Canaan.

Towns for the Levites

35 On the plains of Moab by
the Jordan across from
Jericho,[a] the LORD said to Moses,
2"Command the Israelites to give
the Levites towns to live in[a] from
the inheritance the Israelites will
possess. And give them pasture-
lands around the towns. 3Then they
will have towns to live in and
pasture-lands for their cattle,
flocks and all their other livestock.
4"The pasture-lands around the
towns that you give the Levites will
extend out fifteen hundred feet[b]
from the town wall. 5Outside the
town, measure three thousand
feet[c] on the east side, three thousand on the south side, three
thousand on the west and three
thousand on the north, with the
town in the centre. They will have
this area as pasture-land for the
towns.

Cities of Refuge

35:6–34Ref Dt 4:41–43; 19:1–14; Jos 20:1–9

6"Six of the towns you give the
Levites will be cities of refuge, to
which a person who has killed
someone may flee.[b] In addition,
give them forty-two other towns.
7In all you must give the Levites
forty-eight towns, together with
their pasture-lands. 8The towns
you give the Levites from the land
the Israelites possess are to be
given in proportion to the inheritance of each tribe: Take many
towns from a tribe that has many,
but few from one that has few."[c]
9Then the LORD said to Moses:
10"Speak to the Israelites and say to
them: 'When you cross the Jordan
into Canaan,[d] 11select some towns
to be your cities of refuge, to which
a person who has killed someone[e]
accidentally[f] may flee. 12They will
be places of refuge from the
avenger,[g] so that a person accused
of murder may not die before he
stands trial before the assembly.
13These six towns you give will be
your cities of refuge. 14Give three

34:14 *m* Nu 32:33; Jos 14:3
34:17 *n* Jos 14:1
34:18 *o* Nu 1:4,16
34:19 *p* Nu 26:65; *q* Ge 29:35; Dt 33:7
34:20 *r* Ge 49:5
34:21 *s* Ge 49:27; Ps 68:27
34:27 *t* Nu 1:40
35:2 *a* Lev 25:32-34; Jos 14:3,4
35:6 *b* Jos 20:7-9; Jos 21:3,13
35:8 *c* Nu 26:54; Nu 33:54; Jos 21:1-42
35:10 *d* Jos 20:2
35:11 *e* ver 22-25; *f* Ex 21:13; Dt 19:1-13
35:12 *g* Dt 19:6; Jos 20:3

f15 *Jordan of Jericho* was possibly an ancient name for the Jordan River. a1 Hebrew *Jordan of Jericho*; possibly an ancient name for the Jordan River b4 Hebrew *a thousand cubits* (about 450 metres) c5 Hebrew *two thousand cubits* (about 900 metres)

on this side of the Jordan and three in Canaan as cities of refuge. 15 These six towns will be a place of refuge for Israelites, aliens and any other people living among them, so that anyone who has killed another accidentally can flee there.

16 " 'If a man strikes someone with an iron object so that he dies, he is a murderer; the murderer shall be put to death.[h] 17 Or if anyone has a stone in his hand that could kill, and he strikes someone so that he dies, he is a murderer; the murderer shall be put to death. 18 Or if anyone has a wooden object in his hand that could kill, and he hits someone so that he dies, he is a murderer; the murderer shall be put to death. 19 The avenger of blood shall put the murderer to death; when he meets him, he shall put him to death.[i] 20 If anyone with malice aforethought pushes another or throws something at him intentionally[j] so that he dies 21 or if in hostility he hits him with his fist so that he dies, that person shall be put to death; he is a murderer. The avenger of blood shall put the murderer to death when he meets him.

22 " 'But if without hostility someone suddenly pushes another or throws something at him unintentionally[k] 23 or, without seeing him, drops a stone on him that could kill him, and he dies, then since he was not his enemy and he did not intend to harm him, 24 the assembly[l] must judge between him and the avenger of blood according to these regulations. 25 The assembly must protect the one accused of murder from the avenger of blood and send him back to the city of refuge to which he fled. He must stay there until the death of the high priest, who was anointed with holy oil.[m]

26 " 'But if the accused ever goes outside the limits of the city of refuge to which he has fled 27 and the avenger of blood finds him outside the city, the avenger of blood may kill the accused without being guilty of murder. 28 The accused must stay in his city of refuge until the death of the high priest; only after the death of the high priest may he return to his own property.

29 " 'These are to be legal requirements[n] for you throughout the generations to come, wherever you live.

30 " 'Anyone who kills a person is to be put to death as a murderer only on the testimony of witnesses. But no-one is to be put to death on the testimony of only one witness.[o]

31 " 'Do not accept a ransom for the life of a murderer, who deserves to die. He must surely be put to death.

32 " 'Do not accept a ransom for anyone who has fled to a city of refuge and so allow him to go back and live on his own land before the death of the high priest.

33 " 'Do not pollute the land where you are. Bloodshed pollutes the land,[p] and atonement cannot be made for the land on which blood has been shed, except by the blood of the one who shed it. 34 Do not defile the land[q] where you live and where I dwell,[r] for I, the LORD, dwell among the Israelites.' "

Inheritance of Zelophehad's Daughters

36:1–12pp Nu 27:1–11

36 The family heads of the clan of Gilead[a] son of Makir, the son of Manasseh, who were from the clans of the descendants of Joseph, came and spoke before Moses and the leaders,[b] the heads of the Israelite families. 2 They said, "When the LORD commanded my lord to give the land as an inheritance to the Israelites by lot, he ordered you to give the inheritance of our brother Zelophehad[c] to his daughters. 3 Now suppose they marry men from

35:16 h Ex 21:12; Lev 24:17
35:19 i ver 21
35:20 j Ge 4:8; Ex 21:14; Dt 19:11; 2Sa 3:27; 2Sa 20:10
35:22 k ver 11; Ex 21:13
35:24 l ver 12; Jos 20:6
35:25 m Ex 29:7
35:29 n Nu 27:11
35:30 o ver 16; Dt 17:6; Dt 19:15; Mt 18:16; Jn 7:51; 2Co 13:1; Heb 10:28
35:33 p Ge 9:6; Ps 106:38; Mic 4:11
35:34 q Lev 18:24,25; r Ex 29:45
36:1 a Nu 26:29; b Nu 27:2
36:2 c Nu 26:33; Nu 27:1,7

other Israelite tribes; then their inheritance will be taken from our
ancestral inheritance and added to
that of the tribe they marry into.
And so part of the inheritance allotted to us will be taken away. 4When
the Year of Jubilee[d] for the Israelites comes, their inheritance will
be added to that of the tribe into
which they marry, and their property will be taken from the tribal
inheritance of our forefathers."
5Then at the LORD's command
Moses gave this order to the Israelites: "What the tribe of the descendants of Joseph is saying is
right. 6This is what the LORD commands for Zelophehad's daughters:
They may marry anyone they
please as long as they marry within
the tribal clan of their father. 7No
inheritance[e] in Israel is to pass
from tribe to tribe, for every Israelite shall keep the tribal land
inherited from his forefathers.
8Every daughter who inherits land
in any Israelite tribe must marry
someone in her father's tribal
clan,[f] so that every Israelite will
possess the inheritance of his fathers. 9No inheritance may pass
from tribe to tribe, for each Israelite tribe is to keep the land it
inherits."
10So Zelophehad's daughters did
as the LORD commanded Moses.
11Zelophehad's daughters—Mahlah, Tirzah, Hoglah, Milcah and
Noah[g]—married their cousins on
their father's side. 12They married
within the clans of the descendants
of Manasseh son of Joseph, and
their inheritance remained in their
father's clan and tribe.
13These are the commands and
regulations the LORD gave through
Moses[h] to the Israelites on the
plains of Moab by the Jordan
across from Jericho.[a][i]

36:4
d Lev 25:10
36:7
e 1Ki 21:3
36:8
f 1Ch 23:22
36:11
g Nu 26:33; Nu 27:1
36:13
h Lev 26:46; Lev 27:34
i Nu 22:1

a13 Hebrew *Jordan of Jericho*; possibly an ancient name for the Jordan River

DEUTERONOMY

The Command to Leave Horeb

1 These are the words Moses spoke to all Israel in the desert east of the Jordan—that is, in the Arabah—opposite Suph, between Paran and Tophel, Laban, Hazeroth and Dizahab. 2(It takes eleven days to go from Horeb[a] to Kadesh Barnea[b] by the Mount Seir road.)

3In the fortieth year,[c] on the first day of the eleventh month, Moses proclaimed[d] to the Israelites all that the LORD had commanded him concerning them. 4This was after he had defeated Sihon[e] king of the Amorites, who reigned in Heshbon,[f] and at Edrei had defeated Og[g] king of Bashan, who reigned in Ashtaroth.

5East of the Jordan in the territory of Moab, Moses began to expound this law, saying:

6The LORD our God said to us[h] at Horeb,[i] "You have stayed long enough at this mountain. 7Break camp and advance into the hill country of the Amorites; go to all the neighbouring peoples in the Arabah, in the mountains, in the western foothills, in the Negev[j] and along the coast, to the land of the Canaanites and to Lebanon,[k] as far as the great river, the Euphrates. 8See, I have given you this land. Go in and take possession of the land that the LORD swore[l] he would give to your fathers—to Abraham, Isaac and Jacob—and to their descendants after them."

The Appointment of Leaders

9At that time I said to you, "You are too heavy a burden for me to carry alone.[m] 10The LORD your God has increased your numbers so that today you are as many[n] as the stars in the sky.[o] 11May the LORD, the God of your fathers, increase you a thousand times and bless you as he has promised![p] 12But how can I bear your problems and your burdens and your disputes all by myself? 13Choose some wise, understanding and respected men[q] from each of your tribes, and I will set them over you."

14You answered me, "What you propose to do is good."

15So I took[r] the leading men of your tribes, wise and respected men, and appointed them to have authority over you—as commanders of thousands, of hundreds, of fifties and of tens and as tribal officials. 16And I charged your judges at that time: Hear the disputes between your brothers and judge fairly,[s] whether the case is between brother Israelites or between one of them and an alien.[t] 17Do not show partiality[u] in judging; hear both small and great alike. Do not be afraid of any man,[v] for judgment belongs to God. Bring me any case too hard for you, and I will hear it.[w] 18And at that time I told you everything you were to do.

Spies Sent Out

19Then, as the LORD our God commanded us, we set out from Horeb and went towards the hill country of the Amorites through all that vast and dreadful desert[x] that you have seen, and so we reached Kadesh Barnea.[y] 20Then I said to you, "You have reached the hill country of the Amorites, which the LORD our God is giving us. 21See, the LORD your God has given you the land. Go up and take possession of it as the LORD, the God of your

1:2
a Ex 3:1
b Nu 13:26; Dt 9:23

1:3
c Nu 33:38
d Dt 4:1-2

1:4
e Nu 21:21-26
f Nu 21:25
g Nu 21:33-35; Jos 13:12

1:6
h Nu 10:13
i Ex 3:1

1:7
j Jos 10:40
k Dt 11:24

1:8
l Ge 12:7; Ge 15:18; Ge 17:7-8; Ge 26:4; Ge 28:13

1:9
m Ex 18:18

1:10
n Ge 15:5
o Dt 10:22; Dt 28:62

1:11
p Ge 22:17; Ex 32:13

1:13
q Ex 18:21

1:15
r Ex 18:25

1:16
s Dt 16:18; Jn 7:24
t Lev 24:22

1:17
u Lev 19:15; Dt 16:19; Pr 24:23; Jas 2:1
v 2Ch 19:6
w Ex 18:26

1:19
x Dt 8:15; Jer 2:2,6
y ver 2; Nu 13:26

fathers, told you. Do not be afraid;[z] do not be discouraged."

22Then all of you came to me and said, "Let us send men ahead to spy out the land for us and bring back a report about the route we are to take and the towns we will come to."

23The idea seemed good to me; so I selected[a] twelve of you, one man from each tribe. 24They left and went up into the hill country, and came to the Valley of Eshcol[b] and explored it. 25Taking with them some of the fruit of the land, they brought it down to us and reported,[c] "It is a good land that the LORD our God is giving us."

Rebellion Against the LORD

26But you were unwilling to go up;[d] you rebelled against the command of the LORD your God. 27You grumbled[e] in your tents and said, "The LORD hates us; so he brought us out of Egypt to deliver us into the hands of the Amorites to destroy us. 28Where can we go? Our brothers have made us lose heart. They say, 'The people are stronger and taller[f] than we are; the cities are large, with walls up to the sky. We even saw the Anakites[g] there.' "

29Then I said to you, "Do not be terrified; do not be afraid of them. 30The LORD your God, who is going before you, will fight[h] for you, as he did for you in Egypt, before your very eyes, 31and in the desert. There you saw how the LORD your God carried[i] you, as a father carries his son, all the way you went until you reached this place."

32In spite of this, you did not trust[j] in the LORD your God, 33who went ahead of you on your journey, in fire by night and in a cloud by day,[k] to search[l] out places for you to camp and to show you the way you should go.

34When the LORD heard what you said, he was angry and solemnly swore:[m] 35"Not a man of this evil generation shall see the good land[n] I swore to give your forefathers, 36except Caleb son of Jephunneh. He will see it, and I will give him and his descendants the land he set his feet on, because he followed the LORD wholeheartedly.[o]"

37Because of you the LORD became angry[p] with me also and said, "You shall not enter[q] it, either. 38But your assistant, Joshua[r] son of Nun, will enter it. Encourage[s] him, because he will lead[t] Israel to inherit it. 39And the little ones that you said would be taken captive,[u] your children who do not yet know[v] good from bad—they will enter the land. I will give it to them and they will take possession of it. 40But as for you, turn round and set out towards the desert along the route to the Red Sea."[a][w]

41Then you replied, "We have sinned against the LORD. We will go up and fight, as the LORD our God commanded us." So every one of you put on his weapons, thinking it easy to go up into the hill country.

42But the LORD said to me, "Tell them, 'Do not go up and fight, because I will not be with you. You will be defeated by your enemies.' "[x]

43So I told you, but you would not listen. You rebelled against the LORD's command and in your arrogance you marched up into the hill country. 44The Amorites who lived in those hills came out against you; they chased you like a swarm of bees[y] and beat you down from Seir all the way to Hormah. 45You came back and wept before the LORD, but he paid no attention to your weeping and turned a deaf ear to you. 46And so you stayed in Kadesh[z] many days—all the time you spent there.

1:21 z Jos 1:6,9,18
1:23 a Nu 13:1-3
1:24 b Nu 13:21-25
1:25 c Nu 13:27
1:26 d Nu 14:1-4
1:27 e Dt 9:28; Ps 106:25
1:28 f Nu 13:32; g Nu 13:33; Dt 9:1-3
1:30 h Ex 14:14; Dt 3:22; Ne 4:20
1:31 i Dt 32:10-12; Isa 46:3-4; Isa 63:9; Hos 11:3; Ac 13:18
1:32 j Ps 106:24; Jude 1:5
1:33 k Ex 13:21; Ps 78:14; l Nu 10:33
1:34 m Nu 14:23, 28-30
1:35 n Ps 95:11
1:36 o Nu 14:24; Jos 14:9
1:37 p Dt 3:26; Dt 4:21; q Nu 20:12
1:38 r Nu 14:30; s Dt 31:7; t Dt 3:28
1:39 u Nu 14:3; v Isa 7:15-16
1:40 w Nu 14:25
1:42 x Nu 14:41-43
1:44 y Ps 118:12
1:46 z Nu 20:1; Jdg 11:17

a40 Hebrew *Yam Suph*; that is, Sea of Reeds

Wanderings in the Desert

2 Then we turned back and set out towards the desert along the route to the Red Sea,[a][a] as the LORD had directed me. For a long time we made our way around the hill country of Seir.

2Then the LORD said to me, 3"You have made your way around this hill country long enough; now turn north. 4Give the people these orders:[b] 'You are about to pass through the territory of your brothers the descendants of Esau, who live in Seir. They will be afraid of you, but be very careful. 5Do not provoke them to war, for I will not give you any of their land, not even enough to put your foot on. I have given Esau the hill country of Seir as his own.[c] 6You are to pay them in silver for the food you eat and the water you drink.' "

7The LORD your God has blessed you in all the work of your hands. He has watched[d] over your journey through this vast desert. These forty years the LORD your God has been with you, and you have not lacked anything.

8So we went on past our brothers the descendants of Esau, who live in Seir. We turned from the Arabah road, which comes up from Elath and Ezion Geber,[e] and travelled along the desert road of Moab.[f]

9Then the LORD said to me, "Do not harass the Moabites or provoke them to war, for I will not give you any part of their land. I have given Ar[g] to the descendants of Lot[h] as a possession."

10(The Emites[i] used to live there—a people strong and numerous, and as tall as the Anakites.[j] 11Like the Anakites, they too were considered Rephaites, but the Moabites called them Emites. 12Horites used to live in Seir, but the descendants of Esau drove them out. They destroyed the Horites from before them and settled in their place, just as Israel did[k] in the land the LORD gave them as their possession.)

13And the LORD said, "Now get up and cross the Zered Valley." So we crossed the valley.

14Thirty-eight years passed from the time we left Kadesh Barnea[l] until we crossed the Zered Valley. By then, that entire generation[m] of fighting men had perished from the camp, as the LORD had sworn to them.[n] 15The LORD's hand was against them until he had completely eliminated[o] them from the camp.

16Now when the last of these fighting men among the people had died, 17the LORD said to me, 18"Today you are to pass by the region of Moab at Ar. 19When you come to the Ammonites,[p] do not harass them or provoke them to war, for I will not give you possession of any land belonging to the Ammonites. I have given it as a possession to the descendants of Lot.[q]"

20(That too was considered a land of the Rephaites, who used to live there; but the Ammonites called them Zamzummites. 21They were a people strong and numerous, and as tall as the Anakites.[r] The LORD destroyed them from before the Ammonites, who drove them out and settled in their place. 22The LORD had done the same for the descendants of Esau, who lived in Seir,[s] when he destroyed the Horites from before them. They drove them out and have lived in their place to this day. 23And as for the Avvites[t] who lived in villages as far as Gaza, the Caphtorites[u] coming out from Caphtor[b][v] destroyed them and settled in their place.)

Defeat of Sihon King of Heshbon

24"Set out now and cross the Arnon Gorge.[w] See, I have given into your hand Sihon the Amorite, king

2:1 a Nu 21:4
2:4 b Nu 20:14-21
2:5 c Ge 36:8; Jos 24:4
2:7 d Dt 8:2-4
2:8 e 1Ki 9:26; f Jdg 11:18
2:9 g Nu 21:15; h Ge 19:36-38
2:10 i Ge 14:5; j Nu 13:22,33
2:12 k ver 22
2:14 l Nu 13:26; m Nu 14:29-35; n Dt 1:34-35
2:15 o Ps 106:26
2:19 p Ge 19:38; q ver 9
2:21 r ver 10
2:22 s Ge 36:8
2:23 t Jos 13:3; u Ge 10:14; v Am 9:7
2:24 w Nu 21:13-14; Jdg 11:13,18

a1 Hebrew *Yam Suph*; that is, Sea of Reeds
b23 That is, Crete

of Heshbon, and his country. Begin to take possession of it and engage him in battle. 25This very day I will begin to put the terror[x] and fear[y] of you on all the nations under heaven. They will hear reports of you and will tremble[z] and be in anguish because of you."

26From the desert of Kedemoth I sent messengers to Sihon king of Heshbon offering peace and saying, 27"Let us pass through your country. We will stay on the main road; we will not turn aside to the right or to the left.[a] 28Sell us food to eat and water to drink for their price in silver. Only let us pass through on foot[b]—29as the descendants of Esau, who live in Seir, and the Moabites, who live in Ar, did for us—until we cross the Jordan into the land the LORD our God is giving us." 30But Sihon king of Heshbon refused to let us pass through. For the LORD[c] your God had made his spirit stubborn[d] and his heart obstinate in order to give him into your hands, as he has now done.

31The LORD said to me, "See, I have begun to deliver Sihon and his country over to you. Now begin to conquer and possess his land."[e]

32When Sihon and all his army came out to meet us in battle[f] at Jahaz, 33the LORD our God delivered him over to us and we struck him down,[g] together with his sons and his whole army. 34At that time we took all his towns and completely destroyed[c][h] them—men, women and children. We left no survivors. 35But the livestock and the plunder from the towns we had captured we carried off for ourselves. 36From Aroer[i] on the rim of the Arnon Gorge, and from the town in the gorge, even as far as Gilead, not one town was too strong for us. The LORD our God gave[j] us all of them. 37But in accordance with the command of the LORD our God,[k] you did not encroach on any of the land of the Ammonites,[l] neither the land along the course of the Jabbok[m] nor that around the towns in the hills.

Defeat of Og King of Bashan

3 Next we turned and went up along the road towards Bashan, and Og king of Bashan with his whole army marched out to meet us in battle at Edrei.[a] 2The LORD said to me, "Do not be afraid[b] of him, for I have handed him over to you with his whole army and his land. Do to him what you did to Sihon king of the Amorites, who reigned in Heshbon."

3So the LORD our God also gave into our hands Og king of Bashan and all his army. We struck them down, leaving no survivors.[c] 4At that time we took all his cities. There was not one of the sixty cities that we did not take from them—the whole region of Argob, Og's kingdom in Bashan.[d] 5All these cities were fortified with high walls and with gates and bars, and there were also a great many unwalled villages. 6We completely destroyed[a] them, as we had done with Sihon king of Heshbon, destroying[a][e] every city—men, women and children. 7But all the livestock and the plunder from their cities we carried off for ourselves.

8So at that time we took from these two kings of the Amorites the territory east of the Jordan, from the Arnon Gorge as far as Mount Hermon. 9(Hermon is called Sirion[f] by the Sidonians; the Amorites call it Senir.)[g] 10We took all the towns on the plateau, and all Gilead, and all Bashan as far as Salecah[h] and Edrei, towns of Og's kingdom in Bashan. 11(Only Og king of Bashan was left of the remnant of the Rephaites.[i] His bed[b]

2:25 x Dt 11:25 y Jos 2:9,11 z Ex 15:14-16
2:27 a Nu 21:21-22
2:28 b Nu 20:19
2:30 c Jos 11:20 d Ex 4:21 Nu 21:23 Ro 9:18
2:31 e Dt 1:8
2:32 f Nu 21:23
2:33 g Dt 29:7
2:34 h Dt 3:6 Dt 7:2
2:36 i Dt 3:12 Dt 4:48 Jos 13:9 j Ps 44:3
2:37 k ver 18-19 l Nu 21:24 m Ge 32:22 Dt 3:16
3:1 a Nu 21:33
3:2 b Nu 21:34
3:3 c Nu 21:35
3:4 d 1Ki 4:13
3:6 e Dt 2:24,34
3:9 f Dt 4:48 Ps 29:6 g 1Ch 5:23
3:10 h Jos 13:11
3:11 i Ge 14:5

c*34* The Hebrew term refers to the irrevocable giving over of things or persons to the LORD, often by totally destroying them.
a*6* The Hebrew term refers to the irrevocable giving over of things or persons to the LORD, often by totally destroying them.
b*11* Or *sarcophagus*

was made of iron and was more than thirteen feet long and six feet wide.[c] It is still in Rabbah[j] of the Ammonites.)

Division of the Land

12 Of the land that we took over at that time, I gave the Reubenites and the Gadites the territory north of Aroer[k] by the Arnon Gorge, including half the hill country of Gilead, together with its towns. 13 The rest of Gilead and also all of Bashan, the kingdom of Og, I gave to the half-tribe of Manasseh. (The whole region of Argob in Bashan used to be known as a land of the Rephaites. 14 Jair,[l] a descendant of Manasseh, took the whole region of Argob as far as the border of the Geshurites and the Maacathites; it was named after him, so that to this day Bashan is called Havvoth Jair.[d]) 15 And I gave Gilead to Makir.[m] 16 But to the Reubenites and the Gadites I gave the territory extending from Gilead down to the Arnon Gorge (the middle of the gorge being the border) and out to the Jabbok River,[n] which is the border of the Ammonites. 17 Its western border was the Jordan in the Arabah, from Kinnereth[o] to the Sea of the Arabah (the Salt Sea[e][p]), below the slopes of Pisgah.

18 I commanded you at that time: "The LORD your God has given you this land to take possession of it. But all your able-bodied men, armed for battle, must cross over ahead of your brother Israelites.[q] 19 However, your wives, your children and your livestock (I know you have much livestock) may stay in the towns I have given you, 20 until the LORD gives rest to your brothers as he has to you, and they too have taken over the land that the LORD your God is giving them, across the Jordan. After that, each of you may go back to the possession I have given you."

Moses Forbidden to Cross the Jordan

21 At that time I commanded Joshua: "You have seen with your own eyes all that the LORD your God has done to these two kings. The LORD will do the same to all the kingdoms over there where you are going. 22 Do not be afraid[r] of them; the LORD your God himself will fight[s] for you."

23 At that time I pleaded with the LORD: 24 "O Sovereign LORD, you have begun to show to your servant your greatness[t] and your strong hand. For what god[u] is there in heaven or on earth who can do the deeds and mighty works[v] you do?[w] 25 Let me go over and see the good land[x] beyond the Jordan—that fine hill country and Lebanon."

26 But because of you the LORD was angry[y] with me and would not listen to me. "That is enough," the LORD said. "Do not speak to me any more about this matter. 27 Go up to the top of Pisgah and look west and north and south and east. Look at the land with your own eyes, since you are not going to cross this Jordan.[z] 28 But commission[a] Joshua, and encourage and strengthen him, for he will lead this people across[b] and will cause them to inherit the land that you will see." 29 So we stayed in the valley near Beth Peor.[c]

Obedience Commanded

4 Hear now, O Israel, the decrees and laws I am about to teach you. Follow them so that you may live[a] and may go in and take possession of the land that the LORD, the God of your fathers, is giving you. 2 Do not add[b] to what I command you and do not subtract from it, but keep the commands of the LORD your God that I give you.

3:11 j 2Sa 12:26; Jer 49:2
3:12 k Nu 32:32-38; Dt 2:36; Jos 13:8-13
3:14 l Nu 32:41; 1Ch 2:22
3:15 m Nu 32:39-40
3:16 n Nu 21:24
3:17 o Nu 34:11; Jos 13:27; p Ge 14:3; Jos 12:3
3:18 q Nu 32:17
3:22 r Dt 1:29; s Ex 14:14; Dt 20:4
3:24 t Dt 11:2; u Ex 15:11; Ps 86:8; v Ps 71:16,19; w 2Sa 7:22
3:25 x Dt 4:22
3:26 y Dt 1:37; Dt 31:2
3:27 z Nu 27:12
3:28 a Nu 27:18-23; b Dt 31:3,23
3:29 c Dt 4:46; Dt 34:6
4:1 a Dt 5:33; Dt 8:1; Dt 16:20; Dt 30:15-20; Eze 20:11; Ro 10:5
4:2 b Dt 12:32; Jos 1:7; Rev 22:18-19

c 11 Hebrew *nine cubits long and four cubits wide* (about 4 metres long and 1.8 metres wide)
d 14 Or *called the settlements of Jair*
e 17 That is, the Dead Sea

3You saw with your own eyes what the LORD did at Baal Peor.[c] The LORD your God destroyed from among you everyone who followed the Baal of Peor, 4but all of you who held fast to the LORD your God are still alive today.

5See, I have taught you decrees and laws as the LORD my God commanded me, so that you may follow them in the land you are entering to take possession of it. 6Observe them carefully, for this will show your wisdom[d] and understanding to the nations, who will hear about all these decrees and say, "Surely this great nation is a wise and understanding people."[e] 7What other nation is so great[f] as to have their gods near[g] them the way the LORD our God is near us whenever we pray to him? 8And what other nation is so great as to have such righteous decrees and laws as this body of laws I am setting before you today?

9Only be careful,[h] and watch yourselves closely so that you do not forget the things your eyes have seen or let them slip from your heart as long as you live. Teach[i] them to your children[j] and to their children after them. 10Remember the day you stood before the LORD your God at Horeb,[k] when he said to me, "Assemble the people before me to hear my words so that they may learn to revere me as long as they live in the land and may teach them to their children." 11You came near and stood at the foot of the mountain while it blazed with fire[l] to the very heavens, with black clouds and deep darkness. 12Then the LORD spoke[m] to you out of the fire. You heard the sound of words but saw no form; there was only a voice. 13He declared to you his covenant,[n] the Ten Commandments,[o] which he commanded you to follow and then wrote them on two stone tablets. 14And the LORD directed me at that time to teach you the decrees and laws you are to follow in the land that you are crossing the Jordan to possess.

Idolatry Forbidden

15You saw no form[p] of any kind the day the LORD spoke to you at Horeb out of the fire. Therefore watch yourselves very carefully,[q] 16so that you do not become corrupt and make for yourselves an idol,[r] an image of any shape, whether formed like a man or a woman, 17or like any animal on earth or any bird that flies in the air, 18or like any creature that moves along the ground or any fish in the waters below. 19And when you look up to the sky and see the sun,[s] the moon and the stars—all the heavenly array[t]—do not be enticed into bowing down to them and worshipping things the LORD your God has apportioned to all the nations under heaven. 20But as for you, the LORD took you and brought you out of the iron-smelting furnace,[u] out of Egypt, to be the people of his inheritance,[v] as you now are.

21The LORD was angry with me[w] because of you, and he solemnly swore that I would not cross the Jordan and enter the good land the LORD your God is giving you as your inheritance. 22I will die in this land; I will not cross the Jordan; but you are about to cross over and take possession of that good land.[x] 23Be careful not to forget the covenant[y] of the LORD your God that he made with you; do not make for yourselves an idol[z] in the form of anything the LORD your God has forbidden. 24For the LORD your God is a consuming fire,[a] a jealous God.

25After you have had children and grandchildren and have lived in the land a long time—if you then become corrupt and make any kind of idol, doing evil[b] in the eyes of the LORD your God and provoking him to anger, 26I call heaven and

4:3 c Nu 25:1-9; Ps 106:28
4:6 d Dt 30:19-20; Ps 19:7; Pr 1:7; e Job 28:28
4:7 f 2Sa 7:23; g Ps 46:1; Isa 55:6
4:9 h Pr 4:23; i Ge 18:19; Eph 6:4; j Ps 78:5-6
4:10 k Ex 19:9,16
4:11 l Ex 19:18; Heb 12:18-19
4:12 m Ex 20:22; Dt 5:4,22
4:13 n Dt 9:9,11; o Ex 24:12; Ex 31:18; Ex 34:28
4:15 p Isa 40:18; q Jos 23:11
4:16 r Ex 20:4-5; Ex 32:7; Dt 5:8; Ro 1:23
4:19 s Dt 17:3; Job 31:26; t 2Ki 17:16; 2Ki 21:3; Ro 1:25
4:20 u 1Ki 8:51; Jer 11:4; v Ex 19:5; Dt 9:29
4:21 w Nu 20:12; Dt 1:37
4:22 x Dt 3:25
4:23 y ver 9,16; z Ex 20:4
4:24 a Ex 24:17; Dt 9:3; Heb 12:29
4:25 b 2Ki 17:2,17

earth as witnesses against you[c]
this day that you will quickly perish from the land that you are
crossing the Jordan to possess. You
will not live there long but will certainly be destroyed. 27 The LORD
will scatter[d] you among the peoples, and only a few of you will survive among the nations to which
the LORD will drive you. 28 There
you will worship man-made gods[e]
of wood and stone, which cannot
see or hear or eat or smell.[f] 29 But
if from there you seek[g] the LORD
your God, you will find him if you
look for him with all your heart[h]
and with all your soul.[i] 30 When you
are in distress and all these things
have happened to you, then in later
days[j] you will return to the LORD
your God and obey him. 31 For the
LORD your God is a merciful[k] God;
he will not abandon or destroy you
or forget the covenant with your
forefathers, which he confirmed to
them by oath.

The LORD Is God

32 Ask[l] now about the former
days, long before your time, from
the day God created man on the
earth;[m] ask from one end of the
heavens to the other.[n] Has anything so great as this ever happened, or has anything like it ever
been heard of? 33 Has any other people heard the voice of God[a] speaking out of fire, as you have, and
lived?[o] 34 Has any god ever tried to
take for himself one nation out of
another nation,[p] by testings, by
miraculous signs[q] and wonders,[r]
by war, by a mighty hand and an
outstretched arm,[s] or by great and
awesome deeds,[t] like all the
things the LORD your God did for
you in Egypt before your very
eyes?
35 You were shown these things so
that you might know that the LORD
is God; besides him there is no
other.[u] 36 From heaven he made
you hear his voice[v] to discipline
you. On earth he showed you his
great fire, and you heard his words
from out of the fire. 37 Because he
loved[w] your forefathers and chose
their descendants after them, he
brought you out of Egypt by his
Presence and his great strength,[x]
38 to drive out before you nations
greater and stronger than you and
to bring you into their land to give
it to you for your inheritance,[y] as
it is today.
39 Acknowledge and take to heart
this day that the LORD is God in
heaven above and on the earth
below. There is no other.[z] 40 Keep[a]
his decrees and commands, which I
am giving you today, so that it may
go well[b] with you and your children after you and that you may
live long[c] in the land the LORD
your God gives you for all time.

Cities of Refuge

4:41–43Ref Nu 35:6–34; Dt 19:1–14; Jos 20:1–9

41 Then Moses set aside three
cities east of the Jordan, 42 to which
anyone who had killed a person
could flee if he had unintentionally
killed his neighbour without malice
aforethought. He could flee into
one of these cities and save his life.
43 The cities were these: Bezer in
the desert plateau, for the Reubenites; Ramoth in Gilead, for the
Gadites; and Golan in Bashan, for
the Manassites.

Introduction to the Law

44 This is the law Moses set before
the Israelites. 45 These are the
stipulations, decrees and laws
Moses gave them when they came
out of Egypt 46 and were in the valley near Beth Peor east of the Jordan, in the land of Sihon[d] king of
the Amorites, who reigned in Heshbon and was defeated by Moses
and the Israelites as they came out
of Egypt. 47 They took possession of
his land and the land of Og king of

4:26 c Dt 30:18-19; Isa 1:2; Mic 6:2
4:27 d Lev 26:33; Dt 28:36,64; Ne 1:8
4:28 e Dt 28:36,64; 1Sa 26:19; Jer 16:13 f Ps 115:4-8; Ps 135:15-18
4:29 g 2Ch 15:4; Isa 55:6 h Jer 29:13 i Dt 30:1-3,10
4:30 j Dt 31:29; Jer 23:20; Hos 3:5
4:31 k 2Ch 30:9; Ne 9:31; Ps 116:5; Jnh 4:2
4:32 l Dt 32:7; Job 8:8 m Ge 1:27 n Mt 24:31
4:33 o Ex 20:22; Dt 5:24-26
4:34 p Ex 6:6 q Ex 7:3 r Dt 7:19; Dt 26:8 s Ex 13:3 t Dt 34:12
4:35 u Dt 32:39; 1Sa 2:2; Isa 45:5,18
4:36 v Ex 19:9,19
4:37 w Dt 10:15 x Ex 13:3,9,14
4:38 y Dt 7:1; Dt 9:5
4:39 z ver 35; Jos 2:11
4:40 a Lev 22:31; Dt 5:33 b Dt 5:16 c Dt 6:3,18; Eph 6:2-3
4:46 d Nu 21:26; Dt 3:29

[a]33 Or *of a god*

Bashan, the two Amorite kings east of the Jordan. 48This land extended from Aroer[e] on the rim of the Arnon Gorge to Mount Siyon[b][f] (that is, Hermon), 49and included all the Arabah east of the Jordan, as far as the Sea of the Arabah,[c] below the slopes of Pisgah.

The Ten Commandments

5:6–21pp Ex 20:1–17

5 Moses summoned all Israel and said:

Hear, O Israel, the decrees and the laws I declare in your hearing today. Learn them and be sure to follow them. 2The LORD our God made a covenant[a] with us at Horeb. 3It was not with our fathers that the LORD made this covenant, but with us, with all of us who are alive here today.[b] 4The LORD spoke[c] to you face to face out of the fire on the mountain. 5(At that time I stood between[d] the LORD and you to declare to you the word of the LORD, because you were afraid[e] of the fire and did not go up the mountain.) And he said:

6"I am the LORD your God, who brought you out of Egypt, out of the land of slavery.

7"You shall have no other gods before[a] me.

8"You shall not make for yourself an idol in the form of anything in heaven above or on the earth beneath or in the waters below. 9You shall not bow down to them or worship them; for I, the LORD your God, am a jealous God, punishing the children for the sin of the fathers to the third and fourth generation of those who hate me,[f] 10but showing love to a thousand ⌞generations⌟ of those who love me and keep my commandments.[g]

4:48 *e* Dt 2:36 *f* Dt 3:9
5:2 *a* Ex 19:5
5:3 *b* Heb 8:9
5:4 *c* Dt 4:12,33,36
5:5 *d* Gal 3:19 *e* Ex 20:18,21
5:9 *f* Ex 34:7
5:10 *g* Jer 32:18
5:11 *h* Lev 19:12; Mt 5:33-37
5:12 *i* Ex 20:8
5:14 *j* Ge 2:2; Heb 4:4
5:15 *k* Dt 4:34
5:16 *l* Ex 20:12; Lev 19:3; Dt 27:16; Eph 6:2-3*; Col 3:20 *m* Dt 4:40
5:17 *n* Mt 5:21-22*
5:18 *o* Mt 5:27-30; Lk 18:20*; Jas 2:11*

11"You shall not misuse the name of the LORD your God, for the LORD will not hold anyone guiltless who misuses his name.[h]

12"Observe the Sabbath day by keeping it holy,[i] as the LORD your God has commanded you. 13Six days you shall labour and do all your work, 14but the seventh day[j] is a Sabbath to the LORD your God. On it you shall not do any work, neither you, nor your son or daughter, nor your manservant or maidservant, nor your ox, your donkey or any of your animals, nor the alien within your gates, so that your manservant and maidservant may rest, as you do. 15Remember that you were slaves in Egypt and that the LORD your God brought you out of there with a mighty hand and an outstretched arm.[k] Therefore the LORD your God has commanded you to observe the Sabbath day.

16"Honour your father and your mother,[l] as the LORD your God has commanded you, so that you may live long[m] and that it may go well with you in the land the LORD your God is giving you.

17"You shall not murder.[n]

18"You shall not commit adultery.[o]

19"You shall not steal.

20"You shall not give false testimony against your neighbour.

21"You shall not covet your neighbour's wife. You shall not set your desire

[b]48 Hebrew; Syriac (see also Deut. 3:9) *Sirion*
[c]49 That is, the Dead Sea [a]7 Or *besides*

on your neighbour's house or land, his manservant or maidservant, his ox or donkey, or anything that belongs to your neighbour."[p]

22These are the commandments the LORD proclaimed in a loud voice to your whole assembly there on the mountain from out of the fire, the cloud and the deep darkness; and he added nothing more. Then he wrote them on two stone tablets[q] and gave them to me.

23When you heard the voice out of the darkness, while the mountain was ablaze with fire, all the leading men of your tribes and your elders came to me. 24And you said, "The LORD our God has shown us his glory and his majesty, and we have heard his voice from the fire. Today we have seen that a man can live even if God speaks with him.[r] 25But now, why should we die? This great fire will consume us, and we will die if we hear the voice of the LORD our God any longer.[s] 26For what mortal man has ever heard the voice of the living God speaking out of fire, as we have, and survived?[t] 27Go near and listen to all that the LORD our God says. Then tell us whatever the LORD our God tells you. We will listen and obey."

28The LORD heard you when you spoke to me and the LORD said to me, "I have heard what this people said to you. Everything they said was good.[u] 29Oh, that their hearts would be inclined to fear me[v] and keep all my commands[w] always, so that it might go well with them and their children for ever![x]

30"Go, tell them to return to their tents. 31But you stay here[y] with me so that I may give you all the commands, decrees and laws that you are to teach them to follow in the land I am giving them to possess."

32So be careful to do what the LORD your God has commanded you; do not turn aside to the right or to the left.[z] 33Walk in all the way that the LORD your God has commanded you,[a] so that you may live and prosper and prolong your days[b] in the land that you will possess.

5:21 p Ro 7:7* Ro 13:9*
5:22 q Ex 24:12 Ex 31:18 Dt 4:13
5:24 r Ex 19:19
5:25 s Dt 18:16
5:26 t Dt 4:33
5:28 u Dt 18:17
5:29 v Ps 81:8,13 w Dt 11:1 Isa 48:18 x Dt 4:1,40
5:31 y Ex 24:12
5:32 z Dt 17:11,20 Dt 28:14 Jos 1:7 Jos 23:6 Pr 4:27
5:33 a Jer 7:23 b Dt 4:40
6:2 a Ex 20:20 Dt 10:12-13
6:3 b Dt 5:33 c Ex 3:8
6:4 d Mk 12:29* 1Co 8:4
6:5 e Mt 22:37* Mk 12:30* Lk 10:27* f Dt 10:12
6:6 g Dt 11:18
6:7 h Dt 4:9 Dt 11:19 Eph 6:4
6:8 i Ex 13:9,16 Dt 11:18
6:9 j Dt 11:20
6:10 k Jos 24:13

Love the LORD Your God

6 These are the commands, decrees and laws the LORD your God directed me to teach you to observe in the land that you are crossing the Jordan to possess, 2so that you, your children and their children after them may fear[a] the LORD your God as long as you live by keeping all his decrees and commands that I give you, and so that you may enjoy long life. 3Hear, O Israel, and be careful to obey so that it may go well with you and that you may increase greatly[b] in a land flowing with milk and honey,[c] just as the LORD, the God of your fathers, promised you.

4Hear, O Israel: The LORD our God, the LORD is one.[a][d] 5Love[e] the LORD your God with all your heart and with all your soul and with all your strength.[f] 6These commandments that I give you today are to be upon your hearts.[g] 7Impress them on your children. Talk about them when you sit at home and when you walk along the road, when you lie down and when you get up.[h] 8Tie them as symbols on your hands and bind them on your foreheads.[i] 9Write them on the door-frames of your houses and on your gates.[j]

10When the LORD your God brings you into the land he swore to your fathers, to Abraham, Isaac and Jacob, to give you—a land with large, flourishing cities you did not build,[k] 11houses filled with all

a4 Or *The LORD our God is one LORD*; or *The LORD is our God, the LORD is one*; or *The LORD is our God, the LORD alone*

kinds of good things you did not
provide, wells you did not dig, and
vineyards and olive groves you did
not plant—then when you eat and
are satisfied,[l] 12 be careful that
you do not forget the LORD, who
brought you out of Egypt, out of the
land of slavery.
13 Fear the LORD[m] your God,
serve him only[n] and take your
oaths in his name. 14 Do not follow
other gods, the gods of the peoples
around you; 15 for the LORD your
God[o], who is among you, is a jealous God and his anger will burn
against you, and he will destroy you
from the face of the land. 16 Do not
test the LORD your God[p] as you did
at Massah. 17 Be sure to keep the
commands of the LORD your God
and the stipulations and decrees he
has given you.[q] 18 Do what is right
and good in the LORD's sight, so that
it may go well[r] with you and you
may go in and take over the good
land that the LORD promised on
oath to your forefathers, 19 thrust-
ing out all your enemies before
you, as the LORD said.
20 In the future, when your son
asks you,[s] "What is the meaning of
the stipulations, decrees and laws
the LORD our God has commanded
you?" 21 tell him: "We were slaves
of Pharaoh in Egypt, but the LORD
brought us out of Egypt with a
mighty hand. 22 Before our eyes
the LORD sent miraculous signs
and wonders—great and terrible—
upon Egypt and Pharaoh and his
whole household. 23 But he brought
us out from there to bring us in and
give us the land that he promised
on oath to our forefathers. 24 The
LORD commanded us to obey all
these decrees and to fear the LORD
our God,[t] so that we might always
prosper and be kept alive, as is the
case today.[u] 25 And if we are careful to obey all this law before the
LORD our God, as he has commanded us, that will be our righteousness."[v]

6:11 l Dt 8:10
6:13 m Dt 10:20 n Mt 4:10* Lk 4:8
6:15 o Dt 4:24
6:16 p Ex 17:7 Mt 4:7* Lk 4:12*
6:17 q Dt 11:22 Ps 119:4
6:18 r Dt 4:40
6:20 s Ex 13:14
6:24 t Dt 10:12 Jer 32:39 u Ps 41:2
6:25 v Dt 24:13 Ro 10:3,5
7:1 a Dt 31:3 Ac 13:19
7:2 b Ex 23:32 c Dt 13:8
7:3 d Ex 34:15-16 Ezr 9:2
7:4 e Dt 6:15
7:5 f Ex 23:24 Dt 12:2-3
7:6 g Ex 19:5-6 1Pe 2:9 h Ps 50:5 Jer 2:3 i Dt 14:2
7:7 j Dt 10:22
7:8 k Dt 10:15 l Ex 32:13 m Ex 13:14
7:9 n Dt 4:35 o 1Co 1:9 2Ti 2:13 p Ne 1:5 Da 9:4

Driving Out the Nations

7 When the LORD your God
brings you into the land you
are entering to possess and drives
out before you many nations[a]—the
Hittites, Girgashites, Amorites,
Canaanites, Perizzites, Hivites and
Jebusites, seven nations larger and
stronger than you—2 and when the
LORD your God has delivered them
over to you and you have defeated
them, then you must destroy them
totally.[a] Make no treaty[b] with
them, and show them no mercy.[c]
3 Do not intermarry with them.[d] Do
not give your daughters to their
sons or take their daughters for
your sons, 4 for they will turn your
sons away from following me to
serve other gods, and the LORD's
anger will burn against you and
will quickly destroy[e] you. 5 This is
what you are to do to them: Break
down their altars, smash their
sacred stones, cut down their
Asherah poles[b] and burn their idols
in the fire.[f] 6 For you are a people
holy[g] to the LORD your God.[h] The
LORD your God has chosen[i] you
out of all the peoples on the face of
the earth to be his people, his treasured possession.
7 The LORD did not set his affection on you and choose you because
you were more numerous than
other peoples, for you were the
fewest of all peoples.[j] 8 But it was
because the LORD loved[k] you and
kept the oath he swore[l] to your
forefathers that he brought you out
with a mighty hand and redeemed
you from the land of slavery,[m]
from the power of Pharaoh king of
Egypt. 9 Know therefore that the
LORD your God is God;[n] he is the
faithful God,[o] keeping his covenant of love[p] to a thousand generations of those who love him and
keep his commands. 10 But

a2 The Hebrew term refers to the irrevocable giving over of things or persons to the LORD, often by totally destroying them; also in verse 26.
b5 That is, symbols of the goddess Asherah; here and elsewhere in Deuteronomy

those who hate him he will
repay to their face by
destruction;
he will not be slow to repay to
their face those who hate
him.

11Therefore, take care to follow the
commands, decrees and laws I give
you today.
12If you pay attention to these
laws and are careful to follow
them, then the LORD your God will
keep his covenant of love with you,
as he swore to your forefathers.[q]
13He will love you and bless you[r]
and increase your numbers. He
will bless the fruit of your womb,
the crops of your land—your grain,
new wine and oil—the calves of
your herds and the lambs of your
flocks in the land that he swore
to your forefathers to give you.[s]
14You will be blessed more than any
other people; none of your men or
women will be childless, nor any
of your livestock without young.[t]
15The LORD will keep you free from
every disease.[u] He will not inflict
on you the horrible diseases you
knew in Egypt, but he will inflict
them on all who hate you. 16You
must destroy all the peoples the
LORD your God gives over to you.
Do not look on them with pity[v] and
do not serve their gods, for that will
be a snare[w] to you.
17You may say to yourselves,
"These nations are stronger than
we are. How can we drive them
out?[x]" 18But do not be afraid[y] of
them; remember well what the
LORD your God did to Pharaoh and
to all Egypt.[z] 19You saw with your
own eyes the great trials, the miraculous signs and wonders, the
mighty hand and outstretched arm,
with which the LORD your God
brought you out. The LORD your
God will do the same to all the peoples you now fear.[a] 20Moreover,
the LORD your God will send the
hornet[b] among them until even the
survivors who hide from you have
perished. 21Do not be terrified by
them, for the LORD your God, who
is among you,[c] is a great and awesome God.[d] 22The LORD your God
will drive out those nations before
you, little by little.[e] You will not be
allowed to eliminate them all at
once, or the wild animals will multiply around you. 23But the LORD
your God will deliver them over to
you, throwing them into great confusion until they are destroyed.
24He will give their kings into your
hand, and you will wipe out their
names from under heaven. No-one
will be able to stand up against
you;[f] you will destroy them. 25The
images of their gods you are to
burn[g] in the fire. Do not covet[h]
the silver and gold on them, and do
not take it for yourselves, or you
will be ensnared[i] by it, for it is
detestable[j] to the LORD your God.
26Do not bring a detestable thing
into your house or you, like it,
will be set apart for destruction.[k]
Utterly abhor and detest it, for it is
set apart for destruction.

Do Not Forget the LORD

8 Be careful to follow every
command I am giving you today, so that you may live[a] and increase and may enter and possess
the land that the LORD promised on
oath to your forefathers. 2Remem-
ber how the LORD your God led[b]
you all the way in the desert these
forty years, to humble you and to
test you in order to know what was
in your heart, whether or not you
would keep his commands. 3He
humbled you, causing you to hunger and then feeding you with
manna,[c] which neither you nor
your fathers had known, to teach
you that man does not live on bread
alone but on every word that comes
from the mouth of the LORD.[d]
4Your clothes did not wear out and
your feet did not swell during these
forty years.[e] 5Know then in your
heart that as a man disciplines his

7:12 q Lev 26:3-13; Dt 28:1-14; Ps 105:8-9
7:13 r Jn 14:21; s Dt 28:4
7:14 t Ex 23:26
7:15 u Ex 15:26
7:16 v ver 2; Ex 23:33; w Jdg 8:27
7:17 x Nu 33:53
7:18 y Dt 31:6; z Ps 105:5
7:19 a Dt 4:34
7:20 b Ex 23:28; Jos 24:12
7:21 c Jos 3:10; d Dt 10:17; Ne 9:32
7:22 e Ex 23:28-30
7:24 f Jos 23:9
7:25 g Ex 32:20; 1Ch 14:12; h Jos 7:21; i Jdg 8:27; j Dt 17:1
7:26 k Lev 27:28-29
8:1 a Dt 4:1
8:2 b Am 2:10
8:3 c Ex 16:12,14,35; d Ex 16:2-3; Mt 4:4*; Lk 4:4*
8:4 e Dt 29:5; Ne 9:21

son, so the LORD your God disciplines you.[f]

6Observe the commands of the LORD your God, walking in his ways and revering him.[g] 7For the LORD your God is bringing you into a good land—a land with streams and pools of water, with springs flowing in the valleys and hills;[h] 8a land with wheat and barley, vines and fig-trees, pomegranates, olive oil and honey; 9a land where bread will not be scarce and you will lack nothing; a land where the rocks are iron and you can dig copper out of the hills.

10When you have eaten and are satisfied,[i] praise the LORD your God for the good land he has given you. 11Be careful that you do not forget the LORD your God, failing to observe his commands, his laws and his decrees that I am giving you this day. 12Otherwise, when you eat and are satisfied, when you build fine houses and settle down,[j] 13and when your herds and flocks grow large and your silver and gold increase and all you have is multiplied, 14then your heart will become proud and you will forget[k] the LORD your God, who brought you out of Egypt, out of the land of slavery. 15He led you through the vast and dreadful desert,[l] that thirsty and waterless land, with its venomous snakes[m] and scorpions. He brought you water out of hard rock.[n] 16He gave you manna to eat in the desert, something your fathers had never known,[o] to humble and to test you so that in the end it might go well with you. 17You may say to yourself,[p] "My power and the strength of my hands have produced this wealth for me." 18But remember the LORD your God, for it is he who gives you the ability to produce wealth,[q] and so confirms his covenant, which he swore to your forefathers, as it is today.

19If you ever forget the LORD your God and follow other gods and worship and bow down to them, I testify against you today that you will surely be destroyed.[r] 20Like the nations the LORD destroyed before you, so you will be destroyed for not obeying the LORD your God.

Not Because of Israel's Righteousness

9 Hear, O Israel. You are now about to cross the Jordan to go in and dispossess nations greater and stronger than you,[a] with large cities that have walls up to the sky.[b] 2The people are strong and tall—Anakites! You know about them and have heard it said: "Who can stand up against the Anakites?"[c] 3But be assured today that the LORD your God is the one who goes across ahead of you[d] like a devouring fire.[e] He will destroy them; he will subdue them before you. And you will drive them out and annihilate them quickly,[f] as the LORD has promised you.

4After the LORD your God has driven them out before you, do not say to yourself,[g] "The LORD has brought me here to take possession of this land because of my righteousness." No, it is on account of the wickedness of these nations[h] that the LORD is going to drive them out before you. 5It is not because of your righteousness or your integrity[i] that you are going in to take possession of their land; but on account of the wickedness of these nations, the LORD your God will drive them out before you, to accomplish what he swore[j] to your fathers, to Abraham, Isaac and Jacob. 6Understand, then, that it is not because of your righteousness that the LORD your God is giving you this good land to possess, for you are a stiff-necked people.[k]

The Golden Calf

7Remember this and never forget how you provoked the LORD your God to anger in the desert.

8:5 f 2Sa 7:14; Pr 3:11-12; Heb 12:5-11; Rev 3:19
8:6 g Dt 5:33
8:7 h Dt 11:9-12
8:10 i Dt 6:10-12
8:12 j Hos 13:6
8:14 k Ps 106:21
8:15 l Jer 2:6; m Nu 21:6; n Nu 20:11; Ps 78:15; Ps 114:8
8:16 o Ex 16:15
8:17 p Dt 9:4,7,24
8:18 q Pr 10:22; Hos 2:8
8:19 r Dt 4:26; Dt 30:18
9:1 a Dt 4:38; Dt 11:23,31; b Dt 1:28
9:2 c Nu 13:22,28, 32-33
9:3 d Dt 31:3; Jos 3:11; e Dt 4:24; Heb 12:29; f Ex 23:31; Dt 7:23-24
9:4 g Dt 8:17; h Lev 18:21, 24-30; Dt 18:9-14
9:5 i Tit 3:5; j Ge 12:7; Ge 13:15; Ge 15:7; Ge 17:8; Ge 26:4
9:6 k ver 13; Ex 32:9; Dt 31:27

From the day you left Egypt until
you arrived here, you have been rebellious against the LORD. 8 At Horeb you aroused the LORD's wrath
so that he was angry enough to destroy you.[l] 9 When I went up on the
mountain to receive the tablets of
stone, the tablets of the covenant
that the LORD had made with you, I
stayed on the mountain forty days
and forty nights; I ate no bread and
drank no water.[m] 10 The LORD gave
me two stone tablets inscribed by
the finger of God.[n] On them were
all the commandments the LORD
proclaimed to you on the mountain
out of the fire, on the day of the
assembly.

11 At the end of the forty days and
forty nights, the LORD gave me the
two stone tablets, the tablets of the
covenant. 12 Then the LORD told
me, "Go down from here at once,
because your people whom you
brought out of Egypt have become
corrupt.[o] They have turned away
quickly[p] from what I commanded
them and have made a cast idol for
themselves."

13 And the LORD said to me, "I
have seen this people[q], and they
are a stiff-necked people indeed!
14 Let me alone,[r] so that I may destroy them and blot out[s] their
name from under heaven. And I
will make you into a nation
stronger and more numerous than
they."

15 So I turned and went down from
the mountain while it was ablaze
with fire. And the two tablets of the
covenant were in my hands.[a][t]
16 When I looked, I saw that you had
sinned against the LORD your God;
you had made for yourselves an
idol cast in the shape of a calf.[u]
You had turned aside quickly from
the way that the LORD had commanded you. 17 So I took the two
tablets and threw them out of
my hands, breaking them to pieces
before your eyes.

18 Then once again I fell[v] prostrate before the LORD for forty
days and forty nights; I ate no
bread and drank no water, because
of all the sin you had committed,
doing what was evil in the LORD's
sight and so provoking him to
anger. 19 I feared the anger and
wrath of the LORD, for he was angry
enough with you to destroy you.[w]
But again the LORD listened to
me.[x] 20 And the LORD was angry
enough with Aaron to destroy him,
but at that time I prayed for Aaron
too. 21 Also I took that sinful thing
of yours, the calf you had made,
and burned it in the fire. Then I
crushed it and ground it to powder
as fine as dust and threw the dust
into a stream that flowed down the
mountain.[y]

22 You also made the LORD angry
at Taberah,[z] at Massah[a] and at
Kibroth Hattaavah.[b]

23 And when the LORD sent you out
from Kadesh Barnea, he said, "Go
up and take possession of the land
I have given you." But you rebelled
against the command of the LORD
your God. You did not trust[c] him
or obey him. 24 You have been rebellious against the LORD ever since I
have known you.[d]

25 I lay prostrate before the LORD
those forty days and forty nights
because the LORD had said he
would destroy you.[e] 26 I prayed to
the LORD and said, "O Sovereign
LORD, do not destroy your people,
your own inheritance that you redeemed by your great power and
brought out of Egypt with a mighty
hand.[f] 27 Remember your servants
Abraham, Isaac and Jacob. Overlook the stubbornness of this people, their wickedness and their
sin. 28 Otherwise, the country from
which you brought us will say, 'Because the LORD was not able to take
them into the land he had promised
them, and because he hated them,
he brought them out to put them to
death in the desert.'[g] 29 But they

9:8 l Ex 32:7-10; Ps 106:19
9:9 m Ex 24:12,15,18; Ex 34:28
9:10 n Ex 31:18; Dt 4:13
9:12 o Ex 32:7-8; Dt 31:29; p Jdg 2:17
9:13 q ver 6; Ex 32:9; Dt 10:16
9:14 r Ex 32:10; s Nu 14:12; Dt 29:20
9:15 t Ex 19:18; Ex 32:15
9:16 u Ex 32:19
9:18 v Ex 34:28
9:19 w Ex 32:10-11,14; x Dt 10:10
9:21 y Ex 32:20
9:22 z Nu 11:3; a Ex 17:7; b Nu 11:34
9:23 c Ps 106:24
9:24 d ver 7; Dt 31:27
9:25 e ver 18
9:26 f Ex 32:11
9:28 g Ex 32:12; Nu 14:16

a 15 Or *And I had the two tablets of the covenant with me, one in each hand*

are your people, your inheritance[h]
that you brought out by your great
power and your outstretched
arm.[i]"

Tablets Like the First Ones

10 At that time the LORD said
to me, "Chisel out two stone
tablets[a] like the first ones and
come up to me on the mountain.
Also make a wooden chest.[a] 2I will
write on the tablets the words that
were on the first tablets, which you
broke. Then you are to put them in
the chest."[b]
3So I made the ark out of acacia
wood[c] and chiselled[d] out two
stone tablets like the first ones,
and I went up on the mountain
with the two tablets in my hands.
4The LORD wrote on these tablets
what he had written before, the
Ten Commandments he had proclaimed[e] to you on the mountain,
out of the fire, on the day of the
assembly. And the LORD gave
them to me. 5Then I came back
down the mountain[f] and put the
tablets in the ark[g] I had made, as
the LORD commanded me, and they
are there now.[h]
6(The Israelites travelled from
the wells of the Jaakanites to Mose-
rah.[i] There Aaron died and was
buried, and Eleazar his son succeeded him as priest.[j] 7From there
they travelled to Gudgodah and on
to Jotbathah, a land with streams of
water.[k] 8At that time the LORD set
apart the tribe of Levi[l] to carry
the ark of the covenant of the LORD,
to stand before the LORD to minister[m] and to pronounce blessings[n]
in his name, as they still do today.
9That is why the Levites have no
share or inheritance among their
brothers; the LORD is their inheritance,[o] as the LORD your God told
them.)
10Now I had stayed on the mountain forty days and nights, as I
did the first time, and the LORD
listened to me at this time also. It
was not his will to destroy you.[p]
11"Go," the LORD said to me, "and
lead the people on their way, so
that they may enter and possess the
land that I swore to their fathers to
give them."

Fear the LORD

12And now, O Israel, what does
the LORD your God ask of you[q] but
to fear the LORD your God, to walk
in all his ways, to love him,[r] to
serve the LORD your God with
all your heart[s] and with all your
soul, 13and to observe the LORD's
commands and decrees that I am
giving you today for your own
good?
14To the LORD your God belong
the heavens, even the highest heavens,[t] the earth and everything in
it.[u] 15Yet the LORD set his affection
on your forefathers and loved[v]
them, and he chose you, their descendants, above all the nations,
as it is today. 16Circumcise[w] your
hearts, therefore, and do not be
stiff-necked[x] any longer. 17For the
LORD your God is God of gods[y] and
Lord of lords, the great God,
mighty and awesome, who shows
no partiality[z] and accepts no
bribes. 18He defends the cause of
the fatherless and the widow,[a] and
loves the alien, giving him food and
clothing. 19And you are to love
those who are aliens, for you yourselves were aliens in Egypt.[b]
20Fear the LORD your God and
serve him.[c] Hold fast[d] to him and
take your oaths in his name.[e] 21He
is your praise;[f] he is your God,
who performed for you those great
and awesome wonders[g] you saw
with your own eyes. 22Your forefathers who went down into Egypt
were seventy in all,[h] and now
the LORD your God has made you
as numerous as the stars in the
sky.[i]

9:29 *h* Dt 4:20; 1Ki 8:51 *i* Dt 4:34; Ne 1:10
10:1 *a* Ex 25:10; Ex 34:1-2
10:2 *b* Ex 25:16,21; Dt 4:13
10:3 *c* Ex 25:5,10; Ex 37:1-9 *d* Ex 34:4
10:4 *e* Ex 20:1
10:5 *f* Ex 34:29 *g* Ex 40:20 *h* 1Ki 8:9
10:6 *i* Nu 33:30-31, 38 *j* Nu 20:25-28
10:7 *k* Nu 33:32-34
10:8 *l* Nu 3:6 *m* Dt 18:5 *n* Dt 21:5
10:9 *o* Nu 18:20; Dt 18:1-2; Eze 44:28
10:10 *p* Ex 33:17; Ex 34:28; Dt 9:18-19,25
10:12 *q* Mic 6:8 *r* Dt 5:33; Dt 6:13; Mt 22:37 *s* Dt 6:5
10:14 *t* 1Ki 8:27 *u* Ex 19:5
10:15 *v* Dt 4:37
10:16 *w* Jer 4:4 *x* Dt 9:6
10:17 *y* Jos 22:22; Da 2:47 *z* Ac 10:34; Ro 2:11; Eph 6:9
10:18 *a* Ps 68:5
10:19 *b* Lev 19:34
10:20 *c* Mt 4:10 *d* Dt 11:22 *e* Ps 63:11
10:21 *f* Ex 15:2; Jer 17:14 *g* Ps 106:21-22
10:22 *h* Ge 46:26-27 *i* Ge 15:5; Dt 1:10

a1 That is, an ark

Love and Obey the LORD

11 Love[a] the LORD your God
and keep his requirements,
his decrees, his laws and his commands always.[b] 2Remember today
that your children were not the
ones who saw and experienced the
discipline of the LORD your God:[c]
his majesty, his mighty hand, his
outstretched arm; 3the signs he
performed and the things he did in
the heart of Egypt, both to Pharaoh
king of Egypt and to his whole
country; 4what he did to the Egyptian army, to its horses and chariots, how he overwhelmed them
with the waters of the Red Sea[a][d]
as they were pursuing you, and how
the LORD brought lasting ruin on
them. 5It was not your children who
saw what he did for you in the
desert until you arrived at this
place, 6and what he did[e] to Dathan
and Abiram, sons of Eliab the Reubenite, when the earth opened its
mouth right in the middle of all Israel and swallowed them up with
their households, their tents and
every living thing that belonged to
them. 7But it was your own eyes
that saw all these great things the
LORD has done.

8Observe therefore all the commands I am giving you today, so
that you may have the strength to
go in and take over the land that
you are crossing the Jordan to possess,[f] 9and so that you may live
long[g] in the land that the LORD
swore[h] to your forefathers to give
to them and their descendants, a
land flowing with milk and honey.[i]
10The land you are entering to take
over is not like the land of Egypt,
from which you have come, where
you planted your seed and irri-
gated it by foot as in a vegetable
garden. 11But the land you are
crossing the Jordan to take possession of is a land of mountains and
valleys that drinks rain from
heaven.[j] 12It is a land the LORD
your God cares for; the eyes[k] of
the LORD your God are continually
on it from the beginning of the year
to its end.

13So if you faithfully obey[l] the
commands I am giving you today—
to love[m] the LORD your God and
to serve him with all your heart
and with all your soul—14then I
will send rain[n] on your land in its
season, both autumn and spring
rains,[o] so that you may gather in
your grain, new wine and oil. 15I
will provide grass[p] in the fields for
your cattle, and you will eat and be
satisfied.[q]

16Be careful, or you will be enticed to turn away and worship
other gods and bow down to them.[r]
17Then the LORD's anger[s] will burn
against you, and he will shut[t] the
heavens so that it will not rain and
the ground will yield no produce,
and you will soon perish[u] from the
good land the LORD is giving you.
18Fix these words of mine in your
hearts and minds; tie them as symbols on your hands and bind them
on your foreheads.[v] 19Teach them
to your children,[w] talking about
them when you sit at home and
when you walk along the road,
when you lie down and when you
get up.[x] 20Write them on the door-
frames of your houses and on your
gates,[y] 21so that your days and the
days of your children may be
many[z] in the land that the LORD
swore to give your forefathers, as
many as the days that the heavens
are above the earth.[a]

22If you carefully observe[b] all
these commands I am giving you
to follow—to love the LORD your
God, to walk in all his ways and to
hold fast[c] to him—23then the LORD
will drive out all these nations
before you, and you will dispossess
nations larger and stronger than
you.[d] 24Every place where you set
your foot will be yours:[e] Your
territory will extend from the
desert to Lebanon, and from the

11:1 *a* Dt 10:12 *b* Zec 3:7
11:2 *c* Dt 5:24; Dt 8:5
11:4 *d* Ex 14:27
11:6 *e* Nu 16:1-35
11:8 *f* Jos 1:7
11:9 *g* Dt 4:40; Pr 10:27 *h* Dt 9:5 *i* Ex 3:8
11:11 *j* Dt 8:7
11:12 *k* 1Ki 9:3
11:13 *l* Dt 6:17 *m* Dt 10:12
11:14 *n* Lev 26:4; Dt 28:12 *o* Joel 2:23; Jas 5:7
11:15 *p* Ps 104:14 *q* Dt 6:11
11:16 *r* Dt 8:19; Dt 29:18; Job 31:9,27
11:17 *s* Dt 6:15 *t* 1Ki 8:35; 2Ch 6:26 *u* Dt 4:26
11:18 *v* Dt 6:6-8
11:19 *w* Dt 6:7 *x* Dt 4:9-10
11:20 *y* Dt 6:9
11:21 *z* Pr 3:2; Pr 4:10 *a* Ps 72:5
11:22 *b* Dt 6:17 *c* Dt 10:20
11:23 *d* Dt 4:38; Dt 9:1
11:24 *e* Ge 15:18; Ex 23:31; Jos 1:3; Jos 14:9

[a]4 Hebrew *Yam Suph*; that is, Sea of Reeds

Euphrates River to the western sea.[b] 25 No man will be able to stand against you. The LORD your God, as he promised you, will put the terror and fear of you on the whole land, wherever you go.[f]

26 See, I am setting before you today a blessing and a curse[g]— 27 the blessing[h] if you obey the commands of the LORD your God that I am giving you today; 28 the curse if you disobey[i] the commands of the LORD your God and turn from the way that I command you today by following other gods, which you have not known. 29 When the LORD your God has brought you into the land you are entering to possess, you are to proclaim on Mount Gerizim the blessings, and on Mount Ebal the curses.[j] 30 As you know, these mountains are across the Jordan, west of the road,[c] towards the setting sun, near the great trees of Moreh,[k] in the territory of those Canaanites living in the Arabah in the vicinity of Gilgal.[l] 31 You are about to cross the Jordan to enter and take possession[m] of the land the LORD your God is giving you. When you have taken it over and are living there, 32 be sure that you obey all the decrees and laws I am setting before you today.

The One Place of Worship

12 These are the decrees and laws you must be careful to follow in the land that the LORD, the God of your fathers, has given you to possess—as long as you live in the land.[a] 2 Destroy completely all the places on the high mountains and on the hills and under every spreading tree[b] where the nations you are dispossessing worship their gods. 3 Break down their altars, smash[c] their sacred stones and burn their Asherah poles in the fire; cut down the idols of their gods and wipe out their names from those places.

4 You must not worship the LORD your God in their way. 5 But you are to seek the place the LORD your God will choose from among all your tribes to put his Name there for his dwelling.[d] To that place you must go; 6 there bring your burnt offerings and sacrifices, your tithes[e] and special gifts, what you have vowed to give and your freewill offerings, and the firstborn of your herds and flocks. 7 There, in the presence of the LORD your God, you and your families shall eat and shall rejoice[f] in everything you have put your hand to, because the LORD your God has blessed you.

8 You are not to do as we do here today, everyone as he sees fit, 9 since you have not yet reached the resting place and the inheritance the LORD your God is giving you. 10 But you will cross the Jordan and settle in the land the LORD your God is giving[g] you as an inheritance, and he will give you rest from all your enemies around you so that you will live in safety. 11 Then to the place the LORD your God will choose as a dwelling for his Name[h]—there you are to bring everything I command you: your burnt offerings and sacrifices, your tithes and special gifts, and all the choice possessions you have vowed to the LORD. 12 And there rejoice[i] before the LORD your God, you, your sons and daughters, your menservants and maidservants, and the Levites from your towns, who have no allotment or inheritance[j] of their own. 13 Be careful not to sacrifice your burnt offerings anywhere you please. 14 Offer them only at the place the LORD will choose[k] in one of your tribes, and there observe everything I command you.

15 Nevertheless, you may slaughter your animals in any of your towns and eat as much of the meat as you want, as if it were gazelle or

11:25 f Ex 23:27; Dt 7:24
11:26 g Dt 30:1,15,19
11:27 h Dt 28:1-14
11:28 i Dt 28:15
11:29 j Dt 27:12-13; Jos 8:33
11:30 k Ge 12:6; l Jos 4:19
11:31 m Dt 9:1; Jos 1:11
12:1 a Dt 4:9-10; 1Ki 8:40
12:2 b 2Ki 16:4; 2Ki 17:10
12:3 c Nu 33:52; Dt 7:5; Jdg 2:2
12:5 d ver 11,13; 2Ch 7:12,16
12:6 e Dt 14:22-23
12:7 f ver 12,18; Lev 23:40; Dt 14:26
12:10 g Dt 11:31
12:11 h ver 5; Dt 15:20; Dt 16:2
12:12 i ver 7; j Dt 10:9; Dt 14:29
12:14 k ver 11

[b]*24* That is, the Mediterranean [c]*30* Or *Jordan, westward*

deer,[l] according to the blessing
the LORD your God gives you. Both
the ceremonially unclean and the
clean may eat it. 16But you must not
eat the blood;[m] pour it out on the
ground like water.[n] 17You must not
eat in your own towns the tithe of
your grain and new wine and oil,
or the firstborn of your herds
and flocks, or whatever you have
vowed to give, or your freewill
offerings or special gifts. 18In-
stead, you are to eat[o] them in the
presence of the LORD your God
at the place the LORD your God
will choose[p]—you, your sons and
daughters, your menservants and
maidservants, and the Levites
from your towns—and you are to
rejoice[q] before the LORD your God
in everything you put your hand to.
19Be careful not to neglect the Levites[r] as long as you live in your
land.

20When the LORD your God has
enlarged your territory[s] as he
promised[t] you, and you crave
meat and say, "I would like some
meat," then you may eat as much of
it as you want. 21If the place where
the LORD your God chooses to put
his Name is too far away from you,
you may slaughter animals from
the herds and flocks the LORD has
given you, as I have commanded
you, and in your own towns you
may eat as much of them as you
want. 22Eat them as you would gazelle or deer.[u] Both the ceremonially unclean and the clean may eat.
23But be sure you do not eat the
blood,[v] because the blood is the
life, and you must not eat the life
with the meat. 24You must not eat
the blood; pour it out on the ground
like water. 25Do not eat it, so that it
may go well[w] with you and your
children after you, because you
will be doing what is right[x] in the
eyes of the LORD.

26But take your consecrated
things and whatever you have
vowed to give,[y] and go to the place
the LORD will choose. 27Present
your burnt offerings[z] on the altar
of the LORD your God, both the
meat and the blood. The blood of
your sacrifices must be poured beside the altar of the LORD your God,
but you may eat the meat. 28Be
careful to obey all these regulations I am giving you, so that it may
always go well[a] with you and your
children after you, because you
will be doing what is good and right
in the eyes of the LORD your God.

29The LORD your God will cut
off[b] before you the nations you are
about to invade and dispossess. But
when you have driven them out and
settled in their land, 30and after
they have been destroyed before
you, be careful not to be ensnared
by enquiring about their gods, saying, "How do these nations serve
their gods? We will do the same."
31You must not worship the LORD
your God in their way, because in
worshipping their gods, they do
all kinds of detestable things the
LORD hates.[c] They even burn their
sons[d] and daughters in the fire as
sacrifices to their gods.

32See that you do all I command
you; do not add[e] to it or take away
from it.

Worshipping Other Gods

13 If a prophet,[a] or one who
foretells by dreams, ap-
pears among you and announces to
you a miraculous sign or wonder,
2and if the sign or wonder of which
he has spoken takes place, and he
says, "Let us follow other gods"[b]
(gods you have not known) "and let
us worship them," 3you must not
listen to the words of that prophet
or dreamer. The LORD your God is
testing[c] you to find out whether
you love him with all your heart
and with all your soul. 4It is the
LORD your God you must follow,[d]
and him you must revere. Keep his
commands and obey him; serve
him and hold fast[e] to him. 5That
prophet or dreamer must be put to

12:15 l ver 20-23; Dt 14:5; Dt 15:22
12:16 m Ge 9:4; Lev 7:26; Lev 17:10-12; n Dt 15:23
12:18 o Dt 14:23; p ver 5; q ver 7,12
12:19 r Dt 14:27
12:20 s Dt 19:8; t Ge 15:18; Dt 11:24
12:22 u ver 15
12:23 v ver 16; Ge 9:4; Lev 17:11,14
12:25 w Dt 4:40; Isa 3:10; x Ex 15:26; Dt 13:18; 1Ki 11:38
12:26 y ver 17; Nu 5:9-10
12:27 z Lev 1:5,9,13
12:28 a ver 25; Dt 4:40
12:29 b Jos 23:4
12:31 c Dt 9:5; d Dt 18:10; Jer 32:35
12:32 e Dt 4:2; Jos 1:7; Rev 22:18-19
13:1 a Mt 24:24; Mk 13:22; 2Th 2:9
13:2 b ver 6,13
13:3 c Dt 8:2,16
13:4 d 2Ki 23:3; 2Ch 34:31; e Dt 10:20

death, because he preached rebellion against the LORD your God, who brought you out of Egypt and redeemed you from the land of slavery; he has tried to turn you from the way the LORD your God commanded you to follow. You must purge the evil[f] from among you.

6 If your very own brother, or your son or daughter, or the wife you love, or your closest friend secretly entices[g] you, saying, "Let us go and worship other gods" (gods that neither you nor your fathers have known, 7 gods of the peoples around you, whether near or far, from one end of the land to the other), 8 do not yield[h] to him or listen to him. Show him no pity. Do not spare him or shield him. 9 You must certainly put him to death.[i] Your hand must be the first in putting him to death, and then the hands of all the people. 10 Stone him to death, because he tried to turn you away from the LORD your God, who brought you out of Egypt, out of the land of slavery. 11 Then all Israel will hear and be afraid,[j] and no-one among you will do such an evil thing again.

12 If you hear it said about one of the towns the LORD your God is giving you to live in 13 that wicked men[k] have arisen among you and have led the people of their town astray, saying, "Let us go and worship other gods" (gods you have not known), 14 then you must enquire, probe and investigate it thoroughly. And if it is true and it has been proved that this detestable thing has been done among you, 15 you must certainly put to the sword all who live in that town. Destroy it completely,[a] both its people and its livestock. 16 Gather all the plunder of the town into the middle of the public square and completely burn the town and all its plunder as a whole burnt offering to the LORD your God.[l] It is to remain a ruin[m] for ever, never to be rebuilt. 17 None of those condemned things[a] shall be found in your hands, so that the LORD will turn from his fierce anger;[n] he will show you mercy, have compassion[o] on you, and increase your numbers,[p] as he promised[q] on oath to your forefathers, 18 because you obey the LORD your God, keeping all his commands that I am giving you today and doing what is right[r] in his eyes.

13:5 f Dt 17:7,12; 1Co 5:13
13:6 g Dt 17:2-7; Dt 29:18
13:8 h Pr 1:10
13:9 i Dt 17:5,7
13:11 j Dt 19:20
13:13 k ver 2,6; 1Jn 2:19
13:16 l Jos 6:24; m Jos 8:28; Jer 49:2
13:17 n Nu 25:4; o Dt 30:3; p Dt 7:13; q Ge 22:17; Ge 26:4,24; Ge 28:14
13:18 r Dt 12:25,28
14:1 a Lev 19:28; Lev 21:5; Jer 16:6; Jer 41:5; Ro 8:14; Ro 9:8; Gal 3:26
14:2 b Lev 20:26; c Dt 7:6; Dt 26:18-19
14:3 d Eze 4:14
14:4 e Lev 11:2-45; Ac 10:14
14:8 f Lev 11:26-27

Clean and Unclean Food

14:3–20pp Lev 11:1–23

14 You are the children[a] of the LORD your God. Do not cut yourselves or shave the front of your heads for the dead, 2 for you are a people holy to the LORD your God.[b] Out of all the peoples on the face of the earth, the LORD has chosen you to be his treasured possession.[c]

3 Do not eat any detestable thing.[d] 4 These are the animals you may eat:[e] the ox, the sheep, the goat, 5 the deer, the gazelle, the roe deer, the wild goat, the ibex, the antelope and the mountain sheep.[a] 6 You may eat any animal that has a split hoof divided in two and that chews the cud. 7 However, of those that chew the cud or that have a split hoof completely divided you may not eat the camel, the rabbit or the coney.[b] Although they chew the cud, they do not have a split hoof; they are ceremonially unclean for you. 8 The pig is also unclean; although it has a split hoof, it does not chew the cud. You are not to eat their meat or touch their carcasses.[f]

9 Of all the creatures living in the water, you may eat any that has fins and scales. 10 But anything that does not have fins and scales you

[a] *15,17* The Hebrew term refers to the irrevocable giving over of things or persons to the LORD, often by totally destroying them.
[a] *5* The precise identification of some of the birds and animals in this chapter is uncertain.
[b] *7* That is, the hyrax or rock badger

may not eat; for you it is unclean. 11You may eat any clean bird. 12But these you may not eat: the eagle, the vulture, the black vulture, 13the red kite, the black kite, any kind of falcon, 14any kind of raven, 15the horned owl, the screech owl, the gull, any kind of hawk, 16the little owl, the great owl, the white owl, 17the desert owl, the osprey, the cormorant, 18the stork, any kind of heron, the hoopoe and the bat.

19All flying insects that swarm are unclean to you; do not eat them. 20But any winged creature that is clean you may eat.

21Do not eat anything you find already dead.[g] You may give it to an alien living in any of your towns, and he may eat it, or you may sell it to a foreigner. But you are a people holy to the LORD your God.[h]

Do not cook a young goat in its mother's milk.[i]

Tithes

22Be sure to set aside a tenth[j] of all that your fields produce each year. 23Eat the tithe of your grain, new wine and oil, and the firstborn of your herds and flocks in the presence of the LORD your God at the place he will choose as a dwelling for his Name,[k] so that you may learn[l] to revere the LORD your God always. 24But if that place is too distant and you have been blessed by the LORD your God and cannot carry your tithe (because the place where the LORD will choose to put his Name is so far away), 25then exchange your tithe for silver, and take the silver with you and go to the place the LORD your God will choose. 26Use the silver to buy whatever you like: cattle, sheep, wine or other fermented drink, or anything you wish. Then you and your household shall eat there in the presence of the LORD your God and rejoice.[m] 27And do not neglect the Levites[n] living in your towns, for they have no allotment or inheritance of their own.[o]

28At the end of every three years, bring all the tithes of that year's produce and store it in your towns,[p] 29so that the Levites (who have no allotment[q] or inheritance of their own) and the aliens,[r] the fatherless and the widows who live in your towns may come and eat and be satisfied, and so that the LORD your God may bless[s] you in all the work of your hands.

The Year for Cancelling Debts

15:1–11Ref Lev 25:8–38

15 At the end of every seven years you must cancel debts.[a] 2This is how it is to be done: Every creditor shall cancel the loan he has made to his fellow Israelite. He shall not require payment from his fellow Israelite or brother, because the LORD's time for cancelling debts has been proclaimed. 3You may require payment from a foreigner,[b] but you must cancel any debt your brother owes you. 4However, there should be no poor among you, for in the land the LORD your God is giving you to possess as your inheritance, he will richly bless[c] you, 5if only you fully obey the LORD your God and are careful to follow[d] all these commands I am giving you today. 6For the LORD your God will bless you as he has promised, and you will lend to many nations but will borrow from none. You will rule over many nations but none will rule over you.[e]

7If there is a poor man among your brothers in any of the towns of the land that the LORD your God is giving you, do not be hard-hearted or tight-fisted[f] towards your poor brother. 8Rather be open-handed[g] and freely lend him whatever he needs. 9Be careful not to harbour this wicked thought: "The seventh year, the year for cancelling debts,[h] is near," so that you do not

14:21 g Lev 17:15; Lev 22:8 h ver 2 i Ex 23:19; Ex 34:26
14:22 j Lev 27:30; Dt 12:6,17; Ne 10:37
14:23 k Dt 12:5 l Dt 4:10
14:26 m Dt 12:7-8
14:27 n Dt 12:19 o Nu 18:20
14:28 p Dt 26:12
14:29 q ver 27 r Dt 26:12 s Dt 15:10; Mal 3:10
15:1 a Dt 31:10
15:3 b Dt 23:20
15:4 c Dt 28:8
15:5 d Dt 28:1
15:6 e Dt 28:12-13, 44
15:7 f 1Jn 3:17
15:8 g Mt 5:42; Lk 6:34
15:9 h ver 1

show ill will[i] towards your needy
brother and give him nothing. He
may then appeal to the LORD
against you, and you will be found
guilty of sin.[j] 10Give generously to
him and do so without a grudging
heart;[k] then because of this the
LORD your God will bless[l] you in
all your work and in everything
you put your hand to. 11There will
always be poor people in the
land. Therefore I command you
to be open-handed towards your
brothers and towards the poor and
needy in your land.[m]

Freeing Servants

15:12–18pp Ex 21:2–6
15:12–18Ref Lev 25:38–55

12If a fellow Hebrew, a man or
woman, sells himself to you and
serves you six years, in the seventh
year you must let him go free.[n]
13And when you release him, do
not send him away empty-handed.
14Supply him liberally from your
flock, your threshing-floor and
your winepress. Give to him as the
LORD your God has blessed you.
15Remember that you were slaves[o]
in Egypt and the LORD your God redeemed you.[p] That is why I give
you this command today.

16But if your servant says to you,
"I do not want to leave you," because he loves you and your family
and is well off with you, 17then take
an awl and push it through his ear
lobe into the door, and he will become your servant for life. Do the
same for your maidservant.

18Do not consider it a hardship to
set your servant free, because his
service to you these six years has
been worth twice as much as that of
a hired hand. And the LORD your
God will bless you in everything
you do.

The Firstborn Animals

19Set apart for the LORD your
God every firstborn male[q] of your
herds and flocks. Do not put the

15:9
i Mt 20:15
j Dt 24:15
15:10
k 2Co 9:5
l Dt 14:29
Dt 24:19
15:11
m Mt 26:11
Mk 14:7
Jn 12:8
15:12
n Ex 21:2
Lev 25:39
Jer 34:14
15:15
o Dt 5:15
p Dt 16:12
15:19
q Ex 13:2
15:20
r Dt 12:5-7,17,
18
Dt 14:23
15:21
s Lev 22:19-25
15:22
t Dt 12:15,22
15:23
u Dt 12:16
16:1
a Ex 12:2
Ex 13:4
16:2
b Dt 12:5,26
16:3
c Ex 12:8,39
Ex 34:18
d Ex 12:11,15,
19
e Ex 13:3,6-7
16:4
f Ex 12:10
Ex 34:25
16:6
g Ex 12:6
Dt 12:5
16:7
h Ex 12:8
2Ch 35:13

firstborn of your oxen to work, and
do not shear the firstborn of your
sheep. 20Each year you and your
family are to eat them in the presence of the LORD your God at the
place he will choose.[r] 21If an animal has a defect, is lame or blind,
or has any serious flaw, you must
not sacrifice it to the LORD your
God.[s] 22You are to eat it in your
own towns. Both the ceremonially
unclean and the clean may eat it, as
if it were gazelle or deer.[t] 23But
you must not eat the blood; pour it
out on the ground like water.[u]

Passover

16:1–8pp Ex 12:14–20; Lev 23:4–8; Nu 28:16–25

16 Observe the month of
Abib[a] and celebrate the
Passover of the LORD your God,
because in the month of Abib he
brought you out of Egypt by night.
2Sacrifice as the Passover to the
LORD your God an animal from
your flock or herd at the place the
LORD will choose as a dwelling for
his Name.[b] 3Do not eat it with
bread made with yeast, but for
seven days eat unleavened bread,
the bread of affliction,[c] because
you left Egypt in haste[d]—so that
all the days of your life you may remember the time of your departure
from Egypt.[e] 4Let no yeast be
found in your possession in all your
land for seven days. Do not let any
of the meat you sacrifice on the
evening of the first day remain
until morning.[f]

5You must not sacrifice the Passover in any town the LORD your God
gives you 6except in the place he
will choose as a dwelling for his
Name. There you must sacrifice
the Passover in the evening, when
the sun goes down, on the anniver-
sary[a][g] of your departure from
Egypt. 7Roast[h] it and eat it at the
place the LORD your God will
choose. Then in the morning return

[a]6 Or *down, at the time of day*

to your tents. 8For six days eat unleavened bread and on the seventh day hold an assembly[i] to the LORD your God and do no work.

Feast of Weeks

16:9–12pp Lev 23:15–22; Nu 28:26–31

9Count off seven weeks[j] from the time you begin to put the sickle to the standing corn.[k] 10Then celebrate the Feast of Weeks to the LORD your God by giving a freewill offering in proportion to the blessings the LORD your God has given you. 11And rejoice[l] before the LORD your God at the place he will choose as a dwelling for his Name—you, your sons and daughters, your menservants and maidservants, the Levites[m] in your towns, and the aliens, the fatherless and the widows living among you. 12Remember that you were slaves in Egypt,[n] and follow carefully these decrees.

Feast of Tabernacles

16:13–17pp Lev 23:33–43; Nu 29:12–39

13Celebrate the Feast of Tabernacles for seven days after you have gathered the produce of your threshing-floor[o] and your winepress.[p] 14Be joyful[q] at your Feast—you, your sons and daughters, your menservants and maidservants, and the Levites, the aliens, the fatherless and the widows who live in your towns. 15For seven days celebrate the Feast to the LORD your God at the place the LORD will choose. For the LORD your God will bless you in all your harvest and in all the work of your hands, and your joy[r] will be complete.

16Three times a year all your men must appear before the LORD your God at the place he will choose: at the Feast of Unleavened Bread, the Feast of Weeks and the Feast of Tabernacles.[s] No man should appear before the LORD empty-handed:[t] 17Each of you must bring a gift in proportion to the way the LORD your God has blessed you.

Judges

18Appoint judges[u] and officials for each of your tribes in every town the LORD your God is giving you, and they shall judge the people fairly. 19Do not pervert justice[v] or show partiality.[w] Do not accept a bribe,[x] for a bribe blinds the eyes of the wise and twists the words of the righteous. 20Follow justice and justice alone, so that you may live and possess the land the LORD your God is giving you.

Worshipping Other Gods

21Do not set up any wooden Asherah pole[b][y] beside the altar you build to the LORD your God,[z] 22and do not erect a sacred stone,[a] for these the LORD your God hates.

17

Do not sacrifice to the LORD your God an ox or a sheep that has any defect[a] or flaw in it, for that would be detestable to him.[b]

2If a man or woman living among you in one of the towns the LORD gives you is found doing evil in the eyes of the LORD your God in violation of his covenant,[c] 3and contrary to my command[d] has worshipped other gods, bowing down to them or to the sun[e] or the moon or the stars of the sky, 4and this has been brought to your attention, then you must investigate it thoroughly. If it is true and it has been proved that this detestable thing has been done in Israel,[f] 5take the man or woman who has done this evil deed to your city gate and stone that person to death.[g] 6On the testimony of two or three witnesses a man shall be put to death, but no-one shall be put to death on the testimony of only one witness.[h] 7The hands of the witnesses must be the first in putting

16:8 i Ex 12:16; Ex 13:6; Lev 23:8
16:9 j Ex 34:22; Lev 23:15; k Ex 23:16; Nu 28:26
16:11 l Dt 12:7; m Dt 12:12
16:12 n Dt 15:15
16:13 o Lev 23:34; p Ex 23:16
16:14 q ver 11
16:15 r Lev 23:39
16:16 s Ex 23:14,16; t Ex 34:20
16:18 u Dt 1:16
16:19 v Ex 23:2,8; w Lev 19:15; Dt 1:17; x Ecc 7:7
16:21 y Dt 7:5; z Ex 34:13; 2Ki 17:16; 2Ki 21:3; 2Ch 33:3
16:22 a Lev 26:1
17:1 a Mal 1:8,13; b Dt 15:21
17:2 c Dt 13:6-11
17:3 d Jer 7:22-23; e Job 31:26
17:4 f Dt 13:12-14
17:5 g Lev 24:14
17:6 h Nu 35:30; Dt 19:15; Jos 7:25; Mt 18:16; Jn 8:17; 2Co 13:1; 1Ti 5:19; Heb 10:28

b21 Or *Do not plant any tree dedicated to Asherah*

him to death, and then the hands of all the people. You must purge the evil[i] from among you.

Law Courts

8 If cases come before your courts that are too difficult for you to judge—whether bloodshed, lawsuits or assaults[j]—take them to the place the LORD your God will choose.[k] 9 Go to the priests, who are Levites, and to the judge who is in office at that time. Enquire of them and they will give you the verdict.[l] 10 You must act according to the decisions they give you at the place the LORD will choose. Be careful to do everything they direct you to do. 11 Act according to the law they teach you and the decisions they give you. Do not turn aside from what they tell you, to the right or to the left.[m] 12 The man who shows contempt[n] for the judge or for the priest who stands ministering there to the LORD your God must be put to death. You must purge the evil from Israel. 13 All the people will hear and be afraid, and will not be contemptuous again.[o]

The King

14 When you enter the land the LORD your God is giving you and have taken possession of it and settled in it, and you say, "Let us set a king over us like all the nations around us,"[p] 15 be sure to appoint over you the king the LORD your God chooses. He must be from among your own brothers.[q] Do not place a foreigner over you, one who is not a brother Israelite. 16 The king, moreover, must not acquire great numbers of horses for himself[r] or make the people return to Egypt[s] to get more of them,[t] for the LORD has told you, "You are not to go back that way again."[u] 17 He must not take many wives,[v] or his heart will be led astray. He must not accumulate large amounts of silver and gold.

18 When he takes the throne of his kingdom, he is to write[w] for himself on a scroll a copy of this law, taken from that of the priests, who are Levites. 19 It is to be with him, and he is to read it all the days of his life[x] so that he may learn to revere the LORD his God and follow carefully all the words of this law and these decrees 20 and not consider himself better than his brothers and turn from the law[y] to the right or to the left.[z] Then he and his descendants will reign a long time over his kingdom in Israel.

Offerings for Priests and Levites

18 The priests, who are Levites—indeed the whole tribe of Levi—are to have no allotment or inheritance with Israel. They shall live on the offerings made to the LORD by fire, for that is their inheritance.[a] 2 They shall have no inheritance among their brothers; the LORD is their inheritance, as he promised them.

3 This is the share due to the priests from the people who sacrifice a bull or a sheep: the shoulder, the jowls and the inner parts.[b] 4 You are to give them the firstfruits of your grain, new wine and oil, and the first wool from the shearing of your sheep,[c] 5 for the LORD your God has chosen them[d] and their descendants out of all your tribes to stand and minister[e] in the LORD's name always.

6 If a Levite moves from one of your towns anywhere in Israel where he is living, and comes in all earnestness to the place the LORD will choose,[f] 7 he may minister in the name of the LORD his God like all his fellow Levites who serve there in the presence of the LORD. 8 He is to share equally in their benefits even though he has received money from the sale of family possessions.[g]

17:7 i Dt 13:5,9
17:8 j 2Ch 19:10 k Dt 12:5 Hag 2:11
17:9 l Dt 19:17 Eze 44:24
17:11 m Dt 25:1
17:12 n Nu 15:30
17:13 o Dt 13:11 Dt 19:20
17:14 p Dt 11:31 1Sa 8:5,19-20
17:15 q Jer 30:21
17:16 r 1Ki 4:26 1Ki 10:26 s Isa 31:1 Hos 11:5 t 1Ki 10:28 Eze 17:15 u Ex 13:17
17:17 v 1Ki 11:3
17:18 w Dt 31:22,24
17:19 x Jos 1:8
17:20 y 1Ki 15:5 z Dt 5:32
18:1 a Dt 10:9 1Co 9:13
18:3 b Lev 7:28-34
18:4 c Ex 22:29 Nu 18:12
18:5 d Ex 28:1 e Dt 10:8
18:6 f Nu 35:2-3
18:8 g 2Ch 31:4 Ne 12:44,47

Detestable Practices

9 When you enter the land the LORD your God is giving you, do not learn to imitate[h] the detestable ways of the nations there. 10 Let no-one be found among you who sacrifices his son or daughter in[a] the fire, who practises divination[i] or sorcery, interprets omens, engages in witchcraft,[j] 11 or casts spells, or who is a medium or spiritist or who consults the dead. 12 Anyone who does these things is detestable to the LORD, and because of these detestable practices the LORD your God will drive out those nations before you.[k] 13 You must be blameless before the LORD your God.

The Prophet

14 The nations you will dispossess listen to those who practise sorcery or divination. But as for you, the LORD your God has not permitted you to do so. 15 The LORD your God will raise up for you a prophet like me from among your own brothers.[l] You must listen to him. 16 For this is what you asked of the LORD your God at Horeb on the day of the assembly when you said, "Let us not hear the voice of the LORD our God nor see this great fire any more, or we will die."[m]

17 The LORD said to me: "What they say is good. 18 I will raise up for them a prophet like you from among their brothers; I will put my words[n] in his mouth, and he will tell them everything I command him.[o] 19 If anyone does not listen to my words that the prophet speaks in my name, I myself will call him to account.[p] 20 But a prophet who presumes to speak in my name anything I have not commanded him to say, or a prophet who speaks in the name of other gods,[q] must be put to death."[r]

21 You may say to yourselves, "How can we know when a message has not been spoken by the LORD?" 22 If what a prophet proclaims in the name of the LORD does not take place or come true, that is a message the LORD has not spoken.[s] That prophet has spoken presumptuously.[t] Do not be afraid of him.

Cities of Refuge

19:1–14Ref Nu 35:6–34; Dt 4:41–43; Jos 20:1–9

19 When the LORD your God has destroyed the nations whose land he is giving you, and when you have driven them out and settled in their towns and houses,[a] 2 then set aside for yourselves three cities centrally located in the land the LORD your God is giving you to possess. 3 Build roads to them and divide into three parts the land the LORD your God is giving you as an inheritance, so that anyone who kills a man may flee there.

4 This is the rule concerning the man who kills another and flees there to save his life—one who kills his neighbour unintentionally, without malice aforethought. 5 For instance, a man may go into the forest with his neighbour to cut wood, and as he swings his axe to fell a tree, the head may fly off and hit his neighbour and kill him. That man may flee to one of these cities and save his life. 6 Otherwise, the avenger of blood[b] might pursue him in a rage, overtake him if the distance is too great, and kill him even though he is not deserving of death, since he did it to his neighbour without malice aforethought. 7 This is why I command you to set aside for yourselves three cities.

8 If the LORD your God enlarges your territory, as he promised on oath to your forefathers, and gives you the whole land he promised them, 9 because you carefully follow all these laws I command you today—to love the LORD your God

18:9 *h* Dt 12:29-31
18:10 *i* Dt 12:31 *j* Lev 19:31
18:12 *k* Lev 18:24 Dt 9:4
18:15 *l* Jn 1:21 Ac 3:22* Ac 7:37*
18:16 *m* Ex 20:19 Dt 5:23-27
18:18 *n* Isa 51:16 Jn 17:8 *o* Jn 4:25-26 Jn 8:28 Jn 12:49-50
18:19 *p* Ac 3:23*
18:20 *q* Jer 14:14 *r* Dt 13:1-5
18:22 *s* Jer 28:9 *t* ver 20
19:1 *a* Dt 12:29
19:6 *b* Nu 35:12

a 10 Or *who makes his son or daughter pass through*

and to walk always in his ways[c]—
then you are to set aside three more
cities. 10Do this so that innocent
blood will not be shed in your land,
which the LORD your God is giving
you as your inheritance, and so that
you will not be guilty of bloodshed.[d]
11But if a man hates his neighbour and lies in wait for him, assaults and kills him,[e] and then
flees to one of these cities, 12the
elders of his town shall send for
him, bring him back from the city,
and hand him over to the avenger
of blood to die. 13Show him no
pity.[f] You must purge from Israel
the guilt of shedding innocent
blood,[g] so that it may go well with
you.
14Do not move your neighbour's
boundary stone set up by your predecessors in the inheritance you
receive in the land the LORD your
God is giving you to possess.[h]

Witnesses

15One witness is not enough to
convict a man accused of any crime
or offence he may have committed.
A matter must be established by
the testimony of two or three witnesses.[i]
16If a malicious witness[j] takes
the stand to accuse a man of a
crime, 17the two men involved in
the dispute must stand in the presence of the LORD before the priests
and the judges[k] who are in office
at the time. 18The judges must
make a thorough investigation, and
if the witness proves to be a liar,
giving false testimony against his
brother, 19then do to him as he intended to do to his brother.[l] You
must purge the evil from among
you. 20The rest of the people will
hear of this and be afraid,[m] and
never again will such an evil thing
be done among you. 21Show no
pity:[n] life for life, eye for eye,
tooth for tooth, hand for hand, foot
for foot.[o]

Going to War

20 When you go to war against
your enemies and see
horses and chariots and an army
greater than yours,[a] do not be
afraid[b] of them,[c] because the
LORD your God, who brought you
up out of Egypt, will be with you.
2When you are about to go into
battle, the priest shall come forward and address the army. 3He
shall say: "Hear, O Israel, today
you are going into battle against
your enemies. Do not be faint-
hearted[d] or afraid; do not be terrified or give way to panic before
them. 4For the LORD your God is the
one who goes with you to fight[e] for
you against your enemies to give
you victory."
5The officers shall say to the
army: "Has anyone built a new
house and not dedicated[f] it? Let
him go home, or he may die in
battle and someone else may dedicate it. 6Has anyone planted a vineyard and not begun to enjoy it? Let
him go home, or he may die in
battle and someone else enjoy it.
7Has anyone become pledged to a
woman and not married her? Let
him go home, or he may die in
battle and someone else marry
her.[g]" 8Then the officers shall add,
"Is any man afraid or faint-
hearted? Let him go home so that
his brothers will not become disheartened too."[h] 9When the officers have finished speaking to the
army, they shall appoint commanders over it.
10When you march up to attack a
city, make its people an offer of
peace.[i] 11If they accept and open
their gates, all the people in it shall
be subject to forced labour[j] and
shall work for you. 12If they refuse
to make peace and they engage
you in battle, lay siege to that
city. 13When the LORD your God delivers it into your hand, put to the
sword all the men in it.[k] 14As for
the women, the children, the

19:9
c Jos 20:7-8
19:10
d Nu 35:33; Dt 21:1-9
19:11
e Nu 35:16
19:13
f Dt 7:2
g 1Ki 2:31
19:14
h Dt 27:17; Pr 22:28; Hos 5:10
19:15
i Nu 35:30; Dt 17:6; Mt 18:16*; Jn 8:17; 2Co 13:1*; 1Ti 5:19; Heb 10:28
19:16
j Ex 23:1; Ps 27:12
19:17
k Dt 17:9
19:19
l Pr 19:5,9
19:20
m Dt 17:13; Dt 21:21
19:21
n ver 13
o Ex 21:24; Lev 24:20; Mt 5:38*
20:1
a Ps 20:7; Isa 31:1
b Dt 31:6,8
c 2Ch 32:7-8
20:3
d Jos 23:10
20:4
e Dt 1:30; Dt 3:22; Jos 23:10
20:5
f Ne 12:27
20:7
g Dt 24:5
20:8
h Jdg 7:3
20:10
i Lk 14:31-32
20:11
j 1Ki 9:21
20:13
k Nu 31:7

livestock[l] and everything else in
the city, you may take these as plunder for yourselves. And you may
use the plunder the LORD your God
gives you from your enemies.
15This is how you are to treat all the
cities that are at a distance from
you and do not belong to the nations
nearby.
16However, in the cities of the nations the LORD your God is giving
you as an inheritance, do not leave
alive anything that breathes.[m]
17Completely destroy[a] them—the
Hittites, Amorites, Canaanites, Perizzites, Hivites and Jebusites—as
the LORD your God has commanded
you. 18Otherwise, they will teach
you to follow all the detestable
things they do in worshipping their
gods,[n] and you will sin[o] against
the LORD your God.
19When you lay siege to a city for
a long time, fighting against it to
capture it, do not destroy its trees
by putting an axe to them, because
you can eat their fruit. Do not cut
them down. Are the trees of the
field people, that you should besiege them?[b] 20However, you may
cut down trees that you know are
not fruit trees and use them to
build siege works until the city at
war with you falls.

Atonement for an Unsolved Murder

21 If a man is found slain, lying in a field in the land the
LORD your God is giving you to possess, and it is not known who killed
him, 2your elders and judges shall
go out and measure the distance
from the body to the neighbouring
towns. 3Then the elders of the town
nearest the body shall take a heifer
that has never been worked and has
never worn a yoke 4and lead her
down to a valley that has not been
ploughed or planted and where
there is a flowing stream. There in
the valley they are to break the
heifer's neck. 5The priests, the sons
of Levi, shall step forward, for the
LORD your God has chosen them to
minister and to pronounce blessings[a] in the name of the LORD and
to decide all cases of dispute and
assault.[b] 6Then all the elders of the
town nearest the body shall wash
their hands[c] over the heifer whose
neck was broken in the valley, 7and
they shall declare: "Our hands did
not shed this blood, nor did our
eyes see it done. 8Accept this atonement for your people Israel, whom
you have redeemed, O LORD, and
do not hold your people guilty of
the blood of an innocent man." And
the bloodshed will be atoned for.[d]
9So you will purge[e] from yourselves the guilt of shedding innocent blood, since you have done
what is right in the eyes of the
LORD.

Marrying a Captive Woman

10When you go to war against
your enemies and the LORD your
God delivers them into your
hands[f] and you take captives, 11if
you notice among the captives a
beautiful woman and are attracted
to her, you may take her as your
wife. 12Bring her into your home
and make her shave her head,[g]
trim her nails 13and put aside the
clothes she was wearing when captured. After she has lived in your
house and mourned her father and
mother for a full month,[h] then you
may go to her and be her husband
and she shall be your wife. 14If you
are not pleased with her, let her go
wherever she wishes. You must not
sell her or treat her as a slave, since
you have dishonoured her.[i]

The Right of the Firstborn

15If a man has two wives, and he
loves one but not the other, and

20:14 *l* Jos 8:2; Jos 22:8
20:16 *m* Ex 23:31-33; Nu 21:2-3; Dt 7:2; Jos 11:14
20:18 *n* Ex 34:16; Dt 7:4; Dt 12:30-31 *o* Ex 23:33
21:5 *a* 1Ch 23:13 *b* Dt 17:8-11
21:6 *c* Mt 27:24
21:8 *d* Nu 35:33-34
21:9 *e* Dt 19:13
21:10 *f* Jos 21:44
21:12 *g* Lev 14:9; Nu 6:9
21:13 *h* Ps 45:10
21:14 *i* Ge 34:2

a17 The Hebrew term refers to the irrevocable giving over of things or persons to the LORD, often by totally destroying them. b19 Or *down to use in the siege, for the fruit trees are for the benefit of man.*

both bear him sons but the firstborn is the son of the wife he does
not love,[j] 16when he wills his property to his sons, he must not give
the rights of the firstborn to the son
of the wife he loves in preference
to his actual firstborn, the son of
the wife he does not love.[k] 17He
must acknowledge the son of his
unloved wife as the firstborn by
giving him a double share of all he
has. That son is the first sign of his
father's strength.[l] The right of the
firstborn belongs to him.[m]

A Rebellious Son

18If a man has a stubborn and rebellious son who does not obey his
father and mother[n] and will not listen to them when they discipline
him, 19his father and mother shall
take hold of him and bring him to
the elders at the gate of his town.
20They shall say to the elders, "This
son of ours is stubborn and rebellious. He will not obey us. He is a
profligate and a drunkard." 21Then
all the men of his town shall stone
him to death. You must purge the
evil[o] from among you. All Israel
will hear of it and be afraid.[p]

Various Laws

22If a man guilty of a capital offence[q] is put to death and his body
is hung on a tree, 23you must not
leave his body on the tree overnight.[r] Be sure to bury him that
same day, because anyone who is
hung on a tree is under God's
curse.[s] You must not desecrate[t]
the land the LORD your God is giving you as an inheritance.

22 If you see your brother's ox
or sheep straying, do not ignore it but be sure to take it back to
him.[a] 2If the brother does not live
near you or if you do not know who
he is, take it home with you and
keep it until he comes looking for
it. Then give it back to him. 3Do the
same if you find your brother's
donkey or his cloak or anything he
loses. Do not ignore it.
4If you see your brother's donkey[b] or his ox fallen on the road, do
not ignore it. Help him to get it to its
feet.
5A woman must not wear men's
clothing, nor a man wear women's
clothing, for the LORD your God detests anyone who does this.
6If you come across a bird's nest
beside the road, either in a tree or
on the ground, and the mother is
sitting on the young or on the eggs,
do not take the mother with the
young.[c] 7You may take the young,
but be sure to let the mother go, so
that it may go well with you and you
may have a long life.[d]
8When you build a new house,
make a parapet around your roof so
that you may not bring the guilt of
bloodshed on your house if someone falls from the roof.
9Do not plant two kinds of seed in
your vineyard;[e] if you do, not only
the crops you plant but also the
fruit of the vineyard will be defiled.[a]
10Do not plough with an ox and a
donkey yoked together.[f]
11Do not wear clothes of wool and
linen woven together.[g]
12Make tassels on the four corners of the cloak you wear.[h]

Marriage Violations

13If a man takes a wife and, after
lying with her[i], dislikes her 14and
slanders her and gives her a bad
name, saying, "I married this
woman, but when I approached
her, I did not find proof of her virginity," 15then the girl's father and
mother shall bring proof that she
was a virgin to the town elders at
the gate. 16The girl's father will say
to the elders, "I gave my daughter
in marriage to this man, but he dislikes her. 17Now he has slandered
her and said, 'I did not find your

21:15
j Ge 29:33
21:16
k 1Ch 26:10
21:17
l Ge 49:3
m Ge 25:31
21:18
n Pr 1:8; Isa 30:1; Eph 6:1-3
21:21
o Dt 19:19
p Dt 13:11
21:22
q Dt 22:26; Mk 14:64; Ac 23:29
21:23
r Jos 8:29; Jos 10:27; Jn 19:31
s Gal 3:13*
t Lev 18:25; Nu 35:34
22:1
a Ex 23:4-5
22:4
b Ex 23:5
22:6
c Lev 22:28
22:7
d Dt 4:40
22:9
e Lev 19:19
22:10
f 2Co 6:14
22:11
g Lev 19:19
22:12
h Nu 15:37-41; Mt 23:5
22:13
i Dt 24:1

a9 Or *be forfeited to the sanctuary*

daughter to be a virgin.' But here is the proof of my daughter's virginity." Then her parents shall display the cloth before the elders of the town, 18and the elders[j] shall take the man and punish him. 19They shall fine him a hundred shekels of silver[b] and give them to the girl's father, because this man has given an Israelite virgin a bad name. She shall continue to be his wife; he must not divorce her as long as he lives.

20If, however, the charge is true and no proof of the girl's virginity can be found, 21she shall be brought to the door of her father's house and there the men of her town shall stone her to death. She has done a disgraceful thing[k] in Israel by being promiscuous while still in her father's house. You must purge the evil from among you.

22If a man is found sleeping with another man's wife, both the man who slept with her and the woman must die.[l] You must purge the evil from Israel.

23If a man happens to meet in a town a virgin pledged to be married and he sleeps with her, 24you shall take both of them to the gate of that town and stone them to death—the girl because she was in a town and did not scream for help, and the man because he violated another man's wife. You must purge the evil from among you.[m]

25But if out in the country a man happens to meet a girl pledged to be married and rapes her, only the man who has done this shall die. 26Do nothing to the girl; she has committed no sin deserving death. This case is like that of someone who attacks and murders his neighbour, 27for the man found the girl out in the country, and though the betrothed girl screamed, there was no-one to rescue her.

28If a man happens to meet a virgin who is not pledged to be married and rapes her and they are discovered,[n] 29he shall pay the girl's father fifty shekels of silver.[c] He must marry the girl, for he has violated her. He can never divorce her as long as he lives.

30A man is not to marry his father's wife; he must not dishonour his father's bed.[o]

Exclusion From the Assembly

23 No-one who has been emasculated by crushing or cutting may enter the assembly of the LORD.

2No-one born of a forbidden marriage[a] nor any of his descendants may enter the assembly of the LORD, even down to the tenth generation.

3No Ammonite or Moabite or any of his descendants may enter the assembly of the LORD, even down to the tenth generation.[a] 4For they did not come to meet you with bread and water on your way when you came out of Egypt, and they hired Balaam[b] son of Beor from Pethor in Aram Naharaim[b] to pronounce a curse on you. 5However, the LORD your God would not listen to Balaam but turned the curse[c] into a blessing for you, because the LORD your God loves you. 6Do not seek a treaty of friendship with them as long as you live.[d]

7Do not abhor an Edomite, for he is your brother.[e] Do not abhor an Egyptian, because you lived as an alien in his country.[f] 8The third generation of children born to them may enter the assembly of the LORD.

Uncleanness in the Camp

9When you are encamped against your enemies, keep away from everything impure. 10If one of your men is unclean because of a nocturnal emission, he is to go outside the camp and stay there.[g] 11But as

22:18
j Ex 18:21

22:21
k Ge 34:7; Dt 13:5; Dt 23:17-18; Jdg 20:6; 2Sa 13:12

22:22
l Lev 20:10; Jn 8:5

22:24
m ver 21-22; 1Co 5:13*

22:28
n Ex 22:16

22:30
o Lev 18:8; Lev 20:11; Dt 27:20; 1Co 5:1

23:3
a Ne 13:2

23:4
b Nu 22:5-6; Nu 23:7; 2Pe 2:15

23:5
c Pr 26:2

23:6
d Ezr 9:12

23:7
e Ge 25:26; Ob 1:10,12
f Ex 22:21; Ex 23:9; Lev 19:34; Dt 10:19

23:10
g Lev 15:16

b*19* That is, about 2½ pounds (about 1 kilogram)
c*29* That is, about 1¼ pounds (about 0.6 kilogram)
a2 Or *one of illegitimate birth* b4 That is, North-west Mesopotamia

evening approaches he is to wash
himself, and at sunset he may return to the camp.
12Designate a place outside the
camp where you can go to relieve
yourself. 13As part of your equipment have something to dig with,
and when you relieve yourself, dig
a hole and cover up your excrement. 14For the LORD your God
moves[h] about in your camp to protect you and to deliver your enemies to you. Your camp must be
holy,[i] so that he will not see among
you anything indecent and turn
away from you.

Miscellaneous Laws

15If a slave has taken refuge with
you, do not hand him over to his
master.[j] 16Let him live among you
wherever he likes and in whatever
town he chooses. Do not oppress[k]
him.
17No Israelite man[l] or woman is
to become a shrine-prostitute.[m]
18You must not bring the earnings
of a female prostitute or of a male
prostitute[c] into the house of the
LORD your God to pay any vow, because the LORD your God detests
them both.
19Do not charge your brother interest, whether on money or food
or anything else that may earn interest.[n] 20You may charge a foreigner interest, but not a brother
Israelite, so that the LORD your God
may bless[o] you in everything you
put your hand to in the land you are
entering to possess.
21If you make a vow to the LORD
your God, do not be slow to pay it,
for the LORD your God will certainly demand it of you and you will
be guilty of sin.[p] 22But if you refrain from making a vow, you will
not be guilty. 23Whatever your lips
utter you must be sure to do, because you made your vow freely to
the LORD your God with your own
mouth.

23:14
h Lev 26:12
i Ex 3:5

23:15
j 1Sa 30:15

23:16
k Ex 22:21

23:17
l Ge 19:25
2Ki 23:7
m Lev 19:29
Dt 22:21

23:19
n Ex 22:25
Lev 25:35-37

23:20
o Dt 15:10
Dt 28:12

23:21
p Nu 30:1-2
Ecc 5:4-5
Mt 5:33

23:25
q Mt 12:1
Mk 2:23
Lk 6:1

24:1
a Dt 22:13
b Mt 5:31*
Mt 19:7-9
Mk 10:4-5

24:4
c Jer 3:1

24:5
d Dt 20:7

24:7
e Ex 21:16

24:8
f Lev 13:1-46
Lev 14:2

24If you enter your neighbour's
vineyard, you may eat all the
grapes you want, but do not put any
in your basket. 25If you enter your
neighbour's cornfield, you may
pick the ears with your hands, but
you must not put a sickle to his
standing corn.[q]

24

If a man marries a woman
who becomes displeasing
to him[a] because he finds something indecent about her, and he
writes her a certificate of divorce,[b] gives it to her and sends her
from his house, 2and if after she
leaves his house she becomes the
wife of another man, 3and her
second husband dislikes her and
writes her a certificate of divorce,
gives it to her and sends her from
his house, or if he dies, 4then her
first husband, who divorced her, is
not allowed to marry her again
after she has been defiled. That
would be detestable in the eyes of
the LORD. Do not bring sin upon the
land the LORD[c] your God is giving
you as an inheritance.
5If a man has recently married,
he must not be sent to war or have
any other duty laid on him. For one
year he is to be free to stay at home
and bring happiness to the wife he
has married.[d]
6Do not take a pair of millstones—not even the upper one—
as security for a debt, because that
would be taking a man's livelihood
as security.
7If a man is caught kidnapping
one of his brother Israelites and
treats him as a slave or sells him,
the kidnapper must die.[e] You must
purge the evil from among you.
8In cases of leprous[a] diseases be
very careful to do exactly as the
priests, who are Levites, instruct
you. You must follow carefully
what I have commanded them.[f]
9Remember what the LORD your

c18 Hebrew *of a dog*
a8 The Hebrew word was used for various diseases affecting the skin—not necessarily leprosy.

God did to Miriam along the way
after you came out of Egypt.[g]
10 When you make a loan of any
kind to your neighbour, do not go
into his house to get what he is offering as a pledge. 11 Stay outside
and let the man to whom you are
making the loan bring the pledge
out to you. 12 If the man is poor, do
not go to sleep with his pledge in
your possession. 13 Return his cloak
to him by sunset[h] so that he may
sleep in it. Then he will thank you,
and it will be regarded as a righteous act in the sight of the LORD
your God.[i]
14 Do not take advantage of a
hired man who is poor and needy,
whether he is a brother Israelite or
an alien living in one of your
towns.[j] 15 Pay him his wages each
day before sunset, because he is
poor[k] and is counting on it.[l]
Otherwise he may cry to the LORD
against you, and you will be guilty
of sin.[m]
16 Fathers shall not be put to death
for their children, nor children put
to death for their fathers; each is to
die for his own sin.[n]
17 Do not deprive the alien or the
fatherless of justice,[o] or take the
cloak of the widow as a pledge.
18 Remember that you were slaves
in Egypt and the LORD your God redeemed you from there. That is
why I command you to do this.
19 When you are harvesting in
your field and you overlook a sheaf,
do not go back to get it.[p] Leave it
for the alien, the fatherless and the
widow, so that the LORD your God
may bless[q] you in all the work of
your hands. 20 When you beat the
olives from your trees, do not go
over the branches a second time.[r]
Leave what remains for the alien,
the fatherless and the widow.
21 When you harvest the grapes in
your vineyard, do not go over the
vines again. Leave what remains
for the alien, the fatherless and the
widow. 22 Remember that you were
slaves in Egypt. That is why I command you to do this.[s]

25 When men have a dispute,
they are to take it to court
and the judges will decide the
case,[a] acquitting the innocent and
condemning the guilty.[b] 2 If the
guilty man deserves to be beaten,[c]
the judge shall make him lie down
and have him flogged in his presence with the number of lashes his
crime deserves, 3 but he must not
give him more than forty lashes.[d]
If he is flogged more than that,
your brother will be degraded in
your eyes.[e]
4 Do not muzzle an ox while it is
treading out the grain.[f]
5 If brothers are living together
and one of them dies without a son,
his widow must not marry outside
the family. Her husband's brother
shall take her and marry her and
fulfil the duty of a brother-in-law to
her.[g] 6 The first son she bears shall
carry on the name of the dead
brother so that his name will not be
blotted out from Israel.[h]
7 However, if a man does not want
to marry his brother's wife, she
shall go to the elders at the town
gate and say, "My husband's
brother refuses to carry on his
brother's name in Israel. He will
not fulfil the duty of a brother-in-
law to me."[i] 8 Then the elders of his
town shall summon him and talk to
him. If he persists in saying, "I do
not want to marry her," 9 his
brother's widow shall go up to him
in the presence of the elders, take
off one of his sandals,[j] spit in
his face and say, "This is what is
done to the man who will not build
up his brother's family line."
10 That man's line shall be known in
Israel as The Family of the Unsan-
dalled.
11 If two men are fighting and the
wife of one of them comes to rescue her husband from his assailant,
and she reaches out and seizes him

24:9
g Nu 12:10
24:13
h Ex 22:26
i Dt 6:25; Da 4:27
24:14
j Lev 25:35-43; Dt 15:12-18
24:15
k Jer 22:13
l Lev 19:13
m Dt 15:9; Jas 5:4
24:16
n 2Ki 14:6; 2Ch 25:4; Jer 31:29-30; Eze 18:20
24:17
o Dt 1:17; Dt 10:17-18; Dt 16:19
24:19
p Lev 19:9; Lev 23:22
q Pr 19:17
24:20
r Lev 19:10
24:22
s ver 18
25:1
a Dt 19:17
b Dt 1:16-17
25:2
c Lk 12:47-48
25:3
d 2Co 11:24
e Job 18:3
25:4
f Pr 12:10; 1Co 9:9*; 1Ti 5:18*
25:5
g Mt 22:24; Mk 12:19; Lk 20:28
25:6
h Ge 38:9; Ru 4:5,10
25:7
i Ru 4:1-2,5-6
25:9
j Ru 4:7-8,11

by his private parts, 12you shall cut off her hand. Show her no pity.[k]

13Do not have two differing weights in your bag—one heavy, one light.[l] 14Do not have two differing measures in your house—one large, one small. 15You must have accurate and honest weights and measures, so that you may live long[m] in the land the LORD your God is giving you. 16For the LORD your God detests anyone who does these things, anyone who deals dishonestly.[n]

17Remember what the Amalekites[o] did to you along the way when you came out of Egypt. 18When you were weary and worn out, they met you on your journey and cut off all who were lagging behind; they had no fear of God.[p] 19When the LORD your God gives you rest from all the enemies around you in the land he is giving you to possess as an inheritance, you shall blot out the memory of Amalek[q] from under heaven. Do not forget!

Firstfruits and Tithes

26 When you have entered the land that the LORD your God is giving you as an inheritance and have taken possession of it and settled in it, 2take some of the firstfruits[a] of all that you produce from the soil of the land that the LORD your God is giving you and put them in a basket. Then go to the place that the LORD your God will choose as a dwelling for his Name[b] 3and say to the priest in office at the time, "I declare today to the LORD your God that I have come to the land that the LORD swore to our forefathers to give us." 4The priest shall take the basket from your hands and set it down in front of the altar of the LORD your God. 5Then you shall declare before the LORD your God: "My father was a wandering Aramean,[c] and he went down into Egypt with a few people[d] and lived there and became a great nation, powerful and numerous. 6But the Egyptians ill-treated us and made us suffer,[e] putting us to hard labour. 7Then we cried out to the LORD, the God of our fathers, and the LORD heard our voice[f] and saw[g] our misery, toil and oppression. 8So the LORD brought us out of Egypt with a mighty hand and an outstretched arm, with great terror and with miraculous signs and wonders.[h] 9He brought us to this place and gave us this land, a land flowing with milk and honey;[i] 10and now I bring the firstfruits of the soil that you, O LORD, have given me." Place the basket before the LORD your God and bow down before him. 11And you and the Levites[j] and the aliens among you shall rejoice[k] in all the good things the LORD your God has given to you and your household.

12When you have finished setting aside a tenth[l] of all your produce in the third year, the year of the tithe,[m] you shall give it to the Levite, the alien, the fatherless and the widow, so that they may eat in your towns and be satisfied. 13Then say to the LORD your God: "I have removed from my house the sacred portion and have given it to the Levite, the alien, the fatherless and the widow, according to all you commanded. I have not turned aside from your commands nor have I forgotten any of them.[n] 14I have not eaten any of the sacred portion while I was in mourning, nor have I removed any of it while I was unclean,[o] nor have I offered any of it to the dead. I have obeyed the LORD my God; I have done everything you commanded me. 15Look down from heaven,[p] your holy dwelling-place, and bless your people Israel and the land you have given us as you promised on oath to our forefathers, a land flowing with milk and honey."

25:12 *k* Dt 19:13
25:13 *l* Lev 19:35-37; Pr 11:1; Eze 45:10; Mic 6:11
25:15 *m* Ex 20:12
25:16 *n* Pr 11:1
25:17 *o* Ex 17:8
25:18 *p* Ps 36:1; Ro 3:18
25:19 *q* 1Sa 15:2-3
26:2 *a* Ex 22:29; Ex 23:16,19; Nu 18:13; Pr 3:9 *b* Dt 12:5
26:5 *c* Hos 12:12 *d* Ge 43:1-2; Ge 45:7,11; Ge 46:27; Dt 10:22
26:6 *e* Ex 1:11,14
26:7 *f* Ex 2:23-25 *g* Ex 3:9
26:8 *h* Dt 4:34
26:9 *i* Ex 3:8
26:11 *j* Dt 12:7 *k* Dt 16:11
26:12 *l* Lev 27:30 *m* Nu 18:24; Dt 14:28-29; Heb 7:5,9
26:13 *n* Ps 119:141, 153,176
26:14 *o* Lev 7:20; Hos 9:4
26:15 *p* Isa 63:15; Zec 2:13

Follow the LORD's Commands

16 The LORD your God commands
you this day to follow these decrees
and laws; carefully observe them
with all your heart and with all
your soul.[q] 17 You have declared
this day that the LORD is your God
and that you will walk in his ways,
that you will keep his decrees, commands and laws, and that you will
obey him. 18 And the LORD has declared this day that you are his people, his treasured possession[r] as he
promised, and that you are to keep
all his commands. 19 He has declared that he will set you in praise,
fame and honour high above
all the nations[s] he has made and
that you will be a people holy[t] to the
LORD your God, as he promised.

The Altar on Mount Ebal

27 Moses and the elders of Israel commanded the peo-
ple: "Keep all these commands that
I give you today. 2 When you have
crossed the Jordan into the land the
LORD your God is giving you, set up
some large stones and coat them
with plaster.[a] 3 Write on them all
the words of this law when you
have crossed over to enter the land
the LORD your God is giving you, a
land flowing with milk and honey,[b]
just as the LORD, the God of your fathers, promised you. 4 And when
you have crossed the Jordan, set up
these stones on Mount Ebal,[c] as I
command you today, and coat them
with plaster. 5 Build there an altar[d]
to the LORD your God, an altar of
stones. Do not use any iron tool[e]
upon them. 6 Build the altar of the
LORD your God with stones from
the field and offer burnt offerings
on it to the LORD your God. 7 Sacrifice fellowship offerings[a] there,
eating them and rejoicing in the
presence of the LORD your God.
8 And you shall write very clearly
all the words of this law on these
stones you have set up."

Curses From Mount Ebal

9 Then Moses and the priests, who
are Levites, said to all Israel, "Be
silent, O Israel, and listen! You
have now become the people of the
LORD your God.[f] 10 Obey the LORD
your God and follow his commands
and decrees that I give you today."
11 On the same day Moses commanded the people:
12 When you have crossed the Jordan, these tribes shall stand on
Mount Gerizim[g] to bless the people: Simeon, Levi, Judah, Issachar,
Joseph and Benjamin.[h] 13 And
these tribes shall stand on Mount
Ebal to pronounce curses: Reuben,
Gad, Asher, Zebulun, Dan and
Naphtali.
14 The Levites shall recite to all
the people of Israel in a loud voice:

> 15 "Cursed is the man who
> carves an image or casts an
> idol[i]—a thing detestable to
> the LORD, the work of the
> craftsman's hands—and sets it
> up in secret."
> Then all the people shall say,
> "Amen!"
>
> 16 "Cursed is the man who dis-
> honours his father or his
> mother."[j]
> Then all the people shall say,
> "Amen!"
>
> 17 "Cursed is the man who
> moves his neighbour's bound-
> ary stone."[k]
> Then all the people shall say,
> "Amen!"
>
> 18 "Cursed is the man who
> leads the blind astray on the
> road."[l]
> Then all the people shall say,
> "Amen!"
>
> 19 "Cursed is the man who
> withholds justice from the
> alien,[m] the fatherless or the
> widow."[n]
> Then all the people shall say,
> "Amen!"

26:16 q Dt 4:29
26:18 r Ex 6:7; Ex 19:5; Dt 7:6; Dt 14:2; Dt 28:9
26:19 s Dt 4:7-8; Dt 28:1,13,44; t Ex 19:6; Dt 7:6; 1Pe 2:9
27:2 a Jos 8:31
27:3 b Dt 26:9
27:4 c Dt 11:29
27:5 d Jos 8:31; e Ex 20:25
27:9 f Dt 26:18
27:12 g Dt 11:29; h Jos 8:35
27:15 i Ex 20:4; Ex 34:17; Lev 19:4; Lev 26:1; Dt 4:16,23; Dt 5:8; Isa 44:9
27:16 j Ex 20:12; Ex 21:17; Lev 19:3; Lev 20:9
27:17 k Dt 19:14; Pr 22:28
27:18 l Lev 19:14
27:19 m Ex 22:21; Dt 24:19; n Dt 10:18

a7 Traditionally *peace offerings*

20“Cursed is the man who sleeps with his father’s wife, for he dishonours his father’s bed.”[o]
Then all the people shall say, “Amen!”

21“Cursed is the man who has sexual relations with any animal.”[p]
Then all the people shall say, “Amen!”

22“Cursed is the man who sleeps with his sister, the daughter of his father or the daughter of his mother.”[q]
Then all the people shall say, “Amen!”

23“Cursed is the man who sleeps with his mother-in-law.”[r]
Then all the people shall say, “Amen!”

24“Cursed is the man who kills[s] his neighbour secretly.”
Then all the people shall say, “Amen!”

25“Cursed is the man who accepts a bribe to kill an innocent person.”[t]
Then all the people shall say, “Amen!”

26“Cursed is the man who does not uphold the words of this law by carrying them out.”[u]
Then all the people shall say, “Amen!”

Blessings for Obedience

28 If you fully obey the LORD your God and carefully follow all his commands[a] that I give you today, the LORD your God will set you high above all the nations on earth.[b] 2All these blessings will come upon you[c] and accompany you if you obey the LORD your God:

3You will be blessed[d] in the city and blessed in the country.[e]
4The fruit of your womb will be blessed, and the crops of your land and the young of your livestock—the calves of your herds and the lambs of your flocks.[f]
5Your basket and your kneading trough will be blessed.
6You will be blessed when you come in and blessed when you go out.[g]

7The LORD will grant that the enemies who rise up against you will be defeated before you. They will come at you from one direction but flee from you in seven.[h]

8The LORD will send a blessing on your barns and on everything you put your hand to. The LORD your God will bless you in the land he is giving you.

9The LORD will establish you as his holy people,[i] as he promised you on oath, if you keep the commands of the LORD your God and walk in his ways. 10Then all the peoples on earth will see that you are called by the name[j] of the LORD, and they will fear you. 11The LORD will grant you abundant prosperity—in the fruit of your womb, the young of your livestock and the crops of your ground—in the land he swore to your forefathers to give you.[k]

12The LORD will open the heavens, the storehouse of his bounty, to send rain[l] on your land in season and to bless all the work of your hands. You will lend to many nations but will borrow from none.[m] 13The LORD will make you the head, not the tail. If you pay attention to the commands of the LORD your God that I give you this day and carefully follow them, you will always be at the top, never at the bottom. 14Do not turn aside from any of the commands I give you today, to the right or to the left,[n] following other gods and serving them.

Curses for Disobedience

15However, if you do not obey[o] the LORD your God and do not carefully follow all his commands and

27:20 o Lev 18:7; Dt 22:30
27:21 p Lev 18:23
27:22 q Lev 18:9; Lev 20:17
27:23 r Lev 20:14
27:24 s Lev 24:17; Nu 35:31
27:25 t Ex 23:7-8; Dt 10:17; Eze 22:12
27:26 u Jer 11:3; Gal 3:10*
28:1 a Ex 15:26; Lev 26:3; Dt 7:12-26; b Dt 26:19
28:2 c Zec 1:6
28:3 d Ps 128:1,4; e Ge 39:5
28:4 f Ge 49:25; Pr 10:22
28:6 g Ps 121:8
28:7 h Lev 26:8,17
28:9 i Ex 19:6; Dt 7:6
28:10 j 2Ch 7:14
28:11 k Dt 30:9; Pr 10:22
28:12 l Lev 26:4; m Dt 15:3,6
28:14 n Dt 5:32
28:15 o Lev 26:14

decrees I am giving you today, all these curses will come upon you and overtake you:[p]

> 16 You will be cursed in the city and cursed in the country.
> 17 Your basket and your kneading trough will be cursed.
> 18 The fruit of your womb will be cursed, and the crops of your land, and the calves of your herds and the lambs of your flocks.
> 19 You will be cursed when you come in and cursed when you go out.

20 The LORD will send on you curses,[q] confusion and rebuke[r] in everything you put your hand to, until you are destroyed and come to sudden ruin[s] because of the evil you have done in forsaking him.[a] 21 The LORD will plague you with diseases until he has destroyed you from the land you are entering to possess.[t] 22 The LORD will strike you with wasting disease, with fever and inflammation, with scorching heat and drought,[u] with blight and mildew, which will plague you until you perish.[v] 23 The sky over your head will be bronze, the ground beneath you iron.[w] 24 The LORD will turn the rain of your country into dust and powder; it will come down from the skies until you are destroyed.

25 The LORD will cause you to be defeated before your enemies. You will come at them from one direction but flee from them in seven,[x] and you will become a thing of horror to all the kingdoms on earth.[y] 26 Your carcasses will be food for all the birds of the air and the beasts of the earth, and there will be no-one to frighten them away.[z] 27 The LORD will afflict you with the boils of Egypt[a] and with tumours, festering sores and the itch, from which you cannot be cured. 28 The LORD will afflict you with madness, blindness and confusion of mind. 29 At midday you will grope[b] about like a blind man in the dark. You will be unsuccessful in everything you do; day after day you will be oppressed and robbed, with no-one to rescue you.

30 You will be pledged to be married to a woman, but another will take her and ravish her.[c] You will build a house, but you will not live in it.[d] You will plant a vineyard, but you will not even begin to enjoy its fruit.[e] 31 Your ox will be slaughtered before your eyes, but you will eat none of it. Your donkey will be forcibly taken from you and will not be returned. Your sheep will be given to your enemies, and no-one will rescue them. 32 Your sons and daughters will be given to another nation,[f] and you will wear out your eyes watching for them day after day, powerless to lift a hand. 33 A people that you do not know will eat what your land and labour produce, and you will have nothing but cruel oppression all your days.[g] 34 The sights you see will drive you mad. 35 The LORD will afflict your knees and legs with painful boils[h] that cannot be cured, spreading from the soles of your feet to the top of your head.

36 The LORD will drive you and the king[i] you set over you to a nation unknown to you or your fathers.[j] There you will worship other gods, gods of wood and stone.[k] 37 You will become a thing of horror and an object of scorn and ridicule to all the nations where the LORD will drive you.[l]

38 You will sow much seed in the field but you will harvest little,[m] because locusts will devour[n] it. 39 You will plant vineyards and cultivate them but you will not drink the wine or gather the grapes, because worms will eat them.[o] 40 You will have olive trees throughout your country but you will not use the oil, because the olives will drop

28:15 p Jos 23:15; Da 9:11; Mal 2:2
28:20 q Mal 2:2; r Isa 51:20; Isa 66:15; s Dt 4:26
28:21 t Lev 26:25; Jer 24:10
28:22 u Lev 26:16; v Am 4:9
28:23 w Lev 26:19
28:25 x Isa 30:17; y Jer 15:4; Jer 24:9; Eze 23:46
28:26 z Jer 7:33; Jer 16:4; Jer 34:20
28:27 a ver 60-61; 1Sa 5:6
28:29 b Job 5:14; Isa 59:10
28:30 c Job 31:10; Jer 8:10; d Am 5:11; e Jer 12:13
28:32 f ver 41
28:33 g Jer 5:15-17
28:35 h ver 27
28:36 i 2Ki 17:4,6; 2Ki 24:12,14; 2Ki 25:7,11; j Jer 16:13; k Dt 4:28
28:37 l Jer 24:9
28:38 m Mic 6:15; Hag 1:6,9; n Joel 1:4
28:39 o Isa 5:10; Isa 17:10-11

a20 Hebrew *me*

off.[p] 41You will have sons and
daughters but you will not keep
them, because they will go into captivity.[q] 42Swarms of locusts will
take over all your trees and the
crops of your land.
43The alien who lives among you
will rise above you higher and
higher, but you will sink lower and
lower.[r] 44He will lend to you, but
you will not lend to him.[s] He will
be the head, but you will be the
tail.[t]
45All these curses will come upon
you. They will pursue you and overtake you until you are destroyed,[u]
because you did not obey the LORD
your God and observe the commands and decrees he gave you.
46They will be a sign and a wonder
to you and your descendants for
ever.[v] 47Because you did not
serve[w] the LORD your God joyfully
and gladly[x] in the time of prosperity, 48therefore in hunger and
thirst, in nakedness and dire poverty, you will serve the enemies the
LORD sends against you. He will put
an iron yoke[y] on your neck until he
has destroyed you.
49The LORD will bring a nation
against you from far away, from
the ends of the earth,[z] like an
eagle[a] swooping down, a nation
whose language you will not understand, 50a fierce-looking nation
without respect for the old[b] or pity
for the young. 51They will devour
the young of your livestock and the
crops of your land until you are destroyed. They will leave you no
grain, new wine or oil, nor any
calves of your herds or lambs of
your flocks until you are ruined.[c]
52They will lay siege to all the cities
throughout your land until the high
fortified walls in which you trust
fall down. They will besiege all the
cities throughout the land the LORD
your God is giving you.[d]
53Because of the suffering that
your enemy will inflict on you during the siege, you will eat the fruit
of the womb, the flesh of the sons
and daughters the LORD your God
has given you.[e] 54Even the most
gentle and sensitive man among
you will have no compassion on his
own brother or the wife he loves or
his surviving children, 55and he
will not give to one of them any of
the flesh of his children that he is
eating. It will be all he has left because of the suffering that your enemy will inflict on you during the
siege of all your cities. 56The most
gentle and sensitive[f] woman
among you—so sensitive and gentle that she would not venture to
touch the ground with the sole of
her foot—will begrudge the husband she loves and her own son or
daughter 57the afterbirth from her
womb and the children she bears.
For she intends to eat them secretly during the siege and in the
distress that your enemy will inflict on you in your cities.
58If you do not carefully follow
all the words of this law, which are
written in this book, and do not revere[g] this glorious and awesome
name[h]—the LORD your God—59the
LORD will send fearful plagues on
you and your descendants, harsh
and prolonged disasters, and severe and lingering illnesses. 60He
will bring upon you all the diseases
of Egypt[i] that you dreaded, and
they will cling to you. 61The LORD
will also bring on you every kind of
sickness and disaster not recorded
in this Book of the Law, until you
are destroyed.[j] 62You who were as
numerous as the stars in the sky[k]
will be left but few in number, because you did not obey the LORD
your God. 63Just as it pleased[l] the
LORD to make you prosper and increase in number, so it will please[m]
him to ruin and destroy you. You
will be uprooted[n] from the land
you are entering to possess.
64Then the LORD will scatter[o]
you among all nations,[p] from one

28:40 p Mic 6:15
28:41 q ver 32
28:43 r ver 13
28:44 s ver 12; t ver 13
28:45 u ver 15
28:46 v Isa 8:18; Eze 14:8
28:47 w Dt 32:15; x Ne 9:35
28:48 y Jer 28:13-14
28:49 z Jer 5:15; Jer 6:22; a La 4:19; Hos 8:1
28:50 b Isa 47:6
28:51 c ver 33
28:52 d Jer 10:18; Zep 1:14-16, 17
28:53 e Lev 26:29; 2Ki 6:28-29; Jer 19:9; La 2:20; La 4:10
28:56 f ver 54
28:58 g Mal 1:14; h Ex 6:3
28:60 i ver 27
28:61 j Dt 4:25-26
28:62 k Dt 4:27; Dt 10:22; Ne 9:23
28:63 l Jer 32:41; m Pr 1:26; n Jer 12:14; Jer 45:4
28:64 o Lev 26:33; Dt 4:27; p Ne 1:8

end of the earth to the other. There
you will worship other gods—gods
of wood and stone, which neither
you nor your fathers have known.
65 Among those nations you will find
no repose, no resting place for the
sole of your foot. There the LORD
will give you an anxious mind, eyes
weary with longing, and a despairing heart.[q] 66 You will live in constant suspense, filled with dread
both night and day, never sure of
your life. 67 In the morning you will
say, "If only it were evening!" and
in the evening, "If only it were
morning!"—because of the terror
that will fill your hearts and the
sights that your eyes will see.[r]
68 The LORD will send you back in
ships to Egypt on a journey I said
you should never make again.
There you will offer yourselves for
sale to your enemies as male and
female slaves, but no-one will buy
you.

Renewal of the Covenant

29 These are the terms of the
covenant the LORD com-
manded Moses to make with the Israelites in Moab, in addition to the
covenant he had made with them at
Horeb.[a]
2 Moses summoned all the Israelites and said to them:

Your eyes have seen all that the
LORD did in Egypt to Pharaoh, to all
his officials and to all his land.[b]
3 With your own eyes you saw those
great trials, those miraculous signs
and great wonders.[c] 4 But to this
day the LORD has not given you a
mind that understands or eyes that
see or ears that hear.[d] 5 During the
forty years that I led you through
the desert, your clothes did not
wear out, nor did the sandals on
your feet.[e] 6 You ate no bread and
drank no wine or other fermented
drink. I did this so that you might
know that I am the LORD your
God.[f]

7 When you reached this place, Sihon[g] king of Heshbon and Og king
of Bashan came out to fight against
us, but we defeated them.[h] 8 We
took their land and gave it as an inheritance to the Reubenites, the
Gadites and the half-tribe of Manasseh.[i]
9 Carefully follow[j] the terms of
this covenant, so that you may
prosper in everything you do.[k]
10 All of you are standing today in
the presence of the LORD your
God—your leaders and chief men,
your elders and officials, and all
the other men of Israel, 11 together
with your children and your wives,
and the aliens living in your camps
who chop your wood and carry
your water.[l] 12 You are standing
here in order to enter into a covenant with the LORD your God,
a covenant the LORD is making
with you this day and sealing
with an oath, 13 to confirm you this
day as his people,[m] that he may
be your God[n] as he promised you
and as he swore to your fathers,
Abraham, Isaac and Jacob. 14 I am
making this covenant,[o] with its
oath, not only with you 15 who are
standing here with us today in the
presence of the LORD our God but
also with those who are not here
today.[p]
16 You yourselves know how we
lived in Egypt and how we passed
through the countries on the way
here. 17 You saw among them their
detestable images and idols of
wood and stone, of silver and
gold.[q] 18 Make sure there is no man
or woman, clan or tribe among you
today whose heart turns away from
the LORD our God to go and worship the gods of those nations;
make sure there is no root among
you that produces such bitter poison.[r]
19 When such a person hears the
words of this oath, he invokes a
blessing on himself and therefore
thinks, "I will be safe, even though

28:65 q Lev 26:16,36
28:67 r ver 34; Job 7:4
29:1 a Dt 5:2-3
29:2 b Ex 19:4
29:3 c Dt 4:34; Dt 7:19
29:4 d Isa 6:10; Ac 28:26-27; Ro 11:8*; Eph 4:18
29:5 e Dt 8:4
29:6 f Dt 8:3
29:7 g Dt 2:32; Dt 3:1; h Nu 21:21-24, 33-35
29:8 i Nu 32:33; Dt 3:12-13
29:9 j Dt 4:6; Jos 1:7; k 1Ki 2:3
29:11 l Jos 9:21,23, 27
29:13 m Dt 28:9; n Ge 17:7; Ex 6:7
29:14 o Jer 31:31
29:15 p Ac 2:39
29:17 q Dt 28:36
29:18 r Dt 11:16; Heb 12:15

I persist in going my own way." This will bring disaster on the watered land as well as the dry.[a] 20 The LORD will never be willing to forgive him; his wrath and zeal[s] will burn[t] against that man. All the curses written in this book will fall upon him, and the LORD will blot[u] out his name from under heaven. 21 The LORD will single him out from all the tribes of Israel for disaster, according to all the curses of the covenant written in this Book of the Law.

22 Your children who follow you in later generations and foreigners who come from distant lands will see the calamities that have fallen on the land and the diseases with which the LORD has afflicted it.[v] 23 The whole land will be a burning waste[w] of salt[x] and sulphur—nothing planted, nothing sprouting, no vegetation growing on it. It will be like the destruction of Sodom and Gomorrah,[y] Admah and Zeboiim, which the LORD overthrew in fierce anger. 24 All the nations will ask: "Why has the LORD done this to this land?[z] Why this fierce, burning anger?"

25 And the answer will be: "It is because this people abandoned the covenant of the LORD, the God of their fathers, the covenant he made with them when he brought them out of Egypt. 26 They went off and worshipped other gods and bowed down to them, gods they did not know, gods he had not given them. 27 Therefore the LORD's anger burned against this land, so that he brought on it all the curses written in this book.[a] 28 In furious anger and in great wrath the LORD uprooted[b] them from their land and thrust them into another land, as it is now."

29 The secret things belong to the LORD our God, but the things revealed belong to us and to our children for ever, that we may follow all the words of this law.

29:20 s Eze 23:25 t Ps 74:1 Ps 79:5 u Ex 32:33 Dt 9:14
29:22 v Jer 19:8
29:23 w Isa 34:9 x Jer 17:6 y Ge 19:24,25 Zep 2:9
29:24 z 1Ki 9:8 Jer 22:8-9
29:27 a Da 9:11,13,14
29:28 b 1Ki 14:15 2Ch 7:20 Ps 52:5 Pr 2:22
30:1 a ver 15,19 Dt 11:26 b Lev 26:40-45 Dt 28:64 Dt 29:28 1Ki 8:47
30:2 c Dt 4:30 Ne 1:9
30:3 d Ps 126:4 e Ps 147:2 Jer 32:37 Eze 34:13 f Jer 29:14
30:4 g Ne 1:8-9 Isa 43:6
30:5 h Jer 29:14
30:6 i Dt 10:16 Jer 32:39
30:7 j Dt 7:15
30:9 k Dt 28:11 Jer 31:28 Jer 32:41
30:10 l Dt 4:29

Prosperity After Turning to the LORD

30 When all these blessings and curses[a] I have set before you come upon you and you take them to heart wherever the LORD your God disperses you among the nations,[b] 2 and when you and your children return[c] to the LORD your God and obey him with all your heart and with all your soul according to everything I command you today, 3 then the LORD your God will restore your fortunes[a][d] and have compassion on you and gather[e] you again from all the nations where he scattered you.[f] 4 Even if you have been banished to the most distant land under the heavens, from there the LORD your God will gather you and bring you back.[g] 5 He will bring[h] you to the land that belonged to your fathers, and you will take possession of it. He will make you more prosperous and numerous than your fathers. 6 The LORD your God will circumcise your hearts and the hearts of your descendants,[i] so that you may love him with all your heart and with all your soul, and live. 7 The LORD your God will put all these curses on your enemies who hate and persecute you.[j] 8 You will again obey the LORD and follow all his commands I am giving you today. 9 Then the LORD your God will make you most prosperous in all the work of your hands and in the fruit of your womb, the young of your livestock and the crops of your land.[k] The LORD will again delight in you and make you prosperous, just as he delighted in your fathers, 10 if you obey the LORD your God and keep his commands and decrees that are written in this Book of the Law and turn to the LORD your God with all your heart and with all your soul.[l]

a 19 Or *way, in order to add drunkenness to thirst."* a 3 Or *will bring you back from captivity*

The Offer of Life or Death

11Now what I am commanding
you today is not too difficult for
you or beyond your reach.[m] 12It is
not up in heaven, so that you have
to ask, "Who will ascend into
heaven to get it and proclaim it to
us so that we may obey it?"[n] 13Nor
is it beyond the sea, so that you
have to ask, "Who will cross the sea
to get it and proclaim it to us so that
we may obey it?" 14No, the word is
very near you; it is in your mouth
and in your heart so that you may
obey it.

15See, I set before you today life
and prosperity, death and destruction.[o] 16For I command you today
to love the LORD your God, to walk
in his ways, and to keep his commands, decrees and laws; then you
will live and increase, and the LORD
your God will bless you in the land
you are entering to possess.

17But if your heart turns away
and you are not obedient, and if you
are drawn away to bow down to
other gods and worship them, 18I
declare to you this day that you will
certainly be destroyed.[p] You will
not live long in the land you are
crossing the Jordan to enter and
possess.

19This day I call heaven and earth
as witnesses against you[q] that I
have set before you life and death,
blessings and curses.[r] Now choose
life, so that you and your children
may live 20and that you may love[s]
the LORD your God, listen to his
voice, and hold fast to him. For the
LORD is your life,[t] and he will give
you many years in the land he
swore to give to your fathers, Abraham, Isaac and Jacob.

Joshua to Succeed Moses

31 Then Moses went out and
spoke these words to all Israel: 2"I am now a hundred and
twenty years old[a] and I am no
longer able to lead you.[b] The LORD
has said to me, 'You shall not cross
the Jordan.'[c] 3The LORD your God
himself will cross[d] over ahead of
you.[e] He will destroy these nations
before you, and you will take possession of their land. Joshua also
will cross[f] over ahead of you, as
the LORD said. 4And the LORD will
do to them what he did to Sihon and
Og, the kings of the Amorites,
whom he destroyed along with
their land. 5The LORD will deliver[g]
them to you, and you must do to
them all that I have commanded
you. 6Be strong and courageous.[h]
Do not be afraid or terrified[i] because of them, for the LORD your
God goes with you;[j] he will never
leave you[k] nor forsake[l] you."

7Then Moses summoned Joshua
and said[m] to him in the presence of
all Israel, "Be strong and courageous, for you must go with this
people into the land that the LORD
swore to their forefathers to give
them, and you must divide it among
them as their inheritance. 8The
LORD himself goes before you and
will be with you;[n] he will never
leave you nor forsake you. Do not
be afraid; do not be discouraged."

The Reading of the Law

9So Moses wrote down this law
and gave it to the priests, the sons
of Levi, who carried[o] the ark of the
covenant of the LORD, and to all the
elders of Israel. 10Then Moses commanded them: "At the end of every
seven years, in the year for cancelling debts,[p] during the Feast of
Tabernacles,[q] 11when all Israel
comes to appear[r] before the LORD
your God at the place he will
choose, you shall read this law[s] before them in their hearing. 12As-
semble the people—men, women
and children, and the aliens living
in your towns—so that they can listen and learn[t] to fear the LORD
your God and follow carefully all
the words of this law. 13Their children,[u] who do not know this law,
must hear it and learn to fear the

30:11 m Isa 45:19,23
30:12 n Ro 10:6*
30:15 o Dt 11:26
30:18 p Dt 8:19
30:19 q Dt 4:26; r ver 1
30:20 s Dt 6:5; Dt 10:20; t Ps 27:1; Jn 11:25
31:2 a Dt 34:7; b Nu 27:17; 1Ki 3:7; c Dt 3:23,26
31:3 d Nu 27:18; e Dt 9:3; f Dt 3:28
31:5 g Dt 7:2
31:6 h Jos 10:25; 1Ch 22:13; i Dt 7:18; j Dt 1:29; Dt 20:4; k Jos 1:5; l Heb 13:5*
31:7 m Dt 1:38; Dt 3:28
31:8 n Ex 13:21; Ex 33:14
31:9 o ver 25; Nu 4:15; Jos 3:3
31:10 p Dt 15:1; q Lev 23:34
31:11 r Dt 16:16; s Jos 8:34-35; 2Ki 23:2
31:12 t Dt 4:10
31:13 u Dt 11:2; Ps 78:6-7

LORD your God as long as you live
in the land you are crossing the Jordan to possess."

Israel's Rebellion Predicted

14The LORD said to Moses, "Now
the day of your death[v] is near. Call
Joshua and present yourselves at
the Tent of Meeting, where I will
commission him." So Moses and
Joshua came and presented themselves at the Tent of Meeting.
15Then the LORD appeared at the
Tent in a pillar of cloud, and the
cloud stood over the entrance to
the Tent.[w] 16And the LORD said to
Moses: "You are going to rest with
your fathers, and these people will
soon prostitute[x] themselves to the
foreign gods of the land they are
entering. They will forsake[y] me
and break the covenant I made with
them. 17On that day I will become
angry[z] with them and forsake[a]
them; I will hide[b] my face from
them, and they will be destroyed.
Many disasters and difficulties
will come upon them, and on that
day they will ask, 'Have not these
disasters come upon us because
our God is not with us?'[c] 18And I
will certainly hide my face on that
day because of all their wickedness
in turning to other gods.
19"Now write down for yourselves this song and teach it to the
Israelites and make them sing it, so
that it may be a witness for me
against them. 20When I have
brought them into the land flowing
with milk and honey, the land I
promised on oath to their forefathers,[d] and when they eat their
fill and thrive, they will turn to
other gods[e] and worship them, rejecting me and breaking my covenant.[f] 21And when many
disasters and difficulties come
upon them,[g] this song will testify
against them, because it will not be
forgotten by their descendants. I
know what they are disposed to
do,[h] even before I bring them into

31:14 v Nu 27:13; Dt 32:49-50
31:15 w Ex 33:9
31:16 x Jdg 2:12; y Jdg 10:6,13
31:17 z Jdg 2:14,20; a Jdg 6:13; 2Ch 15:2; b Dt 32:20; Isa 1:15; Isa 8:17; c Nu 14:42
31:20 d Dt 6:10-12; e Dt 32:15-17; f ver 16
31:21 g ver 17; h Hos 5:3
31:22 i ver 19
31:23 j ver 7; k Jos 1:6
31:26 l ver 19
31:27 m Ex 32:9; Dt 9:6,24
31:28 n Dt 4:26; Dt 30:19; Dt 32:1
31:29 o Dt 32:5; Jdg 2:19; p Dt 28:15
32:1 a Isa 1:2
32:2 b Isa 55:11; c Ps 72:6

the land I promised them on oath."
22So Moses wrote[i] down this song
that day and taught it to the Israelites.
23The LORD gave this command[j]
to Joshua son of Nun: "Be strong
and courageous,[k] for you will
bring the Israelites into the land I
promised them on oath, and I myself will be with you."
24After Moses finished writing in
a book the words of this law from
beginning to end, 25he gave this
command to the Levites who carried the ark of the covenant of the
LORD: 26"Take this Book of the Law
and place it beside the ark of the
covenant of the LORD your God.
There it will remain as a witness
against you.[l] 27For I know how rebellious and stiff-necked[m] you are.
If you have been rebellious against
the LORD while I am still alive and
with you, how much more will you
rebel after I die! 28Assemble before me all the elders of your tribes
and all your officials, so that I can
speak these words in their hearing
and call heaven and earth to testify
against them.[n] 29For I know that
after my death you are sure to become utterly corrupt[o] and to turn
from the way I have commanded
you. In days to come, disaster[p] will
fall upon you because you will do
evil in the sight of the LORD and
provoke him to anger by what your
hands have made."

The Song of Moses

30And Moses recited the words of
this song from beginning to end in
the hearing of the whole assembly
of Israel:

32 Listen, O heavens,[a] and I
will speak;
hear, O earth, the words of my
mouth.
2Let my teaching fall like rain
and my words descend like
dew,[b]
like showers[c] on new grass,

like abundant rain on tender plants.
3 I will proclaim the name of the LORD.[d]
Oh, praise the greatness[e] of our God!
4 He is the Rock,[f] his works are perfect,[g]
and all his ways are just.
A faithful God[h] who does no wrong,
upright and just is he.
5 They have acted corruptly towards him;
to their shame they are no longer his children,
but a warped and crooked generation.[a][i]
6 Is this the way you repay[j] the LORD,
O foolish and unwise people?[k]
Is he not your Father,[l] your Creator,[b]
who made you and formed you?[m]
7 Remember the days of old;
consider the generations long past.
Ask your father and he will tell you,
your elders, and they will explain to you.[n]
8 When the Most High gave the nations their inheritance,
when he divided all mankind,[o]
he set up boundaries for the peoples
according to the number of the sons of Israel.[c]
9 For the LORD's portion[p] is his people,
Jacob his allotted inheritance.[q]
10 In a desert[r] land he found him,
in a barren and howling waste.
He shielded him and cared for him;
he guarded him as the apple of his eye,[s]
11 like an eagle that stirs up its nest
and hovers over its young,[t]
that spreads its wings to catch them
and carries them on its pinions.
12 The LORD alone led him;
no foreign god was with him.[u]
13 He made him ride on the heights[v] of the land
and fed him with the fruit of the fields.
He nourished him with honey from the rock,
and with oil[w] from the flinty crag,
14 with curds and milk from herd and flock
and with fattened lambs and goats,
with choice rams of Bashan
and the finest grains of wheat.[x]
You drank the foaming blood of the grape.[y]
15 Jeshurun[d] grew fat[z] and kicked;
filled with food, he became heavy and sleek.
He abandoned[a] the God who made him
and rejected the Rock[b] his Saviour.
16 They made him jealous[c] with their foreign gods
and angered[d] him with their detestable idols.
17 They sacrificed to demons, which are not God—
gods they had not known,[e]
gods that recently appeared,[f]
gods your fathers did not fear.
18 You deserted the Rock, who fathered you;
you forgot[g] the God who gave you birth.
19 The LORD saw this and rejected them[h]

32:3 d Ex 33:19 e Dt 3:24
32:4 f ver 15,18,30 g 2Sa 22:31 h Dt 7:9
32:5 i Dt 31:29
32:6 j Ps 116:12 k Ps 74:2 l Dt 1:31 Isa 63:16 m ver 15
32:7 n Ex 13:14
32:8 o Ge 11:8 Ac 17:26
32:9 p Jer 10:16 q 1Ki 8:51,53
32:10 r Jer 2:6 s Ps 17:8 Zec 2:8
32:11 t Ex 19:4
32:12 u ver 39
32:13 v Isa 58:14 w Job 29:6
32:14 x Ps 81:16 Ps 147:14 y Ge 49:11
32:15 z Dt 31:20 a ver 6 Isa 1:4,28 b ver 4
32:16 c 1Co 10:22 d Ps 78:58
32:17 e Dt 28:64 f Jdg 5:8
32:18 g Isa 17:10
32:19 h Jer 44:21-23

[a]5 Or *Corrupt are they and not his children, / a generation warped and twisted to their shame* [b]6 Or *Father, who bought you* [c]8 Masoretic Text; Dead Sea Scrolls (see also Septuagint) *sons of God* [d]15 *Jeshurun* means *the upright one,* that is, Israel.

because he was angered by his sons and daughters.[i]
20"I will hide my face[j] from them," he said,
"and see what their end will be;
for they are a perverse generation,[k]
children who are unfaithful.
21They made me jealous[l] by what is no god
and angered me with their worthless idols.[m]
I will make them envious by those who are not a people;
I will make them angry by a nation that has no understanding.[n]
22For a fire has been kindled by my wrath,
one that burns to the realm of death[e] below.[o]
It will devour the earth and its harvests
and set on fire the foundations of the mountains.

23"I will heap calamities[p] upon them
and expend my arrows[q] against them.
24I will send wasting famine against them,
consuming pestilence[r] and deadly plague;[s]
I will send against them the fangs of wild beasts,[t]
the venom of vipers[u] that glide in the dust.
25In the street the sword will make them childless;
in their homes terror will reign.[v]
Young men and young women will perish,
infants and grey-haired men.[w]
26I said I would scatter[x] them
and blot out their memory from mankind,[y]
27but I dreaded the taunt of the enemy,
lest the adversary misunderstand
and say, 'Our hand has triumphed;
the LORD has not done all this.' "[z]

28They are a nation without sense,
there is no discernment in them.
29If only they were wise and would understand this[a]
and discern what their end will be!
30How could one man chase a thousand,
or two put ten thousand to flight,[b]
unless their Rock had sold them,
unless the LORD had given them up?[c]
31For their rock is not like our Rock,
as even our enemies concede.
32Their vine comes from the vine of Sodom
and from the fields of Gomorrah.
Their grapes are filled with poison,
and their clusters with bitterness.
33Their wine is the venom of serpents,
the deadly poison of cobras.[d]

34"Have I not kept this in reserve
and sealed it in my vaults?[e]
35It is mine to avenge; I will repay.[f]
In due time their foot will slip;[g]
their day of disaster is near
and their doom rushes upon them.[h]"

36The LORD will judge his people
and have compassion on his servants[i]
when he sees their strength is gone
and no-one is left, slave or free.

32:19 [i] Ps 106:40
32:20 [j] Dt 31:17,29 [k] ver 5
32:21 [l] 1Co 10:22 [m] 1Ki 16:13,26 [n] Ro 10:19*
32:22 [o] Ps 18:7-8; Jer 15:14; La 4:11
32:23 [p] Dt 29:21 [q] Ps 7:13; Eze 5:16
32:24 [r] Dt 28:22 [s] Ps 91:6 [t] Lev 26:22 [u] Am 5:18-19
32:25 [v] Eze 7:15 [w] 2Ch 36:17; La 2:21
32:26 [x] Dt 4:27 [y] Ps 34:16
32:27 [z] Isa 10:13
32:29 [a] Dt 5:29; Ps 81:13
32:30 [b] Lev 26:8 [c] Ps 44:12
32:33 [d] Ps 58:4
32:34 [e] Jer 2:22; Hos 13:12
32:35 [f] Ro 12:19*; Heb 10:30* [g] Jer 23:12 [h] Eze 7:8-9
32:36 [i] Dt 30:1-3; Ps 135:14; Joel 2:14

[e]22 Hebrew *to Sheol*

37He will say: "Now where are
their gods,
the rock they took refuge in,[j]
38the gods who ate the fat of their
sacrifices
and drank the wine of their
drink offerings?
Let them rise up to help you!
Let them give you shelter!

39"See now that I myself am
He![k]
There is no god besides me.[l]
I put to death and I bring to
life,[m]
I have wounded and I will
heal,[n]
and no-one can deliver out of
my hand.[o]
40I lift my hand to heaven and
declare:
As surely as I live for ever,
41when I sharpen my flashing
sword[p]
and my hand grasps it in
judgment,
I will take vengeance on my
adversaries
and repay those who hate
me.[q]
42I will make my arrows drunk
with blood,[r]
while my sword devours
flesh:[s]
the blood of the slain and the
captives,
the heads of the enemy
leaders."
43Rejoice,[t] O nations, with his
people,[f,g]
for he will avenge the blood of
his servants;[u]
he will take vengeance on his
enemies
and make atonement for his
land and people.[v]

44Moses came with Joshua[h][w]
son of Nun and spoke all the words
of this song in the hearing of the
people. 45When Moses finished re-
citing all these words to all Israel,
46he said to them, "Take to heart all
the words I have solemnly declared
to you this day,[x] so that you may
command your children to obey
carefully all the words of this law.
47They are not just idle words for
you—they are your life.[y] By them
you will live long in the land you
are crossing the Jordan to possess."

Moses to Die on Mount Nebo

48On that same day the LORD told
Moses, 49"Go up into the Abarim[z]
Range to Mount Nebo in Moab,
across from Jericho, and view Canaan, the land I am giving the Israelites as their own possession.
50There on the mountain that you
have climbed you will die[a] and be
gathered to your people, just as
your brother Aaron died on Mount
Hor and was gathered to his people.
51This is because both of you broke
faith with me in the presence of the
Israelites at the waters of Meribah
Kadesh in the Desert of Zin[b] and
because you did not uphold my
holiness among the Israelites.[c]
52Therefore, you will see the land
only from a distance;[d] you will not
enter[e] the land I am giving to the
people of Israel."

Moses Blesses the Tribes

33:1–29Ref Ge 49:1–28

33 This is the blessing that
Moses the man of God[a]
pronounced on the Israelites before his death. 2He said:

"The LORD came from Sinai[b]
and dawned over them from
Seir;[c]
he shone forth from Mount
Paran.[d]
He came with[a] myriads of holy
ones[e]
from the south, from his
mountain slopes.[b]

[f]43 Or *Make his people rejoice, O nations*
[g]43 Masoretic Text; Dead Sea Scrolls (see also Septuagint) *people, / and let all the angels worship him /*
[h]44 Hebrew *Hoshea*, a variant of *Joshua*
[a]2 Or *from*
[b]2 The meaning of the Hebrew for this phrase is uncertain.

32:37 *j* Jdg 10:14; Jer 2:28
32:39 *k* Isa 41:4; *l* Isa 45:5; *m* 1Sa 2:6; Ps 68:20; *n* Hos 6:1; *o* Ps 50:22
32:41 *p* Isa 34:6; Isa 66:16; Eze 21:9-10; *q* Jer 50:29
32:42 *r* ver 23; *s* Jer 46:10,14
32:43 *t* Ro 15:10*; *u* 2Ki 9:7; *v* Ps 65:3; Ps 85:1; Rev 19:2
32:44 *w* Nu 13:8,16
32:46 *x* Eze 40:4
32:47 *y* Dt 30:20
32:49 *z* Nu 27:12
32:50 *a* Ge 25:8
32:51 *b* Nu 20:11-13; *c* Nu 27:14
32:52 *d* Dt 34:1-3; *e* Dt 1:37
33:1 *a* Jos 14:6
33:2 *b* Ex 19:18; Ps 68:8; *c* Jdg 5:4; *d* Hab 3:3; *e* Da 7:10; Ac 7:53; Rev 5:11

[3]Surely it is you who love[f] the
people;
all the holy ones are in your
hand.[g]
At your feet they all bow
down,[h]
and from you receive
instruction,
[4]the law that Moses gave us,[i]
the possession of the assembly
of Jacob.[j]
[5]He was king over Jeshurun[c]
when the leaders of the people
assembled,
along with the tribes of Israel.

[6]"Let Reuben live and not die,
nor[d] his men be few."

[7]And this he said about Judah:[k]

"Hear, O LORD, the cry of
Judah;
bring him to his people.
With his own hands he defends
his cause.
Oh, be his help against his
foes!"

[8]About Levi he said:

"Your Thummim and Urim[l]
belong
to the man you favoured.
You tested him at Massah;
you contended with him at the
waters of Meribah.[m]
[9]He said of his father and
mother,[n]
'I have no regard for them.'
He did not recognise his
brothers
or acknowledge his own
children,
but he watched over your word
and guarded your covenant.[o]
[10]He teaches your precepts to
Jacob
and your law to Israel.[p]
He offers incense before you
and whole burnt offerings on
your altar.[q]
[11]Bless all his skills, O LORD,
and be pleased with the work
of his hands.[r]

33:3 *f* Hos 11:1 *g* Dt 14:2 *h* Lk 10:39
33:4 *i* Jn 1:17 *j* Ps 119:111
33:7 *k* Ge 49:10
33:8 *l* Ex 28:30 *m* Ex 17:7
33:9 *n* Ex 32:26-29 *o* Mal 2:5
33:10 *p* Lev 10:11; Dt 31:9-13 *q* Ps 51:19
33:11 *r* 2Sa 24:23
33:12 *s* Dt 12:10 *t* Ex 28:12
33:13 *u* Ge 49:25 *v* Ge 27:28
33:15 *w* Hab 3:6
33:16 *x* Ex 3:2
33:17 *y* Nu 23:22 *z* 1Ki 22:11; Ps 44:5
33:18 *a* Ge 49:13-15

Smite the loins of those who
rise up against him;
strike his foes till they rise no
more."

[12]About Benjamin he said:

"Let the beloved of the LORD
rest secure in him,[s]
for he shields him all day
long,
and the one the LORD loves
rests between his
shoulders.[t]"

[13]About Joseph[u] he said:

"May the LORD bless his land
with the precious dew from
heaven above
and with the deep waters that
lie below;[v]
[14]with the best the sun brings
forth
and the finest the moon can
yield;
[15]with the choicest gifts of the
ancient mountains[w]
and the fruitfulness of the
everlasting hills;
[16]with the best gifts of the earth
and its fulness
and the favour of him who
dwelt in the burning bush.[x]
Let all these rest on the head of
Joseph,
on the brow of the prince
among[e] his brothers.
[17]In majesty he is like a firstborn
bull;
his horns are the horns of a
wild ox.[y]
With them he will gore[z] the
nations,
even those at the ends of the
earth.
Such are the ten thousands of
Ephraim;
such are the thousands of
Manasseh."

[18]About Zebulun[a] he said:

[c]5 *Jeshurun* means *the upright one*, that is, Israel; also in verse 26. [d]6 Or *but let* [e]16 Or *of the one separated from*

"Rejoice, Zebulun, in your going
out,
and you, Issachar, in your
tents.
19 They will summon peoples to
the mountain[b]
and there offer sacrifices of
righteousness;[c]
they will feast on the
abundance of the seas,[d]
on the treasures hidden in the
sand."

20 About Gad[e] he said:

"Blessed is he who enlarges
Gad's domain!
Gad lives there like a lion,
tearing at arm or head.
21 He chose the best land for
himself;[f]
the leader's portion was kept
for him.
When the heads of the people
assembled,
he carried out the LORD's
righteous will,[g]
and his judgments concerning
Israel."

22 About Dan[h] he said:

"Dan is a lion's cub,
springing out of Bashan."

23 About Naphtali he said:

"Naphtali is abounding with the
favour of the LORD
and is full of his blessing;
he will inherit southward to
the lake."

24 About Asher[i] he said:

"Most blessed of sons is Asher;
let him be favoured by his
brothers,
and let him bathe his feet in
oil.[j]
25 The bolts of your gates will be
iron and bronze,
and your strength will equal
your days.[k]

26 "There is no-one like the God of
Jeshurun,[l]
who rides on the heavens to
help you[m]

33:19 b Ex 15:17 Isa 2:3 c Ps 4:5 d Isa 60:5,11
33:20 e Ge 49:19
33:21 f Nu 32:1-5, 31-32 g Jos 4:12 Jos 22:1-3
33:22 h Ge 49:16
33:24 i Ge 49:21 j Ge 49:20 Job 29:6
33:25 k Dt 4:40 Dt 32:47
33:26 l Ex 15:11 m Ps 104:3
33:27 n Ps 90:1 o Jos 24:18 p Dt 7:2
33:28 q Nu 23:9 Jer 23:6 r Ge 27:28
33:29 s Ps 144:15 t Ps 18:44 u 2Sa 7:23 v Ps 115:9-11 w Dt 32:13
34:1 a Dt 32:49 b Dt 32:52
34:2 c Dt 11:24
34:3 d Jdg 1:16 Jdg 3:13 2Ch 28:15
34:4 e Ge 28:13 f Ge 12:7 g Dt 3:27
34:5 h Nu 12:7 i Dt 32:50 Jos 1:1-2
34:6 j Dt 3:29 k Jude 1:9
34:7 l Dt 31:2

and on the clouds in his
majesty.
27 The eternal God is your
refuge,[n]
and underneath are the
everlasting arms.
He will drive out your enemy
before you,[o]
saying, 'Destroy him!'[p]
28 So Israel will live in safety
alone;[q]
Jacob's spring is secure
in a land of grain and new wine,
where the heavens drop dew.[r]
29 Blessed are you, O Israel![s]
Who is like you,[t]
a people saved by the LORD?[u]
He is your shield and helper[v]
and your glorious sword.
Your enemies will cower before
you,
and you will trample down
their high places."[f][w]

The Death of Moses

34 Then Moses climbed
Mount Nebo from the
plains of Moab to the top of Pisgah,
across from Jericho.[a] There the
LORD showed[b] him the whole
land—from Gilead to Dan, 2 all of
Naphtali, the territory of Ephraim
and Manasseh, all the land of Judah
as far as the western sea,[a][c] 3 the
Negev and the whole region from
the Valley of Jericho, the City of
Palms,[d] as far as Zoar. 4 Then the
LORD said to him, "This is the land
I promised on oath[e] to Abraham,
Isaac and Jacob when I said, 'I will
give it[f] to your descendants.' I
have let you see it with your eyes,
but you will not cross[g] over into
it."
5 And Moses the servant of the
LORD[h] died[i] there in Moab, as the
LORD had said. 6 He buried him[b] in
Moab, in the valley opposite Beth
Peor,[j] but to this day no-one knows
where his grave is.[k] 7 Moses was a
hundred and twenty years old[l]

[f]29 Or *will tread upon their bodies* [a]2 That is, the Mediterranean [b]6 Or *He was buried*

when he died, yet his eyes were not
weak[m] nor his strength gone. 8 The
Israelites grieved for Moses in the
plains of Moab thirty days, until the
time of weeping and mourning[n]
was over.
9 Now Joshua son of Nun was
filled with the spirit[c] of wisdom[o]
because Moses had laid his hands
on him.[p] So the Israelites listened
to him and did what the LORD had
commanded Moses.
10 Since then, no prophet has risen
in Israel like Moses,[q] whom the
LORD knew face to face,[r] 11 who did
all those miraculous signs and wonders[s] the LORD sent him to do in
Egypt—to Pharaoh and to all his officials[t] and to his whole land. 12 For
no-one has ever shown the mighty
power or performed the awesome
deeds that Moses did in the sight of
all Israel.

34:7
m Ge 27:1
34:8
n Ge 50:3,10
2Sa 11:27
34:9
o Ge 41:38
Isa 11:2
Da 6:3
p Nu 27:18,23
34:10
q Dt 18:15,18
r Ex 33:11
Nu 12:6,8
Dt 5:4
34:11
s Dt 4:34
t Dt 7:19

c9 Or *Spirit*

JOSHUA

The LORD Commands Joshua

1 After the death of Moses the servant of the LORD,[a] the LORD said to Joshua[b] son of Nun, Moses' assistant: 2"Moses my servant is dead. Now then, you and all these people, get ready to cross the Jordan River[c] into the land I am about to give to them—to the Israelites. 3I will give you every place where you set your foot,[d] as I promised Moses. 4Your territory will extend from the desert to Lebanon, and from the great river, the Euphrates[e]—all the Hittite country—to the Great Sea[a] on the west.[f] 5No-one will be able to stand up against you[g] all the days of your life. As I was with[h] Moses, so I will be with you; I will never leave you nor forsake[i] you.

6"Be strong and courageous, because you will lead these people to inherit the land I swore to their forefathers[j] to give them. 7Be strong and very courageous. Be careful to obey all the law my servant Moses gave you; do not turn from it to the right or to the left,[k] that you may be successful wherever you go.[l] 8Do not let this Book of the Law depart from your mouth; meditate on it day and night, so that you may be careful to do everything written in it. Then you will be prosperous and successful.[m] 9Have I not commanded you? Be strong and courageous. Do not be terrified;[n] do not be discouraged, for the LORD your God will be with you wherever you go."[o]

10So Joshua ordered the officers of the people: 11"Go through the camp and tell the people, 'Get your supplies ready. Three days from now you will cross the Jordan here to go in and take possession[p] of the land the LORD your God is giving you for your own.' "

12But to the Reubenites, the Gadites and the half-tribe of Manasseh,[q] Joshua said, 13"Remember the command that Moses the servant of the LORD gave you: 'The LORD your God is giving you rest[r] and has granted you this land.' 14Your wives, your children and your livestock may stay in the land that Moses gave you east of the Jordan, but all your fighting men, fully armed, must cross over ahead of your brothers. You are to help your brothers 15until the LORD gives them rest, as he has done for you, and until they too have taken possession of the land that the LORD your God is giving them. After that, you may go back and occupy your own land, which Moses the servant of the LORD gave you east of the Jordan towards the sunrise."[s]

16Then they answered Joshua, "Whatever you have commanded us we will do, and wherever you send us we will go. 17Just as we fully obeyed Moses, so we will obey you.[t] Only may the LORD your God be with you as he was with Moses. 18Whoever rebels against your word and does not obey your words, whatever you may command them, will be put to death. Only be strong and courageous!"

Rahab and the Spies

2 Then Joshua son of Nun secretly sent two spies[a] from Shittim.[b] "Go, look over the land," he said, "especially Jericho." So they went and entered the house of

1:1 *a* Nu 12:7; Dt 34:5 *b* Ex 24:13; Dt 1:38
1:2 *c* ver 11
1:3 *d* Dt 11:24
1:4 *e* Ge 15:18 *f* Nu 34:2-12
1:5 *g* Dt 7:24 *h* Jos 3:7; Jos 6:27 *i* Dt 31:6-8
1:6 *j* Dt 31:23
1:7 *k* Dt 5:32; Dt 28:14 *l* Jos 11:15
1:8 *m* Dt 29:9; Ps 1:1-3
1:9 *n* Ps 27:1 *o* ver 7; Dt 31:7-8; Jer 1:8
1:11 *p* Joel 3:2
1:12 *q* Nu 32:20-22
1:13 *r* Dt 3:18-20
1:15 *s* Jos 22:1-4
1:17 *t* ver 5,9
2:1 *a* Jas 2:25 *b* Nu 25:1; Jos 3:1

a4 That is, the Mediterranean

a prostitute[a] named Rahab[c] and
stayed there.
2The king of Jericho was told,
"Look! Some of the Israelites have
come here tonight to spy out the
land." 3So the king of Jericho sent
this message to Rahab: "Bring out
the men who came to you and entered your house, because they
have come to spy out the whole
land."
4But the woman had taken the
two men and hidden them.[d] She
said, "Yes, the men came to me, but
I did not know where they had
come from. 5At dusk, when it was
time to close the city gate, the men
left. I don't know which way they
went. Go after them quickly. You
may catch up with them." 6(But she
had taken them up to the roof and
hidden them under the stalks of
flax[e] she had laid out on the
roof.)[f] 7So the men set out in pursuit of the spies on the road that
leads to the fords of the Jordan, and
as soon as the pursuers had gone
out, the gate was shut.
8Before the spies lay down for
the night, she went up on the roof
9and said to them, "I know that the
LORD has given this land to you and
that a great fear[g] of you has fallen
on us, so that all who live in this
country are melting in fear because of you. 10We have heard how
the LORD dried up[h] the water of the
Red Sea[b] for you when you came
out of Egypt,[i] and what you did
to Sihon and Og,[j] the two kings of
the Amorites east of the Jordan,
whom you completely destroyed.[c]
11When we heard of it, our hearts
sank[d] and everyone's courage
failed because of you,[k] for the
LORD your God is God in heaven
above and on the earth[l] below.
12Now then, please swear to me by
the LORD that you will show kindness to my family, because I have
shown kindness to you. Give me a
sure sign[m] 13that you will spare the
lives of my father and mother, my
brothers and sisters, and all who
belong to them, and that you will
save us from death."
14"Our lives for your lives!" the
men assured her. "If you don't tell
what we are doing, we will treat
you kindly and faithfully[n] when
the LORD gives us the land."
15So she let them down by a rope
through the window,[o] for the
house she lived in was part of the
city wall. 16Now she had said to
them, "Go to the hills so that the
pursuers will not find you. Hide
yourselves there three days[p] until
they return, and then go on your
way."[q]
17The men said to her, "This
oath[r] you made us swear will not
be binding on us 18unless, when we
enter the land, you have tied this
scarlet cord in the window through
which you let us down, and unless
you have brought your father and
mother, your brothers and all your
family[s] into your house. 19If anyone goes outside your house into
the street, his blood will be on his
own head;[t] we will not be responsible. As for anyone who is in the
house with you, his blood will be on
our head[u] if a hand is laid on him.
20But if you tell what we are doing,
we will be released from the oath
you made us swear."
21"Agreed," she replied. "Let it
be as you say." So she sent them
away and they departed. And she
tied the scarlet cord in the window.
22When they left, they went into
the hills and stayed there three
days, until the pursuers had
searched all along the road and returned without finding them.
23Then the two men started back.
They went down out of the hills,
forded the river and came to
Joshua son of Nun and told him
everything that had happened to
them. 24They said to Joshua, "The

2:1 *c* Heb 11:31
2:4 *d* 2Sa 17:19-20
2:6 *e* Jas 2:25 *f* Ex 1:17,19; 2Sa 17:19
2:9 *g* Ge 35:5; Ex 23:27; Dt 2:25
2:10 *h* Ex 14:21 *i* Nu 23:22 *j* Nu 21:21,24, 34-35
2:11 *k* Ex 15:14; Jos 5:1; Jos 7:5; Ps 22:14; Isa 13:7 *l* Dt 4:39
2:12 *m* ver 18
2:14 *n* Jdg 1:24; Mt 5:7
2:15 *o* Ac 9:25
2:16 *p* Jas 2:25 *q* Heb 11:31
2:17 *r* Ge 24:8
2:18 *s* ver 12; Jos 6:23
2:19 *t* Eze 33:4 *u* Mt 27:25

a*1* Or possibly *an innkeeper* b*10* Hebrew *Yam Suph*; that is, Sea of Reeds c*10* The Hebrew term refers to the irrevocable giving over of things or persons to the LORD, often by totally destroying them. d*11* Hebrew *melted*

LORD has surely given the whole
land into our hands;[v] all the people
are melting in fear because of us."

Crossing the Jordan

3 Early in the morning Joshua
and all the Israelites set out
from Shittim[a] and went to the Jordan, where they camped before
crossing over. 2After three days
the officers went throughout the
camp,[b] 3giving orders to the people: "When you see the ark of the
covenant[c] of the LORD your God,
and the priests,[d] who are Levites,
carrying it, you are to move out
from your positions and follow it.
4Then you will know which way to
go, since you have never been this
way before. But keep a distance of
about a thousand yards[a] between
you and the ark; do not go near it."
5Joshua told the people, "Consecrate yourselves,[e] for tomorrow
the LORD will do amazing things
among you."
6Joshua said to the priests, "Take
up the ark of the covenant and pass
on ahead of the people." So they
took it up and went ahead of them.
7And the LORD said to Joshua,
"Today I will begin to exalt you[f] in
the eyes of all Israel, so that they
may know that I am with you as
I was with Moses.[g] 8Tell the
priests[h] who carry the ark of the
covenant: 'When you reach the
edge of the Jordan's waters, go and
stand in the river.' "
9Joshua said to the Israelites,
"Come here and listen to the words
of the LORD your God. 10This is how
you will know that the living God[i]
is among you and that he will certainly drive out before you the
Canaanites, Hittites, Hivites,
Perizzites, Girgashites, Amorites
and Jebusites.[j] 11See, the ark of
the covenant of the Lord of all the
earth[k] will go into the Jordan
ahead of you. 12Now then, choose
twelve men[l] from the tribes of Israel, one from each tribe. 13And as
soon as the priests who carry the
ark of the LORD — the Lord of all the
earth[m] — set foot in the Jordan, its
waters flowing downstream[n] will
be cut off and stand up in a heap.[o]"
14So when the people broke camp
to cross the Jordan, the priests
carrying the ark of the covenant[p]
went ahead[q] of them. 15Now the
Jordan is in flood[r] all during harvest. Yet as soon as the priests
who carried the ark reached the
Jordan and their feet touched the
water's edge, 16the water from up-
stream stopped flowing.[s] It piled
up in a heap a great distance away,
at a town called Adam in the vicinity of Zarethan,[t] while the water
flowing down[u] to the Sea of the
Arabah[v] (the Salt Sea[b][w]) was
completely cut off. So the people
crossed over opposite Jericho.
17The priests who carried the ark of
the covenant of the LORD stood
firm on dry ground in the middle
of the Jordan, while all Israel
passed by until the whole nation
had completed the crossing on dry
ground.[x]

4 When the whole nation had finished crossing the Jordan,[a]
the LORD said to Joshua, 2"Choose
twelve men[b] from among the people, one from each tribe, 3and tell
them to take up twelve stones[c]
from the middle of the Jordan from
right where the priests stood and to
carry them over with you and put
them down at the place where you
stay tonight.[d]"
4So Joshua called together the
twelve men he had appointed from
the Israelites, one from each tribe,
5and said to them, "Go over before
the ark of the LORD your God into
the middle of the Jordan. Each of
you is to take up a stone on his
shoulder, according to the number
of the tribes of the Israelites, 6to
serve as a sign among you. In the
future, when your children ask

2:24 v ver 9; Jos 6:2
3:1 a Jos 2:1
3:2 b Jos 1:11
3:3 c Nu 10:33; d Dt 31:9
3:5 e Ex 19:10,14; Lev 20:7; Jos 7:13; 1Sa 16:5; Joel 2:16
3:7 f Jos 4:14; 1Ch 29:25; g Jos 1:5
3:8 h ver 3
3:10 i Dt 5:26; 1Sa 17:26,36; 2Ki 19:4,16; Hos 1:10; Mt 16:16; 1Th 1:9; j Ex 33:2; Dt 7:1
3:11 k ver 13; Job 41:11; Zec 6:5
3:12 l Jos 4:2,4
3:13 m ver 11; n ver 16; o Ex 15:8; Ps 78:13
3:14 p Ps 132:8; q Ac 7:44-45
3:15 r Jos 4:18; 1Ch 12:15
3:16 s Ps 66:6; Ps 74:15; t 1Ki 4:12; 1Ki 7:46; u ver 13; v Dt 1:1; w Ge 14:3
3:17 x Ex 14:22,29
4:1 a Dt 27:2
4:2 b Jos 3:12
4:3 c ver 20; d ver 19

a4 Hebrew *about two thousand cubits* (about 900 metres) b16 That is, the Dead Sea

you, 'What do these stones mean?'[e]
7 tell them that the flow of the Jordan was cut off[f] before the ark of
the covenant of the LORD. When it
crossed the Jordan, the waters of
the Jordan were cut off. These
stones are to be a memorial[g] to the
people of Israel for ever."
8 So the Israelites did as Joshua
commanded them. They took
twelve stones from the middle of
the Jordan, according to the number of the tribes of the Israelites, as
the LORD had told Joshua;[h] and
they carried them over with them
to their camp, where they put them
down. 9 Joshua set up the twelve
stones[i] that had been[a] in the middle of the Jordan at the spot where
the priests who carried the ark of
the covenant had stood. And they
are there to this day.
10 Now the priests who carried
the ark remained standing in the
middle of the Jordan until everything the LORD had commanded
Joshua was done by the people, just
as Moses had directed Joshua. The
people hurried over, 11 and as soon
as all of them had crossed, the ark
of the LORD and the priests came to
the other side while the people
watched. 12 The men of Reuben,
Gad and the half-tribe of Manasseh
crossed over, armed, in front of the
Israelites,[j] as Moses had directed
them. 13 About forty thousand
armed for battle crossed over before the LORD to the plains of Jericho for war.
14 That day the LORD exalted[k]
Joshua in the sight of all Israel; and
they revered him all the days of his
life, just as they had revered
Moses.
15 Then the LORD said to Joshua,
16 "Command the priests carrying
the ark of the Testimony[l] to come
up out of the Jordan."
17 So Joshua commanded the
priests, "Come up out of the Jordan."
18 And the priests came up out of
the river carrying the ark of the

4:6 e ver 21 Ex 12:26 Ex 13:14
4:7 f Jos 3:13 g Ex 12:14
4:8 h ver 20
4:9 i Ge 28:18 Jos 24:26 1Sa 7:12
4:12 j Nu 32:27
4:14 k Jos 3:7
4:16 l Ex 25:22
4:18 m Jos 3:15
4:19 n Jos 5:9
4:20 o ver 3,8
4:21 p ver 6
4:22 q Jos 3:17
4:23 r Ex 14:21
4:24 s 1Ki 8:42-43 2Ki 19:19 Ps 106:8 Jer 10:7 t Ex 15:16 1Ch 29:12 Ps 89:13 u Ex 14:31
5:1 a Nu 13:29 b Jos 2:9-11
5:2 c Ex 4:25

covenant of the LORD. No sooner
had they set their feet on the dry
ground than the waters of the Jordan returned to their place and ran
in flood[m] as before.
19 On the tenth day of the first
month the people went up from the
Jordan and camped at Gilgal[n] on
the eastern border of Jericho.
20 And Joshua set up at Gilgal the
twelve stones[o] they had taken out
of the Jordan. 21 He said to the Israelites, "In the future when your
descendants ask their fathers,
'What do these stones mean?'[p]
22 tell them, 'Israel crossed the Jordan on dry ground.'[q] 23 For the
LORD your God dried up the Jordan
before you until you had crossed
over. The LORD your God did to the
Jordan just what he had done to the
Red Sea[b] when he dried it up before us until we had crossed over.[r]
24 He did this so that all the peoples
of the earth might know[s] that the
hand of the LORD is powerful[t] and
so that you might always fear the
LORD your God.[u]"

Circumcision at Gilgal

5 Now when all the Amorite
kings west of the Jordan and
all the Canaanite kings along the
coast[a] heard how the LORD had
dried up the Jordan before the Israelites until we had crossed over,
their hearts sank[a][b] and they no
longer had the courage to face the
Israelites.
2 At that time the LORD said to
Joshua, "Make flint knives[c] and
circumcise the Israelites again."
3 So Joshua made flint knives and
circumcised the Israelites at Gibeath Haaraloth.[b]
4 Now this is why he did so: All
those who came out of Egypt—all
the men of military age—died in
the desert on the way after leaving

[a]9 Or *Joshua also set up twelve stones*
[b]23 Hebrew *Yam Suph*; that is, Sea of Reeds
[a]1 Hebrew *melted* [b]3 *Gibeath Haaraloth* means *hill of foreskins*.

Egypt.[d] 5All the people that came out had been circumcised, but all the people born in the desert during the journey from Egypt had not. 6The Israelites had moved about in the desert forty years[e] until all the men who were of military age when they left Egypt had died, since they had not obeyed the LORD. For the LORD had sworn to them that they would not see the land that he had solemnly promised their fathers to give us,[f] a land flowing with milk and honey.[g] 7So he raised up their sons in their place, and these were the ones Joshua circumcised. They were still uncircumcised because they had not been circumcised on the way. 8And after the whole nation had been circumcised, they remained where they were in camp until they were healed.[h]

9Then the LORD said to Joshua, "Today I have rolled away the reproach of Egypt from you." So the place has been called Gilgal[c] to this day.

10On the evening of the fourteenth day of the month,[i] while camped at Gilgal on the plains of Jericho, the Israelites celebrated the Passover. 11The day after the Passover, that very day, they ate some of the produce of the land:[j] unleavened bread and roasted grain.[k] 12The manna stopped the day after[d] they ate this food from the land; there was no longer any manna for the Israelites, but that year they ate of the produce of Canaan.[l]

The Fall of Jericho

13Now when Joshua was near Jericho, he looked up and saw a man[m] standing in front of him with a drawn sword[n] in his hand. Joshua went up to him and asked, "Are you for us or for our enemies?"

14"Neither," he replied, "but as commander of the army of the LORD I have now come." Then Joshua fell face down[o] to the ground in reverence, and asked him, "What message does my Lord[e] have for his servant?"

15The commander of the LORD's army replied, "Take off your sandals, for the place where you are standing is holy."[p] And Joshua did so.

6 Now Jericho[a] was tightly shut up because of the Israelites. No-one went out and no-one came in.

2Then the LORD said to Joshua, "See, I have delivered[b] Jericho into your hands, along with its king and its fighting men. 3March around the city once with all the armed men. Do this for six days. 4Make seven priests carry trumpets of rams' horns in front of the ark. On the seventh day, march around the city seven times, with the priests blowing the trumpets.[c] 5When you hear them sound a long blast[d] on the trumpets, make all the people give a loud shout;[e] then the wall of the city will collapse and the people will go up, every man straight in."

6So Joshua son of Nun called the priests and said to them, "Take up the ark of the covenant of the LORD and make seven priests carry trumpets in front of it." 7And he ordered the people, "Advance[f]! March around the city, with the armed guard going ahead of the ark of the LORD."

8When Joshua had spoken to the people, the seven priests carrying the seven trumpets before the LORD went forward, blowing their trumpets, and the ark of the LORD's covenant followed them. 9The armed guard marched ahead of the priests who blew the trumpets, and the rear guard[g] followed the ark. All this time the trumpets were sounding. 10But Joshua had commanded the people, "Do not give a

5:4 d Dt 2:14
5:6 e Dt 2:7 f Nu 14:23, 29-35 Dt 2:14 g Ex 3:8
5:8 h Ge 34:25
5:10 i Ex 12:6
5:11 j Nu 15:19 k Lev 23:14
5:12 l Ex 16:35
5:13 m Ge 18:2 Ge 32:24 n Nu 22:23
5:14 o Ge 17:3
5:15 p Ex 3:5 Ac 7:33
6:1 a Jos 24:11
6:2 b Dt 7:24 Jos 2:9,24 Jos 8:1
6:4 c Lev 25:9 Nu 10:8
6:5 d Ex 19:13 e ver 20 1Sa 4:5 Ps 42:4 Isa 42:13
6:7 f Ex 14:15
6:9 g ver 13 Isa 52:12

c9 *Gilgal* sounds like the Hebrew for *roll*.
d12 Or *the day* e14 Or *lord*

war cry, do not raise your voices,
do not say a word until the day I tell
you to shout. Then shout![h]" 11 So he
had the ark of the LORD carried
around the city, circling it once.
Then the people returned to camp
and spent the night there.
12 Joshua got up early the next
morning and the priests took up the
ark of the LORD. 13 The seven
priests carrying the seven trumpets went forward, marching before the ark of the LORD and
blowing the trumpets. The armed
men went ahead of them and the
rear guard followed the ark of the
LORD, while the trumpets kept
sounding. 14 So on the second day
they marched around the city once
and returned to the camp. They did
this for six days.
15 On the seventh day, they got up
at daybreak and marched around
the city seven times in the same
manner, except that on that day
they circled the city seven times.[i]
16 The seventh time around, when
the priests sounded the trumpet
blast, Joshua commanded the people, "Shout! For the LORD has given
you the city! 17 The city and all that
is in it are to be devoted[a][j] to the
LORD. Only Rahab the prostitute[b]
and all who are with her in her
house shall be spared, because she
hid[k] the spies we sent. 18 But keep
away from the devoted things,[l] so
that you will not bring about your
own destruction by taking any of
them. Otherwise you will make the
camp of Israel liable to destruction[m] and bring trouble[n] on it. 19 All
the silver and gold and the articles
of bronze and iron[o] are sacred to
the LORD and must go into his treasury."
20 When the trumpets sounded,[p]
the people shouted, and at the
sound of the trumpet, when the
people gave a loud shout,[q] the wall
collapsed; so every man charged
straight in, and they took the city.[r]
21 They devoted the city to the LORD
and destroyed[s] with the sword

6:10 h ver 20
6:15 i 1Ki 18:44
6:17 j Lev 27:28; Dt 20:17; k Jos 2:4
6:18 l Jos 7:1; m Jos 7:12; n Jos 7:25,26
6:19 o ver 24; Nu 31:22
6:20 p Jdg 6:34; Jer 4:21; Am 2:2; q ver 5; r Heb 11:30
6:21 s Dt 20:16
6:22 t Jos 2:14; Heb 11:31
6:23 u Jos 2:13
6:24 v ver 19
6:25 w Heb 11:31; x Jos 2:6
6:26 y 1Ki 16:34
6:27 z Ge 39:2; Jos 1:5; a Jos 9:1
7:1 a Jos 6:18

every living thing in it—men and
women, young and old, cattle,
sheep and donkeys.
22 Joshua said to the two men who
had spied out the land, "Go into the
prostitute's house and bring her
out and all who belong to her, in accordance with your oath to her.[t]"
23 So the young men who had done
the spying went in and brought out
Rahab, her father and mother and
brothers and all who belonged to
her.[u] They brought out her entire
family and put them in a place outside the camp of Israel.
24 Then they burned the whole
city and everything in it, but they
put the silver and gold and the articles of bronze and iron[v] into the
treasury of the LORD's house. 25 But
Joshua spared Rahab the prostitute,[w] with her family and all who
belonged to her, because she hid
the men Joshua had sent as spies to
Jericho[x]—and she lives among the
Israelites to this day.
26 At that time Joshua pronounced this solemn oath: "Cursed
before the LORD is the man who
undertakes to rebuild this city, Jericho:

"At the cost of his firstborn son
will he lay its foundations;
at the cost of his youngest
will he set up its gates."[y]

27 So the LORD was with Joshua,[z]
and his fame spread[a] throughout
the land.

Achan's Sin

7 But the Israelites acted unfaithfully in regard to the devoted things;[a][a] Achan son of
Carmi, the son of Zimri,[b] the son of

[a]17 The Hebrew term refers to the irrevocable giving over of things or persons to the LORD, often by totally destroying them; also in verses 18 and 21. [b]17 Or possibly *innkeeper*; also in verses 22 and 25 [a]1 The Hebrew term refers to the irrevocable giving over of things or persons to the LORD, often by totally destroying them; also in verses 11, 12, 13 and 15. [b]1 See Septuagint and 1 Chron. 2:6; Hebrew *Zabdi*; also in verses 17 and 18.

Zerah,[b] of the tribe of Judah, took
some of them. So the LORD's anger
burned against Israel.
2Now Joshua sent men from Jericho to Ai, which is near Beth
Aven[c] to the east of Bethel, and
told them, "Go up and spy out the
region." So the men went up and
spied out Ai.
3When they returned to Joshua,
they said, "Not all the people will
have to go up against Ai. Send two
or three thousand men to take it
and do not weary all the people, for
only a few men are there." 4So
about three thousand men went up;
but they were routed by the men of
Ai,[d] 5who killed about thirty-six of
them. They chased the Israelites
from the city gate as far as the
stone quarries[c] and struck them
down on the slopes. At this the
hearts of the people melted[e] and
became like water.
6Then Joshua tore his clothes[f]
and fell face down to the ground before the ark of the LORD, remaining
there till evening. The elders of Israel did the same, and sprinkled
dust[g] on their heads. 7And Joshua
said, "Ah, Sovereign LORD, why did
you ever bring this people across
the Jordan to deliver us into the
hands of the Amorites to destroy
us?[h] If only we had been content to
stay on the other side of the Jordan! 8O Lord, what can I say, now
that Israel has been routed by its
enemies? 9The Canaanites and the
other people of the country will
hear about this and they will surround us and wipe out our name
from the earth.[i] What then will
you do for your own great name?"
10The LORD said to Joshua, "Stand
up! What are you doing down on
your face? 11Israel has sinned; they
have violated my covenant,[j]
which I commanded them to keep.
They have taken some of the devoted things; they have stolen, they
have lied,[k] they have put them
with their own possessions. 12That
is why the Israelites cannot stand
against their enemies;[l] they turn
their backs and run because they
have been made liable to destruction.[m] I will not be with you any
more unless you destroy whatever
among you is devoted to destruction.
13"Go, consecrate the people.
Tell them, 'Consecrate yourselves[n] in preparation for tomorrow; for this is what the LORD, the
God of Israel, says: That which is
devoted is among you, O Israel.
You cannot stand against your enemies until you remove it.
14" 'In the morning, present yourselves tribe by tribe. The tribe that
the LORD takes[o] shall come forward clan by clan; the clan that the
LORD takes shall come forward
family by family; and the family
that the LORD takes shall come forward man by man. 15He who is
caught with the devoted things
shall be destroyed by fire, along
with all that belongs to him.[p] He
has violated the covenant[q] of the
LORD and has done a disgraceful
thing in Israel!' "[r]
16Early the next morning Joshua
had Israel come forward by tribes,
and Judah was taken. 17The clans of
Judah came forward, and he took
the Zerahites.[s] He had the clan of
the Zerahites come forward by
families, and Zimri was taken.
18Joshua had his family come forward man by man, and Achan son
of Carmi, the son of Zimri, the son
of Zerah, of the tribe of Judah, was
taken.
19Then Joshua said to Achan,
"My son, give glory[t] to the LORD,[d]
the God of Israel, and give him the
praise.[e] Tell[u] me what you have
done; do not hide it from me."
20Achan replied, "It is true! I
have sinned against the LORD, the
God of Israel. This is what I have
done: 21When I saw in the plunder a

7:1 b Jos 22:20
7:2 c Jos 18:12; 1Sa 13:5; 1Sa 14:23
7:4 d Lev 26:17; Dt 28:25
7:5 e Lev 26:36; Jos 2:9,11; Eze 21:7; Na 2:10
7:6 f Ge 37:29 g 1Sa 4:12; 2Sa 13:19; Ne 9:1; Job 2:12; La 2:10; Rev 18:19
7:7 h Ex 5:22
7:9 i Ex 32:12; Dt 9:28
7:11 j Jos 6:17-19 k Ac 5:1-2
7:12 l Nu 14:45; Jdg 2:14 m Jos 6:18
7:13 n Jos 3:5; Jos 6:18
7:14 o Pr 16:33
7:15 p 1Sa 14:39 q ver 11 r Ge 34:7
7:17 s Nu 26:20
7:19 t 1Sa 6:5; Jer 13:16; Jn 9:24* u 1Sa 14:43

c5 Or *as far as Shebarim* d19 A solemn charge to tell the truth e19 Or *and confess to him*

beautiful robe from Babylonia,[f] two hundred shekels[g] of silver and a wedge of gold weighing fifty shekels,[h] I coveted[v] them and took them. They are hidden in the ground inside my tent, with the silver underneath."

22 So Joshua sent messengers, and they ran to the tent, and there it was, hidden in his tent, with the silver underneath. 23 They took the things from the tent, brought them to Joshua and all the Israelites and spread them out before the LORD.

24 Then Joshua, together with all Israel, took Achan son of Zerah, the silver, the robe, the gold wedge, his sons and daughters, his cattle, donkeys and sheep, his tent and all that he had, to the Valley of Achor.[w] 25 Joshua said, "Why have you brought this trouble[x] on us? The LORD will bring trouble on you today."

Then all Israel stoned him,[y] and after they had stoned the rest, they burned them. 26 Over Achan they heaped up a large pile of rocks, which remains to this day. Then the LORD turned from his fierce anger.[z] Therefore that place has been called the Valley of Achor[i][a] ever since.

Ai Destroyed

8 Then the LORD said to Joshua, "Do not be afraid;[a] do not be discouraged.[b] Take the whole army[c] with you, and go up and attack Ai. For I have delivered[d] into your hands the king of Ai, his people, his city and his land. 2 You shall do to Ai and its king as you did to Jericho and its king, except that you may carry off their plunder and livestock for yourselves.[e] Set an ambush behind the city."

3 So Joshua and the whole army moved out to attack Ai. He chose thirty thousand of his best fighting men and sent them out at night 4 with these orders: "Listen carefully. You are to set an ambush behind the city. Don't go very far from it. All of you be on the alert. 5 I and all those with me will advance on the city, and when the men come out against us, as they did before, we will flee from them. 6 They will pursue us until we have lured them away from the city, for they will say, 'They are running away from us as they did before.' So when we flee from them, 7 you are to rise up from ambush and take the city. The LORD your God will give it into your hand.[f] 8 When you have taken the city, set it on fire.[g] Do what the LORD has commanded.[h] See to it; you have my orders."

9 Then Joshua sent them off, and they went to the place of ambush[i] and lay in wait between Bethel and Ai, to the west of Ai—but Joshua spent that night with the people.

10 Early the next morning[j] Joshua mustered his men, and he and the leaders of Israel[k] marched before them to Ai. 11 The entire force that was with him marched up and approached the city and arrived in front of it. They set up camp north of Ai, with the valley between them and the city. 12 Joshua had taken about five thousand men and set them in ambush between Bethel and Ai, to the west of the city. 13 They had the soldiers take up their positions—all those in the camp to the north of the city and the ambush to the west of it. That night Joshua went into the valley.

14 When the king of Ai saw this, he and all the men of the city hurried out early in the morning to meet Israel in battle at a certain place overlooking the Arabah.[l] But he did not know[m] that an ambush had been set against him behind the city. 15 Joshua and all Israel let themselves be driven back[n] before them, and they fled towards

7:21 v Dt 7:25; Eph 5:5; 1Ti 6:10
7:24 w ver 26; Jos 15:7
7:25 x Jos 6:18; y Dt 17:5
7:26 z Nu 25:4; Dt 13:17; a ver 24; Isa 65:10; Hos 2:15
8:1 a Dt 31:6; b Dt 1:21; Dt 7:18; Jos 1:9; c Jos 10:7; d Jos 6:2
8:2 e ver 27; Dt 20:14
8:7 f Jdg 7:7; 1Sa 23:4
8:8 g Jdg 20:29-38; h ver 19
8:9 i 2Ch 13:13
8:10 j Ge 22:3; k Jos 7:6
8:14 l Dt 1:1; m Jdg 20:34
8:15 n Jdg 20:36

f21 Hebrew *Shinar* g21 That is, about 5 pounds (about 2.3 kilograms) h21 That is, about 1¼ pounds (about 0.6 kilogram) i26 *Achor* means *trouble*.

the desert.[o] 16All the men of Ai
were called to pursue them, and
they pursued Joshua and were
lured away[p] from the city. 17Not a
man remained in Ai or Bethel who
did not go after Israel. They left the
city open and went in pursuit of Israel.
18Then the LORD said to Joshua,
"Hold out towards Ai the javelin[q]
that is in your hand,[r] for into your
hand I will deliver the city." So
Joshua held out his javelin[s] towards Ai. 19As soon as he did this,
the men in the ambush rose
quickly[t] from their position and
rushed forward. They entered the
city and captured it and quickly set
it on fire.[u]
20The men of Ai looked back and
saw the smoke of the city rising
against the sky,[v] but they had no
chance to escape in any direction,
for the Israelites who had been
fleeing towards the desert had
turned back against their pursuers.
21For when Joshua and all Israel
saw that the ambush had taken the
city and that smoke was going up
from the city, they turned round
and attacked the men of Ai. 22The
men of the ambush also came out of
the city against them, so that they
were caught in the middle, with Israelites on both sides. Israel cut
them down, leaving them neither
survivors nor fugitives.[w] 23But
they took the king of Ai alive[x] and
brought him to Joshua.
24When Israel had finished killing all the men of Ai in the fields
and in the desert where they had
chased them, and when every one
of them had been put to the sword,
all the Israelites returned to Ai and
killed those who were in it.
25Twelve thousand men and women
fell that day—all the people of Ai.[y]
26For Joshua did not draw back the
hand that held out his javelin until
he had destroyed[a][z] all who lived
in Ai.[a] 27But Israel did carry off
for themselves the livestock and

8:15
o Jos 15:61
Jos 16:1
Jos 18:12

8:16
p Jdg 20:31

8:18
q Job 41:26
Ps 35:3
r Ex 4:2
Ex 14:16
Ex 17:9-12
s ver 26

8:19
t Jdg 20:33
u ver 8

8:20
v Jdg 20:40

8:22
w Dt 7:2
Jos 10:1

8:23
x 1Sa 15:8

8:25
y Dt 20:16-18

8:26
z Nu 21:2
a Ex 17:12

8:27
b ver 2

8:28
c Nu 31:10
d Jos 7:2
Jer 49:3
e Dt 13:16
Jos 10:1
f Ge 35:20

8:29
g Dt 21:23
Jn 19:31
h 2Sa 18:17

8:30
i Dt 11:29
j Ex 20:24

8:31
k Ex 20:25
l Dt 27:6-7

8:32
m Dt 27:8

8:33
n Lev 16:29
o Dt 31:12
p Dt 11:29
Dt 27:11-14

8:34
q Dt 28:61
Dt 31:11
Jos 1:8

plunder of this city, as the LORD
had instructed Joshua.[b]
28So Joshua burned[c] Ai[d] and
made it a permanent heap of
ruins,[e] a desolate place to this
day.[f] 29He hung the king of Ai on a
tree and left him there until evening. At sunset,[g] Joshua ordered
them to take his body from the tree
and throw it down at the entrance
of the city gate. And they raised a
large pile of rocks[h] over it, which
remains to this day.

The Covenant Renewed at Mount Ebal

30Then Joshua built on Mount
Ebal[i] an altar[j] to the LORD, the
God of Israel, 31as Moses the servant of the LORD had commanded
the Israelites. He built it according
to what is written in the Book of
the Law of Moses—an altar of uncut stones, on which no iron tool[k]
had been used. On it they offered
to the LORD burnt offerings and
sacrificed fellowship offerings.[b][l]
32There, in the presence of the Israelites, Joshua copied on stones
the law of Moses, which he had
written.[m] 33All Israel, aliens and
citizens[n] alike, with their elders,
officials and judges, were standing
on both sides of the ark of the covenant of the LORD, facing those who
carried it—the priests, who were
Levites.[o] Half of the people stood
in front of Mount Gerizim and half
of them in front of Mount Ebal,[p] as
Moses the servant of the LORD had
formerly commanded when he
gave instructions to bless the people of Israel.
34Afterwards, Joshua read all the
words of the law—the blessings
and the curses—just as it is written
in the Book of the Law.[q] 35There
was not a word of all that Moses
had commanded that Joshua did

[a]26 The Hebrew term refers to the irrevocable giving over of things or persons to the LORD, often by totally destroying them.
[b]31 Traditionally *peace offerings*

not read to the whole assembly of Israel, including the women and children, and the aliens who lived among them.[r]

The Gibeonite Deception

9 Now when all the kings west of the Jordan heard about these things—those in the hill country, in the western foothills, and along the entire coast of the Great Sea[a][a] as far as Lebanon (the kings of the Hittites, Amorites, Canaanites, Perizzites, Hivites and Jebusites)[b]— 2 they came together to make war against Joshua and Israel.

3 However, when the people of Gibeon[c] heard what Joshua had done to Jericho and Ai, 4 they resorted to a ruse: They went as a delegation whose donkeys were loaded[b] with worn-out sacks and old wineskins, cracked and mended. 5 The men put worn and patched sandals on their feet and wore old clothes. All the bread of their food supply was dry and mouldy. 6 Then they went to Joshua in the camp at Gilgal[d] and said to him and the men of Israel, "We have come from a distant country; make a treaty with us."

7 The men of Israel said to the Hivites,[e] "But perhaps you live near us. How then can we make a treaty[f] with you?"

8 "We are your servants,[g]" they said to Joshua.

But Joshua asked, "Who are you and where do you come from?"

9 They answered: "Your servants have come from a very distant country[h] because of the fame of the LORD your God. For we have heard reports[i] of him: all that he did in Egypt, 10 and all that he did to the two kings of the Amorites east of the Jordan—Sihon king of Heshbon, and Og king of Bashan,[j] who reigned in Ashtaroth.[k] 11 And our elders and all those living in our country said to us, 'Take provisions for your journey; go and meet them and say to them, "We are your servants; make a treaty with us." ' 12 This bread of ours was warm when we packed it at home on the day we left to come to you. But now see how dry and mouldy it is. 13 And these wineskins that we filled were new, but see how cracked they are. And our clothes and sandals are worn out by the very long journey."

14 The men of Israel sampled their provisions but did not enquire[l] of the LORD. 15 Then Joshua made a treaty of peace[m] with them to let them live, and the leaders of the assembly ratified it by oath.

16 Three days after they made the treaty with the Gibeonites, the Israelites heard that they were neighbours, living near them. 17 So the Israelites set out and on the third day came to their cities: Gibeon, Kephirah, Beeroth[n] and Kiriath Jearim.[o] 18 But the Israelites did not attack them, because the leaders of the assembly had sworn an oath[p] to them by the LORD, the God of Israel.

The whole assembly grumbled[q] against the leaders, 19 but all the leaders answered, "We have given them our oath by the LORD, the God of Israel, and we cannot touch them now. 20 This is what we will do to them: We will let them live, so that wrath will not fall on us for breaking the oath we swore to them." 21 They continued, "Let them live,[r] but let them be woodcutters and water-carriers[s] for the entire community." So the leaders' promise to them was kept.

22 Then Joshua summoned the Gibeonites and said, "Why did you deceive us by saying, 'We live a long way[t] from you,' while actually you live near[u] us? 23 You are now under a curse:[v] You will never cease to serve as woodcutters and

8:35 r Ex 12:38; Dt 31:12
9:1 a Nu 34:6 b Ex 3:17; Jos 3:10
9:3 c ver 17; Jos 10:2; 2Sa 2:12; 2Ch 1:3; Isa 28:21
9:6 d Jos 5:10
9:7 e ver 1; Jos 11:19 f Ex 23:32; Dt 7:2
9:8 g Dt 20:11; 2Ki 10:5
9:9 h Dt 20:15 i ver 24; Jos 2:9
9:10 j Nu 21:33 k Nu 21:24,35
9:14 l Nu 27:21
9:15 m Ex 23:32; Jos 11:19; 2Sa 21:2
9:17 n Jos 18:25 o 1Sa 7:1-2
9:18 p Ps 15:4 q Ex 15:24
9:21 r ver 15 s Dt 29:11
9:22 t ver 6 u ver 16
9:23 v Ge 9:25

a1 That is, the Mediterranean   b4 Most Hebrew manuscripts; some Hebrew manuscripts, Vulgate and Syriac (see also Septuagint) *They prepared provisions and loaded their donkeys*

water-carriers for the house of my God."

24 They answered Joshua, "Your servants were clearly told[w] how the LORD your God had commanded his servant Moses to give you the whole land and to wipe out all its inhabitants from before you. So we feared for our lives because of you, and that is why we did this. 25 We are now in your hands.[x] Do to us whatever seems good and right to you."

26 So Joshua saved them from the Israelites, and they did not kill them. 27 That day he made the Gibeonites woodcutters and water-carriers for the community and for the altar of the LORD at the place the LORD would choose.[y] And that is what they are to this day.

The Sun Stands Still

10 Now Adoni-Zedek king of Jerusalem[a] heard that Joshua had taken Ai[b] and totally destroyed[a][c] it, doing to Ai and its king as he had done to Jericho and its king, and that the people of Gibeon had made a treaty of peace[d] with Israel and were living near them. 2 He and his people were very much alarmed at this, because Gibeon was an important city, like one of the royal cities; it was larger than Ai, and all its men were good fighters. 3 So Adoni-Zedek king of Jerusalem appealed to Hoham king of Hebron,[e] Piram king of Jarmuth, Japhia king of Lachish[f] and Debir king of Eglon. 4 "Come up and help me attack Gibeon," he said, "because it has made peace[g] with Joshua and the Israelites."

5 Then the five kings of the Amorites[h]—the kings of Jerusalem, Hebron, Jarmuth, Lachish and Eglon—joined forces. They moved up with all their troops and took up positions against Gibeon and attacked it.

6 The Gibeonites then sent word to Joshua in the camp at Gilgal: "Do not abandon your servants. Come up to us quickly and save us! Help us, because all the Amorite kings from the hill country have joined forces against us."

7 So Joshua marched up from Gilgal with his entire army,[i] including all the best fighting men. 8 The LORD said to Joshua, "Do not be afraid[j] of them; I have given them into your hand. Not one of them will be able to withstand you."

9 After an all-night march from Gilgal, Joshua took them by surprise. 10 The LORD threw them into confusion before Israel,[k] who defeated them in a great victory at Gibeon. Israel pursued them along the road going up to Beth Horon[l] and cut them down all the way to Azekah[m] and Makkedah. 11 As they fled before Israel on the road down from Beth Horon to Azekah, the LORD hurled large hailstones[n] down on them from the sky, and more of them died from the hailstones than were killed by the swords of the Israelites.

12 On the day the LORD gave the Amorites[o] over to Israel, Joshua said to the LORD in the presence of Israel:

"O sun, stand still over Gibeon,
O moon, over the Valley of
Aijalon.[p]"
13 So the sun stood still,[q]
and the moon stopped,
till the nation avenged itself
on[b] its enemies,

as it is written in the Book of Jashar.[r]

The sun stopped[s] in the middle of the sky and delayed going down about a full day. 14 There has never been a day like it before or since, a day when the LORD listened to a man. Surely the LORD was fighting[t] for Israel!

9:24 w ver 9
9:25 x Ge 16:6
9:27 y Dt 12:5
10:1 a Jdg 1:7; b Jos 8:1; c Dt 20:16; Jos 8:22; d Jos 9:15
10:3 e Ge 13:18; f 2Ch 11:9; 2Ch 25:27; Ne 11:30; Isa 36:2; Isa 37:8; Jer 34:7; Mic 1:13
10:4 g Jos 9:15
10:5 h Nu 13:29
10:7 i Jos 8:1
10:8 j Dt 3:2; Jos 1:9
10:10 k Dt 7:23; l Jos 16:3,5; m Jos 15:35
10:11 n Ps 18:12; Isa 28:2,17
10:12 o Am 2:9; p Jdg 1:35; Jdg 12:12
10:13 q Hab 3:11; r 2Sa 1:18; s Isa 38:8
10:14 t ver 42; Ex 14:14; Dt 1:30; Ps 106:43; Ps 136:24

a *1* The Hebrew term refers to the irrevocable giving over of things or persons to the LORD, often by totally destroying them; also in verses 28, 35, 37, 39 and 40. b *13* Or *nation triumphed over*

15 Then Joshua returned with all Israel to the camp at Gilgal.[u]

Five Amorite Kings Killed

16 Now the five kings had fled and hidden in the cave at Makkedah. 17 When Joshua was told that the five kings had been found hiding in the cave at Makkedah, 18 he said, "Roll large rocks up to the mouth of the cave, and post some men there to guard it. 19 But don't stop! Pursue your enemies, attack them from the rear and don't let them reach their cities, for the LORD your God has given them into your hand."

20 So Joshua and the Israelites destroyed them completely[v]—almost to a man—but the few who were left reached their fortified cities. 21 The whole army then returned safely to Joshua in the camp at Makkedah, and no-one uttered a word against the Israelites.

22 Joshua said, "Open the mouth of the cave and bring those five kings out to me." 23 So they brought the five kings out of the cave—the kings of Jerusalem, Hebron, Jarmuth, Lachish and Eglon. 24 When they had brought these kings to Joshua, he summoned all the men of Israel and said to the army commanders who had come with him, "Come here and put your feet[w] on the necks of these kings." So they came forward and placed their feet[x] on their necks.

25 Joshua said to them, "Do not be afraid; do not be discouraged. Be strong and courageous.[y] This is what the LORD will do to all the enemies you are going to fight." 26 Then Joshua struck and killed the kings and hung them on five trees, and they were left hanging on the trees until evening.

27 At sunset[z] Joshua gave the order and they took them down from the trees and threw them into the cave where they had been hiding. At the mouth of the cave they placed large rocks, which are there to this day.

28 That day Joshua took Makkedah. He put the city and its king to the sword and totally destroyed everyone in it. He left no survivors.[a] And he did to the king of Makkedah as he had done to the king of Jericho.[b]

Southern Cities Conquered

29 Then Joshua and all Israel with him moved on from Makkedah to Libnah and attacked it. 30 The LORD also gave that city and its king into Israel's hand. The city and everyone in it Joshua put to the sword. He left no survivors there. And he did to its king as he had done to the king of Jericho.

31 Then Joshua and all Israel with him moved on from Libnah to Lachish; he took up positions against it and attacked it. 32 The LORD handed Lachish over to Israel, and Joshua took it on the second day. The city and everyone in it he put to the sword, just as he had done to Libnah. 33 Meanwhile, Horam king of Gezer[c] had come up to help Lachish, but Joshua defeated him and his army—until no survivors were left.

34 Then Joshua and all Israel with him moved on from Lachish to Eglon; they took up positions against it and attacked it. 35 They captured it that same day and put it to the sword and totally destroyed everyone in it, just as they had done to Lachish.

36 Then Joshua and all Israel with him went up from Eglon to Hebron[d] and attacked it. 37 They took the city and put it to the sword, together with its king, its villages and everyone in it. They left no survivors. Just as at Eglon, they totally destroyed it and everyone in it.

38 Then Joshua and all Israel with him turned round and attacked Debir.[e] 39 They took the city, its king and its villages, and put them to the

10:15 u ver 43
10:20 v Dt 20:16
10:24 w Mal 4:3 x Ps 110:1
10:25 y Dt 31:6
10:27 z Dt 21:23 Jos 8:9,29
10:28 a Dt 20:16 b Jos 6:21
10:33 c Jos 16:3,10 Jdg 1:29 1Ki 9:15
10:36 d Jos 14:13 Jos 15:13 Jdg 1:10
10:38 e Jos 15:15 Jdg 1:11

sword. Everyone in it they totally destroyed. They left no survivors. They did to Debir and its king as they had done to Libnah and its king and to Hebron.

40 So Joshua subdued the whole region, including the hill country, the Negev,[f] the western foothills and the mountain slopes,[g] together with all their kings.[h] He left no survivors. He totally destroyed all who breathed, just as the LORD, the God of Israel, had commanded.[i] 41 Joshua subdued them from Kadesh Barnea[j] to Gaza[k] and from the whole region of Goshen[l] to Gibeon. 42 All these kings and their lands Joshua conquered in one campaign, because the LORD, the God of Israel, fought[m] for Israel.

43 Then Joshua returned with all Israel to the camp at Gilgal.[n]

Northern Kings Defeated

11 When Jabin[a] king of Hazor[b] heard of this, he sent word to Jobab king of Madon, to the kings of Shimron[c] and Acshaph, 2 and to the northern kings who were in the mountains, in the Arabah[d] south of Kinnereth,[e] in the western foothills and in Naphoth Dor[a][f] on the west; 3 to the Canaanites in the east and west; to the Amorites, Hittites, Perizzites and Jebusites in the hill country; and to the Hivites[g] below Hermon in the region of Mizpah.[h] 4 They came out with all their troops and a large number of horses and chariots—a huge army, as numerous as the sand on the seashore.[i] 5 All these kings joined forces[j] and made camp together at the Waters of Merom, to fight against Israel.

6 The LORD said to Joshua, "Do not be afraid of them, because by this time tomorrow I will hand all of them over[k] to Israel, slain. You are to hamstring[l] their horses and burn their chariots."

7 So Joshua and his whole army came against them suddenly at the Waters of Merom and attacked them, 8 and the LORD gave them into the hand of Israel. They defeated them and pursued them all the way to Greater Sidon, to Misrephoth Maim,[m] and to the Valley of Mizpah on the east, until no survivors were left. 9 Joshua did to them as the LORD had directed: He hamstrung their horses and burned their chariots.

10 At that time Joshua turned back and captured Hazor and put its king to the sword. (Hazor had been the head of all these kingdoms.) 11 Everyone in it they put to the sword. They totally destroyed[b] them, not sparing anything that breathed,[n] and he burned up Hazor itself.

12 Joshua took all these royal cities and their kings and put them to the sword. He totally destroyed them, as Moses the servant of the LORD had commanded.[o] 13 Yet Israel did not burn any of the cities built on their mounds—except Hazor, which Joshua burned. 14 The Israelites carried off for themselves all the plunder and livestock of these cities, but all the people they put to the sword until they completely destroyed them, not sparing anyone that breathed.[p] 15 As the LORD commanded his servant Moses, so Moses commanded Joshua, and Joshua did it; he left nothing undone of all that the LORD commanded Moses.[q]

16 So Joshua took this entire land: the hill country, all the Negev, the whole region of Goshen, the western foothills,[r] the Arabah and the mountains of Israel with their foothills, 17 from Mount Halak, which rises towards Seir, to Baal Gad in the Valley of Lebanon[s] below Mount Hermon. He captured all their kings and struck them down, putting them to death.[t] 18 Joshua

10:40 f Ge 12:9; Jos 12:8 g Dt 1:7 h Dt 7:24 i Dt 20:16-17
10:41 j Ge 14:7 k Ge 10:19 l Jos 11:16; Jos 15:51
10:42 m ver 14
10:43 n ver 15; Jos 5:9
11:1 a Jdg 4:2,7,23 b ver 10; 1Sa 12:9 c Jos 19:15
11:2 d Jos 12:3 e Nu 34:11 f Jos 17:11; Jdg 1:27; 1Ki 4:11
11:3 g Dt 7:1; Jdg 3:3,5; 1Ki 9:20 h Ge 31:49; Jos 15:38; Jos 18:26
11:4 i Jdg 7:12; 1Sa 13:5
11:5 j Jdg 5:19
11:6 k Jos 10:8 l 2Sa 8:4
11:8 m Jos 13:6
11:11 n Dt 20:16-17
11:12 o Nu 33:50-52; Dt 7:2
11:14 p Nu 31:11-12
11:15 q Ex 34:11; Jos 1:7
11:16 r Jos 10:41
11:17 s Jos 12:7 t Dt 7:24

a2 Or *in the heights of Dor* b11 The Hebrew term refers to the irrevocable giving over of things or persons to the LORD, often by totally destroying them; also in verses 12, 20 and 21.

waged war against all these kings
for a long time. 19Except for the Hivites living in Gibeon,[u] not one
city made a treaty of peace with the
Israelites, who took them all in
battle. 20For it was the LORD himself who hardened their hearts[v] to
wage war against Israel, so that he
might destroy them totally, exter-
minating them without mercy, as
the LORD had commanded Moses.[w]
21At that time Joshua went and
destroyed the Anakites[x] from the
hill country: from Hebron, Debir
and Anab, from all the hill country
of Judah, and from all the hill country of Israel. Joshua totally destroyed them and their towns. 22No
Anakites were left in Israelite territory; only in Gaza, Gath[y] and
Ashdod[z] did any survive. 23So
Joshua took the entire land,[a] just
as the LORD had directed Moses,
and he gave it as an inheritance[b] to
Israel according to their tribal divisions.[c]

Then the land had rest from war.[d]

List of Defeated Kings

12 These are the kings of the
land whom the Israelites
had defeated and whose territory
they took over east of the Jordan,
from the Arnon Gorge to Mount
Hermon,[a] including all the eastern
side of the Arabah:

2Sihon king of the Amorites,
who reigned in Heshbon. He
ruled from Aroer on the rim of
the Arnon Gorge—from the
middle of the gorge—to the
Jabbok River, which is the border of the Ammonites. This included half of Gilead.[b] 3He
also ruled over the eastern
Arabah from the Sea of Kinnereth[a][c] to the Sea of the Arabah (the Salt Sea[b]), to Beth
Jeshimoth,[d] and then southward below the slopes of Pisgah.

11:19 u Jos 9:3
11:20 v Ex 14:17; Ro 9:18; w Dt 7:16; Jdg 14:4
11:21 x Nu 13:22,33; Dt 9:2
11:22 y 1Sa 17:4; 1Ki 2:39; 1Ch 8:13; z 1Sa 5:1; Isa 20:1
11:23 a Jos 21:43-45; b Dt 1:38; Dt 12:9-10; Dt 25:19; c Nu 26:53; d Jos 14:15
12:1 a Dt 3:8
12:2 b Dt 2:36
12:3 c Jos 11:2; d Jos 13:20
12:4 e Nu 21:21,33; Dt 3:11; f Dt 1:4
12:5 g Dt 3:10; h 1Sa 27:8; i Dt 3:14
12:6 j Nu 32:29,33; Jos 13:8
12:7 k Jos 11:17
12:8 l Jos 11:16
12:9 m Jos 6:2; n Jos 8:29
12:10 o Jos 10:23
12:12 p Jos 10:33
12:14 q Nu 21:1
12:16 r Jos 7:2

4And the territory of Og king of Bashan,[e]
one of the last of the Rephaites,
who reigned in Ashtaroth[f] and
Edrei. 5He ruled over Mount
Hermon, Salecah,[g] all of Bashan to the border of the people
of Geshur[h] and Maacah,[i] and
half of Gilead to the border of
Sihon king of Heshbon.

6Moses, the servant of the LORD,
and the Israelites conquered them.
And Moses the servant of the LORD
gave their land to the Reubenites,
the Gadites and the half-tribe of
Manasseh to be their possession.[j]
7These are the kings of the land
that Joshua and the Israelites conquered on the west side of the Jordan, from Baal Gad in the Valley of
Lebanon[k] to Mount Halak, which
rises towards Seir (their lands
Joshua gave as an inheritance to
the tribes of Israel according to
their tribal divisions—8the hill
country, the western foothills, the
Arabah, the mountain slopes, the
desert and the Negev[l]—the lands
of the Hittites, Amorites, Canaanites, Perizzites, Hivites and Jebusites):

9the king of Jericho[m] one
the king of Ai[n] (near Bethel) one
10the king of Jerusalem[o] one
the king of Hebron one
11the king of Jarmuth one
the king of Lachish one
12the king of Eglon one
the king of Gezer[p] one
13the king of Debir one
the king of Geder one
14the king of Hormah one
the king of Arad[q] one
15the king of Libnah one
the king of Adullam one
16the king of Makkedah one
the king of Bethel[r] one
17the king of Tappuah one

[a]3 That is, Galilee [b]3 That is, the Dead Sea

the king of Hepher[s] one
18the king of Aphek[t] one
the king of Lasharon one
19the king of Madon one
the king of Hazor one
20the king of Shimron
Meron one
the king of Acshaph[u] one
21the king of Taanach one
the king of Megiddo one
22the king of Kedesh[v] one
the king of Jokneam in
Carmel[w] one
23the king of Dor (in
Naphoth Dor[c][x]) one
the king of Goyim in
Gilgal one
24the king of Tirzah one
thirty-one kings in all.[y]

Land Still to Be Taken

13 When Joshua was old and
well advanced in years,[a]
the LORD said to him, "You are very
old, and there are still very large
areas of land to be taken over.

2"This is the land that remains:
all the regions of the Philistines and Geshurites: 3from
the Shihor River[b] on the east
of Egypt to the territory of Ekron[c] on the north, all of it
counted as Canaanite (the territory of the five Philistine
rulers[d] in Gaza, Ashdod, Ashkelon, Gath and Ekron—that
of the Avvites);[e] 4from the
south, all the land of the Canaanites, from Arah of the Sidonians as far as Aphek,[f] the
region of the Amorites,[g] 5the
area of the Gebalites;[a][h] and
all Lebanon[i] to the east, from
Baal Gad below Mount Her-
mon to Lebo[b] Hamath.

6"As for all the inhabitants of the
mountain regions from Lebanon to
Misrephoth Maim,[j] that is, all the
Sidonians, I myself will drive them
out before the Israelites. Be sure to
allocate this land to Israel for an
inheritance, as I have instructed
you,[k] 7and divide it as an inheritance[l] among the nine tribes and
half of the tribe of Manasseh."

Division of the Land East of the Jordan

8The other half of Manasseh,[c] the
Reubenites and the Gadites had received the inheritance that Moses
had given them east of the Jordan,
as he, the servant of the LORD, had
assigned[m] it to them.

9It extended from Aroer[n] on
the rim of the Arnon Gorge,
and from the town in the middle of the gorge, and included
the whole plateau[o] of Medeba
as far as Dibon,[p] 10and all the
towns of Sihon king of the Amorites, who ruled in Heshbon,
out to the border of the Ammonites.[q] 11It also included Gilead, the territory of the people
of Geshur and Maacah, all of
Mount Hermon and all Bashan
as far as Salecah[r]—12that is,
the whole kingdom of Og in Bashan,[s] who had reigned in
Ashtaroth[t] and Edrei and had
survived as one of the last of
the Rephaites.[u] Moses had defeated them and taken over
their land. 13But the Israelites
did not drive out the people of
Geshur[v] and Maacah,[w] so
they continue to live among the
Israelites to this day.

14But to the tribe of Levi he gave
no inheritance, since the offerings
made by fire to the LORD, the God
of Israel, are their inheritance, as
he promised them.[x]

15This is what Moses had given to
the tribe of Reuben, clan by clan:

12:17 s 1Ki 4:10
12:18 t Jos 13:4
12:20 u Jos 11:1
12:22 v Jos 19:37; Jos 20:7; Jos 21:32; w 1Sa 15:12
12:23 x Jos 11:2
12:24 y Ps 135:11; Dt 7:24
13:1 a Ge 24:1; Jos 14:10
13:3 b Jer 2:18; c Jdg 1:18; d Jdg 3:3; e Dt 2:23
13:4 f Jos 12:18; Jos 19:30; g Am 2:10
13:5 h 1Ki 5:18; Ps 83:7; Eze 27:9; i Jos 12:7
13:6 j Jos 11:8; k Nu 33:54
13:7 l Jos 11:23; Ps 78:55
13:8 m Jos 12:6
13:9 n ver 16; Jdg 11:26; o Jer 48:8,21; p Nu 21:30
13:10 q Nu 21:24
13:11 r Jos 12:5
13:12 s Dt 3:11; t Jos 12:4; u Ge 14:5
13:13 v Jos 12:5; w Dt 3:14
13:14 x ver 33; Dt 18:1-2

c23 Or *in the heights of Dor* a5 That is, the area of Byblos b5 Or *to the entrance to*
c8 Hebrew *With it* (that is, with the other half of Manasseh)

16The territory from Aroer[y]
on the rim of the Arnon Gorge,
and from the town in the middle of the gorge, and the whole
plateau past Medeba[z] 17to
Heshbon and all its towns on
the plateau, including Dibon,[a]
Bamoth Baal, Beth Baal
Meon,[b] 18Jahaz,[c] Kedemoth,
Mephaath,[d] 19Kiriathaim,[e] Sibmah, Zereth Shahar on the
hill in the valley, 20Beth Peor,[f]
the slopes of Pisgah, and Beth
Jeshimoth 21—all the towns on
the plateau and the entire
realm of Sihon king of the Amorites, who ruled at Heshbon.
Moses had defeated him and
the Midianite chiefs,[g] Evi, Rekem, Zur, Hur and Reba[h]—
princes allied with Sihon—who
lived in that country. 22In addition to those slain in battle,
the Israelites had put to the
sword Balaam son of Beor,[i]
who practised divination. 23The
boundary of the Reubenites
was the bank of the Jordan.
These towns and their villages
were the inheritance of the
Reubenites, clan by clan.

24This is what Moses had given to
the tribe of Gad, clan by clan:

25The territory of Jazer,[j] all
the towns of Gilead and half
the Ammonite country as far
as Aroer, near Rabbah; 26and
from Heshbon[k] to Ramath
Mizpah and Betonim, and from
Mahanaim to the territory of
Debir;[l] 27and in the valley,
Beth Haram, Beth Nimrah,
Succoth[m] and Zaphon with the
rest of the realm of Sihon king
of Heshbon (the east side of the
Jordan, the territory up to the
end of the Sea of Kinne-
reth[d][n]). 28These towns and
their villages were the inheritance of the Gadites,[o] clan by
clan.

29This is what Moses had given to
the half-tribe of Manasseh, that is,
to half the family of the descendants of Manasseh, clan by clan:

30The territory extending from
Mahanaim[p] and including all
of Bashan, the entire realm of
Og king of Bashan—all the settlements of Jair[q] in Bashan,
sixty towns, 31half of Gilead,
and Ashtaroth and Edrei (the
royal cities of Og in Bashan).
This was for the descendants
of Makir[r] son of Manasseh—
for half of the sons of Makir,
clan by clan.

32This is the inheritance Moses
had given when he was in the plains
of Moab across the Jordan east of
Jericho. 33But to the tribe of Levi,
Moses had given no inheritance;
the LORD, the God of Israel, is their
inheritance,[s] as he promised
them.[t]

Division of the Land West of the Jordan

14 Now these are the areas the
Israelites received as an inheritance in the land of Canaan,
which Eleazar the priest, Joshua
son of Nun and the heads of the
tribal clans of Israel allotted to
them.[a] 2Their inheritances were
assigned by lot[b] to the nine-and-a-
half tribes, as the LORD had commanded through Moses. 3Moses
had granted the two-and-a-half
tribes their inheritance east of the
Jordan[c] but had not granted the
Levites an inheritance among the
rest,[d] 4for the sons of Joseph had
become two tribes—Manasseh and
Ephraim.[e] The Levites received
no share of the land but only towns
to live in, with pasture-lands for
their flocks and herds. 5So the Israelites divided the land, just as the
LORD had commanded Moses.[f]

[d]27 That is, Galilee

13:16 y ver 9; Jos 12:2; z Nu 21:30
13:17 a Nu 32:3; b 1Ch 5:8
13:18 c Nu 21:23; d Jer 48:21
13:19 e Nu 32:37
13:20 f Dt 3:29
13:21 g Nu 25:15; h Nu 31:8
13:22 i Nu 22:5; Nu 31:8
13:25 j Nu 21:32; Jos 21:39
13:26 k Nu 21:25; Jer 49:3; l Jos 10:3
13:27 m Ge 33:17; n Nu 34:11
13:28 o Nu 32:33
13:30 p Ge 32:2; q Nu 32:41
13:31 r Ge 50:23
13:33 s Nu 18:20; t ver 14; Jos 18:7
14:1 a Nu 34:17-18
14:2 b Nu 26:55
14:3 c Nu 32:33; d Jos 13:14
14:4 e Ge 41:52; Ge 48:5
14:5 f Nu 34:13; Nu 35:2; Jos 21:2

Hebron Given to Caleb

6Now the men of Judah approached Joshua at Gilgal, and Caleb son of Jephunneh[g] the Kenizzite said to him, "You know what the LORD said to Moses the man of God at Kadesh Barnea[h] about you and me. 7I was forty years old when Moses the servant of the LORD sent me from Kadesh Barnea to explore the land.[i] And I brought him back a report according to my convictions,[j] 8but my brothers who went up with me made the hearts of the people sink.[a][k] I, however, followed the LORD my God wholeheartedly.[l] 9So on that day Moses swore to me, 'The land on which your feet have walked will be your inheritance and that of your children[m] for ever, because you have followed the LORD my God wholeheartedly.'[b]

10"Now then, just as the LORD promised,[n] he has kept me alive for forty-five years since the time he said this to Moses, while Israel moved about in the desert. So here I am today, eighty-five years old! 11I am still as strong[o] today as the day Moses sent me out; I'm just as vigorous to go out to battle now as I was then. 12Now give me this hill country that the LORD promised me that day. You yourself heard then that the Anakites[p] were there and their cities were large and fortified,[q] but, the LORD helping me, I will drive them out just as he said."

13Then Joshua blessed[r] Caleb son of Jephunneh and gave him Hebron[s] as his inheritance.[t] 14So Hebron has belonged to Caleb son of Jephunneh the Kenizzite ever since, because he followed the LORD, the God of Israel, wholeheartedly. 15(Hebron used to be called Kiriath Arba[u] after Arba,[v] who was the greatest man among the Anakites.)

Then the land had rest[w] from war.

14:6 g Nu 13:6; Nu 14:30; h Nu 13:26
14:7 i Nu 13:17; j Nu 13:30; Nu 14:6-9
14:8 k Nu 13:31; l Nu 14:24
14:9 m Nu 14:24; Dt 1:36
14:10 n Nu 14:30
14:11 o Dt 34:7
14:12 p Nu 13:33; q Nu 13:28
14:13 r Jos 22:6,7; s Jos 10:36; t Jdg 1:20; 1Ch 6:56
14:15 u Ge 23:2; v Jos 15:13; w Jos 11:23
15:1 a Nu 34:3; b Nu 33:36
15:3 c Nu 34:4
15:4 d Nu 34:5; e Ge 15:18
15:5 f Nu 34:10; g Jos 18:15-19
15:6 h Jos 18:19,21; i Jos 18:17
15:7 j Jos 7:24; k 2Sa 17:17; 1Ki 1:9
15:8 l ver 63; Jos 18:16,28; Jdg 1:21; Jdg 19:10
15:9 m Jos 18:15; n 1Ch 13:6

Allotment for Judah

15:15–19pp Jdg 1:11–15

15 The allotment for the tribe of Judah, clan by clan, extended down to the territory of Edom,[a] to the Desert of Zin[b] in the extreme south.

2Their southern boundary started from the bay at the southern end of the Salt Sea,[a] 3crossed south of Scorpion[b] Pass,[c] continued on to Zin and went over to the south of Kadesh Barnea. Then it ran past Hezron up to Addar and curved around to Karka. 4It then passed along to Azmon[d] and joined the Wadi of Egypt,[e] ending at the sea. This is their[c] southern boundary.

5The eastern boundary[f] is the Salt Sea as far as the mouth of the Jordan.

The northern boundary[g] started from the bay of the sea at the mouth of the Jordan, 6went up to Beth Hoglah[h] and continued north of Beth Arabah to the Stone of Bohan[i] son of Reuben. 7The boundary then went up to Debir from the Valley of Achor[j] and turned north to Gilgal, which faces the Pass of Adummim south of the gorge. It continued along to the waters of En Shemesh and came out at En Rogel.[k] 8Then it ran up the Valley of Ben Hinnom along the southern slope of the Jebusite[l] city (that is, Jerusalem). From there it climbed to the top of the hill west of the Hinnom Valley at the northern end of the Valley of Rephaim. 9From the hilltop the boundary headed towards the spring of the waters of Nephtoah,[m] came out at the towns of Mount Ephron and went down towards Baalah[n]

[a]8 Hebrew *melt* [b]9 Deut. 1:36 [a]2 That is, the Dead Sea; also in verse 5 [b]3 Hebrew *Akrabbim* [c]4 Hebrew *your*

(that is, Kiriath Jearim).
[10]Then it curved westward
from Baalah to Mount Seir, ran
along the northern slope of
Mount Jearim (that is, Kesa-
lon), continued down to Beth
Shemesh and crossed to Timnah.[o] [11]It went to the northern
slope of Ekron, turned towards
Shikkeron, passed along to
Mount Baalah and reached
Jabneel.[p] The boundary ended
at the sea.

[12]The western boundary is
the coastline of the Great
Sea.[d][q]
These are the boundaries around
the people of Judah by their clans.

[13]In accordance with the LORD's
command to him, Joshua gave to
Caleb son of Jephunneh a portion in
Judah—Kiriath Arba, that is, Hebron. (Arba was the forefather of
Anak.)[r] [14]From Hebron Caleb
drove out the three Anakites[s]—
Sheshai, Ahiman and Talmai[t]—
descendants of Anak.[u] [15]From
there he marched against the people living in Debir (formerly called
Kiriath Sepher). [16]And Caleb said,
"I will give my daughter Acsah[v] in
marriage to the man who attacks
and captures Kiriath Sepher."
[17]Othniel[w] son of Kenaz, Caleb's
brother, took it; so Caleb gave his
daughter Acsah to him in marriage.
[18]One day when she came to Othniel, she urged him[e] to ask her
father for a field. When she got off
her donkey, Caleb asked her,
"What can I do for you?"

[19]She replied, "Do me a special
favour. Since you have given me
land in the Negev, give me also
springs of water." So Caleb gave
her the upper and lower springs.

[20]This is the inheritance of the
tribe of Judah, clan by clan:

[21]The southernmost towns of the
tribe of Judah in the Negev towards the boundary of Edom were:
Kabzeel, Eder,[x] Jagur,
[22]Kinah, Dimonah, Adadah,
[23]Kedesh, Hazor, Ithnan,
[24]Ziph,[y] Telem, Bealoth, [25]Ha-
zor Hadattah, Kerioth Hez-
ron (that is, Hazor), [26]Amam,
Shema, Moladah,[z] [27]Hazar
Gaddah, Heshmon, Beth Pelet,
[28]Hazar Shual, Beersheba,[a]
Biziothiah, [29]Baalah,[b] Iim,
Ezem, [30]Eltolad,[c] Kesil, Hormah, [31]Ziklag,[d] Madmannah,
Sansannah, [32]Lebaoth, Shilhim,
Ain and Rimmon[e]—a total of
twenty-nine towns and their
villages.

[33]In the western foothills:
Eshtaol,[f] Zorah, Ashnah,
[34]Zanoah,[g] En Gannim, Tappuah, Enam, [35]Jarmuth,[h]
Adullam,[i] Socoh, Azekah,
[36]Shaaraim, Adithaim and Gederah[j] (or Gederothaim)[f]—
fourteen towns and their
villages.

[37]Zenan, Hadashah, Migdal
Gad, [38]Dilean, Mizpah, Joktheel,[k] [39]Lachish,[l] Bozkath,[m]
Eglon, [40]Cabbon, Lahmas, Kit-
lish, [41]Gederoth, Beth Dagon,
Naamah and Makkedah[n]—sixteen towns and their villages.

[42]Libnah, Ether, Ashan,[o]
[43]Iphtah, Ashnah, Nezib, [44]Kei-
lah, Aczib[p] and Mareshah[q]—
nine towns and their villages.

[45]Ekron, with its surrounding settlements and villages;
[46]west of Ekron, all that were in
the vicinity of Ashdod, together with their villages;
[47]Ashdod,[r] its surrounding
settlements and villages; and
Gaza, its settlements and villages, as far as the Wadi of
Egypt[s] and the coastline of the
Great Sea.[t]

[48]In the hill country:
Shamir, Jattir,[u] Socoh,

15:10 o Ge 38:12; Jdg 14:1
15:11 p Jos 19:33
15:12 q Nu 34:6
15:13 r Jos 14:13-15
15:14 s Nu 13:33; t Nu 13:22; u Jdg 1:10,20
15:16 v Jdg 1:12
15:17 w Jdg 3:9,11
15:21 x Ge 35:21
15:24 y 1Sa 23:14
15:26 z 1Ch 4:28
15:28 a Ge 21:31
15:29 b ver 9
15:30 c Jos 19:4
15:31 d 1Sa 27:6
15:32 e Jdg 20:45
15:33 f Jdg 13:25; Jdg 16:31
15:34 g 1Ch 4:18; Ne 3:13
15:35 h Jos 10:3; i 1Sa 22:1
15:36 j 1Ch 12:4
15:38 k 2Ki 14:7
15:39 l Jos 10:3; 2Ki 14:19; m 2Ki 22:1
15:41 n Jos 10:10
15:42 o 1Sa 30:30
15:44 p Jdg 1:31; q Mic 1:15
15:47 r Jos 11:22; s ver 4; t Nu 34:6
15:48 u 1Sa 30:27

[d]12 That is, the Mediterranean; also in verse 47
[e]18 Hebrew and some Septuagint manuscripts; other Septuagint manuscripts (see also note at Judges 1:14) *Othniel, he urged her*
[f]36 Or *Gederah and Gederothaim*

49Dannah, Kiriath Sannah (that
is, Debir[v]), 50Anab, Eshte-
moh,[w] Anim, 51Goshen,[x] Holon and Giloh – eleven towns
and their villages.
52Arab, Dumah,[y] Eshan,
53Janim, Beth Tappuah, Aphe-
kah, 54Humtah, Kiriath Arba
(that is, Hebron) and Zior –
nine towns and their villages.
55Maon, Carmel,[z] Ziph, Juttah, 56Jezreel,[a] Jokdeam, Zanoah, 57Kain, Gibeah[b] and
Timnah – ten towns and their
villages.
58Halhul, Beth Zur,[c] Gedor,
59Maarath, Beth Anoth and El-
tekon – six towns and their villages.
60Kiriath Baal (that is, Kiriath Jearim[d]) and Rabbah[e] –
two towns and their villages.

61In the desert:
Beth Arabah, Middin, Seca-
cah, 62Nibshan, the City of Salt
and En Gedi[f] – six towns and
their villages.
63Judah could not[g] dislodge the
Jebusites[h], who were living in
Jerusalem; to this day the Jebusites live there with the people of
Judah.

Allotment for Ephraim and Manasseh

16 The allotment for Jo-
seph began at the Jor-
dan of Jericho,[a] east of the
waters of Jericho, and went up
from there through the
desert[a] into the hill country of
Bethel. 2It went on from Bethel
(that is, Luz[b]),[b] crossed over
to the territory of the Arkites
in Ataroth, 3descended westward to the territory of the
Japhletites as far as the region
of Lower Beth Horon[c] and on
to Gezer,[d] ending at the sea.
4So Manasseh and Ephraim, the descendants of Joseph, received their
inheritance.[e]

5This was the territory of Ephraim,
clan by clan:
The boundary of their in-
heritance went from Ataroth
Addar[f] in the east to Upper
Beth Horon 6and continued to
the sea. From Micmethath[g] on
the north it curved eastward to
Taanath Shiloh, passing by it to
Janoah on the east. 7Then it
went down from Janoah to Ataroth[h] and Naarah, touched
Jericho and came out at the
Jordan. 8From Tappuah the
border went west to the Kanah
Ravine[i] and ended at the sea.
This was the inheritance of the
tribe of the Ephraimites, clan
by clan. 9It also included all the
towns and their villages that
were set aside for the Ephraimites within the inheritance
of the Manassites.
10They did not dislodge the Canaanites living in Gezer; to this day the
Canaanites live among the people
of Ephraim but are required to do
forced labour.[j]

17 This was the allotment for
the tribe of Manasseh as
Joseph's firstborn,[a] that is, for
Makir,[b] Manasseh's firstborn.
Makir was the ancestor of the Gileadites, who had received Gilead
and Bashan because the Makirites
were great soldiers. 2So this allotment was for the rest of the people
of Manasseh – the clans of Abiezer,[c] Helek, Asriel, Shechem, Hepher and Shemida. These are the
other male descendants of Manasseh son of Joseph by their clans.
3Now Zelophehad son of He-
pher,[d] the son of Gilead, the son of
Makir, the son of Manasseh, had no
sons but only daughters,[e] whose
names were Mahlah, Noah, Hoglah,
Milcah and Tirzah. 4They went to
Eleazar the priest, Joshua son of
Nun, and the leaders and said, "The

15:49 v Jos 10:3
15:50 w Jos 21:14
15:51 x Jos 10:41; Jos 11:16
15:52 y Ge 25:14
15:55 z Jos 12:22
15:56 a Jos 17:16
15:57 b Jos 18:28; Jdg 19:12
15:58 c 1Ch 2:45
15:60 d Jos 18:14 e Dt 3:11
15:62 f 1Sa 23:29
15:63 g Jdg 1:21 h 2Sa 5:6
16:1 a Jos 8:15; Jos 18:12
16:2 b Jos 18:13
16:3 c 2Ch 8:5 d Jos 10:33; 1Ki 9:15
16:4 e Jos 17:14
16:5 f Jos 18:13
16:6 g Jos 17:7
16:7 h 1Ch 7:28
16:8 i Jos 17:9
16:10 j Jos 17:13; Jdg 1:28-29; 1Ki 9:16
17:1 a Ge 41:51 b Ge 50:23
17:2 c Nu 26:30; 1Ch 7:18
17:3 d Nu 27:1 e Nu 26:33

a1 *Jordan of Jericho* was possibly an ancient name for the Jordan River. b2 Septuagint; Hebrew *Bethel to Luz*

LORD commanded Moses to give
us an inheritance among our
brothers." So Joshua gave them an
inheritance along with the brothers
of their father, according to the
LORD's command.[f] 5Manasseh's
share consisted of ten tracts of land
besides Gilead and Bashan east of
the Jordan, 6because the daughters
of the tribe of Manasseh received
an inheritance among the sons. The
land of Gilead belonged to the rest
of the descendants of Manasseh.

7The territory of Manasseh
extended from Asher to Micmethath[g] east of Shechem.[h]
The boundary ran southward
from there to include the people living at En Tappuah. 8(Manasseh had the land of
Tappuah, but Tappuah[i] itself,
on the boundary of Manasseh,
belonged to the Ephraimites.)
9Then the boundary continued
south to the Kanah Ravine.[j]
There were towns belonging to
Ephraim lying among the towns
of Manasseh, but the boundary of Manasseh was the
northern side of the ravine and
ended at the sea. 10On the south
the land belonged to Ephraim,
on the north to Manasseh. The
territory of Manasseh reached
the sea and bordered Asher on
the north and Issachar[k] on the
east.

11Within Issachar and Asher,
Manasseh also had Beth
Shan,[l] Ibleam and the people
of Dor,[m] Endor,[n] Taanach and
Megiddo,[o] together with their
surrounding settlements (the
third in the list is Naphoth[a]).
12Yet the Manassites were not
able[p] to occupy these towns, for
the Canaanites were determined to
live in that region. 13However,
when the Israelites grew stronger,
they subjected the Canaanites to
forced labour but did not drive
them out completely.[q]

14The people of Joseph said to
Joshua, "Why have you given us
only one allotment and one portion
for an inheritance? We are a numerous people and the LORD has
blessed us abundantly."[r]

15"If you are so numerous,"
Joshua answered, "and if the hill
country of Ephraim is too small for
you, go up into the forest and clear
land for yourselves there in the
land of the Perizzites and Rephaites.[s]"

16The people of Joseph replied,
"The hill country is not enough for
us, and all the Canaanites who live
in the plain have iron chariots,[t]
both those in Beth Shan and its settlements and those in the Valley of
Jezreel."

17But Joshua said to the house of
Joseph—to Ephraim and Manasseh—"You are numerous and very
powerful. You will have not only
one allotment 18but the forested hill
country as well. Clear it, and its
farthest limits will be yours;
though the Canaanites have iron
chariots[u] and though they are
strong, you can drive them out."

Division of the Rest of the Land

18 The whole assembly of the
Israelites gathered at Shiloh[a] and set up the Tent of Meeting[b] there. The country was
brought under their control, 2but
there were still seven Israelite
tribes who had not yet received
their inheritance.

3So Joshua said to the Israelites:
"How long will you wait before you
begin to take possession of the land
that the LORD, the God of your fathers, has given you? 4Appoint
three men from each tribe. I will
send them out to make a survey of
the land and to write a description
of it, according to the inheritance
of each.[c] Then they will return to
me. 5You are to divide the land into
seven parts. Judah is to remain in
its territory on the south[d] and the

[a] 11 That is, Naphoth Dor

17:4 *f* Nu 27:5-7
17:7 *g* Jos 16:6 *h* Ge 12:6; Jos 21:21
17:8 *i* Jos 16:8
17:9 *j* Jos 16:8
17:10 *k* Ge 30:18
17:11 *l* 1Sa 31:10; 1Ki 4:12; 1Ch 7:29 *m* Jos 11:2 *n* 1Sa 28:7; Ps 83:10 *o* 1Ki 9:15
17:12 *p* Jdg 1:27
17:13 *q* Jos 16:10
17:14 *r* Nu 26:28-37
17:15 *s* Ge 14:5
17:16 *t* Jdg 1:19; Jdg 4:3,13
17:18 *u* ver 16
18:1 *a* Jos 19:51; Jos 21:2; Jdg 18:31; Jdg 21:12,19; 1Sa 1:3; 1Sa 4:3; Jer 7:12; Jer 26:6 *b* Ex 27:21
18:4 *c* Mic 2:5
18:5 *d* Jos 15:1

house of Joseph in its territory on
the north.[e] 6After you have written descriptions of the seven parts
of the land, bring them here to me
and I will cast lots[f] for you in the
presence of the LORD our God. 7The
Levites, however, do not get a portion among you, because the
priestly service of the LORD is their
inheritance.[g] And Gad, Reuben
and the half-tribe of Manasseh
have already received their inheritance on the east side of the
Jordan. Moses the servant of the
LORD gave it to them.[h]"
8As the men started on their way
to map out the land, Joshua instructed them, "Go and make a survey of the land and write a
description of it. Then return to
me, and I will cast lots for you here
at Shiloh[i] in the presence of the
LORD." 9So the men left and went
through the land. They wrote its description on a scroll, town by town,
in seven parts, and returned to
Joshua in the camp at Shiloh.
10Joshua then cast lots[j] for them in
Shiloh in the presence[k] of the
LORD, and there he distributed the
land to the Israelites according to
their tribal divisions.[l]

Allotment for Benjamin

11The lot came up for the tribe of
Benjamin, clan by clan. Their allotted territory lay between the tribes
of Judah and Joseph:
12On the north side their
boundary began at the Jordan,
passed the northern slope of
Jericho and headed west into
the hill country, coming out at
the desert[m] of Beth Aven.[n]
13From there it crossed to the
south slope of Luz[o] (that is,
Bethel[p]) and went down to Ataroth Addar[q] on the hill south
of Lower Beth Horon.
14From the hill facing Beth
Horon[r] on the south the
boundary turned south along
the western side and came out
at Kiriath Baal (that is, Kiriath
Jearim), a town of the people of
Judah. This was the western
side.
15The southern side began at
the outskirts of Kiriath Jearim
on the west, and the boundary
came out at the spring of the
waters of Nephtoah.[s] 16The
boundary went down to the
foot of the hill facing the Valley of Ben Hinnom, north of the
Valley of Rephaim. It continued down the Hinnom Valley[t] along the southern slope
of the Jebusite city and so to En
Rogel.[u] 17It then curved north,
went to En Shemesh, continued
to Geliloth, which faces the
Pass of Adummim, and ran
down to the Stone of Bohan[v]
son of Reuben. 18It continued to
the northern slope of Beth Arabah[a][w] and on down into the
Arabah. 19It then went to the
northern slope of Beth Hoglah
and came out at the northern
bay of the Salt Sea,[b][x] at the
mouth of the Jordan in the
south. This was the southern
boundary.
20The Jordan formed the
boundary on the eastern side.
These were the boundaries that
marked out the inheritance of the
clans of Benjamin on all sides.[y]

21The tribe of Benjamin, clan by
clan, had the following cities:
Jericho, Beth Hoglah, Emek
Keziz, 22Beth Arabah, Zemaraim, Bethel,[z] 23Avvim, Parah,
Ophrah, 24Kephar Ammoni,
Ophni and Geba[a]—twelve
towns and their villages.
25Gibeon,[b] Ramah,[c] Beeroth,[d] 26Mizpah,[e] Kephirah,
Mozah, 27Rekem, Irpeel, Tara-
lah, 28Zelah,[f] Haeleph, the
Jebusite city[g] (that is, Jerusalem[h]), Gibeah[i] and Kir-

18:5 *e* Jos 16:1-4
18:6 *f* Jos 14:2
18:7 *g* Jos 13:33 *h* Jos 13:8
18:8 *i* ver 1
18:10 *j* Nu 34:13 *k* ver 1 Jer 7:12 *l* Nu 33:54 Jos 19:51
18:12 *m* Jos 16:1 *n* Jos 7:2
18:13 *o* Ge 28:19 *p* Jdg 1:23 *q* Jos 16:5
18:14 *r* Jos 10:10
18:15 *s* Jos 15:9
18:16 *t* Jos 15:8 2Ki 23:10 *u* Jos 15:7
18:17 *v* Jos 15:6
18:18 *w* Jos 15:6
18:19 *x* Ge 14:3
18:20 *y* Jos 21:4,17 1Sa 9:1
18:22 *z* Jos 16:1
18:24 *a* Isa 10:29
18:25 *b* Jos 9:3 *c* Jdg 4:5 *d* Jos 9:17
18:26 *e* Jos 11:3
18:28 *f* 2Sa 21:14 *g* Jos 15:8 *h* Jos 10:1 *i* Jos 15:57

[a]18 Septuagint; Hebrew *slope facing the Arabah*
[b]19 That is, the Dead Sea

iath—fourteen towns and their
villages.
This was the inheritance of Benjamin for its clans.

Allotment for Simeon

19:2–10pp 1Ch 4:28–33

19 The second lot came out for
the tribe of Simeon, clan by
clan. Their inheritance lay within
the territory of Judah.[a] 2It included:
Beersheba[b] (or Sheba),[a]
Moladah, 3Hazar Shual, Balah,
Ezem, 4Eltolad, Bethul, Hormah, 5Ziklag, Beth Marcaboth,
Hazar Susah, 6Beth Lebaoth
and Sharuhen—thirteen towns
and their villages;
7Ain, Rimmon, Ether and
Ashan[c]—four towns and their
villages—8and all the villages
around these towns as far as
Baalath Beer (Ramah in the
Negev).[d]
This was the inheritance of the
tribe of the Simeonites, clan by
clan. 9The inheritance of the Simeonites was taken from the share of
Judah,[e] because Judah's portion
was more than they needed. So the
Simeonites received their inheritance within the territory of Judah.[f]

Allotment for Zebulun

10The third lot came up for Zebulun,[g] clan by clan:
The boundary of their in-
heritance went as far as Sarid.
11Going west it ran to Maralah,
touched Dabbesheth, and extended to the ravine near Jokneam.[h] 12It turned east from
Sarid towards the sunrise to
the territory of Kisloth Tabor
and went on to Daberath and up
to Japhia. 13Then it continued
eastward to Gath Hepher and
Eth Kazin; it came out at Rimmon[i] and turned towards
Neah. 14There the boundary
went round on the north to
Hannathon and ended at the
Valley of Iphtah El. 15Included
were Kattath, Nahalal, Shimron, Idalah and Bethlehem.[j]
There were twelve towns and
their villages.
16These towns and their villages
were the inheritance of Zebulun,[k]
clan by clan.[l]

Allotment for Issachar

17The fourth lot came out for Issa-
char,[m] clan by clan. 18Their terri-
tory included:
Jezreel,[n] Kesulloth, Shu-
nem,[o] 19Hapharaim, Shion,
Anaharath, 20Rabbith, Kishion,
Ebez, 21Remeth, En Gannim,
En Haddah and Beth Pazzez.
22The boundary touched
Tabor,[p] Shahazumah and Beth
Shemesh,[q] and ended at the
Jordan. There were sixteen
towns and their villages.
23These towns and their villages
were the inheritance of the tribe of
Issachar,[r] clan by clan.[s]

Allotment for Asher

24The fifth lot came out for the
tribe of Asher,[t] clan by clan.
25Their territory included:
Helkath, Hali, Beten, Ac-
shaph, 26Allammelech, Amad
and Mishal. On the west the
boundary touched Carmel[u]
and Shihor Libnath. 27It then
turned east towards Beth Dagon, touched Zebulun[v] and the
Valley of Iphtah El, and went
north to Beth Emek and Neiel,
passing Cabul[w] on the left. 28It
went to Abdon,[b] Rehob,[x]
Hammon[y] and Kanah, as far
as Greater Sidon.[z] 29The
boundary then turned back towards Ramah[a] and went to the
fortified city of Tyre,[b] turned
towards Hosah and came out at

19:1 *a* ver 9; Ge 49:7
19:2 *b* Ge 21:14; 1Ki 19:3
19:7 *c* Jos 15:42
19:8 *d* Jos 10:40
19:9 *e* Ge 49:7 *f* Eze 48:24
19:10 *g* Jos 21:7,34
19:11 *h* Jos 12:22
19:13 *i* Jos 15:32
19:15 *j* Ge 35:19
19:16 *k* ver 10; Jos 21:7 *l* Eze 48:26
19:17 *m* Ge 30:18
19:18 *n* Jos 15:56 *o* 1Sa 28:4; 2Ki 4:8
19:22 *p* Jdg 4:6,12; Ps 89:12 *q* Jos 15:10
19:23 *r* Jos 17:10 *s* Ge 49:15; Eze 48:25
19:24 *t* Jos 17:7
19:26 *u* Jos 12:22
19:27 *v* ver 10 *w* 1Ki 9:13
19:28 *x* Jdg 1:31 *y* 1Ch 6:76 *z* Ge 10:19; Jos 11:8
19:29 *a* Jos 18:25 *b* 2Sa 5:11; 2Sa 24:7; Isa 23:1; Jer 25:22; Eze 26:2

[a]2 Or *Beersheba, Sheba*; 1 Chron. 4:28 does not have *Sheba*. [b]28 Some Hebrew manuscripts (see also Joshua 21:30); most Hebrew manuscripts *Ebron*

the sea in the region of Aczib,[c]
30Ummah, Aphek and Rehob.
There were twenty-two towns
and their villages.
31These towns and their villages
were the inheritance of the tribe of
Asher,[d] clan by clan.

Allotment for Naphtali

32The sixth lot came out for Naphtali, clan by clan:
33Their boundary went from
Heleph and the large tree in
Zaanannim, passing Adami
Nekeb and Jabneel to Lakkum
and ending at the Jordan. 34The
boundary ran west through Az-
noth Tabor and came out at
Hukkok. It touched Zebulun on
the south, Asher on the west
and the Jordan[c] on the east.
35The fortified cities were Zid-
dim, Zer, Hammath, Rakkath,
Kinnereth,[e] 36Adamah, Ramah,[f] Hazor,[g] 37Kedesh, Edrei,[h] En Hazor, 38Iron, Migdal
El, Horem, Beth Anath and
Beth Shemesh. There were
nineteen towns and their villages.
39These towns and their villages
were the inheritance of the tribe of
Naphtali, clan by clan.[i]

Allotment for Dan

40The seventh lot came out for the
tribe of Dan, clan by clan. 41The
territory of their inheritance included:
Zorah, Eshtaol, Ir Shemesh,
42Shaalabbin, Aijalon,[j] Ithlah,
43Elon, Timnah,[k] Ekron, 44El-
tekeh, Gibbethon, Baalath,
45Jehud, Bene Berak, Gath
Rimmon,[l] 46Me Jarkon and
Rakkon, with the area facing
Joppa.[m]
47(But the Danites had difficulty
taking possession of their territory,[n] so they went up and attacked Leshem[o], took it, put it to
the sword and occupied it. They
settled in Leshem and named it Dan
after their forefather.)[p]
48These towns and their villages
were the inheritance of the tribe of
Dan,[q] clan by clan.

Allotment for Joshua

49When they had finished dividing the land into its allotted portions, the Israelites gave Joshua
son of Nun an inheritance among
them, 50as the LORD had commanded. They gave him the town
he asked for—Timnath Serah[d][r] in
the hill country of Ephraim. And he
built up the town and settled there.
51These are the territories that
Eleazar the priest, Joshua son of
Nun and the heads of the tribal
clans of Israel assigned by lot at
Shiloh in the presence of the LORD
at the entrance to the Tent of Meeting. And so they finished dividing
the land.[s]

Cities of Refuge

20:1–9Ref Nu 35:9–34; Dt 4:41–43; 19:1–14

20 Then the LORD said to
Joshua: 2"Tell the Israelites to designate the cities of refuge, as I instructed you through
Moses, 3so that anyone who kills a
person accidentally and unintentionally[a] may flee there and find
protection from the avenger of
blood.[b]
4"When he flees to one of these
cities, he is to stand in the entrance
of the city gate[c] and state his case
before the elders[d] of that city.
Then they are to admit him into
their city and give him a place to
live with them. 5If the avenger of
blood pursues him, they must not
surrender the one accused, because he killed his neighbour unintentionally and without malice
aforethought. 6He is to stay in that
city until he has stood trial before

19:29 c Jdg 1:31
19:31 d Ge 30:13; Eze 48:2
19:35 e Jos 11:2
19:36 f Jos 18:25; g Jos 11:1
19:37 h Nu 21:33
19:39 i Dt 33:23; Eze 48:3
19:42 j Jdg 1:35
19:43 k Ge 38:12
19:45 l Jos 21:24; 1Ch 6:69
19:46 m 2Ch 2:16; Jnh 1:3
19:47 n Jdg 18:1; o Jdg 18:7,14; p Jdg 18:27,29
19:48 q Ge 30:6
19:50 r Jos 24:30
19:51 s Jos 14:1; Jos 18:10; Ac 13:19
20:3 a Lev 4:2; b Nu 35:12
20:4 c Ru 4:1; Jer 38:7; d Jos 7:6

[c]34 Septuagint; Hebrew *west, and Judah, the Jordan,* [d]50 Also known as *Timnath Heres* (see Judges 2:9)

the assembly[e] and until the death
of the high priest who is serving at
that time. Then he may go back to
his own home in the town from
which he fled."
7So they set apart Kedesh[f] in
Galilee in the hill country of Naphtali, Shechem[g] in the hill country
of Ephraim, and Kiriath Arba (that
is, Hebron[h]) in the hill country of
Judah.[i] 8On the east side of the
Jordan of Jericho[a] they designated Bezer[j] in the desert on the
plateau in the tribe of Reuben, Ramoth in Gilead[k] in the tribe of Gad,
and Golan in Bashan in the tribe of
Manasseh. 9Any of the Israelites or
any alien living among them who
killed someone accidentally could
flee to these designated cities and
not be killed by the avenger of
blood prior to standing trial before
the assembly.[l]

Towns for the Levites

21:4-39pp 1Ch 6:54-80

21 Now the family heads of
the Levites approached
Eleazar the priest, Joshua son of
Nun, and the heads of the other
tribal families of Israel[a] 2at Shiloh[b] in Canaan and said to them,
"The LORD commanded through
Moses that you give us towns to
live in, with pasture-lands for our
livestock."[c] 3So, as the LORD had
commanded, the Israelites gave
the Levites the following towns and
pasture-lands out of their own inheritance:
4The first lot came out for the Kohathites, clan by clan. The Levites
who were descendants of Aaron the
priest were allotted thirteen towns
from the tribes of Judah, Simeon
and Benjamin.[d] 5The rest of Kohath's descendants were allotted
ten towns from the clans of the
tribes of Ephraim, Dan and half of
Manasseh.[e]
6The descendants of Gershon
were allotted thirteen towns from
the clans of the tribes of Issachar,[f]

20:6 *e* Nu 35:12
20:7 *f* Jos 21:32; 1Ch 6:76 *g* Ge 12:6 *h* Jos 10:36; Jos 21:11 *i* Lk 1:39
20:8 *j* Jos 21:36; 1Ch 6:78 *k* Jos 12:2
20:9 *l* Ex 21:13; Nu 35:15
21:1 *a* Jos 14:1
21:2 *b* Jos 18:1 *c* Nu 35:2-3
21:4 *d* ver 19
21:5 *e* ver 26
21:6 *f* Ge 30:18
21:7 *g* Ex 6:16 *h* Jos 19:10
21:11 *i* Jos 15:13; 1Ch 6:55
21:13 *j* Jos 15:42; 1Ch 6:57
21:14 *k* Jos 15:48 *l* Jos 15:50
21:15 *m* Jos 15:51
21:16 *n* Jos 15:55 *o* Jos 15:10
21:17 *p* Jos 18:24
21:21 *q* Jos 17:7; Jos 20:7

Asher, Naphtali and the half-tribe
of Manasseh in Bashan.
7The descendants of Merari,[g]
clan by clan, received twelve towns
from the tribes of Reuben, Gad and
Zebulun.[h]
8So the Israelites allotted to the
Levites these towns and their
pasture-lands, as the LORD had
commanded through Moses.

9From the tribes of Judah and Simeon they allotted the following
towns by name 10(these towns were
assigned to the descendants of
Aaron who were from the Kohathite clans of the Levites, because
the first lot fell to them):
11They gave them Kiriath
Arba (that is, Hebron[i]), with
its surrounding pasture-land,
in the hill country of Judah.
(Arba was the forefather of
Anak.) 12But the fields and villages around the city they had
given to Caleb son of Jephunneh as his possession.
13So to the descendants of
Aaron the priest they gave
Hebron (a city of refuge for
one accused of murder), Libnah,[j] 14Jattir,[k] Eshtemoa,[l]
15Holon,[m] Debir, 16Ain, Juttah[n]
and Beth Shemesh,[o] together
with their pasture-lands—nine
towns from these two tribes.
17And from the tribe of Benjamin they gave them Gibeon,
Geba,[p] 18Anathoth and Almon,
together with their pasture-
lands—four towns.
19All the towns for the priests, the
descendants of Aaron, were thirteen, together with their pasture-
lands.

20The rest of the Kohathite clans of
the Levites were allotted towns
from the tribe of Ephraim:
21In the hill country of Ephraim they were given She-
chem[q] (a city of refuge for one

[a]8 *Jordan of Jericho* was possibly an ancient name for the Jordan River.

accused of murder) and Gezer,
22Kibzaim and Beth Horon,[r]
together with their pasture-
lands—four towns.[s]
23Also from the tribe of Dan
they received Eltekeh, Gibbethon, 24Aijalon and Gath Rimmon,[t] together with their
pasture-lands—four towns.
25From half the tribe of Manasseh they received Taanach
and Gath Rimmon, together
with their pasture-lands—two
towns.
26All these ten towns and their
pasture-lands were given to the
rest of the Kohathite clans.

27The Levite clans of the Gershonites were given:
from the half-tribe of Manasseh,
Golan in Bashan[u] (a city of
refuge for one accused of murder[v]) and Be Eshtarah, together with their pasture-
lands—two towns;
28from the tribe of Issachar,[w]
Kishion, Daberath, 29Jarmuth
and En Gannim, together
with their pasture-lands—four
towns;
30from the tribe of Asher,[x]
Mishal, Abdon, 31Helkath and
Rehob, together with their pasture-lands—four towns;
32from the tribe of Naphtali,
Kedesh[y] in Galilee (a city of
refuge for one accused of
murder[z]), Hammoth Dor and
Kartan, together with their
pasture-lands—three towns.
33All the towns of the Gershonite[a]
clans were thirteen, together with
their pasture-lands.

34The Merarite clans (the rest of
the Levites) were given:
from the tribe of Zebulun,[b]
Jokneam, Kartah, 35Dimnah
and Nahalal, together with
their pasture-lands—four towns;
36from the tribe of Reuben,
Bezer,[c] Jahaz, 37Kedemoth
and Mephaath, together with
their pasture-lands—four towns;
38from the tribe of Gad,
Ramoth[d] in Gilead (a city of
refuge for one accused of murder), Mahanaim,[e] 39Heshbon
and Jazer, together with their
pasture-lands—four towns in
all.
40All the towns allotted to the Merarite clans, who were the rest of the
Levites, were twelve.
41The towns of the Levites in the
territory held by the Israelites
were forty-eight in all, together
with their pasture-lands.[f] 42Each
of these towns had pasture-lands
surrounding it; this was true for all
these towns.

43So the LORD gave Israel all the
land he had sworn to give their
forefathers,[g] and they took possession[h] of it and settled there.[i]
44The LORD gave them rest[j] on
every side, just as he had sworn to
their forefathers. Not one of their
enemies[k] withstood them; the
LORD handed all their enemies[l]
over to them.[m] 45Not one of all the
LORD's good promises[n] to the
house of Israel failed; every one
was fulfilled.

Eastern Tribes Return Home

22 Then Joshua summoned
the Reubenites, the Gad-
ites and the half-tribe of Manasseh
2and said to them, "You have done
all that Moses the servant of the
LORD commanded,[a] and you have
obeyed me in everything I commanded. 3For a long time now—to
this very day—you have not deserted your brothers but have carried out the mission the LORD your
God gave you. 4Now that the LORD
your God has given your brothers
rest as he promised, return to your
homes[b] in the land that Moses the
servant of the LORD gave you on the
other side of the Jordan.[c] 5But be
very careful to keep the commandment[d] and the law that Moses the

21:22 r Jos 10:10 s 1Sa 1:1
21:24 t Jos 19:45
21:27 u Jos 12:5 v Nu 35:6
21:28 w Ge 30:18
21:30 x Jos 17:7
21:32 y Jos 12:22 z Nu 35:6 Jos 20:7
21:33 a ver 6
21:34 b Jos 19:10 1Ch 6:77
21:36 c Jos 20:8
21:38 d Dt 4:43 e Ge 32:2
21:41 f Nu 35:7
21:43 g Dt 34:4 h Dt 11:31 i Dt 17:14
21:44 j Ex 33:14 Jos 1:13 k Dt 6:19 l Ex 23:31 m Dt 7:24 Dt 21:10
21:45 n Jos 23:14 Ne 9:8
22:2 a Nu 32:25
22:4 b Nu 32:22 Dt 3:20 c Nu 32:18 Jos 1:13-15
22:5 d Isa 43:22

servant of the LORD gave you: to love the LORD your God, to walk in all his ways, to obey his commands,[e] to hold fast to him and to serve him with all your heart and all your soul.[f]"

6 Then Joshua blessed[g] them and sent them away, and they went to their homes. 7 (To the half-tribe of Manasseh Moses had given land in Bashan,[h] and to the other half of the tribe Joshua gave land on the west side[i] of the Jordan with their brothers.) When Joshua sent them home, he blessed them, 8 saying, "Return to your homes with your great wealth—with large herds of livestock,[j] with silver, gold, bronze and iron, and a great quantity of clothing—and divide[k] with your brothers the plunder[l] from your enemies."

9 So the Reubenites, the Gadites and the half-tribe of Manasseh left the Israelites at Shiloh in Canaan to return to Gilead,[m] their own land, which they had acquired in accordance with the command of the LORD through Moses.

10 When they came to Geliloth near the Jordan in the land of Canaan, the Reubenites, the Gadites and the half-tribe of Manasseh built an imposing altar there by the Jordan. 11 And when the Israelites heard that they had built the altar on the border of Canaan at Geliloth near the Jordan on the Israelite side, 12 the whole assembly of Israel gathered at Shiloh[n] to go to war against them.

13 So the Israelites sent Phinehas[o] son of Eleazar,[p] the priest, to the land of Gilead—to Reuben, Gad and the half-tribe of Manasseh. 14 With him they sent ten of the chief men, one for each of the tribes of Israel, each the head of a family division among the Israelite clans.[q]

15 When they went to Gilead—to Reuben, Gad and the half-tribe of Manasseh—they said to them: 16 "The whole assembly of the LORD says: 'How could you break faith[r] with the God of Israel like this? How could you turn away from the LORD and build yourselves an altar in rebellion[s] against him now? 17 Was not the sin of Peor[t] enough for us? Up to this very day we have not cleansed ourselves from that sin, even though a plague fell on the community of the LORD! 18 And are you now turning away from the LORD?

" 'If you rebel against the LORD today, tomorrow he will be angry with the whole community[u] of Israel. 19 If the land you possess is defiled, come over to the LORD's land, where the LORD's tabernacle stands, and share the land with us. But do not rebel against the LORD or against us by building an altar for yourselves, other than the altar of the LORD our God. 20 When Achan son of Zerah acted unfaithfully regarding the devoted things,[a][v] did not wrath[w] come upon the whole community of Israel? He was not the only one who died for his sin.' "[x]

21 Then Reuben, Gad and the half-tribe of Manasseh replied to the heads of the clans of Israel: 22 "The Mighty One, God, the LORD! The Mighty One, God,[y] the LORD![z] He knows![a] And let Israel know! If this has been in rebellion or disobedience to the LORD, do not spare us this day. 23 If we have built our own altar to turn away from the LORD and to offer burnt offerings and grain offerings,[b] or to sacrifice fellowship offerings[b] on it, may the LORD himself call us to account.[c]

24 "No! We did it for fear that some day your descendants might say to ours, 'What do you have to do with the LORD, the God of Israel? 25 The LORD has made the Jordan a boundary between us and

22:5 e Dt 5:29 f Dt 6:6,17
22:6 g Ex 39:43
22:7 h Nu 32:33 Jos 12:5 i Jos 17:2,5
22:8 j Dt 20:14 k Nu 31:27 l Ge 49:27 1Sa 30:16 Isa 9:3
22:9 m Nu 32:26,29
22:12 n Jos 18:1
22:13 o Nu 25:7 p Nu 3:32 Jos 24:33
22:14 q Nu 1:4
22:16 r Dt 13:14 s Dt 12:13-14
22:17 t Nu 25:1-9
22:18 u Lev 10:6 Nu 16:22
22:20 v Jos 7:1 w Ps 7:11 x Jos 7:5
22:22 y Dt 10:17 z Ps 50:1 a 1Ki 8:39 Job 10:7 Ps 44:21 Jer 17:10
22:23 b Jer 41:5 c Dt 12:11 Dt 18:19 1Sa 20:16

a20 The Hebrew term refers to the irrevocable giving over of things or persons to the LORD, often by totally destroying them.
b23 Traditionally *peace offerings*; also in verse 27

you—you Reubenites and Gadites! You have no share in the LORD.' So your descendants might cause ours to stop fearing the LORD.

26"That is why we said, 'Let us get ready and build an altar—but not for burnt offerings or sacrifices.' 27On the contrary, it is to be a witness[d] between us and you and the generations that follow, that we will worship the LORD at his sanctuary with our burnt offerings, sacrifices and fellowship offerings.[e] Then in the future your descendants will not be able to say to ours, 'You have no share in the LORD.'

28"And we said, 'If they ever say this to us, or to our descendants, we will answer: Look at the replica of the LORD's altar, which our fathers built, not for burnt offerings and sacrifices, but as a witness between us and you.'

29"Far be it from us to rebel[f] against the LORD and turn away from him today by building an altar for burnt offerings, grain offerings and sacrifices, other than the altar of the LORD our God that stands before his tabernacle.[g]"

30When Phinehas the priest and the leaders of the community—the heads of the clans of the Israelites—heard what Reuben, Gad and Manasseh had to say, they were pleased. 31And Phinehas son of Eleazar, the priest, said to Reuben, Gad and Manasseh, "Today we know that the LORD is with us,[h] because you have not acted unfaithfully towards the LORD in this matter. Now you have rescued the Israelites from the LORD's hand."

32Then Phinehas son of Eleazar, the priest, and the leaders returned to Canaan from their meeting with the Reubenites and Gadites in Gilead and reported to the Israelites. 33They were glad to hear the report and praised God.[i] And they talked no more about going to war against them to devastate the country where the Reubenites and the Gadites lived.

22:27
d Ge 21:30; Jos 24:27
e Dt 12:6

22:29
f Jos 24:16
g Dt 12:13-14

22:31
h Lev 26:11-12; 2Ch 15:2

22:33
i 1Ch 29:20; Da 2:19; Lk 2:28

22:34
j Ge 21:30

23:1
a Dt 12:9; Jos 21:44
b Jos 13:1

23:2
c Jos 7:6
d Jos 24:1

23:3
e Ex 14:14

23:4
f Jos 19:51
g Nu 34:6

23:5
h Ex 23:30; Nu 33:53

23:6
i Dt 5:32; Jos 1:7

23:7
j Ex 23:13; Ps 16:4; Jer 5:7
k Ex 20:5

23:8
l Dt 10:20

23:9
m Dt 11:23
n Dt 7:24

23:10
o Lev 26:8
p Ex 14:14; Dt 3:22

34And the Reubenites and the Gadites gave the altar this name: A Witness[j] Between Us that the LORD is God.

Joshua's Farewell to the Leaders

23 After a long time had passed and the LORD had given Israel rest[a] from all their enemies around them, Joshua, by then old and well advanced in years,[b] 2summoned all Israel—their elders,[c] leaders, judges and officials[d]—and said to them: "I am old and well advanced in years. 3You yourselves have seen everything the LORD your God has done to all these nations for your sake; it was the LORD your God who fought for you.[e] 4Remember how I have allotted[f] as an inheritance for your tribes all the land of the nations that remain—the nations I conquered—between the Jordan and the Great Sea[a][g] in the west. 5The LORD your God himself will drive them out of your way. He will push them out before you, and you will take possession of their land, as the LORD your God promised you.[h]

6"Be very strong; be careful to obey all that is written in the Book of the Law of Moses, without turning aside to the right or to the left.[i] 7Do not associate with these nations that remain among you; do not invoke the names of their gods or swear[j] by them. You must not serve them or bow down[k] to them. 8But you are to hold fast to the LORD[l] your God, as you have until now.

9"The LORD has driven out before you great and powerful nations;[m] to this day no-one has been able to withstand you.[n] 10One of you routs a thousand,[o] because the LORD your God fights for you,[p] just as he

a4 That is, the Mediterranean

promised. 11 So be very careful to love the LORD[q] your God.

12 "But if you turn away and ally yourselves with the survivors of these nations that remain among you and if you intermarry with them[r] and associate with them,[s] 13 then you may be sure that the LORD your God will no longer drive out these nations before you. Instead, they will become snares[t] and traps for you, whips on your backs and thorns in your eyes,[u] until you perish from this good land, which the LORD your God has given you.

14 "Now I am about to go the way of all the earth.[v] You know with all your heart and soul that not one of all the good promises the LORD your God gave you has failed. Every promise has been fulfilled; not one has failed.[w] 15 But just as every good promise of the LORD your God has come true, so the LORD will bring on you all the evil he has threatened, until he has destroyed you from this good land he has given you.[x] 16 If you violate the covenant of the LORD your God, which he commanded you, and go and serve other gods and bow down to them, the LORD's anger will burn against you, and you will quickly perish from the good land he has given you.[y]"

The Covenant Renewed at Shechem

24 Then Joshua assembled all the tribes of Israel at Shechem. He summoned the elders, leaders, judges and officials of Israel,[a] and they presented themselves before God.

2 Joshua said to all the people, "This is what the LORD, the God of Israel, says: 'Long ago your forefathers, including Terah the father of Abraham and Nahor, lived beyond the River[a] and worshipped other gods.[b] 3 But I took your father Abraham from the land beyond the River and led him throughout Canaan[c] and gave him many descendants.[d] I gave him Isaac,[e] 4 and to Isaac I gave Jacob and Esau.[f] I assigned the hill country of Seir[g] to Esau, but Jacob and his sons went down to Egypt.[h]

5 " 'Then I sent Moses and Aaron,[i] and I afflicted the Egyptians by what I did there, and I brought you out. 6 When I brought your fathers out of Egypt, you came to the sea, and the Egyptians pursued them with chariots and horsemen[b][j] as far as the Red Sea.[c] 7 But they cried to the LORD for help, and he put darkness[k] between you and the Egyptians; he brought the sea over them and covered them.[l] You saw with your own eyes what I did to the Egyptians. Then you lived in the desert for a long time.[m]

8 " 'I brought you to the land of the Amorites who lived east of the Jordan. They fought against you, but I gave them into your hands. I destroyed them from before you, and you took possession of their land.[n] 9 When Balak son of Zippor,[o] the king of Moab, prepared to fight against Israel, he sent for Balaam son of Beor to put a curse on you.[p] 10 But I would not listen to Balaam, so he blessed you[q] again and again, and I delivered you out of his hand.

11 " 'Then you crossed the Jordan[r] and came to Jericho.[s] The citizens of Jericho fought against you, as did also the Amorites, Perizzites, Canaanites, Hittites, Girgashites, Hivites and Jebusites, but I gave them into your hands.[t] 12 I sent the hornet[u] ahead of you, which drove them out before you—also the two Amorite kings. You did not do it with your own sword and bow. 13 So I gave you a land on which you did not toil and cities you did not build; and you live in them

23:11 q Jos 22:5
23:12 r Dt 7:3; s Ex 34:16; Ps 106:34-35
23:13 t Ex 23:33; u Nu 33:55
23:14 v 1Ki 2:2; w Jos 21:45
23:15 x Lev 26:17; Dt 28:15
23:16 y Dt 4:25-26
24:1 a Jos 23:2
24:2 b Ge 11:32
24:3 c Ge 12:1; d Ge 15:5; e Ge 21:3
24:4 f Ge 25:26; g Dt 2:5; h Ge 46:5-6
24:5 i Ex 3:10
24:6 j Ex 14:9
24:7 k Ex 14:20; l Ex 14:28; m Dt 1:46
24:8 n Nu 21:31
24:9 o Nu 22:2; p Nu 22:6
24:10 q Nu 23:11; Dt 23:5
24:11 r Jos 3:16-17; s Jos 6:1; t Ex 23:23; Dt 7:1
24:12 u Ex 23:28; Dt 7:20; Ps 44:3,6-7

[a]2 That is, the Euphrates; also in verses 3, 14 and 15 [b]6 Or *charioteers* [c]6 Hebrew *Yam Suph*; that is, Sea of Reeds

and eat from vineyards and olive groves that you did not plant.’[v]

14 “Now fear the LORD and serve him with all faithfulness.[w] Throw away the gods[x] your forefathers worshipped beyond the River and in Egypt,[y] and serve the LORD. 15 But if serving the LORD seems undesirable to you, then choose for yourselves this day whom you will serve, whether the gods your forefathers served beyond the River, or the gods of the Amorites,[z] in whose land you are living. But as for me and my household, we will serve the LORD.”[a]

16 Then the people answered, “Far be it from us to forsake the LORD to serve other gods! 17 It was the LORD our God himself who brought us and our fathers up out of Egypt, from that land of slavery, and performed those great signs before our eyes. He protected us on our entire journey and among all the nations through which we travelled. 18 And the LORD drove out before us all the nations, including the Amorites, who lived in the land. We too will serve the LORD, because he is our God.”

19 Joshua said to the people, “You are not able to serve the LORD. He is a holy God;[b] he is a jealous God.[c] He will not forgive your rebellion[d] and your sins. 20 If you forsake the LORD[e] and serve foreign gods, he will turn[f] and bring disaster on you and make an end of you,[g] after he has been good to you.”

21 But the people said to Joshua, “No! We will serve the LORD.”

22 Then Joshua said, “You are witnesses against yourselves that you have chosen[h] to serve the LORD.”

“Yes, we are witnesses,” they replied.

23 “Now then,” said Joshua, “throw away the foreign gods[i] that are among you and yield your hearts[j] to the LORD, the God of Israel.”

24 And the people said to Joshua, “We will serve the LORD our God and obey him.”[k]

25 On that day Joshua made a covenant[l] for the people, and there at Shechem he drew up for them decrees and laws.[m] 26 And Joshua recorded these things in the Book of the Law of God.[n] Then he took a large stone[o] and set it up there under the oak near the holy place of the LORD.

27 “See!” he said to all the people. “This stone will be a witness[p] against us. It has heard all the words the LORD has said to us. It will be a witness against you if you are untrue to your God.”

Buried in the Promised Land

24:29–31pp Jdg 2:6–9

28 Then Joshua sent the people away, each to his own inheritance.

29 After these things, Joshua son of Nun, the servant of the LORD, died at the age of a hundred and ten.[q] 30 And they buried him in the land of his inheritance, at Timnath Serah[d][r] in the hill country of Ephraim, north of Mount Gaash.

31 Israel served the LORD throughout the lifetime of Joshua and of the elders[s] who outlived him and who had experienced everything the LORD had done for Israel.

32 And Joseph's bones, which the Israelites had brought up from Egypt,[t] were buried at Shechem in the tract of land[u] that Jacob bought for a hundred pieces of silver[e] from the sons of Hamor, the father of Shechem. This became the inheritance of Joseph's descendants.

33 And Eleazar son of Aaron[v] died and was buried at Gibeah, which had been allotted to his son Phinehas[w] in the hill country of Ephraim.

24:13 v Dt 6:10-11
24:14 w Dt 10:12; Dt 18:13; 1Sa 12:24; 2Co 1:12; x ver 23; y Eze 23:3
24:15 z Jdg 6:10; Ru 1:15; a Ru 1:16; 1Ki 18:21
24:19 b Lev 19:2; Lev 20:26; c Ex 20:5; d Ex 23:21
24:20 e 1Ch 28:9,20; f Ac 7:42; g Jos 23:15
24:22 h Ps 119:30,173
24:23 i ver 14; j 1Ki 8:58; Ps 119:36; Ps 141:4
24:24 k Ex 19:8; Ex 24:3,7; Dt 5:27
24:25 l Ex 24:8; m Ex 15:25
24:26 n Dt 31:24; o Ge 28:18
24:27 p Jos 22:27
24:29 q Jdg 2:8
24:30 r Jos 19:50
24:31 s Jdg 2:7
24:32 t Ge 50:25; Ex 13:19; u Ge 33:19; Jn 4:5; Ac 7:16
24:33 v Jos 22:13; w Ex 6:25

d *30* Also known as *Timnath Heres* (see Judges 2:9) e *32* Hebrew *hundred kesitahs*; a kesitah was a unit of money of unknown weight and value.

JUDGES

Israel Fights the Remaining Canaanites

1:11–15pp Jos 15:15–19

1 After the death[a] of Joshua,
the Israelites asked the LORD,
"Who will be the first[b] to go up and
fight for us against the Canaanites?[c]"
2The LORD answered, "Judah[d] is
to go; I have given the land into
their hands.[e]"
3Then the men of Judah said to
the Simeonites their brothers,
"Come up with us into the territory
allotted to us, to fight against the
Canaanites. We in turn will go with
you into yours." So the Simeonites[f] went with them.
4When Judah attacked, the LORD
gave the Canaanites and Perizzites[g] into their hands and they
struck down ten thousand men at
Bezek.[h] 5It was there that they
found Adoni-Bezek and fought
against him, putting to rout the Canaanites and Perizzites. 6Adoni-
Bezek fled, but they chased him
and caught him, and cut off his
thumbs and big toes.
7Then Adoni-Bezek said, "Seventy kings with their thumbs and
big toes cut off have picked up
scraps under my table. Now God
has paid me back[i] for what I did to
them." They brought him to Jerusalem, and he died there.
8The men of Judah attacked
Jerusalem[j] also and took it. They
put the city to the sword and set it
on fire.
9After that, the men of Judah
went down to fight against the Canaanites living in the hill country,[k]
the Negev[l] and the western foothills. 10They advanced against the
Canaanites living in Hebron[m] (formerly called Kiriath Arba[n]) and
defeated Sheshai, Ahiman and Talmai.[o]
11From there they advanced
against the people living in Debir[p]
(formerly called Kiriath Sepher).
12And Caleb said, "I will give my
daughter Acsah in marriage to the
man who attacks and captures Kiriath Sepher." 13Othniel son of Kenaz, Caleb's younger brother, took
it; so Caleb gave his daughter Acsah to him in marriage.
14One day when she came to Othniel, she urged him[a] to ask her
father for a field. When she got off
her donkey, Caleb asked her,
"What can I do for you?"
15She replied, "Do me a special
favour. Since you have given me
land in the Negev, give me also
springs of water." Then Caleb gave
her the upper and lower springs.
16The descendants of Moses'
father-in-law,[q] the Kenite,[r] went
up from the City of Palms[b][s] with
the men of Judah to live among the
people of the Desert of Judah in the
Negev near Arad.[t]
17Then the men of Judah went
with the Simeonites[u] their
brothers and attacked the Canaanites living in Zephath, and they
totally destroyed[c] the city.
Therefore it was called Hormah.[d][v] 18The men of Judah also
took[e] Gaza,[w] Ashkelon and Ekron—each city with its territory.
19The LORD was with[x] the men of
Judah. They took possession of the
hill country, but they were unable
to drive the people from the plains,

1:1 a Jos 24:29 b Nu 27:21 c ver 27 Jdg 3:1-6
1:2 d Ge 49:8 e ver 4 Jdg 3:28
1:3 f ver 17
1:4 g Ge 13:7 Jos 3:10 h 1Sa 11:8
1:7 i Lev 24:19
1:8 j ver 21 Jos 15:63
1:9 k Nu 13:17 l Nu 21:1
1:10 m Ge 13:18 n Ge 35:27 o Jos 15:14
1:11 p Jos 15:15
1:16 q Nu 10:29 r Ge 15:19 Jdg 4:11 s Dt 34:3 Jdg 3:13 t Nu 21:1
1:17 u ver 3 v Nu 21:3
1:18 w Jos 11:22
1:19 x ver 2

a14 Hebrew; Septuagint and Vulgate *Othniel, he urged her* b16 That is, Jericho
c17 The Hebrew term refers to the irrevocable giving over of things or persons to the LORD, often by totally destroying them. d17 *Hormah* means *destruction.* e18 Hebrew; Septuagint *Judah did not take*

because they had iron chariots.[y]
20As Moses had promised, Hebron[z] was given to Caleb, who
drove from it the three sons of
Anak.[a] 21The Benjamites, however, failed[b] to dislodge the Jebusites, who were living in
Jerusalem;[c] to this day the Jebusites live there with the Benjamites.
22Now the house of Joseph attacked Bethel, and the LORD was
with them. 23When they sent men to
spy out Bethel (formerly called
Luz),[d] 24the spies saw a man coming out of the city and they said to
him, "Show us how to get into the
city and we will see that you are
treated well.[e]" 25So he showed
them, and they put the city to the
sword but spared[f] the man and his
whole family. 26He then went to the
land of the Hittites, where he built
a city and called it Luz, which is its
name to this day.
27But Manasseh did not drive out
the people of Beth Shan or Taanach
or Dor or Ibleam[g] or Megiddo and
their surrounding settlements, for
the Canaanites[h] were determined
to live in that land. 28When Israel
became strong, they pressed the
Canaanites into forced labour but
never drove them out completely.
29Nor did Ephraim drive out the Canaanites living in Gezer,[i] but the
Canaanites continued to live there
among them.[j] 30Neither did Zebulun drive out the Canaanites living
in Kitron or Nahalol, who remained
among them; but they did subject
them to forced labour. 31Nor did
Asher drive out those living in
Acco or Sidon or Ahlab or Aczib[k]
or Helbah or Aphek or Rehob, 32and
because of this the people of Asher
lived among the Canaanite inhabitants of the land. 33Neither did
Naphtali drive out those living in
Beth Shemesh or Beth Anath[l]; but
the Naphtalites too lived among the
Canaanite inhabitants of the land,
and those living in Beth Shemesh
and Beth Anath became forced

1:19 y Jos 17:16
1:20 z Jos 14:9; Jos 15:13-14; a ver 10; Jos 14:13
1:21 b Jos 15:63; c ver 8
1:23 d Ge 28:19
1:24 e Jos 2:12,14
1:25 f Jos 6:25
1:27 g Jos 17:11; h ver 1
1:29 i 1Ki 9:16; j Jos 16:10
1:31 k Jdg 10:6
1:33 l Jos 19:38
1:34 m Ex 3:17
1:35 n Jos 19:42
1:36 o Jos 15:3
2:1 a Jdg 6:11; b ver 5; c Ex 20:2; d Ge 17:8; e Lev 26:42-44; Dt 7:9
2:2 f Ex 23:32; Ex 34:12; Dt 7:2; g Ex 34:13
2:3 h Jos 23:13; i Nu 33:55; j Dt 7:16; Jdg 3:6; Ps 106:36

labourers for them. 34The Amorites[m] confined the Danites to the
hill country, not allowing them to
come down into the plain. 35And the
Amorites were determined also
to hold out in Mount Heres, Aijalon[n] and Shaalbim, but when the
power of the house of Joseph increased, they too were pressed into
forced labour. 36The boundary
of the Amorites was from Scorpion[f] Pass[o] to Sela and beyond.

The Angel of the LORD at Bokim

2 The angel of the LORD[a] went
up from Gilgal to Bokim[b] and
said, "I brought you up out of
Egypt[c] and led you into the land
that I swore to give to your forefathers.[d] I said, 'I will never break
my covenant with you,[e] 2and you
shall not make a covenant with the
people of this land,[f] but you shall
break down their altars.[g]' Yet you
have disobeyed me. Why have you
done this? 3Now therefore I tell
you that I will not drive them out before you;[h] they will be ⌞thorns⌟[i] in
your sides and their gods will be a
snare[j] to you."
4When the angel of the LORD had
spoken these things to all the Israelites, the people wept aloud,
5and they called that place Bokim.[a] There they offered sacrifices to the LORD.

Disobedience and Defeat

2:6–9pp Jos 24:29–31

6After Joshua had dismissed the
Israelites, they went to take possession of the land, each to his own
inheritance. 7The people served
the LORD throughout the lifetime of
Joshua and of the elders who outlived him and who had seen all the
great things the LORD had done for
Israel.
8Joshua son of Nun, the servant
of the LORD, died at the age of a

[f]36 Hebrew *Akrabbim* [a]5 *Bokim* means *weepers.*

hundred and ten. 9 And they buried him in the land of his inheritance, at Timnath Heres[b][k] in the hill country of Ephraim, north of Mount Gaash.

10 After that whole generation had been gathered to their fathers, another generation grew up, who knew neither the LORD nor what he had done for Israel.[l] 11 Then the Israelites did evil in the eyes of the LORD[m] and served the Baals.[n] 12 They forsook the LORD, the God of their fathers, who had brought them out of Egypt. They followed and worshipped various gods[o] of the peoples around them.[p] They provoked the LORD to anger 13 because they forsook him and served Baal and the Ashtoreths.[q] 14 In his anger[r] against Israel the LORD handed them over[s] to raiders who plundered them. He sold them[t] to their enemies all around, whom they were no longer able to resist.[u] 15 Whenever Israel went out to fight, the hand of the LORD was against them to defeat them, just as he had sworn to them. They were in great distress.

16 Then the LORD raised up judges,[c][v] who saved[w] them out of the hands of these raiders. 17 Yet they would not listen to their judges but prostituted[x] themselves to other gods and worshipped them. Unlike their fathers, they quickly turned from the way in which their fathers had walked, the way of obedience to the LORD's commands.[y] 18 Whenever the LORD raised up a judge for them, he was with the judge and saved them out of the hands of their enemies as long as the judge lived; for the LORD had compassion[z] on them as they groaned[a] under those who oppressed and afflicted them. 19 But when the judge died, the people returned to ways even more corrupt[b] than those of their fathers, following other gods and serving and worshipping them.[c] They refused to give up their evil practices and stubborn ways.

20 Therefore the LORD was very angry[d] with Israel and said, "Because this nation has violated the covenant that I laid down for their forefathers and has not listened to me, 21 I will no longer drive out[e] before them any of the nations Joshua left when he died. 22 I will use them to test[f] Israel and see whether they will keep the way of the LORD and walk in it as their forefathers did." 23 The LORD had allowed those nations to remain; he did not drive them out at once by giving them into the hands of Joshua.

3 These are the nations the LORD left to test[a] all those Israelites who had not experienced any of the wars in Canaan 2 (he did this only to teach warfare to the descendants of the Israelites who had not had previous battle experience): 3 the five[b] rulers of the Philistines, all the Canaanites, the Sidonians, and the Hivites living in the Lebanon mountains from Mount Baal Hermon to Lebo[a] Hamath. 4 They were left to test[c] the Israelites to see whether they would obey the LORD's commands, which he had given their forefathers through Moses.

5 The Israelites lived[d] among the Canaanites, Hittites, Amorites, Perizzites, Hivites and Jebusites. 6 They took their daughters in marriage and gave their own daughters to their sons, and served their gods.[e]

Othniel

7 The Israelites did evil in the eyes of the LORD; they forgot the LORD[f] their God and served the Baals and the Asherahs.[g] 8 The anger of the LORD burned against

2:9 k Jos 19:50
2:10 l Ex 5:2; 1Sa 2:12; 1Ch 28:9; Gal 4:8
2:11 m Jdg 3:12; Jdg 4:1; Jdg 6:1; Jdg 10:6; n Jdg 3:7; Jdg 8:33
2:12 o Ps 106:36; p Dt 31:16; Jdg 10:6
2:13 q Jdg 10:6
2:14 r Dt 31:17; s Ps 106:41; t Dt 32:30; Jdg 3:8; u Dt 28:25
2:16 v Ac 13:20; w Ps 106:43
2:17 x Ex 34:15; y ver 7
2:18 z Dt 32:36; Jos 1:5; a Ps 106:44
2:19 b Jdg 3:12; c Jdg 4:1; Jdg 8:33
2:20 d ver 14; Jos 23:16
2:21 e Jos 23:13
2:22 f Dt 8:2,16; Jdg 3:1,14
3:1 a Jdg 2:21-22
3:3 b Jos 13:3
3:4 c Dt 8:2; Jdg 2:22
3:5 d Ps 106:35
3:6 e Ex 34:16; Dt 7:3-4
3:7 f Dt 4:9; g Ex 34:13; Jdg 2:11,13

b9 Also known as *Timnath Serah* (see Joshua 19:50 and 24:30) c16 Or *leaders*; similarly in verses 17–19 a3 Or *to the entrance to*

Israel so that he sold[h] them into
the hands of Cushan-Rishathaim
king of Aram Naharaim,[b] to whom
the Israelites were subject for
eight years. 9But when they cried
out[i] to the LORD, he raised up for
them a deliverer, Othniel[j] son of
Kenaz, Caleb's younger brother,
who saved them. 10The Spirit of the
LORD came upon him,[k] so that he
became Israel's judge[c] and went
to war. The LORD gave Cushan-
Rishathaim king of Aram into the
hands of Othniel, who overpowered
him. 11So the land had peace for
forty years, until Othniel son of Kenaz died.

Ehud

12Once again the Israelites did
evil in the eyes of the LORD,[l] and
because they did this evil the LORD
gave Eglon king of Moab[m] power
over Israel. 13Getting the Ammonites and Amalekites to join him,
Eglon came and attacked Israel,
and they took possession of the City
of Palms.[d][n] 14The Israelites were
subject to Eglon king of Moab for
eighteen years.
15Again the Israelites cried out to
the LORD, and he gave them a deliverer[o]—Ehud, a left-handed man,
the son of Gera the Benjamite. The
Israelites sent him with tribute to
Eglon king of Moab. 16Now Ehud
had made a double-edged sword
about a foot and a half[e] long, which
he strapped to his right thigh under
his clothing. 17He presented the
tribute to Eglon king of Moab, who
was a very fat man.[p] 18After Ehud
had presented the tribute, he sent
on their way the men who had carried it. 19At the idols[f] near Gilgal
he himself turned back and said, "I
have a secret message for you, O
king."
The king said, "Quiet!" And all
his attendants left him.
20Ehud then approached him
while he was sitting alone in the
upper room of his summer palace[g]
and said, "I have a message from
God for you." As the king rose from
his seat, 21Ehud reached with his
left hand, drew the sword from his
right thigh and plunged it into the
king's belly. 22Even the handle sank
in after the blade, which came out
of his back. Ehud did not pull the
sword out, and the fat closed in
over it. 23Then Ehud went out to the
porch;[h] he shut the doors of the
upper room behind him and locked
them.
24After he had gone, the servants
came and found the doors of the
upper room locked. They said, "He
must be relieving himself[q] in the
inner room of the house." 25They
waited to the point of embarrass-
ment,[r] but when he did not open
the doors of the room, they took a
key and unlocked them. There they
saw their lord fallen to the floor,
dead.
26While they waited, Ehud got
away. He passed by the idols and
escaped to Seirah. 27When he arrived there, he blew a trumpet[s] in
the hill country of Ephraim, and the
Israelites went down with him
from the hills, with him leading
them.
28"Follow me," he ordered, "for
the LORD has given Moab, your enemy, into your hands.[t]" So they
followed him down and, taking possession of the fords of the Jordan[u]
that led to Moab, they allowed no-
one to cross over. 29At that time
they struck down about ten thousand Moabites, all vigorous and
strong; not a man escaped. 30That
day Moab was made subject to Israel, and the land had peace[v] for
eighty years.

3:8 h Jdg 2:14
3:9 i ver 15; Jdg 6:6,7; Jdg 10:10; Ps 106:44 j Jdg 1:13
3:10 k Nu 11:25,29; Nu 24:2; Jdg 6:34; Jdg 11:29; Jdg 13:25; Jdg 14:6,19; 1Sa 11:6
3:12 l Jdg 2:11,14 m 1Sa 12:9
3:13 n Jdg 1:16
3:15 o ver 9; Ps 78:34; Ps 107:13
3:17 p ver 12
3:24 q 1Sa 24:3
3:25 r 2Ki 2:17; 2Ki 8:11
3:27 s Jdg 6:34; 1Sa 13:3
3:28 t Jdg 7:9,15 u Jos 2:7; Jdg 7:24; Jdg 12:5
3:30 v ver 11

b8 That is, North-west Mesopotamia
c10 Or *leader* d13 That is, Jericho
e16 Hebrew *a cubit* (about 0.5 metre)
f19 Or *the stone quarries*; also in verse 26
g20 The meaning of the Hebrew for this phrase is uncertain. h23 The meaning of the Hebrew for this word is uncertain.

Shamgar

31 After Ehud came Shamgar son of Anath,[w] who struck down six hundred[x] Philistines with an ox-goad. He too saved Israel.

Deborah

4 After Ehud died, the Israelites once again did evil[a] in the eyes of the LORD. 2 So the LORD sold them into the hands of Jabin, a king of Canaan, who reigned in Hazor.[b] The commander of his army was Sisera,[c] who lived in Harosheth Haggoyim. 3 Because he had nine hundred iron chariots[d] and had cruelly oppressed[e] the Israelites for twenty years, they cried to the LORD for help.

4 Deborah, a prophetess, the wife of Lappidoth, was leading[a] Israel at that time. 5 She held court under the Palm of Deborah between Ramah and Bethel[f] in the hill country of Ephraim, and the Israelites came to her to have their disputes decided. 6 She sent for Barak son of Abinoam[g] from Kedesh in Naphtali and said to him, "The LORD, the God of Israel, commands you: 'Go, take with you ten thousand men of Naphtali and Zebulun and lead the way to Mount Tabor. 7 I will lure Sisera, the commander of Jabin's army, with his chariots and his troops to the Kishon River[h] and give him into your hands.' "

8 Barak said to her, "If you go with me, I will go; but if you don't go with me, I won't go."

9 "Very well," Deborah said, "I will go with you. But because of the way you are going about this,[b] the honour will not be yours, for the LORD will hand Sisera over to a woman." So Deborah went with Barak to Kedesh,[i] 10 where he summoned[j] Zebulun and Naphtali. Ten thousand men followed him, and Deborah also went with him.

11 Now Heber the Kenite had left the other Kenites,[k] the descendants of Hobab,[l] Moses' brother-in-law,[c] and pitched his tent by the great tree in Zaanannim[m] near Kedesh.

12 When they told Sisera that Barak son of Abinoam had gone up to Mount Tabor, 13 Sisera gathered together his nine hundred iron chariots[n] and all the men with him, from Harosheth Haggoyim to the Kishon River.

14 Then Deborah said to Barak, "Go! This is the day the LORD has given Sisera into your hands. Has not the LORD gone ahead[o] of you?" So Barak went down Mount Tabor, followed by ten thousand men. 15 At Barak's advance, the LORD routed[p] Sisera and all his chariots and army by the sword, and Sisera abandoned his chariot and fled on foot. 16 But Barak pursued the chariots and army as far as Harosheth Haggoyim. All the troops of Sisera fell by the sword; not a man was left.[q]

17 Sisera, however, fled on foot to the tent of Jael, the wife of Heber the Kenite, because there were friendly relations between Jabin king of Hazor and the clan of Heber the Kenite.

18 Jael went out to meet Sisera and said to him, "Come, my lord, come right in. Don't be afraid." So he entered her tent, and she put a covering over him.

19 "I'm thirsty," he said. "Please give me some water." She opened a skin of milk,[r] gave him a drink, and covered him up.

20 "Stand in the doorway of the tent," he told her. "If someone comes by and asks you, 'Is anyone here?' say 'No.' "

21 But Jael, Heber's wife, picked up a tent peg and a hammer and went quietly to him while he lay fast asleep, exhausted. She drove the peg through his temple into the ground, and he died.[s]

22 Barak came by in pursuit of

3:31 *w* Jdg 5:6 *x* Jos 23:10
4:1 *a* Jdg 2:19
4:2 *b* Jos 11:1 *c* ver 13,16; 1Sa 12:9; Ps 83:9
4:3 *d* Jdg 1:19 *e* Ps 106:42
4:5 *f* Ge 35:8
4:6 *g* Heb 11:32
4:7 *h* Ps 83:9
4:9 *i* ver 21; Jdg 2:14
4:10 *j* ver 14; Jdg 5:15,18
4:11 *k* Jdg 1:16 *l* Nu 10:29 *m* Jos 19:33
4:13 *n* ver 3
4:14 *o* Dt 9:3; 2Sa 5:24; Ps 68:7
4:15 *p* Jos 10:10; Ps 83:9-10
4:16 *q* Ex 14:28; Ps 83:9
4:19 *r* Jdg 5:25
4:21 *s* Jdg 5:26

[a]4 Traditionally *judging* [b]9 Or *But on the expedition you are undertaking* [c]11 Or *father-in-law*

Sisera, and Jael went out to meet
him. "Come," she said, "I will
show you the man you're looking
for." So he went in with her, and
there lay Sisera with the tent peg
through his temple—dead.
23 On that day God subdued[t] Jabin, the Canaanite king, before
the Israelites. 24 And the hand of
the Israelites grew stronger and
stronger against Jabin, the Canaanite king, until they destroyed him.

The Song of Deborah

5 On that day Deborah and Barak son of Abinoam sang this
song:[a]

2 "When the princes in Israel
take the lead,
when the people willingly
offer[b] themselves—
praise the LORD![c]

3 "Hear this, you kings! Listen,
you rulers!
I will sing to[a] the LORD, I will
sing;
I will make music to[b] the
LORD, the God of Israel.[d]

4 "O LORD, when you went out
from Seir,[e]
when you marched from the
land of Edom,
the earth shook, the heavens
poured,
the clouds poured down
water.[f]
5 The mountains quaked[g] before
the LORD, the One of Sinai,
before the LORD, the God of
Israel.

6 "In the days of Shamgar son of
Anath,[h]
in the days of Jael,[i] the
roads[j] were abandoned;
travellers took to winding
paths.
7 Village life[c] in Israel ceased,
ceased until I,[d] Deborah,
arose,
arose a mother in Israel.
8 When they chose new gods,[k]
war came to the city gates,
and not a shield or spear was
seen
among forty thousand in
Israel.
9 My heart is with Israel's
princes,
with the willing volunteers[l]
among the people.
Praise the LORD!

10 "You who ride on white
donkeys,[m]
sitting on your saddle
blankets,
and you who walk along the
road,
consider 11 the voice of the
singers[e] at the watering
places.
They recite the righteous
acts[n] of the LORD,
the righteous acts of his
warriors[f] in Israel.

"Then the people of the LORD
went down to the city gates.[o]
12 'Wake up,[p] wake up, Deborah!
Wake up, wake up, break out
in song!
Arise, O Barak!
Take captive your captives,[q]
O son of Abinoam.'

13 "Then the men who were left
came down to the nobles;
the people of the LORD
came to me with the mighty.
14 Some came from Ephraim,
whose roots were in
Amalek;[r]
Benjamin was with the people
who followed you.
From Makir captains came
down,
from Zebulun those who bear
a commander's staff.
15 The princes of Issachar were
with Deborah;[s]
yes, Issachar was with Barak,

4:23 *t* Ne 9:24; Ps 18:47
5:1 *a* Ex 15:1
5:2 *b* 2Ch 17:16; Ps 110:3 *c* ver 9
5:3 *d* Ps 27:6
5:4 *e* Dt 33:2 *f* Ps 68:8
5:5 *g* Ex 19:18; Ps 68:8; Ps 97:5; Isa 64:3
5:6 *h* Jdg 3:31 *i* Jdg 4:17 *j* Isa 33:8
5:8 *k* Dt 32:17
5:9 *l* ver 2
5:10 *m* Jdg 10:4; Jdg 12:14
5:11 *n* 1Sa 12:7; Mic 6:5 *o* ver 8
5:12 *p* Ps 57:8 *q* Ps 68:18; Eph 4:8
5:14 *r* Jdg 3:13
5:15 *s* Jdg 4:10

[a]3 Or *of* [b]3 Or / *with song I will praise* [c]7 Or *Warriors* [d]7 Or *you* [e]11 Or *archers*; the meaning of the Hebrew for this word is uncertain. [f]11 Or *villagers*

rushing after him into the
valley.
In the districts of Reuben
there was much searching of
heart.
16 Why did you stay among the
campfires[g]
to hear the whistling for the
flocks?[t]
In the districts of Reuben
there was much searching of
heart.
17 Gilead stayed beyond the
Jordan.
And Dan, why did he linger by
the ships?
Asher remained on the coast[u]
and stayed in his coves.
18 The people of Zebulun risked
their very lives;
so did Naphtali on the heights
of the field.[v]
19 "Kings came[w], they fought;
the kings of Canaan fought
at Taanach by the waters of
Megiddo,[x]
but they carried off no silver,
no plunder.[y]
20 From the heavens[z] the stars
fought,
from their courses they fought
against Sisera.
21 The river Kishon[a] swept them
away,
the age-old river, the river
Kishon.
March on, my soul; be strong!
22 Then thundered the horses'
hoofs—
galloping, galloping go his
mighty steeds.
23 'Curse Meroz,' said the angel of
the LORD.
'Curse its people bitterly,
because they did not come to
help the LORD,
to help the LORD against the
mighty.'

24 "Most blessed of women be
Jael,[b]
the wife of Heber the Kenite,

5:16 t Nu 32:1
5:17 u Jos 19:29
5:18 v Jdg 4:6,10
5:19 w Jos 11:5; Jdg 4:13 x Jdg 1:27 y ver 30
5:20 z Jos 10:11
5:21 a Jdg 4:7
5:24 b Jdg 4:17
5:25 c Jdg 4:19
5:26 d Jdg 4:21
5:28 e Pr 7:6
5:30 f Ex 15:9; 1Sa 30:24
5:31 g 2Sa 23:4; Ps 19:4; Ps 89:36 h Jdg 3:11

most blessed of tent-dwelling
women.
25 He asked for water, and she
gave him milk;[c]
in a bowl fit for nobles she
brought him curdled milk.
26 Her hand reached for the tent
peg,
her right hand for the
workman's hammer.
She struck Sisera, she crushed
his head,
she shattered and pierced his
temple.[d]
27 At her feet he sank,
he fell; there he lay.
At her feet he sank, he fell;
where he sank, there he
fell—dead.

28 "Through the window peered
Sisera's mother;
behind the lattice she cried
out,[e]
'Why is his chariot so long in
coming?
Why is the clatter of his
chariots delayed?'
29 The wisest of her ladies answer
her;
indeed, she keeps saying to
herself,
30 'Are they not finding and
dividing the spoils:[f]
a girl or two for each man,
colourful garments as plunder
for Sisera,
colourful garments
embroidered,
highly embroidered garments
for my neck—
all this as plunder?'

31 "So may all your enemies
perish, O LORD!
But may they who love you be
like the sun[g]
when it rises in its strength."

Then the land had peace[h] for forty years.

g16 Or *saddlebags*

Gideon

6 Again the Israelites did evil in
the eyes of the LORD,[a] and for
seven years he gave them into the
hands of the Midianites.[b] 2Because
the power of Midian was so oppressive,[c] the Israelites prepared shelters for themselves in mountain
clefts, caves and strongholds.[d]
3Whenever the Israelites planted
their crops, the Midianites, Amalekites[e] and other eastern peoples
invaded the country. 4They
camped on the land and ruined the
crops[f] all the way to Gaza and did
not spare a living thing for Israel,
neither sheep nor cattle nor donkeys. 5They came up with their
livestock and their tents like
swarms of locusts.[g] It was impossible to count the men and their
camels;[h] they invaded the land to
ravage it. 6Midian so impoverished
the Israelites that they cried out[i]
to the LORD for help.

7When the Israelites cried to the
LORD because of Midian, 8he sent
them a prophet, who said, "This is
what the LORD, the God of Israel,
says: I brought you up out of
Egypt,[j] out of the land of slavery.
9I snatched you from the power of
Egypt and from the hand of all your
oppressors. I drove them from before you and gave you their land.[k]
10I said to you, 'I am the LORD your
God; do not worship[l] the gods of
the Amorites,[m] in whose land you
live.' But you have not listened to
me."

11The angel of the LORD[n] came
and sat down under the oak in Ophrah that belonged to Joash the Abi-
ezrite,[o] where his son Gideon[p]
was threshing wheat in a winepress
to keep it from the Midianites.
12When the angel of the LORD appeared to Gideon, he said, "The
LORD is with you,[q] mighty warrior."

13"But sir," Gideon replied, "if
the LORD is with us, why has all this
happened to us? Where are all his
wonders that our fathers told[r] us
about when they said, 'Did not the
LORD bring us up out of Egypt?' But
now the LORD has abandoned[s] us
and put us into the hand of Midian."

14The LORD turned to him and
said, "Go in the strength you have[t]
and save Israel out of Midian's
hand. Am I not sending you?"

15"But Lord,"[a] Gideon asked,
"how can I save Israel? My clan is
the weakest in Manasseh, and I am
the least in my family.[u]"

16The LORD answered, "I will be
with you,[v] and you will strike
down all the Midianites together."

17Gideon replied, "If now I have
found favour in your eyes, give me
a sign[w] that it is really you talking
to me. 18Please do not go away until
I come back and bring my offering
and set it before you."

And the LORD said, "I will wait
until you return."

19Gideon went in, prepared a
young goat, and from an ephah[b] of
flour he made bread without yeast.
Putting the meat in a basket and its
broth in a pot, he brought them out
and offered them to him under the
oak.[x]

20The angel of God said to him,
"Take the meat and the unleavened
bread, place them on this rock,[y]
and pour out the broth." And Gideon did so. 21With the tip of the staff
that was in his hand, the angel of
the LORD touched the meat and the
unleavened bread.[z] Fire flared
from the rock, consuming the meat
and the bread. And the angel of the
LORD disappeared. 22When Gideon
realised[a] that it was the angel of
the LORD, he exclaimed, "Ah, Sovereign LORD! I have seen the angel
of the LORD face to face!"[b]

23But the LORD said to him,
"Peace! Do not be afraid.[c] You are
not going to die."

24So Gideon built an altar to the
LORD there and called[d] it The LORD

[a]*15* Or *sir* [b]*19* That is, probably about
3/5 bushel (about 22 litres)

6:1 a Jdg 2:11 b Nu 25:15-18 Nu 31:1-3
6:2 c 1Sa 13:6 Isa 8:21 d Heb 11:38
6:3 e Jdg 3:13
6:4 f Lev 26:16 Dt 28:30,51
6:5 g Jdg 7:12 h Jdg 8:10
6:6 i Jdg 3:9
6:8 j Jdg 2:1
6:9 k Ps 44:2
6:10 l 2Ki 17:35 m Jer 10:2
6:11 n Ge 16:7 o Jos 17:2 p Heb 11:32
6:12 q Jos 1:5 Jdg 13:3 Lk 1:11,28
6:13 r Ps 44:1 s 2Ch 15:2
6:14 t Heb 11:34
6:15 u Ex 3:11 1Sa 9:21
6:16 v Ex 3:12 Jos 1:5
6:17 w ver 36-37 Ge 24:14 Isa 38:7-8
6:19 x Ge 18:7-8
6:20 y Jdg 13:19
6:21 z Lev 9:24
6:22 a Jdg 13:16,21 b Ge 32:30 Ex 33:20 Jdg 13:22
6:23 c Da 10:19
6:24 d Ge 22:14

is Peace. To this day it stands in Ophrah[e] of the Abiezrites.

25 That same night the LORD said to him, "Take the second bull from your father's herd, the one seven years old.[c] Tear down your father's altar to Baal and cut down the Asherah pole[d][f] beside it. 26 Then build a proper kind of[e] altar to the LORD your God on the top of this height. Using the wood of the Asherah pole that you cut down, offer the second[f] bull as a burnt offering."

27 So Gideon took ten of his servants and did as the LORD told him. But because he was afraid of his family and the men of the town, he did it at night rather than in the daytime.

28 In the morning when the men of the town got up, there was Baal's altar,[g] demolished, with the Asherah pole beside it cut down and the second bull sacrificed on the newly-built altar!

29 They asked each other, "Who did this?"

When they carefully investigated, they were told, "Gideon son of Joash did it."

30 The men of the town demanded of Joash, "Bring out your son. He must die, because he has broken down Baal's altar and cut down the Asherah pole beside it."

31 But Joash replied to the hostile crowd around him, "Are you going to plead Baal's cause? Are you trying to save him? Whoever fights for him shall be put to death by morning! If Baal really is a god, he can defend himself when someone breaks down his altar." 32 So that day they called Gideon "Jerub-Baal,[g][h]" saying, "Let Baal contend with him," because he broke down Baal's altar.

33 Now all the Midianites, Amalekites and other eastern peoples[i] joined forces and crossed over the Jordan and camped in the Valley of Jezreel.[j] 34 Then the Spirit of the LORD came upon[k] Gideon, and he blew a trumpet,[l] summoning the Abiezrites to follow him. 35 He sent messengers throughout Manasseh, calling them to arms, and also into Asher, Zebulun and Naphtali,[m] so that they too went up to meet them.

36 Gideon said to God, "If you will save[n] Israel by my hand as you have promised—37 look, I will place a wool fleece on the threshing-floor.[o] If there is dew only on the fleece and all the ground is dry, then I will know[p] that you will save Israel by my hand, as you said." 38 And that is what happened. Gideon rose early the next day; he squeezed the fleece and wrung out the dew—a bowlful of water.

39 Then Gideon said to God, "Do not be angry with me. Let me make just one more request.[q] Allow me one more test with the fleece. This time make the fleece dry and the ground covered with dew." 40 That night God did so. Only the fleece was dry; all the ground was covered with dew.

Gideon Defeats the Midianites

7 Early in the morning, Jerub-Baal[a] (that is, Gideon) and all his men camped at the spring of Harod. The camp of Midian was north of them in the valley near the hill of Moreh.[b] 2 The LORD said to Gideon, "You have too many men for me to deliver Midian into their hands. In order that Israel may not boast against me that her own strength[c] has saved her, 3 announce now to the people, 'Anyone who trembles with fear may turn back and leave Mount Gilead.[d]'" So twenty-two thousand men left, while ten thousand remained.

4 But the LORD said to Gideon, "There are still too many[e] men. Take them down to the water, and

6:24 e Jdg 8:32
6:25 f Ex 34:13; Dt 7:5
6:28 g 1Ki 16:32
6:32 h Jdg 7:1; Jdg 8:29,35; 1Sa 12:11
6:33 i ver 3; j Jos 17:16
6:34 k Jdg 3:10; 1Ch 12:18; 2Ch 24:20; l Jdg 3:27
6:35 m Jdg 4:6
6:36 n ver 14
6:37 o Ex 4:3-7; p Ge 24:14
6:39 q Ge 18:32
7:1 a Jdg 6:32; b Ge 12:6
7:2 c Dt 8:17; 2Co 4:7
7:3 d Dt 20:8
7:4 e 1Sa 14:6

c25 Or *Take a full-grown, mature bull from your father's herd* d25 That is, a symbol of the goddess Asherah; here and elsewhere in Judges
e26 Or *build with layers of stone an*
f26 Or *full-grown*; also in verse 28
g32 *Jerub-Baal* means *let Baal contend.*

I will sift them out for you there. If I say, 'This one shall go with you,' he shall go; but if I say, 'This one shall not go with you,' he shall not go."

5So Gideon took the men down to the water. There the LORD told him, "Separate those who lap the water with their tongues like a dog from those who kneel down to drink." 6Three hundred men lapped with their hands to their mouths. All the rest got down on their knees to drink.

7The LORD said to Gideon, "With the three hundred men that lapped I will save you and give the Midianites into your hands. Let all the other men go, each to his own place."[f] 8So Gideon sent the rest of the Israelites to their tents but kept the three hundred, who took over the provisions and trumpets of the others.

Now the camp of Midian lay below him in the valley. 9During that night the LORD said to Gideon, "Get up, go down against the camp, because I am going to give it into your hands.[g] 10If you are afraid to attack, go down to the camp with your servant Purah 11and listen to what they are saying. Afterwards, you will be encouraged to attack the camp." So he and Purah his servant went down to the outposts of the camp. 12The Midianites, the Amalekites[h] and all the other eastern peoples had settled in the valley, thick as locusts.[i] Their camels[j] could no more be counted than the sand on the seashore.[k]

13Gideon arrived just as a man was telling a friend his dream. "I had a dream," he was saying. "A round loaf of barley bread came tumbling into the Midianite camp. It struck the tent with such force that the tent overturned and collapsed."

14His friend responded, "This can be nothing other than the sword of Gideon son of Joash, the Israelite. God has given the Midianites and the whole camp into his hands."

15When Gideon heard the dream and its interpretation, he worshipped God.[l] He returned to the camp of Israel and called out, "Get up! The LORD has given the Midianite camp into your hands." 16Dividing the three hundred men[m] into three companies,[n] he placed trumpets and empty jars in the hands of all of them, with torches inside.

17"Watch me," he told them. "Follow my lead. When I get to the edge of the camp, do exactly as I do. 18When I and all who are with me blow our trumpets,[o] then from all around the camp blow yours and shout, 'For the LORD and for Gideon.' "

19Gideon and the hundred men with him reached the edge of the camp at the beginning of the middle watch, just after they had changed the guard. They blew their trumpets and broke the jars that were in their hands. 20The three companies blew the trumpets and smashed the jars. Grasping the torches in their left hands and holding in their right hands the trumpets they were to blow, they shouted, "A sword[p] for the LORD and for Gideon!" 21While each man held his position around the camp, all the Midianites ran, crying out as they fled.[q]

22When the three hundred trumpets sounded,[r] the LORD caused the men throughout the camp to turn on each other[s] with their swords. The army fled to Beth Shittah towards Zererah as far as the border of Abel Meholah[t] near Tabbath. 23Israelites from Naphtali, Asher and all Manasseh were called out,[u] and they pursued the Midianites. 24Gideon sent messengers throughout the hill country of Ephraim, saying, "Come down against the Midianites and seize the waters of the Jordan[v] ahead of them as far as Beth Barah."

So all the men of Ephraim were

7:7 f 1Sa 14:6
7:9 g Jos 2:24; Jos 10:8; Jos 11:6
7:12 h Jdg 8:10; i Jdg 6:5; j Jer 49:29; k Jos 11:4
7:15 l 1Sa 15:31
7:16 m Ge 14:15; n 2Sa 18:2
7:18 o Jdg 3:27
7:20 p ver 14
7:21 q 2Ki 7:7
7:22 r Jos 6:20; s 1Sa 14:20; 2Ch 20:23; t 1Ki 4:12; 1Ki 19:16
7:23 u Jdg 6:35
7:24 v Jdg 3:28

called out and they took the waters
of the Jordan as far as Beth Barah.
25 They also captured two of the
Midianite leaders, Oreb and
Zeeb[w]. They killed Oreb at the
rock of Oreb,[x] and Zeeb at the
winepress of Zeeb. They pursued
the Midianites and brought the
heads of Oreb and Zeeb to Gideon,
who was by the Jordan.[y]

Zebah and Zalmunna

8 Now the Ephraimites asked
Gideon, "Why have you
treated us like this? Why didn't you
call us when you went to fight Midian?"[a] And they criticised him
sharply.[b]
2 But he answered them, "What
have I accomplished compared to
you? Aren't the gleanings of Ephraim's grapes better than the full
grape harvest of Abiezer? 3 God
gave Oreb and Zeeb,[c] the Midianite leaders, into your hands. What
was I able to do compared to you?"
At this, their resentment against
him subsided.
4 Gideon and his three hundred
men, exhausted yet keeping up the
pursuit, came to the Jordan[d] and
crossed it. 5 He said to the men of
Succoth,[e] "Give my troops some
bread; they are worn out, and I am
still pursuing Zebah and Zalmunna,[f] the kings of Midian."
6 But the officials of Succoth said,
"Do you already have the hands of
Zebah and Zalmunna in your possession? Why should we give
bread[g] to your troops?"[h]
7 Then Gideon replied, "Just for
that, when the LORD has given
Zebah and Zalmunna[i] into my
hand, I will tear your flesh with
desert thorns and briers."
8 From there he went up to Peniel[a][j] and made the same request
of them, but they answered as the
men of Succoth had. 9 So he said to
the men of Peniel, "When I return
in triumph, I will tear down this
tower."[k]

10 Now Zebah and Zalmunna were
in Karkor with a force of about fifteen thousand men, all that were
left of the armies of the eastern
peoples; a hundred and twenty
thousand swordsmen had fallen.[l]
11 Gideon went up by the route of
the nomads east of Nobah[m] and
Jogbehah[n] and fell upon the unsuspecting army. 12 Zebah and Zalmunna, the two kings of Midian,
fled, but he pursued them and captured them, routing their entire
army.
13 Gideon son of Joash then returned from the battle by the Pass
of Heres. 14 He caught a young man
of Succoth and questioned him, and
the young man wrote down for him
the names of the seventy-seven officials of Succoth, the elders of the
town. 15 Then Gideon came and said
to the men of Succoth, "Here are
Zebah and Zalmunna, about whom
you taunted me by saying, 'Do you
already have the hands of Zebah
and Zalmunna in your possession?
Why should we give bread to your
exhausted men?[o]' " 16 He took the
elders of the town and taught the
men of Succoth a lesson[p] by punishing them with desert thorns and
briers. 17 He also pulled down the
tower of Peniel and killed the men
of the town.[q]
18 Then he asked Zebah and Zalmunna, "What kind of men did you
kill at Tabor?[r]"
"Men like you," they answered,
"each one with the bearing of a
prince."
19 Gideon replied, "Those were
my brothers, the sons of my own
mother. As surely as the LORD
lives, if you had spared their lives,
I would not kill you." 20 Turning to
Jether, his oldest son, he said, "Kill
them!" But Jether did not draw his
sword, because he was only a boy
and was afraid.
21 Zebah and Zalmunna said,

7:25 w Jdg 8:3; Ps 83:11 x Isa 10:26 y Jdg 8:4
8:1 a Jdg 12:1 b 2Sa 19:41
8:3 c Jdg 7:25; Pr 15:1
8:4 d Jdg 7:25
8:5 e Ge 33:17 f Ps 83:11
8:6 g 1Sa 25:11 h ver 15
8:7 i Jdg 7:15
8:8 j Ge 32:30; 1Ki 12:25
8:9 k ver 17
8:10 l Jdg 6:5; Jdg 7:12; Isa 9:4
8:11 m Nu 32:42 n Nu 32:35
8:15 o ver 6
8:16 p ver 7
8:17 q ver 9
8:18 r Jos 19:22; Jdg 4:6

[a] 8 Hebrew *Penuel*, a variant of *Peniel*; also in verses 9 and 17

"Come, do it yourself. 'As is the man, so is his strength.'" So Gideon stepped forward and killed them, and took the ornaments[s] off their camels' necks.

Gideon's Ephod

22 The Israelites said to Gideon, "Rule over us—you, your son and your grandson—because you have saved us out of the hand of Midian."

23 But Gideon told them, "I will not rule over you, nor will my son rule over you. The LORD will rule[t] over you." 24 And he said, "I do have one request, that each of you give me an ear-ring from your share of the plunder." (It was the custom of the Ishmaelites[u] to wear gold ear-rings.)

25 They answered, "We'll be glad to give them." So they spread out a garment, and each man threw a ring from his plunder onto it. 26 The weight of the gold rings he asked for came to seventeen hundred shekels,[b] not counting the ornaments, the pendants and the purple garments worn by the kings of Midian or the chains that were on their camels' necks. 27 Gideon made the gold into an ephod,[v] which he placed in Ophrah, his town. All Israel prostituted themselves by worshipping it there, and it became a snare[w] to Gideon and his family.

Gideon's Death

28 Thus Midian was subdued before the Israelites and did not raise its head again. During Gideon's lifetime, the land enjoyed peace[x] for forty years.

29 Jerub-Baal[y] son of Joash went back home to live. 30 He had seventy sons[z] of his own, for he had many wives. 31 His concubine, who lived in Shechem, also bore him a son, whom he named Abimelech.[a] 32 Gideon son of Joash died at a good old age[b] and was buried in the tomb of his father Joash in Ophrah of the Abiezrites.

8:21 s ver 26; Ps 83:11
8:23 t Ex 16:8; 1Sa 8:7; 1Sa 10:19; 1Sa 12:12
8:24 u Ge 25:13
8:27 v Jdg 17:5; Jdg 18:14 w Dt 7:16; Ps 106:39
8:28 x Jdg 5:31
8:29 y Jdg 7:1
8:30 z Jdg 9:2,5,18, 24
8:31 a Jdg 9:1
8:32 b Ge 25:8
8:33 c Jdg 2:11,13, 19 d Jdg 9:4 e Jdg 9:27,46
8:34 f Jdg 3:7; Dt 4:9; Ps 78:11,42
8:35 g Jdg 9:16
9:1 a Jdg 8:31
9:2 b Ge 29:14; Jdg 8:30
9:4 c Jdg 8:33 d Jdg 11:3; 2Ch 13:7
9:5 e ver 2; Jdg 8:30 f 2Ki 11:2
9:7 g Dt 11:29; Dt 27:12; Jn 4:20

33 No sooner had Gideon died than the Israelites again prostituted themselves to the Baals.[c] They set up Baal-Berith[d] as their god[e] and 34 did not remember[f] the LORD their God, who had rescued them from the hands of all their enemies on every side. 35 They also failed to show kindness to the family of Jerub-Baal (that is, Gideon) for all the good things he had done for them.[g]

Abimelech

9 Abimelech[a] son of Jerub-Baal went to his mother's brothers in Shechem and said to them and to all his mother's clan, 2 "Ask all the citizens of Shechem, 'Which is better for you: to have all seventy of Jerub-Baal's sons rule over you, or just one man?' Remember, I am your flesh and blood.[b]"

3 When the brothers repeated all this to the citizens of Shechem, they were inclined to follow Abimelech, for they said, "He is our brother." 4 They gave him seventy shekels[a] of silver from the temple of Baal-Berith,[c] and Abimelech used it to hire reckless adventurers,[d] who became his followers. 5 He went to his father's home in Ophrah and on one stone murdered his seventy brothers,[e] the sons of Jerub-Baal. But Jotham, the youngest son of Jerub-Baal, escaped by hiding.[f] 6 Then all the citizens of Shechem and Beth Millo gathered beside the great tree at the pillar in Shechem to crown Abimelech king.

7 When Jotham was told about this, he climbed up on the top of Mount Gerizim[g] and shouted to them, "Listen to me, citizens of Shechem, so that God may listen to you. 8 One day the trees went out to anoint a king for themselves. They said to the olive tree, 'Be our king.'

9 "But the olive tree answered,

[b] 26 That is, about 43 pounds (about 19.5 kilograms) [a] 4 That is, about 1¾ pounds (about 0.8 kilogram)

'Should I give up my oil, by which both gods and men are honoured, to hold sway over the trees?'

10"Next, the trees said to the fig-tree, 'Come and be our king.'

11"But the fig-tree replied, 'Should I give up my fruit, so good and sweet, to hold sway over the trees?'

12"Then the trees said to the vine, 'Come and be our king.'

13"But the vine answered, 'Should I give up my wine,[h] which cheers both gods and men, to hold sway over the trees?'

14"Finally all the trees said to the thornbush, 'Come and be our king.'

15"The thornbush said to the trees, 'If you really want to anoint me king over you, come and take refuge in my shade;[i] but if not, then let fire come out[j] of the thornbush and consume the cedars of Lebanon!'[k]

16"Now if you have acted honourably and in good faith when you made Abimelech king, and if you have been fair to Jerub-Baal and his family, and if you have treated him as he deserves—17and to think that my father fought for you, risked his life to rescue you from the hand of Midian 18(but today you have revolted against my father's family, murdered his seventy sons[l] on a single stone, and made Abimelech, the son of his slave girl, king over the citizens of Shechem because he is your brother)—19if then you have acted honourably and in good faith towards Jerub-Baal and his family today, may Abimelech be your joy, and may you be his, too! 20But if you have not, let fire come out[m] from Abimelech and consume you, citizens of Shechem and Beth Millo, and let fire come out from you, citizens of Shechem and Beth Millo, and consume Abimelech!"

21Then Jotham fled, escaping to Beer, and he lived there because he was afraid of his brother Abimelech.

22After Abimelech had governed Israel for three years, 23God sent an evil spirit[n] between Abimelech and the citizens of Shechem, who acted treacherously against Abimelech. 24God did this in order that the crime against Jerub-Baal's seventy sons, the shedding[o] of their blood, might be avenged[p] on their brother Abimelech and on the citizens of Shechem, who had helped him[q] murder his brothers. 25In opposition to him these citizens of Shechem set men on the hilltops to ambush and rob everyone who passed by, and this was reported to Abimelech.

26Now Gaal son of Ebed moved with his brothers into Shechem, and its citizens put their confidence in him. 27After they had gone out into the fields and gathered the grapes and trodden[r] them, they held a festival in the temple of their god.[s] While they were eating and drinking, they cursed Abimelech. 28Then Gaal son of Ebed said, "Who[t] is Abimelech, and who is Shechem, that we should be subject to him? Isn't he Jerub-Baal's son, and isn't Zebul his deputy? Serve the men of Hamor,[u] Shechem's father! Why should we serve Abimelech? 29If only this people were under my command![v] Then I would get rid of him. I would say to Abimelech, 'Call out your whole army!' "[b]

30When Zebul the governor of the city heard what Gaal son of Ebed said, he was very angry. 31Under cover he sent messengers to Abimelech, saying, "Gaal son of Ebed and his brothers have come to Shechem and are stirring up the city against you. 32Now then, during the night you and your men should come and lie in wait[w] in the fields. 33In the morning at sunrise, advance against the city. When Gaal and his men come out against

9:13 h Ecc 2:3
9:15 i Isa 30:2 j ver 20 k Isa 2:13
9:18 l ver 5-6 Jdg 8:30
9:20 m ver 15
9:23 n 1Sa 16:14,23 1Sa 18:10 1Ki 22:22 Isa 19:14 Isa 33:1
9:24 o Nu 35:33 1Ki 2:32 p ver 56-57 q Dt 27:25
9:27 r Am 9:13 s Jdg 8:33
9:28 t 1Sa 25:10 1Ki 12:16 u Ge 34:2,6
9:29 v 2Sa 15:4
9:32 w Jos 8:2

b29 Septuagint; Hebrew *him." Then he said to Abimelech, "Call out your whole army!"*

you, do whatever your hand finds to
do.[x]"
34So Abimelech and all his troops
set out by night and took up concealed positions near Shechem in
four companies. 35Now Gaal son of
Ebed had gone out and was standing at the entrance to the city gate
just as Abimelech and his soldiers
came out from their hiding-place.[y]
36When Gaal saw them, he said to
Zebul, "Look, people are coming
down from the tops of the mountains!"
Zebul replied, "You mistake the
shadows of the mountains for
men."
37But Gaal spoke up again: "Look,
people are coming down from the
centre of the land, and a company
is coming from the direction of the
soothsayers' tree."
38Then Zebul said to him, "Where
is your big talk now, you who said,
'Who is Abimelech that we should
be subject to him?' Aren't these the
men you ridiculed?[z] Go out and
fight them!"
39So Gaal led out[c] the citizens of
Shechem and fought Abimelech.
40Abimelech chased him, and many
fell wounded in the flight—all the
way to the entrance to the gate.
41Abimelech stayed in Arumah,
and Zebul drove Gaal and his
brothers out of Shechem.
42The next day the people of Shechem went out to the fields, and
this was reported to Abimelech.
43So he took his men, divided them
into three companies[a] and set an
ambush in the fields. When he saw
the people coming out of the city,
he rose to attack them. 44Abime-
lech and the companies with him
rushed forward to a position at the
entrance to the city gate. Then two
companies rushed upon those in
the fields and struck them down.
45All that day Abimelech pressed
his attack against the city until he
had captured it and killed its people. Then he destroyed the city[b]
and scattered salt[c] over it.
46On hearing this, the citizens in
the tower of Shechem went into the
stronghold of the temple[d] of El-
Berith. 47When Abimelech heard
that they had assembled there, 48he
and all his men went up Mount Zalmon.[e] He took an axe and cut off
some branches, which he lifted to
his shoulders. He ordered the men
with him, "Quick! Do what you
have seen me do!" 49So all the men
cut branches and followed Abimelech. They piled them against the
stronghold and set it on fire over
the people inside. So all the people
in the tower of Shechem, about a
thousand men and women, also
died.
50Next Abimelech went to Thebez[f] and besieged it and captured
it. 51Inside the city, however, was a
strong tower, to which all the men
and women—all the people of the
city—fled. They locked themselves in and climbed up on the
tower roof. 52Abimelech went to
the tower and stormed it. But as he
approached the entrance to the
tower to set it on fire, 53a woman
dropped an upper millstone on his
head and cracked his skull.[g]
54Hurriedly he called to his
armour-bearer, "Draw your sword
and kill me,[h] so that they can't say,
'A woman killed him.'" So his servant ran him through, and he died.
55When the Israelites saw that Abimelech was dead, they went home.
56Thus God repaid the wickedness that Abimelech had done to his
father by murdering his seventy
brothers. 57God also made the men
of Shechem pay for all their wickedness.[i] The curse of Jotham son
of Jerub-Baal came on them.

Tola

10 After the time of Abimelech a man of Issachar,[a]
Tola son of Puah,[b] the son of Dodo,
rose to save[c] Israel. He lived in

9:33 x 1Sa 10:7
9:35 y Ps 32:7; Jer 49:10
9:38 z ver 28-29
9:43 a Jdg 7:16
9:45 b ver 20; 2Ki 3:25; c Dt 29:23
9:46 d Jdg 8:33
9:48 e Ps 68:14
9:50 f 2Sa 11:21
9:53 g 2Sa 11:21
9:54 h 1Sa 31:4; 2Sa 1:9
9:57 i ver 20
10:1 a Ge 30:18; b Ge 46:13; c Jdg 2:16; Jdg 6:14

c39 Or *Gaal went out in the sight of*

Shamir, in the hill country of Ephraim. 2He led[a] Israel for twenty-three years; then he died, and was buried in Shamir.

Jair

3He was followed by Jair of Gilead, who led Israel for twenty-two years. 4He had thirty sons, who rode thirty donkeys. They controlled thirty towns in Gilead, which to this day are called Havvoth Jair.[b][d] 5When Jair died, he was buried in Kamon.

Jephthah

6Again the Israelites did evil in the eyes of the LORD.[e] They served the Baals and the Ashtoreths,[f] and the gods of Aram, the gods of Sidon, the gods of Moab, the gods of the Ammonites and the gods of the Philistines.[g] And because the Israelites forsook the LORD[h] and no longer served him, 7he became angry[i] with them. He sold them[j] into the hands of the Philistines and the Ammonites, 8who that year shattered and crushed them. For eighteen years they oppressed all the Israelites on the east side of the Jordan in Gilead, the land of the Amorites. 9The Ammonites also crossed the Jordan to fight against Judah, Benjamin and the house of Ephraim; and Israel was in great distress. 10Then the Israelites cried out to the LORD, "We have sinned against you, forsaking our God and serving the Baals."[k]

11The LORD replied, "When the Egyptians,[l] the Amorites, the Ammonites,[m] the Philistines,[n] 12the Sidonians, the Amalekites and the Maonites[c] oppressed you[o] and you cried to me for help, did I not save you from their hands? 13But you have forsaken me and served other gods, so I will no longer save you. 14Go and cry out to the gods you have chosen. Let them save you when you are in trouble![p]"

15But the Israelites said to the LORD, "We have sinned. Do with us whatever you think best,[q] but please rescue us now." 16Then they got rid of the foreign gods among them and served the LORD.[r] And he could bear Israel's misery[s] no longer.[t]

17When the Ammonites were called to arms and camped in Gilead, the Israelites assembled and camped at Mizpah.[u] 18The leaders of the people of Gilead said to each other, "Whoever will launch the attack against the Ammonites will be the head[v] of all those living in Gilead."

11

Jephthah[a] the Gileadite was a mighty warrior.[b] His father was Gilead; his mother was a prostitute. 2Gilead's wife also bore him sons, and when they were grown up, they drove Jephthah away. "You are not going to get any inheritance in our family," they said, "because you are the son of another woman." 3So Jephthah fled from his brothers and settled in the land of Tob,[c] where a group of adventurers[d] gathered around him and followed him.

4Some time later, when the Ammonites[e] made war on Israel, 5the elders of Gilead went to get Jephthah from the land of Tob. 6"Come," they said, "be our commander, so we can fight the Ammonites."

7Jephthah said to them, "Didn't you hate me and drive me from my father's house?[f] Why do you come to me now, when you're in trouble?"

8The elders of Gilead said to him, "Nevertheless, we are turning to you now; come with us to fight the Ammonites, and you will be our head[g] over all who live in Gilead."

9Jephthah answered, "Suppose you take me back to fight the

10:4 d Nu 32:41
10:6 e Jdg 2:11 f Jdg 2:13 g Jdg 2:12 h Dt 32:15
10:7 i Dt 31:17 j Dt 32:30 Jdg 2:14 1Sa 12:9
10:10 k 1Sa 12:10
10:11 l Ex 14:30 m Nu 21:21 Jdg 3:13 n Jdg 3:31
10:12 o Ps 106:42
10:14 p Dt 32:37
10:15 q 1Sa 3:18 2Sa 15:26
10:16 r Jos 24:23 Jer 18:8 s Isa 63:9 t Dt 32:36 Ps 106:44-45
10:17 u Ge 31:49 Jdg 11:29
10:18 v Jdg 11:8,9
11:1 a Heb 11:32 b Jdg 6:12
11:3 c 2Sa 10:6,8 d Jdg 9:4
11:4 e Jdg 10:9
11:7 f Ge 26:27
11:8 g Jdg 10:18

a2 Traditionally *judged*; also in verse 3
b4 Or *called the settlements of Jair*
c12 Hebrew; some Septuagint manuscripts *Midianites*

Ammonites and the LORD gives
them to me—will I really be your
head?"
10 The elders of Gilead replied,
"The LORD is our witness;[h] we will
certainly do as you say." 11 So Jephthah went with the elders of Gilead,
and the people made him head and
commander over them. And he repeated all his words before the
LORD in Mizpah.[i]
12 Then Jephthah sent messengers to the Ammonite king with the
question: "What do you have
against us that you have attacked
our country?"
13 The king of the Ammonites answered Jephthah's messengers,
"When Israel came up out of Egypt,
they took away my land from the
Arnon to the Jabbok,[j] all the way
to the Jordan. Now give it back
peaceably."
14 Jephthah sent back messengers to the Ammonite king, 15 saying:

"This is what Jephthah says:
Israel did not take the land of
Moab[k] or the land of the Ammonites.[l] 16 But when they
came up out of Egypt, Israel
went through the desert to the
Red Sea[a][m] and on to Kadesh.[n]
17 Then Israel sent messengers[o] to the king of Edom, saying, 'Give us permission to go
through your country,'[p] but
the king of Edom would not listen. They sent also to the king
of Moab, and he refused.[q] So
Israel stayed at Kadesh.
18 "Next they travelled
through the desert, skirted the
lands of Edom[r] and Moab,
passed along the eastern side[s]
of the country of Moab, and
camped on the other side of the
Arnon.[t] They did not enter the
territory of Moab, for the Arnon was its border.
19 "Then Israel sent mes-
sengers to Sihon king of the
Amorites, who ruled in Heshbon, and said to him, 'Let us
pass through your country to
our own place.'[u] 20 Sihon, however, did not trust Israel[b] to
pass through his territory. He
mustered all his men and
encamped at Jahaz and fought
with Israel.[v]
21 "Then the LORD, the God of
Israel, gave Sihon and all his
men into Israel's hands, and
they defeated them. Israel took
over all the land of the Amorites who lived in that country,
22 capturing all of it from the
Arnon to the Jabbok and from
the desert to the Jordan.[w]
23 "Now since the LORD, the
God of Israel, has driven the
Amorites out before his people
Israel, what right have you to
take it over? 24 Will you not take
what your god Chemosh[x]
gives you? Likewise, whatever
the LORD our God has given us,
we will possess. 25 Are you better than Balak son of Zippor,[y]
king of Moab? Did he ever
quarrel with Israel or fight
with them?[z] 26 For three hundred years Israel occupied[a]
Heshbon, Aroer, the surrounding settlements and all the
towns along the Arnon. Why
didn't you retake them during
that time? 27 I have not wronged
you, but you are doing me
wrong by waging war against
me. Let the LORD, the
Judge,[c][b] decide[c] the dispute
this day between the Israelites
and the Ammonites."

28 The king of Ammon, however,
paid no attention to the message
Jephthah sent him.
29 Then the Spirit[d] of the LORD
came upon Jephthah. He crossed

11:10 *h* Ge 31:50; Jer 42:5
11:11 *i* Jos 11:3; Jdg 10:17; Jdg 20:1; 1Sa 10:17
11:13 *j* Ge 32:22; Nu 21:24
11:15 *k* Dt 2:9 *l* Dt 2:19
11:16 *m* Nu 14:25; Dt 1:40 *n* Nu 20:1
11:17 *o* Nu 20:14 *p* Nu 20:18,21 *q* Jos 24:9
11:18 *r* Nu 21:4 *s* Dt 2:8 *t* Nu 21:13
11:19 *u* Nu 21:21-22; Dt 2:26-27
11:20 *v* Nu 21:23; Dt 2:32
11:22 *w* Dt 2:36
11:24 *x* Nu 21:29; Jos 3:10; 1Ki 11:7
11:25 *y* Nu 22:2 *z* Jos 24:9
11:26 *a* Nu 21:25
11:27 *b* Ge 18:25 *c* Ge 16:5; Ge 31:53; 1Sa 24:12,15
11:29 *d* Nu 11:25; Jdg 3:10; Jdg 6:34; Jdg 14:6,19; Jdg 15:14; 1Sa 11:6; 1Sa 16:13; Isa 11:2

a *16* Hebrew *Yam Suph*; that is, Sea of Reeds
b *20* Or *however, would not make an agreement for Israel* c *27* Or *Ruler*

Gilead and Manasseh, passed through Mizpah of Gilead, and from there he advanced against the Ammonites. 30 And Jephthah made a vow[e] to the LORD: "If you give the Ammonites into my hands, 31 whatever comes out of the door of my house to meet me when I return in triumph from the Ammonites will be the LORD's, and I will sacrifice it as a burnt offering."

32 Then Jephthah went over to fight the Ammonites, and the LORD gave them into his hands. 33 He devastated twenty towns from Aroer to the vicinity of Minnith,[f] as far as Abel Keramim. Thus Israel subdued Ammon.

34 When Jephthah returned to his home in Mizpah, who should come out to meet him but his daughter, dancing to the sound of tambourines![g] She was an only child. Except for her he had neither son nor daughter. 35 When he saw her, he tore his clothes and cried, "Oh! My daughter! You have made me miserable and wretched, because I have made a vow to the LORD that I cannot break.[h]"

36 "My father," she replied, "you have given your word to the LORD. Do to me just as you promised,[i] now that the LORD has avenged you of your enemies,[j] the Ammonites. 37 But grant me this one request," she said. "Give me two months to roam the hills and weep with my friends, because I will never marry."

38 "You may go," he said. And he let her go for two months. She and the girls went into the hills and wept because she would never marry. 39 After the two months, she returned to her father and he did to her as he had vowed. And she was a virgin.

From this comes the Israelite custom 40 that each year the young women of Israel go out for four days to commemorate the daughter of Jephthah the Gileadite.

11:30
e Ge 28:20

11:33
f Eze 27:17

11:34
g Ex 15:20
Jer 31:4

11:35
h Nu 30:2
Ecc 5:2,4,5

11:36
i Lk 1:38
j 2Sa 18:19

12:1
a Jdg 8:1

12:3
b 1Sa 19:5
1Sa 28:21
Job 13:14

12:5
c Jos 22:11
Jdg 3:28

Jephthah and Ephraim

12 The men of Ephraim called out their forces, crossed over to Zaphon and said to Jephthah, "Why did you go to fight the Ammonites without calling us to go with you?[a] We're going to burn down your house over your head."

2 Jephthah answered, "I and my people were engaged in a great struggle with the Ammonites, and although I called, you didn't save me out of their hands. 3 When I saw that you wouldn't help, I took my life in my hands[b] and crossed over to fight the Ammonites, and the LORD gave me the victory over them. Now why have you come up today to fight me?"

4 Jephthah then called together the men of Gilead and fought against Ephraim. The Gileadites struck them down because the Ephraimites had said, "You Gileadites are renegades from Ephraim and Manasseh." 5 The Gileadites captured the fords of the Jordan[c] leading to Ephraim, and whenever a survivor of Ephraim said, "Let me cross over," the men of Gilead asked him, "Are you an Ephraimite?" If he replied, "No," 6 they said, "All right, say 'Shibboleth'." If he said, "Sibboleth", because he could not pronounce the word correctly, they seized him and killed him at the fords of the Jordan. Forty-two thousand Ephraimites were killed at that time.

7 Jephthah led[a] Israel for six years. Then Jephthah the Gileadite died, and was buried in a town in Gilead.

Ibzan, Elon and Abdon

8 After him, Ibzan of Bethlehem led Israel. 9 He had thirty sons and thirty daughters. He gave his daughters away in marriage to those outside his clan, and for his sons he brought in thirty young

[a]7 Traditionally *judged*; also in verses 8–14

women as wives from outside his clan. Ibzan led Israel for seven years. 10 Then Ibzan died, and was buried in Bethlehem.

11 After him, Elon the Zebulunite led Israel for ten years. 12 Then Elon died, and was buried in Aijalon in the land of Zebulun.

13 After him, Abdon son of Hillel, from Pirathon, led Israel. 14 He had forty sons and thirty grandsons,[d] who rode on seventy donkeys.[e] He led Israel for eight years. 15 Then Abdon son of Hillel died, and was buried at Pirathon in Ephraim, in the hill country of the Amalekites.[f]

The Birth of Samson

13 Again the Israelites did evil in the eyes of the LORD, so the LORD delivered them into the hands of the Philistines[a] for forty years.

2 A certain man of Zorah,[b] named Manoah, from the clan of the Danites, had a wife who was sterile and remained childless. 3 The angel of the LORD[c] appeared to her[d] and said, "You are sterile and childless, but you are going to conceive and have a son.[e] 4 Now see to it that you drink no wine or other fermented drink and that you do not eat anything unclean,[f] 5 because you will conceive and give birth to a son. No razor[g] may be used on his head, because the boy is to be a Nazirite,[h] set apart to God from birth, and he will begin[i] the deliverance of Israel from the hands of the Philistines."

6 Then the woman went to her husband and told him, "A man of God[j] came to me. He looked like an angel of God,[k] very awesome. I didn't ask him where he came from, and he didn't tell me his name. 7 But he said to me, 'You will conceive and give birth to a son. Now then, drink no wine or other fermented drink and do not eat anything unclean, because the boy will be a Nazirite of God from birth until the day of his death.' "

8 Then Manoah prayed to the LORD: "O Lord, I beg you, let the man of God you sent to us come again to teach us how to bring up the boy who is to be born."

9 God heard Manoah, and the angel of God came again to the woman while she was out in the field; but her husband Manoah was not with her. 10 The woman hurried to tell her husband, "He's here! The man who appeared to me the other day!"

11 Manoah got up and followed his wife. When he came to the man, he said, "Are you the one who talked to my wife?"

"I am," he said.

12 So Manoah asked him, "When your words are fulfilled, what is to be the rule for the boy's life and work?"

13 The angel of the LORD answered, "Your wife must do all that I have told her. 14 She must not eat anything that comes from the grapevine, nor drink any wine or other fermented drink[l] nor eat anything unclean.[m] She must do everything I have commanded her."

15 Manoah said to the angel of the LORD, "We would like you to stay until we prepare a young goat[n] for you."

16 The angel of the LORD replied, "Even though you detain me, I will not eat any of your food. But if you prepare a burnt offering,[o] offer it to the LORD." (Manoah did not realise that it was the angel of the LORD.)

17 Then Manoah enquired of the angel of the LORD, "What is your name,[p] so that we may honour you when your word comes true?"

18 He replied, "Why do you ask my name?[q] It is beyond understanding."[a] 19 Then Manoah took a young goat, together with the grain

[a] 18 Or *is wonderful*

12:14 d Jdg 10:4 e Jdg 5:10
12:15 f Jdg 5:14
13:1 a Jdg 2:11 1Sa 12:9
13:2 b Jos 15:33 Jos 19:41
13:3 c ver 6,8 Jdg 6:12 d ver 10 e Lk 1:13
13:4 f ver 14 Nu 6:2-4 Lk 1:15
13:5 g Nu 6:5 1Sa 1:11 h Nu 6:2,13 i 1Sa 7:13
13:6 j ver 8 1Sa 2:27 1Sa 9:6 k ver 17-18 Mt 28:3
13:14 l Nu 6:4 m ver 4
13:15 n ver 3 Jdg 6:19
13:16 o Jdg 6:20
13:17 p Ge 32:29
13:18 q Isa 9:6

offering, and sacrificed it on a rock[r]
to the LORD. And the LORD did an
amazing thing while Manoah and
his wife watched: 20As the flame[s]
blazed up from the altar towards
heaven, the angel of the LORD ascended in the flame. Seeing this,
Manoah and his wife fell with their
faces to the ground.[t] 21When the
angel of the LORD did not show himself again to Manoah and his wife,
Manoah realised[u] that it was the
angel of the LORD.

22"We are doomed[v] to die!" he
said to his wife. "We have seen[w]
God!"

23But his wife answered, "If the
LORD had meant to kill us, he would
not have accepted a burnt offering
and grain offering from our hands,
nor shown us all these things or
now told us this."[x]

24The woman gave birth to a boy
and named him Samson.[y] He
grew[z] and the LORD blessed him,[a]
25and the Spirit of the LORD began
to stir[b] him while he was in Mahaneh Dan,[c] between Zorah and Eshtaol.

Samson's Marriage

14 Samson went down to Timnah[a] and saw there a
young Philistine woman. 2When he
returned, he said to his father and
mother, "I have seen a Philistine
woman in Timnah; now get her for
me as my wife."[b]

3His father and mother replied,
"Isn't there an acceptable woman
among your relatives or among all
our people?[c] Must you go to the uncircumcised[d] Philistines to get a
wife?[e]"

But Samson said to his father,
"Get her for me. She's the right one
for me." 4(His parents did not know
that this was from the LORD, who
was seeking an occasion to confront the Philistines;[f] for at that
time they were ruling over Israel.)[g] 5Samson went down to Timnah together with his father and

13:19 r Jdg 6:20
13:20 s Lev 9:24 t 1Ch 21:16 Eze 1:28 Mt 17:6
13:21 u ver 16 Jdg 6:22
13:22 v Dt 5:26 w Ge 32:30 Jdg 6:22
13:23 x Ps 25:14
13:24 y Heb 11:32 z 1Sa 3:19 a Lk 1:80
13:25 b Jdg 3:10 c Jdg 18:12
14:1 a Ge 38:12
14:2 b Ge 21:21 Ge 34:4
14:3 c Ge 24:4 d Dt 7:3 e Ex 34:16
14:4 f Jos 11:20 g Jdg 13:1
14:6 h Jdg 3:10 Jdg 13:25
14:12 i 1Ki 10:1 Eze 17:2 j Ge 29:27 k Ge 45:22 2Ki 5:5
14:15 l Jdg 16:5 Ecc 7:26

mother. As they approached the
vineyards of Timnah, suddenly a
young lion came roaring towards
him. 6The Spirit of the LORD came
upon him in power[h] so that he tore
the lion apart with his bare hands
as he might have torn a young goat.
But he told neither his father nor
his mother what he had done. 7Then
he went down and talked with the
woman, and he liked her.

8Some time later, when he went
back to marry her, he turned aside
to look at the lion's carcass. In it
was a swarm of bees and some
honey, 9which he scooped out with
his hands and ate as he went along.
When he rejoined his parents, he
gave them some, and they too ate it.
But he did not tell them that he had
taken the honey from the lion's carcass.

10Now his father went down to
see the woman. And Samson made
a feast there, as was customary for
bridegrooms. 11When he appeared,
he was given thirty companions.

12"Let me tell you a riddle,[i]"
Samson said to them. "If you can
give me the answer within the
seven days of the feast,[j] I will give
you thirty linen garments and
thirty sets of clothes.[k] 13If you
can't tell me the answer, you must
give me thirty linen garments and
thirty sets of clothes."

"Tell us your riddle," they said.
"Let's hear it."

14He replied,

"Out of the eater, something to
eat;
out of the strong, something
sweet."

For three days they could not give
the answer.

15On the fourth[a] day, they said to
Samson's wife, "Coax[l] your husband into explaining the riddle for
us, or we will burn you and your

[a] *15* Some Septuagint manuscripts and Syriac; Hebrew *seventh*

father's household to death.[m] Did
you invite us here to rob us?"
16Then Samson's wife threw herself on him, sobbing, "You hate me!
You don't really love me.[n] You've
given my people a riddle, but you
haven't told me the answer."
"I haven't even explained it to my
father or mother," he replied, "so
why should I explain it to you?"
17She cried the whole seven days[o]
of the feast. So on the seventh day
he finally told her, because she continued to press him. She in turn explained the riddle to her people.
18Before sunset on the seventh
day the men of the town said to him,

"What is sweeter than honey?
What is stronger than a
lion?"[p]

Samson said to them,

"If you had not ploughed with
my heifer,
you would not have solved my
riddle."

19Then the Spirit of the LORD
came upon him in power.[q] He went
down to Ashkelon, struck down
thirty of their men, stripped them
of their belongings and gave their
clothes to those who had explained
the riddle. Burning with anger,[r]
he went up to his father's house.
20And Samson's wife was given to
the friend[s] who had attended him
at his wedding.

Samson's Vengeance on the Philistines

15 Later on, at the time of
wheat harvest, Samson
took a young goat[a] and went to
visit his wife. He said, "I'm going to
my wife's room." But her father
would not let him go in.
2"I was so sure you thoroughly
hated her," he said, "that I gave her
to your friend.[b] Isn't her younger
sister more attractive? Take her instead."
3Samson said to them, "This time
I have a right to get even with the
Philistines; I will really harm
them." 4So he went out and caught
three hundred foxes and tied them
tail to tail in pairs. He then fastened a torch to every pair of tails,
5lit the torches and let the foxes
loose in the standing corn of the
Philistines. He burned up the
shocks and standing corn, together
with the vineyards and olive
groves.
6When the Philistines asked,
"Who did this?" they were told,
"Samson, the Timnite's son-in-law,
because his wife was given to his
friend."
So the Philistines went up and
burned her and her father to
death.[c] 7Samson said to them,
"Since you've acted like this, I
won't stop until I get my revenge on
you." 8He attacked them viciously
and slaughtered many of them.
Then he went down and stayed
in a cave in the rock of Etam.
9The Philistines went up and
camped in Judah, spreading out
near Lehi.[d] 10The men of Judah
asked, "Why have you come to fight
us?"
"We have come to take Samson
prisoner," they answered, "to do to
him as he did to us."
11Then three thousand men from
Judah went down to the cave in the
rock of Etam and said to Samson,
"Don't you realise that the Philistines are rulers over us?[e] What
have you done to us?"
He answered, "I merely did to
them what they did to me."
12They said to him, "We've come
to tie you up and hand you over to
the Philistines."
Samson said, "Swear to me that
you won't kill me yourselves."
13"Agreed," they answered. "We
will only tie you up and hand
you over to them. We will not kill
you." So they bound him with two
new ropes and led him up from the
rock. 14As he approached Lehi, the

14:15 m Jdg 15:6
14:16 n Jdg 16:15
14:17 o Est 1:5
14:18 p ver 14
14:19 q Nu 11:25; Jdg 3:10; Jdg 6:34; Jdg 11:29; Jdg 13:25; Jdg 15:14; 1Sa 11:6; 1Sa 16:13; 1Ki 18:46; 2Ch 24:20; Isa 11:2 r 1Sa 11:6
14:20 s Jdg 15:2,6; Jn 3:29
15:1 a Ge 38:17
15:2 b Jdg 14:20
15:6 c Jdg 14:15
15:9 d ver 14,17,19
15:11 e Jdg 13:1; Jdg 14:4; Ps 106:40-42

Philistines came towards him shouting. The Spirit of the LORD came upon him in power.[f] The ropes on his arms became like charred flax, and the bindings dropped from his hands. [15]Finding a fresh jaw-bone of a donkey, he grabbed it and struck down a thousand men.[g]

[16]Then Samson said,

"With a donkey's jaw-bone
 I have made donkeys of
  them.[a]
With a donkey's jaw-bone
 I have killed a thousand men."

[17]When he finished speaking, he threw away the jaw-bone; and the place was called Ramath Lehi.[b]

[18]Because he was very thirsty, he cried out to the LORD,[h] "You have given your servant this great victory. Must I now die of thirst and fall into the hands of the uncircumcised?" [19]Then God opened up the hollow place in Lehi, and water came out of it. When Samson drank, his strength returned and he revived.[i] So the spring was called En Hakkore,[c] and it is still there in Lehi.

[20]Samson led[d] Israel for twenty years[j] in the days of the Philistines.

Samson and Delilah

16 One day Samson went to Gaza, where he saw a prostitute. He went in to spend the night with her. [2]The people of Gaza were told, "Samson is here!" So they surrounded the place and lay in wait for him all night at the city gate.[a] They made no move during the night, saying, "At dawn we'll kill him."

[3]But Samson lay there only until the middle of the night. Then he got up and took hold of the doors of the city gate, together with the two posts, and tore them loose, bar and all. He lifted them to his shoulders and carried them to the top of the hill that faces Hebron.[b]

[4]Some time later, he fell in love[c] with a woman in the Valley of Sorek whose name was Delilah. [5]The rulers of the Philistines[d] went to her and said, "See if you can lure[e] him into showing you the secret of his great strength and how we can overpower him so that we may tie him up and subdue him. Each one of us will give you eleven hundred shekels[a] of silver."[f]

[6]So Delilah said to Samson, "Tell me the secret of your great strength and how you can be tied up and subdued."

[7]Samson answered her, "If anyone ties me with seven fresh thongs[b] that have not been dried, I'll become as weak as any other man."

[8]Then the rulers of the Philistines brought her seven fresh thongs that had not been dried, and she tied him with them. [9]With men hidden in the room,[g] she called to him, "Samson, the Philistines are upon you!" But he snapped the thongs as easily as a piece of string snaps when it comes close to a flame. So the secret of his strength was not discovered.

[10]Then Delilah said to Samson, "You have made a fool of me;[h] you lied to me. Come now, tell me how you can be tied."

[11]He said, "If anyone ties me securely with new ropes[i] that have never been used, I'll become as weak as any other man."

[12]So Delilah took new ropes and tied him with them. Then, with men hidden in the room, she called to him, "Samson, the Philistines are upon you!" But he snapped the ropes off his arms as if they were threads.

15:14 *f* Jdg 3:10; Jdg 14:19; 1Sa 11:6
15:15 *g* Lev 26:8; Jos 23:10; Jdg 3:31
15:18 *h* Jdg 16:28
15:19 *i* Ge 45:27; Isa 40:29
15:20 *j* Jdg 13:1; Jdg 16:31; Heb 11:32
16:2 *a* 1Sa 23:26; Ps 118:10-12; Ac 9:24
16:3 *b* Jos 10:36
16:4 *c* Ge 24:67
16:5 *d* Jos 13:3; *e* Ex 10:7; Jdg 14:15; *f* ver 18
16:9 *g* ver 12
16:10 *h* ver 13
16:11 *i* Jdg 15:13

[a]16 Or *made a heap or two*; the Hebrew for *donkey* sounds like the Hebrew for *heap*.
[b]17 *Ramath Lehi* means *jaw-bone hill.*
[c]19 *En Hakkore* means *caller's spring.*
[d]20 Traditionally *judged*
[a]5 That is, about 28 pounds (about 13 kilograms)
[b]7 Or *bow-strings*; also in verses 8 and 9

13 Delilah then said to Samson, "Until now, you have been making a fool of me and lying to me. Tell me how you can be tied."

He replied, "If you weave the seven braids of my head into the fabric ⌊on the loom⌋ and tighten it with the pin, I'll become as weak as any other man." So while he was sleeping, Delilah took the seven braids of his head, wove them into the fabric 14 and[c] tightened it with the pin.

Again she called to him, "Samson, the Philistines are upon you!"[j] He awoke from his sleep and pulled up the pin and the loom, with the fabric.

15 Then she said to him, "How can you say, 'I love you,'[k] when you won't confide in me? This is the third time[l] you have made a fool of me and haven't told me the secret of your great strength.[m]" 16 With such nagging she prodded him day after day until he was tired to death.

17 So he told her everything.[n] "No razor has ever been used on my head," he said, "because I have been a Nazirite[o] set apart to God since birth. If my head were shaved, my strength would leave me, and I would become as weak as any other man."

18 When Delilah saw that he had told her everything, she sent word to the rulers of the Philistines[p], "Come back once more; he has told me everything." So the rulers of the Philistines returned with the silver in their hands. 19 Having put him to sleep on her lap, she called a man to shave off the seven braids of his hair, and so began to subdue him.[d] And his strength left him.[q]

20 Then she called, "Samson, the Philistines are upon you!"

He awoke from his sleep and thought, "I'll go out as before and shake myself free." But he did not know that the LORD had left him.[r]

21 Then the Philistines[s] seized him, gouged out his eyes[t] and took him down to Gaza. Binding him with bronze shackles, they set him to grinding[u] in the prison. 22 But the hair on his head began to grow again after it had been shaved.

The Death of Samson

23 Now the rulers of the Philistines assembled to offer a great sacrifice to Dagon[v] their god and to celebrate, saying, "Our god has delivered Samson, our enemy, into our hands."

24 When the people saw him, they praised their god,[w] saying,

"Our god has delivered our
 enemy
 into our hands,[x]
the one who laid waste our land
 and multiplied our slain."

25 While they were in high spirits,[y] they shouted, "Bring out Samson to entertain us." So they called Samson out of the prison, and he performed for them.

When they stood him among the pillars, 26 Samson said to the servant who held his hand, "Put me where I can feel the pillars that support the temple, so that I may lean against them." 27 Now the temple was crowded with men and women; all the rulers of the Philistines were there, and on the roof[z] were about three thousand men and women watching Samson perform. 28 Then Samson prayed to the LORD,[a] "O Sovereign LORD, remember me. O God, please strengthen me just once more, and let me with one blow get revenge[b] on the Philistines for my two eyes." 29 Then Samson reached towards the two central pillars on which the temple stood. Bracing himself against them, his right hand on the one and his left hand on the other, 30 Samson said, "Let me die with the Philistines!" Then he pushed with

16:14 *j* ver 9,20
16:15 *k* Jdg 14:16 *l* Nu 24:10 *m* ver 5
16:17 *n* Mic 7:5 *o* Nu 6:2,5; Jdg 13:5
16:18 *p* Jos 13:3; 1Sa 5:8
16:19 *q* Pr 7:26-27
16:20 *r* Nu 14:42; Jos 7:12; 1Sa 16:14; 1Sa 18:12; 1Sa 28:15
16:21 *s* Jer 47:1 *t* Nu 16:14 *u* Job 31:10; Isa 47:2
16:23 *v* 1Sa 5:2; 1Ch 10:10
16:24 *w* Da 5:4 *x* 1Sa 31:9; 1Ch 10:9
16:25 *y* Jdg 9:27; Ru 3:7; Est 1:10
16:27 *z* Dt 22:8; Jos 2:8
16:28 *a* Jdg 15:18 *b* Jer 15:15

c 13,14 Some Septuagint manuscripts; Hebrew "*⌊I can⌋ if you weave the seven braids of my head into the fabric ⌊on the loom⌋.*" 14 *So she* d 19 Hebrew; some Septuagint manuscripts *and he began to weaken*

all his might, and down came the
temple on the rulers and all the
people in it. Thus he killed many
more when he died than while he
lived.
31 Then his brothers and his
father's whole family went down to
get him. They brought him back
and buried him between Zorah and
Eshtaol in the tomb of Manoah[c] his
father. He had led[e][d] Israel twenty
years.[e]

Micah's Idols

17 Now a man named Micah[a]
from the hill country of
Ephraim 2 said to his mother, "The
eleven hundred shekels[a] of silver
that were taken from you and about
which I heard you utter a curse – I
have that silver with me; I took it."
Then his mother said, "The LORD
bless you,[b] my son!"
3 When he returned the eleven
hundred shekels of silver to his
mother, she said, "I solemnly consecrate my silver to the LORD for
my son to make a carved image and
a cast idol.[c] I will give it back to
you."
4 So he returned the silver to his
mother, and she took two hundred
shekels[b] of silver and gave them to
a silversmith, who made them into
the image and the idol.[d] And they
were put in Micah's house.
5 Now this man Micah had a
shrine,[e] and he made an ephod[f]
and some idols[g] and installed[h] one
of his sons as his priest.[i] 6 In those
days Israel had no king;[j] everyone
did as he saw fit.[k]
7 A young Levite from Bethlehem
in Judah,[l] who had been living
within the clan of Judah, 8 left that
town in search of some other place
to stay. On his way[c] he came to Micah's house in the hill country of
Ephraim.
9 Micah asked him, "Where are
you from?"
"I'm a Levite from Bethlehem in
Judah," he said, "and I'm looking
for a place to stay."
10 Then Micah said to him, "Live
with me and be my father and
priest,[m] and I'll give you ten shekels[d] of silver a year, your clothes
and your food." 11 So the Levite
agreed to live with him, and the
young man was to him like one of
his sons. 12 Then Micah installed[n]
the Levite, and the young man became his priest and lived in his
house. 13 And Micah said, "Now I
know that the LORD will be good to
me, since this Levite has become
my priest."

Danites Settle in Laish

18 In those days Israel had no
king.[a]
And in those days the tribe of the
Danites was seeking a place of
their own where they might settle,
because they had not yet come into
an inheritance among the tribes of
Israel.[b] 2 So the Danites[c] sent five
warriors from Zorah and Eshtaol to
spy out the land and explore it.
These men represented all their
clans. They told them, "Go, explore
the land."[d]
The men entered the hill country
of Ephraim and came to the house
of Micah,[e] where they spent the
night. 3 When they were near Micah's house, they recognised the
voice of the young Levite; so they
turned in there and asked him,
"Who brought you here? What are
you doing in this place? Why are
you here?"
4 He told them what Micah had
done for him, and said, "He has
hired me and I am his priest.[f]"
5 Then they said to him, "Please
enquire of God[g] to learn whether
our journey will be successful."
6 The priest answered them, "Go

16:31 c Jdg 13:2 d Ru 1:1; 1Sa 4:18 e Jdg 15:20
17:1 a Jdg 18:2,13
17:2 b Ru 2:20; 1Sa 15:13; 2Sa 2:5
17:3 c Ex 20:4,23; Ex 34:17; Lev 19:4
17:4 d Ex 32:4; Isa 17:8
17:5 e Isa 44:13; Eze 8:10 f Jdg 8:27 g Ge 31:19; Jdg 18:14 h Nu 16:10 i Ex 29:9; Jdg 18:24
17:6 j Jdg 18:1; Jdg 19:1; Jdg 21:25 k Dt 12:8
17:7 l Jdg 19:1; Ru 1:1-2; Mic 5:2; Mt 2:1
17:10 m Jdg 18:19
17:12 n Nu 16:10
18:1 a Jdg 17:6; Jdg 19:1 b Jos 19:47
18:2 c Jdg 13:25 d Jos 2:1 e Jdg 17:1
18:4 f Jdg 17:12
18:5 g 1Ki 22:5

e31 Traditionally *judged*
a2 That is, about 28 pounds (about 13 kilograms)
b4 That is, about 5 pounds (about 2.3 kilograms)
c8 Or *To carry on his profession*
d10 That is, about 4 ounces (about 115 grams)

in peace[h]. Your journey has the
LORD's approval."
7 So the five men left and came to
Laish,[i] where they saw that the
people were living in safety, like
the Sidonians, unsuspecting and secure. And since their land lacked
nothing, they were prosperous.[a]
Also, they lived a long way from
the Sidonians[j] and had no relationship with anyone else.[b]
8 When they returned to Zorah
and Eshtaol, their brothers asked
them, "How did you find things?"
9 They answered, "Come on, let's
attack them! We have seen that the
land is very good. Aren't you going
to do something? Don't hesitate to
go there and take it over.[k] 10 When
you get there, you will find an unsuspecting people and a spacious
land that God has put into your
hands, a land that lacks nothing[l]
whatever.[m]"
11 Then six hundred men[n] from
the clan of the Danites,[o] armed for
battle, set out from Zorah and Eshtaol. 12 On their way they set up
camp near Kiriath Jearim in Judah.
This is why the place west of Kiriath Jearim is called Mahaneh
Dan[c][p] to this day. 13 From there
they went on to the hill country of
Ephraim and came to Micah's
house.
14 Then the five men who had
spied out the land of Laish said to
their brothers, "Do you know that
one of these houses has an ephod,
other household gods, a carved image and a cast idol?[q] Now you
know what to do." 15 So they turned
in there and went to the house of
the young Levite at Micah's place
and greeted him. 16 The six hundred
Danites,[r] armed for battle, stood
at the entrance to the gate. 17 The
five men who had spied out the land
went inside and took the carved image, the ephod, the other household
gods[s] and the cast idol while the
priest and the six hundred armed
men stood at the entrance to the
gate.

18:6 h 1Ki 22:6
18:7 i Jos 19:47 j ver 28
18:9 k Nu 13:30; 1Ki 22:3
18:10 l ver 7,27; Dt 8:9 m 1Ch 4:40
18:11 n ver 16,17 o Jdg 13:2
18:12 p Jdg 13:25
18:14 q Ge 31:19; Jdg 17:5
18:16 r ver 11
18:17 s Ge 31:19; Mic 5:13
18:18 t Isa 46:2; Jer 43:11; Hos 10:5
18:19 u Job 21:5; Job 29:9; Job 40:4; Mic 7:16 v Jdg 17:10
18:26 w Ps 18:17; Ps 35:10
18:27 x ver 7,10 y Ge 49:17; Jos 19:47
18:28 z ver 7

18 When these men went into Micah's house and took[t] the carved
image, the ephod, the other household gods and the cast idol, the
priest said to them, "What are you
doing?"
19 They answered him, "Be
quiet![u] Don't say a word. Come
with us, and be our father and
priest.[v] Isn't it better that you
serve a tribe and clan in Israel as
priest rather than just one man's
household?" 20 Then the priest was
glad. He took the ephod, the other
household gods and the carved image and went along with the people.
21 Putting their little children, their
livestock and their possessions in
front of them, they turned away
and left.
22 When they had gone some distance from Micah's house, the men
who lived near Micah were called
together and overtook the Danites.
23 As they shouted after them, the
Danites turned and said to Micah,
"What's the matter with you that
you called out your men to fight?"
24 He replied, "You took the gods
I made, and my priest, and went
away. What else do I have? How
can you ask, 'What's the matter
with you?' "
25 The Danites answered, "Don't
argue with us, or some hot-
tempered men will attack you, and
you and your family will lose your
lives." 26 So the Danites went their
way, and Micah, seeing that they
were too strong for him,[w] turned
round and went back home.
27 Then they took what Micah had
made, and his priest, and went on to
Laish, against a peaceful and unsuspecting people.[x] They attacked
them with the sword and burned
down their city.[y] 28 There was no-
one to rescue them because they
lived a long way from Sidon[z] and
had no relationship with anyone

[a] 7 The meaning of the Hebrew for this clause is uncertain. [b] 7 Hebrew; some Septuagint manuscripts *with the Arameans* [c] *12 Mahaneh Dan* means *Dan's camp.*

else. The city was in a valley near Beth Rehob.[a]

The Danites rebuilt the city and settled there. [29]They named it Dan[b] after their forefather Dan, who was born to Israel—though the city used to be called Laish.[c] [30]There the Danites set up for themselves the idols, and Jonathan son of Gershom,[d] the son of Moses,[d] and his sons were priests for the tribe of Dan until the time of the captivity of the land. [31]They continued to use the idols Micah had made, all the time the house of God[e] was in Shiloh.[f]

A Levite and His Concubine

19 In those days Israel had no king.

Now a Levite who lived in a remote area in the hill country of Ephraim[a] took a concubine from Bethlehem in Judah.[b] [2]But she was unfaithful to him. She left him and went back to her father's house in Bethlehem, Judah. After she had been there for four months, [3]her husband went to her to persuade her to return. He had with him his servant and two donkeys. She took him into her father's house, and when her father saw him, he gladly welcomed him. [4]His father-in-law, the girl's father, prevailed upon him to stay; so he remained with him three days, eating and drinking,[c] and sleeping there.

[5]On the fourth day they got up early and he prepared to leave, but the girl's father said to his son-in-law, "Refresh yourself[d] with something to eat; then you can go." [6]So the two of them sat down to eat and drink together. Afterwards the girl's father said, "Please stay tonight and enjoy yourself.[e]" [7]And when the man got up to go, his father-in-law persuaded him, so he stayed there that night. [8]On the morning of the fifth day, when he rose to go, the girl's father said, "Refresh yourself. Wait till afternoon!" So the two of them ate together.

[9]Then when the man, with his concubine and his servant, got up to leave, his father-in-law, the girl's father, said, "Now look, it's almost evening. Spend the night here; the day is nearly over. Stay and enjoy yourself. Early tomorrow morning you can get up and be on your way home." [10]But, unwilling to stay another night, the man left and went towards Jebus[f] (that is, Jerusalem), with his two saddled donkeys and his concubine.

[11]When they were near Jebus and the day was almost gone, the servant said to his master, "Come, let's stop at this city of the Jebusites[g] and spend the night."

[12]His master replied, "No. We won't go into an alien city, whose people are not Israelites. We will go on to Gibeah." [13]He added, "Come, let's try to reach Gibeah or Ramah[h] and spend the night in one of those places." [14]So they went on, and the sun set as they neared Gibeah in Benjamin.[i] [15]There they stopped to spend the night. They went and sat in the city square,[j] but no-one took them into his home for the night.

[16]That evening[k] an old man from the hill country of Ephraim,[l] who was living in Gibeah (the men of the place were Benjamites), came in from his work in the fields. [17]When he looked and saw the traveller in the city square, the old man asked, "Where are you going? Where did you come from?"[m]

[18]He answered, "We are on our way from Bethlehem in Judah to a remote area in the hill country of Ephraim where I live. I have been to Bethlehem in Judah and now I am going to the house of the LORD.[n] No-one has taken me into his house. [19]We have both straw

18:28 a Nu 13:21; 2Sa 10:6
18:29 b Ge 14:14; c Jos 19:47; 1Ki 15:20
18:30 d Ex 2:22; Jdg 17:3,5
18:31 e Jdg 19:18; f Jos 18:1; Jer 7:14
19:1 a Jdg 18:1; b Ru 1:1
19:4 c Ex 32:6
19:5 d ver 8; Ge 18:5
19:6 e ver 9,22; Jdg 16:25
19:10 f Ge 10:16; Jos 15:8; 1Ch 11:4-5
19:11 g Jos 3:10
19:13 h Jos 18:25
19:14 i 1Sa 10:26; Isa 10:29
19:15 j Ge 19:2
19:16 k Ps 104:23; l ver 1
19:17 m Ge 29:4
19:18 n Jdg 18:31

d30 An ancient Hebrew scribal tradition, some Septuagint manuscripts and Vulgate; Masoretic Text *Manasseh*

and fodder[o] for our donkeys and
bread and wine[p] for ourselves
your servants—me, your maidservant, and the young man with
us. We don't need anything."
20"You are welcome at my
house," the old man said. "Let me
supply whatever you need. Only
don't spend the night in the
square." 21So he took him into his
house and fed his donkeys. After
they had washed their feet, they
had something to eat and drink.[q]
22While they were enjoying
themselves,[r] some of the wicked
men[s] of the city surrounded the
house. Pounding on the door, they
shouted to the old man who owned
the house, "Bring out the man who
came to your house so we can have
sex with him.[t]"
23The owner of the house went
outside[u] and said to them, "No, my
friends, don't be so vile. Since this
man is my guest, don't do this disgraceful thing.[v] 24Look, here is my
virgin daughter,[w] and his concubine. I will bring them out to you
now, and you can use them and do
to them whatever you wish. But to
this man, don't do such a disgraceful thing."
25But the men would not listen to
him. So the man took his concubine
and sent her outside to them, and
they raped her and abused her[x]
throughout the night, and at dawn
they let her go. 26At daybreak the
woman went back to the house
where her master was staying, fell
down at the door and lay there until
daylight.
27When her master got up in the
morning and opened the door of the
house and stepped out to continue
on his way, there lay his concubine,
fallen in the doorway of the house,
with her hands on the threshold.
28He said to her, "Get up; let's go."
But there was no answer. Then the
man put her on his donkey and set
out for home.
29When he reached home, he took
a knife[y] and cut up his concubine,

19:19
o Ge 24:25
p Ge 14:18

19:21
q Ge 24:32-33
Lk 7:44

19:22
r Jdg 16:25
s Dt 13:13
t Ge 19:4-5
Jdg 20:5
Ro 1:26-27

19:23
u Ge 19:6
v Ge 34:7
Lev 19:29
Dt 22:21
Jdg 20:6
2Sa 13:12
Ro 1:27

19:24
w Ge 19:8
Dt 21:14

19:25
x 1Sa 31:4

19:29
y Ge 22:6
z Jdg 20:6
1Sa 11:7

19:30
a Hos 9:9
b Jdg 20:7
Pr 13:10

20:1
a Jdg 21:5
b 1Sa 3:20
2Sa 3:10
1Ki 4:25
c 1Sa 11:7
d 1Sa 7:5

20:2
e Jdg 8:10

20:4
f Jos 15:57
g Jdg 19:15

20:5
h Jdg 19:22
i Jdg 19:25-26

20:6
j Jdg 19:29
k Jos 7:15
Jdg 19:23

20:7
l Jdg 19:30

20:9
m Lev 16:8

limb by limb, into twelve parts and
sent them into all the areas of Israel.[z] 30Everyone who saw it said,
"Such a thing has never been seen
or done, not since the day the Israelites came up out of Egypt.[a]
Think about it! Consider it! Tell us
what to do![b]"

Israelites Fight the Benjamites

20 Then all the Israelites[a]
from Dan to Beersheba[b]
and from the land of Gilead came
out as one man[c] and assembled[d]
before the LORD in Mizpah. 2The
leaders of all the people of the
tribes of Israel took their places in
the assembly of the people of God,
four hundred thousand soldiers[e]
armed with swords. 3(The Benjamites heard that the Israelites had
gone up to Mizpah.) Then the Israelites said, "Tell us how this
awful thing happened."
4So the Levite, the husband of the
murdered woman, said, "I and my
concubine came to Gibeah[f] in
Benjamin to spend the night.[g]
5During the night the men of Gibeah came after me and surrounded
the house, intending to kill me.[h]
They raped my concubine, and she
died.[i] 6I took my concubine, cut
her into pieces and sent one piece
to each region of Israel's inheritance,[j] because they committed
this lewd and disgraceful act[k] in
Israel. 7Now, all you Israelites,
speak up and give your verdict.[l]"
8All the people rose as one man,
saying, "None of us will go home.
No, not one of us will return to his
house. 9But now this is what we'll
do to Gibeah: We'll go up against
it as the lot directs.[m] 10We'll take
ten men out of every hundred from
all the tribes of Israel, and a hundred from a thousand, and a thousand from ten thousand, to get
provisions for the army. Then,
when the army arrives at Gibeah[a]

[a] *10* One Hebrew manuscript; most Hebrew manuscripts *Geba*, a variant of *Gibeah*

in Benjamin, it can give them what
they deserve for all this vileness
done in Israel." 11So all the men of
Israel got together and united as
one man[n] against the city.
12The tribes of Israel sent men
throughout the tribe of Benjamin,
saying, "What about this awful
crime that was committed among
you? 13Now surrender those
wicked men[o] of Gibeah so that we
may put them to death and purge
the evil from Israel.[p]"
But the Benjamites would not listen to their fellow Israelites.
14From their towns they came together at Gibeah to fight against
the Israelites. 15At once the Benjamites mobilised twenty-six thousand swordsmen from their towns,
in addition to seven hundred chosen men from those living in Gibeah. 16Among all these soldiers
there were seven hundred chosen
men who were left-handed,[q] each
of whom could sling a stone at a
hair and not miss.
17Israel, apart from Benjamin,
mustered four hundred thousand
swordsmen, all of them fighting
men.
18The Israelites went up to
Bethel[b] and enquired of God.[r]
They said, "Who of us shall go first
to fight[s] against the Benjamites?"
The LORD replied, "Judah shall
go first."
19The next morning the Israelites
got up and pitched camp near Gibeah. 20The men of Israel went out to
fight the Benjamites and took up
battle positions against them at
Gibeah. 21The Benjamites came out
of Gibeah and cut down twenty-two
thousand Israelites[t] on the battlefield that day. 22But the men of Israel encouraged one another and
again took up their positions where
they had stationed themselves the
first day. 23The Israelites went up
and wept before the LORD until evening,[u] and they enquired of the
LORD. They said, "Shall we go up
again to battle[v] against the Benjamites, our brothers?"
The LORD answered, "Go up
against them."
24Then the Israelites drew near
to Benjamin the second day. 25This
time, when the Benjamites came
out from Gibeah to oppose them,
they cut down another eighteen
thousand Israelites,[w] all of them
armed with swords.
26Then the Israelites, all the people, went up to Bethel, and there
they sat weeping before the
LORD.[x] They fasted that day until
evening and presented burnt offerings and fellowship offerings[c] to
the LORD.[y] 27And the Israelites enquired of the LORD. (In those days
the ark of the covenant of God[z]
was there, 28with Phinehas son of
Eleazar,[a] the son of Aaron, ministering before it.)[b] They asked,
"Shall we go up again to battle with
Benjamin our brother, or not?"
The LORD responded, "Go, for tomorrow I will give them into your
hands.[c]"
29Then Israel set an ambush[d]
around Gibeah. 30They went up
against the Benjamites on the third
day and took up positions against
Gibeah as they had done before.
31The Benjamites came out to meet
them and were drawn away[e] from
the city. They began to inflict casualties on the Israelites as before, so
that about thirty men fell in the
open field and on the roads – the
one leading to Bethel and the other
to Gibeah.
32While the Benjamites were saying, "We are defeating them as before,"[f] the Israelites were saying,
"Let's retreat and draw them away
from the city to the roads."
33All the men of Israel moved
from their places and took up positions at Baal Tamar, and the Israelite ambush charged out of its

20:11 *n* ver 1
20:13 *o* Dt 13:13; Jdg 19:22 *p* Dt 17:12
20:16 *q* Jdg 3:15; 1Ch 12:2
20:18 *r* ver 26-27; Nu 27:21 *s* ver 23,28
20:21 *t* ver 25
20:23 *u* Jos 7:6 *v* ver 18
20:25 *w* ver 21
20:26 *x* ver 23 *y* Jdg 21:4
20:27 *z* Jos 18:1
20:28 *a* Jos 24:33 *b* Dt 18:5 *c* Jdg 7:9
20:29 *d* Jos 8:2,4
20:31 *e* Jos 8:16
20:32 *f* ver 39

b18 Or *to the house of God*; also in verse 26
c26 Traditionally *peace offerings*

place[g] on the west[d] of Gibeah.[e] [34]Then ten thousand of Israel's finest men made a frontal attack on Gibeah. The fighting was so heavy that the Benjamites did not realise[h] how near disaster was.[i] [35]The LORD defeated Benjamin[j] before Israel, and on that day the Israelites struck down 25,100 Benjamites, all armed with swords. [36]Then the Benjamites saw that they were beaten.

Now the men of Israel had given way[k] before Benjamin, because they relied on the ambush they had set near Gibeah. [37]The men who had been in ambush made a sudden dash into Gibeah, spread out and put the whole city to the sword.[l] [38]The men of Israel had arranged with the ambush that they should send up a great cloud of smoke[m] from the city, [39]and then the men of Israel would turn in the battle.

The Benjamites had begun to inflict casualties on the men of Israel (about thirty), and they said, "We are defeating them as in the first battle."[n] [40]But when the column of smoke began to rise from the city, the Benjamites turned and saw the smoke of the whole city going up into the sky.[o] [41]Then the men of Israel turned on them, and the men of Benjamin were terrified, because they realised that disaster had come upon them. [42]So they fled before the Israelites in the direction of the desert, but they could not escape the battle. And the men of Israel who came out of the towns cut them down there. [43]They surrounded the Benjamites, chased them and easily[f] overran them in the vicinity of Gibeah on the east. [44]Eighteen thousand Benjamites fell, all of them valiant fighters.[p] [45]As they turned and fled towards the desert to the rock of Rimmon,[q] the Israelites cut down five thousand men along the roads. They kept pressing after the Benjamites as far as Gidom and struck down two thousand more.

20:33 *g* Jos 8:19
20:34 *h* Jos 8:14 *i* Isa 47:11
20:35 *j* 1Sa 9:21
20:36 *k* Jos 8:15
20:37 *l* Jos 8:19
20:38 *m* Jos 8:20
20:39 *n* ver 32
20:40 *o* Jos 8:20
20:44 *p* Ps 76:5
20:45 *q* Jos 15:32 Jdg 21:13
20:48 *r* Jdg 21:23
21:1 *a* Jos 9:18 *b* Jdg 20:1 *c* ver 7,18
21:4 *d* Jdg 20:26 2Sa 24:25
21:5 *e* Jdg 5:23 Jdg 20:1
21:7 *f* ver 1

[46]On that day twenty-five thousand Benjamite swordsmen fell, all of them valiant fighters. [47]But six hundred men turned and fled into the desert to the rock of Rimmon, where they stayed for four months. [48]The men of Israel went back to Benjamin and put all the towns to the sword, including the animals and everything else they found. All the towns they came across they set on fire.[r]

Wives for the Benjamites

21 The men of Israel had taken an oath[a] at Mizpah:[b] "Not one of us will give[c] his daughter in marriage to a Benjamite."

[2]The people went to Bethel,[a] where they sat before God until evening, raising their voices and weeping bitterly. [3]"O LORD, the God of Israel," they cried, "why has this happened to Israel? Why should one tribe be missing from Israel today?"

[4]Early the next day the people built an altar and presented burnt offerings and fellowship offerings.[b][d]

[5]Then the Israelites asked, "Who from all the tribes of Israel[e] has failed to assemble before the LORD?" For they had taken a solemn oath that anyone who failed to assemble before the LORD at Mizpah should certainly be put to death.

[6]Now the Israelites grieved for their brothers, the Benjamites. "Today one tribe is cut off from Israel," they said. [7]"How can we provide wives for those who are left, since we have taken an oath[f] by the LORD not to give them any of our daughters in marriage?" [8]Then they asked, "Which one of the

[d]33 Some Septuagint manuscripts and Vulgate; the meaning of the Hebrew for this word is uncertain. [e]33 Hebrew *Geba*, a variant of *Gibeah* [f]43 The meaning of the Hebrew for this word is uncertain. [a]2 Or *to the house of God* [b]4 Traditionally *peace offerings*

tribes of Israel failed to assemble before the LORD at Mizpah?" They discovered that no-one from Jabesh Gilead[g] had come to the camp for the assembly. 9For when they counted the people, they found that none of the people of Jabesh Gilead were there.

10So the assembly sent twelve thousand fighting men with instructions to go to Jabesh Gilead and put to the sword those living there, including the women and children. 11"This is what you are to do," they said. "Kill every male and every woman who is not a virgin.[h]" 12They found among the people living in Jabesh Gilead four hundred young women who had never slept with a man, and they took them to the camp at Shiloh[i] in Canaan.

13Then the whole assembly sent an offer of peace[j] to the Benjamites at the rock of Rimmon.[k] 14So the Benjamites returned at that time and were given the women of Jabesh Gilead who had been spared. But there were not enough for all of them.

15The people grieved for Benjamin,[l] because the LORD had made a gap in the tribes of Israel. 16And the elders of the assembly said, "With the women of Benjamin destroyed, how shall we provide wives for the men who are left? 17The Benjamite survivors must have heirs," they said, "so that a tribe of Israel will not be wiped out. 18We can't give them our daughters as wives, since we Israelites have taken this oath: 'Cursed be anyone who gives[m] a wife to a Benjamite.' 19But look, there is the annual festival of the LORD in Shiloh,[n] to the north of Bethel, and east of the road that goes from Bethel to Shechem, and to the south of Lebonah."

20So they instructed the Benjamites, saying, "Go and hide in the vineyards 21and watch. When the girls of Shiloh come out to join in the dancing,[o] then rush from the vineyards and each of you seize a wife from the girls of Shiloh and go to the land of Benjamin. 22When their fathers or brothers complain to us, we will say to them, 'Do us a kindness by helping them, because we did not get wives for them during the war, and you are innocent, since you did not give[p] your daughters to them.' "

23So that is what the Benjamites did. While the girls were dancing, each man caught one and carried her off to be his wife. Then they returned to their inheritance and rebuilt the towns and settled in them.[q]

24At that time the Israelites left that place and went home to their tribes and clans, each to his own inheritance.

25In those days Israel had no king; everyone did as he saw fit.[r]

21:8 g 1Sa 11:1; 1Sa 31:11
21:11 h Nu 31:17-18
21:12 i Jos 18:1
21:13 j Dt 20:10; k Jdg 20:47
21:15 l ver 6
21:18 m ver 1
21:19 n Jos 18:1; Jdg 18:31; 1Sa 1:3
21:21 o Ex 15:20; Jdg 11:34
21:22 p ver 1,18
21:23 q Jdg 20:48
21:25 r Dt 12:8; Jdg 17:6; Jdg 18:1; Jdg 19:1

RUTH

Naomi and Ruth

1 In the days when the judges ruled,[a][a] there was a famine in the land,[b] and a man from Bethlehem in Judah, together with his wife and two sons, went to live for a while in the country of Moab.[c] 2 The man's name was Elimelech, his wife's name Naomi, and the names of his two sons were Mahlon and Kilion. They were Ephrathites from Bethlehem,[d] Judah. And they went to Moab and lived there.

3 Now Elimelech, Naomi's husband, died, and she was left with her two sons. 4 They married Moabite women, one named Orpah and the other Ruth.[e] After they had lived there about ten years, 5 both Mahlon and Kilion also died, and Naomi was left without her two sons and her husband.

6 When she heard in Moab that the LORD had come to the aid of his people[f] by providing food[g] for them, Naomi and her daughters-in-law prepared to return home from there. 7 With her two daughters-in-law she left the place where she had been living and set out on the road that would take them back to the land of Judah.

8 Then Naomi said to her two daughters-in-law, "Go back, each of you, to your mother's home. May the LORD show kindness[h] to you, as you have shown to your dead[i] and to me. 9 May the LORD grant that each of you will find rest[j] in the home of another husband."

Then she kissed them and they wept aloud 10 and said to her, "We will go back with you to your people."

11 But Naomi said, "Return home, my daughters. Why would you come with me? Am I going to have any more sons, who could become your husbands?[k] 12 Return home, my daughters; I am too old to have another husband. Even if I thought there was still hope for me—even if I had a husband tonight and then gave birth to sons—13 would you wait until they grew up? Would you remain unmarried for them? No, my daughters. It is more bitter for me than for you, because the LORD's hand has gone out against me![l]"

14 At this they wept again. Then Orpah kissed her mother-in-law[m] good-bye, but Ruth clung to her.[n]

15 "Look," said Naomi, "your sister-in-law is going back to her people and her gods.[o] Go back with her."

16 But Ruth replied, "Don't urge me to leave you[p] or to turn back from you. Where you go I will go, and where you stay I will stay. Your people will be my people and your God my God.[q] 17 Where you die I will die, and there I will be buried. May the LORD deal with me, be it ever so severely,[r] if anything but death separates you and me." 18 When Naomi realised that Ruth was determined to go with her, she stopped urging her.[s]

19 So the two women went on until they came to Bethlehem. When they arrived in Bethlehem, the whole town was stirred[t] because of them, and the women exclaimed, "Can this be Naomi?"

20 "Don't call me Naomi,"[b] she told them. "Call me Mara,[c] because the Almighty[d][u] has made my life very bitter.[v] 21 I went away full, but the LORD has brought me

1:1 *a* Jdg 2:16-18 *b* Ge 12:10; Ps 105:16 *c* Jdg 3:30
1:2 *d* Ge 35:19
1:4 *e* Mt 1:5
1:6 *f* Ex 4:31; Jer 29:10; Zep 2:7 *g* Ps 132:15; Mt 6:11
1:8 *h* Ru 2:20; 2Ti 1:16 *i* ver 5
1:9 *j* Ru 3:1
1:11 *k* Ge 38:11; Dt 25:5
1:13 *l* Jdg 2:15; Job 4:5; Job 19:21; Ps 32:4
1:14 *m* Ru 2:11 *n* Pr 17:17; Pr 18:24
1:15 *o* Jos 24:14; Jdg 11:24
1:16 *p* 2Ki 2:2 *q* Ru 2:11,12
1:17 *r* 1Sa 3:17; 1Sa 25:22; 2Sa 19:13; 2Ki 6:31
1:18 *s* Ac 21:14
1:19 *t* Mt 21:10
1:20 *u* Ex 6:3 *v* ver 13; Job 6:4

[a] *1* Traditionally *judged* [b] *20* *Naomi* means *pleasant*; also in verse 21. [c] *20* *Mara* means *bitter.* [d] *20* Hebrew *Shaddai*; also in verse 21

back empty.[w] Why call me Naomi? The LORD has afflicted[e] me; the Almighty has brought misfortune upon me."

22So Naomi returned from Moab accompanied by Ruth the Moabitess, her daughter-in-law, arriving in Bethlehem as the barley harvest[x] was beginning.[y]

Ruth Meets Boaz

2 Now Naomi had a relative[a] on her husband's side, from the clan of Elimelech,[b] a man of standing, whose name was Boaz.[c]

2And Ruth the Moabitess said to Naomi, "Let me go to the fields and pick up the leftover grain[d] behind anyone in whose eyes I find favour."

Naomi said to her, "Go ahead, my daughter." 3So she went out and began to glean in the fields behind the harvesters. As it turned out, she found herself working in a field belonging to Boaz, who was from the clan of Elimelech.

4Just then Boaz arrived from Bethlehem and greeted the harvesters, "The LORD be with you![e]"

"The LORD bless you![f]" they called back.

5Boaz asked the foreman of his harvesters, "Whose young woman is that?"

6The foreman replied, "She is the Moabitess[g] who came back from Moab with Naomi. 7She said, 'Please let me glean and gather among the sheaves behind the harvesters.' She went into the field and has worked steadily from morning till now, except for a short rest in the shelter."

8So Boaz said to Ruth, "My daughter, listen to me. Don't go and glean in another field and don't go away from here. Stay here with my servant girls. 9Watch the field where the men are harvesting, and follow along after the girls. I have told the men not to touch you. And whenever you are thirsty, go and get a drink from the water jars the men have filled."

10At this, she bowed down with her face to the ground.[h] She exclaimed, "Why have I found such favour in your eyes that you notice me[i]—a foreigner?[j]"

11Boaz replied, "I've been told all about what you have done for your mother-in-law[k] since the death of your husband—how you left your father and mother and your homeland and came to live with a people you did not know before.[l] 12May the LORD repay you for what you have done. May you be richly rewarded by the LORD,[m] the God of Israel, under whose wings[n] you have come to take refuge.[o]"

13"May I continue to find favour in your eyes, my lord," she said. "You have given me comfort and have spoken kindly to your servant—though I do not have the standing of one of your servant girls."

14At mealtime Boaz said to her, "Come over here. Have some bread and dip it in the wine vinegar."

When she sat down with the harvesters, he offered her some roasted grain. She ate all she wanted and had some left over.[p] 15As she got up to glean, Boaz gave orders to his men, "Even if she gathers among the sheaves, don't embarrass her. 16Rather, pull out some stalks for her from the bundles and leave them for her to pick up, and don't rebuke her."

17So Ruth gleaned in the field until evening. Then she threshed the barley she had gathered, and it amounted to about an ephah.[a] 18She carried it back to town, and her mother-in-law saw how much she had gathered. Ruth also brought out and gave her what she had left over[q] after she had eaten enough.

19Her mother-in-law asked her,

1:21 w Job 1:21
1:22 x Ex 9:31; Ru 2:23 y 2Sa 21:9
2:1 a Ru 3:2,12 b Ru 1:2 c Ru 4:21
2:2 d ver 7; Lev 19:9; Lev 23:22; Dt 24:19
2:4 e Jdg 6:12; Lk 1:28; 2Th 3:16 f Ps 129:7-8
2:6 g Ru 1:22
2:10 h 1Sa 25:23 i Ps 41:1 j Dt 15:3
2:11 k Ru 1:14 l Ru 1:16-17
2:12 m 1Sa 24:19 n Ps 17:8; Ps 36:7; Ps 57:1; Ps 61:4; Ps 63:7; Ps 91:4 o Ru 1:16
2:14 p ver 18
2:18 q ver 14

e21 Or *has testified against* a17 That is, probably about 3/5 bushel (about 22 litres)

"Where did you glean today? Where did you work? Blessed be the man who took notice of you![r]"

Then Ruth told her mother-in-law about the one at whose place she had been working. "The name of the man I worked with today is Boaz," she said.

20"The LORD bless him!" Naomi said to her daughter-in-law. "He has not stopped showing his kindness[s] to the living and the dead." She added, "That man is our close relative; he is one of our kinsman-redeemers.[t]"

21Then Ruth the Moabitess said, "He even said to me, 'Stay with my workers until they finish harvesting all my grain.' "

22Naomi said to Ruth her daughter-in-law, "It will be good for you, my daughter, to go with his girls, because in someone else's field you might be harmed."

23So Ruth stayed close to the servant girls of Boaz to glean until the barley and wheat harvests[u] were finished. And she lived with her mother-in-law.

Ruth and Boaz at the Threshing-Floor

3 One day Naomi her mother-in-law said to her, "My daughter, should I not try to find a home**[a]**[a] for you, where you will be well provided for? 2Is not Boaz, with whose servant girls you have been, a kinsman[b] of ours? Tonight he will be winnowing barley on the threshing-floor. 3Wash and perfume yourself,[c] and put on your best clothes. Then go down to the threshing-floor, but don't let him know you are there until he has finished eating and drinking. 4When he lies down, note the place where he is lying. Then go and uncover his feet and lie down. He will tell you what to do."

5"I will do whatever you say,"[d] Ruth answered. 6So she went down to the threshing-floor and did everything her mother-in-law told her to do.

7When Boaz had finished eating and drinking and was in good spirits,[e] he went over to lie down at the far end of the grain pile. Ruth approached quietly, uncovered his feet and lay down. 8In the middle of the night something startled the man, and he turned and discovered a woman lying at his feet.

9"Who are you?" he asked.

"I am your servant Ruth," she said. "Spread the corner of your garment[f] over me, since you are a kinsman-redeemer.[g]"

10"The LORD bless you, my daughter," he replied. "This kindness is greater than that which you showed earlier: You have not run after the younger men, whether rich or poor. 11And now, my daughter, don't be afraid. I will do for you all you ask. All my fellow townsmen know that you are a woman of noble character.[h] 12Although it is true that I am near of kin, there is a kinsman-redeemer[i] nearer than[j] I. 13Stay here for the night, and in the morning if he wants to redeem,[k] good; let him redeem. But if he is not willing, as surely as the LORD lives[l] I will do it. Lie here until morning."

14So she lay at his feet until morning, but got up before anyone could be recognised; and he said, "Don't let it be known that a woman came to the threshing-floor."[m]

15He also said, "Bring me the shawl you are wearing and hold it out." When she did so, he poured into it six measures of barley and put it on her. Then he**[b]** went back to town.

16When Ruth came to her mother-in-law, Naomi asked, "How did it go, my daughter?"

Then she told her everything Boaz had done for her 17and added,

2:19 r ver 10; Ps 41:1
2:20 s Ru 3:10; 2Sa 2:5; Pr 17:17; t Ru 3:9,12; Ru 4:1,14
2:23 u Dt 16:9
3:1 a Ru 1:9
3:2 b Dt 25:5-10; Ru 2:1
3:3 c 2Sa 14:2
3:5 d Eph 6:1; Col 3:20
3:7 e Jdg 19:6,9,22; 2Sa 13:28; 1Ki 21:7; Est 1:10
3:9 f Eze 16:8; g ver 12; Ru 2:20
3:11 h Pr 12:4; Pr 31:10
3:12 i ver 9; j Ru 4:1
3:13 k Dt 25:5; Ru 4:5; Mt 22:24; l Jdg 8:19; Jer 4:2
3:14 m Ro 14:16; 2Co 8:21

a*1* Hebrew *find rest* (see Ruth 1:9) **b***15* Most Hebrew manuscripts; many Hebrew manuscripts, Vulgate and Syriac *she*

"He gave me these six measures
of barley, saying, 'Don't go
back to your mother-in-law empty-
handed.'"
18Then Naomi said, "Wait, my
daughter, until you find out what
happens. For the man will not rest
until the matter is settled today."[n]

Boaz Marries Ruth

4 Meanwhile Boaz went up to
the town gate and sat there.
When the kinsman-redeemer he
had mentioned[a] came along, Boaz
said, "Come over here, my friend,
and sit down." So he went over and
sat down.
2Boaz took ten of the elders[b] of
the town and said, "Sit here," and
they did so. 3Then he said to the
kinsman-redeemer, "Naomi, who
has come back from Moab, is selling the piece of land that belonged
to our brother Elimelech. 4I
thought I should bring the matter
to your attention and suggest that
you buy it in the presence of these
seated here and in the presence of
the elders of my people. If you will
redeem it, do so. But if you[a] will
not, tell me, so I will know. For no-
one has the right to do it except
you,[c] and I am next in line."
"I will redeem it," he said.
5Then Boaz said, "On the day you
buy the land from Naomi and from
Ruth the Moabitess, you acquire[b]
the dead man's widow, in order to
maintain the name of the dead with
his property."[d]
6At this, the kinsman-redeemer
said, "Then I cannot redeem[e] it because I might endanger my own estate. You redeem it yourself. I
cannot do it."
7(Now in earlier times in Israel,
for the redemption and transfer of
property to become final, one party
took off his sandal and gave it to the
other. This was the method of legal-
ising transactions in Israel.)[f]
8So the kinsman-redeemer said
to Boaz, "Buy it yourself." And he
removed his sandal.
9Then Boaz announced to the elders and all the people, "Today you
are witnesses that I have bought
from Naomi all the property of Elimelech, Kilion and Mahlon. 10I
have also acquired Ruth the Moabitess, Mahlon's widow, as my
wife, in order to maintain the name
of the dead with his property, so
that his name will not disappear
from among his family or from the
town records.[g] Today you are witnesses!"
11Then the elders and all those at
the gate said, "We are witnesses.[h]
May the LORD make the woman
who is coming into your home like
Rachel and Leah,[i] who together
built up the house of Israel. May
you have standing in Ephrathah[j]
and be famous in Bethlehem.
12Through the offspring the LORD
gives you by this young woman,
may your family be like that of
Perez,[k] whom Tamar bore to Judah."

The Genealogy of David

4:18–22pp 1Ch 2:5–15; Mt 1:3–6; Lk 3:31–33

13So Boaz took Ruth and she became his wife. Then he went to her,
and the LORD enabled her to conceive,[l] and she gave birth to a son.
14The women[m] said to Naomi:
"Praise be to the LORD, who this day
has not left you without a kinsman-
redeemer. May he become famous
throughout Israel! 15He will renew
your life and sustain you in your
old age. For your daughter-in-law,
who loves you and who is better to
you than seven sons,[n] has given
him birth."
16Then Naomi took the child, laid
him in her lap and cared for him.
17The women living there said,
"Naomi has a son." And they named

3:18 *n* Ps 37:3-5
4:1 *a* Ru 3:12
4:2 *b* 1Ki 21:8; Pr 31:23
4:4 *c* Lev 25:25; Jer 32:7-8
4:5 *d* Ge 38:8; Dt 25:5-6; Ru 3:13; Mt 22:24
4:6 *e* Lev 25:25; Ru 3:13
4:7 *f* Dt 25:7-9
4:10 *g* Dt 25:6
4:11 *h* Dt 25:9 *i* Ps 127:3; Ps 128:3 *j* Ge 35:16
4:12 *k* ver 18; Ge 38:29
4:13 *l* Ge 29:31; Ge 33:5; Ru 3:11
4:14 *m* Lk 1:58
4:15 *n* Ru 1:16-17; Ru 2:11-12; 1Sa 1:8

[a]4 Many Hebrew manuscripts, Septuagint, Vulgate and Syriac; most Hebrew manuscripts *he*
[b]5 Hebrew; Vulgate and Syriac *Naomi, you acquire Ruth the Moabitess,*

him Obed. He was the father of Jesse,[o] the father of David.

[18]This, then, is the family line of Perez[p]:

Perez was the father of Hezron,
[19]Hezron the father of Ram,
Ram the father of Amminadab,[q]
[20]Amminadab the father of Nahshon,
Nahshon the father of Salmon,[c]
[21]Salmon the father of Boaz,[r]
Boaz the father of Obed,
[22]Obed the father of Jesse,
and Jesse the father of David.

4:17 *o* ver 22 1Sa 16:1,18 1Ch 2:12,13
4:18 *p* Mt 1:3-6
4:19 *q* Ex 6:23
4:21 *r* Ru 2:1

[c]*20* A few Hebrew manuscripts, some Septuagint manuscripts and Vulgate (see also verse 21 and Septuagint of 1 Chron. 2:11); most Hebrew manuscripts *Salma*

1 SAMUEL

The Birth of Samuel

1 There was a certain man from
Ramathaim, a Zuphite[a] from
the hill country[a] of Ephraim,
whose name was Elkanah[b] son of
Jeroham, the son of Elihu, the son
of Tohu, the son of Zuph, an Ephraimite. 2He had two wives;[c] one was
called Hannah and the other Peninnah. Peninnah had children, but
Hannah had none.
3Year after year[d] this man went
up from his town to worship[e] and
sacrifice to the LORD Almighty at
Shiloh,[f] where Hophni and Phinehas, the two sons of Eli, were
priests of the LORD. 4Whenever the
day came for Elkanah to sacrifice,[g] he would give portions of the
meat to his wife Peninnah and to all
her sons and daughters. 5But to
Hannah he gave a double portion
because he loved her, and the LORD
had closed her womb.[h] 6And because the LORD had closed her
womb, her rival kept provoking her
in order to irritate her.[i] 7This went
on year after year. Whenever Hannah went up to the house of the
LORD, her rival provoked her till
she wept and would not eat. 8Elka-
nah her husband would say to her,
"Hannah, why are you weeping?
Why don't you eat? Why are you
downhearted? Don't I mean more
to you than ten sons?[j]"
9Once when they had finished
eating and drinking in Shiloh, Hannah stood up. Now Eli the priest
was sitting on a chair by the doorpost of the LORD's temple.[b][k] 10In
bitterness of soul[l] Hannah wept
much and prayed to the LORD.
11And she made a vow, saying,
"O LORD Almighty, if you will only
look upon your servant's misery
and remember[m] me, and not forget
your servant but give her a son,
then I will give him to the LORD for
all the days of his life, and no
razor[n] will ever be used on his
head."
12As she kept on praying to the
LORD, Eli observed her mouth.
13Hannah was praying in her heart,
and her lips were moving but her
voice was not heard. Eli thought
she was drunk 14and said to her,
"How long will you keep on getting
drunk? Get rid of your wine."
15"Not so, my lord," Hannah replied, "I am a woman who is deeply
troubled. I have not been drinking
wine or beer; I was pouring[o] out
my soul to the LORD. 16Do not take
your servant for a wicked woman;
I have been praying here out of my
great anguish and grief."
17Eli answered, "Go in peace,[p]
and may the God of Israel grant
you what you have asked of him.[q]"
18She said, "May your servant
find favour in your eyes.[r]" Then
she went her way and ate something, and her face was no longer
downcast.[s]
19Early the next morning they
arose and worshipped before the
LORD and then went back to their
home at Ramah. Elkanah lay with
Hannah his wife, and the LORD remembered[t] her. 20So in the course
of time Hannah conceived and
gave birth to a son. She named[u]
him Samuel,[c] saying, "Because I
asked the LORD for him."

Hannah Dedicates Samuel

21When the man Elkanah went up
with all his family to offer the annual[v] sacrifice to the LORD and to

1:1 a Jos 17:17-18 b 1Ch 6:27,34
1:2 c Dt 21:15-17 Lk 2:36
1:3 d ver 21 Ex 23:14 Ex 34:23 Lk 2:41 e Dt 12:5-7 f Jos 18:1
1:4 g Dt 12:17-18
1:5 h Ge 16:1 Ge 30:2
1:6 i Job 24:21
1:8 j Ru 4:15
1:9 k 1Sa 3:3
1:10 l Job 7:11
1:11 m Ge 8:1 Ge 28:20 Ge 29:32 n Nu 6:1-21 Jdg 13:5
1:15 o Ps 42:4 Ps 62:8 La 2:19
1:17 p Jdg 18:6 1Sa 25:35 2Ki 5:19 Mk 5:34 q Ps 20:3-5
1:18 r Ru 2:13 s Ecc 9:7 Ro 15:13
1:19 t Ge 4:1 Ge 30:22
1:20 u Ge 41:51-52 Ex 2:10,22 Mt 1:21
1:21 v ver 3

[a]1 Or *from Ramathaim Zuphim* [b]9 That is, tabernacle [c]20 *Samuel* sounds like the Hebrew for *heard of God.*

fulfil his vow,[w] 22Hannah did not
go. She said to her husband, "After
the boy is weaned, I will take him
and present[x] him before the LORD,
and he will live there always."
23"Do what seems best to you,"
Elkanah her husband told her.
"Stay here until you have weaned
him; only may the LORD make
good[y] his[d] word." So the woman
stayed at home and nursed her son
until she had weaned him.
24After he was weaned, she took
the boy with her, young as he was,
along with a three-year-old bull,[e][z]
an ephah[f] of flour and a skin of
wine, and brought him to the house
of the LORD at Shiloh. 25When they
had slaughtered the bull, they
brought the boy to Eli, 26and she
said to him, "As surely as you live,
my lord, I am the woman who stood
here beside you praying to the
LORD. 27I prayed[a] for this child,
and the LORD has granted me what
I asked of him. 28So now I give him
to the LORD. For his whole life[b] he
shall be given over to the LORD."
And he worshipped the LORD there.

Hannah's Prayer

2 Then Hannah prayed and
said:[a]

"My heart rejoices[b] in the
LORD;
in the LORD my horn[a][c] is
lifted high.
My mouth boasts over my
enemies,
for I delight in your
deliverance.

2"There is no-one holy[b][d] like
the LORD;
there is no-one besides you;
there is no Rock[e] like our
God.

3"Do not keep talking so proudly
or let your mouth speak such
arrogance,[f]
for the LORD is a God who
knows,
and by him deeds[g] are
weighed.[h]

4"The bows of the warriors are
broken,[i]
but those who stumbled are
armed with strength.
5Those who were full hire
themselves out for food,
but those who were hungry
hunger no more.
She who was barren[j] has borne
seven children,
but she who has had many
sons pines away.

6"The LORD brings death and
makes alive;[k]
he brings down to the grave[c]
and raises up.[l]
7The LORD sends poverty and
wealth;[m]
he humbles and he exalts.[n]
8He raises[o] the poor from the
dust
and lifts the needy from the
ash heap;
he seats them with princes
and has them inherit a throne
of honour.[p]

"For the foundations[q] of the
earth are the LORD's;
upon them he has set the
world.
9He will guard the feet[r] of his
saints,
but the wicked will be
silenced in darkness.[s]

"It is not by strength[t] that one
prevails;
10 those who oppose the LORD
will be shattered.[u]
He will thunder[v] against them
from heaven;
the LORD will judge[w] the ends
of the earth.

1:21 w Dt 12:11
1:22 x ver 11,28; Lk 2:22
1:23 y ver 17; Nu 30:7
1:24 z Nu 15:8-10; Dt 12:5; Jos 18:1
1:27 a ver 11-13; Ps 66:19-20
1:28 b ver 11,22; Ge 24:26,52
2:1 a Lk 1:46-55 b Ps 9:14; Ps 13:5 c Ps 89:17,24; Ps 92:10; Isa 12:2-3
2:2 d Ex 15:11; Lev 19:2 e Dt 32:30-31; 2Sa 22:2,32
2:3 f Pr 8:13 g 1Sa 16:7; 1Ki 8:39 h Pr 16:2; Pr 24:11-12
2:4 i Ps 37:15
2:5 j Ps 113:9; Jer 15:9
2:6 k Dt 32:39 l Isa 26:19
2:7 m Dt 8:18 n Job 5:11; Ps 75:7
2:8 o Ps 113:7-8 p Job 36:7 q Job 38:4
2:9 r Ps 91:12 s Mt 8:12 t Ps 33:16-17
2:10 u Ps 2:9 v Ps 18:13 w Ps 96:13

[d]23 Masoretic Text; Dead Sea Scrolls, Septuagint and Syriac *your* [e]24 Dead Sea Scrolls, Septuagint and Syriac; Masoretic Text *with three bulls* [f]24 That is, probably about 3/5 bushel (about 22 litres) [a]1 *Horn* here symbolises strength; also in verse 10. [b]2 Or *no Holy One* [c]6 Hebrew *Sheol*

"He will give strength[x] to his
king
and exalt the horn[y] of his
anointed."

11Then Elkanah went home to Ramah, but the boy ministered[z] before the LORD under Eli the priest.

Eli's Wicked Sons

12Eli's sons were wicked men;
they had no regard[a] for the LORD.
13Now it was the practice of the
priests with the people that whenever anyone offered a sacrifice and
while the meat[b] was being boiled,
the servant of the priest would
come with a three-pronged fork in
his hand. 14He would plunge it into
the pan or kettle or cauldron or pot,
and the priest would take for himself whatever the fork brought up.
This is how they treated all the Israelites who came to Shiloh. 15But
even before the fat was burned, the
servant of the priest would come
and say to the man who was sacrificing, "Give the priest some meat
to roast; he won't accept boiled
meat from you, but only raw."
16If the man said to him, "Let the
fat be burned up first, and then
take whatever you want," the servant would then answer, "No, hand
it over now; if you don't, I'll take it
by force."
17This sin of the young men was
very great in the LORD's sight, for
they[d] were treating the LORD's offering with contempt.[c]
18But Samuel was ministering[d]
before the LORD—a boy wearing a
linen ephod.[e] 19Each year his
mother made him a little robe and
took it to him when she went up
with her husband to offer the annual[f] sacrifice. 20Eli would bless
Elkanah and his wife, saying, "May
the LORD give you children by this
woman to take the place of the one
she prayed[g] for and gave to the
LORD." Then they would go home.
21And the LORD was gracious to
Hannah;[h] she conceived and gave
birth to three sons and two daughters. Meanwhile, the boy Samuel
grew[i] up in the presence of the
LORD.
22Now Eli, who was very old,
heard about everything his sons
were doing to all Israel and how
they slept with the women[j] who
served at the entrance to the Tent
of Meeting. 23So he said to them,
"Why do you do such things? I hear
from all the people about these
wicked deeds of yours. 24No, my
sons; it is not a good report that I
hear spreading among the LORD's
people. 25If a man sins against another man, God[e] may mediate for
him; but if a man sins against the
LORD, who will[k] intercede[l] for
him?" His sons, however, did not
listen to their father's rebuke, for it
was the LORD's will to put them to
death.
26And the boy Samuel continued
to grow[m] in stature and in favour
with the LORD and with men.

Prophecy Against the House of Eli

27Now a man of God[n] came to Eli
and said to him, "This is what the
LORD says: 'Did I not clearly reveal
myself to your father's house when
they were in Egypt under Pharaoh?
28I chose[o] your father out of all the
tribes of Israel to be my priest, to
go up to my altar, to burn incense,
and to wear an ephod[p] in my presence. I also gave your father's
house all the offerings made with
fire by the Israelites. 29Why do
you[f] scorn my sacrifice and offering[q] that I prescribed for my
dwelling?[r] Why do you honour
your sons more than me by fatten-
ing yourselves on the choice parts
of every offering made by my
people Israel?'
30"Therefore the LORD, the God
of Israel, declares: 'I promised that
your house and your father's house

2:10 x Ps 21:1 y Ps 89:24
2:11 z ver 18; 1Sa 3:1
2:12 a Jer 2:8; Jer 9:6
2:13 b Lev 7:29-34
2:17 c Mal 2:7-9
2:18 d ver 11; 1Sa 3:1 e ver 28
2:19 f 1Sa 1:3
2:20 g 1Sa 1:11, 27-28; Lk 2:34
2:21 h Ge 21:1 i ver 26; Jdg 13:24; 1Sa 3:19; Lk 2:40
2:22 j Ex 38:8
2:25 k Nu 15:30; Jos 11:20 l Dt 1:17; 1Sa 3:14; Heb 10:26
2:26 m ver 21; Lk 2:52
2:27 n Ex 4:14-16; 1Ki 13:1
2:28 o Ex 28:1 p Lev 8:7-8
2:29 q ver 12-17 r Dt 12:5; Mt 10:37

d17 Or *men* e25 Or *the judges*
f29 The Hebrew is plural.

would minister before me for
ever.[s]' But now the LORD declares:
'Far be it from me! Those who
honour me I will honour,[t] but those
who despise[u] me will be disdained.
31The time is coming when I will
cut short your strength and the
strength of your father's house, so
that there will not be an old man in
your family line[v] 32and you will
see distress in my dwelling. Although good will be done to Israel,
in your family line there will never
be an old man.[w] 33Every one of you
that I do not cut off from my altar
will be spared only to blind your
eyes with tears and to grieve your
heart, and all your descendants will
die in the prime of life.

34" 'And what happens to your
two sons, Hophni and Phinehas,
will be a sign to you – they will both
die[x] on the same day.[y] 35I will
raise up for myself a faithful
priest,[z] who will do according to
what is in my heart and mind. I will
firmly establish his house, and he
will minister before my anointed[a]
one always. 36Then everyone left in
your family line will come and bow
down before him for a piece of silver and a crust of bread and plead,
"Appoint me to some priestly office so that I can have food to
eat.[b]" ' "

The LORD Calls Samuel

3 The boy Samuel ministered[a]
before the LORD under Eli. In
those days the word of the LORD
was rare;[b] there were not many
visions.[c]

2One night Eli, whose eyes[d]
were becoming so weak that he
could barely see, was lying down in
his usual place. 3The lamp[e] of God
had not yet gone out, and Samuel
was lying down in the temple[a] of
the LORD, where the ark of God
was. 4Then the LORD called Samuel.

Samuel answered, "Here I am.[f]"
5And he ran to Eli and said, "Here
I am; you called me."

2:30 s Ex 29:9 t Ps 50:23 Ps 91:15 u Mal 2:9
2:31 v 1Sa 4:11-18 1Sa 22:16-20
2:32 w 1Ki 2:26-27 Zec 8:4
2:34 x 1Sa 4:11 y 1Ki 13:3
2:35 z 1Sa 12:3 1Ki 2:35 a 1Sa 16:13 2Sa 7:11,27 1Ki 11:38
2:36 b 1Ki 2:27
3:1 a 1Sa 2:11 b Ps 74:9 c Am 8:11
3:2 d 1Sa 4:15
3:3 e Lev 24:1-4
3:4 f Isa 6:8
3:7 g Ac 19:12
3:11 h 2Ki 21:12 Jer 19:3
3:12 i 1Sa 2:27-36
3:13 j 1Sa 2:12,17, 22,29-31
3:14 k Lev 15:30-31 1Sa 2:25 Isa 22:14

But Eli said, "I did not call; go
back and lie down." So he went and
lay down.

6Again the LORD called,
"Samuel!" And Samuel got up and
went to Eli and said, "Here I am;
you called me."

"My son," Eli said, "I did not call;
go back and lie down."

7Now Samuel did not yet know
the LORD: The word of the LORD had
not yet been revealed[g] to him.

8The LORD called Samuel a third
time, and Samuel got up and went
to Eli and said, "Here I am; you
called me."

Then Eli realised that the LORD
was calling the boy. 9So Eli told
Samuel, "Go and lie down, and if he
calls you, say, 'Speak, LORD, for
your servant is listening.' " So
Samuel went and lay down in his
place.

10The LORD came and stood there,
calling as at the other times,
"Samuel! Samuel!"

Then Samuel said, "Speak, for
your servant is listening."

11And the LORD said to Samuel:
"See, I am about to do something in
Israel that will make the ears of
everyone who hears of it tingle.[h]
12At that time I will carry out
against Eli everything[i] I spoke
against his family – from beginning to end. 13For I told him that I
would judge his family for ever because of the sin he knew about; his
sons made themselves contemptible,[b] and he failed to restrain[j]
them. 14Therefore, I swore to the
house of Eli, 'The guilt of Eli's
house will never be atoned[k] for by
sacrifice or offering.' "

15Samuel lay down until morning
and then opened the doors of the
house of the LORD. He was afraid to
tell Eli the vision, 16but Eli called
him and said, "Samuel, my son."

Samuel answered, "Here I am."

[a]3 That is, tabernacle [b]13 Masoretic Text; an ancient Hebrew scribal tradition and Septuagint *sons blasphemed God*

17“What was it he said to you?” Eli asked. “Do not hide it from me. May God deal with you, be it ever so severely,[l] if you hide from me anything he told you.” 18So Samuel told him everything, hiding nothing from him. Then Eli said, “He is the LORD; let him do what is good in his eyes.”[m]

19The LORD was with[n] Samuel as he grew[o] up, and he let none[p] of his words fall to the ground. 20And all Israel from Dan to Beersheba[q] recognised that Samuel was attested as a prophet of the LORD. 21The LORD continued to appear at Shiloh, and there he revealed[r] himself to Samuel through his word.

4 And Samuel’s word came to all Israel.

The Philistines Capture the Ark

Now the Israelites went out to fight against the Philistines. The Israelites camped at Ebenezer,[a] and the Philistines at Aphek.[b] 2The Philistines deployed their forces to meet Israel, and as the battle spread, Israel was defeated by the Philistines, who killed about four thousand of them on the battlefield. 3When the soldiers returned to camp, the elders of Israel asked, “Why[c] did the LORD bring defeat upon us today before the Philistines? Let us bring the ark[d] of the LORD’s covenant from Shiloh, so that it[a] may go with us and save us from the hand of our enemies.”

4So the people sent men to Shiloh, and they brought back the ark of the covenant of the LORD Almighty, who is enthroned between the cherubim.[e] And Eli’s two sons, Hophni and Phinehas, were there with the ark of the covenant of God.

5When the ark of the LORD’s covenant came into the camp, all Israel raised such a great shout[f] that the ground shook. 6Hearing the uproar, the Philistines asked, “What’s all this shouting in the Hebrew camp?”

When they learned that the ark of the LORD had come into the camp, 7the Philistines were afraid.[g] “A god has come into the camp,” they said. “We’re in trouble! Nothing like this has happened before. 8Woe to us! Who will deliver us from the hand of these mighty gods? They are the gods who struck the Egyptians with all kinds of plagues in the desert. 9Be strong, Philistines! Be men, or you will be subject to the Hebrews, as they[h] have been to you. Be men, and fight!”

10So the Philistines fought, and the Israelites were defeated[i] and every man fled to his tent. The slaughter was very great; Israel lost thirty thousand foot soldiers. 11The ark of God was captured, and Eli’s two sons, Hophni and Phinehas, died.[j]

Death of Eli

12That same day a Benjamite ran from the battle line and went to Shiloh, his clothes torn and dust[k] on his head. 13When he arrived, there was Eli[l] sitting on his chair by the side of the road, watching, because his heart feared for the ark of God. When the man entered the town and told what had happened, the whole town sent up a cry.

14Eli heard the outcry and asked, “What is the meaning of this uproar?”

The man hurried over to Eli, 15who was ninety-eight years old and whose eyes[m] were set so that he could not see. 16He told Eli, “I have just come from the battle line; I fled from it this very day.”

Eli asked, “What happened, my son?”

17The man who brought the news replied, “Israel fled before the Philistines, and the army has suffered heavy losses. Also your two

3:17 l Ru 1:17; 2Sa 3:35
3:18 m Job 2:10; Isa 39:8
3:19 n Ge 21:22; Ge 39:2; o 1Sa 2:21; p 1Sa 9:6
3:20 q Jdg 20:1
3:21 r ver 10
4:1 a 1Sa 7:12; b Jos 12:18; 1Sa 29:1
4:3 c Jos 7:7; d Nu 10:35; Jos 6:7
4:4 e Ex 25:22; 2Sa 6:2
4:5 f Jos 6:5,10
4:7 g Ex 15:14
4:9 h Jdg 13:1; 1Co 16:13
4:10 i ver 2; Dt 28:25; 2Sa 18:17; 2Ki 14:12
4:11 j 1Sa 2:34; Ps 78:61,64
4:12 k Jos 7:6; 2Sa 1:2; 2Sa 15:32; Ne 9:1; Job 2:12
4:13 l ver 18; 1Sa 1:9
4:15 m 1Sa 3:2

[a]3 Or *he*

sons, Hophni and Phinehas, are dead, and the ark of God has been captured."

18 When he mentioned the ark of God, Eli fell backwards off his chair by the side of the gate. His neck was broken and he died, for he was an old man and heavy. He had led[b][n] Israel for forty years.

19 His daughter-in-law, the wife of Phinehas, was pregnant and near the time of delivery. When she heard the news that the ark of God had been captured and that her father-in-law and her husband were dead, she went into labour and gave birth, but was overcome by her labour pains. 20 As she was dying, the women attending her said, "Don't despair; you have given birth to a son." But she did not respond or pay any attention.

21 She named the boy Ichabod,[c][o] saying, "The glory[p] has departed from Israel"—because of the capture of the ark of God and the deaths of her father-in-law and her husband. 22 She said, "The glory has departed from Israel, for the ark of God has been captured."

The Ark in Ashdod and Ekron

5 After the Philistines had captured the ark of God, they took it from Ebenezer[a] to Ashdod.[b] 2 Then they carried the ark into Dagon's temple and set it beside Dagon.[c] 3 When the people of Ashdod rose early the next day, there was Dagon, fallen[d] on his face on the ground before the ark of the LORD! They took Dagon and put him back in his place. 4 But the following morning when they rose, there was Dagon, fallen on his face on the ground before the ark of the LORD! His head and hands had been broken[e] off and were lying on the threshold; only his body remained. 5 That is why to this day neither the priests of Dagon nor any others who enter Dagon's temple at Ashdod step on the threshold.[f]

6 The LORD's hand[g] was heavy upon the people of Ashdod and its vicinity; he brought devastation[h] upon them and afflicted them with tumours.[a][i] 7 When the men of Ashdod saw what was happening, they said, "The ark of the god of Israel must not stay here with us, because his hand is heavy upon us and upon Dagon our god." 8 So they called together all the rulers of the Philistines and asked them, "What shall we do with the ark of the god of Israel?"

They answered, "Have the ark of the god of Israel moved to Gath.[j]" So they moved the ark of the God of Israel.

9 But after they had moved it, the LORD's hand was against that city, throwing it into a great panic.[k] He afflicted the people of the city, both young and old, with an outbreak of tumours.[b] 10 So they sent the ark of God to Ekron.

As the ark of God was entering Ekron, the people of Ekron cried out, "They have brought the ark of the god of Israel round to us to kill us and our people." 11 So they called together all the rulers[l] of the Philistines and said, "Send the ark of the god of Israel away; let it go back to its own place, or it[c] will kill us and our people." For death had filled the city with panic; God's hand was very heavy upon it. 12 Those who did not die were afflicted with tumours, and the outcry of the city went up to heaven.

The Ark Returned to Israel

6 When the ark of the LORD had been in Philistine territory for seven months, 2 the Philistines called for the priests and the diviners[a] and said, "What shall we do with the ark of the LORD? Tell us

4:18 *n* ver 13
4:21 *o* Ge 35:18 *p* Ps 26:8; Jer 2:11
5:1 *a* 1Sa 4:1; 1Sa 7:12 *b* Jos 13:3
5:2 *c* Jdg 16:23
5:3 *d* Isa 19:1; Isa 46:7
5:4 *e* Eze 6:6; Mic 1:7
5:5 *f* Zep 1:9
5:6 *g* ver 7; Ex 9:3; Ps 32:4; Ac 13:11 *h* ver 11; Ps 78:66 *i* Dt 28:27; 1Sa 6:5
5:8 *j* ver 11
5:9 *k* ver 6,11; Dt 2:15; 1Sa 7:13; Ps 78:66
5:11 *l* ver 6,8-9
6:2 *a* Ge 41:8; Ex 7:11; Isa 2:6

b18 Traditionally *judged* c21 *Ichabod* means *no glory.* a6 Hebrew; Septuagint and Vulgate *tumours. And rats appeared in their land, and death and destruction were throughout the city* b9 Or *with tumours in the groin* (see Septuagint) c11 Or *he*

how we should send it back to its place."

3They answered, "If you return the ark of the god of Israel, do not send it away empty,[b] but by all means send a guilt offering[c] to him. Then you will be healed, and you will know why his hand[d] has not been lifted from you."

4The Philistines asked, "What guilt offering should we send to him?"

They replied, "Five gold tumours and five gold rats, according to the number[e] of the Philistine rulers, because the same plague has struck both you and your rulers. 5Make models of the tumours[f] and of the rats that are destroying the country, and pay honour[g] to Israel's god. Perhaps he will lift his hand from you and your gods and your land. 6Why do you harden[h] your hearts as the Egyptians and Pharaoh did? When he[a] treated them harshly, did they[i] not send the Israelites out so that they could go on their way?

7"Now then, get a new cart[j] ready, with two cows that have calved and have never been yoked.[k] Hitch the cows to the cart, but take their calves away and pen them up. 8Take the ark of the LORD and put it on the cart, and in a chest beside it put the gold objects you are sending back to him as a guilt offering. Send it on its way, 9but keep watching it. If it goes up to its own territory, towards Beth Shemesh,[l] then the LORD has brought this great disaster on us. But if it does not, then we shall know that it was not his hand that struck us and that it happened to us by chance."

10So they did this. They took two such cows and hitched them to the cart and penned up their calves. 11They placed the ark of the LORD on the cart and along with it the chest containing the gold rats and the models of the tumours. 12Then the cows went straight up towards Beth Shemesh, keeping on the road and lowing all the way; they did not turn to the right or to the left. The rulers of the Philistines followed them as far as the border of Beth Shemesh.

13Now the people of Beth Shemesh were harvesting their wheat in the valley, and when they looked up and saw the ark, they rejoiced at the sight. 14The cart came to the field of Joshua of Beth Shemesh, and there it stopped beside a large rock. The people chopped up the wood of the cart and sacrificed the cows as a burnt offering[m] to the LORD. 15The Levites[n] took down the ark of the LORD, together with the chest containing the gold objects, and placed them on the large rock. On that day the people of Beth Shemesh offered burnt offerings and made sacrifices to the LORD. 16The five rulers of the Philistines saw all this and then returned that same day to Ekron.

17These are the gold tumours the Philistines sent as a guilt offering to the LORD—one each[o] for Ashdod, Gaza, Ashkelon, Gath and Ekron. 18And the number of the gold rats was according to the number of Philistine towns belonging to the five rulers—the fortified towns with their country villages. The large rock, on which[b] they set the ark of the LORD, is a witness to this day in the field of Joshua of Beth Shemesh.

19But God struck down[p] some of the men of Beth Shemesh, putting seventy[c] of them to death because they had looked[q] into the ark of the LORD. The people mourned because of the heavy blow the LORD had dealt them, 20and the men of Beth Shemesh asked, "Who can stand[r] in the presence of the LORD, this holy[s] God? To whom will the ark go up from here?"

6:3
b Ex 23:15; Dt 16:16
c Lev 5:15
d ver 9

6:4
e ver 17-18; Jos 13:3; Jdg 3:3

6:5
f 1Sa 5:6-11
g Jos 7:19; Isa 42:12; Jn 9:24; Rev 14:7

6:6
h Ex 7:13; Ex 8:15; Ex 9:34; Ex 14:17
i Ex 12:31,33

6:7
j 2Sa 6:3
k Nu 19:2

6:9
l ver 3; Jos 15:10; Jos 21:16

6:14
m 2Sa 24:22; 1Ki 19:21

6:15
n Jos 3:3

6:17
o ver 4

6:19
p 2Sa 6:7
q Ex 19:21; Nu 4:5,15,20

6:20
r 2Sa 6:9; Mal 3:2; Rev 6:17
s Lev 11:45

a*6* That is, God
b*18* A few Hebrew manuscripts (see also Septuagint); most Hebrew manuscripts *villages as far as Greater Abel, where*
c*19* A few Hebrew manuscripts; most Hebrew manuscripts and Septuagint *50,070*

21Then they sent messengers to
the people of Kiriath Jearim,[t] saying, "The Philistines have returned
the ark of the LORD. Come down
7 and take it up to your place."
1So the men of Kiriath Jearim
came and took up the ark of the
LORD. They took it to Abinadab's[a]
house on the hill and consecrated
Eleazar his son to guard the ark of
the LORD.

Samuel Subdues the Philistines at Mizpah

2It was a long time, twenty years
in all, that the ark remained at Kiriath Jearim, and all the people of Israel mourned and sought after the
LORD. 3And Samuel said to the
whole house of Israel, "If you are
returning[b] to the LORD with all
your hearts, then rid[c] yourselves
of the foreign gods and the Ashtoreths[d] and commit[e] yourselves to
the LORD and serve him only,[f] and
he will deliver you out of the hand
of the Philistines." 4So the Israelites put away their Baals and Ashtoreths, and served the LORD only.
5Then Samuel said, "Assemble
all Israel at Mizpah[g] and I will intercede with the LORD for you."
6When they had assembled at Mizpah, they drew water and poured[h]
it out before the LORD. On that day
they fasted and there they confessed, "We have sinned against
the LORD." And Samuel was
leader[a][i] of Israel at Mizpah.
7When the Philistines heard that
Israel had assembled at Mizpah,
the rulers of the Philistines came
up to attack them. And when the Israelites heard of it, they were
afraid[j] because of the Philistines.
8They said to Samuel, "Do not stop
crying[k] out to the LORD our God
for us, that he may rescue us from
the hand of the Philistines." 9Then
Samuel[l] took a suckling lamb and
offered it up as a whole burnt offering to the LORD. He cried out to the
LORD on Israel's behalf, and the
LORD answered him.[m]
10While Samuel was sacrificing
the burnt offering, the Philistines
drew near to engage Israel in
battle. But that day the LORD thundered[n] with loud thunder against
the Philistines and threw them into
such a panic[o] that they were
routed before the Israelites. 11The
men of Israel rushed out of Mizpah and pursued the Philistines,
slaughtering them along the way to
a point below Beth Car.
12Then Samuel took a stone[p] and
set it up between Mizpah and Shen.
He named it Ebenezer,[b] saying,
"Thus far has the LORD helped us."
13So the Philistines were subdued[q]
and did not invade Israelite territory again.
Throughout Samuel's lifetime,
the hand of the LORD was against
the Philistines. 14The towns from
Ekron to Gath that the Philistines
had captured from Israel were restored to her, and Israel delivered
the neighbouring territory from
the power of the Philistines. And
there was peace between Israel
and the Amorites.
15Samuel[r] continued as judge
over Israel all the days of his life.
16From year to year he went on a
circuit from Bethel to Gilgal to
Mizpah, judging Israel in all those
places. 17But he always went back
to Ramah,[s] where his home was,
and there he also judged Israel.
And he built an altar[t] there to the
LORD.

Israel Asks for a King

8 When Samuel grew old, he appointed[a] his sons as judges
for Israel. 2The name of his firstborn was Joel and the name of his
second was Abijah, and they
served at Beersheba.[b] 3But his
sons did not walk in his ways. They
turned aside after dishonest gain

6:21 t Jos 9:17; Jos 15:9,60; 1Ch 13:5-6
7:1 a 2Sa 6:3
7:3 b Dt 30:10; Isa 55:7; Hos 6:1; c Ge 35:2; Jos 24:14; d Jdg 2:12-13; 1Sa 31:10; e Joel 2:12; f Dt 6:13; Mt 4:10; Lk 4:8
7:5 g Jdg 20:1
7:6 h Ps 62:8; La 2:19; i Jdg 10:10; Ne 9:1; Ps 106:6
7:7 j 1Sa 17:11
7:8 k 1Sa 12:19,23; Isa 37:4; Jer 15:1
7:9 l Ps 99:6; m Jer 15:1
7:10 n 1Sa 2:10; 2Sa 22:14-15; o Jos 10:10
7:12 p Ge 35:14; Jos 4:9
7:13 q Jdg 13:1,5; 1Sa 13:5
7:15 r ver 6; 1Sa 12:11
7:17 s 1Sa 1:19; 1Sa 8:4; t Jdg 21:4
8:1 a Dt 16:18-19
8:2 b Ge 22:19; 1Ki 19:3; Am 5:4-5

a6 Traditionally *judge* b12 *Ebenezer* means *stone of help.*

and accepted bribes[c] and perverted justice.
4So all the elders of Israel gathered together and came to Samuel
at Ramah.[d] 5They said to him,
"You are old, and your sons do not
walk in your ways; now appoint a
king[e] to lead[a] us, such as all the
other nations have."
6But when they said, "Give us a
king to lead us," this displeased[f]
Samuel; so he prayed to the LORD.
7And the LORD told him: "Listen to
all that the people are saying to
you; it is not you they have rejected, but they have rejected me
as their king.[g] 8As they have done
from the day I brought them up out
of Egypt until this day, forsaking
me and serving other gods, so they
are doing to you. 9Now listen to
them; but warn them solemnly and
let them know[h] what the king who
will reign over them will do."
10Samuel told all the words of the
LORD to the people who were asking him for a king. 11He said, "This
is what the king who will reign over
you will do: He will take[i] your
sons and make them serve with his
chariots and horses, and they will
run in front of his chariots.[j]
12Some he will assign to be commanders[k] of thousands and commanders of fifties, and others to
plough his ground and reap his
harvest, and still others to make
weapons of war and equipment for
his chariots. 13He will take your
daughters to be perfumers and
cooks and bakers. 14He will take the
best of your[l] fields and vineyards[m]
and olive groves and give them
to his attendants. 15He will take a
tenth of your grain and of your vin-
tage and give it to his officials and
attendants. 16Your menservants and
maidservants and the best of your
cattle[b] and donkeys he will take
for his own use. 17He will take a
tenth of your flocks, and you yourselves will become his slaves.
18When that day comes, you will
cry out for relief from the king you
have chosen, and the LORD will not
answer[n] you in that day."
19But the people refused[o] to listen to Samuel. "No!" they said. "We
want a king over us. 20Then we
shall be like all the other nations,[p]
with a king to lead us and to go out
before us and fight our battles."
21When Samuel heard all that the
people said, he repeated[q] it before
the LORD. 22The LORD answered,
"Listen[r] to them and give them a
king."
Then Samuel said to the men of
Israel, "Everyone is to go back to
his town."

8:3 c Ex 23:8; Dt 16:19; Ps 15:5
8:4 d 1Sa 7:17
8:5 e Dt 17:14-20
8:6 f 1Sa 15:11
8:7 g Ex 16:8; 1Sa 10:19
8:9 h ver 11-18; 1Sa 10:25
8:11 i 1Sa 10:25; 1Sa 14:52; j Dt 17:16; 2Sa 15:1
8:12 k 1Sa 22:7
8:14 l Eze 46:18; m 1Ki 21:7,15
8:18 n Pr 1:28; Isa 1:15; Mic 3:4
8:19 o Isa 66:4; Jer 44:16
8:20 p ver 5
8:21 q Jdg 11:11
8:22 r ver 7
9:1 a 1Sa 14:51; 1Ch 8:33; 1Ch 9:39
9:2 b 1Sa 10:24; c 1Sa 10:23
9:4 d Jos 24:33; e 2Ki 4:42
9:5 f 1Sa 1:1; g 1Sa 10:2
9:6 h Dt 33:1; 1Ki 13:1; i 1Sa 3:19

Samuel Anoints Saul

9 There was a Benjamite, a man
of standing, whose name was
Kish[a] son of Abiel, the son of
Zeror, the son of Becorath, the son
of Aphiah of Benjamin. 2He had a
son named Saul, an impressive
young man without equal[b] among
the Israelites—a head taller[c] than
any of the others.
3Now the donkeys belonging to
Saul's father Kish were lost, and
Kish said to his son Saul, "Take one
of the servants with you and go and
look for the donkeys." 4So he
passed through the hill[d] country of
Ephraim and through the area
around Shalisha,[e] but they did not
find them. They went on into the
district of Shaalim, but the donkeys
were not there. Then he passed
through the territory of Benjamin,
but they did not find them.
5When they reached the district
of Zuph,[f] Saul said to the servant
who was with him, "Come, let's go
back, or my father will stop thinking about the donkeys and start
worrying[g] about us."
6But the servant replied, "Look,
in this town there is a man of God;[h]
he is highly respected, and everything[i] he says comes true. Let's go

[a]5 Traditionally *judge;* also in verses 6 and 20
[b]16 Septuagint; Hebrew *young men*

there now. Perhaps he will tell us what way to take."

7 Saul said to his servant, "If we go, what can we give the man? The food in our sacks is gone. We have no gift[j] to take to the man of God. What do we have?"

8 The servant answered him again. "Look," he said, "I have a quarter of a shekel[a] of silver. I will give it to the man of God so that he will tell us what way to take." 9 (Formerly in Israel, if a man went to enquire of God, he would say, "Come, let us go to the seer," because the prophet of today used to be called a seer.)[k]

10 "Good," Saul said to his servant. "Come, let's go." So they set out for the town where the man of God was.

11 As they were going up the hill to the town, they met some girls coming out to draw[l] water, and they asked them, "Is the seer here?"

12 "He is," they answered. "He's ahead of you. Hurry now; he has just come to our town today, for the people have a sacrifice[m] at the high place.[n] 13 As soon as you enter the town, you will find him before he goes up to the high place to eat. The people will not begin eating until he comes, because he must bless the sacrifice; afterwards, those who are invited will eat. Go up now; you should find him about this time."

14 They went up to the town, and as they were entering it, there was Samuel, coming towards them on his way up to the high place.

15 Now the day before Saul came, the LORD had revealed this to Samuel: 16 "About this time tomorrow I will send you a man from the land of Benjamin. Anoint[o] him leader over my people Israel; he will deliver[p] my people from the hand of the Philistines. I have looked upon my people, for their cry has reached me."

17 When Samuel caught sight of Saul, the LORD said to him, "This[q] is the man I spoke to you about; he will govern my people."

18 Saul approached Samuel in the gateway and asked, "Would you please tell me where the seer's house is?"

19 "I am the seer," Samuel replied. "Go up ahead of me to the high place, for today you are to eat with me, and in the morning I will let you go and will tell you all that is in your heart. 20 As for the donkeys[r] you lost three days ago, do not worry about them; they have been found. And to whom is all the desire[s] of Israel turned, if not to you and all your father's family?"

21 Saul answered, "But am I not a Benjamite, from the smallest tribe[t] of Israel, and is not my clan the least of all the clans of the tribe of Benjamin?[u] Why do you say such a thing to me?"

22 Then Samuel brought Saul and his servant into the hall and seated them at the head of those who were invited—about thirty in number. 23 Samuel said to the cook, "Bring the piece of meat I gave you, the one I told you to lay aside."

24 So the cook took up the leg[v] with what was on it and set it in front of Saul. Samuel said, "Here is what has been kept for you. Eat, because it was set aside for you for this occasion, from the time I said, 'I have invited guests.'" And Saul dined with Samuel that day.

25 After they came down from the high place to the town, Samuel talked with Saul on the roof[w] of his house. 26 They rose about daybreak and Samuel called to Saul on the roof, "Get ready, and I will send you on your way." When Saul got ready, he and Samuel went outside together. 27 As they were going down to the edge of the town,

9:7 j 1Ki 14:3; 2Ki 5:5,15; 2Ki 8:8
9:9 k 2Sa 24:11; 2Ki 17:13; 1Ch 9:22; 1Ch 26:28; 1Ch 29:29; Isa 30:10; Am 7:12
9:11 l Ge 24:11,13
9:12 m Nu 28:11-15; 1Sa 7:17; n Ge 31:54; 1Sa 10:5; 1Ki 3:2
9:16 o 1Sa 10:1; p Ex 3:7-9
9:17 q 1Sa 16:12
9:20 r ver 3; s 1Sa 8:5; 1Sa 12:13
9:21 t 1Sa 15:17; u Jdg 20:35,46
9:24 v Lev 7:32-34; Nu 18:18
9:25 w Dt 22:8; Ac 10:9

a8 That is, about 1/10 ounce (about 3 grams)

Samuel said to Saul, "Tell the servant to go on ahead of us"—and the
servant did so—"but you stay here
awhile, so that I may give you a
message from God."

10 Then Samuel took a flask[a]
of oil and poured it on
Saul's head and kissed him, saying,
"Has not the LORD anointed[b] you
leader over his inheritance?[a][c]
2When you leave me today, you will
meet two men near Rachel's
tomb,[d] at Zelzah on the border of
Benjamin. They will say to you,
'The donkeys[e] you set out to look
for have been found. And now your
father has stopped thinking about
them and is worried[f] about you.
He is asking, "What shall I do about
my son?"'
3"Then you will go on from there
until you reach the great tree of
Tabor. Three men going up to God
at Bethel[g] will meet you there. One
will be carrying three young goats,
another three loaves of bread, and
another a skin of wine. 4They will
greet you and offer you two loaves
of bread, which you will accept
from them.
5"After that you will go to Gibeah
of God, where there is a Philistine
outpost.[h] As you approach the
town, you will meet a procession of
prophets coming down from the
high place[i] with lyres, tambourines, flutes and harps[j] being
played before them, and they will
be prophesying.[k] 6The Spirit[l] of
the LORD will come upon you in
power, and you will prophesy with
them; and you will be changed into
a different person. 7Once these
signs are fulfilled, do whatever[m]
your hand finds to do, for God is
with[n] you.
8"Go down ahead of me to Gilgal.[o] I will surely come down to
you to sacrifice burnt offerings
and fellowship offerings,[b] but you
must wait seven days until I come
to you and tell you what you are to
do."

10:1 a 1Sa 16:13; 2Ki 9:1,3,6 b Ps 2:12 c Dt 32:9; Ps 78:62,71
10:2 d Ge 35:20 e 1Sa 9:4 f 1Sa 9:5
10:3 g Ge 28:22; Ge 35:7-8
10:5 h 1Sa 13:3 i 1Sa 9:12 j 2Ki 3:15 k 1Sa 19:20; 1Co 14:1
10:6 l ver 10; Nu 11:25; 1Sa 19:23-24
10:7 m Ecc 9:10 n Jos 1:5; Jdg 6:12; Heb 13:5
10:8 o 1Sa 11:14-15
10:9 p ver 6
10:10 q ver 5-6; 1Sa 19:20
10:11 r Mt 13:54; Jn 7:15 s 1Sa 19:24
10:14 t 1Sa 14:50
10:16 u 1Sa 9:20
10:17 v Jdg 20:1; 1Sa 7:5
10:18 w Jdg 6:8-9

Saul Made King

9As Saul turned to leave Samuel,
God changed[p] Saul's heart, and all
these signs were fulfilled that day.
10When they arrived at Gibeah, a
procession of prophets met him;
the Spirit of God came upon him in
power, and he joined in their prophesying.[q] 11When all those who had
formerly known him saw him
prophesying with the prophets,
they asked each other, "What is
this[r] that has happened to the son
of Kish? Is Saul also among the
prophets?"[s]
12A man who lived there answered, "And who is their father?"
So it became a saying: "Is Saul also
among the prophets?" 13After Saul
stopped prophesying, he went to
the high place.
14Now Saul's uncle[t] asked him
and his servant, "Where have you
been?"
"Looking for the donkeys," he
said. "But when we saw they were
not to be found, we went to
Samuel."
15Saul's uncle said, "Tell me what
Samuel said to you."
16Saul replied, "He assured us
that the donkeys[u] had been
found." But he did not tell his uncle
what Samuel had said about the
kingship.
17Samuel summoned the people
of Israel to the LORD at Mizpah[v]
18and said to them, "This is what
the LORD, the God of Israel, says: 'I
brought Israel up out of Egypt, and
I delivered you from the power of
Egypt and all the kingdoms that oppressed[w] you.' 19But you have now
rejected your God, who saves
you out of all your calamities and

[a]1 Hebrew; Septuagint and Vulgate *over his people Israel? You will reign over the LORD's people and save them from the power of their enemies round about. And this will be a sign to you that the LORD has anointed you leader over his inheritance:* [b]8 Traditionally *peace offerings*

distresses. And you have said,
'No, set a king[x] over us.' So now
present[y] yourselves before the
LORD by your tribes and clans."
20When Samuel brought all the
tribes of Israel near, the tribe of
Benjamin was chosen. 21Then he
brought forward the tribe of Benjamin, clan by clan, and Matri's clan
was chosen. Finally Saul son of
Kish was chosen. But when they
looked for him, he was not to be
found. 22So they enquired[z] further
of the LORD, "Has the man come
here yet?"
And the LORD said, "Yes, he has
hidden himself among the bag-
gage."
23They ran and brought him out,
and as he stood among the people
he was a head taller[a] than any of
the others. 24Samuel said to all the
people, "Do you see the man the
LORD has chosen?[b] There is no-one
like him among all the people."
Then the people shouted, "Long
live[c] the king!"
25Samuel explained to the people
the regulations[d] of the kingship.
He wrote them down on a scroll and
deposited it before the LORD. Then
Samuel dismissed the people, each
to his own home.
26Saul also went to his home in
Gibeah,[e] accompanied by valiant
men whose hearts God had
touched. 27But some troublemakers[f] said, "How can this fellow save us?" They despised him
and brought him no gifts.[g] But
Saul kept silent.

Saul Rescues the City of Jabesh

11 Nahash[a] the Ammonite went
up and besieged Jabesh
Gilead.[b] And all the men of Jabesh said to him, "Make a treaty[c]
with us, and we will be subject
to you."
2But Nahash the Ammonite replied, "I will make a treaty with you
only on the condition that I gouge[d]
out the right eye of every one of
you and so bring disgrace[e] on all
Israel."
3The elders of Jabesh said to him,
"Give us seven days so that we can
send messengers throughout Israel; if no-one comes to rescue us,
we will surrender to you."
4When the messengers came to
Gibeah[f] of Saul and reported
these terms to the people, they all
wept[g] aloud. 5Just then Saul was
returning from the fields, behind
his oxen, and he asked, "What is
wrong with the people? Why are
they weeping?" Then they repeated to him what the men of Jabesh had said.
6When Saul heard their words,
the Spirit[h] of God came upon him
in power, and he burned with
anger. 7He took a pair of oxen, cut
them into pieces, and sent the
pieces by messengers throughout
Israel,[i] proclaiming, "This is what
will be done to the oxen of anyone[j]
who does not follow Saul and
Samuel." Then the terror of the
LORD fell on the people, and they
turned out as one man. 8When Saul
mustered[k] them at Bezek,[l] the
men of Israel numbered three hundred thousand and the men of Judah thirty thousand.
9They told the messengers who
had come, "Say to the men of Jabesh Gilead, 'By the time the sun is
hot tomorrow, you will be delivered.' " When the messengers went
and reported this to the men of Jabesh, they were elated. 10They said
to the Ammonites, "Tomorrow we
will surrender[m] to you, and you can
do to us whatever seems good to
you."
11The next day Saul separated his
men into three divisions;[n] during
the last watch of the night they
broke into the camp of the Ammonites and slaughtered them until
the heat of the day. Those who survived were scattered, so that no
two of them were left together.

10:19 x 1Sa 8:5-7; 1Sa 12:12 y Jos 7:14; Jos 24:1
10:22 z 1Sa 23:2,4, 9-11
10:23 a 1Sa 9:2
10:24 b Dt 17:15; 2Sa 21:6 c 1Ki 1:25,34, 39
10:25 d Dt 17:14-20; 1Sa 8:11-18
10:26 e 1Sa 11:4
10:27 f Dt 13:13 g 1Ki 10:25; 2Ch 17:5
11:1 a 1Sa 12:12 b Jdg 21:8 c 1Ki 20:34; Eze 17:13
11:2 d Nu 16:14 e 1Sa 17:26
11:4 f 1Sa 10:5,26; 1Sa 15:34 g Jdg 2:4; 1Sa 30:4
11:6 h Jdg 3:10; Jdg 6:34; Jdg 13:25; Jdg 14:6; 1Sa 10:10; 1Sa 16:13
11:7 i Jdg 19:29 j Jdg 21:5
11:8 k Jdg 20:2 l Jdg 1:4
11:10 m ver 3
11:11 n Jdg 7:16

Saul Confirmed as King

12 The people then said to Samuel, "Who[o] was it that asked, 'Shall Saul reign over us?' Bring these men to us and we will put them to death."

13 But Saul said, "No-one shall be put to death today,[p] for this day the LORD has rescued[q] Israel."

14 Then Samuel said to the people, "Come, let us go to Gilgal[r] and there reaffirm the kingship.[s]" 15 So all the people went to Gilgal[t] and confirmed Saul as king in the presence of the LORD. There they sacrificed fellowship offerings[a] before the LORD, and Saul and all the Israelites held a great celebration.

Samuel's Farewell Speech

12 Samuel said to all Israel, "I have listened[a] to everything you said to me and have set a king[b] over you. 2 Now you have a king as your leader.[c] As for me, I am old and grey, and my sons are here with you. I have been your leader from my youth until this day. 3 Here I stand. Testify against me in the presence of the LORD and his anointed.[d] Whose ox have I taken? Whose donkey[e] have I taken? Whom have I cheated? Whom have I oppressed? From whose hand have I accepted a bribe[f] to make me shut my eyes? If I have done[g] any of these, I will make it right."

4 "You have not cheated or oppressed us," they replied. "You have not taken anything from anyone's hand."

5 Samuel said to them, "The LORD is witness against you, and also his anointed is witness this day, that you have not found anything[h] in my hand.[i]"

"He is witness," they said.

6 Then Samuel said to the people, "It is the LORD who appointed Moses and Aaron and brought[j] your forefathers up out of Egypt. 7 Now then, stand here, because I am going to confront[k] you with evidence before the LORD as to all the righteous acts performed by the LORD for you and your fathers.

8 "After Jacob entered Egypt, they cried[l] to the LORD for help, and the LORD sent[m] Moses and Aaron, who brought your forefathers out of Egypt and settled them in this place.

9 "But they forgot[n] the LORD their God; so he sold them into the hands of Sisera,[o] the commander of the army of Hazor, and into the hands of the Philistines[p] and the king of Moab,[q] who fought against them. 10 They cried out to the LORD and said, 'We have sinned; we have forsaken[r] the LORD and served the Baals and the Ashtoreths.[s] But now deliver us from the hands of our enemies, and we will serve you.' 11 Then the LORD sent Jerub-Baal,[a][t] Barak,[b][u] Jephthah[v] and Samuel,[c] and he delivered you from the hands of your enemies on every side, so that you lived securely.

12 "But when you saw that Nahash[w] king[x] of the Ammonites was moving against you, you said to me, 'No, we want a king to rule[y] over us'—even though the LORD your God was your king. 13 Now here is the king[z] you have chosen, the one you asked[a] for; see, the LORD has set a king over you. 14 If you fear[b] the LORD and serve and obey him and do not rebel against his commands, and if both you and the king who reigns over you follow the LORD your God—good! 15 But if you do not obey the LORD, and if you rebel against[c] his commands, his hand will be against you, as it was against your fathers.

16 "Now then, stand still and see[d] this great thing the LORD is about to do before your eyes! 17 Is it not

[a]15 Traditionally *peace offerings*
[a]11 Also called *Gideon*
[b]11 Some Septuagint manuscripts and Syriac; Hebrew *Bedan*
[c]11 Hebrew; some Septuagint manuscripts and Syriac *Samson*

11:12 o 1Sa 10:27; Lk 19:27
11:13 p 2Sa 19:22; q Ex 14:13; 1Sa 19:5
11:14 r 1Sa 10:8; s 1Sa 10:25
11:15 t 1Sa 10:8,17
12:1 a 1Sa 8:7; b 1Sa 10:24; 1Sa 11:15
12:2 c 1Sa 8:5
12:3 d 1Sa 10:1; 1Sa 24:6; 2Sa 1:14; e Nu 16:15; f Dt 16:19; g Ac 20:33
12:5 h Ac 23:9; Ac 24:20; i Ex 22:4
12:6 j Ex 6:26; Mic 6:4
12:7 k Isa 1:18; Mic 6:1-5
12:8 l Ex 2:23; m Ex 3:10; Ex 4:16
12:9 n Jdg 3:7; o Jdg 4:2; p Jdg 10:7; Jdg 13:1; q Jdg 3:12
12:10 r Jdg 10:10,15; s Jdg 2:13
12:11 t Jdg 6:14,32; u Jdg 4:6; v Jdg 11:1
12:12 w 1Sa 11:1; x 1Sa 8:5; y Jdg 8:23; 1Sa 8:6,19
12:13 z 1Sa 8:5; Hos 13:11; a 1Sa 10:24
12:14 b Jos 24:14
12:15 c ver 9; Jos 24:20; Isa 1:20
12:16 d Ex 14:13

wheat harvest[e] now? I will call[f]
upon the LORD to send thunder and
rain.[g] And you will realise what an
evil[h] thing you did in the eyes of
the LORD when you asked for a
king."
18Then Samuel called upon the
LORD, and that same day the LORD
sent thunder and rain. So all the
people stood in awe[i] of the LORD
and of Samuel.
19The people all said to Samuel,
"Pray[j] to the LORD your God for
your servants so that we will not
die, for we have added to all our
other sins the evil of asking for a
king."
20"Do not be afraid," Samuel replied. "You have done all this evil;
yet do not turn away from the
LORD, but serve the LORD with all
your heart. 21Do not turn away
after useless[k] idols.[l] They can do
you no good, nor can they rescue
you, because they are useless.
22For the sake[m] of his great name[n]
the LORD will not reject[o] his people, because the LORD was pleased
to make[p] you his own. 23As for me,
far be it from me that I should sin
against the LORD by failing to
pray[q] for you. And I will teach[r]
you the way that is good and right.
24But be sure to fear[s] the LORD and
serve him faithfully with all your
heart; consider[t] what great[u]
things he has done for you. 25Yet if
you persist[v] in doing evil, both you
and your king will be swept[w]
away."

Samuel Rebukes Saul

13 Saul was ⌊thirty⌋[a] years old
when he became king, and
he reigned over Israel for ⌊forty-⌋[b]
two years.
2Saul[c] chose three thousand
men from Israel; two thousand
were with him at Michmash and in
the hill country of Bethel, and a
thousand were with Jonathan at
Gibeah[a] in Benjamin. The rest of

12:17 e 1Sa 7:9-10; f Jas 5:18; g Pr 26:1; h 1Sa 8:6-7
12:18 i Ex 14:31
12:19 j ver 23; Ex 9:28; Jas 5:18; 1Jn 5:16
12:21 k Isa 41:24,29; Jer 16:19; Hab 2:18; l Dt 11:16
12:22 m Ps 106:8; n Jos 7:9; o 1Ki 6:13; p Dt 7:7; 1Pe 2:9
12:23 q Ro 1:9-10; Col 1:9; 2Ti 1:3; r 1Ki 8:36; Ps 34:11; Pr 4:11
12:24 s Ecc 12:13; t Isa 5:12; u Dt 10:21
12:25 v 1Sa 31:1-5; w Jos 24:20
13:2 a 1Sa 10:26
13:3 b 1Sa 10:5
13:4 c Ge 34:30
13:5 d Jos 11:4
13:6 e Jdg 6:2
13:7 f Nu 32:33
13:8 g 1Sa 10:8
13:9 h 2Sa 24:25; 1Ki 3:4
13:10 i 1Sa 15:13
13:11 j ver 2,5,16,23

the men he sent back to their
homes.
3Jonathan attacked the Philistine
outpost[b] at Geba, and the Philistines heard about it. Then Saul had
the trumpet blown throughout the
land and said, "Let the Hebrews
hear!" 4So all Israel heard the
news: "Saul has attacked the Philistine outpost, and now Israel
has become an offence[c] to the
Philistines." And the people were
summoned to join Saul at Gilgal.
5The Philistines assembled to
fight Israel, with three thousand[d]
chariots, six thousand charioteers,
and soldiers as numerous as the
sand[d] on the seashore. They went
up and camped at Michmash, east
of Beth Aven. 6When the men of Israel saw that their situation was
critical and that their army was
hard pressed, they hid in caves and
thickets, among the rocks, and in
pits and cisterns.[e] 7Some Hebrews
even crossed the Jordan to the land
of Gad[f] and Gilead.
Saul remained at Gilgal, and all
the troops with him were quaking
with fear. 8He waited for seven[g]
days, the time set by Samuel; but
Samuel did not come to Gilgal, and
Saul's men began to scatter. 9So he
said, "Bring me the burnt offering
and the fellowship offerings."[e]
And Saul offered[h] up the burnt offering. 10Just as he finished making
the offering, Samuel[i] arrived, and
Saul went out to greet him.
11"What have you done?" asked
Samuel.
Saul replied, "When I saw that
the men were scattering, and that
you did not come at the set time,
and that the Philistines were as-
sembling at Michmash,[j] 12I
thought, 'Now the Philistines will

a1 A few late manuscripts of the Septuagint; Hebrew does not have *thirty*. **b**1 See the round number in Acts 13:21; Hebrew does not have *forty-*. **c**1,2 Or *and when he had reigned over Israel for two years, 2he* **d**5 Some Septuagint manuscripts and Syriac; Hebrew *thirty thousand* **e**9 Traditionally *peace offerings*

come down against me at Gilgal, and I have not sought the LORD's favour.[k] So I felt compelled to offer the burnt offering."

13"You acted foolishly,[l]" Samuel said. "You have not kept[m] the command the LORD your God gave you; if you had, he would have established your kingdom over Israel for all time. 14But now your kingdom[n] will not endure; the LORD has sought out a man after his own heart[o] and appointed[p] him leader of his people, because you have not kept the LORD's command."

15Then Samuel left Gilgal[f] and went up to Gibeah[q] in Benjamin, and Saul counted the men who were with him. They numbered about six hundred.

Israel Without Weapons

16Saul and his son Jonathan and the men with them were staying in Gibeah[g] of Benjamin, while the Philistines camped at Michmash. 17Raiding[r] parties went out from the Philistine camp in three detachments. One turned towards Ophrah[s] in the vicinity of Shual, 18another towards Beth Horon,[t] and the third towards the borderland overlooking the Valley of Zeboim[u] facing the desert.

19Not a blacksmith[v] could be found in the whole land of Israel, because the Philistines had said, "Otherwise the Hebrews will make swords or spears!" 20So all Israel went down to the Philistines to have their ploughshares, mattocks, axes and sickles[h] sharpened. 21The price was two thirds of a shekel[i] for sharpening ploughshares and mattocks, and a third of a shekel[j] for sharpening forks and axes and for repointing goads.

22So on the day of the battle not a soldier with Saul and Jonathan[w] had a sword or spear[x] in his hand; only Saul and his son Jonathan had them.

Jonathan Attacks the Philistines

23Now a detachment of Philistines had gone out to the pass[y] at Michmash.

14

1One day Jonathan son of Saul said to the young man bearing his armour, "Come, let's go over to the Philistine outpost on the other side." But he did not tell his father.

2Saul was staying on the outskirts of Gibeah[a] under a pomegranate tree in Migron.[b] With him were about six hundred men, 3among whom was Ahijah, who was wearing an ephod. He was a son of Ichabod's[c] brother Ahitub[d] son of Phinehas, the son of Eli,[e] the LORD's priest in Shiloh. No-one was aware that Jonathan had left.

4On each side of the pass[f] that Jonathan intended to cross to reach the Philistine outpost was a cliff; one was called Bozez, and the other Seneh. 5One cliff stood to the north towards Michmash, the other to the south towards Geba.

6Jonathan said to his young armour-bearer, "Come, let's go over to the outpost of those uncircumcised[g] fellows. Perhaps the LORD will act on our behalf. Nothing[h] can hinder the LORD from saving, whether by many[i] or by few.[j]"

7"Do all that you have in mind," his armour-bearer said. "Go ahead; I am with you heart and soul."

8Jonathan said, "Come, then; we will cross over towards the men and let them see us. 9If they say to us, 'Wait there until we come to you,' we will stay where we are and not go up to them. 10But if they say, 'Come up to us,' we will climb up, because that will be our sign[k] that

13:12 k Jer 26:19
13:13 l 2Ch 16:9; m 1Sa 15:23,24
13:14 n 1Sa 15:28; o Ac 7:46; Ac 13:22; p 2Sa 6:21
13:15 q 1Sa 14:2
13:17 r 1Sa 14:15; s Jos 18:23
13:18 t Jos 18:13-14; u Ne 11:34
13:19 v 2Ki 24:14; Jer 24:1
13:22 w 1Ch 9:39; x Jdg 5:8
13:23 y 1Sa 14:4
14:2 a 1Sa 13:15; b Isa 10:28
14:3 c 1Sa 4:21; d 1Sa 22:11,20; e 1Sa 2:28
14:4 f 1Sa 13:23
14:6 g 1Sa 17:26,36; Jer 9:26; h Heb 11:34; i Jdg 7:4; j 1Sa 17:46-47
14:10 k Ge 24:14; Jdg 6:36-37

[f]15 Hebrew; Septuagint *Gilgal and went his way; the rest of the people went after Saul to meet the army, and they went out of Gilgal* [g]16 Two Hebrew manuscripts; most Hebrew manuscripts *Geba*, a variant of *Gibeah* [h]20 Septuagint; Hebrew *ploughshares* [i]21 Hebrew *pim*; that is, about ¼ ounce (about 8 grams) [j]21 That is, about ⅛ ounce (about 4 grams)

the LORD has given them into our
hands."
11 So both of them showed themselves to the Philistine outpost.
"Look!" said the Philistines. "The
Hebrews are crawling out of the
holes they were hiding[l] in." 12 The
men of the outpost shouted to Jonathan and his armour-bearer, "Come
up to us and we'll teach you a
lesson.[m]"
So Jonathan said to his armour-
bearer, "Climb up after me; the
LORD has given them into the
hand[n] of Israel."
13 Jonathan climbed up, using his
hands and feet, with his armour-
bearer right behind him. The Philistines fell before Jonathan, and his
armour-bearer followed and killed
behind him. 14 In that first attack
Jonathan and his armour-bearer
killed some twenty men in an area
of about half an acre.[a]

Israel Routs the Philistines

15 Then panic[o] struck the whole
army – those in the camp and field,
and those in the outposts and raiding[p] parties – and the ground
shook. It was a panic sent by God.[b]
16 Saul's lookouts[q] at Gibeah in
Benjamin saw the army melting
away in all directions. 17 Then Saul
said to the men who were with him,
"Muster the forces and see who has
left us." When they did, it was Jonathan and his armour-bearer who
were not there.
18 Saul said to Ahijah, "Bring[r] the
ark of God." (At that time it was
with the Israelites.)[c] 19 While Saul
was talking to the priest, the tumult
in the Philistine camp increased
more and more. So Saul said to the
priest,[s] "Withdraw your hand."
20 Then Saul and all his men assembled and went to the battle.
They found the Philistines in total
confusion, striking[t] each other
with their swords. 21 Those Hebrews who had previously been
with the Philistines and had gone
up with them to their camp went[u]
over to the Israelites who were
with Saul and Jonathan. 22 When all
the Israelites who had hidden[v] in
the hill country of Ephraim heard
that the Philistines were on the run,
they joined the battle in hot pursuit. 23 So the LORD rescued[w] Israel
that day, and the battle moved on
beyond Beth Aven.[x]

Jonathan Eats Honey

24 Now the men of Israel were in
distress that day, because Saul had
bound the people under an oath,[y]
saying, "Cursed be any man who
eats food before evening comes,
before I have avenged myself on
my enemies!" So none of the troops
tasted food.
25 The entire army[d] entered the
woods, and there was honey on the
ground. 26 When they went into the
woods, they saw the honey oozing
out, yet no-one put his hand to his
mouth, because they feared the
oath. 27 But Jonathan had not heard
that his father had bound the people with the oath, so he reached out
the end of the staff that was in his
hand and dipped it into the honeycomb.[z] He raised his hand to his
mouth, and his eyes brightened.[e]
28 Then one of the soldiers told him,
"Your father bound the army under
a strict oath, saying, 'Cursed be any
man who eats food today!' That is
why the men are faint."
29 Jonathan said, "My father has
made trouble[a] for the country. See
how my eyes brightened[f] when I
tasted a little of this honey. 30 How
much better it would have been if
the men had eaten today some of
the plunder they took from their
enemies. Would not the slaughter

14:11 l 1Sa 13:6
14:12 m 1Sa 17:43-44 n 2Sa 5:24
14:15 o Ge 35:5; 2Ki 7:5-7 p 1Sa 13:17
14:16 q 2Sa 18:24
14:18 r 1Sa 30:7
14:19 s Nu 27:21
14:20 t Jdg 7:22; 2Ch 20:23
14:21 u 1Sa 29:4
14:22 v 1Sa 13:6
14:23 w Ex 14:30; Ps 44:6-7 x 1Sa 13:5
14:24 y Jos 6:26
14:27 z ver 43; 1Sa 30:12
14:29 a Jos 7:25; 1Ki 18:18

[a] 14 Hebrew *half a yoke*; a "yoke" was the land ploughed by a yoke of oxen in one day.
[b] 15 Or *a terrible panic*
[c] 18 Hebrew; Septuagint *"Bring the ephod." (At that time he wore the ephod before the Israelites.)*
[d] 25 Or *Now all the people of the land*
[e] 27 Or *his strength was renewed*
[f] 29 Or *my strength was renewed*

of the Philistines have been even
greater?"
31That day, after the Israelites
had struck down the Philistines
from Michmash to Aijalon,[b] they
were exhausted. 32They pounced
on the plunder[c] and, taking sheep,
cattle and calves, they butchered
them on the ground and ate them,
together with the blood.[d] 33Then
someone said to Saul, "Look, the
men are sinning against the LORD
by eating meat that has blood in it."
"You have broken faith," he said.
"Roll a large stone over here at
once." 34Then he said, "Go out
among the men and tell them, 'Each
of you bring me your cattle and
sheep, and slaughter them here and
eat them. Do not sin against the
LORD by eating meat with blood
still in it.' "
So everyone brought his ox that
night and slaughtered it there.
35Then Saul built an altar[e] to the
LORD; it was the first time he had
done this.
36Saul said, "Let us go down after
the Philistines by night and plunder them till dawn, and let us not
leave one of them alive."
"Do whatever seems best to
you," they replied.
But the priest said, "Let us enquire of God here."
37So Saul asked God, "Shall I go
down after the Philistines? Will you
give them into Israel's hand?" But
God did not answer[f] him that day.
38Saul therefore said, "Come
here, all you who are leaders of the
army, and let us find out what sin
has been committed[g] today. 39As
surely as the LORD who rescues Israel lives,[h] even if it lies with my
son Jonathan, he must die." But not
one of the men said a word.
40Saul then said to all the Israelites, "You stand over there; I and
Jonathan my son will stand over
here."
"Do what seems best to you," the
men replied.
41Then Saul prayed to the LORD,
the God of Israel, "Give[i] me the
right[j] answer."[g] And Jonathan
and Saul were taken by lot, and the
men were cleared. 42Saul said,
"Cast the lot between me and Jonathan my son." And Jonathan was
taken.
43Then Saul said to Jonathan,
"Tell me what you have done."[k]
So Jonathan told him, "I merely
tasted a little honey[l] with the end
of my staff. And now must I die?"
44Saul said, "May God deal with
me, be it ever so severely,[m] if you
do not die, Jonathan.[n]"
45But the men said to Saul,
"Should Jonathan die—he who has
brought about this great deliverance in Israel? Never! As surely as
the LORD lives, not a hair[o] of his
head shall fall to the ground, for he
did this today with God's help." So
the men rescued[p] Jonathan, and he
was not put to death.
46Then Saul stopped pursuing the
Philistines, and they withdrew to
their own land.
47After Saul had assumed rule
over Israel, he fought against their
enemies on every side: Moab, the
Ammonites,[q] Edom, the kings[h] of
Zobah,[r] and the Philistines. Wherever he turned, he inflicted punishment on them.[i] 48He fought
valiantly and defeated the Amalekites,[s] delivering Israel from the
hands of those who had plundered
them.

Saul's Family

49Saul's sons were Jonathan,
Ishvi and Malki-Shua.[t] The name
of his older daughter was Merab,
and that of the younger was Michal.[u] 50His wife's name was Ahinoam daughter of Ahimaaz. The
name of the commander of Saul's

14:31 b Jos 10:12
14:32 c 1Sa 15:19 d Ge 9:4; Lev 3:17; Lev 7:26; Lev 17:10-14; Lev 19:26; Dt 12:16, 23-24
14:35 e 1Sa 7:17
14:37 f 1Sa 10:22; 1Sa 28:6,15
14:38 g Jos 7:11; 1Sa 10:19
14:39 h 2Sa 12:5
14:41 i Ac 1:24 j Pr 16:33
14:43 k Jos 7:19 l ver 27
14:44 m Ru 1:17 n ver 39
14:45 o 1Ki 1:52; Lk 21:18; Ac 27:34 p 2Sa 14:11
14:47 q 1Sa 11:1-13 r ver 52; 2Sa 10:6
14:48 s 1Sa 15:2,7
14:49 t 1Sa 31:2; 1Ch 8:33 u 1Sa 18:17-20

g41 Hebrew; Septuagint *"Why have you not answered your servant today? If the fault is in me or my son Jonathan, respond with Urim, but if the men of Israel are at fault, respond with Thummim."* h47 Masoretic Text; Dead Sea Scrolls and Septuagint *king* i47 Hebrew; Septuagint *he was victorious*

army was Abner son of Ner, and
Ner was Saul's uncle. 51Saul's
father Kish[v] and Abner's father
Ner were sons of Abiel.
52All the days of Saul there was
bitter war with the Philistines, and
whenever Saul saw a mighty or
brave man, he took[w] him into his
service.

The LORD Rejects Saul as King

15 Samuel said to Saul, "I am
the one the LORD sent to
anoint[a] you king over his people
Israel; so listen now to the message
from the LORD. 2This is what the
LORD Almighty says: 'I will punish
the Amalekites[b] for what they did
to Israel when they waylaid them
as they came up from Egypt. 3Now
go, attack the Amalekites and totally[c] destroy[a] everything that
belongs to them. Do not spare
them; put to death men and women,
children and infants, cattle and
sheep, camels and donkeys.' "
4So Saul summoned the men and
mustered them at Telaim—two
hundred thousand foot soldiers and
ten thousand men from Judah.
5Saul went to the city of Amalek
and set an ambush in the ravine.
6Then he said to the Kenites,[d] "Go
away, leave the Amalekites so that
I do not destroy you along with
them; for you showed kindness to
all the Israelites when they came
up out of Egypt." So the Kenites
moved away from the Amalekites.
7Then Saul attacked the Amalekites[e] all the way from Havilah to
Shur,[f] to the east of Egypt. 8He
took Agag king of the Amalekites
alive,[g] and all his people he totally
destroyed with the sword. 9But
Saul and the army spared[h] Agag
and the best of the sheep and cattle,
the fat calves[b] and lambs—everything that was good. These they
were unwilling to destroy completely, but everything that was despised and weak they totally
destroyed.
10Then the word of the LORD
came to Samuel: 11"I am grieved[i]
that I have made Saul king, because
he has turned[j] away from me and
has not carried out my instructions."[k] Samuel was troubled,[l]
and he cried out to the LORD all that
night.
12Early in the morning Samuel
got up and went to meet Saul, but he
was told, "Saul has gone to Carmel.[m] There he has set up a monument in his own honour and has
turned and gone on down to Gilgal."
13When Samuel reached him,
Saul said, "The LORD bless you! I
have carried out the LORD's instructions."
14But Samuel said, "What then is
this bleating of sheep in my ears?
What is this lowing of cattle that I
hear?"
15Saul answered, "The soldiers
brought them from the Amalekites; they spared the best of the
sheep and cattle to sacrifice to the
LORD your God, but we totally destroyed the rest."
16"Stop!" Samuel said to Saul.
"Let me tell you what the LORD said
to me last night."
"Tell me," Saul replied.
17Samuel said, "Although you
were once small[n] in your own
eyes, did you not become the head
of the tribes of Israel? The LORD
anointed you king over Israel.
18And he sent you on a mission, saying, 'Go and completely destroy
those wicked people, the Amalekites; make war on them until you
have wiped them out.' 19Why did
you not obey the LORD? Why did
you pounce on the plunder[o] and do
evil in the eyes of the LORD?"
20"But I did obey[p] the LORD,"
Saul said. "I went on the mission
the LORD assigned me. I completely
destroyed the Amalekites and

14:51 v 1Sa 9:1
14:52 w 1Sa 8:11
15:1 a 1Sa 9:16
15:2 b Ex 17:8-14; Nu 24:20; Dt 25:17-19
15:3 c Nu 24:20; Dt 20:16-18; Jos 6:17; 1Sa 22:19
15:6 d Ex 18:10,19; Nu 10:29-32; Nu 24:22; Jdg 1:16; Jdg 4:1
15:7 e 1Sa 14:48; f Ge 16:7; Ge 25:17-18; Ex 15:22
15:8 g 1Sa 30:1
15:9 h ver 3,15
15:11 i Ge 6:6; 2Sa 24:16; j Jos 22:16; k 1Sa 13:13; 1Ki 9:6-7; l ver 35
15:12 m Jos 15:55
15:17 n 1Sa 9:21
15:19 o 1Sa 14:32
15:20 p ver 13

a3 The Hebrew term refers to the irrevocable giving of things or persons to the LORD, often by totally destroying them; also in verses 8, 9, 15, 18, 20 and 21. b9 Or *the grown bulls*; the meaning of the Hebrew for this phrase is uncertain.

brought back Agag their king. 21The soldiers took sheep and cattle from the plunder, the best of what was devoted to God, in order to sacrifice them to the LORD your God at Gilgal."

22But Samuel replied:

"Does the LORD delight in burnt
offerings and sacrifices
as much as in obeying the
voice of the LORD?
To obey is better than
sacrifice,[q]
and to heed is better than the
fat of rams.
23For rebellion is like the sin of
divination,[r]
and arrogance like the evil of
idolatry.
Because you have rejected[s] the
word of the LORD,
he has rejected you as king."

24Then Saul said to Samuel, "I have sinned.[t] I violated the LORD's command and your instructions. I was afraid[u] of the people and so I gave in to them. 25Now I beg you, forgive[v] my sin and come back with me, so that I may worship the LORD."

26But Samuel said to him, "I will not go back with you. You have rejected[w] the word of the LORD, and the LORD has rejected you as king over Israel!"

27As Samuel turned to leave, Saul caught hold of the hem of his robe, and it tore.[x] 28Samuel said to him, "The LORD has torn[y] the kingdom of Israel from you today and has given it to one of your neighbours—to one better than you. 29He who is the Glory of Israel does not lie[z] or change[a] his mind; for he is not a man, that he should change his mind."

30Saul replied, "I have sinned. But please honour[b] me before the elders of my people and before Israel; come back with me, so that I may worship the LORD your God." 31So Samuel went back with Saul, and Saul worshipped the LORD.

32Then Samuel said, "Bring me Agag king of the Amalekites."

Agag came to him confidently,[c] thinking, "Surely the bitterness of death is past."

33But Samuel said,

"As your sword has made
women childless,
so will your mother be
childless among women."[c]

And Samuel put Agag to death before the LORD at Gilgal.

34Then Samuel left for Ramah,[d] but Saul went up to his home in Gibeah[e] of Saul. 35Until the day Samuel[f] died, he did not go to see Saul again, though Samuel mourned[g] for him. And the LORD was grieved that he had made Saul king over Israel.

Samuel Anoints David

16 The LORD said to Samuel, "How long will you mourn[a] for Saul, since I have rejected[b] him as king over Israel? Fill your horn with oil[c] and be on your way; I am sending you to Jesse[d] of Bethlehem. I have chosen[e] one of his sons to be king."

2But Samuel said, "How can I go? Saul will hear about it and kill me."

The LORD said, "Take a heifer with you and say, 'I have come to sacrifice to the LORD.' 3Invite Jesse to the sacrifice, and I will show[f] you what to do. You are to anoint[g] for me the one I indicate."

4Samuel did what the LORD said. When he arrived at Bethlehem,[h] the elders of the town trembled when they met him. They asked, "Do you come in peace?[i]"

5Samuel replied, "Yes, in peace; I have come to sacrifice to the LORD. Consecrate[j] yourselves and come to the sacrifice with me." Then he consecrated Jesse and his sons and invited them to the sacrifice.

6When they arrived, Samuel saw

15:22 q Ps 40:6-8; Ps 51:16; Isa 1:11-15; Jer 7:22; Hos 6:6; Mic 6:6-8; Mt 12:7; Mk 12:33; Heb 10:6-9
15:23 r Dt 18:10; s 1Sa 13:13
15:24 t 2Sa 12:13; u Pr 29:25; Isa 51:12-13
15:25 v Ex 10:17
15:26 w 1Sa 13:14
15:27 x 1Ki 11:11,31
15:28 y 1Sa 28:17; 1Ki 11:31
15:29 z 1Ch 29:11; Tit 1:2; a Nu 23:19; Eze 24:14
15:30 b Isa 29:13; Jn 5:44; Jn 12:43
15:33 c Ge 9:6; Jdg 1:7
15:34 d 1Sa 7:17; e 1Sa 11:4
15:35 f 1Sa 19:24; g 1Sa 16:1
16:1 a 1Sa 15:35; b 1Sa 15:23; c 2Ki 9:1; d Ru 4:17; 1Sa 9:16; e Ps 78:70; Ac 13:22
16:3 f Ex 4:15; g Dt 17:15; 1Sa 9:16
16:4 h Ge 48:7; Lk 2:4; i 1Ki 2:13; 2Ki 9:17
16:5 j Ex 19:10,22

c32 Or *him trembling, yet*

Eliab[k] and thought, "Surely the LORD's anointed stands here before the LORD."

7But the LORD said to Samuel, "Do not consider his appearance or his height, for I have rejected him. The LORD does not look at the things man looks at. Man looks at the outward appearance,[l] but the LORD looks at the heart."[m]

8Then Jesse called Abinadab[n] and made him pass in front of Samuel. But Samuel said, "The LORD has not chosen this one either." 9Jesse then made Shammah pass by, but Samuel said, "Nor has the LORD chosen this one." 10Jesse made seven of his sons pass before Samuel, but Samuel said to him, "The LORD has not chosen these." 11So he asked Jesse, "Are these all[o] the sons you have?"

"There is still the youngest," Jesse answered, "but he is tending the sheep."

Samuel said, "Send for him; we will not sit down[a] until he arrives."

12So he[p] sent and had him brought in. He was ruddy, with a fine appearance and handsome[q] features.

Then the LORD said, "Rise and anoint him; he is the one."

13So Samuel took the horn of oil and anointed him in the presence of his brothers, and from that day on the Spirit of the LORD[r] came upon David in power.[s] Samuel then went to Ramah.

David in Saul's Service

14Now the Spirit of the LORD had departed[t] from Saul, and an evil[b] spirit[u] from the LORD tormented him.

15Saul's attendants said to him, "See, an evil spirit from God is tormenting you. 16Let our lord command his servants here to search for someone who can play the harp.[v] He will play when the evil spirit from God comes upon you, and you will feel better."

17So Saul said to his attendants, "Find someone who plays well and bring him to me."

18One of the servants answered, "I have seen a son of Jesse of Bethlehem who knows how to play the harp. He is a brave man and a warrior. He speaks well and is a fine-looking man. And the LORD is with[w] him."

19Then Saul sent messengers to Jesse and said, "Send me your son David, who is with the sheep." 20So Jesse took a donkey loaded with bread,[x] a skin of wine and a young goat and sent them with his son David to Saul.

21David came to Saul and entered his service.[y] Saul liked him very much, and David became one of his armour-bearers. 22Then Saul sent word to Jesse, saying, "Allow David to remain in my service, for I am pleased with him."

23Whenever the spirit from God came upon Saul, David would take his harp and play. Then relief would come to Saul; he would feel better, and the evil spirit[z] would leave him.

David and Goliath

17 Now the Philistines gathered their forces for war and assembled[a] at Socoh in Judah. They pitched camp at Ephes Dammim, between Socoh[b] and Azekah. 2Saul and the Israelites assembled and camped in the Valley of Elah[c] and drew up their battle line to meet the Philistines. 3The Philistines occupied one hill and the Israelites another, with the valley between them.

4A champion named Goliath,[d] who was from Gath, came out of the Philistine camp. He was over nine feet[a] tall. 5He had a bronze helmet on his head and wore a coat

16:6 k 1Sa 17:13
16:7 l Ps 147:10; m 1Ki 8:39; 1Ch 28:9; Isa 55:8
16:8 n 1Sa 17:13
16:11 o 1Sa 17:12
16:12 p 1Sa 9:17; q Ge 39:6; 1Sa 17:42
16:13 r Nu 27:18; Jdg 11:29; s 1Sa 10:1,6, 9-10; 1Sa 11:6
16:14 t Jdg 16:20; u Jdg 9:23; 1Sa 18:10
16:16 v ver 23; 1Sa 18:10; 1Sa 19:9; 2Ki 3:15
16:18 w 1Sa 3:19; 1Sa 17:32-37
16:20 x 1Sa 10:27; Pr 18:16
16:21 y Ge 41:46; Pr 22:29
16:23 z ver 14-16
17:1 a 1Sa 13:5; b Jos 15:35; 2Ch 28:18
17:2 c 1Sa 21:9
17:4 d Jos 11:21-22; 2Sa 21:19

a *11* Some Septuagint manuscripts; Hebrew *not gather round* b *14* Or *injurious*; also in verses 15, 16 and 23 a *4* Hebrew *was six cubits and a span* (about 3 metres)

of scale armour of bronze weighing
five thousand shekels;[b] 6on his
legs he wore bronze greaves, and a
bronze javelin[e] was slung on his
back. 7His spear shaft was like a
weaver's rod,[f] and its iron point
weighed six hundred shekels.[c] His
shield-bearer[g] went ahead of him.
8Goliath stood and shouted to the
ranks of Israel, "Why do you come
out and line up for battle? Am I not
a Philistine, and are you not the servants of Saul? Choose[h] a man and
have him come down to me. 9If he
is able to fight and kill me, we will
become your subjects; but if I overcome him and kill him, you will become our subjects and serve us."
10Then the Philistine said, "This
day I defy[i] the ranks of Israel!
Give me a man and let us fight each
other." 11On hearing the Philistine's words, Saul and all the Israelites were dismayed and terrified.
12Now David was the son of an
Ephrathite named Jesse,[j] who was
from Bethlehem[k] in Judah. Jesse
had eight[l] sons, and in Saul's time
he was old and well advanced in
years. 13Jesse's three oldest sons
had followed Saul to the war: The
firstborn was Eliab;[m] the second,
Abinadab; and the third, Shammah.[n] 14David was the youngest.
The three oldest followed Saul,
15but David went back and forth
from Saul to tend his father's
sheep[o] at Bethlehem.
16For forty days the Philistine
came forward every morning and
evening and took his stand.
17Now Jesse said to his son
David, "Take this ephah[d] of
roasted grain[p] and these ten
loaves of bread for your brothers
and hurry to their camp. 18Take
along these ten cheeses to the commander of their unit.[e] See how
your brothers[q] are and bring back
some assurance[f] from them.
19They are with Saul and all the
men of Israel in the Valley of Elah,
fighting against the Philistines."
20Early in the morning David left
the flock with a shepherd, loaded
up and set out, as Jesse had directed. He reached the camp as the
army was going out to its battle positions, shouting the war cry. 21Is-
rael and the Philistines were
drawing up their lines facing each
other. 22David left his things with
the keeper of supplies, ran to the
battle lines and greeted his
brothers. 23As he was talking with
them, Goliath, the Philistine champion from Gath, stepped out from
his lines and shouted his usual[r] de-
fiance, and David heard it. 24When
the Israelites saw the man, they all
ran from him in great fear.
25Now the Israelites had been
saying, "Do you see how this man
keeps coming out? He comes out to
defy Israel. The king will give
great wealth to the man who kills
him. He will also give him his
daughter[s] in marriage and will exempt his father's family from taxes
in Israel."
26David asked the men standing
near him, "What will be done for
the man who kills this Philistine
and removes this disgrace[t] from
Israel? Who is this uncircumcised[u] Philistine that he should
defy[v] the armies of the living[w]
God?"
27They repeated to him what they
had been saying and told him, "This
is what will be done for the man
who kills him."
28When Eliab, David's oldest
brother, heard him speaking with
the men, he burned with anger[x] at
him and asked, "Why have you
come down here? And with whom
did you leave those few sheep in
the desert? I know how conceited
you are and how wicked your heart
is; you came down only to watch
the battle."
29"Now what have I done?" said

17:6 e ver 45
17:7 f 2Sa 21:19 g ver 41
17:8 h 1Sa 8:17
17:10 i ver 26,45 2Sa 21:21
17:12 j Ru 4:17 1Ch 2:13-15 k Ge 35:19 l 1Sa 16:11
17:13 m 1Sa 16:6 n 1Sa 16:9
17:15 o 1Sa 16:19
17:17 p 1Sa 25:18
17:18 q Ge 37:14
17:23 r ver 8-10
17:25 s Jos 15:16 1Sa 18:17
17:26 t 1Sa 11:2 u 1Sa 14:6 v ver 10 w Dt 5:26
17:28 x Ge 37:4,8,11 Pr 18:19 Mt 10:36

b5 That is, about 125 pounds (about 57 kilograms)
c7 That is, about 15 pounds (about 7 kilograms)
d17 That is, probably about 3/5 bushel (about 22 litres) e18 Hebrew *thousand*
f18 Or *some token*; or *some pledge of spoils*

David. "Can't I even speak?" 30He then turned away to someone else and brought up the same matter, and the men answered him as before. 31What David said was overheard and reported to Saul, and Saul sent for him.

32David said to Saul, "Let no-one lose heart[y] on account of this Philistine; your servant will go and fight him."

33Saul replied,[z] "You are not able to go out against this Philistine and fight him; you are only a boy, and he has been a fighting man from his youth."

34But David said to Saul, "Your servant has been keeping his father's sheep. When a lion[a] or a bear came and carried off a sheep from the flock, 35I went after it, struck it and rescued the sheep from its mouth. When it turned on me, I seized it by its hair, struck it and killed it. 36Your servant has killed both the lion and the bear; this uncircumcised Philistine will be like one of them, because he has defied the armies of the living God. 37The LORD who delivered[b] me from the paw of the lion[c] and the paw of the bear will deliver me from the hand of this Philistine."

Saul said to David, "Go, and the LORD be with[d] you."

38Then Saul dressed David in his own tunic. He put a coat of armour on him and a bronze helmet on his head. 39David fastened on his sword over the tunic and tried walking around, because he was not used to them.

"I cannot go in these," he said to Saul, "because I am not used to them." So he took them off. 40Then he took his staff in his hand, chose five smooth stones from the stream, put them in the pouch of his shepherd's bag and, with his sling in his hand, approached the Philistine.

41Meanwhile, the Philistine, with his shield-bearer in front of him, kept coming closer to David. 42He looked David over and saw that he was only a boy, ruddy and handsome,[e] and he despised[f] him. 43He said to David, "Am I a dog,[g] that you come at me with sticks?" And the Philistine cursed David by his gods. 44"Come here," he said, "and I'll give your flesh to the birds of the air and the beasts of the field![h]"

45David said to the Philistine, "You come against me with sword and spear and javelin, but I come against you in the name[i] of the LORD Almighty, the God of the armies of Israel, whom you have defied.[j] 46This day the LORD will hand you over to me, and I'll strike you down and cut off your head. Today I will give the carcasses[k] of the Philistine army to the birds of the air and the beasts of the earth, and the whole world[l] will know that there is a God in Israel.[m] 47All those gathered here will know that it is not by sword[n] or spear that the LORD saves;[o] for the battle[p] is the LORD's, and he will give all of you into our hands."

48As the Philistine moved closer to attack him, David ran quickly towards the battle line to meet him. 49Reaching into his bag and taking out a stone, he slung it and struck the Philistine on the forehead. The stone sank into his forehead, and he fell face down on the ground.

50So David triumphed over the Philistine with a sling[q] and a stone; without a sword in his hand he struck down the Philistine and killed him.

51David ran and stood over him. He took hold of the Philistine's sword and drew it from the scabbard. After he killed him, he cut[r] off his head with the sword.[s]

When the Philistines saw that their hero was dead, they turned and ran. 52Then the men of Israel and Judah surged forward with a shout and pursued the Philistines

17:32
y Dt 20:3; 1Sa 16:18

17:33
z Nu 13:31

17:34
a Jer 49:19; Am 3:12

17:37
b 2Co 1:10
c 2Ti 4:17
d 1Sa 20:13; 1Ch 22:11,16

17:42
e 1Sa 16:12
f Ps 123:3-4; Pr 16:18

17:43
g 1Sa 24:14; 2Sa 3:8; 2Sa 9:8; 2Ki 8:13

17:44
h 1Ki 20:10-11

17:45
i 2Sa 22:33,35; 2Ch 32:8; Ps 124:8; Heb 11:32-34
j ver 10

17:46
k Dt 28:26
l Jos 4:24; 1Ki 8:43; Isa 52:10
m 1Ki 18:36; 2Ki 19:19; Isa 37:20

17:47
n Hos 1:7; Zec 4:6
o 1Sa 14:6; 2Ch 14:11
p 2Ch 20:15; Ps 44:6-7

17:50
q 2Sa 23:21

17:51
r Heb 11:34
s 1Sa 21:9

to the entrance of Gath[g] and to the gates of Ekron.[t] Their dead were strewn along the Shaaraim[u] road to Gath and Ekron. 53When the Israelites returned from chasing the Philistines, they plundered their camp. 54David took the Philistine's head and brought it to Jerusalem, and he put the Philistine's weapons in his own tent.

55As Saul watched David[v] going out to meet the Philistine, he said to Abner, commander of the army, "Abner, whose son is that young man?"

Abner replied, "As surely as you live, O king, I don't know."

56The king said, "Find out whose son this young man is."

57As soon as David returned from killing the Philistine, Abner took him and brought him before Saul, with David still holding the Philistine's head.

58"Whose son are you, young man?" Saul asked him.

David said, "I am the son of your servant Jesse[w] of Bethlehem."

Saul's Jealousy of David

18 After David had finished talking with Saul, Jonathan became one in spirit with David, and he loved[a] him as himself.[b] 2From that day Saul kept David with him and did not let him return to his father's house. 3And Jonathan made a covenant[c] with David because he loved him as himself. 4Jonathan took off the robe[d] he was wearing and gave it to David, along with his tunic, and even his sword, his bow and his belt.

5Whatever Saul sent him to do, David did it so successfully[a] that Saul gave him a high rank in the army. This pleased all the people, and Saul's officers as well.

6When the men were returning home after David had killed the Philistine, the women came out from all the towns of Israel to meet King Saul with singing and dancing,[e] with joyful songs and with tambourines[f] and lutes. 7As they danced, they sang:[g]

"Saul has slain his thousands,
  and David his tens[h] of
    thousands."

8Saul was very angry; this refrain galled him. "They have credited David with tens of thousands," he thought, "but me with only thousands. What more can he get but the kingdom?[i]" 9And from that time on Saul kept a jealous eye on David.

10The next day an evil[b] spirit[j] from God came forcefully upon Saul. He was prophesying in his house, while David was playing the harp, as he usually[k] did. Saul had a spear in his hand 11and he hurled it, saying to himself,[l] "I'll pin David to the wall." But David eluded[m] him twice.

12Saul was afraid[n] of David, because the LORD[o] was with[p] David but had left Saul. 13So he sent David away from him and gave him command over a thousand men, and David led[q] the troops in their campaigns.[r] 14In everything he did he had great success,[c][s] because the LORD was with[t] him. 15When Saul saw how successful[d] he was, he was afraid of him. 16But all Israel and Judah loved David, because he led them in their campaigns.[u]

17Saul said to David, "Here is my elder daughter[v] Merab. I will give her to you in marriage; only serve me bravely and fight the battles[w] of the LORD." For Saul said to himself,[x] "I will not raise a hand against him. Let the Philistines do that!"

18But David said to Saul, "Who am I,[y] and what is my family or my father's clan in Israel, that I should become the king's son-in-law?[z]" 19So[e] when the time came for

17:52 t Jos 15:11 u Jos 15:36
17:55 v 1Sa 16:21
17:58 w ver 12
18:1 a 2Sa 1:26 b Ge 44:30
18:3 c 1Sa 20:8,16, 17,42
18:4 d Ge 41:42
18:6 e Ex 15:20 f Jdg 11:34 Ps 68:25
18:7 g Ex 15:21 h 1Sa 21:11 1Sa 29:5
18:8 i 1Sa 15:8
18:10 j 1Sa 16:14 k 1Sa 19:7
18:11 l 1Sa 20:7,33 m 1Sa 19:10
18:12 n ver 15,29 o 1Sa 16:13 p 1Sa 28:15
18:13 q ver 16 Nu 27:17 r 2Sa 5:2
18:14 s Ge 39:3 t Ge 39:2,23 Jos 6:27 1Sa 16:18
18:16 u ver 5
18:17 v 1Sa 17:25 w Nu 21:14 1Sa 25:28 x ver 25
18:18 y 1Sa 9:21 2Sa 7:18 z ver 23

g52 Some Septuagint manuscripts; Hebrew *a valley* a5 Or *wisely* b10 Or *injurious* c14 Or *he was very wise* d15 Or *wise* e19 Or *However,*

Merab,[a] Saul's daughter, to be
given to David, she was given in
marriage to Adriel of Meholah.[b]
20Now Saul's daughter Michal[c]
was in love with David, and when
they told Saul about it, he was
pleased. 21"I will give her to him,"
he thought, "so that she may be a
snare[d] to him and so that the hand
of the Philistines may be against
him." So Saul said to David, "Now
you have a second opportunity to
become my son-in-law."
22Then Saul ordered his attendants: "Speak to David privately and
say, 'Look, the king is pleased with
you, and his attendants all like you;
now become his son-in-law.' "
23They repeated these words to
David. But David said, "Do you
think it is a small matter to become
the king's son-in-law? I'm only a
poor man and little known."
24When Saul's servants told him
what David had said, 25Saul replied,
"Say to David, 'The king wants no
other price[e] for the bride than a
hundred Philistine foreskins, to
take revenge on his enemies.' "
Saul's plan[f] was to have David fall
by the hands of the Philistines.
26When the attendants told David
these things, he was pleased to become the king's son-in-law. So before the allotted time elapsed,
27David and his men went out and
killed two hundred Philistines. He
brought their foreskins and presented the full number to the king
so that he might become the king's
son-in-law. Then Saul gave him his
daughter Michal[g] in marriage.
28When Saul realised that the
LORD was with David and that his
daughter Michal loved David,
29Saul became still more afraid of
him, and he remained his enemy
for the rest of his days.
30The Philistine commanders
continued to go out to battle, and as
often as they did, David met with
more success[f][h] than the rest of
Saul's officers, and his name became well known.

18:19 a 2Sa 21:8 b Jdg 7:22
18:20 c ver 28
18:21 d ver 17,26
18:25 e Ge 34:12 Ex 22:17 1Sa 14:24 f ver 17
18:27 g ver 13 2Sa 3:14
18:30 h ver 5 2Sa 11:1
19:1 a 1Sa 18:1 b 1Sa 18:9
19:3 c 1Sa 20:12
19:4 d 1Sa 20:32 Pr 31:8,9 Jer 18:20 e Ge 42:22 Pr 17:13
19:5 f 1Sa 11:13 1Sa 17:49-50 1Ch 11:14 g Dt 19:10-13 1Sa 20:32 Mt 27:4
19:7 h 1Sa 16:21 1Sa 18:2,13
19:9 i 1Sa 16:14 1Sa 18:10-11
19:10 j 1Sa 18:11
19:11 k Ps 59 Title

Saul Tries to Kill David

19 Saul told his son Jonathan[a]
and all the attendants to
kill[b] David. But Jonathan was very
fond of David 2and warned him,
"My father Saul is looking for a
chance to kill you. Be on your
guard tomorrow morning; go into
hiding and stay there. 3I will go out
and stand with my father in the
field where you are. I'll speak[c] to
him about you and will tell you
what I find out."
4Jonathan spoke[d] well of David
to Saul his father and said to him,
"Let not the king do wrong[e] to his
servant David; he has not wronged
you, and what he has done has ben-
efited you greatly. 5He took his life
in his hands when he killed the Philistine. The LORD won a great victory[f] for all Israel, and you saw it
and were glad. Why then would you
do wrong to an innocent[g] man like
David by killing him for no reason?"
6Saul listened to Jonathan and
took this oath: "As surely as the
LORD lives, David will not be put to
death."
7So Jonathan called David and
told him the whole conversation.
He brought him to Saul, and David
was with Saul as before.[h]
8Once more war broke out, and
David went out and fought the Philistines. He struck them with such
force that they fled before him.
9But an evil[a] spirit[i] from the
LORD came upon Saul as he was sitting in his house with his spear in
his hand. While David was playing
the harp, 10Saul tried to pin him to
the wall with his spear, but David
eluded[j] him as Saul drove the
spear into the wall. That night
David made good his escape.
11Saul sent men to David's house
to watch[k] it and to kill him in the
morning. But Michal, David's wife,
warned him, "If you don't run for

f30 Or *David acted more wisely*
a9 Or *injurious*

your life tonight, tomorrow you'll be killed." 12So Michal let David down through a window,[l] and he fled and escaped. 13Then Michal took an idol[b] and laid it on the bed, covering it with a garment and putting some goats' hair at the head.

14When Saul sent the men to capture David, Michal said,[m] "He is ill."

15Then Saul sent the men back to see David and told them, "Bring him up to me in his bed so that I may kill him." 16But when the men entered, there was the idol in the bed, and at the head was some goats' hair.

17Saul said to Michal, "Why did you deceive me like this and send my enemy away so that he escaped?"

Michal told him, "He said to me, 'Let me get away. Why should I kill you?' "

18When David had fled and made his escape, he went to Samuel at Ramah[n] and told him all that Saul had done to him. Then he and Samuel went to Naioth and stayed there. 19Word came to Saul: "David is in Naioth at Ramah"; 20so he sent men to capture him. But when they saw a group of prophets[o] prophesying, with Samuel standing there as their leader, the Spirit of God came upon[p] Saul's men and they also prophesied.[q] 21Saul was told about it, and he sent more men, and they prophesied too. Saul sent men a third time, and they also prophesied. 22Finally, he himself left for Ramah and went to the great cistern at Secu. And he asked, "Where are Samuel and David?"

"Over in Naioth at Ramah," they said.

23So Saul went to Naioth at Ramah. But the Spirit of God came even upon him, and he walked along prophesying[r] until he came to Naioth. 24He stripped[s] off his robes and also prophesied in Samuel's presence. He lay that way all that day and night. This is why people say, "Is Saul also among the prophets?"[t]

David and Jonathan

20 Then David fled from Naioth at Ramah and went to Jonathan and asked, "What have I done? What is my crime? How have I wronged[a] your father, that he is trying to take my life?"

2"Never!" Jonathan replied. "You are not going to die! Look, my father doesn't do anything, great or small, without confiding in me. Why should he hide this from me? It's not so!"

3But David took an oath[b] and said, "Your father knows very well that I have found favour in your eyes, and he has said to himself, 'Jonathan must not know this or he will be grieved.' Yet as surely as the LORD lives and as you live, there is only a step between me and death."

4Jonathan said to David, "Whatever you want me to do, I'll do for you."

5So David said, "Look, tomorrow is the New Moon festival,[c] and I am supposed to dine with the king; but let me go and hide[d] in the field until the evening of the day after tomorrow. 6If your father misses me at all, tell him, 'David earnestly asked my permission to hurry to Bethlehem,[e] his home town, because an annual[f] sacrifice is being made there for his whole clan.' 7If he says, 'Very well,' then your servant is safe. But if he loses his temper,[g] you can be sure that he is determined to harm me. 8As for you, show kindness to your servant, for you have brought him into a covenant[h] with you before the LORD. If I am guilty, then kill[i] me yourself! Why hand me over to your father?"

9"Never!" Jonathan said. "If I had the least inkling that my father

19:12 l Jos 2:15; Ac 9:25
19:14 m Jos 2:4
19:18 n 1Sa 7:17
19:20 o ver 11,14; Jn 7:32,45; p Nu 11:25; q 1Sa 10:5; Joel 2:28
19:23 r 1Sa 10:13
19:24 s 2Sa 6:20; Isa 20:2; Mic 1:8; t 1Sa 10:11
20:1 a 1Sa 24:9
20:3 b Dt 6:13
20:5 c Nu 10:10; Nu 28:11; d 1Sa 19:2
20:6 e 1Sa 17:58; f Dt 12:5
20:7 g 1Sa 25:17
20:8 h 1Sa 18:3; 1Sa 23:18; i 2Sa 14:32

b 13 Hebrew *teraphim*; also in verse 16

was determined to harm you, wouldn't I tell you?"

10 David asked, "Who will tell me if your father answers you harshly?"

11 "Come," Jonathan said, "let's go out into the field." So they went there together.

12 Then Jonathan said to David: "By the LORD, the God of Israel, I will surely sound out my father by this time the day after tomorrow! If he is favourably disposed towards you, will I not send you word and let you know? 13 But if my father is inclined to harm you, may the LORD deal with me, be it ever so severely,[j] if I do not let you know and send you away safely. May the LORD be with[k] you as he has been with my father. 14 But show me unfailing kindness like that of the LORD as long as I live, so that I may not be killed, 15 and do not ever cut off your kindness from my family[l]—not even when the LORD has cut off every one of David's enemies from the face of the earth."

16 So Jonathan made a covenant[m] with the house of David, saying, "May the LORD call David's enemies to account." 17 And Jonathan made David reaffirm his oath[n] out of love for him, because he loved him as he loved himself.

18 Then Jonathan said to David: "Tomorrow is the New Moon festival. You will be missed, because your seat will be empty.[o] 19 The day after tomorrow, towards evening, go to the place where you hid[p] when this trouble began, and wait by the stone Ezel. 20 I will shoot three arrows to the side of it, as though I were shooting at a target. 21 Then I will send a boy and say, 'Go, find the arrows.' If I say to him, 'Look, the arrows are on this side of you; bring them here,' then come, because, as surely as the LORD lives, you are safe; there is no danger. 22 But if I say to the boy, 'Look, the arrows are beyond[q] you,' then you must go, because the LORD has sent you away. 23 And about the matter you and I discussed—remember, the LORD is witness[r] between you and me for ever."

24 So David hid in the field, and when the New Moon festival came, the king sat down to eat. 25 He sat in his customary place by the wall, opposite Jonathan,[a] and Abner sat next to Saul, but David's place was empty.[s] 26 Saul said nothing that day, for he thought, "Something must have happened to David to make him ceremonially unclean—surely he is unclean.[t]" 27 But the next day, the second day of the month, David's place was empty again. Then Saul said to his son Jonathan, "Why hasn't the son of Jesse come to the meal, either yesterday or today?"

28 Jonathan answered, "David earnestly asked me for permission[u] to go to Bethlehem. 29 He said, 'Let me go, because our family is observing a sacrifice in the town and my brother has ordered me to be there. If I have found favour in your eyes, let me go to see my brothers.' That is why he has not come to the king's table."

30 Saul's anger flared up at Jonathan and he said to him, "You son of a perverse and rebellious woman! Don't I know that you have sided with the son of Jesse to your own shame and to the shame of the mother who bore you? 31 As long as the son of Jesse lives on this earth, neither you nor your kingdom will be established. Now send and bring him to me, for he must die!"

32 "Why[v] should he be put to death? What[w] has he done?" Jonathan asked his father. 33 But Saul hurled his spear at him to kill him. Then Jonathan knew that his father intended[x] to kill David.

34 Jonathan got up from the table in fierce anger; on that second day of the month he did not eat, because

20:13 j Ru 1:17; 1Sa 3:17 k Jos 1:5; 1Sa 17:37; 1Sa 18:12; 1Ch 22:11,16
20:15 l 2Sa 9:7
20:16 m 1Sa 25:22
20:17 n 1Sa 18:3
20:18 o ver 5,25
20:19 p 1Sa 19:2
20:22 q ver 37
20:23 r ver 14-15; Ge 31:50
20:25 s ver 18
20:26 t Lev 7:20-21; Lev 15:5; 1Sa 16:5
20:28 u ver 6
20:32 v 1Sa 19:4; Mt 27:23 w Ge 31:36; Lk 23:22
20:33 x ver 7; 1Sa 18:11,17

a25 Septuagint; Hebrew *wall. Jonathan arose*

he was grieved at his father's
shameful treatment of David.
35 In the morning Jonathan went
out to the field for his meeting with
David. He had a small boy with
him, 36 and he said to the boy, "Run
and find the arrows I shoot." As the
boy ran, he shot an arrow beyond
him. 37 When the boy came to the
place where Jonathan's arrow had
fallen, Jonathan called out after
him, "Isn't the arrow beyond[y]
you?" 38 Then he shouted, "Hurry!
Go quickly! Don't stop!" The boy
picked up the arrow and returned
to his master. 39 (The boy knew
nothing of all this; only Jonathan
and David knew.) 40 Then Jonathan
gave his weapons to the boy and
said, "Go, carry them back to
town."
41 After the boy had gone, David
got up from the south side ⌊of the
stone⌋ and bowed down before Jonathan three times, with his face to
the ground. Then they kissed each
other and wept together—but
David wept the most.
42 Jonathan said to David, "Go in
peace,[z] for we have sworn friendship[a] with each other in the name
of the LORD, saying, 'The LORD is
witness between you and me, and
between your descendants and my
descendants for ever.'" Then
David left, and Jonathan went back
to the town.

David at Nob

21 David went to Nob,[a] to
Ahimelech the priest. Ahimelech trembled[b] when he met
him, and asked, "Why are you
alone? Why is no-one with you?"
2 David answered Ahimelech the
priest, "The king charged me with
a certain matter and said to me,
'No-one is to know anything about
your mission and your instructions.' As for my men, I have told
them to meet me at a certain place.
3 Now then, what have you to hand?
Give me five loaves of bread, or
whatever you can find."
4 But the priest answered David,
"I don't have any ordinary bread[c]
to hand; however, there is some
consecrated[d] bread here—provided the men have kept[e] themselves
from women."
5 David replied, "Indeed women
have been kept from us, as usual
whenever[a] I set out. The men's
things[b] are holy[f] even on mis-
sions that are not holy. How much
more so today!" 6 So the priest gave
him the consecrated bread,[g] since
there was no bread there except
the bread of the Presence that had
been removed from before the
LORD and replaced by hot bread on
the day it was taken away.
7 Now one of Saul's servants was
there that day, detained before the
LORD; he was Doeg[h] the Edomite,[i]
Saul's head shepherd.
8 David asked Ahimelech, "Don't
you have a spear or sword here? I
haven't brought my sword or any
other weapon, because the king's
business was urgent."
9 The priest replied, "The sword[j]
of Goliath the Philistine, whom you
killed in the Valley of Elah,[k] is
here; it is wrapped in a cloth behind
the ephod. If you want it, take it;
there is no sword here but that
one."
David said, "There is none like it;
give it to me."

David at Gath

10 That day David fled from Saul
and went[l] to Achish king of Gath.
11 But the servants of Achish said to
him, "Isn't this David, the king of
the land? Isn't he the one they sing
about in their dances:

"'Saul has slain his thousands,
and David his tens of
thousands'?"[m]

20:37 y ver 22
20:42 z ver 22; 1Sa 1:17 a 2Sa 1:26; Pr 18:24
21:1 a 1Sa 14:3; 1Sa 22:9,19; Ne 11:32; Isa 10:32 b 1Sa 16:4
21:4 c Lev 24:8-9 d Ex 25:30; Mt 12:4 e Ex 19:15
21:5 f 1Th 4:4
21:6 g Lev 24:8-9; Mt 12:3-4; Mk 2:25-28; Lk 6:1-5
21:7 h 1Sa 22:9,22 i 1Sa 14:47; Ps 52 Title
21:9 j 1Sa 17:51 k 1Sa 17:2
21:10 l 1Sa 27:2
21:11 m 1Sa 18:7; 1Sa 29:5; Ps 56 Title

a5 Or *from us in the past few days since* b5 Or *bodies*

12David took these words to heart and was very much afraid of Achish king of Gath. 13So he feigned insanity[n] in their presence; and while he was in their hands he acted like a madman, making marks on the doors of the gate and letting saliva run down his beard.

14Achish said to his servants, "Look at the man! He is insane! Why bring him to me? 15Am I so short of madmen that you have to bring this fellow here to carry on like this in front of me? Must this man come into my house?"

David at Adullam and Mizpah

22 David left Gath and escaped to the cave[a] of Adullam. When his brothers and his father's household heard about it, they went down to him there. 2All those who were in distress or in debt or discontented gathered[b] round him, and he became their leader. About four hundred men were with him.

3From there David went to Mizpah in Moab and said to the king of Moab, "Would you let my father and mother come and stay with you until I learn what God will do for me?" 4So he left them with the king of Moab, and they stayed with him as long as David was in the stronghold.

5But the prophet Gad[c] said to David, "Do not stay in the stronghold. Go into the land of Judah." So David left and went to the forest of Hereth.

Saul Kills the Priests of Nob

6Now Saul heard that David and his men had been discovered. And Saul, spear in hand, was seated[d] under the tamarisk[e] tree on the hill at Gibeah, with all his officials standing round him. 7Saul said to them, "Listen, men of Benjamin! Will the son of Jesse give all of you fields and vineyards? Will he make all of you commanders[f] of thousands and commanders of hundreds? 8Is that why you have all conspired against me? No-one tells me when my son makes a covenant[g] with the son of Jesse. None of you is concerned[h] about me or tells me that my son has incited my servant to lie in wait for me, as he does today."

9But Doeg[i] the Edomite, who was standing with Saul's officials, said, "I saw the son of Jesse come to Ahimelech son of Ahitub at Nob.[j] 10Ahimelech enquired[k] of the LORD for him; he also gave him provisions[l] and the sword of Goliath the Philistine."

11Then the king sent for the priest Ahimelech son of Ahitub and his father's whole family, who were the priests at Nob, and they all came to the king. 12Saul said, "Listen now, son of Ahitub."

"Yes, my lord," he answered.

13Saul said to him, "Why have you conspired[m] against me, you and the son of Jesse, giving him bread and a sword and enquiring of God for him, so that he has rebelled against me and lies in wait for me, as he does today?"

14Ahimelech answered the king, "Who[n] of all your servants is as loyal as David, the king's son-in-law, captain of your bodyguard and highly respected in your household? 15Was that day the first time I enquired of God for him? Of course not! Let not the king accuse your servant or any of his father's family, for your servant knows nothing at all about this whole affair."

16But the king said, "You shall surely die, Ahimelech, you and your father's whole family."

17Then the king ordered the guards at his side: "Turn and kill the priests of the LORD, because they too have sided with David. They knew he was fleeing, yet they did not tell me."

21:13 *n* Ps 34 Title
22:1 *a* 2Sa 23:13; Ps 57 Title; Ps 142 Title
22:2 *b* 1Sa 23:13; 1Sa 25:13; 2Sa 15:20
22:5 *c* 2Sa 24:11; 1Ch 21:9; 1Ch 29:29; 2Ch 29:25
22:6 *d* Jdg 4:5 *e* Ge 21:33
22:7 *f* 1Sa 8:14
22:8 *g* 1Sa 18:3; 1Sa 20:16 *h* 1Sa 23:21
22:9 *i* 1Sa 21:7; Ps 52 Title *j* 1Sa 21:1
22:10 *k* Nu 27:21; 1Sa 10:22 *l* 1Sa 21:6
22:13 *m* ver 8
22:14 *n* 1Sa 19:4

But the king's officials were not willing[o] to raise a hand to strike the priests of the LORD.

18The king then ordered Doeg, "You turn and strike down the priests." So Doeg the Edomite turned and struck them down. That day he killed eighty-five men who wore the linen ephod.[p] 19He also put to the sword[q] Nob, the town of the priests, with its men and women, its children and infants, and its cattle, donkeys and sheep.

20But Abiathar,[r] son of Ahimelech son of Ahitub, escaped and fled to join David.[s] 21He told David that Saul had killed the priests of the LORD. 22Then David said to Abiathar: "That day, when Doeg[t] the Edomite was there, I knew he would be sure to tell Saul. I am responsible for the death of your father's whole family. 23Stay with me; don't be afraid; the man who is seeking your life[u] is seeking mine also. You will be safe with me."

David Saves Keilah

23 When David was told, "Look, the Philistines are fighting against Keilah[a] and are looting the threshing-floors," 2he enquired[b] of the LORD, saying, "Shall I go and attack these Philistines?"

The LORD answered him, "Go, attack the Philistines and save Keilah."

3But David's men said to him, "Here in Judah we are afraid. How much more, then, if we go to Keilah against the Philistine forces!"

4Once again David enquired of the LORD, and the LORD answered him, "Go down to Keilah, for I am going to give the Philistines into your hand.[c]" 5So David and his men went to Keilah, fought the Philistines and carried off their livestock. He inflicted heavy losses on the Philistines and saved the people of Keilah. 6(Now Abiathar[d] son of Ahimelech had brought the ephod down with him when he fled to David at Keilah.)

Saul Pursues David

7Saul was told that David had gone to Keilah, and he said, "God has handed him over to me, for David has imprisoned himself by entering a town with gates and bars." 8And Saul called up all his forces for battle, to go down to Keilah to besiege David and his men.

9When David learned that Saul was plotting against him, he said to Abiathar[e] the priest, "Bring the ephod." 10David said, "O LORD, God of Israel, your servant has heard definitely that Saul plans to come to Keilah and destroy the town on account of me. 11Will the citizens of Keilah surrender me to him? Will Saul come down, as your servant has heard? O LORD, God of Israel, tell your servant."

And the LORD said, "He will."

12Again David asked, "Will the citizens of Keilah surrender[f] me and my men to Saul?"

And the LORD said, "They will."

13So David and his men,[g] about six hundred in number, left Keilah and kept moving from place to place. When Saul was told that David had escaped from Keilah, he did not go there.

14David stayed in the desert strongholds and in the hills of the Desert of Ziph.[h] Day after day Saul searched[i] for him, but God did not[j] give David into his hands.

15While David was at Horesh in the Desert of Ziph, he learned that Saul had come out to take his life. 16And Saul's son Jonathan went to David at Horesh and helped him to find strength[k] in God. 17"Don't be afraid," he said. "My father Saul will not lay a hand on you. You shall

22:17 o Ex 1:17
22:18 p 1Sa 2:18,31
22:19 q 1Sa 15:3
22:20 r 1Sa 23:6,9; 1Sa 30:7; 1Ki 2:22,26,27; s 1Sa 2:32
22:22 t 1Sa 21:7
22:23 u 1Ki 2:26
23:1 a Jos 15:44
23:2 b ver 4,12; 1Sa 30:8; 2Sa 5:19,23
23:4 c Jos 8:7; Jdg 7:7
23:6 d 1Sa 22:20
23:9 e ver 6; 1Sa 22:20; 1Sa 30:7
23:12 f ver 20
23:13 g 1Sa 22:2; 1Sa 25:13
23:14 h Jos 15:24,55; i Ps 54:3-4; j Ps 32:7
23:16 k 1Sa 30:6

be king[l] over Israel, and I will be second to you. Even my father Saul knows this." 18 The two of them made a covenant[m] before the LORD. Then Jonathan went home, but David remained at Horesh.

19 The Ziphites[n] went up to Saul at Gibeah and said, "Is not David hiding among us[o] in the strongholds at Horesh, on the hill of Hakilah,[p] south of Jeshimon? 20 Now, O king, come down whenever it pleases you to do so, and we will be responsible for handing[q] him over to the king."

21 Saul replied, "The LORD bless you for your concern[r] for me. 22 Go and make further preparation. Find out where David usually goes and who has seen him there. They tell me he is very crafty. 23 Find out about all the hiding-places he uses and come back to me with definite information.[a] Then I will go with you; if he is in the area, I will track him down among all the clans of Judah."

24 So they set out and went to Ziph ahead of Saul. Now David and his men were in the Desert of Maon,[s] in the Arabah south of Jeshimon. 25 Saul and his men began the search, and when David was told about it, he went down to the rock and stayed in the Desert of Maon. When Saul heard this, he went into the Desert of Maon in pursuit of David.

26 Saul[t] was going along one side of the mountain, and David and his men were on the other side, hurrying to get away from Saul. As Saul and his forces were closing in on David and his men to capture them, 27 a messenger came to Saul, saying, "Come quickly! The Philistines are raiding the land." 28 Then Saul broke off his pursuit of David and went to meet the Philistines. That is why they call this place Sela Hammahlekoth.[b] 29 And David went up from there and lived in the strongholds of En Gedi.[u]

23:17 l 1Sa 20:31; 1Sa 24:20
23:18 m 1Sa 18:3; 1Sa 20:16,42; 2Sa 9:1; 2Sa 21:7
23:19 n 1Sa 26:1; o Ps 54 Title; p 1Sa 26:3
23:20 q ver 12
23:21 r 1Sa 22:8
23:24 s Jos 15:55; 1Sa 25:2
23:26 t Ps 17:9
23:29 u 2Ch 20:2
24:1 a 1Sa 23:28-29
24:2 b 1Sa 26:2
24:3 c Ps 57 Title; Ps 142 Title; d Jdg 3:24
24:4 e 1Sa 25:28-30; f 1Sa 23:17; 1Sa 26:8
24:5 g 2Sa 24:10
24:6 h 1Sa 26:11
24:8 i 1Sa 25:23-24

David Spares Saul's Life

24 After Saul returned from pursuing the Philistines, he was told, "David is in the Desert of En Gedi.[a]" 2 So Saul took three thousand chosen men from all Israel and set out to look[b] for David and his men near the Crags of the Wild Goats.

3 He came to the sheep pens along the way; a cave[c] was there, and Saul went in to relieve[d] himself. David and his men were far back in the cave. 4 The men said, "This is the day the LORD spoke[e] of when he said[a] to you, 'I will give your enemy into your hands for you to deal with as you wish.' "[f] Then David crept up unnoticed and cut off a corner of Saul's robe.

5 Afterwards, David was conscience-stricken[g] for having cut off a corner of his robe. 6 He said to his men, "The LORD forbid that I should do such a thing to my master, the LORD's anointed,[h] or lift my hand against him; for he is the anointed of the LORD." 7 With these words David rebuked his men and did not allow them to attack Saul. And Saul left the cave and went his way.

8 Then David went out of the cave and called out to Saul, "My lord the king!" When Saul looked behind him, David bowed down and prostrated himself with his face to the ground.[i] 9 He said to Saul, "Why do you listen when men say, 'David is bent on harming you'? 10 This day you have seen with your own eyes how the LORD gave you into my hands in the cave. Some urged me to kill you, but I spared you; I said, 'I will not lift my hand against my master, because he is the LORD's anointed.' 11 See, my father, look at this piece of your robe in my hand! I cut off the corner of your robe but did not kill you. Now understand

a23 Or *me at Nacon* b28 *Sela Hammahlekoth* means *rock of parting.* a4 Or *"Today the LORD is saying*

and recognise that I am not guilty[j]
of wrongdoing or rebellion. I have
not wronged you, but you are hunting[k] me down to take my life.
12 May the LORD judge[l] between
you and me. And may the LORD
avenge[m] the wrongs you have done
to me, but my hand will not touch
you. 13 As the old saying goes, 'From
evildoers come evil deeds,[n]' so my
hand will not touch you.

14 "Against whom has the king of
Israel come out? Whom are you
pursuing? A dead dog?[o] A flea?[p]
15 May the LORD be our judge[q] and
decide between us. May he consider my cause and uphold[r] it;
may he vindicate[s] me by delivering[t] me from your hand."

16 When David finished saying
this, Saul asked, "Is that your
voice,[u] David my son?" And he
wept aloud. 17 "You are more righteous than I,"[v] he said. "You have
treated me well,[w] but I have
treated you badly. 18 You have just
now told me of the good you did to
me; the LORD gave[x] me into your
hands, but you did not kill me.
19 When a man finds his enemy,
does he let him get away unharmed? May the LORD reward you
well for the way you treated me today. 20 I know that you will surely
be king[y] and that the kingdom[z] of
Israel will be established in your
hands. 21 Now swear[a] to me by the
LORD that you will not cut off my
descendants or wipe out my name
from my father's family.[b]"

22 So David gave his oath to Saul.
Then Saul returned home, but
David and his men went up to the
stronghold.[c]

David, Nabal and Abigail

25 Now Samuel died,[a] and all
Israel assembled and
mourned[b] for him; and they
buried him at his home in Ramah.[c]

Then David moved down into the
Desert of Maon.[a] 2 A certain man in
Maon,[d] who had property there at
Carmel, was very wealthy. He had
a thousand goats and three thousand sheep, which he was shearing
in Carmel. 3 His name was Nabal
and his wife's name was Abigail.[e]
She was an intelligent and beautiful woman, but her husband, a Ca-
lebite,[f] was surly and mean in his
dealings.

4 While David was in the desert,
he heard that Nabal was shearing
sheep. 5 So he sent ten young men
and said to them, "Go up to Nabal at
Carmel and greet him in my name.
6 Say to him: 'Long life to you! Good
health[g] to you and your household!
And good health to all that is
yours![h]

7 " 'Now I hear that it is sheep-
shearing time. When your shepherds were with us, we did not
ill-treat[i] them, and the whole time
they were at Carmel nothing of
theirs was missing. 8 Ask your own
servants and they will tell you.
Therefore be favourable towards
my young men, since we come at a
festive time. Please give your servants and your son David whatever[j] you can find for them.' "

9 When David's men arrived, they
gave Nabal this message in David's
name. Then they waited.

10 Nabal answered David's servants, "Who[k] is this David? Who is
this son of Jesse? Many servants
are breaking away from their masters these days. 11 Why should I take
my bread[l] and water, and the meat
I have slaughtered for my shearers, and give it to men coming from
who knows where?"

12 David's men turned round and
went back. When they arrived, they
reported every word. 13 David said
to his men, "Put on your swords!"
So they put on their swords, and
David put on his. About four hundred men went[m] up with David,
while two hundred stayed with the
supplies.[n]

24:11 *j* Ps 7:3 *k* 1Sa 23:14,23; 1Sa 26:20
24:12 *l* Ge 16:5; Ge 31:53; Job 5:8 *m* Jdg 11:27; 1Sa 26:10
24:13 *n* Mt 7:20
24:14 *o* 1Sa 17:43; 2Sa 9:8 *p* 1Sa 26:20
24:15 *q* ver 12 *r* Ps 35:1,23; Mic 7:9 *s* Ps 43:1 *t* Ps 119:134, 154
24:16 *u* 1Sa 26:17
24:17 *v* Ge 38:26; 1Sa 26:21 *w* Mt 5:44
24:18 *x* 1Sa 26:23
24:20 *y* 1Sa 23:17 *z* 1Sa 13:14
24:21 *a* Ge 21:23; 2Sa 21:1-9 *b* 1Sa 20:14-15
24:22 *c* 1Sa 23:29
25:1 *a* 1Sa 28:3 *b* Nu 20:29; Dt 34:8 *c* Ge 21:21; 2Ch 33:20
25:2 *d* Jos 15:55; 1Sa 23:24
25:3 *e* Pr 31:10 *f* Jos 15:13
25:6 *g* Ps 122:7; Lk 10:5 *h* 1Ch 12:18
25:7 *i* ver 15
25:8 *j* Ne 8:10
25:10 *k* Jdg 9:28
25:11 *l* Jdg 8:6
25:13 *m* 1Sa 23:13 *n* 1Sa 30:24

a 1 Some Septuagint manuscripts; Hebrew *Paran*

14One of the servants told Nabal's
wife Abigail: "David sent messengers from the desert to give our
master his greetings,[o] but he
hurled insults at them. 15Yet these
men were very good to us. They did
not ill-treat[p] us, and the whole
time we were out in the fields near
them nothing was missing.[q]
16Night and day they were a wall[r]
around us all the time we were herd-
ing our sheep near them. 17Now
think it over and see what you
can do, because disaster is hanging over our master and his whole
household. He is such a wicked[s]
man that no-one can talk to him."

18Abigail lost no time. She took
two hundred loaves of bread, two
skins of wine, five dressed sheep,
five seahs[b] of roasted grain, a hundred cakes of raisins[t] and two
hundred cakes of pressed figs, and
loaded them on donkeys.[u] 19Then
she told her servants, "Go on
ahead;[v] I'll follow you." But she
did not tell her husband Nabal.

20As she came riding her donkey
into a mountain ravine, there were
David and his men descending towards her, and she met them.
21David had just said, "It's been
useless—all my watching over this
fellow's property in the desert so
that nothing of his was missing. He
has paid[w] me back evil for good.
22May God deal with David,[c] be it
ever so severely,[x] if by morning I
leave alive one male[y] of all who belong to him!"

23When Abigail saw David, she
quickly got off her donkey and
bowed down before David with her
face to the ground.[z] 24She fell at
his feet and said: "My lord, let the
blame be on me alone. Please let
your servant speak to you; hear
what your servant has to say. 25May
my lord pay no attention to that
wicked man Nabal. He is just like
his name—his name is Fool,[a] and
folly goes with him. But as for me,
your servant, I did not see the men
my master sent.

25:14 o 1Sa 13:10
25:15 p ver 7 q ver 21
25:16 r Ex 14:22 Job 1:10
25:17 s 1Sa 20:7
25:18 t 1Ch 12:40 u 2Sa 16:1
25:19 v Ge 32:20
25:21 w Ps 109:5
25:22 x 1Sa 3:17 1Sa 20:13 y 1Ki 14:10 1Ki 21:21 2Ki 9:8
25:23 z 1Sa 20:41
25:25 a Pr 14:16
25:26 b ver 33 c Heb 10:30 d 2Sa 18:32
25:27 e Ge 33:11 1Sa 30:26
25:28 f ver 24 g 2Sa 7:11,26 h 1Sa 18:17 i 1Sa 24:11
25:29 j Jer 10:18
25:30 k 1Sa 13:14
25:31 l Ge 40:14
25:32 m Ge 24:27 Ex 18:10 Lk 1:68
25:33 n ver 26

26"Now since the LORD has kept
you, my master, from bloodshed[b]
and from avenging[c] yourself with
your own hands, as surely as the
LORD lives and as you live, may
your enemies and all who intend to
harm my master be like Nabal.[d]
27And let this gift,[e] which your servant has brought to my master, be
given to the men who follow you.
28Please forgive[f] your servant's
offence, for the LORD will certainly
make a lasting[g] dynasty for my
master, because he fights the
LORD's battles.[h] Let no wrongdoing[i] be found in you as long as
you live. 29Even though someone is
pursuing you to take your life, the
life of my master will be bound securely in the bundle of the living by
the LORD your God. But the lives of
your enemies he will hurl[j] away as
from the pocket of a sling. 30When
the LORD has done for my master
every good thing he promised concerning him and has appointed him
leader[k] over Israel, 31my master
will not have on his conscience the
staggering burden of needless
bloodshed or of having avenged
himself. And when the LORD has
brought my master success, remember[l] your servant."

32David said to Abigail, "Praise[m]
be to the LORD, the God of Israel,
who has sent you today to meet me.
33May you be blessed for your good
judgment and for keeping me from
bloodshed[n] this day and from
avenging myself with my own
hands. 34Otherwise, as surely as the
LORD, the God of Israel, lives, who
has kept me from harming you, if
you had not come quickly to meet
me, not one male belonging to Nabal would have been left alive by
daybreak."

35Then David accepted from her
hand what she had brought to him
and said, "Go home in peace. I have

[b] *18* That is, probably about a bushel (about 37 litres) [c] *22* Some Septuagint manuscripts; Hebrew *with David's enemies*

heard your words and granted[o]
your request."
36 When Abigail went to Nabal, he
was in the house holding a banquet
like that of a king. He was in high[p]
spirits and very drunk.[q] So she
told[r] him nothing until daybreak.
37 Then in the morning, when Nabal
was sober, his wife told him all
these things, and his heart failed
him and he became like a stone.
38 About ten days later, the LORD
struck[s] Nabal and he died.
39 When David heard that Nabal
was dead, he said, "Praise be to the
LORD, who has upheld my cause
against Nabal for treating me with
contempt. He has kept his servant
from doing wrong and has brought
Nabal's wrongdoing down on his
own head."
Then David sent word to Abigail,
asking her to become his wife.
40 His servants went to Carmel and
said to Abigail, "David has sent us
to you to take you to become his
wife."
41 She bowed down with her face
to the ground and said, "Here is
your maidservant, ready to serve
you and wash the feet of my master's servants." 42 Abigail[t] quickly
got on a donkey and, attended by
her five maids, went with David's
messengers and became his wife.
43 David had also married Ahinoam[u] of Jezreel, and they both
were his wives.[v] 44 But Saul had
given his daughter Michal, David's
wife, to Paltiel[d][w] son of Laish, who
was from Gallim.[x]

David Again Spares Saul's Life

26 The Ziphites[a] went to Saul
at Gibeah and said, "Is not
David hiding[b] on the hill of Hakilah, which faces Jeshimon?"
2 So Saul went down to the Desert
of Ziph, with his three thousand
chosen men of Israel, to search[c]
there for David. 3 Saul made his
camp beside the road on the hill of
Hakilah facing Jeshimon, but
David stayed in the desert. When
he saw that Saul had followed him
there, 4 he sent out scouts and
learned that Saul had definitely
arrived.[a]
5 Then David set out and went to
the place where Saul had camped.
He saw where Saul and Abner[d] son
of Ner, the commander of the
army, had lain down. Saul was lying
inside the camp, with the army encamped around him.
6 David then asked Ahimelech the
Hittite and Abishai son of Zeruiah,[e] Joab's brother, "Who will go
down into the camp with me to
Saul?"
"I'll go with you," said Abishai.
7 So David and Abishai went to
the army by night, and there was
Saul, lying asleep inside the camp
with his spear stuck in the ground
near his head. Abner and the soldiers were lying round him.
8 Abishai said to David, "Today
God has given your enemy into
your hands. Now let me pin him to
the ground with one thrust of my
spear; I won't strike him twice."
9 But David said to Abishai,
"Don't destroy him! Who can lay a
hand on the LORD's anointed[f] and
be guiltless?[g] 10 As surely as the
LORD lives," he said, "the LORD himself will strike[h] him; either his
time[i] will come and he will die,[j]
or he will go into battle and perish.
11 But the LORD forbid that I should
lay a hand on the LORD's anointed.
Now get the spear and water jug
that are near his head, and let's go."
12 So David took the spear and
water jug near Saul's head, and
they left. No-one saw or knew about
it, nor did anyone wake up. They
were all sleeping, because the
LORD had put them into a deep
sleep.[k]
13 Then David crossed over to the
other side and stood on top of the
hill some distance away; there was

25:35 o Ge 19:21; 1Sa 20:42; 2Ki 5:19
25:36 p 2Sa 13:23 q Pr 20:1; Isa 5:11,22; Hos 4:11 r ver 19
25:38 s 1Sa 26:10; 2Sa 6:7
25:42 t Ge 24:61-67
25:43 u Jos 15:56 v 1Sa 27:3; 1Sa 30:5
25:44 w 2Sa 3:15 x Isa 10:30
26:1 a 1Sa 23:19 b Ps 54 Title
26:2 c 1Sa 13:2; 1Sa 24:2
26:5 d 1Sa 14:50; 1Sa 17:55
26:6 e Jdg 7:10-11; 1Ch 2:16
26:9 f 2Sa 1:14 g 1Sa 24:5
26:10 h 1Sa 25:38; Ro 12:19 i Ge 47:29; Dt 31:14; Ps 37:13 j 1Sa 31:6; 2Sa 1:1
26:12 k Ge 2:21; Ge 15:12

d 44 Hebrew *Palti*, a variant of *Paltiel*
a 4 Or *had come to Nacon*

a wide space between them. 14He
called out to the army and to Abner
son of Ner, “Aren’t you going to
answer me, Abner?”
Abner replied, “Who are you who
calls to the king?”
15David said, “You’re a man,
aren’t you? And who is like you in
Israel? Why didn’t you guard your
lord the king? Someone came to destroy your lord the king. 16What
you have done is not good. As
surely as the LORD lives, you and
your men deserve to die, because
you did not guard your master, the
LORD’s anointed. Look around you.
Where are the king’s spear and
water jug that were near his head?”
17Saul recognised David’s voice
and said, “Is that your voice,[l]
David my son?”
David replied, “Yes it is, my lord
the king.” 18And he added, “Why is
my lord pursuing his servant?
What have I done, and what
wrong[m] am I guilty of? 19Now let
my lord the king listen to his servant’s words. If the LORD has incited you against me, then may he
accept an offering.[n] If, however,
men have done it, may they be
cursed before the LORD! They have
now driven me from my share in
the LORD’s inheritance[o] and have
said, ‘Go, serve other gods.’ 20Now
do not let my blood fall to the
ground far from the presence of
the LORD. The king of Israel has
come out to look for a flea[p]—as
one hunts a partridge in the mountains.”
21Then Saul said, “I have
sinned.[q] Come back, David my
son. Because you considered my
life precious[r] today, I will not try
to harm you again. Surely I have
acted like a fool and have erred
greatly.”
22“Here is the king’s spear,”
David answered. “Let one of your
young men come over and get it.
23The LORD rewards[s] every man
for his righteousness[t] and faithfulness. The LORD gave you into my
hands today, but I would not lay a
hand on the LORD’s anointed. 24As
surely as I valued your life today,
so may the LORD value my life and
deliver[u] me from all trouble.”
25Then Saul said to David, “May
you be blessed, my son David; you
will do great things and surely triumph.”
So David went on his way, and
Saul returned home.

David Among the Philistines

27 But David thought to himself, “One of these days I
shall be destroyed by the hand of
Saul. The best thing I can do is to
escape to the land of the Philistines. Then Saul will give up
searching for me anywhere in Israel, and I will slip out of his hand.”
2So David and the six hundred
men[a] with him left and went[b] over
to Achish[c] son of Maoch king of
Gath. 3David and his men settled in
Gath with Achish. Each man had
his family with him, and David had
his two wives:[d] Ahinoam of Jezreel and Abigail of Carmel, the
widow of Nabal. 4When Saul was
told that David had fled to Gath, he
no longer searched for him.
5Then David said to Achish, “If I
have found favour in your eyes, let
a place be assigned to me in one of
the country towns, that I may live
there. Why should your servant
live in the royal city with you?”
6So on that day Achish gave him
Ziklag,[e] and it has belonged to the
kings of Judah ever since. 7David
lived[f] in Philistine territory for a
year and four months.
8Now David and his men went up
and raided the Geshurites,[g] the
Girzites and the Amalekites.[h]
(From ancient times these peoples
had lived in the land extending to
Shur[i] and Egypt.) 9Whenever
David attacked an area, he did not
leave a man or woman alive,[j] but
took sheep and cattle, donkeys and

26:17 l 1Sa 24:16
26:18 m 1Sa 24:9, 11-14
26:19 n 2Sa 16:11; o 2Sa 14:16
26:20 p 1Sa 24:14
26:21 q Ex 9:27; 1Sa 15:24; r 1Sa 24:17
26:23 s Ps 62:12; t Ps 7:8; Ps 18:20,24
26:24 u Ps 54:7
27:2 a 1Sa 25:13; b 1Sa 21:10; c 1Ki 2:39
27:3 d 1Sa 25:43; 1Sa 30:3
27:6 e Jos 15:31; Jos 19:5; Ne 11:28
27:7 f 1Sa 29:3
27:8 g Jos 13:2,13; h Ex 17:8; 1Sa 15:7-8; i Ex 15:22
27:9 j 1Sa 15:3

camels, and clothes. Then he returned to Achish.
10When Achish asked, "Where
did you go raiding today?" David
would say, "Against the Negev of
Judah" or "Against the Negev of
Jerahmeel[k]" or "Against the
Negev of the Kenites.[l]" 11He did
not leave a man or woman alive to
be brought to Gath, for he thought,
"They might inform on us and say,
'This is what David did.' " And such
was his practice as long as he lived
in Philistine territory. 12Achish
trusted David and said to himself,
"He has become so odious to his
people, the Israelites, that he will
be my servant for ever."

Saul and the Witch of Endor

28 In those days the Philistines gathered[a] their
forces to fight against Israel.
Achish said to David, "You must
understand that you and your men
will accompany me in the army."
2David said, "Then you will see
for yourself what your servant can
do."
Achish replied, "Very well, I
will make you my bodyguard for
life."
3Now Samuel was dead,[b] and all
Israel had mourned for him and
buried him in his own town of Ramah.[c] Saul had expelled the mediums and spiritists[d] from the
land.
4The Philistines assembled and
came and set up camp at Shunem,[e]
while Saul gathered all the Israelites and set up camp at Gilboa.[f]
5When Saul saw the Philistine
army, he was afraid; terror filled
his heart. 6He enquired[g] of the
LORD, but the LORD did not answer
him by dreams[h] or Urim[i] or
prophets. 7Saul then said to his attendants, "Find me a woman who is
a medium,[j] so that I may go and
enquire of her."
"There is one in Endor,[k]" they
said.
8So Saul disguised[l] himself, putting on other clothes, and at night
he and two men went to the woman.
"Consult[m] a spirit for me," he said,
"and bring up for me the one I
name."
9But the woman said to him,
"Surely you know what Saul has
done. He has cut off[n] the mediums
and spiritists from the land. Why
have you set a trap for my life to
bring about my death?"
10Saul swore to her by the LORD,
"As surely as the LORD lives, you
will not be punished for this."
11Then the woman asked, "Whom
shall I bring up for you?"
"Bring up Samuel," he said.
12When the woman saw Samuel,
she cried out at the top of her voice
and said to Saul, "Why have you deceived me? You are Saul!"
13The king said to her, "Don't be
afraid. What do you see?"
The woman said, "I see a spirit[a]
coming up out of the ground."
14"What does he look like?" he
asked.
"An old man wearing a robe[o] is
coming up," she said.
Then Saul knew it was Samuel,
and he bowed down and prostrated
himself with his face to the ground.
15Samuel said to Saul, "Why have
you disturbed me by bringing me
up?"
"I am in great distress," Saul
said. "The Philistines are fighting
against me, and God has turned[p]
away from me. He no longer answers me, either by prophets or by
dreams. So I have called on you to
tell me what to do."
16Samuel said, "Why do you consult me, now that the LORD has
turned away from you and become
your enemy? 17The LORD has done
what he predicted through me. The
LORD has torn[q] the kingdom out of
your hands and given it to one of

27:10 k 1Sa 30:29; 1Ch 2:9,25 l Jdg 1:16
28:1 a 1Sa 29:1
28:3 b 1Sa 25:1 c 1Sa 7:17 d Ex 22:18; Lev 19:31; Lev 20:27; Dt 18:10-11; 1Sa 15:23
28:4 e Jos 19:18; 2Ki 4:8 f 1Sa 31:1,3
28:6 g 1Sa 14:37; 1Ch 10:13-14; Pr 1:28 h Nu 12:6 i Ex 28:30; Nu 27:21
28:7 j Ac 16:16 k Jos 17:11
28:8 l 2Ch 18:29; 2Ch 35:22 m Dt 18:10-11; 1Ch 10:13; Isa 8:19
28:9 n ver 3
28:14 o 1Sa 15:27; 1Sa 24:8
28:15 p ver 6; 1Sa 18:12
28:17 q 1Sa 15:28

a13 Or *see spirits*; or *see gods*

your neighbours—to David. [18]Because you did not obey[r] the LORD or carry out his fierce wrath[s] against the Amalekites, the LORD has done this to you today. [19]The LORD will hand over both Israel and you to the Philistines, and tomorrow you and your sons[t] will be with me. The LORD will also hand over the army of Israel to the Philistines."

[20]Immediately Saul fell full length on the ground, filled with fear because of Samuel's words. His strength was gone, for he had eaten nothing all that day and night.

[21]When the woman came to Saul and saw that he was greatly shaken, she said, "Look, your maidservant has obeyed you. I took my life[u] in my hands and did what you told me to do. [22]Now please listen to your servant and let me give you some food so that you may eat and have the strength to go on your way."

[23]He refused[v] and said, "I will not eat."

But his men joined the woman in urging him, and he listened to them. He got up from the ground and sat on the couch.

[24]The woman had a fattened calf at the house, which she slaughtered at once. She took some flour, kneaded it and baked bread without yeast. [25]Then she set it before Saul and his men, and they ate. That same night they got up and left.

Achish Sends David Back to Ziklag

29 The Philistines gathered[a] all their forces at Aphek,[b] and Israel camped by the spring in Jezreel.[c] [2]As the Philistine rulers marched with their units of hundreds and thousands, David and his men were marching at the rear[d] with Achish. [3]The commanders of the Philistines asked, "What about these Hebrews?"

Achish replied, "Is this not David, who was an officer of Saul king of Israel? He has already been with me for over a year,[e] and from the day he left Saul until now, I have found no fault in him."

[4]But the Philistine commanders were angry with him and said, "Send[f] the man back, that he may return to the place you assigned him. He must not go with us into battle, or he will turn[g] against us during the fighting. How better could he regain his master's favour than by taking the heads of our own men? [5]Isn't this the David they sang about in their dances:

" 'Saul has slain his thousands,
and David his tens of
thousands'?"[h]

[6]So Achish called David and said to him, "As surely as the LORD lives, you have been reliable, and I would be pleased to have you serve with me in the army. From the day[i] you came to me until now, I have found no fault in you, but the rulers[j] don't approve of you. [7]Turn back and go in peace; do nothing to displease the Philistine rulers."

[8]"But what have I done?" asked David. "What have you found against your servant from the day I came to you until now? Why can't I go and fight against the enemies of my lord the king?"

[9]Achish answered, "I know that you have been as pleasing in my eyes as an angel[k] of God; nevertheless, the Philistine commanders[l] have said, 'He must not go up with us into battle.' [10]Now get up early, along with your master's servants who have come with you, and leave[m] in the morning as soon as it is light."

[11]So David and his men got up early in the morning to go back to the land of the Philistines, and the Philistines went up to Jezreel.

28:18
r 1Sa 15:20
s 1Ki 20:42

28:19
t 1Sa 31:2

28:21
u Jdg 12:3; 1Sa 19:5; Job 13:14

28:23
v 2Ki 5:13

29:1
a 1Sa 28:1
b Jos 12:18; 1Sa 4:1
c 2Ki 9:30

29:2
d 1Sa 28:2

29:3
e 1Sa 27:7; Da 6:5

29:4
f 1Ch 12:19
g 1Sa 14:21

29:5
h 1Sa 18:7; 1Sa 21:11

29:6
i 1Sa 27:8-12
j ver 3

29:9
k 2Sa 14:17,20; 2Sa 19:27
l ver 4

29:10
m 1Ch 12:19

David Destroys the Amalekites

30 David and his men reached Ziklag[a] on the third day. Now the Amalekites[b] had raided the Negev and Ziklag. They had attacked Ziklag and burned it, 2and had taken captive the women and all who were in it, both young and old. They killed none of them, but carried them off as they went on their way.

3When David and his men came to Ziklag, they found it destroyed by fire and their wives and sons and daughters taken captive. 4So David and his men wept aloud until they had no strength left to weep. 5David's two wives[c] had been captured—Ahinoam of Jezreel and Abigail, the widow of Nabal of Carmel. 6David was greatly distressed because the men were talking of stoning[d] him; each one was bitter in spirit because of his sons and daughters. But David found strength[e] in the LORD his God.

7Then David said to Abiathar[f] the priest, the son of Ahimelech, "Bring me the ephod.[g]" Abiathar brought it to him, 8and David enquired[h] of the LORD, "Shall I pursue this raiding party? Will I overtake them?"

"Pursue them," he answered. "You will certainly overtake them and succeed[i] in the rescue."

9David and the six hundred men[j] with him came to the Besor Ravine, where some stayed behind, 10for two hundred men were too exhausted[k] to cross the ravine. But David and four hundred men continued the pursuit.

11They found an Egyptian in a field and brought him to David. They gave him water to drink and food to eat—12part of a cake of pressed figs and two cakes of raisins. He ate and was revived,[l] for he had not eaten any food or drunk any water for three days and three nights.

13David asked him, "To whom do you belong, and where do you come from?"

He said, "I am an Egyptian, the slave of an Amalekite. My master abandoned me when I became ill three days ago. 14We raided the Negev of the Kerethites[m] and the territory belonging to Judah and the Negev of Caleb.[n] And we burned[o] Ziklag."

15David asked him, "Can you lead me down to this raiding party?"

He answered, "Swear to me before God that you will not kill me or hand me over to my master, and I will take you down to them."

16He led David down, and there they were, scattered over the countryside, eating, drinking and revelling[p] because of the great amount of plunder[q] they had taken from the land of the Philistines and from Judah. 17David fought[r] them from dusk until the evening of the next day, and none of them got away, except four hundred young men who rode off on camels and fled.[s] 18David recovered[t] everything the Amalekites had taken, including his two wives. 19Nothing was missing: young or old, boy or girl, plunder or anything else they had taken. David brought everything back. 20He took all the flocks and herds, and his men drove them ahead of the other livestock, saying, "This is David's plunder."

21Then David came to the two hundred men who had been too exhausted[u] to follow him and who were left behind at the Besor Ravine. They came out to meet David and the people with him. As David and his men approached, he greeted them. 22But all the evil men and troublemakers among David's followers said, "Because they did not go out with us, we will not share with them the plunder we recovered. However, each man may take his wife and children and go."

23David replied, "No, my brothers, you must not do that with

30:1 a 1Sa 29:4,11 b 1Sa 15:7 1Sa 27:8
30:5 c 1Sa 25:43 2Sa 2:2
30:6 d Ex 17:4 Jn 8:59 e Ps 27:14 Ps 56:3-4,11 Ro 4:20
30:7 f 1Sa 22:20 g 1Sa 23:9
30:8 h 1Sa 23:2 i ver 18
30:9 j 1Sa 27:2
30:10 k ver 9,21
30:12 l Jdg 15:19
30:14 m 2Sa 8:18 1Ki 1:38,44 Eze 25:16 Zep 2:5 n ver 16 Jos 14:13 Jos 15:13 o ver 1
30:16 p Lk 12:19 q ver 14
30:17 r 1Sa 11:11 s 1Sa 15:3
30:18 t Ge 14:16
30:21 u ver 10

what the LORD has given us. He has protected us and handed over to us the forces that came against us. 24 Who will listen to what you say? The share of the man who stayed with the supplies is to be the same as that of him who went down to the battle. All shall share alike.[v]" 25 David made this a statute and ordinance for Israel from that day to this.

26 When David arrived in Ziklag, he sent some of the plunder to the elders of Judah, who were his friends, saying, "Here is a present for you from the plunder of the LORD's enemies."

27 He sent it to those who were in Bethel,[w] Ramoth[x] Negev and Jattir;[y] 28 to those in Aroer,[z] Siphmoth, Eshtemoa[a] 29 and Racal; to those in the towns of the Jerahmeelites[b] and the Kenites;[c] 30 to those in Hormah,[d] Bor Ashan,[e] Athach 31 and Hebron;[f] and to those in all the other places where David and his men had roamed.

Saul Takes His Life

31:1–13pp 2Sa 1:4–12; 1Ch 10:1–12

31 Now the Philistines fought against Israel; the Israelites fled before them, and many fell slain on Mount Gilboa.[a] 2 The Philistines pressed hard after Saul and his sons, and they killed his sons Jonathan, Abinadab and Malki-Shua. 3 The fighting grew fierce around Saul, and when the archers overtook him, they wounded[b] him critically.

4 Saul said to his armour-bearer, "Draw your sword and run me through,[c] or these uncircumcised[d] fellows will come and run me through and abuse me."

But the armour-bearer was terrified and would not do it; so Saul took his own sword and fell on it. 5 When the armour-bearer saw that Saul was dead, he too fell on his sword and died with him. 6 So Saul and his three sons and his armour-bearer and all his men died together that same day.

7 When the Israelites along the valley and those across the Jordan saw that the Israelite army had fled and that Saul and his sons had died, they abandoned their towns and fled. And the Philistines came and occupied them.

8 The next day, when the Philistines came to strip the dead, they found Saul and his three sons fallen on Mount Gilboa. 9 They cut off his head and stripped off his armour, and they sent messengers throughout the land of the Philistines to proclaim the news[e] in the temple of their idols and among their people.[f] 10 They put his armour in the temple of the Ashtoreths[g] and fastened his body to the wall of Beth Shan.[h]

11 When the people of Jabesh Gilead[i] heard of what the Philistines had done to Saul, 12 all their valiant men journeyed through the night to Beth Shan. They took down the bodies of Saul and his sons from the wall of Beth Shan and went to Jabesh, where they burned[j] them. 13 Then they took their bones[k] and buried them under a tamarisk[l] tree at Jabesh, and they fasted[m] seven days.[n]

30:24
v Nu 31:27 Jos 22:8

30:27
w Jos 7:2
x Jos 19:8
y Jos 15:48

30:28
z Jos 13:16
a Jos 15:50

30:29
b 1Sa 27:10
c Jdg 1:16 1Sa 15:6

30:30
d Nu 14:45 Jdg 1:17
e Jos 15:42

30:31
f Jos 14:13 2Sa 2:1,4

31:1
a 1Sa 28:4 1Ch 10:1-12

31:3
b 2Sa 1:6

31:4
c Jdg 9:54 2Sa 1:6,10
d 1Sa 14:6

31:9
e 2Sa 1:20
f Jdg 16:24

31:10
g Jdg 2:12-13
h 2Sa 21:12

31:11
i 1Sa 11:1

31:12
j 2Sa 2:4-7 Am 6:10

31:13
k 2Sa 21:12-14
l 1Sa 22:6
m 2Sa 1:12
n Ge 50:10

2 SAMUEL

David Hears of Saul's Death

1:4–12pp 1Sa 31:1–13; 1Ch 10:1–12

1 After the death[a] of Saul,
David returned from defeating[b] the Amalekites and stayed in
Ziklag two days. 2On the third day
a man[c] arrived from Saul's camp,
with his clothes torn and with dust
on his head.[d] When he came to
David, he fell to the ground to pay
him honour.

3"Where have you come from?"
David asked him.

He answered, "I have escaped
from the Israelite camp."

4"What happened?" David asked.
"Tell me."

He said, "The men fled from the
battle. Many of them fell and died.
And Saul and his son Jonathan are
dead."

5Then David said to the young
man who brought him the report,
"How do you know that Saul and his
son Jonathan are dead?"

6"I happened to be on Mount Gilboa,[e]" the young man said, "and
there was Saul, leaning on his
spear, with the chariots and riders
almost upon him. 7When he turned
round and saw me, he called out to
me, and I said, 'What can I do?'

8"He asked me, 'Who are you?'

" 'An Amalekite,[f]' I answered.

9"Then he said to me, 'Stand over
me and kill me! I am in the throes
of death, but I'm still alive.'

10"So I stood over him and killed
him, because I knew that after he
had fallen he could not survive.
And I took the crown[g] that was on
his head and the band on his arm
and have brought them here to my
lord."

11Then David and all the men
with him took hold of their clothes
and tore[h] them. 12They mourned
and wept and fasted till evening for
Saul and his son Jonathan, and for
the army of the LORD and the house
of Israel, because they had fallen
by the sword.

13David said to the young man
who brought him the report,
"Where are you from?"

"I am the son of an alien, an Amalekite,[i]" he answered.

14David asked him, "Why were
you not afraid to lift your hand to
destroy the LORD's anointed?[j]"

15Then David called one of his
men and said, "Go, strike him
down!"[k] So he struck him down,
and he died.[l] 16For David had said
to him, "Your blood be on your own
head.[m] Your own mouth testified
against you when you said, 'I killed
the LORD's anointed.' "

David's Lament for Saul and Jonathan

17David took up this lament[n]
concerning Saul and his son Jonathan, 18and ordered that the men of
Judah be taught this lament of the
bow (it is written in the Book of Jashar):[o]

19"Your glory, O Israel, lies
slain on your heights.
How the mighty have fallen![p]

20"Tell it not in Gath,[q]
proclaim it not in the
streets of Ashkelon,
lest the daughters of the
Philistines[r] be glad,
lest the daughters of the
uncircumcised rejoice.[s]

21"O mountains of Gilboa,[t]
may you have neither dew
nor rain,
nor fields that yield
offerings[u] ⌞of grain⌟.

1:1 a 1Sa 31:6 b 1Sa 30:17
1:2 c 2Sa 4:10 d 1Sa 4:12
1:6 e 1Sa 28:4 1Sa 31:2-4
1:8 f 1Sa 15:2 1Sa 30:13,17
1:10 g Jdg 9:54 2Ki 11:12
1:11 h Ge 37:29 2Sa 3:31 2Sa 13:31
1:13 i ver 8
1:14 j 1Sa 24:6 1Sa 26:9
1:15 k 2Sa 4:12 l 2Sa 4:10
1:16 m Lev 20:9 2Sa 3:28-29 1Ki 2:32 Mt 27:24-25 Ac 18:6
1:17 n 2Ch 35:25
1:18 o Jos 10:13 1Sa 31:3
1:19 p ver 27
1:20 q Mic 1:10 r 1Sa 31:8 s Ex 15:20 1Sa 18:6
1:21 t ver 6 1Sa 31:1 u Eze 31:15

For there the shield of the
mighty was defiled,
the shield of Saul—no longer
rubbed with oil.[v]
22From the blood[w] of the slain,
from the flesh of the mighty,
the bow[x] of Jonathan did not
turn back,
the sword of Saul did not
return unsatisfied.

23"Saul and Jonathan—
in life they were loved and
gracious,
and in death they were not
parted.
They were swifter than
eagles,[y]
they were stronger than
lions.[z]

24"O daughters of Israel,
weep for Saul,
who clothed you in scarlet and
finery,
who adorned your garments
with ornaments of gold.

25"How the mighty have fallen
in battle!
Jonathan lies slain on your
heights.
26I grieve for you, Jonathan my
brother;[a]
you were very dear to me.
Your love for me was
wonderful,[b]
more wonderful than that of
women.

27"How the mighty have fallen!
The weapons of war have
perished!"[c]

David Anointed King Over Judah

2 In the course of time, David
enquired[a] of the LORD. "Shall
I go up to one of the towns of Ju-
dah?" he asked.
The LORD said, "Go up."
David asked, "Where shall I go?"
"To Hebron,"[b] the LORD an-
swered.

1:21 v Isa 21:5
1:22 w Isa 34:3,7 x Dt 32:42 1Sa 18:4
1:23 y Dt 28:49 Jer 4:13 z Jdg 14:18
1:26 a 1Sa 20:42 b 1Sa 18:1
1:27 c ver 19,25 1Sa 2:4
2:1 a 1Sa 23:2, 11-12 b Ge 13:18 1Sa 30:31
2:2 c 1Sa 25:43 1Sa 30:5 d 1Sa 25:42
2:3 e 1Sa 27:2 1Sa 30:9
2:4 f 1Sa 30:31 g 1Sa 2:35 2Sa 5:3-5 h 1Sa 31:11-13
2:5 i 1Sa 23:21
2:6 j Ex 34:6 1Ti 1:16
2:8 k 1Sa 14:50 l Ge 32:2
2:9 m Nu 32:26 n Jdg 1:32 o 1Ch 12:29
2:11 p 2Sa 5:5
2:12 q Jos 18:25
2:13 r 2Sa 8:16 1Ch 2:16 1Ch 11:6

2So David went up there with his
two wives,[c] Ahinoam of Jezreel
and Abigail,[d] the widow of Nabal
of Carmel. 3David also took the
men who were with him,[e] each
with his family, and they settled in
Hebron and its towns. 4Then the
men of Judah came to Hebron[f]
and there they anointed[g] David
king over the house of Judah.
When David was told that it was
the men of Jabesh Gilead[h] who had
buried Saul, 5he sent messengers to
the men of Jabesh Gilead to say to
them, "The LORD bless[i] you for
showing this kindness to Saul your
master by burying him. 6May the
LORD now show you kindness and
faithfulness,[j] and I too will show
you the same favour because you
have done this. 7Now then, be
strong and brave, for Saul your
master is dead, and the house of
Judah has anointed me king over
them."

War Between the Houses of David and Saul

3:2–5pp 1Ch 3:1–4

8Meanwhile, Abner[k] son of Ner,
the commander of Saul's army, had
taken Ish-Bosheth son of Saul and
brought him over to Mahanaim.[l]
9He made him king over Gilead,[m]
Ashuri[a][n] and Jezreel, and also
over Ephraim, Benjamin and all
Israel.[o]
10Ish-Bosheth son of Saul was
forty years old when he became
king over Israel, and he reigned
two years. The house of Judah,
however, followed David. 11The
length of time David was king in
Hebron over the house of Judah
was seven years and six months.[p]
12Abner son of Ner, together with
the men of Ish-Bosheth son of Saul,
left Mahanaim and went to Gibeon.[q] 13Joab[r] son of Zeruiah and
David's men went out and met
them at the pool of Gibeon. One

a9 Or *Asher*

group sat down on one side of the
pool and one group on the other
side.
14 Then Abner said to Joab, "Let's
have some of the young men get up
and fight hand to hand in front of
us."
"All right, let them do it," Joab
said.
15 So they stood up and were
counted off—twelve men for Benjamin and Ish-Bosheth son of Saul,
and twelve for David. 16 Then each
man grabbed his opponent by the
head and thrust his dagger into his
opponent's side, and they fell down
together. So that place in Gibeon
was called Helkath Hazzurim.[b]
17 The battle that day was very
fierce, and Abner and the men of
Israel were defeated[s] by David's
men.
18 The three sons of Zeruiah[t]
were there: Joab,[u] Abishai[v] and
Asahel.[w] Now Asahel was as fleet-
footed as a wild gazelle.[x] 19 He
chased Abner, turning neither to
the right nor to the left as he pursued him. 20 Abner looked behind
him and asked, "Is that you, Asahel?"
"It is," he answered.
21 Then Abner said to him, "Turn
aside to the right or to the left; take
on one of the young men and strip
him of his weapons." But Asahel
would not stop chasing him.
22 Again Abner warned Asahel,
"Stop chasing me! Why should I
strike you down? How could I look
your brother Joab in the face?"[y]
23 But Asahel refused to give up
the pursuit; so Abner thrust the
butt of his spear into Asahel's stomach,[z] and the spear came out
through his back. He fell there and
died on the spot. And every man
stopped when he came to the place
where Asahel had fallen and died.[a]
24 But Joab and Abishai pursued
Abner, and as the sun was setting,
they came to the hill of Ammah,
near Giah on the way to the wasteland of Gibeon. 25 Then the men of

2:17 s 2Sa 3:1
2:18 t 2Sa 3:39 u 2Sa 3:30 v 1Sa 26:6 w 1Ch 2:16 x 1Ch 12:8
2:22 y 2Sa 3:27
2:23 z 2Sa 3:27; 2Sa 4:6 a 2Sa 20:12
2:26 b Dt 32:42; Jer 46:10,14
2:28 c 2Sa 18:16 d Jdg 3:27
2:29 e ver 8
2:32 f Ge 49:29
3:1 a 1Ki 14:30 b 2Sa 5:10 c 2Sa 2:17
3:2 d 1Sa 25:43; 1Ch 3:1-3

Benjamin rallied behind Abner.
They formed themselves into a
group and took their stand on top of
a hill.
26 Abner called out to Joab, "Must
the sword devour[b] for ever? Don't
you realise that this will end in bitterness? How long before you order your men to stop pursuing their
brothers?"
27 Joab answered, "As surely as
God lives, if you had not spoken,
the men would have continued the
pursuit of their brothers until
morning."[c]
28 So Joab[c] blew the trumpet,[d]
and all the men came to a halt; they
no longer pursued Israel, nor did
they fight any more.
29 All that night Abner and his
men marched through the Arabah.
They crossed the Jordan, continued through the whole Bithron[d]
and came to Mahanaim.[e]
30 Then Joab returned from pursuing Abner and assembled all his
men. Besides Asahel, nineteen of
David's men were found missing.
31 But David's men had killed 360
Benjamites who were with Abner.
32 They took Asahel and buried him
in his father's tomb[f] at Bethlehem. Then Joab and his men
marched all night and arrived at
Hebron by daybreak.

3 The war between the house of
Saul and the house of David
lasted a long time.[a] David grew
stronger and stronger,[b] while the
house of Saul grew weaker and
weaker.[c]
2 Sons were born to David in Hebron:
His firstborn was Amnon
the son of Ahinoam[d] of Jezreel;
3 his second, Kileab the son of

[b]16 *Helkath Hazzurim* means *field of daggers* or *field of hostilities.* [c]27 Or *spoken this morning, the men would not have taken up the pursuit of their brothers; or spoken, the men would have given up the pursuit of their brothers by morning* [d]29 Or *morning*; or *ravine*; the meaning of the Hebrew for this word is uncertain.

Abigail[e] the widow of Nabal
of Carmel;
the third, Absalom[f] the son
of Maacah daughter of Talmai king of Geshur;[g]
4the fourth, Adonijah[h] the
son of Haggith;
the fifth, Shephatiah the son
of Abital;
5and the sixth, Ithream the
son of David's wife Eglah.
These were born to David in
Hebron.

Abner Goes Over to David

6During the war between the
house of Saul and the house of
David, Abner had been strengthening his own position in the house of
Saul. 7Now Saul had had a concubine[i] named Rizpah[j] daughter of
Aiah. And Ish-Bosheth said to Abner, "Why did you sleep with my
father's concubine?"
8Abner was very angry because
of what Ish-Bosheth said and he answered, "Am I a dog's head[k]—on
Judah's side? This very day I am
loyal to the house of your father
Saul and to his family and friends.
I haven't handed you over to David.
Yet now you accuse me of an offence involving this woman! 9May
God deal with Abner, be it ever so
severely, if I do not do for David
what the LORD promised[l] him on
oath 10and transfer the kingdom
from the house of Saul and establish David's throne over Israel and
Judah from Dan to Beersheba."[m]
11Ish-Bosheth did not dare to say
another word to Abner, because he
was afraid of him.
12Then Abner sent messengers
on his behalf to say to David,
"Whose land is it? Make an agreement with me, and I will help you
bring all Israel over to you."
13"Good," said David. "I will
make an agreement with you. But I
demand one thing of you: Do not
come into my presence unless you
bring Michal daughter of Saul

3:3
e 1Sa 25:42
f 2Sa 13:1,28
g 1Sa 27:8
2Sa 13:37
2Sa 14:32
2Sa 15:8

3:4
h 1Ki 1:5,11

3:7
i 2Sa 16:21-22
j 2Sa 21:8-11

3:8
k 1Sa 24:14
2Sa 9:8
2Sa 16:9

3:9
l 1Sa 15:28
1Ki 19:2

3:10
m Jdg 20:1
1Sa 3:20

3:13
n Ge 43:5
1Sa 18:20

3:14
o 1Sa 18:27

3:15
p Dt 24:1-4
q 1Sa 25:44

3:16
r 2Sa 16:5
2Sa 19:16

3:17
s Jdg 11:11

3:18
t 1Sa 9:16
u 1Sa 15:28
2Sa 8:6

3:19
v 1Sa 10:20-21
1Ch 12:2,16,
29

3:21
w ver 10,12
x 1Ki 11:37

when you come to see me."[n]
14Then David sent messengers to
Ish-Bosheth son of Saul, demanding, "Give me my wife Michal,[o]
whom I betrothed to myself for the
price of a hundred Philistine foreskins."
15So Ish-Bosheth gave orders and
had her taken away from her husband[p] Paltiel[q] son of Laish. 16Her
husband, however, went with her,
weeping behind her all the way to
Bahurim.[r] Then Abner said to
him, "Go back home!" So he went
back.
17Abner conferred with the elders[s] of Israel and said, "For some
time you have wanted to make
David your king. 18Now do it! For
the LORD promised David, 'By my
servant David I will rescue my people Israel from the hand of the Philistines[t] and from the hand of all
their enemies.[u]' "
19Abner also spoke to the Benjamites in person. Then he went to
Hebron to tell David everything
that Israel and the whole house of
Benjamin[v] wanted to do. 20When
Abner, who had twenty men with
him, came to David at Hebron,
David prepared a feast for him and
his men. 21Then Abner said to
David, "Let me go at once and assemble all Israel for my lord the
king, so that they may make a compact[w] with you, and that you may
rule over all that your heart desires."[x] So David sent Abner away,
and he went in peace.

Joab Murders Abner

22Just then David's men and Joab
returned from a raid and brought
with them a great deal of plunder.
But Abner was no longer with
David in Hebron, because David
had sent him away, and he had gone
in peace. 23When Joab and all the
soldiers with him arrived, he was
told that Abner son of Ner had

come to the king and that the king
had sent him away and that he had
gone in peace.
24So Joab went to the king and
said, "What have you done? Look,
Abner came to you. Why did you let
him go? Now he is gone! 25You
know Abner son of Ner; he came to
deceive you and observe your
movements and find out everything you are doing."
26Joab then left David and sent
messengers after Abner, and they
brought him back from the well of
Sirah. But David did not know it.
27Now when Abner[y] returned to
Hebron, Joab took him aside into
the gateway, as though to speak
with him privately. And there, to
avenge the blood of his brother Asahel, Joab stabbed him in the stomach, and he died.[z]
28Later, when David heard about
this, he said, "I and my kingdom
are for ever innocent[a] before the
LORD concerning the blood of Abner son of Ner. 29May his blood[b]
fall upon the head of Joab and upon
all his father's house![c] May Joab's
house never be without someone
who has a running sore[d] or leprosy[a] or who leans on a crutch or
who falls by the sword or who lacks
food."
30(Joab and his brother Abishai
murdered Abner because he had
killed their brother Asahel in the
battle of Gibeon.)
31Then David said to Joab and all
the people with him, "Tear your
clothes and put on sackcloth[e] and
walk in mourning[f] in front of Abner." King David himself walked
behind the bier. 32They buried Abner in Hebron, and the king wept[g]
aloud at Abner's tomb. All the people wept also.
33The king sang this lament[h] for
Abner:

"Should Abner have died as the
lawless die?
34 Your hands were not bound,
your feet were not fettered.

3:27 y 2Sa 2:8 z 2Sa 2:22 2Sa 20:9-10 1Ki 2:5
3:28 a ver 37 Dt 21:9
3:29 b Lev 20:9 c 1Ki 2:31-33 d Lev 15:2
3:31 e 2Sa 1:2,11 Ps 30:11 Isa 20:2 f Ge 37:34
3:32 g Nu 14:1 Pr 24:17
3:33 h 2Sa 1:17
3:35 i Ru 1:17 1Sa 3:17 j 1Sa 31:13 2Sa 1:12 2Sa 12:17 Jer 16:7
3:37 k ver 28
3:38 l 2Sa 1:19
3:39 m 2Sa 2:18 n 2Sa 19:5-7 o 1Ki 2:5-6, 33-34 Ps 41:10 Ps 101:8
4:1 a 2Sa 3:27 Ezr 4:4
4:2 b Jos 9:17 Jos 18:25
4:3 c Ne 11:33
4:4 d 1Sa 18:1 e 1Sa 31:1-4

You fell as one falls before
wicked men."

And all the people wept over him
again.
35Then they all came and urged
David to eat something while it was
still day; but David took an oath,
saying, "May God deal with me, be
it ever so severely,[i] if I taste
bread[j] or anything else before the
sun sets!"
36All the people took note and
were pleased; indeed, everything
the king did pleased them. 37So
on that day all the people and all
Israel knew that the king had no
part[k] in the murder of Abner son
of Ner.
38Then the king said to his men,
"Do you not realise that a prince
and a great man has fallen[l] in Israel this day? 39And today, though I
am the anointed king, I am weak,
and these sons of Zeruiah[m] are too
strong for me.[n] May the LORD repay[o] the evildoer according to his
evil deeds!"

Ish-Bosheth Murdered

4 When Ish-Bosheth son of Saul
heard that Abner[a] had died
in Hebron, he lost courage, and all
Israel became alarmed. 2Now
Saul's son had two men who were
leaders of raiding bands. One
was named Baanah and the other
Recab; they were sons of Rimmon
the Beerothite from the tribe
of Benjamin—Beeroth[b] is considered part of Benjamin, 3be-
cause the people of Beeroth fled
to Gittaim[c] and have lived there
as aliens to this day.
4(Jonathan[d] son of Saul had a son
who was lame in both feet. He was
five years old when the news[e]
about Saul and Jonathan came

a29 The Hebrew word was used for various diseases affecting the skin—not necessarily leprosy.

from Jezreel. His nurse picked him up and fled, but as she hurried to leave, he fell and became crippled.[f] His name was Mephibosheth.)[g]

5Now Recab and Baanah, the sons of Rimmon the Beerothite, set out for the house of Ish-Bosheth,[h] and they arrived there in the heat of the day while he was taking his noonday rest. 6They went into the inner part of the house as if to get some wheat, and they stabbed[i] him in the stomach. Then Recab and his brother Baanah slipped away.

7They had gone into the house while he was lying on the bed in his bedroom. After they stabbed and killed him, they cut off his head. Taking it with them, they travelled all night by way of the Arabah. 8They brought the head of Ish-Bosheth to David at Hebron and said to the king, "Here is the head of Ish-Bosheth son of Saul,[j] your enemy, who tried to take your life. This day the LORD has avenged my lord the king against Saul and his offspring."

9David answered Recab and his brother Baanah, the sons of Rimmon the Beerothite, "As surely as the LORD lives, who has delivered[k] me out of all trouble, 10when a man told me, 'Saul is dead,' and thought he was bringing good news, I seized him and put him to death in Ziklag.[l] That was the reward I gave him for his news! 11How much more—when wicked men have killed an innocent man in his own house and on his own bed—should I not now demand his blood[m] from your hand and rid the earth of you!"

12So David gave an order to his men, and they killed them.[n] They cut off their hands and feet and hung the bodies by the pool in Hebron. But they took the head of Ish-Bosheth and buried it in Abner's tomb at Hebron.

4:4 f Lev 21:18 g 2Sa 9:3,6; 1Ch 8:34; 1Ch 9:40
4:5 h 2Sa 2:8
4:6 i 2Sa 2:23
4:8 j 1Sa 24:4; 1Sa 25:29
4:9 k Ge 48:16; 1Ki 1:29
4:10 l 2Sa 1:2-16
4:11 m Ge 9:5; Ps 9:12
4:12 n 2Sa 1:15
5:1 a 2Sa 19:43 b 1Ch 11:1
5:2 c 1Sa 18:5,13,16 d 1Sa 16:1; 2Sa 7:7 e 1Sa 25:30
5:3 f 2Sa 3:21 g 2Sa 2:4
5:4 h Lk 3:23 i 1Ki 2:11; 1Ch 3:4 j 1Ch 26:31; 1Ch 29:27
5:5 k 2Sa 2:11; 1Ch 3:4
5:6 l Jdg 1:8 m Jos 15:8
5:7 n 2Sa 6:12,16; 1Ki 2:10

David Becomes King Over Israel

5:1-3pp 1Ch 11:1-3

5 All the tribes of Israel[a] came to David at Hebron and said, "We are your own flesh and blood.[b] 2In the past, while Saul was king over us, you were the one who led Israel on their military campaigns.[c] And the LORD said to you, 'You shall shepherd[d] my people Israel, and you shall become their ruler.[e]' "

3When all the elders of Israel had come to King David at Hebron, the king made a compact[f] with them at Hebron before the LORD, and they anointed[g] David king over Israel.

4David was thirty years old[h] when he became king, and he reigned[i] for forty[j] years. 5In Hebron he reigned over Judah for seven years and six months,[k] and in Jerusalem he reigned over all Israel and Judah for thirty-three years.

David Conquers Jerusalem

5:6-10pp 1Ch 11:4-9
5:11-16pp 1Ch 3:5-9; 14:1-7

6The king and his men marched to Jerusalem[l] to attack the Jebusites,[m] who lived there. The Jebusites said to David, "You will not get in here; even the blind and the lame can ward you off." They thought, "David cannot get in here." 7Nevertheless, David captured the fortress of Zion, the City of David.[n]

8On that day, David said, "Anyone who conquers the Jebusites will have to use the water shaft[a] to reach those 'lame and blind' who are David's enemies."[b] That is why they say, "The 'blind and lame' will not enter the palace."

9David then took up residence in the fortress and called it the City of David. He built up the area around

[a] 8 Or *use scaling hooks* [b] 8 Or *are hated by David*

it, from the supporting terraces[c][o]
inward. 10And he became more and
more powerful,[p] because the LORD
God Almighty was with him.
11Now Hiram[q] king of Tyre sent
messengers to David, along with
cedar logs and carpenters and
stonemasons, and they built a palace for David. 12And David knew
that the LORD had established him
as king over Israel and had exalted
his kingdom for the sake of his people Israel.
13After he left Hebron, David
took more concubines and wives[r]
in Jerusalem, and more sons and
daughters were born to him.
14These are the names of the children born to him there:[s] Shammua, Shobab, Nathan, Solomon,
15Ibhar, Elishua, Nepheg, Japhia,
16Elishama, Eliada and Eliphelet.

David Defeats the Philistines

5:17–25pp 1Ch 14:8–17

17When the Philistines heard that
David had been anointed king over
Israel, they went up in full force to
search for him, but David heard
about it and went down to the
stronghold.[t] 18Now the Philistines
had come and spread out in the Valley of Rephaim;[u] 19so David enquired[v] of the LORD, "Shall I go
and attack the Philistines? Will you
hand them over to me?"
The LORD answered him, "Go, for
I will surely hand the Philistines
over to you."
20So David went to Baal Perazim,
and there he defeated them. He
said, "As waters break out, the
LORD has broken out against my enemies before me." So that place
was called Baal Perazim.[d][w] 21The
Philistines abandoned their idols
there, and David and his men carried them off.[x]
22Once more the Philistines came
up and spread out in the Valley of
Rephaim; 23so David enquired of
the LORD, and he answered, "Do not
go straight up, but circle round

5:9 o ver 7; 1Ki 9:15,24
5:10 p 2Sa 3:1
5:11 q 1Ki 5:1,18; 1Ch 14:1
5:13 r Dt 17:17; 1Ch 3:9
5:14 s 1Ch 3:5
5:17 t 2Sa 23:14; 1Ch 11:16
5:18 u Jos 15:8; Jos 17:15; Jos 18:16
5:19 v 1Sa 23:2; 2Sa 2:1
5:20 w Isa 28:21
5:21 x Dt 7:5; 1Ch 14:12; Isa 46:2
5:24 y 2Ki 7:6; z Jdg 4:14
5:25 a Isa 28:21; b 1Ch 14:16
6:2 a Jos 15:9; b 1Sa 4:4; 1Sa 7:1; c Lev 24:16; Isa 63:14; d Ps 99:1; e Ex 25:22; 1Ch 13:5-6
6:3 f Nu 7:4-9; 1Sa 6:7
6:5 g 1Sa 18:6-7; Ezr 3:10; Ps 150:5
6:6 h Nu 4:15, 19-20; 1Ch 13:9
6:7 i 1Ch 15:13-15

behind them and attack them in
front of the balsam trees. 24As soon
as you hear the sound[y] of marching in the tops of the balsam trees,
move quickly, because that will
mean the LORD has gone out in
front[z] of you to strike the Philistine army." 25So David did as the
LORD commanded him, and he
struck down the Philistines all the
way from Gibeon[e][a] to Gezer.[b]

The Ark Brought to Jerusalem

6:1–11pp 1Ch 13:1–14
6:12–19pp 1Ch 15:25–16:3

6 David again brought together
out of Israel chosen men,
thirty thousand in all. 2He and all
his men set out from Baalah[a] of Judah[a] to bring up from there the
ark[b] of God, which is called by the
Name,[b][c] the name of the LORD
Almighty, who is enthroned[d] between the cherubim[e] that are on
the ark. 3They set the ark of God on
a new cart[f] and brought it from
the house of Abinadab, which was
on the hill. Uzzah and Ahio, sons of
Abinadab, were guiding the new
cart 4with the ark of God on it,[c]
and Ahio was walking in front of it.
5David and the whole house of Israel were celebrating with all their
might before the LORD, with
songs[d] and with harps, lyres, tambourines, sistrums and cymbals.[g]
6When they came to the
threshing-floor of Nacon, Uzzah
reached out and took hold of[h] the
ark of God, because the oxen stumbled. 7The LORD's anger burned
against Uzzah because of his irrev-
erent act;[i] therefore God struck

[c]9 Or *the Millo* [d]20 *Baal Perazim* means *the lord who breaks out.* [e]25 Septuagint (see also 1 Chron. 14:16); Hebrew *Geba* [a]2 That is, Kiriath Jearim; Hebrew *Baale Judah*, a variant of *Baalah of Judah* [b]2 Hebrew; Septuagint and Vulgate do not have *the Name.* [c]3,4 Dead Sea Scrolls and some Septuagint manuscripts; Masoretic Text *cart* [4]*and they brought it with the ark of God from the house of Abinadab, which was on the hill* [d]5 See Dead Sea Scrolls, Septuagint and 1 Chron. 13:8; Masoretic Text *celebrating before the LORD with all kinds of instruments made of pine.*

him down[j] and he died there beside the ark of God.
8 Then David was angry because
the LORD's wrath[k] had broken out
against Uzzah, and to this day that
place is called Perez Uzzah.[e][l]
9 David was afraid of the LORD
that day and said, "How[m] can the
ark of the LORD ever come to me?"
10 He was not willing to take the ark
of the LORD to be with him in the
City of David. Instead, he took it
aside to the house of Obed-Edom[n]
the Gittite. 11 The ark of the LORD
remained in the house of Obed-
Edom the Gittite for three months,
and the LORD blessed him and his
entire household.[o]
12 Now King David[p] was told,
"The LORD has blessed the household of Obed-Edom and everything
he has, because of the ark of God."
So David went down and brought
up the ark of God from the house of
Obed-Edom to the City of David
with rejoicing. 13 When those who
were carrying the ark of the LORD
had taken six steps, he sacrificed[q]
a bull and a fattened calf. 14 David,
wearing a linen ephod,[r] danced[s]
before the LORD with all his might,
15 while he and the entire house of
Israel brought up the ark of the
LORD with shouts and the sound of
trumpets.[t]
16 As the ark of the LORD was entering the City of David,[u] Michal
daughter of Saul watched from a
window. And when she saw King
David leaping and dancing before
the LORD, she despised him in her
heart.
17 They brought the ark of the
LORD and set it in its place inside
the tent that David had pitched for
it,[v] and David sacrificed burnt offerings[w] and fellowship offerings[f] before the LORD. 18 After he
had finished sacrificing[x] the burnt
offerings and fellowship offerings,
he blessed the people in the name
of the LORD Almighty. 19 Then he
gave a loaf of bread, a cake of dates
and a cake of raisins[y] to each
person in the whole crowd of Israelites, both men and women.[z]
And all the people went to their
homes.
20 When David returned home to
bless his household, Michal daughter of Saul came out to meet him
and said, "How the king of Israel
has distinguished himself today,
disrobing[a] in the sight of the slave
girls of his servants as any vulgar
fellow would."
21 David said to Michal, "It was
before the LORD, who chose me
rather than your father or anyone
from his house when he appointed[b] me ruler over the LORD's
people Israel—I will celebrate before the LORD. 22 I will become even
more undignified than this, and I
will be humiliated in my own eyes.
But by these slave girls you spoke
of, I will be held in honour."
23 And Michal daughter of Saul
had no children to the day of her
death.

God's Promise to David

7:1-17pp 1Ch 17:1-15

7 After the king was settled in
his palace[a] and the LORD had
given him rest from all his enemies
around him, 2 he said to Nathan the
prophet, "Here I am, living in a palace[b] of cedar, while the ark of God
remains in a tent."[c]
3 Nathan replied to the king,
"Whatever you have in mind, go
ahead and do it, for the LORD is with
you."
4 That night the word of the LORD
came to Nathan, saying:
5 "Go and tell my servant
David, 'This is what the LORD
says: Are you[d] the one to build
me a house to dwell in?[e] 6 I
have not dwelt in a house from
the day I brought the Israelites
up out of Egypt to this day. I

6:7 j Ex 19:22; 1Sa 6:19
6:8 k Ps 7:11; l Ge 38:29
6:9 m Ps 119:120
6:10 n 1Ch 13:13; 1Ch 26:4-5
6:11 o Ge 30:27; Ge 39:5
6:12 p 1Ki 8:1; 1Ch 15:25
6:13 q 1Ki 8:5,62
6:14 r Ex 19:6; 1Sa 2:18; s Ex 15:20
6:15 t Ps 47:5; Ps 98:6
6:16 u 2Sa 5:7
6:17 v 1Ch 15:1; 2Ch 1:4; w Lev 1:1-17; 1Ki 8:62-64
6:18 x 1Ki 8:22
6:19 y Hos 3:1; z Ne 8:10
6:20 a ver 14,16
6:21 b 1Sa 13:14; 1Sa 15:28
7:1 a 1Ch 17:1
7:2 b 2Sa 5:11; c Ex 26:1; Ac 7:45-46
7:5 d 1Ki 8:19; 1Ch 22:8; e 1Ki 5:3-5

e8 *Perez Uzzah* means *the outbreak against Uzzah.* f17 Traditionally *peace offerings*; also in verse 18

have been moving from place
to place with a tent[f] as my
dwelling.[g] 7Wherever I have
moved with all the Israelites,[h]
did I ever say to any of their
rulers whom I commanded to
shepherd[i] my people Israel,
"Why have you not built me a
house of cedar?[j]" '
8"Now then, tell my servant
David, 'This is what the LORD
Almighty says: I took you from
the pasture and from following
the flock[k] to be ruler[l] over
my people Israel.[m] 9I have
been with you wherever you
have gone,[n] and I have cut off
all your enemies from before
you.[o] Now I will make your
name great, like the names of
the greatest men of the earth.
10And I will provide a place for
my people Israel and will
plant[p] them so that they can
have a home of their own and
no longer be disturbed.
Wicked[q] people shall not oppress them any more,[r] as they
did at the beginning 11and have
done ever since the time I appointed leaders[a][s] over my people Israel. I will also give you
rest from all your enemies.[t]
" 'The LORD declares to you
that the LORD himself will establish[u] a house[v] for you:
12When your days are over and
you rest[w] with your fathers, I
will raise up your offspring to
succeed you, who will come
from your own body,[x] and I
will establish his kingdom.
13He is the one who will build
a house for my Name,[y] and
I will establish the throne of
his kingdom for ever.[z] 14I will
be his father, and he shall be
my son.[a] When he does wrong,
I will punish him with the
rod[b] of men, with floggings
inflicted by men. 15But my
love will never be taken away
from him, as I took it away
from Saul,[c] whom I removed
from before you. 16Your house
and your kingdom shall endure
for ever before me;[b] your
throne[d] shall be established
for ever.[e]' "

17Nathan reported to David all
the words of this entire revelation.

David's Prayer

7:18–29pp 1Ch 17:16–27

18Then King David went in and
sat before the LORD, and he said:

"Who am I,[f] O Sovereign
LORD, and what is my family,
that you have brought me this
far? 19And as if this were not
enough in your sight, O Sovereign LORD, you have also spoken about the future of the
house of your servant. Is this
your usual way of dealing with
man,[g] O Sovereign LORD?
20"What more can David say
to you? For you know[h] your
servant,[i] O Sovereign LORD.
21For the sake of your word and
according to your will, you
have done this great thing and
made it known to your servant.
22"How great[j] you are,[k] O
Sovereign LORD! There is no-
one like you, and there is no
God[l] but you, as we have
heard with our own ears.[m]
23And who is like your people
Israel[n]—the one nation on
earth that God went out to redeem as a people for himself,
and to make a name for himself, and to perform great and
awesome wonders[o] by driving
out nations and their gods from
before your people, whom you
redeemed[p] from Egypt?[c]
24You have established your
people Israel as your very
own[q] for ever, and you,

7:6 *f* Ex 40:18,34 *g* 1Ki 8:16
7:7 *h* Dt 23:14 *i* 2Sa 5:2 *j* Lev 26:11-12
7:8 *k* 1Sa 16:11 *l* 2Sa 6:21 *m* Ps 78:70-72; 2Co 6:18*
7:9 *n* 2Sa 5:10 *o* Ps 18:37-42
7:10 *p* Ex 15:17; Isa 5:1-7 *q* Ps 89:22-23 *r* Isa 60:18
7:11 *s* Jdg 2:16; 1Sa 12:9-11 *t* ver 1 *u* 1Sa 25:28 *v* ver 27
7:12 *w* 1Ki 2:1 *x* Ps 132:11-12
7:13 *y* 1Ki 5:5; 1Ki 8:19,29 *z* Isa 9:7
7:14 *a* Ps 89:26; Heb 1:5* *b* Ps 89:30-33
7:15 *c* 1Sa 15:23,28
7:16 *d* Ps 89:36-37 *e* ver 13
7:18 *f* Ex 3:11; 1Sa 18:18
7:19 *g* Isa 55:8-9
7:20 *h* Jn 21:17 *i* 1Sa 16:7
7:22 *j* Ps 48:1; Ps 86:10; Jer 10:6 *k* Dt 3:24 *l* Ex 15:11 *m* Ex 10:2; Ps 44:1
7:23 *n* Dt 4:32-38 *o* Dt 10:21 *p* Dt 9:26; Dt 15:15
7:24 *q* Dt 26:18

[a]11 Traditionally *judges* [b]16 Some Hebrew manuscripts and Septuagint; most Hebrew manuscripts *you* [c]23 See Septuagint and 1 Chron. 17:21; Hebrew *wonders for your land and before your people, whom you redeemed from Egypt, from the nations and their gods.*

O LORD, have become their God.[r]

25“And now, LORD God, keep for ever the promise you have made concerning your servant and his house. Do as you promised, 26so that your name will be great for ever. Then men will say, ‘The LORD Almighty is God over Israel!’ And the house of your servant David will be established before you.

27“O LORD Almighty, God of Israel, you have revealed this to your servant, saying, ‘I will build a house for you.’ So your servant has found courage to offer you this prayer. 28O Sovereign LORD, you are God! Your words are trustworthy,[s] and you have promised these good things to your servant. 29Now be pleased to bless the house of your servant, that it may continue for ever in your sight; for you, O Sovereign LORD, have spoken, and with your blessing[t] the house of your servant will be blessed for ever.”

David's Victories

8:1–14pp 1Ch 18:1–13

8 In the course of time, David defeated the Philistines and subdued them, and he took Metheg Ammah from the control of the Philistines.

2David also defeated the Moabites.[a] He made them lie down on the ground and measured them off with a length of cord. Every two lengths of them were put to death, and the third length was allowed to live. So the Moabites became subject to David and brought tribute.

3Moreover, David fought Hadadezer[b] son of Rehob, king of Zobah,[c] when he went to restore his control along the Euphrates River. 4David captured a thousand of his chariots, seven thousand charioteers[a] and twenty thousand foot soldiers. He hamstrung[d] all but a hundred of the chariot horses.

5When the Arameans of Damascus[e] came to help Hadadezer king of Zobah, David struck down twenty-two thousand of them. 6He put garrisons in the Aramean kingdom of Damascus, and the Arameans became subject to him and brought tribute. The LORD gave David victory wherever he went.[f]

7David took the gold shields[g] that belonged to the officers of Hadadezer and brought them to Jerusalem. 8From Tebah[b] and Berothai,[h] towns that belonged to Hadadezer, King David took a great quantity of bronze.

9When Tou[c] king of Hamath[i] heard that David had defeated the entire army of Hadadezer, 10he sent his son Joram[d] to King David to greet him and congratulate him on his victory in battle over Hadadezer, who had been at war with Tou. Joram brought with him articles of silver and gold and bronze.

11King David dedicated[j] these articles to the LORD, as he had done with the silver and gold from all the nations he had subdued: 12Edom[e] and Moab,[k] the Ammonites[l] and the Philistines,[m] and Amalek.[n] He also dedicated the plunder taken from Hadadezer son of Rehob, king of Zobah.

13And David became famous[o] after he returned from striking down eighteen thousand Edomites[f] in the Valley of Salt.[p]

14He put garrisons throughout Edom, and all the Edomites[q] became subject to David.[r] The LORD

7:24 r Ex 6:6-7; Ps 48:14
7:28 s Ex 34:6; Jn 17:17
7:29 t Nu 6:23-27
8:2 a Ge 19:37; Nu 24:17
8:3 b 2Sa 10:16,19; c 1Sa 14:47
8:4 d Jos 11:9
8:5 e 1Ki 11:24
8:6 f ver 14; 2Sa 3:18; 2Sa 7:9
8:7 g 1Ki 10:16
8:8 h Eze 47:16
8:9 i 1Ki 8:65; 2Ch 8:4
8:11 j 1Ki 7:51; 1Ch 26:26
8:12 k ver 2; l 2Sa 10:14; m 2Sa 5:25; n 1Sa 27:8
8:13 o 2Sa 7:9; p 2Ki 14:7; 1Ch 18:12
8:14 q Nu 24:17-18; r Ge 27:29, 37-40

a*4* Septuagint (see also Dead Sea Scrolls and 1 Chron. 18:4); Masoretic Text *captured seventeen hundred of his charioteers* b*8* See some Septuagint manuscripts (see also 1 Chron. 18:8); Hebrew *Betah.* c*9* Hebrew *Toi,* a variant of *Tou;* also in verse 10 d*10* A variant of *Hadoram* e*12* Some Hebrew manuscripts, Septuagint and Syriac (see also 1 Chron. 18:11); most Hebrew manuscripts *Aram* f*13* A few Hebrew manuscripts, Septuagint and Syriac (see also 1 Chron. 18:12); most Hebrew manuscripts *Aram* (that is, Arameans)

gave David victory wherever he
went.[s]

David's Officials

8:15–18pp 1Ch 18:14–17

15 David reigned over all Israel,
doing what was just and right for
all his people. 16 Joab[t] son of Zeruiah was over the army; Jehoshaphat[u] son of Ahilud was recorder;
17 Zadok[v] son of Ahitub and Ahimelech son of Abiathar were priests;
Seraiah was secretary;[w] 18 Benaiah[x] son of Jehoiada was over
the Kerethites[y] and Pelethites;
and David's sons were royal advisers.[g]

David and Mephibosheth

9 David asked, "Is there anyone
still left of the house of Saul to
whom I can show kindness for Jonathan's sake?"[a]
2 Now there was a servant of
Saul's household named Ziba.[b]
They called him to appear before
David, and the king said to him,
"Are you Ziba?"
"Your servant," he replied.
3 The king asked, "Is there no-one
still left of the house of Saul to
whom I can show God's kindness?"
Ziba answered the king, "There
is still a son of Jonathan;[c] he is
crippled[d] in both feet."
4 "Where is he?" the king asked.
Ziba answered, "He is at the
house of Makir[e] son of Ammiel in
Lo Debar."
5 So King David had him brought
from Lo Debar, from the house of
Makir son of Ammiel.
6 When Mephibosheth son of Jonathan, the son of Saul, came to
David, he bowed down to pay him
honour.[f]
David said, "Mephibosheth!"
"Your servant," he replied.
7 "Don't be afraid," David said to
him, "for I will surely show you
kindness for the sake of your
father Jonathan. I will restore to
you all the land that belonged to
your grandfather Saul, and you will
always eat at my table.[g]"
8 Mephibosheth bowed down and
said, "What is your servant, that
you should notice a dead dog[h] like
me?"
9 Then the king summoned Ziba,
Saul's servant, and said to him, "I
have given your master's grandson
everything that belonged to Saul
and his family. 10 You and your sons
and your servants are to farm the
land for him and bring in the crops,
so that your master's grandson[i]
may be provided for. And Mephibosheth, grandson of your master,
will always eat at my table." (Now
Ziba had fifteen sons and twenty
servants.)
11 Then Ziba said to the king,
"Your servant will do whatever my
lord the king commands his servant to do." So Mephibosheth ate at
David's[a] table like one of the
king's sons.[j]
12 Mephibosheth had a young son
named Mica, and all the members
of Ziba's household were servants
of Mephibosheth.[k] 13 And Mephibosheth lived in Jerusalem, because
he always ate at the king's table,
and he was crippled in both feet.

David Defeats the Ammonites

10:1–19pp 1Ch 19:1–19

10 In the course of time, the
king of the Ammonites
died, and his son Hanun succeeded
him as king. 2 David thought, "I will
show kindness to Hanun son of Nahash,[a] just as his father showed
kindness to me." So David sent a
delegation to express his sympathy
to Hanun concerning his father.
When David's men came to the
land of the Ammonites, 3 the Ammonite nobles said to Hanun their
lord, "Do you think David is honouring your father by sending men
to you to express sympathy? Hasn't
David sent them to you to explore

8:14 s ver 6
8:16 t 2Sa 19:13; 1Ch 11:6 u 2Sa 20:24; 1Ki 4:3
8:17 v 2Sa 15:24,29; 1Ch 16:39; 1Ch 24:3 w 1Ki 4:3; 2Ki 12:10
8:18 x 2Sa 20:23; 1Ki 1:8,38; 1Ch 18:17 y 1Sa 30:14
9:1 a 1Sa 20:14-17, 42
9:2 b 2Sa 16:1-4; 2Sa 19:17,26, 29
9:3 c 1Sa 20:14 d 2Sa 4:4
9:4 e 2Sa 17:27-29
9:6 f 2Sa 16:4; 2Sa 19:24-30
9:7 g ver 1,3; 2Sa 12:8; 2Sa 19:28; 1Ki 2:7; 2Ki 25:29
9:8 h 2Sa 16:9
9:10 i ver 7,11,13; 2Sa 19:28
9:11 j Job 36:7; Ps 113:8
9:12 k 1Ch 8:34
10:2 a 1Sa 11:1

g18 Or *were priests* a11 Septuagint; Hebrew *my*

the city and spy it out and overthrow it?" 4So Hanun seized
David's men, shaved off half of
each man's beard,[b] cut off their
garments in the middle at the buttocks,[c] and sent them away.
5When David was told about this,
he sent messengers to meet the
men, for they were greatly humiliated. The king said, "Stay at Jericho till your beards have grown,
and then come back."
6When the Ammonites realised
that they had become an offence
to[d] David's nostrils, they hired
twenty thousand Aramean[e] foot
soldiers from Beth Rehob[f] and Zobah, as well as the king of Maacah[g]
with a thousand men, and also
twelve thousand men from Tob.
7On hearing this, David sent Joab
out with the entire army of fighting
men. 8The Ammonites came out
and drew up in battle formation at
the entrance to their city gate,
while the Arameans of Zobah and
Rehob and the men of Tob and Maacah were by themselves in the open
country.
9Joab saw that there were battle
lines in front of him and behind
him; so he selected some of the best
troops in Israel and deployed them
against the Arameans. 10He put the
rest of the men under the command
of Abishai his brother and deployed them against the Ammonites. 11Joab said, "If the Arameans
are too strong for me, then you are
to come to my rescue; but if the
Ammonites are too strong for you,
then I will come to rescue you. 12Be
strong[h] and let us fight bravely for
our people and the cities of our
God. The LORD will do what is good
in his sight."[i]
13Then Joab and the troops with
him advanced to fight the Arameans, and they fled before him.
14When the Ammonites saw that
the Arameans were fleeing, they
fled before Abishai and went inside
the city. So Joab returned from
fighting the Ammonites and came
to Jerusalem.
15After the Arameans saw that
they had been routed by Israel,
they regrouped. 16Hadadezer had
Arameans brought from beyond
the River;[a] they went to Helam,
with Shobach the commander of
Hadadezer's army leading them.
17When David was told of this, he
gathered all Israel, crossed the Jordan and went to Helam. The Arameans formed their battle lines to
meet David and fought against
him. 18But they fled before Israel,
and David killed seven hundred of
their charioteers and forty thousand of their foot soldiers.[b] He
also struck down Shobach the commander of their army, and he died
there. 19When all the kings who
were vassals of Hadadezer saw
that they had been defeated by
Israel, they made peace with the
Israelites and became subject[j] to
them.
So the Arameans[k] were afraid to
help the Ammonites any more.

David and Bathsheba

11 In the spring,[a] at the time
when kings go off to war,
David sent Joab[b] out with the
king's men and the whole Israelite
army.[c] They destroyed the Ammonites and besieged Rabbah.[d] But
David remained in Jerusalem.
2One evening David got up from
his bed and walked around on the
roof[e] of the palace. From the roof
he saw[f] a woman bathing. The
woman was very beautiful, 3and
David sent someone to find out
about her. The man said, "Isn't this
Bathsheba,[g] the daughter of
Eliam[h] and the wife of Uriah[i] the
Hittite?" 4Then David sent messengers to get her.[j] She came to
him, and he slept[k] with her.
(She had purified herself from her

[a]16 That is, the Euphrates [b]18 Some Septuagint manuscripts (see also 1 Chron. 19:18); Hebrew *horsemen*

10:4
b Lev 19:27; Isa 15:2; Jer 48:37
c Isa 20:4

10:6
d Ge 34:30
e 2Sa 8:5
f Jdg 18:28
g Dt 3:14

10:12
h Dt 31:6; 1Co 16:13; Eph 6:10
i Jdg 10:15; 1Sa 3:18; Ne 4:14

10:19
j 2Sa 8:6
k 1Ki 11:25; 2Ki 5:1

11:1
a 1Ki 20:22,26
b 2Sa 2:18
c 1Ch 20:1
d 2Sa 12:26-28

11:2
e Dt 22:8; Jos 2:8
f Mt 5:28

11:3
g 1Ch 3:5
h 2Sa 23:34
i 2Sa 23:39

11:4
j Lev 20:10; Ps 51 Title; Jas 1:14-15
k Dt 22:22

uncleanness.)[l] Then[a] she went back home. 5The woman conceived and sent word to David, saying, "I am pregnant."

6So David sent this word to Joab: "Send me Uriah[m] the Hittite." And Joab sent him to David. 7When Uriah came to him, David asked him how Joab was, how the soldiers were and how the war was going. 8Then David said to Uriah, "Go down to your house and wash your feet."[n] So Uriah left the palace, and a gift from the king was sent after him. 9But Uriah slept at the entrance to the palace with all his master's servants and did not go down to his house.

10When David was told, "Uriah did not go home," he asked him, "Haven't you just come from a distance? Why didn't you go home?"

11Uriah said to David, "The ark[o] and Israel and Judah are staying in tents, and my master Joab and my lord's men are camped in the open fields. How could I go to my house to eat and drink and lie with my wife? As surely as you live, I will not do such a thing!"

12Then David said to him, "Stay here one more day, and tomorrow I will send you back." So Uriah remained in Jerusalem that day and the next. 13At David's invitation, he ate and drank with him, and David made him drunk. But in the evening Uriah went out to sleep on his mat among his master's servants; he did not go home.

14In the morning David wrote a letter[p] to Joab and sent it with Uriah. 15In it he wrote, "Put Uriah in the front line where the fighting is fiercest. Then withdraw from him so that he will be struck down[q] and die.[r]"

16So while Joab had the city under siege, he put Uriah at a place where he knew the strongest defenders were. 17When the men of the city came out and fought against Joab, some of the men in David's army fell; moreover, Uriah the Hittite died.

18Joab sent David a full account of the battle. 19He instructed the messenger: "When you have finished giving the king this account of the battle, 20the king's anger may flare up, and he may ask you, 'Why did you get so close to the city to fight? Didn't you know they would shoot arrows from the wall? 21Who killed Abimelech[s] son of Jerub-Besheth?[b] Didn't a woman throw an upper millstone on him from the wall,[t] so that he died in Thebez? Why did you get so close to the wall?' If he asks you this, then say to him, 'Also, your servant Uriah the Hittite is dead.' "

22The messenger set out, and when he arrived he told David everything Joab had sent him to say. 23The messenger said to David, "The men overpowered us and came out against us in the open, but we drove them back to the entrance to the city gate. 24Then the archers shot arrows at your servants from the wall, and some of the king's men died. Moreover, your servant Uriah the Hittite is dead."

25David told the messenger, "Say this to Joab: 'Don't let this upset you; the sword devours one as well as another. Press the attack against the city and destroy it.' Say this to encourage Joab."

26When Uriah's wife heard that her husband was dead, she mourned for him. 27After the time of mourning was over, David had her brought to his house, and she became his wife and bore him a son. But the thing David had done displeased[u] the LORD.

11:4 l Lev 15:25-30; Lev 18:19
11:6 m 1Ch 11:41
11:8 n Ge 18:4; Ge 43:24; Lk 7:44
11:11 o 2Sa 7:2
11:14 p 1Ki 21:8
11:15 q 2Sa 12:9; r 2Sa 12:12
11:21 s Jdg 8:31; t Jdg 9:50-54
11:27 u 2Sa 12:9; Ps 51:4-5

[a]4 Or *with her. When she purified herself from her uncleanness,* [b]21 Also known as *Jerub-Baal* (that is, Gideon)

Nathan Rebukes David

11:1; 12:29-31pp 1Ch 20:1-3

12 The LORD sent Nathan[a] to David.[b] When he came to him,[c] he said, "There were two men in a certain town, one rich and the other poor. 2The rich man had a very large number of sheep and cattle, 3but the poor man had nothing except one little ewe lamb that he had bought. He raised it, and it grew up with him and his children. It shared his food, drank from his cup and even slept in his arms. It was like a daughter to him.

4"Now a traveller came to the rich man, but the rich man refrained from taking one of his own sheep or cattle to prepare a meal for the traveller who had come to him. Instead, he took the ewe lamb that belonged to the poor man and prepared it for the one who had come to him."

5David[d] burned with anger against the man and said to Nathan, "As surely as the LORD lives, the man who did this deserves to die! 6He must pay for that lamb four times over,[e] because he did such a thing and had no pity."

7Then Nathan said to David, "You are the man! This is what the LORD, the God of Israel, says: 'I anointed[f] you[g] king over Israel, and I delivered you from the hand of Saul. 8I gave your master's house to you,[h] and your master's wives into your arms. I gave you the house of Israel and Judah. And if all this had been too little, I would have given you even more. 9Why did you despise[i] the word of the LORD by doing what is evil in his eyes? You struck down[j] Uriah the Hittite with the sword and took his wife to be your own. You killed him with the sword of the Ammonites. 10Now, therefore, the sword[k] shall never depart from your house, because you despised me and took the wife of Uriah the Hittite to be your own.'

11"This is what the LORD says: 'Out of your own household I am going to bring calamity upon you.[l] Before your very eyes I will take your wives and give them to one who is close to you, and he will lie with your wives in broad daylight. 12You did it in secret,[m] but I will do this thing in broad daylight[n] before all Israel.' "

13Then David said to Nathan, "I have sinned[o] against the LORD."

Nathan replied, "The LORD has taken away[p] your sin.[q] You are not going to die.[r] 14But because by doing this you have made the enemies of the LORD show utter contempt,[a][s] the son born to you will die."

15After Nathan had gone home, the LORD struck[t] the child that Uriah's wife had borne to David, and he became ill. 16David pleaded with God for the child. He fasted and went into his house and spent the nights lying[u] on the ground. 17The elders of his household stood beside him to get him up from the ground, but he refused, and he would not eat any food with them.[v]

18On the seventh day the child died. David's servants were afraid to tell him that the child was dead, for they thought, "While the child was still living, we spoke to David but he would not listen to us. How can we tell him the child is dead? He may do something desperate."

19David noticed that his servants were whispering among themselves and he realised that the child was dead. "Is the child dead?" he asked.

"Yes," they replied, "he is dead."

20Then David got up from the ground. After he had washed,[w] put on lotions and changed his clothes,[x] he went into the house of

12:1 a 2Sa 7:2; 1Ki 20:35-41 b Ps 51 Title c 2Sa 14:4
12:5 d 1Ki 20:40
12:6 e Ex 22:1; Lk 19:8
12:7 f 1Sa 16:13 g 1Ki 20:42
12:8 h 2Sa 9:7
12:9 i Nu 15:31; 1Sa 15:19 j 2Sa 11:15
12:10 k 2Sa 13:28; 2Sa 18:14-15; 1Ki 2:25
12:11 l Dt 28:30; 2Sa 16:21-22
12:12 m 2Sa 11:4-15 n 2Sa 16:22
12:13 o Ge 13:13; Nu 22:34; 1Sa 15:24; 2Sa 24:10 p Ps 32:1-5; Ps 51:1,9; Ps 103:12; Zec 3:4,9 q Pr 28:13; Mic 7:18-19 r Lev 20:10; Lev 24:17
12:14 s Isa 52:5; Ro 2:24
12:15 t 1Sa 25:38
12:16 u 2Sa 13:31; Ps 5:7
12:17 v 2Sa 3:35
12:20 w Mt 6:17 x Job 1:20

a14 Masoretic Text; an ancient Hebrew scribal tradition *this you have shown utter contempt for the LORD*

the LORD and worshipped. Then he went to his own house, and at his request they served him food, and he ate.

21 His servants asked him, "Why are you acting in this way? While the child was alive, you fasted and wept,[y] but now that the child is dead, you get up and eat!"

22 He answered, "While the child was still alive, I fasted and wept. I thought, 'Who knows?[z] The LORD may be gracious to me and let the child live.'[a] 23 But now that he is dead, why should I fast? Can I bring him back again? I will go to him,[b] but he will not return to me."[c]

24 Then David comforted his wife Bathsheba,[d] and he went to her and lay with her. She gave birth to a son, and they named him Solomon.[e] The LORD loved him; 25 and because the LORD loved him, he sent word through Nathan the prophet to name him Jedidiah.[b][f]

26 Meanwhile Joab fought against Rabbah[g] of the Ammonites and captured the royal citadel. 27 Joab then sent messengers to David, saying, "I have fought against Rabbah and taken its water supply. 28 Now muster the rest of the troops and besiege the city and capture it. Otherwise I shall take the city, and it will be named after me."

29 So David mustered the entire army and went to Rabbah, and attacked and captured it. 30 He took the crown[h] from the head of their king[c]—its weight was a talent[d] of gold, and it was set with precious stones—and it was placed on David's head. He took a great quantity of plunder from the city 31 and brought out the people who were there, consigning them to labour with saws and with iron picks and axes, and he made them work at brickmaking.[e] He did this to all the Ammonite[i] towns. Then David and his entire army returned to Jerusalem.

12:21 y Jdg 20:26
12:22 z Jnh 3:9; a Isa 38:1-5
12:23 b Ge 37:35; c 1Sa 31:13; 2Sa 13:39; Job 7:10; Job 10:21
12:24 d 1Ki 1:11; e 1Ki 1:10; 1Ch 22:9; 1Ch 28:5; Mt 1:6
12:25 f Ne 13:26
12:26 g Dt 3:11; 1Ch 20:1-3
12:30 h 1Ch 20:2; Est 8:15; Ps 21:3; Ps 132:18
12:31 i 1Sa 14:47
13:1 a 2Sa 3:2; b 2Sa 14:27; 1Ch 3:9; c 2Sa 3:3
13:3 d 1Sa 16:9
13:9 e Ge 45:1

Amnon and Tamar

13 In the course of time, Amnon[a] son of David fell in love with Tamar,[b] the beautiful sister of Absalom[c] son of David.

2 Amnon became frustrated to the point of illness on account of his sister Tamar, for she was a virgin, and it seemed impossible for him to do anything to her.

3 Now Amnon had a friend named Jonadab son of Shimeah,[d] David's brother. Jonadab was a very shrewd man. 4 He asked Amnon, "Why do you, the king's son, look so haggard morning after morning? Won't you tell me?"

Amnon said to him, "I'm in love with Tamar, my brother Absalom's sister."

5 "Go to bed and pretend to be ill," Jonadab said. "When your father comes to see you, say to him, 'I would like my sister Tamar to come and give me something to eat. Let her prepare the food in my sight so that I may watch her and then eat it from her hand.' "

6 So Amnon lay down and pretended to be ill. When the king came to see him, Amnon said to him, "I would like my sister Tamar to come and make some special bread in my sight, so that I may eat from her hand."

7 David sent word to Tamar at the palace: "Go to the house of your brother Amnon and prepare some food for him." 8 So Tamar went to the house of her brother Amnon, who was lying down. She took some dough, kneaded it, made the bread in his sight and baked it. 9 Then she took the pan and served him the bread, but he refused to eat.

"Send everyone out of here,"[e] Amnon said. So everyone left him. 10 Then Amnon said to Tamar,

[b]25 *Jedidiah* means *loved by the LORD*.
[c]30 Or *of Milcom* (that is, Molech)
[d]30 That is, about 75 pounds (about 34 kilograms)
[e]31 The meaning of the Hebrew for this clause is uncertain.

"Bring the food here into my bedroom so that I may eat from your
hand." And Tamar took the bread
she had prepared and brought it to
her brother Amnon in his bedroom.
11 But when she took it to him to eat,
he grabbed[f] her and said, "Come
to bed with me, my sister."[g]
12 "Don't, my brother!" she said to
him. "Don't force me. Such a thing
should not be done in Israel![h]
Don't do this wicked thing.[i]
13 What about me?[j] Where could I
get rid of my disgrace? And what
about you? You would be like one of
the wicked fools in Israel. Please
speak to the king; he will not keep
me from being married to you."
14 But he refused to listen to her,
and since he was stronger than she,
he raped her.[k]
15 Then Amnon hated her with intense hatred. In fact, he hated her
more than he had loved her. Amnon
said to her, "Get up and get out!"
16 "No!" she said to him. "Sending
me away would be a greater wrong
than what you have already done to
me."
But he refused to listen to her.
17 He called his personal servant
and said, "Get this woman out of
here and bolt the door after her."
18 So his servant put her out and
bolted the door after her. She was
wearing a richly ornamented[a]
robe,[l] for this was the kind of garment the virgin daughters of the
king wore. 19 Tamar put ashes[m] on
her head and tore the ornamented
robe she was wearing. She put her
hand on her head and went away,
weeping aloud as she went.
20 Her brother Absalom said to
her, "Has that Amnon, your
brother, been with you? Be quiet
now, my sister; he is your brother.
Don't take this thing to heart." And
Tamar lived in her brother Absalom's house, a desolate woman.
21 When King David heard all this,
he was furious.[n] 22 Absalom never
said a word to Amnon, either good
or bad;[o] he hated[p] Amnon because he had disgraced his sister
Tamar.

Absalom Kills Amnon

23 Two years later, when Absalom's sheep-shearers[q] were at
Baal Hazor near the border of Ephraim, he invited all the king's sons
to come there. 24 Absalom went to the
king and said, "Your servant has
had shearers come. Will the king
and his officials please join me?"
25 "No, my son," the king replied.
"All of us should not go; we would
only be a burden to you." Although
Absalom urged him, he still refused to go, but gave him his blessing.
26 Then Absalom said, "If not,
please let my brother Amnon come
with us."
The king asked him, "Why should
he go with you?" 27 But Absalom
urged him, so he sent with him Amnon and the rest of the king's sons.
28 Absalom[r] ordered his men,
"Listen! When Amnon is in high[s]
spirits from drinking wine and I
say to you, 'Strike Amnon down,'
then kill him. Don't be afraid. Have
not I given you this order? Be
strong and brave.[t]" 29 So Absalom's men did to Amnon what Absalom had ordered. Then all the
king's sons got up, mounted their
mules and fled.
30 While they were on their way,
the report came to David: "Absalom has struck down all the king's
sons; not one of them is left." 31 The
king stood up, tore[u] his clothes and
lay down on the ground; and all his
servants stood by with their
clothes torn.
32 But Jonadab son of Shimeah,
David's brother, said, "My lord
should not think that they killed all
the princes; only Amnon is dead.
This has been Absalom's expressed
intention ever since the day that

13:11
f Ge 39:12
g Ge 38:16

13:12
h Lev 20:17; Jdg 20:6
i Ge 34:7; Jdg 19:23

13:13
j Ge 20:12; Lev 18:9; Dt 22:21, 23-24

13:14
k Ge 34:2; Dt 22:25; Eze 22:11

13:18
l Ge 37:23; Jdg 5:30

13:19
m Jos 7:6; 1Sa 4:12; 2Sa 1:2; Est 4:1; Da 9:3

13:21
n Ge 34:7

13:22
o Ge 31:24
p Lev 19:17-18; 1Jn 2:9-11

13:23
q 1Sa 25:7

13:28
r 2Sa 3:3
s Jdg 19:6,9,22; Ru 3:7; 1Sa 25:36
t 2Sa 12:10

13:31
u Nu 14:6; 2Sa 1:11; 2Sa 12:16

a *18* The meaning of the Hebrew for this phrase is uncertain; also in verse 19.

Amnon raped his sister Tamar. 33My lord the king should not be concerned about the report that all the king's sons are dead. Only Amnon is dead."

34Meanwhile, Absalom had fled.

Now the man standing watch looked up and saw many people on the road west of him, coming down the side of the hill. The watchman went and told the king, "I see men in the direction of Horonaim, on the side of the hill."[b]

35Jonadab said to the king, "See, the king's sons are here; it has happened just as your servant said."

36As he finished speaking, the king's sons came in, wailing loudly. The king, too, and all his servants wept very bitterly.

37Absalom fled and went to Talmai[v] son of Ammihud, the king of Geshur. But King David mourned for his son every day.

38After Absalom fled and went to Geshur, he stayed there for three years. 39And the spirit of the king[c] longed to go to Absalom,[w] for he was consoled[x] concerning Amnon's death.

Absalom Returns to Jerusalem

14 Joab[a] son of Zeruiah knew that the king's heart longed for Absalom. 2So Joab sent someone to Tekoa[b] and had a wise woman[c] brought from there. He said to her, "Pretend you are in mourning. Dress in mourning clothes, and don't use any cosmetic lotions.[d] Act like a woman who has spent many days grieving for the dead. 3Then go to the king and speak these words to him." And Joab[e] put the words in her mouth.

4When the woman from Tekoa went[a] to the king, she fell with her face to the ground to pay him honour, and she said, "Help me, O king!"

5The king asked her, "What is troubling you?"

She said, "I am indeed a widow; my husband is dead. 6I your servant had two sons. They got into a fight with each other in the field, and no-one was there to separate them. One struck the other and killed him. 7Now the whole clan has risen up against your servant; they say, 'Hand over the one who struck his brother down, so that we may put him to death[f] for the life of his brother whom he killed; then we will get rid of the heir[g] as well.' They would put out the only burning coal I have left,[h] leaving my husband neither name nor descendant on the face of the earth."

8The king said to the woman, "Go home,[i] and I will issue an order on your behalf."

9But the woman from Tekoa said to him, "My lord the king, let the blame[j] rest on me and on my father's family,[k] and let the king and his throne be without guilt.[l]"

10The king replied, "If anyone says anything to you, bring him to me, and he will not bother you again."

11She said, "Then let the king invoke the LORD his God to prevent the avenger[m] of blood from adding to the destruction, so that my son shall not be destroyed."

"As surely as the LORD lives," he said, "not one hair[n] of your son's head will fall to the ground.[o]"

12Then the woman said, "Let your servant speak a word to my lord the king."

"Speak," he replied.

13The woman said, "Why then have you devised a thing like this against the people of God? When the king says this, does he not convict himself,[p] for the king has not brought back his banished son?[q] 14Like water[r] spilled on the

13:37 v ver 34; 2Sa 3:3; 2Sa 14:23,32
13:39 w 2Sa 14:13; x 2Sa 12:19-23
14:1 a 2Sa 2:18
14:2 b 2Ch 11:6; Ne 3:5; Jer 6:1; Am 1:1; c 2Sa 20:16; d Ru 3:3; 2Sa 12:20; Isa 1:6
14:3 e ver 19
14:7 f Nu 35:19; g Mt 21:38; h Dt 19:10-13
14:8 i 1Sa 25:35
14:9 j 1Sa 25:24; k Mt 27:25; l 1Sa 25:28; 1Ki 2:33
14:11 m Nu 35:12,21; n Mt 10:30; o 1Sa 14:45
14:13 p 2Sa 12:7; 1Ki 20:40; q 2Sa 13:38-39
14:14 r Job 14:11; Ps 58:7; Isa 19:5

b34 Septuagint; Hebrew does not have this sentence. c39 Dead Sea Scrolls and some Septuagint manuscripts; Masoretic Text *But the spirit of David the king* a4 Many Hebrew manuscripts, Septuagint, Vulgate and Syriac; most Hebrew manuscripts *spoke*

ground, which cannot be recovered, so we must die.[s] But God
does not take away life; instead, he
devises ways so that a banished
person[t] may not remain estranged
from him.
15"And now I have come to say
this to my lord the king because the
people have made me afraid. Your
servant thought, 'I will speak to the
king; perhaps he will do what his
servant asks. 16Perhaps the king
will agree to deliver his servant
from the hand of the man who is
trying to cut off both me and my
son from the inheritance[u] God
gave us.'
17"And now your servant says,
'May the word of my lord the king
bring me rest, for my lord the king
is like an angel[v] of God in discerning[w] good and evil. May the LORD
your God be with you.' "
18Then the king said to the woman, "Do not keep from me the answer to what I am going to ask you."
"Let my lord the king speak," the
woman said.
19The king asked, "Isn't the hand
of Joab[x] with you in all this?"
The woman answered, "As
surely as you live, my lord the king,
no-one can turn to the right or to
the left from anything my lord the
king says. Yes, it was your servant
Joab who instructed me to do this
and who put all these words into the
mouth of your servant. 20Your servant Joab did this to change the
present situation. My lord has wisdom[y] like that of an angel of God—
he knows everything that happens
in the land.[z]"
21The king said to Joab, "Very
well, I will do it. Go, bring back the
young man Absalom."
22Joab fell with his face to the
ground to pay him honour, and he
blessed the king.[a] Joab said, "Today your servant knows that he has
found favour in your eyes, my lord
the king, because the king has
granted his servant's request."
23Then Joab went to Geshur and

14:14
s Job 10:8
Job 17:13
Job 30:23
Ps 22:15
Heb 9:27
t Nu 35:15, 25-28
Job 34:15

14:16
u Ex 34:9
1Sa 26:19

14:17
v ver 20
1Sa 29:9
2Sa 19:27
w 1Ki 3:9
Da 2:21

14:19
x ver 3

14:20
y 1Ki 3:12,28
Isa 28:6
z ver 17
2Sa 18:13
2Sa 19:27

14:22
a Ge 47:7

14:26
b 2Sa 18:9
Eze 44:20

14:27
c 2Sa 18:18
d 2Sa 13:1

14:30
e Ex 9:31

14:31
f Jdg 15:5

14:32
g 2Sa 3:3
h 1Sa 20:8

14:33
i Ge 33:4
Lk 15:20

brought Absalom back to Jerusalem. 24But the king said, "He
must go to his own house; he must
not see my face." So Absalom went
to his own house and did not see the
face of the king.
25In all Israel there was not a man
so highly praised for his handsome
appearance as Absalom. From the
top of his head to the sole of his foot
there was no blemish in him.
26Whenever he cut the hair of his
head[b]—he used to cut his hair
from time to time when it became
too heavy for him—he would weigh
it, and its weight was two hundred
shekels[b] by the royal standard.
27Three sons[c] and a daughter
were born to Absalom. The daughter's name was Tamar,[d] and she
became a beautiful woman.
28Absalom lived for two years in
Jerusalem without seeing the
king's face. 29Then Absalom sent
for Joab in order to send him to the
king, but Joab refused to come to
him. So he sent a second time, but
he refused to come. 30Then he said
to his servants, "Look, Joab's field
is next to mine, and he has barley[e]
there. Go and set it on fire." So Absalom's servants set the field on
fire.
31Then Joab did go to Absalom's
house and he said to him, "Why
have your servants set my field on
fire?[f]"
32Absalom said to Joab, "Look, I
sent word to you and said, 'Come
here so that I can send you to the
king to ask, "Why have I come from
Geshur?[g] It would be better for me
if I were still there!" ' Now then, I
want to see the king's face, and if I
am guilty of anything, let him put
me to death."[h]
33So Joab went to the king and
told him this. Then the king summoned Absalom, and he came in
and bowed down with his face to
the ground before the king. And the
king kissed[i] Absalom.

b26 That is, about 5 pounds (about 2.3 kilograms)

Absalom's Conspiracy

15 In the course of time,[a] Absalom provided himself
with a chariot[b] and horses and
with fifty men to run ahead of him.
2He would get up early and stand
by the side of the road leading to
the city gate.[c] Whenever anyone
came with a complaint to be placed
before the king for a decision, Absalom would call out to him, "What
town are you from?" He would answer, "Your servant is from one of
the tribes of Israel." 3Then Absalom would say to him, "Look, your
claims are valid and proper, but
there is no representative of the
king to hear you."[d] 4And Absalom
would add, "If only I were appointed judge in the land![e] Then
everyone who has a complaint or
case could come to me and I would
see that he receives justice."
5Also, whenever anyone approached him to bow down before
him, Absalom would reach out his
hand, take hold of him and kiss him.
6Absalom behaved in this way towards all the Israelites who came
to the king asking for justice, and
so he stole the hearts[f] of the men
of Israel.
7At the end of four[a] years, Absalom said to the king, "Let me go to
Hebron and fulfil a vow I made to
the LORD. 8While your servant was
living at Geshur[g] in Aram, I made
this vow:[h] 'If the LORD takes me
back to Jerusalem, I will worship
the LORD in Hebron.' "[b]
9The king said to him, "Go in
peace." So he went to Hebron.
10Then Absalom sent secret messengers throughout the tribes of Israel to say, "As soon as you hear the
sound of the trumpets,[i] then say,
'Absalom is king in Hebron.' "
11Two hundred men from Jerusalem had accompanied Absalom.
They had been invited as guests
and went quite innocently, knowing nothing about the matter.
12While Absalom was offering
sacrifices, he also sent for Ahithophel[j] the Gilonite, David's
counsellor,[k] to come from Giloh,[l]
his home town. And so the conspiracy gained strength, and Absalom's following kept on
increasing.[m]

David Flees

13A messenger came and told
David, "The hearts of the men of Israel are with Absalom."
14Then David said to all his officials who were with him in Jerusalem, "Come! We must flee,[n] or
none of us will escape from Absalom.[o] We must leave immediately,
or he will move quickly to overtake
us and bring ruin upon us and put
the city to the sword."
15The king's officials answered
him, "Your servants are ready to do
whatever our lord the king
chooses."
16The king set out, with his entire
household following him; but he
left ten concubines[p] to take care of
the palace. 17So the king set out,
with all the people following him,
and they halted at a place some distance away. 18All his men marched
past him, along with all the Kerethites[q] and Pelethites; and all the
six hundred Gittites who had
accompanied him from Gath
marched before the king.
19The king said to Ittai[r] the Gittite, "Why should you come along
with us? Go back and stay with
King Absalom. You are a foreigner,[s] an exile from your homeland. 20You came only yesterday.
And today shall I make you wander[t] about with us, when I do not
know where I am going? Go back,
and take your countrymen. May
kindness and faithfulness[u] be with
you."
21But Ittai replied to the king, "As
surely as the LORD lives, and as my

15:1 a 2Sa 12:11 b 1Sa 8:11; 1Ki 1:5
15:2 c Ge 23:10; 2Sa 19:8
15:3 d Pr 12:2
15:4 e Jdg 9:29
15:6 f Ro 16:18
15:8 g 2Sa 3:3; 2Sa 13:37-38 h Ge 28:20
15:10 i 1Ki 1:34,39; 2Ki 9:13
15:12 j ver 31,34; 2Sa 16:15,23; 1Ch 27:33 k Job 19:14; Ps 41:9; Ps 55:13; Jer 9:4 l Jos 15:51 m Ps 3:1
15:14 n 2Sa 12:11; 1Ki 2:26; Ps 132:1; Ps 3 Title o 2Sa 19:9
15:16 p 2Sa 16:21-22; 2Sa 20:3
15:18 q 1Sa 30:14; 2Sa 8:18; 2Sa 20:7,23; 1Ki 1:38,44; 1Ch 18:17
15:19 r 2Sa 18:2 s Ge 31:15
15:20 t 1Sa 23:13 u 2Sa 2:6

a7 Some Septuagint manuscripts, Syriac and Josephus; Hebrew *forty* b8 Some Septuagint manuscripts; Hebrew does not have *in Hebron.*

lord the king lives, wherever my
lord the king may be, whether it
means life or death, there will your
servant be."[v]
22David said to Ittai, "Go ahead,
march on." So Ittai the Gittite
marched on with all his men and
the families that were with him.
23The whole countryside wept
aloud as all the people passed by.
The king also crossed the Kidron
Valley,[w] and all the people moved
on towards the desert.
24Zadok[x] was there, too, and all
the Levites who were with him
were carrying the ark[y] of the covenant of God. They set down the
ark of God, and Abiathar[z] offered
sacrifices[c] until all the people had
finished leaving the city.
25Then the king said to Zadok,
"Take the ark of God back into the
city. If I find favour in the LORD's
eyes, he will bring me back and let
me see it and his dwelling-place[a]
again. 26But if he says, 'I am not
pleased with you,' then I am ready;
let him do to me whatever seems
good to him.[b]"
27The king also said to Zadok the
priest, "Aren't you a seer?[c] Go
back to the city in peace, with your
son Ahimaaz and Jonathan[d] son of
Abiathar. You and Abiathar take
your two sons with you. 28I will wait
at the fords[e] in the desert until
word comes from you to inform
me." 29So Zadok and Abiathar took
the ark of God back to Jerusalem
and stayed there.
30But David continued up the
Mount of Olives, weeping[f] as he
went; his head[g] was covered and
he was barefoot. All the people with
him covered their heads too and
were weeping as they went up.
31Now David had been told, "Ahithophel[h] is among the conspira-
tors with Absalom." So David
prayed, "O LORD, turn Ahithophel's
counsel into foolishness."
32When David arrived at the summit, where people used to worship
God, Hushai the Arkite[i] was there
to meet him, his robe torn and
dust[j] on his head. 33David said to
him, "If you go with me, you will be
a burden[k] to me. 34But if you return to the city and say to Absalom,
'I will be your servant, O king; I
was your father's servant in the
past, but now I will be your servant,'[l] then you can help me by
frustrating Ahithophel's advice.
35Won't the priests Zadok and Abiathar be there with you? Tell them
anything you hear in the king's palace.[m] 36Their two sons, Ahimaaz
son of Zadok and Jonathan[n] son of
Abiathar, are there with them.
Send them to me with anything you
hear."
37So David's friend Hushai[o] arrived at Jerusalem as Absalom[p]
was entering the city.

David and Ziba

16 When David had gone a
short distance beyond the
summit, there was Ziba,[a] the steward of Mephibosheth, waiting to
meet him. He had a string of donkeys saddled and loaded with two
hundred loaves of bread, a hundred
cakes of raisins, a hundred cakes of
figs and a skin of wine.[b]
2The king asked Ziba, "Why have
you brought these?"
Ziba answered, "The donkeys are
for the king's household to ride on,
the bread and fruit are for the men
to eat, and the wine is to refresh[c]
those who become exhausted in the
desert."
3The king then asked, "Where is
your master's grandson?"[d]
Ziba said to him, "He is staying in
Jerusalem, because he thinks, 'Today the house of Israel will give me
back my grandfather's kingdom.'"
4Then the king said to Ziba, "All
that belonged to Mephibosheth is
now yours."

15:21 v Ru 1:16-17; Pr 17:17
15:23 w 2Ch 29:16
15:24 x 2Sa 8:17; y Nu 4:15; z 1Sa 22:20
15:25 a Ex 15:13; Ps 43:3; Jer 25:30
15:26 b 1Sa 3:18; 2Sa 22:20; 1Ki 10:9
15:27 c 1Sa 9:9; d 2Sa 17:17
15:28 e 2Sa 17:16
15:30 f 2Sa 19:4; Ps 126:6; g Est 6:12; Isa 20:2-4
15:31 h ver 12; 2Sa 16:23; 2Sa 17:14,23
15:32 i Jos 16:2; j 2Sa 1:2
15:33 k 2Sa 19:35
15:34 l 2Sa 16:19
15:35 m 2Sa 17:15-16
15:36 n ver 27; 2Sa 17:17
15:37 o 2Sa 16:16-17; 1Ch 27:33; p 2Sa 16:15
16:1 a 2Sa 9:1-13; b 1Sa 25:18
16:2 c 2Sa 17:27-29
16:3 d 2Sa 9:9-10; 2Sa 19:26-27

c24 Or *Abiathar went up*

"I humbly bow," Ziba said. "May
I find favour in your eyes, my lord
the king."

Shimei Curses David

5As King David approached Bahurim,[e] a man from the same clan
as Saul's family came out from
there. His name was Shimei[f] son
of Gera, and he cursed[g] as he came
out. 6He pelted David and all the
king's officials with stones, though
all the troops and the special guard
were on David's right and left. 7As
he cursed, Shimei said, "Get out, get
out, you man of blood, you scoundrel! 8The LORD has repaid you for
all the blood you shed in the household of Saul, in whose place you
have reigned.[h] The LORD has handed the kingdom over to your son
Absalom. You have come to ruin
because you are a man of blood!"
9Then Abishai[i] son of Zeruiah
said to the king, "Why should this
dead dog curse my lord the king?
Let me go over and cut off his
head."[j]
10But the king said, "What do you
and I have in common, you sons of
Zeruiah?[k] If he is cursing because
the LORD said to him, 'Curse David,'
who can ask, 'Why do you do
this?' "[l]
11David then said to Abishai and
all his officials, "My son,[m] who is of
my own flesh, is trying to take my
life. How much more, then, this
Benjamite! Leave him alone; let
him curse, for the LORD has told
him to.[n] 12It may be that the LORD
will see my distress[o] and repay me
with good[p] for the cursing I am receiving today.[q]"
13So David and his men continued
along the road while Shimei was going along the hillside opposite him,
cursing as he went and throwing
stones at him and showering him
with dirt. 14The king and all the
people with him arrived at their
destination exhausted.[r] And there
he refreshed himself.

16:5
e 2Sa 3:16
f 2Sa 19:16-23; 1Ki 2:8-9,36,44
g Ex 22:28

16:8
h 2Sa 21:9

16:9
i 2Sa 9:8
j Ex 22:28; Lk 9:54

16:10
k 2Sa 19:22
l Ro 9:20

16:11
m 2Sa 12:11
n Ge 45:5

16:12
o Ps 4:1; Ps 25:18
p Dt 23:5; Ro 8:28
q Ps 109:28

16:14
r 2Sa 17:2

16:15
s 2Sa 15:37
t 2Sa 15:12

16:16
u 2Sa 15:37

16:17
v 2Sa 19:25

16:19
w 2Sa 15:34

16:22
x 2Sa 12:11-12; 2Sa 15:16

16:23
y 2Sa 17:14,23
z 2Sa 15:12

17:2
a 2Sa 16:14
b 1Ki 22:31; Zec 13:7

The Advice of Hushai and Ahithophel

15Meanwhile, Absalom[s] and all
the men of Israel came to Jerusalem, and Ahithophel[t] was with
him. 16Then Hushai[u] the Arkite,
David's friend, went to Absalom
and said to him, "Long live the
king! Long live the king!"
17Absalom asked Hushai, "Is this
the love you show your friend?
Why didn't you go with your
friend?"[v]
18Hushai said to Absalom, "No,
the one chosen by the LORD, by
these people and by all the men of
Israel—his I will be, and I will remain with him. 19Furthermore,
whom should I serve? Should I not
serve the son? Just as I served your
father, so I will serve you."[w]
20Absalom said to Ahithophel,
"Give us your advice. What should
we do?"
21Ahithophel answered, "Lie with
your father's concubines whom he
left to take care of the palace. Then
all Israel will hear that you have
made yourself an offence to your
father's nostrils, and the hands of
everyone with you will be strengthened." 22So they pitched a tent for
Absalom on the roof, and he lay
with his father's concubines in the
sight of all Israel.[x]
23Now in those days the advice[y]
Ahithophel gave was like that of
one who enquires of God. That was
how both David[z] and Absalom regarded all of Ahithophel's advice.

17 Ahithophel said to Absalom, "I would[a] choose
twelve thousand men and set out tonight in pursuit of David. 2I would[b]
attack him while he is weary and
weak.[a] I would[b] strike him with
terror, and then all the people with
him will flee. I would[b] strike down
only the king[b] 3and bring all the
people back to you. The death of
the man you seek will mean the

a1 Or *Let me* b2 Or *will*

return of all; all the people will be unharmed." 4 This plan seemed good to Absalom and to all the elders of Israel.

5 But Absalom said, "Summon also Hushai[c] the Arkite, so that we can hear what he has to say." 6 When Hushai came to him, Absalom said, "Ahithophel has given this advice. Should we do what he says? If not, give us your opinion."

7 Hushai replied to Absalom, "The advice Ahithophel has given is not good this time. 8 You know your father and his men; they are fighters, and as fierce as a wild bear robbed of her cubs.[d] Besides, your father is an experienced fighter;[e] he will not spend the night with the troops. 9 Even now, he is hidden in a cave or some other place.[f] If he should attack your troops first,[c] whoever hears about it will say, 'There has been a slaughter among the troops who follow Absalom.' 10 Then even the bravest soldier, whose heart is like the heart of a lion,[g] will melt[h] with fear, for all Israel knows that your father is a fighter and that those with him are brave.[i]

11 "So I advise you: Let all Israel, from Dan to Beersheba[j]—as numerous as the sand[k] on the seashore—be gathered to you, with you yourself leading them into battle. 12 Then we will attack him wherever he may be found, and we will fall on him as dew settles on the ground. Neither he nor any of his men will be left alive. 13 If he withdraws into a city, then all Israel will bring ropes to that city, and we will drag it down to the valley[l] until not even a piece of it can be found."

14 Absalom and all the men of Israel said, "The advice[m] of Hushai the Arkite is better than that of Ahithophel."[n] For the LORD had determined to frustrate[o] the good advice of Ahithophel in order to bring disaster[p] on Absalom.[q]

15 Hushai told Zadok and Abiathar, the priests, "Ahithophel has advised Absalom and the elders of Israel to do such and such, but I have advised them to do so and so. 16 Now send a message immediately and tell David, 'Do not spend the night at the fords in the desert;[r] cross over without fail, or the king and all the people with him will be swallowed up.[s]' "

17 Jonathan[t] and Ahimaaz were staying at En Rogel.[u] A servant girl was to go and inform them, and they were to go and tell King David, for they could not risk being seen entering the city. 18 But a young man saw them and told Absalom. So the two of them left quickly and went to the house of a man in Bahurim.[v] He had a well in his courtyard, and they climbed down into it. 19 His wife took a covering and spread it out over the opening of the well and scattered grain over it. No-one knew anything about it.[w]

20 When Absalom's men came to the woman[x] at the house, they asked, "Where are Ahimaaz and Jonathan?"

The woman answered them, "They crossed over the brook."[d] The men searched but found no-one, so they returned to Jerusalem.

21 After the men had gone, the two climbed out of the well and went to inform King David. They said to him, "Set out and cross the river at once; Ahithophel has advised such and such against you." 22 So David and all the people with him set out and crossed the Jordan. By daybreak, no-one was left who had not crossed the Jordan.

23 When Ahithophel saw that his advice[y] had not been followed, he saddled his donkey and set out for his house in his home town. He put his house in order[z] and then

17:5 c 2Sa 15:32
17:8 d Hos 13:8 e 1Sa 16:18
17:9 f Jer 41:9
17:10 g 1Ch 12:8 h Jos 2:9,11 Eze 21:15 i 2Sa 23:8 1Ch 11:11
17:11 j Jdg 20:1 k Ge 12:2 Ge 22:17 Jos 11:4
17:13 l Mic 1:6
17:14 m 2Sa 16:23 n 2Sa 15:12 o 2Sa 15:34 Ne 4:15 p Ps 9:16 q 2Ch 10:8
17:16 r 2Sa 15:28 s 2Sa 15:35
17:17 t 2Sa 15:27,36 u Jos 15:7 Jos 18:16
17:18 v 2Sa 3:16 2Sa 16:5
17:19 w Jos 2:6
17:20 x Ex 1:19 Jos 2:3-5 1Sa 19:12-17
17:23 y 2Sa 15:12 2Sa 16:23 z 2Ki 20:1 Mt 27:5

c9 Or *When some of the men fall at the first attack* d20 Or *"They passed by the sheep pen towards the water."*

hanged himself. So he died and was buried in his father's tomb.

24David went to Mahanaim,[a] and Absalom crossed the Jordan with all the men of Israel. 25Absalom had appointed Amasa[b] over the army in place of Joab. Amasa was the son of a man named Jether,[e][c] an Israelite[f] who had married Abigail,[g] the daughter of Nahash and sister of Zeruiah the mother of Joab. 26The Israelites and Absalom camped in the land of Gilead.

27When David came to Mahanaim, Shobi son of Nahash[d] from Rabbah[e] of the Ammonites, and Makir[f] son of Ammiel from Lo Debar, and Barzillai[g] the Gileadite[h] from Rogelim 28brought bedding and bowls and articles of pottery. They also brought wheat and barley, flour and roasted grain, beans and lentils,[h] 29honey and curds, sheep, and cheese from cows' milk for David and his people to eat.[i] For they said, "The people have become hungry and tired and thirsty in the desert.[j]"

Absalom's Death

18 David mustered the men who were with him and appointed over them commanders of thousands and commanders of hundreds. 2David sent the troops out[a]—a third under the command of Joab, a third under Joab's brother Abishai[b] son of Zeruiah, and a third under Ittai[c] the Gittite. The king told the troops, "I myself will surely march out with you."

3But the men said, "You must not go out; if we are forced to flee, they won't care about us. Even if half of us die, they won't care; but you are worth ten[d] thousand of us.[a] It would be better now for you to give us support from the city."[e]

4The king answered, "I will do whatever seems best to you."

So the king stood beside the gate while all the men marched out in units of hundreds and of thousands.

17:24
a Ge 32:2; 2Sa 2:8

17:25
b 2Sa 19:13; 2Sa 20:4,9-12; 1Ki 2:5,32; 1Ch 12:18
c 1Ch 2:13-17

17:27
d 1Sa 11:1
e Dt 3:11; 2Sa 10:1-2; 2Sa 12:26,29
f 2Sa 9:4
g 2Sa 19:31-39; 1Ki 2:7
h 2Sa 19:31; Ezr 2:61

17:29
i 1Ch 12:40
j 2Sa 16:2; Ro 12:13

18:2
a Jdg 7:16; 1Sa 11:11
b 1Sa 26:6
c 2Sa 15:19

18:3
d 1Sa 18:7
e 2Sa 21:17

18:6
f Jos 17:18

18:9
g 2Sa 14:26

18:11
h 2Sa 3:39
i 1Sa 18:4

5The king commanded Joab, Abishai and Ittai, "Be gentle with the young man Absalom for my sake." And all the troops heard the king giving orders concerning Absalom to each of the commanders.

6The army marched into the field to fight Israel, and the battle took place in the forest[f] of Ephraim. 7There the army of Israel was defeated by David's men, and the casualties that day were great—twenty thousand men. 8The battle spread out over the whole countryside, and the forest claimed more lives that day than the sword.

9Now Absalom happened to meet David's men. He was riding his mule, and as the mule went under the thick branches of a large oak, Absalom's head[g] got caught in the tree. He was left hanging in midair, while the mule he was riding kept on going.

10When one of the men saw this, he told Joab, "I have just seen Absalom hanging in an oak tree."

11Joab said to the man who had told him this, "What! You saw him? Why didn't you strike[h] him to the ground right there? Then I would have had to give you ten shekels[b] of silver and a warrior's belt.[i]"

12But the man replied, "Even if a thousand shekels[c] were weighed out into my hands, I would not lift my hand against the king's son. In our hearing the king commanded you and Abishai and Ittai, 'Protect the young man Absalom for my sake.'[d] 13And if I had put my life in

e25 Hebrew *Ithra,* a variant of *Jether*
f25 Hebrew and some Septuagint manuscripts; other Septuagint manuscripts (see also 1 Chron. 2:17) *Ishmaelite* or *Jezreelite*
g25 Hebrew *Abigal,* a variant of *Abigail*
h28 Most Septuagint manuscripts and Syriac; Hebrew *lentils, and roasted grain*
a3 Two Hebrew manuscripts, some Septuagint manuscripts and Vulgate; most Hebrew manuscripts *care; for now there are ten thousand like us*
b11 That is, about 4 ounces (about 115 grams)
c12 That is, about 25 pounds (about 11 kilograms)
d12 A few Hebrew manuscripts, Septuagint, Vulgate and Syriac; most Hebrew manuscripts may be translated *Absalom, whoever you may be.*

jeopardy[e]—and nothing is hidden
from the king[j]—you would have
kept your distance from me."
14Joab[k] said, "I am not going to
wait like this for you." So he took
three javelins in his hand and
plunged them into Absalom's heart
while Absalom was still alive in the
oak tree. 15And ten of Joab's
armour-bearers surrounded Absalom, struck him and killed him.[l]
16Then Joab[m] sounded the trumpet, and the troops stopped pursuing Israel, for Joab halted them.
17They took Absalom, threw him
into a big pit in the forest and piled
up[n] a large heap of rocks[o] over
him. Meanwhile, all the Israelites
fled to their homes.
18During his life-time Absalom
had taken a pillar and erected it in
the King's Valley[p] as a monument[q] to himself, for he thought,
"I have no son[r] to carry on the
memory of my name." He named
the pillar after himself, and it is
called Absalom's Monument to this
day.

David Mourns

19Now Ahimaaz[s] son of Zadok
said, "Let me run and take the news
to the king that the LORD has delivered him from the hand of his enemies.[t]"
20"You are not the one to take the
news today," Joab told him. "You
may take the news another time,
but you must not do so today, because the king's son is dead."
21Then Joab said to a Cushite,
"Go, tell the king what you have
seen." The Cushite bowed down before Joab and ran off.
22Ahimaaz son of Zadok again
said to Joab, "Come what may,
please let me run behind the Cushite."
But Joab replied, "My son, why
do you want to go? You don't have
any news that will bring you a reward."

18:13 j 2Sa 14:19-20
18:14 k 2Sa 2:18; 2Sa 14:30
18:15 l 2Sa 12:10
18:16 m 2Sa 2:28; 2Sa 20:22
18:17 n Jos 7:26; o Jos 8:29
18:18 p Ge 14:17; q Ge 50:5; Nu 32:42; 1Sa 15:12; r 2Sa 14:27
18:19 s 2Sa 15:36; t ver 31; Jdg 11:36
18:24 u 1Sa 14:16; 2Sa 19:8; 2Ki 9:17; Jer 51:12
18:26 v 1Ki 1:42; Isa 52:7; Isa 61:1
18:27 w 2Ki 9:20

23He said, "Come what may, I
want to run."
So Joab said, "Run!" Then Ahimaaz ran by way of the plain[f] and
outran the Cushite.
24While David was sitting between the inner and outer gates,
the watchman[u] went up to the roof
of the gateway by the wall. As he
looked out, he saw a man running
alone. 25The watchman called out to
the king and reported it.
The king said, "If he is alone, he
must have good news." And the
man came closer and closer.
26Then the watchman saw another man running, and he called
down to the gatekeeper, "Look, another man running alone!"
The king said, "He must be bringing good news,[v] too."
27The watchman said, "It seems
to me that the first one runs like[w]
Ahimaaz son of Zadok."
"He's a good man," the king said.
"He comes with good news."
28Then Ahimaaz called out to the
king, "All is well!" He bowed down
before the king with his face to the
ground and said, "Praise be to the
LORD your God! He has delivered
up the men who lifted their hands
against my lord the king."
29The king asked, "Is the young
man Absalom safe?"
Ahimaaz answered, "I saw great
confusion just as Joab was about to
send the king's servant and me,
your servant, but I don't know what
it was."
30The king said, "Stand aside and
wait here." So he stepped aside and
stood there.
31Then the Cushite arrived and
said, "My lord the king, hear the
good news! The LORD has delivered
you today from all who rose up
against you."
32The king asked the Cushite, "Is
the young man Absalom safe?"

e13 Or *Otherwise, if I had acted treacherously towards him* f23 That is, the plain of the Jordan

The Cushite replied, "May the
enemies of my lord the king and all
who rise up to harm you be like that
young man."[x]
33 The king was shaken. He went
up to the room over the gateway
and wept. As he went, he said: "O
my son Absalom! My son, my son
Absalom! If only I had died[y] instead of you—O Absalom, my son,
my son!"[z]

19 Joab was told, "The king is
weeping and mourning for
Absalom." 2 And for the whole army
the victory that day was turned into
mourning, because on that day the
troops heard it said, "The king is
grieving for his son." 3 The men
stole into the city that day as men
steal in who are ashamed when
they flee from battle. 4 The king
covered his face and cried aloud,
"O my son Absalom! O Absalom,
my son, my son!"
5 Then Joab went into the house to
the king and said, "Today you have
humiliated all your men, who have
just saved your life and the lives of
your sons and daughters and the
lives of your wives and concubines.
6 You love those who hate you and
hate those who love you. You have
made it clear today that the commanders and their men mean nothing to you. I see that you would be
pleased if Absalom were alive today and all of us were dead. 7 Now
go out and encourage your men. I
swear by the LORD that if you don't
go out, not a man will be left with
you by nightfall. This will be worse
for you than all the calamities that
have come upon you from your
youth till now."[a]
8 So the king got up and took his
seat in the gateway. When the men
were told, "The king is sitting in the
gateway,[b]" they all came before
him.

David Returns to Jerusalem

Meanwhile, the Israelites had
fled to their homes. 9 Throughout
the tribes of Israel, the people were
all arguing with each other, saying,
"The king delivered us from the
hand of our enemies; he is the one
who rescued us from the hand of
the Philistines.[c] But now he has
fled the country because of Absalom;[d] 10 and Absalom, whom we
anointed to rule over us, has died in
battle. So why do you say nothing
about bringing the king back?"
11 King David sent this message
to Zadok[e] and Abiathar, the
priests: "Ask the elders of Judah,
'Why should you be the last to bring
the king back to his palace, since
what is being said throughout Israel has reached the king at his
quarters? 12 You are my brothers,
my own flesh and blood. So why
should you be the last to bring back
the king?' 13 And say to Amasa,[f]
'Are you not my own flesh and
blood?[g] May God deal with me, be
it ever so severely,[h] if from now on
you are not the commander of my
army in place of Joab.[i]'"
14 He won over the hearts of all
the men of Judah as though they
were one man. They sent word to
the king, "Return, you and all your
men." 15 Then the king returned and
went as far as the Jordan.
Now the men of Judah had come
to Gilgal[j] to go out and meet the
king and bring him across the Jordan. 16 Shimei[k] son of Gera, the
Benjamite from Bahurim, hurried
down with the men of Judah to
meet King David. 17 With him were
a thousand Benjamites, along with
Ziba,[l] the steward of Saul's household,[m] and his fifteen sons and
twenty servants. They rushed to
the Jordan, where the king was.
18 They crossed at the ford to take
the king's household over and to do
whatever he wished.
When Shimei son of Gera crossed
the Jordan, he fell prostrate before
the king 19 and said to him, "May my
lord not hold me guilty. Do not remember how your servant did
wrong on the day my lord the king

18:32
x Jdg 5:31; 1Sa 25:26
18:33
y Ex 32:32
z Ge 43:14; 2Sa 19:4; Ro 9:3
19:7
a Pr 14:28
19:8
b 2Sa 15:2
19:9
c 2Sa 8:1-14
d 2Sa 15:14
19:11
e 2Sa 15:24
19:13
f 2Sa 17:25
g Ge 29:14
h Ru 1:17; 1Ki 19:2; 1Ki 8:16
i 2Sa 2:13
19:15
j Jos 5:9; 1Sa 11:15
19:16
k 2Sa 16:5-13; 1Ki 2:8
19:17
l 2Sa 9:2; 2Sa 16:1-2
m Ge 43:16

left Jerusalem.[n] May the king put
it out of his mind. 20 For I your servant know that I have sinned, but
today I have come here as the first
of the whole house of Joseph to
come down and meet my lord the
king."
21 Then Abishai[o] son of Zeruiah
said, "Shouldn't Shimei be put to
death for this? He cursed[p] the
LORD's anointed."[q]
22 David replied, "What do you
and I have in common, you sons of
Zeruiah?[r] This day you have become my adversaries! Should anyone be put to death in Israel
today?[s] Do I not know that today I
am king over Israel?" 23 So the king
said to Shimei, "You shall not die."
And the king promised him on
oath.[t]
24 Mephibosheth,[u] Saul's grandson, also went down to meet the
king. He had not taken care of his
feet or trimmed his moustache or
washed his clothes from the day
the king left until the day he returned safely. 25 When he came
from Jerusalem to meet the king,
the king asked him, "Why didn't
you go with me,[v] Mephibosheth?"
26 He said, "My lord the king,
since I your servant am lame,[w] I
said, 'I will have my donkey saddled and will ride on it, so that I can
go with the king.' But Ziba[x] my
servant betrayed me. 27 And he has
slandered your servant to my lord
the king. My lord the king is like an
angel[y] of God; so do whatever
pleases you. 28 All my grandfather's
descendants deserved nothing but
death[z] from my lord the king, but
you gave your servant a place
among those who eat at your
table.[a] So what right do I have to
make any more appeals to the
king?"
29 The king said to him, "Why say
more? I order you and Ziba to divide the fields."
30 Mephibosheth said to the king,
"Let him take everything, now that
my lord the king has arrived home
safely."
31 Barzillai[b] the Gileadite also
came down from Rogelim to cross
the Jordan with the king and to
send him on his way from there.
32 Now Barzillai was a very old man,
eighty years of age. He had provided for the king during his stay in
Mahanaim, for he was a very
wealthy[c] man. 33 The king said to
Barzillai, "Cross over with me and
stay with me in Jerusalem, and I
will provide for you."
34 But Barzillai answered the
king, "How many more years shall
I live, that I should go up to Jerusalem with the king? 35 I am now
eighty[d] years old. Can I tell the difference between what is good and
what is not? Can your servant taste
what he eats and drinks? Can I still
hear the voices of men and women
singers?[e] Why should your servant be an added[f] burden to my
lord the king? 36 Your servant will
cross over the Jordan with the king
for a short distance, but why should
the king reward me in this way?
37 Let your servant return, that I
may die in my own town near the
tomb of my father[g] and mother.
But here is your servant Kimham.[h] Let him cross over with my
lord the king. Do for him whatever
pleases you."
38 The king said, "Kimham shall
cross over with me, and I will do for
him whatever pleases you. And
anything you desire from me I will
do for you."
39 So all the people crossed the
Jordan, and then the king crossed
over. The king kissed Barzillai and
gave him his blessing,[i] and Barzillai returned to his home.
40 When the king crossed over to
Gilgal, Kimham crossed with him.
All the troops of Judah and half the
troops of Israel had taken the king
over.
41 Soon all the men of Israel were
coming to the king and saying to
him, "Why did our brothers, the

19:19
n 1Sa 22:15
2Sa 16:6-8

19:21
o 1Sa 26:6
p Ex 22:28
q 1Sa 12:3
1Sa 26:9
2Sa 16:7-8

19:22
r 2Sa 2:18
2Sa 16:10
s 1Sa 11:13

19:23
t 1Ki 2:8,42

19:24
u 2Sa 4:4
2Sa 9:6-10

19:25
v 2Sa 16:17

19:26
w Lev 21:18
x 2Sa 9:2

19:27
y 1Sa 29:9
2Sa 14:17,20

19:28
z 2Sa 16:8
2Sa 21:6-9
a 2Sa 9:7,13

19:31
b 2Sa 17:27-29,
27
1Ki 2:7

19:32
c 1Sa 25:2
2Sa 17:27

19:35
d Ps 90:10
e 2Ch 35:25
Ezr 2:65
Ecc 2:8
Ecc 12:1
Isa 5:11-12
f 2Sa 15:33

19:37
g Ge 49:29
1Ki 2:7
h ver 40
Jer 41:17

19:39
i Ge 31:55
Ge 47:7

men of Judah, steal the king away
and bring him and his household
across the Jordan, together with all
his men?"[j]
42All the men of Judah answered
the men of Israel, "We did this because the king is closely related to
us. Why are you angry about it?
Have we eaten any of the king's
provisions? Have we taken anything for ourselves?"
43Then the men of Israel[k] answered the men of Judah, "We have
ten shares in the king; and besides,
we have a greater claim on David
than you have. So why do you treat
us with contempt? Were we not the
first to speak of bringing back our
king?"
But the men of Judah responded
even more harshly than the men of
Israel.

Sheba Rebels Against David

20 Now a troublemaker named
Sheba son of Bicri, a Benjamite, happened to be there.
He sounded the trumpet and
shouted,

"We have no share[a] in David,[b]
no part in Jesse's son![c]
Every man to his tent,
O Israel!"

2So all the men of Israel deserted
David to follow Sheba son of Bicri.
But the men of Judah stayed by
their king all the way from the Jordan to Jerusalem.
3When David returned to his palace in Jerusalem, he took the ten
concubines[d] he had left to take
care of the palace and put them in
a house under guard. He provided
for them, but did not lie with them.
They were kept in confinement till
the day of their death, living as
widows.
4Then the king said to Amasa,[e]
"Summon the men of Judah to
come to me within three days, and
be here yourself." 5But when Amasa went to summon Judah, he took

19:41
j Jdg 8:1
Jdg 12:1

19:43
k 2Sa 5:1

20:1
a Ge 31:14
b Ge 29:14
1Ki 12:16
c 1Sa 22:7-8
2Ch 10:16

20:3
d 2Sa 15:16
2Sa 16:21-22

20:4
e 2Sa 17:25
2Sa 19:13

20:6
f 2Sa 21:17

20:7
g 1Sa 30:14
2Sa 8:18
2Sa 15:18
1Ki 1:38

20:8
h Jos 9:3
i 2Sa 2:18

20:10
j Jdg 3:21
2Sa 2:23
2Sa 3:27
k 1Ki 2:5

20:12
l 2Sa 2:23

20:14
m Nu 21:16

longer than the time the king had
set for him.
6David said to Abishai,[f] "Now
Sheba son of Bicri will do us more
harm than Absalom did. Take your
master's men and pursue him, or he
will find fortified cities and escape
from us." 7So Joab's men and the
Kerethites[g] and Pelethites and all
the mighty warriors went out under the command of Abishai. They
marched out from Jerusalem to
pursue Sheba son of Bicri.
8While they were at the great
rock in Gibeon,[h] Amasa came to
meet them. Joab[i] was wearing his
military tunic, and strapped over it
at his waist was a belt with a dagger
in its sheath. As he stepped forward, it dropped out of its sheath.
9Joab said to Amasa, "How are
you, my brother?" Then Joab took
Amasa by the beard with his right
hand to kiss him. 10Amasa was not
on his guard against the dagger[j] in
Joab[k]'s hand, and Joab plunged it
into his belly, and his intestines
spilled out on the ground. Without
being stabbed again, Amasa died.
Then Joab and his brother Abishai
pursued Sheba son of Bicri.
11One of Joab's men stood beside
Amasa and said, "Whoever favours
Joab, and whoever is for David, let
him follow Joab!" 12Amasa lay wallowing in his blood in the middle of
the road, and the man saw that all
the troops came to a halt[l] there.
When he realised that everyone
who came up to Amasa stopped, he
dragged him from the road into a
field and threw a garment over
him. 13After Amasa had been removed from the road, all the men
went on with Joab to pursue Sheba
son of Bicri.
14Sheba passed through all the
tribes of Israel to Abel Beth Maacah[a] and through the entire region
of the Berites,[m] who gathered
together and followed him. 15All
the troops with Joab came and

[a] *14* Or *Abel, even Beth Maacah*; also in verse 15

besieged Sheba in Abel Beth Maacah.[n] They built a siege ramp[o] up
to the city, and it stood against the
outer fortifications. While they
were battering the wall to bring it
down, [16]a wise woman[p] called
from the city, "Listen! Listen! Tell
Joab to come here so that I can
speak to him." [17]He went towards
her, and she asked, "Are you
Joab?"
"I am," he answered.
She said, "Listen to what your
servant has to say."
"I'm listening," he said.
[18]She continued, "Long ago they
used to say, 'Get your answer at
Abel,' and that settled it. [19]We are
the peaceful[q] and faithful in Israel. You are trying to destroy a
city that is a mother in Israel. Why
do you want to swallow up the
LORD's inheritance?"[r]
[20]"Far be it from me!" Joab replied, "Far be it from me to swallow
up or destroy! [21]That is not the
case. A man named Sheba son of
Bicri, from the hill country of Ephraim, has lifted up his hand against
the king, against David. Hand over
this one man, and I'll withdraw
from the city."
The woman said to Joab, "His
head[s] will be thrown to you from
the wall."
[22]Then the woman went to all the
people with her wise advice,[t] and
they cut off the head of Sheba
son of Bicri and threw it to Joab.
So he sounded the trumpet, and
his men dispersed from the city,
each returning to his home. And
Joab went back to the king in Jerusalem.
[23]Joab[u] was over Israel's entire
army; Benaiah son of Jehoiada was
over the Kerethites and Pelethites;
[24]Adoniram[b][v] was in charge of
forced labour; Jehoshaphat[w] son
of Ahilud was recorder; [25]Sheva
was secretary; Zadok[x] and Abiathar were priests; [26]and Ira the Jai-
rite was David's priest.

20:15
n 1Ki 15:20; 2Ki 15:29
o 2Ki 19:32; Isa 37:33; Jer 6:6; Jer 32:24

20:16
p 2Sa 14:2

20:19
q Dt 2:26
r 1Sa 26:19; 2Sa 21:3

20:21
s 2Sa 4:8

20:22
t Ecc 9:13

20:23
u 2Sa 2:28; 2Sa 8:16-18; 2Sa 24:2

20:24
v 1Ki 4:6; 1Ki 5:14; 1Ki 12:18; 2Ch 10:18
w 2Sa 8:16; 1Ki 4:3

20:25
x 1Sa 2:35; 2Sa 8:17

21:1
a Ge 12:10; Dt 32:24
b Ex 32:11

21:2
c Jos 9:15

21:3
d 1Sa 26:19; 2Sa 20:19

21:4
e Nu 35:33-34

21:6
f Nu 25:4
g 1Sa 10:24

21:7
h 2Sa 4:4
i 1Sa 18:3; 1Sa 20:8,15; 2Sa 9:7

21:8
j 2Sa 3:7

The Gibeonites Avenged

21 During the reign of David,
there was a famine[a] for
three successive years; so David
sought[b] the face of the LORD. The
LORD said, "It is on account of Saul
and his blood-stained house; it is
because he put the Gibeonites to
death."
[2]The king summoned the Gibeonites[c] and spoke to them. (Now the
Gibeonites were not a part of Israel
but were survivors of the Amorites; the Israelites had sworn to
⌞spare⌟ them, but Saul in his zeal for
Israel and Judah had tried to annihilate them.) [3]David asked the
Gibeonites, "What shall I do for
you? How shall I make amends so
that you will bless the LORD's inheritance?"[d]
[4]The Gibeonites answered him,
"We have no right to demand silver
or gold from Saul or his family, nor
do we have the right to put anyone
in Israel to death."[e]
"What do you want me to do for
you?" David asked.
[5]They answered the king, "As for
the man who destroyed us and plotted against us so that we have been
decimated and have no place anywhere in Israel, [6]let seven of his
male descendants be given to us to
be killed and exposed[f] before the
LORD at Gibeah of Saul – the LORD's
chosen[g] one."
So the king said, "I will give them
to you."
[7]The king spared Mephibosheth[h] son of Jonathan, the son of
Saul, because of the oath[i] before
the LORD between David and Jonathan son of Saul. [8]But the king took
Armoni and Mephibosheth, the two
sons of Aiah's daughter Rizpah,[j]
whom she had borne to Saul, together with the five sons of Saul's
daughter Merab,[a] whom she had

[b]*24* Some Septuagint manuscripts (see also 1 Kings 4:6 and 5:14); Hebrew *Adoram*
[a]*8* Two Hebrew manuscripts, some Septuagint manuscripts and Syriac (see also 1 Samuel 18:19); most Hebrew and Septuagint manuscripts *Michal*

borne to Adriel son of Barzillai the
Meholathite.[k] 9He handed them
over to the Gibeonites, who killed
and exposed them on a hill before
the LORD. All seven of them fell together; they were put to death[l]
during the first days of harvest,
just as the barley harvest was beginning.[m]
10Rizpah daughter of Aiah took
sackcloth and spread it out for herself on a rock. From the beginning
of the harvest till the rain poured
down from the heavens on the
bodies, she did not let the birds of
the air touch them by day or the
wild animals by night.[n] 11When
David was told what Aiah's daughter Rizpah, Saul's concubine, had
done, 12he went and took the bones
of Saul[o] and his son Jonathan from
the citizens of Jabesh Gilead.
(They had taken them secretly
from the public square at Beth
Shan,[p] where the Philistines had
hung[q] them after they struck Saul
down on Gilboa.) 13David brought
the bones of Saul and his son Jonathan from there, and the bones of
those who had been killed and exposed were gathered up.
14They buried the bones of Saul
and his son Jonathan in the tomb of
Saul's father Kish, at Zela[r] in Benjamin, and did everything the king
commanded. After that,[s] God answered prayer[t] on behalf of the
land.

Wars Against the Philistines

21:15–22pp 1Ch 20:4–8

15Once again there was a battle
between the Philistines[u] and Israel. David went down with his men
to fight against the Philistines, and
he became exhausted. 16And Ishbi-
Benob, one of the descendants of
Rapha, whose bronze spearhead
weighed three hundred shekels[b]
and who was armed with a new
⌊sword⌋, said he would kill David.
17But Abishai[v] son of Zeruiah
came to David's rescue; he struck
the Philistine down and killed him.
Then David's men swore to him,
saying, "Never again will you go
out with us to battle, so that the
lamp[w] of Israel will not be extinguished.[x]"
18In the course of time, there was
another battle with the Philistines,
at Gob. At that time Sibbecai[y] the
Hushathite killed Saph, one of the
descendants of Rapha.
19In another battle with the Philistines at Gob, Elhanan son of
Jaare-Oregim[c] the Bethlehemite
killed Goliath[d] the Gittite, who had
a spear with a shaft like a weaver's
rod.[z]
20In still another battle, which
took place at Gath, there was a
huge man with six fingers on each
hand and six toes on each foot—
twenty-four in all. He also was descended from Rapha. 21When he
taunted Israel, Jonathan son of
Shimeah,[a] David's brother, killed
him.
22These four were descendants
of Rapha in Gath, and they fell at
the hands of David and his men.

David's Song of Praise

22:1–51pp Ps 18:1–50

22 David sang[a] to the LORD
the words of this song when
the LORD delivered him from the
hand of all his enemies and from
the hand of Saul. 2He said:

"The LORD is my rock,[b] my
fortress[c] and my
deliverer;[d]
3 my God is my rock, in whom I
take refuge,[e]
my shield[f] and the horn[a][g] of
my salvation.
He is my stronghold,[h] my
refuge and my saviour—
from violent men you save
me.

21:8 k 1Sa 18:19
21:9 l 2Sa 16:8; m Ru 1:22
21:10 n ver 8; Dt 21:23; 1Sa 17:44
21:12 o 1Sa 31:11-13; p Jos 17:11; q 1Sa 31:10
21:14 r Jos 18:28; s Jos 7:26; t 2Sa 24:25
21:15 u 2Sa 5:25
21:17 v 2Sa 20:6; w 1Ki 11:36; x 2Sa 18:3
21:18 y 1Ch 11:29; 1Ch 20:4; 1Ch 27:11
21:19 z 1Sa 17:7
21:21 a 1Sa 16:9
22:1 a Ex 15:1; Jdg 5:1; Ps 18:2-50
22:2 b Dt 32:4; Ps 71:3; c Ps 31:3; Ps 91:2; d Ps 144:2
22:3 e Dt 32:37; Jer 16:19; f Ge 15:1; g Lk 1:69; h Ps 9:9

b16 That is, about 7½ pounds (about 3.5 kilograms)
c19 Or *son of Jair the weaver*
d19 Hebrew and Septuagint; 1 Chron. 20:5 *son of Jair killed Lahmi the brother of Goliath*
a3 *Horn* here symbolises strength.

4 I call to the LORD, who is
 worthy[i] of praise,
and I am saved from my
 enemies.
5 "The waves[j] of death swirled
 about me;
the torrents of destruction
 overwhelmed me.
6 The cords of the grave[b][k]
 coiled around me;
the snares of death confronted
 me.
7 In my distress[l] I called[m] to the
 LORD;
I called out to my God.
From his temple he heard my
 voice;
my cry came to his ears.
8 "The earth[n] trembled and
 quaked,[o]
the foundations[p] of the
 heavens[c] shook;
they trembled because he was
 angry.
9 Smoke rose from his nostrils;
consuming fire[q] came from
 his mouth,
burning coals blazed out of it.
10 He parted the heavens and
 came down;
dark clouds[r] were under his
 feet.
11 He mounted the cherubim and
 flew;
he soared[d] on the wings of
 the wind.[s]
12 He made darkness his canopy
 around him—
the dark[e] rain clouds of the
 sky.
13 Out of the brightness of his
 presence
bolts of lightning[t] blazed
 forth.
14 The LORD thundered[u] from
 heaven;
the voice of the Most High
 resounded.
15 He shot arrows[v] and scattered
 ⌊the enemies⌋,
bolts of lightning and routed
 them.
16 The valleys of the sea were
 exposed
and the foundations of the
 earth laid bare
at the rebuke[w] of the LORD,
 at the blast of breath from his
 nostrils.
17 "He reached down from on
 high[x] and took hold of me;
he drew[y] me out of deep
 waters.
18 He rescued me from my
 powerful enemy,
from my foes, who were too
 strong for me.
19 They confronted me in the day
 of my disaster,
but the LORD was my
 support.[z]
20 He brought me out into a
 spacious[a] place;
he rescued[b] me because he
 delighted[c] in me.[d]
21 "The LORD has dealt with me
 according to my
 righteousness;[e]
according to the cleanness of
 my hands[f] he has
 rewarded me.
22 For I have kept[g] the ways of
 the LORD;
I have not done evil by
 turning from my God.
23 All his laws are before me;[h]
I have not turned[i] away from
 his decrees.
24 I have been blameless[j] before
 him
and have kept myself from
 sin.
25 The LORD has rewarded me
 according to my
 righteousness,[k]
according to my cleanness[f] in
 his sight.

22:4 *i* Ps 48:1; Ps 96:4
22:5 *j* Ps 69:14-15; Ps 93:4; Jnh 2:3
22:6 *k* Ps 116:3
22:7 *l* Ps 120:1 *m* Ps 34:6,15; Ps 116:4
22:8 *n* Jdg 5:4; Ps 97:4 *o* Ps 77:18 *p* Job 26:11
22:9 *q* Ps 97:3; Heb 12:29
22:10 *r* 1Ki 8:12; Na 1:3
22:11 *s* Ps 104:3
22:13 *t* ver 9
22:14 *u* 1Sa 2:10
22:15 *v* Dt 32:23
22:16 *w* Na 1:4
22:17 *x* Ps 144:7 *y* Ex 2:10
22:19 *z* Ps 23:4
22:20 *a* Ps 31:8 *b* Ps 118:5 *c* Ps 22:8 *d* 2Sa 15:26
22:21 *e* 1Sa 26:23 *f* Ps 24:4
22:22 *g* Ge 18:19; Ps 128:1; Pr 8:32
22:23 *h* Dt 6:4-9; Ps 119:30-32 *i* Ps 119:102
22:24 *j* Ge 6:9; Eph 1:4
22:25 *k* ver 21

b *6* Hebrew *Sheol* c *8* Hebrew; Vulgate and Syriac (see also Psalm 18:7) *mountains*
d *11* Many Hebrew manuscripts (see also Psalm 18:10); most Hebrew manuscripts *appeared*
e *12* Septuagint and Vulgate (see also Psalm 18:11); Hebrew *massed* f *25* Hebrew; Septuagint and Vulgate (see also Psalm 18:24) *to the cleanness of my hands*

26"To the faithful you show
yourself faithful,
to the blameless you show
yourself blameless,
27to the pure[l] you show yourself
pure,
but to the crooked you show
yourself shrewd.[m]
28You save the humble,[n]
but your eyes are on the
haughty to bring them
low.[o]
29You are my lamp,[p] O LORD;
the LORD turns my darkness
into light.
30With your help I can advance
against a troop;[g]
with my God I can scale a
wall.
31"As for God, his way is
perfect;[q]
the word of the LORD is
flawless.[r]
He is a shield
for all who take refuge in him.
32For who is God besides the
LORD?
And who is the Rock[s] except
our God?
33It is God who arms me with
strength[h]
and makes my way perfect.
34He makes my feet like the feet
of a deer;[t]
he enables me to stand on the
heights.[u]
35He trains my hands[v] for battle;
my arms can bend a bow of
bronze.
36You give me your shield[w] of
victory;
you stoop down to make me
great.
37You broaden the path[x] beneath
me,
so that my ankles do not turn
over.

38"I pursued my enemies and
crushed them;
I did not turn back till they
were destroyed.
39I crushed[y] them completely,
and they could not rise;
they fell beneath my feet.
40You armed me with strength
for battle;
you made my adversaries bow
at my feet.[z]
41You made my enemies turn
their backs[a] in flight,
and I destroyed my foes.
42They cried for help,[b] but there
was no-one to save
them—[c]
to the LORD, but he did not
answer.
43I beat them as fine as the dust
of the earth;
I pounded and trampled[d]
them like mud[e] in the
streets.

44"You have delivered[f] me from
the attacks of my people;
you have preserved[g] me as
the head of nations.
People[h] I did not know are
subject to me,
45 and foreigners come
cringing[i] to me;
as soon as they hear me, they
obey me.
46They all lose heart;
they come trembling[i][j] from
their strongholds.

47"The LORD lives! Praise be to
my Rock!
Exalted be God, the Rock, my
Saviour![k]
48He is the God who avenges
me,[l]
who puts the nations under
me,
49 who sets me free from my
enemies.[m]
You exalted me above my foes;
from violent men you rescued
me.
50Therefore I will praise you,
O LORD, among the nations;

22:27 l Mt 5:8 m Lev 26:23-24
22:28 n Ex 3:8 Ps 72:12-13 o Isa 2:12,17 Isa 5:15
22:29 p Ps 27:1
22:31 q Dt 32:4 Mt 5:48 r Ps 12:6 Ps 119:140 Pr 30:5-6
22:32 s 1Sa 2:2
22:34 t Hab 3:19 u Dt 32:13
22:35 v Ps 144:1
22:36 w Eph 6:16
22:37 x Pr 4:11
22:39 y Mal 4:3
22:40 z Ps 44:5
22:41 a Ex 23:27
22:42 b Isa 1:15 c Ps 50:22
22:43 d Mic 7:10 e Isa 10:6 Mic 7:10
22:44 f 2Sa 3:1 g Dt 28:13 h 2Sa 8:1-14 Isa 55:3-5
22:45 i Ps 66:3 Ps 81:15
22:46 j Mic 7:17
22:47 k Ps 89:26
22:48 l Ps 94:1 Ps 144:2 1Sa 25:39
22:49 m Ps 140:1,4

g30 Or *can run through a barricade* h33 Dead Sea Scrolls, some Septuagint manuscripts, Vulgate and Syriac (see also Psalm 18:32); Masoretic Text *who is my strong refuge* i46 Some Septuagint manuscripts and Vulgate (see also Psalm 18:45); Masoretic Text *they arm themselves.*

I will sing praises to your
name.[n]
51 He gives his king great
victories;[o]
he shows unfailing kindness to
his anointed,[p]
to David[q] and his descendants
for ever."

The Last Words of David

23

These are the last words of David:

"The oracle of David son of
Jesse,
the oracle of the man exalted[a]
by the Most High,
the man anointed[b] by the God
of Jacob,
Israel's singer of songs:[a]

2 "The Spirit[c] of the LORD spoke
through me;
his word was on my tongue.
3 The God of Israel spoke,
the Rock[d] of Israel said to
me:
'When one rules over men in
righteousness,[e]
when he rules in the fear of
God,[f]
4 he is like the light of morning
at sunrise[g]
on a cloudless morning,
like the brightness after rain
that brings the grass from the
earth.'

5 "Is not my house right with
God?
Has he not made with me an
everlasting covenant,[h]
arranged and secured in every
part?
Will he not bring to fruition my
salvation
and grant me my every
desire?
6 But evil men are all to be cast
aside like thorns,[i]
which are not gathered with
the hand.

22:50
n Ro 15:9*

22:51
o Ps 144:9-10
p Ps 89:20
q 2Sa 7:13
r Ps 89:24,29

23:1
a 2Sa 7:8-9
Ps 78:70-71
Ps 89:27
b 1Sa 16:12-13
Ps 89:20

23:2
c Mt 22:43
2Pe 1:21

23:3
d Dt 32:4
2Sa 22:2,32
e Ps 72:3
f 2Ch 19:7,9
Isa 11:1-5

23:4
g Jdg 5:31
Ps 89:36

23:5
h Ps 89:29
Isa 55:3

23:6
i Mt 13:40-41

23:9
j 1Ch 27:4
k 1Ch 8:4

23:13
l 1Sa 22:1
m 2Sa 5:18

7 Whoever touches thorns
uses a tool of iron or the shaft
of a spear;
they are burned up where
they lie."

David's Mighty Men

23:8-39pp 1Ch 11:10-41

8 These are the names of David's
mighty men:
Josheb-Basshebeth,[b] a Tahke-
monite,[c] was chief of the Three; he
raised his spear against eight hundred men, whom he killed[d] in one
encounter.
9 Next to him was Eleazar son of
Dodai[j] the Ahohite.[k] As one of the
three mighty men, he was with
David when they taunted the Philistines gathered ⌞at Pas Dammim,⌟[e]
for battle. Then the men of Israel
retreated, 10 but he stood his ground
and struck down the Philistines till
his hand grew tired and froze to the
sword. The LORD brought about a
great victory that day. The troops
returned to Eleazar, but only to
strip the dead.
11 Next to him was Shammah son
of Agee the Hararite. When the
Philistines banded together at a
place where there was a field full
of lentils, Israel's troops fled from
them. 12 But Shammah took his
stand in the middle of the field. He
defended it and struck the Philistines down, and the LORD brought
about a great victory.
13 During harvest time, three of
the thirty chief men came down to
David at the cave of Adullam,[l]
while a band of Philistines was encamped in the Valley of Rephaim.[m]
14 At that time David was in the

a *1* Or *Israel's beloved singer* b *8* Hebrew; some Septuagint manuscripts suggest *Ish-Bosheth,* that is, *Esh-Baal* (see also 1 Chron. 11:11 *Jashobeam*). c *8* Probably a variant of *Hacmonite* (see 1 Chron. 11:11) d *8* Some Septuagint manuscripts (see also 1 Chron. 11:11); Hebrew and other Septuagint manuscripts *Three; it was Adino the Eznite who killed eight hundred men* e *9* See 1 Chron. 11:13; Hebrew *gathered there.*

stronghold,[n] and the Philistine
garrison was at Bethlehem.[o]
15 David longed for water and said,
"Oh, that someone would get me a
drink of water from the well near
the gate of Bethlehem!" 16 So the
three mighty men broke through
the Philistine lines, drew water
from the well near the gate of Bethlehem and carried it back to David.
But he refused to drink it; instead,
he poured[p] it out before the LORD.
17 "Far be it from me, O LORD, to do
this!" he said. "Is it not the blood[q] of
men who went at the risk of their
lives?" And David would not drink it.
Such were the exploits of the
three mighty men.
18 Abishai[r] the brother of Joab
son of Zeruiah was chief of the
Three.[f] He raised his spear
against three hundred men, whom
he killed, and so he became as famous as the Three. 19 Was he not
held in greater honour than the
Three? He became their commander, even though he was not included among them.
20 Benaiah[s] son of Jehoiada was a
valiant fighter from Kabzeel,[t]
who performed great exploits. He
struck down two of Moab's best
men. He also went down into a pit
on a snowy day and killed a lion.
21 And he struck down a huge Egyptian. Although the Egyptian had a
spear in his hand, Benaiah went
against him with a club. He
snatched the spear from the Egyptian's hand and killed him with his
own spear. 22 Such were the exploits
of Benaiah son of Jehoiada; he too
was as famous as the three mighty
men. 23 He was held in greater honour than any of the Thirty, but he
was not included among the Three.
And David put him in charge of his
bodyguard.

24 Among the Thirty were:
Asahel[u] the brother of Joab,
Elhanan son of Dodo from
Bethlehem,

23:14 *n* 1Sa 22:4-5 *o* Ru 1:19
23:16 *p* Ge 35:14
23:17 *q* Lev 17:10-12
23:18 *r* 2Sa 10:10,14 1Ch 11:20
23:20 *s* 2Sa 8:18 2Sa 20:23 *t* Jos 15:21
23:24 *u* 2Sa 2:18
23:25 *v* Jdg 7:1 1Ch 11:27
23:26 *w* 1Ch 27:10
23:27 *x* Jos 21:18
23:28 *y* 1Ch 27:13 *z* 2Ki 25:23 Ne 7:26
23:29 *a* Jos 15:57
23:30 *b* Jdg 12:13 *c* Jos 24:30
23:31 *d* 2Sa 3:16
23:34 *e* 2Sa 11:3 *f* 2Sa 15:12
23:35 *g* Jos 12:22
23:36 *h* 1Sa 14:47
23:38 *i* 2Sa 20:26 1Ch 2:53
23:39 *j* 2Sa 11:3

25 Shammah the Harodite,[v]
Elika the Harodite,
26 Helez[w] the Paltite,
Ira son of Ikkesh from Tekoa,
27 Abiezer from Anathoth,[x]
Mebunnai[g] the Hushathite,
28 Zalmon the Ahohite,
Maharai[y] the Netopha-
thite,[z]
29 Heled[h] son of Baanah the
Netophathite,
Ithai son of Ribai from Gibeah[a] in Benjamin,
30 Benaiah the Pirathonite,[b]
Hiddai[i] from the ravines of
Gaash,[c]
31 Abi-Albon the Arbathite,
Azmaveth the Barhumite,[d]
32 Eliahba the Shaalbonite,
the sons of Jashen,
Jonathan 33 son of[j] Shammah
the Hararite,
Ahiam son of Sharar[k] the
Hararite,
34 Eliphelet son of Ahasbai the
Maacathite,
Eliam[e] son of Ahithophel[f]
the Gilonite,
35 Hezro the Carmelite,[g]
Paarai the Arbite,
36 Igal son of Nathan from Zobah,[h]
the son of Hagri,[l]
37 Zelek the Ammonite,
Naharai the Beerothite, the
armour-bearer of Joab son
of Zeruiah,
38 Ira the Ithrite,[i]
Gareb the Ithrite
39 and Uriah[j] the Hittite.
There were thirty-seven in all.

[f] *18* Most Hebrew manuscripts (see also 1 Chron. 11:20); two Hebrew manuscripts and Syriac *Thirty* [g] *27* Hebrew; some Septuagint manuscripts (see also 1 Chron. 11:29) *Sibbecai* [h] *29* Some Hebrew manuscripts and Vulgate (see also 1 Chron. 11:30); most Hebrew manuscripts *Heleb* [i] *30* Hebrew; some Septuagint manuscripts (see also 1 Chron. 11:32) *Hurai* [j] *33* Some Septuagint manuscripts (see also 1 Chron. 11:34); Hebrew does not have *son of.* [k] *33* Hebrew; some Septuagint manuscripts (see also 1 Chron. 11:35) *Sacar* [l] *36* Some Septuagint manuscripts (see also 1 Chron. 11:38); Hebrew *Haggadi*

David Counts the Fighting Men

24:1–17pp 1Ch 21:1–17

24 Again[a] the anger of the LORD burned against Israel, and he incited David against them, saying, "Go and take a census of[b] Israel and Judah."

2 So the king said to Joab[c] and the army commanders[a] with him, "Go throughout the tribes of Israel from Dan to Beersheba[d] and enrol the fighting men, so that I may know how many there are."

3 But Joab replied to the king, "May the LORD your God multiply the troops a hundred times over,[e] and may the eyes of my lord the king see it. But why does my lord the king want to do such a thing?"

4 The king's word, however, overruled Joab and the army commanders; so they left the presence of the king to enrol the fighting men of Israel.

5 After crossing the Jordan, they camped near Aroer,[f] south of the town in the gorge, and then went through Gad and on to Jazer.[g] 6 They went to Gilead and the region of Tahtim Hodshi, and on to Dan Jaan and around towards Sidon.[h] 7 Then they went towards the fortress of Tyre[i] and all the towns of the Hivites and Canaanites. Finally, they went on to Beersheba[j] in the Negev[k] of Judah.

8 After they had gone through the entire land, they came back to Jerusalem at the end of nine months and twenty days.

9 Joab reported the number of the fighting men to the king: In Israel there were eight hundred thousand able-bodied men who could handle a sword, and in Judah five hundred thousand.[l]

10 David was conscience-stricken[m] after he had counted the fighting men, and he said to the LORD, "I have sinned[n] greatly in what I have done. Now, O LORD, I beg you, take away the guilt of your servant. I have done a very foolish thing.[o]"

11 Before David got up the next morning, the word of the LORD had come to Gad[p] the prophet, David's seer:[q] 12 "Go and tell David, 'This is what the LORD says: I am giving you three options. Choose one of them for me to carry out against you.' "

13 So Gad went to David and said to him, "Shall there come upon you three[b] years of famine[r] in your land? Or three months of fleeing from your enemies while they pursue you? Or three days of plague[s] in your land? Now then, think it over and decide how I should answer the one who sent me."

14 David said to Gad, "I am in deep distress. Let us fall into the hands of the LORD, for his mercy[t] is great; but do not let me fall into the hands of men."

15 So the LORD sent a plague on Israel from that morning until the end of the time designated, and seventy thousand of the people from Dan to Beersheba died.[u] 16 When the angel stretched out his hand to destroy Jerusalem, the LORD was grieved[v] because of the calamity and said to the angel who was afflicting the people, "Enough! Withdraw your hand." The angel of the LORD[w] was then at the threshing-floor of Araunah the Jebusite.

17 When David saw the angel who was striking down the people, he said to the LORD, "I am the one who has sinned and done wrong. These are but sheep.[x] What have they done? Let your hand fall upon me and my family."[y]

24:1 *a* Jos 9:15 *b* 1Ch 27:23
24:2 *c* 2Sa 20:23 *d* Jdg 20:1; 2Sa 3:10
24:3 *e* Dt 1:11
24:5 *f* Dt 2:36; Jos 13:9 *g* Nu 21:32
24:6 *h* Ge 10:19; Jos 19:28; Jdg 1:31
24:7 *i* Jos 19:29 *j* Ge 21:22-33 *k* Dt 1:7; Jos 11:3
24:9 *l* Nu 1:44-46; 1Ch 21:5
24:10 *m* 1Sa 24:5 *n* 2Sa 12:13 *o* Nu 12:11; 1Sa 13:13
24:11 *p* 1Sa 22:5 *q* 1Sa 9:9; 1Ch 29:29
24:13 *r* Dt 28:38-42, 48; Eze 14:21 *s* Lev 26:25
24:14 *t* Ne 9:28; Ps 51:1; Ps 103:8,13; Ps 130:4
24:15 *u* 1Ch 27:24
24:16 *v* Ge 6:6; 1Sa 15:11 *w* Ex 12:23; Ac 12:23
24:17 *x* Ps 74:1 *y* Jnh 1:12

a2 Septuagint (see also verse 4 and 1 Chron. 21:2); Hebrew *Joab the army commander*
b13 Septuagint (see also 1 Chron. 21:12); Hebrew *seven*

David Builds an Altar

24:18–25pp 1Ch 21:18–26

18 On that day Gad went to David and said to him, "Go up and build an altar to the LORD on the threshing-floor of Araunah the Jebusite." 19 So David went up, as the LORD had commanded through Gad. 20 When Araunah looked and saw the king and his men coming towards him, he went out and bowed down before the king with his face to the ground.

21 Araunah said, "Why has my lord the king come to his servant?"

"To buy your threshing-floor," David answered, "so that I can build an altar to the LORD, that the plague on the people may be stopped."[z]

22 Araunah said to David, "Let my lord the king take whatever pleases him and offer it up. Here are oxen[a] for the burnt offering, and here are threshing-sledges and ox yokes for the wood. 23 O king, Araunah gives[b] all this to the king." Araunah also said to him, "May the LORD your God accept you."

24 But the king replied to Araunah, "No, I insist on paying you for it. I will not sacrifice to the LORD my God burnt offerings that cost me nothing."[c]

So David bought the threshing-floor and the oxen and paid fifty shekels[c] of silver for them. 25 David built an altar[d] to the LORD there and sacrificed burnt offerings and fellowship offerings.[d] Then the LORD answered prayer[e] on behalf of the land, and the plague on Israel was stopped.

24:21 z Nu 16:44-50
24:22 a 1Sa 6:14; 1Ki 19:21
24:23 b Eze 20:40-41
24:24 c Mal 1:13-14
24:25 d 1Sa 7:17; e 2Sa 21:14

c24 That is, about 1¼ pounds (about 0.6 kilogram)
d25 Traditionally *peace offerings*

1 KINGS

Adonijah Sets Himself Up as King

1 When King David was old and well advanced in years, he could not keep warm even when they put covers over him. 2 So his servants said to him, "Let us look for a young virgin to attend the king and take care of him. She can lie beside him so that our lord the king may keep warm."

3 Then they searched throughout Israel for a beautiful girl and found Abishag, a Shunammite,[a] and brought her to the king. 4 The girl was very beautiful; she took care of the king and waited on him, but the king had no intimate relations with her.

5 Now Adonijah,[b] whose mother was Haggith, put himself forward and said, "I will be king." So he got chariots[c] and horses[a] ready, with fifty men to run ahead of him. 6 (His father had never interfered[d] with him by asking, "Why do you behave as you do?" He was also very handsome and was born next after Absalom.)

7 Adonijah conferred with Joab[e] son of Zeruiah and with Abiathar[f] the priest, and they gave him their support. 8 But Zadok[g] the priest, Benaiah[h] son of Jehoiada, Nathan[i] the prophet, Shimei[j] and Rei[b] and David's special guard[k] did not join Adonijah.

9 Adonijah then sacrificed sheep, cattle and fattened calves at the Stone of Zoheleth near En Rogel.[l] He invited all his brothers, the king's sons, and all the men of Judah who were royal officials, 10 but he did not invite Nathan the prophet or Benaiah or the special guard or his brother Solomon.[m]

11 Then Nathan asked Bathsheba,[n] Solomon's mother, "Have you not heard that Adonijah,[o] the son of Haggith, has become king without our lord David's knowing it? 12 Now then, let me advise[p] you how you can save your own life and the life of your son Solomon. 13 Go in to King David and say to him, 'My lord the king, did you not swear[q] to me your servant: "Surely Solomon your son shall be king after me, and he will sit on my throne"? Why then has Adonijah become king?' 14 While you are still there talking to the king, I will come in and confirm what you have said."

15 So Bathsheba went to see the aged king in his room, where Abishag[r] the Shunammite was attending him. 16 Bathsheba bowed low and knelt before the king.

"What is it you want?" the king asked.

17 She said to him, "My lord, you yourself swore[s] to me your servant by the LORD your God: 'Solomon your son shall become king after me, and he will sit on my throne.' 18 But now Adonijah has become king, and you, my lord the king, do not know about it. 19 He has sacrificed[t] great numbers of cattle, fattened calves, and sheep, and has invited all the king's sons, Abiathar the priest and Joab the commander of the army, but he has not invited Solomon your servant. 20 My lord the king, the eyes of all Israel are on you, to learn from you who will sit on the throne of my lord the king after him. 21 Otherwise, as soon as my lord the king is laid to rest[u] with his fathers, I and my son Solomon will be treated as criminals."

1:3 a Jos 19:18
1:5 b 2Sa 3:4; c 2Sa 15:1
1:6 d 2Sa 3:3-4
1:7 e 1Ki 2:22,28; 1Ch 11:6; f 1Sa 22:20; 2Sa 20:25
1:8 g 2Sa 20:25; h 2Sa 8:18; i 2Sa 12:1; j 1Ki 4:18; k 2Sa 23:8
1:9 l 2Sa 17:17
1:10 m 2Sa 12:24
1:11 n 2Sa 12:24; o 2Sa 3:4
1:12 p Pr 15:22
1:13 q ver 30; 1Ch 22:9-13
1:15 r ver 1
1:17 s ver 13,30
1:19 t ver 9
1:21 u Dt 31:16; 1Ki 2:10

[a] 5 Or *charioteers* [b] 8 Or *and his friends*

22While she was still speaking
with the king, Nathan the prophet
arrived. 23And they told the king,
"Nathan the prophet is here." So he
went before the king and bowed
with his face to the ground.

24Nathan said, "Have you, my
lord the king, declared that Adonijah shall be king after you, and that
he will sit on your throne? 25Today
he has gone down and sacrificed
great numbers of cattle, fattened
calves, and sheep. He has invited
all the king's sons, the commanders
of the army and Abiathar the
priest. At this very moment they
are eating and drinking with him
and saying, 'Long live King Adonijah!' 26But me your servant, and
Zadok the priest, and Benaiah son
of Jehoiada, and your servant Solomon he did not invite.[v] 27Is this
something my lord the king has
done without letting his servants
know who should sit on the throne
of my lord the king after him?"

David Makes Solomon King

1:28–53pp 1Ch 29:21–25

28Then King David said, "Call in
Bathsheba." So she came into the
king's presence and stood before
him.

29The king then took an oath: "As
surely as the LORD lives, who has
delivered me out of every trouble,[w] 30I will surely carry out today
what I swore[x] to you by the LORD,
the God of Israel: Solomon your son
shall be king after me, and he will
sit on my throne in my place."

31Then Bathsheba bowed low
with her face to the ground and,
kneeling before the king, said,
"May my lord King David live for
ever!"

32King David said, "Call in Zadok
the priest, Nathan the prophet and
Benaiah son of Jehoiada." When
they came before the king, 33he
said to them: "Take your lord's servants with you and set Solomon my
son on my own mule[y] and take him
down to Gihon.[z] 34There shall
Zadok the priest and Nathan the
prophet anoint[a] him king over Israel. Blow the trumpet[b] and shout,
'Long live King Solomon!' 35Then
you are to go up with him, and he is
to come and sit on my throne and
reign in my place. I have appointed
him ruler over Israel and Judah."

36Benaiah son of Jehoiada answered the king, "Amen! May the
LORD, the God of my lord the king,
so declare it. 37As the LORD was
with my lord the king, so may he be
with[c] Solomon to make his throne
even greater[d] than the throne of
my lord King David!"

38So Zadok[e] the priest, Nathan
the prophet, Benaiah son of Jehoiada, the Kerethites[f] and the Pelethites went down and put Solomon
on King David's mule and escorted
him to Gihon.[g] 39Zadok the priest
took the horn of oil[h] from the
sacred tent and anointed Solomon.
Then they sounded the trumpet
and all the people shouted,[i] "Long
live King Solomon!" 40And all the
people went up after him, playing
flutes and rejoicing greatly, so that
the ground shook with the sound.

41Adonijah and all the guests who
were with him heard it as they
were finishing their feast. On hearing the sound of the trumpet, Joab
asked, "What's the meaning of all
the noise in the city?"

42Even as he was speaking, Jonathan[j] son of Abiathar the priest
arrived. Adonijah said, "Come in.
A worthy man like you must be
bringing good news."[k]

43"Not at all!" Jonathan answered. "Our lord King David has
made Solomon king. 44The king has
sent with him Zadok the priest, Nathan the prophet, Benaiah son of
Jehoiada, the Kerethites and the
Pelethites, and they have put him
on the king's mule, 45and Zadok the
priest and Nathan the prophet have
anointed him king at Gihon. From
there they have gone up cheering,
and the city resounds[l] with it.

1:26 v ver 8,10
1:29 w 2Sa 4:9
1:30 x ver 13,17
1:33 y 2Sa 20:6-7 z 2Ch 32:30 2Ch 33:14
1:34 a 1Sa 10:1 1Sa 16:3,12 1Ki 19:16 2Ki 9:3,13 b ver 25 2Sa 5:3 2Sa 15:10
1:37 c Jos 1:5,17 1Sa 20:13 d ver 47
1:38 e ver 8 f 2Sa 8:18 g ver 33
1:39 h Ex 30:23-32 Ps 89:20 i ver 34 1Sa 10:24
1:42 j 2Sa 15:27,36 k 2Sa 18:26
1:45 l ver 40

That's the noise you hear. 46Moreover, Solomon has taken his seat on the royal throne. 47Also, the royal officials have come to congratulate our lord King David, saying, 'May your God make Solomon's name more famous than yours and his throne greater[m] than yours!' And the king bowed in worship on his bed 48and said, 'Praise be to the LORD, the God of Israel, who has allowed my eyes to see a successor[n] on my throne today.' "

49At this, all Adonijah's guests rose in alarm and dispersed. 50But Adonijah, in fear of Solomon, went and took hold of the horns[o] of the altar. 51Then Solomon was told, "Adonijah is afraid of King Solomon and is clinging to the horns of the altar. He says, 'Let King Solomon swear to me today that he will not put his servant to death with the sword.' "

52Solomon replied, "If he shows himself to be a worthy man, not a hair[p] of his head will fall to the ground; but if evil is found in him, he will die." 53Then King Solomon sent men, and they brought him down from the altar. And Adonijah came and bowed down to King Solomon, and Solomon said, "Go to your home."

David's Charge to Solomon

2:10–12pp 1Ch 29:26–28

2 When the time drew near for David to die,[a] he gave a charge to Solomon his son.

2"I am about to go the way of all the earth,"[b] he said. "So be strong,[c] show yourself a man, 3and observe[d] what the LORD your God requires: Walk in his ways, and keep his decrees and commands, his laws and requirements, as written in the Law of Moses, so that you may prosper[e] in all you do and wherever you go, 4and that the LORD may keep his promise[f] to me: 'If your descendants watch how they live, and if they walk faithfully[g] before me with all their heart and soul, you will never fail to have a man on the throne of Israel.'

5"Now you yourself know what Joab[h] son of Zeruiah did to me—what he did to the two commanders of Israel's armies, Abner[i] son of Ner and Amasa[j] son of Jether. He killed them, shedding their blood in peacetime as if in battle, and with that blood stained the belt round his waist and the sandals on his feet. 6Deal with him according to your wisdom,[k] but do not let his grey head go down to the grave[a] in peace.

7"But show kindness to the sons of Barzillai[l] of Gilead and let them be among those who eat at your table.[m] They stood by me when I fled from your brother Absalom.

8"And remember, you have with you Shimei[n] son of Gera, the Benjamite from Bahurim, who called down bitter curses on me the day I went to Mahanaim. When he came down to meet me at the Jordan, I swore[o] to him by the LORD: 'I will not put you to death by the sword.' 9But now, do not consider him innocent. You are a man of wisdom;[p] you will know what to do to him. Bring his grey head down to the grave in blood."

10Then David rested with his fathers and was buried[q] in the City of David.[r] 11He had reigned[s] for forty years over Israel—seven years in Hebron and thirty-three in Jerusalem. 12So Solomon sat on the throne[t] of his father David, and his rule was firmly established.[u]

Solomon's Throne Established

13Now Adonijah, the son of Haggith, went to Bathsheba, Solomon's mother. Bathsheba asked him, "Do you come peacefully?"[v]

He answered, "Yes, peacefully."

1:47 *m* ver 37; Ge 47:31
1:48 *n* 2Sa 7:12; 1Ki 3:6
1:50 *o* 1Ki 2:28
1:52 *p* 1Sa 14:45; 2Sa 14:11
2:1 *a* Ge 47:29; Dt 31:14
2:2 *b* Jos 23:14 *c* Dt 31:7,23; Jos 1:6
2:3 *d* Dt 17:14-20; Jos 1:7 *e* 1Ch 22:13
2:4 *f* 2Sa 7:13,25; 1Ki 8:25 *g* 2Ki 20:3; Ps 132:12
2:5 *h* 2Sa 2:18; 2Sa 18:5,12,14 *i* 2Sa 3:27 *j* 2Sa 20:10
2:6 *k* ver 9
2:7 *l* 2Sa 17:27; 2Sa 19:31-39 *m* 2Sa 9:7
2:8 *n* 2Sa 16:5-13 *o* 2Sa 19:18-23
2:9 *p* ver 6
2:10 *q* Ac 2:29; Ac 13:36 *r* 2Sa 5:7
2:11 *s* 2Sa 5:4,5
2:12 *t* 1Ch 29:23 *u* 2Ch 1:1
2:13 *v* 1Sa 16:4

a6 Hebrew *Sheol*; also in verse 9

14Then he added, "I have something to say to you."

"You may say it," she replied.

15"As you know," he said, "the kingdom was mine. All Israel looked to me as their king. But things changed, and the kingdom has gone to my brother; for it has come to him from the LORD. 16Now I have one request to make of you. Do not refuse me."

"You may make it," she said.

17So he continued, "Please ask King Solomon—he will not refuse you—to give me Abishag[w] the Shunammite as my wife."

18"Very well," Bathsheba replied, "I will speak to the king for you."

19When Bathsheba went to King Solomon to speak to him for Adonijah, the king stood up to meet her, bowed down to her and sat down on his throne. He had a throne brought for the king's mother,[x] and she sat down at his right hand.[y]

20"I have one small request to make of you," she said. "Do not refuse me."

The king replied, "Make it, my mother; I will not refuse you."

21So she said, "Let Abishag[z] the Shunammite be given in marriage to your brother Adonijah."

22King Solomon answered his mother, "Why do you request Abishag[a] the Shunammite for Adonijah? You might as well request the kingdom for him—after all, he is my older brother[b]—yes, for him and for Abiathar the priest and Joab son of Zeruiah!"

23Then King Solomon swore by the LORD: "May God deal with me, be it ever so severely,[c] if Adonijah does not pay with his life for this request! 24And now, as surely as the LORD lives—he who has established me securely on the throne of my father David and has founded a dynasty for me as he promised[d]—Adonijah shall be put to death today!" 25So King Solomon gave orders to Benaiah[e] son of Jehoiada, and he struck down Adonijah and he died.

26To Abiathar[f] the priest the king said, "Go back to your fields in Anathoth.[g] You deserve to die, but I will not put you to death now, because you carried the ark[h] of the Sovereign LORD before my father David and shared all my father's hardships."[i] 27So Solomon removed Abiathar from the priesthood of the LORD, fulfilling[j] the word the LORD had spoken at Shiloh about the house of Eli.

28When the news reached Joab, who had conspired with Adonijah though not with Absalom, he fled to the tent of the LORD and took hold of the horns[k] of the altar. 29King Solomon was told that Joab had fled to the tent of the LORD and was beside the altar. Then Solomon ordered Benaiah[l] son of Jehoiada, "Go, strike him down!"

30So Benaiah entered the tent of the LORD and said to Joab, "The king says, 'Come out![m]' "

But he answered, "No, I will die here."

Benaiah reported to the king, "This is how Joab answered me."

31Then the king commanded Benaiah, "Do as he says. Strike him down and bury him, and so clear me and my father's house of the guilt of the innocent blood[n] that Joab shed. 32The LORD will repay[o] him for the blood he shed,[p] because without the knowledge of my father David he attacked two men and killed them with the sword. Both of them—Abner son of Ner, commander of Israel's army, and Amasa[q] son of Jether, commander of Judah's army—were better[r] men and more upright than he. 33May the guilt of their blood rest on the head of Joab and his descendants for ever. But on David and his descendants, his house and his throne, may there be the LORD's peace for ever."

34So Benaiah son of Jehoiada went up and struck down Joab and

2:17 w 1Ki 1:3
2:19 x 1Ki 15:13 y Ps 45:9
2:21 z 1Ki 1:3
2:22 a 2Sa 12:8 1Ki 1:3 b 1Ch 3:2
2:23 c Ru 1:17
2:24 d 2Sa 7:11 1Ch 22:10
2:25 e 2Sa 8:18
2:26 f 1Sa 22:20 g Jos 21:18 h 2Sa 15:24 i 1Sa 23:6
2:27 j 1Sa 2:27-36
2:28 k 1Ki 1:7,50
2:29 l ver 25
2:30 m Ex 21:14
2:31 n Nu 35:33 Dt 19:13 Dt 21:8-9
2:32 o Jdg 9:57 Ps 7:16 p Jdg 9:24 q 2Sa 3:27 2Sa 20:10 r 2Ch 21:13

killed him, and he was buried on his own land[b] in the desert. 35The king put Benaiah[s] son of Jehoiada over the army in Joab's position and replaced Abiathar with Zadok[t] the priest.

36Then the king sent for Shimei[u] and said to him, "Build yourself a house in Jerusalem and live there, but do not go anywhere else. 37The day you leave and cross the Kidron Valley,[v] you can be sure you will die; your blood will be on your own head."[w]

38Shimei answered the king, "What you say is good. Your servant will do as my lord the king has said." And Shimei stayed in Jerusalem for a long time.

39But three years later, two of Shimei's slaves ran off to Achish[x] son of Maacah, king of Gath, and Shimei was told, "Your slaves are in Gath." 40At this, he saddled his donkey and went to Achish at Gath in search of his slaves. So Shimei went away and brought the slaves back from Gath.

41When Solomon was told that Shimei had gone from Jerusalem to Gath and had returned, 42the king summoned Shimei and said to him, "Did I not make you swear by the LORD and warn you, 'On the day you leave to go anywhere else, you can be sure you will die'? At that time you said to me, 'What you say is good. I will obey.' 43Why then did you not keep your oath to the LORD and obey the command I gave you?"

44The king also said to Shimei, "You know in your heart all the wrong[y] you did to my father David. Now the LORD will repay you for your wrongdoing. 45But King Solomon will be blessed, and David's throne will remain secure[z] before the LORD for ever."

46Then the king gave the order to Benaiah son of Jehoiada, and he went out and struck Shimei down and killed him.

The kingdom was now firmly established[a] in Solomon's hands.

Solomon Asks for Wisdom

3:4–15pp 2Ch 1:2–13

3 Solomon made an alliance with Pharaoh king of Egypt and married[a] his daughter.[b] He brought her to the City of David[c] until he finished building his palace[d] and the temple of the LORD, and the wall around Jerusalem. 2The people, however, were still sacrificing at the high places,[e] because a temple had not yet been built for the Name of the LORD. 3Solomon showed his love[f] for the LORD by walking according to the statutes[g] of his father David, except that he offered sacrifices and burned incense on the high places.

4The king went to Gibeon[h] to offer sacrifices, for that was the most important high place, and Solomon offered a thousand burnt offerings on that altar. 5At Gibeon the LORD appeared[i] to Solomon during the night in a dream,[j] and God said, "Ask for whatever you want me to give you."

6Solomon answered, "You have shown great kindness to your servant, my father David, because he was faithful[k] to you and righteous and upright in heart. You have continued this great kindness to him and have given him a son[l] to sit on his throne this very day.

7"Now, O LORD my God, you have made your servant king in place of my father David. But I am only a little child[m] and do not know how to carry out my duties. 8Your servant is here among the people you have chosen,[n] a great people, too numerous to count or number.[o] 9So give your servant a discerning[p] heart to govern your people and to distinguish[q] between right and wrong. For who is able[r] to govern this great people of yours?"

2:35 *s* 1Ki 4:4 *t* ver 27 1Ch 29:22
2:36 *u* ver 8 2Sa 16:5
2:37 *v* 2Sa 15:23 *w* Lev 20:9 Jos 2:19 2Sa 1:16
2:39 *x* 1Sa 27:2
2:44 *y* 1Sa 25:39 2Sa 16:5-13 Eze 17:19
2:45 *z* 2Sa 7:13 Pr 25:5
2:46 *a* ver 12 2Ch 1:1
3:1 *a* 1Ki 7:8 *b* 1Ki 9:24 *c* 2Sa 5:7 *d* 1Ki 7:1 1Ki 9:15,19
3:2 *e* Lev 17:3-5 Dt 12:2,4-5 1Ki 22:43
3:3 *f* Dt 6:5 Ps 31:23 1Co 8:3 *g* 1Ki 2:3 1Ki 9:4 1Ki 11:4,6,38
3:4 *h* 1Ch 16:39
3:5 *i* 1Ki 9:2 *j* Nu 12:6 Mt 1:20
3:6 *k* 1Ki 2:4 1Ki 9:4 *l* 1Ki 1:48
3:7 *m* Nu 27:17 1Ch 29:1
3:8 *n* Dt 7:6 *o* Ge 15:5
3:9 *p* 2Sa 14:17 Jas 1:5 *q* Pr 2:3-9 Heb 5:14 *r* Ps 72:1-2

b34 Or *buried in his tomb*

10 The Lord was pleased that Solomon had asked for this. 11 So God
said to him, "Since you have
asked[s] for this and not for long life
or wealth for yourself, nor have
asked for the death of your enemies but for discernment in administering justice, 12 I will do what you
have asked.[t] I will give you a
wise[u] and discerning heart, so that
there will never have been anyone
like you, nor will there ever be.
13 Moreover, I will give you what
you have not[v] asked for—both
riches and honour[w]—so that in
your lifetime you will have no
equal[x] among kings. 14 And if you
walk[y] in my ways and obey my
statutes and commands as David
your father did, I will give you a
long life."[z] 15 Then Solomon
awoke[a]—and he realised it had
been a dream.

He returned to Jerusalem, stood
before the ark of the Lord's covenant and sacrificed burnt offerings[b] and fellowship offerings.[a][c]
Then he gave a feast[d] for all his
court.

A Wise Ruling

16 Now two prostitutes came to
the king and stood before him.
17 One of them said, "My lord, this
woman and I live in the same
house. I had a baby while she was
there with me. 18 The third day after
my child was born, this woman also
had a baby. We were alone; there
was no-one in the house but the two
of us.

19 "During the night this woman's
son died because she lay on him.
20 So she got up in the middle of the
night and took my son from my side
while I your servant was asleep.
She put him by her breast and put
her dead son by my breast. 21 The
next morning, I got up to nurse my
son—and he was dead! But when I
looked at him closely in the morning light, I saw that it wasn't the son
I had borne."

22 The other woman said, "No!
The living one is my son; the dead
one is yours."

But the first one insisted, "No!
The dead one is yours; the living
one is mine." And so they argued
before the king.

23 The king said, "This one says,
'My son is alive and your son is
dead,' while that one says, 'No!
Your son is dead and mine is
alive.' "

24 Then the king said, "Bring me a
sword." So they brought a sword
for the king. 25 He then gave an order: "Cut the living child in two and
give half to one and half to the
other."

26 The woman whose son was
alive was filled with compassion[e]
for her son and said to the king,
"Please, my lord, give her the living baby! Don't kill him!"

But the other said, "Neither I nor
you shall have him. Cut him in
two!"

27 Then the king gave his ruling:
"Give the living baby to the first
woman. Do not kill him; she is his
mother."

28 When all Israel heard the verdict the king had given, they held
the king in awe, because they saw
that he had wisdom[f] from God to
administer justice.

Solomon's Officials and Governors

4 So King Solomon ruled over all
Israel. 2 And these were his
chief officials:

Azariah[a] son of Zadok—the
priest;
3 Elihoreph and Ahijah, sons of
Shisha—secretaries;
Jehoshaphat[b] son of Ahilud—
recorder;
4 Benaiah[c] son of Jehoiada—
commander-in-chief;
Zadok[d] and Abiathar—priests;

3:11 s Jas 4:3
3:12 t 1Jn 5:14-15 u 1Ki 4:29,30,31 1Ki 5:12 1Ki 10:23 Ecc 1:16
3:13 v Mt 6:33 Eph 3:20 w 1Ki 4:21-24 Pr 3:1-2,16 x 1Ki 10:23
3:14 y ver 6 Pr 3:1-2,16 z Ps 61:6 Ps 91:16
3:15 a Ge 41:7 b 1Ki 8:65 c Mk 6:21 d Est 1:3,9 Da 5:1
3:26 e Ge 43:30 Isa 49:15 Jer 31:20 Hos 11:8
3:28 f ver 9,11-12 Col 2:3
4:2 a 1Ch 6:10
4:3 b 2Sa 8:16
4:4 c 1Ki 2:35 d 1Ki 2:27

a15 Traditionally *peace offerings*

5 Azariah son of Nathan—in charge of the district officers;
Zabud son of Nathan—a priest and personal adviser to the king;
6 Ahishar—in charge of the palace;
Adoniram son of Abda—in charge of forced labour.

7 Solomon also had twelve district
governors over all Israel, who supplied provisions for the king and
the royal household. Each one had
to provide supplies for one month
in the year. 8 These are their names:

Ben-Hur—in the hill country[e] of Ephraim;
9 Ben-Deker—in Makaz, Shaalbim,[f] Beth Shemesh[g] and Elon Bethhanan;
10 Ben-Hesed—in Arubboth (Socoh[h] and all the land of Hepher[i] were his);
11 Ben-Abinadab—in Naphoth Dor[a][j] (he was married to Taphath daughter of Solomon);
12 Baana son of Ahilud—in Taanach and Megiddo, and in all of Beth Shan[k] next to Zarethan[l] below Jezreel, from Beth Shan to Abel Meholah[m] across to Jokmeam;[n]
13 Ben-Geber—in Ramoth Gilead (the settlements of Jair[o] son of Manasseh in Gilead were his, as well as the district of Argob in Bashan and its sixty large walled cities[p] with bronze gate bars);
14 Ahinadab son of Iddo—in Mahanaim;[q]
15 Ahimaaz[r]—in Naphtali (he had married Basemath daughter of Solomon);
16 Baana son of Hushai[s]—in Asher and in Aloth;
17 Jehoshaphat son of Paruah—in Issachar;
18 Shimei[t] son of Ela—in Benjamin;
19 Geber son of Uri—in Gilead (the country of Sihon king of the Amorites and the country of Og[u] king of Bashan). He was the only governor over the district.

Solomon's Daily Provisions

20 The people of Judah and Israel
were as numerous as the sand[v] on
the seashore; they ate, they drank
and they were happy. 21 And Solomon ruled[w] over all the kingdoms
from the River[b][x] to the land of the
Philistines, as far as the border of
Egypt.[y] These countries brought
tribute[z] and were Solomon's subjects all his life.
22 Solomon's daily provisions
were thirty cors[c] of fine flour and
sixty cors[d] of meal, 23 ten head of
stall-fed cattle, twenty of pasture-
fed cattle and a hundred sheep and
goats, as well as deer, gazelles,
roebucks and choice fowl. 24 For
he ruled over all the kingdoms
west of the River, from Tiphsah[a]
to Gaza, and had peace[b] on all
sides. 25 During Solomon's lifetime
Judah and Israel, from Dan to
Beersheba,[c] lived in safety,[d] each
man under his own vine and fig-
tree.[e]
26 Solomon had four[e] thousand
stalls for chariot horses,[f] and
twelve thousand horses.[f]
27 The district officers,[g] each in
his month, supplied provisions for
King Solomon and all who came to
the king's table. They saw to it that
nothing was lacking. 28 They also
brought to the proper place their
quotas of barley and straw for the
chariot horses and the other
horses.

4:8 *e* Jos 24:33
4:9 *f* Jdg 1:35 *g* Jos 21:16
4:10 *h* Jos 15:35 *i* Jos 12:17
4:11 *j* Jos 11:2
4:12 *k* Jos 17:11 Jdg 5:19 *l* Jos 3:16 *m* 1Ki 19:16 *n* 1Ch 6:68
4:13 *o* Nu 32:41 *p* Dt 3:4
4:14 *q* Jos 13:26
4:15 *r* 2Sa 15:27
4:16 *s* 2Sa 15:32
4:18 *t* 1Ki 1:8
4:19 *u* Dt 3:8-10
4:20 *v* Ge 22:17 Ge 32:12 1Ki 3:8
4:21 *w* 2Ch 9:26 Ps 72:11 *x* Jos 1:4 Ps 72:8 *y* Ge 15:18 *z* Ps 68:29
4:24 *a* Ps 72:11 *b* 1Ch 22:9
4:25 *c* Jdg 20:1 *d* Jer 23:6 *e* Mic 4:4 Zec 3:10
4:26 *f* 1Ki 10:26 2Ch 1:14
4:27 *g* ver 7

a *11* Or *in the heights of Dor* b *21* That is, the Euphrates; also in verse 24 c *22* That is, probably about 180 bushels (about 6.6 kilolitres) d *22* That is, probably about 365 bushels (about 13.2 kilolitres) e *26* Some Septuagint manuscripts (see also 2 Chron. 9:25); Hebrew *forty* f *26* Or *charioteers*

Solomon's Wisdom

29 God gave Solomon wisdom[h]
and very great insight, and a
breadth of understanding as measureless as the sand on the seashore.
30 Solomon's wisdom was greater
than the wisdom of all the men
of the East,[i] and greater than all
the wisdom of Egypt.[j] 31 He was
wiser[k] than any other man, including Ethan the Ezrahite—wiser than
Heman, Calcol and Darda, the sons
of Mahol. And his fame spread to
all the surrounding nations. 32 He
spoke three thousand proverbs[l]
and his songs[m] numbered a thousand and five. 33 He described plant
life, from the cedar of Lebanon to
the hyssop that grows out of walls.
He also taught about animals and
birds, reptiles and fish. 34 Men of all
nations came to listen to Solomon's
wisdom, sent by all the kings[n] of
the world, who had heard of his
wisdom.

Preparations for Building the Temple

5:1–16pp 2Ch 2:1–18

5 When Hiram[a] king of Tyre
heard that Solomon had been
anointed king to succeed his father
David, he sent his envoys to Solomon, because he had always been
on friendly terms with David.
2 Solomon sent back this message to
Hiram:

3 "You know that because of
the wars[b] waged against my
father David from all sides, he
could not build a temple for the
Name of the LORD his God until
the LORD put his enemies under his feet. 4 But now the LORD
my God has given me rest[c] on
every side, and there is no adversary or disaster. 5 I intend,
therefore, to build a temple[d]
for the Name of the LORD my
God, as the LORD told my
father David, when he said,
'Your son whom I will put on
the throne in your place will
build the temple for my
Name.'[e]
6 "So give orders that cedars
of Lebanon be cut for me. My
men will work with yours, and
I will pay you for your men
whatever wages you set. You
know that we have no-one so
skilled in felling timber as the
Sidonians."

7 When Hiram heard Solomon's
message, he was greatly pleased
and said, "Praise be to the LORD today, for he has given David a wise
son to rule over this great nation."
8 So Hiram sent word to Solomon:

"I have received the mes-
sage you sent me and will do all
you want in providing the cedar and pine logs. 9 My men will
haul them down from Lebanon
to the sea[f], and I will float
them in rafts by sea to the
place you specify. There I will
separate them and you can
take them away. And you are to
grant my wish by providing
food[g] for my royal household."

10 In this way Hiram kept Solomon supplied with all the cedar
and pine logs he wanted, 11 and Solomon gave Hiram twenty thousand
cors[a] of wheat as food for his
household, in addition to twenty
thousand baths[b,c] of pressed olive
oil. Solomon continued to do this
for Hiram year after year. 12 The
LORD gave Solomon wisdom,[h] just
as he had promised him. There
were peaceful relations between
Hiram and Solomon, and the two of
them made a treaty.[i]
13 King Solomon conscripted
labourers[j] from all Israel—thirty
thousand men. 14 He sent them off
to Lebanon in shifts of ten thousand

4:29 h 1Ki 3:12
4:30 i Ge 25:6; j Ac 7:22
4:31 k 1Ki 3:12; 1Ch 2:6; 1Ch 6:33; 1Ch 15:19; Ps 89 Title
4:32 l Pr 1:1; Ecc 12:9; m SS 1:1
4:34 n 1Ki 10:1; 2Ch 9:23
5:1 a ver 10,18; 2Sa 5:11; 1Ch 14:1
5:3 b 1Ch 22:8; 1Ch 28:3
5:4 c 1Ki 4:24; 1Ch 22:9
5:5 d 1Ch 17:12; e 2Sa 7:13; 1Ch 22:10
5:9 f Ezr 3:7; g Eze 27:17; Ac 12:20
5:12 h 1Ki 3:12; i Am 1:9
5:13 j 1Ki 9:15

a *11* That is, probably about 121,000 bushels (about 4,400 kilolitres) b *11* Septuagint (see also 2 Chron. 2:10); Hebrew *twenty cors* c *11* That is, about 97,000 gallons (about 440 kilolitres) a month, so that they spent one month in Lebanon and two months at home. Adoniram[k] was in charge of the forced labour. 15 Solomon had seventy thousand carriers and eighty thousand stonecutters in the hills, 16 as well as thirty-three hundred[d] foremen[l] who supervised the project and directed the workmen. 17 At the king's command they removed from the quarry[m] large blocks of quality stone[n] to provide a foundation of dressed stone for the temple. 18 The craftsmen of Solomon and Hiram and the men of Gebal[e][o] cut and prepared the timber and stone for the building of the temple.

Solomon Builds the Temple

6:1–29pp 2Ch 3:1–14

6 In the four hundred and eightieth[a] year after the Israelites had come out of Egypt, in the fourth year of Solomon's reign over Israel, in the month of Ziv, the second month, he began to build the temple of the LORD.[a]

2 The temple[b] that King Solomon built for the LORD was sixty cubits long, twenty wide and thirty high.[b] 3 The portico at the front of the main hall of the temple extended the width of the temple, that is twenty cubits,[c] and projected ten cubits[d] from the front of the temple. 4 He made narrow clerestory windows[c] in the temple. 5 Against the walls of the main hall and inner sanctuary he built a structure around the building, in which there were side rooms.[d] 6 The lowest floor was five cubits[e] wide, the middle floor six cubits[f] and the third floor seven.[g] He made offset ledges around the outside of the temple so that nothing would be inserted into the temple walls.

7 In building the temple, only blocks dressed[e] at the quarry were used, and no hammer, chisel or any other iron tool[f] was heard at the temple site while it was being built.

8 The entrance to the lowest[h] floor was on the south side of the temple; a stairway led up to the middle level and from there to the third. 9 So he built the temple and completed it, roofing it with beams and cedar[g] planks. 10 And he built the side rooms all along the temple. The height of each was five cubits, and they were attached to the temple by beams of cedar.

11 The word of the LORD came to Solomon: 12 "As for this temple you are building, if you follow my decrees, carry out my regulations and keep all my commands and obey them, I will fulfil through you the promise[h] I gave to David your father. 13 And I will live among the Israelites and will not abandon[i] my people Israel."

14 So Solomon built the temple and completed[j] it. 15 He lined its interior walls with cedar boards, panelling them from the floor of the temple to the ceiling,[k] and covered the floor of the temple with planks of pine. 16 He partitioned off twenty cubits[i] at the rear of the temple with cedar boards from floor to ceiling to form within the temple an inner sanctuary, the Most Holy Place.[l] 17 The main hall in front of this room was forty cubits[j] long. 18 The inside of the temple was cedar,[m] carved with gourds and open flowers. Everything was cedar; no stone was to be seen.

19 He prepared the inner sanctuary[n] within the temple to set the

5:14 *k* 1Ki 4:6; 2Ch 10:18
5:16 *l* 1Ki 9:23
5:17 *m* 1Ki 6:7; *n* 1Ch 22:2
5:18 *o* Jos 13:5
6:1 *a* Ac 7:47
6:2 *b* Eze 41:1
6:4 *c* Eze 40:16; Eze 41:16
6:5 *d* ver 16,19-21; Eze 41:5-6
6:7 *e* Ex 20:25; *f* Dt 27:5
6:9 *g* ver 14,38
6:12 *h* 2Sa 7:12-16; 1Ki 2:4; 1Ki 9:5
6:13 *i* Ex 25:8; Lev 26:11; Dt 31:6; Heb 13:5
6:14 *j* ver 9,38
6:15 *k* 1Ki 7:7
6:16 *l* Ex 26:33; Lev 16:2; 1Ki 8:6
6:18 *m* 1Ki 7:24; Ps 74:6
6:19 *n* 1Ki 8:6

d *16* Hebrew; some Septuagint manuscripts (see also 2 Chron. 2:2, 18) *thirty-six hundred*
e *18* That is, Byblos
a *1* Hebrew; Septuagint *four hundred and fortieth*
b *2* That is, about 90 feet (about 27 metres) long and 30 feet (about 9 metres) wide and 45 feet (about 13.5 metres) high
c *3* That is, about 30 feet (about 9 metres)
d *3* That is, about 15 feet (about 4.5 metres)
e *6* That is, about 7½ feet (about 2.3 metres); also in verses 10 and 24
f *6* That is, about 9 feet (about 2.7 metres)
g *6* That is, about 10½ feet (about 3.2 metres)
h *8* Septuagint; Hebrew *middle*
i *16* That is, about 30 feet (about 9 metres)
j *17* That is, about 60 feet (about 18 metres)

ark of the covenant[o] of the LORD
there. 20The inner sanctuary[p] was
twenty cubits long, twenty wide
and twenty high.[k] He overlaid the
inside with pure gold, and he also
overlaid the altar of cedar. 21Solo-
mon covered the inside of the temple with pure gold, and he extended
gold chains across the front of the
inner sanctuary, which was overlaid with gold. 22So he overlaid the
whole interior with gold. He also
overlaid with gold the altar that belonged to the inner sanctuary.
23In the inner sanctuary he made
a pair of cherubim[q] of olive wood,
each ten cubits[l] high. 24One wing
of the first cherub was five cubits
long, and the other wing five cubits—ten cubits from wing tip to
wing tip. 25The second cherub also
measured ten cubits, for the two
cherubim were identical in size and
shape. 26The height of each cherub
was ten cubits. 27He placed the
cherubim[r] inside the innermost
room of the temple, with their
wings spread out. The wing of one
cherub touched one wall, while the
wing of the other touched the other
wall, and their wings touched each
other in the middle of the room.
28He overlaid the cherubim with
gold.
29On the walls all round the temple, in both the inner and outer
rooms, he carved cherubim,[s] palm
trees and open flowers. 30He also
covered the floors of both the inner
and outer rooms of the temple with
gold.
31For the entrance of the inner
sanctuary he made doors of olive
wood with five-sided jambs. 32And
on the two olive wood doors he
carved cherubim, palm trees and
open flowers, and overlaid the
cherubim and palm trees with
beaten gold. 33In the same way he
made four-sided jambs of olive
wood for the entrance to the main
hall. 34He also made two pine doors,
each having two leaves that turned
in sockets. 35He carved cherubim,
palm trees and open flowers on
them and overlaid them with gold
hammered evenly over the carv-
ings.
36And he built the inner courtyard of three courses[t] of dressed
stone and one course of trimmed
cedar beams.
37The foundation of the temple of
the LORD was laid in the fourth
year, in the month of Ziv. 38In the
eleventh year in the month of Bul,
the eighth month, the temple was
finished in all its details according
to its specifications.[u] He had spent
seven years building it.

Solomon Builds His Palace

7 It took Solomon thirteen
years, however, to complete
the construction of his palace.[a]
2He built the Palace[b] of the Forest
of Lebanon[c] a hundred cubits long,
fifty wide and thirty high,[a] with
four rows of cedar columns supporting trimmed cedar beams. 3It
was roofed with cedar above the
beams that rested on the columns—forty-five beams, fifteen to
a row. 4Its windows were placed
high in sets of three, facing each
other. 5All the doorways had rectangular frames; they were in the
front part in sets of three, facing
each other.[b]
6He made a colonnade fifty cubits long and thirty wide.[c] In front
of it was a portico, and in front of
that were pillars and an overhanging roof.
7He built the throne hall, the Hall
of Justice, where he was to judge,[d]
and he covered it with cedar
from floor to ceiling.[d][e] 8And the palace in which he was to live, set farther back, was similar in design.

6:19 o 1Sa 3:3
6:20 p Eze 41:3-4
6:23 q Ex 37:1-9
6:27 r Ex 25:20; Ex 37:9; 1Ki 8:7; 2Ch 5:8
6:29 s ver 32,35
6:36 t 1Ki 7:12; Ezr 6:4
6:38 u Heb 8:5
7:1 a 1Ki 9:10; 2Ch 8:1
7:2 b 2Sa 7:2; c 1Ki 10:17; 2Ch 9:16
7:7 d Ps 122:5; Pr 20:8; e 1Ki 6:15

k20 That is, about 30 feet (about 9 metres) long, wide and high l23 That is, about 15 feet (about 4.5 metres) a2 That is, about 150 feet (about 46 metres) long, 75 feet (about 23 metres) wide and 45 feet (about 13.5 metres) high
b5 The meaning of the Hebrew for this verse is uncertain. c6 That is, about 75 feet (about 23 metres) long and 45 feet (about 13.5 metres) wide d7 Vulgate and Syriac; Hebrew *floor*

Solomon also made a palace like this hall for Pharaoh's daughter, whom he had married.[f]

9 All these structures, from the outside to the great courtyard and from foundation to eaves, were made of blocks of high-grade stone cut to size and trimmed with a saw on their inner and outer faces. 10 The foundations were laid with large stones of good quality, some measuring ten cubits[e] and some eight.[f] 11 Above were high-grade stones, cut to size, and cedar beams. 12 The great courtyard was surrounded by a wall of three courses[g] of dressed stone and one course of trimmed cedar beams, as was the inner courtyard of the temple of the LORD with its portico.

The Temple's Furnishings

7:23–26pp 2Ch 4:2–5
7:38–51pp 2Ch 4:6,10–5:1

13 King Solomon sent to Tyre and brought Huram,[g][h] 14 whose mother was a widow from the tribe of Naphtali and whose father was a man of Tyre and a craftsman in bronze. Huram was highly skilled[i] and experienced in all kinds of bronze work. He came to King Solomon and did all[j] the work assigned to him.

15 He cast two bronze pillars,[k] each eighteen cubits high and twelve cubits round,[h] by line. 16 He also made two capitals[l] of cast bronze to set on the tops of the pillars; each capital was five cubits[i] high. 17 A network of interwoven chains festooned the capitals on top of the pillars, seven for each capital. 18 He made pomegranates in two rows[j] encircling each network to decorate the capitals on top of the pillars.[k] He did the same for each capital. 19 The capitals on top of the pillars in the portico were in the shape of lilies, four cubits[l] high. 20 On the capitals of both pillars, above the bowl-shaped part next to the network, were the two hundred pomegranates[m] in rows all around. 21 He erected the pillars at the portico of the temple. The pillar to the south he named Jakin[m] and the one to the north Boaz.[n][n] 22 The capitals on top were in the shape of lilies. And so the work on the pillars was completed.

23 He made the Sea[o] of cast metal, circular in shape, measuring ten cubits[o] from rim to rim and five cubits high. It took a line of thirty cubits[p] to measure round it. 24 Below the rim, gourds encircled it—ten to a cubit. The gourds were cast in two rows in one piece with the Sea.

25 The Sea stood on twelve bulls,[p] three facing north, three facing west, three facing south and three facing east. The Sea rested on top of them, and their hindquarters were towards the centre. 26 It was a handbreadth[q] in thickness, and its rim was like the rim of a cup, like a lily blossom. It held two thousand baths.[r]

27 He also made ten movable stands[q] of bronze; each was four cubits long, four wide and three high.[s] 28 This is how the stands were made: They had side panels attached to uprights. 29 On the panels between the uprights were lions, bulls and cherubim—and on the uprights as well. Above and below the lions and bulls were

7:8 *f* 1Ki 3:1; 2Ch 8:11
7:12 *g* 1Ki 6:36
7:13 *h* 2Ch 2:13
7:14 *i* Ex 31:2-5; Ex 35:31; Ex 36:1; 2Ch 2:14 *j* 2Ch 4:11,16
7:15 *k* 2Ki 25:17; 2Ch 3:15; 2Ch 4:12; 2Ch 52:17,21
7:16 *l* 2Ki 25:17
7:20 *m* 2Ch 3:16; 2Ch 4:13; Jer 52:23
7:21 *n* 1Ki 6:3; 2Ch 3:17
7:23 *o* 2Ki 25:13; 1Ch 18:8; Jer 52:17
7:25 *p* 2Ch 4:4-5; Jer 52:20
7:27 *q* ver 38; 2Ch 4:14

[e] *10* That is, about 15 feet (about 4.5 metres)
[f] *10* That is, about 12 feet (about 3.7 metres)
[g] *13* Hebrew *Hiram*, a variant of *Huram*; also in verses 40 and 45
[h] *15* That is, about 27 feet (about 8.2 metres) high and 18 feet (about 5.5 metres) round
[i] *16* That is, about 7½ feet (about 2.3 metres); also in verse 23
[j] *18* Two Hebrew manuscripts and Septuagint; most Hebrew manuscripts *made the pillars, and there were two rows*
[k] *18* Many Hebrew manuscripts and Syriac; most Hebrew manuscripts *pomegranates*
[l] *19* That is, about 6 feet (about 1.8 metres); also in verse 38
[m] *21* *Jakin* probably means *he establishes.*
[n] *21* *Boaz* probably means *in him is strength.*
[o] *23* That is, about 15 feet (about 4.5 metres)
[p] *23* That is, about 45 feet (about 13.7 metres)
[q] *26* That is, about 3 inches (about 8 centimetres)
[r] *26* That is, probably about 9,700 gallons (about 44 kilolitres); the Septuagint does not have this sentence.
[s] *27* That is, about 6 feet (about 1.8 metres) long and wide and about 4½ feet (about 1.4 metres) high

wreaths of hammered work. 30 Each
stand[r] had four bronze wheels
with bronze axles, and each had a
basin resting on four supports, cast
with wreaths on each side. 31 On the
inside of the stand there was an
opening that had a circular frame
one cubit[t] deep. This opening was
round, and with its basework it
measured a cubit and a half.[u]
Around its opening there was engraving. The panels of the stands
were square, not round. 32 The four
wheels were under the panels, and
the axles of the wheels were attached to the stand. The diameter
of each wheel was a cubit and a
half. 33 The wheels were made like
chariot wheels; the axles, rims,
spokes and hubs were all of cast
metal.
34 Each stand had four handles,
one on each corner, projecting
from the stand. 35 At the top of the
stand there was a circular band
half a cubit[v] deep. The supports
and panels were attached to the top
of the stand. 36 He engraved cherubim, lions and palm trees on the
surfaces of the supports and on the
panels, in every available space,
with wreaths all around. 37 This is
the way he made the ten stands.
They were all cast in the same
moulds and were identical in size
and shape.
38 He then made ten bronze
basins,[s] each holding forty baths[w]
and measuring four cubits across,
one basin to go on each of the ten
stands. 39 He placed five of the
stands on the south side of the temple and five on the north. He placed
the Sea on the south side, at the
south-east corner of the temple.
40 He also made the basins and shovels and sprinkling bowls.
So Huram finished all the work
he had undertaken for King Solomon in the temple of the LORD:

41 the two pillars;
the two bowl-shaped capitals
on top of the pillars;
the two sets of network decorating the two bowl-shaped
capitals on top of the pillars;
42 the four hundred pomegranates for the two sets of
network (two rows of
pomegranates for each network, decorating the bowl-
shaped capitals[t] on top of
the pillars);
43 the ten stands with their ten
basins;
44 the Sea and the twelve bulls
under it;
45 the pots, shovels and sprinkling bowls.[u]

All these objects that Huram
made for King Solomon for the
temple of the LORD were of burnished bronze. 46 The king had them
cast in clay moulds in the plain[v] of
the Jordan between Succoth[w] and
Zarethan.[x] 47 Solomon left all these
things unweighed,[y] because there
were so many; the weight of the
bronze was not determined.
48 Solomon also made all the furnishings that were in the LORD's
temple:

the golden altar;
the golden table[z] on which
was the bread of the Presence;[a]
49 the lampstands[b] of pure gold
(five on the right and five on
the left, in front of the inner
sanctuary);
the gold floral work and lamps
and tongs;
50 the pure gold dishes, wick
trimmers, sprinkling bowls,
dishes and censers;[c]
and the gold sockets for the
doors of the innermost
room, the Most Holy Place,
and also for the doors of the
main hall of the temple.

7:30 r 2Ki 16:17
7:38 s Ex 30:18; 2Ch 4:6
7:42 t ver 20
7:45 u Ex 27:3
7:46 v 2Ch 4:17; w Ge 33:17; Jos 13:27; x Jos 3:16
7:47 y 1Ch 22:3
7:48 z Ex 37:10; a Ex 25:30
7:49 b Ex 25:31-38
7:50 c 2Ki 25:13

t *31* That is, about 1½ feet (about 0.5 metre)
u *31* That is, about 2¼ feet (about 0.7 metre); also in verse 32
v *35* That is, about ¾ foot (about 0.2 metre)
w *38* That is, about 195 gallons (about 880 litres)

51When all the work King Solomon had done for the temple of the
LORD was finished, he brought in
the things his father David had
dedicated[d]—the silver and gold
and the furnishings—and he placed
them in the treasuries of the LORD's
temple.

The Ark Brought to the Temple

8:1–21pp 2Ch 5:2–6:11

8 Then King Solomon summoned into his presence at
Jerusalem the elders of Israel, all
the heads of the tribes and the
chiefs[a] of the Israelite families, to
bring up the ark[b] of the LORD's
covenant from Zion, the City of
David.[c] 2All the men of Israel
came together to King Solomon at
the time of the festival[d] in the
month of Ethanim, the seventh
month.[e]
3When all the elders of Israel had
arrived, the priests[f] took up the
ark, 4and they brought up the ark of
the LORD and the Tent of Meeting[g]
and all the sacred furnishings in it.
The priests and Levites carried
them up, 5and King Solomon and
the entire assembly of Israel that
had gathered about him were before the ark, sacrificing[h] so many
sheep and cattle that they could not
be recorded or counted.
6The priests then brought the ark
of the LORD's covenant[i] to its place
in the inner sanctuary of the temple, the Most Holy Place, and put it
beneath the wings of the cherubim.[j] 7The cherubim spread their
wings over the place of the ark and
overshadowed the ark and its
carrying poles. 8These poles were
so long that their ends could be
seen from the Holy Place in front
of the inner sanctuary, but not
from outside the Holy Place; and
they are still there today.[k] 9There
was nothing in the ark except the
two stone tablets[l] that Moses had
placed in it at Horeb, where the
LORD made a covenant with the
Israelites after they came out of
Egypt.
10When the priests withdrew
from the Holy Place, the cloud[m]
filled the temple of the LORD. 11And
the priests could not perform
their service because of the cloud,
for the glory of the LORD filled his
temple.
12Then Solomon said, "The LORD
has said that he would dwell in a
dark cloud;[n] 13I have indeed built a
magnificent temple for you, a place
for you to dwell[o] for ever."
14While the whole assembly of Israel was standing there, the king
turned round and blessed[p] them.
15Then he said:

"Praise be to the LORD,[q] the
God of Israel, who with his own
hand has fulfilled what he
promised with his own mouth
to my father David. For he
said, 16'Since the day I brought
my people Israel out of Egypt,
I have not chosen a city in
any tribe of Israel to have a
temple built for my Name[r]
to be there, but I have chosen[s] David[t] to rule my people
Israel.'
17"My father David had it in
his heart to build a temple[u] for
the Name of the LORD, the God
of Israel. 18But the LORD said to
my father David, 'Because it
was in your heart to build a
temple for my Name, you did
well to have this in your heart.
19Nevertheless, you[v] are not
the one to build the temple, but
your son, who is your own flesh
and blood—he is the one who
will build the temple for my
Name.'[w]
20"The LORD has kept the
promise he made: I have succeeded David my father and
now I sit on the throne of Israel, just as the LORD promised, and I have built[x] the
temple for the Name of the

7:51 d 2Sa 8:11
8:1 a Nu 7:2; b 2Sa 6:17; c 2Sa 5:7
8:2 d 2Ch 7:8; e Lev 23:34
8:3 f Nu 7:9; Jos 3:3
8:4 g 1Ki 3:4; 2Ch 1:3
8:5 h 2Sa 6:13
8:6 i 2Sa 6:17; j 1Ki 6:19,27
8:8 k Ex 25:13-15
8:9 l Ex 24:7-8; Ex 25:21; Ex 40:20; Dt 10:2-5; Heb 9:4
8:10 m Ex 40:34-35; 2Ch 7:1-2
8:12 n Ps 18:11; Ps 97:2
8:13 o Ex 15:17; 2Sa 7:13; Ps 132:13
8:14 p 2Sa 6:18
8:15 q 2Sa 7:12-13; 1Ch 29:10, 20; Ne 9:5; Lk 1:68
8:16 r Dt 12:5; s 1Sa 16:1; t 2Sa 7:4-6,8
8:17 u 2Sa 7:2; 1Ch 17:1
8:19 v 2Sa 7:5; w 2Sa 7:13; 1Ki 5:3,5
8:20 x 1Ch 28:6

LORD, the God of Israel. 21I
have provided a place there for
the ark, in which is the covenant of the LORD that he made
with our fathers when he
brought them out of Egypt."

Solomon's Prayer of Dedication

8:22–53pp 2Ch 6:12-40

22Then Solomon stood before the
altar of the LORD in front of the
whole assembly of Israel, spread
out his hands[y] towards heaven
23and said:

"O LORD, God of Israel, there
is no God like[z] you in heaven
above or on earth below—you
who keep your covenant of
love[a] with your servants who
continue wholeheartedly in
your way. 24You have kept your
promise to your servant David
my father; with your mouth
you have promised and with
your hand you have fulfilled
it—as it is today.

25"Now LORD, God of Israel,
keep for your servant David
my father the promises[b] you
made to him when you said,
'You shall never fail to have a
man to sit before me on the
throne of Israel, if only your
sons are careful in all they do
to walk before me as you have
done.' 26And now, O God of Israel, let your word that you
promised[c] your servant David
my father come true.

27"But will God really dwell[d]
on earth? The heavens, even
the highest heaven, cannot
contain[e] you. How much less
this temple I have built! 28Yet
give attention to your servant's
prayer and his plea for mercy,
O LORD my God. Hear the cry
and the prayer that your servant is praying in your presence this day. 29May your eyes
be open[f] towards[g] this temple night and day, this place of
which you said, 'My Name[h]
shall be there,' so that you will
hear the prayer your servant
prays towards this place.
30Hear the supplication of your
servant and of your people Israel when they pray towards
this place. Hear from heaven,
your dwelling-place, and when
you hear, forgive.[i]

31"When a man wrongs his
neighbour and is required to
take an oath and he comes and
swears the oath[j] before your
altar in this temple, 32then hear
from heaven and act. Judge
between your servants, condemning the guilty and bringing down on his own head what
he has done. Declare the innocent not guilty, and so establish
his innocence.[k]

33"When your people Israel
have been defeated[l] by an
enemy because they have
sinned[m] against you, and when
they turn back to you and confess your name, praying and
making supplication to you in
this temple, 34then hear from
heaven and forgive the sin of
your people Israel and bring
them back to the land you gave
to their fathers.

35"When the heavens are
shut up and there is no rain[n]
because your people have
sinned against you, and when
they pray towards this place
and confess your name and
turn from their sin because
you have afflicted them, 36then
hear from heaven and forgive
the sin of your servants, your
people Israel. Teach[o] them the
right way[p] to live, and send
rain on the land you gave your
people for an inheritance.

37"When famine[q] or plague
comes to the land, or blight[r]
or mildew, locusts or grasshoppers, or when an enemy be-
sieges them in any of their
cities, whatever disaster or
disease may come, 38and when

8:22
y Ex 9:29; Ezr 9:5

8:23
z 1Sa 2:2; 2Sa 7:22
a Dt 7:9,12; Ne 1:5; Ne 9:32; Da 9:4

8:25
b 1Ki 2:4

8:26
c 2Sa 7:25

8:27
d Ac 7:48
e 2Ch 2:6; Ps 139:7-16; Isa 66:1; Jer 23:24

8:29
f 2Ch 7:15; Ne 1:6
g Da 6:10
h Dt 12:11

8:30
i Ps 85:2

8:31
j Ex 22:11

8:32
k Dt 25:1

8:33
l Lev 26:17; Dt 28:25
m Lev 26:39

8:35
n Lev 26:19; Dt 28:24

8:36
o 1Sa 12:23; Ps 25:4; Ps 94:12
p Ps 5:8; Ps 27:11; Jer 6:16

8:37
q Lev 26:26
r Dt 28:22

a prayer or plea is made by any
of your people Israel—each
one aware of the afflictions of
his own heart, and spreading
out his hands towards this temple—39 then hear from heaven,
your dwelling-place. Forgive
and act; deal with each man according to all he does, since
you know[s] his heart (for you
alone know the hearts of all
men), 40 so that they will fear[t]
you all the time they live in the
land you gave our fathers.
41 "As for the foreigner who
does not belong to your people
Israel but has come from a distant land because of your
name—42 for men will hear of
your great name and your
mighty hand[u] and your outstretched arm—when he
comes and prays towards this
temple, 43 then hear from
heaven, your dwelling-place,
and do whatever the foreigner
asks of you, so that all the peoples of the earth may know[v]
your name and fear[w] you, as do
your own people Israel, and
may know that this house I
have built bears your Name.
44 "When your people go to
war against their enemies,
wherever you send them, and
when they pray to the LORD towards the city you have chosen
and the temple I have built for
your Name, 45 then hear from
heaven their prayer and their
plea, and uphold their cause.
46 "When they sin against
you—for there is no-one who
does not sin[x]—and you become angry with them and give
them over to the enemy, who
takes them captive[y] to his own
land, far away or near; 47 and if
they have a change of heart in
the land where they are held
captive, and repent and plead[z]
with you in the land of their
conquerors and say, 'We have
sinned, we have done wrong,
we have acted wickedly';[a]
48 and if they turn back to you
with all their heart[b] and soul
in the land of their enemies
who took them captive, and
pray[c] to you towards the land
you gave their fathers, towards the city you have chosen
and the temple[d] I have built
for your Name; 49 then from
heaven, your dwelling-place,
hear their prayer and their
plea, and uphold their cause.
50 And forgive your people, who
have sinned against you; forgive all the offences they have
committed against you, and
cause their conquerors to show
them mercy;[e] 51 for they are
your people and your inheritance,[f] whom you brought out
of Egypt, out of that iron-
smelting furnace.[g]
52 "May your eyes be open to
your servant's plea and to the
plea of your people Israel, and
may you listen to them whenever they cry out to you. 53 For
you singled them out from all
the nations of the world to be
your own inheritance,[h] just as
you declared through your servant Moses when you, O Sovereign LORD, brought our fathers
out of Egypt."

54 When Solomon had finished all
these prayers and supplications to
the LORD, he rose from before the
altar of the LORD, where he had
been kneeling with his hands
spread out towards heaven. 55 He
stood and blessed[i] the whole assembly of Israel in a loud voice,
saying:

56 "Praise be to the LORD, who
has given rest[j] to his people
Israel just as he promised.
Not one word has failed of all
the good promises[k] he gave
through his servant Moses.
57 May the LORD our God be
with us as he was with our fathers; may he never leave us

8:39 s 1Sa 16:7; 1Ch 28:9; Ps 11:4; Jer 17:10; Jn 2:24; Ac 1:24
8:40 t Ps 130:4
8:42 u Dt 3:24
8:43 v 1Sa 17:46; 2Ki 19:19; w Ps 102:15
8:46 x Pr 20:9; Ecc 7:20; Ro 3:9; 1Jn 1:8-10; y Lev 26:33-39; Dt 28:64
8:47 z Lev 26:40; Ne 1:6; a Ps 106:6; Da 9:5
8:48 b Dt 4:29; Jer 29:12-14; c Da 6:10; d Jnh 2:4
8:50 e 2Ch 30:9; Ps 106:46
8:51 f Dt 4:20; Dt 9:29; Ne 1:10; g Jer 11:4
8:53 h Ex 19:5; Dt 9:26-29
8:55 i ver 14; 2Sa 6:18
8:56 j Dt 12:10; k Jos 21:45; Jos 23:15

nor forsake[l] us. 58May he turn
our hearts[m] to him, to walk in
all his ways and to keep the
commands, decrees and regulations he gave our fathers.
59And may these words of
mine, which I have prayed before the LORD, be near to the
LORD our God day and night,
that he may uphold the cause of
his servant and the cause of his
people Israel according to each
day's need, 60so that all the peoples[n] of the earth may know
that the LORD is God and that
there is no other.[o] 61But your
hearts must be fully committed[p] to the LORD our God, to
live by his decrees and obey his
commands, as at this time."

The Dedication of the Temple

8:62–66pp 2Ch 7:1–10

62Then the king and all Israel
with him offered sacrifices before
the LORD. 63Solomon offered a sacrifice of fellowship offerings[a] to
the LORD: twenty-two thousand
cattle and a hundred and twenty
thousand sheep and goats. So the
king and all the Israelites dedicated
the temple of the LORD.
64On that same day the king consecrated the middle part of the
courtyard in front of the temple of
the LORD, and there he offered
burnt offerings, grain offerings
and the fat of the fellowship offerings, because the bronze altar[q]
before the LORD was too small to
hold the burnt offerings, the grain
offerings and the fat of the
fellowship offerings.
65So Solomon observed the festival[r] at that time, and all Israel
with him—a vast assembly, people
from Lebo[b] Hamath[s] to the Wadi
of Egypt.[t] They celebrated it before the LORD our God for seven
days and seven days more, fourteen days in all. 66On the following
day he sent the people away. They
blessed the king and then went

8:57 *l* Dt 31:6; Jos 1:5; Heb 13:5
8:58 *m* Ps 119:36
8:60 *n* Jos 4:24; 1Sa 17:46 *o* Dt 4:35; 1Ki 18:39; Jer 10:10-12
8:61 *p* 1Ki 11:4; 1Ki 15:3,14; 2Ki 20:3
8:64 *q* 2Ch 4:1
8:65 *r* ver 2; Lev 23:34 *s* Nu 34:8; Jos 13:5; Jdg 3:3; 2Ki 14:25 *t* Ge 15:18
9:1 *a* 1Ki 7:1; 2Ch 8:6
9:2 *b* 1Ki 3:5
9:3 *c* 2Ki 20:5; Ps 10:17 *d* Dt 11:12; 1Ki 8:29
9:4 *e* Ge 17:1 *f* 1Ki 15:5
9:5 *g* 1Ch 22:10 *h* 2Sa 7:15; 1Ki 2:4
9:6 *i* 2Sa 7:14
9:7 *j* 2Ki 17:23; 2Ki 25:21 *k* Jer 7:14 *l* Ps 44:14 *m* Dt 28:37

home, joyful and glad in heart for
all the good things the LORD had
done for his servant David and his
people Israel.

The LORD Appears to Solomon

9:1–9pp 2Ch 7:11–22

9 When Solomon had finished[a]
building the temple of the
LORD and the royal palace, and had
achieved all he had desired to do,
2the LORD appeared[b] to him a
second time, as he had appeared to
him at Gibeon. 3The LORD said to
him:

"I have heard[c] the prayer
and plea you have made before
me; I have consecrated this
temple, which you have built,
by putting my Name there for
ever. My eyes[d] and my heart
will always be there.
4"As for you, if you walk before me in integrity of heart[e]
and uprightness, as David[f]
your father did, and do all I
command and observe my decrees and laws, 5I will establish[g] your royal throne over
Israel for ever, as I promised
David your father when I said,
'You shall never fail[h] to have a
man on the throne of Israel.'
6"But if you[a] or your sons
turn away[i] from me and do not
observe the commands and decrees I have given you[a] and go
off to serve other gods and
worship them, 7then I will cut
off Israel from the land[j] I
have given them and will reject this temple I have consecrated for my Name.[k] Israel
will then become a byword[l]
and an object of ridicule[m]
among all peoples. 8And
though this temple is now imposing, all who pass by will be

[a]63 Traditionally *peace offerings*; also in verse 64
[b]65 Or *from the entrance to*
[a]6 The Hebrew is plural.

appalled and will scoff and say,
'Why has the LORD done such a
thing to this land and to this
temple?'[n] 9People will answer,
'Because they have forsaken
the LORD their God, who
brought their fathers out of
Egypt, and have embraced
other gods, worshipping and
serving them—that is why the
LORD brought all this disaster
on them.'"

Solomon's Other Activities

9:10–28pp 2Ch 8:1–18

10At the end of twenty years, during which Solomon built these two
buildings—the temple of the LORD
and the royal palace—11King Solomon gave twenty towns in Galilee
to Hiram king of Tyre, because
Hiram had supplied him with all
the cedar and pine and gold[o] he
wanted. 12But when Hiram went
from Tyre to see the towns that Solomon had given him, he was not
pleased with them. 13"What kind
of towns are these you have given
me, my brother?" he asked. And
he called them the Land of Cabul,[b][p]
a name they have to this day.
14Now Hiram had sent to the king 120
talents[c] of gold.
15Here is the account of the
forced labour King Solomon conscripted[q] to build the LORD's temple, his own palace, the supporting
terraces,[d][r] the wall of Jerusalem,
and Hazor,[s] Megiddo and Gezer.[t]
16(Pharaoh king of Egypt had attacked and captured Gezer. He had
set it on fire. He killed its Canaanite inhabitants and then gave it as a
wedding gift to his daughter, Solomon's wife. 17And Solomon rebuilt
Gezer.) He built up Lower Beth
Horon,[u] 18Baalath,[v] and Tadmor[e]
in the desert, within his land, 19as
well as all his store cities[w] and the
towns for his chariots[x] and for his
horses[f]—whatever he desired to
build in Jerusalem, in Lebanon and
throughout all the territory he
ruled.
20All the people left from the Amorites, Hittites, Perizzites, Hivites
and Jebusites (these peoples were
not Israelites), 21that is, their descendants[y] remaining in the land,
whom the Israelites could not
exterminate[g][z]—these Solomon conscripted for his slave labour
force,[a] as it is to this day. 22But Solomon did not make slaves[b] of any
of the Israelites; they were his
fighting men, his government officials, his officers, his captains, and
the commanders of his chariots
and charioteers. 23They were also
the chief officials[c] in charge of
Solomon's projects—550 officials
supervising the men who did the
work.
24After Pharaoh's daughter[d] had
come up from the City of David to
the palace Solomon had built for
her, he constructed the supporting
terraces.[e]
25Three[f] times a year Solomon
sacrificed burnt offerings and fellowship offerings[h] on the altar he
had built for the LORD, burning incense before the LORD along with
them, and so fulfilled the temple
obligations.
26King Solomon also built ships[g]
at Ezion Geber,[h] which is near
Elath in Edom, on the shore of
the Red Sea.[i] 27And Hiram sent
his men—sailors[i] who knew the
sea—to serve in the fleet with Solomon's men. 28They sailed to Ophir[j]
and brought back 420 talents[j] of
gold, which they delivered to King
Solomon.

9:8 n Dt 29:24; Jer 22:8-9
9:11 o 2Ch 8:2
9:13 p Jos 19:27
9:15 q Jos 16:10; 1Ki 5:13 r ver 24; 2Sa 5:9 s Jos 19:36 t Jos 17:11
9:17 u Jos 16:3; 2Ch 8:5
9:18 v Jos 19:44
9:19 w ver 1 x 1Ki 4:26
9:21 y Ge 9:25-26 z Jos 15:63; Jos 17:12; Jdg 1:21,27,29 a Ezr 2:55,58
9:22 b Lev 25:39
9:23 c 1Ki 5:16
9:24 d 1Ki 3:1; 1Ki 7:8 e 2Sa 5:9; 1Ki 11:27; 2Ch 32:5
9:25 f Ex 23:14; 2Ch 8:12-13,16
9:26 g 1Ki 22:48 h Nu 33:35; Dt 2:8
9:27 i 1Ki 10:11; Eze 27:8
9:28 j 1Ch 29:4

b13 *Cabul* sounds like the Hebrew for *good-for-nothing.* c14 That is, about 4 tons (about 4 metric tons) d15 Or *the Millo*; also in verse 24 e18 The Hebrew may also be read *Tamar.* f19 Or *charioteers* g21 The Hebrew term refers to the irrevocable giving over of things or persons to the LORD, often by totally destroying them. h25 Traditionally *peace offerings* i26 Hebrew *Yam Suph*; that is, Sea of Reeds j28 That is, about 14 tons (about 14.5 metric tons)

The Queen of Sheba Visits Solomon

10:1–13pp 2Ch 9:1–12

10 When the queen of Sheba[a]
heard about the fame of
Solomon and his relation to the
name of the LORD, she came to test
him with hard questions.[b] 2Arriv-
ing at Jerusalem with a very great
caravan—with camels carrying
spices, large quantities of gold, and
precious stones—she came to Solomon and talked with him about all
that she had on her mind. 3Solomon
answered all her questions; nothing was too hard for the king to explain to her. 4When the queen of
Sheba saw all the wisdom of Solomon and the palace he had built,
5the food on his table,[c] the seating
of his officials, the attending servants in their robes, his cupbearers, and the burnt offerings he
made at[a] the temple of the LORD,
she was overwhelmed.
6She said to the king, "The report
I heard in my own country about
your achievements and your wisdom is true. 7But I did not believe
these things until I came and saw
with my own eyes. Indeed, not even
half was told me; in wisdom and
wealth[d] you have far exceeded the
report I heard. 8How happy your
men must be! How happy your
officials, who continually stand before you and hear[e] your wisdom!
9Praise[f] be to the LORD your God,
who has delighted in you and
placed you on the throne of Israel.
Because of the LORD's eternal love
for Israel, he has made you king, to
maintain justice[g] and righteousness."
10And she gave the king 120 talents[b] of gold,[h] large quantities of
spices, and precious stones. Never
again were so many spices brought
in as those the queen of Sheba gave
to King Solomon.
11(Hiram's ships brought gold
from Ophir;[i] and from there they
brought great cargoes of almug-
wood[c] and precious stones. 12The
king used the almug-wood to make
supports for the temple of the LORD
and for the royal palace, and to
make harps and lyres for the musicians. So much almug-wood has
never been imported or seen since
that day.)
13King Solomon gave the queen
of Sheba all she desired and asked
for, besides what he had given her
out of his royal bounty. Then she
left and returned with her retinue
to her own country.

Solomon's Splendour

10:14–29pp 2Ch 1:14–17; 9:13–28

14The weight of the gold[j] that
Solomon received yearly was 666
talents,[d] 15not including the revenues from merchants and traders
and from all the Arabian kings and
the governors of the land.
16King Solomon made two hundred large shields[k] of hammered
gold; six hundred bekas[e] of gold
went into each shield. 17He also
made three hundred small shields
of hammered gold, with three
minas[f] of gold in each shield. The
king put them in the Palace of the
Forest of Lebanon.[l]
18Then the king made a great
throne inlaid with ivory and overlaid with fine gold. 19The throne
had six steps, and its back had a
rounded top. On both sides of the
seat were armrests, with a lion
standing beside each of them.
20Twelve lions stood on the six
steps, one at either end of each
step. Nothing like it had ever been
made for any other kingdom. 21All
King Solomon's goblets were gold,
and all the household articles in the
Palace of the Forest of Lebanon
were pure gold. Nothing was made

10:1 *a* Ge 10:7,28; Mt 12:42; Lk 11:31 *b* Jdg 14:12
10:5 *c* 1Ch 26:16
10:7 *d* 1Ch 29:25
10:8 *e* Pr 8:34
10:9 *f* 1Ki 5:7 *g* 2Sa 8:15; Ps 33:5; Ps 72:2
10:10 *h* ver 2
10:11 *i* Ge 10:29; 1Ki 9:27-28
10:14 *j* 1Ki 9:28
10:16 *k* 1Ki 14:26-28
10:17 *l* 1Ki 7:2

a5 Or *the ascent by which he went up to*
b10 That is, about 4 tons (about 4 metric tons)
c11 Probably a variant of *algum-wood*; also in verse 12
d14 That is, about 22½ tons (about 23 metric tons)
e16 That is, about 7½ pounds (about 3.5 kilograms)
f17 That is, about 3¾ pounds (about 1.7 kilograms)

of silver, because silver was considered of little value in Solomon's
days. 22 The king had a fleet of trading ships[g][m] at sea along with the
ships of Hiram. Once every three
years it returned carrying gold,
silver and ivory, and apes and
baboons.
23 King Solomon was greater in
riches[n] and wisdom[o] than all the
other kings of the earth. 24 The
whole world sought audience with
Solomon to hear the wisdom[p] God
had put in his heart. 25 Year after
year, everyone who came brought
a gift—articles of silver and gold,
robes, weapons and spices, and
horses and mules.
26 Solomon accumulated chariots
and horses;[q] he had fourteen hundred chariots and twelve thousand
horses,[h] which he kept in the chariot cities and also with him in Jerusalem. 27 The king made silver as
common[r] in Jerusalem as stones,
and cedar as plentiful as sycamore-
fig trees in the foothills. 28 Solomon's horses were imported from
Egypt[i] and from Kue[j]—the royal
merchants purchased them from
Kue.[j] 29 They imported a chariot
from Egypt for six hundred shekels[k] of silver, and a horse for a
hundred and fifty.[l] They also exported them to all the kings of the
Hittites[s] and of the Arameans.

Solomon's Wives

11 King Solomon, however,
loved many foreign
women[a] besides Pharaoh's daughter—Moabites, Ammonites, Edomites, Sidonians and Hittites.
2 They were from nations about
which the LORD had told the Israelites, "You must not intermarry[b]
with them, because they will surely
turn your hearts after their gods."
Nevertheless, Solomon held fast to
them in love. 3 He had seven hundred wives of royal birth and three
hundred concubines, and his wives
led him astray. 4 As Solomon grew
old, his wives turned his heart after
other gods, and his heart was not
fully devoted[c] to the LORD his God,
as the heart of David his father had
been. 5 He followed Ashtoreth[d] the
goddess of the Sidonians, and Molech[a][e] the detestable god of the
Ammonites. 6 So Solomon did evil in
the eyes of the LORD; he did not follow the LORD completely, as David
his father had done.
7 On a hill east[f] of Jerusalem,
Solomon built a high place for Chemosh[g] the detestable god of Moab,
and for Molech[h] the detestable
god of the Ammonites. 8 He did the
same for all his foreign wives, who
burned incense and offered sacrifices to their gods.
9 The LORD became angry with
Solomon because his heart had
turned away from the LORD, the
God of Israel, who had appeared[i]
to him twice. 10 Although he had forbidden Solomon to follow other
gods,[j] Solomon did not keep the
LORD's command.[k] 11 So the LORD
said to Solomon, "Since this is your
attitude and you have not kept my
covenant and my decrees, which
I commanded you, I will most
certainly tear[l] the kingdom away
from you and give it to one of your
subordinates. 12 Nevertheless, for
the sake of David your father, I will
not do it during your lifetime. I will
tear it out of the hand of your son.
13 Yet I will not tear the whole kingdom from him, but will give him
one tribe[m] for the sake[n] of David
my servant and for the sake of
Jerusalem, which I have chosen."[o]

Solomon's Adversaries

14 Then the LORD raised up
against Solomon an adversary,

10:22 m 1Ki 9:26
10:23 n 1Ki 3:13 o 1Ki 4:30
10:24 p 1Ki 3:9,12,28
10:26 q Dt 17:16 1Ki 4:26 1Ki 9:19 2Ch 1:14 2Ch 9:25
10:27 r Dt 17:17
10:29 s 2Ki 7:6-7
11:1 a Dt 17:17 Ne 13:26
11:2 b Ex 34:16 Dt 7:3-4
11:4 c 1Ki 8:61 1Ki 9:4
11:5 d ver 33 Jdg 2:13 2Ki 23:13 e ver 7
11:7 f 2Ki 23:13 g Nu 21:29 Jdg 11:24 h Lev 20:2-5 Ac 7:43
11:9 i ver 2-3 1Ki 3:5 1Ki 9:2
11:10 j 1Ki 9:6 k 1Ki 6:12
11:11 l ver 31 1Ki 12:15-16 2Ki 17:21
11:13 m 1Ki 12:20 n 2Sa 7:15 o Dt 12:11

[g]22 Hebrew *of ships of Tarshish*
[h]26 Or *charioteers* [i]28 Or possibly *Muzur*, a region in Cilicia; also in verse 29 [j]28 Probably *Cilicia* [k]29 That is, about 15 pounds (about 7 kilograms) [l]29 That is, about 3¾ pounds (about 1.7 kilograms) [a]5 Hebrew *Milcom*; also in verse 33

Hadad the Edomite, from the royal line of Edom. 15Earlier when David was fighting with Edom, Joab the commander of the army, who had gone up to bury the dead, had struck down all the men in Edom.[p] 16Joab and all the Israelites stayed there for six months, until they had destroyed all the men in Edom. 17But Hadad, still only a boy, fled to Egypt with some Edomite officials who had served his father. 18They set out from Midian and went to Paran.[q] Then taking men from Paran with them, they went to Egypt, to Pharaoh king of Egypt, who gave Hadad a house and land and provided him with food.

19Pharaoh was so pleased with Hadad that he gave him a sister of his own wife, Queen Tahpenes, in marriage. 20The sister of Tahpenes bore him a son named Genubath, whom Tahpenes brought up in the royal palace. There Genubath lived with Pharaoh's own children.

21While he was in Egypt, Hadad heard that David rested with his fathers and that Joab the commander of the army was also dead. Then Hadad said to Pharaoh, "Let me go, so that I may return to my own country."

22"What have you lacked here that you want to go back to your own country?" Pharaoh asked.

"Nothing," Hadad replied, "but do let me go!"

23And God raised up against Solomon another adversary,[r] Rezon son of Eliada, who had fled from his master, Hadadezer[s] king of Zobah. 24He gathered men around him and became the leader of a band of rebels when David destroyed the forces[b] ⌊of Zobah⌋; the rebels went to Damascus,[t] where they settled and took control. 25Rezon was Israel's adversary as long as Solomon lived, adding to the trouble caused by Hadad. So Rezon ruled in Aram[u] and was hostile towards Israel.

11:15 p Dt 20:13; 2Sa 8:14; 1Ch 18:12
11:18 q Nu 10:12
11:23 r ver 14; s 2Sa 8:3
11:24 t 2Sa 8:5; 2Sa 10:8,18
11:25 u 2Sa 10:19
11:26 v 2Sa 20:21; 1Ki 12:2; 2Ch 13:6
11:27 w 1Ki 9:24
11:28 x Ru 2:1; y Pr 22:29
11:29 z 1Ki 12:15; 1Ki 14:2; 2Ch 9:29
11:30 a 1Sa 15:27
11:31 b ver 11
11:33 c ver 5-7; d 1Ki 3:3

Jeroboam Rebels Against Solomon

26Also, Jeroboam son of Nebat rebelled[v] against the king. He was one of Solomon's officials, an Ephraimite from Zeredah, and his mother was a widow named Zeruah.

27Here is the account of how he rebelled against the king: Solomon had built the supporting terraces[c][w] and had filled in the gap in the wall of the city of David his father. 28Now Jeroboam was a man of standing,[x] and when Solomon saw how well[y] the young man did his work, he put him in charge of the whole labour force of the house of Joseph.

29About that time Jeroboam was going out of Jerusalem, and Ahijah[z] the prophet of Shiloh met him on the way, wearing a new cloak. The two of them were alone out in the country, 30and Ahijah took hold of the new cloak he was wearing and tore[a] it into twelve pieces. 31Then he said to Jeroboam, "Take ten pieces for yourself, for this is what the LORD, the God of Israel, says: 'See, I am going to tear[b] the kingdom out of Solomon's hand and give you ten tribes. 32But for the sake of my servant David and the city of Jerusalem, which I have chosen out of all the tribes of Israel, he will have one tribe. 33I will do this because they have[d] forsaken me and worshipped[c] Ashtoreth the goddess of the Sidonians, Chemosh the god of the Moabites, and Molech the god of the Ammonites, and have not walked in my ways, nor done what is right in my eyes, nor kept my statutes[d] and laws as David, Solomon's father, did.

34" 'But I will not take the whole kingdom out of Solomon's hand; I have made him ruler all the days of

b24 Hebrew *destroyed them* c27 Or *the Millo*
d33 Hebrew; Septuagint, Vulgate and Syriac *because he has*

his life for the sake of David my servant, whom I chose and who observed my commands and statutes. 35I will take the kingdom from his son's hands and give you ten tribes. 36I will give one tribe[e] to his son so that David my servant may always have a lamp[f] before me in Jerusalem, the city where I chose to put my Name. 37However, as for you, I will take you, and you will rule over all that your heart desires;[g] you will be king over Israel. 38If you do whatever I command you and walk in my ways and do what is right in my eyes by keeping my statutes[h] and commands, as David my servant did, I will be with you. I will build you a dynasty[i] as enduring as the one I built for David and will give Israel to you. 39I will humble David's descendants because of this, but not for ever.' "

40Solomon tried to kill Jeroboam, but Jeroboam fled to Egypt, to Shishak[j] the king, and stayed there until Solomon's death.

Solomon's Death

11:41–43pp 2Ch 9:29–31

41As for the other events of Solomon's reign—all he did and the wisdom he displayed—are they not written in the book of the annals of Solomon? 42Solomon reigned in Jerusalem over all Israel for forty years. 43Then he rested with his fathers and was buried in the city of David his father. And Rehoboam[k] his son succeeded him as king.

Israel Rebels Against Rehoboam

12:1–24pp 2Ch 10:1–11:4

12 Rehoboam went to Shechem, for all the Israelites had gone there to make him king. 2When Jeroboam son of Nebat heard this (he was still in Egypt, where he had fled[a] from King Solomon), he returned from[a] Egypt. 3So they sent for Jeroboam, and he and the whole assembly of Israel went to Rehoboam and said to him: 4"Your father put a heavy yoke[b] on us, but now lighten the harsh labour and the heavy yoke he put on us, and we will serve you."

5Rehoboam answered, "Go away for three days and then come back to me." So the people went away.

6Then King Rehoboam consulted the elders[c] who had served his father Solomon during his lifetime. "How would you advise me to answer these people?" he asked.

7They replied, "If today you will be a servant to these people and serve them and give them a favourable answer,[d] they will always be your servants."

8But Rehoboam rejected the advice the elders gave him and consulted the young men who had grown up with him and were serving him. 9He asked them, "What is your advice? How should we answer these people who say to me, 'Lighten the yoke your father put on us'?"

10The young men who had grown up with him replied, "Tell these people who have said to you, 'Your father put a heavy yoke on us, but make our yoke lighter'—tell them, 'My little finger is thicker than my father's waist. 11My father laid on you a heavy yoke; I will make it even heavier. My father scourged you with whips; I will scourge you with scorpions.' "

12Three days later Jeroboam and all the people returned to Rehoboam, as the king had said, "Come back to me in three days." 13The king answered the people harshly. Rejecting the advice given him by the elders, 14he followed the advice of the young men and said, "My father made your yoke heavy; I will make it even heavier. My father scourged[e] you with whips; I will scourge you with scorpions." 15So the king did not listen to the people,

11:36
e ver 13; 1Ki 12:17
f 1Ki 15:4; 2Ki 8:19
11:37
g 2Sa 3:21
11:38
h Dt 17:19
i Jos 1:5; 2Sa 7:11,27
11:40
j 2Ch 12:2
11:43
k 1Ki 14:21; Mt 1:7
12:2
a 1Ki 11:40
12:4
b 1Sa 8:11-18; 1Ki 4:20-28
12:6
c 1Ki 4:2
12:7
d Pr 15:1
12:14
e Ex 1:14; Ex 5:5-9, 16-18

a2 Or *he remained in*

for this turn of events was from the LORD,[f] to fulfil the word the LORD had spoken to Jeroboam son of Nebat through Ahijah[g] the Shilonite. 16When all Israel saw that the king refused to listen to them, they answered the king:

> "What share do we have in
> David,
> what part in Jesse's son?
> To your tents, O Israel![h]
> Look after your own house,
> O David!"

So the Israelites went home. 17But as for the Israelites who were living in the towns of Judah,[i] Rehoboam still ruled over them.

18King Rehoboam sent out Adoniram,[b][j] who was in charge of forced labour, but all Israel stoned him to death. King Rehoboam, however, managed to get into his chariot and escape to Jerusalem. 19So Israel has been in rebellion against the house of David[k] to this day.

20When all the Israelites heard that Jeroboam had returned, they sent and called him to the assembly and made him king over all Israel. Only the tribe of Judah remained loyal to the house of David.[l]

21When Rehoboam arrived in Jerusalem, he mustered the whole house of Judah and the tribe of Benjamin—a hundred and eighty thousand fighting men—to make war[m] against the house of Israel and to regain the kingdom for Rehoboam son of Solomon.

22But this word of God came to Shemaiah[n] the man of God: 23"Say to Rehoboam son of Solomon king of Judah, to the whole house of Judah and Benjamin, and to the rest of the people, 24'This is what the LORD says: Do not go up to fight against your brothers, the Israelites. Go home, every one of you, for this is my doing.' " So they obeyed the word of the LORD and went home again, as the LORD had ordered.

12:15 f ver 24; Dt 2:30; Jdg 14:4; 2Ch 22:7; 2Ch 25:20 g 1Ki 11:29
12:16 h 2Sa 20:1
12:17 i 1Ki 11:13,36
12:18 j 2Sa 20:24; 1Ki 4:6; 1Ki 5:14
12:19 k 2Ki 17:21
12:20 l 1Ki 11:13,32
12:21 m 2Ch 11:1
12:22 n 2Ch 12:5-7
12:25 o Jdg 9:45 p Jdg 8:8,17
12:27 q Dt 12:5-6
12:28 r Ex 32:4; 2Ki 10:29; 2Ki 17:16 s Ex 32:8
12:29 t Ge 28:19 u Jdg 18:27-31
12:30 v 1Ki 13:34; 2Ki 17:21
12:31 w 1Ki 13:32 x Nu 3:10; 1Ki 13:33; 2Ki 17:32; 2Ch 11:14-15; 2Ch 13:9
12:32 y Lev 23:33-34; Nu 29:12
12:33 z Nu 15:39; 1Ki 13:1; Am 7:13
13:1 a 2Ki 23:17 b 1Ki 12:32-33

Golden Calves at Bethel and Dan

25Then Jeroboam fortified Shechem[o] in the hill country of Ephraim and lived there. From there he went out and built up Peniel.[c][p]

26Jeroboam thought to himself, "The kingdom is now likely to revert to the house of David. 27If these people go up to offer sacrifices at the temple of the LORD in Jerusalem,[q] they will again give their allegiance to their lord, Rehoboam king of Judah. They will kill me and return to King Rehoboam."

28After seeking advice, the king made two golden calves.[r] He said to the people, "It is too much for you to go up to Jerusalem. Here are your gods, O Israel, who brought you up out of Egypt."[s] 29One he set up in Bethel,[t] and the other in Dan.[u] 30And this thing became a sin;[v] the people went even as far as Dan to worship the one there.

31Jeroboam built shrines[w] on high places and appointed priests[x] from all sorts of people, even though they were not Levites. 32He instituted a festival on the fifteenth day of the eighth[y] month, like the festival held in Judah, and offered sacrifices on the altar. This he did in Bethel, sacrificing to the calves he had made. And at Bethel he also installed priests at the high places he had made. 33On the fifteenth day of the eighth month, a month of his own choosing, he offered sacrifices on the altar he had built at Bethel.[z] So he instituted the festival for the Israelites and went up to the altar to make offerings.

The Man of God From Judah

13 By the word of the LORD a man of God[a] came from Judah to Bethel,[b] as Jeroboam was standing by the altar to make an

[b] 18 Some Septuagint manuscripts and Syriac (see also 1 Kings 4:6 and 5:14); Hebrew *Adoram*
[c] 25 Hebrew *Penuel*, a variant of *Peniel*

offering. 2He cried out against the
altar by the word of the LORD: "O
altar, altar! This is what the LORD
says: 'A son named Josiah[c] will be
born to the house of David. On you
he will sacrifice the priests of the
high places who now make offerings here, and human bones will be
burned on you.' " 3That same day
the man of God gave a sign:[d] "This
is the sign the LORD has declared:
The altar will be split apart and the
ashes on it will be poured out."
4When King Jeroboam heard
what the man of God cried out
against the altar at Bethel, he
stretched out his hand from the
altar and said, "Seize him!" But the
hand he stretched out towards
the man shrivelled up, so that he
could not pull it back. 5Also, the altar
was split apart and its ashes poured
out according to the sign given by
the man of God by the word of
the LORD.
6Then the king said to the man of
God, "Intercede[e] with the LORD
your God and pray for me that my
hand may be restored." So the man
of God interceded with the LORD,
and the king's hand was restored
and became as it was before.
7The king said to the man of God,
"Come home with me and have
something to eat, and I will give
you a gift."[f]
8But the man of God answered
the king, "Even if you were to give
me half your possessions,[g] I would
not go with you, nor would I eat
bread[h] or drink water here. 9For I
was commanded by the word of the
LORD: 'You must not eat bread or
drink water or return by the way
you came.' " 10So he took another
road and did not return by the way
he had come to Bethel.
11Now there was a certain old
prophet living in Bethel, whose
sons came and told him all that the
man of God had done there that
day. They also told their father
what he had said to the king.
12Their father asked them, "Which
way did he go?" And his sons
showed him which road the man of
God from Judah had taken. 13So he
said to his sons, "Saddle the donkey for me." And when they had
saddled the donkey for him, he
mounted it 14and rode after the
man of God. He found him sitting
under an oak tree and asked, "Are
you the man of God who came
from Judah?"
"I am," he replied.
15So the prophet said to him,
"Come home with me and eat."
16The man of God said, "I cannot
turn back and go with you, nor can
I eat bread[i] or drink water with
you in this place. 17I have been told
by the word of the LORD: 'You must
not eat bread or drink water there
or return by the way you came.' "
18The old prophet answered, "I
too am a prophet, as you are. And
an angel said to me by the word of
the LORD: 'Bring him back with you
to your house so that he may eat
bread and drink water.' " (But he
was lying[j] to him.) 19So the man of
God returned with him and ate and
drank in his house.
20While they were sitting at the
table, the word of the LORD came to
the old prophet who had brought
him back. 21He cried out to the man
of God who had come from Judah,
"This is what the LORD says: 'You
have defied[k] the word of the LORD
and have not kept the command the
LORD your God gave you. 22You
came back and ate bread and drank
water in the place where he told
you not to eat or drink. Therefore
your body will not be buried in the
tomb of your fathers.' "
23When the man of God had finished eating and drinking, the
prophet who had brought him back
saddled his donkey for him. 24As he
went on his way, a lion[l] met him on
the road and killed him, and his
body was thrown down on the road,
with both the donkey and the lion
standing beside it. 25Some people
who passed by saw the body thrown

13:2 c 2Ki 23:15-16, 20
13:3 d Jdg 6:17; Isa 7:14; Jn 2:11; 1Co 1:22
13:6 e Ex 8:8; Ex 9:28; Ex 10:17; Lk 6:27-28; Ac 8:24; Jas 5:16
13:7 f 1Sa 9:7; 2Ki 5:15
13:8 g Nu 22:18; Nu 24:13; h ver 16
13:16 i ver 8
13:18 j Dt 13:3
13:21 k ver 26
13:24 l 1Ki 20:36

down there, with the lion standing beside the body, and they went and reported it in the city where the old prophet lived.

26 When the prophet who had brought him back from his journey heard of it, he said, "It is the man of God who defied the word of the LORD. The LORD has given him over to the lion, which has mauled him and killed him, as the word of the LORD had warned him."

27 The prophet said to his sons, "Saddle the donkey for me," and they did so. 28 Then he went out and found the body thrown down on the road, with the donkey and the lion standing beside it. The lion had neither eaten the body nor mauled the donkey. 29 So the prophet picked up the body of the man of God, laid it on the donkey, and brought it back to his own city to mourn for him and bury him. 30 Then he laid the body in his own tomb, and they mourned over him and said, "Oh, my brother!"[m]

31 After burying him, he said to his sons, "When I die, bury me in the grave where the man of God is buried; lay my bones[n] beside his bones. 32 For the message he declared by the word of the LORD against the altar in Bethel and against all the shrines on the high places[o] in the towns of Samaria[p] will certainly come true."[q]

33 Even after this, Jeroboam did not change his evil ways, but once more appointed priests for the high places from all sorts[r] of people. Anyone who wanted to become a priest he consecrated for the high places. 34 This was the sin[s] of the house of Jeroboam that led to its downfall and to its destruction[t] from the face of the earth.

Ahijah's Prophecy Against Jeroboam

14 At that time Abijah son of Jeroboam became ill, 2 and Jeroboam said to his wife, "Go, disguise yourself, so that you won't be recognised as the wife of Jeroboam. Then go to Shiloh. Ahijah[a] the prophet is there—the one who told me I would be king over this people. 3 Take ten loaves of bread[b] with you, some cakes and a jar of honey, and go to him. He will tell you what will happen to the boy." 4 So Jeroboam's wife did what he said and went to Ahijah's house in Shiloh.

Now Ahijah could not see; his sight was gone because of his age. 5 But the LORD had told Ahijah, "Jeroboam's wife is coming to ask you about her son, for he is ill, and you are to give her such and such an answer. When she arrives, she will pretend to be someone else."

6 So when Ahijah heard the sound of her footsteps at the door, he said, "Come in, wife of Jeroboam. Why this pretence? I have been sent to you with bad news. 7 Go, tell Jeroboam that this is what the LORD, the God of Israel, says: 'I raised you up from among the people and made you a leader[c] over my people Israel. 8 I tore[d] the kingdom away from the house of David and gave it to you, but you have not been like my servant David, who kept my commands and followed me with all his heart, doing only what was right[e] in my eyes. 9 You have done more evil than all who lived before you. You have made for yourself other gods, idols[f] made of metal; you have provoked me to anger and thrust me behind your back.[g]

10 " 'Because of this, I am going to bring disaster on the house of Jeroboam. I will cut off from Jeroboam every last male in Israel—slave or free.[h] I will burn up the house of Jeroboam as one burns dung, until it is all gone.[i] 11 Dogs[j] will eat those belonging to Jeroboam who die in the city, and the birds of the

13:30 m Jer 22:18
13:31 n 2Ki 23:18
13:32 o ver 2; Lev 26:30 p 1Ki 16:24,28 q 2Ki 23:16
13:33 r 1Ki 12:31; 2Ch 11:15; 2Ch 13:9
13:34 s 1Ki 12:30 t 1Ki 14:10
14:2 a 1Sa 28:8; 2Sa 14:2; 1Ki 11:29
14:3 b 1Sa 9:7
14:7 c 2Sa 12:7-8; 1Ki 16:2
14:8 d 1Ki 11:31,33,38 e 1Ki 15:5
14:9 f Ex 34:17; 1Ki 12:28; 2Ch 11:15 g Ne 9:26; Ps 50:17; Eze 23:35
14:10 h Dt 32:36; 1Ki 21:21; 2Ki 9:8-9; 2Ki 14:26 i 1Ki 15:29
14:11 j 1Ki 16:4; 1Ki 21:24

air will feed on those who die in the
country. The LORD has spoken!'
12"As for you, go back home.
When you set foot in your city,
the boy will die. 13All Israel will
mourn for him and bury him. He
is the only one belonging to
Jeroboam who will be buried, because he is the only one in the
house of Jeroboam in whom the
LORD, the God of Israel, has found
anything good.[k]
14"The LORD will raise up for
himself a king over Israel who will
cut off the family of Jeroboam.
This is the day! What? Yes, even
now.[a] 15And the LORD will strike
Israel, so that it will be like a reed
swaying in the water. He will uproot[l] Israel from this good land
that he gave to their forefathers
and scatter them beyond the
River,[b] because they provoked[m]
the LORD to anger by making Asherah[n] poles.[c] 16And he will give
Israel up because of the sins[o]
Jeroboam has committed and has
caused Israel to commit."
17Then Jeroboam's wife got up
and left and went to Tirzah.[p] As
soon as she stepped over the
threshold of the house, the boy
died. 18They buried him, and all Israel mourned for him, as the LORD
had said through his servant the
prophet Ahijah.
19The other events of Jeroboam's
reign, his wars and how he ruled,
are written in the book of the annals of the kings of Israel. 20He
reigned for twenty-two years and
then rested with his fathers. And
Nadab his son succeeded him as
king.

Rehoboam King of Judah

14:21,25–31pp 2Ch 12:9–16

21Rehoboam son of Solomon was
king in Judah. He was forty-one
years old when he became king,
and he reigned for seventeen years
in Jerusalem, the city the LORD had

14:13
k 2Ch 12:12
2Ch 19:3
14:15
l Dt 29:28
2Ki 15:29
2Ki 17:6
Ps 52:5
m Jos 23:15-16
n Ex 34:13
Dt 12:3
14:16
o 1Ki 12:30
1Ki 13:34
1Ki 15:30,34
1Ki 16:2
14:17
p ver 12
1Ki 15:33
1Ki 16:6-9
14:21
q ver 31
1Ki 11:1
2Ch 12:13
14:22
r 2Ch 12:1
s Dt 32:21
Ps 78:58
1Co 10:22
14:23
t Dt 16:22
2Ki 17:9-10
Eze 16:24-25
u Dt 12:2
Isa 57:5
14:24
v Dt 23:17
1Ki 15:12
2Ki 23:7
14:25
w 1Ki 11:40
2Ch 12:2
14:26
x 1Ki 15:15,18
y 1Ki 10:17
14:30
z 1Ki 12:21
1Ki 15:6
14:31
a ver 21
2Ch 12:16

chosen out of all the tribes of Israel
in which to put his Name. His
mother's name was Naamah; she
was an Ammonite.[q]
22Judah[r] did evil in the eyes of
the LORD. By the sins they committed they stirred up his jealous
anger[s] more than their fathers
had done. 23They also set up for
themselves high places, sacred
stones[t] and Asherah poles on
every high hill and under every
spreading tree.[u] 24There were
even male shrine-prostitutes[v] in
the land; the people engaged in all
the detestable practices of the
nations the LORD had driven out
before the Israelites.
25In the fifth year of King Rehoboam, Shishak king of Egypt attacked[w] Jerusalem. 26He carried
off the treasures of the temple[x] of
the LORD and the treasures of the
royal palace. He took everything,
including all the gold shields[y]
Solomon had made. 27So King
Rehoboam made bronze shields to
replace them and assigned these to
the commanders of the guard on
duty at the entrance to the royal
palace. 28Whenever the king went
to the LORD's temple, the guards
bore the shields, and afterwards
they returned them to the guardroom.
29As for the other events of Rehoboam's reign, and all he did, are
they not written in the book of the
annals of the kings of Judah?
30There was continual warfare[z]
between Rehoboam and Jeroboam.
31And Rehoboam rested with his
fathers and was buried with them
in the City of David. His mother's
name was Naamah; she was an
Ammonite.[a] And Abijah[d] his son
succeeded him as king.

[a] *14* The meaning of the Hebrew for this sentence is uncertain. [b] *15* That is, the Euphrates
[c] *15* That is, symbols of the goddess Asherah; here and elsewhere in 1 Kings [d] *31* Some Hebrew manuscripts and Septuagint (see also 2 Chron. 12:16); most Hebrew manuscripts *Abijam*

Abijah King of Judah

15:1–2,6–8pp 2Ch 13:1–2,22–14:1

15 In the eighteenth year of
the reign of Jeroboam son
of Nebat, Abijah[a] became king of
Judah, 2and he reigned in Jerusalem for three years. His mother's
name was Maacah[a] daughter of
Abishalom.[b]
3He committed all the sins his
father had done before him; his
heart was not fully devoted[b] to the
LORD his God, as the heart of David
his forefather had been. 4Never-
theless, for David's sake the LORD
his God gave him a lamp[c] in Jerusalem by raising up a son to succeed him and by making Jerusalem
strong. 5For David had done what
was right in the eyes of the LORD
and had not failed to keep[d] any of
the LORD's commands all the days
of his life—except in the case of
Uriah[e] the Hittite.
6There was war[f] between Rehoboam[c] and Jeroboam throughout
⌞Abijah's⌟ lifetime. 7As for the other
events of Abijah's reign, and all he
did, are they not written in the book
of the annals of the kings of Judah?
There was war between Abijah and
Jeroboam. 8And Abijah rested with
his fathers and was buried in the
City of David. And Asa his son succeeded him as king.

Asa King of Judah

15:9–22pp 2Ch 14:2–3; 15:16–16:6
15:23–24pp 2Ch 16:11–17:1

9In the twentieth year of Jeroboam king of Israel, Asa became
king of Judah, 10and he reigned in
Jerusalem for forty-one years. His
grandmother's name was Maacah[g]
daughter of Abishalom.
11Asa did what was right in the
eyes of the LORD, as his father
David had done. 12He expelled the
male shrine-prostitutes[h] from the
land and got rid of all the idols his
fathers had made. 13He even deposed his grandmother Maacah
from her position as queen mother,
because she had made a repulsive
Asherah pole. Asa cut the pole
down[i] and burned it in the Kidron
Valley. 14Although he did not remove the high places, Asa's heart
was fully committed[j] to the LORD
all his life. 15He brought into the
temple of the LORD the silver and
gold and the articles that he and his
father had dedicated.[k]
16There was war[l] between Asa
and Baasha king of Israel throughout their reigns. 17Baasha king of
Israel went up against Judah and
fortified Ramah[m] to prevent anyone from leaving or entering the
territory of Asa king of Judah.
18Asa then took all the silver and
gold that was left in the treasuries
of the LORD's temple[n] and of his
own palace. He entrusted it to his
officials and sent[o] them to Ben-
Hadad[p] son of Tabrimmon, the son
of Hezion, the king of Aram, who
was ruling in Damascus. 19"Let
there be a treaty between me and
you," he said, "as there was between my father and your father.
See, I am sending you a gift of
silver and gold. Now break your
treaty with Baasha king of Israel so
that he will withdraw from me."
20Ben-Hadad agreed with King
Asa and sent the commanders of
his forces against the towns of Israel. He conquered[q] Ijon, Dan,
Abel Beth Maacah and all Kinnereth in addition to Naphtali. 21When
Baasha heard this, he stopped
building Ramah and withdrew to
Tirzah. 22Then King Asa issued an
order to all Judah—no-one was
exempt—and they carried away
from Ramah the stones and timber
Baasha had been using there. With
them King Asa built up Geba[r] in
Benjamin, and also Mizpah.
23As for all the other events of

15:2 *a* 2Ch 11:20; 2Ch 13:2
15:3 *b* 1Ki 11:4; Ps 119:80
15:4 *c* 2Sa 21:17; 1Ki 11:36; 2Ch 21:7
15:5 *d* 1Ki 9:4; 1Ki 14:8; *e* 2Sa 11:2-27; 2Sa 12:9
15:6 *f* 1Ki 14:30
15:10 *g* ver 2
15:12 *h* 1Ki 14:24; 1Ki 22:46
15:13 *i* Ex 32:20
15:14 *j* ver 3; 1Ki 8:61; 1Ki 22:43
15:15 *k* 1Ki 7:51
15:16 *l* ver 32
15:17 *m* Jos 18:25; 1Ki 12:27
15:18 *n* ver 15; 1Ki 14:26; *o* 2Ki 12:18; *p* 1Ki 11:23-24
15:20 *q* Jdg 18:29; 2Sa 20:14; 2Ki 15:29
15:22 *r* Jos 18:24; Jos 21:17

a1 Some Hebrew manuscripts and Septuagint (see also 2 Chron. 12:16); most Hebrew manuscripts *Abijam*; also in verses 7 and 8 **b**2 A variant of *Absalom*; also in verse 10 **c**6 Most Hebrew manuscripts; some Hebrew manuscripts and Syriac *Abijam* (that is, Abijah)

Asa's reign, all his achievements,
all he did and the cities he built, are
they not written in the book of the
annals of the kings of Judah? In his
old age, however, his feet became
diseased. 24Then Asa rested with
his fathers and was buried with
them in the city of his father David.
And Jehoshaphat[s] his son succeeded him as king.

Nadab King of Israel

25Nadab son of Jeroboam became
king of Israel in the second year of
Asa king of Judah, and he reigned
over Israel for two years. 26He did
evil in the eyes of the LORD, walking in the ways of his father[t] and
in his sin, which he had caused
Israel to commit.
27Baasha son of Ahijah of the
house of Issachar plotted against
him, and he struck him down[u] at
Gibbethon,[v] a Philistine town,
while Nadab and all Israel were besieging it. 28Baasha killed Nadab in
the third year of Asa king of Judah
and succeeded him as king.
29As soon as he began to reign, he
killed Jeroboam's whole family.[w]
He did not leave Jeroboam anyone
that breathed, but destroyed them
all, according to the word of the
LORD given through his servant
Ahijah the Shilonite—30because of
the sins[x] Jeroboam had committed
and had caused Israel to commit,
and because he provoked the LORD,
the God of Israel, to anger.
31As for the other events of Nadab's reign, and all he did, are they
not written in the book of the annals of the kings of Israel? 32There
was war[y] between Asa and Baasha
king of Israel throughout their
reigns.

Baasha King of Israel

33In the third year of Asa king of
Judah, Baasha son of Ahijah became king of all Israel in Tirzah,
and he reigned for twenty-four
years. 34He did evil[z] in the eyes of
the LORD, walking in the ways of
Jeroboam and in his sin, which he
had caused Israel to commit.

16 Then the word of the LORD
came to Jehu[a] son of Hanani[b] against Baasha: 2"I lifted
you up from the dust[c] and made
you leader[d] of my people Israel,
but you walked in the ways of Jeroboam and caused[e] my people Israel to sin and to provoke me to
anger by their sins. 3So I am about
to consume Baasha and his house,[f]
and I will make your house like that
of Jeroboam son of Nebat. 4Dogs[g]
will eat those belonging to Baasha
who die in the city, and the birds of
the air will feed on those who die in
the country."
5As for the other events of Baasha's reign, what he did and his
achievements, are they not written
in the book of the annals[h] of the
kings of Israel? 6Baasha rested
with his fathers and was buried in
Tirzah.[i] And Elah his son succeeded him as king.
7Moreover, the word of the LORD
came[j] through the prophet Jehu[k]
son of Hanani to Baasha and his
house, because of all the evil he had
done in the eyes of the LORD, provoking him to anger by the things
he did, and becoming like the house
of Jeroboam—and also because he
destroyed it.

Elah King of Israel

8In the twenty-sixth year of Asa
king of Judah, Elah son of Baasha
became king of Israel, and he
reigned in Tirzah for two years.
9Zimri, one of his officials, who
had command of half his chariots,
plotted against him. Elah was in
Tirzah at the time, getting drunk[l]
in the home of Arza, the man in
charge[m] of the palace at Tirzah.
10Zimri came in, struck him down
and killed him in the twenty-
seventh year of Asa king of Judah.
Then he succeeded him as king.
11As soon as he began to reign

15:24 s Mt 1:8
15:26 t 1Ki 12:30; 1Ki 14:16
15:27 u 1Ki 14:14; v Jos 19:44; Jos 21:23
15:29 w 1Ki 14:10,14
15:30 x 1Ki 14:9,16
15:32 y ver 16
15:34 z ver 26; 1Ki 12:28-29; 1Ki 13:33; 1Ki 14:16
16:1 a ver 7; 2Ch 19:2; 2Ch 20:34; b 2Ch 16:7
16:2 c 1Sa 2:8; d 1Ki 14:7-9; e 1Ki 15:34
16:3 f ver 11; 1Ki 14:10; 1Ki 15:29; 1Ki 21:22
16:4 g 1Ki 14:11
16:5 h 1Ki 14:19; 1Ki 15:31
16:6 i 1Ki 14:17; 1Ki 15:33
16:7 j 1Ki 15:27,29; k ver 1
16:9 l 2Ki 9:30-33; m 1Ki 18:3

and was seated on the throne, he
killed off Baasha's whole family.[n]
He did not spare a single male,
whether relative or friend. 12So
Zimri destroyed the whole family
of Baasha, in accordance with the
word of the LORD spoken against
Baasha through the prophet Jehu—
13because of all the sins Baasha and
his son Elah had committed and
had caused Israel to commit, so
that they provoked the LORD, the
God of Israel, to anger by their
worthless idols.[o]
14As for the other events of
Elah's reign, and all he did, are they
not written in the book of the annals of the kings of Israel?

Zimri King of Israel

15In the twenty-seventh year of
Asa king of Judah, Zimri reigned in
Tirzah for seven days. The army
was encamped near Gibbethon,[p] a
Philistine town. 16When the Israelites in the camp heard that Zimri
had plotted against the king and
murdered him, they proclaimed
Omri, the commander of the army,
king over Israel that very day there
in the camp. 17Then Omri and all
the Israelites with him withdrew
from Gibbethon and laid siege to
Tirzah. 18When Zimri saw that the
city was taken, he went into the
citadel of the royal palace and set
the palace on fire around him. So he
died, 19because of the sins he had
committed, doing evil in the eyes of
the LORD and walking in the ways
of Jeroboam and in the sin he had
committed and had caused Israel to
commit.
20As for the other events of
Zimri's reign, and the rebellion he
carried out, are they not written in
the book of the annals of the kings
of Israel?

Omri King of Israel

21Then the people of Israel were
split into two factions; half supported Tibni son of Ginath for king,
and the other half supported Omri.
22But Omri's followers proved
stronger than those of Tibni son
of Ginath. So Tibni died and Omri
became king.
23In the thirty-first year of Asa
king of Judah, Omri became king of
Israel, and he reigned for twelve
years, six of them in Tirzah.[q] 24He
bought the hill of Samaria from
Shemer for two talents[a] of silver
and built a city on the hill, calling it
Samaria,[r] after Shemer, the name
of the former owner of the hill.
25But Omri did evil[s] in the eyes
of the LORD and sinned more than
all those before him. 26He walked in
all the ways of Jeroboam son of Nebat and in his sin, which he had
caused[t] Israel to commit, so that
they provoked the LORD, the God of
Israel, to anger by their worthless
idols.[u]
27As for the other events of
Omri's reign, what he did and the
things he achieved, are they not
written in the book of the annals of
the kings of Israel? 28Omri rested
with his fathers and was buried
in Samaria. And Ahab his son
succeeded him as king.

Ahab Becomes King of Israel

29In the thirty-eighth year of Asa
king of Judah, Ahab son of Omri became king of Israel, and he reigned
in Samaria over Israel for twenty-
two years. 30Ahab son of Omri did
more[v] evil in the eyes of the LORD
than any of those before him. 31He
not only considered it trivial to
commit the sins of Jeroboam son of
Nebat, but he also married[w] Jezebel daughter[x] of Ethbaal king of
the Sidonians, and began to serve
Baal[y] and worship him. 32He set up
an altar for Baal in the temple[z] of
Baal that he built in Samaria.
33Ahab also made an Asherah pole[a]
and did more[b] to provoke the
LORD, the God of Israel, to anger

16:11 n ver 3
16:13 o Dt 32:21; 1Sa 12:21; Isa 41:29
16:15 p Jos 19:44; 1Ki 15:27
16:23 q 1Ki 15:21
16:24 r 1Ki 13:32; Jn 4:4
16:25 s Dt 4:25; Mic 6:16
16:26 t ver 19; u Dt 32:21
16:30 v ver 25; 1Ki 14:9
16:31 w Dt 7:3; 1Ki 11:2; x Jdg 18:7; 2Ki 9:34; y 2Ki 10:18; 2Ki 17:16
16:32 z 2Ki 10:21,27; 2Ki 11:18
16:33 a 2Ki 13:6; b ver 29,30; 1Ki 14:9; 1Ki 21:25

a24 That is, about 150 pounds (about 70 kilograms)

than did all the kings of Israel before him.

34 In Ahab's time, Hiel of Bethel rebuilt Jericho. He laid its foundations at the cost of his firstborn son Abiram, and he set up its gates at the cost of his youngest son Segub, in accordance with the word of the LORD spoken by Joshua son of Nun.[c]

Elijah Fed by Ravens

17 Now Elijah[a] the Tishbite, from Tishbe[a] in Gilead,[b] said to Ahab, "As the LORD, the God of Israel, lives, whom I serve, there will be neither dew nor rain[c] in the next few years except at my word."

2 Then the word of the LORD came to Elijah: 3 "Leave here, turn eastward and hide in the Kerith Ravine, east of the Jordan. 4 You will drink from the brook, and I have ordered the ravens[d] to feed you there."

5 So he did what the LORD had told him. He went to the Kerith Ravine, east of the Jordan, and stayed there. 6 The ravens brought him bread and meat in the morning[e] and bread and meat in the evening, and he drank from the brook.

The Widow at Zarephath

7 Some time later the brook dried up because there had been no rain in the land. 8 Then the word of the LORD came to him: 9 "Go at once to Zarephath[f] of Sidon and stay there. I have commanded a widow[g] in that place to supply you with food." 10 So he went to Zarephath. When he came to the town gate, a widow was there gathering sticks. He called to her and asked, "Would you bring me a little water in a jar so I may have a drink?"[h] 11 As she was going to get it, he called, "And bring me, please, a piece of bread."

12 "As surely as the LORD your God lives," she replied, "I don't have any bread—only a handful of flour in a jar and a little oil[i] in a jug. I am gathering a few sticks to take home and make a meal for myself and my son, that we may eat it—and die."

13 Elijah said to her, "Don't be afraid. Go home and do as you have said. But first make a small cake of bread for me from what you have and bring it to me, and then make something for yourself and your son. 14 For this is what the LORD, the God of Israel, says: 'The jar of flour will not be used up and the jug of oil will not run dry until the day the LORD gives rain on the land.'"

15 She went away and did as Elijah had told her. So there was food every day for Elijah and for the woman and her family. 16 For the jar of flour was not used up and the jug of oil did not run dry, in keeping with the word of the LORD spoken by Elijah.

17 Some time later the son of the woman who owned the house became ill. He grew worse and worse, and finally stopped breathing. 18 She said to Elijah, "What do you have against me, man of God? Did you come to remind me of my sin[j] and kill my son?"

19 "Give me your son," Elijah replied. He took him from her arms, carried him to the upper room where he was staying, and laid him on his bed. 20 Then he cried out to the LORD, "O LORD my God, have you brought tragedy also upon this widow I am staying with, by causing her son to die?" 21 Then he stretched[k] himself out on the boy three times and cried to the LORD, "O LORD my God, let this boy's life return to him!"

22 The LORD heard Elijah's cry, and the boy's life returned to him, and he lived. 23 Elijah picked up the child and carried him down from the room into the house. He gave him to his mother and said, "Look, your son is alive!"

24 Then the woman said to Elijah,

16:34
c Jos 6:26

17:1
a Mal 4:5; Jas 5:17
b Jdg 12:4
c Dt 10:8; 1Ki 18:1; 2Ki 3:14; Lk 4:25

17:4
d Ge 8:7

17:6
e Ex 16:8

17:9
f Ob 1:20
g Lk 4:26

17:10
h Ge 24:17; Jn 4:7

17:12
i ver 1; 2Ki 4:2

17:18
j 2Ki 3:13; Lk 5:8

17:21
k 2Ki 4:34; Ac 20:10

[a] 1 Or *Tishbite, of the settlers*

"Now I know[l] that you are a man of God and that the word of the LORD from your mouth is the truth."[m]

Elijah and Obadiah

18 After a long time, in the third[a] year, the word of the LORD came to Elijah: "Go and present yourself to Ahab, and I will send rain[b] on the land." 2So Elijah went to present himself to Ahab.

Now the famine was severe in Samaria, 3and Ahab had summoned Obadiah, who was in charge[c] of his palace. (Obadiah was a devout believer[d] in the LORD. 4While Jezebel[e] was killing off the LORD's prophets, Obadiah had taken a hundred prophets and hidden[f] them in two caves, fifty in each, and had supplied them with food and water.) 5Ahab had said to Obadiah, "Go through the land to all the springs and valleys. Maybe we can find some grass to keep the horses and mules alive so we will not have to kill any of our animals." 6So they divided the land they were to cover, Ahab going in one direction and Obadiah in another.

7As Obadiah was walking along, Elijah met him. Obadiah recognised[g] him, bowed down to the ground, and said, "Is it really you, my lord Elijah?"

8"Yes," he replied. "Go tell your master, 'Elijah is here.' "

9"What have I done wrong," asked Obadiah, "that you are handing your servant over to Ahab to be put to death? 10As surely as the LORD your God lives, there is not a nation or kingdom where my master has not sent someone to look[h] for you. And whenever a nation or kingdom claimed you were not there, he made them swear they could not find you. 11But now you tell me to go to my master and say, 'Elijah is here.' 12I don't know where the Spirit[i] of the LORD may carry you when I leave you. If I go and tell Ahab and he doesn't find you, he will kill me. Yet I your servant have worshipped the LORD since my youth. 13Haven't you heard, my lord, what I did while Jezebel was killing the prophets of the LORD? I hid a hundred of the LORD's prophets in two caves, fifty in each, and supplied them with food and water. 14And now you tell me to go to my master and say, 'Elijah is here.' He will kill me!"

15Elijah said, "As the LORD Almighty lives, whom I serve, I will surely present[j] myself to Ahab today."

Elijah on Mount Carmel

16So Obadiah went to meet Ahab and told him, and Ahab went to meet Elijah. 17When he saw Elijah, he said to him, "Is that you, you troubler[k] of Israel?"

18"I have not made trouble for Israel," Elijah replied. "But you[l] and your father's family have. You have abandoned[m] the LORD's commands and have followed the Baals. 19Now summon the people from all over Israel to meet me on Mount Carmel.[n] And bring the four hundred and fifty prophets of Baal and the four hundred prophets of Asherah, who eat at Jezebel's table."

20So Ahab sent word throughout all Israel and assembled the prophets on Mount Carmel. 21Elijah went before the people and said, "How long will you waver[o] between two opinions? If the LORD is God, follow him; but if Baal is God, follow him."

But the people said nothing.

22Then Elijah said to them, "I am the only one of the LORD's prophets left,[p] but Baal has four hundred and fifty prophets.[q] 23Get two bulls for us. Let them choose one for themselves, and let them cut it into pieces and put it on the wood but not set fire to it. I will prepare the other bull and put it on the wood but not set fire to it. 24Then you call

17:24 l Jn 3:2; Jn 16:30 m Ps 119:43; Jn 17:17
18:1 a 1Ki 17:1; Lk 4:25; Jas 5:17 b Dt 28:12
18:3 c 1Ki 16:9 d Ne 7:2
18:4 e 2Ki 9:7 f ver 13; Isa 16:3
18:7 g 2Ki 1:8
18:10 h 1Ki 17:3
18:12 i 2Ki 2:16; Eze 3:14; Ac 8:39
18:15 j 1Ki 17:1
18:17 k Jos 7:25; 1Ki 21:20; Ac 16:20
18:18 l 1Ki 16:31,33; 1Ki 21:25 m 2Ch 15:2
18:19 n Jos 19:26
18:21 o Jos 24:15; 2Ki 17:41; Mt 6:24
18:22 p 1Ki 19:10 q ver 19

on the name of your god, and I will
call on the name of the LORD. The
god who answers by fire[r]—he is
God."
Then all the people said, "What
you say is good."
25 Elijah said to the prophets of
Baal, "Choose one of the bulls and
prepare it first, since there are so
many of you. Call on the name of
your god, but do not light the fire."
26 So they took the bull given them
and prepared it.
Then they called on the name
of Baal from morning till noon.
"O Baal, answer us!" they shouted.
But there was no response;[s] no-
one answered. And they danced
around the altar they had made.
27 At noon Elijah began to taunt
them. "Shout louder!" he said.
"Surely he is a god! Perhaps he is
deep in thought, or busy, or travelling. Maybe he is sleeping and must
be awakened."[t] 28 So they shouted
louder and slashed[u] themselves
with swords and spears, as was
their custom, until their blood
flowed. 29 Midday passed, and they
continued their frantic prophesying until the time for the evening
sacrifice.[v] But there was no response, no-one answered, no-one
paid attention.[w]
30 Then Elijah said to all the people, "Come here to me." They came
to him, and he repaired the altar[x]
of the LORD, which was in ruins.
31 Elijah took twelve stones, one for
each of the tribes descended from
Jacob, to whom the word of the
LORD had come, saying, "Your
name shall be Israel."[y] 32 With the
stones he built an altar in the
name[z] of the LORD, and he dug a
trench round it large enough to
hold two seahs[a] of seed. 33 He arranged[a] the wood, cut the bull into
pieces and laid it on the wood. Then
he said to them, "Fill four large jars
with water and pour it on the offering and on the wood."
34 "Do it again," he said, and they
did it again.

18:24 r ver 38; 1Ch 21:26
18:26 s Ps 115:4-5; Jer 10:5; 1Co 8:4; 1Co 12:2
18:27 t Hab 2:19
18:28 u Lev 19:28; Dt 14:1
18:29 v Ex 29:41 w ver 26
18:30 x 1Ki 19:10
18:31 y Ge 32:28; Ge 35:10; 2Ki 17:34
18:32 z Col 3:17
18:33 a Ge 22:9; Lev 1:6-8
18:36 b Ex 3:6; Mt 22:32 c 1Ki 8:43; 2Ki 19:19 d Nu 16:28
18:38 e Lev 9:24; Jdg 6:21; 1Ch 21:26; 2Ch 7:1; Job 1:16
18:39 f ver 24
18:40 g Jdg 4:7 h Dt 13:5; Dt 18:20; 2Ki 10:24-25
18:42 i ver 19-20; Jas 5:18
18:44 j Lk 12:54

"Do it a third time," he ordered,
and they did it the third time. 35 The
water ran down around the altar
and even filled the trench.
36 At the time of sacrifice, the
prophet Elijah stepped forward
and prayed: "O LORD, God of Abraham,[b] Isaac and Israel, let it be
known[c] today that you are God in
Israel and that I am your servant
and have done all these things at
your command.[d] 37 Answer me,
O LORD, answer me, so these people will know that you, O LORD, are
God, and that you are turning their
hearts back again."
38 Then the fire[e] of the LORD fell
and burned up the sacrifice, the
wood, the stones and the soil, and
also licked up the water in the
trench.
39 When all the people saw this,
they fell prostrate and cried, "The
LORD—he is God! The LORD—he is
God!"[f]
40 Then Elijah commanded them,
"Seize the prophets of Baal. Don't
let anyone get away!" They seized
them, and Elijah had them brought
down to the Kishon Valley[g] and
slaughtered[h] there.
41 And Elijah said to Ahab, "Go,
eat and drink, for there is the sound
of a heavy rain." 42 So Ahab went off
to eat and drink, but Elijah climbed
to the top of Carmel, bent down to
the ground and put his face between his knees.[i]
43 "Go and look towards the sea,"
he told his servant. And he went up
and looked.
"There is nothing there," he said.
Seven times Elijah said, "Go
back."
44 The seventh time the servant
reported, "A cloud[j] as small as a
man's hand is rising from the sea."
So Elijah said, "Go and tell Ahab,
'Hitch up your chariot and go down
before the rain stops you.'"
45 Meanwhile, the sky grew black

a32 That is, probably about 26 pints (about 15 litres)

with clouds, the wind rose, a heavy
rain came on and Ahab rode off to
Jezreel. 46The power[k] of the LORD
came upon Elijah and, tucking his
cloak into his belt,[l] he ran ahead of
Ahab all the way to Jezreel.

Elijah Flees to Horeb

19 Now Ahab told Jezebel
everything Elijah had done
and how he had killed[a] all the
prophets with the sword. 2So Jezebel sent a messenger to Elijah to
say, "May the gods deal with me, be
it ever so severely,[b] if by this time
tomorrow I do not make your life
like that of one of them."
3Elijah was afraid[a] and ran[c] for
his life. When he came to Beersheba in Judah, he left his servant
there, 4while he himself went a
day's journey into the desert. He
came to a broom tree, sat down under it and prayed that he might die.
"I have had enough, LORD," he said.
"Take my life;[d] I am no better than
my ancestors." 5Then he lay down
under the tree and fell asleep.[e]
All at once an angel touched him
and said, "Get up and eat." 6He
looked around, and there by his
head was a cake of bread baked
over hot coals, and a jar of water.
He ate and drank and then lay down
again.
7The angel of the LORD came
back a second time and touched
him and said, "Get up and eat, for
the journey is too much for you."
8So he got up and ate and drank.
Strengthened by that food, he travelled for forty[f] days and forty
nights until he reached Horeb,[g]
the mountain of God. 9There he
went into a cave[h] and spent the
night.

The LORD Appears to Elijah

And the word of the LORD came
to him: "What are you doing here,
Elijah?"
10He replied, "I have been very
zealous[i] for the LORD God
Almighty. The Israelites have rejected your covenant, broken down
your altars, and put your prophets
to death with the sword. I am the
only one left,[j] and now they are
trying to kill me too."
11The LORD said, "Go out and
stand on the mountain[k] in the presence of the LORD, for the LORD is
about to pass by."
Then a great and powerful
wind[l] tore the mountains apart
and shattered the rocks before the
LORD, but the LORD was not in the
wind. After the wind there was an
earthquake, but the LORD was not
in the earthquake. 12After the
earthquake came a fire, but the
LORD was not in the fire. And after
the fire came a gentle whisper.[m]
13When Elijah heard it, he pulled
his cloak over his face[n] and went
out and stood at the mouth of the
cave.
Then a voice said to him, "What
are you doing here, Elijah?"
14He replied, "I have been very
zealous for the LORD God
Almighty. The Israelites have rejected your covenant, broken down
your altars, and put your prophets
to death with the sword. I am the
only one left,[o] and now they are
trying to kill me too."
15The LORD said to him, "Go back
the way you came, and go to the
Desert of Damascus. When you get
there, anoint Hazael[p] king over
Aram. 16Also, anoint[q] Jehu son of
Nimshi king over Israel, and anoint
Elisha[r] son of Shaphat from Abel
Meholah to succeed you as prophet.
17Jehu will put to death any who
escape the sword of Hazael,[s] and
Elisha will put to death any who
escape the sword of Jehu. 18Yet I
reserve[t] seven thousand in Israel—all whose knees have not
bowed down to Baal and all whose
mouths have not kissed[u] him."

18:46 k 2Ki 3:15 l 2Ki 4:29; 2Ki 9:1
19:1 a 1Ki 18:40
19:2 b 1Ki 20:10; 2Ki 6:31; Ru 1:17
19:3 c Ge 31:21
19:4 d Nu 11:15; Jer 20:18; Jnh 4:8
19:5 e Ge 28:11
19:8 f Ex 24:18; Ex 34:28; Dt 9:9-11,18; Mt 4:2 g Ex 3:1
19:9 h Ex 33:22
19:10 i Nu 25:13 j 1Ki 18:4,22; Ro 11:3*
19:11 k Ex 24:12 l Eze 1:4; Eze 37:7
19:12 m Job 4:16; Zec 4:6
19:13 n ver 9; Ex 3:6
19:14 o ver 10
19:15 p 2Ki 8:7-15
19:16 q 2Ki 9:1-3,6 r ver 21; 2Ki 2:9,15
19:17 s 2Ki 8:12,29; 2Ki 9:14; 2Ki 13:3,7,22
19:18 t Ro 11:4* u Hos 13:2

[a]3 Or *Elijah saw*

The Call of Elisha

[19]So Elijah went from there and found Elisha son of Shaphat. He was ploughing with twelve yoke of oxen, and he himself was driving the twelfth pair. Elijah went up to him and threw his cloak[v] around him. [20]Elisha then left his oxen and ran after Elijah. "Let me kiss my father and mother good-bye,"[w] he said, "and then I will come with you."

"Go back," Elijah replied. "What have I done to you?"

[21]So Elisha left him and went back. He took his yoke of oxen[x] and slaughtered them. He burned the ploughing equipment to cook the meat and gave it to the people, and they ate. Then he set out to follow Elijah and became his attendant.[y]

Ben-Hadad Attacks Samaria

20 Now Ben-Hadad[a] king of Aram mustered his entire army. Accompanied by thirty-two kings with their horses and chariots, he went up and besieged Samaria and attacked it. [2]He sent messengers into the city to Ahab king of Israel, saying, "This is what Ben-Hadad says: [3]'Your silver and gold are mine, and the best of your wives and children are mine.' "

[4]The king of Israel answered, "Just as you say, my lord the king. I and all I have are yours."

[5]The messengers came again and said, "This is what Ben-Hadad says: 'I sent to demand your silver and gold, your wives and your children. [6]But about this time tomorrow I am going to send my officials to search your palace and the houses of your officials. They will seize everything you value and carry it away.' "

[7]The king of Israel summoned all the elders of the land and said to them, "See how this man is looking for trouble![b] When he sent for my wives and my children, my silver and my gold, I did not refuse him."

[8]The elders and the people all answered, "Don't listen to him or agree to his demands."

[9]So he replied to Ben-Hadad's messengers, "Tell my lord the king, 'Your servant will do all you demanded the first time, but this demand I cannot meet.' " They left and took the answer back to Ben-Hadad.

[10]Then Ben-Hadad sent another message to Ahab: "May the gods deal with me, be it ever so severely, if enough dust[c] remains in Samaria to give each of my men a handful."

[11]The king of Israel answered, "Tell him: 'One who puts on his armour should not boast[d] like one who takes it off.' "

[12]Ben-Hadad heard this message while he and the kings were drinking[e] in their tents,[a] and he ordered his men: "Prepare to attack." So they prepared to attack the city.

Ahab Defeats Ben-Hadad

[13]Meanwhile a prophet came to Ahab king of Israel and announced, "This is what the LORD says: 'Do you see this vast army? I will give it into your hand today, and then you will know[f] that I am the LORD.' "

[14]"But who will do this?" asked Ahab.

The prophet replied, "This is what the LORD says: 'The young officers of the provincial commanders will do it.' "

"And who will start[g] the battle?" he asked.

The prophet answered, "You will."

[15]So Ahab summoned the young officers of the provincial commanders, 232 men. Then he assembled the rest of the Israelites, 7,000 in all. [16]They set

19:19 *v* 2Ki 2:8,14
19:20 *w* Mt 8:21-22; Lk 9:61
19:21 *x* 2Sa 24:22; *y* ver 16
20:1 *a* 1Ki 15:18; 1Ki 22:31; 2Ki 6:24
20:7 *b* 2Ki 5:7
20:10 *c* 2Sa 22:43; 1Ki 19:2
20:11 *d* Pr 27:1; Jer 9:23
20:12 *e* ver 16; 1Ki 16:9
20:13 *f* ver 28; Ex 6:7
20:14 *g* Jdg 1:1

[a]12 Or *in Succoth*; also in verse 16

out at noon while Ben-Hadad and the 32 kings allied with him were in their tents getting drunk.[h] 17 The young officers of the provincial commanders went out first.

Now Ben-Hadad had dispatched scouts, who reported, "Men are advancing from Samaria."

18 He said, "If they have come out for peace, take them alive; if they have come out for war, take them alive."

19 The young officers of the provincial commanders marched out of the city with the army behind them 20 and each one struck down his opponent. At that, the Arameans fled, with the Israelites in pursuit. But Ben-Hadad king of Aram escaped on horseback with some of his horsemen. 21 The king of Israel advanced and overpowered the horses and chariots and inflicted heavy losses on the Arameans.

22 Afterwards, the prophet[i] came to the king of Israel and said, "Strengthen your position and see what must be done, because next spring[j] the king of Aram will attack you again."

23 Meanwhile, the officials of the king of Aram advised him, "Their gods are gods[k] of the hills. That is why they were too strong for us. But if we fight them on the plains, surely we will be stronger than they. 24 Do this: Remove all the kings from their commands and replace them with other officers. 25 You must also raise an army like the one you lost—horse for horse and chariot for chariot—so we can fight Israel on the plains. Then surely we will be stronger than they." He agreed with them and acted accordingly.

26 The next spring[l] Ben-Hadad mustered the Arameans and went up to Aphek[m] to fight against Israel. 27 When the Israelites were also mustered and given provisions, they marched out to meet them. The Israelites camped opposite them like two small flocks of goats, while the Arameans covered the countryside.[n]

28 The man of God came up and told the king of Israel, "This is what the LORD says: 'Because the Arameans think the LORD is a god of the hills and not a god[o] of the valleys, I will deliver this vast army into your hands, and you will know[p] that I am the LORD.'"

29 For seven days they camped opposite each other, and on the seventh day the battle was joined. The Israelites inflicted a hundred thousand casualties on the Aramean foot soldiers in one day. 30 The rest of them escaped to the city of Aphek,[q] where the wall collapsed on twenty-seven thousand of them. And Ben-Hadad fled to the city and hid[r] in an inner room.

31 His officials said to him, "Look, we have heard that the kings of the house of Israel are merciful. Let us go to the king of Israel with sackcloth[s] round our waists and ropes round our heads. Perhaps he will spare your life."

32 Wearing sackcloth round their waists and ropes round their heads, they went to the king of Israel and said, "Your servant Ben-Hadad says: 'Please let me live.'"

The king answered, "Is he still alive? He is my brother."

33 The men took this as a good sign and were quick to pick up his word. "Yes, your brother Ben-Hadad!" they said.

"Go and get him," the king said.

When Ben-Hadad came out, Ahab had him come up into his chariot.

34 "I will return the cities[t] my father took from your father," Ben-Hadad offered. "You may set up your own market areas in Damascus,[u] as my father did in Samaria."

⌞Ahab said,⌟ "On the basis of a treaty[v] I will set you free." So he made a treaty with him, and let him go.

20:16 h ver 12; 1Ki 16:9
20:22 i ver 13; j ver 26; 2Sa 11:1
20:23 k 1Ki 14:23; Ro 1:21-23
20:26 l ver 22; m 2Ki 13:17
20:27 n Jdg 6:6; 1Sa 13:6
20:28 o ver 23; p ver 13
20:30 q ver 26; r 1Ki 22:25; 2Ch 18:24
20:31 s Ge 37:34
20:34 t 1Ki 15:20; u Jer 49:23-27; v Ex 23:32

A Prophet Condemns Ahab

35 By the word of the LORD one of the sons of the prophets said to his companion, "Strike me with your weapon," but the man refused.[w]

36 So the prophet said, "Because you have not obeyed the LORD, as soon as you leave me a lion[x] will kill you." And after the man went away, a lion found him and killed him.

37 The prophet found another man and said, "Strike me, please." So the man struck him and wounded him. 38 Then the prophet went and stood by the road waiting for the king. He disguised himself with his headband down over his eyes. 39 As the king passed by, the prophet called out to him, "Your servant went into the thick of the battle, and someone came to me with a captive and said, 'Guard this man. If he is missing, it will be your life for his life,[y] or you must pay a talent[b] of silver.' 40 While your servant was busy here and there, the man disappeared."

"That is your sentence," the king of Israel said. "You have pronounced it yourself."

41 Then the prophet quickly removed the headband from his eyes, and the king of Israel recognised him as one of the prophets. 42 He said to the king, "This is what the LORD says: 'You have set free a man I had determined should die.[c][z] Therefore it is your life for his life,[a] your people for his people.' " 43 Sullen and angry,[b] the king of Israel went to his palace in Samaria.

Naboth's Vineyard

21 Some time later there was an incident involving a vineyard belonging to Naboth[a] the Jezreelite. The vineyard was in Jezreel,[b] close to the palace of Ahab king of Samaria. 2 Ahab said to Naboth, "Let me have your vineyard to use for a vegetable garden, since it is close to my palace. In exchange I will give you a better vineyard or, if you prefer, I will pay you whatever it is worth."

3 But Naboth replied, "The LORD forbid that I should give you the inheritance[c] of my fathers."

4 So Ahab went home, sullen and angry[d] because Naboth the Jezreelite had said, "I will not give you the inheritance of my fathers." He lay on his bed sulking and refused to eat.

5 His wife Jezebel came in and asked him, "Why are you so sullen? Why won't you eat?"

6 He answered her, "Because I said to Naboth the Jezreelite, 'Sell me your vineyard; or if you prefer, I will give you another vineyard in its place.' But he said, 'I will not give you my vineyard.' "

7 Jezebel his wife said, "Is this how you act as king over Israel? Get up and eat! Cheer up. I'll get you the vineyard[e] of Naboth the Jezreelite."

8 So she wrote letters in Ahab's name, placed his seal[f] on them, and sent them to the elders and nobles who lived in Naboth's city with him. 9 In those letters she wrote:

> "Proclaim a day of fasting and seat Naboth in a prominent place among the people. 10 But seat two scoundrels[g] opposite him and have them testify that he has cursed[h] both God and the king. Then take him out and stone him to death."

11 So the elders and nobles who lived in Naboth's city did as Jezebel directed in the letters she had written to them. 12 They proclaimed a fast[i] and seated Naboth in a prominent place among the people. 13 Then two scoundrels came and sat opposite him and brought charges against Naboth before the

20:35 w 1Ki 13:21; 2Ki 2:3-7
20:36 x 1Ki 13:24
20:39 y 2Ki 10:24
20:42 z Jer 48:10; a ver 39; Jos 2:14; 1Ki 22:31-37
20:43 b 1Ki 21:4
21:1 a 2Ki 9:21; b 1Ki 18:45-46
21:3 c Lev 25:23; Nu 36:7; Eze 46:18
21:4 d 1Ki 20:43
21:7 e 1Sa 8:14
21:8 f Ge 38:18; Est 3:12; Est 8:8,10
21:10 g Ac 6:11; h Ex 22:28; Lev 24:15-16
21:12 i Isa 58:4

b39 That is, about 75 pounds (about 34 kilograms)
c42 The Hebrew term refers to the irrevocable giving over of things or persons to the LORD, often by totally destroying them.

people, saying, "Naboth has cursed
both God and the king." So they
took him outside the city and
stoned him to death.[j] 14Then they
sent word to Jezebel: "Naboth has
been stoned and is dead."
15As soon as Jezebel heard that
Naboth had been stoned to death,
she said to Ahab, "Get up and take
possession of the vineyard[k] of Naboth the Jezreelite that he refused
to sell you. He is no longer alive,
but dead." 16When Ahab heard that
Naboth was dead, he got up and
went down to take possession of
Naboth's vineyard.
17Then the word of the LORD
came to Elijah the Tishbite: 18"Go
down to meet Ahab king of Israel,
who rules in Samaria. He is now in
Naboth's vineyard, where he has
gone to take possession of it. 19Say
to him, 'This is what the LORD says:
Have you not murdered a man and
seized his property?' Then say to
him, 'This is what the LORD says: In
the place where dogs licked up Naboth's blood,[l] dogs[m] will lick up
your blood—yes, yours!' "
20Ahab said to Elijah, "So you
have found me, my enemy!"[n]
"I have found you," he answered,
"because you have sold[o] yourself
to do evil in the eyes of the LORD.
21'I am going to bring disaster on
you. I will consume your descendants and cut off from Ahab every
last male[p] in Israel—slave or free.
22I will make your house[q] like that
of Jeroboam son of Nebat and that
of Baasha son of Ahijah, because
you have provoked me to anger and
have caused Israel to sin.'[r]
23"And also concerning Jezebel
the LORD says: 'Dogs[s] will devour
Jezebel by the wall of[a] Jezreel.'
24"Dogs[t] will eat those belonging to Ahab who die in the city, and
the birds of the air will feed on
those who die in the country."
25(There was never[u] a man like
Ahab, who sold himself to do evil in
the eyes of the LORD, urged on by
Jezebel his wife. 26He behaved in
the vilest manner by going after
idols, like the Amorites[v] the LORD
drove out before Israel.)
27When Ahab heard these words,
he tore his clothes, put on sackcloth[w] and fasted. He lay in sackcloth and went around meekly.
28Then the word of the LORD
came to Elijah the Tishbite:
29"Have you noticed how Ahab has
humbled himself before me? Because he has humbled himself, I
will not bring this disaster in his
day, but I will bring it on his house
in the days of his son."[x]

Micaiah Prophesies Against Ahab

22:1-28pp 2Ch 18:1-27

22 For three years there was
no war between Aram and
Israel. 2But in the third year Jehoshaphat king of Judah went
down to see the king of Israel. 3The
king of Israel had said to his officials, "Don't you know that Ramoth
Gilead[a] belongs to us and yet we
are doing nothing to retake it from
the king of Aram?"
4So he asked Jehoshaphat, "Will
you go with me to fight[b] against
Ramoth Gilead?"
Jehoshaphat replied to the king
of Israel, "I am as you are, my people as your people, my horses as
your horses." 5But Jehoshaphat
also said to the king of Israel, "First
seek the counsel[c] of the LORD."
6So the king of Israel brought together the prophets—about four
hundred men—and asked them,
"Shall I go to war against Ramoth
Gilead, or shall I refrain?"
"Go,"[d] they answered, "for the
Lord will give it into the king's
hand."
7But Jehoshaphat asked, "Is
there not a prophet[e] of the LORD
here whom we can enquire of?"

21:13 j 2Ki 9:26
21:15 k 1Sa 8:14
21:19 l 2Ki 9:26 Ps 9:12 Isa 14:20 m 1Ki 22:38
21:20 n 1Ki 18:17 o ver 25 2Ki 17:17 Ro 7:14
21:21 p 1Ki 14:10 2Ki 9:8
21:22 q 1Ki 15:29 1Ki 16:3 r 1Ki 12:30
21:23 s 2Ki 9:10, 34-36
21:24 t 1Ki 14:11 1Ki 16:4
21:25 u ver 20 1Ki 16:33
21:26 v Ge 15:16 Lev 18:25-30 2Ki 21:11
21:27 w Ge 37:34 2Sa 3:31 2Ki 6:30
21:29 x 2Ki 9:26
22:3 a Dt 4:43 Jos 21:38
22:4 b 2Ki 3:7
22:5 c Ex 33:7 2Ki 3:11
22:6 d 1Ki 18:19
22:7 e 2Ki 3:11

a*23* Most Hebrew manuscripts; a few Hebrew manuscripts, Vulgate and Syriac (see also 2 Kings 9:26) *the plot of ground at*

8The king of Israel answered Jehoshaphat, "There is still one man
through whom we can enquire of
the LORD, but I hate[f] him because
he never prophesies anything
good[g] about me, but always bad.
He is Micaiah son of Imlah."
"The king should not say that,"
Jehoshaphat replied.
9So the king of Israel called one
of his officials and said, "Bring Micaiah son of Imlah at once."
10Dressed in their royal robes,
the king of Israel and Jehoshaphat
king of Judah were sitting on their
thrones at the threshing-floor[h] by
the entrance of the gate of Samaria,
with all the prophets prophesying
before them. 11Now Zedekiah son
of Kenaanah had made iron horns[i]
and he declared, "This is what the
LORD says: 'With these you will
gore the Arameans until they are
destroyed.' "
12All the other prophets were
prophesying the same thing. "Attack Ramoth Gilead and be victorious," they said, "for the LORD will
give it into the king's hand."
13The messenger who had gone
to summon Micaiah said to him,
"Look, as one man the other prophets are predicting success for the
king. Let your word agree with
theirs, and speak favourably."
14But Micaiah said, "As surely as
the LORD lives, I can tell him only
what the LORD tells me."[j]
15When he arrived, the king
asked him, "Micaiah, shall we go to
war against Ramoth Gilead, or
shall I refrain?"
"Attack and be victorious," he
answered, "for the LORD will give it
into the king's hand."
16The king said to him, "How
many times must I make you swear
to tell me nothing but the truth in
the name of the LORD?"
17Then Micaiah answered, "I saw
all Israel scattered on the hills like
sheep without a shepherd,[k] and
the LORD said, 'These people have
no master. Let each one go home in
peace.' "
18The king of Israel said to Jehoshaphat, "Didn't I tell you that he
never prophesies anything good
about me, but only bad?"
19Micaiah continued, "Therefore
hear the word of the LORD: I saw
the LORD sitting on his throne[l]
with all the host[m] of heaven standing round him on his right and on
his left. 20And the LORD said, 'Who
will entice Ahab into attacking Ramoth Gilead and going to his death
there?'
"One suggested this, and another
that. 21Finally, a spirit came forward, stood before the LORD and
said, 'I will entice him.'
22" 'By what means?' the LORD
asked.
" 'I will go out and be a lying[n]
spirit in the mouths of all his
prophets,' he said.
" 'You will succeed in enticing
him,' said the LORD. 'Go and do it.'
23"So now the LORD has put a lying spirit in the mouths of all these
prophets[o] of yours. The LORD has
decreed disaster for you."
24Then Zedekiah[p] son of Kenaanah went up and slapped[q] Micaiah
in the face. "Which way did the
spirit from[a] the LORD go when he
went from me to speak to you?" he
asked.
25Micaiah replied, "You will find
out on the day you go to hide[r] in an
inner room."
26The king of Israel then ordered,
"Take Micaiah and send him back
to Amon the ruler of the city and to
Joash the king's son 27and say, 'This
is what the king says: Put this fellow in prison[s] and give him nothing but bread and water until I
return safely.' "
28Micaiah declared, "If you ever
return safely, the LORD has not spoken[t] through me." Then he added,
"Mark my words, all you people!"

22:8 f Am 5:10 g Isa 5:20
22:10 h ver 6
22:11 i Dt 33:17 Zec 1:18-21
22:14 j Nu 22:18 Nu 24:13 1Ki 18:10,15
22:17 k ver 34-36 Nu 27:17 Mt 9:36
22:19 l Isa 6:1 Eze 1:26 Da 7:9 m Job 1:6 Job 2:1 Ps 103:20-21 Mt 18:10 Heb 1:7,14
22:22 n Jdg 9:23 1Sa 16:14 1Sa 18:10 1Sa 19:9 Eze 14:9 2Th 2:11
22:23 o Eze 14:9
22:24 p ver 11 q Ac 23:2
22:25 r 1Ki 20:30
22:27 s 2Ch 16:10
22:28 t Dt 18:22

a24 Or *Spirit of*

Ahab Killed at Ramoth Gilead

22:29–36pp 2Ch 18:28–34

29 So the king of Israel and Jehoshaphat king of Judah went up to Ramoth Gilead. 30 The king of Israel said to Jehoshaphat, "I will enter the battle in disguise,[u] but you wear your royal robes." So the king of Israel disguised himself and went into battle.

31 Now the king of Aram had ordered his thirty-two chariot commanders, "Do not fight with anyone, small or great, except the king[v] of Israel." 32 When the chariot commanders saw Jehoshaphat, they thought, "Surely this is the king of Israel." So they turned to attack him, but when Jehoshaphat cried out, 33 the chariot commanders saw that he was not the king of Israel and stopped pursuing him.

34 But someone drew his bow[w] at random and hit the king of Israel between the sections of his armour. The king told his chariot driver, "Wheel round and get me out of the fighting. I've been wounded." 35 All day long the battle raged, and the king was propped up in his chariot facing the Arameans. The blood from his wound ran onto the floor of the chariot, and that evening he died. 36 As the sun was setting, a cry spread through the army: "Every man to his town; everyone to his land!"[x]

37 So the king died and was brought to Samaria, and they buried him there. 38 They washed the chariot at a pool in Samaria (where the prostitutes bathed),[b] and the dogs[y] licked up his blood, as the word of the LORD had declared.

39 As for the other events of Ahab's reign, including all he did, the palace he built and inlaid with ivory,[z] and the cities he fortified, are they not written in the book of the annals of the kings of Israel? 40 Ahab rested with his fathers. And Ahaziah his son succeeded him as king.

Jehoshaphat King of Judah

22:41–50pp 2Ch 20:31–21:1

41 Jehoshaphat son of Asa became king of Judah in the fourth year of Ahab king of Israel. 42 Jehoshaphat was thirty-five years old when he became king, and he reigned in Jerusalem for twenty-five years. His mother's name was Azubah daughter of Shilhi. 43 In everything he walked in the ways of his father Asa[a] and did not stray from them; he did what was right in the eyes of the LORD. The high places,[b] however, were not removed, and the people continued to offer sacrifices and burn incense there. 44 Jehoshaphat was also at peace with the king of Israel.

45 As for the other events of Jehoshaphat's reign, the things he achieved and his military exploits, are they not written in the book of the annals of the kings of Judah? 46 He rid the land of the rest of the male shrine-prostitutes[c] who remained there even after the reign of his father Asa. 47 There was then no king[d] in Edom; a deputy ruled.

48 Now Jehoshaphat built a fleet of trading ships[c][e] to go to Ophir for gold, but they never set sail—they were wrecked at Ezion Geber. 49 At that time Ahaziah son of Ahab said to Jehoshaphat, "Let my men sail with your men," but Jehoshaphat refused.

50 Then Jehoshaphat rested with his fathers and was buried with them in the city of David his father. And Jehoram his son succeeded him.

Ahaziah King of Israel

51 Ahaziah son of Ahab became king of Israel in Samaria in the seventeenth year of Jehoshaphat king

22:30 *u* 2Ch 35:32
22:31 *v* 2Sa 17:2
22:34 *w* 2Ch 35:23
22:36 *x* 2Ki 14:12
22:38 *y* 1Ki 21:19
22:39 *z* 2Ch 9:17; Am 3:15
22:43 *a* 2Ch 17:3; *b* 1Ki 3:2; 1Ki 15:14; 2Ki 12:3
22:46 *c* Dt 23:17; 1Ki 14:24; 1Ki 15:12
22:47 *d* 2Sa 8:14; 2Ki 3:9; 2Ki 8:20
22:48 *e* 1Ki 9:26; 1Ki 10:22

b38 Or *Samaria and cleaned the weapons*
c48 Hebrew *of ships of Tarshish*

of Judah, and he reigned over Israel for two years. 52He did evil[f] in
the eyes of the LORD, because he
walked in the ways of his father
and mother and in the ways of
Jeroboam son of Nebat, who caused
Israel to sin. 53He served and
worshipped Baal[g] and provoked
the LORD, the God of Israel, to
anger, just as his father[h] had done.

22:52
f 1Ki 15:26
1Ki 21:25

22:53
g Jdg 2:11
h 1Ki 16:30-32

2 KINGS

The LORD's Judgment on Ahaziah

1 After Ahab's death, Moab[a] rebelled against Israel. 2Now
Ahaziah had fallen through the lattice of his upper room in Samaria
and injured himself. So he sent
messengers,[b] saying to them, "Go
and consult Baal-Zebub,[c] the god
of Ekron,[d] to see if I will recover[e]
from this injury."
3But the angel[f] of the LORD said
to Elijah[g] the Tishbite, "Go up and
meet the messengers of the king of
Samaria and ask them, 'Is it because there is no God in Israel[h]
that you are going off to consult
Baal-Zebub, the god of Ekron?'
4Therefore this is what the LORD
says: 'You will not leave[i] the bed
you are lying on. You will certainly
die!' " So Elijah went.
5When the messengers returned
to the king, he asked them, "Why
have you come back?"
6"A man came to meet us," they
replied. "And he said to us, 'Go
back to the king who sent you and
tell him, "This is what the LORD
says: Is it because there is no God
in Israel that you are sending men
to consult Baal-Zebub, the god of
Ekron? Therefore you will not
leave the bed you are lying on. You
will certainly die!" ' "
7The king asked them, "What
kind of man was it who came to
meet you and told you this?"
8They replied, "He was a man
with a garment of hair[j] and with a
leather belt round his waist."
The king said, "That was Elijah
the Tishbite."
9Then he sent[k] to Elijah a captain[l] with his company of fifty
men. The captain went up to Elijah,
who was sitting on the top of a hill,

1:1 a Ge 19:37 2Sa 8:2 2Ki 3:5
1:2 b ver 16 c Mk 3:22 d 1Sa 6:2 Isa 2:6 Isa 14:29 Mt 10:25 e Jdg 18:5 2Ki 8:7-10
1:3 f ver 15 Ge 16:7 g 1Ki 17:1 h 1Sa 28:8
1:4 i ver 6,16 Ps 41:8
1:8 j 1Ki 18:7 Zec 13:4 Mt 3:4 Mk 1:6
1:9 k 2Ki 6:14 l Ex 18:25 Isa 3:3
1:10 m 1Ki 18:38 Lk 9:54 Rev 11:5 Rev 13:13
1:13 n 1Sa 26:21 Ps 72:14
1:15 o ver 3 p Isa 51:12 Isa 57:11 Jer 1:17 Eze 2:6
1:16 q ver 2 r ver 4
1:17 s 2Ki 8:15 Jer 20:6 Jer 28:17

and said to him, "Man of God, the
king says, 'Come down!' "
10Elijah answered the captain,
"If I am a man of God, may fire
come down from heaven and consume you and your fifty men!"
Then the fire[m] fell from heaven
and consumed the captain and his
men.
11At this the king sent to Elijah
another captain with his fifty men.
The captain said to him, "Man of
God, this is what the king says,
'Come down at once!' "
12"If I am a man of God," Elijah
replied, "may fire come down from
heaven and consume you and your
fifty men!" Then the fire of God
fell from heaven and consumed
him and his fifty men.
13So the king sent a third captain
with his fifty men. This third captain went up and fell on his knees
before Elijah. "Man of God," he
begged, "please have respect for
my life[n] and the lives of these fifty
men, your servants! 14See, fire has
fallen from heaven and consumed
the first two captains and all their
men. But now have respect for my
life!"
15The angel[o] of the LORD said to
Elijah, "Go down with him; do not
be afraid[p] of him." So Elijah got up
and went down with him to the
king.
16He told the king, "This is what
the LORD says: Is it because there is
no God in Israel for you to consult
that you have sent messengers[q] to
consult Baal-Zebub, the god of Ekron? Because you have done this,
you will never leave[r] the bed you
are lying on. You will certainly
die!" 17So he died,[s] according to
the word of the LORD that Elijah
had spoken.
Because Ahaziah had no son,

Joram[a][t] succeeded him as king in
the second year of Jehoram son of
Jehoshaphat king of Judah. 18As for
all the other events of Ahaziah's
reign, and what he did, are they not
written in the book of the annals of
the kings of Israel?

Elijah Taken Up to Heaven

2 When the LORD was about to
take[a] Elijah up to heaven in a
whirlwind,[b] Elijah and Elisha[c]
were on their way from Gilgal.[d]
2Elijah said to Elisha, "Stay here;[e]
the LORD has sent me to Bethel."
But Elisha said, "As surely as the
LORD lives and as you live, I will not
leave you."[f] So they went down to
Bethel.
3The company[g] of the prophets
at Bethel came out to Elisha and
asked, "Do you know that the LORD
is going to take your master from
you today?"
"Yes, I know," Elisha replied,
"but do not speak of it."
4Then Elijah said to him, "Stay
here, Elisha; the LORD has sent me
to Jericho.[h]"
And he replied, "As surely as the
LORD lives and as you live, I will not
leave you." So they went to Jericho.
5The company[i] of the prophets
at Jericho went up to Elisha and
asked him, "Do you know that the
LORD is going to take your master
from you today?"
"Yes, I know," he replied, "but do
not speak of it."
6Then Elijah said to him, "Stay
here;[j] the LORD has sent me to the
Jordan."[k]
And he replied, "As surely as the
LORD lives and as you live, I will not
leave you."[l] So the two of them
walked on.
7Fifty men of the company of the
prophets went and stood at a distance, facing the place where Elijah and Elisha had stopped at the
Jordan. 8Elijah took his cloak,[m]
rolled it up and struck[n] the water
with it. The water divided[o] to the
right and to the left, and the two of
them crossed over on dry[p] ground.
9When they had crossed, Elijah
said to Elisha, "Tell me, what can I
do for you before I am taken from
you?"
"Let me inherit a double[q] portion of your spirit,"[r] Elisha replied.
10"You have asked a difficult
thing," Elijah said, "yet if you see
me when I am taken from you, it
will be yours—otherwise not."
11As they were walking along
and talking together, suddenly a
chariot of fire[s] and horses of fire
appeared and separated the two
of them, and Elijah went up to
heaven[t] in a whirlwind.[u] 12Elisha
saw this and cried out, "My father!
My father! The chariots[v] and
horsemen of Israel!" And Elisha
saw him no more. Then he took hold
of his own clothes and tore[w] them
apart.
13He picked up the cloak that had
fallen from Elijah and went back
and stood on the bank of the Jordan. 14Then he took the cloak[x] that
had fallen from him and struck[y]
the water with it. "Where now is the
LORD, the God of Elijah?" he asked.
When he struck the water, it divided to the right and to the left, and
he crossed over.
15The company[z] of the prophets
from Jericho, who were watching,
said, "The spirit[a] of Elijah is resting on Elisha." And they went to
meet him and bowed to the ground
before him. 16"Look," they said,
"we your servants have fifty able
men. Let them go and look for your
master. Perhaps the Spirit[b] of the
LORD has picked him up[c] and set
him down on some mountain or in
some valley."
"No," Elisha replied, "do not send
them."
17But they persisted until he was
too ashamed[d] to refuse. So he said,
"Send them." And they sent fifty

1:17
t 2Ki 3:1; 2Ki 8:16

2:1
a Ge 5:24; Heb 11:5
b ver 11; 1Ki 19:11; Isa 5:28; Isa 66:15; Jer 4:13; Na 1:3
c 1Ki 19:16,21
d Dt 11:30; 2Ki 4:38

2:2
e ver 6
f Ru 1:16; 1Sa 1:26; 2Ki 4:30

2:3
g 1Sa 10:5; 2Ki 4:1,38

2:4
h Jos 3:16; Jos 6:26

2:5
i ver 3

2:6
j ver 2
k Jos 3:15
l Ru 1:16

2:8
m 1Ki 19:19
n ver 14
o Ex 14:21
p Ex 14:22,29

2:9
q Dt 21:17
r Nu 11:17

2:11
s 2Ki 6:17; Ps 68:17; Ps 104:3,4; Isa 66:15; Hab 3:8; Zec 6:1
t Ge 5:24
u ver 1

2:12
v 2Ki 6:17; 2Ki 13:14
w Ge 37:29

2:14
x 1Ki 19:19
y ver 8

2:15
z ver 7; 1Sa 10:5
a Nu 11:17

2:16
b 1Ki 18:12
c Ac 8:39

2:17
d 2Ki 8:11

[a]17 Hebrew *Jehoram*, a variant of *Joram*

men, who searched for three days
but did not find him. 18When they
returned to Elisha, who was staying in Jericho, he said to them,
"Didn't I tell you not to go?"

Healing of the Water

19The men of the city said to Elisha, "Look, our lord, this town is
well situated, as you can see, but
the water is bad and the land is unproductive."
20"Bring me a new bowl," he said,
"and put salt in it." So they brought
it to him.
21Then he went out to the spring
and threw[e] the salt into it, saying,
"This is what the LORD says: 'I have
healed this water. Never again will
it cause death or make the land unproductive.' " 22And the water has
remained wholesome[f] to this day,
according to the word Elisha had
spoken.

Elisha Is Jeered

23From there Elisha went up to
Bethel. As he was walking along
the road, some youths came out of
the town and jeered[g] at him. "Go
on up, you baldhead!" they said.
"Go on up, you baldhead!" 24He
turned round, looked at them and
called down a curse[h] on them in
the name[i] of the LORD. Then two
bears came out of the woods and
mauled forty-two of the youths.
25And he went on to Mount Carmel[j] and from there returned to
Samaria.

Moab Revolts

3 Joram[a][a] son of Ahab became
king of Israel in Samaria in the
eighteenth year of Jehoshaphat
king of Judah, and he reigned for
twelve years. 2He did evil[b] in the
eyes of the LORD, but not as his
father[c] and mother had done. He
got rid of the sacred stone[d] of Baal
that his father had made. 3Never-
theless he clung to the sins[e] of

2:21 *e* Ex 15:25; 2Ki 4:41; 2Ki 6:6
2:22 *f* Ex 15:25
2:23 *g* Ex 22:28; 2Ch 36:16; Job 19:18; Ps 31:18
2:24 *h* Ge 4:11; Ne 13:25-27; *i* Dt 18:19
2:25 *j* 1Ki 18:20; 2Ki 4:25
3:1 *a* 2Ki 1:17
3:2 *b* 1Ki 15:26; *c* 1Ki 16:30-32; *d* Ex 23:24; 2Ki 10:18, 26-28
3:3 *e* 1Ki 12:28-32; 1Ki 14:9,16
3:4 *f* Ge 19:37; 2Ki 1:1; *g* Ezr 7:17; Isa 16:1
3:5 *h* 2Ki 1:1
3:7 *i* 1Ki 22:4
3:9 *j* 1Ki 22:47
3:11 *k* Ge 25:22; 1Ki 22:7; *l* Ge 20:7; *m* 1Ki 19:16
3:12 *n* Nu 11:17

Jeroboam son of Nebat, which he
had caused Israel to commit; he did
not turn away from them.
4Now Mesha king of Moab[f]
raised sheep, and he had to supply
the king of Israel with a hundred
thousand lambs[g] and with the wool
of a hundred thousand rams. 5But
after Ahab died, the king of Moab
rebelled[h] against the king of Israel. 6So at that time King Joram
set out from Samaria and mobilised
all Israel. 7He also sent this message to Jehoshaphat king of Judah:
"The king of Moab has rebelled
against me. Will you go with me to
fight[i] against Moab?"
"I will go with you," he replied. "I
am as you are, my people as your
people, my horses as your horses."
8"By what route shall we attack?"
he asked.
"Through the Desert of Edom,"
he answered.
9So the king of Israel set out with
the king of Judah and the king of
Edom.[j] After a roundabout march
of seven days, the army had no
more water for themselves or for
the animals with them.
10"What!" exclaimed the king of
Israel. "Has the LORD called us
three kings together only to hand
us over to Moab?"
11But Jehoshaphat asked, "Is
there no prophet of the LORD here,
that we may enquire[k] of the LORD
through him?"
An officer of the king of Israel
answered, "Elisha[l] son of Shaphat
is here. He used to pour water on
the hands of Elijah."[b][m]
12Jehoshaphat said, "The word[n]
of the LORD is with him." So the
king of Israel and Jehoshaphat and
the king of Edom went down to
him.
13Elisha said to the king of Israel,
"What do we have to do with each
other? Go to the prophets of your

[a]*1* Hebrew *Jehoram*, a variant of *Joram*; also in verse 6 [b]*11* That is, he was Elijah's personal servant.

father and the prophets of your
mother."
"No," the king of Israel answered, "because it was the LORD
who called us three kings together
to hand us over to Moab."
14Elisha said, "As surely as the
LORD Almighty lives, whom I
serve, if I did not have respect for
the presence of Jehoshaphat king
of Judah, I would not look at you or
even notice you. 15But now bring
me a harpist."[o]
While the harpist was playing,
the hand[p] of the LORD came upon
Elisha 16and he said, "This is what
the LORD says: Make this valley full
of ditches. 17For this is what the
LORD says: You will see neither
wind nor rain, yet this valley will
be filled with water,[q] and you,
your cattle and your other animals
will drink. 18This is an easy[r] thing
in the eyes of the LORD; he will also
hand Moab over to you. 19You will
overthrow every fortified city and
every major town. You will cut
down every good tree, stop up all
the springs, and ruin every good
field with stones."
20The next morning, about the
time[s] for offering the sacrifice,
there it was—water flowing from
the direction of Edom! And the land
was filled with water.[t]
21Now all the Moabites had heard
that the kings had come to fight
against them; so every man, young
and old, who could bear arms was
called up and stationed on the border. 22When they got up early in the
morning, the sun was shining on
the water. To the Moabites across
the way, the water looked red—like
blood. 23"That's blood!" they said.
"Those kings must have fought and
slaughtered each other. Now to the
plunder, Moab!"
24But when the Moabites came to
the camp of Israel, the Israelites
rose up and fought them until they
fled. And the Israelites invaded the
land and slaughtered the Moabites.
25They destroyed the towns, and
each man threw a stone on every
good field until it was covered.
They stopped up all the springs and
cut down every good tree. Only Kir
Hareseth[u] was left with its stones
in place, but men armed with slings
surrounded it and attacked it as
well.
26When the king of Moab saw that
the battle had gone against him, he
took with him seven hundred
swordsmen to break through to
the king of Edom, but they failed.
27Then he took his firstborn[v] son,
who was to succeed him as king,
and offered him as a sacrifice on
the city wall. The fury against Israel was great; they withdrew and
returned to their own land.

The Widow's Oil

4 The wife of a man from the
company[a] of the prophets
cried out to Elisha, "Your servant
my husband is dead, and you know
that he revered the LORD. But now
his creditor[b] is coming to take my
two boys as his slaves."
2Elisha replied to her, "How can
I help you? Tell me, what do you
have in your house?"
"Your servant has nothing there
at all," she said, "except a little
oil."[c]
3Elisha said, "Go round and ask
all your neighbours for empty jars.
Don't ask for just a few. 4Then go
inside and shut the door behind you
and your sons. Pour oil into all the
jars, and as each is filled, put it to
one side."
5She left him and afterwards
shut the door behind her and her
sons. They brought the jars to her
and she kept pouring. 6When all the
jars were full, she said to her son,
"Bring me another one."
But he replied, "There is not a jar
left." Then the oil stopped flowing.
7She went and told the man of
God,[d] and he said, "Go, sell the oil
and pay your debts. You and your
sons can live on what is left."

3:15
o 1Sa 16:23
p Jer 15:17; Eze 1:3
3:17
q Ps 107:35; Isa 32:2; Isa 35:6; Isa 41:18
3:18
r Ge 18:14; 2Ki 20:10; Isa 49:6; Jer 32:17,27; Mk 10:27
3:20
s Ex 29:39-40
t Ex 17:6
3:25
u ver 19; Isa 15:1; Isa 16:7; Jer 48:31,36
3:27
v Dt 12:31; 2Ki 16:3; 2Ki 21:6; 2Ch 28:3; Ps 106:38; Jer 19:4-5; Am 2:1; Mic 6:7
4:1
a 1Sa 10:5; 2Ki 2:3
b Ex 22:26; Lev 25:39-43; Ne 5:3-5; Job 22:6; Job 24:9
4:2
c 1Ki 17:12
4:7
d 1Ki 12:22

The Shunammite's Son Restored to Life

8One day Elisha went to Shunem.[e] And a well-to-do woman was
there, who urged him to stay for a
meal. So whenever he came by, he
stopped there to eat. 9She said to
her husband, "I know that this man
who often comes our way is a holy
man of God. 10Let's make a small
room on the roof and put in it a
bed and a table, a chair and a lamp
for him. Then he can stay[f] there
whenever he comes to us."
11One day when Elisha came, he
went up to his room and lay down
there. 12He said to his servant Gehazi, "Call the Shunammite."[g] So
he called her, and she stood before
him. 13Elisha said to him, "Tell her,
'You have gone to all this trouble
for us. Now what can be done for
you? Can we speak on your behalf
to the king or the commander of the
army?' "

She replied, "I have a home
among my own people."
14"What can be done for her?"
Elisha asked.

Gehazi said, "Well, she has no son
and her husband is old."
15Then Elisha said, "Call her." So
he called her, and she stood in the
doorway. 16"About this time[h] next
year," Elisha said, "you will hold a
son in your arms."

"No, my lord," she objected.
"Don't mislead your servant, O
man of God!"
17But the woman became pregnant, and the next year about that
same time she gave birth to a son,
just as Elisha had told her.
18The child grew, and one day he
went out to his father, who was
with the reapers.[i] 19"My head! My
head!" he said to his father.

His father told a servant, "Carry
him to his mother." 20After the servant had lifted him up and carried
him to his mother, the boy sat on
her lap until noon, and then he died.
21She went up and laid him on the
bed[j] of the man of God, then shut
the door and went out.
22She called her husband and
said, "Please send me one of the
servants and a donkey so I can
go to the man of God quickly and
return."
23"Why go to him today?" he
asked. "It's not the New Moon[k] or
the Sabbath."

"It's all right," she said.
24She saddled the donkey and
said to her servant, "Lead on; don't
slow down for me unless I tell you."
25So she set out and came to the
man of God at Mount Carmel.[l]

When he saw her in the distance,
the man of God said to his servant
Gehazi, "Look! There's the Shunammite! 26Run to meet her and
ask her, 'Are you all right? Is your
husband all right? Is your child all
right?' "

"Everything is all right," she
said.
27When she reached the man of
God at the mountain, she took hold
of his feet. Gehazi came over to
push her away, but the man of God
said, "Leave her alone! She is in
bitter distress,[m] but the LORD has
hidden it from me and has not told
me why."
28"Did I ask you for a son, my
lord?" she said. "Didn't I tell you,
'Don't raise my hopes'?"
29Elisha said to Gehazi, "Tuck
your cloak into your belt,[n] take my
staff[o] in your hand and run. If you
meet anyone, do not greet him, and
if anyone greets you, do not answer. Lay my staff on the boy's
face."
30But the child's mother said, "As
surely as the LORD lives and as you
live, I will not leave you." So he got
up and followed her.
31Gehazi went on ahead and laid
the staff on the boy's face, but
there was no sound or response. So
Gehazi went back to meet Elisha
and told him, "The boy has not
awakened."
32When Elisha reached the house,

4:8 e Jos 19:18
4:10 f Mt 10:41; Ro 12:13
4:12 g 2Ki 8:1
4:16 h Ge 18:10
4:18 i Ru 2:3
4:21 j ver 32
4:23 k Nu 10:10; 1Ch 23:31; Ps 81:3
4:25 l 1Ki 18:20; 2Ki 2:25
4:27 m 1Sa 1:15
4:29 n 1Ki 18:46; 2Ki 2:8,14; 2Ki 9:1; o Ex 4:2; Ex 7:19; Ex 14:16

there was the boy lying dead on his
couch.[p] 33He went in, shut the door
on the two of them and prayed[q] to
the LORD. 34Then he got on the bed
and lay upon the boy, mouth to
mouth, eyes to eyes, hands to
hands. As he stretched[r] himself
out upon him, the boy's body grew
warm. 35Elisha turned away and
walked back and forth in the room
and then got onto the bed and
stretched out upon him once more.
The boy sneezed seven times[s] and
opened his eyes.[t]
36Elisha summoned Gehazi and
said, "Call the Shunammite." And
he did. When she came, he said,
"Take your son."[u] 37She came in,
fell at his feet and bowed to the
ground. Then she took her son and
went out.

Death in the Pot

38Elisha returned to Gilgal[v] and
there was a famine[w] in that region.
While the company of the prophets
was meeting with him, he said to
his servant, "Put on the large pot
and cook some stew for these men."
39One of them went out into the
fields to gather herbs and found a
wild vine. He gathered some of its
gourds and filled the fold of his
cloak. When he returned, he cut
them up into the pot of stew, though
no-one knew what they were. 40The
stew was poured out for the men,
but as they began to eat it, they
cried out, "O man of God, there is
death in the pot!" And they could
not eat it.
41Elisha said, "Get some flour."
He put it into the pot and said,
"Serve it to the people to eat." And
there was nothing harmful in the
pot.[x]

Feeding of a Hundred

42A man came from Baal Shali-
shah,[y] bringing the man of God
twenty loaves[z] of barley bread[a]
baked from the first ripe corn,
along with some ears of new corn.

4:32 p ver 21
4:33 q 1Ki 17:20; Mt 6:6
4:34 r 1Ki 17:21; Ac 20:10
4:35 s Jos 6:15; t 2Ki 8:5
4:36 u Heb 11:35
4:38 v 2Ki 2:1; w Lev 26:26; 2Ki 8:1
4:41 x Ex 15:25; 2Ki 2:21
4:42 y 1Sa 9:4; z Mt 14:17; Mt 15:36; a 1Sa 9:7
4:43 b Lk 9:13; c Mt 14:20; Jn 6:12
5:1 a Ge 10:22; 2Sa 10:19; b Ex 4:6; Nu 12:10; Lk 4:27
5:2 c 2Ki 6:23; 2Ki 13:20; 2Ki 24:2
5:3 d Ge 20:7
5:5 e ver 22; Ge 24:53; Jdg 14:12; 1Sa 9:7
5:7 f 2Ki 19:14; g Ge 30:2; h Dt 32:39; 1Sa 2:6

"Give it to the people to eat," Elisha
said.
43"How can I set this before a
hundred men?" his servant asked.
But Elisha answered, "Give it to
the people to eat.[b] For this is what
the LORD says: 'They will eat and
have some left over.[c]'" 44Then he
set it before them, and they ate and
had some left over, according to
the word of the LORD.

Naaman Healed of Leprosy

5 Now Naaman was commander
of the army of the king of
Aram.[a] He was a great man in the
sight of his master and highly regarded, because through him the
LORD had given victory to Aram.
He was a valiant soldier, but he had
leprosy.[a][b]
2Now bands[c] from Aram had
gone out and had taken captive a
young girl from Israel, and she
served Naaman's wife. 3She said to
her mistress, "If only my master
would see the prophet[d] who is in
Samaria! He would cure him of his
leprosy."
4Naaman went to his master and
told him what the girl from Israel
had said. 5"By all means, go," the
king of Aram replied. "I will send a
letter to the king of Israel." So
Naaman left, taking with him ten
talents[b] of silver, six thousand
shekels[c] of gold and ten sets of
clothing.[e] 6The letter that he took
to the king of Israel read: "With
this letter I am sending my servant
Naaman to you so that you may
cure him of his leprosy."
7As soon as the king of Israel
read the letter,[f] he tore his robes
and said, "Am I God?[g] Can I kill
and bring back to life?[h] Why does
this fellow send someone to me to
be cured of his leprosy? See how

[a]*1* The Hebrew word was used for various diseases affecting the skin—not necessarily leprosy; also in verses 3, 6, 7, 11 and 27.
[b]*5* That is, about 750 pounds (about 340 kilograms)
[c]*5* That is, about 150 pounds (about 70 kilograms)

he is trying to pick a quarrel[i]
with me!"
8When Elisha the man of God
heard that the king of Israel had
torn his robes, he sent him this
message: "Why have you torn your
robes? Make the man come to me
and he will know that there is a
prophet[j] in Israel." 9So Naaman
went with his horses and chariots
and stopped at the door of Elisha's
house. 10Elisha sent a messenger to
say to him, "Go, wash[k] yourself
seven times[l] in the Jordan, and
your flesh will be restored and you
will be cleansed."
11But Naaman went away angry
and said, "I thought that he would
surely come out to me and stand
and call on the name of the LORD his
God, wave his hand[m] over the spot
and cure me of my leprosy. 12Are
not Abana and Pharpar, the rivers
of Damascus, better than any of the
waters[n] of Israel? Couldn't I wash
in them and be cleansed?" So he
turned and went off in a rage.[o]
13Naaman's servants went to him
and said, "My father,[p] if the
prophet had told you to do some
great thing, would you not have
done it? How much more, then,
when he tells you, 'Wash and be
cleansed'?" 14So he went down and
dipped himself in the Jordan seven
times,[q] as the man of God had told
him, and his flesh was restored[r]
and became clean like that of a
young boy.[s]
15Then Naaman and all his attendants went back to the man of
God[t]. He stood before him and
said, "Now I know[u] that there is no
God in all the world except in Israel. Please accept now a gift[v]
from your servant."
16The prophet answered, "As
surely as the LORD lives, whom I
serve, I will not accept a thing."
And even though Naaman urged
him, he refused.[w]
17"If you will not," said Naaman,
"please let me, your servant, be
given as much earth[x] as a pair of
mules can carry, for your servant
will never again make burnt offerings and sacrifices to any other god
but the LORD. 18But may the LORD
forgive your servant for this one
thing: When my master enters the
temple of Rimmon to bow down and
he is leaning[y] on my arm and I bow
there also—when I bow down in the
temple of Rimmon, may the LORD
forgive your servant for this."
19"Go in peace,"[z] Elisha said.
After Naaman had travelled
some distance, 20Gehazi, the servant of Elisha the man of God, said
to himself, "My master was too
easy on Naaman, this Aramean, by
not accepting from him what he
brought. As surely as the LORD[a]
lives, I will run after him and get
something from him."
21So Gehazi hurried after Naaman. When Naaman saw him running towards him, he got down
from the chariot to meet him. "Is
everything all right?" he asked.
22"Everything is all right," Gehazi answered. "My master sent
me to say, 'Two young men from
the company of the prophets have
just come to me from the hill country of Ephraim. Please give them a
talent[d] of silver and two sets of
clothing.' "[b]
23"By all means, take two talents," said Naaman. He urged Gehazi to accept them, and then tied
up the two talents of silver in two
bags, with two sets of clothing. He
gave them to two of his servants,
and they carried them ahead of Gehazi. 24When Gehazi came to the
hill, he took the things from the servants and put them away in the
house. He sent the men away and
they left. 25Then he went in and
stood before his master Elisha.
"Where have you been, Gehazi?"
Elisha asked.
"Your servant didn't go anywhere," Gehazi answered.
26But Elisha said to him, "Was not

5:7 i 1Ki 20:7
5:8 j 1Ki 22:7
5:10 k Jn 9:7; l Ge 33:3; Lev 14:7
5:11 m Ex 7:19
5:12 n Isa 8:6; o Pr 14:17,29; Pr 19:11; Pr 29:11
5:13 p 2Ki 6:21; 2Ki 13:14
5:14 q Ge 33:3; Lev 14:7; Jos 6:15; r Ex 4:7; s Job 33:25; Lk 4:27
5:15 t Jos 2:11; u Jos 4:24; 1Sa 17:46; Da 2:47; v 1Sa 9:7; 1Sa 25:27
5:16 w ver 20,26; Ge 14:23; Da 5:17
5:17 x Ex 20:24
5:18 y 2Ki 7:2
5:19 z 1Sa 1:17; Ac 15:33
5:20 a Ex 20:7
5:22 b ver 5; Ge 45:22

d22 That is, about 75 pounds (about 34 kilograms)

my spirit with you when the man got down from his chariot to meet you? Is this the time[c] to take money, or to accept clothes, olive groves, vineyards, flocks, herds, or menservants and maidservants?[d] 27Naaman's leprosy[e] will cling to you and to your descendants for ever." Then Gehazi[f] went from Elisha's presence and he was leprous, as white as snow.[g]

An Axe-Head Floats

6 The company[a] of the prophets said to Elisha, "Look, the place where we meet with you is too small for us. 2Let us go to the Jordan, where each of us can get a pole; and let us build a place there for us to live."

And he said, "Go."

3Then one of them said, "Won't you please come with your servants?"

"I will," Elisha replied. 4And he went with them.

They went to the Jordan and began to cut down trees. 5As one of them was cutting down a tree, the iron axe-head fell into the water. "Oh, my lord," he cried out, "it was borrowed!"

6The man of God asked, "Where did it fall?" When he showed him the place, Elisha cut a stick and threw[b] it there, and made the iron float. 7"Lift it out," he said. Then the man reached out his hand and took it.

Elisha Traps Blinded Arameans

8Now the king of Aram was at war with Israel. After conferring with his officers, he said, "I will set up my camp in such and such a place."

9The man of God sent word to the king[c] of Israel: "Beware of passing that place, because the Arameans are going down there." 10So the king of Israel checked on the place indicated by the man of God. Time and again Elisha warned[d] the king, so that he was on his guard in such places.

11This enraged the king of Aram. He summoned his officers and demanded of them, "Will you not tell me which of us is on the side of the king of Israel?"

12"None of us, my lord the king[e]," said one of his officers, "but Elisha, the prophet who is in Israel, tells the king of Israel the very words you speak in your bedroom."

13"Go, find out where he is," the king ordered, "so that I can send men and capture him." The report came back: "He is in Dothan."[f] 14Then he sent[g] horses and chariots and a strong force there. They went by night and surrounded the city.

15When the servant of the man of God got up and went out early the next morning, an army with horses and chariots had surrounded the city. "Oh, my lord, what shall we do?" the servant asked.

16"Don't be afraid,"[h] the prophet answered. "Those who are with us are more[i] than those who are with them."

17And Elisha prayed, "O LORD, open his eyes so that he may see." Then the LORD opened the servant's eyes, and he looked and saw the hills full of horses and chariots[j] of fire all round Elisha.

18As the enemy came down towards him, Elisha prayed to the LORD, "Strike these people with blindness."[k] So he struck them with blindness, as Elisha had asked.

19Elisha told them, "This is not the road and this is not the city. Follow me, and I will lead you to the man you are looking for." And he led them to Samaria.

20After they entered the city, Elisha said, "LORD, open the eyes of these men so that they can see." Then the LORD opened their eyes and they looked, and there they were, inside Samaria.

5:26 c ver 16 d Jer 45:5
5:27 e Nu 12:10; 2Ki 15:5 f Col 3:5 g Ex 4:6
6:1 a 1Sa 10:5; 2Ki 4:38
6:6 b Ex 15:25; 2Ki 2:21
6:9 c ver 12
6:10 d Jer 11:18
6:12 e ver 9
6:13 f Ge 37:17
6:14 g 2Ki 1:9
6:16 h Ge 15:1 i 2Ch 32:7; Ps 55:18; Ro 8:31; 1Jn 4:4
6:17 j 2Ki 2:11,12; Ps 68:17; Zec 6:1-7
6:18 k Ge 19:11; Ac 13:11

21 When the king of Israel saw them, he asked Elisha, "Shall I kill them, my father?[l] Shall I kill them?"

22 "Do not kill them," he answered. "Would you kill men you have captured[m] with your own sword or bow? Set food and water before them so that they may eat and drink and then go back to their master." 23 So he prepared a great feast for them, and after they had finished eating and drinking, he sent them away, and they returned to their master. So the bands[n] from Aram stopped raiding Israel's territory.

Famine in Besieged Samaria

24 Some time later, Ben-Hadad[o] king of Aram mobilised his entire army and marched up and laid siege[p] to Samaria. 25 There was a great famine[q] in the city; the siege lasted so long that a donkey's head sold for eighty shekels[a] of silver, and a quarter of a cab[b] of seed pods[c][r] for five shekels.[d]

26 As the king of Israel was passing by on the wall, a woman cried to him, "Help me, my lord the king!"

27 The king replied, "If the LORD does not help you, where can I get help for you? From the threshing-floor? From the winepress?" 28 Then he asked her, "What's the matter?"

She answered, "This woman said to me, 'Give up your son so that we may eat him today, and tomorrow we'll eat my son.' 29 So we cooked my son and ate[s] him. The next day I said to her, 'Give up your son so that we may eat him,' but she had hidden him."

30 When the king heard the woman's words, he tore[t] his robes. As he went along the wall, the people looked, and there, underneath, he had sackcloth[u] on his body. 31 He said, "May God deal with me, be it ever so severely, if the head of Elisha son of Shaphat remains on his shoulders today!"

32 Now Elisha was sitting in his house, and the elders[v] were sitting with him. The king sent a messenger ahead, but before he arrived, Elisha said to the elders, "Don't you see how this murderer[w] is sending someone to cut off my head?[x] Look, when the messenger comes, shut the door and hold it shut against him. Is not the sound of his master's footsteps behind him?"

33 While he was still talking to them, the messenger came down to him. And ⌊the king⌋ said, "This disaster is from the LORD. Why should I wait[y] for the LORD any longer?"

7 Elisha said, "Hear the word of the LORD. This is what the LORD says: About this time tomorrow, a seah[a] of flour will sell for a shekel[b] and two seahs[c] of barley for a shekel[a] at the gate of Samaria."

2 The officer on whose arm the king was leaning[b] said to the man of God, "Look, even if the LORD should open the floodgates[c] of the heavens, could this happen?"

"You will see it with your own eyes," answered Elisha, "but you will not eat[d] any of it!"

The Siege Lifted

3 Now there were four men with leprosy[d][e] at the entrance of the city gate. They said to each other, "Why stay here until we die? 4 If we say, 'We'll go into the city'—the famine is there, and we will die. And if we stay here, we will die. So let's go over to the camp of the Arameans and surrender. If they spare

6:21 *l* 2Ki 5:13
6:22 *m* Dt 20:11; 2Ch 28:8-15; Ro 12:20
6:23 *n* 2Ki 5:2
6:24 *o* 1Ki 15:18; 1Ki 20:1; 2Ki 8:7 *p* Dt 28:52
6:25 *q* Lev 26:26; Ru 1:1 *r* Isa 36:12
6:29 *s* Lev 26:29; Dt 28:53-55
6:30 *t* 2Ki 18:37; Isa 22:15 *u* Ge 37:34; 1Ki 21:27
6:32 *v* Eze 8:1; Eze 14:1; Eze 20:1 *w* 1Ki 18:4 *x* ver 31
6:33 *y* Lev 24:11; Job 2:9; Job 14:14; Isa 40:31
7:1 *a* ver 16
7:2 *b* 2Ki 5:18 *c* ver 19; Ge 7:11; Ps 78:23; Mal 3:10 *d* ver 17
7:3 *e* Lev 13:45-46; Nu 5:1-4

[a] 25 That is, about 2 pounds (about 1 kilogram)
[b] 25 That is, probably about ½ pint (about 0.3 litre)
[c] 25 Or *of dove's dung*
[d] 25 That is, about 2 ounces (about 55 grams)
[a] 1 That is, probably about 13 pints (about 7.3 litres); also in verses 16 and 18
[b] 1 That is, about ⅖ ounce (about 11 grams); also in verses 16 and 18
[c] 1 That is, probably about 13 quarts (about 15 litres); also in verses 16 and 18
[d] 3 The Hebrew word is used for various diseases affecting the skin—not necessarily leprosy; also in verse 8.

us, we live; if they kill us, then we
die."
5At dusk they got up and went to
the camp of the Arameans. When
they reached the edge of the camp,
not a man was there, 6for the Lord
had caused the Arameans to hear
the sound[f] of chariots and horses
and a great army, so that they said
to one another, "Look, the king of
Israel has hired[g] the Hittite[h] and
Egyptian kings to attack us!" 7So
they got up and fled[i] in the dusk
and abandoned their tents and their
horses and donkeys. They left the
camp as it was and ran for their
lives.
8The men who had leprosy[j]
reached the edge of the camp and
entered one of the tents. They ate
and drank, and carried away silver,
gold and clothes, and went off and
hid them. They returned and entered
another tent and took some
things from it and hid them also.
9Then they said to each other,
"We're not doing right. This is a
day of good news and we are keeping
it to ourselves. If we wait until
daylight, punishment will overtake
us. Let's go at once and report this
to the royal palace."
10So they went and called out to
the city gatekeepers and told them,
"We went into the Aramean camp
and not a man was there—not a
sound of anyone—only tethered
horses and donkeys, and the tents
left just as they were." 11The gatekeepers
shouted the news, and it
was reported within the palace.
12The king got up in the night and
said to his officers, "I will tell you
what the Arameans have done to
us. They know we are starving; so
they have left the camp to hide[k] in
the countryside, thinking, 'They
will surely come out, and then we
will take them alive and get into the
city.'"
13One of his officers answered,
"Make some men take five of the
horses that are left in the city.
Their plight will be like that of all
the Israelites left here—yes, they
will only be like all these Israelites
who are doomed. So let us send
them to find out what happened."
14So they selected two chariots
with their horses, and the king sent
them after the Aramean army. He
commanded the drivers, "Go and
find out what has happened."
15They followed them as far as the
Jordan, and they found the whole
road strewn with the clothing and
equipment the Arameans had
thrown away in their headlong
flight. So the messengers returned
and reported to the king. 16Then the
people went out and plundered[l]
the camp of the Arameans. So a
seah of flour sold for a shekel, and
two seahs of barley sold for a
shekel,[m] as the LORD had said.
17Now the king had put the officer
on whose arm he leaned in
charge of the gate, and the people
trampled him in the gateway, and
he died,[n] just as the man of God
had foretold when the king came
down to his house. 18It happened as
the man of God had said to the king:
"About this time tomorrow, a seah
of flour will sell for a shekel and
two seahs of barley for a shekel at
the gate of Samaria."
19The officer had said to the man
of God, "Look, even if the LORD
should open the floodgates[o] of the
heavens, could this happen?" The
man of God had replied, "You will
see it with your own eyes, but you
will not eat any of it!" 20And that is
exactly what happened to him, for
the people trampled him in the
gateway, and he died.

The Shunammite's Land Restored

8 Now Elisha had said to the
woman[a] whose son he had restored
to life, "Go away with your
family and stay for a while wherever
you can, because the LORD has
decreed a famine[b] in the land that
will last seven years."[c] 2The

7:6
f Ex 14:24; 2Sa 5:24; Eze 1:24
g 2Sa 10:6; Jer 46:21
h Nu 13:29

7:7
i Jdg 7:21; Ps 48:4-6; Pr 28:1; Isa 30:17

7:8
j Isa 33:23; Isa 35:6

7:12
k Jos 8:4; 2Ki 6:25-29

7:16
l Isa 33:4,23
m ver 1

7:17
n ver 2; 2Ki 6:32

7:19
o ver 2

8:1
a 2Ki 4:8-37
b Lev 26:26; Dt 28:22; Ru 1:1
c Ge 12:10; Ps 105:16; Hag 1:11

woman proceeded to do as the man
of God said. She and her family
went away and stayed in the land of
the Philistines for seven years.
3At the end of the seven years she
came back from the land of the
Philistines and went to the king to
beg for her house and land. 4The
king was talking to Gehazi, the servant of the man of God, and had
said, "Tell me about all the great
things Elisha has done." 5Just as
Gehazi was telling the king how Elisha had restored[d] the dead to life,
the woman whose son Elisha had
brought back to life came to beg
the king for her house and land.
Gehazi said, "This is the woman,
my lord the king, and this is her son
whom Elisha restored to life." 6The
king asked the woman about it, and
she told him.
Then he assigned an official to
her case and said to him, "Give
back everything that belonged to
her, including all the income from
her land from the day she left the
country until now."

Hazael Murders Ben-Hadad

7Elisha went to Damascus,[e] and
Ben-Hadad[f] king of Aram was ill.
When the king was told, "The man
of God has come all the way up
here," 8he said to Hazael,[g] "Take a
gift[h] with you and go to meet the
man of God. Consult[i] the LORD
through him; ask him, 'Will I recover from this illness?' "
9Hazael went to meet Elisha, taking with him as a gift forty camel-
loads of all the finest wares of
Damascus. He went in and stood
before him, and said, "Your son
Ben-Hadad king of Aram has sent
me to ask, 'Will I recover from this
illness?' "
10Elisha answered, "Go and say
to him, 'You will certainly recover';[j] but[a] the LORD has revealed to me that he will in fact
die." 11He stared at him with
a fixed gaze until Hazael felt

8:5 d 2Ki 4:35
8:7 e 2Sa 8:5; 1Ki 11:24 f 2Ki 6:24
8:8 g 1Ki 19:15 h Ge 32:20; 1Sa 9:7; 2Ki 1:2 i Jdg 18:5
8:10 j Isa 38:1
8:11 k Jdg 3:25 l Lk 19:41
8:12 m 1Ki 19:17; 2Ki 10:32; 2Ki 12:17; 2Ki 13:3,7 n Ps 137:9; Isa 13:16; Hos 13:16; Na 3:10; Lk 19:44 o Ge 34:29 p 2Ki 15:16; Am 1:13
8:13 q 1Sa 17:43; 2Sa 3:8 r 1Ki 19:15
8:15 s 2Ki 1:17
8:16 t 2Ki 1:17; 2Ki 3:1 u 2Ch 21:1-4
8:18 v ver 26; 2Ki 11:1
8:19 w Ge 6:13 x 2Sa 21:17; 2Sa 7:13; 1Ki 11:36; Rev 21:23

ashamed.[k] Then the man of God
began to weep.[l]
12"Why is my lord weeping?"
asked Hazael.
"Because I know the harm[m] you
will do to the Israelites," he answered. "You will set fire to their
fortified places, kill their young
men with the sword, dash[n] their
little children[o] to the ground, and
rip open[p] their pregnant women."
13Hazael said, "How could your
servant, a mere dog,[q] accomplish
such a feat?"
"The LORD has shown me that
you will become king[r] of Aram,"
answered Elisha.
14Then Hazael left Elisha and returned to his master. When Ben-
Hadad asked, "What did Elisha say
to you?" Hazael replied, "He told
me that you would certainly recover." 15But the next day he took a
thick cloth, soaked it in water and
spread it over the king's face, so
that he died.[s] Then Hazael succeeded him as king.

Jehoram King of Judah

8:16-24pp 2Ch 21:5-10,20

16In the fifth year of Joram[t] son
of Ahab king of Israel, when Jehoshaphat was king of Judah, Jehoram[u] son of Jehoshaphat began his
reign as king of Judah. 17He was
thirty-two years old when he became king, and he reigned in Jerusalem for eight years. 18He walked
in the ways of the kings of Israel, as
the house of Ahab had done, for he
married a daughter[v] of Ahab. He
did evil in the eyes of the LORD.
19Nevertheless, for the sake of his
servant David, the LORD was not
willing to destroy[w] Judah. He had
promised to maintain a lamp[x] for
David and his descendants for
ever.
20In the time of Jehoram, Edom
rebelled against Judah and set up

[a]10 The Hebrew may also be read *Go and say, 'You will certainly not recover,' for.*

its own king.[y] 21So Jehoram[b] went
to Zair with all his chariots. The
Edomites surrounded him and his
chariot commanders, but he rose
up and broke through by night; his
army, however, fled back home.
22To this day Edom has been in
rebellion[z] against Judah. Libnah[a]
revolted at the same time.
23As for the other events of Jehoram's reign, and all he did, are they
not written in the book of the annals of the kings of Judah? 24Jeho-
ram rested with his fathers and
was buried with them in the City of
David. And Ahaziah his son succeeded him as king.

Ahaziah King of Judah

8:25–29pp 2Ch 22:1–6

25In the twelfth[b] year of Joram
son of Ahab king of Israel, Ahaziah
son of Jehoram king of Judah began to reign. 26Ahaziah was twenty-
two years old when he became
king, and he reigned in Jerusalem
for one year. His mother's name
was Athaliah,[c] a granddaughter of
Omri[d] king of Israel. 27He walked
in the ways of the house of Ahab[e]
and did evil[f] in the eyes of the
LORD, as the house of Ahab had
done, for he was related by marriage to Ahab's family.
28Ahaziah went with Joram son of
Ahab to war against Hazael king
of Aram at Ramoth Gilead.[g] The
Arameans wounded Joram; 29so
King Joram returned to Jezreel[h] to
recover from the wounds the
Arameans had inflicted on him
at Ramoth[c] in his battle with
Hazael[i] king of Aram.
Then Ahaziah son of Jehoram
king of Judah went down to Jezreel
to see Joram son of Ahab, because
he had been wounded.

Jehu Anointed King of Israel

9 The prophet Elisha summoned
a man from the company[a] of
the prophets and said to him, "Tuck
your cloak into your belt,[b] take
this flask of oil[c] with you and go to
Ramoth Gilead.[d] 2When you get
there, look for Jehu son of Jehoshaphat, the son of Nimshi. Go to him,
get him away from his companions
and take him into an inner room.
3Then take the flask and pour the
oil[e] on his head and declare, 'This
is what the LORD says: I anoint you
king over Israel.' Then open the
door and run; don't delay!"
4So the young man, the prophet,
went to Ramoth Gilead. 5When he
arrived, he found the army officers
sitting together. "I have a message
for you, commander," he said.
"For which of us?" asked Jehu.
"For you, commander," he replied.
6Jehu got up and went into the
house. Then the prophet poured the
oil[f] on Jehu's head and declared,
"This is what the LORD, the God of
Israel, says: 'I anoint you king over
the LORD's people Israel. 7You are
to destroy the house of Ahab your
master, and I will avenge[g] the
blood of my servants[h] the prophets and the blood of all the LORD's
servants shed by Jezebel.[i] 8The
whole house[j] of Ahab will perish.
I will cut off from Ahab every last
male[k] in Israel—slave or free. 9I
will make the house of Ahab like
the house of Jeroboam[l] son of Nebat and like the house of Baasha[m]
son of Ahijah. 10As for Jezebel,
dogs[n] will devour her on the plot of
ground at Jezreel, and no-one will
bury her.' " Then he opened the
door and ran.
11When Jehu went out to his fellow officers, one of them asked
him, "Is everything all right? Why
did this madman[o] come to you?"
"You know the man and the sort
of things he says," Jehu replied.
12"That's not true!" they said.
"Tell us."
Jehu said, "Here is what he told

8:20 y 1Ki 22:47
8:22 z Ge 27:40; a Nu 33:20; Jos 21:13; 2Ki 19:8
8:25 b 2Ki 9:29
8:26 c ver 18; d 1Ki 16:23
8:27 e 1Ki 16:30; f 1Ki 15:26
8:28 g Dt 4:43; 1Ki 22:3,29
8:29 h 2Ki 9:15; i 1Ki 19:15,17
9:1 a 1Sa 10:5; b 2Ki 4:29; c 1Sa 10:1; d 2Ki 8:28
9:3 e 1Ki 19:16
9:6 f 1Ki 19:16; 2Ch 22:7
9:7 g Ge 4:24; Rev 6:10; h Dt 32:43; i 1Ki 18:4; 1Ki 21:15
9:8 j 2Ki 10:17; k Dt 32:36; 1Sa 25:22; 1Ki 21:21; 2Ki 14:26
9:9 l 1Ki 14:10; 1Ki 15:29; 1Ki 16:3,11; m 1Ki 16:3
9:10 n ver 35-36; 1Ki 21:23
9:11 o Jer 29:26; Jn 10:20; Ac 26:24

[b]21 Hebrew *Joram*, a variant of *Jehoram*; also in verses 23 and 24 [c]29 Hebrew *Ramah*, a variant of *Ramoth*

me: 'This is what the LORD says: I anoint you king over Israel.' "

13 They hurried and took their cloaks and spread[p] them under him on the bare steps. Then they blew the trumpet[q] and shouted, "Jehu is king!"

Jehu Kills Joram and Ahaziah

9:21–29pp 2Ch 22:7–9

14 So Jehu son of Jehoshaphat, the son of Nimshi, conspired against Joram. (Now Joram and all Israel had been defending Ramoth Gilead[r] against Hazael king of Aram, 15 but King Joram[a] had returned to Jezreel to recover[s] from the wounds the Arameans had inflicted on him in the battle with Hazael king of Aram.) Jehu said, "If this is the way you feel, don't let anyone slip out of the city to go and tell the news in Jezreel." 16 Then he got into his chariot and rode to Jezreel, because Joram was resting there and Ahaziah[t] king of Judah had gone down to see him.

17 When the lookout[u] standing on the tower in Jezreel saw Jehu's troops approaching, he called out, "I see some troops coming."

"Get a horseman," Joram ordered. "Send him to meet them and ask, 'Do you come in peace?[v]' "

18 The horseman rode off to meet Jehu and said, "This is what the king says: 'Do you come in peace?' "

"What do you have to do with peace?" Jehu replied. "Fall in behind me."

The lookout reported, "The messenger has reached them, but he isn't coming back."

19 So the king sent out a second horseman. When he came to them he said, "This is what the king says: 'Do you come in peace?' "

Jehu replied, "What do you have to do with peace? Fall in behind me."

20 The lookout reported, "He has reached them, but he isn't coming back either. The driving is like[w] that of Jehu son of Nimshi—he drives like a madman."

21 "Hitch up my chariot," Joram ordered. And when it was hitched up, Joram king of Israel and Ahaziah king of Judah rode out, each in his own chariot, to meet Jehu. They met him at the plot of ground that had belonged to Naboth[x] the Jezreelite. 22 When Joram saw Jehu he asked, "Have you come in peace, Jehu?"

"How can there be peace," Jehu replied, "as long as all the idolatry and witchcraft of your mother Jezebel[y] abound?"

23 Joram turned about and fled, calling out to Ahaziah, "Treachery,[z] Ahaziah!"

24 Then Jehu drew his bow[a] and shot Joram between the shoulders. The arrow pierced his heart and he slumped down in his chariot. 25 Jehu said to Bidkar, his chariot officer, "Pick him up and throw him on the field that belonged to Naboth the Jezreelite. Remember how you and I were riding together in chariots behind Ahab his father when the LORD made this prophecy[b] about him: 26 'Yesterday I saw the blood of Naboth[c] and the blood of his sons, declares the LORD, and I will surely make you pay for it on this plot of ground, declares the LORD.'[b] Now then, pick him up and throw him on that plot, in accordance with the word of the LORD."[d]

27 When Ahaziah king of Judah saw what had happened, he fled up the road to Beth Haggan.[c] Jehu chased him, shouting, "Kill him too!" They wounded him in his chariot on the way up to Gur near Ibleam,[e] but he escaped to Megiddo[f] and died there. 28 His servants took him by chariot[g] to Jerusalem and buried him with his fathers in his tomb in the City of

9:13 *p* Mt 21:8; Lk 19:36 *q* 2Sa 15:10; 1Ki 1:34,39
9:14 *r* Dt 4:43; 2Ki 8:28
9:15 *s* 2Ki 8:29
9:16 *t* 2Ch 22:7
9:17 *u* Isa 21:6 *v* 1Sa 16:4
9:20 *w* 2Sa 18:27
9:21 *x* ver 26; 1Ki 21:1-7, 15-19
9:22 *y* 1Ki 16:30-33; 1Ki 18:19; 2Ch 21:13; Rev 2:20
9:23 *z* 2Ki 11:14
9:24 *a* 1Ki 22:34
9:25 *b* 1Ki 21:19-22, 24-29
9:26 *c* 1Ki 21:19 *d* 1Ki 21:29
9:27 *e* Jdg 1:27 *f* 2Ki 23:29
9:28 *g* 2Ki 14:20; 2Ki 23:30

[a] *15* Hebrew *Jehoram*, a variant of *Joram*; also in verses 17 and 21–24 [b] *26* See 1 Kings 21:19.
[c] *27* Or *fled by way of the garden house*

David. 29(In the eleventh[h] year of Joram son of Ahab, Ahaziah had become king of Judah.)

Jezebel Killed

30Then Jehu went to Jezreel. When Jezebel heard about it, she painted[i] her eyes, arranged her hair and looked out of a window. 31As Jehu entered the gate, she asked, "Have you come in peace, Zimri,[j] you murderer of your master?"[d]

32He looked up at the window and called out, "Who is on my side? Who?" Two or three eunuchs looked down at him. 33"Throw her down!" Jehu said. So they threw her down, and some of her blood spattered the wall and the horses as they trampled her underfoot.[k]

34Jehu went in and ate and drank. "Take care of that cursed woman," he said, "and bury her, for she was a king's daughter."[l] 35But when they went out to bury her, they found nothing except her skull, her feet and her hands. 36They went back and told Jehu, who said, "This is the word of the LORD that he spoke through his servant Elijah the Tishbite: On the plot of ground at Jezreel dogs[m] will devour Jezebel's flesh.[e][n] 37Jezebel's body will be like refuse[o] on the ground in the plot at Jezreel, so that no-one will be able to say, 'This is Jezebel.' "

Ahab's Family Killed

10 Now there were in Samaria[a] seventy sons[b] of the house of Ahab. So Jehu wrote letters and sent them to Samaria: to the officials of Jezreel,[a][c] to the elders and to the guardians[d] of Ahab's children. He said, 2"As soon as this letter reaches you, since your master's sons are with you and you have chariots and horses, a fortified city and weapons, 3choose the best and most worthy of your master's sons and set him on his father's throne. Then fight for your master's house."

4But they were terrified and said, "If two kings could not resist him, how can we?"

5So the palace administrator, the city governor, the elders and the guardians sent this message to Jehu: "We are your servants[e] and we will do anything you say. We will not appoint anyone as king; you do whatever you think best."

6Then Jehu wrote them a second letter, saying, "If you are on my side and will obey me, take the heads of your master's sons and come to me in Jezreel by this time tomorrow."

Now the royal princes, seventy of them, were with the leading men of the city, who were bringing them up. 7When the letter arrived, these men took the princes and slaughtered all seventy[f] of them. They put their heads[g] in baskets and sent them to Jehu in Jezreel. 8When the messenger arrived, he told Jehu, "They have brought the heads of the princes."

Then Jehu ordered, "Put them in two piles at the entrance of the city gate until morning."

9The next morning Jehu went out. He stood before all the people and said, "You are innocent. It was I who conspired against my master and killed him, but who killed all these? 10Know then, that not a word the LORD has spoken against the house of Ahab will fail. The LORD has done what he promised[h] through his servant Elijah."[i] 11So Jehu[j] killed everyone in Jezreel who remained of the house of Ahab, as well as all his chief men, his close friends and his priests, leaving him no survivor.[k]

12Jehu then set out and went towards Samaria. At Beth Eked of the Shepherds, 13he met some relatives

9:29 h 2Ki 8:25
9:30 i Jer 4:30; Eze 23:40
9:31 j 1Ki 16:9-10
9:33 k Ps 7:5
9:34 l 1Ki 16:31; 1Ki 21:25
9:36 m Ps 68:23; Jer 15:3; n 1Ki 21:23
9:37 o Ps 83:10; Isa 5:25; Jer 8:2; Jer 9:22; Jer 16:4; Jer 25:33; Zep 1:17
10:1 a 1Ki 13:32; b Jdg 8:30; c 1Ki 21:1; d ver 5
10:5 e Jos 9:8; 1Ki 20:4,32
10:7 f 1Ki 21:21; g 2Sa 4:8
10:10 h 2Ki 9:7-10; i 1Ki 21:29
10:11 j Hos 1:4; k ver 14; Job 18:19

[d]31 Or *"Did Zimri have peace, who murdered his master?"* [e]36 See 1 Kings 21:23.
[a]1 Hebrew; some Septuagint manuscripts and Vulgate *of the city*

of Ahaziah king of Judah and asked, “Who are you?”

They said, “We are relatives of Ahaziah,[l] and we have come down to greet the families of the king and of the queen mother.[m]”

14“Take them alive!” he ordered. So they took them alive and slaughtered them by the well of Beth Eked—forty-two men. He left no survivor.

15After he left there, he came upon Jehonadab[n] son of Recab,[o] who was on his way to meet him. Jehu greeted him and said, “Are you in accord with me, as I am with you?”

“I am,” Jehonadab answered.

“If so,” said Jehu, “give me your hand.”[p] So he did, and Jehu helped him up into the chariot. 16Jehu said, “Come with me and see my zeal[q] for the LORD.” Then he made him ride in his chariot.

17When Jehu came to Samaria, he killed all who were left there of Ahab’s family;[r] he destroyed them, according to the word of the LORD spoken to Elijah.

Ministers of Baal Killed

18Then Jehu brought all the people together and said to them, “Ahab served[s] Baal a little; Jehu will serve him much. 19Now summon[t] all the prophets of Baal, all his ministers and all his priests. See that no-one is missing, because I am going to hold a great sacrifice for Baal. Anyone who fails to come will no longer live.” But Jehu was acting deceptively in order to destroy the ministers of Baal.

20Jehu said, “Call an assembly[u] in honour of Baal.” So they proclaimed it. 21Then he sent word throughout Israel, and all the ministers of Baal came; not one stayed away. They crowded into the temple of Baal until it was full from one end to the other. 22And Jehu said to the keeper of the wardrobe, “Bring robes for all the ministers of Baal.”

10:13
l 2Ki 8:24,29; 2Ch 22:8
m 1Ki 2:19

10:15
n Jer 35:6, 14-19
o 1Ch 2:55; Jer 35:2
p Ezr 10:19; Eze 17:18

10:16
q Nu 25:13; 1Ki 19:10

10:17
r 2Ki 9:8

10:18
s Jdg 2:11; 1Ki 16:31-32

10:19
t 1Ki 18:19; 1Ki 22:6

10:20
u Ex 32:5; Joel 1:14

10:24
v 1Ki 20:39

10:25
w Ex 22:20; 2Ki 11:18
x 1Ki 18:40

10:26
y 1Ki 14:23

10:27
z 1Ki 16:32

10:28
a 1Ki 19:17

10:29
b 1Ki 12:30
c 1Ki 12:28-29
d 1Ki 12:32

10:30
e ver 35; 2Ki 15:12

10:31
f Pr 4:23
g 1Ki 12:30

10:32
h 2Ki 13:25
i 1Ki 19:17; 2Ki 8:12

So he brought out robes for them. 23Then Jehu and Jehonadab son of Recab went into the temple of Baal. Jehu said to the ministers of Baal, “Look around and see that no servants of the LORD are here with you—only ministers of Baal.” 24So they went in to make sacrifices and burnt offerings. Now Jehu had posted eighty men outside with this warning: “If one of you lets any of the men I am placing in your hands escape, it will be your life for his life.”[v]

25As soon as Jehu had finished making the burnt offering, he ordered the guards and officers: “Go in and kill[w] them; let no-one escape.”[x] So they cut them down with the sword. The guards and officers threw the bodies out and then entered the inner shrine of the temple of Baal. 26They brought the sacred stone[y] out of the temple of Baal and burned it. 27They demolished the sacred stone of Baal and tore down the temple[z] of Baal, and people have used it for a latrine to this day.

28So Jehu[a] destroyed Baal worship in Israel. 29However, he did not turn away from the sins[b] of Jeroboam son of Nebat, which he had caused Israel to commit—the worship of the golden calves[c] at Bethel[d] and Dan.

30The LORD said to Jehu, “Because you have done well in accomplishing what is right in my eyes and have done to the house of Ahab all I had in mind to do, your descendants will sit on the throne of Israel to the fourth generation.”[e] 31Yet Jehu was not careful[f] to keep the law of the LORD, the God of Israel, with all his heart. He did not turn away from the sins[g] of Jeroboam, which he had caused Israel to commit.

32In those days the LORD began to reduce[h] the size of Israel. Hazael[i] overpowered the Israelites throughout their territory 33east of the Jordan in all the land of Gilead

(the region of Gad, Reuben and Manasseh), from Aroer[j] by the Arnon
Gorge through Gilead to Bashan.
34 As for the other events of
Jehu's reign, all he did, and all his
achievements, are they not written
in the book of the annals[k] of the
kings of Israel?
35 Jehu rested with his fathers
and was buried in Samaria. And Jehoahaz his son succeeded him as
king. 36 The time that Jehu reigned
over Israel in Samaria was twenty-eight years.

Athaliah and Joash

11:1-21pp 2Ch 22:10-23:21

11 When Athaliah[a] the
mother of Ahaziah saw that
her son was dead, she proceeded to
destroy the whole royal family.
2 But Jehosheba, the daughter of
King Jehoram[a] and sister of Ahaziah, took Joash[b] son of Ahaziah and
stole him away from among the
royal princes, who were about to be
murdered. She put him and his
nurse in a bedroom to hide him
from Athaliah; so he was not
killed.[c] 3 He remained hidden with
his nurse at the temple of the LORD
for six years while Athaliah ruled
the land.
4 In the seventh year Jehoiada
sent for the commanders of units of
a hundred, the Carites[d] and the
guards and had them brought to
him at the temple of the LORD. He
made a covenant with them and put
them under oath at the temple of
the LORD. Then he showed them the
king's son. 5 He commanded them,
saying, "This is what you are to do:
You who are in the three companies
that are going on duty on the Sabbath[e]—a third of you guarding the
royal palace,[f] 6 a third at the Sur
Gate, and a third at the gate behind
the guard, who take turns guarding
the temple—7 and you who are in
the other two companies that normally go off Sabbath duty are all
to guard the temple for the king.
8 Station yourselves round the king,
each man with his weapon in his
hand. Anyone who approaches
your ranks[b] must be put to death.
Stay close to the king wherever he
goes."
9 The commanders of units of a
hundred did just as Jehoiada the
priest ordered. Each one took his
men—those who were going on
duty on the Sabbath and those who
were going off duty—and came to
Jehoiada the priest. 10 Then he gave
the commanders the spears and
shields[g] that had belonged to King
David and that were in the temple
of the LORD. 11 The guards, each
with his weapon in his hand, stationed themselves round the king—
near the altar and the temple, from
the south side to the north side of
the temple.
12 Jehoiada brought out the king's
son and put the crown on him; he
presented him with a copy of the
covenant[h] and proclaimed him
king. They anointed[i] him, and the
people clapped their hands[j] and
shouted, "Long live the king!"[k]
13 When Athaliah heard the noise
made by the guards and the people,
she went to the people at the temple
of the LORD. 14 She looked and there
was the king, standing by the pillar,[l] as the custom was. The officers and the trumpeters were
beside the king, and all the people
of the land were rejoicing and
blowing trumpets.[m] Then Athaliah
tore[n] her robes and called out,
"Treason! Treason!"[o]
15 Jehoiada the priest ordered the
commanders of units of a hundred,
who were in charge of the troops:
"Bring her out between the ranks[c]
and put to the sword anyone who
follows her." For the priest had
said, "She must not be put to death
in the temple[p] of the LORD." 16 So
they seized her as she reached the

10:33 *j* Nu 32:34 Dt 2:36 Jdg 11:26 Isa 17:2
10:34 *k* 1Ki 15:31
11:1 *a* 2Ki 8:18
11:2 *b* ver 21 2Ki 12:1 *c* Jdg 9:5
11:4 *d* ver 19
11:5 *e* 1Ch 9:25 *f* 1Ki 14:27
11:10 *g* 2Sa 8:7 1Ch 18:7
11:12 *h* Ex 25:16 2Ki 23:3 *i* 1Sa 9:16 1Ki 1:39 *j* Ps 47:1 Ps 98:8 Isa 55:12 *k* 1Sa 10:24
11:14 *l* 1Ki 7:15 2Ki 23:3 2Ch 34:31 *m* 1Ki 1:39 *n* Ge 37:29 *o* 2Ki 9:23
11:15 *p* 1Ki 2:30

a2 Hebrew *Joram*, a variant of *Jehoram*
b8 Or *approaches the precincts* c15 Or *out from the precincts*

place where the horses enter[q] the palace grounds, and there she was put to death.[r]

[17]Jehoiada then made a covenant[s] between the LORD and the king and people that they would be the LORD's people. He also made a covenant between the king and the people.[t] [18]All the people of the land went to the temple[u] of Baal and tore it down. They smashed[v] the altars and idols to pieces and killed Mattan the priest[w] of Baal in front of the altars.

Then Jehoiada the priest posted guards at the temple of the LORD. [19]He took with him the commanders of hundreds, the Carites,[x] the guards and all the people of the land, and together they brought the king down from the temple of the LORD and went into the palace, entering by way of the gate of the guards. The king then took his place on the royal throne, [20]and all the people of the land rejoiced.[y] And the city was quiet, because Athaliah had been slain with the sword at the palace.

[21]Joash[d] was seven years old when he began his reign.

Joash Repairs the Temple

12:1–21pp 2Ch 24:1–14,23–27

12 In the seventh year of Jehu, Joash[a][a] became king, and he reigned in Jerusalem for forty years. His mother's name was Zibiah; she was from Beersheba. [2]Joash did what was right in the eyes of the LORD all the years Jehoiada the priest instructed him. [3]The high places,[b] however, were not removed; the people continued to offer sacrifices and burn incense there.

[4]Joash said to the priests, "Collect[c] all the money that is brought as sacred offerings[d] to the temple of the LORD—the money collected in the census,[e] the money received from personal vows and the money brought voluntarily[f] to the temple. [5]Let every priest receive the money from one of the treasurers, and let it be used to repair whatever damage is found in the temple."

[6]But by the twenty-third year of King Joash the priests still had not repaired the temple. [7]Therefore King Joash summoned Jehoiada the priest and the other priests and asked them, "Why aren't you repairing the damage done to the temple? Take no more money from your treasurers, but hand it over for repairing the temple." [8]The priests agreed that they would not collect any more money from the people and that they would not repair the temple themselves.

[9]Jehoiada the priest took a chest and bored a hole in its lid. He placed it beside the altar, on the right side as one enters the temple of the LORD. The priests who guarded the entrance[g] put into the chest all the money[h] that was brought to the temple of the LORD. [10]Whenever they saw that there was a large amount of money in the chest, the royal secretary[i] and the high priest came, counted the money that had been brought into the temple of the LORD and put it into bags. [11]When the amount had been determined, they gave the money to the men appointed to supervise the work on the temple. With it they paid those who worked on the temple of the LORD—the carpenters and builders, [12]the masons and stonecutters.[j] They purchased timber and dressed stone for the repair of the temple of the LORD, and met all the other expenses of restoring the temple.

[13]The money brought into the temple was not spent for making silver basins, wick trimmers, sprinkling bowls, trumpets or any other articles of gold[k] or silver for

11:16 q Ne 3:28; Jer 31:40 r Ge 4:14
11:17 s Ex 24:8; 2Sa 5:3; 2Ch 15:12; 2Ch 23:3; 2Ch 29:10; 2Ch 34:31; Ezr 10:3 t 2Ki 23:3; Jer 34:8
11:18 u 1Ki 16:32 v Dt 12:3 w 1Ki 18:40; 2Ki 10:25; 2Ki 23:20
11:19 x ver 4
11:20 y Pr 11:10; Pr 28:12; Pr 29:2
12:1 a 2Ki 11:2
12:3 b 1Ki 3:3; 2Ki 14:4; 2Ki 15:35; 2Ki 18:4
12:4 c 2Ki 22:4 d Ex 35:5 e Ex 30:12 f Ex 35:29; 1Ch 29:3-9
12:9 g Jer 35:4 h 2Ch 24:8; Mk 12:41; Lk 21:1
12:10 i 2Sa 8:17
12:12 j 2Ki 22:5-6
12:13 k 1Ki 7:48-51; 2Ch 24:14

d21 Hebrew *Jehoash*, a variant of *Joash*
a1 Hebrew *Jehoash*, a variant of *Joash*; also in verses 2, 4, 6, 7 and 18

the temple of the LORD; 14it was paid to the workmen, who used it to repair the temple. 15They did not require an accounting from those to whom they gave the money to pay the workers, because they acted with complete honesty.[l] 16The money from the guilt offerings[m] and sin offerings[n] was not brought into the temple of the LORD; it belonged[o] to the priests.

17About this time Hazael[p] king of Aram went up and attacked Gath and captured it. Then he turned to attack Jerusalem. 18But Joash king of Judah took all the sacred objects dedicated by his fathers—Jehoshaphat, Jehoram and Ahaziah, the kings of Judah—and the gifts he himself had dedicated and all the gold found in the treasuries of the temple of the LORD and of the royal palace, and he sent[q] them to Hazael king of Aram, who then withdrew[r] from Jerusalem.

19As for the other events of the reign of Joash, and all he did, are they not written in the book of the annals of the kings of Judah? 20His officials[s] conspired against him and assassinated[t] him at Beth Millo,[u] on the road down to Silla. 21The officials who murdered him were Jozabad son of Shimeath and Jehozabad son of Shomer. He died and was buried with his fathers in the City of David. And Amaziah his son succeeded him as king.

Jehoahaz King of Israel

13 In the twenty-third year of Joash son of Ahaziah king of Judah, Jehoahaz son of Jehu became king of Israel in Samaria, and he reigned for seventeen years. 2He did evil[a] in the eyes of the LORD by following the sins of Jeroboam son of Nebat, which he had caused Israel to commit, and he did not turn away from them. 3So the LORD's anger[b] burned against Israel, and for a long time he kept them under the power[c] of Hazael king of Aram and Ben-Hadad[d] his son.

4Then Jehoahaz sought[e] the LORD's favour, and the LORD listened to him, for he saw[f] how severely the king of Aram was oppressing[g] Israel. 5The LORD provided a deliverer[h] for Israel, and they escaped from the power of Aram. So the Israelites lived in their own homes as they had before. 6But they did not turn away from the sins[i] of the house of Jeroboam, which he had caused Israel to commit; they continued in them. Also, the Asherah pole[a][j] remained standing in Samaria.

7Nothing had been left[k] of the army of Jehoahaz except fifty horsemen, ten chariots and ten thousand foot soldiers, for the king of Aram had destroyed the rest and made them like the dust[l] at threshing time.

8As for the other events of the reign of Jehoahaz, all he did and his achievements, are they not written in the book of the annals of the kings of Israel? 9Jehoahaz rested with his fathers and was buried in Samaria. And Jehoash[b] his son succeeded him as king.

Jehoash King of Israel

10In the thirty-seventh year of Joash king of Judah, Jehoash son of Jehoahaz became king of Israel in Samaria, and he reigned for sixteen years. 11He did evil in the eyes of the LORD and did not turn away from any of the sins of Jeroboam son of Nebat, which he had caused Israel to commit; he continued in them.

12As for the other events of the reign of Jehoash, all he did and his achievements, including his war against Amaziah[m] king of Judah, are they not written in the book of the annals[n] of the kings of Israel?

[a]6 That is, a symbol of the goddess Asherah; here and elsewhere in 2 Kings [b]9 Hebrew *Joash*, a variant of *Jehoash*; also in verses 12–14 and 25

12:15
l 2Ki 22:7; 1Co 4:2
12:16
m Lev 5:14-19; Nu 18:9
n Lev 4:1-35
o Lev 7:7
12:17
p 2Ki 8:12
12:18
q 1Ki 15:18; 2Ch 21:16-17
r 1Ki 15:21
12:20
s 2Ki 14:5
t 2Ch 24:25
u Jdg 9:6
13:2
a 1Ki 12:26-33
13:3
b Dt 31:17; Jdg 2:14
c 1Ki 8:12; 1Ki 12:17; 1Ki 19:17
d ver 24
13:4
e Dt 4:29; Ps 78:34
f Ex 3:7; Dt 26:7
g 2Ki 14:26
13:5
h ver 25; 2Ki 14:25,27
13:6
i 1Ki 12:30
j 1Ki 16:33
13:7
k 2Ki 10:32-33
l 2Sa 22:43
13:12
m 2Ki 14:15
n 1Ki 15:31

13Jehoash rested with his fathers, and Jeroboam[o] succeeded him on the throne. Jehoash was buried in Samaria with the kings of Israel.

14Now Elisha was suffering from the illness from which he died. Jehoash king of Israel went down to see him and wept over him. "My father! My father!" he cried. "The chariots[p] and horsemen of Israel!"

15Elisha said, "Get a bow and some arrows,"[q] and he did so. 16"Take the bow in your hands," he said to the king of Israel. When he had taken it, Elisha put his hands on the king's hands.

17"Open the east window," he said, and he opened it. "Shoot!"[r] Elisha said, and he shot. "The LORD's arrow of victory, the arrow of victory over Aram!" Elisha declared. "You will completely destroy the Arameans at Aphek."[s]

18Then he said, "Take the arrows," and the king took them. Elisha told him, "Strike the ground." He struck it three times and stopped. 19The man of God was angry with him and said, "You should have struck the ground five or six times; then you would have defeated Aram and completely destroyed it. But now you will defeat it only three times."[t]

20Elisha died and was buried.

Now Moabite raiders[u] used to enter the country every spring. 21Once while some Israelites were burying a man, suddenly they saw a band of raiders; so they threw the man's body into Elisha's tomb. When the body touched Elisha's bones, the man came to life[v] and stood up on his feet.

22Hazael king of Aram oppressed[w] Israel throughout the reign of Jehoahaz. 23But the LORD was gracious to them and had compassion and showed concern for them because of his covenant[x] with Abraham, Isaac and Jacob. To this day he has been unwilling to destroy[y] them or banish them from his presence.[z]

24Hazael king of Aram died, and Ben-Hadad[a] his son succeeded him as king. 25Then Jehoash son of Jehoahaz recaptured from Ben-Hadad son of Hazael the towns he had taken in battle from his father Jehoahaz. Three times[b] Jehoash defeated him, and so he recovered[c] the Israelite towns.

Amaziah King of Judah

14:1–7pp 2Ch 25:1–4,11–12
14:8–22pp 2Ch 25:17–26:2

14 In the second year of Jehoash[a] son of Jehoahaz king of Israel, Amaziah son of Joash king of Judah began to reign. 2He was twenty-five years old when he became king, and he reigned in Jerusalem for twenty-nine years. His mother's name was Jehoaddin; she was from Jerusalem. 3He did what was right in the eyes of the LORD, but not as his father David had done. In everything he followed the example of his father Joash. 4The high places,[a] however, were not removed; the people continued to offer sacrifices and burn incense there.

5After the kingdom was firmly in his grasp, he executed[b] the officials[c] who had murdered his father the king. 6Yet he did not put the sons of the assassins to death, in accordance with what is written in the Book of the Law[d] of Moses where the LORD commanded: "Fathers shall not be put to death for their children, nor children put to death for their fathers; each is to die for his own sins."[b][e]

7He was the one who defeated ten thousand Edomites in the Valley of Salt[f] and captured Sela[g] in battle, calling it Joktheel, the name it has to this day.

8Then Amaziah sent messengers to Jehoash son of Jehoahaz, the son of Jehu, king of Israel, with the

13:13 *o* 2Ki 14:23; Hos 1:1
13:14 *p* 2Ki 2:12
13:15 *q* 1Sa 20:20
13:17 *r* Jos 8:18 *s* 1Ki 20:26
13:19 *t* ver 25
13:20 *u* 2Ki 3:7; 2Ki 24:2
13:21 *v* Mt 27:52
13:22 *w* 1Ki 19:17; 2Ki 8:12
13:23 *x* Ge 13:16-17; Ex 2:24 *y* Dt 29:20 *z* Ex 33:15; 2Ki 14:27; 2Ki 17:18; 2Ki 24:3,20
13:24 *a* ver 3
13:25 *b* ver 18,19 *c* 2Ki 10:32
14:4 *a* 2Ki 12:3; 2Ki 16:4
14:5 *b* 2Ki 21:24 *c* 2Ki 12:20
14:6 *d* Dt 28:61 *e* Nu 26:11; Job 21:20; Jer 31:30; Jer 44:3; Eze 18:4,20
14:7 *f* 2Sa 8:13; 2Ch 25:11 *g* Jdg 1:36

a*1* Hebrew *Joash,* a variant of *Jehoash*; also in verses 13, 23 and 27 b6 Deut. 24:16

challenge: "Come, meet me face to
face."
9But Jehoash king of Israel replied to Amaziah king of Judah: "A
thistle[h] in Lebanon sent a message
to a cedar in Lebanon, 'Give your
daughter to my son in marriage.'
Then a wild beast in Lebanon came
along and trampled the thistle
underfoot. 10You have indeed defeated Edom and now you are arrogant.[i] Glory in your victory, but
stay at home! Why ask for trouble
and cause your own downfall and
that of Judah also?"
11Amaziah, however, would not
listen, so Jehoash king of Israel
attacked. He and Amaziah king of
Judah faced each other at Beth
Shemesh[j] in Judah. 12Judah was
routed by Israel, and every man
fled to his home.[k] 13Jehoash king
of Israel captured Amaziah king of
Judah, the son of Joash, the son of
Ahaziah, at Beth Shemesh. Then
Jehoash went to Jerusalem and
broke down the wall[l] of Jerusalem
from the Ephraim Gate[m] to the
Corner Gate[n]—a section about six
hundred feet long.[c] 14He took all
the gold and silver and all the articles found in the temple of the
LORD and in the treasuries of the
royal palace. He also took hostages
and returned to Samaria.
15As for the other events of the
reign of Jehoash, what he did and
his achievements, including his
war[o] against Amaziah king of Judah, are they not written in the
book of the annals of the kings of
Israel? 16Jehoash rested with his
fathers and was buried in Samaria
with the kings of Israel. And Jeroboam his son succeeded him as
king.
17Amaziah son of Joash king of
Judah lived for fifteen years after
the death of Jehoash son of Jehoahaz king of Israel. 18As for the
other events of Amaziah's reign,
are they not written in the book of
the annals of the kings of Judah?
19They conspired[p] against him
in Jerusalem, and he fled to Lachish,[q] but they sent men after
him to Lachish and killed him
there. 20He was brought back by
horse[r] and was buried in Jerusalem with his fathers, in the City
of David.
21Then all the people of Judah
took Azariah,[d][s] who was sixteen
years old, and made him king in
place of his father Amaziah. 22He
was the one who rebuilt Elath[t] and
restored it to Judah after Amaziah
rested with his fathers.

Jeroboam II King of Israel

23In the fifteenth year of Amaziah son of Joash king of Judah,
Jeroboam[u] son of Jehoash king of
Israel became king in Samaria, and
he reigned for forty-one years.
24He did evil in the eyes of the LORD
and did not turn away from any of
the sins of Jeroboam son of Nebat,
which he had caused Israel to
commit.[v] 25He was the one who
restored the boundaries of Israel
from Lebo[e] Hamath[w] to the Sea of
the Arabah,[f][x] in accordance with
the word of the LORD, the God of Israel, spoken through his servant
Jonah[y] son of Amittai, the prophet
from Gath Hepher.
26The LORD had seen how bitterly
everyone in Israel, whether slave
or free,[z] was suffering;[a] there
was no-one to help them.[b] 27And
since the LORD had not said he
would blot out[c] the name of Israel
from under heaven, he saved[d]
them by the hand of Jeroboam son
of Jehoash.
28As for the other events of Jeroboam's reign, all he did, and his
military achievements, including
how he recovered for Israel both
Damascus[e] and Hamath,[f] which
had belonged to Yaudi,[g] are they
not written in the book of the

14:9 h Jdg 9:8-15
14:10 i Dt 8:14; 2Ch 26:16; 2Ch 32:25
14:11 j Jos 15:10
14:12 k 2Sa 18:17
14:13 l 1Ki 3:1; 2Ch 33:14; 2Ch 36:19; Jer 39:2 m Ne 8:16; Ne 12:39 n 2Ch 25:23; Jer 31:38; Zec 14:10
14:15 o 2Ki 13:12
14:19 p 2Ki 12:20 q Jos 10:3; 2Ki 18:14,17
14:20 r 2Ki 9:28
14:21 s 2Ki 15:1; 2Ch 26:23
14:22 t 1Ki 9:26; 2Ki 16:6
14:23 u 2Ki 13:13
14:24 v 1Ki 15:30
14:25 w Nu 13:21; 1Ki 8:65 x Dt 3:17 y Jnh 1:1; Mt 12:39
14:26 z Dt 32:36 a 2Ki 13:4 b Ps 18:41; Ps 22:11; Ps 72:12; Ps 107:12; Isa 63:5; La 1:7
14:27 c 2Ki 13:23 d Jdg 6:14
14:28 e 2Sa 8:5; 1Ki 11:24 f 2Ch 8:3

[c]13 Hebrew *four hundred cubits* (about 180 metres) [d]21 Also called *Uzziah*
[e]25 Or *from the entrance to* [f]25 That is, the Dead Sea [g]28 Or *Judah*

annals[g] of the kings of Israel? [29]Jeroboam rested with his fathers, the kings of Israel. And Zechariah his son succeeded him as king.

Azariah King of Judah

15:1–7pp 2Ch 26:3–4,21–23

15 In the twenty-seventh year of Jeroboam king of Israel, Azariah[a] son of Amaziah king of Judah began to reign. [2]He was sixteen years old when he became king, and he reigned in Jerusalem for fifty-two years. His mother's name was Jecoliah; she was from Jerusalem. [3]He did what was right in the eyes of the LORD, just as his father Amaziah had done. [4]The high places, however, were not removed; the people continued to offer sacrifices and burn incense there.

[5]The LORD afflicted[b] the king with leprosy[a] until the day he died, and he lived in a separate house.[b][c] Jotham[d] the king's son had charge of the palace[e] and governed the people of the land.

[6]As for the other events of Azariah's reign, and all he did, are they not written in the book of the annals of the kings of Judah? [7]Azariah rested[f] with his fathers and was buried near them in the City of David. And Jotham[g] his son succeeded him as king.

Zechariah King of Israel

[8]In the thirty-eighth year of Azariah king of Judah, Zechariah son of Jeroboam became king of Israel in Samaria, and he reigned for six months. [9]He did evil[h] in the eyes of the LORD, as his fathers had done. He did not turn away from the sins of Jeroboam son of Nebat, which he had caused Israel to commit.

[10]Shallum son of Jabesh conspired against Zechariah. He attacked him in front of the people,[c] assassinated[i] him and succeeded him as king. [11]The other events of Zechariah's reign are written in the book of the annals[j] of the kings of Israel. [12]So the word of the LORD spoken to Jehu was fulfilled:[k] "Your descendants will sit on the throne of Israel to the fourth generation."[d]

Shallum King of Israel

[13]Shallum son of Jabesh became king in the thirty-ninth year of Uzziah king of Judah, and he reigned in Samaria[l] for one month. [14]Then Menahem son of Gadi went from Tirzah[m] up to Samaria. He attacked Shallum son of Jabesh in Samaria, assassinated[n] him and succeeded him as king.

[15]The other events of Shallum's reign, and the conspiracy he led, are written in the book of the annals[o] of the kings of Israel.

[16]At that time Menahem, starting out from Tirzah, attacked Tiphsah[p] and everyone in the city and its vicinity, because they refused to open[q] their gates. He sacked Tiphsah and ripped open all the pregnant women.

Menahem King of Israel

[17]In the thirty-ninth year of Azariah king of Judah, Menahem son of Gadi became king of Israel, and he reigned in Samaria for ten years. [18]He did evil in the eyes of the LORD. During his entire reign he did not turn away from the sins of Jeroboam son of Nebat, which he had caused Israel to commit.

[19]Then Pul[e][r] king of Assyria invaded the land, and Menahem gave him a thousand talents[f] of silver to gain his support and strengthen his own hold on the kingdom. [20]Menahem exacted this money from

14:28
g 1Ki 15:31

15:1
a ver 32
2Ki 14:21

15:5
b Ge 12:17
c Lev 13:46
d 2Ch 27:1
e Ge 41:40

15:7
f Isa 6:1
Isa 14:28
g ver 5

15:9
h 1Ki 15:26

15:10
i 2Ki 12:20

15:11
j 1Ki 15:31

15:12
k 2Ki 10:30

15:13
l ver 1,8

15:14
m 1Ki 14:17
n 2Ki 12:20

15:15
o 1Ki 15:31

15:16
p 1Ki 4:24
q 2Ki 8:12
Hos 13:16

15:19
r 1Ch 5:6,26

[a]5 The Hebrew word was used for various diseases affecting the skin—not necessarily leprosy. [b]5 Or *in a house where he was relieved of responsibility* [c]10 Hebrew; some Septuagint manuscripts *in Ibleam*
[d]12 2 Kings 10:30 [e]19 Also called *Tiglath-Pileser* [f]19 That is, about 34 tons (about 34 metric tons)

Israel. Every wealthy man had to contribute fifty shekels[g] of silver to be given to the king of Assyria. So the king of Assyria withdrew[s] and stayed in the land no longer.

[21]As for the other events of Menahem's reign, and all he did, are they not written in the book of the annals of the kings of Israel? [22]Menahem rested with his fathers. And Pekahiah his son succeeded him as king.

Pekahiah King of Israel

[23]In the fiftieth year of Azariah king of Judah, Pekahiah son of Menahem became king of Israel in Samaria, and he reigned for two years. [24]Pekahiah did evil in the eyes of the LORD. He did not turn away from the sins of Jeroboam son of Nebat, which he had caused Israel to commit. [25]One of his chief officers, Pekah[t] son of Remaliah, conspired against him. Taking fifty men of Gilead with him, he assassinated[u] Pekahiah, along with Argob and Arieh, in the citadel of the royal palace at Samaria. So Pekah killed Pekahiah and succeeded him as king.

[26]The other events of Pekahiah's reign, and all he did, are written in the book of the annals of the kings of Israel.

Pekah King of Israel

[27]In the fifty-second year of Azariah king of Judah, Pekah[v] son of Remaliah[w] became king of Israel in Samaria, and he reigned for twenty years. [28]He did evil in the eyes of the LORD. He did not turn away from the sins of Jeroboam son of Nebat, which he had caused Israel to commit.

[29]In the time of Pekah king of Israel, Tiglath-Pileser[x] king of Assyria came and took Ijon,[y] Abel Beth Maacah, Janoah, Kedesh and Hazor. He took Gilead and Galilee, including all the land of Naphtali,[z] and deported[a] the people to Assyria. [30]Then Hoshea[b] son of Elah conspired against Pekah son of Remaliah. He attacked and assassinated[c] him, and then succeeded him as king in the twentieth year of Jotham son of Uzziah.

[31]As for the other events of Pekah's reign, and all he did, are they not written in the book of the annals of the kings of Israel?

Jotham King of Judah

15:33–38pp 2Ch 27:1–4,7–9

[32]In the second year of Pekah son of Remaliah king of Israel, Jotham[d] son of Uzziah king of Judah began to reign. [33]He was twenty-five years old when he became king, and he reigned in Jerusalem for sixteen years. His mother's name was Jerusha daughter of Zadok. [34]He did what was right[e] in the eyes of the LORD, just as his father Uzziah had done. [35]The high places,[f] however, were not removed; the people continued to offer sacrifices and burn incense there. Jotham rebuilt the Upper Gate[g] of the temple of the LORD.

[36]As for the other events of Jotham's reign, and what he did, are they not written in the book of the annals of the kings of Judah? [37](In those days the LORD began to send Rezin[h] king of Aram and Pekah son of Remaliah against Judah.) [38]Jotham rested with his fathers and was buried with them in the City of David, the city of his father. And Ahaz his son succeeded him as king.

Ahaz King of Judah

16:1–20pp 2Ch 28:1–27

16 In the seventeenth year of Pekah son of Remaliah, Ahaz[a] son of Jotham king of Judah began to reign. [2]Ahaz was twenty years old when he became king, and he reigned in Jerusalem for sixteen years. Unlike David his

15:20 s 2Ki 12:18
15:25 t 2Ch 28:6; Isa 7:1 u 2Ki 12:20
15:27 v 2Ch 28:6; Isa 7:1 w Isa 7:4
15:29 x 2Ki 16:7; 2Ki 17:6; 1Ch 5:26; 2Ch 28:20; Jer 50:17 y 1Ki 15:20 z 2Ki 16:9; 2Ki 17:24; 2Ch 16:4; Isa 9:1 a 2Ki 24:14-16; 1Ch 5:22; Isa 14:6,17; Isa 36:17; Isa 45:13
15:30 b 2Ki 17:1 c 2Ki 12:20
15:32 d 1Ch 5:17
15:34 e ver 3; 1Ki 14:8; 2Ch 26:4-5
15:35 f 2Ki 12:3 g 2Ch 23:20
15:37 h 2Ki 16:5; Isa 7:1
16:1 a Isa 1:1; Isa 14:28

[g]20 That is, about 1¼ pounds (about 0.6 kilogram)

father, he did not do what was
right[b] in the eyes of the LORD his
God. 3He walked in the ways of the
kings of Israel and even sacrificed
his son[c] in[a] the fire, following the
detestable[d] ways of the nations the
LORD had driven out before the Israelites. 4He offered sacrifices and
burned incense at the high places,
on the hilltops and under every
spreading tree.[e]
5Then Rezin[f] king of Aram and
Pekah son of Remaliah king of Israel marched up to fight against
Jerusalem and besieged Ahaz, but
they could not overpower him. 6At
that time, Rezin[g] king of Aram recovered Elath[h] for Aram by driving out the men of Judah. Edomites
then moved into Elath and have
lived there to this day.
7Ahaz sent messengers to say to
Tiglath-Pileser[i] king of Assyria,
"I am your servant and vassal.
Come up and save[j] me out of the
hand of the king of Aram and of the
king of Israel who are attacking
me." 8And Ahaz took the silver and
gold found in the temple of the
LORD and in the treasuries of the
royal palace and sent it as a gift[k]
to the king of Assyria. 9The king
of Assyria complied by attacking
Damascus[l] and capturing it. He
deported its inhabitants to Kir[m]
and put Rezin to death.
10Then King Ahaz went to Damascus to meet Tiglath-Pileser
king of Assyria. He saw an altar in
Damascus and sent to Uriah[n] the
priest a sketch of the altar, with de-
tailed plans for its construction.
11So Uriah the priest built an altar
in accordance with all the plans
that King Ahaz had sent from Damascus and finished it before King
Ahaz returned. 12When the king
came back from Damascus and
saw the altar, he approached it and
presented offerings[b][o] on it. 13He
offered up his burnt offering[p] and
grain offering, poured out his drink
offering, and sprinkled the blood of
his fellowship offerings[c][q] on the

16:2
b 1Ki 14:8
16:3
c Lev 18:21; 2Ki 21:6
d Lev 18:3; Dt 9:4; Dt 12:31
16:4
e Dt 12:2; Eze 6:13
16:5
f 2Ki 15:37; Isa 7:1,4
16:6
g Isa 9:12
h 2Ki 14:22; 2Ch 26:2
16:7
i 2Ki 15:29
j Isa 2:6; Jer 2:18; Eze 16:28; Hos 10:6
16:8
k 2Ki 12:18
16:9
l 2Ki 15:29
m Isa 22:6; Am 1:5; Am 9:7
16:10
n Isa 8:2
16:12
o 2Ch 26:16
16:13
p Lev 6:8-13
q Lev 7:11-21
16:14
r 2Ch 4:1
16:15
s Ex 29:38-41
t 1Sa 9:9
16:17
u 1Ki 7:27
16:18
v Eze 16:28
17:1
a 2Ki 15:30

altar. 14The bronze altar[r] that
stood before the LORD he brought
from the front of the temple—from
between the new altar and the temple of the LORD—and put it on the
north side of the new altar.
15King Ahaz then gave these orders to Uriah the priest: "On the
large new altar, offer the morning[s] burnt offering and the evening grain offering, the king's
burnt offering and his grain offering, and the burnt offering of all
the people of the land, and their
grain offering and their drink offering. Sprinkle on the altar all the
blood of the burnt offerings and
sacrifices. But I will use the bronze
altar for seeking guidance."[t]
16And Uriah the priest did just as
King Ahaz had ordered.
17King Ahaz took away the side
panels and removed the basins
from the movable stands. He removed the Sea from the bronze
bulls that supported it and set it on
a stone base.[u] 18He took away the
Sabbath canopy[d] that had been
built at the temple and removed the
royal entrance outside the temple
of the LORD, in deference to the
king of Assyria.[v]
19As for the other events of the
reign of Ahaz, and what he did, are
they not written in the book of
the annals of the kings of Judah?
20Ahaz rested with his fathers and
was buried with them in the City of
David. And Hezekiah his son succeeded him as king.

Hoshea Last King of Israel

17:3-7pp 2Ki 18:9-12

17 In the twelfth year of Ahaz
king of Judah, Hoshea[a]
son of Elah became king of Israel in
Samaria, and he reigned for nine
years. 2He did evil in the eyes of the

[a]3 Or *even made his son pass through*
[b]12 Or *and went up* [c]13 Traditionally *peace offerings* [d]18 Or *the dais of his throne* (see Septuagint)

LORD, but not like the kings of Israel who preceded him.

3Shalmaneser[b] king of Assyria came up to attack Hoshea, who had been Shalmaneser's vassal and had paid him tribute. 4But the king of Assyria discovered that Hoshea was a traitor, for he had sent envoys to So[a] king of Egypt, and he no longer paid tribute to the king of Assyria, as he had done year by year. Therefore Shalmaneser seized him and put him in prison. 5The king of Assyria invaded the entire land, marched against Samaria and laid siege[c] to it for three years. 6In the ninth year of Hoshea, the king of Assyria captured Samaria[d] and deported[e] the Israelites to Assyria. He settled them in Halah, in Gozan[f] on the Habor River and in the towns of the Medes.

Israel Exiled Because of Sin

7All this took place because the Israelites had sinned[g] against the LORD their God, who had brought them up out of Egypt[h] from under the power of Pharaoh king of Egypt. They worshipped other gods 8and followed the practices of the nations[i] the LORD had driven out before them, as well as the practices that the kings of Israel had introduced. 9The Israelites secretly did things against the LORD their God that were not right. From watchtower to fortified city[j] they built themselves high places in all their towns. 10They set up sacred stones and Asherah poles[k] on every high hill and under every spreading tree.[l] 11At every high place they burned incense, as the nations whom the LORD had driven out before them had done. They did wicked things that provoked the LORD to anger. 12They worshipped idols,[m] though the LORD had said, "You shall not do this."[b] 13The LORD warned Israel and Judah through all his prophets and seers:[n] "Turn from your evil ways.[o] Observe my commands and decrees, in accordance with the entire Law that I commanded your fathers to obey and that I delivered to you through my servants the prophets."

14But they would not listen and were as stiff-necked[p] as their fathers, who did not trust in the LORD their God. 15They rejected his decrees and the covenant[q] he had made with their fathers and the warnings he had given them. They followed worthless idols[r] and themselves became worthless. They imitated the nations[s] around them although the LORD had ordered them, "Do not do as they do," and they did the things the LORD had forbidden them to do.

16They forsook all the commands of the LORD their God and made for themselves two idols cast in the shape of calves,[t] and an Asherah[u] pole. They bowed down to all the starry hosts,[v] and they worshipped Baal.[w] 17They sacrificed[x] their sons and daughters in[c] the fire. They practised divination and sorcery[y] and sold[z] themselves to do evil in the eyes of the LORD, provoking him to anger.

18So the LORD was very angry with Israel and removed them from his presence. Only the tribe of Judah was left, 19and even Judah did not keep the commands of the LORD their God. They followed the practices Israel had introduced.[a] 20Therefore the LORD rejected all the people of Israel; he afflicted them and gave them into the hands of plunderers,[b] until he thrust them from his presence.

21When he tore[c] Israel away from the house of David, they made Jeroboam son of Nebat their king.[d] Jeroboam enticed Israel away from following the LORD and

17:3 *b* 2Ki 18:9-12; Hos 10:14
17:5 *c* Hos 13:16
17:6 *d* Hos 13:16 *e* Dt 28:36,64; 2Ki 18:10-11 *f* 1Ch 5:26
17:7 *g* Jos 23:16; Jdg 6:10 *h* Ex 14:15-31
17:8 *i* Lev 18:3; Dt 18:9; 2Ki 16:3
17:9 *j* 2Ki 18:8
17:10 *k* Ex 34:13; Mic 5:14 *l* 1Ki 14:23
17:12 *m* Ex 20:4
17:13 *n* 1Sa 9:9 *o* Jer 18:11; Jer 25:5; Jer 35:15
17:14 *p* Ex 32:9; Dt 31:27; Ac 7:51
17:15 *q* Dt 29:25 *r* Dt 32:21; Ro 1:21-23 *s* Dt 12:30-31
17:16 *t* 1Ki 12:28 *u* 1Ki 14:15,23 *v* 2Ki 21:3 *w* 1Ki 16:31
17:17 *x* Dt 18:10-12; 2Ki 16:3 *y* Lev 19:26 *z* 1Ki 21:20
17:19 *a* 1Ki 14:22-23; 2Ki 16:3
17:20 *b* 2Ki 15:29
17:21 *c* 1Ki 11:11 *d* 1Ki 12:20

[a]4 Or *to Sais, to the*; *So* is possibly an abbreviation for *Osorkon*. [b]12 Exodus 20:4, 5
[c]17 Or *They made their sons and daughters pass through*

caused them to commit a great sin.
22 The Israelites persisted in all the
sins of Jeroboam and did not turn
away from them 23 until the LORD
removed them from his presence,
as he had warned through all his
servants the prophets. So the people of Israel were taken from their
homeland into exile in Assyria, and
they are still there.

Samaria Resettled

24 The king of Assyria[e] brought
people from Babylon, Cuthah,
Avva, Hamath and Sepharvaim[f]
and settled them in the towns of
Samaria to replace the Israelites.
They took over Samaria and lived
in its towns. 25 When they first lived
there, they did not worship the
LORD; so he sent lions[g] among
them and they killed some of the
people. 26 It was reported to the
king of Assyria: "The people you
deported and resettled in the towns
of Samaria do not know what the
god of that country requires. He
has sent lions among them, which
are killing them off, because the
people do not know what he requires."
27 Then the king of Assyria gave
this order: "Make one of the priests
you took captive from Samaria go
back to live there and teach the
people what the god of the land requires." 28 So one of the priests who
had been exiled from Samaria
came to live in Bethel and taught
them how to worship the LORD.
29 Nevertheless, each national
group made its own gods in the several towns[h] where they settled,
and set them up in the shrines[i]
the people of Samaria had made at
the high places.[j] 30 The men from
Babylon made Succoth Benoth,
the men from Cuthah made
Nergal, and the men from Hamath
made Ashima; 31 the Avvites made
Nibhaz and Tartak, and the
Sepharvites burned their children
in the fire as sacrifices to

17:24 e Ezr 4:2,10 f 2Ki 18:34
17:25 g Ge 37:20
17:29 h Jer 2:28 i 1Ki 12:31 j Mic 4:5
17:31 k 2Ki 19:37 l ver 24
17:32 m 1Ki 12:31
17:34 n Ge 32:28 Ge 35:10 1Ki 18:31
17:35 o Ex 20:5 Jdg 6:10
17:36 p Ex 3:20 Ex 6:6 Ps 136:12
17:37 q Dt 5:32
17:38 r Dt 4:23 Dt 6:12
17:41 s ver 32-33 1Ki 18:21 Mt 6:24
18:1 a Isa 1:1 2Ch 28:27

Adrammelech[k] and Anammelech,
the gods of Sepharvaim.[l] 32 They
worshipped the LORD, but they also
appointed all sorts[m] of their own
people to officiate for them as
priests in the shrines at the high
places. 33 They worshipped the
LORD, but they also served their
own gods in accordance with the
customs of the nations from which
they had been brought.
34 To this day they persist in their
former practices. They neither
worship the LORD nor adhere to the
decrees and ordinances, the laws
and commands that the LORD gave
the descendants of Jacob, whom he
named Israel.[n] 35 When the LORD
made a covenant with the Israelites, he commanded them: "Do not
worship[o] any other gods or bow
down to them, serve them or sacrifice to them. 36 But the LORD, who
brought you up out of Egypt with
mighty power and outstretched
arm,[p] is the one you must worship.
To him you shall bow down and to
him offer sacrifices. 37 You must always be careful[q] to keep the decrees and ordinances, the laws and
commands he wrote for you. Do not
worship other gods. 38 Do not forget[r] the covenant I have made
with you, and do not worship other
gods. 39 Rather, worship the LORD
your God; it is he who will deliver you from the hand of all your
enemies."
40 They would not listen, however, but persisted in their former
practices. 41 Even while these people were worshipping the LORD,[s]
they were serving their idols. To
this day their children and grandchildren continue to do as their
fathers did.

Hezekiah King of Judah

18:2–4pp 2Ch 29:1–2; 31:1
18:5–7pp 2Ch 31:20–21
18:9–12pp 2Ki 17:3–7

18 In the third year of Hoshea
son of Elah king of Israel,
Hezekiah[a] son of Ahaz king of

Judah began to reign. 2He was
twenty-five years old when he became king, and he reigned in Jerusalem for twenty-nine years.[b] His
mother's name was Abijah[a]
daughter of Zechariah. 3He did
what was right in the eyes of
the LORD, just as his father David[c]
had done. 4He removed[d] the
high places, smashed the sacred
stones[e] and cut down the Asherah
poles. He broke into pieces the
bronze snake[f] Moses had made,
for up to that time the Israelites
had been burning incense to it. (It
was called[b] Nehushtan.[c])
5Hezekiah trusted[g] in the LORD,
the God of Israel. There was no-one
like him among all the kings of Judah, either before him or after him.
6He held fast[h] to the LORD and did
not cease to follow him; he kept the
commands the LORD had given
Moses. 7And the LORD was with
him; he was successful[i] in whatever he undertook. He rebelled[j]
against the king of Assyria and did
not serve him. 8From watchtower
to fortified city,[k] he defeated the
Philistines, as far as Gaza and its
territory.
9In King Hezekiah's fourth
year,[l] which was the seventh year
of Hoshea son of Elah king of Israel, Shalmaneser king of Assyria
marched against Samaria and laid
siege to it. 10At the end of three
years the Assyrians took it. So Samaria was captured in Hezekiah's
sixth year, which was the ninth
year of Hoshea king of Israel. 11The
king[m] of Assyria deported Israel to
Assyria and settled them in Halah,
in Gozan on the Habor River, and in
towns of the Medes. 12This happened because they had not obeyed
the LORD their God, but had violated his covenant[n]—all that Moses
the servant of the LORD commanded.[o] They neither listened to
the commands[p] nor carried them
out.
13In the fourteenth year of King
Hezekiah's reign, Sennacherib king
of Assyria attacked all the fortified cities of Judah[q] and captured them. 14So Hezekiah king of
Judah sent this message to the king
of Assyria at Lachish: "I have done
wrong.[r] Withdraw from me, and I
will pay whatever you demand of
me." The king of Assyria exacted
from Hezekiah king of Judah three
hundred talents[d] of silver and
thirty talents[e] of gold. 15So Hezekiah gave[s] him all the silver that
was found in the temple of the LORD
and in the treasuries of the royal
palace.
16At this time Hezekiah king of
Judah stripped off the gold with
which he had covered the doors
and doorposts of the temple of the
LORD, and gave it to the king of
Assyria.

Sennacherib Threatens Jerusalem

18:13, 17–37pp Isa 36:1–22
18:17–35pp 2Ch 32:9–19

17The king of Assyria sent his supreme commander,[t] his chief officer and his field commander with a
large army, from Lachish to King
Hezekiah at Jerusalem. They came
up to Jerusalem and stopped at the
aqueduct of the Upper Pool,[u] on
the road to the Washerman's Field.
18They called for the king; and Eliakim[v] son of Hilkiah the palace
administrator, Shebna[w] the secretary, and Joah son of Asaph the
recorder went out to them.
19The field commander said to
them, "Tell Hezekiah:

" 'This is what the great king,
the king of Assyria, says: On
what are you basing this confidence of yours? 20You say you
have strategy and military
strength—but you speak only
empty words. On whom are

18:2 *b* Isa 38:5
18:3 *c* Isa 38:5
18:4 *d* 2Ch 31:1 *e* Ex 23:24 *f* Nu 21:9
18:5 *g* 2Ki 19:10; 2Ki 23:25
18:6 *h* Dt 10:20; Jos 23:8
18:7 *i* Ge 39:3; 1Sa 18:14 *j* 2Ki 16:7
18:8 *k* 2Ki 17:9; Isa 14:29
18:9 *l* Isa 1:1
18:11 *m* Isa 37:12
18:12 *n* 2Ki 17:15 *o* Da 9:6,10 *p* 1Ki 9:6
18:13 *q* 2Ch 32:1; Isa 1:7; Mic 1:9
18:14 *r* Isa 24:5
18:15 *s* 1Ki 15:18; 2Ki 16:8
18:17 *t* Isa 20:1 *u* 2Ki 20:20; 2Ch 32:4,30; Isa 7:3
18:18 *v* 2Ki 19:2; Isa 22:20 *w* Isa 22:15

[a]2 Hebrew *Abi*, a variant of *Abijah* [b]4 Or *He called it* [c]4 *Nehushtan* sounds like the Hebrew for *bronze* and *snake* and *unclean thing*.
[d]*14* That is, about 10 tons (about 10 metric tons)
[e]*14* That is, about 1 ton (about 1 metric ton)

you depending, that you rebel against me? 21 Look now, you are depending on Egypt,[x] that splintered reed of a staff,[y] which pierces a man's hand and wounds him if he leans on it! Such is Pharaoh king of Egypt to all who depend on him. 22 And if you say to me, "We are depending on the LORD our God"—isn't he the one whose high places and altars Hezekiah removed, saying to Judah and Jerusalem, "You must worship before this altar in Jerusalem"?

23 " 'Come now, make a bargain with my master, the king of Assyria: I will give you two thousand horses—if you can put riders on them! 24 How can you repulse one officer[z] of the least of my master's officials, even though you are depending on Egypt for chariots and horsemen?[f] 25 Furthermore, have I come to attack and destroy this place without word from the LORD?[a] The LORD himself told me to march against this country and destroy it.' "

26 Then Eliakim son of Hilkiah, and Shebna and Joah said to the field commander, "Please speak to your servants in Aramaic,[b] since we understand it. Don't speak to us in Hebrew in the hearing of the people on the wall."

27 But the commander replied, "Was it only to your master and you that my master sent me to say these things, and not to the men sitting on the wall—who, like you, will have to eat their own filth and drink their own urine?"

28 Then the commander stood and called out in Hebrew: "Hear the word of the great king, the king of Assyria! 29 This is what the king says: Do not let Hezekiah deceive[c] you. He cannot deliver you from my hand. 30 Do not let Hezekiah persuade you to trust in the LORD when he says, 'The LORD will surely deliver us; this city will not be given into the hand of the king of Assyria.'

31 "Do not listen to Hezekiah. This is what the king of Assyria says: Make peace with me and come out to me. Then every one of you will eat from his own vine and fig-tree[d] and drink water from his own cistern,[e] 32 until I come and take you to a land like your own, a land of grain and new wine, a land of bread and vineyards, a land of olive trees and honey. Choose life[f] and not death!

"Do not listen to Hezekiah, for he is misleading you when he says, 'The LORD will deliver us.' 33 Has the god[g] of any nation ever delivered his land from the hand of the king of Assyria? 34 Where are the gods of Hamath[h] and Arpad?[i] Where are the gods of Sepharvaim, Hena and Ivvah? Have they rescued Samaria from my hand? 35 Who of all the gods of these countries has been able to save his land from me? How then can the LORD deliver Jerusalem from my hand?"[j]

36 But the people remained silent and said nothing in reply, because the king had commanded, "Do not answer him."

37 Then Eliakim son of Hilkiah the palace administrator, Shebna the secretary and Joah son of Asaph the recorder went to Hezekiah, with their clothes torn,[k] and told him what the field commander had said.

Jerusalem's Deliverance Foretold

19:1–13pp Isa 37:1–13

19 When King Hezekiah heard this, he tore[a] his clothes and put on sackcloth and went into the temple of the LORD. 2 He sent

[f] 24 Or *charioteers*

18:21 *x* Isa 20:5; Eze 29:6 *y* Isa 30:5,7
18:24 *z* Isa 10:8
18:25 *a* 2Ki 19:6,22
18:26 *b* Ezr 4:7
18:29 *c* 2Ki 19:10
18:31 *d* Nu 13:23; 1Ki 4:25 *e* Jer 14:3; La 4:4
18:32 *f* Dt 8:7-9; Dt 30:19
18:33 *g* 2Ki 19:12; Isa 10:10-11
18:34 *h* 2Ki 17:24; 2Ki 19:13 *i* Isa 10:9
18:35 *j* Ps 2:1-2
18:37 *k* 2Ki 6:30
19:1 *a* Ge 37:34; 1Ki 21:27; 2Ch 32:20-22

Eliakim the palace administrator,
Shebna the secretary and the leading priests, all wearing sackcloth,
to the prophet Isaiah[b] son of Amoz.
3They told him, "This is what Hezekiah says: This day is a day of distress and rebuke and disgrace, as
when children come to the point of
birth and there is no strength to deliver them. 4It may be that the LORD
your God will hear all the words of
the field commander, whom his
master, the king of Assyria, has
sent to ridicule[c] the living God,
and that he will rebuke[d] him for
the words the LORD your God has
heard. Therefore pray for the remnant that still survives."
5When King Hezekiah's officials
came to Isaiah, 6Isaiah said to
them, "Tell your master, 'This is
what the LORD says: Do not be
afraid of what you have heard—
those words with which the underlings of the king of Assyria have
blasphemed[e] me. 7Listen! I am going to put such a spirit in him that
when he hears a certain report, he
will return to his own country, and
there I will have him cut down with
the sword.[f]' "
8When the field commander
heard that the king of Assyria had
left Lachish,[g] he withdrew and
found the king fighting against
Libnah.
9Now Sennacherib received a report that Tirhakah, the Cushite[a]
king ⌊of Egypt⌋, was marching out to
fight against him. So he again sent
messengers to Hezekiah with this
word: 10"Say to Hezekiah king of
Judah: Do not let the god you depend[h] on deceive[i] you when he
says, 'Jerusalem will not be handed
over to the king of Assyria.'
11Surely you have heard what the
kings of Assyria have done to all
the countries, destroying them
completely. And will you be delivered? 12Did the gods of the nations
that were destroyed by my forefathers deliver[j] them: the gods of
Gozan,[k] Haran,[l] Rezeph and the
people of Eden who were in Tel Assar? 13Where is the king of Hamath,
the king of Arpad, the king of the
city of Sepharvaim, or of Hena or
Ivvah?"[m]

Hezekiah's Prayer

19:14–19pp Isa 37:14–20

14Hezekiah received the letter
from the messengers and read it.
Then he went up to the temple of
the LORD and spread it out before
the LORD. 15And Hezekiah prayed
to the LORD: "O LORD, God of Israel, enthroned between the cherubim,[n] you alone are God over all
the kingdoms of the earth. You
have made heaven and earth.
16Give ear,[o] O LORD, and hear;[p]
open your eyes,[q] O LORD, and see;
listen to the words Sennacherib has
sent to insult the living God.
17"It is true, O LORD, that the Assyrian kings have laid waste these
nations and their lands. 18They
have thrown their gods into the fire
and destroyed them, for they were
not gods[r] but only wood and stone,
fashioned by men's hands.[s] 19Now,
O LORD our God, deliver us from
his hand, so that all kingdoms[t] on
earth may know[u] that you alone,
O LORD, are God."

Isaiah Prophesies Sennacherib's Fall

19:20–37pp Isa 37:21–38
19:35–37pp 2Ch 32:20–21

20Then Isaiah son of Amoz sent a
message to Hezekiah: "This is what
the LORD, the God of Israel, says: I
have heard[v] your prayer concerning Sennacherib king of Assyria.
21This is the word that the LORD has
spoken against him:

" 'The Virgin Daughter[w] of Zion
despises you and mocks[x] you.
The Daughter of Jerusalem
tosses her head[y] as you flee.
22Who is it you have insulted and
blasphemed?

a9 That is, from the upper Nile region

19:2 b Isa 1:1
19:4 c 2Ki 18:35 d 2Sa 16:12
19:6 e 2Ki 18:25
19:7 f ver 37
19:8 g 2Ki 18:14
19:10 h 2Ki 18:5 i 2Ki 18:29
19:12 j 2Ki 18:33 k 2Ki 17:6 l Ge 11:31
19:13 m 2Ki 18:34
19:15 n Ex 25:22
19:16 o Ps 31:2 p 1Ki 8:29 q ver 4 2Ch 6:40
19:18 r Isa 44:9-11 Jer 10:3-10 s Ps 115:4 Ac 17:29
19:19 t 1Ki 8:43 u Ps 83:18
19:20 v 2Ki 20:5
19:21 w Jer 14:17 La 2:13 x Ps 22:7-8 y Job 16:4 Ps 109:25

Against whom have you raised
your voice
and lifted your eyes in pride?
Against the Holy One[z] of
Israel!
23 By your messengers
you have heaped insults on the
Lord.
And you have said,[a]
"With my many chariots[b]
I have ascended the heights of
the mountains,
the utmost heights of Lebanon.
I have cut down its tallest
cedars,
the choicest of its pines.
I have reached its remotest
parts,
the finest of its forests.
24 I have dug wells in foreign
lands
and drunk the water there.
With the soles of my feet
I have dried up all the streams
of Egypt."

25 " 'Have you not heard?[c]
Long ago I ordained it.
In days of old I planned[d] it;
now I have brought it to pass,
that you have turned fortified
cities
into piles of stone.[e]
26 Their people, drained of power,
are dismayed[f] and put to
shame.
They are like plants in the field,
like tender green shoots,[g]
like grass sprouting on the roof,
scorched[h] before it grows up.

27 " 'But I know[i] where you stay
and when you come and go
and how you rage against me.
28 Because you rage against me
and your insolence has
reached my ears,
I will put my hook[j] in your
nose
and my bit[k] in your mouth,
and I will make you return[l]
by the way you came.'

29 "This will be the sign[m] for you,
O Hezekiah:

This year you will eat what
grows by itself,[n]
and the second year what
springs from that.
But in the third year sow and
reap,
plant vineyards[o] and eat their
fruit.
30 Once more a remnant of the
house of Judah
will take root[p] below and bear
fruit above.
31 For out of Jerusalem will come
a remnant,
and out of Mount Zion a band
of survivors.
The zeal[q] of the LORD Almighty
will accomplish this.

32 "Therefore this is what the
LORD says concerning the king of
Assyria:

"He will not enter this city
or shoot an arrow here.
He will not come before it with
shield
or build a siege ramp against
it.
33 By the way that he came he will
return;[r]
he will not enter this city,
declares the LORD.
34 I will defend[s] this city and
save it,
for my sake and for the sake
of David[t] my servant."

35 That night the angel of the
LORD[u] went out and put to death a
hundred and eighty-five thousand
men in the Assyrian camp. When
the people got up the next morning—there were all the dead
bodies![v] 36 So Sennacherib king of
Assyria broke camp and withdrew.
He returned to Nineveh[w] and
stayed there.
37 One day, while he was worshipping in the temple of his god Nis-
roch, his sons Adrammelech and
Sharezer cut him down with the
sword,[x] and they escaped to the
land of Ararat.[y] And Esarhaddon[z]
his son succeeded him as king.

19:22 z Ps 71:22; Isa 5:24
19:23 a Isa 10:18; b Ps 20:7
19:25 c Isa 40:21,28; d Isa 10:5; Isa 45:7; e Mic 1:6
19:26 f Ps 6:10; g Isa 4:2; h Ps 129:6
19:27 i Ps 139:1-4
19:28 j Eze 19:9; Eze 29:4; k Isa 30:28; l ver 33
19:29 m 2Ki 20:8-9; Lk 2:12; n Lev 25:5; o Ps 107:37
19:30 p 2Ch 32:22-23
19:31 q Isa 9:7
19:33 r ver 28
19:34 s 2Ki 20:6; t 1Ki 11:12-13
19:35 u Ex 12:23; v Job 24:24
19:36 w Ge 10:11; Jnh 1:2
19:37 x ver 7; y Ge 8:4; z Ezr 4:2

Hezekiah's Illness

20:1–11pp 2Ch 32:24–26; Isa 38:1–8

20 In those days Hezekiah became ill and was at the
point of death. The prophet Isaiah
son of Amoz went to him and said,
"This is what the LORD says: Put
your house in order, because you
are going to die; you will not recover."
2Hezekiah turned his face to the
wall and prayed to the LORD, 3"Remember,[a] O LORD, how I have
walked before you faithfully[b] and
with wholehearted devotion and
have done what is good in your
eyes." And Hezekiah wept bitterly.
4Before Isaiah had left the middle court, the word of the LORD
came to him: 5"Go back and tell
Hezekiah, the leader of my people,
'This is what the LORD, the God of
your father David, says: I have
heard[c] your prayer and seen your
tears;[d] I will heal you. On the third
day from now you will go up to the
temple of the LORD. 6I will add fifteen years to your life. And I will
deliver you and this city from the
hand of the king of Assyria. I will
defend[e] this city for my sake and
for the sake of my servant David.' "
7Then Isaiah said, "Prepare a
poultice of figs." They did so and
applied it to the boil,[f] and he recovered.
8Hezekiah had asked Isaiah,
"What will be the sign that the LORD
will heal me and that I will go up to
the temple of the LORD on the third
day from now?"
9Isaiah answered, "This is the
LORD's sign[g] to you that the LORD
will do what he has promised: Shall
the shadow go forward ten steps, or
shall it go back ten steps?"
10"It is a simple matter for the
shadow to go forward ten steps,"
said Hezekiah. "Rather, have it go
back ten steps."
11Then the prophet Isaiah called
upon the LORD, and the LORD made
the shadow go back[h] the ten steps
it had gone down on the stairway of
Ahaz.

Envoys From Babylon

20:12–19pp Isa 39:1–8
20:20–21pp 2Ch 32:32–33

12At that time Merodach-Baladan
son of Baladan king of Babylon
sent Hezekiah letters and a gift, because he had heard of Hezekiah's
illness. 13Hezekiah received the
messengers and showed them all
that was in his storehouses—the
silver, the gold, the spices and the
fine oil—his armoury and everything found among his treasures.
There was nothing in his palace or
in all his kingdom that Hezekiah
did not show them.
14Then Isaiah the prophet went to
King Hezekiah and asked, "What
did those men say, and where did
they come from?"
"From a distant land," Hezekiah
replied. "They came from Babylon."
15The prophet asked, "What did
they see in your palace?"
"They saw everything in my palace," Hezekiah said. "There is
nothing among my treasures that I
did not show them."
16Then Isaiah said to Hezekiah,
"Hear the word of the LORD: 17The
time will surely come when everything in your palace, and all that
your fathers have stored up until
this day, will be carried off to Babylon.[i] Nothing will be left, says the
LORD. 18And some of your descendants,[j] your own flesh and blood,
that will be born to you, will be
taken away, and they will become
eunuchs in the palace of the king of
Babylon."
19"The word of the LORD you have
spoken is good," Hezekiah replied.
For he thought, "Will there not be
peace and security in my lifetime?"
20As for the other events of Hezekiah's reign, all his achievements
and how he made the pool[k] and the
tunnel by which he brought water

20:3
a Ne 13:22
b 2Ki 18:3-6

20:5
c 1Sa 9:16; 1Ki 9:3; 2Ki 19:20
d Ps 39:12; Ps 56:8

20:6
e 2Ki 19:34

20:7
f Isa 38:21

20:9
g Dt 13:2; Jer 44:29

20:11
h Jos 10:13

20:17
i 2Ki 24:13; 2Ki 25:13; 2Ch 36:10; Jer 27:22; Jer 52:17-23

20:18
j 2Ki 24:15; 2Ch 33:11; Da 1:3

20:20
k Ne 3:16

into the city, are they not written in the book of the annals of the kings of Judah? 21 Hezekiah rested with his fathers. And Manasseh his son succeeded him as king.

Manasseh King of Judah

21:1–10pp 2Ch 33:1–10
21:17–18pp 2Ch 33:18–20

21 Manasseh was twelve years old when he became king, and he reigned in Jerusalem for fifty-five years. His mother's name was Hephzibah.[a] 2 He did evil[b] in the eyes of the LORD, following the detestable practices[c] of the nations the LORD had driven out before the Israelites. 3 He rebuilt the high places[d] his father Hezekiah had destroyed; he also erected altars to Baal[e] and made an Asherah pole, as Ahab king of Israel had done. He bowed down to all the starry hosts[f] and worshipped them. 4 He built altars[g] in the temple of the LORD, of which the LORD had said, "In Jerusalem I will put my Name."[h] 5 In both courts[i] of the temple of the LORD, he built altars to all the starry hosts. 6 He sacrificed his own son[j] in**a** the fire, practised sorcery and divination, and consulted mediums and spiritists.[k] He did much evil in the eyes of the LORD, provoking him to anger.

7 He took the carved Asherah pole[l] he had made and put it in the temple, of which the LORD had said to David and to his son Solomon, "In this temple and in Jerusalem, which I have chosen out of all the tribes of Israel, I will put my Name[m] for ever. 8 I will not again[n] make the feet of the Israelites wander from the land I gave their forefathers, if only they will be careful to do everything I commanded them and will keep the whole Law that my servant Moses[o] gave them." 9 But the people did not listen. Manasseh led them astray, so that they did more evil[p] than the nations[q] the LORD had destroyed before the Israelites.

10 The LORD said through his servants the prophets: 11 "Manasseh king of Judah has committed these detestable sins. He has done more evil[r] than the Amorites[s] who preceded him and has led Judah into sin with his idols. 12 Therefore this is what the LORD, the God of Israel, says: I am going to bring such disaster[t] on Jerusalem and Judah that the ears of everyone who hears of it will tingle.[u] 13 I will stretch out over Jerusalem the measuring line used against Samaria and the plumb-line[v] used against the house of Ahab. I will wipe[w] out Jerusalem as one wipes out a dish, wiping it and turning it upside-down. 14 I will forsake[x] the remnant[y] of my inheritance and hand them over to their enemies. They will be looted and plundered by all their foes, 15 because they have done evil[z] in my eyes and have provoked[a] me to anger from the day their forefathers came out of Egypt until this day."

16 Moreover, Manasseh also shed so much innocent blood[b] that he filled Jerusalem from end to end—besides the sin that he had caused Judah to commit, so that they did evil in the eyes of the LORD.

17 As for the other events of Manasseh's reign, and all he did, including the sin he committed, are they not written in the book of the annals of the kings of Judah? 18 Manasseh rested with his fathers and was buried in his palace garden,[c] the garden of Uzza. And Amon his son succeeded him as king.

Amon King of Judah

21:19–24pp 2Ch 33:21–25

19 Amon was twenty-two years old when he became king, and he reigned in Jerusalem for two years. His mother's name was

21:1 a Isa 62:4
21:2 b Jer 15:4; c 2Ki 16:3
21:3 d 2Ki 18:4; e Jdg 6:28, 1Ki 16:32; f Dt 17:3, 2Ki 17:16
21:4 g Jer 32:34; h 2Sa 7:13, 1Ki 8:29
21:5 i 1Ki 7:12, 2Ki 23:12
21:6 j Lev 18:21, Dt 18:10, 2Ki 16:3, 2Ki 17:17; k Lev 19:31
21:7 l Dt 16:21, 2Ki 23:4; m 2Sa 7:13, 1Ki 8:29, 1Ki 9:3, 2Ki 23:27, Jer 32:34
21:8 n 2Sa 7:10; o 2Ki 18:12
21:9 p Pr 29:12; q Dt 9:4
21:11 r 2Ki 24:3-4; s Ge 15:16, 1Ki 21:26
21:12 t 2Ki 23:26, 2Ki 24:3, Jer 15:4; u 1Sa 3:11, Jer 19:3
21:13 v Isa 34:11, La 2:8, Am 7:7-9; w 2Ki 23:27
21:14 x Ps 78:58-60; y 2Ki 19:4, Mic 2:12
21:15 z Ex 32:22; a Jer 25:7
21:16 b 2Ki 24:4
21:18 c ver 26

a6 Or *He made his own son pass through*

Meshullemeth daughter of Haruz; she was from Jotbah. 20He did evil[d] in the eyes of the LORD, as his father Manasseh had done. 21He walked in all the ways of his father; he worshipped the idols his father had worshipped, and bowed down to them. 22He forsook the LORD, the God of his fathers, and did not walk[e] in the way of the LORD.

23Amon's officials conspired against him and assassinated[f] the king in his palace. 24Then the people of the land killed[g] all who had plotted against King Amon, and they made Josiah his son king in his place.

25As for the other events of Amon's reign, and what he did, are they not written in the book of the annals of the kings of Judah? 26He was buried in his grave in the garden[h] of Uzza. And Josiah his son succeeded him as king.

The Book of the Law Found

22:1–20pp 2Ch 34:1–2,8–28

22 Josiah was eight years old when he became king, and he reigned in Jerusalem for thirty-one years. His mother's name was Jedidah daughter of Adaiah; she was from Bozkath.[a] 2He did what was right[b] in the eyes of the LORD and walked in all the ways of his father David, not turning aside to the right[c] or to the left.

3In the eighteenth year of his reign, King Josiah sent the secretary, Shaphan[d] son of Azaliah, the son of Meshullam, to the temple of the LORD. He said: 4"Go up to Hilkiah the high priest and make him get ready the money that has been brought into the temple of the LORD, which the doorkeepers have collected[e] from the people. 5Make them entrust it to the men appointed to supervise the work on the temple. And make these men pay the workers who repair[f] the temple of the LORD—6the carpenters, the builders and the masons. Also make them purchase timber and dressed stone to repair the temple.[g] 7But they need not account for the money entrusted to them, because they are acting faithfully."[h]

8Hilkiah the high priest said to Shaphan the secretary, "I have found the Book of the Law[i] in the temple of the LORD." He gave it to Shaphan, who read it. 9Then Shaphan the secretary went to the king and reported to him: "Your officials have paid out the money that was in the temple of the LORD and have entrusted it to the workers and supervisors at the temple." 10Then Shaphan the secretary informed the king, "Hilkiah the priest has given me a book." And Shaphan read from it in the presence of the king.[j]

11When the king heard the words of the Book of the Law, he tore his robes. 12He gave these orders to Hilkiah the priest, Ahikam[k] son of Shaphan, Acbor son of Micaiah, Shaphan the secretary and Asaiah the king's attendant: 13"Go and enquire of the LORD for me and for the people and for all Judah about what is written in this book that has been found. Great is the LORD's anger[l] that burns against us because our fathers have not obeyed the words of this book; they have not acted in accordance with all that is written there concerning us."

14Hilkiah the priest, Ahikam, Acbor, Shaphan and Asaiah went to speak to the prophetess Huldah, who was the wife of Shallum son of Tikvah, the son of Harhas, keeper of the wardrobe. She lived in Jerusalem, in the Second District.

15She said to them, "This is what the LORD, the God of Israel, says: Tell the man who sent you to me, 16'This is what the LORD says: I am going to bring disaster[m] on this place and its people, according to everything written in the book[n] the king of Judah has read.

21:20 *d* ver 2-6
21:22 *e* 1Ki 11:33
21:23 *f* 2Ki 12:20; 2Ch 33:24-25
21:24 *g* 2Ki 14:5
21:26 *h* ver 18
22:1 *a* Jos 15:39
22:2 *b* Dt 17:19 *c* Dt 5:32
22:3 *d* 2Ch 34:20; Jer 39:14
22:4 *e* 2Ki 12:4-5
22:5 *f* 2Ki 12:5, 11-14
22:6 *g* 2Ki 12:11-12
22:7 *h* 2Ki 12:15
22:8 *i* Dt 31:24
22:10 *j* Jer 36:21
22:12 *k* 2Ki 25:22; Jer 26:24
22:13 *l* Dt 29:24-28; Dt 31:17
22:16 *m* Dt 31:29; Jos 23:15 *n* Dt 29:27; Da 9:11

17Because they have forsaken[o] me
and burned incense to other gods
and provoked me to anger by all the
idols their hands have made,[a] my
anger will burn against this place
and will not be quenched.' 18Tell the
king of Judah, who sent you to enquire[p] of the LORD, 'This is what
the LORD, the God of Israel, says
concerning the words you heard:
19Because your heart was responsive and you humbled[q] yourself
before the LORD when you heard
what I have spoken against this
place and its people, that they
would become accursed[r] and laid
waste,[s] and because you tore your
robes and wept in my presence, I
have heard you, declares the LORD.
20Therefore I will gather you to
your fathers, and you will be buried
in peace.[t] Your eyes will not see
all the disaster I am going to bring
on this place.' "

So they took her answer back to the king.

Josiah Renews the Covenant

23:1–3pp 2Ch 34:29–32
23:4–20Ref 2Ch 34:3–7,33
23:21–23pp 2Ch 35:1,18–19
23:28–30pp 2Ch 35:20–36:1

23 Then the king called together all the elders of Judah and Jerusalem. 2He went up to
the temple of the LORD with the
men of Judah, the people of Jerusalem, the priests and the prophets—all the people from the least to
the greatest. He read[a] in their
hearing all the words of the Book of
the Covenant, which had been
found in the temple of the LORD.
3The king stood by the pillar and renewed the covenant[b] in the presence of the LORD—to follow[c] the
LORD and keep his commands,
regulations and decrees with all his
heart and all his soul, thus confirming the words of the covenant
written in this book. Then all the
people pledged themselves to the
covenant.
4The king ordered Hilkiah the
high priest, the priests next in rank
and the doorkeepers[d] to remove[e]
from the temple of the LORD all the
articles made for Baal and Asherah
and all the starry hosts. He burned
them outside Jerusalem in the
fields of the Kidron Valley and took
the ashes to Bethel. 5He did away
with the pagan priests appointed
by the kings of Judah to burn incense on the high places of the
towns of Judah and on those around
Jerusalem—those who burned incense to Baal, to the sun and moon,
to the constellations and to all the
starry hosts.[f] 6He took the Asherah pole from the temple of the
LORD to the Kidron Valley outside
Jerusalem and burned it there. He
ground it to powder and scattered
the dust over the graves of the
common people.[g] 7He also tore
down the quarters of the male
shrine-prostitutes,[h] which were in
the temple of the LORD and where
women did weaving for Asherah.
8Josiah brought all the priests
from the towns of Judah and desecrated the high places, from
Geba[i] to Beersheba, where the
priests had burned incense. He
broke down the shrines[a] at the
gates—at the entrance to the Gate
of Joshua, the city governor, which
is on the left of the city gate. 9Al-
though the priests of the high
places did not serve[j] at the altar of
the LORD in Jerusalem, they ate unleavened bread with their fellow
priests.
10He desecrated Topheth,[k]
which was in the Valley of Ben Hinnom,[l] so no-one could use it to sacrifice his son[m] or daughter in[b] the
fire to Molech. 11He removed from
the entrance to the temple of the
LORD the horses that the kings of
Judah had dedicated to the sun.
They were in the court near
the room of an official named

22:17 o Dt 29:25-27
22:18 p 2Ch 34:26; Jer 21:2
22:19 q Ex 10:3; 1Ki 21:29; Ps 51:17; Isa 57:15; Mic 6:8; r Jer 26:6; s Lev 26:31
22:20 t Isa 57:1
23:2 a Dt 31:11; 2Ki 22:8
23:3 b 2Ki 11:14,17; c Dt 13:4
23:4 d 2Ki 25:18; e 2Ki 21:7
23:5 f 2Ki 21:3; Jer 8:2
23:6 g Jer 26:23
23:7 h 1Ki 14:24; 1Ki 15:12; Eze 16:16
23:8 i 1Ki 15:22
23:9 j Eze 44:10-14
23:10 k Isa 30:33; Jer 7:31,32; Jer 19:6; l Jos 15:8; m Lev 18:21; Dt 18:10

a17 Or *by everything they have done*
a8 Or *high places* b10 Or *to make his son or daughter pass through*

Nathan-Melech. Josiah then burned the chariots dedicated to the sun.[n]

12 He pulled down the altars the kings of Judah had erected on the roof[o] near the upper room of Ahaz, and the altars Manasseh had built in the two courts[p] of the temple of the LORD. He removed them from there, smashed them to pieces and threw the rubble into the Kidron Valley. 13 The king also desecrated the high places that were east of Jerusalem on the south of the Hill of Corruption—the ones Solomon[q] king of Israel had built for Ashtoreth the vile goddess of the Sidonians, for Chemosh the vile god of Moab, and for Molech[c] the detestable god of the people of Ammon. 14 Josiah smashed[r] the sacred stones and cut down the Asherah poles and covered the sites with human bones.

15 Even the altar[s] at Bethel, the high place made by Jeroboam[t] son of Nebat, who had caused Israel to sin—even that altar and high place he demolished. He burned the high place and ground it to powder, and burned the Asherah pole also. 16 Then Josiah[u] looked around, and when he saw the tombs that were there on the hillside, he had the bones removed from them and burned on the altar to defile it, in accordance with the word of the LORD proclaimed by the man of God who foretold these things.

17 The king asked, "What is that tombstone I see?"

The men of the city said, "It marks the tomb of the man of God who came from Judah and pronounced against the altar of Bethel the very things you have done to it."

18 "Leave it alone," he said. "Don't let anyone disturb his bones[v]." So they spared his bones and those of the prophet who had come from Samaria.

19 Just as he had done at Bethel, Josiah removed and defiled all the shrines at the high places that the kings of Israel had built in the towns of Samaria that had provoked the LORD to anger. 20 Josiah slaughtered[w] all the priests of those high places on the altars and burned human bones[x] on them. Then he went back to Jerusalem.

21 The king gave this order to all the people: "Celebrate the Passover[y] to the LORD your God, as it is written in this Book of the Covenant." 22 Not since the days of the judges who led Israel, nor throughout the days of the kings of Israel and the kings of Judah, had any such Passover been observed. 23 But in the eighteenth year of King Josiah, this Passover was celebrated to the LORD in Jerusalem.

24 Furthermore, Josiah got rid of the mediums and spiritists,[z] the household gods,[a] the idols and all the other detestable things seen in Judah and Jerusalem. This he did to fulfil the requirements of the law written in the book that Hilkiah the priest had discovered in the temple of the LORD. 25 Neither before nor after Josiah was there a king like him who turned[b] to the LORD as he did—with all his heart and with all his soul and with all his strength, in accordance with all the Law of Moses.

26 Nevertheless, the LORD did not turn away from the heat of his fierce anger, which burned against Judah because of all that Manasseh[c] had done to provoke him to anger. 27 So the LORD said, "I will remove[d] Judah also from my presence[e] as I removed Israel, and I will reject Jerusalem, the city I chose, and this temple, about which I said, 'There shall my Name be.'[d]"

28 As for the other events of Josiah's reign, and all he did, are they not written in the book of the annals of the kings of Judah?

29 While Josiah was king, Pharaoh Neco[f] king of Egypt went up to the Euphrates River to help the king of

23:11 n Dt 4:19
23:12 o Jer 19:13; Zep 1:5 p 2Ki 21:5
23:13 q 1Ki 11:7
23:14 r Ex 23:24; Dt 7:5,25
23:15 s 1Ki 13:1-3 t 1Ki 12:33
23:16 u 1Ki 13:2
23:18 v 1Ki 13:31
23:20 w Ex 22:20; 2Ki 10:25; 2Ki 11:18 x 1Ki 13:2
23:21 y Ex 12:11; Nu 9:2; Dt 16:1-8
23:24 z Lev 19:31; Dt 18:11; 2Ki 21:6 a Ge 31:19
23:25 b 2Ki 18:5
23:26 c 2Ki 21:12; Jer 15:4
23:27 d 2Ki 21:13 e 2Ki 18:11
23:29 f Jer 46:2

c 13 Hebrew *Milcom* d 27 1 Kings 8:29

Assyria. King Josiah marched out
to meet him in battle, but Neco
faced him and killed him at
Megiddo.[g] 30Josiah's servants
brought his body in a chariot[h]
from Megiddo to Jerusalem and
buried him in his own tomb. And
the people of the land took Jehoahaz son of Josiah and anointed him
and made him king in place of his
father.

Jehoahaz King of Judah

23:31–34pp 2Ch 36:2–4

31Jehoahaz[i] was twenty-three
years old when he became king,
and he reigned in Jerusalem for
three months. His mother's name
was Hamutal[j] daughter of Jeremiah; she was from Libnah. 32He
did evil in the eyes of the LORD, just
as his fathers had done. 33Pharaoh
Neco put him in chains at Riblah[k]
in the land of Hamath[e][l] so that he
might not reign in Jerusalem, and
he imposed on Judah a levy of a
hundred talents[f] of silver and a
talent[g] of gold. 34Pharaoh Neco
made Eliakim[m] son of Josiah king
in place of his father Josiah and
changed Eliakim's name to Jehoiakim. But he took Jehoahaz and carried him off to Egypt, and there he
died.[n] 35Jehoiakim paid Pharaoh
Neco the silver and gold he demanded. In order to do so, he taxed
the land and exacted the silver and
gold from the people of the land
according to their assessments.[o]

Jehoiakim King of Judah

23:36–24:6pp 2Ch 36:5–8

36Jehoiakim[p] was twenty-five
years old when he became king,
and he reigned in Jerusalem for
eleven years. His mother's name
was Zebidah daughter of Pedaiah;
she was from Rumah. 37And he did
evil in the eyes of the LORD, just as
his fathers had done.

24 During Jehoiakim's reign,
Nebuchadnezzar[a] king of
Babylon invaded the land, and
Jehoiakim became his vassal for
three years. But then he changed
his mind and rebelled against
Nebuchadnezzar. 2The LORD sent
Babylonian,[a] Aramean,[b] Moabite
and Ammonite raiders against him.
He sent them to destroy[c] Judah,
in accordance with the word of
the LORD proclaimed by his servants the prophets. 3Surely these
things happened to Judah according to the LORD's command,[d] in
order to remove them from his
presence because of the sins of
Manasseh[e] and all he had done,
4including the shedding of innocent blood.[f] For he had filled Jerusalem with innocent blood, and
the LORD was not willing to forgive.
5As for the other events of Jehoiakim's reign, and all he did, are
they not written in the book of the
annals of the kings of Judah? 6Je-
hoiakim rested[g] with his fathers.
And Jehoiachin his son succeeded
him as king.
7The king of Egypt[h] did not
march out from his own country
again, because the king of Babylon[i] had taken all his territory,
from the Wadi of Egypt to the
Euphrates River.

Jehoiachin King of Judah

24:8–17pp 2Ch 36:9–10

8Jehoiachin[j] was eighteen years
old when he became king, and he
reigned in Jerusalem for three
months. His mother's name was
Nehushta daughter of Elnathan;
she was from Jerusalem. 9He did
evil in the eyes of the LORD, just as
his father had done.
10At that time the officers of
Nebuchadnezzar[k] king of Babylon

23:29 g Zec 12:11
23:30 h 2Ki 9:28
23:31 i 1Ch 3:15; Jer 22:11 j 2Ki 24:18
23:33 k 2Ki 25:6 l 1Ki 8:65
23:34 m 1Ch 3:15; 2Ch 36:5-8 n Jer 22:12; Eze 19:3-4
23:35 o ver 33
23:36 p Jer 26:1
24:1 a Jer 25:1,9; Da 1:1
24:2 b Jer 35:11 c Jer 25:9
24:3 d 2Ki 18:25 e 2Ki 21:12; 2Ki 23:26
24:4 f 2Ki 21:16
24:6 g Jer 22:19
24:7 h Ge 15:18 i Jer 37:5-7; Jer 46:2
24:8 j 1Ch 3:16
24:10 k Da 1:1

e33 Hebrew; Septuagint (see also 2 Chron. 36:3) *Neco at Riblah in Hamath removed him*
f33 That is, about 3½ tons (about 3.4 metric tons)
g33 That is, about 75 pounds (about 34 kilograms)
a2 Or *Chaldean*

advanced on Jerusalem and laid siege to it, 11and Nebuchadnezzar himself came up to the city while his officers were besieging it. 12Jehoiachin king of Judah, his mother, his attendants, his nobles and his officials all surrendered[l] to him.

In the eighth year of the reign of the king of Babylon, he took Jehoiachin prisoner. 13As the LORD had declared,[m] Nebuchadnezzar removed all the treasures[n] from the temple of the LORD and from the royal palace, and took away all the gold articles[o] that Solomon[p] king of Israel had made for the temple of the LORD. 14He carried into exile[q] all Jerusalem: all the officers and fighting men, and all the craftsmen and artisans—a total of ten thousand. Only the poorest[r] people of the land were left.

15Nebuchadnezzar took Jehoiachin captive to Babylon. He also took from Jerusalem to Babylon the king's mother,[s] his wives, his officials and the leading men[t] of the land. 16The king of Babylon also deported to Babylon the entire force of seven thousand fighting men, strong and fit for war, and a thousand craftsmen and artisans.[u] 17He made Mattaniah, Jehoiachin's uncle, king in his place and changed his name to Zedekiah.[v]

Zedekiah King of Judah

24:18–20pp 2Ch 36:11–16; Jer 52:1–3

18Zedekiah[w] was twenty-one years old when he became king, and he reigned in Jerusalem for eleven years. His mother's name was Hamutal[x] daughter of Jeremiah; she was from Libnah. 19He did evil in the eyes of the LORD, just as Jehoiakim had done. 20It was because of the LORD's anger that all this happened to Jerusalem and Judah, and in the end he thrust[y] them from his presence.

The Fall of Jerusalem

25:1–12pp Jer 39:1–10
25:1–21pp 2Ch 36:17–20; Jer 52:4–27
25:22–26pp Jer 40:7–9; 41:1–3, 16–18

Now Zedekiah rebelled against the king of Babylon.

25 So in the ninth year of Zedekiah's reign, on the tenth day of the tenth month, Nebuchadnezzar[a] king of Babylon marched against Jerusalem with his whole army. He encamped outside the city and built siege works[b] all around it. 2The city was kept under siege until the eleventh year of King Zedekiah. 3By the ninth day of the ⌞fourth⌟[a] month the famine[c] in the city had become so severe that there was no food for the people to eat. 4Then the city wall was broken through,[d] and the whole army fled at night through the gate between the two walls near the king's garden, though the Babylonians[b] were surrounding[e] the city. They fled towards the Arabah,[c] 5but the Babylonian[d] army pursued the king and overtook him in the plains of Jericho. All his soldiers were separated from him and scattered,[f] 6and he was captured.[g] He was taken to the king of Babylon at Riblah,[h] where sentence was pronounced on him. 7They killed the sons of Zedekiah before his eyes. Then they put out his eyes, bound him with bronze shackles and took him to Babylon.[i]

8On the seventh day of the fifth month, in the nineteenth year of Nebuchadnezzar king of Babylon, Nebuzaradan commander of the imperial guard, an official of the king of Babylon, came to Jerusalem. 9He set fire[j] to the temple of the LORD, the royal palace and all the houses of Jerusalem. Every important building he burned down.[k] 10The whole Babylonian army, under the commander of the imperial guard, broke down the walls[l]

24:12 *l* 2Ki 25:27; Jer 22:24-30; Jer 24:1; Jer 25:1; Jer 29:2; Jer 52:28
24:13 *m* 2Ki 20:17; *n* 2Ki 25:15; Isa 39:6; *o* 2Ki 25:14; Jer 20:5; *p* 1Ki 7:51
24:14 *q* Jer 24:1; Jer 52:28; *r* 2Ki 25:12; Jer 40:7; Jer 52:16
24:15 *s* Jer 22:24-28; *t* Est 2:6; Eze 17:12-14
24:16 *u* Jer 52:28
24:17 *v* 1Ch 3:15; 2Ch 36:11; Jer 37:1
24:18 *w* Jer 52:1; *x* 2Ki 23:31
24:20 *y* Dt 4:26; Dt 29:27
25:1 *a* Jer 34:1-7; *b* Eze 24:2
25:3 *c* Jer 14:18; La 4:9
25:4 *d* Eze 33:21; *e* Jer 4:17
25:5 *f* Eze 12:14
25:6 *g* Jer 34:21-22; *h* 2Ki 23:33
25:7 *i* Jer 21:7; Jer 32:4-5; Eze 12:11
25:9 *j* Isa 60:7; *k* Ps 74:3-8; Jer 2:15; Am 2:5; Mic 3:12
25:10 *l* Ne 1:3

a3 See Jer. 52:6. b4 Or *Chaldeans*; also in verses 13, 25 and 26 c4 Or *the Jordan Valley* d5 Or *Chaldean*; also in verses 10 and 24

around Jerusalem. 11 Nebuzaradan the commander of the guard carried into exile[m] the people who remained in the city, along with the rest of the populace and those who had gone over to the king of Babylon.[n] 12 But the commander left behind some of the poorest people[o] of the land to work the vineyards and fields.

13 The Babylonians broke up the bronze pillars, the movable stands and the bronze Sea that were at the temple of the LORD and they carried the bronze to Babylon. 14 They also took away the pots, shovels, wick trimmers, dishes and all the bronze articles[p] used in the temple service. 15 The commander of the imperial guard took away the censers and sprinkling bowls—all that were made of pure gold or silver. 16 The bronze from the two pillars, the Sea and the movable stands, which Solomon had made for the temple of the LORD, was more than could be weighed. 17 Each pillar[q] was twenty-seven feet[e] high. The bronze capital on top of one pillar was four and a half feet[f] high and was decorated with a network and pomegranates of bronze all around. The other pillar, with its network, was similar.

18 The commander of the guard took as prisoners Seraiah[r] the chief priest, Zephaniah[s] the priest next in rank and the three doorkeepers. 19 Of those still in the city, he took the officer in charge of the fighting men and five royal advisers. He also took the secretary who was chief officer in charge of conscripting the people of the land and sixty of his men who were found in the city. 20 Nebuzaradan the commander took them all and brought them to the king of Babylon at Riblah. 21 There at Riblah, in the land of Hamath, the king had them executed.

So Judah went into captivity, away from her land.[t]

22 Nebuchadnezzar king of Babylon appointed Gedaliah[u] son of Ahikam, the son of Shaphan, to be over the people he had left behind in Judah. 23 When all the army officers and their men heard that the king of Babylon had appointed Gedaliah as governor, they came to Gedaliah at Mizpah—Ishmael son of Nethaniah, Johanan son of Kareah, Seraiah son of Tanhumeth the Netophathite, Jaazaniah the son of the Maacathite, and their men. 24 Gedaliah took an oath to reassure them and their men. "Do not be afraid of the Babylonian officials," he said. "Settle down in the land and serve the king of Babylon, and it will go well with you."

25 In the seventh month, however, Ishmael son of Nethaniah, the son of Elishama, who was of royal blood, came with ten men and assassinated Gedaliah and also the men of Judah and the Babylonians who were with him at Mizpah. 26 At this, all the people from the least to the greatest, together with the army officers, fled to Egypt[v] for fear of the Babylonians.

Jehoiachin Released

25:27–30pp Jer 52:31–34

27 In the thirty-seventh year of the exile of Jehoiachin king of Judah, in the year Evil-Merodach[g] became king of Babylon, he released Jehoiachin[w] from prison on the twenty-seventh day of the twelfth month. 28 He spoke kindly to him and gave him a seat of honour[x] higher than those of the other kings who were with him in Babylon. 29 So Jehoiachin put aside his prison clothes and for the rest of his life ate regularly at the king's table.[y] 30 Day by day the king gave Jehoiachin a regular allowance as long as he lived.[z]

25:11 *m* 2Ki 24:14 *n* 2Ki 24:1
25:12 *o* 2Ki 24:14
25:14 *p* Ex 27:3; 1Ki 7:47-50
25:17 *q* 1Ki 7:15-22
25:18 *r* 1Ch 6:14; Ezr 7:1; Ne 11:11 *s* Jer 21:1; Jer 29:25
25:21 *t* Ge 12:7; Dt 28:64; Jos 23:13; 2Ki 23:27
25:22 *u* Jer 39:14; Jer 40:5,7
25:26 *v* Isa 30:2; Jer 43:7
25:27 *w* 2Ki 24:12; Jer 52:31-34
25:28 *x* Ezr 5:5; Ne 2:1; Da 2:48
25:29 *y* 2Sa 9:7
25:30 *z* Est 2:9; Jer 28:4

e17 Hebrew *eighteen cubits* (about 8.2 metres)
f17 Hebrew *three cubits* (about 1.4 metres)
g27 Also called *Amel-Marduk*

1 CHRONICLES

Historical Records From Adam to Abraham

To Noah's Sons

1 Adam,[a] Seth, Enosh, 2 Kenan,[b] Mahalalel,[c] Jared,[d]
3 Enoch,[e] Methuselah,[f] Lamech,[g]
Noah.[h]

4 The sons of Noah:[a][i]
Shem, Ham and Japheth.[j]

The Japhethites

1:5–7pp Ge 10:2–5

5 The sons[b] of Japheth:
Gomer, Magog, Madai, Javan, Tubal, Meshech and Tiras.
6 The sons of Gomer:
Ashkenaz, Riphath[c] and Togarmah.
7 The sons of Javan:
Elishah, Tarshish, the Kittim and the Rodanim.

The Hamites

1:8–16pp Ge 10:6–20

8 The sons of Ham:
Cush, Mizraim,[d] Put and Canaan.
9 The sons of Cush:
Seba, Havilah, Sabta, Raamah and Sabteca.
The sons of Raamah:
Sheba and Dedan.
10 Cush was the father[e] of
Nimrod, who grew to be a mighty warrior on earth.
11 Mizraim was the father of
the Ludites, Anamites, Lehabites, Naphtuhites, 12 Path-
rusites, Casluhites (from whom the Philistines came) and Caphtorites.
13 Canaan was the father of
Sidon his firstborn,[f] and of
the Hittites, 14 Jebusites,
Amorites, Girgashites, 15 Hivites, Arkites, Sinites, 16 Ar-
vadites, Zemarites and Hamathites.

The Semites

1:17–23pp Ge 10:21–31; 11:10–27

17 The sons of Shem:
Elam, Asshur, Arphaxad, Lud and Aram.
The sons of Aram:[g]
Uz, Hul, Gether and Meshech.
18 Arphaxad was the father of
Shelah, and Shelah the father of Eber.
19 Two sons were born to Eber:
One was named Peleg,[h] because in his time the earth was divided; his brother was named Joktan.
20 Joktan was the father of
Almodad, Sheleph, Hazarmaveth, Jerah, 21 Hadoram,
Uzal, Diklah, 22 Obal,[i] Abi-
mael, Sheba, 23 Ophir, Havi-
lah and Jobab. All these were sons of Joktan.

24 Shem,[k] Arphaxad,[j] Shelah,
25 Eber, Peleg, Reu,

1:1 *a* Ge 5:1-32; Lk 3:36-38
1:2 *b* Ge 5:9; *c* Ge 5:12; *d* Ge 5:15
1:3 *e* Ge 5:18; Jude 1:14; *f* Ge 5:21; *g* Ge 5:25; *h* Ge 5:29
1:4 *i* Ge 6:10; Ge 10:1; *j* Ge 5:32
1:24 *k* Ge 10:21-25; Lk 3:34-36

a4 Septuagint; Hebrew does not have *The sons of Noah:* b5 *Sons* may mean *descendants* or *successors* or *nations*; also in verses 6–10, 17 and 20. c6 Many Hebrew manuscripts and Vulgate (see also Septuagint and Gen. 10:3); most Hebrew manuscripts *Diphath* d8 That is, Egypt; also in verse 11 e10 *Father* may mean *ancestor* or *predecessor* or *founder*; also in verses 11, 13, 18 and 20. f13 Or *of the Sidonians, the foremost* g17 One Hebrew manuscript and some Septuagint manuscripts (see also Gen. 10:23); most Hebrew manuscripts do not have this line. h19 *Peleg* means *division.* i22 Some Hebrew manuscripts and Syriac (see also Gen. 10:28); most Hebrew manuscripts *Ebal* j24 Hebrew; some Septuagint manuscripts *Arphaxad, Cainan* (see also note at Gen. 11:10)

[26]Serug, Nahor, Terah
[27]and Abram (that is, Abraham).

The Family of Abraham

[28]The sons of Abraham:
Isaac and Ishmael.

Descendants of Hagar

1:29–31pp Ge 25:12–16

[29]These were their descendants:
Nebaioth the firstborn of Ishmael, Kedar, Adbeel,
Mibsam, [30]Mishma, Dumah,
Massa, Hadad, Tema, [31]Je-
tur, Naphish and Kedemah. These were the sons of Ishmael.

Descendants of Keturah

1:32–33pp Ge 25:1–4

[32]The sons born to Keturah, Abraham's concubine:[l]
Zimran, Jokshan, Medan, Midian, Ishbak and Shuah.
The sons of Jokshan:
Sheba and Dedan.[m]
[33]The sons of Midian:
Ephah, Epher, Hanoch, Abida and Eldaah.
All these were descendants of Keturah.

Descendants of Sarah

1:35–37pp Ge 36:10–14

[34]Abraham[n] was the father of Isaac.[o]
The sons of Isaac:
Esau and Israel.[p]

Esau's Sons

[35]The sons of Esau:[q]
Eliphaz, Reuel,[r] Jeush, Jalam and Korah.
[36]The sons of Eliphaz:
Teman, Omar, Zepho,[k] Gatam and Kenaz;
by Timna: Amalek.[l][s]
[37]The sons of Reuel:[t]
Nahath, Zerah, Shammah and Mizzah.

1:32 *l* Ge 22:24 *m* Ge 10:7
1:34 *n* Lk 3:34 *o* Ge 21:2-3; Mt 1:2; Ac 7:8 *p* Ge 17:5; Ge 25:25-26
1:35 *q* Ge 36:19 *r* Ge 36:4
1:36 *s* Ex 17:14
1:37 *t* Ge 36:17
1:40 *u* Ge 36:2
1:45 *v* Ge 36:11

The People of Seir in Edom

1:38–42pp Ge 36:20–28

[38]The sons of Seir:
Lotan, Shobal, Zibeon, Anah, Dishon, Ezer and Dishan.
[39]The sons of Lotan:
Hori and Homam. Timna was Lotan's sister.
[40]The sons of Shobal:
Alvan,[m] Manahath, Ebal, Shepho and Onam.
The sons of Zibeon:
Aiah and Anah.[u]
[41]The son of Anah:
Dishon.
The sons of Dishon:
Hemdan,[n] Eshban, Ithran and Keran.
[42]The sons of Ezer:
Bilhan, Zaavan and Akan.[o]
The sons of Dishan:[p]
Uz and Aran.

The Rulers of Edom

1:43–54pp Ge 36:31–43

[43]These were the kings who reigned in Edom before any Israelite king reigned:[q]
Bela son of Beor, whose city was named Dinhabah.
[44]When Bela died, Jobab son of Zerah from Bozrah succeeded him as king.
[45]When Jobab died, Husham from the land of the Temanites[v] succeeded him as king.
[46]When Husham died, Hadad son of Bedad, who defeated Midian in the country of

[k]36 Many Hebrew manuscripts, some Septuagint manuscripts and Syriac (see also Gen. 36:11); most Hebrew manuscripts *Zephi* [l]36 Some Septuagint manuscripts (see also Gen. 36:12); Hebrew *Gatam, Kenaz, Timna and Amalek* [m]40 Many Hebrew manuscripts and some Septuagint manuscripts (see also Gen. 36:23); most Hebrew manuscripts *Alian* [n]41 Many Hebrew manuscripts and some Septuagint manuscripts (see also Gen. 36:26); most Hebrew manuscripts *Hamran* [o]42 Many Hebrew and Septuagint manuscripts (see also Gen. 36:27); most Hebrew manuscripts *Zaavan, Jaakan* [p]42 Hebrew *Dishon*, a variant of *Dishan* [q]43 Or *before an Israelite king reigned over them*

Moab, succeeded him as
king. His city was named
Avith.
47 When Hadad died, Samlah
from Masrekah succeeded
him as king.
48 When Samlah died, Shaul from
Rehoboth on the river[r] succeeded him as king.
49 When Shaul died, Baal-Hanan
son of Acbor succeeded him
as king.
50 When Baal-Hanan died, Hadad
succeeded him as king. His
city was named Pau,[s] and
his wife's name was Mehe-
tabel daughter of Matred,
the daughter of Me-Zahab.
51 Hadad also died.

The chiefs of Edom were:
Timna, Alvah, Jetheth,
52 Oholibamah, Elah, Pinon,
53 Kenaz, Teman, Mibzar,
54 Magdiel and Iram. These
were the chiefs of Edom.

Israel's Sons

2:1–2pp Ge 35:23–26

2

These were the sons of Israel:
Reuben, Simeon, Levi,
Judah, Issachar, Zebulun,
2 Dan, Joseph, Benjamin,
Naphtali, Gad and Asher.

Judah

2:5–15pp Ru 4:18–22; Mt 1:3–6

To Hezron's Sons

3 The sons of Judah:[a]
Er, Onan and Shelah.[b]
These three were born to
him by a Canaanite woman,
the daughter of Shua.[c] Er,
Judah's firstborn, was
wicked in the LORD's sight;
so the LORD put him to
death.[d] 4 Tamar,[e] Judah's
daughter-in-law,[f] bore him
Perez[g] and Zerah. Judah
had five sons in all.

2:3
a Ge 29:35
Ge 38:2-10
b Ge 38:5
c Ge 38:2
d Nu 26:19

2:4
e Ge 38:11-30
f Ge 11:31
g Ge 38:29

2:5
h Ge 46:12
i Nu 26:21

2:7
j Jos 7:1
k Jos 6:18

2:9
l Nu 26:21

2:10
m Lk 3:32-33
n Ex 6:23
o Nu 1:7

2:12
p Ru 2:1
q Ru 4:17

2:13
r Ru 4:17
s 1Sa 16:6

2:16
t 1Sa 26:6
u 2Sa 2:18
v 2Sa 2:13

2:17
w 2Sa 17:25

5 The sons of Perez:[h]
Hezron[i] and Hamul.
6 The sons of Zerah:
Zimri, Ethan, Heman, Calcol
and Darda[a]—five in all.
7 The son of Carmi:
Achar,[b][j] who brought trouble on Israel by violating
the ban on taking devoted
things.[c][k]
8 The son of Ethan:
Azariah.
9 The sons born to Hezron[l]
were:
Jerahmeel, Ram and Ca-
leb.[d]

From Ram Son of Hezron

10 Ram[m] was the father of
Amminadab[n], and Ammina-
dab the father of Nahshon,[o]
the leader of the people of
Judah. 11 Nahshon was the
father of Salmon,[e] Salmon
the father of Boaz, 12 Boaz[p]
the father of Obed and Obed
the father of Jesse.[q]
13 Jesse[r] was the father of
Eliab[s] his firstborn; the
second son was Abinadab,
the third Shimea, 14 the
fourth Nethanel, the fifth
Raddai, 15 the sixth Ozem
and the seventh David.
16 Their sisters were Ze-
ruiah[t] and Abigail. Ze-
ruiah's[u] three sons were
Abishai, Joab[v] and Asahel.
17 Abigail was the mother of
Amasa,[w] whose father was
Jether the Ishmaelite.

r *48* Possibly the Euphrates s *50* Many Hebrew manuscripts, some Septuagint manuscripts, Vulgate and Syriac (see also Gen. 36:39); most Hebrew manuscripts *Pai* a *6* Many Hebrew manuscripts, some Septuagint manuscripts and Syriac (see also 1 Kings 4:31); most Hebrew manuscripts *Dara* b *7* *Achar* means *trouble*; *Achar* is called *Achan* in Joshua.
c *7* The Hebrew term refers to the irrevocable giving over of things or persons to the LORD, often by totally destroying them. d *9* Hebrew *Kelubai*, a variant of *Caleb* e *11* Septuagint (see also Ruth 4:21); Hebrew *Salma*

Caleb Son of Hezron

18Caleb son of Hezron had children by his wife Azubah
(and by Jerioth). These were
her sons: Jesher, Shobab
and Ardon. 19When Azubah
died, Caleb[x] married Ephrath, who bore him Hur.
20Hur was the father of Uri,
and Uri the father of Be-
zalel.[y]

21Later, Hezron lay with the
daughter of Makir the
father of Gilead[z] (he had
married her when he was
sixty years old), and she
bore him Segub. 22Segub
was the father of Jair,
who controlled twenty-three
towns in Gilead. 23(But Geshur and Aram captured
Havvoth Jair,[f][a] as well as
Kenath[b] with its sur-
rounding settlements—sixty
towns.) All these were descendants of Makir the
father of Gilead.

24After Hezron died in Caleb
Ephrathah, Abijah the wife
of Hezron bore him Ash-
hur[c] the father[g] of Tekoa.

Jerahmeel Son of Hezron

25The sons of Jerahmeel the firstborn of Hezron:
Ram his firstborn, Bunah,
Oren, Ozem and[h] Ahijah.
26Jerahmeel had another
wife, whose name was Ata-
rah; she was the mother of
Onam.

27The sons of Ram the firstborn of Jerahmeel:
Maaz, Jamin and Eker.

28The sons of Onam:
Shammai and Jada.
The sons of Shammai:
Nadab and Abishur.

29Abishur's wife was named Abihail, who bore him Ahban and Molid.

30The sons of Nadab:
Seled and Appaim. Seled died without children.

31The son of Appaim:
Ishi, who was the father of Sheshan.
Sheshan was the father of Ahlai.

32The sons of Jada, Shammai's brother:
Jether and Jonathan. Jether died without children.

33The sons of Jonathan:
Peleth and Zaza.
These were the descendants of Jerahmeel.

34Sheshan had no sons—only daughters.
He had an Egyptian servant
named Jarha. 35Sheshan
gave his daughter in mar-
riage to his servant Jarha,
and she bore him Attai.

36Attai was the father of Nathan,
Nathan the father of Zabad,[d]
37Zabad the father of Ephlal,
Ephlal the father of Obed,
38Obed the father of Jehu,
Jehu the father of Azariah,
39Azariah the father of Helez,
Helez the father of Eleasah,
40Eleasah the father of Sismai,
Sismai the father of Shallum,
41Shallum the father of Jekamiah, and Jekamiah the father of Elishama.

The Clans of Caleb

42The sons of Caleb[e] the brother of Jerahmeel:
Mesha his firstborn, who was the father of Ziph, and his son Mareshah,[i] who was the father of Hebron.

2:19 x ver 42,50
2:20 y Ex 31:2
2:21 z Nu 27:1
2:23 a Nu 32:41; Dt 3:14; Jos 13:30 b Nu 32:42
2:24 c 1Ch 4:5
2:36 d 1Ch 11:41
2:42 e ver 19

f23 Or *captured the settlements of Jair*
g24 *Father* may mean *civic leader* or *military leader*; also in verses 42, 45, 49–52 and possibly elsewhere.
h25 Or *Oren and Ozem, by*
i42 The meaning of the Hebrew for this phrase is uncertain.

43The sons of Hebron:
Korah, Tappuah, Rekem and
Shema. 44Shema was the
father of Raham, and Raham
the father of Jorkeam. Rekem was the father of Shammai. 45The son of Shammai
was Maon[f], and Maon was
the father of Beth Zur.[g]
46Caleb's concubine Ephah was
the mother of Haran, Moza
and Gazez. Haran was the
father of Gazez.
47The sons of Jahdai:
Regem, Jotham, Geshan, Pelet, Ephah and Shaaph.
48Caleb's concubine Maacah
was the mother of Sheber
and Tirhanah. 49She also
gave birth to Shaaph the
father of Madmannah[h] and
to Sheva the father of Mac-
benah and Gibea. Caleb's
daughter was Acsah.[i]
50These were the descend-
ants of Caleb.

The sons of Hur[j] the firstborn of Ephrathah:
Shobal the father of Kiriath
Jearim,[k] 51Salma the father
of Bethlehem, and Hareph
the father of Beth Gader.
52The descendants of Shobal the
father of Kiriath Jearim
were:
Haroeh, half the Manaha-
thites, 53and the clans of Kiriath Jearim: the Ithrites,[l]
Puthites, Shumathites and
Mishraites. From these descended the Zorathites and
Eshtaolites.
54The descendants of Salma:
Bethlehem, the Netopha-
thites,[m] Atroth Beth Joab,
half the Manahathites, the
Zorites, 55and the clans of
scribes[j] who lived at Jabez:
the Tirathites, Shimeathites
and Sucathites. These are
the Kenites[n] who came
from Hammath,[o] the father
of the house of Recab.[k][p]

2:45
f Jos 15:55
g Jos 15:58

2:49
h Jos 15:31
i Jos 15:16

2:50
j 1Ch 4:4
k ver 19

2:53
l 2Sa 23:38

2:54
m Ezr 2:22
Ne 7:26
Ne 12:28

2:55
n Ge 15:19
Jdg 1:16
Jdg 4:11
o Jos 19:35
p 2Ki 10:15,23
Jer 35:2-19

3:1
a 1Ch 14:3
1Ch 28:5
b Jos 15:56
c 1Sa 25:42

3:2
d 1Ki 2:22

3:4
e 2Sa 5:4
1Ch 29:27
f 2Sa 2:11
2Sa 5:5

3:5
g 2Sa 11:3
2Sa 12:24

3:9
h 2Sa 13:1
i 1Ch 14:4

3:10
j 1Ki 11:43
1Ki 14:21-31
2Ch 12:16
k 2Ch 17:1-21:3

The Sons of David

3:1–4pp 2Sa 3:2–5
3:5–8pp 2Sa 5:14–16; 1Ch 14:4–7

3 These were the sons of
David[a] born to him in Hebron:
The firstborn was Amnon
the son of Ahinoam of Jezreel;[b]
the second, Daniel the son of
Abigail[c] of Carmel;
2the third, Absalom the son of
Maacah daughter of Talmai
king of Geshur;
the fourth, Adonijah[d] the
son of Haggith;
3the fifth, Shephatiah the son
of Abital;
and the sixth, Ithream, by
his wife Eglah.
4These six were born to
David in Hebron,[e] where he
reigned for seven years and
six months.[f]
David reigned in Jerusalem for
thirty-three years, 5and these were
the children born to him there:
Shammua,[a] Shobab, Nathan
and Solomon. These four
were by Bathsheba[b][g]
daughter of Ammiel. 6There
were also Ibhar, Elishua,[c]
Eliphelet, 7Nogah, Nepheg,
Japhia, 8Elishama, Eliada
and Eliphelet—nine in all.
9All these were the sons of
David, besides his sons
by his concubines. And
Tamar[h] was their sister.[i]

The Kings of Judah

10Solomon's son was Reho-
boam,[j]
Abijah his son,
Asa his son,
Jehoshaphat[k] his son,

[j]55 Or *of the Sopherites* [k]55 Or *father of Beth Recab* [a]5 Hebrew *Shimea,* a variant of *Shammua* [b]5 One Hebrew manuscript and Vulgate (see also Septuagint and 2 Sam. 11:3); most Hebrew manuscripts *Bathshua* [c]6 Two Hebrew manuscripts (see also 2 Sam. 5:15 and 1 Chron. 14:5); most Hebrew manuscripts *Elishama*

11 Jehoram[d][l] his son,
Ahaziah[m] his son,
Joash[n] his son,
12 Amaziah[o] his son,
Azariah his son,
Jotham[p] his son,
13 Ahaz[q] his son,
Hezekiah[r] his son,
Manasseh[s] his son,
14 Amon[t] his son,
Josiah[u] his son.
15 The sons of Josiah:
Johanan the firstborn,
Jehoiakim[v] the second son,
Zedekiah[w] the third,
Shallum[x] the fourth.
16 The successors of Jehoiakim:
Jehoiachin[e][y] his son,
and Zedekiah.[z]

The Royal Line After the Exile

17 The descendants of Jehoiachin the captive:
Shealtiel[a] his son, 18 Malkiram, Pedaiah, Shenazzar,[b] Jekamiah, Hoshama and Nedabiah.[c]
19 The sons of Pedaiah:
Zerubbabel[d] and Shimei.
The sons of Zerubbabel:
Meshullam and Hananiah.
Shelomith was their sister.
20 There were also five others:
Hashubah, Ohel, Berekiah, Hasadiah and Jushab-Hesed.
21 The descendants of Hananiah:
Pelatiah and Jeshaiah, and the sons of Rephaiah, of Arnan, of Obadiah and of Shecaniah.
22 The descendants of Shecaniah:
Shemaiah and his sons:
Hattush,[e] Igal, Bariah, Neariah and Shaphat—six in all.
23 The sons of Neariah:
Elioenai, Hizkiah and Azrikam—three in all.
24 The sons of Elioenai:
Hodaviah, Eliashib, Pelaiah, Akkub, Johanan, Delaiah and Anani—seven in all.

3:11
l 2Ki 8:16-24; 2Ch 21:1
m 2Ch 22:1-10
n 2Ki 11:1-12:21

3:12
o 2Ki 14:1-22; 2Ch 25:1-28
p Isa 1:1; Hos 1:1; Mic 1:1

3:13
q 2Ki 16:1-20; 2Ch 28:1; Isa 7:1
r 2Ki 18:1-20:21; 2Ch 29:1; Jer 26:19
s 2Ch 33:1

3:14
t 2Ki 21:19-26; 2Ch 33:21; Zep 1:1
u 2Ch 34:1; Jer 1:2; Jer 3:6; Jer 25:3

3:15
v 2Ki 23:34
w Jer 37:1
x 2Ki 23:31

3:16
y 2Ki 24:6,8; Mt 1:11
z 2Ki 24:18

3:17
a Ezr 3:2

3:18
b Ezr 1:8; Ezr 5:14
c Jer 22:30

3:19
d Ezr 2:2; Ezr 3:2; Ezr 5:2; Ne 7:7; Ne 12:1; Hag 1:1; Hag 2:2; Zec 4:6

3:22
e Ezr 8:2-3

4:1
a Ge 29:35; Ge 46:12; 1Ch 2:3
b Nu 26:21

4:4
c 1Ch 2:50
d Ru 1:19

4:5
e 1Ch 2:24

Other Clans of Judah

4 The descendants of Judah:[a]
Perez, Hezron,[b] Carmi, Hur and Shobal.
2 Reaiah son of Shobal was the father of Jahath, and Jahath the father of Ahumai and Lahad. These were the clans of the Zorathites.
3 These were the sons[a] of Etam:
Jezreel, Ishma and Idbash. Their sister was named Hazzelelponi. 4 Penuel was the father of Gedor, and Ezer the father of Hushah.
These were the descendants of Hur,[c] the firstborn of Ephrathah and father[b] of Bethlehem.[d]
5 Ashhur[e] the father of Tekoa had two wives, Helah and Naarah.
6 Naarah bore him Ahuzzam, Hepher, Temeni and Haahashtari. These were the descendants of Naarah.
7 The sons of Helah:
Zereth, Zohar, Ethnan, 8 and Koz, who was the father of Anub and Hazzobebah and of the clans of Aharhel son of Harum.

9 Jabez was more honourable than his brothers. His mother had named him Jabez,[c] saying, "I gave birth to him in pain." 10 Jabez cried out to the God of Israel, "Oh, that you would bless me and enlarge my territory! Let your hand be with me, and keep me from harm so that I will be free from pain." And God granted his request.

11 Kelub, Shuhah's brother, was the father of Mehir, who was the father of Eshton.

[d] 11 Hebrew *Joram*, a variant of *Jehoram*
[e] 16 Hebrew *Jeconiah*, a variant of *Jehoiachin*; also in verse 17
[a] 3 Some Septuagint manuscripts (see also Vulgate); Hebrew *father*
[b] 4 *Father* may mean *civic leader* or *military leader*; also in verses 12, 14, 17, 18 and possibly elsewhere.
[c] 9 *Jabez* sounds like the Hebrew for *pain*.

12 Eshton was the father of
Beth Rapha, Paseah and Te-
hinnah the father of Ir
Nahash.[d] These were the men
of Recah.

13 The sons of Kenaz:
Othniel[f] and Seraiah.
The sons of Othniel:
Hathath and Meonothai.[e]
14 Meonothai was the father
of Ophrah.
Seraiah was the father of Joab,
the father of Ge Harashim.[f]
It was called this because
its people were craftsmen.
15 The sons of Caleb son of Jephunneh:
Iru, Elah and Naam.
The son of Elah:
Kenaz.
16 The sons of Jehallelel:
Ziph, Ziphah, Tiria and Asa-
rel.
17 The sons of Ezrah:
Jether, Mered, Epher and
Jalon. One of Mered's wives
gave birth to Miriam,[g]
Shammai and Ishbah the
father of Eshtemoa. 18 (His
Judean wife gave birth to Je-
red the father of Gedor, Heber the father of Soco, and
Jekuthiel the father of Zanoah.[h]) These were the children of Pharaoh's daughter
Bithiah, whom Mered had
married.
19 The sons of Hodiah's wife, the
sister of Naham:
the father of Keilah[i] the
Garmite, and Eshtemoa the
Maacathite.[j]
20 The sons of Shimon:
Amnon, Rinnah, Ben-Hanan
and Tilon.
The descendants of Ishi:
Zoheth and Ben-Zoheth.
21 The sons of Shelah[k] son of Judah:
Er the father of Lecah, Laa-
dah the father of Mareshah
and the clans of the linen
workers at Beth Ashbea,

4:13
f Jos 15:17
4:17
g Ex 15:20
4:18
h Jos 15:34
4:19
i Jos 15:44
j Dt 3:14
4:21
k Ge 38:5
4:24
l Ge 29:33
m Nu 26:12
4:28
n Ge 21:14
o Jos 15:26
4:29
p Jos 15:29
4:30
q Nu 14:45
4:31
r Jos 15:36
4:32
s Nu 34:11
t Jos 15:42

22 Jokim, the men of Cozeba,
and Joash and Saraph, who
ruled in Moab and Jashubi
Lehem. (These records are
from ancient times.) 23 They
were the potters who lived
at Netaim and Gederah;
they stayed there and
worked for the king.

Simeon

4:28–33pp Jos 19:2–10

24 The descendants of Simeon:[l]
Nemuel, Jamin, Jarib,[m]
Zerah and Shaul;
25 Shallum was Shaul's son,
Mibsam his son and Mishma
his son.
26 The descendants of Mishma:
Hammuel his son, Zaccur
his son and Shimei his son.
27 Shimei had sixteen sons and six
daughters, but his brothers did not
have many children; so their entire
clan did not become as numerous
as the people of Judah. 28 They lived
in Beersheba,[n] Moladah,[o] Hazar
Shual, 29 Bilhah, Ezem,[p] Tolad,
30 Bethuel, Hormah,[q] Ziklag,
31 Beth Marcaboth, Hazar Susim,
Beth Biri and Shaaraim.[r] These
were their towns until the reign of
David. 32 Their surrounding villages were Etam, Ain,[s] Rimmon,
Token and Ashan[t]—five towns—
33 and all the villages around these
towns as far as Baalath.[g] These
were their settlements. And they
kept a genealogical record.

34 Meshobab, Jamlech, Joshah
son of Amaziah, 35 Joel, Jehu
son of Joshibiah, the son of Seraiah, the son of Asiel, 36 also
Elioenai, Jaakobah, Jesho-
haiah, Asaiah, Adiel, Jesimiel,
Benaiah, 37 and Ziza son of

[d] 12 Or *of the city of Nahash* [e] 13 Some Septuagint manuscripts and Vulgate; Hebrew does not have *and Meonothai.* [f] 14 *Ge Harashim* means *valley of craftsmen.* [g] 33 Some Septuagint manuscripts (see also Joshua 19:8); Hebrew *Baal*

Shiphi, the son of Allon, the son
of Jedaiah, the son of Shimri,
the son of Shemaiah.

38 The men listed above by name
were leaders of their clans. Their
families increased greatly, 39 and
they went to the outskirts of Gedor[u] to the east of the valley in
search of pasture for their flocks.
40 They found rich, good pasture,
and the land was spacious, peaceful
and quiet.[v] Some Hamites had
lived there formerly.

41 The men whose names were
listed came in the days of Hezekiah
king of Judah. They attacked the
Hamites in their dwellings and also
the Meunites[w] who were there and
completely destroyed[h] them, as is
evident to this day. Then they settled in their place, because there
was pasture for their flocks. 42 And
five hundred of these Simeonites,
led by Pelatiah, Neariah, Rephaiah
and Uzziel, the sons of Ishi, invaded
the hill country of Seir.[x] 43 They
killed the remaining Amalekites[y]
who had escaped, and they have
lived there to this day.

Reuben

5 The sons of Reuben[a] the firstborn of Israel (he was the
firstborn, but when he defiled his
father's marriage bed,[b] his rights
as firstborn were given to the sons
of Joseph[c] son of Israel;[d] so he
could not be listed in the genealogical record in accordance with his
birthright,[e] 2 and though Judah[f]
was the strongest of his brothers
and a ruler[g] came from him, the
rights of the firstborn[h] belonged
to Joseph)—3 the sons of Reuben[i]
the firstborn of Israel:

Hanoch, Pallu,[j] Hezron and
Carmi.

4 The descendants of Joel:
Shemaiah his son, Gog his
son,
Shimei his son, 5 Micah his
son,
Reaiah his son, Baal his son,
6 and Beerah his son, whom
Tiglath-Pileser[a][k] king of
Assyria took into exile.
Beerah was a leader of the
Reubenites.

7 Their relatives by clans,[l]
listed according to their genealogical records:
Jeiel the chief, Zechariah,
8 and Bela son of Azaz, the
son of Shema, the son of
Joel. They settled in the area
from Aroer[m] to Nebo and
Baal Meon.[n] 9 To the east
they occupied the land up to
the edge of the desert that
extends to the Euphrates
River, because their livestock had increased in Gilead.[o]

10 During Saul's reign they
waged war against the Hagrites[p], who were defeated at
their hands; they occupied
the dwellings of the Hag-
rites throughout the entire
region east of Gilead.

Gad

11 The Gadites[q] lived next to
them in Bashan, as far as
Salecah:[r]
12 Joel was the chief, Shapham
the second, then Janai and
Shaphat, in Bashan.
13 Their relatives, by families,
were:
Michael, Meshullam, Sheba,
Jorai, Jacan, Zia and Eber—
seven in all.
14 These were the sons of Abihail son of Huri, the son of
Jaroah, the son of Gilead, the
son of Michael, the son of Je-
shishai, the son of Jahdo, the
son of Buz.
15 Ahi son of Abdiel, the son of

4:39 u Jos 15:58
4:40 v Jdg 18:7-10
4:41 w 2Ch 20:1; 2Ch 26:7
4:42 x Ge 14:6
4:43 y 1Sa 15:8; 1Sa 30:17; 2Sa 8:12; Est 3:1; Est 9:16
5:1 a Ge 29:32 b Ge 35:22; Ge 49:4 c Ge 48:16,22; Ge 49:26 d Ge 48:5 e 1Ch 26:10
5:2 f Ge 49:10,12 g 1Sa 9:16; 1Sa 12:12; 2Sa 6:21; 1Ch 11:2; 2Ch 7:18; Ps 60:7; Mic 5:2; Mt 2:6 h Ge 25:31
5:3 i Ge 29:32; Ge 46:9; Ex 6:14; Nu 26:5-11 j Nu 26:5
5:6 k ver 26; 2Ki 15:19; 2Ki 16:10; 2Ch 28:20
5:7 l ver 17
5:8 m Nu 32:34 n Jos 13:17
5:9 o Nu 32:26; Jos 22:9
5:10 p ver 18-21
5:11 q Jos 13:24-28 r Dt 3:10; Jos 13:11

h41 The Hebrew term refers to the irrevocable giving over of things or persons to the LORD, often by totally destroying them. a6 Hebrew *Tilgath-Pilneser*, a variant of *Tiglath-Pileser*; also in verse 26

Guni, was head of their family.
16 The Gadites lived in Gilead, in
Bashan and its outlying villages, and on all the pasture-
lands of Sharon as far as
they extended.
17 All these were entered in the
genealogical records during the
reigns of Jotham[s] king of Judah
and Jeroboam[t] king of Israel.

18 The Reubenites, the Gadites
and the half-tribe of Manasseh had
44,760 men ready for military service[u]—able-bodied men who could
handle shield and sword, who could
use a bow, and who were trained
for battle. 19 They waged war
against the Hagrites, Jetur,[v] Naphish and Nodab. 20 They were
helped[w] in fighting them, and God
handed the Hagrites and all their
allies over to them, because they
cried[x] out to him during the battle.
He answered their prayers, because they trusted[y] in him. 21 They
seized the livestock of the Hagrites—fifty thousand camels, two
hundred and fifty thousand sheep
and two thousand donkeys. They
also took one hundred thousand
people captive, 22 and many others
fell slain, because the battle[z] was
God's. And they occupied the land
until the exile.[a]

The Half-Tribe of Manasseh

23 The people of the half-tribe of
Manasseh were numerous; they
settled in the land from Bashan to
Baal Hermon, that is, to Senir
(Mount Hermon).[b]
24 These were the heads of their
families: Epher, Ishi, Eliel, Azriel,
Jeremiah, Hodaviah and Jahdiel.
They were brave warriors, famous
men, and heads of their families.
25 But they were unfaithful[c] to the
God of their fathers and prostituted[d] themselves to the gods of
the peoples of the land, whom God
had destroyed before them. 26 So
the God of Israel stirred up the
spirit of Pul[e] king of Assyria (that
is, Tiglath-Pileser[f] king of Assyria), who took the Reubenites,
the Gadites and the half-tribe of
Manasseh into exile. He took them
to Halah,[g] Habor, Hara and the
river of Gozan, where they are to
this day.

Levi

6 The sons of Levi:[a]
Gershon, Kohath and Mer-
ari.
2 The sons of Kohath:
Amram, Izhar, Hebron and
Uzziel.
3 The children of Amram:
Aaron, Moses and Miriam.
The sons of Aaron:
Nadab, Abihu,[b] Eleazar and
Ithamar.
4 Eleazar was the father of
Phinehas,
Phinehas the father of Abishua,
5 Abishua the father of Bukki,
Bukki the father of Uzzi,
6 Uzzi the father of Zerahiah,
Zerahiah the father of Meraioth,
7 Meraioth the father of
Amariah,
Amariah the father of Ahitub,
8 Ahitub the father of Zadok,[c]
Zadok the father of Ahi-
maaz,
9 Ahimaaz the father of Azariah,
Azariah the father of Johanan,
10 Johanan the father of Azariah[d] (it was he who served
as priest in the temple Solomon built in Jerusalem),
11 Azariah the father of Amariah,
Amariah the father of Ahitub,
12 Ahitub the father of Zadok,
Zadok the father of Shallum,
13 Shallum the father of
Hilkiah,[e]

5:17 s 2Ki 15:32 t 2Ki 14:16,28
5:18 u Nu 1:3
5:19 v ver 10 Ge 25:15 1Ch 1:31
5:20 w Ps 37:40 x 1Ki 8:44 2Ch 13:14 2Ch 14:11 Ps 20:7-9 Ps 22:5 y Ps 26:1 Da 6:23
5:22 z 2Ch 32:8 a 2Ki 15:29 2Ki 17:6
5:23 b Dt 3:8,9 SS 4:8
5:25 c Dt 32:15-18 2Ki 17:7 1Ch 9:1 2Ch 26:16 d Ex 34:15
5:26 e 2Ki 15:19 f 2Ki 15:29 g 2Ki 17:6 2Ki 18:11
6:1 a Ge 46:11 Ex 6:16 Nu 26:57 1Ch 23:6
6:3 b Lev 10:1
6:8 c 2Sa 8:17 2Sa 15:27 Ezr 7:2
6:10 d 1Ki 4:2 1Ki 6:1 2Ch 3:1 2Ch 26:17-18
6:13 e 2Ki 22:1-20 2Ch 34:9 2Ch 35:8

Hilkiah the father of Azariah,
14 Azariah the father of Seraiah,[f]
and Seraiah the father of Jehozadak.
15 Jehozadak[g] was deported when the LORD sent Judah and Jerusalem into exile by the hand of Nebuchadnezzar.

16 The sons of Levi:[h]
Gershon,[a] Kohath and Merari.[i]
17 These are the names of the sons of Gershon:
Libni and Shimei.
18 The sons of Kohath:
Amram, Izhar, Hebron and Uzziel.
19 The sons of Merari:[j]
Mahli and Mushi.
These are the clans of the Levites listed according to their fathers:
20 Of Gershon:
Libni his son, Jehath his son,
Zimmah his son, 21 Joah his son,
Iddo his son, Zerah his son
and Jeatherai his son.
22 The descendants of Kohath:
Amminadab his son, Korah[k] his son,
Assir his son, 23 Elkanah his son,
Ebiasaph his son, Assir his son,
24 Tahath his son, Uriel[l] his son,
Uzziah his son and Shaul his son.
25 The descendants of Elkanah:
Amasai, Ahimoth,
26 Elkanah his son,[b] Zophai his son,
Nahath his son, 27 Eliab his son,
Jeroham his son, Elkanah[m] his son
and Samuel[n] his son.[c]
28 The sons of Samuel:
Joel[d][o] the firstborn
and Abijah the second son.

29 The descendants of Merari:
Mahli, Libni his son,
Shimei his son, Uzzah his son,
30 Shimea his son, Haggiah his son
and Asaiah his son.

The Temple Musicians

6:54–80pp Jos 21:4–39

31 These are the men[p] David put in charge of the music[q] in the house of the LORD after the ark came to rest there. 32 They ministered with music before the tabernacle, the Tent of Meeting, until Solomon built the temple of the LORD in Jerusalem. They performed their duties according to the regulations laid down for them.
33 Here are the men who served, together with their sons:
From the Kohathites:
Heman,[r] the musician,
the son of Joel,[s] the son of Samuel,
34 the son of Elkanah,[t] the son of Jeroham,
the son of Eliel, the son of Toah,
35 the son of Zuph, the son of Elkanah,
the son of Mahath, the son of Amasai,
36 the son of Elkanah, the son of Joel,
the son of Azariah, the son of Zephaniah,
37 the son of Tahath, the son of Assir,
the son of Ebiasaph, the son of Korah,[u]
38 the son of Izhar,[v] the son of Kohath,

6:14 *f* 2Ki 25:18; Ezr 2:2; Ne 11:11
6:15 *g* 2Ki 25:18; Ne 12:1; Hag 1:1,14; Hag 2:2,4; Zec 6:11
6:16 *h* Ge 29:34; Ex 6:16; Nu 3:17-20 *i* Nu 26:57
6:19 *j* Ge 46:11; 1Ch 23:21; 1Ch 24:26
6:22 *k* Ex 6:24
6:24 *l* 1Ch 15:5
6:27 *m* 1Sa 1:1 *n* 1Sa 1:20
6:28 *o* ver 33; 1Sa 8:2
6:31 *p* 1Ch 25:1; 2Ch 29:25-26; Ne 12:45 *q* 1Ch 9:33; 1Ch 15:19; Ezr 3:10; Ps 68:25
6:33 *r* 1Ki 4:31; 1Ch 15:17; 1Ch 25:1 *s* ver 28
6:34 *t* 1Sa 1:1
6:37 *u* Ex 6:24
6:38 *v* Ex 6:21

[a] *16* Hebrew *Gershom*, a variant of *Gershon*; also in verses 17, 20, 43, 62 and 71 [b] *26* Some Hebrew manuscripts, Septuagint and Syriac; most Hebrew manuscripts *Ahimoth 26 and Elkanah. The sons of Elkanah:* [c] *27* Some Septuagint manuscripts (see also 1 Sam. 1:19, 20 and 1 Chron. 6:33, 34); Hebrew does not have *and Samuel his son.* [d] *28* Some Septuagint manuscripts and Syriac (see also 1 Sam. 8:2 and 1 Chron. 6:33); Hebrew does not have *Joel.*

the son of Levi, the son of Israel;
39and Heman's associate Asaph,[w] who served at his right hand:
Asaph son of Berekiah, the son of Shimea,[x]
40the son of Michael, the son of Baaseiah,[e]
the son of Malkijah, 41the son of Ethni,
the son of Zerah, the son of Adaiah,
42the son of Ethan, the son of Zimmah,
the son of Shimei, 43the son of Jahath,
the son of Gershon, the son of Levi;
44and from their associates, the Merarites, at his left hand:
Ethan son of Kishi, the son of Abdi,
the son of Malluch, 45the son of Hashabiah,
the son of Amaziah, the son of Hilkiah,
46the son of Amzi, the son of Bani,
the son of Shemer, 47the son of Mahli,
the son of Mushi, the son of Merari,
the son of Levi.

48Their fellow Levites[y] were assigned to all the other duties of the tabernacle, the house of God.
49But Aaron and his descendants were the ones who presented offerings on the altar[z] of burnt offering and on the altar of incense[a] in connection with all that was done in the Most Holy Place, making atonement for Israel, in accordance with all that Moses the servant of God had commanded.

50These were the descendants of Aaron:
Eleazar his son, Phinehas his son,
Abishua his son, 51Bukki his son,
Uzzi his son, Zerahiah his son,
52Meraioth his son, Amariah his son,
Ahitub his son, 53Zadok[b] his son
and Ahimaaz his son.

54These were the locations of their settlements[c] allotted as their territory (they were assigned to the descendants of Aaron who were from the Kohathite clan, because the first lot was for them):
55They were given Hebron in Judah with its surrounding pasture-lands.
56But the fields and villages around the city were given to Caleb son of Jephunneh.[d]
57So the descendants of Aaron were given Hebron (a city of refuge), and Libnah,[f][e] Jattir,[f] Eshtemoa,
58Hilen, Debir,[g]
59Ashan,[h] Juttah[g] and Beth Shemesh, together with their pasture-lands.
60And from the tribe of Benjamin they were given Gibeon,[h] Geba, Alemeth and Anathoth,[i] together with their pasture-lands.
These towns, which were distributed among the Kohathite clans, were thirteen in all.
61The rest of Kohath's descendants were allotted ten towns from the clans of half the tribe of Manasseh.
62The descendants of Gershon, clan by clan, were allotted thirteen towns from the tribes of Issachar, Asher and Naphtali, and from the part of the tribe of Manasseh that is in Bashan.
63The descendants of Merari, clan by clan, were allotted twelve

6:39 w 1Ch 25:1,9 2Ch 29:13 Ne 11:17 x 1Ch 15:17
6:48 y 1Ch 23:32
6:49 z Ex 27:1-8 a Ex 30:1-7,10 2Ch 26:18
6:53 b 2Sa 8:17
6:54 c Nu 31:10
6:56 d Jos 14:13 Jos 15:13
6:57 e Nu 33:20 f Jos 15:48
6:58 g Jos 10:3
6:59 h Jos 15:42
6:60 i Jer 1:1

e40 Most Hebrew manuscripts; some Hebrew manuscripts, one Septuagint manuscript and Syriac *Maaseiah* f57 See Joshua 21:13; Hebrew *given the cities of refuge: Hebron, Libnah.* g59 Syriac (see also Septuagint and Joshua 21:16); Hebrew does not have *Juttah.* h60 See Joshua 21:17; Hebrew does not have *Gibeon.*

towns from the tribes of Reuben,
Gad and Zebulun.
64So the Israelites gave the Levites these towns[j] and their
pasture-lands. 65From the tribes of
Judah, Simeon and Benjamin they
allotted the previously named
towns.
66Some of the Kohathite clans
were given as their territory towns
from the tribe of Ephraim.
67In the hill country of Ephraim they were given Shechem
(a city of refuge), and
Gezer,[i][k] 68Jokmeam,[l] Beth
Horon,[m] 69Aijalon[n] and Gath
Rimmon,[o] together with their
pasture-lands.
70And from half the tribe of
Manasseh the Israelites gave
Aner and Bileam, together
with their pasture-lands, to the
rest of the Kohathite clans.

71The Gershonites[p] received
the following:
From the clan of the half-tribe
of Manasseh
they received Golan in Bashan[q] and also Ashtaroth,
together with their pasture-
lands;
72from the tribe of Issachar
they received Kedesh, Da-
berath,[r] 73Ramoth and
Anem, together with their
pasture-lands;
74from the tribe of Asher
they received Mashal, Ab-
don,[s] 75Hukok[t] and Rehob,[u] together with their
pasture-lands;
76and from the tribe of Naphtali
they received Kedesh in
Galilee, Hammon[v] and Kiriathaim,[w] together with
their pasture-lands.

77The Merarites (the rest of the
Levites) received the following:
From the tribe of Zebulun
they received Jokneam,
Kartah,[j] Rimmono and
Tabor, together with their
pasture-lands;
78from the tribe of Reuben
across the Jordan east of
Jericho
they received Bezer[x] in the
desert, Jahzah, 79Kede-
moth[y] and Mephaath, to-
gether with their
pasture-lands;
80and from the tribe of Gad
they received Ramoth
in Gilead,[z] Mahanaim,[a]
81Heshbon and Jazer,[b] together with their pasture-
lands.[c]

Issachar

7 The sons of Issachar:[a]
Tola, Puah,[b] Jashub and
Shimron—four in all.
2The sons of Tola:
Uzzi, Rephaiah, Jeriel, Jah-
mai, Ibsam and Samuel—
heads of their families.
During the reign of David,
the descendants of Tola
listed as fighting men in
their genealogy numbered
22,600.
3The son of Uzzi:
Izrahiah.
The sons of Izrahiah:
Michael, Obadiah, Joel and
Isshiah. All five of them
were chiefs. 4According to
their family genealogy, they
had 36,000 men ready for
battle, for they had many
wives and children.
5The relatives who were fighting men belonging to all the
clans of Issachar, as listed in
their genealogy, were 87,000
in all.

Benjamin

6Three sons of Benjamin:[c]
Bela, Beker and Jediael.

6:64 j Nu 35:1-8; Jos 21:3, 41-42
6:67 k Jos 10:33
6:68 l 1Ki 4:12; m Jos 10:10
6:69 n Jos 10:12; o Jos 19:45
6:71 p 1Ch 23:7; q Jos 20:8
6:72 r Jos 19:12
6:74 s Jos 19:28
6:75 t Jos 19:34; u Nu 13:21
6:76 v Jos 19:28; w Nu 32:37
6:78 x Jos 20:8
6:79 y Dt 2:26
6:80 z Jos 20:8; a Ge 32:2
6:81 b Nu 21:32; c 2Ch 11:14
7:1 a Ge 30:18; Nu 26:23; b Ge 46:13
7:6 c Ge 46:21; Nu 26:38; 1Ch 8:1-40

i67 See Joshua 21:21; Hebrew *given the cities of refuge: Shechem, Gezer.*
j77 See Septuagint and Joshua 21:34; Hebrew does not have *Jokneam, Kartah.*

7The sons of Bela:
Ezbon, Uzzi, Uzziel, Jerimoth and Iri, heads of families—five in all. Their genealogical record listed 22,034 fighting men.
8The sons of Beker:
Zemirah, Joash, Eliezer, Elioenai, Omri, Jeremoth, Abijah, Anathoth and Alemeth. All these were the sons of Beker. 9Their genealogical record listed the heads of families and 20,200 fighting men.
10The son of Jediael:
Bilhan.
The sons of Bilhan:
Jeush, Benjamin, Ehud, Kenaanah, Zethan, Tarshish and Ahishahar. 11All these sons of Jediael were heads of families. There were 17,200 fighting men ready to go out to war.
12The Shuppites and Huppites were the descendants of Ir, and the Hushites the descendants of Aher.

Naphtali

13The sons of Naphtali:[d]
Jahziel, Guni, Jezer and Shillem[a]—the descendants of Bilhah.

Manasseh

14The descendants of Manasseh:[e]
Asriel was his descendant through his Aramean concubine. She gave birth to Makir the father of Gilead.[f] 15Makir took a wife from among the Huppites and Shuppites. His sister's name was Maacah.
Another descendant was named Zelophehad,[g] who had only daughters.
16Makir's wife Maacah gave birth to a son and named him Peresh. His brother was named Sheresh, and his sons were Ulam and Rakem.
17The son of Ulam:
Bedan.
These were the sons of Gilead[h] son of Makir, the son of Manasseh. 18His sister Hammoleketh gave birth to Ishhod, Abiezer[i] and Mahlah.
19The sons of Shemida were:
Ahian, Shechem, Likhi and Aniam.

Ephraim

20The descendants of Ephraim:[j]
Shuthelah, Bered his son,
Tahath his son, Eleadah his son,
Tahath his son, 21Zabad his son
and Shuthelah his son.
Ezer and Elead were killed by the native-born men of Gath, when they went down to seize their livestock. 22Their father Ephraim mourned for them many days, and his relatives came to comfort him. 23Then he lay with his wife again, and she became pregnant and gave birth to a son. He named him Beriah,[b] because there had been misfortune in his family. 24His daughter was Sheerah, who built Lower and Upper Beth Horon[k] as well as Uzzen Sheerah.
25Rephah was his son, Resheph his son,[c]
Telah his son, Tahan his son,

7:13 d Ge 30:8; Ge 46:24
7:14 e Ge 41:51; Jos 17:1; 1Ch 5:23; f Nu 26:30
7:15 g Nu 26:33; Nu 36:1-12
7:17 h Nu 26:30; 1Sa 12:11
7:18 i Jos 17:2
7:20 j Ge 41:52; Nu 1:33; Nu 26:35
7:24 k Jos 10:10; Jos 16:3,5

a13 Some Hebrew and Septuagint manuscripts (see also Gen. 46:24 and Num. 26:49); most Hebrew manuscripts *Shallum* b23 *Beriah* sounds like the Hebrew for *misfortune.* c25 Some Septuagint manuscripts; Hebrew does not have *his son.*

26 Ladan his son, Ammihud his son,
Elishama his son, 27 Nun his son
and Joshua his son.

28 Their lands and settlements included Bethel and its surrounding villages, Naaran to the east, Gezer[l] and its villages to the west, and Shechem and its villages all the way to Ayyah and its villages. 29 Along the borders of Manasseh were Beth Shan,[m] Taanach, Megiddo and Dor,[n] together with their villages. The descendants of Joseph son of Israel lived in these towns.

Asher

30 The sons of Asher:[o]
Imnah, Ishvah, Ishvi and Beriah. Their sister was Serah.
31 The sons of Beriah:
Heber and Malkiel, who was the father of Birzaith.
32 Heber was the father of Japhlet, Shomer and Hotham and of their sister Shua.
33 The sons of Japhlet:
Pasach, Bimhal and Ashvath.
These were Japhlet's sons.
34 The sons of Shomer:
Ahi, Rohgah,[d] Hubbah and Aram.
35 The sons of his brother Helem:
Zophah, Imna, Shelesh and Amal.
36 The sons of Zophah:
Suah, Harnepher, Shual, Beri, Imrah, 37 Bezer, Hod, Shamma, Shilshah, Ithran[e] and Beera.
38 The sons of Jether:
Jephunneh, Pispah and Ara.
39 The sons of Ulla:
Arah, Hanniel and Rizia.

40 All these were descendants of Asher—heads of families, choice men, brave warriors and outstanding leaders. The number of men ready for battle, as listed in their genealogy, was 26,000.

7:28 *l* Jos 10:33; Jos 16:7
7:29 *m* Jos 17:11; *n* Jos 11:2
7:30 *o* Ge 46:17; Nu 1:40; Nu 26:44
8:1 *a* Ge 46:21; 1Ch 7:6
8:3 *b* Ge 46:21
8:4 *c* 2Sa 23:9
8:6 *d* Jdg 3:12-30; 1Ch 2:52
8:12 *e* Ezr 2:33; Ne 6:2; Ne 7:37; Ne 11:35
8:13 *f* Jos 10:12; *g* Jos 11:22

The Genealogy of Saul the Benjamite

8:28-38pp 1Ch 9:34-44

8 Benjamin[a] was the father of Bela his firstborn,
Ashbel the second son, Aharah the third,
2 Nohah the fourth and Rapha the fifth.
3 The sons of Bela were:
Addar,[b] Gera, Abihud,[a] 4 Abishua, Naaman, Ahoah,[c] 5 Gera, Shephuphan and Huram.
6 These were the descendants of Ehud,[d] who were heads of families of those living in Geba and were deported to Manahath:
7 Naaman, Ahijah and Gera, who deported them and who was the father of Uzza and Ahihud.
8 Sons were born to Shaharaim in Moab after he had divorced his wives Hushim and Baara. 9 By his wife Hodesh he had Jobab, Zibia, Mesha, Malcam, 10 Jeuz, Sakia and Mirmah. These were his sons, heads of families. 11 By Hushim he had Abitub and Elpaal.
12 The sons of Elpaal:
Eber, Misham, Shemed (who built Ono[e] and Lod with its surrounding villages), 13 and Beriah and Shema, who were heads of families of those living in Aijalon[f] and who drove out the inhabitants of Gath.[g]
14 Ahio, Shashak, Jeremoth, 15 Zebadiah, Arad, Eder, 16 Michael, Ishpah and Joha were the sons of Beriah.
17 Zebadiah, Meshullam, Hizki, Heber, 18 Ishmerai, Izliah and Jobab were the sons of Elpaal.

[d] 34 Or *of his brother Shomer: Rohgah*
[e] 37 Possibly a variant of *Jether*
[a] 3 Or *Gera the father of Ehud*

19 Jakim, Zicri, Zabdi, 20 Elienai,
Zillethai, Eliel, 21 Adaiah, Be-
raiah and Shimrath were the
sons of Shimei.
22 Ishpan, Eber, Eliel, 23 Abdon,
Zicri, Hanan, 24 Hananiah,
Elam, Anthothijah, 25 Iph-
deiah and Penuel were the
sons of Shashak.
26 Shamsherai, Shehariah, Athaliah, 27 Jaareshiah, Elijah and
Zicri were the sons of Jeroham.
28 All these were heads of families, chiefs as listed in their genealogy, and they lived in Jerusalem.

29 Jeiel[b] the father[c] of Gibeon
lived in Gibeon.[h]
His wife's name was Maa-
cah, 30 and his firstborn son
was Abdon, followed by Zur,
Kish, Baal, Ner,[d] Nadab,
31 Gedor, Ahio, Zeker 32 and
Mikloth, who was the father
of Shimeah. They too lived
near their relatives in Jerusalem.
33 Ner[i] was the father of Kish,[j]
Kish the father of Saul[k],
and Saul the father of Jonathan, Malki-Shua, Abinadab
and Esh-Baal.[e][l]
34 The son of Jonathan:[m]
Merib-Baal,[f][n] who was the
father of Micah.
35 The sons of Micah:
Pithon, Melech, Tarea and
Ahaz.
36 Ahaz was the father of Jehoaddah, Jehoaddah was the
father of Alemeth, Azma-
veth and Zimri, and Zimri
was the father of Moza.
37 Moza was the father of
Binea; Raphah was his son,
Eleasah his son and Azel his
son.
38 Azel had six sons, and these
were their names:
Azrikam, Bokeru, Ishmael,
Sheariah, Obadiah and Ha-
nan. All these were the sons
of Azel.

8:29 *h* Jos 9:3
8:33 *i* 1Sa 28:19 *j* 1Sa 9:1 *k* 1Sa 14:49 *l* 2Sa 2:8
8:34 *m* 2Sa 9:12 *n* 2Sa 4:4
8:40 *o* Nu 26:38
9:1 *a* 1Ch 5:25
9:2 *b* Jos 9:27 Ezr 2:70 *c* Ezr 2:43,58 Ezr 8:20 Ne 7:60
9:4 *d* Ge 38:29 Ge 46:12

39 The sons of his brother Eshek:
Ulam his firstborn, Jeush
the second son and Eliphelet
the third. 40 The sons of Ulam
were brave warriors who
could handle the bow. They
had many sons and grand-
sons—150 in all.
All these were the descendants of Benjamin.[o]

9 All Israel was listed in the genealogies in the book of the
kings of Israel.

The People in Jerusalem

9:1–17pp Ne 11:3–19

The people of Judah were taken
captive to Babylon because of their
unfaithfulness.[a] 2 Now the first to
resettle on their own property in
their own towns[b] were some Israelites, priests, Levites and temple servants.[c]
3 Those from Judah, from Benjamin, and from Ephraim and Manasseh who lived in Jerusalem were:
4 Uthai son of Ammihud, the son
of Omri, the son of Imri, the
son of Bani, a descendant of
Perez son of Judah.[d]
5 Of the Shilonites:
Asaiah the firstborn and his
sons.
6 Of the Zerahites:
Jeuel.
The people from Judah numbered 690.
7 Of the Benjamites:
Sallu son of Meshullam, the
son of Hodaviah, the son of
Hassenuah;
8 Ibneiah son of Jeroham;
Elah son of Uzzi, the son of
Micri; and Meshullam son
of Shephatiah, the son of
Reuel, the son of Ibnijah.

[b]29 Some Septuagint manuscripts (see also 1 Chron. 9:35); Hebrew does not have *Jeiel.*
[c]29 *Father* may mean *civic leader* or *military leader.*
[d]30 Some Septuagint manuscripts (see also 1 Chron. 9:36); Hebrew does not have *Ner.*
[e]33 Also known as *Ish-Bosheth*
[f]34 Also known as *Mephibosheth*

9The people from Benjamin,
as listed in their genealogy,
numbered 956. All these
men were heads of their
families.
10Of the priests:
Jedaiah; Jehoiarib; Jakin;
11Azariah son of Hilkiah, the
son of Meshullam, the son of
Zadok, the son of Meraioth,
the son of Ahitub, the official in charge of the house of
God;
12Adaiah son of Jeroham, the
son of Pashhur,[e] the son of
Malkijah; and Maasai son of
Adiel, the son of Jahzerah,
the son of Meshullam, the
son of Meshillemith, the son
of Immer.
13The priests, who were heads
of families, numbered 1,760.
They were able men, re-
sponsible for ministering in
the house of God.
14Of the Levites:
Shemaiah son of Hasshub,
the son of Azrikam, the son
of Hashabiah, a Merarite;
15Bakbakkar, Heresh, Galal
and Mattaniah[f] son of Mica,
the son of Zicri, the son of
Asaph; 16Obadiah son of Shemaiah, the son of Galal, the
son of Jeduthun; and Berekiah son of Asa, the son of
Elkanah, who lived in the villages of the Netophathites.[g]
17The gatekeepers:[h]
Shallum, Akkub, Talmon,
Ahiman and their brothers,
Shallum their chief 18being
stationed at the King's
Gate[i] on the east, up to the
present time. These were
the gatekeepers belonging
to the camp of the Levites.
19Shallum[j] son of Kore, the
son of Ebiasaph, the son of
Korah, and his fellow gatekeepers from his family (the
Korahites) were responsible
for guarding the thresholds
of the Tent[a] just as their fathers had been responsible
for guarding the entrance to
the dwelling of the LORD.
20In earlier times Phinehas[k]
son of Eleazar was in charge
of the gatekeepers, and the
LORD was with him. 21Zecha-
riah[l] son of Meshelemiah
was the gatekeeper at the
entrance to the Tent of
Meeting.
22Altogether, those chosen to be
gatekeepers[m] at the thresholds
numbered 212. They were registered by genealogy in their villages. The gatekeepers had been
assigned to their positions of trust
by David and Samuel the seer.[n]
23They and their descendants were
in charge of guarding the gates of
the house of the LORD—the house
called the Tent. 24The gatekeepers
were on the four sides: east, west,
north and south. 25Their brothers in
their villages had to come from
time to time and share their duties
for seven-day[o] periods. 26But the
four principal gatekeepers, who
were Levites, were entrusted with
the responsibility for the rooms
and treasuries[p] in the house of
God. 27They would spend the night
stationed round the house of God,[q]
because they had to guard it; and
they had charge of the key[r] for
opening it each morning.
28Some of them were in charge of
the articles used in the temple service; they counted them when they
were brought in and when they
were taken out. 29Others were assigned to take care of the furnishings and all the other articles of the
sanctuary,[s] as well as the flour
and wine, and the oil, incense and
spices. 30But some[t] of the priests
took care of mixing the spices. 31A
Levite named Mattithiah, the firstborn son of Shallum the Korahite,
was entrusted with the responsibility for baking the offering bread.

a19 That is, the temple; also in verses 21 and 23

9:12 e Ezr 2:38; Ezr 10:22; Ne 10:3; Jer 21:1; Jer 38:1
9:15 f 2Ch 20:14; Ne 11:22
9:16 g Ne 12:28
9:17 h ver 22; 1Ch 26:1; 2Ch 8:14; 2Ch 31:14; Ezr 2:42; Ne 7:45
9:18 i 1Ch 26:14; Eze 43:1; Eze 46:1
9:19 j Jer 35:4
9:20 k Nu 25:7-13
9:21 l 1Ch 26:2,14
9:22 m ver 17; 1Ch 26:1-2; 2Ch 31:15,18; n 1Sa 9:9
9:25 o 2Ki 11:5; 2Ch 23:8
9:26 p 1Ch 26:22
9:27 q Nu 3:38; 1Ch 23:30-32; r Isa 22:22
9:29 s Nu 3:28; 1Ch 23:29
9:30 t Ex 30:23-25

32Some of their Kohathite brothers
were in charge of preparing for
every Sabbath the bread set out on
the table.[u]
33Those who were musicians,[v]
heads of Levite families, stayed in
the rooms of the temple and were
exempt from other duties because
they were responsible for the work
day and night.[w]
34All these were heads of Levite
families, chiefs as listed in their
genealogy, and they lived in
Jerusalem.

The Genealogy of Saul

9:34–44pp 1Ch 8:28–38

35Jeiel[x] the father[b] of Gibeon
lived in Gibeon.
His wife's name was Maa-
cah, 36and his firstborn son
was Abdon, followed by Zur,
Kish, Baal, Ner, Nadab,
37Gedor, Ahio, Zechariah
and Mikloth. 38Mikloth was
the father of Shimeam. They
too lived near their relatives
in Jerusalem.
39Ner[y] was the father of Kish,[z]
Kish the father of Saul, and
Saul the father of Jona-
than,[a] Malki-Shua, Abinadab and Esh-Baal.[c][b]
40The son of Jonathan:
Merib-Baal,[d][c] who was the
father of Micah.
41The sons of Micah:
Pithon, Melech, Tahrea and
Ahaz.[e]
42Ahaz was the father of Jadah, Jadah[f] was the father
of Alemeth, Azmaveth and
Zimri, and Zimri was the
father of Moza. 43Moza was
the father of Binea; Re-
phaiah was his son, Eleasah
his son and Azel his son.
44Azel had six sons, and these
were their names:
Azrikam, Bokeru, Ishmael,
Sheariah, Obadiah and Ha-
nan. These were the sons of
Azel.

9:32
u Lev 24:5-8
1Ch 23:29
2Ch 13:11

9:33
v 1Ch 6:31
1Ch 25:1-31
w Ps 134:1

9:35
x 1Ch 8:29

9:39
y 1Ch 8:33
z 1Sa 9:1
a 1Sa 13:22
b 2Sa 2:8

9:40
c 2Sa 4:4

10:10
a Jdg 16:23

10:11
b Jdg 21:8

Saul Takes His Life

10:1–12pp 1Sa 31:1–13; 2Sa 1:4–12

10 Now the Philistines fought
against Israel; the Israelites fled before them, and many fell
slain on Mount Gilboa. 2The Philistines pressed hard after Saul and
his sons, and they killed his sons
Jonathan, Abinadab and Malki-
Shua. 3The fighting grew fierce
around Saul, and when the archers
overtook him, they wounded him.
4Saul said to his armour-bearer,
"Draw your sword and run me
through, or these uncircumcised
fellows will come and abuse me."
But his armour-bearer was terrified and would not do it; so Saul
took his own sword and fell on it.
5When the armour-bearer saw that
Saul was dead, he too fell on his
sword and died. 6So Saul and his
three sons died, and all his house
died together.
7When all the Israelites in the
valley saw that the army had fled
and that Saul and his sons had died,
they abandoned their towns and
fled. And the Philistines came and
occupied them.
8The next day, when the Philistines came to strip the dead, they
found Saul and his sons fallen on
Mount Gilboa. 9They stripped him
and took his head and his armour,
and sent messengers throughout
the land of the Philistines to proclaim the news among their idols
and their people. 10They put his armour in the temple of their gods
and hung up his head in the temple
of Dagon.[a]
11When all the inhabitants of Jabesh Gilead[b] heard of everything
the Philistines had done to Saul,
12all their valiant men went and

[b]35 *Father* may mean *civic leader* or *military leader.* [c]39 Also known as *Ish-Bosheth*
[d]40 Also known as *Mephibosheth* [e]41 Vulgate and Syriac (see also Septuagint and 1 Chron. 8:35); Hebrew does not have *and Ahaz.*
[f]42 Some Hebrew manuscripts and Septuagint (see also 1 Chron. 8:36); most Hebrew manuscripts *Jarah, Jarah*

took the bodies of Saul and his sons and brought them to Jabesh. Then they buried their bones under the great tree in Jabesh, and they fasted seven days.

13 Saul died[c] because he was unfaithful[d] to the LORD; he did not keep[e] the word of the LORD, and even consulted a medium[f] for guidance, 14 and did not enquire of the LORD. So the LORD put him to death and turned[g] the kingdom[h] over to David son of Jesse.

David Becomes King Over Israel

11:1–3pp 2Sa 5:1–3

11 All Israel[a] came together to David at Hebron[b] and said, "We are your own flesh and blood. 2 In the past, even while Saul was king, you were the one who led Israel on their military campaigns.[c] And the LORD your God said to you, 'You will shepherd[d] my people Israel, and you will become their ruler.[e]' "

3 When all the elders of Israel had come to King David at Hebron, he made a compact with them at Hebron before the LORD, and they anointed[f] David king over Israel, as the LORD had promised through Samuel.

David Conquers Jerusalem

11:4–9pp 2Sa 5:6–10

4 David and all the Israelites marched to Jerusalem (that is, Jebus). The Jebusites[g] who lived there 5 said to David, "You will not get in here." Nevertheless, David captured the fortress of Zion, the City of David.

6 David had said, "Whoever leads the attack on the Jebusites will become commander-in-chief." Joab[h] son of Zeruiah went up first, and so he received the command.

7 David then took up residence in the fortress, and so it was called the City of David. 8 He built up the city around it, from the supporting terraces[a][i] to the surrounding wall, while Joab restored the rest of the city. 9 And David became more and more powerful,[j] because the LORD Almighty was with him.

David's Mighty Men

11:10–41pp 2Sa 23:8–39

10 These were the chiefs of David's mighty men—they, together with all Israel,[k] gave his kingship strong support to extend it over the whole land, as the LORD had promised[l]— 11 this is the list of David's mighty men:[m]

Jashobeam,[b] a Hacmonite, was chief of the officers;[c] he raised his spear against three hundred men, whom he killed in one encounter.

12 Next to him was Eleazar son of Dodai the Ahohite, one of the three mighty men. 13 He was with David at Pas Dammim when the Philistines gathered there for battle. At a place where there was a field full of barley, the troops fled from the Philistines. 14 But they took their stand in the middle of the field. They defended it and struck the Philistines down, and the LORD brought about a great victory.[n]

15 Three of the thirty chiefs came down to David to the rock at the cave of Adullam, while a band of Philistines was encamped in the Valley[o] of Rephaim. 16 At that time David was in the stronghold,[p] and the Philistine garrison was at Bethlehem. 17 David longed for water and said, "Oh, that someone would get me a drink of water from the well near the gate of Bethlehem!" 18 So the Three broke through the Philistine lines, drew water from the well near the gate of Bethlehem and carried it back to David. But he refused to drink it; instead, he poured[q] it out before the LORD. 19 "God forbid that I should do this!"

10:13 c 2Sa 1:1 d 1Sa 15:23 1Ch 5:25 e 1Sa 13:13 f Lev 19:31 Lev 20:6 Dt 18:9-14 1Sa 28:7
10:14 g 1Ch 12:23 h 1Sa 13:14 1Sa 15:28
11:1 a 1Ch 9:1 b Ge 13:18 Ge 23:19
11:2 c 1Sa 18:5,16 d Ps 78:71 Mt 2:6 e 1Ch 5:2
11:3 f 1Sa 16:1-13
11:4 g Ge 10:16 Ge 15:18-21 Jos 3:10 Jos 15:8 Jdg 1:21 Jdg 19:10
11:6 h 2Sa 2:13 2Sa 8:16
11:8 i 2Sa 5:9 2Ch 32:5
11:9 j 2Sa 3:1 Est 9:4
11:10 k ver 1 l ver 3 1Ch 12:23
11:11 m 2Sa 17:10
11:14 n Ex 14:30 1Sa 11:13
11:15 o 1Ch 14:9 Isa 17:5
11:16 p 2Sa 5:17
11:18 q Dt 12:16

a8 Or *the Millo* b11 Possibly a variant of *Jashob-Baal* c11 Or *Thirty*; some Septuagint manuscripts *Three* (see also 2 Sam. 23:8)

he said. "Should I drink the blood of
these men who went at the risk of
their lives?" Because they risked
their lives to bring it back, David
would not drink it.
Such were the exploits of the
three mighty men.
20Abishai[r] the brother of Joab
was chief of the Three. He raised
his spear against three hundred
men, whom he killed, and so he became as famous as the Three. 21He
was doubly honoured above the
Three and became their commander, even though he was not included among them.
22Benaiah son of Jehoiada was a
valiant fighter from Kabzeel,[s]
who performed great exploits. He
struck down two of Moab's best
men. He also went down into a pit
on a snowy day and killed a lion.[t]
23And he struck down an Egyptian
who was seven and a half feet[d] tall.
Although the Egyptian had a spear
like a weaver's rod[u] in his hand,
Benaiah went against him with a
club. He snatched the spear from
the Egyptian's hand and killed him
with his own spear. 24Such were the
exploits of Benaiah son of Jehoiada; he too was as famous as the
three mighty men. 25He was held in
greater honour than any of the
Thirty, but he was not included
among the Three. And David put
him in charge of his bodyguard.

26The mighty men were:
Asahel[v] the brother of Joab,
Elhanan son of Dodo from Bethlehem,
27Shammoth[w] the Harorite,
Helez the Pelonite,
28Ira son of Ikkesh from Tekoa,
Abiezer[x] from Anathoth,
29Sibbecai[y] the Hushathite,
Ilai the Ahohite,
30Maharai the Netophathite,
Heled son of Baanah the Netophathite,
31Ithai son of Ribai from Gibeah in Benjamin,
Benaiah[z] the Pirathonite,[a]
32Hurai from the ravines of Gaash,
Abiel the Arbathite,
33Azmaveth the Baharumite,
Eliahba the Shaalbonite,
34the sons of Hashem the Gizonite,
Jonathan son of Shagee the Hararite,
35Ahiam son of Sacar the Hararite,
Eliphal son of Ur,
36Hepher the Mekerathite,
Ahijah the Pelonite,
37Hezro the Carmelite,
Naarai son of Ezbai,
38Joel the brother of Nathan,
Mibhar son of Hagri,
39Zelek the Ammonite,
Naharai the Berothite, the armour-bearer of Joab son of Zeruiah,
40Ira the Ithrite,
Gareb the Ithrite,
41Uriah[b] the Hittite,
Zabad[c] son of Ahlai,
42Adina son of Shiza the Reubenite, who was chief of the Reubenites, and the thirty with him,
43Hanan son of Maacah,
Joshaphat the Mithnite,
44Uzzia the Ashterathite,[d]
Shama and Jeiel the sons of Hotham the Aroerite,
45Jediael son of Shimri,
his brother Joha the Tizite,
46Eliel the Mahavite,
Jeribai and Joshaviah the sons of Elnaam,
Ithmah the Moabite,
47Eliel, Obed and Jaasiel the Mezobaite.

Warriors Join David

12 These were the men who
came to David at Ziklag,[a]
while he was banished from the
presence of Saul son of Kish (they
were among the warriors who

11:20 r 1Sa 26:6
11:22 s Jos 15:21 t 1Sa 17:36
11:23 u 1Sa 17:7
11:26 v 2Sa 2:18
11:27 w 1Ch 27:8
11:28 x 1Ch 27:12
11:29 y 2Sa 21:18
11:31 z 1Ch 27:14 a Jdg 12:13
11:41 b 2Sa 11:6 c 1Ch 2:36
11:44 d Dt 1:4
12:1 a Jos 15:31 1Sa 27:2-6

d23 Hebrew *five cubits* (about 2.3 metres)

helped him in battle; 2they were
armed with bows and were able to
shoot arrows or to sling stones
right-handed or left-handed;[b] they
were kinsmen of Saul[c] from the
tribe of Benjamin):

3Ahiezer their chief and Joash
the sons of Shemaah the Gibea-
thite; Jeziel and Pelet the sons
of Azmaveth; Beracah, Jehu
the Anathothite, 4and Ishmaiah
the Gibeonite, a mighty man
among the Thirty, who was a
leader of the Thirty; Jeremiah,
Jahaziel, Johanan, Jozabad the
Gederathite,[d] 5Eluzai, Jerimoth, Bealiah, Shemariah and
Shephatiah the Haruphite; 6El-
kanah, Isshiah, Azarel, Joezer
and Jashobeam the Korahites;
7and Joelah and Zebadiah the
sons of Jeroham from Gedor.[e]

8Some Gadites[f] defected to
David at his stronghold in the
desert. They were brave warriors,
ready for battle and able to handle
the shield and spear. Their faces
were the faces of lions,[g] and they
were as swift as gazelles[h] in the
mountains.

9Ezer was the chief,
Obadiah the second in command, Eliab the third,
10Mishmannah the fourth, Jeremiah the fifth,
11Attai the sixth, Eliel the seventh,
12Johanan the eighth, Elzabad
the ninth,
13Jeremiah the tenth and Mac-
bannai the eleventh.

14These Gadites were army commanders; the least was a match for
a hundred,[i] and the greatest for a
thousand.[j] 15It was they who
crossed the Jordan in the first
month when it was overflowing all
its banks,[k] and they put to flight
everyone living in the valleys, to
the east and to the west.

16Other Benjamites[l] and some
men from Judah also came to
David in his stronghold. 17David
went out to meet them and said to
them, "If you have come to me in
peace, to help me, I am ready to
have you unite with me. But if you
have come to betray me to my enemies when my hands are free
from violence, may the God of our
fathers see it and judge you."

18Then the Spirit[m] came upon
Amasai,[n] chief of the Thirty, and
he said:

"We are yours, O David!
We are with you, O son of
Jesse!
Success,[o] success to you,
and success to those who help
you,
for your God will help you."

So David received them and
made them leaders of his raiding
bands.

19Some of the men of Manasseh
defected to David when he went
with the Philistines to fight against
Saul. (He and his men did not help
the Philistines because, after con-
sultation, their rulers sent him
away. They said, "It will cost us our
heads if he deserts to his master
Saul.")[p] 20When David went to Ziklag,[q] these were the men of Manasseh who defected to him: Adnah,
Jozabad, Jediael, Michael, Jozabad,
Elihu and Zillethai, leaders of units
of a thousand in Manasseh. 21They
helped David against raiding
bands, for all of them were brave
warriors, and they were commanders in his army. 22Day after day
men came to help David, until he
had a great army, like the army of
God.[a]

Others Join David at Hebron

23These are the numbers of the
men armed for battle who came to
David at Hebron[r] to turn[s] Saul's
kingdom over to him, as the LORD
had said:[t]
24men of Judah, carrying shield

12:2 b Jdg 3:15; Jdg 20:16; c 2Sa 3:19
12:4 d Jos 15:36
12:7 e Jos 15:58
12:8 f Ge 30:11; g 2Sa 17:10; h 2Sa 2:18
12:14 i Lev 26:8; j Dt 32:30
12:15 k Jos 3:15
12:16 l 2Sa 3:19
12:18 m Jdg 3:10; Jdg 6:34; 1Ch 28:12; 2Ch 15:1; 2Ch 20:14; 2Ch 24:20; n 2Sa 17:25; o 1Sa 25:5-6
12:19 p 1Sa 29:2-11
12:20 q 1Sa 27:6
12:23 r 2Sa 2:3-4; s 1Ch 10:14; t 1Sa 16:1; 1Ch 11:10

a22 Or *a great and mighty army*

and spear—6,800 armed for battle;
[25]men of Simeon, warriors ready for battle—7,100;
[26]men of Levi—4,600, [27]including Jehoiada, leader of the family of Aaron with 3,700 men, [28]and Zadok,[u] a brave young warrior, with 22 officers from his family;
[29]men of Benjamin,[v] Saul's kinsmen—3,000, most[w] of whom had remained loyal to Saul's house until then;
[30]men of Ephraim, brave warriors, famous in their own clans—20,800;
[31]men of half the tribe of Manasseh, designated by name to come and make David king—18,000;
[32]men of Issachar, who understood the times and knew what Israel should do[x]—200 chiefs, with all their relatives under their command;
[33]men of Zebulun, experienced soldiers prepared for battle with every type of weapon, to help David with undivided loyalty—50,000;
[34]men of Naphtali—1,000 officers, together with 37,000 men carrying shields and spears;
[35]men of Dan, ready for battle—28,600;
[36]men of Asher, experienced soldiers prepared for battle—40,000;
[37]and from east of the Jordan, men of Reuben, Gad, and the half-tribe of Manasseh, armed with every type of weapon—120,000.

[38]All these were fighting men who volunteered to serve in the ranks. They came to Hebron fully determined to make David king over all Israel.[y] All the rest of the Israelites were also of one mind to make David king. [39]The men spent three days there with David, eating and drinking,[z] for their families had supplied provisions for them. [40]Also, their neighbours from as far away as Issachar, Zebulun and Naphtali came bringing food on donkeys, camels, mules and oxen. There were plentiful supplies[a] of flour, fig cakes, raisin[b] cakes, wine, oil, cattle and sheep, for there was joy[c] in Israel.

Bringing Back the Ark

13:1–14pp 2Sa 6:1–11

13 David conferred with each of his officers, the commanders of thousands and commanders of hundreds. [2]He then said to the whole assembly of Israel, "If it seems good to you and if it is the will of the LORD our God, let us send word far and wide to the rest of our brothers throughout the territories of Israel, and also to the priests and Levites who are with them in their towns and pasturelands, to come and join us. [3]Let us bring the ark of our God back to us,[a] for we did not enquire[b] of[a] it[b] during the reign of Saul." [4]The whole assembly agreed to do this, because it seemed right to all the people.

[5]So David assembled all the Israelites,[c] from the Shihor River[d] in Egypt to Lebo[c] Hamath,[e] to bring the ark of God from Kiriath Jearim.[f] [6]David and all the Israelites with him went to Baalah[g] of Judah (Kiriath Jearim) to bring up from there the ark of God the LORD, who is enthroned between the cherubim[h]—the ark that is called by the Name.

[7]They moved the ark of God from Abinadab's[i] house on a new cart, with Uzzah and Ahio guiding it. [8]David and all the Israelites were celebrating with all their might before God, with songs and with harps, lyres, tambourines, cymbals and trumpets.[j]

[9]When they came to the

12:28
u 2Sa 8:17; 1Ch 6:8; 1Ch 15:11; 1Ch 16:39; 1Ch 27:17
12:29
v 2Sa 3:19
w 2Sa 2:8-9
12:32
x Est 1:13
12:38
y 2Sa 5:1-3; 1Ch 9:1
12:39
z 2Sa 3:20; Isa 25:6-8
12:40
a 2Sa 16:1; 2Sa 17:29
b 1Sa 25:18
c 1Ch 29:22
13:3
a 1Sa 7:1-2
b 2Ch 1:5
13:5
c 1Ch 11:1; 1Ch 15:3
d Jos 13:3
e Nu 13:21
f 1Sa 6:21; 1Sa 7:2
13:6
g Jos 15:9; 2Sa 6:2
h Ex 25:22; 2Ki 19:15
13:7
i Nu 4:15; 1Sa 7:1
13:8
j 2Sa 6:5; 1Ch 15:16,19,24; 2Ch 5:12; Ps 92:3

[a]3 Or *we neglected* [b]3 Or *him* [c]5 Or *to the entrance to*

threshing-floor of Kidon, Uzzah
reached out his hand to steady the
ark, because the oxen stumbled.
10The LORD's anger[k] burned
against Uzzah, and he struck him
down[l] because he had put his hand
on the ark. So he died there before
God.
11Then David was angry because
the LORD's wrath had broken out
against Uzzah, and to this day that
place is called Perez Uzzah.[d][m]
12David was afraid of God that
day and asked, "How can I ever
bring the ark of God to me?" 13He
did not take the ark to be with him
in the City of David. Instead, he
took it aside to the house of Obed-
Edom[n] the Gittite. 14The ark of
God remained with the family of
Obed-Edom in his house for three
months, and the LORD blessed his
household[o] and everything he had.

David's House and Family

14:1–7pp 2Sa 5:11–16; 1Ch 3:5–8

14 Now Hiram king of Tyre
sent messengers to David,
along with cedar logs,[a] stonemasons and carpenters to build a
palace for him. 2And David knew
that the LORD had established him
as king over Israel and that his
kingdom had been highly exalted[b]
for the sake of his people Israel.
3In Jerusalem David took more
wives and became the father of
more sons[c] and daughters. 4These
are the names of the children born
to him there:[d] Shammua, Shobab,
Nathan, Solomon, 5Ibhar, Elishua,
Elpelet, 6Nogah, Nepheg, Japhia,
7Elishama, Beeliada[a] and Eliphelet.

David Defeats the Philistines

14:8–17pp 2Sa 5:17–25

8When the Philistines heard that
David had been anointed king over
all Israel,[e] they went up in full
force to search for him, but David
heard about it and went out to meet
them. 9Now the Philistines had
come and raided the Valley[f] of
Rephaim; 10so David enquired of
God: "Shall I go and attack the
Philistines? Will you hand them
over to me?"
The LORD answered him, "Go, I
will hand them over to you."
11So David and his men went up
to Baal Perazim,[g] and there he defeated them. He said, "As waters
break out, God has broken out
against my enemies by my hand."
So that place was called Baal Perazim.[b] 12The Philistines had abandoned their gods there, and David
gave orders to burn[h] them in the
fire.[i]
13Once more the Philistines
raided the valley;[j] 14so David enquired of God again, and God answered him, "Do not go straight up,
but circle round them and attack
them in front of the balsam trees.
15As soon as you hear the sound of
marching in the tops of the balsam
trees, move out to battle, because
that will mean God has gone out in
front of you to strike the Philistine
army." 16So David did as God commanded him, and they struck down
the Philistine army, all the way
from Gibeon[k] to Gezer.[l]
17So David's fame[m] spread
throughout every land, and the
LORD made all the nations fear[n]
him.

The Ark Brought to Jerusalem

15:25–16:3pp 2Sa 6:12–19

15 After David had constructed buildings for himself in the City of David, he
prepared[a] a place for the ark of
God and pitched[b] a tent for it.
2Then David said, "No-one but the
Levites[c] may carry[d] the ark of
God, because the LORD chose them
to carry the ark of the LORD and to
minister[e] before him for ever."
3David assembled all Israel[f] in

13:10 k 1Ch 15:13,15 l Lev 10:2
13:11 m 1Ch 15:13 Ps 7:11
13:13 n 1Ch 15:18,24 1Ch 16:38 1Ch 26:4-5,15
13:14 o 2Sa 6:11 1Ch 26:4-5
14:1 a 2Ch 2:3 Ezr 3:7
14:2 b Nu 24:7 Dt 26:19
14:3 c 1Ch 3:1
14:4 d 1Ch 3:9
14:8 e 1Ch 11:1
14:9 f ver 13 Jos 15:8 1Ch 11:15
14:11 g Isa 28:21
14:12 h Ex 32:20 i Jos 7:15
14:13 j ver 9
14:16 k Jos 9:3 l Jos 10:33
14:17 m Jos 6:27 2Ch 26:8 n Ex 15:14-16 Dt 2:25
15:1 a Ps 132:1-18 b 1Ch 16:1 1Ch 17:1
15:2 c Nu 4:15 Dt 10:8 2Ch 5:5 d Dt 31:9 e 1Ch 23:13
15:3 f 1Ki 8:1 1Ch 13:5

d11 *Perez Uzzah* means *outbreak against Uzzah.*
a7 A variant of *Eliada* b11 *Baal Perazim* means *the lord who breaks out.*

Jerusalem to bring up the ark of the LORD to the place he had prepared for it. 4He called together the descendants of Aaron and the Levites:

5From the descendants of Kohath,
Uriel the leader and 120 relatives;
6from the descendants of Merari,
Asaiah the leader and 220 relatives;
7from the descendants of Gershon,[a]
Joel the leader and 130 relatives;
8from the descendants of Elizaphan,[g]
Shemaiah the leader and 200 relatives;
9from the descendants of Hebron,[h]
Eliel the leader and 80 relatives;
10from the descendants of Uzziel,
Amminadab the leader and 112 relatives.

11Then David summoned Zadok[i] and Abiathar[j] the priests, and Uriel, Asaiah, Joel, Shemaiah, Eliel and Amminadab the Levites. 12He said to them, "You are the heads of the Levitical families; you and your fellow Levites are to consecrate[k] yourselves and bring up the ark of the LORD, the God of Israel, to the place I have prepared for it. 13It was because you, the Levites,[l] did not bring it up the first time that the LORD our God broke out in anger against us.[m] We did not enquire of him about how to do it in the prescribed way." 14So the priests and Levites consecrated themselves in order to bring up the ark of the LORD, the God of Israel. 15And the Levites carried the ark of God with the poles on their shoulders, as Moses had commanded[n] in accordance with the word of the LORD.

16David told the leaders of the Levites to appoint their brothers as singers[o] to sing joyful songs, accompanied by musical instruments: lyres, harps and cymbals.[p]

17So the Levites appointed Heman[q] son of Joel; from his brothers, Asaph[r] son of Berekiah; and from their brothers the Merarites,[s] Ethan son of Kushaiah; 18and with them their brothers next in rank: Zechariah,[b] Jaaziel, Shemiramoth, Jehiel, Unni, Eliab, Benaiah, Maaseiah, Mattithiah, Eliphelehu, Mikneiah, Obed-Edom[t] and Jeiel,[c] the gatekeepers.

19The musicians Heman,[u] Asaph and Ethan were to sound the bronze cymbals; 20Zechariah, Aziel, Shemiramoth, Jehiel, Unni, Eliab, Maaseiah and Benaiah were to play the lyres according to *alamoth*,[d] 21and Mattithiah, Eliphelehu, Mikneiah, Obed-Edom, Jeiel and Azaziah were to play the harps, directing according to *sheminith*.[e] 22Kenaniah the head Levite was in charge of the singing; that was his responsibility because he was skilful at it.

23Berekiah and Elkanah were to be doorkeepers for the ark. 24Shebaniah, Joshaphat, Nethanel, Amasai, Zechariah, Benaiah and Eliezer the priests were to blow trumpets[v] before the ark of God. Obed-Edom and Jehiah were also to be doorkeepers for the ark.

25So David and the elders of Israel and the commanders of units of a thousand went to bring up the ark[w] of the covenant of the LORD from the house of Obed-Edom, with rejoicing. 26Because God had helped the Levites who were carrying the ark of the covenant of the LORD, seven bulls and seven rams[x]

15:8 g Ex 6:22
15:9 h Ex 6:18
15:11 i 1Ch 12:28 j 1Sa 22:20
15:12 k Ex 19:14-15 Lev 11:44 2Ch 35:6
15:13 l 1Ki 8:4 m 2Sa 6:3 1Ch 13:7-10
15:15 n Ex 25:14 Nu 4:5,15
15:16 o Ps 68:25 p 1Ch 13:8 1Ch 25:1 Ne 12:27,36
15:17 q 1Ch 6:33 r 1Ch 6:39 s 1Ch 6:44
15:18 t 1Ch 26:4-5
15:19 u 1Ch 25:6
15:24 v ver 28 1Ch 16:6 2Ch 7:6
15:25 w 1Ch 13:13 2Ch 1:4
15:26 x Nu 23:1-4,29

a7 Hebrew *Gershom*, a variant of *Gershon*
b18 Three Hebrew manuscripts and most Septuagint manuscripts (see also verse 20 and 1 Chron. 16:5); most Hebrew manuscripts *Zechariah son and* or *Zechariah, Ben and*
c18 Hebrew; Septuagint (see also verse 21) *Jeiel and Azaziah*
d20 Probably a musical term
e21 Probably a musical term

were sacrificed. 27Now David was
clothed in a robe of fine linen, as
were all the Levites who were
carrying the ark, and as were the
singers, and Kenaniah, who was in
charge of the singing of the choirs.
David also wore a linen ephod. 28So
all Israel brought up the ark of the
covenant of the LORD with shouts,
with the sounding of rams' horns[y]
and trumpets, and of cymbals, and
the playing of lyres and harps.
29As the ark of the covenant of
the LORD was entering the City of
David, Michal daughter of Saul
watched from a window. And when
she saw King David dancing and
celebrating, she despised him in
her heart.

16 They brought the ark of
God and set it inside the
tent that David had pitched[a] for it,
and they presented burnt offerings
and fellowship offerings[a] before
God. 2After David had finished sacrificing the burnt offerings and fellowship offerings, he blessed[b] the
people in the name of the LORD.
3Then he gave a loaf of bread, a
cake of dates and a cake of raisins
to each Israelite man and woman.
4He appointed some of the Levites to minister[c] before the ark of
the LORD, to make petition, to give
thanks, and to praise the LORD, the
God of Israel: 5Asaph was the
chief, Zechariah second, then Jeiel,
Shemiramoth, Jehiel, Mattithiah,
Eliab, Benaiah, Obed-Edom and
Jeiel. They were to play the lyres
and harps, Asaph was to sound the
cymbals, 6and Benaiah and Jahaziel the priests were to blow the
trumpets regularly before the ark
of the covenant of God.

David's Psalm of Thanks

16:8–22pp Ps 105:1–15
16:23–33pp Ps 96:1–13
16:34–36pp Ps 106:1,47–48

7That day David first committed
to Asaph and his associates this
psalm[d] of thanks to the LORD:

15:28 y 1Ch 13:8
16:1 a 1Ch 15:1
16:2 b Ex 39:43
16:4 c 1Ch 15:2
16:7 d 2Sa 23:1
16:8 e ver 34; Ps 136:1; f 2Ki 19:19
16:9 g Ex 15:1
16:11 h 1Ch 28:9; 2Ch 7:14; Ps 24:6; Ps 119:2,58
16:12 i Ps 77:11; j Ps 78:43
16:14 k Isa 26:9
16:16 l Ge 12:7; Ge 15:18; Ge 17:2; Ge 22:16-18; Ge 26:3; Ge 28:13; Ge 35:11
16:17 m Ge 35:9-12
16:18 n Ge 13:14-17
16:19 o Ge 34:30; Dt 7:7

8Give thanks[e] to the LORD, call
on his name;
make known among the
nations[f] what he has done.
9Sing to him, sing praise[g] to
him;
tell of all his wonderful acts.
10Glory in his holy name;
let the hearts of those who
seek the LORD rejoice.
11Look to the LORD and his
strength;
seek[h] his face always.
12Remember[i] the wonders he
has done,
his miracles,[j] and the
judgments he pronounced,
13O descendants of Israel his
servant,
O sons of Jacob, his chosen
ones.

14He is the LORD our God;
his judgments[k] are in all the
earth.
15He remembers[b] his covenant
for ever,
the word he commanded, for a
thousand generations,
16the covenant[l] he made with
Abraham,
the oath he swore to Isaac.
17He confirmed it to Jacob[m] as a
decree,
to Israel as an everlasting
covenant:
18"To you I will give the land of
Canaan[n]
as the portion you will
inherit."

19When they were but few in
number,[o]
few indeed, and strangers in
it,
20they[c] wandered from nation to
nation,
from one kingdom to another.

a*1* Traditionally *peace offerings*; also in verse 2
b*15* Some Septuagint manuscripts (see also Psalm 105:8); Hebrew *Remember*
c*18–20* One Hebrew manuscript, Septuagint and Vulgate (see also Psalm 105:12); most Hebrew manuscripts *inherit, / 19though you are but few in number, / few indeed, and strangers in it." / 20They*

21 He allowed no man to oppress
them;
for their sake he rebuked
kings:[p]
22 "Do not touch my anointed
ones;
do my prophets[q] no harm."
23 Sing to the LORD, all the earth;
proclaim his salvation day
after day.
24 Declare his glory among the
nations,
his marvellous deeds among
all peoples.
25 For great is the LORD and most
worthy of praise;[r]
he is to be feared[s] above all
gods.[t]
26 For all the gods of the nations
are idols,
but the LORD made the
heavens.[u]
27 Splendour and majesty are
before him;
strength and joy in his
dwelling-place.
28 Ascribe to the LORD, O families
of nations,
ascribe to the LORD glory and
strength,[v]
29 ascribe to the LORD the glory
due to his name.
Bring an offering and come
before him;
worship the LORD in the
splendour of his[d]
holiness.[w]
30 Tremble[x] before him, all the
earth!
The world is firmly
established; it cannot be
moved.
31 Let the heavens rejoice, let the
earth be glad;[y]
let them say among the
nations, "The LORD
reigns![z]"
32 Let the sea resound, and all that
is in it;[a]
let the fields be jubilant, and
everything in them!
33 Then the trees[b] of the forest
will sing,
they will sing for joy before
the LORD,
for he comes to judge[c] the
earth.
34 Give thanks[d] to the LORD, for
he is good;[e]
his love endures for ever.[f]
35 Cry out, "Save us, O God our
Saviour;[g]
gather us and deliver us from
the nations,
that we may give thanks to your
holy name,
that we may glory in your
praise."
36 Praise be to the LORD, the God
of Israel,[h]
from everlasting to
everlasting.

Then all the people said "Amen"
and "Praise the LORD."

37 David left Asaph and his associates before the ark of the covenant
of the LORD to minister there regularly, according to each day's
requirements.[i] 38 He also left
Obed-Edom[j] and his sixty-eight
associates to minister with them.
Obed-Edom son of Jeduthun, and
also Hosah,[k] were gatekeepers.

39 David left Zadok[l] the priest
and his fellow priests before the
tabernacle of the LORD at the high
place in Gibeon[m] 40 to present burnt
offerings to the LORD on the altar of
burnt offering regularly, morning
and evening, in accordance with
everything written in the Law[n] of
the LORD, which he had given Israel. 41 With them were Heman[o]
and Jeduthun and the rest of those
chosen and designated by name to
give thanks to the LORD, "for his
love endures for ever." 42 Heman
and Jeduthun were responsible for
the sounding of the trumpets and
cymbals and for the playing of the
other instruments for sacred
song.[p] The sons of Jeduthun were
stationed at the gate.

16:21 p Ge 12:17; Ge 20:3; Ex 7:15-18
16:22 q Ge 20:7
16:25 r Ps 48:1; s Ps 76:7; Ps 89:7; t Dt 32:39
16:26 u Lev 19:4; Ps 102:25
16:28 v Ps 29:1-2
16:29 w Ps 29:1-2
16:30 x Ps 114:7
16:31 y Isa 44:23; Isa 49:13; z Ps 93:1
16:32 a Ps 98:7
16:33 b Isa 55:12; c Ps 96:10; Ps 98:9
16:34 d ver 8; e Na 1:7; f 2Ch 5:13; 2Ch 7:3; Ezr 3:11; Ps 136:1-26; Jer 33:11
16:35 g Mic 7:7
16:36 h Dt 27:15; 1Ki 8:15; Ps 72:18-19
16:37 i 2Ch 8:14
16:38 j 1Ch 13:13; k 1Ch 26:10
16:39 l 2Sa 8:17; 1Ch 15:11; m 1Ki 3:4; 2Ch 1:3
16:40 n Ex 29:38; Nu 28:1-8
16:41 o 1Ch 6:33; 1Ch 25:1-6; 2Ch 5:13
16:42 p 2Ch 7:6

[d]29 Or *LORD with the splendour of*

43Then all the people left, each for his own home, and David returned home to bless his family.

God's Promise to David

17:1–15pp 2Sa 7:1–17

17 After David was settled in his palace, he said to Nathan the prophet, "Here I am, living in a palace of cedar, while the ark of the covenant of the LORD is under a tent.[a]"

2Nathan replied to David, "Whatever you have in mind,[b] do it, for God is with you."

3That night the word of God came to Nathan, saying:

4"Go and tell my servant David, 'This is what the LORD says: You[c] are not the one to build me a house to dwell in. 5I have not dwelt in a house from the day I brought Israel up out of Egypt to this day. I have moved from one tent site to another, from one dwelling-place to another. 6Wherever I have moved with all the Israelites, did I ever say to any of their leaders[a] whom I commanded to shepherd my people, "Why have you not built me a house of cedar?" '

7"Now then, tell my servant David, 'This is what the LORD Almighty says: I took you from the pasture and from following the flock, to be ruler[d] over my people Israel. 8I have been with you wherever you have gone, and I have cut off all your enemies from before you. Now I will make your name like the names of the greatest men of the earth. 9And I will provide a place for my people Israel and will plant them so that they can have a home of their own and no longer be disturbed. Wicked people will not oppress them any more, as they did at the beginning 10and have done ever since the time I appointed leaders[e] over my people Israel. I will also subdue all your enemies.

" 'I declare to you that the LORD will build a house for you: 11When your days are over and you go to be with your fathers, I will raise up your offspring to succeed you, one of your own sons, and I will establish his kingdom. 12He is the one who will build[f] a house for me, and I will establish his throne for ever.[g] 13I will be his father,[h] and he will be my son.[i] I will never take my love away from him, as I took it away from your predecessor. 14I will set him over my house and my kingdom for ever; his throne[j] will be established for ever.[k]' "

15Nathan reported to David all the words of this entire revelation.

David's Prayer

17:16–27pp 2Sa 7:18–29

16Then King David went in and sat before the LORD, and he said:

"Who am I, O LORD God, and what is my family, that you have brought me this far? 17And as if this were not enough in your sight, O God, you have spoken about the future of the house of your servant. You have looked on me as though I were the most exalted of men, O LORD God.

18"What more can David say to you for honouring your servant? For you know your servant, 19O LORD. For the sake[l] of your servant and according to your will, you have done this great thing and made known all these great promises.[m]

20"There is no-one like you, O LORD, and there is no God but you,[n] as we have heard

17:1 *a* 1Ch 15:1
17:2 *b* 2Ch 6:7
17:4 *c* 1Ch 28:3
17:7 *d* 2Sa 6:21
17:10 *e* Jdg 2:16
17:12 *f* 1Ki 5:5 *g* 2Ch 7:18
17:13 *h* 2Co 6:18 *i* Lk 1:32; Heb 1:5
17:14 *j* 1Ki 2:12; 1Ch 28:5 *k* Ps 132:11; Jer 33:17
17:19 *l* 2Sa 7:16-17; 2Ki 20:6; Isa 9:7; Isa 37:35; Isa 55:3 *m* 2Sa 7:25
17:20 *n* Ex 8:10; Ex 9:14; Ex 15:11; Isa 44:6; Isa 46:9

[a]6 Traditionally *judges*; also in verse 10

with our own ears. 21And who is like your people Israel—the one nation on earth whose God went out to redeem[o] a people for himself, and to make a name for yourself, and to perform great and awesome wonders by driving out nations from before your people, whom you redeemed from Egypt? 22You made your people Israel your very own for ever,[p] and you, O LORD, have become their God.

23"And now, LORD, let the promise[q] you have made concerning your servant and his house be established for ever. Do as you promised, 24so that it will be established and that your name will be great for ever. Then men will say, 'The LORD Almighty, the God over Israel, is Israel's God!' And the house of your servant David will be established before you.

25"You, my God, have revealed to your servant that you will build a house for him. So your servant has found courage to pray to you. 26O LORD, you are God! You have promised these good things to your servant. 27Now you have been pleased to bless the house of your servant, that it may continue for ever in your sight;[r] for you, O LORD, have blessed it, and it will be blessed for ever."

David's Victories

18:1–13pp 2Sa 8:1–14

18 In the course of time, David defeated the Philistines and subdued them, and he took Gath and its surrounding villages from the control of the Philistines.

2David also defeated the Moabites,[a] and they became subject to him and brought tribute.

3Moreover, David fought Hadadezer king of Zobah,[b] as far as Hamath, when he went to establish his control along the Euphrates River.[c] 4David captured a thousand of his chariots, seven thousand charioteers and twenty thousand foot soldiers. He hamstrung[d] all but a hundred of the chariot horses.

5When the Arameans of Damascus[e] came to help Hadadezer king of Zobah, David struck down twenty-two thousand of them. 6He put garrisons in the Aramean kingdom of Damascus, and the Arameans became subject to him and brought tribute. The LORD gave David victory everywhere he went.

7David took the gold shields carried by the officers of Hadadezer and brought them to Jerusalem. 8From Tebah[a] and Cun, towns that belonged to Hadadezer, David took a great quantity of bronze, which Solomon used to make the bronze Sea,[f] the pillars and various bronze articles.

9When Tou king of Hamath heard that David had defeated the entire army of Hadadezer king of Zobah, 10he sent his son Hadoram to King David to greet him and congratulate him on his victory in battle over Hadadezer, who had been at war with Tou. Hadoram brought all kinds of articles of gold and silver and bronze.

11King David dedicated these articles to the LORD, as he had done with the silver and gold he had taken from all these nations: Edom[g] and Moab, the Ammonites and the Philistines, and Amalek.[h]

12Abishai son of Zeruiah struck down eighteen thousand Edomites[i] in the Valley of Salt. 13He put garrisons in Edom, and all the Edomites became subject to David. The LORD gave David victory everywhere he went.

17:21 *o* Ex 6:6
17:22 *p* Ex 19:5-6
17:23 *q* 1Ki 8:25
17:27 *r* Ps 16:11 Ps 21:6
18:2 *a* Nu 21:29
18:3 *b* 1Ch 19:6 *c* Ge 2:14
18:4 *d* Ge 49:6
18:5 *e* 2Ki 16:9 1Ch 19:6
18:8 *f* 1Ki 7:23 2Ch 4:12, 15-16
18:11 *g* Nu 24:18 *h* Nu 24:20
18:12 *i* 1Ki 11:15

a8 Hebrew *Tibhath*, a variant of *Tebah*

David's Officials

18:14–17pp 2Sa 8:15–18

14 David reigned[j] over all Israel,[k] doing what was just and right for all his people. 15 Joab[l] son of Zeruiah was over the army; Jehoshaphat son of Ahilud was recorder; 16 Zadok[m] son of Ahitub and Ahimelech[b][n] son of Abiathar were priests; Shavsha was secretary; 17 Benaiah son of Jehoiada was over the Kerethites and Pelethites;[o] and David's sons were chief officials at the king's side.

The Battle Against the Ammonites

19:1–19pp 2Sa 10:1–19

19 In the course of time, Nahash king of the Ammonites[a] died, and his son succeeded him as king. 2 David thought, "I will show kindness to Hanun son of Nahash, because his father showed kindness to me." So David sent a delegation to express his sympathy to Hanun concerning his father.

When David's men came to Hanun in the land of the Ammonites to express sympathy to him, 3 the Ammonite nobles said to Hanun, "Do you think David is honouring your father by sending men to you to express sympathy? Haven't his men come to you to explore and spy out[b] the country and overthrow it?" 4 So Hanun seized David's men, shaved them, cut off their garments in the middle at the buttocks, and sent them away.

5 When someone came and told David about the men, he sent messengers to meet them, for they were greatly humiliated. The king said, "Stay at Jericho till your beards have grown, and then come back."

6 When the Ammonites realised that they had become an offence to[c] David's nostrils, Hanun and the Ammonites sent a thousand talents[a] of silver to hire chariots and charioteers from Aram Naharaim,[b] Aram Maacah and Zobah.[d] 7 They hired thirty-two thousand chariots and charioteers, as well as the king of Maacah with his troops, who came and camped near Medeba,[e] while the Ammonites were mustered from their towns and moved out for battle.

8 On hearing this, David sent Joab out with the entire army of fighting men. 9 The Ammonites came out and drew up in battle formation at the entrance to their city, while the kings who had come were by themselves in the open country.

10 Joab saw that there were battle lines in front of him and behind him; so he selected some of the best troops in Israel and deployed them against the Arameans. 11 He put the rest of the men under the command of Abishai[f] his brother, and they were deployed against the Ammonites. 12 Joab said, "If the Arameans are too strong for me, then you are to rescue me; but if the Ammonites are too strong for you, then I will rescue you. 13 Be strong and let us fight bravely for our people and the cities of our God. The LORD will do what is good in his sight."

14 Then Joab and the troops with him advanced to fight the Arameans, and they fled before him. 15 When the Ammonites saw that the Arameans were fleeing, they too fled before his brother Abishai and went inside the city. So Joab went back to Jerusalem.

16 After the Arameans saw that they had been routed by Israel, they sent messengers and had Arameans brought from beyond the River,[c] with Shophach the commander of Hadadezer's army leading them.

17 When David was told of this, he gathered all Israel[g] and crossed

18:14 j 1Ch 29:26 k 1Ch 11:1
18:15 l 2Sa 5:6-8 1Ch 11:6
18:16 m 2Sa 8:17 1Ch 6:8 n 1Ch 24:6
18:17 o 1Sa 30:14 2Sa 8:18 2Sa 15:18
19:1 a Ge 19:38 Jdg 10:17-11:33 2Ch 20:1-2 Zep 2:8-11
19:3 b Nu 21:32
19:6 c Ge 34:30 d 1Ch 18:3,5,9
19:7 e Nu 21:30 Jos 13:9,16
19:11 f 1Sa 26:6
19:17 g 1Ch 9:1

b16 Some Hebrew manuscripts, Vulgate and Syriac (see also 2 Sam. 8:17); most Hebrew manuscripts *Abimelech* a6 That is, about 34 tons (about 34 metric tons) b6 That is, North-west Mesopotamia c16 That is, the Euphrates

the Jordan; he advanced against them and formed his battle lines opposite them. David formed his lines to meet the Arameans in battle, and they fought against him. 18 But they fled before Israel, and David killed seven thousand of their charioteers and forty thousand of their foot soldiers. He also killed Shophach the commander of their army.

19 When the vassals of Hadadezer saw that they had been defeated by Israel, they made peace with David and became subject to him.

So the Arameans were not willing to help the Ammonites any more.

The Capture of Rabbah

20:1–3pp 2Sa 11:1; 12:29–31

20 In the spring, at the time when kings go off to war, Joab led out the armed forces. He laid waste the land of the Ammonites and went to Rabbah[a] and besieged it, but David remained in Jerusalem. Joab attacked Rabbah and left it in ruins.[b] 2 David took the crown from the head of their king[a]—its weight was found to be a talent[b] of gold, and it was set with precious stones—and it was placed on David's head. He took a great quantity of plunder from the city 3 and brought out the people who were there, consigning them to labour with saws and with iron picks and axes.[c] David did this to all the Ammonite towns. Then David and his entire army returned to Jerusalem.

War With the Philistines

2:4–8pp 2Sa 21:15–22

4 In the course of time, war broke out with the Philistines, at Gezer.[d] At that time Sibbecai the Hushathite killed Sippai, one of the descendants of the Rephaites,[e] and the Philistines were subjugated.

5 In another battle with the Philistines, Elhanan son of Jair killed Lahmi the brother of Goliath the Gittite, who had a spear with a shaft like a weaver's rod.[f]

6 In still another battle, which took place at Gath, there was a huge man with six fingers on each hand and six toes on each foot—twenty-four in all. He also was descended from Rapha. 7 When he taunted Israel, Jonathan son of Shimea, David's brother, killed him.

8 These were descendants of Rapha in Gath, and they fell at the hands of David and his men.

David Numbers the Fighting Men

2.:1–26pp 2Sa 24:1–25

21 Satan[a] rose up against Israel and incited David to take a census[b] of Israel. 2 So David said to Joab and the commanders of the troops, "Go and count[c] the Israelites from Beersheba to Dan. Then report back to me so that I may know how many there are."

3 But Joab replied, "May the LORD multiply his troops a hundred times over.[d] My lord the king, are they not all my lord's subjects? Why does my lord want to do this? Why should he bring guilt on Israel?"

4 The king's word, however, overruled Joab; so Joab left and went throughout Israel and then came back to Jerusalem. 5 Joab reported the number of the fighting men to David: In all Israel[e] there were one million one hundred thousand men who could handle a sword, including four hundred and seventy thousand in Judah.

6 But Joab did not include Levi and Benjamin in the numbering, because the king's command was repulsive to him. 7 This command was also evil in the sight of God; so he punished Israel.

8 Then David said to God, "I have

[a]2 Or *of Milcom,* that is, Molech [b]2 That is, about 75 pounds (about 34 kilograms)

20:1 a Dt 3:11; 2Sa 12:26 b Am 1:13-15
20:3 c Dt 29:11
20:4 d Jos 10:33 e Ge 14:5
20:5 f 1Sa 17:7
21:1 a 2Ch 18:21; Ps 109:6 b 2Ch 14:8; 2Ch 25:5
21:2 c 1Ch 27:23-24
21:3 d Dt 1:11
21:5 e 1Ch 9:1

sinned greatly by doing this. Now,
I beg you, take away the guilt of
your servant. I have done a very
foolish thing."
9The LORD said to Gad,[f] David's
seer,[g] 10"Go and tell David, 'This is
what the LORD says: I am giving
you three options. Choose one of
them for me to carry out against
you.' "
11So Gad went to David and said
to him, "This is what the LORD says:
'Take your choice: 12three years of
famine,[h] three months of being
swept away[a] before your enemies,
with their swords overtaking you,
or three days of the sword[i] of the
LORD[j]—days of plague in the land,
with the angel of the LORD ravaging
every part of Israel.' Now then, decide how I should answer the one
who sent me."
13David said to Gad, "I am in deep
distress. Let me fall into the hands
of the LORD, for his mercy[k] is very
great; but do not let me fall into the
hands of men."
14So the LORD sent a plague on Israel, and seventy thousand men of
Israel fell dead.[l] 15And God sent
an angel[m] to destroy Jerusalem.[n]
But as the angel was doing so, the
LORD saw it and was grieved[o] because of the calamity and said to
the angel who was destroying[p] the
people, "Enough! Withdraw your
hand." The angel of the LORD was
then standing at the threshing-
floor of Araunah[b] the Jebusite.
16David looked up and saw the
angel of the LORD standing between heaven and earth, with a
drawn sword in his hand extended
over Jerusalem. Then David and
the elders, clothed in sackcloth, fell
face down.[q]
17David said to God, "Was it not I
who ordered the fighting men to be
counted? I am the one who has
sinned and done wrong. These are
but sheep.[r] What have they done?
O LORD my God, let your hand fall
upon me and my family,[s] but do
not let this plague remain on your
people."
18Then the angel of the LORD ordered Gad to tell David to go up and
build an altar to the LORD on the
threshing-floor[t] of Araunah the
Jebusite. 19So David went up in
obedience to the word that Gad had
spoken in the name of the LORD.
20While Araunah was threshing
wheat,[u] he turned and saw the
angel; his four sons who were with
him hid themselves. 21Then David
approached, and when Araunah
looked and saw him, he left the
threshing-floor and bowed down
before David with his face to the
ground.
22David said to him, "Let me have
the site of your threshing-floor so
that I can build an altar to the LORD,
that the plague on the people may
be stopped. Sell it to me at the full
price."
23Araunah said to David, "Take
it! Let my lord the king do whatever pleases him. Look, I will give
the oxen for the burnt offerings,
the threshing-sledges for the wood,
and the wheat for the grain offering. I will give all this."
24But King David replied to
Araunah, "No, I insist on paying the
full price. I will not take for the
LORD what is yours, or sacrifice
a burnt offering that costs me
nothing."
25So David paid Araunah six hundred shekels[c] of gold for the site.
26David built an altar to the LORD
there and sacrificed burnt offerings and fellowship offerings.[d] He
called on the LORD, and the LORD
answered him with fire[v] from
heaven on the altar of burnt offering.
27Then the LORD spoke to the
angel, and he put his sword back
into its sheath. 28At that time, when

21:9 f 1Sa 22:5 g 1Sa 9:9
21:12 h Dt 32:24 i Eze 30:25 j Ge 19:13
21:13 k Ps 6:4 Ps 86:15 Ps 130:4,7
21:14 l 1Ch 27:24
21:15 m Ge 32:1 n Ps 125:2 o Ge 6:6 Ex 32:14 p Ge 19:13
21:16 q Nu 14:5 Jos 7:6
21:17 r 2Sa 7:8 Ps 74:1 s Jnh 1:12
21:18 t 2Ch 3:1
21:20 u Jdg 6:11
21:26 v Lev 9:24 Jdg 6:21

[a]12 Hebrew; Septuagint and Vulgate (see also 2 Sam. 24:13) *of fleeing* [b]15 Hebrew *Ornan*, a variant of *Araunah*; also in verses 18–28
[c]25 That is, about 15 pounds (about 7 kilograms)
[d]26 Traditionally *peace offerings*

David saw that the LORD had answered him on the threshing-floor of Araunah the Jebusite, he offered sacrifices there. 29 The tabernacle of the LORD, which Moses had made in the desert, and the altar of burnt offering were at that time on the high place at Gibeon.[w] 30 But David could not go before it to enquire of God, because he was afraid of the sword of the angel of the LORD.

22 Then David said, "The house of the LORD God[a] is to be here, and also the altar of burnt offering for Israel."

Preparations for the Temple

2 So David gave orders to assemble the aliens[b] living in Israel, and from among them he appointed stonecutters[c] to prepare dressed stone for building the house of God. 3 He provided a large amount of iron to make nails for the doors of the gateways and for the fittings, and more bronze than could be weighed.[d] 4 He also provided more cedar logs[e] than could be counted, for the Sidonians and Tyrians had brought large numbers of them to David.

5 David said, "My son Solomon is young[f] and inexperienced, and the house to be built for the LORD should be of great magnificence and fame and splendour in the sight of all the nations. Therefore I will make preparations for it." So David made extensive preparations before his death.

6 Then he called for his son Solomon and charged him to build[g] a house for the LORD, the God of Israel. 7 David said to Solomon: "My son, I had it in my heart[h] to build[i] a house for the Name[j] of the LORD my God. 8 But this word of the LORD came to me: 'You have shed much blood and have fought many wars.[k] You are not to build a house for my Name,[l] because you have shed much blood on the earth in my sight. 9 But you will have a son who will be a man of peace[m] and rest, and I will give him rest from all his enemies on every side. His name will be Solomon,[a][n] and I will grant Israel peace and quiet[o] during his reign. 10 He is the one who will build a house for my Name.[p] He will be my son,[q] and I will be his father. And I will establish the throne of his kingdom over Israel for ever.'[r]

11 "Now, my son, the LORD be with[s] you, and may you have success and build the house of the LORD your God, as he said you would. 12 May the LORD give you discretion and understanding[t] when he puts you in command over Israel, so that you may keep the law of the LORD your God. 13 Then you will have success if you are careful to observe the decrees and laws[u] that the LORD gave to Moses for Israel. Be strong and courageous.[v] Do not be afraid or discouraged.

14 "I have taken great pains to provide for the temple of the LORD a hundred thousand talents[b] of gold, a million talents[c] of silver, quantities of bronze and iron too great to be weighed, and wood and stone. And you may add to them.[w] 15 You have many workmen: stonecutters, masons and carpenters, as well as men skilled in every kind of work 16 in gold and silver, bronze and iron—craftsmen[x] beyond number. Now begin the work, and the LORD be with you."

17 Then David ordered[y] all the leaders of Israel to help his son Solomon. 18 He said to them, "Is not the LORD your God with you? And has he not granted you rest[z] on every side?[a] For he has handed the inhabitants of the land over to me, and the land is subject to the LORD and to his people. 19 Now devote your heart and soul to seeking the LORD your God.[b] Begin to build the sanctuary of the LORD God, so that

21:29 w 1Ki 3:4; 1Ch 16:39
22:1 a Ge 28:17; 1Ch 21:18-29; 2Ch 3:1
22:2 b 1Ki 9:21; Isa 56:6; c 1Ki 5:17-18
22:3 d ver 14; 1Ki 7:47; 1Ch 29:2-5
22:4 e 1Ki 5:6
22:5 f 1Ki 3:7; 1Ch 29:1
22:6 g Ac 7:47
22:7 h 1Ch 17:2; i 2Sa 7:2; 1Ki 8:17; j Dt 12:5,11
22:8 k 1Ki 5:3; l 1Ch 28:3
22:9 m 1Ki 5:4; n 2Sa 12:24; o 1Ki 4:20
22:10 p 1Ch 17:12; q 2Sa 7:13; r 2Sa 7:14; 2Ch 6:15
22:11 s ver 16
22:12 t 1Ki 3:9-12; 2Ch 1:10
22:13 u 1Ch 28:7; v Dt 31:6; Jos 1:6-9; 1Ch 28:20
22:14 w ver 3; 1Ch 29:2-5,19
22:16 x ver 11; 2Ch 2:7
22:17 y 1Ch 28:1-6
22:18 z ver 9; 1Ch 23:25; a 2Sa 7:1
22:19 b ver 7; 1Ki 8:6; 1Ch 28:9; 2Ch 5:7; 2Ch 7:14

a9 *Solomon* sounds like and may be derived from the Hebrew for *peace*. b14 That is, about 3,395 tons (about 3,450 metric tons) c14 That is, about 33,950 tons (about 34,500 metric tons)

you may bring the ark of the covenant of the LORD and the sacred
articles belonging to God into the
temple that will be built for the
Name of the LORD."

The Levites

23 When David was old and
full of years, he made his
son Solomon[a] king over Israel.[b]
2He also gathered together all
the leaders of Israel, as well as the
priests and Levites. 3The Levites
thirty years old or more[c] were
counted, and the total number of
men was thirty-eight thousand.[d]
4David said, "Of these, twenty-four
thousand are to supervise[e] the
work of the temple of the LORD and
six thousand are to be officials and
judges.[f] 5Four thousand are to be
gatekeepers and four thousand are
to praise the LORD with the musical
instruments[g] I have provided for
that purpose."[h]
6David divided[i] the Levites into
groups corresponding to the sons
of Levi: Gershon, Kohath and
Merari.

Gershonites

7Belonging to the Gershonites:
Ladan and Shimei.
8The sons of Ladan:
Jehiel the first, Zetham and
Joel—three in all.
9The sons of Shimei:
Shelomoth, Haziel and Ha-
ran—three in all.
These were the heads of the
families of Ladan.
10And the sons of Shimei:
Jahath, Ziza,[a] Jeush and Beriah.
These were the sons of
Shimei—four in all.
11Jahath was the first and Ziza
the second, but Jeush and
Beriah did not have many
sons; so they were counted
as one family with one as-
signment.

23:1
a 1Ki 1:33-39
1Ch 28:5
b 1Ki 1:30
1Ch 29:28

23:3
c ver 24
Nu 8:24
d Nu 4:3-49

23:4
e Ezr 3:8
f 1Ch 26:29
2Ch 19:8

23:5
g 1Ch 15:16
h Ne 12:45

23:6
i 2Ch 8:14
2Ch 29:25

23:12
j Ex 6:18

23:13
k Ex 6:20
Ex 28:1
l Ex 30:7-10
Dt 21:5
m Nu 6:23

23:14
n Dt 33:1

23:15
o Ex 18:4

23:16
p 1Ch 26:24-28

23:19
q 1Ch 24:23

23:21
r 1Ch 24:26

Kohathites

12The sons of Kohath:[j]
Amram, Izhar, Hebron and
Uzziel—four in all.
13The sons of Amram:[k]
Aaron and Moses.
Aaron was set apart,[l] he
and his descendants for
ever, to consecrate the most
holy things, to offer sacrifices before the LORD, to
minister before him and to
pronounce blessings[m] in his
name for ever. 14The sons of
Moses the man[n] of God
were counted as part of the
tribe of Levi.
15The sons of Moses:
Gershom and Eliezer.[o]
16The descendants of Ger-
shom:[p]
Shubael was the first.
17The descendants of Eliezer:
Rehabiah was the first.
Eliezer had no other sons,
but the sons of Rehabiah
were very numerous.
18The sons of Izhar:
Shelomith was the first.
19The sons of Hebron:[q]
Jeriah the first, Amariah the
second, Jahaziel the third
and Jekameam the fourth.
20The sons of Uzziel:
Micah the first and Isshiah
the second.

Merarites

21The sons of Merari:[r]
Mahli and Mushi.
The sons of Mahli:
Eleazar and Kish.
22Eleazar died without having
sons: he had only daughters.
Their cousins, the sons of
Kish, married them.
23The sons of Mushi:
Mahli, Eder and Jerimoth—
three in all.

a*10* One Hebrew manuscript, Septuagint and Vulgate (see also verse 11); most Hebrew manuscripts *Zina*

24These were the descendants of
Levi by their families—the heads
of families as they were registered
under their names and counted in-
dividually, that is, the workers
twenty years old or more[s] who
served in the temple of the LORD.
25For David had said, "Since the
LORD, the God of Israel, has
granted rest[t] to his people and has
come to dwell in Jerusalem for
ever, 26the Levites no longer need to
carry the tabernacle or any of the
articles used in its service."[u] 27Ac-
cording to the last instructions of David, the Levites were counted from
those twenty years old or more.
28The duty of the Levites was to
help Aaron's descendants in the
service of the temple of the LORD:
to be in charge of the courtyards,
the side rooms, the purification[v]
of all sacred things and the per-
formance of other duties at the
house of God. 29They were in
charge of the bread set out on the
table,[w] the flour for the grain offerings,[x] the unleavened wafers,
the baking and the mixing, and all
measurements of quantity and
size.[y] 30They were also to stand
every morning to thank and praise
the LORD. They were to do the same
in the evening[z] 31and whenever
burnt offerings were presented to
the LORD on Sabbaths and at New
Moon[a] festivals and at appointed
feasts.[b] They were to serve before
the LORD regularly in the proper
number and in the way prescribed
for them.
32And so the Levites[c] carried out
their responsibilities for the Tent
of Meeting,[d] for the Holy Place
and, under their brothers the descendants of Aaron, for the service
of the temple of the LORD.[e]

The Divisions of Priests

24 These were the divisions[a]
of the sons of Aaron:[b]
The sons of Aaron were Nadab,
Abihu, Eleazar and Ithamar.[c] 2But
Nadab and Abihu died before their
father did,[d] and they had no sons;
so Eleazar and Ithamar served
as the priests. 3With the help of
Zadok[e] a descendant of Eleazar
and Ahimelech a descendant of Ithamar, David separated them into
divisions for their appointed order
of ministering. 4A larger number of
leaders were found among Eleazar's descendants than among Ithamar's, and they were divided
accordingly: sixteen heads of families from Eleazar's descendants
and eight heads of families from
Ithamar's descendants. 5They divided them impartially by drawing
lots,[f] for there were officials of
the sanctuary and officials of God
among the descendants of both
Eleazar and Ithamar.
6The scribe Shemaiah son of Nethanel, a Levite, recorded their
names in the presence of the king
and of the officials: Zadok the
priest, Ahimelech[g] son of Abiathar
and the heads of families of the
priests and of the Levites—one
family being taken from Eleazar
and then one from Ithamar.

7The first lot fell to Jehoiarib,
the second to Jedaiah,[h]
8the third to Harim,[i]
the fourth to Seorim,
9the fifth to Malkijah,
the sixth to Mijamin,
10the seventh to Hakkoz,
the eighth to Abijah,[j]
11the ninth to Jeshua,
the tenth to Shecaniah,
12the eleventh to Eliashib,
the twelfth to Jakim,
13the thirteenth to Huppah,
the fourteenth to Jeshebeab,
14the fifteenth to Bilgah,
the sixteenth to Immer,[k]
15the seventeenth to Hezir,[l]
the eighteenth to Happizzez,
16the nineteenth to Pethahiah,
the twentieth to Jehezkel,
17the twenty-first to Jakin,
the twenty-second to Gamul,

23:24 s Nu 4:3; Nu 10:17,21
23:25 t 1Ch 22:9
23:26 u Nu 4:5,15; Nu 7:9; Dt 10:8
23:28 v 2Ch 29:15; Ne 13:9; Mal 3:3
23:29 w Ex 25:30; x Lev 2:4-7; Lev 6:20-23; y Lev 19:35-36; 1Ch 9:29,32
23:30 z 1Ch 9:33; Ps 134:1
23:31 a 2Ki 4:23; b Lev 23:4; Nu 28:9-29:39; Isa 1:13-14; Col 2:16
23:32 c Nu 1:53; 1Ch 6:48; d Nu 3:6-8,38; e 2Ch 23:18; 2Ch 31:2; Eze 44:14
24:1 a 1Ch 23:6; 1Ch 28:13; 2Ch 5:11; 2Ch 8:14; 2Ch 23:8; 2Ch 31:2; 2Ch 35:4,5; Ezr 6:18; b Nu 3:2-4; c Ex 6:23
24:2 d Lev 10:1-2; Nu 3:4
24:3 e 2Sa 8:17
24:5 f ver 31; 1Ch 25:8
24:6 g 1Ch 18:16
24:7 h Ezr 2:36; Ne 12:6
24:8 i Ezr 2:39; Ne 10:5
24:10 j Ne 12:4,17; Lk 1:5
24:14 k Jer 20:1
24:15 l Ne 10:20

18 the twenty-third to Delaiah
and the twenty-fourth to Maaziah.

19 This was their appointed order
of ministering when they entered
the temple of the LORD, according
to the regulations prescribed for
them by their forefather Aaron, as
the LORD, the God of Israel, had
commanded him.

The Rest of the Levites

20 As for the rest of the descendants
of Levi:[m]
from the sons of Amram: Shubael;
from the sons of Shubael:
Jehdeiah.
21 As for Rehabiah,[n] from his
sons:
Isshiah was the first.
22 From the Izharites: Shelomoth;
from the sons of Shelomoth:
Jahath.
23 The sons of Hebron:[o] Jeriah
the first,[a] Amariah the
second, Jahaziel the third
and Jekameam the fourth.
24 The son of Uzziel: Micah;
from the sons of Micah: Shamir.
25 The brother of Micah: Isshiah;
from the sons of Isshiah:
Zechariah.
26 The sons of Merari:[p] Mahli
and Mushi.
The son of Jaaziah: Beno.
27 The sons of Merari:
from Jaaziah: Beno, Sho-
ham, Zaccur and Ibri.
28 From Mahli: Eleazar, who had
no sons.
29 From Kish: the son of Kish:
Jerahmeel.
30 And the sons of Mushi: Mahli,
Eder and Jerimoth.

These were the Levites, according to their families. 31 They also
cast lots,[q] just as their brothers
the descendants of Aaron did, in
the presence of King David and of
Zadok, Ahimelech, and the heads of
families of the priests and of the
Levites. The families of the oldest
brother were treated the same as
those of the youngest.

The Singers

25 David, together with the
commanders of the army,
set apart some of the sons of
Asaph,[a] Heman[b] and Jeduthun[c]
for the ministry of prophesying,[d]
accompanied by harps, lyres
and cymbals.[e] Here is the list of
the men[f] who performed this
service:[g]

2 From the sons of Asaph:
Zaccur, Joseph, Nethaniah
and Asarelah. The sons of
Asaph were under the supervision of Asaph, who prophesied under the king's
supervision.
3 As for Jeduthun, from his
sons:[h]
Gedaliah, Zeri, Jeshaiah,
Shimei,[a] Hashabiah and
Mattithiah, six in all, under
the supervision of their
father Jeduthun, who prophesied, using the harp[i] in
thanking and praising the
LORD.
4 As for Heman, from his sons:
Bukkiah, Mattaniah, Uzziel,
Shubael and Jerimoth;
Hananiah, Hanani, Eliathah,
Giddalti and Romamti-Ezer;
Joshbekashah, Mallothi, Hothir and Mahazioth. 5 All these
were sons of Heman the
king's seer. They were given
to him through the promises
of God to exalt him.[b] God
gave Heman fourteen sons
and three daughters.

24:20 m 1Ch 23:6
24:21 n 1Ch 23:17
24:23 o 1Ch 23:19
24:26 p 1Ch 6:19; 1Ch 23:21
24:31 q ver 5
25:1 a 1Ch 6:39; b 1Ch 6:33; c 1Ch 16:41,42; Ne 11:17; d 1Sa 10:5; 2Ki 3:15; e 1Ch 15:16; f 1Ch 6:31; g 2Ch 5:12; 2Ch 8:14; 2Ch 34:12; 2Ch 35:15; Ezr 3:10
25:3 h 1Ch 16:41-42; i Ge 4:21; Ps 33:2

a23 Two Hebrew manuscripts and some Septuagint manuscripts (see also 1 Chron. 23:19); most Hebrew manuscripts *The sons of Jeriah:*
a3 One Hebrew manuscript and some Septuagint manuscripts (see also verse 17); most Hebrew manuscripts do not have *Shimei.* b5 Hebrew *exalt the horn*

6All these men were under the
supervision of their fathers[j] for
the music of the temple of the
LORD, with cymbals, lyres and
harps, for the ministry at the house
of God. Asaph, Jeduthun and Heman[k] were under the supervision
of the king.[l] 7Along with their
relatives—all of them trained and
skilled in music for the LORD—they
numbered 288. 8Young and old
alike, teacher as well as student,
cast lots[m] for their duties.

9The first lot, which was for
Asaph,[n] fell to Joseph,
his sons and relatives,[c] 12[d]
the second to Gedaliah,
he and his relatives and
sons, 12
10the third to Zaccur,
his sons and relatives, 12
11the fourth to Izri,[e]
his sons and relatives, 12
12the fifth to Nethaniah,
his sons and relatives, 12
13the sixth to Bukkiah,
his sons and relatives, 12
14the seventh to Jesarelah,[f]
his sons and relatives, 12
15the eighth to Jeshaiah,
his sons and relatives, 12
16the ninth to Mattaniah,
his sons and relatives, 12
17the tenth to Shimei,
his sons and relatives, 12
18the eleventh to Azarel,[g]
his sons and relatives, 12
19the twelfth to Hashabiah,
his sons and relatives, 12
20the thirteenth to Shubael,
his sons and relatives, 12
21the fourteenth to
Mattithiah,
his sons and relatives, 12
22the fifteenth to Jerimoth,
his sons and relatives, 12
23the sixteenth to Hananiah,
his sons and relatives, 12
24the seventeenth to
Joshbekashah,
his sons and relatives, 12
25the eighteenth to Hanani,
his sons and relatives, 12
26the nineteenth to Mallothi,
his sons and relatives, 12
27the twentieth to Eliathah,
his sons and relatives, 12
28the twenty-first to Hothir,
his sons and relatives, 12
29the twenty-second to
Giddalti,
his sons and relatives, 12
30the twenty-third to
Mahazioth,
his sons and relatives, 12
31the twenty-fourth to
Romamti-Ezer,
his sons and relatives, 12[o]

The Gatekeepers

26 The divisions of the gatekeepers:[a]

From the Korahites: Meshe-
lemiah son of Kore, one of
the sons of Asaph.
2Meshelemiah had sons:
Zechariah[b] the firstborn,
Jediael the second,
Zebadiah the third,
Jathniel the fourth,
3Elam the fifth,
Jehohanan the sixth
and Eliehoenai the seventh.
4Obed-Edom also had sons:
Shemaiah the firstborn,
Jehozabad the second,
Joah the third,
Sacar the fourth,
Nethanel the fifth,
5Ammiel the sixth,
Issachar the seventh
and Peullethai the eighth.
(For God had blessed Obed-
Edom.[c])
6His son Shemaiah also had
sons, who were leaders in
their father's family be-
cause they were very ca-
pable men. 7The sons of

25:6 j 1Ch 15:16 k 1Ch 15:19 l 2Ch 23:18 2Ch 29:25
25:8 m 1Ch 26:13
25:9 n 1Ch 6:39
25:31 o 1Ch 9:33
26:1 a 1Ch 9:17
26:2 b 1Ch 9:21
26:5 c 2Sa 6:10 1Ch 13:13 1Ch 16:38

c9 See Septuagint; Hebrew does not have *his sons and relatives.* d9 See the total in verse 7; Hebrew does not have *twelve.* e11 A variant of *Zeri* f14 A variant of *Asarelah* g18 A variant of *Uzziel*

Shemaiah: Othni, Rephael,
Obed and Elzabad; his relatives Elihu and Semakiah
were also able men. 8All
these were descendants of
Obed-Edom; they and their
sons and their relatives
were capable men with the
strength to do the work—descendants of Obed-Edom, 62
in all.
9Meshelemiah had sons and
relatives, who were able
men—18 in all.
10Hosah the Merarite had sons:
Shimri the first (although he
was not the firstborn, his
father had appointed him
the first),[d] 11Hilkiah the
second, Tabaliah the third
and Zechariah the fourth.
The sons and relatives of
Hosah were 13 in all.
12These divisions of the gatekeepers, through their chief men,
had duties for ministering[e] in the
temple of the LORD, just as their
relatives had. 13Lots[f] were cast for
each gate, according to their families, young and old alike.
14The lot for the East Gate[g] fell
to Shelemiah.[a] Then lots were cast
for his son Zechariah,[h] a wise
counsellor, and the lot for the
North Gate fell to him. 15The lot for
the South Gate fell to Obed-
Edom,[i] and the lot for the storehouse fell to his sons. 16The lots for
the West Gate and the Shalleketh
Gate on the upper road fell to Shup-
pim and Hosah.
Guard was alongside guard:
17There were six Levites a day on
the east, four a day on the north,
four a day on the south and two at
a time at the storehouse. 18As for
the court to the west, there were
four at the road and two at the court
itself.
19These were the divisions of the
gatekeepers who were descendants of Korah and Merari.[j]

26:10 d Dt 21:16; 1Ch 5:1
26:12 e 1Ch 9:22
26:13 f 1Ch 24:5,31; 1Ch 25:8
26:14 g 1Ch 9:18; h 1Ch 9:21
26:15 i 1Ch 13:13; 2Ch 25:24
26:19 j 2Ch 35:15; Ne 7:1; Eze 44:11
26:20 k 2Ch 24:5; l 1Ch 28:12
26:21 m 1Ch 23:7; 1Ch 29:8
26:22 n 1Ch 9:26
26:23 o Nu 3:27
26:24 p 1Ch 23:16
26:25 q 1Ch 23:18
26:26 r 2Sa 8:11
26:28 s 1Sa 9:9
26:29 t Dt 17:8-13; 1Ch 23:4; Ne 11:16

The Treasurers and Other Officials

20Their fellow Levites[k] were[b] in
charge of the treasuries of the
house of God and the treasuries for
the dedicated things.[l]
21The descendants of Ladan, who
were Gershonites through Ladan
and who were heads of families belonging to Ladan the Gershonite,[m]
were Jehieli, 22the sons of Jehieli,
Zetham and his brother Joel. They
were in charge of the treasuries[n]
of the temple of the LORD.
23From the Amramites, the Izharites, the Hebronites and the
Uzzielites:[o]
24Shubael,[p] a descendant of
Gershom son of Moses, was
the officer in charge of the
treasuries. 25His relatives
through Eliezer: Rehabiah
his son, Jeshaiah his son, Joram his son, Zicri his son and
Shelomith[q] his son. 26Shelo-
mith and his relatives were
in charge of all the treasuries for the things dedicated[r] by King David, by
the heads of families who
were the commanders of
thousands and commanders
of hundreds, and by the
other army commanders.
27Some of the plunder taken
in battle they dedicated for
the repair of the temple of
the LORD. 28And everything
dedicated by Samuel the
seer[s] and by Saul son of
Kish, Abner son of Ner and
Joab son of Zeruiah, and all
the other dedicated things
were in the care of Shelomith and his relatives.
29From the Izharites: Kenaniah
and his sons were assigned
duties away from the tem-
ple, as officials and judges[t]
over Israel.

[a] 14 A variant of *Meshelemiah* [b] 20 Septuagint; Hebrew *As for the Levites, Ahijah was*

30From the Hebronites: Hashabiah[u] and his relatives—
seventeen hundred able
men—were responsible in
Israel west of the Jordan for
all the work of the LORD and
for the king's service. 31As
for the Hebronites,[v] Jeriah
was their chief according to
the genealogical records of
their families. In the fortieth[w] year of David's reign a
search was made in the
records, and capable men
among the Hebronites were
found at Jazer in Gilead.
32Jeriah had two thousand
seven hundred relatives,
who were able men and
heads of families, and King
David put them in charge of
the Reubenites, the Gadites
and the half-tribe of Manasseh for every matter per-
taining to God and for the
affairs of the king.

Army Divisions

27 This is the list of the Israelites—heads of families,
commanders of thousands and commanders of hundreds, and their
officers, who served the king in
all that concerned the army divisions that were on duty month by
month throughout the year. Each
division consisted of 24,000 men.
2In charge of the first division,
for the first month, was Jashobeam[a] son of Zabdiel. There
were 24,000 men in his division. 3He was a descendant of
Perez and chief of all the army
officers for the first month.
4In charge of the division for the
second month was Dodai[b] the
Ahohite; Mikloth was the
leader of his division. There
were 24,000 men in his division.
5The third army commander, for
the third month, was Be-
naiah[c] son of Jehoiada the
priest. He was chief and there
were 24,000 men in his division. 6This was the Benaiah
who was a mighty man among
the Thirty and was over the
Thirty. His son Ammizabad
was in charge of his division.
7The fourth, for the fourth month,
was Asahel[d] the brother of
Joab; his son Zebadiah was his
successor. There were 24,000
men in his division.
8The fifth, for the fifth month,
was the commander Sham-
huth[e] the Izrahite. There
were 24,000 men in his division.
9The sixth, for the sixth month,
was Ira[f] the son of Ikkesh the
Tekoite. There were 24,000
men in his division.
10The seventh, for the seventh
month, was Helez[g] the Pelonite, an Ephraimite. There
were 24,000 men in his division.
11The eighth, for the eighth month,
was Sibbecai[h] the Hushathite,
a Zerahite. There were 24,000
men in his division.
12The ninth, for the ninth month,
was Abiezer[i] the Anathothite,
a Benjamite. There were
24,000 men in his division.
13The tenth, for the tenth month,
was Maharai[j] the Netophathite, a Zerahite. There were
24,000 men in his division.
14The eleventh, for the eleventh
month, was Benaiah[k] the Pirathonite, an Ephraimite. There
were 24,000 men in his division.
15The twelfth, for the twelfth
month, was Heldai[l] the Netophathite, from the family of
Othniel.[m] There were 24,000
men in his division.

Officers of the Tribes

16The officers over the tribes of
Israel:

26:30 u 1Ch 27:17
26:31 v 1Ch 23:19 w 2Sa 5:4
27:2 a 2Sa 23:8 1Ch 11:11
27:4 b 2Sa 23:9
27:5 c 2Sa 23:20
27:7 d 2Sa 2:18 1Ch 11:26
27:8 e 1Ch 11:27
27:9 f 2Sa 23:26 1Ch 11:28
27:10 g 2Sa 23:26 1Ch 11:27
27:11 h 2Sa 21:18
27:12 i 2Sa 23:27 1Ch 11:28
27:13 j 2Sa 23:28 1Ch 11:30
27:14 k 1Ch 11:31
27:15 l 2Sa 23:29 m Jos 15:17

over the Reubenites: Eliezer
son of Zicri;
over the Simeonites: Shephatiah son of Maacah;
17over Levi: Hashabiah[n] son of
Kemuel;
over Aaron: Zadok;[o]
18over Judah: Elihu, a brother of
David;
over Issachar: Omri son of Michael;
19over Zebulun: Ishmaiah son of
Obadiah;
over Naphtali: Jerimoth son of
Azriel;
20over the Ephraimites: Hoshea
son of Azaziah;
over half the tribe of Manasseh: Joel son of Pedaiah;
21over the half-tribe of Manasseh in Gilead: Iddo son of
Zechariah;
over Benjamin: Jaasiel son of
Abner;
22over Dan: Azarel son of Jeroham.
These were the officers over the
tribes of Israel.

23David did not take the number
of the men twenty years old or
less,[p] because the LORD had promised to make Israel as numerous as
the stars[q] in the sky. 24Joab son of
Zeruiah began to count the men
but did not finish. Wrath came on
Israel on account of this numbering,[r] and the number was not
entered in the book[a] of the annals
of King David.

The King's Overseers

25Azmaveth son of Adiel was in
charge of the royal storehouses.
Jonathan son of Uzziah was in
charge of the storehouses in the
outlying districts, in the towns, the
villages and the watchtowers.
26Ezri son of Kelub was in charge
of the field workers who farmed
the land.
27Shimei the Ramathite was in
charge of the vineyards.
Zabdi the Shiphmite was in

27:17
n 1Ch 26:30
o 2Sa 8:17
1Ch 12:28
27:23
p 1Ch 21:2-5
q Ge 15:5
27:24
r 2Sa 24:15
1Ch 21:7
27:28
s 1Ki 10:27
2Ch 1:15
27:31
t 1Ch 5:10
27:33
u 2Sa 15:12
v 2Sa 15:37
27:34
w 1Ki 1:7
x 1Ch 11:6
28:1
a 1Ch 11:10
1Ch 27:1-31

charge of the produce of the vineyards for the wine vats.
28Baal-Hanan the Gederite was
in charge of the olive and
sycamore-fig[s] trees in the western
foothills.
Joash was in charge of the supplies of olive oil.
29Shitrai the Sharonite was in
charge of the herds grazing in
Sharon.
Shaphat son of Adlai was in
charge of the herds in the valleys.
30Obil the Ishmaelite was in
charge of the camels.
Jehdeiah the Meronothite was in
charge of the donkeys.
31Jaziz the Hagrite[t] was in
charge of the flocks.
All these were the officials in
charge of King David's property.

32Jonathan, David's uncle, was a
counsellor, a man of insight and a
scribe. Jehiel son of Hacmoni took
care of the king's sons.
33Ahithophel[u] was the king's
counsellor.
Hushai[v] the Arkite was the
king's friend. 34Ahithophel was
succeeded by Jehoiada son of
Benaiah and by Abiathar.[w]
Joab[x] was the commander of the
royal army.

David's Plans for the Temple

28 David summoned all the
officials[a] of Israel to assemble at Jerusalem: the officers
over the tribes, the commanders
of the divisions in the service of
the king, the commanders of thousands and commanders of hundreds, and the officials in charge
of all the property and livestock
belonging to the king and his sons,
together with the palace officials,
the mighty men and all the brave
warriors.
2King David rose to his feet and
said: "Listen to me, my brothers
and my people. I had it in my

[a]24 Septuagint; Hebrew *number*

heart[b] to build a house as a place of
rest for the ark of the covenant of
the LORD, for the footstool[c] of our
God, and I made plans to build it.
3But God said to me,[d] 'You are not
to build a house for my Name,[e] because you are a warrior and have
shed blood.'[f]

4"Yet the LORD, the God of Israel,
chose me[g] from my whole family[h]
to be king over Israel for ever. He
chose Judah[i] as leader, and from
the house of Judah he chose my
family, and from my father's sons
he was pleased to make me king
over all Israel. 5Of all my sons—
and the LORD has given me
many[j]—he has chosen my son Solomon[k] to sit on the throne of the
kingdom of the LORD over Israel.
6He said to me, 'Solomon your son
is the one who will build my house
and my courts, for I have chosen
him to be my son,[l] and I will be his
father. 7I will establish his kingdom for ever if he is unswerving in
carrying out my commands and
laws,[m] as is being done at this
time.'

8"So now I charge you in the sight
of all Israel and of the assembly of
the LORD, and in the hearing of our
God: Be careful to follow all the
commands[n] of the LORD your God,
that you may possess this good land
and pass it on as an inheritance to
your descendants for ever.[o]

9"And you, my son Solomon, acknowledge the God of your father,
and serve him with wholehearted
devotion[p] and with a willing mind,
for the LORD searches every
heart[q] and understands every mo-
tive behind the thoughts. If you
seek him,[r] he will be found by you;
but if you forsake[s] him, he will reject[t] you for ever. 10Consider now,
for the LORD has chosen you to
build a temple as a sanctuary. Be
strong and do the work."

11Then David gave his son Solomon the plans[u] for the portico of
the temple, its buildings, its storerooms, its upper parts, its inner
rooms and the place of atonement.
12He gave him the plans of all that
the Spirit[v] had put in his mind for
the courts of the temple of the LORD
and all the surrounding rooms, for
the treasuries of the temple of God
and for the treasuries for the dedicated things.[w] 13He gave him instructions for the divisions[x] of the
priests and Levites, and for all the
work of serving in the temple of the
LORD, as well as for all the articles
to be used in its service. 14He designated the weight of gold for all the
gold articles to be used in various
kinds of service, and the weight of
silver for all the silver articles to
be used in various kinds of service:
15the weight of gold for the gold
lampstands[y] and their lamps, with
the weight for each lampstand and
its lamps; and the weight of silver
for each silver lampstand and its
lamps, according to the use of each
lampstand; 16the weight of gold for
each table[z] for consecrated bread;
the weight of silver for the silver
tables; 17the weight of pure gold for
the forks, sprinkling bowls[a] and
pitchers; the weight of gold for
each gold dish; the weight of silver
for each silver dish; 18and the
weight of the refined gold for the
altar of incense.[b] He also gave him
the plan for the chariot,[c] that is,
the cherubim of gold that spread
their wings and shelter[d] the ark of
the covenant of the LORD.

19"All this," David said, "I have in
writing from the hand of the LORD
upon me, and he gave me understanding in all the details[e] of the
plan.[f]"

20David also said to Solomon his
son, "Be strong and courageous,[g]
and do the work. Do not be afraid or
discouraged, for the LORD God, my
God, is with you. He will not fail
you or forsake[h] you until all the
work for the service of the temple
of the LORD is finished.[i] 21The divisions of the priests and Levites are
ready for all the work on the temple of God, and every willing man

28:2 b 1Ch 17:2 c Ps 99:5 Ps 132:7
28:3 d 2Sa 7:5 e 1Ch 22:8 f 1Ki 5:3 1Ch 17:4
28:4 g 1Ch 17:23,27 2Ch 6:6 h 1Sa 16:1-13 i Ge 49:10 1Ch 5:2
28:5 j 1Ch 3:1 k 1Ch 22:9 1Ch 23:1
28:6 l 2Sa 7:13 1Ch 22:9-10
28:7 m 1Ch 22:13
28:8 n Dt 6:1 o Dt 4:1
28:9 p 1Ch 29:19 q 1Sa 16:7 Ps 7:9 r Ps 40:16 Jer 29:13 s Jos 24:20 2Ch 15:2 t Ps 44:23
28:11 u Ex 25:9
28:12 v 1Ch 12:18 w 1Ch 26:20
28:13 x 1Ch 24:1
28:15 y Ex 25:31
28:16 z Ex 25:23
28:17 a Ex 27:3
28:18 b Ex 30:1-10 c Ex 25:18-22 d Ex 25:20
28:19 e 1Ki 6:38 f Ex 25:9
28:20 g Dt 31:6 1Ch 22:13 2Ch 19:11 Hag 2:4 h Dt 4:31 Jos 24:20 i 1Ki 6:14 2Ch 7:11

skilled[j] in any craft will help you
in all the work. The officials and all
the people will obey your every
command."

Gifts for Building the Temple

29 Then King David said to
the whole assembly: "My
son Solomon, the one whom God
has chosen, is young and inexperienced.[a] The task is great, because
this palatial structure is not for
man but for the LORD God. 2With all
my resources I have provided for
the temple of my God—gold[b] for
the gold work, silver for the silver,
bronze for the bronze, iron for the
iron and wood for the wood, as well
as onyx for the settings, turquoise,[a][c] stones of various colours, and all kinds of fine stone and
marble—all of these in large quantities.[d] 3Besides, in my devotion to
the temple of my God I now give
my personal treasures of gold and
silver for the temple of my God,
over and above everything I have
provided[e] for this holy temple:
4three thousand talents[b] of gold
(gold of Ophir)[f] and seven thousand talents[c] of refined silver,[g]
for the overlaying of the walls of
the buildings, 5for the gold work
and the silver work, and for all the
work to be done by the craftsmen.
Now, who is willing to consecrate
himself today to the LORD?"

6Then the leaders of families, the
officers of the tribes of Israel, the
commanders of thousands and
commanders of hundreds, and the
officials[h] in charge of the king's
work gave willingly.[i] 7They[j]
gave towards the work on the temple of God five thousand talents[d]
and ten thousand darics[e] of gold,
ten thousand talents[f] of silver,
eighteen thousand talents[g] of
bronze and a hundred thousand
talents[h] of iron. 8Any who had
precious stones[k] gave them to
the treasury of the temple of the
LORD in the custody of Jehiel the
Gershonite.[l] 9The people rejoiced
at the willing response of their
leaders, for they had given freely
and wholeheartedly[m] to the LORD.
David the king also rejoiced
greatly.

David's Prayer

10David praised the LORD in the
presence of the whole assembly,
saying,

"Praise be to you, O LORD,
God of our father Israel,
from everlasting to
everlasting.
11Yours, O LORD, is the greatness
and the power[n]
and the glory and the majesty
and the splendour,
for everything in heaven and
earth is yours.[o]
Yours, O LORD, is the kingdom;
you are exalted as head over
all.[p]
12Wealth and honour[q] come from
you;
you are the ruler[r] of all
things.
In your hands are strength and
power
to exalt and give strength to
all.
13Now, our God, we give you
thanks,
and praise your glorious name.

14"But who am I, and who are my
people, that we should be able to
give as generously as this? Everything comes from you, and we have
given you only what comes from
your hand. 15We are aliens and
strangers[s] in your sight, as were
all our forefathers. Our days on
earth are like a shadow,[t] without

28:21 j Ex 35:25-36:5
29:1 a 1Ki 3:7; 1Ch 22:5; 2Ch 13:7
29:2 b ver 7,14,16; Ezr 1:4; Ezr 6:5; Hag 2:8; c Isa 54:11; d 1Ch 22:2-5
29:3 e 2Ch 24:10; 2Ch 31:3; 2Ch 35:8
29:4 f Ge 10:29; g 1Ch 22:14
29:6 h 1Ch 27:1; 1Ch 28:1; i ver 9; Ex 25:1-8; Ex 35:20-29; Ex 36:2; 2Ch 24:10; Ezr 7:15
29:7 j Ex 25:2; Ne 7:70-71
29:8 k Ex 35:27; l 1Ch 26:21
29:9 m 1Ki 8:61; 2Co 9:7
29:11 n Ps 24:8; Ps 59:17; Ps 62:11; o Ps 89:11; p Rev 5:12-13
29:12 q 2Ch 1:12; r 2Ch 20:6; Ro 11:36
29:15 s Ps 39:12; Heb 11:13; t Job 14:2

[a]2 The meaning of the Hebrew for this word is uncertain. [b]4 That is, about 100 tons (about 100 metric tons) [c]4 That is, about 240 tons (about 240 metric tons) [d]7 That is, about 170 tons (about 170 metric tons)
[e]7 That is, about 185 pounds (about 84 kilograms)
[f]7 That is, about 340 tons (about 345 metric tons)
[g]7 That is, about 610 tons (about 620 metric tons)
[h]7 That is, about 3,400 tons (about 3,450 metric tons)

hope. 16O LORD our God, as for all this abundance that we have provided for building you a temple for your Holy Name, it comes from your hand, and all of it belongs to you. 17I know, my God, that you test the heart[u] and are pleased with integrity. All these things have I given willingly and with honest intent. And now I have seen with joy how willingly your people who are here have given to you.[v] 18O LORD, God of our fathers Abraham, Isaac and Israel, keep this desire in the hearts of your people for ever, and keep their hearts loyal to you. 19And give my son Solomon the wholehearted devotion[w] to keep your commands, requirements and decrees[x] and to do everything to build the palatial structure for which I have provided."[y]

20Then David said to the whole assembly, "Praise the LORD your God." So they all praised the LORD, the God of their fathers; they bowed low and fell prostrate before the LORD and the king.

Solomon Acknowledged as King

29:21–25pp 1Ki 1:28–53

21The next day they made sacrifices to the LORD and presented burnt offerings to him:[z] a thousand bulls, a thousand rams and a thousand male lambs, together with their drink offerings, and other sacrifices in abundance for all Israel. 22They ate and drank with great joy[a] in the presence of the LORD that day.

Then they acknowledged Solomon son of David as king a second time, anointing him before the LORD to be ruler and Zadok[b] to be priest. 23So Solomon sat on the throne[c] of the LORD as king in place of his father David. He prospered and all Israel obeyed him. 24All the officers and mighty men, as well as all of King David's sons, pledged their submission to King Solomon.

25The LORD highly exalted Solomon in the sight of all Israel and bestowed on him royal splendour[d] such as no king over Israel ever had before.[e]

The Death of David

29:26–28pp 1Ki 2:10–12

26David son of Jesse was king[f] over all Israel. 27He ruled over Israel for forty years—seven in Hebron and thirty-three in Jerusalem.[g] 28He died[h] at a good old age, having enjoyed long life, wealth and honour. His son Solomon succeeded him as king.[i]

29As for the events of King David's reign, from beginning to end, they are written in the records of Samuel the seer,[j] the records of Nathan[k] the prophet and the records of Gad[l] the seer, 30together with the details of his reign and power, and the circumstances that surrounded him and Israel and the kingdoms of all the other lands.

29:17
u Ps 139:23; Pr 15:11; Pr 17:3; Jer 11:20; Jer 17:10
v 1Ch 28:9; Ps 15:1-5

29:19
w 1Ch 28:9
x Ps 72:1
y 1Ch 22:14

29:21
z 1Ki 8:62

29:22
a 1Ch 23:1
b 1Ki 1:33-39

29:23
c 1Ki 2:12

29:25
d 2Ch 1:1,12
e 1Ki 3:13; Ecc 2:9

29:26
f 1Ch 18:14

29:27
g 2Sa 5:4-5; 1Ki 2:11; 1Ch 3:4

29:28
h Ge 15:15; Ac 13:36
i 1Ch 23:1

29:29
j 1Sa 9:9
k 2Sa 7:2
l 1Sa 22:5

2 CHRONICLES

Solomon Asks for Wisdom

1:2–13pp 1Ki 3:4–15
1:14–17pp 1Ki 10:26–29; 2Ch 9:25–28

1 Solomon son of David established[a] himself firmly over
his kingdom, for the LORD his God
was with[b] him and made him exceedingly great.[c]
2 Then Solomon spoke to all
Israel[d]—to the commanders of
thousands and commanders of
hundreds, to the judges and to all
the leaders in Israel, the heads of
families—3 and Solomon and the
whole assembly went to the high
place at Gibeon, for God's Tent of
Meeting[e] was there, which
Moses[f] the LORD's servant had
made in the desert. 4 Now David
had brought up the ark[g] of God
from Kiriath Jearim to the place he
had prepared for it, because he had
pitched a tent[h] for it in Jerusalem.
5 But the bronze altar[i] that Bezalel[j] son of Uri, the son of Hur,
had made was in Gibeon in front
of the tabernacle of the LORD; so
Solomon and the assembly enquired[k] of him there. 6 Solomon
went up to the bronze altar before
the LORD in the Tent of Meeting
and offered a thousand burnt offerings on it.
7 That night God appeared[l] to
Solomon and said to him, "Ask
for whatever you want me to give
you."
8 Solomon answered God, "You
have shown great kindness to
David my father and have made
me[m] king in his place. 9 Now, LORD
God, let your promise[n] to my
father David be confirmed, for you
have made me king over a people
who are as numerous as the dust of
the earth.[o] 10 Give me wisdom and
knowledge, that I may lead[p] this
people, for who is able to govern
this great people of yours?"
11 God said to Solomon, "Since
this is your heart's desire and you
have not asked for wealth,[q] riches
or honour, nor for the death of your
enemies, and since you have not
asked for a long life but for wisdom
and knowledge to govern my people over whom I have made you
king, 12 therefore wisdom and
knowledge will be given you. And I
will also give you wealth, riches
and honour,[r] such as no king who
was before you ever had and none
after you will have.[s]"
13 Then Solomon went to Jerusalem from the high place at
Gibeon, from before the Tent
of Meeting. And he reigned over
Israel.
14 Solomon accumulated chariots[t] and horses; he had fourteen
hundred chariots and twelve thousand horses,[a] which he kept in the
chariot cities and also with him in
Jerusalem. 15 The king made silver
and gold[u] as common in Jerusalem
as stones, and cedar as plentiful as
sycamore-fig trees in the foothills.
16 Solomon's horses were imported
from Egypt[b] and from Kue[c]—the
royal merchants purchased them
from Kue. 17 They imported a chariot[v] from Egypt for six hundred
shekels[d] of silver, and a horse
for a hundred and fifty.[e] They
also exported them to all the
kings of the Hittites and of the
Arameans.

1:1 *a* 1Ki 2:12,26; 2Ch 12:1 *b* Ge 21:22; Ge 39:2; Nu 14:43 *c* 1Ch 29:25
1:2 *d* 1Ch 9:1; 1Ch 28:1
1:3 *e* Ex 36:8 *f* Ex 40:18
1:4 *g* 2Sa 6:2; 1Ch 15:25 *h* 2Sa 6:17; 1Ch 15:1
1:5 *i* Ex 38:2 *j* Ex 31:2 *k* 1Ch 13:3
1:7 *l* 2Ch 7:12
1:8 *m* 1Ch 23:1; 1Ch 28:5
1:9 *n* 2Sa 7:25; 1Ki 8:25 *o* Ge 12:2
1:10 *p* Nu 27:17; 2Sa 5:2; Pr 8:15-16
1:11 *q* Dt 17:17
1:12 *r* 1Ch 29:12 *s* 1Ch 29:25; 2Ch 9:22; Ne 13:26
1:14 *t* 1Sa 8:11; 1Ki 4:26; 1Ki 9:19
1:15 *u* 1Ki 9:28; Isa 60:5
1:17 *v* SS 1:9

[a] *14* Or *charioteers* [b] *16* Or possibly *Muzur*, a region in Cilicia; also in verse 17
[c] *16* Probably Cilicia [d] *17* That is, about 15 pounds (about 7 kilograms)
[e] *17* That is, about 3¾ pounds (about 1.7 kilograms)

Preparations for Building the Temple

2:1–18pp 1Ki 5:1–16

2 Solomon gave orders to build a
temple[a] for the Name of the
LORD and a royal palace for himself.[b] 2He conscripted seventy
thousand men as carriers and
eighty thousand as stonecutters in
the hills and thirty-six hundred as
foremen over them.[c]
3Solomon sent this message to
Hiram[a][d] king of Tyre:

"Send me cedar logs[e] as you
did for my father David when
you sent him cedar to build a
palace to live in. 4Now I am
about to build a temple[f] for
the Name of the LORD my God
and to dedicate it to him for
burning fragrant incense[g] before him, for setting out the
consecrated bread[h] regularly,
and for making burnt offerings[i] every morning and evening and on Sabbaths[j] and
New Moons and at the ap-
pointed feasts of the LORD our
God. This is a lasting ordinance
for Israel.
5"The temple I am going to
build will be great,[k] because
our God is greater than all
other gods.[l] 6But who is able
to build a temple for him, since
the heavens, even the highest
heavens, cannot contain him?[m]
Who then am I[n] to build a temple for him, except as a place to
burn sacrifices before him?
7"Send me, therefore, a man
skilled to work in gold and silver, bronze and iron, and in
purple, crimson and blue yarn,
and experienced in the art of
engraving, to work in Judah
and Jerusalem with my skilled
craftsmen,[o] whom my father
David provided.
8"Send me also cedar, pine
and algum[b] logs from Lebanon, for I know that your men
are skilled in cutting timber
there. My men shall work with
yours 9to provide me with
plenty of timber, because the
temple I build must be large
and magnificent. 10I will give
your servants, the woodsmen
who cut the timber, twenty
thousand cors[c] of ground
wheat, twenty thousand cors
of barley, twenty thousand
baths[d] of wine and twenty
thousand baths of olive oil.[p]"

11Hiram king of Tyre replied by
letter to Solomon:

"Because the LORD loves[q]
his people, he has made you
their king."

12And Hiram added:

"Praise be to the LORD, the
God of Israel, who made
heaven and earth![r] He has
given King David a wise son,
endowed with intelligence and
discernment, who will build
a temple for the LORD and a
palace for himself.
13"I am sending you Huram-
Abi,[s] a man of great skill,
14whose mother was from
Dan[t] and whose father was
from Tyre. He is trained[u] to
work in gold and silver, bronze
and iron, stone and wood, and
with purple and blue[v] and
crimson yarn and fine linen.
He is experienced in all kinds
of engraving and can execute
any design given to him. He
will work with your craftsmen
and with those of my lord,
David your father.
15"Now let my lord send his
servants the wheat and barley
and the olive oil[w] and wine he

2:1 *a* Dt 12:5 *b* Ecc 2:4
2:2 *c* ver 18; 2Ch 10:4
2:3 *d* 2Sa 5:11 *e* 1Ch 14:1
2:4 *f* ver 1; Dt 12:5 *g* Ex 30:7 *h* Ex 25:30 *i* Ex 29:42; 2Ch 13:11 *j* Nu 28:9-10
2:5 *k* 1Ch 22:5; Ps 135:5 *l* 1Ch 16:25
2:6 *m* 1Ki 8:27; 2Ch 6:18; Jer 23:24 *n* Ex 3:11
2:7 *o* ver 13-14; Ex 35:31; 1Ch 22:16
2:10 *p* Ezr 3:7
2:11 *q* 1Ki 10:9; 2Ch 9:8
2:12 *r* Ne 9:6; Ps 8:3; Ps 33:6; Ps 102:25
2:13 *s* 1Ki 7:13
2:14 *t* Ex 31:6 *u* Ex 35:31 *v* Ex 35:35
2:15 *w* ver 10; Ezr 3:7

[a]3 Hebrew *Huram*, a variant of *Hiram*; also in verses 11 and 12 [b]8 Probably a variant of *almug*; possibly juniper [c]*10* That is, probably about 120,000 bushels (about 4,400 kilolitres) [d]*10* That is, probably about 95,000 gallons (about 440 kilolitres)

promised, [16]and we will cut all the logs from Lebanon that you need and will float them in rafts by sea down to Joppa.[x] You can then take them up to Jerusalem."

[17]Solomon took a census of all the aliens[y] who were in Israel, after the census[z] his father David had taken; and they were found to be 153,600. [18]He assigned[a] 70,000 of them to be carriers and 80,000 to be stonecutters in the hills, with 3,600 foremen over them to keep the people working.

Solomon Builds the Temple

3:1–14pp 1Ki 6:1–29

3 Then Solomon began to build[a] the temple of the LORD[b] in Jerusalem on Mount Moriah, where the LORD had appeared to his father David. It was on the threshing-floor of Araunah[a][c] the Jebusite, the place provided by David. [2]He began building on the second day of the second month in the fourth year of his reign.[d]

[3]The foundation Solomon laid for building the temple of God was sixty cubits long and twenty cubits wide[b][e] (using the cubit of the old standard). [4]The portico at the front of the temple was twenty cubits[c] long across the width of the building and twenty cubits[d] high.

He overlaid the inside with pure gold. [5]He panelled the main hall with pine and covered it with fine gold and decorated it with palm tree[f] and chain designs. [6]He adorned the temple with precious stones. And the gold he used was gold of Parvaim. [7]He overlaid the ceiling beams, door-frames, walls and doors of the temple with gold, and he carved cherubim[g] on the walls.

[8]He built the Most Holy Place,[h] its length corresponding to the width of the temple—twenty cubits long and twenty cubits wide. He overlaid the inside with six hundred talents[e] of fine gold. [9]The gold nails[i] weighed fifty shekels.[f] He also overlaid the upper parts with gold.

[10]In the Most Holy Place he made a pair[j] of sculptured cherubim and overlaid them with gold. [11]The total wing-span of the cherubim was twenty cubits. One wing of the first cherub was five cubits[g] long and touched the temple wall, while its other wing, also five cubits long, touched the wing of the other cherub. [12]Similarly one wing of the second cherub was five cubits long and touched the other temple wall, and its other wing, also five cubits long, touched the wing of the first cherub. [13]The wings of these cherubim[k] extended twenty cubits. They stood on their feet, facing the main hall.[h]

[14]He made the curtain[l] of blue, purple and crimson yarn and fine linen, with cherubim[m] worked into it.

[15]In the front of the temple he made two pillars,[n] which ⌞together⌟ were thirty-five cubits[i] long, each with a capital[o] on top measuring five cubits. [16]He made interwoven chains[j][p] and put them on top of the pillars. He also made a hundred pomegranates[q] and attached them to the chains. [17]He erected the pillars in the front of the temple, one to the south and one to the north. The one to the south he named Jakin[k] and the one to the north Boaz.[l]

2:16 x Jos 19:46; Jnh 1:3
2:17 y 1Ch 22:2; z 2Sa 24:2
2:18 a ver 2; 1Ch 22:2; 2Ch 8:8
3:1 a Ac 7:47; b Ge 28:17; c 2Sa 24:18; 1Ch 21:18
3:2 d Ezr 5:11
3:3 e Eze 41:2
3:5 f Eze 40:16
3:7 g Ge 3:24; 1Ki 6:29-35; Eze 41:18
3:8 h Ex 26:33
3:9 i Ex 26:32
3:10 j Ex 25:18
3:13 k Ex 25:18
3:14 l Ex 26:31,33; Heb 9:3; m Ge 3:24
3:15 n 1Ki 7:15; Rev 3:12; o 1Ki 7:22
3:16 p 1Ki 7:17; q 1Ki 7:20

a*1* Hebrew *Ornan*, a variant of *Araunah*
b*3* That is, about 90 feet (about 27 metres) long and 30 feet (about 9 metres) wide
c*4* That is, about 30 feet (about 9 metres); also in verses 8, 11 and 13
d*4* Some Septuagint and Syriac manuscripts; Hebrew *and a hundred and twenty*
e*8* That is, about 20 tons (about 21 metric tons)
f*9* That is, about 1¼ pounds (about 0.6 kilogram)
g*11* That is, about 7½ feet (about 2.3 metres); also in verse 15
h*13* Or *facing inward*
i*15* That is, about 52 feet (about 16 metres)
j*16* Or possibly *made chains in the inner sanctuary*; the meaning of the Hebrew for this phrase is uncertain.
k*17* *Jakin* probably means *he establishes.*
l*17* *Boaz* probably means *in him is strength.*

The Temple's Furnishings

4:2–6,10–5:1pp 1Ki 7:23–26,38–51

4 He made a bronze altar[a]
twenty cubits long, twenty cubits wide and ten cubits high.[a] 2He
made the Sea[b] of cast metal, circular in shape, measuring ten cubits
from rim to rim and five cubits[b]
high. It took a line of thirty cubits[c]
to measure round it. 3Below the
rim, figures of bulls encircled it—
ten to a cubit.[d] The bulls were cast
in two rows in one piece with the
Sea.

4The Sea stood on twelve bulls,
three facing north, three facing
west, three facing south and three
facing east.[c] The Sea rested on top
of them, and their hindquarters
were towards the centre. 5It was a
handbreadth[e] in thickness, and its
rim was like the rim of a cup, like
a lily blossom. It held three thousand baths.[f]

6He then made ten basins[d] for
washing and placed five on the
south side and five on the north. In
them the things to be used for the
burnt offerings[e] were rinsed, but
the Sea was to be used by the
priests for washing.

7He made ten gold lampstands[f]
according to the specifications[g]
for them and placed them in the
temple, five on the south side and
five on the north.

8He made ten tables[h] and placed
them in the temple, five on the
south side and five on the north. He
also made a hundred gold sprinkling bowls.[i]

9He made the courtyard[j] of the
priests, and the large court and the
doors for the court, and overlaid
the doors with bronze. 10He placed
the Sea on the south side, at the
south-east corner.

11He also made the pots and shovels and sprinkling bowls.

So Huram finished[k] the work he
had undertaken for King Solomon
in the temple of God:

12the two pillars;
the two bowl-shaped capitals
on top of the pillars;
the two sets of network decorating the two bowl-shaped
capitals on top of the pillars;
13the four hundred pomegranates for the two sets of
network (two rows of
pomegranates for each network, decorating the bowl-
shaped capitals on top of the
pillars);
14the stands[l] with their basins;
15the Sea and the twelve bulls
under it;
16the pots, shovels, meat forks
and all related articles.

All the objects that Huram-Abi[m]
made for King Solomon for the
temple of the LORD were of polished bronze. 17The king had them
cast in clay moulds in the plain of
the Jordan between Succoth[n] and
Zarethan.[g] 18All these things that
Solomon made amounted to so
much that the weight of the
bronze[o] was not determined.

19Solomon also made all the furnishings that were in God's temple:

the golden altar;
the tables[p] on which was the
bread of the Presence;
20the lampstands[q] of pure gold
with their lamps, to burn in
front of the inner sanctuary
as prescribed;
21the gold floral work and lamps
and tongs (they were solid
gold);
22the pure gold wick trimmers,
sprinkling bowls, dishes[r]
and censers;[s] and the gold
doors of the temple: the inner doors to the Most Holy

4:1 *a* Ex 20:24; Ex 27:1-2; Ex 40:6; 1Ki 8:64; 2Ki 16:14
4:2 *b* Rev 4:6; Rev 15:2
4:4 *c* Nu 2:3-25; Eze 48:30-34; Rev 21:13
4:6 *d* Ex 30:18; *e* Ne 13:5,9; Eze 40:38
4:7 *f* Ex 25:31; *g* Ex 25:40
4:8 *h* Ex 25:23; *i* Nu 4:14
4:9 *j* 1Ki 6:36; 2Ki 21:5; 2Ch 33:5
4:11 *k* 1Ki 7:14
4:14 *l* 1Ki 7:27-30
4:16 *m* 1Ki 7:13
4:17 *n* Ge 33:17
4:18 *o* 1Ki 7:23
4:19 *p* Ex 25:23,30
4:20 *q* Ex 25:31
4:22 *r* Nu 7:14; *s* Lev 10:1

a*1* That is, about 30 feet (about 9 metres) long and wide, and about 15 feet (about 4.5 metres) high
b*2* That is, about 7½ feet (about 2.3 metres)
c*2* That is, about 45 feet (about 13.5 metres)
d*3* That is, about 1½ feet (about 0.5 metre)
e*5* That is, about 3 inches (about 8 centimetres)
f*5* That is, about 14,500 gallons (about 66 kilolitres)
g*17* Hebrew *Zeredatha*, a variant of *Zarethan*

Place and the doors of the main hall.

5 When all the work Solomon had done for the temple of the LORD was finished,[a] he brought in the things his father David had dedicated[b]—the silver and gold and all the furnishings—and he placed them in the treasuries of God's temple.

The Ark Brought to the Temple

5:2–6:11pp 1Ki 8:1–21

2 Then Solomon summoned to Jerusalem the elders of Israel, all the heads of the tribes and the chiefs of the Israelite families, to bring up the ark[c] of the LORD's covenant from Zion, the City of David. 3 And all the men of Israel[d] came together to the king at the time of the festival in the seventh month.

4 When all the elders of Israel had arrived, the Levites took up the ark, 5 and they brought up the ark and the Tent of Meeting and all the sacred furnishings in it. The priests, who were Levites,[e] carried them up; 6 and King Solomon and the entire assembly of Israel that had gathered about him were before the ark, sacrificing so many sheep and cattle that they could not be recorded or counted.

7 The priests then brought the ark[f] of the LORD's covenant to its place in the inner sanctuary of the temple, the Most Holy Place, and put it beneath the wings of the cherubim. 8 The cherubim[g] spread their wings over the place of the ark and covered the ark and its carrying poles. 9 These poles were so long that their ends, extending from the ark, could be seen from in front of the inner sanctuary, but not from outside the Holy Place; and they are still there today. 10 There was nothing in the ark except[h] the two tablets[i] that Moses had placed in it at Horeb, where the LORD made a covenant with the Israelites after they came out of Egypt.

11 The priests then withdrew from the Holy Place. All the priests who were there had consecrated themselves, regardless of their divisions.[j] 12 All the Levites who were musicians[k]—Asaph, Heman, Jeduthun and their sons and relatives—stood on the east side of the altar, dressed in fine linen and playing cymbals, harps and lyres. They were accompanied by 120 priests sounding trumpets.[l] 13 The trumpeters and singers joined in unison, as with one voice, to give praise and thanks to the LORD. Accompanied by trumpets, cymbals and other instruments, they raised their voices in praise to the LORD and sang:

"He is good;
  his love endures for ever."[m]

Then the temple of the LORD was filled with a cloud, 14 and the priests could not perform[n] their service because of the cloud,[o] for the glory[p] of the LORD filled the temple of God.

6 Then Solomon said, "The LORD has said that he would dwell in a dark cloud;[a] 2 I have built a magnificent temple for you, a place for you to dwell for ever.[b]"

3 While the whole assembly of Israel was standing there, the king turned round and blessed them. 4 Then he said:

"Praise be to the LORD, the God of Israel, who with his hands has fulfilled what he promised with his mouth to my father David. For he said, 5 'Since the day I brought my people out of Egypt, I have not chosen a city in any tribe of Israel to have a temple built for my Name to be there, nor have I chosen anyone to be the leader over my people Israel. 6 But now I have chosen Jerusalem[c] for my Name[d] to be

5:1 a 1Ki 6:14 b 2Sa 8:11
5:2 c Nu 3:31; 2Sa 6:12; 1Ch 15:25
5:3 d 1Ch 9:1; 2Ch 7:8-10
5:5 e Nu 3:31; 1Ch 15:2
5:7 f Rev 11:19
5:8 g Ge 3:24
5:10 h Heb 9:4 i Ex 16:34; Dt 10:2
5:11 j 1Ch 24:1
5:12 k 1Ki 10:12; 1Ch 25:1; Ps 68:25 l 1Ch 13:8; 1Ch 15:24
5:13 m 1Ch 16:34,41; 2Ch 7:3; 2Ch 20:21; Ezr 3:11; Ps 100:5; Ps 136:1; Jer 33:11
5:14 n Ex 40:35; Rev 15:8 o Ex 19:16 p Ex 29:43; 2Ch 7:2
6:1 a Ex 19:9; 1Ki 8:12-50
6:2 b Ezr 6:12; Ezr 7:15; Ps 135:21
6:6 c Dt 12:5; Isa 14:1 d Ex 20:24; 2Ch 12:13

there, and I have chosen
David[e] to rule my people
Israel.’
7“My father David had it in
his heart[f] to build a temple for
the Name of the LORD, the God
of Israel. 8But the LORD said to
my father David, ‘Because it
was in your heart to build a
temple for my Name, you did
well to have this in your heart.
9Nevertheless, you are not the
one to build the temple, but
your son, who is your own flesh
and blood—he is the one who
will build the temple for my
Name.’
10“The LORD has kept the
promise he made. I have succeeded David my father and
now I sit on the throne of Israel, just as the LORD promised, and I have built the
temple for the Name of the
LORD, the God of Israel.
11There I have placed the ark,
in which is the covenant[g] of
the LORD that he made with the
people of Israel.”

Solomon’s Prayer of Dedication

6:12–40pp 1Ki 8:22–53
6:41–42pp Ps 132:8–10

12Then Solomon stood before the
altar of the LORD in front of the
whole assembly of Israel and
spread out his hands. 13Now he had
made a bronze platform,[h] five cubits[a] long, five cubits wide and
three cubits[b] high, and had placed
it in the centre of the outer court.
He stood on the platform and then
knelt down[i] before the whole assembly of Israel and spread out his
hands towards heaven. 14He said:

“O LORD, God of Israel, there
is no God like you[j] in heaven
or on earth—you who keep
your covenant of love[k] with
your servants who continue
wholeheartedly in your way.
15You have kept your promise
to your servant David my
father; with your mouth you
have promised[l] and with your
hand you have fulfilled it—as it
is today.
16“Now LORD, God of Israel,
keep for your servant David
my father the promises you
made to him when you said,
‘You shall never fail[m] to have a
man to sit before me on the
throne of Israel, if only your
sons are careful in all they do
to walk before me according to
my law,[n] as you have done.’
17And now, O LORD, God of Israel, let your word that you
promised your servant David
come true.
18“But will God really dwell[o]
on earth with men? The heavens,[p] even the highest heavens, cannot contain you. How
much less this temple that I
have built! 19Yet give attention
to your servant’s prayer and
his plea for mercy, O LORD my
God. Hear the cry and the
prayer that your servant is
praying in your presence.
20May your eyes[q] be open towards this temple day and
night, this place of which you
said you would put your
Name[r] there. May you hear[s]
the prayer your servant prays
towards this place. 21Hear the
supplications of your servant
and of your people Israel when
they pray towards this place.
Hear from heaven, your
dwelling-place; and when you
hear, forgive.[t]
22“When a man wrongs his
neighbour and is required to
take an oath[u] and he comes
and swears the oath before
your altar in this temple, 23then
hear from heaven and act.
Judge between your servants,
repaying[v] the guilty by bringing down on his own head what

6:6 e 1Ch 28:4
6:7 f 1Sa 10:7; 1Ch 17:2; 1Ch 28:2; Ac 7:46
6:11 g Dt 10:2; 2Ch 5:10; Ps 25:10; Ps 50:5
6:13 h Ne 8:4; i Ps 95:6
6:14 j Ex 8:10; Ex 15:11; k Dt 7:9
6:15 l 1Ch 22:10
6:16 m 2Sa 7:13,15; 1Ki 2:4; 2Ch 7:18; 2Ch 23:3; n Ps 132:12
6:18 o Rev 21:3; p 2Ch 2:6; Ps 11:4; Isa 40:22; Isa 66:1; Ac 7:49
6:20 q Ex 3:16; Ps 34:15; r Dt 12:11; s 2Ch 7:14; 2Ch 30:20
6:21 t Ps 51:1; Isa 33:24; Isa 40:2; Isa 43:25; Isa 44:22; Isa 55:7; Mic 7:18
6:22 u Ex 22:11
6:23 v Isa 3:11; Isa 65:6; Mt 16:27

a *13* That is, about 7½ feet (about 2.3 metres)
b *13* That is, about 4½ feet (about 1.4 metres)

he has done. Declare the innocent not guilty and so establish his innocence.

24 "When your people Israel have been defeated[w] by an enemy because they have sinned against you and when they turn back and confess your name, praying and making supplication before you in this temple, 25 then hear from heaven and forgive the sin of your people Israel and bring them back to the land you gave to them and their fathers.

26 "When the heavens are shut up and there is no rain[x] because your people have sinned against you, and when they pray towards this place and confess your name and turn from their sin because you have afflicted them, 27 then hear from heaven and forgive[y] the sin of your servants, your people Israel. Teach them the right way to live, and send rain on the land that you gave your people for an inheritance.

28 "When famine[z] or plague comes to the land, or blight or mildew, locusts or grasshoppers, or when enemies besiege them in any of their cities, whatever disaster or disease may come, 29 and when a prayer or plea is made by any of your people Israel—each one aware of his afflictions and pains, and spreading out his hands towards this temple— 30 then hear from heaven, your dwelling-place. Forgive,[a] and deal with each man according to all he does, since you know his heart (for you alone know the hearts of men),[b] 31 so that they will fear you[c] and walk in your ways all the time they live in the land that you gave our fathers.

32 "As for the foreigner who does not belong to your people Israel but has come[d] from a distant land because of your great name and your mighty hand[e] and your outstretched arm—when he comes and prays towards this temple, 33 then hear from heaven, your dwelling-place, and do whatever the foreigner[f] asks of you, so that all the peoples of the earth may know your name and fear you, as do your own people Israel, and may know that this house that I have built bears your Name.

34 "When your people go to war against their enemies,[g] wherever you send them, and when they pray[h] to you towards this city you have chosen and the temple I have built for your Name, 35 then hear from heaven their prayer and their plea, and uphold their cause.

36 "When they sin against you—for there is no-one who does not sin[i]—and you become angry with them and give them over to the enemy, who takes them captive[j] to a land far away or near; 37 and if they have a change of heart[k] in the land where they are held captive, and repent and plead with you in the land of their captivity and say, 'We have sinned, we have done wrong and acted wickedly'; 38 and if they turn back to you with all their heart and soul in the land of their captivity where they were taken, and pray towards the land that you gave their fathers, towards the city you have chosen and towards the temple that I have built for your Name; 39 then from heaven, your dwelling-place, hear their prayer and their pleas, and uphold their cause. And forgive your people, who have sinned against you.

40 "Now, my God, may your eyes be open and your ears

6:24 w Lev 26:17
6:26 x Lev 26:19; Dt 11:17; Dt 28:24; 2Sa 1:21; 1Ki 17:1
6:27 y ver 30,39; 2Ch 7:14
6:28 z 2Ch 20:9
6:30 a ver 27; b 1Sa 16:7; 1Ch 28:9; Ps 7:9; Ps 44:21; Pr 16:2; Pr 17:3
6:31 c Ps 103:11,13; Pr 8:13
6:32 d 2Ch 9:6; Jn 12:20; Ac 8:27; e Ex 3:19,20
6:33 f 2Ch 7:14
6:34 g Dt 28:7; h 1Ch 5:20
6:36 i Job 15:14; Ps 143:2; Ecc 7:20; Jer 17:9; Jas 3:1; 1Jn 1:8-10; j Lev 26:44
6:37 k 2Ch 7:14; 2Ch 33:12,19,23; Jer 29:13

attentive[l] to the prayers offered in this place.

41 "Now arise,[m] O LORD God,
and come to your resting place,[n]
you and the ark of your might.
May your priests,[o] O LORD God, be clothed with salvation,
may your saints rejoice in your goodness.[p]
42 O LORD God, do not reject your anointed one.
Remember the great love[q] promised to David your servant."

The Dedication of the Temple

7:1–10pp 1Ki 8:62–66

7 When Solomon finished praying, fire[a] came down from heaven and consumed the burnt offering and the sacrifices, and the glory of the LORD filled[b] the temple.[c] 2 The priests could not enter[d] the temple of the LORD because the glory[e] of the LORD filled it. 3 When all the Israelites saw the fire coming down and the glory of the LORD above the temple, they knelt on the pavement with their faces to the ground, and they worshipped and gave thanks to the LORD, saying,

"He is good;
his love endures for ever."[f]

4 Then the king and all the people offered sacrifices before the LORD. 5 And King Solomon offered a sacrifice of twenty-two thousand head of cattle and a hundred and twenty thousand sheep and goats. So the king and all the people dedicated the temple of God. 6 The priests took their positions, as did the Levites[g] with the LORD's musical instruments,[h] which King David had made for praising the LORD and which were used when he gave thanks, saying, "His love endures for ever." Opposite the Levites, the priests blew their trumpets, and all the Israelites were standing.

7 Solomon consecrated the middle part of the courtyard in front of the temple of the LORD, and there he offered burnt offerings and the fat of the fellowship offerings,[a] because the bronze altar he had made could not hold the burnt offerings, the grain offerings and the fat portions.

8 So Solomon observed the festival[i] at that time for seven days, and all Israel with him—a vast assembly, people from Lebo[b] Hamath to the Wadi of Egypt.[j] 9 On the eighth day they held an assembly, for they had celebrated the dedication of the altar for seven days and the festival[k] for seven days more. 10 On the twenty-third day of the seventh month he sent the people to their homes, joyful and glad in heart for the good things the LORD had done for David and Solomon and for his people Israel.

The LORD Appears to Solomon

7:11–22pp 1Ki 9:1–9

11 When Solomon had finished the temple of the LORD and the royal palace, and had succeeded in carrying out all he had in mind to do in the temple of the LORD and in his own palace, 12 the LORD appeared to him at night and said:

"I have heard your prayer and have chosen this place for myself[l] as a temple for sacrifices.

13 "When I shut up the heavens so that there is no rain,[m] or command locusts to devour the land or send a plague among my people, 14 if my people, who are called by my name, will humble[n] themselves and pray and seek my face[o] and turn[p] from their wicked ways, then

6:40 *l* 2Ch 7:15; Ne 1:6,11; Ps 17:1,6
6:41 *m* Isa 33:10 *n* 1Ch 28:2 *o* Ps 132:16 *p* Ps 116:12
6:42 *q* Ps 89:24,28; Isa 55:3
7:1 *a* Lev 9:24; 1Ki 18:38 *b* Ex 16:10 *c* Ps 26:8
7:2 *d* 1Ki 8:11 *e* Ex 29:43; Ex 40:35; 2Ch 5:14
7:3 *f* 1Ch 16:34; 2Ch 5:13; 2Ch 20:21
7:6 *g* 1Ch 15:16 *h* 2Ch 5:12
7:8 *i* 2Ch 30:26 *j* Ge 15:18
7:9 *k* Lev 23:36
7:12 *l* Dt 12:5
7:13 *m* 2Ch 6:26-28; Am 4:7
7:14 *n* Lev 26:41; 2Ch 6:37; Jas 4:10 *o* 1Ch 16:11 *p* Isa 55:7; Zec 1:4

[a]7 Traditionally *peace offerings* [b]8 Or *from the entrance to*

will I hear from heaven and
will forgive[q] their sin and will
heal[r] their land. 15Now my
eyes will be open and my ears
attentive to the prayers offered in this place.[s] 16I have
chosen[t] and consecrated this
temple so that my Name may
be there for ever. My eyes and
my heart will always be there.
17"As for you, if you walk before me[u] as David your father
did, and do all I command, and
observe my decrees and laws,
18I will establish your royal
throne, as I covenanted with
David your father when I said,
'You shall never fail to have a
man[v] to rule over Israel.'[w]
19"But if you[c] turn away[x]
and forsake[y] the decrees and
commands I have given you[c]
and go off to serve other gods
and worship them, 20then I will
uproot[z] Israel from my land,[a]
which I have given them, and
will reject this temple which I
have consecrated for my
Name. I will make it a byword
and an object of ridicule[b]
among all peoples. 21And
though this temple is now so
imposing, all who pass by will
be appalled and say,[c] 'Why has
the LORD done such a thing to
this land and to this temple?'
22People will answer, 'Because
they have forsaken the LORD,
the God of their fathers, who
brought them out of Egypt, and
have embraced other gods,
worshipping and serving
them—that is why he brought
all this disaster on them.'"

Solomon's Other Activities

8:1–18pp 1Ki 9:10–28

8 At the end of twenty years, during which Solomon built the
temple of the LORD and his own palace, 2Solomon rebuilt the villages
that Hiram[a] had given him, and
settled Israelites in them. 3Solomon
then went to Hamath Zobah and
captured it. 4He also built up Tadmor in the desert and all the
store cities he had built in Hamath.
5He rebuilt Upper Beth Horon[a]
and Lower Beth Horon as fortified
cities, with walls and with gates
and bars, 6as well as Baalath and all
his store cities, and all the cities for
his chariots and for his horses[b]—
whatever he desired to build
in Jerusalem, in Lebanon and
throughout all the territory that he
ruled.
7All the people left from the Hittites, Amorites, Perizzites, Hivites
and Jebusites[b] (these peoples
were not Israelites), 8that is, their
descendants remaining in the land,
whom the Israelites had not
destroyed—these Solomon conscripted[c] for his slave labour
force, as it is to this day. 9But Solomon did not make slaves of the Israelites for his work; they were his
fighting men, commanders of
his captains, and commanders
of his chariots and charioteers.
10They were also King Solomon's
chief officials—two hundred and
fifty officials supervising the men.
11Solomon brought Pharaoh's
daughter[d] up from the City of
David to the palace he had built for
her, for he said, "My wife must not
live in the palace of David king of
Israel, because the places the ark
of the LORD has entered are holy."
12On the altar[e] of the LORD that
he had built in front of the portico,
Solomon sacrificed burnt offerings
to the LORD, 13according to the
daily requirement[f] for offerings
commanded by Moses for Sabbaths,[g] New Moons and the three[h]
annual feasts—the Feast of Unleavened Bread, the Feast of
Weeks[i] and the Feast of Tabernacles. 14In keeping with the ordinance of his father David, he

7:14 q 2Ch 6:27 r 2Ch 30:20 Isa 30:26 Isa 57:18
7:15 s 2Ch 6:40
7:16 t ver 12 2Ch 6:6
7:17 u 1Ki 9:4
7:18 v 2Ch 6:16 w 2Sa 7:13 2Ch 13:5
7:19 x Dt 28:15 y Lev 26:14,33
7:20 z Dt 29:28 a 1Ki 14:15 b Dt 28:37
7:21 c Dt 29:24
8:5 a 1Ch 7:24 2Ch 14:7
8:7 b Ge 10:16
8:8 c 1Ki 4:6 1Ki 9:21
8:11 d 1Ki 3:1 1Ki 7:8
8:12 e 1Ki 8:64 2Ch 4:1 2Ch 15:8
8:13 f Ex 29:38 Nu 28:3 g Nu 28:9 h Ex 23:14 Dt 16:16 i Ex 23:16

c19 The Hebrew is plural. a2 Hebrew *Huram*, a variant of *Hiram*; also in verse 18 b6 Or *charioteers*

appointed the divisions[j] of the priests for their duties and the Levites[k] to lead the praise and to assist the priests according to each day's requirement. He also appointed the gatekeepers[l] by divisions for the various gates, because this was what David the man of God[m] had ordered.[n] [15]They did not deviate from the king's commands to the priests or to the Levites in any matter, including that of the treasuries.

[16]All Solomon's work was carried out, from the day the foundation of the temple of the LORD was laid until its completion. So the temple of the LORD was finished.

[17]Then Solomon went to Ezion Geber and Elath on the coast of Edom. [18]And Hiram sent him ships commanded by his own officers, men who knew the sea. These with Solomon's men, sailed to Ophir and brought back four hundred and fifty talents[c] of gold,[o] which they delivered to King Solomon.

The Queen of Sheba Visits Solomon

9:1–12pp 1Ki 10:1–13

9 When the queen of Sheba[a] heard of Solomon's fame, she came to Jerusalem to test him with hard questions. Arriving with a very great caravan—with camels carrying spices, large quantities of gold, and precious stones—she came to Solomon and talked with him about all she had on her mind. [2]Solomon answered all her questions; nothing was too hard for him to explain to her. [3]When the queen of Sheba saw the wisdom of Solomon,[b] as well as the palace he had built, [4]the food on his table, the seating of his officials, the attending servants in their robes, the cupbearers in their robes and the burnt offerings he made at[a] the temple of the LORD, she was overwhelmed.

[5]She said to the king, "The report I heard in my own country about your achievements and your wisdom is true. [6]But I did not believe what they said until I came[c] and saw with my own eyes. Indeed, not even half the greatness of your wisdom was told me; you have far exceeded the report I heard. [7]How happy your men must be! How happy your officials, who continually stand before you and hear your wisdom! [8]Praise be to the LORD your God, who has delighted in you and placed you on his throne[d] as king to rule for the LORD your God. Because of the love of your God for Israel and his desire to uphold them for ever, he has made you king[e] over them, to maintain justice and righteousness."

[9]Then she gave the king 120 talents[b] of gold,[f] large quantities of spices, and precious stones. There had never been such spices as those the queen of Sheba gave to King Solomon.

[10](The men of Hiram and the men of Solomon brought gold from Ophir;[g] they also brought algum-wood[c] and precious stones. [11]The king used the algum-wood to make steps for the temple of the LORD and for the royal palace, and to make harps and lyres for the musicians. Nothing like them had ever been seen in Judah.)

[12]King Solomon gave the queen of Sheba all she desired and asked for; he gave her more than she had brought to him. Then she left and returned with her retinue to her own country.

Solomon's Splendour

9:13–28pp 1Ki 10:14–29; 2Ch 1:14–17

[13]The weight of the gold that Solomon received yearly was 666 talents,[d] [14]not including the revenues brought in by merchants and

8:14
j 1Ch 24:1
k 1Ch 25:1
l 1Ch 9:17; 1Ch 26:1
m Ne 12:24,36
n 1Ch 23:6; Ne 12:45

8:18
o 2Ch 9:9

9:1
a Ge 10:7; Eze 23:42; Mt 12:42; Lk 11:31

9:3
b 1Ki 5:12

9:6
c 2Ch 6:32

9:8
d 1Ki 2:12; 1Ch 17:14; 1Ch 28:5; 1Ch 29:23; 2Ch 13:8
e 2Ch 2:11

9:9
f 2Ch 8:18

9:10
g 2Ch 8:18

c*18* That is, about 17 tons (about 16 metric tons)
a*4* Or *the ascent by which he went up to*
b*9* That is, about 4 tons (about 4 metric tons)
c*10* Probably a variant of *almug-wood*
d*13* That is, about 23 tons (about 23 metric tons)

traders. Also all the kings of Arabia[h] and the governors of the land brought gold and silver to Solomon.
15King Solomon made two hundred large shields of hammered gold; six hundred bekas[e] of hammered gold went into each shield. 16He also made three hundred small shields[i] of hammered gold, with three hundred bekas[f] of gold in each shield. The king put them in the Palace of the Forest of Lebanon.[j]

17Then the king made a great throne inlaid with ivory[k] and overlaid with pure gold. 18The throne had six steps, and a footstool of gold was attached to it. On both sides of the seat were armrests, with a lion standing beside each of them. 19Twelve lions stood on the six steps, one at either end of each step. Nothing like it had ever been made for any other kingdom. 20All King Solomon's goblets were gold, and all the household articles in the Palace of the Forest of Lebanon were pure gold. Nothing was made of silver, because silver was considered of little value in Solomon's day. 21The king had a fleet of trading ships[g] manned by Hiram's[h] men. Once every three years it returned, carrying gold, silver and ivory, and apes and baboons.

22King Solomon was greater in riches and wisdom than all the other kings of the earth.[l] 23All the kings[m] of the earth sought audience with Solomon to hear the wisdom God had put in his heart. 24Year after year, everyone who came brought a gift[n]—articles of silver and gold, and robes, weapons and spices, and horses and mules.

25Solomon had four thousand stalls for horses and chariots,[o] and twelve thousand horses,[i] which he kept in the chariot cities and also with him in Jerusalem. 26He ruled[p] over all the kings from the River[j][q] to the land of the Philistines, as far as the border of Egypt.[r] 27The king made silver as common in Jerusalem as stones, and cedar as plentiful as sycamore-fig trees in the foothills. 28Solomon's horses were imported from Egypt[k] and from all other countries.

9:14 *h* 2Ch 17:11; Isa 21:13; Jer 25:24; Eze 27:21; Eze 30:5
9:16 *i* 2Ch 12:9; *j* 1Ki 7:2
9:17 *k* 1Ki 22:39
9:22 *l* 1Ki 3:13; 2Ch 1:12
9:23 *m* 1Ki 4:34
9:24 *n* 2Ch 32:23; Ps 45:12; Ps 68:29; Ps 72:10; Isa 18:7
9:25 *o* 1Sa 8:11; 1Ki 4:26
9:26 *p* 1Ki 4:21; *q* Ps 72:8-9; *r* Ge 15:18-21
9:29 *s* 2Sa 7:2; 1Ch 29:29; *t* 1Ki 11:29; *u* 2Ch 10:2
9:31 *v* 1Ki 2:10
10:2 *a* 2Ch 9:29; *b* 1Ki 11:40
10:3 *c* 1Ch 9:1
10:4 *d* 2Ch 2:2
10:6 *e* Job 8:8-9; Job 12:12; Job 15:10; Job 32:7

Solomon's Death

9:29–31pp 1Ki 11:41–43

29As for the other events of Solomon's reign, from beginning to end, are they not written in the records of Nathan[s] the prophet, in the prophecy of Ahijah[t] the Shilonite and in the visions of Iddo the seer concerning Jeroboam[u] son of Nebat? 30Solomon reigned in Jerusalem over all Israel for forty years. 31Then he rested with his fathers and was buried in the city of David[v] his father. And Rehoboam his son succeeded him as king.

Israel Rebels Against Rehoboam

10:1–11:4pp 1Ki 12:1–24

10 Rehoboam went to Shechem, for all the Israelites had gone there to make him king. 2When Jeroboam[a] son of Nebat heard this (he was in Egypt, where he had fled[b] from King Solomon), he returned from Egypt. 3So they sent for Jeroboam, and he and all Israel[c] went to Rehoboam and said to him: 4"Your father put a heavy yoke on us,[d] but now lighten the harsh labour and the heavy yoke he put on us, and we will serve you."

5Rehoboam answered, "Come back to me in three days." So the people went away.

6Then King Rehoboam consulted the elders[e] who had served his father Solomon during his lifetime. "How would you advise me to answer these people?" he asked.

[e]15 That is, about 7½ pounds (about 3.5 kilograms)
[f]16 That is, about 3¾ pounds (about 1.7 kilograms)
[g]21 Hebrew *of ships that could go to Tarshish*
[h]21 Hebrew *Huram*, a variant of *Hiram*
[i]25 Or *charioteers* [j]26 That is, the Euphrates
[k]28 Or possibly *Muzur*, a region in Cilicia

7They replied, "If you will be
kind to these people and please
them and give them a favourable
answer,[f] they will always be your
servants."
8But Rehoboam rejected[g] the
advice the elders[h] gave him and
consulted the young men who had
grown up with him and were serving him. 9He asked them, "What is
your advice? How should we answer these people who say to me,
'Lighten the yoke your father put
on us'?"
10The young men who had grown
up with him replied, "Tell the people who have said to you, 'Your
father put a heavy yoke on us, but
make our yoke lighter' – tell them,
'My little finger is thicker than my
father's waist. 11My father laid on
you a heavy yoke; I will make it
even heavier. My father scourged
you with whips; I will scourge you
with scorpions.'"
12Three days later Jeroboam and
all the people returned to Rehoboam, as the king had said, "Come
back to me in three days." 13The
king answered them harshly. Rejecting the advice of the elders,
14he followed the advice of the
young men and said, "My father
made your yoke heavy; I will make
it even heavier. My father
scourged you with whips; I will
scourge you with scorpions." 15So
the king did not listen to the people,
for this turn of events was from
God,[i] to fulfil the word that the
LORD had spoken to Jeroboam son
of Nebat through Ahijah the Shilonite.[j]
16When all Israel[k] saw that the
king refused to listen to them, they
answered the king:

"What share do we have in
David,[l]
what part in Jesse's son?
To your tents, O Israel!
Look after your own house,
O David!"

So all the Israelites went home.

10:7 f Pr 15:1
10:8 g 2Sa 17:14 h Pr 13:20
10:15 i 2Ch 11:4 2Ch 25:16-20 j 1Ki 11:29
10:16 k 1Ch 9:1 l ver 19 2Sa 20:1
10:18 m 1Ki 5:14
11:1 a 1Ki 12:21
11:2 b 2Ch 12:5-7,15
11:4 c 2Ch 28:8-11
11:14 d Nu 35:2-5

17But as for the Israelites who were
living in the towns of Judah, Rehoboam still ruled over them.
18King Rehoboam sent out Adoniram,[a][m] who was in charge of
forced labour, but the Israelites
stoned him to death. King Rehoboam, however, managed to get
into his chariot and escape to Jerusalem. 19So Israel has been in rebellion against the house of David to
this day.

11 When Rehoboam arrived in
Jerusalem,[a] he mustered
the house of Judah and Benjamin –
a hundred and eighty thousand
fighting men – to make war against
Israel and to regain the kingdom
for Rehoboam.
2But this word of the LORD came
to Shemaiah[b] the man of God:
3"Say to Rehoboam son of Solomon
king of Judah and to all the Israelites in Judah and Benjamin, 4'This
is what the LORD says: Do not go up
to fight against your brothers.[c] Go
home, every one of you, for this is
my doing.'" So they obeyed the
words of the LORD and turned back
from marching against Jeroboam.

Rehoboam Fortifies Judah

5Rehoboam lived in Jerusalem
and built up towns for defence in
Judah: 6Bethlehem, Etam, Tekoa,
7Beth Zur, Soco, Adullam, 8Gath,
Mareshah, Ziph, 9Adoraim, Lachish, Azekah, 10Zorah, Aijalon and
Hebron. These were fortified cities
in Judah and Benjamin. 11He
strengthened their defences and
put commanders in them, with supplies of food, olive oil and wine.
12He put shields and spears in all
the cities, and made them very
strong. So Judah and Benjamin
were his.
13The priests and Levites from
all their districts throughout Israel
sided with him. 14The Levites[d]
even abandoned their pasture-

[a]18 Hebrew *Hadoram*, a variant of *Adoniram*

lands and property,[e] and came to
Judah and Jerusalem because Jeroboam and his sons had rejected
them as priests of the LORD. 15And
he appointed[f] his own priests[g] for
the high places and for the goat[h]
and calf[i] idols he had made.
16Those from every tribe of Israel[j]
who set their hearts on seeking the
LORD, the God of Israel, followed
the Levites to Jerusalem to offer
sacrifices to the LORD, the God of
their fathers. 17They strengthened[k] the kingdom of Judah and
supported Rehoboam son of Solomon for three years, walking in the
ways of David and Solomon during
this time.

Rehoboam's Family

18Rehoboam married Mahalath,
who was the daughter of David's
son Jerimoth and of Abihail, the
daughter of Jesse's son Eliab. 19She
bore him sons: Jeush, Shemariah
and Zaham. 20Then he married
Maacah[l] daughter of Absalom,
who bore him Abijah,[m] Attai, Ziza
and Shelomith. 21Rehoboam loved
Maacah daughter of Absalom more
than any of his other wives and concubines. In all he had eighteen
wives[n] and sixty concubines,
twenty-eight sons and sixty daughters.
22Rehoboam appointed Abijah[o]
son of Maacah to be the chief
prince among his brothers, in order
to make him king. 23He acted
wisely, dispersing some of his sons
throughout the districts of Judah
and Benjamin, and to all the fortified cities. He gave them abundant
provisions and took many wives for
them.

Shishak Attacks Jerusalem

12:9–16pp 1Ki 14:21, 25–31

12 After Rehoboam's position
as king was established[a]
and he had become strong,[b] he and
all Israel[a] with him abandoned the
law of the LORD. 2Because they had
been unfaithful[c] to the LORD, Shishak[d] king of Egypt attacked Jerusalem in the fifth year of King
Rehoboam. 3With twelve hundred
chariots and sixty thousand horsemen and the innumerable troops of
Libyans, Sukkites and Cushites[b][e]
that came with him from Egypt, 4he
captured the fortified cities[f] of
Judah and came as far as Jerusalem.
5Then the prophet Shemaiah[g]
came to Rehoboam and to the leaders of Judah who had assembled in
Jerusalem for fear of Shishak, and
he said to them, "This is what the
LORD says: 'You have abandoned
me; therefore I now abandon[h] you
to Shishak.'"
6The leaders of Israel and the
king humbled themselves and said,
"The LORD is just."[i]
7When the LORD saw that they
humbled themselves, this word of
the LORD came to Shemaiah: "Since
they have humbled themselves, I
will not destroy them but will soon
give them deliverance.[j] My wrath
will not be poured out on Jerusalem
through Shishak. 8They will, however, become subject[k] to him, so
that they may learn the difference
between serving me and serving
the kings of other lands."
9When Shishak king of Egypt attacked Jerusalem, he carried off
the treasures of the temple of the
LORD and the treasures of the royal
palace. He took everything, including the gold shields[l] that Solomon
had made. 10So King Rehoboam
made bronze shields to replace
them and assigned these to the
commanders of the guard on duty
at the entrance to the royal palace.
11Whenever the king went to the
LORD's temple, the guards went
with him, bearing the shields, and
afterwards they returned them to
the guardroom.
12Because Rehoboam humbled

11:14 e 2Ch 13:9
11:15 f 1Ki 13:33 g 1Ki 12:31 h Lev 17:7 i 1Ki 12:28 2Ch 13:8
11:16 j 2Ch 15:9
11:17 k 2Ch 12:1
11:20 l 1Ki 15:2 m 2Ch 13:2
11:21 n Dt 17:17
11:22 o Dt 21:15-17
12:1 a ver 13 b 2Ch 11:17
12:2 c 1Ki 14:22-24 d 1Ki 11:40
12:3 e 2Ch 16:8 Na 3:9
12:4 f 2Ch 11:10
12:5 g 2Ch 11:2 h Dt 28:15 2Ch 15:2
12:6 i Ex 9:27 Da 9:14
12:7 j 1Ki 21:29 Ps 78:38
12:8 k Dt 28:48
12:9 l 2Ch 9:16

a*1* That is, Judah, as frequently in 2 Chronicles
b*3* That is, people from the upper Nile region

himself, the LORD's anger turned
from him, and he was not totally destroyed. Indeed, there was some
good[m] in Judah.
13King Rehoboam established
himself firmly in Jerusalem and
continued as king. He was forty-
one years old when he became
king, and he reigned for seventeen
years in Jerusalem, the city the
LORD had chosen out of all the
tribes of Israel in which to put his
Name.[n] His mother's name was
Naamah; she was an Ammonite.
14He did evil because he had not set
his heart on seeking the LORD.
15As for the events of Rehoboam's reign, from beginning to
end, are they not written in the
records of Shemaiah[o] the prophet
and of Iddo the seer that deal with
genealogies? There was continual
warfare between Rehoboam and
Jeroboam. 16Rehoboam rested with
his fathers and was buried in the
City of David. And Abijah[p] his son
succeeded him as king.

Abijah King of Judah

13:1–2,22–14:1pp 1Ki 15:1–2,6–8

13 In the eighteenth year of
the reign of Jeroboam, Abijah became king of Judah, 2and he
reigned in Jerusalem for three
years. His mother's name was Maacah,[a] a daughter[b] of Uriel of Gibeah.
There was war between Abijah[a]
and Jeroboam.[b] 3Abijah went into
battle with a force of four hundred
thousand able fighting men, and
Jeroboam drew up a battle line
against him with eight hundred
thousand able troops.
4Abijah stood on Mount Zemaraim,[c] in the hill country of Ephraim, and said, "Jeroboam and all
Israel,[d] listen to me! 5Don't you
know that the LORD, the God of Israel, has given the kingship of Israel to David and his descendants
for ever[e] by a covenant of salt?[f]
6Yet Jeroboam son of Nebat, an
official of Solomon son of David, rebelled[g] against his master. 7Some
worthless scoundrels[h] gathered
around him and opposed Rehoboam son of Solomon when he was
young and indecisive and not
strong enough to resist them.
8"And now you plan to resist the
kingdom of the LORD, which is in
the hands of David's descendants.
You are indeed a vast army and
have with you the golden calves[i]
that Jeroboam made to be your
gods. 9But didn't you drive out the
priests of the LORD,[j] the sons of
Aaron, and the Levites, and make
priests of your own as the peoples
of other lands do? Whoever comes
to consecrate himself with a young
bull[k] and seven rams may become
a priest of what are not gods.[l]
10"As for us, the LORD is our God,
and we have not forsaken him. The
priests who serve the LORD are
sons of Aaron, and the Levites assist them. 11Every morning and
evening[m] they present burnt offerings and fragrant incense to the
LORD. They set out the bread on the
ceremonially clean table[n] and
light the lamps on the gold lampstand every evening. We are observing the requirements of the
LORD our God. But you have forsaken him. 12God is with us; he is
our leader. His priests with their
trumpets will sound the battle cry
against you.[o] Men of Israel, do not
fight against the LORD,[p] the God
of your fathers, for you will not
succeed."
13Now Jeroboam had sent troops
round to the rear, so that while he
was in front of Judah the ambush[q]
was behind them. 14Judah turned
and saw that they were being attacked at both front and rear. Then
they cried out[r] to the LORD. The
priests blew their trumpets 15and
the men of Judah raised the battle

12:12 m 1Ki 14:13; 2Ch 19:3
12:13 n Dt 12:5; 2Ch 6:6
12:15 o 2Ch 9:29; 2Ch 11:2
12:16 p 2Ch 11:20
13:2 a 2Ch 11:20; b 1Ki 15:6
13:4 c Jos 18:22; d 1Ch 11:1
13:5 e 2Sa 7:13; f Lev 2:13; Nu 18:19
13:6 g 1Ki 11:26
13:7 h Jdg 9:4
13:8 i 1Ki 12:28; 2Ch 11:15
13:9 j 2Ch 11:14-15; k Ex 29:35-36; l Jer 2:11
13:11 m Ex 29:39; 2Ch 2:4; n Lev 24:5-9
13:12 o Nu 10:8-9; p Ac 5:39
13:13 q Jos 8:9
13:14 r 2Ch 14:11

[a]2 Most Septuagint manuscripts and Syriac (see also 2 Chron. 11:20 and 1 Kings 15:2); Hebrew *Micaiah* [b]2 Or *granddaughter*

cry. At the sound of their battle
cry, God routed Jeroboam and all
Israel[s] before Abijah and Judah.
16 The Israelites fled before Judah,
and God delivered[t] them into their
hands. 17 Abijah and his men inflicted heavy losses on them, so
that there were five hundred thousand casualties among Israel's able
men. 18 The men of Israel were subdued on that occasion, and the men
of Judah were victorious because
they relied[u] on the LORD, the God
of their fathers.
19 Abijah pursued Jeroboam and
took from him the towns of Bethel,
Jeshanah and Ephron, with their
surrounding villages. 20 Jeroboam
did not regain power during the
time of Abijah. And the LORD
struck him down and he died.
21 But Abijah grew in strength.
He married fourteen wives and had
twenty-two sons and sixteen
daughters.
22 The other events of Abijah's
reign, what he did and what he said,
are written in the annotations of
the prophet Iddo.

14 And Abijah rested with his
fathers and was buried in
the City of David. Asa his son succeeded him as king, and in his days
the country was at peace for ten
years.

Asa King of Judah

14:2–3pp 1Ki 15:11–12

2 Asa did what was good and right
in the eyes of the LORD his God. 3 He
removed the foreign altars and the
high places, smashed the sacred
stones and cut down the Asherah
poles.[a][a] 4 He commanded Judah to
seek the LORD, the God of their fathers, and to obey his laws and
commands. 5 He removed the high
places and incense altars[b] in every
town in Judah, and the kingdom
was at peace under him. 6 He built
up the fortified cities of Judah,
since the land was at peace. No-one
was at war with him during those
years, for the LORD gave him rest.[c]
7 "Let us build up these towns," he
said to Judah, "and put walls round
them, with towers, gates and bars.
The land is still ours, because we
have sought the LORD our God; we
sought him and he has given us rest
on every side." So they built and
prospered.
8 Asa had an army of three hundred thousand men from Judah,
equipped with large shields and
with spears, and two hundred and
eighty thousand from Benjamin,
armed with small shields and with
bows. All these were brave fighting
men.
9 Zerah the Cushite[d] marched out
against them with a vast army[b]
and three hundred chariots, and
came as far as Mareshah.[e] 10 Asa
went out to meet him, and they took
up battle positions in the Valley of
Zephathah near Mareshah.
11 Then Asa called[f] to the LORD
his God and said, "LORD, there is
no-one like you to help the powerless against the mighty. Help us,
O LORD our God, for we rely[g] on
you, and in your name[h] we have
come against this vast army.
O LORD, you are our God; do not let
man prevail[i] against you."
12 The LORD struck down[j] the
Cushites before Asa and Judah.
The Cushites fled, 13 and Asa and
his army pursued them as far as
Gerar.[k] Such a great number of
Cushites fell that they could not recover; they were crushed before
the LORD and his forces. The men of
Judah carried off a large amount of
plunder. 14 They destroyed all the
villages around Gerar, for the terror[l] of the LORD had fallen upon
them. They plundered all these villages, since there was much booty
there. 15 They also attacked the
camps of the herdsmen and carried
off droves of sheep and goats and

a3 That is, symbols of the goddess Asherah; here and elsewhere in 2 Chronicles b9 Hebrew *with an army of a thousand thousands* or *with an army of thousands upon thousands*

13:15 s 2Ch 14:12
13:16 t 2Ch 16:8
13:18 u 1Ch 5:20; 2Ch 14:11; Ps 22:5
14:3 a Ex 34:13; Dt 7:5; 1Ki 15:12-14
14:5 b 2Ch 34:4,7
14:6 c 1Ch 22:9; 2Ch 15:15
14:9 d 2Ch 12:3; 2Ch 16:8; e 2Ch 11:8
14:11 f 2Ch 13:14; g 2Ch 13:18; h 1Sa 17:45; i 1Sa 14:6; Ps 9:19
14:12 j 2Ch 13:15
14:13 k Ge 10:19
14:14 l Ge 35:5; 2Ch 17:10

camels. Then they returned to
Jerusalem.

Asa's Reform

15:16–19pp 1Ki 15:13–16

15 The Spirit of God came
upon[a] Azariah son of
Oded. 2He went out to meet Asa and
said to him, "Listen to me, Asa and
all Judah and Benjamin. The LORD
is with you[b] when you are with
him.[c] If you seek[d] him, he will be
found by you, but if you forsake
him, he will forsake you.[e] 3For a
long time Israel was without the
true God, without a priest to
teach[f] and without the law.[g] 4But
in their distress they turned to the
LORD, the God of Israel, and sought
him,[h] and he was found by them.
5In those days it was not safe to
travel about,[i] for all the inhabitants of the lands were in great
turmoil. 6One nation was being
crushed by another and one city by
another,[j] because God was troubling them with every kind of distress. 7But as for you, be strong[k]
and do not give up, for your work
will be rewarded."[l]
8When Asa heard these words
and the prophecy of Azariah son
of[a] Oded the prophet, he took courage. He removed the detestable
idols from the whole land of Judah
and Benjamin and from the towns
he had captured[m] in the hills of
Ephraim. He repaired the altar[n] of
the LORD that was in front of the
portico of the LORD's temple.
9Then he assembled all Judah
and Benjamin and the people from
Ephraim, Manasseh and Simeon
who had settled among them, for
large numbers[o] had come over to
him from Israel when they saw that
the LORD his God was with him.
10They assembled at Jerusalem
in the third month of the fifteenth
year of Asa's reign. 11At that time
they sacrificed to the LORD seven
hundred head of cattle and seven
thousand sheep and goats from the
plunder[p] they had brought back.
12They entered into a covenant[q] to
seek the LORD,[r] the God of their fathers, with all their heart and soul.
13All who would not seek the LORD,
the God of Israel, were to be put to
death,[s] whether small or great,
man or woman. 14They took an oath
to the LORD with loud acclamation,
with shouting and with trumpets
and horns. 15All Judah rejoiced
about the oath because they had
sworn it wholeheartedly. They
sought God[t] eagerly, and he was
found by them. So the LORD gave
them rest[u] on every side.
16King Asa also deposed his
grandmother Maacah from her position as queen mother, because
she had made a repulsive Asherah
pole.[v] Asa cut the pole down, broke
it up and burned it in the Kidron
Valley. 17Although he did not remove the high places from Israel,
Asa's heart was fully committed ⌞to
the LORD⌟ all his life. 18He brought
into the temple of God the silver
and gold and the articles that he
and his father had dedicated.
19There was no more war until
the thirty-fifth year of Asa's reign.

Asa's Last Years

16:1–6pp 1Ki 15:17–22
16:11–17:1pp 1Ki 15:23–24

16 In the thirty-sixth year of
Asa's reign Baasha[a] king
of Israel went up against Judah and
fortified Ramah to prevent anyone
from leaving or entering the territory of Asa king of Judah.
2Asa then took the silver and gold
out of the treasuries of the LORD's
temple and of his own palace and
sent it to Ben-Hadad king of Aram,
who was ruling in Damascus. 3"Let
there be a treaty[b] between me and
you," he said, "as there was between my father and your father.
See, I am sending you silver and
gold. Now break your treaty with

15:1
a Nu 11:25,26; Nu 24:2; 2Ch 20:14; 2Ch 24:20
15:2
b ver 4,15; 2Ch 20:17
c Jas 4:8
d Jer 29:13
e 1Ch 28:9; 2Ch 24:20
15:3
f Lev 10:11
g 2Ch 17:9; La 2:9
15:4
h Dt 4:29
15:5
i Jdg 5:6
15:6
j Mt 24:7
15:7
k Jos 1:7,9
l Ps 58:11
15:8
m 2Ch 13:19
n 2Ch 8:12
15:9
o 2Ch 11:16-17
15:11
p 2Ch 14:13
15:12
q 2Ki 11:17; 2Ch 23:16; 2Ch 34:31
r 1Ch 16:11
15:13
s Ex 22:20; Dt 13:9-16
15:15
t Dt 4:29
u 1Ch 22:9; 2Ch 14:7
15:16
v Ex 34:13; 2Ch 14:2-5
16:1
a Jer 41:9
16:3
b 2Ch 20:35

[a]8 Vulgate and Syriac (see also Septuagint and verse 1); Hebrew does not have *Azariah son of.*

Baasha king of Israel so that he will withdraw from me."

4Ben-Hadad agreed with King Asa and sent the commanders of his forces against the towns of Israel. They conquered Ijon, Dan, Abel Maim[a] and all the store cities of Naphtali. 5When Baasha heard this, he stopped building Ramah and abandoned his work. 6Then King Asa brought all the men of Judah, and they carried away from Ramah the stones and timber Baasha had been using. With them he built up Geba and Mizpah.

7At that time Hanani[c] the seer came to Asa king of Judah and said to him: "Because you relied on the king of Aram and not on the LORD your God, the army of the king of Aram has escaped from your hand. 8Were not the Cushites[b][d] and Libyans a mighty army with great numbers of chariots and horsemen[c]? Yet when you relied on the LORD, he delivered[e] them into your hand. 9For the eyes[f] of the LORD range throughout the earth to strengthen those whose hearts are fully committed to him. You have done a foolish[g] thing, and from now on you will be at war."

10Asa was angry with the seer because of this; he was so enraged that he put him in prison. At the same time Asa brutally oppressed some of the people.

11The events of Asa's reign, from beginning to end, are written in the book of the kings of Judah and Israel. 12In the thirty-ninth year of his reign Asa was afflicted with a disease in his feet. Though his disease was severe, even in his illness he did not seek help from the LORD,[h] but only from the physicians. 13Then in the forty-first year of his reign Asa died and rested with his fathers. 14They buried him in the tomb that he had cut out for himself in the City of David. They laid him on a bier covered with spices and various blended perfumes,[i] and they made a huge fire[j] in his honour.

Jehoshaphat King of Judah

17 Jehoshaphat his son succeeded him as king and strengthened himself against Israel. 2He stationed troops in all the fortified cities of Judah and put garrisons in Judah and in the towns of Ephraim that his father Asa had captured.[a]

3The LORD was with Jehoshaphat because in his early years he walked in the ways that his father David[b] had followed. He did not consult the Baals 4but sought[c] the God of his father and followed his commands rather than the practices of Israel. 5The LORD established the kingdom under his control; and all Judah brought gifts[d] to Jehoshaphat, so that he had great wealth and honour.[e] 6His heart was devoted[f] to the ways of the LORD; furthermore, he removed the high places[g] and the Asherah poles[h] from Judah.[i]

7In the third year of his reign he sent his officials Ben-Hail, Obadiah, Zechariah, Nethanel and Micaiah to teach[j] in the towns of Judah. 8With them were certain Levites[k]—Shemaiah, Nethaniah, Zebadiah, Asahel, Shemiramoth, Jehonathan, Adonijah, Tobijah and Tob-Adonijah—and the priests Elishama and Jehoram. 9They taught throughout Judah, taking with them the Book of the Law[l] of the LORD; they went round to all the towns of Judah and taught the people.

10The fear[m] of the LORD fell on all the kingdoms of the lands surrounding Judah, so that they did not make war with Jehoshaphat. 11Some Philistines brought Jehoshaphat gifts and silver as tribute, and the Arabs[n] brought him

16:7
c 1Ki 16:1
16:8
d 2Ch 12:3; 2Ch 14:9
e 2Ch 13:16
16:9
f Pr 15:3; Jer 16:17; Zec 4:10
g 1Sa 13:13
16:12
h Jer 17:5-6
16:14
i Ge 50:2; Jn 19:39-40
j 2Ch 21:19; Jer 34:5
17:2
a 2Ch 15:8
17:3
b 1Ki 22:43
17:4
c 1Ki 12:28; 2Ch 22:9
17:5
d 1Sa 10:27
e 2Ch 18:1
17:6
f 1Ki 8:61; 2Ch 15:17
g 1Ki 15:14; 2Ch 19:3; 2Ch 20:33
h Ex 34:13
i 2Ch 21:12
17:7
j Lev 10:11; Dt 6:4-9; 2Ch 15:3; 2Ch 35:3
17:8
k 2Ch 19:8; Ne 8:7-8
17:9
l Dt 6:4-9; Dt 28:61
17:10
m Ge 35:5; Dt 2:25; 2Ch 14:14
17:11
n 2Ch 9:14; 2Ch 26:8

a4 Also known as *Abel Beth Maacah*
b8 That is, people from the upper Nile region
c8 Or *charioteers*

flocks:[o] seven thousand seven hundred rams and seven thousand seven hundred goats.

12Jehoshaphat became more and more powerful; he built forts and store cities in Judah 13and had large supplies in the towns of Judah. He also kept experienced fighting men in Jerusalem. 14Their enrolment[p] by families was as follows:

From Judah, commanders of units of 1,000:
Adnah the commander, with 300,000 fighting men;
15next, Jehohanan the commander, with 280,000;
16next, Amasiah son of Zicri, who volunteered[q] himself for the service of the LORD, with 200,000.
17From Benjamin:[r]
Eliada, a valiant soldier, with 200,000 men armed with bows and shields;
18next, Jehozabad, with 180,000 men armed for battle.

19These were the men who served the king, besides those he stationed in the fortified cities[s] throughout Judah.[t]

Micaiah Prophesies Against Ahab

18:1–27pp 1Ki 22:1–28

18 Now Jehoshaphat had great wealth and honour,[a] and he allied[b] himself with Ahab[c] by marriage. 2Some years later he went down to visit Ahab in Samaria. Ahab slaughtered many sheep and cattle for him and the people with him and urged him to attack Ramoth Gilead. 3Ahab king of Israel asked Jehoshaphat king of Judah, "Will you go with me against Ramoth Gilead?"

Jehoshaphat replied, "I am as you are, and my people as your people; we will join you in the war." 4But Jehoshaphat also said to the king of Israel, "First seek the counsel of the LORD."

5So the king of Israel brought together the prophets—four hundred men—and asked them, "Shall we go to war against Ramoth Gilead, or shall I refrain?"

"Go," they answered, "for God will give it into the king's hand."

6But Jehoshaphat asked, "Is there not a prophet of the LORD here whom we can enquire of?"

7The king of Israel answered Jehoshaphat, "There is still one man through whom we can enquire of the LORD, but I hate him because he never prophesies anything good about me, but always bad. He is Micaiah son of Imlah."

"The king should not say that," Jehoshaphat replied.

8So the king of Israel called one of his officials and said, "Bring Micaiah son of Imlah at once."

9Dressed in their royal robes, the king of Israel and Jehoshaphat king of Judah were sitting on their thrones at the threshing-floor by the entrance to the gate of Samaria, with all the prophets prophesying before them. 10Now Zedekiah son of Kenaanah had made iron horns, and he declared, "This is what the LORD says: 'With these you will gore the Arameans until they are destroyed.' "

11All the other prophets were prophesying the same thing. "Attack Ramoth Gilead[d] and be victorious," they said, "for the LORD will give it into the king's hand."

12The messenger who had gone to summon Micaiah said to him, "Look, as one man the other prophets are predicting success for the king. Let your word agree with theirs, and speak favourably."

13But Micaiah said, "As surely as the LORD lives, I can tell him only what my God says."[e]

14When he arrived, the king asked him, "Micaiah, shall we go to war against Ramoth Gilead, or shall I refrain?"

17:11 o 2Ch 21:16
17:14 p 2Sa 24:2
17:16 q Jdg 5:9; 1Ch 29:9
17:17 r Nu 1:36
17:19 s 2Ch 11:10; t 2Ch 25:5
18:1 a 2Ch 17:5; b 2Ch 19:1-3; 2Ch 22:3; c 2Ch 21:6
18:11 d 2Ch 22:5
18:13 e Nu 22:18,20, 35

"Attack and be victorious," he
answered, "for they will be given
into your hand."
15The king said to him, "How
many times must I make you swear
to tell me nothing but the truth in
the name of the LORD?"
16Then Micaiah answered, "I saw
all Israel[f] scattered on the hills
like sheep without a shepherd,[g]
and the LORD said, 'These people
have no master. Let each one go
home in peace.' "
17The king of Israel said to Jehoshaphat, "Didn't I tell you that he
never prophesies anything good
about me, but only bad?"
18Micaiah continued, "Therefore
hear the word of the LORD: I saw
the LORD sitting on his throne[h]
with all the host of heaven standing
on his right and on his left. 19And
the LORD said, 'Who will entice
Ahab king of Israel into attacking
Ramoth Gilead and going to his
death there?'
"One suggested this, and another
that. 20Finally, a spirit came forward, stood before the LORD and
said, 'I will entice him.'
" 'By what means?' the LORD
asked.
21" 'I will go and be a lying spirit[i]
in the mouths of all his prophets,'
he said.
" 'You will succeed in enticing
him,' said the LORD. 'Go and do it.'
22"So now the LORD has put a lying spirit in the mouths of these
prophets of yours.[j] The LORD has
decreed disaster for you."
23Then Zedekiah son of Kenaanah went up and slapped[k] Micaiah
in the face. "Which way did the
spirit from[a] the LORD go when he
went from me to speak to you?" he
asked.
24Micaiah replied, "You will find
out on the day you go to hide in an
inner room."
25The king of Israel then ordered,
"Take Micaiah and send him back
to Amon the ruler of the city and to
Joash the king's son, 26and say,
'This is what the king says: Put this
fellow in prison[l] and give him
nothing but bread and water until I
return safely.' "
27Micaiah declared, "If you ever
return safely, the LORD has not spoken through me." Then he added,
"Mark my words, all you people!"

Ahab Killed at Ramoth Gilead

18:28–34pp 1Ki 22:29–36

28So the king of Israel and Jehoshaphat king of Judah went up to
Ramoth Gilead. 29The king of Israel
said to Jehoshaphat, "I will enter
the battle in disguise, but you wear
your royal robes." So the king of Israel disguised[m] himself and went
into battle.
30Now the king of Aram had ordered his chariot commanders,
"Do not fight with anyone, small or
great, except the king of Israel."
31When the chariot commanders
saw Jehoshaphat, they thought,
"This is the king of Israel." So they
turned to attack him, but Jehoshaphat cried out,[n] and the LORD
helped him. God drew them away
from him, 32for when the chariot
commanders saw that he was not
the king of Israel, they stopped
pursuing him.
33But someone drew his bow at
random and hit the king of Israel
between the sections of his armour.
The king told the chariot driver,
"Wheel around and get me out of
the fighting. I've been wounded."
34All day long the battle raged, and
the king of Israel propped himself
up in his chariot facing the Arameans until evening. Then at sunset he died.[o]

19 When Jehoshaphat king of
Judah returned safely to
his palace in Jerusalem, 2Jehu[a] the
seer, the son of Hanani, went out to
meet him and said to the king,
"Should you help the wicked[b] and
love[a] those who hate the LORD?[c]

18:16 f 1Ch 9:1 g Nu 27:17 Eze 34:5-8
18:18 h Da 7:9
18:21 i 1Ch 21:1 Job 1:6 Zec 3:1 Jn 8:44
18:22 j Job 12:16 Isa 19:14 Eze 14:9
18:23 k Jer 20:2 Mk 14:65 Ac 23:2
18:26 l 2Ch 16:10 Heb 11:36
18:29 m 1Sa 28:8
18:31 n 2Ch 13:14
18:34 o 2Ch 22:5
19:2 a 1Ki 16:1 b 2Ch 16:2-9 c Ps 139:21-22

[a]23. Or *Spirit of* [a]2 Or *and make alliances with*

Because of this, the wrath[d] of the LORD is upon you. 3There is, however, some good[e] in you, for you have rid the land of the Asherah poles[f] and have set your heart on seeking God.[g]"

Jehoshaphat Appoints Judges

4Jehoshaphat lived in Jerusalem, and he went out again among the people from Beersheba to the hill country of Ephraim and turned them back to the LORD, the God of their fathers. 5He appointed judges[h] in the land, in each of the fortified cities of Judah. 6He told them, "Consider carefully what you do,[i] because you are not judging for man[j] but for the LORD, who is with you whenever you give a verdict. 7Now let the fear of the LORD be upon you. Judge carefully, for with the LORD our God there is no injustice[k] or partiality[l] or bribery."

8In Jerusalem also, Jehoshaphat appointed some of the Levites, priests and heads of Israelite families to administer[m] the law of the LORD and to settle disputes. And they lived in Jerusalem. 9He gave them these orders: "You must serve faithfully and wholeheartedly in the fear of the LORD. 10In every case that comes before you from your fellow countrymen who live in the cities—whether bloodshed or other concerns of the law, commands, decrees or ordinances—you are to warn them not to sin against the LORD;[n] otherwise his wrath will come on you and your brothers. Do this, and you will not sin.

11"Amariah the chief priest will be over you in any matter concerning the LORD, and Zebadiah son of Ishmael, the leader of the tribe of Judah, will be over you in any matter concerning the king, and the Levites will serve as officials before you. Act with courage,[o] and may the LORD be with those who do well."

Jehoshaphat Defeats Moab and Ammon

20 After this, the Moabites and Ammonites with some of the Meunites[a][a] came to make war on Jehoshaphat.

2Some men came and told Jehoshaphat, "A vast army is coming against you from Edom,[b] from the other side of the Sea.[c] It is already in Hazazon Tamar[b]" (that is, En Gedi). 3Alarmed, Jehoshaphat resolved to enquire of the LORD, and he proclaimed a fast[c] for all Judah. 4The people of Judah came together to seek help from the LORD; indeed, they came from every town in Judah to seek him.

5Then Jehoshaphat stood up in the assembly of Judah and Jerusalem at the temple of the LORD in the front of the new courtyard 6and said:

"O LORD, God of our fathers,[d] are you not the God who is in heaven?[e] You rule over all the kingdoms[f] of the nations. Power and might are in your hand, and no-one can withstand you. 7O our God, did you not drive out the inhabitants of this land before your people Israel and give it for ever to the descendants of Abraham your friend?[g] 8They have lived in it and have built in it a sanctuary[h] for your Name, saying, 9'If calamity comes upon us, whether the sword of judgment, or plague or famine,[i] we will stand in your presence before this temple that bears your Name and will cry out to you in our distress, and you will hear us and save us.'

[a]1 Some Septuagint manuscripts; Hebrew *Ammonites* [b]2 One Hebrew manuscript; most Hebrew manuscripts, Septuagint and Vulgate *Aram* [c]2 That is, the Dead Sea

19:2 d 2Ch 24:18; 2Ch 32:25; Ps 7:11
19:3 e 1Ki 14:13; 2Ch 12:12; f 2Ch 17:6; g 2Ch 18:1; 2Ch 20:35; 2Ch 25:7; Ezr 7:10
19:5 h Ge 47:6; Ex 18:26
19:6 i Lev 19:15; j Dt 1:17; Dt 16:18-20; Dt 17:8-13
19:7 k Ge 18:25; Dt 32:4; l Dt 10:17; Job 34:19; Ro 2:11; Col 3:25
19:8 m 2Ch 17:8-9
19:10 n Dt 17:8-13
19:11 o 1Ch 28:20
20:1 a 1Ch 4:41
20:2 b Ge 14:7
20:3 c 1Sa 7:6; 2Ch 19:3; Ezr 8:21; Jer 36:9; Jnh 3:5,7
20:6 d Mt 6:9; e Dt 4:39; f 1Ch 29:11-12
20:7 g Isa 41:8; Jas 2:23
20:8 h 2Ch 6:20
20:9 i 2Ch 6:28

10"But now here are men from Ammon, Moab and Mount Seir, whose territory you would not allow Israel to invade when they came from Egypt;[j] so they turned away from them and did not destroy them. 11See how they are repaying us by coming to drive us out of the possession[k] you gave us as an inheritance. 12O our God, will you not judge them?[l] For we have no power to face this vast army that is attacking us. We do not know what to do, but our eyes are upon you.[m]"

13All the men of Judah, with their wives and children and little ones, stood there before the LORD.

14Then the Spirit[n] of the LORD came upon Jahaziel son of Zechariah, the son of Benaiah, the son of Jeiel, the son of Mattaniah, a Levite and descendant of Asaph, as he stood in the assembly.

15He said: "Listen, King Jehoshaphat and all who live in Judah and Jerusalem! This is what the LORD says to you: 'Do not be afraid or discouraged[o] because of this vast army. For the battle[p] is not yours, but God's. 16Tomorrow march down against them. They will be climbing up by the Pass of Ziz, and you will find them at the end of the gorge in the Desert of Jeruel. 17You will not have to fight this battle. Take up your positions; stand firm and see[q] the deliverance the LORD will give you, O Judah and Jerusalem. Do not be afraid; do not be discouraged. Go out to face them tomorrow, and the LORD will be with you.' "

18Jehoshaphat bowed[r] with his face to the ground, and all the people of Judah and Jerusalem fell down in worship before the LORD. 19Then some Levites from the Kohathites and Korahites stood up and praised the LORD, the God of Israel, with a very loud voice.

20:10
j Nu 20:14-21; Dt 2:4-6,9, 18-19

20:11
k Ps 83:1-12

20:12
l Jdg 11:27
m Ps 25:15; Ps 121:1-2

20:14
n 2Ch 15:1

20:15
o 2Ch 32:7
p Ex 14:13-14; 1Sa 17:47

20:17
q Ex 14:13; 2Ch 15:2

20:18
r Ex 4:31

20:20
s Isa 7:9
t Ge 39:3; Pr 16:3

20:21
u 1Ch 16:29; Ps 29:2
v 2Ch 5:13; Ps 136:1

20:22
w Jdg 7:22; 2Ch 13:13

20:23
x Ge 19:38
y 2Ch 21:8
z Jdg 7:22; 1Sa 14:20; Eze 38:21

20Early in the morning they left for the Desert of Tekoa. As they set out, Jehoshaphat stood and said, "Listen to me, Judah and people of Jerusalem! Have faith[s] in the LORD your God and you will be upheld; have faith in his prophets and you will be successful.[t]" 21After consulting the people, Jehoshaphat appointed men to sing to the LORD and to praise him for the splendour of his[d] holiness[u] as they went out at the head of the army, saying:

"Give thanks to the LORD,
for his love endures for
ever."[v]

22As they began to sing and praise, the LORD set ambushes[w] against the men of Ammon and Moab and Mount Seir who were invading Judah, and they were defeated. 23The men of Ammon[x] and Moab rose up against the men from Mount Seir[y] to destroy and annihilate them. After they finished slaughtering the men from Seir, they helped to destroy one another.[z]

24When the men of Judah came to the place that overlooks the desert and looked towards the vast army, they saw only dead bodies lying on the ground; no-one had escaped. 25So Jehoshaphat and his men went to carry off their plunder, and they found among them a great amount of equipment and clothing[e] and also articles of value—more than they could take away. There was so much plunder that it took three days to collect it. 26On the fourth day they assembled in the Valley of Beracah, where they praised the LORD. This is why it is called the Valley of Beracah[f] to this day.

27Then, led by Jehoshaphat, all the men of Judah and Jerusalem returned joyfully to Jerusalem, for the LORD had given them cause to

[d]21 Or *him with the splendour of* [e]25 Some Hebrew manuscripts and Vulgate; most Hebrew manuscripts *corpses*
[f]26 *Beracah* means *praise.*

rejoice over their enemies. 28They
entered Jerusalem and went to the
temple of the LORD with harps and
lutes and trumpets.
29The fear[a] of God came upon all
the kingdoms of the countries
when they heard how the LORD had
fought[b] against the enemies of Israel. 30And the kingdom of Jehoshaphat was at peace, for his God had
given him rest[c] on every side.

The End of Jehoshaphat's Reign

20:31–21:1pp 1Ki 22:41–50

31So Jehoshaphat reigned over
Judah. He was thirty-five years old
when he became king of Judah, and
he reigned in Jerusalem for
twenty-five years. His mother's
name was Azubah daughter of
Shilhi. 32He walked in the ways of
his father Asa and did not stray
from them; he did what was right in
the eyes of the LORD. 33The high
places,[d] however, were not removed, and the people still had not
set their hearts on the God of their
fathers.
34The other events of Jehoshaphat's reign, from beginning to
end, are written in the annals of
Jehu[e] son of Hanani, which are recorded in the book of the kings of
Israel.
35Later, Jehoshaphat king of Judah made an alliance[f] with Ahaziah king of Israel, who was guilty of
wickedness.[g] 36He agreed with
him to construct a fleet of trading
ships.[g] After these were built at
Ezion Geber, 37Eliezer son of Doda-
vahu of Mareshah prophesied
against Jehoshaphat, saying, "Because you have made an alliance
with Ahaziah, the LORD will destroy
what you have made." The ships[h]
were wrecked and were not able to
set sail to trade.[h]

21 Then Jehoshaphat rested
with his fathers and was
buried with them in the City of
David. And Jehoram[a] his son succeeded him as king. 2Jehoram's
brothers, the sons of Jehoshaphat,
were Azariah, Jehiel, Zechariah,
Azariahu, Michael and Shephatiah.
All these were sons of Jehoshaphat
king of Israel.[a] 3Their father had
given them many gifts[b] of silver
and gold and articles of value, as
well as fortified cities[c] in Judah,
but he had given the kingdom to Jehoram because he was his firstborn
son.

Jehoram King of Judah

21:5–10,20pp 2Ki 8:16–24

4When Jehoram established[d]
himself firmly over his father's
kingdom, he put all his brothers[e]
to the sword along with some of the
princes of Israel. 5Jehoram was
thirty-two years old when he became king, and he reigned in Jerusalem for eight years. 6He walked
in the ways of the kings of Israel,[f]
as the house of Ahab had done, for
he married a daughter of Ahab.[g]
He did evil in the eyes of the LORD.
7Nevertheless, because of the covenant the LORD had made with
David,[h] the LORD was not willing to
destroy the house of David.[i] He
had promised to maintain a lamp[j]
for him and his descendants for
ever.
8In the time of Jehoram, Edom[k]
rebelled against Judah and set up
its own king. 9So Jehoram went
there with his officers and all his
chariots. The Edomites surrounded
him and his chariot commanders,
but he rose up and broke through
by night. 10To this day Edom has
been in rebellion against Judah.
Libnah[l] revolted at the same
time, because Jehoram had forsaken the LORD, the God of his fathers. 11He had also built high
places on the hills of Judah and had
caused the people of Jerusalem to

20:29 a Ge 35:5 Dt 2:25 2Ch 14:14 2Ch 17:10 b Ex 14:14
20:30 c 1Ch 22:9 2Ch 14:6-7 2Ch 15:15
20:33 d 2Ch 17:6 2Ch 19:3
20:34 e 1Ki 16:1
20:35 f 2Ch 16:3 g 2Ch 19:1-3
20:37 h 1Ki 9:26 2Ch 9:21
21:1 a 1Ch 3:11
21:3 b 2Ch 11:23 c 2Ch 11:10
21:4 d 1Ki 2:12 e Jdg 9:5
21:6 f 1Ki 12:28-30 g 2Ch 18:1 2Ch 22:3
21:7 h 2Sa 7:13 i 2Sa 7:15 2Ch 23:3 j 2Sa 21:17 1Ki 11:36
21:8 k 2Ch 20:22-23
21:10 l Nu 33:20

g36 Hebrew *of ships that could go to Tarshish*
h37 Hebrew *sail for Tarshish* a2 That is, Judah, as frequently in 2 Chronicles

prostitute themselves and had led
Judah astray.
12Jehoram received a letter from
Elijah[m] the prophet, which said:

"This is what the LORD, the God
of your father[n] David, says:
'You have not walked in the
ways of your father Jehoshaphat or of Asa[o] king of Judah.
13But you have walked in the
ways of the kings of Israel, and
you have led Judah and the
people of Jerusalem to prostitute themselves, just as the
house of Ahab did.[p] You have
also murdered your own
brothers, members of your
father's house, men who were
better[q] than you. 14So now the
LORD is about to strike your
people, your sons, your wives
and everything that is yours,
with a heavy blow. 15You yourself will be very ill with a lingering disease[r] of the bowels,
until the disease causes your
bowels to come out.'"

16The LORD aroused against Jehoram the hostility of the Philistines
and of the Arabs[s] who lived near
the Cushites. 17They attacked Judah, invaded it and carried off all
the goods found in the king's palace, together with his sons and
wives. Not a son was left to him except Ahaziah,[b] the youngest.[t]
18After all this, the LORD afflicted
Jehoram with an incurable disease
of the bowels. 19In the course of
time, at the end of the second year,
his bowels came out because of
the disease, and he died in great
pain. His people made no fire in
his honour,[u] as they had for his
fathers.
20Jehoram was thirty-two years
old when he became king, and he
reigned in Jerusalem for eight
years. He passed away, to no-one's
regret, and was buried[v] in the City
of David, but not in the tombs of the
kings.

21:12
m 2Ki 1:16-17
n 2Ch 17:3-6
o 2Ch 14:2

21:13
p ver 6,11
1Ki 16:29-33
q ver 4
1Ki 2:32

21:15
r ver 18-19
Nu 12:10

21:16
s 2Ch 17:10-11
2Ch 22:1
2Ch 26:7

21:17
t 2Ki 12:18
2Ch 22:1
2Ch 25:23
Joel 3:5

21:19
u 2Ch 16:14

21:20
v 2Ch 24:25
2Ch 28:27
2Ch 33:20
Jer 22:18,28

22:1
a 2Ch 33:25
2Ch 36:1
b 2Ch 23:20-21
2Ch 26:1
c 2Ch 21:16-17

22:3
d 2Ch 18:1
e 2Ch 21:6

22:5
f 2Ch 18:11,34

22:6
g 1Ki 19:15
2Ki 8:13-15
2Ki 9:15

22:7
h 2Ki 9:16
2Ch 10:15

22:8
i 2Ki 10:13

Ahaziah King of Judah

22:1–6pp 2Ki 8:25–29
22:7–9pp 2Ki 9:21–29

22 The people[a] of Jerusalem[b] made Ahaziah, Jehoram's youngest son, king in his
place, since the raiders,[c] who
came with the Arabs into the camp,
had killed all the older sons. So
Ahaziah son of Jehoram king of Judah began to reign.
2Ahaziah was twenty-two[a] years
old when he became king, and he
reigned in Jerusalem for one year.
His mother's name was Athaliah, a
granddaughter of Omri.
3He too walked[d] in the ways of
the house of Ahab,[e] for his mother
encouraged him in doing wrong.
4He did evil in the eyes of the LORD,
as the house of Ahab had done, for
after his father's death they became his advisers, to his undoing.
5He also followed their counsel
when he went with Joram[b] son of
Ahab king of Israel to war against
Hazael king of Aram at Ramoth
Gilead.[f] The Arameans wounded
Joram; 6so he returned to Jezreel to
recover from the wounds they had
inflicted on him at Ramoth[c] in his
battle with Hazael[g] king of Aram.
Then Ahaziah[d] son of Jehoram
king of Judah went down to Jezreel
to see Joram son of Ahab because
he had been wounded.
7Through Ahaziah's[h] visit to Joram, God brought about Ahaziah's
downfall. When Ahaziah arrived,
he went out with Joram to meet
Jehu son of Nimshi, whom the LORD
had anointed to destroy the house
of Ahab. 8While Jehu was execut-
ing judgment on the house of
Ahab,[i] he found the princes of Judah and the sons of Ahaziah's relatives, who had been attending

[b]17 Hebrew *Jehoahaz*, a variant of *Ahaziah*
[a]2 Some Septuagint manuscripts and Syriac (see also 2 Kings 8:26); Hebrew *forty-two*
[b]5 Hebrew *Jehoram*, a variant of *Joram*; also in verses 6 and 7 [c]6 Hebrew *Ramah*, a variant of *Ramoth* [d]6 Some Hebrew manuscripts, Septuagint, Vulgate and Syriac (see also 2 Kings 8:29); most Hebrew manuscripts *Azariah*

Ahaziah, and he killed them. 9He
then went in search of Ahaziah, and
his men captured him while he
was hiding[j] in Samaria. He was
brought to Jehu and put to death.
They buried him, for they said, "He
was a son of Jehoshaphat, who
sought[k] the LORD with all his
heart." So there was no-one in the
house of Ahaziah powerful enough
to retain the kingdom.

Athaliah and Joash

22:10–23:21pp 2Ki 11:1–21

10When Athaliah the mother of
Ahaziah saw that her son was dead,
she proceeded to destroy the whole
royal family of the house of Judah.
11But Jehosheba,[e] the daughter of
King Jehoram, took Joash son of
Ahaziah and stole him away from
among the royal princes who were
about to be murdered and put him
and his nurse in a bedroom. Because Jehosheba,[e] the daughter of
King Jehoram and wife of the
priest Jehoiada, was Ahaziah's sister, she hid the child from Athaliah
so that she could not kill him. 12He
remained hidden with them at the
temple of God for six years while
Athaliah ruled the land.

23 In the seventh year Jehoiada showed his strength.
He made a covenant with the commanders of units of a hundred:
Azariah son of Jeroham, Ishmael
son of Jehohanan, Azariah son of
Obed, Maaseiah son of Adaiah, and
Elishaphat son of Zicri. 2They went
throughout Judah and gathered the
Levites[a] and the heads of Israelite
families from all the towns. When
they came to Jerusalem, 3the whole
assembly made a covenant[b] with
the king at the temple of God.

Jehoiada said to them, "The
king's son shall reign, as the LORD
promised concerning the descendants of David.[c] 4Now this is what
you are to do: A third of you priests
and Levites who are going on duty
on the Sabbath are to keep watch at
the doors, 5a third of you at the
royal palace and a third at the
Foundation Gate, and all the other
men are to be in the courtyards of
the temple of the LORD. 6No-one is
to enter the temple of the LORD except the priests and Levites on
duty; they may enter because they
are consecrated, but all the other
men are to guard[d] what the LORD
has assigned to them.[a] 7The Levites are to station themselves
round the king, each man with his
weapons in his hand. Anyone who
enters the temple must be put to
death. Stay close to the king wherever he goes."

8The Levites and all the men of
Judah did just as Jehoiada the
priest ordered.[e] Each one took his
men—those who were going on
duty on the Sabbath and those who
were going off duty—for Jehoiada
the priest had not released any of
the divisions.[f] 9Then he gave the
commanders of units of a hundred
the spears and the large and small
shields that had belonged to King
David and that were in the temple
of God. 10He stationed all the men,
each with his weapon in his hand,
round the king—near the altar and
the temple, from the south side to
the north side of the temple.

11Jehoiada and his sons brought
out the king's son and put the
crown on him; they presented him
with a copy[g] of the covenant and
proclaimed him king. They
anointed him and shouted, "Long
live the king!"

12When Athaliah heard the noise
of the people running and cheering
the king, she went to them at the
temple of the LORD. 13She looked,
and there was the king,[h] standing
by his pillar[i] at the entrance. The
officers and the trumpeters were

22:9 *j* Jdg 9:5 *k* 2Ch 17:4
23:2 *a* Nu 35:2-5
23:3 *b* 2Ki 11:17 *c* 2Sa 7:12; 1Ki 2:4; 2Ch 6:16; 2Ch 7:18; 2Ch 21:7
23:6 *d* 1Ch 23:28-29; Zec 3:7
23:8 *e* 2Ki 11:9 *f* 1Ch 24:1
23:11 *g* Ex 25:16; Dt 17:18; 1Sa 10:24
23:13 *h* 1Ki 1:41 *i* 1Ki 7:15

e*11* Hebrew *Jehoshabeath*, a variant of *Jehosheba*
a*6* Or *to observe the LORD's command* ⌞*not to enter*⌟

beside the king, and all the people
of the land were rejoicing and
blowing trumpets, and singers with
musical instruments were leading
the praises. Then Athaliah tore her
robes and shouted, "Treason! Treason!"
14Jehoiada the priest sent out the
commanders of units of a hundred,
who were in charge of the troops,
and said to them: "Bring her out between the ranks[b] and put to the
sword anyone who follows her."
For the priest had said, "Do not
put her to death at the temple
of the LORD." 15So they seized her
as she reached the entrance of
the Horse Gate[j] on the palace
grounds, and there they put her
to death.
16Jehoiada then made a covenant[k] that he and the people and
the king[c] would be the LORD's people. 17All the people went to the
temple of Baal and tore it down.
They smashed the altars and idols
and killed[l] Mattan the priest of
Baal in front of the altars.
18Then Jehoiada placed the over-
sight of the temple of the LORD in
the hands of the priests, who were
Levites,[m] to whom David had made
assignments in the temple,[n] to
present the burnt offerings of the
LORD as written in the Law of
Moses, with rejoicing and singing,
as David had ordered. 19He also stationed doorkeepers[o] at the gates
of the LORD's temple so that no-one
who was in any way unclean might
enter.
20He took with him the commanders of hundreds, the nobles, the rulers of the people and all the people
of the land and brought the king
down from the temple of the LORD.
They went into the palace through
the Upper Gate[p] and seated the
king on the royal throne, 21and all
the people of the land rejoiced.
And the city was quiet, because
Athaliah had been slain with the
sword.[q]

23:15
j Ne 3:28
Jer 31:40
23:16
k 2Ch 29:10
2Ch 34:31
Ne 9:38
23:17
l Dt 13:6-9
23:18
m 1Ch 23:28-32
2Ch 5:5
n 1Ch 23:6
1Ch 25:6
23:19
o 1Ch 9:22
23:20
p 2Ki 15:35
23:21
q 2Ch 22:1
24:2
a 2Ch 25:2
2Ch 26:5
24:5
b Ex 30:16
Ne 10:32-33
Mt 17:24
c 1Ch 11:1
d 1Ch 26:20
24:6
e Ex 30:12-16
Nu 1:50
24:10
f Ex 25:2
1Ch 29:3,6,9

Joash Repairs the Temple

24:1–14pp 2Ki 12:1–16
24:23–27pp 2Ki 12:17–21

24 Joash was seven years old
when he became king, and
he reigned in Jerusalem for forty
years. His mother's name was Zibiah; she was from Beersheba. 2Jo-
ash did what was right in the eyes
of the LORD[a] all the years of Jehoiada the priest. 3Jehoiada chose two
wives for him, and he had sons and
daughters.
4Some time later Joash decided
to restore the temple of the LORD.
5He called together the priests and
Levites and said to them, "Go to the
towns of Judah and collect the
money[b] due annually from all Israel,[c] to repair the temple of your
God. Do it now." But the Levites[d]
did not act at once.
6Therefore the king summoned
Jehoiada the chief priest and said
to him, "Why haven't you required
the Levites to bring in from Judah
and Jerusalem the tax imposed by
Moses the servant of the LORD and
by the assembly of Israel for the
Tent of the Testimony?"[e]
7Now the sons of that wicked
woman Athaliah had broken into
the temple of God and had used
even its sacred objects for the
Baals.
8At the king's command, a chest
was made and placed outside, at the
gate of the temple of the LORD. 9A
proclamation was then issued in
Judah and Jerusalem that they
should bring to the LORD the tax
that Moses the servant of God had
required of Israel in the desert.
10All the officials and all the people brought their contributions
gladly,[f] dropping them into the
chest until it was full. 11Whenever
the chest was brought in by the Levites to the king's officials and they
saw that there was a large amount

[b]14 Or *out from the precincts* [c]16 Or *covenant between ⌞the LORD⌟ and the people and the king that they* (see 2 Kings 11:17)

of money, the royal secretary and
the officer of the chief priest would
come and empty the chest and
carry it back to its place. They did
this regularly and collected a great
amount of money. 12 The king and
Jehoiada gave it to the men who
carried out the work required for
the temple of the LORD. They
hired[g] masons and carpenters to
restore the LORD's temple, and also
workers in iron and bronze to repair the temple.
13 The men in charge of the work
were diligent, and the repairs pro-
gressed under them. They rebuilt
the temple of God according to its
original design and reinforced it.
14 When they had finished, they
brought the rest of the money to
the king and Jehoiada, and with it
were made articles for the LORD's
temple: articles for the service and
for the burnt offerings, and also
dishes and other objects of gold
and silver. As long as Jehoiada
lived, burnt offerings were presented continually in the temple of
the LORD.
15 Now Jehoiada was old and full
of years, and he died at the age of
a hundred and thirty. 16 He was
buried with the kings in the City
of David, because of the good he
had done in Israel for God and his
temple.

The Wickedness of Joash

17 After the death of Jehoiada, the
officials of Judah came and paid
homage to the king, and he listened
to them. 18 They abandoned[h] the
temple of the LORD, the God of their
fathers, and worshipped Asherah
poles and idols.[i] Because of their
guilt, God's anger[j] came upon Judah and Jerusalem. 19 Although the
LORD sent prophets to the people to
bring them back to him, and though
they testified against them, they
would not listen.[k]
20 Then the Spirit[l] of God came
upon Zechariah[m] son of Jehoiada
the priest. He stood before the people and said, "This is what God
says: 'Why do you disobey the
LORD's commands? You will not
prosper.[n] Because you have forsaken the LORD, he has forsaken[o]
you.' "
21 But they plotted against him,
and by order of the king they
stoned[p] him to death[q] in the courtyard of the LORD's temple.[r] 22 King
Joash did not remember the kindness Zechariah's father Jehoiada
had shown him but killed his son,
who said as he lay dying, "May the
LORD see this and call you to account."[s]
23 At the turn of the year,[a] the
army of Aram marched against Joash; it invaded Judah and Jerusalem and killed all the leaders of
the people.[t] They sent all the plunder to their king in Damascus. 24 Although the Aramean army had
come with only a few men,[u] the
LORD delivered into their hands a
much larger army.[v] Because Judah had forsaken the LORD, the God
of their fathers, judgment was executed on Joash. 25 When the Arameans withdrew, they left Joash
severely wounded. His officials
conspired against him for murdering the son of Jehoiada the priest,
and they killed him in his bed. So he
died and was buried[w] in the City of
David, but not in the tombs of the
kings.
26 Those who conspired against
him were Zabad,[b] son of Shimeath
an Ammonite woman, and Jehozabad, son of Shimrith[c][x] a Moabite
woman.[y] 27 The account of his sons,
the many prophecies about him,
and the record of the restoration of
the temple of God are written in the
annotations on the book of the
kings. And Amaziah his son succeeded him as king.

24:12 g 2Ch 34:11
24:18 h ver 4; Jos 24:20; 2Ch 7:19 i Ex 34:13; 1Ki 14:23; 2Ch 33:3; Jer 17:2 j Jos 22:20; 2Ch 19:2
24:19 k Nu 11:29; Jer 7:25; Zec 1:4
24:20 l Jdg 3:10; 1Ch 12:18; 2Ch 20:14 m Mt 23:35; Lk 11:51 n Nu 14:41 o Dt 31:17; 2Ch 15:2
24:21 p Jos 7:25; Ac 7:58-59 q Ne 9:26; Jer 26:21 r Jer 20:2; Mt 23:35
24:22 s Ge 9:5
24:23 t 2Ki 12:17-18
24:24 u 2Ch 14:9; 2Ch 16:8; 2Ch 20:2,12 v Lev 26:23-25; Dt 28:25
24:25 w 2Ch 21:20
24:26 x 2Ki 12:21 y Ru 1:4

a23 Probably in the spring b26 A variant of *Jozabad* c26 A variant of *Shomer*

Amaziah King of Judah

25:1–4pp 2Ki 14:1–6
25:11–12pp 2Ki 14:7
25:17–28pp 2Ki 14:8–20

25 Amaziah was twenty-five years old when he became king, and he reigned in Jerusalem for twenty-nine years. His mother's name was Jehoaddin;[a] she was from Jerusalem. 2He did what was right in the eyes of the LORD, but not wholeheartedly.[a] 3After the kingdom was firmly in his control, he executed the officials who had murdered his father the king. 4Yet he did not put their sons to death, but acted in accordance with what is written in the Law, in the Book of Moses,[b] where the LORD commanded: "Fathers shall not be put to death for their children, nor children put to death for their fathers; each is to die for his own sins."[b][c]

5Amaziah called the people of Judah together and assigned them according to their families to commanders of thousands and commanders of hundreds for all Judah and Benjamin. He then mustered[d] those twenty years old[e] or more and found that there were three hundred thousand men ready for military service,[f] able to handle the spear and shield. 6He also hired a hundred thousand fighting men from Israel for a hundred talents[c] of silver.

7But a man of God came to him and said, "O king, these troops from Israel[g] must not march with you, for the LORD is not with Israel—not with any of the people of Ephraim. 8Even if you go and fight courageously in battle, God will overthrow you before the enemy, for God has the power to help or to overthrow."[h]

9Amaziah asked the man of God, "But what about the hundred talents I paid for these Israelite troops?"

The man of God replied, "The LORD can give you much more than that."[i] 10So Amaziah dismissed the troops who had come to him from Ephraim and sent them home. They were furious with Judah and left for home in a great rage.[j]

11Amaziah then marshalled his strength and led his army to the Valley of Salt, where he killed ten thousand men of Seir. 12The army of Judah also captured ten thousand men alive, took them to the top of a cliff and threw them down so that all were dashed to pieces.[k]

13Meanwhile the troops that Amaziah had sent back and had not allowed to take part in the war raided Judean towns from Samaria to Beth Horon. They killed three thousand people and carried off great quantities of plunder.

14When Amaziah returned from slaughtering the Edomites, he brought back the gods of the people of Seir. He set them up as his own gods,[l] bowed down to them and burned sacrifices to them. 15The anger of the LORD burned against Amaziah, and he sent a prophet to him, who said, "Why do you consult this people's gods, which could not save[m] their own people from your hand?"

16While he was still speaking, the king said to him, "Have we appointed you an adviser to the king? Stop! Why be struck down?"

So the prophet stopped but said, "I know that God has determined to destroy you, because you have done this and have not listened to my counsel."

17After Amaziah king of Judah consulted his advisers, he sent this challenge to Jehoash[d] son of Jehoahaz, the son of Jehu, king of Israel: "Come, meet me face to face."

25:2 *a* ver 14; 1Ki 8:61; 2Ch 24:2
25:4 *b* Dt 28:61 *c* Nu 26:11; Dt 24:16
25:5 *d* 2Sa 24:2 *e* Ex 30:14 *f* Nu 1:3; 1Ch 21:1; 2Ch 17:14-19
25:7 *g* 2Ch 16:2-9; 2Ch 19:1-3
25:8 *h* 2Ch 14:11; 2Ch 20:6
25:9 *i* Dt 8:18; Pr 10:22
25:10 *j* ver 13
25:12 *k* Ps 141:6; Ob 1:3
25:14 *l* Ex 20:3; 2Ch 28:23; Isa 44:15
25:15 *m* Ps 96:5; Isa 36:20

[a]*1* Hebrew *Jehoaddan*, a variant of *Jehoaddin*
[b]*4* Deut. 24:16 [c]*6* That is, about 3 1/3 tons (about 3.4 metric tons); also in verse 9
[d]*17* Hebrew *Joash*, a variant of *Jehoash*; also in verses 18, 21, 23 and 25

[18]But Jehoash king of Israel replied to Amaziah king of Judah, "A thistle[n] in Lebanon sent a message to a cedar in Lebanon, 'Give your daughter to my son in marriage.' Then a wild beast in Lebanon came along and trampled the thistle underfoot. [19]You say to yourself that you have defeated Edom, and now you are arrogant and proud. But stay at home! Why ask for trouble and cause your own downfall and that of Judah also?"

[20]Amaziah, however, would not listen, for God so worked that he might hand them over to ⌊Jehoash⌋, because they sought the gods of Edom.[o] [21]So Jehoash king of Israel attacked. He and Amaziah king of Judah faced each other at Beth Shemesh in Judah. [22]Judah was routed by Israel, and every man fled to his home. [23]Jehoash king of Israel captured Amaziah king of Judah, the son of Joash, the son of Ahaziah,[e] at Beth Shemesh. Then Jehoash brought him to Jerusalem and broke down the wall of Jerusalem from the Ephraim Gate[p] to the Corner Gate[q]—a section about six hundred feet[f] long. [24]He took all the gold and silver and all the articles found in the temple of God that had been in the care of Obed-Edom,[r] together with the palace treasures and the hostages, and returned to Samaria.

[25]Amaziah son of Joash king of Judah lived for fifteen years after the death of Jehoash son of Jehoahaz king of Israel. [26]As for the other events of Amaziah's reign, from beginning to end, are they not written in the book of the kings of Judah and Israel? [27]From the time that Amaziah turned away from following the LORD, they conspired against him in Jerusalem and he fled to Lachish[s], but they sent men after him to Lachish and killed him there. [28]He was brought back by horse and was buried with his fathers in the City of Judah.

25:18 n Jdg 9:8-15
25:20 o 1Ki 12:15; 2Ch 10:15; 2Ch 22:7
25:23 p 2Ki 14:13; Ne 8:16; Ne 12:39; q 2Ch 26:9; Jer 31:38
25:24 r 1Ch 26:15
25:27 s Jos 10:3
26:1 a 2Ch 22:1
26:5 b 2Ch 15:2; 2Ch 24:2; Da 1:17; c 2Ch 27:6
26:6 d Isa 2:6; Isa 11:14; Isa 14:29; Jer 25:20; e Am 1:8; Am 3:9
26:7 f 2Ch 21:16; g 2Ch 20:1
26:8 h Ge 19:38; 2Ch 17:11
26:9 i 2Ki 14:13; 2Ch 25:23; j Ne 2:13; Ne 3:13

Uzziah King of Judah

26:1–4pp 2Ki 14:21–22; 15:1–3
26:21–23pp 2Ki 15:5–7

26 Then all the people of Judah[a] took Uzziah,[a] who was sixteen years old, and made him king in place of his father Amaziah. [2]He was the one who rebuilt Elath and restored it to Judah after Amaziah rested with his fathers.

[3]Uzziah was sixteen years old when he became king, and he reigned in Jerusalem for fifty-two years. His mother's name was Jecoliah; she was from Jerusalem. [4]He did what was right in the eyes of the LORD, just as his father Amaziah had done. [5]He sought God during the days of Zechariah, who instructed him in the fear[b] of God.[b] As long as he sought the LORD, God gave him success.[c]

[6]He went to war against the Philistines[d] and broke down the walls of Gath, Jabneh and Ashdod.[e] He then rebuilt towns near Ashdod and elsewhere among the Philistines. [7]God helped him against the Philistines and against the Arabs[f] who lived in Gur Baal and against the Meunites.[g] [8]The Ammonites[h] brought tribute to Uzziah, and his fame spread as far as the border of Egypt, because he had become very powerful.

[9]Uzziah built towers in Jerusalem at the Corner Gate,[i] at the Valley Gate[j] and at the angle of the wall, and he fortified them. [10]He also built towers in the desert and dug many cisterns, because he had much livestock in the foothills and in the plain. He had people working his fields and vineyards in the hills and in the fertile lands, for he loved the soil.

[11]Uzziah had a well-trained army, ready to go out by divisions

[e]23 Hebrew *Jehoahaz*, a variant of *Ahaziah*
[f]23 Hebrew *four hundred cubits* (about 180 metres)
[a]1 Also called *Azariah*
[b]5 Many Hebrew manuscripts, Septuagint and Syriac; other Hebrew manuscripts *vision*

according to their numbers as mustered by Jeiel the secretary and Maaseiah the officer under the direction of Hananiah, one of the royal officials. 12The total number of family leaders over the fighting men was 2,600. 13Under their command was an army of 307,500 men trained for war, a powerful force to support the king against his enemies. 14Uzziah provided shields, spears, helmets, coats of armour, bows and slingstones for the entire army.[k] 15In Jerusalem he made machines designed by skilful men for use on the towers and on the corner defences to shoot arrows and hurl large stones. His fame spread far and wide, for he was greatly helped until he became powerful.

16But after Uzziah became powerful, his pride[l] led to his downfall.[m] He was unfaithful[n] to the LORD his God, and entered the temple of the LORD to burn incense[o] on the altar of incense. 17Azariah[p] the priest with eighty other courageous priests of the LORD followed him in. 18They confronted him and said, "It is not right for you, Uzziah, to burn incense to the LORD. That is for the priests,[q] the descendants[r] of Aaron,[s] who have been consecrated to burn incense.[t] Leave the sanctuary, for you have been unfaithful; and you will not be honoured by the LORD God."

19Uzziah, who had a censer in his hand ready to burn incense, became angry. While he was raging at the priests in their presence before the incense altar in the LORD's temple, leprosy[c][u] broke out on his forehead. 20When Azariah the chief priest and all the other priests looked at him, they saw that he had leprosy on his forehead, so they hurried him out. Indeed, he himself was eager to leave, because the LORD had afflicted him.

21King Uzziah had leprosy until the day he died. He lived in a separate house[d][v]—leprous, and excluded from the temple of the LORD. Jotham his son had charge of the palace and governed the people of the land.

22The other events of Uzziah's reign, from beginning to end, are recorded by the prophet Isaiah[w] son of Amoz. 23Uzziah[x] rested with his fathers and was buried near them in a field for burial that belonged to the kings, for people said, "He had leprosy." And Jotham his son succeeded him as king.[y]

Jotham King of Judah

27:1–4,7–9pp 2Ki 15:33–38

27 Jotham[a] was twenty-five years old when he became king, and he reigned in Jerusalem for sixteen years. His mother's name was Jerusha daughter of Zadok. 2He did what was right in the eyes of the LORD, just as his father Uzziah had done, but unlike him he did not enter the temple of the LORD. The people, however, continued their corrupt practices. 3Jotham rebuilt the Upper Gate of the temple of the LORD and did extensive work on the wall at the hill of Ophel.[b] 4He built towns in the Judean hills and forts and towers in the wooded areas.

5Jotham made war on the king of the Ammonites[c] and conquered them. That year the Ammonites paid him a hundred talents[a] of silver, ten thousand cors[b] of wheat and ten thousand cors of barley. The Ammonites brought him the same amount also in the second and third years.

6Jotham grew powerful[d] because he walked steadfastly before the LORD his God.

7The other events in Jotham's reign, including all his wars and the

26:14 k Jer 46:4
26:16 l 2Ki 14:10 m Dt 32:15 2Ch 25:19 n 1Ch 5:25 o 2Ki 16:12
26:17 p 1Ki 4:2 1Ch 6:10
26:18 q Nu 16:39 r Nu 18:1-7 s Ex 30:7 t 1Ch 6:49
26:19 u Nu 12:10 2Ki 5:25-27
26:21 v Ex 4:6 Lev 13:46 Lev 14:8 Nu 5:2 Nu 19:12
26:22 w 2Ki 15:1 Isa 1:1 Isa 6:1
26:23 x Isa 1:1 Isa 6:1 y 2Ki 14:21 2Ki 15:7 Am 1:1
27:1 a 2Ki 15:5,32 1Ch 3:12
27:3 b 2Ch 33:14 Ne 3:26
27:5 c Ge 19:38
27:6 d 2Ch 26:5

c*19* The Hebrew word was used for various diseases affecting the skin—not necessarily leprosy; also in verses 20, 21 and 23. d*21* Or *in a house where he was relieved of responsibilities*
a*5* That is, about 3 ⅓ tons (about 3.4 metric tons)
b*5* That is, probably about 60,500 bushels (about 2,200 kilolitres)

other things he did, are written in the book of the kings of Israel and Judah. 8He was twenty-five years old when he became king, and he reigned in Jerusalem for sixteen years. 9Jotham rested with his fathers and was buried in the City of David. And Ahaz his son succeeded him as king.

Ahaz King of Judah

28:1–27pp 2Ki 16:1–20

28 Ahaz[a] was twenty years old when he became king, and he reigned in Jerusalem for sixteen years. Unlike David his father, he did not do what was right in the eyes of the LORD. 2He walked in the ways of the kings of Israel and also made cast idols[b] for worshipping the Baals. 3He burned sacrifices in the Valley of Ben Hinnom[c] and sacrificed his sons[d] in the fire, following the detestable[e] ways of the nations that the LORD had driven out before the Israelites. 4He offered sacrifices and burned incense at the high places, on the hilltops and under every spreading tree.

5Therefore the LORD his God handed him over to the king of Aram.[f] The Arameans defeated him and took many of his people as prisoners and brought them to Damascus.

He was also given into the hands of the king of Israel, who inflicted heavy casualties on him. 6In one day Pekah[g] son of Remaliah killed a hundred and twenty thousand soldiers in Judah[h]—because Judah had forsaken the LORD, the God of their fathers. 7Zicri, an Ephraimite warrior, killed Maaseiah the king's son, Azrikam the officer in charge of the palace, and Elkanah, second to the king. 8The Israelites took captive from their kinsmen[i] two hundred thousand wives, sons and daughters. They also took a great deal of plunder, which they carried back to Samaria.[j]

9But a prophet of the LORD named Oded was there, and he went out to meet the army when it returned to Samaria. He said to them, "Because the LORD, the God of your fathers, was angry[k] with Judah, he gave them into your hand. But you have slaughtered them in a rage that reaches to heaven.[l] 10And now you intend to make the men and women of Judah and Jerusalem your slaves.[m] But aren't you also guilty of sins against the LORD your God? 11Now listen to me! Send back your fellow countrymen that you have taken as prisoners, for the LORD's fierce anger rests on you.[n]"

12Then some of the leaders in Ephraim—Azariah son of Jehohanan, Berekiah son of Meshillemoth, Jehizkiah son of Shallum, and Amasa son of Hadlai—confronted those who were arriving from the war. 13"You must not bring those prisoners here," they said, "or we will be guilty before the LORD. Do you intend to add to our sin and guilt? For our guilt is already great, and his fierce anger rests on Israel."

14So the soldiers gave up the prisoners and plunder in the presence of the officials and all the assembly. 15The men designated by name took the prisoners, and from the plunder they clothed all who were naked. They provided them with clothes and sandals, food and drink,[o] and healing balm. All those who were weak they put on donkeys. So they took them back to their fellow countrymen at Jericho, the City of Palms,[p] and returned to Samaria.

16At that time King Ahaz sent to the king[a] of Assyria[q] for help.

28:1
a 1Ch 3:13; Isa 1:1
28:2
b Ex 34:17; 2Ch 22:3
28:3
c Jos 15:8; 2Ki 23:10
d Lev 18:21; 2Ki 3:27; 2Ch 33:6; Eze 20:26
e Dt 18:9; 2Ch 33:2
28:5
f Isa 7:1
28:6
g 2Ki 15:25,27
h ver 8; Isa 9:21; Isa 11:13
28:8
i Dt 28:25-41; 2Ch 11:4
j 2Ch 29:9
28:9
k 2Ch 25:15; Isa 10:6; Isa 47:6; Zec 1:15
l Ezr 9:6; Rev 18:5
28:10
m Lev 25:39-46
28:11
n 2Ch 11:4; Jas 2:13
28:15
o 2Ki 6:22; Pr 25:21-22
p Dt 34:3; Jdg 1:16
28:16
q 2Ki 16:7

[a]*16* One Hebrew manuscript, Septuagint and Vulgate (see also 2 Kings 16:7); most Hebrew manuscripts *kings*

17The Edomites[r] had again come
and attacked Judah and carried
away prisoners,[s] 18while the Philistines[t] had raided towns in the
foothills and in the Negev of Judah.
They captured and occupied Beth
Shemesh, Aijalon[u] and Gederoth,
as well as Soco, Timnah and Gimzo,
with their surrounding villages.
19The LORD had humbled Judah because of Ahaz king of Israel,[b] for
he had promoted wickedness in Judah and had been most unfaithful[v]
to the LORD. 20Tiglath-Pileser[c][w]
king of Assyria came to him, but
gave him trouble instead of help.[x]
21Ahaz took some of the things
from the temple of the LORD and
from the royal palace and from the
princes and presented them to the
king of Assyria, but that did not
help him.

22In his time of trouble King Ahaz
became even more unfaithful[y] to
the LORD. 23He offered sacrifices to
the gods[z] of Damascus, who had
defeated him; for he thought,
"Since the gods of the kings of
Aram have helped them, I will
sacrifice to them so that they will
help me."[a] But they were his
downfall and the downfall of all
Israel.

24Ahaz gathered together the furnishings from the temple of God[b]
and took them away.[d] He shut the
doors[c] of the LORD's temple and
set up altars[d] at every street corner in Jerusalem. 25In every town
in Judah he built high places to
burn sacrifices to other gods and
provoked the LORD, the God of his
fathers, to anger.

26The other events of his reign
and all his ways, from beginning to
end, are written in the book of the
kings of Judah and Israel. 27Ahaz
rested[e] with his fathers and was
buried[f] in the city of Jerusalem,
but he was not placed in the tombs
of the kings of Israel. And Hezekiah his son succeeded him as
king.

28:17 r Ps 137:7; Isa 34:5 s 2Ch 29:9
28:18 t Eze 16:27,57 u Jos 10:12
28:19 v 2Ch 21:2
28:20 w 2Ki 15:29; 1Ch 5:6 x 2Ki 16:7
28:22 y Jer 5:3
28:23 z 2Ch 25:14 a Jer 44:17-18
28:24 b 2Ki 16:18 c 2Ch 29:7 d 2Ch 30:14
28:27 e Isa 14:28-32 f 2Ch 21:20; 2Ch 24:25
29:1 a 1Ch 3:13
29:2 b 2Ch 28:1; 2Ch 34:2
29:3 c 2Ch 28:24
29:5 d 2Ch 35:6
29:6 e Ps 106:6-47; Jer 2:27 f 1Ch 5:25; Eze 8:16
29:8 g Dt 28:25; 2Ch 24:18 h Jer 18:16; Jer 19:8; Jer 25:9,18
29:9 i 2Ch 28:5-8,17
29:10 j 2Ch 15:12; 2Ch 23:16
29:11 k Nu 3:6; Nu 8:6,14 l 1Ch 15:2

Hezekiah Purifies the Temple

29:1–2pp 2Ki 18:2–3

29 Hezekiah[a] was twenty-
five years old when he became king, and he reigned in
Jerusalem for twenty-nine years.
His mother's name was Abijah
daughter of Zechariah. 2He did
what was right in the eyes of the
LORD, just as his father David[b] had
done.

3In the first month of the first
year of his reign, he opened the
doors of the temple of the LORD and
repaired[c] them. 4He brought in the
priests and the Levites, assembled
them in the square on the east side
5and said, "Listen to me, Levites!
Consecrate[d] yourselves now and
consecrate the temple of the LORD,
the God of your fathers. Remove all
defilement from the sanctuary.
6Our fathers[e] were unfaithful;[f]
they did evil in the eyes of the LORD
our God and forsook him. They
turned their faces away from the
LORD's dwelling-place and turned
their backs on him. 7They also shut
the doors of the portico and put out
the lamps. They did not burn incense or present any burnt offerings at the sanctuary to the God of
Israel. 8Therefore, the anger of the
LORD has fallen on Judah and Jerusalem; he has made them an object
of dread and horror[g] and scorn,[h]
as you can see with your own eyes.
9This is why our fathers have fallen
by the sword and why our sons and
daughters and our wives are in captivity.[i] 10Now I intend to make a
covenant[j] with the LORD, the God
of Israel, so that his fierce anger
will turn away from us. 11My sons,
do not be negligent now, for the
LORD has chosen you to stand before him and serve him,[k] to minister[l] before him and to burn
incense."

b19 That is, Judah, as frequently in 2 Chronicles
c20 Hebrew *Tilgath-Pilneser*, a variant of *Tiglath-Pileser* **d**24 Or *and cut them up*

12Then these Levites[m] set to
work:
from the Kohathites,
Mahath son of Amasai and
Joel son of Azariah;
from the Merarites,
Kish son of Abdi and Azariah
son of Jehallelel;
from the Gershonites,
Joah son of Zimmah and
Eden[n] son of Joah;
13from the descendants of Elizaphan,
Shimri and Jeiel;
from the descendants of
Asaph,[o]
Zechariah and Mattaniah;
14from the descendants of Heman,
Jehiel and Shimei;
from the descendants of Jeduthun,
Shemaiah and Uzziel.
15When they had assembled their
brothers and consecrated themselves, they went in to purify[p] the
temple of the LORD, as the king had
ordered, following the word of the
LORD. 16The priests went into the
sanctuary of the LORD to purify it.
They brought out to the courtyard
of the LORD's temple everything
unclean that they found in the temple of the LORD. The Levites took it
and carried it out to the Kidron Valley.[q] 17They began the consecration on the first day of the first
month, and by the eighth day of the
month they reached the portico of
the LORD. For eight more days they
consecrated the temple of the LORD
itself, finishing in the sixteenth day
of the first month.
18Then they went in to King Hezekiah and reported: "We have purified the entire temple of the LORD,
the altar of burnt offering with all
its utensils, and the table for setting out the consecrated bread,
with all its articles. 19We have prepared and consecrated all the articles[r] that King Ahaz removed in
his unfaithfulness while he was

29:12
m Nu 3:17-20
n 2Ch 31:15

29:13
o 1Ch 6:39

29:15
p ver 5
1Ch 23:28
2Ch 30:12

29:16
q 2Sa 15:23

29:19
r 2Ch 28:24

29:21
s Lev 4:13-14

29:22
t Lev 4:18

29:23
u Lev 4:15

29:24
v Ex 29:36
Lev 4:26

29:25
w 1Ch 25:6
2Ch 8:14
x 1Sa 22:5
2Sa 24:11

29:26
y 1Ch 15:16
z 1Ch 15:24
1Ch 23:5
2Ch 5:12

29:27
a 2Ch 23:18

king. They are now in front of the
LORD's altar."
20Early the next morning King
Hezekiah gathered the city officials together and went up to the
temple of the LORD. 21They brought
seven bulls, seven rams, seven
male lambs and seven male goats
as a sin offering[s] for the kingdom,
for the sanctuary and for Judah.
The king commanded the priests,
the descendants of Aaron, to offer
these on the altar of the LORD. 22So
they slaughtered the bulls, and the
priests took the blood and sprinkled it on the altar; next they
slaughtered the rams and sprinkled their blood on the altar; then
they slaughtered the lambs and
sprinkled their blood[t] on the altar.
23The goats for the sin offering
were brought before the king and
the assembly, and they laid their
hands[u] on them. 24The priests then
slaughtered the goats and presented their blood on the altar for a
sin offering to atone[v] for all Israel,
because the king had ordered the
burnt offering and the sin offering
for all Israel.
25He stationed the Levites in the
temple of the LORD with cymbals,
harps and lyres in the way prescribed by David[w] and Gad[x] the
king's seer and Nathan the
prophet; this was commanded by
the LORD through his prophets. 26So
the Levites stood ready with
David's instruments,[y] and the
priests with their trumpets.[z]
27Hezekiah gave the order to sacrifice the burnt offering on the
altar. As the offering began, singing to the LORD began also, accompanied by trumpets and the
instruments[a] of David king of Israel. 28The whole assembly bowed
in worship, while the singers sang
and the trumpeters played. All this
continued until the sacrifice of the
burnt offering was completed.
29When the offerings were finished, the king and everyone
present with him knelt down and

worshipped.[b] 30 King Hezekiah and his officials ordered the Levites to praise the LORD with the words of David and of Asaph the seer. So they sang praises with gladness and bowed their heads and worshipped.

31 Then Hezekiah said, "You have now dedicated yourselves to the LORD. Come and bring sacrifices[c] and thank-offerings to the temple of the LORD." So the assembly brought sacrifices and thank-offerings, and all whose hearts were willing[d] brought burnt offerings.

32 The number of burnt offerings the assembly brought was seventy bulls, a hundred rams and two hundred male lambs—all of them for burnt offerings to the LORD. 33 The animals consecrated as sacrifices amounted to six hundred bulls and three thousand sheep and goats. 34 The priests, however, were too few to skin all the burnt offerings;[e] so their kinsmen the Levites helped them until the task was finished and until other priests had been consecrated,[f] for the Levites had been more conscientious in consecrating themselves than the priests had been. 35 There were burnt offerings in abundance, together with the fat[g] of the fellowship offerings[a][h] and the drink offerings[i] that accompanied the burnt offerings.

So the service of the temple of the LORD was re-established. 36 Hezekiah and all the people rejoiced at what God had brought about for his people, because it was done so quickly.

Hezekiah Celebrates the Passover

30 Hezekiah sent word to all Israel and Judah and also wrote letters to Ephraim and Manasseh,[a] inviting them to come to the temple of the LORD in Jerusalem and celebrate the Passover[b] to the LORD, the God of Israel. 2 The king and his officials and the whole assembly in Jerusalem decided to celebrate[c] the Passover in the second month. 3 They had not been able to celebrate it at the regular time because not enough priests had consecrated[d] themselves and the people had not assembled in Jerusalem. 4 The plan seemed right both to the king and to the whole assembly. 5 They decided to send a proclamation throughout Israel, from Beersheba to Dan,[e] calling the people to come to Jerusalem and celebrate the Passover to the LORD, the God of Israel. It had not been celebrated in large numbers according to what was written.

6 At the king's command, couriers went throughout Israel and Judah with letters from the king and from his officials, which read:

> "People of Israel, return to the LORD, the God of Abraham, Isaac and Israel, that he may return to you who are left, who have escaped from the hand of the kings of Assyria. 7 Do not be like your fathers[f] and brothers, who were unfaithful to the LORD, the God of their fathers, so that he made them an object of horror,[g] as you see. 8 Do not be stiff-necked,[h] as your fathers were; submit to the LORD. Come to the sanctuary, which he has consecrated for ever. Serve the LORD your God, so that his fierce anger[i] will turn away from you. 9 If you return[j] to the LORD, then your brothers and your children will be shown compassion[k] by their captors and will come back to this land, for the LORD your God is gracious and compassionate.[l] He will not turn his face from you if you return to him."

10 The couriers went from town to

29:29 b 2Ch 20:18
29:31 c Heb 13:15-16 d Ex 25:2; Ex 35:22
29:34 e 2Ch 35:11 f 2Ch 30:3,15
29:35 g Ex 29:13; Lev 3:16 h Lev 7:11-21 i Nu 15:5-10
30:1 a Ge 41:52 b Ex 12:11; Nu 28:16
30:2 c Nu 9:10
30:3 d 2Ch 29:34
30:5 e Jdg 20:1
30:7 f Ps 78:8,57; Ps 106:6; Eze 20:18 g 2Ch 29:8
30:8 h Ex 32:9 i Nu 25:4; 2Ch 29:10
30:9 j Dt 30:2-5; Isa 1:16; Isa 55:7 k 1Ki 8:50; Ps 106:46 l Ex 34:6-7; Dt 4:31; Mic 7:18

a 35 Traditionally *peace offerings*

town in Ephraim and Manasseh, as far as Zebulun, but the people scorned and ridiculed[m] them. 11Nevertheless, some men of Asher, Manasseh and Zebulun humbled themselves and went to Jerusalem.[n] 12Also in Judah the hand of God was on the people to give them unity[o] of mind to carry out what the king and his officials had ordered, following the word of the LORD.

13A very large crowd of people assembled in Jerusalem to celebrate the Feast of Unleavened Bread[p] in the second month. 14They removed the altars[q] in Jerusalem and cleared away the incense altars and threw them into the Kidron Valley.[r]

15They slaughtered the Passover lamb on the fourteenth day of the second month. The priests and the Levites were ashamed and consecrated[s] themselves and brought burnt offerings to the temple of the LORD. 16Then they took up their regular positions[t] as prescribed in the Law of Moses the man of God. The priests sprinkled the blood handed to them by the Levites. 17Since many in the crowd had not consecrated themselves, the Levites had to kill[u] the Passover lambs for all those who were not ceremonially clean and could not consecrate ⌞their lambs⌟ to the LORD. 18Although most of the many people who came from Ephraim, Manasseh, Issachar and Zebulun had not purified themselves,[v] yet they ate the Passover, contrary to what was written. But Hezekiah prayed for them, saying, "May the LORD, who is good, pardon everyone 19who sets his heart on seeking God—the LORD, the God of his fathers—even if he is not clean according to the rules of the sanctuary." 20And the LORD heard[w] Hezekiah and healed[x] the people.[y]

21The Israelites who were present in Jerusalem celebrated the Feast of Unleavened Bread[z] for seven days with great rejoicing, while the Levites and priests sang to the LORD every day, accompanied by the LORD's instruments of praise.[a]

22Hezekiah spoke encouragingly to all the Levites, who showed good understanding of the service of the LORD. For the seven days they ate their assigned portion and offered fellowship offerings[b] and praised the LORD, the God of their fathers.

23The whole assembly then agreed to celebrate[a] the festival seven more days; so for another seven days they celebrated joyfully. 24Hezekiah king of Judah provided[b] a thousand bulls and seven thousand sheep and goats for the assembly, and the officials provided them with a thousand bulls and ten thousand sheep and goats. A great number of priests consecrated themselves. 25The entire assembly of Judah rejoiced, along with the priests and Levites and all who had assembled from Israel[c], including the aliens who had come from Israel and those who lived in Judah. 26There was great joy in Jerusalem, for since the days of Solomon[d] son of David king of Israel there had been nothing like this in Jerusalem. 27The priests and the Levites stood to bless[e] the people, and God heard them, for their prayer reached heaven, his holy dwelling-place.

31 When all this had ended, the Israelites who were there went out to the towns of Judah, smashed the sacred stones and cut down[a] the Asherah poles. They destroyed the high places and the altars throughout Judah and Benjamin and in Ephraim and Manasseh. After they had destroyed all of them, the Israelites returned to their own towns and to their own property.

[a]21 Or *priests praised the LORD every day with resounding instruments belonging to the LORD.*
[b]22 Traditionally *peace offerings*

30:10 m 2Ch 36:16
30:11 n ver 25
30:12 o Jer 32:39; Eze 11:19; Php 2:13
30:13 p Nu 28:16
30:14 q 2Ch 28:24; r 2Sa 15:23
30:15 s 2Ch 29:34
30:16 t 2Ch 35:10
30:17 u 2Ch 29:34
30:18 v Ex 12:43-49; Nu 9:6-10
30:20 w 2Ch 6:20; x 2Ch 7:14; Mal 4:2; y Jas 5:16
30:21 z Ex 12:15,17; Ex 13:6
30:23 a 1Ki 8:65; 2Ch 7:9
30:24 b 1Ki 8:5; 2Ch 29:34; 2Ch 35:7; Ezr 6:17; Ezr 8:35
30:25 c ver 11
30:26 d 2Ch 7:8
30:27 e Ex 39:43; Nu 6:23; Dt 26:15; 2Ch 23:18; Ps 68:5
31:1 a 2Ki 18:4; 2Ch 32:12; Isa 36:7

Contributions for Worship

31:20–21pp 2Ki 18:5–7

2 Hezekiah[b] assigned the priests and Levites to divisions[c]—each of them according to their duties as priests or Levites—to offer burnt offerings and fellowship offerings,[a] to minister,[d] to give thanks and to sing praises[e] at the gates of the LORD's dwelling.[f] 3 The king contributed[g] from his own possessions for the morning and evening burnt offerings and for the burnt offerings on the Sabbaths, New Moons and appointed feasts as written in the Law of the LORD.[h] 4 He ordered the people living in Jerusalem to give the portion[i] due to the priests and Levites so that they could devote themselves to the Law of the LORD. 5 As soon as the order went out, the Israelites generously gave the firstfruits[j] of their grain, new wine,[k] oil and honey and all that the fields produced. They brought a great amount, a tithe of everything. 6 The men of Israel and Judah who lived in the towns of Judah also brought a tithe[l] of their herds and flocks and a tithe of the holy things dedicated to the LORD their God, and they piled them in heaps.[m] 7 They began doing this in the third month and finished in the seventh month.[n] 8 When Hezekiah and his officials came and saw the heaps, they praised the LORD and blessed[o] his people Israel.

9 Hezekiah asked the priests and Levites about the heaps; 10 and Azariah the chief priest, from the family of Zadok,[p] answered, "Since the people began to bring their contributions to the temple of the LORD, we have had enough to eat and plenty to spare, because the LORD has blessed his people, and this great amount is left over."[q]

11 Hezekiah gave orders to prepare storerooms in the temple of the LORD, and this was done. 12 Then they faithfully brought in the contributions, tithes and dedicated gifts. Conaniah,[r] a Levite, was in charge of these things, and his brother Shimei was next in rank. 13 Jehiel, Azaziah, Nahath, Asahel, Jerimoth, Jozabad,[s] Eliel, Ismakiah, Mahath and Benaiah were supervisors under Conaniah and Shimei his brother, by appointment of King Hezekiah and Azariah the official in charge of the temple of God.

14 Kore son of Imnah the Levite, keeper of the East Gate, was in charge of the freewill offerings given to God, distributing the contributions made to the LORD and also the consecrated gifts. 15 Eden,[t] Miniamin, Jeshua, Shemaiah, Amariah and Shecaniah assisted him faithfully in the towns[u] of the priests, distributing to their fellow priests according to their divisions, old and young alike.

16 In addition, they distributed to the males three years old or more whose names were in the genealogical records[v]—all who would enter the temple of the LORD to perform the daily duties of their various tasks, according to their responsibilities and their divisions. 17 And they distributed to the priests enrolled by their families in the genealogical records and likewise to the Levites twenty years old or more, according to their responsibilities and their divisions. 18 They included all the little ones, the wives, and the sons and daughters of the whole community listed in these genealogical records. For they were faithful in consecrating themselves.

19 As for the priests, the descendants of Aaron, who lived on the farm lands around their towns or in any other towns,[w] men were designated by name to distribute

31:2
b 2Ch 29:9
c 1Ch 24:1
d 1Ch 15:2
e Ps 7:17; Ps 9:2; Ps 47:6; Ps 71:22
f 1Ch 23:28-32

31:3
g 1Ch 29:3; 2Ch 35:7; Eze 45:17
h Nu 28:1-29:40

31:4
i Nu 18:8; Dt 18:8; Ne 13:10; Mal 2:7

31:5
j Nu 18:12,24; Ne 13:12; Eze 44:30
k Dt 12:17

31:6
l Lev 27:30; Ne 13:10-12
m Dt 14:28; Ru 3:7

31:7
n Ex 23:16

31:8
o Ps 144:13-15

31:10
p 2Sa 8:17
q Ex 36:5; Eze 44:30; Mal 3:10-12

31:12
r 2Ch 35:9

31:13
s 2Ch 35:9

31:15
t 2Ch 29:12
u Jos 21:9-19

31:16
v 1Ch 23:3; Ezr 3:4

31:19
w ver 12-15; Lev 25:34; Nu 35:2-5

a2 Traditionally *peace offerings*

portions to every male among
them and to all who were recorded
in the genealogies of the Levites.
20This is what Hezekiah did
throughout Judah, doing what was
good and right and faithful[x] before the LORD his God. 21In everything that he undertook in the
service of God's temple and in
obedience to the law and the commands, he sought his God and
worked wholeheartedly. And so he
prospered.[y]

Sennacherib Threatens Jerusalem

32:9–19pp 2Ki 18:17–35; Isa 36:2–20
32:20–21pp 2Ki 19:35–37; Isa 37:36–38

32 After all that Hezekiah had
so faithfully done, Sen-
nacherib[a] king of Assyria came
and invaded Judah. He laid siege to
the fortified cities, thinking to conquer them for himself. 2When Hezekiah saw that Sennacherib had
come and that he intended to make
war on Jerusalem,[b] 3he consulted
with his officials and military staff
about blocking off the water from
the springs outside the city, and
they helped him. 4A large force of
men assembled, and they blocked
all the springs[c] and the stream
that flowed through the land. "Why
should the kings[a] of Assyria come
and find plenty of water?" they
said. 5Then he worked hard repairing all the broken sections of the
wall[d] and building towers on it. He
built another wall outside that one
and reinforced the supporting terraces[b][e] of the City of David. He
also made large numbers of weapons[f] and shields.
6He appointed military officers
over the people and assembled
them before him in the square at
the city gate and encouraged them
with these words: 7"Be strong and
courageous.[g] Do not be afraid or
discouraged[h] because of the king
of Assyria and the vast army with
him, for there is a greater power
with us than with him.[i] 8With him
is only the arm of flesh,[j] but with
us[k] is the LORD our God to help us
and to fight our battles."[l] And the
people gained confidence from
what Hezekiah the king of Judah
said.
9Later, when Sennacherib king of
Assyria and all his forces were laying siege to Lachish,[m] he sent his
officers to Jerusalem with this
message for Hezekiah king of Judah and for all the people of Judah
who were there:

> 10"This is what Sennacherib
> king of Assyria says: On what
> are you basing your con-
> fidence,[n] that you remain
> in Jerusalem under siege?
> 11When Hezekiah says, 'The
> LORD our God will save us from
> the hand of the king of As-
> syria,' he is misleading[o] you,
> to let you die of hunger and
> thirst. 12Did not Hezekiah him-
> self remove this god's high
> places and altars, saying to Ju-
> dah and Jerusalem, 'You must
> worship before one altar[p] and
> burn sacrifices on it'?
> 13"Do you not know what I
> and my fathers have done to all
> the peoples of the other lands?
> Were the gods of those nations
> ever able to deliver their land
> from my hand?[q] 14Who of all
> the gods of these nations that
> my fathers destroyed has been
> able to save his people from
> me? How then can your god de-
> liver you from my hand? 15Now
> do not let Hezekiah deceive[r]
> you and mislead you like this.
> Do not believe him, for no god
> of any nation or kingdom has
> been able to deliver[s] his peo-
> ple from my hand or the hand
> of my fathers.[t] How much
> less will your god deliver you
> from my hand!"

a4 Hebrew; Septuagint and Syriac *king*
b5 Or *the Millo*

31:20 x 2Ki 20:3; 2Ki 22:2
31:21 y Dt 29:9
32:1 a 2Ki 18:13-19; Isa 36:1; Isa 37:9,17,37
32:2 b Isa 22:7; Jer 1:15
32:4 c 2Ki 18:17; 2Ki 20:20; Isa 22:9,11; Na 3:14
32:5 d 2Ch 25:23; Isa 22:10; e 1Ki 9:24; 1Ch 11:8; f Isa 22:8
32:7 g Dt 31:6; 1Ch 22:13; h 2Ch 20:15; i Nu 14:9; 2Ki 6:16
32:8 j Job 40:9; Isa 52:10; Jer 17:5; Jer 32:21; k Dt 3:22; 1Sa 17:45; 2Ch 13:12; l 1Ch 5:22; 2Ch 20:17; Ps 20:7; Isa 28:6
32:9 m Jos 10:3,31
32:10 n Eze 29:16
32:11 o Isa 37:10
32:12 p 2Ch 31:1
32:13 q ver 15
32:15 r Isa 37:10; s Da 3:15; t Ex 5:2

16Sennacherib's officers spoke further against the LORD God and against his servant Hezekiah. 17The king also wrote letters[u] insulting[v] the LORD, the God of Israel, and saying this against him: "Just as the gods[w] of the peoples of the other lands did not rescue their people from my hand, so the god of Hezekiah will not rescue his people from my hand." 18Then they called out in Hebrew to the people of Jerusalem who were on the wall, to terrify them and make them afraid in order to capture the city. 19They spoke about the God of Jerusalem as they did about the gods of the other peoples of the world—the work of men's hands.[x]

20King Hezekiah and the prophet Isaiah son of Amoz cried out in prayer to heaven about this. 21And the LORD sent an angel,[y] who annihilated all the fighting men and the leaders and officers in the camp of the Assyrian king. So he withdrew to his own land in disgrace. And when he went into the temple of his god, some of his sons cut him down with the sword.[z]

22So the LORD saved Hezekiah and the people of Jerusalem from the hand of Sennacherib king of Assyria and from the hand of all others. He took care of them[c] on every side. 23Many brought offerings to Jerusalem for the LORD and valuable gifts[a] for Hezekiah king of Judah. From then on he was highly regarded by all the nations.

Hezekiah's Pride, Success and Death

32:24–33pp 2Ki 20:1–21; Isa 37:21–38; 38:1–8

24In those days Hezekiah became ill and was at the point of death. He prayed to the LORD, who answered him and gave him a miraculous sign. 25But Hezekiah's heart was proud[b] and he did not respond to the kindness shown him; therefore the LORD's wrath[c] was on him and on Judah and Jerusalem. 26Then Hezekiah repented[d] of the pride of his heart, as did the people of Jerusalem; therefore the LORD's wrath did not come upon them during the days of Hezekiah.[e]

27Hezekiah had very great riches and honour,[f] and he made treasuries for his silver and gold and for his precious stones, spices, shields and all kinds of valuables. 28He also made buildings to store the harvest of grain, new wine and oil; and he made stalls for various kinds of cattle, and pens for the flocks. 29He built villages and acquired great numbers of flocks and herds, for God had given him very great riches.[g]

30It was Hezekiah who blocked[h] the upper outlet of the Gihon[i] spring and channelled the water down to the west side of the City of David. He succeeded in everything he undertook. 31But when envoys were sent by the rulers of Babylon[j] to ask him about the miraculous sign[k] that had occurred in the land, God left him to test[l] him and to know everything that was in his heart.

32The other events of Hezekiah's reign and his acts of devotion are written in the vision of the prophet Isaiah son of Amoz in the book of the kings of Judah and Israel. 33Hezekiah rested with his fathers and was buried on the hill where the tombs of David's descendants are. All Judah and the people of Jerusalem honoured him when he died. And Manasseh his son succeeded him as king.

Manasseh King of Judah

33:1–10pp 2Ki 21:1–10
33:18–20pp 2Ki 21:17–18

33 Manasseh[a] was twelve years old when he became king, and he reigned in Jerusalem for fifty-five years. 2He did evil in

32:17 u Isa 37:14 v Ps 74:22; Isa 37:4,17 w 2Ki 19:12
32:19 x 2Ki 19:18; Ps 115:4,4-8; Isa 2:8; Isa 17:8
32:21 y Ge 19:13 z 2Ki 19:7
32:23 a 2Ch 9:24; 2Ch 17:5; Isa 45:14; Zec 14:16-17
32:25 b 2Ki 14:10; 2Ch 26:16 c 2Ch 19:2; 2Ch 24:18
32:26 d Jer 26:18-19 e 2Ch 34:27,28; Isa 39:8
32:27 f 1Ch 29:12
32:29 g 1Ch 29:12
32:30 h 2Ki 18:17 i 1Ki 1:33
32:31 j Isa 39:1 k ver 24; Isa 38:7 l Ge 22:1; Dt 8:16
33:1 a 1Ch 3:13

c22 Hebrew; Septuagint and Vulgate *He gave them rest*

the eyes of the LORD,[b] following the detestable[c] practices of the nations the LORD had driven out before the Israelites. 3He rebuilt the high places his father Hezekiah had demolished; he also erected altars to the Baals and made Asherah poles.[d] He bowed down[e] to all the starry hosts and worshipped them. 4He built altars in the temple of the LORD, of which the LORD had said, "My Name[f] will remain in Jerusalem for ever." 5In both courts of the temple of the LORD,[g] he built altars to all the starry hosts. 6He sacrificed his sons[h] in[a] the fire in the Valley of Ben Hinnom, practised sorcery, divination and witchcraft, and consulted mediums[i] and spiritists.[j] He did much evil in the eyes of the LORD, provoking him to anger.

7He took the carved image he had made and put it in God's temple,[k] of which God had said to David and to his son Solomon, "In this temple and in Jerusalem, which I have chosen out of all the tribes of Israel, I will put my Name for ever. 8I will not again make the feet of the Israelites leave the land[l] I assigned to your forefathers, if only they will be careful to do everything that I commanded them concerning all the laws, decrees and ordinances given through Moses." 9But Manasseh led Judah and the people of Jerusalem astray, so that they did more evil than the nations the LORD had destroyed before the Israelites.[m]

10The LORD spoke to Manasseh and his people, but they paid no attention. 11So the LORD brought against them the army commanders of the king of Assyria, who took Manasseh prisoner,[n] put a hook in his nose, bound him with bronze shackles[o] and took him to Babylon. 12In his distress he sought the favour of the LORD his God and humbled[p] himself greatly before the God of his fathers. 13And when he prayed to him, the LORD was moved by his entreaty and listened to his plea; so he brought him back to Jerusalem and to his kingdom. Then Manasseh knew that the LORD is God.

14Afterwards he rebuilt the outer wall of the City of David, west of the Gihon[q] spring in the valley, as far as the entrance of the Fish Gate[r] and encircling the hill of Ophel;[s] he also made it much higher. He stationed military commanders in all the fortified cities in Judah.

15He got rid of the foreign gods and removed[t] the image from the temple of the LORD, as well as all the altars he had built on the temple hill and in Jerusalem; and he threw them out of the city. 16Then he restored the altar of the LORD and sacrificed fellowship offerings[b] and thank-offerings[u] on it, and told Judah to serve the LORD, the God of Israel. 17The people, however, continued to sacrifice at the high places, but only to the LORD their God.

18The other events of Manasseh's reign, including his prayer to his God and the words the seers spoke to him in the name of the LORD, the God of Israel, are written in the annals of the kings of Israel.[c] 19His prayer and how God was moved by his entreaty, as well as all his sins and unfaithfulness, and the sites where he built high places and set up Asherah poles and idols before he humbled[v] himself—all are written in the records of the seers.[d][w] 20Manasseh rested with his fathers and was buried[x] in his palace. And Amon his son succeeded him as king.

33:2 b Jer 15:4 c Dt 18:9; 2Ch 28:3
33:3 d Dt 16:21-22 e Dt 17:3; 2Ch 31:1
33:4 f 2Ch 7:16
33:5 g 2Ch 4:9
33:6 h Lev 18:21; Dt 18:10; 2Ch 28:3 i Lev 19:31 j 1Sa 28:13
33:7 k 2Ch 7:16
33:8 l 2Sa 7:10
33:9 m Jer 15:4
33:11 n Dt 28:36 o Ps 149:8
33:12 p 2Ch 6:37; 2Ch 32:26; 1Pe 5:6
33:14 q 1Ki 1:33 r Ne 3:3; Ne 12:39; Zep 1:10 s 2Ch 27:3; Ne 3:26
33:15 t ver 3-7; 2Ki 23:12
33:16 u Lev 7:11-18
33:19 v 2Ch 6:37 w 2Ki 21:17
33:20 x 2Ki 21:18; 2Ch 21:20

a6 Or *He made his sons pass through*
b16 Traditionally *peace offerings*
c18 That is, Judah, as frequently in 2 Chronicles
d19 One Hebrew manuscript and Septuagint; most Hebrew manuscripts *of Hozai*

Amon King of Judah

33:21–25pp 2Ki 21:19–24

21 Amon[y] was twenty-two years
old when he became king, and he
reigned in Jerusalem for two
years. 22 He did evil in the eyes of
the LORD, as his father Manasseh
had done. Amon worshipped and
offered sacrifices to all the idols
Manasseh had made. 23 But unlike
his father Manasseh, he did not
humble[z] himself before the LORD;
Amon increased his guilt.
24 Amon's officials conspired
against him and assassinated him
in his palace. 25 Then the people[a] of
the land killed all who had plotted
against King Amon, and they made
Josiah his son king in his place.

Josiah's Reforms

34:1–2pp 2Ki 22:1–2
34:3–7Ref 2Ki 23:4–20
34:8–13pp 2Ki 22:3–7

34 Josiah[a] was eight years
old when he became king,[b]
and he reigned in Jerusalem for
thirty-one years. 2 He did what was
right in the eyes of the LORD and
walked in the ways of his father
David,[c] not turning aside to the
right or to the left.
3 In the eighth year of his reign,
while he was still young, he began
to seek the God[d] of his father
David. In his twelfth year he began
to purge Judah and Jerusalem of
high places, Asherah poles, carved
idols and cast images. 4 Under his
direction the altars of the Baals
were torn down; he cut to pieces
the incense altars that were above
them, and smashed the Asherah
poles,[e] the idols and the images.
These he broke to pieces and scattered over the graves of those who
had sacrificed to them.[f] 5 He
burned[g] the bones of the priests on
their altars, and so he purged Judah and Jerusalem. 6 In the towns of
Manasseh, Ephraim and Simeon, as
far as Naphtali, and in the ruins
around them, 7 he tore down the
altars and the Asherah poles and
crushed the idols to powder[h] and
cut to pieces all the incense altars
throughout Israel. Then he went
back to Jerusalem.
8 In the eighteenth year of Josiah's reign, to purify the land and
the temple, he sent Shaphan son of
Azaliah and Maaseiah the ruler of
the city, with Joah son of Joahaz,
the recorder, to repair the temple
of the LORD his God.
9 They went to Hilkiah[i] the high
priest and gave him the money that
had been brought into the temple of
God, which the Levites who were
the doorkeepers had collected
from the people of Manasseh, Ephraim and the entire remnant of Israel and from all the people of
Judah and Benjamin and the inhabitants of Jerusalem. 10 Then they
entrusted it to the men appointed to
supervise the work on the LORD's
temple. These men paid the workers who repaired and restored the
temple. 11 They also gave money[j]
to the carpenters and builders to
purchase dressed stone, and timber for joists and beams for the
buildings that the kings of Judah
had allowed to fall into ruin.[k]
12 The men did the work faithfully.[l] Over them to direct them
were Jahath and Obadiah, Levites
descended from Merari, and Zechariah and Meshullam, descended
from Kohath. The Levites—all who
were skilled in playing musical instruments—[m] 13 had charge of the
labourers[n] and supervised all the
workers from job to job. Some of
the Levites were secretaries,
scribes and doorkeepers.

The Book of the Law Found

34:14–28pp 2Ki 22:8–20
34:29–32pp 2Ki 23:1–3

14 While they were bringing out
the money that had been taken into
the temple of the LORD, Hilkiah the
priest found the Book of the Law of
the LORD that had been given

33:21 y 1Ch 3:14
33:23 z ver 12; Ex 10:3; 2Ch 7:14; Ps 18:27; Ps 147:6; Pr 3:34
33:25 a 2Ch 22:1
34:1 a 1Ch 3:14; b Zep 1:1
34:2 c 2Ch 29:2
34:3 d 1Ki 13:2; 1Ch 16:11; 2Ch 15:2; 2Ch 33:17,22
34:4 e Ex 34:13; f Ex 32:20; Lev 26:30; 2Ki 23:11; Mic 1:5
34:5 g 1Ki 13:2
34:7 h Ex 32:20; 2Ch 31:1
34:9 i 1Ch 6:13; 2Ch 35:8
34:11 j 2Ch 24:12; k 2Ch 33:4-7
34:12 l 2Ki 12:15; m 1Ch 25:1
34:13 n 1Ch 23:4

through Moses. 15 Hilkiah said to
Shaphan the secretary, "I have
found the Book of the Law[o] in the
temple of the LORD." He gave it to
Shaphan.
16 Then Shaphan took the book to
the king and reported to him: "Your
officials are doing everything that
has been committed to them.
17 They have paid out the money
that was in the temple of the LORD
and have entrusted it to the supervisors and workers." 18 Then Shaphan the secretary informed the
king, "Hilkiah the priest has given
me a book." And Shaphan read
from it in the presence of the king.
19 When the king heard the words
of the Law,[p] he tore[q] his robes.
20 He gave these orders to Hilkiah,
Ahikam son of Shaphan[r], Abdon
son of Micah,[a] Shaphan the secretary and Asaiah the king's attendant: 21 "Go and enquire of the LORD
for me and for the remnant in Israel and Judah about what is written in this book that has been
found. Great is the LORD's anger
that is poured out[s] on us because
our fathers have not kept the word
of the LORD; they have not acted in
accordance with all that is written
in this book."
22 Hilkiah and those the king had
sent with him[b] went to speak to the
prophetess[t] Huldah, who was the
wife of Shallum son of Tokhath,[c]
the son of Hasrah,[d] keeper of the
wardrobe. She lived in Jerusalem,
in the Second District.
23 She said to them, "This is what
the LORD, the God of Israel, says:
Tell the man who sent you to me,
24 'This is what the LORD says: I am
going to bring disaster[u] on this
place and its people[v]—all the
curses[w] written in the book that
has been read in the presence of
the king of Judah. 25 Because they
have forsaken me[x] and burned incense to other gods and provoked
me to anger by all that their hands
have made,[e] my anger will be
poured out on this place and will
not be quenched.' 26 Tell the king of
Judah, who sent you to enquire of
the LORD, 'This is what the LORD,
the God of Israel, says concerning the words you heard: 27 Because
your heart was responsive[y] and
you humbled[z] yourself before God
when you heard what he spoke
against this place and its people,
and because you humbled yourself
before me and tore your robes and
wept in my presence, I have heard
you, declares the LORD. 28 Now I will
gather you to your fathers,[a] and
you will be buried in peace. Your
eyes will not see all the disaster I
am going to bring on this place and
on those who live here.' "[b]
So they took her answer back to
the king.
29 Then the king called together
all the elders of Judah and Jerusalem. 30 He went up to the temple
of the LORD[c] with the men of Judah, the people of Jerusalem, the
priests and the Levites—all the
people from the least to the greatest. He read in their hearing all the
words of the Book of the Covenant,
which had been found in the temple
of the LORD. 31 The king stood by his
pillar[d] and renewed the covenant[e] in the presence of the
LORD—to follow[f] the LORD and
keep his commands, regulations
and decrees with all his heart and
all his soul, and to obey the words
of the covenant written in this
book.
32 Then he made everyone in
Jerusalem and Benjamin pledge
themselves to it; the people of Jerusalem did this in accordance with
the covenant of God, the God of
their fathers.
33 Josiah removed all the detestable[g] idols from all the territory
belonging to the Israelites, and he
made all who were present in Israel

34:15 o 2Ki 22:8; Ezr 7:6; Ne 8:1
34:19 p Dt 28:3-68; q Jos 7:6; Isa 36:22; Isa 37:1
34:20 r 2Ki 22:3
34:21 s 2Ch 29:8; La 2:4; La 4:11; Eze 36:18
34:22 t Ex 15:20; Ne 6:14
34:24 u Pr 16:4; Isa 3:9; Jer 40:2; Jer 42:10; Jer 44:2,11; v 2Ch 36:14-20; w Dt 28:15-68
34:25 x 2Ch 33:3-6; Jer 22:9
34:27 y 2Ch 12:7; 2Ch 32:26; z Ex 10:3; 2Ch 6:37
34:28 a 2Ch 35:20-25; b 2Ch 32:26
34:30 c 2Ki 23:2; Ne 8:1-3
34:31 d 1Ki 7:15; 2Ki 11:14; e 2Ki 11:17; 2Ch 23:16; 2Ch 29:10; f Dt 13:4
34:33 g ver 3-7; Dt 18:9

a 20 Also called *Acbor son of Micaiah* b 22 One Hebrew manuscript, Vulgate and Syriac; most Hebrew manuscripts do not have *had sent with him.* c 22 Also called *Tikvah* d 22 Also called *Harhas* e 25 Or *by everything they have done*

serve the LORD their God. As long as he lived, they did not fail to follow the LORD, the God of their fathers.

Josiah Celebrates the Passover

35:1,18–19pp 2Ki 23:21–23

35 Josiah celebrated the Passover[a] to the LORD in Jerusalem, and the Passover lamb was slaughtered on the fourteenth day of the first month. 2 He appointed the priests to their duties and encouraged them in the service of the LORD's temple. 3 He said to the Levites, who instructed[b] all Israel and who had been consecrated to the LORD: "Put the sacred ark in the temple that Solomon son of David king of Israel built. It is not to be carried about on your shoulders. Now serve the LORD your God and his people Israel. 4 Prepare yourselves by families in your divisions,[c] according to the directions written by David king of Israel and by his son Solomon.

5 "Stand in the holy place with a group of Levites for each subdivision of the families of your fellow countrymen, the lay people. 6 Slaughter the Passover lambs, consecrate yourselves[d] and prepare ⌞the lambs⌟ for your fellow countrymen, doing what the LORD commanded through Moses."

7 Josiah provided for all the lay people who were there a total of thirty thousand sheep and goats for the Passover offerings,[e] and also three thousand cattle—all from the king's own possessions.[f]

8 His officials also contributed[g] voluntarily to the people and the priests and Levites. Hilkiah,[h] Zechariah and Jehiel, the administrators of God's temple, gave the priests two thousand six hundred Passover offerings and three hundred cattle. 9 Also Conaniah[i] along with Shemaiah and Nethanel, his brothers, and Hashabiah, Jeiel and Jozabad,[j] the leaders of the Levites, provided five thousand Passover offerings and five hundred head of cattle for the Levites.

10 The service was arranged and the priests stood in their places with the Levites in their divisions[k] as the king had ordered.[l] 11 The Passover lambs were slaughtered,[m] and the priests sprinkled the blood handed to them, while the Levites skinned the animals. 12 They set aside the burnt offerings to give them to the subdivisions of the families of the people to offer to the LORD, as is written in the Book of Moses. They did the same with the cattle. 13 They roasted the Passover animals over the fire as prescribed,[n] and boiled the holy offerings in pots, caldrons and pans and served them quickly to all the people. 14 After this, they made preparations for themselves and for the priests, because the priests, the descendants of Aaron, were sacrificing the burnt offerings and the fat portions[o] until nightfall. So the Levites made preparations for themselves and for the Aaronic priests.

15 The musicians,[p] the descendants of Asaph, were in the places prescribed by David, Asaph, Heman and Jeduthun the king's seer. The gatekeepers at each gate did not need to leave their posts, because their fellow Levites made the preparations for them.

16 So at that time the entire service of the LORD was carried out for the celebration of the Passover and the offering of burnt offerings on the altar of the LORD, as King Josiah had ordered. 17 The Israelites who were present celebrated the Passover at that time and observed the Feast of Unleavened Bread for seven days. 18 The Passover had not been observed like this in Israel since the days of the prophet Samuel; and none of the kings of Israel had ever celebrated such a Passover as did Josiah, with the

35:1
a Ex 12:1-30; Nu 9:3; Nu 28:16

35:3
b Dt 33:10; 1Ch 23:26; 2Ch 5:7; 2Ch 17:7

35:4
c ver 10; 1Ch 9:10-13; 1Ch 24:1; 2Ch 8:14; Ezr 6:18

35:6
d Lev 11:44; 2Ch 29:5,15

35:7
e 2Ch 30:24
f 2Ch 31:3

35:8
g 1Ch 29:3; 2Ch 29:31-36
h 1Ch 6:13

35:9
i 2Ch 31:12
j 2Ch 31:13

35:10
k ver 4; Ezr 6:18
l 2Ch 30:16

35:11
m 2Ch 29:22,34; 2Ch 30:17

35:13
n Ex 12:2-11; Lev 6:25; 1Sa 2:13-15

35:14
o Ex 29:13

35:15
p 1Ch 25:1; 1Ch 26:12-19; 2Ch 29:30; Ne 12:46; Ps 68:25

priests, the Levites and all Judah and Israel who were there with the people of Jerusalem. [19]This Passover was celebrated in the eighteenth year of Josiah's reign.

The Death of Josiah

35:20–36:1pp 2Ki 23:28–30

[20]After all this, when Josiah had set the temple in order, Neco king of Egypt went up to fight at Carchemish[q] on the Euphrates,[r] and Josiah marched out to meet him in battle. [21]But Neco sent messengers to him saying, "What quarrel is there between you and me, O king of Judah? It is not you I am attacking at this time, but the house with which I am at war. God has told[s] me to hurry; so stop opposing God, who is with me, or he will destroy you."

[22]Josiah, however, would not turn away from him, but disguised[t] himself to engage him in battle. He would not listen to what Neco had said at God's command but went to fight him on the plain of Megiddo.

[23]Archers[u] shot King Josiah, and he told his officers, "Take me away; I am badly wounded." [24]So they took him out of his chariot, put him in the other chariot he had and brought him to Jerusalem, where he died. He was buried in the tombs of his fathers, and all Judah and Jerusalem mourned for him.

[25]Jeremiah composed laments for Josiah, and to this day all the men and women singers commemorate Josiah in the laments.[v] These became a tradition in Israel and are written in the Laments.

[26]The other events of Josiah's reign and his acts of devotion, according to what is written in the Law of the LORD—[27]all the events, from beginning to end, are written in the book of the kings of Israel and Judah.

36 [1]And the people of the land took Jehoahaz son of Josiah and made him king in Jerusalem in place of his father.

35:20 *q* Isa 10:9; Jer 46:2 *r* Ge 2:14
35:21 *s* 1Ki 13:18; 2Ki 18:25
35:22 *t* Jdg 5:19; 1Sa 28:8; 2Ch 18:29
35:23 *u* 1Ki 22:34
35:25 *v* Jer 22:10, 15-16
36:4 *a* Jer 22:10-12
36:5 *b* Jer 22:18; Jer 26:1; Jer 35:1
36:6 *c* Jer 25:9; Jer 27:6; Eze 29:18 *d* 2Ch 33:11; Eze 19:9; Da 1:1
36:7 *e* 2Ki 24:13; Ezr 1:7; Da 1:2
36:9 *f* Jer 22:24-28; Jer 52:31

Jehoahaz King of Judah

36:2–4pp 2Ki 23:31–34

[2]Jehoahaz[a] was twenty-three years old when he became king, and he reigned in Jerusalem for three months. [3]The king of Egypt dethroned him in Jerusalem and imposed on Judah a levy of a hundred talents[b] of silver and a talent[c] of gold. [4]The king of Egypt made Eliakim, a brother of Jehoahaz, king over Judah and Jerusalem and changed Eliakim's name to Jehoiakim. But Neco[a] took Eliakim's brother Jehoahaz and carried him off to Egypt.

Jehoiakim King of Judah

36:5–8pp 2Ki 23:36–24:6

[5]Jehoiakim[b] was twenty-five years old when he became king, and he reigned in Jerusalem for eleven years. He did evil in the eyes of the LORD his God. [6]Nebuchadnezzar[c] king of Babylon attacked him and bound him with bronze shackles to take him to Babylon.[d] [7]Nebuchadnezzar also took to Babylon articles from the temple of the LORD and put them in his temple[d] there.[e]

[8]The other events of Jehoiakim's reign, the detestable things he did and all that was found against him, are written in the book of the kings of Israel and Judah. And Jehoiachin his son succeeded him as king.

Jehoiachin King of Judah

36:9–10pp 2Ki 24:8–17

[9]Jehoiachin[f] was eighteen[e] years old when he became king, and he reigned in Jerusalem for

[a]2 Hebrew *Joahaz,* a variant of *Jehoahaz;* also in verse 4 [b]3 That is, about 3 ⅓ tons (about 3.4 metric tons) [c]3 That is, about 75 pounds (about 34 kilograms) [d]7 Or *palace* [e]9 One Hebrew manuscript, some Septuagint manuscripts and Syriac (see also 2 Kings 24:8); most Hebrew manuscripts *eight*

three months and ten days. He did evil in the eyes of the LORD. 10In the spring, King Nebuchadnezzar sent for him and brought him to Babylon,[g] together with articles of value from the temple of the LORD, and he made Jehoiachin's uncle,[f] Zedekiah, king over Judah and Jerusalem.

Zedekiah King of Judah

36:11–16pp 2Ki 24:18–20; Jer 52:1–3

11Zedekiah[h] was twenty-one years old when he became king, and he reigned in Jerusalem for eleven years. 12He did evil in the eyes of the LORD[i] his God and did not humble[j] himself before Jeremiah the prophet, who spoke the word of the LORD. 13He also rebelled against King Nebuchadnezzar, who had made him take an oath[k] in God's name. He became stiff-necked[l] and hardened his heart and would not turn to the LORD, the God of Israel. 14Furthermore, all the leaders of the priests and the people became more and more unfaithful,[m] following all the detestable practices of the nations and defiling the temple of the LORD, which he had consecrated in Jerusalem.

The Fall of Jerusalem

36:17–20pp 2Ki 25:1–21; Jer 52:4–27
36:22–23pp Ezr 1:1–3

15The LORD, the God of their fathers, sent word to them through his messengers[n] again and again,[o] because he had pity on his people and on his dwelling-place. 16But they mocked God's messengers, despised his words and scoffed[p] at his prophets until the wrath[q] of the LORD was aroused against his people and there was no remedy.[r] 17He brought up against them the king of the Babylonians,[g] who killed their young men with the sword in the sanctuary, and spared neither young man[s] nor young woman, old man or aged. God handed all of them over to Nebuchadnezzar.[t] 18He carried to Babylon all the articles[u] from the temple of God, both large and small, and the treasures of the LORD's temple and the treasures of the king and his officials. 19They set fire[v] to God's temple[w] and broke down the wall[x] of Jerusalem; they burned all the palaces and destroyed[y] everything of value there.[z]

20He carried into exile[a] to Babylon the remnant who escaped from the sword, and they became servants[b] to him and his sons until the kingdom of Persia came to power. 21The land enjoyed its sabbath rests;[c] all the time of its desolation it rested,[d] until the seventy years[e] were completed in fulfilment of the word of the LORD spoken by Jeremiah.

22In the first year of Cyrus[f] king of Persia, in order to fulfil the word of the LORD spoken by Jeremiah, the LORD moved the heart of Cyrus king of Persia to make a proclamation throughout his realm and to put it in writing:

23"This is what Cyrus king of Persia says:

"'The LORD, the God of heaven, has given me all the kingdoms of the earth and he has appointed[g] me to build a temple for him at Jerusalem in Judah. Anyone of his people among you—may the LORD his God be with him, and let him go up.'"

36:10 *g* ver 18 2Ki 20:17 Ezr 1:7 Jer 22:25 Jer 24:1 Jer 29:1 Jer 37:1 Eze 17:12
36:11 *h* 2Ki 24:17 Jer 27:1 Jer 28:1
36:12 *i* Jer 37:1-39:18 *j* Dt 8:3 2Ch 7:14 2Ch 33:23 Jer 21:3-7
36:13 *k* Eze 17:13 *l* 2Ki 17:14 2Ch 30:8
36:14 *m* 1Ch 5:25
36:15 *n* Isa 5:4 Isa 44:26 Jer 7:25 Hag 1:13 Zec 1:4 Mal 2:7 Mal 3:1 *o* Jer 7:13,25 Jer 25:3-4 Jer 35:14,15 Jer 44:4-6
36:16 *p* 2Ki 2:23 Pr 1:25 Jer 5:13 *q* Ezr 5:12 Pr 1:30-31 *r* 2Ch 30:10 Pr 29:1 Zec 1:2
36:17 *s* Jer 6:11 *t* Ezr 5:12 Jer 32:28
36:18 *u* ver 7,10
36:19 *v* Jer 11:16 Jer 17:27 Jer 21:10,14 Jer 22:7 Jer 32:29 Jer 39:8 La 4:11 Eze 20:47 Am 2:5 Zec 11:1 *w* 1Ki 9:8-9 *x* 2Ki 14:13 *y* La 2:6 *z* Ps 79:1-3
36:20 *a* Lev 26:44 2Ki 24:14 Ezr 2:1 Ne 7:6 *b* Jer 27:7
36:21 *c* Lev 25:4 Lev 26:34 *d* 1Ch 22:9 *e* Jer 1:1 Jer 25:11 Jer 27:22 Jer 29:10 Jer 40:1 Da 9:2 Zec 1:12 Zec 7:5
36:22 *f* Isa 44:28 Isa 45:1,13 Jer 25:12 Jer 29:10 Da 1:21 Da 6:28 Da 10:1 **36:23** *g* Jdg 4:10

f10 Hebrew *brother*, that is, relative (see 2 Kings 24:17) g17 Or *Chaldeans*

EZRA

Cyrus Helps the Exiles to Return

1:1–3pp 2Ch 36:22–23

1 In the first year of Cyrus king
of Persia, in order to fulfil the
word of the LORD spoken by Jeremiah,[a] the LORD moved the heart[b]
of Cyrus king of Persia to make a
proclamation throughout his realm
and to put it in writing:

2 "This is what Cyrus king of
Persia says:

" 'The LORD, the God of
heaven, has given me all the
kingdoms of the earth and he
has appointed[c] me to build[d] a
temple for him at Jerusalem in
Judah. 3 Anyone of his people
among you—may his God be
with him, and let him go up to
Jerusalem in Judah and build
the temple of the LORD, the God
of Israel, the God who is in
Jerusalem. 4 And the people of
any place where survivors[e]
may now be living are to provide him with silver and gold,
with goods and livestock, and
with freewill offerings[f] for
the temple of God in Jerusalem.' "[g]

5 Then the family heads of Judah
and Benjamin,[h] and the priests
and Levites—everyone whose
heart God had moved[i]—prepared
to go up and build the house[j] of the
LORD in Jerusalem. 6 All their
neighbours assisted them with articles of silver and gold, with goods
and livestock, and with valuable
gifts, in addition to all the freewill
offerings. 7 Moreover, King Cyrus
brought out the articles belonging
to the temple of the LORD, which
Nebuchadnezzar had carried away
from Jerusalem and had placed in
the temple of his god.[a][k] 8 Cyrus
king of Persia had them brought by
Mithredath the treasurer, who
counted them out to Sheshbazzar[l]
the prince of Judah.
9 This was the inventory:

gold dishes	30
silver dishes	1,000
silver pans[b]	29
10 gold bowls	30
matching silver bowls	410
other articles	1,000

11 In all, there were 5,400 articles
of gold and of silver. Sheshbazzar
brought all these along when the
exiles came up from Babylon to
Jerusalem.

The List of the Exiles Who Returned

2:1–70pp Ne 7:6–73

2 Now these are the people of
the province who came up
from the captivity of the exiles,[a]
whom Nebuchadnezzar king of
Babylon[b] had taken captive to
Babylon (they returned to Jerusalem and Judah, each to his own
town,[c] 2 in company with Zerubbabel,[d] Jeshua,[e] Nehemiah,
Seraiah,[f] Reelaiah, Mordecai,
Bilshan, Mispar, Bigvai, Rehum
and Baanah):

The list of the men of the people of Israel:

3 the descendants of Parosh[g]	2,172
4 of Shephatiah	372
5 of Arah	775
6 of Pahath-Moab (through the line of Jeshua and Joab)	2,812
7 of Elam	1,254

[a]7 Or *gods* [b]9 The meaning of the Hebrew for this word is uncertain.

1:1 *a* Jer 25:11-12; Jer 29:10-14 *b* 2Ch 36:22,23
1:2 *c* Isa 44:28; Isa 45:13 *d* Ezr 5:13
1:4 *e* Isa 10:20-22 *f* Nu 15:3; Ps 50:14; Ps 54:6; Ps 116:17 *g* Ezr 4:3; Ezr 5:13; Ezr 6:3,14
1:5 *h* Ezr 4:1; Ne 11:4 *i* ver 1; Ex 35:20-22; 2Ch 36:22; Hag 1:14; Php 2:13 *j* Ps 127:1
1:7 *k* 2Ki 24:13; 2Ch 36:7,10; Ezr 5:14; Ezr 6:5
1:8 *l* Ezr 5:14
2:1 *a* 2Ch 36:20; Ne 7:6 *b* 2Ki 24:16; 2Ki 25:12 *c* Ne 7:73
2:2 *d* 1Ch 3:19 *e* Ezr 3:2 *f* Ne 10:2
2:3 *g* Ezr 8:3

8 of Zattu 945
9 of Zaccai 760
10 of Bani 642
11 of Bebai 623
12 of Azgad 1,222
13 of Adonikam[h] 666
14 of Bigvai 2,056
15 of Adin 454
16 of Ater (through
Hezekiah) 98
17 of Bezai 323
18 of Jorah 112
19 of Hashum 223
20 of Gibbar 95

21 the men of Bethlehem[i] 123
22 of Netophah 56
23 of Anathoth 128
24 of Azmaveth 42
25 of Kiriath Jearim,[a]
Kephirah and Beeroth 743
26 of Ramah[j] and Geba 621
27 of Michmash 122
28 of Bethel and Ai[k] 223
29 of Nebo 52
30 of Magbish 156
31 of the other Elam 1,254
32 of Harim 320
33 of Lod, Hadid and Ono 725
34 of Jericho[l] 345
35 of Senaah 3,630

36 The priests:

the descendants of Jedaiah[m]
(through the family of
Jeshua) 973
37 of Immer[n] 1,052
38 of Pashhur[o] 1,247
39 of Harim[p] 1,017

40 The Levites:[q]

the descendants of Jeshua[r]
and Kadmiel (through the
line of Hodaviah) 74

41 The singers:[s]

the descendants of Asaph 128

42 The gatekeepers[t] of the
temple:

the descendants of
Shallum, Ater, Talmon,
Akkub, Hatita and
Shobai 139

43 The temple servants:[u]

the descendants of
Ziha, Hasupha, Tabbaoth,
44 Keros, Siaha, Padon,
45 Lebanah, Hagabah, Akkub,
46 Hagab, Shalmai, Hanan,
47 Giddel, Gahar, Reaiah,
48 Rezin, Nekoda, Gazzam,
49 Uzza, Paseah, Besai,
50 Asnah, Meunim, Nephussim,
51 Bakbuk, Hakupha, Harhur,
52 Bazluth, Mehida, Harsha,
53 Barkos, Sisera, Temah,
54 Neziah and Hatipha

55 The descendants of the servants of Solomon:

the descendants of
Sotai, Hassophereth,
Peruda,
56 Jaala, Darkon, Giddel,
57 Shephatiah, Hattil,
Pokereth-Hazzebaim and
Ami

58 The temple servants[v] and
the descendants of the
servants of Solomon 392

59 The following came up
from the towns of Tel Melah,
Tel Harsha, Kerub, Addon and
Immer, but they could not
show that their families were
descended[w] from Israel:

60 The descendants of
Delaiah, Tobiah and
Nekoda 652

61 And from among the priests:

The descendants of
Hobaiah, Hakkoz and
Barzillai (a man who had
married a daughter of
Barzillai the Gileadite[x] and
was called by that name).

62 These searched for their
family records, but they could
not find them and so were excluded from the priesthood[y]
as unclean. 63 The governor ordered them not to eat any of the

[a] 25 See Septuagint (see also Neh. 7:29); Hebrew *Kiriath Arim.*

2:13 [h] Ezr 8:13
2:21 [i] Mic 5:2
2:26 [j] Jos 18:25
2:28 [k] Ge 12:8
2:34 [l] 1Ki 16:34; 2Ch 28:15
2:36 [m] 1Ch 24:7
2:37 [n] 1Ch 24:14
2:38 [o] 1Ch 9:12
2:39 [p] 1Ch 24:8
2:40 [q] Ge 29:34; Nu 3:9; Dt 18:6-7; 1Ch 16:4; Ezr 7:7; Ezr 8:15; Ne 12:24 [r] Ezr 3:9
2:41 [s] 1Ch 15:16
2:42 [t] 1Sa 3:15; 1Ch 9:17
2:43 [u] 1Ch 9:2; Ne 11:21
2:58 [v] 1Ki 9:21; 1Ch 9:2
2:59 [w] Nu 1:18
2:61 [x] 2Sa 17:27
2:62 [y] Nu 3:10; Nu 16:39-40

most sacred food[z] until there was a priest ministering with the Urim and Thummim.[a]

64 The whole company numbered 42,360, 65 besides their 7,337 menservants and maidservants; and they also had 200 men and women singers.[b] 66 They had 736 horses,[c] 245 mules, 67 435 camels and 6,720 donkeys.

68 When they arrived at the house of the LORD in Jerusalem, some of the heads of the families[d] gave freewill offerings towards the rebuilding of the house of God on its site. 69 According to their ability they gave to the treasury for this work 61,000 drachmas[b] of gold, 5,000 minas[c] of silver and 100 priestly garments.

70 The priests, the Levites, the singers, the gatekeepers and the temple servants settled in their own towns, along with some of the other people, and the rest of the Israelites settled in their towns.[e]

Rebuilding the Altar

3 When the seventh month came and the Israelites had settled in their towns,[a] the people assembled[b] as one man in Jerusalem. 2 Then Jeshua[c] son of Jozadak[d] and his fellow priests and Zerubbabel son of Shealtiel[e] and his associates began to build the altar of the God of Israel to sacrifice burnt offerings on it, in accordance with what is written in the Law of Moses[f] the man of God. 3 Despite their fear[g] of the peoples around them, they built the altar on its foundation and sacrificed burnt offerings on it to the LORD, both the morning and evening sacrifices.[h] 4 Then in accordance with what is written, they celebrated the Feast of Tabernacles[i] with the required number of burnt offerings prescribed for each day. 5 After that, they presented the regular burnt offerings, the New Moon[j] sacrifices and the sacrifices for all the appointed sacred feasts of the LORD,[k] as well as those brought as freewill offerings to the LORD. 6 On the first day of the seventh month they began to offer burnt offerings to the LORD, though the foundation of the LORD's temple had not yet been laid.

Rebuilding the Temple

7 Then they gave money to the masons and carpenters, and gave food and drink and oil to the people of Sidon and Tyre, so that they would bring cedar logs[l] by sea from Lebanon[m] to Joppa, as authorised by Cyrus[n] king of Persia.

8 In the second month of the second year after their arrival at the house of God in Jerusalem, Zerubbabel[o] son of Shealtiel, Jeshua son of Jozadak and the rest of their brothers (the priests and the Levites and all who had returned from the captivity to Jerusalem) began the work, appointing Levites twenty[p] years of age and older to supervise the building of the house of the LORD. 9 Jeshua[q] and his sons and brothers and Kadmiel and his sons (descendants of Hodaviah[a]) and the sons of Henadad and their sons and brothers—all Levites—joined together in supervising those working on the house of God.

10 When the builders laid[r] the foundation of the temple of the LORD, the priests in their vestments and with trumpets,[s] and the Levites (the sons of Asaph) with cymbals, took their places to praise[t] the LORD, as prescribed by David[u] king of Israel.[v] 11 With praise and thanksgiving they sang to the LORD:

2:63 z Lev 2:3,10 a Ex 28:30 Nu 27:21
2:65 b 2Sa 19:35
2:66 c Isa 66:20
2:68 d Ex 25:2
2:70 e ver 1 1Ch 9:2 Ne 11:3-4
3:1 a Ne 7:73 Ne 8:1 b Lev 23:24
3:2 c Ezr 2:2 Ne 12:1,8 Hag 2:2 d Hag 1:1 Zec 6:11 e 1Ch 3:17 f Ex 20:24 Dt 12:5-6
3:3 g Ezr 4:4 Da 9:25 h Ex 29:39 Nu 28:1-8
3:4 i Ex 23:16 Nu 29:12-38 Ne 8:14-18 Zec 14:16-19
3:5 j Nu 28:3,11,14 Col 2:16 k Lev 23:1-44 Nu 29:39
3:7 l 1Ch 14:1 m Isa 35:2 n Ezr 1:2-4 Ezr 6:3
3:8 o Zec 4:9 p 1Ch 23:24
3:9 q Ezr 2:40
3:10 r Ezr 5:16 s Nu 10:2 1Ch 16:6 t 1Ch 25:1 u 1Ch 6:31 v Zec 6:12

b69 That is, about 1,100 pounds (about 500 kilograms) c69 That is, about 2 ⅘ tons (about 2.9 metric tons) a9 Hebrew *Yehudah*, probably a variant of *Hodaviah*

"He is good;
his love to Israel endures for
ever."[w]

And all the people gave a great
shout[x] of praise to the LORD, because the foundation of the house
of the LORD was laid. 12But many of
the older priests and Levites and
family heads, who had seen the former temple,[y] wept aloud when
they saw the foundation of this
temple being laid, while many
others shouted for joy. 13No-one
could distinguish the sound of the
shouts of joy[z] from the sound of
weeping, because the people made
so much noise. And the sound was
heard far away.

Opposition to the Rebuilding

4 When the enemies of Judah
and Benjamin heard that the
exiles were building a temple for
the LORD, the God of Israel, 2they
came to Zerubbabel and to the
heads of the families and said, "Let
us help you build because, like you,
we seek your God and have been
sacrificing to him since the time of
Esarhaddon[a] king of Assyria, who
brought us here."[b]
3But Zerubbabel, Jeshua and the
rest of the heads of the families of
Israel answered, "You have no part
with us in building a temple to our
God. We alone will build it for the
LORD, the God of Israel, as King Cyrus, the king of Persia, commanded
us."[c]
4Then the peoples around them
set out to discourage the people of
Judah and make them afraid to go
on building.[a][d] 5They hired counsellors to work against them and
frustrate their plans during the entire reign of Cyrus king of Persia
and down to the reign of Darius
king of Persia.

*Later Opposition Under Xerxes
and Artaxerxes*

6At the beginning of the reign
of Xerxes,[b][e] they lodged an
accusation against the people of
Judah and Jerusalem.[f]
7And in the days of Artaxerxes[g]
king of Persia, Bishlam, Mithredath, Tabeel and the rest of his
associates wrote a letter to
Artaxerxes. The letter was written
in Aramaic script and in the Aramaic[h] language.[c,d]
8Rehum the commanding officer
and Shimshai the secretary wrote a
letter against Jerusalem to Artaxerxes the king as follows:

9Rehum the commanding officer and Shimshai the secretary, together with the rest of
their associates[i]—the judges
and officials over the men
from Tripolis, Persia,[e] Erech
and Babylon, the Elamites of
Susa, 10and the other people
whom the great and honourable Ashurbanipal[f] deported
and settled in the city of Samaria and elsewhere in Trans-
Euphrates.[j]

11(This is a copy of the letter they
sent him.)

To King Artaxerxes,
From your servants, the men
of Trans-Euphrates:

12The king should know that
the Jews who came up to us
from you have gone to Jerusalem and are rebuilding that
rebellious and wicked city.
They are restoring the walls
and repairing the founda-
tions.[k]
13Furthermore, the king
should know that if this city is
built and its walls are restored,
no more taxes, tribute or
duty[l] will be paid, and the
royal revenues will suffer.

3:11 w 1Ch 16:34,41; 2Ch 7:3; Ps 107:1; Ps 118:1 x Ne 12:24
3:12 y Hag 2:3,9
3:13 z Job 8:21; Ps 27:6; Isa 16:9
4:2 a 2Ki 17:24; 2Ki 19:37 b 2Ki 17:41
4:3 c Ezr 1:1-4; Ne 2:20
4:4 d Ezr 3:3
4:6 e Est 1:1; Da 9:1 f Est 3:13; Est 9:5
4:7 g Ezr 7:1; Ne 2:1 h 2Ki 18:26; Isa 36:11; Da 2:4
4:9 i Ezr 5:6; Ezr 6:6,13
4:10 j ver 17; Ne 4:2
4:12 k Ezr 5:3,9
4:13 l Ezr 7:24; Ne 5:4

a4 Or *and troubled them as they built*
b6 Hebrew *Ahasuerus*, a variant of Xerxes' Persian name
c7 Or *written in Aramaic and translated*
d7 The text of Ezra 4:8–6:18 is in Aramaic.
e9 Or *officials, magistrates and governors over the men from*
f10 Aramaic *Osnappar*, a variant of *Ashurbanipal*

14 Now since we are under obligation to the palace and it is not proper for us to see the king dishonoured, we are sending this message to inform the king, 15 so that a search may be made in the archives[m] of your predecessors. In these records you will find that this city is a rebellious city, troublesome to kings and provinces, a place of rebellion from ancient times. That is why this city was destroyed.[n] 16 We inform the king that if this city is built and its walls are restored, you will be left with nothing in Trans-Euphrates.

17 The king sent this reply:

To Rehum the commanding officer, Shimshai the secretary and the rest of their associates living in Samaria and elsewhere in Trans-Euphrates:[o]

Greetings.

18 The letter you sent us has been read and translated in my presence. 19 I issued an order and a search was made, and it was found that this city has a long history of revolt[p] against kings and has been a place of rebellion and sedition. 20 Jerusalem has had powerful kings ruling over the whole of Trans-Euphrates,[q] and taxes, tribute and duty were paid to them. 21 Now issue an order to these men to stop work, so that this city will not be rebuilt until I so order. 22 Be careful not to neglect this matter. Why let this threat grow, to the detriment of the royal interests?[r]

23 As soon as the copy of the letter of King Artaxerxes was read to Rehum and Shimshai the secretary and their associates,[s] they went immediately to the Jews in Jerusalem and compelled them by force to stop.

24 Thus the work on the house of God in Jerusalem came to a standstill until the second year of the reign of Darius[t] king of Persia.

Tattenai's Letter to Darius

5 Now Haggai[a] the prophet and Zechariah[b] the prophet, a descendant of Iddo, prophesied[c] to the Jews in Judah and Jerusalem in the name of the God of Israel, who was over them. 2 Then Zerubbabel[d] son of Shealtiel and Jeshua[e] son of Jozadak set to work[f] to rebuild the house of God in Jerusalem. And the prophets of God were with them, helping them.

3 At that time Tattenai,[g] governor of Trans-Euphrates, and Shethar-Bozenai[h] and their associates went to them and asked, "Who authorised you to rebuild this temple and restore this structure?"[i] 4 They also asked, "What are the names of the men constructing this building?"[a] 5 But the eye of their God[j] was watching over the elders of the Jews, and they were not stopped until a report could go to Darius and his written reply be received.

6 This is a copy of the letter that Tattenai, governor of Trans-Euphrates, and Shethar-Bozenai and their associates, the officials of Trans-Euphrates, sent to King Darius. 7 The report they sent him read as follows:

To King Darius:

Cordial greetings.

8 The king should know that we went to the district of Judah, to the temple of the great God. The people are building it with large stones and placing the timbers in the walls. The work[k] is being carried on with diligence and is making rapid progress under their direction.

4:15
m Ezr 5:17; Ezr 6:1
n Est 3:8

4:17
o ver 10

4:19
p 2Ki 18:7

4:20
q Ge 15:18-21; Ex 23:31; Jos 1:4; 1Ki 4:21; 1Ch 18:3; Ps 72:8-11

4:22
r Da 6:2

4:23
s ver 9

4:24
t Ne 2:1-8; Da 9:25; Hag 1:1,15; Zec 1:1

5:1
a Ezr 6:14; Hag 1:1,3,12; Hag 2:1,10,20
b Zec 1:1; Zec 7:1
c Hag 1:14-2:9; Zec 4:9-10; Zec 8:9

5:2
d 1Ch 3:19; Hag 1:14; Hag 2:21; Zec 4:6-10
e Ezr 2:2; Ezr 3:2
f ver 8; Hag 2:2-5

5:3
g Ezr 6:6
h Ezr 6:6
i ver 9; Ezr 1:3; Ezr 4:12

5:5
j 2Ki 25:28; Ezr 7:6,9,28; Ezr 8:18,22,31; Ne 2:8,18; Ps 33:18; Isa 66:14

5:8
k ver 2

a4 See Septuagint; Aramaic 4*We told them the names of the men constructing this building.*

9We questioned the elders
and asked them, "Who authorised you to rebuild this temple
and restore this structure?"[l]
10We also asked them their
names, so that we could write
down the names of their leaders for your information.
11This is the answer they
gave us:

"We are the servants of the
God of heaven and earth, and
we are rebuilding the temple[m]
that was built many years ago,
one that a great king of Israel
built and finished. 12But because our fathers angered[n]
the God of heaven, he handed
them over to Nebuchadnezzar
the Chaldean, king of Babylon,
who destroyed this temple and
deported the people to Babylon.[o]
13"However, in the first year
of Cyrus king of Babylon, King
Cyrus issued a decree[p] to rebuild this house of God. 14He
even removed from the temple[b] of Babylon the gold and
silver articles of the house of
God, which Nebuchadnezzar
had taken from the temple in
Jerusalem and brought to the
temple[b] in Babylon.[q]
"Then King Cyrus gave them
to a man named Sheshbazzar,[r]
whom he had appointed governor, 15and he told him, 'Take
these articles and go and deposit them in the temple in
Jerusalem. And rebuild the
house of God on its site.' 16So
this Sheshbazzar came and laid
the foundations of the house of
God[s] in Jerusalem. From that
day to the present it has been
under construction but is not
yet finished."

17Now if it pleases the king,
let a search be made in the
royal archives[t] of Babylon to
see if King Cyrus did in fact
issue a decree to rebuild this
house of God in Jerusalem.
Then let the king send us his
decision in this matter.

The Decree of Darius

6 King Darius then issued an order, and they searched in the
archives[a] stored in the treasury at
Babylon. 2A scroll was found in the
citadel of Ecbatana in the province
of Media, and this was written on it:

Memorandum:

3In the first year of King Cyrus, the king issued a decree
concerning the temple of God
in Jerusalem:

Let the temple be rebuilt as a
place to present sacrifices, and
let its foundations be laid.[b] It
is to be ninety feet[a] high and
ninety feet wide, 4with three
courses[c] of large stones and
one of timbers. The costs are to
be paid by the royal treasury.[d]
5Also, the gold[e] and silver articles of the house of God,
which Nebuchadnezzar took
from the temple in Jerusalem
and brought to Babylon, are to
be returned to their places in
the temple in Jerusalem; they
are to be deposited in the house
of God.[f]

6Now then, Tattenai,[g] governor of Trans-Euphrates, and
Shethar-Bozenai[h] and you,
their fellow officials of that
province, stay away from
there. 7Do not interfere with
the work on this temple of God.
Let the governor of the Jews
and the Jewish elders rebuild
this house of God on its site.
8Moreover, I hereby decree
what you are to do for these
elders of the Jews in the construction of this house of God:
The expenses of these men

5:9 l Ezr 4:12
5:11 m 1Ki 6:1; 2Ch 3:1-2
5:12 n 2Ch 36:16; o Dt 21:10; Dt 28:36; 2Ki 24:1; 2Ki 25:8,9,11; Jer 1:3
5:13 p Ezr 1:1
5:14 q Ezr 1:7; Ezr 6:5; Da 5:2; r 1Ch 3:18
5:16 s Ezr 3:10; Ezr 6:15
5:17 t Ezr 4:15; Ezr 6:1,2
6:1 a Ezr 4:15; Ezr 5:17
6:3 b Ezr 3:10; Hag 2:3
6:4 c 1Ki 6:36; d ver 8; Ezr 7:20
6:5 e 1Ch 29:2; f Ezr 1:7; Ezr 5:14
6:6 g Ezr 5:3; h Ezr 5:3

b14 Or *palace* a3 Aramaic *sixty cubits* (about 27 metres)

are to be fully paid out of the royal treasury,[i] from the revenues[j] of Trans-Euphrates, so that the work will not stop. 9 Whatever is needed—young bulls, rams, male lambs for burnt offerings[k] to the God of heaven, and wheat, salt, wine and oil, as requested by the priests in Jerusalem—must be given them daily without fail, 10 so that they may offer sacrifices pleasing to the God of heaven and pray for the well-being of the king and his sons.[l]

11 Furthermore, I decree that if anyone changes this edict, a beam is to be pulled from his house and he is to be lifted up and impaled[m] on it. And for this crime his house is to be made a pile of rubble.[n] 12 May God, who has caused his Name to dwell there,[o] overthrow any king or people who lifts a hand to change this decree or to destroy this temple in Jerusalem.

I Darius[p] have decreed it. Let it be carried out with diligence.

Completion and Dedication of the Temple

13 Then, because of the decree King Darius had sent, Tattenai, governor of Trans-Euphrates, and Shethar-Bozenai and their associates[q] carried it out with diligence. 14 So the elders of the Jews continued to build and prosper under the preaching[r] of Haggai the prophet and Zechariah, a descendant of Iddo. They finished building the temple according to the command of the God of Israel and the decrees of Cyrus,[s] Darius[t] and Artaxerxes,[u] kings of Persia. 15 The temple was completed on the third day of the month Adar, in the sixth year of the reign of King Darius.[v]

16 Then the people of Israel—the priests, the Levites and the rest of the exiles—celebrated the dedication[w] of the house of God with joy. 17 For the dedication of this house of God they offered[x] a hundred bulls, two hundred rams, four hundred male lambs and, as a sin offering for all Israel, twelve male goats, one for each of the tribes of Israel. 18 And they installed the priests in their divisions[y] and the Levites in their groups[z] for the service of God at Jerusalem, according to what is written in the Book of Moses.[a]

The Passover

19 On the fourteenth day of the first month, the exiles celebrated the Passover.[b] 20 The priests and Levites had purified themselves and were all ceremonially clean. The Levites slaughtered[c] the Passover lamb for all the exiles, for their brothers the priests and for themselves. 21 So the Israelites who had returned from the exile ate it, together with all who had separated themselves[d] from the unclean practices[e] of their Gentile neighbours in order to seek the LORD,[f] the God of Israel. 22 For seven days they celebrated with joy the Feast of Unleavened Bread,[g] because the LORD had filled them with joy by changing the attitude[h] of the king of Assyria, so that he assisted them in the work on the house of God, the God of Israel.

Ezra Comes to Jerusalem

7 After these things, during the reign of Artaxerxes[a] king of Persia, Ezra son of Seraiah, the son of Azariah, the son of Hilkiah,[b] 2 the son of Shallum, the son of Zadok,[c] the son of Ahitub,[d] 3 the son of Amariah, the son of Azariah, the son of Meraioth, 4 the son of Zerahiah, the son of Uzzi, the son of Bukki, 5 the son of Abishua, the son of Phinehas, the son of Eleazar, the

6:8 *i* ver 4 *j* 1Sa 9:20
6:9 *k* Lev 1:3,10
6:10 *l* Ezr 7:23; 1Ti 2:1-2
6:11 *m* Dt 21:22-23; Est 2:23; Est 5:14; Est 9:14 *n* Ezr 7:26; Da 2:5; Da 3:29
6:12 *o* Ex 20:24; Dt 12:5; 1Ki 9:3; 2Ch 6:2 *p* ver 14
6:13 *q* Ezr 4:9
6:14 *r* Ezr 5:1 *s* Ezr 1:1-4 *t* ver 12 *u* Ezr 7:1; Ne 2:1
6:15 *v* Zec 1:1; Zec 4:9
6:16 *w* 1Ki 8:63; 2Ch 7:5
6:17 *x* 2Sa 6:13; 2Ch 29:21; 2Ch 30:24; Ezr 8:35
6:18 *y* 1Ch 23:6; 2Ch 35:4; Lk 1:5 *z* 1Ch 24:1 *a* Nu 3:6-9; Nu 8:9-11; Nu 18:1-32
6:19 *b* Ex 12:11; Nu 28:16
6:20 *c* 2Ch 30:15,17; 2Ch 35:11
6:21 *d* Ezr 9:1; Ne 9:2 *e* Dt 18:9; Ezr 9:11; Eze 36:25 *f* 1Ch 22:19; Ps 14:2
6:22 *g* Ex 12:17 *h* Ezr 1:1
7:1 *a* Ezr 4:7; Ezr 6:14; Ne 2:1 *b* 2Ki 22:4
7:2 *c* 1Ki 1:8; 1Ch 6:8 *d* Ne 11:11

son of Aaron the chief priest—6this
Ezra[e] came up from Babylon. He
was a teacher well versed in the
Law of Moses, which the LORD, the
God of Israel, had given. The king
had granted him everything he
asked, for the hand of the LORD his
God was on him.[f] 7Some of the Israelites, including priests, Levites,
singers, gatekeepers and temple
servants, also came up to Jerusalem in the seventh year of King
Artaxerxes.[g]
8Ezra arrived in Jerusalem in the
fifth month of the seventh year of
the king. 9He had begun his journey from Babylon on the first day
of the first month, and he arrived in
Jerusalem on the first day of the
fifth month, for the gracious hand
of his God was on him.[h] 10For Ezra
had devoted himself to the study
and observance of the Law of the
LORD, and to teaching[i] its decrees
and laws in Israel.

King Artaxerxes' Letter to Ezra

11This is a copy of the letter King
Artaxerxes had given to Ezra the
priest and teacher, a man learned
in matters concerning the commands and decrees of the LORD for
Israel:

12[a]Artaxerxes, king of kings,[j]

To Ezra the priest, a teacher of
the Law of the God of heaven:

Greetings.

13Now I decree that any of
the Israelites in my kingdom,
including priests and Levites,
who wish to go to Jerusalem
with you, may go. 14You are
sent by the king and his seven
advisers[k] to enquire about Judah and Jerusalem with regard
to the Law of your God, which
is in your hand. 15Moreover,
you are to take with you the
silver and gold that the king
and his advisers have freely
given[l] to the God of Israel,
whose dwelling[m] is in Jerusalem, 16together with all the
silver and gold[n] you may obtain from the province of Babylon, as well as the freewill
offerings of the people and
priests for the temple of their
God in Jerusalem.[o] 17With this
money be sure to buy bulls,
rams and male lambs,[p] together with their grain offerings and drink offerings,[q] and
sacrifice[r] them on the altar of
the temple of your God in Jerusalem.
18You and your brother Jews
may then do whatever seems
best with the rest of the silver
and gold, in accordance with
the will of your God. 19De-
liver[s] to the God of Jerusalem
all the articles entrusted to you
for worship in the temple of
your God. 20And anything else
needed for the temple of your
God that you may have occasion to supply, you may provide from the royal treasury.[t]
21Now I, King Artaxerxes,
order all the treasurers of
Trans-Euphrates to provide
with diligence whatever Ezra
the priest, a teacher of the Law
of the God of heaven, may ask
of you—22up to a hundred
talents[b] of silver, a hundred cors[c] of wheat, a hundred
baths[d] of wine, a hundred
baths[d] of olive oil, and salt
without limit. 23Whatever the
God of heaven has prescribed,
let it be done with diligence for
the temple of the God of
heaven. Why should there be
wrath against the realm of the
king and of his sons?[u] 24You
are also to know that you have
no authority to impose taxes,
tribute or duty[v] on any of the

7:6 e Ne 12:36 f Ezr 5:5 Isa 41:20
7:7 g Ezr 8:1
7:9 h ver 6
7:10 i ver 25 Dt 33:10 Ne 8:1-8
7:12 j Eze 26:7 Da 2:37
7:14 k Est 1:14
7:15 l 1Ch 29:6 m 1Ch 29:6,9 2Ch 6:2
7:16 n Ezr 8:25 o Zec 6:10
7:17 p 2Ki 3:4 q Nu 15:5-12 r Dt 12:5-11
7:19 s Ezr 5:14 Jer 27:22
7:20 t Ezr 6:4
7:23 u Ezr 6:10
7:24 v Ezr 4:13

a *12* The text of Ezra 7:12–26 is in Aramaic.
b *22* That is, about 3 1/3 tons (about 3.4 metric tons)
c *22* That is, probably about 600 bushels (about 22 kilolitres)
d *22* That is, probably about 500 gallons (about 2.2 kilolitres)

priests, Levites, singers, gatekeepers, temple servants or
other workers at this house of
God.[w]
25 And you, Ezra, in accordance with the wisdom of your
God, which you possess, appoint[x] magistrates and judges
to administer justice to all the
people of Trans-Euphrates—
all who know the laws of your
God. And you are to teach[y] any
who do not know them. 26 Whoever does not obey the law of
your God and the law of the
king must surely be punished
by death, banishment, confiscation of property, or imprisonment.[z]

27 Praise be to the LORD, the God
of our fathers, who has put it into
the king's heart[a] to bring honour[b]
to the house of the LORD in Jerusalem in this way 28 and who has extended his good favour[c] to me
before the king and his advisers
and all the king's powerful officials. Because the hand of the LORD
my God was on me,[d] I took courage
and gathered leading men from Israel to go up with me.

List of the Family Heads Returning With Ezra

8 These are the family heads
and those registered with
them who came up with me from
Babylon during the reign of King
Artaxerxes:[a]

2 of the descendants of Phinehas, Gershom;
of the descendants of Ithamar, Daniel;
of the descendants of David, Hattush
3 of the descendants of Shecaniah;[b]
of the descendants of Parosh,[c] Zechariah, and with him were registered 150 men;
4 of the descendants of Pahath-Moab,[d] Eliehoenai son of Zerahiah, and with him 200 men;
5 of the descendants of Zattu,[a] Shecaniah son of Jahaziel, and with him 300 men;
6 of the descendants of Adin,[e] Ebed son of Jonathan, and with him 50 men;
7 of the descendants of Elam, Jeshaiah son of Athaliah, and with him 70 men;
8 of the descendants of Shephatiah, Zebadiah son of Michael, and with him 80 men;
9 of the descendants of Joab, Obadiah son of Jehiel, and with him 218 men;
10 of the descendants of Bani,[b] Shelomith son of Josiphiah, and with him 160 men;
11 of the descendants of Bebai, Zechariah son of Bebai, and with him 28 men;
12 of the descendants of Azgad, Johanan son of Hakkatan, and with him 110 men;
13 of the descendants of Adonikam,[f] the last ones, whose names were Eliphelet, Jeuel and Shemaiah, and with them 60 men;
14 of the descendants of Bigvai, Uthai and Zaccur, and with them 70 men.

The Return to Jerusalem

15 I assembled them at the canal
that flows towards Ahava,[g] and we
camped there three days. When I
checked among the people and the
priests, I found no Levites[h] there.
16 So I summoned Eliezer, Ariel,
Shemaiah, Elnathan, Jarib, Elnathan, Nathan, Zechariah and Meshullam, who were leaders, and
Joiarib and Elnathan, who were
men of learning, 17 and I sent them
to Iddo, the leader in Casiphia. I
told them what to say to Iddo and

7:24 w Ezr 8:36
7:25 x Ex 18:21,26; Dt 16:18 y ver 10; Lev 10:11
7:26 z Ezr 6:11
7:27 a Ezr 1:1; Ezr 6:22 b 1Ch 29:12
7:28 c 2Ki 25:28 d Ezr 5:5; Ezr 9:9
8:1 a Ezr 7:7
8:3 b 1Ch 3:22 c Ezr 2:3
8:4 d Ezr 2:6
8:6 e Ezr 2:15; Ne 7:20; Ne 10:16
8:13 f Ezr 2:13
8:15 g ver 21,31 h Ezr 2:40; Ezr 7:7

a5 Some Septuagint manuscripts (also 1 Esdras 8:32); Hebrew does not have *Zattu*.
b10 Some Septuagint manuscripts (also 1 Esdras 8:36); Hebrew does not have *Bani*.

his kinsmen, the temple servants[i]
in Casiphia, so that they might
bring attendants to us for the house
of our God. 18Because the gracious
hand of our God was on us,[j] they
brought us Sherebiah, a capable
man, from the descendants of
Mahli son of Levi, the son of Israel,
and Sherebiah's sons and brothers,
18 men; 19and Hashabiah, together
with Jeshaiah from the descendants of Merari, and his brothers
and nephews, 20 men. 20They also
brought 220 of the temple servants[k]—a body that David and the
officials had established to assist
the Levites. All were registered by
name.

21There, by the Ahava Canal,[l] I
proclaimed a fast, so that we might
humble ourselves before our God
and ask him for a safe journey[m] for
us and our children, with all our
possessions. 22I was ashamed to ask
the king for soldiers[n] and horsemen to protect us from enemies on
the road, because we had told the
king, "The gracious hand of our
God is on everyone[o] who looks to
him, but his great anger is against
all who forsake him.[p]" 23So we
fasted[q] and petitioned our God
about this, and he answered our
prayer.

24Then I set apart twelve of the
leading priests, together with Sherebiah,[r] Hashabiah and ten of
their brothers, 25and I weighed
out[s] to them the offering of silver
and gold and the articles that the
king, his advisers, his officials and
all Israel present there had do-
nated for the house of our God. 26I
weighed out to them 650 talents[c]
of silver, silver articles weighing
100 talents,[d] 100 talents[d] of gold,
2720 bowls of gold valued at 1,000
darics,[e] and two fine articles of
polished bronze, as precious as
gold.

28I said to them, "You as well as
these articles are consecrated to
the LORD.[t] The silver and gold are
a freewill offering to the LORD, the
God of your fathers. 29Guard them
carefully until you weigh them out
in the chambers of the house of
the LORD in Jerusalem before the
leading priests and the Levites and
the family heads of Israel." 30Then
the priests and Levites received the
silver and gold and sacred articles
that had been weighed out to be
taken to the house of our God in
Jerusalem.

31On the twelfth day of the first
month we set out from the Ahava
Canal[u] to go to Jerusalem. The
hand of our God was on us, and he
protected us from enemies and
bandits along the way. 32So we arrived in Jerusalem, where we
rested three days.[v]

33On the fourth day, in the house
of our God, we weighed out the silver and gold and the sacred articles
into the hands of Meremoth[w] son
of Uriah, the priest. Eleazar son of
Phinehas was with him, and so
were the Levites Jozabad son of
Jeshua and Noadiah son of Binnui.[x]
34Everything was accounted for by
number and weight, and the entire
weight was recorded at that time.

35Then the exiles who had returned from captivity sacrificed
burnt offerings to the God of Israel: twelve bulls for all Israel,
ninety-six rams, seventy-seven
male lambs and, as a sin offering,
twelve male goats.[y] All this was a
burnt offering to the LORD. 36They
also delivered the king's orders[z]
to the royal satraps and to the governors of Trans-Euphrates who
then gave assistance to the people
and to the house of God.[a]

Ezra's Prayer About Intermarriage

9 After these things had been
done, the leaders came to me
and said, "The people of Israel,
including the priests and the

8:17 i Ezr 2:43
8:18 j Ezr 5:5
8:20 k 1Ch 9:2; Ezr 2:43
8:21 l ver 15; 2Ch 20:3; m Ps 5:8; Ps 107:7
8:22 n Ne 2:9; Ezr 7:6,9,28; o Ezr 5:5; p Dt 31:17; 2Ch 15:2
8:23 q 2Ch 20:3; 2Ch 33:13
8:24 r ver 18
8:25 s ver 33; Ezr 7:15,16
8:28 t Lev 21:6; Lev 22:2-3
8:31 u ver 15
8:32 v Ge 40:13; Ne 2:11
8:33 w Ne 3:4,21; x Ne 3:24
8:35 y 2Ch 29:21; Ezr 6:17
8:36 z Ezr 7:21-24; a Est 9:3

c26 That is, about 22 tons (about 22 metric tons)
d26 That is, about 3 ⅓ tons (about 3.4 metric tons)
e27 That is, about 19 pounds (about 8.5 kilograms)

Levites, have not kept themselves
separate[a] from the neighbouring
peoples with their detestable
practices, like those of the Canaanites, Hittites, Perizzites, Jebusites,
Ammonites,[b] Moabites, Egyptians
and Amorites.[c] 2They have taken
some of their daughters[d] as wives
for themselves and their sons,
and have mingled the holy race[e]
with the peoples around them.
And the leaders and officials have
led the way in this unfaithfulness."[f]

3When I heard this, I tore my tunic and cloak, pulled hair from my
head and beard and sat down appalled. 4Then everyone who trembled[g] at the words of the God of
Israel gathered round me because
of this unfaithfulness of the exiles.
And I sat there appalled until the
evening sacrifice.

5Then, at the evening sacrifice,[h]
I rose from my self-abasement,
with my tunic and cloak torn, and
fell on my knees with my hands
spread out to the LORD my God 6and
prayed:

"O my God, I am too ashamed
and disgraced to lift up my
face to you, my God, because
our sins are higher than our
heads and our guilt has
reached to the heavens.[i]
7From the days of our forefathers[j] until now, our guilt
has been great. Because of our
sins, we and our kings and our
priests have been subjected to
the sword[k] and captivity,[l] to
pillage and humiliation[m] at the
hand of foreign kings, as it is
today.

8"But now, for a brief moment, the LORD our God has
been gracious[n] in leaving us a
remnant[o] and giving us a firm
place[p] in his sanctuary, and so
our God gives light to our
eyes[q] and a little relief in our
bondage. 9Though we are
slaves,[r] our God has not deserted us in our bondage. He
has shown us kindness[s] in
the sight of the kings of Persia: He has granted us new
life to rebuild the house of
our God and repair its ruins,[t]
and he has given us a wall
of protection in Judah and
Jerusalem.

10"But now, O our God, what
can we say after this? For we
have disregarded the com-
mands[u] 11you gave through
your servants the prophets
when you said: 'The land you
are entering to possess is a
land polluted[v] by the corruption of its peoples. By their detestable practices[w] they have
filled it with their impurity
from one end to the other.
12Therefore, do not give your
daughters in marriage to their
sons or take their daughters
for your sons. Do not seek a
treaty of friendship with
them[x] at any time, that you
may be strong and eat the good
things of the land and leave it
to your children as an everlasting inheritance.'

13"What has happened to us
is a result of our evil deeds and
our great guilt, and yet, our
God, you have punished us less
than our sins have deserved[y]
and have given us a remnant
like this. 14Shall we again break
your commands and inter-
marry[z] with the peoples who
commit such detestable practices? Would you not be angry
enough with us to destroy us,[a]
leaving us no remnant[b] or survivor? 15O LORD, God of Israel,
you are righteous![c] We are
left this day as a remnant. Here
we are before you in our guilt,
though because of it not one of
us can stand[d] in your presence.[e]"

9:1 a Ezr 6:21; Ne 9:2 b Ge 19:38 c Ex 13:5
9:2 d Ex 34:16 e Ex 22:31 f Ezr 10:2
9:4 g Ezr 10:3
9:5 h Ex 29:41
9:6 i 2Ch 28:9; Job 42:6; Ps 38:4; Rev 18:5
9:7 j 2Ch 29:6 k Eze 21:1-32 l Dt 28:64 m Dt 28:37
9:8 n Ps 25:16; Isa 33:2 o Ge 45:7 p Ecc 12:11; Isa 22:23 q Ps 13:3
9:9 r Ex 1:14; Ne 9:36 s Ezr 7:28 t Ps 69:35; Isa 43:1; Jer 32:44
9:10 u Dt 11:8; Isa 1:19-20
9:11 v Lev 18:25-28 w Dt 9:4
9:12 x Ex 34:15; Dt 7:3; Dt 23:6
9:13 y Job 11:6; Ps 103:10
9:14 z Ne 13:27 a Dt 9:8 b Dt 9:14
9:15 c Ge 18:25; Ps 51:4; Jer 12:1; Da 9:7 d Ne 9:33; Ps 130:3; Mal 3:2 e 1Ki 8:47

The People's Confession of Sin

10 While Ezra was praying
and confessing,[a] weeping
and throwing himself down before
the house of God, a large crowd of
Israelites—men, women and children—gathered round him. They
too wept bitterly. 2Then Shecaniah
son of Jehiel, one of the descendants of Elam, said to Ezra, "We
have been unfaithful[b] to our God
by marrying foreign women from
the peoples around us. But in spite
of this, there is still hope for Israel.[c] 3Now let us make a covenant[d] before our God to send
away[e] all these women and their
children, in accordance with the
counsel of my lord and of those who
fear the commands of our God. Let
it be done according to the Law.
4Rise up; this matter is in your
hands. We will support you, so take
courage and do it."
5So Ezra rose up and put the leading priests and Levites and all Israel under oath[f] to do what had
been suggested. And they took the
oath. 6Then Ezra withdrew from
before the house of God and went
to the room of Jehohanan son of Eliashib. While he was there, he ate no
food and drank no water,[g] because
he continued to mourn over the unfaithfulness of the exiles.
7A proclamation was then issued
throughout Judah and Jerusalem
for all the exiles to assemble in
Jerusalem. 8Anyone who failed to
appear within three days would
forfeit all his property, in accordance with the decision of the officials and elders, and would himself
be expelled from the assembly of
the exiles.

9Within the three days, all the
men of Judah and Benjamin[h] had
gathered in Jerusalem. And on the
twentieth day of the ninth month,
all the people were sitting in the
square before the house of God,
greatly distressed by the occasion
and because of the rain. 10Then
Ezra the priest stood up and said to
them, "You have been unfaithful;
you have married foreign women,
adding to Israel's guilt. 11Now
make confession to the LORD, the
God of your fathers, and do his will.
Separate yourselves from the peoples around you and from your foreign wives."[i]
12The whole assembly responded
with a loud voice:[j] "You are right!
We must do as you say. 13But there
are many people here and it is the
rainy season; so we cannot stand
outside. Besides, this matter cannot be taken care of in a day or two,
because we have sinned greatly in
this thing. 14Let our officials act for
the whole assembly. Then let
everyone in our towns who has
married a foreign woman come at a
set time, along with the elders and
judges[k] of each town, until the
fierce anger[l] of our God in this
matter is turned away from us."
15Only Jonathan son of Asahel and
Jahzeiah son of Tikvah, supported
by Meshullam and Shabbethai[m] the
Levite, opposed this.
16So the exiles did as was proposed. Ezra the priest selected men
who were family heads, one from
each family division, and all of
them designated by name. On the
first day of the tenth month they
sat down to investigate the cases,
17and by the first day of the first
month they finished dealing with
all the men who had married foreign women.

Those Guilty of Intermarriage

18Among the descendants of the
priests, the following had
married foreign women:[n]

From the descendants of
Jeshua[o] son of Jozadak, and
his brothers:
Maaseiah, Eliezer, Jarib and
Gedaliah. 19(They all gave
their hands[p] in pledge to
put away their wives, and
for their guilt they each

10:1 a 2Ch 20:9 Da 9:20
10:2 b Ezr 9:2 Ne 13:27 c Dt 30:8-10
10:3 d 2Ch 34:31 e Ex 34:16 Dt 7:2-3 Ezr 9:4
10:5 f Ne 5:12 Ne 13:25
10:6 g Ex 34:28 Dt 9:18
10:9 h Ezr 1:5
10:11 i ver 3 Dt 24:1 Ne 9:2 Mal 2:10-16
10:12 j Jos 6:5
10:14 k Dt 16:18 l Nu 25:4 2Ch 29:10 2Ch 30:8
10:15 m Ne 11:16
10:18 n Jdg 3:6 o Ezr 2:2
10:19 p 2Ki 10:15

presented a ram from the flock as a guilt offering.)[q]

20 From the descendants of Immer:[r]
Hanani and Zebadiah.

21 From the descendants of Harim:[s]
Maaseiah, Elijah, Shemaiah, Jehiel and Uzziah.

22 From the descendants of Pashhur:[t]
Elioenai, Maaseiah, Ishmael, Nethanel, Jozabad and Elasah.

23 Among the Levites:[u]

Jozabad, Shimei, Kelaiah (that is Kelita), Pethahiah, Judah and Eliezer.

24 From the singers:
Eliashib.[v]

From the gatekeepers:
Shallum, Telem and Uri.

25 And among the other Israelites:

From the descendants of Parosh:[w]
Ramiah, Izziah, Malkijah, Mijamin, Eleazar, Malkijah and Benaiah.

26 From the descendants of Elam:[x]
Mattaniah, Zechariah, Jehiel, Abdi, Jeremoth and Elijah.

27 From the descendants of Zattu:
Elioenai, Eliashib, Mattaniah, Jeremoth, Zabad and Aziza.

28 From the descendants of Bebai:
Jehohanan, Hananiah, Zabbai and Athlai.

29 From the descendants of Bani:
Meshullam, Malluch, Adaiah, Jashub, Sheal and Jeremoth.

30 From the descendants of Pahath-Moab:
Adna, Kelal, Benaiah, Maaseiah, Mattaniah, Bezalel, Binnui and Manasseh.

31 From the descendants of Harim:
Eliezer, Ishijah, Malkijah, Shemaiah, Shimeon,
32 Benjamin, Malluch and Shemariah.

33 From the descendants of Hashum:
Mattenai, Mattattah, Zabad, Eliphelet, Jeremai, Manasseh and Shimei.

34 From the descendants of Bani:
Maadai, Amram, Uel,
35 Benaiah, Bedeiah, Keluhi,
36 Vaniah, Meremoth, Eliashib,
37 Mattaniah, Mattenai and Jaasu.

38 From the descendants of Binnui:[a]
Shimei,
39 Shelemiah, Nathan, Adaiah,
40 Macnadebai, Shashai, Sharai,
41 Azarel, Shelemiah, Shemariah,
42 Shallum, Amariah and Joseph.

43 From the descendants of Nebo:
Jeiel, Mattithiah, Zabad, Zebina, Jaddai, Joel and Benaiah.

44 All these had married foreign women, and some of them had children by these wives.[b]

10:19 q Lev 5:15; Lev 6:6
10:20 r 1Ch 24:14
10:21 s 1Ch 24:8
10:22 t 1Ch 9:12
10:23 u Ne 8:7; Ne 9:4
10:24 v Ne 3:1; Ne 12:10; Ne 13:7,28
10:25 w Ezr 2:3
10:26 x ver 2

[a] 37,38 See Septuagint (also 1 Esdras 9:34); Hebrew *Jaasu* [38] *and Bani and Binnui,*
[b] 44 Or *and they sent them away with their children*

NEHEMIAH

Nehemiah's Prayer

1 The words of Nehemiah son of Hacaliah:

In the month of Kislev[a] in the twentieth year, while I was in the citadel of Susa, 2Hanani,[b] one of my brothers, came from Judah with some other men, and I questioned them about the Jewish remnant[c] that survived the exile, and also about Jerusalem.

3They said to me, "Those who survived the exile and are back in the province are in great trouble and disgrace. The wall of Jerusalem is broken down, and its gates have been burned with fire.[d]"

4When I heard these things, I sat down and wept.[e] For some days I mourned and fasted[f] and prayed before the God of heaven. 5Then I said:

"O LORD, God of heaven, the great and awesome God,[g] who keeps his covenant of love[h] with those who love him and obey his commands, 6let your ear be attentive and your eyes open to hear[i] the prayer[j] your servant is praying before you day and night for your servants, the people of Israel. I confess the sins we Israelites, including myself and my father's house, have committed against you. 7We have acted very wickedly[k] towards you. We have not obeyed the commands, decrees and laws you gave your servant Moses.

8"Remember[l] the instruction you gave your servant Moses, saying, 'If you are unfaithful, I will scatter[m] you among the nations, 9but if you return to me and obey my commands, then even if your exiled people are at the farthest horizon, I will gather[n] them from there and bring them to the place I have chosen as a dwelling for my Name.'[o]

10"They are your servants and your people, whom you redeemed by your great strength and your mighty hand.[p] 11O Lord, let your ear be attentive[q] to the prayer of this your servant and to the prayer of your servants who delight in revering your name. Give your servant success today by granting him favour in the presence of this man."

I was cupbearer[r] to the king.

1:1 a Ne 10:1; Zec 7:1
1:2 b Ne 7:2; c Jer 52:28
1:3 d 2Ki 25:10; Ne 2:3,13,17
1:4 e Ps 137:1; f Ezr 9:4
1:5 g Dt 7:21; Ne 4:14; h Ex 20:6; Da 9:4
1:6 i 1Ki 8:29; j Da 9:17
1:7 k Dt 28:14-15; Ps 106:6
1:8 l 2Ki 20:3; m Lev 26:33
1:9 n Dt 30:4; o 1Ki 8:48; Jer 29:14
1:10 p Ex 32:11; Dt 9:29
1:11 q ver 6; r Ge 40:1
2:1 a Ezr 7:1
2:3 b 1Ki 1:31; Da 2:4; Da 5:10; Da 6:6,21; c Ps 137:6; d Ne 1:3

Artaxerxes Sends Nehemiah to Jerusalem

2 In the month of Nisan in the twentieth year of King Artaxerxes,[a] when wine was brought for him, I took the wine and gave it to the king. I had not been sad in his presence before; 2so the king asked me, "Why does your face look so sad when you are not ill? This can be nothing but sadness of heart."

I was very much afraid, 3but I said to the king, "May the king live for ever![b] Why should my face not look sad when the city[c] where my fathers are buried lies in ruins, and its gates have been destroyed by fire?[d]"

4The king said to me, "What is it you want?"

Then I prayed to the God of heaven, 5and I answered the king, "If it pleases the king and if your servant has found favour in his sight, let him send me to the city in Judah where my fathers are buried so that I can rebuild it."

6 Then the king[e], with the queen sitting beside him, asked me, "How long will your journey take, and when will you get back?" It pleased the king to send me; so I set a time.

7 I also said to him, "If it pleases the king, may I have letters to the governors of Trans-Euphrates,[f] so that they will provide me safe-conduct until I arrive in Judah? 8 And may I have a letter to Asaph, keeper of the king's forest, so he will give me timber to make beams for the gates of the citadel[g] by the temple and for the city wall and for the residence I will occupy?" And because the gracious hand of my God was upon me,[h] the king granted my requests. 9 So I went to the governors of Trans-Euphrates and gave them the king's letters. The king had also sent army officers and cavalry[i] with me.

10 When Sanballat[j] the Horonite and Tobiah[k] the Ammonite official heard about this, they were very much disturbed that someone had come to promote the welfare of the Israelites.[l]

Nehemiah Inspects Jerusalem's Walls

11 I went to Jerusalem, and after staying there three days[m] 12 I set out during the night with a few men. I had not told anyone what my God had put in my heart to do for Jerusalem. There were no mounts with me except the one I was riding on.

13 By night I went out through the Valley Gate[n] towards the Jackal[a] Well and the Dung Gate,[o] examining the walls[p] of Jerusalem, which had been broken down, and its gates, which had been destroyed by fire. 14 Then I moved on towards the Fountain Gate[q] and the King's Pool,[r] but there was not enough room for my mount to get through; 15 so I went up the valley by night, examining the wall. Finally, I turned back and re-entered through the Valley Gate. 16 The officials did not know where I had gone or what I was doing, because as yet I had said nothing to the Jews or the priests or nobles or officials or any others who would be doing the work.

17 Then I said to them, "You see the trouble we are in: Jerusalem lies in ruins, and its gates have been burned with fire.[s] Come, let us rebuild the wall[t] of Jerusalem, and we will no longer be in disgrace.[u]" 18 I also told them about the gracious hand of my God upon me[v] and what the king had said to me.

They replied, "Let us start rebuilding." So they began this good work.

19 But when Sanballat the Horonite, Tobiah the Ammonite official and Geshem[w] the Arab heard about it, they mocked and ridiculed us.[x] "What is this you are doing?" they asked. "Are you rebelling against the king?"

20 I answered them by saying, "The God of heaven will give us success. We his servants will start rebuilding, but as for you, you have no share[y] in Jerusalem or any claim or historic right to it."

Builders of the Wall

3 Eliashib[a] the high priest and his fellow priests went to work and rebuilt[b] the Sheep Gate.[c] They dedicated it and set its doors in place, building as far as the Tower of the Hundred, which they dedicated, and as far as the Tower of Hananel.[d] 2 The men of Jericho[e] built the adjoining section, and Zaccur son of Imri built next to them.

3 The Fish Gate[f] was rebuilt by the sons of Hassenaah. They laid its beams and put its doors and bolts and bars in place. 4 Meremoth son of Uriah, the son of Hakkoz,

2:6 e Ne 5:14; Ne 13:6
2:7 f Ezr 8:36
2:8 g Ne 7:2; h ver 18; Ezr 5:5; Ezr 7:6
2:9 i Ezr 8:22
2:10 j ver 19; Ne 4:1,7; k Ne 4:3; Ne 13:4-7; l Est 10:3
2:11 m Ge 40:13
2:13 n 2Ch 26:9; o Ne 3:13; p Ne 1:3
2:14 q Ne 3:15; r 2Ki 18:17
2:17 s Ne 1:3; t Ps 102:16; Isa 30:13; Isa 58:12; u Eze 5:14
2:18 v 2Sa 2:7
2:19 w Ne 6:1,2,6; x Ps 44:13-16
2:20 y Ezr 4:3
3:1 a Ezr 10:24; b Isa 58:12; c ver 32; Ne 12:39; d Ne 12:39; Jer 31:38; Zec 14:10
3:2 e Ne 7:36
3:3 f 2Ch 33:14; Ne 12:39

a *13* Or *Serpent* or *Fig*

repaired the next section. Next to him Meshullam son of Berekiah, the son of Meshezabel, made repairs, and next to him Zadok son of Baana also made repairs. 5The next section was repaired by the men of Tekoa,[g] but their nobles would not put their shoulders to the work under their supervisors.[a]

6The Jeshanah[b] Gate[h] was repaired by Joiada son of Paseah and Meshullam son of Besodeiah. They laid its beams and put its doors and bolts and bars in place. 7Next to them, repairs were made by men from Gibeon[i] and Mizpah—Melatiah of Gibeon and Jadon of Meronoth—places under the authority of the governor of Trans-Euphrates. 8Uzziel son of Harhaiah, one of the goldsmiths, repaired the next section; and Hananiah, one of the perfume-makers, made repairs next to that. They restored[c] Jerusalem as far as the Broad Wall.[j] 9Rephaiah son of Hur, ruler of a half-district of Jerusalem, repaired the next section. 10Adjoining this, Jedaiah son of Harumaph made repairs opposite his house, and Hattush son of Hashabneiah made repairs next to him. 11Malkijah son of Harim and Hasshub son of Pahath-Moab repaired another section and the Tower of the Ovens.[k] 12Shallum son of Hallohesh, ruler of a half-district of Jerusalem, repaired the next section with the help of his daughters.

13The Valley Gate[l] was repaired by Hanun and the residents of Zanoah.[m] They rebuilt it and put its doors and bolts and bars in place. They also repaired five hundred yards[d] of the wall as far as the Dung Gate.[n]

14The Dung Gate was repaired by Malkijah son of Recab, ruler of the district of Beth Hakkerem.[o] He rebuilt it and put its doors and bolts and bars in place.

3:5
g 2Sa 14:2
3:6
h Ne 12:39
3:7
i Jos 9:3; Ne 2:7
3:8
j Ne 12:38
3:11
k Ne 12:38
3:13
l 2Ch 26:9
m Jos 15:34
n Ne 2:13
3:14
o Jer 6:1
3:15
p Isa 8:6; Jn 9:7
3:16
q Jos 15:58
r Ac 2:29
3:17
s Jos 15:44
3:21
t Ezr 8:33
3:24
u Ezr 8:33

15The Fountain Gate was repaired by Shallun son of Col-Hozeh, ruler of the district of Mizpah. He rebuilt it, roofing it over and putting its doors and bolts and bars in place. He also repaired the wall of the Pool of Siloam,[e][p] by the King's Garden, as far as the steps going down from the City of David. 16Beyond him, Nehemiah son of Azbuk, ruler of a half-district of Beth Zur,[q] made repairs up to a point opposite the tombs[f][r] of David, as far as the artificial pool and the House of the Heroes.

17Next to him, the repairs were made by the Levites under Rehum son of Bani. Beside him, Hashabiah, ruler of half the district of Keilah,[s] carried out repairs for his district. 18Next to him, the repairs were made by their countrymen under Binnui[g] son of Henadad, ruler of the other half-district of Keilah. 19Next to him, Ezer son of Jeshua, ruler of Mizpah, repaired another section, from a point facing the ascent to the armoury as far as the angle. 20Next to him, Baruch son of Zabbai zealously repaired another section, from the angle to the entrance of the house of Eliashib the high priest. 21Next to him, Meremoth[t] son of Uriah, the son of Hakkoz, repaired another section, from the entrance of Eliashib's house to the end of it.

22The repairs next to him were made by the priests from the surrounding region. 23Beyond them, Benjamin and Hasshub made repairs in front of their house; and next to them, Azariah son of Maaseiah, the son of Ananiah, made repairs beside his house. 24Next to him, Binnui[u] son of Henadad repaired another section, from

a5 Or *their Lord* or *the governor* b6 Or *Old*
c8 Or *They left out part of* d13 Hebrew *a thousand cubits* (about 450 metres)
e15 Hebrew *Shelah*, a variant of *Shiloah*, that is, *Siloam* f16 Hebrew; Septuagint, some Vulgate manuscripts and Syriac *tomb* g18 Two Hebrew manuscripts and Syriac (see also Septuagint and verse 24); most Hebrew manuscripts *Bavvai*

Azariah's house to the angle and the corner, 25and Palal son of Uzai worked opposite the angle and the tower projecting from the upper palace near the court of the guard.[v] Next to him, Pedaiah son of Parosh[w] 26and the temple servants[x] living on the hill of Ophel[y] made repairs up to a point opposite the Water Gate[z] towards the east and the projecting tower. 27Next to them, the men of Tekoa[a] repaired another section, from the great projecting tower[b] to the wall of Ophel.

28Above the Horse Gate,[c] the priests made repairs, each in front of his own house. 29Next to them, Zadok son of Immer made repairs opposite his house. Next to him, Shemaiah son of Shecaniah, the guard at the East Gate, made repairs. 30Next to him, Hananiah son of Shelemiah, and Hanun, the sixth son of Zalaph, repaired another section. Next to them, Meshullam son of Berekiah made repairs opposite his living quarters. 31Next to him, Malkijah, one of the goldsmiths, made repairs as far as the house of the temple servants and the merchants, opposite the Inspection Gate, and as far as the room above the corner; 32and between the room above the corner and the Sheep Gate[d] the goldsmiths and merchants made repairs.

Opposition to the Rebuilding

4 When Sanballat[a] heard that we were rebuilding the wall, he became angry and was greatly incensed. He ridiculed the Jews, 2and in the presence of his associates[b] and the army of Samaria, he said, "What are those feeble Jews doing? Will they restore their wall? Will they offer sacrifices? Will they finish in a day? Can they bring the stones back to life from those heaps of rubble[c]—burned as they are?"

3Tobiah[d] the Ammonite, who was at his side, said, "What they are building—if even a fox climbed up on it, he would break down their wall of stones!"[e]

4Hear us, O our God, for we are despised.[f] Turn their insults back on their own heads. Give them over as plunder in a land of captivity. 5Do not cover up their guilt[g] or blot out their sins from your sight,[h] for they have thrown insults in the face of[a] the builders.

6So we rebuilt the wall till all of it reached half its height, for the people worked with all their heart.

7But when Sanballat, Tobiah,[i] the Arabs, the Ammonites and the men of Ashdod heard that the repairs to Jerusalem's walls had gone ahead and that the gaps were being closed, they were very angry. 8They all plotted together[j] to come and fight against Jerusalem and stir up trouble against it. 9But we prayed to our God and posted a guard day and night to meet this threat.

10Meanwhile, the people in Judah said, "The strength of the labourers[k] is giving out, and there is so much rubble that we cannot rebuild the wall."

11Also our enemies said, "Before they know it or see us, we will be right there among them and will kill them and put an end to the work."

12Then the Jews who lived near them came and told us ten times over, "Wherever you turn, they will attack us."

13Therefore I stationed some of the people behind the lowest points of the wall at the exposed places, posting them by families, with their swords, spears and bows. 14After I looked things over, I stood up and said to the nobles, the

3:25 v Jer 32:2; Jer 37:21; Jer 39:14 w Ezr 2:3
3:26 x Ne 7:46; Ne 11:21 y 2Ch 33:14 z Ne 8:1,3,16; Ne 12:37
3:27 a ver 5 b Ps 48:12
3:28 c 2Ki 11:16; 2Ch 23:15; Jer 31:40
3:32 d ver 1; Jn 5:2
4:1 a Ne 2:10
4:2 b Ezr 4:9-10 c Ps 79:1; Jer 26:18
4:3 d Ne 2:10 e Job 13:12; Job 15:3
4:4 f Ps 44:13; Ps 79:12; Ps 123:3-4; Jer 33:24
4:5 g Isa 2:9; La 1:22 h 2Ki 14:27; Ps 51:1; Ps 69:27-28; Ps 109:14; Jer 18:23
4:7 i Ne 2:10
4:8 j Ps 2:2; Ps 83:1-18
4:10 k 1Ch 23:4

[a]5 Or *have provoked you to anger before*

officials and the rest of the people, "Don't be afraid[l] of them. Remember[m] the Lord, who is great and awesome,[n] and fight[o] for your brothers, your sons and your daughters, your wives and your homes."

15When our enemies heard that we were aware of their plot and that God had frustrated it,[p] we all returned to the wall, each to his own work.

16From that day on, half of my men did the work, while the other half were equipped with spears, shields, bows and armour. The officers posted themselves behind all the people of Judah 17who were building the wall. Those who carried materials did their work with one hand and held a weapon[q] in the other, 18and each of the builders wore his sword at his side as he worked. But the man who sounded the trumpet[r] stayed with me.

19Then I said to the nobles, the officials and the rest of the people, "The work is extensive and spread out, and we are widely separated from each other along the wall. 20Wherever you hear the sound of the trumpet,[s] join us there. Our God will fight[t] for us!"

21So we continued the work with half the men holding spears, from the first light of dawn till the stars came out. 22At that time I also said to the people, "Have every man and his helper stay inside Jerusalem at night, so that they can serve us as guards by night and workmen by day." 23Neither I nor my brothers nor my men nor the guards with me took off our clothes; each had his weapon, even when he went for water.[b]

Nehemiah Helps the Poor

5 Now the men and their wives raised a great outcry against their Jewish brothers. 2Some were saying, "We and our sons and daughters are numerous; in order for us to eat and stay alive, we must get grain."

3Others were saying, "We are mortgaging our fields,[a] our vineyards and our homes to get grain during the famine."[b]

4Still others were saying, "We have had to borrow money to pay the king's tax[c] on our fields and vineyards. 5Although we are of the same flesh and blood[d] as our countrymen and though our sons are as good as theirs, yet we have to subject our sons and daughters to slavery.[e] Some of our daughters have already been enslaved, but we are powerless, because our fields and our vineyards belong to others."[f]

6When I heard their outcry and these charges, I was very angry. 7I pondered them in my mind and then accused the nobles and officials. I told them, "You are exacting usury[g] from your own countrymen!" So I called together a large meeting to deal with them 8and said: "As far as possible, we have bought[h] back our Jewish brothers who were sold to the Gentiles. Now you are selling your brothers, only for them to be sold back to us!" They kept quiet, because they could find nothing to say.[i]

9So I continued, "What you are doing is not right. Shouldn't you walk in the fear of our God to avoid the reproach[j] of our Gentile enemies? 10I and my brothers and my men are also lending the people money and grain. But let the exacting of usury stop![k] 11Give back to them immediately their fields, vineyards, olive groves and houses, and also the usury[l] you are charging them—the hundredth part of the money, grain, new wine and oil."

4:14 l Ge 28:15; Nu 14:9; Dt 1:29; m Ne 1:8; n Ne 1:5; o 2Sa 10:12
4:15 p 2Sa 17:14; Job 5:12
4:17 q Ps 149:6
4:18 r Nu 10:2
4:20 s Eze 33:3; t Ex 14:14; Dt 1:30; Dt 20:4; Jos 10:14
5:3 a Ps 109:11; b Ge 47:23
5:4 c Ezr 4:13
5:5 d Ge 29:14; e Lev 25:39-43, 47; 2Ki 4:1; Isa 50:1; f Dt 15:7-11; 2Ki 4:1
5:7 g Ex 22:25-27; Lev 25:35-37; Dt 23:19-20; Dt 24:10-13
5:8 h Lev 25:47; i Jer 34:8
5:9 j Isa 52:5
5:10 k Ex 22:25
5:11 l Isa 58:6

b23 The meaning of the Hebrew for this clause is uncertain.

12"We will give it back," they said. "And we will not demand anything more from them. We will do as you say."

Then I summoned the priests and made the nobles and officials take an oath[m] to do what they had promised. 13I also shook[n] out the folds of my robe and said, "In this way may God shake out of his house and possessions every man who does not keep this promise. So may such a man be shaken out and emptied!"

At this the whole assembly said, "Amen,"[o] and praised the LORD. And the people did as they had promised.

14Moreover, from the twentieth year of King Artaxerxes,[p] when I was appointed to be their governor[q] in the land of Judah, until his thirty-second year—twelve years—neither I nor my brothers ate the food allotted to the governor. 15But the earlier governors—those preceding me—placed a heavy burden on the people and took forty shekels[a] of silver from them in addition to food and wine. Their assistants also lorded it over the people. But out of reverence for God[r] I did not act like that. 16Instead,[s] I devoted myself to the work on this wall. All my men were assembled there for the work; we[b] did not acquire any land.

17Furthermore, a hundred and fifty Jews and officials ate at my table, as well as those who came to us from the surrounding nations. 18Each day one ox, six choice sheep and some poultry[t] were prepared for me, and every ten days an abundant supply of wine of all kinds. In spite of all this, I never demanded the food allotted to the governor, because the demands were heavy on these people.

19Remember[u] me with favour, O my God, for all I have done for these people.

5:12 *m* Ezr 10:5
5:13 *n* Mt 10:14; Ac 18:6 *o* Dt 27:15-26
5:14 *p* Ne 2:6; Ne 13:6 *q* Ge 42:6; Ezr 6:7; Jer 40:7; Hag 1:1
5:15 *r* Ge 20:11
5:16 *s* 2Th 3:7-10
5:18 *t* 1Ki 4:23
5:19 *u* Ge 8:1; 2Ki 20:3; Ne 1:8; Ne 13:14,22,31
6:1 *a* Ne 2:10 *b* Ne 2:19
6:2 *c* 1Ch 8:12
6:5 *d* Ne 2:10
6:6 *e* Ne 2:19

Further Opposition to the Rebuilding

6 When word came to Sanballat, Tobiah,[a] Geshem[b] the Arab and the rest of our enemies that I had rebuilt the wall and not a gap was left in it—though up to that time I had not set the doors in the gates—2Sanballat and Geshem sent me this message: "Come, let us meet together in one of the villages[a] on the plain of Ono.[c]"

But they were scheming to harm me; 3so I sent messengers to them with this reply: "I am carrying on a great project and cannot go down. Why should the work stop while I leave it and go down to you?" 4Four times they sent me the same message, and each time I gave them the same answer.

5Then, the fifth time, Sanballat[d] sent his assistant to me with the same message, and in his hand was an unsealed letter 6in which was written:

> "It is reported among the nations—and Geshem[b][e] says it is true—that you and the Jews are plotting to revolt, and therefore you are building the wall. Moreover, according to these reports you are about to become their king 7and have even appointed prophets to make this proclamation about you in Jerusalem: 'There is a king in Judah!' Now this report will get back to the king; so come, let us confer together."

8I sent him this reply: "Nothing like what you are saying is happening; you are just making it up out of your head."

9They were all trying to frighten us, thinking, "Their hands will get too weak for the work, and it will not be completed."

a*15* That is, about 1 pound (about 0.5 kilogram)
b*16* Most Hebrew manuscripts; some Hebrew manuscripts, Septuagint, Vulgate and Syriac *I*
a2 Or *in Kephirim* b6 Hebrew *Gashmu*, a variant of *Geshem*

⌞But I prayed,⌟ "Now strengthen my hands."

10One day I went to the house of Shemaiah son of Delaiah, the son of Mehetabel, who was shut in at his home. He said, "Let us meet in the house of God, inside the temple[f], and let us close the temple doors, because men are coming to kill you—by night they are coming to kill you."

11But I said, "Should a man like me run away? Or should one like me go into the temple to save his life? I will not go!" 12I realised that God had not sent him, but that he had prophesied against me[g] because Tobiah and Sanballat[h] had hired him. 13He had been hired to intimidate me so that I would commit a sin by doing this, and then they would give me a bad name to discredit me.[i]

14Remember[j] Tobiah and Sanballat,[k] O my God, because of what they have done; remember also the prophetess[l] Noadiah and the rest of the prophets[m] who have been trying to intimidate me.

The Completion of the Wall

15So the wall was completed on the twenty-fifth of Elul, in fifty-two days. 16When all our enemies heard about this, all the surrounding nations were afraid and lost their self-confidence, because they realised that this work had been done with the help of our God.

17Also, in those days the nobles of Judah were sending many letters to Tobiah, and replies from Tobiah kept coming to them. 18For many in Judah were under oath to him, since he was son-in-law to Shecaniah son of Arah, and his son Jehohanan had married the daughter of Meshullam son of Berekiah. 19Moreover, they kept reporting to me his good deeds and then telling him what I said. And Tobiah sent letters to intimidate me.

6:10 f Nu 18:7
6:12 g Eze 13:22-23 h Ne 2:10
6:13 i Jer 20:10
6:14 j Ne 1:8 k Ne 2:10 l Ex 15:20 Eze 13:17-23 Ac 21:9 Rev 2:20 m Ne 13:29 Jer 23:9-40 Zec 13:2-3
7:1 a 1Ch 9:27 1Ch 26:12-19 Ne 6:1,15 b Ps 68:25 c Ne 8:9
7:2 d Ne 1:2 e Ne 10:23 f Ne 2:8 g 1Ki 18:3
7:4 h Ne 11:1
7:6 i 2Ch 36:20 Ezr 2:1-70 Ne 1:2
7:7 j 1Ch 3:19 Ezr 2:2

7 After the wall had been rebuilt and I had set the doors in place, the gatekeepers[a] and the singers[b] and the Levites[c] were appointed. 2I put in charge of Jerusalem my brother Hanani,[d] along with[a] Hananiah[e] the commander of the citadel,[f] because he was a man of integrity and feared[g] God more than most men do. 3I said to them, "The gates of Jerusalem are not to be opened until the sun is hot. While the gatekeepers are still on duty, make them shut the doors and bar them. Also appoint residents of Jerusalem as guards, some at their posts and some near their own houses."

The List of the Exiles Who Returned

7:6–73pp Ezr 2:1–70

4Now the city was large and spacious, but there were few people in it,[h] and the houses had not yet been rebuilt. 5So my God put it into my heart to assemble the nobles, the officials and the common people for registration by families. I found the genealogical record of those who had been the first to return. This is what I found written there:

> 6These are the people of the province who came up from the captivity of the exiles[i] whom Nebuchadnezzar king of Babylon had taken captive (they returned to Jerusalem and Judah, each to his own town, 7in company with Zerubbabel,[j] Jeshua, Nehemiah, Azariah, Raamiah, Nahamani, Mordecai, Bilshan, Mispereth, Bigvai, Nehum and Baanah):
>
> The list of the men of Israel:

8the descendants of Parosh	2,172
9of Shephatiah	372
10of Arah	652

a2 Or *Hanani, that is,*

11 of Pahath-Moab (through the line of Jeshua and Joab) 2,818
12 of Elam 1,254
13 of Zattu 845
14 of Zaccai 760
15 of Binnui 648
16 of Bebai 628
17 of Azgad 2,322
18 of Adonikam 667
19 of Bigvai 2,067
20 of Adin[k] 655
21 of Ater (through Hezekiah) 98
22 of Hashum 328
23 of Bezai 324
24 of Hariph 112
25 of Gibeon 95

26 the men of Bethlehem and Netophah[l] 188
27 of Anathoth[m] 128
28 of Beth Azmaveth 42
29 of Kiriath Jearim, Kephirah[n] and Beeroth[o] 743
30 of Ramah and Geba 621
31 of Michmash 122
32 of Bethel and Ai[p] 123
33 of the other Nebo 52
34 of the other Elam 1,254
35 of Harim 320
36 of Jericho[q] 345
37 of Lod, Hadid and Ono[r] 721
38 of Senaah 3,930

39 The priests:

the descendants of Jedaiah (through the family of Jeshua) 973
40 of Immer 1,052
41 of Pashhur 1,247
42 of Harim 1,017

43 The Levites:

the descendants of Jeshua (through Kadmiel through the line of Hodaviah) 74

44 The singers:[s]

the descendants of Asaph 148

45 The gatekeepers:[t]

the descendants of Shallum, Ater, Talmon, Akkub, Hatita and Shobai 138

46 The temple servants:[u]

the descendants of
Ziha, Hasupha, Tabbaoth,
47 Keros, Sia, Padon,
48 Lebana, Hagaba, Shalmai,
49 Hanan, Giddel, Gahar,
50 Reaiah, Rezin, Nekoda,
51 Gazzam, Uzza, Paseah,
52 Besai, Meunim, Nephussim,
53 Bakbuk, Hakupha, Harhur,
54 Bazluth, Mehida, Harsha,
55 Barkos, Sisera, Temah,
56 Neziah and Hatipha

57 The descendants of the servants of Solomon:

the descendants of
Sotai, Sophereth, Perida,
58 Jaala, Darkon, Giddel,
59 Shephatiah, Hattil, Pokereth-Hazzebaim and Amon

60 The temple servants and the descendants of the servants of Solomon[v] 392

61 The following came up from the towns of Tel Melah, Tel Harsha, Kerub, Addon and Immer, but they could not show that their families were descended from Israel:

62 the descendants of Delaiah, Tobiah and Nekoda 642

63 And from among the priests:

the descendants of Hobaiah, Hakkoz and Barzillai (a man who had married a daughter of Barzillai the Gileadite and was called by that name).
64 These searched for their family records, but they could not find them and so were excluded from the priesthood as unclean. 65 The governor, therefore, ordered them not to

7:20 *k* Ezr 8:6
7:26 *l* 2Sa 23:28; 1Ch 2:54
7:27 *m* Jos 21:18
7:29 *n* Jos 18:26; *o* Jos 18:25
7:32 *p* Ge 12:8
7:36 *q* Ne 3:2
7:37 *r* 1Ch 8:12
7:44 *s* Ne 11:23
7:45 *t* 1Ch 9:17
7:46 *u* Ne 3:26
7:60 *v* 1Ch 9:2

eat any of the most sacred food
until there should be a priest
ministering with the Urim and
Thummim.[w]

66 The whole company num-
bered 42,360, 67 besides their
7,337 menservants and maidservants; and they also had
245 men and women singers.
68 There were 736 horses, 245
mules,[b] 69 435 camels and 6,720
donkeys.

70 Some of the heads of the
families contributed to the
work. The governor gave to the
treasury 1,000 drachmas[c] of
gold, 50 bowls and 530 garments for priests. 71 Some of
the heads of the families[x]
gave to the treasury for the
work 20,000 drachmas[d] of
gold and 2,200 minas[e] of silver. 72 The total given by the
rest of the people was 20,000
drachmas of gold, 2,000
minas[f] of silver and 67 garments for priests.[y]

73 The priests, the Levites,
the gatekeepers, the singers
and the temple servants,[z]
along with certain of the people and the rest of the Israelites, settled in their own
towns.[a]

Ezra Reads the Law

When the seventh month came and
the Israelites had settled in their
8 towns,[b] 1 all the people assembled as one man in the
square before the Water Gate.[a]
They told Ezra the scribe to bring
out the Book of the Law of Moses,[b]
which the LORD had commanded
for Israel.

2 So on the first day of the seventh
month,[c] Ezra the priest brought
the Law[d] before the assembly,
which was made up of men and
women and all who were able to
understand. 3 He read it aloud from

7:65
w Ex 28:30
Ne 8:9

7:71
x 1Ch 29:7

7:72
y Ex 25:2

7:73
z Ne 1:10
Ps 34:22
Ps 103:21
Ps 113:1
Ps 135:1
a Ezr 3:1
Ne 11:1
b Ezr 3:1

8:1
a Ne 3:26
b Dt 28:61
2Ch 34:15
Ezr 7:6

8:2
c Lev 23:23-25
Nu 29:1-6
d Dt 31:11

8:3
e Ne 3:26

8:4
f 2Ch 6:13

8:5
g Jdg 3:20

8:6
h Ex 4:31
Ezr 9:5
1Ti 2:8

8:7
i Ezr 10:23
j Lev 10:11
2Ch 17:7

8:9
k Ne 7:1,65,70
l Dt 12:7,12
Dt 16:14-15

daybreak till noon as he faced the
square before the Water Gate[e] in
the presence of the men, women
and others who could understand.
And all the people listened attentively to the Book of the Law.

4 Ezra the scribe stood on a high
wooden platform[f] built for the occasion. Beside him on his right
stood Mattithiah, Shema, Anaiah,
Uriah, Hilkiah and Maaseiah; and
on his left were Pedaiah, Mishael,
Malkijah, Hashum, Hashbaddanah,
Zechariah and Meshullam.
5 Ezra opened the book. All the
people could see him because he
was standing[g] above them; and as
he opened it, the people all stood
up. 6 Ezra praised the LORD, the
great God; and all the people lifted
their hands[h] and responded,
"Amen! Amen!" Then they bowed
down and worshipped the LORD
with their faces to the ground.

7 The Levites[i]—Jeshua, Bani,
Sherebiah, Jamin, Akkub, Shabbethai, Hodiah, Maaseiah, Kelita,
Azariah, Jozabad, Hanan and Pelaiah—instructed[j] the people in
the Law while the people were
standing there. 8 They read from
the Book of the Law of God, making
it clear[a] and giving the meaning so
that the people could understand
what was being read.

9 Then Nehemiah the governor,
Ezra the priest and scribe, and the
Levites[k] who were instructing the
people said to them all, "This day is
sacred to the LORD your God. Do
not mourn or weep."[l] For all the
people had been weeping as they
listened to the words of the Law.

10 Nehemiah said, "Go and enjoy
choice food and sweet drinks, and

b *68* Some Hebrew manuscripts (see also Ezra 2:66); most Hebrew manuscripts do not have this verse.
c *70* That is, about 19 pounds (about 8.5 kilograms)
d *71* That is, about 375 pounds (about 170 kilograms); also in verse 72
e *71* That is, about 1¼ tons (about 1.3 metric tons)
f *72* That is, about 1 ton (about 1.1 metric tons)
a *8* Or *God, translating it*

send some to those who have nothing[m] prepared. This day is sacred to our Lord. Do not grieve, for the joy[n] of the LORD is your strength."

11 The Levites calmed all the people, saying, "Be still, for this is a sacred day. Do not grieve."

12 Then all the people went away to eat and drink, to send portions of food and to celebrate with great joy,[o] because they now understood the words that had been made known to them.

13 On the second day of the month, the heads of all the families, along with the priests and the Levites, gathered round Ezra the scribe to give attention to the words of the Law. 14 They found written in the Law, which the LORD had commanded through Moses, that the Israelites were to live in booths during the feast of the seventh month 15 and that they should proclaim this word and spread it throughout their towns and in Jerusalem: "Go out into the hill country and bring back branches from olive and wild olive trees, and from myrtles, palms and shade trees, to make booths"—as it is written.[b]

16 So the people went out and brought back branches and built themselves booths on their own roofs, in their courtyards, in the courts of the house of God and in the square by the Water Gate and the one by the Gate of Ephraim.[p] 17 The whole company that had returned from exile built booths and lived in them. From the days of Joshua son of Nun until that day, the Israelites had not celebrated[q] it like this. And their joy was very great.

18 Day after day, from the first day to the last, Ezra read[r] from the Book of the Law of God. They celebrated the feast for seven days, and on the eighth day, in accordance with the regulation,[s] there was an assembly.

8:10
m 1Sa 25:8; Lk 14:12-14
n Lev 23:40; Dt 12:18; Dt 16:11, 14-15

8:12
o Est 9:22

8:16
p 2Ki 14:13; Ne 12:39

8:17
q 2Ch 7:8; 2Ch 8:13; 2Ch 30:21

8:18
r Dt 31:11
s Lev 23:36,40; Nu 29:35

9:1
a Jos 7:6; 1Sa 4:12

9:2
b Ne 13:3,30
c Ezr 10:11; Ps 106:6

9:4
d Ezr 10:23

9:5
e Ps 78:4

9:6
f Dt 6:4
g 2Ki 19:15
h Ge 1:1; Isa 37:16
i Ps 95:5
j Dt 10:14

9:7
k Ge 11:31
l Ge 17:5

9:8
m Ge 15:18-21

The Israelites Confess Their Sins

9 On the twenty-fourth day of the same month, the Israelites gathered together, fasting and wearing sackcloth and having dust on their heads.[a] 2 Those of Israelite descent had separated themselves from all foreigners.[b] They stood in their places and confessed their sins and the wickedness of their fathers.[c] 3 They stood where they were and read from the Book of the Law of the LORD their God for a quarter of the day, and spent another quarter in confession and in worshipping the LORD their God. 4 Standing on the stairs were the Levites[d]—Jeshua, Bani, Kadmiel, Shebaniah, Bunni, Sherebiah, Bani and Kenani—who called with loud voices to the LORD their God. 5 And the Levites—Jeshua, Kadmiel, Bani, Hashabneiah, Sherebiah, Hodiah, Shebaniah and Pethahiah—said: "Stand up and praise the LORD your God,[e] who is from everlasting to everlasting."[a]

"Blessed be your glorious
name, and may it be exalted
above all blessing and praise.
6 You alone are the LORD.[f] You
made the heavens,[g] even the
highest heavens, and all their
starry host, the earth[h] and all
that is on it, the seas[i] and all
that is in them.[j] You give life
to everything, and the multitudes of heaven worship you.

7 "You are the LORD God, who
chose Abram and brought him
out of Ur of the Chaldeans[k]
and named him Abraham.[l]
8 You found his heart faithful to
you, and you made a covenant
with him to give to his descendants the land of the Canaanites,
Hittites, Amorites, Perizzites,
Jebusites and Girgashites.[m]

[b] 15 See Lev. 23:37–40. [a] 5 Or *God for ever and ever*

You have kept your promise[n]
because you are righteous.[o]
9“You saw the suffering of
our forefathers in Egypt;[p] you
heard their cry at the Red
Sea.[b][q] 10You sent miraculous
signs[r] and wonders against
Pharaoh, against all his officials and all the people of his
land, for you knew how arrogantly the Egyptians treated
them. You made a name[s] for
yourself, which remains to this
day. 11You divided the sea before them,[t] so that they
passed through it on dry
ground, but you hurled their
pursuers into the depths, like a
stone into mighty waters.[u]
12By day you led[v] them with a
pillar of cloud,[w] and by night
with a pillar of fire to give
them light on the way they
were to take.
13“You came down on Mount
Sinai;[x] you spoke[y] to them
from heaven. You gave them
regulations and laws that are
just[z] and right, and decrees
and commands that are good.[a]
14You made known to them
your holy Sabbath[b] and gave
them commands, decrees and
laws through your servant
Moses. 15In their hunger you
gave them bread from
heaven[c] and in their thirst you
brought them water from the
rock;[d] you told them to go in
and take possession of the land
you had sworn with uplifted
hand to give them.[e]
16“But they, our forefathers,
became arrogant and stiff-
necked, and did not obey your
commands.[f] 17They refused to
listen and failed to remember[g]
the miracles you performed
among them. They became
stiff-necked and in their rebellion appointed a leader in order
to return to their slavery.[h] But
you are a forgiving God, gracious and compassionate, slow
to anger[i] and abounding in
love.[j] Therefore you did not
desert them,[k] 18even when
they cast for themselves an image of a calf[l] and said, ‘This is
your god, who brought you up
out of Egypt,’ or when they
committed awful blasphemies.
19“Because of your great
compassion you did not abandon them in the desert. By day
the pillar of cloud did not cease
to guide them on their path, nor
the pillar of fire by night to
shine on the way they were to
take. 20You gave your good
Spirit[m] to instruct them. You
did not withhold your manna[n]
from their mouths, and you
gave them water[o] for their
thirst. 21For forty years you
sustained them in the desert;
they lacked nothing,[p] their
clothes did not wear out nor did
their feet become swollen.[q]
22“You gave them kingdoms
and nations, allotting to them
even the remotest frontiers.
They took over the country of
Sihon[c][r] king of Heshbon and
the country of Og king of Bashan.[s] 23You made their sons
as numerous as the stars in the
sky, and you brought them into
the land that you told their fathers to enter and possess.
24Their sons went in and took
possession of the land.[t] You
subdued before them the Canaanites, who lived in the land;
you handed the Canaanites
over to them, along with their
kings and the peoples of the
land, to deal with them as they
pleased. 25They captured fortified cities and fertile land;
they took possession of houses
filled with all kinds of good
things, wells already dug, vineyards, olive groves and fruit

9:8
n Jos 21:45
o Ge 15:6
Ezr 9:15

9:9
p Ex 3:7
q Ex 14:10-30

9:10
r Ex 10:1
s Jer 32:20
Da 9:15

9:11
t Ex 14:21
Ps 78:13
u Ex 15:4-5,10
Heb 11:29

9:12
v Ex 15:13
w Ex 13:21

9:13
x Ex 19:11
y Ex 19:19
z Ps 119:137
a Ex 20:1

9:14
b Ge 2:3
Ex 20:8-11

9:15
c Ex 16:4
Jn 6:31
d Ex 17:6
Nu 20:7-13
e Dt 1:8,21

9:16
f Dt 1:26-33
Dt 31:29

9:17
g Ps 78:42
h Nu 14:1-4
i Ex 34:6
j Nu 14:17-19
k Ps 78:11

9:18
l Ex 32:4

9:20
m Nu 11:17
Isa 63:11,14
n Ex 16:15
o Ex 17:6

9:21
p Dt 2:7
q Dt 8:4

9:22
r Nu 21:21
s Nu 21:33

9:24
t Jos 11:23

b9 Hebrew *Yam Suph*; that is, Sea of Reeds
c22 One Hebrew manuscript and Septuagint; most Hebrew manuscripts *Sihon, that is, the country of the*

trees in abundance. They ate to the full and were well-nourished;[u] they revelled in your great goodness.[v]

26"But they were disobedient and rebelled against you; they put your law behind their backs.[w] They killed your prophets,[x] who had admonished them in order to turn them back to you; they committed awful blasphemies.[y] 27So you handed them over to their enemies,[z] who oppressed them. But when they were oppressed they cried out to you. From heaven you heard them, and in your great compassion[a] you gave them deliverers, who rescued them from the hand of their enemies.

28"But as soon as they were at rest, they again did what was evil in your sight. Then you abandoned them to the hand of their enemies so that they ruled over them. And when they cried out to you again, you heard from heaven, and in your compassion you delivered them[b] time after time.

29"You warned them to return to your law, but they became arrogant[c] and disobeyed your commands. They sinned against your ordinances, by which a man will live if he obeys them.[d] Stubbornly they turned their backs on you, became stiff-necked and refused to listen.[e] 30For many years you were patient with them. By your Spirit you admonished them through your prophets.[f] Yet they paid no attention, so you handed them over to the neighbouring peoples. 31But in your great mercy you did not put an end[g] to them or abandon them, for you are a gracious and merciful God.

32"Now therefore, O our God, the great, mighty[h] and awesome God, who keeps his covenant of love,[i] do not let all this hardship seem trifling in your eyes—the hardship that has come upon us, upon our kings and leaders, upon our priests and prophets, upon our fathers and all your people, from the days of the kings of Assyria until today. 33In all that has happened to us, you have been just;[j] you have acted faithfully, while we did wrong.[k] 34Our kings,[l] our leaders, our priests and our fathers[m] did not follow your law; they did not pay attention to your commands or the warnings you gave them. 35Even while they were in their kingdom, enjoying your great goodness[n] to them in the spacious and fertile land you gave them, they did not serve you[o] or turn from their evil ways.

36"But see, we are slaves[p] today, slaves in the land you gave our forefathers so that they could eat its fruit and the other good things it produces. 37Because of our sins, its abundant harvest goes to the kings you have placed over us. They rule over our bodies and our cattle as they please. We are in great distress.[q]

The Agreement of the People

38"In view of all this, we are making a binding agreement,[r] putting it in writing,[s] and our leaders, our Levites and our priests are affixing their seals to it."

10 Those who sealed it were:

Nehemiah the governor, the son of Hacaliah.

Zedekiah, 2Seraiah,[a] Azariah, Jeremiah,
3Pashhur,[b] Amariah, Malkijah,
4Hattush, Shebaniah, Malluch,

9:25 u Dt 6:10-12 v Nu 13:27 Dt 32:12-15
9:26 w 1Ki 14:9 x Mt 21:35-36 y Jdg 2:12-13
9:27 z Jdg 2:14 a Ps 106:45
9:28 b Ps 106:43
9:29 c Ps 5:5 Isa 2:11 Jer 43:2 d Dt 30:16 e Zec 7:11-12
9:30 f 2Ki 17:13-18 2Ch 36:16
9:31 g Isa 48:9 Jer 4:27
9:32 h Ps 24:8 i Dt 7:9
9:33 j Ge 18:25 k Jer 44:3 Da 9:7-8,14
9:34 l 2Ki 23:11 m Jer 44:17
9:35 n Isa 63:7 o Dt 28:45-48
9:36 p Dt 28:48 Ezr 9:9
9:37 q Dt 28:33 La 5:5
9:38 r 2Ch 23:16 s Isa 44:5
10:2 a Ezr 2:2
10:3 b 1Ch 9:12

5 Harim,[c] Meremoth, Obadiah,
6 Daniel, Ginnethon, Baruch,
7 Meshullam, Abijah, Mijamin,
8 Maaziah, Bilgai and Shemaiah.
These were the priests.

9 The Levites:[d]
Jeshua son of Azaniah,
Binnui of the sons of Henadad, Kadmiel,
10 and their associates:
Shebaniah, Hodiah, Kelita,
Pelaiah, Hanan,
11 Mica, Rehob, Hashabiah,
12 Zaccur, Sherebiah, Shebaniah,
13 Hodiah, Bani and Beninu.

14 The leaders of the people:
Parosh, Pahath-Moab, Elam,
Zattu, Bani,
15 Bunni, Azgad, Bebai,
16 Adonijah, Bigvai, Adin,[e]
17 Ater, Hezekiah, Azzur,
18 Hodiah, Hashum, Bezai,
19 Hariph, Anathoth, Nebai,
20 Magpiash, Meshullam, Hezir,[f]
21 Meshezabel, Zadok, Jaddua,
22 Pelatiah, Hanan, Anaiah,
23 Hoshea, Hananiah,[g] Hasshub,
24 Hallohesh, Pilha, Shobek,
25 Rehum, Hashabnah, Maaseiah,
26 Ahiah, Hanan, Anan,
27 Malluch, Harim and Baanah.

28 "The rest of the people—
priests, Levites, gatekeepers,
singers, temple servants[h] and
all who separated themselves
from the neighbouring peoples[i] for the sake of the Law of
God, together with their wives
and all their sons and daughters who are able to understand—29 all these now join
their brothers the nobles, and
bind themselves with a curse
and an oath[j] to follow the Law
of God given through Moses
the servant of God and to obey
carefully all the commands,
regulations and decrees of the
LORD our Lord.
30 "We promise not to give
our daughters in marriage to
the peoples around us or take
their daughters for our sons.[k]
31 "When the neighbouring
peoples bring merchandise or
grain to sell on the Sabbath,[l]
we will not buy from them on
the Sabbath or on any holy day.
Every seventh year we will
forgo working the land[m] and
will cancel all debts.[n]
32 "We assume the responsibility for carrying out the commands to give a third of a
shekel[a] each year for the service of the house of our God:
33 for the bread set out on the
table;[o] for the regular grain
offerings and burnt offerings;
for the offerings on the Sabbaths, New Moon[p] festivals
and appointed feasts; for the
holy offerings; for sin offerings to make atonement for Israel; and for all the duties of
the house of our God.[q]
34 "We—the priests, the Levites and the people—have
cast lots[r] to determine when
each of our families is to bring
to the house of our God at set
times each year a contribution
of wood[s] to burn on the altar of
the LORD our God, as it is written in the Law.
35 "We also assume responsibility for bringing to the house
of the LORD each year the firstfruits[t] of our crops and of
every fruit tree.[u]
36 "As it is also written in the
Law, we will bring the firstborn[v] of our sons and of our
cattle, of our herds and of our
flocks to the house of our God,
to the priests ministering
there.[w]

10:5 c 1Ch 24:8
10:9 d Ne 12:1
10:16 e Ezr 8:6
10:20 f 1Ch 24:15
10:23 g Ne 7:2
10:28 h Ps 135:1 i 2Ch 6:26 Ne 9:2
10:29 j Nu 5:21 Ps 119:106
10:30 k Ex 34:16 Dt 7:3 Ne 13:23
10:31 l Ne 13:16,18 Jer 17:27 Eze 23:38 Am 8:5 m Ex 23:11 Lev 25:1-7 n Dt 15:1
10:33 o Lev 24:6 p Nu 10:10 Ps 81:3 Isa 1:14 q 2Ch 24:5
10:34 r Lev 16:8 s Ne 13:31
10:35 t Ex 22:29 Ex 23:19 Nu 18:12 u Dt 26:1-11
10:36 v Ex 13:2 Nu 18:14-16 w Ne 13:31

[a] 32 That is, about 1/8 ounce (about 4 grams)

37“Moreover, we will bring to
the storerooms of the house of
our God, to the priests, the first
of our ground meal, of our
⌞grain⌟ offerings, of the fruit of
all our trees and of our new
wine and oil.[x] And we will
bring a tithe[y] of our crops to
the Levites,[z] for it is the Levites who collect the tithes in
all the towns where we work.[a]
38A priest descended from
Aaron is to accompany the Levites when they receive the
tithes, and the Levites are to
bring a tenth of the tithes[b] up
to the house of our God, to the
storerooms of the treasury.
39The people of Israel, including the Levites, are to bring
their contributions of grain,
new wine and oil to the storerooms where the articles for
the sanctuary are kept and
where the ministering priests,
the gatekeepers and the singers stay.

“We will not neglect the
house of our God.”[c]

The New Residents of Jerusalem

11:3–19pp 1Ch 9:1–17

11 Now the leaders of the people settled in Jerusalem,
and the rest of the people cast lots
to bring one out of every ten to live
in Jerusalem,[a] the holy city,[b]
while the remaining nine were to
stay in their own towns.[c] 2The people commended all the men who
volunteered to live in Jerusalem.

3These are the provincial leaders
who settled in Jerusalem (now
some Israelites, priests, Levites,
temple servants and descendants
of Solomon’s servants lived in the
towns of Judah, each on his own
property in the various towns,[d]
4while other people from both Judah and Benjamin[e] lived in Jerusalem):[f]

From the descendants of Judah:

Athaiah son of Uzziah, the son
of Zechariah, the son of Amariah, the son of Shephatiah, the
son of Mahalalel, a descendant
of Perez; 5and Maaseiah son of
Baruch, the son of Col-Hozeh,
the son of Hazaiah, the son of
Adaiah, the son of Joiarib, the
son of Zechariah, a descendant
of Shelah. 6The descendants of
Perez who lived in Jerusalem
totalled 468 able men.

7From the descendants of Benjamin:

Sallu son of Meshullam, the son
of Joed, the son of Pedaiah, the
son of Kolaiah, the son of Maaseiah, the son of Ithiel, the son
of Jeshaiah, 8and his followers,
Gabbai and Sallai—928 men.
9Joel son of Zicri was their
chief officer, and Judah son of
Hassenuah was over the
Second District of the city.

10From the priests:

Jedaiah; the son of Joiarib; Jakin; 11Seraiah[g] son of Hilkiah,
the son of Meshullam, the son
of Zadok, the son of Meraioth,
the son of Ahitub,[h] supervisor
in the house of God, 12and their
associates, who carried on
work for the temple—822 men;
Adaiah son of Jeroham, the son
of Pelaliah, the son of Amzi, the
son of Zechariah, the son of
Pashhur, the son of Malkijah,
13and his associates, who were
heads of families—242 men;
Amashsai son of Azarel, the
son of Ahzai, the son of Meshillemoth, the son of Immer,
14and his[a] associates, who
were able men—128 men.
Their chief officer was Zabdiel
son of Haggedolim.

15From the Levites:

Shemaiah son of Hasshub, the
son of Azrikam, the son of

10:37 x Lev 23:17; Nu 18:12 y Lev 27:30; Nu 18:21 z Dt 14:22-29 a Eze 44:30
10:38 b Nu 18:26
10:39 c Dt 12:6; Ne 13:11,12
11:1 a Ne 7:4 b ver 18; Isa 48:2; Isa 52:1; Isa 64:10; Zec 14:20-21 c Ne 7:73
11:3 d 1Ch 9:2-3; Ezr 2:1
11:4 e Ezr 1:5 f Ezr 2:70
11:11 g 2Ki 25:18; Ezr 2:2 h Ezr 7:2

a *14* Most Septuagint manuscripts; Hebrew *their*

Hashabiah, the son of Bunni;
16 Shabbethai[i] and Jozabad,[j]
two of the heads of the Levites,
who had charge of the outside
work of the house of God;
17 Mattaniah[k] son of Mica, the
son of Zabdi, the son of
Asaph,[l] the director who led
in thanksgiving and prayer;
Bakbukiah, second among his
associates; and Abda son of
Shammua, the son of Galal, the
son of Jeduthun.[m] 18 The Levites in the holy city[n] totalled
284.

19 The gatekeepers:

Akkub, Talmon and their associates, who kept watch at the
gates—172 men.

20 The rest of the Israelites, with
the priests and Levites, were in all
the towns of Judah, each on his ancestral property.
21 The temple servants[o] lived on
the hill of Ophel, and Ziha and
Gishpa were in charge of them.
22 The chief officer of the Levites
in Jerusalem was Uzzi son of Bani,
the son of Hashabiah, the son of
Mattaniah,[p] the son of Mica. Uzzi
was one of Asaph's descendants,
who were the singers responsible
for the service of the house of God.
23 The singers[q] were under the
king's orders, which regulated
their daily activity.
24 Pethahiah son of Meshezabel,
one of the descendants of Zerah[r]
son of Judah, was the king's agent
in all affairs relating to the people.
25 As for the villages with their
fields, some of the people of Judah
lived in Kiriath Arba[s] and its surrounding settlements, in Dibon[t]
and its settlements, in Jekabzeel
and its villages, 26 in Jeshua, in Moladah, in Beth Pelet,[u] 27 in Hazar
Shual, in Beersheba[v] and its settlements, 28 in Ziklag,[w] in Meconah
and its settlements, 29 in En Rimmon, in Zorah,[x] in Jarmuth,[y] 30 Zanoah, Adullam[z] and their villages,
in Lachish[a] and its fields, and in
Azekah[b] and its settlements. So
they were living all the way from
Beersheba[c] to the Valley of Hinnom.
31 The descendants of the Benjamites from Geba[d] lived in Michmash,[e] Aija, Bethel and its settlements, 32 in Anathoth,[f] Nob[g] and
Ananiah, 33 in Hazor,[h] Ramah and
Gittaim,[i] 34 in Hadid, Zeboim[j] and Ne-
ballat, 35 in Lod and Ono,[k] and in
the Valley of the Craftsmen.
36 Some of the divisions of the Levites of Judah settled in Benjamin.

Priests and Levites

12 These were the priests[a]
and Levites who returned
with Zerubbabel[b] son of Shealtiel
and with Jeshua:[c]

Seraiah,[d] Jeremiah, Ezra,
2 Amariah, Malluch, Hattush,
3 Shecaniah, Rehum, Mere-
moth,
4 Iddo,[e] Ginnethon,[a] Abijah,[f]
5 Mijamin,[b] Moadiah, Bilgah,
6 Shemaiah, Joiarib, Jedaiah,[g]
7 Sallu, Amok, Hilkiah and Jedaiah.

These were the leaders of the
priests and their associates in the
days of Jeshua.
8 The Levites were Jeshua, Binnui, Kadmiel, Sherebiah, Judah,
and also Mattaniah,[h] who, together
with his associates, was in charge
of the songs of thanksgiving. 9 Bakbukiah and Unni, their associates,
stood opposite them in the services.
10 Jeshua was the father of Joiakim, Joiakim the father of Eliashib,[i] Eliashib the father of
Joiada, 11 Joiada the father of Jonathan, and Jonathan the father of
Jaddua.
12 In the days of Joiakim, these
were the heads of the priestly
families:

11:16 *i* Ezr 10:15 *j* Ezr 8:33
11:17 *k* 1Ch 9:15 Ne 12:8 *l* 2Ch 5:12 *m* 1Ch 25:1
11:18 *n* Rev 21:2
11:21 *o* Ezr 2:43 Ne 3:26
11:22 *p* 1Ch 9:15
11:23 *q* Ne 7:44
11:24 *r* Ge 38:30
11:25 *s* Ge 35:27 Jos 14:15 *t* Nu 21:30
11:26 *u* Jos 15:27
11:27 *v* Ge 21:14
11:28 *w* 1Sa 27:6
11:29 *x* Jos 15:33 *y* Jos 10:3
11:30 *z* Jos 15:35 *a* Jos 10:3 *b* Jos 10:10 *c* Jos 15:28
11:31 *d* Jos 21:17 Isa 10:29 *e* 1Sa 13:2
11:32 *f* Jos 21:18 Isa 10:30 *g* 1Sa 21:1
11:33 *h* Jos 11:1 *i* 2Sa 4:3
11:34 *j* 1Sa 13:18
11:35 *k* 1Ch 8:12
12:1 *a* Ne 10:1-8 *b* 1Ch 3:19 *c* Ezr 2:2 *d* Ezr 2:2
12:4 *e* Zec 1:1 *f* Lk 1:5
12:6 *g* 1Ch 24:7
12:8 *h* Ne 11:17
12:10 *i* Ezr 10:24

a4 Many Hebrew manuscripts and Vulgate (see also Neh. 12:16); most Hebrew manuscripts *Ginnethoi* **b**5 A variant of *Miniamin*

of Seraiah's family, Meraiah;
of Jeremiah's, Hananiah;
13 of Ezra's, Meshullam;
of Amariah's, Jehohanan;
14 of Malluch's, Jonathan;
of Shecaniah's,[c] Joseph;
15 of Harim's, Adna;
of Meremoth's,[d] Helkai;
16 of Iddo's,[j] Zechariah;
of Ginnethon's, Meshullam;
17 of Abijah's, Zicri;
of Miniamin's and of
Moadiah's, Piltai;
18 of Bilgah's, Shammua;
of Shemaiah's, Jehonathan;
19 of Joiarib's, Mattenai;
of Jedaiah's, Uzzi;
20 of Sallu's, Kallai;
of Amok's, Eber;
21 of Hilkiah's, Hashabiah;
of Jedaiah's, Nethanel.

22 The family heads of the Levites in the days of Eliashib, Joiada, Johanan and Jaddua, as well as those of the priests, were recorded in the reign of Darius the Persian. 23 The family heads among the descendants of Levi up to the time of Johanan son of Eliashib were recorded in the book of the annals. 24 And the leaders of the Levites[k] were Hashabiah, Sherebiah, Jeshua son of Kadmiel, and their associates, who stood opposite them to give praise and thanksgiving, one section responding to the other, as prescribed by David the man of God. 25 Mattaniah, Bakbukiah, Obadiah, Meshullam, Talmon and Akkub were gatekeepers who guarded the storerooms at the gates. 26 They served in the days of Joiakim son of Jeshua, the son of Jozadak, and in the days of Nehemiah the governor and of Ezra the priest and scribe.

Dedication of the Wall of Jerusalem

27 At the dedication[l] of the wall of Jerusalem, the Levites were sought out from where they lived and were brought to Jerusalem to celebrate joyfully the dedication with songs of thanksgiving and with the music of cymbals,[m] harps and lyres.[n] 28 The singers also were brought together from the region around Jerusalem—from the villages of the Netophathites,[o] 29 from Beth Gilgal, and from the area of Geba and Azmaveth, for the singers had built villages for themselves around Jerusalem. 30 When the priests and Levites had purified themselves ceremonially, they purified the people,[p] the gates and the wall.

31 I had the leaders of Judah go up on top[e] of the wall. I also assigned two large choirs to give thanks. One was to proceed on top[f] of the wall to the right, towards the Dung Gate.[q] 32 Hoshaiah and half the leaders of Judah followed them, 33 along with Azariah, Ezra, Meshullam, 34 Judah, Benjamin,[r] Shemaiah, Jeremiah, 35 as well as some priests with trumpets,[s] and also Zechariah son of Jonathan, the son of Shemaiah, the son of Mattaniah, the son of Micaiah, the son of Zaccur, the son of Asaph, 36 and his associates—Shemaiah, Azarel, Milalai, Gilalai, Maai, Nethanel, Judah and Hanani—with musical instruments[t] ⌊prescribed by⌋ David the man of God.[u] Ezra[v] the scribe led the procession. 37 At the Fountain Gate[w] they continued directly up the steps of the City of David on the ascent to the wall and passed above the house of David to the Water Gate[x] on the east.

38 The second choir proceeded in the opposite direction. I followed them on top[g] of the wall, together with half the people—past the

12:16 j ver 4
12:24 k Ezr 2:40
12:27 l Dt 20:5; m 2Sa 6:5; n 1Ch 15:16,28; 1Ch 25:6; Ps 92:3
12:28 o 1Ch 2:54; 1Ch 9:16
12:30 p Ex 19:10; Job 1:5
12:31 q Ne 2:13
12:34 r Ezr 1:5
12:35 s Ezr 3:10
12:36 t 1Ch 15:16; u 2Ch 8:14; v Ezr 7:6
12:37 w Ne 2:14; Ne 3:15; x Ne 3:26

c14 Very many Hebrew manuscripts, some Septuagint manuscripts and Syriac (see also Neh. 12:3); most Hebrew manuscripts *Shebaniah's*
d15 Some Septuagint manuscripts (see also Neh. 12:3); Hebrew *Meraioth's* e31 Or *go alongside* f31 Or *proceed alongside*
g38 Or *them alongside*

Tower of the Ovens[y] to the Broad Wall,[z] 39 over the Gate of Ephraim,[a] the Jeshanah[h] Gate,[b] the Fish Gate,[c] the Tower of Hananel[d] and the Tower of the Hundred,[e] as far as the Sheep Gate.[f] At the Gate of the Guard they stopped.

40 The two choirs that gave thanks then took their places in the house of God; so did I, together with half the officials, 41 as well as the priests—Eliakim, Maaseiah, Miniamin, Micaiah, Elioenai, Zechariah and Hananiah with their trumpets—42 and also Maaseiah, Shemaiah, Eleazar, Uzzi, Jehohanan, Malkijah, Elam and Ezer. The choirs sang under the direction of Jezrahiah. 43 And on that day they offered great sacrifices, rejoicing because God had given them great joy. The women and children also rejoiced. The sound of rejoicing in Jerusalem could be heard far away.

44 At that time men were appointed to be in charge of the storerooms[g] for the contributions, firstfruits and tithes.[h] From the fields around the towns they were to bring into the storerooms the portions required by the Law for the priests and the Levites, for Judah was pleased with the ministering priests and Levites.[i] 45 They performed the service of their God and the service of purification, as did also the singers and gatekeepers, according to the commands of David[j] and his son Solomon.[k] 46 For long ago, in the days of David and Asaph,[l] there had been directors for the singers and for the songs of praise[m] and thanksgiving to God. 47 So in the days of Zerubbabel and of Nehemiah, all Israel contributed the daily portions for the singers and gatekeepers. They also set aside the portion for the other Levites, and the Levites set aside the portion for the descendants of Aaron.[n]

12:38 y Ne 3:11 z Ne 3:8
12:39 a 2Ki 14:13; Ne 8:16 b Ne 3:6 c 2Ch 33:14; Ne 3:3 d Ne 3:1 e Ne 3:1 f Ne 3:1
12:44 g Ne 13:4,13 h Lev 27:30 i Dt 18:8
12:45 j 1Ch 25:1; 2Ch 8:14 k 1Ch 6:31; 1Ch 23:5
12:46 l 2Ch 35:15 m 2Ch 29:27; Ps 137:4
12:47 n Nu 18:21; Dt 18:8
13:1 a ver 23; Dt 23:3
13:2 b Nu 22:3-11 c Nu 23:7; Dt 23:3 d Nu 23:11; Dt 23:4-5
13:3 e ver 23; Ne 9:2
13:4 f Ne 12:44 g Ne 2:10
13:5 h Lev 27:30; Nu 18:21
13:6 i Ne 2:6; Ne 5:14
13:7 j Ezr 10:24
13:8 k Mt 21:12-13; Jn 2:13-16
13:9 l 1Ch 23:28; 2Ch 29:5
13:10 m Dt 12:19

Nehemiah's Final Reforms

13 On that day the Book of Moses was read aloud in the hearing of the people and there it was found written that no Ammonite or Moabite should ever be admitted into the assembly of God,[a] 2 because they had not met the Israelites with food and water but had hired Balaam[b] to call a curse down on them.[c] (Our God, however, turned the curse into a blessing.)[d] 3 When the people heard this law, they excluded from Israel all who were of foreign descent.[e]

4 Before this, Eliashib the priest had been put in charge of the storerooms[f] of the house of our God. He was closely associated with Tobiah,[g] 5 and he had provided him with a large room formerly used to store the grain offerings and incense and temple articles, and also the tithes[h] of grain, new wine and oil prescribed for the Levites, singers and gatekeepers, as well as the contributions for the priests.

6 But while all this was going on, I was not in Jerusalem, for in the thirty-second year of Artaxerxes[i] king of Babylon I had returned to the king. Some time later I asked his permission 7 and came back to Jerusalem. Here I learned about the evil thing Eliashib[j] had done in providing Tobiah a room in the courts of the house of God. 8 I was greatly displeased and threw all Tobiah's household goods out of the room.[k] 9 I gave orders to purify the rooms,[l] and then I put back into them the equipment of the house of God, with the grain offerings and the incense.

10 I also learned that the portions assigned to the Levites had not been given to them,[m] and that all the Levites and singers responsible for the service had gone back to their own fields. 11 So I rebuked the

[h]39 Or *Old*

officials and asked them, "Why is
the house of God neglected?"[n]
Then I called them together and
stationed them at their posts.
12 All Judah brought the tithes[o]
of grain, new wine and oil into the
storerooms.[p] 13 I put Shelemiah the
priest, Zadok the scribe, and a Levite named Pedaiah in charge of
the storerooms and made Hanan
son of Zaccur, the son of Mattaniah,
their assistant, because these men
were considered trustworthy.
They were made responsible for
distributing the supplies to their
brothers.[q]
14 Remember[r] me for this, O my
God, and do not blot out what I have
so faithfully done for the house of
my God and its services.

15 In those days I saw men in Judah treading winepresses on the
Sabbath and bringing in grain and
loading it on donkeys, together
with wine, grapes, figs and all other
kinds of loads. And they were
bringing all this into Jerusalem on
the Sabbath.[s] Therefore I warned
them against selling food on that
day. 16 Men from Tyre who lived in
Jerusalem were bringing in fish
and all kinds of merchandise and
selling them in Jerusalem on the
Sabbath[t] to the people of Judah.
17 I rebuked the nobles of Judah and
said to them, "What is this wicked
thing you are doing—desecrating
the Sabbath day? 18 Didn't your
forefathers do the same things, so
that our God brought all this calamity upon us and upon this city? Now
you are stirring up more wrath
against Israel by desecrating the
Sabbath."[u]
19 When evening shadows fell on
the gates of Jerusalem before the
Sabbath,[v] I ordered the doors to be
shut and not opened until the Sabbath was over. I stationed some of
my own men at the gates so that
no load could be brought in on the
Sabbath day. 20 Once or twice the
merchants and sellers of all kinds of
goods spent the night outside Jerusalem. 21 But I warned them and
said, "Why do you spend the night
by the wall? If you do this again, I
will lay hands on you." From that
time on they no longer came on the
Sabbath. 22 Then I commanded the
Levites to purify themselves and
go and guard the gates in order to
keep the Sabbath day holy.

Remember[w] me for this also,
O my God, and show mercy to me
according to your great love.

23 Moreover, in those days I saw
men of Judah who had married[x]
women from Ashdod, Ammon and
Moab.[y] 24 Half of their children
spoke the language of Ashdod or
the language of one of the other
peoples, and did not know how to
speak the language of Judah. 25 I rebuked them and called curses down
on them. I beat some of the men and
pulled out their hair. I made them
take an oath[z] in God's name and
said: "You are not to give your
daughters in marriage to their
sons, nor are you to take their
daughters in marriage for your
sons or for yourselves. 26 Was it not
because of marriages like these
that Solomon king of Israel sinned?
Among the many nations there was
no king like him.[a] He was loved by
his God,[b] and God made him king
over all Israel, but even he was led
into sin by foreign women.[c] 27 Must
we hear now that you too are doing
all this terrible wickedness and are
being unfaithful to our God by
marrying[d] foreign women?"
28 One of the sons of Joiada son of
Eliashib[e] the high priest was son-
in-law to Sanballat[f] the Horonite.
And I drove him away from me.

29 Remember[g] them, O my God,
because they defiled the priestly
office and the covenant of the
priesthood and of the Levites.

30 So I purified the priests and the

13:11 n Ne 10:37-39; Hag 1:1-9
13:12 o 2Ch 31:6; p 1Ki 7:51; Ne 10:37-39; Mal 3:10
13:13 q Ne 12:44; Ac 6:1-5
13:14 r Ge 8:1
13:15 s Ex 20:8-11; Ex 34:21; Dt 5:12-15; Ne 10:31
13:16 t Ne 10:31
13:18 u Ne 10:31; Jer 17:21-23
13:19 v Lev 23:32
13:22 w Ge 8:1; Ne 12:30
13:23 x Ezr 9:1-2; Mal 2:11; y ver 1; Ne 10:30
13:25 z Ezr 10:5
13:26 a 1Ki 3:13; 2Ch 1:12; b 2Sa 12:25; c 1Ki 11:3
13:27 d Ezr 9:14; Ezr 10:2
13:28 e Ezr 10:24; f Ne 2:10
13:29 g Ne 6:14

Levites of everything foreign,[h] and assigned them duties, each to his own task. [31]I also made provision for contributions of wood[i] at designated times, and for the firstfruits.

Remember[j] me with favour, O my God.

13:30 *h* Ne 10:30

13:31 *i* Ne 10:34 *j* ver 14,22 Ge 8:1

ESTHER

Queen Vashti Deposed

1 This is what happened during
the time of Xerxes,[a][a] the
Xerxes who ruled over 127 provinces[b] stretching from India to
Cush:[b][c] 2At that time King Xerxes
reigned from his royal throne in
the citadel of Susa,[d] 3and in the
third year of his reign he gave a
banquet[e] for all his nobles and officials. The military leaders of Persia and Media, the princes, and the
nobles of the provinces were
present.
4For a full 180 days he displayed
the vast wealth of his kingdom and
the splendour and glory of his majesty. 5When these days were over,
the king gave a banquet, lasting
seven days,[f] in the enclosed garden[g] of the king's palace, for all
the people from the least to the
greatest, who were in the citadel of
Susa. 6The garden had hangings of
white and blue linen, fastened with
cords of white linen and purple material to silver rings on marble pillars. There were couches[h] of gold
and silver on a mosaic pavement of
porphyry, marble, mother-of-pearl
and other costly stones. 7Wine was
served in goblets of gold, each one
different from the other, and the
royal wine was abundant, in keeping with the king's liberality.[i] 8By
the king's command each guest
was allowed to drink in his own
way, for the king instructed all the
wine stewards to serve each man
what he wished.
9Queen Vashti also gave a banquet[j] for the women in the royal
palace of King Xerxes.
10On the seventh day, when King
Xerxes was in high spirits[k] from
wine,[l] he commanded the seven
eunuchs who served him—
Mehuman, Biztha, Harbona,[m] Bigtha,
Abagtha, Zethar and Carcas—11to
bring[n] before him Queen Vashti,
wearing her royal crown, in order
to display her beauty[o] to the people and nobles, for she was lovely
to look at. 12But when the attendants delivered the king's command, Queen Vashti refused to
come. Then the king became furious and burned with anger.[p]
13Since it was customary for the
king to consult experts in matters
of law and justice, he spoke with
the wise men who understood the
times[q] 14and were closest to the
king—Carshena, Shethar, Adma-
tha, Tarshish, Meres, Marsena and
Memucan, the seven nobles[r] of
Persia and Media who had special
access to the king and were highest
in the kingdom.
15"According to law, what must
be done to Queen Vashti?" he
asked. "She has not obeyed the
command of King Xerxes that the
eunuchs have taken to her."
16Then Memucan replied in the
presence of the king and the nobles, "Queen Vashti has done
wrong, not only against the king
but also against all the nobles and
the peoples of all the provinces of
King Xerxes. 17For the queen's conduct will become known to all the
women, and so they will despise
their husbands and say, 'King
Xerxes commanded Queen Vashti
to be brought before him, but she
would not come.' 18This very day
the Persian and Median women of
the nobility who have heard about
the queen's conduct will respond to
all the king's nobles in the same

1:1 *a* Ezr 4:6; Da 9:1 *b* Est 9:30; Da 3:2; Da 6:1 *c* Est 8:9
1:2 *d* Ezr 4:9; Ne 1:1; Est 2:8
1:3 *e* 1Ki 3:15; Est 2:18
1:5 *f* Jdg 14:17 *g* 2Ki 21:18; Est 7:7-8
1:6 *h* Est 7:8; Eze 23:41; Am 3:12; Am 6:4
1:7 *i* Est 2:18; Da 5:2
1:9 *j* 1Ki 3:15
1:10 *k* Jdg 16:25; Ru 3:7 *l* Ge 14:18; Est 3:15; Est 5:6; Est 7:2; Pr 31:4-7; Da 5:1-4 *m* Est 7:9
1:11 *n* SS 2:4 *o* Ps 45:11; Eze 16:14
1:12 *p* Ge 39:19; Est 2:21; Est 7:7; Pr 19:12
1:13 *q* 1Ch 12:32; Jer 10:7; Da 2:12
1:14 *r* 2Ki 25:19; Ezr 7:14

[a]*1* Hebrew *Ahasuerus*, a variant of Xerxes' Persian name; here and throughout Esther
[b]*1* That is, the upper Nile region

way. There will be no end of disrespect and discord.[s]

19"Therefore, if it pleases the king,[t] let him issue a royal decree and let it be written in the laws of Persia and Media, which cannot be repealed,[u] that Vashti is never again to enter the presence of King Xerxes. Also let the king give her royal position to someone else who is better than she. 20Then when the king's edict is proclaimed throughout all his vast realm, all the women will respect their husbands, from the least to the greatest."

21The king and his nobles were pleased with this advice, so the king did as Memucan proposed. 22He sent dispatches to all parts of the kingdom, to each province in its own script and to each people in its own language,[v] proclaiming in each people's tongue that every man should be ruler over his own household.

Esther Made Queen

2 Later when the anger of King Xerxes had subsided,[a] he remembered Vashti and what she had done and what he had decreed about her. 2Then the king's personal attendants proposed, "Let a search be made for beautiful young virgins for the king. 3Let the king appoint commissioners in every province of his realm to bring all these beautiful girls into the harem at the citadel of Susa. Let them be placed under the care of Hegai, the king's eunuch, who is in charge of the women; and let beauty treatments be given to them. 4Then let the girl who pleases the king be queen instead of Vashti." This advice appealed to the king, and he followed it.

5Now there was in the citadel of Susa a Jew of the tribe of Benjamin, named Mordecai son of Jair, the son of Shimei, the son of Kish,[b] 6who had been carried into exile from Jerusalem by Nebuchadnezzar king of Babylon, among those taken captive with Jehoiachin[a][c] king of Judah.[d] 7Mordecai had a cousin named Hadassah, whom he had brought up because she had neither father nor mother. This girl, who was also known as Esther,[e] was lovely[f] in form and features, and Mordecai had taken her as his own daughter when her father and mother died.

8When the king's order and edict had been proclaimed, many girls were brought to the citadel of Susa[g] and put under the care of Hegai. Esther also was taken to the king's palace and entrusted to Hegai, who had charge of the harem. 9The girl pleased him and won his favour.[h] Immediately he provided her with her beauty treatments and special food.[i] He assigned to her seven maids selected from the king's palace and moved her and her maids into the best place in the harem.

10Esther had not revealed her nationality and family background, because Mordecai had forbidden her to do so.[j] 11Every day he walked to and fro near the courtyard of the harem to find out how Esther was and what was happening to her.

12Before a girl's turn came to go in to King Xerxes, she had to complete twelve months of beauty treatments prescribed for the women, six months with oil of myrrh and six with perfumes[k] and cosmetics. 13And this is how she would go to the king: Anything she wanted was given to her to take with her from the harem to the king's palace. 14In the evening she would go there and in the morning return to another part of the harem to the care of Shaashgaz, the king's eunuch who was in charge of the concubines.[l] She would not return to the king unless he was pleased

1:18 s Pr 19:13; Pr 27:15
1:19 t Ecc 8:4; u Est 8:8; Da 6:8,12
1:22 v Ne 13:24; Est 8:9; Eph 5:22-24; 1Ti 2:12
2:1 a Est 1:19-20; Est 7:10
2:5 b 1Sa 9:1; Est 3:2
2:6 c 2Ki 24:6,15; 2Ch 36:10,20; d Da 1:1-5; Da 5:13
2:7 e Ge 41:45; f Ge 39:6
2:8 g ver 3,15; Ne 1:1; Est 1:2; Da 8:2
2:9 h Ge 39:21; i ver 3,12; Ge 37:3; 1Sa 9:22-24; 2Ki 25:30; Eze 16:9-13; Da 1:5
2:10 j ver 20
2:12 k Pr 27:9; SS 1:3; Isa 3:24
2:14 l 1Ki 11:3; SS 6:8; Da 5:2

a6 Hebrew *Jeconiah*, a variant of *Jehoiachin*

with her and summoned her by name.[m]

15 When the turn came for Esther (the girl Mordecai had adopted, the daughter of his uncle Abihail[n]) to go to the king,[o] she asked for nothing other than what Hegai, the king's eunuch who was in charge of the harem, suggested. And Esther won the favour[p] of everyone who saw her. 16 She was taken to King Xerxes in the royal residence in the tenth month, the month of Tebeth, in the seventh year of his reign.

17 Now the king was attracted to Esther more than to any of the other women, and she won his favour and approval more than any of the other virgins. So he set a royal crown on her head and made her queen[q] instead of Vashti. 18 And the king gave a great banquet,[r] Esther's banquet, for all his nobles and officials.[s] He proclaimed a holiday throughout the provinces and distributed gifts with royal liberality.[t]

Mordecai Uncovers a Conspiracy

19 When the virgins were assembled a second time, Mordecai was sitting at the king's gate.[u] 20 But Esther had kept secret her family background and nationality just as Mordecai had told her to do, for she continued to follow Mordecai's instructions as she had done when he was bringing her up.[v]

21 During the time Mordecai was sitting at the king's gate, Bigthana[b] and Teresh, two of the king's officers[w] who guarded the doorway, became angry[x] and conspired to assassinate King Xerxes. 22 But Mordecai found out about the plot and told Queen Esther, who in turn reported it to the king, giving credit to Mordecai. 23 And when the report was investigated and found to be true, the two officials were hanged[y] on a gallows.[c] All this was recorded in the book of the annals[z] in the presence of the king.

Haman's Plot to Destroy the Jews

3 After these events, King Xerxes honoured Haman son of Hammedatha, the Agagite,[a] elevating him and giving him a seat of honour higher than that of all the other nobles. 2 All the royal officials at the king's gate knelt down and paid honour to Haman, for the king had commanded this concerning him. But Mordecai would not kneel down or pay him honour.

3 Then the royal officials at the king's gate asked Mordecai, "Why do you disobey the king's command?"[b] 4 Day after day they spoke to him but he refused to comply.[c] Therefore they told Haman about it to see whether Mordecai's behaviour would be tolerated, for he had told them he was a Jew.

5 When Haman saw that Mordecai would not kneel down or pay him honour, he was enraged.[d] 6 Yet having learned who Mordecai's people were, he scorned the idea of killing only Mordecai. Instead Haman looked for a way[e] to destroy[f] all Mordecai's people, the Jews,[g] throughout the whole kingdom of Xerxes.

7 In the twelfth year of King Xerxes, in the first month, the month of Nisan, they cast the *pur*[h] (that is, the lot[i]) in the presence of Haman to select a day and month. And the lot fell on[a] the twelfth month, the month of Adar.[j]

8 Then Haman said to King Xerxes, "There is a certain people dispersed and scattered among the peoples in all the provinces of your kingdom whose customs[k] are different from those of all other people and who do not obey[l] the king's

2:14 *m* Est 4:11
2:15 *n* Est 9:29 *o* Ps 45:14 *p* Ge 18:3 Ge 30:27 Est 5:8
2:17 *q* Est 1:11 Eze 16:9-13
2:18 *r* 1Ki 3:15 Est 1:3 *s* Ge 40:20 *t* Est 1:7
2:19 *u* ver 21 Est 3:2 Est 4:2 Est 5:13
2:20 *v* ver 10
2:21 *w* Ge 40:2 Est 6:2 *x* Est 1:12 Est 3:5 Est 5:9 Est 7:7
2:23 *y* Ge 40:19 Ps 7:14-16 Pr 26:27 *z* Est 6:1 Est 10:2
3:1 *a* ver 10 Ex 17:8-16 Nu 24:7 Dt 25:17-19 1Sa 14:48 Est 5:11
3:3 *b* Est 5:9 Da 3:12
3:4 *c* Ge 39:10
3:5 *d* Est 2:21 Est 5:9
3:6 *e* Pr 16:25 *f* Ps 74:8 Ps 83:4 *g* Est 9:24
3:7 *h* Est 9:24,26 *i* Lev 16:8 1Sa 10:21 *j* ver 13 Ezr 6:15 Est 9:19
3:8 *k* Ac 16:20-21 *l* Jer 29:7 Da 6:13

b21 Hebrew *Bigthan*, a variant of *Bigthana*
c23 Or *were hung* (or *impaled*) *on poles*; similarly elsewhere in Esther
a7 Septuagint; Hebrew does not have *And the lot fell on.*

laws; it is not in the king's best interest to tolerate them.[m] 9If it pleases the king, let a decree be issued to destroy them, and I will put ten thousand talents[b] of silver into the royal treasury for the men who carry out this business."[n]

10So the king took his signet ring[o] from his finger and gave it to Haman son of Hammedatha, the Agagite, the enemy of the Jews. 11"Keep the money," the king said to Haman, "and do with the people as you please."

12Then on the thirteenth day of the first month the royal secretaries were summoned. They wrote out in the script of each province and in the language[p] of each people all Haman's orders to the king's satraps, the governors of the various provinces and the nobles of the various peoples. These were written in the name of King Xerxes himself and sealed[q] with his own ring. 13Dispatches were sent by couriers to all the king's provinces with the order to destroy, kill and annihilate all the Jews[r]—young and old, women and little children—on a single day, the thirteenth day of the twelfth month, the month of Adar,[s] and to plunder[t] their goods. 14A copy of the text of the edict was to be issued as law in every province and made known to the people of every nationality so that they would be ready for that day.[u]

15Spurred on by the king's command, the couriers went out, and the edict was issued in the citadel of Susa.[v] The king and Haman sat down to drink,[w] but the city of Susa was bewildered.[x]

Mordecai Persuades Esther to Help

4 When Mordecai learned of all that had been done, he tore his clothes,[a] put on sackcloth and ashes,[b] and went out into the city, wailing[c] loudly and bitterly. 2But

3:8 m Ezr 4:15
3:9 n Est 7:4
3:10 o Ge 41:42; Est 7:6; Est 8:2
3:12 p Ne 13:24; q Ge 38:18; 1Ki 21:8; Est 8:8-10
3:13 r 1Sa 15:3; Ezr 4:6; Est 8:10-14; s ver 7; t Est 8:11; Est 9:10
3:14 u Est 8:8; Est 9:1
3:15 v Est 8:14; w Est 1:10; x Est 8:15
4:1 a Nu 14:6; b 2Sa 13:19; Eze 27:30-31; Jnh 3:5-6; c Ex 11:6; Ps 30:11
4:2 d Est 2:19
4:7 e Est 3:9; Est 7:4
4:11 f Est 2:14; g Da 2:9; h Est 5:1,2; Est 8:4

he went only as far as the king's gate,[d] because no-one clothed in sackcloth was allowed to enter it. 3In every province to which the edict and order of the king came, there was great mourning among the Jews, with fasting, weeping and wailing. Many lay in sackcloth and ashes.

4When Esther's maids and eunuchs came and told her about Mordecai, she was in great distress. She sent clothes for him to put on instead of his sackcloth, but he would not accept them. 5Then Esther summoned Hathach, one of the king's eunuchs assigned to attend her, and ordered him to find out what was troubling Mordecai and why.

6So Hathach went out to Mordecai in the open square of the city in front of the king's gate. 7Mordecai told him everything that had happened to him, including the exact amount of money Haman had promised to pay into the royal treasury for the destruction of the Jews.[e] 8He also gave him a copy of the text of the edict for their annihilation, which had been published in Susa, to show to Esther and explain it to her, and he told him to urge her to go into the king's presence to beg for mercy and plead with him for her people.

9Hathach went back and reported to Esther what Mordecai had said. 10Then she instructed him to say to Mordecai, 11"All the king's officials and the people of the royal provinces know that for any man or woman who approaches the king in the inner court without being summoned[f] the king has but one law:[g] that he be put to death. The only exception to this is for the king to extend the gold sceptre[h] to him and spare his life. But thirty days have passed since I was called to go to the king."

[b]9 That is, about 340 tons (about 345 metric tons)

12When Esther's words were reported to Mordecai, 13he sent back
this answer: "Do not think that because you are in the king's house
you alone of all the Jews will escape. 14For if you remain silent[i] at
this time, relief[j] and deliverance[k]
for the Jews will arise from another place, but you and your
father's family will perish. And
who knows but that you have come
to royal position for such a time as
this?"[l]

15Then Esther sent this reply to
Mordecai: 16"Go, gather together
all the Jews who are in Susa, and
fast[m] for me. Do not eat or drink
for three days, night or day. I and
my maids will fast as you do. When
this is done, I will go to the king,
even though it is against the law.
And if I perish, I perish."[n]

17So Mordecai went away and
carried out all of Esther's instructions.

Esther's Request to the King

5 On the third day Esther put on
her royal robes[a] and stood in
the inner court of the palace, in
front of the king's[b] hall. The king
was sitting on his royal throne in
the hall, facing the entrance.
2When he saw Queen Esther standing in the court, he was pleased
with her and held out to her the
gold sceptre that was in his hand.
So Esther approached and touched
the tip of the sceptre.[c]

3Then the king asked, "What is it,
Queen Esther? What is your request? Even up to half the kingdom,[d] it will be given you."

4"If it pleases the king," replied
Esther, "let the king, together with
Haman, come today to a banquet I
have prepared for him."

5"Bring Haman at once," the king
said, "so that we may do what Esther asks."

So the king and Haman went to
the banquet Esther had prepared.
6As they were drinking wine,[e] the
king again asked Esther, "Now
what is your petition? It will be
given you. And what is your request? Even up to half the kingdom,[f] it will be granted."[g]

7Esther replied, "My petition and
my request is this: 8If the king regards me with favour[h] and if it
pleases the king to grant my petition and fulfil my request, let the
king and Haman come tomorrow to
the banquet[i] I will prepare for
them. Then I will answer the king's
question."

Haman's Rage Against Mordecai

9Haman went out that day happy
and in high spirits. But when he
saw Mordecai at the king's gate and
observed that he neither rose nor
showed fear in his presence, he was
filled with rage[j] against Mordecai.[k] 10Nevertheless, Haman restrained himself and went home.

Calling together his friends and
Zeresh,[l] his wife, 11Haman
boasted[m] to them about his vast
wealth, his many sons,[n] and all the
ways the king had honoured him
and how he had elevated him above
the other nobles and officials.
12"And that's not all," Haman
added. "I'm the only person[o]
Queen Esther invited to accompany the king to the banquet she
gave. And she has invited me along
with the king tomorrow. 13But all
this gives me no satisfaction as
long as I see that Jew Mordecai sitting at the king's gate.[p]"

14His wife Zeresh and all his
friends said to him, "Have a gallows built, seventy-five feet[a]
high,[q] and ask the king in the
morning to have Mordecai
hanged[r] on it. Then go with the
king to the dinner and be happy."
This suggestion delighted Haman,
and he had the gallows built.

4:14 *i* Ecc 3:7; Isa 62:1; Am 5:13 *j* Est 9:16,22 *k* Ge 45:7; Dt 28:29 *l* Ge 50:20
4:16 *m* 2Ch 20:3; Est 9:31 *n* Ge 43:14
5:1 *a* Est 4:16; Eze 16:13 *b* Est 6:4; Pr 21:1
5:2 *c* Est 4:11; Est 8:4; Pr 21:1
5:3 *d* Est 7:2; Da 5:16; Mk 6:23
5:6 *e* Est 1:10 *f* Mk 6:23 *g* Est 7:2; Est 9:12
5:8 *h* Est 2:15; Est 7:3; Est 8:5 *i* 1Ki 3:15; Est 6:14
5:9 *j* Est 2:21; Pr 14:17 *k* Est 3:3,5
5:10 *l* Est 6:13
5:11 *m* Pr 13:16 *n* Est 9:7-10,13
5:12 *o* Job 22:29; Pr 16:18; Pr 29:23
5:13 *p* Est 2:19
5:14 *q* Est 7:9 *r* Ezr 6:11; Est 6:4

a *14* Hebrew *fifty cubits* (about 23 metres)

Mordecai Honoured

6 That night the king could not sleep;[a] so he ordered the book of the chronicles,[b] the record of his reign, to be brought in and read to him. 2It was found recorded there that Mordecai had exposed Bigthana and Teresh, two of the king's officers who guarded the doorway, who had conspired to assassinate King Xerxes.

3"What honour and recognition has Mordecai received for this?" the king asked.

"Nothing has been done for him,"[c] his attendants answered.

4The king said, "Who is in the court?" Now Haman had just entered the outer court of the palace to speak to the king about hanging Mordecai on the gallows he had erected for him.

5His attendants answered, "Haman is standing in the court."

"Bring him in," the king ordered.

6When Haman entered, the king asked him, "What should be done for the man the king delights to honour?"

Now Haman thought to himself, "Who is there that the king would rather honour than me?" 7So he answered the king, "For the man the king delights to honour, 8have them bring a royal robe[d] the king has worn and a horse[e] the king has ridden, one with a royal crest placed on its head. 9Then let the robe and horse be entrusted to one of the king's most noble princes. Let them robe the man the king delights to honour, and lead him on the horse through the city streets, proclaiming before him, 'This is what is done for the man the king delights to honour!'[f] "

10"Go at once," the king commanded Haman. "Get the robe and the horse and do just as you have suggested for Mordecai the Jew, who sits at the king's gate. Do not neglect anything you have recommended."

11So Haman got[g] the robe and the horse. He robed Mordecai, and led him on horseback through the city streets, proclaiming before him, "This is what is done for the man the king delights to honour!"

12Afterwards Mordecai returned to the king's gate. But Haman rushed home, with his head covered,[h] in grief, 13and told Zeresh[i] his wife and all his friends everything that had happened to him.

His advisers and his wife Zeresh said to him, "Since Mordecai, before whom your downfall[j] has started, is of Jewish origin, you cannot stand against him—you will surely come to ruin!" 14While they were still talking with him, the king's eunuchs arrived and hurried Haman away to the banquet[k] Esther had prepared.

Haman Hanged

7 So the king and Haman went to dine[a] with Queen Esther, 2and as they were drinking wine[b] on that second day, the king again asked, "Queen Esther, what is your petition? It will be given you. What is your request? Even up to half the kingdom,[c] it will be granted.[d]"

3Then Queen Esther answered, "If I have found favour[e] with you, O king, and if it pleases your majesty, grant me my life—this is my petition. And spare my people—this is my request. 4For I and my people have been sold for destruction and slaughter and annihilation.[f] If we had merely been sold as male and female slaves, I would have kept quiet, because no such distress would justify disturbing the king."[a]

5King Xerxes asked Queen Esther, "Who is he? Where is the man who has dared to do such a thing?"

6Esther said, "The adversary and enemy is this vile Haman."

[a]4 Or *quiet, but the compensation our adversary offers cannot be compared with the loss the king would suffer*

6:1 *a* Da 2:1; Da 6:18 *b* Est 2:23; Est 10:2
6:3 *c* Ecc 9:13-16
6:8 *d* Ge 41:42; Isa 52:1 *e* 1Ki 1:33
6:9 *f* Ge 41:43
6:11 *g* Ge 41:42
6:12 *h* 2Sa 15:30; Jer 14:3,4; Mic 3:7
6:13 *i* Est 5:10 *j* Ps 57:6; Pr 26:27; Pr 28:18
6:14 *k* 1Ki 3:15; Est 5:8
7:1 *a* Ge 40:20-22; Mt 22:1-14
7:2 *b* Est 1:10 *c* Est 5:3 *d* Est 9:12
7:3 *e* Est 2:15
7:4 *f* Est 3:9

Then Haman was terrified before the king and queen. 7The king got up in a rage,[g] left his wine and went out into the palace garden.[h] But Haman, realising that the king had already decided his fate,[i] stayed behind to beg Queen Esther for his life.

8Just as the king returned from the palace garden to the banquet hall, Haman was falling on the couch[j] where Esther was reclining.[k]

The king exclaimed, "Will he even molest the queen while she is with me in the house?"[l]

As soon as the word left the king's mouth, they covered Haman's face.[m] 9Then Harbona,[n] one of the eunuchs attending the king, said, "A gallows seventy-five feet[b] high[o] stands by Haman's house. He had it made for Mordecai, who spoke up to help the king."

The king said, "Hang him on it!"[p] 10So they hanged Haman[q] on the gallows[r] he had prepared for Mordecai.[s] Then the king's fury subsided.[t]

The King's Edict on Behalf of the Jews

8 That same day King Xerxes gave Queen Esther the estate of Haman,[a] the enemy of the Jews. And Mordecai came into the presence of the king, for Esther had told how he was related to her. 2The king took off his signet ring,[b] which he had reclaimed from Haman, and presented it to Mordecai. And Esther appointed him over Haman's estate.[c]

3Esther again pleaded with the king, falling at his feet and weeping. She begged him to put an end to the evil plan of Haman the Agagite, which he had devised against the Jews. 4Then the king extended the gold sceptre[d] to Esther and she arose and stood before him.

5"If it pleases the king," she said, "and if he regards me with favour and thinks it the right thing to do, and if he is pleased with me, let an order be written overruling the dispatches that Haman son of Hammedatha, the Agagite, devised and wrote to destroy the Jews in all the king's provinces. 6For how can I bear to see disaster fall on my people? How can I bear to see the destruction of my family?"[e]

7King Xerxes replied to Queen Esther and to Mordecai the Jew, "Because Haman attacked the Jews, I have given his estate to Esther, and they have hanged him on the gallows. 8Now write another decree[f] in the king's name on behalf of the Jews as seems best to you, and seal it with the king's signet ring[g]—for no document written in the king's name and sealed with his ring can be revoked."[h]

9At once the royal secretaries were summoned—on the twenty-third day of the third month, the month of Sivan. They wrote out all Mordecai's orders to the Jews, and to the satraps, governors and nobles of the 127 provinces stretching from India to Cush.[a][i] These orders were written in the script of each province and the language of each people and also to the Jews in their own script and language.[j] 10Mordecai wrote in the name of King Xerxes, sealed the dispatches with the king's signet ring, and sent them by mounted couriers, who rode fast horses especially bred for the king.

11The king's edict granted the Jews in every city the right to assemble and protect themselves; to destroy, kill and annihilate any armed force of any nationality or province that might attack them and their women and children; and to plunder[k] the property of their enemies. 12The day appointed for the Jews to do this in all the provinces of King Xerxes was the

7:7
g Ge 34:7; Est 1:12; Pr 19:12; Pr 20:1-2
h 2Ki 21:18
i Est 6:13

7:8
j Est 1:6
k Ge 39:14
l Ge 34:7
m Est 6:12

7:9
n Est 1:10
o Est 5:14
p Ps 7:14-16; Ps 9:16; Pr 11:5-6; Pr 26:27; Mt 7:2

7:10
q Pr 10:28
r Est 9:25
s Da 6:24
t Est 2:1

8:1
a Est 2:7; Est 7:6; Pr 22:22-23

8:2
b Ge 41:42; Est 3:10
c Pr 13:22; Da 2:48

8:4
d Est 4:11; Est 5:2

8:6
e Est 7:4; Est 9:1

8:8
f Est 3:12-14
g Ge 41:42
h Est 1:19; Da 6:15

8:9
i Est 1:1
j Est 1:22

8:11
k Est 9:10,15,16

b9 Hebrew *fifty cubits* (about 23 metres)
a9 That is, the upper Nile region

thirteenth day of the twelfth month,
the month of Adar.[l] 13A copy of the
text of the edict was to be issued as
law in every province and made
known to the people of every nationality so that the Jews would be
ready on that day[m] to avenge themselves on their enemies.
14The couriers, riding the royal
horses, raced out, spurred on by
the king's command. And the edict
was also issued in the citadel of
Susa.
15Mordecai[n] left the king's presence wearing royal garments of
blue and white, a large crown of
gold and a purple robe of fine
linen.[o] And the city of Susa held a
joyous celebration.[p] 16For the
Jews it was a time of happiness and
joy,[q] gladness and honour.[r] 17In
every province and in every city,
wherever the edict of the king
went, there was joy[s] and gladness
among the Jews, with feasting and
celebrating. And many people of
other nationalities became Jews
because fear[t] of the Jews had
seized them.[u]

Triumph of the Jews

9 On the thirteenth day of the
twelfth month, the month of
Adar,[a] the edict commanded by
the king was to be carried out. On
this day the enemies of the Jews
had hoped to overpower them, but
now the tables were turned and the
Jews got the upper hand[b] over
those who hated them.[c] 2The Jews
assembled in their cities[d] in all the
provinces of King Xerxes to attack
those seeking their destruction.
No-one could stand against them,[e]
because the people of all the other
nationalities were afraid of them.
3And all the nobles of the provinces, the satraps, the governors
and the king's administrators
helped the Jews,[f] because fear of
Mordecai had seized them. 4Morde-
cai was prominent[g] in the palace;
his reputation spread throughout
the provinces, and he became more
and more powerful.[h]
5The Jews struck down all their
enemies with the sword, killing and
destroying them,[i] and they did
what they pleased to those who
hated them. 6In the citadel of Susa,
the Jews killed and destroyed five
hundred men. 7They also killed
Parshandatha, Dalphon, Aspatha,
8Poratha, Adalia, Aridatha, 9Par-
mashta, Arisai, Aridai and Vaiza-
tha, 10the ten sons[j] of Haman son
of Hammedatha, the enemy of the
Jews. But they did not lay their
hands on the plunder.[k]
11The number of those slain in
the citadel of Susa was reported to
the king that same day. 12The king
said to Queen Esther, "The Jews
have killed and destroyed five hundred men and the ten sons of Haman in the citadel of Susa. What
have they done in the rest of the
king's provinces? Now what is your
petition? It will be given you. What
is your request? It will also be
granted."[l]
13"If it pleases the king," Esther
answered, "give the Jews in Susa
permission to carry out this day's
edict tomorrow also, and let Haman's ten sons[m] be hanged[n] on
gallows."
14So the king commanded that
this be done. An edict was issued in
Susa, and they hanged[o] the ten
sons of Haman. 15The Jews in Susa
came together on the fourteenth
day of the month of Adar, and they
put to death in Susa three hundred
men, but they did not lay their
hands on the plunder.[p]
16Meanwhile, the remainder of
the Jews who were in the king's
provinces also assembled to protect themselves and get relief[q]
from their enemies.[r] They killed
seventy-five thousand of them[s]
but did not lay their hands on the
plunder. 17This happened on the
thirteenth day of the month of
Adar, and on the fourteenth they

8:12 l Est 3:13; Est 9:1
8:13 m Est 3:14
8:15 n Est 9:4; o Ge 41:42; p Est 3:15
8:16 q Ps 97:10-12; r Ps 112:4
8:17 s Est 9:19,27; Ps 35:27; Pr 11:10; t Ex 15:14,16; Dt 11:25; u Est 9:3
9:1 a Est 8:12; b Jer 29:4-7; c Est 3:12-14; Pr 22:22-23
9:2 d ver 15-18; e Est 8:11,17; Ps 71:13,24
9:3 f Ezr 8:36
9:4 g Ex 11:3; h 2Sa 3:1; 1Ch 11:9
9:5 i Ezr 4:6
9:10 j Est 5:11; k Ge 14:23; 1Sa 14:32; Est 3:13; Est 8:11
9:12 l Est 5:6; Est 7:2
9:13 m Est 5:11; n Dt 21:22-23
9:14 o Ezr 6:11
9:15 p Ge 14:23; Est 8:11
9:16 q Est 4:14; r Dt 25:19; s 1Ch 4:43

rested and made it a day of feasting[t] and joy.

Purim Celebrated

18 The Jews in Susa, however, had assembled on the thirteenth and fourteenth, and then on the fifteenth they rested and made it a day of feasting and joy.

19 That is why rural Jews—those living in villages—observe the fourteenth of the month of Adar[u] as a day of joy and feasting, a day for giving presents to each other.[v]

20 Mordecai recorded these events, and he sent letters to all the Jews throughout the provinces of King Xerxes, near and far, 21 to have them celebrate annually the fourteenth and fifteenth days of the month of Adar 22 as the time when the Jews got relief[w] from their enemies, and as the month when their sorrow was turned into joy and their mourning into a day of celebration.[x] He wrote to them to observe the days as days of feasting and joy and giving presents of food[y] to one another and gifts to the poor.

23 So the Jews agreed to continue the celebration they had begun, doing what Mordecai had written to them. 24 For Haman son of Hammedatha, the Agagite,[z] the enemy of all the Jews, had plotted against the Jews to destroy them and had cast the *pur*[a] (that is, the lot[b]) for their ruin and destruction. 25 But when the plot came to the king's attention,[a] he issued written orders that the evil scheme Haman had devised against the Jews should come back on to his own head,[c] and that he and his sons should be hanged[d] on the gallows.[e] 26 (Therefore these days were called Purim, from the word *pur*.[f]) Because of everything written in this letter and because of what they had seen and what had happened to them, 27 the Jews took it upon themselves to establish the custom that they and their descendants and all who join them should without fail observe these two days every year, in the way prescribed and at the time appointed. 28 These days should be remembered and observed in every generation by every family, and in every province and in every city. And these days of Purim should never cease to be celebrated by the Jews, nor should the memory of them die out among their descendants.

29 So Queen Esther, daughter of Abihail,[g] along with Mordecai the Jew, wrote with full authority to confirm this second letter concerning Purim. 30 And Mordecai sent letters to all the Jews in the 127 provinces[h] of the kingdom of Xerxes—words of goodwill and assurance—31 to establish these days of Purim at their designated times, as Mordecai the Jew and Queen Esther had decreed for them, and as they had established for themselves and their descendants in regard to their times of fasting[i] and lamentation.[j] 32 Esther's decree confirmed these regulations about Purim, and it was written down in the records.

The Greatness of Mordecai

10 King Xerxes imposed tribute throughout the empire, to its distant shores.[a] 2 And all his acts of power and might, together with a full account of the greatness of Mordecai[b] to which the king had raised him,[c] are they not written in the book of the annals[d] of the kings of Media and Persia? 3 Mordecai the Jew was second[e] in rank[f] to King Xerxes,[g] pre-eminent among the Jews, and held in high esteem by his many fellow Jews, because he worked for the good of his people and spoke up for the welfare of all the Jews.[h]

9:17 t 1Ki 3:15
9:19 u Est 3:7; v ver 22; Dt 16:11,14; Ne 8:10,12; Est 2:9; Rev 11:10
9:22 w Est 4:14; x Ne 8:12; Ps 30:11-12; y 2Ki 25:30
9:24 z Ex 17:8-16; a Est 3:7; b Lev 16:8
9:25 c Ps 7:16; d Dt 21:22-23; e Est 7:10
9:26 f ver 20; Est 3:7
9:29 g Est 2:15
9:30 h Est 1:1
9:31 i Est 4:16; j Est 4:1-3
10:1 a Ps 72:10; Ps 97:1; Isa 24:15
10:2 b Est 8:15; Est 9:4; c Ge 41:44; d Est 2:23
10:3 e Da 5:7; f Ge 41:43; g Ge 41:40; h Ne 2:10; Jer 29:4-7; Da 6:3

a25 Or *when Esther came before the king*

JOB

Prologue

1 In the land of Uz[a] there lived a man whose name was Job.[b] This man was blameless[c] and upright; he feared God[d] and shunned evil. 2He had seven sons and three daughters,[e] 3and he owned seven thousand sheep, three thousand camels, five hundred yoke of oxen and five hundred donkeys, and had a large number of servants. He was the greatest man[f] among all the people of the East.

4His sons used to take turns holding feasts in their homes, and they would invite their three sisters to eat and drink with them. 5When a period of feasting had run its course, Job would send and have them purified. Early in the morning he would sacrifice a burnt offering[g] for each of them, thinking, "Perhaps my children have sinned[h] and cursed God[i] in their hearts." This was Job's regular custom.

Job's First Test

6One day the angels[a][j] came to present themselves before the LORD, and Satan[b] also came with them.[k] 7The LORD said to Satan, "Where have you come from?"

Satan answered the LORD, "From roaming through the earth and going to and fro in it."[l]

8Then the LORD said to Satan, "Have you considered my servant Job?[m] There is no-one on earth like him; he is blameless and upright, a man who fears God and shuns evil."[n]

9"Does Job fear God for nothing?"[o] Satan replied. 10"Have you not put a hedge around him and his household and everything he has?[p] You have blessed the work of his hands, so that his flocks and herds are spread throughout the land.[q] 11But stretch out your hand and strike everything he has,[r] and he will surely curse you to your face."[s]

12The LORD said to Satan, "Very well, then, everything he has is in your hands, but on the man himself do not lay a finger."

Then Satan went out from the presence of the LORD.

13One day when Job's sons and daughters were feasting and drinking wine at the oldest brother's house, 14a messenger came to Job and said, "The oxen were ploughing and the donkeys were grazing nearby, 15and the Sabeans[t] attacked and carried them off. They put the servants to the sword, and I am the only one who has escaped to tell you!"

16While he was still speaking, another messenger came and said, "The fire of God fell from the sky[u] and burned up the sheep and the servants,[v] and I am the only one who has escaped to tell you!"

17While he was still speaking, another messenger came and said, "The Chaldeans[w] formed three raiding parties and swept down on your camels and carried them off. They put the servants to the sword, and I am the only one who has escaped to tell you!"

18While he was still speaking, yet another messenger came and said, "Your sons and daughters were feasting and drinking wine at the oldest brother's house, 19when suddenly a mighty wind[x] swept in from the desert and struck the four corners of the house. It collapsed

1:1 a Jer 25:20 b Eze 14:14,20 Jas 5:11 c Ge 6:9 Ge 17:1 d Ge 22:12 Ex 18:21
1:2 e Job 42:13
1:3 f Job 29:25
1:5 g Ge 8:20 Job 42:8 h Job 8:4 i 1Ki 21:10,13
1:6 j Job 38:7 k Job 2:1
1:7 l 1Pe 5:8
1:8 m Jos 1:7 Job 42:7-8 n ver 1
1:9 o 1Ti 6:5
1:10 p Ps 34:7 q ver 3 Job 29:6 Job 31:25 Ps 128:1-2
1:11 r Job 19:21 s Job 2:5
1:15 t Ge 10:7 Job 6:19
1:16 u Ge 19:24 v Lev 10:2 Nu 11:1-3
1:17 w Ge 11:28,31
1:19 x Jer 4:11 Jer 13:24

a6 Hebrew *the sons of God* b6 *Satan* means *accuser.*

on them and they are dead, and I am the only one who has escaped to tell you!"

20 At this, Job got up and tore his robe[y] and shaved his head. Then he fell to the ground in worship[z] 21 and said:

"Naked I came from my
mother's womb,
and naked I shall depart.[c][a]
The LORD gave and the LORD
has taken away;[b]
may the name of the LORD be
praised."[c]

22 In all this, Job did not sin by charging God with wrongdoing.[d]

Job's Second Test

2 On another day the angels[a] came to present themselves before the LORD, and Satan also came with them[a] to present himself before him. 2 And the LORD said to Satan, "Where have you come from?"

Satan answered the LORD, "From roaming through the earth and going to and fro in it."

3 Then the LORD said to Satan, "Have you considered my servant Job? There is no-one on earth like him; he is blameless and upright, a man who fears God and shuns evil.[b] And he still maintains his integrity,[c] though you incited me against him to ruin him without any reason."[d]

4 "Skin for skin!" Satan replied. "A man will give all he has for his own life. 5 But stretch out your hand and strike his flesh and bones,[e] and he will surely curse you to your face."[f]

6 The LORD said to Satan, "Very well, then, he is in your hands; but you must spare his life."[g]

7 So Satan went out from the presence of the LORD and afflicted Job with painful sores from the soles of his feet to the top of his head.[h] 8 Then Job took a piece of broken pottery and scraped himself with it as he sat among the ashes.[i]

9 His wife said to him, "Are you still holding on to your integrity? Curse God and die!"

10 He replied, "You are talking like a foolish[b] woman. Shall we accept good from God, and not trouble?"[j]

In all this, Job did not sin in what he said.[k]

Job's Three Friends

11 When Job's three friends, Eliphaz the Temanite,[l] Bildad the Shuhite[m] and Zophar the Naamathite, heard about all the troubles that had come upon him, they set out from their homes and met together by agreement to go and sympathise with him and comfort him.[n] 12 When they saw him from a distance, they could hardly recognise him; they began to weep aloud, and they tore their robes and sprinkled dust on their heads.[o] 13 Then they sat on the ground with him for seven days and seven nights.[p] No-one said a word to him, because they saw how great his suffering was.

Job Speaks

3 After this, Job opened his mouth and cursed the day of his birth. 2 He said:

3 "May the day of my birth
perish,
and the night it was said, 'A
boy is born!'[a]
4 That day—may it turn to
darkness;
may God above not care about
it;
may no light shine upon it.
5 May darkness and deep
shadow[a][b] claim it once
more;

1:20 y Ge 37:29; z 1Pe 5:6
1:21 a Ecc 5:15; 1Ti 6:7; b 1Sa 2:7; c Job 2:10; Eph 5:20; 1Th 5:18
1:22 d Job 2:10
2:1 a Job 1:6
2:3 b Job 1:1,8; c Job 27:6; d Job 9:17
2:5 e Job 19:20; f Job 1:11
2:6 g Job 1:12
2:7 h Dt 28:35; Job 7:5
2:8 i Job 42:6; Jer 6:26; Eze 27:30; Mt 11:21
2:10 j Job 1:21; k Job 1:22; Ps 39:1; Jas 1:12; Jas 5:11
2:11 l Ge 36:11; Jer 49:7; m Ge 25:2; n Job 42:11; Ro 12:15
2:12 o Jos 7:6; Ne 9:1; La 2:10; Eze 27:30
2:13 p Ge 50:10; Eze 3:15
3:3 a Job 10:18-19; Jer 20:14-18
3:5 b Job 10:21,22; Ps 23:4; Jer 2:6; Jer 13:16

c21 Or *shall return there* a1 Hebrew *the sons of God* b10 The Hebrew word rendered *foolish* denotes moral deficiency. a5 Or *and the shadow of death*

may a cloud settle over it;
may blackness overwhelm its
light.
6 That night—may thick
darkness[c] seize it;
may it not be included among
the days of the year
nor be entered in any of the
months.
7 May that night be barren;
may no shout of joy be heard
in it.
8 May those who curse days[b]
curse that day,
those who are ready to rouse
Leviathan.[d]
9 May its morning stars become
dark;
may it wait for daylight in
vain
and not see the first rays of
dawn,[e]
10 for it did not shut the doors of
the womb on me
to hide trouble from my eyes.

11 "Why did I not perish at birth,
and die as I came from the
womb?[f]
12 Why were there knees to
receive me[g]
and breasts that I might be
nursed?
13 For now I would be lying
down[h] in peace;
I would be asleep and at rest[i]
14 with kings and counsellors of
the earth,[j]
who built for themselves
places now lying in ruins,[k]
15 with rulers[l] who had gold,
who filled their houses with
silver.[m]
16 Or why was I not hidden in the
ground like a stillborn
child,[n]
like an infant who never saw
the light of day?
17 There the wicked cease from
turmoil,
and there the weary are at
rest.[o]
18 Captives also enjoy their ease;
they no longer hear the slave
driver's shout.[p]
19 The small and the great are
there,
and the slave is freed from his
master.

20 "Why is light given to those in
misery,
and life to the bitter of soul,[q]
21 to those who long for death that
does not come,[r]
who search for it more than
for hidden treasure,[s]
22 who are filled with gladness
and rejoice when they reach
the grave?
23 Why is life given to a man
whose way is hidden,
whom God has hedged in?[t]
24 For sighing comes to me
instead of food;[u]
my groans pour out like
water.[v]
25 What I feared has come upon
me;
what I dreaded[w] has happened
to me.
26 I have no peace, no quietness;
I have no rest,[x] but only
turmoil."

Eliphaz

4 Then Eliphaz the Temanite
replied:

2 "If someone ventures a word
with you, will you be
impatient?
But who can keep from
speaking?[a]
3 Think how you have instructed
many,
how you have strengthened
feeble hands.[b]
4 Your words have supported
those who stumbled;
you have strengthened
faltering knees.[c]
5 But now trouble comes to you,
and you are discouraged;

3:6 *c* Job 23:17
3:8 *d* Job 41:1,8,10,25
3:9 *e* Job 41:18
3:11 *f* Job 10:18
3:12 *g* Ge 30:3; Isa 66:12
3:13 *h* Job 17:13 *i* Job 7:8-10,21; Job 10:22; Job 14:10-12; Job 19:27; Job 21:13,23
3:14 *j* Job 12:17 *k* Job 15:28
3:15 *l* Job 12:21 *m* Job 27:17
3:16 *n* Ps 58:8; Ecc 6:3
3:17 *o* Job 17:16
3:18 *p* Job 39:7
3:20 *q* 1Sa 1:10; Jer 20:18; Eze 27:30-31
3:21 *r* Rev 9:6 *s* Pr 2:4
3:23 *t* Job 19:6,8,12; Ps 88:8; La 3:7
3:24 *u* Job 6:7; Job 33:20 *v* Ps 42:3,4
3:25 *w* Job 30:15
3:26 *x* Job 7:4,14
4:2 *a* Job 32:20
4:3 *b* Isa 35:3; Heb 12:12
4:4 *c* Isa 35:3; Heb 12:12

b8 Or *the sea*

it strikes[d] you, and you are
dismayed.[e]
6 Should not your piety be your
confidence[f]
and your blameless[g] ways
your hope?

7 "Consider now: Who, being
innocent, has ever
perished?[h]
Where were the upright ever
destroyed?[i]
8 As I have observed, those who
plough evil[j]
and those who sow trouble
reap it.[k]
9 At the breath of God[l] they are
destroyed;
at the blast of his anger they
perish.[m]
10 The lions may roar and growl,
yet the teeth of the great lions
are broken.[n]
11 The lion perishes for lack of
prey,[o]
and the cubs of the lioness are
scattered.
12 "A word was secretly brought
to me,
my ears caught a whisper[p] of
it.[q]
13 Amid disquieting dreams in the
night,
when deep sleep falls on
men,[r]
14 fear and trembling seized me
and made all my bones
shake.[s]
15 A spirit glided past my face,
and the hair on my body stood
on end.
16 It stopped,
but I could not tell what it
was.
A form stood before my eyes,
and I heard a hushed voice:
17 'Can a mortal be more righteous
than God?[t]
Can a man be more pure than
his Maker?[u]
18 If God places no trust in his
servants,
if he charges his angels with
error,[v]

4:5 d Job 19:21 e Job 6:14
4:6 f Pr 3:26 g Job 1:1
4:7 h Job 36:7 i Job 8:20 Ps 37:25
4:8 j Job 15:35 k Pr 22:8 Hos 10:13 Gal 6:7-8
4:9 l Job 15:30 Isa 30:33 2Th 2:8 m Job 40:13
4:10 n Job 5:15 Ps 58:6
4:11 o Job 27:14 Ps 34:10
4:12 p Job 26:14 q Job 33:14
4:13 r Job 33:15
4:14 s Jer 23:9 Hab 3:16
4:17 t Job 9:2 u Job 35:10
4:18 v Job 15:15
4:19 w Job 10:9 x Job 22:16 y Ge 2:7
4:20 z Job 14:2,20 Job 20:7 Ps 90:5-6
4:21 a Job 8:22 b Job 18:21 Job 36:12
5:1 a Job 15:15
5:2 b Pr 12:16
5:3 c Ps 37:35 Jer 12:2 d Job 24:18
5:4 e Job 4:11 f Am 5:12
5:5 g Job 18:8-10
5:7 h Job 14:1
5:8 i Ps 35:23 Ps 50:15
5:9 j Job 42:3 Ps 40:5

19 how much more those who live
in houses of clay,[w]
whose foundations[x] are in the
dust,[y]
who are crushed more readily
than a moth!
20 Between dawn and dusk they
are broken to pieces;
unnoticed, they perish for
ever.[z]
21 Are not the cords of their tent
pulled up,[a]
so that they die without
wisdom?'[a][b]

5 "Call if you will, but who will
answer you?
To which of the holy ones[a]
will you turn?
2 Resentment kills a fool,
and envy slays the simple.[b]
3 I myself have seen a fool taking
root,[c]
but suddenly his house was
cursed.[d]
4 His children are far from
safety,[e]
crushed in court[f] without a
defender.
5 The hungry consume his
harvest,[g]
taking it even from among
thorns,
and the thirsty pant after his
wealth.
6 For hardship does not spring
from the soil,
nor does trouble sprout from
the ground.
7 Yet man is born to trouble[h]
as surely as sparks fly
upward.
8 "But if it were I, I would appeal
to God;
I would lay my cause before
him.[i]
9 He performs wonders that
cannot be fathomed,[j]
miracles that cannot be
counted.
10 He bestows rain on the earth;

a 21 Some interpreters end the quotation after verse 17.

he sends water upon the
countryside.[k]
11 The lowly he sets on high,[l]
and those who mourn are
lifted to safety.
12 He thwarts the plans[m] of the
crafty,
so that their hands achieve no
success.
13 He catches the wise in their
craftiness,[n]
and the schemes of the wily
are swept away.
14 Darkness[o] comes upon them in
the daytime;
at noon they grope as in the
night.[p]
15 He saves the needy[q] from the
sword in their mouth;
he saves them from the
clutches of the powerful.[r]
16 So the poor have hope,
and injustice shuts its
mouth.[s]

17 "Blessed is the man whom God
corrects;[t]
so do not despise the
discipline[u] of the
Almighty.[a][v]
18 For he wounds, but he also
binds up;[w]
he injures, but his hands also
heal.[x]
19 From six calamities he will
rescue you;
in seven no harm will befall
you.[y]
20 In famine[z] he will ransom you
from death,
and in battle from the stroke
of the sword.[a]
21 You will be protected from the
lash of the tongue,[b]
and need not fear[c] when
destruction comes.
22 You will laugh at destruction
and famine,
and need not fear the beasts
of the earth.[d]
23 For you will have a covenant
with the stones[e] of the
field,
and the wild animals will be at
peace with you.[f]
24 You will know that your tent is
secure;
you will take stock of your
property and find nothing
missing.[g]
25 You will know that your
children will be many,[h]
and your descendants like the
grass of the earth.[i]
26 You will come to the grave in
full vigour,[j]
like sheaves gathered in
season.

27 "We have examined this, and it
is true.
So hear it and apply it to
yourself."

Job

6

Then Job replied:

2 "If only my anguish could be
weighed
and all my misery be placed
on the scales![a]
3 It would surely outweigh the
sand[b] of the seas—
no wonder my words have
been impetuous.[c]
4 The arrows[d] of the Almighty
are in me,[e]
my spirit drinks[f] in their
poison;
God's terrors[g] are marshalled
against me.[h]
5 Does a wild donkey bray when
it has grass,
or an ox bellow when it has
fodder?
6 Is tasteless food eaten without
salt,
or is there flavour in the white
of an egg?[a]
7 I refuse to touch it;
such food makes me ill.[i]
8 "Oh, that I might have my
request,

5:10 k Job 36:28
5:11 l Ps 113:7-8
5:12 m Ne 4:15; Ps 33:10
5:13 n 1Co 3:19*
5:14 o Job 12:25; p Dt 28:29
5:15 q Ps 35:10; r Job 4:10
5:16 s Ps 107:42
5:17 t Jas 1:12; u Ps 94:12; Pr 3:11; v Heb 12:5-11
5:18 w Isa 30:26; x 1Sa 2:6
5:19 y Ps 34:19; Ps 91:10
5:20 z Ps 33:19; a Ps 144:10
5:21 b Ps 31:20; c Ps 91:5
5:22 d Ps 91:13; Eze 34:25
5:23 e Ps 91:12; f Isa 11:6-9
5:24 g Job 8:6
5:25 h Ps 112:2; i Ps 72:16; Isa 44:3-4
5:26 j Ge 15:15
6:2 a Job 31:6
6:3 b Pr 27:3; c Job 23:2
6:4 d Ps 38:2; e Job 16:12,13; f Job 21:20; g Job 30:15; h Ps 88:15-18
6:7 i Job 3:24

[a] 17 Hebrew *Shaddai*; here and throughout Job
[a] 6 The meaning of the Hebrew for this phrase is uncertain.

that God would grant what I
hope for,[j]
9 that God would be willing to
crush me,
to let loose his hand and cut
me off![k]
10 Then I would still have this
consolation—
my joy in unrelenting pain—
that I had not denied the
words[l] of the Holy One.[m]

11 "What strength do I have, that I
should still hope?
What prospects, that I should
be patient?[n]
12 Do I have the strength of stone?
Is my flesh bronze?
13 Do I have any power to help
myself,[o]
now that success has been
driven from me?

14 "A despairing man[p] should
have the devotion[q] of his
friends,
even though he forsakes the
fear of the Almighty.
15 But my brothers are as
undependable as
intermittent streams,[r]
as the streams that overflow
16 when darkened by thawing ice
and swollen with melting
snow,
17 but that cease to flow in the dry
season,
and in the heat[s] vanish from
their channels.
18 Caravans turn aside from their
routes;
they go up into the wasteland
and perish.
19 The caravans of Tema[t] look
for water,
the travelling merchants of
Sheba look in hope.
20 They are distressed, because
they had been confident;
they arrive there, only to be
disappointed.[u]
21 Now you too have proved to be
of no help;
you see something dreadful
and are afraid.[v]
22 Have I ever said, 'Give
something on my behalf,
pay a ransom for me from
your wealth,
23 deliver me from the hand of the
enemy,
ransom me from the clutches
of the ruthless'?

24 "Teach me, and I will be
quiet;[w]
show me where I have been
wrong.
25 How painful are honest
words![x]
But what do your arguments
prove?
26 Do you mean to correct what I
say,
and treat the words of a
despairing man as wind?[y]
27 You would even cast lots[z] for
the fatherless
and barter away your friend.

28 "But now be so kind as to look
at me.
Would I lie to your face?[a]
29 Relent, do not be unjust;
reconsider, for my integrity is
at stake.[b][b]
30 Is there any wickedness on my
lips?[c]
Can my mouth not discern[d]
malice?

7

"Does not man have hard
service[a] on earth?[b]
Are not his days like those of
a hired man?[c]
2 Like a slave longing for the
evening shadows,
or a hired man waiting
eagerly for his wages,[d]
3 so I have been allotted months
of futility,
and nights of misery have
been assigned to me.[e]
4 When I lie down I think, 'How
long before I get up?'[f]
The night drags on, and I toss
till dawn.

6:8 j Job 14:13
6:9 k Nu 11:15; 1Ki 19:4
6:10 l Job 22:22; Job 23:12; m Lev 19:2; Isa 57:15
6:11 n Job 21:4
6:13 o Job 26:2
6:14 p Job 4:5; q Job 15:4
6:15 r Ps 38:11; Jer 15:18
6:17 s Job 24:19
6:19 t Ge 25:15; Isa 21:14
6:20 u Jer 14:3
6:21 v Ps 38:11
6:24 w Ps 39:1
6:25 x Ecc 12:11
6:26 y Job 8:2; Job 15:3
6:27 z Joel 3:3; Na 3:10; 2Pe 2:3
6:28 a Job 27:4; Job 33:1,3; Job 36:3,4
6:29 b Job 23:7,10; Job 34:5,36; Job 42:6
6:30 c Job 27:4; d Job 12:11
7:1 a Job 14:14; Isa 40:2; b Job 5:7; c Job 14:6
7:2 d Lev 19:13
7:3 e Job 16:7; Ps 6:6
7:4 f Dt 28:67

b29 Or *my righteousness still stands*

5My body is clothed with
worms[g] and scabs,
my skin is broken and
festering.

6"My days are swifter than a
weaver's shuttle,[h]
and they come to an end
without hope.[i]
7Remember, O God, that my life
is but a breath;[j]
my eyes will never see
happiness again.[k]
8The eye that now sees me will
see me no longer;
you will look for me, but I will
be no more.[l]
9As a cloud vanishes and is gone,
so he who goes down to the
grave[a][m] does not return.[n]
10He will never come to his house
again;
his place[o] will know him no
more.[p]

11"Therefore I will not keep
silent;[q]
I will speak out in the anguish
of my spirit,
I will complain in the
bitterness of my soul.[r]
12Am I the sea, or the monster of
the deep,[s]
that you put me under guard?
13When I think my bed will
comfort me
and my couch will ease my
complaint,[t]
14even then you frighten me with
dreams
and terrify[u] me with visions,
15so that I prefer strangling and
death,[v]
rather than this body of mine.
16I despise my life;[w] I would not
live for ever.
Let me alone; my days have
no meaning.

17"What is man that you make so
much of him,
that you give him so much
attention,[x]
18that you examine him every
morning

7:5 g Job 17:14; Isa 14:11
7:6 h Job 9:25; i Job 13:15; Job 17:11,15
7:7 j Ps 78:39; Jas 4:14; k Job 9:25
7:8 l Job 20:7,9,21
7:9 m Job 11:8; n 2Sa 12:23; Job 30:15
7:10 o Job 27:21,23; p Job 8:18
7:11 q Ps 40:9; r 1Sa 1:10
7:12 s Eze 32:2-3
7:13 t Job 9:27
7:14 u Job 9:34
7:15 v 1Ki 19:4
7:16 w Job 9:21; Job 10:1
7:17 x Ps 8:4; Ps 144:3; Heb 2:6
7:18 y Job 14:3
7:19 z Job 9:18
7:20 a Job 35:6; b Job 16:12
7:21 c Job 10:14; d Job 10:9; Ps 104:29
8:2 a Job 6:26
8:3 b Dt 32:4; 2Ch 19:7; Ro 3:5; c Ge 18:25
8:4 d Job 1:19
8:5 e Job 11:13
8:6 f Ps 7:6; g Job 5:24
8:7 h Job 42:12
8:8 i Dt 4:32; Dt 32:7; Job 15:18

and test him every moment?[y]
19Will you never look away from
me,
or let me alone even for an
instant?[z]
20If I have sinned, what have I
done to you,[a]
O watcher of men?
Why have you made me your
target?[b]
Have I become a burden to
you?[b]
21Why do you not pardon my
offences
and forgive my sins?[c]
For I shall soon lie down in the
dust;[d]
you will search for me, but I
shall be no more."

Bildad

8

Then Bildad the Shuhite replied:

2"How long will you say such
things?
Your words are a blustering
wind.[a]
3Does God pervert justice?[b]
Does the Almighty pervert
what is right?[c]
4When your children sinned
against him,
he gave them over to the
penalty of their sin.[d]
5But if you will look to God
and plead[e] with the Almighty,
6if you are pure and upright,
even now he will rouse
himself on your behalf[f]
and restore you to your
rightful place.[g]
7Your beginnings will seem
humble,
so prosperous[h] will your
future be.

8"Ask the former generations[i]
and find out what their fathers
learned,

[a]9 Hebrew *Sheol* [b]20 A few manuscripts of the Masoretic Text, an ancient Hebrew scribal tradition and Septuagint; most manuscripts of the Masoretic Text *I have become a burden to myself.*

9 for we were born only
yesterday and know
nothing,[j]
and our days on earth are but
a shadow.[k]
10 Will they not instruct you and
tell you?
Will they not bring forth
words from their
understanding?
11 Can papyrus grow tall where
there is no marsh?
Can reeds thrive without
water?
12 While still growing and uncut,
they wither more quickly than
grass.[l]
13 Such is the destiny of all who
forget God;[m]
so perishes the hope of the
godless.[n]
14 What he trusts in is fragile;[a]
what he relies on is a spider's
web.[o]
15 He leans on his web,[p] but it
gives way;
he clings to it, but it does not
hold.[q]
16 He is like a well-watered plant
in the sunshine,
spreading its shoots[r] over the
garden;[s]
17 it entwines its roots around a
pile of rocks
and looks for a place among
the stones.
18 But when it is torn from its
spot,
that place disowns it and says,
'I never saw you.'[t]
19 Surely its life withers[u] away,
and[b] from the soil other
plants grow.[v]

20 "Surely God does not reject a
blameless[w] man
or strengthen the hands of
evildoers.[x]
21 He will yet fill your mouth with
laughter[y]
and your lips with shouts of
joy.[z]
22 Your enemies will be clothed in
shame,[a]
and the tents of the wicked
will be no more."[b]

Job

9

Then Job replied:

2 "Indeed, I know that this is
true.
But how can a mortal be
righteous before God?[a]
3 Though one wished to dispute
with him,
he could not answer him one
time out of a thousand.[b]
4 His wisdom[c] is profound, his
power is vast.[d]
Who has resisted him and
come out unscathed?[e]
5 He moves mountains without
their knowing it
and overturns them in his
anger.[f]
6 He shakes the earth[g] from its
place
and makes its pillars
tremble.[h]
7 He speaks to the sun and it does
not shine;
he seals off the light of the
stars.[i]
8 He alone stretches out the
heavens[j]
and treads on the waves of the
sea.[k]
9 He is the Maker of the Bear
and Orion,
the Pleiades and the
constellations of the
south.[l]
10 He performs wonders[m] that
cannot be fathomed,
miracles that cannot be
counted.[n]
11 When he passes me, I cannot
see him;
when he goes by, I cannot
perceive him.[o]

8:9 j Ge 47:9 k 1Ch 29:15 Job 7:6
8:12 l Ps 129:6 Jer 17:6
8:13 m Ps 9:17 n Job 11:20 Job 13:16 Job 15:34 Pr 10:28
8:14 o Isa 59:5
8:15 p Job 27:18 q Ps 49:11
8:16 r Ps 80:11 s Ps 37:35 Jer 11:16
8:18 t Job 7:8 Ps 37:36
8:19 u Job 20:5 v Ecc 1:4
8:20 w Job 1:1 x Job 21:30
8:21 y Job 5:22 z Ps 126:2 Ps 132:16
8:22 a Ps 35:26 Ps 109:29 Ps 132:18 b Job 18:6,14, 21
9:2 a Job 4:17 Ps 143:2 Ro 3:20
9:3 b Job 10:2 Job 40:2
9:4 c Job 11:6 d Job 36:5 e 2Ch 13:12
9:5 f Mic 1:4
9:6 g Isa 2:21 Hag 2:6 Heb 12:26 h Job 26:11
9:7 i Isa 13:10 Eze 32:8
9:8 j Ge 1:6 Ps 104:2-3 k Job 38:16 Ps 77:19
9:9 l Ge 1:16 Job 38:31 Am 5:8
9:10 m Ps 71:15 n Job 5:9
9:11 o Job 23:8-9 Job 35:14

a 14 The meaning of the Hebrew for this word is uncertain. b 19 Or *Surely all the joy it has / is that*

12If he snatches away, who can
stop him?[p]
Who can say to him, 'What are
you doing?'[q]
13God does not restrain his anger;
even the cohorts of Rahab[r]
cowered at his feet.

14"How then can I dispute with
him?
How can I find words to argue
with him?
15Though I were innocent, I could
not answer him;[s]
I could only plead[t] with my
Judge for mercy.
16Even if I summoned him and he
responded,
I do not believe he would give
me a hearing.
17He would crush me[u] with a
storm[v]
and multiply[w] my wounds for
no reason.[x]
18He would not let me regain my
breath
but would overwhelm me with
misery.[y]
19If it is a matter of strength, he
is mighty!
And if it is a matter of justice,
who will summon him?[a]
20Even if I were innocent, my
mouth would condemn me;
if I were blameless, it would
pronounce me guilty.

21"Although I am blameless,[z]
I have no concern for myself;
I despise my own life.[a]
22It is all the same; that is why I
say,
'He destroys both the
blameless and the
wicked.'[b]
23When a scourge[c] brings sudden
death,
he mocks the despair of the
innocent.[d]
24When a land falls into the hands
of the wicked,[e]
he blindfolds its judges.[f]
If it is not he, then who is it?

25"My days are swifter than a
runner;[g]
they fly away without a
glimpse of joy.
26They skim past like boats of
papyrus,[h]
like eagles swooping down on
their prey.[i]
27If I say, 'I will forget my
complaint,[j]
I will change my expression,
and smile,'
28I still dread[k] all my sufferings,
for I know you will not hold
me innocent.[l]
29Since I am already found guilty,
why should I struggle in
vain?[m]
30Even if I washed myself with
soap[b]
and my hands[n] with washing
soda,[o]
31you would plunge me into a
slime pit
so that even my clothes would
detest me.

32"He is not a man like me that I
might answer him,[p]
that we might confront each
other in court.[q]
33If only there were someone to
arbitrate between us,[r]
to lay his hand upon us both,
34someone to remove God's rod
from me,[s]
so that his terror would
frighten me no more.
35Then I would speak up without
fear of him,
but as it now stands with me, I
cannot.[t]

10

"I loathe my very life;[a]
therefore I will give free
rein to my complaint
and speak out in the bitterness
of my soul.[b]
2I will say to God: Do not
condemn me,
but tell me what charges[c] you
have against me.

9:12 p Job 11:10 q Isa 45:9 Ro 9:20
9:13 r Job 26:12 Ps 89:10 Isa 30:7 Isa 51:9
9:15 s Job 10:15 t Job 8:5
9:17 u Job 16:12 v Job 30:22 w Job 16:14 x Job 2:3
9:18 y Job 7:19 Job 27:2
9:21 z Job 1:1 a Job 7:16
9:22 b Job 10:8 Ecc 9:2,3 Eze 21:3
9:23 c Heb 11:36 d Job 24:1,12
9:24 e Job 10:3 Job 16:11 f Job 12:6
9:25 g Job 7:6
9:26 h Isa 18:2 i Hab 1:8
9:27 j Job 7:11
9:28 k Job 3:25 Ps 119:120 l Job 7:21
9:29 m Ps 37:33
9:30 n Job 31:7 o Jer 2:22
9:32 p Ro 9:20 q Ps 143:2 Ecc 6:10
9:33 r 1Sa 2:25
9:34 s Job 13:21 Ps 39:10
9:35 t Job 13:21
10:1 a 1Ki 19:4 b Job 7:11
10:2 c Job 9:29

a19 See Septuagint; Hebrew *me.* b30 Or *snow*

3 Does it please you to oppress me,[d]
to spurn the work of your hands,[e]
while you smile on the schemes of the wicked?[f]
4 Do you have eyes of flesh?
Do you see as a mortal sees?[g]
5 Are your days like those of a mortal
or your years like those of a man,[h]
6 that you must search out my faults
and probe after my sin[i]—
7 though you know that I am not guilty
and that no-one can rescue me from your hand?

8 "Your hands shaped[j] me and made me.
Will you now turn and destroy me?
9 Remember that you moulded me like clay.[k]
Will you now turn me to dust again?[l]
10 Did you not pour me out like milk
and curdle me like cheese,
11 clothe me with skin and flesh
and knit me together[m] with bones and sinews?
12 You gave me life[n] and showed me kindness,
and in your providence watched over my spirit.

13 "But this is what you concealed in your heart,
and I know that this was in your mind:[o]
14 If I sinned, you would be watching me
and would not let my offence go unpunished.[p]
15 If I am guilty—woe to me![q]
Even if I am innocent, I cannot lift my head,[r]
for I am full of shame
and drowned in[a] my affliction.

10:3 d Job 9:22 e Job 14:15; Ps 138:8; Isa 64:8 f Job 21:16; Job 22:18
10:4 g 1Sa 16:7
10:5 h Ps 90:2,4; 2Pe 3:8
10:6 i Job 14:16
10:8 j Ps 119:73
10:9 k Isa 64:8 l Ge 2:7
10:11 m Ps 139:13,15
10:12 n Job 33:4
10:13 o Job 23:13
10:14 p Job 7:21
10:15 q Job 9:13; Isa 3:11 r Job 9:15
10:16 s Isa 38:13; La 3:10 t Job 5:9
10:17 u Job 16:8 v Ru 1:21
10:18 w Job 3:11
10:20 x Job 14:1 y Job 7:19 z Job 7:16
10:21 a 2Sa 12:23; Job 3:13; Job 16:22 b Ps 23:4; Ps 88:12
11:2 a Job 8:2
11:3 b Job 17:2; Job 21:3
11:4 c Job 6:10 d Job 10:7

16 If I hold my head high, you stalk me like a lion[s]
and again display your awesome power against me.[t]
17 You bring new witnesses against me[u]
and increase your anger towards me;[v]
your forces come against me wave upon wave.

18 "Why then did you bring me out of the womb?[w]
I wish I had died before any eye saw me.
19 If only I had never come into being,
or had been carried straight from the womb to the grave!
20 Are not my few days[x] almost over?[y]
Turn away from me[z] so that I can have a moment's joy
21 before I go to the place of no return,[a]
to the land of gloom and deep shadow,[b][b]
22 to the land of deepest night,
of deep shadow and disorder,
where even the light is like darkness."

Zophar

11

Then Zophar the Naamathite replied:

2 "Are all these words to go unanswered?[a]
Is this talker to be vindicated?
3 Will your idle talk reduce men to silence?
Will no-one rebuke you when you mock?[b]
4 You say to God, 'My beliefs are flawless[c]
and I am pure[d] in your sight.'
5 Oh, how I wish that God would speak,
that he would open his lips against you

[a] 15 Or *and aware of* [b] 21 Or *and the shadow of death*; also in verse 22

6and disclose to you the secrets
of wisdom,[e]
for true wisdom has two sides.
Know this: God has even
forgotten some of your
sin.[f]

7"Can you fathom[g] the
mysteries of God?
Can you probe the limits of
the Almighty?
8They are higher than the
heavens[h]—what can you
do?
They are deeper than the
depths of the grave[a]—what
can you know?
9Their measure is longer than
the earth
and wider than the sea.

10"If he comes along and confines
you in prison
and convenes a court, who can
oppose him?[i]
11Surely he recognises deceitful
men;
and when he sees evil, does he
not take note?[j]
12But a witless man can no more
become wise
than a wild donkey's colt can
be born a man.[b]

13"Yet if you devote your heart[k]
to him
and stretch out your hands to
him,[l]
14if you put away the sin that is
in your hand
and allow no evil[m] to dwell in
your tent,[n]
15then you will lift up your face[o]
without shame;
you will stand firm and
without fear.
16You will surely forget your
trouble,[p]
recalling it only as waters
gone by.[q]
17Life will be brighter than
noonday,[r]
and darkness will become like
morning.
18You will be secure, because
there is hope;
you will look about you and
take your rest[s] in safety.[t]
19You will lie down, with no-one
to make you afraid,[u]
and many will court your
favour.[v]
20But the eyes of the wicked will
fail,[w]
and escape will elude them;[x]
their hope will become a dying
gasp."[y]

Job

12

Then Job replied:

2"Doubtless you are the people,
and wisdom will die with
you![a]
3But I have a mind as well as
you;
I am not inferior to you.
Who does not know all these
things?[b]

4"I have become a laughing-
stock[c] to my friends,
though I called upon God and
he answered[d]—
a mere laughing-stock, though
righteous and blameless![e]
5Men at ease have contempt for
misfortune
as the fate of those whose feet
are slipping.
6The tents of marauders are
undisturbed,[f]
and those who provoke God
are secure[g]—
those who carry their god in
their hands.[a]

7"But ask the animals, and they
will teach you,
or the birds of the air, and
they will tell you;
8or speak to the earth, and it will
teach you,

11:6 e Job 9:4 f Ezr 9:13; Job 15:5
11:7 g Ecc 3:11; Ro 11:33
11:8 h Job 22:12
11:10 i Job 9:12; Rev 3:7
11:11 j Job 34:21-25; Ps 10:14
11:13 k 1Sa 7:3; Ps 78:8 l Ps 88:9
11:14 m Ps 101:4 n Job 22:23
11:15 o Job 22:26; 1Jn 3:21
11:16 p Isa 65:16 q Job 22:11
11:17 r Job 22:28; Ps 37:6; Isa 58:8,10
11:18 s Ps 3:5 t Lev 26:6; Pr 3:24
11:19 u Lev 26:6 v Isa 45:14
11:20 w Dt 28:65; Job 17:5 x Job 27:22; Job 34:22 y Job 8:13
12:2 a Job 17:10
12:3 b Job 13:2
12:4 c Job 21:3 d Ps 91:15 e Job 6:29
12:6 f Job 22:18 g Job 9:24; Job 21:9

[a]8 Hebrew *than Sheol* [b]12 Or *wild donkey can be born tame* [a]6 Or *secure / in what God's hand brings them*

or let the fish of the sea
inform you.
9 Which of all these does not
know
that the hand of the LORD has
done this?[h]
10 In his hand is the life of every
creature
and the breath of all
mankind.[i]
11 Does not the ear test words
as the tongue tastes food?[j]
12 Is not wisdom found among the
aged?[k]
Does not long life bring
understanding?[l]

13 "To God belong wisdom[m] and
power;[n]
counsel and understanding are
his.[o]
14 What he tears down[p] cannot be
rebuilt;[q]
the man he imprisons cannot
be released.
15 If he holds back the waters,[r]
there is drought;[s]
if he lets them loose, they
devastate the land.[t]
16 To him belong strength and
victory;
both deceived and deceiver
are his.[u]
17 He leads counsellors away
stripped[v]
and makes fools of judges.[w]
18 He takes off the shackles[x] put
on by kings
and ties a loincloth[b] round
their waist.
19 He leads priests away stripped
and overthrows men long
established.[y]
20 He silences the lips of trusted
advisers
and takes away the
discernment of elders.[z]
21 He pours contempt on nobles
and disarms the mighty.
22 He reveals the deep things of
darkness[a]
and brings deep shadows[b]
into the light.[c]
23 He makes nations great, and
destroys them;[d]
he enlarges nations,[e] and
disperses them.
24 He deprives the leaders of the
earth of their reason;
he sends them wandering
through a trackless waste.[f]
25 They grope in darkness with no
light;[g]
he makes them stagger like
drunkards.[h]

13 "My eyes have seen all
this,
my ears have heard and
understood it.
2 What you know, I also know;
I am not inferior to you.[a]
3 But I desire to speak to the
Almighty
and to argue my case with
God.[b]
4 You, however, smear me with
lies;[c]
you are worthless physicians,
all of you!
5 If only you would be altogether
silent!
For you, that would be
wisdom.[d]
6 Hear now my argument;
listen to the plea of my lips.
7 Will you speak wickedly on
God's behalf?
Will you speak deceitfully for
him?[e]
8 Will you show him partiality?[f]
Will you argue the case for
God?
9 Would it turn out well if he
examined you?
Could you deceive him as you
might deceive men?[g]
10 He would surely rebuke you
if you secretly showed
partiality.
11 Would not his splendour[h]
terrify you?
Would not the dread of him
fall on you?

12:9 h Isa 41:20
12:10 i Job 27:3; Job 33:4; Ac 17:28
12:11 j Job 34:3
12:12 k Job 15:10; l Job 32:7,9
12:13 m Job 11:6; n Job 9:4; o Job 32:8; Job 38:36
12:14 p Job 19:10; q Job 37:7; Isa 25:2
12:15 r 1Ki 8:35; s 1Ki 17:1; t Ge 7:11
12:16 u Job 13:7,9
12:17 v Job 19:9; w Job 3:14
12:18 x Ps 116:16
12:19 y Job 24:12,22; Job 34:20,28; Job 35:9
12:20 z Job 32:9
12:22 a 1Co 4:5; b Job 3:5; c Da 2:22
12:23 d Jer 25:9; e Ps 107:38; Isa 9:3; Isa 26:15
12:24 f Ps 107:40
12:25 g Job 5:14; h Ps 107:27; Isa 24:20
13:2 a Job 12:3
13:3 b Job 23:3-4
13:4 c Ps 119:69; Jer 23:32
13:5 d Pr 17:28
13:7 e Job 36:4
13:8 f Lev 19:15
13:9 g Job 12:16; Gal 6:7
13:11 h Job 31:23

b18 Or *shackles of kings / and ties a belt*

12Your maxims are proverbs of ashes;
your defences are defences of clay.
13“Keep silent and let me speak;
then let come to me what may.
14Why do I put myself in jeopardy
and take my life in my hands?
15Though he slay me, yet will I hope[i] in him;[j]
I will surely[a] defend my ways to his face.[k]
16Indeed, this will turn out for my deliverance,[l]
for no godless man would dare come before him!
17Listen carefully to my words;[m]
let your ears take in what I say.
18Now that I have prepared my case,[n]
I know I will be vindicated.
19Can anyone bring charges against me?[o]
If so, I will be silent and die.[p]

20“Only grant me these two things, O God,
and then I will not hide from you:
21Withdraw your hand[q] far from me,
and stop frightening me with your terrors.
22Then summon me and I will answer,[r]
or let me speak, and you reply.[s]
23How many wrongs and sins have I committed?[t]
Show me my offence and my sin.
24Why do you hide your face[u]
and consider me your enemy?[v]
25Will you torment a wind-blown leaf?[w]
Will you chase after dry chaff?[x]
26For you write down bitter things against me
and make me inherit the sins of my youth.[y]
27You fasten my feet in shackles;[z]
you keep close watch on all my paths
by putting marks on the soles of my feet.

28“So man wastes away like something rotten,
like a garment eaten by moths.[a]

14

“Man born of woman
is of few days and full of trouble.[a]
2He springs up like a flower[b] and withers away;[c]
like a fleeting shadow,[d] he does not endure.
3Do you fix your eye on such a one?[e]
Will you bring him[a] before you for judgment?[f]
4Who can bring what is pure[g] from the impure?[h]
No-one![i]
5Man's days are determined;
you have decreed the number of his months[j]
and have set limits he cannot exceed.
6So look away from him and let him alone,[k]
till he has put in his time like a hired man.[l]

7“At least there is hope for a tree:
If it is cut down, it will sprout again,
and its new shoots will not fail.
8Its roots may grow old in the ground
and its stump die in the soil,
9yet at the scent of water it will bud
and put forth shoots like a plant.
10But man dies and is laid low;
he breathes his last and is no more.[m]

13:15 i Job 7:6 j Ps 23:4; Pr 14:32 k Job 27:5
13:16 l Isa 12:1
13:17 m Job 21:2
13:18 n Job 23:4
13:19 o Job 40:4; Isa 50:8 p Job 10:8
13:21 q Ps 39:10
13:22 r Job 14:15 s Job 9:16
13:23 t 1Sa 26:18
13:24 u Dt 32:20; Ps 13:1; Isa 8:17 v Job 19:11; La 2:5
13:25 w Lev 26:36 x Job 21:18; Isa 42:3
13:26 y Ps 25:7
13:27 z Job 33:11
13:28 a Isa 50:9; Jas 5:2
14:1 a Job 5:7; Ecc 2:23
14:2 b Jas 1:10 c Ps 90:5-6 d Job 8:9
14:3 e Ps 8:4; Ps 144:3 f Ps 143:2
14:4 g Ps 51:10 h Eph 2:1-3 i Jn 3:6; Ro 5:12
14:5 j Job 21:21
14:6 k Job 7:19 l Job 7:1,2; Ps 39:13
14:10 m Job 13:19

[a]15 Or *He will surely slay me; I have no hope — / yet I will*
[a]3 Septuagint, Vulgate and Syriac; Hebrew *me*

11 As water disappears from the
sea
or a river bed becomes
parched and dry,[n]
12 so man lies down and does not
rise;
till the heavens are no more,[o]
men will not awake
or be roused from their
sleep.[p]

13 "If only you would hide me in
the grave[b]
and conceal me till your anger
has passed![q]
If only you would set me a time
and then remember me!
14 If a man dies, will he live
again?
All the days of my hard
service
I will wait for my renewal[c] to
come.
15 You will call and I will answer
you;[r]
you will long for the creature
your hands have made.
16 Surely then you will count my
steps[s]
but not keep track of my sin.[t]
17 My offences will be sealed up
in a bag;[u]
you will cover over my sin.[v]

18 "But as a mountain erodes and
crumbles
and as a rock is moved from
its place,
19 as water wears away stones
and torrents wash away the
soil,
so you destroy man's hope.[w]
20 You overpower him once for all,
and he is gone;
you change his countenance
and send him away.
21 If his sons are honoured, he
does not know it;
if they are brought low, he
does not see it.[x]
22 He feels but the pain of his own
body
and mourns only for himself."

Eliphaz

15 Then Eliphaz the Temanite replied:

2 "Would a wise man answer with
empty notions
or fill his belly with the hot
east wind?[a]
3 Would he argue with useless
words,
with speeches that have no
value?
4 But you even undermine piety
and hinder devotion to God.
5 Your sin prompts your mouth;
you adopt the tongue of the
crafty.[b]
6 Your own mouth condemns you,
not mine;
your own lips testify against
you.[c]

7 "Are you the first man ever
born?[d]
Were you brought forth before
the hills?[e]
8 Do you listen in on God's
council?[f]
Do you limit wisdom to
yourself?
9 What do you know that we do
not know?
What insights do you have that
we do not have?[g]
10 The grey-haired and the aged[h]
are on our side,
men even older than your
father.
11 Are God's consolations[i] not
enough for you,
words[j] spoken gently to
you?[k]
12 Why has your heart[l] carried
you away,
and why do your eyes flash,
13 so that you vent your rage
against God
and pour out such words from
your mouth?

14 "What is man, that he could be
pure,

14:11 *n* Isa 19:5
14:12 *o* Rev 20:11; Rev 21:1 *p* Ac 3:21
14:13 *q* Isa 26:20
14:15 *r* Job 13:22
14:16 *s* Ps 139:1-3; Pr 5:21; Jer 32:19 *t* Job 10:6
14:17 *u* Dt 32:34 *v* Hos 13:12
14:19 *w* Job 7:6
14:21 *x* Ecc 9:5; Isa 63:16
15:2 *a* Job 6:26
15:5 *b* Job 5:13
15:6 *c* Lk 19:22
15:7 *d* Job 38:21 *e* Ps 90:2; Pr 8:25
15:8 *f* Ro 11:34; 1Co 2:11
15:9 *g* Job 13:2
15:10 *h* Job 32:6-7
15:11 *i* 2Co 1:3-4 *j* Zec 1:13 *k* Job 36:16
15:12 *l* Job 11:13

b13 Hebrew *Sheol* c14 Or *release*

or one born of woman,[m] that
he could be righteous?[n]
15If God places no trust in his
holy ones,
if even the heavens are not
pure in his eyes,[o]
16how much less man, who is vile
and corrupt,[p]
who drinks up evil like
water![q]

17"Listen to me and I will explain
to you;
let me tell you what I have
seen,
18what wise men have declared,
hiding nothing received from
their fathers[r]
19(to whom alone the land was
given
when no alien passed among
them):
20All his days the wicked man
suffers torment,
the ruthless through all the
years stored up for him.[s]
21Terrifying sounds fill his ears;[t]
when all seems well,
marauders attack him.[u]
22He despairs of escaping the
darkness;
he is marked for the sword.[v]
23He wanders about[w]—food for
vultures;[a]
he knows the day of darkness
is at hand.[x]
24Distress and anguish fill him
with terror;
they overwhelm him, like a
king poised to attack,
25because he shakes his fist at
God
and vaunts himself against the
Almighty,[y]
26defiantly charging against him
with a thick, strong shield.

27"Though his face is covered
with fat
and his waist bulges with
flesh,[z]
28he will inhabit ruined towns
and houses where no-one
lives,[a]
houses crumbling to rubble.[b]
29He will no longer be rich and
his wealth will not
endure,[c]
nor will his possessions spread
over the land.
30He will not escape the
darkness;[d]
a flame[e] will wither his
shoots,
and the breath of God's
mouth[f] will carry him
away.
31Let him not deceive himself by
trusting what is
worthless,[g]
for he will get nothing in
return.
32Before his time[h] he will be
paid in full,[i]
and his branches will not
flourish.[j]
33He will be like a vine stripped
of its unripe grapes,[k]
like an olive tree shedding its
blossoms.
34For the company of the godless
will be barren,
and fire will consume the
tents of those who love
bribes.[l]
35They conceive trouble and give
birth to evil;[m]
their womb fashions deceit."

Job

16

Then Job replied:

2"I have heard many things like
these;
miserable comforters are you
all![a]
3Will your long-winded speeches
never end?
What ails you that you keep on
arguing?[b]
4I also could speak like you,
if you were in my place;
I could make fine speeches
against you

15:14 m Job 14:4 Job 25:4 n Pr 20:9 Ecc 7:20
15:15 o Job 4:18 Job 25:5
15:16 p Ps 14:1 q Job 34:7 Pr 19:28
15:18 r Job 8:8
15:20 s Job 24:1 Job 27:13-23
15:21 t Job 18:11 Job 20:25 u Job 27:20 1Th 5:3
15:22 v Job 19:29 Job 27:14
15:23 w Ps 59:15 Ps 109:10 x Job 18:12
15:25 y Job 36:9
15:27 z Ps 17:10
15:28 a Isa 5:9 b Job 3:14
15:29 c Job 27:16-17
15:30 d Job 5:14 e Job 22:20 f Job 4:9
15:31 g Isa 59:4
15:32 h Ecc 7:17 i Job 22:16 Ps 55:23 j Job 18:16
15:33 k Hab 3:17
15:34 l Job 8:22
15:35 m Ps 7:14 Isa 59:4 Hos 10:13
16:2 a Job 13:4
16:3 b Job 6:26

[a]23 Or *about, looking for food*

and shake my head[c] at you.
5But my mouth would encourage
you;
comfort from my lips would
bring you relief.

6"Yet if I speak, my pain is not
relieved;
and if I refrain, it does not go
away.
7Surely, O God, you have worn
me out;[d]
you have devastated my entire
household.
8You have bound me—and it has
become a witness;
my gauntness[e] rises up and
testifies against me.[f]
9God assails me and tears[g] me
in his anger
and gnashes his teeth at me;[h]
my opponent fastens on me
his piercing eyes.[i]
10Men open their mouths[j] to jeer
at me;
they strike my cheek[k] in
scorn
and unite together against
me.[l]
11God has turned me over to evil
men
and thrown me into the
clutches of the wicked.[m]
12All was well with me, but he
shattered me;
he seized me by the neck and
crushed me.[n]
He has made me his target;[o]
13 his archers surround me.
Without pity, he pierces[p] my
kidneys
and spills my gall on the
ground.
14Again and again[q] he bursts
upon me;
he rushes at me like a
warrior.[r]

15"I have sewed sackcloth[s] over
my skin
and buried my brow in the
dust.
16My face is red with weeping,
deep shadows ring my eyes;
17yet my hands have been free of
violence[t]
and my prayer is pure.

18"O earth, do not cover my
blood;[u]
may my cry never be laid to
rest![v]
19Even now my witness[w] is in
heaven;
my advocate is on high.
20My intercessor is my friend[a]
as my eyes pour out[x] tears to
God;
21on behalf of a man he pleads[y]
with God
as a man pleads for his friend.

22"Only a few years will pass
before I go on the journey of
no return.[z]

17

1My spirit is broken,
my days are cut short,
the grave awaits me.[a]
2Surely mockers[b] surround me;
my eyes must dwell on their
hostility.

3"Give me, O God, the pledge
you demand.[c]
Who else will put up security[d]
for me?[e]
4You have closed their minds to
understanding;
therefore you will not let them
triumph.
5If a man denounces his friends
for reward,
the eyes of his children will
fail.[f]

6"God has made me a byword[g]
to everyone,
a man in whose face people
spit.
7My eyes have grown dim with
grief;[h]
my whole frame is but a
shadow.
8Upright men are appalled at
this;
the innocent are aroused[i]
against the ungodly.

16:4 c Ps 22:7; Ps 109:25; La 2:15; Zep 2:15; Mt 27:39
16:7 d Job 7:3
16:8 e Job 19:20; f Job 10:17
16:9 g Hos 6:1; h Ps 35:16; La 2:16; Ac 7:54; i Job 13:24
16:10 j Ps 22:13; k Isa 50:6; La 3:30; Mic 5:1; Ac 23:2; l Ps 35:15
16:11 m Job 1:15,17
16:12 n Job 9:17; o La 3:12
16:13 p Job 20:24
16:14 q Job 9:17; r Joel 2:7
16:15 s Ge 37:34
16:17 t Isa 59:6; Jnh 3:8
16:18 u Isa 26:21; v Ps 66:18-19
16:19 w Ge 31:50; Ro 1:9; 1Th 2:5
16:20 x La 2:19
16:21 y Ps 9:4
16:22 z Ecc 12:5
17:1 a Ps 88:3-4
17:2 b 1Sa 1:6-7
17:3 c Ps 119:122; d Pr 6:1; e Isa 38:14
17:5 f Job 11:20
17:6 g Job 30:9
17:7 h Job 16:8
17:8 i Job 22:19

a20 Or *My friends treat me with scorn*

9 Nevertheless, the righteous[j]
will hold to their ways,
and those with clean hands[k]
will grow stronger.
10 "But come on, all of you, try
again!
I will not find a wise man
among you.[l]
11 My days have passed, my plans
are shattered,
and so are the desires of my
heart.[m]
12 These men turn night into day;
in the face of darkness they
say, 'Light is near.'
13 If the only home I hope for is
the grave,[a][n]
if I spread out my bed in
darkness,
14 if I say to corruption,[o] 'You are
my father,'
and to the worm,[p] 'My
mother' or 'My sister',
15 where then is my hope?[q]
Who can see any hope for me?
16 Will it go down to the gates of
death?[b][r]
Will we descend together into
the dust?"

Bildad

18 Then Bildad the Shuhite replied:

2 "When will you end these
speeches?
Be sensible, and then we can
talk.
3 Why are we regarded as cattle
and considered stupid in your
sight?[a]
4 You who tear yourself[b] to
pieces in your anger,
is the earth to be abandoned
for your sake?
Or must the rocks be moved
from their place?
5 "The lamp of the wicked is
snuffed out;[c]
the flame of his fire stops
burning.
6 The light in his tent becomes
dark;
the lamp beside him goes out.
7 The vigour of his step is
weakened;[d]
his own schemes[e] throw him
down.[f]
8 His feet thrust him into a net[g]
and he wanders into its mesh.
9 A trap seizes him by the heel;
a snare holds him fast.
10 A noose is hidden for him on
the ground;
a trap lies in his path.
11 Terrors startle him on every
side[h]
and dog[i] his every step.
12 Calamity is hungry[j] for him;
disaster is ready for him when
he falls.
13 It eats away parts of his skin;
death's firstborn devours his
limbs.[k]
14 He is torn from the security of
his tent[l]
and marched off to the king of
terrors.
15 Fire resides[a] in his tent;
burning sulphur[m] is scattered
over his dwelling.
16 His roots dry up below[n]
and his branches wither
above.[o]
17 The memory of him perishes
from the earth;
he has no name in the land.[p]
18 He is driven from light into
darkness[q]
and is banished from the
world.
19 He has no offspring[r] or
descendants[s] among his
people,
no survivor where once he
lived.[t]
20 Men of the west are appalled at
his fate;[u]
men of the east are seized
with horror.
21 Surely such is the dwelling[v] of
an evil man;

17:9 j Pr 4:18 k Job 22:30
17:10 l Job 12:2
17:11 m Job 7:6
17:13 n Job 3:13
17:14 o Job 13:28 Job 30:28,30 Ps 16:10 p Job 21:26
17:15 q Job 7:6
17:16 r Job 3:17-19 Jnh 2:6
18:3 a Ps 73:22
18:4 b Job 13:14
18:5 c Job 21:17 Pr 13:9 Pr 20:20 Pr 24:20
18:7 d Pr 4:12 e Job 5:13 f Job 15:6
18:8 g Job 22:10 Ps 9:15 Ps 35:7
18:11 h Job 15:21 Jer 6:25 Jer 20:3 i Job 20:8
18:12 j Isa 8:21
18:13 k Zec 14:12
18:14 l Job 8:22
18:15 m Ps 11:6
18:16 n Isa 5:24 Hos 9:1-16 Am 2:9 o Job 15:30 Mal 4:1
18:17 p Ps 34:16 Pr 2:22 Pr 10:7
18:18 q Job 5:14
18:19 r Jer 22:30 s Isa 14:22 t Job 27:14-15
18:20 u Ps 37:13 Jer 50:27,31
18:21 v Job 21:28

a *13* Hebrew *Sheol* b *16* Hebrew *to Sheol*
a *15* Or *Nothing he had remains*

such is the place of one who
knows not God."[w]

Job

19 Then Job replied:

2"How long will you torment me
and crush me with words?
3Ten times now you have
reproached me;
shamelessly you attack me.
4If it is true that I have gone
astray,
my error[a] remains my
concern alone.
5If indeed you would exalt
yourselves above me[b]
and use my humiliation
against me,
6then know that God has
wronged me[c]
and drawn his net[d] around
me.

7"Though I cry, 'I've been
wronged!' I get no
response;[e]
though I call for help, there is
no justice.[f]
8He has blocked my way so that
I cannot pass;[g]
he has shrouded my paths in
darkness.[h]
9He has stripped[i] me of my
honour
and removed the crown from
my head.[j]
10He tears me down[k] on every
side till I am gone;
he uproots my hope[l] like a
tree.[m]
11His anger[n] burns against me;
he counts me among his
enemies.[o]
12His troops advance in force;[p]
they build a siege ramp[q]
against me
and encamp around my tent.

13"He has alienated my brothers[r]
from me;
my acquaintances are
completely estranged from
me.[s]
14My kinsmen have gone away;
my friends have forgotten me.
15My guests and my maidservants
count me a stranger;
they look upon me as an alien.
16I summon my servant, but he
does not answer,
though I beg him with my own
mouth.
17My breath is offensive to my
wife;
I am loathsome to my own
brothers.
18Even the little boys[t] scorn me;
when I appear, they ridicule
me.
19All my intimate friends[u] detest
me;[v]
those I love have turned
against me.
20I am nothing but skin and
bones;[w]
I have escaped by only the
skin of my teeth.[a]

21"Have pity on me, my friends,
have pity,
for the hand of God has struck
me.
22Why do you pursue[x] me as God
does?
Will you never get enough of
my flesh?[y]

23"Oh, that my words were
recorded,
that they were written on a
scroll,[z]
24that they were inscribed with
an iron tool on[b] lead,
or engraved in rock for ever!
25I know that my Redeemer[c] [a]
lives,[b]
and that in the end he will
stand upon the earth.[d]
26And after my skin has been
destroyed,
yet[e] in[f] my flesh I will see
God;[c]
27I myself will see him

[a]20 Or *only my gums* [b]24 Or *and*
[c]25 Or *defender* [d]25 Or *upon my grave*
[e]26 Or *And after I awake, / though this ⌊body⌋ has been destroyed, / then* [f]26 Or */ apart from*

18:21 *w* Jer 9:3; 1Th 4:5
19:4 *a* Job 6:24
19:5 *b* Ps 35:26; Ps 38:16; Ps 55:12
19:6 *c* Job 27:2; *d* Job 18:8
19:7 *e* Job 30:20; *f* Job 9:24; Hab 1:2-4
19:8 *g* Job 3:23; La 3:7; *h* Job 30:26
19:9 *i* Job 12:17; *j* Ps 89:39,44; La 5:16
19:10 *k* Job 12:14; *l* Job 7:6; *m* Job 24:20
19:11 *n* Job 16:9; *o* Job 13:24
19:12 *p* Job 16:13; *q* Job 30:12
19:13 *r* Ps 69:8; *s* Job 16:7; Ps 88:8
19:18 *t* 2Ki 2:23
19:19 *u* Ps 55:12-13; *v* Ps 38:11
19:20 *w* Job 33:21; Ps 102:5
19:22 *x* Job 13:25; Job 16:11; *y* Ps 69:26
19:23 *z* Isa 30:8
19:25 *a* Ps 78:35; Pr 23:11; Isa 43:14; Jer 50:34; *b* Job 16:19
19:26 *c* Ps 17:15; Mt 5:8; 1Co 13:12; 1Jn 3:2

with my own eyes—I, and not
another.
How my heart yearns[d] within
me!

28"If you say, 'How we will hound
him,
since the root of the trouble
lies in him,'[g]
29you should fear the sword
yourselves;
for wrath will bring
punishment by the sword,[e]
and then you will know that
there is judgment."[h] [f]

Zophar

20 Then Zophar the Naamathite replied:

2"My troubled thoughts prompt
me to answer
because I am greatly
disturbed.
3I hear a rebuke[a] that
dishonours me,
and my understanding inspires
me to reply.

4"Surely you know how it has
been from of old,
ever since man[a] was placed
on the earth,
5that the mirth of the wicked is
brief,
the joy of the godless lasts but
a moment.[b]
6Though his pride reaches to the
heavens
and his head touches the
clouds,[c]
7he will perish for ever,[d] like
his own dung;
those who have seen him will
say, 'Where is he?'[e]
8Like a dream[f] he flies away,[g]
no more to be found,
banished[h] like a vision of the
night.[i]
9The eye that saw him will not
see him again;
his place will look on him no
more.[j]

10His children[k] must make
amends to the poor;
his own hands must give back
his wealth.[l]
11The youthful vigour[m] that fills
his bones
will lie with him in the dust.[n]

12"Though evil is sweet in his
mouth
and he hides it under his
tongue,
13though he cannot bear to let it
go
and keeps it in his mouth,[o]
14yet his food will turn sour in his
stomach;
it will become the venom of
serpents within him.
15He will spit out the riches he
swallowed;
God will make his stomach
vomit them up.
16He will suck the poison[p] of
serpents;
the fangs of an adder will kill
him.[q]
17He will not enjoy the streams,
the rivers flowing with
honey[r] and cream.[s]
18What he toiled for he must give
back uneaten;
he will not enjoy the profit
from his trading.
19For he has oppressed the poor
and left them destitute;[t]
he has seized houses he did
not build.

20"Surely he will have no respite
from his craving;[u]
he cannot save himself by his
treasure.
21Nothing is left for him to
devour;
his prosperity will not
endure.[v]
22In the midst of his plenty,
distress will overtake him;
the full force of misery will
come upon him.

19:27 d Ps 73:26
19:29 e Job 15:22 f Job 22:4 Ps 1:5 Ps 9:7
20:3 a Job 19:3
20:5 b Job 8:12 Ps 37:35-36 Ps 73:19
20:6 c Isa 14:13-14 Ob 1:3-4
20:7 d Job 4:20 e Job 7:10 Job 8:18
20:8 f Ps 73:20 g Job 27:21-23 h Job 18:18 i Ps 90:5
20:9 j Job 7:8
20:10 k Job 5:4 l Job 27:16-17
20:11 m Job 13:26 n Job 21:26
20:13 o Nu 11:18-20
20:16 p Dt 32:32 q Dt 32:24
20:17 r Dt 32:13 s Job 29:6
20:19 t Job 24:4,14 Job 35:9
20:20 u Ecc 5:12-14
20:21 v Job 15:29

g28 Many Hebrew manuscripts, Septuagint and Vulgate; most Hebrew manuscripts *me*
h29 Or / *that you may come to know the Almighty*
a4 Or *Adam*

23When he has filled his belly,
God will vent his burning
anger against him
and rain down his blows upon
him.[w]
24Though he flees[x] from an iron
weapon,
a bronze-tipped arrow pierces
him.
25He pulls it out of his back,
the gleaming point out of his
liver.
Terrors[y] will come over him;[z]
26 total darkness[a] lies in wait
for his treasures.
A fire unfanned will consume
him[b]
and devour what is left in his
tent.
27The heavens will expose his
guilt;
the earth will rise up against
him.[c]
28A flood will carry off his
house,[d]
rushing waters[b] on the day of
God's wrath.[e]
29Such is the fate God allots the
wicked,
the heritage appointed for
them by God."[f]

Job

21

Then Job replied:

2"Listen carefully to my words;
let this be the consolation you
give me.
3Bear with me while I speak,
and after I have spoken, mock
on.[a]
4"Is my complaint directed to
man?
Why should I not be
impatient?[b]
5Look at me and be astonished;
clap your hand over your
mouth.[c]
6When I think about this, I am
terrified;
trembling seizes my body.
7Why do the wicked live on,
growing old and increasing in
power?[d]
8They see their children
established around them,
their offspring before their
eyes.[e]
9Their homes are safe and free
from fear;[f]
the rod of God is not upon
them.
10Their bulls never fail to breed;
their cows calve and do not
miscarry.[g]
11They send forth their children
as a flock;
their little ones dance about.
12They sing to the music of
tambourine and harp;
they make merry to the sound
of the flute.[h]
13They spend their years in
prosperity[i]
and go down to the grave[a] in
peace.[b]
14Yet they say to God, 'Leave us
alone![j]
We have no desire to know
your ways.[k]
15Who is the Almighty, that we
should serve him?
What would we gain by
praying to him?'[l]
16But their prosperity is not in
their own hands,
so I stand aloof from the
counsel of the wicked.
17"Yet how often is the lamp of
the wicked snuffed out?[m]
How often does calamity come
upon them,
the fate God allots in his
anger?
18How often are they like straw
before the wind,
like chaff[n] swept away by a
gale?
19⌊It is said,⌋ 'God stores up a
man's punishment for his
sons.'[o]
Let him repay the man
himself, so that he will
know it!

20:23 *w* Ps 78:30-31
20:24 *x* Isa 24:18; Am 5:19
20:25 *y* Job 18:11; *z* Job 16:13
20:26 *a* Job 18:18; *b* Ps 21:9
20:27 *c* Dt 31:28
20:28 *d* Dt 28:31; *e* Job 21:17,20, 30
20:29 *f* Job 27:13
21:3 *a* Job 16:10
21:4 *b* Job 6:11
21:5 *c* Jdg 18:19; Job 29:9; Job 40:4
21:7 *d* Job 12:6; Ps 73:3; Jer 12:1; Hab 1:13
21:8 *e* Ps 17:14
21:9 *f* Ps 73:5
21:10 *g* Ex 23:26
21:12 *h* Ps 81:2
21:13 *i* Job 36:11
21:14 *j* Job 22:17; *k* Pr 1:29
21:15 *l* Ex 5:2; Job 34:9; Mal 3:14
21:17 *m* Job 18:5
21:18 *n* Job 13:25; Ps 1:4
21:19 *o* Ex 20:5; Jer 31:29; Eze 18:2

b28 Or *The possessions in his house will be carried off, / washed away*
a13 Hebrew *Sheol*
b13 Or *in an instant*

20Let his own eyes see his
destruction;
let him drink[p] of the wrath of
the Almighty.[c][q]
21For what does he care about the
family he leaves behind
when his allotted months[r]
come to an end?

22"Can anyone teach knowledge to
God,[s]
since he judges even the
highest?[t]
23One man dies in full vigour,
completely secure and at ease,
24his body[d] well nourished,
his bones rich with marrow.[u]
25Another man dies in bitterness
of soul,
never having enjoyed anything
good.
26Side by side they lie in the dust,
and worms cover them both.[v]

27"I know full well what you are
thinking,
the schemes by which you
would wrong me.
28You say, 'Where now is the
great man's[w] house,
the tents where wicked men
lived?'[x]
29Have you never questioned
those who travel?
Have you paid no regard to
their accounts—
30that the evil man is spared from
the day of calamity,[y]
that he is delivered from[e] the
day of wrath?[z]
31Who denounces his conduct to
his face?
Who repays him for what he
has done?
32He is carried to the grave,
and watch is kept over his
tomb.
33The soil in the valley is sweet to
him;[a]
all men follow after him,
and a countless throng goes[f]
before him.[b]

34"So how can you console me[c]
with your nonsense?
Nothing is left of your
answers but falsehood!"

21:20 *p* Ps 75:8; Isa 51:17 *q* Jer 25:15; Rev 14:10
21:21 *r* Job 14:5
21:22 *s* Job 35:11; Job 36:22; Isa 40:13-14; Ro 11:34 *t* Ps 82:1
21:24 *u* Pr 3:8
21:26 *v* Job 24:20; Ecc 9:2-3; Isa 14:11
21:28 *w* Job 1:3; Job 12:21; Job 31:37 *x* Job 8:22
21:30 *y* Pr 16:4 *z* Job 20:22,28; 2Pe 2:9
21:33 *a* Job 3:22; Job 17:16; Job 24:24 *b* Job 3:19
21:34 *c* Job 16:2
22:2 *a* Lk 17:10
22:4 *b* Job 14:3; Job 19:29; Ps 143:2
22:5 *c* Job 11:6; Job 15:5
22:6 *d* Ex 22:26; Dt 24:6,17; Eze 18:12,16
22:7 *e* Job 31:17,21,31
22:8 *f* Isa 3:3; Isa 9:15
22:9 *g* Job 24:3,21
22:11 *h* Job 5:14 *i* Ps 69:1-2; Ps 124:4-5; La 3:54

Eliphaz

22

Then Eliphaz the Temanite
replied:

2"Can a man be of benefit to
God?[a]
Can even a wise man benefit
him?
3What pleasure would it give the
Almighty if you were
righteous?
What would he gain if your
ways were blameless?

4"Is it for your piety that he
rebukes you
and brings charges against
you?[b]
5Is not your wickedness great?
Are not your sins[c] endless?
6You demanded security[d] from
your brothers for no
reason;
you stripped men of their
clothing, leaving them
naked.
7You gave no water to the weary
and you withheld food from
the hungry,[e]
8though you were a powerful
man, owning land—
an honoured man,[f] living on
it.
9And you sent widows away
empty-handed[g]
and broke the strength of the
fatherless.
10That is why snares are all
around you,
why sudden peril terrifies you,
11why it is so dark[h] that you
cannot see,
and why a flood of water
covers you.[i]

[c]*17–20* Verses 17 and 18 may be taken as exclamations and 19 and 20 as declarations.
[d]*24* The meaning of the Hebrew for this word is uncertain.
[e]*30* Or *man is reserved for the day of calamity, / that he is brought forth to*
[f]*33* Or */ as a countless throng went*

12"Is not God in the heights of
heaven?[j]
And see how lofty are the
highest stars!
13Yet you say, 'What does God
know?[k]
Does he judge through such
darkness?[l]
14Thick clouds[m] veil him, so he
does not see us
as he goes about in the vaulted
heavens.'
15Will you keep to the old path
that evil men have trod?
16They were carried off before
their time,[n]
their foundations washed away
by a flood.[o]
17They said to God, 'Leave us
alone!
What can the Almighty do to
us?'[p]
18Yet it was he who filled their
houses with good things,[q]
so I stand aloof from the
counsel of the wicked.[r]

19"The righteous see their ruin
and rejoice;[s]
the innocent mock[t] them,
saying,
20'Surely our foes are destroyed,
and fire[u] devours their
wealth.'

21"Submit to God and be at peace
with him;
in this way prosperity will
come to you.[v]
22Accept instruction from his
mouth
and lay up his words in your
heart.
23If you return[w] to the Almighty,
you will be restored:[x]
If you remove wickedness far
from your tent[y]
24and assign your nuggets to the
dust,
your gold of Ophir to the
rocks in the ravines,[z]
25then the Almighty will be your
gold,
the choicest silver for you.[a]
26Surely then you will find
delight in the Almighty[b]
and will lift up your face to
God.
27You will pray to him,[c] and he
will hear you,
and you will fulfil your vows.
28What you decide on will be
done,
and light will shine on your
ways.
29When men are brought low and
you say, 'Lift them up!'
then he will save the
downcast.[d]
30He will deliver even one who is
not innocent,
who will be delivered through
the cleanness of your
hands."[e]

Job

23 Then Job replied:

2"Even today my complaint[a] is
bitter;[b]
his hand[a] is heavy in spite
of[b] my groaning.
3If only I knew where to find
him;
if only I could go to his
dwelling!
4I would state my case[c] before
him
and fill my mouth with
arguments.
5I would find out what he would
answer me,
and consider what he would
say.
6Would he oppose me with great
power?[d]
No, he would not press
charges against me.
7There an upright man could
present his case before
him,[e]
and I would be delivered for
ever from my judge.

[a]2 Septuagint and Syriac; Hebrew / *the hand on me* [b]2 Or *heavy on me in*

22:12 j Job 11:8
22:13 k Ps 10:11; Isa 29:15; l Eze 8:12
22:14 m Job 26:9
22:16 n Job 15:32; o Job 14:19; Mt 7:26-27
22:17 p Job 21:15
22:18 q Job 12:6; r Job 21:16
22:19 s Ps 58:10; Ps 107:42; t Ps 52:6
22:20 u Job 15:30
22:21 v Ps 34:8-10
22:23 w Job 8:5; Isa 31:6; Zec 1:3; x Isa 19:22; Ac 20:32; y Job 11:14
22:24 z Job 31:25
22:25 a Isa 33:6
22:26 b Job 27:10; Isa 58:14
22:27 c Job 33:26; Job 34:28; Isa 58:9
22:29 d Mt 23:12; 1Pe 5:5
22:30 e Job 42:7-8
23:2 a Job 7:11; b Job 6:3
23:4 c Job 13:18
23:6 d Job 9:4
23:7 e Job 13:3

8"But if I go to the east, he is not
there;
if I go to the west, I do not
find him.
9When he is at work in the north,
I do not see him;
when he turns to the south, I
catch no glimpse of him.[f]
10But he knows the way that I
take;
when he has tested me,[g] I
shall come forth as gold.[h]
11My feet have closely followed
his steps;[i]
I have kept to his way without
turning aside.[j]
12I have not departed from the
commands of his lips;[k]
I have treasured the words of
his mouth more than my
daily bread.[l]

13"But he stands alone, and who
can oppose him?
He does whatever he
pleases.[m]
14He carries out his decree
against me,
and many such plans he still
has in store.[n]
15That is why I am terrified
before him;
when I think of all this, I fear
him.
16God has made my heart faint;[o]
the Almighty[p] has terrified
me.
17Yet I am not silenced by the
darkness,[q]
by the thick darkness that
covers my face.

24

"Why does the Almighty
not set times for
judgment?[a]
Why must those who know
him look in vain for such
days?[b]
2Men move boundary stones;[c]
they pasture flocks they have
stolen.
3They drive away the orphan's
donkey
and take the widow's ox in
pledge.[d]
4They thrust the needy from the
path
and force all the poor[e] of the
land into hiding.[f]
5Like wild donkeys in the desert,
the poor go about their
labour[g] of foraging food;
the wasteland provides food
for their children.
6They gather fodder in the fields
and glean in the vineyards of
the wicked.
7Lacking clothes, they spend the
night naked;
they have nothing to cover
themselves in the cold.[h]
8They are drenched by mountain
rains
and hug[i] the rocks for lack of
shelter.
9The fatherless[j] child is
snatched from the breast;
the infant of the poor is seized
for a debt.
10Lacking clothes, they go about
naked;
they carry the sheaves, but
still go hungry.
11They crush olives among the
terraces;[a]
they tread the winepresses,
yet suffer thirst.
12The groans of the dying rise
from the city,
and the souls of the wounded
cry out for help.[k]
But God charges no-one with
wrongdoing.[l]

13"There are those who rebel
against the light,[m]
who do not know its ways
or stay in its paths.[n]
14When daylight is gone, the
murderer rises up
and kills the poor and needy;
in the night he steals forth
like a thief.[o]
15The eye of the adulterer
watches for dusk;[p]
he thinks, 'No eye will see
me,'[q]

[a]*11* Or *olives between the millstones*; the meaning of the Hebrew for this word is uncertain.

23:9 f Job 9:11
23:10 g Ps 66:10; Ps 139:1-3; h 1Pe 1:7
23:11 i Ps 17:5; j Ps 44:18
23:12 k Job 6:10; l Jn 4:32,34
23:13 m Ps 115:3
23:14 n 1Th 3:3
23:16 o Dt 20:3; Ps 22:14; Jer 51:46; p Job 27:2
23:17 q Job 19:8
24:1 a Jer 46:10; b Ac 1:7
24:2 c Dt 19:14; Dt 27:17; Pr 23:10
24:3 d Dt 24:6,10,12,17; Job 22:6
24:4 e Job 29:12; Job 30:25; Ps 41:1; f Pr 28:28
24:5 g Ps 104:23
24:7 h Ex 22:27; Job 22:6
24:8 i La 4:5
24:9 j Dt 24:17
24:12 k Eze 26:15; l Job 9:23
24:13 m Jn 3:19-20; n Isa 5:20
24:14 o Ps 10:9
24:15 p Pr 7:8-9; q Ps 10:11

and he keeps his face
concealed.
16In the dark, men break into
houses,[r]
but by day they shut
themselves in;
they want nothing to do with
the light.[s]
17For all of them, deep darkness
is their morning;[b]
they make friends with the
terrors of darkness.[c]

18"Yet they are foam[t] on the
surface of the water;[u]
their portion of the land is
cursed,
so that no-one goes to the
vineyards.
19As heat and drought snatch
away the melted snow,[v]
so the grave[d][w] snatches away
those who have sinned.
20The womb forgets them,
the worm feasts on them;
evil men are no longer
remembered[x]
but are broken like a tree.[y]
21They prey on the barren and
childless woman,
and to the widow show no
kindness.[z]
22But God drags away the mighty
by his power;
though they become
established, they have no
assurance of life.[a]
23He may let them rest in a
feeling of security,[b]
but his eyes are on their
ways.[c]
24For a little while they are
exalted, and then they are
gone;[d]
they are brought low and
gathered up like all others;
they are cut off like ears of
corn.[e]

25"If this is not so, who can prove
me false
and reduce my words to
nothing?"[f]

Bildad

25

Then Bildad the Shuhite replied:

2"Dominion and awe belong to
God;[a]
he establishes order in the
heights of heaven.
3Can his forces be numbered?
Upon whom does his light not
rise?[b]
4How then can a man be
righteous before God?
How can one born of woman
be pure?[c]
5If even the moon[d] is not bright
and the stars are not pure in
his eyes,[e]
6how much less man, who is but
a maggot—
a son of man,[f] who is only a
worm!"[g]

Job

26

Then Job replied:

2"How you have helped the
powerless![a]
How you have saved the arm
that is feeble![b]
3What advice you have offered
to one without wisdom!
And what great insight you
have displayed!
4Who has helped you utter these
words?
And whose spirit spoke from
your mouth?

5"The dead are in deep
anguish,[c]
those beneath the waters and
all that live in them.
6Death[a][d] is naked before God;
Destruction[b] lies uncovered.[e]
7He spreads out the northern
⌞skies⌟[f] over empty space;
he suspends the earth over
nothing.

24:16 r Ex 22:2; Mt 6:19; s Jn 3:20
24:18 t Job 9:26; u Job 22:16
24:19 v Job 6:17; w Job 21:13
24:20 x Job 18:17; Pr 10:7; y Ps 31:12; Da 4:14
24:21 z Job 22:9
24:22 a Dt 28:66
24:23 b Job 12:6; c Job 11:11
24:24 d Job 14:21; Ps 37:10; e Isa 17:5
24:25 f Job 6:28; Job 27:4
25:2 a Job 9:4; Rev 1:6
25:3 b Jas 1:17
25:4 c Job 4:17; Job 14:4
25:5 d Job 31:26; e Job 15:15
25:6 f Job 7:17; g Ps 22:6
26:2 a Job 6:12; b Ps 71:9
26:5 c Ps 88:10
26:6 d Ps 139:8; e Job 41:11; Pr 15:11; Heb 4:13
26:7 f Job 9:8

b17 Or *them, their morning is like the shadow of death* c17 Or *of the shadow of death*
d19 Hebrew *Sheol* a6 Hebrew *Sheol*
b6 Hebrew *Abaddon*

a tempest snatches him away
in the night.[v]
21 The east wind carries him off,
and he is gone;
it sweeps him out of his
place.[w]
22 It hurls itself against him
without mercy[x]
as he flees headlong from its
power.[y]
23 It claps its hands in derision
and hisses him out of his
place.[z]

28

"There is a mine for
silver
and a place where gold is
refined.
2 Iron is taken from the earth,
and copper is smelted from
ore.[a]
3 Man puts an end to the
darkness;[b]
he searches the farthest
recesses
for ore in the blackest
darkness.
4 Far from where people dwell he
cuts a shaft,
in places forgotten by the foot
of man;
far from men he dangles and
sways.
5 The earth, from which food
comes,[c]
is transformed below as by
fire;
6 sapphires[a] come from its
rocks,
and its dust contains nuggets
of gold.
7 No bird of prey knows that
hidden path,
no falcon's eye has seen it.
8 Proud beasts do not set foot on
it,
and no lion prowls there.
9 Man's hand assaults the flinty
rock
and lays bare the roots of the
mountains.
10 He tunnels through the rock;
his eyes see all its treasures.
11 He searches[b] the sources of
the rivers
and brings hidden things to
light.
12 "But where can wisdom be
found?[d]
Where does understanding
dwell?
13 Man does not comprehend its
worth;[e]
it cannot be found in the land
of the living.
14 The deep says, 'It is not in me';
the sea says, 'It is not with
me.'
15 It cannot be bought with the
finest gold,
nor can its price be weighed
in silver.[f]
16 It cannot be bought with the
gold of Ophir,
with precious onyx or
sapphires.
17 Neither gold nor crystal can
compare with it,
nor can it be had for jewels of
gold.[g]
18 Coral and jasper are not worthy
of mention;
the price of wisdom is beyond
rubies.[h]
19 The topaz of Cush cannot
compare with it;
it cannot be bought with pure
gold.[i]
20 "Where then does wisdom come
from?
Where does understanding
dwell?[j]
21 It is hidden from the eyes of
every living thing,
concealed even from the birds
of the air.
22 Destruction[c][k] and Death say,
'Only a rumour of it has
reached our ears.'
23 God understands the way to it
and he alone knows where it
dwells,[l]

27:20 *v* Job 20:8
27:21 *w* Job 7:10; Job 21:18
27:22 *x* Jer 13:14; Eze 5:11; Eze 24:14 *y* Job 11:20
27:23 *z* Job 18:18
28:2 *a* Dt 8:9
28:3 *b* Ecc 1:13
28:5 *c* Ps 104:14
28:12 *d* Ecc 7:24
28:13 *e* Pr 3:15; Mt 13:44-46
28:15 *f* Pr 3:13-14; Pr 8:10-11; Pr 16:16
28:17 *g* Pr 16:16
28:18 *h* Pr 3:15
28:19 *i* Pr 8:19
28:20 *j* ver 23,28
28:22 *k* Job 26:6
28:23 *l* Pr 8:22-31

a6 Or *lapis lazuli*; also in verse 16
b11 Septuagint, Aquila and Vulgate; Hebrew *He dams up* c22 Hebrew *Abaddon*

8He wraps up the waters[g] in his
clouds,[h]
yet the clouds do not burst
under their weight.
9He covers the face of the full
moon,
spreading his clouds[i] over it.
10He marks out the horizon on the
face of the waters[j]
for a boundary between light
and darkness.[k]
11The pillars of the heavens
quake,
aghast at his rebuke.
12By his power he churned up the
sea;[l]
by his wisdom[m] he cut Rahab
to pieces.
13By his breath the skies became
fair;
his hand pierced the gliding
serpent.[n]
14And these are but the outer
fringe of his works;
how faint the whisper we hear
of him!
Who then can understand the
thunder of his power?"[o]

27

And Job continued his discourse:[a]

2"As surely as God lives, who
has denied me justice,[b]
the Almighty, who has made
me taste bitterness of
soul,[c]
3as long as I have life within me,
the breath of God[d] in my
nostrils,
4my lips will not speak
wickedness,
and my tongue will utter no
deceit.[e]
5I will never admit you are in
the right;
till I die, I will not deny my
integrity.[f]
6I will maintain my
righteousness and never let
go of it;
my conscience will not
reproach me as long as I
live.[g]

26:8 g Pr 30:4 h Job 37:11
26:9 i Job 22:14; Ps 97:2
26:10 j Pr 8:27,29 k Job 38:8-11
26:12 l Ex 14:21; Isa 51:15; Jer 31:35 m Job 12:13
26:13 n Isa 27:1
26:14 o Job 36:29
27:1 a Job 29:1
27:2 b Job 34:5 c Job 9:18
27:3 d Job 32:8; Job 33:4
27:4 e Job 6:28
27:5 f Job 2:9; Job 13:15
27:6 g Job 2:3
27:8 h Job 8:13 i Job 11:20; Lk 12:20
27:9 j Job 35:12; Pr 1:28; Isa 1:15; Jer 14:12; Mic 3:4
27:10 k Job 22:26
27:13 l Job 15:20; Job 20:29
27:14 m Dt 28:41; Job 15:22; Hos 9:13 n Job 20:10
27:15 o Ps 78:64
27:16 p Zec 9:3
27:17 q Pr 28:8; Ecc 2:26
27:18 r Job 8:14 s Isa 1:8
27:19 t Job 7:8
27:20 u Job 15:21

7"May my enemies be like the
wicked,
my adversaries like the
unjust!
8For what hope has the godless[h]
when he is cut off,
when God takes away his
life?[i]
9Does God listen to his cry
when distress comes upon
him?[j]
10Will he find delight in the
Almighty?[k]
Will he call upon God at all
times?
11"I will teach you about the
power of God;
the ways of the Almighty I
will not conceal.
12You have all seen this
yourselves.
Why then this meaningless
talk?
13"Here is the fate God allots to
the wicked,
the heritage a ruthless man
receives from the
Almighty:[l]
14However many his children,
their fate is the sword;[m]
his offspring will never have
enough to eat.[n]
15The plague will bury those who
survive him,
and their widows will not
weep for them.[o]
16Though he heaps up silver like
dust
and clothes like piles of clay,[p]
17what he lays up the righteous
will wear,[q]
and the innocent will divide
his silver.
18The house he builds is like a
moth's cocoon,[r]
like a hut[s] made by a
watchman.
19He lies down wealthy, but will
do so no more;[t]
when he opens his eyes, all is
gone.
20Terrors overtake him like a
flood;[u]

24 for he views the ends of the earth[m]
and sees everything under the heavens.[n]
25 When he established the force of the wind
and measured out the waters,[o]
26 when he made a decree for the rain
and a path for the thunderstorm,[p]
27 then he looked at wisdom and appraised it;
he confirmed it and tested it.
28 And he said to man,
'The fear of the Lord—that is wisdom,
and to shun evil is understanding.[q]' "

29 Job continued his discourse:[a]

2 "How I long for the months gone by,
for the days when God watched over me,[b]
3 when his lamp shone upon my head
and by his light I walked through darkness![c]
4 Oh, for the days when I was in my prime,
when God's intimate friendship blessed my house,[d]
5 when the Almighty was still with me
and my children were around me,
6 when my path was drenched with cream[e]
and the rock[f] poured out for me streams of olive oil.[g]

7 "When I went to the gate[h] of the city
and took my seat in the public square,
8 the young men saw me and stepped aside
and the old men rose to their feet;
9 the chief men refrained from speaking
and covered their mouths with their hands;[i]
10 the voices of the nobles were hushed,
and their tongues stuck to the roof of their mouths.[j]
11 Whoever heard me spoke well of me,
and those who saw me commended me,
12 because I rescued the poor[k] who cried for help,
and the fatherless[l] who had none to assist him.[m]
13 The man who was dying blessed me;[n]
I made the widow's[o] heart sing.
14 I put on righteousness[p] as my clothing;
justice was my robe and my turban.
15 I was eyes[q] to the blind
and feet to the lame.
16 I was a father to the needy;[r]
I took up the case of the stranger.
17 I broke the fangs of the wicked
and snatched the victims from their teeth.[s]

18 "I thought, 'I shall die in my own house,
my days as numerous as the grains of sand.[t]
19 My roots will reach to the water,[u]
and the dew will lie all night on my branches.
20 My glory will remain fresh in me,
the bow[v] ever new in my hand.'[w]

21 "Men listened to me expectantly,
waiting in silence for my counsel.
22 After I had spoken, they spoke no more;
my words fell gently on their ears.[x]

28:24 m Ps 33:13-14 n Pr 15:3
28:25 o Job 12:15 Ps 135:7
28:26 p Job 37:3,8,11 Job 38:25,27
28:28 q Dt 4:6 Ps 111:10 Pr 1:7 Pr 9:10
29:1 a Job 13:12 Job 27:1
29:2 b Jer 31:28
29:3 c Job 11:17
29:4 d Ps 25:14 Pr 3:32
29:6 e Job 20:17 f Ps 81:16 g Dt 32:13
29:7 h Job 31:21
29:9 i Job 21:5
29:10 j Ps 137:6
29:12 k Job 24:4 l Job 31:17,21 m Ps 72:12 Pr 21:13
29:13 n Job 31:20 o Job 22:9
29:14 p Job 27:6 Ps 132:9 Isa 59:17 Isa 61:10 Eph 6:14
29:15 q Nu 10:31
29:16 r Job 24:4 Pr 29:7
29:17 s Ps 3:7
29:18 t Ps 30:6
29:19 u Job 18:16 Jer 17:8
29:20 v Ps 18:34 w Ge 49:24
29:22 x Dt 32:2

23They waited for me as for
showers
and drank in my words as the
spring rain.
24When I smiled at them, they
scarcely believed it;
the light of my face was
precious to them.[a]
25I chose the way for them and
sat as their chief;
I dwelt as a king[y] among his
troops;
I was like one who comforts
mourners.[z]

30

"But now they mock me,[a]
men younger than I,
whose fathers I would have
disdained
to put with my sheep dogs.
2Of what use was the strength of
their hands to me,
since their vigour had gone
from them?
3Haggard from want and hunger,
they roamed[a] the parched
land
in desolate wastelands at
night.
4In the brush they gathered salt
herbs,
and their food[b] was the root
of the broom tree.
5They were banished from their
fellow-men,
shouted at as if they were
thieves.
6They were forced to live in the
dry stream beds,
among the rocks and in holes
in the ground.
7They brayed among the bushes
and huddled in the
undergrowth.
8A base and nameless brood,
they were driven out of the
land.

9"And now their sons mock me[b]
in song;[c]
I have become a byword[d]
among them.
10They detest me and keep their
distance;
they do not hesitate to spit in
my face.[e]
11Now that God has unstrung my
bow and afflicted me,[f]
they throw off restraint[g] in
my presence.
12On my right the tribe[c] attacks;
they lay snares for my feet,[h]
they build their siege ramps
against me.[i]
13They break up my road;[j]
they succeed in destroying
me—
without anyone's helping
them.[d]
14They advance as through a
gaping breach;
amid the ruins they come
rolling in.
15Terrors overwhelm me;[k]
my dignity is driven away as
by the wind,
my safety vanishes like a
cloud.[l]

16"And now my life ebbs away;[m]
days of suffering grip me.
17Night pierces my bones;
my gnawing pains never rest.
18In his great power ⌊God⌋
becomes like clothing to
me;[e]
he binds me like the neck of
my garment.
19He throws me into the mud,[n]
and I am reduced to dust and
ashes.

20"I cry out to you, O God, but
you do not answer;[o]
I stand up, but you merely
look at me.
21You turn on me ruthlessly;[p]
with the might of your hand[q]
you attack me.[r]
22You snatch me up and drive me
before the wind;[s]
you toss me about in the
storm.[t]

29:25
y Job 1:3
Job 31:37
z Job 4:4

30:1
a Job 12:4

30:9
b Ps 69:11
c Job 12:4
La 3:14,63
d Job 17:6

30:10
e Nu 12:14
Dt 25:9
Isa 50:6
Mt 26:67

30:11
f Ru 1:21
g Ps 32:9

30:12
h Ps 140:4-5
i Job 19:12

30:13
j Isa 3:12

30:15
k Job 31:23
Ps 55:4-5
l Job 3:25
Hos 13:3

30:16
m Job 3:24
Ps 22:14
Ps 42:4

30:19
n Ps 69:2,14

30:20
o Job 19:7

30:21
p Job 19:6,22
q Job 16:9,14
r Job 10:3

30:22
s Job 27:21
t Job 9:17

[a]*24* The meaning of the Hebrew for this clause is uncertain. [a]*3* Or *gnawed* [b]*4* Or *fuel* [c]*12* The meaning of the Hebrew for this word is uncertain. [d]*13* Or *me. / 'No-one can help him,' ⌊they say⌋,* [e]*18* Hebrew; Septuagint *⌊God⌋ grasps my clothing*

23 I know you will bring me down
to death,[u]
to the place appointed for all
the living.[v]

24 "Surely no-one lays a hand on a
broken man
when he cries for help in his
distress.[w]
25 Have I not wept for those in
trouble?
Has not my soul grieved for
the poor?[x]
26 Yet when I hoped for good, evil
came;
when I looked for light, then
came darkness.[y]
27 The churning inside me never
stops;[z]
days of suffering confront me.
28 I go about blackened,[a] but not
by the sun;
I stand up in the assembly and
cry for help.[b]
29 I have become a brother of
jackals,[c]
a companion of owls.[d]
30 My skin grows black and
peels;[e]
my body burns with fever.[f]
31 My harp is tuned to mourning,[g]
and my flute to the sound of
wailing.

31

"I made a covenant with
my eyes
not to look lustfully at a girl.[a]
2 For what is man's lot from God
above,
his heritage from the
Almighty on high?[b]
3 Is it not ruin[c] for the wicked,
disaster for those who do
wrong?[d]
4 Does he not see my ways[e]
and count my every step?[f]

5 "If I have walked in falsehood
or my foot has hurried after
deceit[g]—
6 let God weigh me in honest
scales[h]
and he will know that I am
blameless—
7 if my steps have turned from
the path,[i]
if my heart has been led by
my eyes,
or if my hands[j] have been
defiled,
8 then may others eat what I have
sown,[k]
and may my crops be
uprooted.[l]

9 "If my heart has been enticed[m]
by a woman,
or if I have lurked at my
neighbour's door,
10 then may my wife grind
another man's grain,
and may other men sleep with
her.[n]
11 For that would have been
shameful,
a sin to be judged.[o]
12 It is a fire[p] that burns to
Destruction;[a][q]
it would have uprooted my
harvest.[r]

13 "If I have denied justice to my
menservants and
maidservants
when they had a grievance
against me,[s]
14 what will I do when God
confronts me?
What will I answer when
called to account?
15 Did not he who made me in the
womb make them?
Did not the same one form us
both within our mothers?[t]

16 "If I have denied the desires of
the poor[u]
or let the eyes of the widow[v]
grow weary,
17 if I have kept my bread to
myself,
not sharing it with the
fatherless[w]—
18 but from my youth I reared him
as would a father,

30:23 u Job 9:22; Job 10:8 v Job 3:19
30:24 w Job 19:7
30:25 x Job 24:4; Ps 35:13-14; Ro 12:15
30:26 y Job 3:25-26; Job 19:8; Jer 8:15
30:27 z La 2:11
30:28 a Ps 38:6; Ps 42:9; Ps 43:2 b Job 19:7
30:29 c Ps 44:19 d Ps 102:6; Mic 1:8
30:30 e La 4:8 f Ps 102:3
30:31 g Isa 24:8
31:1 a Mt 5:28
31:2 b Job 20:29
31:3 c Job 21:30 d Job 34:22
31:4 e 2Ch 16:9 f Pr 5:21
31:5 g Mic 2:11
31:6 h Job 6:2; Job 27:5-6
31:7 i Job 23:11 j Job 9:30
31:8 k Lev 26:16; Job 20:18 l Mic 6:15
31:9 m Job 24:15
31:10 n Dt 28:30; Jer 8:10
31:11 o Ge 38:24; Lev 20:10; Dt 22:22-24
31:12 p Job 15:30 q Job 26:6 r Job 20:28
31:13 s Dt 24:14-15
31:15 t Job 10:3
31:16 u Job 5:16; Job 20:19 v Job 22:9
31:17 w Job 22:7 Job 29:12

a12 Hebrew *Abaddon*

and from my birth I guided
the widow—
19if I have seen anyone perishing
for lack of clothing,[x]
or a needy[y] man without a
garment,
20and his heart did not bless me
for warming him with the
fleece from my sheep,
21if I have raised my hand
against the fatherless,[z]
knowing that I had influence
in court,
22then let my arm fall from the
shoulder,
let it be broken off at the
joint.[a]
23For I dreaded destruction from
God,
and for fear of his splendour[b]
I could not do such things.

24"If I have put my trust in gold[c]
or said to pure gold, 'You are
my security,'[d]
25if I have rejoiced over my great
wealth,[e]
the fortune my hands had
gained,
26if I have regarded the sun[f] in
its radiance
or the moon moving in
splendour,
27so that my heart was secretly
enticed
and my hand offered them a
kiss of homage,
28then these also would be sins to
be judged,[g]
for I would have been
unfaithful to God on high.

29"If I have rejoiced at my
enemy's misfortune[h]
or gloated over the trouble
that came to him[i]—
30I have not allowed my mouth to
sin
by invoking a curse against
his life—
31if the men of my household
have never said,
'Who has not had his fill of
Job's meat?'[j]—
32but no stranger had to spend
the night in the street,
for my door was always open
to the traveller[k]—
33if I have concealed[l] my sin as
men do,[b]
by hiding[m] my guilt in my
heart
34because I so feared the crowd[n]
and so dreaded the contempt
of the clans
that I kept silent and would
not go outside—

35("Oh, that I had someone to
hear me![o]
I sign now my defence—let
the Almighty answer me;
let my accuser[p] put his
indictment in writing.
36Surely I would wear it on my
shoulder,
I would put it on like a crown.
37I would give him an account of
my every step;
like a prince[q] I would
approach him.)—
38"if my land cries out against
me[r]
and all its furrows are wet
with tears,
39if I have devoured its yield
without payment[s]
or broken the spirit of its
tenants,[t]
40then let briers[u] come up
instead of wheat
and weeds instead of barley."

The words of Job are ended.

Elihu

32 So these three men stopped
answering Job, because he
was righteous in his own eyes.[a]
2But Elihu son of Barakel the Bu-
zite,[b] of the family of Ram, became very angry with Job for
justifying himself rather than
God.[c] 3He was also angry with the
three friends, because they had

31:19 x Job 22:6 y Job 24:4
31:21 z Job 22:9
31:22 a Job 38:15
31:23 b Job 13:11
31:24 c Job 22:25 d Mt 6:24 Mk 10:24
31:25 e Ps 62:10
31:26 f Eze 8:16
31:28 g Dt 17:2-7
31:29 h Ob 1:12 i Pr 17:5 Pr 24:17-18
31:31 j Job 22:7
31:32 k Ge 19:2-3 Ro 12:13
31:33 l Pr 28:13 m Ge 3:8
31:34 n Ex 23:2
31:35 o Job 19:7 Job 30:28 p Job 27:7 Job 35:14
31:37 q Job 1:3 Job 29:25
31:38 r Ge 4:10
31:39 s 1Ki 21:19 t Lev 19:13 Jas 5:4
31:40 u Ge 3:18
32:1 a Job 10:7 Job 33:9
32:2 b Ge 22:21 c Job 27:5 Job 30:21

b33 Or *as Adam did*

found no way to refute Job, and yet
had condemned him.[a] 4 Now Elihu
had waited before speaking to Job
because they were older than he.
5 But when he saw that the three
men had nothing more to say, his
anger was aroused.

6 So Elihu son of Barakel the Bu-
zite said:

"I am young in years,
and you are old;[d]
that is why I was fearful,
not daring to tell you what I
know.
7 I thought, 'Age should speak;
advanced years should teach
wisdom.'
8 But it is the spirit[b] in a man,
the breath of the Almighty,[e]
that gives him
understanding.[f]
9 It is not only the old[c] who are
wise,[g]
not only the aged who
understand what is right.

10 "Therefore I say: Listen to me;
I too will tell you what I know.
11 I waited while you spoke,
I listened to your reasoning;
while you were searching for
words,
12 I gave you my full attention.
But not one of you has proved
Job wrong;
none of you has answered his
arguments.
13 Do not say, 'We have found
wisdom;[h]
let God refute him, not man.'
14 But Job has not marshalled his
words against me,
and I will not answer him with
your arguments.

15 "They are dismayed and have
no more to say;
words have failed them.
16 Must I wait, now that they are
silent,
now that they stand there with
no reply?
17 I too will have my say;
I too will tell what I know.
18 For I am full of words,
and the spirit within me
compels me;
19 inside I am like bottled-up wine,
like new wineskins ready to
burst.
20 I must speak and find relief;
I must open my lips and reply.
21 I will show partiality[i] to
no-one,[j]
nor will I flatter any man;
22 for if I were skilled in flattery,
my Maker would soon take me
away.

33

"But now, Job, listen to
my words;
pay attention to everything I
say.[a]
2 I am about to open my mouth;
my words are on the tip of my
tongue.
3 My words come from an
upright heart;
my lips sincerely speak what I
know.[b]
4 The Spirit of God has made me;[c]
the breath of the Almighty[d]
gives me life.
5 Answer me[e] then, if you can;
prepare[f] yourself and
confront me.
6 I am just like you before God;
I too have been taken from
clay.[g]
7 No fear of me should alarm
you,
nor should my hand be heavy
upon you.[h]

8 "But you have said in my
hearing—
I heard the very words—
9 'I am pure[i] and without sin;[j]
I am clean and free from
guilt.
10 Yet God has found fault with
me;
he considers me his enemy.[k]
11 He fastens my feet in
shackles;[l]

32:6 d Job 15:10
32:8 e Job 27:3; Job 33:4 f Pr 2:6
32:9 g 1Co 1:26
32:13 h Jer 9:23
32:21 i Lev 19:15; Job 13:10 j Mt 22:16
33:1 a Job 13:6
33:3 b Job 6:28; Job 27:4; Job 36:4
33:4 c Ge 2:7; Job 10:3 d Job 27:3
33:5 e ver 32 f Job 13:18
33:6 g Job 4:19
33:7 h Job 9:34; Job 13:21; 2Co 2:4
33:9 i Job 10:7 j Job 13:23; Job 16:17
33:10 k Job 13:24
33:11 l Job 13:27

a 3 Masoretic Text; an ancient Hebrew scribal tradition *Job, and so had condemned God*
b 8 Or *Spirit*; also in verse 18 c 9 Or *many*; or *great*

he keeps close watch on all
my paths.'[m]

12"But I tell you, in this you are
not right,
for God is greater than man.[n]
13Why do you complain to him[o]
that he answers none of man's
words?[a]
14For God does speak[p]—now one
way, now another—
though man may not perceive
it.
15In a dream,[q] in a vision of the
night,
when deep sleep falls on men
as they slumber in their beds,
16he may speak[r] in their ears
and terrify them with
warnings,
17to turn man from wrongdoing
and keep him from pride,
18to preserve his soul from the
pit,[b][s]
his life from perishing by the
sword.[c][t]
19Or a man may be chastened on
a bed of pain
with constant distress in his
bones,[u]
20so that his very being finds
food[v] repulsive
and his soul loathes the
choicest meal.[w]
21His flesh wastes away to
nothing,
and his bones, once hidden,
now stick out.[x]
22His soul draws near to the pit,[d]
and his life to the messengers
of death.[e][y]

23"Yet if there is an angel on his
side
as a mediator, one out of a
thousand,
to tell a man what is right for
him,[z]
24to be gracious to him and say,
'Spare him from going down
to the pit;[f][a]
I have found a ransom for
him'—
25then his flesh is renewed like a
child's;
it is restored as in the days of
his youth.[b]
26He prays to God and finds
favour with him,[c]
he sees God's face and shouts
for joy;[d]
he is restored by God to his
righteous state.[e]
27Then he comes to men and says,
'I have sinned,[f] and perverted
what was right,[g]
but I did not get what I
deserved.[h]
28He redeemed my soul from
going down to the pit,[g]
and I shall live to enjoy the
light.'[i]

29"God does all these things to a
man[j]—
twice, even three times—
30to turn back his soul from the
pit,[h]
that the light of life[k] may
shine on him.

31"Pay attention, Job, and listen
to me;
be silent, and I will speak.
32If you have anything to say,
answer me;
speak up, for I want you to be
cleared.
33But if not, then listen to me;
be silent, and I will teach you
wisdom.[l]"

34

Then Elihu said:

2"Hear my words, you wise men;
listen to me, you men of
learning.
3For the ear tests words
as the tongue tastes food.[a]
4Let us discern for ourselves
what is right;
let us learn together what is
good.[b]

33:11 m Job 14:16
33:12 n Ecc 7:20
33:13 o Job 40:2; Isa 45:9
33:14 p Ps 62:11
33:15 q Job 4:13
33:16 r Job 36:10,15
33:18 s ver 22,24,28, 30; t Job 15:22
33:19 u Job 30:17
33:20 v Ps 107:18; w Job 3:24; Job 6:6
33:21 x Job 16:8; Job 19:20
33:22 y Ps 88:3
33:23 z Mic 6:8
33:24 a Isa 38:17
33:25 b 2Ki 5:14
33:26 c Job 34:28; d Job 22:26; e Ps 50:15; Ps 51:12
33:27 f 2Sa 12:13; g Lk 15:21; h Ro 6:21
33:28 i Job 22:28
33:29 j 1Co 12:6; Eph 1:11; Php 2:13
33:30 k Ps 56:13
33:33 l Ps 34:11
34:3 a Job 12:11
34:4 b 1Th 5:21

[a]13 Or *that he does not answer for any of his actions* [b]18 Or *preserve him from the grave* [c]18 Or *from crossing the River* [d]22 Or *He draws near to the grave* [e]22 Or *to the dead* [f]24 Or *grave* [g]28 Or *redeemed me from going down to the grave* [h]30 Or *turn him back from the grave*

5 "Job says, 'I am innocent,[c]
but God denies me justice.[d]
6 Although I am right,
I am considered a liar;
although I am guiltless,
his arrow inflicts an incurable
wound.'[e]
7 What man is like Job,
who drinks scorn like water?[f]
8 He keeps company with
evildoers;
he associates with wicked
men.[g]
9 For he says, 'It profits a man
nothing
when he tries to please God.'[h]

10 "So listen to me, you men of
understanding.
Far be it from God to do
evil,[i]
from the Almighty to do
wrong.[j]
11 He repays a man for what he
has done;[k]
he brings upon him what his
conduct deserves.[l]
12 It is unthinkable that God would
do wrong,
that the Almighty would
pervert justice.[m]
13 Who appointed him over the
earth?
Who put him in charge of the
whole world?[n]
14 If it were his intention
and he withdrew his spirit[a]
and breath,[o]
15 all mankind would perish
together
and man would return to the
dust.[p]

16 "If you have understanding,
hear this;
listen to what I say.
17 Can he who hates justice
govern?[q]
Will you condemn the just and
mighty One?[r]
18 Is he not the One who says to
kings, 'You are worthless,'
and to nobles, 'You are
wicked,'[s]

34:5 c Job 33:9 d Job 27:2
34:6 e Job 6:4
34:7 f Job 15:16
34:8 g Job 22:15; Ps 50:18
34:9 h Job 21:15; Job 35:3
34:10 i Ge 18:25 j Dt 32:4; Job 8:3; Ro 9:14
34:11 k Ps 62:12; Mt 16:27; Ro 2:6; 2Co 5:10 l Jer 32:19; Eze 33:20
34:12 m Job 8:3
34:13 n Job 38:4,6
34:14 o Ps 104:29
34:15 p Ge 3:19; Job 9:22
34:17 q 2Sa 23:3-4 r Job 40:8
34:18 s Ex 22:28
34:19 t Dt 10:17; Ac 10:34 u Lev 19:15 v Job 10:3
34:20 w Ex 12:29 x Job 12:19
34:21 y Job 31:4; Pr 15:3
34:22 z Ps 139:12 a Am 9:2-3
34:23 b Job 11:11
34:24 c Job 12:19 d Da 2:21
34:27 e Ps 28:5; Isa 5:12 f 1Sa 15:11
34:28 g Ex 22:23; Job 35:9; Jas 5:4
34:30 h Pr 29:2-12

19 who shows no partiality[t] to
princes
and does not favour the rich
over the poor,[u]
for they are all the work of his
hands?[v]
20 They die in an instant, in the
middle of the night;[w]
the people are shaken and
they pass away;
the mighty are removed
without human hand.[x]

21 "His eyes are on the ways of
men;
he sees their every step.[y]
22 There is no dark place,[z] no
deep shadow,[a]
where evildoers can hide.
23 God has no need to examine
men further,
that they should come before
him for judgment.[b]
24 Without enquiry he shatters the
mighty[c]
and sets up others in their
place.[d]
25 Because he takes note of their
deeds,
he overthrows them in the
night and they are crushed.
26 He punishes them for their
wickedness
where everyone can see them,
27 because they turned from
following him[e]
and had no regard for any of
his ways.[f]
28 They caused the cry of the poor
to come before him,
so that he heard the cry of the
needy.[g]
29 But if he remains silent, who
can condemn him?
If he hides his face, who can
see him?
Yet he is over man and nation
alike,
30 to keep a godless man from
ruling,
from laying snares for the
people.[h]

[a] *14* Or *Spirit*

31 "Suppose a man says to God,
'I am guilty but will offend no more.
32 Teach me what I cannot see;[i]
if I have done wrong, I will not do so again.'[j]
33 Should God then reward you on your terms,
when you refuse to repent?[k]
You must decide, not I;
so tell me what you know.

34 "Men of understanding declare,
wise men who hear me say to me,
35 'Job speaks without knowledge;[l]
his words lack insight.'
36 Oh, that Job might be tested to the utmost
for answering like a wicked man![m]
37 To his sin he adds rebellion;
scornfully he claps his hands[n] among us
and multiplies his words against God."[o]

35

Then Elihu said:

2 "Do you think this is just?
You say, 'I shall be cleared by God.'[a]
3 Yet you ask him, 'What profit is it to me,[b]
and what do I gain by not sinning?'[a]

4 "I would like to reply to you
and to your friends with you.
5 Look up at the heavens[b] and see;
gaze at the clouds so high above you.[c]
6 If you sin, how does that affect him?
If your sins are many, what does that do to him?[d]
7 If you are righteous, what do you give to him,[e]
or what does he receive[f] from your hand?[g]
8 Your wickedness affects only a man like yourself,
and your righteousness only the sons of men.

9 "Men cry out[h] under a load of oppression;
they plead for relief from the arm of the powerful.[i]
10 But no-one says, 'Where is God my Maker,[j]
who gives songs in the night,[k]
11 who teaches[l] more to us than to[c] the beasts of the earth
and makes us wiser than[d] the birds of the air?'
12 He does not answer[m] when men cry out
because of the arrogance of the wicked.
13 Indeed, God does not listen to their empty plea;
the Almighty pays no attention to it.[n]
14 How much less, then, will he listen
when you say that you do not see him,[o]
that your case[p] is before him
and you must wait for him,
15 and further, that his anger never punishes
and he does not take the least notice of wickedness.[e]
16 So Job opens his mouth with empty talk;
without knowledge he multiplies words."[q]

36

Elihu continued:

2 "Bear with me a little longer
and I will show you
that there is more to be said on God's behalf.
3 I get my knowledge from afar;
I will ascribe justice to my Maker.[a]
4 Be assured that my words are not false;[b]

34:32 *i* Job 35:11; Ps 25:4 *j* Job 33:27
34:33 *k* Job 41:11
34:35 *l* Job 35:16; Job 38:2
34:36 *m* Job 22:15
34:37 *n* Job 27:23 *o* Job 23:2
35:3 *a* Job 9:29-31; Job 34:9
35:5 *b* Ge 15:5 *c* Job 22:12
35:6 *d* Pr 8:36
35:7 *e* Ro 11:35 *f* Pr 9:12 *g* Job 22:2-3; Lk 17:10
35:9 *h* Ex 2:23 *i* Job 12:19
35:10 *j* Job 27:10; Isa 51:13 *k* Ps 42:8; Ps 149:5; Ac 16:25
35:11 *l* Ps 94:12
35:12 *m* Pr 1:28
35:13 *n* Job 27:9; Pr 15:29; Isa 1:15; Jer 11:11
35:14 *o* Job 9:11 *p* Ps 37:6
35:16 *q* Job 34:35,37
36:3 *a* Job 8:3; Job 37:23
36:4 *b* Job 33:3

[a] 2 Or *My righteousness is more than God's*
[b] 3 Or *you*
[c] 11 Or *teaches us by*
[d] 11 Or *us wise by*
[e] 15 Symmachus, Theodotion and Vulgate; the meaning of the Hebrew for this word is uncertain.

one perfect in knowledge[c] is
with you.

5 "God is mighty, but does not
despise men;[d]
he is mighty, and firm in his
purpose.[e]
6 He does not keep the wicked
alive[f]
but gives the afflicted their
rights.[g]
7 He does not take his eyes off
the righteous;[h]
he enthrones them with
kings[i]
and exalts them for ever.
8 But if men are bound in
chains,[j]
held fast by cords of
affliction,
9 he tells them what they have
done—
that they have sinned
arrogantly.[k]
10 He makes them listen[l] to
correction
and commands them to repent
of their evil.[m]
11 If they obey and serve him,[n]
they will spend the rest of
their days in prosperity
and their years in
contentment.
12 But if they do not listen,
they will perish by the
sword[a][o]
and die without knowledge.[p]

13 "The godless in heart[q] harbour
resentment;
even when he fetters them,
they do not cry for help.
14 They die in their youth,
among male prostitutes of the
shrines.[r]
15 But those who suffer he
delivers in their suffering;
he speaks to them in their
affliction.

16 "He is wooing[s] you from the
jaws of distress
to a spacious place free from
restriction,
to the comfort of your table[t]
laden with choice food.
17 But now you are laden with the
judgment due to the
wicked;
judgment and justice have
taken hold of you.[u]
18 Be careful that no-one entices
you by riches;
do not let a large bribe turn
you aside.[v]
19 Would your wealth
or even all your mighty
efforts
sustain you so you would not
be in distress?
20 Do not long for the night,[w]
to drag people away from
their homes.[b]
21 Beware of turning to evil,[x]
which you seem to prefer to
affliction.[y]

22 "God is exalted in his power.
Who is a teacher like him?[z]
23 Who has prescribed his ways
for him,[a]
or said to him, 'You have done
wrong'?[b]
24 Remember to extol his work,[c]
which men have praised in
song.[d]
25 All mankind has seen it;
men gaze on it from afar.
26 How great is God—beyond our
understanding![e]
The number of his years is
past finding out.[f]

27 "He draws up the drops of
water,
which distil as rain to the
streams;[c][g]
28 the clouds pour down their
moisture
and abundant showers fall on
mankind.[h]
29 Who can understand how he
spreads out the clouds,
how he thunders from his
pavilion?[i]

36:4 c Job 37:5,16,23
36:5 d Ps 22:24; e Job 12:13
36:6 f Job 8:22; g Job 5:15
36:7 h Ps 33:18; i Ps 113:8
36:8 j Ps 107:10,14
36:9 k Job 15:25
36:10 l Job 33:16; m 2Ki 17:13
36:11 n Isa 1:19
36:12 o Job 15:22; p Job 4:21
36:13 q Ro 2:5
36:14 r Dt 23:17
36:16 s Hos 2:14; t Ps 23:5
36:17 u Job 22:11
36:18 v Job 34:33
36:20 w Job 34:20,25
36:21 x Ps 66:18; y Heb 11:25
36:22 z Isa 40:13; 1Co 2:16
36:23 a Job 34:13; b Job 8:3
36:24 c Ps 92:5; Ps 138:5; d Ps 59:16; Rev 15:3
36:26 e 1Co 13:12; f Job 10:5; Ps 90:2; Ps 102:24; Heb 1:12
36:27 g Job 38:28; Ps 147:8
36:28 h Job 5:10
36:29 i Job 26:14; Job 37:16

a 12 Or *will cross the River* b 20 The meaning of the Hebrew for verses 18–20 is uncertain. c 27 Or *distil from the mist as rain*

30 See how he scatters his
lightning about him,
bathing the depths of the sea.
31 This is the way he governs[d] the
nations[j]
and provides food in
abundance.[k]
32 He fills his hands with lightning
and commands it to strike its
mark.[l]
33 His thunder announces the
coming storm;
even the cattle make known
its approach.[e]

37 "At this my heart pounds
and leaps from its place.
2 Listen! Listen to the roar of his
voice,
to the rumbling that comes
from his mouth.[a]
3 He unleashes his lightning
beneath the whole heaven
and sends it to the ends of the
earth.
4 After that comes the sound of
his roar;
he thunders with his majestic
voice.
When his voice resounds,
he holds nothing back.
5 God's voice thunders in
marvellous ways;
he does great things beyond
our understanding.[b]
6 He says to the snow,[c] 'Fall on
the earth,'
and to the rain shower, 'Be a
mighty downpour.'[d]
7 So that all men he has made
may know his work,
he stops every man from his
labour.[a][e]
8 The animals take cover;
they remain in their dens.[f]
9 The tempest comes out from its
chamber,
the cold from the driving
winds.
10 The breath of God produces ice,
and the broad waters become
frozen.[g]
11 He loads the clouds with
moisture;
he scatters his lightning
through them.[h]
12 At his direction they swirl
around
over the face of the whole
earth
to do whatever he commands
them.[i]
13 He brings the clouds to punish
men,[j]
or to water his earth[b] and
show his love.[k]

14 "Listen to this, Job;
stop and consider God's
wonders.
15 Do you know how God controls
the clouds
and makes his lightning flash?
16 Do you know how the clouds
hang poised,
those wonders of him who is
perfect in knowledge?[l]
17 You who swelter in your clothes
when the land lies hushed
under the south wind,
18 can you join him in spreading
out the skies,[m]
hard as a mirror of cast
bronze?

19 "Tell us what we should say to
him;
we cannot draw up our case
because of our darkness.
20 Should he be told that I want to
speak?
Would any man ask to be
swallowed up?
21 Now no-one can look at the sun,
bright as it is in the skies
after the wind has swept them
clean.
22 Out of the north he comes in
golden splendour;
God comes in awesome
majesty.
23 The Almighty is beyond our
reach and exalted in
power;[n]

36:31 *j* Job 37:13 *k* Ps 136:25; Ac 14:17
36:32 *l* Job 37:12,15
37:2 *a* Ps 29:3-9
37:5 *b* Job 5:9
37:6 *c* Job 38:22 *d* Job 36:27
37:7 *e* Job 12:14
37:8 *f* Job 38:40; Ps 104:22
37:10 *g* Job 38:29-30; Ps 147:17
37:11 *h* Job 36:27,29
37:12 *i* Ps 148:8
37:13 *j* 1Sa 12:17 *k* Ex 9:18; 1Ki 18:45; Job 38:27
37:16 *l* Job 36:4
37:18 *m* Job 9:8; Ps 104:2; Isa 44:24
37:23 *n* Job 9:4; Job 36:4; 1Ti 6:16

[d]31 Or *nourishes* [e]33 Or *announces his coming— / the One zealous against evil*
[a]7 Or / *he fills all men with fear by his power*
[b]13 Or *to favour them*

in his justice[o] and great
righteousness, he does not
oppress.[p]
24Therefore, men revere him,[q]
for does he not have regard
for all the wise[r] in
heart?"[c]

The LORD Speaks

38 Then the LORD answered
Job out of the storm.[a] He
said:

2"Who is this that darkens my
counsel
with words without
knowledge?[b]
3Brace yourself like a man;
I will question you,
and you shall answer me.[c]

4"Where were you when I laid
the earth's foundation?[d]
Tell me, if you understand.
5Who marked off its
dimensions?[e] Surely you
know!
Who stretched a measuring
line across it?
6On what were its footings set,
or who laid its cornerstone[f]—
7while the morning stars sang
together
and all the angels[a] shouted
for joy?

8"Who shut up the sea behind
doors[g]
when it burst forth from the
womb,[h]
9when I made the clouds its
garment
and wrapped it in thick
darkness,
10when I fixed limits for it[i]
and set its doors and bars in
place,[j]
11when I said, 'This far you may
come and no farther;
here is where your proud
waves halt'?[k]

12"Have you ever given orders to
the morning,
or shown the dawn its place,

37:23 o Job 8:3 p Isa 63:9 Eze 18:23,32
37:24 q Mt 10:28 r Mt 11:25
38:1 a Job 40:6
38:2 b Job 35:16 Job 42:3 1Ti 1:7
38:3 c Job 40:7
38:4 d Ps 104:5 Pr 8:29
38:5 e Pr 8:29 Isa 40:12
38:6 f Job 26:7
38:8 g Jer 5:22 h Ge 1:9-10
38:10 i Ps 33:7 Ps 104:9 j Job 26:10
38:11 k Ps 89:9
38:13 l Ps 104:35
38:15 m Job 18:5 n Ps 10:15
38:16 o Ps 77:19
38:17 p Ps 9:13
38:18 q Job 28:24
38:20 r Job 26:10
38:21 s Job 15:7
38:22 t Job 37:6
38:23 u Isa 30:30 Eze 13:11 v Ex 9:18 Jos 10:11 Rev 16:21

13that it might take the earth by
the edges
and shake the wicked[l] out of
it?
14The earth takes shape like clay
under a seal;
its features stand out like
those of a garment.
15The wicked are denied their
light,[m]
and their upraised arm is
broken.[n]

16"Have you journeyed to the
springs of the sea
or walked in the recesses of
the deep?[o]
17Have the gates of death[p] been
shown to you?
Have you seen the gates of the
shadow of death?[b]
18Have you comprehended the
vast expanses of the
earth?[q]
Tell me, if you know all this.

19"What is the way to the abode
of light?
And where does darkness
reside?
20Can you take them to their
places?
Do you know the paths[r] to
their dwellings?
21Surely you know, for you were
already born![s]
You have lived so many years!

22"Have you entered the
storehouses of the snow[t]
or seen the storehouses of the
hail,
23which I reserve for times of
trouble,[u]
for days of war and battle?[v]
24What is the way to the place
where the lightning is
dispersed,
or the place where the east
winds are scattered over
the earth?

c24 Or *for he does not have regard for any who think they are wise.* a7 Hebrew *the sons of God* b17 Or *gates of deep shadows*

25Who cuts a channel for the
torrents of rain,
and a path for the
thunderstorm,[w]
26to water[x] a land where no man
lives,
a desert with no-one in it,
27to satisfy a desolate wasteland
and make it sprout with
grass?[y]
28Does the rain have a father?[z]
Who fathers the drops of dew?
29From whose womb comes the
ice?
Who gives birth to the frost
from the heavens[a]
30when the waters become hard
as stone,
when the surface of the deep
is frozen?[b]

31"Can you bind the beautiful[c]
Pleiades?
Can you loose the cords of
Orion?[c]
32Can you bring forth the
constellations in their
seasons[d]
or lead out the Bear[e] with its
cubs?
33Do you know the laws[d] of the
heavens?
Can you set up ⌞God's[f]⌟
dominion over the earth?

34"Can you raise your voice to the
clouds
and cover yourself with a
flood of water?[e]
35Do you send the lightning bolts
on their way?[f]
Do they report to you, 'Here
we are'?
36Who endowed the heart[g] with
wisdom[g]
or gave understanding[h] to the
mind?[h]
37Who has the wisdom to count
the clouds?
Who can tip over the water
jars of the heavens
38when the dust becomes hard
and the clods of earth stick
together?

39"Do you hunt the prey for the
lioness
and satisfy the hunger of the
lions[i]
40when they crouch in their
dens[j]
or lie in wait in a thicket?
41Who provides food for the
raven[k]
when its young cry out to God
and wander about for lack of
food?[l]

39 "Do you know when the
mountain goats[a] give
birth?
Do you watch when the doe
bears her fawn?
2Do you count the months till
they bear?
Do you know the time they
give birth?
3They crouch down and bring
forth their young;
their labour pains are ended.
4Their young thrive and grow
strong in the wilds;
they leave and do not return.

5"Who let the wild donkey[b] go
free?
Who untied his ropes?
6I gave him the wasteland[c] as
his home,
the salt flats as his habitat.[d]
7He laughs at the commotion in
the town;
he does not hear a driver's
shout.[e]
8He ranges the hills for his
pasture
and searches for any green
thing.

9"Will the wild ox[f] consent to
serve you?
Will he stay by your manger
at night?
10Can you hold him to the furrow
with a harness?

38:25 *w* Job 28:26
38:26 *x* Job 36:27
38:27 *y* Ps 104:14; Ps 107:35
38:28 *z* Ps 147:8; Jer 14:22
38:29 *a* Ps 147:16-17
38:30 *b* Job 37:10
38:31 *c* Job 9:9; Am 5:8
38:33 *d* Ps 148:6; Jer 31:36
38:34 *e* Job 22:11; Job 36:27-28
38:35 *f* Job 36:32; Job 37:3
38:36 *g* Job 9:4; *h* Job 32:8; Ps 51:6; Ecc 2:26
38:39 *i* Ps 104:21
38:40 *j* Job 37:8
38:41 *k* Lk 12:24; *l* Ps 147:9; Mt 6:26
39:1 *a* Dt 14:5
39:5 *b* Job 6:5; Job 11:12; Job 24:5
39:6 *c* Job 24:5; Ps 107:34; Jer 2:24; *d* Hos 8:9
39:7 *e* Job 3:18
39:9 *f* Nu 23:22; Dt 33:17

c31 Or *the twinkling*; or *the chains of the*
d32 Or *the morning star in its season*
e32 Or *out Leo* f33 Or *his*; or *their*
g36 The meaning of the Hebrew for this word is uncertain. h36 The meaning of the Hebrew for this word is uncertain.

Will he till the valleys behind you?
11 Will you rely on him for his great strength?
Will you leave your heavy work to him?
12 Can you trust him to bring in your grain
and gather it to your threshing-floor?

13 "The wings of the ostrich flap joyfully,
but they cannot compare with the pinions and feathers of the stork.
14 She lays her eggs on the ground
and lets them warm in the sand,
15 unmindful that a foot may crush them,
that some wild animal may trample them.
16 She treats her young harshly,[g]
as if they were not hers;
she cares not that her labour was in vain,
17 for God did not endow her with wisdom
or give her a share of good sense.[h]
18 Yet when she spreads her feathers to run,
she laughs at horse and rider.

19 "Do you give the horse his strength
or clothe his neck with a flowing mane?
20 Do you make him leap like a locust,[i]
striking terror with his proud snorting?[j]
21 He paws fiercely, rejoicing in his strength,
and charges into the fray.[k]
22 He laughs at fear, afraid of nothing;
he does not shy away from the sword.
23 The quiver rattles against his side,
along with the flashing spear and lance.
24 In frenzied excitement he eats up the ground;
he cannot stand still when the trumpet sounds.[l]
25 At the blast of the trumpet[m] he snorts, 'Aha!'
He catches the scent of battle from afar,
the shout of commanders and the battle cry.[n]

26 "Does the hawk take flight by your wisdom
and spread his wings towards the south?
27 Does the eagle soar at your command
and build his nest on high?[o]
28 He dwells on a cliff and stays there at night;
a rocky crag is his stronghold.
29 From there he seeks out his food;[p]
his eyes detect it from afar.
30 His young ones feast on blood,
and where the slain are, there is he."[q]

40

The LORD said to Job:[a]

2 "Will the one who contends with the Almighty correct him?
Let him who accuses God answer him!"

3 Then Job answered the LORD:

4 "I am unworthy[b]—how can I reply to you?
I put my hand over my mouth.[c]
5 I spoke once, but I have no answer[d]—
twice, but I will say no more."[e]

6 Then the LORD spoke to Job out
of the storm:[f]

7 "Brace yourself like a man;
I will question you,
and you shall answer me.[g]

8 "Would you discredit my justice?[h]
Would you condemn me to justify yourself?

39:16 g La 4:3
39:17 h Job 35:11
39:20 i Joel 2:4-5; j Jer 8:16
39:21 k Jer 8:6
39:24 l Jer 4:5,19; Eze 7:14; Am 3:6
39:25 m Jos 6:5; n Am 1:14; Am 2:2
39:27 o Jer 49:16; Ob 1:4
39:29 p Job 9:26
39:30 q Mt 24:28; Lk 17:37
40:1 a Job 10:2; Job 13:3; Job 23:4; Job 31:35; Job 33:13
40:4 b Job 42:6; c Job 29:9
40:5 d Job 9:3; e Job 9:15
40:6 f Job 38:1
40:7 g Job 38:3; Job 42:4
40:8 h Job 27:2; Ro 3:3

9Do you have an arm like God's,[i]
and can your voice thunder like his?[j]
10Then adorn yourself with glory and splendour,
and clothe yourself in honour and majesty.[k]
11Unleash the fury of your wrath,[l]
look at every proud man and bring him low,[m]
12look at every proud man and humble him,[n]
crush[o] the wicked where they stand.
13Bury them all in the dust together;
shroud their faces in the grave.
14Then I myself will admit to you
that your own right hand can save you.[p]

15"Look at the behemoth,[a]
which I made along with you
and which feeds on grass like an ox.
16What strength he has in his loins,
what power in the muscles of his belly!
17His tail[b] sways like a cedar;
the sinews of his thighs are close-knit.
18His bones are tubes of bronze,
his limbs like rods of iron.
19He ranks first among the works of God,[q]
yet his Maker can approach him with his sword.
20The hills bring him their produce,[r]
and all the wild animals play[s] nearby.
21Under the lotus plant he lies,
hidden among the reeds in the marsh.
22The lotuses conceal him in their shadow;
the poplars by the stream[t] surround him.
23When the river rages, he is not alarmed;
he is secure, though the Jordan should surge against his mouth.
24Can anyone capture him by the eyes,[c]
or trap him and pierce his nose?[u]

41

"Can you pull in the leviathan[a][a] with a fishhook
or tie down his tongue with a rope?
2Can you put a cord through his nose
or pierce his jaw with a hook?[b]
3Will he keep begging you for mercy?
Will he speak to you with gentle words?
4Will he make an agreement with you
for you to take him as your slave for life?[c]
5Can you make a pet of him like a bird
or put him on a leash for your girls?
6Will traders barter for him?
Will they divide him up among the merchants?
7Can you fill his hide with harpoons
or his head with fishing spears?
8If you lay a hand on him,
you will remember the struggle and never do it again!
9Any hope of subduing him is false;
the mere sight of him is overpowering.
10No-one is fierce enough to rouse him.[d]
Who then is able to stand against me?[e]
11Who has a claim against me that I must pay?[f]

40:9 *i* 2Ch 32:8 *j* Job 37:5; Ps 29:3-4
40:10 *k* Ps 93:1; Ps 104:1
40:11 *l* Isa 42:25; Na 1:6 *m* Isa 2:11,12, 17; Da 4:37
40:12 *n* 1Sa 2:7 *o* Isa 13:11; Isa 63:2-3,6
40:14 *p* Ps 20:6; Ps 60:5; Ps 108:6
40:19 *q* Job 41:33
40:20 *r* Ps 104:14 *s* Ps 104:26
40:22 *t* Isa 44:4
40:24 *u* Job 41:2,7,26
41:1 *a* Job 3:8; Ps 104:26; Isa 27:1
41:2 *b* Isa 37:29
41:4 *c* Ex 21:6
41:10 *d* Job 3:8 *e* Jer 50:44
41:11 *f* Ro 11:35

a *15* Possibly the hippopotamus or the elephant
b *17* Possibly trunk
c *24* Or *by a water hole*
a *1* Possibly the crocodile

Everything under heaven
belongs to me.[g]

12 "I will not fail to speak of his
limbs,
his strength and his graceful
form.
13 Who can strip off his outer
coat?
Who would approach him with
a bridle?
14 Who dares open the doors of his
mouth,
ringed about with his
fearsome teeth?
15 His back has[b] rows of shields
tightly sealed together;
16 each is so close to the next
that no air can pass between.
17 They are joined fast to one
another;
they cling together and cannot
be parted.
18 His snorting throws out flashes
of light;
his eyes are like the rays of
dawn.[h]
19 Firebrands stream from his
mouth;
sparks of fire shoot out.
20 Smoke pours from his nostrils
as from a boiling pot over a
fire of reeds.
21 His breath[i] sets coals ablaze,
and flames dart from his
mouth.[j]
22 Strength resides in his neck;
dismay goes before him.
23 The folds of his flesh are
tightly joined;
they are firm and immovable.
24 His chest is hard as rock,
hard as a lower millstone.
25 When he rises up, the mighty
are terrified;
they retreat before his
thrashing.
26 The sword that reaches him has
no effect,
nor does the spear or the dart
or the javelin.
27 Iron he treats like straw
and bronze like rotten wood.
28 Arrows do not make him flee;
slingstones are like chaff to
him.
29 A club seems to him but a piece
of straw;
he laughs at the rattling of the
lance.
30 His undersides are jagged
potsherds,
leaving a trail in the mud like
a threshing-sledge.[k]
31 He makes the depths churn like
a boiling cauldron
and stirs up the sea like a pot
of ointment.
32 Behind him he leaves a
glistening wake;
one would think the deep had
white hair.
33 Nothing on earth is his
equal[l]—
a creature without fear.
34 He looks down on all that are
haughty;
he is king over all that are
proud.[m]"

Job

42 Then Job replied to the LORD:

2 "I know that you can do all
things;[a]
no plan of yours can be
thwarted.[b]
3 ⌊You asked,⌋ 'Who is this that
obscures my counsel
without knowledge?'[c]
Surely I spoke of things I did
not understand,
things too wonderful for me to
know.[d]

4 ⌊"You said,⌋ 'Listen now, and I
will speak;
I will question you,
and you shall answer me.'[e]
5 My ears had heard of you[f]
but now my eyes have seen
you.[g]
6 Therefore I despise myself[h]
and repent in dust and
ashes."[i]

41:11 g Ex 19:5; Dt 10:14; Ps 24:1; Ps 50:12; 1Co 10:26
41:18 h Job 3:9
41:21 i Isa 40:7; j Ps 18:8
41:30 k Isa 41:15
41:33 l Job 40:19
41:34 m Job 28:8
42:2 a Ge 18:14; Mt 19:26; b 2Ch 20:6
42:3 c Job 38:2; d Ps 40:5; Ps 131:1; Ps 139:6
42:4 e Job 38:3; Job 40:7
42:5 f Job 26:14; Ro 10:17; g Jdg 13:22; Isa 6:5; Eph 1:17-18
42:6 h Job 40:4; i Ezr 9:6

b15 Or *His pride is his*

Epilogue

[7]After the LORD had said these
things to Job, he said to Eliphaz the
Temanite, "I am angry with you
and your two friends,[j] because
you have not spoken of me what is
right, as my servant Job has. [8]So
now take seven bulls and seven
rams[k] and go to my servant Job
and sacrifice a burnt offering[l] for
yourselves. My servant Job will
pray for you, and I will accept his
prayer[m] and not deal with you according
to your folly.[n] You have
not spoken of me what is right, as
my servant Job has." [9]So Eliphaz
the Temanite, Bildad the Shuhite
and Zophar the Naamathite did
what the LORD told them; and the
LORD accepted Job's prayer.

[10]After Job had prayed for his
friends, the LORD made him prosperous
again[o] and gave him twice
as much as he had before.[p] [11]All
his brothers and sisters and everyone
who had known him before[q]
came and ate with him in his house.

42:7
j Job 32:3

42:8
k Nu 23:1,29
l Job 1:5
m Ge 20:17
Jas 5:15-16
1Jn 5:16
n Job 22:30

42:10
o Dt 30:3
Ps 14:7
p Job 1:3
Ps 85:1-3
Ps 126:5-6

42:11
q Job 19:13

42:17
r Ge 15:15
Ge 25:8

They comforted and consoled him
over all the trouble the LORD had
brought upon him, and each one
gave him a piece of silver[a] and a
gold ring.

[12]The LORD blessed the latter
part of Job's life more than the
first. He had fourteen thousand
sheep, six thousand camels, a thousand
yoke of oxen and a thousand
donkeys. [13]And he also had seven
sons and three daughters. [14]The
first daughter he named Jemimah,
the second Keziah and the third
Keren-Happuch. [15]Nowhere in all
the land were there found women
as beautiful as Job's daughters,
and their father granted them
an inheritance along with their
brothers.

[16]After this, Job lived a hundred
and forty years; he saw his children
and their children to the
fourth generation. [17]And so he died,
old and full of years.[r]

[a]*11* Hebrew *him a kesitah*; a kesitah was a unit of money of unknown weight and value.

PSALMS

Book I: Psalms 1–41

Psalm 1

1 Blessed is the man
who does not walk[a] in the counsel of the wicked
or stand in the way of sinners
or sit[b] in the seat of mockers.
2 But his delight[c] is in the law of the LORD,[d]
and on his law he meditates[e] day and night.
3 He is like a tree[f] planted by streams of water,[g]
which yields its fruit[h] in season
and whose leaf does not wither.
Whatever he does prospers.[i]

4 Not so the wicked!
They are like chaff[j]
that the wind blows away.
5 Therefore the wicked will not stand[k] in the judgment,[l]
nor sinners in the assembly of the righteous.

6 For the LORD watches over[m] the way of the righteous,
but the way of the wicked will perish.[n]

Psalm 2

1 Why do the nations conspire[a]
and the peoples plot[a] in vain?
2 The kings[b] of the earth take their stand
and the rulers gather together against the LORD
and against his Anointed[c] One.[b][d]
3 "Let us break their chains,"
they say,
"and throw off their fetters."[e]

4 The One enthroned in heaven laughs;[f]
the Lord scoffs at them.
5 Then he rebukes them in his anger
and terrifies them in his wrath,[g] saying,
6 "I have installed my King[c]
on Zion, my holy hill."

7 I will proclaim the decree of the LORD:

He said to me, "You are my Son;[d]
today I have become your Father.[e][h]
8 Ask of me,
and I will make the nations your inheritance,
the ends of the earth[i] your possession.
9 You will rule them with an iron sceptre;[f][j]
you will dash them to pieces[k] like pottery.[l]"

10 Therefore, you kings, be wise;
be warned, you rulers of the earth.
11 Serve the LORD with fear
and rejoice[m] with trembling.[n]
12 Kiss the Son,[o] lest he be angry
and you be destroyed in your way,
for his wrath[p] can flare up in a moment.
Blessed are all who take refuge[q] in him.

Psalm 3

A psalm of David. When he fled from his son Absalom.[a]

1 O LORD, how many are my foes!
How many rise up against me!

[a]1 Hebrew; Septuagint *rage* [b]2 Or *anointed one* [c]6 Or *king* [d]7 Or *son*; also in verse 12 [e]7 Or *have begotten you* [f]9 Or *will break them with a rod of iron*

1:1 *a* Pr 4:14 *b* Ps 26:4 Jer 15:17
1:2 *c* Ps 119:16,35 *d* Ps 119:1 *e* Jos 1:8
1:3 *f* Ps 128:3 *g* Jer 17:8 *h* Eze 47:12 *i* Ge 39:3
1:4 *j* Job 21:18 Isa 17:13
1:5 *k* Ps 5:5 *l* Ps 9:7-8,16
1:6 *m* Ps 37:18 2Ti 2:19 *n* Ps 9:6
2:1 *a* Ps 21:11
2:2 *b* Ps 48:4 *c* Jn 1:41 *d* Ps 74:18,23 Ac 4:25-26*
2:3 *e* Jer 5:5
2:4 *f* Ps 37:13 Ps 59:8 Pr 1:26
2:5 *g* Ps 21:9 Ps 78:49-50
2:7 *h* Ac 13:33* Heb 1:5*
2:8 *i* Ps 22:27
2:9 *j* Rev 12:5 *k* Ps 89:23 *l* Rev 2:27*
2:11 *m* Heb 12:28 *n* Ps 119:119-120
2:12 *o* Jn 5:23 *p* Rev 6:16 *q* Ps 34:8 Ro 9:33
3 Title *a* 2Sa 15:14

2 Many are saying of me,
"God will not deliver him.[b]"
Selah[a]
3 But you are a shield[c] around me, O LORD;
you bestow glory on me and lift[b] up my head.[d]
4 To the LORD I cry aloud,
and he answers me from his holy hill.[e] *Selah*
5 I lie down and sleep;[f]
I wake again, because the LORD sustains me.
6 I will not fear[g] the tens of thousands
drawn up against me on every side.
7 Arise,[h] O LORD!
Deliver me,[i] O my God!
Strike[j] all my enemies on the jaw;
break the teeth[k] of the wicked.
8 From the LORD comes deliverance.[l]
May your blessing be on your people. *Selah*

Psalm 4

For the director of music. With stringed instruments. A psalm of David.

1 Answer me when I call to you,
O my righteous God.
Give me relief from my distress;
be merciful[a] to me and hear my prayer.[b]
2 How long, O men, will you turn my glory into shame?[a]
How long will you love delusions and seek false gods?[b][c] *Selah*
3 Know that the LORD has set apart the godly[d] for himself;
the LORD will hear[e] when I call to him.
4 In your anger do not sin;[f]
when you are on your beds,[g]

3:2 *b* Ps 71:11
3:3 *c* Ge 15:1 Ps 28:7 *d* Ps 27:6
3:4 *e* Ps 2:6
3:5 *f* Lev 26:6 Pr 3:24
3:6 *g* Ps 27:3
3:7 *h* Ps 7:6 *i* Ps 6:4 *j* Job 16:10 *k* Ps 58:6
3:8 *l* Isa 43:3,11
4:1 *a* Ps 25:16 *b* Ps 17:6
4:2 *c* Ps 31:6
4:3 *d* Ps 31:23 *e* Ps 6:8
4:4 *f* Eph 4:26* *g* Ps 77:6
4:5 *h* Dt 33:19 Ps 37:3
4:6 *i* Nu 6:25
4:7 *j* Ac 14:17 *k* Isa 9:3
4:8 *l* Ps 3:5 *m* Lev 25:18
5:2 *a* Ps 3:4 *b* Ps 84:3
5:3 *c* Ps 88:13
5:4 *d* Ps 11:5 Ps 92:15
5:5 *e* Ps 73:3 *f* Ps 1:5 *g* Ps 11:5
5:6 *h* Ps 55:23 Rev 21:8
5:7 *i* Ps 138:2

search your hearts and be silent. *Selah*
5 Offer right sacrifices
and trust in the LORD.[h]
6 Many are asking, "Who can show us any good?"
Let the light of your face shine upon us,[i] O LORD.
7 You have filled my heart[j] with greater joy[k]
than when their grain and new wine abound.
8 I will lie down and sleep[l] in peace,
for you alone, O LORD,
make me dwell in safety.[m]

Psalm 5

For the director of music. For flutes. A psalm of David.

1 Give ear to my words, O LORD,
consider my sighing.
2 Listen to my cry for help,[a]
my King and my God,[b]
for to you I pray.
3 In the morning,[c] O LORD, you hear my voice;
in the morning I lay my requests before you
and wait in expectation.
4 You are not a God who takes pleasure in evil;
with you the wicked[d] cannot dwell.
5 The arrogant[e] cannot stand[f] in your presence;
you hate[g] all who do wrong.
6 You destroy those who tell lies;[h]
bloodthirsty and deceitful men
the LORD abhors.
7 But I, by your great mercy,
will come into your house;
in reverence will I bow down[i]
towards your holy temple.

a2 A word of uncertain meaning, occurring frequently in the Psalms; possibly a musical term
b3 Or *LORD, / my Glorious One, who lifts*
a2 Or *you dishonour my Glorious One*
b2 Or *seek lies*

8 Lead me, O LORD, in your
righteousness[j]
because of my enemies—
make straight your way[k]
before me.

9 Not a word from their mouth
can be trusted;
their heart is filled with
destruction.
Their throat is an open grave;[l]
with their tongue they speak
deceit.[m]
10 Declare them guilty, O God!
Let their intrigues be their
downfall.
Banish them for their many
sins,[n]
for they have rebelled[o]
against you.

11 But let all who take refuge in
you be glad;
let them ever sing for joy.[p]
Spread your protection over
them,
that those who love your
name[q] may rejoice in
you.[r]
12 For surely, O LORD, you bless
the righteous;
you surround them[s] with your
favour as with a shield.

Psalm 6

For the director of music. With stringed instruments. According to *sheminith*.[a] A psalm of David.

1 O LORD, do not rebuke me in
your anger[a]
or discipline me in your
wrath.
2 Be merciful to me, LORD, for I
am faint;
O LORD, heal me,[b] for my
bones are in agony.[c]
3 My soul is in anguish.[d]
How long,[e] O LORD, how long?

4 Turn, O LORD, and deliver me;
save me because of your
unfailing love.[f]
5 No-one remembers you when he
is dead.

5:8 j Ps 31:1 k Ps 27:11
5:9 l Lk 11:44 m Ro 3:13*
5:10 n Ps 9:16 o Ps 107:11
5:11 p Ps 2:12 q Ps 69:36 r Isa 65:13
5:12 s Ps 32:7
6:1 a Ps 38:1
6:2 b Hos 6:1 c Ps 22:14 Ps 31:10
6:3 d Jn 12:27 e Ps 90:13
6:4 f Ps 17:13
6:5 g Ps 30:9 Ps 88:10-12 Ecc 9:10 Isa 38:18
6:6 h Ps 69:3 i Ps 42:3
6:7 j Ps 31:9
6:8 k Ps 119:115 l Mt 7:23 Lk 13:27
6:9 m Ps 116:1
6:10 n Ps 71:24 Ps 73:19
7:1 a Ps 31:15
7:2 b Isa 38:13 c Ps 50:22
7:3 d 1Sa 24:11 Isa 59:3

Who praises you from his
grave?[b][g]

6 I am worn out[h] from groaning;
all night long I flood my bed
with weeping
and drench my couch with
tears.[i]
7 My eyes grow weak[j] with
sorrow;
they fail because of all my
foes.

8 Away from me,[k] all you who do
evil,[l]
for the LORD has heard my
weeping.
9 The LORD has heard my cry for
mercy;[m]
the LORD accepts my prayer.
10 All my enemies will be ashamed
and dismayed;
they will turn back in sudden
disgrace.[n]

Psalm 7

A *shiggaion*[a] of David, which he sang to the LORD concerning Cush, a Benjamite.

1 O LORD my God, I take refuge
in you;
save and deliver me from all
who pursue me,[a]
2 or they will tear me like a lion[b]
and rip me to pieces with
no-one to rescue[c] me.

3 O LORD my God, if I have done
this
and there is guilt on my
hands[d]—
4 if I have done evil to him who
is at peace with me
or without cause have robbed
my foe—
5 then let my enemy pursue and
overtake me;
let him trample my life to the
ground

[a]Title: Probably a musical term [b]5 Hebrew *Sheol* [a]Title: Probably a literary or musical term

and make me sleep in the
dust. *Selah*

6 Arise,[e] O LORD, in your anger;
rise up against the rage of my
enemies.[f]
Awake,[g] my God; decree
justice.
7 Let the assembled peoples
gather round you.
Rule over them from on high;
8 let the LORD judge the peoples.
Judge me, O LORD, according to
my righteousness,[h]
according to my integrity,
O Most High.
9 O righteous God,[i]
who searches minds and
hearts,[j]
bring to an end the violence of
the wicked
and make the righteous
secure.[k]

10 My shield[b] is God Most High,
who saves the upright in
heart.[l]
11 God is a righteous judge,[m]
a God who expresses his
wrath every day.
12 If he does not relent,
he[c] will sharpen his sword;[n]
he will bend and string his
bow.
13 He has prepared his deadly
weapons;
he makes ready his flaming
arrows.

14 He who is pregnant with evil
and conceives trouble gives
birth[o] to disillusionment.
15 He who digs a hole and scoops
it out
falls into the pit he has
made.[p]
16 The trouble he causes recoils on
himself;
his violence comes down on
his own head.

17 I will give thanks to the LORD
because of his
righteousness[q]
and will sing praise[r] to the
name of the LORD Most
High.

Psalm 8

For the director of music. According to *gittith*.[a] A psalm of David.

1 O LORD, our Lord,
how majestic is your name in
all the earth!

You have set your glory
above the heavens.[a]
2 From the lips of children and
infants
you have ordained praise[b][b]
because of your enemies,
to silence the foe[c] and the
avenger.

3 When I consider your
heavens,[d]
the work of your fingers,
the moon and the stars,[e]
which you have set in place,
4 what is man that you are
mindful of him,
the son of man that you care
for him?[f]
5 You made him a little lower
than the heavenly beings[c]
and crowned him with glory
and honour.[g]

6 You made him ruler[h] over the
works of your hands;
you put everything under his
feet:[i][j]
7 all flocks and herds,
and the beasts of the field,
8 the birds of the air,
and the fish of the sea,
all that swim the paths of the
seas.

9 O LORD, our Lord,
how majestic is your name in
all the earth![k]

7:6 *e* Ps 94:2 *f* Ps 138:7 *g* Ps 44:23
7:8 *h* Ps 18:20; Ps 96:13
7:9 *i* Jer 11:20 *j* 1Ch 28:9; Ps 26:2; Rev 2:23 *k* Ps 37:23
7:10 *l* Ps 125:4
7:11 *m* Ps 50:6
7:12 *n* Dt 32:41
7:14 *o* Job 15:35; Isa 59:4; Jas 1:15
7:15 *p* Job 4:8
7:17 *q* Ps 71:15-16 *r* Ps 9:2
8:1 *a* Ps 57:5; Ps 113:4; Ps 148:13
8:2 *b* Mt 21:16* *c* Ps 44:16; 1Co 1:27
8:3 *d* Ps 89:11 *e* Ps 136:9
8:4 *f* Job 7:17; Ps 144:3; Heb 2:6
8:5 *g* Ps 21:5; Ps 103:4
8:6 *h* Ge 1:28 *i* Heb 2:6-8* *j* 1Co 15:25, 27*; Eph 1:22
8:9 *k* ver 1

[b]10 Or *sovereign* [c]12 Or *If a man does not repent, / God* [a]Title: Probably a musical term [b]2 Or *strength* [c]5 Or *than God*

Psalm 9[a]

For the director of music. To ⌞the tune of⌟ "The Death of the Son". A psalm of David.

1 I will praise you, O LORD, with
all my heart;[a]
I will tell of all your
wonders.[b]
2 I will be glad and rejoice[c] in
you;
I will sing praise to your
name,[d] O Most High.

3 My enemies turn back;
they stumble and perish
before you.
4 For you have upheld my right
and my cause;[e]
you have sat on your throne,
judging righteously.[f]
5 You have rebuked the nations
and destroyed the wicked;
you have blotted out their
name[g] for ever and ever.
6 Endless ruin has overtaken the
enemy,
you have uprooted their cities;
even the memory of them[h]
has perished.

7 The LORD reigns for ever;
he has established his throne[i]
for judgment.
8 He will judge the world in
righteousness;[j]
he will govern the peoples
with justice.
9 The LORD is a refuge for the
oppressed,
a stronghold in times of
trouble.[k]
10 Those who know your name[l]
will trust in you,
for you, LORD, have never
forsaken[m] those who seek
you.

11 Sing praises to the LORD,
enthroned in Zion;[n]
proclaim among the nations[o]
what he has done.[p]
12 For he who avenges blood[q]
remembers;
he does not ignore the cry of
the afflicted.

9:1 a Ps 86:12 b Ps 26:7
9:2 c Ps 5:11 d Ps 92:1; Ps 83:18
9:4 e Ps 140:12 f 1Pe 2:23
9:5 g Pr 10:7
9:6 h Ps 34:16
9:7 i Ps 89:14
9:8 j Ps 96:13
9:9 k Ps 32:7
9:10 l Ps 91:14 m Ps 37:28
9:11 n Ps 76:2 o Ps 107:22 p Ps 105:1
9:12 q Ge 9:5
9:13 r Ps 38:19
9:14 s Ps 106:2 t Ps 13:5; Ps 51:12
9:15 u Ps 7:15-16 v Ps 35:8; Ps 57:6
9:17 w Ps 49:14 x Job 8:13; Ps 50:22
9:18 y Ps 71:5; Pr 23:18 z Ps 12:5
9:20 a Ps 62:9; Isa 31:3
10:1 a Ps 22:1,11 b Ps 13:1

13 O LORD, see how my enemies[r]
persecute me!
Have mercy and lift me up
from the gates of death,
14 that I may declare your
praises[s]
in the gates of the Daughter of
Zion
and there rejoice in your
salvation.[t]

15 The nations have fallen into the
pit they have dug;[u]
their feet are caught in the net
they have hidden.[v]
16 The LORD is known by his
justice;
the wicked are ensnared by
the work of their hands.
Higgaion.[b] *Selah*

17 The wicked return to the
grave,[c][w]
all the nations that forget
God.[x]
18 But the needy will not always
be forgotten,
nor the hope[y] of the
afflicted[z] ever perish.

19 Arise, O LORD, let not man
triumph;
let the nations be judged in
your presence.
20 Strike them with terror,
O LORD;
let the nations know they are
but men.[a]
Selah

Psalm 10[a]

1 Why, O LORD, do you stand far
off?[a]
Why do you hide yourself[b] in
times of trouble?

[a]Psalms 9 and 10 may have been originally a single acrostic poem, the stanzas of which begin with the successive letters of the Hebrew alphabet. In the Septuagint they constitute one psalm. [b]16 Or *Meditation*; possibly a musical notation [c]17 Hebrew *Sheol* [a]Psalms 9 and 10 may have been originally a single acrostic poem, the stanzas of which begin with the successive letters of the Hebrew alphabet. In the Septuagint they constitute one psalm.

2 In his arrogance the wicked
man hunts down the weak,
who are caught in the schemes
he devises.
3 He boasts[c] of the cravings of
his heart;
he blesses the greedy and
reviles the LORD.
4 In his pride the wicked does not
seek him;
in all his thoughts there is no
room for God.[d]
5 His ways are always
prosperous;
he is haughty and your laws
are far from him;
he sneers at all his enemies.
6 He says to himself, "Nothing
will shake me;
I'll always be happy[e] and
never have trouble."
7 His mouth is full of curses[f]
and lies and threats;[g]
trouble and evil are under his
tongue.[h]
8 He lies in wait near the
villages;
from ambush he murders the
innocent,[i]
watching in secret for his
victims.
9 He lies in wait like a lion in
cover;
he lies in wait to catch the
helpless;[j]
he catches the helpless and
drags them off in his net.
10 His victims are crushed, they
collapse;
they fall under his strength.
11 He says to himself, "God has
forgotten;[k]
he covers his face and never
sees."

12 Arise, LORD! Lift up your
hand,[l] O God.
Do not forget the helpless.[m]
13 Why does the wicked man
revile God?
Why does he say to himself,
"He won't call me to account"?

10:3 c Ps 94:4
10:4 d Ps 14:1; Ps 36:1
10:6 e Rev 18:7
10:7 f Ro 3:14*; g Ps 73:8; h Ps 140:3
10:8 i Ps 94:6
10:9 j Ps 17:12; Ps 59:3; Ps 140:5
10:11 k Job 22:13
10:12 l Ps 17:7; Mic 5:9; m Ps 9:12
10:14 n Ps 22:11; o Ps 37:5; p Ps 68:5
10:15 q Ps 37:17
10:16 r Ps 29:10; s Dt 8:20
10:17 t 1Ch 29:18; Ps 34:15
10:18 u Ps 82:3; v Ps 9:9
11:1 a Ps 56:11
11:2 b Ps 7:13; c Ps 64:3-4
11:3 d Ps 82:5
11:4 e Ps 18:6; f Ps 103:19; g Ps 33:13; h Ps 34:15-16

14 But you, O God, do see trouble[n]
and grief;
you consider it to take it in
hand.
The victim commits himself to
you;[o]
you are the helper[p] of the
fatherless.
15 Break the arm of the wicked
and evil man;[q]
call him to account for his
wickedness
that would not be found out.
16 The LORD is King for ever and
ever;[r]
the nations[s] will perish from
his land.
17 You hear, O LORD, the desire of
the afflicted;[t]
you encourage them, and you
listen to their cry,
18 defending the fatherless[u] and
the oppressed,[v]
in order that man, who is of
the earth, may terrify no
more.

Psalm 11

For the director of music. Of David.

1 In the LORD I take refuge.[a]
How then can you say to me:
"Flee like a bird to your
mountain.
2 For look, the wicked bend their
bows;
they set their arrows[b] against
the strings
to shoot from the shadows
at the upright in heart.[c]
3 When the foundations[d] are
being destroyed,
what can the righteous do?"[a]

4 The LORD is in his holy
temple;[e]
the LORD is on his heavenly
throne.[f]
He observes the sons of men;[g]
his eyes examine[h] them.

[a]3 Or *what is the Righteous One doing*

5 The LORD examines the righteous,[i]
but the wicked[b] and those who love violence
his soul hates.[j]
6 On the wicked he will rain fiery coals and burning sulphur;[k]
a scorching wind[l] will be their lot.

7 For the LORD is righteous,[m]
he loves justice;[n]
upright men will see his face.[o]

Psalm 12

For the director of music. According to *sheminith*.[a] A psalm of David.

1 Help, LORD, for the godly are no more;[a]
the faithful have vanished from among men.
2 Everyone lies to his neighbour;
their flattering lips speak with deception.[b]

3 May the LORD cut off all flattering lips
and every boastful tongue[c]
4 that says, "We will triumph with our tongues;
we own our lips[b]—who is our master?"

5 "Because of the oppression of the weak
and the groaning of the needy,
I will now arise," says the LORD.
"I will protect them[d] from those who malign them."
6 And the words of the LORD are flawless,[e]
like silver refined in a furnace of clay,
purified seven times.

7 O LORD, you will keep us safe
and protect us from such people for ever.[f]
8 The wicked freely strut[g] about
when what is vile is honoured among men.

Psalm 13

For the director of music. A psalm of David.

1 How long, O LORD? Will you forget me for ever?
How long will you hide your face[a] from me?
2 How long must I wrestle with my thoughts[b]
and every day have sorrow in my heart?
How long will my enemy triumph over me?[c]

3 Look on me and answer,[d] O LORD my God.
Give light to my eyes,[e] or I will sleep in death;[f]
4 my enemy will say, "I have overcome him,[g]"
and my foes will rejoice when I fall.

5 But I trust in your unfailing love;[h]
my heart rejoices in your salvation.[i]
6 I will sing[j] to the LORD,
for he has been good to me.

Psalm 14

14:1–7pp Ps 53:1–6

For the director of music. Of David.

1 The fool[a] says in his heart,
"There is no God."[a]
They are corrupt, their deeds are vile;
there is no-one who does good.

2 The LORD looks down from heaven[b]
on the sons of men
to see if there are any who understand,[c]
any who seek God.
3 All have turned aside,
they have together become corrupt;[d]

11:5 *i* Ge 22:1; Jas 1:12 *j* Ps 5:5
11:6 *k* Eze 38:22 *l* Jer 4:11-12
11:7 *m* Ps 7:9,11; Ps 45:7 *n* Ps 33:5 *o* Ps 17:15
12:1 *a* Isa 57:1
12:2 *b* Ps 10:7; Ps 41:6; Ps 55:21; Ro 16:18
12:3 *c* Da 7:8; Rev 13:5
12:5 *d* Ps 10:18; Ps 34:6
12:6 *e* 2Sa 22:31; Ps 18:30; Pr 30:5
12:7 *f* Ps 37:28
12:8 *g* Ps 55:10-11
13:1 *a* Job 13:24; Ps 44:24
13:2 *b* Ps 42:4 *c* Ps 42:9
13:3 *d* Ps 5:1 *e* Ezr 9:8 *f* Jer 51:39
13:4 *g* Ps 25:2
13:5 *h* Ps 52:8 *i* Ps 9:14
13:6 *j* Ps 116:7
14:1 *a* Ps 10:4
14:2 *b* Ps 33:13 *c* Ps 92:6
14:3 *d* Ps 58:3

[b]5 Or *The LORD, the Righteous One, examines the wicked, /* [a]Title: Probably a musical term [b]4 Or */ our lips are our ploughshares* [a]1 The Hebrew words rendered *fool* in Psalms denote one who is morally deficient.

there is no-one who does good,[e]
not even one.[f]

4 Will evildoers never learn—[g]
those who devour my people[h]
as men eat bread
and who do not call on the
LORD?[i]
5 There they are, overwhelmed
with dread,
for God is present in the
company of the righteous.
6 You evildoers frustrate the
plans of the poor,
but the LORD is their refuge.[j]

7 Oh, that salvation for Israel
would come out of Zion!
When the LORD restores the
fortunes[k] of his people,
let Jacob rejoice and Israel be
glad!

Psalm 15

A psalm of David.

1 LORD, who may dwell in your
sanctuary?[a]
Who may live on your holy
hill?[b]

2 He whose walk is blameless
and who does what is
righteous,
who speaks the truth[c] from his
heart
3 and has no slander[d] on his
tongue,
who does his neighbour no
wrong
and casts no slur on his
fellow-man,
4 who despises a vile man
but honours[e] those who fear
the LORD,
who keeps his oath[f]
even when it hurts,
5 who lends his money without
usury[g]
and does not accept a bribe[h]
against the innocent.

He who does these things
will never be shaken.[i]

Psalm 16

A *miktam*[a] of David.

1 Keep me safe,[a] O God,
for in you I take refuge.[b]

2 I said to the LORD, "You are my
Lord;
apart from you I have no good
thing."[c]
3 As for the saints who are in the
land,[d]
they are the glorious ones in
whom is all my delight.[b]
4 The sorrows[e] of those will
increase
who run after other gods.[f]
I will not pour out their
libations of blood
or take up their names[g] on
my lips.

5 LORD, you have assigned me my
portion[h] and my cup;[i]
you have made my lot secure.
6 The boundary lines have fallen
for me in pleasant places;
surely I have a delightful
inheritance.[j]

7 I will praise the LORD, who
counsels me;[k]
even at night[l] my heart
instructs me.
8 I have set the LORD always
before me.
Because he is at my right
hand,[m]
I shall not be shaken.

9 Therefore my heart is glad[n]
and my tongue rejoices;
my body also will rest
secure,[o]
10 because you will not abandon
me to the grave,[c]
nor will you let your Holy
One[d] see decay.[p]
11 You have made known[e] to me
the path of life;[q]

[a]Title: Probably a literary or musical term
[b]3 Or *As for the pagan priests who are in the land / and the nobles in whom all delight, I said:*
[c]10 Hebrew *Sheol* [d]10 Or *your faithful one*
[e]11 Or *You will make known*

14:3 *e* Ps 143:2 *f* Ro 3:10-12*
14:4 *g* Ps 82:5 *h* Ps 27:2 *i* Ps 79:6 Isa 64:7
14:6 *j* Ps 9:9 Ps 40:17
14:7 *k* Ps 53:6
15:1 *a* Ps 27:5-6 *b* Ps 24:3-5
15:2 *c* Ps 24:4 Zec 8:3,16 Eph 4:25
15:3 *d* Ex 23:1
15:4 *e* Ac 28:10 *f* Jdg 11:35
15:5 *g* Ex 22:25 *h* Ex 23:8 Dt 16:19 *i* 2Pe 1:10
16:1 *a* Ps 17:8 *b* Ps 7:1
16:2 *c* Ps 73:25
16:3 *d* Ps 101:6
16:4 *e* Ps 32:10 *f* Ps 106:37-38 *g* Ex 23:13
16:5 *h* Ps 73:26 *i* Ps 23:5
16:6 *j* Ps 78:55 Jer 3:19
16:7 *k* Ps 73:24 *l* Ps 77:6
16:8 *m* Ps 73:23
16:9 *n* Ps 4:7 Ps 30:11 *o* Ps 4:8
16:10 *p* Ac 13:35*
16:11 *q* Mt 7:14

you will fill me with joy in
your presence,[r]
with eternal pleasures[s] at
your right hand.

Psalm 17

A prayer of David.

1 Hear, O LORD, my righteous
plea;
listen to my cry.[a]
Give ear to my prayer—
it does not rise from deceitful
lips.[b]
2 May my vindication come from
you;
may your eyes see what is
right.
3 Though you probe my heart and
examine me at night,
though you test me,[c] you will
find nothing;[d]
I have resolved that my mouth
will not sin.[e]
4 As for the deeds of men—
by the word of your lips
I have kept myself
from the ways of the violent.
5 My steps have held to your
paths;[f]
my feet have not slipped.[g]
6 I call on you, O God, for you
will answer me;[h]
give ear to me[i] and hear my
prayer.[j]
7 Show the wonder of your great
love,[k]
you who save by your right
hand[l]
those who take refuge in you
from their foes.
8 Keep me as the apple of your
eye;[m]
hide me in the shadow of your
wings
9 from the wicked who assail me,
from my mortal enemies who
surround me.[n]
10 They close up their callous
hearts,[o]
and their mouths speak with
arrogance.[p]
11 They have tracked me down,
they now surround me,[q]
with eyes alert, to throw me to
the ground.
12 They are like a lion[r] hungry
for prey,
like a great lion crouching in
cover.
13 Rise up, O LORD, confront them,
bring them down;[s]
rescue me from the wicked by
your sword.
14 O LORD, by your hand save me
from such men,
from men of this world[t]
whose reward is in this life.

You still the hunger of those
you cherish;
their sons have plenty,
and they store up wealth[u] for
their children.
15 And I—in righteousness I shall
see your face;
when I awake, I shall be
satisfied with seeing your
likeness.[v]

Psalm 18

18:Title–50pp 2Sa 22:1–51

For the director of music. Of David the servant of the LORD. He sang to the LORD the words of this song when the LORD delivered him from the hand of all his enemies and from the hand of Saul. He said:

1 I love you, O LORD, my
strength.

2 The LORD is my rock,[a] my
fortress and my deliverer;
my God is my rock, in whom I
take refuge.
He is my shield[b] and the
horn[a] of my salvation,[c]
my stronghold.
3 I call to the LORD, who is
worthy of praise,[d]
and I am saved from my
enemies.

16:11 r Ac 2:25-28* s Ps 36:7-8
17:1 a Ps 61:1 b Isa 29:13
17:3 c Ps 26:2 Ps 66:10 d Job 23:10 Jer 50:20 e Ps 39:1
17:5 f Ps 44:18 Ps 119:133 g Ps 18:36
17:6 h Ps 86:7 i Ps 116:2 j Ps 88:2
17:7 k Ps 31:21 l Ps 20:6
17:8 m Dt 32:10
17:9 n Ps 31:20 Ps 109:3
17:10 o Ps 73:7 p 1Sa 2:3
17:11 q Ps 37:14 Ps 88:17
17:12 r Ps 7:2 Ps 10:9
17:13 s Ps 7:12 Ps 22:20 Ps 73:18
17:14 t Lk 16:8 u Ps 73:3-7
17:15 v Nu 12:8 Ps 4:6-7 Ps 16:11 1Jn 3:2
18:2 a Ps 19:14 b Ps 59:11 c Ps 75:10
18:3 d Ps 48:1

a2 *Horn* here symbolises strength.

4The cords of death[e] entangled me;
the torrents[f] of destruction overwhelmed me.
5The cords of the grave[b] coiled around me;
the snares of death[g] confronted me.
6In my distress I called to the LORD;
I cried to my God for help.
From his temple he heard my voice;[h]
my cry came before him, into his ears.
7The earth trembled and quaked,[i]
and the foundations of the mountains shook;
they trembled because he was angry.[j]
8Smoke rose from his nostrils;
consuming fire[k] came from his mouth,
burning coals blazed out of it.
9He parted the heavens and came down;[l]
dark clouds were under his feet.
10He mounted the cherubim[m] and flew;
he soared on the wings of the wind.[n]
11He made darkness his covering,[o] his canopy around him—
the dark rain clouds of the sky.
12Out of the brightness of his presence[p] clouds advanced,
with hailstones and bolts of lightning.[q]
13The LORD thundered[r] from heaven;
the voice of the Most High resounded.[c]
14He shot his arrows and scattered ⌞the enemies⌟,
great bolts of lightning and routed them.[s]
15The valleys of the sea were exposed
and the foundations of the earth laid bare
at your rebuke,[t] O LORD,
at the blast of breath from your nostrils.

16He reached down from on high and took hold of me;
he drew me out of deep waters.[u]
17He rescued me from my powerful enemy,
from my foes, who were too strong for me.[v]
18They confronted me in the day of my disaster,
but the LORD was my support.[w]
19He brought me out into a spacious place;[x]
he rescued me because he delighted in me.[y]

20The LORD has dealt with me according to my righteousness;
according to the cleanness of my hands[z] he has rewarded me.
21For I have kept the ways of the LORD;[a]
I have not done evil by turning[b] from my God.
22All his laws are before me;[c]
I have not turned away from his decrees.
23I have been blameless before him
and have kept myself from sin.
24The LORD has rewarded me according to my righteousness,[d]
according to the cleanness of my hands in his sight.

25To the faithful[e] you show yourself faithful,
to the blameless you show yourself blameless,

18:4 *e* Ps 116:3 *f* Ps 124:4
18:5 *g* Ps 116:3
18:6 *h* Ps 34:15
18:7 *i* Jdg 5:4 *j* Ps 68:7-8
18:8 *k* Ps 50:3
18:9 *l* Ps 144:5
18:10 *m* Ps 80:1 *n* Ps 104:3
18:11 *o* Dt 4:11 Ps 97:2
18:12 *p* Ps 104:2 *q* Ps 97:3
18:13 *r* Ps 29:3 Ps 104:7
18:14 *s* Ps 144:6
18:15 *t* Ps 76:6 Ps 106:9
18:16 *u* Ps 144:7
18:17 *v* Ps 35:10
18:18 *w* Ps 59:16
18:19 *x* Ps 31:8 *y* Ps 118:5
18:20 *z* Ps 24:4
18:21 *a* 2Ch 34:33 *b* Ps 119:102
18:22 *c* Ps 119:30
18:24 *d* 1Sa 26:23
18:25 *e* 1Ki 8:32 Ps 62:12 Mt 5:7

[b]5 Hebrew *Sheol* [c]13 Some Hebrew manuscripts and Septuagint (see also 2 Samuel 22:14); most Hebrew manuscripts *resounded, / amid hailstones and bolts of lightning*

26 to the pure you show yourself
pure,
but to the crooked you show
yourself shrewd.[f]
27 You save the humble
but bring low those whose
eyes are haughty.[g]
28 You, O LORD, keep my lamp
burning;
my God turns my darkness
into light.[h]
29 With your help[i] I can advance
against a troop;[d]
with my God I can scale a
wall.

30 As for God, his way is perfect;[j]
the word of the LORD is
flawless.[k]
He is a shield
for all who take refuge[l] in
him.
31 For who is God besides the
LORD?[m]
And who is the Rock[n] except
our God?
32 It is God who arms me with
strength[o]
and makes my way perfect.
33 He makes my feet like the feet
of a deer;[p]
he enables me to stand on the
heights.[q]
34 He trains my hands for battle;[r]
my arms can bend a bow of
bronze.
35 You give me your shield of
victory,
and your right hand sustains[s]
me;
you stoop down to make me
great.
36 You broaden the path beneath
me,
so that my ankles do not turn
over.

37 I pursued my enemies[t] and
overtook them;
I did not turn back till they
were destroyed.
38 I crushed them so that they
could not rise;[u]
they fell beneath my feet.[v]
39 You armed me with strength
for battle;
you made my adversaries bow
at my feet.
40 You made my enemies turn
their backs[w] in flight,
and I destroyed[x] my foes.
41 They cried for help, but there
was no-one to save
them[y]—
to the LORD, but he did not
answer.[z]
42 I beat them as fine as dust
borne on the wind;
I poured them out like mud in
the streets.

43 You have delivered me from
the attacks of the people;
you have made me the head of
nations;[a]
people I did not know[b] are
subject to me.
44 As soon as they hear me, they
obey me;
foreigners[c] cringe before me.
45 They all lose heart;
they come trembling from
their strongholds.[d]

46 The LORD lives! Praise be to my
Rock!
Exalted be God my Saviour![e]
47 He is the God who avenges me,
who subdues nations[f] under
me,
48 who saves[g] me from my
enemies.
You exalted me above my foes;
from violent men you rescued
me.
49 Therefore I will praise you
among the nations, O LORD;
I will sing[h] praises to your
name.[i]
50 He gives his king great
victories;
he shows unfailing kindness to
his anointed,
to David[j] and his descendants
for ever.[k]

18:26 f Pr 3:34
18:27 g Pr 6:17
18:28 h Job 18:6; Job 29:3
18:29 i Heb 11:34
18:30 j Dt 32:4; Rev 15:3; k Ps 12:6; l Ps 17:7
18:31 m Dt 32:39; Dt 86:8; Isa 45:5,6,14,18,21; n Dt 32:31; 1Sa 2:2
18:32 o Isa 45:5
18:33 p Hab 3:19; q Dt 32:13
18:34 r Ps 144:1
18:35 s Ps 119:116
18:37 t Ps 37:20; Ps 44:5
18:38 u Ps 36:12; v Ps 47:3
18:40 w Ps 21:12; x Ps 94:23
18:41 y Ps 50:22; z Job 27:9; Pr 1:28
18:43 a 2Sa 8:1-14; b Isa 52:15; Isa 55:5
18:44 c Ps 66:3
18:45 d Mic 7:17
18:46 e Ps 51:14
18:47 f Ps 47:3
18:48 g Ps 59:1
18:49 h Ps 108:1; i Ro 15:9*
18:50 j Ps 144:10; k Ps 89:4

d29 Or *can run through a barricade*

Psalm 19

For the director of music. A psalm of David.

1 The heavens[a] declare[b] the glory of God;
the skies proclaim the work of his hands.
2 Day after day they pour forth speech;
night after night they display knowledge.[c]
3 There is no speech or language
where their voice is not heard.[a]
4 Their voice[b] goes out into all the earth,
their words to the ends of the world.[d]
In the heavens he has pitched a tent[e] for the sun,
5 which is like a bridegroom coming forth from his pavilion,
like a champion rejoicing to run his course.
6 It rises at one end of the heavens
and makes its circuit to the other;[f]
nothing is hidden from its heat.

7 The law of the LORD is perfect,
reviving the soul.[g]
The statutes of the LORD are trustworthy,[h]
making wise the simple.[i]
8 The precepts of the LORD are right,[j]
giving joy to the heart.
The commands of the LORD are radiant,
giving light to the eyes.
9 The fear of the LORD is pure,
enduring for ever.
The ordinances of the LORD are sure
and altogether righteous.[k]
10 They are more precious than gold,[l]
than much pure gold;
they are sweeter than honey,
than honey from the comb.
11 By them is your servant warned;
in keeping them there is great reward.
12 Who can discern his errors?
Forgive my hidden faults.[m]
13 Keep your servant also from wilful sins;
may they not rule over me.
Then will I be blameless,
innocent of great transgression.

14 May the words of my mouth
and the meditation of my heart
be pleasing[n] in your sight,
O LORD, my Rock[o] and my Redeemer.[p]

Psalm 20

For the director of music. A psalm of David.

1 May the LORD answer you when you are in distress;
may the name of the God of Jacob[a] protect you.[b]
2 May he send you help from the sanctuary[c]
and grant you support from Zion.
3 May he remember[d] all your sacrifices
and accept your burnt offerings.[e] *Selah*
4 May he give you the desire of your heart[f]
and make all your plans succeed.
5 We will shout for joy when you are victorious
and will lift up our banners[g] in the name of our God.
May the LORD grant all your requests.[h]

6 Now I know that the LORD saves his anointed;[i]
he answers him from his holy heaven

19:1 a Isa 40:22 b Ps 50:6 Ro 1:19
19:2 c Ps 74:16
19:4 d Ro 10:18* e Ps 104:2
19:6 f Ps 113:3 Ecc 1:5
19:7 g Ps 23:3 h Ps 93:5 Ps 111:7 i Ps 119:98-100
19:8 j Ps 12:6 Ps 119:128
19:9 k Ps 119:138, 142
19:10 l Pr 8:10
19:12 m Ps 51:2 Ps 90:8 Ps 139:6
19:14 n Ps 104:34 o Ps 18:2 p Isa 47:4
20:1 a Ps 46:7,11 b Ps 91:14
20:2 c Ps 3:4
20:3 d Ac 10:4 e Ps 51:19
20:4 f Ps 21:2 Ps 145:16,19
20:5 g Ps 9:14 Ps 60:4 h 1Sa 1:17
20:6 i Ps 28:8 Ps 41:11 Isa 58:9

a3 Or *They have no speech, there are no words; / no sound is heard from them* b4 Septuagint, Jerome and Syriac; Hebrew *line*

with the saving power of his right hand.
7Some trust in chariots and some in horses,[j]
but we trust in the name of the LORD our God.[k]
8They are brought to their knees and fall,
but we rise up[l] and stand firm.[m]

9O LORD, save the king!
Answer[a] us[n] when we call!

Psalm 21

For the director of music. A psalm of David.

1O LORD, the king rejoices in your strength.
How great is his joy in the victories you give![a]
2You have granted him the desire of his heart[b]
and have not withheld the request of his lips. *Selah*
3You welcomed him with rich blessings
and placed a crown of pure gold[c] on his head.
4He asked you for life, and you gave it to him—
length of days, for ever and ever.[d]
5Through the victories[e] you gave, his glory is great;
you have bestowed on him splendour and majesty.
6Surely you have granted him eternal blessings
and made him glad with the joy[f] of your presence.[g]
7For the king trusts in the LORD;
through the unfailing love of the Most High
he will not be shaken.

8Your hand will lay hold[h] on all your enemies;
your right hand will seize your foes.
9At the time of your appearing
you will make them like a fiery furnace.
In his wrath the LORD will swallow them up,
and his fire will consume them.[i]
10You will destroy their descendants from the earth,
their posterity from mankind.[j]
11Though they plot evil[k] against you
and devise wicked schemes,[l]
they cannot succeed;
12for you will make them turn their backs[m]
when you aim at them with drawn bow.

13Be exalted, O LORD, in your strength;
we will sing and praise your might.

Psalm 22

For the director of music. To ⌊the tune of⌋ "The Doe of the Morning". A psalm of David.

1My God, my God, why have you forsaken me?[a]
Why are you so far[b] from saving me,
so far from the words of my groaning?
2O my God, I cry out by day, but you do not answer,
by night,[c] and am not silent.

3Yet you are enthroned as the Holy One;[d]
you are the praise[e] of Israel.[a]
4In you our fathers put their trust;
they trusted and you delivered them.
5They cried to you and were saved;
in you they trusted and were not disappointed.[f]

6But I am a worm[g] and not a man,

[a]9 Or *save! / O King, answer* [a]3 Or *Yet you are holy, / enthroned on the praises of Israel*

20:7 j Ps 33:17 Isa 31:1 k 2Ch 32:8
20:8 l Mic 7:8 m Ps 37:23
20:9 n Ps 3:7 Ps 17:6
21:1 a Ps 59:16-17
21:2 b Ps 37:4
21:3 c 2Sa 12:30
21:4 d Ps 61:5-6 Ps 91:16 Ps 133:3
21:5 e Ps 18:50
21:6 f Ps 43:4 g 1Ch 17:27
21:8 h Isa 10:10
21:9 i Ps 50:3 La 2:2 Mal 4:1
21:10 j Dt 28:18 Ps 37:28
21:11 k Ps 2:1 l Ps 10:2
21:12 m Ps 7:12-13 Ps 18:40
22:1 a Mt 27:46* Mk 15:34* b Ps 10:1
22:2 c Ps 42:3
22:3 d Ps 99:9 e Dt 10:21
22:5 f Isa 49:23
22:6 g Job 25:6 Isa 41:14

scorned by men[h] and
despised[i] by the people.
7 All who see me mock me;
they hurl insults,[j] shaking
their heads:[k]
8 "He trusts in the LORD;
let the LORD rescue him.[l]
Let him deliver him,
since he delights[m] in him."

9 Yet you brought me out of the
womb;[n]
you made me trust in you
even at my mother's breast.
10 From birth[o] I was cast upon
you;
from my mother's womb you
have been my God.
11 Do not be far from me,
for trouble is near
and there is no-one to help.[p]

12 Many bulls[q] surround me;
strong bulls of Bashan[r]
encircle me.
13 Roaring lions[s] tearing their
prey
open their mouths wide[t]
against me.
14 I am poured out like water,
and all my bones are out of
joint.[u]
My heart has turned to wax;
it has melted away[v] within
me.
15 My strength is dried up like a
potsherd,
and my tongue sticks to the
roof of my mouth;[w]
you lay me[b] in the dust[x] of
death.
16 Dogs[y] have surrounded me;
a band of evil men has
encircled me,
they have pierced[c][z] my
hands and my feet.
17 I can count all my bones;
people stare[a] and gloat over
me.[b]
18 They divide my garments
among them
and cast lots[c] for my clothing.

22:6 h Ps 31:11 i Isa 49:7 Isa 53:3
22:7 j Mt 27:39,44 k Mk 15:29
22:8 l Ps 91:14 m Mt 27:43
22:9 n Ps 71:6
22:10 o Isa 46:3
22:11 p Ps 72:12
22:12 q Ps 68:30 r Dt 32:14
22:13 s Ps 17:12 t Ps 35:21
22:14 u Ps 31:10 v Job 30:16 Da 5:6
22:15 w Ps 38:10 Jn 19:28 x Ps 104:29
22:16 y Ps 59:6 z Isa 53:5 Zec 12:10 Jn 19:34
22:17 a Lk 23:35 b Lk 23:27
22:18 c Mt 27:35* Lk 23:34 Jn 19:24*
22:19 d Ps 70:5
22:20 e Ps 35:17
22:22 f Heb 2:12*
22:23 g Ps 86:12 Ps 135:19 h Ps 33:8
22:24 i Ps 69:17 j Heb 5:7
22:25 k Ps 35:18 l Ecc 5:4
22:26 m Ps 107:9 n Ps 40:16
22:27 o Ps 2:8 p Ps 86:9
22:28 q Ps 47:7-8

19 But you, O LORD, be not far off;
O my Strength, come quickly[d]
to help me.
20 Deliver my life from the sword,
my precious life[e] from the
power of the dogs.
21 Rescue me from the mouth of
the lions;
save[d] me from the horns of
the wild oxen.

22 I will declare your name to my
brothers;
in the congregation I will
praise you.[f]
23 You who fear the LORD, praise
him![g]
All you descendants of Jacob,
honour him!
Revere him,[h] all you
descendants of Israel!
24 For he has not despised or
disdained
the suffering of the afflicted
one;
he has not hidden his face[i]
from him
but has listened to his cry for
help.[j]

25 From you comes the theme of
my praise in the great
assembly;[k]
before those who fear you[e]
will I fulfil my vows.[l]
26 The poor will eat[m] and be
satisfied;
they who seek the LORD will
praise him—[n]
may your hearts live for ever!
27 All the ends of the earth[o]
will remember and turn to the
LORD,
and all the families of the
nations
will bow down before him,[p]
28 for dominion belongs to the
LORD[q]
and he rules over the nations.

b15 Or / *I am laid* **c**16 Some Hebrew manuscripts, Septuagint and Syriac; most Hebrew manuscripts / *like the lion,* **d**21 Or / *you have heard* **e**25 Hebrew *him*

29 All the rich[r] of the earth will
feast and worship;
all who go down to the dust[s]
will kneel before him—
those who cannot keep
themselves alive.
30 Posterity[t] will serve him;
future generations will be told
about the Lord.
31 They will proclaim his
righteousness
to a people yet unborn[u]—
for he has done it.

Psalm 23

A psalm of David.

1 The LORD is my shepherd,[a] I
shall not be in want.[b]
2 He makes me lie down in
green pastures,
he leads me beside quiet
waters,[c]
3 he restores my soul.[d]
He guides me in paths of
righteousness[e]
for his name's sake.
4 Even though I walk
through the valley of the
shadow of death,[a][f]
I will fear no evil,[g]
for you are with me;[h]
your rod and your staff,
they comfort me.

5 You prepare a table before me
in the presence of my
enemies.
You anoint my head with oil;[i]
my cup[j] overflows.
6 Surely goodness and love will
follow me
all the days of my life,
and I will dwell in the house of
the LORD
for ever.

Psalm 24

Of David. A psalm.

1 The earth is the LORD's,[a] and
everything in it,
the world, and all who live in
it;[b]

22:29 r Ps 45:12 s Isa 26:19
22:30 t Ps 102:28
22:31 u Ps 78:6
23:1 a Isa 40:11 Jn 10:11 1Pe 2:25 b Php 4:19
23:2 c Eze 34:14 Rev 7:17
23:3 d Ps 19:7 e Ps 5:8 Ps 85:13
23:4 f Job 10:21-22 g Ps 3:6 Ps 27:1 h Isa 43:2
23:5 i Ps 92:10 j Ps 16:5
24:1 a Ex 9:29 Job 41:11 Ps 89:11 b 1Co 10:26*
24:3 c Ps 2:6 d Ps 15:1 Ps 65:4
24:4 e Job 17:9 f Mt 5:8
24:6 g Ps 27:8
24:7 h Isa 26:2 i Ps 97:6 1Co 2:8
24:8 j Ps 76:3-6
25:1 a Ps 86:4
25:2 b Ps 41:11

2 for he founded it upon the seas
and established it upon the
waters.
3 Who may ascend the hill[c] of
the LORD?
Who may stand in his holy
place?[d]
4 He who has clean hands[e] and a
pure heart,[f]
who does not lift up his soul to
an idol
or swear by what is false.[a]
5 He will receive blessing from
the LORD
and vindication from God his
Saviour.
6 Such is the generation of those
who seek him,
who seek your face,[g] O God
of Jacob.[b] *Selah*
7 Lift up your heads, O you
gates;[h]
be lifted up, you ancient
doors,
that the King of glory[i] may
come in.
8 Who is this King of glory?
The LORD strong and mighty,
the LORD mighty in battle.[j]
9 Lift up your heads, O you gates;
lift them up, you ancient
doors,
that the King of glory may
come in.
10 Who is he, this King of glory?
The LORD Almighty—
he is the King of glory. *Selah*

Psalm 25[a]

Of David.

1 To you, O LORD, I lift up my
soul;[a]
2 in you I trust,[b] O my God.
Do not let me be put to shame,
nor let my enemies triumph
over me.
3 No-one whose hope is in you

[a]4 Or *through the darkest valley* [a]4 Or *swear falsely* [b]6 Two Hebrew manuscripts and Syriac (see also Septuagint); most Hebrew manuscripts *face, Jacob* [a]This psalm is an acrostic poem, the verses of which begin with the successive letters of the Hebrew alphabet.

will ever be put to shame,[c]
but they will be put to shame
who are treacherous without
excuse.

4 Show me your ways, O LORD,
teach me your paths;[d]
5 guide me in your truth and
teach me,
for you are God my Saviour,
and my hope is in you all day
long.
6 Remember, O LORD, your great
mercy and love,[e]
for they are from of old.
7 Remember not the sins of my
youth[f]
and my rebellious ways;
according to your love[g]
remember me,
for you are good, O LORD.

8 Good and upright[h] is the LORD;
therefore he instructs[i]
sinners in his ways.
9 He guides[j] the humble in what
is right
and teaches them[k] his way.
10 All the ways of the LORD are
loving and faithful[l]
for those who keep the
demands of his covenant.[m]
11 For the sake of your name,[n]
O LORD,
forgive my iniquity, though it
is great.
12 Who, then, is the man that fears
the LORD?
He will instruct him in the
way[o] chosen for him.
13 He will spend his days in
prosperity,[p]
and his descendants will
inherit the land.[q]
14 The LORD confides[r] in those
who fear him;
he makes his covenant
known[s] to them.
15 My eyes are ever on the LORD,[t]
for only he will release my
feet from the snare.

16 Turn to me[u] and be gracious to
me,
for I am lonely and afflicted.
17 The troubles of my heart have
multiplied;
free me from my anguish.[v]
18 Look upon my affliction and my
distress[w]
and take away all my sins.
19 See how my enemies[x] have
increased
and how fiercely they hate
me!
20 Guard my life[y] and rescue me;
let me not be put to shame,
for I take refuge in you.
21 May integrity[z] and uprightness
protect me,
because my hope is in you.

22 Redeem Israel,[a] O God,
from all their troubles!

Psalm 26

Of David.

1 Vindicate me, O LORD,
for I have led a blameless
life;[a]
I have trusted[b] in the LORD
without wavering.[c]
2 Test me,[d] O LORD, and try me,
examine my heart and my
mind;[e]
3 for your love is ever before me,
and I walk continually[f] in
your truth.
4 I do not sit[g] with deceitful
men,
nor do I consort with
hypocrites;
5 I abhor[h] the assembly of
evildoers
and refuse to sit with the
wicked.
6 I wash my hands in innocence,[i]
and go about your altar,
O LORD,
7 proclaiming aloud your praise
and telling of all your
wonderful deeds.[j]
8 I love[k] the house where you
live, O LORD,
the place where your glory
dwells.

25:3 c Isa 49:23
25:4 d Ex 33:13
25:6 e Ps 103:17 Isa 63:7,15
25:7 f Job 13:26 Jer 3:25 g Ps 51:1
25:8 h Ps 92:15 i Ps 32:8
25:9 j Ps 23:3 k Ps 27:11
25:10 l Ps 40:11 m Ps 103:18
25:11 n Ps 31:3 Ps 79:9
25:12 o Ps 37:23
25:13 p Pr 19:23 q Ps 37:11
25:14 r Pr 3:32 s Jn 7:17
25:15 t Ps 141:8
25:16 u Ps 69:16
25:17 v Ps 107:6
25:18 w 2Sa 16:12
25:19 x Ps 3:1
25:20 y Ps 86:2
25:21 z Ps 41:12
25:22 a Ps 130:8
26:1 a Ps 7:8 Pr 20:7 b Ps 28:7 c 2Ki 20:3 Heb 10:23
26:2 d Ps 17:3 e Ps 7:9
26:3 f 2Ki 20:3
26:4 g Ps 1:1
26:5 h Ps 31:6 Ps 139:21
26:6 i Ps 73:13
26:7 j Ps 9:1
26:8 k Ps 27:4

9 Do not take away my soul along
with sinners,
my life with bloodthirsty
men,[l]
10 in whose hands are wicked
schemes,
whose right hands are full of
bribes.[m]
11 But I lead a blameless life;
redeem me[n] and be merciful
to me.

12 My feet stand on level ground;[o]
in the great assembly[p] I will
praise the LORD.

Psalm 27

Of David.

1 The LORD is my light[a] and my
salvation[b]—
whom shall I fear?
The LORD is the stronghold of
my life—
of whom shall I be afraid?[c]
2 When evil men advance against
me
to devour my flesh,[a]
when my enemies and my foes
attack me,
they will stumble and fall.[d]
3 Though an army besiege me,
my heart will not fear;[e]
though war break out against
me,
even then will I be confident.[f]

4 One thing[g] I ask of the LORD,
this is what I seek:
that I may dwell in the house of
the LORD
all the days of my life,[h]
to gaze upon the beauty of the
LORD
and to seek him in his temple.
5 For in the day of trouble
he will keep me safe in his
dwelling;
he will hide me[i] in the shelter
of his tabernacle
and set me high upon a rock.[j]
6 Then my head will be exalted[k]
above the enemies who
surround me;
at his tabernacle will I
sacrifice[l] with shouts of
joy;
I will sing and make music to
the LORD.

7 Hear my voice when I call,
O LORD;
be merciful to me and answer
me.[m]
8 My heart says of you, "Seek
his[b] face!"
Your face, LORD, I will seek.
9 Do not hide your face[n] from
me,
do not turn your servant away
in anger;
you have been my helper.
Do not reject me or forsake me,
O God my Saviour.
10 Though my father and mother
forsake me,
the LORD will receive me.
11 Teach me your way, O LORD;
lead me in a straight path[o]
because of my oppressors.
12 Do not hand me over to the
desire of my foes,
for false witnesses[p] rise up
against me,
breathing out violence.

13 I am still confident of this:
I will see the goodness of the
LORD[q]
in the land of the living.[r]
14 Wait[s] for the LORD;
be strong and take heart
and wait for the LORD.

Psalm 28

Of David.

1 To you I call, O LORD my Rock;
do not turn a deaf ear to me.
For if you remain silent,[a]
I shall be like those who have
gone down to the pit.[b]
2 Hear my cry for mercy[c]
as I call to you for help,
as I lift up my hands

26:9 l Ps 28:3
26:10 m 1Sa 8:3
26:11 n Ps 69:18
26:12 o Ps 27:11; Ps 40:2 p Ps 22:22
27:1 a Isa 60:19 b Ex 15:2 c Ps 118:6
27:2 d Ps 9:3; Ps 14:4
27:3 e Ps 3:6 f Job 4:6
27:4 g Ps 90:17 h Ps 23:6; Ps 26:8
27:5 i Ps 17:8; Ps 31:20 j Ps 40:2
27:6 k Ps 3:3 l Ps 107:22
27:7 m Ps 13:3
27:9 n Ps 69:17
27:11 o Ps 5:8; Ps 25:4; Ps 86:11
27:12 p Mt 26:60; Ac 9:1
27:13 q Ps 31:19 r Jer 11:19; Eze 26:20
27:14 s Ps 40:1
28:1 a Ps 83:1 b Ps 88:4
28:2 c Ps 138:2; Ps 140:6

a2 Or *to slander me*
b8 Or *To you, O my heart, he has said, "Seek my*

towards your Most Holy
Place.[d]

[3]Do not drag me away with the
wicked,
with those who do evil,
who speak cordially with their
neighbours
but harbour malice in their
hearts.[e]
[4]Repay them for their deeds
and for their evil work;
repay them for what their
hands have done[f]
and bring back upon them
what they deserve.[g]
[5]Since they show no regard for
the works of the LORD
and what his hands have
done,[h]
he will tear them down
and never build them up
again.

[6]Praise be to the LORD,
for he has heard my cry for
mercy.
[7]The LORD is my strength[i] and
my shield;
my heart trusts[j] in him, and I
am helped.
My heart leaps for joy
and I will give thanks to him
in song.[k]

[8]The LORD is the strength of his
people,
a fortress of salvation for his
anointed one.[l]
[9]Save your people and bless your
inheritance;[m]
be their shepherd[n] and carry
them[o] for ever.

Psalm 29

A psalm of David.

[1]Ascribe to the LORD,[a] O mighty
ones,
ascribe to the LORD glory[b]
and strength.
[2]Ascribe to the LORD the glory
due to his name;
worship the LORD in the
splendour of his[a]
holiness.[c]

[3]The voice[d] of the LORD is over
the waters;
the God of glory thunders,[e]
the LORD thunders over the
mighty waters.
[4]The voice of the LORD is
powerful;[f]
the voice of the LORD is
majestic.
[5]The voice of the LORD breaks
the cedars;
the LORD breaks in pieces the
cedars of Lebanon.[g]
[6]He makes Lebanon skip[h] like a
calf,
Sirion[b][i] like a young wild ox.
[7]The voice of the LORD strikes
with flashes of lightning.
[8]The voice of the LORD shakes
the desert;
the LORD shakes the Desert of
Kadesh.[j]
[9]The voice of the LORD twists the
oaks[c]
and strips the forests bare.
And in his temple all cry,
"Glory!"[k]

[10]The LORD sits[d] enthroned over
the flood;[l]
the LORD is enthroned as King
for ever.[m]
[11]The LORD gives strength to his
people;[n]
the LORD blesses his people
with peace.[o]

Psalm 30

A psalm. A song. For the dedication of
the temple.[a] Of David.

[1]I will exalt you, O LORD,
for you lifted me out of the
depths
and did not let my enemies
gloat over me.[a]

28:2 *d* Ps 5:7
28:3 *e* Ps 12:2; Ps 26:9; Jer 9:8
28:4 *f* 2Ti 4:14; Rev 22:12 *g* Rev 18:6
28:5 *h* Isa 5:12
28:7 *i* Ps 18:1 *j* Ps 13:5 *k* Ps 40:3; Ps 69:30
28:8 *l* Ps 20:6
28:9 *m* Dt 9:29; Ezr 1:4 *n* Isa 40:11 *o* Dt 1:31; Dt 32:11
29:1 *a* 1Ch 16:28 *b* Ps 96:7-9
29:2 *c* 2Ch 20:21
29:3 *d* Job 37:5 *e* Ps 18:13
29:4 *f* Ps 68:33
29:5 *g* Jdg 9:15
29:6 *h* Ps 114:4 *i* Dt 3:9
29:8 *j* Nu 13:26
29:9 *k* Ps 26:8
29:10 *l* Ge 6:17 *m* Ps 10:16
29:11 *n* Ps 28:8 *o* Ps 37:11
30:1 *a* Ps 25:2; Ps 28:9

[a]2 Or *LORD with the splendour of* [b]6 That is, Mount Hermon [c]9 Or *LORD makes the deer give birth* [d]10 Or *sat* [a]Title: Or *palace*

2 O LORD my God, I called to you
for help[b]
and you healed me.[c]
3 O LORD, you brought me up
from the grave;[b]
you spared me from going
down into the pit.[d]
4 Sing to the LORD, you saints[e] of
his;
praise his holy name.[f]
5 For his anger[g] lasts only a
moment,
but his favour lasts a lifetime;
weeping may remain for a
night,
but rejoicing comes in the
morning.[h]
6 When I felt secure, I said,
"I shall never be shaken."
7 O LORD, when you favoured me,
you made my mountain[c]
stand firm;
but when you hid your face,[i]
I was dismayed.
8 To you, O LORD, I called;
to the Lord I cried for mercy:
9 "What gain is there in my
destruction,[d]
in my going down into the pit?
Will the dust praise you?
Will it proclaim your
faithfulness?[j]
10 Hear, O LORD, and be merciful
to me;
O LORD, be my help."
11 You turned my wailing into
dancing;
you removed my sackcloth
and clothed me with joy,[k]
12 that my heart may sing to you
and not be silent.
O LORD my God, I will give
you thanks[l] for ever.[m]

Psalm 31

31:1–4pp Ps 71:1–3

For the director of music. A psalm of David.

1 In you, O LORD, I have taken
refuge;
let me never be put to shame;
deliver me in your
righteousness.
2 Turn your ear to me,
come quickly to my rescue;[a]
be my rock of refuge,[b]
a strong fortress to save me.
3 Since you are my rock and my
fortress,[c]
for the sake of your name[d]
lead and guide me.
4 Free me from the trap that is
set for me,
for you are my refuge.[e]
5 Into your hands I commit my
spirit;[f]
redeem me, O LORD, the God
of truth.
6 I hate those who cling to
worthless idols;
I trust in the LORD.[g]
7 I will be glad and rejoice in
your love,
for you saw my affliction[h]
and knew the anguish[i] of my
soul.
8 You have not handed me over[j]
to the enemy
but have set my feet in a
spacious place.
9 Be merciful to me, O LORD, for
I am in distress;
my eyes grow weak with
sorrow,[k]
my soul and my body with
grief.
10 My life is consumed by anguish
and my years by groaning;[l]
my strength fails because of my
affliction,[a]
and my bones grow weak.[m]
11 Because of all my enemies,
I am the utter contempt of my
neighbours;[n]
I am a dread to my friends—
those who see me on the street
flee from me.
12 I am forgotten by them as
though I were dead;[o]

30:2 *b* Ps 88:13 *c* Ps 6:2
30:3 *d* Ps 28:1; Ps 86:13
30:4 *e* Ps 149:1 *f* Ps 97:12
30:5 *g* Ps 103:9 *h* 2Co 4:17
30:7 *i* Dt 31:17; Ps 104:29
30:9 *j* Ps 6:5
30:11 *k* Ps 4:7; Jer 31:4,13
30:12 *l* Ps 16:9 *m* Ps 44:8
31:2 *a* Ps 71:2 *b* Ps 18:2
31:3 *c* Ps 18:2 *d* Ps 23:3
31:4 *e* Ps 25:15
31:5 *f* Lk 23:46; Ac 7:59
31:6 *g* Jnh 2:8
31:7 *h* Ps 90:14 *i* Ps 10:14; Jn 10:27
31:8 *j* Dt 32:30
31:9 *k* Ps 6:7
31:10 *l* Ps 13:2 *m* Ps 38:3; Ps 39:11
31:11 *n* Job 19:13; Ps 38:11; Ps 64:8; Isa 53:4
31:12 *o* Ps 88:4

b3 Hebrew *Sheol* c7 Or *hill country*
d9 Or *there if I am silenced* a10 Or *guilt*

I have become like broken
pottery.
13For I hear the slander of many;
there is terror on every side;[p]
they conspire against me
and plot to take my life.[q]

14But I trust[r] in you, O LORD;
I say, "You are my God."
15My times[s] are in your hands;
deliver me from my enemies
and from those who pursue
me.
16Let your face shine[t] on your
servant;
save me in your unfailing
love.
17Let me not be put to shame,[u]
O LORD,
for I have cried out to you;
but let the wicked be put to
shame
and lie silent[v] in the grave.[b]
18Let their lying lips[w] be
silenced,
for with pride and contempt
they speak arrogantly[x]
against the righteous.

19How great is your goodness,[y]
which you have stored up for
those who fear you,
which you bestow in the sight
of men[z]
on those who take refuge in
you.
20In the shelter of your presence
you hide[a] them
from the intrigues of men;[b]
in your dwelling you keep them
safe
from accusing tongues.

21Praise be to the LORD,
for he showed his wonderful
love[c] to me
when I was in a besieged
city.[d]
22In my alarm[e] I said,
"I am cut off from your
sight!"
Yet you heard my cry[f] for
mercy
when I called to you for help.

31:13
p Jer 20:3,10
La 2:22
q Mt 27:1

31:14
r Ps 140:6

31:15
s Job 24:1
Ps 143:9

31:16
t Nu 6:25
Ps 4:6

31:17
u Ps 25:2-3
v Ps 115:17

31:18
w Ps 120:2
x Ps 94:4

31:19
y Ro 11:22
z Isa 64:4

31:20
a Ps 27:5
b Job 5:21

31:21
c Ps 17:7
d 1Sa 23:7

31:22
e Ps 116:11
f La 3:54

31:23
g Ps 34:9
h Ps 145:20
i Ps 94:2

31:24
j Ps 27:14

32:1
a Ps 85:2

32:2
b Ro 4:7-8*
2Co 5:19
c Jn 1:47

32:3
d Ps 31:10

32:4
e Job 33:7

32:5
f Pr 28:13
g Ps 103:12
h Lev 26:40

32:6
i Ps 69:13
Isa 55:6
j Isa 43:2

32:7
k Ps 9:9

23Love the LORD, all his saints![g]
The LORD preserves the
faithful,[h]
but the proud he pays back[i]
in full.
24Be strong and take heart,[j]
all you who hope in the LORD.

Psalm 32

Of David. A *maskil*.[a]

1Blessed is he
whose transgressions are
forgiven,
whose sins are covered.[a]
2Blessed is the man
whose sin the LORD does not
count against him[b]
and in whose spirit is no
deceit.[c]

3When I kept silent,
my bones wasted away[d]
through my groaning all day
long.
4For day and night
your hand was heavy[e] upon
me;
my strength was sapped
as in the heat of summer.
Selah
5Then I acknowledged my sin to
you
and did not cover up my
iniquity.
I said, "I will confess[f]
my transgressions[g] to the
LORD"—
and you forgave
the guilt of my sin.[h] *Selah*
6Therefore let everyone who is
godly pray to you
while you may be found;[i]
surely when the mighty waters
rise,
they will not reach him.[j]
7You are my hiding-place;
you will protect me from
trouble[k]

[b]17 Hebrew *Sheol*
[a]Title: Probably a literary or musical term

and surround me with songs
of deliverance.[l] *Selah*

8 I will instruct[m] you and teach
you in the way you should
go;
I will counsel you and watch
over[n] you.
9 Do not be like the horse or the
mule,
which have no understanding
but must be controlled by bit
and bridle[o]
or they will not come to you.
10 Many are the woes of the
wicked,[p]
but the LORD's unfailing love
surrounds the man who
trusts[q] in him.

11 Rejoice in the LORD[r] and be
glad, you righteous;
sing, all you who are upright
in heart!

Psalm 33

1 Sing joyfully to the LORD, you
righteous;
it is fitting[a] for the upright[b]
to praise him.
2 Praise the LORD with the harp;
make music to him on the
ten-stringed lyre.[c]
3 Sing to him a new song;[d]
play skilfully, and shout for
joy.

4 For the word of the LORD is
right[e] and true;
he is faithful in all he does.
5 The LORD loves righteousness
and justice;[f]
the earth is full of his
unfailing love.[g]

6 By the word[h] of the LORD were
the heavens made,
their starry host by the breath
of his mouth.
7 He gathers the waters of the
sea into jars;**a**
he puts the deep into
storehouses.

8 Let all the earth fear the LORD;
let all the people of the world
revere him.[i]
9 For he spoke, and it came to be;
he commanded,[j] and it stood
firm.
10 The LORD foils the plans of the
nations;[k]
he thwarts the purposes of the
peoples.
11 But the plans of the LORD stand
firm for ever,
the purposes[l] of his heart
through all generations.

12 Blessed is the nation whose God
is the LORD,[m]
the people he chose[n] for his
inheritance.
13 From heaven the LORD looks
down
and sees all mankind;[o]
14 from his dwelling-place[p] he
watches
all who live on earth—
15 he who forms[q] the hearts of all,
who considers everything they
do.[r]
16 No king is saved by the size of
his army;[s]
no warrior escapes by his
great strength.
17 A horse[t] is a vain hope for
deliverance;
despite all its great strength it
cannot save.
18 But the eyes[u] of the LORD are
on those who fear him,
on those whose hope is in his
unfailing love,[v]
19 to deliver them from death
and keep them alive in
famine.[w]

20 We wait[x] in hope for the LORD;
he is our help and our shield.
21 In him our hearts rejoice,[y]
for we trust in his holy name.
22 May your unfailing love rest
upon us, O LORD,
even as we put our hope in
you.

32:7 *l* Ex 15:1
32:8 *m* Ps 25:8 *n* Ps 33:18
32:9 *o* Pr 26:3
32:10 *p* Ro 2:9 *q* Pr 16:20
32:11 *r* Ps 64:10
33:1 *a* Ps 147:1 *b* Ps 32:11
33:2 *c* Ps 92:3
33:3 *d* Ps 96:1
33:4 *e* Ps 19:8
33:5 *f* Ps 11:7 *g* Ps 119:64
33:6 *h* Heb 11:3
33:8 *i* Ps 67:7 Ps 96:9
33:9 *j* Ge 1:3 Ps 148:5
33:10 *k* Isa 8:10
33:11 *l* Job 23:13
33:12 *m* Ps 144:15 *n* Ex 19:5 Dt 7:6
33:13 *o* Job 28:24 Ps 11:4
33:14 *p* 1Ki 8:39
33:15 *q* Job 10:8 *r* Jer 32:19
33:16 *s* Ps 44:6
33:17 *t* Ps 20:7 Pr 21:31
33:18 *u* Job 36:7 Ps 34:15 *v* Ps 147:11
33:19 *w* Job 5:20
33:20 *x* Ps 130:6
33:21 *y* Zec 10:7 Jn 16:22

a7 Or *sea as into a heap*

Psalm 34[a]

Of David. When he pretended to be insane before Abimelech, who drove him away, and he left.

1I will extol the LORD at all times;[a]
his praise will always be on my lips.
2My soul will boast[b] in the LORD;
let the afflicted hear and rejoice.[c]
3Glorify the LORD with me;
let us exalt[d] his name together.

4I sought the LORD,[e] and he answered me;
he delivered me from all my fears.
5Those who look to him are radiant;[f]
their faces are never covered with shame.[g]
6This poor man called, and the LORD heard him;
he saved him out of all his troubles.
7The angel of the LORD[h] encamps around those who fear him,
and he delivers them.

8Taste and see that the LORD is good;[i]
blessed is the man who takes refuge[j] in him.
9Fear the LORD, you his saints,
for those who fear him lack nothing.[k]
10The lions may grow weak and hungry,
but those who seek the LORD lack no good thing.[l]

11Come, my children, listen to me;
I will teach you[m] the fear of the LORD.
12Whoever of you loves life[n]
and desires to see many good days,
13keep your tongue from evil
and your lips from speaking lies.[o]
14Turn from evil and do good;[p]
seek peace[q] and pursue it.

15The eyes of the LORD[r] are on the righteous[s]
and his ears are attentive to their cry;
16the face of the LORD is against[t] those who do evil,[u]
to cut off the memory[v] of them from the earth.

17The righteous cry out, and the LORD hears[w] them;
he delivers them from all their troubles.
18The LORD is close[x] to the broken-hearted[y]
and saves those who are crushed in spirit.

19A righteous man may have many troubles,[z]
but the LORD delivers him from them all;[a]
20he protects all his bones,
not one of them will be broken.[b]

21Evil will slay the wicked;[c]
the foes of the righteous will be condemned.
22The LORD redeems[d] his servants;
no-one will be condemned who takes refuge in him.

Psalm 35

Of David.

1Contend, O LORD, with those who contend with me;
fight[a] against those who fight against me.
2Take up shield and buckler;
arise[b] and come to my aid.
3Brandish spear and javelin[a]
against those who pursue me.
Say to my soul,
"I am your salvation."

4May those who seek my life

34:1 a Ps 71:6; Eph 5:20
34:2 b Jer 9:24; 1Co 1:31; c Ps 119:74
34:3 d Lk 1:46
34:4 e Mt 7:7
34:5 f Ps 36:9; g Ps 25:3
34:7 h 2Ki 6:17; Da 6:22
34:8 i 1Pe 2:3; j Ps 2:12
34:9 k Ps 23:1
34:10 l Ps 84:11
34:11 m Ps 32:8
34:12 n 1Pe 3:10
34:13 o 1Pe 2:22
34:14 p Ps 37:27; q Heb 12:14
34:15 r Ps 33:18; s Job 36:7
34:16 t Lev 17:10; Jer 44:11; u 1Pe 3:10-12*; v Pr 10:7
34:17 w Ps 145:19
34:18 x Ps 145:18; y Isa 57:15
34:19 z ver 17; a ver 4,6; Pr 24:16
34:20 b Jn 19:36*
34:21 c Ps 94:23
34:22 d 1Ki 1:29; Ps 71:23
35:1 a Ps 43:1
35:2 b Ps 62:2

[a]This psalm is an acrostic poem, the verses of which begin with the successive letters of the Hebrew alphabet.
[a]3 Or *and block the way*

be disgraced[c] and put to
shame;
may those who plot my ruin
be turned back in dismay.
5 May they be like chaff[d] before
the wind,
with the angel of the LORD
driving them away;
6 may their path be dark and
slippery,
with the angel of the LORD
pursuing them.
7 Since they hid their net for me
without cause
and without cause dug a pit
for me,
8 may ruin overtake them by
surprise—[e]
may the net they hid entangle
them,
may they fall into the pit,[f] to
their ruin.
9 Then my soul will rejoice[g] in
the LORD
and delight in his salvation.[h]
10 My whole being will exclaim,
"Who is like you,[i] O LORD?
You rescue the poor from those
too strong[j] for them,
the poor and needy[k] from
those who rob them."

11 Ruthless witnesses[l] come
forward;
they question me on things I
know nothing about.
12 They repay me evil for good[m]
and leave my soul forlorn.
13 Yet when they were ill, I put on
sackcloth
and humbled myself with
fasting.[n]
When my prayers returned to
me unanswered,
14 I went about mourning
as though for my friend or
brother.
I bowed my head in grief
as though weeping for my
mother.
15 But when I stumbled, they
gathered in glee;
attackers gathered against me
when I was unaware.
They slandered[o] me without
ceasing.
16 Like the ungodly they
maliciously mocked;[b]
they gnashed their teeth[p] at
me.
17 O Lord, how long[q] will you look
on?
Rescue my life from their
ravages,
my precious life[r] from these
lions.
18 I will give you thanks in the
great assembly;[s]
among throngs of people I will
praise you.[t]

19 Let not those gloat over me
who are my enemies without
cause;
let not those who hate me
without reason[u]
maliciously wink the eye.[v]
20 They do not speak peaceably,
but devise false accusations
against those who live quietly
in the land.
21 They gape[w] at me and say,
"Aha! Aha![x]
With our own eyes we have
seen it."
22 O LORD, you have seen[y] this; be
not silent.
Do not be far[z] from me,
O Lord.
23 Awake,[a] and rise to my
defence!
Contend for me, my God and
Lord.
24 Vindicate me in your
righteousness, O LORD my
God;
do not let them gloat over me.
25 Do not let them think, "Aha,
just what we wanted!"
or say, "We have swallowed
him up."[b]
26 May all who gloat over my
distress
be put to shame[c] and
confusion;

35:4 c Ps 70:2
35:5 d Job 21:18; Ps 1:4; Isa 29:5
35:8 e 1Th 5:3; f Ps 9:15
35:9 g Lk 1:47; h Isa 61:10
35:10 i Ex 15:11; j Ps 18:17; k Ps 37:14
35:11 l Ps 27:12
35:12 m Jn 10:32
35:13 n Job 30:25; Ps 69:10
35:15 o Job 30:1,8
35:16 p Job 16:9; La 2:16
35:17 q Hab 1:13; r Ps 22:20
35:18 s Ps 22:25; t Ps 22:22
35:19 u Ps 38:19; Ps 69:4; Jn 15:25*; v Ps 13:4; Pr 6:13
35:21 w Ps 22:13; x Ps 40:15
35:22 y Ex 3:7; z Ps 10:1; Ps 28:1
35:23 a Ps 44:23
35:25 b La 2:16
35:26 c Ps 40:14; Ps 109:29

b16 Septuagint; Hebrew may mean *ungodly circle of mockers.*

may all who exalt themselves
over me[d]
be clothed with shame and
disgrace.
27 May those who delight in my
vindication[e]
shout for joy[f] and gladness;
may they always say, "The LORD
be exalted,
who delights[g] in the well-
being of his servant."
28 My tongue will speak of your
righteousness[h]
and of your praises all day
long.

Psalm 36

For the director of music. Of David the servant of the LORD.

1 An oracle is within my heart
concerning the sinfulness of
the wicked:[a]
There is no fear of God
before his eyes.[a]
2 For in his own eyes he flatters
himself
too much to detect or hate his
sin.
3 The words of his mouth[b] are
wicked and deceitful;
he has ceased to be wise[c] and
to do good.[d]
4 Even on his bed he plots evil;[e]
he commits himself to a sinful
course[f]
and does not reject what is
wrong.[g]

5 Your love, O LORD, reaches to
the heavens,
your faithfulness to the skies.
6 Your righteousness is like the
mighty mountains,
your justice like the great
deep.[h]
O LORD, you preserve both man
and beast.
7 How priceless is your
unfailing love!
Both high and low among men
find[b] refuge in the shadow of
your wings.[i]

35:26
d Ps 38:16

35:27
e Ps 9:4
f Ps 32:11
g Ps 40:16
Ps 147:11

35:28
h Ps 51:14

36:1
a Ro 3:18*

36:3
b Ps 10:7
c Ps 94:8
d Jer 4:22

36:4
e Pr 4:16
Mic 2:1
f Isa 65:2
g Ps 52:3
Ro 12:9

36:6
h Job 11:8
Ps 77:19
Ro 11:33

36:7
i Ru 2:12
Ps 17:8

36:8
j Ps 65:4
k Job 20:17
Rev 22:1

36:9
l Jer 2:13
m 1Pe 2:9

36:12
n Ps 140:10

37:1
a Pr 23:17-18
b Ps 73:3

37:2
c Ps 90:6

37:3
d Dt 30:20
e Isa 40:11
Jn 10:9

37:4
f Isa 58:14

37:5
g Ps 4:5
Ps 55:22
Pr 16:3
1Pe 5:7

37:6
h Mic 7:9
i Job 11:17

37:7
j Ps 62:5
La 3:26
k Ps 40:1

8 They feast in the abundance of
your house;[j]
you give them drink from
your river[k] of delights.
9 For with you is the fountain of
life;[l]
in your light[m] we see light.

10 Continue your love to those who
know you,
your righteousness to the
upright in heart.
11 May the foot of the proud not
come against me,
nor the hand of the wicked
drive me away.
12 See how the evildoers lie
fallen—
thrown down, not able to
rise![n]

Psalm 37[a]

Of David.

1 Do not fret because of evil men
or be envious[a] of those who
do wrong;[b]
2 for like the grass they will soon
wither,
like green plants they will
soon die away.[c]

3 Trust in the LORD and do good;
dwell in the land[d] and enjoy
safe pasture.[e]
4 Delight[f] yourself in the LORD
and he will give you the
desires of your heart.
5 Commit your way to the LORD;
trust in him[g] and he will do
this:
6 He will make your
righteousness[h] shine like
the dawn,[i]
the justice of your cause like
the noonday sun.

7 Be still[j] before the LORD and
wait patiently[k] for him;

[a] 1 Or *heart: / Sin proceeds from the wicked.*
[b] 7 Or *love, O God! / Men find*; or *love! / Both heavenly beings and men / find*
[a] This psalm is an acrostic poem, the stanzas of which begin with the successive letters of the Hebrew alphabet.

do not fret when men succeed
in their ways,
when they carry out their
wicked schemes.
8Refrain from anger[l] and turn
from wrath;
do not fret—it leads only to
evil.
9For evil men will be cut off,
but those who hope in the
LORD will inherit the land.[m]
10A little while, and the wicked
will be no more;[n]
though you look for them, they
will not be found.
11But the meek will inherit the
land[o]
and enjoy great peace.

12The wicked plot against the
righteous
and gnash their teeth[p] at
them;
13but the Lord laughs at the
wicked,
for he knows their day is
coming.[q]

14The wicked draw the sword
and bend the bow[r]
to bring down the poor and
needy,[s]
to slay those whose ways are
upright.
15But their swords will pierce
their own hearts,[t]
and their bows will be broken.

16Better the little that the
righteous have
than the wealth[u] of many
wicked;
17for the power of the wicked will
be broken,[v]
but the LORD upholds the
righteous.
18The days of the blameless are
known to the LORD,[w]
and their inheritance will
endure for ever.
19In times of disaster they will
not wither;
in days of famine they will
enjoy plenty.

20But the wicked will perish:
The LORD's enemies will be
like the beauty of the
fields,
they will vanish—vanish like
smoke.[x]

21The wicked borrow and do not
repay,
but the righteous give
generously;[y]
22those the LORD blesses will
inherit the land,
but those he curses[z] will be
cut off.

23If the LORD delights[a] in a
man's way,
he makes his steps firm;[b]
24though he stumble, he will not
fall,[c]
for the LORD upholds[d] him
with his hand.

25I was young and now I am old,
yet I have never seen the
righteous forsaken[e]
or their children begging
bread.
26They are always generous and
lend freely;
their children will be
blessed.[f]

27Turn from evil and do good;[g]
then you will dwell in the land
for ever.
28For the LORD loves the just
and will not forsake his
faithful ones.

They will be protected for ever,
but the offspring of the
wicked will be cut off;[h]
29the righteous will inherit the
land[i]
and dwell in it for ever.

30The mouth of the righteous man
utters wisdom,
and his tongue speaks what is
just.
31The law of his God is in his
heart;[j]
his feet do not slip.[k]

37:8 l Eph 4:31; Col 3:8
37:9 m Isa 57:13; Isa 60:21
37:10 n Job 7:10; Job 24:24
37:11 o Mt 5:5
37:12 p Ps 35:16
37:13 q 1Sa 26:10; Ps 2:4
37:14 r Ps 11:2; s Ps 35:10
37:15 t Ps 9:16
37:16 u Pr 15:16
37:17 v Job 38:15; Ps 10:15
37:18 w Ps 1:6
37:20 x Ps 102:3
37:21 y Ps 112:5
37:22 z Job 5:3; Pr 3:33
37:23 a Ps 147:11; b 1Sa 2:9
37:24 c Pr 24:16; d Ps 145:14; Ps 147:6
37:25 e Heb 13:5
37:26 f Ps 147:13
37:27 g Ps 34:14
37:28 h Ps 21:10; Isa 14:20
37:29 i ver 9; Pr 2:21
37:31 j Dt 6:6; Ps 40:8; Isa 51:7; k ver 23

32The wicked lie in wait[l] for the
righteous,
seeking their very lives;
33but the LORD will not leave
them in their power
or let them be condemned
when brought to trial.[m]

34Wait for the LORD[n]
and keep his way.
He will exalt you to inherit the
land;
when the wicked are cut off,
you will see[o] it.

35I have seen a wicked and
ruthless man
flourishing[p] like a green tree
in its native soil,
36but he soon passed away and
was no more;
though I looked for him, he
could not be found.[q]

37Consider the blameless, observe
the upright;
there is a future[b] for the man
of peace.[r]
38But all sinners will be
destroyed;
the future[c] of the wicked will
be cut off.[s]

39The salvation[t] of the righteous
comes from the LORD;
he is their stronghold in time
of trouble.[u]
40The LORD helps[v] them and
delivers[w] them;
he delivers them from the
wicked and saves them,
because they take refuge in
him.

Psalm 38

A psalm of David. A petition.

1O LORD, do not rebuke me in
your anger
or discipline me in your
wrath.[a]
2For your arrows[b] have pierced
me,
and your hand has come down
upon me.

37:32 *l* Ps 10:8
37:33 *m* Ps 109:31; 2Pe 2:9
37:34 *n* Ps 27:14 *o* Ps 52:6
37:35 *p* Job 5:3
37:36 *q* Job 20:5
37:37 *r* Isa 57:1-2
37:38 *s* Ps 1:4
37:39 *t* Ps 3:8 *u* Ps 9:9
37:40 *v* 1Ch 5:20 *w* Isa 31:5
38:1 *a* Ps 6:1
38:2 *b* Job 6:4; Ps 32:4
38:3 *c* Ps 6:2; Isa 1:6
38:4 *d* Ezr 9:6
38:5 *e* Ps 69:5
38:6 *f* Job 30:28; Ps 35:14; Ps 42:9
38:7 *g* Ps 102:3
38:8 *h* Ps 22:1
38:9 *i* Job 3:24; Ps 6:6; Ps 10:17
38:10 *j* Ps 31:10 *k* Ps 6:7
38:11 *l* Ps 31:11
38:12 *m* Ps 140:5 *n* Ps 35:4; Ps 54:3 *o* Ps 35:20
38:15 *p* Ps 39:7 *q* Ps 17:6

3Because of your wrath there is
no health in my body;
my bones[c] have no soundness
because of my sin.
4My guilt has overwhelmed me
like a burden too heavy to
bear.[d]

5My wounds fester and are
loathsome
because of my sinful folly.[e]
6I am bowed down and brought
very low;
all day long I go about
mourning.[f]
7My back is filled with searing
pain;[g]
there is no health in my body.
8I am feeble and utterly
crushed;
I groan[h] in anguish of heart.

9All my longings lie open before
you, O Lord;
my sighing[i] is not hidden
from you.
10My heart pounds, my strength
fails[j] me;
even the light has gone from
my eyes.[k]
11My friends and companions
avoid me because of my
wounds;[l]
my neighbours stay far away.
12Those who seek my life set
their traps,[m]
those who would harm me talk
of my ruin;[n]
all day long they plot
deception.[o]

13I am like a deaf man, who
cannot hear,
like a mute, who cannot open
his mouth;
14I have become like a man who
does not hear,
whose mouth can offer no
reply.
15I wait[p] for you, O LORD;
you will answer,[q] O Lord my
God.

[b]37 Or *there will be posterity* [c]38 Or *posterity*

16For I said, "Do not let them
gloat[r]
or exalt themselves over me
when my foot slips."[s]

17For I am about to fall,
and my pain is ever with me.
18I confess my iniquity;[t]
I am troubled by my sin.
19Many are those who are my
vigorous enemies;[u]
those who hate me without
reason[v] are numerous.
20Those who repay my good with
evil[w]
slander me when I pursue
what is good.

21O LORD, do not forsake me;
be not far[x] from me, O my
God.
22Come quickly to help me,[y]
O Lord my Saviour.[z]

Psalm 39

For the director of music. For Jeduthun. A psalm of David.

1I said, "I will watch my ways[a]
and keep my tongue from
sin;[b]
I will put a muzzle on my mouth
as long as the wicked are in
my presence."
2But when I was silent[c] and
still,
not even saying anything good,
my anguish increased.
3My heart grew hot within me,
and as I meditated, the fire
burned;
then I spoke with my tongue:

4"Show me, O LORD, my life's
end
and the number of my days;[d]
let me know how fleeting is
my life.[e]
5You have made my days[f] a
mere handbreadth;
the span of my years is as
nothing before you.
Each man's life is but a
breath.[g] *Selah*

38:16 r Ps 35:26 s Ps 13:4
38:18 t Ps 32:5
38:19 u Ps 18:17 v Ps 35:19
38:20 w Ps 35:12 1Jn 3:12
38:21 x Ps 35:22
38:22 y Ps 40:13 z Ps 27:1
39:1 a 1Ki 2:4 b Job 2:10 Jas 3:2
39:2 c Ps 38:13
39:4 d Ps 90:12 e Ps 103:14
39:5 f Ps 89:45 g Ps 62:9
39:6 h 1Pe 1:24 i Ps 127:2 j Lk 12:20
39:7 k Ps 38:15
39:8 l Ps 51:9 m Ps 44:13
39:9 n Job 2:10
39:10 o Job 9:34 Ps 32:4
39:11 p 2Pe 2:16 q Job 13:28
39:12 r 1Pe 2:11 s Heb 11:13
39:13 t Job 10:21 Job 14:10
40:1 a Ps 27:14 b Ps 34:15
40:2 c Ps 69:14

6Man is a mere phantom[h] as he
goes to and fro:
He bustles about, but only in
vain;[i]
he heaps up wealth, not
knowing who will get it.[j]

7"But now, Lord, what do I look
for?
My hope is in you.[k]
8Save me[l] from all my
transgressions;[m]
do not make me the scorn of
fools.
9I was silent; I would not open
my mouth,[n]
for you are the one who has
done this.
10Remove your scourge from me;
I am overcome by the blow of
your hand.[o]
11You rebuke[p] and discipline
men for their sin;
you consume their wealth like
a moth[q]—
each man is but a breath.
Selah

12"Hear my prayer, O LORD,
listen to my cry for help;
be not deaf to my weeping.
For I dwell with you as an
alien,[r]
a stranger,[s] as all my fathers
were.
13Look away from me, that I may
rejoice again
before I depart and am no
more."[t]

Psalm 40

40:13–17pp Ps 70:1–5

For the director of music. Of David. A psalm.

1I waited patiently[a] for the
LORD;
he turned to me and heard my
cry.[b]
2He lifted me out of the slimy
pit,
out of the mud and mire;[c]

he set my feet on a rock[d]
and gave me a firm place to
stand.
3 He put a new song[e] in my
mouth,
a hymn of praise to our God.
Many will see and fear
and put their trust in the
LORD.

4 Blessed is the man[f]
who makes the LORD his
trust,[g]
who does not look to the proud,
to those who turn aside to
false gods.[a]
5 Many, O LORD my God,
are the wonders[h] you have
done.
The things you planned for us
no-one can recount[i] to you;
were I to speak and tell of
them,
they would be too many to
declare.

6 Sacrifice and offering you did
not desire,[j]
but my ears you have
pierced;[b,c]
burnt offerings[k] and sin
offerings
you did not require.
7 Then I said, "Here I am, I have
come—
it is written about me in the
scroll.[d]
8 I desire to do your will,[l] O my
God;
your law is within my heart."[m]

9 I proclaim righteousness in the
great assembly;[n]
I do not seal my lips,
as you know,[o] O LORD.
10 I do not hide your righteousness
in my heart;
I speak of your faithfulness[p]
and salvation.
I do not conceal your love and
your truth
from the great assembly.[q]

11 Do not withhold your mercy
from me, O LORD;
may your love[r] and your
truth[s] always protect me.
12 For troubles[t] without number
surround me;
my sins have overtaken me,
and I cannot see.[u]
They are more than the hairs of
my head,[v]
and my heart fails[w] within
me.

13 Be pleased, O LORD, to save me;
O LORD, come quickly to help
me.[x]
14 May all who seek to take my
life
be put to shame and
confusion;
may all who desire my ruin[y]
be turned back in disgrace.
15 May those who say to me, "Aha!
Aha!"
be appalled at their own
shame.
16 But may all who seek you
rejoice and be glad in you;
may those who love your
salvation always say,
"The LORD be exalted!"[z]

17 Yet I am poor and needy;
may the Lord think of me.
You are my help and my
deliverer;
O my God, do not delay.[a]

Psalm 41

For the director of music. A psalm
of David.

1 Blessed is he who has regard
for the weak;[a]
the LORD delivers him in times
of trouble.
2 The LORD will protect him and
preserve his life;
he will bless him in the land[b]

40:2 *d* Ps 27:5
40:3 *e* Ps 33:3
40:4 *f* Ps 34:8 *g* Ps 84:12
40:5 *h* Ps 136:4 *i* Ps 139:18 Isa 55:8
40:6 *j* 1Sa 15:22 Am 5:22 *k* Isa 1:11
40:8 *l* Jn 4:34 *m* Ps 37:31
40:9 *n* Ps 22:25 *o* Jos 22:22 Ps 119:13
40:10 *p* Ps 89:1 *q* Ac 20:20
40:11 *r* Pr 20:28 *s* Ps 43:3
40:12 *t* Ps 116:3 *u* Ps 38:4 *v* Ps 69:4 *w* Ps 73:26
40:13 *x* Ps 70:1
40:14 *y* Ps 35:4
40:16 *z* Ps 35:27
40:17 *a* Ps 70:5
41:1 *a* Ps 82:3-4 Pr 14:21
41:2 *b* Ps 37:22

a4 Or *to falsehood* b6 Hebrew; Septuagint *but a body you have prepared for me* (see also Symmachus and Theodotion) c6 Or *opened* d7 Or *come / with the scroll written for me*

and not surrender him to the
desire of his foes.[c]
3 The LORD will sustain him on
his sick-bed
and restore him from his bed
of illness.

4 I said, "O LORD, have mercy[d]
on me;
heal me, for I have sinned[e]
against you."
5 My enemies say of me in
malice,
"When will he die and his
name perish?[f]"
6 Whenever one comes to see
me,
he speaks falsely,[g] while his
heart gathers slander;[h]
then he goes out and spreads
it abroad.

7 All my enemies whisper
together[i] against me;
they imagine the worst for
me, saying,
8 "A vile disease has beset him;
he will never get up from the
place where he lies."
9 Even my close friend,[j] whom I
trusted,
he who shared my bread,
has lifted up his heel against
me.[k]

10 But you, O LORD, have mercy on
me;
raise me up,[l] that I may
repay them.
11 I know that you are pleased
with me,[m]
for my enemy does not
triumph over me.[n]
12 In my integrity you uphold me[o]
and set me in your presence
for ever.[p]

13 Praise be to the LORD, the God
of Israel,[q]
from everlasting to
everlasting.
Amen and Amen.[r]

41:2 *c* Ps 27:12
41:4 *d* Ps 6:2 *e* Ps 51:4
41:5 *f* Ps 38:12
41:6 *g* Ps 12:2 *h* Pr 26:24
41:7 *i* Ps 56:5; Ps 71:10-11
41:9 *j* 2Sa 15:12; Ps 55:12 *k* Job 19:19; Ps 55:20; Mt 26:23; Jn 13:18*
41:10 *l* Ps 3:3
41:11 *m* Ps 147:11 *n* Ps 25:2
41:12 *o* Ps 37:17 *p* Job 36:7
41:13 *q* Ps 72:18 *r* Ps 89:52; Ps 106:48
42:1 *a* Ps 119:131
42:2 *b* Ps 63:1 *c* Jer 10:10 *d* Ps 43:4
42:3 *e* Ps 80:5 *f* Ps 79:10
42:4 *g* Isa 30:29 *h* Ps 100:4
42:5 *i* Ps 38:6; Ps 77:3 *j* La 3:24 *k* Ps 44:3
42:7 *l* Ps 88:7; Jnh 2:3
42:8 *m* Ps 57:3

Book II: Psalms 42–72

Psalm 42[a]

For the director of music. A *maskil*[b] of the Sons of Korah.

1 As the deer pants for streams
of water,
so my soul pants[a] for you,
O God.
2 My soul thirsts[b] for God, for
the living God.[c]
When can I go[d] and meet with
God?
3 My tears[e] have been my food
day and night,
while men say to me all day
long,
"Where is your God?"[f]
4 These things I remember
as I pour out my soul:
how I used to go with the
multitude,
leading the procession to the
house of God,[g]
with shouts of joy and
thanksgiving[h]
among the festive throng.

5 Why are you downcast,[i] O my
soul?
Why so disturbed within me?
Put your hope in God,[j]
for I will yet praise him,
my Saviour[k] and 6 my God.

My[c] soul is downcast within
me;
therefore I will remember you
from the land of the Jordan,
the heights of Hermon—from
Mount Mizar.
7 Deep calls to deep
in the roar of your waterfalls;
all your waves and breakers
have swept over me.[l]

8 By day the LORD directs his
love,[m]

aIn many Hebrew manuscripts Psalms 42 and 43 constitute one psalm. **b**Title: Probably a literary or musical term **c**5,6 A few Hebrew manuscripts, Septuagint and Syriac; most Hebrew manuscripts *praise him for his saving help.* / 6*O my God, my*

at night[n] his song[o] is with
me—
a prayer to the God of my life.

9 I say to God my Rock,
"Why have you forgotten me?
Why must I go about
mourning,[p]
oppressed by the enemy?"
10 My bones suffer mortal agony
as my foes taunt me,
saying to me all day long,
"Where is your God?"

11 Why are you downcast, O my
soul?
Why so disturbed within me?
Put your hope in God,
for I will yet praise him,
my Saviour and my God.[q]

Psalm 43[a]

1 Vindicate me, O God,
and plead my cause[a] against
an ungodly nation;
rescue me from deceitful and
wicked men.[b]
2 You are God my stronghold.
Why have you rejected[c] me?
Why must I go about mourning,
oppressed by the enemy?[d]
3 Send forth your light[e] and your
truth,
let them guide me;
let them bring me to your holy
mountain,[f]
to the place where you dwell.[g]
4 Then will I go to the altar[h] of
God,
to God, my joy and my
delight.
I will praise you with the
harp,[i]
O God, my God.

5 Why are you downcast, O my
soul?
Why so disturbed within me?
Put your hope in God,
for I will yet praise him,
my Saviour and my God.[j]

42:8 *n* Job 35:10 *o* Ps 63:6; Ps 149:5
42:9 *p* Ps 38:6
42:11 *q* Ps 43:5
43:1 *a* 1Sa 24:15; Ps 26:1; Ps 35:1 *b* Ps 5:6
43:2 *c* Ps 44:9 *d* Ps 42:9
43:3 *e* Ps 36:9 *f* Ps 42:4 *g* Ps 84:1
43:4 *h* Ps 26:6 *i* Ps 33:2
43:5 *j* Ps 42:6
44:1 *a* Ex 12:26; Ps 78:3
44:2 *b* Ps 78:55 *c* Ex 15:17 *d* Ps 80:9
44:3 *e* Dt 8:17; Jos 24:12 *f* Ps 77:15 *g* Dt 4:37; Dt 7:7-8
44:4 *h* Ps 74:12
44:5 *i* Ps 108:13
44:6 *j* Ps 33:16
44:7 *k* Ps 136:24 *l* Ps 53:5
44:8 *m* Ps 34:2 *n* Ps 30:12
44:9 *o* Ps 74:1 *p* Ps 60:1,10
44:10 *q* Lev 26:17; Jos 7:8; Ps 89:41

Psalm 44

For the director of music. Of the Sons of Korah. A *maskil*.[a]

1 We have heard with our ears,
O God;
our fathers have told us[a]
what you did in their days,
in days long ago.
2 With your hand you drove out[b]
the nations
and planted[c] our fathers;
you crushed the peoples
and made our fathers
flourish.[d]
3 It was not by their sword[e] that
they won the land,
nor did their arm bring them
victory;
it was your right hand, your
arm,[f]
and the light of your face, for
you loved[g] them.

4 You are my King[h] and my God,
who decrees[b] victories for
Jacob.
5 Through you we push back our
enemies;
through your name we
trample[i] our foes.
6 I do not trust in my bow,[j]
my sword does not bring me
victory;
7 but you give us victory[k] over
our enemies,
you put our adversaries to
shame.[l]
8 In God we make our boast[m] all
day long,
and we will praise your name
for ever.[n] *Selah*

9 But now you have rejected[o]
and humbled us;
you no longer go out with our
armies.[p]
10 You made us retreat[q] before
the enemy,
and our adversaries have
plundered us.

[a]In many Hebrew manuscripts Psalms 42 and 43 constitute one psalm. [a]Title: Probably a literary or musical term [b]4 Septuagint, Aquila and Syriac; Hebrew *King, O God; / command*

11You gave us up to be devoured
like sheep[r]
and have scattered us among
the nations.[s]
12You sold your people for a
pittance,[t]
gaining nothing from their
sale.

13You have made us a reproach to
our neighbours,[u]
the scorn[v] and derision of
those around us.
14You have made us a byword
among the nations;
the peoples shake their
heads[w] at us.
15My disgrace is before me all
day long,
and my face is covered with
shame
16at the taunts of those who
reproach and revile[x] me,
because of the enemy, who is
bent on revenge.

17All this happened to us,
though we had not forgotten[y]
you
or been false to your
covenant.
18Our hearts had not turned[z]
back;
our feet had not strayed from
your path.
19But you crushed[a] us and made
us a haunt for jackals
and covered us over with deep
darkness.[b]

20If we had forgotten[c] the name
of our God
or spread out our hands to a
foreign god,[d]
21would not God have discovered
it,
since he knows the secrets of
the heart?[e]
22Yet for your sake we face death
all day long;
we are considered as sheep to
be slaughtered.[f]

23Awake,[g] O Lord! Why do you
sleep?[h]

44:11
r Ro 8:36
s Dt 4:27; Dt 28:64; Ps 106:27
44:12
t Isa 52:3; Jer 15:13
44:13
u Ps 79:4; Ps 80:6
v Dt 28:37
44:14
w Ps 109:25; Jer 24:9
44:16
x Ps 74:10
44:17
y Ps 78:7,57; Da 9:13
44:18
z Job 23:11
44:19
a Ps 51:8
b Job 3:5
44:20
c Ps 78:11
d Dt 6:14; Ps 81:9
44:21
e Ps 139:1-2; Jer 17:10
44:22
f Isa 53:7; Ro 8:36*
44:23
g Ps 7:6
h Ps 78:65
i Ps 77:7
44:24
j Job 13:24
k Ps 42:9
44:25
l Ps 119:25
44:26
m Ps 35:2
n Ps 25:22
45:2
a Lk 4:22
45:3
b Heb 4:12; Rev 1:16
c Isa 9:6
45:4
d Rev 6:2
45:6
e Ps 93:2; Ps 98:9
45:7
f Ps 33:5

Rouse yourself! Do not reject
us for ever.[i]
24Why do you hide your face[j]
and forget our misery and
oppression?[k]

25We are brought down to the
dust;[l]
our bodies cling to the ground.
26Rise up[m] and help us;
redeem[n] us because of your
unfailing love.

Psalm 45

For the director of music. To ⌊the tune of⌋ "Lilies". Of the Sons of Korah. A *maskil*.[a] A wedding song.

1My heart is stirred by a noble
theme
as I recite my verses for the
king;
my tongue is the pen of a
skilful writer.

2You are the most excellent of
men
and your lips have been
anointed with grace,[a]
since God has blessed you for
ever.
3Gird your sword[b] upon your
side, O mighty one;[c]
clothe yourself with splendour
and majesty.
4In your majesty ride forth
victoriously[d]
on behalf of truth, humility
and righteousness;
let your right hand display
awesome deeds.
5Let your sharp arrows pierce
the hearts of the king's
enemies;
let the nations fall beneath
your feet.
6Your throne, O God, will last
for ever and ever;[e]
a sceptre of justice will be the
sceptre of your kingdom.
7You love righteousness[f] and
hate wickedness;

[a]Title: Probably a literary or musical term

therefore God, your God, has
set you above your
companions
by anointing[g] you with the oil
of joy.[h]
8All your robes are fragrant[i]
with myrrh and aloes and
cassia;
from palaces adorned with
ivory
the music of the strings makes
you glad.
9Daughters of kings[j] are among
your honoured women;
at your right hand[k] is the
royal bride in gold of
Ophir.

10Listen, O daughter, consider
and give ear:
Forget your people[l] and your
father's house.
11The king is enthralled by your
beauty;
honour[m] him, for he is your
lord.[n]
12The Daughter of Tyre will come
with a gift,[b][o]
men of wealth will seek your
favour.

13All glorious[p] is the princess
within ⌊her chamber⌋;
her gown is interwoven with
gold.
14In embroidered garments she is
led to the king;[q]
her virgin companions follow
her
and are brought to you.
15They are led in with joy and
gladness;
they enter the palace of the
king.

16Your sons will take the place of
your fathers;
you will make them princes
throughout the land.
17I will perpetuate your memory
through all generations;[r]
therefore the nations will
praise you[s] for ever and
ever.

Psalm 46

For the director of music. Of the Sons of Korah. According to *alamoth*.[a] A song.

1God is our refuge[a] and
strength,
an ever-present[b] help in
trouble.
2Therefore we will not fear,[c]
though the earth give way[d]
and the mountains fall[e] into
the heart of the sea,
3though its waters roar[f] and
foam
and the mountains quake with
their surging. *Selah*

4There is a river whose streams
make glad the city of
God,[g]
the holy place where the Most
High dwells.
5God is within her,[h] she will not
fall;
God will help[i] her at break of
day.
6Nations[j] are in uproar,
kingdoms[k] fall;
he lifts his voice, the earth
melts.[l]

7The LORD Almighty is with us;[m]
the God of Jacob is our
fortress.[n] *Selah*

8Come and see the works of the
LORD,[o]
the desolations[p] he has
brought on the earth.
9He makes wars[q] cease to the
ends of the earth;
he breaks the bow[r] and
shatters the spear,
he burns the shields[b] with
fire.[s]
10"Be still, and know that I am
God;[t]
I will be exalted[u] among the
nations,
I will be exalted in the earth."

45:7 g Isa 61:1 h Ps 21:6 Heb 1:8-9*
45:8 i SS 1:3
45:9 j SS 6:8 k 1Ki 2:19
45:10 l Dt 21:13
45:11 m Ps 95:6 n Isa 54:5
45:12 o Ps 22:29 Isa 49:23
45:13 p Isa 61:10
45:14 q SS 1:4
45:17 r Mal 1:11 s Ps 138:4
46:1 a Ps 9:9 Ps 14:6 b Dt 4:7
46:2 c Ps 23:4 d Ps 82:5 e Ps 18:7
46:3 f Ps 93:3
46:4 g Ps 48:1,8 Isa 60:14
46:5 h Isa 12:6 Eze 43:7 i Ps 37:40
46:6 j Ps 2:1 k Ps 68:32 l Mic 1:4
46:7 m 2Ch 13:12 n Ps 9:9
46:8 o Ps 66:5 p Isa 61:4
46:9 q Isa 2:4 r Ps 76:3 s Eze 39:9
46:10 t Ps 100:3 u Isa 2:11

[b]12 Or *A Tyrian robe is among the gifts* [a]Title: Probably a musical term [b]9 Or *chariots*

11 The LORD Almighty is with us;
the God of Jacob is our
fortress. *Selah*

Psalm 47

For the director of music. Of the Sons of Korah. A psalm.

1 Clap your hands,[a] all you
nations;
shout to God with cries of
joy.[b]
2 How awesome[c] is the LORD
Most High,
the great King[d] over all the
earth!
3 He subdued[e] nations under us,
peoples under our feet.
4 He chose our inheritance[f] for
us,
the pride of Jacob, whom he
loved. *Selah*
5 God has ascended amid shouts
of joy,
the LORD amid the sounding of
trumpets.[g]
6 Sing praises[h] to God, sing
praises;
sing praises to our King, sing
praises.
7 For God is the King of all the
earth;[i]
sing to him a psalm[a][j] of
praise.
8 God reigns[k] over the nations;
God is seated on his holy
throne.
9 The nobles of the nations
assemble
as the people of the God of
Abraham,
for the kings[b] of the earth
belong to God;[l]
he is greatly exalted.[m]

Psalm 48

A song. A psalm of the Sons of Korah.

1 Great is the LORD,[a] and most
worthy of praise,
in the city of our God,[b] his
holy mountain.[c]
2 It is beautiful[d] in its loftiness,
the joy of the whole earth.
Like the utmost heights of
Zaphon[a] is Mount Zion,
the[b] city of the Great King.[e]
3 God is in her citadels;
he has shown himself to be
her fortress.[f]
4 When the kings joined forces,
when they advanced
together,[g]
5 they saw ⌞her⌟ and were
astounded;
they fled in terror.[h]
6 Trembling seized them there,
pain like that of a woman in
labour.
7 You destroyed them like ships
of Tarshish
shattered by an east wind.[i]
8 As we have heard,
so have we seen
in the city of the LORD
Almighty,
in the city of our God:
God makes her secure for
ever.[j] *Selah*
9 Within your temple, O God,
we meditate on your unfailing
love.[k]
10 Like your name,[l] O God,
your praise reaches to the
ends of the earth;[m]
your right hand is filled with
righteousness.
11 Mount Zion rejoices,
the villages of Judah are glad
because of your judgments.[n]
12 Walk about Zion, go round her,
count her towers,
13 consider well her ramparts,
view her citadels,[o]
that you may tell of them to
the next generation.[p]
14 For this God is our God for
ever and ever;
he will be our guide[q] even to
the end.

[a]7 Or *a maskil* (probably a literary or musical term) [b]9 Or *shields* [a]2 *Zaphon* can refer to a sacred mountain or the direction north.
[b]2 Or *earth, / Mount Zion, on the northern side / of the*

47:1 *a* Ps 98:8; Isa 55:12 *b* Ps 106:47
47:2 *c* Dt 7:21 *d* Mal 1:14
47:3 *e* Ps 18:39,47
47:4 *f* 1Pe 1:4
47:5 *g* Ps 68:33; Ps 98:6
47:6 *h* Ps 68:4; Ps 89:18
47:7 *i* Zec 14:9 *j* Col 3:16
47:8 *k* 1Ch 16:31
47:9 *l* Ps 72:11; Ps 89:18 *m* Ps 97:9
48:1 *a* Ps 96:4 *b* Ps 46:4 *c* Isa 2:2-3; Mic 4:1; Zec 8:3
48:2 *d* Ps 50:2; La 2:15 *e* Mt 5:35
48:3 *f* Ps 46:7
48:4 *g* 2Sa 10:1-19
48:5 *h* Ex 15:16
48:7 *i* Jer 18:17; Eze 27:26
48:8 *j* Ps 87:5
48:9 *k* Ps 26:3
48:10 *l* Dt 28:58; Jos 7:9 *m* Isa 41:10
48:11 *n* Ps 97:8
48:13 *o* ver 3; Ps 122:7 *p* Ps 78:6
48:14 *q* Ps 23:4

Psalm 49

For the director of music. Of the Sons of Korah. A psalm.

[1]Hear this, all you peoples;[a]
listen, all who live in this
world,[b]
[2]both low and high,
rich and poor alike:
[3]My mouth will speak words of
wisdom;[c]
the utterance from my heart
will give understanding.[d]
[4]I will turn my ear to a
proverb;[e]
with the harp I will expound
my riddle:[f]

[5]Why should I fear[g] when evil
days come,
when wicked deceivers
surround me—
[6]those who trust in their wealth[h]
and boast of their great
riches?
[7]No man can redeem the life of
another
or give to God a ransom for
him—
[8]the ransom for a life is costly,
no payment is ever enough—[i]
[9]that he should live on[j] for ever
and not see decay.

[10]For all can see that wise men
die;[k]
the foolish and the senseless
alike perish
and leave their wealth to
others.[l]
[11]Their tombs will remain their
houses[a] for ever,
their dwellings for endless
generations,
though they had[b] named[m]
lands after themselves.

[12]But man, despite his riches,
does not endure;
he is[c] like the beasts that
perish.

[13]This is the fate of those who
trust in themselves,[n]
and of their followers, who
approve their sayings.
Selah
[14]Like sheep they are destined
for the grave,[d][o]
and death will feed on them.
The upright will rule[p] over
them in the morning;
their forms will decay in the
grave,[d]
far from their princely
mansions.
[15]But God will redeem my life[e]
from the grave;[q]
he will surely take me to
himself.[r] *Selah*
[16]Do not be overawed when a
man grows rich,
when the splendour of his
house increases;
[17]for he will take nothing with
him when he dies,
his splendour will not descend
with him.[s]
[18]Though while he lived he
counted himself blessed—[t]
and men praise you when you
prosper—
[19]he will join the generation of
his fathers,[u]
who will never see the light[v]
⌞of life⌟.
[20]A man who has riches without
understanding
is like the beasts that perish.[w]

Psalm 50

A psalm of Asaph.

[1]The Mighty One, God, the
LORD,[a]
speaks and summons the earth
from the rising of the sun to
the place where it sets.[b]
[2]From Zion, perfect in beauty,[c]
God shines forth.[d]
[3]Our God comes[e] and will not
be silent;

[a]*11* Septuagint and Syriac; Hebrew *In their thoughts their houses will remain* [b]*11* Or */ for they have* [c]*12* Hebrew; Septuagint and Syriac read verse 12 the same as verse 20. [d]*14* Hebrew *Sheol*; also in verse 15 [e]*15* Or *soul*

49:1 a Ps 78:1 b Ps 33:8
49:3 c Ps 37:30 d Ps 119:130
49:4 e Ps 78:2 f Nu 12:8
49:5 g Ps 23:4
49:6 h Job 31:24
49:8 i Mt 16:26
49:9 j Ps 22:29 Ps 89:48
49:10 k Ecc 2:16 l Ecc 2:18,21
49:11 m Ge 4:17 Dt 3:14
49:13 n Lk 12:20
49:14 o Job 24:19 Ps 9:17 p Da 7:18 Mal 4:3 1Co 6:2 Rev 2:26
49:15 q Ps 56:13 Hos 13:14 r Ps 73:24
49:17 s Ps 17:14 1Ti 6:7
49:18 t Dt 29:19 Lk 12:19
49:19 u Ge 15:15 v Job 33:30
49:20 w Ecc 3:19
50:1 a Jos 22:22 b Ps 113:3
50:2 c Ps 48:2 d Dt 33:2 Ps 80:1
50:3 e Ps 96:13

a fire devours before him,[f]
and around him a tempest
rages.
4 He summons the heavens
above,
and the earth,[g] that he may
judge his people:
5 "Gather to me my consecrated
ones,[h]
who made a covenant[i] with
me by sacrifice."
6 And the heavens proclaim[j] his
righteousness,
for God himself is judge.[k]
Selah
7 "Hear, O my people, and I will
speak,
O Israel, and I will testify[l]
against you:
I am God, your God.[m]
8 I do not rebuke you for your
sacrifices
or your burnt offerings,[n]
which are ever before me.
9 I have no need of a bull[o] from
your stall
or of goats from your pens,
10 for every animal of the forest is
mine,
and the cattle on a thousand
hills.[p]
11 I know every bird in the
mountains,
and the creatures of the field
are mine.
12 If I were hungry I would not
tell you,
for the world[q] is mine, and all
that is in it.
13 Do I eat the flesh of bulls
or drink the blood of goats?
14 Sacrifice thank-offerings[r] to
God,
fulfil your vows[s] to the Most
High,
15 and call[t] upon me in the day of
trouble;
I will deliver you, and you will
honour[u] me."

16 But to the wicked, God says:

"What right have you to recite
my laws

50:3 f Ps 97:3; Da 7:10
50:4 g Dt 4:26; Isa 1:2
50:5 h Ps 30:4; i Ex 24:7
50:6 j Ps 89:5; k Ps 75:7
50:7 l Ps 81:8; m Ex 20:2
50:8 n Ps 40:6; Hos 6:6
50:9 o Ps 69:31
50:10 p Ps 104:24
50:12 q Ex 19:5
50:14 r Heb 13:15; s Dt 23:21
50:15 t Ps 81:7; u Ps 22:23
50:16 v Isa 29:13
50:17 w Ne 9:26; Ro 2:21-22
50:18 x Ro 1:32; 1Ti 5:22
50:19 y Ps 10:7; Ps 52:2
50:20 z Mt 10:21
50:21 a Ecc 8:11; Isa 42:14; b Ps 90:8
50:22 c Job 8:13; Ps 9:17; d Ps 7:2
50:23 e Ps 85:13; f Ps 91:16
51:1 a Ac 3:19; b Isa 43:25; Col 2:14
51:2 c 1Jn 1:9; d Heb 9:14
51:3 e Isa 59:12

or take my covenant on your
lips?[v]
17 You hate my instruction
and cast my words behind[w]
you.
18 When you see a thief, you join[x]
with him;
you throw in your lot with
adulterers.
19 You use your mouth for evil
and harness your tongue to
deceit.[y]
20 You speak continually against
your brother[z]
and slander your own mother's
son.
21 These things you have done and
I kept silent;[a]
you thought I was altogether[a]
like you.
But I will rebuke you
and accuse[b] you to your face.

22 "Consider this, you who forget
God,[c]
or I will tear you to pieces,
with none to rescue:[d]
23 He who sacrifices thank-
offerings honours
me,
and he prepares the way[e]
so that I may show him[b] the
salvation of God.[f]"

Psalm 51

For the director of music. A psalm of David. When the prophet Nathan came to him after David had committed adultery with Bathsheba.

1 Have mercy on me, O God,
according to your unfailing
love;
according to your great
compassion
blot out[a] my transgressions.[b]
2 Wash away[c] all my iniquity
and cleanse[d] me from my sin.

3 For I know my transgressions,
and my sin is always before
me.[e]

a 21 Or *thought the 'I AM' was*
b 23 Or *and to him who considers his way / I will show*

4Against you, you only, have I sinned
and done what is evil in your sight,[f]
so that you are proved right when you speak
and justified when you judge.[g]
5Surely I was sinful[h] at birth,
sinful from the time my mother conceived me.
6Surely you desire truth in the inner parts;[a]
you teach[b] me wisdom[i] in the inmost place.[j]

7Cleanse me with hyssop,[k] and I shall be clean;
wash me, and I shall be whiter than snow.[l]
8Let me hear joy and gladness;[m]
let the bones you have crushed rejoice.
9Hide your face from my sins[n]
and blot out all my iniquity.

10Create in me a pure heart,[o] O God,
and renew a steadfast spirit within me.[p]
11Do not cast me from your presence
or take your Holy Spirit[q] from me.
12Restore to me the joy of your salvation[r]
and grant me a willing spirit, to sustain me.

13Then I will teach transgressors your ways,[s]
and sinners will turn back to you.[t]
14Save me from bloodguilt,[u] O God,
the God who saves me,[v]
and my tongue will sing of your righteousness.[w]
15O Lord, open my lips,[x]
and my mouth will declare your praise.
16You do not delight in sacrifice,[y] or I would bring it;
you do not take pleasure in burnt offerings.
17The sacrifices of God are[c] a broken spirit;
a broken and contrite heart,[z]
O God, you will not despise.

18In your good pleasure make Zion[a] prosper;
build up the walls of Jerusalem.
19Then there will be righteous sacrifices,[b]
whole burnt offerings[c] to delight you;
then bulls[d] will be offered on your altar.

51:4 [f] Ge 20:6; Lk 15:21 [g] Ro 3:4*
51:5 [h] Job 14:4
51:6 [i] Pr 2:6 [j] Ps 15:2
51:7 [k] Lev 14:4; Heb 9:19 [l] Isa 1:18
51:8 [m] Isa 35:10
51:9 [n] Jer 16:17
51:10 [o] Ps 78:37; Ac 15:9 [p] Eze 18:31
51:11 [q] Eph 4:30
51:12 [r] Ps 13:5
51:13 [s] Ac 9:21-22 [t] Ps 22:27
51:14 [u] 2Sa 12:9 [v] Ps 25:5 [w] Ps 35:28
51:15 [x] Ps 9:14
51:16 [y] 1Sa 15:22; Ps 40:6
51:17 [z] Ps 34:18
51:18 [a] Ps 102:16; Isa 51:3
51:19 [b] Ps 4:5 [c] Ps 66:13 [d] Ps 66:15
52 Title [a] 1Sa 22:9
52:1 [b] Ps 94:4
52:2 [c] Ps 57:4 [d] Ps 50:19
52:3 [e] Jer 9:5
52:4 [f] Ps 120:2,3
52:5 [g] Isa 22:19 [h] Pr 2:22 [i] Ps 27:13
52:6 [j] Job 22:19; Ps 37:34; Ps 40:3

Psalm 52

For the director of music. A *maskil*[a] of David. When Doeg the Edomite[a] had gone to Saul and told him: "David has gone to the house of Ahimelech."

1Why do you boast of evil, you mighty man?
Why do you boast[b] all day long,
you who are a disgrace in the eyes of God?
2Your tongue plots destruction;
it is like a sharpened razor,[c]
you who practise deceit.[d]
3You love evil rather than good,
falsehood[e] rather than speaking the truth. *Selah*
4You love every harmful word,
O you deceitful tongue![f]

5Surely God will bring you down to everlasting ruin:
He will snatch you up and tear[g] you from your tent;
he will uproot[h] you from the land of the living.[i] *Selah*
6The righteous will see and fear;
they will laugh[j] at him, saying,
7"Here now is the man
who did not make God his stronghold

[a]6 The meaning of the Hebrew for this phrase is uncertain. [b]6 Or *you desired . . . ; / you taught* [c]17 Or *My sacrifice, O God, is* [a]Title: Probably a literary or musical term

but trusted in his great wealth[k]
and grew strong by destroying others!"

8 But I am like an olive tree[l]
flourishing in the house of God;
I trust[m] in God's unfailing love
for ever and ever.
9 I will praise you for ever[n] for
what you have done;
in your name I will hope, for
your name is good.[o]
I will praise you in the
presence of your saints.

Psalm 53

53:1–6pp Ps 14:1–7

For the director of music. According to *mahalath*.[a] A *maskil*[b] of David.

1 The fool[a] says in his heart,
"There is no God."[b]
They are corrupt, and their
ways are vile;
there is no-one who does good.

2 God looks down from heaven[c]
on the sons of men
to see if there are any who
understand,
any who seek God.[d]
3 Everyone has turned away,
they have together become
corrupt;
there is no-one who does good,
not even one.[e]

4 Will the evildoers never learn—
those who devour my people
as men eat bread
and who do not call on God?
5 There they were, overwhelmed
with dread,
where there was nothing to
dread.[f]
God scattered the bones[g] of
those who attacked you;
you put them to shame, for
God despised them.

6 Oh, that salvation for Israel
would come out of Zion!
When God restores the
fortunes of his people,

52:7 k Ps 49:6
52:8 l Jer 11:16; m Ps 13:5
52:9 n Ps 30:12; o Ps 54:6
53:1 a Ps 14:1-7; Ro 3:10; b Ps 10:4
53:2 c Ps 33:13; d 2Ch 15:2
53:3 e Ro 3:10-12*
53:5 f Lev 26:17; g Eze 6:5
54:1 a Ps 20:1; b 2Ch 20:6
54:2 c Ps 5:1; Ps 55:1
54:3 d Ps 86:14; e Ps 40:14; f Ps 36:1
54:4 g Ps 118:7; h Ps 41:12
54:5 i Ps 94:23; j Ps 89:49; Ps 143:12
54:6 k Ps 50:14; l Ps 52:9
54:7 m Ps 34:6; n Ps 59:10
55:1 a Ps 27:9; Ps 61:1
55:2 b Ps 66:19; c Ps 77:3; Isa 38:14

let Jacob rejoice and Israel be
glad!

Psalm 54

For the director of music. With stringed instruments. A *maskil*[a] of David. When the Ziphites had gone to Saul and said, "Is not David hiding among us?"

1 Save me, O God, by your
name;[a]
vindicate me by your might.[b]
2 Hear my prayer, O God;[c]
listen to the words of my
mouth.

3 Strangers are attacking me;[d]
ruthless men seek my life[e]—
men without regard for God.[f]
Selah

4 Surely God is my help;[g]
the Lord is the one who
sustains me.[h]

5 Let evil recoil[i] on those who
slander me;
in your faithfulness[j] destroy
them.

6 I will sacrifice a freewill
offering[k] to you;
I will praise your name,
O LORD,
for it is good.[l]
7 For he has delivered me[m] from
all my troubles,
and my eyes have looked in
triumph on my foes.[n]

Psalm 55

For the director of music. With stringed instruments. A *maskil*[a] of David.

1 Listen to my prayer, O God,
do not ignore my plea;[a]
2 hear me and answer me.[b]
My thoughts trouble me and I
am distraught[c]
3 at the voice of the enemy,

[a]Title: Probably a musical term
[b]Title: Probably a literary or musical term
[a]Title: Probably a literary or musical term
[a]Title: Probably a literary or musical term

at the stares of the wicked;
for they bring down suffering
upon me[d]
and revile me in their anger.[e]

4My heart is in anguish within
me;
the terrors[f] of death assail
me.
5Fear and trembling[g] have beset
me;
horror has overwhelmed me.
6I said, "Oh, that I had the wings
of a dove!
I would fly away and be at
rest—
7I would flee far away
and stay in the desert; *Selah*
8I would hurry to my place of
shelter,
far from the tempest and
storm.[h]"

9Confuse the wicked, O Lord,
confound their speech,
for I see violence and strife[i]
in the city.
10Day and night they prowl about
on its walls;
malice and abuse are within it.
11Destructive forces[j] are at
work in the city;
threats and lies[k] never leave
its streets.

12If an enemy were insulting me,
I could endure it;
if a foe were raising himself
against me,
I could hide from him.
13But it is you, a man like myself,
my companion, my close
friend,[l]
14with whom I once enjoyed
sweet fellowship
as we walked with the throng
at the house of God.[m]

15Let death take my enemies by
surprise;[n]
let them go down alive to the
grave,[b][o]
for evil finds lodging among
them.

16But I call to God,
and the LORD saves me.
17Evening,[p] morning[q] and noon
I cry out in distress,
and he hears my voice.
18He ransoms me unharmed
from the battle waged against
me,
even though many oppose me.
19God, who is enthroned for
ever,[r]
will hear[s] them and afflict
them— *Selah*
men who never change their
ways
and have no fear of God.

20My companion attacks his
friends;[t]
he violates his covenant.[u]
21His speech is smooth as butter,
yet war is in his heart;
his words are more soothing
than oil,[v]
yet they are drawn swords.[w]

22Cast your cares on the LORD
and he will sustain you;[x]
he will never let the righteous
fall.[y]
23But you, O God, will bring down
the wicked
into the pit[z] of corruption;
bloodthirsty and deceitful men[a]
will not live out half their
days.[b]
But as for me, I trust in you.[c]

Psalm 56

For the director of music. To the tune of "A Dove on Distant Oaks". Of David. A *miktam*.[a] When the Philistines had seized him in Gath.

1Be merciful to me, O God, for
men hotly pursue me;[a]
all day long they press their
attack.
2My slanderers pursue me all
day long;[b]
many are attacking me in
their pride.[c]

55:3 d 2Sa 16:6-8; Ps 17:9; e Ps 71:11
55:4 f Ps 116:3
55:5 g Job 21:6; Ps 119:120
55:8 h Isa 4:6
55:9 i Jer 6:7
55:11 j Ps 5:9; k Ps 10:7
55:13 l 2Sa 15:12; Ps 41:9
55:14 m Ps 42:4
55:15 n Ps 64:7; o Nu 16:30,33
55:17 p Ps 141:2; Ac 3:1; q Ps 5:3
55:19 r Dt 33:27; s Ps 78:59
55:20 t Ps 7:4; u Ps 89:34
55:21 v Pr 5:3; w Ps 28:3; Ps 57:4; Ps 59:7
55:22 x Ps 37:5; Mt 6:25-34; 1Pe 5:7; y Ps 37:24
55:23 z Ps 73:18; a Ps 5:6; b Job 15:32; Pr 10:27; c Ps 25:2
56:1 a Ps 57:1-3
56:2 b Ps 57:3; c Ps 35:1

b15 Hebrew *Sheol*
aTitle: Probably a literary or musical term

[3]When I am afraid,[d]
I will trust in you.
[4]In God, whose word I praise,
in God I trust; I will not be afraid.
What can mortal man do to me?[e]

[5]All day long they twist my words;[f]
they are always plotting to harm me.
[6]They conspire,[g] they lurk,
they watch my steps,
eager to take my life.[h]
[7]On no account let them escape;
in your anger, O God, bring down the nations.[i]
[8]Record my lament;
list my tears on your scroll[b]—
are they not in your record?[j]

[9]Then my enemies will turn back[k]
when I call for help.[l]
By this I will know that God is for me.[m]
[10]In God, whose word I praise,
in the LORD, whose word I praise—
[11]in God I trust; I will not be afraid.
What can man do to me?
[12]I am under vows[n] to you, O God;
I will present my thank-offerings to you.
[13]For you have delivered me[c] from death[o]
and my feet from stumbling,
that I may walk before God
in the light of life.[d][p]

Psalm 57

57:7–11pp Ps 108:1–5

For the director of music. ⌞To the tune of,⌟ "Do Not Destroy". Of David. A *miktam*.[a] When he had fled from Saul into the cave.

[1]Have mercy on me, O God,
have mercy on me,
for in you my soul takes refuge.[a]
I will take refuge in the shadow of your wings[b]
until the disaster has passed.[c]

[2]I cry out to God Most High,
to God, who fulfils ⌞his purpose⌟ for me.[d]
[3]He sends from heaven and saves me,[e]
rebuking those who hotly pursue me;[f] *Selah*
God sends his love and his faithfulness.[g]

[4]I am in the midst of lions;[h]
I lie among ravenous beasts—
men whose teeth are spears and arrows,
whose tongues are sharp swords.[i]

[5]Be exalted, O God, above the heavens;
let your glory be over all the earth.[j]

[6]They spread a net for my feet—
I was bowed down[k] in distress.
They dug a pit[l] in my path—
but they have fallen into it themselves.[m] *Selah*

[7]My heart is steadfast, O God,
my heart is steadfast;[n]
I will sing and make music.
[8]Awake, my soul!
Awake, harp and lyre![o]
I will awaken the dawn.
[9]I will praise you, O Lord, among the nations;
I will sing of you among the peoples.
[10]For great is your love, reaching to the heavens;
your faithfulness reaches to the skies.[p]

[11]Be exalted, O God, above the heavens;

56:3 *d* Ps 55:4-5
56:4 *e* Ps 118:6; Heb 13:6
56:5 *f* Ps 41:7
56:6 *g* Ps 59:3 *h* Ps 71:10
56:7 *i* Ps 36:12; Ps 55:23
56:8 *j* Mal 3:16
56:9 *k* Ps 9:3 *l* Ps 102:2 *m* Ro 8:31
56:12 *n* Ps 50:14
56:13 *o* Ps 116:8 *p* Job 33:30
57:1 *a* Ps 2:12 *b* Ps 17:8 *c* Isa 26:20
57:2 *d* Ps 138:8
57:3 *e* Ps 18:9,16 *f* Ps 56:1 *g* Ps 40:11
57:4 *h* Ps 35:17 *i* Ps 55:21; Pr 30:14
57:5 *j* Ps 108:5
57:6 *k* Ps 145:14 *l* Ps 35:7 *m* Ps 7:15; Pr 28:10
57:7 *n* Ps 108:1
57:8 *o* Ps 16:9; Ps 30:12; Ps 150:3
57:10 *p* Ps 36:5; Ps 103:11

[b]8 Or *I put my tears in your wineskin*
[c]13 Or *my soul* [d]13 Or *the land of the living*
[a]Title: Probably a literary or musical term

let your glory be over all the
earth.[q]

Psalm 58

For the director of music. ⌞To the tune
of⌟ "Do Not Destroy". Of David.
A *miktam*.[a]

1 Do you rulers indeed speak
justly?[a]
Do you judge uprightly among
men?
2 No, in your heart you devise
injustice,
and your hands mete out
violence on the earth.[b]
3 Even from birth the wicked go
astray;
from the womb they are
wayward and speak lies.
4 Their venom is like the venom
of a snake,[c]
like that of a cobra that has
stopped its ears,
5 that will not heed the tune of
the charmer,
however skilful the enchanter
may be.

6 Break the teeth in their mouths,
O God;[d]
tear out, O LORD, the fangs of
the lions![e]
7 Let them vanish like water that
flows away;[f]
when they draw the bow, let
their arrows be blunted.[g]
8 Like a slug melting away as it
moves along,
like a stillborn child,[h] may
they not see the sun.

9 Before your pots can feel ⌞the
heat of⌟ the thorns[i]—
whether they be green or
dry—the wicked will be
swept away.[b][j]
10 The righteous will be glad when
they are avenged,[k]
when they bathe their feet in
the blood of the wicked.[l]
11 Then men will say,
"Surely the righteous still are
rewarded;
surely there is a God who
judges the earth."[m]

Psalm 59

For the director of music. ⌞To the tune
of⌟ "Do Not Destroy". Of David.
A *miktam*.[a] When Saul had sent men
to watch David's house in order to
kill him.

1 Deliver me from my enemies,
O God;[a]
protect me from those who
rise up against me.
2 Deliver me from evildoers
and save me from bloodthirsty
men.[b]

3 See how they lie in wait for me!
Fierce men conspire[c] against
me
for no offence or sin of mine,
O LORD.
4 I have done no wrong, yet they
are ready to attack me.[d]
Arise to help me; look on my
plight!
5 O LORD God Almighty, the God
of Israel,
rouse yourself to punish all
the nations;
show no mercy to wicked
traitors.[e] *Selah*

6 They return at evening,
snarling like dogs,[f]
and prowl about the city.
7 See what they spew from their
mouths—
they spew out swords[g] from
their lips,
and they say, "Who can hear
us?"[h]
8 But you, O LORD, laugh at
them;[i]
you scoff at all those nations.[j]

9 O my Strength, I watch for you;
you, O God, are my fortress,[k]
10 my loving God.

57:11 q ver 5
58:1 a Ps 82:2
58:2 b Ps 94:20; Mal 3:15
58:4 c Ps 140:3; Ecc 10:11
58:6 d Ps 3:7; e Job 4:10
58:7 f Jos 7:5; Ps 112:10; g Ps 64:3
58:8 h Job 3:16
58:9 i Ps 118:12; j Pr 10:25
58:10 k Ps 64:10; Ps 91:8; l Ps 68:23
58:11 m Ps 9:8; Ps 18:20
59:1 a Ps 143:9
59:2 b Ps 139:19
59:3 c Ps 56:6
59:4 d Ps 35:19,23
59:5 e Jer 18:23
59:6 f ver 14
59:7 g Ps 57:4; h Ps 10:11
59:8 i Ps 37:13; Pr 1:26; j Ps 2:4
59:9 k Ps 9:9; Ps 62:2

[a]Title: Probably a literary or musical term
[b]9 The meaning of the Hebrew for this verse is uncertain. [a]Title: Probably a literary or musical term

God will go before me
and will let me gloat over
those who slander me.
11But do not kill them, O Lord our
shield,[b] [l]
or my people will forget.[m]
In your might make them
wander about,
and bring them down.[n]
12For the sins of their mouths,[o]
for the words of their lips,[p]
let them be caught in their
pride.[q]
For the curses and lies they
utter,
13 consume them in wrath,
consume them till they are no
more.[r]
Then it will be known to the
ends of the earth
that God rules over Jacob.[s]
Selah
14They return at evening,
snarling like dogs,
and prowl about the city.
15They wander about for food[t]
and howl if not satisfied.
16But I will sing of your
strength,[u]
in the morning[v] I will sing of
your love;[w]
for you are my fortress,
my refuge in times of
trouble.[x]

17O my Strength, I sing praise to
you;
you, O God, are my fortress,
my loving God.

Psalm 60

60:5–12pp Ps 108:6–13

For the director of music. To ⌊the tune of⌋ "The Lily of the Covenant". A *miktam*[a] of David. For teaching. When he fought Aram Naharaim[b] and Aram Zobah,[c] and when Joab returned and struck down twelve thousand Edomites in the Valley of Salt.

1You have rejected us,[a] O God,
and burst forth upon us;
you have been angry[b]—now
restore us![c]
2You have shaken the land[d] and
torn it open;
mend its fractures,[e] for it is
quaking.
3You have shown your people
desperate times;[f]
you have given us wine that
makes us stagger.[g]

4But for those who fear you, you
have raised a banner
to be unfurled against the
bow. *Selah*

5Save us and help us with your
right hand,[h]
that those you love[i] may be
delivered.
6God has spoken from his
sanctuary:
"In triumph I will parcel out
Shechem[j]
and measure off the Valley of
Succoth.
7Gilead[k] is mine, and Manasseh
is mine;
Ephraim is my helmet,
Judah[l] my sceptre.[m]
8Moab is my washbasin,
upon Edom I toss my sandal;
over Philistia I shout in
triumph.[n]"

9Who will bring me to the
fortified city?
Who will lead me to Edom?
10Is it not you, O God, you who
have rejected us
and no longer go out with our
armies?[o]
11Give us aid against the enemy,
for the help of man is
worthless.[p]
12With God we shall gain the
victory,
and he will trample down our
enemies.[q]

59:11 *l* Ps 84:9 *m* Dt 4:9 *n* Ps 106:27
59:12 *o* Ps 10:7 *p* Pr 12:13 *q* Zep 3:11
59:13 *r* Ps 104:35 *s* Ps 83:18
59:15 *t* Job 15:23
59:16 *u* Ps 21:13 *v* Ps 88:13 *w* Ps 101:1 *x* Ps 46:1
60:1 *a* 2Sa 5:20; Ps 44:9 *b* Ps 79:5 *c* Ps 80:3
60:2 *d* Ps 18:7 *e* 2Ch 7:14
60:3 *f* Ps 71:20 *g* Isa 51:17; Jer 25:16
60:5 *h* Ps 17:7; Ps 108:6 *i* Ps 127:2
60:6 *j* Ge 12:6
60:7 *k* Jos 13:31 *l* Dt 33:17 *m* Ge 49:10
60:8 *n* 2Sa 8:1
60:10 *o* Jos 7:12; Ps 44:9; Ps 108:11
60:11 *p* Ps 146:3
60:12 *q* Nu 24:18; Ps 44:5

[b]*11* Or *sovereign* [a]Title: Probably a literary or musical term [b]Title: That is, Arameans of North-west Mesopotamia [c]Title: That is, Arameans of central Syria

Psalm 61

For the director of music. With stringed instruments. Of David.

1Hear my cry, O God;[a]
listen to my prayer.[b]

2From the ends of the earth I call to you,
I call as my heart grows faint;[c]
lead me to the rock[d] that is higher than I.
3For you have been my refuge,[e]
a strong tower against the foe.[f]
4I long to dwell[g] in your tent for ever
and take refuge in the shelter of your wings.[h] *Selah*
5For you have heard my vows,[i] O God;
you have given me the heritage of those who fear your name.[j]
6Increase the days of the king's life,
his years for many generations.[k]
7May he be enthroned in God's presence for ever;[l]
appoint your love and faithfulness to protect him.[m]

8Then will I ever sing praise to your name[n]
and fulfil my vows day after day.

Psalm 62

For the director of music. For Jeduthun. A psalm of David.

1My soul finds rest[a] in God alone;
my salvation comes from him.
2He alone is my rock[b] and my salvation;
he is my fortress, I shall never be shaken.

3How long will you assault a man?
Would all of you throw him down—
this leaning wall,[c] this tottering fence?
4They fully intend to topple him from his lofty place;
they take delight in lies.
With their mouths they bless,
but in their hearts they curse.[d] *Selah*

5Find rest, O my soul, in God alone;
my hope comes from him.
6He alone is my rock and my salvation;
he is my fortress, I shall not be shaken.
7My salvation and my honour depend on God;[a]
he is my mighty rock, my refuge.[e]
8Trust in him at all times, O people;
pour out your hearts to him,[f]
for God is our refuge. *Selah*

9Lowborn men are but a breath,[g]
the highborn are but a lie;
if weighed on a balance,[h] they are nothing;
together they are only a breath.
10Do not trust in extortion
or take pride in stolen goods;[i]
though your riches increase,
do not set your heart on them.[j]

11One thing God has spoken,
two things have I heard:
that you, O God, are strong,
12 and that you, O Lord, are loving.
Surely you will reward each person
according to what he has done.[k]

61:1 a Ps 64:1 b Ps 86:6
61:2 c Ps 77:3 d Ps 18:2
61:3 e Ps 62:7 f Pr 18:10
61:4 g Ps 23:6 h Ps 91:4
61:5 i Ps 56:12 j Ps 86:11
61:6 k Ps 21:4
61:7 l Ps 41:12 m Ps 40:11
61:8 n Ps 65:1 Ps 71:22
62:1 a Ps 33:20
62:2 b Ps 89:26
62:3 c Isa 30:13
62:4 d Ps 28:3
62:7 e Ps 46:1 Ps 85:9 Jer 3:23
62:8 f 1Sa 1:15 Ps 42:4 La 2:19
62:9 g Ps 39:5,11 h Isa 40:15
62:10 i Isa 61:8 j Job 31:25 1Ti 6:6-10
62:12 k Job 34:11 Mt 16:27

a7 Or / *God Most High is my salvation and my honour*

Psalm 63

A psalm of David. When he was in the Desert of Judah.

[1]O God, you are my God,
earnestly I seek you;
my soul thirsts for you,[a]
my body longs for you,
in a dry and weary land
where there is no water.

[2]I have seen you in the sanctuary[b]
and beheld your power and your glory.
[3]Because your love is better than life,[c]
my lips will glorify you.
[4]I will praise you as long as I live,[d]
and in your name I will lift up my hands.[e]
[5]My soul will be satisfied as with the richest of foods;[f]
with singing lips my mouth will praise you.

[6]On my bed I remember you;
I think of you through the watches of the night.[g]
[7]Because you are my help,[h]
I sing in the shadow of your wings.
[8]My soul clings to you;
your right hand upholds me.[i]

[9]They who seek my life will be destroyed;[j]
they will go down to the depths of the earth.[k]
[10]They will be given over to the sword
and become food for jackals.

[11]But the king will rejoice in God;
all who swear by God's name will praise him,[l]
while the mouths of liars will be silenced.

Psalm 64

For the director of music. A psalm of David.

[1]Hear me, O God, as I voice my complaint;[a]
protect my life from the threat of the enemy.[b]
[2]Hide me from the conspiracy of the wicked,[c]
from that noisy crowd of evildoers.

[3]They sharpen their tongues like swords
and aim their words like deadly arrows.[d]
[4]They shoot from ambush at the innocent man;[e]
they shoot at him suddenly, without fear.[f]

[5]They encourage each other in evil plans,
they talk about hiding their snares;
they say, "Who will see them?"[a][g]
[6]They plot injustice and say,
"We have devised a perfect plan!"
Surely the mind and heart of man are cunning.

[7]But God will shoot them with arrows;
suddenly they will be struck down.
[8]He will turn their own tongues against them[h]
and bring them to ruin;
all who see them will shake their heads[i] in scorn.

[9]All mankind will fear;
they will proclaim the works of God
and ponder what he has done.[j]
[10]Let the righteous rejoice in the LORD
and take refuge in him;[k]
let all the upright in heart praise him![l]

63:1 a Ps 42:2; Ps 84:2
63:2 b Ps 27:4
63:3 c Ps 69:16
63:4 d Ps 104:33; e Ps 28:2
63:5 f Ps 36:8
63:6 g Ps 42:8
63:7 h Ps 27:9
63:8 i Ps 18:35
63:9 j Ps 40:14; k Ps 55:15
63:11 l Dt 6:13; Ps 21:1; Isa 45:23
64:1 a Ps 55:2; b Ps 140:1
64:2 c Ps 56:6; Ps 59:2
64:3 d Ps 58:7
64:4 e Ps 11:2; f Ps 55:19
64:5 g Ps 10:11
64:8 h Ps 9:3; Pr 18:7; i Ps 22:7
64:9 j Jer 51:10
64:10 k Ps 25:20; l Ps 32:11

[a]5 Or *us*

Psalm 65

For the director of music. A psalm of David. A song.

1 Praise awaits[a] you, O God, in Zion;
to you our vows will be fulfilled.[a]
2 O you who hear prayer,
to you all men will come.[b]
3 When we were overwhelmed by sins,[c]
you forgave[b] our transgressions.[d]
4 Blessed are those you choose[e]
and bring near to live in your courts!
We are filled with the good things of your house,[f]
of your holy temple.

5 You answer us with awesome deeds of righteousness,
O God our Saviour,[g]
the hope of all the ends of the earth
and of the farthest seas,[h]
6 who formed the mountains by your power,
having armed yourself with strength,[i]
7 who stilled the roaring of the seas,[j]
the roaring of their waves,
and the turmoil of the nations.[k]
8 Those living far away fear your wonders;
where morning dawns and evening fades
you call forth songs of joy.

9 You care for the land and water it;[l]
you enrich it abundantly.
The streams of God are filled with water
to provide the people with corn,[m]
for so you have ordained it.[c]
10 You drench its furrows
and level its ridges;
you soften it with showers
and bless its crops.

65:1 *a* Ps 116:18
65:2 *b* Isa 66:23
65:3 *c* Ps 38:4 *d* Heb 9:14
65:4 *e* Ps 4:3; Ps 33:12 *f* Ps 36:8
65:5 *g* Ps 85:4 *h* Ps 107:23
65:6 *i* Ps 93:1
65:7 *j* Mt 8:26 *k* Isa 17:12-13
65:9 *l* Ps 68:9-10 *m* Ps 46:4; Ps 104:14
65:12 *n* Job 28:26
65:13 *o* Ps 144:13 *p* Ps 72:16 *q* Ps 98:8; Isa 55:12
66:1 *a* Ps 100:1
66:2 *b* Ps 79:9
66:3 *c* Ps 65:5 *d* Ps 18:44
66:4 *e* Ps 22:27 *f* Ps 67:3
66:5 *g* Ps 106:22
66:6 *h* Ex 14:22
66:7 *i* Ps 145:13 *j* Ps 11:4 *k* Ps 140:8
66:8 *l* Ps 98:4

11 You crown the year with your bounty,
and your carts overflow with abundance.
12 The grasslands of the desert overflow;[n]
the hills are clothed with gladness.
13 The meadows are covered with flocks[o]
and the valleys are mantled with corn;[p]
they shout for joy and sing.[q]

Psalm 66

For the director of music. A song. A psalm.

1 Shout with joy to God, all the earth![a]
2 Sing the glory of his name;[b]
make his praise glorious!
3 Say to God, "How awesome are your deeds![c]
So great is your power
that your enemies cringe[d] before you.
4 All the earth bows down[e] to you;
they sing praise[f] to you,
they sing praise to your name." *Selah*

5 Come and see what God has done,
how awesome his works[g] on man's behalf!
6 He turned the sea into dry land,[h]
they passed through the waters on foot—
come, let us rejoice in him.
7 He rules for ever[i] by his power,
his eyes watch[j] the nations—
let not the rebellious[k] rise up against him. *Selah*

8 Praise[l] our God, O peoples,
let the sound of his praise be heard;

[a] *1* Or *befits*; the meaning of the Hebrew for this word is uncertain. [b] *3* Or *made atonement for*
[c] *9* Or *for that is how you prepare the land*

9 he has preserved our lives
and kept our feet from
slipping.[m]
10 For you, O God, tested us;
you refined us like silver.[n]
11 You brought us into prison
and laid burdens[o] on our
backs.
12 You let men ride over our
heads;[p]
we went through fire and
water,
but you brought us to a place
of abundance.[q]

13 I will come to your temple with
burnt offerings
and fulfil my vows[r] to you—
14 vows my lips promised and my
mouth spoke
when I was in trouble.
15 I will sacrifice fat animals to
you
and an offering of rams;
I will offer bulls and goats.[s]
Selah

16 Come and listen,[t] all you who
fear God;
let me tell[u] you what he has
done for me.
17 I cried out to him with my
mouth;
his praise was on my tongue.
18 If I had cherished sin in my
heart,
the Lord would not have
listened;[v]
19 but God has surely listened
and heard my voice[w] in
prayer.
20 Praise be to God,
who has not rejected[x] my
prayer
or withheld his love from me!

Psalm 67

For the director of music. With stringed instruments. A psalm. A song.

1 May God be gracious to us and
bless us
and make his face shine upon
us,[a] *Selah*
2 that your ways may be known
on earth,
your salvation[b] among all
nations.[c]

3 May the peoples praise you,
O God;
may all the peoples praise
you.
4 May the nations be glad and
sing for joy,
for you rule the peoples
justly[d]
and guide the nations of the
earth. *Selah*
5 May the peoples praise you,
O God;
may all the peoples praise
you.

6 Then the land will yield its
harvest,[e]
and God, our God, will bless
us.
7 God will bless us,
and all the ends of the earth
will fear him.[f]

Psalm 68

For the director of music. Of David. A psalm. A song.

1 May God arise, may his
enemies be scattered;
may his foes flee[a] before him.
2 As smoke[b] is blown away by
the wind,
may you blow them away;
as wax melts[c] before the fire,
may the wicked perish before
God.
3 But may the righteous be glad
and rejoice[d] before God;
may they be happy and joyful.

4 Sing to God, sing praise to his
name,[e]
extol him who rides on the
clouds[a] [f]—
his name is the LORD[g]—
and rejoice before him.

66:9 m Ps 121:3
66:10 n Ps 17:3; Isa 48:10; Zec 13:9; 1Pe 1:6-7
66:11 o La 1:13
66:12 p Isa 51:23; q Isa 43:2
66:13 r Ecc 5:4
66:15 s Nu 6:14; Ps 51:19
66:16 t Ps 34:11; u Ps 71:15,24
66:18 v Job 36:21; Isa 1:15; Jas 4:3
66:19 w Ps 116:1-2
66:20 x Ps 22:24; Ps 68:35
67:1 a Nu 6:24-26; Ps 4:6
67:2 b Isa 52:10; c Tit 2:11
67:4 d Ps 96:10-13
67:6 e Lev 26:4; Ps 85:12; Eze 34:27
67:7 f Ps 33:8
68:1 a Nu 10:35; Isa 33:3
68:2 b Hos 13:3; c Isa 9:18; Mic 1:4
68:3 d Ps 32:11
68:4 e Ps 66:2; f Dt 33:26; g Ex 6:3; Ps 83:18

a4 Or / *prepare the way for him who rides through the deserts*

5 A father to the fatherless,[h] a
defender of widows,[i]
is God in his holy dwelling.[j]
6 God sets the lonely in
families,[b][k]
he leads forth the prisoners[l]
with singing;
but the rebellious live in a
sun-scorched land.[m]

7 When you went out[n] before
your people, O God,
when you marched through
the wasteland, *Selah*
8 the earth shook,
the heavens poured down
rain,[o]
before God, the One of Sinai,[p]
before God, the God of Israel.
9 You gave abundant showers,[q]
O God;
you refreshed your weary
inheritance.
10 Your people settled in it,
and from your bounty, O God,
you provided[r] for the poor.

11 The Lord announced the word,
and great was the company of
those who proclaimed it:
12 "Kings and armies flee[s] in
haste;
in the camps men divide the
plunder.
13 Even while you sleep among the
campfires,[c][t]
the wings of ⌞my⌟ dove are
sheathed with silver,
its feathers with shining gold."
14 When the Almighty[d]
scattered[u] the kings in the
land,
it was like snow fallen on
Zalmon.

15 The mountains of Bashan are
majestic mountains;
rugged are the mountains of
Bashan.
16 Why gaze in envy, O rugged
mountains,
at the mountain where God
chooses[v] to reign,
where the LORD himself will
dwell for ever?

68:5 *h* Ps 10:14 *i* Dt 10:18 *j* Dt 26:15
68:6 *k* Ps 113:9 *l* Ac 12:6 *m* Ps 107:34
68:7 *n* Ex 13:21 Jdg 4:14
68:8 *o* Jdg 5:4 *p* Ex 19:16,18
68:9 *q* Dt 11:11
68:10 *r* Ps 74:19
68:12 *s* Jos 10:16
68:13 *t* Ge 49:14
68:14 *u* Jos 10:10
68:16 *v* Dt 12:5
68:17 *w* Dt 33:2 Da 7:10
68:18 *x* Jdg 5:12 *y* Eph 4:8*
68:19 *z* Ps 65:5 *a* Ps 55:22
68:20 *b* Ps 56:13
68:21 *c* Ps 110:5 Hab 3:13
68:22 *d* Nu 21:33
68:23 *e* Ps 58:10 *f* 1Ki 21:19
68:24 *g* Ps 63:2
68:25 *h* Jdg 11:34 1Ch 13:8
68:26 *i* Ps 26:12 Isa 48:1
68:27 *j* 1Sa 9:21

17 The chariots of God are tens of
thousands
and thousands of thousands;[w]
the Lord ⌞has come⌟ from Sinai
into his sanctuary.
18 When you ascended on high,
you led captives[x] in your
train;
you received gifts from men,[y]
even from[e] the rebellious—
that you,[f] O LORD God, might
dwell there.
19 Praise be to the Lord, to God
our Saviour,[z]
who daily bears our burdens.[a]
Selah
20 Our God is a God who saves;
from the Sovereign LORD
comes escape from death.[b]

21 Surely God will crush the
heads[c] of his enemies,
the hairy crowns of those who
go on in their sins.
22 The Lord says, "I will bring
them from Bashan;
I will bring them from the
depths of the sea,[d]
23 that you may plunge your feet
in the blood of your foes,[e]
while the tongues of your
dogs[f] have their share."

24 Your procession has come into
view, O God,
the procession of my God and
King into the sanctuary.[g]
25 In front are the singers, after
them the musicians;
with them are the maidens
playing tambourines.[h]
26 Praise God in the great
congregation;
praise the LORD in the
assembly of Israel.[i]
27 There is the little tribe[j] of
Benjamin, leading them,
there the great throng of
Judah's princes,
and there the princes of
Zebulun and of Naphtali.

[b]6 Or *the desolate in a homeland* [c]13 Or *saddlebags* [d]14 Hebrew *Shaddai* [e]18 Or *gifts for men, / even* [f]18 Or *they*

28 Summon your power, O God;[g]
show us your strength, O God,
as you have done before.
29 Because of your temple at
Jerusalem
kings will bring you gifts.[k]
30 Rebuke the beast among the
reeds,
the herd of bulls[l] among the
calves of the nations.
Humbled, may it bring bars of
silver.
Scatter the nations[m] who
delight in war.
31 Envoys will come from Egypt;[n]
Cush[h] will submit herself to
God.

32 Sing to God, O kingdoms of the
earth,
sing praise to the Lord, *Selah*
33 to him who rides[o] the ancient
skies above,
who thunders with mighty
voice.[p]
34 Proclaim the power[q] of God,
whose majesty is over Israel,
whose power is in the skies.
35 You are awesome, O God, in
your sanctuary;
the God of Israel gives power
and strength to his
people.[r]

Praise be to God![s]

Psalm 69

For the director of music. To ⌊the tune of⌋ "Lilies". Of David.

1 Save me, O God,
for the waters have come up
to my neck.[a]
2 I sink in the miry depths,[b]
where there is no foothold.
I have come into the deep
waters;
the floods engulf me.
3 I am worn out calling for help;[c]
my throat is parched.
My eyes fail,[d]
looking for my God.
4 Those who hate me without
reason[e]
outnumber the hairs of my
head;
many are my enemies without
cause,[f]
those who seek to destroy me.
I am forced to restore
what I did not steal.

5 You know my folly,[g] O God;
my guilt is not hidden from
you.[h]

6 May those who hope in you
not be disgraced because of
me,
O Lord, the LORD Almighty;
may those who seek you
not be put to shame because
of me,
O God of Israel.
7 For I endure scorn for your
sake,[i]
and shame covers my face.[j]
8 I am a stranger to my brothers,
an alien to my own mother's
sons;[k]
9 for zeal for your house
consumes me,[l]
and the insults of those who
insult you fall on me.[m]
10 When I weep and fast,[n]
I must endure scorn;
11 when I put on sackcloth,[o]
people make sport of me.
12 Those who sit at the gate mock
me,
and I am the song of the
drunkards.[p]

13 But I pray to you, O LORD,
in the time of your favour;[q]
in your great love,[r] O God,
answer me with your sure
salvation.
14 Rescue me from the mire,
do not let me sink;
deliver me from those who hate
me,
from the deep waters.[s]
15 Do not let the floodwaters[t]
engulf me

68:29 *k* Ps 72:10
68:30 *l* Ps 22:12 *m* Ps 89:10
68:31 *n* Isa 19:19; Isa 45:14
68:33 *o* Ps 18:10 *p* Ps 29:4
68:34 *q* Ps 29:1
68:35 *r* Ps 29:11 *s* Ps 66:20
69:1 *a* Jnh 2:5
69:2 *b* Ps 40:2
69:3 *c* Ps 6:6 *d* Ps 119:82; Isa 38:14
69:4 *e* Jn 15:25* *f* Ps 35:19; Ps 38:19
69:5 *g* Ps 38:5 *h* Ps 44:21
69:7 *i* Jer 15:15 *j* Ps 44:15
69:8 *k* Ps 31:11; Isa 53:3
69:9 *l* Jn 2:17* *m* Ps 89:50-51; Ro 15:3
69:10 *n* Ps 35:13
69:11 *o* Ps 35:13
69:12 *p* Job 30:9
69:13 *q* Isa 49:8; 2Co 6:2 *r* Ps 51:1
69:14 *s* ver 2; Ps 144:7
69:15 *t* Ps 124:4-5

[g] *28* Many Hebrew manuscripts, Septuagint and Syriac; most Hebrew manuscripts *Your God has summoned power for you* [h] *31* That is, the upper Nile region

or the depths swallow me up[u]
or the pit close its mouth over
me.
16 Answer me, O LORD, out of the
goodness of your love;[v]
in your great mercy turn to
me.
17 Do not hide your face[w] from
your servant;
answer me quickly, for I am
in trouble.[x]
18 Come near and rescue me;
redeem[y] me because of my
foes.

19 You know how I am scorned,[z]
disgraced and shamed;
all my enemies are before
you.
20 Scorn has broken my heart
and has left me helpless;
I looked for sympathy, but
there was none,
for comforters,[a] but I found
none.[b]
21 They put gall in my food
and gave me vinegar for my
thirst.[c]

22 May the table set before them
become a snare;
may it become retribution
and[a] a trap.
23 May their eyes be darkened so
that they cannot see,
and their backs be bent for
ever.[d]
24 Pour out your wrath[e] on them;
let your fierce anger overtake
them.
25 May their place be deserted;[f]
let there be no-one to dwell in
their tents.[g]
26 For they persecute those you
wound
and talk about the pain of
those you hurt.[h]
27 Charge them with crime upon
crime;[i]
do not let them share in your
salvation.[j]
28 May they be blotted out of the
book of life[k]
and not be listed with the
righteous.[l]

29 I am in pain and distress;
may your salvation, O God,
protect me.[m]

30 I will praise God's name in
song[n]
and glorify him[o] with
thanksgiving.
31 This will please the LORD more
than an ox,
more than a bull with its horns
and hoofs.[p]
32 The poor will see and be
glad[q] —
you who seek God, may your
hearts live![r]
33 The LORD hears the needy[s]
and does not despise his
captive people.

34 Let heaven and earth praise
him,
the seas and all that move in
them,[t]
35 for God will save Zion[u]
and rebuild the cities of
Judah.[v]
Then people will settle there
and possess it;
36 the children of his servants
will inherit it,
and those who love his name
will dwell there.[w]

Psalm 70

70:1–5pp Ps 40:13–17

For the director of music. Of David.
A petition.

1 Hasten, O God, to save me;
O LORD, come quickly to help
me.[a]
2 May those who seek my life[b]
be put to shame and
confusion;
may all who desire my ruin
be turned back in disgrace.[c]
3 May those who say to me, "Aha!
Aha!"
turn back because of their
shame.
4 But may all who seek you
rejoice and be glad in you;

69:15 *u* Nu 16:33
69:16 *v* Ps 63:3
69:17 *w* Ps 27:9 *x* Ps 66:14
69:18 *y* Ps 49:15
69:19 *z* Ps 22:6
69:20 *a* Job 16:2 *b* Isa 63:5
69:21 *c* Mt 27:34 Mk 15:23 Jn 19:28-30
69:23 *d* Isa 6:9-10 Ro 11:9-10*
69:24 *e* Ps 79:6
69:25 *f* Mt 23:38 *g* Ac 1:20*
69:26 *h* Isa 53:4 Zec 1:15
69:27 *i* Ne 4:5 *j* Ps 109:14 Isa 26:10
69:28 *k* Ex 32:32-33 Lk 10:20 Php 4:3 *l* Eze 13:9
69:29 *m* Ps 59:1 Ps 70:5
69:30 *n* Ps 28:7 *o* Ps 34:3
69:31 *p* Ps 50:9-13
69:32 *q* Ps 34:2 *r* Ps 22:26
69:33 *s* Ps 12:5 Ps 68:6
69:34 *t* Ps 96:11 Ps 148:1 Isa 44:23 Isa 49:13 Isa 55:12
69:35 *u* Ob 1:17 *v* Ps 51:18 Isa 44:26
69:36 *w* Ps 37:29 Ps 102:28
70:1 *a* Ps 40:13
70:2 *b* Ps 35:4 *c* Ps 35:26

a22 Or *snare / and their fellowship become*

may those who love your
salvation always say,
"Let God be exalted!"

5 Yet I am poor and needy;[d]
come quickly to me,[e] O God.
You are my help and my
deliverer;
O LORD, do not delay.

Psalm 71

71:1–3pp Ps 31:1–4

1 In you, O LORD, I have taken
refuge;
let me never be put to
shame.[a]
2 Rescue me and deliver me in
your righteousness;
turn your ear[b] to me and save
me.
3 Be my rock of refuge,
to which I can always go;
give the command to save me,
for you are my rock and my
fortress.[c]
4 Deliver me, O my God, from
the hand of the wicked,[d]
from the grasp of evil and
cruel men.

5 For you have been my hope,
O Sovereign LORD,
my confidence[e] since my
youth.
6 From my birth[f] I have relied
on you;
you brought me forth from my
mother's womb.[g]
I will ever praise[h] you.
7 I have become like a portent[i]
to many,
but you are my strong
refuge.[j]
8 My mouth[k] is filled with your
praise,
declaring your splendour[l] all
day long.

9 Do not cast[m] me away when I
am old;[n]
do not forsake me when my
strength is gone.
10 For my enemies speak against
me;
those who wait to kill[o] me
conspire[p] together.
11 They say, "God has forsaken
him;
pursue him and seize him,
for no-one will rescue[q] him."
12 Be not far[r] from me, O God;
come quickly, O my God, to
help[s] me.
13 May my accusers perish in
shame;
may those who want to harm
me
be covered with scorn and
disgrace.[t]

14 But as for me, I shall always
have hope;[u]
I will praise you more and
more.
15 My mouth will tell[v] of your
righteousness,
of your salvation all day long,
though I know not its
measure.
16 I will come and proclaim your
mighty acts,[w] O Sovereign
LORD;
I will proclaim your
righteousness, yours alone.
17 Since my youth, O God, you
have taught[x] me,
and to this day I declare your
marvellous deeds.[y]
18 Even when I am old and grey,[z]
do not forsake me, O God,
till I declare your power to the
next generation,
your might to all who are to
come.[a]

19 Your righteousness reaches to
the skies,[b] O God,
you who have done great
things.[c]
Who, O God, is like you?[d]
20 Though you have made me see
troubles,[e] many and bitter,
you will restore[f] my life
again;

70:5 *d* Ps 40:17 *e* Ps 141:1
71:1 *a* Ps 25:2-3 Ps 31:1
71:2 *b* Ps 17:6
71:3 *c* Ps 18:2 Ps 31:2-3 Ps 44:4
71:4 *d* Ps 140:4
71:5 *e* Job 4:6 Jer 17:7
71:6 *f* Ps 22:10 *g* Ps 22:9 Isa 46:3 *h* Ps 9:1 Ps 34:1 Ps 52:9 Ps 119:164 Ps 145:2
71:7 *i* Isa 8:18 1Co 4:9 *j* 2Sa 22:3 Ps 61:3
71:8 *k* Ps 51:15 Ps 63:5 *l* Ps 35:28 Ps 96:6 Ps 104:1
71:9 *m* Ps 51:11 *n* ver 18 Ps 92:14 Isa 46:4
71:10 *o* Ps 10:8 Ps 59:3 Pr 1:18 *p* Ps 31:13 Ps 56:6 Mt 12:14
71:11 *q* Ps 7:2
71:12 *r* Ps 35:22 Ps 38:21 *s* Ps 38:22 Ps 70:1
71:13 *t* ver 24
71:14 *u* Ps 130:7
71:15 *v* Ps 35:28 Ps 40:5
71:16 *w* Ps 106:2
71:17 *x* Dt 4:5 *y* Ps 26:7
71:18 *z* ver 9 *a* Ps 22:30,31 Ps 78:4
71:19 *b* Ps 36:5 Ps 57:10

71:19 *c* Ps 126:2 Lk 1:49 *d* Ps 35:10
71:20 *e* Ps 60:3 *f* Hos 6:2

from the depths of the earth
you will again bring me up.
21 You will increase my honour[g]
and comfort[h] me once again.

22 I will praise you with the harp[i]
for your faithfulness, O my God;
I will sing praise to you with the lyre,[j]
O Holy One of Israel.[k]
23 My lips will shout for joy
when I sing praise to you—
I, whom you have redeemed.[l]
24 My tongue will tell of your righteous acts
all day long,[m]
for those who wanted to harm me[n]
have been put to shame and confusion.

Psalm 72

Of Solomon.

1 Endow the king with your justice, O God,
the royal son with your righteousness.
2 He will[a] judge your people in righteousness,[a]
your afflicted ones with justice.
3 The mountains will bring prosperity to the people,
the hills the fruit of righteousness.
4 He will defend the afflicted among the people
and save the children of the needy;[b]
he will crush the oppressor.

5 He will endure[b] as long as the sun,
as long as the moon, through all generations.
6 He will be like rain[c] falling on a mown field,
like showers watering the earth.
7 In his days the righteous will flourish;[d]
prosperity will abound till the moon is no more.
8 He will rule from sea to sea
and from the River[c][e] to the ends of the earth.[d][f]
9 The desert tribes will bow before him
and his enemies will lick the dust.
10 The kings of Tarshish and of distant shores
will bring tribute to him;
the kings of Sheba[g] and Seba
will present him gifts.[h]
11 All kings will bow down to him
and all nations will serve him.

12 For he will deliver the needy who cry out,
the afflicted who have no-one to help.
13 He will take pity on the weak and the needy
and save the needy from death.
14 He will rescue[i] them from oppression and violence,
for precious[j] is their blood in his sight.

15 Long may he live!
May gold from Sheba[k] be given to him.
May people ever pray for him
and bless him all day long.
16 Let corn abound throughout the land;
on the tops of the hills may it sway.
Let its fruit flourish like Lebanon;[l]
let it thrive like the grass of the field.
17 May his name endure for ever;[m]
may it continue as long as the sun.[n]

All nations will be blessed through him,
and they will call him blessed.[o]

71:21 g Ps 18:35 h Ps 23:4 Ps 86:17 Isa 12:1 Isa 49:13
71:22 i Ps 33:2 j Ps 92:3 Ps 144:9 k 2Ki 19:22
71:23 l Ps 103:4
71:24 m Ps 35:28 n ver 13
72:2 a Isa 9:7 Isa 11:4-5 Isa 32:1
72:4 b Isa 11:4
72:6 c Dt 32:2 Hos 6:3
72:7 d Ps 92:12 Isa 2:4
72:8 e Ex 23:31 f Zec 9:10
72:10 g Ge 10:7 h 2Ch 9:24
72:14 i Ps 69:18 j 1Sa 26:21 Ps 116:15
72:15 k Isa 60:6
72:16 l Ps 104:16
72:17 m Ex 3:15 n Ps 89:36 o Ge 12:3 Lk 1:48

a2 Or *May he*; similarly in verses 3–11 and 17
b5 Septuagint; Hebrew *You will be feared*
c8 That is, the Euphrates
d8 Or *the end of the land*

[18]Praise be to the LORD God, the
God of Israel,[p]
who alone does marvellous
deeds.[q]
[19]Praise be to his glorious name
for ever;
may the whole earth be filled
with his glory.[r]
Amen and Amen.[s]

[20]This concludes the prayers of
David son of Jesse.

Book III: Psalms 73–89

Psalm 73

A psalm of Asaph.

[1]Surely God is good to Israel,
to those who are pure in
heart.[a]
[2]But as for me, my feet had
almost slipped;
I had nearly lost my foothold.
[3]For I envied[b] the arrogant
when I saw the prosperity of
the wicked.[c]
[4]They have no struggles;
their bodies are healthy and
strong.[a]
[5]They are free[d] from the
burdens common to man;
they are not plagued by
human ills.
[6]Therefore pride is their
necklace;[e]
they clothe themselves with
violence.[f]
[7]From their callous hearts[g]
comes iniquity;[b]
the evil conceits of their
minds know no limits.
[8]They scoff, and speak with
malice;
in their arrogance[h] they
threaten oppression.
[9]Their mouths lay claim to
heaven,
and their tongues take
possession of the earth.

72:18
p 1Ch 29:10; Ps 41:13; Ps 106:48
q Job 5:9
72:19
r Nu 14:21; Ne 9:5
s Ps 41:13
73:1
a Mt 5:8
73:3
b Ps 37:1; Pr 23:17
c Job 21:7; Jer 12:1
73:5
d Job 21:9
73:6
e Ge 41:42
f Ps 109:18
73:7
g Ps 17:10
73:8
h Ps 17:10; Jude 16
73:12
i Ps 49:6
73:13
j Job 21:15; Job 34:9
k Ps 26:6
73:16
l Ecc 8:17
73:17
m Ps 77:13
n Ps 37:38
73:18
o Ps 35:6
73:19
p Isa 47:11
73:20
q Job 20:8
r Ps 78:65
73:22
s Ps 49:10; Ps 92:6
t Ecc 3:18

[10]Therefore their people turn to
them
and drink up waters in
abundance.[c]
[11]They say, "How can God know?
Does the Most High have
knowledge?"
[12]This is what the wicked are
like—
always carefree, they increase
in wealth.[i]
[13]Surely in vain[j] have I kept my
heart pure;
in vain have I washed my
hands in innocence.[k]
[14]All day long I have been
plagued;
I have been punished every
morning.
[15]If I had said, "I will speak
thus,"
I would have betrayed your
children.
[16]When I tried to understand[l] all
this,
it was oppressive to me
[17]till I entered the sanctuary[m] of
God;
then I understood their final
destiny.[n]
[18]Surely you place them on
slippery ground;[o]
you cast them down to ruin.
[19]How suddenly[p] are they
destroyed,
completely swept away by
terrors!
[20]As a dream[q] when one
awakes,[r]
so when you arise, O Lord,
you will despise them as
fantasies.
[21]When my heart was grieved
and my spirit embittered,
[22]I was senseless[s] and ignorant;
I was a brute beast[t] before
you.

[a]4 With a different word division of the Hebrew; Masoretic Text *struggles at their death; / their bodies are healthy* [b]7 Syriac (see also Septuagint); Hebrew *Their eyes bulge with fat* [c]10 The meaning of the Hebrew for this verse is uncertain.

23 Yet I am always with you;
you hold me by my right hand.
24 You guide[u] me with your counsel,[v]
and afterwards you will take me into glory.
25 Whom have I in heaven but you?
And earth has nothing I desire besides you.[w]
26 My flesh and my heart[x] may fail,[y]
but God is the strength of my heart
and my portion for ever.
27 Those who are far from you will perish;[z]
you destroy all who are unfaithful to you.
28 But as for me, it is good to be near God.[a]
I have made the Sovereign LORD my refuge;
I will tell of all your deeds.[b]

Psalm 74

A *maskil*[a] of Asaph.

1 Why have you rejected us for ever,[a] O God?
Why does your anger smoulder against the sheep of your pasture?[b]
2 Remember the people you purchased[c] of old,[d]
the tribe of your inheritance, whom you redeemed[e]—
Mount Zion, where you dwelt.[f]
3 Turn your steps towards these everlasting ruins,
all this destruction the enemy has brought on the sanctuary.
4 Your foes roared[g] in the place where you met with us;
they set up their standards[h] as signs.
5 They behaved like men wielding axes
to cut through a thicket of trees.[i]
6 They smashed all the carved[j] panelling
with their axes and hatchets.
7 They burned your sanctuary to the ground;
they defiled the dwelling-place of your Name.
8 They said in their hearts, "We will crush[k] them completely!"
They burned every place where God was worshipped in the land.
9 We are given no miraculous signs;
no prophets[l] are left,
and none of us knows how long this will be.

10 How long will the enemy mock you, O God?
Will the foe revile[m] your name for ever?
11 Why do you hold back your hand, your right hand?[n]
Take it from the folds of your garment and destroy them!

12 But you, O God, are my king[o] from of old;
you bring salvation upon the earth.
13 It was you who split open the sea[p] by your power;
you broke the heads of the monster[q] in the waters.
14 It was you who crushed the heads of Leviathan
and gave him as food to the creatures of the desert.
15 It was you who opened up springs[r] and streams;
you dried up[s] the ever-flowing rivers.
16 The day is yours, and yours also the night;
you established the sun and moon.[t]
17 It was you who set all the boundaries[u] of the earth;
you made both summer and winter.[v]

73:24 u Ps 48:14 v Ps 32:8
73:25 w Php 3:8
73:26 x Ps 84:2 y Ps 40:12
73:27 z Ps 119:155
73:28 a Heb 10:22 Jas 4:8 b Ps 40:5
74:1 a Dt 29:20 Ps 44:23 b Ps 79:13 Ps 95:7 Ps 100:3
74:2 c Ex 15:16 d Dt 32:7 e Ex 15:13 f Ps 68:16
74:4 g La 2:7 h Nu 2:2
74:5 i Jer 46:22
74:6 j 1Ki 6:18
74:8 k Ps 83:4
74:9 l 1Sa 3:1
74:10 m Ps 44:16
74:11 n La 2:3
74:12 o Ps 44:4
74:13 p Ex 14:21 q Isa 51:9 Eze 29:3
74:15 r Ex 17:6 Nu 20:11 s Jos 2:10 Jos 3:13
74:16 t Ge 1:16 Ps 136:7-9
74:17 u Dt 32:8 Ac 17:26 v Ge 8:22

[a] Title: Probably a literary or musical term

18 Remember how the enemy has
mocked you, O LORD,
how foolish people[w] have
reviled your name.
19 Do not hand over the life of
your dove to wild beasts;
do not forget the lives of your
afflicted[x] people for ever.
20 Have regard for your
covenant,[y]
because haunts of violence fill
the dark places of the land.
21 Do not let the oppressed[z]
retreat in disgrace;
may the poor and needy[a]
praise your name.
22 Rise up, O God, and defend
your cause;
remember how fools[b] mock
you all day long.
23 Do not ignore the clamour of
your adversaries,[c]
the uproar of your enemies,
which rises continually.

Psalm 75

For the director of music. ⌞To the tune of⌟ "Do Not Destroy". A psalm of Asaph. A song.

1 We give thanks to you, O God,
we give thanks, for your
Name is near;[a]
men tell of your wonderful
deeds.[b]
2 You say, "I choose the
appointed time;
it is I who judge uprightly.
3 When the earth and all its
people quake,[c]
it is I who hold its pillars[d]
firm. *Selah*
4 To the arrogant I say, 'Boast no
more,'
and to the wicked, 'Do not lift
up your horns.[e]
5 Do not lift your horns against
heaven;
do not speak with outstretched
neck.' "
6 No-one from the east or the
west
or from the desert can exalt a
man.
7 But it is God who judges:[f]
He brings one down, he exalts
another.[g]
8 In the hand of the LORD is a cup
full of foaming wine mixed[h]
with spices;
he pours it out, and all the
wicked of the earth
drink it down to its very
dregs.[i]

9 As for me, I will declare[j] this
for ever;
I will sing praise to the God of
Jacob.
10 I will cut off the horns of all
the wicked,
but the horns of the righteous
shall be lifted up.[k]

Psalm 76

For the director of music. With stringed instruments. A psalm of Asaph. A song.

1 In Judah God is known;
his name is great in Israel.
2 His tent is in Salem,[a]
his dwelling-place in Zion.
3 There he broke the flashing
arrows,
the shields and the swords, the
weapons of war.[b] *Selah*

4 You are resplendent with light,
more majestic than mountains
rich with game.
5 Valiant men lie plundered,
they sleep their last sleep;[c]
not one of the warriors
can lift his hands.
6 At your rebuke, O God of Jacob,
both horse and chariot[d] lie
still.
7 You alone are to be feared.[e]
Who can stand[f] before you
when you are angry?[g]
8 From heaven you pronounced
judgment,
and the land feared[h] and was
quiet—

74:18 w Dt 32:6; Ps 39:8
74:19 x Ps 9:18
74:20 y Ge 17:7; Ps 106:45
74:21 z Ps 103:6; a Ps 35:10
74:22 b Ps 53:1
74:23 c Ps 65:7
75:1 a Ps 145:18; b Ps 44:1; Ps 71:16
75:3 c Isa 24:19; d 1Sa 2:8
75:4 e Zec 1:21
75:7 f Ps 50:6; g 1Sa 2:7; Ps 147:6; Da 2:21
75:8 h Pr 23:30; i Job 21:20; Jer 25:15
75:9 j Ps 40:10
75:10 k Ps 89:17; Ps 92:10; Ps 148:14
76:2 a Ge 14:18
76:3 b Ps 46:9
76:5 c Ps 13:3
76:6 d Ex 15:1
76:7 e 1Ch 16:25; f Ezr 9:15; Rev 6:17; g Ps 2:5; Na 1:6
76:8 h 1Ch 16:30; 2Ch 20:29-30

9when you, O God, rose up to
judge,[i]
to save all the afflicted of the
land. *Selah*
10Surely your wrath against men
brings you praise,[j]
and the survivors of your
wrath are restrained.[a]
11Make vows to the LORD your
God and fulfil them;[k]
let all the neighbouring lands
bring gifts[l] to the One to be
feared.
12He breaks the spirit of rulers;
he is feared by the kings of
the earth.

Psalm 77

For the director of music. For
Jeduthun. Of Asaph. A psalm.

1I cried out to God[a] for help;
I cried out to God to hear me.
2When I was in distress,[b] I
sought the Lord;
at night I stretched out
untiring hands[c]
and my soul refused to be
comforted.[d]

3I remembered you, O God, and
I groaned;
I mused, and my spirit grew
faint.[e] *Selah*
4You kept my eyes from closing;
I was too troubled to speak.
5I thought about the former
days,[f]
the years of long ago;
6I remembered my songs in the
night.
My heart mused and my spirit
enquired:

7"Will the Lord reject for ever?
Will he never show his
favour[g] again?
8Has his unfailing love vanished
for ever?
Has his promise[h] failed for
all time?
9Has God forgotten to be
merciful?[i]
Has he in anger withheld his
compassion?[j]" *Selah*

10Then I thought, "To this I will
appeal:
the years of the right hand[k]
of the Most High."
11I will remember the deeds of
the LORD;
yes, I will remember your
miracles[l] of long ago.
12I will meditate on all your
works
and consider all your mighty
deeds.

13Your ways, O God, are holy.
What god is so great as our
God?[m]
14You are the God who performs
miracles;
you display your power among
the peoples.
15With your mighty arm you
redeemed your people,[n]
the descendants of Jacob and
Joseph. *Selah*

16The waters[o] saw you, O God,
the waters saw you and
writhed;[p]
the very depths were
convulsed.
17The clouds poured down
water,[q]
the skies resounded with
thunder;
your arrows flashed back and
forth.
18Your thunder was heard in the
whirlwind,
your lightning lit up the
world;
the earth trembled and
quaked.[r]
19Your path led through the sea,[s]
your way through the mighty
waters,
though your footprints were
not seen.

76:9 i Ps 9:8
76:10 j Ex 9:16; Ro 9:17
76:11 k Ps 50:14; Ecc 5:4-5; l 2Ch 32:23; Ps 68:29
77:1 a Ps 3:4
77:2 b Ps 50:15; Isa 26:9,16; c Job 11:13; d Ge 37:35
77:3 e Ps 143:4
77:5 f Dt 32:7; Ps 44:1; Ps 143:5; Isa 51:9
77:7 g Ps 85:1
77:8 h 2Pe 3:9
77:9 i Ps 25:6; Ps 40:11; Ps 51:1; j Isa 49:15
77:10 k Ps 31:22
77:11 l Ps 143:5
77:13 m Ex 15:11; Ps 71:19; Ps 86:8
77:15 n Ex 6:6; Dt 9:29
77:16 o Ex 14:21,28; Hab 3:8; p Ps 114:4; Hab 3:10
77:17 q Jdg 5:4
77:18 r Jdg 5:4
77:19 s Hab 3:15

a10 Or *Surely the wrath of men brings you praise, / and with the remainder of wrath you arm yourself*

20 You led your people[t] like a
flock[u]
by the hand of Moses and
Aaron.

Psalm 78

A *maskil*[a] of Asaph.

1 O my people, hear my
teaching;[a]
listen to the words of my
mouth.
2 I will open my mouth in
parables,[b]
I will utter hidden things,
things from of old—
3 what we have heard and known,
what our fathers have told
us.[c]
4 We will not hide them from
their children;[d]
we will tell the next
generation
the praiseworthy deeds[e] of the
LORD,
his power, and the wonders he
has done.
5 He decreed statutes[f] for
Jacob[g]
and established the law in
Israel,
which he commanded our
forefathers
to teach their children,
6 so that the next generation
would know them,
even the children yet to be
born,[h]
and they in turn would tell
their children.
7 Then they would put their trust
in God
and would not forget[i] his
deeds
but would keep his
commands.[j]
8 They would not be like their
forefathers[k]—
a stubborn[l] and rebellious[m]
generation,
whose hearts were not loyal to
God,
whose spirits were not faithful
to him.
9 The men of Ephraim, though
armed with bows,[n]
turned back on the day of
battle;[o]
10 they did not keep God's
covenant[p]
and refused to live by his law.
11 They forgot what he had done,[q]
the wonders he had shown
them.
12 He did miracles[r] in the sight of
their fathers
in the land of Egypt,[s] in the
region of Zoan.[t]
13 He divided the sea[u] and led
them through;
he made the water stand firm
like a wall.[v]
14 He guided them with the cloud
by day
and with light from the fire all
night.[w]
15 He split the rocks[x] in the
desert
and gave them water as
abundant as the seas;
16 he brought streams out of a
rocky crag
and made water flow down
like rivers.

17 But they continued to sin[y]
against him,
rebelling in the desert against
the Most High.
18 They wilfully put God to the
test[z]
by demanding the food they
craved.[a]
19 They spoke against God,[b]
saying,
"Can God spread a table in the
desert?
20 When he struck the rock, water
gushed out,[c]
and streams flowed
abundantly.
But can he also give us food?
Can he supply meat[d] for his
people?"

[a]Title: Probably a literary or musical term

77:20 t Ex 13:21 u Ps 78:52 Isa 63:11
78:1 a Isa 51:4 Isa 55:3
78:2 b Ps 49:4 Mt 13:35*
78:3 c Ps 44:1
78:4 d Dt 11:19 e Ps 26:7 Ps 71:17
78:5 f Ps 19:7 Ps 81:5 g Ps 147:19
78:6 h Ps 22:31 Ps 102:18
78:7 i Dt 6:12 j Dt 5:29
78:8 k 2Ch 30:7 l Ex 32:9 m ver 37 Isa 30:9
78:9 n ver 57 1Ch 12:2 o Jdg 20:39
78:10 p 2Ki 17:15
78:11 q Ps 106:13
78:12 r Ps 106:22 s Ex 7-12 t Nu 13:22
78:13 u Ex 14:21 Ps 136:13 v Ex 15:8
78:14 w Ex 13:21 Ps 105:39
78:15 x Nu 20:11 1Co 10:4
78:17 y Dt 9:22 Isa 63:10 Heb 3:16
78:18 z 1Co 10:9 a Ex 16:2 Nu 11:4
78:19 b Nu 21:5
78:20 c Nu 20:11 d Nu 11:18

21When the LORD heard them, he
was very angry;
his fire broke out[e] against
Jacob,
and his wrath rose against
Israel,
22for they did not believe in God
or trust[f] in his deliverance.
23Yet he gave a command to the
skies above
and opened the doors of the
heavens;[g]
24he rained down manna[h] for the
people to eat,
he gave them the grain of
heaven.
25Men ate the bread of angels;
he sent them all the food they
could eat.
26He let loose the east wind[i]
from the heavens
and led forth the south wind
by his power.
27He rained meat down on them
like dust,
flying birds like sand on the
seashore.
28He made them come down
inside their camp,
all around their tents.
29They ate till they had more than
enough,[j]
for he had given them what
they craved.
30But before they turned from
the food they craved,
even while it was still in their
mouths,[k]
31God's anger rose against them;
he put to death the sturdiest[l]
among them,
cutting down the young men
of Israel.

32In spite of all this, they kept on
sinning;
in spite of his wonders,[m] they
did not believe.[n]
33So he ended their days in
futility[o]
and their years in terror.
34Whenever God slew them, they
would seek[p] him;
they eagerly turned to him
again.
35They remembered that God was
their Rock,[q]
that God Most High was their
Redeemer.[r]
36But then they would flatter him
with their mouths,[s]
lying to him with their
tongues;
37their hearts were not loyal[t] to
him,
they were not faithful to his
covenant.
38Yet he was merciful;[u]
he forgave[v] their iniquities[w]
and did not destroy them.
Time after time he restrained
his anger
and did not stir up his full
wrath.
39He remembered that they were
but flesh,[x]
a passing breeze[y] that does
not return.

40How often they rebelled[z]
against him in the desert[a]
and grieved him[b] in the
wasteland!
41Again and again they put God to
the test;[c]
they vexed the Holy One of
Israel.[d]
42They did not remember his
power—
the day he redeemed them
from the oppressor,
43the day he displayed his
miraculous signs in Egypt,
his wonders in the region of
Zoan.
44He turned their rivers to
blood;[e]
they could not drink from
their streams.
45He sent swarms of flies[f] that
devoured them,
and frogs[g] that devastated
them.
46He gave their crops to the
grasshopper,
their produce to the locust.[h]

78:21 e Nu 11:1
78:22 f Dt 1:32; Heb 3:19
78:23 g Ge 7:11; Mal 3:10
78:24 h Ex 16:4; Jn 6:31*
78:26 i Nu 11:31
78:29 j Nu 11:20
78:30 k Nu 11:33
78:31 l Isa 10:16
78:32 m ver 11; n ver 22
78:33 o Nu 14:29,35
78:34 p Hos 5:15
78:35 q Dt 32:4; r Dt 9:26
78:36 s Eze 33:31
78:37 t ver 8; Ac 8:21
78:38 u Ex 34:6; v Isa 48:10; w Nu 14:18,20
78:39 x Ge 6:3; Ps 103:14; y Job 7:7; Jas 4:14
78:40 z Heb 3:16; a Ps 95:8; Ps 106:14; b Eph 4:30
78:41 c Nu 14:22; d 2Ki 19:22; Ps 89:18
78:44 e Ex 7:20-21; Ps 105:29
78:45 f Ex 8:24; Ps 105:31; g Ex 8:2,6
78:46 h Ex 10:13

47He destroyed their vines with hail[i]
and their sycamore-figs with sleet.
48He gave over their cattle to the hail,
their livestock[j] to bolts of lightning.
49He unleashed against them his hot anger,[k]
his wrath, indignation and hostility—
a band of destroying angels.
50He prepared a path for his anger;
he did not spare them from death
but gave them over to the plague.
51He struck down all the firstborn of Egypt,[l]
the firstfruits of manhood in the tents of Ham.[m]
52But he brought his people out like a flock;[n]
he led them like sheep through the desert.
53He guided them safely, so they were unafraid;
but the sea engulfed[o] their enemies.[p]
54Thus he brought them to the border of his holy land,
to the hill country his right hand[q] had taken.
55He drove out nations[r] before them
and allotted their lands to them as an inheritance;[s]
he settled the tribes of Israel in their homes.

56But they put God to the test
and rebelled against the Most High;
they did not keep his statutes.
57Like their fathers[t] they were disloyal and faithless,
as unreliable as a faulty bow.[u]
58They angered him[v] with their high places;[w]
they aroused his jealousy with their idols.[x]
59When God heard them, he was very angry;
he rejected Israel[y] completely.
60He abandoned the tabernacle of Shiloh,[z]
the tent he had set up among men.
61He sent ⌊the ark of⌋ his might[a] into captivity,[b]
his splendour into the hands of the enemy.
62He gave his people over to the sword;
he was very angry with his inheritance.
63Fire consumed[c] their young men,
and their maidens had no wedding songs;[d]
64their priests were put to the sword,[e]
and their widows could not weep.
65Then the Lord awoke as from sleep,[f]
as a man wakes from the stupor of wine.
66He beat back his enemies;
he put them to everlasting shame.[g]
67Then he rejected the tents of Joseph,
he did not choose the tribe of Ephraim;
68but he chose the tribe of Judah,
Mount Zion,[h] which he loved.
69He built his sanctuary like the heights,
like the earth that he established for ever.
70He chose David[i] his servant
and took him from the sheep pens;
71from tending the sheep he brought him
to be the shepherd[j] of his people Jacob,
of Israel his inheritance.
72And David shepherded them with integrity of heart;[k]
with skilful hands he led them.

78:47 i Ex 9:23; Ps 105:32
78:48 j Ex 9:25
78:49 k Ex 15:7
78:51 l Ex 12:29; Ps 135:8 m Ps 105:23; Ps 106:22
78:52 n Ps 77:20
78:53 o Ex 14:28 p Ps 106:10
78:54 q Ex 15:17; Ps 44:3
78:55 r Ps 44:2 s Jos 13:7
78:57 t Eze 20:27 u Hos 7:16
78:58 v Jdg 2:12 w Lev 26:30 x Ex 20:4; Dt 32:21
78:59 y Dt 32:19
78:60 z Jos 18:1
78:61 a Ps 132:8 b 1Sa 4:17
78:63 c Nu 11:1 d Jer 7:34; Jer 16:9
78:64 e 1Sa 4:17; 1Sa 22:18
78:65 f Ps 44:23
78:66 g 1Sa 5:6
78:68 h Ps 87:2
78:70 i 1Sa 16:1
78:71 j 2Sa 5:2; Ps 28:9
78:72 k 1Ki 9:4

Psalm 79

A psalm of Asaph.

1O God, the nations have invaded
your inheritance;[a]
they have defiled your holy
temple,
they have reduced Jerusalem
to rubble.[b]
2They have given the dead
bodies of your servants
as food to the birds of the air,
the flesh of your saints to the
beasts of the earth.[c]
3They have poured out blood like
water
all around Jerusalem,
and there is no-one to bury the
dead.[d]
4We are objects of reproach to
our neighbours,
of scorn and derision to those
around us.[e]

5How long,[f] O LORD? Will you
be angry[g] for ever?
How long will your jealousy
burn like fire?[h]
6Pour out your wrath[i] on the
nations
that do not acknowledge[j] you,
on the kingdoms
that do not call on your
name;[k]
7for they have devoured Jacob
and destroyed his homeland.
8Do not hold against us the sins
of the fathers;[l]
may your mercy come quickly
to meet us,
for we are in desperate need.[m]

9Help us,[n] O God our Saviour,
for the glory of your name;
deliver us and forgive our sins
for your name's sake.[o]
10Why should the nations say,
"Where is their God?"[p]
Before our eyes, make known
among the nations
that you avenge[q] the
outpoured blood of your
servants.
11May the groans of the prisoners
come before you;
by the strength of your arm
preserve those condemned to
die.
12Pay back into the laps[r] of our
neighbours seven times[s]
the reproach they have hurled
at you, O Lord.
13Then we your people, the sheep
of your pasture,[t]
will praise you for ever;[u]
from generation to generation
we will recount your praise.

Psalm 80

For the director of music. To ⌊the tune of⌋ "The Lilies of the Covenant". Of Asaph. A psalm.

1Hear us, O Shepherd of Israel,
you who lead Joseph like a
flock;[a]
you who sit enthroned between
the cherubim,[b] shine forth
2 before Ephraim, Benjamin and
Manasseh.[c]
Awaken[d] your might;
come and save us.

3Restore[e] us,[f] O God;
make your face shine upon us,
that we may be saved.

4O LORD God Almighty,
how long will your anger
smoulder
against the prayers of your
people?
5You have fed them with the
bread of tears;
you have made them drink
tears by the bowlful.[g]
6You have made us a source of
contention to our
neighbours,
and our enemies mock us.[h]

7Restore us, O God Almighty;
make your face shine upon us,
that we may be saved.

8You brought a vine[i] out of
Egypt;
you drove out[j] the nations
and planted it.
9You cleared the ground for it,

79:1 a Ps 74:2 b 2Ki 25:9
79:2 c Dt 28:26 Jer 7:33
79:3 d Jer 16:4
79:4 e Ps 44:13 Ps 80:6
79:5 f Ps 74:10 g Ps 74:1 Ps 85:5 h Dt 29:20 Ps 89:46 Zep 3:8
79:6 i Ps 69:24 Rev 16:1 j Jer 10:25 2Th 1:8 k Ps 14:4
79:8 l Isa 64:9 m Ps 116:6 Ps 142:6
79:9 n 2Ch 14:11 o Ps 25:11 Ps 31:3 Jer 14:7
79:10 p Ps 42:10 q Ps 94:1
79:12 r Isa 65:6 Jer 32:18 s Ge 4:15
79:13 t Ps 74:1 Ps 95:7 u Ps 44:8
80:1 a Ps 77:20 b Ex 25:22
80:2 c Nu 2:18-24 d Ps 35:23
80:3 e Ps 85:4 La 5:21 f Nu 6:25
80:5 g Ps 42:3 Isa 30:20
80:6 h Ps 79:4
80:8 i Isa 5:1-2 Jer 2:21 j Jos 13:6 Ac 7:45

and it took root and filled the
land.
10 The mountains were covered
with its shade,
the mighty cedars with its
branches.
11 It sent out its boughs to the
Sea,[a]
its shoots as far as the
River.[b][k]

12 Why have you broken down its
walls[l]
so that all who pass by pick its
grapes?
13 Boars from the forest ravage[m]
it
and the creatures of the field
feed on it.
14 Return to us, O God Almighty!
Look down from heaven and
see![n]
Watch over this vine,
15 the root your right hand has
planted,
the son[c] you have raised up
for yourself.

16 Your vine is cut down, it is
burned with fire;
at your rebuke[o] your people
perish.
17 Let your hand rest on the man
at your right hand,
the son of man you have
raised up for yourself.
18 Then we will not turn away
from you;
revive us, and we will call on
your name.

19 Restore us, O LORD God
Almighty;
make your face shine upon us,
that we may be saved.

Psalm 81

For the director of music. According to *gittith*.[a] Of Asaph.

1 Sing for joy to God our
strength;
shout aloud to the God of
Jacob![a]

80:11 *k* Ps 72:8
80:12 *l* Ps 89:40; Isa 5:5
80:13 *m* Jer 5:6
80:14 *n* Isa 63:15
80:16 *o* Ps 39:11; Ps 76:6
81:1 *a* Ps 66:1
81:2 *b* Ex 15:20 *c* Ps 92:3
81:5 *d* Ex 11:4 *e* Ps 114:1
81:6 *f* Isa 9:4
81:7 *g* Ex 2:23; Ps 50:15 *h* Ex 19:19 *i* Ex 17:7
81:8 *j* Ps 50:7
81:9 *k* Ex 20:3; Dt 32:12; Isa 43:12
81:10 *l* Ex 20:2 *m* Ps 107:9
81:11 *n* Ex 32:1-6
81:12 *o* Ac 7:42; Ro 1:24

2 Begin the music, strike the
tambourine,[b]
play the melodious harp[c] and
lyre.
3 Sound the ram's horn at the
New Moon,
and when the moon is full, on
the day of our Feast;
4 this is a decree for Israel,
an ordinance of the God of
Jacob.
5 He established it as a statute
for Joseph
when he went out against
Egypt,[d]
where we heard a language we
did not understand.[b][e]

6 He says, "I removed the burden
from their shoulders;[f]
their hands were set free from
the basket.
7 In your distress you called[g]
and I rescued you,
I answered[h] you out of a
thundercloud;
I tested you at the waters of
Meribah.[i] *Selah*
8 "Hear, O my people,[j] and I will
warn you—
if you would but listen to me,
O Israel!
9 You shall have no foreign god[k]
among you;
you shall not bow down to an
alien god.
10 I am the LORD your God,
who brought you up out of
Egypt.[l]
Open wide your mouth and I
will fill[m] it.

11 "But my people would not listen
to me;
Israel would not submit to
me.[n]
12 So I gave them over[o] to their
stubborn hearts
to follow their own devices.

[a]*11* Probably the Mediterranean [b]*11* That is, the Euphrates [c]*15* Or *branch* [a]Title: Probably a musical term [b]*5* Or / *and we heard a voice we had not known*

13"If my people would but listen
to me,[p]
if Israel would follow my
ways,
14how quickly would I subdue[q]
their enemies
and turn my hand against[r]
their foes!
15Those who hate the LORD would
cringe before him,
and their punishment would
last for ever.
16But you would be fed with the
finest of wheat;[s]
with honey from the rock I
would satisfy you."

Psalm 82

A psalm of Asaph.

1God presides in the great
assembly;
he gives judgment[a] among
the "gods":

2"How long will you[a] defend the
unjust
and show partiality[b] to the
wicked?[c] *Selah*
3Defend the cause of the weak
and fatherless;[d]
maintain the rights of the
poor[e] and oppressed.
4Rescue the weak and needy;
deliver them from the hand of
the wicked.

5"They know nothing, they
understand nothing.[f]
They walk about in
darkness;[g]
all the foundations[h] of the
earth are shaken.

6"I said, 'You are "gods";[i]
you are all sons of the Most
High.'
7But you will die[j] like mere
men;
you will fall like every other
ruler."

8Rise up,[k] O God, judge the
earth,
for all the nations are your
inheritance.[l]

Psalm 83

A song. A psalm of Asaph.

1O God, do not keep silent;[a]
be not quiet, O God, be not
still.
2See how your enemies are
astir,[b]
how your foes rear their
heads.[c]
3With cunning they conspire[d]
against your people;
they plot against those you
cherish.
4"Come," they say, "let us
destroy[e] them as a nation,
that the name of Israel be
remembered[f] no more."

5With one mind they plot
together;[g]
they form an alliance against
you—
6the tents of Edom[h] and the
Ishmaelites,
of Moab[i] and the Hagrites,[j]
7Gebal,[a][k] Ammon and Amalek,
Philistia, with the people of
Tyre.[l]
8Even Assyria has joined them
to lend strength to the
descendants of Lot.[m] *Selah*

9Do to them as you did to
Midian,[n]
as you did to Sisera and Jabin
at the river Kishon,[o]
10who perished at Endor
and became like refuse[p] on
the ground.
11Make their nobles like Oreb and
Zeeb,[q]
all their princes like Zebah
and Zalmunna,[r]
12who said, "Let us take
possession[s]
of the pasture-lands of God."

13Make them like tumble-weed,
O my God,

81:13 p Dt 5:29; Isa 48:18
81:14 q Ps 47:3; r Am 1:8
81:16 s Dt 32:14
82:1 a Ps 58:11; Isa 3:13
82:2 b Dt 1:17; c Ps 58:1-2; Pr 18:5
82:3 d Dt 24:17; e Jer 22:16
82:5 f Ps 14:4; Mic 3:1; g Isa 59:9; h Ps 11:3
82:6 i Jn 10:34*
82:7 j Ps 49:12; Eze 31:14
82:8 k Ps 12:5; l Ps 2:8; Rev 11:15
83:1 a Ps 28:1; Ps 35:22
83:2 b Ps 2:1; Isa 17:12; c Jdg 8:28; Ps 81:15
83:3 d Ps 31:13
83:4 e Est 3:6; f Jer 11:19
83:5 g Ps 2:2
83:6 h Ps 137:7; i 2Ch 20:1; j Ge 25:16
83:7 k Jos 13:5; l Eze 27:3
83:8 m Dt 2:9
83:9 n Jdg 7:1-23; o Jdg 4:23-24
83:10 p Zep 1:17
83:11 q Jdg 7:25; r Jdg 8:12,21
83:12 s 2Ch 20:11

a2 The Hebrew is plural. a7 That is, Byblos

like chaff[t] before the wind.
14 As fire consumes the forest
or a flame sets the mountains ablaze,[u]
15 so pursue them with your tempest
and terrify them with your storm.[v]
16 Cover their faces with shame[w]
so that men will seek your name, O LORD.

17 May they ever be ashamed and dismayed;
may they perish in disgrace.[x]
18 Let them know that you, whose name is the LORD—
that you alone are the Most High over all the earth.[y]

Psalm 84

For the director of music. According to *gittith*.[a] Of the Sons of Korah. A psalm.

1 How lovely is your dwelling-place,[a]
O LORD Almighty!
2 My soul yearns,[b] even faints,
for the courts of the LORD;
my heart and my flesh cry out
for the living God.

3 Even the sparrow has found a home,
and the swallow a nest for herself,
where she may have her young—
a place near your altar,[c]
O LORD Almighty, my King and my God.[d]
4 Blessed are those who dwell in your house;
they are ever praising you.
Selah

5 Blessed are those whose strength[e] is in you,
who have set their hearts on pilgrimage.[f]
6 As they pass through the Valley of Baca,
they make it a place of springs;

83:13 t Ps 35:5 Isa 17:13
83:14 u Dt 32:22 Isa 9:18
83:15 v Job 9:17
83:16 w Ps 109:29 Ps 132:18
83:17 x Ps 35:4
83:18 y Ps 59:13
84:1 a Ps 27:4 Ps 43:3 Ps 132:5
84:2 b Ps 42:1-2
84:3 c Ps 43:4 d Ps 5:2
84:5 e Ps 81:1 f Jer 31:6
84:6 g Joel 2:23
84:7 h Pr 4:18 i Dt 16:16
84:9 j Ps 59:11 k 1Sa 16:6 Ps 2:2 Ps 132:17
84:10 l 1Ch 23:5
84:11 m Isa 60:19 Rev 21:23 n Ge 15:1 o Ps 34:10
84:12 p Ps 2:12
85:1 a Ps 14:7 Jer 30:18 Eze 39:25
85:2 b Nu 14:19 c Ps 78:38
85:3 d Ps 106:23 e Ex 32:12 Dt 13:17 Ps 78:38 Jnh 3:9
85:4 f Ps 80:3,7

the autumn[g] rains also cover it with pools.[b]
7 They go from strength to strength,[h]
till each appears[i] before God in Zion.

8 Hear my prayer, O LORD God Almighty;
listen to me, O God of Jacob.
Selah
9 Look upon our shield,[c][j] O God;
look with favour on your anointed one.[k]

10 Better is one day in your courts
than a thousand elsewhere;
I would rather be a doorkeeper[l] in the house of my God
than dwell in the tents of the wicked.
11 For the LORD God is a sun[m] and shield;[n]
the LORD bestows favour and honour;
no good thing does he withhold[o]
from those whose walk is blameless.

12 O LORD Almighty,
blessed[p] is the man who trusts in you.

Psalm 85

For the director of music. Of the Sons of Korah. A psalm.

1 You showed favour to your land, O LORD;
you restored the fortunes[a] of Jacob.
2 You forgave[b] the iniquity[c] of your people
and covered all their sins.
Selah
3 You set aside all your wrath[d]
and turned from your fierce anger.[e]

4 Restore[f] us again, O God our Saviour,

[a]Title: Probably a musical term
[b]6 Or *blessings* [c]9 Or *sovereign*

and put away your displeasure
towards us.
5Will you be angry with us for
ever?[g]
Will you prolong your anger
through all generations?
6Will you not revive[h] us again,
that your people may rejoice
in you?
7Show us your unfailing love,
O LORD,
and grant us your salvation.
8I will listen to what God the
LORD will say;
he promises peace[i] to his
people, his saints—
but let them not return to
folly.
9Surely his salvation[j] is near
those who fear him,
that his glory[k] may dwell in
our land.

10Love and faithfulness[l] meet
together;
righteousness[m] and peace kiss
each other.
11Faithfulness springs forth from
the earth,
and righteousness[n] looks
down from heaven.
12The LORD will indeed give what
is good,[o]
and our land will yield[p] its
harvest.
13Righteousness goes before him
and prepares the way for his
steps.

Psalm 86

A prayer of David.

1Hear, O LORD, and answer[a] me,
for I am poor and needy.
2Guard my life, for I am devoted
to you.
You are my God; save your
servant
who trusts in you.[b]
3Have mercy[c] on me, O Lord,
for I call[d] to you all day long.
4Bring joy to your servant,
for to you, O Lord,
I lift[e] up my soul.
5You are forgiving and good,
O Lord,
abounding in love[f] to all who
call to you.
6Hear my prayer, O LORD;
listen to my cry for mercy.
7In the day of my trouble[g] I will
call to you,
for you will answer me.

8Among the gods there is none
like you,[h] O Lord;
no deeds can compare with
yours.
9All the nations you have made
will come and worship[i]
before you, O Lord;
they will bring glory[j] to your
name.
10For you are great and do
marvellous deeds;[k]
you alone[l] are God.

11Teach me your way,[m] O LORD,
and I will walk in your truth;
give me an undivided[n] heart,
that I may fear your name.
12I will praise you, O Lord my
God, with all my heart;
I will glorify your name for
ever.
13For great is your love towards
me;
you have delivered me from
the depths of the grave.[a]

14The arrogant are attacking me,
O God;
a band of ruthless men seeks
my life—
men without regard for you.[o]
15But you, O Lord, are a
compassionate and
gracious[p] God,
slow to anger, abounding in
love and faithfulness.[q]
16Turn to me and have mercy on
me;
grant your strength to your
servant

a13 Hebrew *Sheol*

85:5 g Ps 79:5
85:6 h Ps 80:18; Hab 3:2
85:8 i Zec 9:10
85:9 j Isa 46:13; k Zec 2:5
85:10 l Ps 89:14; Pr 3:3; m Ps 72:2-3; Isa 32:17
85:11 n Isa 45:8
85:12 o Ps 84:11; Jas 1:17; p Lev 26:4; Ps 67:6; Zec 8:12
86:1 a Ps 17:6
86:2 b Ps 25:2; Ps 31:14
86:3 c Ps 4:1; Ps 57:1; d Ps 88:9
86:4 e Ps 25:1; Ps 143:8
86:5 f Ex 34:6; Ne 9:17; Ps 103:8; Ps 145:8; Joel 2:13; Jnh 4:2
86:7 g Ps 50:15
86:8 h Ex 15:11; Dt 3:24; Ps 89:6
86:9 i Ps 66:4; Rev 15:4; j Isa 43:7
86:10 k Ps 72:18; l Dt 6:4; Mk 12:29; 1Co 8:4
86:11 m Ps 25:5; n Jer 32:39
86:14 o Ps 54:3
86:15 p Ps 103:8; q Ex 34:6; Ne 9:17; Joel 2:13

and save the son of your
maidservant.[b][r]
17Give me a sign of your
goodness,
that my enemies may see it
and be put to shame,
for you, O LORD, have helped
me and comforted me.

Psalm 87

Of the Sons of Korah. A psalm. A song.

1He has set his foundation on the
holy mountain;
2 the LORD loves the gates of
Zion[a]
more than all the dwellings of
Jacob.
3Glorious things are said of you,
O city of God:[b] *Selah*
4"I will record Rahab[a][c] and
Babylon
among those who acknowledge
me—
Philistia too, and Tyre[d], along
with Cush[b]—
and will say, 'This[c] one was
born in Zion.[e]' "
5Indeed, of Zion it will be said,
"This one and that one were
born in her,
and the Most High himself
will establish her."
6The LORD will write in the
register[f] of the peoples:
"This one was born in Zion."
Selah
7As they make music[g] they will
sing,
"All my fountains[h] are in
you."

Psalm 88

A song. A psalm of the Sons of Korah.
For the director of music. According to
mahalath leannoth.[a] A *maskil*[b] of
Heman the Ezrahite.

1O LORD, the God who saves
me,[a]
day and night I cry out[b]
before you.

86:16
r Ps 116:16
87:2
a Ps 78:68
87:3
b Ps 46:4
Isa 60:1
87:4
c Job 9:13
d Ps 45:12
e Isa 19:25
87:6
f Ps 69:28
Isa 4:3
Eze 13:9
87:7
g Ps 149:3
h Ps 36:9
88:1
a Ps 51:14
b Ps 22:2
Ps 27:9
Lk 18:7
88:3
c Ps 107:18,26
88:4
d Ps 28:1
88:5
e Ps 31:22
Isa 53:8
88:6
f Ps 69:15
La 3:55
88:7
g Ps 42:7
88:8
h Job 19:13
Ps 31:11
i Jer 32:2
88:9
j Ps 38:10
k Ps 86:3
l Job 11:13
Ps 143:6
88:10
m Ps 6:5
88:11
n Ps 30:9

2May my prayer come before
you;
turn your ear to my cry.
3For my soul is full of trouble
and my life draws near the
grave.[c][c]
4I am counted among those who
go down to the pit;[d]
I am like a man without
strength.
5I am set apart with the dead,
like the slain who lie in the
grave,
whom you remember no more,
who are cut off[e] from your
care.
6You have put me in the lowest
pit,
in the darkest depths.[f]
7Your wrath lies heavily upon
me;
you have overwhelmed me
with all your waves.[g] *Selah*
8You have taken from me my
closest friends[h]
and have made me repulsive
to them.
I am confined[i] and cannot
escape;
9 my eyes[j] are dim with grief.

I call[k] to you, O LORD, every
day;
I spread out my hands[l] to
you.
10Do you show your wonders to
the dead?
Do those who are dead rise up
and praise you?[m] *Selah*
11Is your love declared in the
grave,
your faithfulness[n] in
Destruction?[d]
12Are your wonders known in the
place of darkness,

[b]16 Or *save your faithful son* [a]4 A poetic name for Egypt [b]4 That is, the upper Nile region [c]4 Or *"O Rahab and Babylon, / Philistia, Tyre and Cush, / I will record concerning those who acknowledge me: / 'This* [a]Title: Possibly a tune, "The Suffering of Affliction" [b]Title: Probably a literary or musical term [c]3 Hebrew *Sheol* [d]11 Hebrew *Abaddon*

or your righteous deeds in the
land of oblivion?
13 But I cry to you for help,[o]
O LORD;
in the morning[p] my prayer
comes before you.[q]
14 Why, O LORD, do you reject[r]
me
and hide your face[s] from me?
15 From my youth I have been
afflicted and close to death;
I have suffered your terrors[t]
and am in despair.
16 Your wrath has swept over me;
your terrors have destroyed
me.
17 All day long they surround me
like a flood;[u]
they have completely engulfed
me.
18 You have taken my
companions[v] and loved
ones from me;
the darkness is my closest
friend.

Psalm 89

A *maskil*[a] of Ethan the Ezrahite.

1 I will sing[a] of the LORD's great
love for ever;
with my mouth I will make
your faithfulness known[b]
through all generations.
2 I will declare that your love
stands firm for ever,
that you established your
faithfulness in heaven
itself.[c]
3 You said, "I have made a
covenant with my chosen
one,
I have sworn to David my
servant,
4 'I will establish your line for
ever
and make your throne firm
through all generations.' "[d]
Selah
5 The heavens[e] praise your
wonders, O LORD,
your faithfulness too, in the
assembly of the holy ones.
6 For who in the skies above can
compare with the LORD?
Who is like the LORD among
the heavenly beings?[f]
7 In the council of the holy ones
God is greatly feared;
he is more awesome than all
who surround him.[g]
8 O LORD God Almighty, who is
like you?[h]
You are mighty, O LORD, and
your faithfulness surrounds
you.
9 You rule over the surging sea;
when its waves mount up, you
still them.[i]
10 You crushed Rahab[j] like one of
the slain;
with your strong arm you
scattered[k] your enemies.
11 The heavens are yours, and
yours also the earth;[l]
you founded the world and all
that is in it.[m]
12 You created the north and the
south;
Tabor[n] and Hermon[o] sing for
joy[p] at your name.
13 Your arm is endued with power;
your hand is strong, your right
hand exalted.
14 Righteousness and justice are
the foundation of your
throne;[q]
love and faithfulness go
before you.
15 Blessed are those who have
learned to acclaim you,
who walk in the light[r] of your
presence, O LORD.
16 They rejoice in your name[s] all
day long;
they exult in your
righteousness.
17 For you are their glory and
strength,
and by your favour you exalt
our horn.[b][t]

88:13 o Ps 30:2 p Ps 5:3 q Ps 119:147
88:14 r Ps 43:2 s Job 13:24 Ps 13:1
88:15 t Job 6:4
88:17 u Ps 22:16 Ps 124:4
88:18 v ver 8 Job 19:13 Ps 38:11
89:1 a Ps 59:16 Ps 101:1 b Ps 36:5 Ps 40:10
89:2 c Ps 36:5
89:4 d 2Sa 7:12-16 1Ki 8:16 Ps 132:11-12 Isa 9:7 Lk 1:33
89:5 e Ps 19:1
89:6 f Ps 113:5
89:7 g Ps 47:2
89:8 h Ps 71:19
89:9 i Ps 65:7
89:10 j Ps 87:4 k Ps 68:1
89:11 l 1Ch 29:11 Ps 24:1 m Ge 1:1
89:12 n Jos 19:22 o Dt 3:8 Jos 12:1 p Ps 98:8
89:14 q Ps 97:2
89:15 r Ps 44:3
89:16 s Ps 105:3
89:17 t Ps 75:10 Ps 92:10 Ps 148:14

[a] Title: Probably a literary or musical term
[b] 17 *Horn* here symbolises strong one.

[18]Indeed, our shield[c] belongs to
the LORD,
our king[u] to the Holy One of
Israel.

[19]Once you spoke in a vision,
to your faithful people you
said:
"I have bestowed strength on a
warrior;
I have exalted a young man
from among the people.
[20]I have found David[v] my
servant;[w]
with my sacred oil I have
anointed[x] him.
[21]My hand will sustain him;
surely my arm will strengthen
him.[y]
[22]No enemy will subject him to
tribute;
no wicked man will oppress[z]
him.
[23]I will crush his foes before
him[a]
and strike down his
adversaries.[b]
[24]My faithful love will be with
him,[c]
and through my name his
horn[d] will be exalted.
[25]I will set his hand over the sea,
his right hand over the
rivers.[d]
[26]He will call out to me, 'You are
my Father,[e]
my God, the Rock my
Saviour.'[f]
[27]I will also appoint him my
firstborn,[g]
the most exalted[h] of the
kings[i] of the earth.
[28]I will maintain my love to him
for ever,
and my covenant with him will
never fail.[j]
[29]I will establish his line for ever,
his throne as long as the
heavens endure.[k]

[30]"If his sons forsake my law
and do not follow my statutes,
[31]if they violate my decrees
and fail to keep my
commands,
[32]I will punish their sin with the
rod,
their iniquity with flogging;[l]
[33]but I will not take my love from
him,[m]
nor will I ever betray my
faithfulness.
[34]I will not violate my covenant
or alter what my lips have
uttered.[n]
[35]Once for all, I have sworn by
my holiness—
and I will not lie to David—
[36]that his line will continue for
ever
and his throne endure before
me like the sun;
[37]it will be established for ever
like the moon,
the faithful witness in the
sky." *Selah*

[38]But you have rejected,[o] you
have spurned,
you have been very angry
with your anointed one.
[39]You have renounced the
covenant with your servant
and have defiled his crown in
the dust.[p]
[40]You have broken through all his
walls[q]
and reduced his strongholds[r]
to ruins.
[41]All who pass by have plundered
him;
he has become the scorn of his
neighbours.[s]
[42]You have exalted the right hand
of his foes;
you have made all his enemies
rejoice.[t]
[43]You have turned back the edge
of his sword
and have not supported him in
battle.[u]
[44]You have put an end to his
splendour
and cast his throne to the
ground.
[45]You have cut short the days of
his youth;

89:18 u Ps 47:9
89:20 v Ac 13:22 w Ps 78:70 x 1Sa 16:1,12
89:21 y Ps 18:35
89:22 z 2Sa 7:10
89:23 a Ps 18:40 b 2Sa 7:9
89:24 c 2Sa 7:15
89:25 d Ps 72:8
89:26 e 2Sa 7:14 f 2Sa 22:47
89:27 g Col 1:18 h Nu 24:7 i Rev 1:5 Rev 19:16
89:28 j ver 33-34 Isa 55:3
89:29 k ver 4,36 Dt 11:21 Jer 33:17
89:32 l 2Sa 7:14
89:33 m 2Sa 7:15
89:34 n Nu 23:19
89:38 o Dt 32:19 1Ch 28:9 Ps 44:9
89:39 p La 5:16
89:40 q Ps 80:12 r La 2:2
89:41 s Ps 44:13
89:42 t Ps 13:2 Ps 80:6
89:43 u Ps 44:10

c18 Or *sovereign* d24 *Horn* here symbolises strength.

you have covered him with a
mantle of shame.[v] *Selah*
46 How long, O LORD? Will you
hide yourself for ever?
How long will your wrath
burn like fire?[w]
47 Remember how fleeting is my
life.[x]
For what futility you have
created all men!
48 What man can live and not see
death,
or save himself from the
power of the grave?[e][y]
Selah
49 O Lord, where is your former
great love,
which in your faithfulness you
swore to David?
50 Remember, Lord, how your
servant has[f] been
mocked,[z]
how I bear in my heart the
taunts of all the nations,
51 the taunts with which your
enemies have mocked,
O LORD,
with which they have mocked
every step of your anointed
one.[a]
52 Praise be to the LORD for ever!
Amen and Amen.[b]

Book IV: Psalms 90–106

Psalm 90

A prayer of Moses the man of God.

1 Lord, you have been our
dwelling-place[a]
throughout all generations.
2 Before the mountains were
born[b]
or you brought forth the earth
and the world,
from everlasting to
everlasting you are God.[c]
3 You turn men back to dust,
saying, "Return to dust,
O sons of men."[d]
4 For a thousand years in your
sight
are like a day that has just
gone by,
or like a watch in the night.[e]
5 You sweep men away[f] in the
sleep of death;
they are like the new grass of
the morning—
6 though in the morning it
springs up new,
by evening it is dry and
withered.[g]

7 We are consumed by your
anger
and terrified by your
indignation.
8 You have set our iniquities
before you,
our secret sins[h] in the light of
your presence.
9 All our days pass away under
your wrath;
we finish our years with a
moan.[i]
10 The length of our days is
seventy years—
or eighty, if we have the
strength;
yet their span[a] is but trouble
and sorrow,
for they quickly pass, and we
fly away.[j]
11 Who knows the power of your
anger?
For your wrath is as great as
the fear that is due to
you.[k]
12 Teach us to number our days[l]
aright,
that we may gain a heart of
wisdom.[m]
13 Relent, O LORD! How long[n] will
it be?
Have compassion on your
servants.[o]
14 Satisfy[p] us in the morning with
your unfailing love,
that we may sing for joy[q] and
be glad all our days.[r]

89:45 *v* Ps 44:15; Ps 109:29
89:46 *w* Ps 79:5
89:47 *x* Job 7:7; Ps 39:5
89:48 *y* Ps 22:29; Ps 49:9
89:50 *z* Ps 69:19
89:51 *a* Ps 74:10
89:52 *b* Ps 41:13; Ps 72:19
90:1 *a* Dt 33:27; Eze 11:16
90:2 *b* Job 15:7; Pr 8:25 *c* Ps 102:24-27
90:3 *d* Ge 3:19; Job 34:15
90:4 *e* 2Pe 3:8
90:5 *f* Ps 73:20; Isa 40:6
90:6 *g* Mt 6:30; Jas 1:10
90:8 *h* Ps 19:12
90:9 *i* Ps 78:33
90:10 *j* Job 20:8
90:11 *k* Ps 76:7
90:12 *l* Ps 39:4 *m* Dt 32:29
90:13 *n* Ps 6:3 *o* Dt 32:36; Ps 135:14
90:14 *p* Ps 103:5 *q* Ps 85:6 *r* Ps 31:7

e48 Hebrew *Sheol* f50 Or *your servants have*
a10 Or *yet the best of them*

15Make us glad for as many days
as you have afflicted us,
for as many years as we have
seen trouble.
16May your deeds be shown to
your servants,
your splendour to their
children.[s]
17May the favour[b] of the Lord
our God rest upon us;
establish the work of our
hands for us—
yes, establish the work of our
hands.[t]

Psalm 91

1He who dwells in the shelter[a]
of the Most High
will rest in the shadow[b] of the
Almighty.[a]
2I will say[b] of the LORD, "He is
my refuge[c] and my
fortress,
my God, in whom I trust."
3Surely he will save you from
the fowler's snare[d]
and from the deadly
pestilence.[e]
4He will cover you with his
feathers,
and under his wings you will
find refuge;[f]
his faithfulness will be your
shield[g] and rampart.
5You will not fear[h] the terror of
night,
nor the arrow that flies by
day,
6nor the pestilence that stalks in
the darkness,
nor the plague that destroys at
midday.
7A thousand may fall at your
side,
ten thousand at your right
hand,
but it will not come near you.
8You will only observe with your
eyes
and see the punishment of the
wicked.[i]
9If you make the Most High your
dwelling—
even the LORD, who is my
refuge—
10then no harm[j] will befall you,
no disaster will come near
your tent.
11For he will command his
angels[k] concerning you
to guard you in all your
ways;[l]
12they will lift you up in their
hands,
so that you will not strike your
foot against a stone.[m]
13You will tread upon the lion and
the cobra;
you will trample the great lion
and the serpent.[n]
14"Because he loves me," says the
LORD, "I will rescue him;
I will protect him, for he
acknowledges my name.
15He will call upon me, and I will
answer him;
I will be with him in trouble,
I will deliver him and honour
him.[o]
16With long life[p] will I satisfy
him
and show him my salvation.[q]"

Psalm 92

A psalm. A song. For the Sabbath day.

1It is good to praise the LORD
and make music to your
name,[a] O Most High,[b]
2to proclaim your love in the
morning[c]
and your faithfulness at night,
3to the music of the ten-stringed
lyre
and the melody of the harp.[d]
4For you make me glad by your
deeds, O LORD;
I sing for joy at the work of
your hands.[e]
5How great are your works,[f]
O LORD,

90:16 s Ps 44:1; Hab 3:2
90:17 t Isa 26:12
91:1 a Ps 31:20; b Ps 17:8
91:2 c Ps 142:5
91:3 d Ps 124:7; Pr 6:5; e 1Ki 8:37
91:4 f Ps 17:8; g Ps 35:2
91:5 h Job 5:21
91:8 i Ps 37:34; Ps 58:10; Mal 1:5
91:10 j Pr 12:21
91:11 k Heb 1:14; l Ps 34:7
91:12 m Mt 4:6*; Lk 4:10-11*
91:13 n Da 6:22; Lk 10:19
91:15 o 1Sa 2:30; Ps 50:15; Jn 12:26
91:16 p Dt 6:2; Ps 21:4; q Ps 50:23
92:1 a Ps 147:1; b Ps 135:3
92:2 c Ps 89:1
92:3 d 1Sa 10:5; Ne 12:27; Ps 33:2
92:4 e Ps 8:6; Ps 143:5
92:5 f Rev 15:3

[b]17 Or *beauty*
[b]2 Or *He says*
[a]1 Hebrew *Shaddai*

how profound your thoughts![g]
6 The senseless man[h] does not
know,
fools do not understand,
7 that though the wicked spring
up like grass
and all evildoers flourish,
they will be for ever destroyed.

8 But you, O LORD, are exalted
for ever.

9 For surely your enemies,
O LORD,
surely your enemies will
perish;
all evildoers will be
scattered.[i]
10 You have exalted my horn[a][j]
like that of a wild ox;
fine oils[k] have been poured
upon me.
11 My eyes have seen the defeat of
my adversaries;
my ears have heard the rout
of my wicked foes.[l]

12 The righteous will flourish like
a palm tree,
they will grow like a cedar of
Lebanon;[m]
13 planted in the house of the
LORD,
they will flourish in the courts
of our God.[n]
14 They will still bear fruit[o] in old
age,
they will stay fresh and green,
15 proclaiming, "The LORD is
upright;
he is my Rock, and there is no
wickedness in him.[p]"

Psalm 93

1 The LORD reigns,[a] he is robed
in majesty;[b]
the LORD is robed in majesty
and is armed with strength.[c]
The world is firmly established;
it cannot be moved.[d]
2 Your throne was established
long ago;
you are from all eternity.[e]

3 The seas[f] have lifted up,
O LORD,
the seas have lifted up their
voice;
the seas have lifted up their
pounding waves.
4 Mightier than the thunder[g] of
the great waters,
mightier than the breakers of
the sea—
the LORD on high is mighty.

5 Your statutes stand firm;
holiness[h] adorns your house
for endless days, O LORD.

Psalm 94

1 O LORD, the God who avenges,[a]
O God who avenges, shine
forth.[b]
2 Rise up, O Judge[c] of the earth;
pay back[d] to the proud what
they deserve.
3 How long will the wicked,
O LORD,
how long will the wicked be
jubilant?

4 They pour out arrogant[e] words;
all the evildoers are full of
boasting.[f]
5 They crush your people,[g]
O LORD;
they oppress your inheritance.
6 They slay the widow and the
alien;
they murder the fatherless.
7 They say, "The LORD does not
see;[h]
the God of Jacob pays no
heed."

8 Take heed, you senseless ones[i]
among the people;
you fools, when will you
become wise?
9 Does he who implanted the ear
not hear?
Does he who formed the eye
not see?[j]
10 Does he who disciplines nations
not punish?

92:5 g Ps 40:5; Ps 139:17; Isa 28:29; Ro 11:33
92:6 h Ps 73:22
92:9 i Ps 68:1; Ps 89:10
92:10 j Ps 89:17; k Ps 23:5
92:11 l Ps 54:7; Ps 91:8
92:12 m Ps 1:3; Ps 52:8; Jer 17:8; Hos 14:6
92:13 n Ps 100:4
92:14 o Jn 15:2
92:15 p Job 34:10
93:1 a Ps 97:1; b Ps 104:1; c Ps 65:6; d Ps 96:10
93:2 e Ps 45:6
93:3 f Ps 96:11
93:4 g Ps 65:7
93:5 h Ps 29:2
94:1 a Na 1:2; Ro 12:19; b Ps 80:1
94:2 c Ge 18:25; d Ps 31:23
94:4 e Ps 31:18; f Ps 52:1
94:5 g Isa 3:15
94:7 h Job 22:14; Ps 10:11
94:8 i Ps 92:6
94:9 j Ex 4:11; Pr 20:12

a *10 Horn* here symbolises strength.

Does he who teaches[k] man lack knowledge?
11The LORD knows the thoughts of man;
he knows that they are futile.[l]

12Blessed is the man you discipline,[m] O LORD,
the man you teach[n] from your law;
13you grant him relief from days of trouble,
till a pit[o] is dug for the wicked.
14For the LORD will not reject his people;[p]
he will never forsake his inheritance.
15Judgment will again be founded on righteousness,[q]
and all the upright in heart will follow it.

16Who will rise up[r] for me against the wicked?
Who will take a stand for me against evildoers?[s]
17Unless the LORD had given me help,[t]
I would soon have dwelt in the silence of death.
18When I said, "My foot is slipping,[u]"
your love, O LORD, supported me.
19When anxiety was great within me,
your consolation brought joy to my soul.

20Can a corrupt throne be allied with you—
one that brings on misery by its decrees?[v]
21They band together[w] against the righteous
and condemn the innocent[x] to death.
22But the LORD has become my fortress,
and my God the rock in whom I take refuge.[y]
23He will repay[z] them for their sins
and destroy them for their wickedness;
the LORD our God will destroy them.

Psalm 95

1Come, let us sing for joy to the LORD;
let us shout aloud[a] to the Rock[b] of our salvation.
2Let us come before him[c] with thanksgiving
and extol him with music[d] and song.

3For the LORD is the great God,[e]
the great King above all gods.[f]
4In his hand are the depths of the earth,
and the mountain peaks belong to him.
5The sea is his, for he made it,
and his hands formed the dry land.[g]

6Come, let us bow down[h] in worship,
let us kneel[i] before the LORD our Maker;[j]
7for he is our God
and we are the people of his pasture,[k]
the flock under his care.

Today, if you hear his voice,
8 do not harden your hearts as you did at Meribah,[a][l]
as you did that day at Massah[b] in the desert,
9where your fathers tested[m] and tried me,
though they had seen what I did.
10For forty years[n] I was angry with that generation;
I said, "They are a people whose hearts go astray,
and they have not known my ways."

[a]8 *Meribah* means *quarrelling.* [b]8 *Massah* means *testing.*

94:10 k Job 35:11; Isa 28:26
94:11 l 1Co 3:20*
94:12 m Job 5:17; Heb 12:5; n Dt 8:3
94:13 o Ps 55:23
94:14 p 1Sa 12:22; Ps 37:28; Ro 11:2
94:15 q Ps 97:2
94:16 r Nu 10:35; Ps 17:13; s Ps 59:2
94:17 t Ps 124:2
94:18 u Ps 38:16
94:20 v Ps 58:2
94:21 w Ps 56:6; x Ps 106:38; Pr 17:15,26
94:22 y Ps 18:2; Ps 59:9
94:23 z Ps 7:16
95:1 a Ps 81:1; b 2Sa 22:47
95:2 c Mic 6:6; d Ps 81:2; Eph 5:19
95:3 e Ps 48:1; Ps 145:3; f Ps 96:4; Ps 97:9
95:5 g Ge 1:9; Ps 146:6
95:6 h Php 2:10; i 2Ch 6:13; j Ps 100:3; Ps 149:2; Isa 17:7; Da 6:10-11; Hos 8:14
95:7 k Ps 74:1; Ps 79:13
95:8 l Ex 17:7
95:9 m Nu 14:22; Ps 78:18; 1Co 10:9
95:10 n Ac 7:36; Heb 3:17

11 So I declared on oath[o] in my
anger,
"They shall never enter my
rest."[p]

Psalm 96

96:1–13pp 1Ch 16:23–33

1 Sing to the LORD[a] a new song;
sing to the LORD, all the earth.
2 Sing to the LORD, praise his
name;
proclaim his salvation[b] day
after day.
3 Declare his glory among the
nations,
his marvellous deeds among
all peoples.

4 For great is the LORD and most
worthy of praise;[c]
he is to be feared[d] above all
gods.[e]
5 For all the gods of the nations
are idols,
but the LORD made the
heavens.[f]
6 Splendour and majesty are
before him;
strength and glory[g] are in his
sanctuary.

7 Ascribe to the LORD,[h]
O families of nations,[i]
ascribe to the LORD glory and
strength.
8 Ascribe to the LORD the glory
due to his name;
bring an offering[j] and come
into his courts.
9 Worship the LORD in the
splendour of his[a]
holiness;[k]
tremble[l] before him, all the
earth.[m]

10 Say among the nations, "The
LORD reigns.[n]"
The world is firmly
established, it cannot be
moved;[o]
he will judge the peoples with
equity.[p]
11 Let the heavens rejoice, let the
earth be glad;[q]
let the sea resound, and all
that is in it;
12 let the fields be jubilant, and
everything in them.
Then all the trees of the forest[r]
will sing for joy;[s]
13 they will sing before the LORD,
for he comes,
he comes to judge[t] the earth.
He will judge the world in
righteousness
and the peoples in his truth.

Psalm 97

1 The LORD reigns,[a] let the earth
be glad;[b]
let the distant shores rejoice.
2 Clouds and thick darkness[c]
surround him;
righteousness and justice are
the foundation of his
throne.[d]
3 Fire[e] goes before[f] him
and consumes[g] his foes on
every side.
4 His lightning lights up the
world;
the earth sees and trembles.[h]
5 The mountains melt[i] like wax
before the LORD,
before the Lord of all the
earth.[j]
6 The heavens proclaim his
righteousness,[k]
and all the peoples see his
glory.[l]

7 All who worship images[m] are
put to shame,[n]
those who boast in idols—
worship him,[o] all you gods!

8 Zion hears and rejoices
and the villages of Judah are
glad
because of your judgments,[p]
O LORD.
9 For you, O LORD, are the Most
High over all the earth;[q]
you are exalted[r] far above all
gods.

95:11 o Nu 14:23 p Dt 1:35 Heb 4:3,5*
96:1 a 1Ch 16:23
96:2 b Ps 71:15
96:4 c Ps 18:3 Ps 145:3 d Ps 89:7 e Ps 95:3
96:5 f Ps 115:15
96:6 g Ps 29:1
96:7 h Ps 29:1 i Ps 22:27
96:8 j Ps 45:12 Ps 72:10
96:9 k Ps 29:2 l Ps 114:7 m Ps 33:8
96:10 n Ps 97:1 o Ps 93:1 p Ps 67:4
96:11 q Ps 97:1 Ps 98:7 Isa 49:13
96:12 r Isa 44:23 s Ps 65:13
96:13 t Rev 19:11
97:1 a Ps 96:10 b Ps 96:11
97:2 c Ex 19:9 Ps 18:11 d Ps 89:14
97:3 e Da 7:10 f Hab 3:5 g Ps 18:8
97:4 h Ps 104:32
97:5 i Ps 46:2,6 Mic 1:4 j Jos 3:11
97:6 k Ps 50:6 l Ps 19:1
97:7 m Lev 26:1 n Jer 10:14 o Heb 1:6
97:8 p Ps 48:11
97:9 q Ps 83:18 Ps 95:3 r Ex 18:11

a9 Or *LORD with the splendour of*

10 Let those who love the LORD
hate evil,[s]
for he guards the lives of his
faithful ones[t]
and delivers[u] them from the
hand of the wicked.[v]
11 Light is shed[w] upon the
righteous
and joy on the upright in
heart.
12 Rejoice in the LORD, you who
are righteous,
and praise his holy name.[x]

Psalm 98

A psalm.

1 Sing to the LORD a new song,[a]
for he has done marvellous
things;[b]
his right hand[c] and his holy
arm[d]
have worked salvation for
him.
2 The LORD has made his
salvation known[e]
and revealed his righteousness
to the nations.
3 He has remembered[f] his love
and his faithfulness to the
house of Israel;
all the ends of the earth have
seen
the salvation of our God.
4 Shout for joy[g] to the LORD, all
the earth,
burst into jubilant song with
music;
5 make music to the LORD with
the harp,[h]
with the harp and the sound of
singing,[i]
6 with trumpets[j] and the blast of
the ram's horn—
shout for joy before the LORD,
the King.[k]
7 Let the sea resound, and
everything in it,
the world, and all who live in
it.[l]
8 Let the rivers clap their hands,
let the mountains[m] sing
together for joy;

97:10
s Ps 34:14; Am 5:15; Ro 12:9
t Pr 2:8
u Da 3:28
v Ps 37:40; Jer 15:21

97:11
w Job 22:28

97:12
x Ps 30:4

98:1
a Ps 96:1
b Ps 96:3
c Ex 15:6
d Isa 52:10

98:2
e Isa 52:10

98:3
f Lk 1:54

98:4
g Isa 44:23

98:5
h Ps 92:3
i Isa 51:3

98:6
j Nu 10:10
k Ps 47:7

98:7
l Ps 24:1

98:8
m Isa 55:12

98:9
n Ps 96:10

99:1
a Ps 97:1
b Ex 25:22

99:2
c Ps 48:1
d Ps 97:9; Ps 113:4

99:3
e Ps 76:1

99:4
f Ps 11:7
g Ps 98:9

99:5
h Ps 132:7

99:6
i Ex 24:6
j Jer 15:1
k 1Sa 7:9

99:7
l Ex 33:9

99:8
m Nu 14:20

9 let them sing before the LORD,
for he comes to judge the
earth.
He will judge the world in
righteousness
and the peoples with equity.[n]

Psalm 99

1 The LORD reigns,[a]
let the nations tremble;
he sits enthroned between the
cherubim,[b]
let the earth shake.
2 Great is the LORD[c] in Zion;
he is exalted[d] over all the
nations.
3 Let them praise your great and
awesome name[e]—
he is holy.
4 The King is mighty, he loves
justice[f]—
you have established equity;[g]
in Jacob you have done
what is just and right.
5 Exalt[h] the LORD our God
and worship at his footstool;
he is holy.
6 Moses[i] and Aaron were among
his priests,
Samuel[j] was among those
who called on his name;
they called on the LORD
and he answered[k] them.
7 He spoke to them from the
pillar of cloud;[l]
they kept his statutes and the
decrees he gave them.
8 O LORD our God,
you answered them;
you were to Israel[a] a forgiving
God,[m]
though you punished their
misdeeds.[b]
9 Exalt the LORD our God
and worship at his holy
mountain,
for the LORD our God is holy.

[a] 8 Hebrew *them* [b] 8 Or / *an avenger of the wrongs done to them*

Psalm 100

A psalm. For giving thanks.

1 Shout for joy[a] to the LORD, all
the earth.
2 Worship the LORD with
gladness;
come before him[b] with joyful
songs.
3 Know that the LORD is God.[c]
It is he who made us,[d] and we
are his;[a]
we are his people, the sheep of
his pasture.[e]

4 Enter his gates with
thanksgiving
and his courts with praise;
give thanks to him and praise
his name.[f]
5 For the LORD is good[g] and his
love endures for ever;[h]
his faithfulness[i] continues
through all generations.

Psalm 101

Of David. A psalm.

1 I will sing of your love[a] and
justice;
to you, O LORD, I will sing
praise.
2 I will be careful to lead a
blameless life—
when will you come to me?

I will walk in my house
with blameless heart.
3 I will set before my eyes
no vile thing.[b]

The deeds of faithless men I
hate;[c]
they shall not cling to me.
4 Men of perverse heart[d] shall
be far from me;
I will have nothing to do with
evil.

5 Whoever slanders his
neighbour[e] in secret,
him will I put to silence;
whoever has haughty eyes[f] and
a proud heart,
him will I not endure.

6 My eyes will be on the faithful
in the land,
that they may dwell with me;
he whose walk is blameless[g]
will minister to me.

7 No-one who practises deceit
will dwell in my house;
no-one who speaks falsely
will stand in my presence.

8 Every morning[h] I will put to
silence
all the wicked[i] in the land;
I will cut off every evildoer[j]
from the city of the LORD.[k]

Psalm 102

A prayer of an afflicted man. When he is faint and pours out his lament before the LORD.

1 Hear my prayer, O LORD;
let my cry for help[a] come to
you.
2 Do not hide your face[b] from
me
when I am in distress.
Turn your ear to me;
when I call, answer me
quickly.

3 For my days vanish like
smoke;[c]
my bones burn like glowing
embers.
4 My heart is blighted and
withered like grass;[d]
I forget to eat my food.
5 Because of my loud groaning
I am reduced to skin and
bones.
6 I am like a desert owl,[e]
like an owl among the ruins.
7 I lie awake;[f] I have become
like a bird alone[g] on a roof.
8 All day long my enemies taunt
me;
those who rail against me use
my name as a curse.
9 For I eat ashes as my food
and mingle my drink with
tears[h]

100:1 a Ps 98:4
100:2 b Ps 95:2
100:3 c Ps 46:10; d Job 10:3; e Ps 74:1; Eze 34:31
100:4 f Ps 116:17
100:5 g 1Ch 16:34; Ps 25:8; h Ezr 3:11; Ps 106:1; i Ps 119:90
101:1 a Ps 51:14; Ps 89:1; Ps 145:7
101:3 b Dt 15:9; c Ps 40:4
101:4 d Pr 11:20
101:5 e Ps 50:20; f Ps 10:5; Pr 6:17
101:6 g Ps 119:1
101:8 h Jer 21:12; i Ps 75:10; j Ps 118:10-12; k Ps 46:4
102:1 a Ex 2:23
102:2 b Ps 69:17
102:3 c Jas 4:14
102:4 d Ps 37:2
102:6 e Job 30:29; Isa 34:11
102:7 f Ps 77:4; g Ps 38:11
102:9 h Ps 42:3

a3 Or *and not we ourselves*

10 because of your great wrath,[i]
for you have taken me up and
thrown me aside.
11 My days are like the evening
shadow;[j]
I wither away like grass.

12 But you, O LORD, sit enthroned
for ever;[k]
your renown endures[l]
through all generations.
13 You will arise and have
compassion[m] on Zion,
for it is time to show favour to
her;
the appointed time has come.
14 For her stones are dear to your
servants;
her very dust moves them to
pity.
15 The nations will fear[n] the name
of the LORD,
all the kings[o] of the earth will
revere your glory.
16 For the LORD will rebuild Zion
and appear in his glory.[p]
17 He will respond to the prayer[q]
of the destitute;
he will not despise their plea.

18 Let this be written[r] for a
future generation,
that a people not yet created[s]
may praise the LORD:
19 "The LORD looked down[t] from
his sanctuary on high,
from heaven he viewed the
earth,
20 to hear the groans of the
prisoners[u]
and release those condemned
to death."
21 So the name of the LORD will be
declared[v] in Zion
and his praise in Jerusalem
22 when the peoples and the
kingdoms
assemble to worship the LORD.

23 In the course of my life[a] he
broke my strength;
he cut short my days.
24 So I said:
"Do not take me away, O my
God, in the midst of my
days;
your years go on[w] through all
generations.
25 In the beginning[x] you laid the
foundations of the earth,
and the heavens are the work
of your hands.
26 They will perish,[y] but you
remain;
they will all wear out like a
garment.
Like clothing you will change
them
and they will be discarded.
27 But you remain the same,[z]
and your years will never end.
28 The children of your servants[a]
will live in your presence;
their descendants[b] will be
established before you."

Psalm 103

Of David.

1 Praise the LORD, O my soul;[a]
all my inmost being, praise his
holy name.
2 Praise the LORD, O my soul,
and forget not all his
benefits—
3 who forgives all your sins[b]
and heals[c] all your diseases,
4 who redeems your life from the
pit
and crowns you with love and
compassion,
5 who satisfies your desires with
good things
so that your youth is renewed
like the eagle's.[d]
6 The LORD works righteousness
and justice for all the
oppressed.
7 He made known[e] his ways[f] to
Moses,
his deeds[g] to the people of
Israel:

102:10 i Ps 38:3
102:11 j Job 14:2
102:12 k Ps 9:7; l Ps 135:13
102:13 m Isa 60:10
102:15 n 1Ki 8:43; o Ps 138:4
102:16 p Isa 60:1-2
102:17 q Ne 1:6
102:18 r Ro 15:4; s Ps 22:31
102:19 t Dt 26:15
102:20 u Ps 79:11
102:21 v Ps 22:22
102:24 w Ps 90:2; Isa 38:10
102:25 x Ge 1:1; Heb 1:10-12*
102:26 y Isa 34:4; Mt 24:35; 2Pe 3:7-10; Rev 20:11
102:27 z Mal 3:6; Heb 13:8; Jas 1:17
102:28 a Ps 69:36; b Ps 89:4
103:1 a Ps 104:1
103:3 b Ps 130:8; c Ex 15:26
103:5 d Isa 40:31
103:7 e Ps 99:7; Ps 147:19; f Ex 33:13; g Ps 106:22

a 23 Or *By his power*

8The LORD is compassionate and
gracious,[h]
slow to anger, abounding in
love.
9He will not always accuse,
nor will he harbour his anger
for ever;[i]
10he does not treat us as our sins
deserve[j]
or repay us according to our
iniquities.
11For as high as the heavens are
above the earth,
so great is his love[k] for those
who fear him;
12as far as the east is from the
west,
so far has he removed our
transgressions[l] from us.
13As a father has compassion[m] on
his children,
so the LORD has compassion on
those who fear him;
14for he knows how we are
formed,[n]
he remembers that we are
dust.
15As for man, his days are like
grass,[o]
he flourishes like a flower[p] of
the field;
16the wind blows[q] over it and it
is gone,
and its place[r] remembers it
no more.
17But from everlasting to
everlasting
the LORD's love is with those
who fear him,
and his righteousness with
their children's children—
18with those who keep his
covenant
and remember to obey his
precepts.[s]
19The LORD has established his
throne in heaven,
and his kingdom rules[t] over
all.
20Praise the LORD, you his
angels,[u]
you mighty ones[v] who do his
bidding,
who obey his word.
21Praise the LORD, all his
heavenly hosts,[w]
you his servants who do his
will.
22Praise the LORD, all his works[x]
everywhere in his dominion.

Praise the LORD, O my soul.

Psalm 104

1Praise the LORD, O my soul.[a]

O LORD my God, you are very
great;
you are clothed with splendour
and majesty.
2He wraps[b] himself in light as
with a garment;
he stretches out the heavens[c]
like a tent
3 and lays the beams[d] of his
upper chambers on their
waters.
He makes the clouds[e] his
chariot
and rides on the wings of the
wind.[f]
4He makes winds his
messengers,[a][g]
flames of fire[h] his servants.

5He set the earth[i] on its
foundations;
it can never be moved.
6You covered it[j] with the deep[k]
as with a garment;
the waters stood above the
mountains.
7But at your rebuke[l] the waters
fled,
at the sound of your thunder
they took to flight;
8they flowed over the mountains,
they went down into the
valleys,
to the place you assigned[m] for
them.
9You set a boundary they cannot
cross;
never again will they cover
the earth.

103:8 h Ex 34:6; Ps 86:15; Jas 5:11
103:9 i Ps 30:5; Isa 57:16; Jer 3:5,12; Mic 7:18
103:10 j Ezr 9:13
103:11 k Ps 57:10
103:12 l 2Sa 12:13
103:13 m Mal 3:17
103:14 n Isa 29:16
103:15 o Ps 90:5; p Job 14:2; Jas 1:10; 1Pe 1:24
103:16 q Isa 40:7; r Job 7:10
103:18 s Dt 7:9
103:19 t Ps 47:2
103:20 u Ps 148:2; Heb 1:14; v Ps 29:1
103:21 w 1Ki 22:19
103:22 x Ps 145:10
104:1 a Ps 103:22
104:2 b Da 7:9; c Isa 40:22
104:3 d Am 9:6; e Isa 19:1; f Ps 18:10
104:4 g Ps 148:8; Heb 1:7*; h 2Ki 2:11
104:5 i Job 26:7; Ps 24:1-2
104:6 j Ge 7:19; k Ge 1:2
104:7 l Ps 18:15
104:8 m Ps 33:7

a4 Or *angels*

10 He makes springs[n] pour water
into the ravines;
it flows between the
mountains.
11 They give water to all the
beasts of the field;
the wild donkeys quench their
thirst.
12 The birds of the air[o] nest by
the waters;
they sing among the branches.
13 He waters the mountains[p] from
his upper chambers;
the earth is satisfied by the
fruit of his work.
14 He makes grass grow[q] for the
cattle,
and plants for man to
cultivate—
bringing forth food[r] from the
earth:
15 wine[s] that gladdens the heart
of man,
oil[t] to make his face shine,
and bread that sustains his
heart.
16 The trees of the LORD are well
watered,
the cedars of Lebanon that he
planted.
17 There the birds[u] make their
nests;
the stork has its home in the
pine trees.
18 The high mountains belong to
the wild goats;
the crags are a refuge for the
conies.[b][v]
19 The moon marks off the
seasons,[w]
and the sun[x] knows when to
go down.
20 You bring darkness,[y] it
becomes night,[z]
and all the beasts of the
forest[a] prowl.
21 The lions roar for their prey
and seek their food from
God.[b]
22 The sun rises, and they steal
away;
they return and lie down in
their dens.[c]

104:10 [n] Ps 107:33; Isa 41:18
104:12 [o] Mt 8:20
104:13 [p] Ps 147:8; Jer 10:13
104:14 [q] Job 38:27; Ps 147:8 [r] Ge 1:30; Job 28:5
104:15 [s] Jdg 9:13 [t] Ps 23:5; Ps 92:10; Lk 7:46
104:17 [u] ver 12
104:18 [v] Pr 30:26
104:19 [w] Ge 1:14 [x] Ps 19:6
104:20 [y] Isa 45:7 [z] Ps 74:16 [a] Ps 50:10
104:21 [b] Job 38:39; Ps 145:15; Joel 1:20
104:22 [c] Job 37:8
104:23 [d] Ge 3:19
104:24 [e] Ps 40:5 [f] Pr 3:19
104:25 [g] Ps 69:34
104:26 [h] Ps 107:23; Eze 27:9 [i] Job 41:1
104:27 [j] Job 36:31; Ps 136:25; Ps 145:15; Ps 147:9
104:28 [k] Ps 145:16
104:29 [l] Dt 31:17 [m] Job 34:14; Ecc 12:7
104:31 [n] Ge 1:31
104:32 [o] Ps 97:4 [p] Ex 19:18 [q] Ps 144:5
104:33 [r] Ps 63:4

23 Then man goes out to his
work,[d]
to his labour until evening.
24 How many are your works,[e]
O LORD!
In wisdom you made[f] them
all;
the earth is full of your
creatures.
25 There is the sea,[g] vast and
spacious,
teeming with creatures
beyond number—
living things both large and
small.
26 There the ships[h] go to and fro,
and the leviathan,[i] which you
formed to frolic there.
27 These all look to you
to give them their food[j] at
the proper time.
28 When you give it to them,
they gather it up;
when you open your hand,
they are satisfied[k] with good
things.
29 When you hide your face,[l]
they are terrified;
when you take away their
breath,
they die and return to the
dust.[m]
30 When you send your Spirit,
they are created,
and you renew the face of the
earth.
31 May the glory of the LORD
endure for ever;
may the LORD rejoice in his
works[n]—
32 he who looks at the earth, and it
trembles,[o]
who touches the mountains,[p]
and they smoke.[q]
33 I will sing[r] to the LORD all my
life;
I will sing praise to my God as
long as I live.
34 May my meditation be pleasing
to him,

[b] *18* That is, the hyrax or rock badger

as I rejoice[s] in the LORD.
35But may sinners vanish[t] from the earth
and the wicked be no more.

Praise the LORD, O my soul.

Praise the LORD.[c][u]

Psalm 105

105:1–15pp 1Ch 16:8–22

1Give thanks to the LORD,[a] call on his name;[b]
make known among the nations what he has done.
2Sing to him,[c] sing praise to him;
tell of all his wonderful acts.
3Glory in his holy name;
let the hearts of those who seek the LORD rejoice.
4Look to the LORD and his strength;
seek his face[d] always.
5Remember the wonders[e] he has done,
his miracles, and the judgments he pronounced,[f]
6O descendants of Abraham his servant,[g]
O sons of Jacob, his chosen[h] ones.
7He is the LORD our God;
his judgments are in all the earth.
8He remembers his covenant[i] for ever,
the word he commanded, for a thousand generations,
9the covenant he made with Abraham,[j]
the oath he swore to Isaac.
10He confirmed it[k] to Jacob as a decree,
to Israel as an everlasting covenant:
11"To you I will give the land of Canaan[l]
as the portion you will inherit."
12When they were but few in number,[m]
few indeed, and strangers in it,[n]
13they wandered from nation to nation,
from one kingdom to another.
14He allowed no-one to oppress[o] them;
for their sake he rebuked kings:[p]
15"Do not touch[q] my anointed ones;
do my prophets no harm."
16He called down famine[r] on the land
and destroyed all their supplies of food;
17and he sent a man before them—
Joseph, sold as a slave.[s]
18They bruised his feet with shackles,[t]
his neck was put in irons,
19till what he foretold[u] came to pass,
till the word of the LORD proved him true.
20The king sent and released him,
the ruler of peoples set him free.[v]
21He made him master of his household,
ruler over all he possessed,
22to instruct his princes[w] as he pleased
and teach his elders wisdom.
23Then Israel entered Egypt;[x]
Jacob lived as an alien in the land of Ham.
24The LORD made his people very fruitful;
he made them too numerous[y] for their foes,
25whose hearts he turned[z] to hate his people,
to conspire[a] against his servants.
26He sent Moses[b] his servant,
and Aaron, whom he had chosen.[c]

104:34 *s* Ps 9:2 **104:35** *t* Ps 37:38 *u* Ps 105:45; Ps 106:48 **105:1** *a* 1Ch 16:34 *b* Ps 99:6 **105:2** *c* Ps 96:1 **105:4** *d* Ps 27:8 **105:5** *e* Ps 40:5 *f* Ps 77:11 **105:6** *g* ver 42 *h* Ps 106:5 **105:8** *i* Ps 106:45; Lk 1:72 **105:9** *j* Ge 12:7; Ge 17:2; Ge 22:16-18; Gal 3:15-18 **105:10** *k* Ge 28:13-15 **105:11** *l* Ge 13:15; Ge 15:18 **105:12** *m* Ge 34:30; Dt 7:7 *n* Ge 23:4; Heb 11:9 **105:14** *o* Ge 35:5 *p* Ge 12:17-20 **105:15** *q* Ge 26:11 **105:16** *r* Ge 41:54; Lev 26:26; Isa 3:1; Eze 4:16 **105:17** *s* Ge 37:28; Ge 45:5; Ac 7:9 **105:18** *t* Ge 40:15 **105:19** *u* Ge 40:20-22 **105:20** *v* Ge 41:14 **105:22** *w* Ge 41:43-44 **105:23** *x* Ge 46:6; Ac 13:17 **105:24** *y* Ex 1:7,9 **105:25** *z* Ex 4:21 *a* Ex 1:6-10; Ac 7:19 **105:26** *b* Ex 3:10 *c* Nu 16:5; Nu 17:5-8

c35 Hebrew *Hallelu Yah*; in the Septuagint this line stands at the beginning of Psalm 105.

27They performed[d] his
miraculous signs among
them,
his wonders in the land of
Ham.
28He sent darkness[e] and made
the land dark—
for had they not rebelled
against his words?
29He turned their waters into
blood,[f]
causing their fish to die.[g]
30Their land teemed with frogs,[h]
which went up into the
bedrooms of their rulers.
31He spoke, and there came
swarms of flies,[i]
and gnats[j] throughout their
country.
32He turned their rain into hail,[k]
with lightning throughout
their land;
33he struck down their vines[l]
and fig-trees
and shattered the trees of
their country.
34He spoke, and the locusts
came,[m]
grasshoppers without number;
35they ate up every green thing in
their land,
ate up the produce of their
soil.
36Then he struck down all the
firstborn[n] in their land,
the firstfruits of all their
manhood.

37He brought out Israel, laden
with silver and gold,[o]
and from among their tribes
no-one faltered.
38Egypt was glad when they left,
because dread of Israel[p] had
fallen on them.
39He spread out a cloud[q] as a
covering,
and a fire to give light at
night.[r]
40They asked,[s] and he brought
them quail[t]
and satisfied them with the
bread of heaven.[u]

105:27 *d* Ex 7:8-12:51
105:28 *e* Ex 10:22
105:29 *f* Ps 78:44 *g* Ex 7:21
105:30 *h* Ex 8:2,6
105:31 *i* Ex 8:21-24 *j* Ex 8:16-18
105:32 *k* Ex 9:22-25
105:33 *l* Ps 78:47
105:34 *m* Ex 10:4,12-15
105:36 *n* Ex 12:29
105:37 *o* Ex 12:35
105:38 *p* Ex 12:33; Ex 15:16
105:39 *q* Ex 13:21 *r* Ne 9:12; Ps 78:14
105:40 *s* Ps 78:18,24 *t* Ex 16:13 *u* Jn 6:31
105:41 *v* Ex 17:6; Nu 20:11; Ps 78:15-16; 1Co 10:4
105:42 *w* Ge 15:13-16
105:43 *x* Ex 15:1-18; Ps 106:12
105:44 *y* Jos 13:6-7
105:45 *z* Dt 4:40; Dt 6:21-24
106:1 *a* Ps 100:5; Ps 105:1
106:2 *b* Ps 145:4,12
106:3 *c* Ps 15:2
106:4 *d* Ps 119:132
106:5 *e* Ps 1:3 *f* Ps 118:15
106:6 *g* Da 9:5

41He opened the rock,[v] and water
gushed out;
like a river it flowed in the
desert.
42For he remembered his holy
promise[w]
given to his servant Abraham.
43He brought out his people with
rejoicing,[x]
his chosen ones with shouts of
joy;
44he gave them the lands of the
nations,[y]
and they fell heir to what
others had toiled for—
45that they might keep his
precepts
and observe his laws.[z]

Praise the LORD.[a]

Psalm 106

106:1,47–48pp 1Ch 16:34–36

1Praise the LORD.[a]

Give thanks to the LORD, for he
is good;[a]
his love endures for ever.
2Who can proclaim the mighty
acts[b] of the LORD
or fully declare his praise?
3Blessed are they who maintain
justice,
who constantly do what is
right.[c]
4Remember me,[d] O LORD, when
you show favour to your
people,
come to my aid when you save
them,
5that I may enjoy the
prosperity[e] of your chosen
ones,
that I may share in the joy[f]
of your nation
and join your inheritance in
giving praise.

6We have sinned,[g] even as our
fathers did;

[a]45 Hebrew *Hallelu Yah* [a]1 Hebrew *Hallelu Yah*; also in verse 48

we have done wrong and acted
wickedly.
7 When our fathers were in
Egypt,
they gave no thought to your
miracles;
they did not remember[h] your
many kindnesses,
and they rebelled by the sea,[i]
the Red Sea.[b]
8 Yet he saved them for his
name's sake,[j]
to make his mighty power
known.
9 He rebuked[k] the Red Sea, and
it dried up;[l]
he led them through[m] the
depths as through a
desert.
10 He saved them[n] from the hand
of the foe;
from the hand of the enemy
he redeemed them.[o]
11 The waters covered[p] their
adversaries;
not one of them survived.
12 Then they believed his promises
and sang his praise.[q]

13 But they soon forgot[r] what he
had done
and did not wait for his
counsel.
14 In the desert they gave in to
their craving;
in the wasteland they put God
to the test.[s]
15 So he gave them[t] what they
asked for,
but sent a wasting disease[u]
upon them.

16 In the camp they grew
envious[v] of Moses
and of Aaron, who was
consecrated to the LORD.
17 The earth opened[w] up and
swallowed Dathan;
it buried the company of
Abiram.
18 Fire blazed[x] among their
followers;
a flame consumed the wicked.
19 At Horeb they made a calf[y]
and worshipped an idol cast
from metal.
20 They exchanged their Glory[z]
for an image of a bull, which
eats grass.
21 They forgot the God[a] who
saved them,
who had done great things[b] in
Egypt,
22 miracles in the land of Ham[c]
and awesome deeds by the
Red Sea.
23 So he said he would destroy[d]
them—
had not Moses, his chosen one,
stood in the breach[e] before him
to keep his wrath from
destroying them.

24 Then they despised the pleasant
land;[f]
they did not believe[g] his
promise.
25 They grumbled[h] in their tents
and did not obey the LORD.
26 So he swore[i] to them with
uplifted hand
that he would make them fall
in the desert,[j]
27 make their descendants fall
among the nations
and scatter[k] them throughout
the lands.

28 They yoked themselves to the
Baal of Peor[l]
and ate sacrifices offered to
lifeless gods;
29 they provoked the LORD to
anger by their wicked
deeds;
and a plague broke out among
them.
30 But Phinehas stood up and
intervened,
and the plague was checked.[m]
31 This was credited to him[n] as
righteousness
for endless generations to
come.

106:7 h Ps 78:11,42 i Ex 14:11-12
106:8 j Ex 9:16
106:9 k Ps 18:15 l Ex 14:21 Na 1:4 m Isa 63:11-14
106:10 n Ex 14:30 o Ps 107:2
106:11 p Ex 14:28 Ex 15:5
106:12 q Ex 15:1-21
106:13 r Ex 15:24
106:14 s 1Co 10:9
106:15 t Nu 11:31 u Isa 10:16
106:16 v Nu 16:1-3
106:17 w Dt 11:6
106:18 x Nu 16:35
106:19 y Ex 32:4
106:20 z Jer 2:11 Ro 1:23
106:21 a Ps 78:11 b Dt 10:21
106:22 c Ps 105:27
106:23 d Ex 32:10 e Ex 32:11-14
106:24 f Dt 8:7 Eze 20:6 g Heb 3:18-19
106:25 h Nu 14:2
106:26 i Eze 20:15 Heb 3:11 j Nu 14:28-35
106:27 k Lev 26:33 Ps 44:11
106:28 l Nu 25:2-3 Hos 9:10
106:30 m Nu 25:8
106:31 n Nu 25:11-13

b7 Hebrew *Yam Suph*; that is, Sea of Reeds; also in verses 9 and 22

32By the waters of Meribah[o] they
angered the LORD,
and trouble came to Moses
because of them;
33for they rebelled against the
Spirit of God,
and rash words came from
Moses' lips.[c][p]

34They did not destroy[q] the
peoples
as the LORD had commanded[r]
them,
35but they mingled[s] with the
nations
and adopted their customs.
36They worshipped their idols,[t]
which became a snare to
them.
37They sacrificed their sons[u]
and their daughters to
demons.
38They shed innocent blood,
the blood of their sons[v] and
daughters,
whom they sacrificed to the
idols of Canaan,
and the land was desecrated
by their blood.
39They defiled themselves[w] by
what they did;
by their deeds they
prostituted[x] themselves.

40Therefore the LORD was angry[y]
with his people
and abhorred his inheritance.[z]
41He handed them over[a] to the
nations,
and their foes ruled over
them.
42Their enemies oppressed them
and subjected them to their
power.
43Many times he delivered them,
but they were bent on
rebellion[b]
and they wasted away in their
sin.

44But he took note of their
distress
when he heard their cry;[c]
45for their sake he remembered
his covenant[d]

106:32 o Nu 20:2-13; Ps 81:7
106:33 p Nu 20:8-12
106:34 q Jdg 1:21; r Dt 7:16
106:35 s Jdg 3:5-6
106:36 t Jdg 2:12
106:37 u 2Ki 16:3; 2Ki 17:17
106:38 v Nu 35:33
106:39 w Eze 20:18; x Lev 17:7; Nu 15:39
106:40 y Jdg 2:14; Ps 78:59; z Dt 9:29
106:41 a Jdg 2:14; Ne 9:27
106:43 b Jdg 2:16-19
106:44 c Jdg 3:9; Jdg 10:10
106:45 d Lev 26:42; Ps 105:8; e Jdg 2:18
106:46 f Ezr 9:9; Jer 42:12
106:47 g Ps 147:2
106:48 h Ps 41:13
107:1 a Ps 106:1
107:2 b Ps 106:10
107:3 c Ps 106:47; Isa 43:5-6
107:4 d Nu 14:33; Nu 32:13
107:6 e Ps 50:15
107:7 f Ezr 8:21

and out of his great love[e] he
relented.
46He caused them to be pitied[f]
by all who held them captive.

47Save us, O LORD our God,
and gather us[g] from the
nations,
that we may give thanks to your
holy name
and glory in your praise.

48Praise be to the LORD, the God
of Israel,
from everlasting to
everlasting.
Let all the people say,
"Amen!"[h]

Praise the LORD.

Book V: Psalms 107–150

Psalm 107

1Give thanks to the LORD,[a] for
he is good;
his love endures for ever.
2Let the redeemed[b] of the LORD
say this—
those he redeemed from the
hand of the foe,
3those he gathered[c] from the
lands,
from east and west, from
north and south.[a]

4Some wandered in desert[d]
wastelands,
finding no way to a city where
they could settle.
5They were hungry and thirsty,
and their lives ebbed away.
6Then they cried out[e] to the
LORD in their trouble,
and he delivered them from
their distress.
7He led them by a straight way[f]
to a city where they could
settle.
8Let them give thanks to the
LORD for his unfailing love
and his wonderful deeds for men,

c33 Or *against his spirit, / and rash words came from his lips* a3 Hebrew *north and the sea*

9for he satisfies[g] the thirsty
and fills the hungry with good things.[h]
10Some sat in darkness[i] and the deepest gloom,
prisoners suffering in iron chains,[j]
11for they had rebelled[k] against the words of God
and despised the counsel[l] of the Most High.
12So he subjected them to bitter labour;
they stumbled, and there was no-one to help.[m]
13Then they cried to the LORD in their trouble,
and he saved them from their distress.
14He brought them out of darkness and the deepest gloom
and broke away their chains.[n]
15Let them give thanks to the LORD for his unfailing love
and his wonderful deeds for men,
16for he breaks down gates of bronze
and cuts through bars of iron.
17Some became fools through their rebellious ways
and suffered affliction[o] because of their iniquities.
18They loathed all food[p]
and drew near the gates of death.[q]
19Then they cried to the LORD in their trouble,
and he saved them from their distress.
20He sent forth his word[r] and healed them;[s]
he rescued[t] them from the grave.[u]
21Let them give thanks to the LORD for his unfailing love
and his wonderful deeds for men.
22Let them sacrifice thank-offerings[v]
and tell of his works[w] with songs of joy.

23Others went out on the sea in ships;
they were merchants on the mighty waters.
24They saw the works of the LORD,
his wonderful deeds in the deep.
25For he spoke[x] and stirred up a tempest[y]
that lifted high the waves.[z]
26They mounted up to the heavens and went down to the depths;
in their peril their courage melted[a] away.
27They reeled and staggered like drunken men;
they were at their wits' end.
28Then they cried out to the LORD in their trouble,
and he brought them out of their distress.
29He stilled the storm[b] to a whisper;
the waves[c] of the sea were hushed.
30They were glad when it grew calm,
and he guided them to their desired haven.
31Let them give thanks to the LORD for his unfailing love
and his wonderful deeds for men.
32Let them exalt him in the assembly[d] of the people
and praise him in the council of the elders.

33He turned rivers into a desert,[e]
flowing springs into thirsty ground,
34and fruitful land into a salt waste,[f]
because of the wickedness of those who lived there.
35He turned the desert into pools of water[g]
and the parched ground into flowing springs;
36there he brought the hungry to live,

107:9 g Ps 22:26; Lk 1:53 h Ps 34:10
107:10 i Lk 1:79 j Job 36:8
107:11 k Ps 106:7; La 3:42 l 2Ch 36:16
107:12 m Ps 22:11
107:14 n Ps 116:16; Lk 13:16; Ac 12:7
107:17 o Isa 65:6-7; La 3:39
107:18 p Job 33:20 q Job 33:22; Ps 9:13; Ps 88:3
107:20 r Mt 8:8 s Ps 103:3 t Job 33:28 u Ps 30:3; Ps 49:15
107:22 v Lev 7:12; Ps 50:14; Ps 116:17 w Ps 9:11; Ps 73:28; Ps 118:17
107:25 x Ps 105:31 y Jnh 1:4 z Ps 93:3
107:26 a Ps 22:14
107:29 b Mt 8:26 c Ps 89:9
107:32 d Ps 22:22,25; Ps 35:18
107:33 e 1Ki 17:1; Ps 74:15
107:34 f Ge 13:10; Ge 14:3; Ge 19:25
107:35 g Ps 114:8; Isa 41:18

and they founded a city where
they could settle.
37They sowed fields and planted
vineyards[h]
that yielded a fruitful harvest;
38he blessed them, and their
numbers greatly
increased,[i]
and he did not let their herds
diminish.

39Then their numbers
decreased,[j] and they were
humbled
by oppression, calamity and
sorrow;
40he who pours contempt on
nobles[k]
made them wander in a
trackless waste.[l]
41But he lifted the needy[m] out of
their affliction
and increased their families
like flocks.
42The upright see and rejoice,[n]
but all the wicked shut their
mouths.[o]

43Whoever is wise,[p] let him heed
these things
and consider the great love[q]
of the LORD.

Psalm 108

108:1–5pp Ps 57:7–11
108:6–13pp Ps 60:5–12

A song. A psalm of David.

1My heart is steadfast, O God;
I will sing and make music
with all my soul.
2Awake, harp and lyre!
I will awaken the dawn.
3I will praise you, O LORD,
among the nations;
I will sing of you among the
peoples.
4For great is your love, higher
than the heavens;
your faithfulness reaches to
the skies.
5Be exalted, O God, above the
heavens,
and let your glory be over all
the earth.[a]

6Save us and help us with your
right hand,
that those you love may be
delivered.
7God has spoken from his
sanctuary:
"In triumph I will parcel out
Shechem
and measure off the Valley of
Succoth.
8Gilead is mine, Manasseh is
mine;
Ephraim is my helmet,
Judah[b] my sceptre.
9Moab is my washbasin,
upon Edom I toss my sandal;
over Philistia I shout in
triumph."

10Who will bring me to the
fortified city?
Who will lead me to Edom?
11Is it not you, O God, you who
have rejected us
and no longer go out with our
armies?[c]
12Give us aid against the enemy,
for the help of man is
worthless.
13With God we shall gain the
victory,
and he will trample down our
enemies.

Psalm 109

For the director of music. Of David.
A psalm.

1O God, whom I praise,
do not remain silent,[a]
2for wicked and deceitful men
have opened their mouths
against me;
they have spoken against me
with lying tongues.[b]
3With words of hatred[c] they
surround me;
they attack me without
cause.[d]
4In return for my friendship
they accuse me,
but I am a man of prayer.[e]
5They repay me evil for good,[f]
and hatred for my friendship.

107:37 h Isa 65:21
107:38 i Ge 12:2; Ge 17:16,20; Ex 1:7
107:39 j 2Ki 10:32; Eze 5:12
107:40 k Job 12:21; l Job 12:24
107:41 m 1Sa 2:8; Ps 113:7-9
107:42 n Job 22:19; o Job 5:16; Ps 63:11; Ro 3:19
107:43 p Jer 9:12; Hos 14:9; q Ps 64:9
108:5 a Ps 57:5
108:8 b Ge 49:10
108:11 c Ps 44:9
109:1 a Ps 83:1
109:2 b Ps 52:4; Ps 120:2
109:3 c Ps 69:4; d Ps 35:7; Jn 15:25
109:4 e Ps 69:13
109:5 f Ps 35:12; Ps 38:20

6Appoint[a] an evil man[b] to
oppose him;
let an accuser[c][g] stand at his
right hand.
7When he is tried, let him be
found guilty,
and may his prayers
condemn[h] him.
8May his days be few;
may another take his place[i]
of leadership.
9May his children be fatherless
and his wife a widow.[j]
10May his children be wandering
beggars;
may they be driven[d] from
their ruined homes.
11May a creditor seize all he has;
may strangers plunder the
fruits of his labour.[k]
12May no-one extend kindness to
him
or take pity[l] on his fatherless
children.
13May his descendants be cut
off,[m]
their names blotted out[n] from
the next generation.
14May the iniquity of his fathers[o]
be remembered before the
LORD;
may the sin of his mother
never be blotted out.
15May their sins always remain
before the LORD,
that he may cut off the
memory[p] of them from the
earth.

16For he never thought of doing a
kindness,
but hounded to death the poor
and the needy[q] and the
broken-hearted.[r]
17He loved to pronounce a
curse—
may it[e] come on him;[s]
he found no pleasure in
blessing—
may it be[f] far from him.
18He wore cursing[t] as his
garment;
it entered into his body like
water,[u]
into his bones like oil.
19May it be like a cloak wrapped
about him,
like a belt tied for ever round
him.
20May this be the LORD's
payment[v] to my accusers,
to those who speak evil[w] of
me.

21But you, O Sovereign LORD,
deal well with me for your
name's sake;[x]
out of the goodness of your
love,[y] deliver me.
22For I am poor and needy,
and my heart is wounded
within me.
23I fade away like an evening
shadow;[z]
I am shaken off like a locust.
24My knees give[a] way from
fasting;
my body is thin and gaunt.
25I am an object of scorn[b] to my
accusers;
when they see me, they shake
their heads.[c]

26Help me,[d] O LORD my God;
save me in accordance with
your love.
27Let them know[e] that it is your
hand,
that you, O LORD, have done it.
28They may curse,[f] but you will
bless;
when they attack they will be
put to shame,
but your servant will rejoice.[g]
29My accusers will be clothed
with disgrace
and wrapped in shame[h] as in
a cloak.
30With my mouth I will greatly
extol the LORD;
in the great throng[i] I will
praise him.

109:6 g Zec 3:1
109:7 h Pr 28:9
109:8 i Ac 1:20*
109:9 j Ex 22:24
109:11 k Job 5:5
109:12 l Isa 9:17
109:13 m Job 18:19; Ps 37:28; n Pr 10:7
109:14 o Ex 20:5; Ne 4:5; Jer 18:23
109:15 p Job 18:17; Ps 34:16
109:16 q Ps 37:14,32; r Ps 34:18
109:17 s Pr 14:14; Eze 35:6
109:18 t Ps 73:6; u Nu 5:22
109:20 v Ps 94:23; 2Ti 4:14; w Ps 71:10
109:21 x Ps 79:9; y Ps 69:16
109:23 z Ps 102:11
109:24 a Heb 12:12
109:25 b Ps 22:6; c Mt 27:39; Mk 15:29
109:26 d Ps 119:86
109:27 e Job 37:7
109:28 f 2Sa 16:12; g Isa 65:14
109:29 h Ps 35:26; Ps 132:18
109:30 i Ps 35:18; Ps 111:1

a6 Or ⌊*They say:*⌋ "*Appoint* (with quotation marks at the end of verse 19) b6 Or *the Evil One* c6 Or *let Satan* d10 Septuagint; Hebrew *sought* e17 Or *curse, / and it has* f17 Or *blessing, / and it is*

31 For he stands at the right
hand[j] of the needy one,
to save his life from those who
condemn him.

Psalm 110

Of David. A psalm.

1 The LORD says[a] to my Lord:
"Sit at my right hand
until I make your enemies
a footstool for your feet."[b]
2 The LORD will extend your
mighty sceptre[c] from Zion;
you will rule in the midst of
your enemies.
3 Your troops will be willing
on your day of battle.
Arrayed in holy majesty,[d]
from the womb of the dawn
you will receive the dew of
your youth.[a]
4 The LORD has sworn
and will not change his mind:[e]
"You are a priest for ever,[f]
in the order of Melchizedek.[g]"
5 The Lord is at your right
hand;[h]
he will crush kings[i] on the
day of his wrath.[j]
6 He will judge nations,[k] heaping
up the dead[l]
and crushing the rulers[m] of
the whole earth.
7 He will drink from a brook
beside the way;[b]
therefore he will lift up his
head.[n]

Psalm 111[a]

1 Praise the LORD.[b]

I will extol the LORD with all
my heart
in the council of the upright
and in the assembly.
2 Great are the works[a] of the
LORD;
they are pondered by all who
delight in them.
3 Glorious and majestic are his
deeds,
and his righteousness endures
for ever.
4 He has caused his wonders to
be remembered;
the LORD is gracious and
compassionate.[b]
5 He provides food[c] for those
who fear him;
he remembers his covenant
for ever.
6 He has shown his people the
power of his works,
giving them the lands of other
nations.
7 The works of his hands are
faithful and just;
all his precepts are
trustworthy.[d]
8 They are steadfast for ever[e]
and ever,
done in faithfulness and
uprightness.
9 He provided redemption[f] for
his people;
he ordained his covenant for
ever—
holy and awesome[g] is his
name.

10 The fear of the LORD is the
beginning of wisdom;[h]
all who follow his precepts
have good understanding.[i]
To him belongs eternal
praise.[j]

Psalm 112[a]

1 Praise the LORD.[b]

Blessed is the man who fears
the LORD,[a]
who finds great delight[b] in
his commands.

2 His children will be mighty in
the land;

109:31 j Ps 16:8; Ps 73:23; Ps 121:5
110:1 a Mt 22:44*; Mk 12:36*; Lk 20:42*; Ac 2:34* b 1Co 15:25
110:2 c Ps 45:6
110:3 d Jdg 5:2; Ps 96:9
110:4 e Nu 23:19 f Heb 5:6*; Heb 7:21* g Heb 7:15-17*
110:5 h Ps 16:8 i Ps 2:12 j Ps 2:5; Ro 2:5
110:6 k Isa 2:4 l Isa 66:24 m Ps 68:21
110:7 n Ps 27:6
111:2 a Ps 92:5; Ps 143:5
111:4 b Ps 103:8
111:5 c Mt 6:26, 31-33
111:7 d Ps 19:7; Rev 15:3
111:8 e Isa 40:8; Mt 5:18
111:9 f Lk 1:68 g Ps 99:3; Lk 1:49
111:10 h Pr 9:10 i Ecc 12:13 j Ps 145:2
112:1 a Ps 128:1 b Ps 119:14,16, 47,92

[a] 3 Or / *your young men will come to you like the dew* [b] 7 Or / *The One who grants succession will set him in authority* [a] This psalm is an acrostic poem, the lines of which begin with the successive letters of the Hebrew alphabet.
[b] 1 Hebrew *Hallelu Yah* [a] This psalm is an acrostic poem, the lines of which begin with the successive letters of the Hebrew alphabet.
[b] 1 Hebrew *Hallelu Yah*

the generation of the upright
will be blessed.
3 Wealth and riches are in his
house,
and his righteousness endures
for ever.
4 Even in darkness light dawns[c]
for the upright,
for the gracious and
compassionate and
righteous[d] man.[c]
5 Good will come to him who is
generous and lends freely,[e]
who conducts his affairs with
justice.
6 Surely he will never be shaken;
a righteous man will be
remembered[f] for ever.
7 He will have no fear of bad
news;
his heart is steadfast,[g]
trusting in the LORD.
8 His heart is secure, he will have
no fear;
in the end he will look in
triumph on his foes.[h]
9 He has scattered abroad his
gifts to the poor,[i]
his righteousness endures for
ever;
his horn[d] will be lifted[j] high
in honour.
10 The wicked man will see[k] and
be vexed,
he will gnash his teeth[l] and
waste away;[m]
the longings of the wicked will
come to nothing.[n]

Psalm 113

1 Praise the LORD.[a]

Praise, O servants of the
LORD,[a]
praise the name of the LORD.
2 Let the name of the LORD be
praised,
both now and for evermore.[b]
3 From the rising of the sun[c] to
the place where it sets,
the name of the LORD is to be
praised.

112:4 c Job 11:17 d Ps 97:11
112:5 e Ps 37:21,26
112:6 f Pr 10:7
112:7 g Ps 57:7 Pr 1:33
112:8 h Ps 59:10
112:9 i 2Co 9:9* j Ps 75:10
112:10 k Ps 86:17 l Ps 37:12 m Ps 58:7-8 n Pr 11:7
113:1 a Ps 135:1
113:2 b Da 2:20
113:3 c Isa 59:19 Mal 1:11
113:4 d Ps 99:2 e Ps 8:1 Ps 97:9
113:5 f Ps 89:6 g Ps 103:19
113:6 h Ps 11:4 Ps 138:6 Isa 57:15
113:7 i 1Sa 2:8 j Ps 107:41
113:8 k Job 36:7
113:9 l 1Sa 2:5 Ps 68:6 Isa 54:1
114:1 a Ex 13:3
114:3 b Ex 14:21 Ps 77:16 c Jos 3:16
114:7 d Ps 96:9
114:8 e Ex 17:6 Nu 20:11 Ps 107:35

4 The LORD is exalted[d] over all
the nations,
his glory above the heavens.[e]
5 Who is like the LORD our God,[f]
the One who sits enthroned[g]
on high,
6 who stoops down to look[h]
on the heavens and the earth?
7 He raises the poor[i] from the
dust
and lifts the needy[j] from the
ash heap;
8 he seats them[k] with princes,
with the princes of their
people.
9 He settles the barren[l] woman
in her home
as a happy mother of children.

Praise the LORD.

Psalm 114

1 When Israel came out of
Egypt,[a]
the house of Jacob from a
people of foreign tongue,
2 Judah became God's sanctuary,
Israel his dominion.

3 The sea looked and fled,[b]
the Jordan turned back;[c]
4 the mountains skipped like
rams,
the hills like lambs.

5 Why was it, O sea, that you fled,
O Jordan, that you turned
back,
6 you mountains, that you skipped
like rams,
you hills, like lambs?

7 Tremble, O earth,[d] at the
presence of the Lord,
at the presence of the God of
Jacob,
8 who turned the rock into a pool,
the hard rock into springs of
water.[e]

c4 Or / *for ˌthe LORDˌ is gracious and compassionate and righteous* d9 *Horn* here symbolises dignity. a1 Hebrew *Hallelu Yah*; also in verse 9

Psalm 115

115:4-11pp Ps 135:15-20

1Not to us, O LORD, not to us
but to your name be the
glory,[a]
because of your love and
faithfulness.

2Why do the nations say,
"Where is their God?"[b]
3Our God is in heaven;[c]
he does whatever pleases
him.[d]
4But their idols are silver and
gold,
made by the hands of men.[e]
5They have mouths, but cannot
speak,[f]
eyes, but they cannot see;
6they have ears, but cannot hear,
noses, but they cannot smell;
7they have hands, but cannot
feel,
feet, but they cannot walk;
nor can they utter a sound
with their throats.
8Those who make them will be
like them,
and so will all who trust in
them.

9O house of Israel, trust in the
LORD—
he is their help and shield.
10O house of Aaron,[g] trust in the
LORD—
he is their help and shield.
11You who fear him, trust in the
LORD—
he is their help and shield.

12The LORD remembers us and
will bless us:
He will bless the house of
Israel,
he will bless the house of
Aaron,
13he will bless those who fear[h]
the LORD—
small and great alike.

14May the LORD make you
increase,[i]
both you and your children.
15May you be blessed by the
LORD,
the Maker of heaven[j] and
earth.

16The highest heavens belong to
the LORD,[k]
but the earth he has given[l] to
man.
17It is not the dead[m] who praise
the LORD,
those who go down to silence;
18it is we who extol the LORD,
both now and for evermore.[n]

Praise the LORD.[a]

Psalm 116

1I love the LORD,[a] for he heard
my voice;
he heard my cry[b] for mercy.
2Because he turned his ear[c] to
me,
I will call on him as long as I
live.

3The cords of death[d] entangled
me,
the anguish of the grave[a]
came upon me;
I was overcome by trouble
and sorrow.
4Then I called on the name[e] of
the LORD:
"O LORD, save me![f]"
5The LORD is gracious and
righteous;[g]
our God is full of compassion.
6The LORD protects the
simple-hearted;
when I was in great need,[h] he
saved me.

7Be at rest[i] once more, O my
soul,
for the LORD has been good[j]
to you.

8For you, O LORD, have delivered
my soul[k] from death,
my eyes from tears,
my feet from stumbling,

[a]*18* Hebrew *Hallelu Yah* [a]*3* Hebrew *Sheol*

115:1 *a* Ps 96:8; Isa 48:11; Eze 36:32
115:2 *b* Ps 42:3; Ps 79:10
115:3 *c* Ps 103:19; *d* Ps 135:6; Da 4:35
115:4 *e* Dt 4:28; Jer 10:3-5
115:5 *f* Jer 10:5
115:10 *g* Ps 118:3
115:13 *h* Ps 128:1,4
115:14 *i* Dt 1:11
115:15 *j* Ge 1:1; Ge 14:19; Ps 96:5
115:16 *k* Ps 89:11; *l* Ps 8:6-8
115:17 *m* Ps 6:5; Ps 88:10-12; Isa 38:18
115:18 *n* Ps 113:2; Da 2:20
116:1 *a* Ps 18:1; *b* Ps 66:19
116:2 *c* Ps 40:1
116:3 *d* Ps 18:4-5
116:4 *e* Ps 118:5; *f* Ps 22:20
116:5 *g* Ezr 9:15; Ne 9:8; Ps 103:8; Ps 145:17
116:6 *h* Ps 19:7; Ps 79:8
116:7 *i* Jer 6:16; Mt 11:29; *j* Ps 13:6
116:8 *k* Ps 56:13

9that I may walk before the
LORD
in the land of the living.[l]
10I believed;[m] therefore[b] I said,
"I am greatly afflicted."
11And in my dismay I said,
"All men are liars."[n]

12How can I repay the LORD
for all his goodness to me?
13I will lift up the cup of
salvation
and call on the name[o] of the
LORD.
14I will fulfil my vows[p] to the
LORD
in the presence of all his
people.

15Precious in the sight[q] of the
LORD
is the death of his saints.
16O LORD, truly I am your
servant;[r]
I am your servant, the son of
your maidservant;[c][s]
you have freed me from my
chains.

17I will sacrifice a thank-
offering[t] to you
and call on the name of the
LORD.
18I will fulfil my vows to the
LORD
in the presence of all his
people,
19in the courts[u] of the house of
the LORD—
in your midst, O Jerusalem.

Praise the LORD.[d]

Psalm 117

1Praise the LORD, all you
nations;[a]
extol him, all you peoples.
2For great is his love towards us,
and the faithfulness of the
LORD[b] endures for ever.

Praise the LORD.[d]

Psalm 118

1Give thanks to the LORD,[a] for
he is good;
his love endures for ever.[b]

2Let Israel say:[c]
"His love endures for ever."
3Let the house of Aaron say:
"His love endures for ever."
4Let those who fear the LORD
say:
"His love endures for ever."

5In my anguish[d] I cried to the
LORD,
and he answered[e] by setting
me free.
6The LORD is with me;[f] I will
not be afraid.
What can man do to me?[g]
7The LORD is with me; he is my
helper.[h]
I will look in triumph on my
enemies.[i]

8It is better to take refuge in the
LORD[j]
than to trust in man.[k]
9It is better to take refuge in the
LORD
than to trust in princes.[l]

10All the nations surrounded me,
but in the name of the LORD I
cut them off.[m]
11They surrounded me[n] on every
side,[o]
but in the name of the LORD I
cut them off.
12They swarmed around me like
bees,[p]
but they died out as quickly as
burning thorns;[q]
in the name of the LORD I cut
them off.
13I was pushed back and about to
fall,
but the LORD helped me.[r]
14The LORD is my strength[s] and
my song;
he has become my salvation.[t]

15Shouts of joy[u] and victory

b10 Or *believed even when* c16 Or *servant, your faithful son* d19,2 Hebrew *Hallelu Yah*

116:9 *l* Ps 27:13
116:10 *m* 2Co 4:13*
116:11 *n* Ro 3:4
116:13 *o* Ps 16:5; Ps 80:18
116:14 *p* Ps 22:25; Jnh 2:9
116:15 *q* Ps 72:14
116:16 *r* Ps 119:125; Ps 143:12; *s* Ps 86:16
116:17 *t* Lev 7:12; Ps 50:14
116:19 *u* Ps 96:8; Ps 135:2
117:1 *a* Ro 15:11*
117:2 *b* Ps 100:5
118:1 *a* 1Ch 16:8; *b* Ps 106:1; Ps 136:1
118:2 *c* Ps 115:9
118:5 *d* Ps 120:1; *e* Ps 18:19
118:6 *f* Heb 13:6*; *g* Ps 27:1; Ps 56:4
118:7 *h* Ps 54:4; *i* Ps 59:10
118:8 *j* Ps 40:4; *k* Jer 17:5
118:9 *l* Ps 146:3
118:10 *m* Ps 18:40
118:11 *n* Ps 88:17; *o* Ps 3:6
118:12 *p* Dt 1:44; *q* Ps 58:9
118:13 *r* Ps 86:17; Ps 140:4
118:14 *s* Ex 15:2; *t* Isa 12:2
118:15 *u* Ps 68:3

resound in the tents of the
righteous:
"The LORD's right hand[v] has
done mighty things!
16 The LORD's right hand is lifted
high;
the LORD's right hand has done
mighty things!"

17 I will not die[w] but live,
and will proclaim[x] what the
LORD has done.
18 The LORD has chastened me
severely,
but he has not given me over
to death.[y]

19 Open for me the gates[z] of
righteousness;
I will enter and give thanks to
the LORD.
20 This is the gate of the LORD
through which the righteous
may enter.[a]
21 I will give you thanks, for you
answered me;[b]
you have become my
salvation.

22 The stone the builders rejected
has become the capstone;[c]
23 the LORD has done this,
and it is marvellous in our
eyes.
24 This is the day the LORD has
made;
let us rejoice and be glad in it.

25 O LORD, save us;
O LORD, grant us success.
26 Blessed is he who comes[d] in
the name of the LORD.
From the house of the LORD
we bless you.[a]
27 The LORD is God,
and he has made his light
shine[e] upon us.
With boughs in hand, join in the
festal procession
up[b] to the horns of the altar.

28 You are my God, and I will give
thanks;
you are my God,[f] and I will
exalt[g] you.

118:15
v Ps 89:13
118:17
w Ps 6:5
Hab 1:12
x Ex 15:6
Ps 73:28
118:18
y 2Co 6:9
118:19
z Isa 26:2
118:20
a Ps 24:7
Isa 35:8
Rev 22:14
118:21
b Ps 116:1
118:22
c Mt 21:42
Mk 12:10
Lk 20:17*
Ac 4:11*
1Pe 2:7*
118:26
d Mt 21:9*
Mk 11:9*
Lk 13:35*
Lk 19:38
Jn 12:13*
118:27
e 1Pe 2:9
118:28
f Isa 25:1
g Ex 15:2
119:1
a Ps 128:1
119:2
b Dt 6:5
119:3
c 1Jn 3:9
1Jn 5:18
119:9
d 2Ch 6:16
119:10
e 2Ch 15:15
f ver 21,118
119:11
g Ps 37:31
Lk 2:19,51
119:12
h ver 26

29 Give thanks to the LORD, for he
is good;
his love endures for ever.

Psalm 119[a]

א Aleph

1 Blessed are they whose ways
are blameless,
who walk[a] according to the
law of the LORD.
2 Blessed are they who keep his
statutes
and seek him with all their
heart.[b]
3 They do nothing wrong;[c]
they walk in his ways.
4 You have laid down precepts
that are to be fully obeyed.
5 Oh, that my ways were
steadfast
in obeying your decrees!
6 Then I would not be put to
shame
when I consider all your
commands.
7 I will praise you with an
upright heart
as I learn your righteous laws.
8 I will obey your decrees;
do not utterly forsake me.

ב Beth

9 How can a young man keep his
way pure?
By living according to your
word.[d]
10 I seek you with all my heart;[e]
do not let me stray from your
commands.[f]
11 I have hidden your word in my
heart[g]
that I might not sin against
you.
12 Praise be to you, O LORD;
teach me your decrees.[h]
13 With my lips I recount

[a]26 The Hebrew is plural. [b]27 Or *Bind the festal sacrifice with ropes / and take it* [a]This psalm is an acrostic poem; the verses of each stanza begin with the same letter of the Hebrew alphabet.

all the laws that come from
your mouth.[i]
14 I rejoice in following your
statutes
as one rejoices in great riches.
15 I meditate on your precepts[j]
and consider your ways.
16 I delight[k] in your decrees;
I will not neglect your word.

ג Gimel

17 Do good to your servant,[l] and I
will live;
I will obey your word.
18 Open my eyes that I may see
wonderful things in your law.
19 I am a stranger on earth;[m]
do not hide your commands
from me.
20 My soul is consumed[n] with
longing
for your laws[o] at all times.
21 You rebuke the arrogant, who
are cursed
and who stray[p] from your
commands.
22 Remove from me scorn[q] and
contempt,
for I keep your statutes.
23 Though rulers sit together and
slander me,
your servant will meditate on
your decrees.
24 Your statutes are my delight;
they are my counsellors.

ד Daleth

25 I am laid low in the dust;[r]
preserve my life[s] according
to your word.
26 I recounted my ways and you
answered me;
teach me your decrees.[t]
27 Let me understand the teaching
of your precepts;
then I will meditate on your
wonders.[u]
28 My soul is weary with sorrow;[v]
strengthen me[w] according to
your word.
29 Keep me from deceitful ways;
be gracious to me through
your law.

119:13 *i* Ps 40:9
119:15 *j* Ps 1:2
119:16 *k* Ps 1:2
119:17 *l* Ps 13:6; Ps 116:7
119:19 *m* 1Ch 29:15; Ps 39:12; 2Co 5:6; Heb 11:13
119:20 *n* Ps 42:2; Ps 84:2; *o* Ps 63:1
119:21 *p* ver 10
119:22 *q* Ps 39:8
119:25 *r* Ps 44:25; *s* Ps 143:11
119:26 *t* Ps 25:4; Ps 27:11; Ps 86:11
119:27 *u* Ps 145:5
119:28 *v* Ps 107:26; *w* Ps 20:2; 1Pe 5:10
119:31 *x* Dt 11:22
119:33 *y* ver 12
119:36 *z* 1Ki 8:58; *a* Eze 33:31; Mk 7:21-22; Lk 12:15; Heb 13:5
119:37 *b* Ps 71:20; Isa 33:15
119:38 *c* 2Sa 7:25
119:40 *d* ver 20
119:42 *e* Pr 27:11

30 I have chosen the way of truth;
I have set my heart on your
laws.
31 I hold fast[x] to your statutes,
O LORD;
do not let me be put to shame.
32 I run in the path of your
commands,
for you have set my heart
free.

ה He

33 Teach me,[y] O LORD, to follow
your decrees;
then I will keep them to the
end.
34 Give me understanding, and I
will keep your law
and obey it with all my heart.
35 Direct me in the path of your
commands,
for there I find delight.
36 Turn my heart[z] towards your
statutes
and not towards selfish gain.[a]
37 Turn my eyes away from
worthless things;
preserve my life[b] according
to your word.[b]
38 Fulfil your promise[c] to your
servant,
so that you may be feared.
39 Take away the disgrace I dread,
for your laws are good.
40 How I long[d] for your precepts!
Preserve my life in your
righteousness.

ו Waw

41 May your unfailing love come
to me, O LORD,
your salvation according to
your promise;
42 then I will answer[e] the one who
taunts me,
for I trust in your word.
43 Do not snatch the word of truth
from my mouth,

b37 Two manuscripts of the Masoretic Text and Dead Sea Scrolls; most manuscripts of the Masoretic Text *life in your way*

for I have put my hope in your
laws.
44I will always obey your law,
for ever and ever.
45I will walk about in freedom,
for I have sought out your
precepts.
46I will speak of your statutes
before kings[f]
and will not be put to shame,
47for I delight in your commands
because I love them.
48I lift up my hands to[c] your
commands, which I love,
and I meditate on your
decrees.

ז Zayin

49Remember your word to your
servant,
for you have given me hope.
50My comfort in my suffering is
this:
Your promise preserves my
life.[g]
51The arrogant mock me[h]
without restraint,
but I do not turn[i] from your
law.
52I remember[j] your ancient
laws, O LORD,
and I find comfort in them.
53Indignation grips me[k] because
of the wicked,
who have forsaken your law.[l]
54Your decrees are the theme of
my song
wherever I lodge.
55In the night I remember[m] your
name, O LORD,
and I will keep your law.
56This has been my practice:
I obey your precepts.

ח Heth

57You are my portion,[n] O LORD;
I have promised to obey your
words.
58I have sought your face with all
my heart;
be gracious to me[o] according
to your promise.[p]
59I have considered my ways[q]
and have turned my steps to
your statutes.
60I will hasten and not delay
to obey your commands.
61Though the wicked bind me
with ropes,
I will not forget[r] your law.
62At midnight[s] I rise to give you
thanks
for your righteous laws.
63I am a friend to all who fear
you,[t]
to all who follow your
precepts.
64The earth is filled with your
love,[u] O LORD;
teach me your decrees.

ט Teth

65Do good to your servant
according to your word,
O LORD.
66Teach me knowledge and good
judgment,
for I believe in your
commands.
67Before I was afflicted I went
astray,[v]
but now I obey your word.
68You are good,[w] and what you do
is good;
teach me your decrees.[x]
69Though the arrogant have
smeared me with lies,[y]
I keep your precepts with all
my heart.
70Their hearts are callous[z] and
unfeeling,
but I delight in your law.
71It was good for me to be
afflicted
so that I might learn your
decrees.
72The law from your mouth is
more precious to me
than thousands of pieces of
silver and gold.[a]

י Yodh

73Your hands made me[b] and
formed me;

[c]48 Or *for*

119:46 f Mt 10:18; Ac 26:1-2
119:50 g Ro 15:4
119:51 h Jer 20:7; i ver 157; Job 23:11; Ps 44:18
119:52 j Ps 103:18
119:53 k Ezr 9:3; l Ps 89:30
119:55 m Ps 63:6
119:57 n Ps 16:5; La 3:24
119:58 o 1Ki 13:6; p ver 41
119:59 q Lk 15:17-18
119:61 r Ps 140:5
119:62 s Ac 16:25
119:63 t Ps 101:6-7
119:64 u Ps 33:5
119:67 v Jer 31:18-19; Heb 12:11
119:68 w Ps 106:1; Ps 107:1; Mt 19:17; x ver 12
119:69 y Job 13:4; Ps 109:2
119:70 z Ps 17:10; Isa 6:10; Ac 28:27
119:72 a Ps 19:10; Pr 8:10-11,19
119:73 b Job 10:8; Ps 100:3; Ps 138:8; Ps 139:13-16

give me understanding to
learn your commands.
74 May those who fear you
rejoice[c] when they see me,
for I have put my hope in your
word.
75 I know, O LORD, that your laws
are righteous,
and in faithfulness[d] you have
afflicted me.
76 May your unfailing love be my
comfort,
according to your promise to
your servant.
77 Let your compassion[e] come to
me that I may live,
for your law is my delight.
78 May the arrogant[f] be put to
shame for wronging me
without cause;[g]
but I will meditate on your
precepts.
79 May those who fear you turn to
me,
those who understand your
statutes.
80 May my heart be blameless
towards your decrees,
that I may not be put to
shame.

כ Kaph

81 My soul faints[h] with longing
for your salvation,
but I have put my hope in
your word.
82 My eyes fail,[i] looking for your
promise;
I say, "When will you comfort
me?"
83 Though I am like a wineskin in
the smoke,
I do not forget your decrees.
84 How long[j] must your servant
wait?
When will you punish my
persecutors?
85 The arrogant dig pitfalls[k] for
me,
contrary to your law.
86 All your commands are
trustworthy;[l]
help me,[m] for men persecute
me without cause.[n]
87 They almost wiped me from the
earth,
but I have not forsaken[o] your
precepts.
88 Preserve my life according to
your love,
and I will obey the statutes of
your mouth.

ל Lamedh

89 Your word, O LORD, is eternal;[p]
it stands firm in the heavens.
90 Your faithfulness[q] continues
through all generations;
you established the earth, and
it endures.[r]
91 Your laws endure[s] to this day,
for all things serve you.
92 If your law had not been my
delight,
I would have perished in my
affliction.
93 I will never forget your
precepts,
for by them you have
preserved my life.
94 Save me, for I am yours;
I have sought out your
precepts.
95 The wicked are waiting to
destroy me,
but I will ponder your
statutes.
96 To all perfection I see a limit;
but your commands are
boundless.

מ Mem

97 Oh, how I love your law!
I meditate[t] on it all day long.
98 Your commands make me
wiser[u] than my enemies,
for they are ever with me.
99 I have more insight than all my
teachers,
for I meditate on your
statutes.
100 I have more understanding
than the elders,
for I obey your precepts.[v]

119:74 c Ps 34:2
119:75 d Heb 12:5-11
119:77 e ver 41
119:78 f Jer 50:32 g ver 86,161
119:81 h Ps 84:2
119:82 i Ps 69:3 La 2:11
119:84 j Ps 39:4 Rev 6:10
119:85 k Ps 35:7 Jer 18:20,22
119:86 l Ps 35:19 m Ps 109:26 n ver 78
119:87 o Isa 58:2
119:89 p Mt 24:34-35 1Pe 1:25
119:90 q Ps 36:5 r Ps 148:6 Ecc 1:4
119:91 s Jer 33:25
119:97 t Ps 1:2
119:98 u Dt 4:6
119:100 v Job 32:7-9

101 I have kept my feet[w] from
every evil path
so that I might obey your
word.
102 I have not departed from your
laws,
for you yourself have taught
me.
103 How sweet are your words to
my taste,
sweeter than honey[x] to my
mouth![y]
104 I gain understanding from your
precepts;
therefore I hate every wrong
path.[z]

נ Nun

105 Your word is a lamp to my feet
and a light[a] for my path.
106 I have taken an oath[b] and
confirmed it,
that I will follow your
righteous laws.
107 I have suffered much;
preserve my life, O LORD,
according to your word.
108 Accept, O LORD, the willing
praise of my mouth,[c]
and teach me your laws.
109 Though I constantly take my
life in my hands,[d]
I will not forget your law.
110 The wicked have set a snare[e]
for me,
but I have not strayed[f] from
your precepts.
111 Your statutes are my heritage
for ever;
they are the joy of my heart.
112 My heart is set on keeping
your decrees
to the very end.[g]

ס Samekh

113 I hate double-minded men,[h]
but I love your law.
114 You are my refuge and my
shield;[i]
I have put my hope[j] in your
word.

119:101 w Pr 1:15
119:103 x Ps 19:10; Pr 8:11 y Pr 24:13-14
119:104 z ver 128
119:105 a Pr 6:23
119:106 b Ne 10:29
119:108 c Hos 14:2; Heb 13:15
119:109 d Jdg 12:3; Job 13:14
119:110 e Ps 140:5; Ps 141:9 f ver 10
119:112 g ver 33
119:113 h Jas 1:8
119:114 i Ps 32:7; Ps 91:1 j ver 74
119:115 k Ps 6:8; Ps 139:19; Mt 7:23
119:116 l Ps 54:4 m Ps 25:2; Ro 5:5; Ro 9:33
119:119 n Eze 22:18,19
119:120 o Hab 3:16
119:122 p Job 17:3
119:123 q ver 82
119:124 r ver 12
119:125 s Ps 116:16
119:127 t Ps 19:10
119:128 u ver 104,163

115 Away from me,[k] you evildoers,
that I may keep the commands
of my God!
116 Sustain me[l] according to your
promise, and I shall live;
do not let my hopes be
dashed.[m]
117 Uphold me, and I shall be
delivered;
I shall always have regard for
your decrees.
118 You reject all who stray from
your decrees,
for their deceitfulness is in
vain.
119 All the wicked of the earth you
discard like dross;[n]
therefore I love your statutes.
120 My flesh trembles[o] in fear of
you;
I stand in awe of your laws.

ע Ayin

121 I have done what is righteous
and just;
do not leave me to my
oppressors.
122 Ensure your servant's
well-being;[p]
let not the arrogant oppress
me.
123 My eyes fail, looking for your
salvation,
looking for your righteous
promise.[q]
124 Deal with your servant
according to your love
and teach me your decrees.[r]
125 I am your servant;[s] give me
discernment
that I may understand your
statutes.
126 It is time for you to act,
O LORD;
your law is being broken.
127 Because I love your commands
more than gold,[t] more than
pure gold,
128 and because I consider all your
precepts right,
I hate every wrong path.[u]

פ Pe

129 Your statutes are wonderful;
therefore I obey them.
130 The unfolding of your words
gives light;[v]
it gives understanding to the
simple.[w]
131 I open my mouth and pant,[x]
longing for your commands.[y]
132 Turn to me and have mercy[z]
on me,
as you always do to those who
love your name.
133 Direct my footsteps according
to your word;[a]
let no sin rule[b] over me.
134 Redeem me from the
oppression of men,[c]
that I may obey your precepts.
135 Make your face shine[d] upon
your servant
and teach me your decrees.
136 Streams of tears[e] flow from
my eyes,
for your law is not obeyed.[f]

צ Tsadhe

137 Righteous are you,[g] O LORD,
and your laws are right.[h]
138 The statutes you have laid
down are righteous;[i]
they are fully trustworthy.
139 My zeal wears me out,[j]
for my enemies ignore your
words.
140 Your promises have been
thoroughly tested,[k]
and your servant loves them.
141 Though I am lowly and
despised,[l]
I do not forget your precepts.
142 Your righteousness is
everlasting
and your law is true.[m]
143 Trouble and distress have
come upon me,
but your commands are my
delight.
144 Your statutes are for ever
right;
give me understanding[n] that I
may live.

119:130 v Pr 6:23 w Ps 19:7
119:131 x Ps 42:1 y ver 20
119:132 z Ps 25:16 Ps 106:4
119:133 a Ps 17:5 b Ps 19:13 Ro 6:12
119:134 c Ps 142:6 Lk 1:74
119:135 d Nu 6:25 Ps 4:6
119:136 e Jer 9:1,18 f Eze 9:4
119:137 g Ezr 9:15 Jer 12:1 h Ne 9:13
119:138 i Ps 19:7
119:139 j Ps 69:9 Jn 2:17
119:140 k Ps 12:6
119:141 l Ps 22:6
119:142 m Ps 19:7
119:144 n Ps 19:9
119:147 o Ps 5:3 Ps 57:8 Ps 108:2
119:148 p Ps 63:6
119:151 q Ps 34:18 Ps 145:18 r ver 142
119:152 s Lk 21:33
119:153 t La 5:1 u Pr 3:1
119:154 v Mic 7:9 w 1Sa 24:15
119:155 x Job 5:4
119:156 y 2Sa 24:14
119:157 z Ps 7:1
119:158 a Ps 139:21

ק Qoph

145 I call with all my heart; answer
me, O LORD,
and I will obey your decrees.
146 I call out to you; save me
and I will keep your statutes.
147 I rise before dawn[o] and cry
for help;
I have put my hope in your
word.
148 My eyes stay open through the
watches of the night,[p]
that I may meditate on your
promises.
149 Hear my voice in accordance
with your love;
preserve my life, O LORD,
according to your laws.
150 Those who devise wicked
schemes are near,
but they are far from your
law.
151 Yet you are near,[q] O LORD,
and all your commands are
true.[r]
152 Long ago I learned from your
statutes
that you established them to
last for ever.[s]

ר Resh

153 Look upon my suffering[t] and
deliver me,
for I have not forgotten[u] your
law.
154 Defend my cause[v] and redeem
me;[w]
preserve my life according to
your promise.
155 Salvation is far from the
wicked,
for they do not seek out[x] your
decrees.
156 Your compassion is great,
O LORD;
preserve my life[y] according
to your laws.
157 Many are the foes who
persecute me,[z]
but I have not turned from
your statutes.
158 I look on the faithless with
loathing,[a]

for they do not obey your
word.
159 See how I love your precepts;
preserve my life, O LORD,
according to your love.
160 All your words are true;
all your righteous laws are
eternal.

ש Sin and Shin

161 Rulers persecute me[b] without
cause,
but my heart trembles at your
word.
162 I rejoice in your promise
like one who finds great
spoil.[c]
163 I hate and abhor falsehood
but I love your law.
164 Seven times a day I praise you
for your righteous laws.
165 Great peace[d] have they who
love your law,
and nothing can make them
stumble.
166 I wait for your salvation,[e]
O LORD,
and I follow your commands.
167 I obey your statutes,
for I love them greatly.
168 I obey your precepts and your
statutes,
for all my ways are known[f] to
you.

ת Taw

169 May my cry come[g] before you,
O LORD;
give me understanding
according to your word.
170 May my supplication come[h]
before you;
deliver me[i] according to your
promise.
171 May my lips overflow with
praise,[j]
for you teach me[k] your
decrees.
172 May my tongue sing of your
word,
for all your commands are
righteous.
173 May your hand be ready to
help[l] me,
for I have chosen[m] your
precepts.
174 I long for your salvation,[n]
O LORD,
and your law is my delight.
175 Let me live[o] that I may praise
you,
and may your laws sustain me.
176 I have strayed like a lost
sheep.[p]
Seek your servant,
for I have not forgotten your
commands.

Psalm 120

A song of ascents.

1 I call on the LORD in my
distress,[a]
and he answers me.
2 Save me, O LORD, from lying
lips[b]
and from deceitful tongues.[c]

3 What will he do to you,
and what more besides,
O deceitful tongue?
4 He will punish you with a
warrior's sharp arrows,[d]
with burning coals of the
broom tree.

5 Woe to me that I dwell in
Meshech,
that I live among the tents of
Kedar![e]
6 Too long have I lived
among those who hate peace.
7 I am a man of peace;
but when I speak, they are for
war.

Psalm 121

A song of ascents.

1 I lift up my eyes to the hills—
where does my help come
from?
2 My help comes from the LORD,
the Maker of heaven and
earth.[a]

119:161 b 1Sa 24:11
119:162 c 1Sa 30:16
119:165 d Pr 3:2 Isa 26:3,12 Isa 32:17
119:166 e Ge 49:18
119:168 f Pr 5:21
119:169 g Ps 18:6
119:170 h Ps 28:2 i Ps 31:2
119:171 j Ps 51:15 k Ps 94:12
119:173 l Ps 37:24 m Jos 24:22
119:174 n ver 166
119:175 o Isa 55:3
119:176 p Isa 53:6
120:1 a Ps 102:2 Jnh 2:2
120:2 b Pr 12:22 c Ps 52:4
120:4 d Ps 45:5
120:5 e Ge 25:13 Jer 49:28
121:2 a Ps 115:15 Ps 124:8

[3]He will not let your foot slip—
he who watches over you will not slumber;
[4]indeed, he who watches over Israel
will neither slumber nor sleep.

[5]The LORD watches over[b] you—
the LORD is your shade at your right hand;
[6]the sun[c] will not harm you by day,
nor the moon by night.

[7]The LORD will keep you from all harm[d]—
he will watch over your life;
[8]the LORD will watch over your coming and going
both now and for evermore.[e]

Psalm 122

A song of ascents. Of David.

[1]I rejoiced with those who said to me,
"Let us go to the house of the LORD."
[2]Our feet are standing
in your gates, O Jerusalem.

[3]Jerusalem is built like a city
that is closely compacted together.
[4]That is where the tribes go up,
the tribes of the LORD,
to praise the name of the LORD
according to the statute given to Israel.
[5]There the thrones for judgment stand,
the thrones of the house of David.

[6]Pray for the peace of Jerusalem:
"May those who love[a] you be secure.
[7]May there be peace within your walls
and security within your citadels."
[8]For the sake of my brothers and friends,
I will say, "Peace be within you."
[9]For the sake of the house of the LORD our God,
I will seek your prosperity.[b]

Psalm 123

A song of ascents.

[1]I lift up my eyes to you,
to you whose throne[a] is in heaven.
[2]As the eyes of slaves look to the hand of their master,
as the eyes of a maid look to the hand of her mistress,
so our eyes look to the LORD[b] our God,
till he shows us his mercy.

[3]Have mercy on us, O LORD,
have mercy on us,
for we have endured much contempt.
[4]We have endured much ridicule from the proud,
much contempt from the arrogant.

Psalm 124

A song of ascents. Of David.

[1]If the LORD had not been on our side—
let Israel say[a]—
[2]if the LORD had not been on our side
when men attacked us,
[3]when their anger flared against us,
they would have swallowed us alive;
[4]the flood would have engulfed us,
the torrent would have swept over us,
[5]the raging waters
would have swept us away.

[6]Praise be to the LORD,
who has not let us be torn by their teeth.
[7]We have escaped like a bird
out of the fowler's snare;[b]

121:5 *b* Isa 25:4
121:6 *c* Ps 91:5; Isa 49:10; Rev 7:16
121:7 *d* Ps 41:2; Ps 91:10-12
121:8 *e* Dt 28:6
122:6 *a* Ps 51:18
122:9 *b* Ne 2:10
123:1 *a* Ps 11:4; Ps 121:1; Ps 141:8
123:2 *b* Ps 25:15
124:1 *a* Ps 129:1
124:7 *b* Ps 91:3; Pr 6:5

the snare has been broken,
and we have escaped.
8Our help is in the name of the LORD,
the Maker of heaven[c] and earth.

Psalm 125

A song of ascents.

1Those who trust in the LORD are like Mount Zion,
which cannot be shaken[a] but endures for ever.
2As the mountains surround Jerusalem,
so the LORD surrounds[b] his people
both now and for evermore.
3The sceptre of the wicked will not remain[c]
over the land allotted to the righteous,
for then the righteous might use
their hands to do evil.[d]
4Do good, O LORD,[e] to those who are good,
to those who are upright in heart.[f]
5But those who turn[g] to crooked ways[h]
the LORD will banish with the evildoers.

Peace be upon Israel.[i]

Psalm 126

A song of ascents.

1When the LORD brought back[a] the captives to[a] Zion,
we were like men who dreamed.[b]
2Our mouths were filled with laughter,
our tongues with songs of joy.[b]
Then it was said among the nations,
"The LORD has done great things[c] for them."
3The LORD has done great things for us,
and we are filled with joy.[d]
4Restore our fortunes,[c] O LORD,
like streams in the Negev.[e]
5Those who sow in tears
will reap with songs of joy.[f]
6He who goes out weeping,
carrying seed to sow,
will return with songs of joy,
carrying sheaves with him.

Psalm 127

A song of ascents. Of Solomon.

1Unless the LORD builds[a] the house,
its builders labour in vain.
Unless the LORD watches[b] over the city,
the watchmen stand guard in vain.
2In vain you rise early
and stay up late,
toiling for food[c] to eat—
for he grants sleep[d] to[a] those he loves.
3Sons are a heritage from the LORD,
children a reward[e] from him.
4Like arrows in the hands of a warrior
are sons born in one's youth.
5Blessed is the man
whose quiver is full of them.
They will not be put to shame
when they contend with their enemies[f] in the gate.

Psalm 128

A song of ascents.

1Blessed are all who fear the LORD,[a]
who walk in his ways.[b]
2You will eat the fruit of your labour;[c]

124:8 c Ge 1:1; Ps 121:2; Ps 134:3
125:1 a Ps 46:5
125:2 b Ps 121:8; Zec 2:4-5
125:3 c Ps 89:22; Pr 22:8; Isa 14:5 d 1Sa 24:10; Ps 55:20
125:4 e Ps 119:68 f Ps 7:10; Ps 36:10; Ps 94:15
125:5 g Job 23:11 h Pr 2:15; Isa 59:8 i Ps 128:6
126:1 a Ps 85:1; Hos 6:11
126:2 b Job 8:21; Ps 51:14 c Ps 71:19
126:3 d Isa 25:9
126:4 e Isa 35:6; Isa 43:19
126:5 f Isa 35:10
127:1 a Ps 78:69 b Ps 121:4
127:2 c Ge 3:17 d Job 11:18
127:3 e Ge 33:5
127:5 f Pr 27:11
128:1 a Ps 112:1 b Ps 119:1-3
128:2 c Isa 3:10

a1 Or *LORD restored the fortunes of* b1 Or *men restored to health* c4 Or *Bring back our captives* a2 Or *eat— / for while they sleep he provides for*

blessings and prosperity[d] will
be yours.
3 Your wife will be like a fruitful
vine[e]
within your house;
your sons will be like olive
shoots[f]
round your table.
4 Thus is the man blessed
who fears the LORD.

5 May the LORD bless you from
Zion[g]
all the days of your life;
may you see the prosperity of
Jerusalem,
6 and may you live to see your
children's children.[h]

Peace be upon Israel.[i]

Psalm 129

A song of ascents.

1 They have greatly oppressed
me from my youth[a]—
let Israel say[b]—
2 they have greatly oppressed me
from my youth,
but they have not gained the
victory[c] over me.
3 Ploughmen have ploughed my
back
and made their furrows long.
4 But the LORD is righteous;[d]
he has cut me free from the
cords of the wicked.

5 May all who hate Zion[e]
be turned back in shame.[f]
6 May they be like grass on the
roof,
which withers[g] before it can
grow;
7 with it the reaper cannot fill his
hands,
nor the one who gathers fill
his arms.
8 May those who pass by not say,
"The blessing of the LORD be
upon you;
we bless you[h] in the name of
the LORD."

Psalm 130

A song of ascents.

1 Out of the depths[a] I cry to you,
O LORD;
2 O Lord, hear my voice.[b]
Let your ears be attentive[c]
to my cry for mercy.

3 If you, O LORD, kept a record of
sins,
O Lord, who could stand?[d]
4 But with you there is
forgiveness;[e]
therefore you are feared.[f]

5 I wait for the LORD,[g] my soul
waits,
and in his word[h] I put my
hope.
6 My soul waits for the Lord
more than watchmen[i] wait
for the morning,
more than watchmen wait for
the morning.[j]

7 O Israel, put your hope[k] in the
LORD,
for with the LORD is unfailing
love
and with him is full
redemption.
8 He himself will redeem[l] Israel
from all their sins.

Psalm 131

A song of ascents. Of David.

1 My heart is not proud,[a]
O LORD,
my eyes are not haughty;
I do not concern myself with
great matters
or things too wonderful for
me.
2 But I have stilled and quietened
my soul;
like a weaned child with its
mother,
like a weaned child is my
soul[b] within me.

3 O Israel, put your hope[c] in the
LORD
both now and for evermore.

128:2 d Ecc 8:12
128:3 e Eze 19:10 f Ps 52:8 Ps 144:12
128:5 g Ps 20:2 Ps 134:3
128:6 h Ge 50:23 Job 42:16 i Ps 125:5
129:1 a Ps 88:15 Hos 2:15 b Ps 124:1
129:2 c Mt 16:18
129:4 d Ps 119:137
129:5 e Mic 4:11 f Ps 71:13
129:6 g Ps 37:2
129:8 h Ru 2:4 Ps 118:26
130:1 a Ps 42:7 Ps 69:2 La 3:55
130:2 b Ps 28:2 c 2Ch 6:40 Ps 64:1
130:3 d Ps 76:7 Ps 143:2
130:4 e Ex 34:7 Isa 55:7 Jer 33:8 f 1Ki 8:40
130:5 g Ps 27:14 Ps 33:20 Isa 8:17 h Ps 119:81
130:6 i Ps 63:6 j Ps 119:147
130:7 k Ps 131:3
130:8 l Lk 1:68
131:1 a Ps 101:5 Ro 12:16
131:2 b Mt 18:3 1Co 14:20
131:3 c Ps 130:7

Psalm 132

132:8–10pp 2Ch 6:41–42

A song of ascents.

1O LORD, remember David
and all the hardships he
endured.

2He swore an oath to the LORD
and made a vow to the Mighty
One of Jacob:[a]
3"I will not enter my house
or go to my bed—
4I will allow no sleep to my eyes,
no slumber to my eyelids,
5till I find a place[b] for the LORD,
a dwelling for the Mighty One
of Jacob."

6We heard it in Ephrathah,[c]
we came upon it in the fields
of Jaar:[a,b][d]
7"Let us go to his dwelling-
place;[e]
let us worship at his
footstool[f]—
8arise, O LORD,[g] and come to
your resting place,
you and the ark of your might.
9May your priests be clothed
with righteousness;[h]
may your saints sing for joy."

10For the sake of David your
servant,
do not reject your anointed
one.

11The LORD swore an oath to
David,[i]
a sure oath that he will not
revoke:
"One of your own descendants[j]
I will place on your throne—
12if your sons keep my covenant
and the statutes I teach them,
then their sons shall sit
on your throne[k] for ever and
ever."

13For the LORD has chosen Zion,[l]
he has desired it for his
dwelling:
14"This is my resting place for
ever and ever;[m]
here I will sit enthroned, for I
have desired it—

132:2 *a* Ge 49:24
132:5 *b* Ac 7:46
132:6 *c* 1Sa 17:12 *d* 1Sa 7:2
132:7 *e* Ps 5:7 *f* Ps 99:5
132:8 *g* Nu 10:35 Ps 78:61
132:9 *h* Job 29:14 Isa 61:3,10
132:11 *i* Ps 89:3-4,35 *j* 2Sa 7:12
132:12 *k* Lk 1:32 Ac 2:30
132:13 *l* Ps 48:1-2
132:14 *m* Ps 68:16
132:15 *n* Ps 107:9 Ps 147:14
132:16 *o* 2Ch 6:41
132:17 *p* Eze 29:21 Lk 1:69 *q* 1Ki 11:36 2Ch 21:7
132:18 *r* Ps 35:26 Ps 109:29
133:1 *a* Ge 13:8 Heb 13:1
133:2 *b* Ex 30:25
133:3 *c* Dt 4:48 *d* Lev 25:21 Dt 28:8 *e* Ps 42:8
134:1 *a* Ps 135:1-2 *b* 1Ch 9:33
134:2 *c* Ps 28:2 1Ti 2:8

15I will bless her with abundant
provisions;
her poor will I satisfy with
food.[n]
16I will clothe her priests[o] with
salvation,
and her saints shall ever sing
for joy.

17"Here I will make a horn[c]
grow[p] for David
and set up a lamp[q] for my
anointed one.
18I will clothe his enemies with
shame,[r]
but the crown on his head
shall be resplendent."

Psalm 133

A song of ascents. Of David.

1How good and pleasant it is
when brothers live together[a]
in unity!
2It is like precious oil poured on
the head,[b]
running down on the beard,
running down on Aaron's beard,
down upon the collar of his
robes.
3It is as if the dew of Hermon[c]
were falling on Mount Zion.
For there the LORD bestows his
blessing,[d]
even life for evermore.[e]

Psalm 134

A song of ascents.

1Praise the LORD, all you
servants[a] of the LORD
who minister by night[b] in the
house of the LORD.
2Lift up your hands[c] in the
sanctuary
and praise the LORD.

a6 That is, Kiriath Jearim   b6 Or *heard of it in Ephrathah, / we found it in the fields of Jaar.* (and no quotation marks around verses 7–9)
c17 *Horn* here symbolises strong one, that is, king.

3 May the LORD, the Maker of
heaven[d] and earth,
bless you from Zion.[e]

Psalm 135

135:15–20pp Ps 115:4–11

1 Praise the LORD.[a]

Praise the name of the LORD;
praise him, you servants[a] of
the LORD,
2 you who minister in the house[b]
of the LORD,
in the courts[c] of the house of
our God.

3 Praise the LORD, for the LORD is
good;[d]
sing praise to his name, for
that is pleasant.[e]
4 For the LORD has chosen
Jacob[f] to be his own,
Israel to be his treasured
possession.[g]

5 I know that the LORD is great,[h]
that our Lord is greater than
all gods.[i]
6 The LORD does whatever
pleases him,[j]
in the heavens and on the
earth,
in the seas and all their
depths.
7 He makes clouds rise from the
ends of the earth;
he sends lightning with the
rain[k]
and brings out the wind[l] from
his storehouses.[m]

8 He struck down the firstborn[n]
of Egypt,
the firstborn of men and
animals.
9 He sent his signs[o] and wonders
into your midst, O Egypt,
against Pharaoh and all his
servants.[p]
10 He struck down many[q] nations
and killed mighty kings—
11 Sihon[r] king of the Amorites,
Og king of Bashan
and all the kings of Canaan[s]—
12 and he gave their land as an
inheritance,[t]
an inheritance to his people
Israel.

13 Your name, O LORD, endures for
ever,[u]
your renown,[v] O LORD,
through all generations.
14 For the LORD will vindicate his
people
and have compassion on his
servants.[w]

15 The idols of the nations are
silver and gold,
made by the hands of men.
16 They have mouths, but cannot
speak,
eyes, but they cannot see;
17 they have ears, but cannot hear,
nor is there breath in their
mouths.
18 Those who make them will be
like them,
and so will all who trust in
them.

19 O house of Israel, praise the
LORD;
O house of Aaron, praise
the LORD;
20 O house of Levi, praise the
LORD;
you who fear him, praise
the LORD.
21 Praise be to the LORD from
Zion,[x]
to him who dwells in
Jerusalem.

Praise the LORD.

Psalm 136

1 Give thanks to the LORD, for he
is good.[a]
His love endures for ever.[b]
2 Give thanks to the God of
gods.[c]
His love endures for ever.

134:3 d Ps 124:8 e Ps 128:5
135:1 a Ps 113:1 Ps 134:1
135:2 b Lk 2:37 c Ps 116:19
135:3 d Ps 119:68 e Ps 147:1
135:4 f Dt 10:15 1Pe 2:9 g Ex 19:5 Dt 7:6
135:5 h Ps 48:1 i Ps 97:9
135:6 j Ps 115:3
135:7 k Jer 10:13 Zec 10:1 l Job 28:25 m Job 38:22
135:8 n Ex 12:12 Ps 78:51
135:9 o Dt 6:22 p Ps 136:10-15
135:10 q Nu 21:21-25 Ps 136:17-21
135:11 r Nu 21:21 s Jos 12:7-24
135:12 t Ps 78:55
135:13 u Ex 3:15 v Ps 102:12
135:14 w Dt 32:36
135:21 x Ps 134:3
136:1 a Ps 106:1 b 1Ch 16:34 2Ch 20:21
136:2 c Dt 10:17

a1 Hebrew *Hallelu Yah*; also in verses 3 and 21

3 Give thanks to the Lord of
lords:
His love endures for ever.
4 to him who alone does great
wonders,[d]
His love endures for ever.
5 who by his understanding[e]
made the heavens,[f]
His love endures for ever.
6 who spread out the earth[g] upon
the waters,[h]
His love endures for ever.
7 who made the great lights[i]—
His love endures for ever.
8 the sun to govern[j] the day,
His love endures for ever.
9 the moon and stars to govern
the night;
His love endures for ever.

10 to him who struck down the
firstborn[k] of Egypt
His love endures for ever.
11 and brought Israel out[l] from
among them
His love endures for ever.
12 with a mighty hand and
outstretched arm;[m]
His love endures for ever.

13 to him who divided the Red
Sea[a][n] asunder
His love endures for ever.
14 and brought Israel through[o]
the midst of it,
His love endures for ever.
15 but swept Pharaoh and his army
into the Red Sea;[p]
His love endures for ever.

16 to him who led his people
through the desert,[q]
His love endures for ever.
17 who struck down great kings,[r]
His love endures for ever.
18 and killed mighty kings[s]—
His love endures for ever.
19 Sihon king of the Amorites[t]
His love endures for ever.
20 and Og king of Bashan—
His love endures for ever.
21 and gave their land[u] as an
inheritance,
His love endures for ever.
22 an inheritance to his servant
Israel;
His love endures for ever.
23 to the One who remembered
us[v] in our low estate
His love endures for ever.
24 and freed us from our
enemies,[w]
His love endures for ever.
25 and who gives food[x] to every
creature.
His love endures for ever.

26 Give thanks to the God of
heaven.
His love endures for ever.

Psalm 137

1 By the rivers of Babylon[a] we
sat and wept[b]
when we remembered Zion.
2 There on the poplars
we hung our harps,
3 for there our captors asked us
for songs,
our tormentors demanded[c]
songs of joy;
they said, "Sing us one of the
songs of Zion!"

4 How can we sing the songs of
the LORD
while in a foreign land?
5 If I forget you, O Jerusalem,
may my right hand forget ⌊its
skill⌋.
6 May my tongue cling to the
roof[d] of my mouth
if I do not remember you,
if I do not consider Jerusalem
my highest joy.

7 Remember, O LORD, what the
Edomites[e] did
on the day Jerusalem fell.[f]
"Tear it down," they cried,
"tear it down to its
foundations!"

8 O Daughter of Babylon, doomed
to destruction,[g]

136:4 *d* Ps 72:18
136:5 *e* Pr 3:19; Jer 51:15 *f* Ge 1:1
136:6 *g* Ge 1:9; Jer 10:12 *h* Ps 24:2
136:7 *i* Ge 1:14,16
136:8 *j* Ge 1:16
136:10 *k* Ex 12:29; Ps 135:8
136:11 *l* Ex 6:6; Ex 12:51
136:12 *m* Dt 4:34; Ps 44:3
136:13 *n* Ex 14:21; Ps 78:13
136:14 *o* Ex 14:22
136:15 *p* Ex 14:27; Ps 135:9
136:16 *q* Ex 13:18
136:17 *r* Ps 135:9-12
136:18 *s* Dt 29:7
136:19 *t* Nu 21:21-25
136:21 *u* Jos 12:1
136:23 *v* Ps 113:7
136:24 *w* Ps 107:2
136:25 *x* Ps 104:27; Ps 145:15
137:1 *a* Eze 1:1,3 *b* Ne 1:4
137:3 *c* Ps 80:6
137:6 *d* Eze 3:26
137:7 *e* Jer 49:7; La 4:21-22; Eze 25:12 *f* Ob 1:11
137:8 *g* Isa 13:1,19; Jer 25:12,26; Jer 50:15; Rev 18:6

a *13* Hebrew *Yam Suph*; that is, Sea of Reeds; also in verse 15

happy is he who repays you
for what you have done to
us—
9 he who seizes your infants
and dashes them[h] against the
rocks.

Psalm 138

Of David.

1 I will praise you, O LORD, with
all my heart;
before the "gods"[a] I will sing
your praise.
2 I will bow down towards your
holy temple[b]
and will praise your name
for your love and your
faithfulness,
for you have exalted above all
things
your name and your word.[c]
3 When I called, you answered
me;
you made me bold and
stout-hearted.[d]
4 May all the kings of the earth[e]
praise you, O LORD,
when they hear the words of
your mouth.
5 May they sing of the ways of
the LORD,
for the glory of the LORD is
great.
6 Though the LORD is on high, he
looks upon the lowly,[f]
but the proud[g] he knows from
afar.
7 Though I walk[h] in the midst of
trouble,
you preserve my life;
you stretch out your hand
against the anger of my
foes,[i]
with your right hand[j] you
save me.[k]
8 The LORD will fulfil ⌊his
purpose⌋[l] for me;
your love, O LORD, endures for
ever—
do not abandon the works of
your hands.[m]

137:9
h 2Ki 8:12; Isa 13:16

138:1
a Ps 95:3; Ps 96:4

138:2
b 1Ki 8:29; Ps 5:7; Ps 28:2
c Isa 42:21

138:3
d Ps 28:7

138:4
e Ps 102:15

138:6
f Ps 113:6; Isa 57:15
g Pr 3:34; Jas 4:6

138:7
h Ps 23:4
i Jer 51:25
j Ps 20:6
k Ps 71:20

138:8
l Ps 57:2; Php 1:6
m Job 10:3,8; Job 14:15

139:1
a Ps 17:3
b Jer 12:3

139:2
c 2Ki 19:27
d Mt 9:4; Jn 2:24

139:3
e Job 31:4

139:4
f Heb 4:13

139:5
g Ps 34:7

139:6
h Job 42:3; Ro 11:33

139:7
i Jer 23:24; Jnh 1:3

139:8
j Am 9:2-3
k Pr 15:11

139:10
l Ps 23:3

139:12
m Job 34:22; Da 2:22

Psalm 139

For the director of music. Of David.
A psalm.

1 O LORD, you have searched me[a]
and you know[b] me.
2 You know when I sit and when I
rise;[c]
you perceive my thoughts[d]
from afar.
3 You discern my going out and
my lying down;
you are familiar with all my
ways.[e]
4 Before a word is on my tongue
you know it completely,[f]
O LORD.

5 You hem me in[g]—behind and
before;
you have laid your hand upon
me.
6 Such knowledge is too
wonderful for me,
too lofty[h] for me to attain.

7 Where can I go from your
Spirit?
Where can I flee[i] from your
presence?
8 If I go up to the heavens,[j] you
are there;
if I make my bed[k] in the
depths,[a] you are there.
9 If I rise on the wings of the
dawn,
if I settle on the far side of
the sea,
10 even there your hand will guide
me,[l]
your right hand will hold me
fast.
11 If I say, "Surely the darkness
will hide me
and the light become night
around me,"
12 even the darkness will not be
dark[m] to you;
the night will shine like the
day,
for darkness is as light to you.

[a]8 Hebrew *Sheol*

13 For you created my inmost
being;[n]
you knit me together[o] in my
mother's womb.
14 I praise you because I am
fearfully and wonderfully
made;
your works are wonderful,[p]
I know that full well.
15 My frame was not hidden from
you
when I was made in the secret
place.
When I was woven together[q] in
the depths of the earth,[r]
16 your eyes saw my unformed
body.
All the days ordained for me
were written in your book
before one of them came to
be.
17 How precious to[b] me are your
thoughts, O God![s]
How vast is the sum of them!
18 Were I to count them,
they would outnumber the
grains of sand.
When I awake,
I am still with you.
19 If only you would slay the
wicked,[t] O God!
Away from me,[u] you
bloodthirsty men!
20 They speak of you with evil
intent;
your adversaries misuse your
name.[v]
21 Do I not hate those[w] who hate
you, O LORD,
and abhor those who rise up
against you?
22 I have nothing but hatred for
them;
I count them my enemies.
23 Search me,[x] O God, and know
my heart;[y]
test me and know my anxious
thoughts.
24 See if there is any offensive
way in me,
and lead me[z] in the way
everlasting.

Psalm 140

For the director of music. A psalm
of David.

1 Rescue me,[a] O LORD, from evil
men;
protect me from men of
violence,[b]
2 who devise evil plans[c] in their
hearts
and stir up war every day.
3 They make their tongues as
sharp as[d] a serpent's;
the poison of vipers[e] is on
their lips. *Selah*
4 Keep me,[f] O LORD, from the
hands of the wicked;[g]
protect me from men of
violence
who plan to trip my feet.
5 Proud men have hidden a snare
for me;
they have spread out the cords
of their net
and have set traps[h] for me
along my path. *Selah*
6 O LORD, I say to you, "You are
my God."[i]
Hear, O LORD, my cry for
mercy.[j]
7 O Sovereign LORD,[k] my strong
deliverer,
who shields my head in the
day of battle—
8 do not grant the wicked[l] their
desires, O LORD;
do not let their plans succeed,
or they will become proud.
Selah
9 Let the heads of those who
surround me
be covered with the trouble
their lips have caused.[m]
10 Let burning coals fall upon
them;
may they be thrown into the
fire,[n]
into miry pits, never to rise.
11 Let slanderers not be
established in the land;

139:13 n Ps 119:73 o Job 10:11
139:14 p Ps 40:5
139:15 q Job 10:11 r Ps 63:9
139:17 s Ps 40:5
139:19 t Isa 11:4 u Ps 119:115
139:20 v Jude 15
139:21 w 2Ch 19:2 Ps 31:6 Ps 119:113 Ps 119:158
139:23 x Job 31:6 Ps 26:2 y Jer 11:20
139:24 z Ps 5:8 Ps 143:10 Pr 15:9
140:1 a Ps 17:13 b Ps 18:48
140:2 c Ps 36:4 Ps 56:6
140:3 d Ps 57:4 e Ps 58:4 Jas 3:8
140:4 f Ps 141:9 g Ps 71:4
140:5 h Ps 31:4 Ps 35:7
140:6 i Ps 16:2 j Ps 116:1 Ps 143:1
140:7 k Ps 28:8
140:8 l Ps 10:2-3
140:9 m Ps 7:16
140:10 n Ps 11:6 Ps 21:9

b 17 Or *concerning*

may disaster hunt down men
of violence.[o]

12 I know that the LORD secures
justice for the poor
and upholds the cause[p] of the
needy.[q]
13 Surely the righteous will praise
your name[r]
and the upright will live[s]
before you.

Psalm 141

A psalm of David.

1 O LORD, I call to you; come
quickly[a] to me.
Hear my voice[b] when I call to
you.
2 May my prayer be set before
you like incense;[c]
may the lifting up of my
hands[d] be like the evening
sacrifice.[e]

3 Set a guard over my mouth,
O LORD;
keep watch over the door of
my lips.
4 Let not my heart be drawn to
what is evil,
to take part in wicked deeds
with men who are evildoers;
let me not eat of their
delicacies.[f]

5 Let a righteous man[a] strike
me—it is a kindness;
let him rebuke me[g]—it is oil
on my head.[h]
My head will not refuse it.

Yet my prayer is ever against
the deeds of evildoers;
6 their rulers will be thrown
down from the cliffs,
and the wicked will learn that
my words were well
spoken.
7 ⌊They will say,⌋ "As one ploughs
and breaks up the earth,
so our bones have been
scattered at the mouth[i] of
the grave."[b]

8 But my eyes are fixed[j] on you,
O Sovereign LORD;
in you I take refuge[k]—do not
give me over to death.
9 Keep me[l] from the snares they
have laid for me,
from the traps set[m] by
evildoers.
10 Let the wicked fall[n] into their
own nets,
while I pass by in safety.

Psalm 142

A *maskil*[a] of David. When he was in
the cave. A prayer.

1 I cry aloud to the LORD;
I lift up my voice to the LORD
for mercy.[a]
2 I pour out my complaint[b]
before him;
before him I tell my trouble.

3 When my spirit grows faint[c]
within me,
it is you who know my way.
In the path where I walk
men have hidden a snare for
me.
4 Look to my right and see;
no-one is concerned for me.
I have no refuge;
no-one cares[d] for my life.

5 I cry to you, O LORD;
I say, "You are my refuge,[e]
my portion[f] in the land of the
living."[g]
6 Listen to my cry,[h]
for I am in desperate need;[i]
rescue me from those who
pursue me,
for they are too strong for me.
7 Set me free from my prison,[j]
that I may praise your name.

Then the righteous will gather
about me
because of your goodness to
me.[k]

[a]5 Or *Let the Righteous One* [b]7 Hebrew *Sheol*
[a]Title: Probably a literary or musical term

140:11 o Ps 34:21
140:12 p Ps 9:4 q Ps 35:10
140:13 r Ps 97:12 s Ps 11:7
141:1 a Ps 22:19 Ps 70:5 b Ps 143:1
141:2 c Rev 5:8 Rev 8:3 d 1Ti 2:8 e Ex 29:39,41
141:4 f Pr 23:6
141:5 g Pr 9:8 h Ps 23:5
141:7 i Ps 53:5
141:8 j Ps 25:15 k Ps 2:12
141:9 l Ps 140:4 m Ps 38:12
141:10 n Ps 35:8
142:1 a Ps 30:8
142:2 b Isa 26:16
142:3 c Ps 140:5 Ps 143:4,7
142:4 d Ps 31:11 Jer 30:17
142:5 e Ps 46:1 f Ps 16:5 g Ps 27:13
142:6 h Ps 17:1 i Ps 79:8 Ps 116:6
142:7 j Ps 146:7 k Ps 13:6

Psalm 143

A psalm of David.

1 O LORD, hear my prayer,
listen to my cry for mercy;[a]
in your faithfulness[b] and
righteousness[c]
come to my relief.
2 Do not bring your servant into
judgment,
for no-one living is righteous[d]
before you.

3 The enemy pursues me,
he crushes me to the ground;
he makes me dwell in darkness
like those long dead.
4 So my spirit grows faint within
me;
my heart within me is
dismayed.[e]
5 I remember[f] the days of long
ago;
I meditate on all your works
and consider what your hands
have done.
6 I spread out my hands[g] to you;
my soul thirsts for you like a
parched land. *Selah*
7 Answer me quickly,[h] O LORD;
my spirit fails.
Do not hide your face[i] from
me
or I will be like those who go
down to the pit.
8 Let the morning bring me word
of your unfailing love,[j]
for I have put my trust in you.
Show me the way[k] I should go,
for to you I lift up my soul.[l]
9 Rescue me from my enemies,[m]
O LORD,
for I hide myself in you.
10 Teach me to do your will,
for you are my God;
may your good Spirit
lead[n] me on level ground.
11 For your name's sake, O LORD,
preserve my life;[o]
in your righteousness,[p] bring
me out of trouble.
12 In your unfailing love, silence
my enemies;

143:1
a Ps 140:6
b Ps 89:1-2
c Ps 71:2
143:2
d Ps 14:3
Ecc 7:20
Ro 3:20
143:4
e Ps 142:3
143:5
f Ps 77:6
143:6
g Ps 63:1
Ps 88:9
143:7
h Ps 69:17
i Ps 27:9
Ps 28:1
143:8
j Ps 46:5
Ps 90:14
k Ps 27:11
l Ps 25:1-2
143:9
m Ps 31:15
143:10
n Ne 9:20
Ps 23:3
Ps 25:4-5
143:11
o Ps 119:25
p Ps 31:1
143:12
q Ps 52:5
Ps 54:5
r Ps 116:16
144:1
a Ps 18:2,34
144:2
b Ps 59:9
Ps 91:2
c Ps 84:9
144:3
d Ps 8:4
Heb 2:6
144:4
e Ps 39:11
Ps 102:11
144:5
f Ps 18:9
Isa 64:1
g Ps 104:32
144:6
h Ps 7:12-13
Ps 18:14
144:7
i Ps 69:2
j Ps 18:44
144:8
k Ps 12:2
144:9
l Ps 33:2-3

destroy all my foes,[q]
for I am your servant.[r]

Psalm 144

Of David.

1 Praise be to the LORD my
Rock,[a]
who trains my hands for war,
my fingers for battle.
2 He is my loving God and my
fortress,[b]
my stronghold and my
deliverer,
my shield,[c] in whom I take
refuge,
who subdues peoples[a] under
me.

3 O LORD, what is man[d] that you
care for him,
the son of man that you think
of him?
4 Man is like a breath;
his days are like a fleeting
shadow.[e]
5 Part your heavens,[f] O LORD,
and come down;
touch the mountains, so that
they smoke.[g]
6 Send forth lightning and scatter
⌊the enemies⌋;
shoot your arrows[h] and rout
them.
7 Reach down your hand from on
high;
deliver me and rescue me
from the mighty waters,[i]
from the hands of foreigners[j]
8 whose mouths are full of lies,[k]
whose right hands are
deceitful.
9 I will sing a new song to you,
O God;
on the ten-stringed lyre[l] I
will make music to you,
10 to the One who gives victory to
kings,

a2 Many manuscripts of the Masoretic Text, Dead Sea Scrolls, Aquila, Jerome and Syriac; most manuscripts of the Masoretic Text *subdues my people*

who delivers his servant
David[m] from the deadly
sword.

11Deliver me and rescue me
from the hands of foreigners
whose mouths are full of lies,
whose right hands are
deceitful.[n]

12Then our sons in their youth
will be like well-nurtured
plants,[o]
and our daughters will be like
pillars
carved to adorn a palace.
13Our barns will be filled
with every kind of provision.
Our sheep will increase by
thousands,
by tens of thousands in our
fields;
14 our oxen will draw heavy
loads.[b]
There will be no breaching of
walls,
no going into captivity,
no cry of distress in our
streets.
15Blessed are the people[p] of
whom this is true;
blessed are the people whose
God is the LORD.

Psalm 145[a]

A psalm of praise. Of David.

1I will exalt you,[a] my God the
King;[b]
I will praise your name for
ever and ever.
2Every day I will praise[c] you
and extol your name for ever
and ever.

3Great is the LORD and most
worthy of praise;
his greatness no-one can
fathom.[d]
4One generation[e] will commend
your works to another;
they will tell of your mighty
acts.

144:10 *m* Ps 18:50
144:11 *n* Ps 12:2; Isa 44:20
144:12 *o* Ps 128:3
144:15 *p* Ps 33:12
145:1 *a* Ps 30:1; Ps 34:1 *b* Ps 5:2
145:2 *c* Ps 71:6
145:3 *d* Job 5:9; Ps 147:5; Ro 11:33
145:4 *e* Isa 38:19
145:5 *f* Ps 119:27
145:6 *g* Ps 66:3 *h* Dt 32:3
145:7 *i* Isa 63:7 *j* Ps 51:14
145:8 *k* Ps 86:15 *l* Ex 34:6; Nu 14:18
145:9 *m* Ps 100:5
145:10 *n* Ps 19:1 *o* Ps 68:26
145:12 *p* Ps 105:1
145:13 *q* 1Ti 1:17; 2Pe 1:11
145:14 *r* Ps 37:24 *s* Ps 146:8

5They will speak of the glorious
splendour of your majesty,
and I will meditate on your
wonderful works.[b][f]
6They will tell of the power of
your awesome works,[g]
and I will proclaim[h] your
great deeds.
7They will celebrate your
abundant goodness[i]
and joyfully sing of your
righteousness.[j]

8The LORD is gracious and
compassionate,[k]
slow to anger and rich in
love.[l]
9The LORD is good[m] to all;
he has compassion on all he
has made.
10All you have made will praise
you,[n] O LORD;
your saints will extol you.[o]
11They will tell of the glory of
your kingdom
and speak of your might,
12so that all men may know of
your mighty acts[p]
and the glorious splendour of
your kingdom.
13Your kingdom is an everlasting
kingdom,[q]
and your dominion endures
through all generations.

The LORD is faithful to all his
promises
and loving towards all he has
made.[c]
14The LORD upholds[r] all those
who fall
and lifts up all[s] who are
bowed down.
15The eyes of all look to you,

[b]14 Or *our chieftains will be firmly established*
[a]This psalm is an acrostic poem, the verses of which (including verse 13b) begin with the successive letters of the Hebrew alphabet.
[b]5 Dead Sea Scrolls and Syriac (see also Septuagint); Masoretic Text *On the glorious splendour of your majesty / and on your wonderful works I will meditate*
[c]13 One manuscript of the Masoretic Text, Dead Sea Scrolls and Syriac (see also Septuagint); most manuscripts of the Masoretic Text do not have the last two lines of verse 13.

and you give them their food[t]
at the proper time.
16 You open your hand
and satisfy the desires[u] of
every living thing.

17 The LORD is righteous in all his
ways
and loving towards all he has
made.
18 The LORD is near[v] to all who
call on him,[w]
to all who call on him in truth.
19 He fulfils the desires[x] of those
who fear him;
he hears their cry[y] and saves
them.
20 The LORD watches over all who
love him,[z]
but all the wicked he will
destroy.[a]

21 My mouth will speak[b] in praise
of the LORD.
Let every creature[c] praise his
holy name
for ever and ever.

Psalm 146

1 Praise the LORD.[a]

Praise the LORD,[a] O my soul.
2 I will praise the LORD all my
life;[b]
I will sing praise to my God as
long as I live.

3 Do not put your trust in
princes,[c]
in mortal men,[d] who cannot
save.
4 When their spirit departs, they
return to the ground;[e]
on that very day their plans
come to nothing.[f]

5 Blessed is he[g] whose help[h] is
the God of Jacob,
whose hope is in the LORD his
God,
6 the Maker of heaven[i] and
earth,
the sea, and everything in
them—
the LORD, who remains
faithful[j] for ever.
7 He upholds the cause of the
oppressed[k]
and gives food to the hungry.[l]
The LORD sets prisoners free,[m]
8 the LORD gives sight to the
blind,[n]
the LORD lifts up those who are
bowed down,
the LORD loves the righteous.
9 The LORD watches over the
alien
and sustains the fatherless and
the widow,[o]
but he frustrates the ways of
the wicked.

10 The LORD reigns[p] for ever,
your God, O Zion, for all
generations.

Praise the LORD.

Psalm 147

1 Praise the LORD.[a]

How good it is to sing praises to
our God,
how pleasant[a] and fitting to
praise him![b]

2 The LORD builds up
Jerusalem;[c]
he gathers the exiles[d] of
Israel.
3 He heals the broken-hearted
and binds up their wounds.

4 He determines the number of
the stars[e]
and calls them each by name.
5 Great is our Lord[f] and mighty
in power;
his understanding has no
limit.[g]
6 The LORD sustains the humble[h]
but casts the wicked to the
ground.

7 Sing to the LORD[i] with
thanksgiving;

145:15 t Ps 104:27; Ps 136:25
145:16 u Ps 104:28
145:18 v Dt 4:7; w Jn 4:24
145:19 x Ps 37:4; y Pr 15:29
145:20 z Ps 31:23; Ps 97:10; a Ps 9:5
145:21 b Ps 71:8; c Ps 65:2
146:1 a Ps 103:1
146:2 b Ps 104:33
146:3 c Ps 118:9; d Isa 2:22
146:4 e Ps 104:29; Ecc 12:7; f Ps 33:10; 1Co 2:6
146:5 g Ps 144:15; Jer 17:7; h Ps 71:5
146:6 i Ps 115:15; Ac 14:15; Rev 14:7; j Ps 117:2
146:7 k Ps 103:6; l Ps 107:9; m Ps 68:6
146:8 n Mt 9:30
146:9 o Ex 22:22; Dt 10:18; Ps 68:5
146:10 p Ex 15:18; Ps 10:16
147:1 a Ps 135:3; b Ps 33:1
147:2 c Ps 102:16; d Dt 30:3
147:4 e Isa 40:26
147:5 f Ps 48:1; g Isa 40:28
147:6 h Ps 146:8-9
147:7 i Ps 33:3

a1 Hebrew *Hallelu Yah*; also in verse 10
a1 Hebrew *Hallelu Yah*; also in verse 20

make music to our God on the
harp.
8He covers the sky with clouds;
he supplies the earth with
rain[j]
and makes grass grow[k] on the
hills.
9He provides food[l] for the
cattle
and for the young ravens[m]
when they call.

10His pleasure is not in the
strength[n] of the horse,[o]
nor his delight in the legs of a
man;
11the LORD delights in those who
fear him,
who put their hope in his
unfailing love.

12Extol the LORD, O Jerusalem;
praise your God, O Zion,
13for he strengthens the bars of
your gates
and blesses your people within
you.
14He grants peace[p] to your
borders
and satisfies you[q] with the
finest of wheat.

15He sends his command[r] to the
earth;
his word runs swiftly.
16He spreads the snow[s] like wool
and scatters the frost[t] like
ashes.
17He hurls down hail like pebbles.
Who can withstand his icy
blast?
18He sends his word[u] and melts
them;
he stirs up his breezes, and
the waters flow.

19He has revealed his word to
Jacob,
his laws and decrees[v] to
Israel.
20He has done this for no other
nation;[w]
they do not know his laws.

Praise the LORD.

147:8 j Job 38:26 k Ps 104:14
147:9 l Ps 104:27-28 Mt 6:26 m Job 38:41
147:10 n 1Sa 16:7 o Ps 33:16-17
147:14 p Isa 60:17-18 q Ps 132:15
147:15 r Job 37:12
147:16 s Job 37:6 t Job 38:29
147:18 u Ps 33:9
147:19 v Dt 33:4 Mal 4:4
147:20 w Dt 4:7-8, 32-34
148:2 a Ps 103:20
148:4 b Ge 1:7 1Ki 8:27
148:5 c Ge 1:1,6 Ps 33:6,9
148:6 d Job 38:33 Ps 89:37 Jer 33:25
148:7 e Ps 74:13-14
148:8 f Ps 147:15-18
148:9 g Isa 44:23 Isa 49:13 Isa 55:12
148:13 h Isa 12:4 i Ps 8:1 Ps 113:4
148:14 j Ps 75:10

Psalm 148

1Praise the LORD.[a]

Praise the LORD from the
heavens,
praise him in the heights
above.
2Praise him, all his angels,[a]
praise him, all his heavenly
hosts.
3Praise him, sun and moon,
praise him, all you shining
stars.
4Praise him, you highest heavens
and you waters above the
skies.[b]
5Let them praise the name of the
LORD,
for he commanded[c] and they
were created.
6He set them in place for ever
and ever;
he gave a decree[d] that will
never pass away.
7Praise the LORD from the earth,
you great sea creatures[e] and
all ocean depths,
8lightning and hail, snow and
clouds,
stormy winds that do his
bidding,[f]
9you mountains and all hills,[g]
fruit trees and all cedars,
10wild animals and all cattle,
small creatures and flying
birds,
11kings of the earth and all
nations,
you princes and all rulers on
earth,
12young men and maidens,
old men and children.
13Let them praise the name of the
LORD,[h]
for his name alone is exalted;
his splendour is above the
earth and the heavens.[i]
14He has raised up for his people
a horn,[b][j]
the praise of all his saints,

a1 Hebrew *Hallelu Yah*; also in verse 14
b14 *Horn* here symbolises strong one, that is, king.

of Israel, the people close to
his heart.

Praise the LORD.

Psalm 149

1Praise the LORD.[a] [a]

Sing to the LORD a new song,
his praise in the assembly[b] of the saints.

2Let Israel rejoice in their Maker;[c]
let the people of Zion be glad in their King.[d]
3Let them praise his name with dancing
and make music to him with tambourine and harp.[e]
4For the LORD takes delight[f] in his people;
he crowns the humble with salvation.[g]
5Let the saints rejoice[h] in this honour
and sing for joy on their beds.[i]

6May the praise of God be in their mouths[j]
and a double-edged[k] sword in their hands,
7to inflict vengeance on the nations
and punishment on the peoples,
8to bind their kings with fetters,
their nobles with shackles of iron,
9to carry out the sentence written against them.[l]
This is the glory of all his saints.[m]

Praise the LORD.

Psalm 150

1Praise the LORD.[a]

Praise God in his sanctuary;[a]
praise him in his mighty heavens.[b]
2Praise him for his acts of power;[c]
praise him for his surpassing greatness.[d]
3Praise him with the sounding of the trumpet,
praise him with the harp and lyre,[e]
4praise him with tambourine and dancing,[f]
praise him with the strings[g] and flute,
5praise him with the clash of cymbals,[h]
praise him with resounding cymbals.

6Let everything[i] that has breath praise the LORD.

Praise the LORD.

a*1* Hebrew *Hallelu Yah*; also in verse 9
a*1* Hebrew *Hallelu Yah*; also in verse 6

149:1
a Ps 33:2
b Ps 35:18
149:2
c Ps 95:6
d Ps 47:6
Zec 9:9
149:3
e Ps 81:2
Ps 150:4
149:4
f Ps 35:27
g Ps 132:16
149:5
h Ps 132:16
i Job 35:10
149:6
j Ps 66:17
k Heb 4:12
Rev 1:16
149:9
l Dt 7:1
Eze 28:26
m Ps 148:14
150:1
a Ps 102:19
b Ps 19:1
150:2
c Dt 3:24
d Ps 145:5-6
150:3
e Ps 149:3
150:4
f Ex 15:20
g Isa 38:20
150:5
h 1Ch 13:8
1Ch 15:16
150:6
i Ps 145:21

PROVERBS

Prologue: Purpose and Theme

1 The proverbs of Solomon[a] son of David, king of Israel:[b]

2 for attaining wisdom and discipline;
for understanding words of insight;
3 for acquiring a disciplined and prudent life,
doing what is right and just and fair;
4 for giving prudence to the simple,[c]
knowledge and discretion[d] to the young—
5 let the wise listen and add to their learning,[e]
and let the discerning get guidance—
6 for understanding proverbs and parables,[f]
the sayings and riddles[g] of the wise.

7 The fear of the LORD[h] is the beginning of knowledge,
but fools[a] despise wisdom and discipline.

Exhortations to Embrace Wisdom

Warning Against Enticement

8 Listen, my son,[i] to your father's instruction
and do not forsake your mother's teaching.[j]
9 They will be a garland to grace your head
and a chain to adorn your neck.[k]

10 My son, if sinners entice[l] you,
do not give in[m] to them.[n]
11 If they say, "Come along with us;
let's lie in wait[o] for someone's blood,
let's waylay some harmless soul;
12 let's swallow them alive, like the grave,[b]
and whole, like those who go down to the pit;[p]
13 we will get all sorts of valuable things
and fill our houses with plunder;
14 throw in your lot with us,
and we will share a common purse"—
15 my son, do not go along with them,
do not set foot[q] on their paths;[r]
16 for their feet rush into sin,
they are swift to shed blood.[s]
17 How useless to spread a net
in full view of all the birds!
18 These men lie in wait for their own blood;
they waylay only themselves!
19 Such is the end of all who go after ill-gotten gain;
it takes away the lives of those who get it.[t]

Warning Against Rejecting Wisdom

20 Wisdom calls aloud[u] in the street,
she raises her voice in the public squares;
21 at the head of the noisy streets[c] she cries out,

1:1 a 1Ki 4:29-34 b Pr 10:1 Pr 25:1 Ecc 1:1
1:4 c Pr 8:5 d Pr 2:10-11 Pr 8:12
1:5 e Pr 9:9
1:6 f Ps 49:4 Ps 78:2 g Nu 12:8
1:7 h Job 28:28 Ps 111:10 Pr 9:10 Pr 15:33 Ecc 12:13
1:8 i Pr 4:1 j Pr 6:20
1:9 k Pr 4:1-9
1:10 l Ge 39:7 m Dt 13:8 n Pr 16:29 Eph 5:11
1:11 o Ps 10:8
1:12 p Ps 28:1
1:15 q Ps 119:101 r Ps 1:1 Pr 4:14
1:16 s Pr 6:18 Isa 59:7
1:19 t Pr 15:27
1:20 u Pr 8:1 Pr 9:1-3, 13-15

[a]7 The Hebrew words rendered *fool* in Proverbs, and often elsewhere in the Old Testament, denote one who is morally deficient. [b]12 Hebrew *Sheol* [c]21 Hebrew; Septuagint / *on the tops of the walls*

in the gateways of the city she
makes her speech:
22 "How long will you simple
ones[d][v] love your simple
ways?
How long will mockers delight
in mockery
and fools hate knowledge?
23 If you had responded to my
rebuke,
I would have poured out my
heart to you
and made my thoughts known
to you.
24 But since you rejected me when
I called[w]
and no-one gave heed when I
stretched out my hand,
25 since you ignored all my advice
and would not accept my
rebuke,
26 I in turn will laugh[x] at your
disaster;
I will mock when calamity
overtakes you[y]—
27 when calamity overtakes you
like a storm,
when disaster sweeps over
you like a whirlwind,
when distress and trouble
overwhelm you.

28 "Then they will call to me but I
will not answer;[z]
they will look for me but will
not find me.[a]
29 Since they hated knowledge
and did not choose to fear the
LORD,[b]
30 since they would not accept my
advice
and spurned my rebuke,[c]
31 they will eat the fruit of their
ways
and be filled with the fruit of
their schemes.[d]
32 For the waywardness of the
simple will kill them,
and the complacency of fools
will destroy them;[e]
33 but whoever listens to me will
live in safety[f]
and be at ease, without fear of
harm."[g]

1:22 v Pr 8:5 Pr 9:4,16
1:24 w Isa 65:12 Isa 66:4 Jer 7:13 Zec 7:11
1:26 x Ps 2:4 y Pr 6:15 Pr 10:24
1:28 z 1Sa 8:18 Isa 1:15 Jer 11:11 Mic 3:4 a Job 27:9 Pr 8:17 Eze 8:18 Zec 7:13
1:29 b Job 21:14
1:30 c ver 25 Ps 81:11
1:31 d Job 4:8 Pr 14:14 Isa 3:11 Jer 6:19
1:32 e Jer 2:19
1:33 f Ps 25:12 Pr 3:23 g Ps 112:8
2:2 a Pr 22:17
2:4 b Job 3:21 Pr 3:14 Mt 13:44
2:5 c Pr 1:7
2:6 d 1Ki 3:9,12 Jas 1:5
2:7 e Pr 30:5-6 f Ps 84:11
2:8 g 1Sa 2:9 Ps 66:9
2:10 h Pr 14:33
2:11 i Pr 4:6 Pr 6:22
2:13 j Pr 4:19 Jn 3:19

Moral Benefits of Wisdom

2 My son, if you accept my
words
and store up my commands
within you,
2 turning your ear to wisdom
and applying your heart to
understanding,[a]
3 and if you call out for insight
and cry aloud for
understanding,
4 and if you look for it as for
silver
and search for it as for hidden
treasure,[b]
5 then you will understand the
fear of the LORD
and find the knowledge of
God.[c]
6 For the LORD gives wisdom,[d]
and from his mouth come
knowledge and
understanding.
7 He holds victory in store for
the upright,
he is a shield[e] to those whose
walk is blameless,[f]
8 for he guards the course of the
just
and protects the way of his
faithful ones.[g]

9 Then you will understand what
is right and just
and fair—every good path.
10 For wisdom will enter your
heart,[h]
and knowledge will be
pleasant to your soul.
11 Discretion will protect you,
and understanding will guard
you.[i]

12 Wisdom will save you from the
ways of wicked men,
from men whose words are
perverse,
13 who leave the straight paths
to walk in dark ways,[j]
14 who delight in doing wrong

d22 The Hebrew word rendered *simple* in Proverbs generally denotes one without moral direction and inclined to evil.

and rejoice in the
perverseness of evil,[k]
15 whose paths are crooked[l]
and who are devious in their
ways.[m]

16 It will save you also from the
adulteress,[n]
from the wayward wife with
her seductive words,
17 who has left the partner of her
youth
and ignored the covenant she
made before God.[a][o]
18 For her house leads down to
death
and her paths to the spirits of
the dead.[p]
19 None who go to her return
or attain the paths of life.[q]

20 Thus you will walk in the ways
of good men
and keep to the paths of the
righteous.
21 For the upright will live in the
land,[r]
and the blameless will remain
in it;
22 but the wicked will be cut off
from the land,[s]
and the unfaithful will be torn
from it.[t]

Further Benefits of Wisdom

3 My son, do not forget my
teaching,[a]
but keep my commands in
your heart,
2 for they will prolong your life
many years[b]
and bring you prosperity.

3 Let love and faithfulness never
leave you;
bind them around your neck,
write them on the tablet of
your heart.[c]
4 Then you will win favour and a
good name
in the sight of God and man.[d]

5 Trust in the LORD[e] with all
your heart
and lean not on your own
understanding;
6 in all your ways acknowledge
him,
and he will make your paths[f]
straight.[a][g]
7 Do not be wise in your own
eyes;[h]
fear the LORD and shun evil.[i]
8 This will bring health to your
body[j]
and nourishment to your
bones.[k]
9 Honour the LORD with your
wealth,
with the firstfruits[l] of all
your crops;
10 then your barns will be filled[m]
to overflowing,
and your vats will brim over
with new wine.[n]
11 My son, do not despise the
LORD's discipline[o]
and do not resent his rebuke,
12 because the LORD disciplines
those he loves,[p]
as a father[b] the son he
delights in.[q]
13 Blessed is the man who finds
wisdom,
the man who gains
understanding,
14 for she is more profitable than
silver
and yields better returns than
gold.[r]
15 She is more precious than
rubies;[s]
nothing you desire can
compare with her.[t]
16 Long life is in her right hand;
in her left hand are riches and
honour.[u]
17 Her ways are pleasant ways,
and all her paths are peace.[v]
18 She is a tree of life[w] to those
who embrace her;
those who lay hold of her will
be blessed.

2:14 *k* Pr 10:23 Jer 11:15
2:15 *l* Ps 125:5 *m* Pr 21:8
2:16 *n* Pr 5:1-6 Pr 6:20-29 Pr 7:5-27
2:17 *o* Mal 2:14
2:18 *p* Pr 7:27
2:19 *q* Ecc 7:26
2:21 *r* Ps 37:29
2:22 *s* Job 18:17 Ps 37:38 *t* Dt 28:63 Pr 10:30
3:1 *a* Pr 4:5
3:2 *b* Pr 4:10
3:3 *c* Ex 13:9 Pr 6:21 Pr 7:3 2Co 3:3
3:4 *d* 1Sa 2:26 Lk 2:52
3:5 *e* Ps 37:3,5
3:6 *f* 1Ch 28:9 *g* Pr 16:3 Isa 45:13
3:7 *h* Ro 12:16 *i* Job 1:1 Pr 16:6
3:8 *j* Pr 4:22 *k* Job 21:24
3:9 *l* Ex 22:29 Ex 23:19 Dt 26:1-15
3:10 *m* Dt 28:8 *n* Joel 2:24
3:11 *o* Job 5:17
3:12 *p* Pr 13:24 Rev 3:19 *q* Dt 8:5 Heb 12:5-6*
3:14 *r* Job 28:15 Pr 8:19 Pr 16:16
3:15 *s* Job 28:18 *t* Pr 8:11
3:16 *u* Pr 8:18
3:17 *v* Pr 16:7 Mt 11:28-30
3:18 *w* Ge 2:9 Pr 11:30 Rev 2:7

[a]17 Or *covenant of her God* [a]6 Or *will direct your paths.* [b]12 Hebrew; Septuagint / *and he punishes*

19By wisdom the LORD laid the
earth's foundations,[x]
by understanding he set the
heavens[y] in place;
20by his knowledge the deeps
were divided,
and the clouds let drop the
dew.

21My son, preserve sound
judgment and discernment,
do not let them out of your
sight;[z]
22they will be life for you,
an ornament to grace your
neck.[a]
23Then you will go on your way in
safety,
and your foot will not
stumble;[b]
24when you lie down,[c] you will
not be afraid;
when you lie down, your
sleep[d] will be sweet.
25Have no fear of sudden disaster
or of the ruin that overtakes
the wicked,
26for the LORD will be your
confidence
and will keep your foot[e] from
being snared.

27Do not withhold good from
those who deserve it,
when it is in your power to
act.
28Do not say to your neighbour,
"Come back later; I'll give it
tomorrow"—
when you now have it with
you.[f]
29Do not plot harm against your
neighbour,
who lives trustfully near you.
30Do not accuse a man for no
reason—
when he has done you no
harm.

31Do not envy[g] a violent man
or choose any of his ways,
32for the LORD detests a perverse
man[h]
but takes the upright into his
confidence.[i]

3:19 x Ps 104:24 y Pr 8:27-29
3:21 z Pr 4:20-22
3:22 a Pr 1:8-9
3:23 b Ps 37:24 Pr 4:12
3:24 c Lev 26:6 Ps 3:5 d Job 11:18
3:26 e 1Sa 2:9
3:28 f Lev 19:13 Dt 24:15
3:31 g Ps 37:1 Pr 24:1-2
3:32 h Pr 11:20 i Job 29:4 Ps 25:14
3:33 j Dt 11:28 Mal 2:2 k Zec 5:4 l Ps 1:3
3:34 m Jas 4:6* 1Pe 5:5*
4:1 a Pr 1:8
4:4 b Pr 7:2
4:5 c Pr 16:16
4:6 d 2Th 2:10
4:7 e Mt 13:44-46 f Pr 23:23
4:8 g 1Sa 2:30 Pr 3:18
4:9 h Pr 1:8-9
4:10 i Pr 3:2

33The LORD's curse[j] is on the
house of the wicked,[k]
but he blesses the home of the
righteous.[l]
34He mocks proud mockers
but gives grace to the
humble.[m]
35The wise inherit honour,
but fools he holds up to
shame.

Wisdom Is Supreme

4 Listen, my sons,[a] to a
father's instruction;
pay attention and gain
understanding.
2I give you sound learning,
so do not forsake my teaching.
3When I was a boy in my
father's house,
still tender, and an only child
of my mother,
4he taught me and said,
"Lay hold of my words with
all your heart;
keep my commands and you
will live.[b]
5Get wisdom,[c] get
understanding;
do not forget my words or
swerve from them.
6Do not forsake wisdom, and she
will protect you;[d]
love her, and she will watch
over you.
7Wisdom is supreme; therefore
get wisdom.
Though it cost all[e] you have,[a]
get understanding.[f]
8Esteem her, and she will exalt
you;
embrace her, and she will
honour you.[g]
9She will set a garland of grace
on your head
and present you with a crown
of splendour.[h]"

10Listen, my son, accept what I
say,
and the years of your life will
be many.[i]

a7 Or *Whatever else you get*

11 I guide[j] you in the way of wisdom
and lead you along straight paths.
12 When you walk, your steps will not be hampered;
when you run, you will not stumble.[k]
13 Hold on to instruction, do not let it go;
guard it well, for it is your life.[l]
14 Do not set foot on the path of the wicked
or walk in the way of evil men.[m]
15 Avoid it, do not travel on it;
turn from it and go on your way.
16 For they cannot sleep till they do evil;[n]
they are robbed of slumber till they make someone fall.
17 They eat the bread of wickedness
and drink the wine of violence.

18 The path of the righteous[o] is like the first gleam of dawn,
shining ever brighter till the full light of day.[p]
19 But the way of the wicked is like deep darkness;[q]
they do not know what makes them stumble.

20 My son, pay attention to what I say;
listen closely to my words.[r]
21 Do not let them out of your sight,[s]
keep them within your heart;
22 for they are life to those who find them
and health to a man's whole body.[t]
23 Above all else, guard your heart,
for it is the wellspring of life.[u]
24 Put away perversity from your mouth;

4:11 j 1Sa 12:23
4:12 k Job 18:7; Pr 3:23
4:13 l Pr 3:22
4:14 m Ps 1:1; Pr 1:15
4:16 n Ps 36:4; Mic 2:1
4:18 o Isa 26:7; p 2Sa 23:4; Da 12:3; Mt 5:14; Php 2:15
4:19 q Job 18:5; Pr 2:13; Isa 59:9-10; Jn 12:35
4:20 r Pr 5:1
4:21 s Pr 3:21; Pr 7:1-2
4:22 t Pr 3:8; Pr 12:18
4:23 u Mt 12:34; Lk 6:45
4:26 v Heb 12:13*
4:27 w Dt 5:32; Dt 28:14
5:1 a Pr 4:20; Pr 22:17
5:3 b Ps 55:21; Pr 2:16; Pr 7:5
5:4 c Ecc 7:26
5:5 d Pr 7:26-27
5:6 e Pr 30:20
5:7 f Pr 7:24
5:8 g Pr 7:1-27

keep corrupt talk far from your lips.
25 Let your eyes look straight ahead,
fix your gaze directly before you.
26 Make level[b] paths for your feet[v]
and take only ways that are firm.
27 Do not swerve to the right or the left;[w]
keep your foot from evil.

Warning Against Adultery

5 My son, pay attention to my wisdom,
listen well to my words[a] of insight,
2 that you may maintain discretion
and your lips may preserve knowledge.
3 For the lips of an adulteress drip honey,
and her speech is smoother than oil;[b]
4 but in the end she is bitter as gall,[c]
sharp as a double-edged sword.
5 Her feet go down to death;
her steps lead straight to the grave.[a][d]
6 She gives no thought to the way of life;
her paths are crooked, but she knows it not.[e]

7 Now then, my sons, listen[f] to me;
do not turn aside from what I say.
8 Keep to a path far from her,[g]
do not go near the door of her house,
9 lest you give your best strength to others
and your years to one who is cruel,
10 lest strangers feast on your wealth

b26 Or *Consider the*
a5 Hebrew *Sheol*

and your toil enrich another man's house.
11 At the end of your life you will groan,
when your flesh and body are spent.
12 You will say, "How I hated discipline!
How my heart spurned correction![h]
13 I would not obey my teachers
or listen to my instructors.
14 I have come to the brink of utter ruin
in the midst of the whole assembly."

15 Drink water from your own cistern,
running water from your own well.
16 Should your springs overflow in the streets,
your streams of water in the public squares?
17 Let them be yours alone,
never to be shared with strangers.
18 May your fountain[i] be blessed,
and may you rejoice in the wife of your youth.[j]
19 A loving doe, a graceful deer[k]—
may her breasts satisfy you always,
may you ever be captivated by her love.
20 Why be captivated, my son, by an adulteress?
Why embrace the bosom of another man's wife?

21 For a man's ways are in full view[l] of the LORD,
and he examines all his paths.[m]
22 The evil deeds of a wicked man ensnare him;[n]
the cords of his sin hold him fast.[o]
23 He will die for lack of discipline,[p]
led astray by his own great folly.

Warnings Against Folly

6 My son, if you have put up security for your neighbour,[a]
if you have struck hands in pledge[b] for another,
2 if you have been trapped by what you said,
ensnared by the words of your mouth,
3 then do this, my son, to free yourself,
since you have fallen into your neighbour's hands:
Go and humble yourself;
press your plea with your neighbour!
4 Allow no sleep to your eyes,
no slumber to your eyelids.[c]
5 Free yourself, like a gazelle from the hand of the hunter,
like a bird from the snare of the fowler.[d]

6 Go to the ant, you sluggard;[e]
consider its ways and be wise!
7 It has no commander,
no overseer or ruler,
8 yet it stores its provisions in summer
and gathers its food at harvest.[f]

9 How long will you lie there, you sluggard?[g]
When will you get up from your sleep?
10 A little sleep, a little slumber,
a little folding of the hands to rest[h]—
11 and poverty[i] will come on you like a bandit
and scarcity like an armed man.[a]

12 A scoundrel and villain,
who goes about with a corrupt mouth,
13 who winks with his eye,[j]
signals with his feet
and motions with his fingers,

5:12 h Pr 1:29; Pr 12:1
5:18 i SS 4:12-15; j Ecc 9:9; Mal 2:14
5:19 k SS 2:9; SS 4:5
5:21 l Ps 119:168; Hos 7:2; m Job 14:16; Job 31:4; Job 34:21; Pr 15:3; Jer 16:17; Jer 32:19; Heb 4:13
5:22 n Ps 9:16; o Nu 32:23; Ps 7:15-16; Pr 1:31-32
5:23 p Job 4:21; Job 36:12
6:1 a Pr 17:18; b Pr 11:15; Pr 22:26-27
6:4 c Ps 132:4
6:5 d Ps 91:3
6:6 e Pr 20:4
6:8 f Pr 10:4
6:9 g Pr 24:30-34
6:10 h Pr 24:33
6:11 i Pr 24:30-34
6:13 j Ps 35:19

a11 Or *like a vagrant / and scarcity like a beggar*

14 who plots evil[k] with deceit in his heart—
he always stirs up dissension.[l]
15Therefore disaster will overtake him in an instant;
he will suddenly be destroyed—without remedy.[m]
16There are six things the LORD hates,
seven that are detestable to him:
17 haughty eyes,
a lying tongue,[n]
hands that shed innocent blood,[o]
18 a heart that devises wicked schemes,
feet that are quick to rush into evil,[p]
19 a false witness[q] who pours out lies
and a man who stirs up dissension among brothers.[r]

Warning Against Adultery

20My son, keep your father's commands
and do not forsake your mother's teaching.[s]
21Bind them upon your heart for ever;
fasten them around your neck.[t]
22When you walk, they will guide you;
when you sleep, they will watch over you;
when you awake, they will speak to you.
23For these commands are a lamp,
this teaching is a light,[u]
and the corrections of discipline are the way to life,
24keeping you from the immoral woman,
from the smooth tongue of the wayward wife.[v]
25Do not lust in your heart after her beauty
or let her captivate you with her eyes,
26for the prostitute reduces you to a loaf of bread,
and the adulteress preys upon your very life.[w]
27Can a man scoop fire into his lap
without his clothes being burned?
28Can a man walk on hot coals
without his feet being scorched?
29So is he who sleeps[x] with another man's wife;[y]
no-one who touches her will go unpunished.
30Men do not despise a thief if he steals
to satisfy his hunger when he is starving.
31Yet if he is caught, he must pay sevenfold,[z]
though it costs him all the wealth of his house.
32But a man who commits adultery[a] lacks judgment;[b]
whoever does so destroys himself.
33Blows and disgrace are his lot,
and his shame will never[c] be wiped away;
34for jealousy[d] arouses a husband's fury,[e]
and he will show no mercy when he takes revenge.
35He will not accept any compensation;
he will refuse the bribe, however great it is.[f]

Warning Against the Adulteress

7 My son,[a] keep my words
and store up my commands within you.
2Keep my commands and you will live;[b]
guard my teachings as the apple of your eye.
3Bind them on your fingers;
write them on the tablet of your heart.[c]

6:14 k Mic 2:1 l ver 16-19
6:15 m 2Ch 36:16
6:17 n Ps 120:2 Pr 12:22 o Dt 19:10 Isa 1:15 Isa 59:7
6:18 p Ge 6:5
6:19 q Ps 27:12 r ver 12-15
6:20 s Pr 1:8
6:21 t Pr 3:3 Pr 7:1-3
6:23 u Ps 19:8 Ps 119:105
6:24 v Pr 2:16 Pr 7:5
6:26 w Pr 7:22-23 Pr 29:3
6:29 x Ex 20:14 y Pr 2:16-19 Pr 5:8
6:31 z Ex 22:1-14
6:32 a Ex 20:14 b Pr 7:7 Pr 9:4,16
6:33 c Pr 5:9-14
6:34 d Nu 5:14 e Ge 34:7
6:35 f Job 31:9-11 SS 8:7
7:1 a Pr 1:8 Pr 2:1
7:2 b Pr 4:4
7:3 c Dt 6:8 Pr 3:3

4Say to wisdom, "You are my
sister,"
and call understanding your
kinsman;
5they will keep you from the
adulteress,
from the wayward wife with
her seductive words.[d]

6At the window of my house
I looked out through the
lattice.
7I saw among the simple,
I noticed among the young
men,
a youth who lacked
judgment.[e]
8He was going down the street
near her corner,
walking along in the direction
of her house
9at twilight,[f] as the day was
fading,
as the dark of night set in.
10Then out came a woman to
meet him,
dressed like a prostitute and
with crafty intent.
11(She is loud[g] and defiant,
her feet never stay at home;
12now in the street, now in the
squares,
at every corner she lurks.)[h]
13She took hold of him[i] and
kissed him
and with a brazen face she
said:[j]

14"I have fellowship offerings[a][k]
at home;
today I fulfilled my vows.
15So I came out to meet you;
I looked for you and have
found you!
16I have covered my bed
with coloured linens from
Egypt.
17I have perfumed my bed[l]
with myrrh,[m] aloes and
cinnamon.
18Come, let's drink deep of love
till morning;
let's enjoy ourselves with
love![n]

7:5
d ver 21
Job 31:9
Pr 2:16
Pr 6:24

7:7
e Pr 1:22
Pr 6:32

7:9
f Job 24:15

7:11
g Pr 9:13
1Ti 5:13

7:12
h Pr 8:1-36
Pr 23:26-28

7:13
i Ge 39:12
j Pr 1:20

7:14
k Lev 7:11-18

7:17
l Est 1:6
Isa 57:7
Eze 23:41
Am 6:4
m Ge 37:25

7:18
n Ge 39:7

7:21
o Pr 5:3

7:22
p Job 18:10

7:23
q Job 15:22
Job 16:13
r Pr 6:26
Ecc 7:26
Ecc 9:12

7:24
s Pr 1:8-9
Pr 5:7
Pr 8:32

7:25
t Pr 5:7-8

7:27
u Pr 2:18
Pr 5:5
Pr 9:18
Rev 22:15

8:1
a Pr 1:20
Pr 9:3

8:3
b Job 29:7

19My husband is not at home;
he has gone on a long journey.
20He took his purse filled with
money
and will not be home till full
moon."
21With persuasive words she led
him astray;
she seduced him with her
smooth talk.[o]
22All at once he followed her
like an ox going to the
slaughter,
like a deer[b] stepping into a
noose[c][p]
23 till an arrow pierces[q] his
liver,
like a bird darting into a snare,
little knowing it will cost him
his life.[r]

24Now then, my sons, listen[s] to
me;
pay attention to what I say.
25Do not let your heart turn to
her ways
or stray into her paths.[t]
26Many are the victims she has
brought down;
her slain are a mighty throng.
27Her house is a highway to the
grave,[d]
leading down to the chambers
of death.[u]

Wisdom's Call

8 Does not wisdom call out?[a]
Does not understanding raise
her voice?
2On the heights along the way,
where the paths meet, she
takes her stand;
3beside the gates leading into the
city,
at the entrances, she cries
aloud:[b]
4"To you, O men, I call out;
I raise my voice to all
mankind.

[a]14 Traditionally *peace offerings* [b]22 Syriac (see also Septuagint); Hebrew *fool*
[c]22 The meaning of the Hebrew for this line is uncertain. [d]27 Hebrew *Sheol*

5 You who are simple,[c] gain
prudence;[d]
you who are foolish, gain
understanding.
6 Listen, for I have worthy things
to say;
I open my lips to speak what
is right.
7 My mouth speaks what is true,[e]
for my lips detest wickedness.
8 All the words of my mouth are
just;
none of them is crooked or
perverse.
9 To the discerning all of them
are right;
they are faultless to those who
have knowledge.
10 Choose my instruction instead
of silver,
knowledge rather than choice
gold,[f]
11 for wisdom is more precious[g]
than rubies,
and nothing you desire can
compare with her.[h]

12 "I, wisdom, dwell together with
prudence;
I possess knowledge and
discretion.[i]
13 To fear the LORD is to hate
evil;[j]
I hate[k] pride and arrogance,
evil behaviour and perverse
speech.
14 Counsel and sound judgment
are mine;
I have understanding and
power.[l]
15 By me kings reign
and rulers[m] make laws that
are just;
16 by me princes govern,
and all nobles who rule on
earth.[a]
17 I love those who love me,[n]
and those who seek me find
me.[o]
18 With me are riches and
honour,[p]
enduring wealth and
prosperity.[q]
19 My fruit is better than fine
gold;
what I yield surpasses choice
silver.[r]
20 I walk in the way of
righteousness,
along the paths of justice,
21 bestowing wealth on those who
love me
and making their treasuries
full.[s]

22 "The LORD brought me forth as
the first of his works,[b,c]
before his deeds of old;
23 I was appointed[d] from eternity,
from the beginning, before the
world began.
24 When there were no oceans, I
was given birth,
when there were no springs
abounding with water;[t]
25 before the mountains were
settled in place,
before the hills, I was given
birth,[u]
26 before he made the earth or its
fields
or any of the dust of the
world.[v]
27 I was there when he set the
heavens in place,[w]
when he marked out the
horizon on the face of the
deep,
28 when he established the clouds
above
and fixed securely the
fountains of the deep,
29 when he gave the sea its
boundary[x]
so that the waters would not
overstep his command,[y]
and when he marked out the
foundations of the earth.[z]
30 Then I was the craftsman at
his side.[a]
I was filled with delight day
after day,

8:5 c Pr 1:22 d Pr 1:4
8:7 e Ps 37:30 Jn 8:14
8:10 f Pr 3:14-15
8:11 g Job 28:17-19 h Pr 3:13-15
8:12 i Pr 1:4
8:13 j Pr 16:6 k Jer 44:4
8:14 l Pr 21:22 Ecc 7:19
8:15 m Da 2:21 Ro 13:1
8:17 n 1Sa 2:30 Ps 91:14 Jn 14:21-24 o Pr 1:28 Jas 1:5
8:18 p Pr 3:16 q Dt 8:18 Mt 6:33
8:19 r Pr 3:13-14 Pr 10:20
8:21 s Pr 24:4
8:24 t Ge 7:11
8:25 u Job 15:7
8:26 v Ps 90:2
8:27 w Pr 3:19
8:29 x Ge 1:9 Job 38:10 Ps 16:6 y Ps 104:9 z Job 38:5
8:30 a Jn 1:1-3

a 16 Many Hebrew manuscripts and Septuagint; most Hebrew manuscripts *and nobles—all righteous rulers* b 22 Or *way;* or *dominion* c 22 Or *The LORD possessed me at the beginning of his work;* or *The LORD brought me forth at the beginning of his work* d 23 Or *fashioned*

rejoicing always in his
presence,
31 rejoicing in his whole world
and delighting in mankind.[b]

32 "Now then, my sons, listen to
me;
blessed are[c] those who keep
my ways.[d]
33 Listen to my instruction and be
wise;
do not ignore it.
34 Blessed is the man who listens[e]
to me,
watching daily at my doors,
waiting at my doorway.
35 For whoever finds me[f] finds
life
and receives favour from the
LORD.[g]
36 But whoever fails to find me
harms himself;[h]
all who hate me love death."

Invitations of Wisdom and of Folly

9 Wisdom has built[a] her
house;
she has hewn out its seven
pillars.
2 She has prepared her meat and
mixed her wine;
she has also set her table.[b]
3 She has sent out her maids, and
she calls[c]
from the highest point of the
city.[d]
4 "Let all who are simple come in
here!"
she says to those who lack
judgment.[e]
5 "Come, eat my food
and drink the wine I have
mixed.[f]
6 Leave your simple ways and
you will live;[g]
walk in the way of
understanding.

7 "Whoever corrects a mocker
invites insult;
whoever rebukes a wicked
man incurs abuse.[h]
8 Do not rebuke a mocker[i] or he
will hate you;
rebuke a wise man and he will
love you.[j]
9 Instruct a wise man and he will
be wiser still;
teach a righteous man and he
will add to his learning.[k]

10 "The fear of the LORD[l] is the
beginning of wisdom,
and knowledge of the Holy
One is understanding.
11 For through me your days will
be many,
and years will be added to
your life.[m]
12 If you are wise, your wisdom
will reward you;
if you are a mocker, you alone
will suffer."

13 The woman Folly is loud;[n]
she is undisciplined and
without knowledge.[o]
14 She sits at the door of her
house,
on a seat at the highest point
of the city,[p]
15 calling out to those who pass
by,
who go straight on their way.
16 "Let all who are simple come in
here!"
she says to those who lack
judgment.
17 "Stolen water is sweet;
food eaten in secret is
delicious![q]"
18 But little do they know that the
dead are there,
that her guests are in the
depths of the grave.[a][r]

Proverbs of Solomon

10 The proverbs of Solomon:[a]
A wise son brings joy to his
father,[b]
but a foolish son grief to his
mother.

8:31 b Ps 16:3; Ps 104:1-30
8:32 c Lk 11:28; d Ps 119:1-2
8:34 e Pr 3:13,18
8:35 f Pr 3:13-18; g Pr 12:2
8:36 h Pr 15:32
9:1 a Eph 2:20-22; 1Pe 2:5
9:2 b Lk 14:16-23
9:3 c Pr 8:1-3; d ver 14
9:4 e Pr 6:32
9:5 f Isa 55:1
9:6 g Pr 8:35
9:7 h Pr 23:9
9:8 i Pr 15:12; j Ps 141:5
9:9 k Pr 1:5,7
9:10 l Job 28:28; Pr 1:7
9:11 m Pr 3:16; Pr 10:27
9:13 n Pr 7:11; o Pr 5:6
9:14 p ver 3
9:17 q Pr 20:17
9:18 r Pr 2:18; Pr 7:26-27
10:1 a Pr 1:1; b Pr 15:20; Pr 29:3

a18 Hebrew *Sheol*

2 Ill-gotten treasures are of no
value,[c]
but righteousness delivers
from death.[d]

3 The LORD does not let the
righteous go hungry[e]
but he thwarts the craving of
the wicked.

4 Lazy hands make a man poor,[f]
but diligent hands bring
wealth.[g]

5 He who gathers crops in
summer is a wise son,
but he who sleeps during
harvest is a disgraceful
son.

6 Blessings crown the head of the
righteous,
but violence overwhelms the
mouth of the wicked.[a][h]

7 The memory of the righteous[i]
will be a blessing,
but the name of the wicked[j]
will rot.[k]

8 The wise in heart accept
commands,
but a chattering fool comes to
ruin.[l]

9 The man of integrity[m] walks
securely,[n]
but he who takes crooked
paths will be found out.[o]

10 He who winks maliciously[p]
causes grief,
and a chattering fool comes to
ruin.

11 The mouth of the righteous is a
fountain of life,[q]
but violence overwhelms the
mouth of the wicked.[r]

12 Hatred stirs up dissension,
but love covers over all
wrongs.[s]

13 Wisdom is found on the lips of
the discerning,[t]
but a rod is for the back of
him who lacks judgment.[u]

10:2 c Pr 21:6 d Pr 11:4,19
10:3 e Mt 6:25-34
10:4 f Pr 19:15 g Pr 12:24 Pr 13:4 Pr 21:5
10:6 h ver 8,11,14
10:7 i Ps 112:6 j Ps 109:13 k Ps 9:6
10:8 l Mt 7:24-27
10:9 m Isa 33:15 n Ps 23:4 o Pr 28:18
10:10 p Ps 35:19
10:11 q Ps 37:30 Pr 13:12,14, 19 r ver 6
10:12 s Pr 17:9 1Co 13:4-7 1Pe 4:8
10:13 t ver 31 u Pr 26:3
10:14 v Pr 18:6,7
10:15 w Pr 18:11 x Pr 19:7
10:16 y Pr 11:18-19
10:17 z Pr 6:23
10:19 a Pr 17:28 Ecc 5:3 Jas 1:19 Jas 3:2-12
10:21 b Pr 5:22-23 Hos 4:1,6,14
10:22 c Ge 24:35 Ps 37:22
10:23 d Pr 2:14 Pr 15:21
10:24 e Isa 66:4 f Ps 145:17-19 Mt 5:6 1Jn 5:14-15
10:25 g Ps 15:5 h Pr 12:3,7 Mt 7:24-27

14 Wise men store up knowledge,
but the mouth of a fool invites
ruin.[v]

15 The wealth of the rich is their
fortified city,[w]
but poverty is the ruin of the
poor.[x]

16 The wages of the righteous
bring them life,
but the income of the wicked
brings them punishment.[y]

17 He who heeds discipline shows
the way to life,[z]
but whoever ignores
correction leads others
astray.

18 He who conceals his hatred has
lying lips,
and whoever spreads slander
is a fool.

19 When words are many, sin is
not absent,
but he who holds his tongue is
wise.[a]

20 The tongue of the righteous is
choice silver,
but the heart of the wicked is
of little value.

21 The lips of the righteous
nourish many,
but fools die for lack of
judgment.[b]

22 The blessing of the LORD brings
wealth,[c]
and he adds no trouble to it.

23 A fool finds pleasure in evil
conduct,[d]
but a man of understanding
delights in wisdom.

24 What the wicked dreads[e] will
overtake him;
what the righteous desire will
be granted.[f]

25 When the storm has swept by,
the wicked are gone,
but the righteous stand firm[g]
for ever.[h]

[a]6 Or *but the mouth of the wicked conceals violence*; also in verse 11

26 As vinegar to the teeth and
smoke to the eyes,
so is a sluggard to those who
send him.[i]

27 The fear of the LORD adds
length to life,[j]
but the years of the wicked
are cut short.[k]

28 The prospect of the righteous is
joy,
but the hopes of the wicked
come to nothing.[l]

29 The way of the LORD is a refuge
for the righteous,
but it is the ruin of those who
do evil.[m]

30 The righteous will never be
uprooted,
but the wicked will not remain
in the land.[n]

31 The mouth of the righteous
brings forth wisdom,[o]
but a perverse tongue will be
cut out.

32 The lips of the righteous know
what is fitting,[p]
but the mouth of the wicked
only what is perverse.

11

The LORD abhors
dishonest scales,[a]
but accurate weights are his
delight.[b]

2 When pride comes, then comes
disgrace,[c]
but with humility comes
wisdom.[d]

3 The integrity of the upright
guides them,
but the unfaithful are
destroyed by their
duplicity.[e]

4 Wealth is worthless in the day
of wrath,[f]
but righteousness delivers
from death.[g]

5 The righteousness of the
blameless makes a straight
way for them,

10:26
i Pr 26:6
10:27
j Pr 9:10-11
k Job 15:32
10:28
l Job 8:13
Pr 11:7
10:29
m Pr 21:15
10:30
n Ps 37:9,28-29
Pr 2:20-22
10:31
o Ps 37:30
10:32
p Ecc 10:12
11:1
a Lev 19:36
Dt 25:13-16
Pr 20:10,23
b Pr 16:11
11:2
c Pr 16:18
d Pr 18:12
Pr 29:23
11:3
e Pr 13:6
11:4
f Eze 7:19
Zep 1:18
g Ge 7:1
Pr 10:2
11:5
h Pr 5:21-23
11:7
i Pr 10:28
11:8
j Pr 21:18
11:10
k Pr 28:12
11:11
l Pr 29:8
11:12
m Pr 14:21
11:13
n Lev 19:16
Pr 20:19
1Ti 5:13
11:14
o Pr 20:18
p Pr 15:22
Pr 24:6
11:15
q Pr 6:1
11:16
r Pr 31:31

but the wicked are brought
down by their own
wickedness.[h]

6 The righteousness of the
upright delivers them,
but the unfaithful are trapped
by evil desires.

7 When a wicked man dies, his
hope perishes;
all he expected from his
power comes to nothing.[i]

8 The righteous man is rescued
from trouble,
and it comes on the wicked
instead.[j]

9 With his mouth the godless
destroys his neighbour,
but through knowledge the
righteous escape.

10 When the righteous prosper, the
city rejoices;[k]
when the wicked perish, there
are shouts of joy.

11 Through the blessing of the
upright a city is exalted,
but by the mouth of the
wicked it is destroyed.[l]

12 A man who lacks judgment
derides his neighbour,[m]
but a man of understanding
holds his tongue.

13 A gossip betrays a confidence,[n]
but a trustworthy man keeps a
secret.

14 For lack of guidance a nation
falls,[o]
but many advisers make
victory sure.[p]

15 He who puts up security[q] for
another will surely suffer,
but whoever refuses to strike
hands in pledge is safe.

16 A kind-hearted woman gains
respect,[r]
but ruthless men gain only
wealth.

17 A kind man benefits himself,
but a cruel man brings trouble
on himself.

18 The wicked man earns
deceptive wages,
but he who sows righteousness
reaps a sure reward.[s]

19 The truly righteous man attains
life,
but he who pursues evil goes
to his death.

20 The LORD detests men of
perverse heart
but he delights in those whose
ways are blameless.[t]

21 Be sure of this: The wicked will
not go unpunished,
but those who are righteous
will go free.[u]

22 Like a gold ring in a pig's snout
is a beautiful woman who
shows no discretion.

23 The desire of the righteous
ends only in good,
but the hope of the wicked
only in wrath.

24 One man gives freely, yet gains
even more;
another withholds unduly, but
comes to poverty.

25 A generous man will prosper;
he who refreshes others will
himself be refreshed.[v]

26 People curse the man who
hoards grain,
but blessing crowns him who
is willing to sell.

27 He who seeks good finds
goodwill,
but evil comes to him who
searches for it.[w]

28 Whoever trusts in his riches
will fall,[x]
but the righteous will thrive
like a green leaf.[y]

29 He who brings trouble on his
family will inherit only
wind,
and the fool will be servant to
the wise.[z]

30 The fruit of the righteous is a
tree of life,[a]
and he who wins souls is wise.

31 If the righteous receive their
due[b] on earth,
how much more the ungodly
and the sinner!

12

1 Whoever loves discipline
loves knowledge,
but he who hates correction is
stupid.[a]

2 A good man obtains favour
from the LORD,
but the LORD condemns a
crafty man.

3 A man cannot be established
through wickedness,
but the righteous cannot be
uprooted.[b]

4 A wife of noble character is her
husband's crown,
but a disgraceful wife is like
decay in his bones.[c]

5 The plans of the righteous are
just,
but the advice of the wicked is
deceitful.

6 The words of the wicked lie in
wait for blood,
but the speech of the upright
rescues them.[d]

7 Wicked men are overthrown
and are no more,[e]
but the house of the righteous
stands firm.[f]

8 A man is praised according to
his wisdom,
but men with warped minds
are despised.

9 Better to be a nobody and yet
have a servant
than pretend to be somebody
and have no food.

10 A righteous man cares for the
needs of his animal,

11:18 s Hos 10:12-13
11:20 t 1Ch 29:17; Ps 119:1; Pr 12:2,22
11:21 u Pr 16:5
11:25 v Mt 5:7; 2Co 9:6-9
11:27 w Est 7:10; Ps 7:15-16
11:28 x Job 31:24-28; Ps 49:6; Ps 52:7; Mk 10:25; 1Ti 6:17; y Ps 1:3; Ps 92:12-14; Jer 17:8
11:29 z Pr 14:19
11:30 a Jas 5:20
11:31 b Pr 13:21; Jer 25:29; 1Pe 4:18
12:1 a Pr 9:7-9; Pr 15:5,10,12, 32
12:3 b Pr 10:25
12:4 c Pr 14:30
12:6 d Pr 14:3
12:7 e Ps 37:36; f Pr 10:25

but the kindest acts of the wicked are cruel.

11 He who works his land will have abundant food,
but he who chases fantasies lacks judgment.[g]

12 The wicked desire the plunder of evil men,
but the root of the righteous flourishes.

13 An evil man is trapped by his sinful talk,[h]
but a righteous man escapes trouble.[i]

14 From the fruit of his lips a man is filled with good things[j]
as surely as the work of his hands rewards him.[k]

15 The way of a fool seems right to him,[l]
but a wise man listens to advice.

16 A fool shows his annoyance at once,
but a prudent man overlooks an insult.[m]

17 A truthful witness gives honest testimony,
but a false witness tells lies.[n]

18 Reckless words pierce like a sword,[o]
but the tongue of the wise brings healing.[p]

19 Truthful lips endure for ever,
but a lying tongue lasts only a moment.

20 There is deceit in the hearts of those who plot evil,
but joy for those who promote peace.

21 No harm befalls the righteous,[q]
but the wicked have their fill of trouble.

22 The LORD detests lying lips,[r]
but he delights in men who are truthful.[s]

23 A prudent man keeps his knowledge to himself,[t]
but the heart of fools blurts out folly.

24 Diligent hands will rule,
but laziness ends in slave labour.[u]

25 An anxious heart weighs a man down,[v]
but a kind word cheers him up.

26 A righteous man is cautious in friendship,[a]
but the way of the wicked leads them astray.

27 The lazy man does not roast[b] his game,
but the diligent man prizes his possessions.

28 In the way of righteousness there is life;[w]
along that path is immortality.

13 A wise son heeds his father's instruction,
but a mocker does not listen to rebuke.[a]

2 From the fruit of his lips a man enjoys good things,[b]
but the unfaithful have a craving for violence.

3 He who guards his lips[c] guards his life,[d]
but he who speaks rashly will come to ruin.[e]

4 The sluggard craves and gets nothing,
but the desires of the diligent are fully satisfied.

5 The righteous hate what is false,
but the wicked bring shame and disgrace.

6 Righteousness guards the man of integrity,
but wickedness overthrows the sinner.[f]

12:11 g Pr 28:19
12:13 h Pr 18:7; i Pr 21:23; 2Pe 2:9
12:14 j Pr 13:2; Pr 15:23; Pr 18:20; k Isa 3:10-11
12:15 l Pr 14:12; Pr 16:2,25; Lk 18:11
12:16 m Pr 29:11
12:17 n Pr 14:5,25
12:18 o Ps 57:4; p Pr 15:4
12:21 q Ps 91:10
12:22 r Pr 6:17; Rev 22:15; s Pr 11:20
12:23 t Pr 10:14; Pr 13:16
12:24 u Pr 10:4
12:25 v Pr 15:13; Isa 50:4
12:28 w Dt 30:15
13:1 a Pr 10:1
13:2 b Pr 12:14
13:3 c Jas 3:2; d Pr 21:23; e Pr 18:7,20-21
13:6 f Pr 11:3,5

a26 Or *man is a guide to his neighbour*
b27 The meaning of the Hebrew for this word is uncertain.

7 One man pretends to be rich,
yet has nothing;
another pretends to be poor,
yet has great wealth.[g]

8 A man's riches may ransom his
life,
but a poor man hears no
threat.

9 The light of the righteous
shines brightly,
but the lamp of the wicked is
snuffed out.[h]

10 Pride only breeds quarrels,
but wisdom is found in those
who take advice.

11 Dishonest money dwindles
away,[i]
but he who gathers money
little by little makes it
grow.

12 Hope deferred makes the heart
sick,
but a longing fulfilled is a tree
of life.

13 He who scorns instruction will
pay for it,[j]
but he who respects a
command is rewarded.

14 The teaching of the wise is a
fountain of life,[k]
turning a man from the snares
of death.[l]

15 Good understanding wins
favour,
but the way of the unfaithful
is hard.[a]

16 Every prudent man acts out of
knowledge,
but a fool exposes his folly.[m]

17 A wicked messenger falls into
trouble,
but a trustworthy envoy
brings healing.[n]

18 He who ignores discipline
comes to poverty and
shame,
but whoever heeds correction
is honoured.[o]

13:7 *g* 2Co 6:10
13:9 *h* Job 18:5; Pr 4:18-19; Pr 24:20
13:11 *i* Pr 10:2
13:13 *j* Nu 15:31; 2Ch 36:16
13:14 *k* Pr 10:11 *l* Pr 14:27
13:16 *m* Pr 12:23
13:17 *n* Pr 25:13
13:18 *o* Pr 15:5,31-32
13:20 *p* Pr 15:31
13:21 *q* Ps 32:10
13:22 *r* Job 27:17; Ecc 2:26
13:24 *s* Pr 19:18; Pr 22:15; Pr 23:13-14; Pr 29:15,17; Heb 12:7
13:25 *t* Ps 34:10; Pr 10:3
14:1 *a* Pr 24:3
14:3 *b* Pr 12:6
14:5 *c* Pr 6:19; Pr 12:17

19 A longing fulfilled is sweet to
the soul,
but fools detest turning from
evil.

20 He who walks with the wise
grows wise,
but a companion of fools
suffers harm.[p]

21 Misfortune pursues the sinner,
but prosperity is the reward
of the righteous.[q]

22 A good man leaves an
inheritance for his
children's children,
but a sinner's wealth is stored
up for the righteous.[r]

23 A poor man's field may produce
abundant food,
but injustice sweeps it away.

24 He who spares the rod hates his
son,
but he who loves him is
careful to discipline him.[s]

25 The righteous eat to their
hearts' content,
but the stomach of the wicked
goes hungry.[t]

14

1 The wise woman builds
her house,[a]
but with her own hands the
foolish one tears hers down.

2 He whose walk is upright fears
the LORD,
but he whose ways are
devious despises him.

3 A fool's talk brings a rod to his
back,
but the lips of the wise protect
them.[b]

4 Where there are no oxen, the
manger is empty,
but from the strength of an ox
comes an abundant harvest.

5 A truthful witness does not
deceive,
but a false witness pours out
lies.[c]

[a]15 Or *unfaithful does not endure*

6 The mocker seeks wisdom and finds none,
but knowledge comes easily to the discerning.

7 Stay away from a foolish man,
for you will not find knowledge on his lips.

8 The wisdom of the prudent is to give thought to their ways,
but the folly of fools is deception.[d]

9 Fools mock at making amends for sin,
but goodwill is found among the upright.

10 Each heart knows its own bitterness,
and no-one else can share its joy.

11 The house of the wicked will be destroyed,
but the tent of the upright will flourish.[e]

12 There is a way that seems right to a man,[f]
but in the end it leads to death.[g]

13 Even in laughter[h] the heart may ache,
and joy may end in grief.

14 The faithless will be fully repaid for their ways,[i]
and the good man rewarded for his.[j]

15 A simple man believes anything,
but a prudent man gives thought to his steps.

16 A wise man fears the LORD and shuns evil,[k]
but a fool is hotheaded and reckless.

17 A quick-tempered man does foolish things,[l]
and a crafty man is hated.

18 The simple inherit folly,
but the prudent are crowned with knowledge.

14:8
d ver 24

14:11
e Pr 3:33
Pr 12:7

14:12
f Pr 12:15
g Pr 16:25

14:13
h Ecc 2:2

14:14
i Pr 1:31
j Pr 12:14

14:16
k Pr 22:3

14:17
l ver 29

14:19
m Pr 11:29

14:20
n Pr 19:4,7

14:21
o Pr 11:12
p Ps 41:1
Pr 19:17

14:25
q ver 5

14:26
r Pr 18:10
Pr 19:23
Isa 33:6

14:27
s Pr 13:14

14:29
t Ecc 7:8-9
Jas 1:19

14:30
u Pr 12:4

19 Evil men will bow down in the presence of the good,
and the wicked at the gates of the righteous.[m]

20 The poor are shunned even by their neighbours,
but the rich have many friends.[n]

21 He who despises his neighbour sins,[o]
but blessed is he who is kind to the needy.[p]

22 Do not those who plot evil go astray?
But those who plan what is good find[a] love and faithfulness.

23 All hard work brings a profit,
but mere talk leads only to poverty.

24 The wealth of the wise is their crown,
but the folly of fools yields folly.

25 A truthful witness saves lives,
but a false witness is deceitful.[q]

26 He who fears the LORD has a secure fortress,[r]
and for his children it will be a refuge.

27 The fear of the LORD is a fountain of life,
turning a man from the snares of death.[s]

28 A large population is a king's glory,
but without subjects a prince is ruined.

29 A patient man has great understanding,
but a quick-tempered man displays folly.[t]

30 A heart at peace gives life to the body,
but envy rots the bones.[u]

[a] 22 Or *show*

[31]He who oppresses the poor
shows contempt for their Maker,[v]
but whoever is kind to the needy honours God.

[32]When calamity comes, the wicked are brought down,[w]
but even in death the righteous have a refuge.[x]

[33]Wisdom reposes in the heart of the discerning[y]
and even among fools she lets herself be known.[b]

[34]Righteousness exalts a nation,[z]
but sin is a disgrace to any people.

[35]A king delights in a wise servant,
but a shameful servant incurs his wrath.[a]

15 A gentle answer turns away wrath,[a]
but a harsh word stirs up anger.

[2]The tongue of the wise commends knowledge,
but the mouth of the fool gushes folly.[b]

[3]The eyes[c] of the LORD are everywhere,[d]
keeping watch on the wicked and the good.[e]

[4]The tongue that brings healing is a tree of life,
but a deceitful tongue crushes the spirit.

[5]A fool spurns his father's discipline,
but whoever heeds correction shows prudence.[f]

[6]The house of the righteous contains great treasure,[g]
but the income of the wicked brings them trouble.

[7]The lips of the wise spread knowledge;
not so the hearts of fools.

[8]The LORD detests the sacrifice of the wicked,[h]
but the prayer of the upright pleases him.[i]

[9]The LORD detests the way of the wicked
but he loves those who pursue righteousness.[j]

[10]Stern discipline awaits him who leaves the path;
he who hates correction will die.[k]

[11]Death and Destruction[a] lie open before the LORD[l]—
how much more the hearts of men![m]

[12]A mocker resents correction;[n]
he will not consult the wise.

[13]A happy heart makes the face cheerful,
but heartache crushes the spirit.[o]

[14]The discerning heart seeks knowledge,[p]
but the mouth of a fool feeds on folly.

[15]All the days of the oppressed are wretched,
but the cheerful heart has a continual feast.[q]

[16]Better a little with the fear of the LORD
than great wealth with turmoil.[r]

[17]Better a meal of vegetables where there is love
than a fattened calf with hatred.[s]

[18]A hot-tempered man stirs up dissension,[t]
but a patient man calms a quarrel.[u]

[19]The way of the sluggard is blocked with thorns,[v]

14:31 *v* Pr 17:5
14:32 *w* Pr 6:15 *x* Job 13:15; 2Ti 4:18
14:33 *y* Pr 2:6-10
14:34 *z* Pr 11:11
14:35 *a* Mt 24:45-51; Mt 25:14-30
15:1 *a* Pr 25:15
15:2 *b* Pr 12:23
15:3 *c* 2Ch 16:9 *d* Job 31:4; Heb 4:13 *e* Job 34:21; Jer 16:17
15:5 *f* Pr 13:1
15:6 *g* Pr 8:21
15:8 *h* Pr 21:27; Isa 1:11; Jer 6:20 *i* ver 29
15:9 *j* Pr 21:21; 1Ti 6:11
15:10 *k* Pr 1:31-32; Pr 5:12
15:11 *l* Job 26:6; Ps 139:8 *m* 2Ch 6:30; Ps 44:21
15:12 *n* Am 5:10
15:13 *o* Pr 12:25; Pr 17:22; Pr 18:14
15:14 *p* Pr 18:15
15:15 *q* ver 13
15:16 *r* Ps 37:16-17; Pr 16:8; 1Ti 6:6
15:17 *s* Pr 17:1
15:18 *t* Pr 26:21 *u* Ge 13:8
15:19 *v* Pr 22:5

b33 Hebrew; Septuagint and Syriac / *but in the heart of fools she is not known* a11 Hebrew *Sheol and Abaddon*

but the path of the upright is a highway.

20A wise son brings joy to his father,[w]
but a foolish man despises his mother.

21Folly delights a man who lacks judgment,[x]
but a man of understanding keeps a straight course.

22Plans fail for lack of counsel,
but with many advisers they succeed.[y]

23A man finds joy in giving an apt reply[z]—
and how good is a timely word![a]

24The path of life leads upward for the wise
to keep him from going down to the grave.[b]

25The LORD tears down the proud man's house[b]
but he keeps the widow's boundaries intact.[c]

26The LORD detests the thoughts of the wicked,[d]
but those of the pure are pleasing to him.

27A greedy man brings trouble to his family,
but he who hates bribes will live.[e]

28The heart of the righteous weighs its answers,[f]
but the mouth of the wicked gushes evil.

29The LORD is far from the wicked
but he hears the prayer of the righteous.[g]

30A cheerful look brings joy to the heart,
and good news gives health to the bones.

31He who listens to a life-giving rebuke
will be at home among the wise.[h]

32He who ignores discipline despises himself,[i]
but whoever heeds correction gains understanding.

33The fear of the LORD[j] teaches a man wisdom,[c]
and humility comes before honour.[k]

16 To man belong the plans of the heart,
but from the LORD comes the reply of the tongue.[a]

2All a man's ways seem innocent to him,
but motives are weighed by the LORD.[b]

3Commit to the LORD whatever you do,
and your plans will succeed.[c]

4The LORD works out everything for his own ends[d]—
even the wicked for a day of disaster.[e]

5The LORD detests all the proud of heart.[f]
Be sure of this: They will not go unpunished.[g]

6Through love and faithfulness sin is atoned for;
through the fear of the LORD a man avoids evil.[h]

7When a man's ways are pleasing to the LORD,
he makes even his enemies live at peace with him.

8Better a little with righteousness
than much gain[i] with injustice.

9In his heart a man plans his course,
but the LORD determines his steps.[j]

15:20 w Pr 10:1
15:21 x Pr 10:23
15:22 y Pr 11:14
15:23 z Pr 12:14 a Pr 25:11
15:25 b Pr 12:7 c Dt 19:14 Ps 68:5-6 Pr 23:10-11
15:26 d Pr 6:16
15:27 e Ex 23:8 Isa 33:15
15:28 f 1Pe 3:15
15:29 g Ps 145:18-19
15:31 h ver 5
15:32 i Pr 1:7
15:33 j Pr 1:7 k Pr 18:12
16:1 a Pr 19:21
16:2 b Pr 21:2
16:3 c Ps 37:5-6 Pr 3:5-6
16:4 d Isa 43:7 e Ro 9:22
16:5 f Pr 6:16 g Pr 11:20-21
16:6 h Pr 14:16
16:8 i Ps 37:16
16:9 j Jer 10:23

b24 Hebrew *Sheol* c33 Or *Wisdom teaches the fear of the LORD*

10 The lips of a king speak as an
oracle,
and his mouth should not
betray justice.

11 Honest scales and balances are
from the LORD;
all the weights in the bag are
of his making.[k]

12 Kings detest wrongdoing,
for a throne is established
through righteousness.[l]

13 Kings take pleasure in honest
lips;
they value a man who speaks
the truth.[m]

14 A king's wrath is a messenger
of death,[n]
but a wise man will appease it.

15 When a king's face brightens, it
means life;[o]
his favour is like a rain cloud
in spring.

16 How much better to get wisdom
than gold,
to choose understanding
rather than silver![p]

17 The highway of the upright
avoids evil;
he who guards his way guards
his life.

18 Pride goes before destruction,
a haughty spirit before a
fall.[q]

19 Better to be lowly in spirit and
among the oppressed
than to share plunder with the
proud.

20 Whoever gives heed to
instruction prospers,
and blessed is he who trusts in
the LORD.[r]

21 The wise in heart are called
discerning,
and pleasant words promote
instruction.[a][s]

22 Understanding is a fountain of
life to those who have it,[t]
but folly brings punishment to
fools.

23 A wise man's heart guides his
mouth,
and his lips promote
instruction.[b]

24 Pleasant words are a
honeycomb,
sweet to the soul and healing
to the bones.[u]

25 There is a way that seems right
to a man,[v]
but in the end it leads to
death.[w]

26 The labourer's appetite works
for him;
his hunger drives him on.

27 A scoundrel plots evil,
and his speech is like a
scorching fire.[x]

28 A perverse man stirs up
dissension,[y]
and a gossip separates close
friends.[z]

29 A violent man entices his
neighbour
and leads him down a path
that is not good.[a]

30 He who winks with his eye is
plotting perversity;
he who purses his lips is bent
on evil.

31 Grey hair is a crown of
splendour;[b]
it is attained by a righteous
life.

32 Better a patient man than a
warrior,
a man who controls his temper
than one who takes a city.

33 The lot is cast into the lap,
but its every decision is from
the LORD.[c]

16:11 *k* Pr 11:1
16:12 *l* Pr 25:5
16:13 *m* Pr 14:35
16:14 *n* Pr 19:12
16:15 *o* Job 29:24
16:16 *p* Pr 8:10,19
16:18 *q* Pr 11:2; Pr 18:12
16:20 *r* Ps 2:12; Ps 34:8; Pr 19:8; Jer 17:7
16:21 *s* ver 23
16:22 *t* Pr 13:14
16:24 *u* Pr 24:13-14
16:25 *v* Pr 12:15; *w* Pr 14:12
16:27 *x* Jas 3:6
16:28 *y* Pr 15:18; *z* Pr 17:9
16:29 *a* Pr 1:10; Pr 12:26
16:31 *b* Pr 20:29
16:33 *c* Pr 18:18; Pr 29:26

[a] *21* Or *words make a man persuasive*
[b] *23* Or *mouth / and makes his lips persuasive*

17 Better a dry crust with peace and quiet
than a house full of feasting,[a] with strife.[a]

2 A wise servant will rule over a disgraceful son,
and will share the inheritance as one of the brothers.

3 The crucible for silver and the furnace for gold,[b]
but the LORD tests the heart.[c]

4 A wicked man listens to evil lips;
a liar pays attention to a malicious tongue.

5 He who mocks the poor shows contempt for their Maker;[d]
whoever gloats over disaster[e] will not go unpunished.[f]

6 Children's children[g] are a crown to the aged,
and parents are the pride of their children.

7 Arrogant[b] lips are unsuited to a fool—
how much worse lying lips to a ruler!

8 A bribe is a charm to the one who gives it;
wherever he turns, he succeeds.

9 He who covers over an offence promotes love,[h]
but whoever repeats the matter separates close friends.[i]

10 A rebuke impresses a man of discernment
more than a hundred lashes a fool.

11 An evil man is bent only on rebellion;
a merciless official will be sent against him.

12 Better to meet a bear robbed of her cubs
than a fool in his folly.

13 If a man pays back evil[j] for good,
evil will never leave his house.

14 Starting a quarrel is like breaching a dam;
so drop the matter before a dispute breaks out.[k]

15 Acquitting the guilty and condemning the innocent[l]—
the LORD detests them both.[m]

16 Of what use is money in the hand of a fool,
since he has no desire to get wisdom?[n]

17 A friend loves at all times,
and a brother is born for adversity.

18 A man lacking in judgment strikes hands in pledge
and puts up security for his neighbour.[o]

19 He who loves a quarrel loves sin;
he who builds a high gate invites destruction.

20 A man of perverse heart does not prosper;
he whose tongue is deceitful falls into trouble.

21 To have a fool for a son brings grief;
there is no joy for the father of a fool.[p]

22 A cheerful heart is good medicine,
but a crushed spirit dries up the bones.[q]

23 A wicked man accepts a bribe[r] in secret
to pervert the course of justice.

24 A discerning man keeps wisdom in view,
but a fool's eyes[s] wander to the ends of the earth.

25 A foolish son brings grief to his father
and bitterness to the one who bore him.[t]

17:1 a Pr 15:16,17
17:3 b Pr 27:21 c 1Ch 29:17; Ps 26:2; Jer 17:10
17:5 d Pr 14:31 e Job 31:29 f Ob 1:12
17:6 g Pr 13:22
17:9 h Pr 10:12 i Pr 16:28
17:13 j Ps 109:4-5; Jer 18:20
17:14 k Pr 20:3
17:15 l Pr 18:5 m Ex 23:6-7; Isa 5:23
17:16 n Pr 23:23
17:18 o Pr 6:1-5; Pr 11:15; Pr 22:26-27
17:21 p Pr 10:1
17:22 q Ps 22:15; Pr 15:13
17:23 r Ex 23:8
17:24 s Ecc 2:14
17:25 t Pr 10:1

a1 Hebrew *sacrifices* b7 Or *Eloquent*

26 It is not good to punish an
innocent man,[u]
or to flog officials for their
integrity.

27 A man of knowledge uses words
with restraint,
and a man of understanding is
even-tempered.[v]

28 Even a fool is thought wise if he
keeps silent,
and discerning if he holds his
tongue.[w]

18 An unfriendly man
pursues selfish ends;
he defies all sound judgment.

2 A fool finds no pleasure in
understanding
but delights in airing his own
opinions.[a]

3 When wickedness comes, so
does contempt,
and with shame comes
disgrace.

4 The words of a man's mouth are
deep waters,
but the fountain of wisdom is
a bubbling brook.

5 It is not good to be partial to
the wicked[b]
or to deprive the innocent of
justice.[c]

6 A fool's lips bring him strife,
and his mouth invites a
beating.

7 A fool's mouth is his undoing,
and his lips are a snare[d] to
his soul.[e]

8 The words of a gossip are like
choice morsels;
they go down to a man's
inmost parts.[f]

9 One who is slack in his work
is brother to one who
destroys.[g]

10 The name of the LORD is a
strong tower;[h]
the righteous run to it and are
safe.

11 The wealth of the rich is their
fortified city;[i]
they imagine it an unscalable
wall.

12 Before his downfall a man's
heart is proud,
but humility comes before
honour.[j]

13 He who answers before
listening—
that is his folly and his
shame.[k]

14 A man's spirit sustains him in
sickness,
but a crushed spirit who can
bear?[l]

15 The heart of the discerning
acquires knowledge;[m]
the ears of the wise seek it
out.

16 A gift[n] opens the way for the
giver
and ushers him into the
presence of the great.

17 The first to present his case
seems right,
till another comes forward and
questions him.

18 Casting the lot settles disputes[o]
and keeps strong opponents
apart.

19 An offended brother is more
unyielding than a fortified
city,
and disputes are like the
barred gates of a citadel.

20 From the fruit of his mouth a
man's stomach is filled;
with the harvest from his lips
he is satisfied.[p]

21 The tongue has the power of
life and death,
and those who love it will eat
its fruit.[q]

22 He who finds a wife finds what
is good[r]
and receives favour from the
LORD.[s]

17:26 u Pr 18:5
17:27 v Pr 14:29; Jas 1:19
17:28 w Job 13:5
18:2 a Pr 12:23
18:5 b Lev 19:15; Pr 24:23-25; Pr 28:21; c Ps 82:2; Pr 17:15
18:7 d Ps 140:9; e Ps 64:8; Pr 10:14; Pr 12:13; Pr 13:3; Ecc 10:12
18:8 f Pr 26:22
18:9 g Pr 28:24
18:10 h 2Sa 22:3; Ps 61:3
18:11 i Pr 10:15
18:12 j Pr 11:2; Pr 15:33; Pr 16:18
18:13 k Pr 20:25; Jn 7:51
18:14 l Pr 15:13; Pr 17:22
18:15 m Pr 15:14
18:16 n Ge 32:20
18:18 o Pr 16:33
18:20 p Pr 12:14
18:21 q Pr 13:2-3; Mt 12:37
18:22 r Pr 12:4; s Pr 19:14; Pr 31:10

23 A poor man pleads for mercy,
but a rich man answers
harshly.

24 A man of many companions
may come to ruin,
but there is a friend who
sticks closer than a
brother.[t]

19 Better a poor man whose
walk is blameless
than a fool whose lips are
perverse.[a]

2 It is not good to have zeal
without knowledge,
nor to be hasty and miss the
way.[b]

3 A man's own folly ruins his life,
yet his heart rages against the
LORD.

4 Wealth brings many friends,
but a poor man's friend
deserts him.[c]

5 A false witness[d] will not go
unpunished,
and he who pours out lies will
not go free.[e]

6 Many curry favour with a
ruler,[f]
and everyone is the friend of a
man who gives gifts.[g]

7 A poor man is shunned by all
his relatives—
how much more do his friends
avoid him!
Though he pursues them with
pleading,
they are nowhere to be
found.[a][h]

8 He who gets wisdom loves his
own soul;
he who cherishes
understanding prospers.[i]

9 A false witness will not go
unpunished,
and he who pours out lies will
perish.[j]

10 It is not fitting for a fool[k] to
live in luxury—
how much worse for a slave to
rule over princes![l]

11 A man's wisdom gives him
patience;[m]
it is to his glory to overlook an
offence.

12 A king's rage is like the roar of
a lion,
but his favour is like dew[n] on
the grass.[o]

13 A foolish son is his father's
ruin,[p]
and a quarrelsome wife is like
a constant dripping.[q]

14 Houses and wealth are inherited
from parents,[r]
but a prudent wife is from the
LORD.[s]

15 Laziness brings on deep sleep,
and the shiftless man goes
hungry.[t]

16 He who obeys instructions
guards his life,
but he who is contemptuous of
his ways will die.[u]

17 He who is kind to the poor
lends to the LORD,
and he will reward him for
what he has done.[v]

18 Discipline your son, for in that
there is hope;
do not be a willing party to his
death.[w]

19 A hot-tempered man must pay
the penalty;
if you rescue him, you will
have to do it again.

20 Listen to advice and accept
instruction,[x]
and in the end you will be
wise.[y]

21 Many are the plans in a man's
heart,
but it is the LORD's purpose
that prevails.[z]

18:24
t Pr 17:17; Jn 15:13-15

19:1
a Pr 28:6

19:2
b Pr 29:20

19:4
c Pr 14:20

19:5
d Ex 23:1
e Dt 19:19; Pr 21:28

19:6
f Pr 29:26
g Pr 17:8; Pr 18:16

19:7
h ver 4; Ps 38:11

19:8
i Pr 16:20

19:9
j ver 5

19:10
k Pr 26:1
l Pr 30:21-23; Ecc 10:5-7

19:11
m Pr 16:32

19:12
n Ps 133:3
o Pr 16:14-15

19:13
p Pr 10:1
q Pr 21:9

19:14
r 2Co 12:14
s Pr 18:22

19:15
t Pr 6:9; Pr 10:4

19:16
u Pr 16:17; Lk 10:28

19:17
v Mt 10:42; 2Co 9:6-8

19:18
w Pr 13:24; Pr 23:13-14

19:20
x Pr 4:1
y Pr 12:15

19:21
z Ps 33:11; Pr 16:9; Isa 14:24,27

a7 The meaning of the Hebrew for this sentence is uncertain.

22 What a man desires is unfailing love;[b]
better to be poor than a liar.

23 The fear of the LORD leads to life:
Then one rests content,
untouched by trouble.[a]

24 The sluggard buries his hand in the dish;
he will not even bring it back to his mouth![b]

25 Flog a mocker, and the simple will learn prudence;
rebuke a discerning man, and he will gain knowledge.[c]

26 He who robs his father and drives out his mother[d]
is a son who brings shame and disgrace.

27 Stop listening to instruction, my son,
and you will stray from the words of knowledge.

28 A corrupt witness mocks at justice,
and the mouth of the wicked gulps down evil.[e]

29 Penalties are prepared for mockers,
and beatings for the backs of fools.[f]

20

1 Wine is a mocker and beer a brawler;
whoever is led astray by them is not wise.[a]

2 A king's wrath is like the roar of a lion;[b]
he who angers him forfeits his life.[c]

3 It is to a man's honour to avoid strife,
but every fool is quick to quarrel.[d]

4 A sluggard does not plough in season;
so at harvest time he looks but finds nothing.

19:23 a Ps 25:13; Pr 12:21; 1Ti 4:8
19:24 b Pr 26:15
19:25 c Pr 9:9; Pr 21:11
19:26 d Pr 28:24
19:28 e Job 15:16
19:29 f Pr 26:3
20:1 a Pr 31:4
20:2 b Pr 19:12; c Pr 8:36
20:3 d Pr 17:14
20:6 e Ps 12:1
20:7 f Ps 37:25-26; Ps 112:2
20:8 g ver 26; Pr 25:4-5
20:9 h 1Ki 8:46; Ecc 7:20; 1Jn 1:8
20:10 i ver 23; Pr 11:1
20:11 j Mt 7:16
20:12 k Ps 94:9
20:13 l Pr 6:11; Pr 19:15
20:16 m Ex 22:26; n Pr 27:13

5 The purposes of a man's heart are deep waters,
but a man of understanding draws them out.

6 Many a man claims to have unfailing love,
but a faithful man who can find?[e]

7 The righteous man leads a blameless life;
blessed are his children after him.[f]

8 When a king sits on his throne to judge,
he winnows out all evil with his eyes.[g]

9 Who can say, "I have kept my heart pure;
I am clean and without sin"?[h]

10 Differing weights and differing measures—
the LORD detests them both.[i]

11 Even a child is known by his actions,
by whether his conduct is pure[j] and right.

12 Ears that hear and eyes that see—
the LORD has made them both.[k]

13 Do not love sleep or you will grow poor;[l]
stay awake and you will have food to spare.

14 "It's no good, it's no good!" says the buyer;
then off he goes and boasts about his purchase.

15 Gold there is, and rubies in abundance,
but lips that speak knowledge are a rare jewel.

16 Take the garment of one who puts up security for a stranger;
hold it in pledge[m] if he does it for a wayward woman.[n]

b22 Or *A man's greed is his shame*

[17]Food gained by fraud tastes
sweet to a man,[o]
but he ends up with a mouth
full of gravel.

[18]Make plans by seeking advice;
if you wage war, obtain
guidance.[p]

[19]A gossip betrays a confidence;[q]
so avoid a man who talks too
much.

[20]If a man curses his father or
mother,[r]
his lamp will be snuffed out in
pitch darkness.[s]

[21]An inheritance quickly gained
at the beginning
will not be blessed at the end.

[22]Do not say, "I'll pay you back
for this wrong!"[t]
Wait for the LORD, and he will
deliver you.[u]

[23]The LORD detests differing
weights,
and dishonest scales do not
please him.[v]

[24]A man's steps are directed by
the LORD.
How then can anyone
understand his own way?[w]

[25]It is a trap for a man to
dedicate something rashly
and only later to consider his
vows.[x]

[26]A wise king winnows out the
wicked;
he drives the threshing wheel
over them.[y]

[27]The lamp of the LORD searches
the spirit of a man;[a]
it searches out his inmost
being.

[28]Love and faithfulness keep a
king safe;
through love his throne is
made secure.[z]

[29]The glory of young men is their
strength,
grey hair the splendour of the
old.[a]

[30]Blows and wounds cleanse[b]
away evil,
and beatings purge the inmost
being.

20:17 o Pr 9:17
20:18 p Pr 11:14; Pr 24:6
20:19 q Pr 11:13
20:20 r Pr 30:11; s Ex 21:17; Job 18:5
20:22 t Pr 24:29; u Ro 12:19
20:23 v ver 10
20:24 w Jer 10:23
20:25 x Ecc 5:2,4-5
20:26 y ver 8
20:28 z Pr 29:14
20:29 a Pr 16:31
20:30 b Pr 22:15
21:2 a Pr 16:2; Pr 24:12; Lk 16:15
21:3 b 1Sa 15:22; Pr 15:8; Isa 1:11; Hos 6:6; Mic 6:6-8
21:4 c Pr 6:17
21:5 d Pr 10:4; Pr 28:22
21:6 e 2Pe 2:3
21:8 f Pr 2:15
21:9 g Pr 25:24

21

The king's heart is in the
hand of the LORD;
he directs it like a
watercourse wherever he
pleases.

[2]All a man's ways seem right to
him,
but the LORD weighs the
heart.[a]

[3]To do what is right and just
is more acceptable to the LORD
than sacrifice.[b]

[4]Haughty eyes[c] and a proud
heart,
the lamp of the wicked, are
sin!

[5]The plans of the diligent lead to
profit[d]
as surely as haste leads to
poverty.

[6]A fortune made by a lying
tongue
is a fleeting vapour and a
deadly snare.[a][e]

[7]The violence of the wicked will
drag them away,
for they refuse to do what is
right.

[8]The way of the guilty is
devious,[f]
but the conduct of the
innocent is upright.

[9]Better to live on a corner of the
roof
than share a house with a
quarrelsome wife.[g]

[10]The wicked man craves evil;
his neighbour gets no mercy
from him.

[a]27 Or *The spirit of man is the LORD's lamp*
[a]6 Some Hebrew manuscripts, Septuagint and Vulgate; most Hebrew manuscripts *vapour for those who seek death*

[11]When a mocker is punished, the
simple gain wisdom;
when a wise man is instructed,
he gets knowledge.[h]

[12]The Righteous One[b] takes note
of the house of the wicked
and brings the wicked to
ruin.[i]

[13]If a man shuts his ears to the
cry of the poor,
he too will cry out and not be
answered.[j]

[14]A gift given in secret soothes
anger,
and a bribe concealed in the
cloak pacifies great
wrath.[k]

[15]When justice is done, it brings
joy to the righteous
but terror to evildoers.[l]

[16]A man who strays from the
path of understanding
comes to rest in the company
of the dead.[m]

[17]He who loves pleasure will
become poor;
whoever loves wine and oil
will never be rich.[n]

[18]The wicked become a ransom[o]
for the righteous,
and the unfaithful for the
upright.

[19]Better to live in a desert
than with a quarrelsome and
ill-tempered wife.[p]

[20]In the house of the wise are
stores of choice food and
oil,
but a foolish man devours all
he has.

[21]He who pursues righteousness
and love
finds life, prosperity[c] and
honour.[q]

[22]A wise man attacks the city of
the mighty[r]
and pulls down the stronghold
in which they trust.

[23]He who guards his mouth[s] and
his tongue
keeps himself from calamity.[t]

[24]The proud and arrogant[u]
man—"Mocker" is his
name;
he behaves with overweening
pride.

[25]The sluggard's craving will be
the death of him,[v]
because his hands refuse to
work.

[26]All day long he craves for
more,
but the righteous give without
sparing.[w]

[27]The sacrifice of the wicked is
detestable[x]—
how much more so when
brought with evil intent![y]

[28]A false witness will perish,[z]
and whoever listens to him
will be destroyed for
ever.[d]

[29]A wicked man puts up a bold
front,
but an upright man gives
thought to his ways.

[30]There is no wisdom,[a] no
insight, no plan
that can succeed against the
LORD.[b]

[31]The horse is made ready for the
day of battle,
but victory rests with the
LORD.[c]

22 A good name is more
desirable than great
riches;
to be esteemed is better than
silver or gold.[a]

[2]Rich and poor have this in
common:
The LORD is the Maker of
them all.[b]

21:11 h Pr 19:25
21:12 i Pr 14:11
21:13 j Mt 18:30-34 Jas 2:13
21:14 k Pr 18:16 Pr 19:6
21:15 l Pr 10:29
21:16 m Ps 49:14
21:17 n Pr 23:20-21, 29-35
21:18 o Pr 11:8 Isa 43:3
21:19 p ver 9
21:21 q Mt 5:6
21:22 r Ecc 9:15-16
21:23 s Jas 3:2 t Pr 12:13 Pr 13:3
21:24 u Ps 1:1 Pr 1:22 Isa 16:6 Jer 48:29
21:25 v Pr 13:4
21:26 w Ps 37:26 Mt 5:42 Eph 4:28
21:27 x Isa 66:3 Jer 6:20 Am 5:22 y Pr 15:8
21:28 z Pr 19:5
21:30 a Jer 9:23 b Isa 8:10 Ac 5:39
21:31 c Ps 3:8 Ps 33:12-19 Isa 31:1
22:1 a Ecc 7:1
22:2 b Job 31:15

[b]12 Or *The righteous man*
[c]21 Or *righteousness*
[d]28 Or / *but the words of an obedient man will live on*

[3]A prudent man sees danger and takes refuge,[c]
but the simple keep going and suffer for it.[d]
[4]Humility and the fear of the LORD
bring wealth and honour and life.
[5]In the paths of the wicked lie thorns and snares,[e]
but he who guards his soul stays far from them.
[6]Train[a] a child in the way he should go,[f]
and when he is old he will not turn from it.
[7]The rich rule over the poor,
and the borrower is servant to the lender.
[8]He who sows wickedness reaps trouble,[g]
and the rod of his fury will be destroyed.[h]
[9]A generous man will himself be blessed,[i]
for he shares his food with the poor.[j]
[10]Drive out the mocker, and out goes strife;
quarrels and insults are ended.[k]
[11]He who loves a pure heart and whose speech is gracious
will have the king for his friend.[l]
[12]The eyes of the LORD keep watch over knowledge,
but he frustrates the words of the unfaithful.
[13]The sluggard says, "There is a lion outside!"[m]
or, "I will be murdered in the streets!"
[14]The mouth of an adulteress is a deep pit;[n]
he who is under the LORD's wrath will fall into it.[o]

22:3 c Pr 14:16 d Pr 27:12
22:5 e Pr 15:19
22:6 f Eph 6:4
22:8 g Job 4:8 h Ps 125:3
22:9 i 2Co 9:6 j Pr 19:17
22:10 k Pr 18:6 Pr 26:20
22:11 l Pr 16:13 Mt 5:8
22:13 m Pr 26:13
22:14 n Pr 2:16 Pr 5:3-5 Pr 7:5 Pr 23:27 o Ecc 7:26
22:15 p Pr 13:24 Pr 23:14
22:17 q Pr 5:1
22:21 r Lk 1:3-4 1Pe 3:15
22:22 s Zec 7:10 t Ex 23:6 Mal 3:5
22:23 u Ps 12:5 v 1Sa 25:39 Pr 23:10-11
22:25 w 1Co 15:33
22:26 x Pr 11:15

[15]Folly is bound up in the heart of a child,
but the rod of discipline will drive it far from him.[p]
[16]He who oppresses the poor to increase his wealth
and he who gives gifts to the rich—both come to poverty.

Sayings of the Wise

[17]Pay attention and listen to the sayings of the wise;[q]
apply your heart to what I teach,
[18]for it is pleasing when you keep them in your heart
and have all of them ready on your lips.
[19]So that your trust may be in the LORD,
I teach you today, even you.
[20]Have I not written thirty[b] sayings for you,
sayings of counsel and knowledge,
[21]teaching you true and reliable words,[r]
so that you can give sound answers
to him who sent you?
[22]Do not exploit the poor[s] because they are poor
and do not crush the needy in court,[t]
[23]for the LORD will take up their case[u]
and will plunder those who plunder them.[v]
[24]Do not make friends with a hot-tempered man,
do not associate with one easily angered,
[25]or you may learn his ways
and get yourself ensnared.[w]
[26]Do not be a man who strikes hands in pledge[x]
or puts up security for debts;
[27]if you lack the means to pay,

[a]6 Or *Start* [b]20 Or *not formerly written;* or *not written excellent*

your very bed will be
snatched from under you.[y]

28Do not move an ancient
boundary stone[z]
set up by your forefathers.

29Do you see a man skilled in his
work?
He will serve[a] before kings;
he will not serve before
obscure men.

23

1When you sit to dine with
a ruler,
note well what[a] is before you,
2and put a knife to your throat
if you are given to gluttony.
3Do not crave his delicacies,[a]
for that food is deceptive.

4Do not wear yourself out to get
rich;
have the wisdom to show
restraint.
5Cast but a glance at riches, and
they are gone,
for they will surely sprout
wings
and fly off to the sky like an
eagle.[b]

6Do not eat the food of a stingy
man,
do not crave his delicacies;[c]
7for he is the kind of man
who is always thinking about
the cost.[b]
"Eat and drink," he says to you,
but his heart is not with you.
8You will vomit up the little you
have eaten
and will have wasted your
compliments.

9Do not speak to a fool,
for he will scorn the wisdom
of your words.[d]

10Do not move an ancient
boundary stone[e]
or encroach on the fields of
the fatherless,
11for their Defender[f] is strong;
he will take up their case
against you.[g]

22:27 y Pr 17:18
22:28 z Dt 19:14; Pr 23:10
22:29 a Ge 41:46
23:3 a ver 6-8
23:5 b Pr 27:24
23:6 c Ps 141:4
23:9 d Pr 1:7; Pr 9:7; Mt 7:6
23:10 e Dt 19:14; Pr 22:28
23:11 f Job 19:25; g Pr 22:22-23
23:16 h ver 24; Pr 27:11
23:17 i Ps 37:1; Pr 28:14
23:18 j Ps 9:18; Pr 24:14, 19-20
23:20 k Isa 5:11,22; Ro 13:13; Eph 5:18
23:21 l Pr 21:17
23:22 m Lev 19:32; Pr 1:8; Pr 30:17; Eph 6:1-2
23:23 n Pr 4:7
23:24 o ver 15-16; Pr 10:1; Pr 15:20

12Apply your heart to instruction
and your ears to words of
knowledge.

13Do not withhold discipline from
a child;
if you punish him with the
rod, he will not die.
14Punish him with the rod
and save his soul from death.[c]

15My son, if your heart is wise,
then my heart will be glad;
16my inmost being will rejoice
when your lips speak what is
right.[h]

17Do not let your heart envy[i]
sinners,
but always be zealous for the
fear of the LORD.
18There is surely a future hope
for you,
and your hope will not be cut
off.[j]

19Listen, my son, and be wise,
and keep your heart on the
right path.
20Do not join those who drink too
much wine[k]
or gorge themselves on meat,
21for drunkards and gluttons
become poor,[l]
and drowsiness clothes them
in rags.

22Listen to your father, who gave
you life,
and do not despise your
mother when she is old.[m]
23Buy the truth and do not sell it;
get wisdom, discipline and
understanding.[n]
24The father of a righteous man
has great joy;
he who has a wise son delights
in him.[o]
25May your father and mother be
glad;
may she who gave you birth
rejoice!

[a]1 Or *who* [b]7 Or *for as he thinks within himself, / so he is*; or *for as he puts on a feast, / so he is* [c]14 Hebrew *Sheol*

26 My son,[p] give me your heart
and let your eyes keep to my ways,[q]
27 for a prostitute is a deep pit[r]
and a wayward wife is a narrow well.
28 Like a bandit she lies in wait,[s]
and multiplies the unfaithful among men.

29 Who has woe? Who has sorrow?
Who has strife? Who has complaints?
Who has needless bruises?
Who has bloodshot eyes?
30 Those who linger over wine,[t]
who go to sample bowls of mixed wine.
31 Do not gaze at wine when it is red,
when it sparkles in the cup,
when it goes down smoothly!
32 In the end it bites like a snake
and poisons like a viper.
33 Your eyes will see strange sights
and your mind imagine confusing things.
34 You will be like one sleeping on the high seas,
lying on top of the rigging.
35 "They hit me," you will say,
"but I'm not hurt!
They beat me, but I don't feel it!
When will I wake up
so I can find another drink?"

24 Do not envy[a] wicked men,
do not desire their company;
2 for their hearts plot violence,
and their lips talk about making trouble.[b]

3 By wisdom a house is built,[c]
and through understanding it is established;
4 through knowledge its rooms are filled
with rare and beautiful treasures.[d]

5 A wise man has great power,
and a man of knowledge increases strength;

23:26 p Pr 3:1; Pr 5:1-6; q Ps 18:21; Pr 4:4
23:27 r Pr 22:14
23:28 s Pr 7:11-12; Ecc 7:26
23:30 t Ps 75:8; Isa 5:11; Eph 5:18
24:1 a Ps 37:1; Ps 73:3; Pr 3:31-32; Pr 23:17-18
24:2 b Ps 10:7
24:3 c Pr 14:1
24:4 d Pr 8:21
24:6 e Pr 11:14; Pr 20:18; Lk 14:31
24:10 f Job 4:5; Jer 51:46; Heb 12:3
24:11 g Ps 82:4; Isa 58:6-7
24:12 h Pr 21:2; i Job 34:11; Ps 62:12; Ro 2:6*
24:14 j Ps 119:103; Pr 16:24; k Pr 23:18
24:16 l Job 5:19; Ps 34:19; Mic 7:8
24:17 m Ob 1:12; n Job 31:29

6 for waging war you need guidance,
and for victory many advisers.[e]

7 Wisdom is too high for a fool;
in the assembly at the gate he has nothing to say.

8 He who plots evil
will be known as a schemer.
9 The schemes of folly are sin,
and men detest a mocker.

10 If you falter in times of trouble,
how small is your strength![f]

11 Rescue those being led away to death;
hold back those staggering towards slaughter.[g]
12 If you say, "But we knew nothing about this,"
does not he who weighs[h] the heart perceive it?
Does not he who guards your life know it?
Will he not repay each person according to what he has done?[i]

13 Eat honey, my son, for it is good;
honey from the comb is sweet to your taste.
14 Know also that wisdom is sweet to your soul;
if you find it, there is a future hope for you,
and your hope will not be cut off.[j k]

15 Do not lie in wait like an outlaw against a righteous man's house,
do not raid his dwelling-place;
16 for though a righteous man falls seven times, he rises again,
but the wicked are brought down by calamity.[l]

17 Do not gloat[m] when your enemy falls;
when he stumbles, do not let your heart rejoice,[n]
18 or the LORD will see and disapprove

and turn his wrath away from
him.

19Do not fret[o] because of evil
men
or be envious of the wicked,
20for the evil man has no future
hope,
and the lamp of the wicked
will be snuffed out.[p]

21Fear the LORD and the king,[q]
my son,
and do not join with the
rebellious,
22for those two will send sudden
destruction upon them,
and who knows what
calamities they can bring?

Further Sayings of the Wise

23These also are sayings of the
wise:[r]

To show partiality[s] in judging
is not good:[t]
24Whoever says to the guilty,
"You are innocent"[u]—
peoples will curse him and
nations denounce him.
25But it will go well with those
who convict the guilty,
and rich blessing will come
upon them.

26An honest answer
is like a kiss on the lips.

27Finish your outdoor work
and get your fields ready;
after that, build your house.

28Do not testify against your
neighbour without cause,[v]
or use your lips to deceive.
29Do not say, "I'll do to him as he
has done to me;
I'll pay that man back for
what he did."[w]

30I went past the field of the
sluggard,[x]
past the vineyard of the man
who lacks judgment;
31thorns had come up
everywhere,
the ground was covered with
weeds,
and the stone wall was in
ruins.
32I applied my heart to what I
observed
and learned a lesson from
what I saw:
33A little sleep, a little slumber,
a little folding of the hands to
rest[y]—
34and poverty will come on you
like a bandit
and scarcity like an armed
man.[a][z]

More Proverbs of Solomon

25 These are more proverbs[a]
of Solomon, copied by the
men of Hezekiah king of Judah:[b]

2It is the glory of God to conceal
a matter;
to search out a matter is the
glory of kings.[c]

3As the heavens are high and the
earth is deep,
so the hearts of kings are
unsearchable.

4Remove the dross from the
silver,
and out comes material for[a]
the silversmith;
5remove the wicked from the
king's presence,[d]
and his throne will be
established[e] through
righteousness.[f]

6Do not exalt yourself in the
king's presence,
and do not claim a place
among great men;
7it is better for him to say to
you, "Come up here,"[g]
than for him to humiliate you
before a nobleman.

What you have seen with your
eyes

24:19 o Ps 37:1
24:20 p Job 18:5; Pr 13:9; Pr 23:17-18
24:21 q Ro 13:1-5; 1Pe 2:17
24:23 r Pr 1:6 s Lev 19:15 t Pr 28:21
24:24 u Pr 17:15
24:28 v Ps 7:4; Pr 25:18; Eph 4:25
24:29 w Pr 20:22; Mt 5:38-41; Ro 12:17
24:30 x Pr 6:6-11; Pr 26:13-16
24:33 y Pr 6:10
24:34 z Pr 10:4; Ecc 10:18
25:1 a 1Ki 4:32 b Pr 1:1
25:2 c Pr 16:10-15
25:5 d Pr 20:8 e 2Sa 7:13 f Pr 16:12; Pr 29:14
25:7 g Lk 14:7-10

[a]34 Or *like a vagrant / and scarcity like a beggar*
[a]4 Or *comes a vessel from*

8 do not bring[b] hastily to court,
for what will you do in the end
if your neighbour puts you to shame?[h]

9 If you argue your case with a neighbour,
do not betray another man's confidence,
10 or he who hears it may shame you
and you will never lose your bad reputation.

11 A word aptly spoken
is like apples of gold in settings of silver.[i]

12 Like an ear-ring of gold or an ornament of fine gold
is a wise man's rebuke to a listening ear.[j]

13 Like the coolness of snow at harvest time
is a trustworthy messenger to those who send him;
he refreshes the spirit of his masters.[k]

14 Like clouds and wind without rain
is a man who boasts of gifts he does not give.

15 Through patience a ruler can be persuaded,[l]
and a gentle tongue can break a bone.[m]

16 If you find honey, eat just enough—
too much of it, and you will vomit.[n]

17 Seldom set foot in your neighbour's house—
too much of you, and he will hate you.

18 Like a club or a sword or a sharp arrow
is the man who gives false testimony against his neighbour.[o]

19 Like a bad tooth or a lame foot
is reliance on the unfaithful in times of trouble.

20 Like one who takes away a garment on a cold day,
or like vinegar poured on soda,
is one who sings songs to a heavy heart.

21 If your enemy is hungry, give him food to eat;
if he is thirsty, give him water to drink.
22 In doing this, you will heap burning coals[p] on his head,
and the LORD will reward you.[q]

23 As a north wind brings rain,
so a sly tongue brings angry looks.

24 Better to live on a corner of the roof
than share a house with a quarrelsome wife.[r]

25 Like cold water to a weary soul
is good news from a distant land.[s]

26 Like a muddied spring or a polluted well
is a righteous man who gives way to the wicked.

27 It is not good to eat too much honey,[t]
nor is it honourable to seek one's own honour.[u]

28 Like a city whose walls are broken down
is a man who lacks self-control.

26

Like snow in summer or rain[a] in harvest,
honour is not fitting for a fool.[b]

2 Like a fluttering sparrow or a darting swallow,
an undeserved curse does not come to rest.[c]

3 A whip for the horse, a halter for the donkey,[d]

25:8 h Mt 5:25-26
25:11 i ver 12; Pr 15:23
25:12 j ver 11; Ps 141:5; Pr 13:18; Pr 15:31
25:13 k Pr 10:26; Pr 13:17
25:15 l Ecc 10:4; m Pr 15:1
25:16 n ver 27
25:18 o Ps 57:4; Pr 12:18
25:22 p Ps 18:8; q 2Sa 16:12; 2Ch 28:15; Mt 5:44; Ro 12:20*
25:24 r Pr 21:9
25:25 s Pr 15:30
25:27 t ver 16; u Pr 27:2; Mt 23:12
26:1 a 1Sa 12:17; b ver 8; Pr 19:10
26:2 c Nu 23:8; Dt 23:5
26:3 d Ps 32:9

[b]7, 8 Or *nobleman / on whom you had set your eyes.* / [8]*Do not go*

and a rod for the backs of
fools![e]

4Do not answer a fool according
to his folly,
or you will be like him
yourself.[f]

5Answer a fool according to his
folly,
or he will be wise in his own
eyes.[g]

6Like cutting off one's feet or
drinking violence
is the sending of a message by
the hand of a fool.[h]

7Like a lame man's legs that
hang limp
is a proverb in the mouth of a
fool.[i]

8Like tying a stone in a sling
is the giving of honour to a
fool.[j]

9Like a thornbush in a
drunkard's hand
is a proverb in the mouth of a
fool.[k]

10Like an archer who wounds at
random
is he who hires a fool or any
passer-by.

11As a dog returns to its vomit,[l]
so a fool repeats his folly.[m]

12Do you see a man wise in his
own eyes?[n]
There is more hope for a fool
than for him.[o]

13The sluggard says,[p] "There is a
lion in the road,
a fierce lion roaming the
streets!"[q]

14As a door turns on its hinges,
so a sluggard turns on his
bed.[r]

15The sluggard buries his hand in
the dish;
he is too lazy to bring it back
to his mouth.[s]

16The sluggard is wiser in his
own eyes

26:3 e Pr 10:13
26:4 f ver 5; Isa 36:21
26:5 g ver 4; Pr 3:7
26:6 h Pr 10:26
26:7 i ver 9
26:8 j ver 1
26:9 k ver 7
26:11 l 2Pe 2:22*; m Ex 8:15; Ps 85:8
26:12 n Pr 3:7; o Pr 29:20
26:13 p Pr 6:6-11; Pr 24:30-34; q Pr 22:13
26:14 r Pr 6:9
26:15 s Pr 19:24
26:20 t Pr 22:10
26:21 u Pr 14:17; Pr 15:18
26:22 v Pr 18:8
26:24 w Ps 31:18; x Ps 41:6; Pr 10:18; Pr 12:20
26:25 y Ps 28:3; z Jer 9:4-8
26:27 a Ps 7:15; b Est 6:13; c Est 2:23; Est 7:9; Ps 35:8; Ps 141:10; Pr 28:10; Pr 29:6; Isa 50:11
26:28 d Ps 12:3; Pr 29:5

than seven men who answer
discreetly.

17Like one who seizes a dog by
the ears
is a passer-by who meddles in
a quarrel not his own.

18Like a madman shooting
firebrands or deadly arrows
19is a man who deceives his
neighbour
and says, "I was only joking!"

20Without wood a fire goes out;
without gossip a quarrel dies
down.[t]

21As charcoal to embers and as
wood to fire,
so is a quarrelsome man for
kindling strife.[u]

22The words of a gossip are like
choice morsels;
they go down to a man's
inmost parts.[v]

23Like a coating of glaze[a] over
earthenware
are fervent lips with an evil
heart.

24A malicious man disguises
himself with his lips,[w]
but in his heart he harbours
deceit.[x]

25Though his speech is
charming,[y] do not believe
him,
for seven abominations fill his
heart.[z]

26His malice may be concealed by
deception,
but his wickedness will be
exposed in the assembly.

27If a man digs a pit,[a] he will fall
into it;[b]
if a man rolls a stone, it will
roll back on him.[c]

28A lying tongue hates those it
hurts,
and a flattering mouth[d] works
ruin.

[a]23 With a different word division of the Hebrew; Masoretic Text *of silver dross*

27 Do not boast[a] about
tomorrow,
for you do not know what a
day may bring forth.[b]

2 Let another praise you, and not
your own mouth;
someone else, and not your
own lips.[c]

3 Stone is heavy and sand[d] a
burden,
but provocation by a fool is
heavier than both.

4 Anger is cruel and fury
overwhelming,
but who can stand before
jealousy?[e]

5 Better is open rebuke
than hidden love.

6 Wounds from a friend can be
trusted,
but an enemy multiplies
kisses.[f]

7 He who is full loathes honey,
but to the hungry even what is
bitter tastes sweet.

8 Like a bird that strays from its
nest[g]
is a man who strays from his
home.

9 Perfume[h] and incense bring
joy to the heart,
and the pleasantness of one's
friend springs from his
earnest counsel.

10 Do not forsake your friend and
the friend of your father,
and do not go to your
brother's house when
disaster[i] strikes you—
better a neighbour nearby
than a brother far away.

11 Be wise, my son, and bring joy
to my heart;[j]
then I can answer anyone who
treats me with contempt.[k]

12 The prudent see danger and
take refuge,
but the simple keep going and
suffer for it.[l]

27:1 *a* 1Ki 20:11 *b* Mt 6:34 Lk 12:19-20 Jas 4:13-16
27:2 *c* Pr 25:27
27:3 *d* Job 6:3
27:4 *e* Nu 5:14
27:6 *f* Ps 141:5 Pr 28:23
27:8 *g* Isa 16:2
27:9 *h* Est 2:12 Ps 45:8
27:10 *i* Pr 17:17 Pr 18:24
27:11 *j* Pr 10:1 Pr 23:15-16 *k* Ge 24:60
27:12 *l* Pr 22:3
27:13 *m* Pr 20:16
27:15 *n* Est 1:18 Pr 19:13
27:18 *o* 1Co 9:7 *p* Lk 19:12-27
27:20 *q* Pr 30:15-16 Hab 2:5 *r* Ecc 1:8 Ecc 6:7
27:21 *s* Pr 17:3
27:23 *t* Pr 12:10
27:24 *u* Pr 23:5

13 Take the garment of one who
puts up security for a
stranger;
hold it in pledge if he does it
for a wayward woman.[m]

14 If a man loudly blesses his
neighbour early in the
morning,
it will be taken as a curse.

15 A quarrelsome wife is like
a constant dripping[n] on a
rainy day;
16 restraining her is like
restraining the wind
or grasping oil with the hand.

17 As iron sharpens iron,
so one man sharpens another.

18 He who tends a fig-tree will eat
its fruit,[o]
and he who looks after his
master will be honoured.[p]

19 As water reflects a face,
so a man's heart reflects the
man.

20 Death and Destruction[a] are
never satisfied,[q]
and neither are the eyes of
man.[r]

21 The crucible for silver and the
furnace for gold,[s]
but man is tested by the
praise he receives.

22 Though you grind a fool in a
mortar,
grinding him like grain with a
pestle,
you will not remove his folly
from him.

23 Be sure you know the condition
of your flocks,[t]
give careful attention to your
herds;
24 for riches do not endure for
ever,[u]
and a crown is not secure for
all generations.
25 When the hay is removed and
new growth appears

a20 Hebrew *Sheol and Abaddon*

and the grass from the hills is
gathered in,
26 the lambs will provide you with
clothing,
and the goats with the price of
a field.
27 You will have plenty of goats' milk
to feed you and your family
and to nourish your servant
girls.

28

The wicked man flees[a]
though no-one pursues,[b]
but the righteous are as bold
as a lion.[c]

2 When a country is rebellious, it
has many rulers,
but a man of understanding
and knowledge maintains
order.

3 A ruler[a] who oppresses the
poor
is like a driving rain that
leaves no crops.

4 Those who forsake the law
praise the wicked,
but those who keep the law
resist them.

5 Evil men do not understand
justice,
but those who seek the LORD
understand it fully.

6 Better a poor man whose walk
is blameless
than a rich man whose ways
are perverse.[d]

7 He who keeps the law is a
discerning son,
but a companion of gluttons
disgraces his father.[e]

8 He who increases his wealth by
exorbitant interest[f]
amasses it for another,[g] who
will be kind to the poor.[h]

9 If anyone turns a deaf ear to
the law,
even his prayers are
detestable.[i]

10 He who leads the upright along
an evil path
will fall into his own trap,[j]
but the blameless will receive
a good inheritance.

11 A rich man may be wise in his
own eyes,
but a poor man who has
discernment sees through
him.

12 When the righteous triumph,
there is great elation;[k]
but when the wicked rise to
power, men go into
hiding.[l]

13 He who conceals his sins[m] does
not prosper,
but whoever confesses and
renounces them finds
mercy.[n]

14 Blessed is the man who always
fears the LORD,
but he who hardens his heart
falls into trouble.

15 Like a roaring lion or a
charging bear
is a wicked man ruling over a
helpless people.

16 A tyrannical ruler lacks
judgment,
but he who hates ill-gotten
gain will enjoy a long life.

17 A man tormented by the guilt of
murder
will be a fugitive[o] till death;
let no-one support him.

18 He whose walk is blameless is
kept safe,
but he whose ways are
perverse will suddenly
fall.[p]

19 He who works his land will
have abundant food,
but the one who chases
fantasies will have his fill
of poverty.[q]

28:1
a 2Ki 7:7
b Lev 26:17
Ps 53:5
c Ps 138:3

28:6
d Pr 19:1

28:7
e Pr 23:19-21

28:8
f Ex 18:21
g Job 27:17
Pr 13:22
h Ps 112:9
Pr 14:31
Lk 14:12-14

28:9
i Ps 66:18
Ps 109:7
Pr 15:8
Isa 1:13

28:10
j Pr 26:27

28:12
k 2Ki 11:20
l Pr 11:10
Pr 29:2

28:13
m Job 31:33
n Ps 32:1-5
1Jn 1:9

28:17
o Ge 9:6

28:18
p Pr 10:9

28:19
q Pr 12:11

[a] 3 Or *A poor man*

20 A faithful man will be richly blessed,
but one eager to get rich will not go unpunished.[r]

21 To show partiality is not good[s]—
yet a man will do wrong for a piece of bread.[t]

22 A stingy man is eager to get rich
and is unaware that poverty awaits him.[u]

23 He who rebukes a man will in the end gain more favour
than he who has a flattering tongue.[v]

24 He who robs his father or mother[w]
and says, "It's not wrong"—
he is partner to him who destroys.[x]

25 A greedy man stirs up dissension,
but he who trusts in the LORD[y] will prosper.

26 He who trusts in himself is a fool,[z]
but he who walks in wisdom is kept safe.

27 He who gives to the poor will lack nothing,[a]
but he who closes his eyes to them receives many curses.

28 When the wicked rise to power, people go into hiding;[b]
but when the wicked perish, the righteous thrive.

29

A man who remains stiff-necked after many rebukes
will suddenly be destroyed—without remedy.[a]

2 When the righteous thrive, the people rejoice;[b]
when the wicked rule, the people groan.[c]

3 A man who loves wisdom brings joy to his father,[d]
but a companion of prostitutes squanders his wealth.[e]

4 By justice a king gives a country stability,[f]
but one who is greedy for bribes tears it down.

5 Whoever flatters his neighbour
is spreading a net for his feet.

6 An evil man is snared by his own sin,[g]
but a righteous one can sing and be glad.

7 The righteous care about justice for the poor,[h]
but the wicked have no such concern.

8 Mockers stir up a city,
but wise men turn away anger.[i]

9 If a wise man goes to court with a fool,
the fool rages and scoffs, and there is no peace.

10 Bloodthirsty men hate a man of integrity
and seek to kill the upright.[j]

11 A fool gives full vent to his anger,
but a wise man keeps himself under control.[k]

12 If a ruler listens to lies,
all his officials become wicked.

13 The poor man and the oppressor have this in common:
The LORD gives sight to the eyes of both.[l]

14 If a king judges the poor with fairness,
his throne will always be secure.[m]

15 The rod of correction imparts wisdom,
but a child left to himself disgraces his mother.[n]

16 When the wicked thrive, so does sin,

28:20 r ver 22; Pr 10:6; 1Ti 6:9
28:21 s Pr 18:5; t Eze 13:19
28:22 u ver 20; Pr 23:6
28:23 v Pr 27:5-6
28:24 w Pr 19:26; x Pr 18:9
28:25 y Pr 29:25
28:26 z Ps 4:5; Pr 3:5
28:27 a Dt 15:7; Dt 24:19; Pr 19:17; Pr 22:9
28:28 b ver 12
29:1 a 2Ch 36:16; Pr 6:15
29:2 b Est 8:15; c Pr 28:12
29:3 d Pr 10:1; e Pr 5:8-10; Lk 15:11-32
29:4 f Pr 8:15-16
29:6 g Ecc 9:12
29:7 h Job 29:16; Ps 41:1; Pr 31:8-9
29:8 i Pr 11:11; Pr 16:14
29:10 j 1Jn 3:12
29:11 k Pr 12:16; Pr 19:11
29:13 l Pr 22:2; Mt 5:45
29:14 m Ps 72:1-5; Pr 16:12
29:15 n Pr 10:1; Pr 13:24; Pr 17:21,25

but the righteous will see their
downfall.[o]

17Discipline your son, and he will
give you peace;
he will bring delight to your
soul.[p]

18Where there is no revelation,
the people cast off
restraint;
but blessed is he who keeps
the law.[q]

19A servant cannot be corrected
by mere words;
though he understands, he will
not respond.

20Do you see a man who speaks in
haste?
There is more hope for a fool
than for him.[r]

21If a man pampers his servant
from youth,
he will bring grief[a] in the
end.

22An angry man stirs up
dissension,
and a hot-tempered one
commits many sins.[s]

23A man's pride brings him low,
but a man of lowly spirit gains
honour.[t]

24The accomplice of a thief is his
own enemy;
he is put under oath and dare
not testify.[u]

25Fear of man will prove to be a
snare,
but whoever trusts in the
LORD[v] is kept safe.

26Many seek an audience with a
ruler,[w]
but it is from the LORD that
man gets justice.

27The righteous detest the
dishonest;
the wicked detest the
upright.[x]

29:16
o Ps 37:35-36
Ps 58:10
Ps 91:8
Ps 92:11

29:17
p ver 15
Pr 10:1

29:18
q Ps 1:1-2
Ps 119:1-2
Jn 13:17

29:20
r Pr 26:12
Jas 1:19

29:22
s Pr 14:17
Pr 15:18
Pr 26:21

29:23
t Pr 11:2
Pr 15:33
Pr 16:18
Isa 66:2
Mt 23:12

29:24
u Lev 5:1

29:25
v Pr 28:25

29:26
w Pr 19:6

29:27
x ver 10

30:3
a Pr 9:10

30:4
b Ps 24:1-2
Jn 3:13
Eph 4:7-10
c Ps 104:3
Isa 40:12
d Job 26:8
Job 38:8-9
e Ge 1:2
f Rev 19:12

30:5
g Ps 12:6
Ps 18:30
h Ge 15:1
Ps 84:11

30:6
i Dt 4:2
Dt 12:32
Rev 22:18

30:8
j Mt 6:11

30:9
k Jos 24:27
Isa 1:4
Isa 59:13
l Dt 6:12
Dt 8:10-14
Hos 13:6
m Dt 8:12

Sayings of Agur

30 The sayings of Agur son of
Jakeh—an oracle:[a]

This man declared to Ithiel,
to Ithiel and to Ucal:[b]

2"I am the most ignorant of men;
I do not have a man's
understanding.
3I have not learned wisdom,
nor have I knowledge of the
Holy One.[a]
4Who has gone up[b] to heaven
and come down?
Who has gathered up the wind
in the hollow[c] of his
hands?
Who has wrapped up the
waters[d] in his cloak?[e]
Who has established all the
ends of the earth?
What is his name,[f] and the
name of his son?
Tell me if you know!

5"Every word of God is
flawless;[g]
he is a shield[h] to those who
take refuge in him.
6Do not add[i] to his words,
or he will rebuke you and
prove you a liar.

7"Two things I ask of you,
O LORD;
do not refuse me before I die:
8Keep falsehood and lies far
from me;
give me neither poverty nor
riches,
but give me only my daily
bread.[j]
9Otherwise, I may have too
much and disown[k] you
and say, 'Who is the LORD?'[l]
Or I may become poor and
steal,
and so dishonour the name of
my God.[m]

[a]21 The meaning of the Hebrew for this word is uncertain. [a]1 Or *Jakeh of Massa*
[b]1 Masoretic Text; with a different word division of the Hebrew *declared, "I am weary, O God; / I am weary, O God, and faint.*

10"Do not slander a servant to his
master,
or he will curse you, and you
will pay for it.

11"There are those who curse
their fathers
and do not bless their
mothers;[n]
12those who are pure in their own
eyes[o]
and yet are not cleansed of
their filth;[p]
13those whose eyes are ever so
haughty,[q]
whose glances are so
disdainful;
14those whose teeth[r] are swords
and whose jaws are set with
knives[s]
to devour[t] the poor[u] from the
earth,
the needy from among
mankind.[v]

15"The leech has two daughters.
'Give! Give!' they cry.

"There are three things that are
never satisfied,[w]
four that never say, 'Enough!':
16the grave,[c][x] the barren womb,
land, which is never satisfied
with water,
and fire, which never says,
'Enough!'

17"The eye that mocks[y] a father,
that scorns obedience to a
mother,
will be pecked out by the
ravens of the valley,
will be eaten by the vultures.[z]

18"There are three things that are
too amazing for me,
four that I do not understand:
19the way of an eagle in the sky,
the way of a snake on a rock,
the way of a ship on the high
seas,
and the way of a man with a
maiden.

20"This is the way of an
adulteress:
She eats and wipes her mouth
and says, 'I've done nothing
wrong.'[a]

21"Under three things the earth
trembles,
under four it cannot bear up:
22a servant who becomes king,[b]
a fool who is full of food,
23an unloved woman who is
married,
and a maidservant who
displaces her mistress.

24"Four things on earth are small,
yet they are extremely wise:
25Ants are creatures of little
strength,
yet they store up their food in
the summer;[c]
26conies[d][d] are creatures of little
power,
yet they make their home in
the crags;
27locusts[e] have no king,
yet they advance together in
ranks;
28a lizard can be caught with the
hand,
yet it is found in kings'
palaces.

29"There are three things that are
stately in their stride,
four that move with stately
bearing:
30a lion, mighty among beasts,
who retreats before nothing;
31a strutting cock, a he-goat,
and a king with his army
around him.[e]

32"If you have played the fool and
exalted yourself,
or if you have planned evil,
clap your hand over your
mouth![f]
33For as churning the milk
produces butter,
and as twisting the nose
produces blood,
so stirring up anger produces
strife."

30:11
n Pr 20:20

30:12
o Pr 16:2; Lk 18:11
p Jer 2:23,35

30:13
q 2Sa 22:28; Job 41:34; Ps 131:1; Pr 6:17

30:14
r Job 4:11; Job 29:17; Ps 3:7
s Ps 57:4
t Job 24:9; Ps 14:4
u Am 8:4; Mic 2:2
v Job 19:22

30:15
w Pr 27:20

30:16
x Pr 27:20; Isa 5:14; Isa 14:9,11; Hab 2:5

30:17
y Dt 21:18-21; Pr 23:22
z Job 15:23

30:20
a Pr 5:6

30:22
b Pr 19:10; Pr 29:2

30:25
c Pr 6:6-8

30:26
d Ps 104:18

30:27
e Ex 10:4

30:32
f Job 21:5; Job 29:9

c16 Hebrew *Sheol* d26 That is, the hyrax or rock badger e31 Or *king secure against revolt.*

Sayings of King Lemuel

31 The sayings[a] of King Lemuel—an oracle[a] his mother
taught him:

[2]"O my son, O son of my womb,
O son of my vows,[b][b]
[3]do not spend your strength on
women,
your vigour on those who ruin
kings.[c]

[4]"It is not for kings, O Lemuel—
not for kings to drink wine,[d]
not for rulers to crave beer,
[5]lest they drink[e] and forget
what the law decrees,[f]
and deprive all the oppressed
of their rights.
[6]Give beer to those who are
perishing,
wine[g] to those who are in
anguish;
[7]let them drink[h] and forget
their poverty
and remember their misery no
more.

[8]"Speak[i] up for those who
cannot speak for
themselves,
for the rights of all who are
destitute.
[9]Speak up and judge fairly;
defend the rights of the poor
and needy."[j]

Epilogue: The Wife of Noble Character

[10][c]A wife of noble character[k]
who can find?[l]
She is worth far more than
rubies.
[11]Her husband[m] has full
confidence in her
and lacks nothing of value.[n]
[12]She brings him good, not harm,
all the days of her life.
[13]She selects wool and flax
and works with eager hands.[o]
[14]She is like the merchant ships,
bringing her food from afar.
[15]She gets up while it is still
dark;
she provides food for her
family
and portions for her servant
girls.
[16]She considers a field and buys
it;
out of her earnings she plants
a vineyard.
[17]She sets about her work
vigorously;
her arms are strong for her
tasks.
[18]She sees that her trading is
profitable,
and her lamp does not go out
at night.
[19]In her hand she holds the
distaff
and grasps the spindle with
her fingers.
[20]She opens her arms to the poor
and extends her hands to the
needy.[p]
[21]When it snows, she has no fear
for her household;
for all of them are clothed in
scarlet.
[22]She makes coverings for her
bed;
she is clothed in fine linen and
purple.
[23]Her husband is respected at the
city gate,
where he takes his seat among
the elders[q] of the land.
[24]She makes linen garments and
sells them,
and supplies the merchants
with sashes.
[25]She is clothed with strength and
dignity;
she can laugh at the days to
come.
[26]She speaks with wisdom,
and faithful instruction is on
her tongue.[r]
[27]She watches over the affairs of
her household

31:1 *a* Pr 22:17
31:2 *b* Jdg 11:30; Isa 49:15
31:3 *c* Dt 17:17; 1Ki 11:3; Ne 13:26; Pr 5:1-14
31:4 *d* Pr 20:1; Ecc 10:16-17; Isa 5:22
31:5 *e* 1Ki 16:9 *f* Pr 16:12; Hos 4:11
31:6 *g* Ge 14:18
31:7 *h* Est 1:10
31:8 *i* 1Sa 19:4; Job 29:12-17
31:9 *j* Lev 19:15; Dt 1:16; Pr 24:23; Pr 29:7; Isa 1:17; Jer 22:16
31:10 *k* Ru 3:11; Pr 12:4; Pr 18:22 *l* Pr 8:35; Pr 19:14
31:11 *m* Ge 2:18 *n* Pr 12:4
31:13 *o* 1Ti 2:9-10
31:20 *p* Dt 15:11; Eph 4:28; Heb 13:16
31:23 *q* Ex 3:16; Ru 4:1,11; Pr 12:4
31:26 *r* Pr 10:31

a1 Or *of Lemuel king of Massa, which* **b**2 Or */ the answer to my prayers* **c**10 Verses 10–31 are an acrostic, each verse beginning with a successive letter of the Hebrew alphabet.

and does not eat the bread of
idleness.
28Her children arise and call her
blessed;
her husband also, and he
praises her:
29"Many women do noble things,
but you surpass them all."
30Charm is deceptive, and beauty
is fleeting;
but a woman who fears the
LORD is to be praised.
31Give her the reward she has
earned,
and let her works bring her
praise[s] at the city gate.

31:31
s Pr 11:16

ECCLESIASTES

Everything Is Meaningless

1 The words of the Teacher,[a][a] son of David, king of Jerusalem:[b]

2"Meaningless! Meaningless!"
says the Teacher.
"Utterly meaningless!
Everything is meaningless."[c]

3What does man gain from all
his labour
at which he toils under the
sun?[d]
4Generations come and
generations go,
but the earth remains for
ever.[e]
5The sun rises and the sun sets,
and hurries back to where it
rises.[f]
6The wind blows to the south
and turns to the north;
round and round it goes,
ever returning on its course.
7All streams flow into the sea,
yet the sea is never full.
To the place the streams come
from,
there they return again.[g]
8All things are wearisome,
more than one can say.
The eye never has enough of
seeing,[h]
nor the ear its fill of hearing.
9What has been will be again,
what has been done will be
done again;[i]
there is nothing new under the
sun.
10Is there anything of which one
can say,
"Look! This is something
new"?
It was here already, long ago;
it was here before our time.
11There is no remembrance of
men of old,
and even those who are yet to
come
will not be remembered
by those who follow.[j]

Wisdom Is Meaningless

12I, the Teacher,[k] was king over
Israel in Jerusalem. 13I devoted
myself to study and to explore by
wisdom all that is done under
heaven. What a heavy burden God
has laid on men![l] 14I have seen all
the things that are done under the
sun; all of them are meaningless, a
chasing after the wind.[m]

15What is twisted cannot be
straightened;[n]
what is lacking cannot be
counted.

16I thought to myself, "Look, I
have grown and increased in wisdom more than anyone who has
ruled over Jerusalem before me;[o]
I have experienced much of wisdom and knowledge." 17Then I applied myself to the understanding
of wisdom,[p] and also of madness
and folly,[q] but I learned that this,
too, is a chasing after the wind.

18For with much wisdom comes
much sorrow;
the more knowledge, the more
grief.[r]

Pleasures Are Meaningless

2 I thought in my heart, "Come
now, I will test you with pleasure[a] to find out what is good."
But that also proved to be meaningless. 2"Laughter,"[b] I said, "is foolish. And what does pleasure
accomplish?" 3I tried cheering
myself with wine,[c] and embracing

[a]1 Or *leader of the assembly*; also in verses 2 and 12

1:1 a ver 12 Ecc 7:27 Ecc 12:10 b Pr 1:1
1:2 c Ps 39:5-6 Ps 62:9 Ps 144:4 Ecc 12:8 Ro 8:20-21
1:3 d Ecc 2:11,22 Ecc 3:9 Ecc 5:15-16
1:4 e Ps 104:5 Ps 119:90
1:5 f Ps 19:5-6
1:7 g Job 36:28
1:8 h Pr 27:20
1:9 i Ecc 2:12 Ecc 3:15
1:11 j Ecc 2:16
1:12 k ver 1
1:13 l Ge 3:17 Ecc 3:10
1:14 m Ecc 2:11,17
1:15 n Ecc 7:13
1:16 o 1Ki 3:12 1Ki 4:30 Ecc 2:9
1:17 p Ecc 7:23 q Ecc 2:3,12 Ecc 7:25
1:18 r Ecc 2:23 Ecc 12:12
2:1 a Ecc 7:4 Ecc 8:15 Lk 12:19
2:2 b Pr 14:13 Ecc 7:6
2:3 c ver 24-25 Ecc 3:12-13

folly[d]—my mind still guiding me
with wisdom. I wanted to see what
was worth while for men to do under heaven during the few days of
their lives.
4 I undertook great projects: I
built houses for myself[e] and
planted vineyards.[f] 5 I made gardens and parks and planted all
kinds of fruit trees in them. 6 I made
reservoirs to water groves of flourishing trees. 7 I bought male and female slaves and had other slaves
who were born in my house. I also
owned more herds and flocks than
anyone in Jerusalem before me. 8 I
amassed silver and gold[g] for myself, and the treasure of kings and
provinces. I acquired men and
women singers,[h] and a harem[a] as
well—the delights of the heart of
man. 9 I became greater by far than
anyone in Jerusalem before me.[i]
In all this my wisdom stayed with
me.

10 I denied myself nothing my
eyes desired;
I refused my heart no
pleasure.
My heart took delight in all my
work,
and this was the reward for all
my labour.
11 Yet when I surveyed all that my
hands had done
and what I had toiled to
achieve,
everything was meaningless, a
chasing after the wind;[j]
nothing was gained under the
sun.[k]

Wisdom and Folly Are Meaningless

12 Then I turned my thoughts to
consider wisdom,
and also madness and folly.[l]
What more can the king's
successor do
than what has already been
done?[m]

2:3 d Ecc 1:17
2:4 e 1Ki 7:1-12 f SS 8:11
2:8 g 1Ki 9:28; 1Ki 10:10,14,21 h 2Sa 19:35
2:9 i 1Ch 29:25; Ecc 1:16
2:11 j Ecc 1:14 k Ecc 1:3
2:12 l Ecc 1:17 m Ecc 1:9; Ecc 7:25
2:13 n Ecc 7:19; Ecc 9:18 o Ecc 7:11-12
2:14 p Ps 49:10; Pr 17:24; Ecc 3:19; Ecc 6:6; Ecc 7:2; Ecc 9:3,11-12
2:15 q Ecc 6:8
2:16 r Ecc 1:11; Ecc 9:5
2:17 s Ecc 4:2
2:18 t Ps 39:6; Ps 49:10
2:22 u Ecc 1:3; Ecc 3:9

13 I saw that wisdom[n] is better
than folly,[o]
just as light is better than
darkness.
14 The wise man has eyes in his
head,
while the fool walks in the
darkness;
but I came to realise
that the same fate overtakes
them both.[p]
15 Then I thought in my heart,
"The fate of the fool will
overtake me also.
What then do I gain by being
wise?"[q]
I said in my heart,
"This too is meaningless."
16 For the wise man, like the fool,
will not be long
remembered;
in days to come both will be
forgotten.[r]
Like the fool, the wise man too
must die!

Toil Is Meaningless

17 So I hated life, because the
work that is done under the sun was
grievous to me. All of it is meaningless, a chasing after the wind.[s] 18 I
hated all the things I had toiled for
under the sun, because I must leave
them to the one who comes after
me.[t] 19 And who knows whether he
will be a wise man or a fool? Yet he
will have control over all the work
into which I have poured my effort
and skill under the sun. This too is
meaningless. 20 So my heart began
to despair over all my toilsome labour under the sun. 21 For a man
may do his work with wisdom,
knowledge and skill, and then he
must leave all he owns to someone
who has not worked for it. This too
is meaningless and a great misfortune. 22 What does a man get for all
the toil and anxious striving with
which he labours under the sun?[u]

[a] 8 The meaning of the Hebrew for this phrase is uncertain.

23 All his days his work is pain and
grief;[v] even at night his mind does
not rest. This too is meaningless.
24 A man can do nothing better
than to eat and drink[w] and find satisfaction in his work.[x] This too, I
see, is from the hand of God,[y] 25 for
without him, who can eat or find enjoyment? 26 To the man who pleases
him, God gives wisdom, knowledge
and happiness, but to the sinner he
gives the task of gathering and
storing up wealth[z] to hand it over
to the one who pleases God.[a] This
too is meaningless, a chasing after
the wind.

A Time for Everything

3 There is a time[a] for
everything,
and a season for every
activity under heaven:

2 a time to be born and a time
to die,
a time to plant and a time to
uproot,
3 a time to kill and a time to
heal,
a time to tear down and a time
to build,
4 a time to weep and a time to
laugh,
a time to mourn and a time to
dance,
5 a time to scatter stones and a
time to gather them,
a time to embrace and a time
to refrain,
6 a time to search and a time to
give up,
a time to keep and a time to
throw away,
7 a time to tear and a time to
mend,
a time to be silent[b] and a time
to speak,
8 a time to love and a time to
hate,
a time for war and a time for
peace.

9 What does the worker gain from
his toil?[c] 10 I have seen the burden
God has laid on men.[d] 11 He has
made everything beautiful in its
time.[e] He has also set eternity in
the hearts of men; yet they cannot
fathom[f] what God has done from
beginning to end.[g] 12 I know that
there is nothing better for men
than to be happy and do good while
they live. 13 That everyone may eat
and drink,[h] and find satisfaction[i]
in all his toil—this is the gift of
God.[j] 14 I know that everything
God does will endure for ever;
nothing can be added to it and nothing taken from it. God does it so
that men will revere him.[k]

15 Whatever is has already been,[l]
and what will be has been
before;[m]
and God will call the past to
account.[a]

16 And I saw something else under
the sun:

In the place of judgment—
wickedness was
there,
in the place of justice—
wickedness was
there.

17 I thought in my heart,
"God will bring to judgment[n]
both the righteous and the
wicked,
for there will be a time for
every activity,
a time for every deed."[o]

18 I also thought, "As for men, God
tests them so that they may see that
they are like the animals.[p] 19 Man's
fate[q] is like that of the animals; the
same fate awaits them both: As one
dies, so dies the other. All have the
same breath;[b] man has no advantage over the animal. Everything is
meaningless. 20 All go to the same
place; all come from dust, and to
dust all return.[r] 21 Who knows if
the spirit of man rises upward[s]

2:23 v Job 5:7; Job 14:1; Ecc 1:18
2:24 w Ecc 8:15; 1Co 15:32; x Ecc 3:22; y Ecc 3:12-13; Ecc 5:17-19; Ecc 9:7-10
2:26 z Job 27:17; a Pr 13:22
3:1 a ver 11,17; Ecc 8:6
3:7 b Am 5:13
3:9 c Ecc 1:3
3:10 d Ecc 1:13
3:11 e ver 1; f Job 11:7; Ecc 8:17; g Job 28:23; Ro 11:33
3:13 h Ecc 2:3; i Ps 34:12; j Dt 12:7,18; Ecc 2:24; Ecc 5:19
3:14 k Job 23:15; Ecc 5:7; Ecc 7:18; Ecc 8:12-13; Jas 1:17
3:15 l Ecc 6:10; m Ecc 1:9
3:17 n Job 19:29; Ecc 11:9; Mt 16:27; Ro 2:6-8; 2Th 1:6-7; o ver 1
3:18 p Ps 73:22
3:19 q Ecc 2:14
3:20 r Ge 2:7; Ge 3:19; Job 34:15
3:21 s Ecc 12:7

a15 Or *God calls back the past*   b19 Or *spirit*

and if the spirit of the animal[c] goes down into the earth?"

22So I saw that there is nothing better for a man than to enjoy his work,[t] because that is his lot.[u] For who can bring him to see what will happen after him?

Oppression, Toil, Friendlessness

4 Again I looked and saw all the oppression[a] that was taking place under the sun:

I saw the tears of the
 oppressed—
 and they have no comforter;
power was on the side of their
 oppressors—
 and they have no comforter.[b]
2And I declared that the dead,[c]
 who had already died,
are happier than the living,
 who are still alive.[d]
3But better than both
 is he who has not yet been,[e]
who has not seen the evil
 that is done under the sun.[f]

4And I saw that all labour and all achievement spring from man's envy of his neighbour. This too is meaningless, a chasing after the wind.[g]

5The fool folds his hands[h]
 and ruins himself.
6Better one handful with
 tranquillity
 than two handfuls with toil[i]
 and chasing after the wind.

7Again I saw something meaningless under the sun:

8There was a man all alone;
 he had neither son nor
 brother.
There was no end to his toil,
 yet his eyes were not content[j]
 with his wealth.
"For whom am I toiling," he
 asked,
 "and why am I depriving
 myself of enjoyment?"

3:22
t Ecc 2:24
Ecc 5:18
u Job 31:2

4:1
a Ps 12:5
Ecc 3:16
b La 1:16

4:2
c Jer 20:17-18
Jer 22:10
d Job 3:17
Job 10:18

4:3
e Job 3:16
Ecc 6:3
f Job 3:22

4:4
g Ecc 1:14

4:5
h Pr 6:10

4:6
i Pr 15:16-17
Pr 16:8

4:8
j Pr 27:20

5:2
a Jdg 11:35
b Job 6:24
Pr 10:19
Pr 20:25

This too is meaningless—
 a miserable business!

9Two are better than one,
 because they have a good
 return for their work:
10If one falls down,
 his friend can help him up.
But pity the man who falls
 and has no-one to help him up!
11Also, if two lie down together,
 they will keep warm.
But how can one keep warm
 alone?
12Though one may be
 overpowered,
 two can defend themselves.
A cord of three strands is not
 quickly broken.

Advancement Is Meaningless

13Better a poor but wise youth than an old but foolish king who no longer knows how to take warning. 14The youth may have come from prison to the kingship, or he may have been born in poverty within his kingdom. 15I saw that all who lived and walked under the sun followed the youth, the king's successor. 16There was no end to all the people who were before them. But those who came later were not pleased with the successor. This too is meaningless, a chasing after the wind.

Stand in Awe of God

5 Guard your steps when you go to the house of God. Go near to listen rather than to offer the sacrifice of fools, who do not know that they do wrong.

2Do not be quick with your
 mouth,
 do not be hasty in your heart
 to utter anything before God.[a]
God is in heaven
 and you are on earth,
 so let your words be few.[b]

c21 Or *Who knows the spirit of man, which rises upward, or the spirit of the animal, which*

3As a dream[c] comes when there
are many cares,
so the speech of a fool when
there are many words.[d]

4When you make a vow to God, do
not delay in fulfilling it.[e] He has no
pleasure in fools; fulfil your vow.[f]
5It is better not to vow than to make
a vow and not fulfil it.[g] 6Do not let
your mouth lead you into sin. And
do not protest to the ⌊temple⌋ messenger, "My vow was a mistake."
Why should God be angry at what
you say and destroy the work of
your hands? 7Much dreaming and
many words are meaningless.
Therefore stand in awe of God.[h]

Riches Are Meaningless

8If you see the poor oppressed[i]
in a district, and justice and rights
denied, do not be surprised at such
things; for one official is eyed by a
higher one, and over them both are
others higher still. 9The increase
from the land is taken by all; the
king himself profits from the
fields.

10Whoever loves money never has
money enough;
whoever loves wealth is never
satisfied with his income.
This too is meaningless.
11As goods increase,
so do those who consume
them.
And what benefit are they to
the owner
except to feast his eyes on
them?
12The sleep of a labourer is
sweet,
whether he eats little or much,
but the abundance of a rich
man
permits him no sleep.[j]

13I have seen a grievous evil under the sun:[k]

wealth hoarded to the harm of
its owner,

5:3
c Job 20:8
d Ecc 10:14

5:4
e Dt 23:21
Jdg 11:35
Ps 119:60
f Nu 30:2
Ps 66:13-14
Ps 76:11

5:5
g Nu 30:2-4
Pr 20:25
Jnh 2:9
Ac 5:4

5:7
h Ecc 3:14
Ecc 12:13

5:8
i Ps 12:5
Ecc 4:1

5:12
j Job 20:20

5:13
k Ecc 6:1-2

5:15
l Job 1:21
m Ps 49:17
1Ti 6:7
n Ecc 1:3

5:16
o Pr 11:29
Ecc 1:3

5:18
p Ecc 2:3
q Ecc 2:10,24

5:19
r 1Ch 29:12
2Ch 1:12
s Ecc 6:2
t Job 31:2
u Ecc 2:24
Ecc 3:13

5:20
v Dt 12:7,18

6:2
a Ps 17:14
Ecc 5:19
b Ecc 5:13

6:3
c Job 3:16
Ecc 4:3
d Job 3:3

14 or wealth lost through some
misfortune,
so that when he has a son
there is nothing left for him.
15Naked a man comes from his
mother's womb,
and as he comes, so he
departs.[l]
He takes nothing from his
labour[m]
that he can carry in his
hand.[n]

16This too is a grievous evil:

As a man comes, so he departs,
and what does he gain,
since he toils for the wind?[o]
17All his days he eats in darkness,
with great frustration,
affliction and anger.

18Then I realised that it is good
and proper for a man to eat and
drink,[p] and to find satisfaction in
his toilsome labour[q] under the sun
during the few days of life God has
given him—for this is his lot.
19Moreover, when God gives any
man wealth and possessions,[r] and
enables him to enjoy them,[s] to accept his lot[t] and be happy in his
work—this is a gift of God.[u] 20He
seldom reflects on the days of his
life, because God keeps him occupied with gladness of heart.[v]

6 I have seen another evil under
the sun, and it weighs heavily
on men: 2God gives a man wealth,
possessions and honour, so that he
lacks nothing his heart desires, but
God does not enable him to enjoy
them,[a] and a stranger enjoys them
instead. This is meaningless, a
grievous evil.[b]

3A man may have a hundred children and live many years; yet no
matter how long he lives, if he cannot enjoy his prosperity and does
not receive proper burial, I say that
a stillborn[c] child is better off than
he.[d] 4It comes without meaning, it
departs in darkness, and in darkness its name is shrouded. 5Though
it never saw the sun or knew

anything, it has more rest than
does that man—6 even if he lives a
thousand years twice over but
fails to enjoy his prosperity. Do
not all go to the same place?

7 All man's efforts are for his
mouth,
yet his appetite is never
satisfied.[e]
8 What advantage has a wise man
over a fool?[f]
What does a poor man gain
by knowing how to conduct
himself before others?
9 Better what the eye sees
than the roving of the
appetite.
This too is meaningless,
a chasing after the wind.[g]
10 Whatever exists has already
been named,
and what man is has been
known;
no man can contend
with one who is stronger than
he.
11 The more the words,
the less the meaning,
and how does that profit
anyone?

12 For who knows what is good for
a man in life, during the few and
meaningless days[h] he passes
through like a shadow?[i] Who can
tell him what will happen under the
sun after he is gone?

Wisdom

7 A good name is better than
fine perfume,[a]
and the day of death better
than the day of birth.
2 It is better to go to a house of
mourning
than to go to a house of
feasting,
for death[b] is the destiny[c] of
every man;
the living should take this to
heart.
3 Sorrow is better than
laughter,[d]

6:7 e Pr 16:26 Pr 27:20
6:8 f Ecc 2:15
6:9 g Ecc 1:14
6:12 h Job 10:20 i Job 14:2 Ps 39:6 Jas 4:14
7:1 a Pr 22:1 SS 1:3
7:2 b Pr 11:19 c Ps 90:12
7:3 d Pr 14:13
7:4 e Ecc 2:1 Jer 16:8
7:5 f Ps 141:5 Pr 13:18 Pr 15:31-32
7:6 g Ps 58:9 Ps 118:12 h Ecc 2:2
7:7 i Ex 18:21 Ex 23:8 Dt 16:19
7:8 j Pr 14:29 Gal 5:22 Eph 4:2
7:9 k Mt 5:22 Pr 14:17 Jas 1:19
7:11 l Pr 8:10-11 Ecc 2:13 m Ecc 11:7
7:13 n Ecc 2:24 o Ecc 1:15

because a sad face is good for
the heart.
4 The heart of the wise is in the
house of mourning,
but the heart of fools is in the
house of pleasure.[e]
5 It is better to heed a wise man's
rebuke[f]
than to listen to the song of
fools.
6 Like the crackling of thorns[g]
under the pot,
so is the laughter[h] of fools.
This too is meaningless.
7 Extortion turns a wise man into
a fool,
and a bribe[i] corrupts the
heart.
8 The end of a matter is better
than its beginning,
and patience[j] is better than
pride.
9 Do not be quickly provoked[k] in
your spirit,
for anger resides in the lap of
fools.
10 Do not say, "Why were the old
days better than these?"
For it is not wise to ask such
questions.
11 Wisdom, like an inheritance, is
a good thing[l]
and benefits those who see the
sun.[m]
12 Wisdom is a shelter
as money is a shelter,
but the advantage of knowledge
is this:
that wisdom preserves the life
of its possessor.

13 Consider what God has done:[n]

Who can straighten
what he has made crooked?[o]
14 When times are good, be happy;
but when times are bad,
consider:
God has made the one
as well as the other.
Therefore, a man cannot
discover
anything about his future.

[15]In this meaningless life[p] of mine I have seen both of these:

a righteous man perishing in his
righteousness,
and a wicked man living long
in his wickedness.[q]
[16]Do not be over-righteous,
neither be overwise—
why destroy yourself?
[17]Do not be overwicked,
and do not be a fool—
why die before your time?[r]
[18]It is good to grasp the one
and not let go of the other.
The man who fears God[s] will
avoid all ⌞extremes⌟.[a]
[19]Wisdom[t] makes one wise man
more powerful[u]
than ten rulers in a city.
[20]There is not a righteous man[v]
on earth
who does what is right and
never sins.[w]
[21]Do not pay attention to every
word people say,
or you[x] may hear your
servant cursing you—
[22]for you know in your heart
that many times you yourself
have cursed others.

[23]All this I tested by wisdom and I said,

"I am determined to be
wise"[y]—
but this was beyond me.
[24]Whatever wisdom may be,
it is far off and most
profound—
who can discover it?[z]
[25]So I turned my mind to
understand,
to investigate and to search
out wisdom and the scheme
of things[a]
and to understand the stupidity
of wickedness
and the madness of folly.[b]
[26]I find more bitter than death
the woman who is a snare,[c]
whose heart is a trap
and whose hands are chains.
The man who pleases God will
escape her,
but the sinner she will
ensnare.[d]

[27]"Look," says the Teacher,[b][e] "this is what I have discovered:

"Adding one thing to another to
discover the scheme of
things—
[28] while I was still searching
but not finding—
I found one ⌞upright⌟ man among
a thousand,
but not one ⌞upright⌟ woman[f]
among them all.
[29]This only have I found:
God made mankind upright,
but men have gone in search
of many schemes."

8

Who is like the wise man?
Who knows the explanation
of things?
Wisdom brightens a man's face
and changes its hard
appearance.

Obey the King

[2]Obey the king's command, I say, because you took an oath before God. [3]Do not be in a hurry to leave the king's presence.[a] Do not stand up for a bad cause, for he will do whatever he pleases. [4]Since a king's word is supreme, who can say to him, "What are you doing?[b]"

[5]Whoever obeys his command
will come to no harm,
and the wise heart will know
the proper time and
procedure.
[6]For there is a proper time and
procedure for every
matter,[c]
though a man's misery weighs
heavily upon him.

7:15 p Job 7:7 q Ecc 8:12-14 Jer 12:1
7:17 r Job 15:32 Ps 55:23
7:18 s Ecc 3:14
7:19 t Ecc 2:13 u Ecc 9:13-18
7:20 v Ps 14:3 w 1Ki 8:46 2Ch 6:36 Pr 20:9 Ro 3:23
7:21 x Pr 30:10
7:23 y Ecc 1:17 Ro 1:22
7:24 z Job 28:12
7:25 a Job 28:3 b Ecc 1:17
7:26 c Ex 10:7 Jdg 14:15 d Pr 2:16-19 Pr 5:3-5 Pr 7:23 Pr 22:14
7:27 e Ecc 1:1
7:28 f 1Ki 11:3
8:3 a Ecc 10:4
8:4 b Job 9:12 Est 1:19 Da 4:35
8:6 c Ecc 3:1

[a]18 Or *will follow them both* [b]27 Or *leader of the assembly*

7 Since no man knows the future,
who can tell him what is to
come?
8 No man has power over the
wind to contain it;[a]
so no-one has power over the
day of his death.
As no-one is discharged in time
of war,
so wickedness will not release
those who practise it.

9 All this I saw, as I applied my
mind to everything done under the
sun. There is a time when a man
lords it over others to his own[b]
hurt. 10 Then too, I saw the wicked
buried[d]—those who used to come
and go from the holy place and receive praise[c] in the city where
they did this. This too is meaningless.
11 When the sentence for a crime
is not quickly carried out, the
hearts of the people are filled with
schemes to do wrong. 12 Although a
wicked man commits a hundred
crimes and still lives a long time, I
know that it will go better[e] with
God-fearing men,[f] who are reverent before God.[g] 13 Yet because the
wicked do not fear God,[h] it will not
go well with them, and their days[i]
will not lengthen like a shadow.
14 There is something else meaningless that occurs on earth: righteous men who get what the wicked
deserve, and wicked men who get
what the righteous deserve.[j] This
too, I say, is meaningless.[k] 15 So I
commend the enjoyment of life[l],
because nothing is better for a man
under the sun than to eat and
drink[m] and be glad.[n] Then joy will
accompany him in his work all the
days of the life God has given him
under the sun.
16 When I applied my mind to
know wisdom[o] and to observe
man's labour on earth[p]—his eyes
not seeing sleep day or night—
17 then I saw all that God has done.[q]
No-one can comprehend what goes
on under the sun. Despite all his
efforts to search it out, man cannot discover its meaning. Even if
a wise man claims he knows, he
cannot really comprehend it.[r]

A Common Destiny for All

9 So I reflected on all this and
concluded that the righteous
and the wise and what they do are
in God's hands, but no man knows
whether love or hate awaits him.[a]
2 All share a common destiny—the
righteous and the wicked, the good
and the bad,[a] the clean and the unclean, those who offer sacrifices
and those who do not.

As it is with the good man,
so with the sinner;
as it is with those who take
oaths,
so with those who are afraid
to take them.[b]

3 This is the evil in everything
that happens under the sun: The
same destiny overtakes all.[c] The
hearts of men, moreover, are full of
evil and there is madness in their
hearts while they live,[d] and afterwards they join the dead.[e] 4 Anyone who is among the living has
hope[b]—even a live dog is better
off than a dead lion!

5 For the living know that they
will die,
but the dead know nothing;[f]
they have no further reward,
and even the memory of
them[g] is forgotten.[h]
6 Their love, their hate
and their jealousy have long
since vanished;
never again will they have a
part
in anything that happens
under the sun.[i]

8:10 d Ecc 1:11
8:12 e Dt 12:28; Ps 37:11, 18-19; Pr 1:32-33; Isa 3:10-11; f Ex 1:20; g Ecc 3:14
8:13 h Ecc 3:14; Isa 3:11; i Dt 4:40; Job 5:26; Ps 34:12; Isa 65:20
8:14 j Job 21:7; Ps 73:14; Mal 3:15; k Ecc 7:15
8:15 l Ps 42:8; m Ex 32:6; Ecc 2:3; n Ecc 2:24; Ecc 3:12-13; Ecc 5:18; Ecc 9:7
8:16 o Ecc 1:17; p Ecc 1:13
8:17 q Job 28:3; r Job 5:9; Job 28:23; Ecc 3:11; Ro 11:33
9:1 a Dt 33:3; Job 12:10; Ecc 10:14
9:2 b Job 9:22; Ecc 2:14; Ecc 6:6; Ecc 7:2
9:3 c Job 9:22; Ecc 2:14; d Jer 11:8; Jer 13:10; Jer 16:12; Jer 17:9; e Job 21:26
9:5 f Job 14:21; g Ps 9:6; h Ecc 1:11; Ecc 2:16; Isa 26:14
9:6 i Job 21:21

a8 Or *over his spirit to retain it* b9 Or *to their* c10 Some Hebrew manuscripts and Septuagint (Aquila); most Hebrew manuscripts *and are forgotten* a2 Septuagint (Aquila), Vulgate and Syriac; Hebrew does not have *and the bad.* b4 Or *What then is to be chosen? With all who live, there is hope*

7Go, eat your food with gladness,
and drink your wine[j] with a joyful
heart,[k] for it is now that God
favours what you do. 8Always be
clothed in white,[l] and always
anoint your head with oil. 9Enjoy
life with your wife,[m] whom you
love, all the days of this meaningless life that God has given you under the sun—all your meaningless
days. For this is your lot[n] in life
and in your toilsome labour under
the sun. 10Whatever[o] your hand
finds to do, do it with all your
might,[p] for in the grave,[c][q] where
you are going, there is neither
working nor planning nor knowledge nor wisdom.[r]

11I have seen something else under the sun:

The race is not to the swift
  or the battle to the strong,[s]
nor does food come to the
    wise[t]
  or wealth to the brilliant
  or favour to the learned;
but time and chance[u] happen to
    them all.[v]

12Moreover, no man knows when
his hour will come:

As fish are caught in a cruel
    net,
  or birds are taken in a snare,
so men are trapped by evil
    times[w]
  that fall unexpectedly upon
    them.[x]

Wisdom Better Than Folly

13I also saw under the sun this example of wisdom[y] that greatly im-
pressed me: 14There was once a
small city with only a few people in
it. And a powerful king came
against it, surrounded it and built
huge siegeworks against it. 15Now
there lived in that city a man poor
but wise, and he saved the city by
his wisdom. But nobody remembered that poor man.[z] 16So I said,
"Wisdom is better than strength."
But the poor man's wisdom is
despised, and his words are no longer heeded.[a]

17The quiet words of the wise are
    more to be heeded
  than the shouts of a ruler of
    fools.
18Wisdom[b] is better than
    weapons of war,
  but one sinner destroys much
    good.

10

As dead flies give
    perfume a bad smell,
  so a little folly[a] outweighs
    wisdom and honour.
2The heart of the wise inclines to
    the right,
  but the heart of the fool to the
    left.
3Even as he walks along the
    road,
  the fool lacks sense
  and shows everyone[b] how
    stupid he is.
4If a ruler's anger rises against
    you,
  do not leave your post;[c]
  calmness can lay great errors
    to rest.[d]

5There is an evil I have seen
    under the sun,
  the sort of error that arises
    from a ruler:
6Fools are put in many high
    positions,[e]
  while the rich occupy the low
    ones.
7I have seen slaves on
    horseback,
  while princes go on foot like
    slaves.[f]
8Whoever digs a pit may fall into
    it;[g]
  whoever breaks through a wall
    may be bitten by a snake.[h]
9Whoever quarries stones may
    be injured by them;
  whoever splits logs may be
    endangered by them.[i]

10If the axe is dull
  and its edge unsharpened,

[c]10 Hebrew *Sheol*

9:7 j Nu 6:20 k Ecc 2:24 Ecc 8:15
9:8 l Ps 23:5 Rev 3:4
9:9 m Pr 5:18 n Job 31:2
9:10 o 1Sa 10:7 p Ecc 11:6 Ro 12:11 Col 3:23 q Nu 16:33 r Ecc 2:24
9:11 s Am 2:14-15 t Job 32:13 Isa 47:10 Jer 9:23 u Ecc 2:14 v Dt 8:18
9:12 w Pr 29:6 x Ps 73:22 Ecc 2:14 Ecc 8:7
9:13 y 2Sa 20:22
9:15 z Ge 40:14 Ecc 1:11 Ecc 2:16 Ecc 4:13
9:16 a Pr 21:22 Ecc 7:19
9:18 b ver 16
10:1 a Pr 13:16 Pr 18:2
10:3 b Pr 13:16 Pr 18:2
10:4 c Ecc 8:3 d Pr 16:14 Pr 25:15
10:6 e Pr 29:2
10:7 f Pr 19:10
10:8 g Ps 7:15 Ps 57:6 Pr 26:27 h Est 2:23 Ps 9:16 Am 5:19
10:9 i Pr 26:27

more strength is needed
but skill will bring success.

11 If a snake bites before it is charmed,
there is no profit for the charmer.[j]

12 Words from a wise man's mouth are gracious,[k]
but a fool is consumed by his own lips.[l]
13 At the beginning his words are folly;
at the end they are wicked madness—
14 and the fool multiplies words.[m]

No-one knows what is coming—
who can tell him what will happen after him?[n]

15 A fool's work wearies him;
he does not know the way to town.

16 Woe to you, O land whose king was a servant[a][o]
and whose princes feast in the morning.
17 Blessed are you, O land whose king is of noble birth
and whose princes eat at a proper time—
for strength and not for drunkenness.[p]

18 If a man is lazy, the rafters sag;
if his hands are idle, the house leaks.[q]

19 A feast is made for laughter,
and wine[r] makes life merry,
but money is the answer for everything.

20 Do not revile the king[s] even in your thoughts,
or curse the rich in your bedroom,
because a bird of the air may carry your words,
and a bird on the wing may report what you say.

Bread Upon the Waters

11 Cast[a] your bread upon the waters,
for after many days you will find it again.[b]
2 Give portions to seven, yes to eight,
for you do not know what disaster may come upon the land.

3 If clouds are full of water,
they pour rain upon the earth.
Whether a tree falls to the south or to the north,
in the place where it falls,
there will it lie.
4 Whoever watches the wind will not plant;
whoever looks at the clouds will not reap.
5 As you do not know the path of the wind,[c]
or how the body is formed[a] in a mother's womb,[d]
so you cannot understand the work of God,
the Maker of all things.

6 Sow your seed in the morning,
and at evening let not your hands be idle,[e]
for you do not know which will succeed,
whether this or that,
or whether both will do equally well.

Remember Your Creator While Young

7 Light is sweet,
and it pleases the eyes to see the sun.[f]
8 However many years a man may live,
let him enjoy them all.
But let him remember[g] the days of darkness,
for they will be many.
Everything to come is meaningless.

10:11 j Ps 58:5; Isa 3:3
10:12 k Pr 10:32; l Pr 10:14; Pr 14:3; Pr 15:2; Pr 18:7
10:14 m Pr 15:2; Ecc 5:3; Ecc 6:12; Ecc 8:7; n Ecc 9:1
10:16 o Isa 3:4-5,12
10:17 p Dt 14:26; 1Sa 25:36; Pr 31:4
10:18 q Pr 20:4; Pr 24:30-34
10:19 r Ge 14:18; Jdg 9:13
10:20 s Ex 22:28
11:1 a ver 6; Isa 32:20; Hos 10:12; b Dt 24:19; Pr 19:17; Mt 10:42
11:5 c Jn 3:8-10; d Ps 139:14-16
11:6 e Ecc 9:10
11:7 f Ecc 7:11
11:8 g Ecc 12:1

a16 Or *king is a child* a5 Or *know how life* (or *the spirit*) / *enters the body being formed*

9 Be happy, young man, while
 you are young,
 and let your heart give you
 joy in the days of your
 youth.
Follow the ways of your heart
 and whatever your eyes see,
but know that for all these
 things
 God will bring you to
 judgment.[h]
10 So then, banish anxiety[i] from
 your heart
 and cast off the troubles of
 your body,
 for youth and vigour are
 meaningless.[j]

12

Remember[a] your Creator
 in the days of your youth,
before the days of trouble[b]
 come
 and the years approach when
 you will say,
 "I find no pleasure in them"—
2 before the sun and the light
 and the moon and the stars
 grow dark,
 and the clouds return after the
 rain;
3 when the keepers of the house
 tremble,
 and the strong men stoop,
when the grinders cease
 because they are few,
 and those looking through the
 windows grow dim;
4 when the doors to the street are
 closed
 and the sound of grinding
 fades;
when men rise up at the sound
 of birds,
 but all their songs grow
 faint;[c]
5 when men are afraid of heights
 and of dangers in the streets;
when the almond tree blossoms
 and the grasshopper drags
 himself along
 and desire no longer is stirred.
Then man goes to his eternal
 home[d]
 and mourners[e] go about the
 streets.

6 Remember him—before the
 silver cord is severed,
 or the golden bowl is broken;
before the pitcher is shattered
 at the spring,
 or the wheel broken at the
 well,
7 and the dust returns[f] to the
 ground it came from,
 and the spirit returns to God[g]
 who gave it.[h]

8 "Meaningless! Meaningless!"
 says the Teacher.[a]
 "Everything is meaningless!"[i]

The Conclusion of the Matter

9 Not only was the Teacher wise,
but also he imparted knowledge
to the people. He pondered and
searched out and set in order
many proverbs.[j] 10 The Teacher
searched to find just the right
words, and what he wrote was upright and true.[k]

11 The words of the wise are like
goads, their collected sayings like
firmly embedded nails[l]—given by
one Shepherd. 12 Be warned, my
son, of anything in addition to
them.

Of making many books there is
no end, and much study wearies the
body.[m]

13 Now all has been heard;
 here is the conclusion of the
 matter:
Fear God and keep his
 commandments,[n]
 for this is the whole ⌊duty⌋ of
 man.[o]
14 For God will bring every deed
 into judgment,[p]
 including every hidden thing,[q]
 whether it is good or evil.

11:9 *h* Job 19:29; Ecc 2:24; Ecc 3:17; Ecc 12:14; Ro 14:10
11:10 *i* Ps 94:19 *j* Ecc 2:24
12:1 *a* Ecc 11:8 *b* 2Sa 19:35
12:4 *c* Jer 25:10
12:5 *d* Job 17:13; Job 10:21 *e* Jer 9:17; Am 5:16
12:7 *f* Ge 3:19; Job 34:15; Ps 146:4 *g* Ecc 3:21 *h* Job 20:8; Zec 12:1
12:8 *i* Ecc 1:2
12:9 *j* 1Ki 4:32
12:10 *k* Pr 22:20-21
12:11 *l* Ezr 9:8
12:12 *m* Ecc 1:18
12:13 *n* Dt 4:2; Dt 10:12 *o* Mic 6:8
12:14 *p* Ecc 3:17 *q* Mt 10:26; 1Co 4:5

a8 Or *the leader of the assembly*; also in verses 9 and 10

SONG OF SONGS

1 Solomon's Song of Songs.[a]

Beloved[a]

2 Let him kiss me with the kisses
of his mouth—
for your love[b] is more
delightful than wine.
3 Pleasing is the fragrance of
your perfumes;[c]
your name[d] is like perfume
poured out.
No wonder the maidens[e] love
you!
4 Take me away with you—let us
hurry!
Let the king bring me into his
chambers.[f]

Friends

We rejoice and delight in you;[b]
we will praise your love more
than wine.

Beloved

How right they are to adore
you!

5 Dark am I, yet lovely,[g]
O daughters of Jerusalem,[h]
dark like the tents of Kedar,
like the tent curtains of
Solomon.[c]
6 Do not stare at me because I
am dark,
because I am darkened by the
sun.
My mother's sons were angry
with me
and made me take care of the
vineyards;[i]
my own vineyard I have
neglected.
7 Tell me, you whom I love,
where you graze your flock
and where you rest your
sheep[j] at midday.
Why should I be like a veiled
woman
beside the flocks of your
friends?

Friends

8 If you do not know, most
beautiful of women,[k]
follow the tracks of the sheep
and graze your young goats
by the tents of the shepherds.

Lover

9 I liken you, my darling, to a
mare
harnessed to one of the
chariots[l] of Pharaoh.
10 Your cheeks[m] are beautiful
with ear-rings,
your neck with strings of
jewels.[n]
11 We will make you ear-rings of
gold,
studded with silver.

Beloved

12 While the king was at his
table,
my perfume spread its
fragrance.[o]
13 My lover is to me a sachet of
myrrh
resting between my breasts.
14 My lover is to me a cluster of
henna[p] blossoms
from the vineyards of En
Gedi.[q]

1:1
a 1Ki 4:32

1:2
b SS 4:10

1:3
c SS 4:10
d Ecc 7:1
e Ps 45:14

1:4
f Ps 45:15

1:5
g SS 2:14
SS 4:3
h SS 2:7
SS 5:8
SS 5:16

1:6
i Ps 69:8
SS 8:12

1:7
j SS 3:1-4
Isa 13:20

1:8
k SS 5:9
SS 6:1

1:9
l 2Ch 1:17

1:10
m SS 5:13
n Isa 61:10

1:12
o SS 4:11-14

1:14
p SS 4:13
q 1Sa 23:29

a2 Primarily on the basis of the gender of the Hebrew pronouns used, male and female speakers are indicated in the margins by the captions *Lover* and *Beloved* respectively. The words of others are marked *Friends*. In some instances the divisions and their captions are debatable.
b4 The Hebrew is masculine singular.
c5 Or *Salma*

Lover

[15]How beautiful[r] you are, my darling!
Oh, how beautiful!
Your eyes are doves.[s]

Beloved

[16]How handsome you are, my lover!
Oh, how charming!
And our bed is verdant.

Lover

[17]The beams of our house are cedars;[t]
our rafters are firs.

Beloved[a]

2 I am a rose[b][a] of Sharon,[b]
a lily[c] of the valleys.

Lover

[2]Like a lily among thorns
is my darling among the maidens.

Beloved

[3]Like an apple tree among the trees of the forest
is my lover[d] among the young men.
I delight[e] to sit in his shade,
and his fruit is sweet to my taste.[f]
[4]He has taken me to the banquet hall,[g]
and his banner[h] over me is love.
[5]Strengthen me with raisins,
refresh me with apples,[i]
for I am faint with love.[j]
[6]His left arm is under my head,
and his right arm embraces me.[k]
[7]Daughters of Jerusalem, I charge you[l]
by the gazelles and by the does of the field:
Do not arouse or awaken love
until it so desires.[m]

1:15 r SS 4:7 s SS 2:14; SS 4:1; SS 5:2,12; SS 6:9
1:17 t 1Ki 6:9
2:1 a Isa 35:1 b 1Ch 27:29 c SS 5:13; Hos 14:5
2:3 d SS 1:14 e SS 1:4 f SS 4:16
2:4 g Est 1:11 h Nu 1:52
2:5 i SS 7:8 j SS 5:8
2:6 k SS 8:3
2:7 l SS 5:8 m SS 3:5; SS 8:4
2:8 n ver 17; SS 8:14
2:9 o 2Sa 2:18 p ver 17; SS 8:14
2:13 q Isa 28:4; Jer 24:2; Hos 9:10; Mic 7:1; Na 3:12 r SS 7:12
2:14 s Ge 8:8; SS 1:15 t SS 1:5; SS 8:13
2:15 u Jdg 15:4 v SS 1:6 w SS 7:12
2:16 x SS 7:10 y SS 4:5; SS 6:3
2:17 z SS 4:6

[8]Listen! My lover!
Look! Here he comes,
leaping across the mountains,
bounding over the hills.[n]
[9]My lover is like a gazelle[o] or a young stag.[p]
Look! There he stands behind our wall,
gazing through the windows,
peering through the lattice.
[10]My lover spoke and said to me,
"Arise, my darling,
my beautiful one, and come with me.
[11]See! The winter is past;
the rains are over and gone.
[12]Flowers appear on the earth;
the season of singing has come,
the cooing of doves
is heard in our land.
[13]The fig-tree forms its early fruit;[q]
the blossoming[r] vines spread their fragrance.
Arise, come, my darling;
my beautiful one, come with me."

Lover

[14]My dove[s] in the clefts of the rock,
in the hiding-places on the mountainside,
show me your face,
let me hear your voice;
for your voice is sweet,
and your face is lovely.[t]
[15]Catch for us the foxes,[u]
the little foxes
that ruin the vineyards,[v]
our vineyards that are in bloom.[w]

Beloved

[16]My lover is mine and I am his;[x]
he browses among the lilies.[y]
[17]Until the day breaks
and the shadows flee,[z]

[a]*1* Or *Lover* [b]*1* Possibly a member of the crocus family

turn, my lover,[a]
and be like a gazelle
or like a young stag[b]
on the rugged hills.[c][c]

3 All night long on my bed
I looked[a] for the one my heart loves;
I looked for him but did not find him.
2 I will get up now and go about the city,
through its streets and squares;
I will search for the one my heart loves.
So I looked for him but did not find him.
3 The watchmen found me
as they made their rounds in the city.[b]
"Have you seen the one my heart loves?"
4 Scarcely had I passed them
when I found the one my heart loves.
I held him and would not let him go
till I had brought him to my mother's house,[c]
to the room of the one who conceived me.[d]
5 Daughters of Jerusalem, I charge you[e]
by the gazelles and by the does of the field:
Do not arouse or awaken love
until it so desires.[f]

6 Who is this coming up from the desert[g]
like a column of smoke,
perfumed with myrrh[h] and incense
made from all the spices[i] of the merchant?
7 Look! It is Solomon's carriage,
escorted by sixty warriors,[j]
the noblest of Israel,
8 all of them wearing the sword,
all experienced in battle,
each with his sword at his side,
prepared for the terrors of the night.[k]
9 King Solomon made for himself
the carriage;
he made it of wood from Lebanon.
10 Its posts he made of silver,
its base of gold.
Its seat was upholstered with purple,
its interior lovingly inlaid
by[a] the daughters of Jerusalem.
11 Come out, you daughters of Zion,[l]
and look at King Solomon
wearing the crown,
the crown with which his mother crowned him
on the day of his wedding,
the day his heart rejoiced.[m]

Lover

4 How beautiful you are, my darling!
Oh, how beautiful!
Your eyes behind your veil
are doves.[a]
Your hair is like a flock of goats
descending from Mount Gilead.[b]
2 Your teeth are like a flock of sheep just shorn,
coming up from the washing.
Each has its twin;
not one of them is alone.[c]
3 Your lips are like a scarlet ribbon;
your mouth[d] is lovely.
Your temples behind your veil
are like the halves of a pomegranate.[e]
4 Your neck is like the tower[f] of David,
built with elegance;[a]
on it hang a thousand shields,[g]
all of them shields of warriors.
5 Your two breasts[h] are like two fawns,
like twin fawns of a gazelle[i]

2:17 a SS 1:14 b ver 9 c ver 8
3:1 a SS 5:6; Isa 26:9
3:3 b SS 5:7
3:4 c SS 8:2 d SS 6:9
3:5 e SS 2:7 f SS 8:4
3:6 g SS 8:5 h SS 1:13; SS 4:6,14 i Ex 30:34
3:7 j 1Sa 8:11
3:8 k Job 15:22; Ps 91:5
3:11 l Isa 4:4 m Isa 62:5
4:1 a SS 1:15; SS 5:12 b SS 6:5; Mic 7:14
4:2 c SS 6:6
4:3 d SS 5:16 e SS 6:7
4:4 f SS 7:4 g Eze 27:10
4:5 h SS 7:3 i Pr 5:19

c17 Or *the hills of Bether*
a10 Or *its inlaid interior a gift of love / from*
a4 The meaning of the Hebrew for this word is uncertain.

that browse among the lilies.[j]
6Until the day breaks
and the shadows flee,[k]
I will go to the mountain of
myrrh[l]
and to the hill of incense.
7All beautiful[m] you are, my
darling;
there is no flaw in you.

8Come with me from Lebanon,
my bride,[n]
come with me from Lebanon.
Descend from the crest of
Amana,
from the top of Senir,[o] the
summit of Hermon,[p]
from the lions' dens
and the mountain haunts of
the leopards.
9You have stolen my heart, my
sister, my bride;
you have stolen my heart
with one glance of your eyes,
with one jewel of your
necklace.[q]
10How delightful[r] is your love[s],
my sister, my bride!
How much more pleasing is
your love than wine,
and the fragrance of your
perfume than any spice!
11Your lips drop sweetness as the
honeycomb, my bride;
milk and honey are under
your tongue.[t]
The fragrance of your
garments is like that of
Lebanon.[u]
12You are a garden locked up, my
sister, my bride;
you are a spring enclosed, a
sealed fountain.[v]
13Your plants are an orchard of
pomegranates[w]
with choice fruits,
with henna[x] and nard,
14 nard and saffron,
calamus and cinnamon,[y]
with every kind of incense
tree,
with myrrh[z] and aloes
and all the finest spices.[a]
15You are[b] a garden fountain,

4:5 j SS 2:16; SS 6:2-3
4:6 k SS 2:17; l ver 14
4:7 m SS 1:15
4:8 n SS 5:1; o Dt 3:9; p 1Ch 5:23
4:9 q Ge 41:42
4:10 r SS 7:6; s SS 1:2
4:11 t Ps 19:10; SS 5:1; u Hos 14:6
4:12 v Pr 5:15-18
4:13 w SS 6:11; SS 7:12; x SS 1:14
4:14 y Ex 30:23; z SS 3:6; a SS 1:12
4:16 b SS 2:3; SS 5:1
5:1 a SS 4:8; b SS 4:11; Isa 55:1
5:2 c SS 4:7; d SS 6:9
5:5 e ver 13

a well of flowing water
streaming down from
Lebanon.

Beloved

16Awake, north wind,
and come, south wind!
Blow on my garden,
that its fragrance may spread
abroad.
Let my lover come into his
garden
and taste its choice fruits.[b]

Lover

5 I have come into my garden,
my sister, my bride;[a]
I have gathered my myrrh
with my spice.
I have eaten my honeycomb and
my honey;
I have drunk my wine and my
milk.[b]

Friends

Eat, O friends, and drink;
drink your fill, O lovers.

Beloved

2I slept but my heart was awake.
Listen! My lover is knocking:
"Open to me, my sister, my
darling,
my dove, my flawless[c] one.[d]
My head is drenched with dew,
my hair with the dampness of
the night."
3I have taken off my robe—
must I put it on again?
I have washed my feet—
must I soil them again?
4My lover thrust his hand
through the latch-opening;
my heart began to pound for
him.
5I arose to open for my lover,
and my hands dripped with
myrrh,[e]
my fingers with flowing myrrh,
on the handles of the lock.

b15 Or *I am* (spoken by the *Beloved*)

6I opened for my lover,[f]
but my lover had left; he was gone.[g]
My heart sank at his departure.[a]
I looked[h] for him but did not find him.
I called him but he did not answer.
7The watchmen found me
as they made their rounds in the city.[i]
They beat me, they bruised me;
they took away my cloak,
those watchmen of the walls!
8O daughters of Jerusalem, I charge you[j]—
if you find my lover,
what will you tell him?
Tell him I am faint with love.[k]

Friends

9How is your beloved better than others,
most beautiful of women?[l]
How is your beloved better than others,
that you charge us so?

Beloved

10My lover is radiant and ruddy,
outstanding among ten thousand.[m]
11His head is purest gold;
his hair is wavy
and black as a raven.
12His eyes are like doves[n]
by the water streams,
washed in milk,[o]
mounted like jewels.
13His cheeks[p] are like beds of spice[q]
yielding perfume.
His lips are like lilies[r]
dripping with myrrh.
14His arms are rods of gold
set with chrysolite.
His body is like polished ivory
decorated with sapphires.[b][s]
15His legs are pillars of marble
set on bases of pure gold.
His appearance is like Lebanon,[t]
choice as its cedars.
16His mouth[u] is sweetness itself;
he is altogether lovely.
This is my lover,[v] this my friend,
O daughters of Jerusalem.[w]

Friends

6 Where has your lover[a] gone,
most beautiful of women?[b]
Which way did your lover turn,
that we may look for him with you?

Beloved

2My lover has gone[c] down to his garden,[d]
to the beds of spices,[e]
to browse in the gardens
and to gather lilies.
3I am my lover's and my lover is mine;[f]
he browses among the lilies.[g]

Lover

4You are beautiful, my darling, as Tirzah,[h]
lovely as Jerusalem,[i]
majestic as troops with banners.[j]
5Turn your eyes from me;
they overwhelm me.
Your hair is like a flock of goats
descending from Gilead.[k]
6Your teeth are like a flock of sheep
coming up from the washing.
Each has its twin,
not one of them is alone.[l]
7Your temples behind your veil[m]
are like the halves of a pomegranate.[n]
8Sixty queens[o] there may be,
and eighty concubines,[p]
and virgins beyond number;

a6 Or *heart had gone out to him when he spoke*
b14 Or *lapis lazuli*

5:6 f SS 6:1 g SS 6:2 h SS 3:1
5:7 i SS 3:3
5:8 j SS 2:7; SS 3:5 k SS 2:5
5:9 l SS 1:8; SS 6:1
5:10 m Ps 45:2
5:12 n SS 1:15; SS 4:1 o Ge 49:12
5:13 p SS 1:10 q SS 6:2 r SS 2:1
5:14 s Job 28:6
5:15 t 1Ki 4:33; SS 7:4
5:16 u SS 4:3 v SS 7:9 w SS 1:5
6:1 a SS 5:6 b SS 1:8
6:2 c SS 5:6 d SS 4:12 e SS 5:13
6:3 f SS 7:10 g SS 2:16
6:4 h Jos 12:24 i Ps 48:2; Ps 50:2 j ver 10
6:5 k SS 4:1
6:6 l SS 4:2
6:7 m Ge 24:65 n SS 4:3
6:8 o Ps 45:9 p Ge 22:24

9 but my dove,[q] my perfect one,[r] is unique,
the only daughter of her mother,
the favourite of the one who bore her.[s]
The maidens saw her and called her blessed;
the queens and concubines praised her.

Friends

10 Who is this that appears like the dawn,
fair as the moon, bright as the sun,
majestic as the stars in procession?

Lover

11 I went down to the grove of nut trees
to look at the new growth in the valley,
to see if the vines had budded
or the pomegranates were in bloom.[t]
12 Before I realised it,
my desire set me among the royal chariots of my people.[a]

Friends

13 Come back, come back,
O Shulammite;
come back, come back, that we may gaze on you!

Lover

Why would you gaze on the Shulammite
as on the dance[u] of Mahanaim?

7

1 How beautiful your sandalled feet,
O prince's[a] daughter!
Your graceful legs are like jewels,
the work of a craftsman's hands.

6:9 q SS 1:15 r SS 5:2 s SS 3:4
6:11 t SS 7:12
6:13 u Ex 15:20
7:1 a Ps 45:13
7:3 b SS 4:5
7:4 c Ps 144:12; SS 4:4 d Nu 21:26 e SS 5:15
7:5 f Isa 35:2
7:6 g SS 1:15 h SS 4:10
7:7 i SS 4:5
7:8 j SS 2:5
7:9 k SS 5:16
7:10 l Ps 45:11 m SS 2:16; SS 6:3

2 Your navel is a rounded goblet
that never lacks blended wine.
Your waist is a mound of wheat
encircled by lilies.
3 Your breasts[b] are like two fawns,
twins of a gazelle.
4 Your neck is like an ivory tower.[c]
Your eyes are the pools of Heshbon[d]
by the gate of Bath Rabbim.
Your nose is like the tower of Lebanon[e]
looking towards Damascus.
5 Your head crowns you like Mount Carmel.[f]
Your hair is like royal tapestry;
the king is held captive by its tresses.
6 How beautiful[g] you are and how pleasing,
O love, with your delights![h]
7 Your stature is like that of the palm,
and your breasts[i] like clusters of fruit.
8 I said, "I will climb the palm tree;
I will take hold of its fruit."
May your breasts be like the clusters of the vine,
the fragrance of your breath like apples,[j]
9 and your mouth like the best wine.

Beloved

May the wine go straight to my lover,[k]
flowing gently over lips and teeth.[a]
10 I belong to my lover,
and his desire[l] is for me.[m]

[a]12 Or *among the chariots of Amminadab*; or *among the chariots of the people of the prince*
[a]9 Septuagint, Aquila, Vulgate and Syriac; Hebrew *lips of sleepers*

[11]Come, my lover, let us go to the
countryside,
let us spend the night in the
villages.[b]
[12]Let us go early to the
vineyards[n]
to see if the vines have
budded,[o]
if their blossoms[p] have opened,
and if the pomegranates[q] are
in bloom[r]—
there I will give you my love.
[13]The mandrakes[s] send out their
fragrance,
and at our door is every
delicacy,
both new and old,
that I have stored up for you,
my lover.[t]

8 If only you were to me like a
brother,
who was nursed at my
mother's breasts!
Then, if I found you outside,
I would kiss you,
and no-one would despise me.
[2]I would lead you
and bring you to my mother's
house[a]—
she who has taught me.
I would give you spiced wine to
drink,
the nectar of my
pomegranates.
[3]His left arm is under my head
and his right arm embraces
me.[b]
[4]Daughters of Jerusalem, I
charge you:
Do not arouse or awaken love
until it so desires.[c]

Friends

[5]Who is this coming up from the
desert[d]
leaning on her lover?

Beloved

Under the apple tree I roused
you;
there your mother conceived[e]
you,
there she who was in labour
gave you birth.
[6]Place me like a seal over your
heart,
like a seal on your arm;
for love[f] is as strong as death,
its jealousy[a][g] unyielding as
the grave.[b]
It burns like blazing fire,
like a mighty flame.[c]
[7]Many waters cannot quench
love;
rivers cannot wash it away.
If one were to give
all the wealth of his house for
love,
it[d] would be utterly scorned.[h]

Friends

[8]We have a young sister,
and her breasts are not yet
grown.
What shall we do for our sister
for the day she is spoken for?
[9]If she is a wall,
we will build towers of silver
on her.
If she is a door,
we will enclose her with
panels of cedar.

Beloved

[10]I am a wall,
and my breasts are like
towers.
Thus I have become in his eyes
like one bringing contentment.
[11]Solomon had a vineyard[i] in
Baal Hamon;
he let out his vineyard to
tenants.
Each was to bring for its fruit
a thousand shekels[e][j] of
silver.
[12]But my own vineyard[k] is mine
to give;

7:12
n SS 1:6
o SS 2:15
p SS 2:13
q SS 4:13
r SS 6:11

7:13
s Ge 30:14
t SS 4:16

8:2
a SS 3:4

8:3
b SS 2:6

8:4
c SS 2:7
SS 3:5

8:5
d SS 3:6
e SS 3:4

8:6
f SS 1:2
g Nu 5:14

8:7
h Pr 6:35

8:11
i Ecc 2:4
j Isa 7:23

8:12
k SS 1:6

[b]11 Or *henna bushes* [a]6 Or *ardour*
[b]6 Hebrew *Sheol* [c]6 Or / *like the very flame of the LORD* [d]7 Or *he* [e]11 That is, about 25 pounds (about 11.5 kilograms); also in verse 12

the thousand shekels are for
you, O Solomon,
and two hundred[f] are for
those who tend its fruit.

Lover

13 You who dwell in the gardens
with friends in attendance,
let me hear your voice!

8:14
l Pr 5:19
m SS 2:9
n SS 2:8,17

Beloved

14 Come away, my lover,
and be like a gazelle[l]
or like a young stag[m]
on the spice-laden
mountains.[n]

f *12* That is, about 5 pounds (about 2.3 kilograms)

ISAIAH

1 The vision[a] concerning Judah and Jerusalem[b] that Isaiah son of Amoz saw[c] during the reigns of Uzziah,[d] Jotham, Ahaz[e] and Hezekiah, kings of Judah.

A Rebellious Nation

2Hear, O heavens! Listen,
O earth!
For the LORD has spoken:[f]
"I reared children and brought
them up,
but they have rebelled[g]
against me.
3The ox knows his master,
the donkey his owner's
manger,
but Israel does not know,[h]
my people do not understand."

4Ah, sinful nation,
a people loaded with guilt,
a brood of evildoers,[i]
children given to corruption!
They have forsaken the LORD;
they have spurned the Holy
One[j] of Israel
and turned their backs on him.

5Why should you be beaten any
more?
Why do you persist in
rebellion?[k]
Your whole head is injured,
your whole heart afflicted.[l]
6From the sole of your foot to
the top of your head
there is no soundness[m]—
only wounds and bruises
and open sores,
not cleansed or bandaged[n]
or soothed with oil.[o]

7Your country is desolate,[p]
your cities burned with fire;
your fields are being stripped
by foreigners
right before you,
laid waste as when overthrown
by strangers.
8The Daughter of Zion is left
like a shelter in a vineyard,
like a hut[q] in a field of melons,
like a city under siege.
9Unless the LORD Almighty
had left us some survivors,[r]
we would have become like
Sodom,
we would have been like
Gomorrah.[s]

10Hear the word of the LORD,[t]
you rulers of Sodom;[u]
listen to the law[v] of our God,
you people of Gomorrah!
11"The multitude of your
sacrifices—
what are they to me?" says the
LORD.
"I have more than enough of
burnt offerings,
of rams and the fat of fattened
animals;[w]
I have no pleasure
in the blood of bulls[x] and
lambs and goats.[y]
12When you come to appear
before me,
who has asked this of you,[z]
this trampling of my courts?
13Stop bringing meaningless
offerings![a]
Your incense[b] is detestable to
me.
New Moons, Sabbaths and
convocations[c]—
I cannot bear your evil
assemblies.
14Your New Moon festivals and
your appointed feasts[d]
my soul hates.
They have become a burden to
me;
I am weary[e] of bearing them.
15When you spread out your
hands in prayer,

1:1 *a* Nu 12:6 *b* Isa 40:9 *c* Isa 2:1 *d* 2Ch 26:22 *e* 2Ki 16:1
1:2 *f* Mic 1:2 *g* Isa 30:1,9 Isa 65:2
1:3 *h* Jer 8:7 Jer 9:3,6
1:4 *i* Isa 14:20 *j* Isa 5:19,24
1:5 *k* Isa 31:6 *l* Isa 33:6,24
1:6 *m* Ps 38:3 *n* Isa 30:26 Jer 8:22 *o* Lk 10:34
1:7 *p* Lev 26:34
1:8 *q* Job 27:18
1:9 *r* Isa 10:20-22 Isa 37:4, 31-32 *s* Ge 19:24 Ro 9:29*
1:10 *t* Isa 28:14 *u* Isa 3:9 Eze 16:49 Ro 9:29 Rev 11:8 *v* Isa 8:20
1:11 *w* Ps 50:8 *x* Jer 6:20 *y* 1Sa 15:22 Mal 1:10
1:12 *z* Ex 23:17
1:13 *a* Isa 66:3 *b* Jer 7:9 *c* 1Ch 23:31
1:14 *d* Lev 23:1-44 Nu 28:11-29:39 Isa 29:1 *e* Isa 7:13 Isa 43:22,24

I will hide[f] my eyes from
you;
even if you offer many prayers,
I will not listen.
Your hands are full of blood;[g]
16 wash and make yourselves
clean.
Take your evil deeds
out of my sight![h]
Stop doing wrong,[i]
17 learn to do right!
Seek justice,[j]
encourage the oppressed.[a]
Defend the cause of the
fatherless,[k]
plead the case of the widow.

18"Come now, let us reason
together,"[l]
says the LORD.
"Though your sins are like
scarlet,
they shall be as white as
snow;[m]
though they are red as crimson,
they shall be like wool.
19If you are willing and obedient,
you will eat the best from the
land;[n]
20but if you resist and rebel,
you will be devoured by the
sword."[o]
For the mouth of the LORD
has spoken.[p]

21See how the faithful city
has become a harlot![q]
She once was full of justice;
righteousness used to dwell in
her—
but now murderers!
22Your silver has become dross,
your choice wine is diluted
with water.
23Your rulers are rebels,
companions of thieves;
they all love bribes[r]
and chase after gifts.
They do not defend the cause of
the fatherless;
the widow's case does not
come before them.[s]

24Therefore the Lord, the LORD
Almighty,
the Mighty One of Israel,
declares:
"Ah, I will get relief from my
foes
and avenge[t] myself on my
enemies.
25I will turn my hand against you;
I will thoroughly purge away
your dross
and remove all your
impurities.[u]
26I will restore your judges as in
days of old,[v]
your counsellors as at the
beginning.
Afterwards you will be called
the City of Righteousness,[w]
the Faithful City."[x]

27Zion will be redeemed with
justice,
her penitent ones with
righteousness.[y]
28But rebels and sinners will both
be broken,
and those who forsake the
LORD will perish.[z]

29"You will be ashamed because
of the sacred oaks[a]
in which you have delighted;
you will be disgraced because
of the gardens[b]
that you have chosen.
30You will be like an oak with
fading leaves,
like a garden without water.
31The mighty man will become
tinder
and his work a spark;
both will burn together,
with no-one to quench the fire.[c]"

The Mountain of the LORD

2:1–4pp Mic 4:1–3

2 This is what Isaiah son of Amoz saw concerning Judah and Jerusalem:[a]

2In the last days
the mountain[b] of the LORD's
temple will be established

1:15 f Isa 8:17; Isa 59:2; Mic 3:4; g Isa 59:3
1:16 h Isa 52:11; i Isa 55:7; Jer 25:5
1:17 j Zep 2:3; k Ps 82:3
1:18 l Isa 41:1; Isa 43:9,26; m Ps 51:7; Rev 7:14
1:19 n Dt 30:15-16; Isa 55:2
1:20 o Isa 3:25; Isa 65:12; p Isa 34:16; Isa 40:5; Isa 58:14; Mic 4:4
1:21 q Isa 57:3-9; Jer 2:20
1:23 r Ex 23:8; s Isa 10:2; Jer 5:28; Eze 22:6-7; Zec 7:10
1:24 t Isa 35:4; Isa 59:17; Isa 61:2; Isa 63:4
1:25 u Eze 22:22; Mal 3:3
1:26 v Jer 33:7,11; w Isa 33:5; Isa 62:1; Zec 8:3; x Isa 60:14; Isa 62:2
1:27 y Isa 35:10; Isa 62:12; Isa 63:4
1:28 z Ps 9:5; Isa 24:20; Isa 66:24; 2Th 1:8-9
1:29 a Isa 57:5; b Isa 65:3; Isa 66:17
1:31 c Isa 5:24; Isa 9:18-19; Isa 26:11; Isa 33:14; Isa 66:15-16, 24
2:1 a Isa 1:1
2:2 b Isa 27:13 Isa 56:7 Isa 66:20 Mic 4:7

a17 Or / *rebuke the oppressor*

as chief among the mountains;
it will be raised above the hills,
and all nations will stream to it.

3 Many peoples will come and say,

"Come, let us go up to the mountain of the LORD,
to the house of the God of Jacob.
He will teach us his ways,
so that we may walk in his paths."
The law[c] will go out from Zion,
the word of the LORD from Jerusalem.[d]
4 He will judge between the nations
and will settle disputes for many peoples.
They will beat their swords into ploughshares
and their spears into pruning hooks.[e]
Nation will not take up sword against nation,[f]
nor will they train for war any more.

5 Come, O house of Jacob,[g]
let us walk in the light[h] of the LORD.

The Day of the LORD

6 You have abandoned[i] your people,
the house of Jacob.
They are full of superstitions from the East;
they practise divination like the Philistines[j]
and clasp hands[k] with pagans.[l]
7 Their land is full of silver and gold;
there is no end to their treasures.
Their land is full of horses;[m]
there is no end to the chariots.[n]
8 Their land is full of idols;[o]
they bow down to the work of their hands,
to what their fingers[p] have made.
9 So man will be brought low[q]
and mankind humbled[r]—
do not forgive them.[a][s]

10 Go into the rocks,
hide in the ground
from dread of the LORD
and the splendour of his majesty![t]
11 The eyes of the arrogant man will be humbled
and the pride[u] of men brought low;
the LORD alone will be exalted in that day.

12 The LORD Almighty has a day in store
for all the proud and lofty,
for all that is exalted[v]
(and they will be humbled),[w]
13 for all the cedars of Lebanon, tall and lofty,
and all the oaks of Bashan,[x]
14 for all the towering mountains
and all the high hills,[y]
15 for every lofty tower
and every fortified wall,[z]
16 for every trading ship[b][a]
and every stately vessel.
17 The arrogance of man will be brought low
and the pride of men humbled;
the LORD alone will be exalted in that day,[b]
18 and the idols will totally disappear.[c]

19 Men will flee to caves in the rocks
and to holes in the ground
from the dread of the LORD
and the splendour of his majesty,
when he rises to shake the earth.[d]
20 In that day men will throw away
to the rodents and bats[e]
their idols of silver and idols of gold,

2:3 c Isa 51:4,7 d Lk 24:47
2:4 e Joel 3:10 f Ps 46:9; Isa 9:5; Isa 11:6-9; Isa 32:18; Hos 2:18; Zec 9:10
2:5 g Isa 58:1 h Isa 60:1, 19-20; 1Jn 1:5,7
2:6 i Dt 31:17 j 2Ki 1:2 k Pr 6:1 l 2Ki 16:7
2:7 m Dt 17:16 n Isa 31:1; Mic 5:10
2:8 o Isa 10:9-11 p Isa 17:8
2:9 q Ps 62:9 r Isa 5:15 s Ne 4:5
2:10 t 2Th 1:9; Rev 6:15-16
2:11 u Isa 5:15; Isa 37:23
2:12 v Isa 24:4,21; Mal 4:1 w Job 40:11
2:13 x Zec 11:2
2:14 y Isa 30:25; Isa 40:4
2:15 z Isa 25:2,12
2:16 a 1Ki 10:22
2:17 b ver 11
2:18 c Isa 21:9
2:19 d Heb 12:26
2:20 e Lev 11:19

a9 Or *not raise them up* b16 Hebrew *every ship of Tarshish*

which they made to worship.
21 They will flee to caverns in the rocks
and to the overhanging crags
from dread of the LORD
and the splendour of his majesty,
when he rises to shake the earth.[f]

22 Stop trusting in man,[g]
who has but a breath in his nostrils.
Of what account is he?[h]

Judgment on Jerusalem and Judah

3 See now, the Lord,
the LORD Almighty,
is about to take from Jerusalem and Judah
both supply and support:
all supplies of food[a] and all supplies of water,[b]
2 the hero and warrior,[c]
the judge and prophet,
the soothsayer and elder,[d]
3 the captain of fifty and man of rank,
the counsellor, skilled craftsman and clever enchanter.

4 I will make boys their officials;
mere children will govern them.[e]
5 People will oppress each other –
man against man, neighbour against neighbour.[f]
The young will rise up against the old,
the base against the honourable.

6 A man will seize one of his brothers
at his father's home, and say,
"You have a cloak, you be our leader;
take charge of this heap of ruins!"
7 But in that day he will cry out,
"I have no remedy.[g]

2:21 *f* ver 19
2:22 *g* Ps 146:3 Jer 17:5 *h* Ps 8:4 Ps 144:3 Isa 40:15 Jas 4:14
3:1 *a* Lev 26:26 *b* Isa 5:13 Eze 4:16
3:2 *c* Eze 17:13 *d* 2Ki 24:14 Isa 9:14-15
3:4 *e* Ecc 10:16 *fn*
3:5 *f* Isa 9:19 Jer 9:8 Mic 7:2,6
3:7 *g* Eze 34:4 Hos 5:13
3:8 *h* Isa 1:7 *i* Isa 9:15,17 *j* Ps 73:9,11
3:9 *k* Ge 13:13 *l* Pr 8:36 Ro 6:23
3:10 *m* Dt 28:1-14 *n* Ps 128:2
3:11 *o* Dt 28:15-68
3:12 *p* ver 4 *q* Isa 9:16
3:13 *r* Mic 6:2
3:14 *s* Job 22:4 *t* Job 24:9 Jas 2:6
3:15 *u* Ps 94:5
3:16 *v* SS 3:11

I have no food or clothing in my house;
do not make me the leader of the people."

8 Jerusalem staggers,
Judah is falling;[h]
their words[i] and deeds are against the LORD,
defying[j] his glorious presence.
9 The look on their faces testifies against them;
they parade their sin like Sodom;[k]
they do not hide it.
Woe to them!
They have brought disaster[l] upon themselves.

10 Tell the righteous it will be well[m] with them,
for they will enjoy the fruit of their deeds.[n]
11 Woe to the wicked! Disaster[o] is upon them!
They will be paid back for what their hands have done.

12 Youths[p] oppress my people,
women rule over them.
O my people, your guides lead you astray;[q]
they turn you from the path.

13 The LORD takes his place in court;
he rises to judge[r] the people.
14 The LORD enters into judgment[s]
against the elders and leaders of his people:
"It is you who have ruined my vineyard;
the plunder[t] from the poor is in your houses.
15 What do you mean by crushing my people[u]
and grinding the faces of the poor?"
declares the Lord,
the LORD Almighty.

16 The LORD says,
"The women of Zion[v] are haughty,

walking along with outstretched
necks,
flirting with their eyes,
tripping along with mincing
steps,
with ornaments jingling on
their ankles.
17Therefore the Lord will bring
sores on the heads of the
women of Zion;
the LORD will make their
scalps bald."

18In that day the Lord will snatch
away their finery: the bangles and
headbands and crescent necklaces,[w] 19the ear-rings and bracelets and veils, 20the head-dresses[x]
and ankle chains and sashes, the perfume bottles and charms, 21the signet rings and nose rings, 22the fine
robes and the capes and cloaks, the
purses 23and mirrors, and the linen
garments and tiaras and shawls.

24Instead of fragrance[y] there
will be a stench;
instead of a sash,[z] a rope;
instead of well-dressed hair,
baldness;[a]
instead of fine clothing,
sackcloth;[b]
instead of beauty,[c] branding.
25Your men will fall by the
sword,[d]
your warriors in battle.
26The gates of Zion will lament
and mourn;[e]
destitute, she will sit on the
ground.[f]

4 In that day seven women
will take hold of one man[a]
and say, "We will eat our own
food[b]
and provide our own clothes;
only let us be called by your
name.
Take away our disgrace!"[c]

The Branch of the LORD

2In that day the Branch of the
LORD[d] will be beautiful and glorious, and the fruit[e] of the land will
be the pride and glory of the survivors in Israel. 3Those who are left
in Zion, who remain[f] in Jerusalem,
will be called holy,[g] all who are recorded[h] among the living in Jerusalem. 4The Lord will wash away
the filth[i] of the women of Zion;
he will cleanse the bloodstains[j]
from Jerusalem by a spirit[a] of
judgment[k] and a spirit[a] of fire.[l]
5Then the LORD will create over all
of Mount Zion and over those who
assemble there a cloud of smoke by
day and a glow of flaming fire by
night;[m] over all the glory[n] will be
a canopy. 6It will be a shelter[o] and
shade from the heat of the day, and
a refuge[p] and hiding-place from
the storm and rain.

The Song of the Vineyard

5 I will sing for the one I love
a song about his vineyard:[a]
My loved one had a vineyard
on a fertile hillside.
2He dug it up and cleared it of
stones
and planted it with the
choicest vines.[b]
He built a watchtower in it
and cut out a winepress as
well.
Then he looked for a crop of
good grapes,
but it yielded only bad fruit.[c]

3"Now you dwellers in Jerusalem
and men of Judah,
judge between me and my
vineyard.[d]
4What more could have been
done for my vineyard
than I have done for it?[e]
When I looked for good grapes,
why did it yield only bad?
5Now I will tell you
what I am going to do to my
vineyard:
I will take away its hedge,
and it will be destroyed;
I will break down its wall,[f]

3:18 w Jdg 8:21
3:20 x Ex 39:28
3:24 y Est 2:12 z Pr 31:24 a Isa 22:12 b La 2:10 Eze 27:30-31 c 1Pe 3:3
3:25 d Isa 1:20
3:26 e Jer 14:2 f La 2:10
4:1 a Isa 13:12 b 2Th 3:12 c Ge 30:23
4:2 d Isa 11:1-5 Isa 53:2 Jer 23:5-6 Zec 3:8 Zec 6:12 e Ps 72:16
4:3 f Ro 11:5 g Isa 52:1 Isa 60:21 h Lk 10:20
4:4 i Isa 3:24 j Isa 1:15 k Isa 28:6 l Isa 1:31 Mt 3:11
4:5 m Ex 13:21 n Isa 60:1
4:6 o Ps 27:5 p Isa 25:4
5:1 a Ps 80:8-9
5:2 b Jer 2:21 c Mt 21:19 Mk 11:13 Lk 13:6
5:3 d Mt 21:40
5:4 e 2Ch 36:15 Jer 2:5-7 Mic 6:3-4 Mt 23:37
5:5 f Ps 80:12

a4 Or *the Spirit*

and it will be trampled.[g]
[6]I will make it a wasteland,
neither pruned nor cultivated,
and briers and thorns[h] will
grow there.
I will command the clouds
not to rain on it."

[7]The vineyard[i] of the LORD
Almighty
is the house of Israel,
and the men of Judah
are the garden of his delight.
And he looked for justice,[j] but
saw bloodshed;
for righteousness, but heard
cries of distress.

Woes and Judgments

[8]Woe[k] to you who add house to
house
and join field to field[l]
till no space is left
and you live alone in the land.

[9]The LORD Almighty has declared in my hearing:[m]

"Surely the great houses will
become desolate,[n]
the fine mansions left without
occupants.
[10]A ten-acre[a] vineyard will
produce only a bath[b] of
wine,
a homer[c] of seed only an
ephah[d] of grain."[o]

[11]Woe to those who rise early in
the morning
to run after their drinks,
who stay up late at night
till they are inflamed with
wine.[p]
[12]They have harps and lyres at
their banquets,
tambourines and flutes and
wine,
but they have no regard[q] for
the deeds of the LORD,
no respect for the work of his
hands.[r]
[13]Therefore my people will go
into exile
for lack of understanding;[s]
their men of rank will die of
hunger
and their masses will be
parched with thirst.
[14]Therefore the grave[e][t]
enlarges its appetite
and opens its mouth[u] without
limit;
into it will descend their nobles
and masses
with all their brawlers and
revellers.
[15]So man will be brought low[v]
and mankind humbled,[w]
the eyes of the arrogant[x]
humbled.
[16]But the LORD Almighty will be
exalted by his justice,[y]
and the holy God will show
himself holy[z] by his
righteousness.
[17]Then sheep will graze as in
their own pasture;[a]
lambs will feed[f] among the
ruins of the rich.

[18]Woe to those who draw sin
along with cords of deceit,
and wickedness[b] as with cart
ropes,
[19]to those who say, "Let God
hurry,
let him hasten his work
so that we may see it.
Let it approach,
let the plan of the Holy One of
Israel come,
so that we may know it."[c]

[20]Woe to those who call evil good
and good evil,
who put darkness for light
and light for darkness,[d]
who put bitter for sweet
and sweet for bitter.[e]

[21]Woe to those who are wise in
their own eyes[f]
and clever in their own sight.

5:5 g Isa 28:3,18; La 1:15; Lk 21:24
5:6 h Isa 7:23,24; Heb 6:8
5:7 i Ps 80:8; j Isa 59:15
5:8 k Jer 22:13; l Mic 2:2; Hab 2:9-12
5:9 m Isa 22:14; n Isa 6:11-12; Mt 23:38
5:10 o Lev 26:26
5:11 p Pr 23:29-30
5:12 q Job 34:27; r Ps 28:5; Am 6:5-6
5:13 s Isa 1:3; Hos 4:6
5:14 t Pr 30:16; u Nu 16:30
5:15 v Isa 10:33; w Isa 2:9; x Isa 2:11
5:16 y Isa 28:17; Isa 30:18; Isa 33:5; Isa 61:8; z Isa 29:23
5:17 a Isa 7:25; Zep 2:6,14
5:18 b Isa 59:4-8; Jer 23:14
5:19 c Jer 17:15; Eze 12:22; 2Pe 3:4
5:20 d Mt 6:22-23; Lk 11:34-35; e Am 5:7
5:21 f Pr 3:7; Ro 12:16; 1Co 3:18-20

a *10* Hebrew *ten-yoke*, that is, the land ploughed by 10 yoke of oxen in one day
b *10* That is, probably about 5 gallons (about 22 litres)
c *10* That is, probably about 6 bushels (about 220 litres)
d *10* That is, probably about 3/5 bushel (about 22 litres)
e *14* Hebrew *Sheol*
f *17* Septuagint; Hebrew / *strangers will eat*

22 Woe to those who are heroes at
drinking wine[g]
and champions at mixing
drinks,
23 who acquit the guilty for a
bribe,[h]
but deny justice[i] to the
innocent.[j]
24 Therefore, as tongues of fire
lick up straw
and as dry grass sinks down in
the flames,
so their roots will decay[k]
and their flowers blow away
like dust;
for they have rejected the law
of the LORD Almighty
and spurned the word[l] of the
Holy One of Israel.
25 Therefore the LORD's anger[m]
burns against his people;
his hand is raised and he
strikes them down.
The mountains shake,
and the dead bodies are like
refuse[n] in the streets.

Yet for all this, his anger is not
turned away,[o]
his hand is still upraised.[p]

26 He lifts up a banner for the
distant nations,
he whistles[q] for those at the
ends of the earth.[r]
Here they come,
swiftly and speedily!
27 Not one of them grows tired or
stumbles,
not one slumbers or sleeps;
not a belt is loosened at the
waist,[s]
not a sandal thong is broken.[t]
28 Their arrows are sharp,[u]
all their bows[v] are strung;
their horses' hoofs seem like
flint,
their chariot wheels like a
whirlwind.
29 Their roar is like that of the
lion,[w]
they roar like young lions;
they growl as they seize[x] their
prey
and carry it off with no-one to
rescue.[y]
30 In that day they will roar over
it
like the roaring of the sea.[z]
And if one looks at the land,
he will see darkness and
distress;[a]
even the light will be
darkened[b] by the clouds.

Isaiah's Commission

6 In the year that King Uzziah[a]
died,[b] I saw the Lord[c] seated
on a throne,[d] high and exalted, and
the train of his robe filled the temple. 2 Above him were seraphs,[e]
each with six wings: With two
wings they covered their faces,
with two they covered their feet,[f]
and with two they were flying.
3 And they were calling to one another:

"Holy, holy, holy is the LORD
Almighty;
the whole earth is full of his
glory."[g]

4 At the sound of their voices the
doorposts and thresholds shook
and the temple was filled with
smoke.
5 "Woe to me!" I cried. "I am
ruined! For I am a man of unclean
lips, and I live among a people of
unclean lips,[h] and my eyes have
seen the King,[i] the LORD Almighty."
6 Then one of the seraphs flew to
me with a live coal in his hand,
which he had taken with tongs from
the altar. 7 With it he touched my
mouth and said, "See, this has
touched your lips;[j] your guilt is
taken away and your sin atoned
for.[k]"
8 Then I heard the voice[l] of the
Lord saying, "Whom shall I send?
And who will go for us?"
And I said, "Here am I. Send
me!"
9 He said, "Go[m] and tell this people:

5:22 g Pr 23:20
5:23 h Ex 23:8 i Isa 10:2 j Ps 94:21 Jas 5:6
5:24 k Job 18:16 l Isa 8:6 Isa 30:9,12
5:25 m 2Ki 22:13 n 2Ki 9:37 o Jer 4:8 Da 9:16 p Isa 9:12,17, 21 Isa 10:4
5:26 q Isa 7:18 Zec 10:8 r Dt 28:49 Isa 13:5 Isa 18:3
5:27 s Job 12:18 t Joel 2:7-8
5:28 u Ps 45:5 v Ps 7:12
5:29 w Jer 51:38 Zep 3:3 Zec 11:3 x Isa 10:6 Isa 49:24-25 y Isa 42:22 Mic 5:8
5:30 z Lk 21:25 a Isa 8:22 Jer 4:23-28 b Joel 2:10
6:1 a 2Ch 26:22,23 b 2Ki 15:7 c Jn 12:41 d Rev 4:2
6:2 e Rev 4:8 f Eze 1:11
6:3 g Ps 72:19 Rev 4:8
6:5 h Jer 9:3-8 i Jer 51:57
6:7 j Jer 1:9 k 1Jn 1:7
6:8 l Ac 9:4
6:9 m Eze 3:11

" 'Be ever hearing, but never
understanding;
be ever seeing, but never
perceiving.'[n]
10Make the heart of this people
calloused;[o]
make their ears dull
and close their eyes.[a]
Otherwise they might see with
their eyes,
hear with their ears,[p]
understand with their hearts,
and turn and be healed."[q]

11Then I said, "For how long,
O Lord?"[r]
And he answered:

"Until the cities lie ruined[s]
and without inhabitant,
until the houses are left
deserted
and the fields ruined and
ravaged,
12until the LORD has sent
everyone far away[t]
and the land is utterly
forsaken.[u]
13And though a tenth remains[v] in
the land,
it will again be laid waste.
But as the terebinth and oak
leave stumps when they are
cut down,
so the holy seed will be the
stump in the land."[w]

The Sign of Immanuel

7 When Ahaz son of Jotham, the
son of Uzziah, was king of Judah, King Rezin[a] of Aram[b] and
Pekah[c] son of Remaliah king of Israel marched up to fight against
Jerusalem, but they could not overpower it.
2Now the house of David[d] was
told, "Aram has allied itself with[a]
Ephraim[e]"; so the hearts of Ahaz
and his people were shaken, as the
trees of the forest are shaken by
the wind.
3Then the LORD said to Isaiah,
"Go out, you and your son Shear-
Jashub,[b] to meet Ahaz at the end of
the aqueduct of the Upper Pool, on
the road to the Washerman's
Field.[f] 4Say to him, 'Be careful,
keep calm[g] and don't be afraid.[h]
Do not lose heart[i] because of these
two smouldering stubs[j] of firewood—because of the fierce
anger[k] of Rezin and Aram and of
the son of Remaliah. 5Aram, Ephraim and Remaliah's son have plotted your ruin, saying, 6"Let us
invade Judah; let us tear it apart
and divide it among ourselves, and
make the son of Tabeel king over
it." 7Yet this is what the Sovereign
LORD says:

" 'It will not take place,
it will not happen,[l]
8for the head of Aram is
Damascus,[m]
and the head of Damascus is
only Rezin.
Within sixty-five years
Ephraim will be too
shattered[n] to be a people.
9The head of Ephraim is
Samaria,
and the head of Samaria is
only Remaliah's son.
If you do not stand firm in your
faith,[o]
you will not stand at all.' "[p]

10Again the LORD spoke to Ahaz,
11"Ask the LORD your God for a
sign, whether in the deepest depths
or in the highest heights."
12But Ahaz said, "I will not ask; I
will not put the LORD to the test."
13Then Isaiah said, "Hear now,
you house of David! Is it not
enough to try the patience of men?
Will you try the patience of my
God[q] also? 14Therefore the Lord
himself will give you[c] a sign: The
virgin will be with child and will

6:9 *n* Mt 13:15*; Lk 8:10*
6:10 *o* Dt 32:15; Ps 119:70; *p* Jer 5:21; *q* Mt 13:13-15; Mk 4:12*; Ac 28:26-27*
6:11 *r* Ps 79:5; *s* Lev 26:31
6:12 *t* Dt 28:64; *u* Jer 4:29
6:13 *v* Isa 1:9; *w* Job 14:7
7:1 *a* 2Ki 15:37; *b* 2Ch 28:5; *c* 2Ki 15:25
7:2 *d* ver 13; Isa 22:22; *e* Isa 9:9
7:3 *f* 2Ki 18:17; Isa 36:2
7:4 *g* Isa 30:15; *h* Isa 35:4; *i* Dt 20:3; *j* Zec 3:2; *k* Isa 10:24
7:7 *l* Isa 8:10; Ac 4:25
7:8 *m* Ge 14:15; *n* Isa 17:1-3
7:9 *o* 2Ch 20:20; *p* Isa 8:6-8; Isa 30:12-14
7:13 *q* Isa 25:1

[a]9, 10 Hebrew; Septuagint *'You will be ever hearing, but never understanding; / you will be ever seeing, but never perceiving.' / 10This people's heart has become calloused; / they hardly hear with their ears, / and they have closed their eyes*
[a]2 Or *has set up camp in* [b]3 *Shear-Jashub* means *a remnant will return.* [c]14 The Hebrew is plural.

give birth to a son,[r] and[d] will call
him Immanuel.[e][s] 15He will eat
curds and honey[t] when he knows
enough to reject the wrong and
choose the right. 16But before the
boy knows[u] enough to reject the
wrong and choose the right,
the land of the two kings you dread
will be laid waste.[v] 17The LORD will
bring on you and on your people
and on the house of your father a
time unlike any since Ephraim
broke away[w] from Judah—he will
bring the king of Assyria.[x]"
18In that day the LORD will whis-
tle[y] for flies from the distant
streams of Egypt and for bees from
the land of Assyria.[z] 19They will all
come and settle in the steep ravines
and in the crevices[a] in the rocks,
on all the thornbushes and at all the
water holes. 20In that day the Lord
will use[b] a razor hired from beyond the River[f]—the king of Assyria[c]—to shave your head and
the hair of your legs, and to take off
your beards also. 21In that day, a
man will keep alive a young cow
and two goats. 22And because of the
abundance of the milk they give, he
will have curds to eat. All who remain in the land will eat curds and
honey. 23In that day, in every place
where there were a thousand vines
worth a thousand silver shekels,[g]
there will be only briers and
thorns.[d] 24Men will go there with
bow and arrow, for the land will be
covered with briers and thorns.
25As for all the hills once cultivated
by the hoe, you will no longer go
there for fear of the briers and
thorns; they will become places
where cattle are turned loose and
where sheep run.[e]

Assyria, the LORD's Instrument

8 The LORD said to me, "Take
a large scroll[a] and write on
it with an ordinary pen: Maher-
Shalal-Hash-Baz.[a][b] 2And I will call
in Uriah[c] the priest and Zechariah
son of Jeberekiah as reliable witnesses for me."
3Then I went to the prophetess,
and she conceived and gave birth to
a son. And the LORD said to me,
"Name him Maher-Shalal-Hash-
Baz. 4Before the boy knows[d] how
to say 'My father' or 'My mother',
the wealth of Damascus and the
plunder of Samaria will be carried
off by the king of Assyria.[e]"
5The LORD spoke to me again:

6"Because this people has
rejected[f]
the gently flowing waters of
Shiloah[g]
and rejoices over Rezin
and the son of Remaliah,[h]
7therefore the Lord is about to
bring against them
the mighty floodwaters[i] of
the River[b]—
the king of Assyria[j] with all
his pomp.
It will overflow all its channels,
run over all its banks
8and sweep on into Judah,
swirling over it,
passing through it and
reaching up to the neck.
Its outspread wings will cover
the breadth of your land,
O Immanuel!"[c][k]

9Raise the war cry,[d][l] you
nations, and be shattered!
Listen, all you distant lands.
Prepare[m] for battle, and be
shattered!
Prepare for battle, and be
shattered!
10Devise your strategy, but it will
be thwarted;[n]
propose your plan, but it will
not stand,[o]
for God is with us.[e][p]

7:14 r Lk 1:31 s Isa 8:8,10 Mt 1:23*
7:15 t ver 22
7:16 u Isa 8:4 v Isa 17:3 Hos 5:9,13 Am 1:3-5
7:17 w 1Ki 12:16 x 2Ch 28:20
7:18 y Isa 5:26 z Isa 13:5
7:19 a Isa 2:19
7:20 b Isa 10:15 c Isa 8:7 Isa 10:5
7:23 d Isa 5:6
7:25 e Isa 5:17
8:1 a Isa 30:8 b ver 3 Hab 2:2
8:2 c 2Ki 16:10
8:4 d Isa 7:16 e Isa 7:8
8:6 f Isa 5:24 g Jn 9:7 h Isa 7:1
8:7 i Isa 17:12-13 j Isa 7:20
8:8 k Isa 7:14
8:9 l Isa 17:12-13 m Joel 3:9
8:10 n Job 5:12 o Isa 7:7 p Isa 7:14 Ro 8:31

[d]14 Masoretic Text; Dead Sea Scrolls *and he* or *and they* [e]14 *Immanuel* means *God with us.* [f]20 That is, the Euphrates [g]23 That is, about 25 pounds (about 11.5 kilograms) [a]1 *Maher-Shalal-Hash-Baz* means *quick to the plunder, swift to the spoil*; also in verse 3. [b]7 That is, the Euphrates [c]8 *Immanuel* means *God with us.* [d]9 Or *Do your worst* [e]10 Hebrew *Immanuel*

Fear God

11The LORD spoke to me with his
strong hand upon me,[q] warning
me not to follow[r] the way of this
people. He said:

12"Do not call conspiracy[s]
everything that these people
call conspiracy;[f]
do not fear what they fear,
and do not dread it.[t]
13The LORD Almighty is the one
you are to regard as holy,[u]
he is the one you are to fear,
he is the one you are to
dread,[v]
14and he will be a sanctuary;[w]
but for both houses of Israel
he will be
a stone that causes men to
stumble
and a rock that makes them
fall.[x]
And for the people of Jerusalem
he will be
a trap and a snare.[y]
15Many of them will stumble;[z]
they will fall and be broken,
they will be snared and
captured."

16Bind up the testimony
and seal[a] up the law among
my disciples.
17I will wait[b] for the LORD,
who is hiding[c] his face from
the house of Jacob.
I will put my trust in him.

18Here am I, and the children the
LORD has given me.[d] We are
signs[e] and symbols in Israel from
the LORD Almighty, who dwells on
Mount Zion.[f]
19When men tell you to consult[g]
mediums and spiritists, who whisper and mutter,[h] should not a people enquire of their God? Why
consult the dead on behalf of the
living? 20To the law[i] and to the testimony! If they do not speak according to this word, they have no
light[j] of dawn. 21Distressed and
hungry, they will roam through the
land; when they are famished, they
will become enraged and, looking
upward, will curse[k] their king and
their God. 22Then they will look towards the earth and see only distress and darkness and fearful
gloom, and they will be thrust into
utter darkness.[l]

To Us a Child Is Born

9 Nevertheless, there will be no
more gloom for those who
were in distress. In the past he
humbled the land of Zebulun and
the land of Naphtali,[a] but in the future he will honour Galilee of the
Gentiles, by the way of the sea,
along the Jordan—

2The people walking in darkness
have seen a great light;[b]
on those living in the land of
the shadow of death[a][c]
a light has dawned.[d]
3You have enlarged the nation
and increased their joy;
they rejoice before you
as people rejoice at the
harvest,
as men rejoice
when dividing the plunder.
4For as in the day of Midian's
defeat,[e]
you have shattered
the yoke[f] that burdens them,
the bar across their
shoulders,[g]
the rod of their oppressor.[h]
5Every warrior's boot used in
battle
and every garment rolled in
blood
will be destined for burning,[i]
will be fuel for the fire.
6For to us a child is born,[j]
to us a son is given,[k]
and the government[l] will be
on his shoulders.

8:11 q Eze 3:14 r Eze 2:8
8:12 s Isa 7:2 Isa 30:1 t 1Pe 3:14*
8:13 u Nu 20:12 v Isa 29:23
8:14 w Isa 4:6 Eze 11:16 x Lk 2:34 Ro 9:33* 1Pe 2:8* y Isa 24:17-18
8:15 z Isa 28:13 Isa 59:10 Lk 20:18 Ro 9:32
8:16 a Isa 29:11-12
8:17 b Hab 2:3 c Dt 31:17 Isa 54:8
8:18 d Heb 2:13* e Lk 2:34 f Ps 9:11
8:19 g 1Sa 28:8 h Isa 29:4
8:20 i Isa 1:10 Lk 16:29 j Mic 3:6
8:21 k Rev 16:11
8:22 l ver 20 Isa 5:30
9:1 a 2Ki 15:29
9:2 b Eph 5:8 c Lk 1:79 d Mt 4:15-16*
9:4 e Jdg 7:25 f Isa 14:25 g Isa 10:27 h Isa 14:4 Isa 49:26 Isa 51:13 Isa 54:14
9:5 i Isa 2:4
9:6 j Isa 53:2 Lk 2:11 k Jn 3:16 l Mt 28:18

f12 Or *Do not call for a treaty / every time these people call for a treaty* a2 Or *land of darkness*

And he will be called
Wonderful Counsellor,[b][m]
Mighty God,[n]
Everlasting Father, Prince of
Peace.[o]
7Of the increase of his
government and peace
there will be no end.[p]
He will reign on David's throne
and over his kingdom,
establishing and upholding it
with justice[q] and
righteousness
from that time on and for
ever.
The zeal[r] of the LORD Almighty
will accomplish this.

The LORD's Anger Against Israel

8The Lord has sent a message
against Jacob;
it will fall on Israel.
9All the people will know it—
Ephraim and the inhabitants
of Samaria[s]—
who say with pride
and arrogance[t] of heart,
10"The bricks have fallen down,
but we will rebuild with
dressed stone;
the fig-trees have been felled,
but we will replace them with
cedars."
11But the LORD has strengthened
Rezin's[u] foes against them
and has spurred their enemies
on.
12Arameans[v] from the east and
Philistines[w] from the west
have devoured[x] Israel with
open mouth.

Yet for all this, his anger is not
turned away,
his hand is still upraised.[y]

13But the people have not
returned to him who
struck[z] them,
nor have they sought[a] the
LORD Almighty.

9:6
m Isa 28:29
n Isa 10:21
Isa 11:2
o Isa 26:3,12
Isa 66:12

9:7
p Da 2:44
Lk 1:33
q Isa 11:4
Isa 16:5
Isa 32:1,16
r Isa 37:32
Isa 59:17

9:9
s Isa 7:9
t Isa 46:12

9:11
u Isa 7:8

9:12
v 2Ki 16:6
w 2Ch 28:18
x Ps 79:7
y Isa 5:25

9:13
z Jer 5:3
a Isa 31:1
Hos 7:7,10

9:14
b Isa 19:15
c Rev 18:8

9:15
d Isa 3:2-3

9:16
e Mt 15:14
Mt 23:16,24
f Isa 3:12

9:17
g Jer 18:21
h Isa 27:11
i Isa 10:6
j Isa 1:4
k Mt 12:34
l Isa 5:25

9:18
m Mal 4:1
n Ps 83:14

9:19
o Isa 13:9,13
p Isa 1:31
q Mic 7:2,6

9:20
r Lev 26:26
s Isa 49:26

9:21
t 2Ch 28:6
u Isa 5:25

14So the LORD will cut off from
Israel both head and tail,
both palm branch and reed[b]
in a single day;[c]
15the elders[d] and prominent men
are the head,
the prophets who teach lies
are the tail.
16Those who guide[e] this people
mislead them,
and those who are guided are
led astray.[f]
17Therefore the Lord will take no
pleasure in the young
men,[g]
nor will he pity[h] the
fatherless and widows,
for everyone is ungodly[i] and
wicked,[j]
every mouth speaks vileness.[k]
Yet for all this, his anger is not
turned away,
his hand is still upraised.[l]
18Surely wickedness burns like a
fire;[m]
it consumes briers and thorns,
it sets the forest thickets
ablaze,[n]
so that it rolls upward in a
column of smoke.
19By the wrath[o] of the LORD
Almighty
the land will be scorched
and the people will be fuel for
the fire;[p]
no-one will spare his brother.[q]
20On the right they will devour,
but still be hungry;[r]
on the left they will eat,[s]
but not be satisfied.
Each will feed on the flesh of
his own offspring:[c]
21 Manasseh will feed on
Ephraim, and Ephraim on
Manasseh;
together they will turn against
Judah.[t]
Yet for all this, his anger is not
turned away,
his hand is still upraised.[u]

[b]6 Or *Wonderful, Counsellor*   [c]20 Or *arm*

10 Woe to those who make
unjust laws,
to those who issue oppressive
decrees,[a]
2 to deprive[b] the poor of their
rights
and withhold justice from the
oppressed of my people,[c]
making widows their prey
and robbing the fatherless.
3 What will you do on the day of
reckoning,[d]
when disaster[e] comes from
afar?
To whom will you run for
help?[f]
Where will you leave your
riches?
4 Nothing will remain but to
cringe among the captives[g]
or fall among the slain.[h]

Yet for all this, his anger is not
turned away,[i]
his hand is still upraised.

God's Judgment on Assyria

5 "Woe to the Assyrian,[j] the rod
of my anger,
in whose hand is the club[k] of
my wrath![l]
6 I send him against a godless[m]
nation,
I dispatch him against a
people who anger me,[n]
to seize loot and snatch
plunder,[o]
and to trample them down like
mud in the streets.
7 But this is not what he
intends,[p]
this is not what he has in
mind;
his purpose is to destroy,
to put an end to many nations.
8 'Are not my commanders[q] all
kings?' he says.
9 'Has not Calno[r] fared like
Carchemish?[s]
Is not Hamath like Arpad,
and Samaria[t] like
Damascus?[u]

10:1 *a* Ps 58:2
10:2 *b* Isa 3:14 *c* Isa 5:23
10:3 *d* Job 31:14 Hos 9:7 *e* Lk 19:44 *f* Isa 20:6
10:4 *g* Isa 24:22 *h* Isa 22:2 Isa 34:3 Isa 66:16 *i* Isa 5:25
10:5 *j* Isa 14:25 Zep 2:13 *k* Jer 51:20 *l* Isa 13:3,5,13 Isa 30:30 Isa 66:14
10:6 *m* Isa 9:17 *n* Isa 9:19 *o* Isa 5:29
10:7 *p* Ge 50:20 Ac 4:23-28
10:8 *q* 2Ki 18:24
10:9 *r* Ge 10:10 *s* 2Ch 35:20 *t* 2Ki 17:6 *u* 2Ki 16:9
10:10 *v* 2Ki 19:18
10:12 *w* Isa 28:21-22 Isa 65:7 *x* 2Ki 19:31 *y* Jer 50:18
10:13 *z* Isa 37:24 Da 4:30 *a* Eze 28:4
10:14 *b* Jer 49:16 Ob 1:4 *c* Job 31:25
10:15 *d* Isa 45:9 Ro 9:20-21 *e* ver 5
10:16 *f* ver 18 Isa 17:4 *g* Isa 8:7
10:17 *h* Isa 31:9

10 As my hand seized the
kingdoms of the idols,[v]
kingdoms whose images
excelled those of Jerusalem
and Samaria—
11 shall I not deal with Jerusalem
and her images
as I dealt with Samaria and
her idols?' "

12 When the Lord has finished all
his work[w] against Mount Zion[x]
and Jerusalem, he will say, "I will
punish the king of Assyria[y] for the
wilful pride of his heart and the
haughty look in his eyes. 13 For he
says:

" 'By the strength of my hand I
have done this,[z]
and by my wisdom, because I
have understanding.
I removed the boundaries of
nations,
I plundered their treasures;[a]
like a mighty one I subdued[a]
their kings.
14 As one reaches into a nest,[b]
so my hand reached for the
wealth[c] of the nations;
as men gather abandoned eggs,
so I gathered all the countries;
not one flapped a wing,
or opened its mouth to
chirp.' "
15 Does the axe raise itself above
him who swings it,
or the saw boast against him
who uses it?[d]
As if a rod were to wield him
who lifts it up,
or a club[e] brandish him who
is not wood!
16 Therefore, the Lord, the LORD
Almighty,
will send a wasting disease[f]
upon his sturdy warriors;
under his pomp[g] a fire will be
kindled
like a blazing flame.
17 The Light of Israel will become
a fire,[h]

a *13* Or / *I subdued the mighty,*

their Holy One[i] a flame;
in a single day it will burn and consume
his thorns[j] and his briers.[k]
18The splendour of his forests[l]
and fertile fields
it will completely destroy,
as when a sick man wastes away.
19And the remaining trees of his forests will be so few[m]
that a child could write them down.

The Remnant of Israel

20In that day[n] the remnant of Israel,
the survivors of the house of Jacob,
will no longer rely[o] on him
who struck them down[p]
but will truly rely[q] on the LORD,
the Holy One of Israel.
21A remnant[r] will return,[b] a remnant of Jacob
will return to the Mighty God.[s]
22Though your people, O Israel,
be like the sand by the sea,
only a remnant will return.[t]
Destruction has been decreed,[u]
overwhelming and righteous.
23The Lord, the LORD Almighty,
will carry out
the destruction decreed upon
the whole land.[v]

24Therefore, this is what the Lord, the LORD Almighty, says:

"O my people who live in Zion,[w]
do not be afraid of the Assyrians,
who beat[x] you with a rod
and lift up a club against you,
as Egypt did.
25Very soon[y] my anger against you will end
and my wrath[z] will be directed to their destruction."
26The LORD Almighty will lash[a] them with a whip,

10:17 [i] Isa 37:23 [j] Nu 11:1-3 [k] Isa 9:18
10:18 [l] 2Ki 19:23
10:19 [m] Isa 21:17
10:20 [n] Isa 11:10,11 [o] 2Ki 16:7 [p] 2Ch 28:20 [q] Isa 17:7
10:21 [r] Isa 6:13 [s] Isa 9:6
10:22 [t] Ro 9:27-28 [u] Isa 28:22 Da 9:27
10:23 [v] Isa 28:22 Ro 9:27-28*
10:24 [w] Ps 87:5-6 [x] Ex 5:14
10:25 [y] Isa 17:14 [z] ver 5 Da 11:36
10:26 [a] Isa 37:36-38 [b] Isa 9:4 [c] Ex 14:16
10:27 [d] Isa 9:4 [e] Isa 14:25
10:28 [f] 1Sa 14:2 [g] 1Sa 13:2
10:29 [h] Jos 18:25
10:30 [i] 1Sa 25:44 [j] Ne 11:32
10:32 [k] 1Sa 21:1 [l] Jer 6:23
10:33 [m] Am 2:9
11:1 [a] ver 10 Isa 9:7 Rev 5:5 [b] Isa 4:2

as when he struck down Midian[b] at the rock of Oreb;
and he will raise his staff over the waters,[c]
as he did in Egypt.
27In that day their burden will be lifted from your shoulders,
their yoke[d] from your neck;[e]
the yoke will be broken
because you have grown so fat.[c]
28They enter Aiath;
they pass through Migron;[f]
they store supplies at Michmash.[g]
29They go over the pass, and say,
"We will camp overnight at Geba."
Ramah[h] trembles;
Gibeah of Saul flees.
30Cry out, O Daughter of Gallim![i]
Listen, O Laishah!
Poor Anathoth![j]
31Madmenah is in flight;
the people of Gebim take cover.
32This day they will halt at Nob;[k]
they will shake their fist
at the mount of the Daughter of Zion,[l]
at the hill of Jerusalem.
33See, the Lord, the LORD Almighty,
will lop off the boughs with great power.
The lofty trees will be felled,
the tall[m] ones will be brought low.
34He will cut down the forest thickets with an axe;
Lebanon will fall before the Mighty One.

The Branch From Jesse

11 A shoot will come up from the stump of Jesse;[a]
from his roots a Branch[b] will bear fruit.

b21 Hebrew *shear-jashub*; also in verse 22
c27 Hebrew; Septuagint *broken / from your shoulders*

2 The Spirit[c] of the LORD will
rest on him—
the Spirit of wisdom[d] and of
understanding,
the Spirit of counsel and of
power,[e]
the Spirit of knowledge and of
the fear of the LORD—
3 and he will delight in the fear
of the LORD.

He will not judge by what he
sees with his eyes,[f]
or decide by what he hears
with his ears;[g]
4 but with righteousness[h] he will
judge the needy,
with justice[i] he will give
decisions for the poor[j] of
the earth.
He will strike[k] the earth with
the rod of his mouth;
with the breath[l] of his lips he
will slay the wicked.
5 Righteousness will be his belt
and faithfulness[m] the sash
round his waist.[n]

6 The wolf will live with the
lamb,[o]
the leopard will lie down with
the goat,
the calf and the lion and the
yearling[a] together;
and a little child will lead
them.
7 The cow will feed with the
bear,
their young will lie down
together,
and the lion will eat straw like
the ox.
8 The infant will play near the
hole of the cobra,
and the young child put his
hand into the viper's nest.
9 They will neither harm nor
destroy[p]
on all my holy mountain,
for the earth[q] will be full of
the knowledge[r] of the
LORD
as the waters cover the sea.

11:2
c Isa 42:1
Isa 48:16
Isa 61:1
Mt 3:16
Jn 1:32-33
d Eph 1:17
e 2Ti 1:7

11:3
f Jn 7:24
g Jn 2:25

11:4
h Ps 72:2
i Isa 9:7
j Isa 3:14
k Mal 4:6
l Job 4:9
2Th 2:8

11:5
m Isa 25:1
n Eph 6:14

11:6
o Isa 65:25

11:9
p Job 5:23
q Ps 98:2-3
Isa 52:10
r Isa 45:6,14
Hab 2:14

11:10
s Jn 12:32
t Isa 49:23
Lk 2:32
u Ro 15:12*
v Isa 14:3
Isa 28:12
Isa 32:17-18

11:11
w Isa 10:20
x Isa 19:24
Hos 11:11
Mic 7:12
Zec 10:10
y Ge 10:22
z Isa 42:4,10,
12
Isa 66:19

11:12
a Zep 3:10

11:13
b Jer 3:18
Eze 37:16-17,
22
Hos 1:11

11:14
c Da 11:41
Joel 3:19
d Isa 16:14
Isa 25:10

11:15
e Isa 19:16
f Isa 7:20

11:16
g Isa 19:23
Isa 62:10

10 In that day the Root of Jesse
will stand as a banner[s] for the peoples; the nations[t] will rally to
him,[u] and his place of rest[v] will be
glorious. 11 In that day[w] the Lord
will reach out his hand a second
time to reclaim the remnant that is
left of his people from Assyria,[x]
from Lower Egypt, from Upper
Egypt,[b] from Cush,[c] from Elam,[y]
from Babylonia,[d] from Hamath
and from the islands[z] of the sea.

12 He will raise a banner for the
nations
and gather the exiles of Israel;
he will assemble the scattered
people[a] of Judah
from the four quarters of the
earth.
13 Ephraim's jealousy will vanish,
and Judah's enemies[e] will be
cut off;
Ephraim will not be jealous of
Judah,
nor Judah hostile towards
Ephraim.[b]
14 They will swoop down on the
slopes of Philistia to the
west;
together they will plunder the
people to the east.
They will lay hands on Edom[c]
and Moab,[d]
and the Ammonites will be
subject to them.
15 The LORD will dry up
the gulf of the Egyptian sea;
with a scorching wind he will
sweep his hand[e]
over the Euphrates River.[f][f]
He will break it up into seven
streams
so that men can cross over in
sandals.
16 There will be a highway[g] for
the remnant of his people
that is left from Assyria,
as there was for Israel

a 6 Hebrew; Septuagint *lion will feed*
b 11 Hebrew *from Pathros* c 11 That is, the upper Nile region d 11 Hebrew *Shinar*
e 13 Or *hostility* f 15 Hebrew *the River*

when they came up from
Egypt.[h]

Songs of Praise

12 In that day you will say:

"I will praise[a] you, O LORD.
Although you were angry with
me,
your anger has turned away
and you have comforted me.
2Surely God is my salvation;
I will trust[b] and not be afraid.
The LORD, the LORD, is my
strength and my song;
he has become my
salvation.[c]"
3With joy you will draw water[d]
from the wells of salvation.

4In that day you will say:

"Give thanks to the LORD, call
on his name;[e]
make known among the
nations what he has done,
and proclaim that his name is
exalted.
5Sing[f] to the LORD, for he has
done glorious things;[g]
let this be known to all the
world.
6Shout aloud and sing for joy,
people of Zion,
for great is the Holy One of
Israel[h] among you.[i]"

A Prophecy Against Babylon

13 An oracle concerning Babylon that Isaiah son of
Amoz saw:

2Raise a banner[a] on a bare
hilltop,
shout to them;
beckon to them
to enter the gates of the
nobles.
3I have commanded my holy
ones;
I have summoned my
warriors[b] to carry out my
wrath—
those who rejoice[c] in my
triumph.

4Listen, a noise on the
mountains,
like that of a great
multitude![d]
Listen, an uproar among the
kingdoms,
like nations massing together!
The LORD Almighty is
mustering
an army for war.
5They come from faraway lands,
from the ends of the
heavens[e]—
the LORD and the weapons of his
wrath—
to destroy[f] the whole country.

6Wail,[g] for the day[h] of the LORD
is near;
it will come like destruction
from the Almighty.[a]
7Because of this, all hands will
go limp,
every man's heart will melt.[i]
8Terror[j] will seize them,
pain and anguish will grip
them;
they will writhe like a woman
in labour.
They will look aghast at each
other,
their faces aflame.[k]

9See, the day of the LORD is
coming—
a cruel day, with wrath and
fierce anger—
to make the land desolate
and destroy the sinners within
it.
10The stars of heaven and their
constellations
will not show their light.
The rising sun[l] will be
darkened[m]
and the moon will not give its
light.[n]
11I will punish[o] the world for its
evil,
the wicked for their sins.

11:16 h Ex 14:26-31
12:1 a Isa 25:1
12:2 b Isa 26:3 c Ex 15:2 Ps 118:14
12:3 d Jn 4:10,14
12:4 e Ps 105:1 Isa 24:15
12:5 f Ex 15:1 g Ps 98:1
12:6 h Isa 49:26 i Zep 3:14-17
13:2 a Jer 50:2 Jer 51:27
13:3 b Joel 3:11 c Ps 149:2
13:4 d Joel 3:14
13:5 e Isa 5:26 f Isa 24:1
13:6 g Eze 30:2 h Isa 2:12 Joel 1:15
13:7 i Eze 21:7
13:8 j Isa 21:4 k Na 2:10
13:10 l Isa 24:23 m Isa 5:30 Rev 8:12 n Eze 32:7 Mt 24:29* Mk 13:24*
13:11 o Isa 3:11 Isa 11:4 Isa 26:21

a6 Hebrew *Shaddai*

I will put an end to the
arrogance of the haughty
and will humble the pride of
the ruthless.
12I will make man[p] scarcer than
pure gold,
more rare than the gold of
Ophir.
13Therefore I will make the
heavens tremble;[q]
and the earth will shake from
its place
at the wrath of the LORD
Almighty,
in the day of his burning
anger.
14Like a hunted gazelle,
like sheep without a
shepherd,[r]
each will return to his own
people,
each will flee to his native
land.[s]
15Whoever is captured will be
thrust through;
all who are caught will fall[t]
by the sword.[u]
16Their infants[v] will be dashed to
pieces before their eyes;
their houses will be looted and
their wives ravished.

17See, I will stir up[w] against them
the Medes,
who do not care for silver
and have no delight in gold.[x]
18Their bows will strike down the
young men;
they will have no mercy on
infants
nor will they look with
compassion on children.
19Babylon, the jewel of kingdoms,
the glory[y] of the
Babylonians'[b] pride,
will be overthrown[z] by God
like Sodom and Gomorrah.[a]
20She will never be inhabited[b]
or lived in through all
generations;
no Arab[c] will pitch his tent
there,
no shepherd will rest his
flocks there.

13:12 p Isa 4:1
13:13 q Isa 34:4; Isa 51:6; Hag 2:6
13:14 r 1Ki 22:17; s Jer 50:16
13:15 t Jer 51:4; u Isa 14:19; Jer 50:25
13:16 v Ps 137:9
13:17 w Jer 51:1; x Pr 6:34-35
13:19 y Da 4:30; z Rev 14:8; a Ge 19:24
13:20 b Isa 14:23; Isa 34:10-15; c 2Ch 17:11
13:21 d Rev 18:2
13:22 e Isa 25:2; f Isa 34:13; g Jer 51:33
14:1 a Ps 102:13; Isa 49:10,13; Isa 54:7-8,10; b Isa 41:8; Isa 44:1; Isa 49:7; Zec 1:17; Zec 2:12; c Eph 2:12-19
14:2 d Isa 60:9; e Isa 49:7,23; f Isa 60:14; Isa 61:5
14:3 g Isa 11:10
14:4 h Hab 2:6; i Isa 9:4
14:5 j Ps 125:3
14:6 k Isa 10:14

21But desert creatures[d] will lie
there,
jackals will fill her houses;
there the owls will dwell,
and there the wild goats will
leap about.
22Hyenas will howl in her
strongholds,[e]
jackals[f] in her luxurious
palaces.
Her time is at hand,[g]
and her days will not be
prolonged.

14

The LORD will have
compassion[a] on Jacob;
once again he will choose[b]
Israel
and will settle them in their
own land.
Aliens[c] will join them
and unite with the house of
Jacob.
2Nations will take them
and bring[d] them to their own
place.
And the house of Israel will
possess the nations[e]
as menservants and
maidservants in the LORD's
land.
They will make captives of
their captors
and rule over their
oppressors.[f]

3On the day the LORD gives you
relief[g] from suffering and turmoil
and cruel bondage, 4you will take
up this taunt[h] against the king of
Babylon:

How the oppressor[i] has come
to an end!
How his fury[a] has ended!
5The LORD has broken the rod of
the wicked,[j]
the sceptre of the rulers,
6which in anger struck down
peoples[k]
with unceasing blows,

b19 Or *Chaldeans'* a4 Dead Sea Scrolls, Septuagint and Syriac; the meaning of the word in the Masoretic Text is uncertain.

and in fury subdued nations
with relentless aggression.[l]
7All the lands are at rest and at peace;
they break into singing.[m]
8Even the pine trees[n] and the cedars of Lebanon
exult over you and say,
"Now that you have been laid low,
no woodsman comes to cut us down."

9The grave[b][o] below is all astir
to meet you at your coming;
it rouses the spirits of the departed to greet you—
all those who were leaders in the world;
it makes them rise from their thrones—
all those who were kings over the nations.
10They will all respond,
they will say to you,
"You also have become weak, as we are;
you have become like us."[p]
11All your pomp has been brought down to the grave,
along with the noise of your harps;
maggots are spread out beneath you
and worms[q] cover you.

12How you have fallen[r] from heaven,
O morning star,[s] son of the dawn!
You have been cast down to the earth,
you who once laid low the nations!
13You said in your heart,
"I will ascend[t] to heaven;
I will raise my throne[u]
above the stars of God;
I will sit enthroned on the mount of assembly,
on the utmost heights of the sacred mountain.[c]
14I will ascend above the tops of the clouds;
I will make myself like the Most High."[v]
15But you are brought down to the grave,
to the depths[w] of the pit.

16Those who see you stare at you,
they ponder your fate:[x]
"Is this the man who shook the earth
and made kingdoms tremble,
17the man who made the world a desert,[y]
who overthrew its cities
and would not let his captives go home?"

18All the kings of the nations lie in state,
each in his own tomb.
19But you are cast out[z] of your tomb
like a rejected branch;
you are covered with the slain,
with those pierced by the sword,
those who descend to the stones of the pit.[a]
Like a corpse trampled underfoot,
20 you will not join them in burial,
for you have destroyed your land
and killed your people.

The offspring[b] of the wicked[c]
will never be mentioned[d] again.
21Prepare a place to slaughter his sons
for the sins of their forefathers;[e]
they are not to rise to inherit the land
and cover the earth with their cities.

22"I will rise up against them,"
declares the LORD Almighty.
"I will cut off from Babylon her name and survivors,

14:6 l Isa 47:6
14:7 m Ps 98:1; Ps 126:1-3
14:8 n Eze 31:16
14:9 o Eze 32:21
14:10 p Eze 32:21
14:11 q Isa 51:8
14:12 r Isa 34:4; Lk 10:18; s 2Pe 1:19; Rev 2:28; Rev 8:10; Rev 9:1
14:13 t Da 5:23; Da 8:10; Mt 11:23; u Eze 28:2; 2Th 2:4
14:14 v Isa 47:8; 2Th 2:4
14:15 w Mt 11:23; Lk 10:15
14:16 x Jer 50:23
14:17 y Joel 2:3
14:19 z Isa 22:16-18; a Jer 41:7-9
14:20 b Job 18:19; c Isa 1:4; d Ps 21:10
14:21 e Ex 20:5; Lev 26:39

b9 Hebrew *Sheol*; also in verses 11 and 15
c13 Or *the north*; Hebrew *Zaphon*

her offspring and
descendants,[f]"
declares the LORD.
23"I will turn her into a place for
owls[g]
and into swampland;
I will sweep her with the broom
of destruction,"
declares the LORD Almighty.

A Prophecy Against Assyria

24The LORD Almighty has
sworn,[h]

"Surely, as I have planned, so it
will be,
and as I have purposed, so it
will stand.[i]
25I will crush the Assyrian[j] in
my land;
on my mountains I will
trample him down.
His yoke[k] will be taken from
my people,
and his burden removed from
their shoulders.[l]"
26This is the plan[m] determined
for the whole world;
this is the hand[n] stretched out
over all nations.
27For the LORD Almighty has
purposed, and who can
thwart him?
His hand is stretched out, and
who can turn it back?[o]

A Prophecy Against the Philistines

28This oracle[p] came in the year
King Ahaz[q] died:

29Do not rejoice, all you
Philistines,[r]
that the rod that struck you is
broken;
from the root of that snake will
spring up a viper,[s]
its fruit will be a darting,
venomous serpent.
30The poorest of the poor will
find pasture,
and the needy[t] will lie down
in safety.[u]
But your root I will destroy by
famine;[v]
it will slay[w] your survivors.

31Wail, O gate![x] Howl, O city!
Melt away, all you Philistines!
A cloud of smoke comes from
the north,[y]
and there is not a straggler in
its ranks.
32What answer shall be given
to the envoys[z] of that nation?
"The LORD has established
Zion,[a]
and in her his afflicted people
will find refuge.[b]"

A Prophecy Against Moab

16:6–12pp Jer 48:29–36

15 An oracle concerning
Moab:[a]

Ar in Moab is ruined,[b]
destroyed in a night!
Kir in Moab is ruined,
destroyed in a night!
2Dibon goes up to its temple,
to its high places[c] to weep;
Moab wails over Nebo and
Medeba.
Every head is shaved[d]
and every beard cut off.
3In the streets they wear
sackcloth;
on the roofs and in the public
squares[e]
they all wail,
prostrate with weeping.[f]
4Heshbon and Elealeh[g] cry out,
their voices are heard all the
way to Jahaz.
Therefore the armed men of
Moab cry out,
and their hearts are faint.

5My heart cries out over Moab;[h]
her fugitives flee as far as
Zoar,
as far as Eglath Shelishiyah.
They go up the way to Luhith,
weeping as they go;
on the road to Horonaim[i]
they lament their
destruction.[j]

14:22 f 1Ki 14:10; Job 18:19
14:23 g Isa 34:11-15; Zep 2:14
14:24 h Isa 45:23; i Ac 4:28
14:25 j Isa 10:5,12; k Isa 9:4; l Isa 10:27
14:26 m Isa 23:9; n Ex 15:12
14:27 o 2Ch 20:6; Isa 43:13; Da 4:35
14:28 p Isa 13:1; q 2Ki 16:20
14:29 r 2Ch 26:6; s Isa 11:8
14:30 t Isa 3:15; u Isa 7:21-22; v Isa 8:21; Isa 9:20; Isa 51:19; w Jer 25:16
14:31 x Isa 3:26; y Jer 1:14
14:32 z Isa 37:9; a Ps 87:2,5; Isa 44:28; Isa 54:11; b Isa 4:6; Jas 2:5
15:1 a Isa 11:14; b Jer 48:24,41
15:2 c Jer 48:35; d Lev 21:5
15:3 e Jer 48:38; f Isa 22:4
15:4 g Nu 32:3
15:5 h Jer 48:31; i Jer 48:3,34; j Jer 4:20; Jer 48:5

6 The waters of Nimrim are dried
up[k]
and the grass is withered;[l]
the vegetation is gone
and nothing green is left.
7 So the wealth they have
acquired[m] and stored up
they carry away over the
Ravine of the Poplars.
8 Their outcry echoes along the
border of Moab;
their wailing reaches as far as
Eglaim,
their lamentation as far as
Beer Elim.
9 Dimon's[a] waters are full of
blood,
but I will bring still more
upon Dimon[a]—
a lion[n] upon the fugitives of
Moab
and upon those who remain in
the land.

16 Send lambs[a] as tribute
to the ruler of the land,
from Sela,[b] across the desert,
to the mount of the Daughter
of Zion.[c]
2 Like fluttering birds
pushed from the nest,[d]
so are the women of Moab
at the fords of the Arnon.[e]

3 "Give us counsel,
render a decision.
Make your shadow like night—
at high noon.
Hide the fugitives,[f]
do not betray the refugees.
4 Let the Moabite fugitives stay
with you;
be their shelter from the
destroyer."
The oppressor[g] will come to an
end,
and destruction will cease;
the aggressor will vanish from
the land.
5 In love a throne[h] will be
established;
in faithfulness a man will sit
on it—
one from the house[a] of
David[i]—
one who in judging seeks
justice[j]
and speeds the cause of
righteousness.

6 We have heard of Moab's[k]
pride[l]—
her overweening pride and
conceit,
her pride and her insolence—
but her boasts are empty.
7 Therefore the Moabites wail,[m]
they wail together for Moab.
Lament and grieve
for the men[b][n] of Kir
Hareseth.[o]
8 The fields of Heshbon wither,
the vines of Sibmah also.
The rulers of the nations
have trampled down the
choicest vines,
which once reached Jazer
and spread towards the desert.
Their shoots spread out
and went as far as the sea.
9 So I weep,[p] as Jazer weeps,
for the vines of Sibmah.
O Heshbon, O Elealeh,
I drench you with tears!
The shouts of joy over your
ripened fruit
and over your harvests[q] have
been stilled.
10 Joy and gladness are taken
away from the orchards;[r]
no-one sings or shouts in the
vineyards;
no-one treads[s] out wine at the
presses,[t]
for I have put an end to the
shouting.
11 My heart laments for Moab[u]
like a harp,
my inmost being[v] for Kir
Hareseth.
12 When Moab appears at her high
place,
she only wears herself out;

15:6
k Isa 19:5-7
Jer 48:34
l Joel 1:12
15:7
m Isa 30:6
Jer 48:36
15:9
n 2Ki 17:25
16:1
a 2Ki 3:4
b 2Ki 14:7
c Isa 10:32
16:2
d Pr 27:8
e Nu 21:13-14
Jer 48:20
16:3
f 1Ki 18:4
16:4
g Isa 9:4
16:5
h Da 7:14
Mic 4:7
i Lk 1:32
j Isa 9:7
16:6
k Am 2:1
Zep 2:8
l Ob 1:3
Zep 2:10
16:7
m Jer 48:20
n 1Ch 16:3
o 2Ki 3:25
16:9
p Isa 15:3
q Jer 40:12
16:10
r Isa 24:7-8
s Jdg 9:27
t Job 24:11
16:11
u Isa 15:5
v Isa 63:15
Hos 11:8
Php 2:1

a9 Masoretic Text; Dead Sea Scrolls, some Septuagint manuscripts and Vulgate *Dibon*
a5 Hebrew *tent* b7 Or *"raisin cakes,"* a word play

when she goes to her shrine[w] to
pray,
it is to no avail.[x]

13 This is the word the LORD has
already spoken concerning Moab.
14 But now the LORD says: "Within
three years, as a servant bound by
contract would count them, Moab's
splendour and all her many people
will be despised,[y] and her survivors will be very few and feeble."[z]

An Oracle Against Damascus

17 An oracle concerning Damascus:[a]

"See, Damascus will no longer
be a city
but will become a heap of
ruins.[b]
2 The cities of Aroer will be
deserted
and left to flocks,[c] which will
lie down,
with no-one to make them
afraid.[d]
3 The fortified city will disappear
from Ephraim,
and royal power from
Damascus;
the remnant of Aram will be
like the glory[e] of the
Israelites,"[f]
declares the LORD Almighty.

4 "In that day the glory of Jacob
will fade;
the fat of his body will waste[g]
away.
5 It will be as when a reaper
gathers the standing corn
and harvests[h] the corn with
his arm—
as when a man gleans ears of
corn
in the Valley of Rephaim.
6 Yet some gleanings will
remain,[i]
as when an olive tree is
beaten,[j]
leaving two or three olives on
the topmost branches,
four or five on the fruitful
boughs,"
declares the LORD,
the God of Israel.

7 In that day men will look[k] to
their Maker
and turn their eyes to the
Holy One[l] of Israel.
8 They will not look to the altars,
the work of their hands,[m]
and they will have no regard
for the Asherah poles[a]
and the incense altars their
fingers have made.

9 In that day their strong cities,
which they left because of the
Israelites, will be like places
abandoned to thickets and
undergrowth. And all will be desolation.

10 You have forgotten[n] God your
Saviour;[o]
you have not remembered the
Rock, your fortress.
Therefore, though you set out
the finest plants
and plant imported vines,
11 though on the day you set them
out, you make them grow,
and on the morning[p] when
you plant them, you bring
them to bud,
yet the harvest will be as
nothing[q]
in the day of disease and
incurable pain.[r]

12 Oh, the raging of many
nations—
they rage like the raging
sea![s]
Oh, the uproar of the peoples—
they roar like the roaring of
great waters!
13 Although the peoples roar like
the roar of surging waters,
when he rebukes[t] them they
flee[u] far away,
driven before the wind like
chaff[v] on the hills,

16:12 w Isa 15:2 x 1Ki 18:29
16:14 y Isa 25:10 Jer 48:42 z Isa 21:17
17:1 a Ge 14:15 Jer 49:23 Ac 9:2 b Isa 25:2 Am 1:3 Zec 9:1
17:2 c Isa 7:21 Eze 25:5 d Jer 7:33 Mic 4:4
17:3 e ver 4 Hos 9:11 f Isa 7:8,16 Isa 8:4
17:4 g Isa 10:16
17:5 h ver 11 Jer 51:33 Joel 3:13 Mt 13:30
17:6 i Dt 4:27 Isa 24:13 j Isa 27:12
17:7 k Isa 10:20 l Mic 7:7
17:8 m Isa 2:18,20 Isa 30:22
17:10 n Isa 51:13 o Ps 68:19 Isa 12:2
17:11 p Ps 90:6 q Hos 8:7 r Job 4:8
17:12 s Ps 18:4 Jer 6:23 Lk 21:25
17:13 t Ps 9:5 u Isa 13:14 v Isa 41:2, 15-16

a8 That is, symbols of the goddess Asherah

like tumble-weed before a
gale.[w]
14 In the evening, sudden terror!
Before the morning, they are
gone![x]
This is the portion of those who
loot us,
the lot of those who plunder
us.

A Prophecy Against Cush

18 Woe to the land of
whirring wings[a]
along the rivers of Cush,[b][a]
2 which sends envoys by sea
in papyrus[b] boats over the
water.

Go, swift messengers,
to a people tall and smooth-
skinned,
to a people feared far and
wide,
an aggressive[c] nation of
strange speech,
whose land is divided by
rivers.[d]

3 All you people of the world,
you who live on the earth,
when a banner[e] is raised on the
mountains,
you will see it,
and when a trumpet sounds,
you will hear it.
4 This is what the LORD says to
me:
"I will remain quiet and will
look on from my
dwelling-place,[f]
like shimmering heat in the
sunshine,
like a cloud of dew[g] in the
heat of harvest."
5 For, before the harvest, when
the blossom is gone
and the flower becomes a
ripening grape,
he will cut off the shoots with
pruning knives,
and cut down and take away
the spreading branches.[h]
6 They will all be left to the
mountain birds of prey
and to the wild animals;[i]
the birds will feed on them all
summer,
the wild animals all winter.

7 At that time gifts will be
brought to the LORD Almighty

from a people tall and
smooth-skinned,
from a people feared far and
wide,
an aggressive nation of strange
speech,
whose land is divided by
rivers—
the gifts will be brought to Mount
Zion, the place of the Name of the
LORD Almighty.[j]

A Prophecy About Egypt

19 An oracle[a] concerning
Egypt:[b][c]

See, the LORD rides on a swift
cloud[d]
and is coming to Egypt.
The idols of Egypt tremble
before him,
and the hearts of the
Egyptians melt[e] within
them.

2 "I will stir up Egyptian against
Egyptian—
brother will fight against
brother,[f]
neighbour against neighbour,
city against city,
kingdom against kingdom.[g]
3 The Egyptians will lose heart,
and I will bring their plans to
nothing;
they will consult the idols and
the spirits of the dead,
the mediums and the
spiritists.[h]
4 I will hand the Egyptians over
to the power of a cruel
master,
and a fierce king[i] will rule
over them,"

17:13 w Job 21:18
17:14 x 2Ki 19:35
18:1 a Isa 20:3-5; Eze 30:4-5,9; Zep 2:12; Zep 3:10
18:2 b Ex 2:3; c Ge 10:8-9; 2Ch 12:3; d ver 7
18:3 e Isa 5:26
18:4 f Isa 26:21; Hos 5:15; g Isa 26:19; Hos 14:5
18:5 h Isa 17:10-11; Eze 17:6
18:6 i Isa 56:9; Jer 7:33; Eze 32:4; Eze 39:17
18:7 j Ps 68:31
19:1 a Isa 13:1; Jer 43:12; b Joel 3:19; c Ex 12:12; d Ps 18:10; Ps 104:3; Rev 1:7; e Jos 2:11
19:2 f Jdg 7:22; Mt 10:21,36; g 2Ch 20:23
19:3 h Isa 8:19; Isa 47:13; Da 2:2,10
19:4 i Isa 20:4; Jer 46:26; Eze 29:19

a1 Or *of locusts* b1 That is, the upper Nile region

declares the Lord, the LORD
Almighty.

5 The waters of the river will dry
up,[j]
and the river bed will be
parched and dry.
6 The canals will stink;[k]
the streams of Egypt will
dwindle and dry up.[l]
The reeds and rushes will
wither,[m]
7 also the plants along the Nile,
at the mouth of the river.
Every sown field[n] along the
Nile
will become parched, will blow
away and be no more.
8 The fishermen[o] will groan and
lament,
all who cast hooks[p] into the
Nile;
those who throw nets on the
water
will pine away.
9 Those who work with combed
flax will despair,
the weavers of fine linen[q] will
lose hope.
10 The workers in cloth will be
dejected,
and all the wage earners will
be sick at heart.

11 The officials of Zoan[r] are
nothing but fools;
the wise counsellors of
Pharaoh give senseless
advice.
How can you say to Pharaoh,
"I am one of the wise men,[s]
a disciple of the ancient
kings"?

12 Where are your wise men[t]
now?
Let them show you and make
known
what the LORD Almighty
has planned[u] against Egypt.
13 The officials of Zoan have
become fools,
the leaders of Memphis[a][v] are
deceived;
the cornerstones of her peoples

19:5 j Jer 51:36
19:6 k Ex 7:18 l Isa 37:25 Eze 30:12 m Isa 15:6
19:7 n Isa 23:3
19:8 o Eze 47:10 p Hab 1:15
19:9 q Pr 7:16 Eze 27:7
19:11 r Nu 13:22 s 1Ki 4:30 Ac 7:22
19:12 t 1Co 1:20 u Isa 14:24 Ro 9:17
19:13 v Jer 2:16 Eze 30:13,16
19:14 w Mt 17:17
19:15 x Isa 9:14
19:16 y Jer 51:30 Na 3:13 z Heb 10:31 a Isa 11:15
19:17 b Isa 14:24
19:18 c Zep 3:9
19:19 d Jos 22:10 e Ge 28:18
19:20 f Isa 49:24-26
19:21 g Isa 11:9 h Isa 56:7 Mal 1:11
19:22 i Heb 12:11 j Isa 45:14 Hos 14:1 k Dt 32:39
19:23 l Isa 11:16

have led Egypt astray.
14 The LORD has poured into them
a spirit of dizziness;[w]
they make Egypt stagger in all
that she does,
as a drunkard staggers around
in his vomit.
15 There is nothing Egypt can do—
head or tail, palm branch or
reed.[x]

16 In that day the Egyptians will
be like women.[y] They will shudder
with fear[z] at the uplifted hand[a]
that the LORD Almighty raises
against them. 17 And the land of Judah will bring terror to the Egyptians; everyone to whom Judah is
mentioned will be terrified, because of what the LORD Almighty is
planning[b] against them.
18 In that day five cities in Egypt
will speak the language of Canaan
and swear allegiance[c] to the LORD
Almighty. One of them will be
called the City of Destruction.[b]
19 In that day there will be an
altar[d] to the LORD in the heart of
Egypt, and a monument[e] to the
LORD at its border. 20 It will be a sign
and witness to the LORD Almighty
in the land of Egypt. When they cry
out to the LORD because of their oppressors, he will send them a
saviour and defender, and he will
rescue[f] them. 21 So the LORD will
make himself known to the Egyptians, and in that day they will acknowledge[g] the LORD. They will
worship[h] with sacrifices and grain
offerings; they will make vows to
the LORD and keep them. 22 The
LORD will strike[i] Egypt with a
plague; he will strike them and heal
them. They will turn[j] to the LORD,
and he will respond to their pleas
and heal[k] them.
23 In that day there will be a highway[l] from Egypt to Assyria. The
Assyrians will go to Egypt and the

[a]13 Hebrew *Noph* [b]18 Most manuscripts of the Masoretic Text; some manuscripts of the Masoretic Text, Dead Sea Scrolls and Vulgate *City of the Sun* (that is, Heliopolis)

Egyptians to Assyria. The Egyptians and Assyrians will worship[m]
together. [24]In that day Israel will be
the third, along with Egypt and Assyria, a blessing on the earth. [25]The
LORD Almighty will bless them,
saying, "Blessed be Egypt my people,[n] Assyria my handiwork,[o] and
Israel my inheritance.[p]"

A Prophecy Against Egypt and Cush

20 In the year that the supreme commander,[a] sent
by Sargon king of Assyria, came to
Ashdod and attacked and captured
it—[2]at that time the LORD spoke
through Isaiah son of Amoz.[b] He
said to him, "Take off the sackcloth[c] from your body and the sandals[d] from your feet." And he did
so, going around stripped[e] and
barefoot.[f]

[3]Then the LORD said, "Just as my
servant Isaiah has gone stripped
and barefoot for three years, as a
sign[g] and portent against Egypt
and Cush,[a][h] [4]so the king[i] of Assyria will lead away stripped
and barefoot the Egyptian captives
and Cushite exiles, young and old,
with buttocks bared—to Egypt's
shame.[j] [5]Those who trusted in
Cush and boasted in Egypt[k] will be
afraid and put to shame. [6]In that
day the people who live on this
coast will say, 'See what has happened to those we relied on, those
we fled to for help[l] and deliverance from the king of Assyria! How
then can we escape?[m]' "

A Prophecy Against Babylon

21 An oracle concerning the
Desert[a] by the Sea:

Like whirlwinds sweeping
through the southland,[b]
an invader comes from the
desert,
from a land of terror.

[2]A dire[c] vision has been shown
to me:
The traitor betrays,[d] the
looter takes loot.
Elam,[e] attack! Media, lay
siege!
I will bring to an end all the
groaning she caused.

[3]At this my body is racked with
pain,
pangs seize me, like those of a
woman in labour;[f]
I am staggered by what I hear,
I am bewildered by what I
see.
[4]My heart falters,
fear makes me tremble;
the twilight I longed for
has become a horror to me.
[5]They set the tables,
they spread the rugs,
they eat, they drink![g]
Get up, you officers,
oil the shields!

[6]This is what the Lord says to me:

"Go, post a lookout
and have him report what he
sees.
[7]When he sees chariots[h]
with teams of horses,
riders on donkeys
or riders on camels,
let him be alert,
fully alert."

[8]And the lookout[a][i] shouted,

"Day after day, my lord, I stand
on the watchtower;
every night I stay at my post.
[9]Look, here comes a man in a
chariot
with a team of horses.
And he gives back the answer:
'Babylon[j] has fallen,[k] has
fallen!
All the images of its gods[l]
lie shattered on the ground!' "

[10]O my people, crushed on the
threshing-floor,[m]
I tell you what I have heard

19:23 m Isa 27:13
19:25 n Ps 100:3 o Isa 29:23; Isa 45:11; Isa 60:21; Isa 64:8; Eph 2:10 p Hos 2:23
20:1 a 2Ki 18:17
20:2 b Isa 13:1 c Zec 13:4; Mt 3:4 d Eze 24:17,23 e 1Sa 19:24 f Mic 1:8
20:3 g Isa 8:18 h Isa 37:9; Isa 43:3
20:4 i Isa 19:4 j Isa 47:3; Jer 13:22,26
20:5 k 2Ki 18:21; Isa 30:5
20:6 l Isa 10:3 m Jer 30:15-17; Mt 23:33; 1Th 5:3; Heb 2:3
21:1 a Isa 13:21; Jer 51:43 b Zec 9:14
21:2 c Ps 60:3 d Isa 33:1 e Isa 22:6; Jer 49:34
21:3 f Ps 48:6; Isa 26:17
21:5 g Jer 51:39,57; Da 5:2
21:7 h ver 9
21:8 i Hab 2:1
21:9 j Rev 14:8 k Jer 51:8; Rev 18:2 l Isa 46:1; Jer 50:2; Jer 51:44
21:10 m Jer 51:33

[a]3 That is, the upper Nile region; also in verse 5
[a]8 Dead Sea Scrolls and Syriac; Masoretic Text *A lion*

from the LORD Almighty,
from the God of Israel.

A Prophecy Against Edom

11 An oracle concerning Dumah:[b][n]

Someone calls to me from
Seir,[o]
"Watchman, what is left of the
night?
Watchman, what is left of the
night?"
12 The watchman replies,
"Morning is coming, but also
the night.
If you would ask, then ask;
and come back yet again."

A Prophecy Against Arabia

13 An oracle[p] concerning Arabia:

You caravans of Dedanites,
who camp in the thickets of
Arabia,
14 bring water for the thirsty;
you who live in Tema,[q]
bring food for the fugitives.
15 They flee[r] from the sword,
from the drawn sword,
from the bent bow
and from the heat of battle.

16 This is what the Lord says to
me: "Within one year, as a servant
bound by contract[s] would count it,
all the pomp[t] of Kedar[u] will come
to an end. 17 The survivors of the
bowmen, the warriors of Kedar,
will be few.[v]" The LORD, the God of
Israel, has spoken.

A Prophecy About Jerusalem

22 An oracle[a] concerning the
Valley[b] of Vision:

What troubles you now,
that you have all gone up on
the roofs,
2 O town full of commotion,
O city of tumult and revelry?[c]
Your slain were not killed by
the sword,
nor did they die in battle.
3 All your leaders have fled
together;
they have been captured
without using the bow.
All you who were caught were
taken prisoner together,
having fled while the enemy
was still far away.
4 Therefore I said, "Turn away
from me;
let me weep[d] bitterly.
Do not try to console me
over the destruction of my
people."[e]

5 The Lord, the LORD Almighty,
has a day
of tumult and trampling and
terror[f]
in the Valley of Vision,
a day of battering down walls
and of crying out to the
mountains.
6 Elam[g] takes up the quiver,[h]
with her charioteers and
horses;
Kir[i] uncovers the shield.
7 Your choicest valleys are full of
chariots,
and horsemen are posted at
the city gates;[j]
8 the defences of Judah are
stripped away.

And you looked in that day
to the weapons[k] in the Palace
of the Forest;[l]
9 you saw that the City of David
had many breaches in its
defences;
you stored up water
in the Lower Pool.[m]
10 You counted the buildings in
Jerusalem
and tore down houses to
strengthen the wall.
11 You built a reservoir between
the two walls[n]
for the water of the Old Pool,[o]
but you did not look to the One
who made it,

21:11 n Ge 25:14 o Ge 32:3
21:13 p Isa 13:1
21:14 q Ge 25:15
21:15 r Isa 13:14
21:16 s Isa 16:14 t Isa 17:3 u Ps 120:5 Isa 60:7
21:17 v Isa 10:19
22:1 a Isa 13:1 b Ps 125:2 Jer 21:13 Joel 3:2,12, 14
22:2 c Isa 32:13
22:4 d Isa 15:3 Lk 19:41 e Jer 9:1
22:5 f La 1:5
22:6 g Isa 21:2 h Jer 49:35 i 2Ki 16:9
22:7 j 2Ch 32:1-2
22:8 k 2Ch 32:5 l 1Ki 7:2
22:9 m 2Ch 32:4
22:11 n 2Ki 25:4 Jer 39:4 o 2Ch 32:4

b 11 *Dumah* means *silence* or *stillness*, a word play on *Edom*.

or have regard for the One
who planned it long ago.

12The Lord, the LORD Almighty,
called you on that day
to weep[p] and to wail,
to tear out your hair[q] and put
on sackcloth.[r]
13But see, there is joy and
revelry,
slaughtering of cattle and
killing of sheep,
eating of meat and drinking of
wine![s]
"Let us eat and drink," you say,
"for tomorrow we die!"[t]

14The LORD Almighty has revealed this in my hearing:[u] "Till
your dying day this sin will not be
atoned[v] for," says the Lord, the
LORD Almighty.

15This is what the Lord, the LORD
Almighty, says:

"Go, say to this steward,
to Shebna,[w] who is in charge
of the palace:
16What are you doing here and
who gave you permission
to cut out a grave[x] for
yourself here,
hewing your grave on the
height
and chiselling your resting
place in the rock?
17"Beware, the LORD is about to
take firm hold of you
and hurl you away, O you
mighty man.
18He will roll you up tightly like a
ball
and throw[y] you into a large
country.
There you will die
and there your splendid
chariots will remain—
you disgrace to your master's
house!
19I will depose you from your
office,
and you will be ousted from
your position.

20"In that day I will summon my
servant, Eliakim[z] son of Hilkiah.
21I will clothe him with your robe
and fasten your sash around him
and hand your authority over to
him. He will be a father to those
who live in Jerusalem and to the
house of Judah. 22I will place on his
shoulder the key[a] to the house of
David;[b] what he opens no-one can
shut, and what he shuts no-one can
open.[c] 23I will drive him like a
peg[d] into a firm place;[e] he will be
a seat[a] of honour[f] for the house of
his father. 24All the glory of his
family will hang on him: its offspring and offshoots—all its lesser
vessels, from the bowls to all the
jars.

25"In that day," declares the LORD
Almighty, "the peg[g] driven into
the firm place will give way; it will
be sheared off and will fall, and the
load hanging on it will be cut
down." The LORD has spoken.[h]

A Prophecy About Tyre

23

An oracle concerning Tyre:[a]

Wail, O ships[b] of Tarshish![c]
For Tyre is destroyed
and left without house or
harbour.
From the land of Cyprus[a]
word has come to them.
2Be silent, you people of the
island
and you merchants of Sidon,
whom the seafarers have
enriched.
3On the great waters
came the grain of the Shihor;
the harvest of the Nile[b][d] was
the revenue of Tyre,[e]
and she became the market-
place of the nations.

22:12 p Joel 2:17 q Mic 1:16 r Joel 1:13
22:13 s Isa 5:22; Isa 28:7-8; Isa 56:12; Lk 17:26-29 t 1Co 15:32*
22:14 u Isa 5:9 v Isa 13:11; Isa 26:21; Isa 30:13-14; Eze 24:13
22:15 w 2Ki 18:18; Isa 36:3
22:16 x Mt 27:60
22:18 y Isa 17:13
22:20 z 2Ki 18:18; Isa 36:3
22:22 a Rev 3:7 b Isa 7:2 c Job 12:14
22:23 d Zec 10:4 e Ezr 9:8 f 1Sa 2:7-8; Job 36:7
22:25 g ver 23 h Isa 46:11; Mic 4:4
23:1 a Jos 19:29; 1Ki 5:1; Jer 47:4; Eze 26,27,28; Joel 3:4-8; Am 1:9-10; Zec 9:2-4 b 1Ki 10:22 c Ge 10:4; Isa 2:16 *fn*
23:3 d Isa 19:7 e Eze 27:3

[a]23 Or *throne* [a]1 Hebrew *Kittim*
[b]2,3 Masoretic Text; one Dead Sea Scroll *Sidon, / who cross over the sea; / your envoys* 3*are on the great waters. / The grain of the Shihor, / the harvest of the Nile,*

4 Be ashamed, O Sidon,[f] and you,
O fortress of the sea,
for the sea has spoken:
"I have neither been in labour
nor given birth;
I have neither reared sons nor
brought up daughters."
5 When word comes to Egypt,
they will be in anguish at the
report from Tyre.

6 Cross over to Tarshish;
wail, you people of the island.
7 Is this your city of revelry,[g]
the old, old city,
whose feet have taken her
to settle in far-off lands?
8 Who planned this against Tyre,
the bestower of crowns,
whose merchants are princes,
whose traders are renowned in
the earth?
9 The LORD Almighty planned it,
to bring low[h] the pride of all
glory
and to humble[i] all who are
renowned[j] on the earth.

10 Till[c] your land as along the
Nile,
O Daughter of Tarshish,
for you no longer have a
harbour.
11 The LORD has stretched out his
hand[k] over the sea
and made its kingdoms
tremble.
He has given an order
concerning Phoenicia[d]
that her fortresses be
destroyed.[l]
12 He said, "No more of your
revelling,[m]
O Virgin Daughter[n] of Sidon,
now crushed!
"Up, cross over to Cyprus;[e]
even there you will find no
rest."
13 Look at the land of the
Babylonians,[f]
this people that is now of no
account!
The Assyrians[o] have made it
a place for desert creatures;
they raised up their siege
towers,
they stripped its fortresses
bare
and turned it into a ruin.[p]
14 Wail, you ships of Tarshish;[q]
your fortress is destroyed!

15 At that time Tyre[r] will be forgotten for seventy years, the span
of a king's life. But at the end of
these seventy years, it will happen
to Tyre as in the song of the prostitute:

16 "Take up a harp, walk through
the city,
O prostitute forgotten;
play the harp well, sing many a
song,
so that you will be
remembered."

17 At the end of seventy years, the
LORD will deal with Tyre. She will
return to her hire as a prostitute[s]
and will ply her trade with all the
kingdoms on the face of the earth.
18 Yet her profit and her earnings
will be set apart for the LORD;[t]
they will not be stored up or
hoarded. Her profits will go to
those who live before the LORD,[u]
for abundant food and fine clothes.

The LORD's Devastation of the Earth

24 See, the LORD is going to
lay waste the earth[a]
and devastate it;
he will ruin its face
and scatter its inhabitants—
2 it will be the same
for priest as for people,[b]
for master as for servant,
for mistress as for maid,
for seller as for buyer,[c]
for borrower as for lender,
for debtor as for creditor.[d]

23:4 f Ge 10:15,19
23:7 g Isa 22:2; Isa 32:13
23:9 h Job 40:11; i Isa 13:11; j Isa 5:13; Isa 9:15
23:11 k Ex 14:21; l Isa 25:2; Zec 9:3-4
23:12 m Rev 18:22; n Isa 47:1
23:13 o Isa 10:5; p Isa 10:7
23:14 q Isa 2:16 *fn*
23:15 r Jer 25:22
23:17 s Eze 16:26; Na 3:4; Rev 17:1
23:18 t Ex 28:36; Ps 72:10; u Isa 60:5-9; Mic 4:13
24:1 a ver 20; Isa 2:19-21; Isa 33:9
24:2 b Hos 4:9; c Eze 7:12; d Lev 25:35-37; Dt 23:19-20

c 10 Dead Sea Scrolls and some Septuagint manuscripts; Masoretic Text *Go through*
d 11 Hebrew *Canaan* e 12 Hebrew *Kittim*
f 13 Or *Chaldeans*

3The earth will be completely
laid waste
and totally plundered.[e]
The LORD has spoken
this word.

4The earth dries up and withers,
the world languishes and
withers,
the exalted[f] of the earth
languish.
5The earth is defiled[g] by its
people;
they have disobeyed[h] the
laws,
violated the statutes
and broken the everlasting
covenant.
6Therefore a curse consumes the
earth;
its people must bear their
guilt.
Therefore earth's inhabitants
are burned up,[i]
and very few are left.
7The new wine dries up and the
vine withers;[j]
all the merrymakers groan.[k]
8The gaiety of the tambourines[l]
is stilled,
the noise[m] of the revellers has
stopped,
the joyful harp[n] is silent.[o]
9No longer do they drink wine[p]
with a song;
the beer is bitter[q] to its
drinkers.
10The ruined city lies desolate;
the entrance to every house is
barred.
11In the streets they cry out for
wine;
all joy turns to gloom,[r]
all gaiety is banished from the
earth.
12The city is left in ruins,
its gate is battered to pieces.
13So will it be on the earth
and among the nations,
as when an olive tree is
beaten,[s]
or as when gleanings are left
after the grape harvest.

14They raise their voices, they
shout for joy;[t]
from the west they acclaim
the LORD's majesty.
15Therefore in the east give
glory[u] to the LORD;
exalt[v] the name of the LORD,
the God of Israel,
in the islands of the sea.
16From the ends of the earth we
hear singing:
"Glory[w] to the
Righteous One."

But I said, "I waste away, I
waste away!
Woe to me!
The treacherous betray!
With treachery the
treacherous betray![x]"
17Terror and pit and snare[y] await
you,
O people of the earth.
18Whoever flees at the sound of
terror
will fall into a pit;
whoever climbs out of the pit
will be caught in a snare.

The floodgates of the heavens[z]
are opened,
the foundations of the earth
shake.[a]
19The earth is broken up,
the earth is split asunder,[b]
the earth is thoroughly
shaken.
20The earth reels like a
drunkard,[c]
it sways like a hut in the wind;
so heavy upon it is the guilt of
its rebellion[d]
that it falls—never to rise
again.

21In that day the LORD will
punish[e]
the powers in the heavens
above
and the kings on the earth
below.
22They will be herded together
like prisoners[f] bound in a
dungeon;[g]
they will be shut up in prison

24:3 e Isa 6:11-12
24:4 f Isa 2:12
24:5 g Ge 3:17; Nu 35:33 h Isa 10:6; Isa 59:12
24:6 i Isa 1:31
24:7 j Joel 1:10-12 k Isa 16:8-10
24:8 l Isa 5:12 m Jer 7:34; Jer 16:9; Jer 25:10; Hos 2:11 n Rev 18:22 o Eze 26:13
24:9 p Isa 5:11,22 q Isa 5:20
24:11 r Isa 16:10; Isa 32:13; Jer 14:3
24:13 s Isa 17:6
24:14 t Isa 12:6
24:15 u Isa 66:19 v Isa 25:3; Mal 1:11
24:16 w Isa 28:5 x Isa 21:2; Jer 5:11
24:17 y Jer 48:43
24:18 z Ge 7:11 a Ps 18:7
24:19 b Dt 11:6
24:20 c Isa 19:14 d Isa 1:2,28; Isa 43:27
24:21 e Isa 10:12
24:22 f Isa 10:4 g Isa 42:7,22

and be punished[a] after many
days.[h]
23The moon will be abashed, the
sun[i] ashamed;
for the LORD Almighty will
reign[j]
on Mount Zion[k] and in
Jerusalem,
and before its elders,
gloriously.[l]

Praise to the LORD

25

O LORD, you are my God;
I will exalt you and praise
your name,
for in perfect faithfulness
you have done marvellous
things,[a]
things planned[b] long ago.
2You have made the city a heap
of rubble,[c]
the fortified[d] town a ruin,
the foreigners' stronghold[e] a
city no more;
it will never be rebuilt.
3Therefore strong peoples will
honour you;
cities of ruthless[f] nations will
revere you.
4You have been a refuge[g] for
the poor,
a refuge for the needy in his
distress,
a shelter from the storm
and a shade from the heat.
For the breath of the ruthless[h]
is like a storm driving against
a wall
5 and like the heat of the desert.
You silence[i] the uproar of
foreigners;
as heat is reduced by the
shadow of a cloud,
so the song of the ruthless is
stilled.

6On this mountain[j] the LORD
Almighty will prepare
a feast[k] of rich food for all
peoples,
a banquet of aged wine—
the best of meats and the
finest of wines.[l]
7On this mountain he will
destroy
the shroud[m] that enfolds all
peoples,
the sheet that covers all
nations;
8 he will swallow up death[n] for
ever.
The Sovereign LORD will wipe
away the tears[o]
from all faces;
he will remove the disgrace[p] of
his people
from all the earth.
The LORD has spoken.

9In that day they will say,

"Surely this is our God;[q]
we trusted in him, and he
saved[r] us.
This is the LORD, we trusted in
him;
let us rejoice[s] and be glad in
his salvation."

10The hand of the LORD will rest
on this mountain;
but Moab[t] will be trampled
under him
as straw is trampled down in
the manure.
11They will spread out their
hands in it,
as a swimmer spreads out his
hands to swim.
God will bring down[u] their
pride[v]
despite the cleverness[a] of
their hands.
12He will bring down your high
fortified walls
and lay them low;[w]
he will bring them down to the
ground,
to the very dust.

A Song of Praise

26

In that day this song will be
sung in the land of Judah:

We have a strong city;[a]
God makes salvation

24:22 h Eze 38:8
24:23 i Isa 13:10; j Rev 22:5; k Heb 12:22; l Isa 60:19
25:1 a Ps 98:1; b Nu 23:19
25:2 c Isa 17:1; d Isa 17:3; e Isa 13:22
25:3 f Isa 13:11
25:4 g Isa 4:6; Isa 17:10; Isa 27:5; Isa 33:16; h Isa 29:5; Isa 49:25
25:5 i Jer 51:55
25:6 j Isa 2:2; k Isa 1:19; Mt 8:11; Mt 22:4; l Pr 9:2
25:7 m 2Co 3:15-16; Eph 4:18
25:8 n Hos 13:14; 1Co 15:54-55*; o Isa 30:19; Isa 35:10; Isa 51:11; Isa 65:19; Rev 7:17; Rev 21:4; p Mt 5:11; 1Pe 4:14
25:9 q Isa 40:9; r Ps 20:5; Isa 33:22; Isa 35:4; Isa 49:25; Isa 60:16; s Isa 35:2,10
25:10 t Am 2:1-3
25:11 u Isa 5:25; Isa 14:26; Isa 16:14; v Job 40:12
25:12 w Isa 15:1
26:1 a Isa 14:32

a22 Or *released* a11 The meaning of the Hebrew for this word is uncertain.

its walls[b] and ramparts.
2 Open the gates
that the righteous[c] nation
may enter,
the nation that keeps faith.
3 You will keep in perfect peace
him whose mind is steadfast,
because he trusts in you.
4 Trust[d] in the LORD for ever,
for the LORD, the LORD, is the
Rock eternal.
5 He humbles those who dwell on
high,
he lays the lofty city low;
he levels it to the ground[e]
and casts it down to the dust.
6 Feet trample it down—
the feet of the oppressed,
the footsteps of the poor.[f]

7 The path of the righteous is
level;
O upright One, you make the
way of the righteous
smooth.[g]
8 Yes, LORD, walking in the way
of your laws,[a][h]
we wait for you;
your name[i] and renown
are the desire of our hearts.
9 My soul yearns for you in the
night;
in the morning my spirit
longs[j] for you.
When your judgments come
upon the earth,
the people of the world learn
righteousness.[k]
10 Though grace is shown to the
wicked,
they do not learn
righteousness;
even in a land of uprightness
they go on doing evil[l]
and regard[m] not the majesty
of the LORD.
11 O LORD, your hand is lifted
high,
but they do not see[n] it.
Let them see your zeal for your
people and be put to shame;
let the fire[o] reserved for your
enemies consume them.

26:1
b Isa 60:18

26:2
c Isa 54:14
Isa 58:8
Isa 62:2

26:4
d Isa 12:2
Isa 50:10

26:5
e Isa 25:12

26:6
f Isa 3:15

26:7
g Isa 42:16

26:8
h Isa 56:1
i Isa 12:4

26:9
j Ps 63:1
Ps 78:34
Isa 55:6
k Mt 6:33

26:10
l Isa 32:6
m Isa 22:12-13
Hos 11:7
Jn 5:37-38
Ro 2:4

26:11
n Isa 44:9,18
o Heb 10:27

26:13
p Isa 2:8
Isa 10:5,11
q Isa 63:7

26:14
r Dt 4:28
s Isa 10:3

26:15
t Isa 33:17

26:16
u Hos 5:15

26:17
v Jn 16:21

26:18
w Isa 33:11
Isa 59:4
x Ps 17:14

26:19
y Isa 25:8
Eph 5:14
z Eze 37:1-14
Da 12:2

12 LORD, you establish peace for
us;
all that we have accomplished
you have done for us.
13 O LORD, our God, other lords[p]
besides you have ruled over
us,
but your name alone do we
honour.[q]
14 They are now dead,[r] they live
no more;
those departed spirits do not
rise.
You punished them and brought
them to ruin;[s]
you wiped out all memory of
them.
15 You have enlarged the nation,
O LORD;
you have enlarged the nation.
You have gained glory for
yourself;
you have extended all the
borders[t] of the land.

16 LORD, they came to you in their
distress;[u]
when you disciplined them,
they could barely whisper a
prayer.[b]
17 As a woman with child and
about to give birth[v]
writhes and cries out in her
pain,
so were we in your presence,
O LORD.
18 We were with child, we writhed
in pain,
but we gave birth[w] to wind.
We have not brought salvation[x]
to the earth;
we have not given birth to
people of the world.
19 But your dead[y] will live;
their bodies will rise.
You who dwell in the dust,
wake up and shout for joy.
Your dew is like the dew of the
morning;
the earth will give birth to her
dead.[z]

[a]8 Or *judgments* [b]16 The meaning of the Hebrew for this clause is uncertain.

20Go, my people, enter your
rooms
and shut the doors[a] behind
you;
hide[b] yourselves for a little
while
until his wrath has passed
by.[c]
21See, the LORD is coming[d] out of
his dwelling[e]
to punish[f] the people of the
earth for their sins.
The earth will disclose the
blood[g] shed upon her;
she will conceal her slain no
longer.

Deliverance of Israel

27 In that day,
the LORD will punish with his
sword,[a]
his fierce, great and powerful
sword,
Leviathan[b] the gliding serpent,
Leviathan the coiling serpent;
he will slay the monster[c] of the
sea.

2In that day—
"Sing about a fruitful
vineyard:[d]
3 I, the LORD, watch over it;
I water[e] it continually.
I guard it day and night
so that no-one may harm it.
4 I am not angry.
If only there were briers and
thorns confronting me!
I would march against them in
battle;
I would set them all on fire.[f]
5Or else let them come to me for
refuge;[g]
let them make peace[h] with
me,
yes, let them make peace with
me."
6In days to come Jacob will take
root,
Israel will bud and blossom[i]
and fill all the world with
fruit.[j]

26:20 *a* Ex 12:23 *b* Ps 91:1,4 *c* Ps 30:5; Isa 54:7-8
26:21 *d* Jude 1:14 *e* Mic 1:3 *f* Isa 13:9,11; Isa 30:12-14 *g* Job 16:18; Lk 11:50-51
27:1 *a* Isa 34:6; Isa 66:16 *b* Job 3:8 *c* Ps 74:13
27:2 *d* Jer 2:21
27:3 *e* Isa 58:11
27:4 *f* Isa 10:17; Mt 3:12; Heb 6:8
27:5 *g* Isa 25:4 *h* Job 22:21; Ro 5:1; 2Co 5:20
27:6 *i* Hos 14:5-6 *j* Isa 37:31
27:7 *k* Isa 37:36-38
27:8 *l* Isa 50:1; Isa 54:7
27:9 *m* Ro 11:27* *n* Ex 34:13
27:10 *o* Isa 32:14; Jer 26:6 *p* Isa 17:2
27:11 *q* Dt 32:28; Isa 1:3; Jer 8:7 *r* Dt 32:18; Isa 43:1,7,15; Isa 44:1-2,21,24 *s* Isa 9:17
27:12 *t* Ge 15:18 *u* Dt 30:4; Isa 11:12; Isa 17:6
27:13 *v* Lev 25:9; Mt 24:31 *w* Isa 19:21,25

7Has the LORD struck her
as he struck[k] down those who
struck her?
Has she been killed
as those were killed who killed
her?
8By warfare[a] and exile[l] you
contend with her—
with his fierce blast he drives
her out,
as on a day the east wind
blows.
9By this, then, will Jacob's guilt
be atoned for,
and this will be the full
fruitage of the removal of
his sin:[m]
When he makes all the altar
stones
to be like chalk stones crushed
to pieces,
no Asherah poles[b][n] or incense
altars
will be left standing.
10The fortified city stands
desolate,[o]
an abandoned settlement,
forsaken like the desert;
there the calves graze,
there they lie down;[p]
they strip its branches bare.
11When its twigs are dry, they are
broken off
and women come and make
fires with them.
For this is a people without
understanding;[q]
so their Maker has no
compassion on them,
and their Creator[r] shows
them no favour.[s]

12In that day the LORD will thresh
from the flowing Euphrates[c] to
the Wadi of Egypt,[t] and you, O Israelites, will be gathered[u] up one
by one. 13And in that day a great
trumpet[v] will sound. Those who
were perishing in Assyria and
those who were exiled in Egypt[w]

[a]8 See Septuagint; the meaning of the Hebrew for this word is uncertain. [b]9 That is, symbols of the goddess Asherah [c]12 Hebrew *River*

will come and worship the LORD on
the holy mountain in Jerusalem.

Woe to Ephraim

28 Woe to that wreath, the
pride of Ephraim's[a]
drunkards,
to the fading flower, his
glorious beauty,
set on the head of a fertile
valley[b]—
to that city, the pride of those
laid low by wine![c]
2See, the Lord has one who is
powerful[d] and strong.
Like a hailstorm[e] and a
destructive wind,[f]
like a driving rain and a
flooding[g] downpour,
he will throw it forcefully to
the ground.
3That wreath, the pride of
Ephraim's[h] drunkards,
will be trampled underfoot.
4That fading flower, his glorious
beauty,
set on the head of a fertile
valley,[i]
will be like a fig[j] ripe before
harvest—
as soon as someone sees it and
takes it in his hand,
he swallows it.
5In that day the LORD Almighty
will be a glorious crown,[k]
a beautiful wreath
for the remnant of his people.
6He will be a spirit of justice[l]
to him who sits in judgment,[m]
a source of strength
to those who turn back the
battle[n] at the gate.

7And these also stagger from
wine[o]
and reel[p] from beer:
Priests[q] and prophets[r] stagger
from beer
and are befuddled with wine;
they reel from beer,
they stagger when seeing
visions,[s]
they stumble when rendering
decisions.
8All the tables are covered with
vomit[t]
and there is not a spot without
filth.

9"Who is it he is trying to
teach?[u]
To whom is he explaining his
message?
To children weaned[v] from their
milk,[w]
to those just taken from the
breast?
10For it is:
Do and do, do and do,
rule on rule, rule on rule;[a]
a little here, a little there."
11Very well then, with foreign
lips and strange tongues[x]
God will speak to this
people,[y]
12to whom he said,
"This is the resting-place, let
the weary rest";[z]
and, "This is the place of
repose"—
but they would not listen.
13So then, the word of the LORD to
them will become:
Do and do, do and do,
rule on rule, rule on rule;
a little here, a little there—
so that they will go and fall
backwards,
be injured[a] and snared and
captured.[b]

14Therefore hear the word of the
LORD,[c] you scoffers
who rule this people in
Jerusalem.
15You boast, "We have entered
into a covenant with death,
with the grave[b] we have
made an agreement.
When an overwhelming scourge
sweeps by,[d]
it cannot touch us,

28:1 *a* ver 3 Isa 9:9 *b* ver 4 *c* Hos 7:5
28:2 *d* Isa 40:10 *e* Isa 30:30 Eze 13:11 *f* Isa 29:6 *g* Isa 8:7
28:3 *h* ver 1
28:4 *i* ver 1 *j* Hos 9:10 Na 3:12
28:5 *k* Isa 62:3
28:6 *l* Isa 11:2-4 Isa 32:1,16 *m* Jn 5:30 *n* 2Ch 32:8
28:7 *o* Isa 22:13 *p* Isa 56:10-12 *q* Isa 24:2 *r* Isa 9:15 *s* Isa 29:11 Hos 4:11
28:8 *t* Jer 48:26
28:9 *u* ver 26 Isa 30:20 Isa 48:17 Isa 50:4 Isa 54:13 *v* Ps 131:2 *w* Heb 5:12-13
28:11 *x* Isa 33:19 *y* 1Co 14:21*
28:12 *z* Isa 11:10 Mt 11:28-29
28:13 *a* Mt 21:44 *b* Isa 8:15
28:14 *c* Isa 1:10
28:15 *d* ver 2,18 Isa 8:7-8 Isa 30:28 Da 11:22

a*10* Hebrew / *sav lasav sav lasav / kav lakav kav lakav* (possibly meaningless sounds; perhaps a mimicking of the prophet's words); also in verse 13 **b***15* Hebrew *Sheol*; also in verse 18

for we have made a lie[e] our
refuge
and falsehood[c] our hiding-
place.[f]"

16 So this is what the Sovereign
LORD says:

"See, I lay a stone in Zion,
a tested stone,[g]
a precious cornerstone for a
sure foundation;
the one who trusts will never
be dismayed.[h]
17 I will make justice[i] the
measuring line
and righteousness the
plumb-line;[j]
hail will sweep away your
refuge, the lie,
and water will overflow your
hiding-place.
18 Your covenant with death will
be annulled;
your agreement with the
grave will not stand.[k]
When the overwhelming
scourge sweeps by,[l]
you will be beaten down[m] by
it.
19 As often as it comes it will
carry you away;[n]
morning after morning, by day
and by night,
it will sweep through."

The understanding of this
message
will bring sheer terror.[o]
20 The bed is too short to stretch
out on,
the blanket too narrow to
wrap around you.[p]
21 The LORD will rise up as he did
at Mount Perazim,[q]
he will rouse himself as in the
Valley of Gibeon[r]—
to do his work,[s] his strange
work,
and perform his task, his alien
task.
… stop your mocking,
…ur chains will become
…er;

the Lord, the LORD Almighty,
has told me
of the destruction decreed[t]
against the whole land.[u]

23 Listen and hear my voice;
pay attention and hear what I
say.
24 When a farmer ploughs for
planting, does he plough
continually?
Does he keep on breaking up
and harrowing the soil?
25 When he has levelled the
surface,
does he not sow caraway and
scatter cummin?[v]
Does he not plant wheat in its
place,**[d]**
barley in its plot,**[d]**
and spelt[w] in its field?
26 His God instructs him
and teaches him the right way.
27 Caraway is not threshed with a
sledge,
nor is a cartwheel rolled over
cummin;
caraway is beaten out with a
rod,
and cummin with a stick.
28 Grain must be ground to make
bread;
so one does not go on
threshing it for ever.
Though he drives the wheels of
his threshing-cart over it,
his horses do not grind it.
29 All this also comes from the
LORD Almighty,
wonderful in counsel[x] and
magnificent in wisdom.[y]

Woe to David's City

29 Woe[a] to you, Ariel,
Ariel,[b]
the city where David settled!
Add year to year
and let your cycle of
festivals[c] go on.
2 Yet I will besiege Ariel;
she will mourn and lament,[d]

28:15 e Isa 9:15 f Isa 29:15
28:16 g Ps 118:22 Isa 8:14-15 Mt 21:42 Ac 4:11 Eph 2:20 h Ro 9:33* Ro 10:11* 1Pe 2:6*
28:17 i Isa 5:16 j 2Ki 21:13
28:18 k Isa 7:7 l ver 15 m Da 8:13
28:19 n 2Ki 24:2 o Job 18:11
28:20 p Isa 59:6
28:21 q 1Ch 14:11 r Jos 10:10,12 1Ch 14:16 s Isa 10:12 Lk 19:41-44
28:22 t Isa 10:22 u Isa 10:23
28:25 v Mt 23:23 w Ex 9:32
28:29 x Isa 9:6 y Ro 11:33
29:1 a Isa 22:12-13 b 2Sa 5:9 c Isa 1:14
29:2 d Isa 3:26 La 2:5

c15 Or *false gods* **d**25 The meaning of the Hebrew for this word is uncertain.

she will be to me like an altar
hearth.[a]
3 I will encamp against you all
around;
I will encircle[e] you with
towers
and set up my siege works
against you.
4 Brought low, you will speak
from the ground;
your speech will mumble[f] out
of the dust.
Your voice will come ghostlike
from the earth;
out of the dust your speech
will whisper.

5 But your many enemies will
become like fine dust,
the ruthless hordes like blown
chaff.[g]
Suddenly,[h] in an instant,
6 the LORD Almighty will come
with thunder and earthquake[i]
and great noise,
with windstorm and tempest
and flames of a devouring
fire.
7 Then the hordes of all the
nations[j] that fight against
Ariel,
that attack her and her
fortress and besiege her,
will be as it is with a dream,[k]
with a vision in the night—
8 as when a hungry man dreams
that he is eating,
but he awakens,[l] and his
hunger remains;
as when a thirsty man dreams
that he is drinking,
but he awakens faint, with his
thirst unquenched.
So will it be with the hordes of
all the nations
that fight against Mount Zion.

9 Be stunned and amazed,
blind yourselves and be
sightless;
be drunk,[m] but not from wine,[n]
stagger, but not from beer.
10 The LORD has brought over you
a deep sleep:
He has sealed your eyes[o] (the
prophets);[p]
he has covered your heads
(the seers).[q]

11 For you this whole vision is
nothing but words sealed[r] in a
scroll. And if you give the scroll to
someone who can read, and say to
him, "Read this, please," he will answer, "I can't; it is sealed." 12 Or if
you give the scroll to someone who
cannot read, and say, "Read this,
please," he will answer, "I don't
know how to read."

13 The Lord says:

"These people come near to me
with their mouth
and honour me with their
lips,
but their hearts are far from
me.[s]
Their worship of me
is made up only of rules
taught by men.[b][t]
14 Therefore once more I will
astound these people
with wonder upon wonder;[u]
the wisdom of the wise[v] will
perish,
the intelligence of the
intelligent will vanish.[w]"
15 Woe to those who go to great
depths
to hide their plans from the
LORD,
who do their work in darkness
and think,
"Who sees us?[x] Who will
know?"[y]
16 You turn things upside down,
as if the potter were thought
to be like the clay!
Shall what is formed say to him
who formed it,
"He did not make me"?
Can the pot say of the potter,[z]
"He knows nothing"?

a 2 The Hebrew for *altar hearth* sounds like the Hebrew for *Ariel*. b 13 Hebrew; Septuagint *They worship me in vain; / their teachings are but rules taught by men.*

29:3 e Lk 19:43-44
29:4 f Isa 8:19
29:5 g Isa 17:13 h Isa 17:14 1Th 5:3
29:6 i Mt 24:7 Mk 13:8 Lk 21:11 Rev 11:19
29:7 j Mic 4:11-12 Zec 12:9 k Job 20:8
29:8 l Ps 73:20
29:9 m Isa 51:17 n Isa 51:21-22
29:10 o Ps 69:23 Isa 6:9-10 Ro 11:8* p Mic 3:6 q 1Sa 9:9
29:11 r Isa 8:16 Mt 13:11 Rev 5:1-2
29:13 s Eze 33:31 t Mt 15:8-9* Mk 7:6-7* Col 2:22
29:14 u Hab 1:5 v Jer 8:9 Jer 49:7 w Isa 6:9-10 1Co 1:19*
29:15 x Ps 10:11-13 Ps 94:7 Isa 57:12 y Job 22:13
29:16 z Isa 45:9 Isa 64:8 Ro 9:20-21*

[17]In a very short time, will not
Lebanon be turned into a
fertile field[a]
and the fertile field seem like
a forest?[b]
[18]In that day the deaf[c] will hear
the words of the scroll,
and out of gloom and darkness
the eyes of the blind will see.[d]
[19]Once more the humble[e] will
rejoice in the LORD;
the needy[f] will rejoice in the
Holy One of Israel.
[20]The ruthless will vanish,
the mockers[g] will disappear,
and all who have an eye for
evil[h] will be cut down—
[21]those who with a word make a
man out to be guilty,
who ensnare the defender in
court[i]
and with false testimony
deprive the innocent of
justice.[j]

[22]Therefore this is what the
LORD, who redeemed Abraham,[k]
says to the house of Jacob:

"No longer will Jacob be
ashamed;[l]
no longer will their faces grow
pale.
[23]When they see among them
their children,[m]
the work of my hands,[n]
they will keep my name holy;
they will acknowledge the
holiness of the Holy One of
Jacob,
and will stand in awe of the
God of Israel.
[24]Those who are wayward[o] in
spirit will gain
understanding;[p]
those who complain will
accept instruction."[q]

Woe to the Obstinate Nation

30 "Woe[a] to the obstinate
children,"[b]
declares the LORD,
"to those who carry out plans
that are not mine,
forming an alliance,[c] but not
by my Spirit,
heaping sin upon sin;
[2]who go down to Egypt[d]
without consulting[e] me;
who look for help to Pharaoh's
protection,[f]
to Egypt's shade for refuge.
[3]But Pharaoh's protection will be
to your shame,
Egypt's shade will bring you
disgrace.[g]
[4]Though they have officials in
Zoan[h]
and their envoys have arrived
in Hanes,
[5]everyone will be put to shame
because of a people[i] useless
to them,
who bring neither help nor
advantage,
but only shame and disgrace."

[6]An oracle concerning the animals of the Negev:

Through a land of hardship and
distress,[j]
of lions and lionesses,
of adders and darting
snakes,[k]
the envoys carry their riches on
donkeys' backs,
their treasures[l] on the humps
of camels,
to that unprofitable nation,
[7] to Egypt, whose help is utterly
useless.
Therefore I call her
Rahab the Do-Nothing.

[8]Go now, write it on a tablet for
them,
inscribe it on a scroll,[m]
that for the days to come
it may be an everlasting
witness.
[9]These are rebellious people,
deceitful[n] children,
children unwilling to listen to
the LORD's instruction.[o]
[10]They say to the seers,
"See no more visions[p]!"
and to the prophets,

29:17 a Ps 84:6 b Isa 32:15
29:18 c Mk 7:37 d Isa 32:3; Isa 35:5; Mt 11:5
29:19 e Isa 61:1; Mt 5:5; Mt 11:29 f Isa 14:30; Mt 11:5; Jas 1:9; Jas 2:5
29:20 g Isa 28:22 h Isa 59:4; Mic 2:1
29:21 i Am 5:10,15 j Isa 32:7
29:22 k Isa 41:8; Isa 63:16 l Isa 49:23
29:23 m Isa 49:20-26 n Isa 19:25
29:24 o Isa 28:7; Heb 5:2 p Isa 41:20; Isa 60:16 q Isa 30:21
30:1 a Isa 29:15 b Isa 1:2 c Isa 8:12
30:2 d Isa 31:1 e Nu 27:21 f Isa 36:9
30:3 g Isa 20:4-5; Isa 36:6
30:4 h Isa 19:11
30:5 i ver 7
30:6 j Ex 5:10,21; Isa 8:22; Jer 11:4 k Dt 8:15 l Isa 15:7
30:8 m Isa 8:1; Hab 2:2
30:9 n Isa 28:15; Isa 59:3-4 o Isa 1:10
30:10 p Jer 11:21; Am 7:13

"Give us no more visions of
what is right!
Tell us pleasant things,[q]
prophesy illusions.[r]
11Leave this way,
get off this path,
and stop confronting[s] us
with the Holy One of Israel!"

12Therefore, this is what the Holy
One of Israel says:

"Because you have rejected this
message,[t]
relied on oppression[u]
and depended on deceit,
13this sin will become for you
like a high wall,[v] cracked and
bulging,
that collapses[w] suddenly,[x] in
an instant.
14It will break in pieces like
pottery,[y]
shattered so mercilessly
that among its pieces not a
fragment will be found
for taking coals from a hearth
or scooping water out of a
cistern."

15This is what the Sovereign
LORD, the Holy One of Israel, says:

"In repentance and rest is your
salvation,
in quietness and trust[z] is your
strength,
but you would have none of it.
16You said, 'No, we will flee on
horses.'[a]
Therefore you will flee!
You said, 'We will ride off on
swift horses.'
Therefore your pursuers will
be swift!
17A thousand will flee
at the threat of one;
at the threat of five[b]
you will all flee[c] away,
till you are left
like a flagstaff on a
mountaintop,
like a banner on a hill."

18Yet the LORD longs[d] to be
gracious to you;

30:10 q 1Ki 22:8 r Eze 13:7 Ro 16:18
30:11 s Job 21:14
30:12 t Isa 5:24 u Isa 5:7
30:13 v Ps 62:3 w 1Ki 20:30 x Isa 29:5
30:14 y Ps 2:9 Jer 19:10-11
30:15 z Isa 32:17
30:16 a Isa 31:1,3
30:17 b Lev 26:8 Jos 23:10 c Lev 26:36 Dt 28:25
30:18 d Isa 42:14 2Pe 3:9,15 e Isa 5:16 f Isa 25:9
30:19 g Isa 60:20 Isa 61:3 h Ps 50:15 Isa 58:9 Isa 65:24 Mt 7:7-11
30:20 i 1Ki 22:27 j Ps 74:9 Am 8:11
30:21 k Isa 29:24
30:22 l Ex 32:4
30:23 m Isa 65:21-22 n Ps 65:13
30:24 o Mt 3:12 Lk 3:17
30:25 p Isa 2:15 q Isa 41:18
30:26 r Isa 24:23 Isa 60:19-20 Rev 21:23 Rev 22:5 s Dt 32:39 Isa 1:5
30:27 t Isa 59:19 u Isa 66:14 v Isa 10:5
30:28 w Isa 11:4

he rises to show you
compassion.
For the LORD is a God of
justice.[e]
Blessed are all who wait for
him![f]

19O people of Zion, who live in
Jerusalem, you will weep no
more.[g] How gracious he will be
when you cry for help! As soon as
he hears, he will answer[h] you. 20Al-
though the Lord gives you the
bread[i] of adversity and the water
of affliction, your teachers will be
hidden[j] no more; with your own
eyes you will see them. 21Whether
you turn to the right or to the left,
your ears will hear a voice[k] behind
you, saying, "This is the way; walk
in it." 22Then you will defile your
idols[l] overlaid with silver and
your images covered with gold;
you will throw them away like a
menstrual cloth and say to them,
"Away with you!"

23He will also send you rain[m] for
the seed you sow in the ground, and
the food that comes from the land
will be rich and plentiful. In that
day your cattle will graze in broad
meadows.[n] 24The oxen and donkeys that work the soil will eat fodder and mash, spread out with
fork[o] and shovel. 25In the day of
great slaughter, when the towers[p]
fall, streams of water will flow[q] on
every high mountain and every
lofty hill. 26The moon will shine like
the sun,[r] and the sunlight will be
seven times brighter, like the light
of seven full days, when the LORD
binds up the bruises of his people
and heals[s] the wounds he inflicted.

27See, the Name[t] of the LORD
comes from afar,
with burning anger[u] and
dense clouds of smoke;
his lips are full of wrath,[v]
and his tongue is a consuming
fire.
28His breath[w] is like a rushing
torrent,

rising up to the neck.[x]
He shakes the nations in the
sieve[y] of destruction;
he places in the jaws of the
peoples
a bit[z] that leads them astray.
29 And you will sing
as on the night you celebrate a
holy festival;
your hearts will rejoice
as when people go up with
flutes
to the mountain[a] of the LORD,
to the Rock of Israel.
30 The LORD will cause men to
hear his majestic voice
and will make them see his
arm coming down
with raging anger and
consuming fire,
with cloudburst, thunderstorm
and hail.
31 The voice of the LORD will
shatter Assyria;[b]
with his sceptre he will
strike[c] them down.
32 Every stroke the LORD lays on
them
with his punishing rod
will be to the music of
tambourines and harps,
as he fights them in battle
with the blows of his arm.[d]
33 Topheth[e] has long been
prepared;
it has been made ready for the
king.
Its fire pit has been made deep
and wide,
with an abundance of fire and
wood;
the breath of the LORD,
like a stream of burning
sulphur,[f]
sets it ablaze.

Woe to Those Who Rely on Egypt

31 Woe to those who go down
to Egypt[a] for help,
who rely on horses,
who trust in the multitude of
their chariots[b]
and in the great strength of
their horsemen,
but do not look to the Holy One
of Israel,
or seek help from the LORD.[c]
2 Yet he too is wise[d] and can
bring disaster;[e]
he does not take back his
words.[f]
He will rise up against the
house of the wicked,[g]
against those who help
evildoers.
3 But the Egyptians[h] are men
and not God;[i]
their horses are flesh and not
spirit.
When the LORD stretches out his
hand,[j]
he who helps will stumble,
he who is helped[k] will fall;
both will perish together.

4 This is what the LORD says to
me:

"As a lion[l] growls,
a great lion over his prey—
and though a whole band of
shepherds
is called together against him,
he is not frightened by their
shouts
or disturbed by their
clamour—
so the LORD Almighty will come
down[m]
to do battle on Mount Zion and
on its heights.
5 Like birds hovering overhead,
the LORD Almighty will
shield[n] Jerusalem;
he will shield it and deliver[o] it,
he will 'pass over' it and will
rescue it."

6 Return to him you have so
greatly revolted against, O Israelites. 7 For in that day every one of
you will reject the idols of silver
and gold[p] your sinful hands have
made.

8 "Assyria[q] will fall by a sword
that is not of man;

30:28 x Isa 8:8 y Am 9:9 z 2Ki 19:28 Isa 37:29
30:29 a Ps 42:4
30:31 b Isa 10:5,12 c Isa 11:4
30:32 d Isa 11:15 Eze 32:10
30:33 e 2Ki 23:10 f Ge 19:24
31:1 a Dt 17:16 Isa 30:2,5 b Isa 2:7 c Ps 20:7 Da 9:13
31:2 d Ro 16:27 e Isa 45:7 f Nu 23:19 g Isa 32:6
31:3 h Isa 36:9 i Eze 28:9 2Th 2:4 j Isa 9:17,21 k Isa 30:5-7
31:4 l Nu 24:9 Hos 11:10 Am 3:8 m Isa 42:13
31:5 n Ps 91:4 o Isa 37:35 Isa 38:6
31:7 p Isa 2:20 Isa 30:22
31:8 q Isa 10:12

a sword, not of mortals, will
devour[r] them.
They will flee before the sword
and their young men will be
put to forced labour.[s]
9Their stronghold[t] will fall
because of terror;
at sight of the battle standard
their commanders will
panic,"
declares the LORD,
whose fire[u] is in Zion,
whose furnace is in Jerusalem.

The Kingdom of Righteousness

32 See, a king[a] will reign in
righteousness
and rulers will rule with
justice.[b]
2Each man will be like a
shelter[c] from the wind
and a refuge from the storm,
like streams of water in the
desert
and the shadow of a great
rock in a thirsty land.

3Then the eyes of those who see
will no longer be closed,[d]
and the ears of those who hear
will listen.
4The mind of the rash will know
and understand,[e]
and the stammering tongue
will be fluent and clear.
5No longer will the fool[f] be
called noble
nor the scoundrel be highly
respected.
6For the fool speaks folly,[g]
his mind is busy with evil:
He practises ungodliness[h]
and spreads error[i]
concerning the LORD;
the hungry he leaves empty[j]
and from the thirsty he
withholds water.
7The scoundrel's methods are
wicked,[k]
he makes up evil schemes[l]
to destroy the poor with lies,
even when the plea of the
needy[m] is just.
8But the noble man makes noble
plans,
and by noble deeds[n] he
stands.

The Women of Jerusalem

9You women who are so
complacent,
rise up and listen[o] to me;
you daughters who feel
secure,[p]
hear what I have to say!
10In little more than a year
you who feel secure will
tremble;
the grape harvest will fail,[q]
and the harvest of fruit will
not come.
11Tremble, you complacent
women;
shudder, you daughters who
feel secure!
Strip off your clothes,[r]
put sackcloth round your
waists.
12Beat your breasts[s] for the
pleasant fields,
for the fruitful vines
13and for the land of my people,
a land overgrown with thorns
and briers[t]—
yes, mourn for all houses of
merriment
and for this city of revelry.[u]
14The fortress[v] will be
abandoned,
the noisy city deserted;[w]
citadel and watchtower[x] will
become a wasteland for
ever,
the delight of donkeys,[y] a
pasture for flocks,
15till the Spirit[z] is poured upon
us from on high,
and the desert becomes a
fertile field,[a]
and the fertile field seems like
a forest.[b]
16Justice will dwell in the desert
and righteousness live in the
fertile field.
17The fruit of righteousness will
be peace;[c]

31:8 r Isa 14:25; Isa 37:7 s Ge 49:15
31:9 t Dt 32:31,37 u Isa 10:17
32:1 a Eze 37:24 b Ps 72:1-4; Isa 9:7
32:2 c Isa 4:6
32:3 d Isa 29:18
32:4 e Isa 29:24
32:5 f 1Sa 25:25
32:6 g Pr 19:3 h Isa 9:17 i Isa 9:16 j Isa 3:15
32:7 k Jer 5:26-28 l Mic 7:3 m Isa 61:1
32:8 n Pr 11:25
32:9 o Isa 28:23 p Isa 47:8; Am 6:1; Zep 2:15
32:10 q Isa 5:5-6; Isa 24:7
32:11 r Isa 47:2
32:12 s Na 2:7
32:13 t Isa 5:6 u Isa 22:2
32:14 v Isa 13:22 w Isa 6:11; Isa 27:10 x Isa 34:13 y Ps 104:11
32:15 z Isa 11:2; Joel 2:28 a Ps 107:35; Isa 35:1-2 b Isa 29:17
32:17 c Ps 119:165; Ro 14:17; Jas 3:18

the effect of righteousness
will be quietness and
confidence[d] for ever.
18 My people will live in peaceful
dwelling-places,
in secure homes,
in undisturbed places of rest.[e]
19 Though hail[f] flattens the
forest[g]
and the city is levelled[h]
completely,
20 how blessed you will be,
sowing[i] your seed by every
stream,
and letting your cattle and
donkeys range free.[j]

Distress and Help

33 Woe to you, O destroyer,
you who have not been
destroyed!
Woe to you, O traitor,
you who have not been
betrayed!
When you stop destroying,
you will be destroyed;[a]
when you stop betraying,
you will be betrayed.[b]

2 O LORD, be gracious to us;
we long for you.
Be our strength[c] every
morning,
our salvation[d] in time of
distress.
3 At the thunder of your voice,
the peoples flee;
when you rise up,[e] the nations
scatter.
4 Your plunder, O nations, is
harvested as by young
locusts;
like a swarm of locusts men
pounce on it.
5 The LORD is exalted,[f] for he
dwells on high;
he will fill Zion with justice[g]
and righteousness.[h]
6 He will be the sure foundation
for your times,
a rich store of salvation[i] and
wisdom and knowledge;
the fear[j] of the LORD is the
key to this treasure.[a]
7 Look, their brave men cry aloud
in the streets;
the envoys[k] of peace weep
bitterly.
8 The highways are deserted,
no travellers are on the
roads.[l]
The treaty is broken,
its witnesses[b] are despised,
no-one is respected.
9 The land mourns[c][m] and wastes
away,
Lebanon[n] is ashamed and
withers;[o]
Sharon is like the Arabah,
and Bashan and Carmel drop
their leaves.

10 "Now will I arise,[p]" says the
LORD.
"Now will I be exalted;
now will I be lifted up.
11 You conceive[q] chaff,
you give birth[r] to straw;
your breath is a fire[s] that
consumes you.
12 The peoples will be burned as if
to lime;
like cut thornbushes they will
be set ablaze.[t]"

13 You who are far away,[u] hear[v]
what I have done;
you who are near,
acknowledge my power!
14 The sinners in Zion are
terrified;
trembling[w] grips the godless:
"Who of us can dwell with the
consuming fire?[x]
Who of us can dwell with
everlasting burning?"
15 He who walks righteously[y]
and speaks what is right,[z]
who rejects gain from extortion
and keeps his hand from
accepting bribes,
who stops his ears against plots
of murder

32:17 *d* Isa 30:15
32:18 *e* Hos 2:18-23
32:19 *f* Isa 28:17; Isa 30:30 *g* Isa 10:19; Zec 11:2 *h* Isa 24:10; Isa 27:10
32:20 *i* Ecc 11:1 *j* Isa 30:24
33:1 *a* Hab 2:8; Mt 7:2 *b* Isa 21:2
33:2 *c* Isa 40:10; Isa 51:9; Isa 59:16 *d* Isa 25:9
33:3 *e* Isa 59:16-18
33:5 *f* Ps 97:9 *g* Isa 28:6 *h* Isa 1:26
33:6 *i* Isa 51:6 *j* Isa 11:2-3; Mt 6:33
33:7 *k* 2Ki 18:37
33:8 *l* Jdg 5:6; Isa 35:8
33:9 *m* Isa 3:26 *n* Isa 2:13; Isa 35:2 *o* Isa 24:4
33:10 *p* Ps 12:5; Isa 2:21
33:11 *q* Ps 7:14; Isa 59:4; Jas 1:15 *r* Isa 26:18 *s* Isa 1:31
33:12 *t* Isa 10:17
33:13 *u* Ps 48:10; Ps 49:1 *v* Isa 49:1
33:14 *w* Isa 32:11 *x* Isa 30:30; Heb 12:29
33:15 *y* Isa 58:8 *z* Ps 15:2; Ps 24:4

[a]6 Or *is a treasure from him* [b]8 Dead Sea Scrolls; Masoretic Text / *the cities* [c]9 Or *dries up*

and shuts his eyes[a] against
contemplating evil—
16this is the man who will dwell
on the heights,
whose refuge[b] will be the
mountain fortress.[c]
His bread will be supplied,
and water will not fail[d] him.

17Your eyes will see the king[e] in
his beauty
and view a land that stretches
afar.[f]
18In your thoughts you will
ponder the former terror:[g]
"Where is that chief officer?
Where is the one who took the
revenue?
Where is the officer in charge
of the towers?"
19You will see those arrogant
people no more,
those people of an obscure
speech,
with their strange,
incomprehensible tongue.[h]

20Look upon Zion, the city of our
festivals;
your eyes will see Jerusalem,
a peaceful abode,[i] a tent that
will not be moved;[j]
its stakes will never be pulled
up,
nor any of its ropes broken.
21There the LORD will be our
Mighty One.
It will be like a place of broad
rivers and streams.[k]
No galley with oars will ride
them,
no mighty ship will sail them.
22For the LORD is our judge,[l]
the LORD is our lawgiver,[m]
the LORD is our king;[n]
it is he who will save[o] us.

23Your rigging hangs loose:
The mast is not held secure,
the sail is not spread.
Then an abundance of spoils
will be divided
and even the lame[p] will carry
off plunder.[q]

33:15
a Ps 119:37
33:16
b Isa 25:4
c Isa 26:1
d Isa 49:10
33:17
e Isa 6:5
f Isa 26:15
33:18
g Isa 17:14
33:19
h Isa 28:11
Jer 5:15
33:20
i Isa 32:18
j Ps 46:5
Ps 125:1-2
33:21
k Isa 41:18
Isa 48:18
Isa 66:12
33:22
l Isa 11:4
m Isa 2:3
Jas 4:12
n Ps 89:18
o Isa 25:9
33:23
p 2Ki 7:8
q 2Ki 7:16
33:24
r Isa 30:26
s Jer 50:20
1Jn 1:7-9
34:1
a Isa 41:1
Isa 43:9
b Ps 49:1
c Dt 32:1
34:2
d Isa 13:5
e Isa 30:25
34:3
f Joel 2:20
Am 4:10
g ver 7
Eze 14:19
Eze 35:6
Eze 38:22
34:4
h Isa 13:13
2Pe 3:10
i Eze 32:7-8
j Joel 2:31
Mt 24:29*
Rev 6:13
34:5
k Dt 32:41-42
Jer 46:10
Eze 21:5
l Am 1:11-12
m Isa 24:6
Mal 1:4

24No-one living in Zion will say,
"I am ill";[r]
and the sins of those who
dwell there will be
forgiven.[s]

Judgment Against the Nations

34 Come near, you nations,
and listen;
pay attention, you peoples![a]
Let the earth[b] hear, and all that
is in it,
the world, and all that comes
out of it![c]
2The LORD is angry with all
nations;
his wrath is upon all their
armies.
He will totally destroy[a][d] them,
he will give them over to
slaughter.[e]
3Their slain will be thrown out,
their dead bodies will send up
a stench;[f]
the mountains will be soaked
with their blood.[g]
4All the stars of the heavens will
be dissolved[h]
and the sky rolled up[i] like a
scroll;
all the starry host will fall[j]
like withered leaves from the
vine,
like shrivelled figs from the
fig-tree.

5My sword[k] has drunk its fill in
the heavens;
see, it descends in judgment
on Edom,[l]
the people I have totally
destroyed.[m]
6The sword of the LORD is
bathed in blood,
it is covered with fat—
the blood of lambs and goats,
fat from the kidneys of rams.
For the LORD has a sacrifice in
Bozrah
and a great slaughter in Edom.

a2 The Hebrew term refers to the irrevocable giving over of things or persons to the LORD, often by totally destroying them; also in verse 5.

7 And the wild oxen will fall with
them,
the bull calves and the great
bulls.[n]
Their land will be drenched
with blood,
and the dust will be soaked
with fat.

8 For the LORD has a day of
vengeance,[o]
a year of retribution, to
uphold Zion's cause.
9 Edom's streams will be turned
into pitch,
her dust into burning sulphur;
her land will become blazing
pitch!
10 It will not be quenched night
and day;
its smoke will rise for ever.[p]
From generation to generation
it will lie desolate;[q]
no-one will ever pass through
it again.
11 The desert owl[b][r] and screech
owl[b] will possess it;
the great owl[b] and the raven
will nest there.
God will stretch out over Edom
the measuring line of chaos
and the plumb-line[s] of
desolation.
12 Her nobles will have nothing
there to be called a
kingdom,
all her princes[t] will vanish[u]
away.
13 Thorns will overrun her
citadels,
nettles and brambles her
strongholds.[v]
She will become a haunt for
jackals,[w]
a home for owls.
14 Desert creatures will meet with
hyenas,[x]
and wild goats will bleat to
each other;
there the night creatures will
also repose
and find for themselves places
of rest.
15 The owl will nest there and lay
eggs,
she will hatch them, and care
for her young under the
shadow of her wings;
there also the falcons[y] will
gather,
each with its mate.

16 Look in the scroll[z] of the LORD
and read:

None of these will be missing,
not one will lack her mate.
For it is his mouth[a] that has
given the order,
and his Spirit will gather them
together.
17 He allots their portions;[b]
his hand distributes them by
measure.
They will possess it for ever
and dwell there from
generation to generation.[c]

Joy of the Redeemed

35 The desert[a] and the
parched land will be glad;
the wilderness will rejoice and
blossom.[b]
Like the crocus, 2 it will burst
into bloom;
it will rejoice greatly and
shout for joy.[c]
The glory of Lebanon[d] will be
given to it,
the splendour of Carmel[e] and
Sharon;
they will see the glory of the
LORD,
the splendour of our God.[f]
3 Strengthen the feeble hands,
steady the knees[g] that give
way;
4 say to those with fearful hearts,
"Be strong, do not fear;
your God will come,
he will come with
vengeance;[h]
with divine retribution
he will come to save you."

34:7 n Ps 68:30
34:8 o Isa 63:4
34:10 p Rev 14:10-11; Rev 19:3 q Isa 13:20; Isa 24:1; Eze 29:12; Mal 1:3
34:11 r Zep 2:14; Rev 18:2 s 2Ki 21:13; La 2:8
34:12 t Jer 27:20; Jer 39:6 u Isa 41:11-12
34:13 v Isa 13:22; Isa 32:13 w Ps 44:19; Jer 9:11; Jer 10:22
34:14 x Isa 13:22
34:15 y Dt 14:13
34:16 z Isa 30:8 a Isa 1:20; Isa 58:14
34:17 b Isa 17:14; Jer 13:25 c ver 10
35:1 a Isa 27:10; Isa 41:18-19 b Isa 51:3
35:2 c Isa 25:9; Isa 55:12 d Isa 32:15 e SS 7:5 f Isa 25:9
35:3 g Job 4:4; Heb 12:12
35:4 h Isa 1:24; Isa 34:8

[b] *11* The precise identification of these birds is uncertain.

5Then will the eyes of the blind
be opened[i]
and the ears of the deaf[j]
unstopped.
6Then will the lame[k] leap like a
deer,
and the mute tongue[l] shout
for joy.
Water will gush forth in the
wilderness
and streams[m] in the desert.
7The burning sand will become a
pool,
the thirsty ground bubbling
springs.[n]
In the haunts where jackals[o]
once lay,
grass and reeds and papyrus
will grow.

8And a highway[p] will be there;
it will be called the Way of
Holiness.[q]
The unclean[r] will not journey
on it;
it will be for those who walk
in that Way;
wicked fools will not go about
on it.[a]
9No lion[s] will be there,
nor will any ferocious beast[t]
get up on it;
they will not be found there.
But only the redeemed[u] will
walk there,
10 and the ransomed of the LORD
will return.
They will enter Zion with
singing;
everlasting joy[v] will crown
their heads.
Gladness and joy will overtake
them,
and sorrow and sighing will
flee away.[w]

Sennacherib Threatens Jerusalem

36:1–22pp 2Ki 18:13,17–37; 2Ch 32:9–19

36 In the fourteenth year of
King Hezekiah's reign,
Sennacherib[a] king of Assyria attacked all the fortified cities of Judah and captured them. 2Then the
king of Assyria sent his field commander with a large army from
Lachish to King Hezekiah at
Jerusalem. When the commander
stopped at the aqueduct of the
Upper Pool, on the road to the
Washerman's Field,[b] 3Eliakim[c]
son of Hilkiah the palace administrator, Shebna[d] the secretary, and
Joah son of Asaph the recorder
went out to him.
4The field commander said to
them, "Tell Hezekiah,

" 'This is what the great king,
the king of Assyria, says: On
what are you basing this confidence of yours? 5You say you
have strategy and military
strength—but you speak only
empty words. On whom are
you depending, that you rebel[e]
against me? 6Look now, you are
depending on Egypt,[f] that
splintered reed[g] of a staff,
which pierces a man's hand
and wounds him if he leans on
it! Such is Pharaoh king of
Egypt to all who depend on
him. 7And if you say to me, "We
are depending on the LORD our
God"—isn't he the one whose
high places and altars Hezekiah removed,[h] saying to Judah and Jerusalem, "You must
worship before this altar"?[i]
8" 'Come now, make a bar-
gain with my master, the king
of Assyria: I will give you two
thousand horses—if you can
put riders on them! 9How then
can you repulse one officer
of the least of my master's
officials, even though you
are depending on Egypt[j]
for chariots and horsemen?[k]
10Furthermore, have I come to
attack and destroy this land
without the LORD? The LORD
himself told[l] me to march
against this country and destroy it.' "

[a]8 Or / *the simple will not stray from it*

35:5 *i* Mt 11:5; Jn 9:6-7 *j* Isa 29:18; Isa 50:4
35:6 *k* Mt 15:30; Jn 5:8-9; Ac 3:8 *l* Isa 32:4; Mt 9:32-33; Mt 12:22; Lk 11:14 *m* Isa 41:18; Jn 7:38
35:7 *n* Isa 49:10 *o* Isa 13:22
35:8 *p* Isa 11:16; Isa 33:8; Mt 7:13-14 *q* Isa 4:3; 1Pe 1:15 *r* Isa 52:1
35:9 *s* Isa 30:6 *t* Isa 34:14 *u* Isa 51:11; Isa 62:12; Isa 63:4
35:10 *v* Isa 25:9 *w* Isa 30:19; Isa 51:11; Rev 7:17; Rev 21:4
36:1 *a* 2Ch 32:1
36:2 *b* Isa 7:3
36:3 *c* Isa 22:20-21 *d* 2Ki 18:18
36:5 *e* 2Ki 18:7
36:6 *f* Isa 30:2,5 *g* Eze 29:6-7
36:7 *h* 2Ki 18:4 *i* Dt 12:2-5
36:9 *j* Isa 31:3 *k* Isa 30:2-5
36:10 *l* 1Ki 13:18

11 Then Eliakim, Shebna and Joah said to the field commander, "Please speak to your servants in Aramaic,[m] since we understand it. Don't speak to us in Hebrew in the hearing of the people on the wall."

12 But the commander replied, "Was it only to your master and you that my master sent me to say these things, and not to the men sitting on the wall—who, like you, will have to eat their own filth and drink their own urine?"

13 Then the commander stood and called out in Hebrew,[n] "Hear the words of the great king, the king of Assyria! 14 This is what the king says: Do not let Hezekiah deceive you. He cannot deliver you! 15 Do not let Hezekiah persuade you to trust in the LORD when he says, 'The LORD will surely deliver us; this city will not be given into the hand of the king of Assyria.'[o]

16 "Do not listen to Hezekiah. This is what the king of Assyria says: Make peace with me and come out to me. Then every one of you will eat from his own vine and fig-tree[p] and drink water from his own cistern,[q] 17 until I come and take you to a land like your own—a land of corn and new wine, a land of bread and vineyards.

18 "Do not let Hezekiah mislead you when he says, 'The LORD will deliver us.' Has the god of any nation ever delivered his land from the hand of the king of Assyria? 19 Where are the gods of Hamath and Arpad? Where are the gods of Sepharvaim? Have they rescued Samaria from my hand? 20 Who of all the gods[r] of these countries has been able to save his land from me? How then can the LORD deliver Jerusalem from my hand?"

21 But the people remained silent and said nothing in reply, because the king had commanded, "Do not answer him."[s]

22 Then Eliakim son of Hilkiah the palace administrator, Shebna the secretary, and Joah son of Asaph the recorder went to Hezekiah, with their clothes torn, and told him what the field commander had said.

36:11 m Ezr 4:7
36:13 n 2Ch 32:18
36:15 o Isa 37:10
36:16 p 1Ki 4:25; Zec 3:10; q Pr 5:15
36:20 r 1Ki 20:23
36:21 s Pr 9:7-8; Pr 26:4
37:2 a Isa 1:1
37:3 b Isa 26:18; Isa 66:9; Hos 13:13
37:4 c Isa 36:13, 18-20; d Isa 1:9
37:6 e Isa 7:4
37:7 f ver 9
37:8 g Nu 33:20
37:9 h ver 7

Jerusalem's Deliverance Foretold

37:1–13pp 2Ki 19:1–13

37 When King Hezekiah heard this, he tore his clothes and put on sackcloth and went into the temple of the LORD. 2 He sent Eliakim the palace administrator, Shebna the secretary, and the leading priests, all wearing sackcloth, to the prophet Isaiah son of Amoz.[a] 3 They told him, "This is what Hezekiah says: This day is a day of distress and rebuke and disgrace, as when children come to the point of birth[b] and there is no strength to deliver them. 4 It may be that the LORD your God will hear the words of the field commander, whom his master, the king of Assyria, has sent to ridicule the living God, and that he will rebuke him for the words the LORD your God has heard.[c] Therefore pray for the remnant[d] that still survives."

5 When King Hezekiah's officials came to Isaiah, 6 Isaiah said to them, "Tell your master, 'This is what the LORD says: Do not be afraid[e] of what you have heard—those words with which the underlings of the king of Assyria have blasphemed me. 7 Listen! I am going to put a spirit in him so that when he hears a certain report,[f] he will return to his own country, and there I will have him cut down with the sword.' "

8 When the field commander heard that the king of Assyria had left Lachish, he withdrew and found the king fighting against Libnah.[g]

9 Now Sennacherib received a report[h] that Tirhakah, the Cushite[a] king ⌊of Egypt⌋, was marching out to

a9 That is, from the upper Nile region

fight against him. When he heard it,
he sent messengers to Hezekiah
with this word: 10“Say to Hezekiah
king of Judah: Do not let the god
you depend on deceive you when he
says, ‘Jerusalem will not be handed
over to the king of Assyria.’[i]
11Surely you have heard what the
kings of Assyria have done to all
the countries, destroying them
completely. And will you be delivered?[j] 12Did the gods of the nations that were destroyed by my
forefathers[k] deliver them—the
gods of Gozan, Haran,[l] Rezeph
and the people of Eden who were in
Tel Assar? 13Where is the king of
Hamath, the king of Arpad, the
king of the city of Sepharvaim, or
of Hena or Ivvah?”

Hezekiah’s Prayer

37:14–20pp 2Ki 19:14–19

14Hezekiah received the letter
from the messengers and read it.
Then he went up to the temple of
the LORD and spread it out before
the LORD. 15And Hezekiah prayed
to the LORD: 16“O LORD Almighty,
God of Israel, enthroned between
the cherubim, you alone are God[m]
over all the kingdoms of the earth.
You have made heaven and earth.
17Give ear, O LORD, and hear;[n]
open your eyes, O LORD, and see;[o]
listen to all the words Sennacherib
has sent to insult the living God.

18“It is true, O LORD, that the Assyrian kings have laid waste all
these peoples and their lands.[p]
19They have thrown their gods into
the fire and destroyed them,[q] for
they were not gods[r] but only wood
and stone, fashioned by human
hands. 20Now, O LORD our God, deliver us from his hand, so that all
kingdoms on earth may know that
you alone, O LORD, are God.”[b][s]

Sennacherib’s Fall

37:21–38pp 2Ki 19:20–37; 2Ch 32:20–21

21Then Isaiah son of Amoz[t] sent
a message to Hezekiah: “This is
what the LORD, the God of Israel,
says: Because you have prayed to
me concerning Sennacherib king
of Assyria, 22this is the word the
LORD has spoken against him:

“The Virgin Daughter of Zion
despises and mocks you.
The Daughter of Jerusalem
tosses her head[u] as you flee.
23Who is it you have insulted and
blasphemed?[v]
Against whom have you raised
your voice
and lifted your eyes in pride?[w]
Against the Holy One of
Israel!
24By your messengers
you have heaped insults on the
Lord.
And you have said,
‘With my many chariots
I have ascended the heights of
the mountains,
the utmost heights of
Lebanon.[x]
I have cut down its tallest
cedars,
the choicest of its pines.
I have reached its remotest
heights,
the finest of its forests.
25I have dug wells in foreign
lands[c]
and drunk the water there.
With the soles of my feet
I have dried up all the streams
of Egypt.[y]’

26“Have you not heard?
Long ago I ordained[z] it.
In days of old I planned[a] it;
now I have brought it to pass,
that you have turned fortified
cities
into piles of stone.[b]
27Their people, drained of power,
are dismayed and put to
shame.
They are like plants in the field,
like tender green shoots,

37:10 *i* Isa 36:15
37:11 *j* Isa 36:18-20
37:12 *k* 2Ki 18:11 *l* Ge 11:31; Ge 12:1-4; Ac 7:2
37:16 *m* Dt 10:17; Ps 86:10; Ps 136:2-3
37:17 *n* 2Ch 6:40 *o* Da 9:18
37:18 *p* 2Ki 15:29; Na 2:11-12
37:19 *q* Isa 26:14 *r* Isa 41:24,29
37:20 *s* Ps 46:10
37:21 *t* ver 2
37:22 *u* Job 16:4
37:23 *v* ver 4 *w* Isa 2:11
37:24 *x* Isa 14:8
37:25 *y* Dt 11:10
37:26 *z* Ac 2:23; Ac 4:27-28; 1Pe 2:8 *a* Isa 10:6; Isa 25:1 *b* Isa 25:2

[b] *20* Dead Sea Scrolls (see also 2 Kings 19:19); Masoretic Text *alone are the LORD* [c] *25* Dead Sea Scrolls (see also 2 Kings 19:24); Masoretic Text does not have *in foreign lands.*

like grass sprouting on the
roof,[c]
scorched[d] before it grows up.

28"But I know where you stay
and when you come and go[d]
and how you rage[e] against
me.
29Because you rage against me
and because your insolence[f]
has reached my ears,
I will put my hook in your
nose[g]
and my bit in your mouth,
and I will make you return
by the way you came.[h]

30"This will be the sign for you,
O Hezekiah:

"This year you will eat what
grows by itself,
and the second year what
springs from that.
But in the third year sow and
reap,
plant vineyards and eat their
fruit.
31Once more a remnant of the
house of Judah
will take root below and bear
fruit[i] above.
32For out of Jerusalem will come
a remnant,
and out of Mount Zion a band
of survivors.
The zeal[j] of the LORD Almighty
will accomplish this.

33"Therefore this is what the
LORD says concerning the king of
Assyria:

"He will not enter this city
or shoot an arrow here.
He will not come before it with
shield
or build a siege ramp against
it.
34By the way that he came he will
return;[k]
he will not enter this city,"
declares the LORD.
35"I will defend[l] this city and
save it,
for my sake[m] and for the sake
of David[n] my servant!"

36Then the angel of the LORD
went out and put to death a hundred
and eighty-five thousand men in
the Assyrian[o] camp. When the
people got up the next morning—
there were all the dead bodies! 37So
Sennacherib king of Assyria broke
camp and withdrew. He returned
to Nineveh[p] and stayed there.
38One day, while he was worshipping in the temple of his god Nis-
roch, his sons Adrammelech and
Sharezer cut him down with the
sword, and they escaped to the land
of Ararat.[q] And Esarhaddon his
son succeeded him as king.

Hezekiah's Illness

38:1–8pp 2Ki 20:1–11; 2Ch 32:24–26

38 In those days Hezekiah became ill and was at the
point of death. The prophet Isaiah
son of Amoz[a] went to him and said,
"This is what the LORD says: Put
your house in order,[b] because you
are going to die; you will not recover."
2Hezekiah turned his face to the
wall and prayed to the LORD, 3"Remember, O LORD, how I have
walked[c] before you faithfully and
with wholehearted devotion[d] and
have done what is good in your
eyes.[e]" And Hezekiah wept[f] bitterly.
4Then the word of the LORD came
to Isaiah: 5"Go and tell Hezekiah,
'This is what the LORD, the God of
your father David, says: I have
heard your prayer and seen your
tears; I will add fifteen years[g] to
your life. 6And I will deliver you
and this city from the hand of the
king of Assyria. I will defend[h] this
city.

37:27 c Ps 129:6
37:28 d Ps 139:1-3 e Ps 2:1
37:29 f Isa 10:12 g Isa 30:28; Eze 38:4 h ver 34
37:31 i Isa 27:6
37:32 j Isa 9:7
37:34 k ver 29
37:35 l Isa 31:5; Isa 38:6 m Isa 43:25; Isa 48:9,11 n 2Ki 20:6
37:36 o Isa 10:12
37:37 p Ge 10:11
37:38 q Ge 8:4; Jer 51:27
38:1 a Isa 37:2 b 2Sa 17:23
38:3 c Ne 13:14; Ps 26:3 d 1Ch 29:19 e Dt 6:18 f Ps 6:8
38:5 g 2Ki 18:2
38:6 h Isa 31:5; Isa 37:35

d27 Some manuscripts of the Masoretic Text, Dead Sea Scrolls and some Septuagint manuscripts (see also 2 Kings 19:26); most manuscripts of the Masoretic Text *roof / and terraced fields*

7" 'This is the LORD's sign[i] to you
that the LORD will do what he has
promised: 8I will make the shadow
cast by the sun go back the ten
steps it has gone down on the stairway of Ahaz.' " So the sunlight went
back the ten steps it had gone
down.[j]

9A writing of Hezekiah king of
Judah after his illness and recovery:

10I said, "In the prime of my
life[k]
must I go through the gates of
death[a][l]
and be robbed of the rest of
my years?[m]"
11I said, "I will not again see the
LORD,
the LORD, in the land of the
living;[n]
no longer will I look on
mankind,
or be with those who now
dwell in this world.[b]
12Like a shepherd's tent[o] my
house
has been pulled down[p] and
taken from me.
Like a weaver I have rolled[q] up
my life,
and he has cut me off from
the loom;[r]
day and night[s] you made an
end of me.
13I waited patiently till dawn,
but like a lion he broke[t] all
my bones;[u]
day and night you made an
end of me.
14I cried like a swift or thrush,
I moaned like a mourning
dove.[v]
My eyes grew weak as I looked
to the heavens.
I am troubled; O Lord, come
to my aid!"[w]
15But what can I say?
He has spoken to me, and he
himself has done this.[x]
I will walk humbly[y] all my
years

38:7
i Isa 7:11,14

38:8
j Jos 10:13

38:10
k Ps 102:24
l Ps 107:18
2Co 1:9
m Job 17:11

38:11
n Ps 27:13
Ps 116:9

38:12
o 2Co 5:1,4
2Pe 1:13-14
p Job 4:21
q Heb 1:12
r Job 7:6
s Ps 73:14

38:13
t Ps 51:8
u Job 10:16
Da 6:24

38:14
v Isa 59:11
w Job 17:3

38:15
x Ps 39:9
y 1Ki 21:27
z Job 7:11

38:16
a Ps 119:25

38:17
b Ps 30:3
c Jer 31:34
d Isa 43:25
Mic 7:19

38:18
e Ecc 9:10
f Ps 6:5
Ps 88:10-11
Ps 115:17
g Ps 30:9

38:19
h Dt 6:7
Ps 118:17
Ps 119:175
i Dt 11:19

38:20
j Ps 68:25
k Ps 33:2
l Ps 116:2
m Ps 116:17-19

39:1
a 2Ch 32:31

39:2
b 2Ch 32:31
c 2Ki 18:15

because of this anguish of my
soul.[z]
16Lord, by such things men live;
and my spirit finds life in
them too.
You restored me to health
and let me live.[a]
17Surely it was for my benefit
that I suffered such anguish.
In your love you kept me
from the pit[b] of destruction;
you have put all my sins[c]
behind your back.[d]
18For the grave[c][e] cannot praise
you,
death cannot sing your
praise;[f]
those who go down to the pit[g]
cannot hope for your
faithfulness.
19The living, the living—they
praise[h] you,
as I am doing today;
fathers tell their children[i]
about your faithfulness.
20The LORD will save me,
and we will sing[j] with
stringed instruments[k]
all the days of our lives[l]
in the temple[m] of the LORD.

21Isaiah had said, "Prepare a
poultice of figs and apply it to the
boil, and he will recover."
22Hezekiah had asked, "What will
be the sign that I will go up to the
temple of the LORD?"

Envoys From Babylon

39:1–8pp 2Ki 20:12–19

39 At that time Merodach-
Baladan son of Baladan
king of Babylon[a] sent Hezekiah
letters and a gift, because he had
heard of his illness and recovery.
2Hezekiah received the envoys[b]
gladly and showed them what was
in his storehouses—the silver, the
gold,[c] the spices, the fine oil, his
entire armoury and everything

[a]*10* Hebrew *Sheol* [b]*11* A few Hebrew manuscripts; most Hebrew manuscripts *in the place of cessation* [c]*18* Hebrew *Sheol*

found among his treasures. There
was nothing in his palace or in all
his kingdom that Hezekiah did not
show them.
3 Then Isaiah the prophet went to
King Hezekiah and asked, "What
did those men say, and where did
they come from?"
"From a distant land,[d]" Hezekiah replied. "They came to me
from Babylon."
4 The prophet asked, "What did
they see in your palace?"
"They saw everything in my palace," Hezekiah said. "There is
nothing among my treasures that I
did not show them."
5 Then Isaiah said to Hezekiah,
"Hear the word of the LORD
Almighty: 6 The time will surely
come when everything in your palace, and all that your fathers have
stored up until this day, will be carried off to Babylon.[e] Nothing will
be left, says the LORD. 7 And some of
your descendants, your own flesh
and blood who will be born to you,
will be taken away, and they will
become eunuchs in the palace of
the king of Babylon.[f]"
8 "The word of the LORD you have
spoken is good," Hezekiah replied.
For he thought, "There will be
peace and security in my lifetime.[g]"

Comfort for God's People

40 Comfort, comfort[a] my
people,
says your God.
2 Speak tenderly[b] to Jerusalem,
and proclaim to her
that her hard service has been
completed,[c]
that her sin has been paid for,
that she has received from the
LORD's hand
double[d] for all her sins.

3 A voice of one calling:
"In the desert prepare
the way[e] for the LORD;[a]
make straight in the wilderness
a highway for our God.[b][f]
4 Every valley shall be raised up,
every mountain and hill made
low;
the rough ground shall become
level,[g]
the rugged places a plain.
5 And the glory of the LORD will
be revealed,
and all mankind together will
see it.[h]
For the mouth of the LORD
has spoken."[i]

6 A voice says, "Cry out."
And I said, "What shall I cry?"
"All men are like grass,[j]
and all their glory is like the
flowers of the field.
7 The grass withers and the
flowers fall,
because the breath[k] of the
LORD blows on them.
Surely the people are grass.
8 The grass withers and the
flowers fall,
but the word[l] of our God
stands for ever.[m]"

9 You who bring good tidings[n] to
Zion,
go up on a high mountain.
You who bring good tidings to
Jerusalem,[c]
lift up your voice with a shout,
lift it up, do not be afraid;
say to the towns of Judah,
"Here is your God!"[o]
10 See, the Sovereign LORD
comes[p] with power,
and his arm[q] rules[r] for him.
See, his reward[s] is with him,
and his recompense
accompanies him.
11 He tends his flock like a
shepherd:[t]
He gathers the lambs in his
arms
and carries them close to his
heart;

39:3 *d* Dt 28:49
39:6 *e* 2Ki 24:13; Jer 20:5
39:7 *f* 2Ki 24:15; Da 1:1-7
39:8 *g* 2Ch 32:26
40:1 *a* Isa 12:1; Isa 49:13; Isa 51:3,12; Isa 52:9; Isa 61:2; Isa 66:13; Jer 31:13; Zep 3:14-17; 2Co 1:3
40:2 *b* Isa 35:4 *c* Isa 41:11-13; Isa 49:25 *d* Isa 61:7; Jer 16:18; Zec 9:12; Rev 18:6
40:3 *e* Mal 3:1 *f* Mt 3:3*; Mk 1:3*; Jn 1:23*
40:4 *g* Isa 45:2,13
40:5 *h* Isa 52:10; Lk 3:4-6* *i* Isa 1:20; Isa 58:14
40:6 *j* Job 14:2
40:7 *k* Job 41:21
40:8 *l* Isa 55:11; Isa 59:21 *m* Mt 5:18; 1Pe 1:24-25*
40:9 *n* Isa 52:7-10; Isa 61:1; Ro 10:15 *o* Isa 25:9
40:10 *p* Rev 22:7 *q* Isa 59:16 *r* Isa 9:6-7 *s* Isa 62:11; Rev 22:12
40:11 *t* Eze 34:23; Mic 5:4; Jn 10:11

a3 Or *A voice of one calling in the desert: / "Prepare the way for the LORD* **b**3 Hebrew; Septuagint *make straight the paths of our God* **c**9 Or *O Zion, bringer of good tidings, / go up on a high mountain. / O Jerusalem, bringer of good tidings*

he gently leads those that
have young.

12Who has measured the waters[u]
in the hollow of his hand,[v]
or with the breadth of his
hand marked off the
heavens?[w]
Who has held the dust of the
earth in a basket,
or weighed the mountains on
the scales
and the hills in a balance?
13Who has understood the mind[d]
of the LORD,
or instructed him as his
counsellor?[x]
14Whom did the LORD consult to
enlighten him,
and who taught him the right
way?
Who was it that taught him
knowledge[y]
or showed him the path of
understanding?

15Surely the nations are like a
drop in a bucket;
they are regarded as dust on
the scales;
he weighs the islands as
though they were fine dust.
16Lebanon is not sufficient for
altar fires,
nor its animals[z] enough for
burnt offerings.
17Before him all the nations[a] are
as nothing;[b]
they are regarded by him as
worthless
and less than nothing.[c]

18To whom, then, will you
compare God?[d]
What image[e] will you
compare him to?
19As for an idol,[f] a craftsman
casts it,
and a goldsmith[g] overlays it
with gold[h]
and fashions silver chains for
it.
20A man too poor to present such
an offering
selects wood that will not rot.

40:12 *u* Job 38:10 *v* Pr 30:4 *w* Heb 1:10-12
40:13 *x* Ro 11:34* 1Co 2:16*
40:14 *y* Job 21:22 Col 2:3
40:16 *z* Ps 50:9-11 Mic 6:7 Heb 10:5-9
40:17 *a* Isa 30:28 *b* Isa 29:7 *c* Da 4:35
40:18 *d* Ex 8:10 1Sa 2:2 Isa 46:5 *e* Ac 17:29
40:19 *f* Ps 115:4 *g* Isa 41:7 Jer 10:3 *h* Isa 2:20
40:20 *i* 1Sa 5:3
40:21 *j* Ps 19:1 Ps 50:6 Ac 14:17 *k* Ro 1:19 *l* Isa 48:13 Isa 51:13
40:22 *m* Nu 13:33 Ps 104:2 Isa 42:5 *n* Job 22:14 *o* Job 36:29
40:23 *p* Isa 34:12 *q* Job 12:21 Ps 107:40
40:24 *r* Isa 41:16
40:25 *s* ver 18
40:26 *t* Isa 51:6 *u* Ps 89:11-13 Isa 42:5 *v* Ps 147:4 *w* Isa 34:16
40:27 *x* Job 27:2 Lk 18:7-8
40:28 *y* ver 21

He looks for a skilled craftsman
to set up an idol that will not
topple.[i]

21Do you not know?
Have you not heard?
Has it not been told[j] you from
the beginning?
Have you not understood[k]
since the earth was
founded?[l]
22He sits enthroned above the
circle of the earth,
and its people are like
grasshoppers.[m]
He stretches out the heavens
like a canopy,[n]
and spreads them out like a
tent[o] to live in.
23He brings princes[p] to naught
and reduces the rulers of this
world to nothing.[q]
24No sooner are they planted,
no sooner are they sown,
no sooner do they take root in
the ground,
than he blows[r] on them and
they wither,
and a whirlwind sweeps them
away like chaff.

25"To whom will you compare
me?[s]
Or who is my equal?" says the
Holy One.
26Lift your eyes and look to the
heavens:[t]
Who created[u] all these?
He who brings out the starry
host[v] one by one,
and calls them each by name.
Because of his great power and
mighty strength,
not one of them is missing.[w]

27Why do you say, O Jacob,
and complain, O Israel,
"My way is hidden from the
LORD;
my cause is disregarded by
my God"?[x]
28Do you not know?
Have you not heard?[y]

[d]13 Or *Spirit*; or *spirit*

The LORD is the everlasting[z]
God,
the Creator of the ends of the
earth.
He will not grow tired or
weary,
and his understanding no-one
can fathom.[a]
29He gives strength to the
weary[b]
and increases the power of the
weak.
30Even youths grow tired and
weary,
and young men[c] stumble and
fall;
31but those who hope[d] in the
LORD
will renew their strength.[e]
They will soar on wings like
eagles;[f]
they will run and not grow
weary,
they will walk and not be
faint.[g]

The Helper of Israel

41 "Be silent[a] before me,
you islands![b]
Let the nations renew their
strength!
Let them come forward[c] and
speak;
let us meet together[d] at the
place of judgment.

2"Who has stirred[e] up one from
the east,[f]
calling him in righteousness to
his service?[a]
He hands nations over to him
and subdues kings before him.
He turns them to dust[g] with his
sword,
to wind-blown chaff[h] with his
bow.
3He pursues them and moves on
unscathed,
by a path his feet have not
travelled before.
4Who has done this and carried
it through,
calling forth the generations
from the beginning?[i]
I, the LORD—with the first of
them
and with the last[j]—I am he."

5The islands[k] have seen it and
fear;
the ends of the earth tremble.
They approach and come
forward;
6 each helps the other
and says to his brother, "Be
strong!"
7The craftsman encourages the
goldsmith,[l]
and he who smooths with the
hammer
spurs on him who strikes the
anvil.
He says of the welding, "It is
good."
He nails down the idol so that
it will not topple.

8"But you, O Israel, my servant,
Jacob, whom I have chosen,
you descendants of Abraham[m]
my friend,[n]
9I took you from the ends of the
earth,[o]
from its farthest corners I
called you.
I said, 'You are my servant';
I have chosen[p] you and have
not rejected you.
10So do not fear, for I am with
you;[q]
do not be dismayed, for I am
your God.
I will strengthen you and help[r]
you;
I will uphold you with my
righteous right hand.

11"All who rage[s] against you
will surely be ashamed and
disgraced;[t]
those who oppose[u] you
will be as nothing and
perish.[v]
12Though you search for your
enemies,
you will not find them.[w]

40:28 z Ps 90:2 a Ps 147:5 Ro 11:33
40:29 b Isa 50:4 Jer 31:25
40:30 c Isa 9:17 Jer 6:11 Jer 9:21
40:31 d Lk 18:1 e 2Co 4:16 f Ex 19:4 Ps 103:5 g 2Co 4:1 Heb 12:1-3
41:1 a Hab 2:20 Zec 2:13 b Isa 11:11 c Isa 48:16 d Isa 1:18 Isa 34:1 Isa 50:8
41:2 e Ezr 1:2 f ver 25 Isa 45:1,13 g 2Sa 22:43 h Isa 40:24
41:4 i ver 26 Isa 46:10 j Isa 44:6 Isa 48:12 Rev 1:8,17 Rev 22:13
41:5 k Eze 26:17-18
41:7 l Isa 40:19
41:8 m Isa 29:22 Isa 51:2 Isa 63:16 n 2Ch 20:7 Jas 2:23
41:9 o Isa 11:12 p Dt 7:6
41:10 q Jos 1:9 Isa 43:2,5 Ro 8:31 r ver 13-14 Isa 44:2 Isa 49:8
41:11 s Isa 17:12 t Isa 45:24 u Ex 23:22 v Isa 29:8
41:12 w Ps 37:35-36

a2 Or / *whom victory meets at every step*

Those who wage war against
you
will be as nothing[x] at all.
13For I am the LORD, your God,
who takes hold of your right
hand[y]
and says to you, Do not fear;
I will help[z] you.
14Do not be afraid, O worm
Jacob,
O little Israel,
for I myself will help you,"
declares the LORD,
your Redeemer, the Holy One
of Israel.
15"See, I will make you into a
threshing-sledge,[a]
new and sharp, with many
teeth.
You will thresh the mountains
and crush them,
and reduce the hills to chaff.
16You will winnow[b] them, the
wind will pick them up,
and a gale will blow them
away.
But you will rejoice in the LORD
and glory[c] in the Holy One of
Israel.

17"The poor and needy search for
water,[d]
but there is none;
their tongues are parched with
thirst.
But I the LORD will answer[e]
them;
I, the God of Israel, will not
forsake them.
18I will make rivers flow[f] on
barren heights,
and springs within the valleys.
I will turn the desert[g] into
pools of water,
and the parched ground into
springs.[h]
19I will put in the desert
the cedar and the acacia, the
myrtle and the olive.
I will set pines in the wasteland,
the fir and the cypress
together,[i]
20so that people may see and
know,
may consider and understand,
that the hand of the LORD has
done this,
that the Holy One of Israel
has created[j] it.

21"Present your case," says the
LORD.
"Set forth your arguments,"
says Jacob's King.[k]
22"Bring in ⌊your idols⌋ to tell us
what is going to happen.[l]
Tell us what the former things
were,
so that we may consider them
and know their final outcome.
Or declare to us the things to
come,[m]
23 tell us what the future holds,
so that we may know[n] you are
gods.
Do something, whether good or
bad,[o]
so that we will be dismayed
and filled with fear.
24But you are less than nothing[p]
and your works are utterly
worthless;
he who chooses you is
detestable.[q]

25"I have stirred up one from the
north,[r] and he comes—
one from the rising sun who
calls on my name.
He treads[s] on rulers as if they
were mortar,
as if he were a potter treading
the clay.
26Who told of this from the
beginning, so that we could
know,
or beforehand, so that we
could say, 'He was right'?
No-one told of this,
no-one foretold it,
no-one heard any words[t]
from you.
27I was the first to tell[u] Zion,
'Look, here they are!'
I gave to Jerusalem a
messenger of good
tidings.[v]

41:12 x Isa 17:14
41:13 y Isa 42:6; Isa 45:1; z ver 10
41:15 a Mic 4:13
41:16 b Jer 51:2; c Isa 45:25
41:17 d Isa 43:20; e Isa 30:19
41:18 f Isa 30:25; g Isa 43:19; h Isa 35:7
41:19 i Isa 60:13
41:20 j Job 12:9
41:21 k Isa 43:15
41:22 l Isa 43:9; Isa 45:21; m Isa 46:10
41:23 n Isa 42:9; Isa 44:7-8; Isa 45:3; o Jer 10:5
41:24 p Isa 37:19; Isa 44:9; 1Co 8:4; q Ps 115:8
41:25 r ver 2; s 2Sa 22:43
41:26 t Hab 2:18-19
41:27 u Isa 48:3,16; v Isa 40:9

28I look but there is no-one[w]—
no-one among them to give
counsel,[x]
no-one to give answer when I
ask them.
29See, they are all false!
Their deeds amount to
nothing;[y]
their images are but wind[z]
and confusion.

The Servant of the LORD

42 "Here is my servant,
whom I uphold,
my chosen one[a] in whom I
delight;
I will put my Spirit[b] on him
and he will bring justice to the
nations.
2He will not shout or cry out,
or raise his voice in the
streets.
3A bruised reed he will not
break,
and a smouldering wick he
will not snuff out.
In faithfulness he will bring
forth justice;[c]
4 he will not falter or be
discouraged
till he establishes justice on
earth.
In his law the islands will put
their hope."[d]
5This is what God the LORD
says—
he who created the heavens and
stretched them out,
who spread out the earth and
all that comes out of it,[e]
who gives breath[f] to its people,
and life to those who walk on it:
6"I, the LORD, have called[g] you
in righteousness;[h]
I will take hold of your hand.
I will keep[i] you and will make
you
to be a covenant[j] for the
people
and a light for the Gentiles,[k]
7to open eyes that are blind,[l]
to free[m] captives from
prison[n]
and to release from the
dungeon those who sit in
darkness.
8"I am the LORD; that is my
name![o]
I will not give my glory to
another[p]
or my praise to idols.
9See, the former things have
taken place,
and new things I declare;
before they spring into being
I announce them to you."

Song of Praise to the LORD

10Sing to the LORD a new song,[q]
his praise from the ends of the
earth,[r]
you who go down to the sea, and
all that is in it,[s]
you islands, and all who live in
them.
11Let the desert[t] and its towns
raise their voices;
let the settlements where
Kedar[u] lives rejoice.
Let the people of Sela sing for
joy;
let them shout from the
mountaintops.[v]
12Let them give glory[w] to the
LORD
and proclaim his praise in the
islands.
13The LORD will march out like a
mighty[x] man,
like a warrior he will stir up
his zeal;[y]
with a shout[z] he will raise the
battle cry
and will triumph over his
enemies.[a]
14"For a long time I have kept
silent,
I have been quiet and held
myself back.
But now, like a woman in
childbirth,
I cry out, I gasp and pant.
15I will lay waste[b] the mountains
and hills

41:28
w Isa 50:2
Isa 59:16
Isa 63:5
x Isa 40:13-14

41:29
y ver 24
z Jer 5:13

42:1
a Isa 43:10
Lk 9:35
1Pe 2:4,6
b Isa 11:2
Mt 3:16-17
Jn 3:34

42:3
c Ps 72:2

42:4
d Ge 49:10
Mt 12:18-21*

42:5
e Ps 24:2
f Ac 17:25

42:6
g Isa 43:1
h Jer 23:6
i Isa 26:3
j Isa 49:8
k Lk 2:32
Ac 13:47

42:7
l Isa 35:5
m Isa 49:9
Isa 61:1
n Lk 4:19
2Ti 2:26
Heb 2:14-15

42:8
o Ex 3:15
p Isa 48:11

42:10
q Ps 33:3
Ps 40:3
Ps 98:1
r Isa 49:6
s 1Ch 16:32
Ps 96:11

42:11
t Isa 32:16
u Isa 60:7
v Isa 52:7
Na 1:15

42:12
w Isa 24:15

42:13
x Isa 9:6
y Isa 26:11
z Hos 11:10
a Isa 66:14

42:15
b Eze 38:20

and dry up all their
vegetation;
I will turn rivers into islands
and dry up[c] the pools.
16I will lead[d] the blind[e] by ways
they have not known,
along unfamiliar paths I will
guide them;
I will turn the darkness into
light before them
and make the rough places
smooth.[f]
These are the things I will do;
I will not forsake[g] them.
17But those who trust in idols,
who say to images, 'You are
our gods,'
will be turned back in utter
shame.[h]

Israel Blind and Deaf

18"Hear, you deaf;[i]
look, you blind, and see!
19Who is blind[j] but my servant,[k]
and deaf like the messenger[l]
I send?
Who is blind like the one
committed[m] to me,
blind like the servant of the
LORD?
20You have seen many things, but
have paid no attention;
your ears are open, but you
hear nothing."[n]
21It pleased the LORD
for the sake of his
righteousness
to make his law[o] great and
glorious.
22But this is a people plundered
and looted,
all of them trapped in pits[p]
or hidden away in prisons.[q]
They have become plunder,
with no-one to rescue them;
they have been made loot,
with no-one to say, "Send them
back."
23Which of you will listen to this
or pay close attention[r] in time
to come?
24Who handed Jacob over to
become loot,

42:15
c Isa 50:2
Na 1:4-6
42:16
d Lk 1:78-79
e Isa 32:3
f Lk 3:5
g Heb 13:5
42:17
h Ps 97:7
Isa 1:29
Isa 44:11
Isa 45:16
42:18
i Isa 35:5
42:19
j Isa 43:8
Eze 12:2
k Isa 41:8-9
l Isa 44:26
m Isa 26:3
42:20
n Jer 6:10
42:21
o ver 4
42:22
p Isa 24:18
q Isa 24:22
42:23
r Isa 48:18
42:24
s Isa 30:15
42:25
t 2Ki 25:9
u Isa 29:13
Isa 47:7
Isa 57:1,11
Hos 7:9
43:1
a ver 7
b Ge 32:28
Isa 44:21
c Isa 44:2,6
d Isa 42:6
Isa 45:3-4
43:2
e Isa 8:7
f Dt 31:6,8
g Isa 29:6
Isa 30:27
h Ps 66:12
Da 3:25-27
43:3
i Ex 20:2
j Isa 20:3
k Pr 21:18
43:4
l Isa 63:9
43:5
m Isa 44:2
n Jer 30:10-11

and Israel to the plunderers?
Was it not the LORD,
against whom we have sinned?
For they would not follow[s] his
ways;
they did not obey his law.
25So he poured out on them his
burning anger,
the violence of war.
It enveloped them in flames,[t]
yet they did not
understand;
it consumed them, but they
did not take it to heart.[u]

Israel's Only Saviour

43 But now, this is what the
LORD says—
he who created you, O Jacob,
he who formed[a] you,
O Israel:[b]
"Fear not, for I have
redeemed[c] you;
I have summoned you by
name;[d] you are mine.
2When you pass through the
waters,[e]
I will be with you;[f]
and when you pass through the
rivers,
they will not sweep over you.
When you walk through the
fire,[g]
you will not be burned;
the flames will not set you
ablaze.[h]
3For I am the LORD, your God,[i]
the Holy One of Israel, your
Saviour;
I give Egypt for your ransom,
Cush[a][j] and Seba in your
stead.[k]
4Since you are precious and
honoured in my sight,
and because I love[l] you,
I will give men in exchange for
you,
and people in exchange for
your life.
5Do not be afraid,[m] for I am
with you;[n]

a3 That is, the upper Nile region

I will bring your children[o]
from the east
and gather you from the west.
6I will say to the north, 'Give
them up!'
and to the south,[p] 'Do not hold
them back.'
Bring my sons from afar
and my daughters[q] from the
ends of the earth—
7everyone who is called by my
name,[r]
whom I created for my glory,
whom I formed and made.[s]"

8Lead out those who have eyes
but are blind,[t]
who have ears but are deaf.[u]
9All the nations gather together[v]
and the peoples assemble.
Which of them foretold[w] this
and proclaimed to us the
former things?
Let them bring in their
witnesses to prove they
were right,
so that others may hear and
say, "It is true."
10"You are my witnesses,"
declares the LORD,
"and my servant[x] whom I
have chosen,
so that you may know and
believe me
and understand that I am he.
Before me no god[y] was formed,
nor will there be one after me.
11I, even I, am the LORD,
and apart from me there is no
saviour.[z]
12I have revealed and saved and
proclaimed—
I, and not some foreign god[a]
among you.
You are my witnesses,[b]"
declares the LORD, "that I
am God.
13 Yes, and from ancient days[c] I
am he.
No-one can deliver out of my
hand.
When I act, who can reverse
it?"[d]

43:5 o Isa 41:8
43:6 p Ps 107:3 q 2Co 6:18
43:7 r Isa 56:5; Isa 63:19; Jas 2:7 s ver 1,21; Ps 100:3; Eph 2:10
43:8 t Isa 6:9-10 u Isa 42:20; Eze 12:2
43:9 v Isa 41:1 w Isa 41:26
43:10 x Isa 41:8-9 y Isa 44:6,8
43:11 z Isa 45:21
43:12 a Dt 32:12; Ps 81:9 b Isa 44:8
43:13 c Ps 90:2 d Job 9:12; Isa 14:27
43:14 e Isa 13:14-15 f Isa 23:13
43:16 g Ps 77:19; Isa 11:15; Isa 51:10
43:17 h Ps 118:12; Isa 1:31 i Ex 14:9
43:19 j 2Co 5:17; Rev 21:5 k Ex 17:6; Nu 20:11
43:20 l Isa 13:22 m Isa 48:21
43:21 n Ps 102:18; 1Pe 2:9
43:22 o Isa 30:11

God's Mercy and Israel's Unfaithfulness

14This is what the LORD says—
your Redeemer, the Holy One
of Israel:
"For your sake I will send to
Babylon
and bring down as fugitives[e]
all the Babylonians,[b][f]
in the ships in which they took
pride.
15I am the LORD, your Holy One,
Israel's Creator, your King."

16This is what the LORD says—
he who made a way through
the sea,
a path through the mighty
waters,[g]
17who drew out[h] the chariots and
horses,
the army and reinforcements
together,[i]
and they lay there, never to rise
again,
extinguished, snuffed out like
a wick:
18"Forget the former things;
do not dwell on the past.
19See, I am doing a new thing![j]
Now it springs up; do you not
perceive it?
I am making a way in the
desert[k]
and streams in the wasteland.
20The wild animals honour me,
the jackals[l] and the owls,
because I provide water[m] in the
desert
and streams in the wasteland,
to give drink to my people, my
chosen,
21 the people I formed for
myself
that they may proclaim my
praise.[n]
22"Yet you have not called upon
me, O Jacob,
you have not wearied
yourselves for me,
O Israel.[o]

[b]14 Or *Chaldeans*

23You have not brought me sheep
for burnt offerings,
nor honoured[p] me with your
sacrifices.[q]
I have not burdened you with
grain offerings
nor wearied you with
demands[r] for incense.[s]
24You have not bought any
fragrant calamus[t] for me,
or lavished on me the fat of
your sacrifices.
But you have burdened me with
your sins
and wearied[u] me with your
offences.[v]

25"I, even I, am he who blots out
your transgressions,[w] for my
own sake,[x]
and remembers your sins no
more.[y]
26Review the past for me,
let us argue the matter
together;[z]
state the case[a] for your
innocence.
27Your first father sinned;
your spokesmen[b] rebelled
against me.
28So I will disgrace the
dignitaries of your temple,
and I will consign Jacob to
destruction[c]
and Israel to scorn.[c]

Israel the Chosen

44 "But now listen, O Jacob,
my servant,[a]
Israel, whom I have chosen.
2This is what the LORD says—
he who made you, who formed
you in the womb,
and who will help[b] you:
Do not be afraid, O Jacob, my
servant,
Jeshurun,[c] whom I have
chosen.
3For I will pour water[d] on the
thirsty land,
and streams on the dry
ground;
I will pour out my Spirit[e] on
your offspring,
and my blessing on your
descendants.[f]
4They will spring up like grass
in a meadow,
like poplar trees[g] by flowing
streams.[h]
5One will say, 'I belong to the
LORD';
another will call himself by
the name of Jacob;
still another will write on his
hand,[i] 'The LORD's',[j]
and will take the name Israel.

The LORD, Not Idols

6"This is what the LORD says—
Israel's King[k] and
Redeemer,[l] the LORD
Almighty:
I am the first and I am the
last;[m]
apart from me there is no
God.
7Who then is like me? Let him
proclaim it.
Let him declare and lay out
before me
what has happened since I
established my ancient
people,
and what is yet to come—
yes, let him foretell[n] what
will come.
8Do not tremble, do not be
afraid.
Did I not proclaim this and
foretell it long ago?
You are my witnesses. Is there
any God[o] besides me?
No, there is no other Rock;[p] I
know not one."
9All who make idols are nothing,
and the things they treasure
are worthless.[q]
Those who would speak up for
them are blind;
they are ignorant, to their own
shame.

43:23 p Zec 7:5-6; Mal 1:6-8 q Am 5:25 r Jer 7:22 s Ex 30:35; Lev 2:1
43:24 t Ex 30:23 u Isa 1:14; Isa 7:13 v Mal 2:17
43:25 w Ac 3:19 x Isa 37:35; Eze 36:22 y Isa 38:17; Jer 31:34
43:26 z Isa 1:18 a Isa 41:1; Isa 50:8
43:27 b Isa 9:15; Isa 28:7; Jer 5:31
43:28 c Jer 24:9; Eze 5:15
44:1 a ver 21; Jer 30:10; Jer 46:27-28
44:2 b Isa 41:10 c Dt 32:15
44:3 d Joel 3:18 e Joel 2:28; Ac 2:17 f Isa 61:9; Isa 65:23
44:4 g Lev 23:40 h Job 40:22
44:5 i Ex 13:9 j Zec 8:20-22
44:6 k Isa 41:21 l Isa 43:1 m Isa 41:4; Rev 1:8,17; Rev 22:13
44:7 n Isa 41:22,26
44:8 o Isa 43:10 p Dt 4:35; 1Sa 2:2
44:9 q Isa 41:24

c28 The Hebrew term refers to the irrevocable giving over of things or persons to the LORD, often by totally destroying them.

10 Who shapes a god and casts an idol,
which can profit him nothing?[r]
11 He and his kind will be put to shame;[s]
craftsmen are nothing but men.
Let them all come together and take their stand;
they will be brought down to terror and infamy.[t]

12 The blacksmith[u] takes a tool
and works with it in the coals;
he shapes an idol with hammers,
he forges it with the might of his arm.[v]
He gets hungry and loses his strength;
he drinks no water and grows faint.
13 The carpenter[w] measures with a line
and makes an outline with a marker;
he roughs it out with chisels
and marks it with compasses.
He shapes it in the form of man,[x]
of man in all his glory,
that it may dwell in a shrine.[y]
14 He cut down cedars,
or perhaps took a cypress or oak.
He let it grow among the trees of the forest,
or planted a pine, and the rain made it grow.
15 It is man's fuel[z] for burning;
some of it he takes and warms himself,
he kindles a fire and bakes bread.
But he also fashions a god and worships it;
he makes an idol and bows[a] down to it.
16 Half of the wood he burns in the fire;
over it he prepares his meal,
he roasts his meat and eats his fill.
He also warms himself and says,
"Ah! I am warm; I see the fire."
17 From the rest he makes a god, his idol;
he bows down to it and worships.
He prays[b] to it and says,
"Save[c] me; you are my god."
18 They know nothing, they understand[d] nothing;
their eyes[e] are plastered over so that they cannot see,
and their minds closed so that they cannot understand.
19 No-one stops to think,
no-one has the knowledge or understanding[f] to say,
"Half of it I used for fuel;
I even baked bread over its coals,
I roasted meat and I ate.
Shall I make a detestable[g] thing from what is left?
Shall I bow down to a block of wood?"
20 He feeds on ashes,[h] a deluded[i] heart misleads him;
he cannot save himself, or say,
"Is not this thing in my right hand a lie?[j]"

21 "Remember[k] these things, O Jacob,
for you are my servant, O Israel.
I have made you, you are my servant;[l]
O Israel, I will not forget you.[m]
22 I have swept away[n] your offences like a cloud,
your sins like the morning mist.
Return[o] to me,
for I have redeemed[p] you."

23 Sing for joy,[q] O heavens, for the LORD has done this;
shout aloud, O earth[r] beneath.
Burst into song, you mountains,[s]
you forests and all your trees,

44:10 r Isa 41:29; Jer 10:5; Ac 19:26
44:11 s Isa 1:29; t Isa 42:17
44:12 u Isa 40:19; Isa 41:6-7; v Jer 10:3-5; Ac 17:29
44:13 w Isa 41:7; x Ps 115:4-7; y Jdg 17:4-5
44:15 z ver 19; a 2Ch 25:14
44:17 b 1Ki 18:26; c Isa 45:20
44:18 d Isa 1:3; e Isa 6:9-10
44:19 f Isa 5:13; Isa 27:11; Isa 45:20; g Dt 27:15
44:20 h Ps 102:9; i Job 15:31; Ro 1:21-23,28; 2Th 2:11; 2Ti 3:13; j Isa 59:3,4,13; Ro 1:25
44:21 k Isa 46:8; Zec 10:9; l ver 1-2; m Isa 49:15
44:22 n Isa 43:25; Ac 3:19; o Isa 55:7; p 1Co 6:20
44:23 q Isa 42:10; r Ps 148:7; s Ps 98:8

for the LORD has redeemed
Jacob,
he displays his glory[t] in
Israel.

Jerusalem to Be Inhabited

24"This is what the LORD says—
your Redeemer,[u] who formed
you in the womb:

I am the LORD,
who has made all things,
who alone stretched out the
heavens,[v]
who spread out the earth by
myself,
25who foils[w] the signs of false
prophets
and makes fools of diviners,[x]
who overthrows the learning of
the wise[y]
and turns it into nonsense,[z]
26who carries out the words[a] of
his servants
and fulfils[b] the predictions of
his messengers,

who says of Jerusalem, 'It shall
be inhabited,'
of the towns of Judah, 'They
shall be built,'
and of their ruins, 'I will
restore them,'[c]
27who says to the watery deep,
'Be dry,
and I will dry up your
streams,'
28who says of Cyrus,[d] 'He is my
shepherd
and will accomplish all that I
please;
he will say of Jerusalem,[e]
"Let it be rebuilt,"
and of the temple,[f] "Let its
foundations be laid." '

45 "This is what the LORD
says to his anointed,
to Cyrus, whose right hand I
take hold[a] of
to subdue nations[b] before him
and to strip kings of their
armour,
to open doors before him

44:23
t Isa 61:3
44:24
u Isa 43:14
v Isa 42:5
44:25
w Ps 33:10
x Isa 47:13
y 1Co 1:27
z 2Sa 15:31
1Co 1:19-20
44:26
a Zec 1:6
b Isa 55:11
Mt 5:18
c Isa 49:8-21
44:28
d 2Ch 36:22
e Isa 14:32
f Ezr 1:2-4
45:1
a Ps 73:23
Isa 41:13
Isa 42:6
b Jer 50:35
45:2
c Isa 40:4
d Ps 107:16
Jer 51:30
45:3
e Jer 50:37
f Jer 41:8
g Isa 41:23
h Ex 33:12
Isa 43:1
45:4
i Isa 41:8-9
j Ac 17:23
45:5
k Isa 44:8
l Ps 18:31
m Ps 18:39
45:6
n Isa 43:5
Mal 1:11
o ver 5,18
45:7
p Isa 31:2
Am 3:6
45:8
q Ps 72:6
Joel 3:18
r Ps 85:11
Isa 60:21
Isa 61:10,11
Hos 10:12
s Isa 12:3

so that gates will not be shut:
2I will go before you
and will level[c] the
mountains;[a]
I will break down gates of
bronze
and cut through bars of iron.[d]
3I will give you the treasures[e]
of darkness,
riches stored in secret
places,[f]
so that you may know[g] that I
am the LORD,
the God of Israel, who
summons you by name.[h]
4For the sake of Jacob my
servant,[i]
of Israel my chosen,
I summon you by name
and bestow on you a title of
honour,
though you do not
acknowledge[j] me.
5I am the LORD, and there is no
other;[k]
apart from me there is no
God.[l]
I will strengthen you,[m]
though you have not
acknowledged me,
6so that from the rising of the
sun
to the place of its setting[n]
men may know there is none
besides me.[o]
I am the LORD, and there is no
other.
7I form the light and create
darkness,
I bring prosperity and create
disaster;[p]
I, the LORD, do all these
things.

8"You heavens above, rain[q]
down righteousness;[r]
let the clouds shower it down.
Let the earth open wide,
let salvation[s] spring up,
let righteousness grow with it;
I, the LORD, have created it.

[a]2 Dead Sea Scrolls and Septuagint; the meaning of the word in the Masoretic Text is uncertain.

9"Woe to him who quarrels[t]
with his Maker,
to him who is but a potsherd
among the potsherds on the
ground.
Does the clay say to the
potter,[u]
'What are you making?'
Does your work say,
'He has no hands'?
10Woe to him who says to his
father,
'What have you begotten?'
or to his mother,
'What have you brought to
birth?'

11"This is what the LORD says—
the Holy One of Israel, and its
Maker:
Concerning things to come,
do you question me about my
children,
or give me orders about the
work of my hands?[v]
12It is I who made the earth
and created mankind upon it.
My own hands stretched out the
heavens;[w]
I marshalled their starry
hosts.[x]
13I will raise up Cyrus[b][y] in my
righteousness:
I will make all his ways
straight.
He will rebuild my city
and set my exiles free,
but not for a price or reward,[z]
says the LORD Almighty."

14This is what the LORD says:

"The products of Egypt and the
merchandise of Cush,[c]
and those tall Sabeans—
they will come over to you
and will be yours;
they will trudge behind you,
coming over to you in
chains.[a]
They will bow down before you
and plead[b] with you, saying,
'Surely God is with you,[c] and
there is no other;
there is no other god.' "

45:9
t Job 15:25
u Isa 29:16
Ro 9:20-21*

45:11
v Isa 19:25

45:12
w Ge 2:1
Isa 42:5
x Ne 9:6

45:13
y 2Ch 36:22
Isa 41:2
z Isa 52:3

45:14
a Isa 14:1-2
b Jer 16:19
Zec 8:20-23
c 1Co 14:25

45:15
d Ps 44:24

45:16
e Isa 44:9,11

45:17
f Ro 11:26
g Isa 26:4

45:18
h Ge 1:2
i Ge 1:26
Isa 42:5
j ver 5

45:19
k Isa 48:16
l Isa 41:8
m Dt 30:11

45:20
n Isa 43:9
o Isa 44:19
p Isa 46:1
Jer 10:5
q Isa 44:17
Isa 46:6-7

45:21
r Isa 41:22

15Truly you are a God who
hides[d] himself,
O God and Saviour of Israel.
16All the makers of idols will be
put to shame and
disgraced;[e]
they will go off into disgrace
together.
17But Israel will be saved[f] by the
LORD
with an everlasting
salvation;[g]
you will never be put to shame
or disgraced,
to ages everlasting.

18For this is what the LORD
says—
he who created the heavens,
he is God;
he who fashioned and made the
earth,
he founded it;
he did not create it to be
empty,[h]
but formed it to be
inhabited[i]—
he says:
"I am the LORD,
and there is no other.[j]
19I have not spoken in secret,[k]
from somewhere in a land of
darkness;
I have not said to Jacob's
descendants,[l]
'Seek me in vain.'
I, the LORD, speak the truth;
I declare what is right.[m]

20"Gather together[n] and come;
assemble, you fugitives from
the nations.
Ignorant[o] are those who
carry[p] about idols of wood,
who pray to gods that cannot
save.[q]
21Declare what is to be, present
it—
let them take counsel together.
Who foretold[r] this long ago,
who declared it from the
distant past?

b13 Hebrew *him* c14 That is, the upper Nile region

Was it not I, the LORD?
And there is no God apart
from me,[s]
a righteous God and a Saviour;
there is none but me.
22“Turn[t] to me and be saved,[u]
all you ends of the earth;[v]
for I am God, and there is no
other.
23By myself I have sworn,[w]
my mouth has uttered in all
integrity[x]
a word that will not be
revoked:[y]
Before me every knee will bow;
by me every tongue will
swear.[z]
24They will say of me, ‘In the
LORD alone
are righteousness[a] and
strength.’ ”
All who have raged against him
will come to him and be put to
shame.[b]
25But in the LORD all the
descendants of Israel
will be found righteous and
will exult.[c]

Gods of Babylon

46 Bel[a] bows down, Nebo
stoops low;
their idols are borne by beasts
of burden.[a]
The images that are carried[b]
about are burdensome,
a burden for the weary.
2They stoop and bow down
together;
unable to rescue the burden,
they themselves go off into
captivity.[c]
3“Listen[d] to me, O house of
Jacob,
all you who remain of the
house of Israel,
you whom I have upheld since
you were conceived,
and have carried since your
birth.
4Even to your old age and grey
hairs[e]
I am he,[f] I am he who will
sustain you.
I have made you and I will
carry you;
I will sustain you and I will
rescue you.
5“To whom will you compare me
or count me equal?
To whom will you liken me
that we may be
compared?[g]
6Some pour out gold from their
bags
and weigh out silver on the
scales;
they hire a goldsmith[h] to make
it into a god,
and they bow down and
worship it.[i]
7They lift it to their shoulders
and carry[j] it;
they set it up in its place, and
there it stands.
From that spot it cannot move.
Though one cries out to it, it
does not answer;
it cannot save[k] him from his
troubles.
8“Remember[l] this, fix it in
mind,
take it to heart, you rebels.
9Remember the former things,
those of long ago;[m]
I am God, and there is no
other;
I am God, and there is none
like me.[n]
10I make known the end from the
beginning,
from ancient times,[o] what is
still to come.
I say: My purpose will stand,[p]
and I will do all that I please.
11From the east I summon a bird
of prey;
from a far-off land, a man to
fulfil my purpose.
What I have said, that will I
bring about;
what I have planned, that will
I do.

45:21
s ver 5

45:22
t Zec 12:10
u Nu 21:8-9
2Ch 20:12
v Isa 49:6,12

45:23
w Ge 22:16
x Heb 6:13
y Isa 55:11
z Ps 63:11
Isa 19:18
Ro 14:11*
Php 2:10-11

45:24
a Jer 33:16
b Isa 41:11

45:25
c Isa 41:16

46:1
a Isa 21:9
Jer 50:2
Jer 51:44
b Isa 45:20

46:2
c Jdg 18:17-18
2Sa 5:21

46:3
d ver 12

46:4
e Ps 71:18
f Isa 43:13

46:5
g Isa 40:18,25

46:6
h Isa 40:19
i Isa 44:17

46:7
j ver 1
k Isa 44:17
Isa 45:20

46:8
l Isa 44:21

46:9
m Dt 32:7
n Isa 45:5,21

46:10
o Isa 45:21
p Pr 19:21
Ac 5:39

a1 Or *are but beasts and cattle*

[12]Listen[q] to me, you stubborn-hearted,
you who are far from righteousness.[r]
[13]I am bringing my righteousness near,
it is not far away;
and my salvation will not be delayed.
I will grant salvation to Zion,
my splendour[s] to Israel.

The Fall of Babylon

47 "Go down, sit in the dust,
Virgin Daughter[a] of Babylon;
sit on the ground without a throne,
Daughter of the Babylonians.[a b]
No more will you be called
tender or delicate.[c]
[2]Take millstones[d] and grind[e] flour;
take off your veil.[f]
Lift up your skirts,[g] bare your legs,
and wade through the streams.
[3]Your nakedness[h] will be exposed
and your shame[i] uncovered.
I will take vengeance;[j]
I will spare no-one."

[4]Our Redeemer—the LORD Almighty is his name[k]—
is the Holy One of Israel.

[5]"Sit in silence, go into darkness,[l]
Daughter of the Babylonians;
no more will you be called
queen of kingdoms.[m]
[6]I was angry[n] with my people
and desecrated my inheritance;
I gave them into your hand,[o]
and you showed them no mercy.
Even on the aged
you laid a very heavy yoke.
[7]You said, 'I will continue for ever—
the eternal queen!'[p]
But you did not consider these things
or reflect[q] on what might happen.[r]

[8]"Now then, listen, you wanton creature,
lounging in your security[s]
and saying to yourself,
'I am, and there is none besides me.[t]
I will never be a widow[u]
or suffer the loss of children.'
[9]Both of these will overtake you
in a moment,[v] on a single day:
loss of children[w] and widowhood.
They will come upon you in full measure,
in spite of your many sorceries[x]
and all your potent spells.[y]
[10]You have trusted[z] in your wickedness
and have said, 'No-one sees me.'[a]
Your wisdom[b] and knowledge mislead[c] you
when you say to yourself,
'I am, and there is none besides me.'
[11]Disaster will come upon you,
and you will not know how to conjure it away.
A calamity will fall upon you
that you cannot ward off with a ransom;
a catastrophe you cannot foresee
will suddenly[d] come upon you.

[12]"Keep on, then, with your magic spells
and with your many sorceries,[e]
which you have laboured at since childhood.
Perhaps you will succeed,
perhaps you will cause terror.
[13]All the counsel you have received has only worn you out![f]

46:12 q ver 3 r Ps 119:150 Isa 48:1 Jer 2:5
46:13 s Isa 44:23
47:1 a Isa 23:12 b Ps 137:8 Jer 50:42 Jer 51:33 Zec 2:7 c Dt 28:56
47:2 d Ex 11:5 Mt 24:41 e Jdg 16:21 f Ge 24:65 g Isa 32:11
47:3 h Eze 16:37 Na 3:5 i Isa 20:4 j Isa 34:8
47:4 k Jer 50:34
47:5 l Isa 13:10 m Isa 13:19
47:6 n 2Ch 28:9 o Isa 10:13
47:7 p ver 5 Rev 18:7 q Isa 42:23,25 r Dt 32:29
47:8 s Isa 32:9 t Isa 45:6 Zep 2:15 u Rev 18:7
47:9 v Ps 73:19 1Th 5:3 Rev 18:8-10 w Isa 13:18 x Na 3:4 y Rev 18:23
47:10 z Ps 52:7 Ps 62:10 a Isa 29:15 b Isa 5:21 c Isa 44:20
47:11 d 1Th 5:3
47:12 e ver 9
47:13 f Isa 57:10 Jer 51:58

a1 Or *Chaldeans*; also in verse 5

Let your astrologers[g] come
forward,
those stargazers who make
predictions month by
month,
let them save[h] you from what
is coming upon you.
14Surely they are like stubble;[i]
the fire will burn them up.
They cannot even save
themselves
from the power of the flame.[j]
Here are no coals to warm
anyone;
here is no fire to sit by.
15That is all they can do for you—
these you have laboured with
and trafficked[k] with since
childhood.
Each of them goes on in his
error;
there is not one that can save
you.

Stubborn Israel

48 "Listen to this, O house of
Jacob,
you who are called by the
name of Israel
and come from the line of
Judah,
you who take oaths in the name
of the LORD
and invoke[a] the God of
Israel—
but not in truth[b] or
righteousness—
2you who call yourselves citizens
of the holy city[c]
and rely[d] on the God of
Israel—
the LORD Almighty is his
name:
3I foretold the former things[e]
long ago,
my mouth announced[f] them
and I made them known;
then suddenly I acted, and
they came to pass.
4For I knew how stubborn[g] you
were;
the sinews of your neck[h]
were iron,
your forehead[i] was bronze.
5Therefore I told you these
things long ago;
before they happened I
announced them to you
so that you could not say,
'My idols did them;[j]
my wooden image and metal
god ordained them.'
6You have heard these things;
look at them all.
Will you not admit them?

"From now on I will tell you of
new things,
of hidden things unknown to
you.
7They are created now, and not
long ago;
you have not heard of them
before today.
So you cannot say,
'Yes, I knew of them.'
8You have neither heard nor
understood;
from of old your ear has not
been open.
Well do I know how treacherous
you are;
you were called a rebel[k] from
birth.
9For my own name's sake I delay
my wrath;[l]
for the sake of my praise I
hold it back from you,
so as not to cut you off.[m]
10See, I have refined you, though
not as silver;
I have tested you in the
furnace[n] of affliction.
11For my own sake,[o] for my own
sake, I do this.
How can I let myself be
defamed?[p]
I will not yield my glory to
another.[q]

Israel Freed

12"Listen[r] to me, O Jacob,
Israel, whom I have called:
I am he;
I am the first and I am the
last.[s]

47:13
g Isa 44:25
h ver 15

47:14
i Isa 5:24
Na 1:10
j Isa 10:17
Jer 51:30,32,
58

47:15
k Rev 18:11

48:1
a Isa 58:2
b Jer 4:2

48:2
c Isa 52:1
d Isa 10:20
Mic 3:11
Ro 2:17

48:3
e Isa 41:22
f Isa 45:21

48:4
g Dt 31:27
h Ex 32:9
Ac 7:51
i Eze 3:9

48:5
j Jer 44:15-18

48:8
k Dt 9:7,24
Ps 58:3

48:9
l Ps 78:38
Isa 30:18
m Ne 9:31

48:10
n 1Ki 8:51

48:11
o 1Sa 12:22
Isa 37:35
p Dt 32:27
Jer 14:7,21
Eze 20:9,14,
22,44
q Isa 42:8

48:12
r Isa 46:3
s Isa 41:4
Rev 1:17
Rev 22:13

13 My own hand laid the
foundations of the earth,[t]
and my right hand spread out
the heavens;[u]
when I summon them,
they all stand up together.[v]

14 "Come together,[w] all of you,
and listen:
Which of ⌊the idols⌋ has
foretold these things?
The LORD's chosen ally
will carry out his purpose[x]
against Babylon;
his arm will be against the
Babylonians.[a]
15 I, even I, have spoken;
yes, I have called[y] him.
I will bring him,
and he will succeed in his
mission.

16 "Come near[z] me and listen to
this:

"From the first announcement I
have not spoken in secret;[a]
at the time it happens, I am
there."

And now the Sovereign LORD
has sent[b] me,
with his Spirit.
17 This is what the LORD says—
your Redeemer,[c] the Holy
One[d] of Israel:
"I am the LORD your God,
who teaches you what is best
for you,
who directs[e] you in the way[f]
you should go.
18 If only you had paid attention[g]
to my commands,
your peace[h] would have been
like a river,
your righteousness[i] like the
waves of the sea.
19 Your descendants would have
been like the sand,
your children like its
numberless grains;[j]
their name would never be cut
off[k]
nor destroyed from before
me."

20 Leave Babylon,
flee[l] from the Babylonians!
Announce this with shouts of
joy[m]
and proclaim it.
Send it out to the ends of the
earth;
say, "The LORD has
redeemed[n] his servant
Jacob."
21 They did not thirst[o] when he
led them through the
deserts;
he made water flow[p] for them
from the rock;
he split the rock
and water gushed out.[q]

22 "There is no peace," says the
LORD, "for the wicked."[r]

The Servant of the LORD

49 Listen to me, you islands;
hear this, you distant
nations:
Before I was born[a] the LORD
called[b] me;
from my birth he has made
mention of my name.
2 He made my mouth like a
sharpened sword,[c]
in the shadow of his hand he
hid me;
he made me into a polished
arrow
and concealed me in his
quiver.
3 He said to me, "You are my
servant,[d]
Israel, in whom I will display
my splendour.[e]"
4 But I said, "I have laboured to
no purpose;
I have spent my strength in
vain[f] and for nothing.
Yet what is due to me is in the
LORD's hand,
and my reward[g] is with my
God."

48:13 t Heb 1:10-12 u Ex 20:11 v Isa 40:26
48:14 w Isa 43:9 x Isa 46:10-11
48:15 y Isa 45:1
48:16 z Isa 41:1 a Isa 45:19 b Zec 2:9,11
48:17 c Isa 49:7 d Isa 43:14 e Isa 49:10 f Ps 32:8
48:18 g Dt 32:29 h Ps 119:165 Isa 66:12 i Isa 45:8
48:19 j Ge 22:17 k Isa 56:5 Isa 66:22
48:20 l Jer 50:8 Jer 51:6,45 Zec 2:6-7 Rev 18:4 m Isa 49:13 n Isa 52:9 Isa 63:9
48:21 o Isa 41:17 p Isa 30:25 q Ex 17:6 Nu 20:11 Ps 105:41 Isa 35:6
48:22 r Isa 57:21
49:1 a Isa 44:24 Isa 46:3 Mt 1:20 b Isa 7:14 Isa 9:6 Isa 44:2 Jer 1:5 Gal 1:15
49:2 c Isa 11:4 Rev 1:16
49:3 d Zec 3:8 e Isa 44:23
49:4 f Isa 65:23 g Isa 35:4

a 14 Or *Chaldeans*; also in verse 20

5And now the LORD says—
he who formed me in the
womb to be his servant
to bring Jacob back to him
and gather Israel[h] to himself,
for I am honoured[i] in the eyes
of the LORD
and my God has been my
strength—
6he says:
"It is too small a thing for you
to be my servant
to restore the tribes of Jacob
and bring back those of Israel
I have kept.
I will also make you a light for
the Gentiles,[j]
that you may bring my
salvation to the ends of the
earth."[k]

7This is what the LORD says—
the Redeemer and Holy One
of Israel[l]—
to him who was despised[m] and
abhorred by the nation,
to the servant of rulers:
"Kings[n] will see you and rise up,
princes will see and bow
down,
because of the LORD, who is
faithful,
the Holy One of Israel, who
has chosen you."

Restoration of Israel

8This is what the LORD says:

"In the time of my favour[o] I
will answer you,
and in the day of salvation I
will help you;[p]
I will keep[q] you and will make
you
to be a covenant for the
people,[r]
to restore the land[s]
and to reassign its desolate
inheritances,
9to say to the captives,[t] 'Come
out,'
and to those in darkness, 'Be
free!'

49:5 h Isa 11:12 i Isa 43:4
49:6 j Lk 2:32 k Ac 13:47*
49:7 l Isa 48:17 m Ps 22:6 Ps 69:7-9 n Isa 52:15
49:8 o Ps 69:13 p 2Co 6:2* q Isa 26:3 r Isa 42:6 s Isa 44:26
49:9 t Isa 42:7 Isa 61:1 Lk 4:19 u Isa 41:18
49:10 v Isa 33:16 w Ps 121:6 Rev 7:16 x Isa 14:1 y Isa 35:7
49:11 z Isa 11:16 a Isa 40:4
49:12 b Isa 43:5-6
49:13 c Isa 44:23 d Isa 40:1
49:15 e Isa 44:21
49:16 f SS 8:6 g Ps 48:12-13 Isa 62:6
49:17 h Isa 10:6
49:18 i Isa 43:5 Isa 54:7 Isa 60:4

"They will feed beside the
roads
and find pasture on every
barren hill.[u]
10They will neither hunger nor
thirst,[v]
nor will the desert heat or the
sun beat upon them.[w]
He who has compassion[x] on
them will guide them
and lead them beside springs[y]
of water.
11I will turn all my mountains
into roads,
and my highways[z] will be
raised up.[a]
12See, they will come from
afar[b]—
some from the north, some
from the west,
some from the region of
Aswan."**[a]**

13Shout for joy, O heavens;
rejoice, O earth;
burst into song,
O mountains![c]
For the LORD comforts[d] his
people
and will have compassion on
his afflicted ones.

14But Zion said, "The LORD has
forsaken me,
the Lord has forgotten me."

15"Can a mother forget the baby
at her breast
and have no compassion on
the child she has borne?
Though she may forget,
I will not forget you![e]
16See, I have engraved[f] you on
the palms of my hands;
your walls[g] are ever before
me.
17Your sons hasten back,
and those who laid you waste[h]
depart from you.
18Lift up your eyes and look
around;
all your sons gather[i] and
come to you.

a12 Dead Sea Scrolls; Masoretic Text *Sinim*

As surely as I live,[j]" declares
the LORD,
"you will wear[k] them all as
ornaments;
you will put them on, like a
bride.

19"Though you were ruined and
made desolate[l]
and your land laid waste,[m]
now you will be too small for
your people,[n]
and those who devoured you
will be far away.
20The children born during your
bereavement
will yet say in your hearing,
'This place is too small for us;
give us more space to live
in.'[o]
21Then you will say in your heart,
'Who bore me these?
I was bereaved and barren;
I was exiled and rejected.[p]
Who brought these up?
I was left[q] all alone,
but these – where have they
come from?' "

22This is what the Sovereign
LORD says:

"See, I will beckon to the
Gentiles,
I will lift up my banner[r] to
the peoples;
they will bring your sons in
their arms
and carry your daughters on
their shoulders.[s]
23Kings[t] will be your foster
fathers,
and their queens your nursing
mothers.[u]
They will bow down before you
with their faces to the
ground;
they will lick the dust[v] at
your feet.
Then you will know that I am
the LORD;[w]
those who hope in me will not
be disappointed."

49:18
j Isa 45:23
k Isa 52:1

49:19
l Isa 54:1,3
m Isa 5:6
n Zec 10:10

49:20
o Isa 54:1-3

49:21
p Isa 5:13
q Isa 1:8

49:22
r Isa 11:10
s Isa 60:4

49:23
t Isa 60:3, 10-11
u Isa 60:16
v Ps 72:9
w Mic 7:17

49:24
x Mt 12:29
Lk 11:21

49:25
y Isa 14:2
z Jer 50:33-34
a Isa 25:9
Isa 35:4

49:26
b Isa 9:4
c Isa 9:20
d Rev 16:6
e Eze 39:7

50:1
a Dt 24:1
Jer 3:8
Hos 2:2
b Ne 5:5
Mt 18:25
c Dt 32:30
Isa 52:3

50:2
d Isa 41:28
e Nu 11:23
Isa 59:1
f Ge 18:14
g Ex 14:22
Jos 3:16

24Can plunder be taken from
warriors,[x]
or captives rescued from the
fierce?[b]

25But this is what the LORD says:

"Yes, captives[y] will be taken
from warriors,[z]
and plunder retrieved from
the fierce;
I will contend with those who
contend with you,
and your children I will
save.[a]
26I will make your oppressors[b]
eat[c] their own flesh;
they will be drunk on their
own blood,[d] as with wine.
Then all mankind will know[e]
that I, the LORD, am your
Saviour,
your Redeemer, the Mighty
One of Jacob."

Israel's Sin and the Servant's Obedience

50 This is what the LORD says:

"Where is your mother's
certificate of divorce[a]
with which I sent her away?
Or to which of my creditors
did I sell[b] you?
Because of your sins you were
sold;[c]
because of your
transgressions your mother
was sent away.
2When I came, why was there
no-one?
When I called, why was there
no-one to answer?[d]
Was my arm too short[e] to
ransom you?
Do I lack the strength[f] to
rescue you?
By a mere rebuke I dry up the
sea,[g]
I turn rivers into a desert;
their fish rot for lack of water

[b]24 Dead Sea Scrolls, Vulgate and Syriac (see also Septuagint and verse 25); Masoretic Text *righteous*

and die of thirst.
3I clothe the sky with darkness
and make sackcloth[h] its
covering."

4The Sovereign LORD has given
me an instructed tongue,[i]
to know the word that sustains
the weary.[j]
He wakens me morning by
morning,[k]
wakens my ear to listen like
one being taught.
5The Sovereign LORD has opened
my ears,[l]
and I have not been
rebellious;[m]
I have not drawn back.
6I offered my back to those who
beat[n] me,
my cheeks to those who pulled
out my beard;
I did not hide my face
from mocking and spitting.[o]
7Because the Sovereign LORD
helps[p] me,
I will not be disgraced.
Therefore have I set my face
like flint,[q]
and I know I will not be put to
shame.
8He who vindicates me is near.
Who then will bring charges
against me?[r]
Let us face each other![s]
Who is my accuser?
Let him confront me!
9It is the Sovereign LORD who
helps[t] me.
Who is he who will condemn
me?
They will all wear out like a
garment;
the moths[u] will eat them up.

10Who among you fears the LORD
and obeys the word of his
servant?[v]
Let him who walks in the dark,
who has no light,
trust[w] in the name of the LORD
and rely on his God.
11But now, all you who light fires
and provide yourselves with
flaming torches,[x]
go, walk in the light of your
fires[y]
and of the torches you have
set ablaze.
This is what you shall receive
from my hand:
You will lie down in torment.[z]

Everlasting Salvation for Zion

51 "Listen[a] to me, you who
pursue righteousness[b]
and who seek the LORD:
Look to the rock from which
you were cut
and to the quarry from which
you were hewn;
2look to Abraham,[c] your father,
and to Sarah, who gave you
birth.
When I called him he was but
one,
and I blessed him and made
him many.[d]
3The LORD will surely comfort[e]
Zion
and will look with compassion
on all her ruins;[f]
he will make her deserts like
Eden,[g]
her wastelands like the garden
of the LORD.
Joy and gladness[h] will be found
in her,
thanksgiving and the sound of
singing.

4"Listen to me, my people;[i]
hear me, my nation:
The law will go out from me;
my justice[j] will become a
light to the nations.[k]
5My righteousness draws near
speedily,
my salvation is on the way,[l]
and my arm[m] will bring
justice to the nations.
The islands will look to me
and wait in hope for my arm.
6Lift up your eyes to the
heavens,
look at the earth beneath;
the heavens will vanish like
smoke,[n]

50:3
h Rev 6:12
50:4
i Ex 4:12
j Mt 11:28
k Ps 5:3
Ps 119:147
Ps 143:8
50:5
l Isa 35:5
m Mt 26:39
Jn 8:29
Jn 14:31
Jn 15:10
Ac 26:19
Heb 5:8
50:6
n Isa 53:5
Mt 27:30
Mk 14:65
Mk 15:19
Lk 22:63
o La 3:30
Mt 26:67
50:7
p Isa 42:1
q Eze 3:8-9
50:8
r Isa 43:26
Ro 8:32-34
s Isa 41:1
50:9
t Isa 41:10
u Job 13:28
Isa 51:8
50:10
v Isa 49:3
w Isa 26:4
50:11
x Pr 26:18
y Jas 3:6
z Isa 65:13-15
51:1
a Isa 46:3
b ver 7
Ps 94:15
Ro 9:30-31
51:2
c Isa 29:22
Ro 4:16
Heb 11:11
d Ge 12:2
51:3
e Isa 40:1
f Isa 52:9
g Ge 2:8
h Isa 25:9
Isa 66:10
51:4
i Ps 50:7
j Isa 2:4
k Isa 42:4,6
51:5
l Isa 46:13
m Isa 40:10
Isa 63:1,5
51:6
n Mt 24:35
2Pe 3:10

the earth will wear out like a
garment[o]
and its inhabitants die like
flies.
But my salvation will last for
ever,
my righteousness will never
fail.

7"Hear me, you who know what
is right,[p]
you people who have my law
in your hearts:[q]
Do not fear the reproach of
men
or be terrified by their
insults.[r]
8For the moth will eat them up
like a garment;[s]
the worm will devour them
like wool.
But my righteousness will last
for ever,[t]
my salvation through all
generations."

9Awake, awake! Clothe yourself
with strength,[u]
O arm of the LORD;
awake, as in days gone by,
as in generations of old.[v]
Was it not you who cut Rahab to
pieces,
who pierced that monster[w]
through?
10Was it not you who dried up the
sea,[x]
the waters of the great deep,
who made a road in the depths
of the sea
so that the redeemed might
cross over?
11The ransomed[y] of the LORD will
return.
They will enter Zion with
singing;
everlasting joy will crown
their heads.
Gladness and joy[z] will
overtake them,
and sorrow and sighing will
flee away.[a]

12"I, even I, am he who
comforts[b] you.
Who are you that you fear
mortal men,[c]
the sons of men, who are but
grass,[d]
13that you forget[e] the LORD your
Maker,[f]
who stretched out the
heavens[g]
and laid the foundations of the
earth,
that you live in constant
terror[h] every day
because of the wrath of the
oppressor,
who is bent on destruction?
For where is the wrath of the
oppressor?
14 The cowering prisoners will
soon be set free;
they will not die in their
dungeon,
nor will they lack bread.[i]
15For I am the LORD your God,
who churns up the sea[j] so
that its waves roar—
the LORD Almighty is his
name.
16I have put my words in your
mouth[k]
and covered you with the
shadow of my hand[l]—
I who set the heavens in place,
who laid the foundations of
the earth,
and who say to Zion, 'You are
my people.'"

The Cup of the LORD's Wrath

17Awake, awake![m]
Rise up, O Jerusalem,
you who have drunk from the
hand of the LORD
the cup of his wrath,[n]
you who have drained to its
dregs
the goblet that makes men
stagger.[o]
18Of all the sons[p] she bore
there was none to guide her;[q]
of all the sons she brought up
there was none to take her by
the hand.

51:6 o Ps 102:25-26
51:7 p ver 1 q Ps 37:31 r Mt 5:11 Ac 5:41
51:8 s Isa 50:9 t ver 6
51:9 u Isa 52:1 v Dt 4:34 w Ps 74:13
51:10 x Ex 14:22
51:11 y Isa 35:9 z Jer 33:11 a Rev 7:17
51:12 b 2Co 1:4 c Ps 118:6 Isa 2:22 d Isa 40:6-7 1Pe 1:24
51:13 e Isa 17:10 f Isa 45:11 g Ps 104:2 Isa 48:13 h Isa 7:4
51:14 i Isa 49:10
51:15 j Jer 31:35
51:16 k Dt 18:18 Isa 59:21 l Ex 33:22
51:17 m Isa 52:1 n Job 21:20 Rev 14:10 Rev 16:19 o Ps 60:3
51:18 p Ps 88:18 q Isa 49:21

19These double calamities[r] have
come upon you—
who can comfort you?—
ruin and destruction, famine[s]
and sword—
who can[a] console you?
20Your sons have fainted;
they lie at the head of every
street,[t]
like antelope caught in a net.
They are filled with the wrath
of the LORD
and the rebuke of your God.

21Therefore hear this, you
afflicted one,
made drunk,[u] but not with
wine.
22This is what your Sovereign
LORD says,
your God, who defends[v] his
people:
"See, I have taken out of your
hand
the cup[w] that made you
stagger;
from that cup, the goblet of my
wrath,
you will never drink again.
23I will put it into the hands of
your tormentors,[x]
who said to you,
'Fall prostrate[y] that we may
walk[z] over you.'
And you made your back like
the ground,
like a street to be walked
over."

52 Awake, awake,[a] O Zion,
clothe yourself with
strength.[b]
Put on your garments of
splendour,[c]
O Jerusalem, the holy city.[d]
The uncircumcised and defiled
will not enter you again.[e]
2Shake off your dust;[f]
rise up, sit enthroned,
O Jerusalem.
Free yourself from the chains
on your neck,
O captive Daughter of Zion.

3For this is what the LORD says:

"You were sold for nothing,[g]
and without money[h] you will
be redeemed."

4For this is what the Sovereign
LORD says:

"At first my people went down
to Egypt[i] to live;
lately, Assyria has oppressed
them.

5"And now what do I have here?"
declares the LORD.

"For my people have been taken
away for nothing,
and those who rule them
mock,"[a]
declares the LORD.
"And all day long
my name is constantly
blasphemed.[j]
6Therefore my people will
know[k] my name;
therefore in that day they will
know
that it is I who foretold it.
Yes, it is I."

7How beautiful on the mountains
are the feet of those who
bring good news,[l]
who proclaim peace,[m]
who bring good tidings,
who proclaim salvation,
who say to Zion,
"Your God reigns!"[n]
8Listen! Your watchmen[o] lift up
their voices;
together they shout for joy.
When the LORD returns to Zion,
they will see it with their own
eyes.
9Burst into songs of joy[p]
together,
you ruins[q] of Jerusalem,
for the LORD has comforted his
people,
he has redeemed Jerusalem.[r]

51:19 r Isa 47:9 s Isa 14:30
51:20 t Isa 5:25; Jer 14:16
51:21 u ver 17; Isa 29:9
51:22 v Isa 49:25 w ver 17
51:23 x Isa 49:26; Jer 25:15-17, 26,28; Jer 49:12 y Zec 12:2 z Jos 10:24
52:1 a Isa 51:17 b Isa 51:9 c Ex 28:2,40; Ps 110:3; Zec 3:4 d Ne 11:1; Mt 4:5; Rev 21:2 e Na 1:15; Rev 21:27
52:2 f Isa 29:4
52:3 g Ps 44:12 h Isa 45:13
52:4 i Ge 46:6
52:5 j Eze 36:20; Ro 2:24*
52:6 k Isa 49:23
52:7 l Isa 40:9; Ro 10:15* m Na 1:15; Eph 6:15 n Ps 93:1
52:8 o Isa 62:6
52:9 p Ps 98:4 q Isa 51:3 r Isa 48:20

a19 Dead Sea Scrolls, Septuagint, Vulgate and Syriac; Masoretic Text / *how can I* a5 Dead Sea Scrolls and Vulgate; Masoretic Text *wail*

10The LORD will lay bare his holy
arm
in the sight of all the nations,[s]
and all the ends of the earth
will see
the salvation[t] of our God.
11Depart,[u] depart, go out from
there!
Touch no unclean thing![v]
Come out from it and be pure,[w]
you who carry the vessels of
the LORD.
12But you will not leave in haste[x]
or go in flight;
for the LORD will go before
you,[y]
the God of Israel will be your
rear guard.[z]

The Suffering and Glory of the Servant

13See, my servant[a] will act
wisely;[b]
he will be raised and lifted up
and highly exalted.[b]
14Just as there were many who
were appalled at him[c]—
his appearance was so
disfigured beyond that of
any man
and his form marred beyond
human likeness—
15so will he sprinkle many
nations,[d]
and kings will shut their
mouths because of him.
For what they were not told,
they will see,
and what they have not heard,
they will understand.[c]

53

Who has believed our
message[a]
and to whom has the arm of
the LORD been revealed?[b]
2He grew up before him like a
tender shoot,
and like a root out of dry
ground.
He had no beauty or majesty to
attract us to him,
nothing in his appearance[c]
that we should desire him.

52:10 *s* Isa 66:18 *t* Ps 98:2-3 Lk 3:6
52:11 *u* Isa 48:20 *v* Isa 1:16 2Co 6:17* *w* 2Ti 2:19
52:12 *x* Ex 12:11 *y* Mic 2:13 *z* Ex 14:19
52:13 *a* Isa 42:1 *b* Isa 57:15 Php 2:9
52:15 *c* Ro 15:21* Eph 3:4-5
53:1 *a* Ro 10:16* *b* Jn 12:38*
53:2 *c* Isa 52:14
53:3 *d* ver 4,10 Lk 18:31-33 *e* Ps 22:6 Jn 1:10-11
53:4 *f* Mt 8:17* *g* Jn 19:7
53:5 *h* Ro 4:25 1Co 15:3 Heb 9:28 *i* 1Pe 2:24-25
53:7 *j* Mk 14:61
53:8 *k* Da 9:26 Ac 8:32-33* *l* ver 12

3He was despised and rejected
by men,
a man of sorrows, and familiar
with suffering.[d]
Like one from whom men hide
their faces
he was despised,[e] and we
esteemed him not.

4Surely he took up our
infirmities
and carried our sorrows,[f]
yet we considered him stricken
by God,[g]
smitten by him, and afflicted.
5But he was pierced for our
transgressions,[h]
he was crushed for our
iniquities;
the punishment that brought us
peace was upon him,
and by his wounds we are
healed.[i]
6We all, like sheep, have gone
astray,
each of us has turned to his
own way;
and the LORD has laid on him
the iniquity of us all.

7He was oppressed and afflicted,
yet he did not open his
mouth;[j]
he was led like a lamb to the
slaughter,
and as a sheep before her
shearers is silent,
so he did not open his mouth.
8By oppression[a] and judgment
he was taken away.
And who can speak of his
descendants?
For he was cut off from the
land of the living;[k]
for the transgression[l] of my
people he was stricken.[b]
9He was assigned a grave with
the wicked,

[b]13 Or *will prosper* [c]14 Hebrew *you*
[d]15 Hebrew; Septuagint *so will many nations marvel at him* [a]8 Or *From arrest*
[b]8 Or *away. / Yet who of his generation considered / that he was cut off from the land of the living / for the transgression of my people, / to whom the blow was due?*

and with the rich[m] in his
death,
though he had done no
violence,[n]
nor was any deceit in his
mouth.[o]

10 Yet it was the LORD's will[p] to
crush[q] him and cause him
to suffer,[r]
and though the LORD makes[c]
his life a guilt offering,
he will see his offspring[s] and
prolong his days,
and the will of the LORD will
prosper in his hand.
11 After the suffering[t] of his soul,
he will see the light ⌊of life⌋[d]
and be satisfied;[e]
by his knowledge[f] my
righteous servant will
justify[u] many,
and he will bear their
iniquities.
12 Therefore I will give him a
portion among the great,[g][v]
and he will divide the spoils
with the strong,[h]
because he poured out his life
unto death,[w]
and was numbered with the
transgressors.[x]
For he bore the sin of many,
and made intercession for the
transgressors.

The Future Glory of Zion

54 "Sing, O barren woman,
you who never bore a
child;
burst into song, shout for joy,
you who were never in labour;
because more are the children[a]
of the desolate woman
than of her who has a
husband,[b]"
says the LORD.
2 "Enlarge the place of your
tent,[c]
stretch your tent curtains
wide,
do not hold back;
lengthen your cords,
strengthen your stakes.[d]
3 For you will spread out to the
right and to the left;
your descendants will
dispossess nations
and settle in their desolate[e]
cities.

4 "Do not be afraid; you will not
suffer shame.
Do not fear disgrace; you will
not be humiliated.
You will forget the shame of
your youth
and remember no more the
reproach[f] of your
widowhood.
5 For your Maker is your
husband[g]—
the LORD Almighty is his
name—
the Holy One of Israel is your
Redeemer;[h]
he is called the God of all the
earth.[i]
6 The LORD will call you back[j]
as if you were a wife
deserted[k] and distressed in
spirit—
a wife who married young,
only to be rejected," says your
God.
7 "For a brief moment[l] I
abandoned you,
but with deep compassion I
will bring you back.[m]
8 In a surge of anger[n]
I hid my face from you for a
moment,
but with everlasting kindness[o]
I will have compassion on you,"
says the LORD your Redeemer.

9 "To me this is like the days of
Noah,
when I swore that the waters
of Noah would never again
cover the earth.[p]
So now I have sworn not to be
angry[q] with you,

53:9
m Mt 27:57-60
n Isa 42:1-3
o 1Pe 2:22*

53:10
p Isa 46:10
q ver 5
r ver 3
s Ps 22:30

53:11
t Jn 10:14-18
u Ro 5:18-19

53:12
v Php 2:9
w Mt 26:28,38, 39,42
x Mk 15:27*
Lk 22:37*
Lk 23:32

54:1
a Isa 49:20
b 1Sa 2:5
Gal 4:27*

54:2
c Isa 49:19-20
d Ex 35:18
Ex 39:40

54:3
e Isa 49:19

54:4
f Isa 51:7

54:5
g Jer 3:14
h Isa 48:17
i Isa 6:3

54:6
j Isa 49:14-21
k Isa 50:1-2
Isa 62:4,12

54:7
l Isa 26:20
m Isa 49:18

54:8
n Isa 60:10
o ver 10

54:9
p Ge 8:21
q Isa 12:1

[c]10 Hebrew *though you make* [d]11 Dead Sea Scrolls (see also Septuagint); Masoretic Text does not have *the light ⌊of life⌋*. [e]11 Or (with Masoretic Text) 11*He will see the result of the suffering of his soul / and be satisfied* [f]11 Or *by knowledge of him* [g]12 Or *many* [h]12 Or *numerous*

never to rebuke you again.
10 Though the mountains be
shaken[r]
and the hills be removed,
yet my unfailing love for you
will not be shaken[s]
nor my covenant[t] of peace be
removed,"
says the LORD, who has
compassion[u] on you.

11 "O afflicted[v] city, lashed by
storms[w] and not
comforted,[x]
I will build you with stones of
turquoise,[a][y]
your foundations[z] with
sapphires.[b]
12 I will make your battlements of
rubies,
your gates of sparkling jewels,
and all your walls of precious
stones.
13 All your sons will be taught by
the LORD,[a]
and great will be your
children's peace.[b]
14 In righteousness you will be
established:
Tyranny[c] will be far from you;
you will have nothing to fear.
Terror will be far removed;
it will not come near you.
15 If anyone does attack you, it
will not be my doing;
whoever attacks you will
surrender[d] to you.

16 "See, it is I who created the
blacksmith
who fans the coals into flame
and forges a weapon fit for its
work.
And it is I who have created the
destroyer to work havoc;
17 no weapon forged against you
will prevail,[e]
and you will refute[f] every
tongue that accuses you.
This is the heritage of the
servants of the LORD,
and this is their vindication
from me,"
declares the LORD.

54:10
r Ps 46:2
s Isa 51:6
t Ps 89:34
u ver 8

54:11
v Isa 14:32
w Isa 28:2
Isa 29:6
x Isa 51:19
y 1Ch 29:2
Rev 21:18
z Isa 28:16
Rev 21:19-20

54:13
a Jn 6:45*
b Isa 48:18

54:14
c Isa 9:4

54:15
d Isa 41:11-16

54:17
e Isa 29:8
f Isa 45:24-25

55:1
a Jn 4:14
Jn 7:37
b La 5:4
Mt 13:44
Rev 3:18
c SS 5:1
d Hos 14:4
Mt 10:8
Rev 21:6

55:2
e Ps 22:26
Ecc 6:2
Hos 8:7
f Isa 1:19

55:3
g Lev 18:5
Ro 10:5
h Isa 61:8
i Isa 54:8
j Ac 13:34*

55:4
k Jer 30:9
Eze 34:23-24

55:5
l Isa 49:6
m Isa 60:9

55:6
n Ps 32:6
Isa 49:8
2Co 6:1-2
o Isa 65:24

55:7
p Isa 32:7
Isa 59:7
q Isa 44:22
r Isa 54:10
s Isa 1:18
Isa 40:2

Invitation to the Thirsty

55 "Come, all you who are
thirsty,[a]
come to the waters;
and you who have no money,
come, buy[b] and eat!
Come, buy wine and milk[c]
without money and without
cost.[d]
2 Why spend money on what is
not bread,
and your labour on what does
not satisfy?[e]
Listen, listen to me, and eat
what is good,[f]
and your soul will delight in
the richest of fare.
3 Give ear and come to me;
hear me, that your soul may
live.[g]
I will make an everlasting
covenant[h] with you,
my faithful love[i] promised to
David.[j]
4 See, I have made him a witness
to the peoples,
a leader and commander[k] of
the peoples.
5 Surely you will summon
nations[l] you know not,
and nations that do not know
you will hasten to you,
because of the LORD your God,
the Holy One of Israel,
for he has endowed you with
splendour."[m]

6 Seek the LORD while he may be
found;[n]
call[o] on him while he is near.
7 Let the wicked forsake his way
and the evil man his
thoughts.[p]
Let him turn[q] to the LORD, and
he will have mercy[r] on
him,
and to our God, for he will
freely pardon.[s]

8 "For my thoughts are not your
thoughts,

[a]11 The meaning of the Hebrew for this word is uncertain. [b]11 Or *lapis lazuli*

neither are your ways my
ways,"[t]
declares the LORD.
9"As the heavens are higher than
the earth,[u]
so are my ways higher than
your ways
and my thoughts than your
thoughts.
10As the rain[v] and the snow
come down from heaven,
and do not return to it
without watering the earth
and making it bud and flourish,
so that it yields seed for the
sower and bread for the
eater,[w]
11so is my word that goes out
from my mouth:
It will not return to me
empty,[x]
but will accomplish what I
desire
and achieve the purpose[y] for
which I sent it.
12You will go out in joy
and be led forth in peace;[z]
the mountains and hills
will burst into song before
you,
and all the trees[a] of the field
will clap their hands.[b]
13Instead of the thornbush will
grow the pine tree,
and instead of briers[c] the
myrtle[d] will grow.
This will be for the LORD's
renown,[e]
for an everlasting sign,
which will not be destroyed."

Salvation for Others

56 This is what the LORD says:

"Maintain justice[a]
and do what is right,
for my salvation[b] is close at
hand
and my righteousness will
soon be revealed.
2Blessed[c] is the man who does
this,
the man who holds it fast,
who keeps the Sabbath[d]
without desecrating it,
and keeps his hand from doing
any evil."

3Let no foreigner who has bound
himself to the LORD say,
"The LORD will surely exclude
me from his people."
And let not any eunuch[e]
complain,
"I am only a dry tree."

4For this is what the LORD says:

"To the eunuchs who keep my
Sabbaths,
who choose what pleases me
and hold fast to my
covenant—
5to them I will give within my
temple and its walls[f]
a memorial and a name
better than sons and
daughters;
I will give them an everlasting
name
that will not be cut off.[g]
6And foreigners who bind
themselves to the LORD
to serve[h] him,
to love the name of the LORD,
and to worship him,
all who keep the Sabbath[i]
without desecrating it
and who hold fast to my
covenant—
7these I will bring to my holy
mountain[j]
and give them joy in my house
of prayer.
Their burnt offerings and
sacrifices[k]
will be accepted on my altar;
for my house will be called
a house of prayer for all
nations.[l]"[m]
8The Sovereign LORD declares—
he who gathers the exiles of
Israel:
"I will gather[n] still others to
them
besides those already
gathered."

55:8 t Isa 53:6
55:9 u Ps 103:11
55:10 v Isa 30:23 w 2Co 9:10
55:11 x Isa 45:23 y Isa 44:26
55:12 z Isa 54:10,13 a 1Ch 16:33 b Ps 98:8
55:13 c Isa 5:6 d Isa 41:19 e Isa 63:12
56:1 a Isa 1:17 b Ps 85:9
56:2 c Ps 119:2 d Ex 20:8,10 Isa 58:13
56:3 e Jer 38:7 fn Ac 8:27
56:5 f Isa 26:1 Isa 60:18 g Isa 48:19 Isa 55:13
56:6 h Isa 60:7,10 Isa 61:5 i ver 2,4
56:7 j Isa 2:2 k Ro 12:1 Heb 13:15 l Mt 21:13* Lk 19:46* m Mk 11:17*
56:8 n Isa 11:12 Isa 60:3-11 Jn 10:16

God's Accusation Against the Wicked

9Come, all you beasts of the field,[o]
come and devour, all you beasts of the forest!
10Israel's watchmen[p] are blind,
they all lack knowledge;
they are all mute dogs,
they cannot bark;
they lie around and dream,
they love to sleep.[q]
11They are dogs with mighty appetites;
they never have enough.
They are shepherds[r] who lack understanding;[s]
they all turn to their own way,
each seeks his own gain.[t]
12"Come," each one cries, "let me get wine!
Let us drink our fill of beer!
And tomorrow will be like today,
or even far better."[u]

57 The righteous perish,[a]
and no-one ponders it in his heart;[b]
devout men are taken away,
and no-one understands
that the righteous are taken away
to be spared from evil.[c]
2Those who walk uprightly[d]
enter into peace;
they find rest as they lie in death.

3"But you—come here, you sons of a sorceress,
you offspring of adulterers[e] and prostitutes![f]
4Whom are you mocking?
At whom do you sneer
and stick out your tongue?
Are you not a brood of rebels,
the offspring of liars?
5You burn with lust among the oaks
and under every spreading tree;[g]
you sacrifice your children[h] in the ravines

56:9
o Isa 18:6
Jer 12:9
56:10
p Eze 3:17
q Na 3:18
56:11
r Eze 34:2
s Isa 1:3
t Isa 57:17
Eze 13:19
Mic 3:11
56:12
u Ps 10:6
Lk 12:18-19
57:1
a Ps 12:1
b Isa 42:25
c 2Ki 22:20
57:2
d Isa 26:7
57:3
e Mt 16:4
f Isa 1:21
57:5
g 2Ki 16:4
h Lev 18:21
Ps 106:37-38
Eze 16:20
57:6
i Jer 3:9
j Jer 7:18
k Jer 5:9,29
Jer 9:9
57:7
l Jer 3:6
Eze 16:16
57:8
m Eze 16:26
Eze 23:7
n Eze 23:18
57:9
o Eze 23:16,40
57:10
p Jer 2:25
Jer 18:12
57:11
q Pr 29:25
r Jer 2:32
Jer 3:21
s Ps 50:21

and under the overhanging crags.
6⌞The idols⌟[i] among the smooth stones of the ravines are your portion;
they, they are your lot.
Yes, to them you have poured out drink offerings[j]
and offered grain offerings.
In the light of these things, should I relent?[k]
7You have made your bed on a high and lofty hill;[l]
there you went up to offer your sacrifices.
8Behind your doors and your doorposts
you have put your pagan symbols.
Forsaking me, you uncovered your bed,
you climbed into it and opened it wide;
you made a pact with those whose beds you love,[m]
and you looked on their nakedness.[n]
9You went to Molech[a] with olive oil
and increased your perfumes.
You sent your ambassadors[b][o] far away;
you descended to the grave[c] itself!
10You were wearied by all your ways,
but you would not say, 'It is hopeless.'[p]
You found renewal of your strength,
and so you did not faint.

11"Whom have you so dreaded and feared[q]
that you have been false to me,
and have neither remembered[r] me
nor pondered this in your hearts?
Is it not because I have long been silent[s]

[a]9 Or *to the king* [b]9 Or *idols* [c]9 Hebrew *Sheol*

that you do not fear me?
12 I will expose your righteousness
and your works,[t]
and they will not benefit you.
13 When you cry out[u] for help,
let your collection ⌊of idols⌋
save you!
The wind will carry all of them
off,
a mere breath will blow them
away.
But the man who makes me his
refuge
will inherit the land[v]
and possess my holy
mountain."[w]

Comfort for the Contrite

14 And it will be said:

"Build up, build up, prepare the
road!
Remove the obstacles out of
the way of my people."[x]
15 For this is what the high and
lofty[y] One says—
he who lives for ever,[z] whose
name is holy:
"I live in a high and holy place,
but also with him who is
contrite[a] and lowly in
spirit,[b]
to revive the spirit of the lowly
and to revive the heart of the
contrite.[c]
16 I will not accuse for ever,
nor will I always be angry,[d]
for then the spirit of man would
grow faint before me—
the breath of man that I have
created.
17 I was enraged by his sinful
greed;[e]
I punished him, and hid my
face in anger,
yet he kept on in his wilful
ways.[f]
18 I have seen his ways, but I will
heal[g] him;
I will guide him and restore
comfort[h] to him,
19 creating praise on the lips[i] of
the mourners in Israel.

57:12
t Isa 29:15
Mic 3:2-4,8

57:13
u Jer 22:20
Jer 30:15
v Ps 37:9
w Isa 65:9-11

57:14
x Isa 62:10
Jer 18:15

57:15
y Isa 52:13
z Dt 33:27
a Ps 147:3
b Ps 34:18
Ps 51:17
Isa 66:2
c Isa 61:1

57:16
d Ps 85:5
Ps 103:9
Mic 7:18

57:17
e Isa 56:11
f Isa 1:4

57:18
g Isa 30:26
h Isa 61:1-3

57:19
i Isa 6:7
Heb 13:15
j Eph 2:17
k Ac 2:39

57:20
l Job 18:5-21

57:21
m Isa 59:8
n Isa 48:22

58:1
a Isa 40:6
b Isa 48:8

58:2
c Isa 48:1
Tit 1:16
Jas 4:8
d Isa 29:13

58:3
e Lev 16:29
f Mal 3:14
g Isa 22:13
Zec 7:5-6

58:4
h 1Ki 21:9-13
Isa 59:6
i Isa 59:2

58:5
j Zec 7:5
k 1Ki 21:27

Peace, peace,[j] to those far and
near,"[k]
says the LORD. "And I will heal
them."
20 But the wicked[l] are like the
tossing sea,
which cannot rest,
whose waves cast up mire and
mud.
21 "There is no peace,"[m] says my
God, "for the wicked."[n]

True Fasting

58 "Shout it aloud,[a] do not
hold back.
Raise your voice like a
trumpet.
Declare to my people their
rebellion[b]
and to the house of Jacob their
sins.
2 For day after day they seek[c]
me out;
they seem eager to know my
ways,
as if they were a nation that
does what is right
and has not forsaken the
commands of its God.
They ask me for just decisions
and seem eager for God to
come near[d] them.
3 'Why have we fasted,'[e] they
say,
'and you have not seen it?
Why have we humbled
ourselves,
and you have not noticed?'[f]

"Yet on the day of your fasting,
you do as you please[g]
and exploit all your workers.
4 Your fasting ends in quarrelling
and strife,[h]
and in striking each other with
wicked fists.
You cannot fast as you do today
and expect your voice to be
heard[i] on high.
5 Is this the kind of fast[j] I have
chosen,
only a day for a man to
humble[k] himself?

Is it only for bowing one's head
like a reed
and for lying on sackcloth and
ashes?[l]
Is that what you call a fast,
a day acceptable to the LORD?

6"Is not this the kind of fasting I
have chosen:
to loose the chains of injustice[m]
and untie the cords of the
yoke,
to set the oppressed[n] free
and break every yoke?
7Is it not to share your food with
the hungry[o]
and to provide the poor
wanderer with shelter[p]—
when you see the naked, to
clothe[q] him,
and not to turn away from
your own flesh and blood?[r]
8Then your light will break forth
like the dawn,[s]
and your healing[t] will quickly
appear;
then your righteousness[a] will
go before you,
and the glory of the LORD will
be your rear guard.[u]
9Then you will call,[v] and the
LORD will answer;
you will cry for help, and he
will say: Here am I.

"If you do away with the yoke
of oppression,
with the pointing finger[w] and
malicious talk,[x]
10and if you spend yourselves on
behalf of the hungry
and satisfy the needs of the
oppressed,[y]
then your light[z] will rise in the
darkness,
and your night will become
like the noonday.[a]
11The LORD will guide you
always;
he will satisfy your needs[b] in
a sun-scorched land
and will strengthen your
frame.
You will be like a well-watered
garden,[c]
like a spring[d] whose waters
never fail.
12Your people will rebuild the
ancient ruins[e]
and will raise up the age-old
foundations;[f]
you will be called Repairer of
Broken Walls,
Restorer of Streets with
Dwellings.

13"If you keep your feet from
breaking the Sabbath[g]
and from doing as you please
on my holy day,
if you call the Sabbath a
delight[h]
and the LORD's holy day
honourable,
and if you honour it by not
going your own way
and not doing as you please or
speaking idle words,
14then you will find your joy[i] in
the LORD,
and I will cause you to ride on
the heights[j] of the land
and to feast on the inheritance
of your father Jacob."
The mouth of the LORD
has spoken.[k]

Sin, Confession and Redemption

59 Surely the arm of the
LORD is not too short[a] to
save,
nor his ear too dull to hear.[b]
2But your iniquities have
separated
you from your God;
your sins have hidden his face
from you,
so that he will not hear.[c]
3For your hands are stained with
blood,[d]
your fingers with guilt.
Your lips have spoken lies,
and your tongue mutters
wicked things.
4No-one calls for justice;
no-one pleads his case with
integrity.

58:5 *l* Job 2:8
58:6 *m* Ne 5:10-11 *n* Jer 34:9
58:7 *o* Eze 18:16 Lk 3:11 *p* Isa 16:4 Heb 13:2 *q* Job 31:19-20 Mt 25:36 *r* Ge 29:14 Lk 10:31-32
58:8 *s* Job 11:17 *t* Isa 30:26 *u* Ex 14:19
58:9 *v* Ps 50:15 *w* Pr 6:13 *x* Ps 12:2 Isa 59:13
58:10 *y* Dt 15:7-8 *z* Isa 42:16 *a* Job 11:17
58:11 *b* Ps 107:9 *c* SS 4:15 *d* Jn 4:14
58:12 *e* Isa 49:8 *f* Isa 44:28
58:13 *g* Isa 56:2 *h* Ps 84:2,10
58:14 *i* Job 22:26 *j* Dt 32:13 *k* Isa 1:20
59:1 *a* Nu 11:23 Isa 50:2 *b* Isa 58:9 Isa 65:24
59:2 *c* Isa 1:15 Isa 58:4
59:3 *d* Isa 1:15

a8 Or *your righteous One*

They rely on empty arguments and speak lies;
they conceive trouble and give birth to evil.[e]
5They hatch the eggs of vipers and spin a spider's web.[f]
Whoever eats their eggs will die,
and when one is broken, an adder is hatched.
6Their cobwebs are useless for clothing;
they cannot cover themselves with what they make.[g]
Their deeds are evil deeds,
and acts of violence[h] are in their hands.
7Their feet rush into sin;
they are swift to shed innocent blood.[i]
Their thoughts are evil thoughts;[j]
ruin and destruction mark their ways.[k]
8The way of peace they do not know;
there is no justice in their paths.
They have turned them into crooked roads;
no-one who walks in them will know peace.[l]

9So justice is far from us,
and righteousness does not reach us.
We look for light, but all is darkness;[m]
for brightness, but we walk in deep shadows.
10Like the blind[n] we grope along the wall,
feeling our way like men without eyes.
At midday we stumble[o] as if it were twilight;
among the strong, we are like the dead.[p]
11We all growl like bears;
we moan mournfully like doves.[q]
We look for justice, but find none;
for deliverance, but it is far away.
12For our offences[r] are many in your sight,
and our sins testify[s] against us.
Our offences are ever with us,
and we acknowledge our iniquities:
13rebellion and treachery against the LORD,
turning our backs[t] on our God,
fomenting oppression[u] and revolt,
uttering lies[v] our hearts have conceived.
14So justice is driven back,
and righteousness[w] stands at a distance;
truth[x] has stumbled in the streets,
honesty cannot enter.
15Truth is nowhere to be found,
and whoever shuns evil becomes a prey.

The LORD looked and was displeased
that there was no justice.
16He saw that there was no-one,[y]
he was appalled that there was no-one to intervene;
so his own arm worked salvation[z] for him,
and his own righteousness sustained him.
17He put on righteousness as his breastplate,[a]
and the helmet[b] of salvation on his head;
he put on the garments[c] of vengeance
and wrapped himself in zeal[d] as in a cloak.
18According to what they have done,
so will he repay
wrath to his enemies
and retribution to his foes;
he will repay the islands their due.
19From the west,[e] men will fear the name of the LORD,

59:4 e Job 15:35; Ps 7:14
59:5 f Job 8:14
59:6 g Isa 28:20; h Isa 58:4
59:7 i Pr 6:17; j Mk 7:21-22; k Ro 3:15-17*
59:8 l Isa 57:21; Lk 1:79
59:9 m Isa 5:30; Isa 8:20
59:10 n Dt 28:29; o Isa 8:15; p La 3:6
59:11 q Isa 38:14; Eze 7:16
59:12 r Ezr 9:6; s Isa 3:9
59:13 t Pr 30:9; Mt 10:33; Tit 1:16; u Isa 5:7; v Mk 7:21-22
59:14 w Isa 1:21; x Isa 48:1
59:16 y Isa 41:28; z Ps 98:1; Isa 63:5
59:17 a Eph 6:14; b Eph 6:17; 1Th 5:8; c Isa 63:3; d Isa 9:7
59:19 e Isa 49:12

and from the rising of the
sun,[f] they will revere his
glory.
For he will come like a pent-up
flood
that the breath of the LORD
drives along.[a]

20"The Redeemer will come to
Zion,
to those in Jacob who repent
of their sins,"[g]
declares the LORD.

21"As for me, this is my covenant
with them," says the LORD. "My
Spirit,[h] who is on you, and my
words that I have put in your mouth
will not depart from your mouth, or
from the mouths of your children,
or from the mouths of their descendants from this time on and for
ever," says the LORD.

The Glory of Zion

60 "Arise,[a] shine, for your
light[b] has come,
and the glory of the LORD
rises upon you.
2See, darkness covers the earth
and thick darkness[c] is over
the peoples,
but the LORD rises upon you
and his glory appears over
you.
3Nations[d] will come to your
light,
and kings[e] to the brightness
of your dawn.

4"Lift up your eyes and look
about you:
All assemble[f] and come to
you;
your sons come from afar,
and your daughters[g] are
carried on the arm.[h]
5Then you will look and be
radiant,
your heart will throb and
swell with joy;
the wealth on the seas will be
brought to you,
to you the riches of the
nations will come.
6Herds of camels will cover your
land,
young camels of Midian[i] and
Ephah.[j]
And all from Sheba[k] will come,
bearing gold and incense[l]
and proclaiming the praise[m]
of the LORD.
7All Kedar's[n] flocks will be
gathered to you,
the rams of Nebaioth will
serve you;
they will be accepted as
offerings on my altar,
and I will adorn my glorious
temple.[o]

8"Who are these[p] that fly along
like clouds,
like doves to their nests?
9Surely the islands[q] look to me;
in the lead are the ships of
Tarshish,[a][r]
bringing[s] your sons from afar,
with their silver and gold,
to the honour of the LORD your
God,
the Holy One of Israel,
for he has endowed you with
splendour.[t]

10"Foreigners[u] will rebuild your
walls,
and their kings[v] will serve
you.
Though in anger I struck you,
in favour I will show you
compassion.[w]
11Your gates[x] will always stand
open,
they will never be shut, day or
night,
so that men may bring you the
wealth of the nations[y]—
their kings[z] led in triumphal
procession.
12For the nation or kingdom that
will not serve[a] you will
perish;
it will be utterly ruined.

59:19 f Ps 113:3
59:20 g Ac 2:38-39; Ro 11:26-27*
59:21 h Isa 11:2; Isa 44:3
60:1 a Isa 52:2 b Eph 5:14
60:2 c Jer 13:16; Col 1:13
60:3 d Isa 45:14; Rev 21:24 e Isa 49:23
60:4 f Isa 11:12 g Isa 43:6 h Isa 49:20-22
60:6 i Ge 25:2 j Ge 25:4 k Ps 72:10 l Isa 43:23; Mt 2:11 m Isa 42:10
60:7 n Ge 25:13 o ver 13; Hag 2:3,7,9
60:8 p Isa 49:21
60:9 q Isa 11:11 r Isa 2:16 *fn* s Isa 14:2; Isa 43:6 t Isa 55:5
60:10 u Isa 14:1-2 v Isa 49:23; Rev 21:24 w Isa 54:8
60:11 x ver 18; Isa 62:10; Rev 21:25 y ver 5; Rev 21:26 z Ps 149:8
60:12 a Isa 14:2

a19 Or *When the enemy comes in like a flood, / the Spirit of the LORD will put him to flight*
a9 Or *the trading ships*

13"The glory of Lebanon[b] will
come to you,
the pine, the fir and the
cypress together,[c]
to adorn the place of my
sanctuary;
and I will glorify the place of
my feet.[d]
14The sons of your oppressors[e]
will come bowing before
you;
all who despise you will bow
down[f] at your feet
and will call you the City of the
LORD,
Zion[g] of the Holy One of
Israel.

15"Although you have been
forsaken[h] and hated,
with no-one travelling[i]
through,
I will make you the everlasting
pride[j]
and the joy[k] of all
generations.
16You will drink the milk of
nations
and be nursed[l] at royal
breasts.
Then you will know that I, the
LORD, am your Saviour,
your Redeemer,[m] the Mighty
One of Jacob.
17Instead of bronze I will bring
you gold,
and silver in place of iron.
Instead of wood I will bring you
bronze,
and iron in place of stones.
I will make peace your
governor
and righteousness your ruler.
18No longer will violence be
heard in your land,
nor ruin or destruction within
your borders,
but you will call your walls
Salvation[n]
and your gates Praise.
19The sun will no more be your
light by day,
nor will the brightness of the
moon shine on you,

60:13 [b] Isa 35:2 [c] Isa 41:19 [d] 1Ch 28:2; Ps 132:7
60:14 [e] Isa 14:2 [f] Isa 49:23; Rev 3:9 [g] Heb 12:22
60:15 [h] Isa 1:7-9; Isa 6:12 [i] Isa 33:8 [j] Isa 4:2 [k] Isa 65:18
60:16 [l] Isa 49:23; Isa 66:11,12 [m] Isa 59:20
60:18 [n] Isa 26:1
60:19 [o] Rev 22:5 [p] Zec 2:5; Rev 21:23
60:20 [q] Isa 30:26 [r] Isa 35:10
60:21 [s] Rev 21:27 [t] Ps 37:11,22; Isa 57:13; Isa 61:7 [u] Mt 15:13 [v] Isa 19:25; Isa 29:23; Eph 2:10 [w] Isa 52:1
61:1 [a] Isa 11:2 [b] Ps 45:7 [c] Mt 11:5; Lk 7:22 [d] Isa 57:15 [e] Isa 42:7; Isa 49:9
61:2 [f] Isa 49:8; Lk 4:18-19* [g] Isa 34:8 [h] Isa 57:18; Mt 5:4

for the LORD will be your
everlasting light,[o]
and your God will be your
glory.[p]
20Your sun[q] will never set again,
and your moon will wane no
more;
the LORD will be your
everlasting light,
and your days of sorrow[r] will
end.
21Then will all your people be
righteous[s]
and they will possess[t] the
land for ever.
They are the shoot I have
planted,[u]
the work of my hands,[v]
for the display of my
splendour.[w]
22The least of you will become a
thousand,
the smallest a mighty nation.
I am the LORD;
in its time I will do this
swiftly."

The Year of the LORD's Favour

61 The Spirit[a] of the
Sovereign LORD is on me,
because the LORD has
anointed[b] me
to preach good news to the
poor.[c]
He has sent me to bind up[d] the
broken-hearted,
to proclaim freedom for the
captives[e]
and release from darkness for
the prisoners,[a]
2to proclaim the year of the
LORD's favour[f]
and the day of vengeance[g] of
our God,
to comfort[h] all who mourn,
3 and provide for those who
grieve in Zion—
to bestow on them a crown of
beauty
instead of ashes,
the oil of gladness

[a] *1* Hebrew; Septuagint *the blind*

instead of mourning,
and a garment of praise
instead of a spirit of despair.
They will be called oaks of
righteousness,
a planting of the LORD
for the display of his
splendour.[i]

4They will rebuild the ancient
ruins[j]
and restore the places long
devastated;
they will renew the ruined
cities
that have been devastated for
generations.
5Aliens[k] will shepherd your
flocks;
foreigners will work your
fields and vineyards.
6And you will be called priests[l]
of the LORD,
you will be named ministers
of our God.
You will feed on the wealth[m] of
nations,
and in their riches you will
boast.

7Instead of their shame
my people will receive a
double[n] portion,
and instead of disgrace
they will rejoice in their
inheritance;
and so they will inherit a double
portion in their land,
and everlasting joy will be
theirs.
8"For I, the LORD, love justice;[o]
I hate robbery and iniquity.
In my faithfulness I will reward
them
and make an everlasting
covenant[p] with them.
9Their descendants will be
known among the nations
and their offspring among the
peoples.
All who see them will
acknowledge
that they are a people the
LORD has blessed."

61:3
i Isa 60:20-21

61:4
j Isa 49:8
Eze 36:33
Am 9:14

61:5
k Isa 14:1-2

61:6
l Ex 19:6
1Pe 2:5
m Isa 60:11

61:7
n Isa 40:2
Zec 9:12

61:8
o Ps 11:7
Isa 5:16
p Isa 55:3

61:10
q Isa 25:9
Hab 3:18
r Ps 132:9
Isa 52:1
s Isa 49:18
Rev 21:2

61:11
t Ps 85:11

62:1
a Isa 1:26

62:2
b Isa 52:10
Isa 60:3
c ver 4,12

62:3
d Isa 28:5
Zec 9:16
1Th 2:19

62:4
e Isa 54:6
f Jer 32:41
Zep 3:17
g Jer 3:14
Hos 2:19

10I delight greatly in the LORD;
my soul rejoices[q] in my God.
For he has clothed me with
garments of salvation
and arrayed me in a robe of
righteousness,[r]
as a bridegroom adorns his
head like a priest,
and as a bride[s] adorns herself
with her jewels.
11For as the soil makes the young
plant come up
and a garden causes seeds to
grow,
so the Sovereign LORD will
make righteousness[t] and
praise
spring up before all nations.

Zion's New Name

62 For Zion's sake I will not
keep silent,
for Jerusalem's sake I will not
remain quiet,
till her righteousness[a] shines
out like the dawn,
her salvation like a blazing
torch.
2The nations[b] will see your
righteousness,
and all kings your glory;
you will be called by a new
name[c]
that the mouth of the LORD
will bestow.
3You will be a crown[d] of
splendour in the LORD's
hand,
a royal diadem in the hand of
your God.
4No longer will they call you
Deserted,[e]
or name your land Desolate.
But you will be called
Hephzibah,[a]
and your land Beulah;[b]
for the LORD will take delight[f]
in you,
and your land will be
married.[g]

[a]4 *Hephzibah* means *my delight is in her.*
[b]4 *Beulah* means *married.*

5As a young man marries a
maiden,
so will your sons[c] marry you;
as a bridegroom rejoices over
his bride,
so will your God rejoice[h] over
you.

6I have posted watchmen[i] on
your walls, O Jerusalem;
they will never be silent day
or night.
You who call on the LORD,
give yourselves no rest,
7and give him no rest[j] till he
establishes Jerusalem
and makes her the praise of
the earth.

8The LORD has sworn by his
right hand
and by his mighty arm:
"Never again will I give your
grain[k]
as food for your enemies,
and never again will foreigners
drink the new wine
for which you have toiled;
9but those who harvest it will eat
it
and praise the LORD,
and those who gather the
grapes will drink it
in the courts of my
sanctuary."

10Pass through, pass through the
gates![l]
Prepare the way for the
people.
Build up, build up the
highway![m][n]
Remove the stones.
Raise a banner[o] for the nations.

11The LORD has made
proclamation
to the ends of the earth:
"Say to the Daughter of Zion,[p]
'See, your Saviour comes![q]
See, his reward is with him,
and his recompense
accompanies him.' "[r]
12They will be called[s] the Holy
People,[t]
the Redeemed[u] of the LORD;
and you will be called Sought
After,
the City No Longer
Deserted.[v]

God's Day of Vengeance and Redemption

63 Who is this coming from
Edom,
from Bozrah,[a] with his
garments stained crimson?
Who is this, robed in splendour,
striding forward in the
greatness of his strength?

"It is I, speaking in
righteousness,
mighty to save."[b]

2Why are your garments red,
like those of one treading the
winepress?

3"I have trodden the winepress[c]
alone;
from the nations no-one was
with me.
I trampled them in my anger
and trod them down in my
wrath;[d]
their blood spattered my
garments,[e]
and I stained all my clothing.
4For the day of vengeance was
in my heart,
and the year of my
redemption has come.
5I looked, but there was no-one[f]
to help,
I was appalled that no-one
gave support;
so my own arm[g] worked
salvation for me,
and my own wrath sustained
me.[h]
6I trampled the nations in my
anger;
in my wrath I made them
drunk[i]
and poured their blood[j] on
the ground."

62:5 h Isa 65:19
62:6 i Isa 52:8; Eze 3:17
62:7 j Mt 15:21-28; Lk 18:1-8
62:8 k Dt 28:30-33; Isa 1:7; Jer 5:17
62:10 l Isa 60:11; m Isa 57:14; n Isa 11:16; o Isa 11:10
62:11 p Zec 9:9; Mt 21:5; q Rev 22:12; r Isa 40:10
62:12 s ver 4; t 1Pe 2:9; u Isa 35:9; v Isa 42:16
63:1 a Am 1:12; b Zep 3:17
63:3 c Rev 14:20; Rev 19:15; d Isa 22:5; e Rev 19:13
63:5 f Isa 41:28; g Ps 44:3; Ps 98:1; h Isa 59:16
63:6 i Isa 29:9; j Isa 34:3

c5 Or *Builder*

Praise and Prayer

7I will tell of the kindnesses[k] of
the LORD,
the deeds for which he is to be
praised,
according to all the LORD has
done for us—
yes, the many good things he
has done
for the house of Israel,
according to his compassion[l]
and many kindnesses.
8He said, "Surely they are my
people,[m]
sons who will not be false to
me";
and so he became their
Saviour.
9In all their distress he too was
distressed,
and the angel of his presence[n]
saved them.
In his love and mercy he
redeemed[o] them;
he lifted them up and
carried[p] them
all the days of old.
10Yet they rebelled[q]
and grieved his Holy Spirit.[r]
So he turned and became their
enemy[s]
and he himself fought against
them.
11Then his people recalled[a] the
days of old,
the days of Moses and his
people—
where is he who brought them
through the sea,[t]
with the shepherd of his
flock?
Where is he who set
his Holy Spirit[u] among them,
12who sent his glorious arm of
power
to be at Moses' right hand,
who divided the waters[v] before
them,
to gain for himself everlasting
renown,
13who led[w] them through the
depths?
Like a horse in open country,

63:7 k Isa 54:8 l Ps 51:1 Eph 2:4
63:8 m Isa 51:4
63:9 n Ex 33:14 o Dt 7:7-8 p Dt 1:31
63:10 q Ps 78:40 r Ps 51:11 Ac 7:51 Eph 4:30 s Ps 106:40
63:11 t Ex 14:22,30 u Nu 11:17
63:12 v Ex 14:21-22 Isa 11:15
63:13 w Dt 32:12 x Jer 31:9
63:15 y Dt 26:15 Ps 80:14 z Ps 123:1 a Isa 9:7 Isa 26:11 b Jer 31:20 Hos 11:8
63:16 c Job 14:21 d Isa 41:14 Isa 44:6
63:17 e Isa 29:13 f Nu 10:36
63:18 g Ps 74:3-8
64:1 a Ps 18:9 Ps 144:5 b Mic 1:3 c Ex 19:18

they did not stumble;[x]
14like cattle that go down to the
plain,
they were given rest by the
Spirit of the LORD.
This is how you guided your
people
to make for yourself a
glorious name.
15Look down from heaven[y] and
see
from your lofty throne,[z] holy
and glorious.
Where are your zeal[a] and your
might?
Your tenderness and
compassion[b] are withheld
from us.
16But you are our Father,
though Abraham does not
know us
or Israel acknowledge[c] us;
you, O LORD, are our Father,
our Redeemer[d] from of old is
your name.
17Why, O LORD, do you make us
wander from your ways
and harden our hearts so we
do not revere[e] you?
Return[f] for the sake of your
servants,
the tribes that are your
inheritance.
18For a little while your people
possessed your holy place,
but now our enemies have
trampled down your
sanctuary.[g]
19We are yours from of old;
but you have not ruled over
them,
they have not been called by
your name.[b]

64 Oh, that you would rend
the heavens[a] and come
down,[b]
that the mountains[c] would
tremble before you!
2As when fire sets twigs ablaze

[a]11 Or *But may he recall* [b]19 Or *We are like those you have never ruled, / like those never called by your name*

and causes water to boil,
come down to make your name
known to your enemies
and cause the nations to
quake[d] before you!
3For when you did awesome[e]
things that we did not
expect,
you came down, and the
mountains trembled before
you.
4Since ancient times no-one has
heard,
no ear has perceived,
no eye has seen any God
besides you,
who acts on behalf of those
who wait for him.[f]
5You come to the help of those
who gladly do right,[g]
who remember your ways.
But when we continued to sin
against them,
you were angry.
How then can we be saved?
6All of us have become like one
who is unclean,
and all our righteous[h] acts
are like filthy rags;
we all shrivel up like a leaf,[i]
and like the wind our sins
sweep us away.
7No-one[j] calls on your name
or strives to lay hold of you;
for you have hidden[k] your face
from us
and made us waste away[l]
because of our sins.
8Yet, O LORD, you are our
Father.[m]
We are the clay, you are the
potter;[n]
we are all the work of your
hand.
9Do not be angry[o] beyond
measure, O LORD;
do not remember our sins[p]
for ever.
Oh, look upon us we pray,
for we are all your people.
10Your sacred cities have become
a desert;
even Zion is a desert,
Jerusalem a desolation.
11Our holy and glorious temple,[q]
where our fathers praised
you,
has been burned with fire,
and all that we treasured[r] lies
in ruins.
12After all this, O LORD, will you
hold yourself back?[s]
Will you keep silent[t] and
punish us beyond measure?

Judgment and Salvation

65 "I revealed myself to
those who did not ask for
me;
I was found by those who did
not seek me.[a]
To a nation[b] that did not call on
my name,
I said, 'Here am I, here am I.'
2All day long I have held out my
hands
to an obstinate people,[c]
who walk in ways not good,
pursuing their own
imaginations[d]—
3a people who continually
provoke me
to my very face,[e]
offering sacrifices in gardens[f]
and burning incense on altars
of brick;
4who sit among the graves
and spend their nights keeping
secret vigil;
who eat the flesh of pigs,[g]
and whose pots hold broth of
unclean meat;
5who say, 'Keep away; don't
come near me,
for I am too sacred[h] for you!'
Such people are smoke in my
nostrils,
a fire that keeps burning all
day.
6"See, it stands written before
me;
I will not keep silent[i] but will
pay back[j] in full;
I will pay it back into their
laps[k]—

64:2 d Ps 99:1; Jer 5:22; Jer 33:9
64:3 e Ps 65:5
64:4 f Isa 30:18; 1Co 2:9*
64:5 g Isa 26:8
64:6 h Isa 46:12; Isa 48:1; i Ps 90:5-6
64:7 j Isa 59:4; k Dt 31:18; Isa 1:15; Isa 54:8; l Isa 9:18
64:8 m Isa 63:16; n Isa 29:16
64:9 o Isa 57:17; Isa 60:10; p Isa 43:25
64:11 q Ps 74:3-7; r La 1:7,10
64:12 s Ps 74:10-11; Isa 42:14; t Ps 83:1
65:1 a Hos 1:10; Ro 9:24-26; Ro 10:20*; b Eph 2:12
65:2 c Isa 1:2,23; Ro 10:21*; d Ps 81:11-12; Isa 66:18
65:3 e Job 1:11; f Isa 1:29
65:4 g Lev 11:7
65:5 h Mt 9:11; Lk 7:39; Lk 18:9-12
65:6 i Ps 50:3; j Jer 16:18; k Ps 79:12

7both your sins[l] and the sins of
your fathers,"[m]
says the LORD.
"Because they burned sacrifices
on the mountains
and defied me on the hills,[n]
I will measure into their laps
the full payment for their
former deeds."

8This is what the LORD says:

"As when juice is still found in
a cluster of grapes
and men say, 'Don't destroy it,
there is yet some good in it,'
so will I do on behalf of my
servants;
I will not destroy them all.
9I will bring forth descendants[o]
from Jacob,
and from Judah those who will
possess[p] my mountains;
my chosen people will inherit
them,
and there will my servants
live.[q]
10Sharon[r] will become a pasture
for flocks,
and the Valley of Achor[s] a
resting place for herds,
for my people who seek[t] me.

11"But as for you who forsake[u]
the LORD
and forget my holy mountain,
who spread a table for Fortune
and fill bowls of mixed wine
for Destiny,
12I will destine you for the
sword,[v]
and you will all bend down for
the slaughter;
for I called but you did not
answer,[w]
I spoke but you did not
listen.[x]
You did evil in my sight
and chose what displeases
me."

13Therefore this is what the Sovereign LORD says:

"My servants will eat,[y]
but you will go hungry;
my servants will drink,
but you will go thirsty;[z]
my servants will rejoice,
but you will be put to shame.[a]
14My servants will sing
out of the joy of their hearts,
but you will cry out[b]
from anguish of heart
and wail in brokenness of
spirit.
15You will leave your name
to my chosen ones as a
curse;[c]
the Sovereign LORD will put you
to death,
but to his servants he will give
another name.
16Whoever invokes a blessing in
the land
will do so by the God of
truth;[d]
he who takes an oath in the land
will swear[e] by the God of
truth.
For the past troubles will be
forgotten
and hidden from my eyes.

New Heavens and a New Earth

17"Behold, I will create
new heavens and a new
earth.[f]
The former things will not be
remembered,[g]
nor will they come to mind.
18But be glad and rejoice[h] for
ever
in what I will create,
for I will create Jerusalem to
be a delight
and its people a joy.
19I will rejoice[i] over Jerusalem
and take delight in my people;
the sound of weeping and of
crying[j]
will be heard in it no more.

20"Never again will there be in it
an infant who lives but a few
days,
or an old man who does not
live out his years;[k]
he who dies at a hundred
will be thought a mere youth;

65:7 l Isa 22:14 m Ex 20:5 n Isa 57:7
65:9 o Isa 45:19 p Am 9:11-15 q Isa 32:18
65:10 r Isa 35:2 s Jos 7:26 t Isa 51:1
65:11 u Dt 29:24-25 Isa 1:28
65:12 v Isa 27:1 w Pr 1:24-25 Isa 41:28 Isa 66:4 x 2Ch 36:15-16 Jer 7:13
65:13 y Isa 1:19 z Isa 41:17 a Isa 44:9
65:14 b Mt 8:12 Lk 13:28
65:15 c Zec 8:13
65:16 d Ps 31:5 e Isa 19:18
65:17 f Isa 66:22 2Pe 3:13 g Isa 43:18 Jer 3:16
65:18 h Ps 98:1-9 Isa 25:9
65:19 i Isa 35:10 Isa 62:5 j Isa 25:8 Rev 7:17
65:20 k Ecc 8:13

he who fails to reach[a] a
hundred
will be considered accursed.
21 They will build houses[l] and
dwell in them;
they will plant vineyards and
eat their fruit.[m]
22 No longer will they build houses
and others live in them,
or plant and others eat.
For as the days of a tree,[n]
so will be the days[o] of my
people;
my chosen ones will long enjoy
the works of their hands.
23 They will not toil in vain
or bear children doomed to
misfortune;
for they will be a people
blessed[p] by the LORD,
they and their descendants[q]
with them.
24 Before they call[r] I will answer;
while they are still speaking[s]
I will hear.
25 The wolf and the lamb[t] will
feed together,
and the lion will eat straw like
the ox,
but dust will be the serpent's[u]
food.
They will neither harm nor
destroy
on all my holy mountain,"
says the LORD.

Judgment and Hope

66 This is what the LORD says:
"Heaven is my throne,[a]
and the earth is my footstool.[b]
Where is the house[c] you will
build for me?
Where will my resting place
be?
2 Has not my hand made all these
things,[d]
and so they came into being?"
declares the LORD.
"This is the one I esteem:
he who is humble and contrite
in spirit,[e]
and trembles at my word.[f]
3 But whoever sacrifices a bull[g]
is like one who kills a man,
and whoever offers a lamb,
like one who breaks a dog's
neck;
whoever makes a grain offering
is like one who presents pig's
blood,
and whoever burns memorial
incense,[h]
like one who worships an idol.
They have chosen their own
ways,[i]
and their souls delight in their
abominations;
4 so I also will choose harsh
treatment for them
and will bring upon them what
they dread.[j]
For when I called, no-one
answered,[k]
when I spoke, no-one listened.
They did evil[l] in my sight
and chose what displeases
me."[m]

5 Hear the word of the LORD,
you who tremble at his word;
"Your brothers who hate[n] you,
and exclude you because of
my name, have said,
'Let the LORD be glorified,
that we may see your joy!'
Yet they will be put to
shame.[o]
6 Hear that uproar from the city,
hear that noise from the
temple!
It is the sound of the LORD
repaying[p] his enemies all
they deserve.

7 "Before she goes into labour,[q]
she gives birth;
before the pains come upon her,
she delivers a son.[r]
8 Who has ever heard of such a
thing?
Who has ever seen[s] such
things?

65:21 l Isa 32:18 m Isa 37:30 Am 9:14
65:22 n Ps 92:12-14 o Ps 21:4 Ps 91:16
65:23 p Dt 28:3-12 Isa 61:9 q Ac 2:39
65:24 r Isa 55:6 s Da 9:20-23 Da 10:12
65:25 t Isa 11:6 u Ge 3:14 Mic 7:17
66:1 a Mt 23:22 b 1Ki 8:27 Mt 5:34-35 c 2Sa 7:7 Jn 4:20-21 Ac 7:49* Ac 17:24
66:2 d Isa 40:26 Ac 7:50* e Isa 57:15 Mt 5:3-4 Lk 18:13-14 f Ezr 9:4
66:3 g Isa 1:11 h Lev 2:2 i Isa 57:17
66:4 j Pr 10:24 k Pr 1:24 Jer 7:13 l 2Ki 21:2,4,6 m Isa 65:12
66:5 n Ps 38:20 Isa 60:15 o Lk 13:17
66:6 p Isa 65:6 Joel 3:7
66:7 q Isa 54:1 r Rev 12:5
66:8 s Isa 64:4

a20 Or / *the sinner who reaches*

Can a country be born in a day
or a nation be brought forth in
a moment?
Yet no sooner is Zion in labour
than she gives birth to her
children.
9Do I bring to the moment of
birth[t]
and not give delivery?" says
the LORD.
"Do I close up the womb
when I bring to delivery?"
says your God.
10"Rejoice[u] with Jerusalem and
be glad for her,
all you who love[v] her;
rejoice greatly with her,
all you who mourn over her.
11For you will nurse[w] and be
satisfied
at her comforting breasts;
you will drink deeply
and delight in her overflowing
abundance."

12For this is what the LORD says:

"I will extend peace to her like
a river,[x]
and the wealth[y] of nations
like a flooding stream;
you will nurse and be carried[z]
on her arm
and dandled on her knees.
13As a mother comforts her
child,
so will I comfort[a] you;
and you will be comforted
over Jerusalem."

14When you see this, your heart
will rejoice
and you will flourish like
grass;
the hand of the LORD will be
made known to his
servants,
but his fury[b] will be shown to
his foes.
15See, the LORD is coming with
fire,
and his chariots[c] are like a
whirlwind;
he will bring down his anger
with fury,
and his rebuke[d] with flames
of fire.
16For with fire[e] and with his
sword[f]
the LORD will execute
judgment upon all men,
and many will be those slain
by the LORD.

17"Those who consecrate and purify themselves to go into the
gardens,[g] following the one in
the midst of[a] those who eat the
flesh of pigs[h] and rats and other
abominable things—they will meet
their end[i] together," declares the
LORD.
18"And I, because of their actions
and their imaginations, am about to
come[b] and gather all nations and
tongues, and they will come and see
my glory.
19"I will set a sign[j] among them,
and I will send some of those who
survive to the nations—to Tarshish,[k] to the Libyans[c] and Lyd-
ians[l] (famous as archers), to
Tubal[m] and Greece, and to the distant islands[n] that have not heard of
my fame or seen my glory.[o] They
will proclaim my glory among the
nations. 20And they will bring all
your brothers, from all the nations,
to my holy mountain in Jerusalem
as an offering to the LORD—on
horses, in chariots and wagons, and
on mules and camels," says the
LORD. "They will bring them, as
the Israelites bring their grain
offerings, to the temple of the
LORD in ceremonially clean vessels.[p] 21And I will select some of
them also to be priests[q] and Levites,"
says the LORD.

22"As the new heavens and the
new earth[r] that I make will endure

66:9 *t* Isa 37:3
66:10 *u* Dt 32:43; Ro 15:10 *v* Ps 26:8
66:11 *w* Isa 60:16
66:12 *x* Isa 48:18 *y* Ps 72:3; Isa 60:5; Isa 61:6 *z* Isa 60:4
66:13 *a* Isa 40:1; 2Co 1:4
66:14 *b* Isa 10:5
66:15 *c* Ps 68:17 *d* Ps 9:5
66:16 *e* Isa 30:30 *f* Isa 27:1
66:17 *g* Isa 1:29 *h* Lev 11:7 *i* Ps 37:20; Isa 1:28
66:19 *j* Isa 11:10; Isa 49:22 *k* Isa 2:16 *l* Eze 27:10 *m* Ge 10:2 *n* Isa 11:11 *o* 1Ch 16:24; Isa 24:15
66:20 *p* Isa 52:11
66:21 *q* Ex 19:6; Isa 61:6; 1Pe 2:5,9
66:22 *r* Isa 65:17; Heb 12:26-27; 2Pe 3:13; Rev 21:1

a17 Or *gardens behind one of your temples, and*
b18 The meaning of the Hebrew for this clause is uncertain.
c19 Some Septuagint manuscripts *Put* (Libyans); Hebrew *Pul*

before me," declares the LORD, "so
will your name and descendants
endure.[s] 23From one New Moon to
another and from one Sabbath[t] to
another, all mankind will come and
bow down[u] before me," says the
LORD. 24"And they will go out and
look upon the dead bodies of those
who rebelled against me; their
worm[v] will not die, nor will their
fire be quenched,[w] and they will be
loathsome to all mankind."

66:22 s Jn 10:27-29 1Pe 1:4-5
66:23 t Eze 46:1-3 u Isa 19:21
66:24 v Isa 14:11 w Isa 1:31 Mk 9:48*

JEREMIAH

1 The words of Jeremiah son of Hilkiah, one of the priests at Anathoth[a] in the territory of Benjamin. 2 The word of the LORD came to him in the thirteenth year of the reign of Josiah son of Amon king of Judah, 3 and through the reign of Jehoiakim[b] son of Josiah king of Judah, down to the fifth month of the eleventh year of Zedekiah[c] son of Josiah king of Judah, when the people of Jerusalem went into exile.[d]

The Call of Jeremiah

4 The word of the LORD came to me, saying,

5 "Before I formed you in the
 womb I knew[a][e] you,
 before you were born[f] I set
 you apart;
 I appointed you as a prophet
 to the nations.[g]"

6 "Ah, Sovereign LORD," I said, "I do not know how to speak;[h] I am only a child."[i]

7 But the LORD said to me, "Do not say, 'I am only a child.' You must go to everyone I send you to and say whatever I command you. 8 Do not be afraid[j] of them, for I am with you[k] and will rescue you," declares the LORD.

9 Then the LORD reached out his hand and touched[l] my mouth and said to me, "Now, I have put my words in your mouth.[m] 10 See, today I appoint you over nations and kingdoms to uproot and tear down, to destroy and overthrow, to build and to plant."[n]

11 The word of the LORD came to me: "What do you see, Jeremiah?"[o]

"I see the branch of an almond tree," I replied.

12 The LORD said to me, "You have seen correctly, for I am watching[b] to see that my word is fulfilled."

13 The word of the LORD came to me again: "What do you see?"[p]

"I see a boiling pot, tilting away from the north," I answered.

14 The LORD said to me, "From the north disaster will be poured out on all who live in the land. 15 I am about to summon all the peoples of the northern kingdoms," declares the LORD.

"Their kings will come and set
 up their thrones
 in the entrance of the gates of
 Jerusalem;
 they will come against all her
 surrounding walls
 and against all the towns of
 Judah.[q]
16 I will pronounce my judgments
 on my people
 because of their wickedness[r]
 in forsaking me,[s]
 in burning incense to other
 gods[t]
 and in worshipping what their
 hands have made.

17 "Get yourself ready! Stand up and say to them whatever I command you. Do not be terrified[u] by them, or I will terrify you before them. 18 Today I have made you[v] a fortified city, an iron pillar and a bronze wall to stand against the whole land—against the kings of Judah, its officials, its priests and the people of the land. 19 They will fight against you but will not overcome you, for I am with you[w] and will rescue[x] you," declares the LORD.

1:1 *a* Jos 21:18; 1Ch 6:60; Jer 32:7-9
1:3 *b* 2Ki 23:34 *c* 2Ki 24:17; Jer 39:2 *d* Jer 52:15
1:5 *e* Ps 139:16 *f* Isa 49:1 *g* ver 10; Jer 25:15-26
1:6 *h* Ex 4:10; Ex 6:12 *i* 1Ki 3:7
1:8 *j* Eze 2:6 *k* Jos 1:5; Jer 15:20
1:9 *l* Isa 6:7 *m* Ex 4:12
1:10 *n* Jer 18:7-10; Jer 24:6; Jer 31:4,28
1:11 *o* Jer 24:3; Am 7:8
1:13 *p* Zec 4:2
1:15 *q* Jer 4:16; Jer 9:11
1:16 *r* Dt 28:20 *s* Jer 17:13 *t* Jer 7:9; Jer 19:4
1:17 *u* Eze 2:6
1:18 *v* Isa 50:7
1:19 *w* Jer 20:11 *x* ver 8

[a] 5 Or *chose* [b] 12 The Hebrew for *watching* sounds like the Hebrew for *almond tree.*

Israel Forsakes God

2 The word of the LORD came to
me:
2"Go and proclaim in the hearing of
Jerusalem:

" 'I remember the devotion of
your youth,[a]
how as a bride you loved me
and followed me through the
desert,[b]
through a land not sown.
3Israel was holy[c] to the LORD,[d]
the firstfruits[e] of his harvest;
all who devoured[f] her were
held guilty,[g]
and disaster overtook them,' "
declares the LORD.

4Hear the word of the LORD,
O house of Jacob,
all you clans of the house of
Israel.

5This is what the LORD says:

"What fault did your fathers
find in me,
that they strayed so far from
me?
They followed worthless idols
and became worthless[h]
themselves.
6They did not ask, 'Where is the
LORD,
who brought us up out of
Egypt[i]
and led us through the barren
wilderness,
through a land of deserts[j]
and rifts,[k]
a land of drought and
darkness,[a]
a land where no-one travels
and no-one lives?'
7I brought you into a fertile land
to eat its fruit and rich
produce.[l]
But you came and defiled my
land
and made my inheritance
detestable.[m]
8The priests did not ask,
'Where is the LORD?'
Those who deal with the law did
not know me;[n]
the leaders rebelled against
me.
The prophets prophesied by
Baal,[o]
following worthless idols.[p]

9"Therefore I bring charges[q]
against you again,"
declares the LORD.
"And I will bring charges
against your children's
children.
10Cross over to the coasts of
Kittim[b] and look,
send to Kedar[c] and observe
closely;
see if there has ever been
anything like this:
11Has a nation ever changed its
gods?
(Yet they are not gods[r] at all.)
But my people have exchanged
their[d] Glory[s]
for worthless idols.
12Be appalled at this, O heavens,
and shudder with great
horror,"
declares the LORD.
13"My people have committed two
sins:
They have forsaken me,
the spring of living water,[t]
and have dug their own
cisterns,
broken cisterns that cannot
hold water.
14Is Israel a servant, a slave[u] by
birth?
Why then has he become
plunder?
15Lions[v] have roared;
they have growled at him.
They have laid waste[w] his land;
his towns are burned and
deserted.
16Also, the men of Memphis[e][x]
and Tahpanhes[y]

2:2 a Eze 16:8-14, 60; Hos 2:15 b Dt 2:7
2:3 c Dt 7:6 d Ex 19:6 e Jas 1:18; Rev 14:4 f Isa 41:11; Jer 30:16 g Jer 50:7
2:5 h 2Ki 17:15
2:6 i Hos 13:4 j Dt 8:15 k Dt 32:10
2:7 l Nu 13:27; Dt 8:7-9; Dt 11:10-12 m Ps 106:34-39; Jer 16:18
2:8 n Jer 4:22 o Jer 23:13 p Jer 16:19
2:9 q Eze 20:35-36; Mic 6:2
2:11 r Isa 37:19; Jer 16:20 s Ps 106:20; Ro 1:23
2:13 t Ps 36:9; Jn 4:14
2:14 u Ex 4:22
2:15 v Jer 4:7; Jer 50:17 w Isa 1:7
2:16 x Isa 19:13 y Jer 43:7-9

[a]6 Or *and the shadow of death* [b]10 That is, Cyprus and western coastlands [c]10 The home of Bedouin tribes in the Syro-Arabian desert [d]11 Masoretic Text; an ancient Hebrew scribal tradition *my* [e]16 Hebrew *Noph*

have shaved the crown of your
head.[f]
17Have you not brought this on
yourselves[z]
by forsaking the LORD your
God
when he led you in the way?
18Now why go to Egypt[a]
to drink water from the
Shihor?[g][b]
And why go to Assyria
to drink water from the
River?[h]
19Your wickedness will punish
you;
your backsliding[c] will
rebuke[d] you.
Consider then and realise
how evil and bitter[e] it is for
you
when you forsake the LORD
your God
and have no awe[f] of me,"
declares the Lord,
the LORD Almighty.

20"Long ago you broke off your
yoke[g]
and tore off your bonds;
you said, 'I will not serve you!'
Indeed, on every high hill[h]
and under every spreading
tree[i]
you lay down as a prostitute.
21I had planted[j] you like a choice
vine[k]
of sound and reliable stock.
How then did you turn against
me
into a corrupt,[l] wild vine?
22Although you wash yourself
with soda
and use an abundance of soap,
the stain of your guilt is still
before me,"
declares the Sovereign LORD.
23"How can you say, 'I am not
defiled;[m]
I have not run after the
Baals'?[n]
See how you behaved in the
valley;[o]
consider what you have done.
You are a swift she-camel
running[p] here and there,
24a wild donkey[q] accustomed to
the desert,
sniffing the wind in her
craving—
in her heat who can restrain
her?
Any males that pursue her need
not tire themselves;
at mating time they will find
her.
25Do not run until your feet are
bare
and your throat is dry.
But you said, 'It's no use!
I love foreign gods,[r]
and I must go after them.'

26"As a thief is disgraced[s] when
he is caught,
so the house of Israel is
disgraced—
they, their kings and their
officials,
their priests and their
prophets.
27They say to wood, 'You are my
father,'
and to stone,[t] 'You gave me
birth.'
They have turned their backs to
me
and not their faces;[u]
yet when they are in trouble,[v]
they say,
'Come and save us!'
28Where then are the gods[w] you
made for yourselves?
Let them come if they can
save you
when you are in trouble![x]
For you have as many gods
as you have towns,[y] O Judah.

29"Why do you bring charges
against me?
You have all[z] rebelled against
me,"
declares the LORD.
30"In vain I punished your people;
they did not respond to
correction.

2:17 z Jer 4:18
2:18 a Isa 30:2 b Jos 13:3
2:19 c Jer 3:11,22 d Isa 3:9 Hos 5:5 e Job 20:14 Am 8:10 f Ps 36:1
2:20 g Lev 26:13 h Isa 57:7 Jer 17:2 i Dt 12:2
2:21 j Ex 15:17 k Ps 80:8 l Isa 5:4
2:23 m Pr 30:12 n Jer 9:14 o Jer 7:31 p ver 33 Jer 31:22
2:24 q Jer 14:6
2:25 r Dt 32:16 Jer 3:13 Jer 14:10
2:26 s Jer 48:27
2:27 t Jer 3:9 u Jer 18:17 Jer 32:33 v Jdg 10:10 Isa 26:16
2:28 w Isa 45:20 x Dt 32:37 y 2Ki 17:29 Jer 11:13
2:29 z Jer 5:1 Jer 6:13 Da 9:11

[f] *16* Or *have cracked your skull* [g] *18* That is, a branch of the Nile [h] *18* That is, the Euphrates

Your sword has devoured your
prophets[a]
like a ravening lion.

31"You of this generation, consider the word of the LORD:

"Have I been a desert to Israel
or a land of great darkness?[b]
Why do my people say, 'We are
free to roam;
we will come to you no more'?
32Does a maiden forget her
jewellery,
a bride her wedding
ornaments?
Yet my people have forgotten
me,
days without number.
33How skilled you are at pursuing
love!
Even the worst of women can
learn from your ways.
34On your clothes men find
the lifeblood[c] of the innocent
poor,
though you did not catch them
breaking in.[d]
Yet in spite of all this
35 you say, 'I am innocent;
he is not angry with me.'
But I will pass judgment[e] on
you
because you say, 'I have not
sinned.'[f]
36Why do you go about so much,
changing[g] your ways?
You will be disappointed by
Egypt[h]
as you were by Assyria.
37You will also leave that place
with your hands on your
head,[i]
for the LORD has rejected those
you trust;
you will not be helped[j] by
them.

3 "If a man divorces[a] his wife
and she leaves him and
marries another man,
should he return to her again?
Would not the land be
completely defiled?
But you have lived as a
prostitute with many
lovers[b]—
would you now return to me?"
declares the LORD.
2"Look up to the barren heights
and see.
Is there any place where you
have not been ravished?
By the roadside[c] you sat
waiting for lovers,
sat like a nomad[a] in the
desert.
You have defiled the land[d]
with your prostitution and
wickedness.
3Therefore the showers have
been withheld,[e]
and no spring rains[f] have
fallen.
Yet you have the brazen look of
a prostitute;
you refuse to blush with
shame.[g]
4Have you not just called to me:
'My Father,[h] my friend from
my youth,[i]
5will you always be angry?[j]
Will your wrath continue for
ever?'
This is how you talk,
but you do all the evil you
can."

Unfaithful Israel

6During the reign of King Josiah,
the LORD said to me, "Have you
seen what faithless Israel has
done? She has gone up on every
high hill and under every spreading tree[k] and has committed adultery[l] there. 7I thought that after
she had done all this she would return to me but she did not, and her
unfaithful sister[m] Judah saw it. 8I
gave faithless Israel her certificate of divorce and sent her away
because of all her adulteries. Yet I
saw that her unfaithful sister Judah had no fear;[n] she also went out
and committed adultery. 9Because

[a]2 Or *an Arab*

2:30 a Ne 9:26; Ac 7:52; 1Th 2:15
2:31 b Isa 45:19
2:34 c 2Ki 21:16; d Ex 22:2
2:35 e Jer 25:31; f 1Jn 1:8,10
2:36 g Jer 31:22; h Isa 30:2,3,7
2:37 i 2Sa 13:19; j Jer 37:7
3:1 a Dt 24:1-4; b Jer 2:20,25; Eze 16:26,29
3:2 c Ge 38:14; Eze 16:25; d Jer 2:7
3:3 e Lev 26:19; f Jer 14:4; g Jer 6:15; Jer 8:12; Zep 3:5
3:4 h ver 19; i Jer 2:2
3:5 j Ps 103:9; Isa 57:16
3:6 k Jer 17:2; l Jer 2:20
3:7 m Eze 16:46
3:8 n Eze 16:47; Eze 23:11

Israel's immorality mattered so little to her, she defiled the land[o] and
committed adultery with stone[p]
and wood.[q] 10 In spite of all this, her
unfaithful sister Judah did not return to me with all her heart, but
only in pretence,[r]" declares the
LORD.
11 The LORD said to me, "Faithless
Israel is more righteous[s] than
unfaithful[t] Judah. 12 Go, proclaim
this message towards the north:[u]

" 'Return,[v] faithless Israel,'
    declares the LORD,
  'I will frown on you no longer,
for I am merciful,' declares the
    LORD,
  'I will not be angry[w] for ever.
13 Only acknowledge[x] your guilt—
  you have rebelled against the
    LORD your God,
you have scattered your favours
    to foreign gods[y]
  under every spreading tree,[z]
  and have not obeyed[a] me,' "
    declares the LORD.

14 "Return,[b] faithless people,"
declares the LORD, "for I am your
husband. I will choose you—one
from a town and two from a clan—
and bring you to Zion. 15 Then I will
give you shepherds[c] after my own
heart, who will lead you with
knowledge and understanding. 16 In
those days, when your numbers
have increased greatly in the
land," declares the LORD, "men
will no longer say, 'The ark of
the covenant of the LORD.' It
will never enter their minds or
be remembered;[d] it will not be
missed, nor will another one be
made. 17 At that time they will call
Jerusalem The Throne[e] of the
LORD, and all nations will gather in
Jerusalem to honour[f] the name of
the LORD. No longer will they follow the stubbornness of their evil
hearts.[g] 18 In those days the house
of Judah will join the house of
Israel,[h] and together[i] they will
come from a northern[j] land to the
land[k] I gave your forefathers as an
inheritance.
19 "I myself said,

" 'How gladly would I treat you
    like sons
  and give you a desirable land,
  the most beautiful inheritance
    of any nation.'
I thought you would call me
    'Father'[l]
  and not turn away from
    following me.
20 But like a woman unfaithful to
    her husband,
  so you have been unfaithful to
    me, O house of Israel,"
    declares the LORD.

21 A cry is heard on the barren
    heights,[m]
  the weeping and pleading of
    the people of Israel,
because they have perverted
    their ways
  and have forgotten the LORD
    their God.

22 "Return,[n] faithless people;
  I will cure[o] you of
    backsliding."

"Yes, we will come to you,
  for you are the LORD our God.
23 Surely the ⌞idolatrous⌟
    commotion on the hills
  and mountains is a deception;
surely in the LORD our God
  is the salvation[p] of Israel.
24 From our youth shameful[q] gods
    have consumed
  the fruits of our fathers'
    labour—
their flocks and herds,
  their sons and daughters.
25 Let us lie down in our shame,[r]
  and let our disgrace cover us.
We have sinned against the
    LORD our God,
  both we and our fathers;
from our youth[s] till this day
  we have not obeyed the LORD
    our God."

3:9 o ver 2; p Isa 57:6; q Jer 2:27
3:10 r Jer 12:2
3:11 s Eze 16:52; Eze 23:11; t ver 7
3:12 u 2Ki 17:3-6; v ver 14; Jer 31:21,22; Eze 33:11; w Ps 86:15
3:13 x Dt 30:1-3; Jer 14:20; 1Jn 1:9; y Jer 2:25; z Dt 12:2; a ver 25
3:14 b Hos 2:19
3:15 c Ac 20:28
3:16 d Isa 65:17
3:17 e Jer 17:12; Eze 43:7; f Isa 60:9; g Jer 11:8
3:18 h Hos 1:11; i Isa 11:13; Jer 50:4; j Jer 16:15; Jer 31:8; k Am 9:15
3:19 l ver 4; Isa 63:16
3:21 m ver 2
3:22 n Hos 14:4; o Jer 33:6; Hos 6:1
3:23 p Ps 3:8; Jer 17:14
3:24 q Hos 9:10
3:25 r Ezr 9:6; s Jer 22:21

4 "If you will return[a],
O Israel,
return to me,"
declares the LORD.
"If you put your detestable
idols[b] out of my sight
and no longer go astray,
2and if in a truthful, just and
righteous way
you swear,[c] 'As surely as the
LORD lives,'[d]
then the nations will be
blessed[e] by him
and in him they will glory."

3This is what the LORD says to the
men of Judah and to Jerusalem:

"Break up your unploughed
ground[f]
and do not sow among
thorns.[g]
4Circumcise yourselves to the
LORD,
circumcise your hearts,[h]
you men of Judah and people
of Jerusalem,
or my wrath[i] will break out
and burn like fire
because of the evil you have
done—
burn with no-one to quench[j]
it.

Disaster From the North

5"Announce in Judah and
proclaim in Jerusalem and
say:
'Sound the trumpet throughout
the land!'
Cry aloud and say:
'Gather together!
Let us flee to the fortified
cities!'[k]
6Raise the signal to go to Zion!
Flee for safety without delay!
For I am bringing disaster from
the north,[l]
even terrible destruction."

7A lion[m] has come out of his
lair;
a destroyer of nations has set
out.

4:1
a Jer 3:1,22
Joel 2:12
b Jer 35:15

4:2
c Dt 10:20
Isa 65:16
d Jer 12:16
e Ge 22:18
Gal 3:8

4:3
f Hos 10:12
g Mk 4:18

4:4
h Dt 10:16
Jer 9:26
Ro 2:28-29
i Zep 2:2
j Am 5:6

4:5
k Jos 10:20
Jer 8:14

4:6
l Jer 1:13-15
Jer 50:3

4:7
m 2Ki 24:1
Jer 2:15
n Isa 1:7
o Jer 25:9

4:8
p Isa 22:12
Jer 6:26
q Jer 30:24

4:9
r Isa 29:9

4:10
s 2Th 2:11
t Jer 14:13

4:11
u Eze 17:10
Hos 13:15

4:12
v Jer 1:16

4:13
w Isa 19:1
x Isa 66:15
y Isa 5:28
z Dt 28:49
Hab 1:8

4:14
a Jas 4:8

4:15
b Jer 8:16

4:16
c Eze 21:22

He has left his place
to lay waste[n] your land.
Your towns will lie in ruins[o]
without inhabitant.
8So put on sackcloth,[p]
lament and wail,
for the fierce anger[q] of the
LORD
has not turned away from us.

9"In that day," declares the
LORD,
"the king and the officials will
lose heart,
the priests will be horrified,
and the prophets will be
appalled."[r]

10Then I said, "Ah, Sovereign
LORD, how completely you have deceived[s] this people and Jerusalem
by saying, 'You will have peace,'[t]
when the sword is at our throats."
11At that time this people and
Jerusalem will be told, "A scorching wind[u] from the barren heights
in the desert blows towards my
people, but not to winnow or
cleanse; 12a wind too strong for that
comes from me.[a] Now I pronounce
my judgments[v] against them."

13Look! He advances like the
clouds,[w]
his chariots[x] come like a
whirlwind,[y]
his horses are swifter than
eagles.[z]
Woe to us! We are ruined!
14O Jerusalem, wash[a] the evil
from your heart and be
saved.
How long will you harbour
wicked thoughts?
15A voice is announcing from Dan,[b]
proclaiming disaster from the
hills of Ephraim.
16"Tell this to the nations,
proclaim it to Jerusalem:
'A besieging army is coming
from a distant land,
raising a war cry[c] against the
cities of Judah.

[a]12 Or *comes at my command*

17They surround[d] her like men
guarding a field,
because she has rebelled[e]
against me,' "
declares the LORD.
18"Your own conduct and
actions[f]
have brought this upon you.[g]
This is your punishment.
How bitter[h] it is!
How it pierces to the heart!"

19Oh, my anguish, my anguish![i]
I writhe in pain.
Oh, the agony of my heart!
My heart pounds within me,
I cannot keep silent.[j]
For I have heard the sound of
the trumpet;
I have heard the battle cry.[k]
20Disaster follows disaster;[l]
the whole land lies in ruins.
In an instant my tents[m] are
destroyed,
my shelter in a moment.
21How long must I see the battle
standard
and hear the sound of the
trumpet?

22"My people are fools;[n]
they do not know me.[o]
They are senseless children;
they have no understanding.
They are skilled in doing evil;[p]
they know not how to do
good."[q]

23I looked at the earth,
and it was formless and
empty;[r]
and at the heavens,
and their light was gone.
24I looked at the mountains,
and they were quaking;[s]
all the hills were swaying.
25I looked, and there were no
people;
every bird in the sky had
flown away.[t]
26I looked, and the fruitful land
was a desert;
all its towns lay in ruins
before the LORD, before his
fierce anger.

4:17
d 2Ki 25:1,4
e Jer 5:23

4:18
f Ps 107:17
Isa 50:1
g Jer 2:17
h Jer 2:19

4:19
i Isa 16:11
Isa 22:4
Jer 9:10
j Jer 20:9
k Nu 10:9

4:20
l Ps 42:7
Eze 7:26
m Jer 10:20

4:22
n Jer 10:8
o Jer 2:8
p Jer 13:23
1Co 14:20
q Ro 16:19

4:23
r Ge 1:2

4:24
s Isa 5:25
Eze 38:20

4:25
t Jer 9:10
Jer 12:4
Zep 1:3

4:27
u Jer 5:10,18
Jer 12:12
Jer 30:11
Jer 46:28

4:28
v Jer 12:4,11
Jer 14:2
Hos 4:3
w Isa 5:30
Isa 50:3
x Nu 23:19
y Jer 23:20
Jer 30:24

4:29
z Jer 6:23
a 2Ki 25:4
b ver 7

4:30
c Isa 10:3-4
d Eze 23:40
e 2Ki 9:30
f La 1:2
Eze 23:9,22

4:31
g Jer 13:21
h Isa 42:14
i Isa 1:15
La 1:17

5:1
a 2Ch 16:9
Eze 22:30
b Ge 18:32
c Ge 18:24

27This is what the LORD says:

"The whole land will be ruined,
though I will not destroy[u] it
completely.
28Therefore the earth will
mourn[v]
and the heavens above grow
dark,[w]
because I have spoken and will
not relent,[x]
I have decided and will not
turn back."[y]

29At the sound of horsemen and
archers[z]
every town takes to flight.[a]
Some go into the thickets;
some climb up among the
rocks.
All the towns are deserted;[b]
no-one lives in them.

30What are you doing,[c]
O devastated one?
Why dress yourself in scarlet
and put on jewels[d] of gold?
Why shade your eyes with
paint?[e]
You adorn yourself in vain.
Your lovers[f] despise you;
they seek your life.

31I hear a cry as of a woman in
labour,[g]
a groan as of one bearing her
first child—
the cry of the Daughter of Zion
gasping for breath,[h]
stretching out her hands[i] and
saying,
"Alas! I am fainting;
my life is given over to
murderers."

Not One Is Upright

5 "Go up and down[a] the
streets of Jerusalem,
look around and consider,
search through her squares.
If you can find but one person[b]
who deals honestly and seeks
the truth,
I will forgive[c] this city.

2 Although they say, 'As surely as
the LORD lives,'[d]
still they are swearing
falsely."
3 O LORD, do not your eyes[e] look
for truth?
You struck[f] them, but they
felt no pain;
you crushed them but they
refused correction.[g]
They made their faces harder
than stone[h]
and refused to repent.
4 I thought, "These are only the
poor;
they are foolish,
for they do not know[i] the way
of the LORD,
the requirements of their God.
5 So I will go to the leaders[j]
and speak to them;
surely they know the way of the
LORD,
the requirements of their God."
But with one accord they too
had broken off the yoke
and torn off the bonds.[k]
6 Therefore a lion from the forest
will attack them,
a wolf from the desert will
ravage them,
a leopard[l] will lie in wait near
their towns
to tear to pieces any who
venture out,
for their rebellion is great
and their backslidings many.[m]
7 "Why should I forgive you?
Your children have forsaken
me
and sworn[n] by gods that are
not gods.[o]
I supplied all their needs,
yet they committed adultery[p]
and thronged to the houses of
prostitutes.
8 They are well-fed, lusty
stallions,
each neighing for another
man's wife.[q]
9 Should I not punish them for
this?"[r]
declares the LORD.
"Should I not avenge myself
on such a nation as this?
10 "Go through her vineyards and
ravage them,
but do not destroy them
completely.[s]
Strip off her branches,
for these people do not belong
to the LORD.
11 The house of Israel and the
house of Judah
have been utterly unfaithful[t]
to me,"
declares the LORD.
12 They have lied about the LORD;
they said, "He will do nothing!
No harm will come to us;[u]
we will never see sword or
famine.[v]
13 The prophets[w] are but wind
and the word is not in them;
so let what they say be done to
them."

14 Therefore this is what the LORD
God Almighty says:

"Because the people have
spoken these words,
I will make my words in your
mouth[x] a fire[y]
and these people the wood it
consumes.
15 O house of Israel," declares the
LORD,
"I am bringing a distant
nation[z] against you—
an ancient and enduring nation,
a people whose language[a] you
do not know,
whose speech you do not
understand.
16 Their quivers are like an open
grave;
all of them are mighty
warriors.
17 They will devour[bc] your
harvests and food,
devour[de] your sons and
daughters;
they will devour[f] your flocks
and herds,
devour your vines and
fig-trees.

5:2 d Jer 4:2
5:3 e 2Ch 16:9 f Isa 9:13 g Jer 2:30 Zep 3:2 h Jer 7:26 Jer 19:15 Eze 3:8-9
5:4 i Jer 8:7
5:5 j Mic 3:1,9 k Ps 2:3 Jer 2:20
5:6 l Hos 13:7 m Jer 30:14
5:7 n Jos 23:7 Zep 1:5 o Dt 32:21 Jer 2:11 Gal 4:8 p Nu 25:1
5:8 q Jer 29:23 Eze 22:11
5:9 r ver 29 Jer 9:9
5:10 s Jer 4:27
5:11 t Jer 3:20
5:12 u Jer 23:17 v 2Ch 36:16 Jer 14:13
5:13 w Jer 14:15
5:14 x Jer 1:9 Hos 6:5 y Jer 23:29
5:15 z Dt 28:49 Isa 5:26 Jer 4:16 a Isa 28:11
5:17 b Jer 8:16 c Lev 26:16 d Jer 50:7,17 e Dt 28:32 f Dt 28:31

With the sword they will
destroy
the fortified cities in which
you trust.[g]

18"Yet even in those days," declares the LORD, "I will not destroy[h] you completely. 19And when
the people ask,[i] 'Why has the LORD
our God done all this to us?' you will
tell them, 'As you have forsaken me
and served foreign gods[j] in your
own land, so now you will serve foreigners[k] in a land not your own.'

20"Announce this to the house of
Jacob
and proclaim it in Judah:
21Hear this, you foolish and
senseless people,
who have eyes[l] but do not
see,
who have ears but do not
hear:[m]
22Should you not fear[n] me?"
declares the LORD.
"Should you not tremble in my
presence?
I made the sand a boundary for
the sea,
an everlasting barrier it
cannot cross.
The waves may roll, but they
cannot prevail;
they may roar, but they
cannot cross it.
23But these people have stubborn
and rebellious[o] hearts;
they have turned aside and
gone away.
24They do not say to themselves,
'Let us fear the LORD our God,
who gives autumn and spring
rains[p] in season,
who assures us of the regular
weeks of harvest.'[q]
25Your wrongdoings have kept
these away;
your sins have deprived you
of good.

26"Among my people are wicked
men
who lie in wait[r] like men who
snare birds
and like those who set traps to
catch men.
27Like cages full of birds,
their houses are full of
deceit;[s]
they have become rich[t] and
powerful
28 and have grown fat[u] and
sleek.
Their evil deeds have no limit;
they do not plead the case of
the fatherless[v] to win it,
they do not defend the rights
of the poor.[w]
29Should I not punish them for
this?"
declares the LORD.
"Should I not avenge myself
on such a nation as this?

30"A horrible[x] and shocking
thing
has happened in the land:
31The prophets prophesy lies,[y]
the priests rule by their own
authority,
and my people love it this way.
But what will you do in the
end?

Jerusalem Under Siege

6 "Flee for safety, people of
Benjamin!
Flee from Jerusalem!
Sound the trumpet in Tekoa![a]
Raise the signal over Beth
Hakkerem![b]
For disaster looms out of the
north,[c]
even terrible destruction.
2I will destroy the Daughter of
Zion,
so beautiful and delicate.
3Shepherds[d] with their flocks
will come against her;
they will pitch their tents
round[e] her,
each tending his own portion."

4"Prepare for battle against her!
Arise, let us attack at noon![f]
But, alas, the daylight is fading,
and the shadows of evening
grow long.

5:17 g Dt 28:33
5:18 h Jer 4:27
5:19 i Dt 29:24-26; 1Ki 9:9 j Jer 16:13 k Dt 28:48
5:21 l Isa 6:10; Eze 12:2 m Mt 13:15; Mk 8:18
5:22 n Dt 28:58
5:23 o Dt 21:18
5:24 p Ps 147:8; Joel 2:23 q Ge 8:22; Ac 14:17
5:26 r Ps 10:8; Pr 1:11
5:27 s Jer 9:6 t Jer 12:1
5:28 u Dt 32:15 v Zec 7:10 w Isa 1:23; Jer 7:6
5:30 x Jer 23:14; Hos 6:10
5:31 y Eze 13:6; Mic 2:11
6:1 a 2Ch 11:6 b Ne 3:14 c Jer 4:6
6:3 d Jer 12:10 e 2Ki 25:4; Lk 19:43
6:4 f Jer 15:8

[5]So arise, let us attack at night
and destroy her fortresses!"

[6]This is what the LORD Almighty says:

"Cut down the trees[g]
and build siege ramps[h]
against Jerusalem.
This city must be punished;
it is filled with oppression.
[7]As a well pours out its water,
so she pours out her
wickedness.
Violence[i] and destruction[j]
resound in her;
her sickness and wounds are
ever before me.
[8]Take warning, O Jerusalem,
or I will turn away[k] from you
and make your land desolate
so that no-one can live in it."

[9]This is what the LORD Almighty says:

"Let them glean the remnant of
Israel
as thoroughly as a vine;
pass your hand over the
branches again,
like one gathering grapes."
[10]To whom can I speak and give
warning?
Who will listen to me?
Their ears are closed[a][l]
so that they cannot hear.
The word[m] of the LORD is
offensive to them;
they find no pleasure in it.
[11]But I am full of the wrath[n] of
the LORD,
and I cannot hold it in.[o]

"Pour it out on the children in
the street
and on the young men[p]
gathered together;
both husband and wife will be
caught in it,
and the old, those weighed
down with years.
[12]Their houses will be turned
over to others,[q]
together with their fields and
their wives,[r]
when I stretch out my hand[s]
against those who live in the
land,"
declares the LORD.
[13]"From the least to the greatest,
all are greedy for gain;[t]
prophets and priests alike,
all practise deceit.[u]
[14]They dress the wound of my
people
as though it were not serious.
'Peace, peace,' they say,
when there is no peace.[v]
[15]Are they ashamed of their
loathsome conduct?
No, they have no shame at all;
they do not even know how to
blush.[w]
So they will fall among the
fallen;
they will be brought down
when I punish them,"
says the LORD.

[16]This is what the LORD says:

"Stand at the crossroads and
look;
ask for the ancient paths,[x]
ask where the good way[y] is,
and walk in it,
and you will find rest[z] for
your souls.
But you said, 'We will not
walk in it.'
[17]I appointed watchmen[a] over
you and said,
'Listen to the sound of the
trumpet!'
But you said, 'We will not
listen.'[b]
[18]Therefore hear, O nations;
observe, O witnesses,
what will happen to them.
[19]Hear, O earth:[c]
I am bringing disaster on this
people,
the fruit of their schemes,[d]
because they have not listened
to my words
and have rejected my law.[e]
[20]What do I care about incense
from Sheba

6:6 g Dt 20:19-20 h Jer 32:24
6:7 i Ps 55:9; Eze 7:11,23 j Jer 20:8
6:8 k Eze 23:18; Hos 9:12
6:10 l Ac 7:51 m Jer 20:8
6:11 n Jer 7:20 o Job 32:20; Jer 20:9 p Jer 9:21
6:12 q Dt 28:30 r Jer 8:10; Jer 38:22 s Isa 5:25
6:13 t Isa 56:11 u Jer 8:10
6:14 v Jer 4:10; Jer 8:11; Eze 13:10
6:15 w Jer 3:3; Jer 8:10-12
6:16 x Jer 18:15 y Ps 119:3 z Mt 11:29
6:17 a Eze 3:17 b Jer 11:7-8; Jer 25:4
6:19 c Isa 1:2; Jer 22:29 d Pr 1:31 e Jer 8:9

[a] *10* Hebrew *uncircumcised*

or sweet calamus[f] from a
distant land?
Your burnt offerings are not
acceptable;[g]
your sacrifices[h] do not please
me."[i]

21Therefore this is what the LORD
says:

"I will put obstacles before this
people.
Fathers and sons alike will
stumble[j] over them;
neighbours and friends will
perish."

22This is what the LORD says:

"Look, an army is coming
from the land of the north;[k]
a great nation is being stirred
up
from the ends of the earth.
23They are armed with bow and
spear;
they are cruel and show no
mercy.[l]
They sound like the roaring sea
as they ride on their horses;[m]
they come like men in battle
formation
to attack you, O Daughter of
Zion."

24We have heard reports about
them,
and our hands hang limp.
Anguish[n] has gripped us,
pain like that of a woman in
labour.[o]
25Do not go out to the fields
or walk on the roads,
for the enemy has a sword,
and there is terror on every
side.[p]
26O my people, put on sackcloth[q]
and roll in ashes;[r]
mourn with bitter wailing
as for an only son,[s]
for suddenly the destroyer
will come upon us.

27"I have made you a tester[t] of
metals
and my people the ore,
that you may observe
and test their ways.
28They are all hardened rebels,[u]
going about to slander.[v]
They are bronze and iron;[w]
they all act corruptly.
29The bellows blow fiercely
to burn away the lead with
fire,
but the refining goes on in vain;
the wicked are not purged out.
30They are called rejected silver,
because the LORD has rejected
them."[x]

False Religion Worthless

7 This is the word that came to
Jeremiah from the LORD:
2"Stand[a] at the gate of the LORD's
house and there proclaim this message:
" 'Hear the word of the LORD, all
you people of Judah who come
through these gates to worship the
LORD. 3This is what the LORD
Almighty, the God of Israel, says:
Reform your ways[b] and your actions, and I will let you live in this
place. 4Do not trust in deceptive[c]
words and say, "This is the temple
of the LORD, the temple of the LORD,
the temple of the LORD!" 5If you
really change your ways and your
actions and deal with each other
justly,[d] 6if you do not oppress the
alien, the fatherless or the widow
and do not shed innocent blood[e] in
this place, and if you do not follow
other gods[f] to your own harm,
7then I will let you live in this place,
in the land[g] I gave to your forefathers for ever and ever. 8But
look, you are trusting in deceptive[h]
words that are worthless.
9" 'Will you steal and murder,
commit adultery and perjury,[a]
burn incense to Baal[i] and follow
other gods[j] you have not known,
10and then come and stand before
me in this house,[k] which bears my
Name, and say, "We are safe"—
safe to do all these detestable

6:20 f Ex 30:23 g Am 5:22 h Ps 50:8-10 Jer 7:21 Mic 6:7-8 i Isa 1:11
6:21 j Isa 8:14
6:22 k Jer 1:15 Jer 10:22
6:23 l Isa 13:18 m Jer 4:29
6:24 n Jer 4:19 o Jer 4:31 Jer 50:41-43
6:25 p Jer 49:29
6:26 q Jer 4:8 r Jer 25:34 Mic 1:10 s Zec 12:10
6:27 t Jer 9:7
6:28 u Jer 5:23 v Jer 9:4 w Eze 22:18
6:30 x Ps 119:119 Jer 7:29 Hos 9:17
7:2 a Jer 17:19
7:3 b Jer 18:11 Jer 26:13
7:4 c Mic 3:11
7:5 d Jer 22:3
7:6 e Jer 2:34 Jer 19:4 f Dt 8:19
7:7 g Dt 4:40
7:8 h ver 4
7:9 i Jer 11:13,17 j Ex 20:3
7:10 k Jer 32:34 Eze 23:38-39

a9 Or *and swear by false gods*

things? 11 Has this house,[l] which
bears my Name, become a den of
robbers[m] to you? But I have been
watching![n] declares the LORD.
12 " 'Go now to the place in Shiloh[o] where I first made a dwelling
for my Name, and see what I did[p]
to it because of the wickedness of
my people Israel. 13 While you were
doing all these things, declares the
LORD, I spoke to you again and
again,[q] but you did not listen;[r] I
called[s] you, but you did not answer.[t] 14 Therefore, what I did to
Shiloh I will now do to the house
that bears my Name,[u] the temple[v]
you trust in, the place I gave to you
and your fathers. 15 I will thrust you
from my presence, just as I did all
your brothers, the people of Ephraim.'[w]
16 "So do not pray for this people
nor offer any plea[x] or petition for
them; do not plead with me, for I
will not listen to you. 17 Do you not
see what they are doing in the
towns of Judah and in the streets of
Jerusalem? 18 The children gather
wood, the fathers light the fire, and
the women knead the dough and
make cakes of bread for the Queen
of Heaven.[y] They pour out drink
offerings[z] to other gods to provoke[a] me to anger. 19 But am I the
one they are provoking?[b] declares
the LORD. Are they not rather
harming themselves, to their own
shame?[c]
20 " 'Therefore this is what the
Sovereign LORD says: My anger[d]
and my wrath will be poured[e] out on
this place, on man and beast, on the
trees of the field and on the fruit of
the ground, and it will burn and not
be quenched.[f]
21 " 'This is what the LORD
Almighty, the God of Israel, says:
Go ahead, add your burnt offerings
to your other sacrifices[g] and eat[h]
the meat yourselves! 22 For when I
brought your forefathers out of
Egypt and spoke to them, I did not
just give them commands about
burnt offerings and sacrifices,[i]
23 but I gave them this command:
Obey[j] me, and I will be your God
and you will be my people.[k] Walk
in all the ways I command you, that
it may go well[l] with you. 24 But
they did not listen or pay attention;[m] instead, they followed the
stubborn inclinations of their evil
hearts. They went backward and
not forward. 25 From the time your
forefathers left Egypt until now,
day after day, again and again[n] I
sent you my servants the prophets.[o] 26 But they did not listen to me
or pay attention. They were stiff-
necked and did more evil than their
forefathers.'[p]
27 "When you tell[q] them all this,
they will not listen[r] to you; when
you call to them, they will not
answer. 28 Therefore say to them,
'This is the nation that has not
obeyed the LORD its God or responded to correction. Truth has
perished; it has vanished from
their lips. 29 Cut off[s] your hair and
throw it away; take up a lament on
the barren heights, for the LORD
has rejected and abandoned[t] this
generation that is under his wrath.

The Valley of Slaughter

30 " 'The people of Judah have
done evil in my eyes, declares the
LORD. They have set up their detestable idols[u] in the house that
bears my Name and have defiled[v]
it. 31 They have built the high places
of Topheth[w] in the Valley of Ben
Hinnom to burn their sons and
daughters[x] in the fire—something
I did not command, nor did it enter
my mind.[y] 32 So beware, the days
are coming, declares the LORD,
when people will no longer call it
Topheth or the Valley of Ben Hinnom, but the Valley of Slaughter,[z]
for they will bury[a] the dead in Topheth until there is no more room.
33 Then the carcasses of this people
will become food[b] for the birds of

7:11 *l* Isa 56:7 *m* Mt 21:13* Mk 11:17* Lk 19:46* *n* Jer 29:23
7:12 *o* Jos 18:1 *p* 1Sa 4:10-11, 22 Ps 78:60-64
7:13 *q* 2Ch 36:15 *r* Isa 65:12 *s* Pr 1:24 *t* Jer 35:17
7:14 *u* 1Ki 9:7 *v* ver 4
7:15 *w* Ps 78:67
7:16 *x* Ex 32:10 Dt 9:14 Jer 15:1
7:18 *y* Jer 44:17-19 *z* Jer 19:13 *a* 1Ki 14:9
7:19 *b* Dt 32:21 *c* Jer 9:19
7:20 *d* Jer 42:18 La 2:3-5 *e* Jer 6:11-12 *f* Jer 11:16
7:21 *g* Isa 1:11 Am 5:21-22 *h* Hos 8:13
7:22 *i* 1Sa 15:22 Ps 51:16 Hos 6:6
7:23 *j* Ex 19:5 *k* Lev 26:12 *l* Ex 15:26
7:24 *m* Ps 81:11-12 Jer 11:8
7:25 *n* 2Ch 36:15 *o* Jer 25:4
7:26 *p* Jer 16:12
7:27 *q* Eze 2:7 *r* Eze 3:7
7:29 *s* Job 1:20 Isa 15:2 Mic 1:16 *t* Jer 6:30
7:30 *u* Eze 7:20-22 *v* Jer 32:34
7:31 *w* 2Ki 23:10 *x* Ps 106:38 *y* Jer 19:5
7:32 *z* Jer 19:6 *a* Jer 19:11 **7:33** *b* Dt 28:26

the air and the beasts of the earth,
and there will be no-one to frighten
them away. 34I will bring an end to
the sounds[c] of joy and gladness
and to the voices of bride and
bridegroom[d] in the towns of Judah
and the streets of Jerusalem, for
the land will become desolate.[e]

8 " 'At that time, declares the
LORD, the bones of the kings
and officials of Judah, the bones of
the priests and prophets, and the
bones of the people of Jerusalem
will be removed from their graves.
2They will be exposed to the sun
and the moon and all the stars of
the heavens, which they have loved
and served[a] and which they have
followed and consulted and worshipped. They will not be gathered
up or buried, but will be like refuse
lying on the ground. 3Wherever I
banish them, all the survivors of
this evil nation will prefer death to
life,[b] declares the LORD Almighty.'

Sin and Punishment

4"Say to them, 'This is what the
LORD says:

" 'When men fall down, do they
not get up?[c]
When a man turns away, does
he not return?
5Why then have these people
turned away?
Why does Jerusalem always
turn away?
They cling to deceit;[d]
they refuse to return.[e]
6I have listened attentively,
but they do not say what is
right.
No-one repents[f] of his
wickedness,
saying, "What have I done?"
Each pursues his own course[g]
like a horse charging into
battle.
7Even the stork in the sky
knows her appointed seasons,
and the dove, the swift and the
thrush
observe the time of their
migration.

7:34 *c* Isa 24:8; Eze 26:13 *d* Rev 18:23 *e* Lev 26:34
8:2 *a* 2Ki 23:5; Ac 7:42
8:3 *b* Job 3:22; Rev 9:6
8:4 *c* Pr 24:16
8:5 *d* Jer 5:27 *e* Jer 7:24; Jer 9:6
8:6 *f* Rev 9:20 *g* Ps 14:1-3
8:7 *h* Isa 1:3; Jer 5:4-5
8:8 *i* Ro 2:17
8:9 *j* Jer 6:15 *k* Jer 6:19
8:10 *l* Jer 6:12 *m* Isa 56:11
8:11 *n* Jer 6:14
8:12 *o* Jer 3:3 *p* Ps 52:5-7; Isa 3:9 *q* Jer 6:15
8:13 *r* Joel 1:7 *s* Lk 13:6 *t* Mt 21:19 *u* Jer 5:17

But my people do not know[h]
the requirements of the LORD.
8" 'How can you say, "We are
wise,
for we have the law[i] of the
LORD,"
when actually the lying pen of
the scribes
has handled it falsely?
9The wise[j] will be put to shame;
they will be dismayed and
trapped.
Since they have rejected the
word[k] of the LORD,
what kind of wisdom do they
have?
10Therefore I will give their
wives to other men
and their fields to new
owners.[l]
From the least to the greatest,
all are greedy for gain;[m]
prophets and priests alike,
all practise deceit.
11They dress the wound of my
people
as though it were not serious.
"Peace, peace," they say,
when there is no peace.[n]
12Are they ashamed of their
loathsome conduct?
No, they have no shame[o] at all;
they do not even know how to
blush.
So they will fall among the
fallen;
they will be brought down
when they are punished,[p]
says the LORD.[q]

13" 'I will take away their harvest,
declares the LORD.
There will be no grapes on the
vine.[r]
There will be no figs[s] on the
tree,
and their leaves will wither.[t]
What I have given them
will be taken[u] from them.' "[a]

14"Why are we sitting here?
Gather together!

[a] *13* The meaning of the Hebrew for this sentence is uncertain.

Let us flee to the fortified
cities[v]
and perish there!
For the LORD our God has
doomed us to perish
and given us poisoned water[w]
to drink,
because we have sinned[x]
against him.
15We hoped for peace[y]
but no good has come,
for a time of healing
but there was only terror.[z]
16The snorting of the enemy's
horses
is heard from Dan;[a]
at the neighing of their stallions
the whole land trembles.
They have come to devour
the land and everything in it,
the city and all who live
there."

17"See, I will send venomous
snakes[b] among you,
vipers that cannot be
charmed,[c]
and they will bite you,"
declares the LORD.

18O my Comforter[b] in sorrow,
my heart is faint[d] within me.
19Listen to the cry of my people
from a land far away:[e]
"Is the LORD not in Zion?
Is her King no longer
there?"

"Why have they provoked me to
anger with their images,
with their worthless foreign
idols?"[f]

20"The harvest is past,
the summer has ended,
and we are not saved."

21Since my people are crushed,
I am crushed;
I mourn,[g] and horror grips
me.
22Is there no balm in Gilead?[h]
Is there no physician there?
Why then is there no healing[i]
for the wound of my people?

8:14 *v* Jer 4:5; Jer 35:11 *w* Dt 29:18; Jer 9:15; Jer 23:15 *x* Jer 14:7,20
8:15 *y* ver 11 *z* Jer 14:19
8:16 *a* Jer 4:15
8:17 *b* Nu 21:6; Dt 32:24 *c* Ps 58:5
8:18 *d* La 5:17
8:19 *e* Jer 9:16 *f* Dt 32:21
8:21 *g* Jer 14:17
8:22 *h* Ge 37:25 *i* Jer 30:12
9:1 *a* Jer 13:17; La 2:11,18 *b* Isa 22:4
9:2 *c* Jer 5:7-8; Jer 23:10; Hos 4:2
9:3 *d* Ps 64:3
9:4 *e* Mic 7:5-6 *f* Ge 27:35
9:6 *g* Jer 5:27
9:7 *h* Isa 1:25 *i* Jer 6:27
9:8 *j* ver 3

9

1Oh, that my head were a
spring of water
and my eyes a fountain of
tears!
I would weep[a] day and night
for the slain of my people.[b]
2Oh, that I had in the desert
a lodging place for travellers,
so that I might leave my people
and go away from them;
for they are all adulterers,[c]
a crowd of unfaithful people.

3"They make ready their tongue
like a bow, to shoot lies;[d]
it is not by truth
that they triumph[a] in the
land.
They go from one sin to
another;
they do not acknowledge me,"
declares the LORD.
4"Beware of your friends;
do not trust your brothers.[e]
For every brother is a
deceiver,[b][f]
and every friend a slanderer.
5Friend deceives friend,
and no-one speaks the truth.
They have taught their tongues
to lie;
they weary themselves with
sinning.
6You[c] live in the midst of
deception;[g]
in their deceit they refuse to
acknowledge me,"
declares the LORD.

7Therefore this is what the LORD
Almighty says:

"See, I will refine[h] and test[i]
them,
for what else can I do
because of the sin of my
people?
8Their tongue[j] is a deadly
arrow;
it speaks with deceit.

[b]18 The meaning of the Hebrew for this word is uncertain. [a]3 Or *lies; / they are not valiant for truth* [b]4 Or *a deceiving Jacob* [c]6 That is, Jeremiah (the Hebrew is singular)

With his mouth each speaks
cordially to his neighbour,
but in his heart he sets a
trap[k] for him.
9 Should I not punish them for
this?"
declares the LORD.
"Should I not avenge[l] myself
on such a nation as this?"
10 I will weep and wail for the
mountains
and take up a lament
concerning the desert
pastures.
They are desolate and
untravelled,
and the lowing of cattle is not
heard.
The birds of the air[m] have fled
and the animals are gone.
11 "I will make Jerusalem a heap
of ruins,
a haunt of jackals;[n]
and I will lay waste the towns
of Judah
so that no-one can live there."[o]

12 What man is wise[p] enough to
understand this? Who has been instructed by the LORD and can explain it? Why has the land been
ruined and laid waste like a desert
that no-one can cross?
13 The LORD said, "It is because
they have forsaken my law, which
I set before them; they have not
obeyed me or followed my law.[q]
14 Instead, they have followed[r] the
stubbornness of their hearts;[s]
they have followed the Baals,
as their fathers taught them."
15 Therefore, this is what the LORD
Almighty, the God of Israel, says:
"See, I will make this people eat
bitter food[t] and drink poisoned water.[u] 16 I will scatter them
among nations[v] that neither they
nor their fathers have known,[w] and
I will pursue them with the sword[x]
until I have destroyed them."[y]

17 This is what the LORD Almighty
says:

"Consider now! Call for the
wailing women[z] to come;
send for the most skilful of
them.
18 Let them come quickly
and wail over us
till our eyes overflow with tears
and water streams from our
eyelids.[a]
19 The sound of wailing is heard
from Zion:
'How ruined[b] we are!
How great is our shame!
We must leave our land
because our houses are in
ruins.' "
20 Now, O women, hear the word
of the LORD;
open your ears to the words of
his mouth.
Teach your daughters how to
wail;
teach one another a lament.[c]
21 Death has climbed in through
our windows
and has entered our
fortresses;
it has cut off the children from
the streets
and the young men[d] from the
public squares.

22 Say, "This is what the LORD declares:

" 'The dead bodies of men will
lie
like refuse[e] on the open field,
like cut corn behind the reaper,
with no-one to gather them.' "

23 This is what the LORD says:

"Let not the wise man boast of
his wisdom[f]
or the strong man boast of his
strength[g]
or the rich man boast of his
riches,[h]
24 but let him who boasts boast[i]
about this:
that he understands and knows
me,
that I am the LORD,[j] who
exercises kindness,[k]

9:8 k Jer 5:26
9:9 l Jer 5:9,29
9:10 m Jer 4:25; Jer 12:4; Hos 4:3
9:11 n Isa 34:13; o Isa 25:2; Jer 26:9
9:12 p Ps 107:43; Hos 14:9
9:13 q 2Ch 7:19; Ps 89:30-32
9:14 r Jer 2:8,23; s Jer 7:24
9:15 t La 3:15; u Jer 8:14
9:16 v Lev 26:33; w Dt 28:64; x Eze 5:2; y Jer 44:27; Eze 5:12
9:17 z 2Ch 35:25; Ecc 12:5; Am 5:16
9:18 a Jer 14:17
9:19 b Jer 4:13
9:20 c Isa 32:9-13
9:21 d 2Ch 36:17
9:22 e Jer 8:2
9:23 f Ecc 9:11; g 1Ki 20:11; h Eze 28:4-5
9:24 i 1Co 1:31*; Gal 6:14; j 2Co 10:17*; k Ps 51:1; Mic 7:18

justice and righteousness[l] on
earth,
for in these I delight,"
declares the LORD.

25"The days are coming," declares the LORD, "when I will punish all who are circumcised only in the flesh[m]—26Egypt, Judah, Edom, Ammon, Moab and all who live in the desert in distant places.[d][n] For all these nations are really uncircumcised, and even the whole house of Israel is uncircumcised in heart.[o]"

God and Idols

10:12–16pp Jer 51:15–19

10 Hear what the LORD says to you, O house of Israel. 2This is what the LORD says:

"Do not learn the ways of the
nations[a]
or be terrified by signs in the
sky,
though the nations are
terrified by them.
3For the customs of the peoples
are worthless;
they cut a tree out of the
forest,
and a craftsman[b] shapes it
with his chisel.
4They adorn it with silver and
gold;
they fasten it with hammer
and nails
so that it will not totter.[c]
5Like a scarecrow in a melon
patch,
their idols cannot speak;[d]
they must be carried
because they cannot walk.[e]
Do not fear them;
they can do no harm
nor can they do any good."[f]

6No-one is like you, O LORD;
you are great,[g]
and your name is mighty in
power.
7Who should not revere you,
O King of the nations?[h]
This is your due.
Among all the wise men of the
nations
and in all their kingdoms,
there is no-one like you.
8They are all senseless and
foolish;[i]
they are taught by worthless
wooden idols.
9Hammered silver is brought
from Tarshish
and gold from Uphaz.
What the craftsman and
goldsmith have made[j]
is then dressed in blue and
purple—
all made by skilled workers.
10But the LORD is the true God;
he is the living God, the
eternal King.
When he is angry, the earth
trembles;
the nations cannot endure his
wrath.[k]

11"Tell them this: 'These gods, who did not make the heavens and the earth, will perish[l] from the earth and from under the heavens.' "[a]

12But God made the earth by his
power;
he founded the world by his
wisdom
and stretched out the
heavens[m] by his
understanding.
13When he thunders,[n] the waters
in the heavens roar;
he makes clouds rise from the
ends of the earth.
He sends lightning with the
rain[o]
and brings out the wind from
his storehouses.

14Everyone is senseless and
without knowledge;
every goldsmith is shamed by
his idols.
His images are a fraud;
they have no breath in them.

9:24 *l* Ps 36:6
9:25 *m* Ro 2:8-9
9:26 *n* Jer 25:23 *o* Lev 26:41; Ac 7:51; Ro 2:28
10:2 *a* Lev 20:23
10:3 *b* Isa 40:19
10:4 *c* Isa 41:7
10:5 *d* 1Co 12:2 *e* Ps 115:5,7 *f* Isa 41:24; Isa 46:7
10:6 *g* Ps 48:1
10:7 *h* Ps 22:28; Rev 15:4
10:8 *i* Isa 40:19; Jer 4:22
10:9 *j* Ps 115:4; Isa 40:19
10:10 *k* Ps 76:7
10:11 *l* Ps 96:5; Isa 2:18
10:12 *m* Ge 1:1,8; Job 9:8; Isa 40:22
10:13 *n* Job 36:29 *o* Ps 135:7

[d]26 Or *desert and who clip the hair by their foreheads*
[a]11 The text of this verse is in Aramaic.

15They are worthless,[p] the
objects of mockery;
when their judgment comes,
they will perish.
16He who is the Portion[q] of Jacob
is not like these,
for he is the Maker of all
things,[r]
including Israel, the tribe of his
inheritance[s]—
the LORD Almighty is his
name.[t]

Coming Destruction

17Gather up your belongings[u] to
leave the land,
you who live under siege.
18For this is what the LORD says:
"At this time I will hurl[v] out
those who live in this land;
I will bring distress on them
so that they may be captured."

19Woe to me because of my
injury!
My wound[w] is incurable!
Yet I said to myself,
"This is my sickness, and I
must endure[x] it."
20My tent[y] is destroyed;
all its ropes are snapped.
My sons are gone from me and
are no more;[z]
no-one is left now to pitch my
tent
or to set up my shelter.
21The shepherds are senseless
and do not enquire of the
LORD;
so they do not prosper
and all their flock is
scattered.[a]
22Listen! The report is coming—
a great commotion from the
land of the north!
It will make the towns of Judah
desolate,
a haunt of jackals.[b]

Jeremiah's Prayer

23I know, O LORD, that a man's
life is not his own;
it is not for man to direct his
steps.[c]
24Correct me, LORD, but only with
justice—
not in your anger,[d]
lest you reduce me to
nothing.[e]
25Pour out your wrath on the
nations[f]
that do not acknowledge you,
on the peoples who do not call
on your name.[g]
For they have devoured[h]
Jacob;
they have devoured him
completely
and destroyed his homeland.[i]

The Covenant Is Broken

11 This is the word that came
to Jeremiah from the LORD:
2"Listen to the terms of this covenant and tell them to the people of
Judah and to those who live in Jerusalem. 3Tell them that this is what
the LORD, the God of Israel, says:
'Cursed[a] is the man who does not
obey the terms of this covenant—
4the terms I commanded your forefathers when I brought them out
of Egypt, out of the iron-smelting
furnace.[b]' I said, 'Obey[c] me and
do everything I command you, and
you will be my people,[d] and I will
be your God. 5Then I will fulfil the
oath I swore[e] to your forefathers,
to give them a land flowing with
milk and honey'—the land you
possess today."
I answered, "Amen, LORD."
6The LORD said to me, "Proclaim
all these words in the towns of Judah and in the streets of Jerusalem:
'Listen to the terms of this covenant and follow[f] them. 7From the
time I brought your forefathers up
from Egypt until today, I warned
them again and again,[g] saying,
"Obey me." 8But they did not listen
or pay attention;[h] instead, they followed the stubbornness of their
evil hearts. So I brought on them all
the curses[i] of the covenant I had

10:15 p Isa 41:24; Jer 14:22
10:16 q Dt 32:9; Ps 119:57; r ver 12; s Ps 74:2; t Jer 31:35; Jer 32:18
10:17 u Eze 12:3-12
10:18 v 1Sa 25:29
10:19 w Jer 14:17; x Mic 7:9
10:20 y Jer 4:20; z Jer 31:15; La 1:5
10:21 a Jer 23:2
10:22 b Jer 9:11
10:23 c Pr 20:24
10:24 d Ps 6:1; Ps 38:1; e Jer 30:11
10:25 f Zep 3:8; g Job 18:21; Ps 14:4; h Ps 79:7; Jer 8:16; i Ps 79:6-7
11:3 a Dt 27:26; Gal 3:10
11:4 b Dt 4:20; 1Ki 8:51; c Ex 24:8; d Jer 7:23; Jer 31:33
11:5 e Ex 13:5; Dt 7:12; Ps 105:8-11
11:6 f Dt 15:5; Ro 2:13; Jas 1:22
11:7 g 2Ch 36:15
11:8 h Jer 7:26; i Lev 26:14-43

commanded them to follow but that they did not keep.' "

9 Then the LORD said to me, "There is a conspiracy[j] among the people of Judah and those who live in Jerusalem. 10 They have returned to the sins of their forefathers,[k] who refused to listen to my words. They have followed other gods[l] to serve them. Both the house of Israel and the house of Judah have broken the covenant I made with their forefathers. 11 Therefore this is what the LORD says: 'I will bring on them a disaster[m] they cannot escape. Although they cry[n] out to me, I will not listen[o] to them. 12 The towns of Judah and the people of Jerusalem will go and cry out to the gods to whom they burn incense,[p] but they will not help them at all when disaster[q] strikes. 13 You have as many gods as you have towns, O Judah; and the altars you have set up to burn incense[r] to that shameful[s] god Baal are as many as the streets of Jerusalem.'

14 "Do not pray[t] for this people nor offer any plea or petition for them, because I will not listen[u] when they call to me in the time of their distress.

15 "What is my beloved doing in
my temple
as she works out her evil
schemes with many?
Can consecrated meat avert
⌊your punishment⌋?
When you engage in your
wickedness,
then you rejoice."[a]

16 The LORD called you a thriving
olive tree
with fruit beautiful in form.
But with the roar of a mighty
storm
he will set it on fire,[v]
and its branches will be
broken.[w]

17 The LORD Almighty, who planted[x] you, has decreed disaster for you, because the house of Israel and the house of Judah have done evil and provoked me to anger by burning incense to Baal.[y]

Plot Against Jeremiah

18 Because the LORD revealed their plot to me, I knew it, for at that time he showed me what they were doing. 19 I had been like a gentle lamb led to the slaughter; I did not realise that they had plotted[z] against me, saying,

"Let us destroy the tree and its
fruit;
let us cut him off from the
land of the living,[a]
that his name be
remembered[b] no more."

20 But, O LORD Almighty, you who
judge righteously
and test the heart and mind,[c]
let me see your vengeance upon
them,
for to you I have committed
my cause.

21 "Therefore this is what the LORD says about the men of Anathoth who are seeking your life[d] and saying, 'Do not prophesy in the name of the LORD or you will die[e] by our hands'— 22 therefore this is what the LORD Almighty says: 'I will punish them. Their young men[f] will die by the sword, their sons and daughters by famine. 23 Not even a remnant[g] will be left to them, because I will bring disaster on the men of Anathoth in the year of their punishment.[h]' "

Jeremiah's Complaint

12 You are always
righteous,[a] O LORD,
when I bring a case before
you.
Yet I would speak with you
about your justice:

11:9 j Eze 22:25
11:10 k Dt 9:7; l Jdg 2:12-13
11:11 m 2Ki 22:16; n Jer 14:12; Eze 8:18; o ver 14; Pr 1:28; Isa 1:15; Zec 7:13
11:12 p Jer 44:17; q Dt 32:37
11:13 r Jer 7:9; s Jer 3:24
11:14 t Ex 32:10; u ver 11
11:16 v Jer 21:14; w Isa 27:11; Ro 11:17-24
11:17 x Isa 5:2; Jer 12:2; y Jer 7:9
11:19 z Jer 18:18; Jer 20:10; a Job 28:13; Isa 53:8; b Ps 83:4
11:20 c Ps 7:9
11:21 d Jer 12:6; e Jer 26:8,11; Jer 38:4
11:22 f Jer 18:21
11:23 g Jer 6:9; h Jer 23:12
12:1 a Ezr 9:15

[a] 15 Or *Could consecrated meat avert your punishment? / Then you would rejoice*

Why does the way of the
wicked prosper?[b]
Why do all the faithless live at
ease?
2You have planted[c] them, and
they have taken root;
they grow and bear fruit.
You are always on their lips
but far from their hearts.[d]
3Yet you know me, O LORD;
you see me and test[e] my
thoughts about you.
Drag them off like sheep to be
butchered!
Set them apart for the day of
slaughter![f]
4How long will the land lie
parched[a][g]
and the grass in every field be
withered?[h]
Because those who live in it are
wicked,
the animals and birds have
perished.[i]
Moreover, the people are
saying,
"He will not see what happens
to us."

God's Answer

5"If you have raced with men on
foot
and they have worn you out,
how can you compete with
horses?
If you stumble in safe
country,[b]
how will you manage in the
thickets[j] by[c] the Jordan?
6Your brothers, your own
family—
even they have betrayed you;
they have raised a loud cry
against you.[k]
Do not trust them,
though they speak well of
you.[l]
7"I will forsake my house,
abandon[m] my inheritance;
I will give the one I love
into the hands of her enemies.
8My inheritance has become to
me
like a lion in the forest.
She roars at me;
therefore I hate her.[n]
9Has not my inheritance become
to me
like a speckled bird of prey
that other birds of prey
surround and attack?
Go and gather all the wild
beasts;
bring them to devour.[o]
10Many shepherds[p] will ruin my
vineyard
and trample down my field;
they will turn my pleasant field
into a desolate wasteland.[q]
11It will be made a wasteland,
parched and desolate before
me;[r]
the whole land will be laid
waste
because there is no-one who
cares.
12Over all the barren heights in
the desert
destroyers will swarm,
for the sword of the LORD[s] will
devour
from one end of the land to
the other;[t]
no-one will be safe.
13They will sow wheat but reap
thorns;
they will wear themselves out
but gain nothing.[u]
So bear the shame of your
harvest
because of the LORD's fierce
anger."[v]

14This is what the LORD says: "As
for all my wicked neighbours who
seize the inheritance I gave to my
people Israel, I will uproot[w] them
from their lands and I will uproot
the house of Judah from among
them. 15But after I uproot them, I
will again have compassion and
will bring[x] each of them back to
his own inheritance and his own
country. 16And if they learn well
the ways of my people and swear

12:1 b Jer 5:27-28
12:2 c Jer 11:17; d Isa 29:13; Jer 3:10; Mt 15:8; Tit 1:16
12:3 e Ps 7:9; Ps 11:5; Ps 139:1-4; Jer 11:20; f Jer 17:18
12:4 g Jer 4:28; h Joel 1:10-12; i Jer 4:25; Jer 9:10
12:5 j Jer 49:19; Jer 50:44
12:6 k Pr 26:24-25; Jer 9:4; l Ps 12:2
12:7 m Jer 7:29
12:8 n Hos 9:15; Am 6:8
12:9 o Isa 56:9; Jer 15:3; Eze 23:25
12:10 p Jer 23:1; q Isa 5:1-7
12:11 r ver 4; Isa 42:25; Jer 23:10
12:12 s Jer 47:6; t Jer 3:2
12:13 u Lev 26:20; Dt 28:38; Mic 6:15; Hag 1:6; v Jer 4:26
12:14 w Zec 2:7-9
12:15 x Am 9:14-15

a4 Or *land mourn*   b5 Or *If you put your trust in a land of safety*   c5 Or *the flooding of*

by my name, saying, 'As surely as
the LORD lives'[y]—even as they
once taught my people to swear by
Baal[z]—then they will be established among my people.[a] 17But if
any nation does not listen, I will
completely uproot and destroy[b]
it," declares the LORD.

A Linen Belt

13 This is what the LORD said
to me: "Go and buy a linen
belt and put it round your waist, but
do not let it touch water." 2So I
bought a belt, as the LORD directed,
and put it round my waist.
3Then the word of the LORD came
to me a second time: 4"Take the
belt you bought and are wearing
round your waist, and go now to
Perath[a] and hide it there in a crev-
ice in the rocks." 5So I went and hid
it at Perath, as the LORD told me.[a]
6Many days later the LORD said to
me, "Go now to Perath and get the
belt I told you to hide there." 7So I
went to Perath and dug up the belt
and took it from the place where I
had hidden it, but now it was ruined
and completely useless.
8Then the word of the LORD came
to me: 9"This is what the LORD
says: 'In the same way I will
ruin the pride of Judah and the
great pride[b] of Jerusalem. 10These
wicked people, who refuse to listen
to my words, who follow the stubbornness of their hearts[c] and go
after other gods[d] to serve and worship them, will be like this belt—
completely useless! 11For as a belt
is bound round a man's waist, so I
bound the whole house of Israel
and the whole house of Judah to
me,' declares the LORD, 'to be my
people for my renown[e] and praise
and honour.[f] But they have not listened.'[g]

Wineskins

12"Say to them: 'This is what the
LORD, the God of Israel, says:
Every wineskin should be filled
with wine.' And if they say to you,
'Don't we know that every wineskin should be filled with wine?'
13then tell them, 'This is what the
LORD says: I am going to fill with
drunkenness[h] all who live in this
land, including the kings who sit on
David's throne, the priests, the
prophets and all those living in
Jerusalem. 14I will smash them one
against the other, fathers and
sons alike, declares the LORD. I
will allow no pity or mercy or
compassion[i] to keep me from
destroying[j] them.' "

Threat of Captivity

15Hear and pay attention,
do not be arrogant,
for the LORD has spoken.
16Give glory[k] to the LORD your
God
before he brings the darkness,
before your feet stumble[l]
on the darkening hills.
You hope for light,
but he will turn it to thick
darkness
and change it to deep gloom.[m]
17But if you do not listen,[n]
I will weep in secret
because of your pride;
my eyes will weep bitterly,
overflowing with tears,[o]
because the LORD's flock[p] will
be taken captive.[q]

18Say to the king and to the queen
mother,
"Come down from your
thrones,
for your glorious crowns
will fall from your heads."
19The cities in the Negev will be
shut up,
and there will be no-one to
open them.
All Judah[r] will be carried into
exile,
carried completely away.

a4 Or possibly *the Euphrates*; also in verses 5–7

12:16 y Jer 4:2 z Jos 23:7 a Isa 49:6 Jer 3:17
12:17 b Isa 60:12
13:5 a Ex 40:16
13:9 b Lev 26:19
13:10 c Jer 11:8 Jer 16:12 d Jer 9:14
13:11 e Jer 32:20 Jer 33:9 f Ex 19:5-6 g Jer 7:26
13:13 h Ps 60:3 Ps 75:8 Isa 51:17 Isa 63:6 Jer 51:57
13:14 i Jer 16:5 j Dt 29:20 Eze 5:10
13:16 k Jos 7:19 l Jer 23:12 m Isa 59:9
13:17 n Mal 2:2 o Jer 9:1 p Ps 80:1 Jer 23:1 q Jer 14:18
13:19 r Jer 20:4 Jer 52:30

20Lift up your eyes and see
those who are coming from
the north.[s]
Where is the flock[t] that was
entrusted to you,
the sheep of which you
boasted?
21What will you say when ⌊the
LORD⌋ sets over you
those you cultivated as your
special allies?[u]
Will not pain grip you
like that of a woman in
labour?[v]
22And if you ask yourself,
"Why has this happened to
me?"—
it is because of your many sins[w]
that your skirts have been
torn off
and your body ill-treated.[x]
23Can the Ethiopian[b] change his
skin
or the leopard its spots?
Neither can you do good
who are accustomed to doing
evil.

24"I will scatter you like chaff[y]
driven by the desert wind.[z]
25This is your lot,
the portion[a] I have decreed
for you,"
declares the LORD,
"because you have forgotten me
and trusted in false gods.
26I will pull up your skirts over
your face
that your shame may be
seen[b]—
27your adulteries and lustful
neighings,
your shameless prostitution![c]
I have seen your detestable acts
on the hills and in the fields.[d]
Woe to you, O Jerusalem!
How long will you be
unclean?"[e]

Drought, Famine, Sword

14 This is the word of the
LORD to Jeremiah concern-
ing the drought:

2"Judah mourns,[a]
her cities languish;
they wail for the land,
and a cry goes up from
Jerusalem.
3The nobles send their servants
for water;
they go to the cisterns
but find no water.[b]
They return with their jars
unfilled;
dismayed and despairing,
they cover their heads.[c]
4The ground is cracked
because there is no rain in the
land;[d]
the farmers are dismayed
and cover their heads.
5Even the doe in the field
deserts her newborn fawn
because there is no grass.[e]
6Wild donkeys stand on the
barren heights[f]
and pant like jackals;
their eyesight fails
for lack of pasture."

7Although our sins testify[g]
against us,
O LORD, do something for the
sake of your name.
For our backsliding[h] is great;
we have sinned[i] against you.
8O Hope[j] of Israel,
its Saviour in times of
distress,
why are you like a stranger in
the land,
like a traveller who stays only
a night?
9Why are you like a man taken
by surprise,
like a warrior powerless to
save?[k]
You are among[l] us, O LORD,
and we bear your name;[m]
do not forsake us!

10This is what the LORD says
about this people:

13:20 s Jer 6:22; Hab 1:6 t Jer 23:2
13:21 u Jer 38:22 v Jer 4:31
13:22 w Jer 9:2-6; Jer 16:10-12 x Eze 16:37; Na 3:5-6
13:24 y Ps 1:4 z Lev 26:33
13:25 a Job 20:29; Mt 24:51
13:26 b La 1:8; Eze 16:37; Hos 2:10
13:27 c Jer 2:20 d Eze 6:13 e Hos 8:5
14:2 a Isa 3:26; Jer 8:21
14:3 b 2Ki 18:31; Job 6:19-20 c 2Sa 15:30
14:4 d Jer 3:3
14:5 e Isa 15:6
14:6 f Job 39:5-6; Jer 2:24
14:7 g Hos 5:5 h Jer 5:6 i Jer 8:14
14:8 j Jer 17:13
14:9 k Isa 50:2 l Jer 8:19 m Isa 63:19; Jer 15:16

b23 Hebrew *Cushite* (probably a person from the upper Nile region)

"They greatly love to wander;
they do not restrain their
feet.[n]
So the LORD does not accept[o]
them;
he will now remember[p] their
wickedness
and punish them for their
sins."[q]

11 Then the LORD said to me, "Do
not pray[r] for the well-being of this
people. 12 Although they fast, I will
not listen to their cry;[s] though they
offer burnt offerings[t] and grain
offerings, I will not accept[u] them.
Instead, I will destroy them with
the sword, famine and plague."
13 But I said, "Ah, Sovereign
LORD, the prophets keep telling
them, 'You will not see the sword or
suffer famine.[v] Indeed, I will give
you lasting peace in this place.'"
14 Then the LORD said to me, "The
prophets are prophesying lies[w] in
my name. I have not sent[x] them or
appointed them or spoken to them.
They are prophesying to you false
visions,[y] divinations,[z] idolatries[a]
and the delusions of their own
minds. 15 Therefore, this is what the
LORD says about the prophets who
are prophesying in my name: I did
not send them, yet they are saying,
'No sword or famine will touch this
land.' Those same prophets will
perish[a] by sword and famine.[b]
16 And the people they are prophesying to will be thrown out into the
streets of Jerusalem because of
the famine and sword. There will
be no-one to bury[c] them or their
wives, their sons or their daughters.[d] I will pour out on them the
calamity they deserve.[e]

17 "Speak this word to them:

" 'Let my eyes overflow with
tears[f]
night and day without ceasing;
for my virgin daughter—my
people—
has suffered a grievous
wound,

14:10 n Ps 119:101; Jer 2:25 o Jer 6:20; Am 5:22 p Hos 9:9 q Jer 44:21-23; Hos 8:13
14:11 r Ex 32:10
14:12 s Isa 1:15; Jer 11:11 t Jer 7:21 u Jer 6:20
14:13 v Jer 5:12
14:14 w Jer 27:14 x Jer 23:21,32 y Jer 23:16 z Eze 12:24
14:15 a Eze 14:9 b Jer 5:12-13
14:16 c Ps 79:3 d Jer 7:33 e Pr 1:31
14:17 f Jer 9:1 g Jer 8:21
14:18 h Eze 7:15
14:19 i Jer 7:29 j Jer 30:12-13 k Jer 8:15
14:20 l Da 9:7-8
14:21 m ver 7 n Jer 3:17
14:22 o Ps 135:7
15:1 a Ex 32:11; Nu 14:13-20 b 1Sa 7:9 c Jer 7:16; Eze 14:14,20 d 2Ki 17:20
15:2 e Jer 43:11

a crushing blow.[g]
18 If I go into the country,
I see those slain by the sword;
if I go into the city,
I see the ravages of famine.[h]
Both prophet and priest
have gone to a land they know
not.' "

19 Have you rejected Judah
completely?[i]
Do you despise Zion?
Why have you afflicted us
so that we cannot be healed?[j]
We hoped for peace
but no good has come,
for a time of healing
but there is only terror.[k]
20 O LORD, we acknowledge our
wickedness
and the guilt of our fathers;
we have indeed sinned[l]
against you.
21 For the sake of your name[m] do
not despise us;
do not dishonour your glorious
throne.[n]
Remember your covenant with
us
and do not break it.
22 Do any of the worthless idols of
the nations bring rain?[o]
Do the skies themselves send
down showers?
No, it is you, O LORD our God.
Therefore our hope is in you,
for you are the one who does
all this.

15 Then the LORD said to me:
"Even if Moses[a] and
Samuel[b] were to stand before me,
my heart would not go out to this
people.[c] Send them away from my
presence![d] Let them go! 2 And if
they ask you, 'Where shall we go?'
tell them, 'This is what the LORD
says:

" 'Those destined for death, to
death;
those for the sword, to the
sword;[e]

a14 *Or visions, worthless divinations*

those for starvation, to
starvation;[f]
those for captivity, to
captivity.'[g]

3"I will send four kinds of destroyers[h] against them," declares
the LORD, "the sword to kill and the
dogs to drag away and the birds[i]
of the air and the beasts of the
earth to devour and destroy.[j] 4I
will make them abhorrent[k] to all
the kingdoms of the earth[l] because of what Manasseh[m] son of
Hezekiah king of Judah did in Jerusalem.

5"Who will have pity[n] on you,
O Jerusalem?
Who will mourn for you?
Who will stop to ask how you
are?
6You have rejected[o] me,"
declares the LORD.
"You keep on backsliding.
So I will lay hands[p] on you and
destroy you;
I can no longer show
compassion.
7I will winnow them with a
winnowing fork
at the city gates of the land.
I will bring bereavement and
destruction on my people,[q]
for they have not changed
their ways.
8I will make their widows more
numerous
than the sand of the sea.
At midday I will bring a
destroyer[r]
against the mothers of their
young men;
suddenly I will bring down on
them
anguish and terror.
9The mother of seven will grow
faint[s]
and breathe her last.
Her sun will set while it is still
day;
she will be disgraced and
humiliated.
I will put the survivors to the
sword[t]
before their enemies,"
declares the LORD.

10Alas, my mother, that you gave
me birth,[u]
a man with whom the whole
land strives and contends![v]
I have neither lent[w] nor
borrowed,
yet everyone curses me.

11The LORD said,

"Surely I will deliver you[x] for
a good purpose;
surely I will make your
enemies plead[y] with you
in times of disaster and times
of distress.

12"Can a man break iron—
iron from the north[z]—or
bronze?
13Your wealth and your treasures
I will give as plunder, without
charge,[a]
because of all your sins
throughout your country.[b]
14I will enslave you to your
enemies
in[a] a land you do not know,[c]
for my anger will kindle a fire[d]
that will burn against you."

15You understand, O LORD;
remember me and care for
me.
Avenge me on my
persecutors.[e]
You are long-suffering—do not
take me away;
think of how I suffer reproach
for your sake.[f]
16When your words came, I ate[g]
them;
they were my joy and my
heart's delight,[h]
for I bear your name,[i]
O LORD God Almighty.
17I never sat[j] in the company of
revellers,
never made merry with them;

[a]14 Some Hebrew manuscripts, Septuagint and Syriac (see also Jer. 17:4); most Hebrew manuscripts *I will cause your enemies to bring you / into*

15:2 f Jer 14:12 g Rev 13:10
15:3 h Lev 26:16 i Dt 28:26 j Lev 26:22 Eze 14:21
15:4 k Jer 24:9 Jer 29:18 l Dt 28:25 m 2Ki 21:2 2Ki 23:26-27
15:5 n Isa 51:19 Jer 13:14 Jer 21:7 Na 3:7
15:6 o Jer 6:19 Jer 7:24 p Zep 1:4
15:7 q Jer 18:21
15:8 r Jer 6:4
15:9 s 1Sa 2:5 t Jer 21:7
15:10 u Job 3:1 v Jer 1:19 w Lev 25:36
15:11 x Jer 40:4 y Jer 21:1-2 Jer 37:3 Jer 42:1-3
15:12 z Jer 28:14
15:13 a Ps 44:12 b Jer 17:3
15:14 c Dt 28:36 Jer 16:13 d Dt 32:22 Ps 21:9
15:15 e Jer 12:3 f Ps 69:7-9
15:16 g Eze 3:3 Rev 10:10 h Ps 119:72, 103 i Jer 14:9
15:17 j Ps 1:1 Ps 26:4-5 Jer 16:8

I sat alone because your hand
was on me
and you had filled me with
indignation.
18Why is my pain unending
and my wound grievous and
incurable?[k]
Will you be to me like a
deceptive brook,
like a spring that fails?[l]

19Therefore this is what the LORD
says:

"If you repent, I will restore
you
that you may serve[m] me;
if you utter worthy, not
worthless, words,
you will be my spokesman.
Let this people turn to you,
but you must not turn to them.
20I will make you a wall to this
people,
a fortified wall of bronze;
they will fight against you
but will not overcome you,
for I am with you
to rescue and save you,"[n]
declares the LORD.
21"I will save you from the hands
of the wicked
and redeem[o] you from the
grasp of the cruel."[p]

Day of Disaster

16 Then the word of the LORD
came to me: 2"You must not
marry[a] and have sons or daughters in this place." 3For this is what
the LORD says about the sons and
daughters born in this land and
about the women who are their
mothers and the men who are their
fathers:[b] 4"They will die of deadly
diseases. They will not be mourned
or buried[c] but will be like refuse
lying on the ground.[d] They will
perish by sword and famine, and
their dead bodies will become food
for the birds of the air and the
beasts of the earth."[e]
5For this is what the LORD says:
"Do not enter a house where there
is a funeral meal; do not go to
mourn or show sympathy, because
I have withdrawn my blessing, my
love and my pity from this people,"
declares the LORD. 6"Both high and
low will die in this land.[f] They will
not be buried or mourned, and no-
one will cut[g] himself or shave[h] his
head for them. 7No-one will offer
food to comfort those who mourn[i]
for the dead—not even for a father
or a mother—nor will anyone give
them a drink to console them.
8"And do not enter a house where
there is feasting and sit down to eat
and drink.[j] 9For this is what the
LORD Almighty, the God of Israel,
says: Before your eyes and in your
days I will bring an end to the
sounds[k] of joy and gladness and to
the voices of bride and bridegroom
in this place.[l]
10"When you tell these people all
this and they ask you, 'Why has the
LORD decreed such a great disaster
against us? What wrong have we
done? What sin have we committed
against the LORD our God?'[m] 11then
say to them, 'It is because your
fathers forsook me,' declares the
LORD, 'and followed other gods and
served and worshipped them. They
forsook me and did not keep my
law.[n] 12But you have behaved
more wickedly than your fathers.[o]
See how each of you is following
the stubbornness of his evil heart[p]
instead of obeying me. 13So I will
throw you out of this land into a
land neither you nor your fathers
have known,[q] and there you will
serve other gods[r] day and night,
for I will show you no favour.'[s]
14"However, the days are coming," declares the LORD, "when
men will no longer say, 'As surely
as the LORD lives, who brought the
Israelites up out of Egypt,'[t] 15but
they will say, 'As surely as the
LORD lives, who brought the Israelites up out of the land of the north
and out of all the countries where
he had banished them.'[u] For I will

15:18 k Jer 30:15; Mic 1:9 l Job 6:15
15:19 m Zec 3:7
15:20 n Jer 20:11; Eze 3:8
15:21 o Jer 50:34 p Ge 48:16
16:2 a 1Co 7:26-27
16:3 b Jer 6:21
16:4 c Jer 25:33 d Ps 83:10; Jer 9:22 e Ps 79:1-3; Jer 15:3; Jer 34:20
16:6 f Eze 9:5-6 g Lev 19:28 h Jer 41:5; Jer 47:5
16:7 i Eze 24:17; Hos 9:4
16:8 j Ecc 7:2-4; Jer 15:17
16:9 k Isa 24:8; Eze 26:13; Hos 2:11 l Rev 18:23
16:10 m Dt 29:24; Jer 5:19
16:11 n Dt 29:25-26; 1Ki 9:9; Ps 106:35-43; Jer 22:9
16:12 o Jer 7:26 p Ecc 9:3; Jer 13:10
16:13 q Dt 28:36; Jer 5:19 r Dt 4:28 s Jer 15:5
16:14 t Dt 15:15; Jer 23:7-8
16:15 u Isa 11:11; Jer 23:8

restore[v] them to the land I gave to
their forefathers.
[16]"But now I will send for many
fishermen," declares the LORD,
"and they will catch them.[w] After
that I will send for many hunters,
and they will hunt[x] them down on
every mountain and hill and from
the crevices of the rocks.[y] [17]My
eyes are on all their ways; they are
not hidden[z] from me, nor is their
sin concealed from my eyes.[a] [18]I
will repay them double[b] for their
wickedness and their sin, because
they have defiled my land[c] with
the lifeless forms of their vile images and have filled my inheritance with their detestable idols."

[19]O LORD, my strength and my fortress,
my refuge in time of distress,
to you the nations will come[d]
from the ends of the earth and say,
"Our fathers possessed nothing but false gods,[e]
worthless idols that did them no good.
[20]Do men make their own gods?
Yes, but they are not gods!"[f]

[21]"Therefore I will teach them—
this time I will teach them
my power and might.
Then they will know
that my name is the LORD.

17 "Judah's sin is engraved with an iron tool,[a]
inscribed with a flint point,
on the tablets of their hearts[b]
and on the horns of their altars.
[2]Even their children remember
their altars and Asherah poles[a][c]
beside the spreading trees
and on the high hills.[d]
[3]My mountain in the land
and your[b] wealth and all your treasures
I will give away as plunder,[e]
together with your high places,[f]
because of sin throughout your country.[g]
[4]Through your own fault you will lose
the inheritance[h] I gave you.
I will enslave you to your enemies[i]
in a land[j] you do not know,
for you have kindled my anger,
and it will burn[k] for ever."

[5]This is what the LORD says:

"Cursed is the one who trusts in man,[l]
who depends on flesh for his strength
and whose heart turns away from the LORD.
[6]He will be like a bush in the wastelands;
he will not see prosperity when it comes.
He will dwell in the parched places of the desert,
in a salt[m] land where no-one lives.

[7]"But blessed is the man who trusts[n] in the LORD,
whose confidence is in him.
[8]He will be like a tree planted by the water
that sends out its roots by the stream.
It does not fear when heat comes;
its leaves are always green.
It has no worries in a year of drought[o]
and never fails to bear fruit."[p]

[9]The heart[q] is deceitful above all things
and beyond cure.
Who can understand it?

[10]"I the LORD search the heart[r]
and examine the mind,[s]
to reward[t] a man according to his conduct,
according to what his deeds deserve."[u]

16:15 v Jer 24:6
16:16 w Am 4:2; Hab 1:14-15 x Am 9:3; Mic 7:2 y 1Sa 26:20
16:17 z 1Co 4:5; Heb 4:13 a Pr 15:3
16:18 b Isa 40:2; Rev 18:6 c Nu 35:34; Jer 2:7
16:19 d Isa 2:2; Jer 3:17 e Ps 4:2
16:20 f Ps 115:4-7; Isa 37:19; Jer 2:11
17:1 a Job 19:24 b Pr 3:3; 2Co 3:3
17:2 c 2Ch 24:18 d Jer 2:20
17:3 e 2Ki 24:13 f Jer 26:18; Mic 3:12 g Jer 15:13
17:4 h La 5:2 i Dt 28:48; Jer 12:7 j Jer 16:13 k Jer 7:20; Jer 15:14
17:5 l Isa 2:22; Isa 30:1-3
17:6 m Dt 29:23; Job 39:6
17:7 n Ps 34:8; Ps 40:4; Pr 16:20
17:8 o Jer 14:1-6 p Ps 1:3; Ps 92:12-14
17:9 q Ecc 9:3; Mt 13:15; Mk 7:21-22
17:10 r 1Sa 16:7; Rev 2:23 s Ps 17:3; Ps 139:23; Jer 11:20; Jer 20:12; Ro 8:27 t Ps 62:12; Jer 32:19 u Ro 2:6

[a]2 That is, symbols of the goddess Asherah [b]2,3 Or *hills* / [3]*and the mountains of the land. / Your*

11Like a partridge that hatches
eggs it did not lay
is the man who gains riches
by unjust means.
When his life is half gone, they
will desert him,
and in the end he will prove to
be a fool.[v]

12A glorious throne,[w] exalted
from the beginning,
is the place of our sanctuary.
13O LORD, the hope[x] of Israel,
all who forsake[y] you will be
put to shame.
Those who turn away from you
will be written in the dust
because they have forsaken
the LORD,
the spring of living water.

14Heal me, O LORD, and I shall be
healed;
save me and I shall be saved,
for you are the one I praise.[z]
15They keep saying to me,
"Where is the word of the
LORD?
Let it now be fulfilled!"[a]
16I have not run away from being
your shepherd;
you know I have not desired
the day of despair.
What passes my lips is open
before you.
17Do not be a terror[b] to me;
you are my refuge[c] in the day
of disaster.
18Let my persecutors be put to
shame,
but keep me from shame;
let them be terrified,
but keep me from terror.
Bring on them the day of
disaster;
destroy them with double
destruction.[d]

Keeping the Sabbath Holy

19This is what the LORD said to
me: "Go and stand at the gate of the
people, through which the kings of
Judah go in and out; stand also at
all the other gates of Jerusalem.[e]

17:11 v Lk 12:20
17:12 w Jer 3:17
17:13 x Jer 14:8 y Isa 1:28 Jer 2:17
17:14 z Ps 109:1
17:15 a Isa 5:19 2Pe 3:4
17:17 b Ps 88:15-16 c Jer 16:19 Na 1:7
17:18 d Ps 35:1-8
17:19 e Jer 7:2 Jer 26:2
17:20 f Jer 19:3 g Jer 22:2
17:21 h Nu 15:32-36 Ne 13:15-21 Jn 5:10
17:22 i Ex 20:8 Ex 31:13 Isa 56:2-6 Eze 20:12
17:23 j Jer 7:26 k Jer 19:15 l Jer 7:28
17:25 m 2Sa 7:13 Isa 9:7 Jer 22:2,4 Lk 1:32
17:26 n Jer 32:44 Jer 33:13 Zec 7:7
17:27 o Jer 22:5 p Jer 7:20 q 2Ki 25:9 Am 2:5

20Say to them, 'Hear the word of the
LORD, O kings of Judah and all people of Judah and everyone living
in Jerusalem[f] who come through
these gates.[g] 21This is what the
LORD says: Be careful not to carry
a load on the Sabbath[h] day or bring
it through the gates of Jerusalem.
22Do not bring a load out of your
houses or do any work on the
Sabbath, but keep the Sabbath
day holy, as I commanded your
forefathers.[i] 23Yet they did not
listen or pay attention;[j] they were
stiff-necked[k] and would not listen
or respond to discipline.[l] 24But
if you are careful to obey me, declares the LORD, and bring no load
through the gates of this city on the
Sabbath, but keep the Sabbath day
holy by not doing any work on it,
25then kings who sit on David's
throne[m] will come through the
gates of this city with their officials. They and their officials will
come riding in chariots and on
horses, accompanied by the men of
Judah and those living in Jerusalem, and this city will be inhabited for ever. 26People will come
from the towns of Judah and the
villages around Jerusalem, from
the territory of Benjamin and the
western foothills, from the hill
country and the Negev,[n] bringing
burnt offerings and sacrifices,
grain offerings, incense and thank-
offerings to the house of the LORD.
27But if you do not obey[o] me to
keep the Sabbath day holy by not
carrying any load as you come
through the gates of Jerusalem on
the Sabbath day, then I will kindle
an unquenchable fire[p] in the gates
of Jerusalem that will consume her
fortresses.' "[q]

At the Potter's House

18 This is the word that came
to Jeremiah from the LORD:
2"Go down to the potter's house,
and there I will give you my message." 3So I went down to the

potter's house, and I saw him working at the wheel. 4But the pot he was
shaping from the clay was marred
in his hands; so the potter formed it
into another pot, shaping it as
seemed best to him.

5Then the word of the LORD came
to me: 6"O house of Israel, can I not
do with you as this potter does?"
declares the LORD. "Like clay[a] in
the hand of the potter, so are you in
my hand, O house of Israel. 7If at
any time I announce that a nation
or kingdom is to be uprooted,[b] torn
down and destroyed, 8and if that
nation I warned repents of its evil,
then I will relent[c] and not inflict on
it the disaster[d] I had planned. 9And
if at another time I announce that a
nation or kingdom is to be built[e] up
and planted, 10and if it does evil[f] in
my sight and does not obey me,
then I will reconsider[g] the good I
had intended to do for it.

11"Now therefore say to the people of Judah and those living in
Jerusalem, 'This is what the LORD
says: Look! I am preparing a disaster[h] for you and devising a plan
against you. So turn[i] from your
evil ways,[j] each one of you, and reform your ways and your actions.'
12But they will reply, 'It's no use.[k]
We will continue with our own
plans; each of us will follow the
stubbornness of his evil heart.' "

13Therefore this is what the LORD
says:

"Enquire among the nations:
Who has ever heard anything
like this?[l]
A most horrible[m] thing has
been done
by Virgin Israel.
14Does the snow of Lebanon
ever vanish from its rocky
slopes?
Do its cool waters from distant
sources
ever cease to flow?[a]
15Yet my people have forgotten
me;
they burn incense to worthless
idols,[n]
which made them stumble in
their ways
and in the ancient paths.[o]
They made them walk in
bypaths
and on roads not built up.[p]
16Their land will be laid waste,[q]
an object of lasting scorn;[r]
all who pass by will be appalled
and will shake their heads.[s]
17Like a wind[t] from the east,
I will scatter them before
their enemies;
I will show them my back and
not my face[u]
in the day of their disaster."

18They said, "Come, let's make
plans[v] against Jeremiah; for the
teaching of the law by the priest[w]
will not be lost, nor will counsel
from the wise, nor the word from
the prophets.[x] So come, let's attack him with our tongues[y] and
pay no attention to anything he
says."

19Listen to me, O LORD;
hear what my accusers are
saying!
20Should good be repaid with
evil?
Yet they have dug a pit[z] for
me.
Remember that I stood before
you
and spoke on their behalf[a]
to turn your wrath away from
them.
21So give their children over to
famine;[b]
hand them over to the power
of the sword.
Let their wives be made
childless and widows;[c]
let their men be put to death,
their young men slain by the
sword in battle.
22Let a cry[d] be heard from their
houses

18:6 *a* Isa 45:9; Ro 9:20-21
18:7 *b* Jer 1:10
18:8 *c* Jer 26:13; Jnh 3:8-10 *d* Eze 18:21; Hos 11:8-9
18:9 *e* Jer 1:10; Jer 31:28
18:10 *f* Eze 33:18 *g* 1Sa 2:29-30
18:11 *h* Jer 4:6 *i* 2Ki 17:13; Isa 1:16-19 *j* Jer 7:3
18:12 *k* Isa 57:10; Jer 2:25
18:13 *l* Isa 66:8; Jer 2:10 *m* Jer 5:30
18:15 *n* Jer 10:15 *o* Jer 6:16 *p* Isa 57:14; Isa 62:10
18:16 *q* Jer 25:9 *r* Jer 19:8 *s* Ps 22:7
18:17 *t* Jer 13:24 *u* Jer 2:27
18:18 *v* Jer 11:19 *w* Mal 2:7 *x* Jer 5:13 *y* Ps 52:2
18:20 *z* Ps 35:7; Ps 57:6 *a* Ps 106:23
18:21 *b* Jer 11:22 *c* Ps 109:9
18:22 *d* Jer 6:26

[a]14 The meaning of the Hebrew for this sentence is uncertain.

when you suddenly bring
invaders against them,
for they have dug a pit to
capture me
and have hidden snares[e] for
my feet.
23But you know, O LORD,
all their plots to kill[f] me.
Do not forgive[g] their crimes
or blot out their sins from
your sight.
Let them be overthrown before
you;
deal with them in the time of
your anger.

19 This is what the LORD says:
"Go and buy a clay jar from
a potter.[a] Take along some of the
elders[b] of the people and of the
priests 2and go out to the Valley of
Ben Hinnom,[c] near the entrance
of the Potsherd Gate. There proclaim the words I tell you, 3and
say, 'Hear the word of the LORD,
O kings[d] of Judah and people of
Jerusalem. This is what the LORD
Almighty, the God of Israel, says:
Listen! I am going to bring a disaster[e] on this place that will make
the ears of everyone who hears of
it tingle.[f] 4For they have forsaken[g] me and made this a place of
foreign gods; they have burned
sacrifices[h] in it to gods that neither they nor their fathers nor the
kings of Judah ever knew, and they
have filled this place with the blood
of the innocent.[i] 5They have built
the high places of Baal to burn
their sons[j] in the fire as offerings
to Baal—something I did not command or mention, nor did it enter
my mind.[k] 6So beware, the days
are coming, declares the LORD,
when people will no longer call this
place Topheth or the Valley of Ben
Hinnom,[l] but the Valley of Slaughter.[m]
7" 'In this place I will ruin[a] the
plans of Judah and Jerusalem. I
will make them fall by the sword
before their enemies,[n] at the
hands of those who seek their lives,
and I will give their carcasses[o] as
food[p] to the birds of the air and the
beasts of the earth. 8I will devastate this city and make it an object
of scorn;[q] all who pass by will be
appalled and will scoff because of
all its wounds. 9I will make them
eat[r] the flesh of their sons and
daughters, and they will eat one another's flesh during the stress of
the siege imposed on them by the
enemies[s] who seek their lives.'
10"Then break the jar[t] while
those who go with you are watching, 11and say to them, 'This is what
the LORD Almighty says: I will
smash[u] this nation and this city
just as this potter's jar is smashed
and cannot be repaired. They will
bury[v] the dead in Topheth until
there is no more room. 12This is
what I will do to this place and to
those who live here, declares the
LORD. I will make this city like Topheth. 13The houses[w] in Jerusalem
and those of the kings of Judah will
be defiled like this place, Topheth—all the houses where they
burned incense on the roofs to all
the starry hosts[x] and poured out
drink offerings[y] to other gods.' "
14Jeremiah then returned from
Topheth, where the LORD had sent
him to prophesy, and stood in the
court[z] of the LORD's temple and
said to all the people, 15"This is
what the LORD Almighty, the God
of Israel, says: 'Listen! I am going
to bring on this city and the villages
around it every disaster I pronounced against them, because
they were stiff-necked[a] and would
not listen to my words.' "

Jeremiah and Pashhur

20 When the priest Pashhur
son of Immer,[a] the chief
officer[b] in the temple of the LORD,
heard Jeremiah prophesying these
things, 2he had Jeremiah the
prophet beaten[c] and put in the

a7 The Hebrew for *ruin* sounds like the Hebrew for *jar* (see verses 1 and 10).

18:22 e Ps 140:5
18:23 f Jer 11:21 g Ps 109:14
19:1 a Jer 18:2 b Nu 11:17
19:2 c Jos 15:8
19:3 d Jer 17:20 e Jer 6:19 f 1Sa 3:11
19:4 g Dt 28:20 Isa 65:11 h Lev 18:21 i 2Ki 21:16 Jer 2:34
19:5 j Lev 18:21 Ps 106:37-38 k Jer 7:31 Jer 32:35
19:6 l Jos 15:8 m Jer 7:32
19:7 n Lev 26:17 Dt 28:25 o Jer 16:4 Jer 34:20 p Ps 79:2
19:8 q Jer 18:16
19:9 r Lev 26:29 Dt 28:49-57 La 4:10 s Isa 9:20
19:10 t ver 1
19:11 u Ps 2:9 Isa 30:14 v Jer 7:32
19:13 w Jer 32:29 Jer 52:13 x Dt 4:19 Ac 7:42 y Jer 7:18 Eze 20:28
19:14 z 2Ch 20:5 Jer 26:2
19:15 a Ne 9:16 Jer 7:26 Jer 17:23
20:1 a 1Ch 24:14 b 2Ki 25:18
20:2 c Jer 1:19

stocks[d] at the Upper Gate of Benjamin[e] at the LORD's temple. 3The
next day, when Pashhur released
him from the stocks, Jeremiah
said to him, "The LORD's name for
you is not Pashhur, but Magor-
Missabib.[a][f] 4For this is what the
LORD says: 'I will make you a terror
to yourself and to all your friends;
with your own eyes[g] you will see
them fall by the sword of their enemies. I will hand[h] all Judah over
to the king of Babylon, who will
carry[i] them away to Babylon or
put them to the sword. 5I will hand
over to their enemies all the
wealth[j] of this city—all its products, all its valuables and all the
treasures of the kings of Judah.
They will take it away[k] as plunder
and carry it off to Babylon. 6And
you, Pashhur, and all who live in
your house will go into exile to
Babylon. There you will die and
be buried, you and all your friends
to whom you have prophesied[l]
lies.'"

Jeremiah's Complaint

7O LORD, you deceived[b] me, and
I was deceived;[b]
you overpowered me and
prevailed.
I am ridiculed all day long;
everyone mocks me.
8Whenever I speak, I cry out
proclaiming violence and
destruction.[m]
So the word of the LORD has
brought me
insult and reproach[n] all day
long.
9But if I say, "I will not mention
him
or speak any more in his
name,"
his word is in my heart like a
fire,[o]
a fire shut up in my bones.
I am weary of holding it in;[p]
indeed, I cannot.
10I hear many whispering,
"Terror[q] on every side!
Report[r] him! Let's report
him!"
All my friends[s]
are waiting for me to slip,[t]
saying,
"Perhaps he will be deceived;
then we will prevail[u] over
him
and take our revenge on him."
11But the LORD[v] is with me like a
mighty warrior;
so my persecutors[w] will
stumble and not prevail.[x]
They will fail and be thoroughly
disgraced;[y]
their dishonour will never be
forgotten.
12O LORD Almighty, you who
examine the righteous
and probe the heart and
mind,[z]
let me see your vengeance[a]
upon them,
for to you I have committed[b]
my cause.
13Sing to the LORD!
Give praise to the LORD!
He rescues[c] the life of the
needy
from the hands of the wicked.
14Cursed be the day I was born![d]
May the day my mother bore
me not be blessed!
15Cursed be the man who brought
my father the news,
who made him very glad,
saying,
"A child is born to you—a
son!"
16May that man be like the
towns[e]
the LORD overthrew without
pity.
May he hear wailing in the
morning,
a battle cry at noon.
17For he did not kill me in the
womb,[f]
with my mother as my grave,
her womb enlarged for ever.

a3 *Magor-Missabib* means *terror on every side.*
b7 Or *persuaded*

20:2 d Job 13:27 e Jer 37:13; Jer 38:7; Zec 14:10
20:3 f ver 10
20:4 g Jer 29:21 h Jer 21:10 i Jer 52:27
20:5 j Jer 17:3 k 2Ki 20:17
20:6 l Jer 14:15; La 2:14
20:8 m Jer 6:7 n 2Ch 36:16; Jer 6:10
20:9 o Ps 39:3 p Job 32:18-20; Ac 4:20
20:10 q Ps 31:13; Jer 6:25 r Isa 29:21 s Ps 41:9 t Lk 11:53-54 u 1Ki 19:2
20:11 v Jer 1:8; Ro 8:31 w Jer 17:18 x Jer 15:20 y Jer 23:40
20:12 z Jer 17:10 a Ps 54:7; Ps 59:10 b Ps 62:8; Jer 11:20
20:13 c Ps 35:10
20:14 d Job 3:3; Jer 15:10
20:16 e Ge 19:25
20:17 f Job 10:18-19

18Why did I ever come out of the
womb
to see trouble and sorrow
and to end my days in
shame?[g]

God Rejects Zedekiah's Request

21 The word came to Jeremiah from the LORD when King Zedekiah[a] sent to him Pashhur[b] son of Malkijah and the priest Zephaniah[c] son of Maaseiah. They said: 2"Enquire[d] now of the LORD for us because Nebuchadnezzar[a][e] king of Babylon is attacking us. Perhaps the LORD will perform wonders[f] for us as in times past so that he will withdraw from us."

3But Jeremiah answered them, "Tell Zedekiah, 4'This is what the LORD, the God of Israel, says: I am about to turn[g] against you the weapons of war that are in your hands, which you are using to fight the king of Babylon and the Babylonians[b] who are outside the wall besieging[h] you. And I will gather them inside this city. 5I myself will fight against you with an outstretched hand[i] and a mighty arm in anger and fury and great wrath. 6I will strike down those who live in this city—both men and animals—and they will die of a terrible plague.[j] 7After that, declares the LORD, I will hand over Zedekiah[k] king of Judah, his officials and the people in this city who survive the plague, sword and famine, to Nebuchadnezzar king of Babylon[l] and to their enemies who seek their lives. He will put them to the sword; he will show them no mercy or pity or compassion.'[m]

8"Furthermore, tell the people, 'This is what the LORD says: See, I am setting before you the way of life and the way of death. 9Whoever stays in this city will die by the sword, famine or plague.[n] But whoever goes out and surrenders to the Babylonians who are besieging you will live; he will escape with his life.[o] 10I have determined to do this city harm[p] and not good, declares the LORD. It will be given into the hands[q] of the king of Babylon, and he will destroy it with fire.'[r]

11"Moreover, say to the royal house[s] of Judah, 'Hear the word of the LORD; 12O house of David, this is what the LORD says:

"'Administer justice[t] every
morning;
rescue from the hand of his
oppressor
the one who has been robbed,
or my wrath will break out and
burn like fire
because of the evil you have
done—
burn with no-one to quench[u]
it.
13I am against[v] you, ⌞Jerusalem,⌟
you who live above this
valley[w]
on the rocky plateau,
declares the LORD—
you who say, "Who can come
against us?
Who can enter our refuge?"[x]
14I will punish you as your
deeds[y] deserve,
declares the LORD.
I will kindle a fire[z] in your
forests[a]
that will consume everything
around you.'"

Judgment Against Evil Kings

22 This is what the LORD says: "Go down to the palace of the king of Judah and proclaim this message there: 2'Hear the word of the LORD, O king of Judah, you who sit on David's throne[a]—you, your officials and your people who come through these gates.[b] 3This is what the LORD says: Do what is just[c] and right. Rescue from the hand of his oppressor[d] the one who has been

20:18 g Ps 90:9
21:1 a 2Ki 24:18; Jer 52:1 b Jer 38:1 c 2Ki 25:18; Jer 29:25; Jer 37:3
21:2 d Jer 37:3,7 e 2Ki 25:1 f Ps 44:1-4; Jer 32:17
21:4 g Jer 32:5 h Jer 37:8-10
21:5 i Jer 6:12
21:6 j Jer 14:12
21:7 k 2Ki 25:7; Jer 52:9 l Jer 37:17; Jer 39:5 m 2Ch 36:17; Eze 7:9; Hab 1:6
21:9 n Jer 14:12 o Jer 38:2,17; Jer 39:18; Jer 45:5
21:10 p Jer 44:11,27; Am 9:4 q Jer 32:28; Jer 38:2-3 r Jer 52:13
21:11 s Jer 13:18
21:12 t Jer 22:3 u Isa 1:31
21:13 v Eze 13:8 w Ps 125:2 x Jer 49:4; Ob 1:3-4
21:14 y Isa 3:10-11 z 2Ch 36:19; Jer 52:13 a Eze 20:47
22:2 a Jer 17:25; Lk 1:32 b Jer 17:20
22:3 c Mic 6:8; Zec 7:9 d Ps 72:4; Jer 21:12

a2 Hebrew *Nebuchadrezzar*, of which *Nebuchadnezzar* is a variant; here and often in Jeremiah and Ezekiel b4 Or *Chaldeans*; also in verse 9

robbed. Do no wrong or violence to
the alien, the fatherless or the
widow,[e] and do not shed innocent
blood in this place. 4 For if you are
careful to carry out these commands, then kings[f] who sit on
David's throne will come through
the gates of this palace, riding in
chariots and on horses, accompanied by their officials and their
people. 5 But if you do not obey[g]
these commands, declares the
LORD, I swear[h] by myself that this
palace will become a ruin.' "
6 For this is what the LORD says
about the palace of the king of Judah:

"Though you are like Gilead to
me,
like the summit of Lebanon,
I will surely make you like a
desert,[i]
like towns not inhabited.
7 I will send destroyers[j] against
you,
each man with his weapons,
and they will cut[k] up your fine
cedar beams
and throw them into the fire.

8 "People from many nations will
pass by this city and will ask one
another, 'Why has the LORD done
such a thing to this great city?'[l]
9 And the answer will be: 'Because
they have forsaken the covenant of
the LORD their God and have worshipped and served other gods.[m]' "

10 Do not weep for the dead[n]
⌊king⌋ or mourn[o] his loss;
rather, weep bitterly for him
who is exiled,
because he will never return
nor see his native land again.

11 For this is what the LORD says
about Shallum[a][p] son of Josiah,
who succeeded his father as king of
Judah but has gone from this place:
"He will never return. 12 He will
die[q] in the place where they have
led him captive; he will not see this
land again."

13 "Woe to him who builds[r] his
palace by unrighteousness,
his upper rooms by injustice,
making his countrymen work
for nothing,
not paying[s] them for their
labour.
14 He says, 'I will build myself a
great palace[t]
with spacious upper rooms.'
So he makes large windows in
it,
panels it with cedar[u]
and decorates it in red.
15 "Does it make you a king
to have more and more cedar?
Did not your father have food
and drink?
He did what was right and
just,[v]
so all went well[w] with him.
16 He defended the cause of the
poor and needy,[x]
and so all went well.
Is that not what it means to
know me?"
declares the LORD.
17 "But your eyes and your heart
are set only on dishonest gain,
on shedding innocent blood[y]
and on oppression and
extortion."

18 Therefore this is what the LORD
says about Jehoiakim son of Josiah
king of Judah:

"They will not mourn for him:
'Alas, my brother! Alas, my
sister!'
They will not mourn for him:
'Alas, my master! Alas, his
splendour!'
19 He will have the burial of a
donkey—
dragged away and thrown[z]
outside the gates of
Jerusalem."

20 "Go up to Lebanon and cry out,
let your voice be heard in
Bashan,
cry out from Abarim,[a]

[a] 11 Also called *Jehoahaz*

22:3 e Ex 22:22
22:4 f Jer 17:25
22:5 g Jer 17:27 h Heb 6:13
22:6 i Mic 3:12
22:7 j Jer 4:7 k Isa 10:34
22:8 l Dt 29:25-26 1Ki 9:8-9 Jer 16:10-11
22:9 m 2Ki 22:17 2Ch 34:25
22:10 n Ecc 4:2 o ver 18
22:11 p 2Ki 23:31
22:12 q 2Ki 23:34
22:13 r Mic 3:10 Hab 2:9 s Lev 19:13 Jas 5:4
22:14 t Isa 5:8-9 u 2Sa 7:2
22:15 v 2Ki 23:25 w Ps 128:2 Isa 3:10
22:16 x Ps 72:1-4, 12-13
22:17 y 2Ki 24:4
22:19 z Jer 36:30
22:20 a Nu 27:12

for all your allies are crushed.
21 I warned you when you felt
secure,
but you said, 'I will not listen!'
This has been your way from
your youth;[b]
you have not obeyed[c] me.
22 The wind will drive all your
shepherds away,
and your allies will go into
exile.
Then you will be ashamed and
disgraced
because of all your
wickedness.
23 You who live in 'Lebanon',[b]
who are nestled in cedar
buildings,
how you will groan when pangs
come upon you,
pain[d] like that of a woman in
labour!

24 "As surely as I live," declares
the LORD, "even if you, Jehoiachin[c][e] son of Jehoiakim king of
Judah, were a signet ring on my
right hand, I would still pull you
off. 25 I will hand you over[f] to those
who seek your life, those you
fear—to Nebuchadnezzar king of
Babylon and to the Babylonians.[d]
26 I will hurl[g] you and the mother
who gave you birth into another
country, where neither of you was
born, and there you both will die.
27 You will never come back to the
land you long to return to."

28 Is this man Jehoiachin a
despised, broken pot,[h]
an object no-one wants?
Why will he and his children be
hurled[i] out,
cast into a land[j] they do not
know?
29 O land,[k] land, land,
hear the word of the LORD!
30 This is what the LORD says:
"Record this man as if
childless,[l]
a man who will not prosper[m]
in his lifetime,
for none of his offspring will
prosper,
none will sit on the throne[n] of
David
or rule any more in Judah."

The Righteous Branch

23 "Woe to the shepherds[a]
who are destroying and
scattering[b] the sheep of my pasture!"[c] declares the LORD. 2 Therefore this is what the LORD, the God
of Israel, says to the shepherds who
tend my people: "Because you have
scattered my flock and driven
them away and have not bestowed
care on them, I will bestow punishment on you for the evil[d] you have
done," declares the LORD. 3 "I myself will gather the remnant[e] of
my flock out of all the countries
where I have driven them and will
bring them back to their pasture,
where they will be fruitful and
increase in number. 4 I will place
shepherds[f] over them who will
tend them, and they will no longer
be afraid[g] or terrified, nor will any
be missing,[h]" declares the LORD.

5 "The days are coming,"
declares the LORD,
"when I will raise up to
David[a] a righteous
Branch,[i]
a King who will reign[j] wisely
and do what is just and right[k]
in the land.
6 In his days Judah will be saved
and Israel will live in safety.
This is the name[l] by which he
will be called:
The LORD Our
Righteousness.[m]

7 "So then, the days are coming," declares the LORD, "when people will
no longer say, 'As surely as the
LORD lives, who brought the Israelites up out of Egypt,'[n] 8 but they
will say, 'As surely as the LORD
lives, who brought the descendants

[b]23 That is, the palace in Jerusalem (see 1 Kings 7:2) [c]24 Hebrew *Coniah*, a variant of *Jehoiachin*; also in verse 28 [d]25 Or *Chaldeans*
[a]5 Or *up from David's line*

22:21 b Jer 3:25; Jer 32:30 c Jer 7:23-28
22:23 d Jer 4:31
22:24 e 2Ki 24:6,8; Jer 37:1
22:25 f 2Ki 24:16; Jer 34:20
22:26 g 2Ki 24:8; 2Ch 36:10
22:28 h Ps 31:12; Jer 48:38; Hos 8:8 i Jer 15:1 j Jer 17:4
22:29 k Jer 6:19; Mic 1:2
22:30 l 1Ch 3:18; Mt 1:12 m Jer 10:21 n Ps 94:20
23:1 a Jer 10:21; Eze 34:1-10; Zec 11:15-17 b Isa 56:11 c Eze 34:31
23:2 d Jer 21:12
23:3 e Isa 11:10-12; Jer 32:37; Eze 34:11-16
23:4 f Jer 3:15; Jer 31:10; Eze 34:23 g Jer 30:10; Jer 46:27-28 h Jn 6:39
23:5 i Isa 4:2 j Isa 9:7 k Isa 11:1; Zec 6:12
23:6 l Jer 33:16; Mt 1:21-23 m Ro 3:21-22; 1Co 1:30
23:7 n Jer 16:14

of Israel up out of the land of the north and out of all the countries where he had banished them.' Then they will live in their own land."[o]

Lying Prophets

9 Concerning the prophets:

My heart is broken within me;
  all my bones tremble.
I am like a drunken man,
  like a man overcome by wine,
because of the LORD
  and his holy words.[p]
10 The land is full of adulterers;[q]
  because of the curse[b] the land
    lies parched[c]
  and the pastures[r] in the
    desert are withered.[s]
The ⌞prophets⌟ follow an evil
    course
  and use their power unjustly.
11 "Both prophet and priest are
    godless;[t]
  even in my temple[u] I find
    their wickedness,"
      declares the LORD.
12 "Therefore their path will
    become slippery;[v]
  they will be banished to
    darkness
  and there they will fall.
I will bring disaster on them
  in the year they are
    punished,[w]"
      declares the LORD.
13 "Among the prophets of
    Samaria
  I saw this repulsive thing:
They prophesied by Baal[x]
  and led my people Israel
    astray.
14 And among the prophets of
    Jerusalem
  I have seen something
    horrible:[y]
  They commit adultery and live
    a lie.[z]
They strengthen the hands of
    evildoers,[a]
  so that no-one turns from his
    wickedness.
They are all like Sodom[b] to me;
  the people of Jerusalem are
    like Gomorrah."[c]

15 Therefore, this is what the LORD Almighty says concerning the prophets:

"I will make them eat bitter
    food
  and drink poisoned water,[d]
because from the prophets of
    Jerusalem
  ungodliness has spread
    throughout the land."

16 This is what the LORD Almighty says:

"Do not listen[e] to what the
    prophets are prophesying
    to you;
  they fill you with false hopes.
They speak visions[f] from their
    own minds,
  not from the mouth[g] of the
    LORD.
17 They keep saying to those who
    despise me,
  'The LORD says: You will have
    peace.'[h]
And to all who follow the
    stubbornness[i] of their
    hearts
  they say, 'No harm[j] will come
    to you.'
18 But which of them has stood in
    the council of the LORD
  to see or to hear his word?
  Who has listened and heard
    his word?
19 See, the storm[k] of the LORD
  will burst out in wrath,
a whirlwind swirling down
  on the heads of the wicked.
20 The anger[l] of the LORD will not
    turn back[m]
  until he fully accomplishes
    the purposes of his heart.
In days to come
  you will understand it clearly.
21 I did not send[n] these prophets,
  yet they have run with their
    message;

23:8 o Isa 43:5-6; Am 9:14-15
23:9 p Jer 20:8-9
23:10 q Jer 9:2; r Ps 107:34; Jer 9:10; s Hos 4:2-3
23:11 t Jer 6:13; Jer 8:10; Zep 3:4; u Jer 7:10
23:12 v Ps 35:6; Jer 13:16; w Jer 11:23
23:13 x Jer 2:8
23:14 y Jer 5:30; z Jer 29:23; a Eze 13:22; b Ge 18:20; c Isa 1:9-10; Jer 20:16
23:15 d Jer 8:14; Jer 9:15
23:16 e Jer 27:9-10, 14; Mt 7:15; f Jer 14:14; g Jer 9:20
23:17 h Jer 8:11; i Jer 13:10; j Jer 5:12; Am 9:10; Mic 3:11
23:19 k Jer 25:32; Jer 30:23
23:20 l 2Ki 23:26; m Jer 30:24
23:21 n Jer 14:14; Jer 27:15

b 10 Or *because of these things*   c 10 Or *land mourns*

I did not speak to them,
yet they have prophesied.
22But if they had stood in my
council,
they would have proclaimed
my words to my people
and would have turned[o] them
from their evil ways
and from their evil deeds.

23"Am I only a God nearby,[p]"
declares the LORD,
"and not a God far away?
24Can anyone hide[q] in secret
places
so that I cannot see him?"
declares the LORD.
"Do not I fill heaven and
earth?"[r]
declares the LORD.

25"I have heard what the prophets say who prophesy lies[s] in my
name. They say, 'I had a dream![t] I
had a dream!' 26How long will this
continue in the hearts of these lying prophets, who prophesy the
delusions[u] of their own minds?
27They think the dreams they tell
one another will make my people
forget[v] my name, just as their fathers forgot[w] my name through
Baal worship. 28Let the prophet
who has a dream tell his dream, but
let the one who has my word speak
it faithfully. For what has straw to
do with grain?" declares the LORD.
29"Is not my word like fire,"[x] declares the LORD, "and like a hammer that breaks a rock in pieces?
30"Therefore," declares the LORD,
"I am against[y] the prophets[z] who
steal from one another words
supposedly from me. 31Yes," declares the LORD, "I am against
the prophets who wag their own
tongues and yet declare, 'The LORD
declares.'[a] 32Indeed, I am against
those who prophesy false dreams,[b]"
declares the LORD. "They tell
them and lead my people astray
with their reckless lies, yet I did
not send or appoint them. They
do not benefit[c] these people in the
least," declares the LORD.

23:22 o Jer 25:5; Zec 1:4
23:23 p Ps 139:1-10
23:24 q Job 22:12-14; r 1Ki 8:27
23:25 s Jer 14:14; t ver 28,32; Jer 29:8
23:26 u 1Ti 4:1-2
23:27 v Dt 13:1-3; Jer 29:8; w Jdg 3:7; Jdg 8:33-34
23:29 x Jer 5:14
23:30 y Ps 34:16; z Dt 18:20; Jer 14:15
23:31 a ver 17
23:32 b ver 25; c Jer 7:8; La 2:14
23:33 d Mal 1:1; e ver 39
23:34 f La 2:14; g Zec 13:3
23:35 h Jer 33:3; Jer 42:4
23:36 i Gal 1:7-8; 2Pe 3:16
23:39 j Jer 7:15
23:40 k Jer 20:11; Eze 5:14-15
24:1 a 2Ki 24:16; 2Ch 36:9; Jer 29:2; b Am 8:1-2

False Oracles and False Prophets

33"When these people, or a
prophet or a priest, ask you, 'What
is the oracle[d][d] of the LORD?' say to
them, 'What oracle?[e] I will forsake[e] you, declares the LORD.' 34If
a prophet or a priest or anyone else
claims, 'This is the oracle[f] of the
LORD,' I will punish[g] that man and
his household. 35This is what each
of you keeps on saying to his friend
or relative: 'What is the LORD's
answer?'[h] or 'What has the LORD
spoken?' 36But you must not mention 'the oracle of the LORD' again,
because every man's own word
becomes his oracle and so you
distort[i] the words of the living
God, the LORD Almighty, our God.
37This is what you keep saying to a
prophet: 'What is the LORD's answer to you?' or 'What has the LORD
spoken?' 38Although you claim,
'This is the oracle of the LORD,' this
is what the LORD says: You used the
words, 'This is the oracle of the
LORD,' even though I told you that
you must not claim, 'This is the oracle of the LORD.' 39Therefore, I will
surely forget you and cast[j] you out
of my presence along with the city
I gave to you and your fathers. 40I
will bring upon you everlasting disgrace[k]—everlasting shame that
will not be forgotten."

Two Baskets of Figs

24 After Jehoiachin[a][a] son of
Jehoiakim king of Judah
and the officials, the craftsmen and
the artisans of Judah were carried
into exile from Jerusalem to Babylon by Nebuchadnezzar king of
Babylon, the LORD showed me two
baskets of figs[b] placed in front of
the temple of the LORD. 2One basket
had very good figs, like those that

[d]33 Or *burden* (see Septuagint and Vulgate)
[e]33 Hebrew; Septuagint and Vulgate *'You are the burden*; the Hebrew for *oracle* and *burden* is the same.
[a]1 Hebrew *Jeconiah*, a variant of *Jehoiachin*

ripen early; the other basket had very poor[c] figs, so bad that they could not be eaten.

3Then the LORD asked me, "What do you see,[d] Jeremiah?"

"Figs," I answered. "The good ones are very good, but the poor ones are so bad that they cannot be eaten."

4Then the word of the LORD came to me: 5"This is what the LORD, the God of Israel, says: 'Like these good figs, I regard as good the exiles from Judah, whom I sent away from this place to the land of the Babylonians.**b** 6My eyes will watch over them for their good, and I will bring them back[e] to this land. I will build[f] them up and not tear them down; I will plant them and not uproot them. 7I will give them a heart to know me, that I am the LORD. They will be my people,[g] and I will be their God, for they will return[h] to me with all their heart.[i]

8" 'But like the poor[j] figs, which are so bad that they cannot be eaten,' says the LORD, 'so will I deal with Zedekiah king of Judah, his officials[k] and the survivors[l] from Jerusalem, whether they remain in this land or live in Egypt.[m] 9I will make them abhorrent[n] and an offence to all the kingdoms of the earth, a reproach and a byword,[o] an object of ridicule and cursing,[p] wherever I banish[q] them. 10I will send the sword,[r] famine and plague[s] against them until they are destroyed from the land I gave to them and their fathers.' "

Seventy Years of Captivity

25 The word came to Jeremiah concerning all the people of Judah in the fourth year of Jehoiakim[a] son of Josiah king of Judah, which was the first year of Nebuchadnezzar[b] king of Babylon. 2So Jeremiah the prophet said to all the people of Judah[c] and to all those living in Jerusalem: 3For twenty-three years—from the thirteenth year of Josiah[d] son of Amon king of Judah until this very day—the word of the LORD has come to me and I have spoken to you again and again,[e] but you have not listened.[f]

4And though the LORD has sent all his servants the prophets[g] to you again and again, you have not listened or paid any attention. 5They said, "Turn now, each of you, from your evil ways and your evil practices, and you can stay in the land the LORD gave to you and your fathers for ever and ever. 6Do not follow other gods[h] to serve and worship them; do not provoke me to anger with what your hands have made. Then I will not harm you."

7"But you did not listen to me," declares the LORD, "and you have provoked me with what your hands have made,[i] and you have brought harm[j] to yourselves."

8Therefore the LORD Almighty says this: "Because you have not listened to my words, 9I will summon[k] all the peoples of the north[l] and my servant[m] Nebuchadnezzar king of Babylon," declares the LORD, "and I will bring them against this land and its inhabitants and against all the surrounding nations. I will completely destroy**a** them and make them an object of horror and scorn,[n] and an everlasting ruin. 10I will banish from them the sounds[o] of joy and gladness, the voices of bride and bridegroom,[p] the sound of millstones[q] and the light of the lamp.[r] 11This whole country will become a desolate wasteland,[s] and these nations will serve the king of Babylon for seventy years.[t]

12"But when the seventy years[u] are fulfilled, I will punish the king of Babylon and his nation, the land of the Babylonians,**b** for their guilt," declares the LORD, "and will

b5 Or *Chaldeans* **a**9 The Hebrew term refers to the irrevocable giving over of things or persons to the LORD, often by totally destroying them.
b12 Or *Chaldeans*

24:2 c Isa 5:4
24:3 d Jer 1:11; Am 8:2
24:6 e Jer 29:10; Eze 11:17; f Jer 33:7; Jer 42:10
24:7 g Isa 51:16; Jer 31:33; Heb 8:10; h Jer 32:40; i Eze 11:19
24:8 j Jer 29:17; k Jer 39:6; l Jer 39:9; m Jer 44:1,26
24:9 n Jer 15:4; Jer 34:17; o Dt 28:25; 1Ki 9:7; p Jer 29:18; q Dt 28:37
24:10 r Isa 51:19; s Jer 27:8
25:1 a 2Ki 24:2; Jer 36:1; b 2Ki 24:1
25:2 c Jer 18:11
25:3 d Jer 1:2; e Jer 11:7; Jer 26:5; f Jer 7:26
25:4 g Jer 7:25
25:6 h Dt 8:19
25:7 i Dt 32:21; j 2Ki 21:15
25:9 k Isa 13:3-5; l Jer 1:15; m Jer 27:6; n Jer 18:16
25:10 o Isa 24:8; Eze 26:13; p Jer 7:34; q Ecc 12:3-4; r Rev 18:22-23
25:11 s Jer 4:26-27; Jer 12:11-12; t 2Ch 36:21
25:12 u Jer 29:10

make it desolate[v] for ever. 13 I will bring upon that land all the things I have spoken against it, all that are written in this book and prophesied by Jeremiah against all the nations. 14 They themselves will be enslaved[w] by many nations[x] and great kings; I will repay[y] them according to their deeds and the work of their hands."

The Cup of God's Wrath

15 This is what the LORD, the God of Israel, said to me: "Take from my hand this cup[z] filled with the wine of my wrath and make all the nations to whom I send you drink it. 16 When they drink it, they will stagger[a] and go mad[b] because of the sword I will send among them."

17 So I took the cup from the LORD's hand and made all the nations to whom he sent[c] me drink it: 18 Jerusalem and the towns of Judah, its kings and officials, to make them a ruin and an object of horror and scorn and cursing,[d] as they are today;[e] 19 Pharaoh king of Egypt, his attendants, his officials and all his people, 20 and all the foreign people there; all the kings of Uz;[f] all the kings of the Philistines (those of Ashkelon,[g] Gaza, Ekron, and the people left at Ashdod); 21 Edom, Moab and Ammon;[h] 22 all the kings of Tyre and Sidon;[i] the kings of the coastlands[j] across the sea; 23 Dedan, Tema, Buz and all who are in distant places;[c][k] 24 all the kings of Arabia[l] and all the kings of the foreign people who live in the desert; 25 all the kings of Zimri, Elam[m] and Media; 26 and all the kings of the north,[n] near and far, one after the other—all the kingdoms on the face of the earth. And after all of them, the king of Sheshach[d][o] will drink it too.

27 "Then tell them, 'This is what the LORD Almighty, the God of Israel, says: Drink, get drunk[p] and vomit, and fall to rise no more because of the sword[q] I will send among you.' 28 But if they refuse to take the cup from your hand and drink, tell them, 'This is what the LORD Almighty says: You must drink it! 29 See, I am beginning to bring disaster[r] on the city that bears my Name,[s] and will you indeed go unpunished?[t] You will not go unpunished, for I am calling down a sword upon all[u] who live on the earth, declares the LORD Almighty.'

30 "Now prophesy all these words against them and say to them:

" 'The LORD will roar[v] from on high;
he will thunder[w] from his holy dwelling
and roar mightily against his land.
He will shout like those who tread the grapes,
shout against all who live on the earth.
31 The tumult will resound to the ends of the earth,
for the LORD will bring charges[x] against the nations;
he will bring judgment on all mankind
and put the wicked to the sword,' "
declares the LORD.

32 This is what the LORD Almighty says:

"Look! Disaster is spreading from nation to nation;[y]
a mighty storm[z] is rising from the ends of the earth."

33 At that time those slain[a] by the LORD will be everywhere—from one end of the earth to the other. They will not be mourned or gathered[b] up or buried,[c] but will be like refuse lying on the ground.

34 Weep and wail, you shepherds;
roll[d] in the dust, you leaders of the flock.

25:12 v Isa 13:19-22; Isa 14:22-23
25:14 w Jer 27:7; x Jer 50:9; Jer 51:27-28; y Jer 51:6
25:15 z Isa 51:17; Ps 75:8; Rev 14:10
25:16 a Na 3:11; b Jer 51:7
25:17 c Jer 1:10
25:18 d Jer 24:9; e Jer 44:22
25:20 f Job 1:1; g Jer 47:5
25:21 h Jer 49:1
25:22 i Jer 47:4; j Jer 31:10
25:23 k Jer 9:26; Jer 49:32
25:24 l 2Ch 9:14
25:25 m Ge 10:22
25:26 n Jer 50:3,9; o Jer 51:41
25:27 p ver 16,28; Hab 2:16; q Eze 21:4
25:29 r Jer 13:12-14; s 1Pe 4:17; t Pr 11:31; u ver 30-31
25:30 v Isa 16:10; Isa 42:13; w Joel 3:16; Am 1:2
25:31 x Hos 4:1; Joel 3:2; Mic 6:2
25:32 y Isa 34:2; z Jer 23:19
25:33 a Isa 66:16; Eze 39:17-20; b Jer 16:4; c Ps 79:3
25:34 d Jer 6:26

c23 Or *who clip the hair by their foreheads*
d26 *Sheshach* is a cryptogram for Babylon.

For your time to be
slaughtered[e] has come;
you will fall and be shattered
like fine pottery.
35The shepherds will have
nowhere to flee,
the leaders of the flock no
place to escape.[f]
36Hear the cry of the shepherds,
the wailing of the leaders of
the flock,
for the LORD is destroying
their pasture.
37The peaceful meadows will be
laid waste
because of the fierce anger of
the LORD.
38Like a lion[g] he will leave his
lair,
and their land will become
desolate
because of the sword[e] of the
oppressor
and because of the LORD's
fierce anger.

Jeremiah Threatened With Death

26 Early in the reign of Jehoiakim[a] son of Josiah king
of Judah, this word came from
the LORD: 2"This is what the LORD
says: Stand in the courtyard[b] of the
LORD's house and speak to all the
people of the towns of Judah who
come to worship in the house of
the LORD. Tell[c] them everything
I command you; do not omit[d] a
word. 3Perhaps they will listen and
each will turn[e] from his evil way.
Then I will relent[f] and not bring on
them the disaster I was planning
because of the evil they have done.
4Say to them, 'This is what the LORD
says: If you do not listen[g] to me
and follow my law,[h] which I have
set before you, 5and if you do not
listen to the words of my servants
the prophets, whom I have sent to
you again and again (though you
have not listened[i]), 6then I will
make this house like Shiloh[j] and
this city an object of cursing[k]
among all the nations of the
earth.' "
7The priests, the prophets and all
the people heard Jeremiah speak
these words in the house of the
LORD. 8But as soon as Jeremiah finished telling all the people everything the LORD had commanded
him to say, the priests, the prophets
and all the people seized him and
said, "You must die! 9Why do you
prophesy in the LORD's name that
this house will be like Shiloh
and this city will be desolate and
deserted?"[l] And all the people
crowded around Jeremiah in the
house of the LORD.
10When the officials of Judah
heard about these things, they went
up from the royal palace to the
house of the LORD and took their
places at the entrance of the New
Gate of the LORD's house. 11Then
the priests and the prophets said to
the officials and all the people,
"This man should be sentenced to
death[m] because he has prophesied
against this city. You have heard it
with your own ears!"
12Then Jeremiah said to all the
officials[n] and all the people: "The
LORD sent me to prophesy[o] against
this house and this city all the
things you have heard.[p] 13Now reform[q] your ways and your actions
and obey the LORD your God. Then
the LORD will relent and not bring
the disaster he has pronounced
against you. 14As for me, I am in
your hands;[r] do with me whatever
you think is good and right. 15Be assured, however, that if you put me
to death, you will bring the guilt of
innocent blood on yourselves and
on this city and on those who live in
it, for in truth the LORD has sent me
to you to speak all these words in
your hearing."

25:34 e Isa 34:6; Jer 50:27
25:35 f Job 11:20
25:38 g Jer 4:7
26:1 a 2Ki 23:36
26:2 b Jer 19:14; c Jer 1:17; Mt 28:20; Ac 20:27; d Dt 4:2
26:3 e Jer 36:7; f Jer 18:8
26:4 g Lev 26:14; h 1Ki 9:6
26:5 i Jer 25:4
26:6 j Jos 18:1; k 2Ki 22:19
26:9 l Jer 9:11
26:11 m Dt 18:20; Jer 18:23; Jer 38:4; Mt 26:66; Ac 6:11
26:12 n Jer 1:18; o Am 7:15; Ac 4:18-20; Ac 5:29; p ver 2,15
26:13 q Jer 7:5; Joel 2:12-14
26:14 r Jer 38:5

e *38* Some Hebrew manuscripts and Septuagint (see also Jer. 46:16 and 50:16); most Hebrew manuscripts *anger*

16 Then the officials[s] and all the people said to the priests and the prophets, "This man should not be sentenced to death![t] He has spoken to us in the name of the LORD our God."

17 Some of the elders of the land stepped forward and said to the entire assembly of people, 18 "Micah[u] of Moresheth prophesied in the days of Hezekiah king of Judah. He told all the people of Judah, 'This is what the LORD Almighty says:

" 'Zion[v] will be ploughed like a field,
Jerusalem will become a heap of rubble,[w]
the temple hill[x] a mound overgrown with thickets.'[a][y]

19 "Did Hezekiah king of Judah or anyone else in Judah put him to death? Did not Hezekiah[z] fear the LORD and seek his favour? And did not the LORD relent,[a] so that he did not bring the disaster[b] he pronounced against them? We are about to bring a terrible disaster[c] on ourselves!"

20 (Now Uriah son of Shemaiah from Kiriath Jearim[d] was another man who prophesied in the name of the LORD; he prophesied the same things against this city and this land as Jeremiah did. 21 When King Jehoiakim[e] and all his officers and officials heard his words, the king sought to put him to death. But Uriah heard of it and fled[f] in fear to Egypt. 22 King Jehoiakim, however, sent Elnathan[g] son of Acbor to Egypt, along with some other men. 23 They brought Uriah out of Egypt and took him to King Jehoiakim, who had him struck down with a sword and his body thrown into the burial place of the common people.)

24 Furthermore, Ahikam[h] son of Shaphan supported Jeremiah, and so he was not handed over to the people to be put to death.

26:16
s Ac 23:9
t Ac 5:34-39
Ac 23:29

26:18
u Mic 1:1
v Isa 2:3
w Ne 4:2
Jer 9:11
x Mic 4:1
Zec 8:3
y Jer 17:3

26:19
z 2Ch 32:24-26
Isa 37:14-20
a Ex 32:14
2Sa 24:16
b Jer 44:7
c Hab 2:10

26:20
d Jos 9:17

26:21
e 1Ki 19:2
f Mt 10:23

26:22
g Jer 36:12,25

26:24
h 2Ki 22:12

27:1
a 2Ch 36:11

27:2
b Jer 28:10,13

27:3
c Jer 25:21

27:5
d Dt 9:29
e Ps 115:16

27:6
f Jer 25:9
g Jer 21:7
Eze 29:18-20
h Jer 28:14
Da 2:37-38

27:7
i 2Ch 36:20
j Jer 25:12
k Jer 25:14
Da 5:28

27:9
l Dt 18:11

27:10
m Jer 23:25

27:11
n Jer 21:9

Judah to Serve Nebuchadnezzar

27 Early in the reign of Zedekiah[a][a] son of Josiah king of Judah, this word came to Jeremiah from the LORD: 2 This is what the LORD said to me: "Make a yoke[b] out of straps and crossbars and put it on your neck. 3 Then send word to the kings of Edom, Moab, Ammon,[c] Tyre and Sidon through the envoys who have come to Jerusalem to Zedekiah king of Judah. 4 Give them a message for their masters and say, 'This is what the LORD Almighty, the God of Israel, says: "Tell this to your masters: 5 With my great power and outstretched arm[d] I made the earth and its people and the animals that are on it, and I give[e] it to anyone I please. 6 Now I will hand all your countries over to my servant[f] Nebuchadnezzar[g] king of Babylon; I will make even the wild animals subject to him.[h] 7 All nations will serve[i] him and his son and his grandson until the time[j] for his land comes; then many nations and great kings will subjugate[k] him.

8 " ' "If, however, any nation or kingdom will not serve Nebuchadnezzar king of Babylon or bow its neck under his yoke, I will punish that nation with the sword, famine and plague, declares the LORD, until I destroy it by his hand. 9 So do not listen to your prophets, your diviners, your interpreters of dreams, your mediums[l] or your sorcerers who tell you, 'You will not serve the king of Babylon.' 10 They prophesy lies[m] to you that will only serve to remove you far from your lands; I will banish you and you will perish. 11 But if any nation will bow its neck under the yoke[n] of the king of Babylon and serve him, I will let that nation remain in its own land to till it and to live there, declares the LORD." ' "

[a] *18* Micah 3:12 [a] *1* A few Hebrew manuscripts and Syriac (see also Jer. 27:3, 12 and 28:1); most Hebrew manuscripts *Jehoiakim* (most Septuagint manuscripts do not have this verse.)

12I gave the same message to
Zedekiah king of Judah. I said,
"Bow your neck under the yoke of
the king of Babylon; serve him and
his people, and you will live. 13Why
will you and your people die[o] by
the sword, famine and plague with
which the LORD has threatened any
nation that will not serve the king
of Babylon? 14Do not listen to the
words of the prophets who say to
you, 'You will not serve the king of
Babylon,' for they are prophesying
lies[p] to you. 15'I have not sent[q]
them,' declares the LORD. 'They are
prophesying lies in my name.[r]
Therefore, I will banish you and
you will perish,[s] both you and the
prophets who prophesy to you.' "
16Then I said to the priests and all
these people, "This is what the
LORD says: Do not listen to the
prophets who say, 'Very soon now
the articles[t] from the LORD's
house will be brought back from
Babylon.' They are prophesying
lies to you. 17Do not listen to them.
Serve the king of Babylon, and you
will live. Why should this city become a ruin? 18If they are prophets
and have the word of the LORD,
let them plead[u] with the LORD
Almighty that the furnishings remaining in the house of the LORD
and in the palace of the king of Judah and in Jerusalem not be taken
to Babylon. 19For this is what the
LORD Almighty says about the pillars, the Sea,[v] the movable stands
and the other furnishings[w] that are
left in this city, 20which Nebuchadnezzar king of Babylon did not take
away when he carried[x] Jehoiachin[b][y] son of Jehoiakim king of
Judah into exile from Jerusalem to
Babylon, along with all the nobles
of Judah and Jerusalem—21yes,
this is what the LORD Almighty, the
God of Israel, says about the things
that are left in the house of the
LORD and in the palace of the king
of Judah and in Jerusalem: 22'They
will be taken[z] to Babylon and
there they will remain until the
day[a] I come for them,' declares
the LORD. 'Then I will bring[b] them
back and restore them to this
place.' "

The False Prophet Hananiah

28 In the fifth month of that
same year, the fourth year,
early in the reign of Zedekiah[a]
king of Judah, the prophet Hananiah son of Azzur, who was from
Gibeon,[b] said to me in the house of
the LORD in the presence of the
priests and all the people: 2"This
is what the LORD Almighty, the
God of Israel, says: 'I will break
the yoke[c] of the king of Babylon.
3Within two years I will bring back
to this place all the articles[d] of the
LORD's house that Nebuchadnezzar
king of Babylon removed from
here and took to Babylon. 4I will
also bring back to this place Jehoiachin[e] son of Jehoiakim king of Judah and all the other exiles from
Judah who went to Babylon,' declares the LORD, 'for I will break
the yoke of the king of Babylon.' "
5Then the prophet Jeremiah replied to the prophet Hananiah
before the priests and all the people who were standing in the house
of the LORD. 6He said, "Amen! May
the LORD do so! May the LORD fulfil
the words you have prophesied by
bringing the articles of the LORD's
house and all the exiles back to
this place from Babylon. 7Neverthe-
less, listen to what I have to say in
your hearing and in the hearing of
all the people: 8From early times
the prophets who preceded you and
me have prophesied war, disaster
and plague[f] against many countries and great kingdoms. 9But the
prophet who prophesies peace will
be recognised as one truly sent by
the LORD only if his prediction
comes true.[g]"

27:13 o Eze 18:31
27:14 p Jer 14:14
27:15 q Jer 23:21 r Jer 29:9 s Jer 6:15
27:16 t 2Ki 24:13 2Ch 36:7,10 Jer 28:3 Da 1:2
27:18 u 1Sa 7:8
27:19 v 2Ki 25:13 w Jer 52:17-23
27:20 x 2Ch 36:10 Jer 24:1 y Jer 22:24
27:22 z 2Ki 25:13 a 2Ch 36:21 b Ezr 1:7 Ezr 7:19
28:1 a Jer 27:1,3 b Jos 9:3
28:2 c Jer 27:12
28:3 d 2Ki 24:13
28:4 e Jer 22:24-27
28:8 f Lev 26:14-17 Isa 5:5-7
28:9 g Dt 18:22

[b]20 Hebrew *Jeconiah*, a variant of *Jehoiachin*; also in 28:4 and 29:2

10Then the prophet Hananiah took the yoke[h] off the neck of the prophet Jeremiah and broke it, 11and he said[i] before all the people, "This is what the LORD says: 'In the same way will I break the yoke of Nebuchadnezzar king of Babylon off the neck of all the nations within two years.' " At this, the prophet Jeremiah went on his way.

12Shortly after the prophet Hananiah had broken the yoke off the neck of the prophet Jeremiah, the word of the LORD came to Jeremiah: 13"Go and tell Hananiah, 'This is what the LORD says: You have broken a wooden yoke, but in its place you will get a yoke of iron. 14This is what the LORD Almighty, the God of Israel, says: I will put an iron yoke[j] on the necks of all these nations to make them serve[k] Nebuchadnezzar king of Babylon, and they will serve him. I will even give him control over the wild animals.[l]' "

15Then the prophet Jeremiah said to Hananiah the prophet, "Listen, Hananiah! The LORD has not sent[m] you, yet you have persuaded this nation to trust in lies.[n] 16Therefore, this is what the LORD says: 'I am about to remove you from the face of the earth.[o] This very year you are going to die, because you have preached rebellion[p] against the LORD.' "

17In the seventh month of that same year, Hananiah the prophet died.

A Letter to the Exiles

29 This is the text of the letter that the prophet Jeremiah sent from Jerusalem to the surviving elders among the exiles and to the priests, the prophets and all the other people Nebuchadnezzar had carried into exile from Jerusalem to Babylon.[a] 2(This was after King Jehoiachin[b] and the queen mother, the court officials and the leaders of Judah and Jerusalem, the craftsmen and the artisans had gone into exile from Jerusalem.) 3He entrusted the letter to Elasah son of Shaphan and to Gemariah son of Hilkiah, whom Zedekiah king of Judah sent to King Nebuchadnezzar in Babylon. It said:

4This is what the LORD Almighty, the God of Israel, says to all those I carried[c] into exile from Jerusalem to Babylon: 5"Build[d] houses and settle down; plant gardens and eat what they produce. 6Marry and have sons and daughters; find wives for your sons and give your daughters in marriage, so that they too may have sons and daughters. Increase in number there; do not decrease. 7Also, seek the peace and prosperity of the city to which I have carried you into exile. Pray[e] to the LORD for it, because if it prospers, you too will prosper." 8Yes, this is what the LORD Almighty, the God of Israel, says: "Do not let the prophets and diviners among you deceive[f] you. Do not listen to the dreams you encourage them to have.[g] 9They are prophesying lies[h] to you in my name. I have not sent them," declares the LORD.

10This is what the LORD says: "When seventy years[i] are completed for Babylon, I will come to you and fulfil my gracious promise to bring you back[j] to this place. 11For I know the plans[k] I have for you," declares the LORD, "plans to prosper you and not to harm you, plans to give you hope and a future. 12Then you will call upon me and come and pray to me, and I will listen[l] to you. 13You will seek[m] me and find me when you seek me with all your heart.[n] 14I will be found by you," declares the LORD, "and will bring you back[o]

28:10 h Jer 27:2
28:11 i Jer 14:14; Jer 27:10
28:14 j Dt 28:48; k Jer 25:11; l Jer 27:6
28:15 m Jer 29:31; n Jer 20:6; Jer 29:21; La 2:14; Eze 13:6
28:16 o Ge 7:4; p Dt 13:5; Jer 29:32
29:1 a 2Ch 36:10
29:2 b 2Ki 24:12; Jer 22:24-28
29:4 c Jer 24:5
29:5 d ver 28
29:7 e Ezr 6:10; 1Ti 2:1-2
29:8 f Jer 37:9; g Jer 23:27
29:9 h Jer 14:14; Jer 27:15
29:10 i 2Ch 36:21; Jer 25:12; Da 9:2; j Jer 21:22
29:11 k Ps 40:5
29:12 l Ps 145:19
29:13 m Mt 7:7; n Dt 4:29; Jer 24:7
29:14 o Dt 30:3; Jer 30:3

from captivity.[a] I will gather you from all the nations and places where I have banished you," declares the LORD, "and will bring you back to the place from which I carried you into exile."[p]

15 You may say, "The LORD has raised up prophets for us in Babylon," 16 but this is what the LORD says about the king who sits on David's throne and all the people who remain in this city, your countrymen who did not go with you into exile— 17 yes, this is what the LORD Almighty says: "I will send the sword, famine and plague[q] against them and I will make them like poor figs[r] that are so bad they cannot be eaten. 18 I will pursue them with the sword, famine and plague and will make them abhorrent[s] to all the kingdoms of the earth and an object of cursing and horror,[t] of scorn and reproach, among all the nations where I drive them. 19 For they have not listened to my words,"[u] declares the LORD, "words that I sent to them again and again by my servants the prophets.[v] And you exiles have not listened either," declares the LORD.

20 Therefore, hear the word of the LORD, all you exiles whom I have sent[w] away from Jerusalem to Babylon. 21 This is what the LORD Almighty, the God of Israel, says about Ahab son of Kolaiah and Zedekiah son of Maaseiah, who are prophesying lies[x] to you in my name: "I will hand them over to Nebuchadnezzar king of Babylon, and he will put them to death before your very eyes. 22 Because of them, all the exiles from Judah who are in Babylon will use this curse: 'The LORD treat you like Zedekiah and Ahab, whom the king of Babylon burned[y] in the fire.' 23 For they have done outrageous things in Israel; they have committed adultery[z] with their neighbours' wives and in my name have spoken lies, which I did not tell them to do. I know[a] it and am a witness to it," declares the LORD.

Message to Shemaiah

24 Tell Shemaiah the Nehelamite, 25 "This is what the LORD Almighty, the God of Israel, says: You sent letters in your own name to all the people in Jerusalem, to Zephaniah[b] son of Maaseiah the priest, and to all the other priests. You said to Zephaniah, 26 'The LORD has appointed you priest in place of Jehoiada to be in charge of the house of the LORD; you should put any madman[c] who acts like a prophet into the stocks[d] and neck-irons. 27 So why have you not reprimanded Jeremiah from Anathoth, who poses as a prophet among you? 28 He has sent this message[e] to us in Babylon: It will be a long time.[f] Therefore build[g] houses and settle down; plant gardens and eat what they produce.' "

29 Zephaniah the priest, however, read the letter to Jeremiah the prophet. 30 Then the word of the LORD came to Jeremiah: 31 "Send this message to all the exiles: 'This is what the LORD says about Shemaiah[h] the Nehelamite: Because Shemaiah has prophesied to you, even though I did not send[i] him, and has led you to believe a lie, 32 this is what the LORD says: I will surely punish Shemaiah the Nehelamite and his descendants.[j] He will have no-one left among this people, nor will he see the good[k] things I will do for my people, declares the LORD, because he has preached rebellion[l] against me.' "

[a] 14 Or *will restore your fortunes*

29:14 p Jer 23:3-4
29:17 q Jer 27:8 r Jer 24:8-10
29:18 s Jer 15:4 t Dt 28:25 Jer 42:18
29:19 u Jer 6:19 v Jer 25:4
29:20 w Jer 24:5
29:21 x ver 9 Jer 14:14
29:22 y Da 3:6
29:23 z Jer 23:14 a Heb 4:13
29:25 b 2Ki 25:18 Jer 21:1
29:26 c 2Ki 9:11 Hos 9:7 Jn 10:20 d Jer 20:2
29:28 e ver 1 f ver 10 g ver 5
29:31 h ver 24 i Jer 14:14 Jer 28:15
29:32 j 1Sa 2:30-33 k ver 10 l Jer 28:16

Restoration of Israel

30 This is the word that came
to Jeremiah from the LORD:
2"This is what the LORD, the God of
Israel, says: 'Write[a] in a book all
the words I have spoken to you.
3The days are coming,' declares the
LORD, 'when I will bring[b] my people Israel and Judah back from
captivity[a] and restore[c] them to
the land I gave to their forefathers
to possess,' says the LORD."
4These are the words the LORD
spoke concerning Israel and Judah: 5"This is what the LORD says:

" 'Cries of fear[d] are heard—
terror, not peace.
6Ask and see:
Can a man bear children?
Then why do I see every strong
man
with his hands on his stomach
like a woman in labour,[e]
every face turned deathly
pale?
7How awful that day[f] will be!
None will be like it.
It will be a time of trouble[g] for
Jacob,
but he will be saved[h] out of it.

8" 'In that day,' declares the
LORD Almighty,
'I will break the yoke[i] off
their necks
and will tear off their bonds;
no longer will foreigners
enslave them.[j]
9Instead, they will serve the
LORD their God
and David[k] their king,[l]
whom I will raise up for them.

10" 'So do not fear,[m] O Jacob my
servant;[n]
do not be dismayed, O Israel,'
declares the LORD.
'I will surely save[o] you out of a
distant place,
your descendants from the
land of their exile.
Jacob will again have peace and
security,[p]
and no-one will make him
afraid.
11I am with you and will save
you,'
declares the LORD.
'Though I completely destroy
all the nations
among which I scatter you,
I will not completely destroy[q]
you.
I will discipline[r] you but only
with justice;
I will not let you go entirely
unpunished.'[s]

12"This is what the LORD says:

" 'Your wound is incurable,
your injury beyond healing.[t]
13There is no-one to plead your
cause,
no remedy for your sore,
no healing[u] for you.
14All your allies[v] have forgotten
you;
they care nothing for you.
I have struck you as an enemy[w]
would
and punished you as would the
cruel,[x]
because your guilt is so great
and your sins[y] so many.
15Why do you cry out over your
wound,
your pain that has no cure?
Because of your great guilt and
many sins
I have done these things to
you.

16" 'But all who devour[z] you will
be devoured;
all your enemies will go into
exile.[a]
Those who plunder[b] you will be
plundered;
all who make spoil of you I
will despoil.
17But I will restore you to health
and heal your wounds,'
declares the LORD,

30:2 a Isa 30:8
30:3 b Jer 29:14 c Jer 16:15
30:5 d Jer 6:25
30:6 e Jer 4:31
30:7 f Isa 2:12; Joel 2:11 g Zep 1:15 h ver 10
30:8 i Isa 9:4 j Eze 34:27
30:9 k Isa 55:3-4; Lk 1:69; Ac 2:30; Ac 13:23 l Eze 34:23-24; Eze 37:24; Hos 3:5
30:10 m Isa 43:5; Jer 46:27-28 n Isa 44:2 o Jer 29:14 p Isa 35:9
30:11 q Jer 4:27; Jer 46:28 r Jer 10:24 s Am 9:8
30:12 t Jer 15:18
30:13 u Jer 8:22; Jer 14:19; Jer 46:11
30:14 v Jer 22:20; La 1:2 w Job 13:24 x Job 30:21 y Jer 5:6
30:16 z Isa 33:1; Jer 2:3; Jer 10:25 a Isa 14:2; Joel 3:4-8 b Jer 50:10

[a]3 *Or will restore the fortunes of my people Israel and Judah*

'because you are called an
outcast,[c]
Zion for whom no-one cares.'

18"This is what the LORD says:

" 'I will restore the fortunes[d] of
Jacob's tents
and have compassion[e] on his
dwellings;
the city will be rebuilt[f] on her
ruins,
and the palace will stand in its
proper place.
19From them will come songs[g] of
thanksgiving[h]
and the sound of rejoicing.[i]
I will add to their numbers,[j]
and they will not be
decreased;
I will bring them honour,[k]
and they will not be disdained.
20Their children[l] will be as in
days of old,
and their community will be
established[m] before me;
I will punish all who oppress
them.
21Their leader[n] will be one of
their own;
their ruler will arise from
among them.
I will bring him near[o] and he
will come close to me,
for who is he who will devote
himself
to be close to me?'
declares the LORD.
22" 'So you will be my people,
and I will be your God.' "

23See, the storm[p] of the LORD
will burst out in wrath,
a driving wind swirling down
on the heads of the wicked.
24The fierce anger[q] of the LORD
will not turn back[r]
until he fully accomplishes
the purposes of his heart.
In days to come
you will understand[s] this.

31

"At that time," declares the
LORD, "I will be the God[a]
of all the clans of Israel, and they
will be my people."

2This is what the LORD says:

"The people who survive the
sword
will find favour[b] in the
desert;
I will come to give rest[c] to
Israel."

3The LORD appeared to us in the
past,[a] saying:

"I have loved[d] you with an
everlasting love;
I have drawn[e] you with
loving-kindness.
4I will build you up again
and you will be rebuilt,
O Virgin Israel.
Again you will take up your
tambourines
and go out to dance with the
joyful.[f]
5Again you will plant vineyards
on the hills of Samaria;[g]
the farmers will plant them
and enjoy their fruit.[h]
6There will be a day when
watchmen cry out
on the hills of Ephraim,
'Come, let us go up to Zion,
to the LORD our God.' "[i]

7This is what the LORD says:

"Sing with joy for Jacob;
shout for the foremost[j] of the
nations.
Make your praises heard, and
say,
'O LORD, save[k] your people,
the remnant[l] of Israel.'
8See, I will bring them from the
land of the north[m]
and gather[n] them from the
ends of the earth.
Among them will be the blind[o]
and the lame,[p]
expectant mothers and women
in labour;
a great throng will return.
9They will come with weeping;[q]
they will pray as I bring them
back.

30:17
c Jer 33:24

30:18
d ver 3
Jer 31:23
e Ps 102:13
f Jer 31:4,24,
38

30:19
g Isa 35:10
Isa 51:11
h Isa 51:3
i Ps 126:1-2
Jer 31:4
j Jer 33:22
k Isa 60:9

30:20
l Isa 54:13
Jer 31:17
m Isa 54:14

30:21
n ver 9
o Nu 16:5

30:23
p Jer 23:19

30:24
q Jer 4:8
r Jer 4:28
s Jer 23:19-20

31:1
a Jer 30:22

31:2
b Nu 14:20
c Ex 33:14

31:3
d Dt 4:37
e Hos 11:4

31:4
f Jer 30:19

31:5
g Jer 50:19
h Isa 65:21
Am 9:14

31:6
i Isa 2:3
Jer 50:4-5
Mic 4:2

31:7
j Dt 28:13
Isa 61:9
k Ps 14:7
Ps 28:9
l Isa 37:31

31:8
m Jer 3:18
Jer 23:8
n Dt 30:4
Eze 34:12-14
o Isa 42:16
p Eze 34:16
Mic 4:6

31:9
q Ps 126:5

a3 Or *LORD has appeared to us from afar*

I will lead[r] them beside
streams of water
on a level[s] path where they
will not stumble,
because I am Israel's father,[t]
and Ephraim is my firstborn
son.

10"Hear the word of the LORD,
O nations;
proclaim it in distant
coastlands:[u]
'He who scattered Israel will
gather[v] them
and will watch over his flock
like a shepherd.'[w]
11For the LORD will ransom Jacob
and redeem[x] them from the
hand of those stronger[y]
than they.
12They will come and shout for
joy on the heights[z] of Zion;
they will rejoice in the
bounty[a] of the LORD—
the grain, the new wine and the
oil,[b]
the young of the flocks and
herds.
They will be like a well-watered
garden,[c]
and they will sorrow[d] no
more.
13Then maidens will dance and be
glad,
young men and old as well.
I will turn their mourning[e] into
gladness;
I will give them comfort and
joy[f] instead of sorrow.
14I will satisfy[g] the priests with
abundance,
and my people will be filled
with my bounty,"
declares the LORD.

15This is what the LORD says:

"A voice is heard in Ramah,[h]
mourning and great weeping,
Rachel weeping for her children
and refusing to be
comforted,[i]
because her children are no
more."[j]

16This is what the LORD says:

"Restrain your voice from
weeping
and your eyes from tears,[k]
for your work will be
rewarded,"
declares the LORD.
"They will return[m] from the
land of the enemy.
17So there is hope for your
future,"
declares the LORD.
"Your children will return to
their own land.

18"I have surely heard Ephraim's
moaning:
'You disciplined[n] me like an
unruly calf,[o]
and I have been disciplined.
Restore[p] me, and I will return,
because you are the LORD my
God.
19After I strayed,[q]
I repented;
after I came to understand,
I beat[r] my breast.
I was ashamed and humiliated
because I bore the disgrace of
my youth.'
20Is not Ephraim my dear son,
the child in whom I delight?
Though I often speak against
him,
I still remember[s] him.
Therefore my heart yearns for
him;
I have great compassion[t] for
him,"
declares the LORD.

21"Set up road signs;
put up guideposts.
Take note of the highway,[u]
the road that you take.
Return,[v] O Virgin[w] Israel,
return to your towns.
22How long will you wander,[x]
O unfaithful[y] daughter?
The LORD will create a new
thing on earth—

31:9 r Isa 63:13 s Isa 49:11 t Ex 4:22 Jer 3:4
31:10 u Isa 66:19 Jer 25:22 v Jer 50:19 w Isa 40:11 Eze 34:12
31:11 x Isa 44:23 Isa 48:20 y Ps 142:6
31:12 z Eze 17:23 Mic 4:1 a Joel 3:18 b Hos 2:21-22 c Isa 58:11 d Isa 65:19 Jn 16:22 Rev 7:17
31:13 e Isa 61:3 f Ps 30:11 Isa 51:11
31:14 g ver 25
31:15 h Jos 18:25 i Ge 37:35 j Jer 10:20 Mt 2:17-18*
31:16 k Isa 25:8 Isa 30:19 l Ru 2:12 m Jer 30:3 Eze 11:17
31:18 n Job 5:17 o Hos 4:16 p Ps 80:3
31:19 q Eze 36:31 r Eze 21:12 Lk 18:13
31:20 s Hos 4:4 Hos 11:8 t Isa 55:7 Isa 63:15 Mic 7:18
31:21 u Jer 50:5 v Isa 52:11 w ver 4
31:22 x Jer 2:23 y Jer 3:6

a woman will surround[b] a
man."

23This is what the LORD Almighty, the God of Israel, says:
"When I bring them back from captivity,[c][z] the people in the land of
Judah and in its towns will once
again use these words: 'The LORD
bless you, O righteous dwelling,[a]
O sacred mountain.'[b] 24People will
live[c] together in Judah and all its
towns—farmers and those who
move about with their flocks. 25I
will refresh the weary and satisfy
the faint."[d]

26At this I awoke[e] and looked
around. My sleep had been pleasant to me.

27"The days are coming," declares the LORD, "when I will
plant[f] the house of Israel and the
house of Judah with the offspring
of men and of animals. 28Just as I
watched over them to uproot and
tear down, and to overthrow, destroy and bring disaster,[g] so I will
watch over them to build and to
plant,"[h] declares the LORD. 29"In
those days people will no longer
say,

'The fathers[i] have eaten sour
grapes,
and the children's teeth are
set on edge.'[j]

30Instead, everyone will die for his
own sin;[k] whoever eats sour
grapes—his own teeth will be set
on edge.

31"The time is coming," declares
the LORD,
"when I will make a new
covenant[l]
with the house of Israel
and with the house of Judah.
32It will not be like the covenant[m]
I made with their
forefathers[n]
when I took them by the hand
to lead them out of Egypt,
because they broke my
covenant,
though I was a husband to[d]
them,"[e]
declares the LORD.
33"This is the covenant that I will
make with the house of
Israel
after that time," declares the
LORD.
"I will put my law in their
minds
and write it on their hearts.[o]
I will be their God,
and they will be my people.[p]
34No longer will a man teach[q] his
neighbour,
or a man his brother, saying,
'Know the LORD,'
because they will all know[r] me,
from the least of them to the
greatest,"
declares the LORD.
"For I will forgive[s] their
wickedness
and will remember their sins[t]
no more."

35This is what the LORD says,
he who appoints[u] the sun
to shine by day,
who decrees the moon and stars
to shine by night,[v]
who stirs up the sea
so that its waves roar—
the LORD Almighty is his
name:[w]
36"Only if these decrees[x] vanish
from my sight,"
declares the LORD,
"will the descendants[y] of Israel
ever cease
to be a nation before me."

37This is what the LORD says:
"Only if the heavens above can
be measured[z]
and the foundations of the
earth below be searched
out
will I reject[a] all the
descendants of Israel

31:23 z Jer 30:18 a Isa 1:26 b Ps 48:1 Zec 8:3
31:24 c Zec 8:4-8
31:25 d Jn 4:14
31:26 e Zec 4:1
31:27 f Eze 36:9-11 Hos 2:23
31:28 g Jer 18:8 Jer 44:27 h Jer 1:10
31:29 i La 5:7 j Eze 18:2
31:30 k Isa 3:11 Gal 6:7
31:31 l Jer 32:40 Eze 37:26 Lk 22:20 Heb 8:8-12* Heb 10:16-17
31:32 m Ex 24:8 n Dt 5:3
31:33 o 2Co 3:3 p Jer 24:7 Heb 10:16
31:34 q 1Jn 2:27 r Jn 6:45 s Isa 54:13 Jer 33:8 Jer 50:20 t Ro 11:27 Mic 7:19 Heb 10:17*
31:35 u Ps 136:7-9 v Ge 1:16 w Jer 10:16
31:36 x Isa 54:9-10 Jer 33:20-26 y Ps 89:36-37
31:37 z Jer 33:22 a Jer 33:24-26 Ro 11:1-5

b22 Or *will go about* ⌞*seeking*⌟; or *will protect*
c23 Or *I restore their fortunes* d32 Hebrew; Septuagint and Syriac *covenant, / and I turned away from* e32 Or *was their master*

because of all they have
done,"
declares the LORD.

38"The days are coming," declares the LORD, "when this city will be rebuilt[b] for me from the Tower of Hananel[c] to the Corner Gate.[d] 39The measuring line will stretch from there straight to the hill of Gareb and then turn to Goah. 40The whole valley[e] where dead bodies[f] and ashes are thrown, and all the terraces out to the Kidron Valley[g] on the east as far as the corner of the Horse Gate,[h] will be holy[i] to the LORD. The city will never again be uprooted or demolished."

Jeremiah Buys a Field

32 This is the word that came to Jeremiah from the LORD in the tenth[a] year of Zedekiah king of Judah, which was the eighteenth[b] year of Nebuchadnezzar. 2The army of the king of Babylon was then besieging Jerusalem, and Jeremiah the prophet was confined in the courtyard of the guard[c] in the royal palace of Judah.

3Now Zedekiah king of Judah had imprisoned him there, saying, "Why do you prophesy[d] as you do? You say, 'This is what the LORD says: I am about to hand this city over to the king of Babylon, and he will capture[e] it. 4Zedekiah king of Judah will not escape[f] out of the hands of the Babylonians[a] but will certainly be handed over to the king of Babylon, and will speak with him face to face and see him with his own eyes. 5He will take[g] Zedekiah to Babylon, where he will remain until I deal with him, declares the LORD. If you fight against the Babylonians, you will not succeed.' "[h]

6Jeremiah said, "The word of the LORD came to me: 7Hanamel son of Shallum your uncle is going to come to you and say, 'Buy my field at Anathoth, because as nearest relative it is your right and duty[i] to buy it.'

8"Then, just as the LORD had said, my cousin Hanamel came to me in the courtyard of the guard and said, 'Buy my field at Anathoth in the territory of Benjamin. Since it is your right to redeem it and possess it, buy it for yourself.'

"I knew that this was the word of the LORD; 9so I bought the field at Anathoth from my cousin Hanamel and weighed out for him seventeen shekels[b] of silver.[j] 10I signed and sealed the deed, had it witnessed,[k] and weighed out the silver on the scales. 11I took the deed of purchase—the sealed copy containing the terms and conditions, as well as the unsealed copy—12and I gave this deed to Baruch[l] son of Neriah,[m] the son of Mahseiah, in the presence of my cousin Hanamel and of the witnesses who had signed the deed and of all the Jews sitting in the courtyard of the guard.

13"In their presence I gave Baruch these instructions: 14'This is what the LORD Almighty, the God of Israel, says: Take these documents, both the sealed and unsealed copies of the deed of purchase, and put them in a clay jar so that they will last a long time. 15For this is what the LORD Almighty, the God of Israel, says: Houses, fields and vineyards will again be bought in this land.'[n]

16"After I had given the deed of purchase to Baruch son of Neriah, I prayed to the LORD:

17"Ah, Sovereign LORD,[o] you
have made the heavens and the
earth by your great power and
outstretched arm.[p] Nothing is
too hard[q] for you. 18You show
love[r] to thousands but bring
the punishment for the fathers'
sins into the laps of their children[s] after them. O great and
powerful God, whose name is
the LORD Almighty,[t] 19great

31:38 *b* Jer 30:18 *c* Ne 3:1 *d* 2Ki 14:13; Zec 14:10
31:40 *e* Jer 7:31-32 *f* Jer 8:2 *g* 2Sa 15:23; Jn 18:1 *h* 2Ki 11:16 *i* Joel 3:17; Zec 14:21
32:1 *a* 2Ki 25:1 *b* Jer 25:1; Jer 39:1
32:2 *c* Ne 3:25; Jer 37:21
32:3 *d* Jer 26:8-9 *e* ver 28; Jer 34:2-3
32:4 *f* Jer 38:18,23; Jer 39:5-7; Jer 52:9
32:5 *g* Jer 39:7; Eze 12:13 *h* Jer 21:4
32:7 *i* Lev 25:24-25; Ru 4:3-4; Mt 27:10*
32:9 *j* Ge 23:16
32:10 *k* Ru 4:9
32:12 *l* ver 16; Jer 36:4; Jer 43:3,6; Jer 45:1 *m* Jer 51:59
32:15 *n* ver 43-44; Jer 30:18; Am 9:14-15
32:17 *o* Jer 1:6 *p* 2Ki 19:15; Ps 102:25 *q* Mt 19:26
32:18 *r* Dt 5:10 *s* Ex 20:5 *t* Jer 10:16

a4 Or *Chaldeans*; also in verses 5, 24, 25, 28, 29 and 43   b9 That is, about 7 ounces (about 200 grams)

are your purposes and mighty
are your deeds.[u] Your eyes are
open to all the ways of men;[v]
you reward everyone ac-
cording to his conduct and as
his deeds deserve.[w] 20You performed miraculous signs and
wonders in Egypt[x] and have
continued them to this day,
both in Israel and among all
mankind, and have gained the
renown that is still yours.
21You brought your people Israel out of Egypt with signs
and wonders, by a mighty
hand[y] and an outstretched
arm and with great terror.[z]
22You gave them this land you
had sworn to give to their forefathers, a land flowing with
milk and honey.[a] 23They came
in and took possession[b] of it,
but they did not obey you or
follow your law;[c] they did not
do what you commanded them
to do. So you brought all this
disaster[d] upon them.

24"See how the siege ramps
are built up to take the city.
Because of the sword, famine
and plague,[e] the city will be
handed over to the Babylonians who are attacking it.
What you said[f] has happened,
as you now see. 25And though
the city will be handed over to
the Babylonians, you, O Sovereign LORD, say to me, 'Buy the
field with silver and have the
transaction witnessed.' "

26Then the word of the LORD
came to Jeremiah: 27"I am the
LORD, the God of all mankind.[g] Is
anything too hard for me? 28There-
fore, this is what the LORD says: I
am about to hand this city over to
the Babylonians and to Nebuchadnezzar[h] king of Babylon, who will
capture it.[i] 29The Babylonians who
are attacking this city will come
in and set it on fire; they will burn
it down,[j] along with the houses[k]
where the people provoked
me to anger by burning incense
on the roofs to Baal and by pouring out drink offerings[l] to other
gods.

30"The people of Israel and Judah
have done nothing but evil in my
sight from their youth;[m] indeed,
the people of Israel have done nothing but provoke[n] me with what
their hands have made,[o] declares
the LORD. 31From the day it was
built until now, this city has so
aroused my anger and wrath that I
must remove[p] it from my sight.
32The people of Israel and Judah
have provoked me by all the evil[q]
they have done—they, their kings
and officials, their priests and
prophets, the men of Judah and the
people of Jerusalem. 33They turned
their backs[r] to me and not their
faces; though I taught[s] them again
and again, they would not listen or
respond to discipline. 34They set up
their abominable idols in the house
that bears my Name and defiled[t]
it. 35They built high places for Baal
in the Valley of Ben Hinnom to
sacrifice their sons and daughters[c]
to Molech,[u] though I never commanded, nor did it enter my mind,[v]
that they should do such a detestable thing and so make Judah sin.

36"You are saying about this city,
'By the sword, famine and plague[w]
it will be handed over to the king of
Babylon'; but this is what the LORD,
the God of Israel, says: 37I will
surely gather[x] them from all the
lands where I banish them in my
furious anger and great wrath; I
will bring them back to this place
and let them live in safety.[y] 38They
will be my people,[z] and I will be
their God. 39I will give them single-
ness[a] of heart and action, so that
they will always fear me for their
own good and the good of their children after them. 40I will make an
everlasting covenant[b] with them: I
will never stop doing good to them,

c35 *Or to make their sons and daughters pass through ⌊the fire⌋*

32:19 u Isa 28:29 v Pr 5:21 Jer 16:17 w Jer 17:10 Mt 16:27
32:20 x Ex 9:16
32:21 y Ex 6:6 1Ch 17:21 Da 9:15 z Dt 26:8
32:22 a Ex 3:8 Jer 11:5
32:23 b Ps 44:2 Ps 78:54-55 c Ne 9:26 Jer 11:8 d Da 9:14
32:24 e Jer 14:12 f Dt 4:25-26 Jos 23:15-16
32:27 g Nu 16:22
32:28 h 2Ch 36:17 i ver 3
32:29 j 2Ch 36:19 Jer 21:10 Jer 37:8,10 Jer 52:13 k Jer 19:13 l Jer 44:18
32:30 m Jer 22:21 n Jer 8:19 o Jer 25:7
32:31 p 2Ki 23:27 2Ki 24:3
32:32 q Isa 1:4-6 Da 9:8
32:33 r Jer 2:27 Eze 8:16 s Jer 7:13
32:34 t Jer 7:30
32:35 u Lev 18:21 v Jer 7:31 Jer 19:5
32:36 w ver 24
32:37 x Jer 23:3,6 y Dt 30:3 Eze 34:28
32:38 z Jer 24:7 2Co 6:16*
32:39 a Eze 11:19
32:40 b Isa 55:3

and I will inspire them to fear me, so that they will never turn away from me.[c] 41 I will rejoice in doing them good[d] and will assuredly plant[e] them in this land with all my heart and soul.

42 "This is what the LORD says: As I have brought all this great calamity on this people, so I will give them all the prosperity I have promised[f] them. 43 Once more fields will be bought[g] in this land of which you say, 'It is a desolate waste, without men or animals, for it has been handed over to the Babylonians.' 44 Fields will be bought for silver, and deeds[h] will be signed, sealed and witnessed in the territory of Benjamin, in the villages around Jerusalem, in the towns of Judah and in the towns of the hill country, of the western foothills and of the Negev,[i] because I will restore[j] their fortunes,[d] declares the LORD."

Promise of Restoration

33 While Jeremiah was still confined in the courtyard[a] of the guard, the word of the LORD came to him a second time: 2 "This is what the LORD says, he who made the earth,[b] the LORD who formed it and established it—the LORD is his name:[c] 3 'Call[d] to me and I will answer you and tell you great and unsearchable things you do not know.' 4 For this is what the LORD, the God of Israel, says about the houses in this city and the royal palaces of Judah that have been torn down to be used against the siege[e] ramps[f] and the sword 5 in the fight with the Babylonians:[a] 'They will be filled with the dead bodies of the men I will slay in my anger and wrath.[g] I will hide my face[h] from this city because of all its wickedness.

6 " 'Nevertheless, I will bring health and healing to it; I will heal my people and will let them enjoy abundant peace and security. 7 I will bring Judah[i] and Israel back

32:40
c Jer 24:7
32:41
d Dt 30:9
e Jer 24:6; Jer 31:28; Am 9:15
32:42
f Jer 31:28
32:43
g ver 15
32:44
h ver 10
i Jer 17:26
j Jer 33:7,11, 26
33:1
a Jer 32:2-3; Jer 37:21; Jer 38:28
33:2
b Jer 10:16
c Ex 3:15; Ex 15:3
33:3
d Isa 55:6; Jer 29:12
33:4
e Eze 4:2
f Jer 32:24; Hab 1:10
33:5
g Jer 21:4-7
h Isa 8:17
33:7
i Jer 32:44
j Jer 30:3; Am 9:14
k Isa 1:26
33:8
l Heb 9:13-14
m Jer 31:34; Mic 7:18; Zec 13:1
33:9
n Jer 13:11
o Isa 62:7; Jer 3:17
33:10
p Jer 32:43
33:11
q Isa 51:3
r Lev 7:12
s 1Ch 16:8; Ps 136:1
t 1Ch 16:34; 2Ch 5:13; Ps 100:4-5
33:12
u Jer 32:43
v Isa 65:10; Eze 34:11-15
33:13
w Jer 17:26
x Lev 27:32
33:14
y Jer 29:10

from captivity[b][j] and will rebuild them as they were before.[k] 8 I will cleanse[l] them from all the sin they have committed against me and will forgive[m] all their sins of rebellion against me. 9 Then this city will bring me renown, joy, praise[n] and honour[o] before all nations on earth that hear of all the good things I do for it; and they will be in awe and will tremble at the abundant prosperity and peace I provide for it.'

10 "This is what the LORD says: 'You say about this place, "It is a desolate waste, without men or animals."[p] Yet in the towns of Judah and the streets of Jerusalem that are deserted, inhabited by neither men nor animals, there will be heard once more 11 the sounds of joy and gladness,[q] the voices of bride and bridegroom, and the voices of those who bring thank-offerings[r] to the house of the LORD, saying,

> "Give thanks to the LORD Almighty,
> for the LORD is good;[s]
> his love endures for ever."[t]

For I will restore the fortunes of the land as they were before,' says the LORD.

12 "This is what the LORD Almighty says: 'In this place, desolate[u] and without men or animals—in all its towns there will again be pastures for shepherds to rest their flocks.[v] 13 In the towns of the hill country, of the western foothills and of the Negev,[w] in the territory of Benjamin, in the villages around Jerusalem and in the towns of Judah, flocks will again pass under the hand[x] of the one who counts them,' says the LORD.

14 " 'The days are coming,' declares the LORD, 'when I will fulfil the gracious promise[y] I made to

[d]44 Or *will bring them back from captivity*
[a]5 Or *Chaldeans* [b]7 Or *will restore the fortunes of Judah and Israel*

the house of Israel and to the house
of Judah.

15" 'In those days and at that time
I will make a righteous[z]
Branch[a] sprout from
David's line;
he will do what is just and
right in the land.
16In those days Judah will be
saved[b]
and Jerusalem will live in
safety.
This is the name by which it[c]
will be called:
The LORD Our
Righteousness.'[c]

17For this is what the LORD says:
'David will never fail[d] to have a
man to sit on the throne of the
house of Israel, 18nor will the
priests, who are Levites,[e] ever fail
to have a man to stand before me
continually to offer burnt offerings, to burn grain offerings and to
present sacrifices.[f] "

19The word of the LORD came
to Jeremiah: 20"This is what the
LORD says: 'If you can break my
covenant with the day[g] and my
covenant with the night, so that
day and night no longer come at
their appointed time, 21then my covenant[h] with David my servant—
and my covenant with the Levites
who are priests ministering before
me—can be broken and David will
no longer have a descendant to
reign on his throne.[i] 22I will make
the descendants of David my servant and the Levites who minister
before me as countless[j] as the
stars of the sky and as measureless
as the sand on the seashore.' "

23The word of the LORD came to
Jeremiah: 24"Have you not noticed
that these people are saying,
'The LORD has rejected the two
kingdoms[d][k] he chose'? So they
despise[l] my people and no longer
regard them as a nation.[m] 25This is
what the LORD says: 'If I have not
established my covenant with day
and night[n] and the fixed laws of
heaven and earth,[o] 26then I will reject[p] the descendants of Jacob[q]
and David my servant and will not
choose one of his sons to rule over
the descendants of Abraham, Isaac
and Jacob. For I will restore their
fortunes[e][r] and have compassion
on them.' "

Warning to Zedekiah

34 While Nebuchadnezzar king
of Babylon and all his army
and all the kingdoms and peoples[a]
in the empire he ruled were fighting against Jerusalem[b] and all
its surrounding towns, this word
came to Jeremiah from the LORD:
2"This is what the LORD, the God of
Israel, says: Go to Zedekiah[c] king
of Judah and tell him, 'This is what
the LORD says: I am about to hand
this city over to the king of Babylon, and he will burn it down.[d]
3You will not escape from his grasp
but will surely be captured and
handed over[e] to him. You will see
the king of Babylon with your own
eyes, and he will speak with you
face to face. And you will go to Babylon.

4" 'Yet hear the promise of the
LORD, O Zedekiah king of Judah.
This is what the LORD says concerning you: You will not die by the
sword; 5you will die peacefully. As
people made a funeral fire[f] in honour of your fathers, the former
kings who preceded you, so they
will make a fire in your honour and
lament, "Alas,[g] O master!" I myself make this promise, declares
the LORD.' "

6Then Jeremiah the prophet told
all this to Zedekiah king of Judah,
in Jerusalem, 7while the army of
the king of Babylon was fighting
against Jerusalem and the other
cities of Judah that were still holding out—Lachish[h] and Azekah.[i]
These were the only fortified cities
left in Judah.

c16 Or *he* d24 Or *families* e26 Or *will bring them back from captivity*

33:15 z Ps 72:2; a Isa 4:2; Isa 11:1; Jer 23:5
33:16 b Isa 45:17; c 1Co 1:30
33:17 d 2Sa 7:13; 1Ki 2:4; Ps 89:29-37; Lk 1:33
33:18 e Dt 18:1; f Heb 13:15
33:20 g Ps 89:36
33:21 h Ps 89:34; i 2Ch 7:18
33:22 j Ge 15:5
33:24 k Eze 37:22; l Ne 4:4; m Jer 30:17
33:25 n Jer 31:35-36; o Ps 74:16-17
33:26 p Jer 31:37; q Isa 14:1; r ver 7
34:1 a Jer 27:7; b 2Ki 25:1; Jer 39:1
34:2 c 2Ch 36:11; d ver 22; Jer 32:29; Jer 37:8
34:3 e 2Ki 25:7; Jer 21:7; Jer 32:4
34:5 f 2Ch 16:14; 2Ch 21:19; g Jer 22:18
34:7 h Jos 10:3; i Jos 10:10; 2Ch 11:9

Freedom for Slaves

8 The word came to Jeremiah from the LORD after King Zedekiah had made a covenant with all the people[j] in Jerusalem to proclaim freedom[k] for the slaves. 9 Everyone was to free his Hebrew slaves, both male and female; no-one was to hold a fellow Jew in bondage.[l] 10 So all the officials and people who entered into this covenant agreed that they would free their male and female slaves and no longer hold them in bondage. They agreed, and set them free. 11 But afterwards they changed their minds and took back the slaves they had freed and enslaved them again.

12 Then the word of the LORD came to Jeremiah: 13 "This is what the LORD, the God of Israel, says: I made a covenant with your forefathers[m] when I brought them out of Egypt, out of the land of slavery. I said, 14 'Every seventh year each of you must free any fellow Hebrew who has sold himself to you. After he has served you for six years, you must let him go free.'[a][n] Your fathers, however, did not listen to me or pay attention[o] to me. 15 Recently you repented and did what is right in my sight: Each of you proclaimed freedom to his countrymen.[p] You even made a covenant before me in the house that bears my Name.[q] 16 But now you have turned round[r] and profaned[s] my name; each of you has taken back the male and female slaves you had set free to go where they wished. You have forced them to become your slaves again.

17 "Therefore, this is what the LORD says: You have not obeyed me; you have not proclaimed freedom for your fellow countrymen. So I now proclaim 'freedom' for you,[t] declares the LORD—'freedom' to fall by the sword, plague and famine. I will make you abhorrent to all the kingdoms of the earth.[u] 18 The men who have violated my covenant and have not fulfilled the terms of the covenant they made before me, I will treat like the calf they cut in two and then walked between its pieces.[v] 19 The leaders of Judah and Jerusalem, the court officials,[w] the priests and all the people of the land who walked between the pieces of the calf, 20 I will hand over[x] to their enemies who seek their lives.[y] Their dead bodies will become food for the birds of the air and the beasts of the earth.[z]

21 "I will hand Zedekiah[a] king of Judah and his officials[b] over to their enemies who seek their lives, to the army of the king of Babylon, which has withdrawn[c] from you. 22 I am going to give the order, declares the LORD, and I will bring them back to this city. They will fight against it, take[d] it and burn[e] it down. And I will lay waste the towns of Judah so that no-one can live there."

The Recabites

35 This is the word that came to Jeremiah from the LORD during the reign of Jehoiakim[a] son of Josiah king of Judah: 2 "Go to the Recabite[b] family and invite them to come to one of the side rooms[c] of the house of the LORD and give them wine to drink."

3 So I went to get Jaazaniah son of Jeremiah, the son of Habazziniah, and his brothers and all his sons—the whole family of the Recabites. 4 I brought them into the house of the LORD, into the room of the sons of Hanan son of Igdaliah the man of God.[d] It was next to the room of the officials, which was over that of Maaseiah son of Shallum[e] the door-keeper.[f] 5 Then I set bowls full of wine and some cups before the men of the Recabite family and said to them, "Drink some wine."

6 But they replied, "We do not

34:8
j 2Ki 11:17
k Ex 21:2; Lev 25:10, 39-41; Ne 5:5-8
34:9
l Lev 25:39-46
34:13
m Ex 24:8
34:14
n Ex 21:2
o Dt 15:12; 2Ki 17:14
34:15
p ver 8
q Jer 7:10-11; Jer 32:34
34:16
r Eze 3:20; Eze 18:24
s Ex 20:7; Lev 19:12
34:17
t Mt 7:2; Gal 6:7
u Dt 28:25,64; Jer 29:18
34:18
v Ge 15:10
34:19
w Zep 3:3-4
34:20
x Jer 21:7
y Jer 11:21
z Dt 28:26; Jer 7:33; Jer 19:7
34:21
a Jer 32:4
b Jer 39:6; Jer 52:24-27
c Jer 37:5
34:22
d Jer 39:1-2
e Jer 39:8
35:1
a 2Ch 36:5
35:2
b 2Ki 10:15; 1Ch 2:55
c 1Ki 6:5
35:4
d Dt 33:1
e 1Ch 9:19
f 2Ki 12:9

a 14 Deut. 15:12

drink wine, because our forefather Jonadab[g] son of Recab gave
us this command: 'Neither you nor
your descendants must ever drink
wine.[h] 7Also you must never build
houses, sow seed or plant vineyards; you must never have any of
these things, but must always live
in tents.[i] Then you will live a long
time in the land[j] where you are nomads.' 8We have obeyed everything our forefather[k] Jonadab son
of Recab commanded us. Neither
we nor our wives nor our sons and
daughters have ever drunk wine
9or built houses to live in or had
vineyards, fields or crops.[l] 10We
have lived in tents and have fully
obeyed everything our forefather
Jonadab commanded us. 11But
when Nebuchadnezzar king of Babylon invaded[m] this land, we said,
'Come, we must go to Jerusalem[n]
to escape the Babylonian[a] and
Aramean armies.' So we have remained in Jerusalem."

12Then the word of the LORD
came to Jeremiah, saying: 13"This
is what the LORD Almighty, the God
of Israel, says: Go and tell the men
of Judah and the people of Jerusalem, 'Will you not learn a lesson[o]
and obey my words?' declares the
LORD. 14'Jonadab son of Recab ordered his sons not to drink wine
and this command has been kept.
To this day they do not drink wine,
because they obey their forefather's command. But I have spoken to you again and again,[p] yet
you have not obeyed[q] me. 15Again
and again I sent all my servants the
prophets[r] to you. They said, "Each
of you must turn[s] from your
wicked ways and reform[t] your actions; do not follow other gods to
serve them. Then you shall live in
the land[u] I have given to you and
your fathers." But you have not
paid attention or listened[v] to me.
16The descendants of Jonadab son
of Recab have carried out the command their forefather[w] gave them,
but these people have not obeyed
me.'

17"Therefore, this is what the
LORD God Almighty, the God of Israel, says: 'Listen! I am going to
bring on Judah and on everyone living in Jerusalem every disaster[x] I
pronounced against them. I spoke
to them, but they did not listen;[y] I
called to them, but they did not
answer.'"[z]

18Then Jeremiah said to the family of the Recabites, "This is what
the LORD Almighty, the God of
Israel, says: 'You have obeyed
the command of your forefather
Jonadab and have followed all
his instructions and have done
everything he ordered.' 19There-
fore, this is what the LORD
Almighty, the God of Israel, says:
'Jonadab son of Recab shall never
fail[a] to have a man to serve[b] me.'"

Jehoiakim Burns Jeremiah's Scroll

36 In the fourth year of Jehoiakim[a] son of Josiah king of
Judah, this word came to Jeremiah
from the LORD: 2"Take a scroll[b]
and write on it all the words I have
spoken to you concerning Israel,
Judah and all the other nations
from the time I began speaking to
you in the reign of Josiah[c] till now.
3Perhaps[d] when the people of Judah hear[e] about every disaster I
plan to inflict on them, each of
them will turn[f] from his wicked
way; then I will forgive[g] their
wickedness and their sin."

4So Jeremiah called Baruch[h] son
of Neriah, and while Jeremiah dictated[i] all the words the LORD had
spoken to him, Baruch wrote them
on the scroll.[j] 5Then Jeremiah told
Baruch, "I am restricted; I cannot
go to the LORD's temple. 6So you go
to the house of the LORD on a day of
fasting[k] and read to the people
from the scroll the words of the

35:6 g 2Ki 10:15; h Lev 10:9; Nu 6:2-4; Lk 1:15
35:7 i Heb 11:9; j Ex 20:12; Eph 6:2-3
35:8 k Pr 1:8; Col 3:20
35:9 l 1Ti 6:6
35:11 m 2Ki 24:1; n Jer 8:14
35:13 o Jer 6:10; Jer 32:33
35:14 p Jer 7:13; Jer 25:3; q Isa 30:9
35:15 r Jer 7:25; s Jer 26:3; t Isa 1:16-17; Jer 4:1; Jer 18:11; Eze 18:30; u Jer 25:5; v Jer 7:26
35:16 w Mal 1:6
35:17 x Jos 23:15; Jer 21:4-7; y Pr 1:24; Ro 10:21; z Isa 65:12; Isa 66:4; Jer 7:13
35:19 a Jer 33:17; b Jer 15:19
36:1 a 2Ch 36:5
36:2 b Ex 17:14; Jer 30:2; Hab 2:2; c Jer 1:2; Jer 25:3
36:3 d ver 7; Eze 12:3; e Mk 4:12; f Jer 26:3; Jnh 3:8; Ac 3:19; g Jer 18:8
36:4 h Jer 32:12; i ver 18; j Eze 2:9
36:6 k ver 9

a11 Or *Chaldean*

LORD that you wrote as I dictated.
Read them to all the people of Judah who come in from their towns.
7Perhaps they will bring their petition before the LORD, and each will
turn[l] from his wicked ways, for
the anger[m] and wrath pronounced
against this people by the LORD are
great."
8Baruch son of Neriah did everything Jeremiah the prophet told
him to do; at the LORD's temple he
read the words of the LORD from
the scroll. 9In the ninth month[n] of
the fifth year of Jehoiakim son
of Josiah king of Judah, a time of
fasting[o] before the LORD was
proclaimed for all the people in
Jerusalem and those who had come
from the towns of Judah. 10From
the room of Gemariah son of Shaphan the secretary,[p] which was in
the upper courtyard at the entrance of the New Gate[q] of the
temple, Baruch read to all the people at the LORD's temple the words
of Jeremiah from the scroll.
11When Micaiah son of Gemariah, the son of Shaphan, heard all
the words of the LORD from the
scroll, 12he went down to the secretary's room in the royal palace,
where all the officials were sitting:
Elishama the secretary, Delaiah
son of Shemaiah, Elnathan[r] son of
Acbor, Gemariah son of Shaphan,
Zedekiah son of Hananiah, and all
the other officials. 13After Micaiah
told them everything he had heard
Baruch read to the people from the
scroll, 14all the officials sent Jehudi[s] son of Nethaniah, the son of
Shelemiah, the son of Cushi, to say
to Baruch, "Bring the scroll from
which you have read to the people
and come." So Baruch son of Neriah went to them with the scroll in
his hand. 15They said to him, "Sit
down, please, and read it to us."
So Baruch read it to them.
16When they heard all these words,
they looked at each other in fear
and said to Baruch, "We must report all these words to the king."
17Then they asked Baruch, "Tell us,
how did you come to write all this?
Did Jeremiah dictate it?"
18"Yes," Baruch replied, "he dictated[t] all these words to me, and I
wrote them in ink on the scroll."
19Then the officials said to Baruch, "You and Jeremiah, go and
hide.[u] Don't let anyone know
where you are."
20After they put the scroll in the
room of Elishama the secretary,
they went to the king in the courtyard and reported everything to
him. 21The king sent Jehudi[v] to get
the scroll, and Jehudi brought it
from the room of Elishama the secretary and read it to the king[w] and
all the officials standing beside
him. 22It was the ninth month and
the king was sitting in the winter
apartment,[x] with a fire burning in
the brazier in front of him. 23When-
ever Jehudi had read three or four
columns of the scroll, the king cut
them off with a scribe's knife and
threw them into the brazier, until
the entire scroll was burned in the
fire.[y] 24The king and all his attendants who heard all these words
showed no fear,[z] nor did they tear
their clothes.[a] 25Even though Elnathan, Delaiah and Gemariah urged
the king not to burn the scroll, he
would not listen to them. 26Instead,
the king commanded Jerahmeel, a
son of the king, Seraiah son of
Azriel and Shelemiah son of Abdeel
to arrest[b] Baruch the scribe and
Jeremiah the prophet. But the
LORD had hidden[c] them.
27After the king burned the scroll
containing the words that Baruch
had written at Jeremiah's dic-
tation,[d] the word of the LORD came to
Jeremiah: 28"Take another scroll
and write on it all the words that
were on the first scroll, which Jehoiakim king of Judah burned up.
29Also tell Jehoiakim king of Judah,
'This is what the LORD says: You
burned that scroll and said, "Why
did you write on it that the king of
Babylon would certainly come and

36:7 l Jer 26:3 m Dt 31:17
36:9 n ver 22 o 2Ch 20:3
36:10 p Jer 52:25 q Jer 26:10
36:12 r Jer 26:22
36:14 s ver 21
36:18 t ver 4
36:19 u 1Ki 17:3
36:21 v ver 14 w 2Ki 22:10
36:22 x Am 3:15
36:23 y 1Ki 22:8
36:24 z Ps 36:1 a Ge 37:29; 2Ki 22:11; Isa 37:1
36:26 b Mt 23:34 c Jer 15:21
36:27 d ver 4

destroy this land and cut off both
men and animals from it?"[e]
30Therefore, this is what the LORD
says about Jehoiakim king of Judah: He will have no-one to sit on
the throne of David; his body will
be thrown out[f] and exposed to the
heat by day and the frost by night.
31I will punish him and his children
and his attendants for their wickedness; I will bring on them and
those living in Jerusalem and the
people of Judah every disaster[g] I
pronounced against them, because
they have not listened.' "
32So Jeremiah took another scroll
and gave it to the scribe Baruch son
of Neriah, and as Jeremiah dictated,[h] Baruch wrote[i] on it all the
words of the scroll that Jehoiakim
king of Judah had burned[j] in the
fire. And many similar words were
added to them.

Jeremiah in Prison

37 Zedekiah[a] son of Josiah
was made king[b] of Judah
by Nebuchadnezzar king of Babylon; he reigned in place of Jehoiachin[a][c] son of Jehoiakim. 2Neither
he nor his attendants nor the people
of the land paid any attention[d] to
the words the LORD had spoken
through Jeremiah the prophet.
3King Zedekiah, however, sent
Jehucal son of Shelemiah with the
priest Zephaniah[e] son of Maaseiah
to Jeremiah the prophet with this
message: "Please pray[f] to the
LORD our God for us."
4Now Jeremiah was free to come
and go among the people, for he
had not yet been put in prison.[g]
5Pharaoh's army had marched out
of Egypt,[h] and when the Babylonians[b] who were besieging Jerusalem heard the report about them,
they withdrew[i] from Jerusalem.[j]
6Then the word of the LORD came
to Jeremiah the prophet: 7"This
is what the LORD, the God of Israel, says: Tell the king of Judah,
who sent you to enquire[k] of me,
'Pharaoh's army, which has marched
out to support you, will go back to
its own land, to Egypt.[l] 8Then the
Babylonians will return and attack
this city; they will capture it and
burn[m] it down.'
9"This is what the LORD says: Do
not deceive[n] yourselves, thinking,
'The Babylonians will surely leave
us.' They will not! 10Even if you
were to defeat the entire Babylonian[c] army that is attacking you
and only wounded men were left in
their tents, they would come out
and burn this city down."
11After the Babylonian army had
withdrawn[o] from Jerusalem because of Pharaoh's army, 12Jere-
miah started to leave the city to go
to the territory of Benjamin to get
his share of the property[p] among
the people there. 13But when he
reached the Benjamin Gate, the
captain of the guard, whose name
was Irijah son of Shelemiah, the
son of Hananiah, arrested him and
said, "You are deserting to the Babylonians!"
14"That's not true!" Jeremiah
said. "I am not deserting to the
Babylonians." But Irijah would not
listen to him; instead, he arrested[q]
Jeremiah and brought him to the
officials. 15They were angry with
Jeremiah and had him beaten[r] and
imprisoned in the house[s] of Jonathan the secretary, which they had
made into a prison.
16Jeremiah was put into a vaulted
cell in a dungeon, where he remained a long time. 17Then King
Zedekiah sent for him and had him
brought to the palace, where he
asked[t] him privately,[u] "Is there
any word from the LORD?"
"Yes," Jeremiah replied, "you
will be handed over[v] to the king of
Babylon."
18Then Jeremiah said to King
Zedekiah, "What crime[w] have I

[a]1 Hebrew *Coniah*, a variant of *Jehoiachin*
[b]5 Or *Chaldeans*; also in verses 8, 9, 13 and 14
[c]10 Or *Chaldean*; also in verse 11

36:29 e Isa 30:10
36:30 f Jer 22:19
36:31 g Pr 29:1
36:32 h ver 4; i Ex 34:1; j ver 23
37:1 a 2Ki 24:17; b Eze 17:13; c 2Ki 24:8,12; 2Ch 36:10; Jer 22:24
37:2 d 2Ki 24:19; 2Ch 36:12,14
37:3 e Jer 29:25; Jer 52:24; f 1Ki 13:6; Jer 21:1-2; Jer 42:2
37:4 g ver 15; Jer 32:2
37:5 h Eze 17:15; i Jer 34:21; j 2Ki 24:7
37:7 k 2Ki 22:18; l Jer 2:36; La 4:17
37:8 m Jer 34:22; Jer 39:8
37:9 n Jer 29:8
37:11 o ver 5
37:12 p Jer 32:9
37:14 q Jer 40:4
37:15 r Jer 20:2; s Jer 38:26
37:17 t Jer 15:11; u Jer 38:16; v Jer 21:7
37:18 w 1Sa 26:18; Jn 10:32; Ac 25:8

committed against you or your officials or this people, that you have
put me in prison? 19Where are your
prophets who prophesied to you,
'The king of Babylon will not attack
you or this land'? 20But now, my
lord the king, please listen. Let me
bring my petition before you: Do
not send me back to the house of
Jonathan the secretary, or I shall
die there."
21King Zedekiah then gave orders for Jeremiah to be placed in
the courtyard of the guard and
given bread from the street of the
bakers each day until all the
bread[x] in the city was gone.[y] So
Jeremiah remained in the courtyard of the guard.[z]

Jeremiah Thrown Into a Cistern

38 Shephatiah son of Mattan,
Gedaliah son of Pashhur,
Jehucal[a][a] son of Shelemiah, and
Pashhur son of Malkijah heard
what Jeremiah was telling all the
people when he said, 2"This is what
the LORD says: 'Whoever stays in
this city will die by the sword, famine or plague,[b] but whoever goes
over to the Babylonians[b] will live.
He will escape with his life; he will
live.'[c] 3And this is what the LORD
says: 'This city will certainly be
handed over to the army of the king
of Babylon, who will capture it.' "[d]
4Then the officials[e] said to the
king, "This man should be put to
death.[f] He is discouraging the soldiers who are left in this city, as
well as all the people, by the things
he is saying to them. This man is
not seeking the good of these people but their ruin."
5"He is in your hands," King Zedekiah answered. "The king can do
nothing to oppose you."
6So they took Jeremiah and put
him into the cistern of Malkijah,
the king's son, which was in the
courtyard of the guard.[g] They lowered Jeremiah by ropes into the
cistern; it had no water in it, only
mud, and Jeremiah sank down into
the mud.
7But Ebed-Melech,[h] a Cushite,[c]
an official[d][i] in the royal palace,
heard that they had put Jeremiah
into the cistern. While the king was
sitting in the Benjamin Gate,[j]
8Ebed-Melech went out of the palace and said to him, 9"My lord the
king, these men have acted wickedly in all they have done to Jeremiah the prophet. They have
thrown him into a cistern, where he
will starve to death when there is
no longer any bread[k] in the city."
10Then the king commanded
Ebed-Melech the Cushite, "Take
thirty men from here with you and
lift Jeremiah the prophet out of the
cistern before he dies."
11So Ebed-Melech took the men
with him and went to a room under
the treasury in the palace. He took
some old rags and worn-out clothes
from there and let them down with
ropes to Jeremiah in the cistern.
12Ebed-Melech the Cushite said to
Jeremiah, "Put these old rags and
worn-out clothes under your arms
to pad the ropes." Jeremiah did so,
13and they pulled him up with the
ropes and lifted him out of the cistern. And Jeremiah remained in
the courtyard of the guard.[l]

Zedekiah Questions Jeremiah Again

14Then King Zedekiah sent for
Jeremiah the prophet and had him
brought to the third entrance to the
temple of the LORD. "I am going to
ask you something," the king said
to Jeremiah. "Do not hide[m] anything from me."
15Jeremiah said to Zedekiah, "If I
give you an answer, will you not kill
me? Even if I did give you counsel,
you would not listen to me."
16But King Zedekiah swore this

37:21 x Isa 33:16; Jer 38:9 y 2Ki 25:3; Jer 52:6 z Jer 32:2; Jer 38:6,13,28
38:1 a Jer 37:3
38:2 b Jer 34:17 c Jer 21:9; Jer 39:18; Jer 45:5
38:3 d Jer 21:4,10; Jer 32:3
38:4 e Jer 36:12 f Jer 26:11
38:6 g Jer 37:21
38:7 h Jer 39:16 i Ac 8:27 j Job 29:7
38:9 k Jer 37:21
38:13 l Jer 37:21
38:14 m 1Sa 3:17

a1 Hebrew *Jucal*, a variant of *Jehucal*
b2 Or *Chaldeans*; also in verses 18, 19 and 23
c7 Probably from the upper Nile region
d7 Or *a eunuch*

oath secretly[n] to Jeremiah: "As
surely as the LORD lives, who has
given us breath,[o] I will neither kill
you nor hand you over to those who
are seeking your life."[p]
[17]Then Jeremiah said to Zedekiah, "This is what the LORD God
Almighty, the God of Israel, says:
'If you surrender to the officers of
the king of Babylon, your life will
be spared and this city will not be
burned down; you and your family
will live.[q] [18]But if you will not surrender to the officers of the king
of Babylon, this city will be handed over[r] to the Babylonians and
they will burn[s] it down; you yourself will not escape[t] from their
hands.' "
[19]King Zedekiah said to Jeremiah, "I am afraid[u] of the Jews
who have gone over[v] to the Babylonians, for the Babylonians may
hand me over to them and they will
ill-treat me."
[20]"They will not hand you over,"
Jeremiah replied. "Obey[w] the
LORD by doing what I tell you. Then
it will go well with you, and your
life[x] will be spared. [21]But if you refuse to surrender, this is what the
LORD has revealed to me: [22]All the
women[y] left in the palace of
the king of Judah will be brought
out to the officials of the king of
Babylon. Those women will say to
you:

" 'They misled you and
overcame you—
those trusted friends of yours.
Your feet are sunk in the mud;
your friends have deserted
you.'

[23]"All your wives and children[z]
will be brought out to the Babylonians. You yourself will not escape
from their hands but will be captured[a] by the king of Babylon; and
this city will[e] be burned down."
[24]Then Zedekiah said to Jeremiah, "Do not let anyone know
about this conversation, or you
may die. [25]If the officials hear that
I talked with you, and they come to
you and say, 'Tell us what you said
to the king and what the king said
to you; do not hide it from us or we
will kill you,' [26]then tell them, 'I
was pleading with the king not to
send me back to Jonathan's house[b]
to die there.' "
[27]All the officials did come to
Jeremiah and question him, and he
told them everything the king had
ordered him to say. So they said no
more to him, for no-one had heard
his conversation with the king.
[28]And Jeremiah remained in the
courtyard of the guard[c] until the
day Jerusalem was captured.

The Fall of Jerusalem

39:1–10pp 2Ki 25:1–12; Jer 52:4–16

39
This is how Jerusalem was
taken: [1]In the ninth year of
Zedekiah king of Judah, in the
tenth month, Nebuchadnezzar king
of Babylon marched against Jerusalem with his whole army and laid
siege[a] to it. [2]And on the ninth day
of the fourth month of Zedekiah's
eleventh year, the city wall was
broken through. [3]Then all the officials[b] of the king of Babylon came
and took seats in the Middle Gate:
Nergal-Sharezer of Samgar, Nebo-
Sarsekim[a] a chief officer, Nergal-
Sharezer a high official and all the
other officials of the king of Babylon. [4]When Zedekiah king of Judah and all the soldiers saw them,
they fled; they left the city at night
by way of the king's garden,
through the gate between the two
walls, and headed towards the Arabah.[b]
[5]But the Babylonian[c] army pursued them and overtook Zedekiah[c]
in the plains of Jericho. They captured him and took him to Nebuchadnezzar king of Babylon at
Riblah[d] in the land of Hamath,
where he pronounced sentence on

38:16 *n* Jer 37:17 *o* Isa 42:5; Isa 57:16 *p* ver 4
38:17 *q* 2Ki 24:12; Jer 21:9
38:18 *r* ver 3; Jer 34:3 *s* Jer 37:8 *t* Jer 24:8; Jer 32:4
38:19 *u* Isa 51:12; Jn 12:42 *v* Jer 39:9
38:20 *w* Jer 11:4 *x* Isa 55:3
38:22 *y* Jer 6:12
38:23 *z* 2Ki 25:6 *a* Jer 41:10
38:26 *b* Jer 37:15
38:28 *c* Jer 37:21; Jer 39:14
39:1 *a* 2Ki 25:1; Jer 52:4; Eze 24:2
39:3 *b* Jer 21:4
39:5 *c* Jer 32:4 *d* 2Ki 23:33

[e]23 Or *and you will cause this city to*
[a]3 Or *Nergal-Sharezer, Samgar-Nebo, Sarsekim*
[b]4 Or *the Jordan Valley* [c]5 Or *Chaldean*

him. 6There at Riblah the king of
Babylon slaughtered the sons of
Zedekiah before his eyes and also
killed all the nobles of Judah. 7Then
he put out Zedekiah's eyes[e] and
bound him with bronze shackles to
take him to Babylon.[f]

8The Babyloniansᵈ set fire[g] to
the royal palace and the houses of
the people and broke down the
walls[h] of Jerusalem. 9Nebuzara-
dan commander of the imperial
guard carried into exile to Babylon
the people who remained in the
city, along with those who had gone
over to him, and the rest of the people.[i] 10But Nebuzaradan the commander of the guard left behind in
the land of Judah some of the poor
people, who owned nothing; and at
that time he gave them vineyards
and fields.

11Now Nebuchadnezzar king of
Babylon had given these orders
about Jeremiah through Nebuzaradan commander of the imperial
guard: 12"Take him and look after
him; don't harm[j] him but do for
him whatever he asks." 13So Nebuzaradan the commander of the
guard, Nebushazban a chief officer, Nergal-Sharezer a high
official and all the other officers of
the king of Babylon 14sent and had
Jeremiah taken out of the courtyard of the guard.[k] They handed
him over to Gedaliah son of Ahikam,[l] the son of Shaphan, to take
him back to his home. So he remained among his own people.[m]

15While Jeremiah had been confined in the courtyard of the guard,
the word of the LORD came to him:
16"Go and tell Ebed-Melech[n] the
Cushite, 'This is what the LORD
Almighty, the God of Israel, says: I
am about to fulfil my words against
this city through disaster,[o] not
prosperity. At that time they will
be fulfilled before your eyes. 17But
I will rescue[p] you on that day, declares the LORD; you will not be
handed over to those you fear. 18I
will save you; you will not fall by
the sword[q] but will escape with
your life,[r] because you trust[s] in
me, declares the LORD.' "

Jeremiah Freed

40 The word came to Jeremiah from the LORD after
Nebuzaradan commander of the
imperial guard had released him at
Ramah. He had found Jeremiah
bound in chains among all the captives from Jerusalem and Judah
who were being carried into exile
to Babylon. 2When the commander
of the guard found Jeremiah, he
said to him, "The LORD your God
decreed this disaster for this
place.[a] 3And now the LORD has
brought it about; he has done just
as he said he would. All this happened because you people sinned[b]
against the LORD and did not obey[c]
him. 4But today I am freeing you
from the chains on your wrists.
Come with me to Babylon, if you
like, and I will look after you; but if
you do not want to, then don't come.
Look, the whole country lies before
you; go wherever you please."[d]
5However, before Jeremiah turned
to go,ᵃ Nebuzaradan added, "Go
back to Gedaliah[e] son of Ahikam,
the son of Shaphan, whom the king
of Babylon has appointed over the
towns of Judah, and live with him
among the people, or go anywhere
else you please."[f]

Then the commander gave him
provisions and a present and let
him go. 6So Jeremiah went to Gedaliah son of Ahikam at Mizpah[g]
and stayed with him among the
people who were left behind in the
land.

Gedaliah Assassinated

40:7–9; 41:1–3pp 2Ki 25:22–26

7When all the army officers and
their men who were still in the open
country heard that the king of Babylon had appointed Gedaliah son of

39:7 e Eze 12:13 f Jer 32:5
39:8 g Jer 38:18 h Ne 1:3
39:9 i Jer 40:1
39:12 j Pr 16:7 1Pe 3:13
39:14 k Jer 38:28 l 2Ki 22:12 m Jer 40:5
39:16 n Jer 38:7 o Jer 21:10 Da 9:12
39:17 p Ps 41:1-2
39:18 q Jer 45:5 r Jer 21:9 Jer 38:2 s Jer 17:7
40:2 a Jer 50:7
40:3 b Da 9:11 c Dt 29:24-28 Ro 2:5-9
40:4 d Ge 13:9 Jer 39:11-12
40:5 e 2Ki 25:22 f Jer 39:14
40:6 g Jdg 20:1 1Sa 7:5-17

ᵈ8 Or *Chaldeans* ᵃ5 Or *Jeremiah answered*

Ahikam as governor over the land and had put him in charge of the men, women and children who were the poorest[h] in the land and who had not been carried into exile to Babylon, 8they came to Gedaliah at Mizpah[i]—Ishmael[j] son of Nethaniah, Johanan and Jonathan the sons of Kareah, Seraiah son of Tanhumeth, the sons of Ephai the Netophathite,[k] and Jaazaniah[b] the son of the Maacathite,[l] and their men. 9Gedaliah son of Ahikam, the son of Shaphan, took an oath to reassure them and their men. "Do not be afraid to serve[m] the Babylonians,"[c] he said. "Settle down in the land and serve the king of Babylon, and it will go well with you.[n] 10I myself will stay in Mizpah[o] to represent you before the Babylonians who come to us, but you are to harvest the wine, summer fruit and oil, and put them in your storage jars, and live in the towns you have taken over."[p]

11When all the Jews in Moab,[q] Ammon, Edom and all the other countries heard that the king of Babylon had left a remnant in Judah and had appointed Gedaliah son of Ahikam, the son of Shaphan, as governor over them, 12they all came back to the land of Judah, to Gedaliah at Mizpah, from all the countries where they had been scattered.[r] And they harvested an abundance of wine and summer fruit.

13Johanan son of Kareah and all the army officers still in the open country came to Gedaliah at Mizpah[s] 14and said to him, "Don't you know that Baalis king of the Ammonites[t] has sent Ishmael son of Nethaniah to take your life?" But Gedaliah son of Ahikam did not believe them.

15Then Johanan son of Kareah said privately to Gedaliah in Mizpah, "Let me go and kill Ishmael son of Nethaniah, and no-one will know it. Why should he take your life and cause all the Jews who are gathered around you to be scattered and the remnant of Judah to perish?"

16But Gedaliah son of Ahikam said to Johanan son of Kareah, "Don't do such a thing! What you are saying about Ishmael is not true."

41 In the seventh month Ishmael[a] son of Nethaniah, the son of Elishama, who was of royal blood and had been one of the king's officers, came with ten men to Gedaliah son of Ahikam at Mizpah. While they were eating together there, 2Ishmael[b] son of Nethaniah and the ten men who were with him got up and struck down Gedaliah son of Ahikam, the son of Shaphan, with the sword, killing the one whom the king of Babylon had appointed[c] as governor over the land.[d] 3Ishmael also killed all the Jews who were with Gedaliah at Mizpah, as well as the Babylonian[a] soldiers who were there.

4The day after Gedaliah's assassination, before anyone knew about it, 5eighty men who had shaved off their beards,[e] torn their clothes and cut themselves came from Shechem,[f] Shiloh[g] and Samaria,[h] bringing grain offerings and incense with them to the house of the LORD.[i] 6Ishmael son of Nethaniah went out from Mizpah to meet them, weeping[j] as he went. When he met them, he said, "Come to Gedaliah son of Ahikam." 7When they went into the city, Ishmael son of Nethaniah and the men who were with him slaughtered them and threw them into a cistern. 8But ten of them said to Ishmael, "Don't kill us! We have wheat and barley, oil and honey, hidden in a field."[k] So he let them alone and did not kill them with the others. 9Now the cistern where he threw all the bodies

40:7 h Jer 39:10
40:8 i ver 13; j ver 14; Jer 41:1,2; k 2Sa 23:28; l Dt 3:14
40:9 m Jer 27:11; n Jer 38:20
40:10 o ver 6; p Dt 1:39
40:11 q Nu 25:1
40:12 r Jer 43:5
40:13 s ver 8
40:14 t 2Sa 10:1-19; Jer 25:21; Jer 41:10
41:1 a Jer 40:8
41:2 b Ps 41:9; Ps 109:5; c Jer 40:5; d 2Sa 3:27; 2Sa 20:9-10
41:5 e Lev 19:27; f Ge 33:18; Jdg 9:1-57; 1Ki 12:1; g Jos 18:1; h 1Ki 16:24; i 2Ki 25:9
41:6 j 2Sa 3:16
41:8 k Isa 45:3

b8 Hebrew *Jezaniah*, a variant of *Jaazaniah*
c9 Or *Chaldeans*; also in verse 10
a3 Or *Chaldean*

of the men he had killed along with
Gedaliah was the one King Asa[l]
had made as part of his defence[m]
against Baasha[n] king of Israel.
Ishmael son of Nethaniah filled it
with the dead.
10Ishmael made captives of all
the rest of the people[o] who were
in Mizpah—the king's daughters
along with all the others who were
left there, over whom Nebuzaradan commander of the imperial
guard had appointed Gedaliah son
of Ahikam. Ishmael son of Nethaniah took them captive and set out to
cross over to the Ammonites.[p]
11When Johanan[q] son of Kareah
and all the army officers who were
with him heard about all the crimes
Ishmael son of Nethaniah had committed, 12they took all their men
and went to fight Ishmael son of
Nethaniah. They caught up with
him near the great pool[r] in Gibeon.
13When all the people[s] Ishmael had
with him saw Johanan son of Kareah and the army officers who
were with him, they were glad.
14All the people Ishmael had taken
captive at Mizpah turned and went
over to Johanan son of Kareah.
15But Ishmael son of Nethaniah and
eight of his men escaped[t] from Johanan and fled to the Ammonites.

Flight to Egypt

16Then Johanan son of Kareah
and all the army officers who were
with him led away all the survivors[u] from Mizpah whom he had
recovered from Ishmael son of Nethaniah after he had assassinated
Gedaliah son of Ahikam: the soldiers, women, children and court
officials he had brought from Gibeon. 17And they went on, stopping
at Geruth Kimham[v] near Bethlehem on their way to Egypt[w] 18to escape the Babylonians.[b] They were
afraid[x] of them because Ishmael
son of Nethaniah had killed Gedaliah[y] son of Ahikam, whom the king
of Babylon had appointed as governor over the land.

42

Then all the army officers,
including Johanan[a] son of
Kareah and Jezaniah[a] son of Hoshaiah, and all the people from the
least to the greatest[b] approached
2Jeremiah the prophet and said to
him, "Please hear our petition and
pray[c] to the LORD your God for
this entire remnant.[d] For as you
now see, though we were once
many, now only a few[e] are left.
3Pray that the LORD your God will
tell us where we should go and
what we should do."[f]
4"I have heard you," replied Jeremiah the prophet. "I will certainly
pray[g] to the LORD your God as you
have requested; I will tell you
everything the LORD says and will
keep nothing back from you."[h]
5Then they said to Jeremiah,
"May the LORD be a true and faithful witness[i] against us if we do not
act in accordance with everything
the LORD your God sends you to tell
us. 6Whether it is favourable or un-
favourable, we will obey the LORD
our God, to whom we are sending
you, so that it will go well[j] with us,
for we will obey[k] the LORD our
God."
7Ten days later the word of the
LORD came to Jeremiah. 8So he
called together Johanan son of
Kareah and all the army officers[l]
who were with him and all the people from the least to the greatest.
9He said to them, "This is what the
LORD, the God of Israel, to whom
you sent me to present your petition, says:[m] 10'If you stay in this
land, I will build[n] you up and not
tear you down; I will plant[o] you
and not uproot you,[p] for I am
grieved over the disaster I have
inflicted on you.[q] 11Do not be
afraid of the king of Babylon,[r] whom
you now fear.[s] Do not be afraid of
him, declares the LORD, for I am

41:9 *l* 1Ki 15:22; 2Ch 16:6 *m* Jdg 6:2 *n* 2Ch 16:1
41:10 *o* Jer 40:7,12 *p* Jer 40:14
41:11 *q* Jer 40:8
41:12 *r* 2Sa 2:13
41:13 *s* ver 10
41:15 *t* Job 21:30; Pr 28:17
41:16 *u* Jer 43:4
41:17 *v* 2Sa 19:37 *w* Jer 42:14
41:18 *x* Isa 51:12; Jer 42:16; Lk 12:4-5 *y* Jer 40:5
42:1 *a* Jer 40:13; Jer 41:11 *b* Jer 6:13; Jer 44:12
42:2 *c* Jer 36:7; Ac 8:24; Jas 5:16 *d* Isa 1:9 *e* Lev 26:22; La 1:1
42:3 *f* Ps 86:11; Pr 3:6
42:4 *g* Ex 8:29; 1Sa 12:23 *h* 1Ki 22:14; 1Sa 3:17
42:5 *i* Ge 31:50
42:6 *j* Dt 5:29; Dt 6:3; Jer 7:23 *k* Ex 24:7; Jos 24:24
42:8 *l* ver 1
42:9 *m* 2Ki 22:15
42:10 *n* Jer 24:6 *o* Jer 31:28 *p* Eze 36:36 *q* Jer 18:8
42:11 *r* Jer 27:11 *s* Nu 14:9

b *18* Or *Chaldeans*
a *1* Hebrew; Septuagint (see also 43:2) *Azariah*

with you and will save[t] you and deliver you from his hands.[u] 12 I will show you compassion so that he will have compassion on you and restore you to your land.'[v]

13 "However, if you say, 'We will not stay in this land,' and so disobey[w] the LORD your God, 14 and if you say, 'No, we will go and live in Egypt,[x] where we will not see war or hear the trumpet or be hungry for bread,' 15 then hear the word of the LORD, O remnant of Judah. This is what the LORD Almighty, the God of Israel, says: 'If you are determined to go to Egypt and you do go to settle there, 16 then the sword[y] you fear will overtake you there, and the famine you dread will follow you into Egypt, and there you will die. 17 Indeed, all who are determined to go to Egypt to settle there will die by the sword, famine and plague;[z] not one of them will survive or escape the disaster I will bring on them.' 18 This is what the LORD Almighty, the God of Israel, says: 'As my anger and wrath[a] have been poured out on those who lived in Jerusalem,[b] so will my wrath be poured out on you when you go to Egypt. You will be an object of cursing and horror,[c] of condemnation and reproach; you will never see this place again.'[d]

19 "O remnant of Judah, the LORD has told you, 'Do not go to Egypt.'[e] Be sure of this: I warn you today 20 that you made a fatal mistake[b] when you sent me to the LORD your God and said, 'Pray to the LORD our God for us; tell us everything he says and we will do it.'[f] 21 I have told you today, but you still have not obeyed the LORD your God in all he sent me to tell you.[g] 22 So now, be sure of this: You will die by the sword, famine and plague[h] in the place where you want to go to settle."[i]

43

When Jeremiah finished telling the people all the words of the LORD their God—everything the LORD had sent him to tell them[a]— 2 Azariah son of Hoshaiah and Johanan[b] son of Kareah and all the arrogant men said to Jeremiah, "You are lying! The LORD our God has not sent you to say, 'You must not go to Egypt to settle there.' 3 But Baruch son of Neriah is inciting you against us to hand us over to the Babylonians,[a] so that they may kill us or carry us into exile to Babylon."[c]

4 So Johanan son of Kareah and all the army officers and all the people disobeyed the LORD's command[d] to stay in the land of Judah.[e] 5 Instead, Johanan son of Kareah and all the army officers led away all the remnant of Judah who had come back to live in the land of Judah from all the nations where they had been scattered.[f] 6 They also led away all the men, women and children and the king's daughters whom Nebuzaradan commander of the imperial guard had left with Gedaliah son of Ahikam, the son of Shaphan, and Jeremiah the prophet and Baruch son of Neriah. 7 So they entered Egypt in disobedience to the LORD and went as far as Tahpanhes.[g]

8 In Tahpanhes[h] the word of the LORD came to Jeremiah: 9 "While the Jews are watching, take some large stones with you and bury them in clay in the brick pavement at the entrance to Pharaoh's palace in Tahpanhes. 10 Then say to them, 'This is what the LORD Almighty, the God of Israel, says: I will send for my servant[i] Nebuchadnezzar king of Babylon, and I will set his throne over these stones I have buried here; he will spread his royal canopy above them. 11 He will come and attack Egypt,[j] bringing death to those destined for death, captivity to those destined for captivity, and the sword to those destined for the sword.[k] 12 He[b] will set fire to the temples of the gods[l]

42:11 t Isa 43:5 u Jer 1:8; Ro 8:31
42:12 v Ps 106:44-46
42:13 w Jer 44:16
42:14 x Nu 11:4-5
42:16 y Eze 11:8
42:17 z ver 22; Jer 44:13
42:18 a Dt 29:18-20; Jer 7:20 b 2Ch 36:19; Jer 39:1-9 c Jer 29:18 d Jer 22:10
42:19 e Dt 17:16; Isa 30:7
42:20 f ver 2
42:21 g Eze 2:7; Zec 7:11-12
42:22 h ver 17; Eze 6:11 i Hos 9:6
43:1 a Jer 26:8; Jer 42:9-22
43:2 b Jer 42:1
43:3 c Jer 38:4
43:4 d Jer 42:5-6 e Jer 42:10
43:5 f Jer 40:12
43:7 g Jer 2:16; Jer 44:1
43:8 h Jer 2:16
43:10 i Isa 44:28; Jer 25:9; Jer 27:6
43:11 j Jer 46:13-26; Eze 29:19-20 k Jer 15:2; Jer 44:13; Zec 11:9
43:12 l Jer 46:25; Eze 30:13

b20 Or *you erred in your hearts*
a3 Or *Chaldeans* b12 Or *I*

of Egypt; he will burn their temples
and take their gods captive. As a
shepherd wraps[m] his garment
round him, so will he wrap Egypt
round himself and depart from
there unscathed. [13]There in the
temple of the sun[c] in Egypt he will
demolish the sacred pillars and will
burn down the temples of the gods
of Egypt.' "

Disaster Because of Idolatry

44 This word came to Jeremiah concerning all the
Jews living in Lower Egypt—in
Migdol,[a] Tahpanhes[b] and Memphis[a][c]—and in Upper Egypt:[b][d]
[2]"This is what the LORD Almighty,
the God of Israel, says: You saw the
great disaster I brought on Jerusalem and on all the towns of Judah. Today they lie deserted and in
ruins[e] [3]because of the evil they
have done. They provoked me to
anger by burning incense and by
worshipping other gods[f] that
neither they nor you nor your
fathers[g] ever knew. [4]Again and
again[h] I sent my servants the
prophets,[i] who said, 'Do not do
this detestable thing that I hate!'
[5]But they did not listen or pay attention; they did not turn from
their wickedness or stop burning
incense to other gods.[j] [6]There-
fore, my fierce anger was poured
out; it raged against the towns of
Judah and the streets of Jerusalem
and made them the desolate ruins
they are today.
[7]"Now this is what the LORD God
Almighty, the God of Israel, says:
Why bring such great disaster[k] on
yourselves by cutting off from Judah the men and women,[l] the children and infants, and so leave
yourselves without a remnant?
[8]Why provoke me to anger with
what your hands have made,[m]
burning incense to other gods in
Egypt, where you have come to
live?[n] You will destroy yourselves
and make yourselves an object of
cursing and reproach[o] among all
the nations on earth. [9]Have you forgotten the wickedness committed
by your fathers and by the kings
and queens of Judah and the wickedness committed by you and your
wives in the land of Judah and the
streets of Jerusalem?[p] [10]To this
day they have not humbled themselves or shown reverence, nor
have they followed my law[q] and
the decrees I set before you and
your fathers.[r]
[11]"Therefore, this is what the
LORD Almighty, the God of Israel,
says: I am determined to bring
disaster[s] on you and to destroy all
Judah. [12]I will take away the
remnant[t] of Judah who were determined to go to Egypt to settle
there. They will all perish in Egypt;
they will fall by the sword or die
from famine. From the least to the
greatest, they will die by sword or
famine.[u] They will become an object of cursing and horror, of condemnation and reproach.[v] [13]I will
punish those who live in Egypt with
the sword, famine and plague,[w] as
I punished Jerusalem. [14]None of
the remnant of Judah who have
gone to live in Egypt will escape or
survive to return to the land of Judah, to which they long to return
and live; none will return except a
few fugitives."[x]
[15]Then all the men who knew that
their wives were burning incense
to other gods, along with all the
women who were present—a large
assembly—and all the people living in Lower and Upper Egypt,[c]
said to Jeremiah, [16]"We will not listen[y] to the message you have spoken to us in the name of the LORD!
[17]We will certainly do everything
we said we would:[z] We will burn
incense to the Queen of Heaven[a]
and will pour out drink offerings to
her just as we and our fathers, our

43:12
m Ps 104:2; Ps 109:18-19

44:1
a Ex 14:2
b Jer 43:7,8
c Isa 19:13
d Isa 11:11; Jer 46:14

44:2
e Isa 6:11; Jer 9:11; Jer 34:22

44:3
f ver 8; Dt 13:6-11; Dt 29:26
g Dt 32:17; Jer 19:4

44:4
h Jer 7:13
i Jer 7:25; Jer 25:4; Jer 26:5

44:5
j Jer 11:8-10

44:7
k Jer 26:19
l Jer 51:22

44:8
m Jer 25:6-7
n 1Co 10:22
o Jer 42:18

44:9
p ver 17,21

44:10
q Jos 1:7
r 1Ki 9:6-9

44:11
s Jer 21:10; Am 9:4

44:12
t ver 7
u Isa 1:28
v Jer 29:18; Jer 42:15-18

44:13
w Jer 42:17

44:14
x ver 28; Jer 22:24-27; Ro 9:27

44:16
y Jer 11:8-10

44:17
z Dt 23:23
a ver 25; Jer 7:18

c13 Or *in Heliopolis*
a1 Hebrew *Noph*
b1 Hebrew *in Pathros and Pathros*
c15 Hebrew *in Egypt*

kings and our officials did in the
towns of Judah and in the streets
of Jerusalem. At that time we had
plenty of food and were well off
and suffered no harm.[b] 18But ever
since we stopped burning incense
to the Queen of Heaven and pouring out drink offerings to her, we
have had nothing and have been
perishing by sword and famine.[c]"
19The women added, "When we
burned incense to the Queen of
Heaven[d] and poured out drink offerings to her, did not our husbands
know that we were making cakes
like her image and pouring out
drink offerings to her?"
20Then Jeremiah said to all the
people, both men and women, who
were answering him, 21"Did not the
LORD remember[e] and think about
the incense[f] burned in the towns
of Judah and the streets of Jerusalem[g] by you and your fathers,[h]
your kings and your officials and
the people of the land? 22When the
LORD could no longer endure your
wicked actions and the detestable
things you did, your land became
an object of cursing[i] and a desolate waste without inhabitants,
as it is today.[j] 23Because you have
burned incense and have sinned
against the LORD and have not
obeyed him or followed his law or
his decrees or his stipulations, this
disaster[k] has come upon you, as
you now see."[l]
24Then Jeremiah said to all the
people, including the women,[m]
"Hear the word of the LORD, all you
people of Judah in Egypt.[n] 25This
is what the LORD Almighty, the God
of Israel, says: You and your wives
have shown by your actions what
you promised when you said, 'We
will certainly carry out the vows
we made to burn incense and pour
out drink offerings to the Queen of
Heaven.'[o]
"Go ahead then, do what you
promised! Keep your vows![p] 26But
hear the word of the LORD, all Jews
living in Egypt: 'I swear[q] by my
great name,' says the LORD, 'that
no-one from Judah living anywhere in Egypt shall ever again invoke my name or swear, "As surely
as the Sovereign LORD lives."[r]
27For I am watching over them for
harm,[s] not for good; the Jews in
Egypt will perish by sword and
famine until they are all destroyed.
28Those who escape the sword and
return to the land of Judah from
Egypt will be very few.[t] Then the
whole remnant of Judah who came
to live in Egypt will know whose
word will stand—mine or theirs.[u]
29" 'This will be the sign to you
that I will punish you in this place,'
declares the LORD, 'so that you will
know that my threats of harm
against you will surely stand.'[v]
30This is what the LORD says: 'I am
going to hand Pharaoh[w] Hophra
king of Egypt over to his enemies
who seek his life, just as I handed
Zedekiah[x] king of Judah over to
Nebuchadnezzar king of Babylon,
the enemy who was seeking his
life.' "[y]

A Message to Baruch

45 This is what Jeremiah the
prophet told Baruch[a] son
of Neriah in the fourth year of
Jehoiakim[b] son of Josiah king of
Judah, after Baruch had written
on a scroll the words Jeremiah was
then dictating: 2"This is what the
LORD, the God of Israel, says to
you, Baruch: 3You said, 'Woe to
me! The LORD has added sorrow
to my pain; I am worn out with
groaning[c] and find no rest.' "
4⌞The LORD said,⌟ "Say this to him:
'This is what the LORD says: I will
overthrow what I have built and
uproot what I have planted,[d]
throughout the land.[e] 5Should you
then seek great things for yourself? Seek them not.[f] For I will
bring disaster on all people, declares the LORD, but wherever you
go I will let you escape with your
life.' "[g]

44:17 b Hos 2:5-13
44:18 c Mal 3:13-15
44:19 d Jer 7:18
44:21 e Isa 64:9; Jer 14:10 f Jer 11:13 g ver 9 h Ps 79:8
44:22 i Jer 25:18 j Ge 19:13; Ps 107:33-34
44:23 k Jer 40:2 l 1Ki 9:9; Jer 7:13-15; Da 9:11-12
44:24 m ver 15 n Jer 43:7
44:25 o ver 17 p Eze 20:39
44:26 q Ge 22:16; Isa 48:1; Heb 6:13-17 r Dt 32:40; Ps 50:16
44:27 s Jer 31:28
44:28 t ver 13-14; Isa 10:19 u ver 17,25-26
44:29 v Pr 19:21
44:30 w Jer 46:26; Eze 30:21 x 2Ki 25:1-7 y Jer 39:5
45:1 a Jer 32:12; Jer 36:4,18, 32 b 2Ch 36:5
45:3 c Ps 69:3
45:4 d Jer 11:17 e Isa 5:5-7; Jer 18:7-10
45:5 f Mt 6:25-27, 33 g Jer 21:9; Jer 38:2; Jer 39:18

A Message About Egypt

46 This is the word of the
LORD that came to Jere-
miah the prophet concerning the
nations:[a]

2Concerning Egypt:

This is the message against the
army of Pharaoh Neco[b] king of
Egypt, which was defeated at Carchemish[c] on the Euphrates River
by Nebuchadnezzar king of Babylon in the fourth year of Jehoiakim[d] son of Josiah king of Judah:

3"Prepare your shields,[e] both
large and small,
and march out for battle!
4Harness the horses,
mount the steeds!
Take your positions
with helmets on!
Polish[f] your spears,
put on your armour![g]
5What do I see?
They are terrified,
they are retreating,
their warriors are defeated.
They flee[h] in haste
without looking back,
and there is terror[i] on every
side,"
declares the LORD.
6"The swift cannot flee[j]
nor the strong escape.
In the north by the River
Euphrates
they stumble and fall.[k]

7"Who is this that rises like the
Nile,
like rivers of surging
waters?[l]
8Egypt rises like the Nile,
like rivers of surging waters.
She says, 'I will rise and cover
the earth;
I will destroy cities and their
people.'
9Charge, O horses!
Drive furiously,
O charioteers![m]
March on, O warriors—

46:1 *a* Jer 1:10; Jer 25:15-38
46:2 *b* 2Ki 23:29 *c* 2Ch 35:20 *d* Jer 45:1
46:3 *e* Isa 21:5; Jer 51:11-12
46:4 *f* Eze 21:9-11 *g* 1Sa 17:5,38; 2Ch 26:14; Ne 4:16
46:5 *h* ver 21 *i* Jer 49:29
46:6 *j* Isa 30:16 *k* ver 12,16; Da 11:19
46:7 *l* Jer 47:2
46:9 *m* Jer 47:3 *n* Isa 66:19
46:10 *o* Joel 1:15 *p* Dt 32:42 *q* Zep 1:7
46:11 *r* Jer 8:22 *s* Isa 47:1 *t* Jer 30:13; Mic 1:9
46:12 *u* Isa 19:4; Na 3:8-10
46:13 *v* Isa 19:1
46:14 *w* Jer 43:8
46:15 *x* Isa 66:15-16
46:16 *y* Lev 26:37 *z* ver 6

men of Cush[a] and Put who
carry shields,
men of Lydia[n] who draw the
bow.
10But that day[o] belongs to the
Lord, the LORD Almighty—
a day of vengeance, for
vengeance on his foes.
The sword will devour[p] till it is
satisfied,
till it has quenched its thirst
with blood.
For the Lord, the LORD
Almighty, will offer
sacrifice[q]
in the land of the north by the
River Euphrates.

11"Go up to Gilead and get
balm,[r]
O Virgin[s] Daughter of Egypt.
But you multiply remedies in
vain;
there is no healing[t] for you.
12The nations will hear of your
shame;
your cries will fill the earth.
One warrior will stumble over
another;
both will fall[u] down together."

13This is the message the LORD
spoke to Jeremiah the prophet
about the coming of Nebuchadnezzar king of Babylon to attack
Egypt:[v]

14"Announce this in Egypt, and
proclaim it in Migdol;
proclaim it also in Memphis[b]
and Tahpanhes:[w]
'Take your positions and get
ready,
for the sword devours those
around you.'
15Why will your warriors be laid
low?
They cannot stand, for the
LORD will push them
down.[x]
16They will stumble[y] repeatedly;
they will fall[z] over each
other.

a9 That is, the upper Nile region b14 Hebrew *Noph*; also in verse 19

They will say, 'Get up, let us go back
to our own people and our native lands,
away from the sword of the oppressor.'
17 There they will exclaim,
'Pharaoh king of Egypt is only a loud noise;
he has missed his opportunity.[a]'

18 "As surely as I live," declares the King,[b]
whose name is the LORD Almighty,
"one will come who is like Tabor[c] among the mountains,
like Carmel[d] by the sea.
19 Pack your belongings for exile,[e]
you who live in Egypt,
for Memphis will be laid waste
and lie in ruins without inhabitant.

20 "Egypt is a beautiful heifer,
but a gadfly is coming
against her from the north.[f]
21 The mercenaries[g] in her ranks
are like fattened calves.
They too will turn and flee[h] together,
they will not stand their ground,
for the day[i] of disaster is coming upon them,
the time for them to be punished.
22 Egypt will hiss like a fleeing serpent
as the enemy advances in force;
they will come against her with axes,
like men who cut down trees.
23 They will chop down her forest,"
declares the LORD,
"dense though it be.
They are more numerous than locusts,[j]
they cannot be counted.

46:17 a Isa 19:11-16
46:18 b Jer 48:15 c Jos 19:22 d 1Ki 18:42
46:19 e Isa 20:4
46:20 f ver 24; Jer 47:2
46:21 g 2Ki 7:6 h ver 5 i Ps 37:13
46:23 j Jdg 7:12
46:24 k Jer 1:15
46:25 l Eze 30:14; Na 3:8 m Jer 43:12 n Isa 20:6
46:26 o Jer 44:30 p Eze 32:11 q Eze 29:11-16
46:27 r Isa 41:13; Isa 43:5 s Isa 11:11; Jer 50:19
46:28 t Isa 8:9-10 u Jer 4:27
47:1 a Ge 10:19; Am 1:6; Zec 9:5-7

24 The Daughter of Egypt will be put to shame,
handed over to the people of the north.[k]"

25 The LORD Almighty, the God of
Israel, says: "I am about to bring
punishment on Amon god of
Thebes,[c][l] on Pharaoh, on Egypt
and her gods[m] and her kings, and
on those who rely[n] on Pharaoh. 26 I
will hand them over[o] to those who
seek their lives, to Nebuchadnezzar king[p] of Babylon and his officers. Later, however, Egypt will
be inhabited[q] as in times past,"
declares the LORD.

27 "Do not fear,[r] O Jacob my servant;
do not be dismayed, O Israel.
I will surely save you out of a distant place,
and your descendants from the land of their exile.[s]
Jacob will again have peace and security,
and no-one will make him afraid.
28 Do not fear, O Jacob my servant,
for I am with you,"[t] declares the LORD.
"Though I completely destroy[u] all the nations
among which I scatter you,
I will not completely destroy you.
I will discipline you but only with justice;
I will not let you go entirely unpunished."

A Message About the Philistines

47 This is the word of the LORD that came to Jeremiah the prophet concerning the Philistines before Pharaoh attacked Gaza:[a]

2 This is what the LORD says:

[c] 25 Hebrew *No*

"See how the waters are rising
in the north;[b]
they will become an
overflowing torrent.
They will overflow the land and
everything in it,
the towns and those who live
in them.
The people will cry out;
all who dwell in the land will
wail
3at the sound of the hoofs of
galloping steeds,
at the noise of enemy chariots
and the rumble of their
wheels.
Fathers will not turn to help
their children;
their hands will hang limp.
4For the day has come
to destroy all the Philistines
and to cut off all survivors
who could help Tyre[c] and
Sidon.[d]
The LORD is about to destroy
the Philistines,[e]
the remnant from the coasts
of Caphtor.[a][f]
5Gaza will shave[g] her head in
mourning;
Ashkelon[h] will be silenced.
O remnant on the plain,
how long will you cut
yourselves?

6" 'Ah, sword[i] of the LORD,' ⌊you
cry,⌋
'how long till you rest?
Return to your scabbard;
cease and be still.'
7But how can it rest
when the LORD has
commanded it,
when he has ordered it
to attack Ashkelon and the
coast?"

A Message About Moab

48:29–36pp Isa 16:6–12

48 Concerning Moab:

This is what the LORD Almighty, the God of Israel, says:

47:2 *b* Isa 8:7; Isa 14:31
47:4 *c* Am 1:9-10; Zec 9:2-4 *d* Jer 25:22 *e* Ge 10:14; Joel 3:4 *f* Dt 2:23
47:5 *g* Jer 41:5; Mic 1:16 *h* Jer 25:20
47:6 *i* Jer 12:12
48:1 *a* Nu 32:38 *b* Nu 32:37
48:2 *c* Isa 16:14 *d* Nu 21:25
48:3 *e* Isa 15:5
48:5 *f* Isa 15:5
48:6 *g* Jer 17:6
48:7 *h* Nu 21:29 *i* Isa 46:1-2; Jer 49:3

"Woe to Nebo,[a] for it will be
ruined.
Kiriathaim[b] will be disgraced
and captured;
the stronghold[a] will be
disgraced and shattered.
2Moab will be praised[c] no more;
in Heshbon[b][d] men will plot
her downfall:
'Come, let us put an end to
that nation.'
You too, O Madmen,[c] will be
silenced;
the sword will pursue you.
3Listen to the cries from
Horonaim,[e]
cries of great havoc and
destruction.
4Moab will be broken;
her little ones will cry out.[d]
5They go up the way to Luhith,[f]
weeping bitterly as they go;
on the road down to Horonaim
anguished cries over the
destruction are heard.
6Flee! Run for your lives;
become like a bush[e] in the
desert.[g]
7Since you trust in your deeds
and riches,
you too will be taken captive,
and Chemosh[h] will go into
exile,[i]
together with his priests and
officials.
8The destroyer will come against
every town,
and not a town will escape.
The valley will be ruined
and the plateau destroyed,
because the LORD has spoken.
9Put salt on Moab,
for she will be laid waste;[f]
her towns will become desolate,
with no-one to live in them.

10"A curse on him who is lax in
doing the LORD's work!

[a]4 That is, Crete [a]1 Or / *Misgab*
[b]2 The Hebrew for *Heshbon* sounds like the Hebrew for *plot*. [c]2 The name of the Moabite town Madmen sounds like the Hebrew for *be silenced.* [d]4 Hebrew; Septuagint / *proclaim it to Zoar* [e]6 Or *like Aroer* [f]9 Or *Give wings to Moab, / for she will fly away*

A curse on him who keeps his
sword[j] from bloodshed![k]

11"Moab has been at rest[l] from
youth,
like wine left on its dregs,[m]
not poured from one jar to
another—
she has not gone into exile.
So she tastes as she did,
and her aroma is unchanged.
12But days are coming,"
declares the LORD,
"when I will send men who pour
from jars,
and they will pour her out;
they will empty her jars
and smash her jugs.
13Then Moab will be ashamed[n] of
Chemosh,
as the house of Israel was
ashamed
when they trusted in Bethel.

14"How can you say, 'We are
warriors,[o]
men valiant in battle'?
15Moab will be destroyed and her
towns invaded;
her finest young men will go
down in the slaughter,[p]"
declares the King,[q] whose
name is the LORD
Almighty.[r]
16"The fall of Moab is at hand;[s]
her calamity will come
quickly.
17Mourn for her, all who live
around her,
all who know her fame;
say, 'How broken is the mighty
sceptre,
how broken the glorious staff!'

18"Come down from your glory
and sit on the parched
ground,[t]
O inhabitants of the Daughter
of Dibon,[u]
for he who destroys Moab
will come up against you
and ruin your fortified cities.[v]
19Stand by the road and watch,
you who live in Aroer.[w]

48:10
j Jer 47:6
k 1Ki 20:42
2Ki 13:15-19
48:11
l Zec 1:15
m Zep 1:12
48:13
n Hos 10:6
48:14
o Ps 33:16
48:15
p Jer 50:27
q Jer 46:18
r Jer 51:57
48:16
s Isa 13:22
48:18
t Isa 47:1
u Nu 21:30
Jos 13:9
v ver 8
48:19
w Dt 2:36
48:20
x Isa 16:7
y Nu 21:13
48:21
z Nu 21:23
Isa 15:4
a Jos 13:18
48:22
b Jos 13:9,17
48:23
c Jos 13:17
48:24
d Am 2:2
48:25
e Ps 75:10
f Ps 10:15
Eze 30:21
48:26
g Jer 25:16,27
48:27
h Jer 2:26
i Job 16:4
Jer 18:16
j Mic 7:8-10
48:28
k Ps 55:6-7
l Jdg 6:2
48:29
m Job 40:12
Isa 16:6

Ask the man fleeing and the
woman escaping,
ask them, 'What has
happened?'
20Moab is disgraced, for she is
shattered.
Wail[x] and cry out!
Announce by the Arnon[y]
that Moab is destroyed.
21Judgment has come to the
plateau—
to Holon, Jahzah[z] and
Mephaath,[a]
22 to Dibon,[b] Nebo and Beth
Diblathaim,
23 to Kiriathaim, Beth Gamul and
Beth Meon,[c]
24 to Kerioth[d] and Bozrah—
to all the towns of Moab, far
and near.
25Moab's horn[g][e] is cut off;
her arm[f] is broken,"
declares the LORD.

26"Make her drunk,[g]
for she has defied the LORD.
Let Moab wallow in her vomit;
let her be an object of
ridicule.
27Was not Israel the object of
your ridicule?[h]
Was she caught among
thieves,
that you shake your head[i] in
scorn[j]
whenever you speak of her?
28Abandon your towns and dwell
among the rocks,
you who live in Moab.
Be like a dove[k] that makes its
nest
at the mouth of a cave.[l]

29"We have heard of Moab's
pride[m]—
her overweening pride and
conceit,
her pride and arrogance
and the haughtiness of her
heart.
30I know her insolence but it is
futile,"
declares the LORD,

g25 *Horn* here symbolises strength.

"and her boasts accomplish
nothing.
31Therefore I wail[n] over Moab,
for all Moab I cry out,
I moan for the men of Kir
Hareseth.[o]
32I weep for you, as Jazer weeps,
O vines of Sibmah.[p]
Your branches spread as far as
the sea;
they reached as far as the sea
of Jazer.
The destroyer has fallen
on your ripened fruit and
grapes.
33Joy and gladness are gone
from the orchards and fields
of Moab.
I have stopped the flow of
wine[q] from the presses;
no-one treads them with
shouts of joy.[r]
Although there are shouts,
they are not shouts of joy.
34"The sound of their cry rises
from Heshbon to Elealeh[s] and
Jahaz,[t]
from Zoar[u] as far as
Horonaim[v] and Eglath
Shelishiyah,
for even the waters of Nimrim
are dried up.[w]
35In Moab I will put an end
to those who make offerings
on the high places[x]
and burn incense[y] to their
gods,"
declares the LORD.
36"So my heart laments[z] for
Moab like a flute;
it laments like a flute for the
men of Kir Hareseth.
The wealth they acquired[a] is
gone.
37Every head is shaved[b]
and every beard cut off;
every hand is slashed
and every waist is covered
with sackcloth.[c]
38On all the roofs in Moab
and in the public squares
there is nothing but mourning,
for I have broken Moab

48:31 n Isa 15:5-8 o 2Ki 3:25
48:32 p Isa 16:8-9
48:33 q Isa 16:10 r Joel 1:12
48:34 s Nu 32:3 t Isa 15:4 u Ge 13:10 v Isa 15:5 w Isa 15:6
48:35 x Isa 15:2 Isa 16:12 y Jer 11:13
48:36 z Isa 16:11 a Isa 15:7
48:37 b Isa 15:2 Jer 41:5 c Ge 37:34
48:38 d Jer 22:28
48:40 e Dt 28:49 Hab 1:8 f Isa 8:8
48:41 g Isa 21:3
48:42 h Ps 83:4 Isa 16:14 i ver 2 j ver 26
48:43 k Isa 24:17
48:44 l 1Ki 19:17 Isa 24:18 m Jer 11:23
48:45 n Nu 21:21, 26-28 o Nu 24:17
48:46 p Nu 21:29

like a jar[d] that no-one wants,"
declares the LORD.
39"How shattered she is! How
they wail!
How Moab turns her back in
shame!
Moab has become an object of
ridicule,
an object of horror to all those
around her."

40This is what the LORD says:

"Look! An eagle is swooping[e]
down,
spreading its wings[f] over
Moab.
41Kerioth[h] will be captured
and the strongholds taken.
In that day the hearts of Moab's
warriors
will be like the heart of a
woman in labour.[g]
42Moab will be destroyed[h] as a
nation[i]
because she defied[j] the LORD.
43Terror and pit and snare[k] await
you,
O people of Moab,"
declares the LORD.
44"Whoever flees[l] from the
terror
will fall into a pit,
whoever climbs out of the pit
will be caught in a snare;
for I will bring upon Moab
the year[m] of her punishment,"
declares the LORD.

45"In the shadow of Heshbon
the fugitives stand helpless,
for a fire has gone out from
Heshbon,
a blaze from the midst of
Sihon;[n]
it burns the foreheads of Moab,
the skulls[o] of the noisy
boasters.
46Woe to you, O Moab![p]
The people of Chemosh are
destroyed;
your sons are taken into exile

h41 Or *The cities*

and your daughters into
captivity.

47"Yet I will restore[q] the
fortunes of Moab
in days to come,"
declares the LORD.

Here ends the judgment on Moab.

A Message About Ammon

49 Concerning the Ammonites:[a]

This is what the LORD says:

"Has Israel no sons?
Has she no heirs?
Why then has Molech[a] taken
possession of Gad?
Why do his people live in its
towns?
2But the days are coming,"
declares the LORD,
"when I will sound the battle
cry[b]
against Rabbah[c] of the
Ammonites;
it will become a mound of ruins,
and its surrounding villages
will be set on fire.
Then Israel will drive out
those who drove her out,[d]"
says the LORD.
3"Wail, O Heshbon, for Ai[e] is
destroyed!
Cry out, O inhabitants of
Rabbah!
Put on sackcloth and mourn;
rush here and there inside the
walls,
for Molech will go into exile,[f]
together with his priests and
officials.
4Why do you boast of your
valleys,
boast of your valleys so
fruitful?
O unfaithful daughter,
you trust in your riches[g] and
say,
'Who will attack me?'[h]
5I will bring terror on you

48:47
q Jer 12:15
Jer 49:6,39

49:1
a Am 1:13
Zep 2:8-9

49:2
b Jer 4:19
c Dt 3:11
d Isa 14:2
Eze 21:28-32
Eze 25:2-11

49:3
e Jos 8:28
f Jer 48:7

49:4
g Jer 9:23
1Ti 6:17
h Jer 21:13

49:6
i ver 39
Jer 48:47

49:7
j Ge 25:30
Eze 25:12
k Ge 36:11,15,
34

49:8
l Jer 25:23

49:10
m Mal 1:2-5

49:11
n Hos 14:3

49:12
o Jer 25:15
p Jer 25:28-29

from all those around you,"
declares the Lord,
the LORD Almighty.
"Every one of you will be
driven away,
and no-one will gather the
fugitives.

6"Yet afterwards, I will restore[i]
the fortunes of the
Ammonites,"
declares the LORD.

A Message About Edom

49:9–10pp Ob 5–6
49:14–16pp Ob 1–4

7Concerning Edom:[j]

This is what the LORD Almighty
says:

"Is there no longer wisdom in
Teman?[k]
Has counsel perished from the
prudent?
Has their wisdom decayed?
8Turn and flee, hide in deep
caves,
you who live in Dedan,[l]
for I will bring disaster on Esau
at the time I punish him.
9If grape-pickers came to you,
would they not leave a few
grapes?
If thieves came during the
night,
would they not steal only as
much as they wanted?
10But I will strip Esau bare;
I will uncover his hiding-
places,
so that he cannot conceal
himself.
His children, relatives and
neighbours will perish,
and he will be no more.[m]
11Leave your orphans;[n] I will
protect their lives.
Your widows too can trust in
me."

12This is what the LORD says: "If
those who do not deserve to drink
the cup[o] must drink it, why should
you go unpunished?[p] You will not

[a] *1* Or *their king*; Hebrew *malcam*; also in verse 3

go unpunished, but must drink it.
13I swear[q] by myself," declares the
LORD, "that Bozrah[r] will become a
ruin and an object of horror, of reproach and of cursing; and all its
towns will be in ruins for ever."

14I have heard a message from
the LORD:
An envoy was sent to the
nations to say,
"Assemble yourselves to attack
it!
Rise up for battle!"

15"Now I will make you small
among the nations,
despised among men.
16The terror you inspire
and the pride of your heart
have deceived you,
you who live in the clefts of the
rocks,
who occupy the heights of the
hill.
Though you build your nest[s] as
high as the eagle's,
from there I will bring you
down,"
declares the LORD.
17"Edom will become an object of
horror;[t]
all who pass by will be
appalled and will scoff
because of all its wounds.[u]
18As Sodom and Gomorrah[v] were
overthrown,
along with their neighbouring
towns,"
says the LORD,
"so no-one will live there;
no man will dwell[w] in it.

19"Like a lion coming up from
Jordan's thickets[x]
to a rich pasture-land,
I will chase Edom from its land
in an instant.
Who is the chosen one I will
appoint for this?
Who is like me and who can
challenge me?[y]
And what shepherd can stand
against me?"

49:13 q Ge 22:16 r Ge 36:33 Isa 34:6
49:16 s Job 39:27 Am 9:2
49:17 t ver 13 u Jer 50:13 Eze 35:7
49:18 v Ge 19:24 Dt 29:23 w ver 33
49:19 x Jer 12:5 y Jer 50:44
49:20 z Isa 14:27 a Jer 50:45 b Mal 1:3-4
49:21 c Eze 26:15 d Jer 50:46 Eze 26:18
49:22 e Hos 8:1 f Isa 13:8 Jer 48:40-41
49:23 g Ge 14:15 2Ch 16:2 Ac 9:2 h Isa 10:9 Am 6:2 Zec 9:2 i 2Ki 18:34 j Ge 49:4 Isa 57:20
49:26 k Jer 50:30
49:27 l Jer 43:12 Am 1:4 m 1Ki 15:18

20Therefore, hear what the LORD
has planned against Edom,
what he has purposed[z]
against those who live in
Teman:
The young of the flock[a] will be
dragged away;
he will completely destroy[b]
their pasture because of
them.
21At the sound of their fall the
earth will tremble;[c]
their cry[d] will resound to the
Red Sea.[b]
22Look! An eagle will soar and
swoop[e] down,
spreading its wings over
Bozrah.
In that day the hearts of Edom's
warriors
will be like the heart of a
woman in labour.[f]

A Message About Damascus

23Concerning Damascus:[g]

"Hamath[h] and Arpad[i] are
dismayed,
for they have heard bad news.
They are disheartened,
troubled like[c] the restless
sea.[j]
24Damascus has become feeble,
she has turned to flee
and panic has gripped her;
anguish and pain have seized
her,
pain like that of a woman in
labour.
25Why has the city of renown not
been abandoned,
the town in which I delight?
26Surely, her young men will fall
in the streets;
all her soldiers will be
silenced[k] in that day,"
declares the LORD Almighty.
27"I will set fire[l] to the walls of
Damascus;
it will consume the fortresses
of Ben-Hadad.[m]"

b21 Hebrew *Yam Suph*; that is, Sea of Reeds
c23 Hebrew *on* or *by*

A Message About Kedar and Hazor

28 Concerning Kedar[n] and the
kingdoms of Hazor, which Nebuchadnezzar king of Babylon attacked:

This is what the LORD says:

"Arise, and attack Kedar
and destroy the people of the
East.[o]
29 Their tents and their flocks will
be taken;
their shelters will be carried
off
with all their goods and
camels.
Men will shout to them,
'Terror[p] on every side!'

30 "Flee quickly away!
Stay in deep caves, you who
live in Hazor,"
declares the LORD.
"Nebuchadnezzar king of
Babylon has plotted against
you;
he has devised a plan against
you.

31 "Arise and attack a nation at
ease,
which lives in confidence,"
declares the LORD,
"a nation that has neither gates
nor bars;[q]
its people live alone.
32 Their camels will become
plunder,
and their large herds will be
booty.
I will scatter to the winds those
who are in distant
places[d][r]
and will bring disaster on
them from every side,"
declares the LORD.
33 "Hazor will become a haunt of
jackals,
a desolate[s] place for ever.
No-one will live there;
no man will dwell[t] in it."

A Message About Elam

34 This is the word of the LORD
that came to Jeremiah the prophet
concerning Elam,[u] early in the
reign of Zedekiah[v] king of Judah:

35 This is what the LORD Almighty
says:

"See, I will break the bow[w] of
Elam,
the mainstay of their might.
36 I will bring against Elam the
four winds[x]
from the four quarters of the
heavens;
I will scatter them to the four
winds,
and there will not be a nation
where Elam's exiles do not go.
37 I will shatter Elam before their
foes,
before those who seek their
lives;
I will bring disaster upon them,
even my fierce anger,"[y]
declares the LORD.
"I will pursue them with the
sword[z]
until I have made an end of
them.
38 I will set my throne in Elam
and destroy her king and
officials,"
declares the LORD.

39 "Yet I will restore[a] the
fortunes of Elam
in days to come,"
declares the LORD.

A Message About Babylon

51:15–19pp Jer 10:12–16

50 This is the word the LORD
spoke through Jeremiah
the prophet concerning Babylon[a]
and the land of the Babylonians:[a]

2 "Announce and proclaim[b]
among the nations,
lift up a banner and proclaim
it;

49:28 *n* Ge 25:13 *o* Jdg 6:3
49:29 *p* Jer 6:25 Jer 46:5
49:31 *q* Eze 38:11
49:32 *r* Jer 9:26
49:33 *s* Jer 10:22 *t* ver 18 Jer 51:37
49:34 *u* Ge 10:22 *v* 2Ki 24:18
49:35 *w* Isa 22:6
49:36 *x* ver 32
49:37 *y* Jer 30:24 *z* Jer 9:16
49:39 *a* Jer 48:47
50:1 *a* Ge 10:10 Isa 13:1
50:2 *b* Jer 4:16

[d] *32* Or *who clip the hair by their foreheads*
[a] *1* Or *Chaldeans*; also in verses 8, 25, 35 and 45

keep nothing back, but say,
'Babylon will be captured;[c]
Bel[d] will be put to shame,
Marduk[e] filled with terror.
Her images will be put to
shame
and her idols filled with
terror.'
3A nation from the north will
attack her
and lay waste her land.
No-one will live[f] in it;
both men and animals[g] will
flee away.

4"In those days, at that time,"
declares the LORD,
"the people of Israel and the
people of Judah together[h]
will go in tears[i] to seek[j] the
LORD their God.
5They will ask the way to Zion
and turn their faces towards
it.
They will come[k] and bind
themselves to the LORD
in an everlasting covenant[l]
that will not be forgotten.

6"My people have been lost
sheep;[m]
their shepherds have led them
astray
and caused them to roam on
the mountains.
They wandered over mountain
and hill[n]
and forgot their own resting
place.[o]
7Whoever found them devoured
them;
their enemies said, 'We are
not guilty,[p]
for they sinned against the
LORD, their true pasture,
the LORD, the hope[q] of their
fathers.'

8"Flee[r] out of Babylon;
leave the land of the
Babylonians,
and be like the goats that lead
the flock.
9For I will stir up and bring
against Babylon
an alliance of great nations
from the land of the north.
They will take up their
positions against her,
and from the north she will be
captured.
Their arrows will be like skilled
warriors
who do not return
empty-handed.
10So Babylonia[b] will be
plundered;
all who plunder her will have
their fill,"
declares the LORD.

11"Because you rejoice and are
glad,
you who pillage my
inheritance,[s]
because you frolic like a heifer
threshing corn
and neigh like stallions,
12your mother will be greatly
ashamed;
she who gave you birth will be
disgraced.
She will be the least of the
nations—
a wilderness, a dry land, a
desert.
13Because of the LORD's anger
she will not be inhabited
but will be completely
desolate.
All who pass Babylon will be
horrified and scoff[t]
because of all her wounds.[u]

14"Take up your positions round
Babylon,
all you who draw the bow.[v]
Shoot at her! Spare no arrows,
for she has sinned against the
LORD.
15Shout[w] against her on every
side!
She surrenders, her towers
fall,
her walls[x] are torn down.
Since this is the vengeance[y] of
the LORD,
take vengeance on her;

50:2
c Jer 51:31
d Isa 46:1
e Jer 51:47

50:3
f ver 13
Isa 14:22-23
g Zep 1:3

50:4
h Jer 3:18
Hos 1:11
i Ezr 3:12
Jer 31:9
j Hos 3:5

50:5
k Jer 33:7
l Isa 55:3
Jer 32:40
Heb 8:6-10

50:6
m Isa 53:6
Mt 9:36
Mt 10:6
n Jer 3:6
Eze 34:6
o ver 19

50:7
p Jer 2:3
q Jer 14:8

50:8
r Isa 48:20
Jer 51:6
Rev 18:4

50:11
s Isa 47:6

50:13
t Jer 18:16
u Jer 49:17

50:14
v ver 29,42

50:15
w Jer 51:14
x Jer 51:44,58
y Jer 51:6

[b]10 Or *Chaldea*

do to her[z] as she has done to
others.
16Cut off from Babylon the
sower,
and the reaper with his sickle
at harvest.
Because of the sword[a] of the
oppressor
let everyone return to his own
people,[b]
let everyone flee to his own
land.[c]

17"Israel is a scattered flock
that lions[d] have chased away.
The first to devour him
was the king[e] of Assyria;
the last to crush his bones
was Nebuchadnezzar[f] king[g]
of Babylon."

18Therefore this is what the LORD
Almighty, the God of Israel, says:

"I will punish the king of
Babylon and his land
as I punished the king[h] of
Assyria.[i]
19But I will bring[j] Israel back to
his own pasture
and he will graze on Carmel
and Bashan;
his appetite will be satisfied
on the hills[k] of Ephraim and
Gilead.
20In those days, at that time,"
declares the LORD,
"search will be made for
Israel's guilt,
but there will be none,
and for the sins[l] of Judah,
but none will be found,
for I will forgive[m] the
remnant[n] I spare.

21"Attack the land of Merathaim
and those who live in Pekod.[o]
Pursue, kill and completely
destroy[c] them,"
declares the LORD.
"Do everything I have
commanded you.
22The noise[p] of battle is in the
land,
the noise of great destruction!
23How broken and shattered
is the hammer of the whole
earth!
How desolate[q] is Babylon
among the nations!
24I set a trap[r] for you,
O Babylon,
and you were caught before
you knew it;
you were found and captured[s]
because you opposed[t] the
LORD.
25The LORD has opened his
arsenal
and brought out the weapons[u]
of his wrath,
for the Sovereign LORD
Almighty has work to do
in the land of the Babylonians.[v]
26Come against her from afar.
Break open her granaries;
pile her up like heaps of grain.
Completely destroy[w] her
and leave her no remnant.
27Kill all her young bulls;
let them go down to the
slaughter!
Woe to them! For their day has
come,
the time for them to be
punished.
28Listen to the fugitives and
refugees from Babylon
declaring in Zion[x]
how the LORD our God has
taken vengeance,[y]
vengeance for his temple.

29"Summon archers against
Babylon,
all those who draw the bow.[z]
Encamp all round her;
let no-one escape.
Repay[a] her for her deeds;[b]
do to her as she has done.
For she defied[c] the LORD,
the Holy One of Israel.
30Therefore, her young men[d] will
fall in the streets;
all her soldiers will be
silenced in that day,"
declares the LORD.

50:15 z Ps 137:8; Rev 18:6
50:16 a Jer 25:38 b Isa 13:14 c Jer 51:9
50:17 d Jer 2:15 e 2Ki 17:6 f 2Ki 24:10,14 g 2Ki 25:7
50:18 h Isa 10:12 i Eze 31:3
50:19 j Jer 31:10; Eze 34:13 k Jer 31:5; Jer 33:12
50:20 l Mic 7:18,19 m Jer 31:34 n Isa 1:9
50:21 o Eze 23:23
50:22 p Jer 4:19-21; Jer 51:54
50:23 q Isa 14:16
50:24 r Da 5:30-31 s Jer 51:31 t Job 9:4
50:25 u Isa 13:5 v Jer 51:25,55
50:26 w Isa 14:22-23
50:28 x Isa 48:20; Jer 51:10 y ver 15
50:29 z ver 14 a Rev 18:6 b Jer 51:56 c Isa 47:10
50:30 d Isa 13:18; Jer 49:26

c*21* The Hebrew term refers to the irrevocable giving over of things or persons to the LORD, often by totally destroying them; also in verse 26.

[31]"See, I am against[e] you,
O arrogant one,"
declares the Lord, the LORD Almighty,
"for your day has come,
the time for you to be punished.
[32]The arrogant one will stumble and fall
and no-one will help her up;
I will kindle a fire[f] in her towns
that will consume all who are around her."

[33]This is what the LORD Almighty says:

"The people of Israel are oppressed,[g]
and the people of Judah as well.
All their captors hold them fast,
refusing to let them go.[h]
[34]Yet their Redeemer is strong;
the LORD Almighty[i] is his name.
He will vigorously defend their cause[j]
so that he may bring rest[k] to their land,
but unrest to those who live in Babylon.

[35]"A sword[l] against the Babylonians!"
declares the LORD—
"against those who live in Babylon
and against her officials and wise[m] men!
[36]A sword against her false prophets!
They will become fools.
A sword against her warriors![n]
They will be filled with terror.
[37]A sword against her horses and chariots[o]
and all the foreigners in her ranks!
They will become women.[p]
A sword against her treasures!
They will be plundered.
[38]A drought on[d] her waters!
They will dry[q] up.
For it is a land of idols,[r]
idols that will go mad with terror.

[39]"So desert creatures and hyenas will live there,
and there the owl will dwell.
It will never again be inhabited
or lived in from generation to generation.[s]
[40]As God overthrew Sodom and Gomorrah[t]
along with their neighbouring towns,"
declares the LORD,
"so no-one will live there;
no man will dwell in it.

[41]"Look! An army is coming from the north;[u]
a great nation and many kings
are being stirred up from the ends of the earth.[v]
[42]They are armed with bows[w] and spears;
they are cruel and without mercy.[x]
They sound like the roaring sea[y]
as they ride on their horses;
they come like men in battle formation
to attack you, O Daughter of Babylon.[z]
[43]The king of Babylon has heard reports about them,
and his hands hang limp.
Anguish has gripped him,
pain like that of a woman in labour.
[44]Like a lion coming up from Jordan's thickets
to a rich pasture-land,
I will chase Babylon from its land in an instant.
Who is the chosen[a] one I will appoint for this?
Who is like me and who can challenge me?[b]
And what shepherd can stand against me?"

[d]38 Or *A sword against*

50:31 [e] Jer 21:13
50:32 [f] Jer 21:14; Jer 49:27
50:33 [g] Isa 58:6 [h] Isa 14:17
50:34 [i] Jer 51:19 [j] Jer 15:21; Jer 51:36 [k] Isa 14:7
50:35 [l] Jer 47:6 [m] Da 5:7
50:36 [n] Jer 49:22
50:37 [o] Jer 51:21 [p] Jer 51:30; Na 3:13
50:38 [q] Jer 51:36 [r] ver 2
50:39 [s] Isa 13:19-22; Isa 34:13-15; Jer 51:37; Rev 18:2
50:40 [t] Ge 19:24
50:41 [u] Jer 6:22 [v] Isa 13:4; Jer 51:22-28
50:42 [w] ver 14 [x] Isa 13:18 [y] Isa 5:30 [z] Jer 6:23
50:44 [a] Nu 16:5 [b] Job 41:10; Isa 46:9; Jer 49:19

45Therefore, hear what the LORD
has planned against
Babylon,
what he has purposed[c]
against the land of the
Babylonians:
The young of the flock will be
dragged away;
he will completely destroy
their pasture because of
them.
46At the sound of Babylon's
capture the earth will
tremble;
its cry[d] will resound among
the nations.

51

This is what the LORD says:

"See, I will stir up the spirit of
a destroyer
against Babylon and the
people of Leb Kamai.[a]
2I will send foreigners to
Babylon
to winnow[a] her and to
devastate her land;
they will oppose her on every
side
in the day of her disaster.
3Let not the archer string his
bow,[b]
nor let him put on his
armour.[c]
Do not spare her young men;
completely destroy[b] her
army.
4They will fall[d] down slain in
Babylon,[c]
fatally wounded in her
streets.[e]
5For Israel and Judah have not
been forsaken[f]
by their God, the LORD
Almighty,
though their land[d] is full of
guilt[g]
before the Holy One of Israel.

6"Flee[h] from Babylon!
Run for your lives!
Do not be destroyed because
of her sins.[i]
It is time for the LORD's
vengeance;[j]
he will pay[k] her what she
deserves.
7Babylon was a gold cup[l] in the
LORD's hand;
she made the whole earth
drunk.
The nations drank her wine;
therefore they have now gone
mad.
8Babylon will suddenly fall[m] and
be broken.
Wail over her!
Get balm[n] for her pain;
perhaps she can be healed.

9" 'We would have healed
Babylon,
but she cannot be healed;
let us leave[o] her and each go to
his own land,
for her judgment[p] reaches to
the skies,
it rises as high as the clouds.'
10" 'The LORD has vindicated[q] us;
come, let us tell in Zion
what the LORD our God has
done.'[r]

11"Sharpen the arrows,[s]
take up the shields![t]
The LORD has stirred up the
kings of the Medes,[u]
because his purpose[v] is to
destroy Babylon.
The LORD will take vengeance,
vengeance for his temple.[w]
12Lift up a banner against the
walls of Babylon!
Reinforce the guard,
station the watchmen,
prepare an ambush!
The LORD will carry out his
purpose,
his decree against the people
of Babylon.
13You who live by many waters[x]
and are rich in treasures,[y]

50:45 c Ps 33:11; Isa 14:24; Jer 51:11
50:46 d Rev 18:9-10
51:2 a Isa 41:16; Jer 15:7; Mt 3:12
51:3 b Jer 50:29 c Jer 46:4
51:4 d Isa 13:15 e Jer 49:26; Jer 50:30
51:5 f Isa 54:6-8 g Hos 4:1
51:6 h Jer 50:8 i Nu 16:26; Rev 18:4 j Jer 50:15 k Jer 25:14
51:7 l Jer 25:15-16; Rev 14:8-10; Rev 17:4
51:8 m Isa 21:9; Rev 14:8 n Jer 46:11
51:9 o Isa 13:14; Jer 50:16 p Rev 18:4-5
51:10 q Mic 7:9 r Jer 50:28
51:11 s Jer 50:9 t Jer 46:4 u ver 28 v Jer 50:45 w Jer 50:28
51:13 x Rev 17:1,15 y Isa 45:3; Hab 2:9

a1 *Leb Kamai* is a cryptogram for Chaldea, that is, Babylonia. b3 The Hebrew term refers to the irrevocable giving over of things or persons to the LORD, often by totally destroying them. c4 Or *Chaldea* d5 Or / *and the land* ⌞*of the Babylonians*⌟

your end has come,
the time for you to be cut off.
14 The LORD Almighty has sworn
by himself:[z]
I will surely fill you with men,
as with a swarm of
locusts,[a]
and they will shout[b] in
triumph over you.

15 "He made the earth by his
power;
he founded the world by his
wisdom
and stretched[c] out the
heavens by his
understanding.
16 When he thunders,[d] the waters
in the heavens roar;
he makes clouds rise from the
ends of the earth.
He sends lightning with the rain
and brings out the wind from
his storehouses.[e]

17 "Every man is senseless and
without knowledge;
every goldsmith is shamed by
his idols.
His images are a fraud;[f]
they have no breath in them.
18 They are worthless,[g] the
objects of mockery;
when their judgment comes,
they will perish.
19 He who is the Portion of Jacob
is not like these,
for he is the Maker of all
things,
including the tribe of his
inheritance—
the LORD Almighty is his
name.

20 "You are my war club,[h]
my weapon for battle—
with you I shatter[i] nations,
with you I destroy kingdoms,
21 with you I shatter horse and
rider,[j]
with you I shatter chariot and
driver,
22 with you I shatter man and
woman,
with you I shatter old man and
youth,
with you I shatter young man
and maiden,[k]
23 with you I shatter shepherd and
flock,
with you I shatter farmer and
oxen,
with you I shatter governors
and officials.[l]

24 "Before your eyes I will repay[m]
Babylon and all who live in Babylonia[e] for all the wrong they have
done in Zion," declares the LORD.

25 "I am against you, O destroying
mountain,
you who destroy the whole
earth,"
declares the LORD.
"I will stretch out my hand
against you,
roll you off the cliffs,
and make you a burnt-out
mountain.[n]
26 No rock will be taken from you
for a cornerstone,
nor any stone for a foundation,
for you will be desolate[o] for
ever,"
declares the LORD.

27 "Lift up a banner[p] in the land!
Blow the trumpet among the
nations!
Prepare the nations for battle
against her;
summon against her these
kingdoms:[q]
Ararat,[r] Minni and
Ashkenaz.[s]
Appoint a commander against
her;
send up horses like a swarm
of locusts.
28 Prepare the nations for battle
against her—
the kings of the Medes,[t]
their governors and all their
officials,
and all the countries they rule.
29 The land trembles and writhes,

51:14 z Am 6:8 a ver 27; Na 3:15 b Jer 50:15
51:15 c Ge 1:1; Job 9:8; Ps 104:2
51:16 d Ps 18:11-13 e Ps 135:7; Jnh 1:4
51:17 f Isa 44:20; Hab 2:18-19
51:18 g Jer 18:15
51:20 h Isa 10:5 i Mic 4:13
51:21 j Ex 15:1
51:22 k 2Ch 36:17; Isa 13:17-18
51:23 l ver 57
51:24 m Jer 50:15
51:25 n Zec 4:7
51:26 o ver 29; Isa 13:19-22; Jer 50:12
51:27 p Isa 13:2; Jer 50:2 q Jer 25:14 r Ge 8:4 s Ge 10:3
51:28 t ver 11

e24 Or *Chaldea*; also in verse 35

for the LORD's purposes
against Babylon stand—
to lay waste the land of Babylon
so that no-one will live there.[u]
30Babylon's warriors[v] have
stopped fighting;
they remain in their
strongholds.
Their strength is exhausted;
they have become like
women.[w]
Her dwellings are set on fire;
the bars[x] of her gates are
broken.
31One courier[y] follows another
and messenger follows
messenger
to announce to the king of
Babylon
that his entire city is
captured,
32the river crossings seized,
the marshes set on fire,
and the soldiers terrified.[z]"

33This is what the LORD Almighty, the God of Israel, says:

"The Daughter of Babylon is
like a threshing-floor[a]
at the time it is trampled;
the time to harvest[b] her will
soon come."
34"Nebuchadnezzar[c] king of
Babylon has devoured us,
he has thrown us into
confusion,
he has made us an empty jar.
Like a serpent he has swallowed
us
and filled his stomach with
our delicacies,
and then has spewed us out.
35May the violence done to our
flesh[f] be upon Babylon,"
say the inhabitants of Zion.
"May our blood be on those who
live in Babylonia,"
says Jerusalem.[d]

36Therefore, this is what the
LORD says:

"See, I will defend your cause[e]
and avenge[f] you;

51:29 u ver 43; Isa 13:20
51:30 v Jer 50:36 w Isa 19:16 x Isa 45:2; La 2:9; Na 3:13
51:31 y 2Sa 18:19-31
51:32 z Jer 50:36
51:33 a Isa 21:10 b Isa 17:5; Hos 6:11
51:34 c Jer 50:17
51:35 d ver 24; Ps 137:8
51:36 e Ps 140:12; Jer 50:34; La 3:58 f ver 6; Ro 12:19 g Jer 50:38
51:37 h Isa 13:22; Rev 18:2 i Jer 50:13,39
51:39 j ver 57
51:41 k Jer 25:26 l Isa 13:19
51:42 m Isa 8:7
51:43 n ver 29,62; Isa 13:20; Jer 2:6
51:44 o Isa 46:1 p ver 34 q ver 58; Jer 50:15
51:45 r Rev 18:4 s ver 6; Isa 48:20; Jer 50:8
51:46 t Jer 46:27 u 2Ki 19:7

I will dry up[g] her sea
and make her springs dry.
37Babylon will be a heap of ruins,
a haunt[h] of jackals,
an object of horror and scorn,
a place where no-one lives.[i]
38Her people all roar like young
lions,
they growl like lion cubs.
39But while they are aroused,
I will set out a feast for them
and make them drunk,
so that they shout with
laughter—
then sleep for ever and not
awake,"
declares the LORD.[j]
40"I will bring them down
like lambs to the slaughter,
like rams and goats.
41"How Sheshach[g][k] will be
captured,[l]
the boast of the whole earth
seized!
What a horror Babylon will be
among the nations!
42The sea will rise over Babylon;
its roaring waves[m] will cover
her.
43Her towns will be desolate,
a dry and desert land,
a land where no-one lives,
through which no man
travels.[n]
44I will punish Bel[o] in Babylon
and make him spew out[p] what
he has swallowed.
The nations will no longer
stream to him.
And the wall[q] of Babylon will
fall.
45"Come out[r] of her, my people!
Run[s] for your lives!
Run from the fierce anger of
the LORD.
46Do not lose heart or be afraid[t]
when rumours[u] are heard in
the land;
one rumour comes this year,
another the next,

[f]35 Or *done to us and to our children*
[g]41 *Sheshach* is a cryptogram for Babylon.

rumours of violence in the land
and of ruler against ruler.
47For the time will surely come
when I will punish the idols[v] of Babylon;
her whole land will be disgraced[w]
and her slain will all lie fallen within her.
48Then heaven and earth and all that is in them
will shout[x] for joy over Babylon,
for out of the north[y]
destroyers will attack her,"
declares the LORD.

49"Babylon must fall because of Israel's slain,
just as the slain in all the earth
have fallen because of Babylon.[z]
50You who have escaped the sword,
leave[a] and do not linger!
Remember[b] the LORD in a distant land,
and think on Jerusalem."
51"We are disgraced,[c]
for we have been insulted
and shame covers our faces,
because foreigners have entered
the holy places of the LORD's house."[d]

52"But days are coming," declares the LORD,
"when I will punish her idols,[e]
and throughout her land
the wounded will groan.
53Even if Babylon reaches the sky[f]
and fortifies her lofty stronghold,
I will send destroyers[g] against her,"
declares the LORD.

54"The sound of a cry comes from Babylon,
the sound of great destruction[h]
from the land of the Babylonians.[h]
55The LORD will destroy Babylon;
he will silence her noisy din.
Waves[i] ⌞of enemies⌟ will rage like great waters;
the roar of their voices will resound.
56A destroyer[j] will come against Babylon;
her warriors will be captured,
and their bows will be broken.[k]
For the LORD is a God of retribution;
he will repay[l] in full.
57I will make her officials and wise men drunk,
her governors, officers and warriors as well;
they will sleep[m] for ever and not awake,"
declares the King,[n] whose name is the LORD Almighty.

58This is what the LORD Almighty says:

"Babylon's thick wall[o] will be levelled
and her high gates set on fire;
the peoples[p] exhaust themselves for nothing,
the nations' labour is only fuel for the flames."[q]

59This is the message Jeremiah
gave to the staff officer Seraiah
son of Neriah,[r] the son of Mahseiah, when he went to Babylon
with Zedekiah[s] king of Judah in
the fourth[t] year of his reign.
60Jeremiah had written on a scroll[u]
about all the disasters that would
come upon Babylon—all that had
been recorded concerning Babylon. 61He said to Seraiah, "When
you get to Babylon, see that you
read all these words aloud. 62Then
say, 'O LORD, you have said you will
destroy this place, so that neither

51:47 v ver 52; Isa 46:1-2; Jer 50:2; w Jer 50:12
51:48 x Isa 44:23; Rev 18:20; y ver 11
51:49 z Ps 137:8; Jer 50:29
51:50 a ver 45; b Ps 137:6
51:51 c Ps 44:13-16; Ps 79:4; d La 1:10
51:52 e ver 47
51:53 f Ge 11:4; Isa 14:13-14; g Jer 49:16
51:54 h Jer 50:22
51:55 i Ps 18:4
51:56 j ver 48; k Ps 46:9; l ver 6; Ps 94:1-2; Hab 2:8
51:57 m Ps 76:5; Jer 25:27; n Jer 46:18; Jer 48:15
51:58 o ver 44; p ver 64; q Hab 2:13
51:59 r Jer 36:4; s Jer 52:1; t Jer 28:1
51:60 u Jer 30:2; Jer 36:2

h54 Or *Chaldeans*

man nor animal will live in it; it will be desolate[v] for ever.' 63When you finish reading this scroll, tie a stone to it and throw it into the Euphrates. 64Then say, 'So will Babylon sink to rise no more because of the disaster I will bring upon her. And her people[w] will fall.' "

The words of Jeremiah end[x] here.

The Fall of Jerusalem

52:1–3pp 2Ki 24:18–20; 2Ch 36:11–16
52:4–16pp Jer 39:1–10
52:4–21pp 2Ki 25:1–21; 2Ch 36:17–20

52 Zedekiah[a] was twenty-one years old when he became king, and he reigned in Jerusalem for eleven years. His mother's name was Hamutal daughter of Jeremiah; she was from Libnah.[b] 2He did evil in the eyes of the LORD, just as Jehoiakim[c] had done. 3It was because of the LORD's anger that all this happened to Jerusalem and Judah,[d] and in the end he thrust them from his presence.

Now Zedekiah rebelled[e] against the king of Babylon.

4So in the ninth year of Zedekiah's reign, on the tenth[f] day of the tenth month, Nebuchadnezzar king of Babylon marched against Jerusalem[g] with his whole army. They camped outside the city and built siege works all around it.[h] 5The city was kept under siege until the eleventh year of King Zedekiah.

6By the ninth day of the fourth month the famine in the city had become so severe that there was no food for the people to eat.[i] 7Then the city wall was broken through, and the whole army fled. They left the city at night through the gate between the two walls near the king's garden, though the Babylonians[a] were surrounding the city. They fled towards the Arabah,[b] 8but the Babylonian[c] army pursued King Zedekiah and overtook him in the plains of Jericho. All his soldiers were separated from him and scattered, 9and he was captured.[j]

He was taken to the king of Babylon at Riblah[k] in the land of Hamath,[l] where he pronounced sentence on him. 10There at Riblah the king of Babylon slaughtered the sons[m] of Zedekiah before his eyes; he also killed all the officials of Judah. 11Then he put out Zedekiah's eyes, bound him with bronze shackles and took him to Babylon, where he put him in prison till the day of his death.[n]

12On the tenth day of the fifth[o] month, in the nineteenth year of Nebuchadnezzar king of Babylon, Nebuzaradan[p] commander of the imperial guard, who served the king of Babylon, came to Jerusalem. 13He set fire[q] to the temple[r] of the LORD, the royal palace and all the houses of Jerusalem. Every important building he burned down. 14The whole Babylonian army under the commander of the imperial guard broke down all the walls[s] around Jerusalem. 15Nebuzaradan the commander of the guard carried into exile some of the poorest people and those who remained in the city, along with the rest of the craftsmen[d] and those who had gone over to the king of Babylon. 16But Nebuzaradan left behind[t] the rest of the poorest people of the land to work the vineyards and fields.

17The Babylonians broke up the bronze pillars,[u] the movable stands[v] and the bronze Sea[w] that were at the temple of the LORD and they carried all the bronze to Babylon.[x] 18They also took away the pots, shovels, wick trimmers, sprinkling bowls, dishes and all the bronze articles used in the temple service.[y] 19The commander of the

51:62 *v* Isa 13:20; Jer 50:13,39
51:64 *w* ver 58; *x* Job 31:40
52:1 *a* 2Ki 24:17; *b* Jos 10:29; 2Ki 8:22
52:2 *c* Jer 36:30
52:3 *d* Isa 3:1; *e* Eze 17:12-16
52:4 *f* Zec 8:19; *g* 2Ki 25:1-7; Jer 39:1; *h* Eze 24:1-2
52:6 *i* Isa 3:1
52:9 *j* Jer 32:4; *k* Nu 34:11; *l* Nu 13:21
52:10 *m* Jer 22:30
52:11 *n* Eze 12:13
52:12 *o* Zec 7:5; Zec 8:19; *p* Jer 39:9
52:13 *q* 2Ch 36:19; Ps 74:8; La 2:6; *r* Ps 79:1; Mic 3:12
52:14 *s* Ne 1:3
52:16 *t* Jer 40:6
52:17 *u* 1Ki 7:15; *v* 1Ki 7:27-37; *w* 1Ki 7:23; *x* Jer 27:19-22
52:18 *y* Ex 27:3; 1Ki 7:45

[a]7 Or *Chaldeans*; also in verse 17 [b]7 Or *the Jordan Valley* [c]8 Or *Chaldean*; also in verse 14 [d]15 Or *populace*

imperial guard took away the
basins, censers,[z] sprinkling bowls,
pots, lampstands, dishes and bowls
used for drink offerings—all that
were made of pure gold or silver.
20The bronze from the two pillars, the Sea and the twelve bronze
bulls under it, and the movable
stands, which King Solomon had
made for the temple of the LORD,
was more than could be weighed.[a]
21Each of the pillars was eighteen
cubits high and twelve cubits in
circumference;[e] each was four
fingers thick, and hollow.[b] 22The
bronze capital[c] on the top of the
one pillar was five cubits[f] high
and was decorated with a network
and pomegranates of bronze all
around. The other pillar, with
its pomegranates, was similar.
23There were ninety-six pomegranates on the sides; the total number
of pomegranates[d] above the surrounding network was a hundred.
24The commander of the guard
took as prisoners Seraiah[e] the
chief priest, Zephaniah[f] the priest
next in rank and the three doorkeepers. 25Of those still in the city,
he took the officer in charge of the
fighting men, and seven royal advisers. He also took the secretary
who was chief officer in charge of
conscripting the people of the land
and sixty of his men who were
found in the city. 26Nebuzaradan[g]
the commander took them all and
brought them to the king of Babylon at Riblah. 27There at Riblah, in
the land of Hamath, the king had
them executed.

So Judah went into captivity,
away[h] from her land. 28This is the
number of the people Nebuchadnezzar carried into exile:[i]

in the seventh year, 3,023 Jews;
29in Nebuchadnezzar's eighteenth
year,
832 people from Jerusalem;
30in his twenty-third year,
745 Jews taken into exile by
Nebuzaradan
the commander of the imperial
guard.
There were 4,600 people in all.

Jehoiachin Released

52:31–34pp 2Ki 25:27–30

31In the thirty-seventh year of
the exile of Jehoiachin king of Judah, in the year Evil-Merodach[g]
became king of Babylon, he released Jehoiachin king of Judah
and freed him from prison on the
twenty-fifth day of the twelfth
month. 32He spoke kindly to him
and gave him a seat of honour
higher than those of the other kings
who were with him in Babylon. 33So
Jehoiachin put aside his prison
clothes and for the rest of his life
ate regularly at the king's table.[j]
34Day by day the king of Babylon
gave Jehoiachin a regular allowance[k] as long as he lived, till the
day of his death.

52:19 *z* 1Ki 7:50
52:20 *a* 1Ki 7:47
52:21 *b* 1Ki 7:15
52:22 *c* 1Ki 7:16
52:23 *d* 1Ki 7:20
52:24 *e* 2Ki 25:18 *f* Jer 21:1 Jer 37:3
52:26 *g* ver 12
52:27 *h* Jer 20:4
52:28 *i* 2Ki 24:14-16 2Ch 36:20
52:33 *j* 2Sa 9:7
52:34 *k* 2Sa 9:10

e*21* That is, about 27 feet (about 8.1 metres) high and 18 feet (about 5.5 metres) in circumference
f*22* That is, about 7 ½ feet (about 2.3 metres)
g*31* Also called *Amel-Marduk*

LAMENTATIONS

1 [a] How deserted lies the city,
once so full of people!
How like a widow[a] is she,
who once was great[b] among
the nations!
She who was queen among the
provinces
has now become a slave.[c]

2 Bitterly she weeps[d] at night,
tears are upon her cheeks.
Among all her lovers[e]
there is none to comfort her.
All her friends have betrayed[f]
her;
they have become her
enemies.[g]

3 After affliction and harsh
labour,
Judah has gone into exile.[h]
She dwells among the nations;
she finds no resting place.[i]
All who pursue her have
overtaken her
in the midst of her distress.

4 The roads to Zion mourn,
for no-one comes to her
appointed feasts.
All her gateways are desolate,[j]
her priests groan,
her maidens grieve,
and she is in bitter anguish.[k]

5 Her foes have become her
masters;
her enemies are at ease.
The LORD has brought her
grief[l]
because of her many sins.
Her children have gone into
exile,[m]
captive before the foe.

6 All the splendour has departed
from the Daughter of Zion.[n]
Her princes are like deer
that find no pasture;
in weakness they have fled
before the pursuer.

7 In the days of her affliction and
wandering
Jerusalem remembers all the
treasures
that were hers in days of old.
When her people fell into
enemy hands,
there was no-one to help her.[o]
Her enemies looked at her
and laughed at her
destruction.

8 Jerusalem has sinned[p] greatly
and so has become unclean.
All who honoured her despise
her,
for they have seen her
nakedness;[q]
she herself groans[r]
and turns away.

9 Her filthiness clung to her
skirts;
she did not consider her
future.[s]
Her fall[t] was astounding;
there was none to comfort[u]
her.
"Look, O LORD, on my
affliction,[v]
for the enemy has triumphed."

10 The enemy laid hands
on all her treasures;[w]
she saw pagan nations
enter her sanctuary[x]—
those you had forbidden[y]
to enter your assembly.

11 All her people groan[z]
as they search for bread;[a]
they barter their treasures for
food
to keep themselves alive.

1:1 a Isa 47:8 b 1Ki 4:21 c Isa 3:26; Jer 40:9
1:2 d Ps 6:6 e Jer 3:1 f Jer 4:30; Mic 7:5 g ver 16
1:3 h Jer 13:19 i Dt 28:65
1:4 j Jer 9:11 k Joel 1:8-13
1:5 l Jer 30:15 m Jer 39:9; Jer 52:28-30
1:6 n Jer 13:18
1:7 o Jer 37:7; La 4:17
1:8 p ver 20; Isa 59:2-13 q Jer 13:22,26 r ver 21,22
1:9 s Dt 32:28-29; Isa 47:7; Eze 24:13 t Jer 13:18 u Ecc 4:1; Jer 16:7 v Ps 25:18
1:10 w Isa 64:11 x Ps 74:7-8; Jer 51:51 y Dt 23:3
1:11 z Ps 38:8 a Jer 52:6

[a] This chapter is an acrostic poem, the verses of which begin with the successive letters of the Hebrew alphabet.

“Look, O LORD, and consider,
for I am despised.”

12 “Is it nothing to you, all you
who pass by?[b]
Look around and see.
Is any suffering like my
suffering[c]
that was inflicted on me,
that the LORD brought on me
in the day of his fierce
anger?[d]

13 “From on high he sent fire,
sent it down into my bones.[e]
He spread a net for my feet
and turned me back.
He made me desolate,[f]
faint[g] all the day long.

14 “My sins have been bound into
a yoke;[b][h]
by his hands they were woven
together.
They have come upon my neck
and the Lord has sapped my
strength.
He has handed me over[i]
to those I cannot withstand.

15 “The Lord has rejected
all the warriors in my midst;[j]
he has summoned an army[k]
against me
to[c] crush my young men.[l]
In his winepress the Lord has
trampled
the Virgin Daughter of Judah.

16 “This is why I weep
and my eyes overflow with
tears.[m]
No-one is near to comfort[n] me,
no-one to restore my spirit.
My children are destitute
because the enemy has
prevailed.”[o]

17 Zion stretches out her hands,[p]
but there is no-one to comfort
her.
The LORD has decreed for Jacob
that his neighbours become
his foes;
Jerusalem has become
an unclean thing among them.

18 “The LORD is righteous,
yet I rebelled[q] against his
command.
Listen, all you peoples;
look upon my suffering.[r]
My young men and maidens
have gone into exile.[s]

19 “I called to my allies
but they betrayed me.
My priests and my elders
perished[t] in the city
while they searched for food
to keep themselves alive.

20 “See, O LORD, how distressed[u]
I am!
I am in torment[v] within,
and in my heart I am disturbed,
for I have been most
rebellious.
Outside, the sword bereaves;
inside, there is only death.[w]

21 “People have heard my
groaning,[x]
but there is no-one to comfort
me.[y]
All my enemies have heard of
my distress;
they rejoice[z] at what you
have done.
May you bring the day[a] you
have announced
so that they may become like
me.

22 “Let all their wickedness come
before you;
deal with them
as you have dealt with me
because of all my sins.[b]
My groans are many
and my heart is faint.”

2[a]

How the Lord has covered
the Daughter of Zion
with the cloud of his anger![b][a]
He has hurled down the
splendour of Israel

1:12 *b* Jer 18:16 *c* ver 18 *d* Isa 13:13; Jer 30:24
1:13 *e* Job 30:30 *f* Jer 44:6 *g* Hab 3:16
1:14 *h* Dt 28:48; Isa 47:6 *i* Jer 32:5
1:15 *j* Jer 37:10 *k* Isa 41:2 *l* Isa 28:18; Jer 18:21
1:16 *m* La 2:11,18; La 3:48-49 *n* Ps 69:20; Ecc 4:1 *o* ver 2; Jer 13:17; Jer 14:17
1:17 *p* Jer 4:31
1:18 *q* 1Sa 12:14 *r* ver 12 *s* Dt 28:32,41
1:19 *t* Jer 14:15; La 2:20
1:20 *u* Jer 4:19 *v* La 2:11 *w* Dt 32:25; Eze 7:15
1:21 *x* ver 8 *y* ver 4 *z* La 2:15 *a* Isa 47:11; Jer 30:16
1:22 *b* Ne 4:5
2:1 *a* La 3:44

[b] 14 Most Hebrew manuscripts; Septuagint *He kept watch over my sins* [c] 15 Or *has set a time for me / when he will* [a] This chapter is an acrostic poem, the verses of which begin with the successive letters of the Hebrew alphabet. [b] 1 Or *How the LORD in his anger / has treated the Daughter of Zion with contempt!*

from heaven to earth;
he has not remembered his footstool[b]
in the day of his anger.

2 Without pity[c] the Lord has swallowed[d] up
all the dwellings of Jacob;
in his wrath he has torn down
the strongholds[e] of the Daughter of Judah.
He has brought her kingdom and its princes
down to the ground[f] in dishonour.

3 In fierce anger he has cut off every horn[c][g] of Israel.
He has withdrawn his right hand[h]
at the approach of the enemy.
He has burned in Jacob like a flaming fire
that consumes everything around it.[i]

4 Like an enemy he has strung his bow;[j]
his right hand is ready.
Like a foe he has slain
all who were pleasing to the eye;[k]
he has poured out his wrath like fire[l]
on the tent of the Daughter of Zion.

5 The Lord is like an enemy;[m]
he has swallowed up Israel.
He has swallowed up all her palaces
and destroyed her strongholds.[n]
He has multiplied mourning and lamentation
for the Daughter of Judah.[o]

6 He has laid waste his dwelling like a garden;
he has destroyed his place of meeting.[p]
The LORD has made Zion forget
her appointed feasts and her Sabbaths;[q]
in his fierce anger he has spurned
both king and priest.[r]

7 The Lord has rejected his altar
and abandoned his sanctuary.
He has handed over to the enemy
the walls of her palaces;[s]
they have raised a shout in the house of the LORD
as on the day of an appointed feast.[t]

8 The LORD determined to tear down
the wall around the Daughter of Zion.
He stretched out a measuring line[u]
and did not withhold his hand from destroying.
He made ramparts and walls lament;
together they wasted away.[v]

9 Her gates[w] have sunk into the ground;
their bars he has broken and destroyed.
Her king and her princes are exiled[x] among the nations,
the law[y] is no more,
and her prophets no longer find
visions[z] from the LORD.

10 The elders of the Daughter of Zion
sit on the ground in silence;
they have sprinkled dust on their heads[a]
and put on sackcloth.[b]
The young women of Jerusalem
have bowed their heads to the ground.[c]

11 My eyes fail from weeping,[d]
I am in torment within,[e]
my heart is poured out[f] on the ground
because my people are destroyed,
because children and infants faint[g]
in the streets of the city.

2:1 b Ps 99:5; Ps 132:7
2:2 c La 3:43; d Ps 21:9; e Ps 89:39-40; Mic 5:11; f Isa 25:12
2:3 g Ps 75:5,10; h Ps 74:11; i Isa 42:25; Jer 21:4-5,14
2:4 j Job 16:13; La 3:12-13; k Eze 24:16,25; l Isa 42:25; Jer 7:20
2:5 m Jer 30:14; n ver 2; o Jer 9:17-20
2:6 p Jer 52:13; q La 1:4; Zep 3:18; r La 4:16
2:7 s Ps 74:7-8; Isa 64:11; Jer 33:4-5; t Jer 52:13
2:8 u 2Ki 21:13; Isa 34:11; v Isa 3:26
2:9 w Ne 1:3; x Dt 28:36; 2Ki 24:15; y 2Ch 15:3; z Jer 14:14
2:10 a Job 2:12; b Isa 15:3; c Job 2:13; Isa 3:26
2:11 d La 1:16; La 3:48-51; e La 1:20; f ver 19; Ps 22:14; g La 4:4

c3 Or / *all the strength*; or *every king; horn* here symbolises strength.

[12]They say to their mothers,
"Where is bread and wine?"
as they faint like wounded men
in the streets of the city,
as their lives ebb away
in their mothers' arms.[h]

[13]What can I say for you?
With what can I compare you,
O Daughter of Jerusalem?
To what can I liken you,
that I may comfort you,
O Virgin Daughter of Zion?[i]
Your wound is as deep as the
sea.[j]
Who can heal you?

[14]The visions of your prophets
were false and worthless;
they did not expose your sin
to ward off your captivity.[k]
The oracles they gave you
were false and misleading.[l]

[15]All who pass your way
clap their hands at you;[m]
they scoff[n] and shake their
heads
at the Daughter of Jerusalem:
"Is this the city that was called
the perfection of beauty,[o]
the joy of the whole earth?"[p]

[16]All your enemies open their
mouths
wide against you;[q]
they scoff and gnash their
teeth[r]
and say, "We have swallowed
her up.[s]
This is the day we have waited
for;
we have lived to see it."

[17]The LORD has done what he
planned;
he has fulfilled his word,
which he decreed long ago.[t]
He has overthrown you without
pity,[u]
he has let the enemy gloat
over you,
he has exalted the horn[d] of
your foes.[v]

[18]The hearts of the people
cry out to the Lord.[w]
O wall of the Daughter of Zion,
let your tears[x] flow like a
river
day and night;[y]
give yourself no relief,
your eyes no rest.[z]

[19]Arise, cry out in the night,
as the watches of the night
begin;
pour out your heart[a] like water
in the presence of the Lord.[b]
Lift up your hands to him
for the lives of your children,
who faint[c] from hunger
at the head of every street.

[20]"Look, O LORD, and consider:
Whom have you ever treated
like this?
Should women eat their
offspring,[d]
the children they have cared
for?[e]
Should priest and prophet be
killed[f]
in the sanctuary of the Lord?

[21]"Young and old lie together
in the dust of the streets;
my young men and maidens
have fallen by the sword.[g]
You have slain them in the day
of your anger;
you have slaughtered them
without pity.[h]

[22]"As you summon to a feast day,
so you summoned against me
terrors[i] on every side.
In the day of the LORD's anger
no-one escaped or survived;
those I cared for and reared,[j]
my enemy has destroyed."

3 [a] I am the man who has seen
affliction
by the rod of his wrath.[a]
[2]He has driven me away and
made me walk

2:12 h La 4:4
2:13 i Isa 37:22; j Jer 14:17; La 1:12
2:14 k Isa 58:1; l Jer 2:8; Jer 23:25-32, 33-40; Jer 29:9; Eze 13:3; Eze 22:28
2:15 m Eze 25:6; n Jer 19:8; o Ps 50:2; p Ps 48:2
2:16 q Ps 56:2; La 3:46; r Job 16:9; s Ps 35:25
2:17 t Dt 28:15-45; u ver 2; Eze 5:11; v Ps 89:42
2:18 w Ps 119:145; x La 1:16; y Jer 9:1; z La 3:49
2:19 a 1Sa 1:15; Ps 62:8; b Isa 26:9; c Isa 51:20
2:20 d Dt 28:53; Jer 19:9; e La 4:10; f Ps 78:64; Jer 14:15
2:21 g 2Ch 36:17; Ps 78:62-63; Jer 6:11; h Jer 13:14; La 3:43; Zec 11:6
2:22 i Ps 31:13; Jer 6:25; j Hos 9:13
3:1 a Job 19:21; Ps 88:7

d17 *Horn* here symbolises strength. aThis chapter is an acrostic poem; the verses of each stanza begin with the successive letters of the Hebrew alphabet, and the verses within each stanza begin with the same letter.

in darkness[b] rather than
light;
3indeed, he has turned his hand
against me[c]
again and again, all day long.

4He has made my skin and my
flesh grow old
and has broken my bones.[d]
5He has besieged me and
surrounded me
with bitterness[e] and
hardship.[f]
6He has made me dwell in
darkness
like those long dead.[g]

7He has walled me in so that I
cannot escape;[h]
he has weighed me down with
chains.[i]
8Even when I call out or cry for
help,
he shuts out my prayer.[j]
9He has barred my way with
blocks of stone;
he has made my paths
crooked.[k]

10Like a bear lying in wait,
like a lion in hiding,
11he dragged me from the path
and mangled[l] me
and left me without help.
12He drew his bow[m]
and made me the target[n] for
his arrows.[o]

13He pierced my heart
with arrows from his quiver.[p]
14I became the laughing-stock[q]
of all my people;
they mock me in song[r] all day
long.
15He has filled me with bitter
herbs
and sated me with gall.[s]

16He has broken my teeth with
gravel;[t]
he has trampled me in the
dust.
17I have been deprived of peace;
I have forgotten what
prosperity is.

18So I say, "My splendour is gone
and all that I had hoped from
the LORD."[u]

19I remember my affliction and
my wandering,
the bitterness and the gall.
20I well remember them,
and my soul is downcast[v]
within me.[w]
21Yet this I call to mind
and therefore I have hope:

22Because of the LORD's great
love we are not consumed,
for his compassions never
fail.[x]
23They are new every morning;
great is your faithfulness.[y]
24I say to myself, "The LORD is
my portion;[z]
therefore I will wait for him."

25The LORD is good to those
whose hope is in him,
to the one who seeks him;[a]
26it is good to wait quietly
for the salvation of the LORD.[b]
27It is good for a man to bear the
yoke
while he is young.

28Let him sit alone in silence,[c]
for the LORD has laid it on
him.
29Let him bury his face in the
dust—
there may yet be hope.[d]
30Let him offer his cheek to one
who would strike him,[e]
and let him be filled with
disgrace.

31For men are not cast off
by the Lord for ever.[f]
32Though he brings grief, he will
show compassion,
so great is his unfailing love.[g]
33For he does not willingly bring
affliction
or grief to the children of
men.[h]

34To crush underfoot
all prisoners in the land,
35to deny a man his rights
before the Most High,

3:2 b Jer 4:23
3:3 c Isa 5:25
3:4 d Ps 51:8; Isa 38:13; Jer 50:17
3:5 e ver 19; f Jer 23:15
3:6 g Ps 88:5-6
3:7 h Job 3:23; i Jer 40:4
3:8 j Job 30:20; Ps 22:2
3:9 k Isa 63:17; Hos 2:6
3:11 l Hos 6:1
3:12 m La 2:4; n Job 7:20; o Ps 7:12-13; Ps 38:2
3:13 p Job 6:4
3:14 q Jer 20:7; r Job 30:9
3:15 s Jer 9:15
3:16 t Pr 20:17
3:18 u Job 17:15
3:20 v Ps 42:5; w Ps 42:11
3:22 x Ps 78:38; Mal 3:6
3:23 y Zep 3:5
3:24 z Ps 16:5
3:25 a Isa 25:9; Isa 30:18
3:26 b Ps 37:7; Ps 40:1
3:28 c Jer 15:17
3:29 d Jer 31:17
3:30 e Job 16:10; Isa 50:6
3:31 f Ps 94:14; Isa 54:7
3:32 g Ps 78:38; Hos 11:8
3:33 h Eze 33:11

36 to deprive a man of justice—
would not the Lord see such
things?[i]
37 Who can speak and have it
happen
if the Lord has not decreed
it?[j]
38 Is it not from the mouth of the
Most High
that both calamities and good
things come?[k]
39 Why should any living man
complain
when punished for his sins?[l]

40 Let us examine our ways and
test them,[m]
and let us return to the
LORD.[n]
41 Let us lift up our hearts and our
hands
to God in heaven,[o] and say:
42 "We have sinned and rebelled[p]
and you have not forgiven.[q]

43 "You have covered yourself
with anger and pursued us;
you have slain without pity.[r]
44 You have covered yourself with
a cloud[s]
so that no prayer[t] can get
through.
45 You have made us scum[u] and
refuse
among the nations.

46 "All our enemies have opened
their mouths
wide against us.[v]
47 We have suffered terror and
pitfalls,[w]
ruin and destruction."[x]
48 Streams of tears flow from my
eyes[y]
because my people are
destroyed.[z]

49 My eyes will flow unceasingly,
without relief,[a]
50 until the LORD looks down
from heaven and sees.[b]
51 What I see brings grief to my
soul
because of all the women of
my city.

52 Those who were my enemies
without cause
hunted me like a bird.[c]
53 They tried to end my life in a
pit[d]
and threw stones at me;
54 the waters closed over my
head,[e]
and I thought I was about to
be cut off.

55 I called on your name, O LORD,
from the depths of the pit.[f]
56 You heard my plea:[g] "Do not
close your ears
to my cry for relief."
57 You came near when I called
you,
and you said, "Do not fear."[h]

58 O Lord, you took up my case;[i]
you redeemed my life.[j]
59 You have seen, O LORD, the
wrong done to me.[k]
Uphold my cause!
60 You have seen the depth of
their vengeance,
all their plots against me.[l]

61 O LORD, you have heard their
insults,
all their plots against me—
62 what my enemies whisper and
mutter
against me all day long.[m]
63 Look at them! Sitting or
standing,
they mock me in their songs.

64 Pay them back what they
deserve, O LORD,
for what their hands have
done.[n]
65 Put a veil over their hearts,[o]
and may your curse be on
them!
66 Pursue them in anger and
destroy them
from under the heavens of the
LORD.

4[a] How the gold has lost its
lustre,
the fine gold become dull!

[a]This chapter is an acrostic poem, the verses of which begin with the successive letters of the Hebrew alphabet.

3:36 [i] Jer 22:3; Hab 1:13
3:37 [j] Ps 33:9-11
3:38 [k] Job 2:10; Isa 45:7; Jer 32:42
3:39 [l] Jer 30:15; Mic 7:9
3:40 [m] 2Co 13:5 [n] Ps 119:59; Ps 139:23-24
3:41 [o] Ps 25:1; Ps 28:2
3:42 [p] Da 9:5 [q] Jer 5:7-9
3:43 [r] La 2:2,17,21
3:44 [s] Ps 97:2 [t] ver 8
3:45 [u] 1Co 4:13
3:46 [v] La 2:16
3:47 [w] Jer 48:43 [x] Isa 24:17-18; Isa 51:19
3:48 [y] La 1:16 [z] La 2:11
3:49 [a] Jer 14:17
3:50 [b] Isa 63:15
3:52 [c] Ps 35:7
3:53 [d] Jer 37:16
3:54 [e] Ps 69:2; Jnh 2:3-5
3:55 [f] Ps 130:1; Jnh 2:2
3:56 [g] Ps 55:1
3:57 [h] Isa 41:10
3:58 [i] Jer 51:36 [j] Ps 34:22; Jer 50:34
3:59 [k] Jer 18:19-20
3:60 [l] Jer 11:20; Jer 18:18
3:62 [m] Eze 36:3
3:64 [n] Ps 28:4
3:65 [o] Isa 6:10

The sacred gems are scattered
at the head of every street.[a]

2How the precious sons of Zion,
once worth their weight in
gold,
are now considered as pots of
clay,
the work of a potter's hands!

3Even jackals offer their breasts
to nurse their young,
but my people have become
heartless
like ostriches in the desert.[b]

4Because of thirst the infant's
tongue
sticks to the roof of its
mouth;[c]
the children beg for bread,
but no-one gives it to them.[d]

5Those who once ate delicacies
are destitute in the streets.
Those nurtured in purple[e]
now lie on ash heaps.[f]

6The punishment of my people
is greater than that of
Sodom,[g]
which was overthrown in a
moment
without a hand turned to help
her.

7Their princes were brighter
than snow
and whiter than milk,
their bodies more ruddy than
rubies,
their appearance like
sapphires.[b]

8But now they are blacker[h] than
soot;
they are not recognised in the
streets.
Their skin has shrivelled on
their bones;[i]
it has become as dry as a
stick.

9Those killed by the sword are
better off
than those who die of famine;
racked with hunger, they waste
away
for lack of food from the
field.[j]

10With their own hands
compassionate women
have cooked their own
children,[k]
who became their food
when my people were
destroyed.

11The LORD has given full vent to
his wrath;
he has poured out his fierce
anger.
He kindled a fire[l] in Zion
that consumed her
foundations.[m]

12The kings of the earth did not
believe,
nor did any of the world's
people,
that enemies and foes could
enter
the gates of Jerusalem.[n]

13But it happened because of the
sins of her prophets
and the iniquities of her
priests,[o]
who shed within her
the blood of the righteous.

14Now they grope through the
streets
like men who are blind.[p]
They are so defiled with blood[q]
that no-one dares to touch
their garments.

15"Go away! You are unclean!"
men cry to them.
"Away! Away! Don't touch
us!"
When they flee and wander
about,
people among the nations say,
"They can stay here no
longer."[r]

16The LORD himself has scattered
them;
he no longer watches over
them.[s]

4:1 *a* Eze 7:19
4:3 *b* Job 39:16
4:4 *c* Ps 22:15 *d* La 2:11,12
4:5 *e* Jer 6:2 *f* Am 6:3-7
4:6 *g* Ge 19:25
4:8 *h* Job 30:28 *i* Ps 102:3-5
4:9 *j* Jer 15:2; Jer 16:4
4:10 *k* Lev 26:29; Dt 28:53-57; Jer 19:9; La 2:20; Eze 5:10
4:11 *l* Jer 17:27 *m* Dt 32:22; Jer 7:20; Eze 22:31
4:12 *n* 1Ki 9:9; Jer 21:13
4:13 *o* Jer 5:31; Jer 6:13; Eze 22:28; Mic 3:11
4:14 *p* Isa 59:10 *q* Jer 2:34; Jer 19:4
4:15 *r* Lev 13:46
4:16 *s* Isa 9:14-16

[b]7 Or *lapis lazuli*

The priests are shown no
honour,
the elders[t] no favour.

17 Moreover, our eyes failed,
looking in vain[u] for help;[v]
from our towers we watched
for a nation[w] that could not
save us.

18 Men stalked us at every step,
so we could not walk in our
streets.
Our end was near, our days
were numbered,
for our end had come.[x]

19 Our pursuers were swifter
than eagles[y] in the sky;
they chased us[z] over the
mountains
and lay in wait for us in the
desert.

20 The LORD's anointed,[a] our very
life breath,
was caught in their traps.[b]
We thought that under his
shadow
we would live among the
nations.

21 Rejoice and be glad,
O Daughter of Edom,
you who live in the land of Uz.
But to you also the cup[c] will be
passed;
you will be drunk and stripped
naked.[d]

22 O Daughter of Zion, your
punishment will end;[e]
he will not prolong your exile.
But, O Daughter of Edom, he
will punish your sin
and expose your wickedness.[f]

5 Remember, O LORD, what has
happened to us;
look, and see our disgrace.[a]
2 Our inheritance[b] has been
turned over to aliens,
our homes[c] to foreigners.
3 We have become orphans and
fatherless,
our mothers like widows.[d]
4 We must buy the water we
drink;
our wood can be had only at a
price.[e]
5 Those who pursue us are at our
heels;
we are weary[f] and find no
rest.
6 We submitted to Egypt and
Assyria[g]
to get enough bread.
7 Our fathers sinned and are no
more,
and we bear their
punishment.[h]
8 Slaves[i] rule over us,
and there is none to free us
from their hands.[j]
9 We get our bread at the risk of
our lives
because of the sword in the
desert.
10 Our skin is hot as an oven,
feverish from hunger.[k]
11 Women have been ravished[l] in
Zion,
and virgins in the towns of
Judah.
12 Princes have been hung up by
their hands;
elders are shown no respect.[m]
13 Young men toil at the
millstones;
boys stagger under loads of
wood.
14 The elders are gone from the
city gate;
the young men have stopped
their music.[n]
15 Joy is gone from our hearts;
our dancing has turned to
mourning.[o]
16 The crown[p] has fallen from our
head.
Woe to us, for we have
sinned![q]
17 Because of this our hearts[r] are
faint;
because of these things our
eyes[s] grow dim
18 for Mount Zion, which lies
desolate,[t]
with jackals prowling over it.

4:16 t La 5:12
4:17 u Isa 20:5; Eze 29:16 v La 1:7 w Jer 37:7
4:18 x Eze 7:2-12; Am 8:2
4:19 y Dt 28:49 z Isa 5:26-28
4:20 a 2Sa 19:21 b Jer 39:5; Eze 12:12-13; Eze 19:4,8
4:21 c Jer 25:15 d Isa 34:6-10; Am 1:11-12; Ob 1:16
4:22 e Isa 40:2; Jer 33:8 f Ps 137:7; Mal 1:4
5:1 a Ps 44:13-16; Ps 89:50
5:2 b Ps 79:1 c Zep 1:13
5:3 d Jer 15:8; Jer 18:21
5:4 e Isa 3:1
5:5 f Ne 9:37
5:6 g Hos 9:3
5:7 h Jer 14:20; Jer 16:12
5:8 i Ne 5:15 j Zec 11:6
5:10 k La 4:8-9
5:11 l Zec 14:2
5:12 m La 4:16
5:14 n Isa 24:8; Jer 7:34
5:15 o Jer 25:10
5:16 p Ps 89:39 q Isa 3:11
5:17 r Isa 1:5 s Ps 6:7
5:18 t Mic 3:12

[19]You, O LORD, reign for ever;
your throne endures[u] from
generation to
generation.
[20]Why do you always forget
us?[v]
Why do you forsake us so
long?
[21]Restore[w] us to yourself,
O LORD, that we may
return;
renew our days as of old
[22]unless you have utterly rejected
us
and are angry with us beyond
measure.[x]

5:19
u Ps 45:6
Ps 102:12, 24-27
5:20
v Ps 13:1
Ps 44:24
5:21
w Ps 80:3
5:22
x Isa 64:9

EZEKIEL

The Living Creatures and the Glory of the LORD

1 In the[a] thirtieth year, in the fourth month on the fifth day, while I was among the exiles[a] by the Kebar River, the heavens were opened[b] and I saw visions[c] of God.

2 On the fifth of the month—it was the fifth year of the exile of King Jehoiachin[d]— 3 the word of the LORD came to Ezekiel the priest, the son of Buzi,[b] by the Kebar River in the land of the Babylonians.[c] There the hand of the LORD was upon him.[e]

4 I looked, and I saw a windstorm coming out of the north[f]—an immense cloud with flashing lightning and surrounded by brilliant light. The centre of the fire looked like glowing metal,[g] 5 and in the fire was what looked like four living creatures.[h] In appearance their form was that of a man,[i] 6 but each of them had four faces[j] and four wings. 7 Their legs were straight; their feet were like those of a calf and gleamed like burnished bronze.[k] 8 Under their wings on their four sides they had the hands of a man.[l] All four of them had faces and wings, 9 and their wings touched one another. Each one went straight ahead; they did not turn as they moved.[m]

10 Their faces looked like this: Each of the four had the face of a man, and on the right side each had the face of a lion, and on the left the face of an ox; each also had the face of an eagle.[n] 11 Such were their faces. Their wings[o] were spread out upwards; each had two wings, one touching the wing of another creature on either side, and two wings covering its body. 12 Each one went straight ahead. Wherever the spirit would go, they would go, without turning as they went. 13 The appearance of the living creatures was like burning coals of fire or like torches. Fire moved back and forth among the creatures; it was bright, and lightning[p] flashed out of it. 14 The creatures sped back and forth like flashes of lightning.[q]

15 As I looked at the living creatures, I saw a wheel on the ground beside each creature with its four faces. 16 This was the appearance and structure of the wheels: They sparkled like chrysolite,[r] and all four looked alike. Each appeared to be made like a wheel intersecting a wheel. 17 As they moved, they would go in any one of the four directions the creatures faced; the wheels did not turn[s] about[d] as the creatures went. 18 Their rims were high and awesome, and all four rims were full of eyes[t] all around.

19 When the living creatures moved, the wheels beside them moved; and when the living creatures rose from the ground, the wheels also rose. 20 Wherever the spirit would go, they would go,[u] and the wheels would rise along with them, because the spirit of the living creatures was in the wheels. 21 When the creatures moved, they also moved; when the creatures stood still, they also stood still; and when the creatures rose from the ground, the wheels rose along with them, because the spirit of the living creatures was in the wheels.[v]

22 Spread out above the heads of the living creatures was what looked like an expanse,[w] sparkling like ice, and awesome. 23 Under the

1:1 *a* Eze 11:24-25 *b* Mt 3:16; Ac 7:56 *c* Ex 24:10
1:2 *d* 2Ki 24:15
1:3 *e* 2Ki 3:15; Eze 3:14,22
1:4 *f* Jer 1:14 *g* Eze 8:2
1:5 *h* Rev 4:6 *i* ver 26
1:6 *j* Eze 10:14
1:7 *k* Da 10:6; Rev 1:15
1:8 *l* Eze 10:8
1:9 *m* Eze 10:22
1:10 *n* Eze 10:14; Rev 4:7
1:11 *o* Isa 6:2
1:13 *p* Rev 4:5
1:14 *q* Ps 29:7
1:16 *r* Eze 10:9-11; Da 10:6
1:17 *s* ver 9
1:18 *t* Eze 10:12; Rev 4:6
1:20 *u* ver 12
1:21 *v* Eze 10:17
1:22 *w* Eze 10:1

a1 Or ⌞my⌟ b3 Or *Ezekiel son of Buzi the priest*
c3 Or *Chaldeans* d17 Or *aside*

expanse their wings were stretched out one towards the other, and each had two wings covering its body. 24When the creatures moved, I heard the sound of their wings, like the roar of rushing waters, like the voice[x] of the Almighty,[e] like the tumult of an army.[y] When they stood still, they lowered their wings.

25Then there came a voice from above the expanse over their heads as they stood with lowered wings. 26Above the expanse over their heads was what looked like a throne of sapphire,[f][z] and high above on the throne was a figure like that of a man.[a] 27I saw that from what appeared to be his waist up he looked like glowing metal, as if full of fire, and that from there down he looked like fire; and brilliant light surrounded him.[b] 28Like the appearance of a rainbow[c] in the clouds on a rainy day, so was the radiance around him.[d]

This was the appearance of the likeness of the glory[e] of the LORD. When I saw it, I fell face down,[f] and I heard the voice of one speaking.

Ezekiel's Call

2 He said to me, "Son of man, stand[a] up on your feet and I will speak to you." 2As he spoke, the Spirit came into me and raised me[b] to my feet, and I heard him speaking to me.

3He said: "Son of man, I am sending you to the Israelites, to a rebellious nation that has rebelled against me; they and their fathers have been in revolt against me to this very day.[c] 4The people to whom I am sending you are obstinate and stubborn.[d] Say to them, 'This is what the Sovereign LORD says.' 5And whether they listen or fail to listen[e]—for they are a rebellious house[f]—they will know that a prophet has been among them.[g] 6And you, son of man, do not be afraid[h] of them or their words. Do not be afraid, though briers and thorns[i] are all around you and you live among scorpions. Do not be afraid of what they say or terrified by them, though they are a rebellious house.[j] 7You must speak my words to them, whether they listen or fail to listen, for they are rebellious.[k] 8But you, son of man, listen to what I say to you. Do not rebel like that rebellious house;[l] open your mouth and eat[m] what I give you."

9Then I looked, and I saw a hand[n] stretched out to me. In it was a scroll, 10which he unrolled before me. On both sides of it were written words of lament and mourning and woe.[o]

3 And he said to me, "Son of man, eat what is before you, eat this scroll; then go and speak to the house of Israel." 2So I opened my mouth, and he gave me the scroll to eat.

3Then he said to me, "Son of man, eat this scroll I am giving you and fill your stomach with it." So I ate[a] it, and it tasted as sweet as honey[b] in my mouth.

4He then said to me: "Son of man, go now to the house of Israel and speak my words to them. 5You are not being sent to a people of obscure speech and difficult language,[c] but to the house of Israel—6not to many peoples of obscure speech and difficult language, whose words you cannot understand. Surely if I had sent you to them, they would have listened to you.[d] 7But the house of Israel is not willing to listen to you because they are not willing to listen to me, for the whole house of Israel is hardened and obstinate.[e] 8But I will make you as unyielding and hardened as they are.[f] 9I will make your forehead like the hardest stone, harder than flint. Do not be afraid of them or terrified by them,

1:24 x Eze 10:5; Eze 43:2; Da 10:6; Rev 1:15; Rev 19:6 y 2Ki 7:6
1:26 z Ex 24:10; Eze 10:1 a Rev 1:13
1:27 b Eze 8:2
1:28 c Ge 9:13; Rev 10:1 d Rev 4:2 e Eze 8:4 f Eze 3:23; Da 8:17; Rev 1:17
2:1 a Da 10:11
2:2 b Eze 3:24; Da 8:18
2:3 c Jer 3:25; Eze 20:8-24
2:4 d Eze 3:7
2:5 e Eze 3:11 f Eze 3:27 g Eze 33:33
2:6 h Jer 1:8,17 i Isa 9:18; Mic 7:4 j Eze 3:9
2:7 k Jer 1:7; Eze 3:10-11
2:8 l Isa 50:5 m Jer 15:16; Rev 10:9
2:9 n Eze 8:3
2:10 o Rev 8:13
3:3 a Jer 15:16 b Ps 19:10; Ps 119:103; Rev 10:9-10
3:5 c Isa 28:11; Jnh 1:2
3:6 d Mt 11:21-23
3:7 e Eze 2:4; Jn 15:20-23
3:8 f Jer 1:18

e24 Hebrew *Shaddai* f26 Or *lapis lazuli*

though they are a rebellious house.[g]"

10And he said to me, "Son of man, listen carefully and take to heart all the words I speak to you. 11Go now to your countrymen in exile and speak to them. Say to them, 'This is what the Sovereign LORD says,' whether they listen or fail to listen.[h]"

12Then the Spirit lifted me up,[i] and I heard behind me a loud rumbling sound—May the glory of the LORD be praised in his dwelling-place!—13the sound of the wings of the living creatures brushing against each other and the sound of the wheels beside them, a loud rumbling sound.[j] 14The Spirit then lifted me up and took me away, and I went in bitterness and in the anger of my spirit, with the strong hand of the LORD upon me. 15I came to the exiles who lived at Tel Abib near the Kebar River.[k] And there, where they were living, I sat among them for seven days[l]—overwhelmed.

Warning to Israel

16At the end of seven days the word of the LORD came to me.[m] 17"Son of man, I have made you a watchman[n] for the house of Israel; so hear the word I speak and give them warning from me. 18When I say to a wicked man, 'You will surely die,' and you do not warn him or speak out to dissuade him from his evil ways in order to save his life, that wicked man will die for[a] his sin, and I will hold you accountable for his blood.[o] 19But if you do warn the wicked man and he does not turn from his wickedness or from his evil ways, he will die for his sin; but you will have saved yourself.[p]

20"Again, when a righteous man turns from his righteousness and does evil, and I put a stumbling-block before him, he will die. Since you did not warn him, he will die for his sin. The righteous things he did will not be remembered, and I will hold you accountable for his blood.[q] 21But if you do warn the righteous man not to sin and he does not sin, he will surely live because he took warning, and you will have saved yourself.[r]"

22The hand of the LORD[s] was upon me there, and he said to me, "Get up and go[t] out to the plain,[u] and there I will speak to you." 23So I got up and went out to the plain. And the glory of the LORD was standing there, like the glory I had seen by the Kebar River,[v] and I fell face down.[w]

24Then the Spirit came into me and raised me[x] to my feet. He spoke to me and said: "Go, shut yourself inside your house. 25And you, son of man, they will tie with ropes; you will be bound so that you cannot go out among the people.[y] 26I will make your tongue stick to the roof of your mouth so that you will be silent and unable to rebuke them, though they are a rebellious house.[z] 27But when I speak to you, I will open your mouth and you shall say to them, 'This is what the Sovereign LORD says.'[a] Whoever will listen let him listen, and whoever will refuse let him refuse; for they are a rebellious house.[b]

Siege of Jerusalem Symbolised

4 "Now, son of man, take a clay tablet, put it in front of you and draw the city of Jerusalem on it. 2Then lay siege to it: Erect siege works against it, build a ramp[a] up to it, set up camps against it and put battering-rams around it.[b] 3Then take an iron pan, place it as an iron wall between you and the city and turn your face towards it. It will be under siege, and you shall besiege it. This will be a sign[c] to the house of Israel.[d]

4"Then lie on your left side and

3:9 g Isa 50:7 Eze 2:6 Mic 3:8
3:11 h Eze 2:4-5,7
3:12 i Eze 8:3 Ac 8:39
3:13 j Eze 1:24 Eze 10:5, 16-17
3:15 k Ps 137:1 l Job 2:13
3:16 m Jer 42:7
3:17 n Isa 52:8 Jer 6:17 Eze 33:7-9
3:18 o ver 20 Eze 33:6
3:19 p 2Ki 17:13 Eze 14:14,20 Ac 18:6 Ac 20:26 1Ti 4:14-16
3:20 q Ps 125:5 Eze 18:24 Eze 33:12,18
3:21 r Ac 20:31
3:22 s Eze 1:3 t Ac 9:6 u Eze 8:4
3:23 v Eze 1:1 w Eze 1:28
3:24 x Eze 2:2
3:25 y Eze 4:8
3:26 z Eze 2:5 Eze 24:27 Eze 33:22
3:27 a ver 11 b Eze 12:3 Eze 24:27 Eze 33:22
4:2 a Jer 6:6 b Eze 21:22
4:3 c Isa 8:18 Isa 20:3 Eze 12:3-6 Eze 24:24,27 d Jer 39:1

a*18* Or *in*; also in verses 19 and 20

put the sin of the house of Israel
upon yourself.[a] You are to bear
their sin for the number of days
you lie on your side. 5I have assigned you the same number of
days as the years of their sin. So for
390 days you will bear the sin of the
house of Israel.
6"After you have finished this, lie
down again, this time on your right
side, and bear the sin of the house
of Judah. I have assigned you 40
days, a day for each year.[e] 7Turn
your face towards the siege of
Jerusalem and with bared arm
prophesy against her. 8I will tie you
up with ropes so that you cannot
turn from one side to the other until
you have finished the days of your
siege.[f]
9"Take wheat and barley, beans
and lentils, millet and spelt;[g] put
them in a storage jar and use them
to make bread for yourself. You are
to eat it during the 390 days you lie
on your side. 10Weigh out twenty
shekels[b] of food to eat each day
and eat it at set times. 11Also measure out a sixth of a hin[c] of water
and drink it at set times. 12Eat the
food as you would a barley cake;
bake it in the sight of the people,
using human excrement[h] for
fuel." 13The LORD said, "In this way
the people of Israel will eat defiled
food among the nations where I will
drive them."[i]
14Then I said, "Not so, Sovereign
LORD![j] I have never defiled myself. From my youth until now I
have never eaten anything found
dead[k] or torn by wild animals. No
unclean meat has ever entered my
mouth.[l]"
15"Very well," he said, "I will let
you bake your bread over cow manure instead of human excrement."
16He then said to me: "Son of
man, I will cut off[m] the supply of
food in Jerusalem. The people will
eat rationed food in anxiety and
drink rationed water in despair,[n]
17for food and water will be scarce.
They will be appalled at the sight of
each other and will waste away because of[d] their sin.[o]

5 "Now, son of man, take a sharp
sword and use it as a barber's
razor[a] to shave[b] your head and
your beard.[c] Then take a set of
scales and divide up the hair.
2When the days of your siege come
to an end, burn a third of the hair
with fire inside the city. Take a
third and strike it with the sword
all around the city. And scatter a
third to the wind. For I will pursue
them with drawn sword.[d] 3But
take a few strands of hair and tuck
them away in the folds of your garment.[e] 4Again, take a few of these
and throw them into the fire and
burn them up. A fire will spread
from there to the whole house of
Israel.
5"This is what the Sovereign
LORD says: This is Jerusalem,
which I have set in the centre of the
nations, with countries all around
her. 6Yet in her wickedness she has
rebelled against my laws and decrees more than the nations and
countries around her. She has rejected my laws and has not followed my decrees.[f]
7"Therefore this is what the Sovereign LORD says: You have been
more unruly than the nations
around you and have not followed
my decrees or kept my laws. You
have not even[a] conformed to the
standards of the nations around
you.[g]
8"Therefore this is what the Sovereign LORD says: I myself am
against you, Jerusalem, and I will
inflict punishment on you in the
sight of the nations.[h] 9Because of
all your detestable idols, I will do to
you what I have never done before
and will never do again.[i] 10There-
fore in your midst fathers will eat
their children, and children will eat

4:6 e Nu 14:34; Da 9:24-26; Da 12:11-12
4:8 f Eze 3:25
4:9 g Isa 28:25
4:12 h Isa 36:12
4:13 i Hos 9:3
4:14 j Jer 1:6; Eze 9:8; Eze 20:49; k Lev 11:39; l Ex 22:31; Dt 14:3; Ac 10:14
4:16 m Ps 105:16; Eze 5:16; n ver 10-11; Lev 26:26; Isa 3:1; Eze 12:19
4:17 o Lev 26:39; Eze 24:23; Eze 33:10
5:1 a Isa 7:20; b Eze 44:20; c Lev 21:5
5:2 d ver 12; Lev 26:33
5:3 e Jer 39:10
5:6 f Jer 11:10; Eze 16:47-51; Zec 7:11
5:7 g 2Ch 33:9; Jer 2:10-11; Eze 16:47
5:8 h Eze 15:7
5:9 i Da 9:12; Mt 24:21

a4 Or *your side* b10 That is, about 8 ounces (about 0.2 kilogram) c11 That is, about 1 pint (about 0.6 litre) d17 Or *away in* a7 Most Hebrew manuscripts; some Hebrew manuscripts and Syriac *You have*

their fathers.[j] I will inflict punishment on you and will scatter all
your survivors to the winds.[k]
11Therefore as surely as I live, declares the Sovereign LORD, because
you have defiled my sanctuary
with all your vile images[l] and detestable practices,[m] I myself will
withdraw my favour; I will not look
on you with pity or spare you.[n] 12A
third of your people will die of the
plague or perish by famine inside
you; a third will fall by the sword
outside your walls; and a third I
will scatter to the winds and pursue
with drawn sword.[o]

13"Then my anger will cease and
my wrath[p] against them will subside, and I will be avenged.[q] And
when I have spent my wrath upon
them, they will know that I the
LORD have spoken in my zeal.

14"I will make you a ruin and a reproach among the nations around
you, in the sight of all who pass
by.[r] 15You will be a reproach and a
taunt, a warning and an object of
horror to the nations around you
when I inflict punishment on you in
anger and in wrath and with sting-
ing rebuke.[s] I the LORD have spoken.[t] 16When I shoot at you with
my deadly and destructive arrows
of famine, I will shoot to destroy
you. I will bring more and more
famine upon you and cut off your
supply of food.[u] 17I will send famine and wild beasts against you, and
they will leave you childless.
Plague and bloodshed[v] will sweep
through you, and I will bring the
sword against you. I the LORD have
spoken.[w]"

A Prophecy Against the Mountains of Israel

6 The word of the LORD came to
me: 2"Son of man, set your
face against the mountains[a] of Israel; prophesy against them 3and
say: 'O mountains of Israel, hear
the word of the Sovereign LORD.
This is what the Sovereign LORD
says to the mountains and hills, to
the ravines and valleys:[b] I am
about to bring a sword against you,
and I will destroy your high
places.[c] 4Your altars will be demolished and your incense altars[d]
will be smashed; and I will slay
your people in front of your idols. 5I
will lay the dead bodies of the Israelites in front of their idols, and
I will scatter your bones[e] around
your altars. 6Wherever you live,
the towns will be laid waste and the
high places demolished, so that
your altars will be laid waste and
devastated, your idols[f] smashed
and ruined, your incense altars[g]
broken down, and what you have
made wiped out.[h] 7Your people
will fall slain among you, and you
will know that I am the LORD.

8" 'But I will spare some, for
some of you will escape[i] the sword
when you are scattered among the
lands and nations.[j] 9Then in the
nations where they have been carried captive, those who escape will
remember me—how I have been
grieved[k] by their adulterous
hearts, which have turned away
from me, and by their eyes, which
have lusted after their idols.[l]
They will loathe themselves for the
evil they have done and for all their
detestable practices.[m] 10And they
will know that I am the LORD; I did
not threaten in vain to bring this calamity on them.

11" 'This is what the Sovereign
LORD says: Strike your hands together and stamp your feet and cry
out "Alas!" because of all the
wicked and detestable practices of
the house of Israel, for they will
fall by the sword, famine and
plague.[n] 12He that is far away will
die of the plague, and he that is
near will fall by the sword, and he
that survives and is spared will die
of famine. So will I spend my wrath
upon them.[o] 13And they will know
that I am the LORD, when their
people lie slain among their idols
around their altars, on every high

5:10 j Lev 26:29; La 2:20 k Lev 26:33; Ps 44:11; Eze 12:14; Zec 2:6
5:11 l Eze 7:20 m 2Ch 36:14; Eze 8:6 n Eze 7:4,9
5:12 o ver 2,17; Jer 15:2; Jer 21:9; Eze 6:11-12; Eze 12:14
5:13 p Eze 21:17; Eze 36:6 q Isa 1:24
5:14 r Lev 26:32; Ne 2:17; Ps 74:3-10; Ps 79:1-4
5:15 s 1Ki 9:7; Jer 22:8-9; Jer 24:9 t Eze 25:17
5:16 u Dt 32:24
5:17 v Eze 38:22 w Eze 14:21
6:2 a Eze 36:1
6:3 b Eze 36:4 c Lev 26:30
6:4 d 2Ch 14:5
6:5 e Jer 8:1-2
6:6 f Mic 1:7; Zec 13:2 g Lev 26:30 h Isa 6:11; Eze 5:14
6:8 i Jer 44:28 j Isa 6:13; Jer 44:14; Eze 12:16; Eze 14:22
6:9 k Ps 78:40; Isa 7:13 l Eze 20:7,24 m Eze 20:43; Eze 36:31
6:11 n Eze 5:12; Eze 21:14,17; Eze 25:6
6:12 o Eze 5:12

hill and on all the mountaintops, under every spreading tree and every
leafy oak[p]—places where they offered fragrant incense to all their
idols.[q] 14 And I will stretch out my
hand[r] against them and make the
land a desolate waste from the
desert to Diblah[a]—wherever they
live. Then they will know that I am
the LORD.[s]' "

The End Has Come

7 The word of the LORD came to
me: 2 "Son of man, this is what
the Sovereign LORD says to the land
of Israel: The end![a] The end has
come upon the four corners[b] of the
land. 3 The end is now upon you and
I will unleash my anger against
you. I will judge you according to
your conduct and repay you for all
your detestable practices. 4 I will
not look on you with pity[c] or spare
you; I will surely repay you for
your conduct and the detestable
practices among you. Then you will
know that I am the LORD.

5 "This is what the Sovereign
LORD says: Disaster![d] An unheard-
of[a] disaster is coming. 6 The end
has come! The end has come! It has
roused itself against you. It has
come! 7 Doom has come upon you—
you who dwell in the land. The time
has come, the day is near;[e] there is
panic, not joy, upon the mountains.
8 I am about to pour out my wrath[f]
on you and spend my anger against
you; I will judge you according to
your conduct and repay you for all
your detestable practices.[g] 9 I will
not look on you with pity or spare
you; I will repay you in accordance
with your conduct and the detestable practices among you. Then
you will know that it is I the LORD
who strikes the blow.

10 "The day is here! It has come!
Doom has burst forth, the rod[h] has
budded, arrogance has blossomed!
11 Violence has grown into[b] a rod to
punish wickedness; none of the
people will be left, none of that
crowd—no wealth, nothing of
value.[i] 12 The time has come, the
day has arrived. Let not the buyer
rejoice nor the seller grieve, for
wrath is upon the whole crowd.[j]
13 The seller will not recover the
land he has sold as long as both of
them live, for the vision concerning the whole crowd will not be re-
versed. Because of their sins, not
one of them will preserve his life.[k]
14 Though they blow the trumpet
and get everything ready, no-one
will go into battle, for my wrath is
upon the whole crowd.

15 "Outside is the sword, inside
are plague and famine; those in the
country will die by the sword, and
those in the city will be devoured
by famine and plague.[l] 16 All who
survive and escape will be in the
mountains, moaning like doves[m] of
the valleys, each because of his
sins.[n] 17 Every hand will go limp,[o]
and every knee will become as
weak as water. 18 They will put on
sackcloth and be clothed with terror.[p] Their faces will be covered
with shame and their heads will be
shaved.[q] 19 They will throw their silver into the streets, and their gold
will be an unclean thing. Their silver and gold will not be able to
save them in the day of the LORD's
wrath.[r] They will not satisfy their
hunger or fill their stomachs with
it, for it has made them stumble[s]
into sin.[t] 20 They were proud of
their beautiful jewellery and used
it to make their detestable idols and
vile images.[u] Therefore I will turn
these into an unclean thing for
them. 21 I will hand it all over as
plunder to foreigners and as loot to
the wicked of the earth, and they
will defile it.[v] 22 I will turn my
face[w] away from them, and they

6:13 p Isa 57:5 q 1Ki 14:23; Jer 2:20; Eze 20:28; Hos 4:13
6:14 r Isa 5:25 s Eze 14:13
7:2 a Am 8:2,10 b Rev 7:1; Rev 20:8
7:4 c Eze 5:11
7:5 d 2Ki 21:12
7:7 e Eze 12:23; Zep 1:14
7:8 f Isa 42:25; Eze 9:8; Eze 14:19; Na 1:6 g Eze 20:8,21; Eze 36:19
7:10 h Ps 89:32; Isa 10:5
7:11 i Jer 16:6; Zep 1:18
7:12 j ver 7; Isa 5:13-14; Eze 30:3
7:13 k Lev 25:24-28
7:15 l Dt 32:25; Jer 14:18; La 1:20; Eze 5:12
7:16 m Isa 59:11 n Ezr 9:15; Eze 6:8
7:17 o Isa 13:7; Eze 21:7; Eze 22:14
7:18 p Ps 55:5 q Isa 15:2-3; Eze 27:31; Am 8:10
7:19 r Eze 13:5; Zep 1:7,18 s Eze 14:3 t Pr 11:4
7:20 u Jer 7:30
7:21 v 2Ki 24:13
7:22 w Eze 39:23-24

[a] *14* Most Hebrew manuscripts; a few Hebrew manuscripts *Riblah* [a] *5* Most Hebrew manuscripts; some Hebrew manuscripts and Syriac *Disaster after* [b] *11* Or *The violent one has become*

will desecrate my treasured place; robbers will enter it and desecrate it.

23 "Prepare chains, because the land is full of bloodshed[x] and the city is full of violence. 24 I will bring the most wicked of the nations to take possession of their houses; I will put an end to the pride of the mighty, and their sanctuaries[y] will be desecrated.[z] 25 When terror comes, they will seek peace, but there will be none.[a] 26 Calamity upon calamity[b] will come, and rumour upon rumour. They will try to get a vision from the prophet; the teaching of the law by the priest will be lost, as will the counsel of the elders.[c] 27 The king will mourn, the prince will be clothed with despair,[d] and the hands of the people of the land will tremble. I will deal with them according to their conduct,[e] and by their own standards I will judge them. Then they will know that I am the LORD.[f]"

Idolatry in the Temple

8 In the sixth year, in the sixth month on the fifth day, while I was sitting in my house and the elders[a] of Judah were sitting before[b] me, the hand of the Sovereign LORD came upon me there.[c] 2 I looked, and I saw a figure like that of a man.**a** From what appeared to be his waist down he was like fire, and from there up his appearance was as bright as glowing metal.[d] 3 He stretched out what looked like a hand and took me by the hair of my head. The Spirit lifted me up[e] between earth and heaven and in visions of God he took me to Jerusalem, to the entrance to the north gate of the inner court, where the idol that provokes to jealousy[f] stood. 4 And there before me was the glory[g] of the God of Israel, as in the vision I had seen in the plain.[h]

5 Then he said to me, "Son of man, look towards the north." So I looked, and in the entrance north of the gate of the altar I saw this idol[i] of jealousy.

6 And he said to me, "Son of man, do you see what they are doing—the utterly detestable[j] things the house of Israel is doing here, things that will drive me far from my sanctuary? But you will see things that are even more detestable."

7 Then he brought me to the entrance to the court. I looked, and I saw a hole in the wall. 8 He said to me, "Son of man, now dig into the wall." So I dug into the wall and saw a doorway there.

9 And he said to me, "Go in and see the wicked and detestable things they are doing here." 10 So I went in and looked, and I saw portrayed all over the walls all kinds of crawling things and detestable animals and all the idols of the house of Israel.[k] 11 In front of them stood seventy elders of the house of Israel, and Jaazaniah son of Shaphan was standing among them. Each had a censer[l] in his hand, and a fragrant cloud of incense[m] was rising.

12 He said to me, "Son of man, have you seen what the elders of the house of Israel are doing in the darkness, each at the shrine of his own idol? They say, 'The LORD does not see[n] us; the LORD has forsaken the land.'" 13 Again, he said, "You will see them doing things that are even more detestable."

14 Then he brought me to the entrance to the north gate of the house of the LORD, and I saw women sitting there, mourning for Tammuz. 15 He said to me, "Do you see this, son of man? You will see things that are even more detestable than this."

16 He then brought me into the inner court of the house of the LORD, and there at the entrance to the temple, between the portico and the altar,[o] were about twenty-five men. With their backs towards the temple of the LORD and their faces

7:23 x 2Ki 21:16
7:24 y Eze 24:21 z 2Ch 7:20 Eze 28:7
7:25 a Eze 13:10,16
7:26 b Jer 4:20 c Isa 47:11 Eze 20:1-3 Mic 3:6
7:27 d Ps 109:19 Eze 26:16 e Eze 18:20 f ver 4
8:1 a Eze 14:1 b Eze 33:31 c Eze 1:1-3
8:2 d Eze 1:4,26-27
8:3 e Eze 3:12 Eze 11:1 f Ex 20:5 Dt 32:16
8:4 g Eze 1:28 h Eze 3:22
8:5 i Ps 78:58 Jer 32:34
8:6 j Eze 5:11
8:10 k Ex 20:4
8:11 l Nu 16:17 m Nu 16:35
8:12 n Ps 10:11 Isa 29:15 Eze 9:9
8:16 o Joel 2:17

a2 Or *saw a fiery figure*

towards the east, they were bowing
down to the sun in the east.[p]
17He said to me, "Have you seen
this, son of man? Is it a trivial matter for the house of Judah to do the
detestable things they are doing
here? Must they also fill the land
with violence[q] and continually
provoke me to anger?[r] Look at
them putting the branch to their
nose! 18Therefore I will deal with
them in anger; I will not look on
them with pity[s] or spare them. Although they shout in my ears, I will
not listen[t] to them."

Idolaters Killed

9 Then I heard him call out in a
loud voice, "Bring the guards
of the city here, each with a weapon
in his hand." 2And I saw six men
coming from the direction of the
upper gate, which faces north, each
with a deadly weapon in his hand.
With them was a man clothed in
linen[a] who had a writing kit at his
side. They came in and stood beside
the bronze altar.
3Now the glory[b] of the God of Israel went up from above the cherubim,[c] where it had been, and
moved to the threshold of the temple. Then the LORD called to the
man clothed in linen who had the
writing kit at his side 4and said to
him, "Go throughout the city of
Jerusalem and put a mark[d] on the
foreheads of those who grieve and
lament[e] over all the detestable
things that are done in it.[f]"
5As I listened, he said to the
others, "Follow him through the
city and kill, without showing
pity[g] or compassion. 6Slaughter
old men, young men and maidens,
women and children, but do not
touch anyone who has the mark.
Begin at my sanctuary." So they began with the elders[h] who were in
front of the temple.[i]
7Then he said to them, "Defile
the temple and fill the courts with
the slain. Go!" So they went out and
began killing throughout the city.
8While they were killing and I was
left alone, I fell face down,[j] crying
out, "Ah, Sovereign LORD! Are you
going to destroy the entire remnant
of Israel in this outpouring of your
wrath on Jerusalem?[k]"
9He answered me, "The sin of the
house of Israel and Judah is exceedingly great; the land is full of
bloodshed and the city is full of injustice.[l] They say, 'The LORD has
forsaken the land; the LORD does
not see.'[m] 10So I will not look on
them with pity[n] or spare them, but
I will bring down on their own
heads what they have done.[o]"
11Then the man in linen with the
writing kit at his side brought back
word, saying, "I have done as you
commanded."

The Glory Departs From the Temple

10 I looked, and I saw the likeness of a throne[a] of sapphire[a][b] above the expanse[c] that
was over the heads of the cherubim. 2The LORD said to the man
clothed in linen,[d] "Go in among the
wheels[e] beneath the cherubim.
Fill[f] your hands with burning
coals from among the cherubim
and scatter them over the city."
And as I watched, he went in.
3Now the cherubim were standing on the south side of the temple
when the man went in, and a cloud
filled the inner court. 4Then the
glory of the LORD[g] rose from
above the cherubim and moved
to the threshold of the temple.
The cloud filled the temple, and
the court was full of the radiance of
the glory of the LORD. 5The sound
of the wings of the cherubim could
be heard as far away as the outer
court, like the voice[h] of God
Almighty[b] when he speaks.
6When the LORD commanded the
man in linen, "Take fire from

8:16 p Dt 4:19; Dt 17:3; Job 31:28; Jer 2:27; Eze 11:1,12
8:17 q Eze 9:9; r Eze 16:26
8:18 s Eze 9:10; Eze 24:14; t Isa 1:15; Jer 11:11; Mic 3:4; Zec 7:13
9:2 a Lev 16:4; Eze 10:2; Rev 15:6
9:3 b Eze 10:4; c Eze 11:22
9:4 d Ex 12:7; 2Co 1:22; Rev 7:3; Rev 9:4; e Ps 119:136; Jer 13:17; Eze 21:6; f Ps 119:53
9:5 g Eze 5:11
9:6 h Eze 8:11-13, 16; i 2Ch 36:17; Jer 25:29; 1Pe 4:17
9:8 j Jos 7:6; k Eze 11:13; Am 7:1-6
9:9 l Eze 22:29; m Job 22:13; Eze 8:12
9:10 n Eze 7:4; Eze 8:18; o Isa 65:6; Eze 11:21
10:1 a Rev 4:2; b Ex 24:10; c Eze 1:22
10:2 d Eze 9:2; e Eze 1:15; f Rev 8:5
10:4 g Eze 1:28; Eze 9:3
10:5 h Job 40:9; Eze 1:24

a1 Or *lapis lazuli* b5 Hebrew *El-Shaddai*

among the wheels, from among the cherubim," the man went in and stood beside a wheel. 7 Then one of the cherubim reached out his hand to the fire that was among them. He took up some of it and put it into the hands of the man in linen, who took it and went out. 8 (Under the wings of the cherubim could be seen what looked like the hands of a man.)[i]

9 I looked, and I saw beside the cherubim four wheels, one beside each of the cherubim; the wheels sparkled like chrysolite.[j] 10 As for their appearance, the four of them looked alike; each was like a wheel intersecting a wheel. 11 As they moved, they would go in any one of the four directions the cherubim faced; the wheels did not turn about[c] as the cherubim went. The cherubim went in whatever direction the head faced, without turning as they went. 12 Their entire bodies, including their backs, their hands and their wings, were completely full of eyes,[k] as were their four wheels.[l] 13 I heard the wheels being called "the whirling wheels". 14 Each of the cherubim[m] had four faces:[n] One face was that of a cherub, the second the face of a man, the third the face of a lion, and the fourth the face of an eagle.[o]

15 Then the cherubim rose upwards. These were the living creatures[p] I had seen by the Kebar River. 16 When the cherubim moved, the wheels beside them moved; and when the cherubim spread their wings to rise from the ground, the wheels did not leave their side. 17 When the cherubim stood still, they also stood still; and when the cherubim rose, they rose with them, because the spirit of the living creatures was in them.[q]

18 Then the glory of the LORD departed from over the threshold of the temple and stopped above the cherubim.[r] 19 While I watched, the cherubim spread their wings and rose from the ground, and as they went, the wheels went with them.[s] They stopped at the entrance to the east gate of the LORD's house, and the glory of the God of Israel was above them.

20 These were the living creatures I had seen beneath the God of Israel by the Kebar River,[t] and I realised that they were cherubim. 21 Each had four faces[u] and four wings,[v] and under their wings was what looked like the hands of a man. 22 Their faces had the same appearance as those I had seen by the Kebar River. Each one went straight ahead.

Judgment on Israel's Leaders

11 Then the Spirit lifted me up and brought me to the gate of the house of the LORD that faces east. There at the entrance to the gate were twenty-five men, and I saw among them Jaazaniah son of Azzur and Pelatiah son of Benaiah, leaders of the people.[a] 2 The LORD said to me, "Son of man, these are the men who are plotting evil and giving wicked advice in this city. 3 They say, 'Will it not soon be time to build houses?[a] This city is a cooking pot,[b] and we are the meat.'[c] 4 Therefore prophesy[d] against them; prophesy, son of man."

5 Then the Spirit of the LORD came upon me, and he told me to say: "This is what the LORD says: That is what you are saying, O house of Israel, but I know what is going through your mind.[e] 6 You have killed many people in this city and filled its streets with the dead.[f]

7 "Therefore this is what the Sovereign LORD says: The bodies you have thrown there are the meat and this city is the pot, but I will drive you out of it.[g] 8 You fear the sword, and the sword is what I will bring against you, declares the Sovereign LORD.[h] 9 I will drive you out of

10:8 *i* Eze 1:8
10:9 *j* Eze 1:15-16; Rev 21:20
10:12 *k* Rev 4:6-8; *l* Eze 1:15-21
10:14 *m* 1Ki 7:36; *n* Eze 1:6; *o* Eze 1:10; Rev 4:7
10:15 *p* Eze 1:3,5
10:17 *q* Eze 1:20-21
10:18 *r* Ps 18:10
10:19 *s* Eze 11:1,22
10:20 *t* Eze 1:1
10:21 *u* Eze 41:18; *v* Eze 1:6
11:1 *a* Eze 8:16; Eze 10:19; Eze 43:4-5
11:3 *b* Jer 1:13; Eze 24:3; *c* ver 7,11
11:4 *d* Eze 3:4,17
11:5 *e* Jer 17:10
11:6 *f* Eze 7:23; Eze 22:6
11:7 *g* Eze 24:3-13; Mic 3:2-3
11:8 *h* Pr 10:24

c11 Or *aside*   a3 Or *This is not the time to build houses.*

the city and hand you over[i] to foreigners and inflict punishment on you.[j] 10You will fall by the sword, and I will execute judgment on you at the borders of Israel.[k] Then you will know that I am the LORD. 11This city will not be a pot[l] for you, nor will you be the meat in it; I will execute judgment on you at the borders of Israel. 12And you will know that I am the LORD, for you have not followed my decrees[m] or kept my laws but have conformed to the standards of the nations around you.[n]"

13Now as I was prophesying, Pelatiah[o] son of Benaiah died. Then I fell face down and cried out in a loud voice, "Ah, Sovereign LORD! Will you completely destroy the remnant of Israel?[p]"

14The word of the LORD came to me: 15"Son of man, your brothers—your brothers who are your blood-relatives[b] and the whole house of Israel—are those of whom the people of Jerusalem have said, 'They are[c] far away from the LORD; this land was given to us as our possession.'[q]

Promised Return of Israel

16"Therefore say: 'This is what the Sovereign LORD says: Although I sent them far away among the nations and scattered them among the countries, yet for a little while I have been a sanctuary[r] for them in the countries where they have gone.'

17"Therefore say: 'This is what the Sovereign LORD says: I will gather you from the nations and bring you back from the countries where you have been scattered, and I will give you back the land of Israel again.'[s]

18"They will return to it and remove all its vile images[t] and detestable idols.[u] 19I will give them an undivided heart[v] and put a new spirit in them; I will remove from them their heart of stone[w] and give them a heart of flesh.[x] 20Then they will follow my decrees and be careful to keep my laws.[y] They will be my people, and I will be their God.[z] 21But as for those whose hearts are devoted to their vile images and detestable idols, I will bring down on their own heads what they have done, declares the Sovereign LORD.[a]"

22Then the cherubim, with the wheels beside them, spread their wings, and the glory of the God of Israel was above them.[b] 23The glory[c] of the LORD went up from within the city and stopped above the mountain[d] east of it. 24The Spirit[e] lifted me up and brought me to the exiles in Babylonia[d] in the vision[f] given by the Spirit of God.

Then the vision I had seen went up from me, 25and I told the exiles everything the LORD had shown me.[g]

The Exile Symbolised

12 The word of the LORD came to me: 2"Son of man, you are living among a rebellious people. They have eyes to see but do not see and ears to hear but do not hear, for they are a rebellious people.[a]

3"Therefore, son of man, pack your belongings for exile and in the daytime, as they watch, set out and go from where you are to another place. Perhaps[b] they will understand,[c] though they are a rebellious house.[d] 4During the daytime, while they watch, bring out your belongings packed for exile. Then in the evening, while they are watching, go out like those who go into exile.[e] 5While they watch, dig through the wall and take your belongings out through it. 6Put them on your shoulder as they are watching and carry them out at dusk.

11:9 i Ps 106:41 j Dt 28:36 Eze 5:8
11:10 k 2Ki 14:25
11:11 l ver 3
11:12 m Lev 18:4 Eze 18:9 n Eze 8:10
11:13 o ver 1 p Eze 9:8
11:15 q Eze 33:24
11:16 r Ps 90:1 Ps 91:9 Isa 8:14
11:17 s Jer 3:18 Jer 24:5-6 Eze 28:25 Eze 34:13
11:18 t Eze 5:11 u Eze 37:23
11:19 v Jer 32:39 w Zec 7:12 x Eze 18:31 Eze 36:26 2Co 3:3
11:20 y Ps 105:45 z Eze 14:11 Eze 36:26-28
11:21 a Eze 9:10 Eze 16:43
11:22 b Eze 10:19
11:23 c Eze 8:4 Eze 10:4 d Zec 14:4
11:24 e Eze 8:3 f 2Co 12:2-4
11:25 g Eze 3:4,11
12:2 a Isa 6:10 Eze 2:6-8 Mt 13:15
12:3 b Jer 36:3 c Jer 26:3 d 2Ti 2:25-26
12:4 e ver 12 Jer 39:4

b15 Or *are in exile with you* (see Septuagint and Syriac) c15 Or *those to whom the people of Jerusalem have said, 'Stay* d24 Or *Chaldea*

Cover your face so that you cannot
see the land, for I have made you a
sign[f] to the house of Israel."
7So I did as I was commanded.[g]
During the day I brought out my
things packed for exile. Then in the
evening I dug through the wall with
my hands. I took my belongings out
at dusk, carrying them on my
shoulders while they watched.
8In the morning the word of the
LORD came to me: 9"Son of man, did
not that rebellious house of Israel
ask you, 'What are you doing?'[h]
10"Say to them, 'This is what the
Sovereign LORD says: This oracle
concerns the prince in Jerusalem
and the whole house of Israel who
are there.' 11Say to them, 'I am a
sign to you.'
"As I have done, so it will be done
to them. They will go into exile as
captives.[i]
12"The prince among them will
put his things on his shoulder at
dusk[j] and leave, and a hole will be
dug in the wall for him to go
through. He will cover his face so
that he cannot see the land.[k] 13I
will spread my net[l] for him, and he
will be caught in my snare;[m] I will
bring him to Babylonia, the land of
the Chaldeans, but he will not see[n]
it, and there he will die.[o] 14I will
scatter to the winds all those
around him—his staff and all his
troops—and I will pursue them
with drawn sword.[p]
15"They will know that I am the
LORD, when I disperse them among
the nations and scatter them
through the countries. 16But I will
spare a few of them from the
sword, famine and plague, so that
in the nations where they go they
may acknowledge all their detestable practices. Then they will know
that I am the LORD.[q]"
17The word of the LORD came to
me: 18"Son of man, tremble as you
eat your food,[r] and shudder in fear
as you drink your water. 19Say to
the people of the land: 'This is what
the Sovereign LORD says about
those living in Jerusalem and in the
land of Israel: They will eat their
food in anxiety and drink their
water in despair, for their land will
be stripped of everything[s] in it because of the violence of all who live
there.[t] 20The inhabited towns will
be laid waste and the land will be
desolate. Then you will know that I
am the LORD.[u]' "
21The word of the LORD came to
me: 22"Son of man, what is this
proverb you have in the land of Israel: 'The days go by and every
vision comes to nothing'?[v] 23Say to
them, 'This is what the Sovereign
LORD says: I am going to put an end
to this proverb, and they will no
longer quote it in Israel.' Say to
them, 'The days are near when
every vision will be fulfilled.[w]
24For there will be no more false
visions or flattering divinations[x]
among the people of Israel. 25But I
the LORD will speak what I will, and
it shall be fulfilled without delay.
For in your days, you rebellious
house, I will fulfil whatever I say,
declares the Sovereign LORD.[y]' "
26The word of the LORD came to
me: 27"Son of man, the house of Israel is saying, 'The vision he sees
is for many years from now, and
he prophesies about the distant
future.'[z]
28"Therefore say to them, 'This is
what the Sovereign LORD says:
None of my words will be delayed
any longer; whatever I say will be
fulfilled, declares the Sovereign
LORD.' "

False Prophets Condemned

13 The word of the LORD came
to me: 2"Son of man, prophesy against the prophets of Israel
who are now prophesying. Say to
those who prophesy out of their
own imagination: 'Hear the word
of the LORD![a] 3This is what the
Sovereign LORD says: Woe to the

12:6 f ver 12; Isa 8:18; Isa 20:3; Eze 4:3; Eze 24:24
12:7 g Eze 24:18; Eze 37:10
12:9 h Eze 17:12; Eze 20:49; Eze 24:19
12:11 i 2Ki 25:7; Jer 15:2; Jer 52:15
12:12 j Jer 39:4; k Jer 52:7
12:13 l Eze 17:20; Eze 19:8; Hos 7:12; m Isa 24:17-18; n Jer 39:7; o Jer 52:11; Eze 17:16
12:14 p 2Ki 25:5; Eze 5:10,12
12:16 q Jer 22:8-9; Eze 6:8-10; Eze 14:22
12:18 r La 5:9; Eze 4:16
12:19 s Eze 6:6-14; Mic 7:13; Zec 7:14; t Eze 4:16; Eze 23:33
12:20 u Isa 7:23-24; Jer 4:7
12:22 v Eze 11:3; Am 6:3; 2Pe 3:4
12:23 w Ps 37:13; Joel 2:1; Zep 1:14
12:24 x Jer 14:14; Eze 13:23; Zec 13:2-4
12:25 y Isa 14:24; Hab 1:5
12:27 z Da 10:14
13:2 a ver 17; Jer 23:16; Jer 37:19

foolish[a] prophets[b] who follow their
own spirit and have seen nothing![c]
4 Your prophets, O Israel, are like
jackals among ruins. 5 You have not
gone up to the breaks in the wall to
repair[d] it for the house of Israel so
that it will stand firm in the battle
on the day of the LORD.[e] 6 Their
visions are false and their divinations a lie. They say, "The LORD declares", when the LORD has not sent
them; yet they expect their words
to be fulfilled.[f] 7 Have you not seen
false visions and uttered lying divinations when you say, "The LORD
declares", though I have not spoken?

8 " 'Therefore this is what the
Sovereign LORD says: Because of
your false words and lying visions,
I am against you, declares the Sovereign LORD. 9 My hand will be
against the prophets who see false
visions and utter lying divinations.
They will not belong to the council
of my people or be listed in the
records[g] of the house of Israel, nor
will they enter the land of Israel.
Then you will know that I am the
Sovereign LORD.[h]

10 " 'Because they lead my people
astray,[i] saying, "Peace", when
there is no peace, and because,
when a flimsy wall is built, they
cover it with whitewash,[j] 11 therefore tell those who cover it with
whitewash that it is going to fall.
Rain will come in torrents, and I
will send hailstones hurtling down,
and violent winds will burst
forth.[k] 12 When the wall collapses,
will people not ask you, "Where is
the whitewash you covered it
with?"

13 " 'Therefore this is what the
Sovereign LORD says: In my wrath
I will unleash a violent wind, and in
my anger hailstones[l] and torrents
of rain will fall with destructive
fury.[m] 14 I will tear down the wall
you have covered with whitewash
and will level it to the ground so
that its foundation[n] will be laid
bare. When it[b] falls,[o] you will be
destroyed in it; and you will know
that I am the LORD. 15 So I will spend
my wrath against the wall and
against those who covered it with
whitewash. I will say to you, "The
wall is gone and so are those who
whitewashed it, 16 those prophets of
Israel who prophesied to Jerusalem and saw visions of peace for
her when there was no peace, declares the Sovereign LORD.[p]" '

17 "Now, son of man, set your face
against the daughters[q] of your
people who prophesy out of their
own imagination. Prophesy against
them[r] 18 and say, 'This is what the
Sovereign LORD says: Woe to the
women who sew magic charms on
all their wrists and make veils of
various lengths for their heads in
order to ensnare people. Will you
ensnare the lives of my people but
preserve your own? 19 You have
profaned[s] me among my people
for a few handfuls of barley and
scraps of bread. By lying to my
people, who listen to lies, you have
killed those who should not have
died and have spared those who
should not live.[t]

20 " 'Therefore this is what the
Sovereign LORD says: I am against
your magic charms with which you
ensnare people like birds and I will
tear them from your arms; I will
set free the people that you ensnare
like birds. 21 I will tear off your
veils and save my people from your
hands, and they will no longer fall
prey to your power. Then you will
know that I am the LORD.[u] 22 Because you disheartened the righteous with your lies, when I had
brought them no grief, and because
you encouraged the wicked not to
turn from their evil ways and so
save their lives,[v] 23 therefore you
will no longer see false visions or
practise divination.[w] I will save
my people from your hands. And
then you will know that I am the
LORD.[x]' "

13:3 *b* La 2:14 *c* Jer 23:25-32
13:5 *d* Isa 58:12; Eze 22:30 *e* Eze 7:19
13:6 *f* Jer 28:15; Eze 22:28
13:9 *g* Jer 17:13 *h* Eze 20:38
13:10 *i* Jer 50:6 *j* Eze 7:25; Eze 22:28
13:11 *k* Eze 38:22
13:13 *l* Rev 11:19; Rev 16:21 *m* Ex 9:25; Isa 30:30
13:14 *n* Mic 1:6 *o* Jer 6:15
13:16 *p* Isa 57:21; Jer 6:14
13:17 *q* Rev 2:20 *r* ver 2
13:19 *s* Eze 20:39; Eze 22:26 *t* Pr 28:21
13:21 *u* Ps 91:3
13:22 *v* Jer 23:14; Eze 33:14-16
13:23 *w* ver 6; Eze 12:24 *x* Mic 3:6

[a] 3 Or *wicked* [b] 14 Or *the city*

Idolaters Condemned

14 Some of the elders of Israel
came to me and sat down in
front of me.[a] 2Then the word of the
LORD came to me: 3"Son of man,
these men have set up idols in their
hearts and put wicked stumbling-
blocks[b] before their faces. Should
I let them enquire of me at all?[c]
4Therefore speak to them and tell
them, 'This is what the Sovereign
LORD says: When any Israelite sets
up idols in his heart and puts a
wicked stumbling-block before his
face and then goes to a prophet, I
the LORD will answer him myself
in keeping with his great idolatry.
5I will do this to recapture the
hearts of the people of Israel, who
have all deserted[d] me for their
idols.'[e]
6"Therefore say to the house of
Israel, 'This is what the Sovereign
LORD says: Repent! Turn from
your idols and renounce all your
detestable practices![f]
7" 'When any Israelite or any
alien[g] living in Israel separates
himself from me and sets up idols
in his heart and puts a wicked
stumbling-block before his face
and then goes to a prophet to enquire of me, I the LORD will answer
him myself. 8I will set my face
against[h] that man and make him
an example and a byword.[i] I will
cut him off from my people. Then
you will know that I am the LORD.
9" 'And if the prophet[j] is enticed[k] to utter a prophecy, I the
LORD have enticed that prophet,
and I will stretch out my hand
against him and destroy him from
among my people Israel.[l] 10They
will bear their guilt—the prophet
will be as guilty as the one who consults him. 11Then the people of
Israel will no longer stray[m] from
me, nor will they defile themselves
any more with all their sins. They
will be my people, and I will be
their God, declares the Sovereign
LORD.[n]' "

14:1 [a] Eze 8:1; Eze 20:1
14:3 [b] ver 7; Eze 7:19 [c] Isa 1:15; Eze 20:31
14:5 [d] Zec 11:8 [e] Jer 2:11
14:6 [f] Isa 2:20; Isa 30:22
14:7 [g] Ex 12:48; Ex 20:10
14:8 [h] Eze 15:7 [i] Eze 5:15
14:9 [j] Jer 14:15 [k] Jer 4:10 [l] 1Ki 22:23
14:11 [m] Eze 48:11 [n] Eze 11:19-20; Eze 37:23
14:13 [o] Lev 26:26 [p] Eze 5:16; Eze 6:14; Eze 15:8
14:14 [q] Ge 6:8 [r] ver 20; Eze 28:3; Da 1:6; Da 6:13 [s] Job 1:1 [t] Job 42:9; Jer 15:1; Eze 18:20
14:15 [u] Eze 5:17 [v] Lev 26:22
14:16 [w] Eze 18:20
14:17 [x] Lev 26:25; Eze 5:12; Eze 21:3-4 [y] Eze 25:13; Zep 1:3
14:19 [z] Eze 7:8 [a] Eze 38:22
14:20 [b] ver 14
14:21 [c] Jer 15:3; Eze 5:17; Eze 33:27; Am 4:6-10; Rev 6:8

Judgment Inescapable

12The word of the LORD came to
me: 13"Son of man, if a country sins
against me by being unfaithful and
I stretch out my hand against it to
cut off its food supply[o] and send
famine upon it and kill its men and
their animals,[p] 14even if these three
men—Noah,[q] Daniel[a][r] and Job[s]—
were in it, they could save only
themselves by their righteousness,[t] declares the Sovereign LORD.
15"Or if I send wild beasts[u]
through that country and they
leave it childless and it becomes
desolate so that no-one can pass
through it because of the beasts,[v]
16as surely as I live, declares the
Sovereign LORD, even if these
three men were in it, they could not
save their own sons or daughters.
They alone would be saved, but the
land would be desolate.[w]
17"Or if I bring a sword[x] against
that country and say, 'Let the
sword pass throughout the land,'
and I kill its men and their animals,[y] 18as surely as I live, declares the Sovereign LORD, even if
these three men were in it, they
could not save their own sons or
daughters. They alone would be
saved.
19"Or if I send a plague into that
land and pour out my wrath[z] upon
it through bloodshed, killing its
men and their animals,[a] 20as
surely as I live, declares the Sovereign LORD, even if Noah, Daniel and
Job were in it, they could save neither son nor daughter. They would
save only themselves by their
righteousness.[b]
21"For this is what the Sovereign
LORD says: How much worse will it
be when I send against Jerusalem
my four dreadful judgments—
sword and famine and wild beasts
and plague—to kill its men and
their animals![c] 22Yet there will be

[a]14 Or *Danel*; the Hebrew spelling may suggest a person other than the prophet Daniel; also in verse 20.

some survivors—sons and daughters who will be brought out of it.[d] They will come to you, and when you see their conduct[e] and their actions, you will be consoled regarding the disaster I have brought upon Jerusalem—every disaster I have brought upon it. 23 You will be consoled when you see their conduct and their actions, for you will know that I have done nothing in it without cause, declares the Sovereign LORD.[f]"

Jerusalem, a Useless Vine

15 The word of the LORD came to me: 2 "Son of man, how is the wood of a vine[a] better than that of a branch on any of the trees in the forest? 3 Is wood ever taken from it to make anything useful? Do they make pegs from it to hang things on? 4 And after it is thrown on the fire as fuel and the fire burns both ends and chars the middle, is it then useful for anything?[b] 5 If it was not useful for anything when it was whole, how much less can it be made into something useful when the fire has burned it and it is charred?

6 "Therefore this is what the Sovereign LORD says: As I have given the wood of the vine among the trees of the forest as fuel for the fire, so will I treat the people living in Jerusalem. 7 I will set my face against[c] them. Although they have come out of the fire, the fire will yet consume them. And when I set my face against them, you will know that I am the LORD.[d] 8 I will make the land desolate[e] because they have been unfaithful,[f] declares the Sovereign LORD."

An Allegory of Unfaithful Jerusalem

16 The word of the LORD came to me: 2 "Son of man, confront Jerusalem with her detestable practices[a] 3 and say, 'This is what the Sovereign LORD says to Jerusalem: Your ancestry[b] and birth were in the land of the Canaanites; your father was an Amorite and your mother a Hittite.[c] 4 On the day you were born[d] your cord was not cut, nor were you washed with water to make you clean, nor were you rubbed with salt or wrapped in cloths. 5 No-one looked on you with pity or had compassion enough to do any of these things for you. Rather, you were thrown out into the open field, for on the day you were born you were despised.

6 " 'Then I passed by and saw you kicking about in your blood, and as you lay there in your blood I said to you, "Live!"[a][e] 7 I made you grow[f] like a plant of the field. You grew up and developed and became the most beautiful of jewels.[b] Your breasts were formed and your hair grew, you who were naked and bare.[g]

8 " 'Later I passed by, and when I looked at you and saw that you were old enough for love, I spread the corner of my garment[h] over you and covered your nakedness. I gave you my solemn oath and entered into a covenant with you, declares the Sovereign LORD, and you became mine.[i]

9 " 'I bathed[c] you with water and washed[j] the blood from you and put ointments on you. 10 I clothed you with an embroidered[k] dress and put leather sandals on you. I dressed you in fine linen[l] and covered you with costly garments.[m] 11 I adorned you with jewellery:[n] I put bracelets[o] on your arms and a necklace[p] around your neck, 12 and I put a ring on your nose,[q] earrings on your ears and a beautiful crown[r] on your head. 13 So you were adorned with gold and silver;

14:22 d Eze 12:16; e Eze 20:43
14:23 f Jer 22:8-9
15:2 a Isa 5:1-7; Jer 2:21; Hos 10:1
15:4 b Eze 19:14; Jn 15:6
15:7 c Ps 34:16; Eze 14:8; d Isa 24:18; Am 9:1-4
15:8 e Eze 14:13; f Eze 17:20
16:2 a Eze 20:4; Eze 22:2
16:3 b Eze 21:30; c ver 45
16:4 d Hos 2:3
16:6 e Ex 19:4
16:7 f Dt 1:10; g Ex 1:7
16:8 h Ru 3:9; i Jer 2:2; Hos 2:7,19-20
16:9 j Ru 3:3
16:10 k Ex 26:36; l Eze 27:16; m ver 18
16:11 n Eze 23:40; o Isa 3:19; Eze 23:42; p Ge 41:42
16:12 q Isa 3:21; r Isa 28:5; Jer 13:18

a6 A few Hebrew manuscripts, Septuagint and Syriac; most Hebrew manuscripts *"Live!" And as you lay there in your blood I said to you, "Live!"*
b7 Or *became mature*
c9 Or *I had bathed*

your clothes were of fine linen and
costly fabric and embroidered
cloth. Your food was fine flour,
honey and olive oil.[s] You became
very beautiful and rose to be a
queen.[t] 14And your fame[u] spread
among the nations on account of
your beauty,[v] because the splendour I had given you made your
beauty perfect, declares the Sovereign LORD.
15" 'But you trusted in your
beauty and used your fame to become a prostitute. You lavished
your favours on anyone who passed
by[w] and your beauty became his.[d][x]
16You took some of your garments
to make gaudy high places,
where you carried on your prostitution.[y] Such things should not
happen, nor should they ever occur.
17You also took the fine jewellery
I gave you, the jewellery made
of my gold and silver, and you made
for yourself male idols and engaged in prostitution with them.[z]
18And you took your embroidered clothes to put on them, and
you offered my oil and incense
before them. 19Also the food I provided for you—the fine flour, olive
oil and honey I gave you to eat—
you offered as fragrant incense before them. That is what happened,
declares the Sovereign LORD.[a]
20" 'And you took your sons and
daughters[b] whom you bore to me[c]
and sacrificed them as food to the
idols. Was your prostitution not
enough?[d] 21You slaughtered my
children and sacrificed them[e] to
the idols.[e] 22In all your detestable
practices and your prostitution you
did not remember the days of your
youth,[f] when you were naked and
bare, kicking about in your blood.[g]
23" 'Woe! Woe to you, declares
the Sovereign LORD. In addition
to all your other wickedness,
24you built a mound for yourself
and made a lofty shrine[h] in every
public square.[i] 25At the head of
every street you built your lofty
shrines and degraded your beauty,
offering your body with increasing promiscuity to anyone who
passed by.[j] 26You engaged in prostitution with the Egyptians, your lustful neighbours, and provoked[k] me to
anger with your increasing promiscuity.[l] 27So I stretched out my
hand[m] against you and reduced
your territory; I gave you over to
the greed of your enemies, the
daughters of the Philistines,[n] who
were shocked by your lewd conduct. 28You engaged in prostitution
with the Assyrians[o] too, because
you were insatiable; and even after
that, you still were not satisfied.
29Then you increased your promiscuity to include Babylonia,[f][p] a
land of merchants, but even with
this you were not satisfied.
30" 'How weak-willed you are, declares the Sovereign LORD, when
you do all these things, acting like
a brazen prostitute![q] 31When you
built your mounds at the head of
every street and made your lofty
shrines[r] in every public square,
you were unlike a prostitute, because you scorned payment.
32" 'You adulterous wife! You
prefer strangers to your own husband! 33Every prostitute receives a
fee, but you give gifts[s] to all your
lovers, bribing them to come to you
from everywhere for your illicit
favours.[t] 34So in your prostitution
you are the opposite of others; no-
one runs after you for your
favours. You are the very opposite,
for you give payment and none is
given to you.
35" 'Therefore, you prostitute,
hear the word of the LORD! 36This is
what the Sovereign LORD says: Because you poured out your wealth[g]
and exposed your nakedness in
your promiscuity with your lovers,
and because of all your detestable
idols, and because you gave them

16:13 s 1Sa 10:1 t Dt 32:13-14 1Ki 4:21
16:14 u 1Ki 10:24 v La 2:15
16:15 w ver 25 x Isa 57:8 Jer 2:20 Eze 23:3 Eze 27:3
16:16 y 2Ki 23:7
16:17 z Eze 7:20
16:19 a Hos 2:8
16:20 b Jer 7:31 c Ex 13:2 d Ps 106:37-38 Isa 57:5 Eze 23:37
16:21 e 2Ki 17:17 Jer 19:5
16:22 f Jer 2:2 Hos 11:1 g ver 6
16:24 h ver 31 Isa 57:7 i Ps 78:58 Jer 2:20 Jer 3:2 Eze 20:28
16:25 j ver 15 Pr 9:14
16:26 k Eze 8:17 l Eze 20:8 Eze 23:19-21
16:27 m Eze 20:33 n 2Ch 28:18
16:28 o 2Ki 16:7
16:29 p Eze 23:14-17
16:30 q Jer 3:3
16:31 r ver 24
16:33 s Isa 30:6 Isa 57:9 t Hos 8:9-10

d15 Most Hebrew manuscripts; one Hebrew manuscript (see some Septuagint manuscripts) *by. Such a thing should not happen* e21 Or *and made them pass through ⌞the fire⌟* f29 Or *Chaldea* g36 Or *lust*

your children's blood,[u] 37 therefore I am going to gather all your lovers, with whom you found pleasure, those you loved as well as those you hated. I will gather them against you from all around and will strip you in front of them, and they will see all your nakedness.[v] 38 I will sentence you to the punishment of women who commit adultery and who shed blood;[w] I will bring upon you the blood vengeance of my wrath and jealous anger.[x] 39 Then I will hand you over to your lovers, and they will tear down your mounds and destroy your lofty shrines. They will strip you of your clothes and take your fine jewellery and leave you naked and bare.[y] 40 They will bring a mob against you, who will stone[z] you and hack you to pieces with their swords. 41 They will burn down[a] your houses and inflict punishment on you in the sight of many women.[b] I will put a stop[c] to your prostitution, and you will no longer pay your lovers. 42 Then my wrath against you will subside and my jealous anger will turn away from you; I will be calm and no longer angry.[d]

43 " 'Because you did not remember[e] the days of your youth but enraged me with all these things, I will surely bring down[f] on your head what you have done, declares the Sovereign LORD. Did you not add lewdness to all your other detestable practices?[g]

44 " 'Everyone who quotes proverbs will quote this proverb about you: "Like mother, like daughter." 45 You are a true daughter of your mother, who despised her husband and her children; and you are a true sister of your sisters, who despised their husbands and their children. Your mother was a Hittite and your father an Amorite.[h] 46 Your older sister was Samaria, who lived to the north of you with her daughters; and your younger sister, who lived to the south of you with her daughters, was Sodom.[i] 47 You not only walked in their ways and copied their detestable practices, but in all your ways you soon became more depraved than they.[j] 48 As surely as I live, declares the Sovereign LORD, your sister Sodom and her daughters never did what you and your daughters have done.[k]

49 " 'Now this was the sin of your sister Sodom:[l] She and her daughters were arrogant,[m] overfed and unconcerned; they did not help the poor and needy.[n] 50 They were haughty and did detestable things before me. Therefore I did away with them as you have seen.[o] 51 Samaria did not commit half the sins you did. You have done more detestable things than they, and have made your sisters seem righteous by all these things you have done.[p] 52 Bear your disgrace, for you have furnished some justification for your sisters. Because your sins were more vile than theirs, they appear more righteous than you. So then, be ashamed and bear your disgrace, for you have made your sisters appear righteous.

53 " 'However, I will restore[q] the fortunes of Sodom and her daughters and of Samaria and her daughters, and your fortunes along with them, 54 so that you may bear your disgrace[r] and be ashamed of all you have done in giving them comfort. 55 And your sisters, Sodom with her daughters and Samaria with her daughters, will return to what they were before; and you and your daughters will return to what you were before.[s] 56 You would not even mention your sister Sodom in the day of your pride, 57 before your wickedness was uncovered. Even so, you are now scorned by the daughters of Edom[h][t] and all her neighbours and the daughters of the Philistines—all those around

16:36 u Jer 19:5; Eze 23:10
16:37 v Jer 13:22
16:38 w Eze 23:45; x Lev 20:10; Eze 23:25
16:39 y Eze 23:26; Hos 2:3
16:40 z Jn 8:5,7
16:41 a Dt 13:16; b Eze 23:10; c Eze 23:27,48
16:42 d Isa 54:9; Eze 5:13; Eze 39:29
16:43 e Ps 78:42; f Eze 22:31; g ver 22; Eze 11:21
16:45 h Eze 23:2
16:46 i Ge 13:10-13; Eze 23:4
16:47 j 2Ki 21:9; Eze 5:7
16:48 k Mt 10:15; Mt 11:23-24
16:49 l Ge 13:13; m Ps 138:6; n Eze 18:7,12,16; Lk 12:16-20
16:50 o Ge 18:20-21; Ge 19:5
16:51 p Jer 3:8-11
16:53 q Isa 19:24-25
16:54 r Jer 2:26; Eze 14:22
16:55 s Mal 3:4
16:57 t 2Ki 16:6

[h] 57 Many Hebrew manuscripts and Syriac; most Hebrew manuscripts, Septuagint and Vulgate *Aram*

you who despise you. 58You will
bear the consequences of your
lewdness and your detestable practices, declares the LORD.[u]
59" 'This is what the Sovereign
LORD says: I will deal with you as
you deserve, because you have despised my oath by breaking the
covenant.[v] 60Yet I will remember
the covenant I made with you in the
days of your youth, and I will establish an everlasting covenant[w] with
you. 61Then you will remember
your ways and be ashamed[x] when
you receive your sisters, both those
who are older than you and those
who are younger. I will give them
to you as daughters, but not on the
basis of my covenant with you. 62So
I will establish my covenant with
you, and you will know that I am the
LORD.[y] 63Then, when I make atonement[z] for you for all you have
done, you will remember and be
ashamed and never again open
your mouth[a] because of your humiliation, declares the Sovereign
LORD.[b]' "

Two Eagles and a Vine

17 The word of the LORD came
to me: 2"Son of man, set
forth an allegory and tell the house
of Israel a parable.[a] 3Say to them,
'This is what the Sovereign LORD
says: A great eagle[b] with powerful
wings, long feathers and full plumage of varied colours came to
Lebanon.[c] Taking hold of the top
of a cedar, 4he broke off its topmost
shoot and carried it away to a land
of merchants, where he planted it
in a city of traders.
5" 'He took some of the seed of
your land and put it in fertile soil.
He planted it like a willow by abundant water,[d] 6and it sprouted and
became a low, spreading vine. Its
branches turned towards him, but
its roots remained under it. So it
became a vine and produced
branches and put out leafy boughs.
7" 'But there was another great

16:58
u Eze 23:49
16:59
v Eze 17:19
16:60
w Jer 32:40
Eze 37:26
16:61
x Eze 20:43
16:62
y Jer 24:7
Eze 20:37, 43-44
Hos 2:19-20
16:63
z Ps 65:3
Ps 79:9
a Ro 3:19
b Ps 39:9
Da 9:7-8
17:2
a Eze 20:49
17:3
b Hos 8:1
c Jer 22:23
17:5
d Dt 8:7-9
Isa 44:4
17:7
e Eze 31:4
17:10
f Hos 13:15
17:12
g Eze 12:9
h 2Ki 24:15
i Eze 24:19
17:13
j 2Ch 36:13
17:14
k Eze 29:14
17:15
l Jer 52:3
m Dt 17:16
n Jer 34:3
Jer 38:18
17:16
o Jer 52:11
Eze 12:13
p 2Ki 24:17
17:17
q Jer 37:7
r Eze 4:2
s Isa 36:6
Jer 37:5
Eze 29:6-7

eagle with powerful wings and full
plumage. The vine now sent out its
roots towards him from the plot
where it was planted and stretched
out its branches to him for water.[e]
8It had been planted in good soil by
abundant water so that it would
produce branches, bear fruit and
become a splendid vine.'
9"Say to them, 'This is what the
Sovereign LORD says: Will it
thrive? Will it not be uprooted and
stripped of its fruit so that it withers? All its new growth will wither.
It will not take a strong arm or
many people to pull it up by the
roots. 10Even if it[f] is transplanted,
will it thrive? Will it not wither
completely when the east wind
strikes it—wither away in the plot
where it grew?' "
11Then the word of the LORD
came to me: 12"Say to this rebellious house, 'Do you not know what
these things mean?[g]' Say to them:
'The king of Babylon went to Jerusalem and carried off her king and
her nobles,[h] bringing them back
with him to Babylon.[i] 13Then he
took a member of the royal family
and made a treaty with him, putting
him under oath.[j] He also carried
away the leading men of the land,
14so that the kingdom would be
brought low,[k] unable to rise again,
surviving only by keeping his
treaty. 15But the king rebelled[l]
against him by sending his envoys
to Egypt to get horses and a large
army.[m] Will he succeed? Will he
who does such things escape? Will
he break the treaty and yet escape?[n]
16" 'As surely as I live, declares
the Sovereign LORD, he shall die[o]
in Babylon, in the land of the king
who put him on the throne, whose
oath he despised and whose treaty
he broke.[p] 17Pharaoh[q] with his
mighty army and great horde will
be of no help to him in war, when
ramps[r] are built and siege works
erected to destroy many lives.[s]
18He despised the oath by breaking

the covenant. Because he had given
his hand in pledge[t] and yet did all
these things, he shall not escape.
19" 'Therefore this is what the
Sovereign LORD says: As surely as
I live, I will bring down on his head
my oath that he despised and my
covenant that he broke.[u] 20I will
spread my net[v] for him, and he will
be caught in my snare. I will bring
him to Babylon and execute judgment[w] upon him there because he
was unfaithful to me. 21All his fleeing troops will fall by the sword,[x]
and the survivors[y] will be scattered to the winds.[z] Then you will
know that I the LORD have spoken.
22" 'This is what the Sovereign
LORD says: I myself will take a
shoot from the very top of a cedar
and plant it; I will break off a tender sprig from its topmost shoots
and plant it on a high and lofty
mountain.[a] 23On the mountain
heights of Israel I will plant it; it
will produce branches and bear
fruit and become a splendid cedar.
Birds of every kind will nest in it;
they will find shelter in the shade
of its branches.[b] 24All the trees of
the field[c] will know that I the LORD
bring down the tall tree and make
the low tree grow tall. I dry up the
green tree and make the dry tree
flourish.
" 'I the LORD have spoken, and I
will do it.[d]' "

The Soul Who Sins Will Die

18 The word of the LORD came
to me: 2"What do you peo-
ple mean by quoting this proverb
about the land of Israel:

" 'The fathers eat sour grapes,
and the children's teeth are
set on edge'?[a]

3"As surely as I live, declares the
Sovereign LORD, you will no longer
quote this proverb in Israel. 4For
every living soul belongs to me, the
father as well as the son—both
alike belong to me. The soul who
sins is the one who will die.[b]

5"Suppose there is a righteous
man
who does what is just and
right.
6He does not eat at the
mountain[c] shrines
or look to the idols[d] of the
house of Israel.
He does not defile his
neighbour's wife
or lie with a woman during
her period.
7He does not oppress[e] anyone,
but returns what he took in
pledge[f] for a loan.
He does not commit robbery,
but gives his food to the
hungry
and provides clothing for the
naked.[g]
8He does not lend at usury
or take excessive interest.[a][h]
He withholds his hand from
doing wrong
and judges fairly[i] between
man and man.
9He follows my decrees
and faithfully keeps my laws.
That man is righteous;[j]
he will surely live,[k]
declares the Sovereign LORD.

10"Suppose he has a violent son,
who sheds blood[l] or does any of
these other things[b] 11(though the
father has done none of them):

"He eats at the mountain
shrines.
He defiles his neighbour's wife.
12He oppresses the poor[m] and
needy.
He commits robbery.
He does not return what he took
in pledge.
He looks to the idols.
He does detestable things.[n]
13He lends at usury and takes
excessive interest.[o]

[a]8 Or *take interest*; similarly in verses 13 and 17
[b]10 Or *things to a brother*

17:18 t 1Ch 29:24
17:19 u Eze 16:59
17:20 v Eze 12:13; Eze 32:3; w Jer 2:35; Eze 20:36
17:21 x Eze 12:14; y 2Ki 25:11; z 2Ki 25:5
17:22 a Jer 23:5; Eze 20:40; Eze 36:1,36; Eze 37:22
17:23 b Ps 92:12; Isa 2:2; Eze 31:6; Da 4:12; Hos 14:5-7; Mt 13:32
17:24 c Ps 96:12; d Eze 19:12; Eze 21:26; Eze 22:14; Am 9:11
18:2 a Isa 3:15; Jer 31:29; La 5:7
18:4 b ver 20; Isa 42:5; Ro 6:23
18:6 c Eze 22:9; d Dt 4:19; Eze 6:13; Eze 20:24
18:7 e Ex 22:21; f Ex 22:26; Dt 24:12; g Dt 15:11; Mt 25:36
18:8 h Ex 22:25; Lev 25:35-37; Dt 23:19-20; i Zec 8:16
18:9 j Hab 2:4; k Lev 18:5; Eze 20:11; Am 5:4
18:10 l Ex 21:12
18:12 m Am 4:1; n 2Ki 21:11; Isa 59:6-7; Jer 22:17; Eze 8:6,17
18:13 o Ex 22:25

Will such a man live? He will not! Because he has done all these detestable things, he will surely be put to death and his blood will be on his own head.[p]

14“But suppose this son has a son who sees all the sins his father commits, and though he sees them, he does not do such things:[q]

15“He does not eat at the
 mountain shrines
 or look to the idols of the
 house of Israel.
He does not defile his
 neighbour’s wife.
16He does not oppress anyone
 or require a pledge for a loan.
He does not commit robbery,
 but gives his food to the
 hungry
 and provides clothing for the
 naked.[r]
17He withholds his hand from
 sin[c]
 and takes no usury or
 excessive interest.
He keeps my laws and follows
 my decrees.

He will not die for his father’s sin; he will surely live. 18But his father will die for his own sin, because he practised extortion, robbed his brother and did what was wrong among his people.

19“Yet you ask, ‘Why does the son not share the guilt of his father?’ Since the son has done what is just and right and has been careful to keep all my decrees, he will surely live.[s] 20The soul who sins is the one who will die. The son will not share the guilt of the father, nor will the father share the guilt of the son. The righteousness of the righteous man will be credited to him, and the wickedness of the wicked will be charged against him.[t]

21“But if a wicked man turns away from all the sins he has committed and keeps all my decrees and does what is just and right, he will surely live; he will not die.[u] 22None of the offences he has committed will be remembered against him. Because of the righteous things he has done, he will live.[v] 23Do I take any pleasure in the death of the wicked? declares the Sovereign LORD. Rather, am I not pleased[w] when they turn from their ways and live?[x]

24“But if a righteous man turns from his righteousness and commits sin and does the same detestable things the wicked man does, will he live? None of the righteous things he has done will be remembered. Because of the unfaithfulness he is guilty of and because of the sins he has committed, he will die.[y]

25“Yet you say, ‘The way of the Lord is not just.’ Hear, O house of Israel: Is my way unjust?[z] Is it not your ways that are unjust? 26If a righteous man turns from his righteousness and commits sin, he will die for it; because of the sin he has committed he will die. 27But if a wicked man turns away from the wickedness he has committed and does what is just and right, he will save his life.[a] 28Because he considers all the offences he has committed and turns away from them, he will surely live; he will not die. 29Yet the house of Israel says, ‘The way of the Lord is not just.’ Are my ways unjust, O house of Israel? Is it not your ways that are unjust?

30“Therefore, O house of Israel, I will judge you, each one according to his ways, declares the Sovereign LORD. Repent![b] Turn away from all your offences; then sin will not be your downfall.[c] 31Rid yourselves of all the offences you have committed, and get a new heart[d] and a new spirit. Why will you die, O house of Israel?[e] 32For I take no pleasure in the death of anyone, declares the Sovereign LORD. Repent and live![f]

18:13 p Eze 33:4-5
18:14 q 2Ch 34:21; Pr 23:24
18:16 r Ps 41:1; Isa 58:10
18:19 s Ex 20:5; Dt 5:9; Jer 15:4; Zec 1:3-6
18:20 t Dt 24:16; 1Ki 8:32; 2Ki 14:6; Isa 3:11; Mt 16:27; Ro 2:9
18:21 u Eze 33:12,19
18:22 v Ps 18:20-24; Isa 43:25; Mic 7:19
18:23 w Ps 147:11; x Eze 33:11; 1Ti 2:4
18:24 y 1Sa 15:11; 2Ch 24:17-20; Eze 3:20; Eze 20:27; 2Pe 2:20-22
18:25 z Ge 18:25; Jer 12:1; Eze 33:17; Zep 3:5; Mal 2:17; Mal 3:13-15
18:27 a Isa 1:18
18:30 b Mt 3:2; c Eze 7:3; Eze 33:20; Hos 12:6
18:31 d Ps 51:10; e Isa 1:16-17; Eze 11:19; Eze 36:26
18:32 f Eze 33:11

c17 Septuagint (see also verse 8); Hebrew *from the poor*

A Lament for Israel's Princes

19 "Take up a lament[a] concerning the princes[b] of Israel 2 and say:

" 'What a lioness was your
    mother
  among the lions!
She lay down among the young
    lions
  and reared her cubs.
3 She brought up one of her cubs,
  and he became a strong lion.
He learned to tear the prey
  and he devoured men.
4 The nations heard about him,
  and he was trapped in their
    pit.
They led him with hooks
  to the land of Egypt.[c]

5 " 'When she saw her hope
    unfulfilled,
  her expectation gone,
she took another of her cubs
  and made him a strong lion.[d]
6 He prowled among the lions,
  for he was now a strong lion.
He learned to tear the prey
  and he devoured men.[e]
7 He broke down[a] their
    strongholds
  and devastated[f] their towns.
The land and all who were in it
  were terrified by his roaring.
8 Then the nations[g] came against
    him,
  those from regions round
    about.
They spread their net for him,
  and he was trapped in their
    pit.[h]
9 With hooks they pulled him into
    a cage
  and brought him to the king of
    Babylon.[i]
They put him in prison,
  so his roar was heard no
    longer
  on the mountains of Israel.[j]

10 " 'Your mother was like a vine
    in your vineyard[b]
  planted by the water;
it was fruitful and full of
    branches
  because of abundant water.[k]
11 Its branches were strong,
  fit for a ruler's sceptre.
It towered high
  above the thick foliage,
conspicuous for its height
  and for its many branches.[l]
12 But it was uprooted[m] in fury
  and thrown to the ground.
The east wind made it shrivel,
  it was stripped of its fruit;
its strong branches withered
  and fire consumed them.[n]
13 Now it is planted in the
    desert,[o]
  in a dry and thirsty land.[p]
14 Fire spread from one of its
    main[c] branches
  and consumed[q] its fruit.
No strong branch is left on it
  fit for a ruler's sceptre.'[r]

This is a lament and is to be used as a lament."

Rebellious Israel

20 In the seventh year, in the fifth month on the tenth day, some of the elders of Israel came to enquire of the LORD, and they sat down in front of me.[a]

2 Then the word of the LORD came to me: 3 "Son of man, speak to the elders of Israel and say to them, 'This is what the Sovereign LORD says: Have you come to enquire[b] of me? As surely as I live, I will not let you enquire of me, declares the Sovereign LORD.[c]'

4 "Will you judge them? Will you judge them, son of man? Then confront them with the detestable practices of their fathers[d] 5 and say to them: 'This is what the Sovereign LORD says: On the day I chose[e] Israel, I swore with uplifted hand to the descendants of the house of Jacob and revealed

19:1 *a* Eze 26:17; Eze 27:2,32 *b* 2Ki 24:6
19:4 *c* 2Ki 23:33-34; 2Ch 36:4
19:5 *d* 2Ki 23:34
19:6 *e* 2Ki 24:9; 2Ch 36:9
19:7 *f* Eze 30:12
19:8 *g* 2Ki 24:2 *h* 2Ki 24:11
19:9 *i* 2Ch 36:6 *j* 2Ki 24:15
19:10 *k* Ps 80:8-11
19:11 *l* Eze 31:3; Da 4:11
19:12 *m* Eze 17:10 *n* Isa 27:11; Eze 28:17; Hos 13:15
19:13 *o* Eze 20:35 *p* Hos 2:3
19:14 *q* Eze 20:47 *r* Eze 15:4
20:1 *a* Eze 8:1
20:3 *b* Eze 14:3 *c* Mic 3:7
20:4 *d* Eze 16:2; Eze 22:2; Mt 23:32
20:5 *e* Dt 7:6

[a]7 Targum (see Septuagint); Hebrew *He knew*
[b]10 Two Hebrew manuscripts; most Hebrew manuscripts *your blood* [c]14 Or *from under its*

myself to them in Egypt. With uplifted hand I said to them, "I am the LORD your God.[f]" 6 On that day I swore to them that I would bring them out of Egypt into a land I had searched out for them, a land flowing with milk and honey,[g] the most beautiful of all lands.[h] 7 And I said to them, "Each of you, get rid of the vile images[i] you have set your eyes on, and do not defile yourselves with the idols of Egypt. I am the LORD your God.[j]"

8 " 'But they rebelled against me and would not listen to me; they did not get rid of the vile images they had set their eyes on, nor did they forsake the idols of Egypt.[k] So I said I would pour out my wrath on them and spend my anger against them in Egypt.[l] 9 But for the sake of my name I did what would keep it from being profaned in the eyes of the nations they lived among and in whose sight I had revealed myself to the Israelites by bringing them out of Egypt.[m] 10 Therefore I led them out of Egypt and brought them into the desert.[n] 11 I gave them my decrees and made known to them my laws, for the man who obeys them will live by them.[o] 12 Also I gave them my Sabbaths as a sign[p] between us, so they would know that I the LORD made them holy.

13 " 'Yet the people of Israel rebelled[q] against me in the desert. They did not follow my decrees but rejected my laws—although the man who obeys them will live by them—and they utterly desecrated my Sabbaths. So I said I would pour out my wrath[r] on them and destroy them in the desert.[s] 14 But for the sake of my name I did what would keep it from being profaned in the eyes of the nations in whose sight I had brought them out.[t] 15 Also with uplifted hand I swore to them in the desert that I would not bring them into the land I had given them—a land flowing with milk and honey, most beautiful of all lands[u]—16 because they rejected my laws and did not follow my decrees and desecrated my Sabbaths. For their hearts[v] were devoted to their idols.[w] 17 Yet I looked on them with pity and did not destroy them or put an end to them in the desert. 18 I said to their children in the desert, "Do not follow the statutes of your fathers[x] or keep their laws or defile yourselves with their idols. 19 I am the LORD your God;[y] follow my decrees and be careful to keep my laws.[z] 20 Keep my Sabbaths holy, that they may be a sign between us. Then you will know that I am the LORD your God.[a]"

21 " 'But the children rebelled against me: They did not follow my decrees, they were not careful to keep my laws—although the man who obeys them will live by them—and they desecrated my Sabbaths. So I said I would pour out my wrath on them and spend my anger against them in the desert. 22 But I withheld[b] my hand, and for the sake of my name I did what would keep it from being profaned in the eyes of the nations in whose sight I had brought them out. 23 Also with uplifted hand I swore to them in the desert that I would disperse them among the nations and scatter[c] them through the countries, 24 because they had not obeyed my laws but had rejected my decrees and desecrated my Sabbaths,[d] and their eyes ⌊lusted⌋ after[e] their fathers' idols.[f] 25 I also gave them over[g] to statutes that were not good and laws they could not live by;[h] 26 I let them become defiled through their gifts—the sacrifice of every firstborn[a]—that I might fill them with horror so that they would know that I am the LORD.[i]'

27 "Therefore, son of man, speak to the people of Israel and say to them, 'This is what the Sovereign LORD says: In this also your fathers

20:5 f Ex 6:7
20:6 g Ex 3:8; Jer 32:22 h Dt 8:7; Ps 48:2; Da 8:9
20:7 i Ex 20:4 j Ex 20:2; Lev 18:3; Dt 29:18
20:8 k Eze 7:8 l Isa 63:10
20:9 m Eze 36:22; Eze 39:7
20:10 n Ex 13:18
20:11 o Lev 18:5; Dt 4:7-8; Ro 10:5
20:12 p Ex 31:13
20:13 q Ps 78:40 r Dt 9:8 s Nu 14:29; Ps 95:8-10; Isa 56:6
20:14 t Eze 36:23
20:15 u Ps 95:11; Ps 106:26
20:16 v Nu 15:39 w Am 5:26
20:18 x Zec 1:4
20:19 y Ex 20:2 z Dt 5:32-33; Dt 6:1-2; Dt 8:1; Dt 11:1; Dt 12:1
20:20 a Jer 17:22
20:22 b Ps 78:38
20:23 c Lev 26:33; Dt 28:64
20:24 d ver 13 e Eze 6:9 f ver 16
20:25 g Ps 81:12 h 2Th 2:11
20:26 i 2Ki 17:17

a26 Or—*making every firstborn pass through ⌊the fire⌋*

blasphemed[j] me by forsaking
me:[k] 28 When I brought them into
the land[l] I had sworn to give them
and they saw any high hill or any
leafy tree, there they offered their
sacrifices, made offerings that
provoked me to anger, presented
their fragrant incense and poured
out their drink offerings.[m] 29 Then I
said to them: What is this high
place you go to?' " (It is called Bamah[b] to this day.)

Judgment and Restoration

30 "Therefore say to the house of
Israel: 'This is what the Sovereign
LORD says: Will you defile yourselves[n] the way your fathers did
and lust after their vile images?[o]
31 When you offer your gifts—the
sacrifice of your sons[p] in[c] the
fire—you continue to defile yourselves with all your idols to this
day. Am I to let you enquire of me,
O house of Israel? As surely as I
live, declares the Sovereign LORD, I
will not let you enquire of me.[q]
32 " 'You say, "We want to be like
the nations, like the peoples of the
world, who serve wood and stone."
But what you have in mind will
never happen. 33 As surely as I live,
declares the Sovereign LORD, I will
rule over you with a mighty hand
and an outstretched arm and with
outpoured wrath.[r] 34 I will bring
you from the nations[s] and gather
you from the countries where you
have been scattered—with a
mighty hand and an outstretched
arm and with outpoured wrath.[t]
35 I will bring you into the desert of
the nations and there, face to face,
I will execute judgment[u] upon
you. 36 As I judged your fathers in
the desert of the land of Egypt, so
I will judge you, declares the Sovereign LORD.[v] 37 I will take note of
you as you pass under my rod,[w]
and I will bring you into the bond of
the covenant.[x] 38 I will purge[y] you
of those who revolt and rebel
against me. Although I will bring
them out of the land where they are
living, yet they will not enter the
land of Israel. Then you will know
that I am the LORD.[z]
39 " 'As for you, O house of Israel,
this is what the Sovereign LORD
says: Go and serve your idols,[a]
every one of you! But afterwards
you will surely listen to me and no
longer profane my holy name with
your gifts and idols.[b] 40 For on my
holy mountain, the high mountain
of Israel, declares the Sovereign
LORD, there in the land the entire
house of Israel will serve me, and
there I will accept them. There I
will require your offerings[c] and
your choice gifts,[d] along with all
your holy sacrifices.[d] 41 I will accept you as fragrant incense when
I bring you out from the nations
and gather you from the countries
where you have been scattered,
and I will show myself holy[e]
among you in the sight of the nations.[f] 42 Then you will know that I
am the LORD,[g] when I bring you
into the land of Israel,[h] the land I
had sworn with uplifted hand to
give to your fathers. 43 There you
will remember your conduct and
all the actions by which you have
defiled yourselves, and you will
loathe yourselves for all the evil
you have done.[i] 44 You will know
that I am the LORD, when I deal
with you for my name's sake[j] and
not according to your evil ways and
your corrupt practices, O house
of Israel, declares the Sovereign
LORD.[k]' "

Prophecy Against the South

45 The word of the LORD came to
me: 46 "Son of man, set your face
towards the south; preach against
the south and prophesy against[l]
the forest of the southland.[m] 47 Say
to the southern forest: 'Hear the
word of the LORD. This is what the

20:27 *j* Ro 2:24 *k* Eze 18:24
20:28 *l* Ps 78:55,58 *m* Eze 6:13
20:30 *n* ver 43 *o* Jer 16:12
20:31 *p* Eze 16:20 *q* Ps 106:37-39 Jer 7:31
20:33 *r* Jer 21:5
20:34 *s* 2Co 6:17* *t* Isa 27:12-13 Jer 44:6 La 2:4
20:35 *u* Jer 2:35
20:36 *v* Nu 11:1-35 1Co 10:5-10
20:37 *w* Lev 27:32 Jer 33:13 *x* Eze 16:62
20:38 *y* Eze 34:17-22 Am 9:9-10 *z* Ps 95:11 Jer 44:14 Eze 13:9 Mal 3:3 Heb 4:3
20:39 *a* Jer 44:25 *b* Isa 1:13 Eze 43:7 Am 4:4
20:40 *c* Isa 60:7 *d* Isa 56:7 Mal 3:4
20:41 *e* Eze 28:25 Eze 36:23 *f* Eze 11:17
20:42 *g* Eze 38:23 *h* Eze 34:13 Eze 36:24
20:43 *i* Eze 6:9 Eze 16:61 Hos 5:15
20:44 *j* Eze 36:22 *k* Eze 24:24
20:46 *l* Eze 21:2 Am 7:16 *m* Isa 30:6 Jer 13:19

b29 *Bamah* means *high place.* **c**31 Or—*making your sons pass through* **d**40 Or *and the gifts of your firstfruits*

Sovereign LORD says: I am about to
set fire to you, and it will consume
all your trees, both green and dry.
The blazing flame will not be
quenched, and every face from
south to north will be scorched by
it.[n] 48Everyone will see that I
the LORD have kindled it; it will not
be quenched.[o]' "
49Then I said, "Ah, Sovereign
LORD! They are saying of me, 'Isn't
he just telling parables?[p]' "

Babylon, God's Sword of Judgment

21 The word of the LORD came
to me: 2"Son of man, set
your face against Jerusalem and
preach against the sanctuary.
Prophesy against[a] the land of Israel 3and say to her: 'This is what
the LORD says: I am against you.[b]
I will draw my sword from its scabbard and cut off from you both the
righteous and the wicked.[c] 4Be-
cause I am going to cut off the
righteous and the wicked, my
sword will be unsheathed against
everyone from south to north.[d]
5Then all people will know that I
the LORD have drawn my sword
from its scabbard; it will not return[e] again.'[f]
6"Therefore groan, son of man!
Groan before them with broken
heart and bitter grief.[g] 7And when
they ask you, 'Why are you groaning?' you shall say, 'Because of the
news that is coming. Every heart
will melt and every hand go limp;[h]
every spirit will become faint and
every knee become as weak as
water.' It is coming! It will surely
take place, declares the Sovereign
LORD."
8The word of the LORD came to
me: 9"Son of man, prophesy and
say, 'This is what the Lord says:

" 'A sword, a sword,
sharpened and polished—
10sharpened for the slaughter,[i]
polished to flash like
lightning!

20:47 n Isa 9:18-19 Isa 13:8 Jer 21:14
20:48 o Jer 7:20
20:49 p Mt 13:13 Jn 16:25
21:2 a Eze 20:46
21:3 b Jer 21:13 c ver 9-11 Job 9:22
21:4 d Eze 20:47
21:5 e ver 30 f Na 1:9
21:6 g Isa 22:4
21:7 h Eze 22:14 Eze 7:17
21:10 i Ps 110:5-6 Isa 34:5-6
21:11 j Jer 46:4
21:12 k Jer 31:19
21:14 l Nu 24:10 m Eze 6:11 Eze 30:24
21:15 n 2Sa 17:10 o Ps 22:14
21:17 p ver 14 Eze 22:13 q Eze 5:13

" 'Shall we rejoice in the sceptre
of my son ⌞Judah⌟? The sword despises every such stick.

11" 'The sword is appointed to be
polished,[j]
to be grasped with the hand;
it is sharpened and polished,
made ready for the hand of
the slayer.
12Cry out and wail, son of man,
for it is against my people;
it is against all the princes of
Israel.
They are thrown to the sword
along with my people.
Therefore beat your breast.[k]

13" 'Testing will surely come.
And what if the sceptre ⌞of Judah⌟,
which the sword despises, does not
continue? declares the Sovereign
LORD.'

14"So then, son of man, prophesy
and strike your hands[l]
together.
Let the sword strike twice,
even three times.
It is a sword for slaughter—
a sword for great slaughter,
closing in on them from every
side.[m]
15So that hearts may melt[n]
and the fallen be many,
I have stationed the sword for
slaughter[a]
at all their gates.
Oh! It is made to flash like
lightning,
it is grasped for slaughter.[o]
16O sword, slash to the right,
then to the left,
wherever your blade is turned.
17I too will strike my hands[p]
together,
and my wrath[q] will subside.
I the LORD have spoken."

18The word of the LORD came to
me: 19"Son of man, mark out two
roads for the sword of the king of
Babylon to take, both starting from

[a]15 Septuagint; the meaning of the Hebrew for this word is uncertain.

the same country. Make a sign-
post where the road branches off to
the city. 20Mark out one road for
the sword to come against Rabbah
of the Ammonites[r] and another
against Judah and fortified Jerusalem. 21For the king of Babylon
will stop at the fork in the road, at
the junction of the two roads, to
seek an omen: He will cast lots[s]
with arrows, he will consult his
idols, he will examine the liver.[t]
22Into his right hand will come the
lot for Jerusalem, where he is to set
up battering-rams, to give the command to slaughter, to sound the
battle cry, to set battering-rams
against the gates, to build a ramp
and to erect siege works.[u] 23It will
seem like a false omen to those who
have sworn allegiance to him, but
he will remind[v] them of their guilt
and take them captive.

24"Therefore this is what the Sovereign LORD says: 'Because you
people have brought to mind your
guilt by your open rebellion, revealing your sins in all that you
do—because you have done this,
you will be taken captive.

25" 'O profane and wicked prince
of Israel, whose day has come,
whose time of punishment has
reached its climax,[w] 26this is what
the Sovereign LORD says: Take off
the turban, remove the crown.[x] It
will not be as it was: The lowly will
be exalted and the exalted will be
brought low.[y] 27A ruin! A ruin! I
will make it a ruin! It will not be restored until he comes to whom it
rightfully belongs; to him I will
give it.'[z]

28"And you, son of man, prophesy
and say, 'This is what the Sovereign
LORD says about the Ammonites[a]
and their insults:

" 'A sword,[b] a sword,
drawn for the slaughter,
polished to consume
and to flash like lightning!
29Despite false visions concerning
you
and lying divinations about
you,
it will be laid on the necks
of the wicked who are to be
slain,
whose day has come,
whose time of punishment has
reached its climax.[c]
30Return the sword to its
scabbard.[d]
In the place where you were
created,
in the land of your ancestry,[e]
I will judge you.
31I will pour out my wrath upon
you
and breathe out my fiery
anger[f] against you;
I will hand you over to brutal
men,
men skilled in destruction.[g]
32You will be fuel for the fire,[h]
your blood will be shed in
your land,
you will be remembered[i] no
more;
for I the LORD have spoken.' "

Jerusalem's Sins

22 The word of the LORD came
to me: 2"Son of man, will
you judge her? Will you judge this
city of bloodshed?[a] Then confront
her with all her detestable practices[b] 3and say: 'This is what the
Sovereign LORD says: O city that
brings on herself doom by shedding blood[c] in her midst and defiles herself by making idols, 4you
have become guilty because of the
blood you have shed[d] and have become defiled by the idols you have
made. You have brought your days
to a close, and the end of your years
has come.[e] Therefore I will make
you an object of scorn to the nations and a laughing-stock to all the
countries.[f] 5Those who are near
and those who are far away will
mock you, O infamous city, full of
turmoil.

6" 'See how each of the princes of
Israel who are in you uses his

21:20 r Dt 3:11; Jer 49:2; Am 1:14
21:21 s Pr 16:33; t Nu 22:7; Nu 23:23
21:22 u Eze 4:2; Eze 26:9
21:23 v Nu 5:15
21:25 w Eze 35:5
21:26 x Jer 13:18; y Ps 75:7; Eze 17:24
21:27 z Ps 2:6; Jer 23:5-6; Eze 37:24; Hag 2:21-22
21:28 a Zep 2:8; b Jer 12:12
21:29 c ver 25; Eze 22:28; Eze 35:5
21:30 d Jer 47:6; e Eze 16:3
21:31 f Eze 22:20-21; g Jer 51:20-23
21:32 h Mal 4:1; i Eze 25:10
22:2 a Eze 24:6,9; Na 3:1; b Eze 16:2
22:3 c ver 6,13,27; Eze 23:37,45
22:4 d 2Ki 21:16; e Eze 21:25; f Eze 5:14

power to shed blood.[g] 7 In you they have treated father and mother with contempt;[h] in you they have oppressed the alien and ill-treated the fatherless and the widow.[i] 8 You have despised my holy things and desecrated my Sabbaths.[j] 9 In you are slanderous men[k] bent on shedding blood; in you are those who eat at the mountain shrines[l] and commit lewd acts.[m] 10 In you are those who dishonour their fathers' bed; in you are those who violate women during their period, when they are ceremonially unclean.[n] 11 In you one man commits a detestable offence with his neighbour's wife, another shamefully defiles his daughter-in-law,[o] and another violates his sister,[p] his own father's daughter. 12 In you men accept bribes[q] to shed blood; you take usury and excessive interest[a] and make unjust gain from your neighbours[r] by extortion. And you have forgotten me, declares the Sovereign LORD.

13 " 'I will surely strike my hands[s] together at the unjust gain[t] you have made and at the blood[u] you have shed in your midst. 14 Will your courage endure or your hands be strong in the day I deal with you? I the LORD have spoken,[v] and I will do it.[w] 15 I will disperse you among the nations and scatter[x] you through the countries; and I will put an end to your uncleanness.[y] 16 When you have been defiled[b] in the eyes of the nations, you will know that I am the LORD.' "

17 Then the word of the LORD came to me: 18 "Son of man, the house of Israel has become dross[z] to me; all of them are the copper, tin, iron and lead left inside a furnace. They are but the dross of silver.[a] 19 Therefore this is what the Sovereign LORD says: 'Because you have all become dross, I will gather you into Jerusalem. 20 As men gather silver, copper, iron, lead and tin into a furnace to melt it with a fiery blast, so will I gather you in my anger and my wrath and put you inside the city and melt you.[b] 21 I will gather you and I will blow on you with my fiery wrath, and you will be melted inside her. 22 As silver is melted[c] in a furnace, so you will be melted inside her, and you will know that I the LORD have poured out my wrath upon you.' "[d]

23 Again the word of the LORD came to me: 24 "Son of man, say to the land, 'You are a land that has had no rain or showers[c] in the day of wrath.'[e] 25 There is a conspiracy[f] of her princes[d] within her like a roaring lion tearing its prey; they devour people,[g] take treasures and precious things and make many widows[h] within her. 26 Her priests do violence to my law[i] and profane my holy things; they do not distinguish between the holy and the common;[j] they teach that there is no difference between the unclean and the clean;[k] and they shut their eyes to the keeping of my Sabbaths, so that I am profaned among them.[l] 27 Her officials within her are like wolves tearing their prey; they shed blood and kill people to make unjust gain.[m] 28 Her prophets whitewash[n] these deeds for them by false visions and lying divinations. They say, 'This is what the Sovereign LORD says' – when the LORD has not spoken.[o] 29 The people of the land practise extortion and commit robbery; they oppress the poor and needy and ill-treat the alien,[p] denying them justice.[q]

30 "I looked for a man among them who would build up the wall[r] and stand before me in the gap on behalf of the land so that I would not have to destroy it, but I found none.[s] 31 So I will pour out my wrath on them and consume them with my fiery anger, bringing

22:6 g Isa 1:23
22:7 h Dt 5:16; Dt 27:16; i Ex 22:21-22
22:8 j Eze 23:38-39
22:9 k Lev 19:16; l Eze 18:11; m Hos 4:10,14
22:10 n Lev 18:8,19
22:11 o Lev 18:15; p Lev 18:9; 2Sa 13:14
22:12 q Dt 27:25; Mic 7:3; r Lev 19:13
22:13 s Eze 21:17; t Isa 33:15; u ver 3
22:14 v Eze 24:14; w Eze 17:24; Eze 21:7
22:15 x Dt 4:27; Zec 7:14; y Eze 23:27
22:18 z Ps 119:119; Isa 1:22; a Jer 6:28-30
22:20 b Mal 3:2
22:22 c Isa 1:25; d Eze 20:8,33
22:24 e Eze 24:13
22:25 f Jer 11:9; g Hos 6:9; h Jer 15:8
22:26 i Mal 2:7-8; j Eze 44:23; k Lev 10:10; l 1Sa 2:12-17; Jer 2:8,26; Hag 2:11-14
22:27 m Isa 1:23
22:28 n Eze 13:10; o Eze 13:2,6-7
22:29 p Ex 22:21; Ex 23:9; q Isa 5:7
22:30 r Eze 13:5; s Ps 106:23; Jer 5:1

[a] 12 Or *usury and interest* [b] 16 Or *When I have allotted you your inheritance* [c] 24 Septuagint; Hebrew *has not been cleansed or rained on* [d] 25 Septuagint; Hebrew *prophets*

down[t] on their own heads all they have done, declares the Sovereign LORD.[u]"

Two Adulterous Sisters

23 The word of the LORD came to me: 2"Son of man, there were two women, daughters of the same mother.[a] 3They became prostitutes in Egypt,[b] engaging in prostitution[c] from their youth. In that land their breasts were fondled and their virgin bosoms caressed. 4The older was named Oholah, and her sister was Oholibah. They were mine and gave birth to sons and daughters. Oholah is Samaria, and Oholibah is Jerusalem.

5"Oholah engaged in prostitution while she was still mine; and she lusted after her lovers, the Assyrians[d]—warriors[e] 6clothed in blue, governors and commanders, all of them handsome young men, and mounted horsemen. 7She gave herself as a prostitute to all the elite of the Assyrians and defiled herself with all the idols of everyone she lusted after.[f] 8She did not give up the prostitution she began in Egypt,[g] when during her youth men slept with her, caressed her virgin bosom and poured out their lust upon her.[h]

9"Therefore I handed her over[i] to her lovers, the Assyrians, for whom she lusted.[j] 10They stripped[k] her naked, took away her sons and daughters and killed her with the sword. She became a byword among women,[l] and punishment was inflicted on her.[m]

11"Her sister Oholibah saw this, yet in her lust and prostitution she was more depraved than her sister.[n] 12She too lusted after the Assyrians—governors and commanders, warriors in full dress, mounted horsemen, all handsome young men.[o] 13I saw that she too defiled herself; both of them went the same way.

14"But she carried her prostitution still further. She saw men portrayed on a wall,[p] figures of Chaldeans[a] portrayed in red,[q] 15with belts round their waists and flowing turbans on their heads; all of them looked like Babylonian chariot officers, natives of Chaldea.[b] 16As soon as she saw them, she lusted after them and sent messengers to them in Chaldea. 17Then the Babylonians came to her, to the bed of love, and in their lust they defiled her. After she had been defiled by them, she turned away from them in disgust. 18When she carried on her prostitution openly and exposed her nakedness, I turned away[r] from her in disgust, just as I had turned away from her sister.[s] 19Yet she became more and more promiscuous as she recalled the days of her youth, when she was a prostitute in Egypt. 20There she lusted after her lovers, whose genitals were like those of donkeys and whose emission was like that of horses. 21So you longed for the lewdness of your youth, when in Egypt your bosom was caressed and your young breasts fondled.[c][t]

22"Therefore, Oholibah, this is what the Sovereign LORD says: I will stir up your lovers against you, those you turned away from in disgust, and I will bring them against you from every side[u]—23the Babylonians[v] and all the Chaldeans, the men of Pekod[w] and Shoa and Koa, and all the Assyrians with them, handsome young men, all of them governors and commanders, chariot officers and men of high rank, all mounted on horses.[x] 24They will come against you with weapons,[d] chariots and wagons[y] and with a throng of people; they will take up positions against you

22:31 t Eze 16:43 u Eze 7:8-9 Eze 9:10 Ro 2:8
23:2 a Jer 3:7 Eze 16:45
23:3 b Jos 24:14 c Lev 17:7
23:5 d 2Ki 16:7 Hos 5:13 e Hos 8:9
23:7 f Hos 5:3 Hos 6:10
23:8 g Ex 32:4 h Eze 16:15
23:9 i 2Ki 18:11 j Hos 11:5
23:10 k Hos 2:10 l Eze 16:41 m Eze 16:36
23:11 n Jer 3:8-11 Eze 16:51
23:12 o 2Ki 16:7-15 2Ch 28:16
23:14 p Eze 8:10 q Jer 22:14
23:18 r Ps 78:59 Ps 106:40 Jer 6:8 s Jer 12:8 Am 5:21
23:21 t Eze 16:26
23:22 u Eze 16:37
23:23 v 2Ki 20:14-18 w Jer 50:21 x 2Ki 24:2
23:24 y Jer 47:3 Eze 26:7,10 Na 2:4

a14 Or *Babylonians* b15 Or *Babylonia*; also in verse 16 c21 Syriac (see also verse 3); Hebrew *caressed because of your young breasts*
d24 The meaning of the Hebrew for this word is uncertain.

on every side with large and small shields and with helmets. I will turn you over to them for punishment,[z] and they will punish you according to their standards. 25 I will direct my jealous anger against you, and they will deal with you in fury. They will cut off your noses and your ears, and those of you who are left will fall by the sword. They will take away your sons and daughters,[a] and those of you who are left will be consumed by fire.[b] 26 They will also strip[c] you of your clothes and take your fine jewellery.[d] 27 So I will put a stop[e] to the lewdness and prostitution you began in Egypt. You will not look on these things with longing or remember Egypt any more.

28 "For this is what the Sovereign LORD says: I am about to hand you over[f] to those you hate, to those you turned away from in disgust. 29 They will deal with you in hatred and take away everything you have worked for. They will leave you naked and bare, and the shame of your prostitution will be exposed. Your lewdness and promiscuity[g] 30 have brought this upon you, because you lusted after the nations and defiled yourself with their idols.[h] 31 You have gone the way of your sister; so I will put her cup[i] into your hand.[j]

32 "This is what the Sovereign LORD says:

"You will drink your sister's
 cup,
 a cup large and deep;
it will bring scorn and derision,
 for it holds so much.[k]
33 You will be filled with
 drunkenness and sorrow,
 the cup of ruin and desolation,
 the cup of your sister
 Samaria.[l]
34 You will drink it[m] and drain it
 dry;
 you will dash it to pieces
 and tear your breasts.

I have spoken, declares the Sovereign LORD.

35 "Therefore this is what the Sovereign LORD says: Since you have forgotten[n] me and thrust me behind your back,[o] you must bear the consequences of your lewdness and prostitution."

36 The LORD said to me: "Son of man, will you judge Oholah and Oholibah? Then confront[p] them with their detestable practices,[q] 37 for they have committed adultery and blood is on their hands. They committed adultery with their idols; they even sacrificed their children, whom they bore to me,[e] as food for them.[r] 38 They have also done this to me: At that same time they defiled my sanctuary and desecrated my Sabbaths. 39 On the very day they sacrificed their children to their idols, they entered my sanctuary and desecrated[s] it. That is what they did in my house.[t]

40 "They even sent messengers for men who came from far away,[u] and when they arrived you bathed yourself for them, painted your eyes[v] and put on your jewellery.[w] 41 You sat on an elegant couch,[x] with a table[y] spread before it on which you had placed the incense and oil that belonged to me.

42 "The noise of a carefree crowd was around her; Sabeans[f] were brought from the desert along with men from the rabble, and they put bracelets[z] on the arms of the woman and her sister and beautiful crowns on their heads.[a] 43 Then I said about the one worn out by adultery, 'Now let them use her as a prostitute,[b] for that is all she is.' 44 And they slept with her. As men sleep with a prostitute, so they slept with those lewd women, Oholah and Oholibah. 45 But righteous men will sentence them to the punishment of women who commit adultery and shed blood, because

e37 Or *even made the children they bore to me pass through ⌞the fire⌟* f42 Or *drunkards*

23:24 z Jer 39:5-6
23:25 a ver 47 b Eze 20:47-48
23:26 c Jer 13:22 d Isa 3:18-23 Eze 16:39
23:27 e Eze 16:41
23:28 f Jer 34:20
23:29 g Dt 28:48
23:30 h Eze 6:9
23:31 i Jer 25:15 j 2Ki 21:13
23:32 k Ps 60:3 Isa 51:17 Jer 25:15
23:33 l Jer 25:15-16
23:34 m Ps 75:8 Isa 51:17
23:35 n Isa 17:10 Jer 3:21 o 1Ki 14:9
23:36 p Eze 16:2 q Isa 58:1 Eze 22:2 Mic 3:8
23:37 r Eze 16:36
23:39 s 2Ki 21:4 t Jer 7:10
23:40 u Isa 57:9 v 2Ki 9:30 w Jer 4:30 Eze 16:13-19
23:41 x Est 1:6 Pr 7:17 Am 6:4 y Isa 65:11 Eze 44:16
23:42 z Ge 24:30 a Eze 16:11-12
23:43 b ver 3

they are adulterous and blood is on
their hands.[c]
46"This is what the Sovereign
LORD says: Bring a mob[d] against
them and give them over to terror
and plunder. 47The mob will stone
them and cut them down with their
swords; they will kill their sons and
daughters and burn[e] down their
houses.[f]
48"So I will put an end to lewdness in the land, that all women
may take warning and not imitate
you.[g] 49You will suffer the penalty
for your lewdness and bear the consequences of your sins of idolatry.
Then you will know that I am the
Sovereign LORD.[h]"

The Cooking Pot

24 In the ninth year, in the
tenth month on the tenth
day, the word of the LORD came to
me:[a] 2"Son of man, record this
date, this very date, because the
king of Babylon has laid siege to
Jerusalem this very day.[b] 3Tell
this rebellious house[c] a parable[d]
and say to them: 'This is what the
Sovereign LORD says:

" 'Put on the cooking pot;[e] put
it on
and pour water into it.
4Put into it the pieces of meat,
all the choice pieces—the leg
and the shoulder.
Fill it with the best of these
bones;
5 take the pick of the flock.[f]
Pile wood beneath it for the
bones;
bring it to the boil
and cook the bones in it.[g]

6" 'For this is what the Sovereign
LORD says:

" 'Woe to the city of
bloodshed,[h]
to the pot now encrusted,
whose deposit will not go
away!
Empty it piece by piece
without casting lots[i] for
them.

7" 'For the blood she shed is in
her midst:
She poured it on the bare
rock;
she did not pour it on the
ground,
where the dust would cover
it.[j]
8To stir up wrath and take
revenge
I put her blood on the bare
rock,
so that it would not be
covered.

9" 'Therefore this is what the Sovereign LORD says:

" 'Woe to the city of bloodshed!
I, too, will pile the wood high.
10So heap on the wood
and kindle the fire.
Cook the meat well,
mixing in the spices;
and let the bones be charred.
11Then set the empty pot on the
coals
till it becomes hot and its
copper glows
so its impurities may be melted
and its deposit burned away.[k]
12It has frustrated all efforts;
its heavy deposit has not been
removed,
not even by fire.

13" 'Now your impurity is lewdness. Because I tried to cleanse you
but you would not be cleansed from
your impurity, you will not be clean
again until my wrath against you
has subsided.[l]

14" 'I the LORD have spoken. The
time has come for me to act. I will
not hold back; I will not have pity,
nor will I relent. You will be judged
according to your conduct and your
actions,[m] declares the Sovereign
LORD.[n]' "

23:45 c Lev 20:10 Eze 16:38 Hos 6:5
23:46 d Eze 16:40
23:47 e 2Ch 36:19 f 2Ch 36:17 Eze 16:40-41
23:48 g 2Pe 2:6
23:49 h Eze 7:4 Eze 9:10 Eze 20:38
24:1 a Eze 8:1
24:2 b 2Ki 25:1 Jer 39:1 Jer 52:4
24:3 c Isa 1:2 Eze 2:3,6 d Eze 17:2 Eze 20:49 e Jer 1:13 Eze 11:3
24:5 f Jer 52:10 g Jer 52:24-27
24:6 h Eze 22:2 i Ob 1:11 Na 3:10
24:7 j Lev 17:13
24:11 k Jer 21:10 Eze 22:15
24:13 l Jer 6:28-30 Eze 16:42 Eze 22:24
24:14 m Eze 36:19 n Eze 18:30

Ezekiel's Wife Dies

15 The word of the LORD came to me: 16 "Son of man, with one blow I am about to take away from you the delight of your eyes. Yet do not lament or weep or shed any tears.[o] 17 Groan quietly; do not mourn for the dead. Keep your turban fastened and your sandals on your feet; do not cover the lower part of your face or eat the customary food ⌞of mourners⌟.[p]"

18 So I spoke to the people in the morning, and in the evening my wife died. The next morning I did as I had been commanded.

19 Then the people asked me, "Won't you tell us what these things have to do with us?[q]"

20 So I said to them, "The word of the LORD came to me: 21 Say to the house of Israel, 'This is what the Sovereign LORD says: I am about to desecrate my sanctuary—the stronghold in which you take pride, the delight of your eyes,[r] the object of your affection. The sons and daughters[s] you left behind will fall by the sword.[t] 22 And you will do as I have done. You will not cover the lower part of your face or eat the customary food ⌞of mourners⌟.[u] 23 You will keep your turbans on your heads and your sandals on your feet. You will not mourn[v] or weep but will waste away because of[a] your sins and groan among yourselves.[w] 24 Ezekiel will be a sign[x] to you; you will do just as he has done. When this happens, you will know that I am the Sovereign LORD.'

25 "And you, son of man, on the day I take away their stronghold, their joy and glory, the delight of their eyes, their heart's desire, and their sons and daughters[y] as well—26 on that day a fugitive will come to tell you[z] the news. 27 At that time your mouth will be opened; you will speak with him and will no longer be silent. So you will be a sign to them, and they will know that I am the LORD.[a]"

A Prophecy Against Ammon

25 The word of the LORD came to me: 2 "Son of man, set your face against the Ammonites[a] and prophesy against them.[b] 3 Say to them, 'Hear the word of the Sovereign LORD. This is what the Sovereign LORD says: Because you said "Aha![c]" over my sanctuary when it was desecrated and over the land of Israel when it was laid waste and over the people of Judah when they went into exile,[d] 4 therefore I am going to give you to the people of the East[e] as a possession. They will set up their camps and pitch their tents among you; they will eat your fruit and drink your milk.[f] 5 I will turn Rabbah[g] into a pasture for camels and Ammon into a resting place for sheep.[h] Then you will know that I am the LORD. 6 For this is what the Sovereign LORD says: Because you have clapped your hands and stamped your feet, rejoicing with all the malice of your heart against the land of Israel,[i] 7 therefore I will stretch out my hand[j] against you and give you as plunder to the nations. I will cut you off from the nations and exterminate you from the countries. I will destroy[k] you, and you will know that I am the LORD.[l]' "

A Prophecy Against Moab

8 "This is what the Sovereign LORD says: 'Because Moab[m] and Seir said, "Look, the house of Judah has become like all the other nations," 9 therefore I will expose the flank of Moab, beginning at its frontier towns—Beth Jeshimoth[n], Baal Meon[o] and Kiriathaim[p]—the glory of that land. 10 I will give Moab along with the Ammonites to

[a] 23 Or *away in*

24:16 o Jer 13:17; Jer 16:5; Jer 22:10
24:17 p Jer 16:7
24:19 q Eze 12:9; Eze 37:18
24:21 r Ps 27:4; s Eze 23:25; t Jer 7:14,15; Eze 23:47
24:22 u Jer 16:7
24:23 v Job 27:15; w Ps 78:64
24:24 x Isa 20:3; Eze 4:3; Eze 12:11
24:25 y Jer 11:22
24:26 z 1Sa 4:12; Job 1:15-19
24:27 a Eze 3:26; Eze 33:22
25:2 a Eze 21:28; Zep 2:8-9; b Jer 49:1-6
25:3 c Eze 26:2; Eze 36:2; d Pr 17:5
25:4 e Jdg 6:3; f Dt 28:33,51; Jdg 6:33
25:5 g Dt 3:11; Eze 21:20; h Isa 17:2
25:6 i Ob 1:12; Zep 2:8
25:7 j Zep 1:4; k Eze 21:31; l Am 1:14-15
25:8 m Jer 48:1; Am 2:1
25:9 n Nu 33:49; o Nu 32:3; Jos 13:17; p Nu 32:37; Jos 13:19

the people of the East as a possession, so that the Ammonites will not
be remembered[q] among the nations; 11and I will inflict punishment on Moab. Then they will know
that I am the LORD.' "

A Prophecy Against Edom

12"This is what the Sovereign
LORD says: 'Because Edom[r] took
revenge on the house of Judah and
became very guilty by doing so,
13therefore this is what the Sovereign LORD says: I will stretch out
my hand against Edom and kill its
men and their animals.[s] I will lay
it waste, and from Teman to Dedan[t] they will fall by the sword. 14I
will take vengeance on Edom by
the hand of my people Israel, and
they will deal with Edom in accordance with my anger[u] and my
wrath; they will know my vengeance, declares the Sovereign
LORD.' "

A Prophecy Against Philistia

15"This is what the Sovereign
LORD says: 'Because the Philistines[v] acted in vengeance and took
revenge with malice in their
hearts, and with ancient hostility
sought to destroy Judah, 16there-
fore this is what the Sovereign
LORD says: I am about to stretch out
my hand against the Philistines,[w]
and I will cut off the Kerethites[x]
and destroy those remaining along
the coast. 17I will carry out great
vengeance on them and punish
them in my wrath. Then they will
know that I am the LORD, when I
take vengeance on them.' "

A Prophecy Against Tyre

26 In the eleventh year, on the
first day of the month, the
word of the LORD came to me: 2"Son
of man, because Tyre[a] has said of
Jerusalem, 'Aha![b] The gate to the
nations is broken, and its doors
have swung open to me; now that
she lies in ruins I will prosper,'
3therefore this is what the Sovereign LORD says: I am against you, O
Tyre, and I will bring many nations
against you, like the sea[c] casting
up its waves. 4They will destroy[d]
the walls of Tyre[e] and pull down
her towers; I will scrape away her
rubble and make her a bare rock.
5Out in the sea[f] she will become a
place to spread fishing nets, for I
have spoken, declares the Sovereign LORD. She will become plunder[g] for the nations, 6and her
settlements on the mainland will be
ravaged by the sword. Then they
will know that I am the LORD.

7"For this is what the Sovereign
LORD says: From the north I am going to bring against Tyre Nebuchadnezzar[a][h] king of Babylon,
king of kings,[i] with horses and
chariots,[j] with horsemen and a
great army. 8He will ravage your
settlements on the mainland with
the sword; he will set up siege
works[k] against you, build a ramp[l]
up to your walls and raise his
shields against you. 9He will direct
the blows of his battering-rams
against your walls and demolish
your towers with his weapons.
10His horses will be so many that
they will cover you with dust. Your
walls will tremble at the noise of
the war horses, wagons and chariots[m] when he enters your gates as
men enter a city whose walls have
been broken through. 11The hoofs[n]
of his horses will trample all your
streets; he will kill your people
with the sword, and your strong pillars[o] will fall to the ground.[p]
12They will plunder your wealth
and loot your merchandise; they
will break down your walls and demolish your fine houses and throw
your stones, timber and rubble into
the sea.[q] 13I will put an end[r] to

25:10 q Eze 21:32
25:12 r 2Ch 28:17
25:13 s Eze 29:8; t Jer 25:23
25:14 u Eze 35:11
25:15 v 2Ch 28:18
25:16 w Jer 47:1-7; x 1Sa 30:14; Zep 2:4-5
26:2 a 2Sa 5:11; Isa 23; b Eze 25:3
26:3 c Isa 5:30; Jer 50:42; Jer 51:42
26:4 d Isa 23:1,11; e Am 1:10
26:5 f Eze 27:32; g Eze 29:19
26:7 h Jer 27:6; i Ezr 7:12; Da 2:37; j Eze 23:24; Na 2:3-4
26:8 k Jer 6:6; l Eze 21:22
26:10 m Jer 4:13
26:11 n Isa 5:28; o Jer 43:13; p Isa 26:5
26:12 q Isa 23:8; Eze 27:3-27; Eze 28:8
26:13 r Jer 7:34

a7 Hebrew *Nebuchadrezzar*, of which *Nebuchadnezzar* is a variant; here and often in Ezekiel and Jeremiah

your noisy songs, and the music of
your harps[s] will be heard no
more.[t] 14I will make you a bare
rock, and you will become a place
to spread fishing nets. You will
never be rebuilt,[u] for I the LORD
have spoken, declares the Sovereign LORD.
15"This is what the Sovereign
LORD says to Tyre: Will not the
coastlands[v] tremble[w] at the sound
of your fall, when the wounded
groan and the slaughter takes place
in you? 16Then all the princes of the
coast will step down from their
thrones and lay aside their robes
and take off their embroidered garments. Clothed[x] with terror, they
will sit on the ground, trembling[y]
every moment, appalled[z] at you.
17Then they will take up a lament[a]
concerning you and say to you:

" 'How you are destroyed,
O city of renown,
peopled by men of the sea!
You were a power on the seas,
you and your citizens;
you put your terror
on all who lived there.[b]
18Now the coastlands tremble
on the day of your fall;
the islands in the sea
are terrified at your
collapse.'[c]

19"This is what the Sovereign
LORD says: When I make you a
desolate city, like cities no longer
inhabited, and when I bring the
ocean depths over you and its vast
waters cover you,[d] 20then I will
bring you down with those who go
down to the pit,[e] to the people of
long ago. I will make you dwell in
the earth below, as in ancient ruins,
with those who go down to the pit,
and you will not return or take your
place[b] in the land of the living.[f]
21I will bring you to a horrible end
and you will be no more. You will be
sought, but you will never again be
found, declares the Sovereign
LORD."[g]

26:13 s Isa 14:11 t Jer 25:10 Rev 18:22
26:14 u Job 12:14 Mal 1:4
26:15 v Eze 27:35 w Jer 49:21
26:16 x Job 8:22 y Hos 11:10 z Eze 32:10
26:17 a Eze 19:1 Eze 27:32 b Isa 14:12
26:18 c Isa 23:5 Isa 41:5 Eze 27:35
26:19 d Isa 8:7-8
26:20 e Eze 32:18 Am 9:2 Jnh 2:2,6 f Eze 32:24,30
26:21 g Eze 27:36 Eze 28:19 Rev 18:21
27:3 a ver 33 b Eze 28:2
27:5 c Dt 3:9
27:6 d Nu 21:33 Jer 22:20 Zec 11:2 e Ge 10:4 Isa 23:12
27:7 f Ex 25:4 Jer 10:9
27:8 g Ge 10:18 h 1Ki 9:27
27:9 i Jos 13:5 1Ki 5:18
27:10 j Eze 38:5 k Eze 30:5

A Lament for Tyre

27 The word of the LORD came
to me: 2"Son of man, take
up a lament concerning Tyre. 3Say
to Tyre, situated at the gateway to
the sea,[a] merchant of peoples on
many coasts, 'This is what the Sovereign LORD says:

" 'You say, O Tyre,
"I am perfect in beauty.[b]"
4Your domain was on the high
seas;
your builders brought your
beauty to perfection.
5They made all your timbers
of pine trees from Senir;[a][c]
they took a cedar from Lebanon
to make a mast for you.
6Of oaks[d] from Bashan
they made your oars;
of cypress wood[b] from the
coasts of Cyprus[c][e]
they made your deck, inlaid
with ivory.
7Fine embroidered linen from
Egypt was your sail
and served as your banner;
your awnings were of blue and
purple[f]
from the coasts of Elishah.
8Men of Sidon and Arvad[g] were
your oarsmen;
your skilled men, O Tyre,
were aboard as your
seamen.[h]
9Veteran craftsmen of Gebal[d][i]
were on board
as shipwrights to caulk your
seams.
All the ships of the sea and
their sailors
came alongside to trade for
your wares.

10" 'Men of Persia,[j] Lydia and
Put[k]
served as soldiers in your
army.

[b]20 Septuagint; Hebrew *return, and I will give glory* [a]5 That is, Hermon [b]6 Targum; the Masoretic Text has a different division of the consonants. [c]6 Hebrew *Kittim* [d]9 That is, Byblos

They hung their shields and
helmets on your walls,
bringing you splendour.
11Men of Arvad and Helech
manned your walls on every
side;
men of Gammad
were in your towers.
They hung their shields around
your walls;
they brought your beauty to
perfection.

12" 'Tarshish[l] did business with
you because of your great wealth of
goods;[m] they exchanged silver,
iron, tin and lead for your merchandise.
13" 'Greece, Tubal and Meshech[n]
traded with you; they exchanged
slaves[o] and articles of bronze for
your wares.
14" 'Men of Beth Togarmah[p] exchanged work horses, war horses
and mules for your merchandise.
15" 'The men of Rhodes[e][q] traded
with you, and many coastlands[r]
were your customers; they paid
you with ivory[s] tusks and ebony.
16" 'Aram[f][t] did business with
you because of your many products; they exchanged turquoise,[u]
purple fabric, embroidered work,
fine linen, coral and rubies for your
merchandise.
17" 'Judah and Israel traded with
you; they exchanged wheat from
Minnith[v] and confections,[g] honey, oil and balm for your wares.
18" 'Damascus,[w] because of your
many products and great wealth of
goods, did business with you in
wine from Helbon and wool from
Zahar.
19" 'Danites and Greeks from
Uzal bought your merchandise;
they exchanged wrought iron, cassia and calamus for your wares.
20" 'Dedan traded in saddle blankets with you.
21" 'Arabia and all the princes of
Kedar[x] were your customers; they
did business with you in lambs,
rams and goats.
22" 'The merchants of Sheba[y]
and Raamah traded with you; for
your merchandise they exchanged
the finest of all kinds of spices[z]
and precious stones, and gold.
23" 'Haran,[a] Canneh and Eden[b]
and merchants of Sheba, Asshur
and Kilmad traded with you. 24In
your market-place they traded
with you beautiful garments, blue
fabric, embroidered work and
multicoloured rugs with cords
twisted and tightly knotted.

25" 'The ships of Tarshish[c] serve
as carriers for your wares.
You are filled with heavy cargo
in the heart of the sea.
26Your oarsmen take you
out to the high seas.
But the east wind[d] will break
you to pieces
in the heart of the sea.
27Your wealth,[e] merchandise and
wares,
your mariners, seamen and
shipwrights,
your merchants and all your
soldiers,
and everyone else on board
will sink into the heart of the
sea
on the day of your shipwreck.
28The shorelands will quake[f]
when your seamen cry out.
29All who handle the oars
will abandon their ships;
the mariners and all the seamen
will stand on the shore.
30They will raise their voice
and cry bitterly over you;
they will sprinkle dust[g] on
their heads
and roll[h] in ashes.[i]
31They will shave their heads
because of you
and will put on sackcloth.
They will weep[j] over you with
anguish of soul
and with bitter mourning.[k]

27:12 l Ge 10:4 m ver 18,33
27:13 n Ge 10:2 Isa 66:19 Eze 38:2 o Rev 18:13
27:14 p Ge 10:3 Eze 38:6
27:15 q Ge 10:7 r Jer 25:22 s 1Ki 10:22 Rev 18:12
27:16 t Jdg 10:6 Isa 7:1-8 u Eze 28:13
27:17 v Jdg 11:33
27:18 w Ge 14:15 Eze 47:16-18
27:21 x Ge 25:13 Isa 60:7
27:22 y Ge 10:7,28 1Ki 10:1-2 Isa 60:6 z Ge 43:11
27:23 a 2Ki 19:12 b Isa 37:12
27:25 c Isa 2:16 *fn*
27:26 d Ps 48:7 Jer 18:17
27:27 e Pr 11:4
27:28 f Eze 26:15
27:30 g 2Sa 1:2 h Jer 6:26 i Rev 18:18-19
27:31 j Isa 16:9 k Isa 22:12 Eze 7:18

e *15* Septuagint; Hebrew *Dedan* f *16* Most Hebrew manuscripts; some Hebrew manuscripts and Syriac *Edom* g *17* The meaning of the Hebrew for this word is uncertain.

32As they wail and mourn over you,
they will take up a lament[l] concerning you:
"Who was ever silenced like Tyre,
surrounded by the sea?"
33When your merchandise went out on the seas,
you satisfied many nations;
with your great wealth[m] and your wares
you enriched the kings of the earth.
34Now you are shattered by the sea
in the depths of the waters;
your wares and all your company
have gone down with you.[n]
35All who live in the coastlands[o]
are appalled at you;
their kings shudder with horror
and their faces are distorted with fear.
36The merchants among the nations hiss at you;[p]
you have come to a horrible end
and will be no more.[q]' "

A Prophecy Against the King of Tyre

28 The word of the LORD came to me: 2"Son of man, say to the ruler of Tyre, 'This is what the Sovereign LORD says:

" 'In the pride of your heart
you say, "I am a god;
I sit on the throne[a] of a god
in the heart of the seas."
But you are a man and not a god,
though you think you are as wise as a god.[b]
3Are you wiser than Daniel?[a][c]
Is no secret hidden from you?
4By your wisdom and understanding
you have gained wealth for yourself
and amassed gold and silver
in your treasuries.[d]

5By your great skill in trading
you have increased your wealth,
and because of your wealth
your heart has grown proud.[e]

6" 'Therefore this is what the Sovereign LORD says:

" 'Because you think you are wise,
as wise as a god,
7I am going to bring foreigners against you,
the most ruthless of nations;[f]
they will draw their swords
against your beauty and wisdom
and pierce your shining splendour.
8They will bring you down to the pit,[g]
and you will die a violent death
in the heart of the seas.[h]
9Will you then say, "I am a god,"
in the presence of those who kill you?
You will be but a man, not a god,
in the hands of those who slay you.
10You will die the death of the uncircumcised[i]
at the hands of foreigners.

I have spoken, declares the Sovereign LORD.' "

11The word of the LORD came to
me: 12"Son of man, take up a lament[j] concerning the king of Tyre
and say to him: 'This is what the Sovereign LORD says:

" 'You were the model of perfection,
full of wisdom and perfect in beauty.[k]
13You were in Eden,[l]
the garden of God;[m]

27:32 l Eze 26:17
27:33 m ver 12; Eze 28:4-5
27:34 n Zec 9:4
27:35 o Eze 26:15
27:36 p Jer 18:16; Jer 19:8; Jer 49:17; Jer 50:13; Zep 2:15 q Ps 37:10,36; Eze 26:21
28:2 a Isa 14:13 b Ps 9:20; Ps 82:6-7; Isa 31:3; 2Th 2:4
28:3 c Da 1:20; Da 5:11-12
28:4 d Zec 9:3
28:5 e Job 31:25; Ps 52:7; Ps 62:10; Hos 12:8; Hos 13:6
28:7 f Eze 30:11; Eze 31:12; Eze 32:12; Hab 1:6
28:8 g Eze 32:30 h Eze 27:27
28:10 i Eze 31:18; Eze 32:19,24
28:12 j Eze 19:1 k Eze 27:2-4
28:13 l Ge 2:8 m Eze 31:8-9

a3 Or *Danel*; the Hebrew spelling may suggest a person other than the prophet Daniel.

every precious stone adorned
you:
ruby, topaz and emerald,
chrysolite, onyx and jasper,
sapphire,[b] turquoise[n] and
beryl.[c]
Your settings and mountings[d]
were made of gold;
on the day you were created
they were prepared.
14 You were anointed[o] as a
guardian cherub,[p]
for so I ordained you.
You were on the holy mount of
God;
you walked among the fiery
stones.
15 You were blameless in your
ways
from the day you were
created
till wickedness was found in
you.
16 Through your widespread trade
you were filled with
violence,[q]
and you sinned.
So I drove you in disgrace from
the mount of God,
and I expelled you, O guardian
cherub,[r]
from among the fiery stones.
17 Your heart became proud[s]
on account of your beauty,
and you corrupted your wisdom
because of your splendour.
So I threw you to the earth;
I made a spectacle of you
before kings.
18 By your many sins and
dishonest trade
you have desecrated your
sanctuaries.
So I made a fire come out from
you,
and it consumed you,
and I reduced you to ashes[t] on
the ground
in the sight of all who were
watching.
19 All the nations who knew you
are appalled at you;
you have come to a horrible end
and will be no more.[u]' "

28:13
n Eze 27:16

28:14
o Ex 30:26
Ex 40:9
p Ex 25:17-20

28:16
q Hab 2:17
r Ge 3:24

28:17
s Eze 31:10

28:18
t Mal 4:3

28:19
u Jer 51:64
Eze 26:21
Eze 27:36

28:21
v Eze 6:2
w Ge 10:15
Jer 25:22

28:22
x Eze 39:13
y Eze 30:19

28:23
z Eze 38:22

28:24
a Nu 33:55
Jos 23:13
Eze 2:6

28:25
b Ps 106:47
Jer 32:37
c Isa 11:12
d Eze 20:41
e Jer 23:8
Eze 11:17
Eze 34:27
Eze 37:25

28:26
f Jer 23:6
g Isa 65:21
Jer 32:15
Eze 38:8
Am 9:14-15

A Prophecy Against Sidon

20 The word of the LORD came to
me: 21 "Son of man, set your face
against[v] Sidon;[w] prophesy against
her 22 and say: 'This is what the Sovereign LORD says:

" 'I am against you, O Sidon,
and I will gain glory[x] within
you.
They will know that I am the
LORD,
when I inflict punishment[y] on
her
and show myself holy within
her.
23 I will send a plague upon her
and make blood flow in her
streets.
The slain will fall within her,
with the sword against her on
every side.
Then they will know that I am
the LORD.[z]

24 " 'No longer will the people of
Israel have malicious neighbours
who are painful briers and sharp
thorns.[a] Then they will know that
I am the Sovereign LORD.
25 " 'This is what the Sovereign
LORD says: When I gather[b] the people of Israel from the nations
where they have been scattered,[c] I
will show myself holy[d] among
them in the sight of the nations.
Then they will live in their own
land, which I gave to my servant
Jacob.[e] 26 They will live there in
safety[f] and will build houses and
plant vineyards; they will live in
safety when I inflict punishment
on all their neighbours who maligned them. Then they will know
that I am the LORD their God.[g]' "

A Prophecy Against Egypt

29 In the tenth year, in the
tenth month on the twelfth
day, the word of the LORD came to

[b]13 Or *lapis lazuli* [c]13 The precise identification of some of these precious stones is uncertain. [d]13 The meaning of the Hebrew for this phrase is uncertain.

me:[a] 2"Son of man, set your face against Pharaoh king of Egypt[b] and prophesy against him and against all Egypt.[c] 3Speak to him and say: 'This is what the Sovereign LORD says:

" 'I am against you, Pharaoh[d]
king of Egypt,
you great monster[e] lying
among your streams.
You say, "The Nile is mine;
I made it for myself."
4But I will put hooks[f] in your
jaws
and make the fish of your
streams stick to your
scales.
I will pull you out from among
your streams,
with all the fish sticking to
your scales.[g]
5I will leave you in the desert,
you and all the fish of your
streams.
You will fall on the open field
and not be gathered or picked
up.
I will give you as food
to the beasts of the earth and
the birds of the air.[h]

6Then all who live in Egypt will know that I am the LORD.

" 'You have been a staff of reed[i] for the house of Israel. 7When they grasped you with their hands, you splintered[j] and you tore open their shoulders; when they leaned on you, you broke and their backs were wrenched.[a][k]

8" 'Therefore this is what the Sovereign LORD says: I will bring a sword against you and kill your men and their animals.[l] 9Egypt will become a desolate wasteland. Then they will know that I am the LORD.

" 'Because you said, "The Nile is mine; I made it,[m]" 10therefore I am against you and against your streams, and I will make the land of Egypt a ruin and a desolate waste from Migdol to Aswan,[n] as far as the border of Cush.[b] 11No foot of man or animal will pass through it; no-one will live there for forty years.[o] 12I will make the land of Egypt desolate among devastated lands, and her cities will lie desolate for forty years among ruined cities. And I will disperse the Egyptians among the nations and scatter them through the countries.[p]

13" 'Yet this is what the Sovereign LORD says: At the end of forty years I will gather the Egyptians from the nations where they were scattered. 14I will bring them back from captivity and return them to Upper Egypt,[c][q] the land of their ancestry. There they will be a lowly[r] kingdom. 15It will be the lowliest of kingdoms and will never again exalt itself above the other nations.[s] I will make it so weak that it will never again rule over the nations. 16Egypt will no longer be a source of confidence[t] for the people of Israel but will be a reminder of their sin in turning to her for help. Then they will know that I am the Sovereign LORD.[u]' "

17In the twenty-seventh year, in the first month on the first day, the word of the LORD came to me:[v] 18"Son of man, Nebuchadnezzar[w] king of Babylon drove his army in a hard campaign against Tyre; every head was rubbed bare[x] and every shoulder made raw. Yet he and his army got no reward from the campaign he led against Tyre. 19Therefore this is what the Sovereign LORD says: I am going to give Egypt to Nebuchadnezzar king of Babylon, and he will carry off its wealth. He will loot and plunder the land as pay for his army.[y] 20I have given him Egypt as a reward for his efforts because he and his army did it for me, declares the Sovereign LORD.[z]

29:1 a ver 17; Eze 26:1
29:2 b Jer 25:19; c Isa 19:1-17; Jer 46:2; Eze 30:1-26; Eze 31:1-18; Eze 32:1-32
29:3 d Jer 44:30; e Ps 74:13; Isa 27:1; Eze 32:2
29:4 f 2Ki 19:28; g Eze 38:4
29:5 h Jer 7:33; Jer 34:20; Eze 32:4-6; Eze 39:4
29:6 i 2Ki 18:21; Isa 36:6
29:7 j Isa 36:6; k Eze 17:15-17
29:8 l Eze 14:17; Eze 32:11-13
29:9 m Eze 30:7-8, 13-19
29:10 n Eze 30:6
29:11 o Eze 32:13
29:12 p Jer 46:19; Eze 30:7,23, 26
29:14 q Eze 30:14; r Eze 17:14
29:15 s Zec 10:11
29:16 t Isa 36:4,6; u Isa 30:2; Hos 8:13
29:17 v Eze 24:1
29:18 w Jer 27:6; Eze 26:7-8; x Jer 48:37
29:19 y Jer 43:10-13; Eze 30:4,10, 24-25
29:20 z Isa 10:6-7; Isa 45:1; Jer 25:9

a7 Syriac (see also Septuagint and Vulgate); Hebrew *and you caused their backs to stand*
b10 That is, the upper Nile region
c14 Hebrew *to Pathros*

21 “On that day I will make a
horn[d][a] grow for the house of Israel, and I will open your mouth[b]
among them. Then they will know
that I am the LORD.[c]”

A Lament for Egypt

30 The word of the LORD came
to me: 2 “Son of man, prophesy and say: ‘This is what the Sovereign LORD says:

“ ‘Wail[a] and say,
“Alas for that day!”
3 For the day is near,[b]
the day of the LORD[c] is near—
a day of clouds,
a time of doom for the nations.
4 A sword will come against
Egypt,
and anguish will come upon
Cush.[a]
When the slain fall in Egypt,
her wealth will be carried
away
and her foundations torn
down.[d]

5 Cush and Put,[e] Lydia and all Arabia, Libya[b] and the people[f] of the
covenant land will fall by the sword
along with Egypt.
6 “ ‘This is what the LORD says:

“ ‘The allies of Egypt will fall
and her proud strength will
fail.
From Migdol to Aswan[g]
they will fall by the sword
within her,
declares the Sovereign LORD.
7 “ ‘They will be desolate
among desolate lands,
and their cities will lie
among ruined cities.[h]
8 Then they will know that I am
the LORD,
when I set fire to Egypt
and all her helpers are
crushed.

9 “ ‘On that day messengers will
go out from me in ships to frighten
Cush[i] out of her complacency. Anguish[j] will take hold of them on
the day of Egypt’s doom, for it is
sure to come.[k]

10 “ ‘This is what the Sovereign
LORD says:

“ ‘I will put an end to the hordes
of Egypt
by the hand of Nebuchadnezzar
king of Babylon.[l]
11 He and his army—the most
ruthless of nations[m]—
will be brought in to destroy
the land.
They will draw their swords
against Egypt
and fill the land with the slain.
12 I will dry up[n] the streams of
the Nile[o]
and sell the land to evil men;
by the hand of foreigners
I will lay waste the land and
everything in it.

I the LORD have spoken.

13 “ ‘This is what the Sovereign
LORD says:

“ ‘I will destroy the idols[p]
and put an end to the images
in Memphis.[c][q]
No longer will there be a prince
in Egypt,[r]
and I will spread fear
throughout the land.
14 I will lay[s] waste Upper
Egypt,[d]
set fire to Zoan[t]
and inflict punishment on
Thebes.[e][u]
15 I will pour out my wrath on
Pelusium,[f]
the stronghold of Egypt,
and cut off the hordes of
Thebes.
16 I will set fire to Egypt;
Pelusium will writhe in agony.
Thebes will be taken by storm;

29:21 a Ps 132:17 b Eze 33:22 c Eze 24:27
30:2 a Isa 13:6
30:3 b Eze 7:7; Joel 2:1,11; Ob 1:15 c ver 18; Eze 7:12,19
30:4 d Eze 29:19
30:5 e Eze 27:10 f Jer 25:20
30:6 g Eze 29:10
30:7 h Eze 29:12
30:9 i Isa 18:1-2 j Isa 23:5 k Eze 32:9-10
30:10 l Eze 29:19
30:11 m Eze 28:7
30:12 n Isa 19:6 o Eze 29:9
30:13 p Jer 43:12 q Isa 19:13 r Zec 10:11
30:14 s Eze 29:14 t Ps 78:12,43 u Jer 46:25

d 21 *Horn* here symbolises strength. a 4 That is, the upper Nile region; also in verses 5 and 9
b 5 Hebrew *Cub* c 13 Hebrew *Noph*; also in verse 16 d 14 Hebrew *waste Pathros*
e 14 Hebrew *No*; also in verses 15 and 16
f 15 Hebrew *Sin*; also in verse 16

Memphis will be in constant
distress.
[17]The young men of Heliopolis[g][v]
and Bubastis[h]
will fall by the sword,
and the cities themselves will
go into captivity.
[18]Dark will be the day at
Tahpanhes
when I break the yoke of
Egypt;[w]
there her proud strength will
come to an end.
She will be covered with clouds,
and her villages will go into
captivity.[x]
[19]So I will inflict punishment on
Egypt,
and they will know that I am
the LORD.' "

[20]In the eleventh year, in the first
month on the seventh day, the word
of the LORD came to me:[y] [21]"Son of
man, I have broken the arm[z] of
Pharaoh king of Egypt. It has not
been bound up for healing[a] or put
in a splint so as to become strong
enough to hold a sword. [22]There-
fore this is what the Sovereign
LORD says: I am against Pharaoh
king of Egypt.[b] I will break both
his arms, the good arm as well as
the broken one, and make the
sword fall from his hand.[c] [23]I will
disperse the Egyptians among the
nations and scatter them through
the countries.[d] [24]I will strength-
en[e] the arms of the king of Babylon and put my sword[f] in his
hand, but I will break the arms of
Pharaoh, and he will groan before him like a mortally wounded
man. [25]I will strengthen the arms of
the king of Babylon, but the arms
of Pharaoh will fall limp. Then they
will know that I am the LORD, when
I put my sword into the hand of the
king of Babylon and he brandishes
it against Egypt. [26]I will disperse
the Egyptians among the nations
and scatter them through the countries. Then they will know that I am
the LORD.[g]"

30:17 v Ge 41:45
30:18 w Lev 26:13; x ver 3
30:20 y Eze 26:1; Eze 29:17; Eze 31:1
30:21 z Jer 48:25; a Jer 30:13; Jer 46:11
30:22 b Jer 46:25; c Ps 37:17
30:23 d Eze 29:12
30:24 e Zec 10:6,12; f Eze 21:14; Zep 2:12
30:26 g Eze 29:12
31:1 a Jer 52:5; b Eze 30:20
31:3 c Isa 10:34
31:5 d Eze 17:5
31:6 e Eze 17:23; Mt 13:32
31:8 f Ps 80:10; g Ge 2:8-9

A Cedar in Lebanon

31 In the eleventh year,[a] in
the third month on the first
day, the word of the LORD came to
me:[b] [2]"Son of man, say to Pharaoh
king of Egypt and to his hordes:

" 'Who can be compared with
you in majesty?
[3]Consider Assyria, once a cedar
in Lebanon,
with beautiful branches
overshadowing the forest;
it towered on high,
its top above the thick
foliage.[c]
[4]The waters nourished it,
deep springs made it grow
tall;
their streams flowed
all around its base
and sent their channels
to all the trees of the field.
[5]So it towered higher
than all the trees of the field;
its boughs increased
and its branches grew long,
spreading because of abundant
waters.[d]
[6]All the birds of the air
nested in its boughs,
all the beasts of the field
gave birth under its branches;
all the great nations
lived in its shade.[e]
[7]It was majestic in beauty,
with its spreading boughs,
for its roots went down
to abundant waters.
[8]The cedars[f] in the garden of
God
could not rival it,
nor could the pine trees
equal its boughs,
nor could the plane trees
compare with its branches—
no tree in the garden of God
could match its beauty.[g]
[9]I made it beautiful
with abundant branches,

[g]17 Hebrew *Awen* (or *On*) [h]17 Hebrew *Pi Beseth*

the envy of all the trees of
Eden[h]
in the garden of God.[i]

[10]" 'Therefore this is what the
Sovereign LORD says: Because it
towered on high, lifting its top
above the thick foliage, and because it was proud[j] of its height,
[11]I handed it over to the ruler of the
nations, for him to deal with according to its wickedness. I cast it
aside,[k] [12]and the most ruthless of
foreign nations[l] cut it down and
left it. Its boughs fell on the mountains and in all the valleys;[m] its
branches lay broken in all the ravines of the land. All the nations of
the earth came out from under its
shade and left it.[n] [13]All the birds of
the air settled on the fallen tree,
and all the beasts of the field were
among its branches.[o] [14]Therefore
no other trees by the waters are
ever to tower proudly on high, lifting their tops above the thick foliage. No other trees so well-watered
are ever to reach such a height;
they are all destined for death,[p]
for the earth below, among mortal
men, with those who go down to the
pit.[q]
[15]" 'This is what the Sovereign
LORD says: On the day it was
brought down to the grave[a] I covered the deep springs with mourning for it; I held back its streams,
and its abundant waters were restrained. Because of it I clothed
Lebanon with gloom, and all the
trees of the field withered away. [16]I
made the nations tremble[r] at the
sound of its fall when I brought
it down to the grave with those
who go down to the pit. Then all
the trees[s] of Eden, the choicest
and best of Lebanon, all the trees
that were well-watered, were
consoled[t] in the earth below.[u]
[17]Those who lived in its shade, its
allies among the nations, had also
gone down to the grave with it, join-
ing those killed by the sword.[v]
[18]" 'Which of the trees of Eden
can be compared with you in splendour and majesty? Yet you, too, will
be brought down with the trees of
Eden to the earth below; you will lie
among the uncircumcised,[w] with
those killed by the sword.

" 'This is Pharaoh and all his
hordes, declares the Sovereign
LORD.' "

A Lament for Pharaoh

32 In the twelfth year, in the
twelfth month on the first
day, the word of the LORD came to
me:[a] [2]"Son of man, take up a lament[b] concerning Pharaoh king of
Egypt and say to him:

" 'You are like a lion[c] among
the nations;
you are like a monster in the
seas
thrashing about in your
streams,
churning the water with your
feet
and muddying the streams.[d]

[3]" 'This is what the Sovereign
LORD says:

" 'With a great throng of people
I will cast my net over you,
and they will haul you up in
my net.[e]
[4]I will throw you on the land
and hurl you on the open field.
I will let all the birds of the air
settle on you
and all the beasts of the earth
gorge themselves on you.[f]
[5]I will spread your flesh on the
mountains
and fill the valleys[g] with your
remains.
[6]I will drench the land with your
flowing blood[h]
all the way to the mountains,
and the ravines will be filled
with your flesh.
[7]When I snuff you out, I will
cover the heavens
and darken their stars;

31:9 h Ge 2:8 i Ge 13:10 Eze 28:13
31:10 j Isa 14:13-14 Eze 28:17
31:11 k Da 5:20
31:12 l Eze 28:7 m Eze 32:5 Eze 35:8 n Eze 32:11-12 Da 4:14
31:13 o Isa 18:6 Eze 29:5 Eze 32:4
31:14 p Ps 82:7 q Ps 63:9 Eze 26:20 Eze 32:24
31:16 r Eze 26:15 s Isa 14:8 t Eze 14:22 Eze 32:31 u Isa 14:15 Eze 32:18
31:17 v Ps 9:17
31:18 w Jer 9:26 Eze 32:19,21
32:1 a Eze 31:1 Eze 33:21
32:2 b Eze 19:1 Eze 27:2 c Eze 19:3,6 Na 2:11-13 d Eze 29:3 Eze 34:18
32:3 e Eze 12:13
32:4 f Isa 18:6 Eze 31:12-13
32:5 g Eze 31:12
32:6 h Isa 34:3

[a]15 Hebrew *Sheol*; also in verses 16 and 17

I will cover the sun with a
cloud,
and the moon will not give its
light.[i]
8All the shining lights in the
heavens
I will darken over you;
I will bring darkness over
your land,
declares the Sovereign LORD.
9I will trouble the hearts of
many peoples
when I bring about your
destruction among the
nations,
among[a] lands you have not
known.
10I will cause many peoples to be
appalled at you,
and their kings will shudder
with horror because of you
when I brandish my sword
before them.
On the day[j] of your downfall
each of them will tremble
every moment for his life.[k]

11" 'For this is what the Sovereign
LORD says:

" 'The sword of the king of
Babylon[l]
will come against you.
12I will cause your hordes to fall
by the swords of mighty
men—
the most ruthless of all
nations.[m]
They will shatter the pride of
Egypt,
and all her hordes will be
overthrown.[n]
13I will destroy all her cattle
from beside abundant waters
no longer to be stirred by the
foot of man
or muddied by the hoofs of
cattle.[o]
14Then I will let her waters settle
and make her streams flow
like oil,
declares the Sovereign LORD.
15When I make Egypt desolate
and strip the land of
everything in it,
when I strike down all who live
there,
then they will know that I am
the LORD.[p]'

16"This is the lament[q] they will
chant for her. The daughters of
the nations will chant it; for
Egypt and all her hordes they will
chant it, declares the Sovereign
LORD."

17In the twelfth year, on the fifteenth day of the month, the word
of the LORD came to me:[r] 18"Son of
man, wail for the hordes of Egypt
and consign[s] to the earth below
both her and the daughters of
mighty nations, with those who go
down to the pit.[t] 19Say to them,
'Are you more favoured than
others? Go down and be laid among
the uncircumcised.'[u] 20They will
fall among those killed by the
sword. The sword is drawn; let her
be dragged[v] off with all her
hordes. 21From within the grave[b][w]
the mighty leaders will say of
Egypt and her allies, 'They have
come down and they lie with the uncircumcised, with those killed by
the sword.'

22"Assyria is there with her
whole army; she is surrounded by
the graves of all her slain, all who
have fallen by the sword. 23Their
graves are in the depths of the pit[x]
and her army lies around her
grave. All who had spread terror in
the land of the living are slain,
fallen by the sword.

24"Elam[y] is there, with all her
hordes around her grave. All of
them are slain, fallen by the
sword.[z] All who had spread terror
in the land of the living[a] went
down uncircumcised to the earth
below. They bear their shame with
those who go down to the pit.[b] 25A
bed is made for her among the

32:7 i Isa 13:10; Isa 34:4; Eze 30:3; Joel 2:2,31; Joel 3:15; Mt 24:29; Rev 8:12
32:10 j Jer 46:10; k Eze 26:16; Eze 27:35
32:11 l Jer 46:26
32:12 m Eze 28:7; n Eze 31:11-12
32:13 o Eze 29:8,11
32:15 p Ex 7:5; Ex 14:4,18; Ps 107:33-34; Eze 6:7
32:16 q 2Sa 1:17; 2Ch 35:25; Eze 26:17
32:17 r ver 1
32:18 s Jer 1:10; t Eze 31:14,16; Mic 1:8
32:19 u ver 29-30; Eze 28:10; Eze 31:18
32:20 v Ps 28:3
32:21 w Isa 14:9
32:23 x Isa 14:15
32:24 y Ge 10:22; z Jer 49:37; a Job 28:13; b Eze 26:20

a9 Hebrew; Septuagint *bring you into captivity among the nations, / to* b21 Hebrew *Sheol*; also in verse 27

slain, with all her hordes around her grave. All of them are uncircumcised, killed by the sword. Because their terror had spread in the land of the living, they bear their shame with those who go down to the pit; they are laid among the slain.

26 "Meshech and Tubal[c] are there, with all their hordes around their graves. All of them are uncircumcised, killed by the sword because they spread their terror in the land of the living. 27 Do they not lie with the other uncircumcised warriors who have fallen, who went down to the grave with their weapons of war, whose swords were placed under their heads? The punishment for their sins rested on their bones, though the terror of these warriors had stalked through the land of the living.

28 "You too, O Pharaoh, will be broken and will lie among the uncircumcised, with those killed by the sword.

29 "Edom[d] is there, her kings and all her princes; despite their power, they are laid with those killed by the sword. They lie with the uncircumcised, with those who go down to the pit.[e]

30 "All the princes of the north[f] and all the Sidonians[g] are there; they went down with the slain in disgrace despite the terror caused by their power. They lie uncircumcised with those killed by the sword and bear their shame with those who go down to the pit.

31 "Pharaoh—he and all his army—will see them and he will be consoled[h] for all his hordes that were killed by the sword, declares the Sovereign LORD. 32 Although I had him spread terror in the land of the living, Pharaoh and all his hordes will be laid among the uncircumcised, with those killed by the sword, declares the Sovereign LORD."

32:26 c Ge 10:2; Eze 27:13
32:29 d Isa 34:5-15; Jer 49:7; Eze 35:15; Ob 1:1; e Eze 25:12-14
32:30 f Jer 25:26; Eze 38:6; Eze 39:2; g Jer 25:22; Eze 28:21
32:31 h Eze 14:22; Eze 31:16
33:2 a Jer 12:12; b Eze 3:11
33:3 c Hos 8:1
33:4 d 2Ch 25:16; e Jer 6:17; Eze 18:13; Zec 1:4; Ac 18:6
33:6 f Eze 3:18
33:7 g Jer 26:2; Eze 3:17
33:8 h ver 14; i Eze 18:4
33:9 j Eze 3:17-19
33:10 k Eze 24:23; l Lev 26:39; Eze 4:17

Ezekiel a Watchman

33 The word of the LORD came to me: 2 "Son of man, speak to your countrymen and say to them: 'When I bring the sword[a] against a land, and the people of the land choose one of their men and make him their watchman,[b] 3 and he sees the sword coming against the land and blows the trumpet[c] to warn the people, 4 then if anyone hears the trumpet but does not take warning[d] and the sword comes and takes his life, his blood will be on his own head.[e] 5 Since he heard the sound of the trumpet but did not take warning, his blood will be on his own head. If he had taken warning, he would have saved himself. 6 But if the watchman sees the sword coming and does not blow the trumpet to warn the people and the sword comes and takes the life of one of them, that man will be taken away because of his sin, but I will hold the watchman accountable for his blood.'[f]

7 "Son of man, I have made you a watchman for the house of Israel; so hear the word I speak and give them warning from me.[g] 8 When I say to the wicked, 'O wicked man, you will surely die,[h]' and you do not speak out to dissuade him from his ways, that wicked man will die for[a] his sin, and I will hold you accountable for his blood.[i] 9 But if you do warn the wicked man to turn from his ways and he does not do so, he will die for his sin, but you will be saved yourself.[j]

10 "Son of man, say to the house of Israel, 'This is what you are saying: "Our offences and sins weigh us down, and we are wasting away[k] because of[b] them. How then can we live?[l]"' 11 Say to them, 'As surely as I live, declares the Sovereign LORD, I take no pleasure in the death of the wicked, but rather that they turn from their ways and

[a] 8 Or *in*; also in verse 9 [b] 10 Or *away in*

live.[m] Turn! Turn from your evil ways! Why will you die, O house of Israel?'[n]

12"Therefore, son of man, say to your countrymen, 'The righteousness of the righteous man will not save him when he disobeys, and the wickedness of the wicked man will not cause him to fall when he turns from it. The righteous man, if he sins, will not be allowed to live because of his former righteousness.'[o] 13If I tell the righteous man that he will surely live, but then he trusts in his righteousness and does evil, none of the righteous things he has done will be remembered; he will die for the evil he has done.[p] 14And if I say to the wicked man, 'You will surely die,' but he then turns away from his sin and does what is just[q] and right—15if he gives back what he took in pledge for a loan, returns what he has stolen,[r] follows the decrees that give life, and does no evil, he will surely live; he will not die.[s] 16None of the sins he has committed will be remembered against him. He has done what is just and right; he will surely live.[t]

17"Yet your countrymen say, 'The way of the Lord is not just.' But it is their way that is not just. 18If a righteous man turns from his righteousness and does evil, he will die for it.[u] 19And if a wicked man turns away from his wickedness and does what is just and right, he will live by doing so. 20Yet, O house of Israel, you say, 'The way of the Lord is not just.' But I will judge each of you according to his own ways."

Jerusalem's Fall Explained

21In the twelfth year of our exile, in the tenth month on the fifth day, a man who had escaped[v] from Jerusalem came to me and said, "The city has fallen![w]" 22Now the evening before the man arrived, the hand of the LORD was upon me,[x] and he opened my mouth[y] before the man came to me in the morning. So my mouth was opened and I was no longer silent.[z]

23Then the word of the LORD came to me: 24"Son of man, the people living in those ruins[a] in the land of Israel are saying, 'Abraham was only one man, yet he possessed the land. But we are many; surely the land has been given to us as our possession.'[b] 25Therefore say to them, 'This is what the Sovereign LORD says: Since you eat meat with the blood[c] still in it and look to your idols and shed blood, should you then possess the land?[d] 26You rely on your sword, you do detestable things, and each of you defiles his neighbour's wife.[e] Should you then possess the land?'

27"Say this to them: 'This is what the Sovereign LORD says: As surely as I live, those who are left in the ruins will fall by the sword, those out in the country I will give to the wild animals to be devoured, and those in strongholds and caves will die of a plague.[f] 28I will make the land a desolate waste, and her proud strength will come to an end, and the mountains of Israel will become desolate so that no-one will cross them. 29Then they will know that I am the LORD, when I have made the land a desolate waste because of all the detestable things they have done.'

30"As for you, son of man, your countrymen are talking together about you by the walls and at the doors of the houses, saying to each other, 'Come and hear the message that has come from the LORD.' 31My people come to you, as they usually do, and sit before[g] you to listen to your words, but they do not put them into practice. With their mouths they express devotion, but their hearts are greedy for unjust gain.[h] 32Indeed, to them you are nothing more than one who sings love songs with a beautiful voice and plays an instrument well, for

33:11 m Eze 18:32; 2Pe 3:9 n Eze 18:23
33:12 o 2Ch 7:14; Eze 3:20
33:13 p Eze 18:24; Heb 10:38; 2Pe 2:20-21
33:14 q Eze 18:27
33:15 r Ex 22:1-4; Lev 6:2-5 s Eze 20:11; Lk 19:8
33:16 t Isa 43:25; Eze 18:22
33:18 u Eze 3:20; Eze 18:26
33:21 v Eze 24:26 w 2Ki 25:4,10; Jer 39:1-2; Eze 32:1
33:22 x Eze 1:3 y Lk 1:64 z Eze 3:26-27; Eze 24:27
33:24 a Eze 36:4 b Isa 51:2; Jer 40:7; Eze 11:15; Ac 7:5
33:25 c Ge 9:4; Dt 12:16 d Jer 7:9-10; Eze 22:6,27
33:26 e Eze 22:11
33:27 f 1Sa 13:6; Isa 2:19; Jer 42:22; Eze 39:4
33:31 g Eze 8:1 h Ps 78:36-37; Isa 29:13; Eze 22:27; Mt 13:22; 1Jn 3:18

they hear your words but do not put them into practice.[i]

33 "When all this comes true—and it surely will—then they will know that a prophet has been among them.[j]"

Shepherds and Sheep

34 The word of the LORD came to me: 2 "Son of man, prophesy against the shepherds of Israel; prophesy and say to them: 'This is what the Sovereign LORD says: Woe to the shepherds of Israel who only take care of themselves! Should not shepherds take care of the flock?[a] 3 You eat the curds, clothe yourselves with the wool and slaughter the choice animals, but you do not take care of the flock.[b] 4 You have not strengthened the weak or healed the sick or bound up the injured. You have not brought back the strays or searched for the lost. You have ruled them harshly and brutally.[c] 5 So they were scattered because there was no shepherd,[d] and when they were scattered they became food for all the wild animals.[e] 6 My sheep wandered over all the mountains and on every high hill. They were scattered over the whole earth, and no-one searched or looked for them.[f]

7 " 'Therefore, you shepherds, hear the word of the LORD: 8 As surely as I live, declares the Sovereign LORD, because my flock lacks a shepherd and so has been plundered and has become food for all the wild animals, and because my shepherds did not search for my flock but cared for themselves rather than for my flock, 9 therefore, O shepherds, hear the word of the LORD: 10 This is what the Sovereign LORD says: I am against[g] the shepherds and will hold them accountable for my flock. I will remove them from tending the flock so that the shepherds can no longer feed themselves. I will rescue[h] my flock from their mouths, and it will no longer be food for them.[i]

11 " 'For this is what the Sovereign LORD says: I myself will search for my sheep and look after them. 12 As a shepherd[j] looks after his scattered flock when he is with them, so will I look after my sheep. I will rescue them from all the places where they were scattered on a day of clouds and darkness.[k] 13 I will bring them out from the nations and gather them from the countries, and I will bring them into their own land. I will pasture them on the mountains of Israel, in the ravines and in all the settlements in the land.[l] 14 I will tend them in a good pasture, and the mountain heights of Israel[m] will be their grazing land. There they will lie down in good grazing land, and there they will feed in a rich pasture[n] on the mountains of Israel.[o] 15 I myself will tend my sheep and make them lie down, declares the Sovereign LORD.[p] 16 I will search for the lost and bring back the strays. I will bind up the injured and strengthen the weak,[q] but the sleek and the strong I will destroy. I will shepherd the flock with justice.[r]

17 " 'As for you, my flock, this is what the Sovereign LORD says: I will judge between one sheep and another, and between rams and goats.[s] 18 Is it not enough for you to feed on the good pasture? Must you also trample the rest of your pasture with your feet? Is it not enough for you to drink clear water? Must you also muddy the rest with your feet? 19 Must my flock feed on what you have trampled and drink what you have muddied with your feet?

20 " 'Therefore this is what the Sovereign LORD says to them: See, I myself will judge between the fat sheep and the lean sheep. 21 Because you shove with flank and shoulder, butting all the weak sheep with your horns[t] until you

33:32
i Mk 6:20

33:33
j 1Sa 3:20; Jer 28:9; Eze 2:5

34:2
a Ps 78:70-72; Isa 40:11; Jer 3:15; Jer 23:1; Mic 3:11; Jn 10:11; Jn 21:15-17

34:3
b Isa 56:11; Eze 22:27; Zec 11:16

34:4
c Zec 11:15-17

34:5
d Nu 27:17
e ver 28; Isa 56:9

34:6
f Ps 142:4; 1Pe 2:25

34:10
g Jer 21:13
h Ps 72:14
i 1Sa 2:29-30; Zec 10:3

34:12
j Isa 40:11; Jer 31:10; Lk 19:10
k Eze 30:3

34:13
l Jer 23:3

34:14
m Eze 20:40
n Ps 23:2
o Eze 36:29-30

34:15
p Ps 23:1-2

34:16
q Mic 4:6
r Isa 10:16; Lk 5:32

34:17
s Mt 25:32-33

34:21
t Dt 33:17

have driven them away, [22]I will save my flock, and they will no longer be plundered. I will judge between one sheep and another.[u] [23]I will place over them one shepherd, my servant David, and he will tend[v] them; he will tend them and be their shepherd. [24]I the LORD will be their God,[w] and my servant David will be prince among them. I the LORD have spoken.[x]

[25]" 'I will make a covenant of peace with them and rid the land of wild beasts[y] so that they may live in the desert and sleep in the forests in safety.[z] [26]I will bless[a] them and the places surrounding my hill.[a] I will send down showers in season;[b] there will be showers of blessing.[c] [27]The trees of the field will yield their fruit and the ground will yield its crops; the people will be secure in their land. They will know that I am the LORD, when I break the bars of their yoke[d] and rescue them from the hands of those who enslaved them.[e] [28]They will no longer be plundered by the nations, nor will wild animals devour them. They will live in safety, and no-one will make them afraid.[f] [29]I will provide for them a land renowned[g] for its crops, and they will no longer be victims of famine[h] in the land or bear the scorn[i] of the nations.[j] [30]Then they will know that I, the LORD their God, am with them and that they, the house of Israel, are my people, declares the Sovereign LORD.[k] [31]You my sheep, the sheep of my pasture,[l] are people, and I am your God, declares the Sovereign LORD.' "

A Prophecy Against Edom

35 The word of the LORD came to me: [2]"Son of man, set your face against Mount Seir; prophesy against it [3]and say: 'This is what the Sovereign LORD says: I am against you, Mount Seir, and I will stretch out my hand[a] against you and make you a desolate waste.[b] [4]I will turn your towns into ruins and you will be desolate. Then you will know that I am the LORD.[c]

[5]" 'Because you harboured an ancient hostility and delivered the Israelites over to the sword at the time of their calamity, the time their punishment reached its climax,[d] [6]therefore as surely as I live, declares the Sovereign LORD, I will give you over to bloodshed and it will pursue you.[e] Since you did not hate bloodshed, bloodshed will pursue you. [7]I will make Mount Seir a desolate waste and cut off from it all who come and go. [8]I will fill your mountains with the slain; those killed by the sword will fall on your hills and in your valleys and in all your ravines.[f] [9]I will make you desolate for ever; your towns will not be inhabited. Then you will know that I am the LORD.[g]

[10]" 'Because you have said, "These two nations and countries will be ours and we will take possession[h] of them," even though I the LORD was there, [11]therefore as surely as I live, declares the Sovereign LORD, I will treat you in accordance with the anger[i] and jealousy you showed in your hatred of them and I will make myself known among them when I judge you.[j] [12]Then you will know that I the LORD have heard all the contemptible things you have said against the mountains of Israel. You said, "They have been laid waste and have been given over to us to devour.[k]" [13]You boasted against me and spoke against me without restraint, and I heard it.[l] [14]This is what the Sovereign LORD says: While the whole earth rejoices, I will make you desolate.[m] [15]Because you rejoiced[n] when the inheritance of the house of Israel became desolate, that is how I will

34:22 u Ps 72:12-14; Jer 23:2-3
34:23 v Isa 40:11
34:24 w Eze 36:28; x Jer 30:9
34:25 y Lev 26:6; z Isa 11:6-9; Hos 2:18
34:26 a Ge 12:2; b Ps 68:9; c Dt 11:13-15; Isa 44:3
34:27 d Lev 26:13; e Jer 30:8
34:28 f Jer 30:10; Eze 39:26
34:29 g Isa 4:2; h Eze 36:29; i Eze 36:6; j Eze 36:15
34:30 k Eze 14:11; Eze 37:27
34:31 l Ps 100:3; Jer 23:1
35:3 a Jer 6:12; b Eze 25:12-14
35:4 c ver 9
35:5 d Ps 137:7; Eze 21:29
35:6 e Isa 63:2-6
35:8 f Eze 31:12
35:9 g Jer 49:13
35:10 h Ps 83:12; Eze 36:2,5
35:11 i Eze 25:14; j Ps 9:16; Mt 7:2
35:12 k Jer 50:7
35:13 l Da 11:36
35:14 m Jer 51:48
35:15 n Ob 1:12

[a]26 Or *I will make them and the places surrounding my hill a blessing*

treat you. You will be desolate, O
Mount Seir,[o] you and all of
Edom.[p] Then they will know that I
am the LORD.' "

A Prophecy to the Mountains of Israel

36 "Son of man, prophesy to
the mountains of Israel and
say, 'O mountains of Israel, hear
the word of the LORD. 2This is what
the Sovereign LORD says: The enemy said of you, "Aha![a] The ancient heights[b] have become our
possession.[c]" ' 3Therefore prophesy and say, 'This is what the Sovereign LORD says: Because they
ravaged and hounded you from
every side so that you became the
possession of the rest of the nations
and the object of people's malicious talk and slander,[d] 4there-
fore, O mountains of Israel, hear
the word of the Sovereign LORD:
This is what the Sovereign LORD
says to the mountains and hills, to
the ravines and valleys,[e] to the
desolate ruins and the deserted
towns that have been plundered
and ridiculed by the rest of the
nations around you[f]—5this is what
the Sovereign LORD says: In my
burning zeal I have spoken against
the rest of the nations, and against
Edom, for with glee and with malice in their hearts they made my
land their own possession so that
they might plunder its pasture-
land.'[g] 6Therefore prophesy concerning the land of Israel and say
to the mountains and hills, to the ravines and valleys: 'This is what the
Sovereign LORD says: I speak in my
jealous wrath because you have
suffered the scorn of the nations.[h]
7Therefore this is what the Sovereign LORD says: I swear with uplifted hand that the nations around
you will also suffer scorn.
8" 'But you, O mountains of Israel, will produce branches and
fruit[i] for my people Israel, for
they will soon come home. 9I am
concerned for you and will look on
you with favour; you will be
ploughed and sown, 10and I will
multiply the number of people
upon you, even the whole house of
Israel. The towns will be inhabited
and the ruins rebuilt.[j] 11I will increase the number of men and animals upon you, and they will be
fruitful and become numerous. I
will settle people on you as in the
past[k] and will make you prosper
more than before.[l] Then you will
know that I am the LORD. 12I will
cause people, my people Israel, to
walk upon you. They will possess
you, and you will be their inheritance;[m] you will never again deprive them of their children.
13" 'This is what the Sovereign
LORD says: Because people say to
you, "You devour men[n] and deprive your nation of its children,"
14therefore you will no longer devour men or make your nation
childless, declares the Sovereign
LORD. 15No longer will I make you
hear the taunts of the nations, and
no longer will you suffer the scorn
of the peoples or cause your nation
to fall, declares the Sovereign
LORD.[o]' "
16Again the word of the LORD
came to me: 17"Son of man, when
the people of Israel were living in
their own land, they defiled it by
their conduct and their actions.
Their conduct was like a woman's
monthly uncleanness in my sight.[p]
18So I poured out[q] my wrath on
them because they had shed blood
in the land and because they had
defiled it with their idols. 19I dispersed them among the nations,
and they were scattered[r] through
the countries; I judged them according to their conduct and their
actions.[s] 20And wherever they
went among the nations they profaned[t] my holy name, for it was
said of them, 'These are the LORD's
people, and yet they had to leave
his land.'[u] 21I had concern for my
holy name, which the house of

35:15 o ver 3 p Isa 34:5-6,11; Jer 50:11-13; La 4:21
36:2 a Eze 25:3 b Dt 32:13 c Eze 35:10
36:3 d Ps 44:13-14
36:4 e Eze 6:3 f Dt 11:11; Ps 79:4; Eze 34:28
36:5 g Jer 50:11; Eze 25:12-14; Eze 35:10,15
36:6 h Ps 123:3-4; Eze 34:29
36:8 i Isa 27:6
36:10 j ver 33; Isa 49:17-23
36:11 k Mic 7:14 l Jer 31:28; Eze 16:55
36:12 m Eze 47:14,22
36:13 n Nu 13:32
36:15 o Ps 89:50-51; Eze 34:29
36:17 p Jer 2:7
36:18 q 2Ch 34:21
36:19 r Dt 28:64 s Eze 39:24
36:20 t Ro 2:24 u Isa 52:5; Jer 33:24; Eze 12:16

Israel profaned among the nations where they had gone.[v]

22 “Therefore say to the house of Israel, ‘This is what the Sovereign LORD says: It is not for your sake, O house of Israel, that I am going to do these things, but for the sake of my holy name, which you have profaned[w] among the nations where you have gone.[x] 23 I will show the holiness of my great name, which has been profaned among the nations, the name you have profaned among them. Then the nations will know that I am the LORD, declares the Sovereign LORD, when I show myself holy[y] through you before their eyes.[z]

24 “ ‘For I will take you out of the nations; I will gather you from all the countries and bring you back into your own land.[a] 25 I will sprinkle[b] clean water on you, and you will be clean; I will cleanse[c] you from all your impurities and from all your idols.[d] 26 I will give you a new heart[e] and put a new spirit in you; I will remove from you your heart of stone and give you a heart of flesh.[f] 27 And I will put my Spirit[g] in you and move you to follow my decrees and be careful to keep my laws. 28 You will live in the land I gave your forefathers; you will be my people,[h] and I will be your God.[i] 29 I will save you from all your uncleanness. I will call for the corn and make it plentiful and will not bring famine[j] upon you. 30 I will increase the fruit of the trees and the crops of the field, so that you will no longer suffer disgrace among the nations because of famine.[k] 31 Then you will remember your evil ways and wicked deeds, and you will loathe yourselves for your sins and detestable practices.[l] 32 I want you to know that I am not doing this for your sake, declares the Sovereign LORD. Be ashamed and disgraced for your conduct, O house of Israel![m]

33 “ ‘This is what the Sovereign LORD says: On the day I cleanse you from all your sins, I will resettle your towns, and the ruins will be rebuilt. 34 The desolate land will be cultivated instead of lying desolate in the sight of all who pass through it. 35 They will say, “This land that was laid waste has become like the garden of Eden;[n] the cities that were lying in ruins, desolate and destroyed, are now fortified and inhabited.[o]” 36 Then the nations around you that remain will know that I the LORD have rebuilt what was destroyed and have replanted what was desolate. I the LORD have spoken, and I will do it.’[p]

37 “This is what the Sovereign LORD says: Once again I will yield to the plea of the house of Israel and do this for them: I will make their people as numerous as sheep, 38 as numerous as the flocks for offerings[q] at Jerusalem during her appointed feasts. So will the ruined cities be filled with flocks of people. Then they will know that I am the LORD.”

The Valley of Dry Bones

37 The hand of the LORD was upon me,[a] and he brought me out by the Spirit[b] of the LORD and set me in the middle of a valley;[c] it was full of bones.[d] 2 He led me to and fro among them, and I saw a great many bones on the floor of the valley, bones that were very dry. 3 He asked me, “Son of man, can these bones live?”

I said, “O Sovereign LORD, you alone know.[e]”

4 Then he said to me, “Prophesy to these bones and say to them, ‘Dry bones, hear the word of the LORD![f] 5 This is what the Sovereign LORD says to these bones: I will make breath[a] enter you, and you will come to life.[g] 6 I will attach tendons to you and make flesh come upon you and cover you with skin; I will put breath in you, and you will

36:21 v Ps 74:18; Isa 48:9
36:22 w Ro 2:24*; x Ps 106:8
36:23 y Eze 20:41; z Ps 126:2; Isa 5:16
36:24 a Eze 34:13; Eze 37:21
36:25 b Heb 9:13; Heb 10:22; c Ps 51:2,7; d Zec 13:2
36:26 e Jer 24:7; f Ps 51:10; Eze 11:19
36:27 g Eze 37:14
36:28 h Jer 30:22; i Eze 14:11; Eze 37:14,27
36:29 j Eze 34:29
36:30 k Lev 26:4-5; Eze 34:27; Hos 2:21-22
36:31 l Eze 6:9; Eze 20:43
36:32 m Dt 9:5
36:35 n Joel 2:3; o Isa 51:3
36:36 p Eze 17:22; Eze 22:14; Eze 37:14; Eze 39:27-28
36:38 q 1Ki 8:63; 2Ch 35:7-9
37:1 a Eze 1:3; Eze 8:3; b Eze 11:24; Lk 4:1; Ac 8:39; c Jer 7:32; d Jer 8:2; Eze 40:1
37:3 e Dt 32:39; 1Sa 2:6; Isa 26:19
37:4 f Jer 22:29
37:5 g Ge 2:7; Ps 104:29-30

a5 The Hebrew for this word can also mean *wind* or *spirit* (see verses 6–14).

come to life. Then you will know
that I am the LORD.[h]' "
7So I prophesied as I was commanded. And as I was prophesying,
there was a noise, a rattling sound,
and the bones came together, bone
to bone. 8I looked, and tendons and
flesh appeared on them and skin
covered them, but there was no
breath in them.
9Then he said to me, "Prophesy to
the breath;[i] prophesy, son of man,
and say to it, 'This is what the Sovereign LORD says: Come from the
four winds, O breath, and breathe
into these slain, that they may
live.' " 10So I prophesied as he commanded me, and breath entered
them; they came to life and stood
up on their feet—a vast army.[j]
11Then he said to me: "Son of
man, these bones are the whole
house of Israel. They say, 'Our
bones are dried up and our hope is
gone; we are cut off.'[k] 12Therefore
prophesy and say to them: 'This is
what the Sovereign LORD says: O
my people, I am going to open your
graves and bring you up from
them; I will bring you back to the
land of Israel.[l] 13Then you, my
people, will know that I am the
LORD, when I open your graves and
bring you up from them. 14I will put
my Spirit[m] in you and you will live,
and I will settle you in your own
land. Then you will know that I the
LORD have spoken, and I have done
it, declares the LORD.[n]' "

One Nation Under One King

15The word of the LORD came to
me: 16"Son of man, take a stick of
wood and write on it, 'Belonging to
Judah and the Israelites[o] associated with him.[p]' Then take another
stick of wood, and write on it, 'Ephraim's stick, belonging to Joseph
and all the house of Israel associated with him.' 17Join them together into one stick so that they
will become one in your hand.[q]
18"When your countrymen ask
you, 'Won't you tell us what you
mean by this?'[r] 19say to them,
'This is what the Sovereign LORD
says: I am going to take the stick of
Joseph—which is in Ephraim's
hand—and of the Israelite tribes
associated with him, and join it to
Judah's stick, making them a single
stick of wood, and they will become
one in my hand.'[s] 20Hold before
their eyes the sticks you have written on 21and say to them, 'This is
what the Sovereign LORD says: I
will take the Israelites out of the
nations where they have gone. I
will gather them from all around
and bring them back into their own
land.[t] 22I will make them one nation in the land, on the mountains of
Israel. There will be one king over
all of them and they will never
again be two nations or be divided
into two kingdoms.[u] 23They will no
longer defile[v] themselves with
their idols and vile images or with
any of their offences, for I will save
them from all their sinful backsliding,[b] and I will cleanse them. They
will be my people, and I will be
their God.[w]
24" 'My servant David[x] will be
king over them, and they will all
have one shepherd.[y] They will follow my laws and be careful to keep
my decrees.[z] 25They will live in
the land I gave to my servant
Jacob, the land where your fathers
lived.[a] They and their children
and their children's children will
live there for ever,[b] and David my
servant will be their prince for
ever.[c] 26I will make a covenant of
peace[d] with them; it will be an
everlasting covenant. I will establish them and increase their numbers,[e] and I will put my sanctuary
among them for ever.[f] 27My
dwelling-place[g] will be with them;
I will be their God, and they will be
my people.[h] 28Then the nations will

37:6
h Eze 38:23
Joel 2:27
Joel 3:17

37:9
i Ps 104:30

37:10
j Rev 11:11

37:11
k La 3:54

37:12
l Dt 32:39
1Sa 2:6
Isa 26:19
Hos 13:14
Am 9:14-15

37:14
m Joel 2:28-29
n Eze 36:27-28, 36

37:16
o 1Ki 12:20
2Ch 10:17-19
p Nu 17:2-3
2Ch 15:9

37:17
q ver 24
Isa 11:13
Jer 50:4
Hos 1:11

37:18
r Eze 24:19

37:19
s Zec 10:6

37:21
t Isa 43:5-6
Eze 36:24
Eze 39:27

37:22
u Isa 11:13
Jer 3:18
Hos 1:11

37:23
v Eze 36:25
Eze 43:7
w Eze 11:18
Eze 36:28

37:24
x Hos 3:5
y Isa 40:11
Eze 34:23
z Ps 78:70-71

37:25
a Eze 28:25
b Am 9:15
c Isa 11:1

37:26
d Isa 55:3
e Jer 30:19
f Eze 16:62

37:27
g Lev 26:11
Jn 1:14
h 2Co 6:16*

b*23* Many Hebrew manuscripts (see also Septuagint); most Hebrew manuscripts *all their dwelling-places where they sinned*

know that I the LORD make Israel holy,[i] when my sanctuary is among them for ever.' "

A Prophecy Against Gog

38 The word of the LORD came to me: 2"Son of man, set your face against Gog, of the land of Magog,[a] the chief prince of[a] Meshech and Tubal;[b] prophesy against him 3and say: 'This is what the Sovereign LORD says: I am against you, O Gog, chief prince of[b] Meshech and Tubal.[c] 4I will turn you around, put hooks[d] in your jaws and bring you out with your whole army—your horses, your horsemen fully armed, and a great horde with large and small shields, all of them brandishing their swords.[e] 5Persia, Cush[c][f] and Put[g] will be with them, all with shields and helmets, 6also Gomer[h] with all its troops, and Beth Togarmah[i] from the far north with all its troops—the many nations with you.

7" 'Get ready; be prepared,[j] you and all the hordes gathered about you, and take command of them. 8After many days[k] you will be called to arms. In future years you will invade a land that has recovered from war, whose people were gathered from many nations[l] to the mountains of Israel, which had long been desolate. They had been brought out from the nations, and now all of them live in safety.[m] 9You and all your troops and the many nations with you will go up, advancing like a storm;[n] you will be like a cloud[o] covering the land.

10" 'This is what the Sovereign LORD says: On that day thoughts will come into your mind and you will devise an evil scheme.[p] 11You will say, "I will invade a land of unwalled villages; I will attack a peaceful and unsuspecting people—all of them living without walls and without gates and bars.[q] 12I will plunder and loot and turn my hand against the resettled ruins and the people gathered from the nations, rich in livestock and goods, living at the centre of the land." 13Sheba[r] and Dedan and the merchants of Tarshish and all her villages[d] will say to you, "Have you come to plunder? Have you gathered your hordes to loot, to carry off silver and gold, to take away livestock and goods and to seize much plunder?[s]" '

14"Therefore, son of man, prophesy and say to Gog: 'This is what the Sovereign LORD says: In that day, when my people Israel are living in safety,[t] will you not take notice of it? 15You will come from your place in the far north, you and many nations with you, all of them riding on horses, a great horde, a mighty army.[u] 16You will advance against my people Israel like a cloud[v] that covers the land. In days to come, O Gog, I will bring you against my land, so that the nations may know me when I show myself holy through you before their eyes.[w]

17" 'This is what the Sovereign LORD says: Are you not the one I spoke of in former days by my servants the prophets of Israel? At that time they prophesied for years that I would bring you against them. 18This is what will happen in that day: When Gog attacks the land of Israel, my hot anger will be aroused, declares the Sovereign LORD. 19In my zeal and fiery wrath I declare that at that time there shall be a great earthquake in the land of Israel.[x] 20The fish of the sea, the birds of the air, the beasts of the field, every creature that moves along the ground, and all the people on the face of the earth will tremble at my presence. The mountains will be overturned, the cliffs will crumble and every wall will fall to the ground.[y] 21I will

37:28 i Ex 31:13; Eze 20:12
38:2 a Ge 10:2; b Rev 20:8
38:3 c Eze 39:1
38:4 d 2Ki 19:28; e Eze 29:4; Da 11:40
38:5 f Ge 10:6; g Eze 27:10
38:6 h Ge 10:2; i Eze 27:14
38:7 j Isa 8:9
38:8 k Isa 24:22; l Isa 11:11; m Jer 23:6
38:9 n Isa 28:2; o Jer 4:13; Joel 2:2
38:10 p Ps 36:4; Mic 2:1
38:11 q Jer 49:31; Zec 2:4
38:13 r Eze 27:22; s Isa 10:6; Jer 15:13
38:14 t ver 8; Zec 2:5
38:15 u Eze 39:2
38:16 v ver 9; w Isa 29:23; Eze 39:21
38:19 x Ps 18:7; Eze 5:13; Hag 2:6,21
38:20 y Hos 4:3; Na 1:5

[a]2 Or *the prince of Rosh,* [b]3 Or *Gog, prince of Rosh,* [c]5 That is, the upper Nile region
[d]13 Or *her strong lions*

summon a sword[z] against Gog on all my mountains, declares the Sovereign LORD. Every man's sword will be against his brother.[a] 22I will execute judgment[b] upon him with plague and bloodshed; I will pour down torrents of rain, hailstones[c] and burning sulphur on him and on his troops and on the many nations with him. 23And so I will show my greatness and my holiness, and I will make myself known in the sight of many nations. Then they will know that I am the LORD.[d]'

39

"Son of man, prophesy against Gog and say: 'This is what the Sovereign LORD says: I am against you, O Gog, chief prince of[a] Meshech and Tubal.[a] 2I will turn you around and drag you along. I will bring you from the far north and send you against the mountains of Israel. 3Then I will strike your bow[b] from your left hand and make your arrows[c] drop from your right hand. 4On the mountains of Israel you will fall, you and all your troops and the nations with you. I will give you as food to all kinds of carrion birds and to the wild animals.[d] 5You will fall in the open field, for I have spoken, declares the Sovereign LORD. 6I will send fire[e] on Magog and on those who live in safety in the coastlands,[f] and they will know that I am the LORD.

7" 'I will make known my holy name among my people Israel. I will no longer let my holy name be profaned,[g] and the nations will know that I the LORD am the Holy One in Israel.[h] 8It is coming! It will surely take place, declares the Sovereign LORD. This is the day I have spoken of.

9" 'Then those who live in the towns of Israel will go out and use the weapons for fuel and burn them up—the small and large shields, the bows and arrows, the war clubs and spears. For seven years they will use them for fuel.[i] 10They will not need to gather wood from the fields or cut it from the forests, because they will use the weapons for fuel. And they will plunder those who plundered them and loot those who looted them, declares the Sovereign LORD.[j]

11" 'On that day I will give Gog a burial place in Israel, in the valley of those who travel east towards[b] the Sea.[c] It will block the way of travellers, because Gog and all his hordes will be buried there. So it will be called the Valley of Hamon Gog.[d][k]

12" 'For seven months the house of Israel will be burying them in order to cleanse the land.[l] 13All the people of the land will bury them, and the day I am glorified[m] will be a memorable day for them, declares the Sovereign LORD.

14" 'Men will be regularly employed to cleanse the land. Some will go throughout the land and, in addition to them, others will bury those that remain on the ground. At the end of the seven months they will begin their search. 15As they go through the land and one of them sees a human bone, he will set up a marker beside it until the gravediggers have buried it in the Valley of Hamon Gog. 16(Also a town called Hamonah[e] will be there.) And so they will cleanse the land.'

17"Son of man, this is what the Sovereign LORD says: Call out to every kind of bird[n] and all the wild animals: 'Assemble and come together from all around to the sacrifice I am preparing for you, the great sacrifice on the mountains of Israel. There you will eat flesh and drink blood. 18You will eat the flesh of mighty men and drink the blood of the princes of the earth as if they were rams and lambs, goats and bulls—all of them fattened animals from Bashan.[o] 19At the sacrifice I am preparing for you, you will eat

38:21 z Eze 14:17 a 1Sa 14:20; 2Ch 20:23; Hag 2:22
38:22 b Isa 66:16; Jer 25:31 c Ps 18:12; Rev 16:21
38:23 d Eze 36:23
39:1 a Eze 38:2,3
39:3 b Hos 1:5 c Ps 76:3
39:4 d ver 17-20; Eze 29:5; Eze 33:27
39:6 e Eze 30:8; Am 1:4 f Jer 25:22
39:7 g Ex 20:7 h Isa 12:6; Eze 36:16,23
39:9 i Ps 46:9
39:10 j Isa 14:2; Isa 33:1; Hab 2:8
39:11 k Eze 38:2
39:12 l Dt 21:23
39:13 m Eze 28:22
39:17 n Rev 19:17
39:18 o Ps 22:12; Jer 51:40

a*1* Or *Gog, prince of Rosh,* b*11* Or *of* c*11* That is, the Dead Sea d*11* *Hamon Gog* means *hordes of Gog.* e*16* *Hamonah* means *horde.*

fat till you are glutted and drink
blood till you are drunk. 20At my
table you will eat your fill of horses
and riders, mighty men and soldiers of every kind,' declares the
Sovereign LORD.[p]
21"I will display my glory among
the nations, and all the nations will
see the punishment I inflict and the
hand I lay upon them.[q] 22From that
day forward the house of Israel will
know that I am the LORD their God.
23And the nations will know that the
people of Israel went into exile for
their sin, because they were unfaithful to me. So I hid my face
from them and handed them over
to their enemies, and they all fell
by the sword.[r] 24I dealt with them
according to their uncleanness and
their offences, and I hid my face
from them.[s]
25"Therefore this is what the Sovereign LORD says: I will now bring
Jacob back from captivity[f][t] and
will have compassion[u] on all the
people of Israel, and I will be zealous for my holy name.[v] 26They will
forget their shame and all the unfaithfulness they showed towards
me when they lived in safety[w] in
their land with no-one to make
them afraid.[x] 27When I have
brought them back from the nations and have gathered them from
the countries of their enemies, I
will show myself holy through
them in the sight of many nations.[y]
28Then they will know that I am the
LORD their God, for though I sent
them into exile among the nations,
I will gather them to their own
land, not leaving any behind. 29I
will no longer hide my face from
them, for I will pour out my Spirit[z]
on the house of Israel, declares the
Sovereign LORD."

The New Temple Area

40 In the twenty-fifth year of
our exile, at the beginning
of the year, on the tenth of the
month, in the fourteenth year after
the fall of the city[a]—on that very
day the hand of the LORD was upon
me[b] and he took me there. 2In
visions[c] of God he took me to the
land of Israel and set me on a very
high mountain,[d] on whose south
side were some buildings that
looked like a city. 3He took me
there, and I saw a man whose appearance was like bronze;[e] he was
standing in the gateway with a
linen cord and a measuring rod[f] in
his hand. 4The man said to me, "Son
of man, look with your eyes and
hear with your ears and pay attention to everything I am going to
show you, for that is why you have
been brought here. Tell[g] the house
of Israel everything you see.[h]"

The East Gate to the Outer Court

5I saw a wall completely surrounding the temple area. The
length of the measuring rod in the
man's hand was six long cubits,
each of which was a cubit[a] and a
handbreadth.[b] He measured[i] the
wall; it was one measuring rod
thick and one rod high.
6Then he went to the gate facing
east.[j] He climbed its steps and
measured the threshold of the gate;
it was one rod deep.[c] 7The alcoves[k] for the guards were one rod
long and one rod wide, and the projecting walls between the alcoves
were five cubits thick. And the
threshold of the gate next to the
portico facing the temple was one
rod deep.
8Then he measured the portico of
the gateway; 9it[d] was eight cubits
deep and its jambs were two cubits
thick. The portico of the gateway
faced the temple.

39:20 p Rev 19:17-18
39:21 q Ex 9:16; Isa 37:20; Eze 38:16
39:23 r Isa 1:15; Isa 59:2; Jer 22:8-9; Jer 44:23
39:24 s Jer 2:17,19; Jer 4:18; Eze 36:19
39:25 t Jer 33:7; Eze 34:13; u Jer 30:18; v Isa 27:12-13
39:26 w 1Ki 4:25; x Isa 17:2; Eze 34:28; Mic 4:4
39:27 y Eze 36:23-24; Eze 37:21; Eze 38:16
39:29 z Joel 2:28; Ac 2:17
40:1 a 2Ki 25:7; Jer 39:1-10; Jer 52:4-11; Eze 33:21; b Eze 1:3
40:2 c Da 7:1,7; d Eze 17:22; Rev 21:10
40:3 e Eze 1:7; Da 10:6; Rev 1:15; f Eze 47:3; Zec 2:1-2; Rev 11:1; Rev 21:15
40:4 g Jer 26:2; h Eze 44:5
40:5 i Eze 42:20
40:6 j Eze 8:16
40:7 k ver 36

f25 Or *now restore the fortunes of Jacob*
a5 The common cubit was about 1 ½ feet (about 0.5 metre). b5 That is, about 3 inches (about 8 centimetres) c6 Septuagint; Hebrew *deep, the first threshold, one rod deep* d8, 9 Many Hebrew manuscripts, Septuagint, Vulgate and Syriac; most Hebrew manuscripts *gateway facing the temple; it was one rod deep. 9Then he measured the portico of the gateway; it*

10Inside the east gate were three
alcoves on each side; the three had
the same measurements, and the
faces of the projecting walls on
each side had the same measurements. 11Then he measured the
width of the entrance to the gateway; it was ten cubits and its length
was thirteen cubits. 12In front of
each alcove was a wall one cubit
high, and the alcoves were six cubits square. 13Then he measured
the gateway from the top of the
rear wall of one alcove to the top of
the opposite one; the distance was
twenty-five cubits from one parapet opening to the opposite one.
14He measured along the faces of
the projecting walls all around the
inside of the gateway—sixty cubits. The measurement was up to
the portico[e] facing the courtyard.[f] [l] 15The distance from the
entrance of the gateway to the far
end of its portico was fifty cubits.
16The alcoves and the projecting
walls inside the gateway were sur-
mounted by narrow parapet openings all round, as was the portico;
the openings all round faced inward. The faces of the projecting
walls were decorated with palm
trees.[m]

The Outer Court

17Then he brought me into the
outer court.[n] There I saw some
rooms and a pavement that had
been constructed all round the
court; there were thirty rooms[o]
along the pavement.[p] 18It abutted
the sides of the gateways and was
as wide as they were long; this was
the lower pavement. 19Then he
measured the distance from the inside of the lower gateway to the
outside of the inner court;[q] it was
a hundred cubits[r] on the east side
as well as on the north.

The North Gate

20Then he measured the length
and width of the gate facing north,
leading into the outer court. 21Its alcoves[s]—three on each side—its
projecting walls and its portico had
the same measurements as those of
the first gateway. It was fifty cubits long and twenty-five cubits
wide. 22Its openings, its portico[t]
and its palm tree decorations had
the same measurements as those of
the gate facing east. Seven steps
led up to it, with its portico opposite
them. 23There was a gate to the inner court facing the north gate, just
as there was on the east. He measured from one gate to the opposite
one; it was a hundred cubits.[u]

The South Gate

24Then he led me to the south side
and I saw a gate facing south. He
measured its jambs and its portico,
and they had the same measurements as the others. 25The gateway
and its portico had narrow openings all round, like the openings of
the others. It was fifty cubits long
and twenty-five cubits wide.[v]
26Seven steps led up to it, with its
portico opposite them; it had palm
tree decorations on the faces of the
projecting walls on each side.[w]
27The inner court[x] also had a gate
facing south, and he measured
from this gate to the outer gate on
the south side; it was a hundred cubits.

Gates to the Inner Court

28Then he brought me into the inner court through the south gate,
and he measured the south gate; it
had the same measurements[y] as
the others. 29Its alcoves, its projecting walls and its portico had the
same measurements as the others.
The gateway and its portico had
openings all round. It was fifty cubits long and twenty-five cubits

40:14 l Ex 27:9
40:16 m ver 21-22; 2Ch 3:5; Eze 41:26
40:17 n Rev 11:2; o Eze 41:6; p Eze 42:1
40:19 q Eze 46:1; r ver 23,27
40:21 s ver 7
40:22 t ver 49
40:23 u ver 19
40:25 v ver 33
40:26 w ver 22
40:27 x ver 32
40:28 y ver 35

e 14 Septuagint; Hebrew *projecting wall*
f 14 The meaning of the Hebrew for this verse is uncertain.

wide. 30(The porticoes[z] of the gateways around the inner court were twenty-five cubits wide and five cubits deep.) 31Its portico[a] faced the outer court; palm trees decorated its jambs, and eight steps led up to it.

32Then he brought me to the inner court on the east side, and he measured the gateway; it had the same measurements as the others. 33Its alcoves, its projecting walls and its portico had the same measurements as the others. The gateway and its portico had openings all round. It was fifty cubits long and twenty-five cubits wide. 34Its portico[b] faced the outer court; palm trees decorated the jambs on either side, and eight steps led up to it.

35Then he brought me to the north gate[c] and measured it. It had the same measurements as the others, 36as did its alcoves,[d] its projecting walls and its portico, and it had openings all round. It was fifty cubits long and twenty-five cubits wide. 37Its portico[g] faced the outer court; palm trees decorated the jambs on either side, and eight steps led up to it.

The Rooms for Preparing Sacrifices

38A room with a doorway was by the portico in each of the inner gateways, where the burnt offerings[e] were washed. 39In the portico of the gateway were two tables on each side, on which the burnt offerings,[f] sin offerings[g] and guilt offerings[h] were slaughtered. 40By the outside wall of the portico of the gateway, near the steps at the entrance to the north gateway were two tables, and on the other side of the steps were two tables. 41So there were four tables on one side of the gateway and four on the other—eight tables in all—on which the sacrifices were slaughtered. 42There were also four tables of dressed stone[i] for the burnt offerings, each a cubit and a half long, a cubit and a half wide and a cubit high. On them were placed the utensils for slaughtering the burnt offerings and the other sacrifices.[j] 43And double-pronged hooks, each a handbreadth long, were attached to the wall all around. The tables were for the flesh of the offerings.

Rooms for the Priests

44Outside the inner gate, within the inner court, were two rooms, one[h] at the side of the north gate and facing south, and another at the side of the south[i] gate and facing north. 45He said to me, "The room facing south is for the priests who have charge of the temple,[k] 46and the room facing north[l] is for the priests who have charge of the altar.[m] These are the sons of Zadok,[n] who are the only Levites who may draw near to the LORD to minister before him.[o]"

47Then he measured the court: It was square—a hundred cubits long and a hundred cubits wide. And the altar was in front of the temple.

The Temple

48He brought me to the portico of the temple[p] and measured the jambs of the portico; they were five cubits wide on either side. The width of the entrance was fourteen cubits and its projecting walls were[j] three cubits wide on either side. 49The portico[q] was twenty cubits wide, and twelve[k] cubits from front to back. It was reached by a flight of stairs,[l] and there were pillars[r] on each side of the jambs.

40:30 z ver 21
40:31 a ver 22
40:34 b ver 22
40:35 c Eze 44:4; Eze 47:2
40:36 d ver 7
40:38 e 2Ch 4:6; Eze 42:13
40:39 f Eze 46:2; g Lev 4:3,28; h Lev 7:1
40:42 i Ex 20:25; j ver 39
40:45 k 1Ch 9:23
40:46 l Eze 42:13; m Nu 18:5; n 1Ki 2:35; o Nu 16:5; Eze 43:19; Eze 44:15; Eze 45:4; Eze 48:11
40:48 p 1Ki 6:2
40:49 q ver 22; 1Ki 6:3; r 1Ki 7:15

g37 Septuagint (see also verses 31 and 34); Hebrew *jambs* h44 Septuagint; Hebrew *were rooms for singers, which were* i44 Septuagint; Hebrew *east* j48 Septuagint; Hebrew *entrance was* k49 Septuagint; Hebrew *eleven* l49 Hebrew; Septuagint *Ten steps led up to it*

41 Then the man brought me
to the outer sanctuary[a]
and measured the jambs; the width
of the jambs was six cubits[a] on
each side.[b] 2The entrance was ten
cubits wide, and the projecting
walls on each side of it were five
cubits wide. He also measured the
outer sanctuary; it was forty cubits
long and twenty cubits wide.[b]
3Then he went into the inner
sanctuary and measured the jambs
of the entrance; each was two cubits wide. The entrance was six cubits wide, and the projecting walls
on each side of it were seven cubits
wide. 4And he measured the length
of the inner sanctuary; it was
twenty cubits, and its width was
twenty cubits across the end of the
outer sanctuary.[c] He said to me,
"This is the Most Holy Place.[d]"
5Then he measured the wall of
the temple; it was six cubits thick,
and each side room round the temple was four cubits wide. 6The side
rooms were on three levels, one
above another, thirty[e] on each
level. There were ledges all round
the wall of the temple to serve as
supports for the side rooms, so that
the supports were not inserted into
the wall of the temple.[f] 7The side
rooms all round the temple were
wider at each successive level. The
structure surrounding the temple
was built in ascending stages, so
that the rooms widened as one went
upward. A stairway[g] went up from
the lowest floor to the top floor
through the middle floor.
8I saw that the temple had a
raised base all round it, forming
the foundation of the side rooms. It
was the length of the rod, six long
cubits. 9The outer wall of the side
rooms was five cubits thick. The
open area between the side rooms
of the temple 10and the ⌞priests'⌟
rooms was twenty cubits wide all
round the temple. 11There were
entrances to the side rooms from
the open area, one on the north and
another on the south; and the base

41:1 a ver 23
41:2 b 2Ch 3:3
41:4 c 1Ki 6:20 d Ex 26:33 Heb 9:3-8
41:6 e Eze 40:17 f 1Ki 6:5
41:7 g 1Ki 6:8
41:14 h Eze 40:47
41:15 i Eze 42:3
41:16 j 1Ki 6:4 k ver 25-26 1Ki 6:15 Eze 42:3
41:18 l 1Ki 6:18 m Ex 37:7 2Ch 3:7 n 1Ki 6:29 1Ki 7:36 o Eze 10:21
41:19 p Eze 10:14
41:21 q ver 1

adjoining the open area was five
cubits wide all round.
12The building facing the temple
courtyard on the west side was seventy cubits wide. The wall of the
building was five cubits thick all
round, and its length was ninety
cubits.
13Then he measured the temple;
it was a hundred cubits long, and
the temple courtyard and the building with its walls were also a hundred cubits long. 14The width of the
temple courtyard on the east, including the front of the temple, was
a hundred cubits.[h]
15Then he measured the length of
the building facing the courtyard
at the rear of the temple, including
its galleries[i] on each side; it was a
hundred cubits.
The outer sanctuary, the inner
sanctuary and the portico facing
the court, 16as well as the thresholds and the narrow windows[j] and
galleries round the three of them—
everything beyond and including
the threshold was covered with
wood. The floor, the wall up to the
windows, and the windows were
covered.[k] 17In the space above the
outside of the entrance to the inner
sanctuary and on the walls at regular intervals all round the inner and
outer sanctuary 18were carved[l]
cherubim[m] and palm trees.[n] Palm
trees alternated with cherubim.
Each cherub had two faces:[o] 19the
face of a man towards the palm
tree on one side and the face of a
lion towards the palm tree on the
other. They were carved all round
the whole temple.[p] 20From the
floor to the area above the entrance, cherubim and palm trees
were carved on the wall of the
outer sanctuary.
21The outer sanctuary[q] had a
rectangular door-frame, and the
one at the front of the Most Holy

[a]1 The common cubit was about 1½ feet (about 0.5 metre). [b]1 One Hebrew manuscript and Septuagint; most Hebrew manuscripts *side, the width of the tent*

Place was similar. [22]There was a
wooden altar[r] three cubits high
and two cubits square;[c] its corners, its base[d] and its sides were of
wood. The man said to me, "This is
the table[s] that is before the LORD."
[23]Both the outer sanctuary[t] and
the Most Holy Place had double
doors.[u] [24]Each door had two
leaves—two hinged leaves[v] for
each door. [25]And on the doors of the
outer sanctuary were carved
cherubim and palm trees like those
carved on the walls, and there was
a wooden overhang on the front of
the portico. [26]On the side walls of
the portico were narrow windows
with palm trees carved on each
side. The side rooms of the temple
also had overhangs.[w]

Rooms for the Priests

42 Then the man led me north-
ward into the outer court
and brought me to the rooms[a] opposite the temple courtyard[b] and
opposite the outer wall on the north
side.[c] [2]The building whose door
faced north was a hundred cubits[a]
long and fifty cubits wide. [3]Both in
the section twenty cubits from the
inner court and in the section opposite the pavement of the outer
court, gallery[d] faced gallery at the
three levels.[e] [4]In front of the
rooms was an inner passageway
ten cubits wide and a hundred cubits[b] long. Their doors were on the
north.[f] [5]Now the upper rooms
were narrower, for the galleries
took more space from them than
from the rooms on the lower and
middle floors of the building. [6]The
rooms on the third floor had no pillars, as the courts had; so they were
smaller in floor space than those on
the lower and middle floors. [7]There
was an outer wall parallel to the
rooms and the outer court; it extended in front of the rooms for
fifty cubits. [8]While the row of
rooms on the side next to the outer
court was fifty cubits long, the row
on the side nearest the sanctuary
was a hundred cubits long. [9]The
lower rooms had an entrance[g] on
the east side as one enters them
from the outer court.
[10]On the south side[c] along the
length of the wall of the outer
court, adjoining the temple courtyard and opposite the outer wall,
were rooms[h] [11]with a passageway
in front of them. These were like
the rooms on the north; they had
the same length and width, with
similar exits and dimensions. Similar to the doorways on the north
[12]were the doorways of the rooms
on the south. There was a doorway
at the beginning of the passageway
that was parallel to the corresponding wall extending eastward, by
which one enters the rooms.
[13]Then he said to me, "The
north[i] and south rooms facing the
temple courtyard are the priests'
rooms, where the priests who approach the LORD will eat the most
holy offerings. There they will put
the most holy offerings—the grain
offerings, the sin offerings[j] and
the guilt offerings[k]—for the place
is holy.[l] [14]Once the priests enter
the holy precincts, they are not to
go into the outer court until they
leave behind the garments[m] in
which they minister, for these are
holy. They are to put on other
clothes before they go near the
places that are for the people.[n]"
[15]When he had finished measuring what was inside the temple
area, he led me out by the east
gate[o] and measured the area all
around: [16]He measured the east
side with the measuring rod; it was
five hundred cubits.[d] [17]He measured the north side; it was five hundred cubits[e] by the measuring rod.

41:22 r Ex 30:1 s Ex 25:23; Eze 23:41; Eze 44:16; Mal 1:7,12
41:23 t ver 1 u 1Ki 6:32
41:24 v 1Ki 6:34
41:26 w ver 15-16; Eze 40:16
42:1 a ver 13 b Eze 41:12-14 c Eze 40:17
42:3 d Eze 41:15 e Eze 41:16
42:4 f Eze 46:19
42:9 g Eze 44:5; Eze 46:19
42:10 h ver 1
42:13 i Eze 40:46 j Lev 10:17; Lev 6:25 k Lev 14:13 l Ex 29:31; Lev 6:29; Lev 7:6; Lev 10:12-13; Nu 18:9-10
42:14 m Eze 44:19 n Ex 29:9; Lev 8:7-9
42:15 o Eze 43:1

c22 Septuagint; Hebrew *long* d22 Septuagint; Hebrew *length* a2 The common cubit was about 1½ feet (about 0.5 metre). b4 Septuagint and Syriac; Hebrew *and one cubit* c10 Septuagint; Hebrew *Eastward* d16 See Septuagint of verse 17; Hebrew *rods*; also in verses 18 and 19. e17 Septuagint; Hebrew *rods*

18He measured the south side; it
was five hundred cubits by the
measuring rod. 19Then he turned to
the west side and measured; it was
five hundred cubits by the measuring rod. 20So he measured[p] the
area on all four sides. It had a wall
round it,[q] five hundred cubits long
and five hundred cubits wide,[r] to
separate the holy from the common.[s]

The Glory Returns to the Temple

43 Then the man brought me
to the gate facing east,[a]
2and I saw the glory of the God of
Israel coming from the east. His
voice was like the roar of rushing
waters,[b] and the land was radiant
with his glory.[c] 3The vision I saw
was like the vision I had seen when
he[a] came to destroy the city and
like the visions I had seen by the
Kebar River, and I fell face down.
4The glory[d] of the LORD entered
the temple through the gate facing
east.[e] 5Then the Spirit[f] lifted me
up[g] and brought me into the inner
court, and the glory of the LORD
filled the temple.
6While the man was standing beside me, I heard someone speaking
to me from inside the temple. 7He
said: "Son of man, this is the place
of my throne and the place for the
soles of my feet. This is where I
will live among the Israelites for
ever. The house of Israel will never
again defile my holy name—neither they nor their kings—by their
prostitution[b] and the lifeless
idols[c] of their kings at their high
places.[h] 8When they placed their
threshold next to my threshold and
their doorposts beside my doorposts, with only a wall between me
and them, they defiled my holy
name by their detestable practices.
So I destroyed them in my anger.
9Now let them put away from me
their prostitution and the lifeless
idols of their kings, and I will live
among them for ever.[i]
10"Son of man, describe the temple to the people of Israel, that they
may be ashamed[j] of their sins. Let
them consider the plan, 11and if
they are ashamed of all they have
done, make known to them the design of the temple—its arrangement, its exits and entrances—its
whole design and all its regulations[d] and laws. Write these down
before them so that they may be
faithful to its design and follow all
its regulations.[k]
12"This is the law of the temple:
All the surrounding area[l] on top of
the mountain will be most holy.
Such is the law of the temple.

The Altar

13"These are the measurements
of the altar[m] in long cubits, that cubit being a cubit[e] and a handbreadth:[f] Its gutter is a cubit deep
and a cubit wide, with a rim of one
span[g] around the edge. And this is
the height of the altar: 14From the
gutter on the ground up to the
lower ledge it is two cubits high
and a cubit wide, and from the
smaller ledge up to the larger ledge
it is four cubits high and a cubit
wide. 15The altar hearth is four cubits high, and four horns[n] project
upward from the hearth. 16The
altar hearth is square, twelve cubits long and twelve cubits wide.
17The upper ledge also is square,
fourteen cubits long and fourteen
cubits wide, with a rim of half a cubit and a gutter of a cubit all round.
The steps[o] of the altar face east."
18Then he said to me, "Son of
man, this is what the Sovereign

42:20
p Eze 40:5
q Zec 2:5
r Eze 45:2; Rev 21:16
s Eze 22:26

43:1
a Eze 10:19; Eze 42:15; Eze 44:1; Eze 46:1

43:2
b Rev 1:15
c Isa 6:3; Eze 11:23; Rev 18:1

43:4
d Eze 1:28
e Eze 10:19

43:5
f Eze 11:24
g Eze 3:12; Eze 8:3

43:7
h Lev 26:30

43:9
i Eze 37:26-28

43:10
j Eze 16:61

43:11
k Eze 44:5

43:12
l Eze 40:2

43:13
m 2Ch 4:1

43:15
n Ex 27:2

43:17
o Ex 20:26

[a]3 Some Hebrew manuscripts and Vulgate; most Hebrew manuscripts *I* [b]7 Or *their spiritual adultery*; also in verse 9 [c]7 Or *the corpses*; also in verse 9 [d]11 Some Hebrew manuscripts and Septuagint; most Hebrew manuscripts *regulations and its whole design* [e]13 The common cubit was about 1½ feet (about 0.5 metre).
[f]13 That is, about 3 inches (about 8 centimetres)
[g]13 That is, about 9 inches (about 23 centimetres)

LORD says: These will be the regulations for sacrificing burnt offerings[p] and sprinkling blood[q] upon
the altar when it is built: 19You are
to give a young bull[r] as a sin offering to the priests, who are Levites,
of the family of Zadok,[s] who come
near[t] to minister before me, declares the Sovereign LORD. 20You
are to take some of its blood and put
it on the four horns of the altar and
on the four corners of the upper
ledge[u] and all round the rim, and so
purify the altar[v] and make atonement for it. 21You are to take the
bull for the sin offering and burn
it in the designated part of the temple area outside the sanctuary.[w]
22"On the second day you are to
offer a male goat without defect for
a sin offering, and the altar is to be
purified as it was purified with the
bull. 23When you have finished pu-
rifying it, you are to offer a young
bull and a ram from the flock, both
without defect.[x] 24You are to offer
them before the LORD, and the
priests are to sprinkle salt[y] on
them and sacrifice them as a burnt
offering to the LORD.
25"For seven days[z] you are to
provide a male goat daily for a sin
offering; you are also to provide a
young bull and a ram from the
flock, both without defect.[a] 26For
seven days they are to make atonement for the altar and cleanse it;
thus they will dedicate it. 27At the
end of these days, from the eighth
day[b] on, the priests are to present
your burnt offerings and fellowship offerings[h][c] on the altar. Then
I will accept you, declares the Sovereign LORD."

The Prince, the Levites, the Priests

44 Then the man brought me
back to the outer gate of
the sanctuary, the one facing
east,[a] and it was shut. 2The LORD
said to me, "This gate is to remain
shut. It must not be opened; no-one
may enter through it.[b] It is to remain shut because the LORD, the
God of Israel, has entered through
it. 3The prince himself is the only
one who may sit inside the gateway
to eat in the presence[c] of the LORD.
He is to enter by way of the portico
of the gateway and go out the same
way.[d]"
4Then the man brought me by
way of the north gate to the front of
the temple. I looked and saw the
glory of the LORD filling the temple[e] of the LORD, and I fell face
down.[f]
5The LORD said to me, "Son of
man, look carefully, listen closely
and give attention to everything I
tell you concerning all the regulations regarding the temple of the
LORD. Give attention to the entrance of the temple and all the
exits of the sanctuary.[g] 6Say to the
rebellious house[h] of Israel, 'This is
what the Sovereign LORD says:
Enough of your detestable practices, O house of Israel! 7In addition to all your other detestable
practices, you brought foreigners
uncircumcised in heart[i] and flesh
into my sanctuary, desecrating my
temple while you offered me food,
fat and blood, and you broke my
covenant.[j] 8Instead of carrying
out your duty in regard to my holy
things, you put others in charge of
my sanctuary.[k] 9This is what the
Sovereign LORD says: No foreigner
uncircumcised in heart and flesh is
to enter my sanctuary, not even the
foreigners who live among the
Israelites.[l]
10" 'The Levites who went far
from me when Israel went astray[m]
and who wandered from me after
their idols must bear the consequences of their sin.[n] 11They may
serve in my sanctuary, having
charge of the gates of the temple
and serving in it; they may slaughter the burnt offerings[o] and sacrifices for the people and stand

43:18 p Ex 40:29 q Lev 1:5,11 Heb 9:21-22
43:19 r Lev 4:3 Eze 45:18-19 s Eze 44:15 t Nu 16:40 Eze 40:46
43:20 u ver 17 v Lev 16:19
43:21 w Ex 29:14 Heb 13:11
43:23 x Ex 29:1
43:24 y Lev 2:13 Mk 9:49-50
43:25 z Lev 8:33 a Ex 29:37
43:27 b Lev 9:1 c Lev 17:5
44:1 a Eze 43:1
44:2 b Eze 43:4-5
44:3 c Ex 24:9-11 d Eze 46:2,8
44:4 e Isa 6:4 Rev 15:8 f Eze 1:28 Eze 3:23
44:5 g Eze 40:4 Eze 43:10-11
44:6 h Eze 3:9
44:7 i Lev 26:41 j Ge 17:14 Ex 12:48 Lev 22:25
44:8 k Lev 22:2 Nu 18:7
44:9 l Joel 3:17 Zec 14:21
44:10 m 2Ki 23:8 n Nu 18:23
44:11 o 2Ch 29:34

h27 Traditionally *peace offerings*

before the people and serve them.[p] 12 But because they served them in the presence of their idols and made the house of Israel fall into sin, therefore I have sworn with uplifted hand[q] that they must bear the consequences of their sin, declares the Sovereign LORD.[r] 13 They are not to come near to serve me as priests or come near any of my holy things or my most holy offerings; they must bear the shame[s] of their detestable practices.[t] 14 Yet I will put them in charge of the duties of the temple and all the work that is to be done in it.[u]

15 " 'But the priests, who are Levites and descendants of Zadok and who faithfully carried out the duties of my sanctuary when the Israelites went astray from me, are to come near to minister before me; they are to stand before me to offer sacrifices of fat and blood, declares the Sovereign LORD.[v] 16 They alone are to enter my sanctuary; they alone are to come near my table[w] to minister before me and perform my service.[x]

17 " 'When they enter the gates of the inner court, they are to wear linen clothes;[y] they must not wear any woollen garment while ministering at the gates of the inner court or inside the temple. 18 They are to wear linen turbans[z] on their heads and linen undergarments[a] round their waists. They must not wear anything that makes them perspire.[b] 19 When they go out into the outer court where the people are, they are to take off the clothes they have been ministering in and leave them in the sacred rooms, and put on other clothes, so that they do not consecrate[c] the people by means of their garments.[d]

20 " 'They must not shave their heads or let their hair grow long, but they are to keep the hair of their heads trimmed.[e] 21 No priest is to drink wine when he enters the inner court.[f] 22 They must not marry widows or divorced women; they may marry only virgins of Israelite descent or widows of priests.[g] 23 They are to teach my people the difference between the holy and the common[h] and show them how to distinguish between the unclean and the clean.[i]

24 " 'In any dispute, the priests are to serve as judges[j] and decide it according to my ordinances. They are to keep my laws and my decrees for all my appointed feasts, and they are to keep my Sabbaths holy.[k]

25 " 'A priest must not defile himself by going near a dead person; however, if the dead person was his father or mother, son or daughter, brother or unmarried sister, then he may defile himself.[l] 26 After he is cleansed, he must wait seven days.[m] 27 On the day he goes into the inner court of the sanctuary to minister in the sanctuary, he is to offer a sin offering for himself, declares the Sovereign LORD.

28 " 'I am to be the only inheritance[n] the priests have. You are to give them no possession in Israel; I will be their possession. 29 They will eat the grain offerings, the sin offerings and the guilt offerings; and everything in Israel devoted[a] to the LORD[o] will belong to them.[p] 30 The best of all the firstfruits[q] and of all your special gifts will belong to the priests. You are to give them the first portion of your ground meal[r] so that a blessing[s] may rest on your household.[t] 31 The priests must not eat anything, bird or animal, found dead or torn by wild animals.[u]

Division of the Land

45 " 'When you allot the land as an inheritance,[a] you are to present to the LORD a portion of the land as a sacred district, 25,000

44:11 p Nu 3:5-37; Nu 16:9; 1Ch 26:12-19
44:12 q Ps 106:26; r 2Ki 16:10-16
44:13 s Eze 16:61; t Nu 18:3
44:14 u Nu 18:4; 1Ch 23:28-32
44:15 v Jer 33:18; Eze 40:46; Zec 3:7
44:16 w Eze 41:22; x Nu 18:5
44:17 y Ex 39:27-28; Rev 19:8
44:18 z Ex 28:39; Isa 3:20; a Ex 28:42; b Lev 16:4
44:19 c Lev 6:27; Eze 46:20; d Lev 6:10-11; Eze 42:14
44:20 e Lev 21:5; Nu 6:5
44:21 f Lev 10:9
44:22 g Lev 21:7
44:23 h Eze 22:26; i Mal 2:7
44:24 j Dt 17:8-9; 1Ch 23:4; k 2Ch 19:8
44:25 l Lev 21:1-4
44:26 m Nu 19:14
44:28 n Nu 18:20; Dt 10:9; Dt 18:1-2; Jos 13:33
44:29 o Lev 27:21; p Nu 18:9,14
44:30 q Nu 18:12-13; r Nu 15:18-21; s Mal 3:10; t Ne 10:35-37
44:31 u Ex 22:31; Lev 22:8
45:1 a Eze 47:21-22

a29 The Hebrew term refers to the irrevocable giving over of things or persons to the LORD.

cubits long and 20,000[a] cubits
wide; the entire area will be holy.[b]
2 Of this, a section 500 cubits
square[c] is to be for the sanctuary,
with 50 cubits around it for open
land. 3 In the sacred district, measure off a section 25,000 cubits[b]
long and 10,000 cubits[c] wide. In it
will be the sanctuary, the Most
Holy Place. 4 It will be the sacred
portion of the land for the priests,[d]
who minister in the sanctuary and
who draw near to minister before
the LORD. It will be a place for their
houses as well as a holy place for
the sanctuary.[e] 5 An area 25,000 cubits long and 10,000 cubits wide
will belong to the Levites, who
serve in the temple, as their possession for towns to live in.[d][f]
6 " 'You are to give the city as its
property an area 5,000 cubits wide
and 25,000 cubits long, adjoining
the sacred portion; it will belong to
the whole house of Israel.[g]
7 " 'The prince will have the land
bordering each side of the area
formed by the sacred district and
the property of the city. It will extend westward from the west side
and eastward from the east side,
running lengthwise from the western to the eastern border parallel to
one of the tribal portions.[h] 8 This
land will be his possession in Israel.
And my princes will no longer oppress my people but will allow the
house of Israel to possess the land
according to their tribes.[i]
9 " 'This is what the Sovereign
LORD says: You have gone far
enough, O princes of Israel! Give
up your violence and oppression
and do what is just and right.[j] Stop
dispossessing my people, declares
the Sovereign LORD. 10 You are to
use accurate scales,[k] an accurate
ephah[e][l] and an accurate bath.[f]
11 The ephah[m] and the bath are to be
the same size, the bath containing a
tenth of a homer[g] and the ephah a
tenth of a homer; the homer is to be
the standard measure for both.
12 The shekel[h] is to consist of
twenty gerahs.[n] Twenty shekels
plus twenty-five shekels plus fifteen shekels equal one mina.[i]

Offerings and Holy Days

13 " 'This is the special gift you
are to offer: a sixth of an ephah
from each homer of wheat and a
sixth of an ephah from each homer
of barley. 14 The prescribed portion
of oil, measured by the bath, is a
tenth of a bath from each cor
(which consists of ten baths or one
homer, for ten baths are equivalent
to a homer). 15 Also one sheep is to
be taken from every flock of two
hundred from the well-watered
pastures of Israel. These will be
used for the grain offerings, burnt
offerings[o] and fellowship offerings[j] to make atonement[p] for the
people, declares the Sovereign
LORD. 16 All the people of the land
will participate in this special gift
for the use of the prince in Israel.
17 It will be the duty of the prince to
provide the burnt offerings, grain
offerings and drink offerings at the
festivals, the New Moons and the
Sabbaths[q]—at all the appointed
feasts of the house of Israel. He
will provide the sin offerings, grain
offerings, burnt offerings and fellowship offerings to make atonement for the house of Israel.[r]
18 " 'This is what the Sovereign
LORD says: In the first month[s] on
the first day you are to take a young
bull without defect[t] and purify the
sanctuary.[u] 19 The priest is to take
some of the blood of the sin offering and put it on the doorposts of
the temple, on the four corners of
the upper ledge[v] of the altar[w] and

45:1 *b* Eze 48:8-9,29
45:2 *c* Eze 42:20
45:4 *d* Eze 40:46 *e* Eze 48:10-11
45:5 *f* Eze 48:13
45:6 *g* Eze 48:15-18
45:7 *h* Eze 48:21
45:8 *i* Nu 26:53 Eze 46:18
45:9 *j* Jer 22:3 Zec 7:9-10 Zec 8:16
45:10 *k* Dt 25:15 Pr 11:1 Am 8:4-6 Mic 6:10-11 *l* Lev 19:36
45:11 *m* Isa 5:10
45:12 *n* Ex 30:13 Lev 27:25 Nu 3:47
45:15 *o* Lev 1:4 *p* Lev 6:30
45:17 *q* Lev 23:38 Isa 66:23 *r* 1Ki 8:62 2Ch 31:3 Eze 46:4-12
45:18 *s* Ex 12:2 *t* Lev 22:20 Heb 9:14 *u* Lev 16:16,33
45:19 *v* Eze 43:17 *w* Lev 16:18-19 Eze 43:20

a *1* Septuagint (see also verses 3 and 5 and 48:9); Hebrew *10,000* b *3* That is, about 7 miles (about 11 kilometres) c *3* That is, about 3 miles (about 5 kilometres) d *5* Septuagint; Hebrew *temple; they will have as their possession 20 rooms*
e *10* An ephah was a dry measure. f *10* A bath was a liquid measure. g *11* A homer was a dry measure. h *12* A shekel weighed about 2/5 ounce (about 11.5 grams). i *12* That is, 60 shekels; the common mina was 50 shekels.
j *15* Traditionally *peace offerings;* also in verse 17

on the gateposts of the inner court.
20You are to do the same on the
seventh day of the month for anyone who sins unintentionally[x] or
through ignorance; so you are to
make atonement for the temple.
21" 'In the first month on the fourteenth day you are to observe the
Passover,[y] a feast lasting seven
days, during which you shall eat
bread made without yeast. 22On
that day the prince is to provide a
bull as a sin offering for himself
and for all the people of the land.[z]
23Every day during the seven days
of the Feast he is to provide seven
bulls and seven rams[a] without defect as a burnt offering to the LORD,
and a male goat for a sin offering.[b]
24He is to provide as a grain offering[c] an ephah for each bull and an
ephah for each ram, along with a
hin[k] of oil for each ephah.[d]
25" 'During the seven days of the
Feast,[e] which begins in the seventh month on the fifteenth day, he
is to make the same provision for
sin offerings, burnt offerings,
grain offerings and oil.[f]

46 " 'This is what the Sovereign LORD says: The gate of
the inner court[a] facing east[b] is to
be shut on the six working days, but
on the Sabbath day and on the day
of the New Moon[c] it is to be
opened. 2The prince is to enter
from the outside through the portico[d] of the gateway and stand by
the gatepost. The priests are to sacrifice his burnt offering and his fellowship offerings.[a] He is to
worship at the threshold of the
gateway and then go out, but the
gate will not be shut until evening.[e] 3On the Sabbaths and New
Moons the people of the land are to
worship in the presence of the
LORD at the entrance to that gateway.[f] 4The burnt offering the
prince brings to the LORD on the
Sabbath day is to be six male lambs
and a ram, all without defect. 5The
grain offering given with the ram
is to be an ephah,[b] and the grain
offering with the lambs is to be
as much as he pleases, along with
a hin[c] of oil for each ephah.[g] 6On
the day of the New Moon[h] he is to
offer a young bull, six lambs and a
ram, all without defect. 7He is to
provide as a grain offering one
ephah with the bull, one ephah with
the ram, and with the lambs as
much as he wants to give, along
with a hin of oil with each ephah.[i]
8When the prince enters, he is to go
in through the portico[j] of the gateway, and he is to come out the same
way.[k]
9" 'When the people of the land
come before the LORD at the appointed feasts,[l] whoever enters by
the north gate to worship is to go
out by the south gate; and whoever
enters by the south gate is to go out
by the north gate. No-one is to return through the gate by which he
entered, but each is to go out by the
opposite gate. 10The prince is to be
among them, going in when they go
in and going out when they go out.[m]
11" 'At the festivals and the appointed feasts, the grain offering is
to be an ephah with a bull, an ephah
with a ram, and with the lambs as
much as one pleases, along with a
hin of oil for each ephah.[n] 12When
the prince provides[o] a freewill
offering[p] to the LORD—whether a
burnt offering or fellowship offerings—the gate facing east is to be
opened for him. He shall offer his
burnt offering or his fellowship offerings as he does on the Sabbath
day. Then he shall go out, and after
he has gone out, the gate will be
shut.[q]
13" 'Every day you are to provide
a year-old lamb without defect for
a burnt offering to the LORD; morning by morning you shall provide
it.[r] 14You are also to provide with
it morning by morning a grain

45:20 x Lev 4:27
45:21 y Ex 12:11; Lev 23:5-6
45:22 z Lev 4:14
45:23 a Job 42:8; b Nu 28:16-25
45:24 c Nu 28:12-13; d Eze 46:5-7
45:25 e Dt 16:13; f Lev 23:34-43; Nu 29:12-38
46:1 a Eze 40:19; b 1Ch 9:18; c ver 6; Isa 66:23
46:2 d ver 8; e ver 12; Eze 44:3
46:3 f Lk 1:10
46:5 g ver 11; Eze 45:24
46:6 h ver 1; Nu 10:10
46:7 i Eze 45:24
46:8 j ver 2; k Eze 44:3
46:9 l Ex 23:14; Ex 34:20
46:10 m 2Sa 6:14-15; Ps 42:4
46:11 n ver 5
46:12 o Eze 45:17; p Lev 7:16; q ver 2
46:13 r Ex 29:38; Nu 28:3

k24 That is, probably about 6 pints (about 4 litres)
a2 Traditionally *peace offerings*; also in verse 12
b5 That is, probably about 3/5 bushel (about 22 litres)
c5 That is, probably about 6 pints (about 4 litres)

offering, consisting of a sixth of an
ephah with a third of a hin of oil to
moisten the flour. The presenting
of this grain offering to the LORD is
a lasting ordinance.[s] 15 So the lamb
and the grain offering and the oil
shall be provided morning by
morning for a regular[t] burnt offering.[u]
16 " 'This is what the Sovereign
LORD says: If the prince makes a
gift from his inheritance to one of
his sons, it will also belong to his
descendants; it is to be their property by inheritance.[v] 17 If, however, he makes a gift from his
inheritance to one of his servants,
the servant may keep it until the
year of freedom;[w] then it will revert to the prince. His inheritance
belongs to his sons only; it is theirs.
18 The prince must not take any of
the inheritance[x] of the people,
driving them off their property. He
is to give his sons their inheritance
out of his own property, so that
none of my people will be separated from his property.' "
19 Then the man brought me
through the entrance[y] at the side
of the gate to the sacred rooms
facing north, which belonged to the
priests, and showed me a place at
the western end. 20 He said to me,
"This is the place where the priests
will cook the guilt offering and the
sin offering and bake the grain offering, to avoid bringing them into
the outer court and consecrating[z]
the people."[a]
21 He then brought me to the outer
court and led me round to its four
corners, and I saw in each corner
another court. 22 In the four corners
of the outer court were enclosed[d]
courts, forty cubits long and thirty
cubits wide; each of the courts in
the four corners was the same size.
23 Around the inside of each of the
four courts was a ledge of stone,
with places for fire built all round
under the ledge. 24 He said to me,
"These are the kitchens where
those who minister at the temple
will cook the sacrifices of the people."

46:14 [s] Da 8:11
46:15 [t] Ex 29:42 [u] Ex 29:38; Nu 28:5-6
46:16 [v] 2Ch 21:3
46:17 [w] Lev 25:10
46:18 [x] Lev 25:23; Eze 45:8; Mic 2:1-2
46:19 [y] Eze 42:9
46:20 [z] Lev 6:27 [a] Zec 14:20
47:1 [a] Isa 55:1 [b] Ps 46:4; Joel 3:18; Rev 22:1
47:3 [c] Eze 40:3
47:5 [d] Isa 11:9; Hab 2:14
47:7 [e] ver 12; Rev 22:2
47:8 [f] Dt 3:17; Jos 3:16 [g] Isa 41:18

The River From the Temple

47 The man brought me back
to the entrance of the temple, and I saw water[a] coming out
from under the threshold of the
temple towards the east (for the
temple faced east). The water was
coming down from under the south
side of the temple, south of the
altar.[b] 2 He then brought me out
through the north gate and led me
round the outside to the outer gate
facing east, and the water was
flowing from the south side.
3 As the man went eastward with
a measuring line[c] in his hand, he
measured off a thousand cubits[a]
and then led me through water that
was ankle-deep. 4 He measured off
another thousand cubits and led me
through water that was knee-deep.
He measured off another thousand
and led me through water that was
up to the waist. 5 He measured off
another thousand, but now it was a
river that I could not cross, because the water had risen and was
deep enough to swim in—a river
that no-one could cross.[d] 6 He
asked me, "Son of man, do you see
this?"
Then he led me back to the bank
of the river. 7 When I arrived there,
I saw a great number of trees on
each side of the river.[e] 8 He said to
me, "This water flows towards the
eastern region and goes down into
the Arabah,[b][f] where it enters the
Sea.[c] When it empties into the
Sea,[c] the water there becomes
fresh.[g] 9 Swarms of living creatures will live wherever the river
flows. There will be large numbers
of fish, because this water flows
there and makes the salt water
fresh; so where the river flows

[d]22 The meaning of the Hebrew for this word is uncertain. [a]3 That is, about 1,500 feet (about 460 metres) [b]8 Or *the Jordan Valley*
[c]8 That is, the Dead Sea

everything will live.[h] 10Fishermen[i]
will stand along the shore; from
En Gedi[j] to En Eglaim there will
be places for spreading nets.[k] The
fish will be of many kinds[l]—like
the fish of the Great Sea.[d][m] 11But
the swamps and marshes will not
become fresh; they will be left for
salt.[n] 12Fruit trees of all kinds will
grow on both banks of the river.[o]
Their leaves will not wither,
nor will their fruit[p] fail. Every
month they will bear, because
the water from the sanctuary flows
to them. Their fruit will serve for
food and their leaves for healing.[q]"

The Boundaries of the Land

13This is what the Sovereign
LORD says: "These are the boundaries[r] by which you are to divide
the land for an inheritance among
the twelve tribes of Israel, with two
portions for Joseph.[s] 14You are to
divide it equally among them. Because I swore with uplifted hand to
give it to your forefathers, this land
will become your inheritance.[t]

15"This is to be the boundary of
the land:

"On the north side it will run from
the Great Sea by the Hethlon
road[u] past Lebo[e] Hamath to
Zedad, 16Berothah[f][v] and Sib-
raim (which lies on the border
between Damascus and Ha-
math),[w] as far as Hazer Hatti-
con, which is on the border of
Hauran. 17The boundary will
extend from the sea to Hazar
Enan,[g] along the northern border of Damascus, with the border
of Hamath to the north. This
will be the north boundary.[x]

18"On the east side the boundary
will run between Hauran and
Damascus, along the Jordan
between Gilead and the land of
Israel, to the eastern sea and
as far as Tamar.[h] This will be
the east boundary.

19"On the south side it will run from
Tamar as far as the waters of
Meribah Kadesh,[y] then along
the Wadi ⌞of Egypt⌟[z] to the
Great Sea.[a] This will be the
south boundary.

20"On the west side, the Great Sea
will be the boundary to a point
opposite Lebo[i] Hamath.[b] This
will be the west boundary.[c]

21"You are to distribute this land
among yourselves according to the
tribes of Israel. 22You are to allot it
as an inheritance for yourselves
and for the aliens[d] who have settled among you and who have children. You are to consider them as
native-born Israelites; along with
you they are to be allotted an inheritance among the tribes of Israel.[e] 23In whatever tribe the alien
settles, there you are to give him
his inheritance," declares the Sovereign LORD.

The Division of the Land

48 "These are the tribes,
listed by name: At the
northern frontier, Dan[a] will have
one portion; it will follow the Hethlon road[b] to Lebo[a] Hamath;[c] Hazar Enan and the northern border
of Damascus next to Hamath will
be part of its border from the east
side to the west side.

2"Asher[d] will have one portion;
it will border the territory of Dan
from east to west.

3"Naphtali[e] will have one portion; it will border the territory of
Asher from east to west.

4"Manasseh[f] will have one portion; it will border the territory of
Naphtali from east to west.

47:9 h Isa 12:3; Isa 55:1; Jn 4:14; Jn 7:37-38
47:10 i Mt 4:19; j Jos 15:62; k Eze 26:5; l Ps 104:25; Mt 13:47; m Nu 34:6
47:11 n Dt 29:23
47:12 o ver 7; Rev 22:2; p Ps 1:3; q Ge 2:9; Jer 17:8
47:13 r Nu 34:2-12; s Ge 48:5
47:14 t Ge 12:7; Dt 1:8; Eze 20:5-6
47:15 u Eze 48:1
47:16 v 2Sa 8:8; w Nu 13:21; Eze 48:1
47:17 x Eze 48:1
47:19 y Dt 32:51; z Isa 27:12; a Eze 48:28
47:20 b Eze 48:1; c Nu 34:6
47:22 d Isa 14:1; e Nu 26:55-56; Isa 56:6-7; Ro 10:12; Eph 2:12-16; Eph 3:6; Col 3:11
48:1 a Ge 30:6; b Eze 47:15-17; c Eze 47:20
48:2 d Jos 19:24-31
48:3 e Jos 19:32-39
48:4 f Jos 17:1-11

d10 That is, the Mediterranean; also in verses 15, 19 and 20 e15 Or *past the entrance to* f15, 16 See Septuagint and Ezekiel 48:1; Hebrew *road to go into Zedad,* 16*Hamath, Berothah*
g17 Hebrew *Enon,* a variant of *Enan*
h18 Septuagint and Syriac; Hebrew *Israel. You will measure to the eastern sea* i20 Or *opposite the entrance to* a1 Or *to the entrance to*

5“Ephraim[g] will have one portion; it will border the territory of
Manasseh[h] from east to west.[i]
6“Reuben[j] will have one portion;
it will border the territory of Ephraim from east to west.
7“Judah[k] will have one portion;
it will border the territory of Reuben from east to west.
8“Bordering the territory of Judah from east to west will be the
portion you are to present as a special gift. It will be 25,000 cubits[b]
wide, and its length from east to
west will equal one of the tribal
portions; the sanctuary will be in
the centre of it.[l]
9“The special portion you are to
offer to the LORD will be 25,000 cubits long and 10,000 cubits[c] wide.[m]
10This will be the sacred portion for
the priests. It will be 25,000 cubits
long on the north side, 10,000 cubits
wide on the west side, 10,000 cubits
wide on the east side and 25,000 cubits long on the south side. In the
centre of it will be the sanctuary of
the LORD.[n] 11This will be for the
consecrated priests, the Zadok-
ites,[o] who were faithful in serving me[p] and did not go astray as
the Levites did when the Israelites
went astray.[q] 12It will be a special
gift to them from the sacred portion of the land, a most holy portion, bordering the territory of the
Levites.
13“Alongside the territory of the
priests, the Levites will have an allotment 25,000 cubits long and
10,000 cubits wide. Its total length
will be 25,000 cubits and its width
10,000 cubits.[r] 14They must not
sell or exchange any of it. This is
the best of the land and must not
pass into other hands, because it is
holy to the LORD.[s]
15“The remaining area, 5,000 cubits wide and 25,000 cubits long,
will be for the common use of the
city, for houses and for pasture-
land. The city will be in the centre
of it 16and will have these measurements: the north side 4,500 cubits,
the south side 4,500 cubits, the east
side 4,500 cubits, and the west side
4,500 cubits.[t] 17The pasture-land
for the city will be 250 cubits on the
north, 250 cubits on the south, 250
cubits on the east, and 250 cubits on
the west. 18What remains of the
area, bordering on the sacred portion and running the length of it,
will be 10,000 cubits on the east
side and 10,000 cubits on the west
side. Its produce will supply food
for the workers of the city.[u] 19The
workers from the city who farm it
will come from all the tribes of Israel. 20The entire portion will be a
square, 25,000 cubits on each side.
As a special gift you will set aside
the sacred portion, along with the
property of the city.
21“What remains on both sides of
the area formed by the sacred portion and the city property will belong to the prince. It will extend
eastward from the 25,000 cubits of
the sacred portion to the eastern
border, and westward from the
25,000 cubits to the western border. Both these areas running the
length of the tribal portions will belong to the prince, and the sacred
portion with the temple sanctuary
will be in the centre of them.[v] 22So
the property of the Levites and the
property of the city will lie in the
centre of the area that belongs to
the prince. The area belonging to
the prince will lie between the border of Judah and the border of Benjamin.
23“As for the rest of the tribes:
Benjamin[w] will have one portion;
it will extend from the east side to
the west side.
24“Simeon[x] will have one portion; it will border the territory of
Benjamin from east to west.

48:5 g Jos 16:5-9 h Jos 17:7-10 i Jos 17:17
48:6 j Jos 13:15-21
48:7 k Jos 15:1-63
48:8 l ver 21
48:9 m Eze 45:1
48:10 n ver 21 Eze 45:3-4
48:11 o 2Sa 8:17 p Lev 8:35 q Eze 14:11 Eze 44:15
48:13 r Eze 45:5
48:14 s Lev 25:34 Lev 27:10,28
48:16 t Rev 21:16
48:18 u Eze 45:6
48:21 v ver 8,10 Eze 45:7
48:23 w Jos 18:11-28
48:24 x Ge 29:33 Jos 19:1-9

b8 That is, about 7 miles (about 11 kilometres)
c9 That is, about 3 miles (about 5 kilometres)

[25]"Issachar[y] will have one portion; it will border the territory of
Simeon from east to west.
[26]"Zebulun[z] will have one portion; it will border the territory of
Issachar from east to west.
[27]"Gad[a] will have one portion; it
will border the territory of Zebulun
from east to west.
[28]"The southern boundary of Gad
will run south from Tamar[b] to the
waters of Meribah Kadesh, then
along the Wadi ⌞of Egypt⌟ to the
Great Sea.[d][c]
[29]"This is the land you are to allot
as an inheritance to the tribes of Israel, and these will be their portions," declares the Sovereign
LORD.

The Gates of the City

[30]"These will be the exits of the
city: Beginning on the north side,
which is 4,500 cubits long, [31]the
gates of the city will be named
after the tribes of Israel. The three
gates on the north side will be the
gate of Reuben, the gate of Judah
and the gate of Levi.
[32]"On the east side, which
is 4,500 cubits long, will be three
gates: the gate of Joseph, the gate
of Benjamin and the gate of Dan.
[33]"On the south side, which measures 4,500 cubits, will be three
gates: the gate of Simeon, the gate
of Issachar and the gate of Zebulun.
[34]"On the west side, which is
4,500 cubits long, will be three
gates: the gate of Gad, the gate of
Asher and the gate of Naphtali.
[35]"The distance all around will be
18,000 cubits.

"And the name of the city from
that time on will be:

THE LORD IS THERE.[d]"

48:25 y Jos 19:17-23
48:26 z Jos 19:10-16
48:27 a Jos 13:24-28
48:28 b Ge 14:7 c Eze 47:19
48:35 d Isa 12:6 Isa 24:23 Jer 3:17 Jer 14:9 Jer 33:16 Joel 3:21 Zec 2:10 Rev 21:3

d28 That is, the Mediterranean

DANIEL

Daniel's Training in Babylon

1 In the third year of the reign of
Jehoiakim king of Judah,
Nebuchadnezzar[a] king of Babylon
came to Jerusalem and besieged
it.[b] 2And the Lord delivered Jehoiakim king of Judah into his hand,
along with some of the articles
from the temple of God. These he
carried off to the temple of his god
in Babylonia[a] and put in the
treasure-house of his god.[c]
3Then the king ordered Ashpe-
naz, chief of his court officials, to
bring in some of the Israelites from
the royal family and the nobility[d]—4young men without any
physical defect, handsome, showing aptitude for every kind of
learning, well informed, quick to
understand, and qualified to serve
in the king's palace. He was to
teach them the language and literature of the Babylonians.[b] 5The
king assigned them a daily amount
of food and wine[e] from the king's
table. They were to be trained for
three years, and after that they
were to enter the king's service.[f]
6Among these were some from
Judah: Daniel,[g] Hananiah, Mishael and Azariah. 7The chief official gave them new names: to
Daniel, the name Belteshazzar;[h] to
Hananiah, Shadrach; to Mishael,
Meshach; and to Azariah, Abednego.[i]
8But Daniel resolved not to defile[j] himself with the royal food
and wine, and he asked the chief official for permission not to defile
himself in this way. 9Now God had
caused the official to show favour[k]
and sympathy[l] to Daniel, 10but the
official told Daniel, "I am afraid of
my lord the king, who has assigned
your[c] food and drink. Why should
he see you looking worse than the
other young men of your age? The
king would then have my head because of you."
11Daniel then said to the guard
whom the chief official had appointed over Daniel, Hananiah, Mishael and Azariah, 12"Please test
your servants for ten days: Give us
nothing but vegetables to eat and
water to drink. 13Then compare our
appearance with that of the young
men who eat the royal food, and
treat your servants in accordance
with what you see." 14So he agreed
to this and tested them for ten days.
15At the end of the ten days they
looked healthier and better nourished than any of the young men
who ate the royal food.[m] 16So the
guard took away their choice food
and the wine they were to drink and
gave them vegetables instead.[n]
17To these four young men God
gave knowledge and understanding[o] of all kinds of literature and
learning.[p] And Daniel could
understand visions and dreams of
all kinds.[q]
18At the end of the time[r] set by
the king to bring them in, the chief
official presented them to Nebuchadnezzar. 19The king talked with
them, and he found none equal to
Daniel, Hananiah, Mishael and
Azariah; so they entered the king's
service.[s] 20In every matter of wisdom and understanding about
which the king questioned them, he
found them ten times better than
all the magicians and enchanters in
his whole kingdom.[t]
21And Daniel remained there
until the first year of King Cyrus.[u]

1:1 *a* 2Ki 24:1 *b* 2Ch 36:6
1:2 *c* 2Ch 36:7; Jer 27:19-20; Zec 5:5-11
1:3 *d* 2Ki 20:18; 2Ki 24:15; Isa 39:7
1:5 *e* ver 8,10 *f* ver 19
1:6 *g* Eze 14:14
1:7 *h* Da 4:8; Da 5:12 *i* Da 2:49; Da 3:12
1:8 *j* Eze 4:13-14
1:9 *k* Ge 39:21; Pr 16:7 *l* 1Ki 8:50; Ps 106:46
1:15 *m* Ex 23:25
1:16 *n* ver 12-13
1:17 *o* 1Ki 3:12 *p* Da 2:23; Jas 1:5 *q* Da 2:19,30; Da 7:1; Da 8:1
1:18 *r* ver 5
1:19 *s* Ge 41:46
1:20 *t* 1Ki 4:30; Da 2:13,28
1:21 *u* Da 6:28; Da 10:1

[a]2 Hebrew *Shinar* [b]4 Or *Chaldeans*
[c]10 The Hebrew for *your* and *you* in this verse is plural.

Nebuchadnezzar's Dream

2 In the second year of his reign, Nebuchadnezzar had dreams;[a] his mind was troubled[b] and he could not sleep.[c] 2So the king summoned the magicians,[d] enchanters, sorcerers[e] and astrologers[a][f] to tell him what he had dreamed.[g] When they came in and stood before the king, 3he said to them, "I have had a dream that troubles[h] me and I want to know what it means."[b]

4Then the astrologers answered the king in Aramaic,[c][i] "O king, live for ever![j] Tell your servants the dream, and we will interpret it."

5The king replied to the astrologers, "This is what I have firmly decided: If you do not tell me what my dream was and interpret it, I will have you cut into pieces[k] and your houses turned into piles of rubble.[l] 6But if you tell me the dream and explain it, you will receive from me gifts and rewards and great honour.[m] So tell me the dream and interpret it for me."

7Once more they replied, "Let the king tell his servants the dream, and we will interpret it."

8Then the king answered, "I am certain that you are trying to gain time, because you realise that this is what I have firmly decided: 9If you do not tell me the dream, there is just one penalty[n] for you. You have conspired to tell me misleading and wicked things, hoping the situation will change. So then, tell me the dream, and I will know that you can interpret it for me."[o]

10The astrologers answered the king, "There is not a man on earth who can do what the king asks! No king, however great and mighty, has ever asked such a thing of any magician or enchanter or astrologer.[p] 11What the king asks is too difficult. No-one can reveal it to the king except the gods,[q] and they do not live among men."

12This made the king so angry and furious[r] that he ordered the execution[s] of all the wise men of Babylon. 13So the decree was issued to put the wise men to death, and men were sent to look for Daniel and his friends to put them to death.[t]

14When Arioch, the commander of the king's guard, had gone out to put to death the wise men of Babylon, Daniel spoke to him with wisdom and tact. 15He asked the king's officer, "Why did the king issue such a harsh decree?" Arioch then explained the matter to Daniel. 16At this, Daniel went in to the king and asked for time, so that he might interpret the dream for him.

17Then Daniel returned to his house and explained the matter to his friends Hananiah, Mishael and Azariah.[u] 18He urged them to plead for mercy[v] from the God of heaven concerning this mystery,[w] so that he and his friends might not be executed with the rest of the wise men of Babylon. 19During the night the mystery[x] was revealed to Daniel in a vision.[y] Then Daniel praised the God of heaven 20and said:

"Praise be to the name of God
for ever and ever;[z]
wisdom and power[a] are his.
21He changes times and
seasons;[b]
he sets up kings and deposes[c]
them.
He gives wisdom[d] to the wise
and knowledge to the
discerning.
22He reveals deep and hidden
things;[e]
he knows what lies in
darkness,[f]
and light[g] dwells with him.
23I thank and praise you, O God
of my fathers:[h]

2:1 a Job 33:15,18; Da 4:5 b Ge 41:8 c Est 6:1; Da 6:18
2:2 d Ge 41:8 e Ex 7:11 f ver 10; Da 5:7 g Da 4:6
2:3 h Da 4:5
2:4 i Ezr 4:7 j Da 3:9; Da 5:10
2:5 k ver 12 l Ezr 6:11; Da 3:29
2:6 m ver 48; Da 5:7,16
2:9 n Est 4:11 o Isa 41:22-24
2:10 p ver 27
2:11 q Da 5:11
2:12 r Da 3:13,19 s ver 5
2:13 t Da 1:20
2:17 u Da 1:6
2:18 v Isa 37:4 w Jer 33:3
2:19 x ver 28 y Job 33:15; Da 1:17
2:20 z Ps 113:2; Ps 145:1-2 a Jer 32:19
2:21 b Da 7:25 c Job 12:19; Ps 75:6-7 d Jas 1:5
2:22 e Job 12:22; Ps 25:14; Da 5:11 f Ps 139:11-12; Jer 23:24; Heb 4:13 g Isa 45:7; Jas 1:17
2:23 h Ex 3:15

a2 Or *Chaldeans*; also in verses 4, 5 and 10
b3 Or *was*
c4 The text from here through chapter 7 is in Aramaic.

You have given me wisdom[i]
  and power,
you have made known to me
  what we asked of you,
you have made known to us
  the dream of the king."

Daniel Interprets the Dream

24 Then Daniel went to Arioch,[j] whom the king had appointed to execute the wise men of Babylon, and said to him, "Do not execute the wise men of Babylon. Take me to the king, and I will interpret his dream for him."

25 Arioch took Daniel to the king at once and said, "I have found a man among the exiles from Judah[k] who can tell the king what his dream means."

26 The king asked Daniel (also called Belteshazzar),[l] "Are you able to tell me what I saw in my dream and interpret it?"

27 Daniel replied, "No wise man, enchanter, magician or diviner can explain to the king the mystery he has asked about,[m] 28 but there is a God in heaven who reveals mysteries.[n] He has shown King Nebuchadnezzar what will happen in days to come.[o] Your dream and the visions that passed through your mind[p] as you lay on your bed are these:

29 "As you were lying there, O king, your mind turned to things to come, and the revealer of mysteries showed you what is going to happen. 30 As for me, this mystery has been revealed[q] to me, not because I have greater wisdom than other living men, but so that you, O king, may know the interpretation and that you may understand what went through your mind.

31 "You looked, O king, and there before you stood a large statue—an enormous, dazzling statue,[r] awesome in appearance. 32 The head of the statue was made of pure gold, its chest and arms of silver, its belly and thighs of bronze, 33 its legs of iron, its feet partly of iron and partly of baked clay. 34 While you were watching, a rock was cut out, but not by human hands.[s] It struck the statue on its feet of iron and clay and smashed them.[t] 35 Then the iron, the clay, the bronze, the silver and the gold were broken to pieces at the same time and became like chaff on a threshing-floor in the summer. The wind swept them away[u] without leaving a trace. But the rock that struck the statue became a huge mountain[v] and filled the whole earth.

36 "This was the dream, and now we will interpret it to the king. 37 You, O king, are the king of kings.[w] The God of heaven has given you dominion[x] and power and might and glory; 38 in your hands he has placed mankind and the beasts of the field and the birds of the air. Wherever they live, he has made you ruler over them all.[y] You are that head of gold.

39 "After you, another kingdom will rise, inferior to yours. Next, a third kingdom, one of bronze, will rule over the whole earth. 40 Finally, there will be a fourth kingdom, strong as iron—for iron breaks and smashes everything—and as iron breaks things to pieces, so it will crush and break all the others.[z] 41 Just as you saw that the feet and toes were partly of baked clay and partly of iron, so this will be a divided kingdom; yet it will have some of the strength of iron in it, even as you saw iron mixed with clay. 42 As the toes were partly iron and partly clay, so this kingdom will be partly strong and partly brittle. 43 And just as you saw the iron mixed with baked clay, so the people will be a mixture and will not remain united, any more than iron mixes with clay.

44 "In the time of those kings, the God of heaven will set up a kingdom that will never be destroyed, nor will it be left to another people. It will crush[a] all those kingdoms[b]

2:23 i Da 1:17
2:24 j ver 14
2:25 k Da 1:6; Da 5:13; Da 6:13
2:26 l Da 1:7
2:27 m ver 10
2:28 n Ge 40:8; Am 4:13; o Ge 49:1; Da 10:14; p Da 4:5
2:30 q Isa 45:3; Da 1:17; Am 4:13
2:31 r Hab 1:7
2:34 s Zec 4:6; t ver 44-45; Ps 2:9; Isa 60:12; Da 8:25
2:35 u Ps 1:4; Ps 37:10; Isa 17:13; v Isa 2:3; Mic 4:1
2:37 w Eze 26:7; x Jer 27:7
2:38 y Jer 27:6; Da 4:21-22
2:40 z Da 7:7,23
2:44 a Ps 2:9; 1Co 15:24; b Isa 60:12

and bring them to an end, but it will itself endure for ever.[c] 45 This is the meaning of the vision of the rock[d] cut out of a mountain, but not by human hands[e]—a rock that broke the iron, the bronze, the clay, the silver and the gold to pieces.

"The great God has shown the king what will take place in the future. The dream is true and the interpretation is trustworthy."

46 Then King Nebuchadnezzar fell prostrate[f] before Daniel and paid him honour and ordered that an offering[g] and incense be presented to him. 47 The king said to Daniel, "Surely your God is the God of gods[h] and the Lord of kings[i] and a revealer of mysteries,[j] for you were able to reveal this mystery."

48 Then the king placed Daniel in a high position and lavished many gifts on him. He made him ruler over the entire province of Babylon and placed him in charge of all its wise men.[k] 49 Moreover, at Daniel's request the king appointed Shadrach, Meshach and Abednego administrators over the province of Babylon,[l] while Daniel himself remained at the royal court.

The Image of Gold and the Fiery Furnace

3 King Nebuchadnezzar made an image[a] of gold, ninety feet high and nine feet[a] wide, and set it up on the plain of Dura in the province of Babylon. 2 He then summoned the satraps, prefects, governors, advisers, treasurers, judges, magistrates and all the other provincial officials[b] to come to the dedication of the image he had set up. 3 So the satraps, prefects, governors, advisers, treasurers, judges, magistrates and all the other provincial officials assembled for the dedication of the image that King Nebuchadnezzar had set up, and they stood before it.

4 Then the herald loudly proclaimed, "This is what you are commanded to do, O peoples, nations and men of every language:[c] 5 As soon as you hear the sound of the horn, flute, zither, lyre, harp, pipes and all kinds of music, you must fall down and worship the image of gold that King Nebuchadnezzar has set up.[d] 6 Whoever does not fall down and worship will immediately be thrown into a blazing furnace."[e]

7 Therefore, as soon as they heard the sound of the horn, flute, zither, lyre, harp and all kinds of music, all the peoples, nations and men of every language fell down and worshipped the image of gold that King Nebuchadnezzar had set up.[f]

8 At this time some astrologers[b][g] came forward and denounced the Jews. 9 They said to King Nebuchadnezzar, "O king, live for ever![h] 10 You have issued a decree,[i] O king, that everyone who hears the sound of the horn, flute, zither, lyre, harp, pipes and all kinds of music must fall down and worship the image of gold,[j] 11 and that whoever does not fall down and worship will be thrown into a blazing furnace. 12 But there are some Jews whom you have set over the affairs of the province of Babylon—Shadrach, Meshach and Abednego[k]—who pay no attention[l] to you, O king. They neither serve your gods nor worship the image of gold you have set up."[m]

13 Furious[n] with rage, Nebuchadnezzar summoned Shadrach, Meshach and Abednego. So these men were brought before the king, 14 and Nebuchadnezzar said to them, "Is it true, Shadrach, Meshach and Abednego, that you do not serve my gods[o] or worship the image[p] of gold I have set up? 15 Now when you hear the sound of

2:44 c Ps 145:13; Isa 9:7; Da 4:34; Da 6:26; Da 7:14,27; Mic 4:7,13; Lk 1:33
2:45 d Isa 28:16; e Da 8:25
2:46 f Da 8:17; Ac 10:25; g Ac 14:13
2:47 h Da 11:36; i Da 4:25; j ver 22,28
2:48 k ver 6; Da 4:9; Da 5:11
2:49 l Da 1:7
3:1 a Isa 46:6; Jer 16:20; Hab 2:19
3:2 b ver 27; Da 6:7
3:4 c Da 4:1; Da 6:25
3:5 d ver 10,15
3:6 e ver 11,15,21; Jer 29:22; Da 6:7; Mt 13:42,50; Rev 13:15
3:7 f ver 5
3:8 g Da 2:10
3:9 h Ne 2:3; Da 5:10; Da 6:6
3:10 i Da 6:12; j ver 4-6
3:12 k Da 2:49; l Da 6:13; m Est 3:3
3:13 n Da 2:12
3:14 o Isa 46:1; Jer 50:2; p ver 1

a 1 Aramaic *sixty cubits high and six cubits wide* (about 27 metres high and 2.7 metres wide)
b 8 Or *Chaldeans*

the horn, flute, zither, lyre, harp,
pipes and all kinds of music, if you
are ready to fall down and worship
the image I made, very good. But if
you do not worship it, you will be
thrown immediately into a blazing
furnace. Then what god[q] will be
able to rescue[r] you from my
hand?"
16 Shadrach, Meshach and Abednego[s] replied to the king, "O Nebuchadnezzar, we do not need to
defend ourselves before you in this
matter. 17 If we are thrown into the
blazing furnace, the God we serve
is able to save[t] us from it, and he
will rescue[u] us from your hand, O
king. 18 But even if he does not, we
want you to know, O king, that we
will not serve your gods or worship
the image of gold you have set
up.[v]"
19 Then Nebuchadnezzar was
furious with Shadrach, Meshach
and Abednego, and his attitude towards them changed. He ordered
the furnace to be heated seven[w]
times hotter than usual 20 and commanded some of the strongest soldiers in his army to tie up
Shadrach, Meshach and Abednego
and throw them into the blazing
furnace. 21 So these men, wearing
their robes, trousers, turbans and
other clothes, were bound and
thrown into the blazing furnace.
22 The king's command was so urgent and the furnace so hot that the
flames of the fire killed the soldiers who took up Shadrach, Meshach and Abednego,[x] 23 and these
three men, firmly tied, fell into the
blazing furnace.
24 Then King Nebuchadnezzar
leaped to his feet in amazement and
asked his advisers, "Weren't there
three men that we tied up and
threw into the fire?"
They replied, "Certainly, O
king."
25 He said, "Look! I see four men
walking around in the fire, un-
bound and unharmed, and the
fourth looks like a son of the gods."
26 Nebuchadnezzar then approached the opening of the blazing
furnace and shouted, "Shadrach,
Meshach and Abednego, servants of the Most High God,[y] come
out! Come here!"
So Shadrach, Meshach and Abednego came out of the fire, 27 and the
satraps, prefects, governors and
royal advisers[z] crowded around
them.[a] They saw that the fire[b] had
not harmed their bodies, nor was a
hair of their heads singed; their
robes were not scorched, and there
was no smell of fire on them.
28 Then Nebuchadnezzar said,
"Praise be to the God of Shadrach,
Meshach and Abednego, who has
sent his angel[c] and rescued his
servants! They trusted[d] in him
and defied the king's command and
were willing to give up their lives
rather than serve or worship any
god except their own God.[e]
29 Therefore I decree[f] that the people of any nation or language who
say anything against the God of
Shadrach, Meshach and Abednego
be cut into pieces and their houses
be turned into piles of rubble,[g] for no
other god can save[h] in this way."
30 Then the king promoted Shadrach, Meshach and Abednego in the
province of Babylon.[i]

Nebuchadnezzar's Dream of a Tree

4 King Nebuchadnezzar,

To the peoples, nations
and men of every language,[a]
who live in all the world:

May you prosper greatly![b]

2 It is my pleasure to tell you
about the miraculous signs[c]
and wonders that the Most
High God[d] has performed for
me.

3 How great are his signs,
how mighty his wonders![e]
His kingdom is an eternal
kingdom;

3:15 q Isa 36:18-20 r Ex 5:2 2Ch 32:15
3:16 s Da 1:7
3:17 t Ps 27:1-2 u Job 5:19 Jer 1:8
3:18 v ver 28 Jos 24:15
3:19 w Lev 26:18-28
3:22 x Da 1:7
3:26 y Da 4:2,34
3:27 z ver 2 a Isa 43:2 Heb 11:32-34 b Da 6:23
3:28 c Ps 34:7 Da 6:22 Ac 5:19 d Job 13:15 Ps 26:1 Ps 84:12 Jer 17:7 e ver 18
3:29 f Da 6:26 g Ezr 6:11 h Da 6:27
3:30 i Da 2:49
4:1 a Da 3:4 b Da 6:25
4:2 c Ps 74:9 d Da 3:26
4:3 e Ps 105:27 Da 6:27

his dominion endures[f] from
generation to generation.

4 I, Nebuchadnezzar, was at home in my palace, contented[g] and prosperous. 5 I had a dream[h] that made me afraid. As I was lying in my bed, the images and visions that passed through my mind[i] terrified me. 6 So I commanded that all the wise men of Babylon be brought before me to interpret[j] the dream for me. 7 When the magicians,[k] enchanters, astrologers[a] and diviners[l] came, I told them the dream, but they could not interpret it for me.[m] 8 Finally, Daniel came into my presence and I told him the dream. (He is called Belteshazzar,[n] after the name of my god, and the spirit of the holy gods[o] is in him.)

9 I said, "Belteshazzar, chief[p] of the magicians, I know that the spirit of the holy gods[q] is in you, and no mystery is too difficult for you. Here is my dream; interpret it for me. 10 These are the visions I saw while lying in my bed:[r] I looked, and there before me stood a tree in the middle of the land. Its height was enormous.[s] 11 The tree grew large and strong and its top touched the sky; it was visible to the ends of the earth. 12 Its leaves were beautiful, its fruit abundant, and on it was food for all. Under it the beasts of the field found shelter, and the birds of the air lived in its branches;[t] from it every creature was fed.

13 "In the visions I saw while lying in my bed,[u] I looked, and there before me was a messenger,[b] a holy one,[v] coming down from heaven. 14 He called in a loud voice: 'Cut down the tree and trim off its branches; strip off its leaves and scatter its fruit. Let the animals flee from under it and the birds from its branches.[w] 15 But let the stump and its roots, bound with iron and bronze, remain in the ground, in the grass of the field.

"'Let him be drenched with the dew of heaven, and let him live with the animals among the plants of the earth. 16 Let his mind be changed from that of a man and let him be given the mind of an animal, till seven times[c] pass by for him.[x]

17 "'The decision is announced by messengers, the holy ones declare the verdict, so that the living may know that the Most High[y] is sovereign[z] over the kingdoms of men and gives them to anyone he wishes and sets over them the lowliest[a] of men.'

18 "This is the dream that I, King Nebuchadnezzar, had. Now, Belteshazzar, tell me what it means, for none of the wise men in my kingdom can interpret it for me.[b] But you can,[c] because the spirit of the holy gods is in you."[d]

Daniel Interprets the Dream

19 Then Daniel (also called Belteshazzar) was greatly perplexed for a time, and his thoughts terrified[e] him. So the king said, "Belteshazzar, do not let the dream or its meaning alarm you."

Belteshazzar answered, "My lord, if only the dream applied to your enemies and its meaning to your adversaries! 20 The tree you saw, which grew large and strong, with its top touching the sky, visible to the whole earth, 21 with beautiful leaves and abundant fruit, providing

4:3 f Da 2:44
4:4 g Ps 30:6
4:5 h Da 2:1 i Da 2:28
4:6 j Da 2:2
4:7 k Ge 41:8 l Isa 44:25; Da 2:2 m Da 2:10
4:8 n Da 1:7 o Da 5:11,14
4:9 p Da 2:48 q Da 5:11-12
4:10 r ver 5 s Eze 31:3-4
4:12 t Eze 17:23; Mt 13:32
4:13 u Da 7:1 v ver 23; Dt 33:2; Da 8:13
4:14 w Eze 31:12; Mt 3:10
4:16 x ver 23,32
4:17 y ver 2,25; Ps 83:18 z Jer 27:5-7; Da 2:21; Da 5:18-21 a Da 11:21
4:18 b Ge 41:8; Da 5:8,15 c Ge 41:15 d ver 7-9
4:19 e Da 7:15,28; Da 8:27; Da 10:16-17

[a] 7 Or *Chaldeans* [b] 13 Or *watchman*; also in verses 17 and 23 [c] 16 Or *years*; also in verses 23, 25 and 32

food for all, giving shelter to the beasts of the field, and having nesting places in its branches for the birds of the air— 22 you, O king, are that tree![f] You have become great and strong; your greatness has grown until it reaches the sky, and your dominion extends to distant parts of the earth.[g]

23 "You, O king, saw a messenger, a holy one,[h] coming down from heaven and saying, 'Cut down the tree and destroy it, but leave the stump, bound with iron and bronze, in the grass of the field, while its roots remain in the ground. Let him be drenched with the dew of heaven; let him live like the wild animals, until seven times pass by for him.'[i]

24 "This is the interpretation, O king, and this is the decree[j] the Most High has issued against my lord the king: 25 You will be driven away from people and will live with the wild animals; you will eat grass like cattle and be drenched with the dew of heaven. Seven times will pass by for you until you acknowledge that the Most High[k] is sovereign over the kingdoms of men and gives them to anyone he wishes.[l] 26 The command to leave the stump of the tree with its roots[m] means that your kingdom will be restored to you when you acknowledge that Heaven rules.[n] 27 Therefore, O king, be pleased to accept my advice: Renounce your sins by doing what is right, and your wickedness by being kind to the oppressed.[o] It may be that then your prosperity will continue.[p]"

The Dream Is Fulfilled

28 All this happened[q] to King Nebuchadnezzar. 29 Twelve months later, as the king was walking on the roof of the royal palace of Babylon, 30 he said, "Is not this the great Babylon I have built as the royal residence, by my mighty power and for the glory of my majesty?"[r]

31 The words were still on his lips when a voice came from heaven, "This is what is decreed for you, King Nebuchadnezzar: Your royal authority has been taken from you. 32 You will be driven away from people and will live with the wild animals; you will eat grass like cattle. Seven times will pass by for you until you acknowledge that the Most High is sovereign over the kingdoms of men and gives them to anyone he wishes."

33 Immediately what had been said about Nebuchadnezzar was fulfilled. He was driven away from people and ate grass like cattle. His body was drenched with the dew of heaven until his hair grew like the feathers of an eagle and his nails like the claws of a bird.[s]

34 At the end of that time, I, Nebuchadnezzar, raised my eyes towards heaven, and my sanity was restored. Then I praised the Most High; I honoured and glorified him who lives for ever.[t]

His dominion is an eternal
    dominion;
  his kingdom endures from
    generation to generation.[u]
35 All the peoples of the earth
    are regarded as nothing.[v]
He does as he pleases[w]
    with the powers of heaven
    and the peoples of the earth.
No-one can hold back his hand
    or say to him: "What have
    you done?"[x]

4:22 f 2Sa 12:7 g Jer 27:7; Da 2:37-38; Da 5:18-19
4:23 h ver 13 i Da 5:21
4:24 j Job 40:12; Ps 107:40
4:25 k ver 17; Ps 83:18 l Jer 27:5; Da 5:21
4:26 m ver 15 n Da 2:37
4:27 o Isa 55:6-7 p 1Ki 21:29; Ps 41:3; Eze 18:22
4:28 q Nu 23:19
4:30 r Isa 37:24-25; Da 5:20; Hab 2:4
4:33 s Da 5:20-21
4:34 t Da 12:7; Rev 4:10 u Ps 145:13; Da 2:44; Da 5:21; Da 6:26; Lk 1:33
4:35 v Isa 40:17 w Ps 115:3; Ps 135:6 x Isa 45:9; Ro 9:20

36 At the same time that my sanity was restored, my honour and splendour were returned to me for the glory of my kingdom.[y] My advisers and nobles sought me out, and I was restored to my throne and became even greater than before. 37 Now I, Nebuchadnezzar, praise and exalt and glorify the King of heaven, because everything he does is right and all his ways are just.[z] And those who walk in pride he is able to humble.[a]

The Writing on the Wall

5 King Belshazzar gave a great banquet[a] for a thousand of his nobles and drank wine with them. 2 While Belshazzar was drinking his wine, he gave orders to bring in the gold and silver goblets[b] that Nebuchadnezzar his father[a] had taken from the temple in Jerusalem, so that the king and his nobles, his wives and his concubines might drink from them.[c] 3 So they brought in the gold goblets that had been taken from the temple of God in Jerusalem, and the king and his nobles, his wives and his concubines drank from them. 4 As they drank the wine, they praised the gods of gold and silver, of bronze, iron, wood and stone.[d]

5 Suddenly the fingers of a human hand appeared and wrote on the plaster of the wall, near the lampstand in the royal palace. The king watched the hand as it wrote. 6 His face turned pale and he was so frightened[e] that his knees knocked together and his legs gave way.[f]

7 The king called out for the enchanters, astrologers[b] and diviners[g] to be brought and said to these wise[h] men of Babylon, "Whoever reads this writing and tells me what it means will be clothed in purple and have a gold chain placed around his neck,[i] and he will be made the third highest ruler in the kingdom."[j]

8 Then all the king's wise men came in, but they could not read the writing or tell the king what it meant.[k] 9 So King Belshazzar became even more terrified[l] and his face grew more pale. His nobles were baffled.

10 The queen,[c] hearing the voices of the king and his nobles, came into the banquet hall. "O king, live for ever!"[m] she said. "Don't be alarmed! Don't look so pale! 11 There is a man in your kingdom who has the spirit of the holy gods[n] in him. In the time of your father he was found to have insight and intelligence and wisdom[o] like that of the gods. King Nebuchadnezzar your father—your father the king, I say—appointed him chief of the magicians, enchanters, astrologers and diviners.[p] 12 This man Daniel, whom the king called Belteshazzar,[q] was found to have a keen mind and knowledge and understanding, and also the ability to interpret dreams, explain riddles and solve difficult problems.[r] Call for Daniel, and he will tell you what the writing means."

13 So Daniel was brought before the king, and the king said to him, "Are you Daniel, one of the exiles my father the king brought from Judah?[s] 14 I have heard that the spirit of the gods is in you and that you have insight, intelligence and outstanding wisdom. 15 The wise men and enchanters were brought before me to read this writing and tell me what it means, but they could not explain it. 16 Now I have heard that you are able to give interpretations and to solve difficult problems. If you can read this writing and tell me what it means, you will be clothed in purple and have a gold chain placed around your

4:36 y Pr 22:4
4:37 z Dt 32:4; Ps 33:4-5 a Ex 18:11; Job 40:11-12; Da 5:20,23
5:1 a Est 1:3
5:2 b 2Ki 24:13; Jer 52:19 c Est 1:7; Da 1:2
5:4 d Ps 135:15-18; Hab 2:19; Rev 9:20
5:6 e Da 4:5 f Eze 7:17
5:7 g Isa 44:25 h Da 4:6-7 i Ge 41:42 j Da 2:5-6,48; Da 6:2-3
5:8 k Da 2:10,27
5:9 l Isa 21:4
5:10 m Da 3:9
5:11 n Da 4:8-9,19 o ver 14; Da 1:17 p Da 2:47-48
5:12 q Da 1:7 r ver 14-16; Da 6:3
5:13 s Da 6:13

[a]2 Or *ancestor*; or *predecessor*; also in verses 11, 13 and 18 [b]7 Or *Chaldeans*; also in verse 11 [c]10 Or *queen mother*

neck, and you will be made the
third highest ruler in the kingdom."
17 Then Daniel answered the king,
"You may keep your gifts for yourself and give your rewards to someone else.[t] Nevertheless, I will read
the writing for the king and tell him
what it means.
18 "O king, the Most High God
gave your father Nebuchadnezzar
sovereignty and greatness and
glory and splendour.[u] 19 Because of
the high position he gave him, all
the peoples and nations and men of
every language dreaded and
feared him. Those the king wanted
to put to death, he put to death;[v]
those he wanted to spare, he
spared; those he wanted to promote, he promoted; and those he
wanted to humble, he humbled.
20 But when his heart became arrogant and hardened with pride,[w] he
was deposed from his royal throne
and stripped[x] of his glory.[y] 21 He
was driven away from people and
given the mind of an animal; he
lived with the wild donkeys and ate
grass like cattle; and his body was
drenched with the dew of heaven,
until he acknowledged that the
Most High God is sovereign[z] over
the kingdoms of men and sets over
them anyone he wishes.[a]
22 "But you his son,[d] O Belshazzar, have not humbled[b] yourself,
though you knew all this. 23 Instead,
you have set yourself up against[c]
the Lord of heaven. You had the
goblets from his temple brought to
you, and you and your nobles, your
wives and your concubines drank
wine from them. You praised the
gods of silver and gold, of bronze,
iron, wood and stone, which cannot
see or hear or understand.[d] But
you did not honour the God who
holds in his hand your life[e] and all
your ways.[f] 24 Therefore he sent
the hand that wrote the inscription.
25 "This is the inscription that was
written:

MENE, MENE, TEKEL, PARSIN[e]

26 "This is what these words
mean:

Mene[f]: God has numbered
the days[g] of your
reign and brought it to
an end.[h]
27 *Tekel*[g]: You have been
weighed on the scales
and found wanting.[i]
28 *Peres*[h]: Your kingdom is
divided and given to
the Medes[j] and Per-
sians."[k]

29 Then at Belshazzar's command,
Daniel was clothed in purple, a gold
chain was placed around his neck,
and he was proclaimed the third
highest ruler in the kingdom.
30 That very night Belshazzar,[l]
king of the Babylonians,[i] was
slain,[m] 31 and Darius[n] the Mede
took over the kingdom, at the age of
sixty-two.

Daniel in the Den of Lions

6 It pleased Darius[a] to appoint
120 satraps[b] to rule throughout the kingdom, 2 with three administrators over them, one of
whom was Daniel.[c] The satraps
were made accountable[d] to them
so that the king might not suffer
loss. 3 Now Daniel so distinguished
himself among the administrators
and the satraps by his exceptional
qualities that the king planned to
set him over the whole kingdom.[e]
4 At this, the administrators and the
satraps tried to find grounds for
charges against Daniel in his conduct of government affairs, but
they were unable to do so. They
could find no corruption in him, because he was trustworthy and neither corrupt nor negligent. 5 Finally

5:17 t 2Ki 5:16
5:18 u Jer 27:7; Da 2:37-38
5:19 v Da 2:12-13; Da 3:6
5:20 w Da 4:30; x Jer 13:18; y Job 40:12; Isa 14:13-15
5:21 z Eze 17:24; a Da 4:16-17, 35
5:22 b Ex 10:3; 2Ch 33:23
5:23 c Jer 50:29; d Ps 115:4-8; Hab 2:19; e Job 12:10; f Job 31:4; Jer 10:23
5:26 g Jer 27:7; h Isa 13:6
5:27 i Ps 62:9
5:28 j Isa 13:17; k Da 6:28
5:30 l ver 1; m Isa 21:9; Jer 51:31
5:31 n Da 6:1; Da 9:1
6:1 a Da 5:31; b Est 1:1
6:2 c Da 2:48-49; d Ezr 4:22
6:3 e Ge 41:41; Est 10:3; Da 5:12-14

[d]22 Or *descendant*; or *successor* [e]25 Aramaic *UPARSIN* (that is, *AND PARSIN*) [f]26 *Mene* can mean *numbered* or *mina* (a unit of money).
[g]27 *Tekel* can mean *weighed* or *shekel*.
[h]28 *Peres* (the singular of *Parsin*) can mean *divided* or *Persia* or *a half mina* or *a half shekel*.
[i]30 Or *Chaldeans*

these men said, "We will never find any basis for charges against this man Daniel unless it has something to do with the law of his God."[f]

6 So the administrators and the satraps went as a group to the king and said: "O King Darius, live for ever![g] 7 The royal administrators, prefects, satraps, advisers and governors[h] have all agreed that the king should issue an edict and enforce the decree that anyone who prays to any god or man during the next thirty days, except to you, O king, shall be thrown into the lions' den.[i] 8 Now, O king, issue the decree and put it in writing so that it cannot be altered—in accordance with the laws of the Medes and Persians, which cannot be repealed."[j] 9 So King Darius put the decree in writing.

10 Now when Daniel learned that the decree had been published, he went home to his upstairs room where the windows opened towards[k] Jerusalem. Three times a day he got down on his knees[l] and prayed, giving thanks to his God, just as he had done before.[m] 11 Then these men went as a group and found Daniel praying and asking God for help. 12 So they went to the king and spoke to him about his royal decree: "Did you not publish a decree that during the next thirty days anyone who prays to any god or man except to you, O king, would be thrown into the lions' den?"

The king answered, "The decree stands—in accordance with the laws of the Medes and Persians, which cannot be repealed."[n]

13 Then they said to the king, "Daniel, who is one of the exiles from Judah,[o] pays no attention[p] to you, O king, or to the decree you put in writing. He still prays three times a day." 14 When the king heard this, he was greatly distressed;[q] he was determined to rescue Daniel and made every effort until sundown to save him.

15 Then the men went as a group to the king and said to him, "Remember, O king, that according to the law of the Medes and Persians no decree or edict that the king issues can be changed."[r]

16 So the king gave the order, and they brought Daniel and threw him into the lions' den.[s] The king said to Daniel, "May your God, whom you serve continually, rescue[t] you!"

17 A stone was brought and placed over the mouth of the den, and the king sealed[u] it with his own signet ring and with the rings of his nobles, so that Daniel's situation might not be changed. 18 Then the king returned to his palace and spent the night without eating[v] and without any entertainment being brought to him. And he could not sleep.[w]

19 At the first light of dawn, the king got up and hurried to the lions' den. 20 When he came near the den, he called to Daniel in an anguished voice, "Daniel, servant of the living God, has your God, whom you serve continually, been able to rescue you from the lions?"[x]

21 Daniel answered, "O king, live for ever![y] 22 My God sent his angel,[z] and he shut the mouths of the lions.[a] They have not hurt me, because I was found innocent in his sight.[b] Nor have I ever done any wrong before you, O king."

23 The king was overjoyed and gave orders to lift Daniel out of the den. And when Daniel was lifted from the den, no wound[c] was found on him, because he had trusted[d] in his God.

24 At the king's command, the men who had falsely accused Daniel were brought in and thrown into the lions' den,[e] along with their wives and children.[f] And before they reached the floor of the den, the lions overpowered them and crushed all their bones.[g]

25 Then King Darius wrote to all the peoples, nations and men of

6:5 f Ac 24:13-16
6:6 g Ne 2:3; Da 2:4
6:7 h Da 3:2; i Ps 59:3; Ps 64:2-6; Da 3:6
6:8 j Est 1:19
6:10 k 1Ki 8:48-49; l Ps 95:6; m Ac 5:29
6:12 n Est 1:19; Da 3:8-12
6:13 o Da 2:25; Da 5:13; p Est 3:8; Da 3:12
6:14 q Mk 6:26
6:15 r Est 8:8
6:16 s ver 7; t Job 5:19; Ps 37:39-40
6:17 u Mt 27:66
6:18 v 2Sa 12:17; w Est 6:1; Da 2:1
6:20 x Da 3:17
6:21 y Da 2:4
6:22 z Da 3:28; a Ps 91:11-13; Heb 11:33; b Ac 12:11; 2Ti 4:17
6:23 c Da 3:27; d 1Ch 5:20
6:24 e Dt 19:18-19; Est 7:9-10; Ps 54:5; f Dt 24:16; 2Ki 14:6; g Isa 38:13

every language throughout the
land:

"May you prosper greatly![h]

[26]"I issue a decree that in
every part of my kingdom people must fear and reverence
the God of Daniel.[i]

"For he is the living God
and he endures for ever;
his kingdom will not be
destroyed,
his dominion will never
end.[j]
[27]He rescues and he saves;
he performs signs and
wonders[k]
in the heavens and on the
earth.
He has rescued Daniel
from the power of the
lions."[l]

[28]So Daniel prospered during the
reign of Darius and the reign of Cyrus[a][m] the Persian.

Daniel's Dream of Four Beasts

7 In the first year of Belshazzar[a] king of Babylon, Daniel
had a dream, and visions passed
through his mind[b] as he was lying
on his bed. He wrote[c] down the
substance of his dream.
[2]Daniel said: "In my vision at
night I looked, and there before me
were the four winds of heaven[d]
churning up the great sea. [3]Four
great beasts,[e] each different from
the others, came up out of the sea.
[4]"The first was like a lion,[f] and
it had the wings of an eagle.[g] I
watched until its wings were torn
off and it was lifted from the
ground so that it stood on two feet
like a man, and the heart of a man
was given to it.
[5]"And there before me was a
second beast, which looked like a
bear. It was raised up on one of its
sides, and it had three ribs in its
mouth between its teeth. It was

6:25
h Da 4:1
6:26
i Ps 99:1-3
Da 3:29
j Da 2:44
Da 4:34
6:27
k Da 4:3
l ver 22
6:28
m 2Ch 36:22
Da 1:21
7:1
a Da 5:1
b Da 1:17
c Jer 36:4
7:2
d Rev 7:1
7:3
e Rev 13:1
7:4
f Jer 4:7
g Eze 17:3
7:5
h Da 2:39
7:6
i Rev 13:2
7:7
j Da 2:40
k Rev 12:3
7:8
l Da 8:9
m Rev 9:7
n Ps 12:3
Rev 13:5-6
7:9
o Rev 1:14
p Eze 1:15
Eze 10:6
7:10
q Ps 50:3
Ps 97:3
Isa 30:27
r Dt 33:2
Ps 68:17
Rev 5:11
s Rev 20:11-15
7:11
t Rev 19:20

told, 'Get up and eat your fill of
flesh!'[h]
[6]"After that, I looked, and there
before me was another beast, one
that looked like a leopard.[i] And on
its back it had four wings like those
of a bird. This beast had four heads,
and it was given authority to rule.
[7]"After that, in my vision at night
I looked, and there before me was
a fourth beast—terrifying and
frightening and very powerful. It
had large iron[j] teeth; it crushed
and devoured its victims and trampled underfoot whatever was left.
It was different from all the former
beasts, and it had ten horns.[k]
[8]"While I was thinking about the
horns, there before me was another
horn, a little[l] one, which came up
among them; and three of the first
horns were uprooted before it. This
horn had eyes like the eyes of a
man[m] and a mouth that spoke
boastfully.[n]
[9]"As I looked,

"thrones were set in place,
and the Ancient of Days took
his seat.
His clothing was as white as
snow;
the hair of his head was white
like wool.[o]
His throne was flaming with
fire,
and its wheels[p] were all
ablaze.
[10]A river of fire[q] was flowing,
coming out from before him.[r]
Thousands upon thousands
attended him;
ten thousand times ten
thousand stood before him.
The court was seated,
and the books[s] were opened.

[11]"Then I continued to watch because of the boastful words the
horn was speaking. I kept looking
until the beast was slain and its
body destroyed and thrown into the
blazing fire.[t] [12](The other beasts

[a]28 Or *Darius, that is, the reign of Cyrus*

had been stripped of their authority, but were allowed to live for a period of time.)

13"In my vision at night I looked, and there before me was one like a son of man,[u] coming with the clouds of heaven.[v] He approached the Ancient of Days and was led into his presence. 14He was given authority,[w] glory and sovereign power; all peoples, nations and men of every language worshipped him.[x] His dominion is an everlasting dominion that will not pass away, and his kingdom is one that will never be destroyed.[y]

The Interpretation of the Dream

15"I, Daniel, was troubled in spirit, and the visions that passed through my mind disturbed me.[z] 16I approached one of those standing there and asked him the true meaning of all this.

"So he told me and gave me the interpretation[a] of these things: 17'The four great beasts are four kingdoms that will rise from the earth. 18But the saints of the Most High will receive the kingdom and will possess it for ever—yes, for ever and ever.'[b]

19"Then I wanted to know the true meaning of the fourth beast, which was different from all the others and most terrifying, with its iron teeth and bronze claws—the beast that crushed and devoured its victims and trampled underfoot whatever was left. 20I also wanted to know about the ten horns on its head and about the other horn that came up, before which three of them fell—the horn that looked more imposing than the others and that had eyes and a mouth that spoke boastfully. 21As I watched, this horn was waging war against the saints and defeating them,[c] 22until the Ancient of Days came and pronounced judgment in favour of the saints of the Most High, and the time came when they possessed the kingdom.

23"He gave me this explanation: 'The fourth beast is a fourth kingdom that will appear on earth. It will be different from all the other kingdoms and will devour the whole earth, trampling it down and crushing it.[d] 24The ten horns[e] are ten kings who will come from this kingdom. After them another king will arise, different from the earlier ones; he will subdue three kings. 25He will speak against the Most High[f] and oppress his saints and try to change the set times[g] and the laws. The saints will be handed over to him for a time, times and half a time.[a][h]

26" 'But the court will sit, and his power will be taken away and completely destroyed for ever. 27Then the sovereignty, power and greatness of the kingdoms under the whole heaven will be handed over to the saints, the people of the Most High. His kingdom will be an everlasting[i] kingdom, and all rulers will worship[j] and obey him.'

28"This is the end of the matter. I, Daniel, was deeply troubled[k] by my thoughts, and my face turned pale, but I kept the matter to myself."

Daniel's Vision of a Ram and a Goat

8 In the third year of King Belshazzar's reign, I, Daniel, had a vision, after the one that had already appeared to me. 2In my vision I saw myself in the citadel of Susa[a] in the province of Elam;[b] in the vision I was beside the Ulai Canal. 3I looked up,[c] and there before me was a ram with two horns, standing beside the canal, and the horns were long. One of the horns was longer than the other but grew up later. 4I watched the ram as he charged towards the west and the

7:13 u Mt 8:20* Rev 1:13* v Mt 24:30 Rev 1:7
7:14 w Mt 28:18 x Ps 72:11 Ps 102:22 1Co 15:27 Eph 1:22 y Da 2:44 Heb 12:28 Rev 11:15
7:15 z Da 4:19
7:16 a Da 8:16 Da 9:22 Zec 1:9
7:18 b Isa 60:12-14 Rev 2:26 Rev 20:4
7:21 c Rev 13:7
7:23 d Da 2:40
7:24 e Rev 17:12
7:25 f Isa 37:23 Da 11:36 g Da 2:21 h Da 8:24 Da 12:7 Rev 12:14
7:27 i Da 2:44 Da 4:34 Lk 1:33 Rev 11:15 Rev 22:5 j Ps 22:27 Ps 72:11 Ps 86:9
7:28 k Da 4:19
8:2 a Est 1:2 b Ge 10:22
8:3 c Da 10:5

a25 Or *for a year, two years and half a year*

north and the south. No animal
could stand against him, and none
could rescue from his power. He
did as he pleased[d] and became
great.
5 As I was thinking about this,
suddenly a goat with a prominent
horn between his eyes came from
the west, crossing the whole earth
without touching the ground. 6 He
came towards the two-horned ram
I had seen standing beside the canal and charged at him in great
rage. 7 I saw him attack the ram
furiously, striking the ram and
shattering his two horns. The ram
was powerless to stand against
him; the goat knocked him to the
ground and trampled on him,[e] and
none could rescue the ram from his
power. 8 The goat became very
great, but at the height of his power
his large horn was broken off,[f]
and in its place four prominent
horns grew up towards the four
winds of heaven.[g]
9 Out of one of them came another
horn, which started small but grew
in power to the south and to the east
and towards the Beautiful Land.[h]
10 It grew until it reached[i] the host
of the heavens, and it threw some
of the starry host down to the
earth[j] and trampled[k] on them. 11 It
set itself up to be as great as the
Prince of the host;[l] it took away
the daily sacrifice[m] from him, and
the place of his sanctuary was
brought low.[n] 12 Because of rebellion, the host ⌞of the saints⌟[a] and the
daily sacrifice were given over to
it. It prospered in everything it did,
and truth was thrown to the
ground.
13 Then I heard a holy one[o]
speaking, and another holy one said
to him, "How long will it take for
the vision to be fulfilled[p]—the
vision concerning the daily sacrifice, the rebellion that causes desolation, and the surrender of the
sanctuary and of the host that will
be trampled[q] underfoot?"
14 He said to me, "It will take
2,300 evenings and mornings;
then the sanctuary will be reconse-
crated."[r]

The Interpretation of the Vision

15 While I, Daniel, was watching
the vision[s] and trying to understand it, there before me stood one
who looked like a man.[t] 16 And I
heard a man's voice from the Ulai
calling, "Gabriel,[u] tell this man the
meaning of the vision."
17 As he came near the place
where I was standing, I was terrified and fell prostrate.[v] "Son of
man," he said to me, "understand
that the vision concerns the time of
the end."[w]
18 While he was speaking to me, I
was in a deep sleep, with my face to
the ground.[x] Then he touched me
and raised me to my feet.[y]
19 He said: "I am going to tell you
what will happen later in the time
of wrath, because the vision concerns the appointed time of the
end.[b][z] 20 The two-horned ram that
you saw represents the kings of
Media and Persia. 21 The shaggy
goat is the king of Greece,[a] and the
large horn between his eyes is the
first king.[b] 22 The four horns that
replaced the one that was broken
off represent four kingdoms that
will emerge from his nation but
will not have the same power.
23 "In the latter part of their
reign, when rebels have become
completely wicked, a stern-faced
king, a master of intrigue, will
arise. 24 He will become very
strong, but not by his own power.
He will cause astounding devastation and will succeed in whatever
he does. He will destroy the mighty
men and the holy people.[c] 25 He
will cause deceit to prosper, and he
will consider himself superior.
When they feel secure, he will destroy many and take his stand
against the Prince of princes.[d] Yet

8:4 *d* Da 11:3,16
8:7 *e* Da 7:7
8:8 *f* 2Ch 26:16-21; Da 5:20 *g* Da 7:2; Rev 7:1
8:9 *h* Da 11:16
8:10 *i* Isa 14:13 *j* Rev 12:4 *k* Da 7:7
8:11 *l* Da 11:36-37 *m* Eze 46:13-14 *n* Da 11:31; Da 12:11
8:13 *o* Da 4:23 *p* Da 12:6 *q* Lk 21:24; Rev 11:2
8:14 *r* Da 12:11-12
8:15 *s* ver 1 *t* Da 10:16-18
8:16 *u* Da 9:21; Lk 1:19
8:17 *v* Eze 1:28; Da 2:46; Rev 1:17 *w* Hab 2:3
8:18 *x* Da 10:9 *y* Eze 2:2; Da 10:16-18
8:19 *z* Hab 2:3
8:21 *a* Da 10:20 *b* Da 11:3
8:24 *c* Da 7:25; Da 11:36
8:25 *d* Da 11:36

[a] 12 Or *rebellion, the armies* [b] 19 Or *because the end will be at the appointed time*

he will be destroyed, but not by human power.[e]

26“The vision of the evenings and mornings that has been given you is true,[f] but seal[g] up the vision, for it concerns the distant future.”[h]

27I, Daniel, was exhausted and lay ill for several days. Then I got up and went about the king's business.[i] I was appalled[j] by the vision; it was beyond understanding.

Daniel's Prayer

9 In the first year of Darius[a] son of Xerxes**[a]** (a Mede by descent), who was made ruler over the Babylonian**[b]** kingdom—2in the first year of his reign, I, Daniel, understood from the Scriptures, according to the word of the LORD given to Jeremiah the prophet, that the desolation of Jerusalem would last seventy[b] years. 3So I turned to the Lord God and pleaded with him in prayer and petition, in fasting, and in sackcloth and ashes.[c]

4I prayed to the LORD my God and confessed:

“O Lord, the great and awesome God,[d] who keeps his covenant of love[e] with all who love him and obey his commands, 5we have sinned and done wrong.[f] We have been wicked and have rebelled; we have turned away[g] from your commands and laws.[h] 6We have not listened to your servants the prophets,[i] who spoke in your name to our kings, our princes and our fathers, and to all the people of the land.

7“Lord, you are righteous, but this day we are covered with shame[j]—the men of Judah and people of Jerusalem and all Israel, both near and far, in all the countries where you have scattered[k] us because of our unfaithfulness to you.[l] 8O LORD, we and our kings, our princes and our fathers are covered with shame because we have sinned against you. 9The Lord our God is merciful and forgiving,[m] even though we have rebelled against him;[n] 10we have not obeyed the LORD our God or kept the laws he gave us through his servants the prophets.[o] 11All Israel has transgressed your law and turned away, refusing to obey you.

“Therefore the curses and sworn judgments written in the Law of Moses, the servant of God, have been poured out on us, because we have sinned[p] against you. 12You have fulfilled[q] the words spoken against us and against our rulers by bringing upon us great disaster. Under the whole heaven nothing has ever been done like what has been done to Jerusalem.[r] 13Just as it is written in the Law of Moses, all this disaster has come upon us, yet we have not sought the favour of the LORD our God by turning from our sins and giving attention to your truth.[s] 14The LORD did not hesitate to bring the disaster[t] upon us, for the LORD our God is righteous in everything he does; yet we have not obeyed him.[u]

15“Now, O Lord our God, who brought your people out of Egypt with a mighty hand[v] and who made for yourself a name[w] that endures to this day, we have sinned, we have done wrong. 16O Lord, in keeping with all your righteous acts,[x] turn away your anger and your wrath from Jerusalem,[y] your city, your holy hill.[z] Our sins and the iniquities of our fathers have made

8:25 *e* Da 2:34; Da 11:21
8:26 *f* Da 10:1; *g* Rev 22:10; *h* Da 10:14
8:27 *i* Da 2:48; *j* Da 7:28
9:1 *a* Da 5:31
9:2 *b* 2Ch 36:21; Jer 29:10; Zec 7:5
9:3 *c* Ne 1:4; Jer 29:12
9:4 *d* Dt 7:21; *e* Dt 7:9
9:5 *f* Ps 106:6; *g* Isa 53:6; *h* ver 11; La 1:20
9:6 *i* 2Ch 36:16; Jer 44:5
9:7 *j* Ps 44:15; *k* Dt 4:27; Am 9:9; *l* Jer 3:25
9:9 *m* Ps 130:4; *n* Ne 9:17; Jer 14:7
9:10 *o* 2Ki 17:13-15; 2Ki 18:12
9:11 *p* Isa 1:4-6; Jer 8:5-10
9:12 *q* Isa 44:26; Zec 1:6; *r* Jer 44:2-6; Eze 5:9
9:13 *s* Isa 9:13; Jer 2:30
9:14 *t* Jer 44:27; *u* Ne 9:33
9:15 *v* Jer 32:21; *w* Ne 9:10
9:16 *x* Ps 31:1; *y* Jer 32:32; *z* Zec 8:3

a1 Hebrew *Ahasuerus* **b**1 Or *Chaldean*

Jerusalem and your people an object of scorn[a] to all those around us.

17“Now, our God, hear the prayers and petitions of your servant. For your sake, O Lord, look with favour[b] on your desolate sanctuary. 18Give ear, O God, and hear; open your eyes and see[c] the desolation of the city that bears your Name.[d] We do not make requests of you because we are righteous, but because of your great mercy. 19O Lord, listen! O Lord, forgive![e] O Lord, hear and act! For your sake, O my God, do not delay, because your city and your people bear your Name.”

The Seventy “Sevens”

20While I was speaking and praying, confessing my sin and the sin of my people Israel and making my request to the LORD my God for his holy hill[f]—21while I was still in prayer, Gabriel,[g] the man I had seen in the earlier vision, came to me in swift flight about the time of the evening sacrifice.[h] 22He instructed me and said to me, “Daniel, I have now come to give you insight and understanding. 23As soon as you began to pray, an answer was given, which I have come to tell you, for you are highly esteemed.[i] Therefore, consider the message and understand the vision:[j]

24“Seventy ‘sevens’[c] are decreed for your people and your holy city to finish[d] transgression, to put an end to sin, to atone[k] for wickedness, to bring in everlasting righteousness,[l] to seal up vision and prophecy and to anoint the most holy.[e]

25“Know and understand this: From the issuing of the decree[f] to restore and rebuild[m] Jerusalem until the Anointed One,[g][n] the ruler, comes, there will be seven ‘sevens’, and sixty-two ‘sevens’. It will be rebuilt with streets and a trench, but in times of trouble. 26After the sixty-two ‘sevens’, the Anointed One will be cut off[o] and will have nothing.[h] The people of the ruler who will come will destroy the city and the sanctuary. The end will come like a flood:[p] War will continue until the end, and desolations have been decreed. 27He will confirm a covenant with many for one ‘seven’.[i] In the middle of the ‘seven’[i] he will put an end to sacrifice and offering. And on a wing ⌊of the temple⌋ he will set up an abomination that causes desolation, until the end that is decreed[q] is poured out on him.[j]”[k]

Daniel’s Vision of a Man

10 In the third year of Cyrus[a] king of Persia, a revelation was given to Daniel (who was called Belteshazzar).[b] Its message was true[c] and it concerned a great war.[a] The understanding of the message came to him in a vision.

2At that time I, Daniel, mourned[d] for three weeks. 3I ate no choice food; no meat or wine touched my lips; and I used no lotions at all until the three weeks were over.

4On the twenty-fourth day of the first month, as I was standing on the bank of the great river, the Tigris,[e] 5I looked up and there before me was a man dressed in linen,[f] with a belt of the finest gold[g] round his waist. 6His body was like chrysolite, his face like lightning,[h] his eyes like flaming torches,[i] his arms and legs like the gleam of burnished bronze,[j] and

9:16 a Eze 5:14
9:17 b Nu 6:24-26; Ps 80:19
9:18 c Ps 80:14; d Isa 37:17; Jer 7:10-12; Jer 25:29
9:19 e Ps 44:23
9:20 f ver 3; Ps 145:18; Isa 58:9
9:21 g Da 8:16; Lk 1:19; h Ex 29:39
9:23 i Da 10:19; Lk 1:28; j Da 10:11-12; Mt 24:15
9:24 k Isa 53:10; l Isa 56:1
9:25 m Ezr 4:24; n Jn 4:25
9:26 o Isa 53:8; p Na 1:8
9:27 q Isa 10:22
10:1 a Da 1:21; b Da 1:7; c Da 8:26
10:2 d Ezr 9:4
10:4 e Ge 2:14
10:5 f Eze 9:2; Rev 15:6; g Jer 10:9
10:6 h Mt 17:2; i Rev 19:12; j Rev 1:15

c24 Or *‘weeks’*; also in verses 25 and 26
d24 Or *restrain* e24 Or *Most Holy Place*; or *most holy One* f25 Or *word* g25 Or *an anointed one*; also in verse 26 h26 Or *off and will have no-one*; or *off, but not for himself*
i27 Or *‘week’* j27 Or *it* k27 Or *And one who causes desolation will come upon the pinnacle of the abominable ⌊temple⌋, until the end that is decreed is poured out on the desolated ⌊city⌋*
a1 Or *true and burdensome*

his voice like the sound of a multitude.

7 I, Daniel, was the only one who saw the vision; the men with me did not see it,[k] but such terror overwhelmed them that they fled and hid themselves. 8 So I was left alone,[l] gazing at this great vision; I had no strength left,[m] my face turned deathly pale and I was helpless.[n] 9 Then I heard him speaking, and as I listened to him, I fell into a deep sleep, my face to the ground.[o]

10 A hand touched me[p] and set me trembling on my hands and knees.[q] 11 He said, "Daniel, you who are highly esteemed,[r] consider carefully the words I am about to speak to you, and stand up,[s] for I have now been sent to you." And when he said this to me, I stood up trembling.

12 Then he continued, "Do not be afraid, Daniel. Since the first day that you set your mind to gain understanding and to humble[t] yourself before your God, your words were heard, and I have come in response to them.[u] 13 But the prince of the Persian kingdom resisted me twenty-one days. Then Michael,[v] one of the chief princes, came to help me, because I was detained there with the king of Persia. 14 Now I have come to explain[w] to you what will happen to your people in the future, for the vision concerns a time yet to come.[x]"

15 While he was saying this to me, I bowed with my face towards the ground and was speechless.[y] 16 Then one who looked like a man**[b]** touched my lips, and I opened my mouth and began to speak.[z] I said to the one standing before me, "I am overcome with anguish[a] because of the vision, my lord, and I am helpless. 17 How can I, your servant, talk with you, my lord? My strength is gone and I can hardly breathe."[b]

18 Again the one who looked like a man touched[c] me and gave me strength. 19 "Do not be afraid, O man highly esteemed," he said. "Peace![d] Be strong now; be strong."[e]

When he spoke to me, I was strengthened and said, "Speak, my lord, since you have given me strength."[f]

20 So he said, "Do you know why I have come to you? Soon I will return to fight against the prince of Persia, and when I go, the prince of Greece[g] will come; 21 but first I will tell you what is written in the Book of Truth.[h] (No-one supports me against them except Michael,[i]

11 your prince. 1 And in the first year of Darius[a] the Mede, I took my stand to support and protect him.)

The Kings of the South and the North

2 "Now then, I tell you the truth:[b] Three more kings will appear in Persia, and then a fourth, who will be far richer than all the others. When he has gained power by his wealth, he will stir up everyone against the kingdom of Greece.[c] 3 Then a mighty king will appear, who will rule with great power and do as he pleases.[d] 4 After he has appeared, his empire will be broken up and parcelled out towards the four winds of heaven.[e] It will not go to his descendants, nor will it have the power he exercised, because his empire will be uprooted and given to others.

5 "The king of the South will become strong, but one of his commanders will become even stronger than he and will rule his own kingdom with great power. 6 After some years, they will become allies. The daughter of the king of the South will go to the king of the North to make an alliance,

b16 Most manuscripts of the Masoretic Text; one manuscript of the Masoretic Text, Dead Sea Scrolls and Septuagint *Then something that looked like a man's hand*

10:7 k 2Ki 6:17-20; Ac 9:7
10:8 l Ge 32:24; m Da 8:27; n Hab 3:16
10:9 o Da 8:18
10:10 p Jer 1:9; q Rev 1:17
10:11 r Da 9:23; s Eze 2:1
10:12 t Da 9:3; u Da 9:20
10:13 v ver 21; Da 12:1; Jude 1:9
10:14 w Da 9:22; x Da 2:28; Da 8:26; Hab 2:3
10:15 y Eze 24:27; Lk 1:20
10:16 z Isa 6:7; Jer 1:9; Da 8:15-18; a Isa 21:3
10:17 b Da 4:19
10:18 c ver 16
10:19 d Jdg 6:23; Isa 35:4; e Jos 1:9; f Isa 6:1-8
10:20 g Da 8:21; Da 11:2
10:21 h Da 11:2; i ver 13; Jude 1:9
11:1 a Da 5:31
11:2 b Da 10:21; c Da 10:20
11:3 d Da 8:4,21
11:4 e Da 7:2; Da 8:22

but she will not retain her power, and he and his power[a] will not last. In those days she will be handed over, together with her royal escort and her father[b] and the one who supported her.

7 "One from her family line will arise to take her place. He will attack the forces of the king of the North[f] and enter his fortress; he will fight against them and be victorious. 8 He will also seize their gods,[g] their metal images and their valuable articles of silver and gold and carry them off to Egypt.[h] For some years he will leave the king of the North alone. 9 Then the king of the North will invade the realm of the king of the South but will retreat to his own country. 10 His sons will prepare for war and assemble a great army, which will sweep on like an irresistible flood[i] and carry the battle as far as his fortress.

11 "Then the king of the South will march out in a rage and fight against the king of the North, who will raise a large army, but it will be defeated.[j] 12 When the army is carried off, the king of the South will be filled with pride and will slaughter many thousands, yet he will not remain triumphant. 13 For the king of the North will muster another army, larger than the first; and after several years, he will advance with a huge army fully equipped.

14 "In those times many will rise against the king of the South. The violent men among your own people will rebel in fulfilment of the vision, but without success. 15 Then the king of the North will come and build up siege ramps[k] and will capture a fortified city. The forces of the South will be powerless to resist; even their best troops will not have the strength to stand. 16 The invader will do as he pleases;[l] no-one will be able to stand against him.[m] He will establish himself in the Beautiful Land and will have the power to destroy it.[n] 17 He will determine to come with the might of his entire kingdom and will make an alliance with the king of the South. And he will give him a daughter in marriage in order to overthrow the kingdom, but his plans[c] will not succeed[o] or help him. 18 Then he will turn his attention to the coastlands[p] and will take many of them, but a commander will put an end to his insolence and will turn his insolence back upon him.[q] 19 After this, he will turn back towards the fortresses of his own country but will stumble and fall,[r] to be seen no more.[s]

20 "His successor will send out a tax collector to maintain the royal splendour.[t] In a few years, however, he will be destroyed, yet not in anger or in battle.

21 "He will be succeeded by a contemptible[u] person who has not been given the honour of royalty.[v] He will invade the kingdom when its people feel secure, and he will seize it through intrigue. 22 Then an overwhelming army will be swept away before him; both it and a prince of the covenant will be destroyed.[w] 23 After coming to an agreement with him, he will act deceitfully,[x] and with only a few people he will rise to power. 24 When the richest provinces feel secure, he will invade them and will achieve what neither his fathers nor his forefathers did. He will distribute plunder, loot and wealth among his followers.[y] He will plot the overthrow of fortresses—but only for a time.

25 "With a large army he will stir up his strength and courage against the king of the South. The king of the South will wage war with a large and very powerful army, but he will not be able to stand because of the plots devised

11:7 f ver 6
11:8 g Isa 37:19; Isa 46:1-2 h Jer 43:12
11:10 i Isa 8:8; Jer 46:8; Da 9:26
11:11 j Da 8:7-8
11:15 k Eze 4:2
11:16 l Da 8:4 m Jos 1:5; Da 8:7 n Da 8:9
11:17 o Ps 20:4
11:18 p Isa 66:19; Jer 25:22 q Hos 12:14
11:19 r Ps 27:2 s Ps 37:36; Eze 26:21
11:20 t Isa 60:17
11:21 u Da 4:17 v Da 8:25
11:22 w Da 8:10-11
11:23 x Da 8:25
11:24 y Ne 9:25

a6 Or *offspring* b6 Or *child* (see Vulgate and Syriac) c17 Or *but she*

against him. 26 Those who eat from the king's provisions will try to destroy him; his army will be swept away, and many will fall in battle. 27 The two kings, with their hearts bent on evil,[z] will sit at the same table and lie[a] to each other, but to no avail, because an end will still come at the appointed time.[b] 28 The king of the North will return to his own country with great wealth, but his heart will be set against the holy covenant. He will take action against it and then return to his own country.

29 "At the appointed time he will invade the South again, but this time the outcome will be different from what it was before. 30 Ships of the western coastlands[d][c] will oppose him, and he will lose heart. Then he will turn back and vent his fury against the holy covenant. He will return and show favour to those who forsake the holy covenant.

31 "His armed forces will rise up to desecrate the temple fortress and will abolish the daily sacrifice. Then they will set up the abomination that causes desolation.[d] 32 With flattery he will corrupt those who have violated the covenant, but the people who know their God will firmly resist[e] him.

33 "Those who are wise will instruct[f] many, though for a time they will fall by the sword or be burned or captured or plundered.[g] 34 When they fall, they will receive a little help, and many who are not sincere[h] will join them. 35 Some of the wise will stumble, so that they may be refined,[i] purified and made spotless until the time of the end, for it will still come at the appointed time.

The King Who Exalts Himself

36 "The king will do as he pleases. He will exalt and magnify himself above every god and will say unheard-of things[j] against the God of gods.[k] He will be successful until the time of wrath[l] is completed, for what has been determined must take place. 37 He will show no regard for the gods of his fathers or for the one desired by women, nor will he regard any god, but will exalt himself above them all. 38 Instead of them, he will honour a god of fortresses; a god unknown to his fathers he will honour with gold and silver, with precious stones and costly gifts. 39 He will attack the mightiest fortresses with the help of a foreign god and will greatly honour those who acknowledge him. He will make them rulers over many people and will distribute the land at a price.[e]

40 "At the time of the end the king of the South[m] will engage him in battle, and the king of the North will storm[n] out against him with chariots and cavalry and a great fleet of ships. He will invade many countries and sweep through them like a flood.[o] 41 He will also invade the Beautiful Land. Many countries will fall, but Edom,[p] Moab[q] and the leaders of Ammon will be delivered from his hand. 42 He will extend his power over many countries; Egypt will not escape. 43 He will gain control of the treasures of gold and silver and all the riches of Egypt,[r] with the Libyans[s] and Nubians in submission. 44 But reports from the east and the north will alarm him, and he will set out in a great rage to destroy and annihilate many. 45 He will pitch his royal tents between the seas at[f] the beautiful holy mountain. Yet he will come to his end, and no-one will help him.

The End Times

12 "At that time Michael,[a] the great prince who protects your people, will arise. There will be a time of distress[b] such as has

11:27 z Ps 64:6 a Ps 12:2 Jer 9:5 b Hab 2:3
11:30 c Ge 10:4
11:31 d Da 8:11-13 Da 9:27 Mt 24:15* Mk 13:14*
11:32 e Mic 5:7-9
11:33 f Mal 2:7 g Mt 24:9 Jn 16:2 Heb 11:32-38
11:34 h Mt 7:15 Ro 16:18
11:35 i Ps 78:38 Da 12:10 Zec 13:9 Jn 15:2
11:36 j Rev 13:5-6 k Dt 10:17 Isa 14:13-14 Da 7:25 Da 8:11-12, 25 2Th 2:4 l Isa 10:25 Isa 26:20
11:40 m Isa 21:1 n Isa 5:28 o Eze 38:4
11:41 p Isa 11:14 q Jer 48:47
11:43 r Eze 30:4 s 2Ch 12:3 Na 3:9
12:1 a Da 10:13 b Da 9:12 Mt 24:21 Mk 13:19 Rev 16:18

[d] 30 Hebrew *of Kittim* [e] 39 Or *land for a reward*
[f] 45 Or *the sea and*

not happened from the beginning
of nations until then. But at that
time your people—everyone whose
name is found written in the
book[c]—will be delivered.[d] 2Multi-
tudes who sleep in the dust of
the earth will awake: some to everlasting life, others to shame and
everlasting contempt.[e] 3Those who
are wise[a][f] will shine[g] like the
brightness of the heavens, and those
who lead many to righteousness,
like the stars for ever and ever.[h]
4But you, Daniel, close up and seal[i]
the words of the scroll until the
time of the end.[j] Many will go here
and there to increase knowledge."

5Then I, Daniel, looked, and there
before me stood two others, one on
this bank of the river and one on the
opposite bank.[k] 6One of them said
to the man clothed in linen,[l] who
was above the waters of the river,
"How long will it be before these
astonishing things are fulfilled?"[m]
7The man clothed in linen, who
was above the waters of the river,
lifted his right hand and his left
hand towards heaven, and I heard
him swear by him who lives for
ever,[n] saying, "It will be for a time,
times and half a time.[b][o] When the
power of the holy people[p] has been
finally broken, all these things will
be completed.[q]"
8I heard, but I did not understand. So I asked, "My lord, what
will the outcome of all this be?"
9He replied, "Go your way, Daniel, because the words are closed
up and sealed until the time of the
end.[r] 10Many will be purified,
made spotless and refined,[s] but
the wicked will continue to be
wicked.[t] None of the wicked will
understand, but those who are wise
will understand.[u]
11"From the time that the daily
sacrifice is abolished and the
abomination that causes desolation[v] is set up, there will be 1,290
days. 12Blessed is the one who
waits[w] for and reaches the end of
the 1,335 days.[x]
13"As for you, go your way till the
end. You will rest,[y] and then at the
end of the days you will rise to receive your allotted inheritance.[z]"

12:1 *c* Ex 32:32; Ps 56:8 *d* Jer 30:7
12:2 *e* Isa 26:19; Mt 25:46; Jn 5:28-29
12:3 *f* Da 11:33 *g* Mt 13:43; Jn 5:35 *h* 1Co 15:42
12:4 *i* Isa 8:16 *j* ver 9,13; Rev 22:10
12:5 *k* Da 10:4
12:6 *l* Eze 9:2 *m* Da 8:13
12:7 *n* Rev 10:5-6 *o* Da 7:25 *p* Da 8:24 *q* Lk 21:24; Rev 10:7
12:9 *r* ver 4
12:10 *s* Da 11:35 *t* Isa 32:7; Rev 22:11 *u* Hos 14:9
12:11 *v* Da 8:11; Da 9:27; Mt 24:15*; Mk 13:14*
12:12 *w* Isa 30:18 *x* Da 8:14
12:13 *y* Isa 57:2 *z* Ps 16:5; Rev 14:13

a3 Or *who impart wisdom* b7 Or *a year, two years and half a year*

HOSEA

1 The word of the LORD that
came to Hosea son of Beeri
during the reigns of Uzziah, Jotham, Ahaz and Hezekiah, kings of
Judah,[a] and during the reign of
Jeroboam[b] son of Joash king of
Israel:[c]

Hosea's Wife and Children

2When the LORD began to speak
through Hosea, the LORD said to
him, "Go, take to yourself an adulterous[d] wife and children of unfaithfulness, because the land is
guilty of the vilest adultery[e] in de-
parting from the LORD." 3So he
married Gomer daughter of Dib-
laim, and she conceived and bore
him a son.

4Then the LORD said to Hosea,
"Call him Jezreel,[f] because I will
soon punish the house of Jehu for
the massacre at Jezreel, and I will
put an end to the kingdom of Israel.
5In that day I will break Israel's
bow in the Valley of Jezreel.[g]"

6Gomer[h] conceived again and
gave birth to a daughter. Then the
LORD said to Hosea, "Call her Lo-
Ruhamah,**[a]** for I will no longer
show love to the house of Israel,[i]
that I should at all forgive them.
7Yet I will show love to the house of
Judah; and I will save them—not
by bow,[j] sword or battle, or by
horses and horsemen, but by the
LORD their God.[k]"

8After she had weaned Lo-
Ruhamah, Gomer had another son.
9Then the LORD said, "Call him Lo-
Ammi,**[b]** for you are not my people,
and I am not your God.

10"Yet the Israelites will be like
the sand on the seashore, which
cannot be measured or counted.[l]
In the place where it was said to
them, 'You are not my people', they
will be called 'sons of the living
God'.[m] 11The people of Judah and
the people of Israel will be re-
united,[n] and they will appoint one
leader[o] and will come up out of the
land,[p] for great will be the day of
Jezreel.

2 "Say of your brothers, 'My
people', and of your sisters,
'My loved one'.[a]

Israel Punished and Restored

2"Rebuke your mother,[b] rebuke
her,
for she is not my wife,
and I am not her husband.
Let her remove the adulterous[c]
look from her face
and the unfaithfulness from
between her breasts.
3Otherwise I will strip her naked
and make her as bare as on
the day she was born;[d]
I will make her like a desert,[e]
turn her into a parched land,
and slay her with thirst.
4I will not show my love to her
children,[f]
because they are the children
of adultery.
5Their mother has been
unfaithful
and has conceived them in
disgrace.
She said, 'I will go after my
lovers,[g]
who give me my food and my
water,
my wool and my linen, my oil
and my drink.'[h]
6Therefore I will block her path
with thornbushes;
I will wall her in so that she
cannot find her way.[i]

1:1 *a* Isa 1:1; Mic 1:1 *b* 2Ki 13:13 *c* Am 1:1
1:2 *d* Jer 3:1; Hos 2:2,5; Hos 3:1 *e* Dt 31:16; Jer 3:14; Eze 23:3-21; Hos 5:3
1:4 *f* 2Ki 10:1-14; Hos 2:22
1:5 *g* 2Ki 15:29
1:6 *h* ver 3 *i* Hos 2:4
1:7 *j* Ps 44:6 *k* Zec 4:6
1:10 *l* Ge 22:17; Jer 33:22 *m* ver 9; Ro 9:26*
1:11 *n* Isa 11:12,13 *o* Jer 23:5-8 *p* Eze 37:15-28
2:1 *a* ver 23
2:2 *b* ver 5; Isa 50:1; Hos 1:2 *c* Eze 23:45
2:3 *d* Eze 16:4,22 *e* Isa 32:13-14
2:4 *f* Eze 8:18
2:5 *g* Jer 3:6 *h* Jer 44:17-18
2:6 *i* Job 3:23; Job 19:8; La 3:9

a6 *Lo-Ruhamah* means *not loved.* **b**9 *Lo-Ammi* means *not my people.*

7She will chase after her lovers
but not catch them;
she will look for them but not
find them.[j]
Then she will say,
'I will go back to my husband
as at first,[k]
for then I was better off[l]
than now.'
8She has not acknowledged[m] that
I was the one
who gave her the grain, the
new wine and oil,
who lavished on her the silver
and gold—
which they used for Baal.[n]
9"Therefore I will take away my
grain[o] when it ripens,
and my new wine[p] when it is
ready.
I will take back my wool and
my linen,
intended to cover her
nakedness.
10So now I will expose her
lewdness
before the eyes of her lovers;
no-one will take her out of my
hands.[q]
11I will stop[r] all her celebrations:
her yearly festivals, her New
Moons,
her Sabbath days—all her
appointed feasts.[s]
12I will ruin her vines[t] and her
fig-trees,
which she said were her pay
from her lovers;
I will make them a thicket,[u]
and wild animals will devour
them.[v]
13I will punish her for the days
she burned incense to the
Baals;[w]
she decked herself with rings
and jewellery,[x]
and went after her lovers,[y]
but me she forgot,[z]"
declares the LORD.
14"Therefore I am now going to
allure her;
I will lead her into the desert
and speak tenderly to her.

2:7 j Hos 5:13 k Jer 2:2 Jer 3:1 l Eze 16:8
2:8 m Isa 1:3 n Eze 16:15-19 Hos 8:4
2:9 o Hos 8:7 p Hos 9:2
2:10 q Eze 16:37
2:11 r Jer 7:34 s Isa 1:14 Jer 16:9 Hos 3:4 Am 8:10
2:12 t Isa 7:23 Jer 8:13 u Isa 5:6 v Hos 13:8
2:13 w Hos 11:2 x Eze 16:17 y Hos 4:13 z Hos 4:6 Hos 8:14 Hos 13:6
2:15 a Jos 7:24,26 b Ex 15:1-18 c Jer 2:2 d Hos 12:9
2:17 e Ex 23:13 Ps 16:4 f Jos 23:7
2:18 g Job 5:22 h Isa 2:4 i Jer 23:6 Eze 34:25
2:19 j Isa 62:4 k Isa 1:27
2:20 l Jer 31:34 Hos 6:6 Hos 13:4
2:21 m Isa 55:10 Zec 8:12
2:22 n Jer 31:12 Joel 2:19
2:23 o Jer 31:27

15There I will give her back her
vineyards,
and will make the Valley of
Achor[a][a] a door of hope.
There she will sing[b][b] as in the
days of her youth,[c]
as in the day she came up out
of Egypt.[d]

16"In that day," declares the
LORD,
"you will call me 'my
husband';
you will no longer call me 'my
master'.[c]
17I will remove the names of the
Baals from her lips;[e]
no longer will their names be
invoked.[f]
18In that day I will make a
covenant for them
with the beasts of the field
and the birds of the air
and the creatures that move
along the ground.[g]
Bow and sword and battle
I will abolish[h] from the land,
so that all may lie down in
safety.[i]
19I will betroth[j] you to me for
ever;
I will betroth you in[d]
righteousness and justice,[k]
in[e] love and compassion.
20I will betroth you in
faithfulness,
and you will acknowledge[l]
the LORD.

21"In that day I will respond,"
declares the LORD—
"I will respond[m] to the skies,
and they will respond to the
earth;
22and the earth will respond to
the grain,
the new wine and oil,[n]
and they will respond to
Jezreel.[f]
23I will plant[o] her for myself in
the land;

[a]15 *Achor* means *trouble.* [b]15 Or *respond*
[c]16 Hebrew *baal* [d]19 Or *with;* also in verse 20
[e]19 Or *with* [f]22 *Jezreel* means *God plants.*

I will show my love to the one
I called 'Not my loved
one'.[g][p]
I will say to those called 'Not
my people',[h] 'You are my
people';[q]
and they will say, 'You are my
God.[r]' "

Hosea's Reconciliation With His Wife

3 The LORD said to me, "Go,
show your love to your wife
again, though she is loved by another and is an adulteress.[a] Love
her as the LORD loves the Israelites,
though they turn to other gods and
love the sacred raisin cakes.[b]"
2So I bought her for fifteen shekels[a] of silver and about a homer
and a lethek[b] of barley. 3Then I
told her, "You are to live with[c] me
for many days; you must not be a
prostitute or be intimate with any
man, and I will live with[c] you."
4For the Israelites will live for
many days without king or
prince,[c] without sacrifice[d] or sacred stones, without ephod or
idol.[e] 5Afterwards the Israelites
will return and seek the LORD their
God and David their king.[f] They
will come trembling to the LORD
and to his blessings in the last
days.[g]

The Charge Against Israel

4 Hear the word of the LORD,
you Israelites,
because the LORD has a charge
to bring
against you who live in the
land:
"There is no faithfulness, no
love,
no acknowledgment[a] of God
in the land.
2There is only cursing,[a] lying[b]
and murder,[c]
stealing[d] and adultery;
they break all bounds,
and bloodshed follows
bloodshed.
3Because of this the land
mourns,[b][e]
and all who live in it waste
away;[f]
the beasts of the field and the
birds of the air
and the fish of the sea are
dying.[g]

4"But let no man bring a charge,
let no man accuse another,
for your people are like those
who bring charges against a
priest.[h]
5You stumble[i] day and night,
and the prophets stumble with
you.
So I will destroy your
mother[j]—
6 my people are destroyed from
lack of knowledge.[k]

"Because you have rejected
knowledge,
I also reject you as my
priests;
because you have ignored the
law[l] of your God,
I also will ignore your
children.
7The more the priests increased,
the more they sinned against
me;
they exchanged[c] their[d]
Glory[m] for something
disgraceful.[n]
8They feed on the sins of my
people
and relish their wickedness.[o]
9And it will be: Like people, like
priests.[p]
I will punish both of them for
their ways
and repay them for their
deeds.[q]

2:23 p Hos 1:6 q Hos 1:10 r Ro 9:25* 1Pe 2:10
3:1 a Hos 1:2 b 2Sa 6:19
3:4 c Hos 13:11 d Da 11:31 Hos 2:11 e Jdg 17:5-6 Zec 10:2
3:5 f Eze 34:23-24 g Jer 50:4-5
4:1 a Jer 7:28
4:2 b Hos 7:3 Hos 10:4 c Hos 6:9 d Hos 7:1
4:3 e Jer 4:28 f Isa 33:9 g Jer 4:25 Zep 1:3
4:4 h Dt 17:12 Eze 3:26
4:5 i Eze 14:7 j Hos 2:2
4:6 k Hos 2:13 Mal 2:7-8 l Hos 8:1,12
4:7 m Hab 2:16 n Hos 10:1,6 Hos 13:6
4:8 o Isa 56:11 Mic 3:11
4:9 p Isa 24:2 q Jer 5:31 Hos 8:13 Hos 9:9,15

g23 Hebrew *Lo-Ruhamah* h23 Hebrew *Lo-Ammi* a2 That is, about 6 ounces (about 170 grams) b2 That is, probably about 9 bushels (about 330 litres) c3 Or *wait for*
a2 That is, to pronounce a curse upon b3 Or *dries up* c7 Syriac and an ancient Hebrew scribal tradition; Masoretic Text *I will exchange* d7 Masoretic Text; an ancient Hebrew scribal tradition *my*

10 "They will eat but not have
enough;[r]
they will engage in
prostitution but not
increase,
because they have deserted[s]
the LORD
to give themselves 11 to
prostitution,[t]
to old wine and new,
which take away the
understanding[u] 12 of my
people.
They consult a wooden idol[v]
and are answered by a stick of
wood.[w]
A spirit of prostitution leads
them astray;[x]
they are unfaithful to their
God.
13 They sacrifice on the
mountaintops
and burn offerings on the
hills,
under oak,[y] poplar and
terebinth,
where the shade is pleasant.[z]
Therefore your daughters turn
to prostitution[a]
and your daughters-in-law to
adultery.[b]

14 "I will not punish your
daughters
when they turn to
prostitution,
nor your daughters-in-law
when they commit adultery,
because the men themselves
consort with harlots[c]
and sacrifice with
shrine-prostitutes—
a people without
understanding will come to
ruin!

15 "Though you commit adultery,
O Israel,
let not Judah become guilty.

"Do not go to Gilgal;[d]
do not go up to Beth Aven.[e]
And do not swear, 'As surely
as the LORD lives!'

4:10
r Lev 26:26; Mic 6:14
s Hos 7:14; Hos 9:17

4:11
t Hos 5:4
u Pr 20:1

4:12
v Jer 2:27
w Hab 2:19
x Isa 44:20

4:13
y Isa 1:29
z Jer 3:6; Hos 11:2
a Jer 2:20; Am 7:17
b Hos 2:13

4:14
c ver 11

4:15
d Hos 9:15; Hos 12:11; Am 4:4

4:16
e Isa 5:17; Isa 7:25

4:19
f Hos 12:1; Hos 13:15
g Isa 1:29

5:1
a Hos 6:9; Hos 9:8

5:2
b Hos 4:2
c Hos 9:15

5:3
d Hos 6:10

5:4
e Hos 4:11
f Hos 4:6

5:5
g Hos 7:10

16 The Israelites are stubborn,
like a stubborn heifer.
How then can the LORD pasture
them
like lambs[e] in a meadow?
17 Ephraim is joined to idols;
leave him alone!
18 Even when their drinks are
gone,
they continue their
prostitution;
their rulers dearly love
shameful ways.
19 A whirlwind[f] will sweep them
away,
and their sacrifices will bring
them shame.[g]

Judgment Against Israel

5 "Hear this, you priests!
Pay attention, you Israelites!
Listen, O royal house!
This judgment is against you:
You have been a snare[a] at
Mizpah,
a net spread out on Tabor.
2 The rebels are deep in
slaughter.[b]
I will discipline all of them.[c]
3 I know all about Ephraim;
Israel is not hidden from me.
Ephraim, you have now turned
to prostitution;
Israel is corrupt.[d]

4 "Their deeds do not permit
them
to return to their God.
A spirit of prostitution[e] is in
their heart;
they do not acknowledge[f] the
LORD.
5 Israel's arrogance testifies[g]
against them;
the Israelites, even Ephraim,
stumble in their sin;
Judah also stumbles with
them.

e15 *Beth Aven* means *house of wickedness* (a name for Bethel, which means *house of God*).

6 When they go with their flocks
and herds
to seek the LORD,[h]
they will not find him;
he has withdrawn[i] himself
from them.
7 They are unfaithful[j] to the
LORD;
they give birth to
illegitimate[k] children.
Now their New Moon festivals
will devour[l] them and their
fields.

8 "Sound the trumpet in Gibeah,[m]
the horn in Ramah.[n]
Raise the battle cry in Beth
Aven;[a][o]
lead on, O Benjamin.
9 Ephraim will be laid waste
on the day of reckoning.[p]
Among the tribes of Israel
I proclaim what is certain.[q]
10 Judah's leaders are like those
who move boundary stones.[r]
I will pour out my wrath[s] on
them
like a flood of water.
11 Ephraim is oppressed,
trampled in judgment,
intent on pursuing idols.[b][t]
12 I am like a moth[u] to Ephraim,
like rot to the people of Judah.

13 "When Ephraim saw his
sickness,
and Judah his sores,
then Ephraim turned to
Assyria,[v]
and sent to the great king for
help.[w]
But he is not able to cure[x] you,
not able to heal your sores.[y]
14 For I will be like a lion[z] to
Ephraim,
like a great lion to Judah.
I will tear them to pieces and
go away;
I will carry them off, with
no-one to rescue them.[a]
15 Then I will go back to my place
until they admit their guilt.
And they will seek my face;[b]
in their misery[c] they will
earnestly seek me.[d]"

5:6 *h* Mic 6:6-7 *i* Pr 1:28 Isa 1:15 Eze 8:6
5:7 *j* Hos 6:7 *k* Hos 2:4 *l* Hos 2:11-12
5:8 *m* Hos 9:9 Hos 10:9 *n* Isa 10:29 *o* Hos 4:15
5:9 *p* Isa 37:3 Hos 9:11-17 *q* Isa 46:10 Zec 1:6
5:10 *r* Dt 19:14 *s* Eze 7:8
5:11 *t* Hos 9:16 Mic 6:16
5:12 *u* Isa 51:8
5:13 *v* Hos 7:11 Hos 8:9 *w* Hos 10:6 *x* Hos 14:3 *y* Jer 30:12
5:14 *z* Am 3:4 *a* Mic 5:8
5:15 *b* Hos 3:5 *c* Jer 2:27 *d* Isa 64:9
6:1 *a* Hos 5:14 *b* Dt 32:39 Jer 30:17 Hos 14:4
6:2 *c* Ps 30:5
6:3 *d* Joel 2:23 *e* Ps 72:6
6:4 *f* Hos 11:8 *g* Hos 7:1 Hos 13:3
6:5 *h* Jer 1:9-10 Jer 23:29 *i* Heb 4:12
6:6 *j* Isa 1:11 Mt 9:13* Mt 12:7* *k* Hos 2:20
6:7 *l* Hos 8:1 *m* Hos 5:7

Israel Unrepentant

6 "Come, let us return to the
LORD.
He has torn us to pieces[a]
but he will heal us;
he has injured us
but he will bind up our
wounds.[b]
2 After two days he will revive
us;[c]
on the third day he will
restore us,
that we may live in his
presence.
3 Let us acknowledge the LORD;
let us press on to acknowledge
him.
As surely as the sun rises,
he will appear;
he will come to us like the
winter rains,[d]
like the spring rains that
water the earth.[e]"

4 "What can I do with you,
Ephraim?[f]
What can I do with you,
Judah?
Your love is like the morning
mist,
like the early dew that
disappears.[g]
5 Therefore I cut you in pieces
with my prophets,
I killed you with the words of
my mouth;[h]
my judgments flashed like
lightning upon you.[i]
6 For I desire mercy, not
sacrifice,[j]
and acknowledgment[k] of God
rather than burnt offerings.
7 Like Adam,[a] they have broken
the covenant[l]—
they were unfaithful[m] to me
there.
8 Gilead is a city of wicked men,
stained with footprints of
blood.

[a]8 *Beth Aven* means *house of wickedness* (a name for Bethel, which means *house of God*).
[b]11 The meaning of the Hebrew for this word is uncertain.
[a]7 Or *As at Adam*; or *Like men*

9 As marauders lie in ambush for
a man,
so do bands of priests;
they murder on the road to
Shechem,
committing shameful crimes.[n]
10 I have seen a horrible[o] thing
in the house of Israel.
There Ephraim is given to
prostitution
and Israel is defiled.[p]

11 "Also for you, Judah,
a harvest[q] is appointed.

"Whenever I would restore the
fortunes of my people,

7 1 whenever I would heal
Israel,
the sins of Ephraim are
exposed
and the crimes of Samaria
revealed.[a]
They practise deceit,[b]
thieves break into houses,[c]
bandits rob in the streets;
2 but they do not realise
that I remember[d] all their
evil deeds.
Their sins engulf them;[e]
they are always before me.

3 "They delight the king with
their wickedness,
the princes with their lies.[f]
4 They are all adulterers,[g]
burning like an oven
whose fire the baker need not
stir
from the kneading of the
dough till it rises.
5 On the day of the festival of our
king
the princes become inflamed
with wine,[h]
and he joins hands with the
mockers.
6 Their hearts are like an oven;[i]
they approach him with
intrigue.
Their passion smoulders all
night;
in the morning it blazes like a
flaming fire.
7 All of them are hot as an oven;
they devour their rulers.
All their kings fall,
and none of them calls[j] on
me.

8 "Ephraim mixes[k] with the
nations;
Ephraim is a flat cake not
turned over.
9 Foreigners sap his strength,[l]
but he does not realise it.
His hair is sprinkled with grey,
but he does not notice.
10 Israel's arrogance testifies
against him,[m]
but despite all this
he does not return to the LORD
his God
or search[n] for him.

11 "Ephraim is like a dove,[o]
easily deceived and
senseless—
now calling to Egypt,
now turning to Assyria.[p]
12 When they go, I will throw my
net[q] over them;
I will pull them down like
birds of the air.
When I hear them flocking
together,
I will catch them.
13 Woe[r] to them,
because they have strayed[s]
from me!
Destruction to them,
because they have rebelled
against me!
I long to redeem them
but they speak lies against
me.[t]
14 They do not cry out to me from
their hearts[u]
but wail upon their beds.
They gather together[a] for
grain and new wine[v]
but turn away from me.[w]
15 I trained them and strengthened
them,
but they plot evil[x] against me.

6:9 n Jer 7:9-10; Eze 22:9; Hos 7:1
6:10 o Jer 5:30; p Hos 5:3
6:11 q Jer 51:33; Joel 3:13
7:1 a Hos 6:4; b ver 13; c Hos 4:2
7:2 d Jer 14:10; Hos 8:13; e Jer 2:19
7:3 f Hos 4:2; Mic 7:3
7:4 g Jer 9:2
7:5 h Isa 28:1,7
7:6 i Ps 21:9
7:7 j ver 16
7:8 k ver 11; Ps 106:35; Hos 5:13
7:9 l Isa 1:7; Hos 8:7
7:10 m Hos 5:5; n Isa 9:13
7:11 o Hos 11:11; p Hos 5:13; Hos 12:1
7:12 q Eze 12:13
7:13 r Hos 9:12; s Jer 14:10; Eze 34:4-6; Hos 9:17; t ver 1; Mt 23:37
7:14 u Jer 3:10; v Am 2:8; w Hos 13:16
7:15 x Na 1:9,11

[a] 14 Most Hebrew manuscripts; some Hebrew manuscripts and Septuagint *They slash themselves*

16They do not turn to the Most
High;
they are like a faulty bow.[y]
Their leaders will fall by the
sword
because of their insolent
words.
For this they will be ridiculed[z]
in the land of Egypt.[a]

Israel to Reap the Whirlwind

8 "Put the trumpet to your
lips!
An eagle[a] is over the house
of the LORD
because the people have broken
my covenant
and rebelled against my law.[b]
2Israel cries out to me,
'O our God, we acknowledge
you!'
3But Israel has rejected what is
good;
an enemy will pursue him.
4They set up kings without my
consent;
they choose princes without
my approval.[c]
With their silver and gold
they make idols[d] for
themselves
to their own destruction.
5Throw out your calf-idol,
O Samaria![e]
My anger burns against them.
How long will they be incapable
of purity?[f]
6 They are from Israel!
This calf—a craftsman has
made it;
it is not God.
It will be broken in pieces,
that calf of Samaria.

7"They sow the wind
and reap the whirlwind.[g]
The stalk has no head;
it will produce no flour.
Were it to yield grain,
foreigners would swallow it
up.[h]
8Israel is swallowed up;[i]
now she is among the nations
like a worthless[j] thing.
9For they have gone up to
Assyria
like a wild donkey wandering
alone.
Ephraim has sold herself to
lovers.
10Although they have sold
themselves among the
nations,
I will now gather them
together.[k]
They will begin to waste away[l]
under the oppression of the
mighty king.

11"Though Ephraim built many
altars for sin offerings,
these have become altars for
sinning.[m]
12I wrote for them the many
things of my law,
but they regarded them as
something alien.
13They offer sacrifices given to
me
and they eat[n] the meat,
but the LORD is not pleased
with them.
Now he will remember[o] their
wickedness
and punish their sins:[p]
They will return to Egypt.[q]
14Israel has forgotten[r] his Maker
and built palaces;
Judah has fortified many
towns.
But I will send fire upon their
cities
that will consume their
fortresses."[s]

Punishment for Israel

9 Do not rejoice, O Israel;
do not be jubilant[a] like the
other nations.
For you have been unfaithful[b]
to your God;
you love the wages of a
prostitute
at every threshing-floor.
2Threshing-floors and
winepresses will not feed
the people;
the new wine[c] will fail them.

7:16 y Ps 78:9,57 z Eze 23:32 a Hos 9:3
8:1 a Dt 28:49 Jer 4:13 b Hos 4:6 Hos 6:7
8:4 c Hos 13:10 d Hos 2:8
8:5 e Hos 10:5 f Jer 13:27
8:7 g Pr 22:8 Isa 66:15 Hos 10:12-13 Na 1:3 h Hos 2:9
8:8 i Jer 51:34 j Jer 22:28
8:10 k Eze 16:37 Eze 22:20 l Jer 42:2
8:11 m Hos 10:1 Hos 12:11
8:13 n Jer 7:21 o Hos 7:2 p Hos 4:9 q Hos 9:3,6
8:14 r Dt 32:18 Hos 2:13 s Jer 17:27
9:1 a Isa 22:12-13 b Hos 10:5
9:2 c Hos 2:9

3 They will not remain[d] in the
LORD's land;
Ephraim will return to Egypt[e]
and eat unclean[a] food in
Assyria.[f]
4 They will not pour out wine
offerings to the LORD,
nor will their sacrifices
please[g] him.
Such sacrifices will be to them
like the bread of mourners;
all who eat them will be
unclean.[h]
This food will be for
themselves;
it will not come into the
temple of the LORD.

5 What will you do[i] on the day of
your appointed feasts,[j]
on the festival days of the
LORD?
6 Even if they escape from
destruction,
Egypt will gather them,
and Memphis[k] will bury
them.
Their treasures of silver will be
taken over by briers,
and thorns[l] will overrun their
tents.
7 The days of punishment[m] are
coming,
the days of reckoning are at
hand.
Let Israel know this.
Because your sins[n] are so
many
and your hostility so great,
the prophet is considered a
fool,[o]
the inspired man a maniac.
8 The prophet, along with my
God,
is the watchman over
Ephraim,[b]
yet snares[p] await him on all his
paths,
and hostility in the house of
his God.
9 They have sunk deep into
corruption,
as in the days of Gibeah.[q]
God will remember[r] their
wickedness
and punish them for their sins.

10 "When I found Israel,
it was like finding grapes in
the desert;
when I saw your fathers,
it was like seeing the early
fruit on the fig-tree.
But when they came to Baal
Peor,[s]
they consecrated themselves
to that shameful idol[t]
and became as vile as the
thing they loved.
11 Ephraim's glory will fly away
like a bird[u]—
no birth, no pregnancy, no
conception.[v]
12 Even if they bring up children,
I will bereave them of every
one.
Woe[w] to them
when I turn away from
them![x]
13 I have seen Ephraim, like Tyre,
planted in a pleasant place.[y]
But Ephraim will bring out
their children to the slayer."

14 Give them, O LORD—
what will you give them?
Give them wombs that miscarry
and breasts that are dry.[z]

15 "Because of all their
wickedness in Gilgal,[a]
I hated them there.
Because of their sinful deeds,[b]
I will drive them out of my
house.
I will no longer love them;
all their leaders are
rebellious.[c]
16 Ephraim[d] is blighted,
their root is withered,
they yield no fruit.[e]
Even if they bear children,
I will slay[f] their cherished
offspring."

9:3 *d* Lev 25:23 *e* Hos 8:13 *f* Eze 4:13 Hos 7:11
9:4 *g* Jer 6:20 Hos 8:13 *h* Hag 2:13-14
9:5 *i* Isa 10:3 Jer 5:31 *j* Hos 2:11
9:6 *k* Isa 19:13 *l* Isa 5:6 Hos 10:8
9:7 *m* Isa 34:8 Jer 10:15 Mic 7:4 *n* Jer 16:18 *o* Isa 44:25 La 2:14 Eze 14:9-10
9:8 *p* Hos 5:1
9:9 *q* Jdg 19:16-30 Hos 5:8 Hos 10:9 *r* Hos 8:13
9:10 *s* Nu 25:1-5 Ps 106:28-29 *t* Jer 11:13 Hos 4:14
9:11 *u* Hos 4:7 Hos 10:5 *v* ver 14
9:12 *w* Hos 7:13 *x* Dt 31:17
9:13 *y* Eze 27:3
9:14 *z* ver 11 Lk 23:29
9:15 *a* Hos 4:15 *b* Hos 7:2 *c* Isa 1:23 Hos 4:9 Hos 5:2
9:16 *d* Hos 5:11 *e* Hos 8:7 *f* ver 12

a3 That is, ceremonially unclean b8 Or *The prophet is the watchman over Ephraim, / the people of my God*

[17]My God will reject them
because they have not
obeyed[g] him;
they will be wanderers among
the nations.[h]

10

Israel was a spreading
vine;[a]
he brought forth fruit for
himself.
As his fruit increased,
he built more altars;[b]
as his land prospered,
he adorned his sacred
stones.[c]
[2]Their heart is deceitful,[d]
and now they must bear their
guilt.[e]
The LORD will demolish their
altars[f]
and destroy their sacred
stones.[g]

[3]Then they will say, "We have no
king
because we did not revere the
LORD.
But even if we had a king,
what could he do for us?"
[4]They make many promises,
take false oaths[h]
and make agreements;[i]
therefore lawsuits spring up
like poisonous weeds in a
ploughed field.
[5]The people who live in Samaria
fear
for the calf-idol of Beth Aven.[a][j]
Its people will mourn over it,
and so will its idolatrous
priests,[k]
those who had rejoiced over its
splendour,
because it is taken from them
into exile.[l]
[6]It will be carried to Assyria[m]
as tribute for the great king.[n]
Ephraim will be disgraced;[o]
Israel will be ashamed of its
wooden idols.[b]
[7]Samaria and its king will float
away[p]
like a twig on the surface of
the waters.

9:17
g Hos 4:10
h Dt 28:65
Hos 7:13

10:1
a Eze 15:2
b 1Ki 14:23
c Hos 8:11
Hos 12:11

10:2
d 1Ki 18:21
e Hos 13:16
f ver 8
g Mic 5:13

10:4
h Hos 4:2
i Eze 17:19
Am 5:7

10:5
j Hos 5:8
k 2Ki 23:5
l Hos 8:5
Hos 9:1,3,11

10:6
m Hos 11:5
n Hos 5:13
o Isa 30:3
Hos 4:7

10:7
p Hos 13:11

10:8
q 1Ki 12:28-30
Hos 4:13
r Hos 9:6
s ver 2
Isa 32:13
t Lk 23:30*
Rev 6:16

10:9
u Hos 5:8

10:10
v Eze 5:13
Hos 4:9

10:12
w Pr 11:18
x Jer 4:3
y Hos 12:6
z Isa 45:8

10:13
a Job 4:8
Hos 7:3
Hos 11:12
Gal 6:7-8

[8]The high places of
wickedness[c][q] will be
destroyed—
it is the sin of Israel.
Thorns[r] and thistles will grow
up
and cover their altars.[s]
Then they will say to the
mountains, "Cover us!"
and to the hills, "Fall on us!"[t]

[9]"Since the days of Gibeah,[u] you
have sinned, O Israel,
and there you have
remained.[d]
Did not war overtake
the evildoers in Gibeah?
[10]When I please, I will punish[v]
them;
nations will be gathered
against them
to put them in bonds for their
double sin.
[11]Ephraim is a trained heifer
that loves to thresh;
so I will put a yoke
on her fair neck.
I will drive Ephraim,
Judah must plough,
and Jacob must break up the
ground.
[12]Sow for yourselves
righteousness,[w]
reap the fruit of unfailing
love,
and break up your unploughed
ground;[x]
for it is time to seek[y] the
LORD,
until he comes
and showers righteousness[z]
on you.
[13]But you have planted
wickedness,
you have reaped evil,[a]
you have eaten the fruit of
deception.
Because you have depended on
your own strength

[a]5 *Beth Aven* means *house of wickedness* (a name for Bethel, which means *house of God*).
[b]6 Or *its counsel*
[c]8 Hebrew *aven*, a reference to Beth Aven (a derogatory name for Bethel)
[d]9 Or *there a stand was taken*

and on your many warriors,[b]
14the roar of battle will rise
against your people,
so that all your fortresses will
be devastated[c]—
as Shalman devastated Beth
Arbel on the day of battle,
when mothers were dashed to
the ground with their
children.[d]
15Thus will it happen to you,
O Bethel,
because your wickedness is
great.
When that day dawns,
the king of Israel will be
completely destroyed.[e]

God's Love for Israel

11 "When Israel was a child,
I loved him,
and out of Egypt I called my
son.[a]
2But the more I[a] called Israel,
the further they went from
me.[b]
They sacrificed to the Baals[b]
and they burned incense to
images.[c]
3It was I who taught Ephraim to
walk,
taking them by the arms;[d]
but they did not realise
it was I who healed[e] them.
4I led them with cords of human
kindness,
with ties of love;[f]
I lifted the yoke[g] from their
neck
and bent down to feed[h] them.
5"Will they not return to Egypt[i]
and will not Assyria[j] rule
over them
because they refuse to repent?
6Swords[k] will flash in their
cities,
will destroy the bars of their
gates
and put an end to their plans.
7My people are determined to
turn from me.[l]
Even if they call to the Most
High,

10:13 *b* Ps 33:16
10:14 *c* Isa 17:3 *d* Hos 13:16
10:15 *e* ver 7
11:1 *a* Ex 4:22 Hos 12:9,13 Hos 13:4 Mt 2:15*
11:2 *b* Hos 2:13 *c* 2Ki 17:15 Isa 65:7 Jer 18:15
11:3 *d* Dt 1:31 Hos 7:15 *e* Jer 30:17
11:4 *f* Jer 31:2-3 *g* Lev 26:13 *h* Ex 16:32 Ps 78:25
11:5 *i* Hos 7:16 *j* Hos 10:6
11:6 *k* Hos 13:16
11:7 *l* Jer 3:6-7 Jer 8:5
11:8 *m* Hos 6:4 *n* Ge 14:8
11:9 *o* Dt 13:17 Jer 30:11 *p* Mal 3:6 *q* Nu 23:19
11:10 *r* Hos 6:1-3
11:11 *s* Isa 11:11 *t* Eze 28:26
11:12 *u* Hos 4:2
12:1 *a* Eze 17:10 *b* 2Ki 17:4

he will by no means exalt
them.
8"How can I give you up,
Ephraim?[m]
How can I hand you over,
Israel?
How can I treat you like
Admah?
How can I make you like
Zeboiim?[n]
My heart is changed within me;
all my compassion is aroused.
9I will not carry out my fierce
anger,[o]
nor will I turn and devastate[p]
Ephraim.
For I am God, and not man[q]—
the Holy One among you.
I will not come in wrath.[c]
10They will follow the LORD;
he will roar like a lion.
When he roars,
his children will come
trembling from the west.[r]
11They will come trembling
like birds from Egypt,
like doves from Assyria.[s]
I will settle them in their
homes,"[t]
declares the LORD.

Israel's Sin

12Ephraim has surrounded me
with lies,[u]
the house of Israel with
deceit.
And Judah is unruly against
God,
even against the faithful Holy
One.

12 1Ephraim feeds on the
wind;[a]
he pursues the east wind all
day
and multiplies lies and
violence.
He makes a treaty with Assyria
and sends olive oil to Egypt.[b]

[a]2 Some Septuagint manuscripts; Hebrew *they*
[b]2 Septuagint; Hebrew *them* [c]9 Or *come against any city*

2The LORD has a charge[c] to
bring against Judah;
he will punish Jacob[a]
according to his ways
and repay him according to
his deeds.[d]
3In the womb he grasped his
brother's heel;[e]
as a man he struggled[f] with
God.
4He struggled with the angel and
overcame him;
he wept and begged for his
favour.
He found him at Bethel[g]
and talked with him there—
5the LORD God Almighty,
the LORD is his name[h] of
renown!
6But you must return to your
God;
maintain love and justice,[i]
and wait for your God
always.[j]

7The merchant uses dishonest
scales;[k]
he loves to defraud.
8Ephraim boasts,
"I am very rich; I have
become wealthy.[l]
With all my wealth they will not
find in me
any iniquity or sin."

9"I am the LORD your God,
⌞who brought you⌟ out of[b]
Egypt;[m]
I will make you live in tents[n]
again,
as in the days of your
appointed feasts.
10I spoke to the prophets,
gave them many visions
and told parables[o] through
them."[p]

11Is Gilead wicked?[q]
Its people are worthless!
Do they sacrifice bulls in
Gilgal?[r]
Their altars will be like piles
of stones
on a ploughed field.[s]
12Jacob fled to the country of
Aram;[c][t]
Israel served to get a wife,
and to pay for her he tended
sheep.[u]
13The LORD used a prophet to
bring Israel up from Egypt,
by a prophet he cared for
him.[v]
14But Ephraim has bitterly
provoked him to anger;
his Lord will leave upon him
the guilt of his bloodshed[w]
and will repay him for his
contempt.[x]

The LORD's Anger Against Israel

13 When Ephraim spoke,
men trembled;[a]
he was exalted[b] in Israel.
But he became guilty of Baal
worship[c] and died.
2Now they sin more and more;
they make idols for
themselves from their
silver,[d]
cleverly fashioned images,
all of them the work of
craftsmen.
It is said of these people,
"They offer human sacrifice
and kiss[a] the calf-idols.[e]"
3Therefore they will be like the
morning mist,
like the early dew that
disappears,[f]
like chaff[g] swirling from a
threshing-floor,[h]
like smoke[i] escaping through
a window.

4"But I am the LORD your God,
⌞who brought you⌟ out of[b]
Egypt.[j]
You shall acknowledge no God
but me,[k]
no Saviour[l] except me.
5I cared for you in the desert,

12:2 c Mic 6:2 d Hos 4:9
12:3 e Ge 25:26 f Ge 32:24-29
12:4 g Ge 28:12-15 Ge 35:15
12:5 h Ex 3:15
12:6 i Mic 6:8 j Hos 6:1-3 Hos 10:12 Mic 7:7
12:7 k Am 8:5
12:8 l Ps 62:10 Rev 3:17
12:9 m Lev 23:43 Hos 11:1 n Ne 8:17
12:10 o Eze 20:49 p 2Ki 17:13 Jer 7:25
12:11 q Hos 6:8 r Hos 4:15 s Hos 8:11
12:12 t Ge 28:5 u Ge 29:18
12:13 v Ex 13:3 Isa 63:11-14
12:14 w Eze 18:13 x Da 11:18
13:1 a Jdg 12:1 b Jdg 8:1 c Hos 11:2
13:2 d Isa 46:6 Jer 10:4 e Isa 44:17-20
13:3 f Hos 6:4 g Isa 17:13 h Da 2:35 i Ps 68:2
13:4 j Hos 12:9 k Ex 20:3 l Isa 43:11 Isa 45:21-22

a2 *Jacob* means *he grasps the heel* (figuratively, *he deceives*). b9 Or *God / ever since you were in* c12 That is, North-west Mesopotamia
a2 Or "*Men who sacrifice / kiss* b4 Or *God / ever since you were in*

in the land of burning heat.
[6]When I fed them, they were satisfied;
when they were satisfied, they became proud;
then they forgot me.[m]
[7]So I will come upon them like a lion,
like a leopard I will lurk by the path.
[8]Like a bear robbed of her cubs,[n]
I will attack them and rip them open.
Like a lion I will devour them;
a wild animal will tear them apart.[o]

[9]"You are destroyed, O Israel,
because you are against me,[p]
against your helper.[q]
[10]Where is your king,[r] that he may save you?
Where are your rulers in all your towns,
of whom you said,
'Give me a king and princes'?[s]
[11]So in my anger I gave you a king,
and in my wrath I took him away.[t]
[12]The guilt of Ephraim is stored up,
his sins are kept on record.[u]
[13]Pains as of a woman in childbirth[v] come to him,
but he is a child without wisdom;
when the time arrives,
he does not come to the opening of the womb.[w]

[14]"I will ransom them from the power of the grave;[c][x]
I will redeem them from death.
Where, O death, are your plagues?
Where, O grave,[c] is your destruction?[y]

"I will have no compassion,
[15] even though he thrives[z] among his brothers.

13:6 m Dt 32:12-15 Hos 2:13
13:8 n 2Sa 17:8 o Ps 50:22
13:9 p Jer 2:17-19 q Dt 33:29
13:10 r 2Ki 17:4 s 1Sa 8:6 Hos 8:4
13:11 t 1Ki 14:10 Hos 10:7
13:12 u Dt 32:34
13:13 v Isa 13:8 Mic 4:9-10 w Isa 66:9
13:14 x Ps 49:15 Eze 37:12-13 y 1Co 15:55*
13:15 z Hos 10:1 a Eze 19:12 b Jer 51:36 c Jer 20:5
13:16 d Hos 10:2 e Hos 7:14 f Hos 11:6 g 2Ki 8:12 Hos 10:14 h 2Ki 15:16 Isa 13:16
14:1 a Hos 5:5
14:2 b Mic 7:18-19 c Heb 13:15
14:3 d Ps 33:17 Isa 31:1 e Hos 8:6 f Ps 10:14 Ps 68:5
14:4 g Hos 6:1 h Zep 3:17
14:5 i SS 2:1 j Isa 35:2 k Job 29:19
14:6 l Ps 52:8 Jer 11:16

An east wind[a] from the LORD will come,
blowing in from the desert;
his spring will fail
and his well dry up.[b]
His storehouse will be plundered[c]
of all its treasures.
[16]The people of Samaria must bear their guilt,[d]
because they have rebelled[e] against their God.
They will fall by the sword;[f]
their little ones will be dashed[g] to the ground,
their pregnant women[h] ripped open."

Repentance to Bring Blessing

14 Return, O Israel, to the LORD your God.
Your sins have been your downfall![a]
[2]Take words with you
and return to the LORD.
Say to him:
"Forgive all our sins
and receive us graciously,[b]
that we may offer the fruit of our lips.[a][c]
[3]Assyria cannot save us;
we will not mount war-horses.[d]
We will never again say 'Our gods'[e]
to what our own hands have made,
for in you the fatherless[f] find compassion."

[4]"I will heal[g] their waywardness
and love them freely,[h]
for my anger has turned away from them.
[5]I will be like the dew to Israel;
he will blossom like a lily.[i]
Like a cedar of Lebanon[j]
he will send down his roots;[k]
[6] his young shoots will grow.
His splendour will be like an olive tree,[l]

[c]14 Hebrew *Sheol* [a]2 Or *offer our lips as sacrifices of bulls*

his fragrance like a cedar of
Lebanon.[m]
7Men will dwell again in his
shade.[n]
He will flourish like the corn.
He will blossom like a vine,
and his fame will be like the
wine[o] from Lebanon.[p]
8O Ephraim, what more have I[b]
to do with idols?[q]
I will answer him and care for
him.
I am like a green pine tree;
your fruitfulness comes from
me."

9Who is wise?[r] He will realise
these things.
Who is discerning? He will
understand them.[s]
The ways of the LORD are
right;[t]
the righteous walk[u] in them,
but the rebellious stumble in
them.

14:6 m SS 4:11
14:7 n Ps 91:1-4 o Hos 2:22 p Eze 17:23
14:8 q ver 3
14:9 r Ps 107:43 s Pr 10:29 Isa 1:28 t Ps 111:7-8 Zep 3:5 Ac 13:10 u Isa 26:7

[b]8 Or *What more has Ephraim*

JOEL

1 The word of the LORD that came[a] to Joel[b] son of Pethuel.

An Invasion of Locusts

2 Hear this,[c] you elders;
listen, all who live in the land.[d]
Has anything like this ever happened in your days
or in the days of your forefathers?[e]
3 Tell it to your children,[f]
and let your children tell it to their children,
and their children to the next generation.
4 What the locust swarm has left
the great locusts have eaten;
what the great locusts have left
the young locusts have eaten;
what the young locusts have left
other locusts[a] have eaten.[g]

5 Wake up, you drunkards, and weep!
Wail, all you drinkers of wine;[h]
wail because of the new wine,
for it has been snatched from your lips.
6 A nation has invaded my land,
powerful and without number;[i]
it has the teeth[j] of a lion,
the fangs of a lioness.
7 It has laid waste[k] my vines
and ruined my fig-trees.[l]
It has stripped off their bark
and thrown it away,
leaving their branches white.

8 Mourn like a virgin[b] in sackcloth[m]
grieving for the husband[c] of her youth.
9 Grain offerings and drink offerings[n]
are cut off from the house of the LORD.
The priests are in mourning,
those who minister before the LORD.
10 The fields are ruined,
the ground is dried up;[d][o]
the grain is destroyed,
the new wine[p] is dried up,
the oil fails.
11 Despair, you farmers,[q]
wail, you vine growers;
grieve for the wheat and the barley,
because the harvest of the field is destroyed.[r]
12 The vine is dried up
and the fig-tree is withered;
the pomegranate, the palm and the apple tree—
all the trees of the field—are dried up.[s]
Surely the joy of mankind
is withered away.

A Call to Repentance

13 Put on sackcloth,[t] O priests, and mourn;
wail, you who minister[u] before the altar.
Come, spend the night in sackcloth,
you who minister before my God;
for the grain offerings and drink offerings[v]
are withheld from the house of your God.
14 Declare a holy fast;[w]
call a sacred assembly.
Summon the elders
and all who live in the land

1:1 *a* Jer 1:2 *b* Ac 2:16
1:2 *c* Hos 5:1 *d* Hos 4:1 *e* Joel 2:2
1:3 *f* Ex 10:2; Ps 78:4
1:4 *g* Dt 28:39; Na 3:15
1:5 *h* Joel 3:3
1:6 *i* Joel 2:2,11, 25 *j* Rev 9:8
1:7 *k* Isa 5:6 *l* Am 4:9
1:8 *m* ver 13; Isa 22:12; Am 8:10
1:9 *n* Hos 9:4; Joel 2:14,17
1:10 *o* Isa 24:4 *p* Hos 9:2
1:11 *q* Jer 14:3-4; Am 5:16 *r* Isa 17:11
1:12 *s* Hag 2:19
1:13 *t* Jer 4:8 *u* Joel 2:17 *v* ver 9
1:14 *w* 2Ch 20:3

a4 The precise meaning of the four Hebrew words used here for locusts is uncertain. b8 Or *young woman* c8 Or *betrothed* d10 Or *ground mourns*

to the house of the LORD your
God,
and cry out[x] to the LORD.

15 Alas for that[y] day!
For the day of the LORD[z] is
near;
it will come like destruction
from the Almighty.[e]

16 Has not the food been cut off[a]
before our very eyes—
joy and gladness
from the house of our God?[b]

17 The seeds are shrivelled
beneath the clods.[f][c]
The storehouses are in ruins,
the granaries have been
broken down,
for the grain has dried up.

18 How the cattle moan!
The herds mill about
because they have no pasture;
even the flocks of sheep are
suffering.

19 To you, O LORD, I call,[d]
for fire[e] has devoured the
open pastures[f]
and flames have burned up all
the trees of the field.

20 Even the wild animals pant for
you;[g]
the streams of water have
dried up[h]
and fire has devoured the
open pastures.

An Army of Locusts

2 Blow the trumpet[a] in Zion;[b]
sound the alarm on my holy
hill.
Let all who live in the land
tremble,
for the day of the LORD[c] is
coming.
It is close at hand[d]—
2 a day of darkness[e] and
gloom,[f]
a day of clouds and blackness.
Like dawn spreading across the
mountains
a large and mighty army[g]
comes,
such as never was of old[h]
nor ever will be in ages to
come.

3 Before them fire devours,
behind them a flame blazes.
Before them the land is like the
garden of Eden,[i]
behind them, a desert
waste[j]—
nothing escapes them.

4 They have the appearance of
horses;[k]
they gallop along like cavalry.

5 With a noise like that of
chariots[l]
they leap over the
mountaintops,
like a crackling fire[m]
consuming stubble,
like a mighty army drawn up
for battle.

6 At the sight of them, nations
are in anguish;[n]
every face turns pale.[o]

7 They charge like warriors;
they scale walls like soldiers.
They all march in line,
not swerving[p] from their
course.

8 They do not jostle each other;
each marches straight ahead.
They plunge through defences
without breaking ranks.

9 They rush upon the city;
they run along the wall.
They climb into the houses;
like thieves they enter through
the windows.[q]

10 Before them the earth shakes,[r]
the sky trembles,
the sun and moon are
darkened,[s]
and the stars no longer shine.[t]

11 The LORD[u] thunders
at the head of his army;
his forces are beyond number,
and mighty are those who
obey his command.
The day of the LORD is great;[v]
it is dreadful.
Who can endure it?[w]

1:14 x Jnh 3:8
1:15 y Jer 30:7 z Isa 13:6,9 Joel 2:1,11, 31
1:16 a Isa 3:7 b Dt 12:7
1:17 c Isa 17:10-11
1:19 d Ps 50:15 e Am 7:4 f Jer 9:10
1:20 g Ps 104:21 h 1Ki 17:7
2:1 a Jer 4:5 b ver 15 c Joel 1:15 Zep 1:14-16 d Ob 1:15
2:2 e Am 5:18 f Da 9:12 g Joel 1:6 h Joel 1:2
2:3 i Ge 2:8 j Ps 105:34-35
2:4 k Rev 9:7
2:5 l Rev 9:9 m Isa 5:24 Isa 30:30
2:6 n Isa 13:8 o Na 2:10
2:7 p Isa 5:27
2:9 q Jer 9:21
2:10 r Ps 18:7 s Mt 24:29 t Isa 13:10 Eze 32:8
2:11 u Joel 1:15 v Zep 1:14 Rev 18:8 w Eze 22:14

e15 Hebrew *Shaddai* f17 The meaning of the Hebrew for this word is uncertain.

Rend Your Heart

12"Even now," declares the LORD,
"return[x] to me with all your heart,
with fasting and weeping and mourning."

13Rend your heart[y]
and not your garments.[z]
Return to the LORD your God,
for he is gracious and compassionate,
slow to anger and abounding in love,[a]
and he relents from sending calamity.[b]
14Who knows? He may turn[c] and have pity
and leave behind a blessing[d]—
grain offerings and drink offerings[e]
for the LORD your God.

15Blow the trumpet[f] in Zion,
declare a holy fast,[g]
call a sacred assembly.[h]
16Gather the people,
consecrate[i] the assembly;
bring together the elders,
gather the children,
those nursing at the breast.
Let the bridegroom[j] leave his room
and the bride her chamber.
17Let the priests, who minister before the LORD,
weep between the temple porch and the altar.[k]
Let them say, "Spare your people, O LORD.
Do not make your inheritance an object of scorn,[l]
a byword among the nations.
Why should they say among the peoples,
'Where is their God?[m]' "

The LORD's Answer

18Then the LORD will be jealous[n] for his land
and take pity on his people.

19The LORD will reply[a] to them:

"I am sending you grain, new wine and oil,[o]
enough to satisfy you fully;
never again will I make you
an object of scorn[p] to the nations.

20"I will drive the northern army[q] far from you,
pushing it into a parched and barren land,
with its front columns going into the eastern[r] sea[b]
and those in the rear into the western sea.[c]
And its stench[s] will go up;
its smell will rise."

Surely he has done great things.[d]
21 Be not afraid,[t] O land;
be glad and rejoice.
Surely the LORD has done great things.[u]
22 Be not afraid, O wild animals,
for the open pastures are becoming green.[v]
The trees are bearing their fruit;
the fig-tree and the vine yield their riches.[w]
23Be glad, O people of Zion,
rejoice[x] in the LORD your God,
for he has given you
the autumn rains in righteousness.[e]
He sends you abundant showers,
both autumn and spring rains,[y] as before.
24The threshing-floors will be filled with grain;
the vats will overflow[z] with new wine[a] and oil.

25"I will repay you for the years
the locusts have eaten—

2:12 x Jer 4:1; Hos 12:6
2:13 y Ps 34:18; Isa 57:15; z Job 1:20; a Ex 34:6; b Jer 18:8
2:14 c Jer 26:3; d Hag 2:19; e Joel 1:13
2:15 f Nu 10:2; g Jer 36:9; h Joel 1:14
2:16 i Ex 19:10,22; j Ps 19:5
2:17 k Eze 8:16; Mt 23:35; l Dt 9:26-29; Ps 44:13; m Ps 42:3
2:18 n Zec 1:14
2:19 o Jer 31:12; p Eze 34:29
2:20 q Jer 1:14-15; r Zec 14:8; s Isa 34:3
2:21 t Isa 54:4; Zep 3:16-17; u Ps 126:3
2:22 v Ps 65:12; w Joel 1:18-20
2:23 x Ps 149:2; Isa 12:6; Isa 41:16; Hab 3:18; Zec 10:7; y Lev 26:4
2:24 z Lev 26:10; Mal 3:10; a Am 9:13

[a]18, 19 Or *LORD was jealous . . . / and took pity . . . / 19The LORD replied* [b]20 That is, the Dead Sea [c]20 That is, the Mediterranean [d]20 Or *rise. / Surely it has done great things."* [e]23 Or */ the teacher for righteousness:*

the great locust and the young
locust,
the other locusts and the
locust swarm[f] —
my great army that I sent
among you.
26 You will have plenty to eat,
until you are full,[b]
and you will praise[c] the name
of the LORD your God,
who has worked wonders[d] for
you;
never again will my people be
shamed.
27 Then you will know that I am in
Israel,
that I am the LORD[e] your God,
and that there is no other;
never again will my people be
shamed.

The Day of the LORD

28 "And afterwards,
I will pour out my Spirit[f] on
all people.
Your sons and daughters will
prophesy,
your old men will dream
dreams,
your young men will see
visions.
29 Even on my servants,[g] both
men and women,
I will pour out my Spirit in
those days.
30 I will show wonders in the
heavens[h]
and on the earth,[i]
blood and fire and billows of
smoke.
31 The sun will be turned to
darkness[j]
and the moon to blood
before the coming of the great
and dreadful day of the
LORD.[k]
32 And everyone who calls
on the name of the LORD will
be saved;[l]
for on Mount Zion[m] and in
Jerusalem
there will be deliverance,[n]
as the LORD has said,
among the survivors[o]
whom the LORD calls.

The Nations Judged

3 "In those days and at that
time,
when I restore the fortunes[a]
of Judah and Jerusalem,
2 I will gather all nations
and bring them down to the
Valley of Jehoshaphat.[a]
There I will enter into
judgment[b] against them
concerning my inheritance,
my people Israel,
for they scattered my people
among the nations
and divided up my land.
3 They cast lots for my people
and traded boys for
prostitutes;
they sold girls for wine[c]
that they might drink.

4 "Now what have you against me,
O Tyre and Sidon[d] and all you regions of Philistia? Are you repaying me for something I have done?
If you are paying me back, I will
swiftly and speedily return on your
own heads what you have done.[e]
5 For you took my silver and my
gold and carried off my finest
treasures to your temples.[f] 6 You
sold the people of Judah and Jerusalem to the Greeks, that you might
send them far from their homeland.

7 "See, I am going to rouse them
out of the places to which you sold
them,[g] and I will return on your
own heads what you have done. 8 I
will sell your sons[h] and daughters
to the people of Judah,[i] and they
will sell them to the Sabeans, a nation far away." The LORD has spoken.

9 Proclaim this among the
nations:

2:26 *b* Lev 26:5 *c* Isa 62:9 *d* Ps 126:3; Isa 25:1
2:27 *e* Joel 3:17
2:28 *f* Eze 39:29
2:29 *g* 1Co 12:13; Gal 3:28
2:30 *h* Lk 21:11 *i* Mk 13:24-25
2:31 *j* Mt 24:29 *k* Isa 13:9-10; Mal 4:1,5
2:32 *l* Ac 2:17-21*; Ro 10:13* *m* Isa 46:13 *n* Ob 1:17 *o* Isa 11:11; Mic 4:7; Ro 9:27
3:1 *a* Jer 16:15
3:2 *b* Eze 36:5
3:3 *c* Am 2:6
3:4 *d* Mt 11:21 *e* Isa 34:8
3:5 *f* 2Ch 21:16-17
3:7 *g* Isa 43:5-6; Jer 23:8
3:8 *h* Isa 60:14 *i* Isa 14:2

f 25 The precise meaning of the four Hebrew words used here for locusts is uncertain.
a 2 *Jehoshaphat* means *the LORD judges*; also in verse 12.

Prepare for war![j]
Rouse the warriors![k]
Let all the fighting men draw near and attack.
10 Beat your ploughshares into swords
and your pruning hooks[l] into spears.
Let the weakling[m] say,
"I am strong!"
11 Come quickly, all you nations from every side,
and assemble[n] there.

Bring down your warriors,[o] O LORD!

12 "Let the nations be roused;
let them advance into the Valley of Jehoshaphat,
for there I will sit
to judge[p] all the nations on every side.
13 Swing the sickle,
for the harvest[q] is ripe.
Come, trample the grapes,
for the winepress[r] is full
and the vats overflow—
so great is their wickedness!"

14 Multitudes, multitudes
in the valley of decision!
For the day of the LORD[s] is near
in the valley of decision.
15 The sun and moon will be darkened,
and the stars no longer shine.
16 The LORD will roar from Zion
and thunder from Jerusalem;[t]
the earth and the sky will tremble.[u]
But the LORD will be a refuge for his people,
a stronghold[v] for the people of Israel.

Blessings for God's People

17 "Then you will know that I, the LORD your God,[w]
dwell in Zion,[x] my holy hill.
Jerusalem will be holy;
never again will foreigners invade her.

18 "In that day the mountains will drip new wine,
and the hills will flow with milk;[y]
all the ravines of Judah will run with water.[z]
A fountain will flow out of the LORD's house[a]
and will water the valley of acacias.[b b]
19 But Egypt will be desolate,
Edom a desert waste,
because of violence[c] done to the people of Judah,
in whose land they shed innocent blood.
20 Judah will be inhabited for ever[d]
and Jerusalem through all generations.
21 Their bloodguilt, which I have not pardoned,
I will pardon.[e]"

The LORD dwells in Zion!

3:9 j Isa 8:9 k Jer 46:4
3:10 l Isa 2:4 Mic 4:3 m Zec 12:8
3:11 n Eze 38:15-16 Zep 3:8 o Isa 13:3
3:12 p Isa 2:4
3:13 q Hos 6:11 Mt 13:39 Rev 14:15-19 r Rev 14:20
3:14 s Isa 34:2-8 Joel 1:15
3:16 t Am 1:2 u Eze 38:19 v Jer 16:19
3:17 w Joel 2:27 x Isa 4:3
3:18 y Ex 3:8 z Isa 30:25 Isa 35:6 a Rev 22:1-2 b Eze 47:1 Am 9:13
3:19 c Ob 1:10
3:20 d Am 9:15
3:21 e Eze 36:25

[b] 18 Or *Valley of Shittim*

AMOS

1 The words of Amos, one of the
shepherds of Tekoa[a]—what
he saw concerning Israel two years
before the earthquake,[b] when Uzziah[c] was king of Judah and Jeroboam[d] son of Jehoash[a] was king
of Israel.[e]
²He said:

"The LORD roars[f] from Zion
and thunders from
Jerusalem;[g]
the pastures of the shepherds
dry up,[b]
and the top of Carmel[h]
withers."[i]

Judgment on Israel's Neighbours

³This is what the LORD says:

"For three sins of Damascus,[j]
even for four, I will not turn
back ⌊my wrath⌋.[k]
Because she threshed Gilead
with sledges having iron teeth,
⁴I will send fire[l] upon the house
of Hazael
that will consume the
fortresses[m] of Ben-Hadad.[n]
⁵I will break down the gate[o] of
Damascus;
I will destroy the king who is
in[c] the Valley of Aven[d]
and the one who holds the
sceptre in Beth Eden.
The people of Aram will go
into exile to Kir,[p]"
says the LORD.

⁶This is what the LORD says:

"For three sins of Gaza,[q]
even for four, I will not turn
back ⌊my wrath⌋.
Because she took captive whole
communities
and sold them to Edom,[r]
⁷I will send fire upon the walls
of Gaza
that will consume her
fortresses.
⁸I will destroy the king[e] of
Ashdod[s]
and the one who holds the
sceptre in Ashkelon.
I will turn my hand[t] against
Ekron,
till the last of the Philistines[u]
is dead,"
says the Sovereign LORD.[v]

⁹This is what the LORD says:

"For three sins of Tyre,[w]
even for four, I will not turn
back ⌊my wrath⌋.
Because she sold whole
communities of captives to
Edom,
disregarding a treaty of
brotherhood,
¹⁰I will send fire upon the walls
of Tyre
that will consume her
fortresses.[x]"

¹¹This is what the LORD says:

"For three sins of Edom,[y]
even for four, I will not turn
back ⌊my wrath⌋.
Because he pursued his brother
with a sword,
stifling all compassion,[f]
because his anger raged
continually
and his fury flamed
unchecked,[z]
¹²I will send fire upon Teman[a]
that will consume the
fortresses of Bozrah."

¹³This is what the LORD says:

1:1 a 2Sa 14:2 b Zec 14:5 c 2Ch 26:23 d 2Ki 14:23 e Hos 1:1
1:2 f Isa 42:13 g Joel 3:16 h Am 9:3 i Jer 12:4
1:3 j Isa 8:4; Isa 17:1-3 k Am 2:6
1:4 l Jer 49:27 m Jer 17:27 n 1Ki 20:1; 2Ki 6:24
1:5 o Jer 51:30 p 2Ki 16:9
1:6 q 1Sa 6:17; Zep 2:4 r Ob 1:11
1:8 s 2Ch 26:6 t Ps 81:14 u Eze 25:16 v Isa 14:28-32; Zep 2:4-7
1:9 w 1Ki 5:1; 1Ki 9:11-14; Isa 23:1-18; Jer 25:22; Joel 3:4; Mt 11:21
1:10 x Zec 9:1-4
1:11 y Nu 20:14-21; 2Ch 28:17; Jer 49:7-22 z Eze 25:12-14
1:12 a Ob 1:9-10

[a]1 Hebrew *Joash*, a variant of *Jehoash*
[b]2 Or *shepherds mourn*
[c]5 Or *the inhabitants of*
[d]5 *Aven* means *wickedness.*
[e]8 Or *inhabitants*
[f]11 Or *sword / and destroyed his allies*

"For three sins of Ammon,[b]
even for four, I will not turn
back ⌊my wrath⌋.
Because he ripped open the
pregnant women[c] of Gilead
in order to extend his borders,
14I will set fire to the walls of
Rabbah[d]
that will consume her
fortresses
amid war cries[e] on the day of
battle,
amid violent winds on a
stormy day.
15Her king[g] will go into exile,
he and his officials together,"
says the LORD.

2 This is what the LORD says:

"For three sins of Moab,
even for four, I will not turn
back ⌊my wrath⌋.
Because he burned, as if to
lime,
the bones of Edom's king,
2I will send fire upon Moab
that will consume the
fortresses of Kerioth.[a]
Moab will go down in great
tumult
amid war cries and the blast
of the trumpet.
3I will destroy her ruler[a]
and kill all her officials with
him,"[b]
says the LORD.

4This is what the LORD says:

"For three sins of Judah,[c]
even for four, I will not turn
back ⌊my wrath⌋.
Because they have rejected the
law[d] of the LORD
and have not kept his
decrees,[e]
because they have been led
astray[f] by false gods,[b][g]
the gods[c] their ancestors
followed,[h]
5I will send fire upon Judah
that will consume the
fortresses of Jerusalem.[i]"

1:13
b Jer 49:1-6
Eze 21:28
Eze 25:2-7
c Hos 13:16
1:14
d Dt 3:11
e Am 2:2
2:3
a Ps 2:10
b Isa 40:23
2:4
c 2Ki 17:19
Hos 12:2
d Jer 6:19
e Eze 20:24
f Isa 9:16
g Isa 28:15
h 2Ki 22:13
Jer 16:12
2:5
i Jer 17:27
Hos 8:14
2:6
j Joel 3:3
Am 8:6
2:7
k Am 5:11-12
Am 8:4
2:8
l Ex 22:26
m Am 4:1
Am 6:6
2:9
n Nu 21:23-26
Jos 10:12
o Eze 17:9
Mal 4:1
2:10
p Ex 20:2
Am 3:1
q Dt 2:7
r Ex 3:8
Am 9:7
2:11
s Dt 18:18
Jer 7:25
t Nu 6:2-3
Jdg 13:5
2:12
u Isa 30:10
Jer 11:21
Am 7:12-13
Mic 2:6

Judgment on Israel

6This is what the LORD says:

"For three sins of Israel,
even for four, I will not turn
back ⌊my wrath⌋.
They sell the righteous for
silver,
and the needy for a pair of
sandals.[j]
7They trample on the heads of
the poor
as upon the dust of the ground
and deny justice to the
oppressed.
Father and son use the same
girl
and so profane my holy
name.[k]
8They lie down beside every
altar
on garments taken in pledge.[l]
In the house of their god
they drink wine[m] taken as
fines.

9"I destroyed the Amorite[n]
before them,
though he was tall as the
cedars
and strong as the oaks.
I destroyed his fruit above
and his roots[o] below.

10"I brought you up out of
Egypt,[p]
and I led you for forty years
in the desert[q]
to give you the land of the
Amorites.[r]
11I also raised up prophets[s] from
among your sons
and Nazirites[t] from among
your young men.
Is this not true, people of
Israel?"
declares the LORD.
12"But you made the Nazirites
drink wine
and commanded the prophets
not to prophesy.[u]

[g]15 Or / *Molech*; Hebrew *malcam* [a]2 Or *of her cities* [b]4 Or *by lies* [c]4 Or *lies*

13 “Now then, I will crush you
as a cart crushes when loaded
with grain.
14 The swift will not escape,
the strong[v] will not muster
their strength,
and the warrior will not save
his life.[w]
15 The archer[x] will not stand his
ground,
the fleet-footed soldier will not
get away,
and the horseman will not
save his life.
16 Even the bravest warriors[y]
will flee naked on that day,”
declares the LORD.

Witnesses Summoned Against Israel

3 Hear this word the LORD has
spoken against you, O people
of Israel—against the whole family
I brought up out of Egypt:[a]

2 “You only have I chosen[b]
of all the families of the earth;
therefore I will punish you
for all your sins.[c]”

3 Do two walk together
unless they have agreed to do
so?
4 Does a lion roar in the thicket
when he has no prey?[d]
Does he growl in his den
when he has caught nothing?
5 Does a bird fall into a trap on
the ground
where no snare has been set?
Does a trap spring up from the
earth
when there is nothing to
catch?
6 When a trumpet sounds in a
city,
do not the people tremble?
When disaster comes to a city,
has not the LORD caused it?[e]

7 Surely the Sovereign LORD does
nothing
without revealing his plan[f]
to his servants the prophets.[g]

8 The lion has roared—
who will not fear?
The Sovereign LORD has
spoken—
who can but prophesy?[h]

9 Proclaim to the fortresses of
Ashdod
and to the fortresses of Egypt:
“Assemble yourselves on the
mountains of Samaria;[i]
see the great unrest within
her
and the oppression among her
people.”
10 “They do not know how to do
right,[j]” declares the LORD,
“who hoard plunder[k] and loot
in their fortresses.”[l]

11 Therefore this is what the Sovereign LORD says:

“An enemy will overrun the land;
he will pull down your
strongholds
and plunder your
fortresses.[m]”

12 This is what the LORD says:

“As a shepherd saves from the
lion's[n] mouth
only two leg bones or a piece
of an ear,
so will the Israelites be saved,
those who sit in Samaria
on the edge of their beds
and in Damascus on their
couches.[a][o]”

13 “Hear this and testify[p] against
the house of Jacob,” declares the
Lord, the LORD God Almighty.

14 “On the day I punish Israel for
her sins,
I will destroy the altars of
Bethel;[q]
the horns of the altar will be
cut off
and fall to the ground.
15 I will tear down the winter
house[r]

2:14 v Jer 9:23 w Ps 33:16 Isa 30:16-17
2:15 x Eze 39:3
2:16 y Jer 48:41
3:1 a Am 2:10
3:2 b Dt 7:6 Lk 12:47 c Jer 14:10
3:4 d Ps 104:21 Hos 5:14
3:6 e Isa 14:24-27 Isa 45:7
3:7 f Ge 18:17 Da 9:22 Jn 15:15 Rev 10:7 g Jer 23:22
3:8 h Jer 20:9 Jnh 1:1-3 Jnh 3:1-3 Ac 4:20
3:9 i Am 4:1 Am 6:1
3:10 j Jer 4:22 Am 5:7 Am 6:12 k Hab 2:8 l Zep 1:9
3:11 m Am 2:5 Am 6:14
3:12 n 1Sa 17:34 o Am 6:4
3:13 p Eze 2:7
3:14 q Am 5:5-6
3:15 r Jer 36:22

a 12 The meaning of the Hebrew for this line is uncertain.

along with the summer
house;[s]
the houses adorned with ivory[t]
will be destroyed
and the mansions will be
demolished,"
declares the LORD.

Israel Has Not Returned to God

4 Hear this word, you cows of
Bashan[a] on Mount
Samaria,[b]
you women who oppress the
poor and crush the needy
and say to your husbands,
"Bring us some drinks![c]"
[2]The Sovereign LORD has sworn
by his holiness:
"The time will surely come
when you will be taken away[d]
with hooks,
the last of you with fish-hooks.
[3]You will each go straight out
through breaks in the wall,[e]
and you will be cast out
towards Harmon,"[a]
declares the LORD.
[4]"Go to Bethel and sin;
go to Gilgal[f] and sin yet
more.
Bring your sacrifices every
morning,[g]
your tithes[h] every three
years.[b][i]
[5]Burn leavened bread[j] as a
thank-offering
and brag about your freewill
offerings[k]—
boast about them, you
Israelites,
for this is what you love to
do,"
declares the Sovereign
LORD.

[6]"I gave you empty stomachs[c]
in every city
and lack of bread in every
town,
yet you have not returned to
me,"
declares the LORD.[l]

[7]"I also withheld rain from you
when the harvest was still
three months away.
I sent rain on one town,
but withheld it from another.[m]
One field had rain;
another had none and dried
up.
[8]People staggered from town to
town for water[n]
but did not get enough to
drink,
yet you have not returned[o] to
me,"
declares the LORD.[p]

[9]"Many times I struck your
gardens and vineyards,
I struck them with blight and
mildew.[q]
Locusts devoured your fig and
olive trees,[r]
yet you have not returned[s] to
me,"
declares the LORD.

[10]"I sent plagues[t] among you
as I did to Egypt.
I killed your young men with
the sword,
along with your captured
horses.
I filled your nostrils with the
stench of your camps,
yet you have not returned to
me,"
declares the LORD.[u]

[11]"I overthrew some of you
as I[d] overthrew Sodom and
Gomorrah.[v]
You were like a burning stick
snatched from the fire,
yet you have not returned to
me,"
declares the LORD.

[12]"Therefore this is what I will do
to you, Israel,
and because I will do this to
you,

3:15 s Jdg 3:20 t 1Ki 22:39
4:1 a Ps 22:12 Eze 39:18 b Am 3:9 c Am 2:8 Am 5:11 Am 8:6
4:2 d Am 6:8
4:3 e Eze 12:5
4:4 f Hos 4:15 g Nu 28:3 h Dt 14:28 i Eze 20:39 Am 5:21-22
4:5 j Lev 7:13 k Lev 22:18-21
4:6 l Isa 3:1 Jer 5:3 Hag 2:17
4:7 m Ex 9:4,26 Dt 11:17 2Ch 7:13
4:8 n Eze 4:16-17 o Jer 3:7 p Jer 14:4
4:9 q Dt 28:22 r Joel 1:7 s Jer 3:10 Hag 2:17
4:10 t Ex 9:3 Dt 28:27 u Isa 9:13
4:11 v Ge 19:24 Jer 23:14

[a]3 Masoretic Text; with a different word division of the Hebrew (see Septuagint) *out, O mountain of oppression* [b]4 Or *tithes on the third day* [c]6 Hebrew *you cleanness of teeth* [d]11 Hebrew *God*

prepare to meet your God,
O Israel."

13 He who forms the mountains,[w]
creates the wind,
and reveals his thoughts[x] to man,
he who turns dawn to darkness,
and treads the high places of the earth[y]—
the LORD God Almighty is his name.[z]

A Lament and Call to Repentance

5 Hear this word, O house of Israel, this lament[a] I take up
concerning you:

2 "Fallen is Virgin[b] Israel,
never to rise again,
deserted in her own land,
with no-one to lift her up.[c]"

3 This is what the Sovereign LORD
says:

"The city that marches out a thousand strong for Israel
will have only a hundred left;
the town that marches out a hundred strong
will have only ten left.[d]"

4 This is what the LORD says to the
house of Israel:

"Seek me and live;[e]
5 do not seek Bethel,
do not go to Gilgal,[f]
do not journey to Beersheba.[g]
For Gilgal will surely go into exile,
and Bethel will be reduced to nothing.[a][h]"
6 Seek[i] the LORD and live,[j]
or he will sweep through the house of Joseph like a fire;[k]
it will devour,
and Bethel[l] will have no-one to quench it.

7 You who turn justice into bitterness[m]
and cast righteousness to the ground

8 (he who made the Pleiades and Orion,[n]
who turns blackness into dawn[o]
and darkens day into night,[p]
who calls for the waters of the sea
and pours them out over the face of the land—
the LORD is his name[q]—
9 he flashes destruction on the stronghold
and brings the fortified city to ruin),[r]
10 you hate the one who reproves in court[s]
and despise him who tells the truth.[t]

11 You trample on the poor[u]
and force him to give you grain.
Therefore, though you have built stone mansions,[v]
you will not live in them;
though you have planted lush vineyards,
you will not drink their wine.[w]
12 For I know how many are your offences
and how great your sins.

You oppress the righteous and take bribes
and you deprive the poor of justice in the courts.[x]
13 Therefore the prudent man keeps quiet in such times,
for the times are evil.

14 Seek good, not evil,
that you may live.
Then the LORD God Almighty will be with you,
just as you say he is.
15 Hate evil,[y] love good;
maintain justice in the courts.
Perhaps the LORD God Almighty will have mercy[z]
on the remnant[a] of Joseph.

16 Therefore this is what the Lord,
the LORD God Almighty, says:

[a]5 Or *grief*; or *wickedness*; Hebrew *aven*, a reference to Beth Aven (a derogatory name for Bethel)

4:13 w Ps 65:6 x Da 2:28 y Mic 1:3 z Isa 47:4 Am 5:8,27 Am 9:6
5:1 a Eze 19:1
5:2 b Jer 14:17 c Jer 50:32 Am 8:14
5:3 d Isa 6:13 Am 6:9
5:4 e Isa 55:3 Jer 29:13
5:5 f 1Sa 11:14 Am 4:4 g Am 8:14 h 1Sa 7:16
5:6 i Isa 55:6 j ver 14 k Dt 4:24 l Am 3:14
5:7 m Am 6:12
5:8 n Job 9:9 o Isa 42:16 p Ps 104:20 Am 8:9 q Ps 104:6-9 Am 4:13
5:9 r Mic 5:11
5:10 s Isa 29:21 t 1Ki 22:8
5:11 u Am 8:6 v Am 3:15 w Mic 6:15
5:12 x Isa 5:23 Am 2:6-7
5:15 y Ps 97:10 Ro 12:9 z Joel 2:14 a Mic 5:7,8

"There will be wailing[b] in all the streets
and cries of anguish in every public square.
The farmers[c] will be summoned to weep
and the mourners to wail.
17There will be wailing in all the vineyards,
for I will pass through[d] your midst,"
says the LORD.[e]

The Day of the LORD

18Woe to you who long
for the day of the LORD![f]
Why do you long for the day of the LORD?
That day will be darkness,[g]
not light.[h]
19It will be as though a man fled from a lion
only to meet a bear,
as though he entered his house
and rested his hand on the wall
only to have a snake bite him.[i]
20Will not the day of the LORD be darkness, not light—
pitch-dark, without a ray of brightness?[j]

21"I hate, I despise your religious feasts;[k]
I cannot stand your assemblies.[l]
22Even though you bring me burnt offerings and grain offerings,
I will not accept them.
Though you bring choice fellowship offerings,[b]
I will have no regard for them.[mn]
23Away with the noise of your songs!
I will not listen to the music of your harps.[o]
24But let justice[p] roll on like a river,
righteousness like a never-failing stream![q]

25"Did you bring me sacrifices[r] and offerings
for forty years[s] in the desert,
O house of Israel?
26You have lifted up the shrine of your king,
the pedestal of your idols,
the star of your god—[c]
which you made for yourselves.
27Therefore I will send you into exile beyond Damascus,"
says the LORD, whose name is God Almighty.[t]

Woe to the Complacent

6 Woe to you[a] who are complacent in Zion,
and to you who feel secure on Mount Samaria,
you notable men of the foremost nation,
to whom the people of Israel come![b]
2Go to Calneh[c] and look at it;
go from there to great Hamath,[d]
and then go down to Gath[e] in Philistia.
Are they better off than[f] your two kingdoms?
Is their land larger than yours?
3You put off the evil day
and bring near a reign of terror.[g]
4You lie on beds inlaid with ivory
and lounge on your couches.
You dine on choice lambs
and fattened calves.[h]
5You strum away on your harps[i] like David
and improvise on musical instruments.[j]
6You drink wine[k] by the bowlful
and use the finest lotions,

5:16 b Jer 9:17 c Joel 1:11
5:17 d Ex 12:12 e Isa 16:10 Jer 48:33
5:18 f Joel 1:15 g Joel 2:2 h Isa 5:19,30 Jer 30:7
5:19 i Job 20:24 Isa 24:17-18 Jer 15:2-3 Jer 48:44
5:20 j Isa 13:10 Zep 1:15
5:21 k Lev 26:31 l Isa 1:11-16
5:22 m Am 4:4 Mic 6:6-7 n Isa 66:3
5:23 o Am 6:5
5:24 p Jer 22:3 q Mic 6:8
5:25 r Isa 43:23 s Dt 32:17
5:27 t Am 4:13 Ac 7:42-43*
6:1 a Lk 6:24 b Isa 32:9-11
6:2 c Ge 10:10 d 2Ki 18:34 e 2Ch 26:6 f Na 3:8
6:3 g Isa 56:12 Am 9:10
6:4 h Eze 34:2-3 Am 3:12
6:5 i Isa 5:12 Am 5:23 j 1Ch 15:16
6:6 k Am 2:8

b22 Traditionally *peace offerings* c26 Or *lifted up Sakkuth your king / and Kaiwan your idols, / your star-gods*; Septuagint *lifted up the shrine of Molech / and the star of your god Rephan, / their idols*

but you do not grieve[l] over
the ruin of Joseph.
7 Therefore you will be among
the first to go into exile;
your feasting and lounging
will end.

The LORD *Abhors the Pride of Israel*

8 The Sovereign LORD has sworn by himself[m]—the LORD God Almighty declares:

"I abhor[n] the pride of Jacob[o]
and detest his fortresses;
I will deliver up[p] the city
and everything in it.[q]"

9 If ten[r] men are left in one house, they too will die. 10 And if a relative who is to burn the bodies[s] comes to carry them out of the house and asks anyone still hiding there, "Is anyone with you?" and he says, "No," then he will say, "Hush![t] We must not mention the name of the LORD."

11 For the LORD has given the
command,
and he will smash the great
house[u] into pieces
and the small house into
bits.[v]

12 Do horses run on the rocky
crags?
Does one plough there with
oxen?
But you have turned justice into
poison[w]
and the fruit of righteousness
into bitterness[x]—
13 you who rejoice in the conquest
of Lo Debar[a]
and say, "Did we not take
Karnaim[b] by our own
strength?[y]"
14 For the LORD God Almighty
declares,
"I will stir up a nation[z]
against you, O house of
Israel,

6:6 [l] Eze 9:4
6:8 [m] Ge 22:16; Heb 6:13 [n] Lev 26:30 [o] Ps 47:4 [p] Am 4:2 [q] Dt 32:19
6:9 [r] Am 5:3
6:10 [s] 1Sa 31:12 [t] Am 8:3
6:11 [u] Am 3:15 [v] Isa 55:11
6:12 [w] Hos 10:4 [x] Am 5:7
6:13 [y] Job 8:15; Isa 28:14-15
6:14 [z] Jer 5:15 [a] 1Ki 8:65 [b] Am 3:11
7:1 [a] Am 8:1 [b] Joel 1:4
7:2 [c] Ex 10:15 [d] Isa 37:4 [e] Eze 11:13
7:3 [f] Dt 32:36; Jer 26:19; Jnh 3:10 [g] Hos 11:8
7:4 [h] Isa 66:16 [i] Dt 32:22
7:5 [j] ver 1-2; Joel 2:17
7:6 [k] Jnh 3:10
7:8 [l] Jer 1:11,13 [m] Isa 28:17; La 2:8; Am 8:2 [n] 2Ki 21:13 [o] Jer 15:6; Eze 7:2-9
7:9 [p] Lev 26:31 [q] 2Ki 15:9; Isa 63:18; Hos 10:8

that will oppress you all the
way
from Lebo[c] Hamath[a] to the
valley of the Arabah.[b]"

Locusts, Fire and a Plumb-Line

7 This is what the Sovereign LORD showed me:[a] He was preparing swarms of locusts[b] after the king's share had been harvested and just as the second crop was coming up. 2 When they had stripped the land clean,[c] I cried out, "Sovereign LORD, forgive! How can Jacob survive?[d] He is so small![e]"

3 So the LORD relented.[f]

"This will not happen," the LORD said.[g]

4 This is what the Sovereign LORD showed me: The Sovereign LORD was calling for judgment by fire;[h] it dried up the great deep and devoured[i] the land. 5 Then I cried out, "Sovereign LORD, I beg you, stop! How can Jacob survive? He is so small![j]"

6 So the LORD relented.[k]

"This will not happen either," the Sovereign LORD said.

7 This is what he showed me: the Lord was standing by a wall that had been built true to plumb, with a plumb-line in his hand. 8 And the LORD asked me, "What do you see,[l] Amos?[m]"

"A plumb-line,[n]" I replied.

Then the Lord said, "Look, I am setting a plumb-line among my people Israel; I will spare them no longer.[o]

9 "The high places of Isaac will
be destroyed
and the sanctuaries[p] of Israel
will be ruined;
with my sword I will rise
against the house of
Jeroboam.[q]"

a 13 *Lo Debar* means *nothing.* b 13 *Karnaim* means *horns*; *horn* here symbolises strength.
c 14 Or *from the entrance to*

Amos and Amaziah

[10]Then Amaziah the priest of
Bethel[r] sent a message to Jeroboam[s] king of Israel: "Amos is
raising a conspiracy[t] against you
in the very heart of Israel. The land
cannot bear all his words.[u] [11]For
this is what Amos is saying:

"'Jeroboam will die by the
sword,
and Israel will surely go into
exile,
away from their native land.'"

[12]Then Amaziah said to Amos,
"Get out, you seer! Go back to the
land of Judah. Earn your bread
there and do your prophesying
there.[v] [13]Don't prophesy any more
at Bethel, because this is the king's
sanctuary and the temple of the
kingdom.[w]"
[14]Amos answered Amaziah, "I
was neither a prophet[x] nor a
prophet's son, but I was a shepherd,
and I also took care of sycamore-
fig trees. [15]But the LORD took me
from tending the flock[y] and said to
me, 'Go, prophesy to my people Israel.'[z] [16]Now then, hear the word
of the LORD. You say,

"'Do not prophesy against[a]
Israel,
and stop preaching against the
house of Isaac.'

[17]"Therefore this is what the
LORD says:

"'Your wife will become a
prostitute[b] in the city,
and your sons and daughters
will fall by the sword.
Your land will be measured and
divided up,
and you yourself will die in a
pagan[a] country.
And Israel will certainly go into
exile,
away from their native
land.[c]'"

A Basket of Ripe Fruit

8 This is what the Sovereign
LORD showed me: a basket of
ripe fruit. [2]"What do you see,[a]
Amos?[b]" he asked.
"A basket of ripe fruit," I answered.
Then the LORD said to me, "The
time is ripe for my people Israel; I
will spare them no longer.[c]
[3]"In that day," declares the Sovereign LORD, "the songs in the temple will turn to wailing.[a][d] Many,
many bodies—flung everywhere!
Silence![e]"

[4]Hear this, you who trample the
needy
and do away with the poor[f] of
the land,[g]

[5]saying,

"When will the New Moon be
over
that we may sell grain,
and the Sabbath be ended
that we may market wheat?"—
skimping the measure,
boosting the price
and cheating with dishonest
scales,[h]
[6]buying the poor with silver
and the needy for a pair of
sandals,
selling even the sweepings
with the wheat.[i]

[7]The LORD has sworn by the
Pride of Jacob:[j] "I will never forget[k] anything they have done.

[8]"Will not the land tremble[l] for
this,
and all who live in it mourn?
The whole land will rise like the
Nile;
it will be stirred up and then
sink
like the river of Egypt.[m]

[9]"In that day," declares the Sovereign LORD,

[a]17 Hebrew *an unclean* [a]3 Or *"the temple singers will wail*

7:10 *r* 1Ki 12:32 *s* 2Ki 14:23 *t* Jer 38:4 *u* Jer 26:8-11
7:12 *v* Mt 8:34
7:13 *w* Am 2:12 Ac 4:18
7:14 *x* 2Ki 2:5 2Ki 4:38
7:15 *y* 2Sa 7:8 *z* Jer 7:1-2 Eze 2:3-4
7:16 *a* Eze 20:46 Mic 2:6
7:17 *b* Hos 4:13 *c* 2Ki 17:6 Eze 4:13 Hos 9:3
8:2 *a* Jer 24:3 *b* Am 7:8 *c* Eze 7:2-9
8:3 *d* Am 5:16 *e* Am 5:23 Am 6:10
8:4 *f* Pr 30:14 *g* Ps 14:4 Am 2:7
8:5 *h* 2Ki 4:23 Ne 13:15-16 Hos 12:7 Mic 6:10-11
8:6 *i* Am 2:6
8:7 *j* Am 6:8 *k* Hos 8:13
8:8 *l* Hos 4:3 *m* Ps 18:7 Jer 46:8 Am 9:5

"I will make the sun go down at
noon
and darken the earth in broad
daylight.[n]
10 I will turn your religious feasts
into mourning
and all your singing into
weeping.
I will make all of you wear
sackcloth[o]
and shave your heads.
I will make that time like
mourning for an only son[p]
and the end of it like a bitter
day.[q]

11 "The days are coming,"
declares the Sovereign
LORD,
"when I will send a famine
through the land—
not a famine of food or a thirst
for water,
but a famine of hearing the
words of the LORD.[r]
12 Men will stagger from sea to
sea
and wander from north to
east,
searching for the word of the
LORD,
but they will not find it.[s]

13 "In that day

"the lovely young women and
strong young men
will faint because of thirst.[t]
14 They who swear by the shame[b]
of Samaria,
or say, 'As surely as your god
lives, O Dan',[u]
or, 'As surely as the god[c] of
Beersheba[v] lives'—
they will fall,
never to rise again.[w]"

Israel to Be Destroyed

9 I saw the Lord standing by the
altar, and he said:

"Strike the tops of the pillars
so that the thresholds shake.
Bring them down on the heads[a]
of all the people;
those who are left I will kill
with the sword.
Not one will get away,
none will escape.
2 Though they dig down to the
depths of the grave,[a][b]
from there my hand will take
them.
Though they climb up to the
heavens,[c]
from there I will bring them
down.[d]
3 Though they hide themselves on
the top of Carmel,[e]
there I will hunt them down
and seize them.[f]
Though they hide from me at
the bottom of the sea,
there I will command the
serpent to bite them.[g]
4 Though they are driven into
exile by their enemies,
there I will command the
sword[h] to slay them.
I will fix my eyes upon them
for evil[i] and not for good.[j]"[k]

5 The Lord, the LORD Almighty,
he who touches the earth and
it melts,[l]
and all who live in it mourn—
the whole land rises like the
Nile,
then sinks like the river of
Egypt[m]—
6 he who builds his lofty palace[b]
in the heavens
and sets its foundation[c] on
the earth,
who calls for the waters of the
sea
and pours them out over the
face of the land—
the LORD is his name.[n]

7 "Are not you Israelites
the same to me as the
Cushites?"[d][o]
declares the LORD.

8:9 n Job 5:14; Isa 59:9-10; Jer 15:9; Am 5:8; Mic 3:6
8:10 o Jer 48:37; p Jer 6:26; Zec 12:10; q Eze 7:18
8:11 r 1Sa 3:1; 2Ch 15:3; Eze 7:26
8:12 s Eze 20:3,31
8:13 t Isa 41:17; Hos 2:3
8:14 u 1Ki 12:29; v Am 5:5; w Am 5:2
9:1 a Ps 68:21
9:2 b Ps 139:8; c Jer 51:53; d Ob 1:4
9:3 e Am 1:2; f Ps 139:8-10; g Jer 16:16-17
9:4 h Lev 26:33; Eze 5:12; i Jer 21:10; j Jer 39:16; k Jer 44:11
9:5 l Ps 46:2; Mic 1:4; m Am 8:8
9:6 n Ps 104:1-3, 5-6,13; Am 5:8
9:7 o Isa 20:4; Isa 43:3

b14 Or *by Ashima*; or *by the idol* c14 Or *power*
a2 Hebrew *to Sheol* b6 The meaning of the Hebrew for this phrase is uncertain.
c6 The meaning of the Hebrew for this word is uncertain. d7 That is, people from the upper Nile region

"Did I not bring Israel up from
Egypt,
the Philistines from
Caphtor[e][p]
and the Arameans from Kir?[q]

[8]"Surely the eyes of the
Sovereign LORD
are on the sinful kingdom.
I will destroy it
from the face of the earth—
yet I will not totally destroy
the house of Jacob,"
declares the LORD.[r]
[9]"For I will give the command,
and I will shake the house of
Israel
among all the nations
as grain[s] is shaken in a sieve,[t]
and not a pebble will reach the
ground.
[10]All the sinners among my
people
will die by the sword,
all those who say,
'Disaster will not overtake or
meet us.'[u]

Israel's Restoration

[11]"In that day I will restore
David's fallen tent.
I will repair its broken places,
restore its ruins,
and build it as it used to be,[v]
[12]so that they may possess the
remnant of Edom[w]
and all the nations that bear
my name,[f][x]"
declares the LORD,
who will do these things.[y]

[13]"The days are coming," declares the LORD,

"when the reaper will be
overtaken by the
ploughman[z]
and the planter by the one
treading grapes.
New wine will drip from the
mountains
and flow from all the hills.[a]
[14]I will bring back my exiled[g]
people Israel;
they will rebuild the ruined
cities[b] and live in them.
They will plant vineyards and
drink their wine;
they will make gardens and
eat their fruit.[c]
[15]I will plant[d] Israel in their own
land,
never again to be uprooted
from the land I have given
them,"
says the LORD your God.[e]

9:7 p Dt 2:23; Jer 47:4 q 2Ki 16:9; Isa 22:6; Am 1:5; Am 2:10
9:8 r Jer 44:27
9:9 s Lk 22:31 t Isa 30:28
9:10 u Am 6:3
9:11 v Ps 80:12
9:12 w Nu 24:18 x Isa 43:7 y Ac 15:16-17*
9:13 z Lev 26:5 a Joel 3:18
9:14 b Isa 61:4 c Jer 30:18; Jer 31:28; Eze 28:25-26
9:15 d Isa 60:21 e Jer 24:6; Eze 34:25-28; Eze 37:12,25

[e]7 That is, Crete [f]12 Hebrew; Septuagint *so that the remnant of men / and all the nations that bear my name may seek ⌞the Lord⌟* [g]14 Or *will restore the fortunes of my*

OBADIAH

1The vision of Obadiah.

1-4pp Jer 49:14-16
5-6pp Jer 49:9-10

This is what the Sovereign LORD says about Edom[a]—

We have heard a message from the LORD:
An envoy[b] was sent to the nations to say,
"Rise, and let us go against her for battle"[c]—

2"See, I will make you small among the nations;
you will be utterly despised.
3The pride[d] of your heart has deceived you,
you who live in the clefts of the rocks[a]
and make your home on the heights,
you who say to yourself,
'Who can bring me down to the ground?'[e]
4Though you soar like the eagle
and make your nest[f] among the stars,
from there I will bring you down,"[g]
declares the LORD.[h]
5"If thieves came to you,
if robbers in the night—
Oh, what a disaster awaits you—
would they not steal only as much as they wanted?
If grape pickers came to you,
would they not leave a few grapes?[i]
6But how Esau will be ransacked,
his hidden treasures pillaged!
7All your allies[j] will force you to the border;
your friends will deceive and overpower you;
those who eat your bread[k] will set a trap for you,[b]
but you will not detect it.

8"In that day," declares the LORD,
"will I not destroy[l] the wise men of Edom,
men of understanding in the mountains of Esau?
9Your warriors, O Teman,[m] will be terrified,
and everyone in Esau's mountains
will be cut down in the slaughter.
10Because of the violence[n] against your brother Jacob,[o]
you will be covered with shame;
you will be destroyed for ever.[p]
11On the day you stood aloof
while strangers carried off his wealth
and foreigners entered his gates
and cast lots[q] for Jerusalem,
you were like one of them.
12You should not look down on your brother
in the day of his misfortune,
nor rejoice[r] over the people of Judah
in the day of their destruction,[s]
nor boast so much
in the day of their trouble.[t]
13You should not march through the gates of my people
in the day of their disaster,
nor look down on them in their calamity[u]
in the day of their disaster,

1 *a* Isa 63:1-6; Jer 49:7-22; Eze 25:12-14; Am 1:11-12 *b* Isa 18:2 *c* Jer 6:4-5
3 *d* Isa 16:6 *e* Isa 14:13-15; Rev 18:7
4 *f* Hab 2:9 *g* Isa 14:13 *h* Job 20:6
5 *i* Dt 24:21
7 *j* Jer 30:14 *k* Ps 41:9
8 *l* Job 5:12; Isa 29:14
9 *m* Ge 36:11,34
10 *n* Joel 3:19 *o* Ps 137:7; Am 1:11-12 *p* Eze 35:9
11 *q* Na 3:10
12 *r* Eze 35:15 *s* Pr 17:5 *t* Mic 4:11
13 *u* Eze 35:5

a3 Or *of Sela* b7 The meaning of the Hebrew for this clause is uncertain.

nor seize their wealth
in the day of their disaster.
14 You should not wait at the crossroads
to cut down their fugitives,
nor hand over their survivors
in the day of their trouble.

15 "The day of the LORD is near[v]
for all nations.
As you have done, it will be done to you;
your deeds[w] will return upon your own head.
16 Just as you drank on my holy hill,
so all the nations will drink[x] continually;
they will drink and drink
and be as if they had never been.
17 But on Mount Zion will be deliverance;[y]
it will be holy,[z]
and the house of Jacob
will possess its inheritance.
18 The house of Jacob will be a fire
and the house of Joseph a flame;
the house of Esau will be stubble,
and they will set it on fire and consume[a] it.
There will be no survivors
from the house of Esau."
The LORD has spoken.

19 People from the Negev will occupy
the mountains of Esau,
and people from the foothills will possess
the land of the Philistines.[b]
They will occupy the fields of Ephraim and Samaria,[c]
and Benjamin will possess Gilead.
20 This company of Israelite exiles who are in Canaan
will possess ⌊the land⌋ as far as Zarephath;[d]
the exiles from Jerusalem who are in Sepharad
will possess the towns of the Negev.[e]
21 Deliverers will go up on[c] Mount Zion
to govern the mountains of Esau.
And the kingdom will be the LORD's.[f]

c21 Or *from*

15
v Eze 30:3
w Jer 50:29
Hab 2:8

16
x Jer 25:15
Jer 49:12

17
y Am 9:11-15
z Isa 4:3

18
a Zec 12:6

19
b Isa 11:14
c Jer 31:5

20
d 1Ki 17:9-10
e Jer 33:13

21
f Ps 22:28
Zec 14:9,16
Rev 11:15

JONAH

Jonah Flees From the LORD

1 The word of the LORD came to
Jonah[a] son of Amittai:[b] 2"Go
to the great city of Nineveh[c] and
preach against it, because its wickedness has come up before me."
3But Jonah ran[d] away from the
LORD and headed for Tarshish. He
went down to Joppa,[e] where he
found a ship bound for that port.
After paying the fare, he went
aboard and sailed for Tarshish to
flee from the LORD.
4Then the LORD sent a great wind
on the sea, and such a violent storm
arose that the ship threatened to
break up.[f] 5All the sailors were
afraid and each cried out to his own
god. And they threw the cargo into
the sea to lighten the ship.[g]
But Jonah had gone below deck,
where he lay down and fell into a
deep sleep. 6The captain went to
him and said, "How can you sleep?
Get up and call[h] on your god!
Maybe he will take notice of us, and
we will not perish."[i]
7Then the sailors said to each
other, "Come, let us cast lots to find
out who is responsible for this calamity."[j] They cast lots and the lot
fell on Jonah.
8So they asked him, "Tell us, who
is responsible for making all this
trouble for us? What do you do?
Where do you come from? What is
your country? From what people
are you?"
9He answered, "I am a Hebrew
and I worship the LORD, the God of
heaven,[k] who made the sea and the
land.[l]"
10This terrified them and they
asked, "What have you done?"
(They knew he was running away
from the LORD, because he had already told them so.)

1:1 a Mt 12:39-41 b 2Ki 14:25
1:2 c Ge 10:11
1:3 d Ps 139:7 e Jos 19:46 Ac 9:36,43
1:4 f Ps 107:23-26
1:5 g Ac 27:18-19
1:6 h Jnh 3:8 i Ps 107:28
1:7 j Jos 7:10-18 1Sa 14:42
1:9 k Ac 17:24 l Ps 146:6
1:12 m 2Sa 24:17 1Ch 21:17
1:13 n Pr 21:30
1:14 o Dt 21:8 p Ps 115:3
1:15 q Ps 107:29 Lk 8:24
1:16 r Mk 4:41
1:17 s Mt 12:40 Mt 16:4 Lk 11:30
2:2 a Ps 18:6 Ps 120:1
2:3 b Ps 88:6 c Ps 42:7

11The sea was getting rougher
and rougher. So they asked him,
"What should we do to you to make
the sea calm down for us?"
12"Pick me up and throw me into
the sea," he replied, "and it will become calm. I know that it is my
fault that this great storm has come
upon you."[m]
13Instead, the men did their best
to row back to land. But they could
not, for the sea grew even wilder
than before.[n] 14Then they cried to
the LORD, "O LORD, please do not
let us die for taking this man's life.
Do not hold us accountable for
killing an innocent man,[o] for
you, O LORD, have done as you
pleased."[p] 15Then they took Jonah
and threw him overboard, and the
raging sea grew calm.[q] 16At this
the men greatly feared[r] the LORD,
and they offered a sacrifice to the
LORD and made vows to him.
17But the LORD provided a great
fish to swallow Jonah,[s] and Jonah
was inside the fish three days and
three nights.

Jonah's Prayer

2 From inside the fish Jonah
prayed to the LORD his God.
2He said:

"In my distress I called to the
LORD,[a]
and he answered me.
From the depths of the grave[a]
I called for help,
and you listened to my cry.
3You hurled me into the deep,[b]
into the very heart of the seas,
and the currents swirled about
me;
all your waves and breakers
swept over me.[c]

a2 Hebrew *Sheol*

4 I said, 'I have been banished
from your sight;[d]
yet I will look again
towards your holy temple.'
5 The engulfing waters
threatened me,[b]
the deep surrounded me;
seaweed was wrapped around
my head.[e]
6 To the roots of the mountains I
sank down;
the earth beneath barred me
in for ever.
But you brought my life up
from the pit,
O LORD my God.

7 "When my life was ebbing
away,
I remembered[f] you, LORD,
and my prayer[g] rose to you,
to your holy temple.[h]

8 "Those who cling to worthless
idols[i]
forfeit the grace that could be
theirs.
9 But I, with a song of
thanksgiving,
will sacrifice[j] to you.
What I have vowed[k] I will
make good.
Salvation[l] comes from the
LORD."

10 And the LORD commanded the
fish, and it vomited Jonah onto dry
land.

Jonah Goes to Nineveh

3 Then the word of the LORD
came to Jonah[a] a second time:
2 "Go to the great city of Nineveh
and proclaim to it the message I
give you."
3 Jonah obeyed the word of the
LORD and went to Nineveh. Now
Nineveh was a very important
city—a visit required three days.
4 On the first day, Jonah started into
the city. He proclaimed: "Forty
more days and Nineveh will be
overturned." 5 The Ninevites believed God. They declared a fast,
and all of them, from the greatest
to the least, put on sackcloth.[b]
6 When the news reached the king
of Nineveh, he rose from his
throne, took off his royal robes,
covered himself with sackcloth
and sat down in the dust.[c] 7 Then he
issued a proclamation in Nineveh:

"By the decree of the king and
his nobles:

Do not let any man or beast,
herd or flock, taste anything;
do not let them eat or drink.[d]
8 But let man and beast be covered with sackcloth. Let everyone call[e] urgently on God. Let
them give up their evil ways
and their violence. 9 Who
knows?[f] God may yet relent
and with compassion turn[g]
from his fierce anger so that
we will not perish."

10 When God saw what they did
and how they turned from their evil
ways, he had compassion[h] and did
not bring upon them the destruction[i] he had threatened.[j]

Jonah's Anger at the LORD's Compassion

4 But Jonah was greatly displeased and became angry.[a]
2 He prayed to the LORD, "O LORD, is
this not what I said when I was still
at home? That is why I was so quick
to flee to Tarshish. I knew[b] that
you are a gracious and compassionate God, slow to anger and abounding in love,[c] a God who relents
from sending calamity.[d] 3 Now,
O LORD, take away my life,[e] for it
is better for me to die[f] than to
live."
4 But the LORD replied, "Have you
any right to be angry?"[g]
5 Jonah went out and sat down at
a place east of the city. There he
made himself a shelter, sat in its
shade and waited to see what would

2:4 d Ps 31:22
2:5 e Ps 69:1-2
2:7 f Ps 77:11-12; g 2Ch 30:27; h Ps 11:4; Ps 18:6
2:8 i 2Ki 17:15; Jer 10:8
2:9 j Ps 50:14,23; Hos 14:2; k Ecc 5:4-5; l Ps 3:8
3:1 a Jnh 1:1
3:5 b Da 9:3; Lk 11:32
3:6 c Job 2:8,13; Eze 27:30-31
3:7 d 2Ch 20:3
3:8 e Ps 130:1; Jnh 1:6
3:9 f 2Sa 12:22; g Joel 2:14
3:10 h Am 7:6; i Jer 18:8; j Ex 32:14
4:1 a ver 4; Lk 15:28
4:2 b Jer 20:7-8; c Ex 34:6; Ps 86:5,15; d Joel 2:13
4:3 e 1Ki 19:4; f Job 7:15
4:4 g Mt 20:11-15

b5 Or *waters were at my throat*

happen to the city. [6]Then the LORD
God provided a vine and made it
grow up over Jonah to give shade
for his head to ease his discomfort,
and Jonah was very happy about
the vine. [7]But at dawn the next day
God provided a worm, which
chewed the vine so that it withered.[h] [8]When the sun rose, God
provided a scorching east wind,
and the sun blazed on Jonah's head
so that he grew faint. He wanted to
die, and said, "It would be better
for me to die than to live."
[9]But God said to Jonah, "Do you
have a right to be angry about the
vine?"
"I do," he said. "I am angry
enough to die."
[10]But the LORD said, "You have
been concerned about this vine,
though you did not tend it or make
it grow. It sprang up overnight and
died overnight. [11]But Nineveh[i]
has more than a hundred and
twenty thousand people who cannot tell their right hand from their
left, and many cattle as well.
Should I not be concerned[j] about
that great city?"

4:7
h Joel 1:12

4:11
i Jnh 1:2
Jnh 3:2
j Jnh 3:10

MICAH

1 The word of the LORD that
came to Micah of Moresheth[a]
during the reigns of Jotham,[b]
Ahaz[c] and Hezekiah, kings of Judah[d]—the vision[e] he saw concerning Samaria and Jerusalem.

2 Hear, O peoples, all of you,[f]
listen, O earth[g] and all who
are in it,
that the Sovereign LORD may
witness[h] against you,
the Lord from his holy
temple.[i]

Judgment Against Samaria and Jerusalem

3 Look! The LORD is coming from
his dwelling-place;[j]
he comes down and treads the
high places of the earth.[k]
4 The mountains melt[l] beneath
him
and the valleys split apart,[m]
like wax before the fire,
like water rushing down a
slope.
5 All this is because of Jacob's
transgression,
because of the sins of the
house of Israel.
What is Jacob's transgression?
Is it not Samaria?[n]
What is Judah's high place?
Is it not Jerusalem?

6 "Therefore I will make Samaria
a heap of rubble,
a place for planting vineyards.
I will pour her stones[o] into the
valley
and lay bare her foundations.[p]
7 All her idols[q] will be broken to
pieces;
all her temple gifts will be
burned with fire;
I will destroy all her images.[r]

1:1 *a* Jer 26:18 *b* 1Ch 3:12 *c* 1Ch 3:13 *d* Hos 1:1 *e* Isa 1:1
1:2 *f* Ps 50:7 *g* Jer 6:19 *h* Ge 31:50 Dt 4:26 Isa 1:2 *i* Ps 11:4
1:3 *j* Isa 18:4 *k* Am 4:13
1:4 *l* Ps 46:2,6 *m* Nu 16:31 Na 1:5
1:5 *n* Am 8:14
1:6 *o* Am 5:11 *p* Eze 13:14
1:7 *q* Eze 6:6 *r* Dt 9:21 *s* Dt 23:17-18
1:8 *t* Isa 15:3
1:9 *u* Jer 46:11 *v* 2Ki 18:13 *w* Isa 3:26
1:11 *x* Eze 23:29
1:12 *y* Jer 14:19
1:13 *z* Jos 10:3

Since she gathered her gifts
from the wages of
prostitutes,[s]
as the wages of prostitutes
they will again be used."

Weeping and Mourning

8 Because of this I will weep[t]
and wail;
I will go about barefoot and
naked.
I will howl like a jackal
and moan like an owl.
9 For her wound[u] is incurable;
it has come to Judah.[v]
It[a] has reached the very gate[w]
of my people,
even to Jerusalem itself.
10 Tell it not in Gath;[b]
weep not at all.[c]
In Beth Ophrah[d]
roll in the dust.
11 Pass on in nakedness[x] and
shame,
you who live in Shaphir.[e]
Those who live in Zaanan[f]
will not come out.
Beth Ezel is in mourning;
its protection is taken from
you.
12 Those who live in Maroth[g]
writhe in pain,
waiting for relief,[y]
because disaster has come from
the LORD,
even to the gate of Jerusalem.
13 You who live in Lachish,[h][z]
harness the team to the
chariot.

[a]9 Or *He* [b]10 *Gath* sounds like the Hebrew for *tell.* [c]10 Hebrew; Septuagint may suggest *not in Acco.* The Hebrew for *in Acco* sounds like the Hebrew for *weep.* [d]10 *Beth Ophrah* means *house of dust.* [e]11 *Shaphir* means *pleasant.* [f]11 *Zaanan* sounds like the Hebrew for *come out.* [g]12 *Maroth* sounds like the Hebrew for *bitter.* [h]13 *Lachish* sounds like the Hebrew for *team.*

You were the beginning of sin
to the Daughter of Zion,
for the transgressions of Israel
were found in you.
14Therefore you will give parting
gifts[a]
to Moresheth Gath.
The town of Aczib[i][b] will prove
deceptive[c]
to the kings of Israel.
15I will bring a conqueror against
you
who live in Mareshah.[j][d]
He who is the glory of Israel
will come to Adullam.[e]
16Shave[f] your heads in mourning
for the children in whom you
delight;
make yourselves as bald as the
vulture,
for they will go from you into
exile.

Man's Plans and God's

2 Woe to those who plan
iniquity,
to those who plot evil on their
beds![a]
At morning's light they carry it
out
because it is in their power to
do it.
2They covet fields[b] and seize
them,
and houses, and take them.
They defraud[c] a man of his
home,
a fellow-man of his
inheritance.

3Therefore, the LORD says:

"I am planning disaster[d]
against this people,
from which you cannot save
yourselves.
You will no longer walk
proudly,[e]
for it will be a time of
calamity.
4In that day men will ridicule
you;
they will taunt you with this
mournful song:
'We are utterly ruined;[f]
my people's possession is
divided up.
He takes it from me!
He assigns our fields to
traitors.' "
5Therefore you will have no-one
in the assembly of the LORD
to divide the land[g] by lot.

False Prophets

6"Do not prophesy," their
prophets say.
"Do not prophesy about these
things;
disgrace[h] will not overtake
us.[i]"
7Should it be said, O house of
Jacob:
"Is the Spirit of the LORD
angry?
Does he do such things?"

"Do not my words do good[j]
to him whose ways are
upright?[k]
8Lately my people have risen up
like an enemy.
You strip off the rich robe
from those who pass by
without a care,
like men returning from
battle.
9You drive the women of my
people
from their pleasant homes.[l]
You take away my blessing
from their children for ever.
10Get up, go away!
For this is not your resting
place,[m]
because it is defiled,[n]
it is ruined, beyond all
remedy.
11If a liar and deceiver[o] comes
and says,
'I will prophesy for you plenty
of wine and beer,'

1:14 *a* 2Ki 16:8 *b* Jos 15:44 *c* Jer 15:18
1:15 *d* Jos 15:44 *e* Jos 12:15
1:16 *f* Job 1:20
2:1 *a* Ps 36:4
2:2 *b* Isa 5:8 *c* Jer 22:17
2:3 *d* Jer 18:11 Am 3:1-2 *e* Isa 2:12
2:4 *f* Jer 4:13
2:5 *g* Jos 18:4
2:6 *h* Mic 6:16 *i* Am 2:12
2:7 *j* Ps 119:65 *k* Ps 15:2 Ps 84:11
2:9 *l* Jer 10:20
2:10 *m* Dt 12:9 *n* Lev 18:25-29 Ps 106:38-39
2:11 *o* Jer 5:31

i14 *Aczib* means *deception*. j15 *Mareshah* sounds like the Hebrew for *conqueror*.

he would be just the prophet
for this people![p]

Deliverance Promised

12“I will surely gather all of you,
O Jacob;
I will surely bring together
the remnant[q] of Israel.
I will bring them together like
sheep in a pen,
like a flock in its pasture;
the place will throng with
people.
13One who breaks open the way
will go up before[r] them;
they will break through the
gate and go out.
Their king will pass through
before them,
the LORD at their head.”

Leaders and Prophets Rebuked

3 Then I said,

“Listen, you leaders[a] of Jacob,
you rulers of the house of
Israel.
Should you not know justice,
2 you who hate good and love
evil;
who tear the skin from my
people
and the flesh from their
bones;[b]
3who eat my people’s flesh,[c]
strip off their skin
and break their bones in
pieces;[d]
who chop them up like meat for
the pan,
like flesh for the pot.[e]”

4Then they will cry out to the
LORD,
but he will not answer them.[f]
At that time he will hide his
face[g] from them
because of the evil they have
done.

5This is what the LORD says:

“As for the prophets
who lead my people astray,[h]
if one feeds them,
they proclaim ‘peace’;
if he does not,
they prepare to wage war
against him.
6Therefore night will come over
you, without visions,
and darkness, without
divination.[i]
The sun will set for the
prophets,[j]
and the day will go dark for
them.
7The seers will be ashamed[k]
and the diviners disgraced.[l]
They will all cover their faces
because there is no answer
from God.”

8But as for me, I am filled with
power,
with the Spirit of the LORD,
and with justice and might,
to declare to Jacob his
transgression,
to Israel his sin.[m]
9Hear this, you leaders of the
house of Jacob,
you rulers of the house of
Israel,
who despise justice
and distort all that is right;[n]
10who build[o] Zion with
bloodshed,[p]
and Jerusalem with
wickedness.[q]
11Her leaders judge for a bribe,
her priests teach for a price,
and her prophets tell fortunes
for money.[r]
Yet they lean upon the LORD
and say,
“Is not the LORD among us?
No disaster will come upon
us.”[s]
12Therefore because of you,
Zion will be ploughed like a
field,
Jerusalem will become a heap
of rubble,[t]
the temple hill a mound
overgrown with thickets.

2:11 p Isa 30:10
2:12 q Mic 4:7; Mic 5:7; Mic 7:18
2:13 r Isa 52:12
3:1 a Jer 5:5
3:2 b Ps 53:4; Eze 22:27
3:3 c Ps 14:4; d Zep 3:3; e Eze 11:7
3:4 f Ps 18:41; Isa 1:15; g Dt 31:17
3:5 h Isa 3:12; Isa 9:16
3:6 i Isa 8:19-22; j Isa 29:10
3:7 k Mic 7:16; l Isa 44:25
3:8 m Isa 58:1
3:9 n Ps 58:1-2; Isa 1:23
3:10 o Jer 22:13; p Hab 2:12; q Eze 22:27
3:11 r Isa 1:23; Jer 6:13; Hos 4:8,18; s Jer 7:4
3:12 t Jer 26:18

The Mountain of the L*ORD*

4:1–3pp Isa 2:1–4

4 In the last days
the mountain[a] of the LORD's
temple will be established
as chief among the mountains;
it will be raised above the
hills,[b]
and peoples will stream to it.[c]

[2]Many nations will come and say,

"Come, let us go up to the
mountain of the LORD,[d]
to the house of the God of
Jacob.[e]
He will teach us his ways,[f]
so that we may walk in his
paths."
The law will go out from Zion,
the word of the LORD from
Jerusalem.
[3]He will judge between many
peoples
and will settle disputes for
strong nations far and
wide.[g]
They will beat their swords into
ploughshares
and their spears into pruning
hooks.[h]
Nation will not take up sword
against nation,
nor will they train for war any
more.[i]
[4]Every man will sit under his
own vine
and under his own fig-tree,[j]
and no-one will make them
afraid,[k]
for the LORD Almighty has
spoken.[l]
[5]All the nations may walk
in the name of their gods;[m]
we will walk in the name of the
LORD
our God for ever and ever.[n]

The L*ORD's Plan*

[6]"In that day," declares the LORD,

"I will gather the lame;
I will assemble the exiles[o]
and those I have brought to
grief.[p]
[7]I will make the lame a
remnant,[q]
those driven away a strong
nation.
The LORD will rule over them in
Mount Zion
from that day and for ever.[r]
[8]As for you, O watchtower of the
flock,
O stronghold[a] of the
Daughter of Zion,
the former dominion will be
restored[s] to you;
kingship will come to the
Daughter of Jerusalem."

[9]Why do you now cry aloud—
have you no king?[t]
Has your counsellor perished,
that pain seizes you like that
of a woman in labour?[u]
[10]Writhe in agony, O Daughter of
Zion,
like a woman in labour,
for now you must leave the city
to camp in the open field.
You will go to Babylon;[v]
there you will be rescued.
There the LORD will redeem[w]
you
out of the hand of your
enemies.

[11]But now many nations
are gathered against you.
They say, "Let her be defiled,
let our eyes gloat[x] over Zion!"
[12]But they do not know
the thoughts of the LORD;
they do not understand his
plan,[y]
he who gathers them like
sheaves to the threshing-
floor.

[13]"Rise and thresh, O Daughter of
Zion,
for I will give you horns of
iron;
I will give you hoofs of bronze

4:1
a Zec 8:3
b Eze 17:22
c Ps 22:27
Ps 86:9
Jer 3:17

4:2
d Jer 31:6
e Zec 2:11
Zec 14:16
f Ps 25:8-9
Isa 54:13

4:3
g Isa 11:4
h Joel 3:10
i Isa 2:4

4:4
j 1Ki 4:25
k Lev 26:6
l Isa 1:20
Zec 3:10

4:5
m 2Ki 17:29
n Jos 24:14-15
Isa 26:8
Zec 10:12

4:6
o Ps 147:2
p Eze 34:13,16
Eze 37:21
Zep 3:19

4:7
q Mic 2:12
r Da 7:14
Lk 1:33
Rev 11:15

4:8
s Isa 1:26

4:9
t Jer 8:19
u Jer 30:6

4:10
v 2Ki 20:18
Isa 43:14
w Isa 48:20

4:11
x La 2:16
Ob 1:12

4:12
y Isa 55:8
Ro 11:33-34

[a]8 Or *hill*

and you will break to pieces
many nations."[z]

You will devote their ill-gotten
gains to the LORD,
their wealth to the Lord of all
the earth.

A Promised Ruler From Bethlehem

5 Marshal your troops, O city
of troops,[a]
for a siege is laid against us.
They will strike Israel's ruler
on the cheek[a] with a rod.

2 "But you, Bethlehem[b]
Ephrathah,[c]
though you are small among
the clans[b] of Judah,
out of you will come for me
one who will be ruler over
Israel,
whose origins[c] are from of
old,[d]
from ancient times."[d][e]

3 Therefore Israel will be
abandoned
until the time when she who is
in labour gives birth
and the rest of his brothers
return
to join the Israelites.

4 He will stand and shepherd his
flock[f]
in the strength of the LORD,
in the majesty of the name of
the LORD his God.
And they will live securely, for
then his greatness[g]
will reach to the ends of the
earth.
5 And he will be their peace.[h]

Deliverance and Destruction

When the Assyrian invades[i]
our land
and marches through our
fortresses,
we will raise against him seven
shepherds,
even eight leaders of men.[j]

6 They will rule[e] the land of
Assyria with the sword,
the land of Nimrod[k] with
drawn sword.[f][l]
He will deliver us from the
Assyrian
when he invades our land
and marches into our
borders.[m]

7 The remnant[n] of Jacob will be
in the midst of many peoples
like dew from the LORD,
like showers on the grass,[o]
which do not wait for man
or linger for mankind.
8 The remnant of Jacob will be
among the nations,
in the midst of many peoples,
like a lion among the beasts of
the forest,[p]
like a young lion among flocks
of sheep,
which mauls and mangles[q] as it
goes,
and no-one can rescue.[r]
9 Your hand will be lifted up[s] in
triumph over your enemies,
and all your foes will be
destroyed.

10 "In that day," declares the
LORD,

"I will destroy your horses
from among you
and demolish your chariots.[t]
11 I will destroy the cities[u] of
your land
and tear down all your
strongholds.[v]
12 I will destroy your witchcraft
and you will no longer cast
spells.[w]
13 I will destroy your carved
images
and your sacred stones from
among you;
you will no longer bow down
to the work of your hands.[x]

4:13 z Da 2:44
5:1 a La 3:30
5:2 b Jn 7:42 c Ge 48:7 d Ps 102:25 e Mt 2:6*
5:4 f Isa 40:11 Isa 49:9 Eze 34:11-15, 23 Mic 7:14 g Isa 52:13 Lk 1:32
5:5 h Isa 9:6 Lk 2:14 Col 1:19-20 i Isa 8:7 j Isa 10:24-27
5:6 k Ge 10:8 l Zep 2:13 m Na 2:11-13
5:7 n Mic 2:12 o Isa 44:4
5:8 p Ge 49:9 q Mic 4:13 Zec 10:5 r Ps 50:22 Hos 5:14
5:9 s Ps 10:12
5:10 t Hos 14:3 Zec 9:10
5:11 u Isa 6:11 v Hos 10:14 Am 5:9
5:12 w Dt 18:10-12 Isa 2:6 Isa 8:19
5:13 x Eze 6:9 Zec 13:2

a1 Or *Strengthen your walls, O walled city*
b2 Or *rulers* c2 Hebrew *goings out*
d2 Or *from days of eternity* e6 Or *crush*
f6 Or *Nimrod in its gates*

14 I will uproot from among you
your Asherah poles[g][y]
and demolish your cities.
15 I will take vengeance[z] in anger
and wrath
upon the nations that have not
obeyed me."

The LORD's Case Against Israel

6 Listen to what the LORD says:

"Stand up, plead your case
before the mountains;[a]
let the hills hear what you
have to say.
2 Hear,[b] O mountains, the LORD's
accusation;[c]
listen, you everlasting
foundations of the earth.
For the LORD has a case against
his people;
he is lodging a charge[d]
against Israel.

3 "My people, what have I done to
you?
How have I burdened[e] you?
Answer me.
4 I brought you up out of Egypt
and redeemed you from the
land of slavery.[f]
I sent Moses[g] to lead you,
also Aaron[h] and Miriam.[i]
5 My people, remember
what Balak[j] king of Moab
counselled
and what Balaam son of Beor
answered.
Remember ⌊your journey⌋ from
Shittim[k] to Gilgal,[l]
that you may know the
righteous acts[m] of the
LORD."

6 With what shall I come before
the LORD
and bow down before the
exalted God?
Shall I come before him with
burnt offerings,
with calves a year old?[n]
7 Will the LORD be pleased with
thousands of rams,[o]
with ten thousand rivers of
oil?[p]
Shall I offer my firstborn[q] for
my transgression,
the fruit of my body for the
sin of my soul?[r]
8 He has showed you, O man,
what is good.
And what does the LORD
require of you?
To act justly[s] and to love
mercy
and to walk humbly[t] with
your God.[u]

Israel's Guilt and Punishment

9 Listen! The LORD is calling to
the city—
and to fear your name is
wisdom—
"Heed the rod and the One
who appointed it.[a]
10 Am I still to forget, O wicked
house,
your ill-gotten treasures
and the short ephah,[b] which is
accursed?[v]
11 Shall I acquit a man with
dishonest scales,[w]
with a bag of false weights?
12 Her rich men are violent;[x]
her people are liars[y]
and their tongues speak
deceitfully.[z]
13 Therefore, I have begun to
destroy[a] you,
to ruin you because of your
sins.
14 You will eat but not be
satisfied;[b]
your stomach will still be
empty.[c]
You will store up but save
nothing,[c]
because what you save I will
give to the sword.
15 You will plant but not harvest;[d]

5:14 y Ex 34:13
5:15 z Isa 65:12
6:1 a Ps 50:1; Eze 6:2
6:2 b Dt 32:1; c Hos 12:2; d Ps 50:7
6:3 e Jer 2:5
6:4 f Dt 7:8; g Ex 4:16; h Ps 77:20; i Ex 15:20
6:5 j Nu 22:5-6; k Nu 25:1; l Jos 5:9-10; m Jdg 5:11; 1Sa 12:7
6:6 n Ps 40:6-8; Ps 51:16-17
6:7 o Isa 40:16; p Ps 50:8-10; q Lev 18:21; r 2Ki 16:3
6:8 s Isa 1:17; Jer 22:3; t Isa 57:15; u Dt 10:12-13; 1Sa 15:22; Hos 6:6
6:10 v Eze 45:9-10; Am 3:10; Am 8:4-6
6:11 w Lev 19:36; Hos 12:7
6:12 x Isa 1:23; y Isa 3:8; z Jer 9:3
6:13 a Isa 1:7; Isa 6:11
6:14 b Isa 9:20; c Isa 30:6
6:15 d Dt 28:38; Jer 12:13

g *14* That is, symbols of the goddess Asherah
a *9* The meaning of the Hebrew for this line is uncertain. b *10* An ephah was a dry measure.
c *14* The meaning of the Hebrew for this word is uncertain.

you will press olives but not
use the oil on yourselves,
you will crush grapes but not
drink the wine.[e]
16You have observed the statutes
of Omri[f]
and all the practices of
Ahab's[g] house,
and you have followed their
traditions.[h]
Therefore I will give you over
to ruin[i]
and your people to derision;
you will bear the scorn[j] of
the nations."[d]

Israel's Misery

7 What misery is mine!
I am like one who gathers
summer fruit
at the gleaning of the
vineyard;
there is no cluster of grapes to
eat,
none of the early figs that I
crave.
2The godly have been swept
from the land;[a]
not one upright man remains.
All men lie in wait to shed
blood;[b]
each hunts his brother with a
net.[c]
3Both hands are skilled in doing
evil;[d]
the ruler demands gifts,
the judge accepts bribes,
the powerful dictate what they
desire—
they all conspire together.
4The best of them is like a
brier,[e]
the most upright worse than a
thorn hedge.
The day of your watchmen has
come,
the day God visits you.
Now is the time of their
confusion.[f]
5Do not trust a neighbour;
put no confidence in a
friend.[g]
Even with her who lies in your
embrace
be careful of your words.
6For a son dishonours his father,
a daughter rises up against
her mother,[h]
a daughter-in-law against her
mother-in-law—
a man's enemies are the
members of his own
household.[i]

7But as for me, I watch in hope[j]
for the LORD,
I wait for God my Saviour;
my God will hear[k] me.

Israel Will Rise

8Do not gloat over me,[l] my
enemy!
Though I have fallen, I will
rise.[m]
Though I sit in darkness,
the LORD will be my light.[n]
9Because I have sinned against
him,
I will bear the LORD's wrath,[o]
until he pleads my case
and establishes my right.
He will bring me out into the
light;
I will see his righteousness.[p]
10Then my enemy will see it
and will be covered with
shame,[q]
she who said to me,
"Where is the LORD your
God?"
My eyes will see her downfall;[r]
even now she will be
trampled[s] underfoot
like mire in the streets.

11The day for building your
walls[t] will come,
the day for extending your
boundaries.
12In that day people will come to
you
from Assyria and the cities of
Egypt,

6:15
e Am 5:11
Zep 1:13
6:16
f 1Ki 16:25
g 1Ki 16:29-33
h Jer 7:24
i Jer 25:9
j Jer 51:51
7:2
a Ps 12:1
b Mic 3:10
c Jer 5:26
7:3
d Pr 4:16
7:4
e Eze 2:6
f Isa 22:5
Hos 9:7
7:5
g Jer 9:4
7:6
h Eze 22:7
i Mt 10:35-36*
7:7
j Ps 130:5
Isa 25:9
k Ps 4:3
7:8
l Pr 24:17
m Ps 37:24
Am 9:11
n Isa 9:2
7:9
o La 3:39-40
p Isa 46:13
7:10
q Ps 35:26
r Isa 51:23
s Zec 10:5
7:11
t Isa 54:11

d16 Septuagint; Hebrew *scorn due to my people*

even from Egypt to the
Euphrates
and from sea to sea
and from mountain to
mountain.[u]
13The earth will become desolate
because of its inhabitants,
as the result of their deeds.[v]

Prayer and Praise

14Shepherd[w] your people with
your staff,[x]
the flock of your inheritance,
which lives by itself in a forest,
in fertile pasture-lands.[a]
Let them feed in Bashan and
Gilead[y]
as in days long ago.

15"As in the days when you came
out of Egypt,
I will show them my
wonders.[z]"

16Nations will see and be
ashamed,[a]
deprived of all their power.
They will lay their hands on
their mouths
and their ears will become
deaf.

7:12
u Isa 19:23-25

7:13
v Isa 3:10-11

7:14
w Mic 5:4
x Ps 23:4
y Jer 50:19

7:15
z Ex 3:20
Ps 78:12

7:16
a Isa 26:11

7:17
b Isa 25:3
Isa 49:23
Isa 59:19

7:18
c Isa 43:25
Jer 50:20
d Ps 103:8-13
e Mic 2:12
f Ex 34:9
g Ps 103:9
h Jer 32:41

7:19
i Isa 43:25
j Jer 31:34

7:20
k Dt 7:8
Lk 1:72

17They will lick dust like a snake,
like creatures that crawl on
the ground.
They will come trembling out of
their dens;
they will turn in fear[b] to the
LORD our God
and will be afraid of you.
18Who is a God like you,
who pardons sin[c] and forgives[d]
the transgression
of the remnant[e] of his
inheritance?[f]
You do not stay angry[g] for
ever
but delight to show mercy.[h]
19You will again have compassion
on us;
you will tread our sins
underfoot
and hurl all our iniquities[i]
into the depths of the sea.[j]
20You will be true to Jacob,
and show mercy to Abraham,
as you pledged on oath to our
fathers[k]
in days long ago.

a14 Or *in the middle of Carmel*

NAHUM

1 An oracle[a] concerning Nineveh.[b] The book of the vision of Nahum the Elkoshite.

The LORD's Anger Against Nineveh

2 The LORD is a jealous[c] and
  avenging God;
 the LORD takes vengeance[d]
  and is filled with wrath.
The LORD takes vengeance on
  his foes
 and maintains his wrath
  against his enemies.
3 The LORD is slow to anger[e] and
  great in power;
 the LORD will not leave the
  guilty unpunished.[f]
His way is in the whirlwind and
  the storm,
 and clouds[g] are the dust of
  his feet.
4 He rebukes the sea and dries it
  up;
 he makes all the rivers run
  dry.
Bashan and Carmel[h] wither
 and the blossoms of Lebanon
  fade.
5 The mountains quake[i] before
  him
 and the hills melt away.[j]
The earth trembles at his
  presence,
 the world and all who live in
  it.
6 Who can withstand his
  indignation?
 Who can endure[k] his fierce
  anger?
His wrath is poured out like
  fire;[l]
 the rocks are shattered[m]
  before him.

7 The LORD is good,[n]
 a refuge in times of trouble.

1:1 *a* Isa 13:1; Isa 19:1; Jer 23:33-34; *b* Jnh 1:2; Na 2:8; Zep 2:13
1:2 *c* Ex 20:5; *d* Dt 32:41; Ps 94:1
1:3 *e* Ne 9:17; *f* Ex 34:7; *g* Ps 104:3
1:4 *h* Isa 33:9
1:5 *i* Ex 19:18; *j* Mic 1:4
1:6 *k* Mal 3:2; *l* Jer 10:10; *m* 1Ki 19:11
1:7 *n* Jer 33:11; *o* Ps 1:6
1:10 *p* 2Sa 23:6; *q* Isa 5:24; Mal 4:1
1:12 *r* Isa 10:34; *s* Isa 54:6-8; La 3:31-32
1:13 *t* Isa 9:4
1:14 *u* Isa 14:22; *v* Mic 5:13

He cares for[o] those who trust
  in him,
8 but with an overwhelming
  flood
he will make an end of
  ⌊Nineveh⌋;
 he will pursue his foes into
  darkness.

9 Whatever they plot against the
  LORD
 he[a] will bring to an end;
 trouble will not come a second
  time.
10 They will be entangled among
  thorns[p]
 and drunk from their wine;
 they will be consumed like dry
  stubble.[b][q]
11 From you, ⌊O Nineveh,⌋ has one
  come forth
 who plots evil against the
  LORD
 and counsels wickedness.

12 This is what the LORD says:

"Although they have allies and
  are numerous,
 they will be cut off[r] and pass
  away.
Although I have afflicted you,
  ⌊O Judah,⌋
 I will afflict you no more.[s]
13 Now I will break their yoke[t]
  from your neck
 and tear your shackles away."

14 The LORD has given a command
  concerning you, ⌊Nineveh⌋:
 "You will have no descendants
  to bear your name.[u]
I will destroy the carved
  images[v] and cast idols
 that are in the temple of your
  gods.

[a] 9 Or *What do you foes plot against the LORD? / He* [b] *10* The meaning of the Hebrew for this verse is uncertain.

I will prepare your grave,[w]
for you are vile."

15Look, there on the mountains,
the feet of one who brings
good news,[x]
who proclaims peace![y]
Celebrate your festivals,[z]
O Judah,
and fulfil your vows.
No more will the wicked invade
you;[a]
they will be completely
destroyed.

Nineveh to Fall

2 An attacker[a] advances
against you, ⌞Nineveh⌟.
Guard the fortress,
watch the road,
brace yourselves,
marshal all your strength!

2The LORD will restore[b] the
splendour[c] of Jacob
like the splendour of Israel,
though destroyers have laid
them waste
and have ruined their vines.
3The shields of his soldiers are
red;
the warriors are clad in
scarlet.[d]
The metal on the chariots
flashes
on the day they are made
ready;
the spears of pine are
brandished.**a**
4The chariots[e] storm through
the streets,
rushing back and forth
through the squares.
They look like flaming torches;
they dart about like lightning.

5He summons his picked troops,
yet they stumble[f] on their
way.
They dash to the city wall;
the protective shield is put in
place.
6The river gates[g] are thrown
open

1:14
w Eze 32:22-23
1:15
x Isa 40:9
Ro 10:15
y Isa 52:7
z Lev 23:2-4
a Isa 52:1
2:1
a Jer 51:20
2:2
b Eze 37:23
c Isa 60:15
2:3
d Eze 23:14-15
2:4
e Jer 4:13
2:5
f Jer 46:12
2:6
g Na 3:13
2:7
h Isa 59:11
i Isa 32:12
2:10
j Isa 29:22
2:11
k Isa 5:29
2:12
l Jer 51:34
2:13
m Jer 21:13
Na 3:5
n Ps 46:9
3:1
a Eze 22:2
Mic 3:10

and the palace collapses.
7It is decreed**b** that ⌞the city⌟
be exiled and carried away.
Its slave girls moan[h] like doves
and beat upon their breasts.[i]
8Nineveh is like a pool,
and its water is draining away.
"Stop! Stop!" they cry,
but no-one turns back.
9Plunder the silver!
Plunder the gold!
The supply is endless,
the wealth from all its
treasures!
10She is pillaged, plundered,
stripped!
Hearts melt, knees give way,
bodies tremble, every face
grows pale.[j]

11Where now is the lions' den,[k]
the place where they fed their
young,
where the lion and lioness went,
and the cubs, with nothing to
fear?
12The lion killed[l] enough for his
cubs
and strangled the prey for his
mate,
filling his lairs with the kill
and his dens with the prey.

13"I am against[m] you,"
declares the LORD Almighty.
"I will burn up your chariots in
smoke,[n]
and the sword will devour
your young lions.
I will leave you no prey on the
earth.
The voices of your messengers
will no longer be heard."

Woe to Nineveh

3 Woe to the city of blood,[a]
full of lies,
full of plunder,
never without victims!

a3 Hebrew; Septuagint and Syriac / *the horsemen rush to and fro* **b**7 The meaning of the Hebrew for this word is uncertain.

2 The crack of whips,
the clatter of wheels,
galloping horses
and jolting chariots!
3 Charging cavalry,
flashing swords
and glittering spears!
Many casualties,
piles of dead,
bodies without number,
people stumbling over the corpses[b]—
4 all because of the wanton lust of a harlot,
alluring, the mistress of sorceries,[c]
who enslaved nations by her prostitution[d]
and peoples by her witchcraft.

5 "I am against[e] you," declares the LORD Almighty.
"I will lift your skirts[f] over your face.
I will show the nations your nakedness[g]
and the kingdoms your shame.
6 I will pelt you with filth,[h]
I will treat you with contempt[i]
and make you a spectacle.[j]
7 All who see you will flee from you and say,
'Nineveh[k] is in ruins—who will mourn for her?'[l]
Where can I find anyone to comfort[m] you?"

8 Are you better than[n] Thebes,[a][o]
situated on the Nile,[p]
with water around her?
The river was her defence,
the waters her wall.
9 Cush[b][q] and Egypt were her boundless strength;
Put[r] and Libya[s] were among her allies.
10 Yet she was taken captive[t]
and went into exile.
Her infants were dashed[u] to pieces
at the head of every street.
Lots were cast for her nobles,
and all her great men were put in chains.
11 You too will become drunk;[v]
you will go into hiding[w]
and seek refuge from the enemy.

12 All your fortresses are like fig-trees
with their first ripe fruit;
when they are shaken,
the figs[x] fall into the mouth of the eater.
13 Look at your troops—
they are all women![y]
The gates[z] of your land
are wide open to your enemies;
fire has consumed their bars.[a]

14 Draw water for the siege,[b]
strengthen your defences![c]
Work the clay,
tread the mortar,
repair the brickwork!
15 There the fire will devour you;
the sword will cut you down
and, like grasshoppers, consume you.
Multiply like grasshoppers,
multiply like locusts![d]
16 You have increased the number of your merchants
till they are more than the stars of the sky,
but like locusts they strip the land
and then fly away.
17 Your guards are like locusts,[e]
your officials like swarms of locusts
that settle in the walls on a cold day—
but when the sun appears they fly away,
and no-one knows where.

3:3 b 2Ki 19:35; Isa 34:3
3:4 c Isa 47:9; d Isa 23:17; Eze 16:25-29
3:5 e Na 2:13; f Jer 13:22; g Isa 47:3
3:6 h Job 9:31; i 1Sa 2:30; Jer 51:37; j Isa 14:16
3:7 k Na 1:1; l Jer 15:5; m Isa 51:19
3:8 n Am 6:2; o Jer 46:25; p Isa 19:6-9
3:9 q 2Ch 12:3; r Eze 27:10; s Eze 30:5
3:10 t Isa 20:4; u Isa 13:16; Hos 13:16
3:11 v Isa 49:26; w Isa 2:10
3:12 x Isa 28:4
3:13 y Isa 19:16; Jer 50:37; z Na 2:6; a Isa 45:2
3:14 b 2Ch 32:4; c Na 2:1
3:15 d Joel 1:4
3:17 e Jer 51:27

a8 Hebrew *No Amon*   b9 That is, the upper Nile region

[18]O king of Assyria, your
shepherds[c] slumber;[f]
your nobles lie down to rest.[g]
Your people are scattered[h] on
the mountains
with no-one to gather them.
[19]Nothing can heal your wound;[i]
your injury is fatal.
Everyone who hears the news
about you
claps his hands[j] at your fall,
for who has not felt
your endless cruelty?

3:18
[f] Ps 76:5-6
[g] Isa 56:10
[h] 1Ki 22:17

3:19
[i] Jer 30:13
Mic 1:9
[j] Job 27:23
La 2:15
Zep 2:15

[c]*18* Or *rulers*

HABAKKUK

1 The oracle[a] that Habakkuk the prophet received.

Habakkuk's Complaint

2 How long, O LORD, must I call
for help,
but you do not listen?[b]
Or cry out to you, "Violence!"
but you do not save?[c]
3 Why do you make me look at
injustice?
Why do you tolerate[d] wrong?
Destruction and violence[e] are
before me;
there is strife,[f] and conflict
abounds.
4 Therefore the law[g] is
paralysed,
and justice never prevails.
The wicked hem in the
righteous,
so that justice is perverted.[h]

The LORD's Answer

5 "Look at the nations and
watch—
and be utterly amazed.[i]
For I am going to do something
in your days
that you would not believe,
even if you were told.[j]
6 I am raising up the
Babylonians,[a][k]
that ruthless and impetuous
people,
who sweep across the whole
earth
to seize dwelling-places not
their own.[l]
7 They are a feared and dreaded
people;[m]
they are a law to themselves
and promote their own honour.
8 Their horses are swifter[n] than
leopards,
fiercer than wolves at dusk.
Their cavalry gallops headlong;
their horsemen come from
afar.
They fly like a vulture
swooping to devour;
9 they all come bent on
violence.
Their hordes[b] advance like a
desert wind
and gather prisoners[o] like
sand.
10 They deride kings
and scoff at rulers.[p]
They laugh at all fortified
cities;
they build earthen ramps and
capture them.
11 Then they sweep past like the
wind[q] and go on—
guilty men, whose own
strength is their god."[r]

Habakkuk's Second Complaint

12 O LORD, are you not from
everlasting?
My God, my Holy One,[s] we
will not die.
O LORD, you have appointed[t]
them to execute judgment;
O Rock, you have ordained
them to punish.
13 Your eyes are too pure to look
on evil;
you cannot tolerate wrong.[u]
Why then do you tolerate the
treacherous?
Why are you silent while the
wicked
swallow up those more
righteous than themselves?
14 You have made men like fish in
the sea,
like sea creatures that have no
ruler.
15 The wicked foe pulls all of them
up with hooks,[v]

1:1 *a* Na 1:1
1:2 *b* Ps 13:1-2; Ps 22:1-2 *c* Jer 14:9
1:3 *d* ver 13 *e* Jer 20:8 *f* Ps 55:9
1:4 *g* Ps 119:126 *h* Job 19:7; Isa 1:23; Isa 5:20; Eze 9:9
1:5 *i* Isa 29:9 *j* Ac 13:41*
1:6 *k* 2Ki 24:2 *l* Jer 13:20
1:7 *m* Isa 18:7; Jer 39:5-9
1:8 *n* Jer 4:13
1:9 *o* Hab 2:5
1:10 *p* 2Ch 36:6
1:11 *q* Jer 4:11-12 *r* Da 4:30
1:12 *s* Isa 31:1 *t* Isa 10:6
1:13 *u* La 3:34-36
1:15 *v* Isa 19:8

[a]6 Or *Chaldeans* [b]9 The meaning of the Hebrew for this word is uncertain.

he catches them in his net,[w]
he gathers them up in his drag-net;
and so he rejoices and is glad.
16Therefore he sacrifices to his net
and burns incense[x] to his drag-net,
for by his net he lives in luxury
and enjoys the choicest food.
17Is he to keep on emptying his net,
destroying nations without mercy?[y]

2 I will stand at my watch[a]
and station myself on the ramparts;[b]
I will look to see what he will say[c] to me,
and what answer I am to give to this complaint.[a][d]

The LORD's Answer

2Then the LORD replied:

"Write[e] down the revelation
and make it plain on tablets
so that a herald[b] may run with it.
3For the revelation awaits an appointed time;
it speaks of the end[f]
and will not prove false.
Though it linger, wait[g] for it;
it[c] will certainly come and will not delay.[h]

4"See, he is puffed up;
his desires are not upright—
but the righteous will live by his faith[d][i]—
5indeed, wine[j] betrays him;
he is arrogant and never at rest.
Because he is as greedy as the grave[e]
and like death is never satisfied,[k]
he gathers to himself all the nations
and takes captive all the peoples.

1:15 w Jer 16:16
1:16 x Jer 44:8
1:17 y Isa 14:6; Isa 19:8
2:1 a Isa 21:8; b Ps 48:13; c Ps 85:8; d Ps 5:3
2:2 e Rev 1:19
2:3 f Da 8:17; Da 10:14; g Ps 27:14; h Eze 12:25; Heb 10:37-38
2:4 i Ro 1:17*; Gal 3:11*; Heb 10:37-38*
2:5 j Pr 20:1; k Pr 27:20; Pr 30:15-16
2:6 l Isa 14:4; m Am 2:8
2:7 n Pr 29:1
2:8 o Isa 33:1; Zec 2:8-9; p ver 17
2:9 q Jer 22:13
2:10 r Jer 26:19; s ver 16
2:11 t Jos 24:27; Lk 19:40
2:12 u Mic 3:10
2:13 v Isa 50:11; w Isa 47:13
2:14 x Nu 14:21; y Isa 11:9

6"Will not all of them taunt[l] him
with ridicule and scorn, saying,

" 'Woe to him who piles up stolen goods
and makes himself wealthy by extortion![m]
How long must this go on?'
7Will not your debtors[f] suddenly arise?
Will they not wake up and make you tremble?
Then you will become their victim.[n]
8Because you have plundered many nations,
the peoples who are left will plunder you.[o]
For you have shed man's blood;[p]
you have destroyed lands and cities and everyone in them.

9"Woe to him who builds[q] his realm by unjust gain
to set his nest on high,
to escape the clutches of ruin!
10You have plotted the ruin[r] of many peoples,
shaming[s] your own house and forfeiting your life.
11The stones[t] of the wall will cry out,
and the beams of the woodwork will echo it.

12"Woe to him who builds a city with bloodshed[u]
and establishes a town by crime!
13Has not the LORD Almighty determined
that the people's labour is only fuel for the fire,[v]
that the nations exhaust themselves for nothing?[w]
14For the earth will be filled with the knowledge of the glory[x] of the LORD,
as the waters cover the sea.[y]

[a]1 Or *and what to answer when I am rebuked*
[b]2 Or *so that whoever reads it*
[c]3 Or *Though he linger, wait for him; / he*
[d]4 Or *faithfulness*
[e]5 Hebrew *Sheol*
[f]7 Or *creditors*

15“Woe to him who gives drink to
his neighbours,
pouring it from the wineskin
till they are drunk,
so that he can gaze on their
naked bodies.
16You will be filled with shame[z]
instead of glory.
Now it is your turn! Drink and
be exposed![g][a]
The cup[b] from the LORD’s right
hand is coming round to
you,
and disgrace will cover your
glory.
17The violence[c] you have done to
Lebanon will overwhelm
you,
and your destruction of
animals will terrify you.[d]
For you have shed man’s
blood;[e]
you have destroyed lands and
cities and everyone in
them.

18“Of what value is an idol,[f]
since a man has carved it?
Or an image that teaches lies?
For he who makes it trusts in
his own creation;
he makes idols that cannot
speak.[g]
19Woe to him who says to wood,
‘Come to life!’
Or to lifeless stone, ‘Wake
up!’[h]
Can it give guidance?
It is covered with gold and
silver;[i]
there is no breath in it.
20But the LORD is in his holy
temple;[j]
let all the earth be silent[k]
before him.”

Habakkuk’s Prayer

3 A prayer of Habakkuk the prophet. On *shigionoth*.[a]

2LORD, I have heard[a] of your
fame;
I stand in awe[b] of your deeds,
O LORD.

2:16 z ver 10 a La 4:21 b Isa 51:22
2:17 c Jer 51:35 d Jer 50:15 e ver 8
2:18 f Jer 5:21 g Ps 115:4-5 Jer 10:14
2:19 h 1Ki 18:27 i Jer 10:4
2:20 j Ps 11:4 k Isa 41:1
3:2 a Ps 44:1 b Ps 119:120 c Ps 85:6 d Isa 54:8
3:3 e Ps 48:10
3:6 f Ps 114:1-6
3:7 g Jdg 7:24-25 h Ex 15:14
3:8 i Ex 7:20 j Ps 68:17
3:9 k Ps 7:12-13
3:10 l Ps 98:7 m Ps 93:3
3:11 n Jos 10:13 o Ps 18:14

Renew[c] them in our day,
in our time make them known;
in wrath remember mercy.[d]
3God came from Teman,
the Holy One from Mount
Paran. *Selah*[b]
His glory covered the heavens
and his praise filled the
earth.[e]
4His splendour was like the
sunrise;
rays flashed from his hand,
where his power was hidden.
5Plague went before him;
pestilence followed his steps.
6He stood, and shook the earth;
he looked, and made the
nations tremble.
The ancient mountains
crumbled
and the age-old hills
collapsed.[f]
His ways are eternal.
7I saw the tents of Cushan in
distress,
the dwellings of Midian[g] in
anguish.[h]
8Were you angry with the
rivers,[i] O LORD?
Was your wrath against the
streams?
Did you rage against the sea
when you rode with your
horses
and your victorious chariots?[j]
9You uncovered your bow,
you called for many arrows.[k]
Selah
You split the earth with rivers;
10 the mountains saw you and
writhed.
Torrents of water swept by;
the deep roared[l]
and lifted its waves[m] on high.
11Sun and moon stood still[n] in the
heavens
at the glint of your flying
arrows,[o]

g16 Masoretic Text; Dead Sea Scrolls, Aquila, Vulgate and Syriac (see also Septuagint) *and stagger* a1 Probably a literary or musical term b3 A word of uncertain meaning; possibly a musical term; also in verses 9 and 13

at the lightning of your
flashing spear.
12In wrath you strode through the
earth
and in anger you threshed[p]
the nations.
13You came out to deliver[q] your
people,
to save your anointed one.
You crushed[r] the leader of the
land of wickedness,
you stripped him from head to
foot. *Selah*
14With his own spear you pierced
his head
when his warriors stormed out
to scatter us,[s]
gloating as though about to
devour
the wretched[t] who were in
hiding.
15You trampled the sea with your
horses,
churning the great waters.[u]

16I heard and my heart pounded,
my lips quivered at the sound;

3:12
p Isa 41:15
3:13
q Ps 20:6
Ps 28:8
r Ps 68:21
Ps 110:6
3:14
s Jdg 7:22
t Ps 64:2-5
3:15
u Ex 15:8
Ps 77:19
3:17
v Joel 1:10-12, 18
w Jer 5:17
3:18
x Isa 61:10
Php 4:4
3:19
y Dt 33:29
Ps 46:1-5
z Dt 32:13
2Sa 22:34
Ps 18:33

decay crept into my bones,
and my legs trembled.
Yet I will wait patiently for the
day of calamity
to come on the nation invading
us.
17Though the fig-tree does not bud
and there are no grapes on the
vines,
though the olive crop fails
and the fields produce no
food,[v]
though there are no sheep in
the pen
and no cattle in the stalls,[w]
18yet I will rejoice in the LORD,[x]
I will be joyful in God my
Saviour.

19The Sovereign LORD is my
strength;[y]
he makes my feet like the feet
of a deer,
he enables me to go on the
heights.[z]

For the director of music. On
my stringed instruments.

ZEPHANIAH

1 The word of the LORD that came to Zephaniah son of Cushi, the son of Gedaliah, the son of Amariah, the son of Hezekiah, during the reign of Josiah[a] son of Amon king of Judah:

Warning of Coming Destruction

2"I will sweep away everything
from the face of the earth,"[b]
declares the LORD.
3"I will sweep away both men
and animals;
I will sweep away the birds of
the air[c]
and the fish of the sea.
The wicked will have only
heaps of rubble[a]
when I cut off man from the
face of the earth,"[d]
declares the LORD.

Against Judah

4"I will stretch out my hand[e]
against Judah
and against all who live in
Jerusalem.
I will cut off from this place
every remnant of Baal,[f]
the names of the pagan and
the idolatrous priests[g]—
5those who bow down on the
roofs
to worship the starry host,
those who bow down and swear
by the LORD
and who also swear by
Molech,[b][h]
6those who turn back from
following[i] the LORD
and neither seek[j] the LORD
nor enquire[k] of him.
7Be silent[l] before the Sovereign
LORD,
for the day of the LORD[m] is
near.
The LORD has prepared a
sacrifice;[n]
he has consecrated those he
has invited.
8On the day of the LORD's
sacrifice
I will punish[o] the princes
and the king's sons[p]
and all those clad
in foreign clothes.
9On that day I will punish
all who avoid stepping on the
threshold,[c]
who fill the temple of their gods
with violence and deceit.[q]

10"On that day," declares the
LORD,
"a cry will go up from the
Fish Gate,[r]
wailing from the New Quarter,
and a loud crash from the
hills.
11Wail,[s] you who live in the
market district;[d]
all your merchants will be
wiped out,
all who trade with[e] silver will
be ruined.[t]
12At that time I will search
Jerusalem with lamps
and punish those who are
complacent,[u]
who are like wine left on its
dregs,[v]
who think, 'The LORD will do
nothing,[w]
either good or bad.'
13Their wealth will be
plundered,[x]
their houses demolished.
They will build houses
but not live in them;

1:1 [a] 2Ki 22:1; 2Ch 34:1-35:25
1:2 [b] Ge 6:7
1:3 [c] Jer 4:25 [d] Hos 4:3
1:4 [e] Jer 6:12 [f] Mic 5:13 [g] Hos 10:5
1:5 [h] Jer 5:7
1:6 [i] Isa 1:4; Jer 2:13 [j] Isa 9:13 [k] Hos 7:7
1:7 [l] Hab 2:20; Zec 2:13 [m] ver 14; Isa 13:6 [n] Isa 34:6; Jer 46:10
1:8 [o] Isa 24:21 [p] Jer 39:6
1:9 [q] Am 3:10
1:10 [r] 2Ch 33:14
1:11 [s] Jas 5:1 [t] Hos 9:6
1:12 [u] Am 6:1 [v] Jer 48:11 [w] Eze 8:12
1:13 [x] Jer 15:13

[a]3 The meaning of the Hebrew for this line is uncertain. [b]5 Hebrew *Malcam*, that is, Milcom [c]9 See 1 Samuel 5:5. [d]11 Or *the Mortar* [e]11 Or *in*

they will plant vineyards
but not drink the wine.[y]

The Great Day of the LORD

14"The great day of the LORD[z] is
near[a]—
near and coming quickly.
Listen! The cry on the day of
the LORD will be bitter,
the shouting of the warrior
there.
15That day will be a day of wrath,
a day of distress and anguish,
a day of trouble and ruin,
a day of darkness and gloom,
a day of clouds and
blackness,[b]
16a day of trumpet and battle cry[c]
against the fortified cities
and against the corner
towers.[d]
17I will bring distress on the
people
and they will walk like blind[e]
men,
because they have sinned
against the LORD.
Their blood will be poured out[f]
like dust
and their entrails like filth.[g]
18Neither their silver nor their
gold
will be able to save them
on the day of the LORD's
wrath.[h]
In the fire of his jealousy
the whole world will be
consumed,[i]
for he will make a sudden end
of all who live in the earth.[j]"

2 Gather together,[a] gather
together,
O shameful[b] nation,
2before the appointed time
arrives
and that day sweeps on like
chaff,[c]
before the fierce anger[d] of the
LORD comes upon you,
before the day of the LORD's
wrath comes upon you.
3Seek[e] the LORD, all you humble
of the land,
you who do what he
commands.
Seek righteousness, seek
humility;[f]
perhaps you will be
sheltered[g]
on the day of the LORD's
anger.

Against Philistia

4Gaza[h] will be abandoned
and Ashkelon left in ruins.
At midday Ashdod will be
emptied
and Ekron uprooted.
5Woe to you who live by the sea,
O Kerethite[i] people;
the word of the LORD is against
you,[j]
O Canaan, land of the
Philistines.

"I will destroy you,
and none will be left."[k]

6The land by the sea, where the
Kerethites[a] dwell,
will be a place for shepherds
and sheep pens.[l]
7It will belong to the remnant of
the house of Judah;
there they will find pasture.
In the evening they will lie
down
in the houses of Ashkelon.
The LORD their God will care
for them;
he will restore their
fortunes.[b][m]

Against Moab and Ammon

8"I have heard the insults[n] of
Moab
and the taunts of the
Ammonites,
who insulted[o] my people
and made threats against their
land.
9Therefore, as surely as I live,"
declares the LORD Almighty,
the God of Israel,

1:13 y Dt 28:30,39; Am 5:11; Mic 6:15
1:14 z ver 7; Joel 1:15; a Eze 7:7
1:15 b Isa 22:5; Joel 2:2
1:16 c Jer 4:19; d Isa 2:15
1:17 e Isa 59:10; f Ps 79:3; g Jer 9:22
1:18 h Eze 7:19; i ver 2-3; Zep 3:8; j Ge 6:7
2:1 a 2Ch 20:4; Joel 1:14; b Jer 3:3; Jer 6:15
2:2 c Isa 17:13; Hos 13:3; d La 4:11
2:3 e Am 5:6; f Ps 45:4; Am 5:14-15; g Ps 57:1
2:4 h Am 1:6,7-8; Zec 9:5-7
2:5 i Eze 25:16; j Am 3:1; k Isa 14:30
2:6 l Isa 5:17
2:7 m Ps 126:4; Jer 32:44
2:8 n Jer 48:27; o Eze 25:3

a6 The meaning of the Hebrew for this word is uncertain. b7 Or *will bring back their captives*

"surely Moab[p] will become like
Sodom,[q]
the Ammonites[r] like
Gomorrah—
a place of weeds and salt pits,
a wasteland for ever.
The remnant of my people will
plunder[s] them;
the survivors of my nation
will inherit their land.[t]"

10This is what they will get in
return for their pride,[u]
for insulting[v] and mocking
the people of the LORD
Almighty.
11The LORD will be awesome[w] to
them
when he destroys all the
gods[x] of the land.
The nations on every shore will
worship him,[y]
every one in its own land.

Against Cush

12"You too, O Cushites,[c][z]
will be slain by my sword.[a]"

Against Assyria

13He will stretch out his hand
against the north
and destroy Assyria,
leaving Nineveh[b] utterly
desolate
and dry as the desert.[c]
14Flocks and herds will lie down
there,
creatures of every kind.
The desert owl[d] and the
screech owl
will roost on her columns.
Their calls will echo through
the windows,
rubble will be in the
doorways,
the beams of cedar will be
exposed.
15This is the carefree[e] city
that lived in safety.[f]
She said to herself,
"I am, and there is none
besides me."[g]
What a ruin she has become,
a lair for wild beasts!
All who pass by her scoff[h]
and shake their fists.

The Future of Jerusalem

3 Woe to the city of
oppressors,[a]
rebellious and defiled![b]
2She obeys[c] no-one,
she accepts no correction.[d]
She does not trust in the LORD,
she does not draw near[e] to
her God.
3Her officials are roaring lions,
her rulers are evening
wolves,[f]
who leave nothing for the
morning.
4Her prophets are arrogant;
they are treacherous[g] men.
Her priests profane the
sanctuary
and do violence to the law.[h]
5The LORD within her is
righteous;
he does no wrong.[i]
Morning by morning he
dispenses his justice,
and every new day he does not
fail,
yet the unrighteous know no
shame.

6"I have cut off nations;
their strongholds are
demolished.
I have left their streets
deserted,
with no-one passing through.
Their cities are destroyed;[j]
no-one will be left—no-one at
all.
7I said to the city,
'Surely you will fear me
and accept correction!'
Then her dwelling would not be
cut off,
nor all my punishments come
upon her.
But they were still eager
to act corruptly[k] in all they
did.

2:9 *p* Isa 15:1-16:14; Jer 48:1-47 *q* Dt 29:23 *r* Jer 49:1-6; Eze 25:1-7 *s* Isa 11:14 *t* Am 2:1-3
2:10 *u* Isa 16:6 *v* Jer 48:27
2:11 *w* Joel 2:11 *x* Zep 1:4 *y* Zep 3:9
2:12 *z* Isa 18:1; Isa 20:4 *a* Jer 46:10
2:13 *b* Na 1:1 *c* Mic 5:6
2:14 *d* Isa 14:23
2:15 *e* Isa 32:9 *f* Isa 47:8 *g* Eze 28:2 *h* Na 3:19
3:1 *a* Jer 6:6 *b* Eze 23:30
3:2 *c* Jer 22:21 *d* Jer 7:28 *e* Ps 73:28; Jer 5:3
3:3 *f* Eze 22:27
3:4 *g* Jer 9:4 *h* Eze 22:26
3:5 *i* Dt 32:4
3:6 *j* Lev 26:31
3:7 *k* Hos 9:9

c12 That is, people from the upper Nile region

8 Therefore wait[l] for me,"
declares the LORD,
"for the day I will stand up to
testify.[a]
I have decided to assemble the
nations,[m]
to gather the kingdoms
and to pour out my wrath on
them—
all my fierce anger.
The whole world will be
consumed[n]
by the fire of my jealous
anger.

9 "Then will I purify the lips of
the peoples,
that all of them may call[o] on
the name of the LORD
and serve[p] him shoulder to
shoulder.
10 From beyond the rivers of
Cush[b][q]
my worshippers, my scattered
people,
will bring me offerings.[r]
11 On that day you will not be put
to shame[s]
for all the wrongs you have
done to me,
because I will remove from this
city
those who rejoice in their
pride.
Never again will you be
haughty
on my holy hill.
12 But I will leave within you
the meek[t] and humble,
who trust[u] in the name of the
LORD.
13 The remnant[v] of Israel will do
no wrong;[w]
they will speak no lies,[x]
nor will deceit be found in
their mouths.
They will eat and lie down[y]
and no-one will make them
afraid.[z]"

14 Sing, O Daughter of Zion;[a]
shout aloud,[b] O Israel!

3:8
l Ps 27:14
m Joel 3:2
n Zep 1:18

3:9
o Zep 2:11
p Isa 19:18

3:10
q Ps 68:31
r Isa 60:7

3:11
s Joel 2:26-27

3:12
t Isa 14:32
u Na 1:7

3:13
v Isa 10:21
Mic 4:7
w Ps 119:3
x Rev 14:5
y Eze 34:15
Zep 2:7
z Eze 34:25-28

3:14
a Zec 2:10
b Isa 12:6

3:15
c Eze 37:26-28
d Isa 54:14

3:16
e Job 4:3
Isa 35:3-4
Heb 12:12

3:17
f Isa 63:1
g Isa 62:4

3:19
h Eze 34:16
Mic 4:6
i Isa 60:18

3:20
j Jer 29:14
Eze 37:12
k Isa 56:5
Isa 66:22
l Joel 3:1

Be glad and rejoice with all
your heart,
O Daughter of Jerusalem!
15 The LORD has taken away your
punishment,
he has turned back your
enemy.
The LORD, the King of Israel, is
with you;[c]
never again will you fear[d]
any harm.
16 On that day they will say to
Jerusalem,
"Do not fear, O Zion;
do not let your hands hang
limp.[e]
17 The LORD your God is with you,
he is mighty to save.[f]
He will take great delight[g] in
you,
he will quiet you with his love,
he will rejoice over you with
singing."

18 "The sorrows for the appointed
feasts
I will remove from you;
they are a burden and a
reproach to you.[c]
19 At that time I will deal
with all who oppressed you;
I will rescue the lame
and gather those who have
been scattered.[h]
I will give them praise[i] and
honour
in every land where they were
put to shame.
20 At that time I will gather you;
at that time I will bring[j] you
home.
I will give you honour[k] and
praise
among all the peoples of the
earth
when I restore your fortunes[d][l]
before your very eyes,"
says the LORD.

[a] *8* Septuagint and Syriac; Hebrew *will rise up to plunder* [b] *10* That is, the upper Nile region [c] *18* Or *"I will gather you who mourn for the appointed feasts; / your reproach is a burden to you* [d] *20* Or *I bring back your captives*

HAGGAI

A Call to Build the House of the LORD

1 In the second year of King Darius,[a] on the first day of the
sixth month, the word of the LORD
came through the prophet Haggai[b]
to Zerubbabel[c] son of Shealtiel,
governor[d] of Judah, and to
Joshua[a][e] son of Jehozadak,[f] the
high priest:
2This is what the LORD Almighty
says: "These people say, 'The time
has not yet come for the LORD's
house to be built.' "
3Then the word of the LORD came
through the prophet Haggai:[g] 4"Is
it a time for you yourselves to be
living in your panelled houses,[h]
while this house remains a ruin?[i]"
5Now this is what the LORD
Almighty says: "Give careful
thought[j] to your ways. 6You have
planted much, but have harvested
little.[k] You eat, but never have
enough. You drink, but never have
your fill. You put on clothes, but
are not warm. You earn wages,[l]
only to put them in a purse with
holes in it."
7This is what the LORD Almighty
says: "Give careful thought to your
ways. 8Go up into the mountains
and bring down timber and build
the house, so that I may take pleasure[m] in it and be honoured," says
the LORD. 9"You expected much,
but see, it turned out to be little.
What you brought home, I blew
away. Why?" declares the LORD
Almighty. "Because of my house,
which remains a ruin,[n] while each
of you is busy with his own house.
10Therefore, because of you the
heavens have withheld their dew
and the earth its crops.[o] 11I called
for a drought[p] on the fields and the
mountains, on the grain, the new
wine, the oil and whatever the
ground produces, on men and cattle, and on the labour of your
hands.[q]"
12Then Zerubbabel[r] son of Shealtiel, Joshua son of Jehozadak, the
high priest, and the whole remnant[s] of the people obeyed[t] the
voice of the LORD their God and the
message of the prophet Haggai, because the LORD their God had sent
him. And the people feared[u] the
LORD.
13Then Haggai, the LORD's messenger, gave this message of the
LORD to the people: "I am with[v]
you," declares the LORD. 14So the
LORD stirred up the spirit of Zerubbabel[w] son of Shealtiel, governor
of Judah, and the spirit of Joshua
son of Jehozadak, the high priest,
and the spirit of the whole remnant[x] of the people. They came
and began work on the house of the
LORD Almighty, their God, 15on the
twenty-fourth day of the sixth
month[y] in the second year of King
Darius.

The Promised Glory of the New House

2 On the twenty-first day of the
seventh month, the word of the
LORD came through the prophet
Haggai: 2"Speak to Zerubbabel son
of Shealtiel, governor of Judah, to
Joshua son of Jehozadak, the high
priest, and to the remnant of the
people. Ask them, 3'Who of you is
left who saw this house[a] in its former glory? How does it look to you
now? Does it not seem to you like
nothing?[b] 4But now be strong, O
Zerubbabel,' declares the LORD.

1:1 a Ezr 4:24 b Ezr 5:1 c Mt 1:12-13 d Ezr 5:3 e Ezr 2:2 f 1Ch 6:15; Ezr 3:2
1:3 g Ezr 5:1
1:4 h 2Sa 7:2 i ver 9; Jer 33:12
1:5 j La 3:40
1:6 k Dt 28:38 l Hag 2:16; Zec 8:10
1:8 m Ps 132:13-14
1:9 n ver 4
1:10 o Lev 26:19; Dt 28:23
1:11 p Dt 28:22; 1Ki 17:1 q Hag 2:17
1:12 r ver 1 s ver 14; Isa 1:9; Hag 2:2 t Isa 50:10 u Dt 31:12
1:13 v Mt 28:20; Ro 8:31
1:14 w Ezr 5:2 x ver 12
1:15 y ver 1
2:3 a Ezr 3:12 b Zec 4:10

[a]1 A variant of *Jeshua*; here and elsewhere in Haggai

'Be strong,[c] O Joshua son of Jehozadak, the high priest. Be strong, all you people of the land,' declares the LORD, 'and work. For I am with[d] you,' declares the LORD Almighty. 5'This is what I covenanted with you when you came out of Egypt.[e] And my Spirit[f] remains among you. Do not fear.'

6"This is what the LORD Almighty says: 'In a little while[g] I will once more shake the heavens and the earth,[h] the sea and the dry land. 7I will shake all nations, and the desired of all nations will come, and I will fill this house[i] with glory,' says the LORD Almighty. 8'The silver is mine and the gold is mine,' declares the LORD Almighty. 9'The glory[j] of this present house will be greater than the glory of the former house,' says the LORD Almighty. 'And in this place I will grant peace,' declares the LORD Almighty."

Blessings for a Defiled People

10On the twenty-fourth day of the ninth month,[k] in the second year of Darius, the word of the LORD came to the prophet Haggai: 11"This is what the LORD Almighty says: 'Ask the priests[l] what the law says: 12If a person carries consecrated meat in the fold of his garment, and that fold touches some bread or stew, some wine, oil or other food, does it become consecrated?[m]' "

The priests answered, "No."

13Then Haggai said, "If a person defiled by contact with a dead body touches one of these things, does it become defiled?"

"Yes," the priests replied, "it becomes defiled.[n]"

14Then Haggai said, " 'So it is with this people and this nation in my sight,' declares the LORD. 'Whatever they do and whatever they offer[o] there is defiled.

2:4 c 1Ch 28:20; Zec 8:9; Eph 6:10 d 2Sa 5:10; Ac 7:9
2:5 e Ex 29:46 f Ne 9:20; Isa 63:11
2:6 g Isa 10:25 h Heb 12:26*
2:7 i Isa 60:7
2:9 j Ps 85:9
2:10 k ver 1
2:11 l Lev 10:10-11; Dt 17:8-11; Mal 2:7
2:12 m Lev 6:27; Mt 23:19
2:13 n Lev 22:4-6
2:14 o Isa 1:13
2:15 p Hag 1:5 q Ezr 3:10 r Ezr 4:24
2:16 s Hag 1:6
2:17 t Hag 1:11 u Dt 28:22; 1Ki 8:37; Am 4:9 v Am 4:6
2:18 w Zec 8:9
2:21 x Ezr 5:2
2:22 y Da 2:44 z Mic 5:10 a Jdg 7:22
2:23 b Isa 43:10

15" 'Now give careful thought[p] to this from this day on[a]—consider how things were before one stone was laid[q] on another in the LORD's temple.[r] 16When anyone came to a heap of twenty measures, there were only ten. When anyone went to a wine vat to draw fifty measures, there were only twenty.[s] 17I struck all the work of your hands[t] with blight,[u] mildew and hail, yet you did not turn to me,' declares the LORD.[v] 18'From this day on, from this twenty-fourth day of the ninth month, give careful thought to the day when the foundation[w] of the LORD's temple was laid. Give careful thought: 19Is there yet any seed left in the barn? Until now, the vine and the fig-tree, the pomegranate and the olive tree have not borne fruit.

" 'From this day on I will bless you.' "

Zerubbabel the LORD's Signet Ring

20The word of the LORD came to Haggai a second time on the twenty-fourth day of the month: 21"Tell Zerubbabel[x] governor of Judah that I will shake the heavens and the earth. 22I will overturn royal thrones and shatter the power of the foreign kingdoms.[y] I will overthrow chariots[z] and their drivers; horses and their riders will fall, each by the sword of his brother.[a]

23" 'On that day,' declares the LORD Almighty, 'I will take you, my servant[b] Zerubbabel son of Shealtiel,' declares the LORD, 'and I will make you like my signet ring, for I have chosen you,' declares the LORD Almighty."

[a]15 Or *to the days past*

ZECHARIAH

A Call to Return to the LORD

1 In the eighth month of the second year of Darius,[a] the word of the LORD came to the prophet Zechariah[b] son of Berekiah,[c] the son of Iddo:[d]

2“The LORD was very angry[e] with your forefathers. 3Therefore tell the people: This is what the LORD Almighty says: ‘Return to me,’ declares the LORD Almighty, ‘and I will return to you,’[f] says the LORD Almighty. 4Do not be like your forefathers,[g] to whom the earlier prophets proclaimed: This is what the LORD Almighty says: ‘Turn from your evil ways[h] and your evil practices.’ But they would not listen or pay attention to me,[i] declares the LORD. 5Where are your forefathers now? And the prophets, do they live for ever? 6But did not my words and my decrees, which I commanded my servants the prophets, overtake your forefathers?

“Then they repented and said, ‘The LORD Almighty has done to us what our ways and practices deserve,[j] just as he determined to do.’ ”

The Man Among the Myrtle Trees

7On the twenty-fourth day of the eleventh month, the month of Shebat, in the second year of Darius, the word of the LORD came to the prophet Zechariah son of Berekiah, the son of Iddo.

8During the night I had a vision—and there before me was a man riding a red[k] horse! He was standing among the myrtle trees in a ravine. Behind him were red, brown and white horses.[l]

9I asked, “What are these, my lord?”

The angel[m] who was talking with me answered, “I will show you what they are.”

10Then the man standing among the myrtle trees explained, “They are the ones the LORD has sent to go throughout the earth.”[n]

11And they reported to the angel of the LORD, who was standing among the myrtle trees, “We have gone throughout the earth and found the whole world at rest and in peace.”[o]

12Then the angel of the LORD said, “LORD Almighty, how long will you withhold mercy from Jerusalem and from the towns of Judah, which you have been angry with these seventy[p] years?” 13So the LORD spoke kind and comforting words to the angel who talked with me.[q]

14Then the angel who was speaking to me said, “Proclaim this word: This is what the LORD Almighty says: ‘I am very jealous[r] for Jerusalem and Zion, 15but I am very angry with the nations that feel secure.[s] I was only a little angry, but they added to the calamity.’[t]

16“Therefore, this is what the LORD says: ‘I will return[u] to Jerusalem with mercy, and there my house will be rebuilt. And the measuring line[v] will be stretched out over Jerusalem,’ declares the LORD Almighty.

17“Proclaim further: This is what the LORD Almighty says: ‘My towns will again overflow with prosperity, and the LORD will again comfort[w] Zion and choose[x] Jerusalem.’ ”[y]

1:1 a Ezr 4:24; Ezr 6:15; b Ezr 5:1; c Mt 23:35; Lk 11:51; d ver 7; Ne 12:4
1:2 e 2Ch 36:16
1:3 f Mal 3:7; Jas 4:8
1:4 g 2Ch 36:15; h Ps 106:6; i 2Ch 24:19; Ps 78:8; Jer 6:17
1:6 j Jer 12:14-17; La 2:17
1:8 k Rev 6:4; l Zec 6:2-7
1:9 m Zec 4:1,4-5
1:10 n Zec 6:5-8
1:11 o Isa 14:7
1:12 p Da 9:2
1:13 q Zec 4:1
1:14 r Joel 2:18; Zec 8:2
1:15 s Jer 48:11; t Ps 123:3-4; Am 1:11
1:16 u Zec 8:3; v Zec 2:1-2
1:17 w Isa 51:3; x Isa 14:1; y Zec 2:12

Four Horns and Four Craftsmen

18Then I looked up—and there before me were four horns! 19I asked the angel who was speaking to me, "What are these?"

He answered me, "These are the horns[z] that scattered Judah, Israel and Jerusalem."

20Then the LORD showed me four craftsmen. 21I asked, "What are these coming to do?"

He answered, "These are the horns that scattered Judah so that no-one could raise his head, but the craftsmen have come to terrify them and throw down these horns of the nations who lifted up their horns[a] against the land of Judah to scatter its people."[b]

A Man With a Measuring Line

2 Then I looked up—and there before me was a man with a measuring line in his hand! 2I asked, "Where are you going?"

He answered me, "To measure Jerusalem, to find out how wide and how long it is."[a]

3Then the angel who was speaking to me left, and another angel came to meet him 4and said to him: "Run, tell that young man, 'Jerusalem will be a city without walls[b] because of the great number[c] of men and livestock in it. 5And I myself will be a wall[d] of fire around it,' declares the LORD, 'and I will be its glory[e] within.'

6"Come! Come! Flee from the land of the north," declares the LORD, "for I have scattered you to the four winds of heaven,"[f] declares the LORD.

7"Come, O Zion! Escape, you who live in the Daughter of Babylon!"[g] 8For this is what the LORD Almighty says: "After he has honoured me and has sent me against the nations that have plundered you—for whoever touches you touches the apple of his eye[h]—9I will surely raise my hand against them so that their slaves will plunder them.[a][i] Then you will know that the LORD Almighty has sent me.[j]

10"Shout and be glad, O Daughter of Zion.[k] For I am coming,[l] and I will live among you,"[m] declares the LORD. 11"Many nations will be joined with the LORD in that day and will become my people. I will live among you and you will know that the LORD Almighty has sent me to you. 12The LORD will inherit[n] Judah as his portion in the holy land and will again choose[o] Jerusalem. 13Be still[p] before the LORD, all mankind, because he has roused himself from his holy dwelling."

Clean Garments for the High Priest

3 Then he showed me Joshua[a][a] the high priest standing before the angel of the LORD, and Satan[b][b] standing at his right side to accuse him. 2The LORD said to Satan, "The LORD rebuke you,[c] Satan! The LORD, who has chosen[d] Jerusalem, rebuke you! Is not this man a burning stick snatched from the fire?"[e]

3Now Joshua was dressed in filthy clothes as he stood before the angel. 4The angel said to those who were standing before him, "Take off his filthy clothes."

Then he said to Joshua, "See, I have taken away your sin,[f] and I will put rich garments[g] on you."

5Then I said, "Put a clean turban[h] on his head." So they put a clean turban on his head and clothed him, while the angel of the LORD stood by.

6The angel of the LORD gave this charge to Joshua: 7"This is what the LORD Almighty says: 'If you will walk in my ways and keep my requirements, then you will govern my house[i] and have charge of my

1:19 z Am 6:13
1:21 a Ps 75:4; b Ps 75:10
2:2 a Eze 40:3; Rev 21:15
2:4 b Eze 38:11; c Isa 49:20; Jer 30:19; Jer 33:22
2:5 d Isa 26:1; e Rev 21:23
2:6 f Eze 17:21
2:7 g Isa 48:20
2:8 h Dt 32:10
2:9 i Isa 14:2; j Zec 4:9
2:10 k Zep 3:14; l Zec 9:9; m Lev 26:12; Zec 8:3
2:12 n Dt 32:9; Ps 33:12; Jer 10:16; o Zec 1:17
2:13 p Hab 2:20
3:1 a Hag 1:1; Zec 6:11; b Ps 109:6
3:2 c Jude 1:9; d Isa 14:1; e Am 4:11; Jude 1:23
3:4 f Eze 36:25; Mic 7:18; g Isa 52:1; Rev 19:8
3:5 h Ex 29:6
3:7 i Dt 17:8-11; Eze 44:15-16

[a]8, 9 Or *says after ... eye: 9"I ... plunder them."*
[a]1 A variant of *Jeshua*; here and elsewhere in Zechariah [b]1 *Satan* means *accuser.*

courts, and I will give you a place among these standing here.

8" 'Listen, O high priest Joshua and your associates seated before you, who are men symbolic[j] of things to come: I am going to bring my servant, the Branch.[k] 9See, the stone I have set in front of Joshua! There are seven eyes[c] on that one stone,[l] and I will engrave an inscription on it,' says the LORD Almighty, 'and I will remove the sin[m] of this land in a single day.

10" 'In that day each of you will invite his neighbour to sit under his vine and fig-tree,[n]' declares the LORD Almighty."

The Gold Lampstand and the Two Olive Trees

4 Then the angel who talked with me returned and wakened[a] me, as a man is wakened from his sleep.[b] 2He asked me, "What do you see?"[c]

I answered, "I see a solid gold lampstand[d] with a bowl at the top and seven lights[e] on it, with seven channels to the lights. 3Also there are two olive trees[f] by it, one on the right of the bowl and the other on its left."

4I asked the angel who talked with me, "What are these, my lord?"

5He answered, "Do you not know what these are?"

"No, my lord," I replied.[g]

6So he said to me, "This is the word of the LORD to Zerubbabel:[h] 'Not by might nor by power, but by my Spirit,'[i] says the LORD Almighty.

7"What[a] are you, O mighty mountain? Before Zerubbabel you will become level ground.[j] Then he will bring out the capstone[k] to shouts of 'God bless it! God bless it!' "

8Then the word of the LORD came to me: 9"The hands of Zerubbabel have laid the foundation[l] of this temple; his hands will also complete it.[m] Then you will know that the LORD Almighty has sent me[n] to you.

10"Who despises the day of small things?[o] Men will rejoice when they see the plumb-line in the hand of Zerubbabel.

"(These seven are the eyes[p] of the LORD, which range throughout the earth.)"

11Then I asked the angel, "What are these two olive trees[q] on the right and the left of the lampstand?"

12Again I asked him, "What are these two olive branches beside the two gold pipes that pour out golden oil?"

13He replied, "Do you not know what these are?"

"No, my lord," I said.

14So he said, "These are the two who are anointed[r] to[b] serve the Lord of all the earth."

The Flying Scroll

5 I looked again—and there before me was a flying scroll![a]

2He asked me, "What do you see?"

I answered, "I see a flying scroll, thirty feet long and fifteen feet wide."[a]

3And he said to me, "This is the curse[b] that is going out over the whole land; for according to what it says on one side, every thief[c] will be banished, and according to what it says on the other, everyone who swears falsely[d] will be banished. 4The LORD Almighty declares, 'I will send it out, and it will enter the house of the thief and the house of him who swears falsely by my name. It will remain in his house and destroy it, both its timbers and its stones.[e]' "

3:8 j Eze 12:11 k Isa 4:2
3:9 l Isa 28:16 m Jer 50:20
3:10 n 1Ki 4:25 Mic 4:4
4:1 a Da 8:18 b Jer 31:26
4:2 c Jer 1:13 d Ex 25:31 Rev 1:12 e Rev 4:5
4:3 f ver 11 Rev 11:4
4:5 g Zec 1:9
4:6 h Ezr 5:2 i Isa 11:2-4 Hos 1:7
4:7 j Jer 51:25 k Ps 118:22
4:9 l Ezr 3:11 m Ezr 3:8 Ezr 6:15 Zec 6:12 n Zec 2:9
4:10 o Hag 2:3 p Zec 3:9 Rev 5:6
4:11 q ver 3 Rev 11:4
4:14 r Ex 29:7 Ex 40:15 Da 9:24-26 Zec 3:1-7
5:1 a Eze 2:9 Rev 5:1
5:3 b Isa 24:6 Isa 43:28 Mal 3:9 Mal 4:6 c Ex 20:15 Mal 3:8 d Isa 48:1
5:4 e Lev 14:34-45 Hab 2:9-11 Mal 3:5

c9 Or *facets* a7 Or *Who* b14 Or *two who bring oil and* a2 Hebrew *twenty cubits long and ten cubits wide* (about 9 metres long and 4.5 metres wide)

The Woman in a Basket

5 Then the angel who was speaking to me came forward and said to me, "Look up and see what this is that is appearing."

6 I asked, "What is it?"

He replied, "It is a measuring basket."[b] And he added, "This is the iniquity[c] of the people throughout the land."

7 Then the cover of lead was raised, and there in the basket sat a woman! 8 He said, "This is wickedness," and he pushed her back into the basket and pushed the lead cover down over its mouth.[f]

9 Then I looked up—and there before me were two women, with the wind in their wings! They had wings like those of a stork,[g] and they lifted up the basket between heaven and earth.

10 "Where are they taking the basket?" I asked the angel who was speaking to me.

11 He replied, "To the country of Babylonia[d][h] to build a house[i] for it. When it is ready, the basket will be set there in its place."[j]

Four Chariots

6 I looked up again—and there before me were four chariots[a] coming out from between two mountains—mountains of bronze! 2 The first chariot had red horses, the second black,[b] 3 the third white,[c] and the fourth dappled—all of them powerful. 4 I asked the angel who was speaking to me, "What are these, my lord?"

5 The angel answered me, "These are the four spirits[a][d] of heaven, going out from standing in the presence of the Lord of the whole world. 6 The one with the black horses is going towards the north country, the one with the white horses towards the west,[b] and the one with the dappled horses towards the south."

7 When the powerful horses went out, they were straining to go throughout the earth.[e] And he said, "Go throughout the earth!" So they went throughout the earth.

8 Then he called to me, "Look, those going towards the north country have given my Spirit[c] rest[f] in the land of the north."

A Crown for Joshua

9 The word of the LORD came to me: 10 "Take ⌊silver and gold⌋ from the exiles Heldai, Tobijah and Jedaiah, who have arrived from Babylon.[g] Go the same day to the house of Josiah son of Zephaniah. 11 Take the silver and gold and make a crown,[h] and set it on the head of the high priest, Joshua[i] son of Jehozadak.[j] 12 Tell him this is what the LORD Almighty says: 'Here is the man whose name is the Branch,[k] and he will branch out from his place and build the temple of the LORD.[l] 13 It is he who will build the temple of the LORD, and he will be clothed with majesty and will sit and rule on his throne. And he will be a priest[m] on his throne. And there will be harmony between the two.' 14 The crown will be given to Heldai,[d] Tobijah, Jedaiah and Hen[e] son of Zephaniah as a memorial in the temple of the LORD. 15 Those who are far away will come and help to build the temple of the LORD,[n] and you will know that the LORD Almighty has sent me to you.[o] This will happen if you diligently obey[p] the LORD your God."

Justice and Mercy, Not Fasting

7 In the fourth year of King Darius, the word of the LORD came to Zechariah on the fourth day of the ninth month, the month of Kislev.[a] 2 The people of Bethel

5:8 *f* Mic 6:11
5:9 *g* Lev 11:19
5:11 *h* Ge 10:10 *i* Jer 29:5,28 *j* Da 1:2
6:1 *a* ver 5
6:2 *b* Rev 6:5
6:3 *c* Rev 6:2
6:5 *d* Eze 37:9; Mt 24:31; Rev 7:1
6:7 *e* Zec 1:10
6:8 *f* Eze 5:13; Eze 24:13
6:10 *g* Ezr 7:14-16; Jer 28:6
6:11 *h* Ps 21:3 *i* Zec 3:1 *j* Ezr 3:2
6:12 *k* Isa 4:2; Zec 3:8 *l* Ezr 3:8-10; Zec 4:6-9
6:13 *m* Ps 110:4
6:15 *n* Isa 60:10 *o* Zec 2:9-11 *p* Isa 58:12; Jer 7:23; Zec 3:7
7:1 *a* Ne 1:1

b6 Hebrew *an ephah*; also in verses 7–11
c6 Or *appearance*
d11 Hebrew *Shinar*
a5 Or *winds*
b6 Or *horses after them*
c8 Or *spirit*
d14 Syriac; Hebrew *Helem*
e14 Or *and the gracious one, the*

had sent Sharezer and Regem-
Melech, together with their men,
to entreat[b] the LORD 3by asking
the priests of the house of the
LORD Almighty and the prophets,
"Should I mourn[c] and fast in the
fifth[d] month, as I have done for so
many years?"

4Then the word of the LORD
Almighty came to me: 5"Ask all the
people of the land and the priests,
'When you fasted[e] and mourned in
the fifth and seventh months for
the past seventy years, was it
really for me that you fasted? 6And
when you were eating and drinking, were you not just feasting
for yourselves? 7Are these not
the words the LORD proclaimed
through the earlier prophets[f]
when Jerusalem and its surrounding towns were at rest[g] and prosperous, and the Negev and the
western foothills[h] were settled?' "

8And the word of the LORD came
again to Zechariah: 9"This is what
the LORD Almighty says: 'Administer true justice;[i] show mercy and
compassion to one another. 10Do
not oppress the widow or the
fatherless, the alien[j] or the poor.
In your hearts do not think evil of
each other.'[k]

11"But they refused to pay attention; stubbornly they turned their
backs and stopped up their ears.[l]
12They made their hearts as hard as
flint[m] and would not listen to the
law or to the words that the LORD
Almighty had sent by his Spirit
through the earlier prophets.[n] So
the LORD Almighty was very
angry.[o]

13" 'When I called, they did not
listen;[p] so when they called, I
would not listen,'[q] says the LORD
Almighty.[r] 14'I scattered[s] them
with a whirlwind[t] among all the
nations, where they were strangers. The land was left so desolate
behind them that no-one could
come or go. This is how they made
the pleasant land desolate.[u]' "

The LORD Promises to Bless Jerusalem

8 Again the word of the LORD
Almighty came to me. 2This
is what the LORD Almighty says:
"I am very jealous for Zion; I
am burning with jealousy for
her."

3This is what the LORD says: "I
will return[a] to Zion and dwell in
Jerusalem.[b] Then Jerusalem will
be called the City of Truth, and the
mountain of the LORD Almighty
will be called the Holy Mountain."

4This is what the LORD Almighty
says: "Once again men and women
of ripe old age will sit in the streets
of Jerusalem,[c] each with cane in
hand because of his age. 5The city
streets will be filled with boys and
girls playing there.[d]"

6This is what the LORD Almighty
says: "It may seem marvellous to
the remnant of this people at that
time,[e] but will it seem marvellous
to me?[f]" declares the LORD
Almighty.

7This is what the LORD Almighty
says: "I will save my people from
the countries of the east and the
west.[g] 8I will bring them back[h]
to live in Jerusalem; they will be
my people,[i] and I will be faithful
and righteous to them as their
God."

9This is what the LORD Almighty
says: "You who now hear these
words spoken by the prophets[j]
who were there when the foundation was laid for the house of the
LORD Almighty, let your hands
be strong[k] so that the temple
may be built. 10Before that time
there were no wages[l] for man or
beast. No-one could go about
his business safely because of his
enemy, for I had turned every
man against his neighbour. 11But
now I will not deal with the remnant of this people as I did in
the past,"[m] declares the LORD
Almighty.

7:2 b Jer 26:19; Zec 8:21
7:3 c Zec 12:12-14; d Jer 52:12-14; Zec 8:19
7:5 e Isa 58:5
7:7 f Zec 1:4; g Jer 22:21; h Jer 17:26
7:9 i Zec 8:16
7:10 j Ex 22:21; k Ex 22:22; Isa 1:17
7:11 l Jer 8:5; Jer 11:10; Jer 17:23
7:12 m Jer 17:1; Eze 11:19; n Ne 9:29; o Da 9:12
7:13 p Pr 1:24; q Isa 1:15; Jer 11:11; Jer 14:12; Mic 3:4; r Pr 1:28
7:14 s Dt 4:27; Dt 28:64-67; t Jer 23:19; u Jer 44:6
8:3 a Zec 1:16; b Zec 2:10
8:4 c Isa 65:20
8:5 d Jer 30:20; Jer 31:13
8:6 e Ps 118:23; Ps 126:1-3; f Jer 32:17,27
8:7 g Ps 107:3; Isa 11:11; Isa 43:5
8:8 h Zec 10:10; i Eze 11:19-20; Eze 36:28; Zec 2:11
8:9 j Ezr 5:1; k Hag 2:4
8:10 l Hag 1:6
8:11 m Isa 12:1

12"The seed will grow well, the
vine will yield its fruit,[n] the
ground will produce its crops,[o]
and the heavens will drop their
dew.[p] I will give all these things as
an inheritance[q] to the remnant of
this people. 13As you have been an
object of cursing[r] among the nations, O Judah and Israel, so will I
save you, and you will be a blessing.[s] Do not be afraid, but let your
hands be strong."
14This is what the LORD Almighty
says: "Just as I had determined to
bring disaster[t] upon you and
showed no pity when your fathers
angered me," says the LORD
Almighty, 15"so now I have determined to do good[u] again to Jerusalem and Judah. Do not be afraid.
16These are the things you are to
do: Speak the truth[v] to each other,
and render true and sound judgment in your courts;[w] 17do not plot
evil[x] against your neighbour, and
do not love to swear falsely.[y] I hate
all this," declares the LORD.
18Again the word of the LORD
Almighty came to me. 19This is
what the LORD Almighty says: "The
fasts of the fourth,[z] fifth,[a] seventh[b] and tenth[c] months will become joyful[d] and glad occasions
and happy festivals for Judah.
Therefore love truth[e] and peace."
20This is what the LORD Almighty
says: "Many peoples and the inhabitants of many cities will yet come,
21and the inhabitants of one city
will go to another and say, 'Let us
go at once to entreat[f] the LORD and
seek the LORD Almighty. I myself
am going.' 22And many peoples and
powerful nations will come to Jerusalem to seek the LORD Almighty
and to entreat him."[g]
23This is what the LORD Almighty
says: "In those days ten men from
all languages and nations will take
firm hold of one Jew by the hem of
his robe and say, 'Let us go with
you, because we have heard that
God is with you.' "[h]

8:12 n Joel 2:22 o Ps 67:6 p Ge 27:28 q Ob 1:17
8:13 r Jer 42:18 s Ge 12:2
8:14 t Jer 31:28 Eze 24:14
8:15 u ver 13 Jer 29:11 Mic 7:18-20
8:16 v Ps 15:2 Eph 4:25 w Zec 7:9
8:17 x Pr 3:29 y Pr 6:16-19
8:19 z Jer 39:2 a Jer 52:12 b 2Ki 25:25 c Jer 52:4 d Ps 30:11 e ver 16
8:21 f Zec 7:2
8:22 g Ps 117:1 Isa 60:3 Zec 2:11
8:23 h Isa 45:14 1Co 14:25
9:1 a Isa 17:1
9:2 b Jer 49:23 c Eze 28:1-19
9:3 d Job 27:16 Eze 28:4
9:4 e Isa 23:1 Eze 26:3-5 Eze 28:18
9:8 f Isa 52:1 Isa 54:14

Judgment on Israel's Enemies

An Oracle

9 The word of the LORD is
against the land of Hadrach
and will rest upon
Damascus[a]—
for the eyes of men and all the
tribes of Israel
are on the LORD—[a]
2and upon Hamath[b] too, which
borders on it,
and upon Tyre[c] and Sidon,
though they are very
skilful.
3Tyre has built herself a
stronghold;
she has heaped up silver like
dust,
and gold like the dirt of the
streets.[d]
4But the Lord will take away her
possessions
and destroy her power on the
sea,
and she will be consumed by
fire.[e]
5Ashkelon will see it and fear;
Gaza will writhe in agony,
and Ekron too, for her hope
will wither.
Gaza will lose her king
and Ashkelon will be deserted.
6Foreigners will occupy Ashdod,
and I will cut off the pride of
the Philistines.
7I will take the blood from their
mouths,
the forbidden food from
between their teeth.
Those who are left will belong
to our God
and become leaders in Judah,
and Ekron will be like the
Jebusites.
8But I will defend my house
against marauding forces.
Never again will an oppressor
overrun my people,
for now I am keeping watch.[f]

[a]1 Or *Damascus. / For the eye of the LORD is on all mankind, / as well as on the tribes of Israel.*

The Coming of Zion's King

9Rejoice greatly, O Daughter of
Zion!
Shout, Daughter of Jerusalem!
See, your king[b] comes to you,
righteous and having
salvation,[g]
gentle and riding on a donkey,
on a colt, the foal of a
donkey.[h]
10I will take away the chariots
from Ephraim
and the war-horses from
Jerusalem,
and the battle-bow will be
broken.[i]
He will proclaim peace to the
nations.
His rule will extend from sea
to sea
and from the River[c] to the
ends of the earth.[d][j]
11As for you, because of the blood
of my covenant[k] with you,
I will free your prisoners[l]
from the waterless pit.
12Return to your fortress,[m]
O prisoners of hope;
even now I announce that I
will restore twice as much
to you.
13I will bend Judah as I bend my
bow
and fill it with Ephraim.[n]
I will rouse your sons, O Zion,
against your sons, O Greece,[o]
and make you like a warrior's
sword.[p]

The LORD Will Appear

14Then the LORD will appear over
them;[q]
his arrow will flash like
lightning.[r]
The Sovereign LORD will sound
the trumpet;
he will march in the storms[s]
of the south,
15 and the LORD Almighty will
shield[t] them.
They will destroy
and overcome with
slingstones.

9:9
g Isa 9:6-7
Isa 43:3-11
Jer 23:5-6
Zep 3:14-15
Zec 2:10
h Mt 21:5*
Jn 12:15*

9:10
i Hos 1:7
Hos 2:18
Mic 4:3
Mic 5:10
Zec 10:4
j Ps 72:8

9:11
k Ex 24:8
l Isa 42:7

9:12
m Joel 3:16

9:13
n Isa 49:2
o Joel 3:6
p Jer 51:20

9:14
q Isa 31:5
r Ps 18:14
Hab 3:11
s Isa 21:1
Isa 66:15

9:15
t Isa 37:35
Zec 12:8
u Ex 27:2

9:16
v Isa 62:3
Jer 31:11

10:2
a Eze 21:21
b Eze 34:5
Hos 3:4
Mt 9:36

10:3
c Jer 25:34

10:4
d Isa 22:23
e Zec 9:10

They will drink and roar as
with wine;
they will be full like a bowl
used for sprinkling[e] the
corners[u] of the altar.
16The LORD their God will save
them on that day
as the flock of his people.
They will sparkle in his land
like jewels in a crown.[v]
17How attractive and beautiful
they will be!
Grain will make the young
men thrive,
and new wine the young
women.

The LORD Will Care for Judah

10 Ask the LORD for rain in
the springtime;
it is the LORD who makes the
storm clouds.
He gives showers of rain to
men,
and plants of the field to
everyone.
2The idols[a] speak deceit,
diviners see visions that lie;
they tell dreams that are false,
they give comfort in vain.
Therefore the people wander
like sheep
oppressed for lack of a
shepherd.[b]

3"My anger burns against the
shepherds,
and I will punish the leaders;[c]
for the LORD Almighty will care
for his flock, the house of
Judah,
and make them like a proud
horse in battle.
4From Judah will come the
cornerstone,
from him the tent peg,[d]
from him the battle-bow,[e]
from him every ruler.
5Together they[a] will be like
mighty men

b9 Or *King* c10 That is, the Euphrates
d10 Or *the end of the land* e15 Or *bowl, / like*
a4, 5 Or *ruler, all of them together. / 5They*

trampling the muddy streets
in battle.[f]
Because the LORD is with them,
they will fight and overthrow
the horsemen.[g]

6"I will strengthen the house of
Judah
and save the house of Joseph.
I will restore them
because I have compassion on
them.[h]
They will be as though
I had not rejected them,
for I am the LORD their God
and I will answer[i] them.
7The Ephraimites will become
like mighty men,
and their hearts will be glad
as with wine.[j]
Their children will see it and be
joyful;
their hearts will rejoice in the
LORD.
8I will signal[k] for them
and gather them in.
Surely I will redeem them;
they will be as numerous[l] as
before.
9Though I scatter them among
the peoples,
yet in distant lands they will
remember me.[m]
They and their children will
survive,
and they will return.
10I will bring them back from
Egypt
and gather them from
Assyria.[n]
I will bring them to Gilead[o]
and Lebanon,
and there will not be room[p]
enough for them.
11They will pass through the sea
of trouble;
the surging sea will be
subdued
and all the depths of the Nile
will dry up.[q]
Assyria's pride[r] will be
brought down
and Egypt's sceptre[s] will pass
away.

12I will strengthen them in the
LORD
and in his name they will
walk,[t]"
declares the LORD.

11 Open your doors,
O Lebanon,[a]
so that fire may devour your
cedars!
2Wail, O pine tree, for the cedar
has fallen;
the stately trees are ruined!
Wail, oaks of Bashan;
the dense forest[b] has been cut
down!
3Listen to the wail of the
shepherds:
their rich pastures are
destroyed!
Listen to the roar of the lions;
the lush thicket of the Jordan
is ruined![c]

Two Shepherds

4This is what the LORD my God
says: "Pasture the flock marked
for slaughter. 5Their buyers
slaughter them and go unpunished.
Those who sell them say, 'Praise
the LORD, I am rich!' Their own
shepherds do not spare them.[d]
6For I will no longer have pity on
the people of the land," declares
the LORD. "I will hand everyone
over to his neighbour[e] and his
king. They will oppress the land,
and I will not rescue them from
their hands."[f]

7So I pastured the flock marked
for slaughter, particularly the oppressed of the flock. Then I took
two staffs and called one Favour
and the other Union, and I pastured
the flock. 8In one month I got rid of
the three shepherds.

The flock detested me, and I
grew weary of them 9and said, "I
will not be your shepherd. Let the
dying die, and the perishing perish.[g] Let those who are left eat one
another's flesh."

10Then I took my staff called Favour[h] and broke it, revoking[i] the

10:5 f 2Sa 22:43 g Am 2:15 Hag 2:22
10:6 h Zec 8:7-8 i Zec 13:9
10:7 j Zec 9:15
10:8 k Isa 5:26 l Jer 33:22 Eze 36:11
10:9 m Eze 6:9
10:10 n Isa 11:11 o Jer 50:19 p Isa 49:19
10:11 q Isa 19:5-7 Isa 51:10 r Zep 2:13 s Eze 30:13
10:12 t Mic 4:5
11:1 a Eze 31:3
11:2 b Isa 32:19
11:3 c Jer 2:15 Jer 50:44
11:5 d Jer 50:7 Eze 34:2-3
11:6 e Zec 14:13 f Isa 9:19-21 Jer 13:14 Mic 5:8 Mic 7:2-6
11:9 g Jer 15:2 Jer 43:11
11:10 h ver 7 i Ps 89:39 Jer 14:21

covenant I had made with all the nations. 11It was revoked on that day, and so the afflicted of the flock who were watching me knew it was the word of the LORD.

12I told them, "If you think it best, give me my pay; but if not, keep it." So they paid me thirty pieces of silver.[j]

13And the LORD said to me, "Throw it to the potter"—the handsome price at which they priced me! So I took the thirty pieces of silver and threw them into the house of the LORD to the potter.[k]

14Then I broke my second staff called Union, breaking the brotherhood between Judah and Israel.

15Then the LORD said to me, "Take again the equipment of a foolish shepherd. 16For I am going to raise up a shepherd over the land who will not care for the lost, or seek the young, or heal the injured, or feed the healthy, but will eat the meat of the choice sheep, tearing off their hoofs.

17"Woe to the worthless
shepherd,[l]
who deserts the flock!
May the sword strike his arm[m]
and his right eye!
May his arm be completely
withered,
his right eye totally
blinded!"[n]

Jerusalem's Enemies to Be Destroyed

An Oracle

12 This is the word of the LORD concerning Israel. The LORD, who stretches out the heavens,[a] who lays the foundation of the earth,[b] and who forms the spirit of man[c] within him, declares: 2"I am going to make Jerusalem a cup[d] that sends all the surrounding peoples reeling.[e] Judah[f] will be besieged as well as Jerusalem. 3On that day, when all the nations[g] of the earth are gathered against her, I will make Jerusalem an immovable rock[h] for all the nations. All who try to move it will injure[i] themselves. 4On that day I will strike every horse with panic and its rider with madness," declares the LORD. "I will keep a watchful eye over the house of Judah, but I will blind all the horses of the nations.[j] 5Then the leaders of Judah will say in their hearts, 'The people of Jerusalem are strong, because the LORD Almighty is their God.'

6"On that day I will make the leaders of Judah like a brazier[k] in a woodpile, like a flaming torch among sheaves. They will consume[l] right and left all the surrounding peoples, but Jerusalem will remain intact in her place.

7"The LORD will save the dwellings of Judah first, so that the honour of the house of David and of Jerusalem's inhabitants may not be greater than that of Judah.[m] 8On that day the LORD will shield[n] those who live in Jerusalem, so that the feeblest among them will be like David, and the house of David will be like God,[o] like the Angel of the LORD going before[p] them. 9On that day I will set out to destroy all the nations that attack Jerusalem.[q]

Mourning for the One They Pierced

10"And I will pour out on the house of David and the inhabitants of Jerusalem a spirit[a] of grace and supplication.[r] They will look on[b] me, the one they have pierced,[s] and they will mourn for him as one mourns for an only child, and grieve bitterly for him as one grieves for a firstborn son. 11On that day the weeping in Jerusalem will be great, like the weeping of Hadad Rimmon in the plain of Megiddo.[t] 12The land will mourn,[u]

11:12 *j* Ex 21:32 Mt 26:15
11:13 *k* Mt 27:9-10* Ac 1:18-19
11:17 *l* Jer 23:1 *m* Eze 30:21-22 *n* Jer 23:1
12:1 *a* Isa 42:5 Jer 51:15 *b* Ps 102:25 Heb 1:10 *c* Isa 57:16
12:2 *d* Ps 75:8 *e* Isa 51:23 *f* Zec 14:14
12:3 *g* Zec 14:2 *h* Da 2:34-35 *i* Mt 21:44
12:4 *j* Ps 76:6
12:6 *k* Isa 10:17-18 Zec 11:1 *l* Ob 1:18
12:7 *m* Jer 30:18 Am 9:11
12:8 *n* Joel 3:16 Zec 9:15 *o* Ps 82:6 *p* Mic 7:8
12:9 *q* Zec 14:2-3
12:10 *r* Isa 44:3 Eze 39:29 Joel 2:28-29 *s* Jn 19:34,37* Rev 1:7
12:11 *t* 2Ki 23:29
12:12 *u* Mt 24:30 Rev 1:7

a10 Or *the Spirit* b10 Or *to*

each clan by itself, with their wives by themselves: the clan of the house of David and their wives, the clan of the house of Nathan and their wives, [13]the clan of the house of Levi and their wives, the clan of Shimei and their wives, [14]and all the rest of the clans and their wives.

Cleansing From Sin

13 "On that day a fountain[a] will be opened to the house of David and the inhabitants of Jerusalem, to cleanse[b] them from sin and impurity.

[2]"On that day, I will banish the names of the idols[c] from the land, and they will be remembered no more," declares the LORD Almighty. "I will remove both the prophets[d] and the spirit of impurity from the land. [3]And if anyone still prophesies, his father and mother, to whom he was born, will say to him, 'You must die, because you have told lies in the LORD's name.' When he prophesies, his own parents will stab him.[e]

[4]"On that day every prophet will be ashamed[f] of his prophetic vision. He will not put on a prophet's garment[g] of hair[h] in order to deceive. [5]He will say, 'I am not a prophet. I am a farmer; the land has been my livelihood since my youth.'[a][i] [6]If someone asks him, 'What are these wounds on your body?'[b] he will answer, 'The wounds I was given at the house of my friends.'

The Shepherd Struck, the Sheep Scattered

[7]"Awake, O sword,[j] against my
shepherd,[k]
against the man who is close
to me!"
declares the LORD Almighty.
"Strike the shepherd,
and the sheep will be
scattered,[l]
and I will turn my hand
against the little ones.
[8]In the whole land," declares the
LORD,
"two-thirds will be struck
down and perish;
yet one-third will be left in
it.[m]
[9]This third I will bring into the
fire;[n]
I will refine them like silver[o]
and test them like gold.
They will call[p] on my name
and I will answer[q] them;
I will say, 'They are my
people,'[r]
and they will say, 'The LORD is
our God.[s]'"

The LORD Comes and Reigns

14 A day of the LORD[a] is coming when your plunder will be divided among you.

[2]I will gather all the nations to Jerusalem to fight against it; the city will be captured, the houses ransacked, and the women raped. Half of the city will go into exile, but the rest of the people will not be taken from the city.[b]

[3]Then the LORD will go out and fight[c] against those nations, as he fights in the day of battle. [4]On that day his feet will stand on the Mount of Olives,[d] east of Jerusalem, and the Mount of Olives will be split in two from east to west, forming a great valley, with half of the mountain moving north and half moving south. [5]You will flee by my mountain valley, for it will extend to Azel. You will flee as you fled from the earthquake[a][e] in the days of Uzziah king of Judah. Then the LORD my God will come,[f] and all the holy ones with him.[g]

[6]On that day there will be no light,[h] no cold or frost. [7]It will be a

13:1 *a* Jer 17:13 *b* Ps 51:2; Heb 9:14
13:2 *c* Ex 23:13; Eze 36:25; Hos 2:17 *d* 1Ki 22:22; Jer 23:14-15
13:3 *e* Dt 13:6-11; Dt 18:20; Jer 23:34; Eze 14:9
13:4 *f* Jer 6:15; Mic 3:6-7 *g* Mt 3:4 *h* 2Ki 1:8; Isa 20:2
13:5 *i* Am 7:14
13:7 *j* Jer 47:6 *k* Isa 40:11; Isa 53:4; Eze 37:24 *l* Mt 26:31*; Mk 14:27*
13:8 *m* Eze 5:2-4,12
13:9 *n* Mal 3:2 *o* Isa 48:10; 1Pe 1:6-7 *p* Ps 50:15 *q* Zec 10:6 *r* Jer 30:22 *s* Jer 29:12
14:1 *a* Isa 13:9; Mal 4:1
14:2 *b* Isa 13:6; Zec 13:8
14:3 *c* Zec 9:14-15
14:4 *d* Eze 11:23
14:5 *e* Am 1:1 *f* Isa 29:6; Isa 66:15-16 *g* Mt 16:27; Mt 25:31
14:6 *h* Isa 13:10; Jer 4:23

a5 Or *farmer; a man sold me in my youth*
b6 Or *wounds between your hands*
a5 Or [5]*My mountain valley will be blocked and will extend to Azel. It will be blocked as it was blocked because of the earthquake*

unique[i] day, without daytime or
night-time[j]—a day known to the
LORD. When evening comes, there
will be light.[k]
8On that day living water[l] will
flow out from Jerusalem, half to
the eastern[m] sea[b] and half to the
western sea,[c] in summer and in
winter.
9The LORD will be king over the
whole earth.[n] On that day there
will be one LORD, and his name the
only name.[o]
10The whole land, from Geba[p] to
Rimmon, south of Jerusalem, will
become like the Arabah. But Jerusalem will be raised up[q] and remain in its place,[r] from the
Benjamin Gate to the site of the
First Gate, to the Corner Gate, and
from the Tower of Hananel to the
royal winepresses. 11It will be inhabited; never again will it be destroyed. Jerusalem will be
secure.[s]
12This is the plague with which
the LORD will strike all the nations
that fought against Jerusalem:
Their flesh will rot while they are
still standing on their feet, their
eyes will rot in their sockets, and
their tongues will rot in their
mouths.[t] 13On that day men will be
stricken by the LORD with great
panic. Each man will seize the hand
of another, and they will attack
each other.[u] 14Judah[v] too will
fight at Jerusalem. The wealth of
all the surrounding nations will
be collected[w]—great quantities
of gold and silver and clothing.

14:7
i Jer 30:7
j Rev 21:23-25
Rev 22:5
k Isa 30:26

14:8
l Eze 47:1-12
Jn 7:38
Rev 22:1-2
m Joel 2:20

14:9
n Dt 6:4
Isa 45:24
Rev 11:15
o Eph 4:5-6

14:10
p 1Ki 15:22
q Jer 30:18
Am 9:11
r Zec 12:6

14:11
s Eze 34:25-28

14:12
t Lev 26:16
Dt 28:22

14:13
u Zec 11:6

14:14
v Zec 12:2
w Isa 23:18

14:15
x ver 12

14:16
y Isa 60:6-9

14:17
z Jer 14:4
Am 4:7

14:18
a ver 12

14:20
b Eze 46:20
c Zec 9:15

14:21
d Ro 14:6-7
e Ne 8:10
f Zec 9:8
g Eze 44:9

15A similar plague[x] will strike the
horses and mules, the camels and
donkeys, and all the animals in
those camps.
16Then the survivors from all the
nations that have attacked Jerusalem will go up year after year
to worship the King, the LORD
Almighty, and to celebrate the
Feast of Tabernacles.[y] 17If any of
the peoples of the earth do not go
up to Jerusalem to worship the
King, the LORD Almighty, they will
have no rain.[z] 18If the Egyptian
people do not go up and take part,
they will have no rain. The LORD[d]
will bring on them the plague he inflicts on the nations that do not go
up to celebrate the Feast of Tabernacles.[a] 19This will be the punishment of Egypt and the punishment
of all the nations that do not go up
to celebrate the Feast of Tabernacles.
20On that day HOLY TO THE LORD
will be inscribed on the bells of the
horses, and the cooking pots[b] in
the LORD's house will be like the sacred bowls[c] in front of the altar.
21Every pot in Jerusalem and Judah will be holy[d] to the LORD
Almighty, and all who come to sacrifice will take some of the pots and
cook in them. And on that day[e]
there will no longer be a Canaanite[e][f] in the house of the LORD
Almighty.[g]

b8 That is, the Dead Sea c8 That is, the Mediterranean d18 Or *part, then the LORD*
e21 Or *merchant*

MALACHI

1 An oracle:[a] The word[b] of the LORD to Israel through Malachi.[a]

Jacob Loved, Esau Hated

2 “I have loved[c] you,” says the LORD.

“But you ask, ‘How have you loved us?’

“Was not Esau Jacob’s brother?” the LORD says. “Yet I have loved Jacob,[d] 3 but Esau I have hated, and I have turned his mountains into a wasteland[e] and left his inheritance to the desert jackals.[f]”

4 Edom may say, “Though we have been crushed, we will rebuild[g] the ruins.”

But this is what the LORD Almighty says: “They may build, but I will demolish. They will be called the Wicked Land, a people always under the wrath of the LORD.[h] 5 You will see it with your own eyes and say, ‘Great[i] is the LORD—even beyond the borders of Israel!’[j]

Blemished Sacrifices

6 “A son honours his father, and a servant his master. If I am a father, where is the honour due to me? If I am a master, where is the respect[k] due to me?” says the LORD Almighty.[l] “It is you, O priests, who show contempt for my name.

“But you ask, ‘How have we shown contempt for your name?’

7 “You place defiled food[m] on my altar.

“But you ask, ‘How have we defiled you?’

“By saying that the LORD’s table is contemptible. 8 When you bring blind animals for sacrifice, is that not wrong? When you sacrifice crippled or diseased animals,[n] is that not wrong? Try offering them to your governor! Would he be pleased with you? Would he accept you?” says the LORD Almighty.[o]

9 “Now implore God to be gracious to us. With such offerings[p] from your hands, will he accept you?”—says the LORD Almighty.

10 “Oh, that one of you would shut the temple doors, so that you would not light useless fires on my altar! I am not pleased[q] with you,” says the LORD Almighty, “and I will accept no offering[r] from your hands. 11 My name will be great among the nations, from the rising to the setting of the sun. In every place incense[s] and pure offerings will be brought to my name, because my name will be great among the nations,” says the LORD Almighty.

12 “But you profane it by saying of the Lord’s table, ‘It is defiled’, and of its food,[t] ‘It is contemptible.’ 13 And you say, ‘What a burden!’[u] and you sniff at it contemptuously,” says the LORD Almighty.

“When you bring injured, crippled or diseased animals and offer them as sacrifices, should I accept them from your hands?” says the LORD. 14 “Cursed is the cheat who has an acceptable male in his flock and vows to give it, but then sacrifices a blemished animal[v] to the Lord. For I am a great king,[w]” says the LORD Almighty, “and my name is to be feared among the nations.

Admonition for the Priests

2 “And now this admonition is for you, O priests.[a] 2 If you do not listen, and if you do not set your heart to honour my name,” says the LORD Almighty, “I will send a

1:1 *a* Na 1:1 *b* 1Pe 4:11
1:2 *c* Dt 4:37 *d* Ro 9:13*
1:3 *e* Isa 34:10 *f* Eze 35:3-9
1:4 *g* Isa 9:10 *h* Eze 25:12-14
1:5 *i* Ps 35:27 Mic 5:4 *j* Am 1:11-12
1:6 *k* Isa 1:2 *l* Job 5:17
1:7 *m* ver 12 Lev 21:6
1:8 *n* Lev 22:22 Dt 15:21 *o* Isa 43:23
1:9 *p* Lev 23:33-44
1:10 *q* Hos 5:6 *r* Isa 1:11-14 Jer 14:12
1:11 *s* Isa 60:6-7 Rev 8:3
1:12 *t* ver 7
1:13 *u* Isa 43:22-24
1:14 *v* Lev 22:18-21 *w* 1Ti 6:15
2:1 *a* ver 7

[a] 1 *Malachi* means *my messenger*.

curse[b] upon you, and I will curse your blessings. Yes, I have already cursed them, because you have not set your heart to honour me.

3“Because of you I will rebuke[a] your descendants;[b] I will spread on your faces the offal[c] from your festival sacrifices, and you will be carried off with it.[d] 4And you will know that I have sent you this admonition so that my covenant with Levi[e] may continue,” says the LORD Almighty. 5“My covenant was with him, a covenant[f] of life and peace,[g] and I gave them to him; this called for reverence and he revered me and stood in awe of my name. 6True instruction[h] was in his mouth and nothing false was found on his lips. He walked with me in peace and uprightness, and turned many from sin.[i]

7“For the lips of a priest[j] ought to preserve knowledge, and from his mouth men should seek instruction[k]—because he is the messenger[l] of the LORD Almighty. 8But you have turned from the way and by your teaching have caused many to stumble;[m] you have violated the covenant with Levi,” says the LORD Almighty. 9“So I have caused you to be despised[n] and humiliated before all the people, because you have not followed my ways but have shown partiality in matters of the law.”

Judah Unfaithful

10Have we not all one Father?[c][o] Did not one God create us? Why do we profane the covenant[p] of our fathers by breaking faith with one another?

11Judah has broken faith. A detestable thing has been committed in Israel and in Jerusalem: Judah has desecrated the sanctuary the LORD loves, by marrying[q] the daughter of a foreign god.[r] 12As for the man who does this, whoever he may be, may the LORD cut him off[s] from the tents of Jacob[d]—even though he brings offerings[t] to the LORD Almighty.

13Another thing you do: You flood the LORD’s altar with tears. You weep and wail because he no longer pays attention[u] to your offerings or accepts them with pleasure from your hands. 14You ask, “Why?” It is because the LORD is acting as the witness between you and the wife of your youth,[v] because you have broken faith with her, though she is your partner, the wife of your marriage covenant.

15Has not ⌊the LORD⌋ made them one?[w] In flesh and spirit they are his. And why one? Because he was seeking godly offspring.[e][x] So guard yourself in your spirit, and do not break faith with the wife of your youth.

16“I hate divorce,[y]” says the LORD God of Israel, “and I hate a man’s covering himself[f] with violence as well as with his garment,” says the LORD Almighty.

So guard yourself in your spirit, and do not break faith.

The Day of Judgment

17You have wearied[z] the LORD with your words.

“How have we wearied him?” you ask.

By saying, “All who do evil are good in the eyes of the LORD, and he is pleased with them” or “Where is the God of justice?”

3 “See, I will send my messenger, who will prepare the way before me.[a] Then suddenly the Lord you are seeking will come to his temple; the messenger of the covenant, whom you desire, will come,” says the LORD Almighty.

[a]3 Or *cut off* (see Septuagint) [b]3 Or *will blight your corn* [c]10 Or *father* [d]12 Or 12*May the LORD cut off from the tents of Jacob anyone who gives testimony on behalf of the man who does this* [e]15 Or 15*But the one ⌊who is our father⌋ did not do this, not as long as life remained in him. And what was he seeking? An offspring from God* [f]16 Or *his wife*

2:2 *b* Dt 28:20
2:3 *c* Ex 29:14 *d* 1Ki 14:10
2:4 *e* Nu 3:12
2:5 *f* Dt 33:9 *g* Nu 25:12
2:6 *h* Dt 33:10 *i* Jer 23:22; Jas 5:19-20
2:7 *j* Jer 18:18 *k* Lev 10:11 *l* Nu 27:21
2:8 *m* Jer 18:15
2:9 *n* 1Sa 2:30
2:10 *o* 1Co 8:6 *p* Ex 19:5
2:11 *q* Ne 13:23 *r* Ezr 9:1; Jer 3:7-9
2:12 *s* Eze 24:21 *t* Mal 1:10
2:13 *u* Jer 14:12
2:14 *v* Pr 5:18
2:15 *w* Ge 2:24; Mt 19:4-6 *x* 1Co 7:14
2:16 *y* Dt 24:1; Mt 5:31-32; Mt 19:4-9
2:17 *z* Isa 43:24
3:1 *a* Isa 40:3; Mt 11:10*; Mk 1:2*; Lk 7:27*

2 But who can endure[b] the day of his coming? Who can stand when he appears? For he will be like a refiner's fire[c] or a launderer's soap. 3 He will sit as a refiner and purifier of silver;[d] he will purify[e] the Levites and refine them like gold and silver. Then the LORD will have men who will bring offerings in righteousness, 4 and the offerings[f] of Judah and Jerusalem will be acceptable to the LORD, as in days gone by, as in former years.[g]

5 "So I will come near to you for judgment. I will be quick to testify against sorcerers, adulterers and perjurers,[h] against those who defraud labourers of their wages,[i] who oppress the widows[j] and the fatherless, and deprive aliens of justice, but do not fear me," says the LORD Almighty.

Robbing God

6 "I the LORD do not change.[k] So you, O descendants of Jacob, are not destroyed. 7 Ever since the time of your forefathers you have turned away[l] from my decrees and have not kept them. Return to me, and I will return to you,"[m] says the LORD Almighty.

"But you ask, 'How are we to return?'

8 "Will a man rob God? Yet you rob me.

"But you ask, 'How do we rob you?'

"In tithes[n] and offerings. 9 You are under a curse—the whole nation of you—because you are robbing me. 10 Bring the whole tithe into the storehouse,[o] that there may be food in my house. Test me in this," says the LORD Almighty, "and see if I will not throw open the floodgates[p] of heaven and pour out so much blessing that you will not have room enough for it. 11 I will prevent pests from devouring your crops, and the vines in your fields will not cast their fruit," says the LORD Almighty. 12 "Then all the nations will call you blessed,[q] for yours will be a delightful land,"[r] says the LORD Almighty.

13 "You have said harsh things[s] against me," says the LORD.

"Yet you ask, 'What have we said against you?'

14 "You have said, 'It is futile[t] to serve God. What did we gain by carrying out his requirements and going about like mourners[u] before the LORD Almighty? 15 But now we call the arrogant blessed. Certainly the evildoers[v] prosper, and even those who challenge God escape.' "

16 Then those who feared the LORD talked with each other, and the LORD listened and heard.[w] A scroll[x] of remembrance was written in his presence concerning those who feared the LORD and honoured his name.

17 "They will be mine," says the LORD Almighty, "in the day when I make up my treasured possession.[a][y] I will spare[z] them, just as in compassion a man spares his son who serves him. 18 And you will again see the distinction between the righteous[a] and the wicked, between those who serve God and those who do not.

The Day of the LORD

4 "Surely the day is coming;[a] it will burn like a furnace. All the arrogant and every evildoer will be stubble,[b] and that day that is coming will set them on fire," says the LORD Almighty. "Not a root or a branch will be left to them. 2 But for you who revere my name, the sun of righteousness[c] will rise with healing[d] in its wings. And you will go out and leap[e] like calves released from the stall. 3 Then you will trample[f] down the wicked; they will be ashes[g] under the soles of your feet on the day when I do

3:2 b Eze 22:14; Rev 6:17; c Zec 13:9; Mt 3:10-12
3:3 d Da 12:10; e Isa 1:25
3:4 f 2Ch 7:12; Ps 51:19; Mal 1:11; g 2Ch 7:3
3:5 h Jer 7:9; i Lev 19:13; Jas 5:4; j Ex 22:22
3:6 k Nu 23:19; Jas 1:17
3:7 l Jer 7:26; Ac 7:51; m Zec 1:3
3:8 n Ne 13:10-12
3:10 o Ne 13:12; p 2Ki 7:2
3:12 q Isa 61:9; r Isa 62:4
3:13 s Mal 2:17
3:14 t Ps 73:13; u Isa 58:3
3:15 v Jer 7:10
3:16 w Ps 34:15; x Ps 56:8
3:17 y Dt 7:6; z Ps 103:13; Isa 26:20
3:18 a Ge 18:25
4:1 a Joel 2:31; b Isa 5:24; Ob 1:18
4:2 c Lk 1:78; Eph 5:14; d Isa 30:26; e Isa 35:6
4:3 f Job 40:12; g Eze 28:18

a17 Or *Almighty, "my treasured possession, in the day when I act*

these things," says the LORD
Almighty.
[4]"Remember the law[h] of my servant Moses, the decrees and
laws I gave him at Horeb for all
Israel.
[5]"See, I will send you the prophet
Elijah[i] before that great and
dreadful day of the LORD comes.[j]
[6]He will turn the hearts of
the fathers to their children,[k]
and the hearts of the children to
their fathers; or else I will
come and strike[l] the land with a
curse."[m]

4:4 *h* Ps 147:19
4:5 *i* Mt 11:14 *j* Joel 2:31
4:6 *k* Lk 1:17 *l* Isa 11:4 Rev 19:15 *m* Zec 5:3

THE NEW TESTAMENT

MATTHEW

The Genealogy of Jesus

1:1–17pp Lk 3:23–38
1:3–6pp Ru 4:18–22
1:7–11pp 1Ch 3:10–17

1 A record of the genealogy of Jesus Christ the son of David,[a] the son of Abraham:[b]

[2]Abraham was the father of Isaac,[c]
Isaac the father of Jacob,[d]
Jacob the father of Judah and his brothers,[e]
[3]Judah the father of Perez and Zerah, whose mother was Tamar,[f]
Perez the father of Hezron,
Hezron the father of Ram,
[4]Ram the father of Amminadab,
Amminadab the father of Nahshon,
Nahshon the father of Salmon,
[5]Salmon the father of Boaz, whose mother was Rahab,
Boaz the father of Obed, whose mother was Ruth,
Obed the father of Jesse,
[6]and Jesse the father of King David.[g]

David was the father of Solomon, whose mother had been Uriah's wife,[h]
[7]Solomon the father of Rehoboam,
Rehoboam the father of Abijah,
Abijah the father of Asa,
[8]Asa the father of Jehoshaphat,
Jehoshaphat the father of Jehoram,
Jehoram the father of Uzziah,
[9]Uzziah the father of Jotham,
Jotham the father of Ahaz,
Ahaz the father of Hezekiah,
[10]Hezekiah the father of Manasseh,[i]
Manasseh the father of Amon,
Amon the father of Josiah,
[11]and Josiah the father of Jeconiah[a] and his brothers at the time of the exile to Babylon.[j]

[12]After the exile to Babylon:
Jeconiah was the father of Shealtiel,[k]
Shealtiel the father of Zerubbabel,[l]
[13]Zerubbabel the father of Abiud,
Abiud the father of Eliakim,
Eliakim the father of Azor,
[14]Azor the father of Zadok,
Zadok the father of Akim,
Akim the father of Eliud,
[15]Eliud the father of Eleazar,
Eleazar the father of Matthan,
Matthan the father of Jacob,
[16]and Jacob the father of Joseph, the husband of Mary,[m] of whom was born Jesus, who is called Christ.[n]

[17]Thus there were fourteen generations in all from Abraham to David, fourteen from David to the exile to Babylon, and fourteen from the exile to the Christ.[b]

The Birth of Jesus Christ

[18]This is how the birth of Jesus Christ came about: His mother Mary was pledged to be married to Joseph, but before they came together, she was found to be with

1:1
a 2Sa 7:12-16; Isa 9:6,7; Isa 11:1; Jer 23:5,6; Mt 9:27; Lk 1:32,69; Ro 1:3; Rev 22:16
b Ge 22:18; Gal 3:16
1:2
c Ge 21:3,12
d Ge 25:26
e Ge 29:35
1:3
f Ge 38:27-30
1:6
g 1Sa 16:1; 1Sa 17:12
h 2Sa 12:24
1:10
i 2Ki 20:21
1:11
j 2Ki 24:14-16; Jer 27:20; Da 1:1,2
1:12
k 1Ch 3:17
l 1Ch 3:19; Ezr 3:2
1:16
m Lk 1:27
n Mt 27:17

[a]*11* That is, Jehoiachin; also in verse 12
[b]*17* Or *Messiah.* "The Christ" (Greek) and "the Messiah" (Hebrew) both mean "the Anointed One".

child through the Holy Spirit.[o]
19Because Joseph her husband was
a righteous man and did not want to
expose her to public disgrace, he
had in mind to divorce[p] her quietly.
20But after he had considered
this, an angel of the Lord appeared
to him in a dream and said, "Joseph
son of David, do not be afraid to
take Mary home as your wife, because what is conceived in her is
from the Holy Spirit. 21She will
give birth to a son, and you are to
give him the name Jesus,[c][q] because he will save his people from
their sins."[r]
22All this took place to fulfil what
the Lord had said through the
prophet: 23"The virgin will be with
child and will give birth to a son,
and they will call him Immanuel"[d][s]—which means, "God with
us."
24When Joseph woke up, he did
what the angel of the Lord had commanded him and took Mary home
as his wife. 25But he had no union
with her until she gave birth to a
son. And he gave him the name
Jesus.[t]

The Visit of the Magi

2 After Jesus was born in Bethlehem in Judea,[a] during the
time of King Herod,[b] Magi[a] from
the east came to Jerusalem 2and
asked, "Where is the one who has
been born king of the Jews?[c] We
saw his star[d] in the east[b] and have
come to worship him."
3When King Herod heard this he
was disturbed, and all Jerusalem
with him. 4When he had called together all the people's chief priests
and teachers of the law, he asked
them where the Christ[c] was to be
born. 5"In Bethlehem[e] in Judea,"
they replied, "for this is what the
prophet has written:

6" 'But you, Bethlehem, in the
land of Judah,
are by no means least among
the rulers of Judah;
for out of you will come a ruler
who will be the shepherd of
my people Israel.'[d]"[f]

7Then Herod called the Magi secretly and found out from them the
exact time the star had appeared.
8He sent them to Bethlehem and
said, "Go and make a careful
search for the child. As soon as you
find him, report to me, so that I too
may go and worship him."
9After they had heard the king,
they went on their way, and the star
they had seen in the east[e] went
ahead of them until it stopped over
the place where the child was.
10When they saw the star, they
were overjoyed. 11On coming to the
house, they saw the child with his
mother Mary, and they bowed
down and worshipped him.[g] Then
they opened their treasures and
presented him with gifts[h] of gold
and of incense and of myrrh. 12And
having been warned[i] in a dream[j]
not to go back to Herod, they returned to their country by another
route.

The Escape to Egypt

13When they had gone, an angel[k]
of the Lord appeared to Joseph in a
dream.[l] "Get up," he said, "take
the child and his mother and escape
to Egypt. Stay there until I tell you,
for Herod is going to search for the
child to kill him."
14So he got up, took the child and
his mother during the night and left
for Egypt, 15where he stayed until
the death of Herod. And so was fulfilled what the Lord had said
through the prophet: "Out of Egypt
I called my son."[f][m]
16When Herod realised that he
had been outwitted by the Magi, he

1:18 *o* Lk 1:35
1:19 *p* Dt 24:1
1:21 *q* Lk 1:31 *r* Lk 2:11 Ac 5:31 Ac 13:23,28
1:23 *s* Isa 7:14 Isa 8:8,10
1:25 *t* ver 21
2:1 *a* Lk 2:4-7 *b* Lk 1:5
2:2 *c* Jer 23:5 Mt 27:11 Mk 15:2 Jn 1:49 Jn 18:33-37 *d* Nu 24:17
2:5 *e* Jn 7:42
2:6 *f* Mic 5:2 2Sa 5:2
2:11 *g* Isa 60:3 *h* Ps 72:10
2:12 *i* Heb 11:7 *j* ver 13,19,22 Mt 27:19
2:13 *k* Ac 5:19 *l* ver 12,19,22
2:15 *m* Hos 11:1 Ex 4:22,23

c21 *Jesus* is the Greek form of *Joshua,* which means *the LORD saves.* d23 Isaiah 7:14
a1 Traditionally *Wise Men* b2 Or *star when it rose* c4 Or *Messiah* d6 Micah 5:2
e9 Or *seen when it rose* f15 Hosea 11:1

was furious, and he gave orders to
kill all the boys in Bethlehem and
its vicinity who were two years old
and under, in accordance with the
time he had learned from the Magi.
17Then what was said through the
prophet Jeremiah was fulfilled:

18"A voice is heard in Ramah,
 weeping and great mourning,
Rachel weeping for her children
 and refusing to be comforted,
because they are no more."[g][n]

The Return to Nazareth

19After Herod died, an angel of
the Lord appeared in a dream[o] to
Joseph in Egypt 20and said, "Get up,
take the child and his mother and
go to the land of Israel, for those
who were trying to take the child's
life are dead."
21So he got up, took the child and
his mother and went to the land of
Israel. 22But when he heard that Ar-
chelaus was reigning in Judea in
place of his father Herod, he was
afraid to go there. Having been
warned in a dream,[p] he withdrew
to the district of Galilee,[q] 23and he
went and lived in a town called Nazareth.[r] So was fulfilled[s] what was
said through the prophets: "He will
be called a Nazarene."[t]

John the Baptist Prepares the Way

3:1–12pp Mk 1:3–8; Lk 3:2–17

3 In those days John the Baptist[a] came, preaching in the
Desert of Judea 2and saying, "Repent, for the kingdom of heaven[b]
is near." 3This is he who was spoken of through the prophet Isaiah:

"A voice of one calling in the
 desert,
'Prepare the way for the Lord,
 make straight paths for
 him.' "[a][c]

4John's clothes were made of
camel's hair, and he had a leather
belt round his waist.[d] His food was
locusts[e] and wild honey. 5People
went out to him from Jerusalem
and all Judea and the whole region
of the Jordan. 6Confessing their
sins, they were baptised by him in
the Jordan River.
7But when he saw many of the
Pharisees and Sadducees coming
to where he was baptising, he said
to them: "You brood of vipers![f]
Who warned you to flee from the
coming wrath?[g] 8Produce fruit in
keeping with repentance.[h] 9And do
not think you can say to yourselves,
'We have Abraham as our father.' I
tell you that out of these stones God
can raise up children for Abraham.
10The axe is already at the root of
the trees, and every tree that does
not produce good fruit will be cut
down and thrown into the fire.[i]
11"I baptise you with[b] water for
repentance. But after me will come
one who is more powerful than I,
whose sandals I am not fit to carry.
He will baptise you with the Holy
Spirit[j] and with fire.[k] 12His winnowing fork is in his hand, and he
will clear his threshing-floor, gathering his wheat into the barn and
burning up the chaff with unquenchable fire."[l]

The Baptism of Jesus

3:13–17pp Mk 1:9–11; Lk 3:21,22; Jn 1:31–34

13Then Jesus came from Galilee
to the Jordan to be baptised by
John.[m] 14But John tried to deter
him, saying, "I need to be baptised
by you, and do you come to me?"
15Jesus replied, "Let it be so now;
it is proper for us to do this to fulfil
all righteousness." Then John consented.
16As soon as Jesus was baptised,
he went up out of the water. At that
moment heaven was opened, and
he saw the Spirit of God[n] descending like a dove and lighting on him.
17And a voice from heaven[o] said,

2:18 *n* Jer 31:15
2:19 *o* ver 12,13,22
2:22 *p* ver 12,13,19; Mt 27:19 *q* Lk 2:39
2:23 *r* Lk 1:26; Jn 1:45,46 *s* Mt 1:22 *t* Mk 1:24
3:1 *a* Lk 1:13,57-66; Lk 3:2-19
3:2 *b* Da 2:44; Mt 4:17; Mt 6:10; Lk 11:20; Lk 21:31; Jn 3:3,5; Ac 1:3,6
3:3 *c* Isa 40:3; Mal 3:1; Lk 1:76; Jn 1:23
3:4 *d* 2Ki 1:8 *e* Lev 11:22
3:7 *f* Mt 12:34; Mt 23:33 *g* Ro 1:18; 1Th 1:10
3:8 *h* Ac 26:20
3:10 *i* Mt 7:19; Lk 13:6-9; Jn 15:2,6
3:11 *j* Mk 1:8 *k* Isa 4:4; Ac 2:3,4
3:12 *l* Mt 13:30
3:13 *m* Mk 1:4
3:16 *n* Isa 11:2; Isa 42:1
3:17 *o* Mt 17:5; Jn 12:28

g*18* Jer. 31:15 a*3* Isaiah 40:3 b*11* Or *in*

"This is my Son,[p] whom I love; with him I am well pleased."[q]

The Temptation of Jesus

4:1–11pp Mk 1:12,13; Lk 4:1–13

4 Then Jesus was led by the Spirit into the desert to be tempted by the devil. 2 After fasting for forty days and forty nights,[a] he was hungry. 3 The tempter[b] came to him and said, "If you are the Son of God,[c] tell these stones to become bread."

4 Jesus answered, "It is written: 'Man does not live on bread alone, but on every word that comes from the mouth of God.'[a]"[d]

5 Then the devil took him to the holy city[e] and had him stand on the highest point of the temple. 6 "If you are the Son of God," he said, "throw yourself down. For it is written:

" 'He will command his angels
concerning you,
and they will lift you up in
their hands,
so that you will not strike your
foot against a stone.'[b]"[f]

7 Jesus answered him, "It is also written: 'Do not put the Lord your God to the test.'[c]"[g]

8 Again, the devil took him to a very high mountain and showed him all the kingdoms of the world and their splendour. 9 "All this I will give you," he said, "if you will bow down and worship me."

10 Jesus said to him, "Away from me, Satan![h] For it is written: 'Worship the Lord your God, and serve him only.'[d]"[i]

11 Then the devil left him, and angels came and attended him.[j]

Jesus Begins to Preach

12 When Jesus heard that John had been put in prison,[k] he returned to Galilee.[l] 13 Leaving Nazareth, he went and lived in Capernaum,[m] which was by the lake in the area of Zebulun and Naphtali— 14 to fulfil what was said through the prophet Isaiah:

15 "Land of Zebulun and land of
Naphtali,
the way to the sea, along the
Jordan,
Galilee of the Gentiles—
16 the people living in darkness
have seen a great light;
on those living in the land of
the shadow of death
a light has dawned."[e][n]

17 From that time on Jesus began to preach, "Repent, for the kingdom of heaven[o] is near."

The Calling of the First Disciples

4:18–22pp Mk 1:16–20; Lk 5:2–11; Jn 1:35–42

18 As Jesus was walking beside the Sea of Galilee,[p] he saw two brothers, Simon called Peter[q] and his brother Andrew. They were casting a net into the lake, for they were fishermen. 19 "Come, follow me,"[r] Jesus said, "and I will make you fishers of men." 20 At once they left their nets and followed him.

21 Going on from there, he saw two other brothers, James son of Zebedee and his brother John.[s] They were in a boat with their father Zebedee, preparing their nets. Jesus called them, 22 and immediately they left the boat and their father and followed him.

Jesus Heals the Sick

23 Jesus went throughout Galilee,[t] teaching in their synagogues,[u] preaching the good news[v] of the kingdom,[w] and healing every disease and sickness among the people.[x] 24 News about him spread all over Syria,[y] and people brought to him all who were ill with various diseases, those suffering severe pain, the demon-possessed,[z] those having

3:17 *p* Ps 2:7; 2Pe 1:17,18 *q* Isa 42:1; Mt 12:18; Mt 17:5; Mk 1:11; Mk 9:7; Lk 9:35
4:2 *a* Ex 34:28; 1Ki 19:8
4:3 *b* 1Th 3:5 *c* Mt 3:17; Jn 5:25; Ac 9:20
4:4 *d* Dt 8:3
4:5 *e* Ne 11:1; Da 9:24; Mt 27:53
4:6 *f* Ps 91:11,12
4:7 *g* Dt 6:16
4:10 *h* 1Ch 21:1 *i* Dt 6:13
4:11 *j* Mt 26:53; Lk 22:43; Heb 1:14
4:12 *k* Mt 14:3 *l* Mk 1:14
4:13 *m* Mk 1:21; Lk 4:23,31; Jn 2:12; Jn 4:46,47
4:16 *n* Isa 9:1,2; Lk 2:32
4:17 *o* Mt 3:2
4:18 *p* Mt 15:29; Mk 7:31; Jn 6:1 *q* Mt 16:17,18
4:19 *r* Mk 10:21,28, 52
4:21 *s* Mt 20:20
4:23 *t* Mk 1:39; Lk 4:15,44 *u* Mt 9:35; Mt 13:54; Mk 1:21; Lk 4:15; Jn 6:59 *v* Mk 1:14 *w* Mt 3:2; Ac 20:25 *x* Mt 8:16; Mt 15:30; Ac 10:38
4:24 *y* Lk 2:2 *z* Mt 8:16,28; Mt 9:32; Mt 15:22; Mk 1:32; Mk 5:15,16, 18

[a] *4* Deut. 8:3 [b] *6* Psalm 91:11,12
[c] *7* Deut. 6:16 [d] *10* Deut. 6:13 [e] *16* Isaiah 9:1,2

seizures,[a] and the paralysed,[b] and
he healed them. 25Large crowds
from Galilee, the Decapolis,[f] Jerusalem, Judea and the region across
the Jordan followed him.[c]

The Beatitudes

5:3–12pp Lk 6:20–23

5 Now when he saw the crowds,
he went up on a mountainside
and sat down. His disciples came to
him, 2and he began to teach them,
saying:

3"Blessed are the poor in spirit,
for theirs is the kingdom of
heaven.[a]
4Blessed are those who mourn,
for they will be comforted.[b]
5Blessed are the meek,
for they will inherit the
earth.[c]
6Blessed are those who hunger
and thirst for
righteousness,
for they will be filled.[d]
7Blessed are the merciful,
for they will be shown mercy.
8Blessed are the pure in heart,[e]
for they will see God.[f]
9Blessed are the peacemakers,
for they will be called sons of
God.[g]
10Blessed are those who are
persecuted because of
righteousness,[h]
for theirs is the kingdom of
heaven.

11"Blessed are you when people
insult you,[i] persecute you and
falsely say all kinds of evil against
you because of me. 12Rejoice and
be glad,[j] because great is your reward in heaven, for in the same
way they persecuted the prophets
who were before you.[k]

Salt and Light

13"You are the salt of the earth.
But if the salt loses its saltiness,
how can it be made salty again? It
is no longer good for anything,
except to be thrown out and
trampled by men.[l]
14"You are the light of the
world.[m] A city on a hill cannot be
hidden. 15Neither do people light a
lamp and put it under a bowl. Instead they put it on its stand, and it
gives light to everyone in the
house.[n] 16In the same way, let your
light shine before men, that they
may see your good deeds and
praise[o] your Father in heaven.

The Fulfilment of the Law

17"Do not think that I have come
to abolish the Law or the Prophets;
I have not come to abolish them but
to fulfil them.[p] 18I tell you the
truth, until heaven and earth disappear, not the smallest letter, not the
least stroke of a pen, will by any
means disappear from the Law
until everything is accomplished.[q]
19Anyone who breaks one of the
least of these commandments[r]
and teaches others to do the same
will be called least in the kingdom
of heaven, but whoever practises
and teaches these commands will
be called great in the kingdom of
heaven. 20For I tell you that unless
your righteousness surpasses that
of the Pharisees and the teachers of
the law, you will certainly not enter
the kingdom of heaven.

Murder

5:25,26pp Lk 12:58,59

21"You have heard that it was
said to the people long ago, 'Do not
murder,[a][s] and anyone who murders will be subject to judgment.'
22But I tell you that anyone who is
angry with his brother[b] will be
subject to judgment.[t] Again, anyone who says to his brother,
'Raca,'[c] is answerable to the Sanhedrin.[u] But anyone who says,

4:24 *a* Mt 17:15 *b* Mt 8:6; Mt 9:2; Mk 2:3
4:25 *c* Mk 3:7,8; Lk 6:17
5:3 *a* ver 10,19; Mt 25:34
5:4 *b* Isa 61:2,3; Rev 7:17
5:5 *c* Ps 37:11; Ro 4:13
5:6 *d* Isa 55:1,2
5:8 *e* Ps 24:3,4 *f* Heb 12:14; Rev 22:4
5:9 *g* ver 44,45; Ro 8:14
5:10 *h* 1Pe 3:14
5:11 *i* 1Pe 4:14
5:12 *j* Ac 5:41; 1Pe 4:13,16 *k* Mt 23:31,37; Ac 7:52; 1Th 2:15
5:13 *l* Mk 9:50; Lk 14:34,35
5:14 *m* Jn 8:12
5:15 *n* Mk 4:21; Lk 8:16
5:16 *o* Mt 9:8
5:17 *p* Ro 3:31
5:18 *q* Lk 16:17
5:19 *r* Jas 2:10
5:21 *s* Ex 20:13; Dt 5:17
5:22 *t* 1Jn 3:15 *u* Mt 26:59

[f] *25* That is, the Ten Cities
[a] *21* Exodus 20:13
[b] 22 Some manuscripts *brother without cause*
[c] 22 An Aramaic term of contempt

'You fool!' will be in danger of the
fire of hell.[v]
23"Therefore, if you are offering
your gift at the altar and there remember that your brother has
something against you, 24leave
your gift there in front of the altar.
First go and be reconciled to your
brother; then come and offer your
gift.
25"Settle matters quickly with
your adversary who is taking you
to court. Do it while you are still
with him on the way, or he may
hand you over to the judge, and the
judge may hand you over to the officer, and you may be thrown into
prison. 26I tell you the truth, you
will not get out until you have paid
the last penny.[d]

Adultery

27"You have heard that it was
said, 'Do not commit adultery.'[e][w]
28But I tell you that anyone who
looks at a woman lustfully has already committed adultery with her
in his heart.[x] 29If your right eye
causes you to sin,[y] gouge it out and
throw it away. It is better for you to
lose one part of your body than for
your whole body to be thrown into
hell. 30And if your right hand
causes you to sin, cut it off and
throw it away. It is better for you to
lose one part of your body than for
your whole body to go into hell.

Divorce

31"It has been said, 'Anyone who
divorces his wife must give her a
certificate of divorce.'[f][z] 32But I
tell you that anyone who divorces
his wife, except for marital unfaithfulness, causes her to become
an adulteress, and anyone who
marries the divorced woman commits adultery.[a]

Oaths

33"Again, you have heard that it
was said to the people long ago, 'Do
not break your oath,[b] but keep the
oaths you have made to the Lord.'[c]
34But I tell you, Do not swear at
all:[d] either by heaven, for it is
God's throne;[e] 35or by the earth,
for it is his footstool; or by Jerusalem, for it is the city of the Great
King.[f] 36And do not swear by your
head, for you cannot make even one
hair white or black. 37Simply let
your 'Yes' be 'Yes', and your 'No',
'No';[g] anything beyond this comes
from the evil one.[h]

An Eye for an Eye

38"You have heard that it was
said, 'Eye for eye, and tooth for
tooth.'[g][i] 39But I tell you, Do not resist an evil person. If someone
strikes you on the right cheek, turn
to him the other also.[j] 40And if
someone wants to sue you and take
your tunic, let him have your cloak
as well. 41If someone forces you to
go one mile, go with him two miles.
42Give to the one who asks you, and
do not turn away from the one who
wants to borrow from you.[k]

Love for Enemies

43"You have heard that it was
said, 'Love your neighbour[h][l] and
hate your enemy.'[m] 44But I tell you:
Love your enemies[i] and pray for
those who persecute you,[n] 45that
you may be sons[o] of your Father in
heaven. He causes his sun to rise on
the evil and the good, and sends
rain on the righteous and the unrighteous.[p] 46If you love those who
love you, what reward will you
get?[q] Are not even the tax collectors doing that? 47And if you greet
only your brothers, what are you
doing more than others? Do not
even pagans do that? 48Be perfect,
therefore, as your heavenly Father
is perfect.[r]

5:22 v Jas 3:6
5:27 w Ex 20:14; Dt 5:18
5:28 x Pr 6:25
5:29 y Mt 18:6,8,9; Mk 9:42-47
5:31 z Dt 24:1-4
5:32 a Lk 16:18
5:33 b Lev 19:12 c Nu 30:2; Dt 23:21; Mt 23:16-22
5:34 d Jas 5:12 e Isa 66:1; Mt 23:22
5:35 f Ps 48:2
5:37 g Jas 5:12 h Mt 6:13; Mt 13:19,38; Jn 17:15; 2Th 3:3; 1Jn 2:13,14; 1Jn 3:12; 1Jn 5:18,19
5:38 i Ex 21:24; Lev 24:20; Dt 19:21
5:39 j Lk 6:29; Ro 12:17,19; 1Co 6:7; 1Pe 3:9
5:42 k Dt 15:8; Lk 6:30
5:43 l Lev 19:18 m Dt 23:6
5:44 n Lk 6:27,28; Lk 23:34; Ac 7:60; Ro 12:14; 1Co 4:12; 1Pe 2:23
5:45 o ver 9 p Job 25:3
5:46 q Lk 6:32
5:48 r Lev 19:2; 1Pe 1:16

[d] *26* Greek *kodrantes* [e] *27* Exodus 20:14
[f] *31* Deut. 24:1 [g] *38* Exodus 21:24; Lev. 24:20 and Deut. 19:21 [h] *43* Lev. 19:18 [i] *44* Some late manuscripts *enemies, bless those who curse you, do good to those who hate you*

Giving to the Needy

6 "Be careful not to do your 'acts
of righteousness' before men,
to be seen by them.[a] If you do, you
will have no reward from your
Father in heaven.
2"So when you give to the needy,
do not announce it with trumpets,
as the hypocrites do in the synagogues and on the streets, to be
honoured by men. I tell you the
truth, they have received their reward in full. 3But when you give to
the needy, do not let your left hand
know what your right hand is doing, 4so that your giving may be in
secret. Then your Father, who sees
what is done in secret, will reward
you.[b]

Prayer

6:9–13pp Lk 11:2–4

5"And when you pray, do not be
like the hypocrites, for they love to
pray standing[c] in the synagogues
and on the street corners to be seen
by men. I tell you the truth, they
have received their reward in full.
6But when you pray, go into your
room, close the door and pray to
your Father,[d] who is unseen. Then
your Father, who sees what is done
in secret, will reward you. 7And
when you pray, do not keep on bab-
bling[e] like pagans, for they think
they will be heard because of their
many words.[f] 8Do not be like
them, for your Father knows what
you need[g] before you ask him.
9"This, then, is how you should
pray:

" 'Our Father in heaven,
hallowed be your name,
10your kingdom[h] come,
your will be done[i]
on earth as it is in heaven.
11Give us today our daily bread.[j]
12Forgive us our debts,
as we also have forgiven our
debtors.[k]
13And lead us not into
temptation,[l]
but deliver us from the evil
one.'[a] [m]

14For if you forgive men when they
sin against you, your heavenly
Father will also forgive you.[n] 15But
if you do not forgive men their sins,
your Father will not forgive your
sins.[o]

Fasting

16"When you fast, do not look
sombre[p] as the hypocrites do, for
they disfigure their faces to show
men they are fasting. I tell you the
truth, they have received their reward in full. 17But when you fast,
put oil on your head and wash your
face, 18so that it will not be obvious
to men that you are fasting, but
only to your Father, who is unseen;
and your Father, who sees what is
done in secret, will reward you.[q]

Treasures in Heaven

6:22,23pp Lk 11:34–36

19"Do not store up for yourselves
treasures on earth,[r] where moth
and rust destroy,[s] and where
thieves break in and steal. 20But
store up for yourselves treasures
in heaven,[t] where moth and rust
do not destroy, and where thieves
do not break in and steal.[u] 21For
where your treasure is, there your
heart will be also.[v]
22"The eye is the lamp of the
body. If your eyes are good, your
whole body will be full of light.
23But if your eyes are bad, your
whole body will be full of darkness.
If then the light within you is darkness, how great is that darkness!
24"No-one can serve two masters.
Either he will hate the one and love
the other, or he will be devoted to
the one and despise the other. You
cannot serve both God and
Money.[w]

6:1 *a* Mt 23:5
6:4 *b* ver 6,18; Col 3:23,24
6:5 *c* Mk 11:25; Lk 18:10-14
6:6 *d* 2Ki 4:33
6:7 *e* Ecc 5:2 *f* 1Ki 18:26-29
6:8 *g* ver 32
6:10 *h* Mt 3:2 *i* Mt 26:39
6:11 *j* Pr 30:8
6:12 *k* Mt 18:21-35
6:13 *l* Jas 1:13 *m* Mt 5:37
6:14 *n* Mt 18:21-35; Mk 11:25,26; Eph 4:32; Col 3:13
6:15 *o* Mt 18:35
6:16 *p* Isa 58:5
6:18 *q* ver 4,6
6:19 *r* Pr 23:4; Heb 13:5 *s* Jas 5:2,3
6:20 *t* Mt 19:21; Lk 12:33; Lk 18:22; 1Ti 6:19 *u* Lk 12:33
6:21 *v* Lk 12:34
6:24 *w* Lk 16:13

a13 Or *from evil*; some late manuscripts *one, / for yours is the kingdom and the power and the glory for ever. Amen.*

Do Not Worry

6:25–33pp Lk 12:22–31

25“Therefore I tell you, do not worry[x] about your life, what you will eat or drink; or about your body, what you will wear. Is not life more important than food, and the body more important than clothes? 26Look at the birds of the air; they do not sow or reap or store away in barns, and yet your heavenly Father feeds them.[y] Are you not much more valuable than they?[z] 27Who of you by worrying can add a single hour to his life?[b][a]

28“And why do you worry about clothes? See how the lilies of the field grow. They do not labour or spin. 29Yet I tell you that not even Solomon in all his splendour[b] was dressed like one of these. 30If that is how God clothes the grass of the field, which is here today and tomorrow is thrown into the fire, will he not much more clothe you, O you of little faith?[c] 31So do not worry, saying, ‘What shall we eat?’ or ‘What shall we drink?’ or ‘What shall we wear?’ 32For the pagans run after all these things, and your heavenly Father knows that you need them.[d] 33But seek first his kingdom and his righteousness, and all these things will be given to you as well.[e] 34Therefore do not worry about tomorrow, for tomorrow will worry about itself. Each day has enough trouble of its own.

Judging Others

7:3–5pp Lk 6:41,42

7 “Do not judge, or you too will be judged.[a] 2For in the same way as you judge others, you will be judged, and with the measure you use, it will be measured to you.[b]

3“Why do you look at the speck of sawdust in your brother’s eye and pay no attention to the plank in your own eye? 4How can you say to your brother, ‘Let me take the speck out of your eye,’ when all the time there is a plank in your own eye? 5You hypocrite, first take the plank out of your own eye, and then you will see clearly to remove the speck from your brother’s eye.

6“Do not give dogs what is sacred; do not throw your pearls to pigs. If you do, they may trample them under their feet, and then turn and tear you to pieces.

Ask, Seek, Knock

7:7–11pp Lk 11:9–13

7“Ask and it will be given to you;[c] seek and you will find; knock and the door will be opened to you. 8For everyone who asks receives; he who seeks finds;[d] and to him who knocks, the door will be opened.

9“Which of you, if his son asks for bread, will give him a stone? 10Or if he asks for a fish, will give him a snake? 11If you, then, though you are evil, know how to give good gifts to your children, how much more will your Father in heaven give good gifts to those who ask him! 12So in everything, do to others what you would have them do to you,[e] for this sums up the Law and the Prophets.[f]

The Narrow and Wide Gates

13“Enter through the narrow gate.[g] For wide is the gate and broad is the road that leads to destruction, and many enter through it. 14But small is the gate and narrow the road that leads to life, and only a few find it.

A Tree and Its Fruit

15“Watch out for false prophets.[h] They come to you in sheep’s clothing, but inwardly they are ferocious wolves.[i] 16By their fruit you will recognise them.[j] Do people pick grapes from thornbushes, or figs from thistles?[k] 17Likewise

6:25 *x* ver 27,28,31, 34; Lk 10:41; Lk 12:11,22; Php 4:6; 1Pe 5:7
6:26 *y* Job 38:41; Ps 147:9 *z* Mt 10:29-31
6:27 *a* Ps 39:5
6:29 *b* 1Ki 10:4-7
6:30 *c* Mt 8:26; Mt 14:31; Mt 16:8
6:32 *d* ver 8
6:33 *e* Mt 19:29; Mk 10:29-30
7:1 *a* Lk 6:37; Ro 14:4,10,13; 1Co 4:5; Jas 4:11,12
7:2 *b* Mk 4:24; Lk 6:38
7:7 *c* Mt 21:22; Mk 11:24; Jn 14:13,14; Jn 15:7,16; Jn 16:23,24; Jas 1:5-8; Jas 4:2,3; 1Jn 3:22; 1Jn 5:14,15
7:8 *d* Pr 8:17; Jer 29:12,13
7:12 *e* Lk 6:31 *f* Ro 13:8-10; Gal 5:14
7:13 *g* Lk 13:24
7:15 *h* Jer 23:16; Mt 24:24; Mk 13:22; Lk 6:26; 2Pe 2:1; 1Jn 4:1; Rev 16:13 *i* Ac 20:29
7:16 *j* Mt 12:33; Lk 6:44 *k* Jas 3:12

b27 Or *single cubit to his height*

every good tree bears good fruit, but a bad tree bears bad fruit. 18A good tree cannot bear bad fruit, and a bad tree cannot bear good fruit. 19Every tree that does not bear good fruit is cut down and thrown into the fire.[l] 20Thus, by their fruit you will recognise them.

21"Not everyone who says to me, 'Lord, Lord,'[m] will enter the kingdom of heaven, but only he who does the will of my Father who is in heaven.[n] 22Many will say to me on that day,[o] 'Lord, Lord, did we not prophesy in your name, and in your name drive out demons and perform many miracles?'[p] 23Then I will tell them plainly, 'I never knew you. Away from me, you evildoers!'[q]

The Wise and Foolish Builders

7:24–27pp Lk 6:47–49

24"Therefore everyone who hears these words of mine and puts them into practice[r] is like a wise man who built his house on the rock. 25The rain came down, the streams rose, and the winds blew and beat against that house; yet it did not fall, because it had its foundation on the rock. 26But everyone who hears these words of mine and does not put them into practice is like a foolish man who built his house on sand. 27The rain came down, the streams rose, and the winds blew and beat against that house, and it fell with a great crash."

28When Jesus had finished saying these things,[s] the crowds were amazed at his teaching,[t] 29because he taught as one who had authority, and not as their teachers of the law.

The Man With Leprosy

8:2–4pp Mk 1:40–44; Lk 5:12–14

8 When he came down from the mountainside, large crowds followed him. 2A man with leprosy[a][a] came and knelt before him[b] and said, "Lord, if you are willing, you can make me clean."

3Jesus reached out his hand and touched the man. "I am willing," he said. "Be clean!" Immediately he was cured[b] of his leprosy. 4Then Jesus said to him, "See that you don't tell anyone.[c] But go, show yourself to the priest and offer the gift Moses commanded,[d] as a testimony to them."

The Faith of the Centurion

8:5–13pp Lk 7:1–10

5When Jesus had entered Capernaum, a centurion came to him, asking for help. 6"Lord," he said, "my servant lies at home paralysed and in terrible suffering."

7Jesus said to him, "I will go and heal him."

8The centurion replied, "Lord, I do not deserve to have you come under my roof. But just say the word, and my servant will be healed.[e] 9For I myself am a man under authority, with soldiers under me. I tell this one, 'Go,' and he goes; and that one, 'Come,' and he comes. I say to my servant, 'Do this,' and he does it."

10When Jesus heard this, he was astonished and said to those following him, "I tell you the truth, I have not found anyone in Israel with such great faith.[f] 11I say to you that many will come from the east and the west,[g] and will take their places at the feast with Abraham, Isaac and Jacob in the kingdom of heaven.[h] 12But the subjects of the kingdom[i] will be thrown outside, into the darkness, where there will be weeping and gnashing of teeth."[j]

13Then Jesus said to the centurion, "Go! It will be done just as you believed it would."[k] And his servant was healed at that very hour.

7:19 l Mt 3:10
7:21 m Hos 8:2; Mt 25:11 n Ro 2:13; Jas 1:22
7:22 o Mt 10:15 p 1Co 13:1-3
7:23 q Ps 6:8; Mt 25:12,41; Lk 13:25-27
7:24 r Jas 1:22-25
7:28 s Mt 11:1; Mt 13:53; Mt 19:1; Mt 26:1 t Mt 13:54; Mk 1:22; Mk 6:2; Lk 4:32; Jn 7:46
8:2 a Lk 5:12 b Mt 9:18; Mt 15:25; Mt 18:26; Mt 20:20
8:4 c Mt 9:30; Mk 5:43; Mk 7:36; Mk 8:30 d Lev 14:2-32
8:8 e Ps 107:20
8:10 f Mt 15:28
8:11 g Ps 107:3; Isa 49:12; Isa 59:19; Mal 1:11 h Lk 13:29
8:12 i Mt 13:38 j Mt 13:42,50; Mt 22:13; Mt 24:51; Mt 25:30; Lk 13:28
8:13 k Mt 9:22

[a]2 The Greek word was used for various diseases affecting the skin—not necessarily leprosy.
[b]3 Greek *made clean*

Jesus Heals Many

8:14–16pp Mk 1:29–34; Lk 4:38–41

14 When Jesus came into Peter's house, he saw Peter's mother-in-law lying in bed with a fever. 15 He touched her hand and the fever left her, and she got up and began to wait on him.

16 When evening came, many who were demon-possessed were brought to him, and he drove out the spirits with a word and healed all the sick.[l] 17 This was to fulfil[m] what was spoken through the prophet Isaiah:

"He took up our infirmities
and carried our diseases."[c][n]

The Cost of Following Jesus

8:19–22pp Lk 9:57–60

18 When Jesus saw the crowd around him, he gave orders to cross to the other side of the lake.[o] 19 Then a teacher of the law came to him and said, "Teacher, I will follow you wherever you go."

20 Jesus replied, "Foxes have holes and birds of the air have nests, but the Son of Man[p] has nowhere to lay his head."

21 Another disciple said to him, "Lord, first let me go and bury my father."

22 But Jesus told him, "Follow me,[q] and let the dead bury their own dead."

Jesus Calms the Storm

8:23–27pp Mk 4:36–41; Lk 8:22–25
8:23–27Ref Mt 14:22–33

23 Then he got into the boat and his disciples followed him. 24 Without warning, a furious storm came up on the lake, so that the waves swept over the boat. But Jesus was sleeping. 25 The disciples went and woke him, saying, "Lord, save us! We're going to drown!"

26 He replied, "You of little faith,[r] why are you so afraid?" Then he got up and rebuked the winds and the waves, and it was completely calm.[s]

27 The men were amazed and asked, "What kind of man is this? Even the winds and the waves obey him!"

The Healing of Two Demon-possessed Men

8:28–34pp Mk 5:1–17; Lk 8:26–37

28 When he arrived at the other side in the region of the Gadarenes,[d] two demon-possessed[t] men coming from the tombs met him. They were so violent that no-one could pass that way. 29 "What do you want with us,[u] Son of God?" they shouted. "Have you come here to torture us before the appointed time?"[v]

30 Some distance from them a large herd of pigs was feeding. 31 The demons begged Jesus, "If you drive us out, send us into the herd of pigs."

32 He said to them, "Go!" So they came out and went into the pigs, and the whole herd rushed down the steep bank into the lake and died in the water. 33 Those tending the pigs ran off, went into the town and reported all this, including what had happened to the demon-possessed men. 34 Then the whole town went out to meet Jesus. And when they saw him, they pleaded with him to leave their region.[w]

Jesus Heals a Paralytic

9:2–8pp Mk 2:3–12; Lk 5:18–26

9 Jesus stepped into a boat, crossed over and came to his own town.[a] 2 Some men brought to him a paralytic,[b] lying on a mat. When Jesus saw their faith,[c] he said to the paralytic, "Take heart,[d] son; your sins are forgiven."[e]

3 At this, some of the teachers of the law said to themselves, "This fellow is blasphemer!"[f]

[c]17 Isaiah 53:4 [d]28 Some manuscripts *Gergesenes*; others *Gerasenes*

8:16 *l* Mt 4:23,24
8:17 *m* Mt 1:22 *n* Isa 53:4
8:18 *o* Mk 4:35
8:20 *p* Da 7:13 Mt 12:8,32, 40 Mt 16:13,27, 28 Mt 17:9 Mt 19:28 Mk 2:10 Mk 8:31
8:22 *q* Mt 4:19
8:26 *r* Mt 6:30 *s* Ps 65:7 Ps 89:9 Ps 107:29
8:28 *t* Mt 4:24
8:29 *u* Jdg 11:12 2Sa 16:10 1Ki 17:18 Mk 1:24 Lk 4:34 Jn 2:4 *v* 2Pe 2:4
8:34 *w* Lk 5:8 Ac 16:39
9:1 *a* Mt 4:13
9:2 *b* Mt 4:24 *c* ver 22 *d* Jn 16:33 *e* Lk 7:48
9:3 *f* Mt 26:65 Jn 10:33

[4]Knowing their thoughts,[g] Jesus said, "Why do you entertain evil thoughts in your hearts? [5]Which is easier: to say, 'Your sins are forgiven,' or to say, 'Get up and walk'? [6]But so that you may know that the Son of Man[h] has authority on earth to forgive sins. . . ." Then he said to the paralytic, "Get up, take your mat and go home." [7]And the man got up and went home. [8]When the crowd saw this, they were filled with awe; and they praised God,[i] who had given such authority to men.

The Calling of Matthew

9:9–13pp Mk 2:14–17; Lk 5:27–32

[9]As Jesus went on from there, he saw a man named Matthew sitting at the tax collector's booth. "Follow me," he told him, and Matthew got up and followed him.

[10]While Jesus was having dinner at Matthew's house, many tax collectors and "sinners" came and ate with him and his disciples. [11]When the Pharisees saw this, they asked his disciples, "Why does your teacher eat with tax collectors and 'sinners'?"[j]

[12]On hearing this, Jesus said, "It is not the healthy who need a doctor, but the sick. [13]But go and learn what this means: 'I desire mercy, not sacrifice.'[a][k] For I have not come to call the righteous, but sinners."[l]

Jesus Questioned About Fasting

9:14–17pp Mk 2:18–22; Lk 5:33–39

[14]Then John's disciples came and asked him, "How is it that we and the Pharisees fast,[m] but your disciples do not fast?"

[15]Jesus answered, "How can the guests of the bridegroom mourn while he is with them?[n] The time will come when the bridegroom will be taken from them; then they will fast.[o]

[16]"No-one sews a patch of unshrunk cloth on an old garment, for the patch will pull away from the garment, making the tear worse. [17]Neither do men pour new wine into old wineskins. If they do, the skins will burst, the wine will run out and the wineskins will be ruined. No, they pour new wine into new wineskins, and both are preserved."

A Dead Girl and a Sick Woman

9:18–26pp Mk 5:22–43; Lk 8:41–56

[18]While he was saying this, a ruler came and knelt before him[p] and said, "My daughter has just died. But come and put your hand on her,[q] and she will live." [19]Jesus got up and went with him, and so did his disciples.

[20]Just then a woman who had been subject to bleeding for twelve years came up behind him and touched the edge of his cloak.[r] [21]She said to herself, "If I only touch his cloak, I will be healed." [22]Jesus turned and saw her. "Take heart, daughter," he said, "your faith has healed you."[s] And the woman was healed from that moment.[t]

[23]When Jesus entered the ruler's house and saw the flute players and the noisy crowd,[u] [24]he said, "Go away. The girl is not dead[v] but asleep."[w] But they laughed at him. [25]After the crowd had been put outside, he went in and took the girl by the hand, and she got up. [26]News of this spread through all that region.[x]

Jesus Heals the Blind and Mute

[27]As Jesus went on from there, two blind men followed him, calling out, "Have mercy on us, Son of David!"[y]

[28]When he had gone indoors, the blind men came to him, and he asked them, "Do you believe that I am able to do this?"

"Yes, Lord," they replied.

9:4 g Ps 94:11; Mt 12:25; Lk 6:8; Lk 9:47; Lk 11:17
9:6 h Mt 8:20
9:8 i Mt 5:16; Mt 15:31; Lk 7:16; Lk 13:13; Lk 17:15; Lk 23:47; Jn 15:8; Ac 4:21; Ac 11:18; Ac 21:20
9:11 j Mt 11:19; Lk 5:30; Lk 15:2; Gal 2:15
9:13 k Hos 6:6; Mic 6:6-8; Mt 12:7; l 1Ti 1:15
9:14 m Lk 18:12
9:15 n Jn 3:29; o Ac 13:2,3; Ac 14:23
9:18 p Mt 8:2; q Mk 5:23
9:20 r Mt 14:36; Mk 3:10
9:22 s Mk 10:52; Lk 7:50; Lk 17:19; Lk 18:42; t Mt 15:28
9:23 u 2Ch 35:25; Jer 9:17,18
9:24 v Ac 20:10; w Jn 11:11-14
9:26 x Mt 4:24
9:27 y Mt 15:22; Mk 10:47; Lk 18:38-39

[a]13 Hosea 6:6

29 Then he touched their eyes and
said, "According to your faith will
it be done to you";[z] 30 and their
sight was restored. Jesus warned
them sternly, "See that no-one
knows about this."[a] 31 But they
went out and spread the news about
him all over that region.[b]
32 While they were going out, a
man who was demon-possessed[c]
and could not talk[d] was brought
to Jesus. 33 And when the demon
was driven out, the man who had
been mute spoke. The crowd was
amazed and said, "Nothing like this
has ever been seen in Israel."[e]
34 But the Pharisees said, "It is by
the prince of demons that he drives
out demons."[f]

The Workers Are Few

35 Jesus went through all the
towns and villages, teaching in
their synagogues, preaching the
good news of the kingdom and healing every disease and sickness.[g]
36 When he saw the crowds, he had
compassion on them,[h] because
they were harassed and helpless,
like sheep without a shepherd.[i]
37 Then he said to his disciples, "The
harvest[j] is plentiful but the workers are few.[k] 38 Ask the Lord of the
harvest, therefore, to send out
workers into his harvest field."

Jesus Sends Out the Twelve

10:2–4pp Mk 3:16–19; Lk 6:14–16; Ac 1:13
10:9–15pp Mk 6:8–11; Lk 9:3–5; 10:4–12
10:19–22pp Mk 13:11–13; Lk 21:12–17
10:26–33pp Lk 12:2–9
10:34,35pp Lk 12:51–53

10 He called his twelve disciples to him and gave
them authority to drive out evil[a]
spirits[a] and to heal every disease
and sickness.
2 These are the names of the
twelve apostles: first, Simon (who
is called Peter) and his brother Andrew; James son of Zebedee, and
his brother John; 3 Philip and
Bartholomew; Thomas and Matthew the tax collector; James son of
Alphaeus, and Thaddaeus; 4 Simon
the Zealot and Judas Iscariot, who
betrayed him.[b]
5 These twelve Jesus sent out
with the following instructions:
"Do not go among the Gentiles or
enter any town of the Samaritans.[c]
6 Go rather to the lost sheep of Israel.[d] 7 As you go, preach this message: 'The kingdom of heaven[e] is
near.' 8 Heal the sick, raise the
dead, cleanse those who have leprosy,[b] drive out demons. Freely
you have received, freely give. 9 Do
not take along any gold or silver or
copper in your belts;[f] 10 take no
bag for the journey, or extra tunic,
or sandals or a staff; for the worker
is worth his keep.[g]
11 "Whatever town or village you
enter, search for some worthy person there and stay at his house until
you leave. 12 As you enter the home,
give it your greeting.[h] 13 If the
home is deserving, let your peace
rest on it; if it is not, let your peace
return to you. 14 If anyone will not
welcome you or listen to your
words, shake the dust off your
feet[i] when you leave that home or
town. 15 I tell you the truth, it will be
more bearable for Sodom and Gomorrah[j] on the day of judgment[k]
than for that town.[l] 16 I am sending
you out like sheep among wolves.[m]
Therefore be as shrewd as snakes
and as innocent as doves.[n]
17 "Be on your guard against men;
they will hand you over to the local
councils[o] and flog you in their
synagogues.[p] 18 On my account you
will be brought before governors
and kings[q] as witnesses to them
and to the Gentiles. 19 But when
they arrest you, do not worry about

9:29 z ver 22
9:30 a Mt 8:4
9:31 b ver 26; Mk 7:36
9:32 c Mt 4:24; d Mt 12:22-24
9:33 e Mk 2:12
9:34 f Mt 12:24; Lk 11:15
9:35 g Mt 4:23
9:36 h Mt 14:14; i Nu 27:17; Eze 34:5,6; Zec 10:2; Mk 6:34
9:37 j Jn 4:35; k Lk 10:2
10:1 a Mk 3:13-15; Lk 9:1
10:4 b Mt 26:14-16, 25,47; Jn 13:2,26,27
10:5 c 2Ki 17:24; Lk 9:52; Jn 4:4-26,39, 40; Ac 8:5,25
10:6 d Jer 50:6; Mt 15:24
10:7 e Mt 3:2
10:9 f Lk 22:35
10:10 g 1Ti 5:18
10:12 h 1Sa 25:6
10:14 i Ne 5:13; Lk 10:11; Ac 13:51
10:15 j 2Pe 2:6; k Mt 12:36; 2Pe 2:9; 1Jn 4:17; l Mt 11:22,24
10:16 m Lk 10:3; n Ro 16:19
10:17 o Mt 5:22; p Mt 23:34; Mk 13:9; Ac 5:40; Ac 26:11
10:18 q Ac 25:24-26

[a] *1* Greek *unclean* [b] *8* The Greek word was used for various diseases affecting the skin—not necessarily leprosy.

what to say or how to say it.[r] At that time you will be given what to say, [20]for it will not be you speaking, but the Spirit of your Father[s] speaking through you.

[21]"Brother will betray brother to death, and a father his child; children will rebel against their parents[t] and have them put to death. [22]All men will hate you because of me, but he who stands firm to the end will be saved.[u] [23]When you are persecuted in one place, flee to another. I tell you the truth, you will not finish going through the cities of Israel before the Son of Man comes.

[24]"A student is not above his teacher, nor a servant above his master.[v] [25]It is enough for the student to be like his teacher, and the servant like his master. If the head of the house has been called Beelzebub,[c][w] how much more the members of his household!

[26]"So do not be afraid of them. There is nothing concealed that will not be disclosed, or hidden that will not be made known.[x] [27]What I tell you in the dark, speak in the daylight; what is whispered in your ear, proclaim from the roofs. [28]Do not be afraid of those who kill the body but cannot kill the soul. Rather, be afraid of the One[y] who can destroy both soul and body in hell. [29]Are not two sparrows sold for a penny?[d] Yet not one of them will fall to the ground apart from the will of your Father. [30]And even the very hairs of your head are all numbered.[z] [31]So don't be afraid; you are worth more than many sparrows.[a]

[32]"Whoever acknowledges me before men,[b] I will also acknowledge him before my Father in heaven. [33]But whoever disowns me before men, I will disown him before my Father in heaven.[c]

[34]"Do not suppose that I have come to bring peace to the earth. I did not come to bring peace, but a sword. [35]For I have come to turn

" 'a man against his father,
  a daughter against her mother,
a daughter-in-law against her
    mother-in-law[d]—
[36] a man's enemies will be the
    members of his own
    household.'[e][e]

[37]"Anyone who loves his father or mother more than me is not worthy of me; anyone who loves his son or daughter more than me is not worthy of me;[f] [38]and anyone who does not take his cross and follow me is not worthy of me.[g] [39]Whoever finds his life will lose it, and whoever loses his life for my sake will find it.[h]

[40]"He who receives you receives me,[i] and he who receives me receives the one who sent me.[j] [41]Anyone who receives a prophet because he is a prophet will receive a prophet's reward, and anyone who receives a righteous man because he is a righteous man will receive a righteous man's reward. [42]And if anyone gives even a cup of cold water to one of these little ones because he is my disciple, I tell you the truth, he will certainly not lose his reward."[k]

Jesus and John the Baptist

11:2–19pp Lk 7:18–35

11 After Jesus had finished instructing his twelve disciples,[a] he went on from there to teach and preach in the towns of Galilee.[a]

[2]When John heard in prison[b] what Christ was doing, he sent his disciples [3]to ask him, "Are you the one who was to come,[c] or should we expect someone else?"

[4]Jesus replied, "Go back and report to John what you hear and see: [5]The blind receive sight, the lame

10:19 r Ex 4:12
10:20 s Ac 4:8
10:21 t ver 35,36; Mic 7:6
10:22 u Mt 24:13; Mk 13:13
10:24 v Lk 6:40; Jn 13:16; Jn 15:20
10:25 w Mk 3:22
10:26 x Mk 4:22; Lk 8:17
10:28 y Isa 8:12,13; Heb 10:31
10:30 z 1Sa 14:45; 2Sa 14:11; Lk 21:18; Ac 27:34
10:31 a Mt 12:12
10:32 b Ro 10:9
10:33 c Mk 8:38; 2Ti 2:12
10:35 d ver 21
10:36 e Mic 7:6
10:37 f Lk 14:26
10:38 g Mt 16:24; Lk 14:27
10:39 h Lk 17:33; Jn 12:25
10:40 i Mt 18:5; Gal 4:14; j Lk 9:48; Jn 12:44; Jn 13:20
10:42 k Mt 25:40; Mk 9:41; Heb 6:10
11:1 a Mt 7:28
11:2 b Mt 14:3
11:3 c Ps 118:26; Jn 11:27; Heb 10:37

c25 Greek *Beezeboul* or *Beelzeboul* d29 Greek *an assarion* e36 Micah 7:6 a1 Greek *in their towns*

walk, those who have leprosy[b] are
cured, the deaf hear, the dead are
raised, and the good news is
preached to the poor.[d] 6Blessed is
the man who does not fall away on
account of me."[e]

7As John's[f] disciples were leaving, Jesus began to speak to the
crowd about John: "What did you
go out into the desert to see? A reed
swayed by the wind? 8If not, what
did you go out to see? A man
dressed in fine clothes? No, those
who wear fine clothes are in kings'
palaces. 9Then what did you go out
to see? A prophet?[g] Yes, I tell
you, and more than a prophet.
10This is the one about whom it is
written:

"'I will send my messenger
ahead of you,
who will prepare your way
before you.'[c][h]

11I tell you the truth: Among those
born of women there has not risen
anyone greater than John the Baptist; yet he who is least in the kingdom of heaven is greater than he.
12From the days of John the Baptist
until now, the kingdom of heaven
has been forcefully advancing, and
forceful men lay hold of it. 13For all
the Prophets and the Law prophesied until John. 14And if you are
willing to accept it, he is the Elijah
who was to come.[i] 15He who has
ears, let him hear.[j]

16"To what can I compare this
generation? They are like children
sitting in the market-places and
calling out to others:

17"'We played the flute for you,
and you did not dance;
we sang a dirge,
and you did not mourn.'

18For John came neither eating[k]
nor drinking,[l] and they say, 'He
has a demon.' 19The Son of Man
came eating and drinking, and they
say, 'Here is a glutton and a drunkard, a friend of tax collectors and
"sinners".'[m] But wisdom is proved
right by her actions."

11:5 d Isa 35:4-6; Isa 61:1; Lk 4:18,19
11:6 e Mt 13:21
11:7 f Mt 3:1
11:9 g Mt 21:26; Lk 1:76
11:10 h Mal 3:1; Mk 1:2
11:14 i Mal 4:5; Mt 17:10-13; Mk 9:11-13; Lk 1:17; Jn 1:21
11:15 j Mt 13:9,43; Mk 4:23; Lk 14:35; Rev 2:7
11:18 k Mt 3:4; l Lk 1:15
11:19 m Mt 9:11
11:21 n Mk 6:45; Lk 9:10; Jn 12:21; o Mt 15:21; Lk 6:17; Ac 12:20; p Jnh 3:5-9
11:22 q ver 24; Mt 10:15
11:23 r Mt 4:13; s Isa 14:13-15
11:24 t Mt 10:15
11:25 u Lk 22:42; Jn 11:41; v 1Co 1:26-29
11:27 w Mt 28:18; x Jn 3:35; Jn 13:3; Jn 17:2; y Jn 10:15
11:28 z Jn 7:37
11:29 a Jn 13:15; Php 2:5; 1Pe 2:21; 1Jn 2:6

Woe on Unrepentant Cities

11:21-23pp Lk 10:13-15

20Then Jesus began to denounce
the cities in which most of his miracles had been performed, because
they did not repent. 21"Woe to you,
Korazin! Woe to you, Bethsaida![n]
If the miracles that were performed in you had been performed
in Tyre and Sidon,[o] they would
have repented long ago in sackcloth and ashes.[p] 22But I tell you, it
will be more bearable for Tyre and
Sidon on the day of judgment than
for you.[q] 23And you, Capernaum,[r]
will you be lifted up to the skies?
No, you will go down to the
depths.[d][s] If the miracles that
were performed in you had been
performed in Sodom, it would have
remained to this day. 24But I tell
you that it will be more bearable
for Sodom on the day of judgment
than for you."[t]

Rest for the Weary

11:25-27pp Lk 10:21,22

25At that time Jesus said, "I
praise you, Father,[u] Lord of
heaven and earth, because you
have hidden these things from the
wise and learned, and revealed
them to little children.[v] 26Yes,
Father, for this was your good
pleasure.

27"All things have been committed to me[w] by my Father.[x] No-one
knows the Son except the Father,
and no-one knows the Father except the Son and those to whom the
Son chooses to reveal him.[y]

28"Come to me,[z] all you who are
weary and burdened, and I will
give you rest. 29Take my yoke upon
you and learn from me,[a] for I am
gentle and humble in heart, and you

[b]5 The Greek word was used for various diseases affecting the skin—not necessarily leprosy. [c]*10* Mal. 3:1 [d]*23* Greek *Hades*

will find rest for your souls.[b] 30For my yoke is easy and my burden is light."[c]

Lord of the Sabbath

12:1–8pp Mk 2:23–28; Lk 6:1–5
12:9–14pp Mk 3:1–6; Lk 6:6–11

12 At that time Jesus went through the cornfields on the Sabbath. His disciples were hungry and began to pick some ears of corn[a] and eat them. 2When the Pharisees saw this, they said to him, "Look! Your disciples are doing what is unlawful on the Sabbath."[b]

3He answered, "Haven't you read what David did when he and his companions were hungry?[c] 4He entered the house of God, and he and his companions ate the consecrated bread—which was not lawful for them to do, but only for the priests.[d] 5Or haven't you read in the Law that on the Sabbath the priests in the temple desecrate the day[e] and yet are innocent? 6I tell you that one**[a]** greater than the temple is here.[f] 7If you had known what these words mean, 'I desire mercy, not sacrifice,'**[b]**[g] you would not have condemned the innocent. 8For the Son of Man[h] is Lord of the Sabbath."

9Going on from that place, he went into their synagogue, 10and a man with a shrivelled hand was there. Looking for a reason to accuse Jesus, they asked him, "Is it lawful to heal on the Sabbath?"[i]

11He said to them, "If any of you has a sheep and it falls into a pit on the Sabbath, will you not take hold of it and lift it out?[j] 12How much more valuable is a man than a sheep![k] Therefore it is lawful to do good on the Sabbath."

13Then he said to the man, "Stretch out your hand." So he stretched it out and it was completely restored, just as sound as the other. 14But the Pharisees went out and plotted how they might kill Jesus.[l]

God's Chosen Servant

15Aware of this, Jesus withdrew from that place. Many followed him, and he healed all their sick,[m] 16warning them not to tell who he was.[n] 17This was to fulfil what was spoken through the prophet Isaiah:

18"Here is my servant whom I
have chosen,
the one I love, in whom I
delight;[o]
I will put my Spirit on him,
and he will proclaim justice to
the nations.
19He will not quarrel or cry out;
no-one will hear his voice in
the streets.
20A bruised reed he will not
break,
and a smouldering wick he
will not snuff out,
till he leads justice to victory.
21 In his name the nations will
put their hope."**[c]**[p]

Jesus and Beelzebub

12:25–29pp Mk 3:23–27; Lk 11:17–22

22Then they brought him a demon-possessed man who was blind and mute, and Jesus healed him, so that he could both talk and see.[q] 23All the people were astonished and said, "Could this be the Son of David?"[r]

24But when the Pharisees heard this, they said, "It is only by Beelzebub,**[d]**[s] the prince of demons, that this fellow drives out demons."[t]

25Jesus knew their thoughts[u] and said to them, "Every kingdom divided against itself will be ruined, and every city or household divided against itself will not stand. 26If Satan[v] drives out Satan, he is divided against himself. How then can his kingdom stand? 27And

11:29 *b* Jer 6:16
11:30 *c* 1Jn 5:3
12:1 *a* Dt 23:25
12:2 *b* ver 10; Lk 13:14; Lk 14:3; Jn 5:10; Jn 7:23; Jn 9:16
12:3 *c* 1Sa 21:6
12:4 *d* Lev 24:5,9
12:5 *e* Nu 28:9,10; Jn 7:22,23
12:6 *f* ver 41,42
12:7 *g* Hos 6:6; Mic 6:6-8; Mt 9:13
12:8 *h* Mt 8:20
12:10 *i* ver 2; Lk 13:14; Lk 14:3; Jn 9:16
12:11 *j* Lk 14:5
12:12 *k* Mt 10:31
12:14 *l* Mt 26:4; Mt 27:1; Mk 3:6; Lk 6:11; Jn 5:18; Jn 11:53
12:15 *m* Mt 4:23
12:16 *n* Mt 8:4
12:18 *o* Mt 3:17
12:21 *p* Isa 42:1-4
12:22 *q* Mt 4:24; Mt 9:32-33
12:23 *r* Mt 9:27
12:24 *s* Mk 3:22; *t* Mt 9:34
12:25 *u* Mt 9:4
12:26 *v* Mt 4:10

a6 Or *something*; also in verses 41 and 42
b7 Hosea 6:6 **c**21 Isaiah 42:1–4 **d**24 Greek *Beezeboul* or *Beelzeboul*; also in verse 27

if I drive out demons by Beelzebub,
by whom do your people[w] drive
them out? So then, they will be your
judges. 28But if I drive out demons
by the Spirit of God, then the kingdom of God has come upon you.
29"Or again, how can anyone enter a strong man's house and carry
off his possessions unless he first
ties up the strong man? Then he
can rob his house.
30"He who is not with me is
against me, and he who does not
gather with me scatters.[x] 31And so
I tell you, every sin and blasphemy
will be forgiven men, but the blasphemy against the Spirit will not be
forgiven.[y] 32Anyone who speaks a
word against the Son of Man will be
forgiven, but anyone who speaks
against the Holy Spirit will not be
forgiven, either in this age[z] or in
the age to come.[a]
33"Make a tree good and its fruit
will be good, or make a tree bad and
its fruit will be bad, for a tree is
recognised by its fruit.[b] 34You
brood of vipers,[c] how can you who
are evil say anything good? For out
of the overflow of the heart the
mouth speaks.[d] 35The good man
brings good things out of the good
stored up in him, and the evil man
brings evil things out of the evil
stored up in him. 36But I tell you
that men will have to give account
on the day of judgment for every
careless word they have spoken.
37For by your words you will be ac-
quitted, and by your words you will
be condemned."

The Sign of Jonah

12:39–42pp Lk 11:29–32
12:43–45pp Lk 11:24–26

38Then some of the Pharisees and
teachers of the law said to him,
"Teacher, we want to see a miraculous sign from you."[e]
39He answered, "A wicked and
adulterous generation asks for a
miraculous sign! But none will be
given it except the sign of the
prophet Jonah.[f] 40For as Jonah
was three days and three nights in
the belly of a huge fish,[g] so the Son
of Man[h] will be three days and
three nights in the heart of the
earth.[i] 41The men of Nineveh[j]
will stand up at the judgment with
this generation and condemn it; for
they repented at the preaching of
Jonah,[k] and now one[e] greater
than Jonah is here. 42The Queen of
the South will rise at the judgment
with this generation and condemn
it; for she came[l] from the ends of
the earth to listen to Solomon's wisdom, and now one greater than Solomon is here.
43"When an evil[f] spirit comes
out of a man, it goes through arid
places seeking rest and does not
find it. 44Then it says, 'I will return
to the house I left.' When it arrives,
it finds the house unoccupied,
swept clean and put in order.
45Then it goes and takes with it
seven other spirits more wicked
than itself, and they go in and live
there. And the final condition of
that man is worse than the first.[m]
That is how it will be with this
wicked generation."

Jesus' Mother and Brothers

12:46–50pp Mk 3:31–35; Lk 8:19–21

46While Jesus was still talking
to the crowd, his mother[n] and
brothers[o] stood outside, wanting
to speak to him. 47Someone told
him, "Your mother and brothers
are standing outside, wanting to
speak to you."[g]
48He replied to him, "Who is my
mother, and who are my brothers?"
49Pointing to his disciples, he said,
"Here are my mother and my
brothers. 50For whoever does the
will of my Father in heaven[p] is my
brother and sister and mother."

12:27 w Ac 19:13
12:30 x Mk 9:40; Lk 11:23
12:31 y Mk 3:28,29; Lk 12:10
12:32 z Tit 2:12; a Mk 10:30; Lk 20:34,35; Eph 1:21; Heb 6:5
12:33 b Mt 7:16,17; Lk 6:43,44
12:34 c Mt 3:7; Mt 23:33; d Mt 15:18; Lk 6:45
12:38 e Mt 16:1; Mk 8:11,12; Lk 11:16; Jn 2:18; Jn 6:30; 1Co 1:22
12:39 f Mt 16:4; Lk 11:29
12:40 g Jnh 1:17; h Mt 8:20; i Mt 16:21
12:41 j Jnh 1:2; k Jnh 3:5
12:42 l 1Ki 10:1; 2Ch 9:1
12:45 m 2Pe 2:20
12:46 n Mt 1:18; Mt 2:11,13,14,20; Lk 1:43; Lk 2:33,34,48,51; Jn 2:1,5; Jn 19:25,26; o Mt 13:55; Jn 2:12; Jn 7:3,5; Ac 1:14; 1Co 9:5; Gal 1:19
12:50 p Jn 15:14

[e]41 Or *something*; also in verse 42 [f]43 Greek *unclean* [g]47 Some manuscripts do not have verse 47.

The Parable of the Sower

13:1–15pp Mk 4:1–12; Lk 8:4–10
13:16,17pp Lk 10:23,24
13:18–23pp Mk 4:13–20; Lk 8:11–15

13 That same day Jesus went
out of the house[a] and sat
by the lake. 2Such large crowds
gathered round him that he got into
a boat[b] and sat in it, while all the
people stood on the shore. 3Then he
told them many things in parables,
saying: "A farmer went out to sow
his seed. 4As he was scattering the
seed, some fell along the path, and
the birds came and ate it up. 5Some
fell on rocky places, where it did
not have much soil. It sprang up
quickly, because the soil was shallow. 6But when the sun came up,
the plants were scorched, and they
withered because they had no root.
7Other seed fell among thorns,
which grew up and choked the
plants. 8Still other seed fell on good
soil, where it produced a crop—a
hundred,[c] sixty or thirty times
what was sown. 9He who has ears,
let him hear."[d]

10The disciples came to him and
asked, "Why do you speak to the
people in parables?"

11He replied, "The knowledge of
the secrets of the kingdom of
heaven has been given to you,[e] but
not to them. 12Whoever has will be
given more, and he will have an
abundance. Whoever does not
have, even what he has will be
taken from him.[f] 13This is why I
speak to them in parables:

"Though seeing, they do not
see;
though hearing, they do not
hear or understand.[g]

14In them is fulfilled the prophecy
of Isaiah:

" 'You will be ever hearing but
never understanding;
you will be ever seeing but
never perceiving.
15For this people's heart has
become calloused;
they hardly hear with their
ears,
and they have closed their
eyes.
Otherwise they might see with
their eyes,
hear with their ears,
understand with their hearts
and turn, and I would heal
them.'[a][h]

16But blessed are your eyes because they see, and your ears
because they hear.[i] 17For I tell
you the truth, many prophets and
righteous men longed to see what
you see[j] but did not see it, and to
hear what you hear but did not
hear it.

18"Listen then to what the parable of the sower means: 19When
anyone hears the message about
the kingdom[k] and does not understand it, the evil one[l] comes and
snatches away what was sown in
his heart. This is the seed sown
along the path. 20The one who received the seed that fell on rocky
places is the man who hears the
word and at once receives it with
joy. 21But since he has no root, he
lasts only a short time. When trouble or persecution comes because
of the word, he quickly falls
away.[m] 22The one who received the
seed that fell among the thorns is
the man who hears the word, but
the worries of this life and the deceitfulness of wealth[n] choke it,
making it unfruitful. 23But the one
who received the seed that fell on
good soil is the man who hears the
word and understands it. He produces a crop, yielding a hundred,
sixty or thirty times what was
sown."[o]

The Parable of the Weeds

24Jesus told them another parable: "The kingdom of heaven is
like[p] a man who sowed good seed

13:1 a ver 36; Mt 9:28
13:2 b Lk 5:3
13:8 c Ge 26:12
13:9 d Mt 11:15
13:11 e Mt 11:25; Mt 16:17; Mt 19:11; Jn 6:65; 1Co 2:10,14; Col 1:27; 1Jn 2:20,27
13:12 f Mt 25:29; Lk 19:26
13:13 g Dt 29:4; Jer 5:21; Eze 12:2
13:15 h Isa 6:9,10; Jn 12:40; Ac 28:26,27; Ro 11:8
13:16 i Mt 16:17
13:17 j Jn 8:56; Heb 11:13; 1Pe 1:10-12
13:19 k Mt 4:23; l Mt 5:37
13:21 m Mt 11:6
13:22 n Mt 19:23; 1Ti 6:9,10,17
13:23 o ver 8
13:24 p ver 31,33,45, 47; Mt 18:23; Mt 20:1; Mt 22:2; Mt 25:1; Mk 4:26,30

a *15* Isaiah 6:9,10

in his field. 25But while everyone
was sleeping, his enemy came and
sowed weeds among the wheat, and
went away. 26When the wheat
sprouted and formed ears, then the
weeds also appeared.
27"The owner's servants came to
him and said, 'Sir, didn't you sow
good seed in your field? Where
then did the weeds come from?'
28" 'An enemy did this,' he replied.
"The servants asked him, 'Do you
want us to go and pull them up?'
29" 'No,' he answered, 'because
while you are pulling the weeds,
you may root up the wheat with
them. 30Let both grow together
until the harvest. At that time I will
tell the harvesters: First collect the
weeds and tie them in bundles to be
burned; then gather the wheat and
bring it into my barn.' "[q]

The Parables of the Mustard Seed and the Yeast

13:31,32pp Mk 4:30–32
13:31–33pp Lk 13:18–21

31He told them another parable:
"The kingdom of heaven is like[r] a
mustard seed,[s] which a man took
and planted in his field. 32Though it
is the smallest of all your seeds, yet
when it grows, it is the largest of
garden plants and becomes a tree,
so that the birds of the air come and
perch in its branches."[t]
33He told them still another parable: "The kingdom of heaven is
like[u] yeast that a woman took and
mixed into a large amount[b] of
flour[v] until it worked all through
the dough."[w]
34Jesus spoke all these things to
the crowd in parables; he did not
say anything to them without using
a parable.[x] 35So was fulfilled what
was spoken through the prophet:

"I will open my mouth in
  parables,
I will utter things hidden since
  the creation of the
  world."[c][y]

13:30 [q] Mt 3:12
13:31 [r] ver 24 [s] Mt 17:20; Lk 17:6
13:32 [t] Ps 104:12; Eze 17:23; Eze 31:6; Da 4:12
13:33 [u] ver 24 [v] Ge 18:6 [w] Gal 5:9
13:34 [x] Mk 4:33; Jn 16:25
13:35 [y] Ps 78:2; Ro 16:25,26; 1Co 2:7; Eph 3:9; Col 1:26
13:36 [z] Mt 15:15
13:37 [a] Mt 8:20
13:38 [b] Jn 8:44,45; 1Jn 3:10
13:39 [c] Joel 3:13 [d] Mt 24:3; Mt 28:20 [e] Rev 14:15
13:41 [f] Mt 8:20 [g] Mt 24:31
13:42 [h] ver 50; Mt 8:12
13:43 [i] Da 12:3 [j] Mt 11:15
13:44 [k] ver 24 [l] Isa 55:1; Php 3:7,8
13:45 [m] ver 24
13:47 [n] ver 24 [o] Mt 22:10

The Parable of the Weeds Explained

36Then he left the crowd and
went into the house. His disciples
came to him and said, "Explain to
us the parable[z] of the weeds in the
field."
37He answered, "The one who
sowed the good seed is the Son of
Man.[a] 38The field is the world, and
the good seed stands for the sons of
the kingdom. The weeds are the
sons of the evil one,[b] 39and the enemy who sows them is the devil.
The harvest[c] is the end of the
age,[d] and the harvesters are
angels.[e]
40"As the weeds are pulled up and
burned in the fire, so it will be at
the end of the age. 41The Son of
Man[f] will send out his angels,[g]
and they will weed out of his kingdom everything that causes sin and
all who do evil. 42They will throw
them into the fiery furnace, where
there will be weeping and gnashing
of teeth.[h] 43Then the righteous will
shine like the sun[i] in the kingdom
of their Father. He who has ears,
let him hear.[j]

The Parables of the Hidden Treasure and the Pearl

44"The kingdom of heaven is
like[k] treasure hidden in a field.
When a man found it, he hid it
again, and then in his joy went and
sold all he had and bought that
field.[l]
45"Again, the kingdom of heaven
is like[m] a merchant looking for fine
pearls. 46When he found one of
great value, he went away and sold
everything he had and bought it.

The Parable of the Net

47"Once again, the kingdom of
heaven is like[n] a net that was let
down into the lake and caught all
kinds[o] of fish. 48When it was full,

[b]*33* Greek *three satas* (probably about 3/5 bushel or 22 litres) [c]*35* Psalm 78:2

the fishermen pulled it up on the shore. Then they sat down and collected the good fish in baskets, but threw the bad away. [49]This is how it will be at the end of the age. The angels will come and separate the wicked from the righteous[p] [50]and throw them into the fiery furnace, where there will be weeping and gnashing of teeth.[q]

[51]"Have you understood all these things?" Jesus asked.

"Yes," they replied.

[52]He said to them, "Therefore every teacher of the law who has been instructed about the kingdom of heaven is like the owner of a house who brings out of his storeroom new treasures as well as old."

A Prophet Without Honour

13:54–58pp Mk 6:1–6

[53]When Jesus had finished these parables,[r] he moved on from there. [54]Coming to his home town, he began teaching the people in their synagogue,[s] and they were amazed.[t] "Where did this man get this wisdom and these miraculous powers?" they asked. [55]"Isn't this the carpenter's son?[u] Isn't his mother's[v] name Mary, and aren't his brothers James, Joseph, Simon and Judas? [56]Aren't all his sisters with us? Where then did this man get all these things?" [57]And they took offence[w] at him.

But Jesus said to them, "Only in his home town and in his own house is a prophet without honour."[x]

[58]And he did not do many miracles there because of their lack of faith.

John the Baptist Beheaded

14:1–12pp Mk 6:14–29

14 At that time Herod[a] the tetrarch heard the reports about Jesus,[b] [2]and he said to his attendants, "This is John the Baptist;[c] he has risen from the dead! That is why miraculous powers are at work in him."

13:49 p Mt 25:32
13:50 q Mt 8:12
13:53 r Mt 7:28
13:54 s Mt 4:23; t Mt 7:28
13:55 u Lk 3:23; Jn 6:42; v Mt 12:46
13:57 w Jn 6:61; x Lk 4:24; Jn 4:44
14:1 a Mk 8:15; Lk 3:1,19; Lk 13:31; Lk 23:7,8; Ac 4:27; Ac 12:1; b Lk 9:7-9
14:2 c Mt 3:1
14:3 d Mt 4:12; Mt 11:2; e Lk 3:19,20
14:4 f Lev 18:16; Lev 20:21
14:5 g Mt 11:9
14:10 h Mt 17:12
14:12 i Ac 8:2
14:14 j Mt 9:36; k Mt 4:23
14:17 l Mt 16:9

[3]Now Herod had arrested John and bound him and put him in prison[d] because of Herodias, his brother Philip's wife,[e] [4]for John had been saying to him: "It is not lawful for you to have her."[f] [5]Herod wanted to kill John, but he was afraid of the people, because they considered him a prophet.[g]

[6]On Herod's birthday the daughter of Herodias danced for them and pleased Herod so much [7]that he promised with an oath to give her whatever she asked. [8]Prompted by her mother, she said, "Give me here on a platter the head of John the Baptist." [9]The king was distressed, but because of his oaths and his dinner guests, he ordered that her request be granted [10]and had John beheaded[h] in the prison. [11]His head was brought in on a platter and given to the girl, who carried it to her mother. [12]John's disciples came and took his body and buried it.[i] Then they went and told Jesus.

Jesus Feeds the Five Thousand

14:13–21pp Mk 6:32–44; Lk 9:10–17; Jn 6:1–13
14:13–21Ref Mt 15:32–38

[13]When Jesus heard what had happened, he withdrew by boat privately to a solitary place. Hearing of this, the crowds followed him on foot from the towns. [14]When Jesus landed and saw a large crowd, he had compassion on them[j] and healed their sick.[k]

[15]As evening approached, the disciples came to him and said, "This is a remote place, and it's already getting late. Send the crowds away, so that they can go to the villages and buy themselves some food."

[16]Jesus replied, "They do not need to go away. You give them something to eat."

[17]"We have here only five loaves[l] of bread and two fish," they answered.

18“Bring them here to me,” he
said. 19And he directed the people
to sit down on the grass. Taking the
five loaves and the two fish and
looking up to heaven, he gave
thanks and broke the loaves.[m]
Then he gave them to the disciples,
and the disciples gave them to the
people. 20They all ate and were satisfied, and the disciples picked up
twelve basketfuls of broken pieces
that were left over. 21The number
of those who ate was about five
thousand men, besides women and
children.

Jesus Walks on the Water

14:22–33pp Mk 6:45–51; Jn 6:15–21
14:34–36pp Mk 6:53–56

22Immediately Jesus made the
disciples get into the boat and go on
ahead of him to the other side,
while he dismissed the crowd.
23After he had dismissed them, he
went up on a mountainside by himself to pray.[n] When evening came,
he was there alone, 24but the boat
was already a considerable distance[a] from land, buffeted by the
waves because the wind was
against it.

25During the fourth watch of the
night Jesus went out to them, walking on the lake. 26When the disciples saw him walking on the lake,
they were terrified. “It’s a ghost,”[o]
they said, and cried out in fear.

27But Jesus immediately said to
them: “Take courage![p] It is I.
Don’t be afraid.”[q]

28“Lord, if it’s you,” Peter replied, “tell me to come to you on the
water.”

29“Come,” he said.

Then Peter got down out of the
boat, walked on the water and came
towards Jesus. 30But when he saw
the wind, he was afraid and, beginning to sink, cried out, “Lord, save
me!”

31Immediately Jesus reached out
his hand and caught him. “You of

14:19
m 1Sa 9:13; Mt 26:26; Mk 8:6; Lk 24:30; Ac 2:42; Ac 27:35; 1Ti 4:4
14:23
n Lk 3:21
14:26
o Lk 24:37
14:27
p Mt 9:2; Ac 23:11
q Da 10:12; Mt 17:7; Mt 28:10; Lk 1:13,30; Lk 2:10; Ac 18:9; Ac 23:11; Rev 1:17
14:31
r Mt 6:30
14:33
s Ps 2:7; Mt 4:3
14:36
t Mt 9:20
15:2
a Lk 11:38
15:4
b Ex 20:12; Dt 5:16; Eph 6:2
c Ex 21:17; Lev 20:9
15:9
d Col 2:20-22
e Isa 29:13; Mal 2:2

little faith,”[r] he said, “why did you
doubt?”

32And when they climbed into the
boat, the wind died down. 33Then
those who were in the boat worshipped him, saying, “Truly you
are the Son of God.”[s]

34When they had crossed over,
they landed at Gennesaret. 35And
when the men of that place recognised Jesus, they sent word to all
the surrounding country. People
brought all their sick to him 36and
begged him to let the sick just
touch the edge of his cloak,[t] and
all who touched him were healed.

Clean and Unclean

15:1–20pp Mk 7:1–23

15 Then some Pharisees and
teachers of the law came to
Jesus from Jerusalem and asked,
2“Why do your disciples break the
tradition of the elders? They don’t
wash their hands before they
eat!”[a]

3Jesus replied, “And why do you
break the command of God for the
sake of your tradition? 4For God
said, ‘Honour your father and
mother’[a][b] and ‘Anyone who
curses his father or mother must
be put to death.’[b][c] 5But you say
that if a man says to his father or
mother, ‘Whatever help you might
otherwise have received from me
is a gift devoted to God,’ 6he is not
to ‘honour his father’[c] with it. Thus
you nullify the word of God for the
sake of your tradition. 7You hypocrites! Isaiah was right when he
prophesied about you:

8“ ‘These people honour me with
their lips,
but their hearts are far from
me.
9They worship me in vain;
their teachings are but rules
taught by men.’[d]”[d][e]

[a]24 Greek *many stadia* [a]4 Exodus 20:12; Deut. 5:16 [b]4 Exodus 21:17; Lev. 20:9
[c]6 Some manuscripts *father or his mother*
[d]9 Isaiah 29:13

10 Jesus called the crowd to him and said, "Listen and understand. 11 What goes into a man's mouth does not make him 'unclean',[f] but what comes out of his mouth, that is what makes him 'unclean'."[g]

12 Then the disciples came to him and asked, "Do you know that the Pharisees were offended when they heard this?"

13 He replied, "Every plant that my heavenly Father has not planted[h] will be pulled up by the roots. 14 Leave them; they are blind guides.[e][i] If a blind man leads a blind man, both will fall into a pit."[j]

15 Peter said, "Explain the parable to us."[k]

16 "Are you still so dull?"[l] Jesus asked them. 17 "Don't you see that whatever enters the mouth goes into the stomach and then out of the body? 18 But the things that come out of the mouth come from the heart,[m] and these make a man 'unclean'. 19 For out of the heart come evil thoughts, murder, adultery, sexual immorality, theft, false testimony, slander.[n] 20 These are what make a man 'unclean';[o] but eating with unwashed hands does not make him 'unclean'."

The Faith of the Canaanite Woman

15:21–28pp Mk 7:24–30

21 Leaving that place, Jesus withdrew to the region of Tyre and Sidon.[p] 22 A Canaanite woman from that vicinity came to him, crying out, "Lord, Son of David,[q] have mercy on me! My daughter is suffering terribly from demon-possession."[r]

23 Jesus did not answer a word. So his disciples came to him and urged him, "Send her away, for she keeps crying out after us."

24 He answered, "I was sent only to the lost sheep of Israel."[s]

25 The woman came and knelt before him.[t] "Lord, help me!" she said.

26 He replied, "It is not right to take the children's bread and toss it to their dogs."

27 "Yes, Lord," she said, "but even the dogs eat the crumbs that fall from their masters' table."

28 Then Jesus answered, "Woman, you have great faith![u] Your request is granted." And her daughter was healed from that very hour.

Jesus Feeds the Four Thousand

15:29–31pp Mk 7:31–37
15:32–39pp Mk 8:1–10
15:32–39Ref Mt 14:13–21

29 Jesus left there and went along the Sea of Galilee. Then he went up on a mountainside and sat down. 30 Great crowds came to him, bringing the lame, the blind, the crippled, the mute and many others, and laid them at his feet; and he healed them.[v] 31 The people were amazed when they saw the mute speaking, the crippled made well, the lame walking and the blind seeing. And they praised the God of Israel.[w]

32 Jesus called his disciples to him and said, "I have compassion for these people;[x] they have already been with me three days and have nothing to eat. I do not want to send them away hungry, or they may collapse on the way."

33 His disciples answered, "Where could we get enough bread in this remote place to feed such a crowd?"

34 "How many loaves do you have?" Jesus asked.

"Seven," they replied, "and a few small fish."

35 He told the crowd to sit down on the ground. 36 Then he took the seven loaves and the fish, and when he had given thanks, he broke them[y] and gave them to the disciples, and they in turn to the people. 37 They all ate and were satisfied. Afterwards the disciples picked up seven basketfuls of

15:11 f Ac 10:14,15 g ver 18
15:13 h Isa 60:21; Isa 61:3; Jn 15:2
15:14 i Mt 23:16,24; Ro 2:19 j Lk 6:39
15:15 k Mt 13:36
15:16 l Mt 16:9
15:18 m Mt 12:34; Lk 6:45; Jas 3:6
15:19 n Gal 5:19-21
15:20 o Ro 14:14
15:21 p Mt 11:21
15:22 q Mt 9:27 r Mt 4:24
15:24 s Mt 10:6,23; Ro 15:8
15:25 t Mt 8:2
15:28 u Mt 9:22
15:30 v Mt 4:23
15:31 w Mt 9:8
15:32 x Mt 9:36
15:36 y Mt 14:19

e 14 Some manuscripts *guides of the blind*

broken pieces that were left over.[z]
38The number of those who ate was
four thousand, besides women and
children. 39After Jesus had sent the
crowd away, he got into the boat
and went to the vicinity of Magadan.

The Demand for a Sign

16:1–12pp Mk 8:11–21

16 The Pharisees and Sadducees[a] came to Jesus and
tested him by asking him to show
them a sign from heaven.[b]
2He replied,[a] "When evening
comes, you say, 'It will be fair
weather, for the sky is red,' 3and in
the morning, 'Today it will be
stormy, for the sky is red and over-
cast.' You know how to interpret
the appearance of the sky, but you
cannot interpret the signs of the
times.[c] 4A wicked and adulterous
generation looks for a miraculous
sign, but none will be given it except the sign of Jonah."[d] Jesus
then left them and went away.

The Yeast of the Pharisees and Sadducees

5When they went across the lake,
the disciples forgot to take bread.
6"Be careful," Jesus said to them.
"Be on your guard against the yeast
of the Pharisees and Sadducees."[e]
7They discussed this among
themselves and said, "It is because
we didn't bring any bread."
8Aware of their discussion, Jesus
asked, "You of little faith,[f] why
are you talking among yourselves
about having no bread? 9Do you
still not understand? Don't you remember the five loaves for the five
thousand, and how many basketfuls you gathered?[g] 10Or the seven
loaves for the four thousand, and
how many basketfuls you gathered?[h] 11How is it you don't understand that I was not talking to you
about bread? But be on your guard
against the yeast of the Pharisees and Sadducees." 12Then they
understood that he was not telling
them to guard against the yeast
used in bread, but against the
teaching of the Pharisees and Sadducees.[i]

Peter's Confession of Christ

16:13–16pp Mk 8:27–29; Lk 9:18–20

13When Jesus came to the region
of Caesarea Philippi, he asked his
disciples, "Who do people say the
Son of Man is?"
14They replied, "Some say John
the Baptist;[j] others say Elijah;
and still others, Jeremiah or one of
the prophets."[k]
15"But what about you?" he
asked. "Who do you say I am?"
16Simon Peter answered, "You
are the Christ,[b] the Son of the living God."[l]
17Jesus replied, "Blessed are
you, Simon son of Jonah, for this
was not revealed to you by man,[m]
but by my Father in heaven. 18And
I tell you that you are Peter,[c][n] and
on this rock I will build my
church,[o] and the gates of Hades[d]
will not overcome it.[e] 19I will give
you the keys[p] of the kingdom of
heaven; whatever you bind on
earth will be[f] bound in heaven,
and whatever you loose on earth
will be[f] loosed in heaven."[q]
20Then he warned his disciples not
to tell anyone[r] that he was the
Christ.

Jesus Predicts His Death

16:21–28pp Mk 8:31–9:1; Lk 9:22–27

21From that time on Jesus began
to explain to his disciples that he
must go to Jerusalem and suffer
many things[s] at the hands of the
elders, chief priests and teachers
of the law, and that he must be
killed and on the third day[t] be
raised to life.[u]

15:37 z Mt 16:10
16:1 a Ac 4:1 b Mt 12:38
16:3 c Lk 12:54-56
16:4 d Mt 12:39
16:6 e Lk 12:1
16:8 f Mt 6:30
16:9 g Mt 14:17-21
16:10 h Mt 15:34-38
16:12 i Ac 4:1
16:14 j Mt 3:1 Mt 14:2 k Mk 6:15 Jn 1:21
16:16 l Mt 4:3 Ps 42:2 Jn 11:27 Ac 14:15 2Co 6:16 1Th 1:9 1Ti 3:15 Heb 10:31 Heb 12:22
16:17 m 1Co 15:50 Gal 1:16 Eph 6:12 Heb 2:14
16:18 n Jn 1:42 o Eph 2:20
16:19 p Isa 22:22 Rev 3:7 q Mt 18:18 Jn 20:23
16:20 r Mk 8:30
16:21 s Mk 10:34 Lk 17:25 t Jn 2:19 u Mt 17:22,23 Mk 9:31 Lk 9:22 Lk 18:31-33 Lk 24:6,7

[a]2 Some early manuscripts do not have the rest of verse 2 and all of verse 3. [b]16 Or *Messiah*; also in verse 20 [c]18 *Peter* means *rock.* [d]18 Or *hell* [e]18 Or *not prove stronger than it* [f]19 Or *have been*

22 Peter took him aside and began
to rebuke him. "Never, Lord!" he
said. "This shall never happen to
you!"
23 Jesus turned and said to Peter,
"Get behind me, Satan![v] You are a
stumbling-block to me; you do not
have in mind the things of God, but
the things of men."
24 Then Jesus said to his disciples,
"If anyone would come after me, he
must deny himself and take up his
cross and follow me.[w] 25 For whoever wants to save his life[g] will
lose it, but whoever loses his life
for me will find it.[x] 26 What good
will it be for a man if he gains the
whole world, yet forfeits his soul?
Or what can a man give in exchange for his soul? 27 For the Son
of Man[y] is going to come[z] in his
Father's glory with his angels, and
then he will reward each person according to what he has done.[a] 28 I
tell you the truth, some who are
standing here will not taste death
before they see the Son of Man
coming in his kingdom."

The Transfiguration

17:1–8pp Lk 9:28–36
17:1–13pp Mk 9:2–13

17 After six days Jesus took
with him Peter, James and
John the brother of James, and
led them up a high mountain by
themselves. 2 There he was transfigured before them. His face shone
like the sun, and his clothes became as white as the light. 3 Just
then there appeared before them
Moses and Elijah, talking with
Jesus.
4 Peter said to Jesus, "Lord, it is
good for us to be here. If you wish,
I will put up three shelters—one
for you, one for Moses and one for
Elijah."
5 While he was still speaking, a
bright cloud enveloped them, and a
voice from the cloud said, "This is
my Son, whom I love; with him I am
well pleased.[a] Listen to him!"[b]

16:23
v Mt 4:10
16:24
w Mt 10:38; Lk 14:27
16:25
x Jn 12:25
16:27
y Mt 8:20
z Ac 1:11
a Job 34:11; Ps 62:12; Jer 17:10; Ro 2:6; 2Co 5:10; Rev 22:12
17:5
a Mt 3:17; 2Pe 1:17
b Ac 3:22,23
17:7
c Mt 14:27
17:9
d Mk 8:30
e Mt 8:20
f Mt 16:21
17:11
g Mal 4:6; Lk 1:16,17
17:12
h Mt 11:14
i Mt 14:3,10
j Mt 16:21
17:15
k Mt 4:24

6 When the disciples heard this,
they fell face down to the ground,
terrified. 7 But Jesus came and
touched them. "Get up," he said.
"Don't be afraid."[c] 8 When they
looked up, they saw no-one except
Jesus.
9 As they were coming down the
mountain, Jesus instructed them,
"Don't tell anyone[d] what you have
seen, until the Son of Man[e] has
been raised from the dead."[f]
10 The disciples asked him,
"Why then do the teachers of the
law say that Elijah must come
first?"
11 Jesus replied, "To be sure, Elijah comes and will restore all
things.[g] 12 But I tell you, Elijah has
already come,[h] and they did not
recognise him, but have done to
him everything they wished.[i] In
the same way the Son of Man is
going to suffer[j] at their hands."
13 Then the disciples understood
that he was talking to them about
John the Baptist.

The Healing of a Boy With a Demon

17:14–19pp Mk 9:14–28; Lk 9:37–42

14 When they came to the crowd, a
man approached Jesus and knelt
before him. 15 "Lord, have mercy on
my son," he said. "He has seizures[k] and is suffering greatly. He
often falls into the fire or into the
water. 16 I brought him to your disciples, but they could not heal him."
17 "O unbelieving and perverse
generation," Jesus replied, "how
long shall I stay with you? How
long shall I put up with you? Bring
the boy here to me." 18 Jesus rebuked the demon, and it came out
of the boy, and he was healed from
that moment.
19 Then the disciples came to
Jesus in private and asked, "Why
couldn't we drive it out?"

[g] 25 The Greek word means either *life* or *soul*; also in verse 26.

20He replied, "Because you have so little faith. I tell you the truth, if you have faith[l] as small as a mustard seed,[m] you can say to this mountain, 'Move from here to there' and it will move.[n] Nothing will be impossible for you."[a]

22When they came together in Galilee, he said to them, "The Son of Man[o] is going to be betrayed into the hands of men. 23They will kill him,[p] and on the third day[q] he will be raised to life."[r] And the disciples were filled with grief.

The Temple Tax

24After Jesus and his disciples arrived in Capernaum, the collectors of the two-drachma tax[s] came to Peter and asked, "Doesn't your teacher pay the temple tax?"[b]

25"Yes, he does," he replied.

When Peter came into the house, Jesus was the first to speak. "What do you think, Simon?" he asked. "From whom do the kings of the earth collect duty and taxes[t]—from their own sons or from others?"

26"From others," Peter answered.

"Then the sons are exempt," Jesus said to him. 27"But so that we may not offend[u] them, go to the lake and throw out your line. Take the first fish you catch; open its mouth and you will find a four-drachma coin. Take it and give it to them for my tax and yours."

The Greatest in the Kingdom of Heaven

18:1–5pp Mk 9:33–37; Lk 9:46–48

18 At that time the disciples came to Jesus and asked, "Who is the greatest in the kingdom of heaven?"

2He called a little child and had him stand among them. 3And he said: "I tell you the truth, unless you change and become like little children,[a] you will never enter the kingdom of heaven.[b] 4Therefore, whoever humbles himself like this child is the greatest in the kingdom of heaven.[c]

5"And whoever welcomes a little child like this in my name welcomes me.[d] 6But if anyone causes one of these little ones who believe in me to sin,[e] it would be better for him to have a large millstone hung around his neck and to be drowned in the depths of the sea.[f]

7"Woe to the world because of the things that cause people to sin! Such things must come, but woe to the man through whom they come![g] 8If your hand or your foot causes you to sin,[h] cut it off and throw it away. It is better for you to enter life maimed or crippled than to have two hands or two feet and be thrown into eternal fire. 9And if your eye causes you to sin,[i] gouge it out and throw it away. It is better for you to enter life with one eye than to have two eyes and be thrown into the fire of hell.[j]

The Parable of the Lost Sheep

18:12–14pp Lk 15:4–7

10"See that you do not look down on one of these little ones. For I tell you that their angels[k] in heaven always see the face of my Father in heaven.[a]

12"What do you think? If a man owns a hundred sheep, and one of them wanders away, will he not leave the ninety-nine on the hills and go to look for the one that wandered off? 13And if he finds it, I tell you the truth, he is happier about that one sheep than about the ninety-nine that did not wander off. 14In the same way your Father in heaven is not willing that any of these little ones should be lost.

17:20 l Mt 21:21 m Mt 13:31 Mk 11:23 Lk 17:6 n 1Co 13:2
17:22 o Mt 8:20
17:23 p Ac 2:23 Ac 3:13 q Mt 16:21 r Mt 16:21
17:24 s Ex 30:13
17:25 t Mt 22:17-21 Ro 13:7
17:27 u Jn 6:61
18:3 a Mt 19:14 1Pe 2:2 b Mt 3:2
18:4 c Mk 9:35
18:5 d Mt 10:40
18:6 e Mt 5:29 f Mk 9:42 Lk 17:2
18:7 g Lk 17:1
18:8 h Mt 5:29 Mk 9:43,45
18:9 i Mt 5:29 j Mt 5:22
18:10 k Ge 48:16 Ps 34:7 Ac 12:11,15 Heb 1:14

a20 Some manuscripts *you.* 21*But this kind does not go out except by prayer and fasting.*
b24 Greek *the two drachmas*
a10 Some manuscripts *heaven.* 11*The Son of Man came to save what was lost.*

A Brother Who Sins Against You

15“If your brother sins against
you,[b] go and show him his fault,[l]
just between the two of you. If he
listens to you, you have won your
brother over. 16But if he will not listen, take one or two others along, so
that ‘every matter may be established by the testimony of two or
three witnesses.’[c][m] 17If he refuses
to listen to them, tell it to the
church;[n] and if he refuses to listen
even to the church, treat him as you
would a pagan or a tax collector.[o]
18“I tell you the truth, whatever
you bind on earth will be[d] bound in
heaven, and whatever you loose on
earth will be[d] loosed in heaven.[p]
19“Again, I tell you that if two of
you on earth agree about anything
you ask for, it will be done for you[q]
by my Father in heaven. 20For
where two or three come together
in my name, there am I with them.”

The Parable of the Unmerciful Servant

21Then Peter came to Jesus and
asked, “Lord, how many times shall
I forgive my brother when he
sins against me?[r] Up to seven
times?”[s]
22Jesus answered, “I tell you, not
seven times, but seventy-seven
times.[e][t]
23“Therefore, the kingdom of
heaven is like[u] a king who wanted
to settle accounts[v] with his servants. 24As he began the settlement, a man who owed him ten
thousand talents[f] was brought to
him. 25Since he was not able to
pay,[w] the master ordered that he
and his wife and his children and
all that he had be sold[x] to repay the
debt.
26“The servant fell on his knees
before him.[y] ‘Be patient with me,’
he begged, ‘and I will pay back
everything.’ 27The servant’s master took pity on him, cancelled the
debt and let him go.

18:15
l Lev 19:17
Lk 17:3
Gal 6:1
Jas 5:19,20

18:16
m Nu 35:30
Dt 17:6
Dt 19:15
Jn 8:17
2Co 13:1
1Ti 5:19
Heb 10:28

18:17
n 1Co 6:1-6
o Ro 16:17
2Th 3:6,14

18:18
p Mt 16:19
Jn 20:23

18:19
q Mt 7:7

18:21
r Mt 6:14
s Lk 17:4

18:22
t Ge 4:24

18:23
u Mt 13:24
v Mt 25:19

18:25
w Lk 7:42
x Lev 25:39
2Ki 4:1
Ne 5:5,8

18:26
y Mt 8:2

18:35
z Mt 6:14
Jas 2:13

19:1
a Mt 7:28

19:2
b Mt 4:23

19:3
c Mt 5:31

19:4
d Ge 1:27
Ge 5:2

28“But when that servant went
out, he found one of his fellow-
servants who owed him a hundred
denarii.[g] He grabbed him and began to choke him. ‘Pay back what
you owe me!’ he demanded.
29“His fellow-servant fell to his
knees and begged him, ‘Be patient
with me, and I will pay you back.’
30“But he refused. Instead, he
went off and had the man thrown
into prison until he could pay the
debt. 31When the other servants
saw what had happened, they were
greatly distressed and went and
told their master everything that
had happened.
32“Then the master called the
servant in. ‘You wicked servant,’
he said, ‘I cancelled all that debt of
yours because you begged me to.
33Shouldn’t you have had mercy on
your fellow-servant just as I had on
you?’ 34In anger his master turned
him over to the jailers to be tortured, until he should pay back all
he owed.
35“This is how my heavenly
Father will treat each of you unless
you forgive your brother from
your heart.”[z]

Divorce

19:1–9pp Mk 10:1–12

19 When Jesus had finished
saying these things,[a] he
left Galilee and went into the region of Judea to the other side of
the Jordan. 2Large crowds followed him, and he healed them[b]
there.
3Some Pharisees came to him to
test him. They asked, “Is it lawful
for a man to divorce his wife[c] for
any and every reason?”
4“Haven’t you read,” he replied,
“that at the beginning the Creator
‘made them male and female’,[a][d]

[b]15 Some manuscripts do not have *against you.*
[c]16 Deut. 19:15 [d]18 Or *have been*
[e]22 Or *seventy times seven* [f]24 That is, millions of pounds [g]28 That is, a few pounds
[a]4 Gen. 1:27

5and said, 'For this reason a man
will leave his father and mother
and be united to his wife, and the
two will become one flesh'[b]?[e] 6So
they are no longer two, but one.
Therefore what God has joined together, let man not separate."
7"Why then," they asked, "did
Moses command that a man give
his wife a certificate of divorce and
send her away?"[f]
8Jesus replied, "Moses permitted
you to divorce your wives because
your hearts were hard. But it was
not this way from the beginning. 9I
tell you that anyone who divorces
his wife, except for marital unfaithfulness, and marries another
woman commits adultery."[g]
10The disciples said to him, "If
this is the situation between a husband and wife, it is better not to
marry."
11Jesus replied, "Not everyone
can accept this word, but only those
to whom it has been given.[h] 12For
some are eunuchs because they
were born that way; others were
made that way by men; and others
have renounced marriage[c] because of the kingdom of heaven.
The one who can accept this should
accept it."

The Little Children and Jesus

19:13–15pp Mk 10:13–16; Lk 18:15–17

13Then little children were
brought to Jesus for him to place
his hands on them[i] and pray for
them. But the disciples rebuked
those who brought them.
14Jesus said, "Let the little children come to me, and do not hinder
them, for the kingdom of heaven
belongs[j] to such as these."[k]
15When he had placed his hands on
them, he went on from there.

The Rich Young Man

19:16–29pp Mk 10:17–30; Lk 18:18–30

16Now a man came up to Jesus
and asked, "Teacher, what good
thing must I do to get eternal
life[l]?"[m]
17"Why do you ask me about what
is good?" Jesus replied. "There is
only One who is good. If you want
to enter life, obey the commandments."[n]
18"Which ones?" the man enquired.
Jesus replied, " 'Do not murder,
do not commit adultery,[o] do not
steal, do not give false testimony,
19honour your father and mother,'[d][p] and 'love your neighbour
as yourself.'[e]"[q]
20"All these I have kept," the
young man said. "What do I still
lack?"
21Jesus answered, "If you want to
be perfect,[r] go, sell your possessions and give to the poor,[s] and
you will have treasure in heaven.[t]
Then come, follow me."
22When the young man heard
this, he went away sad, because he
had great wealth.
23Then Jesus said to his disciples,
"I tell you the truth, it is hard for a
rich man[u] to enter the kingdom of
heaven. 24Again I tell you, it is easier for a camel to go through the
eye of a needle than for a rich man
to enter the kingdom of God."
25When the disciples heard this,
they were greatly astonished and
asked, "Who then can be saved?"
26Jesus looked at them and said,
"With man this is impossible, but
with God all things are possible."[v]
27Peter answered him, "We have
left everything to follow you![w]
What then will there be for us?"
28Jesus said to them, "I tell you
the truth, at the renewal of all
things, when the Son of Man sits on
his glorious throne,[x] you who have
followed me will also sit on twelve
thrones, judging the twelve tribes
of Israel.[y] 29And everyone who has
left houses or brothers or sisters or

19:5 e Ge 2:24; 1Co 6:16; Eph 5:31
19:7 f Dt 24:1-4; Mt 5:31
19:9 g Mt 5:32; Lk 16:18
19:11 h Mt 13:11; 1Co 7:7-9,17
19:13 i Mk 5:23
19:14 j Mt 25:34; k Mt 18:3; 1Pe 2:2
19:16 l Mt 25:46; m Lk 10:25
19:17 n Lev 18:5
19:18 o Jas 2:11
19:19 p Ex 20:12-16; Dt 5:16-20; q Lev 19:18; Mt 5:43
19:21 r Mt 5:48; s Lk 12:33; Ac 2:45; Ac 4:34-35; t Mt 6:20
19:23 u Mt 13:22; 1Ti 6:9,10
19:26 v Ge 18:14; Job 42:2; Jer 32:17; Zec 8:6; Lk 1:37; Lk 18:27; Ro 4:21
19:27 w Mt 4:19
19:28 x Mt 20:21; Mt 25:31; y Lk 22:28-30; Rev 3:21; Rev 4:4; Rev 20:4

b*5* Gen. 2:24 c*12* Or *have made themselves eunuchs* d*19* Exodus 20:12–16; Deut. 5:16–20
e*19* Lev. 19:18

father or mother[f] or children or fields for my sake will receive a hundred times as much and will inherit eternal life.[z] 30But many who are first will be last, and many who are last will be first.[a]

The Parable of the Workers in the Vineyard

20 "For the kingdom of heaven is like[a] a landowner who went out early in the morning to hire men to work in his vineyard.[b] 2He agreed to pay them a denarius for the day and sent them into his vineyard.

3"About the third hour he went out and saw others standing in the market-place doing nothing. 4He told them, 'You also go and work in my vineyard, and I will pay you whatever is right.' 5So they went.

"He went out again about the sixth hour and the ninth hour and did the same thing. 6About the eleventh hour he went out and found still others standing around. He asked them, 'Why have you been standing here all day long doing nothing?'

7" 'Because no-one has hired us,' they answered.

"He said to them, 'You also go and work in my vineyard.'

8"When evening came,[c] the owner of the vineyard said to his foreman, 'Call the workers and pay them their wages, beginning with the last ones hired and going on to the first.'

9"The workers who were hired about the eleventh hour came and each received a denarius. 10So when those came who were hired first, they expected to receive more. But each one of them also received a denarius. 11When they received it, they began to grumble[d] against the landowner. 12'These men who were hired last worked only one hour,' they said, 'and you have made them equal to us who have borne the burden of the work and the heat[e] of the day.'

13"But he answered one of them, 'Friend,[f] I am not being unfair to you. Didn't you agree to work for a denarius? 14Take your pay and go. I want to give the man who was hired last the same as I gave you. 15Don't I have the right to do what I want with my own money? Or are you envious because I am generous?'[g]

16"So the last will be first, and the first will be last."[h]

Jesus Again Predicts His Death

20:17–19pp Mk 10:32–34; Lk 18:31–33

17Now as Jesus was going up to Jerusalem, he took the twelve disciples aside and said to them, 18"We are going up to Jerusalem,[i] and the Son of Man[j] will be betrayed to the chief priests and the teachers of the law.[k] They will condemn him to death 19and will turn him over to the Gentiles to be mocked and flogged[l] and crucified.[m] On the third day[n] he will be raised to life!"[o]

A Mother's Request

20:20–28pp Mk 10:35–45

20Then the mother of Zebedee's sons[p] came to Jesus with her sons and, kneeling down,[q] asked a favour of him.

21"What is it you want?" he asked.

She said, "Grant that one of these two sons of mine may sit at your right and the other at your left in your kingdom."[r]

22"You don't know what you are asking," Jesus said to them. "Can you drink the cup[s] I am going to drink?"

"We can," they answered.

23Jesus said to them, "You will indeed drink from my cup,[t] but to sit at my right or left is not for me to grant. These places belong to those

19:29 z Mt 6:33; Mt 25:46
19:30 a Mt 20:16; Mk 10:31; Lk 13:30
20:1 a Mt 13:24; b Mt 21:28,33
20:8 c Lev 19:13; Dt 24:15
20:11 d Jnh 4:1
20:12 e Jnh 4:8; Lk 12:55; Jas 1:11
20:13 f Mt 22:12; Mt 26:50
20:15 g Dt 15:9; Mk 7:22
20:16 h Mt 19:30
20:18 i Lk 9:51; j Mt 8:20; k Mt 16:21; Mt 27:1,2
20:19 l Mt 16:21; m Ac 2:23; n Mt 16:21; o Mt 16:21
20:20 p Mt 4:21; q Mt 8:2
20:21 r Mt 19:28
20:22 s Isa 51:17,22; Jer 49:12; Mt 26:39,42; Mk 14:36; Lk 22:42; Jn 18:11
20:23 t Ac 12:2; Rev 1:9

f29 Some manuscripts *mother or wife*

for whom they have been prepared
by my Father."
24When the ten heard about this,
they were indignant[u] with the two
brothers. 25Jesus called them together and said, "You know that the
rulers of the Gentiles lord it over
them, and their high officials exercise authority over them. 26Not so
with you. Instead, whoever wants
to become great among you must
be your servant,[v] 27and whoever
wants to be first must be your
slave—28just as the Son of Man[w]
did not come to be served, but to
serve,[x] and to give his life as a ransom[y] for many."

Two Blind Men Receive Sight

20:29-34pp Mk 10:46-52; Lk 18:35-43

29As Jesus and his disciples were
leaving Jericho, a large crowd followed him. 30Two blind men were
sitting by the roadside, and when
they heard that Jesus was going
by, they shouted, "Lord, Son of
David,[z] have mercy on us!"
31The crowd rebuked them and
told them to be quiet, but they
shouted all the louder, "Lord, Son
of David, have mercy on us!"
32Jesus stopped and called them.
"What do you want me to do for
you?" he asked.
33"Lord," they answered, "we
want our sight."
34Jesus had compassion on them
and touched their eyes. Immediately they received their sight and
followed him.

The Triumphal Entry

21:1-9pp Mk 11:1-10; Lk 19:29-38
21:4-9pp Jn 12:12-15

21 As they approached Jerusalem and came to Beth-
phage on the Mount of Olives,[a]
Jesus sent two disciples, 2saying to
them, "Go to the village ahead of
you, and at once you will find a donkey tied there, with her colt by her.
Untie them and bring them to me.
3If anyone says anything to you,

20:24
u Lk 22:24,25
20:26
v Mt 23:11
Mk 9:35
20:28
w Mt 8:20
x Lk 22:27
Jn 13:13-16
2Co 8:9
Php 2:7
y Isa 53:10
Mt 26:28
1Ti 2:6
Tit 2:14
Heb 9:28
1Pe 1:18,19
20:30
z Mt 9:27
21:1
a Mt 24:3
Mt 26:30
Mk 14:26
Lk 19:37
Lk 21:37
Lk 22:39
Jn 8:1
Ac 1:12
21:5
b Zec 9:9
Isa 62:11
21:8
c 2Ki 9:13
21:9
d ver 15
Mt 9:27
e Ps 118:26
Mt 23:39
f Lk 2:14
21:11
g Lk 7:16,39
Lk 24:19
Jn 1:21,25
Jn 6:14
Jn 7:40
21:12
h Dt 14:26
i Ex 30:13
j Lev 1:14
21:13
k Isa 56:7
l Jer 7:11

tell him that the Lord needs them,
and he will send them right away."
4This took place to fulfil what
was spoken through the prophet:

5"Say to the Daughter of Zion,
'See, your king comes to you,
gentle and riding on a donkey,
on a colt, the foal of a
donkey.' "[a][b]

6The disciples went and did as
Jesus had instructed them. 7They
brought the donkey and the colt,
placed their cloaks on them, and
Jesus sat on them. 8A very large
crowd spread their cloaks[c] on the
road, while others cut branches
from the trees and spread them on
the road. 9The crowds that went
ahead of him and those that followed shouted,

"Hosanna[b] to the Son of
David!"[d]
"Blessed is he who comes in the
name of the Lord!"[c][e]
"Hosanna[b] in the highest!"[f]

10When Jesus entered Jerusalem,
the whole city was stirred and
asked, "Who is this?"
11The crowds answered, "This is
Jesus, the prophet[g] from Nazareth
in Galilee."

Jesus at the Temple

21:12-16pp Mk 11:15-18; Lk 19:45-47

12Jesus entered the temple area
and drove out all who were
buying[h] and selling there. He
overturned the tables of the
money-changers[i] and the benches
of those selling doves.[j] 13"It is
written," he said to them, " 'My
house will be called a house of
prayer,'[d][k] but you are making it a
'den of robbers'.[e]"[l]
14The blind and the lame came to
him at the temple, and he healed

a5 Zech. 9:9 b9 A Hebrew expression meaning "Save!" which became an exclamation of praise; also in verse 15 c9 Psalm 118:26 d13 Isaiah 56:7 e13 Jer. 7:11

them.[m] 15But when the chief
priests and the teachers of the law
saw the wonderful things he did
and the children shouting in the
temple area, "Hosanna to the Son of
David,"[n] they were indignant.[o]
16"Do you hear what these children are saying?" they asked him.
"Yes," replied Jesus, "have you
never read,

" 'From the lips of children and
infants
you have ordained praise'[f]?"[p]

17And he left them and went out
of the city to Bethany,[q] where he
spent the night.

The Fig-Tree Withers

21:18–22pp Mk 11:12–14,20–24

18Early in the morning, as he was
on his way back to the city, he was
hungry. 19Seeing a fig-tree by the
road, he went up to it but found
nothing on it except leaves. Then
he said to it, "May you never bear
fruit again!" Immediately the tree
withered.[r]
20When the disciples saw this,
they were amazed. "How did the
fig-tree wither so quickly?" they
asked.
21Jesus replied, "I tell you the
truth, if you have faith and do not
doubt,[s] not only can you do what
was done to the fig-tree, but also
you can say to this mountain, 'Go,
throw yourself into the sea,' and it
will be done. 22If you believe, you
will receive whatever you ask for[t]
in prayer."

The Authority of Jesus Questioned

21:23–27pp Mk 11:27–33; Lk 20:1–8

23Jesus entered the temple
courts, and, while he was teaching,
the chief priests and the elders of
the people came to him. "By what
authority[u] are you doing these
things?" they asked. "And who
gave you this authority?"

21:14 m Mt 4:23
21:15 n ver 9; Mt 9:27; o Lk 19:39
21:16 p Ps 8:2
21:17 q Mt 26:6; Mk 11:1; Lk 24:50; Jn 11:1,18; Jn 12:1
21:19 r Isa 34:4; Jer 8:13
21:21 s Mt 17:20; Lk 17:6; 1Co 13:2; Jas 1:6
21:22 t Mt 7:7
21:23 u Ac 4:7; Ac 7:27
21:26 v Mt 11:9; Mk 6:20
21:28 w ver 33; Mt 20:1
21:31 x Lk 7:29; y Lk 7:50
21:32 z Mt 3:1-12; a Lk 3:12,13; Lk 7:29; b Lk 7:36-50; c Lk 7:30
21:33 d Ps 80:8

24Jesus replied, "I will also ask
you one question. If you answer
me, I will tell you by what authority
I am doing these things. 25John's
baptism—where did it come from?
Was it from heaven, or from men?"
They discussed it among themselves and said, "If we say, 'From
heaven', he will ask, 'Then why
didn't you believe him?' 26But if we
say, 'From men'—we are afraid of
the people, for they all hold that
John was a prophet."[v]
27So they answered Jesus, "We
don't know."
Then he said, "Neither will I tell
you by what authority I am doing
these things.

The Parable of the Two Sons

28"What do you think? There was
a man who had two sons. He went to
the first and said, 'Son, go and work
today in the vineyard.'[w]
29" 'I will not,' he answered, but
later he changed his mind and
went.
30"Then the father went to the
other son and said the same thing.
He answered, 'I will, sir,' but he did
not go.
31"Which of the two did what his
father wanted?"
"The first," they answered.
Jesus said to them, "I tell you the
truth, the tax collectors[x] and the
prostitutes[y] are entering the kingdom of God ahead of you. 32For
John came to you to show you the
way of righteousness,[z] and you did
not believe him, but the tax collectors[a] and the prostitutes[b] did. And
even after you saw this, you did not
repent[c] and believe him.

The Parable of the Tenants

21:33–46pp Mk 12:1–12; Lk 20:9–19

33"Listen to another parable:
There was a landowner who
planted[d] a vineyard. He put a wall
around it, dug a winepress in it and

[f] *16* Psalm 8:2

built a watchtower.[e] Then he rented the vineyard to some farmers and went away on a journey.[f] 34When the harvest time approached, he sent his servants[g] to the tenants to collect his fruit.

35"The tenants seized his servants; they beat one, killed another, and stoned a third.[h] 36Then he sent other servants[i] to them, more than the first time, and the tenants treated them in the same way. 37Last of all, he sent his son to them. 'They will respect my son,' he said.

38"But when the tenants saw the son, they said to each other, 'This is the heir.[j] Come, let's kill him[k] and take his inheritance.'[l] 39So they took him and threw him out of the vineyard and killed him.

40"Therefore, when the owner of the vineyard comes, what will he do to those tenants?"

41"He will bring those wretches to a wretched end,"[m] they replied, "and he will rent the vineyard to other tenants,[n] who will give him his share of the crop at harvest time."

42Jesus said to them, "Have you never read in the Scriptures:

" 'The stone the builders
rejected
has become the capstone;[g]
the Lord has done this,
and it is marvellous in our
eyes'[h]?[o]

43"Therefore I tell you that the kingdom of God will be taken away from you[p] and given to a people who will produce its fruit. 44He who falls on this stone will be broken to pieces, but he on whom it falls will be crushed."[i][q]

45When the chief priests and the Pharisees heard Jesus' parables, they knew he was talking about them. 46They looked for a way to arrest him, but they were afraid of the crowd because the people held that he was a prophet.[r]

21:33 e Isa 5:1-7 f Mt 25:14,15
21:34 g Mt 22:3
21:35 h 2Ch 24:21 Mt 23:34,37 Heb 11:36,37
21:36 i Mt 22:4
21:38 j Heb 1:2 k Mt 12:14 l Ps 2:8
21:41 m Mt 8:11,12 n Ac 13:46 Ac 18:6 Ac 28:28
21:42 o Ps 118:22,23 Ac 4:11 1Pe 2:7
21:43 p Mt 8:12
21:44 q Lk 2:34
21:46 r ver 11,26
22:2 a Mt 13:24
22:3 b Mt 21:34
22:4 c Mt 21:36
22:7 d Lk 19:27
22:9 e Eze 21:21
22:10 f Mt 13:47,48
22:12 g Mt 20:13 Mt 26:50
22:13 h Mt 8:12
22:14 i Rev 17:14

The Parable of the Wedding Banquet

22:2-14Ref Lk 14:16-24

22 Jesus spoke to them again in parables, saying: 2"The kingdom of heaven is like[a] a king who prepared a wedding banquet for his son. 3He sent his servants[b] to those who had been invited to the banquet to tell them to come, but they refused to come.

4"Then he sent some more servants[c] and said, 'Tell those who have been invited that I have prepared my dinner: My oxen and fattened cattle have been slaughtered, and everything is ready. Come to the wedding banquet.'

5"But they paid no attention and went off—one to his field, another to his business. 6The rest seized his servants, ill-treated them and killed them. 7The king was enraged. He sent his army and destroyed those murderers[d] and burned their city.

8"Then he said to his servants, 'The wedding banquet is ready, but those I invited did not deserve to come. 9Go to the street corners[e] and invite to the banquet anyone you find.' 10So the servants went out into the streets and gathered all the people they could find, both good and bad,[f] and the wedding hall was filled with guests.

11"But when the king came in to see the guests, he noticed a man there who was not wearing wedding clothes. 12'Friend,'[g] he asked, 'how did you get in here without wedding clothes?' The man was speechless.

13"Then the king told the attendants, 'Tie him hand and foot, and throw him outside, into the darkness, where there will be weeping and gnashing of teeth.'[h]

14"For many are invited, but few are chosen."[i]

g42 Or *cornerstone* h42 Psalm 118:22,23
i44 Some manuscripts do not have verse 44.

Paying Taxes to Caesar

22:15–22pp Mk 12:13–17; Lk 20:20–26

15Then the Pharisees went out
and laid plans to trap him in his
words. 16They sent their disciples
to him along with the Herodians.[j]
"Teacher," they said, "we know you
are a man of integrity and that you
teach the way of God in accordance
with the truth. You aren't swayed
by men, because you pay no attention to who they are. 17Tell us then,
what is your opinion? Is it right to
pay taxes[k] to Caesar or not?"
18But Jesus, knowing their evil
intent, said, "You hypocrites, why
are you trying to trap me? 19Show
me the coin used for paying the
tax." They brought him a denarius,
20and he asked them, "Whose portrait is this? And whose inscription?"
21"Caesar's," they replied.
Then he said to them, "Give to
Caesar what is Caesar's,[l] and to
God what is God's."
22When they heard this, they
were amazed. So they left him and
went away.[m]

Marriage at the Resurrection

22:23–33pp Mk 12:18–27; Lk 20:27–40

23That same day the Sadducees,[n]
who say there is no resurrection,[o]
came to him with a question.
24"Teacher," they said, "Moses told
us that if a man dies without having
children, his brother must marry
the widow and have children for
him.[p] 25Now there were seven
brothers among us. The first one
married and died, and since he had
no children, he left his wife to his
brother. 26The same thing happened to the second and third
brother, right on down to the seventh. 27Finally, the woman died.
28Now then, at the resurrection,
whose wife will she be of the seven,
since all of them were married to
her?"
29Jesus replied, "You are in error
because you do not know the
Scriptures[q] or the power of God.
30At the resurrection people will
neither marry nor be given in marriage;[r] they will be like the angels
in heaven. 31But about the resurrection of the dead—have you not
read what God said to you, 32'I am
the God of Abraham, the God of
Isaac, and the God of Jacob'[a]?[s]
He is not the God of the dead but of
the living."
33When the crowds heard this,
they were astonished at his teaching.[t]

The Greatest Commandment

22:34–40pp Mk 12:28–31

34Hearing that Jesus had silenced the Sadducees,[u] the Pharisees got together. 35One of them, an
expert in the law,[v] tested him with
this question: 36"Teacher, which is
the greatest commandment in the
Law?"
37Jesus replied: " 'Love the Lord
your God with all your heart and
with all your soul and with all your
mind.'[b][w] 38This is the first and
greatest commandment. 39And the
second is like it: 'Love your neighbour as yourself.'[c][x] 40All the Law
and the Prophets hang on these two
commandments."[y]

Whose Son Is the Christ?

22:41–46pp Mk 12:35–37; Lk 20:41–44

41While the Pharisees were gathered together, Jesus asked them,
42"What do you think about the
Christ?[d] Whose son is he?"
"The son of David,"[z] they replied.
43He said to them, "How is it then
that David, speaking by the Spirit,
calls him 'Lord'? For he says,

44" 'The Lord said to my Lord:
"Sit at my right hand
until I put your enemies
under your feet." '[e][a]

22:16 [j] Mk 3:6
22:17 [k] Mt 17:25
22:21 [l] Ro 13:7
22:22 [m] Mk 12:12
22:23 [n] Ac 4:1 [o] Ac 23:8; 1Co 15:12
22:24 [p] Dt 25:5,6
22:29 [q] Jn 20:9
22:30 [r] Mt 24:38
22:32 [s] Ex 3:6; Ac 7:32
22:33 [t] Mt 7:28
22:34 [u] Ac 4:1
22:35 [v] Lk 7:30; Lk 10:25; Lk 11:45; Lk 14:3
22:37 [w] Dt 6:5
22:39 [x] Lev 19:18; Mt 5:43; Mt 19:19; Gal 5:14
22:40 [y] Mt 7:12
22:42 [z] Mt 9:27
22:44 [a] Ps 110:1; Ac 2:34,35; 1Co 15:25; Heb 1:13; Heb 10:13

[a]*32* Exodus 3:6 [b]*37* Deut. 6:5 [c]*39* Lev. 19:18
[d]*42* Or *Messiah* [e]*44* Psalm 110:1

45If then David calls him 'Lord',
how can he be his son?" 46No-one
could say a word in reply, and from
that day on no-one dared to ask him
any more questions.[b]

Seven Woes

23:1–7pp Mk 12:38,39; Lk 20:45,46
23:37–39pp Lk 13:34,35

23 Then Jesus said to the
crowds and to his disciples:
2"The teachers of the law[a] and the
Pharisees sit in Moses' seat. 3So
you must obey them and do everything they tell you. But do not do
what they do, for they do not practise what they preach. 4They tie up
heavy loads and put them on men's
shoulders, but they themselves are
not willing to lift a finger to move
them.[b]
5"Everything they do is done for
men to see:[c] They make their phyl-
acteries[a][d] wide and the tassels on
their garments[e] long; 6they love
the place of honour at banquets and
the most important seats in the
synagogues;[f] 7they love to be
greeted in the market-places and to
have men call them 'Rabbi'.[g]
8"But you are not to be called
'Rabbi', for you have only one Master and you are all brothers. 9And
do not call anyone on earth 'father',
for you have one Father,[h] and he is
in heaven. 10Nor are you to be
called 'teacher', for you have one
Teacher, the Christ.[b] 11The greatest among you will be your
servant.[i] 12For whoever exalts
himself will be humbled, and whoever humbles himself will be
exalted.[j]
13"Woe to you, teachers of the law
and Pharisees, you hypocrites![k]
You shut the kingdom of heaven in
men's faces. You yourselves do not
enter, nor will you let those enter
who are trying to.[c][l]
15"Woe to you, teachers of the law
and Pharisees, you hypocrites! You
travel over land and sea to win a
single convert,[m] and when he becomes one, you make him twice as
much a son of hell[n] as you are.
16"Woe to you, blind guides![o]
You say, 'If anyone swears by the
temple, it means nothing; but if
anyone swears by the gold of the
temple, he is bound by his oath.'[p]
17You blind fools! Which is greater:
the gold, or the temple that makes
the gold sacred?[q] 18You also say,
'If anyone swears by the altar, it
means nothing; but if anyone
swears by the gift on it, he is bound
by his oath.' 19You blind men!
Which is greater: the gift, or the
altar that makes the gift sacred?[r]
20Therefore, he who swears by the
altar swears by it and by everything on it. 21And he who swears by
the temple swears by it and by the
one who dwells[s] in it. 22And he who
swears by heaven swears by God's
throne and by the one who sits
on it.[t]
23"Woe to you, teachers of the law
and Pharisees, you hypocrites! You
give a tenth[u] of your spices—mint,
dill and cummin. But you have neglected the more important matters
of the law—justice, mercy and
faithfulness.[v] You should have
practised the latter, without neg-
lecting the former. 24You blind
guides![w] You strain out a gnat but
swallow a camel.
25"Woe to you, teachers of the law
and Pharisees, you hypocrites!
You clean the outside of the cup
and dish,[x] but inside they are
full of greed and self-indulgence.[y]
26Blind Pharisee! First clean the inside of the cup and dish, and then
the outside also will be clean.
27"Woe to you, teachers of the law

22:46 b Mk 12:34 Lk 20:40
23:2 a Ezr 7:6,25 Ne 8:4
23:4 b Lk 11:46 Ac 15:10 Gal 6:13
23:5 c Mt 6:1,2,5,16 d Ex 13:9 Dt 6:8 e Nu 15:38 Dt 22:12
23:6 f Lk 11:43 Lk 14:7 Lk 20:46
23:7 g ver 8 Mk 9:5 Mk 10:51 Jn 1:38,49
23:9 h Mal 1:6 Mt 7:11
23:11 i Mt 20:26 Mk 9:35
23:12 j Lk 14:11
23:13 k ver 15,23,25, 27,29 l Lk 11:52
23:15 m Ac 2:11 Ac 6:5 Ac 13:43 n Mt 5:22
23:16 o ver 24 Mt 15:14 p Mt 5:33-35
23:17 q Ex 30:29
23:19 r Ex 29:37
23:21 s 1Ki 8:13 Ps 26:8
23:22 t Ps 11:4 Mt 5:34
23:23 u Lev 27:30 v Mic 6:8 Lk 11:42
23:24 w ver 16
23:25 x Mk 7:4 y Lk 11:39

a5 That is, boxes containing Scripture verses, worn on forehead and arm b10 Or *Messiah* c13 Some manuscripts *to.* 14*Woe to you, teachers of the Law and Pharisees, you hypocrites! You devour widows' houses and for a show make lengthy prayers. Therefore you will be punished more severely.*

and Pharisees, you hypocrites! You
are like whitewashed tombs,[z]
which look beautiful on the outside
but on the inside are full of dead
men's bones and everything unclean. 28In the same way, on the
outside you appear to people
as righteous but on the inside you
are full of hypocrisy and wickedness.
29"Woe to you, teachers of the law
and Pharisees, you hypocrites! You
build tombs for the prophets[a] and
decorate the graves of the righteous. 30And you say, 'If we had
lived in the days of our forefathers,
we would not have taken part with
them in shedding the blood of the
prophets.' 31So you testify against
yourselves that you are the descendants of those who murdered
the prophets.[b] 32Fill up, then, the
measure[c] of the sin of your forefathers!
33"You snakes! You brood of
vipers![d] How will you escape being condemned to hell?[e] 34There-
fore I am sending you prophets and
wise men and teachers. Some of
them you will kill and crucify;[f]
others you will flog in your synagogues[g] and pursue from town to
town.[h] 35And so upon you will
come all the righteous blood that
has been shed on earth, from the
blood of righteous Abel[i] to the
blood of Zechariah son of Bera-
kiah,[j] whom you murdered between the temple and the altar.[k] 36I
tell you the truth, all this will come
upon this generation.[l]
37"O Jerusalem, Jerusalem, you
who kill the prophets and stone
those sent to you,[m] how often I
have longed to gather your children together, as a hen gathers her
chicks under her wings, but you
were not willing. 38Look, your
house is left to you desolate.[n] 39For
I tell you, you will not see me again
until you say, 'Blessed is he
who comes in the name of the
Lord.'[d]"[o]

23:27 [z] Lk 11:44; Ac 23:3
23:29 [a] Lk 11:47,48
23:31 [b] Ac 7:51-52
23:32 [c] 1Th 2:16
23:33 [d] Mt 3:7; Mt 12:34 [e] Mt 5:22
23:34 [f] 2Ch 36:15,16; Lk 11:49 [g] Mt 10:17 [h] Mt 10:23
23:35 [i] Ge 4:8; Heb 11:4 [j] Zec 1:1 [k] 2Ch 24:21
23:36 [l] Mt 10:23; Mt 24:34
23:37 [m] 2Ch 24:21; Mt 5:12
23:38 [n] 1Ki 9:7,8; Jer 22:5
23:39 [o] Ps 118:26; Mt 21:9
24:2 [a] Lk 19:44
24:3 [b] Mt 21:1
24:5 [c] ver 11,23,24; 1Jn 2:18
24:7 [d] Isa 19:2 [e] Ac 11:28
24:9 [f] Mt 10:17 [g] Jn 16:2
24:11 [h] Mt 7:15
24:13 [i] Mt 10:22
24:14 [j] Mt 4:23 [k] Ro 10:18; Col 1:6,23; Lk 2:1; Lk 4:5; Ac 11:28; Ac 17:6; Rev 3:10; Rev 16:14
24:15 [l] Ac 6:13 [m] Da 9:27; Da 11:31; Da 12:11

Signs of the End of the Age

24:1-51pp Mk 13:1-37; Lk 21:5-36

24 Jesus left the temple and
was walking away when his
disciples came up to him to call his
attention to its buildings. 2"Do you
see all these things?" he asked. "I
tell you the truth, not one stone
here will be left on another;[a] every
one will be thrown down."
3As Jesus was sitting on the
Mount of Olives,[b] the disciples
came to him privately. "Tell us,"
they said, "when will this happen,
and what will be the sign of your
coming and of the end of the age?"
4Jesus answered: "Watch out
that no-one deceives you. 5For
many will come in my name, claiming, 'I am the Christ,'[a] and will deceive many.[c] 6You will hear of
wars and rumours of wars, but
see to it that you are not alarmed.
Such things must happen, but the
end is still to come. 7Nation will
rise against nation, and kingdom
against kingdom.[d] There will be
famines[e] and earthquakes in various places. 8All these are the beginning of birth-pains.
9"Then you will be handed over
to be persecuted[f] and put to
death,[g] and you will be hated by all
nations because of me. 10At that
time many will turn away from the
faith and will betray and hate each
other, 11and many false prophets[h]
will appear and deceive many people. 12Because of the increase of
wickedness, the love of most will
grow cold, 13but he who stands firm
to the end will be saved.[i] 14And
this gospel of the kingdom[j] will be
preached in the whole world[k] as a
testimony to all nations, and then
the end will come.
15"So when you see standing in
the holy place[l] 'the abomination
that causes desolation',[b][m] spoken
of through the prophet Daniel—let
the reader understand—16then let

[d] *39* Psalm 118:26 [a] *5* Or *Messiah*; also in verse 23 [b] *15* Daniel 9:27; 11:31; 12:11

those who are in Judea flee to the
mountains. 17 Let no-one on the roof
of his house[n] go down to take anything out of the house. 18 Let no-one
in the field go back to get his cloak.
19 How dreadful it will be in those
days for pregnant women and nursing mothers![o] 20 Pray that your
flight will not take place in winter
or on the Sabbath. 21 For then there
will be great distress, unequalled
from the beginning of the world
until now—and never to be
equalled again.[p] 22 If those days
had not been cut short, no-one
would survive, but for the sake of
the elect[q] those days will be shortened. 23 At that time if anyone says
to you, 'Look, here is the Christ!' or,
'There he is!' do not believe it.[r]
24 For false Christs and false prophets will appear and perform great
signs and miracles[s] to deceive
even the elect—if that were possible. 25 See, I have told you ahead of
time.

26 "So if anyone tells you, 'There
he is, out in the desert,' do not go
out; or, 'Here he is, in the inner
rooms,' do not believe it. 27 For as
lightning[t] that comes from the
east is visible even in the west, so
will be the coming of the Son of
Man.[u] 28 Wherever there is a carcass, there the vultures will
gather.[v]

29 "Immediately after the distress
of those days

" 'the sun will be darkened,
and the moon will not give its
light;
the stars will fall from the sky,
and the heavenly bodies will
be shaken.'[c][w]

30 "At that time the sign of the Son
of Man will appear in the sky, and
all the nations of the earth will
mourn. They will see the Son of
Man coming on the clouds of the
sky,[x] with power and great glory.
31 And he will send his angels[y] with
a loud trumpet call,[z] and they will
gather his elect from the four
winds, from one end of the heavens
to the other.

32 "Now learn this lesson from the
fig-tree: As soon as its twigs get
tender and its leaves come out, you
know that summer is near. 33 Even
so, when you see all these things,
you know that it[d] is near, right at
the door.[a] 34 I tell you the truth, this
generation[e] will certainly not pass
away until all these things have
happened.[b] 35 Heaven and earth
will pass away, but my words will
never pass away.[c]

The Day and Hour Unknown

24:37–39pp Lk 17:26,27
24:45–51pp Lk 12:42–46

36 "No-one knows about that day
or hour, not even the angels in
heaven, nor the Son,[f] but only the
Father.[d] 37 As it was in the days of
Noah,[e] so it will be at the coming
of the Son of Man. 38 For in the days
before the flood, people were eating and drinking, marrying and
giving in marriage,[f] up to the day
Noah entered the ark; 39 and they
knew nothing about what would
happen until the flood came and
took them all away. That is how it
will be at the coming of the Son of
Man. 40 Two men will be in the field;
one will be taken and the other
left.[g] 41 Two women will be grinding with a hand mill; one will be
taken and the other left.[h]

42 "Therefore keep watch, because you do not know on what day
your Lord will come.[i] 43 But understand this: If the owner of the
house had known at what time of
night the thief was coming,[j] he
would have kept watch and would
not have let his house be broken
into. 44 So you also must be ready,[k]
because the Son of Man will come
at an hour when you do not expect
him.

45 "Who then is the faithful and

24:17 n 1Sa 9:25; Mt 10:27; Lk 12:3; Ac 10:9
24:19 o Lk 23:29
24:21 p Da 12:1; Joel 2:2
24:22 q ver 24,31
24:23 r Lk 17:23; Lk 21:8
24:24 s 2Th 2:9-11; Rev 13:13
24:27 t Lk 17:24; u Mt 8:20
24:28 v Lk 17:37
24:29 w Isa 13:10; Isa 34:4; Eze 32:7; Joel 2:10,31; Zep 1:15; Rev 6:12,13; Rev 8:12
24:30 x Da 7:13; Rev 1:7
24:31 y Mt 13:41; z Isa 27:13; Zec 9:14; 1Co 15:52; 1Th 4:16; Rev 8:2; Rev 10:7; Rev 11:15
24:33 a Jas 5:9
24:34 b Mt 16:28; Mt 23:36
24:35 c Mt 5:18
24:36 d Ac 1:7
24:37 e Ge 6:5; Ge 7:6-23
24:38 f Mt 22:30
24:40 g Lk 17:34
24:41 h Lk 17:35
24:42 i Mt 25:13; Lk 12:40
24:43 j Lk 12:39
24:44 k 1Th 5:6

c29 Isaiah 13:10; 34:4 d33 Or *he*
e34 Or *race* f36 Some manuscripts do not have *nor the Son.*

wise servant,[l] whom the master
has put in charge of the servants in
his household to give them their
food at the proper time? 46It will be
good for that servant whose master
finds him doing so when he returns.[m] 47I tell you the truth, he will
put him in charge of all his possessions.[n] 48But suppose that servant
is wicked and says to himself, 'My
master is staying away a long time,'
49and he then begins to beat his
fellow-servants and to eat and
drink with drunkards.[o] 50The master of that servant will come on a
day when he does not expect him
and at an hour he is not aware of.
51He will cut him to pieces and assign him a place with the hypocrites, where there will be weeping
and gnashing of teeth.[p]

The Parable of the Ten Virgins

25 "At that time the kingdom
of heaven will be like[a] ten
virgins who took their lamps[b] and
went out to meet the bridegroom.[c]
2Five of them were foolish and five
were wise.[d] 3The foolish ones took
their lamps but did not take any oil
with them. 4The wise, however,
took oil in jars along with their
lamps. 5The bridegroom was a long
time in coming, and they all became drowsy and fell asleep.[e]
6"At midnight the cry rang out:
'Here's the bridegroom! Come out
to meet him!'
7"Then all the virgins woke up
and trimmed their lamps. 8The
foolish ones said to the wise, 'Give
us some of your oil; our lamps are
going out.'[f]
9" 'No,' they replied, 'there may
not be enough for both us and you.
Instead, go to those who sell oil and
buy some for yourselves.'
10"But while they were on their
way to buy the oil, the bridegroom
arrived. The virgins who were
ready went in with him to the wedding banquet.[g] And the door was
shut.

24:45 l Mt 25:21,23
24:46 m Rev 16:15
24:47 n Mt 25:21,23
24:49 o Lk 21:34
24:51 p Mt 8:12
25:1 a Mt 13:24 b Lk 12:35-38 Ac 20:8 Rev 4:5 c Rev 19:7 Rev 21:2
25:2 d Mt 24:45
25:5 e 1Th 5:6
25:8 f Lk 12:35
25:10 g Rev 19:9
25:13 h Mt 24:42,44 Mk 13:35 Lk 12:40
25:14 i Mt 21:33 Lk 19:12
25:15 j Mt 18:24,25
25:19 k Mt 18:23
25:21 l ver 23 Mt 24:45,47 Lk 16:10
25:23 m ver 21

11"Later the others also came.
'Sir! Sir!' they said. 'Open the door
for us!'
12"But he replied, 'I tell you the
truth, I don't know you.'
13"Therefore keep watch, because you do not know the day or
the hour.[h]

The Parable of the Talents

25:14-30Ref Lk 19:12-27

14"Again, it will be like a man going on a journey,[i] who called his
servants and entrusted his property to them. 15To one he gave five
talents[a] of money, to another two
talents, and to another one talent,
each according to his ability.[j]
Then he went on his journey. 16The
man who had received the five talents went at once and put his
money to work and gained five
more. 17So also, the one with the
two talents gained two more. 18But
the man who had received the one
talent went off, dug a hole in the
ground and hid his master's money.
19"After a long time the master of
those servants returned and settled accounts with them.[k] 20The
man who had received the five talents brought the other five. 'Master,' he said, 'you entrusted me with
five talents. See, I have gained five
more.'
21"His master replied, 'Well
done, good and faithful servant!
You have been faithful with a few
things; I will put you in charge of
many things.[l] Come and share
your master's happiness!'
22"The man with the two talents
also came. 'Master,' he said, 'you
entrusted me with two talents; see,
I have gained two more.'
23"His master replied, 'Well
done, good and faithful servant!
You have been faithful with a few
things; I will put you in charge of
many things.[m] Come and share
your master's happiness!'

a *15* A talent was worth several hundred pounds.

24“Then the man who had received the one talent came. ‘Master,’ he said, ‘I knew that you are a
hard man, harvesting where you
have not sown and gathering where
you have not scattered seed. 25So I
was afraid and went out and hid
your talent in the ground. See, here
is what belongs to you.’
26“His master replied, ‘You
wicked, lazy servant! So you knew
that I harvest where I have not
sown and gather where I have not
scattered seed? 27Well then, you
should have put my money on deposit with the bankers, so that
when I returned I would have received it back with interest.
28“ ‘Take the talent from him and
give it to the one who has the ten
talents. 29For everyone who has
will be given more, and he will have
an abundance. Whoever does not
have, even what he has will be
taken from him.[n] 30And throw that
worthless servant outside, into the
darkness, where there will be
weeping and gnashing of teeth.’[o]

The Sheep and the Goats

31“When the Son of Man comes[p]
in his glory, and all the angels with
him, he will sit on his throne[q] in
heavenly glory. 32All the nations
will be gathered before him, and he
will separate[r] the people one from
another as a shepherd separates
the sheep from the goats.[s] 33He
will put the sheep on his right and
the goats on his left.
34“Then the King will say to those
on his right, ‘Come, you who are
blessed by my Father; take your inheritance, the kingdom[t] prepared
for you since the creation of the
world.[u] 35For I was hungry and you
gave me something to eat, I was
thirsty and you gave me something
to drink, I was a stranger and you
invited me in,[v] 36I needed clothes
and you clothed me,[w] I was sick
and you looked after me,[x] I was in
prison and you came to visit me.’[y]
37“Then the righteous will answer him, ‘Lord, when did we see
you hungry and feed you, or thirsty
and give you something to drink?
38When did we see you a stranger
and invite you in, or needing
clothes and clothe you? 39When did
we see you sick or in prison and go
to visit you?’
40“The King will reply, ‘I tell you
the truth, whatever you did for one
of the least of these brothers of
mine, you did for me.’[z]
41“Then he will say to those on his
left, ‘Depart from me,[a] you who
are cursed, into the eternal fire[b]
prepared for the devil and his
angels.[c] 42For I was hungry and
you gave me nothing to eat, I was
thirsty and you gave me nothing to
drink, 43I was a stranger and you
did not invite me in, I needed
clothes and you did not clothe me,
I was sick and in prison and you did
not look after me.’
44“They also will answer, ‘Lord,
when did we see you hungry or
thirsty or a stranger or needing
clothes or sick or in prison, and did
not help you?’
45“He will reply, ‘I tell you the
truth, whatever you did not do for
one of the least of these, you did not
do for me.’[d]
46“Then they will go away to eternal punishment, but the righteous
to eternal life.[e]”[f]

The Plot Against Jesus

26:2–5pp Mk 14:1,2; Lk 22:1,2

26 When Jesus had finished
saying all these things,[a] he
said to his disciples, 2“As you know,
the Passover[b] is two days away—
and the Son of Man will be handed
over to be crucified.”
3Then the chief priests and the
elders of the people assembled[c] in
the palace of the high priest, whose
name was Caiaphas,[d] 4and they
plotted to arrest Jesus in some sly
way and kill him.[e] 5“But not during

25:29 *n* Mt 13:12; Mk 4:25; Lk 8:18; Lk 19:26
25:30 *o* Mt 8:12
25:31 *p* Mt 16:27; Lk 17:30 *q* Mt 19:28
25:32 *r* Mal 3:18 *s* Eze 34:17,20
25:34 *t* Mt 3:2; Mt 5:3,10,19; Mt 19:14; Ac 20:32; 1Co 15:50; Gal 5:21; Jas 2:5 *u* Heb 4:3; Heb 9:26; Rev 13:8; Rev 17:8
25:35 *v* Job 31:32; Isa 58:7; Eze 18:7; Heb 13:2
25:36 *w* Isa 58:7; Eze 18:7; Jas 2:15,16 *x* Jas 1:27 *y* 2Ti 1:16
25:40 *z* Pr 19:17; Mt 10:40,42; Heb 6:10; Heb 13:2
25:41 *a* Mt 7:23 *b* Isa 66:24; Mt 3:12; Mt 5:22; Mk 9:43,48; Lk 3:17; Jude 7 *c* 2Pe 2:4
25:45 *d* Pr 14:31; Pr 17:5
25:46 *e* Mt 19:29; Jn 3:15,16,36; Jn 17:2,3; Ro 2:7; Gal 6:8; Gal 5:11,13, 20 *f* Da 12:2; Jn 5:29; Ac 24:15; Ro 2:7,8; Gal 6:8
26:1 *a* Mt 7:28
26:2 *b* Jn 11:55; Jn 13:1
26:3 *c* Ps 2:2 *d* ver 57; Jn 11:47-53; Jn 18:13,14, 24,28
26:4 *e* Mt 12:14

the Feast," they said, "or there may
be a riot[f] among the people."

Jesus Anointed at Bethany

26:6–13pp Mk 14:3–9
26:6–13Ref Lk 7:37,38; Jn 12:1–8

6While Jesus was in Bethany[g] in
the home of a man known as Simon
the Leper, 7a woman came to him
with an alabaster jar of very expensive perfume, which she poured on
his head as he was reclining at the
table.
8When the disciples saw this,
they were indignant. "Why this
waste?" they asked. 9"This perfume could have been sold at a high
price and the money given to the
poor."
10Aware of this, Jesus said to
them, "Why are you bothering this
woman? She has done a beautiful
thing to me. 11The poor you will always have with you,[h] but you will
not always have me. 12When she
poured this perfume on my body,
she did it to prepare me for
burial.[i] 13I tell you the truth, wherever this gospel is preached
throughout the world, what she has
done will also be told, in memory of
her."

Judas Agrees to Betray Jesus

26:14–16pp Mk 14:10,11; Lk 22:3–6

14Then one of the Twelve—the
one called Judas Iscariot[j]—went
to the chief priests 15and asked,
"What are you willing to give me if
I hand him over to you?" So they
counted out for him thirty silver
coins.[k] 16From then on Judas
watched for an opportunity to hand
him over.

The Lord's Supper

26:17–19pp Mk 14:12–16; Lk 22:7–13
26:20–24pp Mk 14:17–21
26:26–29pp Mk 14:22–25; Lk 22:17–20; 1Co 11:23–25

17On the first day of the Feast of
Unleavened Bread,[l] the disciples
came to Jesus and asked, "Where
do you want us to make preparations for you to eat the Passover?"
18He replied, "Go into the city to
a certain man and tell him, 'The
Teacher says: My appointed time[m]
is near. I am going to celebrate the
Passover with my disciples at your
house.' " 19So the disciples did as
Jesus had directed them and prepared the Passover.
20When evening came, Jesus was
reclining at the table with the
Twelve. 21And while they were eating, he said, "I tell you the truth,
one of you will betray me."[n]
22They were very sad and began
to say to him one after the other,
"Surely not I, Lord?"
23Jesus replied, "The one who has
dipped his hand into the bowl with
me will betray me.[o] 24The Son of
Man will go just as it is written
about him.[p] But woe to that man
who betrays the Son of Man! It
would be better for him if he had
not been born."
25Then Judas, the one who would
betray him, said, "Surely not I,
Rabbi?"[q]
Jesus answered, "Yes, it is
you."[a]
26While they were eating, Jesus
took bread, gave thanks and broke
it,[r] and gave it to his disciples, saying, "Take and eat; this is my
body."
27Then he took the cup, gave
thanks and offered it to them, saying, "Drink from it, all of you.
28This is my blood of the[b] covenant,[s] which is poured out for
many for the forgiveness of sins.[t]
29I tell you, I will not drink of
this fruit of the vine from now
on until that day when I drink it
anew with you[u] in my Father's
kingdom."
30When they had sung a hymn,
they went out to the Mount of
Olives.[v]

26:5 f Mt 27:24
26:6 g Mt 21:17
26:11 h Dt 15:11
26:12 i Jn 19:40
26:14 j ver 25,47; Mt 10:4
26:15 k Ex 21:32; Zec 11:12
26:17 l Ex 12:18-20
26:18 m Jn 7:6,8,30; Jn 12:23; Jn 13:1; Jn 17:1
26:21 n Lk 22:21-23; Jn 13:21
26:23 o Ps 41:9; Jn 13:18
26:24 p Isa 53; Da 9:26; Mk 9:12; Lk 24:25-27, 46; Ac 17:2,3; Ac 26:22,23
26:25 q Mt 23:7
26:26 r Mt 14:19; 1Co 10:16
26:28 s Ex 24:6-8; Heb 9:20; t Mt 20:28; Mk 1:4
26:29 u Ac 10:41
26:30 v Mt 21:1; Mk 14:26

[a]25 Or "*You yourself have said it*" [b]28 Some manuscripts *the new*

Jesus Predicts Peter's Denial

26:31–35pp Mk 14:27–31; Lk 22:31–34

31 Then Jesus told them, "This very night you will all fall away on account of me,[w] for it is written:

"'I will strike the shepherd,
and the sheep of the flock will
be scattered.'[c][x]

32 But after I have risen, I will go ahead of you into Galilee."[y]

33 Peter replied, "Even if all fall away on account of you, I never will."

34 "I tell you the truth," Jesus answered, "this very night, before the cock crows, you will disown me three times."[z]

35 But Peter declared, "Even if I have to die with you,[a] I will never disown you." And all the other disciples said the same.

Gethsemane

26:36–46pp Mk 14:32–42; Lk 22:40–46

36 Then Jesus went with his disciples to a place called Gethsemane, and he said to them, "Sit here while I go over there and pray." 37 He took Peter and the two sons of Zebedee[b] along with him, and he began to be sorrowful and troubled. 38 Then he said to them, "My soul is overwhelmed with sorrow[c] to the point of death. Stay here and keep watch with me."[d]

39 Going a little farther, he fell with his face to the ground and prayed, "My Father, if it is possible, may this cup[e] be taken from me. Yet not as I will, but as you will."[f]

40 Then he returned to his disciples and found them sleeping. "Could you men not keep watch with me[g] for one hour?" he asked Peter. 41 "Watch and pray so that you will not fall into temptation.[h] The spirit is willing, but the body is weak."

42 He went away a second time and prayed, "My Father, if it is not possible for this cup to be taken away unless I drink it, may your will be done."

43 When he came back, he again found them sleeping, because their eyes were heavy. 44 So he left them and went away once more and prayed the third time, saying the same thing.

45 Then he returned to the disciples and said to them, "Are you still sleeping and resting? Look, the hour[i] is near, and the Son of Man is betrayed into the hands of sinners. 46 Rise, let us go! Here comes my betrayer!"

Jesus Arrested

26:47–56pp Mk 14:43–50; Lk 22:47–53

47 While he was still speaking, Judas, one of the Twelve, arrived. With him was a large crowd armed with swords and clubs, sent from the chief priests and the elders of the people. 48 Now the betrayer had arranged a signal with them: "The one I kiss is the man; arrest him." 49 Going at once to Jesus, Judas said, "Greetings, Rabbi!"[j] and kissed him.

50 Jesus replied, "Friend,[k] do what you came for."[d]

Then the men stepped forward, seized Jesus and arrested him. 51 With that, one of Jesus' companions reached for his sword,[l] drew it out and struck the servant of the high priest, cutting off his ear.[m]

52 "Put your sword back in its place," Jesus said to him, "for all who draw the sword will die by the sword.[n] 53 Do you think I cannot call on my Father, and he will at once put at my disposal more than twelve legions of angels?[o] 54 But how then would the Scriptures be fulfilled[p] that say it must happen in this way?"

55 At that time Jesus said to the crowd, "Am I leading a rebellion, that you have come out with swords and clubs to capture me? Every day

26:31 w Mt 11:6 x Zec 13:7 Jn 16:32
26:32 y Mt 28:7,10,16
26:34 z ver 75 Jn 13:38
26:35 a Jn 13:37
26:37 b Mt 4:21
26:38 c Jn 12:27 d ver 40,41
26:39 e Mt 20:22 f ver 42 Ps 40:6-8 Isa 50:5 Jn 5:30 Jn 6:38
26:40 g ver 38
26:41 h Mt 6:13
26:45 i ver 18
26:49 j ver 25
26:50 k Mt 20:13 Mt 22:12
26:51 l Lk 22:36,38 m Jn 18:10
26:52 n Ge 9:6 Rev 13:10
26:53 o 2Ki 6:17 Da 7:10 Mt 4:11
26:54 p ver 24

c 31 Zech. 13:7 d 50 Or *"Friend, why have you come?"*

I sat in the temple courts teaching,[q] and you did not arrest me.
56 But this has all taken place that
the writings of the prophets might
be fulfilled."[r] Then all the disciples deserted him and fled.

Before the Sanhedrin

26:57–68pp Mk 14:53–65; Jn 18:12,13,19–24

57 Those who had arrested Jesus
took him to Caiaphas,[s] the high
priest, where the teachers of the
law and the elders had assembled.
58 But Peter followed him at a distance, right up to the courtyard of
the high priest.[t] He entered and
sat down with the guards[u] to see
the outcome.
59 The chief priests and the whole
Sanhedrin[v] were looking for false
evidence against Jesus so that they
could put him to death. 60 But they
did not find any, though many false
witnesses[w] came forward.
Finally two[x] came forward 61 and
declared, "This fellow said, 'I am
able to destroy the temple of God
and rebuild it in three days.' "[y]
62 Then the high priest stood up
and said to Jesus, "Are you not going to answer? What is this testimony that these men are bringing
against you?" 63 But Jesus remained silent.[z]
The high priest said to him, "I
charge you under oath[a] by the living God:[b] Tell us if you are the
Christ,[e] the Son of God."
64 "Yes, it is as you say," Jesus replied. "But I say to all of you: In the
future you will see the Son of Man
sitting at the right hand of the
Mighty One[c] and coming on the
clouds of heaven."[d]
65 Then the high priest tore his
clothes[e] and said, "He has spoken
blasphemy! Why do we need any
more witnesses? Look, now you
have heard the blasphemy. 66 What
do you think?"
"He is worthy of death,"[f] they
answered.
67 Then they spat in his face and
struck him with their fists.[g]
Others slapped him 68 and said,
"Prophesy to us, Christ. Who hit
you?"[h]

Peter Disowns Jesus

26:69–75pp Mk 14:66–72; Lk 22:55–62; Jn 18:16–18,25–27

69 Now Peter was sitting out in the
courtyard, and a servant girl came
to him. "You also were with Jesus
of Galilee," she said.
70 But he denied it before them
all. "I don't know what you're talking about," he said.
71 Then he went out to the gateway, where another girl saw him
and said to the people there, "This
fellow was with Jesus of Nazareth."
72 He denied it again, with an
oath: "I don't know the man!"
73 After a little while, those standing there went up to Peter and said,
"Surely you are one of them, for
your accent gives you away."
74 Then he began to call down
curses on himself and he swore to
them, "I don't know the man!"
Immediately a cock crowed.
75 Then Peter remembered the
word Jesus had spoken: "Before
the cock crows, you will disown me
three times."[i] And he went outside
and wept bitterly.

Judas Hangs Himself

27 Early in the morning, all
the chief priests and the
elders of the people came to the decision to put Jesus to death.[a] 2 They
bound him, led him away and
handed him over[b] to Pilate, the
governor.[c]
3 When Judas, who had betrayed
him,[d] saw that Jesus was condemned, he was seized with re-
morse and returned the thirty
silver coins[e] to the chief priests
and the elders. 4 "I have sinned," he
said, "for I have betrayed innocent
blood."

26:55 q Mk 12:35; Lk 21:37; Jn 7:14,28; Jn 18:20
26:56 r ver 24
26:57 s ver 3
26:58 t Jn 18:15; u Jn 7:32,45,46
26:59 v Mt 5:22
26:60 w Ps 27:12; Ps 35:11; Ac 6:13; x Dt 19:15
26:61 y Jn 2:19
26:63 z Mt 27:12,14; a Lev 5:1; b Mt 16:16
26:64 c Ps 110:1; d Da 7:13; Rev 1:7
26:65 e Mk 14:63
26:66 f Lev 24:16; Jn 19:7
26:67 g Mt 16:21; Mt 27:30
26:68 h Lk 22:63-65
26:75 i ver 34; Jn 13:38
27:1 a Mt 12:14; Mk 15:1; Lk 22:66
27:2 b Mt 20:19; c Mk 15:1; Lk 13:1; Ac 3:13; 1Ti 6:13
27:3 d Mt 10:4; e Mt 26:14,15

[e] 63 Or *Messiah*; also in verse 68

"What is that to us?" they replied.
"That's your responsibility."[f]
5So Judas threw the money into
the temple[g] and left. Then he went
away and hanged himself.[h]
6The chief priests picked up the
coins and said, "It is against the law
to put this into the treasury, since it
is blood money." 7So they decided
to use the money to buy the potter's
field as a burial place for foreigners. 8That is why it has been called
the Field of Blood[i] to this day.
9Then what was spoken by Jeremiah the prophet was fulfilled:[j]
"They took the thirty silver coins,
the price set on him by the people
of Israel, 10and they used them to
buy the potter's field, as the Lord
commanded me."[a][k]

Jesus Before Pilate

27:11–26pp Mk 15:2–15; Lk 23:2,3, 18–25; Jn 18:29–19:16

11Meanwhile Jesus stood before
the governor, and the governor
asked him, "Are you the king of the
Jews?"[l]
"Yes, it is as you say," Jesus replied.
12When he was accused by the
chief priests and the elders, he
gave no answer.[m] 13Then Pilate
asked him, "Don't you hear the testimony they are bringing against
you?"[n] 14But Jesus made no reply,[o] not even to a single charge—
to the great amazement of the
governor.
15Now it was the governor's custom at the Feast to release a prisoner[p] chosen by the crowd. 16At
that time they had a notorious prisoner, called Barabbas. 17So when
the crowd had gathered, Pilate
asked them, "Which one do you
want me to release to you: Barabbas, or Jesus who is called
Christ?"[q] 18For he knew it was out
of envy that they had handed Jesus
over to him.
19While Pilate was sitting on the
judge's seat,[r] his wife sent him
this message: "Don't have anything
to do with that innocent[s] man, for
I have suffered a great deal today
in a dream[t] because of him."
20But the chief priests and the
elders persuaded the crowd to ask
for Barabbas and to have Jesus executed.[u]
21"Which of the two do you want
me to release to you?" asked the
governor.
"Barabbas," they answered.
22"What shall I do, then, with
Jesus who is called Christ?"[v] Pilate asked.
They all answered, "Crucify
him!"
23"Why? What crime has he committed?" asked Pilate.
But they shouted all the louder,
"Crucify him!"
24When Pilate saw that he was
getting nowhere, but that instead
an uproar[w] was starting, he took
water and washed his hands[x] in
front of the crowd. "I am innocent
of this man's blood,"[y] he said. "It is
your responsibility!"[z]
25All the people answered, "Let
his blood be on us and on our children!"[a]
26Then he released Barabbas to
them. But he had Jesus flogged,[b]
and handed him over to be crucified.

The Soldiers Mock Jesus

27:27–31pp Mk 15:16–20

27Then the governor's soldiers
took Jesus into the Praetorium[c]
and gathered the whole company
of soldiers round him. 28They
stripped him and put a scarlet robe
on him,[d] 29and then twisted together a crown of thorns and set it
on his head. They put a staff in his
right hand and knelt in front of him
and mocked him. "Hail, king of the
Jews!" they said.[e] 30They spat on
him, and took the staff and struck
him on the head again and again.[f]

27:4 *f* ver 24
27:5 *g* Lk 1:9,21 *h* Ac 1:18
27:8 *i* Ac 1:19
27:9 *j* Mt 1:22
27:10 *k* Zec 11:12,13 Jer 32:6-9
27:11 *l* Mt 2:2
27:12 *m* Mt 26:63 Mk 14:61 Jn 19:9
27:13 *n* Mt 26:62
27:14 *o* Mk 14:61
27:15 *p* Jn 18:39
27:17 *q* ver 22 Mt 1:16
27:19 *r* Jn 19:13 *s* ver 24 *t* Ge 20:6 Nu 12:6 1Ki 3:5 Job 33:14-16 Mt 1:20 Mt 2:12,13, 19,22
27:20 *u* Ac 3:14
27:22 *v* Mt 1:16
27:24 *w* Mt 26:5 *x* Ps 26:6 *y* Dt 21:6-8 *z* ver 4
27:25 *a* Jos 2:19 Ac 5:28
27:26 *b* Isa 53:5 Jn 19:1
27:27 *c* Jn 18:28,33 Jn 19:9
27:28 *d* Jn 19:2
27:29 *e* Isa 53:3 Jn 19:2,3
27:30 *f* Mt 16:21 Mt 26:67

[a] *10* See Zech. 11:12,13; Jer. 19:1–13; 32:6–9.

31 After they had mocked him, they took off the robe and put his own clothes on him. Then they led him away to crucify him.[g]

The Crucifixion

27:33–44pp Mk 15:22–32; Lk 23:33–43; Jn 19:17–24

32 As they were going out,[h] they met a man from Cyrene,[i] named Simon, and they forced him to carry the cross.[j] 33 They came to a place called Golgotha (which means The Place of the Skull).[k] 34 There they offered Jesus wine to drink, mixed with gall;[l] but after tasting it, he refused to drink it. 35 When they had crucified him, they divided up his clothes by casting lots.[b][m] 36 And sitting down, they kept watch[n] over him there. 37 Above his head they placed the written charge against him: THIS IS JESUS, THE KING OF THE JEWS. 38 Two robbers were crucified with him,[o] one on his right and one on his left. 39 Those who passed by hurled insults at him, shaking their heads[p] 40 and saying, "You who are going to destroy the temple and build it in three days,[q] save yourself![r] Come down from the cross, if you are the Son of God!"[s]

41 In the same way the chief priests, the teachers of the law and the elders mocked him. 42 "He saved others," they said, "but he can't save himself! He's the King of Israel![t] Let him come down now from the cross, and we will believe[u] in him. 43 He trusts in God. Let God rescue him[v] now if he wants him, for he said, 'I am the Son of God.' " 44 In the same way the robbers who were crucified with him also heaped insults on him.

The Death of Jesus

27:45–56pp Mk 15:33–41; Lk 23:44–49

45 From the sixth hour until the ninth hour darkness[w] came over all the land. 46 About the ninth hour Jesus cried out in a loud voice, "*Eloi, Eloi,*[c] *lama sabachthani?*"—which means, "My God, my God, why have you forsaken me?"[d][x]

47 When some of those standing there heard this, they said, "He's calling Elijah."

48 Immediately one of them ran and got a sponge. He filled it with wine vinegar,[y] put it on a stick, and offered it to Jesus to drink. 49 The rest said, "Now leave him alone. Let's see if Elijah comes to save him."

50 And when Jesus had cried out again in a loud voice, he gave up his spirit.[z]

51 At that moment the curtain of the temple[a] was torn in two from top to bottom. The earth shook and the rocks split.[b] 52 The tombs broke open and the bodies of many holy people who had died were raised to life. 53 They came out of the tombs, and after Jesus' resurrection they went into the holy city[c] and appeared to many people.

54 When the centurion and those with him who were guarding[d] Jesus saw the earthquake and all that had happened, they were terrified, and exclaimed, "Surely he was the Son[e] of God!"[e]

55 Many women were there, watching from a distance. They had followed Jesus from Galilee to care for his needs.[f] 56 Among them were Mary Magdalene, Mary the mother of James and Joses, and the mother of Zebedee's sons.[g]

The Burial of Jesus

27:57–61pp Mk 15:42–47; Lk 23:50–56; Jn 19:38–42

57 As evening approached, there came a rich man from Arimathea, named Joseph, who had himself become a disciple of Jesus. 58 Going to

27:31 g Isa 53:7
27:32 h Heb 13:12; i Ac 2:10; Ac 6:9; Ac 11:20; Ac 13:1; j Mk 15:21; Lk 23:26
27:33 k Jn 19:17
27:34 l ver 48; Ps 69:21
27:35 m Ps 22:18
27:36 n ver 54
27:38 o Isa 53:12
27:39 p Ps 22:7; Ps 109:25; La 2:15
27:40 q Mt 26:61; Jn 2:19; r ver 42; s Mt 4:3,6
27:42 t Jn 1:49; Jn 12:13; u Jn 3:15
27:43 v Ps 22:8
27:45 w Am 8:9
27:46 x Ps 22:1
27:48 y ver 34; Ps 69:21
27:50 z Jn 19:30
27:51 a Ex 26:31-33; Heb 9:3,8; b ver 54
27:53 c Mt 4:5
27:54 d ver 36; e Mt 4:3; Mt 17:5
27:55 f Lk 8:2,3
27:56 g Mk 15:47; Lk 24:10; Jn 19:25

[b]35 A few late manuscripts *lots that the word spoken by the prophet might be fulfilled: "They divided my garments among themselves and cast lots for my clothing."* (Psalm 22:18) [c]46 Some manuscripts *Eli, Eli* [d]46 Psalm 22:1 [e]54 Or *a son*

Pilate, he asked for Jesus' body,
and Pilate ordered that it be given
to him. 59Joseph took the body,
wrapped it in a clean linen
cloth, 60and placed it in his
own new tomb[h] that he had cut
out of the rock. He rolled a big
stone in front of the entrance to
the tomb and went away. 61Mary
Magdalene and the other Mary
were sitting there opposite the
tomb.

The Guard at the Tomb

62The next day, the one after
Preparation Day, the chief priests
and the Pharisees went to Pilate.
63"Sir," they said, "we remember
that while he was still alive that deceiver said, 'After three days I will
rise again.'[i] 64So give the order for
the tomb to be made secure until
the third day. Otherwise, his disciples may come and steal the body
and tell the people that he has been
raised from the dead. This last deception will be worse than the
first."
65"Take a guard,"[j] Pilate answered. "Go, make the tomb as secure as you know how." 66So they
went and made the tomb secure by
putting a seal[k] on the stone[l] and
posting the guard.[m]

The Resurrection

28:1-8pp Mk 16:1-8; Lk 24:1-10

28 After the Sabbath, at dawn
on the first day of the week,
Mary Magdalene and the other
Mary[a] went to look at the tomb.
2There was a violent earthquake,[b] for an angel[c] of the Lord
came down from heaven and,
going to the tomb, rolled back the
stone and sat on it. 3His appearance was like lightning, and his
clothes were white as snow.[d] 4The
guards were so afraid of him that
they shook and became like dead
men.
5The angel said to the women,
"Do not be afraid,[e] for I know that
you are looking for Jesus, who was
crucified. 6He is not here; he has
risen, just as he said.[f] Come and
see the place where he lay. 7Then
go quickly and tell his disciples:
'He has risen from the dead and is
going ahead of you into Galilee.[g]
There you will see him.' Now I have
told you."
8So the women hurried away
from the tomb, afraid yet filled
with joy, and ran to tell his
disciples. 9Suddenly Jesus met
them.[h] "Greetings," he said. They
came to him, clasped his feet and
worshipped him. 10Then Jesus said
to them, "Do not be afraid. Go and
tell my brothers[i] to go to Galilee;
there they will see me."

The Guards' Report

11While the women were on their
way, some of the guards[j] went into
the city and reported to the chief
priests everything that had happened. 12When the chief priests had
met with the elders and devised a
plan, they gave the soldiers a large
sum of money, 13telling them, "You
are to say, 'His disciples came during the night and stole him away
while we were asleep.' 14If this report gets to the governor,[k] we will
satisfy him and keep you out of
trouble." 15So the soldiers took the
money and did as they were instructed. And this story has been
widely circulated among the Jews
to this very day.

The Great Commission

16Then the eleven disciples went
to Galilee, to the mountain where
Jesus had told them to go.[l] 17When
they saw him, they worshipped
him; but some doubted. 18Then
Jesus came to them and said, "All
authority in heaven and on earth
has been given to me.[m] 19Therefore

27:60 h Mt 27:66; Mt 28:2; Mk 16:4
27:63 i Mt 16:21
27:65 j ver 66; Mt 28:11
27:66 k Da 6:17; l ver 60; Mt 28:2; m Mt 28:11
28:1 a Mt 27:56
28:2 b Mt 27:51; c Jn 20:12
28:3 d Da 10:6; Mk 9:3; Jn 20:12
28:5 e ver 10; Mt 14:27
28:6 f Mt 16:21
28:7 g ver 10,16; Mt 26:32
28:9 h Jn 20:14-18
28:10 i Jn 20:17; Ro 8:29; Heb 2:11-13, 17
28:11 j Mt 27:65,66
28:14 k Mt 27:2
28:16 l ver 7,10; Mt 26:32
28:18 m Da 7:13,14; Lk 10:22; Jn 3:35; Jn 17:2; 1Co 15:27; Eph 1:20-22; Php 2:9,10

go and make disciples of all nations,[n] baptising them in[a] the
name of the Father and of the Son
and of the Holy Spirit,[o] 20and
teaching[p] them to obey everything
I have commanded you. And surely
I am with you[q] always, to the very
end of the age."[r]

28:19 *n* Mk 16:15,16 Lk 24:47 Ac 1:8 Ac 14:21 *o* Ac 2:38 Ac 8:16 Ro 6:3,4

28:20 *p* Ac 2:42 *q* Mt 18:20 Ac 18:10 *r* Mt 13:39

a*19* Or *into*; see Acts 8:16; 19:5; Rom. 6:3; 1 Cor. 1:13; 10:2 and Gal. 3:27.

MARK

John the Baptist Prepares the Way

1:2–8pp Mt 3:1–11; Lk 3:2–16

1 The beginning of the gospel about Jesus Christ, the Son of God.[a][a]

2 It is written in Isaiah the prophet:

> "I will send my messenger
> ahead of you,
> who will prepare your
> way"[b][b]—
> 3 "a voice of one calling in the
> desert,
> 'Prepare the way for the Lord,
> make straight paths for
> him.' "[c][c]

4 And so John[d] came, baptising in the desert region and preaching a baptism of repentance[e] for the forgiveness of sins.[f] 5 The whole Judean countryside and all the people of Jerusalem went out to him. Confessing their sins, they were baptised by him in the Jordan River. 6 John wore clothing made of camel's hair, with a leather belt round his waist, and he ate locusts[g] and wild honey. 7 And this was his message: "After me will come one more powerful than I, the thongs of whose sandals I am not worthy to stoop down and untie.[h] 8 I baptise you with[d] water, but he will baptise you with the Holy Spirit."[i]

The Baptism and Temptation of Jesus

1:9–11pp Mt 3:13–17; Lk 3:21,22
1:12,13pp Mt 4:1–11; Lk 4:1–13

9 At that time Jesus came from Nazareth[j] in Galilee and was baptised by John in the Jordan. 10 As Jesus was coming up out of the water, he saw heaven being torn open and the Spirit descending on him like a dove.[k] 11 And a voice came from heaven: "You are my Son,[l] whom I love; with you I am well pleased."

12 At once the Spirit sent him out into the desert, 13 and he was in the desert for forty days, being tempted by Satan.[m] He was with the wild animals, and angels attended him.

The Calling of the First Disciples

1:16–20pp Mt 4:18–22; Lk 5:2–11; Jn 1:35–42

14 After John was put in prison, Jesus went into Galilee,[n] proclaiming the good news of God.[o] 15 "The time has come,"[p] he said. "The kingdom of God is near. Repent and believe the good news!"[q]

16 As Jesus walked beside the Sea of Galilee, he saw Simon and his brother Andrew casting a net into the lake, for they were fishermen. 17 "Come, follow me," Jesus said, "and I will make you fishers of men." 18 At once they left their nets and followed him.

19 When he had gone a little farther, he saw James son of Zebedee and his brother John in a boat, preparing their nets. 20 Without delay he called them, and they left their father Zebedee in the boat with the hired men and followed him.

Jesus Drives Out an Evil Spirit

1:21–28pp Lk 4:31–37

21 They went to Capernaum, and when the Sabbath came, Jesus went into the synagogue and began to teach.[r] 22 The people were

1:1 *a* Mt 4:3
1:2 *b* Mal 3:1; Mt 11:10; Lk 7:27
1:3 *c* Isa 40:3; Jn 1:23
1:4 *d* Mt 3:1; *e* Ac 13:24; *f* Lk 1:77
1:6 *g* Lev 11:22
1:7 *h* Ac 13:25
1:8 *i* Isa 44:3; Joel 2:28; Ac 1:5; Ac 2:4; Ac 11:16; Ac 19:4-6
1:9 *j* Mt 2:23
1:10 *k* Jn 1:32
1:11 *l* Mt 3:17
1:13 *m* Mt 4:10
1:14 *n* Mt 4:12; *o* Mt 4:23
1:15 *p* Gal 4:4; Eph 1:10; *q* Ac 20:21
1:21 *r* Mt 4:23; Mk 10:1

[a] *1* Some manuscripts do not have *the Son of God.*
[b] *2* Mal. 3:1 [c] *3* Isaiah 40:3 [d] *8* Or *in*

amazed at his teaching, because he taught them as one who had authority, not as the teachers of the law.[s] 23Just then a man in their synagogue who was possessed by an evil[e] spirit cried out, 24"What do you want with us,[t] Jesus of Nazareth?[u] Have you come to destroy us? I know who you are—the Holy One of God!"[v]

25"Be quiet!" said Jesus sternly. "Come out of him!"[w] 26The evil spirit shook the man violently and came out of him with a shriek.[x]

27The people were all so amazed[y] that they asked each other, "What is this? A new teaching—and with authority! He even gives orders to evil spirits and they obey him." 28News about him spread quickly over the whole region[z] of Galilee.

Jesus Heals Many

1:29–31pp Mt 8:14,15; Lk 4:38,39
1:32–34pp Mt 8:16,17; Lk 4:40,41

29As soon as they left the synagogue,[a] they went with James and John to the home of Simon and Andrew. 30Simon's mother-in-law was in bed with a fever, and they told Jesus about her. 31So he went to her, took her hand and helped her up.[b] The fever left her and she began to wait on them.

32That evening after sunset the people brought to Jesus all the sick and demon-possessed.[c] 33The whole town gathered at the door, 34and Jesus healed many who had various diseases.[d] He also drove out many demons, but he would not let the demons speak because they knew who he was.[e]

Jesus Prays in a Solitary Place

1:35–38pp Lk 4:42,43

35Very early in the morning, while it was still dark, Jesus got up, left the house and went off to a solitary place, where he prayed.[f] 36Simon and his companions went to look for him, 37and when they found him, they exclaimed: "Everyone is looking for you!"

38Jesus replied, "Let us go somewhere else—to the nearby villages—so that I can preach there also. That is why I have come."[g] 39So he travelled throughout Galilee, preaching in their synagogues[h] and driving out demons.[i]

A Man With Leprosy

1:40–44pp Mt 8:2–4; Lk 5:12–14

40A man with leprosy[f] came to him and begged him on his knees,[j] "If you are willing, you can make me clean."

41Filled with compassion, Jesus reached out his hand and touched the man. "I am willing," he said. "Be clean!" 42Immediately the leprosy left him and he was cured.

43Jesus sent him away at once with a strong warning: 44"See that you don't tell this to anyone.[k] But go, show yourself to the priest[l] and offer the sacrifices that Moses commanded for your cleansing,[m] as a testimony to them." 45Instead he went out and began to talk freely, spreading the news. As a result, Jesus could no longer enter a town openly but stayed outside in lonely places.[n] Yet the people still came to him from everywhere.[o]

Jesus Heals a Paralytic

2:3–12pp Mt 9:2–8; Lk 5:18–26

2 A few days later, when Jesus again entered Capernaum, the people heard that he had come home. 2So many[a] gathered that there was no room left, not even outside the door, and he preached the word to them. 3Some men came, bringing to him a paralytic,[b] carried by four of them. 4Since they could not get him to Jesus because of the crowd, they made an opening in the roof above Jesus and, after

1:22 s Mt 7:28,29
1:24 t Mt 8:29 u Mt 2:23; Lk 24:19; Ac 24:5 v Lk 1:35; Jn 6:69; Ac 3:14
1:25 w ver 34
1:26 x Mk 9:20
1:27 y Mk 10:24,32
1:28 z Mt 9:26
1:29 a ver 21,23
1:31 b Lk 7:14
1:32 c Mt 4:24
1:34 d Mt 4:23 e Mk 3:12; Ac 16:17,18
1:35 f Lk 3:21
1:38 g Isa 61:1
1:39 h Mt 4:23 i Mt 4:24
1:40 j Mk 10:17
1:44 k Mt 8:4 l Lev 13:49 m Lev 14:1-32
1:45 n Lk 5:15,16 o Mk 2:13; Lk 5:17; Jn 6:2
2:2 a ver 13; Mk 1:45
2:3 b Mt 4:24

e23 Greek *unclean*; also in verses 26 and 27
f40 The Greek word was used for various diseases affecting the skin—not necessarily leprosy.

digging through it, lowered the mat
the paralysed man was lying on.
5When Jesus saw their faith, he
said to the paralytic, "Son, your
sins are forgiven."[c]
6Now some teachers of the law
were sitting there, thinking to
themselves, 7"Why does this fellow
talk like that? He's blaspheming!
Who can forgive sins but God
alone?"[d]
8Immediately Jesus knew in his
spirit that this was what they were
thinking in their hearts, and he said
to them, "Why are you thinking
these things? 9Which is easier: to
say to the paralytic, 'Your sins are
forgiven,' or to say, 'Get up, take
your mat and walk'? 10But that you
may know that the Son of Man[e]
has authority on earth to forgive
sins. . . ." He said to the paralytic,
11"I tell you, get up, take your mat
and go home." 12He got up, took his
mat and walked out in full view of
them all. This amazed everyone and
they praised God,[f] saying, "We have
never seen anything like this!"[g]

The Calling of Levi

2:14–17pp Mt 9:9–13; Lk 5:27–32

13Once again Jesus went out beside the lake. A large crowd came
to him,[h] and he began to teach
them. 14As he walked along, he saw
Levi son of Alphaeus sitting at the
tax collector's booth. "Follow
me,"[i] Jesus told him, and Levi got
up and followed him.
15While Jesus was having dinner
at Levi's house, many tax collectors and "sinners" were eating with
him and his disciples, for there
were many who followed him.
16When the teachers of the law who
were Pharisees[j] saw him eating
with the "sinners" and tax collectors, they asked his disciples: "Why
does he eat with tax collectors and
'sinners'?"[k]
17On hearing this, Jesus said to
them, "It is not the healthy who
need a doctor, but the sick. I have
not come to call the righteous, but
sinners."[l]

Jesus Questioned About Fasting

2:18–22pp Mt 9:14–17; Lk 5:33–38

18Now John's disciples and the
Pharisees were fasting.[m] Some
people came and asked Jesus,
"How is it that John's disciples and
the disciples of the Pharisees are
fasting, but yours are not?"
19Jesus answered, "How can the
guests of the bridegroom fast while
he is with them? They cannot, so
long as they have him with them.
20But the time will come when the
bridegroom will be taken from
them,[n] and on that day they will
fast.
21"No-one sews a patch of unshrunk cloth on an old garment. If
he does, the new piece will pull
away from the old, making the tear
worse. 22And no-one pours new
wine into old wineskins. If he does,
the wine will burst the skins, and
both the wine and the wineskins
will be ruined. No, he pours new
wine into new wineskins."

Lord of the Sabbath

2:23–28pp Mt 12:1–8; Lk 6:1–5
3:1–6pp Mt 12:9–14; Lk 6:6–11

23One Sabbath Jesus was going
through the cornfields, and as his
disciples walked along, they began
to pick some ears of corn.[o] 24The
Pharisees said to him, "Look, why
are they doing what is unlawful on
the Sabbath?"[p]
25He answered, "Have you never
read what David did when he and
his companions were hungry and in
need? 26In the days of Abiathar the
high priest,[q] he entered the house
of God and ate the consecrated
bread, which is lawful only for
priests to eat.[r] And he also gave
some to his companions."[s]
27Then he said to them, "The Sabbath was made for man,[t] not man
for the Sabbath.[u] 28So the Son of
Man[v] is Lord even of the Sabbath."

2:5 *c* Lk 7:48
2:7 *d* Isa 43:25
2:10 *e* Mt 8:20
2:12 *f* Mt 9:8 *g* Mt 9:33
2:13 *h* Mk 1:45 Lk 5:15 Jn 6:2
2:14 *i* Mt 4:19
2:16 *j* Ac 23:9 *k* Mt 9:11
2:17 *l* Lk 19:10 1Ti 1:15
2:18 *m* Mt 6:16-18 Ac 13:2
2:20 *n* Lk 17:22
2:23 *o* Dt 23:25
2:24 *p* Mt 12:2
2:26 *q* 1Ch 24:6 2Sa 8:17 *r* Lev 24:5-9 *s* 1Sa 21:1-6
2:27 *t* Ex 23:12 Dt 5:14 *u* Col 2:16
2:28 *v* Mt 8:20

3 Another time he went into the synagogue,[a] and a man with a shrivelled hand was there. 2Some of them were looking for a reason to accuse Jesus, so they watched him closely[b] to see if he would heal him on the Sabbath.[c] 3Jesus said to the man with the shrivelled hand, "Stand up in front of everyone."

4Then Jesus asked them, "Which is lawful on the Sabbath: to do good or to do evil, to save life or to kill?" But they remained silent.

5He looked round at them in anger and, deeply distressed at their stubborn hearts, said to the man, "Stretch out your hand." He stretched it out, and his hand was completely restored. 6Then the Pharisees went out and began to plot with the Herodians[d] how they might kill Jesus.[e]

Crowds Follow Jesus

3:7–12pp Mt 12:15,16; Lk 6:17–19

7Jesus withdrew with his disciples to the lake, and a large crowd from Galilee followed.[f] 8When they heard all he was doing, many people came to him from Judea, Jerusalem, Idumea, and the regions across the Jordan and around Tyre and Sidon.[g] 9Because of the crowd he told his disciples to have a small boat ready for him, to keep the people from crowding him. 10For he had healed many,[h] so that those with diseases were pushing forward to touch him.[i] 11Whenever the evil[a] spirits saw him, they fell down before him and cried out, "You are the Son of God."[j] 12But he gave them strict orders not to tell who he was.[k]

The Appointing of the Twelve Apostles

3:16–19pp Mt 10:2–4; Lk 6:14–16; Ac 1:13

13Jesus went up on a mountainside and called to him those he wanted, and they came to him.[l] 14He appointed twelve—designating them apostles[b][m]—that they might be with him and that he might send them out to preach 15and to have authority to drive out demons.[n] 16These are the twelve he appointed: Simon (to whom he gave the name Peter);[o] 17James son of Zebedee and his brother John (to them he gave the name Boanerges, which means Sons of Thunder); 18Andrew, Philip, Bartholomew, Matthew, Thomas, James son of Alphaeus, Thaddaeus, Simon the Zealot 19and Judas Iscariot, who betrayed him.

Jesus and Beelzebub

3:23–27pp Mt 12:25–29; Lk 11:17–22

20Then Jesus entered a house, and again a crowd gathered,[p] so that he and his disciples were not even able to eat.[q] 21When his family heard about this, they went to take charge of him, for they said, "He is out of his mind."[r]

22And the teachers of the law who came down from Jerusalem[s] said, "He is possessed by Beelzebub![c][t] By the prince of demons he is driving out demons."[u]

23So Jesus called them and spoke to them in parables:[v] "How can Satan[w] drive out Satan? 24If a kingdom is divided against itself, that kingdom cannot stand. 25If a house is divided against itself, that house cannot stand. 26And if Satan opposes himself and is divided, he cannot stand; his end has come. 27In fact, no-one can enter a strong man's house and carry off his possessions unless he first ties up the strong man. Then he can rob his house.[x] 28I tell you the truth, all the sins and blasphemies of men will be forgiven them. 29But whoever blasphemes against the Holy Spirit will never be forgiven; he is guilty of an eternal sin."[y]

30He said this because they were saying, "He has an evil spirit."

3:1 *a* Mt 4:23; Mk 1:21
3:2 *b* Mt 12:10; *c* Lk 14:1
3:6 *d* Mt 22:16; Mk 12:13; *e* Mt 12:14
3:7 *f* Mt 4:25
3:8 *g* Mt 11:21
3:10 *h* Mt 4:23; *i* Mt 9:20
3:11 *j* Mt 4:3; Mk 1:23,24
3:12 *k* Mt 8:4; Mk 1:24,25, 34; Ac 16:17,18
3:13 *l* Mt 5:1
3:14 *m* Mk 6:30
3:15 *n* Mt 10:1
3:16 *o* Jn 1:42
3:20 *p* ver 7; *q* Mk 6:31
3:21 *r* Jn 10:20; Ac 26:24
3:22 *s* Mt 15:1; *t* Mt 10:25; Mt 11:18; Mt 12:24; Jn 7:20; Jn 8:48,52; Jn 10:20; *u* Mt 9:34
3:23 *v* Mk 4:2; *w* Mt 4:10
3:27 *x* Isa 49:24,25
3:29 *y* Mt 12:31,32; Lk 12:10

[a] *11* Greek *unclean*; also in verse 30 [b] *14* Some manuscripts do not have *designating them apostles.* [c] *22* Greek *Beezeboul* or *Beelzeboul*

Jesus' Mother and Brothers

3:31–35pp Mt 12:46–50; Lk 8:19–21

31 Then Jesus' mother and brothers arrived.[z] Standing outside, they sent someone in to call him. 32 A crowd was sitting around him, and they told him, "Your mother and brothers are outside looking for you."

33 "Who are my mother and my brothers?" he asked.

34 Then he looked at those seated in a circle around him and said, "Here are my mother and my brothers! 35 Whoever does God's will is my brother and sister and mother."

The Parable of the Sower

4:1–12pp Mt 13:1–15; Lk 8:4–10
4:13–20pp Mt 13:18–23; Lk 8:11–15

4 Again Jesus began to teach by the lake.[a] The crowd that gathered round him was so large that he got into a boat and sat in it out on the lake, while all the people were along the shore at the water's edge. 2 He taught them many things by parables,[b] and in his teaching said: 3 "Listen! A farmer went out to sow his seed.[c] 4 As he was scattering the seed, some fell along the path, and the birds came and ate it up. 5 Some fell on rocky places, where it did not have much soil. It sprang up quickly, because the soil was shallow. 6 But when the sun came up, the plants were scorched, and they withered because they had no root. 7 Other seed fell among thorns, which grew up and choked the plants, so that they did not bear grain. 8 Still other seed fell on good soil. It came up, grew and produced a crop, multiplying thirty, sixty, or even a hundred times."[d]

9 Then Jesus said, "He who has ears to hear, let him hear."[e]

10 When he was alone, the Twelve and the others around him asked him about the parables. 11 He told them, "The secret of the kingdom of God[f] has been given to you. But to those on the outside[g] everything is said in parables 12 so that,

> " 'they may be ever seeing but
> never perceiving,
> and ever hearing but never
> understanding;
> otherwise they might turn and
> be forgiven!'[a]"[h]

13 Then Jesus said to them, "Don't you understand this parable? How then will you understand any parable? 14 The farmer sows the word.[i] 15 Some people are like seed along the path, where the word is sown. As soon as they hear it, Satan[j] comes and takes away the word that was sown in them. 16 Others, like seed sown on rocky places, hear the word and at once receive it with joy. 17 But since they have no root, they last only a short time. When trouble or persecution comes because of the word, they quickly fall away. 18 Still others, like seed sown among thorns, hear the word; 19 but the worries of this life, the deceitfulness of wealth[k] and the desires for other things come in and choke the word, making it unfruitful. 20 Others, like seed sown on good soil, hear the word, accept it, and produce a crop—thirty, sixty or even a hundred times what was sown."

A Lamp on a Stand

21 He said to them, "Do you bring in a lamp to put it under a bowl or a bed? Instead, don't you put it on its stand?[l] 22 For whatever is hidden is meant to be disclosed, and whatever is concealed is meant to be brought out into the open.[m] 23 If anyone has ears to hear, let him hear."[n]

24 "Consider carefully what you hear," he continued. "With the measure you use, it will be measured to you—and even more.[o] 25 Whoever has will be given more;

3:31 z ver 21
4:1 a Mk 2:13; Mk 3:7
4:2 b ver 11; Mk 3:23
4:3 c ver 26
4:8 d Jn 15:5; Col 1:6
4:9 e ver 23; Mt 11:15
4:11 f Mt 3:2; g 1Co 5:12,13; Col 4:5; 1Th 4:12; 1Ti 3:7
4:12 h Isa 6:9,10; Mt 13:13-15
4:14 i Mk 16:20; Lk 1:2; Ac 4:31; Ac 8:4; Ac 16:6; Ac 17:11; Php 1:14
4:15 j Mt 4:10
4:19 k Mt 19:23; 1Ti 6:9,10,17; 1Jn 2:15-17
4:21 l Mt 5:15
4:22 m Jer 16:17; Mt 10:26; Lk 8:17; Lk 12:2
4:23 n ver 9; Mt 11:15
4:24 o Mt 7:2; Lk 6:38

[a] *12* Isaiah 6:9,10

whoever does not have, even what
he has will be taken from him."[p]

The Parable of the Growing Seed

26He also said, "This is what the
kingdom of God is like.[q] A man
scatters seed on the ground.
27Night and day, whether he sleeps
or gets up, the seed sprouts and
grows, though he does not know
how. 28All by itself the soil produces corn—first the stalk, then
the ear, then the full grain in the
ear. 29As soon as the grain is ripe,
he puts the sickle to it, because the
harvest has come."[r]

The Parable of the Mustard Seed

4:30–32pp Mt 13:31,32; Lk 13:18,19

30Again he said, "What shall we
say the kingdom of God is like,[s] or
what parable shall we use to describe it? 31It is like a mustard
seed, which is the smallest seed
you plant in the ground. 32Yet when
planted, it grows and becomes the
largest of all garden plants, with
such big branches that the birds of
the air can perch in its shade."
33With many similar parables
Jesus spoke the word to them, as
much as they could understand.[t]
34He did not say anything to them
without using a parable.[u] But
when he was alone with his own disciples, he explained everything.

Jesus Calms the Storm

4:35–41pp Mt 8:18,23–27; Lk 8:22–25

35That day when evening came,
he said to his disciples, "Let us go
over to the other side." 36Leaving
the crowd behind, they took him
along, just as he was, in the boat.[v]
There were also other boats with
him. 37A furious squall came up,
and the waves broke over the boat,
so that it was nearly swamped.
38Jesus was in the stern, sleeping
on a cushion. The disciples woke
him and said to him, "Teacher,
don't you care if we drown?"
39He got up, rebuked the wind
and said to the waves, "Quiet! Be
still!" Then the wind died down and
it was completely calm.
40He said to his disciples, "Why
are you so afraid? Do you still have
no faith?"[w]
41They were terrified and asked
each other, "Who is this? Even the
wind and the waves obey him!"

The Healing of a Demon-possessed Man

5:1–17pp Mt 8:28–34; Lk 8:26–37
5:18–20pp Lk 8:38,39

5 They went across the lake to
the region of the Gerasenes.[a]
2When Jesus got out of the boat,[a] a
man with an evil[b] spirit[b] came
from the tombs to meet him. 3This
man lived in the tombs, and no-one
could bind him any more, not even
with a chain. 4For he had often been
chained hand and foot, but he tore
the chains apart and broke the
irons on his feet. No-one was strong
enough to subdue him. 5Night and
day among the tombs and in the
hills he would cry out and cut himself with stones.
6When he saw Jesus from a distance, he ran and fell on his knees
in front of him. 7He shouted at the
top of his voice, "What do you want
with me,[c] Jesus, Son of the Most
High God?[d] Swear to God that you
won't torture me!" 8For Jesus had
said to him, "Come out of this man,
you evil spirit!"
9Then Jesus asked him, "What is
your name?"
"My name is Legion,"[e] he replied, "for we are many." 10And he
begged Jesus again and again not to
send them out of the area.
11A large herd of pigs was feeding on the nearby hillside. 12The
demons begged Jesus, "Send us

4:25 p Mt 13:12; Mt 25:29
4:26 q Mt 13:24
4:29 r Rev 14:15
4:30 s Mt 13:24
4:33 t Jn 16:12
4:34 u Jn 16:25
4:36 v ver 1; Mk 3:9; Mk 5:2,21; Mk 6:32,45
4:40 w Mt 14:31; Mk 16:14
5:2 a Mk 4:1; b Mk 1:23
5:7 c Mt 8:29; d Mt 4:3; Lk 1:32; Lk 6:35; Ac 16:17; Heb 7:1
5:9 e ver 15

a1 Some manuscripts *Gadarenes*; other manuscripts *Gergesenes* b2 Greek *unclean*; also in verses 8 and 13

among the pigs; allow us to go into
them.” 13 He gave them permission,
and the evil spirits came out and
went into the pigs. The herd, about
two thousand in number, rushed
down the steep bank into the lake
and were drowned.
14 Those tending the pigs ran off
and reported this in the town and
countryside, and the people went
out to see what had happened.
15 When they came to Jesus, they
saw the man who had been possessed by the legion[f] of demons,[g]
sitting there, dressed and in his
right mind; and they were afraid.
16 Those who had seen it told the
people what had happened to the
demon-possessed man—and told
about the pigs as well. 17 Then the
people began to plead with Jesus to
leave their region.
18 As Jesus was getting into the
boat, the man who had been demon-
possessed begged to go with him.
19 Jesus did not let him, but said,
“Go home to your family and tell
them[h] how much the Lord has
done for you, and how he has had
mercy on you.” 20 So the man went
away and began to tell in the Decapolis[c][i] how much Jesus had
done for him. And all the people
were amazed.

A Dead Girl and a Sick Woman

5:22–43pp Mt 9:18–26; Lk 8:41–56

21 When Jesus had again crossed
over by boat to the other side of the
lake,[j] a large crowd gathered
round him while he was by the
lake.[k] 22 Then one of the synagogue
rulers,[l] named Jairus, came there.
Seeing Jesus, he fell at his feet
23 and pleaded earnestly with him,
“My little daughter is dying. Please
come and put your hands on[m] her
so that she will be healed and live.”
24 So Jesus went with him.
A large crowd followed and
pressed around him. 25 And a
woman was there who had been
subject to bleeding[n] for twelve
years. 26 She had suffered a great
deal under the care of many doctors and had spent all she had, yet
instead of getting better she grew
worse. 27 When she heard about
Jesus, she came up behind him in
the crowd and touched his cloak,
28 because she thought, “If I just
touch his clothes,[o] I will be
healed.” 29 Immediately her bleeding stopped and she felt in her body
that she was freed from her suffering.[p]
30 At once Jesus realised that
power[q] had gone out from him. He
turned around in the crowd and
asked, “Who touched my clothes?”
31 “You see the people crowding
against you,” his disciples answered, “and yet you can ask, ‘Who
touched me?’ ”
32 But Jesus kept looking around
to see who had done it. 33 Then the
woman, knowing what had happened to her, came and fell at his
feet and, trembling with fear, told
him the whole truth. 34 He said to
her, “Daughter, your faith has
healed you.[r] Go in peace[s] and be
freed from your suffering.”
35 While Jesus was still speaking,
some men came from the house
of Jairus, the synagogue ruler.[t]
“Your daughter is dead,” they said.
“Why bother the teacher any
more?”
36 Ignoring what they said, Jesus
told the synagogue ruler, “Don’t be
afraid; just believe.”
37 He did not let anyone follow
him except Peter, James and John
the brother of James.[u] 38 When
they came to the home of the synagogue ruler,[v] Jesus saw a commotion, with people crying and
wailing loudly. 39 He went in and
said to them, “Why all this commotion and wailing? The child is not
dead but asleep.”[w] 40 But they
laughed at him.
After he put them all out, he took
the child’s father and mother and

5:15 f ver 9 g ver 16,18 Mt 4:24
5:19 h Mt 8:4
5:20 i Mt 4:25 Mk 7:31
5:21 j Mt 9:1 k Mk 4:1
5:22 l ver 35,36,38 Lk 13:14 Ac 13:15 Ac 18:8,17
5:23 m Mt 19:13 Mk 6:5 Mk 7:32 Mk 8:23 Mk 16:18 Lk 4:40 Lk 13:13 Ac 6:6
5:25 n Lev 15:25-30
5:28 o Mt 9:20
5:29 p ver 34
5:30 q Lk 5:17 Lk 6:19
5:34 r Mt 9:22 s Ac 15:33
5:35 t ver 22
5:37 u Mt 4:21
5:38 v ver 22
5:39 w Mt 9:24

c *20* That is, the Ten Cities

the disciples who were with him, and went in where the child was. 41He took her by the hand[x] and said to her, "*Talitha koum!*" (which means, "Little girl, I say to you, get up!").[y] 42Immediately the girl stood up and walked around (she was twelve years old). At this they were completely astonished. 43He gave strict orders not to let anyone know about this,[z] and told them to give her something to eat.

A Prophet Without Honour

6:1–6pp Mt 13:54–58

6 Jesus left there and went to his home town,[a] accompanied by his disciples. 2When the Sabbath came,[b] he began to teach in the synagogue,[c] and many who heard him were amazed.[d]

"Where did this man get these things?" they asked. "What's this wisdom that has been given him, that he even does miracles! 3Isn't this the carpenter? Isn't this Mary's son and the brother of James, Joseph,[a] Judas and Simon?[e] Aren't his sisters here with us?" And they took offence at him.[f]

4Jesus said to them, "Only in his home town, among his relatives and in his own house is a prophet without honour."[g] 5He could not do any miracles there, except lay his hands on[h] a few sick people and heal them. 6And he was amazed at their lack of faith.

Jesus Sends Out the Twelve

6:7–11pp Mt 10:1,9–14; Lk 9:1,3–5

Then Jesus went round teaching from village to village.[i] 7Calling the Twelve to him,[j] he sent them out two by two[k] and gave them authority over evil[b] spirits.[l]

8These were his instructions: "Take nothing for the journey except a staff—no bread, no bag, no money in your belts. 9Wear sandals but not an extra tunic. 10Whenever you enter a house, stay there until you leave that town. 11And if any place will not welcome you or listen to you, shake the dust off your feet[m] when you leave, as a testimony against them."

12They went out and preached that people should repent.[n] 13They drove out many demons and anointed many sick people with oil[o] and healed them.

John the Baptist Beheaded

6:14–29pp Mt 14:1–12
6:14–16pp Lk 9:7–9

14King Herod heard about this, for Jesus' name had become well known. Some were saying,[c] "John the Baptist[p] has been raised from the dead, and that is why miraculous powers are at work in him."

15Others said, "He is Elijah."[q]

And still others claimed, "He is a prophet,[r] like one of the prophets of long ago."[s]

16But when Herod heard this, he said, "John, the man I beheaded, has been raised from the dead!"

17For Herod himself had given orders to have John arrested, and he had him bound and put in prison.[t] He did this because of Herodias, his brother Philip's wife, whom he had married. 18For John had been saying to Herod, "It is not lawful for you to have your brother's wife."[u] 19So Herodias nursed a grudge against John and wanted to kill him. But she was not able to, 20because Herod feared John and protected him, knowing him to be a righteous and holy man.[v] When Herod heard John, he was greatly puzzled;[d] yet he liked to listen to him.

21Finally the opportune time came. On his birthday Herod gave a banquet[w] for his high officials and military commanders and the

5:41 x Mk 1:31 y Lk 7:14 Ac 9:40
5:43 z Mt 8:4
6:1 a Mt 2:23
6:2 b Mk 1:21 c Mt 4:23 d Mt 7:28
6:3 e Mt 12:46 f Mt 11:6 Jn 6:61
6:4 g Lk 4:24 Jn 4:44
6:5 h Mk 5:23
6:6 i Mt 9:35 Mk 1:39 Lk 13:22
6:7 j Mk 3:13 k Dt 17:6 Lk 10:1 l Mt 10:1
6:11 m Mt 10:14
6:12 n Lk 9:6
6:13 o Jas 5:14
6:14 p Mt 3:1
6:15 q Mal 4:5 r Mt 21:11 s Mt 16:14 Mk 8:28
6:17 t Mt 4:12 Mt 11:2 Lk 3:19,20
6:18 u Lev 18:16 Lev 20:21
6:20 v Mt 11:9 Mt 21:26
6:21 w Est 1:3 Est 2:18

a3 Greek *Joses*, a variant of *Joseph* b7 Greek *unclean* c14 Some early manuscripts *He was saying* d20 Some early manuscripts *he did many things*

leading men of Galilee.[x] 22When
the daughter of Herodias came in
and danced, she pleased Herod and
his dinner guests.
The king said to the girl, "Ask me
for anything you want, and I'll give
it to you." 23And he promised her
with an oath, "Whatever you ask I
will give you, up to half my kingdom."[y]
24She went out and said to her
mother, "What shall I ask for?"
"The head of John the Baptist,"
she answered.
25At once the girl hurried in to
the king with the request: "I want
you to give me right now the head
of John the Baptist on a platter."
26The king was greatly distressed, but because of his oaths
and his dinner guests, he did not
want to refuse her. 27So he immediately sent an executioner with orders to bring John's head. The man
went, beheaded John in the prison,
28and brought back his head on a
platter. He presented it to the girl,
and she gave it to her mother. 29On
hearing of this, John's disciples
came and took his body and laid it
in a tomb.

Jesus Feeds the Five Thousand

6:32–44pp Mt 14:13–21; Lk 9:10–17; Jn 6:5–13
6:32–44Ref Mk 8:2–9

30The apostles[z] gathered round
Jesus and reported to him all they
had done and taught.[a] 31Then, because so many people were coming
and going that they did not even
have a chance to eat,[b] he said to
them, "Come with me by yourselves to a quiet place and get some
rest."
32So they went away by themselves in a boat[c] to a solitary place.
33But many who saw them leaving
recognised them and ran on foot
from all the towns and got there
ahead of them. 34When Jesus
landed and saw a large crowd, he
had compassion on them, because
they were like sheep without a
shepherd.[d] So he began teaching
them many things.
35By this time it was late in the
day, so his disciples came to him.
"This is a remote place," they said,
"and it's already very late. 36Send
the people away so that they can go
to the surrounding countryside and
villages and buy themselves something to eat."
37But he answered, "You give
them something to eat."[e]
They said to him, "That would
take eight months of a man's
wages![e] Are we to go and spend
that much on bread and give it to
them to eat?"
38"How many loaves do you
have?" he asked. "Go and see."
When they found out, they said,
"Five—and two fish."[f]
39Then Jesus directed them to
have all the people sit down in
groups on the green grass. 40So
they sat down in groups of hundreds and fifties. 41Taking the five
loaves and the two fish and looking
up to heaven, he gave thanks and
broke the loaves.[g] Then he gave
them to his disciples to set before
the people. He also divided the two
fish among them all. 42They all ate
and were satisfied, 43and the disciples picked up twelve basketfuls
of broken pieces of bread and fish.
44The number of the men who had
eaten was five thousand.

Jesus Walks on the Water

6:45–51pp Mt 14:22–32; Jn 6:15–21
6:53–56pp Mt 14:34–36

45Immediately Jesus made his
disciples get into the boat[h] and go
on ahead of him to Bethsaida,[i]
while he dismissed the crowd.
46After leaving them, he went up on
a mountainside to pray.[j]
47When evening came, the boat
was in the middle of the lake, and
he was alone on land. 48He saw the
disciples straining at the oars, because the wind was against them.

6:21 *x* Lk 3:1
6:23 *y* Est 5:3,6; Est 7:2
6:30 *z* Mt 10:2; Lk 9:10; Lk 17:5; Lk 22:14; Lk 24:10; Ac 1:2,26 *a* Lk 9:10
6:31 *b* Mk 3:20
6:32 *c* ver 45; Mk 4:36
6:34 *d* Mt 9:36
6:37 *e* 2Ki 4:42-44
6:38 *f* Mt 15:34; Mk 8:5
6:41 *g* Mt 14:19
6:45 *h* ver 32 *i* Mt 11:21
6:46 *j* Lk 3:21

[e]37 Greek *take two hundred denarii*

About the fourth watch of the night
he went out to them, walking on the
lake. He was about to pass by them,
49but when they saw him walking
on the lake, they thought he was a
ghost.[k] They cried out, 50because
they all saw him and were terrified.
Immediately he spoke to them
and said, "Take courage! It is I.
Don't be afraid."[l] 51Then he
climbed into the boat[m] with them,
and the wind died down.[n] They
were completely amazed, 52for
they had not understood about the
loaves; their hearts were hardened.[o]
53When they had crossed over,
they landed at Gennesaret and an-
chored there.[p] 54As soon as they
got out of the boat, people recognised Jesus. 55They ran throughout
that whole region and carried the
sick on mats to wherever they
heard he was. 56And wherever he
went—into villages, towns or
countryside—they placed the sick
in the market-places. They begged
him to let them touch even the edge
of his cloak,[q] and all who touched
him were healed.

Clean and Unclean

7:1-23pp Mt 15:1-20

7 The Pharisees and some of the
teachers of the law who had
come from Jerusalem gathered
round Jesus and 2saw some of his
disciples eating food with hands
that were "unclean",[a] that is, unwashed. 3(The Pharisees and all the
Jews do not eat unless they give
their hands a ceremonial washing,
holding to the tradition of the elders.[b] 4When they come from the
market-place they do not eat unless
they wash. And they observe many
other traditions, such as the washing of cups, pitchers and kettles.[a])[c]
5So the Pharisees and teachers of
the law asked Jesus, "Why don't
your disciples live according to the
tradition of the elders[d] instead of
eating their food with 'unclean'
hands?"
6He replied, "Isaiah was right
when he prophesied about you hypocrites; as it is written:

" 'These people honour me with
their lips,
but their hearts are far from
me.
7They worship me in vain;
their teachings are but rules
taught by men.'[b][e]

8You have let go of the commands
of God and are holding on to the traditions of men."[f]
9And he said to them: "You have
a fine way of setting aside the commands of God in order to observe[c]
your own traditions![g] 10For Moses
said, 'Honour your father and your
mother,'[d][h] and, 'Anyone who
curses his father or mother must
be put to death.'[e][i] 11But you say[j]
that if a man says to his father or
mother: 'Whatever help you might
otherwise have received from me
is Corban' (that is, a gift devoted to
God), 12then you no longer let him
do anything for his father or
mother. 13Thus you nullify the
word of God[k] by your tradition[l]
that you have handed down. And
you do many things like that."
14Again Jesus called the crowd to
him and said, "Listen to me, everyone, and understand this. 15Nothing
outside a man can make him 'unclean' by going into him. Rather, it
is what comes out of a man that
makes him 'unclean'."[f]
17After he had left the crowd and
entered the house, his disciples
asked him[m] about this parable.
18"Are you so dull?" he asked.
"Don't you see that nothing that enters a man from the outside can
make him 'unclean'? 19For it

6:49 *k* Lk 24:37
6:50 *l* Mt 14:27
6:51 *m* ver 32 *n* Mk 4:39
6:52 *o* Mk 8:17-21
6:53 *p* Jn 6:24,25
6:56 *q* Mt 9:20
7:2 *a* Ac 10:14,28 Ac 11:8 Ro 14:14
7:3 *b* ver 5,8,9,13 Lk 11:38
7:4 *c* Mt 23:25 Lk 11:39
7:5 *d* ver 3 Gal 1:14 Col 2:8
7:7 *e* Isa 29:13
7:8 *f* ver 3
7:9 *g* ver 3
7:10 *h* Ex 20:12 Dt 5:16 *i* Ex 21:17 Lev 20:9
7:11 *j* Mt 23:16,18
7:13 *k* Heb 4:12 *l* ver 3
7:17 *m* Mk 9:28

a4 Some early manuscripts *pitchers, kettles and dining couches* b6, 7 Isaiah 29:13 c9 Some manuscripts *set up* d10 Exodus 20:12; Deut. 5:16 e10 Exodus 21:17; Lev. 20:9
f15 Some early manuscripts *'unclean'. 16If anyone has ears to hear, let him hear."*

doesn't go into his heart but into his
stomach, and then out of his body."
(In saying this, Jesus declared all
foods[n] "clean".)[o]
20He went on: "What comes out of
a man is what makes him 'unclean'.
21For from within, out of men's
hearts, come evil thoughts, sexual
immorality, theft, murder, adultery, 22greed,[p] malice, deceit,
lewdness, envy, slander, arrogance
and folly. 23All these evils come
from inside and make a man 'unclean'."

The Faith of a Syro-Phoenician Woman

7:24–30pp Mt 15:21–28

24Jesus left that place and went to
the vicinity of Tyre.[g][q] He entered
a house and did not want anyone to
know it; yet he could not keep his
presence secret. 25In fact, as soon
as she heard about him, a woman
whose little daughter was possessed by an evil[h] spirit[r] came
and fell at his feet. 26The woman
was a Greek, born in Syrian Phoenicia. She begged Jesus to drive the
demon out of her daughter.
27"First let the children eat all
they want," he told her, "for it is not
right to take the children's bread
and toss it to their dogs."
28"Yes, Lord," she replied, "but
even the dogs under the table eat
the children's crumbs."
29Then he told her, "For such a
reply, you may go; the demon has
left your daughter."
30She went home and found her
child lying on the bed, and the demon gone.

The Healing of a Deaf and Mute Man

7:31–37pp Mt 15:29–31

31Then Jesus left the vicinity of
Tyre[s] and went through Sidon,
down to the Sea of Galilee[t] and
into the region of the Decapolis.[i][u]
32There some people brought to
him a man who was deaf and could
hardly talk,[v] and they begged him
to place his hand on[w] the man.
33After he took him aside, away
from the crowd, Jesus put his
fingers into the man's ears. Then
he spat[x] and touched the man's
tongue. 34He looked up to heaven[y]
and with a deep sigh[z] said to him,
"*Ephphatha!*" (which means, "Be
opened!"). 35At this, the man's
ears were opened, his tongue was
loosened and he began to speak
plainly.[a]
36Jesus commanded them not to
tell anyone.[b] But the more he did
so, the more they kept talking
about it. 37People were overwhelmed with amazement. "He has
done everything well," they said.
"He even makes the deaf hear and
the mute speak."

Jesus Feeds the Four Thousand

8:1–9pp Mt 15:32–39
8:1–9Ref Mk 6:32–44
8:11–21pp Mt 16:1–12

8 During those days another
large crowd gathered. Since
they had nothing to eat, Jesus
called his disciples to him and said,
2"I have compassion for these people;[a] they have already been with
me three days and have nothing to
eat. 3If I send them home hungry,
they will collapse on the way, because some of them have come a
long distance."
4His disciples answered, "But
where in this remote place can anyone get enough bread to feed
them?"
5"How many loaves do you
have?" Jesus asked.
"Seven," they replied.
6He told the crowd to sit down on
the ground. When he had taken the
seven loaves and given thanks, he
broke them and gave them to his
disciples to set before the people,
and they did so. 7They had a few

7:19
n Ro 14:1-12
Col 2:16
1Ti 4:3-5
o Ac 10:15
7:22
p Mt 20:15
7:24
q Mt 11:21
7:25
r Mt 4:24
7:31
s ver 24
Mt 11:21
t Mt 4:18
u Mt 4:25
Mk 5:20
7:32
v Mt 9:32
Lk 11:14
w Mk 5:23
7:33
x Mk 8:23
7:34
y Mk 6:41
Jn 11:41
z Mk 8:12
7:35
a Isa 35:5,6
7:36
b Mt 8:4
8:2
a Mt 9:36

[g]24 Many early manuscripts *Tyre and Sidon*
[h]25 Greek *unclean* [i]31 That is, the Ten Cities

small fish as well; he gave thanks
for them also and told the disciples
to distribute them.[b] 8The people
ate and were satisfied. Afterwards
the disciples picked up seven basketfuls of broken pieces that were
left over.[c] 9About four thousand
men were present. And having sent
them away, 10he got into the boat
with his disciples and went to the
region of Dalmanutha.

11The Pharisees came and began
to question Jesus. To test him, they
asked him for a sign from heaven.[d]
12He sighed deeply[e] and said,
"Why does this generation ask for a
miraculous sign? I tell you the
truth, no sign will be given to it."
13Then he left them, got back into
the boat and crossed to the other
side.

The Yeast of the Pharisees and Herod

14The disciples had forgotten to
bring bread, except for one loaf
they had with them in the boat.
15"Be careful," Jesus warned them.
"Watch out for the yeast[f] of the
Pharisees[g] and that of Herod."[h]

16They discussed this with one
another and said, "It is because we
have no bread."

17Aware of their discussion,
Jesus asked them: "Why are you
talking about having no bread? Do
you still not see or understand? Are
your hearts hardened?[i] 18Do you
have eyes but fail to see, and ears
but fail to hear? And don't you remember? 19When I broke the five
loaves for the five thousand, how
many basketfuls of pieces did you
pick up?"

"Twelve,"[j] they replied.

20"And when I broke the seven
loaves for the four thousand, how
many basketfuls of pieces did you
pick up?"

They answered, "Seven."[k]

21He said to them, "Do you still
not understand?"[l]

8:7 b Mt 14:19
8:8 c ver 20
8:11 d Mt 12:38
8:12 e Mk 7:34
8:15 f 1Co 5:6-8 g Lk 12:1 h Mt 14:1 Mk 12:13
8:17 i Isa 6:9,10 Mk 6:52
8:19 j Mt 14:20 Mk 6:41-44 Lk 9:17 Jn 6:13
8:20 k ver 6-9 Mt 15:37
8:21 l Mk 6:52
8:22 m Mt 11:21 n Mk 10:46 Jn 9:1
8:23 o Mk 7:33 p Mk 5:23
8:28 q Mt 3:1 r Mal 4:5
8:29 s Jn 6:69 Jn 11:27
8:30 t Mt 8:4 Mt 16:20 Mt 17:9 Mk 9:9 Lk 9:21
8:31 u Mt 8:20 v Mt 16:21 w Mt 27:1,2 x Ac 2:23 Ac 3:13 y Mt 16:21

The Healing of a Blind Man at Bethsaida

22They came to Bethsaida,[m] and
some people brought a blind man[n]
and begged Jesus to touch him.
23He took the blind man by the hand
and led him outside the village.
When he had spat[o] on the man's
eyes and put his hands on[p] him,
Jesus asked, "Do you see anything?"

24He looked up and said, "I see
people; they look like trees walking
around."

25Once more Jesus put his hands
on the man's eyes. Then his eyes
were opened, his sight was restored, and he saw everything
clearly. 26Jesus sent him home,
saying, "Don't go into the village."[a]

Peter's Confession of Christ

8:27–29pp Mt 16:13–16; Lk 9:18–20

27Jesus and his disciples went on
to the villages around Caesarea
Philippi. On the way he asked them,
"Who do people say I am?"

28They replied, "Some say John
the Baptist;[q] others say Elijah;[r]
and still others, one of the prophets."

29"But what about you?" he
asked. "Who do you say I am?"

Peter answered, "You are the
Christ."[b] [s]

30Jesus warned them not to tell
anyone about him.[t]

Jesus Predicts His Death

8:31–9:1pp Mt 16:21–28; Lk 9:22–27

31He then began to teach them
that the Son of Man[u] must suffer
many things[v] and be rejected by
the elders, chief priests and teachers of the law,[w] and that he must be
killed[x] and after three days[y] rise

a26 Some manuscripts *Don't go and tell anyone in the village* b29 Or *Messiah.* "The Christ" (Greek) and "the Messiah" (Hebrew) both mean "the Anointed One".

again.[z] 32He spoke plainly[a] about this, and Peter took him aside and began to rebuke him.

33But when Jesus turned and looked at his disciples, he rebuked Peter. "Get behind me, Satan!"[b] he said. "You do not have in mind the things of God, but the things of men."

34Then he called the crowd to him along with his disciples and said: "If anyone would come after me, he must deny himself and take up his cross and follow me.[c] 35For whoever wants to save his life[c] will lose it, but whoever loses his life for me and for the gospel will save it.[d] 36What good is it for a man to gain the whole world, yet forfeit his soul? 37Or what can a man give in exchange for his soul? 38If anyone is ashamed of me and my words in this adulterous and sinful generation, the Son of Man[e] will be ashamed of him[f] when he comes[g] in his Father's glory with the holy angels."

9 And he said to them, "I tell you the truth, some who are standing here will not taste death before they see the kingdom of God come[a] with power."[b]

The Transfiguration

9:2–8pp Lk 9:28–36
9:2–13pp Mt 17:1–13

2After six days Jesus took Peter, James and John[c] with him and led them up a high mountain, where they were all alone. There he was transfigured before them. 3His clothes became dazzling white,[d] whiter than anyone in the world could bleach them. 4And there appeared before them Elijah and Moses, who were talking with Jesus.

5Peter said to Jesus, "Rabbi,[e] it is good for us to be here. Let us put up three shelters—one for you, one for Moses and one for Elijah." 6(He did not know what to say, they were so frightened.)

8:31 z Mt 16:21
8:32 a Jn 18:20
8:33 b Mt 4:10
8:34 c Mt 10:38; Lk 14:27
8:35 d Jn 12:25
8:38 e Mt 8:20; f Mt 10:33; Lk 12:9; g 1Th 2:19
9:1 a Mk 13:30; Lk 22:18; b Mt 24:30; Mt 25:31
9:2 c Mt 4:21
9:3 d Mt 28:3
9:5 e Mt 23:7
9:7 f Ex 24:16; g Mt 3:17
9:9 h Mk 8:30; i Mt 8:20
9:12 j Mt 8:20; k Mt 16:21; l Lk 23:11
9:13 m Mt 11:14

7Then a cloud appeared and enveloped them, and a voice came from the cloud:[f] "This is my Son, whom I love. Listen to him!"[g]

8Suddenly, when they looked round, they no longer saw anyone with them except Jesus.

9As they were coming down the mountain, Jesus gave them orders not to tell anyone[h] what they had seen until the Son of Man[i] had risen from the dead. 10They kept the matter to themselves, discussing what "rising from the dead" meant.

11And they asked him, "Why do the teachers of the law say that Elijah must come first?"

12Jesus replied, "To be sure, Elijah does come first, and restores all things. Why then is it written that the Son of Man[j] must suffer much[k] and be rejected?[l] 13But I tell you, Elijah has come,[m] and they have done to him everything they wished, just as it is written about him."

The Healing of a Boy With an Evil Spirit

9:14–28; 30–32pp Mt 17:14–19; 22,23; Lk 9:37–45

14When they came to the other disciples, they saw a large crowd around them and the teachers of the law arguing with them. 15As soon as all the people saw Jesus, they were overwhelmed with wonder and ran to greet him.

16"What are you arguing with them about?" he asked.

17A man in the crowd answered, "Teacher, I brought you my son, who is possessed by a spirit that has robbed him of speech. 18Whenever it seizes him, it throws him to the ground. He foams at the mouth, gnashes his teeth and becomes rigid. I asked your disciples to drive out the spirit, but they could not."

c*35* The Greek word means either *life* or *soul*; also in verse 36.

19"O unbelieving generation," Jesus replied, "how long shall I stay with you? How long shall I put up with you? Bring the boy to me."

20So they brought him. When the spirit saw Jesus, it immediately threw the boy into a convulsion. He fell to the ground and rolled around, foaming at the mouth.[n]

21Jesus asked the boy's father, "How long has he been like this?"

"From childhood," he answered. 22"It has often thrown him into fire or water to kill him. But if you can do anything, take pity on us and help us."

23" 'If you can'?" said Jesus. "Everything is possible for him who believes."[o]

24Immediately the boy's father exclaimed, "I do believe; help me overcome my unbelief!"

25When Jesus saw that a crowd was running to the scene,[p] he rebuked the evil[a] spirit. "You deaf and mute spirit," he said, "I command you, come out of him and never enter him again."

26The spirit shrieked, convulsed him violently and came out. The boy looked so much like a corpse that many said, "He's dead." 27But Jesus took him by the hand and lifted him to his feet, and he stood up.

28After Jesus had gone indoors, his disciples asked him privately,[q] "Why couldn't we drive it out?"

29He replied, "This kind can come out only by prayer."[b]

30They left that place and passed through Galilee. Jesus did not want anyone to know where they were, 31because he was teaching his disciples. He said to them, "The Son of Man[r] is going to be betrayed into the hands of men. They will kill him,[s] and after three days[t] he will rise."[u] 32But they did not understand what he meant[v] and were afraid to ask him about it.

9:20
n Mk 1:26
9:23
o Mt 21:21
Mk 11:23
Jn 11:40
9:25
p ver 15
9:28
q Mk 7:17
9:31
r Mt 8:20
s ver 12
Ac 2:23
Ac 3:13
t Mt 16:21
u Mt 16:21
9:32
v Lk 2:50
Lk 9:45
Lk 18:34
Jn 12:16
9:33
w Mt 4:13
x Mk 1:29
9:34
y Lk 22:24
9:35
z Mt 18:4
Mt 20:26
Mk 10:43
Lk 22:26
9:36
a Mk 10:16
9:37
b Mt 10:40
9:38
c Nu 11:27-29
9:40
d Mt 12:30
Lk 11:23
9:41
e Mt 10:42
9:42
f Mt 5:29
g Mt 18:6
Lk 17:2
9:43
h Mt 5:29
i Mt 5:30
Mt 18:8

Who Is the Greatest?

9:33–37pp Mt 18:1–5; Lk 9:46–48

33They came to Capernaum.[w] When he was in the house,[x] he asked them, "What were you arguing about on the road?" 34But they kept quiet because on the way they had argued about who was the greatest.[y]

35Sitting down, Jesus called the Twelve and said, "If anyone wants to be first, he must be the very last, and the servant of all."[z]

36He took a little child and had him stand among them. Taking him in his arms,[a] he said to them, 37"Whoever welcomes one of these little children in my name welcomes me; and whoever welcomes me does not welcome me but the one who sent me."[b]

Whoever Is Not Against Us Is for Us

9:38–40pp Lk 9:49,50

38"Teacher," said John, "we saw a man driving out demons in your name and we told him to stop, because he was not one of us."[c]

39"Do not stop him," Jesus said. "No-one who does a miracle in my name can in the next moment say anything bad about me, 40for whoever is not against us is for us.[d] 41I tell you the truth, anyone who gives you a cup of water in my name because you belong to Christ will certainly not lose his reward.[e]

Causing to Sin

42"And if anyone causes one of these little ones who believe in me to sin,[f] it would be better for him to be thrown into the sea with a large millstone tied around his neck.[g] 43If your hand causes you to sin,[h] cut it off. It is better for you to enter life maimed than with two hands to go into hell,[i] where the

[a]25 Greek *unclean* [b]29 Some manuscripts *prayer and fasting*

fire never goes out.[c][j] 45 And if your foot causes you to sin,[k] cut it off. It is better for you to enter life crippled than to have two feet and be thrown into hell.[d][l] 47 And if your eye causes you to sin,[m] pluck it out. It is better for you to enter the kingdom of God with one eye than to have two eyes and be thrown into hell,[n] 48 where

"'their worm does not die,
and the fire is not quenched.'[e][o]

49 Everyone will be salted[p] with fire.

50 "Salt is good, but if it loses its saltiness, how can you make it salty again?[q] Have salt in yourselves,[r] and be at peace with each other."[s]

Divorce

10:1–12pp Mt 19:1–9

10 Jesus then left that place and went into the region of Judea and across the Jordan.[a] Again crowds of people came to him, and as was his custom, he taught them.[b]

2 Some Pharisees[c] came and tested him by asking, "Is it lawful for a man to divorce his wife?"

3 "What did Moses command you?" he replied.

4 They said, "Moses permitted a man to write a certificate of divorce and send her away."[d]

5 "It was because your hearts were hard[e] that Moses wrote you this law," Jesus replied. 6 "But at the beginning of creation God 'made them male and female'.[a][f] 7 'For this reason a man will leave his father and mother and be united to his wife,[b] 8 and the two will become one flesh.'[c][g] So they are no longer two, but one. 9 Therefore what God has joined together, let man not separate."

10 When they were in the house again, the disciples asked Jesus about this. 11 He answered, "Anyone who divorces his wife and marries another woman commits adultery against her.[h] 12 And if she divorces her husband and marries another man, she commits adultery."[i]

The Little Children and Jesus

10:13–16pp Mt 19:13–15; Lk 18:15–17

13 People were bringing little children to Jesus to have him touch them, but the disciples rebuked them. 14 When Jesus saw this, he was indignant. He said to them, "Let the little children come to me, and do not hinder them, for the kingdom of God belongs to such as these.[j] 15 I tell you the truth, anyone who will not receive the kingdom of God like a little child will never enter it."[k] 16 And he took the children in his arms,[l] put his hands on them and blessed them.

The Rich Young Man

10:17–31pp Mt 19:16–30; Lk 18:18–30

17 As Jesus started on his way, a man ran up to him and fell on his knees[m] before him. "Good teacher," he asked, "what must I do to inherit eternal life?"[n]

18 "Why do you call me good?" Jesus answered. "No-one is good—except God alone. 19 You know the commandments: 'Do not murder, do not commit adultery, do not steal, do not give false testimony, do not defraud, honour your father and mother.'[d]"[o]

20 "Teacher," he declared, "all these I have kept since I was a boy."

21 Jesus looked at him and loved him. "One thing you lack," he said. "Go, sell everything you have and give to the poor,[p] and you will have

9:43 *j* Mt 25:41
9:45 *k* Mt 5:29 *l* Mt 18:8
9:47 *m* Mt 5:29 *n* Mt 5:29; Mt 18:9
9:48 *o* Isa 66:24; Mt 25:41
9:49 *p* Lev 2:13
9:50 *q* Mt 5:13; Lk 14:34,35 *r* Col 4:6 *s* Ro 12:18; 2Co 13:11; 1Th 5:13
10:1 *a* Mk 1:5; Jn 10:40; Jn 11:7 *b* Mt 4:23; Mk 2:13; Mk 4:2; Mk 6:6,34
10:2 *c* Mk 2:16
10:4 *d* Dt 24:1-4; Mt 5:31
10:5 *e* Ps 95:8; Heb 3:15
10:6 *f* Ge 1:27; Ge 5:2
10:8 *g* Ge 2:24; 1Co 6:16
10:11 *h* Mt 5:32; Lk 16:18
10:12 *i* Ro 7:3; 1Co 7:10,11
10:14 *j* Mt 25:34
10:15 *k* Mt 18:3
10:16 *l* Mk 9:36
10:17 *m* Mk 1:40 *n* Lk 10:25; Ac 20:32
10:19 *o* Ex 20:12-16; Dt 5:16-20
10:21 *p* Ac 2:45

c43 Some manuscripts *out,* 44*where / " 'their worm does not die, / and the fire is not quenched.'*
d45 Some manuscripts *hell,* 46*where / " 'their worm does not die, / and the fire is not quenched.'*
e48 Isaiah 66:24 a6 Gen. 1:27 b7 Some early manuscripts do not have *and be united to his wife.* c8 Gen. 2:24 d19 Exodus 20:12–16; Deut. 5:16–20

treasure in heaven.[q] Then come,
follow me."[r]
22 At this the man's face fell. He
went away sad, because he had
great wealth.
23 Jesus looked around and said to
his disciples, "How hard it is for
the rich[s] to enter the kingdom of
God!"
24 The disciples were amazed at
his words. But Jesus said again,
"Children, how hard it is[e] to enter
the kingdom of God![t] 25 It is easier
for a camel to go through the eye of
a needle than for a rich man to enter the kingdom of God."[u]
26 The disciples were even more
amazed, and said to each other,
"Who then can be saved?"
27 Jesus looked at them and said,
"With man this is impossible, but
not with God; all things are possible with God."[v]
28 Peter said to him, "We have left
everything to follow you!"[w]
29 "I tell you the truth," Jesus replied, "no-one who has left home or
brothers or sisters or mother or
father or children or fields for me
and the gospel 30 will fail to receive
a hundred times as much[x] in this
present age (homes, brothers, sisters, mothers, children and fields—
and with them, persecutions) and
in the age to come,[y] eternal life.[z]
31 But many who are first will be
last, and the last first."[a]

Jesus Again Predicts His Death

10:32–34pp Mt 20:17–19; Lk 18:31–33

32 They were on their way up to
Jerusalem, with Jesus leading the
way, and the disciples were astonished, while those who followed
were afraid. Again he took the
Twelve[b] aside and told them what
was going to happen to him. 33 "We
are going up to Jerusalem,"[c] he
said, "and the Son of Man[d] will be
betrayed to the chief priests and
teachers of the law.[e] They will
condemn him to death and will
hand him over to the Gentiles,

10:21 q Mt 6:20; Lk 12:33; r Mt 4:19
10:23 s Ps 52:7; Ps 62:10; 1Ti 6:9,10,17
10:24 t Mt 7:13,14
10:25 u Lk 12:16-20
10:27 v Mt 19:26
10:28 w Mt 4:19
10:30 x Mt 6:33; y Mt 12:32; z Mt 25:46
10:31 a Mt 19:30
10:32 b Mk 3:16-19
10:33 c Lk 9:51; d Mt 8:20; e Mt 27:1,2
10:34 f Mt 16:21; g Ac 2:23; Ac 3:13; h Mt 16:21; i Mt 16:21
10:37 j Mt 19:28
10:38 k Job 38:2; l Mt 20:22; m Lk 12:50
10:39 n Ac 12:2; Rev 1:9
10:43 o Mk 9:35
10:45 p Mt 20:28; q Mt 20:28

34 who will mock him and spit on
him, flog him[f] and kill him.[g]
Three days later[h] he will rise."[i]

The Request of James and John

10:35–45pp Mt 20:20–28

35 Then James and John, the
sons of Zebedee, came to him.
"Teacher," they said, "we want you
to do for us whatever we ask."
36 "What do you want me to do for
you?" he asked.
37 They replied, "Let one of us sit
at your right and the other at your
left in your glory."[j]
38 "You don't know what you are
asking,"[k] Jesus said. "Can you
drink the cup[l] I drink or be baptised with the baptism I am
baptised with?"[m]
39 "We can," they answered.
Jesus said to them, "You will
drink the cup I drink and be
baptised with the baptism I am
baptised with,[n] 40 but to sit at my
right or left is not for me to grant.
These places belong to those for
whom they have been prepared."
41 When the ten heard about this,
they became indignant with James
and John. 42 Jesus called them together and said, "You know that
those who are regarded as rulers of
the Gentiles lord it over them, and
their high officials exercise authority over them. 43 Not so with you.
Instead, whoever wants to become
great among you must be your servant,[o] 44 and whoever wants to be
first must be slave of all. 45 For even
the Son of Man did not come to be
served, but to serve,[p] and to give
his life as a ransom for many."[q]

Blind Bartimaeus Receives His Sight

10:46–52pp Mt 20:29–34; Lk 18:35–43

46 Then they came to Jericho. As
Jesus and his disciples, together
with a large crowd, were leaving

[e]24 Some manuscripts *is for those who trust in riches*

the city, a blind man, Bartimaeus
(that is, the Son of Timaeus), was
sitting by the roadside begging.
47When he heard that it was Jesus
of Nazareth,[r] he began to shout,
"Jesus, Son of David,[s] have mercy
on me!"
48Many rebuked him and told him
to be quiet, but he shouted all the
more, "Son of David, have mercy
on me!"
49Jesus stopped and said, "Call
him."
So they called to the blind man,
"Cheer up! On your feet! He's calling you." 50Throwing his cloak
aside, he jumped to his feet and
came to Jesus.
51"What do you want me to do for
you?" Jesus asked him.
The blind man said, "Rabbi,[t] I
want to see."
52"Go," said Jesus, "your faith
has healed you."[u] Immediately he
received his sight and followed[v]
Jesus along the road.

The Triumphal Entry

11:1–10pp Mt 21:1–9; Lk 19:29–38
11:7–10pp Jn 12:12–15

11 As they approached Jerusalem and came to Beth-
phage and Bethany[a] at the Mount
of Olives,[b] Jesus sent two of his
disciples, 2saying to them, "Go to
the village ahead of you, and just as
you enter it, you will find a colt tied
there, which no-one has ever ridden.[c] Untie it and bring it here. 3If
anyone asks you, 'Why are you doing this?' tell him, 'The Lord needs
it and will send it back here
shortly.' "
4They went and found a colt outside in the street, tied at a doorway.[d] As they untied it, 5some
people standing there asked, "What
are you doing, untying that colt?"
6They answered as Jesus had told
them to, and the people let them go.
7When they brought the colt to
Jesus and threw their cloaks over
it, he sat on it. 8Many people spread

10:47
r Mk 1:24
s Mt 9:27
10:51
t Mt 23:7
10:52
u Mt 9:22
v Mt 4:19
11:1
a Mt 21:17
b Mt 21:1
11:2
c Nu 19:2
Dt 21:3
1Sa 6:7
11:4
d Mk 14:16
11:9
e Ps 118:25,26
Mt 23:39
11:10
f Lk 2:14
11:11
g Mt 21:12,17
11:13
h Lk 13:6-9
11:17
i Isa 56:7
j Jer 7:11

their cloaks on the road, while
others spread branches they had
cut in the fields. 9Those who went
ahead and those who followed
shouted,

"Hosanna!"[a]

"Blessed is he who comes in the
name of the Lord!"[b][e]

10"Blessed is the coming kingdom
of our father David!"

"Hosanna in the highest!"[f]

11Jesus entered Jerusalem and
went to the temple. He looked
around at everything, but since it
was already late, he went out to
Bethany with the Twelve.[g]

Jesus Clears the Temple

11:12–14pp Mt 21:18–22
11:15–18pp Mt 21:12–16; Lk 19:45–47; Jn 2:13–16

12The next day as they were leaving Bethany, Jesus was hungry.
13Seeing in the distance a fig-tree in
leaf, he went to find out if it had any
fruit. When he reached it, he found
nothing but leaves, because it was
not the season for figs.[h] 14Then he
said to the tree, "May no-one ever
eat fruit from you again." And his
disciples heard him say it.
15On reaching Jerusalem, Jesus
entered the temple area and began
driving out those who were buying
and selling there. He overturned
the tables of the money-changers
and the benches of those selling
doves, 16and would not allow anyone to carry merchandise through
the temple courts. 17And as he
taught them, he said, "Is it not written:

" 'My house will be called
a house of prayer for all
nations'[c]?[i]

But you have made it 'a den of robbers'.[d]"[j]

[a]9 A Hebrew expression meaning "Save!" which became an exclamation of praise; also in verse 10.
[b]9 Psalm 118:25,26 [c]17 Isaiah 56:7
[d]17 Jer. 7:11

18 The chief priests and the teachers of the law heard this and began looking for a way to kill him, for they feared him,[k] because the whole crowd was amazed at his teaching.[l]

19 When evening came, they[e] went out of the city.[m]

The Withered Fig-Tree

11:20–24pp Mt 21:19–22

20 In the morning, as they went along, they saw the fig-tree withered from the roots. 21 Peter remembered and said to Jesus, "Rabbi,[n] look! The fig-tree you cursed has withered!"

22 "Have[f] faith in God," Jesus answered. 23 "I tell you the truth, if anyone says to this mountain, 'Go, throw yourself into the sea,' and does not doubt in his heart but believes that what he says will happen, it will be done for him.[o] 24 Therefore I tell you, whatever you ask for in prayer, believe that you have received it, and it will be yours.[p] 25 And when you stand praying, if you hold anything against anyone, forgive him, so that your Father in heaven may forgive you your sins."[g][q]

The Authority of Jesus Questioned

11:27–33pp Mt 21:23–27; Lk 20:1–8

27 They arrived again in Jerusalem, and while Jesus was walking in the temple courts, the chief priests, the teachers of the law and the elders came to him. 28 "By what authority are you doing these things?" they asked. "And who gave you authority to do this?"

29 Jesus replied, "I will ask you one question. Answer me, and I will tell you by what authority I am doing these things. 30 John's baptism—was it from heaven, or from men? Tell me!"

31 They discussed it among themselves and said, "If we say, 'From heaven', he will ask, 'Then why didn't you believe him?' 32 But if we say, 'From men' . . . ." (They feared the people, for everyone held that John really was a prophet.)[r]

33 So they answered Jesus, "We don't know."

Jesus said, "Neither will I tell you by what authority I am doing these things."

The Parable of the Tenants

12:1–12pp Mt 21:33–46; Lk 20:9–19

12 He then began to speak to them in parables: "A man planted a vineyard.[a] He put a wall around it, dug a pit for the winepress and built a watchtower. Then he rented the vineyard to some farmers and went away on a journey. 2 At harvest time he sent a servant to the tenants to collect from them some of the fruit of the vineyard. 3 But they seized him, beat him and sent him away empty-handed. 4 Then he sent another servant to them; they struck this man on the head and treated him shamefully. 5 He sent still another, and that one they killed. He sent many others; some of them they beat, others they killed.

6 "He had one left to send, a son, whom he loved. He sent him last of all,[b] saying, 'They will respect my son.'

7 "But the tenants said to one another, 'This is the heir. Come, let's kill him, and the inheritance will be ours.' 8 So they took him and killed him, and threw him out of the vineyard.

9 "What then will the owner of the vineyard do? He will come and kill those tenants and give the vineyard to others. 10 Haven't you read this scripture:

11:18
k Mt 21:46; Mk 12:12; Lk 20:19
l Mt 7:28
11:19
m Lk 21:37
11:21
n Mt 23:7
11:23
o Mt 21:21
11:24
p Mt 7:7
11:25
q Mt 6:14
11:32
r Mt 11:9
12:1
a Isa 5:1-7
12:6
b Heb 1:1-3

e 19 Some early manuscripts *he* f 22 Some early manuscripts *If you have* g 25 Some manuscripts *sins.* 26 *But if you do not forgive, neither will your Father who is in heaven forgive your sins.*

> "'The stone the builders
> rejected
> has become the capstone;[a][c]
> [11]the Lord has done this,
> and it is marvellous in our
> eyes'[b]?"[d]

[12]Then they looked for a way to arrest him because they knew he had spoken the parable against them. But they were afraid of the crowd;[e] so they left him and went away.[f]

Paying Taxes to Caesar

12:13–17pp Mt 22:15–22; Lk 20:20–26

[13]Later they sent some of the Pharisees and Herodians[g] to Jesus to catch him[h] in his words. [14]They came to him and said, "Teacher, we know you are a man of integrity. You aren't swayed by men, because you pay no attention to who they are; but you teach the way of God in accordance with the truth. Is it right to pay taxes to Caesar or not? [15]Should we pay or shouldn't we?"

But Jesus knew their hypocrisy. "Why are you trying to trap me?" he asked. "Bring me a denarius and let me look at it." [16]They brought the coin, and he asked them, "Whose portrait is this? And whose inscription?"

"Caesar's," they replied.

[17]Then Jesus said to them, "Give to Caesar what is Caesar's and to God what is God's."[i]

And they were amazed at him.

Marriage at the Resurrection

12:18–27pp Mt 22:23–33; Lk 20:27–38

[18]Then the Sadducees,[j] who say there is no resurrection,[k] came to him with a question. [19]"Teacher," they said, "Moses wrote for us that if a man's brother dies and leaves a wife but no children, the man must marry the widow and have children for his brother.[l] [20]Now there were seven brothers. The first one married and died without leaving any children. [21]The second one married the widow, but he also died, leaving no child. It was the same with the third. [22]In fact, none of the seven left any children. Last of all, the woman died too. [23]At the resurrection[c] whose wife will she be, since the seven were married to her?"

[24]Jesus replied, "Are you not in error because you do not know the Scriptures[m] or the power of God? [25]When the dead rise, they will neither marry nor be given in marriage; they will be like the angels in heaven.[n] [26]Now about the dead rising—have you not read in the book of Moses, in the account of the bush, how God said to him, 'I am the God of Abraham, the God of Isaac, and the God of Jacob'[d]?[o] [27]He is not the God of the dead, but of the living. You are badly mistaken!"

The Greatest Commandment

12:28–34pp Mt 22:34–40

[28]One of the teachers of the law[p] came and heard them debating. Noticing that Jesus had given them a good answer, he asked him, "Of all the commandments, which is the most important?"

[29]"The most important one," answered Jesus, "is this: 'Hear, O Israel, the Lord our God, the Lord is one.[e] [30]Love the Lord your God with all your heart and with all your soul and with all your mind and with all your strength.'[f][q] [31]The second is this: 'Love your neighbour as yourself.'[g][r] There is no commandment greater than these."

[32]"Well said, teacher," the man replied. "You are right in saying that God is one and there is no other but him.[s] [33]To love him with all your heart, with all your understanding and with all your strength, and to love your neighbour as yourself is more important

12:10 *c* Ac 4:11
12:11 *d* Ps 118:22,23
12:12 *e* Mk 11:18 *f* Mt 22:22
12:13 *g* Mt 22:16 Mk 3:6 *h* Mt 12:10
12:17 *i* Ro 13:7
12:18 *j* Ac 4:1 *k* Ac 23:8 1Co 15:12
12:19 *l* Dt 25:5
12:24 *m* 2Ti 3:15-17
12:25 *n* 1Co 15:42,49, 52
12:26 *o* Ex 3:6
12:28 *p* Lk 10:25-28 Lk 20:39
12:30 *q* Dt 6:4,5
12:31 *r* Lev 19:18 Mt 5:43
12:32 *s* Dt 4:35,39 Isa 45:6,14 Isa 46:9

[a]*10* Or *cornerstone* [b]*11* Psalm 118:22,23
[c]*23* Some manuscripts *resurrection, when men rise from the dead,* [d]*26* Exodus 3:6
[e]*29* Or *the Lord our God is one Lord*
[f]*30* Deut. 6:4,5 [g]*31* Lev. 19:18

than all burnt offerings and sacrifices."[t]

34 When Jesus saw that he had answered wisely, he said to him, "You are not far from the kingdom of God."[u] And from then on no-one dared ask him any more questions.[v]

Whose Son Is the Christ?

12:35–37pp Mt 22:41–46; Lk 20:41–44
12:38–40pp Mt 23:1–7; Lk 20:45–47

35 While Jesus was teaching in the temple courts,[w] he asked, "How is it that the teachers of the law say that the Christ[h] is the son of David?[x] 36 David himself, speaking by the Holy Spirit,[y] declared:

" 'The Lord said to my Lord:
"Sit at my right hand
until I put your enemies
under your feet." '[i][z]

37 David himself calls him 'Lord'. How then can he be his son?"

The large crowd[a] listened to him with delight.

38 As he taught, Jesus said, "Watch out for the teachers of the law. They like to walk around in flowing robes and be greeted in the market-places, 39 and have the most important seats in the synagogues and the places of honour at banquets.[b] 40 They devour widows' houses and for a show make lengthy prayers. Such men will be punished most severely."

The Widow's Offering

12:41–44pp Lk 21:1–4

41 Jesus sat down opposite the place where the offerings were put[c] and watched the crowd putting their money into the temple treasury. Many rich people threw in large amounts. 42 But a poor widow came and put in two very small copper coins,[j] worth only a fraction of a penny.[k]

43 Calling his disciples to him, Jesus said, "I tell you the truth, this poor widow has put more into the treasury than all the others. 44 They all gave out of their wealth; but she, out of her poverty, put in everything—all she had to live on."[d]

Signs of the End of the Age

13:1–37pp Mt 24:1–51; Lk 21:5–36

13 As he was leaving the temple, one of his disciples said to him, "Look, Teacher! What massive stones! What magnificent buildings!"

2 "Do you see all these great buildings?" replied Jesus. "Not one stone here will be left on another; every one will be thrown down."[a]

3 As Jesus was sitting on the Mount of Olives[b] opposite the temple, Peter, James, John[c] and Andrew asked him privately, 4 "Tell us, when will these things happen? And what will be the sign that they are all about to be fulfilled?"

5 Jesus said to them: "Watch out that no-one deceives you.[d] 6 Many will come in my name, claiming, 'I am he,' and will deceive many. 7 When you hear of wars and rumours of wars, do not be alarmed. Such things must happen, but the end is still to come. 8 Nation will rise against nation, and kingdom against kingdom. There will be earthquakes in various places, and famines. These are the beginning of birth-pains.

9 "You must be on your guard. You will be handed over to the local councils and flogged in the synagogues.[e] On account of me you will stand before governors and kings as witnesses to them. 10 And the gospel must first be preached to all nations. 11 Whenever you are arrested and brought to trial, do not worry beforehand about what to say. Just say whatever is given you at the time, for it is not you speaking, but the Holy Spirit.[f]

12 "Brother will betray brother to death, and a father his child.

12:33 t 1Sa 15:22; Hos 6:6; Mic 6:6-8; Heb 10:8
12:34 u Mt 3:2; v Mt 22:46; Lk 20:40
12:35 w Mt 26:55; x Mt 9:27
12:36 y 2Sa 23:2; z Ps 110:1; Mt 22:44
12:37 a Jn 12:9
12:39 b Lk 11:43
12:41 c 2Ki 12:9; Jn 8:20
12:44 d 2Co 8:12
13:2 a Lk 19:44
13:3 b Mt 21:1; c Mt 4:21
13:5 d ver 22; Jer 29:8; Eph 5:6; 2Th 2:3,10-12; 1Ti 4:1; 2Ti 3:13; 1Jn 4:6
13:9 e Mt 10:17
13:11 f Mt 10:19,20; Lk 12:11,12

[h] 35 Or *Messiah* [i] 36 Psalm 110:1 [j] 42 Greek *two lepta* [k] 42 Greek *kodrantes*

Children will rebel against their
parents and have them put to
death.[g] 13All men will hate you
because of me,[h] but he who stands
firm to the end will be saved.[i]
14"When you see 'the abomination that causes desolation'[a][j]
standing where it[b] does not belong—let the reader understand—
then let those who are in Judea flee
to the mountains. 15Let no-one on
the roof of his house go down or enter the house to take anything out.
16Let no-one in the field go back to
get his cloak. 17How dreadful it will
be in those days for pregnant
women and nursing mothers![k]
18Pray that this will not take place
in winter, 19because those will be
days of distress unequalled from
the beginning, when God created
the world,[l] until now—and never
to be equalled again.[m] 20If the Lord
had not cut short those days, no-one
would survive. But for the sake of
the elect, whom he has chosen, he
has shortened them. 21At that time
if anyone says to you, 'Look, here is
the Christ!'[c] or, 'Look, there he is!'
do not believe it.[n] 22For false
Christs and false prophets[o] will
appear and perform signs and miracles[p] to deceive the elect—if that
were possible. 23So be on your
guard;[q] I have told you everything
ahead of time.
24"But in those days, following
that distress,

" 'the sun will be darkened,
and the moon will not give its
light;
25the stars will fall from the sky,
and the heavenly bodies will
be shaken.'[d][r]

26"At that time men will see the
Son of Man coming in clouds[s] with
great power and glory. 27And he
will send his angels and gather his
elect from the four winds, from the
ends of the earth to the ends of
the heavens.[t]
28"Now learn this lesson from the
fig-tree: As soon as its twigs get

13:12 g Mic 7:6; Mt 10:21; Lk 12:51-53
13:13 h Jn 15:21; i Mt 10:22
13:14 j Da 9:27; Da 11:31; Da 12:11
13:17 k Lk 23:29
13:19 l Mk 10:6; m Da 9:26; Da 12:1; Joel 2:2
13:21 n Lk 17:23; Lk 21:8
13:22 o Mt 7:15; p Jn 4:48; 2Th 2:9,10
13:23 q 2Pe 3:17
13:25 r Isa 13:10; Isa 34:4; Mt 24:29
13:26 s Da 7:13; Mt 16:27; Rev 1:7
13:27 t Zec 2:6
13:30 u Mk 9:1; v Lk 17:25
13:31 w Mt 5:18
13:32 x Ac 1:7; 1Th 5:1,2
13:33 y 1Th 5:6
13:34 z Mt 25:14
13:37 a Lk 12:35-40
14:1 a Jn 11:55; Jn 13:1; b Mt 12:14
14:3 c Mt 21:17

tender and its leaves come out, you
know that summer is near. 29Even
so, when you see these things happening, you know that it is near,
right at the door. 30I tell you the
truth, this generation[e][u] will certainly not pass away until all these
things have happened.[v] 31Heaven
and earth will pass away, but my
words will never pass away.[w]

The Day and Hour Unknown

32"No-one knows about that day
or hour, not even the angels in
heaven, nor the Son, but only the
Father.[x] 33Be on guard! Be
alert![f][y] You do not know when
that time will come. 34It's like a
man going away: He leaves his
house and puts his servants[z] in
charge, each with his assigned
task, and tells the one at the door to
keep watch.
35"Therefore keep watch because you do not know when the
owner of the house will come
back—whether in the evening, or
at midnight, or when the cock
crows, or at dawn. 36If he comes
suddenly, do not let him find you
sleeping. 37What I say to you, I say
to everyone: 'Watch!' "[a]

Jesus Anointed at Bethany

14:1-11pp Mt 26:2-16
14:1,2,10,11pp Lk 22:1-6
14:3-8Ref Jn 12:1-8

14 Now the Passover[a] and the
Feast of Unleavened Bread
were only two days away, and the
chief priests and the teachers of
the law were looking for some sly
way to arrest Jesus and kill him.[b]
2"But not during the Feast," they
said, "or the people may riot."
3While he was in Bethany,[c] reclining at the table in the home of a
man known as Simon the Leper, a
woman came with an alabaster jar

a *14* Daniel 9:27; 11:31; 12:11 b *14* Or *he*; also in verse 29 c *21* Or *Messiah* d *25* Isaiah 13:10; 34:4 e *30* Or *race* f *33* Some manuscripts *alert and pray*

of very expensive perfume, made of pure nard. She broke the jar and poured the perfume on his head.[d]

4 Some of those present were saying indignantly to one another, "Why this waste of perfume? 5 It could have been sold for more than a year's wages[a] and the money given to the poor." And they rebuked her harshly.

6 "Leave her alone," said Jesus. "Why are you bothering her? She has done a beautiful thing to me. 7 The poor you will always have with you, and you can help them any time you want.[e] But you will not always have me. 8 She did what she could. She poured perfume on my body beforehand to prepare for my burial.[f] 9 I tell you the truth, wherever the gospel is preached throughout the world,[g] what she has done will also be told, in memory of her."

10 Then Judas Iscariot, one of the Twelve,[h] went to the chief priests to betray Jesus to them.[i] 11 They were delighted to hear this and promised to give him money. So he watched for an opportunity to hand him over.

The Lord's Supper

14:12–26pp Mt 26:17–30; Lk 22:7–23
14:22–25pp 1Co 11:23–25

12 On the first day of the Feast of Unleavened Bread, when it was customary to sacrifice the Passover lamb,[j] Jesus' disciples asked him, "Where do you want us to go and make preparations for you to eat the Passover?"

13 So he sent two of his disciples, telling them, "Go into the city, and a man carrying a jar of water will meet you. Follow him. 14 Say to the owner of the house he enters, 'The Teacher asks: Where is my guest room, where I may eat the Passover with my disciples?' 15 He will show you a large upper room,[k] furnished and ready. Make preparations for us there."

14:3 d Lk 7:37-39
14:7 e Dt 15:11
14:8 f Jn 19:40
14:9 g Mt 24:14; Mk 16:15
14:10 h Mk 3:16-19; i Mt 10:4
14:12 j Ex 12:1-11; Dt 16:1-4; 1Co 5:7
14:15 k Ac 1:13
14:20 l Jn 13:18-27
14:21 m Mt 8:20
14:22 n Mt 14:19
14:23 o 1Co 10:16
14:24 p Mt 26:28
14:25 q Mt 3:2
14:26 r Mt 21:1
14:27 s Zec 13:7
14:28 t Mk 16:7

16 The disciples left, went into the city and found things just as Jesus had told them. So they prepared the Passover.

17 When evening came, Jesus arrived with the Twelve. 18 While they were reclining at the table eating, he said, "I tell you the truth, one of you will betray me—one who is eating with me."

19 They were saddened, and one by one they said to him, "Surely not I?"

20 "It is one of the Twelve," he replied, "one who dips bread into the bowl with me.[l] 21 The Son of Man[m] will go just as it is written about him. But woe to that man who betrays the Son of Man! It would be better for him if he had not been born."

22 While they were eating, Jesus took bread, gave thanks and broke it,[n] and gave it to his disciples, saying, "Take it; this is my body."

23 Then he took the cup, gave thanks and offered it to them, and they all drank from it.[o]

24 "This is my blood of the[b] covenant,[p] which is poured out for many," he said to them. 25 "I tell you the truth, I will not drink again of the fruit of the vine until that day when I drink it anew in the kingdom of God."[q]

26 When they had sung a hymn, they went out to the Mount of Olives.[r]

Jesus Predicts Peter's Denial

14:27–31pp Mt 26:31–35

27 "You will all fall away," Jesus told them, "for it is written:

" 'I will strike the shepherd,
and the sheep will be
scattered.'[c][s]

28 But after I have risen, I will go ahead of you into Galilee."[t]

[a] 5 Greek *than three hundred denarii* [b] 24 Some manuscripts *the new* [c] 27 Zech. 13:7

29Peter declared, "Even if all fall away, I will not."

30"I tell you the truth," Jesus answered, "today—yes, tonight—before the cock crows twice[d] you yourself will disown me three times."[u]

31But Peter insisted emphatically, "Even if I have to die with you,[v] I will never disown you." And all the others said the same.

Gethsemane

14:32–42pp Mt 26:36–46; Lk 22:40–46

32They went to a place called Gethsemane, and Jesus said to his disciples, "Sit here while I pray." 33He took Peter, James and John[w] along with him, and he began to be deeply distressed and troubled. 34"My soul is overwhelmed with sorrow to the point of death,"[x] he said to them. "Stay here and keep watch."

35Going a little farther, he fell to the ground and prayed that if possible the hour[y] might pass from him. 36"*Abba*,[e] Father,"[z] he said, "everything is possible for you. Take this cup[a] from me. Yet not what I will, but what you will."[b]

37Then he returned to his disciples and found them sleeping. "Simon," he said to Peter, "are you asleep? Could you not keep watch for one hour? 38Watch and pray so that you will not fall into temptation.[c] The spirit is willing, but the body is weak."[d]

39Once more he went away and prayed the same thing. 40When he came back, he again found them sleeping, because their eyes were heavy. They did not know what to say to him.

41Returning the third time, he said to them, "Are you still sleeping and resting? Enough! The hour[e] has come. Look, the Son of Man is betrayed into the hands of sinners. 42Rise! Let us go! Here comes my betrayer!"

Jesus Arrested

14:43–50pp Mt 26:47–56; Lk 22:47–50; Jn 18:3–11

43Just as he was speaking, Judas,[f] one of the Twelve, appeared. With him was a crowd armed with swords and clubs, sent from the chief priests, the teachers of the law, and the elders.

44Now the betrayer had arranged a signal with them: "The one I kiss is the man; arrest him and lead him away under guard." 45Going at once to Jesus, Judas said, "Rabbi!"[g] and kissed him. 46The men seized Jesus and arrested him. 47Then one of those standing near drew his sword and struck the servant of the high priest, cutting off his ear.

48"Am I leading a rebellion," said Jesus, "that you have come out with swords and clubs to capture me? 49Every day I was with you, teaching in the temple courts,[h] and you did not arrest me. But the Scriptures must be fulfilled."[i] 50Then everyone deserted him and fled.[j]

51A young man, wearing nothing but a linen garment, was following Jesus. When they seized him, 52he fled naked, leaving his garment behind.

Before the Sanhedrin

14:53–65pp Mt 26:57–68; Jn 18:12,13,19–24
14:61–63pp Lk 22:67–71

53They took Jesus to the high priest, and all the chief priests, elders and teachers of the law came together. 54Peter followed him at a distance, right into the courtyard of the high priest.[k] There he sat with the guards and warmed himself at the fire.[l]

55The chief priests and the whole Sanhedrin[m] were looking for evidence against Jesus so that they could put him to death, but they did not find any. 56Many testified falsely against him, but their statements did not agree.

57Then some stood up and gave

14:30 u ver 66-72; Lk 22:34; Jn 13:38
14:31 v Lk 22:33; Jn 13:37
14:33 w Mt 4:21
14:34 x Jn 12:27
14:35 y ver 41; Mt 26:18
14:36 z Ro 8:15; Gal 4:6; a Mt 20:22; b Mt 26:39
14:38 c Mt 6:13; d Ro 7:22,23
14:41 e ver 35; Mt 26:18
14:43 f Mt 10:4
14:45 g Mt 23:7
14:49 h Mt 26:55; i Isa 53:7-12; Mt 1:22
14:50 j ver 27
14:54 k Mt 26:3; l Jn 18:18
14:55 m Mt 5:22

d30 Some early manuscripts do not have *twice*.
e36 Aramaic for *Father*

this false testimony against him:
58“We heard him say, ‘I will destroy
this man-made temple and in three
days will build another,[n] not made
by man.’ ” 59Yet even then their testimony did not agree.

60Then the high priest stood up
before them and asked Jesus, “Are
you not going to answer? What is
this testimony that these men are
bringing against you?” 61But Jesus
remained silent and gave no answer.[o]

Again the high priest asked him,
“Are you the Christ,[f] the Son of
the Blessed One?”[p]

62“I am,” said Jesus. “And you
will see the Son of Man sitting at
the right hand of the Mighty One
and coming on the clouds of
heaven.”[q]

63The high priest tore his
clothes.[r] “Why do we need any
more witnesses?” he asked. 64“You
have heard the blasphemy. What do
you think?”

They all condemned him as worthy of death.[s] 65Then some began
to spit at him; they blindfolded him,
struck him with their fists, and
said, “Prophesy!” And the guards
took him and beat him.[t]

Peter Disowns Jesus

14:66–72pp Mt 26:69–75; Lk 22:56–62; Jn 18:16–18,25–27

66While Peter was below in the
courtyard,[u] one of the servant
girls of the high priest came by.
67When she saw Peter warming
himself,[v] she looked closely at
him.

“You also were with that Nazarene, Jesus,”[w] she said.

68But he denied it. “I don’t know
or understand what you’re talking
about,”[x] he said, and went out into
the entrance.[g]

69When the servant girl saw him
there, she said again to those standing around, “This fellow is one of
them.” 70Again he denied it.[y]

After a little while, those standing near said to Peter, “Surely you
are one of them, for you are a Galilean.”[z]

71He began to call down curses on
himself, and he swore to them, “I
don’t know this man you’re talking
about.”[a]

72Immediately the cock crowed
the second time.[h] Then Peter remembered the word Jesus had spoken to him: “Before the cock crows
twice[i] you will disown me three
times.”[b] And he broke down and
wept.

Jesus Before Pilate

15:2–15pp Mt 27:11–26; Lk 23:2,3,18–25; Jn 18:29–19:16

15 Very early in the morning,
the chief priests, with the
elders, the teachers of the law[a]
and the whole Sanhedrin,[b] reached
a decision. They bound Jesus, led
him away and turned him over to
Pilate.[c]

2“Are you the king of the
Jews?”[d] asked Pilate.

“Yes, it is as you say,” Jesus replied.

3The chief priests accused him of
many things. 4So again Pilate asked
him, “Aren’t you going to answer?
See how many things they are accusing you of.”

5But Jesus still made no reply,[e]
and Pilate was amazed.

6Now it was the custom at the
Feast to release a prisoner whom
the people requested. 7A man
called Barabbas was in prison with
the insurrectionists who had committed murder in the uprising.
8The crowd came up and asked Pilate to do for them what he usually
did.

9“Do you want me to release to
you the king of the Jews?”[f] asked
Pilate, 10knowing it was out of envy
that the chief priests had handed
Jesus over to him. 11But the chief

14:58 n Mk 15:29; Jn 2:19
14:61 o Isa 53:7; Mt 27:12,14; Mk 15:5; Lk 23:9; Jn 19:9; p Mt 16:16; Jn 4:25,26
14:62 q Rev 1:7
14:63 r Lev 10:6; Lev 21:10; Nu 14:6; Ac 14:14
14:64 s Lev 24:16
14:65 t Mt 16:21
14:66 u ver 54
14:67 v ver 54; w Mk 1:24
14:68 x ver 30,72
14:70 y ver 30,68,72; z Ac 2:7
14:71 a ver 30,72
14:72 b ver 30,68
15:1 a Mt 27:1; Lk 22:66; b Mt 5:22; c Mt 27:2
15:2 d ver 9,12,18,26; Mt 2:2
15:5 e Mk 14:61
15:9 f ver 2

f61 Or *Messiah* g68 Some early manuscripts *entrance and the cock crowed* h72 Some early manuscripts do not have *the second time.*
i72 Some early manuscripts do not have *twice.*

priests stirred up the crowd to have
Pilate release Barabbas[g] instead.
12“What shall I do, then, with the
one you call the king of the Jews?”
Pilate asked them.
13“Crucify him!” they shouted.
14“Why? What crime has he committed?” asked Pilate.
But they shouted all the louder,
“Crucify him!”
15Wanting to satisfy the crowd,
Pilate released Barabbas to them.
He had Jesus flogged,[h] and
handed him over to be crucified.

The Soldiers Mock Jesus

15:16–20pp Mt 27:27–31

16The soldiers led Jesus away
into the palace[i] (that is, the Praetorium) and called together the
whole company of soldiers. 17They
put a purple robe on him, then
twisted together a crown of thorns
and set it on him. 18And they began
to call out to him, “Hail, king of the
Jews!”[j] 19Again and again they
struck him on the head with a staff
and spat on him. Falling on their
knees, they paid homage to him.
20And when they had mocked him,
they took off the purple robe and
put his own clothes on him. Then
they led him out[k] to crucify him.

The Crucifixion

15:22–32pp Mt 27:33–44; Lk 23:33–43; Jn 19:17–24

21A certain man from Cyrene,[l]
Simon, the father of Alexander and
Rufus,[m] was passing by on his way
in from the country, and they
forced him to carry the cross.[n]
22They brought Jesus to the place
called Golgotha (which means The
Place of the Skull). 23Then they
offered him wine mixed with
myrrh,[o] but he did not take it.
24And they crucified him. Dividing
up his clothes, they cast lots[p] to
see what each would get.
25It was the third hour when they
crucified him. 26The written notice
of the charge against him read:
THE KING OF THE JEWS.[q] 27They
crucified two robbers with him, one
on his right and one on his left.[a]
29Those who passed by hurled insults at him, shaking their heads[r]
and saying, “So! You who are going
to destroy the temple and build it in
three days,[s] 30come down from the
cross and save yourself!”
31In the same way the chief
priests and the teachers of the law
mocked him[t] among themselves.
“He saved others,” they said, “but
he can’t save himself! 32Let this
Christ,[b][u] this King of Israel,[v]
come down now from the cross,
that we may see and believe.”
Those crucified with him also
heaped insults on him.

The Death of Jesus

15:33–41pp Mt 27:45–56; Lk 23:44–49

33At the sixth hour darkness
came over the whole land until the
ninth hour.[w] 34And at the ninth
hour Jesus cried out in a loud voice,
“*Eloi, Eloi, lama sabachthani?*”—
which means, “My God, my God,
why have you forsaken me?”[c][x]
35When some of those standing
near heard this, they said, “Listen,
he’s calling Elijah.”
36One man ran, filled a sponge
with wine vinegar,[y] put it on a
stick, and offered it to Jesus to
drink. “Now leave him alone. Let’s
see if Elijah comes to take him
down,” he said.
37With a loud cry, Jesus breathed
his last.[z]
38The curtain of the temple was
torn in two from top to bottom.[a]
39And when the centurion,[b] who
stood there in front of Jesus, heard
his cry and[d] saw how he died, he
said, “Surely this man was the
Son[e] of God!”[c]
40Some women were watching
from a distance.[d] Among them

15:11 *g* Ac 3:14
15:15 *h* Isa 53:6
15:16 *i* Jn 18:28,33; Jn 19:9
15:18 *j* ver 2
15:20 *k* Heb 13:12
15:21 *l* Mt 27:32; *m* Ro 16:13; *n* Mt 27:32; Lk 23:26
15:23 *o* ver 36; Ps 69:21; Pr 31:6
15:24 *p* Ps 22:18
15:26 *q* ver 2
15:29 *r* Ps 22:7; Ps 109:25; *s* Mk 14:58; Jn 2:19
15:31 *t* Ps 22:7
15:32 *u* Mk 14:61; *v* ver 2
15:33 *w* Am 8:9
15:34 *x* Ps 22:1
15:36 *y* ver 23; Ps 69:21
15:37 *z* Jn 19:30
15:38 *a* Heb 10:19,20
15:39 *b* ver 45; *c* Mk 1:1,11; Mk 9:7; Mt 4:3
15:40 *d* Ps 38:11

[a]27 Some manuscripts *left,* 28*and the scripture was fulfilled which says, “He was counted with the lawless ones”* (Isaiah 53:12)
[b]32 Or *Messiah* [c]34 Psalm 22:1 [d]39 Some manuscripts do not have *heard his cry and.*
[e]39 Or *a son*

were Mary Magdalene, Mary the
mother of James the younger and
of Joses, and Salome.[e] 41 In Galilee
these women had followed him and
cared for his needs. Many other
women who had come up with him
to Jerusalem were also there.[f]

The Burial of Jesus

15:42–47pp Mt 27:57–61; Lk 23:50–56; Jn 19:38–42

42 It was Preparation Day (that is,
the day before the Sabbath).[g] So as
evening approached, 43 Joseph of
Arimathea, a prominent member
of the Council,[h] who was himself
waiting for the kingdom of God,[i]
went boldly to Pilate and asked for
Jesus' body. 44 Pilate was surprised
to hear that he was already dead.
Summoning the centurion, he
asked him if Jesus had already
died. 45 When he learned from the
centurion[j] that it was so, he gave
the body to Joseph. 46 So Joseph
bought some linen cloth, took down
the body, wrapped it in the linen,
and placed it in a tomb cut out of
rock. Then he rolled a stone against
the entrance of the tomb.[k] 47 Mary
Magdalene and Mary the mother of
Joses[l] saw where he was laid.

The Resurrection

16:1–8pp Mt 28:1–8; Lk 24:1–10

16 When the Sabbath was
over, Mary Magdalene,
Mary the mother of James, and Salome bought spices[a] so that they
might go to anoint Jesus' body.
2 Very early on the first day of the
week, just after sunrise, they were
on their way to the tomb 3 and they
asked each other, "Who will roll the
stone away from the entrance of
the tomb?"[b]

4 But when they looked up, they
saw that the stone, which was very
large, had been rolled away. 5 As
they entered the tomb, they saw a
young man dressed in a white
robe[c] sitting on the right side, and
they were alarmed.

6 "Don't be alarmed," he said.
"You are looking for Jesus the Nazarene,[d] who was crucified. He has
risen! He is not here. See the place
where they laid him. 7 But go, tell
his disciples and Peter, 'He is going
ahead of you into Galilee. There
you will see him,[e] just as he told
you.' "[f]

8 Trembling and bewildered, the
women went out and fled from the
tomb. They said nothing to anyone,
because they were afraid.

[The most reliable early manuscripts and
other ancient witnesses do not have
Mark 16:9–20.]

9 When Jesus rose early on the
first day of the week, he appeared
first to Mary Magdalene,[g] out of
whom he had driven seven demons.
10 She went and told those who had
been with him and who were
mourning and weeping. 11 When
they heard that Jesus was alive and
that she had seen him, they did not
believe it.[h]

12 Afterwards Jesus appeared in a
different form to two of them while
they were walking in the country.[i]
13 These returned and reported it to
the rest; but they did not believe
them either.

14 Later Jesus appeared to the
Eleven as they were eating; he rebuked them for their lack of faith
and their stubborn refusal to believe those who had seen him after
he had risen.[j]

15 He said to them, "Go into all the
world and preach the good news to
all creation.[k] 16 Whoever believes
and is baptised will be saved, but
whoever does not believe will be
condemned.[l] 17 And these signs
will accompany those who believe:
In my name they will drive out demons;[m] they will speak in new
tongues;[n] 18 they will pick up
snakes[o] with their hands; and
when they drink deadly poison, it
will not hurt them at all; they will

15:40 e Mk 16:1; Lk 24:10; Jn 19:25
15:41 f Mt 27:55,56; Lk 8:2,3
15:42 g Mt 27:62; Jn 19:31
15:43 h Mt 5:22; i Mt 3:2; Lk 2:25,38
15:45 j ver 39
15:46 k Mk 16:3
15:47 l ver 40
16:1 a Lk 23:56; Jn 19:39,40
16:3 b Mk 15:46
16:5 c Jn 20:12
16:6 d Mk 1:24
16:7 e Jn 21:1-23; f Mk 14:28
16:9 g Jn 20:11-18
16:11 h ver 13,14; Lk 24:11
16:12 i Lk 24:13-32
16:14 j Lk 24:36-43
16:15 k Mt 28:18-20; Lk 24:47,48
16:16 l Jn 3:16,18,36; Ac 16:31
16:17 m Mk 9:38; Lk 10:17; Ac 5:16; Ac 8:7; Ac 16:18; Ac 19:13-16; n Ac 2:4; Ac 10:46; Ac 19:6; 1Co 12:10,28, 30
16:18 o Lk 10:19; Ac 28:3-5

place their hands on[p] sick people,
and they will get well."
[19]After the Lord Jesus had spoken to them, he was taken up into
heaven[q] and he sat at the right
hand of God.[r] [20]Then the disciples
went out and preached everywhere, and the Lord worked with
them and confirmed his word by
the signs that accompanied it.

16:18 p Ac 6:6
16:19 q Lk 24:50,51 Jn 6:62 Ac 1:9-11 1Ti 3:16

16:19 r Ps 110:1 Ro 8:34 Col 3:1 Heb 1:3 Heb 12:2

LUKE

Introduction

1:1–4Ref Ac 1:1

1 Many have undertaken to
draw up an account of the
things that have been fulfilled[a]
among us, 2just as they were
handed down to us by those who
from the first[a] were eye-
witnesses[b] and servants of the
word.[c] 3Therefore, since I myself
have carefully investigated everything from the beginning, it
seemed good also to me to write an
orderly account[d] for you, most excellent[e] Theophilus,[f] 4so that you
may know the certainty of the
things you have been taught.[g]

The Birth of John the Baptist Foretold

5In the time of Herod king of Judea[h] there was a priest named
Zechariah, who belonged to the
priestly division of Abijah;[i] his
wife Elizabeth was also a descendant of Aaron. 6Both of them were
upright in the sight of God, observing all the Lord's commandments
and regulations blamelessly.[j] 7But
they had no children, because Elizabeth was barren; and they were
both well on in years.

8Once when Zechariah's division
was on duty and he was serving as
priest before God,[k] 9he was chosen
by lot, according to the custom
of the priesthood, to go into the
temple of the Lord and burn
incense.[l] 10And when the time for
the burning of incense came, all
the assembled worshippers were
praying outside.[m]

11Then an angel[n] of the Lord appeared to him, standing at the right
side of the altar of incense.[o]
12When Zechariah saw him, he was
startled and was gripped with
fear.[p] 13But the angel said to him:
"Do not be afraid,[q] Zechariah;
your prayer has been heard. Your
wife Elizabeth will bear you a son,
and you are to give him the name
John.[r] 14He will be a joy and delight to you, and many will rejoice
because of his birth,[s] 15for he will
be great in the sight of the Lord. He
is never to take wine or other fermented drink,[t] and he will be
filled with the Holy Spirit even
from birth.[b][u] 16Many of the people of Israel will he bring back to
the Lord their God. 17And he will go
on before the Lord,[v] in the spirit
and power of Elijah,[w] to turn the
hearts of the fathers to their children[x] and the disobedient to the
wisdom of the righteous—to make
ready a people prepared for the
Lord."

18Zechariah asked the angel,
"How can I be sure of this? I am an
old man and my wife is well on in
years."[y]

19The angel answered, "I am Gabriel.[z] I stand in the presence of
God, and I have been sent to speak
to you and to tell you this good
news. 20And now you will be silent
and not able to speak[a] until the day
this happens, because you did not
believe my words, which will come
true at their proper time."

21Meanwhile, the people were
waiting for Zechariah and wondering why he stayed so long in the
temple. 22When he came out, he
could not speak to them. They realised he had seen a vision in the
temple, for he kept making signs[b]
to them but remained unable to
speak.

[a]1 Or *been surely believed* [b]15 Or *from his mother's womb*

1:2 a Mk 1:1 Jn 15:27 Ac 1:21,22 b Heb 2:3 1Pe 5:1 2Pe 1:16 1Jn 1:1 c Mk 4:14
1:3 d Ac 11:4 e Ac 24:3 Ac 26:25 f Ac 1:1
1:4 g Jn 20:31
1:5 h Mt 2:1 i 1Ch 24:10
1:6 j Ge 7:1 1Ki 9:4
1:8 k 1Ch 24:19 2Ch 8:14
1:9 l Ex 30:7,8 1Ch 23:13 2Ch 29:11
1:10 m Lev 16:17
1:11 n Ac 5:19 o Ex 30:1-10
1:12 p Jdg 6:22,23 Jdg 13:22
1:13 q ver 30 Mt 14:27 r ver 60,63
1:14 s ver 58
1:15 t Nu 6:3 Jdg 13:4 Lk 7:33 u Jer 1:5 Gal 1:15
1:17 v ver 76 w Mt 11:14 x Mal 4:5,6
1:18 y ver 34 Ge 17:17
1:19 z ver 26 Mt 18:10 Da 8:16 Da 9:21
1:20 a Eze 3:26
1:22 b ver 62

23When his time of service was
completed, he returned home.
24After this his wife Elizabeth became pregnant and for five months
remained in seclusion. 25"The Lord
has done this for me," she said. "In
these days he has shown his favour
and taken away my disgrace[c]
among the people."

The Birth of Jesus Foretold

26In the sixth month, God sent the
angel Gabriel[d] to Nazareth,[e] a
town in Galilee, 27to a virgin
pledged to be married to a man
named Joseph,[f] a descendant of
David. The virgin's name was
Mary. 28The angel went to her and
said, "Greetings, you who are
highly favoured! The Lord is with
you."

29Mary was greatly troubled at
his words and wondered what kind
of greeting this might be. 30But the
angel said to her, "Do not be
afraid,[g] Mary, you have found favour with God. 31You will be with
child and give birth to a son, and
you are to give him the name
Jesus.[h] 32He will be great and will
be called the Son of the Most
High.[i] The Lord God will give him
the throne of his father David,
33and he will reign over the house
of Jacob for ever; his kingdom[j]
will never end."[k]

34"How will this be," Mary asked
the angel, "since I am a virgin?"

35The angel answered, "The Holy
Spirit will come upon you,[l] and the
power of the Most High[m] will over-
shadow you. So the holy one[n] to be
born will be called[c] the Son of
God.[o] 36Even Elizabeth your relative is going to have a child in her
old age, and she who was said to
be barren is in her sixth month.
37For nothing is impossible with
God."[p]

38"I am the Lord's servant," Mary
answered. "May it be to me as
you have said." Then the angel
left her.

Mary Visits Elizabeth

39At that time Mary got ready
and hurried to a town in the hill
country of Judea,[q] 40where she
entered Zechariah's home and
greeted Elizabeth. 41When Elizabeth heard Mary's greeting, the
baby leaped in her womb, and
Elizabeth was filled with the Holy
Spirit. 42In a loud voice she exclaimed: "Blessed are you among
women,[r] and blessed is the child
you will bear! 43But why am I so favoured, that the mother of my Lord
should come to me? 44As soon as the
sound of your greeting reached my
ears, the baby in my womb leaped
for joy. 45Blessed is she who has believed that what the Lord has said
to her will be accomplished!"

Mary's Song

1:46–53pp 1Sa 2:1–10

46And Mary said:

"My soul glorifies the Lord[s]
47 and my spirit rejoices in God
my Saviour,[t]
48for he has been mindful
of the humble state of his
servant.[u]
From now on all generations
will call me blessed,[v]
49 for the Mighty One has done
great things[w] for me—
holy is his name.[x]
50His mercy extends to those who
fear him,
from generation to
generation.[y]
51He has performed mighty deeds
with his arm;[z]
he has scattered those who are
proud in their inmost
thoughts.
52He has brought down rulers
from their thrones
but has lifted up the humble.
53He has filled the hungry with
good things[a]
but has sent the rich away
empty.

1:25 c Ge 30:23; Isa 4:1
1:26 d ver 19; e Mt 2:23
1:27 f Mt 1:16,18,20; Lk 2:4
1:30 g ver 13; Mt 14:27
1:31 h Isa 7:14; Mt 1:21,25; Lk 2:21
1:32 i ver 35,76; Mk 5:7
1:33 j Mt 28:18; k Da 2:44; Da 7:14,27; Mic 4:7; Heb 1:8
1:35 l Mt 1:18; m ver 32,76; n Mk 1:24; o Mt 4:3
1:37 p Mt 19:26
1:39 q ver 65
1:42 r Jdg 5:24
1:46 s Ps 34:2,3
1:47 t 1Ti 1:1; 1Ti 2:3
1:48 u Ps 138:6; v Lk 11:27
1:49 w Ps 71:19; x Ps 111:9
1:50 y Ex 20:6; Ps 103:17
1:51 z Ps 98:1; Isa 40:10
1:53 a Ps 107:9

c35 Or *So the child to be born will be called holy,*

54 He has helped his servant Israel,
remembering to be merciful[b]
55 to Abraham and his descendants[c] for ever,
even as he said to our fathers."

56 Mary stayed with Elizabeth for
about three months and then returned home.

The Birth of John the Baptist

57 When it was time for Elizabeth
to have her baby, she gave birth to
a son. 58 Her neighbours and relatives heard that the Lord had
shown her great mercy, and they
shared her joy.
59 On the eighth day they came to
circumcise[d] the child, and they
were going to name him after his
father Zechariah, 60 but his mother
spoke up and said, "No! He is to be
called John."[e]
61 They said to her, "There is no-
one among your relatives who has
that name."
62 Then they made signs[f] to his
father, to find out what he would
like to name the child. 63 He asked
for a writing tablet, and to everyone's astonishment he wrote, "His
name is John."[g] 64 Immediately his
mouth was opened and his tongue
was loosed, and he began to
speak,[h] praising God. 65 The neighbours were all filled with awe, and
throughout the hill country of Judea[i] people were talking about all
these things. 66 Everyone who
heard this wondered about it, asking, "What then is this child going
to be?" For the Lord's hand was
with him.[j]

Zechariah's Song

67 His father Zechariah was filled
with the Holy Spirit and prophesied:[k]

68 "Praise be to the Lord, the God of Israel,[l]
because he has come and has redeemed his people.[m]
69 He has raised up a horn[d][n] of salvation for us
in the house of his servant David[o]
70 (as he said through his holy prophets of long ago),[p]
71 salvation from our enemies
and from the hand of all who hate us—
72 to show mercy to our fathers[q]
and to remember his holy covenant,[r]
73 the oath he swore to our father Abraham:[s]
74 to rescue us from the hand of our enemies,
and to enable us to serve him[t] without fear
75 in holiness and righteousness[u] before him all our days.

76 And you, my child, will be called a prophet[v] of the Most High;[w]
for you will go on before the Lord to prepare the way for him,[x]
77 to give his people the knowledge of salvation
through the forgiveness of their sins,[y]
78 because of the tender mercy of our God,
by which the rising sun[z] will come to us from heaven
79 to shine on those living in darkness
and in the shadow of death,[a]
to guide our feet into the path of peace."

80 And the child grew and became
strong in spirit;[b] and he lived in
the desert until he appeared publicly to Israel.

The Birth of Jesus

2 In those days Caesar Augus-
tus[a] issued a decree that a
census should be taken of the
entire Roman world.[b] (2 This was

1:54 b Ps 98:3
1:55 c Ge 17:19; Ps 132:11; Gal 3:16
1:59 d Ge 17:12; Lev 12:3; Lk 2:21; Php 3:5
1:60 e ver 13,63
1:62 f ver 22
1:63 g ver 13,60
1:64 h ver 20
1:65 i ver 39
1:66 j Ge 39:2; Ac 11:21
1:67 k Joel 2:28
1:68 l Ps 72:18; m Ps 111:9; Lk 7:16
1:69 n 1Sa 2:1,10; Ps 18:2; Ps 89:17; Ps 132:17; Eze 29:21; o Mt 1:1
1:70 p Jer 23:5
1:72 q Mic 7:20; r Ps 105:8,9; Ps 106:45; Eze 16:60
1:73 s Ge 22:16-18
1:74 t Heb 9:14
1:75 u Eph 4:24
1:76 v Mt 11:9; w ver 32,35; x ver 17; Mal 3:1
1:77 y Jer 31:34; Mk 1:4
1:78 z Mal 4:2
1:79 a Isa 9:2; Isa 59:9; Mt 4:16; Ac 26:18
1:80 b Lk 2:40,52
2:1 a Lk 3:1; Mt 22:17; b Mt 24:14

d69 *Horn* here symbolises strength.

the first census that took place
while Quirinius was governor of
Syria.)[c] 3And everyone went to
his own town to register.
4So Joseph also went up from the
town of Nazareth in Galilee to Judea, to Bethlehem[d] the town of
David, because he belonged to the
house and line of David. 5He went
there to register with Mary, who
was pledged to be married to him
and was expecting a child. 6While
they were there, the time came for
the baby to be born, 7and she gave
birth to her firstborn, a son. She
wrapped him in cloths and placed
him in a manger, because there was
no room for them in the inn.

The Shepherds and the Angels

8And there were shepherds living out in the fields near by, keeping watch over their flocks at night.
9An angel[e] of the Lord appeared to
them, and the glory of the Lord
shone around them, and they were
terrified. 10But the angel said to
them, "Do not be afraid.[f] I bring
you good news of great joy that will
be for all the people. 11Today in the
town of David a Saviour[g] has been
born to you; he is Christ[a][h] the
Lord. 12This will be a sign[i] to you:
You will find a baby wrapped in
cloths and lying in a manger."
13Suddenly a great company of
the heavenly host appeared with
the angel, praising God and saying,

14"Glory to God in the highest,
and on earth peace[j] to men
on whom his favour rests."

15When the angels had left them
and gone into heaven, the shepherds said to one another, "Let's go
to Bethlehem and see this thing
that has happened, which the Lord
has told us about."
16So they hurried off and found
Mary and Joseph, and the baby,
who was lying in the manger.
17When they had seen him, they
spread the word concerning what
had been told them about this child,
18and all who heard it were amazed
at what the shepherds said to them.
19But Mary treasured up all these
things and pondered them in her
heart.[k] 20The shepherds returned,
glorifying and praising God[l] for
all the things they had heard and
seen, which were just as they had
been told.

Jesus Presented in the Temple

21On the eighth day, when it was
time to circumcise him,[m] he was
named Jesus, the name the angel
had given him before he had been
conceived.[n]
22When the time of their purification according to the Law of
Moses[o] had been completed, Joseph and Mary took him to Jerusalem to present him to the Lord
23(as it is written in the Law of the
Lord, "Every firstborn male is to be
consecrated to the Lord"[b]),[p] 24and
to offer a sacrifice in keeping with
what is said in the Law of the Lord:
"a pair of doves or two young
pigeons".[c][q]
25Now there was a man in Jerusalem called Simeon, who was
righteous and devout.[r] He was
waiting for the consolation of Israel,[s] and the Holy Spirit was upon
him. 26It had been revealed to him
by the Holy Spirit that he would not
die before he had seen the Lord's
Christ. 27Moved by the Spirit, he
went into the temple courts. When
the parents brought in the child
Jesus to do for him what the custom of the Law required,[t] 28Sim-
eon took him in his arms and
praised God, saying:

29"Sovereign Lord, as you have
promised,[u]
you now dismiss[d] your
servant in peace.[v]

2:2 c Mt 4:24
2:4 d Jn 7:42
2:9 e Lk 1:11; Ac 5:19
2:10 f Mt 14:27
2:11 g Mt 1:21; Jn 4:42; Ac 5:31 h Mt 1:16; Mt 16:16,20; Jn 11:27; Ac 2:36
2:12 i 1Sa 2:34; 2Ki 19:29; Isa 7:14
2:14 j Lk 1:79; Ro 5:1; Eph 2:14,17
2:19 k ver 51
2:20 l Mt 9:8
2:21 m Lk 1:59 n Lk 1:31
2:22 o Lev 12:2-8
2:23 p Ex 13:2,12,15; Nu 3:13
2:24 q Lev 12:8
2:25 r Lk 1:6 s ver 38; Isa 52:9; Lk 23:51
2:27 t ver 22
2:29 u ver 26 v Ac 2:24

a11 Or *Messiah.* "The Christ" (Greek) and "the Messiah" (Hebrew) both mean "the Anointed One"; also in verse 26. b23 Exodus 13:2,12 c24 Lev. 12:8 d29 Or *promised, / now dismiss*

30 For my eyes have seen your
salvation,[w]
31 which you have prepared in
the sight of all people,
32 a light for revelation to the
Gentiles
and for glory to your people
Israel."[x]

33 The child's father and mother
marvelled at what was said about
him. 34 Then Simeon blessed them
and said to Mary, his mother:[y]
"This child is destined to cause the
falling[z] and rising of many in Israel, and to be a sign that will be
spoken against, 35 so that the
thoughts of many hearts will be revealed. And a sword will pierce
your own soul too."

36 There was also a prophetess,[a]
Anna, the daughter of Phanuel, of
the tribe of Asher. She was very
old; she had lived with her husband
seven years after her marriage,
37 and then was a widow until she
was eighty-four.[e][b] She never left
the temple but worshipped night
and day, fasting and praying.[c]
38 Coming up to them at that very
moment, she gave thanks to God
and spoke about the child to all who
were looking forward to the redemption of Jerusalem.[d]

39 When Joseph and Mary had
done everything required by the
Law of the Lord, they returned to
Galilee to their own town of Nazareth.[e] 40 And the child grew and became strong; he was filled with
wisdom, and the grace of God was
upon him.[f]

The Boy Jesus at the Temple

41 Every year his parents went to
Jerusalem for the Feast of the
Passover.[g] 42 When he was twelve
years old, they went up to the
Feast, according to the custom.
43 After the Feast was over, while
his parents were returning home,
the boy Jesus stayed behind in
Jerusalem, but they were unaware
of it. 44 Thinking he was in their

2:30 w Isa 52:10; Lk 3:6
2:32 x Isa 42:6; Isa 49:6; Ac 13:47; Ac 26:23
2:34 y Mt 12:46; z Isa 8:14; Mt 21:44; 1Co 1:23; 2Co 2:16; 1Pe 2:7,8
2:36 a Ac 21:9
2:37 b 1Ti 5:9; c Ac 13:3; Ac 14:23; 1Ti 5:5
2:38 d ver 25; Isa 40:2; Lk 1:68; Lk 24:21
2:39 e ver 51; Mt 2:23
2:40 f ver 52; Lk 1:80
2:41 g Ex 23:15; Dt 16:1-8
2:47 h Mt 7:28
2:48 i Mt 12:46; j Lk 3:23; Lk 4:22
2:49 k Jn 2:16
2:50 l Mk 9:32
2:51 m ver 39; Mt 2:23; n ver 19
2:52 o ver 40; 1Sa 2:26; Lk 1:80
3:1 a Mt 27:2; b Mt 14:1
3:2 c Mt 26:3; Jn 18:13; Ac 4:6; d Mt 3:1; e Lk 1:13
3:3 f ver 16; Mk 1:4

company, they travelled on for a
day. Then they began looking for
him among their relatives and
friends. 45 When they did not find
him, they went back to Jerusalem
to look for him. 46 After three days
they found him in the temple
courts, sitting among the teachers,
listening to them and asking them
questions. 47 Everyone who heard
him was amazed[h] at his understanding and his answers. 48 When
his parents saw him, they were astonished. His mother[i] said to him,
"Son, why have you treated us like
this? Your father[j] and I have been
anxiously searching for you."
49 "Why were you searching for
me?" he asked. "Didn't you know I
had to be in my Father's house?"[k]
50 But they did not understand what
he was saying to them.[l]
51 Then he went down to Nazareth
with them[m] and was obedient to
them. But his mother treasured all
these things in her heart.[n] 52 And
Jesus grew in wisdom and stature,
and in favour with God and men.[o]

John the Baptist Prepares the Way

3:2–10pp Mt 3:1–10; Mk 1:3–5
3:16,17pp Mt 3:11,12; Mk 1:7,8

3 In the fifteenth year of the
reign of Tiberius Caesar—
when Pontius Pilate[a] was governor of Judea, Herod[b] tetrarch of
Galilee, his brother Philip tetrarch
of Iturea and Traconitis, and Lysa-
nias tetrarch of Abilene— 2 during
the high priesthood of Annas and
Caiaphas,[c] the word of God came
to John[d] son of Zechariah[e] in the
desert. 3 He went into all the country around the Jordan, preaching a
baptism of repentance for the forgiveness of sins.[f] 4 As is written in
the book of the words of Isaiah the
prophet:

"A voice of one calling in the
desert,

[e]37 Or *widow for eighty-four years*

'Prepare the way for the Lord,
make straight paths for him.
5 Every valley shall be filled in,
every mountain and hill made
low.
The crooked roads shall become
straight,
the rough ways smooth.
6 And all mankind will see God's
salvation.' "[a][g]

7 John said to the crowds coming
out to be baptised by him, "You
brood of vipers![h] Who warned you
to flee from the coming wrath?[i]
8 Produce fruit in keeping with repentance. And do not begin to say
to yourselves, 'We have Abraham
as our father.'[j] For I tell you that
out of these stones God can raise up
children for Abraham. 9 The axe is
already at the root of the trees, and
every tree that does not produce
good fruit will be cut down and
thrown into the fire."[k]
10 "What should we do then?"[l]
the crowd asked.
11 John answered, "The man with
two tunics should share with him
who has none, and the one who has
food should do the same."[m]
12 Tax collectors also came to be
baptised.[n] "Teacher," they asked,
"what should we do?"
13 "Don't collect any more than
you are required to,"[o] he told
them.
14 Then some soldiers asked him,
"And what should we do?"
He replied, "Don't extort money
and don't accuse people falsely[p]—
be content with your pay."
15 The people were waiting expectantly and were all wondering
in their hearts if John[q] might
possibly be the Christ.[b][r] 16 John
answered them all, "I baptise you
with[c] water.[s] But one more powerful than I will come, the thongs of
whose sandals I am not worthy to
untie. He will baptise you with the
Holy Spirit and with fire.[t] 17 His
winnowing fork[u] is in his hand to
clear his threshing-floor and to
gather the wheat into his barn, but
he will burn up the chaff with
unquenchable fire."[v] 18 And with
many other words John exhorted
the people and preached the good
news to them.
19 But when John rebuked
Herod[w] the tetrarch because of
Herodias, his brother's wife, and
all the other evil things he had
done, 20 Herod added this to them
all: He locked John up in prison.[x]

The Baptism and Genealogy of Jesus

3:21,22pp Mt 3:13–17; Mk 1:9–11
3:23–38pp Mt 1:1–17

21 When all the people were being
baptised, Jesus was baptised too.
And as he was praying,[y] heaven
was opened 22 and the Holy Spirit
descended on him[z] in bodily form
like a dove. And a voice came from
heaven: "You are my Son,[a] whom
I love; with you I am well
pleased."[b]
23 Now Jesus himself was about
thirty years old when he began his
ministry.[c] He was the son, so it
was thought, of Joseph,[d]

the son of Heli, 24 the son of
Matthat,
the son of Levi, the son of
Melki,
the son of Jannai, the son of
Joseph,
25 the son of Mattathias, the son
of Amos,
the son of Nahum, the son of
Esli,
the son of Naggai, 26 the son of
Maath,
the son of Mattathias, the son
of Semein,
the son of Josech, the son of
Joda,
27 the son of Joanan, the son of
Rhesa,

3:6 g Isa 40:3-5; Ps 98:2; Isa 42:16; Isa 52:10; Lk 2:30
3:7 h Mt 12:34; Mt 23:33; i Ro 1:18
3:8 j Isa 51:2; Lk 19:9; Jn 8:33,39; Ac 13:26; Ro 4:1,11,12,16,17; Gal 3:7
3:9 k Mt 3:10
3:10 l ver 12,14; Ac 2:37; Ac 16:30
3:11 m Isa 58:7
3:12 n Lk 7:29
3:13 o Lk 19:8
3:14 p Ex 23:1; Lev 19:11
3:15 q Mt 3:1; r Jn 1:19,20; Ac 13:25
3:16 s ver 3; Mk 1:4; t Jn 1:26,33; Ac 1:5; Ac 11:16; Ac 19:4
3:17 u Isa 30:24; v Mt 13:30; Mt 25:41
3:19 w ver 1
3:20 x Mt 14:3,4; Mk 6:17-18
3:21 y Mt 14:23; Mk 1:35; Mk 6:46; Lk 5:16; Lk 6:12; Lk 9:18,28; Lk 11:1
3:22 z Isa 42:1; Jn 1:32,33; Ac 10:38; a Mt 3:17; b Mt 3:17
3:23 c Mt 4:17; Ac 1:1; d Lk 1:27

a 6 Isaiah 40:3–5 b 15 Or *Messiah* c 16 Or *in*

the son of Zerubbabel,[e] the son
of Shealtiel,
the son of Neri, [28]the son of
Melki,
the son of Addi, the son of
Cosam,
the son of Elmadam, the son
of Er,
[29]the son of Joshua, the son of
Eliezer,
the son of Jorim, the son of
Matthat,
the son of Levi, [30]the son of
Simeon,
the son of Judah, the son of
Joseph,
the son of Jonam, the son of
Eliakim,
[31]the son of Melea, the son of
Menna,
the son of Mattatha, the son
of Nathan,[f]
the son of David, [32]the son of
Jesse,
the son of Obed, the son of
Boaz,
the son of Salmon,[d] the son of
Nahshon,
[33]the son of Amminadab, the son
of Ram,[e]
the son of Hezron, the son of
Perez,[g]
the son of Judah, [34]the son of
Jacob,
the son of Isaac, the son of
Abraham,
the son of Terah, the son of
Nahor,[h]
[35]the son of Serug, the son of
Reu,
the son of Peleg, the son of
Eber,
the son of Shelah, [36]the son of
Cainan,
the son of Arphaxad,[i] the son
of Shem,
the son of Noah, the son of
Lamech,[j]
[37]the son of Methuselah, the son
of Enoch,
the son of Jared, the son of
Mahalalel,
the son of Kenan, [38]the son of
Enosh,
the son of Seth, the son of
Adam,
the son of God.[k]

3:27 e Mt 1:12
3:31 f 2Sa 5:14; 1Ch 3:5
3:33 g Ru 4:18-22; 1Ch 2:10-12
3:34 h Ge 11:24,26
3:36 i Ge 11:12; j Ge 5:28-32
3:38 k Ge 5:1,2,6-9
4:1 a ver 14,18; b Lk 3:3,21; c Lk 2:27
4:2 d Ex 34:28; 1Ki 19:8
4:4 e Dt 8:3
4:5 f Mt 24:14
4:6 g Jn 12:31; Jn 14:30; 1Jn 5:19
4:8 h Dt 6:13
4:11 i Ps 91:11,12
4:12 j Dt 6:16

The Temptation of Jesus

4:1–13pp Mt 4:1–11; Mk 1:12,13

4 Jesus, full of the Holy Spirit,[a]
returned from the Jordan[b]
and was led by the Spirit[c] in the
desert, [2]where for forty days[d] he
was tempted by the devil. He ate
nothing during those days, and at
the end of them he was hungry.
[3]The devil said to him, "If you are
the Son of God, tell this stone to become bread."
[4]Jesus answered, "It is written:
'Man does not live on bread
alone.'[a]"[e]
[5]The devil led him up to a high
place and showed him in an instant
all the kingdoms of the world.[f]
[6]And he said to him, "I will give you
all their authority and splendour,
for it has been given to me,[g] and I
can give it to anyone I want to. [7]So
if you worship me, it will all be
yours."
[8]Jesus answered, "It is written:
'Worship the Lord your God and
serve him only.'[b]"[h]
[9]The devil led him to Jerusalem
and had him stand on the highest
point of the temple. "If you are the
Son of God," he said, "throw yourself down from here. [10]For it is
written:

" 'He will command his angels
concerning you
to guard you carefully;
[11]they will lift you up in their
hands,
so that you will not strike your
foot against a stone.'[c]"[i]

[12]Jesus answered, "It says: 'Do
not put the Lord your God to the
test.'[d]"[j]

[d]32 Some early manuscripts *Sala* [e]33 Some manuscripts *Amminadab, the son of Admin, the son of Arni*; other manuscripts vary widely.
[a]4 Deut. 8:3 [b]8 Deut. 6:13 [c]11 Psalm 91:11,12 [d]12 Deut. 6:16

13When the devil had finished all
this tempting,[k] he left him[l] until
an opportune time.

Jesus Rejected at Nazareth

14Jesus returned to Galilee[m] in
the power of the Spirit, and news
about him spread through the
whole countryside.[n] 15He taught in
their synagogues,[o] and everyone
praised him.

16He went to Nazareth,[p] where
he had been brought up, and on the
Sabbath day he went into the synagogue,[q] as was his custom. And he
stood up to read. 17The scroll of the
prophet Isaiah was handed to him.
Unrolling it, he found the place
where it is written:

> 18"The Spirit of the Lord is on
> me,[r]
> because he has anointed me
> to preach good news to the
> poor.
> He has sent me to proclaim
> freedom for the prisoners
> and recovery of sight for the
> blind,
> to release the oppressed,
> 19 to proclaim the year of the
> Lord's favour."[e][s]

20Then he rolled up the scroll,
gave it back to the attendant and
sat down.[t] The eyes of everyone in
the synagogue were fastened on
him, 21and he began by saying to
them, "Today this scripture is fulfilled in your hearing."

22All spoke well of him and were
amazed at the gracious words that
came from his lips. "Isn't this Joseph's son?" they asked.[u]

23Jesus said to them, "Surely you
will quote this proverb to me:
'Physician, heal yourself! Do here
in your home town[v] what we have
heard that you did in Capernaum.' "[w]

24"I tell you the truth," he continued, "no prophet is accepted in
his home town.[x] 25I assure you that
there were many widows in Israel
in Elijah's time, when the sky was
shut for three and a half years and
there was a severe famine throughout the land.[y] 26Yet Elijah was not
sent to any of them, but to a widow
in Zarephath in the region of Sidon.[z] 27And there were many in Israel with leprosy[f] in the time of
Elisha the prophet, yet not one of
them was cleansed—only Naaman
the Syrian."[a]

28All the people in the synagogue
were furious when they heard this.
29They got up, drove him out of the
town,[b] and took him to the brow of
the hill on which the town was built,
in order to throw him down the
cliff. 30But he walked right through
the crowd and went on his way.[c]

Jesus Drives Out an Evil Spirit

4:31–37pp Mk 1:21–28

31Then he went down to Capernaum,[d] a town in Galilee, and on
the Sabbath began to teach the people. 32They were amazed at his
teaching,[e] because his message
had authority.[f]

33In the synagogue there was a
man possessed by a demon, an
evil[g] spirit. He cried out at the top
of his voice, 34"Ha! What do you
want with us,[g] Jesus of Nazareth?[h] Have you come to destroy
us? I know who you are[i]—the Holy
One of God!"[j]

35"Be quiet!" Jesus said sternly.[k]
"Come out of him!" Then the
demon threw the man down before them all and came out without
injuring him.

36All the people were amazed[l]
and said to each other, "What is this
teaching? With authority[m] and
power he gives orders to evil spirits and they come out!" 37And the
news about him spread throughout
the surrounding area.[n]

4:13 k Heb 4:15; l Jn 14:30
4:14 m Mt 4:12; n Mt 9:26
4:15 o Mt 4:23
4:16 p Mt 2:23; q Mt 13:54
4:18 r Jn 3:34
4:19 s Isa 61:1,2; Lev 25:10
4:20 t ver 17; Mt 26:55
4:22 u Mt 13:54,55; Jn 6:42; Jn 7:15
4:23 v ver 16; w Mk 1:21-28; Mk 2:1-12
4:24 x Mt 13:57; Jn 4:44
4:25 y 1Ki 17:1; 1Ki 18:1; Jas 5:17,18
4:26 z 1Ki 17:8-16; Mt 11:21
4:27 a 2Ki 5:1-14
4:29 b Nu 15:35; Ac 7:58; Heb 13:12
4:30 c Jn 8:59; Jn 10:39
4:31 d ver 23; Mt 4:13
4:32 e Mt 7:28; f ver 36; Mt 7:29
4:34 g Mt 8:29; h Mk 1:24; i Jas 2:19; j ver 41; Mk 1:24
4:35 k ver 39,41; Mt 8:26; Lk 8:24
4:36 l Mt 7:28; m ver 32; Mt 7:29; Mt 10:1
4:37 n ver 14; Mt 9:26

e19 Isaiah 61:1,2 f27 The Greek word was used for various diseases affecting the skin—not necessarily leprosy. g33 Greek *unclean*; also in verse 36

Jesus Heals Many

4:38–41pp Mt 8:14–17
4:38–43pp Mk 1:29–38

38 Jesus left the synagogue and
went to the home of Simon. Now
Simon's mother-in-law was suffering from a high fever, and they
asked Jesus to help her. 39 So he
bent over her and rebuked[o] the
fever, and it left her. She got
up at once and began to wait on
them.
40 When the sun was setting, the
people brought to Jesus all who had
various kinds of sickness, and laying his hands on each one,[p] he
healed them.[q] 41 Moreover, demons came out of many people,
shouting, "You are the Son of
God!"[r] But he rebuked[s] them and
would not allow them to speak,[t]
because they knew he was the
Christ.[h]
42 At daybreak Jesus went out to a
solitary place. The people were
looking for him and when they
came to where he was, they tried to
keep him from leaving them. 43 But
he said, "I must preach the good
news of the kingdom of God[u] to the
other towns also, because that is
why I was sent." 44 And he kept on
preaching in the synagogues of Judea.[i][v]

The Calling of the First Disciples

5:1–11pp Mt 4:18–22; Mk 1:16–20; Jn 1:40–42

5 One day as Jesus was standing
by the Lake of Gennesaret,[a]
with the people crowding round
him and listening to the word of
God,[a] 2 he saw at the water's edge
two boats, left there by the fishermen, who were washing their
nets. 3 He got into one of the
boats, the one belonging to Simon,
and asked him to put out a little
from shore. Then he sat down
and taught the people from the
boat.[b]
4 When he had finished speaking,
he said to Simon, "Put out into deep
water, and let down[b] the nets for a
catch."[c]
5 Simon answered, "Master,[d]
we've worked hard all night and
haven't caught anything.[e] But because you say so, I will let down the
nets."
6 When they had done so, they
caught such a large number of fish
that their nets began to break.[f] 7 So
they signalled to their partners in
the other boat to come and help
them, and they came and filled both
boats so full that they began to
sink.
8 When Simon Peter saw this, he
fell at Jesus' knees and said, "Go
away from me, Lord; I am a sinful
man!"[g] 9 For he and all his companions were astonished at the catch of
fish they had taken, 10 and so were
James and John, the sons of Zebedee, Simon's partners.
Then Jesus said to Simon, "Don't
be afraid;[h] from now on you will
catch men." 11 So they pulled their
boats up on shore, left everything
and followed him.[i]

The Man With Leprosy

5:12–14pp Mt 8:2–4; Mk 1:40–44

12 While Jesus was in one of the
towns, a man came along who was
covered with leprosy.[c][j] When he
saw Jesus, he fell with his face to
the ground and begged him, "Lord,
if you are willing, you can make me
clean."
13 Jesus reached out his hand and
touched the man. "I am willing," he
said. "Be clean!" And immediately
the leprosy left him.
14 Then Jesus ordered him, "Don't
tell anyone,[k] but go, show yourself
to the priest and offer the sacrifices that Moses commanded[l] for

4:39 *o* ver 35,41
4:40 *p* Mk 5:23 *q* Mt 4:23
4:41 *r* Mt 4:3 *s* ver 35 *t* Mt 8:4
4:43 *u* Mt 3:2
4:44 *v* Mt 4:23
5:1 *a* Mk 4:14 Heb 4:12
5:3 *b* Mt 13:2
5:4 *c* Jn 21:6
5:5 *d* Lk 8:24,45 Lk 9:33,49 Lk 17:13 *e* Jn 21:3
5:6 *f* Jn 21:11
5:8 *g* Ge 18:27 Job 42:6 Isa 6:5
5:10 *h* Mt 14:27
5:11 *i* ver 28 Mt 4:19
5:12 *j* Mt 8:2
5:14 *k* Mt 8:4 *l* Lev 14:2-32

h41 Or *Messiah* i44 Or *the land of the Jews*; some manuscripts *Galilee* a1 That is, Sea of Galilee b4 The Greek verb is plural. c12 The Greek word was used for various diseases affecting the skin—not necessarily leprosy.

your cleansing, as a testimony to them."

15 Yet the news about him spread all the more,[m] so that crowds of people came to hear him and to be healed of their sicknesses. 16 But Jesus often withdrew to lonely places and prayed.[n]

Jesus Heals a Paralytic

5:18–26pp Mt 9:2–8; Mk 2:3–12

17 One day as he was teaching, Pharisees and teachers of the law,[o] who had come from every village of Galilee and from Judea and Jerusalem, were sitting there. And the power of the Lord was present for him to heal the sick.[p] 18 Some men came carrying a paralytic on a mat and tried to take him into the house to lay him before Jesus. 19 When they could not find a way to do this because of the crowd, they went up on the roof and lowered him on his mat through the tiles into the middle of the crowd, right in front of Jesus.

20 When Jesus saw their faith, he said, "Friend, your sins are forgiven."[q]

21 The Pharisees and the teachers of the law began thinking to themselves, "Who is this fellow who speaks blasphemy? Who can forgive sins but God alone?"[r]

22 Jesus knew what they were thinking and asked, "Why are you thinking these things in your hearts? 23 Which is easier: to say, 'Your sins are forgiven,' or to say, 'Get up and walk'? 24 But that you may know that the Son of Man[s] has authority on earth to forgive sins. . . ." He said to the paralysed man, "I tell you, get up, take your mat and go home." 25 Immediately he stood up in front of them, took what he had been lying on and went home praising God. 26 Everyone was amazed and gave praise to God.[t] They were filled with awe and said, "We have seen remarkable things today."

5:15 m Mt 9:26
5:16 n Mt 14:23; Lk 3:21
5:17 o Mt 15:1; Lk 2:46; p Mk 5:30; Lk 6:19
5:20 q Lk 7:48,49
5:21 r Isa 43:25
5:24 s Mt 8:20
5:26 t Mt 9:8
5:27 u Mt 4:19
5:28 v ver 11; Mt 4:19
5:29 w Lk 15:1
5:30 x Ac 23:9; y Mt 9:11
5:32 z Jn 3:17
5:33 a Lk 7:18; Jn 1:35; Jn 3:25,26
5:34 b Jn 3:29
5:35 c Lk 9:22; Lk 17:22; Jn 16:5-7

The Calling of Levi

5:27–32pp Mt 9:9–13; Mk 2:14–17

27 After this, Jesus went out and saw a tax collector by the name of Levi sitting at his tax booth. "Follow me,"[u] Jesus said to him, 28 and Levi got up, left everything and followed him.[v]

29 Then Levi held a great banquet for Jesus at his house, and a large crowd of tax collectors[w] and others were eating with them. 30 But the Pharisees and the teachers of the law who belonged to their sect[x] complained to his disciples, "Why do you eat and drink with tax collectors and 'sinners'?"[y]

31 Jesus answered them, "It is not the healthy who need a doctor, but the sick. 32 I have not come to call the righteous, but sinners to repentance."[z]

Jesus Questioned About Fasting

5:33–39pp Mt 9:14–17; Mk 2:18–22

33 They said to him, "John's disciples[a] often fast and pray, and so do the disciples of the Pharisees, but yours go on eating and drinking."

34 Jesus answered, "Can you make the guests of the bridegroom[b] fast while he is with them? 35 But the time will come when the bridegroom will be taken from them;[c] in those days they will fast."

36 He told them this parable: "No-one tears a patch from a new garment and sews it on an old one. If he does, he will have torn the new garment, and the patch from the new will not match the old. 37 And no-one pours new wine into old wineskins. If he does, the new wine will burst the skins, the wine will run out and the wineskins will be ruined. 38 No, new wine must be poured into new wineskins. 39 And no-one after drinking old wine wants the new, for he says, 'The old is better.' "

Lord of the Sabbath

6:1–11pp Mt 12:1–14; Mk 2:23–3:6

6 One Sabbath Jesus was going
through the cornfields, and his
disciples began to pick some ears
of corn, rub them in their hands
and eat the grain.[a] 2Some of the
Pharisees asked, "Why are you doing what is unlawful on the Sabbath?"[b]

3Jesus answered them, "Have
you never read what David did
when he and his companions were
hungry?[c] 4He entered the house of
God, and taking the consecrated
bread, he ate what is lawful only
for priests to eat.[d] And he also
gave some to his companions."
5Then Jesus said to them, "The Son
of Man[e] is Lord of the Sabbath."

6On another Sabbath[f] he went
into the synagogue and was teaching, and a man was there whose
right hand was shrivelled. 7The
Pharisees and the teachers of the
law were looking for a reason to accuse Jesus, so they watched him
closely[g] to see if he would heal on
the Sabbath.[h] 8But Jesus knew
what they were thinking[i] and said
to the man with the shrivelled
hand, "Get up and stand in front of
everyone." So he got up and stood
there.

9Then Jesus said to them, "I ask
you, which is lawful on the Sabbath: to do good or to do evil, to
save life or to destroy it?"

10He looked round at them all,
and then said to the man, "Stretch
out your hand." He did so, and his
hand was completely restored.
11But they were furious[j] and began to discuss with one another
what they might do to Jesus.

The Twelve Apostles

6:13–16pp Mt 10:2–4; Mk 3:16–19; Ac 1:13

12One of those days Jesus went
out to a mountainside to pray, and
spent the night praying to God.[k]
13When morning came, he called
his disciples to him and chose

6:1 *a* Dt 23:25
6:2 *b* Mt 12:2
6:3 *c* 1Sa 21:6
6:4 *d* Lev 24:5,9
6:5 *e* Mt 8:20
6:6 *f* ver 1
6:7 *g* Mt 12:10 *h* Mt 12:2
6:8 *i* Mt 9:4
6:11 *j* Jn 5:18
6:12 *k* Lk 3:21
6:13 *l* Mk 6:30
6:15 *m* Mt 9:9
6:17 *n* Mt 4:25 Mt 11:21 Mk 3:7,8
6:19 *o* Mt 9:20 *p* Mt 14:36 Mk 5:30 Lk 5:17
6:20 *q* Mt 25:34
6:21 *r* Isa 55:1,2 Mt 5:6 *s* Isa 61:2,3 Mt 5:4 Rev 7:17
6:22 *t* Jn 9:22 Jn 16:2 *u* Isa 51:7 *v* Jn 15:21
6:23 *w* Mt 5:12 *x* Mt 5:12
6:24 *y* Jas 5:1 *z* Lk 16:25

twelve of them, whom he also designated apostles:[l] 14Simon (whom
he named Peter), his brother Andrew, James, John, Philip, Bartholomew, 15Matthew,[m] Thomas,
James son of Alphaeus, Simon who
was called the Zealot, 16Judas son
of James, and Judas Iscariot, who
became a traitor.

Blessings and Woes

6:20–23pp Mt 5:3–12

17He went down with them and
stood on a level place. A large
crowd of his disciples was there
and a great number of people from
all over Judea, from Jerusalem,
and from the coast of Tyre and Sidon,[n] 18who had come to hear him
and to be healed of their diseases.
Those troubled by evil[a] spirits
were cured, 19and the people all
tried to touch him,[o] because power
was coming from him and healing
them all.[p]

20Looking at his disciples, he
said:

"Blessed are you who are poor,
for yours is the kingdom of
God.[q]
21Blessed are you who hunger
now,
for you will be satisfied.[r]
Blessed are you who weep now,
for you will laugh.[s]
22Blessed are you when men hate
you,
when they exclude you[t] and
insult you[u]
and reject your name as evil,
because of the Son of Man.[v]

23"Rejoice in that day and leap
for joy,[w] because great is your reward in heaven. For that is how
their fathers treated the prophets.[x]

24"But woe to you who are rich,[y]
for you have already received
your comfort.[z]

[a]18 Greek *unclean*

25 Woe to you who are well fed now,
for you will go hungry.[a]
Woe to you who laugh now,
for you will mourn and weep.[b]
26 Woe to you when all men speak well of you,
for that is how their fathers treated the false prophets.[c]

Love for Enemies

6:29,30pp Mt 5:39–42

27 "But I tell you who hear me: Love your enemies, do good to those who hate you,[d] 28 bless those who curse you, pray for those who ill-treat you.[e] 29 If someone strikes you on one cheek, turn to him the other also. If someone takes your cloak, do not stop him from taking your tunic. 30 Give to everyone who asks you, and if anyone takes what belongs to you, do not demand it back.[f] 31 Do to others as you would have them do to you.[g]

32 "If you love those who love you, what credit is that to you?[h] Even 'sinners' love those who love them. 33 And if you do good to those who are good to you, what credit is that to you? Even 'sinners' do that. 34 And if you lend to those from whom you expect repayment, what credit is that to you?[i] Even 'sinners' lend to 'sinners', expecting to be repaid in full. 35 But love your enemies, do good to them,[j] and lend to them without expecting to get anything back. Then your reward will be great, and you will be sons[k] of the Most High,[l] because he is kind to the ungrateful and wicked. 36 Be merciful,[m] just as your Father[n] is merciful.

Judging Others

6:37–42pp Mt 7:1–5

37 "Do not judge, and you will not be judged.[o] Do not condemn, and you will not be condemned. Forgive, and you will be forgiven.[p] 38 Give, and it will be given to you. A good measure, pressed down, shaken together and running over, will be poured into your lap.[q] For with the measure you use, it will be measured to you."[r]

39 He also told them this parable: "Can a blind man lead a blind man? Will they not both fall into a pit?[s] 40 A student is not above his teacher, but everyone who is fully trained will be like his teacher.[t]

41 "Why do you look at the speck of sawdust in your brother's eye and pay no attention to the plank in your own eye? 42 How can you say to your brother, 'Brother, let me take the speck out of your eye,' when you yourself fail to see the plank in your own eye? You hypocrite, first take the plank out of your eye, and then you will see clearly to remove the speck from your brother's eye.

A Tree and Its Fruit

6:43,44pp Mt 7:16,18,20

43 "No good tree bears bad fruit, nor does a bad tree bear good fruit. 44 Each tree is recognised by its own fruit.[u] People do not pick figs from thorn-bushes, or grapes from briers. 45 The good man brings good things out of the good stored up in his heart, and the evil man brings evil things out of the evil stored up in his heart. For out of the overflow of his heart his mouth speaks.[v]

The Wise and Foolish Builders

6:47–49pp Mt 7:24–27

46 "Why do you call me, 'Lord, Lord,'[w] and do not do what I say?[x] 47 I will show you what he is like who comes to me and hears my words and puts them into practice.[y] 48 He is like a man building a house, who dug down deep and laid the foundation on rock. When the flood came, the torrent struck that house but could not shake it, because it was well built. 49 But the one who hears my words and does

6:25 a Isa 65:13; b Pr 14:13
6:26 c Mt 7:15
6:27 d ver 35; Mt 5:44; Ro 12:20
6:28 e Mt 5:44
6:30 f Dt 15:7,8,10; Pr 21:26
6:31 g Mt 7:12
6:32 h Mt 5:46
6:34 i Mt 5:42
6:35 j ver 27; k Ro 8:14; l Mk 5:7
6:36 m Jas 2:13; n Mt 5:48; Mt 6:1; Lk 11:2; Lk 12:32; Ro 8:15; Eph 4:6; 1Pe 1:17; 1Jn 1:3; 1Jn 3:1
6:37 o Mt 7:1; p Mt 6:14
6:38 q Ps 79:12; Isa 65:6,7; r Mt 7:2; Mk 4:24
6:39 s Mt 15:14
6:40 t Mt 10:24; Jn 13:16
6:44 u Mt 12:33
6:45 v Pr 4:23; Mt 12:34,35; Mk 7:20
6:46 w Jn 13:13; x Mal 1:6; Mt 7:21
6:47 y Lk 8:21; Lk 11:28; Jas 1:22-25

not put them into practice is like a man who built a house on the ground without a foundation. The moment the torrent struck that house, it collapsed and its destruction was complete."

The Faith of the Centurion

7:1–10pp Mt 8:5–13

7 When Jesus had finished saying all this[a] in the hearing of the people, he entered Capernaum. 2 There a centurion's servant, whom his master valued highly, was sick and about to die. 3 The centurion heard of Jesus and sent some elders of the Jews to him, asking him to come and heal his servant. 4 When they came to Jesus, they pleaded earnestly with him, "This man deserves to have you do this, 5 because he loves our nation and has built our synagogue." 6 So Jesus went with them.

He was not far from the house when the centurion sent friends to say to him: "Lord, don't trouble yourself, for I do not deserve to have you come under my roof. 7 That is why I did not even consider myself worthy to come to you. But say the word, and my servant will be healed.[b] 8 For I myself am a man under authority, with soldiers under me. I tell this one, 'Go', and he goes; and that one, 'Come', and he comes. I say to my servant, 'Do this', and he does it."

9 When Jesus heard this, he was amazed at him, and turning to the crowd following him, he said, "I tell you, I have not found such great faith even in Israel." 10 Then the men who had been sent returned to the house and found the servant well.

Jesus Raises a Widow's Son

7:11–16Ref 1Ki 17:17–24; 2Ki 4:32–37; Mk 5:21–24, 35–43; Jn 11:1–44

11 Soon afterwards, Jesus went to a town called Nain, and his disciples and a large crowd went along with him. 12 As he approached the town gate, a dead person was being carried out—the only son of his mother, and she was a widow. And a large crowd from the town was with her. 13 When the Lord[c] saw her, his heart went out to her and he said, "Don't cry."

14 Then he went up and touched the coffin, and those carrying it stood still. He said, "Young man, I say to you, get up!"[d] 15 The dead man sat up and began to talk, and Jesus gave him back to his mother.

16 They were all filled with awe[e] and praised God.[f] "A great prophet[g] has appeared among us," they said. "God has come to help his people."[h] 17 This news about Jesus spread throughout Judea[a] and the surrounding country.[i]

Jesus and John the Baptist

7:18–35pp Mt 11:2–19

18 John's[j] disciples[k] told him about all these things. Calling two of them, 19 he sent them to the Lord to ask, "Are you the one who was to come, or should we expect someone else?"

20 When the men came to Jesus, they said, "John the Baptist sent us to you to ask, 'Are you the one who was to come, or should we expect someone else?' "

21 At that very time Jesus cured many who had diseases, sicknesses[l] and evil spirits, and gave sight to many who were blind. 22 So he replied to the messengers, "Go back and report to John what you have seen and heard: The blind receive sight, the lame walk, those who have leprosy[b] are cured, the deaf hear, the dead are raised, and the good news is preached to the poor.[m] 23 Blessed is the man who

7:1 *a* Mt 7:28
7:7 *b* Ps 107:20
7:13 *c* ver 19; Lk 10:1; Lk 13:15; Lk 17:5; Lk 22:61; Lk 24:34; Jn 11:2
7:14 *d* Mt 9:25; Mk 1:31; Lk 8:54; Jn 11:43; Ac 9:40
7:16 *e* Lk 1:65 *f* Mt 9:8 *g* ver 39; Mt 21:11 *h* Lk 1:68
7:17 *i* Mt 9:26
7:18 *j* Mt 3:1 *k* Lk 5:33
7:21 *l* Mt 4:23
7:22 *m* Isa 29:18,19; Isa 35:5,6; Isa 61:1,2; Lk 4:18

a17 Or *the land of the Jews* **b**22 The Greek word was used for various diseases affecting the skin—not necessarily leprosy.

does not fall away on account of me."

24 After John's messengers left, Jesus began to speak to the crowd about John: "What did you go out into the desert to see? A reed swayed by the wind? 25 If not, what did you go out to see? A man dressed in fine clothes? No, those who wear expensive clothes and indulge in luxury are in palaces. 26 But what did you go out to see? A prophet?[n] Yes, I tell you, and more than a prophet. 27 This is the one about whom it is written:

" 'I will send my messenger
ahead of you,
who will prepare your way
before you.'[c][o]

28 I tell you, among those born of women there is no-one greater than John; yet the one who is least in the kingdom of God[p] is greater than he."

(29 All the people, even the tax collectors, when they heard Jesus' words, acknowledged that God's way was right, because they had been baptised by John.[q] 30 But the Pharisees and experts in the law[r] rejected God's purpose for themselves, because they had not been baptised by John.)

31 "To what, then, can I compare the people of this generation? What are they like? 32 They are like children sitting in the market-place and calling out to each other:

" 'We played the flute for you,
and you did not dance;
we sang a dirge,
and you did not cry.'

33 For John the Baptist came neither eating bread nor drinking wine,[s] and you say, 'He has a demon.' 34 The Son of Man came eating and drinking, and you say, 'Here is a glutton and a drunkard, a friend of tax collectors and "sinners".'[t] 35 But wisdom is proved right by all her children."

Jesus Anointed by a Sinful Woman

7:37–39Ref Mt 26:6–13; Mk 14:3–9; Jn 12:1–8
7:41,42Ref Mt 18:23–34

36 Now one of the Pharisees invited Jesus to have dinner with him, so he went to the Pharisee's house and reclined at the table. 37 When a woman who had lived a sinful life in that town learned that Jesus was eating at the Pharisee's house, she brought an alabaster jar of perfume, 38 and as she stood behind him at his feet weeping, she began to wet his feet with her tears. Then she wiped them with her hair, kissed them and poured perfume on them.

39 When the Pharisee who had invited him saw this, he said to himself, "If this man were a prophet,[u] he would know who is touching him and what kind of woman she is—that she is a sinner."

40 Jesus answered him, "Simon, I have something to tell you."

"Tell me, teacher," he said.

41 "Two men owed money to a certain money-lender. One owed him five hundred denarii,[d] and the other fifty. 42 Neither of them had the money to pay him back, so he cancelled the debts of both. Now which of them will love him more?"

43 Simon replied, "I suppose the one who had the bigger debt cancelled."

"You have judged correctly," Jesus said.

44 Then he turned towards the woman and said to Simon, "Do you see this woman? I came into your house. You did not give me any water for my feet,[v] but she wet my feet with her tears and wiped them with her hair. 45 You did not give me a kiss,[w] but this woman, from the time I entered, has not stopped kissing my feet. 46 You did not put oil on my head,[x] but she has poured perfume on my feet.

c27 Mal. 3:1 d41 A denarius was a coin worth about a day's wages.

7:26 n Mt 11:9
7:27 o Mal 3:1; Mt 11:10; Mk 1:2
7:28 p Mt 3:2
7:29 q Mt 21:32; Mk 1:5; Lk 3:12
7:30 r Mt 22:35
7:33 s Lk 1:15
7:34 t Lk 5:29,30; Lk 15:1,2
7:39 u ver 16; Mt 21:11
7:44 v Ge 18:4; Ge 19:2; Ge 43:24; Jdg 19:21; Jn 13:4-14; 1Ti 5:10
7:45 w Lk 22:47,48; Ro 16:16
7:46 x Ps 23:5; Ecc 9:8

47Therefore, I tell you, her many
sins have been forgiven—for she
loved much. But he who has been
forgiven little loves little."
48Then Jesus said to her, "Your
sins are forgiven."[y]
49The other guests began to say
among themselves, "Who is this
who even forgives sins?"
50Jesus said to the woman, "Your
faith has saved you;[z] go in
peace."[a]

The Parable of the Sower

8:4–15pp Mt 13:2–23; Mk 4:1–20

8 After this, Jesus travelled
about from one town and village to another, proclaiming the
good news of the kingdom of God.[a]
The Twelve were with him, 2and
also some women who had been
cured of evil spirits and diseases:
Mary (called Magdalene)[b] from
whom seven demons had come out;
3Joanna the wife of Chuza, the manager of Herod's[c] household; Su-
sanna; and many others. These
women were helping to support
them out of their own means.
4While a large crowd was gathering and people were coming to
Jesus from town after town, he told
this parable: 5"A farmer went out
to sow his seed. As he was scattering the seed, some fell along the
path; it was trampled on, and the
birds of the air ate it up. 6Some fell
on rock, and when it came up, the
plants withered because they
had no moisture. 7Other seed fell
among thorns, which grew up with
it and choked the plants. 8Still other
seed fell on good soil. It came up
and yielded a crop, a hundred times
more than was sown."
When he said this, he called out,
"He who has ears to hear, let him
hear."[d]
9His disciples asked him what
this parable meant. 10He said, "The
knowledge of the secrets of the
kingdom of God has been given to

7:48 y Mt 9:2
7:50 z Mt 9:22; Mk 5:34; Lk 8:48; a Ac 15:33
8:1 a Mt 4:23
8:2 b Mt 27:55,56
8:3 c Mt 14:1
8:8 d Mt 11:15
8:10 e Mt 13:11; f Isa 6:9; Mt 13:13,14
8:11 g Heb 4:12
8:13 h Mt 11:6
8:14 i Mt 19:23; 1Ti 6:9,10,17
8:16 j Mt 5:15; Mk 4:21; Lk 11:33
8:17 k Mt 10:26; Mk 4:22; Lk 12:2
8:18 l Mt 13:12; Mt 25:29; Lk 19:26
8:20 m Jn 7:5

you,[e] but to others I speak in parables, so that,

" 'though seeing, they may not
see;
though hearing, they may not
understand.'[a][f]

11"This is the meaning of the parable: The seed is the word of God.[g]
12Those along the path are the ones
who hear, and then the devil comes
and takes away the word from their
hearts, so that they may not believe
and be saved. 13Those on the rock
are the ones who receive the word
with joy when they hear it, but they
have no root. They believe for a
while, but in the time of testing
they fall away.[h] 14The seed that
fell among thorns stands for those
who hear, but as they go on their
way they are choked by life's worries, riches[i] and pleasures, and
they do not mature. 15But the seed
on good soil stands for those with a
noble and good heart, who hear the
word, retain it, and by persevering
produce a crop.

A Lamp on a Stand

16"No-one lights a lamp and hides
it in a jar or puts it under a bed. Instead, he puts it on a stand, so that
those who come in can see the
light.[j] 17For there is nothing hidden that will not be disclosed, and
nothing concealed that will not be
known or brought out into the
open.[k] 18Therefore consider carefully how you listen. Whoever has
will be given more; whoever does
not have, even what he thinks he
has will be taken from him."[l]

Jesus' Mother and Brothers

8:19–21pp Mt 12:46–50; Mk 3:31–35

19Now Jesus' mother and
brothers came to see him, but they
were not able to get near him because of the crowd. 20Someone told
him, "Your mother and brothers[m]

[a] *10* Isaiah 6:9

are standing outside, wanting to see you."

21He replied, "My mother and brothers are those who hear God's word and put it into practice."[n]

Jesus Calms the Storm

8:22–25pp Mt 8:23–27; Mk 4:36–41
8:22–25Ref Mk 6:47–52; Jn 6:16–21

22One day Jesus said to his disciples, "Let's go over to the other side of the lake." So they got into a boat and set out. 23As they sailed, he fell asleep. A squall came down on the lake, so that the boat was being swamped, and they were in great danger.

24The disciples went and woke him, saying, "Master, Master,[o] we're going to drown!"

He got up and rebuked[p] the wind and the raging waters; the storm subsided, and all was calm.[q] 25"Where is your faith?" he asked his disciples.

In fear and amazement they asked one another, "Who is this? He commands even the winds and the water, and they obey him."

The Healing of a Demon-possessed Man

8:26–37pp Mt 8:28–34
8:26–39pp Mk 5:1–20

26They sailed to the region of the Gerasenes,[b] which is across the lake from Galilee. 27When Jesus stepped ashore, he was met by a demon-possessed man from the town. For a long time this man had not worn clothes or lived in a house, but had lived in the tombs. 28When he saw Jesus, he cried out and fell at his feet, shouting at the top of his voice, "What do you want with me,[r] Jesus, Son of the Most High God?[s] I beg you, don't torture me!" 29For Jesus had commanded the evil[c] spirit to come out of the man. Many times it had seized him, and though he was chained hand and foot and kept under guard, he had broken his chains and had been driven by the demon into solitary places.

30Jesus asked him, "What is your name?"

"Legion," he replied, because many demons had gone into him. 31And they begged him repeatedly not to order them to go into the Abyss.[t]

32A large herd of pigs was feeding there on the hillside. The demons begged Jesus to let them go into them, and he gave them permission. 33When the demons came out of the man, they went into the pigs, and the herd rushed down the steep bank into the lake[u] and was drowned.

34When those tending the pigs saw what had happened, they ran off and reported this in the town and countryside, 35and the people went out to see what had happened. When they came to Jesus, they found the man from whom the demons had gone out, sitting at Jesus' feet,[v] dressed and in his right mind; and they were afraid. 36Those who had seen it told the people how the demon-possessed[w] man had been cured. 37Then all the people of the region of the Gerasenes asked Jesus to leave them,[x] because they were overcome with fear. So he got into the boat and left.

38The man from whom the demons had gone out begged to go with him, but Jesus sent him away, saying, 39"Return home and tell how much God has done for you." So the man went away and told all over the town how much Jesus had done for him.

A Dead Girl and a Sick Woman

8:40–56pp Mt 9:18–26; Mk 5:22–43

40Now when Jesus returned, a crowd welcomed him, for they were all expecting him. 41Then a

8:21 n Lk 6:47; Lk 11:28; Jn 14:21
8:24 o Lk 5:5; p Lk 4:35,39,41; q Ps 107:29; Jnh 1:15
8:28 r Mt 8:29; s Mk 5:7
8:31 t Rev 9:1,2,11; Rev 11:7; Rev 17:8; Rev 20:1,3
8:33 u ver 22,23
8:35 v Lk 10:39
8:36 w Mt 4:24
8:37 x Ac 16:39

b26 Some manuscripts *Gadarenes*; other manuscripts *Gergesenes*; also in verse 37
c29 Greek *unclean*

man named Jairus, a ruler of the
synagogue,[y] came and fell at
Jesus' feet, pleading with him to
come to his house 42because his
only daughter, a girl of about
twelve, was dying.

As Jesus was on his way, the
crowds almost crushed him. 43And
a woman was there who had been
subject to bleeding[z] for twelve
years,[d] but no-one could heal her.
44She came up behind him and
touched the edge of his cloak,[a] and
immediately her bleeding stopped.

45"Who touched me?" Jesus
asked.

When they all denied it, Peter
said, "Master,[b] the people are
crowding and pressing against
you."

46But Jesus said, "Someone
touched me;[c] I know that power
has gone out from me."[d]

47Then the woman, seeing that
she could not go unnoticed, came
trembling and fell at his feet. In the
presence of all the people, she told
why she had touched him and how
she had been instantly healed.
48Then he said to her, "Daughter,
your faith has healed you.[e] Go in
peace."[f]

49While Jesus was still speaking,
someone came from the house of
Jairus, the synagogue ruler.[g]
"Your daughter is dead," he said.
"Don't bother the teacher any
more."

50Hearing this, Jesus said to Jairus, "Don't be afraid; just believe,
and she will be healed."

51When he arrived at the house of
Jairus, he did not let anyone go in
with him except Peter, John and
James,[h] and the child's father and
mother. 52Meanwhile, all the people were wailing and mourning[i]
for her. "Stop wailing," Jesus said.
"She is not dead but asleep."[j]

53They laughed at him, knowing
that she was dead. 54But he took her
by the hand and said, "My child, get
up!"[k] 55Her spirit returned, and at
once she stood up. Then Jesus told
them to give her something to eat.
56Her parents were astonished, but
he ordered them not to tell anyone
what had happened.[l]

Jesus Sends Out the Twelve

9:3–5pp Mt 10:9–15; Mk 6:8–11
9:7–9pp Mt 14:1,2; Mk 6:14–16

9 When Jesus had called the
Twelve together, he gave
them power and authority to drive
out all demons[a] and to cure diseases,[b] 2and he sent them out to
preach the kingdom of God[c] and to
heal the sick. 3He told them: "Take
nothing for the journey—no staff,
no bag, no bread, no money, no extra tunic.[d] 4Whatever house you
enter, stay there until you leave
that town. 5If people do not welcome you, shake the dust off your
feet when you leave their town, as
a testimony against them."[e] 6So
they set out and went from village
to village, preaching the gospel and
healing people everywhere.

7Now Herod[f] the tetrarch heard
about all that was going on. And he
was perplexed, because some were
saying that John[g] had been raised
from the dead,[h] 8others that Elijah
had appeared,[i] and still others
that one of the prophets of long ago
had come back to life.[j] 9But Herod
said, "I beheaded John. Who, then,
is this I hear such things about?"
And he tried to see him.[k]

Jesus Feeds the Five Thousand

9:10–17pp Mt 14:13–21; Mk 6:32–44; Jn 6:5–13
9:13–17Ref 2Ki 4:42–44

10When the apostles[l] returned,
they reported to Jesus what they
had done. Then he took them with
him and they withdrew by themselves to a town called Bethsaida,[m]
11but the crowds learned about it
and followed him. He welcomed
them and spoke to them about the
kingdom of God,[n] and healed those
who needed healing.

8:41 *y* ver 49; Mk 5:22
8:43 *z* Lev 15:25-30
8:44 *a* Mt 9:20
8:45 *b* Lk 5:5
8:46 *c* Mt 14:36; Mk 3:10 *d* Lk 5:17; Lk 6:19
8:48 *e* Mt 9:22 *f* Ac 15:33
8:49 *g* ver 41
8:51 *h* Mt 4:21
8:52 *i* Lk 23:27 *j* Mt 9:24; Jn 11:11,13
8:54 *k* Lk 7:14
8:56 *l* Mt 8:4
9:1 *a* Mt 10:1 *b* Mt 4:23; Lk 5:17
9:2 *c* Mt 3:2
9:3 *d* Lk 10:4; Lk 22:35
9:5 *e* Mt 10:14
9:7 *f* Mt 14:1 *g* Mt 3:1 *h* ver 19
9:8 *i* Mt 11:14 *j* ver 19; Jn 1:21
9:9 *k* Lk 23:8
9:10 *l* Mk 6:30 *m* Mt 11:21
9:11 *n* ver 2; Mt 3:2

[d] 43 Many manuscripts *years, and she had spent all she had on doctors*

12 Late in the afternoon the Twelve came to him and said, "Send the crowd away so they can go to the surrounding villages and countryside and find food and lodging, because we are in a remote place here."

13 He replied, "You give them something to eat."

They answered, "We have only five loaves of bread and two fish—unless we go and buy food for all this crowd." 14 (About five thousand men were there.)

But he said to his disciples, "Make them sit down in groups of about fifty each." 15 The disciples did so, and everybody sat down. 16 Taking the five loaves and the two fish and looking up to heaven, he gave thanks and broke them.[o] Then he gave them to the disciples to set before the people. 17 They all ate and were satisfied, and the disciples picked up twelve basketfuls of broken pieces that were left over.

Peter's Confession of Christ

9:18–20pp Mt 16:13–16; Mk 8:27–29
9:22–27pp Mt 16:21–28; Mk 8:31–9:1

18 Once when Jesus was praying[p] in private and his disciples were with him, he asked them, "Who do the crowds say I am?"

19 They replied, "Some say John the Baptist;[q] others say Elijah; and still others, that one of the prophets of long ago has come back to life."[r]

20 "But what about you?" he asked. "Who do you say I am?"

Peter answered, "The Christ[a] of God."[s]

21 Jesus strictly warned them not to tell this to anyone.[t] 22 And he said, "The Son of Man[u] must suffer many things[v] and be rejected by the elders, chief priests and teachers of the law,[w] and he must be killed[x] and on the third day[y] be raised to life."[z]

23 Then he said to them all: "If anyone would come after me, he must deny himself and take up his cross daily and follow me.[a] 24 For whoever wants to save his life will lose it, but whoever loses his life for me will save it.[b] 25 What good is it for a man to gain the whole world, and yet lose or forfeit his very self? 26 If anyone is ashamed of me and my words, the Son of Man will be ashamed of him[c] when he comes in his glory and in the glory of the Father and of the holy angels.[d] 27 I tell you the truth, some who are standing here will not taste death before they see the kingdom of God."

The Transfiguration

9:28–36pp Mt 17:1–8; Mk 9:2–8

28 About eight days after Jesus said this, he took Peter, John and James[e] with him and went up onto a mountain to pray.[f] 29 As he was praying, the appearance of his face changed, and his clothes became as bright as a flash of lightning. 30 Two men, Moses and Elijah, 31 appeared in glorious splendour, talking with Jesus. They spoke about his departure,[g] which he was about to bring to fulfilment at Jerusalem. 32 Peter and his companions were very sleepy,[h] but when they became fully awake, they saw his glory and the two men standing with him. 33 As the men were leaving Jesus, Peter said to him, "Master,[i] it is good for us to be here. Let us put up three shelters—one for you, one for Moses and one for Elijah." (He did not know what he was saying.)

34 While he was speaking, a cloud appeared and enveloped them, and they were afraid as they entered the cloud. 35 A voice came from the cloud, saying, "This is my Son, whom I have chosen;[j] listen to him."[k] 36 When the voice had spoken, they found that Jesus was alone. The disciples kept this to

9:16 *o* Mt 14:19
9:18 *p* Lk 3:21
9:19 *q* Mt 3:1 *r* ver 7,8
9:20 *s* Jn 1:49; Jn 6:66-69; Jn 11:27
9:21 *t* Mt 16:20; Mk 8:30
9:22 *u* Mt 8:20 *v* Mt 16:21 *w* Mt 27:1,2 *x* Ac 2:23; Ac 3:13 *y* Mt 16:21 *z* Mt 16:21
9:23 *a* Mt 10:38; Lk 14:27
9:24 *b* Jn 12:25
9:26 *c* Mt 10:33; Lk 12:9; 2Ti 2:12 *d* Mt 16:27
9:28 *e* Mt 4:21 *f* Lk 3:21
9:31 *g* 2Pe 1:15
9:32 *h* Mt 26:43
9:33 *i* Lk 5:5
9:35 *j* Isa 42:1 *k* Mt 3:17

[a]20 Or *Messiah*

themselves, and told no-one at that time what they had seen.[l]

The Healing of a Boy With an Evil Spirit

9:37–42,43–45pp Mt 17:14–18, 22,23; Mk 9:14–27, 30–32

37 The next day, when they came down from the mountain, a large crowd met him. 38 A man in the crowd called out, "Teacher, I beg you to look at my son, for he is my only child. 39 A spirit seizes him and he suddenly screams; it throws him into convulsions so that he foams at the mouth. It scarcely ever leaves him and is destroying him. 40 I begged your disciples to drive it out, but they could not."

41 "O unbelieving and perverse generation,"[m] Jesus replied, "how long shall I stay with you and put up with you? Bring your son here."

42 Even while the boy was coming, the demon threw him to the ground in a convulsion. But Jesus rebuked the evil[b] spirit, healed the boy and gave him back to his father. 43 And they were all amazed at the greatness of God.

While everyone was marvelling at all that Jesus did, he said to his disciples, 44 "Listen carefully to what I am about to tell you: The Son of Man is going to be betrayed into the hands of men."[n] 45 But they did not understand what this meant. It was hidden from them, so that they did not grasp it,[o] and they were afraid to ask him about it.

Who Will Be the Greatest?

9:46–48pp Mt 18:1–5
9:46–50pp Mk 9:33–40

46 An argument started among the disciples as to which of them would be the greatest.[p] 47 Jesus, knowing their thoughts,[q] took a little child and made him stand beside him. 48 Then he said to them, "Whoever welcomes this little child in my name welcomes me; and whoever welcomes me welcomes the one who sent me.[r] For he who is least among you all—he is the greatest."[s]

49 "Master,"[t] said John, "we saw a man driving out demons in your name and we tried to stop him, because he is not one of us."

50 "Do not stop him," Jesus said, "for whoever is not against you is for you."[u]

Samaritan Opposition

51 As the time approached for him to be taken up to heaven,[v] Jesus resolutely set out for Jerusalem.[w] 52 And he sent messengers on ahead, who went into a Samaritan[x] village to get things ready for him; 53 but the people there did not welcome him, because he was heading for Jerusalem. 54 When the disciples James and John[y] saw this, they asked, "Lord, do you want us to call fire down from heaven to destroy them?"[c][z] 55 But Jesus turned and rebuked them, 56 and[d] they went to another village.

The Cost of Following Jesus

9:57–60pp Mt 8:19–22

57 As they were walking along the road,[a] a man said to him, "I will follow you wherever you go."

58 Jesus replied, "Foxes have holes and birds of the air have nests, but the Son of Man[b] has nowhere to lay his head."

59 He said to another man, "Follow me."[c]

But the man replied, "Lord, first let me go and bury my father."

60 Jesus said to him, "Let the dead bury their own dead, but you go and proclaim the kingdom of God."[d]

61 Still another said, "I will follow you, Lord; but first let me go back and say good-bye to my family."[e]

62 Jesus replied, "No-one who

9:36 l Mt 17:9
9:41 m Dt 32:5
9:44 n ver 22
9:45 o Mk 9:32
9:46 p Lk 22:24
9:47 q Mt 9:4
9:48 r Mt 10:40; s Mk 9:35
9:49 t Lk 5:5
9:50 u Mt 12:30; Lk 11:23
9:51 v Mk 16:19; w Lk 13:22; Lk 17:11; Lk 18:31; Lk 19:28
9:52 x Mt 10:5
9:54 y Mt 4:21; z 2Ki 1:10,12
9:57 a ver 51
9:58 b Mt 8:20
9:59 c Mt 4:19
9:60 d Mt 3:2
9:61 e 1Ki 19:20

[b]42 Greek *unclean* [c]54 Some manuscripts *them, even as Elijah did* [d]55, 56 Some manuscripts *them. And he said, "You do not know what kind of spirit you are of, for the Son of Man did not come to destroy men's lives, but to save them."* 56 *And*

puts his hand to the plough and
looks back is fit for service in the
kingdom of God."

Jesus Sends Out the Seventy-two

10:4–12pp Lk 9:3–5
10:13–15,21,22pp Mt 11:21–23,25–27
10:23,24pp Mt 13:16,17

10 After this the Lord[a]
appointed seventy-two[a]
others[b] and sent them two by two[c]
ahead of him to every town and
place where he was about to go.[d]
2He told them, "The harvest is
plentiful, but the workers are few.
Ask the Lord of the harvest, therefore, to send out workers into his
harvest field.[e] 3Go! I am sending
you out like lambs among wolves.[f]
4Do not take a purse or bag or sandals; and do not greet anyone on the
road.
5"When you enter a house, first
say, 'Peace to this house.' 6If a man
of peace is there, your peace will
rest on him; if not, it will return to
you. 7Stay in that house, eating and
drinking whatever they give you,
for the worker deserves his
wages.[g] Do not move around from
house to house.
8"When you enter a town and are
welcomed, eat what is set before
you.[h] 9Heal the sick who are there
and tell them, 'The kingdom of
God[i] is near you.' 10But when you
enter a town and are not welcomed,
go into its streets and say, 11'Even
the dust of your town that sticks to
our feet we wipe off against you.[j]
Yet be sure of this: The kingdom of
God is near.'[k] 12I tell you, it will be
more bearable on that day for
Sodom[l] than for that town.[m]
13"Woe to you,[n] Korazin! Woe to
you, Bethsaida! For if the miracles
that were performed in you had
been performed in Tyre and Sidon,
they would have repented long ago,
sitting in sackcloth[o] and ashes.
14But it will be more bearable for
Tyre and Sidon at the judgment
than for you. 15And you, Capernaum,[p] will you be lifted up to the
skies? No, you will go down to
the depths.[b]
16"He who listens to you listens to
me; he who rejects you rejects me;
but he who rejects me rejects him
who sent me."[q]
17The seventy-two[r] returned with
joy and said, "Lord, even the demons
submit to us in your name."[s]
18He replied, "I saw Satan[t] fall
like lightning from heaven.[u] 19I
have given you authority to trample on snakes[v] and scorpions and
to overcome all the power of the enemy; nothing will harm you. 20How-
ever, do not rejoice that the spirits
submit to you, but rejoice that your
names are written in heaven."[w]
21At that time Jesus, full of joy
through the Holy Spirit, said, "I
praise you, Father, Lord of heaven
and earth, because you have hidden
these things from the wise and
learned, and revealed them to little
children.[x] Yes, Father, for this
was your good pleasure.
22"All things have been committed to me by my Father.[y] No-one
knows who the Son is except the
Father, and no-one knows who the
Father is except the Son and those
to whom the Son chooses to reveal
him."[z]
23Then he turned to his disciples
and said privately, "Blessed are the
eyes that see what you see. 24For I
tell you that many prophets and
kings wanted to see what you see
but did not see it, and to hear what
you hear but did not hear it."[a]

The Parable of the Good Samaritan

10:25–28pp Mt 22:34–40; Mk 12:28–31

25On one occasion an expert in
the law stood up to test Jesus.
"Teacher," he asked, "what must I
do to inherit eternal life?"[b]
26"What is written in the Law?"

10:1 a Lk 7:13 b Lk 9:1,2,51,52 c Mk 6:7 d Mt 10:1
10:2 e Mt 9:37,38 Jn 4:35
10:3 f Mt 10:16
10:7 g Mt 10:10 1Co 9:14 1Ti 5:18
10:8 h 1Co 10:27
10:9 i Mt 3:2 Mt 10:7
10:11 j Mt 10:14 Mk 6:11 k ver 9
10:12 l Mt 10:15 m Mt 11:24
10:13 n Lk 6:24-26 o Rev 11:3
10:15 p Mt 4:13
10:16 q Mt 10:40 Jn 13:20
10:17 r ver 1 s Mk 16:17
10:18 t Mt 4:10 u Isa 14:12 Rev 9:1 Rev 12:8,9
10:19 v Mk 16:18 Ac 28:3-5
10:20 w Ex 32:32 Ps 69:28 Da 12:1 Php 4:3 Heb 12:23 Rev 13:8 Rev 20:12 Rev 21:27
10:21 x 1Co 1:26-29
10:22 y Mt 28:18 z Jn 1:18
10:24 a 1Pe 1:10-12
10:25 b Mt 19:16 Lk 18:18

a*1* Some manuscripts *seventy*; also in verse 17
b*15* Greek *Hades*

he replied. "How do you read it?"

27 He answered: " 'Love the Lord your God with all your heart and with all your soul and with all your strength and with all your mind';[c][c] and, 'Love your neighbour as yourself.'[d]"[d]

28 "You have answered correctly," Jesus replied. "Do this and you will live."[e]

29 But he wanted to justify himself,[f] so he asked Jesus, "And who is my neighbour?"

30 In reply Jesus said: "A man was going down from Jerusalem to Jericho, when he fell into the hands of robbers. They stripped him of his clothes, beat him and went away, leaving him half-dead. 31 A priest happened to be going down the same road, and when he saw the man, he passed by on the other side.[g] 32 So too, a Levite, when he came to the place and saw him, passed by on the other side. 33 But a Samaritan,[h] as he travelled, came where the man was; and when he saw him, he took pity on him. 34 He went to him and bandaged his wounds, pouring on oil and wine. Then he put the man on his own donkey, brought him to an inn and took care of him. 35 The next day he took out two silver coins[e] and gave them to the innkeeper. 'Look after him,' he said, 'and when I return, I will reimburse you for any extra expense you may have.'

36 "Which of these three do you think was a neighbour to the man who fell into the hands of robbers?"

37 The expert in the law replied, "The one who had mercy on him."

Jesus told him, "Go and do likewise."

At the Home of Martha and Mary

38 As Jesus and his disciples were on their way, he came to a village where a woman named Martha[i] opened her home to him. 39 She had a sister called Mary,[j] who sat at the Lord's feet[k] listening to what he said. 40 But Martha was distracted by all the preparations that had to be made. She came to him and asked, "Lord, don't you care[l] that my sister has left me to do the work by myself? Tell her to help me!"

41 "Martha, Martha," the Lord answered, "you are worried[m] and upset about many things, 42 but only one thing is needed.[f][n] Mary has chosen what is better, and it will not be taken away from her."

Jesus' Teaching on Prayer

11:2–4pp Mt 6:9–13
11:9–13pp Mt 7:7–11

11 One day Jesus was praying[a] in a certain place. When he finished, one of his disciples said to him, "Lord,[b] teach us to pray, just as John taught his disciples."

2 He said to them, "When you pray, say:

" 'Father,[a]
hallowed be your name,
your kingdom[c] come.[b]
3 Give us each day our daily
bread.
4 Forgive us our sins,
for we also forgive everyone
who sins against us.[c][d]
And lead us not into
temptation.' "[d][e]

5 Then he said to them, "Suppose one of you has a friend, and he goes to him at midnight and says, 'Friend, lend me three loaves of bread, 6 because a friend of mine on a journey has come to me, and I have nothing to set before him.'

7 "Then the one inside answers, 'Don't bother me. The door is already locked, and my children are

10:27 *c* Dt 6:5 *d* Lev 19:18; Mt 5:43
10:28 *e* Lev 18:5; Ro 7:10
10:29 *f* Lk 16:15
10:31 *g* Lev 21:1-3
10:33 *h* Mt 10:5
10:38 *i* Jn 11:1; Jn 12:2
10:39 *j* Jn 11:1; Jn 12:3 *k* Lk 8:35
10:40 *l* Mk 4:38
10:41 *m* Mt 6:25-34; Lk 12:11,22
10:42 *n* Ps 27:4
11:1 *a* Lk 3:21 *b* Jn 13:13
11:2 *c* Mt 3:2
11:4 *d* Mt 18:35; Mk 11:25 *e* Mt 26:41; Jas 1:13

[c]27 Deut. 6:5 [d]27 Lev. 19:18 [e]35 Greek *two denarii* [f]42 Some manuscripts *but few things are needed—or only one* [a]2 Some manuscripts *Our Father in heaven* [b]2 Some manuscripts *come. May your will be done on earth as it is in heaven.* [c]4 Greek *everyone who is indebted to us* [d]4 Some manuscripts *temptation but deliver us from the evil one*

with me in bed. I can't get up and
give you anything.' 8 I tell you,
though he will not get up and give
him the bread because he is his
friend, yet because of the man's
boldness[e] he will get up and give
him as much as he needs.[f]
9 "So I say to you: Ask and it will
be given to you;[g] seek and you will
find; knock and the door will be
opened to you. 10 For everyone who
asks receives; he who seeks finds;
and to him who knocks, the door
will be opened.
11 "Which of you fathers, if your
son asks for[f] a fish, will give him
a snake instead? 12 Or if he asks for
an egg, will give him a scorpion?
13 If you then, though you are evil,
know how to give good gifts to your
children, how much more will your
Father in heaven give the Holy
Spirit to those who ask him!"

Jesus and Beelzebub

11:14,15, 17–22, 24–26pp Mt 12:22,24–29, 43–45
11:17–22pp Mk 3:23–27

14 Jesus was driving out a demon
that was mute. When the demon
left, the man who had been mute
spoke, and the crowd was
amazed.[h] 15 But some of them said,
"By Beelzebub,[g][i] the prince of
demons, he is driving out demons."[j] 16 Others tested him by
asking for a sign from heaven.[k]
17 Jesus knew their thoughts[l]
and said to them: "Any kingdom
divided against itself will be
ruined, and a house divided against
itself will fall. 18 If Satan[m] is divided against himself, how can his
kingdom stand? I say this because
you claim that I drive out demons
by Beelzebub. 19 Now if I drive out
demons by Beelzebub, by whom do
your followers drive them out? So
then, they will be your judges.
20 But if I drive out demons by the
finger of God,[n] then the kingdom
of God[o] has come to you.
21 "When a strong man, fully
armed, guards his own house, his
possessions are safe. 22 But when
someone stronger attacks and
overpowers him, he takes away the
armour in which the man trusted
and divides up the spoils.
23 "He who is not with me is
against me, and he who does not
gather with me, scatters.[p]
24 "When an evil[h] spirit comes
out of a man, it goes through arid
places seeking rest and does not
find it. Then it says, 'I will return to
the house I left.' 25 When it arrives,
it finds the house swept clean and
put in order. 26 Then it goes and
takes seven other spirits more
wicked than itself, and they go in
and live there. And the final condition of that man is worse than the
first."[q]
27 As Jesus was saying these
things, a woman in the crowd
called out, "Blessed is the mother
who gave you birth and nursed
you."[r]
28 He replied, "Blessed rather are
those who hear the word of God[s]
and obey it."[t]

The Sign of Jonah

11:29–32pp Mt 12:39–42

29 As the crowds increased, Jesus
said, "This is a wicked generation.
It asks for a miraculous sign,[u] but
none will be given it except the sign
of Jonah.[v] 30 For as Jonah was a
sign to the Ninevites, so also will
the Son of Man be to this generation. 31 The Queen of the South will
rise at the judgment with the men
of this generation and condemn
them; for she came from the ends
of the earth to listen to Solomon's
wisdom,[w] and now one[i] greater
than Solomon is here. 32 The men of
Nineveh will stand up at the judgment with this generation and condemn it; for they repented at the

11:8 *f* Lk 18:1-6
11:9 *g* Mt 7:7
11:14 *h* Mt 9:32,33
11:15 *i* Mk 3:22 *j* Mt 9:34
11:16 *k* Mt 12:38
11:17 *l* Mt 9:4
11:18 *m* Mt 4:10
11:20 *n* Ex 8:19 *o* Mt 3:2
11:23 *p* Mt 12:30 Mk 9:40 Lk 9:50
11:26 *q* 2Pe 2:20
11:27 *r* Lk 23:29
11:28 *s* Heb 4:12 *t* Pr 8:32 Lk 6:47 Lk 8:21 Jn 14:21
11:29 *u* ver 16 Mt 12:38 *v* Jnh 1:17 Mt 16:4
11:31 *w* 1Ki 10:1 2Ch 9:1

e8 Or *persistence* f11 Some manuscripts *for bread, will give him a stone; or if he asks for* g15 Greek *Beezeboul* or *Beelzeboul*; also in verses 18 and 19 h24 Greek *unclean* i31 Or *something*; also in verse 32

preaching of Jonah,[x] and now one greater than Jonah is here.

The Lamp of the Body

11:34,35pp Mt 6:22,23

33“No-one lights a lamp and puts it in a place where it will be hidden, or under a bowl. Instead he puts it on its stand, so that those who come in may see the light.[y] 34Your eye is the lamp of your body. When your eyes are good, your whole body also is full of light. But when they are bad, your body also is full of darkness. 35See to it, then, that the light within you is not darkness. 36Therefore, if your whole body is full of light, and no part of it dark, it will be completely lighted, as when the light of a lamp shines on you.”

Six Woes

37When Jesus had finished speaking, a Pharisee invited him to eat with him; so he went in and reclined at the table.[z] 38But the Pharisee, noticing that Jesus did not first wash before the meal,[a] was surprised.

39Then the Lord[b] said to him, “Now then, you Pharisees clean the outside of the cup and dish, but inside you are full of greed and wickedness.[c] 40You foolish people![d] Did not the one who made the outside make the inside also? 41But give what is inside ⌊the dish⌋[j] to the poor,[e] and everything will be clean for you.[f]

42“Woe to you Pharisees, because you give God a tenth[g] of your mint, rue and all other kinds of garden herbs, but you neglect justice and the love of God.[h] You should have practised the latter without leaving the former undone.[i]

43“Woe to you Pharisees, because you love the most important seats in the synagogues and greetings in the market-places.[j]

44“Woe to you, because you are like unmarked graves,[k] which men walk over without knowing it.”

45One of the experts in the law[l] answered him, “Teacher, when you say these things, you insult us also.”

46Jesus replied, “And you experts in the law, woe to you, because you load people down with burdens they can hardly carry, and you yourselves will not lift one finger to help them.[m]

47“Woe to you, because you build tombs for the prophets, and it was your forefathers who killed them. 48So you testify that you approve of what your forefathers did; they killed the prophets, and you build their tombs.[n] 49Because of this, God in his wisdom[o] said, ‘I will send them prophets and apostles, some of whom they will kill and others they will persecute.’[p] 50Therefore this generation will be held responsible for the blood of all the prophets that has been shed since the beginning of the world, 51from the blood of Abel[q] to the blood of Zechariah,[r] who was killed between the altar and the sanctuary. Yes, I tell you, this generation will be held responsible for it all.[s]

52“Woe to you experts in the law, because you have taken away the key to knowledge. You yourselves have not entered, and you have hindered those who were entering.”[t]

53When Jesus left there, the Pharisees and the teachers of the law began to oppose him fiercely and to besiege him with questions, 54waiting to catch him in something he might say.[u]

Warnings and Encouragements

12:2–9pp Mt 10:26–33

12 Meanwhile, when a crowd of many thousands had gathered, so that they were trampling on one another, Jesus began to speak first to his disciples,

j41 Or *what you have*

11:32 x Jnh 3:5
11:33 y Mt 5:15; Mk 4:21; Lk 8:16
11:37 z Lk 7:36; Lk 14:1
11:38 a Mk 7:3,4
11:39 b Lk 7:13; c Mt 23:25,26; Mk 7:20-23
11:40 d Lk 12:20; 1Co 15:36
11:41 e Lk 12:33; f Ac 10:15
11:42 g Lk 18:12; h Dt 6:5; Mic 6:8; i Mt 23:23
11:43 j Mt 23:6,7; Mk 12:38-39; Lk 14:7; Lk 20:46
11:44 k Mt 23:27
11:45 l Mt 22:35
11:46 m Mt 23:4
11:48 n Mt 23:29-32; Ac 7:51-53
11:49 o 1Co 1:24,30; Col 2:3; p Mt 23:34
11:51 q Ge 4:8; r 2Ch 24:20,21; s Mt 23:35,36
11:52 t Mt 23:13
11:54 u Mt 12:10; Mk 12:13

saying: "Be on your guard against
the yeast of the Pharisees, which is
hypocrisy.[a] 2There is nothing concealed that will not be disclosed, or
hidden that will not be made
known.[b] 3What you have said in the
dark will be heard in the daylight,
and what you have whispered in the
ear in the inner rooms will be proclaimed from the roofs.
4"I tell you, my friends,[c] do not
be afraid of those who kill the body
and after that can do no more. 5But
I will show you whom you should
fear: Fear him who, after the killing of the body, has power to throw
you into hell. Yes, I tell you, fear
him.[d] 6Are not five sparrows sold
for two pennies?[a] Yet not one of
them is forgotten by God. 7Indeed,
the very hairs of your head are all
numbered.[e] Don't be afraid; you
are worth more than many sparrows.[f]
8"I tell you, whoever acknowledges me before men, the Son of
Man will also acknowledge him before the angels of God.[g] 9But he
who disowns me before men will be
disowned[h] before the angels of
God. 10And everyone who speaks a
word against the Son of Man[i] will
be forgiven, but anyone who blasphemes against the Holy Spirit will
not be forgiven.[j]
11"When you are brought before
synagogues, rulers and authorities,
do not worry about how you will defend yourselves or what you will
say,[k] 12for the Holy Spirit will
teach you at that time what you
should say."[l]

The Parable of the Rich Fool

13Someone in the crowd said to
him, "Teacher, tell my brother to
divide the inheritance with me."
14Jesus replied, "Man, who appointed me a judge or an arbiter between you?" 15Then he said to them,
"Watch out! Be on your guard
against all kinds of greed; a man's
life does not consist in the abundance of his possessions."[m]
16And he told them this parable:
"The ground of a certain rich man
produced a good crop. 17He thought
to himself, 'What shall I do? I have
no place to store my crops.'
18"Then he said, 'This is what I'll
do. I will tear down my barns and
build bigger ones, and there I will
store all my grain and my goods.
19And I'll say to myself, "You have
plenty of good things laid up for
many years. Take life easy; eat,
drink and be merry." '
20"But God said to him, 'You
fool![n] This very night your life will
be demanded from you.[o] Then who
will get what you have prepared for
yourself?'[p]
21"This is how it will be with anyone who stores up things for himself but is not rich towards God."[q]

Do Not Worry

12:22–31pp Mt 6:25–33

22Then Jesus said to his disciples:
"Therefore I tell you, do not worry
about your life, what you will eat;
or about your body, what you will
wear. 23Life is more than food, and
the body more than clothes. 24Con-
sider the ravens: They do not sow
or reap, they have no storeroom or
barn; yet God feeds them.[r] And
how much more valuable you are
than birds! 25Who of you by worrying can add a single hour to his
life?[b] 26Since you cannot do this
very little thing, why do you worry
about the rest?
27"Consider how the lilies grow.
They do not labour or spin. Yet I
tell you, not even Solomon in all his
splendour[s] was dressed like one of
these. 28If that is how God clothes
the grass of the field, which is here
today, and tomorrow is thrown into
the fire, how much more will he

12:1 *a* Mt 16:6,11,12 Mk 8:15
12:2 *b* Mk 4:22 Lk 8:17
12:4 *c* Jn 15:14,15
12:5 *d* Heb 10:31
12:7 *e* Mt 10:30 *f* Mt 12:12
12:8 *g* Lk 15:10
12:9 *h* Mk 8:38 2Ti 2:12
12:10 *i* Mt 8:20 *j* Mt 12:31,32 Mk 3:28-29 1Jn 5:16
12:11 *k* Mt 10:17,19 Mk 13:11 Lk 21:12,14
12:12 *l* Ex 4:12 Mt 10:20 Mk 13:11 Lk 21:15
12:15 *m* Job 20:20 Job 31:24 Ps 62:10
12:20 *n* Jer 17:11 Lk 11:40 *o* Job 27:8 *p* Ps 39:6 Ps 49:10
12:21 *q* ver 33
12:24 *r* Job 38:41 Ps 147:9
12:27 *s* 1Ki 10:4-7

a6 Greek *two assaria*
b25 Or *single cubit to his height*

clothe you, O you of little faith![t]
29And do not set your heart on what
you will eat or drink; do not worry
about it. 30For the pagan world runs
after all such things, and your
Father[u] knows that you need
them.[v] 31But seek his kingdom,[w]
and these things will be given to
you as well.[x]
32"Do not be afraid,[y] little flock,
for your Father has been pleased to
give you the kingdom.[z] 33Sell your
possessions and give to the poor.[a]
Provide purses for yourselves that
will not wear out, a treasure in
heaven[b] that will not be exhausted, where no thief comes near
and no moth destroys.[c] 34For
where your treasure is, there your
heart will be also.[d]

Watchfulness

12:35,36pp Mt 25:1–13; Mk 13:33–37
12:39,40; 42–46pp Mt 24:43–51

35"Be dressed ready for service
and keep your lamps burning,
36like men waiting for their master
to return from a wedding banquet,
so that when he comes and knocks
they can immediately open the
door for him. 37It will be good for
those servants whose master finds
them watching when he comes.[e] I
tell you the truth, he will dress himself to serve, will have them recline
at the table and will come and wait
on them.[f] 38It will be good for
those servants whose master finds
them ready, even if he comes in the
second or third watch of the night.
39But understand this: If the owner
of the house had known at what
hour the thief[g] was coming, he
would not have let his house be
broken into. 40You also must be
ready,[h] because the Son of Man
will come at an hour when you do
not expect him."
41Peter asked, "Lord, are you telling this parable to us, or to everyone?"
42The Lord[i] answered, "Who
then is the faithful and wise manager, whom the master puts in
charge of his servants to give them
their food allowance at the proper
time? 43It will be good for that servant whom the master finds doing
so when he returns. 44I tell you the
truth, he will put him in charge of
all his possessions. 45But suppose
the servant says to himself, 'My
master is taking a long time in coming,' and he then begins to beat the
menservants and maidservants
and to eat and drink and get drunk.
46The master of that servant will
come on a day when he does not expect him and at an hour he is not
aware of.[j] He will cut him to
pieces and assign him a place with
the unbelievers.
47"That servant who knows his
master's will and does not get
ready or does not do what his master wants will be beaten with many
blows.[k] 48But the one who does not
know and does things deserving
punishment will be beaten with few
blows.[l] From everyone who has
been given much, much will be demanded; and from the one who has
been entrusted with much, much
more will be asked.

Not Peace but Division

12:51–53pp Mt 10:34–36

49"I have come to bring fire on
the earth, and how I wish it were
already kindled! 50But I have a
baptism[m] to undergo, and how
distressed I am until it is completed![n] 51Do you think I came to
bring peace on earth? No, I tell you,
but division. 52From now on there
will be five in one family divided
against each other, three against
two and two against three. 53They
will be divided, father against
son and son against father,
mother against daughter and
daughter against mother, mother-
in-law against daughter-in-law and
daughter-in-law against mother-in-
law."[o]

12:28 t Mt 6:30
12:30 u Lk 6:36; v Mt 6:8
12:31 w Mt 3:2; x Mt 19:29
12:32 y Mt 14:27; z Mt 25:34
12:33 a Mt 19:21; Ac 2:45; b Mt 6:20; c Jas 5:2
12:34 d Mt 6:21
12:37 e Mt 24:42,46; Mt 25:13; f Mt 20:28
12:39 g Mt 6:19; 1Th 5:2; 2Pe 3:10; Rev 3:3; Rev 16:15
12:40 h Mk 13:33; Lk 21:36
12:42 i Lk 7:13
12:46 j ver 40
12:47 k Dt 25:2
12:48 l Lev 5:17; Nu 15:27-30
12:50 m Mk 10:38; n Jn 19:30
12:53 o Mic 7:6; Mt 10:21

Interpreting the Times

54He said to the crowd: "When
you see a cloud rising in the west,
immediately you say, 'It's going to
rain,' and it does.[p] 55And when the
south wind blows, you say, 'It's going to be hot,' and it is. 56Hypo-
crites! You know how to interpret
the appearance of the earth and the
sky. How is it that you don't know
how to interpret this present
time?[q]
57"Why don't you judge for yourselves what is right? 58As you are
going with your adversary to the
magistrate, try hard to be reconciled to him on the way, or he may
drag you off to the judge, and the
judge turn you over to the officer,
and the officer throw you into
prison.[r] 59I tell you, you will not
get out until you have paid the last
penny."[c] [s]

Repent or Perish

13 Now there were some
present at that time who
told Jesus about the Galileans
whose blood Pilate[a] had mixed
with their sacrifices. 2Jesus answered, "Do you think that these
Galileans were worse sinners than
all the other Galileans because
they suffered this way?[b] 3I tell
you, no! But unless you repent, you
too will all perish. 4Or those eighteen who died when the tower in Siloam[c] fell on them—do you think
they were more guilty than all the
others living in Jerusalem? 5I tell
you, no! But unless you repent,[d]
you too will all perish."
6Then he told this parable: "A
man had a fig-tree, planted in his
vineyard, and he went to look for
fruit on it, but did not find any.[e]
7So he said to the man who took
care of the vineyard, 'For three
years now I've been coming to look
for fruit on this fig-tree and haven't
found any. Cut it down![f] Why
should it use up the soil?'
8" 'Sir,' the man replied, 'leave it

12:54 p Mt 16:2
12:56 q Mt 16:3
12:58 r Mt 5:25
12:59 s Mt 5:26; Mk 12:42
13:1 a Mt 27:2
13:2 b Jn 9:2,3
13:4 c Jn 9:7,11
13:5 d Mt 3:2; Ac 2:38
13:6 e Isa 5:2; Jer 8:13; Mt 21:19
13:7 f Mt 3:10
13:10 g Mt 4:23
13:11 h ver 16
13:13 i Mk 5:23
13:14 j Mt 12:2; Lk 14:3 k Mk 5:22 l Ex 20:9
13:15 m Lk 14:5
13:16 n Lk 3:8; Lk 19:9 o Mt 4:10
13:17 p Isa 66:5
13:18 q Mt 3:2 r Mt 13:24
13:19 s Lk 17:6

alone for one more year, and I'll dig
round it and fertilise it. 9If it bears
fruit next year, fine! If not, then
cut it down.' "

A Crippled Woman Healed on the Sabbath

10On a Sabbath Jesus was teaching in one of the synagogues,[g]
11and a woman was there who had
been crippled by a spirit for eighteen years.[h] She was bent over and
could not straighten up at all.
12When Jesus saw her, he called her
forward and said to her, "Woman,
you are set free from your in-
firmity." 13Then he put his hands
on her,[i] and immediately she
straightened up and praised God.
14Indignant because Jesus had
healed on the Sabbath,[j] the synagogue ruler[k] said to the people,
"There are six days for work.[l] So
come and be healed on those days,
not on the Sabbath."
15The Lord answered him, "You
hypocrites! Doesn't each of you on
the Sabbath untie his ox or donkey
from the stall and lead it out to give
it water?[m] 16Then should not this
woman, a daughter of Abraham,[n]
whom Satan[o] has kept bound for
eighteen long years, be set free on
the Sabbath day from what bound
her?"
17When he said this, all his opponents were humiliated,[p] but the
people were delighted with all the
wonderful things he was doing.

The Parables of the Mustard Seed and the Yeast

13:18,19pp Mk 4:30–32
13:18–21pp Mt 13:31–33

18Then Jesus asked, "What is the
kingdom of God[q] like?[r] What
shall I compare it to? 19It is like a
mustard seed, which a man took
and planted in his garden. It grew
and became a tree,[s] and the

[c]59 Greek *lepton*

birds of the air perched in its branches."[t]

20Again he asked, "What shall I compare the kingdom of God to? 21It is like yeast that a woman took and mixed into a large amount[a] of flour until it worked all through the dough."[u]

The Narrow Door

22Then Jesus went through the towns and villages, teaching as he made his way to Jerusalem.[v] 23Someone asked him, "Lord, are only a few people going to be saved?"

He said to them, 24"Make every effort to enter through the narrow door,[w] because many, I tell you, will try to enter and will not be able to. 25Once the owner of the house gets up and closes the door, you will stand outside knocking and pleading, 'Sir, open the door for us.'

"But he will answer, 'I don't know you or where you come from.'[x]

26"Then you will say, 'We ate and drank with you, and you taught in our streets.'

27"But he will reply, 'I don't know you or where you come from. Away from me, all you evildoers!'[y]

28"There will be weeping there, and gnashing of teeth,[z] when you see Abraham, Isaac and Jacob and all the prophets in the kingdom of God, but you yourselves thrown out. 29People will come from east and west[a] and north and south, and will take their places at the feast in the kingdom of God. 30Indeed there are those who are last who will be first, and first who will be last."[b]

Jesus' Sorrow for Jerusalem

13:34,35pp Mt 23:37–39
13:34,35Ref Lk 19:41

31At that time some Pharisees came to Jesus and said to him, "Leave this place and go somewhere else. Herod[c] wants to kill you."

32He replied, "Go tell that fox, 'I will drive out demons and heal people today and tomorrow, and on the third day I will reach my goal.'[d] 33In any case, I must keep going today and tomorrow and the next day—for surely no prophet[e] can die outside Jerusalem!

34"O Jerusalem, Jerusalem, you who kill the prophets and stone those sent to you, how often I have longed to gather your children together, as a hen gathers her chicks under her wings,[f] but you were not willing! 35Look, your house is left to you desolate.[g] I tell you, you will not see me again until you say, 'Blessed is he who comes in the name of the Lord.'[b]"[h]

Jesus at a Pharisee's House

14:8–10Ref Pr 25:6,7

14 One Sabbath, when Jesus went to eat in the house of a prominent Pharisee,[a] he was being carefully watched.[b] 2There in front of him was a man suffering from dropsy. 3Jesus asked the Pharisees and experts in the law,[c] "Is it lawful to heal on the Sabbath or not?"[d] 4But they remained silent. So taking hold of the man, he healed him and sent him away.

5Then he asked them, "If one of you has a son[a] or an ox that falls into a well on the Sabbath day, will you not immediately pull him out?"[e] 6And they had nothing to say.

7When he noticed how the guests picked the places of honour at the table,[f] he told them this parable: 8"When someone invites you to a wedding feast, do not take the place of honour, for a person more distinguished than you may have been invited. 9If so, the host who invited both of you will come and say to you, 'Give this man your seat.' Then, humiliated, you will have to take the least important place.

13:19 *t* Mt 13:32
13:21 *u* 1Co 5:6
13:22 *v* Lk 9:51
13:24 *w* Mt 7:13
13:25 *x* Mt 7:23; Mt 25:10-12
13:27 *y* Mt 7:23; Mt 25:41
13:28 *z* Mt 8:12
13:29 *a* Mt 8:11
13:30 *b* Mt 19:30
13:31 *c* Mt 14:1
13:32 *d* Heb 2:10
13:33 *e* Mt 21:11
13:34 *f* Mt 23:37
13:35 *g* Jer 12:17; Jer 22:5 *h* Ps 118:26; Mt 21:9; Lk 19:38
14:1 *a* Lk 7:36; Lk 11:37 *b* Mt 12:10
14:3 *c* Mt 22:35 *d* Mt 12:2
14:5 *e* Lk 13:15
14:7 *f* Lk 11:43

[a]21 Greek *three satas* (probably about ⅗ bushel or 22 litres) [b]35 Psalm 118:26 [a]5 Some manuscripts *donkey*

10But when you are invited, take
the lowest place, so that when your
host comes, he will say to you,
'Friend, move up to a better place.'
Then you will be honoured in the
presence of all your fellow guests.
11For everyone who exalts himself
will be humbled, and he who humbles himself will be exalted."[g]
12Then Jesus said to his host,
"When you give a luncheon or dinner, do not invite your friends, your
brothers or relatives, or your rich
neighbours; if you do, they may
invite you back and so you will be
repaid. 13But when you give a
banquet, invite the poor, the crippled, the lame, the blind,[h] 14and
you will be blessed. Although they
cannot repay you, you will be repaid at the resurrection of the
righteous."[i]

The Parable of the Great Banquet

14:16–24Ref Mt 22:2–14

15When one of those at the table
with him heard this, he said to
Jesus, "Blessed is the man who will
eat at the feast[j] in the kingdom of
God."[k]
16Jesus replied: "A certain man
was preparing a great banquet and
invited many guests. 17At the time
of the banquet he sent his servant
to tell those who had been invited,
'Come, for everything is now
ready.'
18"But they all alike began to
make excuses. The first said, 'I
have just bought a field, and I must
go and see it. Please excuse me.'
19"Another said, 'I have just
bought five yoke of oxen, and I'm
on my way to try them out. Please
excuse me.'
20"Still another said, 'I have just
got married, so I can't come.'
21"The servant came back and reported this to his master. Then the
owner of the house became angry
and ordered his servant, 'Go out
quickly into the streets and alleys
of the town and bring in the poor,
the crippled, the blind and the
lame.'[l]
22" 'Sir,' the servant said, 'what
you ordered has been done, but
there is still room.'
23"Then the master told his servant, 'Go out to the roads and country lanes and make them come in,
so that my house will be full. 24I tell
you, not one of those men who were
invited will get a taste of my banquet.' "[m]

The Cost of Being a Disciple

25Large crowds were travelling
with Jesus, and turning to them he
said: 26"If anyone comes to me and
does not hate his father and
mother, his wife and children, his
brothers and sisters—yes, even his
own life—he cannot be my disciple.[n] 27And anyone who does not
carry his cross and follow me cannot be my disciple.[o]
28"Suppose one of you wants to
build a tower. Will he not first sit
down and estimate the cost to see if
he has enough money to complete
it? 29For if he lays the foundation
and is not able to finish it, everyone
who sees it will ridicule him, 30say-
ing, 'This fellow began to build and
was not able to finish.'
31"Or suppose a king is about to
go to war against another king. Will
he not first sit down and consider
whether he is able with ten thousand men to oppose the one coming
against him with twenty thousand?
32If he is not able, he will send a delegation while the other is still a
long way off and will ask for terms
of peace. 33In the same way, any of
you who does not give up everything he has cannot be my disciple.[p]
34"Salt is good, but if it loses its
saltiness, how can it be made salty
again?[q] 35It is fit neither for the
soil nor for the manure heap; it is
thrown out.[r]

14:11 g Mt 23:12; Lk 18:14
14:13 h ver 21
14:14 i Ac 24:15
14:15 j Isa 25:6; Mt 26:29; Lk 13:29; Rev 19:9; k Mt 3:2
14:21 l ver 13
14:24 m Mt 21:43; Ac 13:46
14:26 n Mt 10:37; Jn 12:25
14:27 o Mt 10:38; Lk 9:23
14:33 p Php 3:7,8
14:34 q Mk 9:50
14:35 r Mt 5:13

"He who has ears to hear, let him hear."[s]

The Parable of the Lost Sheep

15:4–7pp Mt 18:12–14

15 Now the tax collectors[a] and "sinners" were all gathering round to hear him. 2But the Pharisees and the teachers of the law muttered, "This man welcomes sinners, and eats with them."[b]

3Then Jesus told them this parable:[c] 4"Suppose one of you has a hundred sheep and loses one of them. Does he not leave the ninety-nine in the open country and go after the lost sheep until he finds it?[d] 5And when he finds it, he joyfully puts it on his shoulders 6and goes home. Then he calls his friends and neighbours together and says, 'Rejoice with me; I have found my lost sheep.'[e] 7I tell you that in the same way there will be more rejoicing in heaven over one sinner who repents than over ninety-nine righteous persons who do not need to repent.[f]

The Parable of the Lost Coin

8"Or suppose a woman has ten silver coins[a] and loses one. Does she not light a lamp, sweep the house and search carefully until she finds it? 9And when she finds it, she calls her friends and neighbours together and says, 'Rejoice with me; I have found my lost coin.'[g] 10In the same way, I tell you, there is rejoicing in the presence of the angels of God over one sinner who repents."[h]

The Parable of the Lost Son

11Jesus continued: "There was a man who had two sons.[i] 12The younger one said to his father, 'Father, give me my share of the estate.'[j] So he divided his property[k] between them.

13"Not long after that, the younger son got together all he had, set off for a distant country and there squandered his wealth[l] in wild living. 14After he had spent everything, there was a severe famine in that whole country, and he began to be in need. 15So he went and hired himself out to a citizen of that country, who sent him to his fields to feed pigs.[m] 16He longed to fill his stomach with the pods that the pigs were eating, but no-one gave him anything.

17"When he came to his senses, he said, 'How many of my father's hired men have food to spare, and here I am starving to death! 18I will set out and go back to my father and say to him: Father, I have sinned[n] against heaven and against you. 19I am no longer worthy to be called your son; make me like one of your hired men.' 20So he got up and went to his father.

"But while he was still a long way off, his father saw him and was filled with compassion for him; he ran to his son, threw his arms around him and kissed him.[o]

21"The son said to him, 'Father, I have sinned against heaven and against you.[p] I am no longer worthy to be called your son.'[b]

22"But the father said to his servants, 'Quick! Bring the best robe[q] and put it on him. Put a ring on his finger[r] and sandals on his feet. 23Bring the fattened calf and kill it. Let's have a feast and celebrate. 24For this son of mine was dead and is alive again;[s] he was lost and is found.' So they began to celebrate.[t]

25"Meanwhile, the older son was in the field. When he came near the house, he heard music and dancing. 26So he called one of the servants and asked him what was going on. 27'Your brother has come,' he replied, 'and your father has killed

14:35
s Mt 11:15

15:1
a Lk 5:29

15:2
b Mt 9:11

15:3
c Mt 13:3

15:4
d Ps 23; Ps 119:176; Jer 31:10; Eze 34:11-16; Lk 5:32; Lk 19:10

15:6
e ver 9

15:7
f ver 10

15:9
g ver 6

15:10
h ver 7

15:11
i Mt 21:28

15:12
j Dt 21:17
k ver 30

15:13
l ver 30; Lk 16:1

15:15
m Lev 11:7

15:18
n Lev 26:40; Mt 3:2

15:20
o Ge 45:14,15; Ge 46:29; Ac 20:37

15:21
p Ps 51:4

15:22
q Zec 3:4; Rev 6:11
r Ge 41:42

15:24
s Eph 2:1,5; Eph 5:14; 1Ti 5:6
t ver 32

[a] 8 Greek *ten drachmas*, each worth about a day's wages [b] 21 Some early manuscripts *son. Make me like one of your hired men.*

the fattened calf because he has
him back safe and sound.’
28“The older brother became
angry[u] and refused to go in. So his
father went out and pleaded with
him. 29But he answered his father,
‘Look! All these years I’ve been
slaving for you and never disobeyed your orders. Yet you never
gave me even a young goat so I
could celebrate with my friends.
30But when this son of yours who
has squandered your property[v]
with prostitutes[w] comes home, you
kill the fattened calf for him!’
31“ ‘My son,’ the father said, ‘you
are always with me, and everything I have is yours. 32But we had
to celebrate and be glad, because
this brother of yours was dead and
is alive again; he was lost and is
found.’ ”[x]

The Parable of the Shrewd Manager

16 Jesus told his disciples:
“There was a rich man
whose manager was accused of
wasting his possessions.[a] 2So he
called him in and asked him, ‘What
is this I hear about you? Give an account of your management, because you cannot be manager any
longer.’
3“The manager said to himself,
‘What shall I do now? My master is
taking away my job. I’m not strong
enough to dig, and I’m ashamed to
beg—4I know what I’ll do so that,
when I lose my job here, people will
welcome me into their houses.’
5“So he called in each one of his
master’s debtors. He asked the
first, ‘How much do you owe my
master?’
6“ ‘Eight hundred gallons[a] of olive oil,’ he replied.
“The manager told him, ‘Take
your bill, sit down quickly, and
make it four hundred.’
7“Then he asked the second, ‘And
how much do you owe?’
“ ‘A thousand bushels[b] of
wheat,’ he replied.
“He told him, ‘Take your bill and
make it eight hundred.’
8“The master commended the
dishonest manager because he had
acted shrewdly. For the people of
this world[b] are more shrewd[c] in
dealing with their own kind than
are the people of the light.[d] 9I tell
you, use worldly wealth[e] to gain
friends for yourselves, so that
when it is gone, you will be welcomed into eternal dwellings.[f]
10“Whoever can be trusted with
very little can also be trusted with
much,[g] and whoever is dishonest
with very little will also be dishonest with much. 11So if you have
not been trustworthy in handling
worldly wealth,[h] who will trust
you with true riches? 12And if you
have not been trustworthy with
someone else’s property, who will
give you property of your own?
13“No servant can serve two masters. Either he will hate the one and
love the other, or he will be devoted
to the one and despise the other.
You cannot serve both God and
Money.”[i]
14The Pharisees, who loved
money,[j] heard all this and were
sneering at Jesus.[k] 15He said to
them, “You are the ones who justify
yourselves[l] in the eyes of men, but
God knows your hearts.[m] What is
highly valued among men is detestable in God’s sight.

Additional Teachings

16“The Law and the Prophets
were proclaimed until John.[n]
Since that time, the good news of
the kingdom of God is being
preached,[o] and everyone is forcing his way into it. 17It is easier for
heaven and earth to disappear than
for the least stroke of a pen to drop
out of the Law.[p]

15:28 *u* Jnh 4:1
15:30 *v* ver 12,13 *w* Pr 29:3
15:32 *x* ver 24; Mal 3:17
16:1 *a* Lk 15:13,30
16:8 *b* Ps 17:14 *c* Ps 18:26 *d* Jn 12:36; Eph 5:8; 1Th 5:5
16:9 *e* ver 11,13 *f* Mt 19:21; Lk 12:33
16:10 *g* Mt 25:21,23; Lk 19:17
16:11 *h* ver 9,13
16:13 *i* ver 9,11; Mt 6:24
16:14 *j* 1Ti 3:3 *k* Lk 23:35
16:15 *l* Lk 10:29 *m* 1Sa 16:7; Rev 2:23
16:16 *n* Mt 11:12,13 *o* Mt 4:23
16:17 *p* Mt 5:18

a6 Greek *one hundred batous* (probably about 3 kilolitres)   b7 Greek *one hundred korous* (probably about 35 kilolitres)

18"Anyone who divorces his wife and marries another woman commits adultery, and the man who marries a divorced woman commits adultery.[q]

The Rich Man and Lazarus

19"There was a rich man who was dressed in purple and fine linen and lived in luxury every day.[r] 20At his gate was laid a beggar[s] named Lazarus, covered with sores 21and longing to eat what fell from the rich man's table.[t] Even the dogs came and licked his sores.

22"The time came when the beggar died and the angels carried him to Abraham's side. The rich man also died and was buried. 23In hell,[c] where he was in torment, he looked up and saw Abraham far away, with Lazarus by his side. 24So he called to him, 'Father Abraham,[u] have pity on me and send Lazarus to dip the tip of his finger in water and cool my tongue, because I am in agony in this fire.'[v]

25"But Abraham replied, 'Son, remember that in your lifetime you received your good things, while Lazarus received bad things,[w] but now he is comforted here and you are in agony.[x] 26And besides all this, between us and you a great chasm has been fixed, so that those who want to go from here to you cannot, nor can anyone cross over from there to us.'

27"He answered, 'Then I beg you, father, send Lazarus to my father's house, 28for I have five brothers. Let him warn them,[y] so that they will not also come to this place of torment.'

29"Abraham replied, 'They have Moses[z] and the Prophets;[a] let them listen to them.'

30" 'No, father Abraham,'[b] he said, 'but if someone from the dead goes to them, they will repent.'

31"He said to him, 'If they do not listen to Moses and the Prophets, they will not be convinced even if someone rises from the dead.' "

Sin, Faith, Duty

17 Jesus said to his disciples: "Things that cause people to sin[a] are bound to come, but woe to that person through whom they come.[b] 2It would be better for him to be thrown into the sea with a millstone tied round his neck than for him to cause one of these little ones[c] to sin.[d] 3So watch yourselves.

"If your brother sins, rebuke him,[e] and if he repents, forgive him.[f] 4If he sins against you seven times in a day, and seven times comes back to you and says, 'I repent,' forgive him."[g]

5The apostles[h] said to the Lord,[i] "Increase our faith!"

6He replied, "If you have faith as small as a mustard seed,[j] you can say to this mulberry tree, 'Be uprooted and planted in the sea,' and it will obey you.[k]

7"Suppose one of you had a servant ploughing or looking after the sheep. Would he say to the servant when he comes in from the field, 'Come along now and sit down to eat'? 8Would he not rather say, 'Prepare my supper, get yourself ready and wait on me[l] while I eat and drink; after that you may eat and drink'? 9Would he thank the servant because he did what he was told to do? 10So you also, when you have done everything you were told to do, should say, 'We are unworthy servants; we have only done our duty.' "[m]

Ten Healed of Leprosy

11Now on his way to Jerusalem,[n] Jesus travelled along the border between Samaria and Galilee.[o] 12As he was going into a village, ten

[c]23 Greek *Hades*

16:18 q Mt 5:31,32 Mt 19:9 Mk 10:11 Ro 7:2,3 1Co 7:10,11
16:19 r Eze 16:49
16:20 s Ac 3:2
16:21 t Mt 15:27
16:24 u ver 30 Lk 3:8 v Mt 5:22
16:25 w Ps 17:14 x Lk 6:21,24,25
16:28 y Ac 2:40 Ac 20:23 1Th 4:6
16:29 z Lk 24:27,44 Jn 5:45-47 Ac 15:21 a Lk 4:17 Jn 1:45
16:30 b ver 24 Lk 3:8
17:1 a Mt 5:29 b Mt 18:7
17:2 c Mk 10:24 Lk 10:21 d Mt 5:29
17:3 e Mt 18:15 f Eph 4:32 Col 3:13
17:4 g Mt 18:21,22
17:5 h Mk 6:30 i Lk 7:13
17:6 j Mt 13:31 Mt 17:20 Lk 13:19 k Mt 21:21 Mk 9:23
17:8 l Lk 12:37
17:10 m 1Co 9:16
17:11 n Lk 9:51 o Lk 9:51,52 Jn 4:3,4

men who had leprosy[a][p] met him. They stood at a distance[q] 13and called out in a loud voice, "Jesus, Master,[r] have pity on us!"

14When he saw them, he said, "Go, show yourselves to the priests."[s] And as they went, they were cleansed.

15One of them, when he saw he was healed, came back, praising God[t] in a loud voice. 16He threw himself at Jesus' feet and thanked him—and he was a Samaritan.[u]

17Jesus asked, "Were not all ten cleansed? Where are the other nine? 18Was no-one found to return and give praise to God except this foreigner?" 19Then he said to him, "Rise and go; your faith has made you well."[v]

The Coming of the Kingdom of God

17:26,27pp Mt 24:37–39

20Once, having been asked by the Pharisees when the kingdom of God would come,[w] Jesus replied, "The kingdom of God does not come with your careful observation, 21nor will people say, 'Here it is,' or 'There it is,'[x] because the kingdom of God is within[b] you."

22Then he said to his disciples, "The time is coming when you will long to see one of the days of the Son of Man,[y] but you will not see it.[z] 23Men will tell you, 'There he is!' or 'Here he is!' Do not go running off after them.[a] 24For the Son of Man in his day[c] will be like the lightning,[b] which flashes and lights up the sky from one end to the other. 25But first he must suffer many things[c] and be rejected[d] by this generation.[e]

26"Just as it was in the days of Noah,[f] so also will it be in the days of the Son of Man. 27People were eating, drinking, marrying and being given in marriage up to the day Noah entered the ark. Then the flood came and destroyed them all.

28"It was the same in the days of Lot.[g] People were eating and drinking, buying and selling, planting and building. 29But the day Lot left Sodom, fire and sulphur rained down from heaven and destroyed them all.

30"It will be just like this on the day the Son of Man is revealed.[h] 31On that day no-one who is on the roof of his house, with his goods inside, should go down to get them. Likewise, no-one in the field should go back for anything.[i] 32Remember Lot's wife![j] 33Whoever tries to keep his life will lose it, and whoever loses his life will preserve it.[k] 34I tell you, on that night two people will be in one bed; one will be taken and the other left. 35Two women will be grinding grain together; one will be taken and the other left."[d][l]

37"Where, Lord?" they asked.

He replied, "Where there is a dead body, there the vultures will gather."[m]

The Parable of the Persistent Widow

18 Then Jesus told his disciples a parable to show them that they should always pray and not give up.[a] 2He said: "In a certain town there was a judge who neither feared God nor cared about men. 3And there was a widow in that town who kept coming to him with the plea, 'Grant me justice[b] against my adversary.'

4"For some time he refused. But finally he said to himself, 'Even though I don't fear God or care about men, 5yet because this widow keeps bothering me, I will see that she gets justice, so that she won't eventually wear me out with her coming!' "[c]

17:12 p Mt 8:2; q Lev 13:45,46
17:13 r Lk 5:5
17:14 s Lev 14:2; Mt 8:4
17:15 t Mt 9:8
17:16 u Mt 10:5
17:19 v Mt 9:22
17:20 w Mt 3:2
17:21 x ver 23
17:22 y Mt 8:20; z Mt 9:15; Lk 5:35
17:23 a Mt 24:23; Mk 13:21; Lk 21:8
17:24 b Mt 24:27
17:25 c Mt 16:21; d Lk 9:22; Lk 18:32; e Mk 13:30; Lk 21:32
17:26 f Ge 7:6-24
17:28 g Ge 19:1-28
17:30 h Mt 10:23; Mt 16:27; Mt 24:3,27,37,39; Mt 25:31; 1Co 1:7; 1Th 2:19; 2Th 1:7; 2Th 2:8; 2Pe 3:4; Rev 1:7
17:31 i Mt 24:17,18; Mk 13:15-16
17:32 j Ge 19:26
17:33 k Jn 12:25
17:35 l Mt 24:41
17:37 m Mt 24:28
18:1 a Isa 40:31; Lk 11:5-8; Ac 1:14; Ro 12:12; Eph 6:18; Col 4:2; 1Th 5:17
18:3 b Isa 1:17
18:5 c Lk 11:8

[a]*12* The Greek word was used for various diseases affecting the skin—not necessarily leprosy. [b]*21* Or *among* [c]*24* Some manuscripts do not have *in his day.* [d]*35* Some manuscripts *left.* 36*Two men will be in the field; one will be taken and the other left.*

6 And the Lord[d] said, "Listen to
what the unjust judge says. 7 And
will not God bring about justice for
his chosen ones, who cry out[e] to
him day and night? Will he keep
putting them off? 8 I tell you, he will
see that they get justice, and
quickly. However, when the Son of
Man[f] comes,[g] will he find faith on
the earth?"

The Parable of the Pharisee and the Tax Collector

9 To some who were confident of
their own righteousness[h] and
looked down on everybody else,[i]
Jesus told this parable: 10 "Two men
went up to the temple to pray,[j] one
a Pharisee and the other a tax collector. 11 The Pharisee stood up[k]
and prayed about[a] himself: 'God, I
thank you that I am not like other
men—robbers, evildoers, adulterers—or even like this tax collector. 12 I fast[l] twice a week and
give a tenth[m] of all I get.'
13 "But the tax collector stood at a
distance. He would not even look
up to heaven, but beat his breast[n]
and said, 'God, have mercy on me,
a sinner.'[o]
14 "I tell you that this man, rather
than the other, went home justified
before God. For everyone who exalts himself will be humbled, and
he who humbles himself will be
exalted."[p]

The Little Children and Jesus

18:15–17pp Mt 19:13–15; Mk 10:13–16

15 People were also bringing
babies to Jesus to have him touch
them. When the disciples saw this,
they rebuked them. 16 But Jesus
called the children to him and said,
"Let the little children come to me,
and do not hinder them, for the
kingdom of God belongs to such as
these. 17 I tell you the truth, anyone
who will not receive the kingdom of
God like a little child[q] will never
enter it."

The Rich Ruler

18:18–30pp Mt 19:16–29; Mk 10:17–30

18 A certain ruler asked him,
"Good teacher, what must I do to
inherit eternal life?"[r]
19 "Why do you call me good?"
Jesus answered. "No-one is good—
except God alone. 20 You know
the commandments: 'Do not commit adultery, do not murder, do
not steal, do not give false testimony, honour your father and
mother.'[b]"[s]
21 "All these I have kept since I
was a boy," he said.
22 When Jesus heard this, he said
to him, "You still lack one thing.
Sell everything you have and give
to the poor,[t] and you will have
treasure in heaven.[u] Then come,
follow me."
23 When he heard this, he became
very sad, because he was a man of
great wealth. 24 Jesus looked at him
and said, "How hard it is for the
rich to enter the kingdom of God![v]
25 Indeed, it is easier for a camel to
go through the eye of a needle than
for a rich man to enter the kingdom
of God."
26 Those who heard this asked,
"Who then can be saved?"
27 Jesus replied, "What is impossible with men is possible with
God."[w]
28 Peter said to him, "We have left
all we had to follow you!"[x]
29 "I tell you the truth," Jesus said
to them, "no-one who has left home
or wife or brothers or parents or
children for the sake of the kingdom of God 30 will fail to receive
many times as much in this age
and, in the age to come,[y] eternal
life."[z]

Jesus Again Predicts His Death

18:31–33pp Mt 20:17–19; Mk 10:32–34

31 Jesus took the Twelve aside
and told them, "We are going up to
Jerusalem,[a] and everything that is

18:6 d Lk 7:13
18:7 e Ex 22:23; Ps 88:1; Rev 6:10
18:8 f Mt 8:20; g Mt 16:27
18:9 h Lk 16:15; i Isa 65:5
18:10 j Ac 3:1
18:11 k Mt 6:5; Mk 11:25
18:12 l Isa 58:3; Mt 9:14; m Mal 3:8; Lk 11:42
18:13 n Isa 66:2; Jer 31:19; Lk 23:48; o Lk 5:32; 1Ti 1:15
18:14 p Mt 23:12; Lk 14:11
18:17 q Mt 11:25; Mt 18:3
18:18 r Lk 10:25
18:20 s Ex 20:12-16; Dt 5:16-20; Ro 13:9
18:22 t Ac 2:45; u Mt 6:20
18:24 v Pr 11:28
18:27 w Mt 19:26
18:28 x Mt 4:19
18:30 y Mt 12:32; z Mt 25:46
18:31 a Lk 9:51

a *11* Or *to* b *20* Exodus 20:12–16; Deut. 5:16–20

written by the prophets[b] about the
Son of Man[c] will be fulfilled. 32He
will be turned over to the Gentiles.[d] They will mock him, insult
him, spit on him, flog him[e] and kill
him.[f] 33On the third day[g] he will
rise again."[h]
34The disciples did not understand any of this. Its meaning was
hidden from them, and they did not
know what he was talking about.[i]

A Blind Beggar Receives His Sight

18:35–43pp Mt 20:29–34; Mk 10:46–52

35As Jesus approached Jericho,[j]
a blind man was sitting by the roadside begging. 36When he heard the
crowd going by, he asked what was
happening. 37They told him, "Jesus
of Nazareth is passing by."[k]
38He called out, "Jesus, Son of
David,[l] have mercy[m] on me!"
39Those who led the way rebuked
him and told him to be quiet, but he
shouted all the more, "Son of
David, have mercy on me!"[n]
40Jesus stopped and ordered the
man to be brought to him. When he
came near, Jesus asked him,
41"What do you want me to do for
you?"
"Lord, I want to see," he replied.
42Jesus said to him, "Receive
your sight; your faith has healed
you."[o] 43Immediately he received
his sight and followed Jesus, praising God. When all the people saw it,
they also praised God.[p]

Zacchaeus the Tax Collector

19 Jesus entered Jericho[a]
and was passing through.
2A man was there by the name
of Zacchaeus; he was a chief tax
collector and was wealthy. 3He
wanted to see who Jesus was, but
being a short man he could not,
because of the crowd. 4So he ran
ahead and climbed a sycamore-
fig[b] tree to see him, since Jesus
was coming that way.[c]
5When Jesus reached the spot, he
looked up and said to him, "Zacchaeus, come down immediately. I
must stay at your house today." 6So
he came down at once and welcomed him gladly.
7All the people saw this and began to mutter, "He has gone to be
the guest of a 'sinner'."[d]
8But Zacchaeus stood up and said
to the Lord,[e] "Look, Lord! Here
and now I give half of my possessions to the poor, and if I have
cheated anybody out of anything,[f]
I will pay back four times the
amount."[g]
9Jesus said to him, "Today salvation has come to this house, because this man, too, is a son of Abraham.[h] 10For the Son of Man came
to seek and to save what was lost."[i]

The Parable of the Ten Minas

19:12–27Ref Mt 25:14–30

11While they were listening to
this, he went on to tell them a parable, because he was near Jerusalem and the people thought that
the kingdom of God[j] was going to
appear at once.[k] 12He said: "A man
of noble birth went to a distant
country to have himself appointed
king and then to return. 13So he
called ten of his servants[l] and
gave them ten minas.[a] 'Put this
money to work,' he said, 'until I
come back.'
14"But his subjects hated him and
sent a delegation after him to say,
'We don't want this man to be our
king.'
15"He was made king, however,
and returned home. Then he sent
for the servants to whom he had
given the money, in order to find
out what they had gained with it.
16"The first one came and said,
'Sir, your mina has earned ten
more.'
17" 'Well done, my good servant!'[m] his master replied. 'Because you have been trustworthy in

18:31 b Ps 22; Isa 53; c Mt 8:20
18:32 d Lk 23:1; e Mt 16:21; f Ac 2:23
18:33 g Mt 16:21; h Mt 16:21
18:34 i Mk 9:32; Lk 9:45
18:35 j Lk 19:1
18:37 k Lk 19:4
18:38 l ver 39; Mt 9:27; m Mt 17:15; Lk 18:13
18:39 n ver 38
18:42 o Mt 9:22
18:43 p Mt 9:8; Lk 13:17
19:1 a Lk 18:35
19:4 b 1Ki 10:27; 1Ch 27:28; Isa 9:10; c Lk 18:37
19:7 d Mt 9:11
19:8 e Lk 7:13; f Lk 3:12,13; g Ex 22:1; Lev 6:4,5; Nu 5:7; 2Sa 12:6
19:9 h Lk 3:8; Lk 13:16; Ro 4:16; Gal 3:7
19:10 i Eze 34:12,16; Jn 3:17
19:11 j Mt 3:2; k Lk 17:20; Ac 1:6
19:13 l Mk 13:34
19:17 m Pr 27:18

a13 A mina was about three months' wages.

a very small matter, take charge of ten cities.'[n]

18"The second came and said, 'Sir, your mina has earned five more.'

19"His master answered, 'You take charge of five cities.'

20"Then another servant came and said, 'Sir, here is your mina; I have kept it laid away in a piece of cloth. 21I was afraid of you, because you are a hard man. You take out what you did not put in and reap what you did not sow.'[o]

22"His master replied, 'I will judge you by your own words,[p] you wicked servant! You knew, did you, that I am a hard man, taking out what I did not put in, and reaping what I did not sow?[q] 23Why then didn't you put my money on deposit, so that when I came back, I could have collected it with interest?'

24"Then he said to those standing by, 'Take his mina away from him and give it to the one who has ten minas.'

25" 'Sir,' they said, 'he already has ten!'

26"He replied, 'I tell you that to everyone who has, more will be given, but as for the one who has nothing, even what he has will be taken away.[r] 27But those enemies of mine who did not want me to be a king over them—bring them here and kill them in front of me.' "

The Triumphal Entry

19:29–38pp Mt 21:1–9; Mk 11:1–10
19:35–38pp Jn 12:12–15

28After Jesus had said this, he went on ahead, going up to Jerusalem.[s] 29As he approached Bethphage and Bethany[t] at the hill called the Mount of Olives,[u] he sent two of his disciples, saying to them, 30"Go to the village ahead of you, and as you enter it, you will find a colt tied there, which no-one has ever ridden. Untie it and bring it here. 31If anyone asks you, 'Why are you untying it?' tell him, 'The Lord needs it.' "

32Those who were sent ahead went and found it just as he had told them.[v] 33As they were untying the colt, its owners asked them, "Why are you untying the colt?"

34They replied, "The Lord needs it."

35They brought it to Jesus, threw their cloaks on the colt and put Jesus on it. 36As he went along, people spread their cloaks[w] on the road.

37When he came near the place where the road goes down the Mount of Olives,[x] the whole crowd of disciples began joyfully to praise God in loud voices for all the miracles they had seen:

38"Blessed is the king who comes
in the name of the Lord!"[b][y]

"Peace in heaven and glory in
the highest!"[z]

39Some of the Pharisees in the crowd said to Jesus, "Teacher, rebuke your disciples!"[a]

40"I tell you," he replied, "if they keep quiet, the stones will cry out."[b]

41As he approached Jerusalem and saw the city, he wept over it[c] 42and said, "If you, even you, had only known on this day what would bring you peace—but now it is hidden from your eyes. 43The days will come upon you when your enemies will build an embankment against you and encircle you and hem you in on every side.[d] 44They will dash you to the ground, you and the children within your walls.[e] They will not leave one stone on another,[f] because you did not recognise the time of God's coming[g] to you."

Jesus at the Temple

19:45,46pp Mt 21:12–16; Mk 11:15–18; Jn 2:13–16

45Then he entered the temple area and began driving out those

b38 Psalm 118:26

19:17 n Lk 16:10
19:21 o Mt 25:24
19:22 p 2Sa 1:16; Job 15:6; q Mt 25:26
19:26 r Mt 13:12; Mt 25:29; Lk 8:18
19:28 s Mk 10:32; Lk 9:51
19:29 t Mt 21:17; u Mt 21:1
19:32 v Lk 22:13
19:36 w 2Ki 9:13
19:37 x Mt 21:1
19:38 y Ps 118:26; Lk 13:35; z Lk 2:14
19:39 a Mt 21:15,16
19:40 b Hab 2:11
19:41 c Isa 22:4; Lk 13:34,35
19:43 d Isa 29:3; Jer 6:6; Eze 4:2; Eze 26:8; Lk 21:20
19:44 e Ps 137:9; f Mt 24:2; Mk 13:2; Lk 21:6; g 1Pe 2:12

who were selling. 46"It is written,"
he said to them, " 'My house will be
a house of prayer';[c][h] but you have
made it 'a den of robbers'.[d]"[i]
47Every day he was teaching at
the temple.[j] But the chief priests,
the teachers of the law and the
leaders among the people were trying to kill him.[k] 48Yet they could
not find any way to do it, because
all the people hung on his words.

The Authority of Jesus Questioned

20:1–8pp Mt 21:23–27; Mk 11:27–33

20 One day as he was teaching
the people in the temple
courts[a] and preaching the gospel,[b] the chief priests and the
teachers of the law, together with
the elders, came up to him. 2"Tell
us by what authority you are doing
these things," they said. "Who gave
you this authority?"[c]
3He replied, "I will also ask
you a question. Tell me, 4John's
baptism[d]—was it from heaven, or
from men?"
5They discussed it among themselves and said, "If we say, 'From
heaven', he will ask, 'Why didn't
you believe him?' 6But if we say,
'From men', all the people[e] will
stone us, because they are persuaded that John was a prophet."[f]
7So they answered, "We don't
know where it was from."
8Jesus said, "Neither will I tell
you by what authority I am doing
these things."

The Parable of the Tenants

20:9–19pp Mt 21:33–46; Mk 12:1–12

9He went on to tell the people this
parable: "A man planted a vineyard,[g] rented it to some farmers
and went away for a long time.[h]
10At harvest time he sent a servant
to the tenants so they would give
him some of the fruit of the vineyard. But the tenants beat him and
sent him away empty-handed. 11He
sent another servant, but that one
also they beat and treated shamefully and sent away empty-handed.
12He sent still a third, and they
wounded him and threw him out.
13"Then the owner of the vineyard said, 'What shall I do? I will
send my son, whom I love;[i] perhaps they will respect him.'
14"But when the tenants saw him,
they talked the matter over. 'This is
the heir,' they said. 'Let's kill him,
and the inheritance will be ours.'
15So they threw him out of the vineyard and killed him.
"What then will the owner of the
vineyard do to them? 16He will
come and kill those tenants[j] and
give the vineyard to others."
When the people heard this, they
said, "May this never be!"
17Jesus looked directly at them
and asked, "Then what is the meaning of that which is written:

" 'The stone the builders
rejected
has become the
capstone'[a,b]?[k]

18Everyone who falls on that stone
will be broken to pieces, but he on
whom it falls will be crushed."[l]
19The teachers of the law and the
chief priests looked for a way to
arrest him[m] immediately, because
they knew he had spoken this parable against them. But they were
afraid of the people.[n]

Paying Taxes to Caesar

20:20–26pp Mt 22:15–22; Mk 12:13–17

20Keeping a close watch on him,
they sent spies, who pretended to
be honest. They hoped to catch
Jesus in something he said[o] so
that they might hand him over to
the power and authority of the
governor.[p] 21So the spies questioned

19:46 h Isa 56:7 i Jer 7:11
19:47 j Mt 26:55 k Mt 12:14 Mk 11:18
20:1 a Mt 26:55 b Lk 8:1
20:2 c Jn 2:18 Ac 4:7 Ac 7:27
20:4 d Mk 1:4
20:6 e Lk 7:29 f Mt 11:9
20:9 g Isa 5:1-7 h Mt 25:14
20:13 i Mt 3:17
20:16 j Lk 19:27
20:17 k Ps 118:22 Ac 4:11
20:18 l Isa 8:14,15
20:19 m Lk 19:47 n Mk 11:18
20:20 o Mt 12:10 p Mt 27:2

c46 Isaiah 56:7 d46 Jer. 7:11
a17 Or *cornerstone* b17 Psalm 118:22

him: "Teacher, we know that you
speak and teach what is right, and
that you do not show partiality but
teach the way of God in accordance
with the truth.[q] 22Is it right for us
to pay taxes to Caesar or not?"
23He saw through their duplicity
and said to them, 24"Show me a denarius. Whose portrait and inscription are on it?"
25"Caesar's," they replied.
He said to them, "Then give to
Caesar what is Caesar's,[r] and to
God what is God's."
26They were unable to trap him in
what he had said there in public.
And astonished by his answer, they
became silent.

The Resurrection and Marriage

20:27–40pp Mt 22:23–33; Mk 12:18–27

27Some of the Sadducees,[s] who
say there is no resurrection,[t]
came to Jesus with a question.
28"Teacher," they said, "Moses
wrote for us that if a man's brother
dies and leaves a wife but no children, the man must marry the
widow and have children for his
brother.[u] 29Now there were seven
brothers. The first one married a
woman and died childless. 30The
second 31and then the third married her, and in the same way the
seven died, leaving no children.
32Finally, the woman died too.
33Now then, at the resurrection
whose wife will she be, since the
seven were married to her?"
34Jesus replied, "The people of
this age marry and are given in
marriage. 35But those who are considered worthy of taking part in
that age[v] and in the resurrection
from the dead will neither marry
nor be given in marriage, 36and
they can no longer die; for they are
like the angels. They are God's children,[w] since they are children of
the resurrection. 37But in the account of the bush, even Moses
showed that the dead rise, for he
calls the Lord 'the God of Abraham,
and the God of Isaac, and the God
of Jacob'.[c][x] 38He is not the God of
the dead, but of the living, for to
him all are alive."
39Some of the teachers of the law
responded, "Well said, teacher!"
40And no-one dared to ask him any
more questions.[y]

Whose Son Is the Christ?

20:41–47pp Mt 22:41–23:7; Mk 12:35–40

41Then Jesus said to them, "How
is it that they say the Christ[d] is the
Son of David?[z] 42David himself declares in the Book of Psalms:

" 'The Lord said to my Lord:
"Sit at my right hand
43until I make your enemies
a footstool for your feet." '[e][a]

44David calls him 'Lord'. How then
can he be his son?"
45While all the people were listening, Jesus said to his disciples,
46"Beware of the teachers of the
law. They like to walk around in
flowing robes and love to be
greeted in the market-places and
have the most important seats in
the synagogues and the places of
honour at banquets.[b] 47They devour widows' houses and for a show
make lengthy prayers. Such men
will be punished most severely."

The Widow's Offering

21:1–4pp Mk 12:41–44

21 As he looked up, Jesus saw
the rich putting their gifts
into the temple treasury.[a] 2He also
saw a poor widow put in two very
small copper coins.[a] 3"I tell you
the truth," he said, "this poor
widow has put in more than all the
others. 4All these people gave their
gifts out of their wealth; but she out
of her poverty put in all she had to
live on."[b]

20:21 q Jn 3:2
20:25 r Lk 23:2; Ro 13:7
20:27 s Ac 4:1; t Ac 23:8; 1Co 15:12
20:28 u Dt 25:5
20:35 v Mt 12:32
20:36 w Jn 1:12; 1Jn 3:1-2
20:37 x Ex 3:6
20:40 y Mt 22:46; Mk 12:34
20:41 z Mt 1:1
20:43 a Ps 110:1; Mt 22:44
20:46 b Lk 11:43
21:1 a Mt 27:6; Jn 8:20
21:4 b 2Co 8:12

[c]37 Exodus 3:6 [d]41 Or *Messiah* [e]43 Psalm 110:1 [a]2 Greek *two lepta*

Signs of the End of the Age

21:5–36pp Mt 24; Mk 13
21:12–17pp Mt 10:17–22

5 Some of his disciples were remarking about how the temple was adorned with beautiful stones and with gifts dedicated to God. But Jesus said, 6 "As for what you see here, the time will come when not one stone will be left on another;[c] every one of them will be thrown down."

7 "Teacher," they asked, "when will these things happen? And what will be the sign that they are about to take place?"

8 He replied: "Watch out that you are not deceived. For many will come in my name, claiming, 'I am he,' and 'The time is near.' Do not follow them.[d] 9 When you hear of wars and revolutions, do not be frightened. These things must happen first, but the end will not come right away."

10 Then he said to them: "Nation will rise against nation, and kingdom against kingdom.[e] 11 There will be great earthquakes, famines and pestilences in various places, and fearful events and great signs from heaven.[f]

12 "But before all this, they will lay hands on you and persecute you. They will deliver you to synagogues and prisons, and you will be brought before kings and governors, and all on account of my name. 13 This will result in your being witnesses to them.[g] 14 But make up your mind not to worry beforehand how you will defend yourselves.[h] 15 For I will give you[i] words and wisdom that none of your adversaries will be able to resist or contradict. 16 You will be betrayed even by parents, brothers, relatives and friends,[j] and they will put some of you to death. 17 All men will hate you because of me.[k] 18 But not a hair of your head will perish.[l] 19 By standing firm you will gain life.[m]

20 "When you see Jerusalem being surrounded by armies,[n] you will know that its desolation is near. 21 Then let those who are in Judea flee to the mountains, let those in the city get out, and let those in the country not enter the city.[o] 22 For this is the time of punishment[p] in fulfilment[q] of all that has been written. 23 How dreadful it will be in those days for pregnant women and nursing mothers! There will be great distress in the land and wrath against this people. 24 They will fall by the sword and will be taken as prisoners to all the nations. Jerusalem will be trampled[r] on by the Gentiles until the times of the Gentiles are fulfilled.

25 "There will be signs in the sun, moon and stars. On the earth, nations will be in anguish and perplexity at the roaring and tossing of the sea.[s] 26 Men will faint from terror, apprehensive of what is coming on the world, for the heavenly bodies will be shaken.[t] 27 At that time they will see the Son of Man[u] coming in a cloud[v] with power and great glory. 28 When these things begin to take place, stand up and lift up your heads, because your redemption is drawing near."[w]

29 He told them this parable: "Look at the fig-tree and all the trees. 30 When they sprout leaves, you can see for yourselves and know that summer is near. 31 Even so, when you see these things happening, you know that the kingdom of God[x] is near.

32 "I tell you the truth, this generation[b][y] will certainly not pass away until all these things have happened. 33 Heaven and earth will pass away, but my words will never pass away.[z]

34 "Be careful, or your hearts will be weighed down with dissipation, drunkenness and the anxieties of life,[a] and that day will close on you unexpectedly[b] like a trap. 35 For it will come upon all those who live on

21:6 c Lk 19:44
21:8 d Lk 17:23
21:10 e 2Ch 15:6; Isa 19:2
21:11 f Isa 29:6; Joel 2:30
21:13 g Php 1:12
21:14 h Lk 12:11
21:15 i Lk 12:12
21:16 j Lk 12:52,53
21:17 k Jn 15:21
21:18 l Mt 10:30
21:19 m Mt 10:22
21:20 n Lk 19:43
21:21 o Lk 17:31
21:22 p Isa 63:4; Da 9:24-27; Hos 9:7 q Mt 1:22
21:24 r Isa 5:5; Isa 63:18; Da 8:13; Rev 11:2
21:25 s 2Pe 3:10,12
21:26 t Mt 24:29
21:27 u Mt 8:20 v Rev 1:7
21:28 w Lk 18:7
21:31 x Mt 3:2
21:32 y Lk 11:50; Lk 17:25
21:33 z Mt 5:18
21:34 a Mk 4:19 b Lk 12:40,46; 1Th 5:2-7

b32 Or *race*

the face of the whole earth. 36Be always on the watch, and pray[c] that
you may be able to escape all that
is about to happen, and that you
may be able to stand before the Son
of Man."
37Each day Jesus was teaching at
the temple,[d] and each evening he
went out[e] to spend the night on the
hill called the Mount of Olives,[f]
38and all the people came early in
the morning to hear him at the temple.[g]

Judas Agrees to Betray Jesus

22:1,2pp Mt 26:2–5; Mk 14:1,2,10,11

22 Now the Feast of Unleavened Bread, called the
Passover, was approaching,[a] 2and
the chief priests and the teachers
of the law were looking for some
way to get rid of Jesus,[b] for they
were afraid of the people. 3Then
Satan[c] entered Judas, called Iscariot,[d] one of the Twelve. 4And Judas
went to the chief priests and the officers of the temple guard[e] and
discussed with them how he might
betray Jesus. 5They were delighted
and agreed to give him money.[f]
6He consented, and watched for an
opportunity to hand Jesus over to
them when no crowd was present.

The Last Supper

22:7–13pp Mt 26:17–19; Mk 14:12–16
22:17–20pp Mt 26:26–29; Mk 14:22–25; 1Co 11:23–25
22:21–23pp Mt 26:21–24; Mk 14:18–21; Jn 13:21–30
22:25–27pp Mt 20:25–28; Mk 10:42–45
22:33,34pp Mt 26:33–35; Mk 14:29–31; Jn 13:37,38

7Then came the day of Unleavened Bread on which the Passover
lamb had to be sacrificed.[g] 8Jesus
sent Peter and John,[h] saying, "Go
and make preparations for us to eat
the Passover."
9"Where do you want us to prepare for it?" they asked.
10He replied, "As you enter the
city, a man carrying a jar of water
will meet you. Follow him to the
house that he enters, 11and say to
the owner of the house, 'The
Teacher asks: Where is the guest
room, where I may eat the Passover with my disciples?' 12He will
show you a large upper room,
all furnished. Make preparations
there."
13They left and found things just
as Jesus had told them.[i] So they
prepared the Passover.
14When the hour came, Jesus
and his apostles[j] reclined at the
table.[k] 15And he said to them, "I
have eagerly desired to eat this
Passover with you before I suffer.[l] 16For I tell you, I will not eat
it again until it finds fulfilment in
the kingdom of God."[m]
17After taking the cup, he gave
thanks and said, "Take this and divide it among you. 18For I tell you I
will not drink again of the fruit of
the vine until the kingdom of God
comes."
19And he took bread, gave thanks
and broke it,[n] and gave it to them,
saying, "This is my body given for
you; do this in remembrance of
me."
20In the same way, after the supper he took the cup, saying, "This
cup is the new covenant[o] in my
blood, which is poured out for you.
21But the hand of him who is going
to betray me is with mine on the
table.[p] 22The Son of Man[q] will go
as it has been decreed,[r] but woe to
that man who betrays him." 23They
began to question among themselves which of them it might be
who would do this.
24Also a dispute arose among
them as to which of them was considered to be greatest.[s] 25Jesus
said to them, "The kings of the Gentiles lord it over them; and those
who exercise authority over them
call themselves Benefactors. 26But
you are not to be like that. Instead,
the greatest among you should be
like the youngest,[t] and the one
who rules like the one who
serves.[u] 27For who is greater, the
one who is at the table or the one
who serves? Is it not the one who is
at the table? But I am among you as

21:36 c Mt 26:41
21:37 d Mt 26:55; e Mk 11:19; f Mt 21:1
21:38 g Jn 8:2
22:1 a Jn 11:55
22:2 b Mt 12:14
22:3 c Mt 4:10; Jn 13:2; d Mt 10:4
22:4 e ver 52; Ac 4:1; Ac 5:24
22:5 f Zec 11:12
22:7 g Ex 12:18-20; Dt 16:5-8; Mk 14:12
22:8 h Ac 3:1,11; Ac 4:13,19; Ac 8:14
22:13 i Lk 19:32
22:14 j Mk 6:30; k Mt 26:20; Mk 14:17,18
22:15 l Mt 16:21
22:16 m Lk 14:15; Rev 19:9
22:19 n Mt 14:19
22:20 o Ex 24:8; Isa 42:6; Jer 31:31-34; Zec 9:11; 2Co 3:6; Heb 8:6; Heb 9:15
22:21 p Ps 41:9
22:22 q Mt 8:20; r Ac 2:23; Ac 4:28
22:24 s Mk 9:34; Lk 9:46
22:26 t 1Pe 5:5; u Mk 9:35; Lk 9:48

one who serves.[v] [28]You are those
who have stood by me in my trials.
[29]And I confer on you a kingdom,[w]
just as my Father conferred one on
me, [30]so that you may eat and drink
at my table in my kingdom[x] and sit
on thrones, judging the twelve
tribes of Israel.[y]
[31]"Simon, Simon, Satan has
asked[z] to sift you[a] as wheat.[a]
[32]But I have prayed for you,[b]
Simon, that your faith may not fail.
And when you have turned back,
strengthen your brothers."[c]
[33]But he replied, "Lord, I am
ready to go with you to prison and
to death."[d]
[34]Jesus answered, "I tell you,
Peter, before the cock crows today,
you will deny three times that you
know me."
[35]Then Jesus asked them, "When
I sent you without purse, bag or
sandals,[e] did you lack anything?"
"Nothing," they answered.
[36]He said to them, "But now if
you have a purse, take it, and also
a bag; and if you don't have a
sword, sell your cloak and buy one.
[37]It is written: 'And he was numbered with the transgressors';[b][f]
and I tell you that this must be
fulfilled in me. Yes, what is written about me is reaching its fulfilment."
[38]The disciples said, "See, Lord,
here are two swords."
"That is enough," he replied.

Jesus Prays on the Mount of Olives

22:40-46pp Mt 26:36-46; Mk 14:32-42

[39]Jesus went out as usual[g] to the
Mount of Olives,[h] and his disciples
followed him. [40]On reaching the
place, he said to them, "Pray that
you will not fall into temptation."[i]
[41]He withdrew about a stone's
throw beyond them, knelt down[j]
and prayed, [42]"Father, if you are
willing, take this cup[k] from me;
yet not my will, but yours be
done."[l] [43]An angel from heaven
appeared to him and strengthened
him.[m] [44]And being in anguish, he
prayed more earnestly, and his
sweat was like drops of blood falling to the ground.[c]
[45]When he rose from prayer and
went back to the disciples, he found
them asleep, exhausted from sorrow. [46]"Why are you sleeping?" he
asked them. "Get up and pray so
that you will not fall into temptation."[n]

Jesus Arrested

22:47-53pp Mt 26:47-56; Mk 14:43-50; Jn 18:3-11

[47]While he was still speaking a
crowd came up, and the man who
was called Judas, one of the
Twelve, was leading them. He approached Jesus to kiss him, [48]but
Jesus asked him, "Judas, are you
betraying the Son of Man with a
kiss?"
[49]When Jesus' followers saw
what was going to happen, they
said, "Lord, should we strike with
our swords?"[o] [50]And one of them
struck the servant of the high
priest, cutting off his right ear.
[51]But Jesus answered, "No more
of this!" And he touched the man's
ear and healed him.
[52]Then Jesus said to the chief
priests, the officers of the temple
guard,[p] and the elders, who had
come for him, "Am I leading a rebellion, that you have come with
swords and clubs? [53]Every day I
was with you in the temple
courts,[q] and you did not lay a hand
on me. But this is your hour[r]—
when darkness reigns."[s]

Peter Disowns Jesus

22:55-62pp Mt 26:69-75; Mk 14:66-72; Jn 18:16-18,25-27

[54]Then seizing him, they led him
away and took him into the house of
the high priest.[t] Peter followed at
a distance.[u] [55]But when they had

22:27 v Mt 20:28; Lk 12:37
22:29 w Mt 25:34; 2Ti 2:12
22:30 x Lk 14:15; y Mt 19:28
22:31 z Job 1:6-12; a Am 9:9
22:32 b Jn 17:9,15; Ro 8:34; c Jn 21:15-17
22:33 d Jn 11:16
22:35 e Mt 10:9,10; Lk 9:3; Lk 10:4
22:37 f Isa 53:12
22:39 g Lk 21:37; h Mt 21:1
22:40 i Mt 6:13
22:41 j Lk 18:11
22:42 k Mt 20:22; l Mt 26:39
22:43 m Mt 4:11; Mk 1:13
22:46 n ver 40
22:49 o ver 38
22:52 p ver 4
22:53 q Mt 26:55; r Jn 12:27; s Mt 8:12; Jn 1:5; Jn 3:20
22:54 t Mt 26:57; Mk 14:53; u Mt 26:58; Mk 14:54; Jn 18:15

[a]*31* The Greek is plural. [b]*37* Isaiah 53:12
[c]*44* Some early manuscripts do not have verses 43 and 44.

kindled a fire in the middle of the
courtyard and had sat down together, Peter sat down with them.
56A servant girl saw him seated
there in the firelight. She looked
closely at him and said, "This man
was with him."
57But he denied it. "Woman, I
don't know him," he said.
58A little later someone else saw
him and said, "You also are one of
them."
"Man, I am not!" Peter replied.
59About an hour later another as-
serted, "Certainly this fellow was
with him, for he is a Galilean."[v]
60Peter replied, "Man, I don't
know what you're talking about!"
Just as he was speaking, the cock
crowed. 61The Lord[w] turned and
looked straight at Peter. Then
Peter remembered the word the
Lord had spoken to him: "Before
the cock crows today, you will disown me three times."[x] 62And he
went outside and wept bitterly.

The Guards Mock Jesus

22:63–65pp Mt 26:67,68; Mk 14:65; Jn 18:22,23

63The men who were guarding
Jesus began mocking and beating
him. 64They blindfolded him and
demanded, "Prophesy! Who hit
you?" 65And they said many other
insulting things to him.[y]

Jesus Before Pilate and Herod

22:67–71pp Mt 26:63–66; Mk 14:61–63; Jn 18:19–21
23:2,3pp Mt 27:11–14; Mk 15:2–5; Jn 18:29–37
23:18–25pp Mt 27:15–26; Mk 15:6–15; Jn 18:39–19:16

66At daybreak the council[z] of the
elders of the people, both the chief
priests and teachers of the law, met
together,[a] and Jesus was led before them. 67"If you are the
Christ,"[d] they said, "tell us."
Jesus answered, "If I tell you,
you will not believe me, 68and if I
asked you, you would not answer.[b]
69But from now on, the Son of Man
will be seated at the right hand of
the mighty God."[c]
70They all asked, "Are you then
the Son of God?"[d]
He replied, "You are right in saying I am."[e]
71Then they said, "Why do we
need any more testimony? We have
heard it from his own lips."

23 Then the whole assembly
rose and led him off to Pilate.[a] 2And they began to accuse
him, saying, "We have found this
man subverting our nation.[b] He
opposes payment of taxes to Caesar[c] and claims to be Christ,[a] a
king."[d]
3So Pilate asked Jesus, "Are you
the king of the Jews?"
"Yes, it is as you say," Jesus replied.
4Then Pilate announced to the
chief priests and the crowd, "I find
no basis for a charge against this
man."[e]
5But they insisted, "He stirs up
the people all over Judea[b] by his
teaching. He started in Galilee[f]
and has come all the way here."
6On hearing this, Pilate asked if
the man was a Galilean.[g] 7When he
learned that Jesus was under
Herod's jurisdiction, he sent him to
Herod,[h] who was also in Jerusalem at that time.
8When Herod saw Jesus, he was
greatly pleased, because for a long
time he had been wanting to see
him.[i] From what he had heard
about him, he hoped to see him perform some miracle. 9He plied him
with many questions, but Jesus
gave him no answer.[j] 10The chief
priests and the teachers of the law
were standing there, vehemently
accusing him. 11Then Herod and
his soldiers ridiculed and mocked
him. Dressing him in an elegant
robe,[k] they sent him back to Pilate.
12That day Herod and Pilate became friends[l]—before this they
had been enemies.

22:59 v Lk 23:6
22:61 w Lk 7:13 x ver 34
22:65 y Mt 16:21
22:66 z Mt 5:22 a Mt 27:1 Mk 15:1
22:68 b Lk 20:3-8
22:69 c Mk 16:19
22:70 d Mt 4:3 e Mt 27:11 Lk 23:3
23:1 a Mt 27:2 Mk 15:1 Jn 18:28
23:2 b ver 14 c Lk 20:22 d Jn 19:12
23:4 e ver 14,22,41 Mt 27:23 Jn 18:38 1Ti 6:13 2Co 5:21
23:5 f Mk 1:14
23:6 g Lk 22:59
23:7 h Mt 14:1 Lk 3:1
23:8 i Lk 9:9
23:9 j Mk 14:61
23:11 k Mk 15:17-19 Jn 19:2,3
23:12 l Ac 4:27

[d]67 Or *Messiah* [a]2 Or *Messiah*; also in verses 35 and 39 [b]5 Or *over the land of the Jews*

[13]Pilate called together the chief
priests, the rulers and the people,
[14]and said to them, "You brought
me this man as one who was inciting the people to rebellion. I have
examined him in your presence
and have found no basis for your
charges against him.[m] [15]Neither
has Herod, for he sent him back to
us; as you can see, he has done
nothing to deserve death. [16]There-
fore, I will punish him[n] and then
release him."[c]
[18]With one voice they cried out,
"Away with this man! Release Barabbas to us!"[o] ([19]Barabbas had
been thrown into prison for an insurrection in the city, and for murder.)
[20]Wanting to release Jesus, Pilate
appealed to them again. [21]But they
kept shouting, "Crucify him! Crucify him!"
[22]For the third time he spoke to
them: "Why? What crime has this
man committed? I have found in
him no grounds for the death penalty. Therefore I will have him punished and then release him."[p]
[23]But with loud shouts they in-
sistently demanded that he be crucified, and their shouts prevailed.
[24]So Pilate decided to grant their
demand. [25]He released the man
who had been thrown into prison
for insurrection and murder, the
one they asked for, and surrendered Jesus to their will.

The Crucifixion

23:33–43pp Mt 27:33–44; Mk 15:22–32; Jn 19:17–24

[26]As they led him away, they
seized Simon from Cyrene,[q] who
was on his way in from the country,
and put the cross on him and made
him carry it behind Jesus.[r] [27]A
large number of people followed
him, including women who
mourned and wailed[s] for him.
[28]Jesus turned and said to them,
"Daughters of Jerusalem, do not
weep for me; weep for yourselves
and for your children.[t] [29]For the
time will come when you will say,
'Blessed are the barren women,
the wombs that never bore and
the breasts that never nursed!'[u]
[30]Then

"'they will say to the
mountains, "Fall on us!"
and to the hills "Cover
us!"'[d][v]

[31]For if men do these things when
the tree is green, what will happen
when it is dry?"[w]
[32]Two other men, both criminals,
were also led out with him to be executed.[x] [33]When they came to the
place called the Skull, there they
crucified him, along with the criminals—one on his right, the other on
his left. [34]Jesus said, "Father,[y] forgive them, for they do not know
what they are doing."[e][z] And they
divided up his clothes by casting
lots.[a]
[35]The people stood watching, and
the rulers even sneered at him.[b]
They said, "He saved others; let
him save himself if he is the Christ
of God, the Chosen One."[c]
[36]The soldiers also came up and
mocked him.[d] They offered him
wine vinegar[e] [37]and said, "If you
are the king of the Jews,[f] save
yourself."
[38]There was a written notice
above him, which read: THIS IS THE
KING OF THE JEWS.[g]
[39]One of the criminals who hung
there hurled insults at him: "Aren't
you the Christ? Save yourself and
us!"[h]
[40]But the other criminal rebuked
him. "Don't you fear God," he said,
"since you are under the same sentence? [41]We are punished justly,
for we are getting what our deeds
deserve. But this man has done
nothing wrong."[i]

23:14 m ver 4
23:16 n ver 22; Mt 27:26; Jn 19:1; Ac 16:37; 2Co 11:23,24
23:18 o Ac 3:13,14
23:22 p ver 16
23:26 q Mt 27:32; r Mk 15:21; Jn 19:17
23:27 s Lk 8:52
23:28 t Lk 19:41-44; Lk 21:23,24
23:29 u Mt 24:19
23:30 v Hos 10:8; Isa 2:19; Rev 6:16
23:31 w Eze 20:47
23:32 x Isa 53:12; Mt 27:38; Mk 15:27; Jn 19:18
23:34 y Mt 11:25; z Mt 5:44; a Ps 22:18
23:35 b Ps 22:17; c Isa 42:1
23:36 d Ps 22:7; e Ps 69:21; Mt 27:48
23:37 f Lk 4:3,9
23:38 g Mt 2:2
23:39 h ver 35,37
23:41 i ver 4

c16 Some manuscripts *him."* [17]*Now he was obliged to release one man to them at the Feast.*
d30 Hosea 10:8 e34 Some early manuscripts do not have this sentence.

42Then he said, "Jesus, remember me when you come into your
kingdom.[f][j]"
43Jesus answered him, "I tell you
the truth, today you will be with me
in paradise."[k]

Jesus' Death

23:44–49pp Mt 27:45–56; Mk 15:33–41

44It was now about the sixth hour,
and darkness came over the whole
land until the ninth hour,[l] 45for the
sun stopped shining. And the curtain of the temple[m] was torn in
two.[n] 46Jesus called out with a loud
voice,[o] "Father, into your hands I
commit my spirit."[p] When he had
said this, he breathed his last.[q]
47The centurion, seeing what had
happened, praised God[r] and said,
"Surely this was a righteous man."
48When all the people who had
gathered to witness this sight saw
what took place, they beat their
breasts[s] and went away. 49But all
those who knew him, including the
women who had followed him from
Galilee,[t] stood at a distance,[u]
watching these things.

Jesus' Burial

23:50–56pp Mt 27:57–61; Mk 15:42–47; Jn 19:38–42

50Now there was a man named Joseph, a member of the Council, a
good and upright man, 51who had
not consented to their decision and
action. He came from the Judean
town of Arimathea and he was waiting for the kingdom of God.[v] 52Go-
ing to Pilate, he asked for Jesus'
body. 53Then he took it down,
wrapped it in linen cloth and placed
it in a tomb cut in the rock, one in
which no-one had yet been laid. 54It
was Preparation Day,[w] and the
Sabbath was about to begin.
55The women who had come with
Jesus from Galilee[x] followed Joseph and saw the tomb and how his
body was laid in it. 56Then they
went home and prepared spices
and perfumes.[y] But they rested on
the Sabbath in obedience to the
commandment.[z]

23:42 *j* Mt 16:27
23:43 *k* 2Co 12:3,4; Rev 2:7
23:44 *l* Am 8:9
23:45 *m* Ex 26:31-33; Heb 9:3,8 *n* Heb 10:19,20
23:46 *o* Mt 27:50 *p* Ps 31:5; 1Pe 2:23 *q* Jn 19:30
23:47 *r* Mt 9:8
23:48 *s* Lk 18:13
23:49 *t* Lk 8:2 *u* Ps 38:11
23:51 *v* Lk 2:25,38
23:54 *w* Mt 27:62
23:55 *x* ver 49
23:56 *y* Mk 16:1; Lk 24:1 *z* Ex 12:16; Ex 20:10
24:1 *a* Lk 23:56
24:3 *b* ver 23,24
24:4 *c* Jn 20:12
24:6 *d* Mt 17:22,23; Mk 9:30-31; Lk 9:22; Lk 24:44
24:7 *e* Mt 8:20 *f* Mt 16:21
24:8 *g* Jn 2:22
24:10 *h* Lk 8:1-3 *i* Mk 6:30
24:11 *j* Mk 16:11
24:12 *k* Jn 20:3-7 *l* Jn 20:10
24:13 *m* Mk 16:12

The Resurrection

24:1–10pp Mt 28:1–8; Mk 16:1–8; Jn 20:1–8

24 On the first day of the
week, very early in the morning, the women took the spices
they had prepared[a] and went to
the tomb. 2They found the stone
rolled away from the tomb, 3but
when they entered, they did not
find the body of the Lord Jesus.[b]
4While they were wondering
about this, suddenly two men in
clothes that gleamed like lightning[c] stood beside them. 5In their
fright the women bowed down with
their faces to the ground, but the
men said to them, "Why do you look
for the living among the dead? 6He
is not here; he has risen! Remember how he told you, while he was
still with you in Galilee:[d] 7'The Son
of Man[e] must be delivered into the
hands of sinful men, be crucified
and on the third day be raised
again.' "[f] 8Then they remembered
his words.[g]
9When they came back from the
tomb, they told all these things to
the Eleven and to all the others. 10It
was Mary Magdalene, Joanna,
Mary the mother of James, and the
others with them[h] who told this to
the apostles.[i] 11But they did not
believe[j] the women, because their
words seemed to them like nonsense. 12Peter, however, got up and
ran to the tomb. Bending over, he
saw the strips of linen lying by
themselves,[k] and he went away,[l]
wondering to himself what had
happened.

On the Road to Emmaus

13Now that same day two of them
were going to a village called Emmaus, about seven miles[a] from
Jerusalem.[m] 14They were talking
with each other about everything
that had happened. 15As they talked
and discussed these things with

[f]42 Some manuscripts *come with your kingly power* [a]13 Greek *sixty stadia* (about 11 kilometres)

each other, Jesus himself came up and walked along with them;[n] 16but they were kept from recognising him.[o]

17He asked them, "What are you discussing together as you walk along?"

They stood still, their faces downcast. 18One of them, named Cleopas,[p] asked him, "Are you only a visitor to Jerusalem and do not know the things that have happened there in these days?"

19"What things?" he asked.

"About Jesus of Nazareth,"[q] they replied. "He was a prophet,[r] powerful in word and deed before God and all the people. 20The chief priests and our rulers[s] handed him over to be sentenced to death, and they crucified him; 21but we had hoped that he was the one who was going to redeem Israel.[t] And what is more, it is the third day[u] since all this took place. 22In addition, some of our women amazed us.[v] They went to the tomb early this morning 23but didn't find his body. They came and told us that they had seen a vision of angels, who said he was alive. 24Then some of our companions went to the tomb and found it just as the women had said, but him they did not see."[w]

25He said to them, "How foolish you are, and how slow of heart to believe all that the prophets have spoken! 26Did not the Christ[b] have to suffer these things and then enter his glory?"[x] 27And beginning with Moses[y] and all the Prophets,[z] he explained to them what was said in all the Scriptures concerning himself.[a]

28As they approached the village to which they were going, Jesus acted as if he were going further. 29But they urged him strongly, "Stay with us, for it is nearly evening; the day is almost over." So he went in to stay with them.

30When he was at the table with them, he took bread, gave thanks, broke it[b] and began to give it to them. 31Then their eyes were opened and they recognised him,[c] and he disappeared from their sight. 32They asked each other, "Were not our hearts burning within us[d] while he talked with us on the road and opened the Scriptures[e] to us?"

33They got up and returned at once to Jerusalem. There they found the Eleven and those with them, assembled together 34and saying, "It is true! The Lord has risen and has appeared to Simon."[f] 35Then the two told what had happened on the way, and how Jesus was recognised by them when he broke the bread.[g]

Jesus Appears to the Disciples

36While they were still talking about this, Jesus himself stood among them and said to them, "Peace be with you."[h]

37They were startled and frightened, thinking they saw a ghost.[i] 38He said to them, "Why are you troubled, and why do doubts rise in your minds? 39Look at my hands and my feet. It is I myself! Touch me and see;[j] a ghost does not have flesh and bones, as you see I have."

40When he had said this, he showed them his hands and feet. 41And while they still did not believe it because of joy and amazement, he asked them, "Do you have anything here to eat?" 42They gave him a piece of broiled fish, 43and he took it and ate it in their presence.[k]

44He said to them, "This is what I told you while I was still with you:[l] Everything must be fulfilled[m] that is written about me in the Law of Moses,[n] the Prophets and the Psalms."[o]

24:15 n ver 36
24:16 o Jn 20:14; Jn 21:4
24:18 p Jn 19:25
24:19 q Mk 1:24; r Mt 21:11
24:20 s Lk 23:13
24:21 t Lk 1:68; Lk 2:38; Lk 21:28; u Mt 16:21
24:22 v ver 1-10
24:24 w ver 12
24:26 x Heb 2:10; 1Pe 1:11
24:27 y Ge 3:15; Nu 21:9; Dt 18:15; z Isa 7:14; Isa 9:6; Isa 40:10,11; Isa 53; Eze 34:23; Da 9:24; Mic 7:20; Mal 3:1; a Jn 1:45
24:30 b Mt 14:19
24:31 c ver 16
24:32 d Ps 39:3; e ver 27,45
24:34 f 1Co 15:5
24:35 g ver 30,31
24:36 h Jn 20:19,21, 26; Jn 14:27
24:37 i Mk 6:49
24:39 j Jn 20:27; 1Jn 1:1
24:43 k Ac 10:41
24:44 l Lk 9:45; Lk 18:34; m Mt 16:21; Lk 9:22,44; Lk 18:31-33; Lk 22:37; n ver 27; o Ps 2; Ps 16; Ps 22; Ps 69; Ps 72; Ps 110; Ps 118

b26 Or *Messiah*; also in verse 46

45 Then he opened their minds so
they could understand the Scriptures. 46 He told them, "This is what
is written: The Christ will suffer
and rise from the dead on the third
day, 47 and repentance and forgiveness of sins will be preached in his
name[p] to all nations,[q] beginning
at Jerusalem. 48 You are witnesses[r]
of these things. 49 I am going to send
you what my Father has prom-
ised;[s] but stay in the city until you
have been clothed with power from
on high."

24:47 p Ac 5:31; Ac 10:43; Ac 13:38; q Mt 28:19
24:48 r Ac 1:8; Ac 2:32; Ac 5:32; Ac 13:31; 1Pe 5:1
24:49 s Jn 14:16; Ac 1:4
24:50 t Mt 21:17
24:51 u 2Ki 2:11

The Ascension

50 When he had led them out to the
vicinity of Bethany,[t] he lifted up
his hands and blessed them.
51 While he was blessing them, he
left them and was taken up into
heaven.[u] 52 Then they worshipped
him and returned to Jerusalem
with great joy. 53 And they stayed
continually at the temple,[v] praising God.

24:53 v Ac 2:46

JOHN

The Word Became Flesh

1 In the beginning was the
Word,[a] and the Word was with
God,[b] and the Word was God.[c] 2He
was with God in the beginning.[d]
3Through him all things were
made; without him nothing was
made that has been made.[e] 4In him
was life,[f] and that life was the
light[g] of men. 5The light shines in
the darkness, but the darkness has
not understood[a] it.[h]
6There came a man who was sent
from God; his name was John.[i]
7He came as a witness to testify[j]
concerning that light, so that
through him all men might believe.[k] 8He himself was not the
light; he came only as a witness to
the light. 9The true light[l] that
gives light to every man[m] was coming into the world.[b]
10He was in the world, and though
the world was made through him,[n]
the world did not recognise him.
11He came to that which was his
own, but his own did not receive
him. 12Yet to all who received him,
to those who believed[o] in his
name,[p] he gave the right to become children of God[q]—13chil-
dren born not of natural descent,[c]
nor of human decision or a husband's will, but born of God.[r]
14The Word became flesh[s] and
made his dwelling among us. We
have seen his glory, the glory of the
One and Only,[d] who came from the
Father, full of grace and truth.[t]
15John testifies[u] concerning
him. He cries out, saying, "This
was he of whom I said, 'He who
comes after me has surpassed me
because he was before me.' "[v]
16From the fulness[w] of his grace
we have all received one blessing
after another. 17For the law was
given through Moses;[x] grace and
truth came through Jesus Christ.[y]
18No-one has ever seen God,[z] but
God the One and Only,[e,f][a] who is
at the Father's side, has made him
known.

John the Baptist Denies Being the Christ

19Now this was John's testimony
when the Jews[b] of Jerusalem sent
priests and Levites to ask him who
he was. 20He did not fail to confess,
but confessed freely, "I am not the
Christ."[g][c]
21They asked him, "Then who are
you? Are you Elijah?"[d]
He said, "I am not."
"Are you the Prophet?"[e]
He answered, "No."
22Finally they said, "Who are
you? Give us an answer to take
back to those who sent us. What do
you say about yourself?"
23John replied in the words of
Isaiah the prophet, "I am the voice
of one calling in the desert,[f] 'Make
straight the way for the Lord.'[h] "[g]
24Now some Pharisees who had
been sent 25questioned him, "Why
then do you baptise if you are not
the Christ, nor Elijah, nor the
Prophet?"
26"I baptise with[i] water," John
replied, "but among you stands one
you do not know. 27He is the one
who comes after me,[h] the thongs

1:1 *a* Rev 19:13 *b* Jn 17:5; 1Jn 1:2 *c* Php 2:6 **1:2** *d* Ge 1:1 **1:3** *e* 1Co 8:6; Col 1:16; Heb 1:2 **1:4** *f* Jn 5:26; Jn 11:25; Jn 14:6 *g* Jn 8:12 **1:5** *h* Jn 3:19 **1:6** *i* Mt 3:1 **1:7** *j* ver 15,19,32 *k* ver 12 **1:9** *l* 1Jn 2:8 *m* Isa 49:6 **1:10** *n* Heb 1:2 **1:12** *o* ver 7 *p* 1Jn 3:23 *q* Gal 3:26 **1:13** *r* Jn 3:6; Jas 1:18; 1Pe 1:23; 1Jn 3:9 **1:14** *s* Gal 4:4; Php 2:7,8; 1Ti 3:16; Heb 2:14 *t* Jn 14:6 **1:15** *u* ver 7 *v* ver 30; Mt 3:11 **1:16** *w* Eph 1:23; Col 1:19 **1:17** *x* Jn 7:19 *y* ver 14 **1:18** *z* Ex 33:20; Jn 6:46; Col 1:15; 1Ti 6:16 *a* Jn 3:16,18; 1Jn 4:9 **1:19** *b* Jn 2:18; Jn 5:10,16; Jn 6:41,52 **1:20** *c* Jn 3:28; Lk 3:15,16

1:21 *d* Mt 11:14 *e* Dt 18:15 **1:23** *f* Mt 3:1 *g* Isa 40:3
1:27 *h* ver 15,30

[a]5 Or *darkness, and the darkness has not overcome* [b]9 Or *This was the true light that gives light to every man who comes into the world* [c]13 Greek *of bloods* [d]14 Or *the Only Begotten* [e]18 Or *the Only Begotten* [f]18 Some manuscripts *but the only* (or *only begotten*) *Son* [g]20 Or *Messiah.* "The Christ" (Greek) and "the Messiah" (Hebrew) both mean "the Anointed One"; also in verse 25. [h]23 Isaiah 40:3 [i]26 Or *in*; also in verses 31 and 33

of whose sandals I am not worthy to
untie."
28 This all happened at Bethany
on the other side of the Jordan,[i]
where John was baptising.

Jesus the Lamb of God

29 The next day John saw Jesus
coming towards him and said,
"Look, the Lamb of God,[j] who
takes away the sin of the world!
30 This is the one I meant when I
said, 'A man who comes after me
has surpassed me because he was
before me.'[k] 31 I myself did not
know him, but the reason I came
baptising with water was that he
might be revealed to Israel."
32 Then John gave this testimony:
"I saw the Spirit come down from
heaven as a dove and remain on
him.[l] 33 I would not have known
him, except that the one who sent
me to baptise with water[m] told me,
'The man on whom you see the
Spirit come down and remain is he
who will baptise with the Holy
Spirit.'[n] 34 I have seen and I testify
that this is the Son of God."[o]

Jesus' First Disciples

1:40–42pp Mt 4:18–22; Mk 1:16–20; Lk 5:2–11

35 The next day John[p] was there
again with two of his disciples.
36 When he saw Jesus passing by, he
said, "Look, the Lamb of God!"[q]
37 When the two disciples heard
him say this, they followed Jesus.
38 Turning round, Jesus saw them
following and asked, "What do you
want?"
They said, "Rabbi"[r] (which
means Teacher), "where are you
staying?"
39 "Come," he replied, "and you
will see."
So they went and saw where he
was staying, and spent that day
with him. It was about the tenth
hour.
40 Andrew, Simon Peter's brother,
was one of the two who heard what

1:28 *i* Jn 3:26; Jn 10:40
1:29 *j* ver 36; Isa 53:7; 1Pe 1:19; Rev 5:6
1:30 *k* ver 15,27
1:32 *l* Mt 3:16; Mk 1:10
1:33 *m* Mk 1:4 *n* Mt 3:11; Mk 1:8
1:34 *o* ver 49; Mt 4:3
1:35 *p* Mt 3:1
1:36 *q* ver 29
1:38 *r* ver 49; Mt 23:7
1:41 *s* Jn 4:25
1:42 *t* Ge 17:5,15 *u* Mt 16:18
1:43 *v* Mt 10:3; Jn 6:5-7; Jn 12:21,22; Jn 14:8,9 *w* Mt 4:19
1:44 *x* Mt 11:21; Jn 12:21
1:45 *y* Jn 21:2 *z* Lk 24:27 *a* Lk 24:27 *b* Mt 2:23; Mk 1:24 *c* Lk 3:23
1:46 *d* Jn 7:41,42,52
1:47 *e* Ro 9:4,6 *f* Ps 32:2
1:49 *g* ver 38; Mt 23:7 *h* ver 34; Mt 4:3 *i* Mt 2:2; Mt 27:42; Jn 12:13
1:51 *j* Mt 3:16 *k* Ge 28:12 *l* Mt 8:20

John had said and who had followed
Jesus. 41 The first thing Andrew did
was to find his brother Simon and
tell him, "We have found the Messiah" (that is, the Christ).[s] 42 And
he brought him to Jesus.
Jesus looked at him and said,
"You are Simon son of John. You
will be called[t] Cephas" (which,
when translated, is Peter[j]).[u]

Jesus Calls Philip and Nathanael

43 The next day Jesus decided
to leave for Galilee. Finding Philip,[v] he said to him, "Follow me."[w]
44 Philip, like Andrew and Peter,
was from the town of Bethsaida.[x]
45 Philip found Nathanael[y] and told
him, "We have found the one Moses
wrote about in the Law,[z] and about
whom the prophets also wrote[a]—
Jesus of Nazareth,[b] the son of Joseph."[c]
46 "Nazareth! Can anything good
come from there?"[d] Nathanael
asked.
"Come and see," said Philip.
47 When Jesus saw Nathanael approaching, he said of him, "Here is
a true Israelite,[e] in whom there is
nothing false."[f]
48 "How do you know me?" Nathanael asked.
Jesus answered, "I saw you while
you were still under the fig-tree
before Philip called you."
49 Then Nathanael declared,
"Rabbi,[g] you are the Son of God;[h]
you are the King of Israel."[i]
50 Jesus said, "You believe[k] because I told you I saw you under the
fig-tree. You shall see greater
things than that." 51 He then added,
"I tell you[l] the truth, you[l] shall
see heaven open,[j] and the angels
of God ascending and descending[k]
on the Son of Man."[l]

[j]42 Both *Cephas* (Aramaic) and *Peter* (Greek) mean *rock*. [k]50 Or *Do you believe . . . ?*
[l]51 The Greek is plural.

Jesus Changes Water to Wine

2 On the third day a wedding took place at Cana in Galilee.[a] Jesus' mother[b] was there, 2and Jesus and his disciples had also been invited to the wedding. 3When the wine was gone, Jesus' mother said to him, "They have no more wine."

4"Dear woman,[c] why do you involve me?"[d] Jesus replied. "My time[e] has not yet come."

5His mother said to the servants, "Do whatever he tells you."[f]

6Nearby stood six stone water jars, the kind used by the Jews for ceremonial washing,[g] each holding from twenty to thirty gallons.[a]

7Jesus said to the servants, "Fill the jars with water"; so they filled them to the brim.

8Then he told them, "Now draw some out and take it to the master of the banquet."

They did so, 9and the master of the banquet tasted the water that had been turned into wine.[h] He did not realise where it had come from, though the servants who had drawn the water knew. Then he called the bridegroom aside 10and said, "Everyone brings out the choice wine first and then the cheaper wine after the guests have had too much to drink; but you have saved the best till now."

11This, the first of his miraculous signs,[i] Jesus performed at Cana in Galilee. He thus revealed his glory,[j] and his disciples put their faith in him.[k]

Jesus Clears the Temple

2:14–16pp Mt 21:12,13; Mk 11:15–17; Lk 19:45,46

12After this he went down to Capernaum[l] with his mother and brothers[m] and his disciples. There they stayed for a few days.

13When it was almost time for the Jewish Passover,[n] Jesus went up to Jerusalem.[o] 14In the temple courts he found men selling cattle, sheep and doves, and others sitting at tables exchanging money. 15So he made a whip out of cords, and drove all from the temple area, both sheep and cattle; he scattered the coins of the money-changers and overturned their tables. 16To those who sold doves he said, "Get these out of here! How dare you turn my Father's house[p] into a market!"

17His disciples remembered that it is written: "Zeal for your house will consume me."[b][q]

18Then the Jews demanded of him, "What miraculous sign can you show us to prove your authority to do all this?"[r]

19Jesus answered them, "Destroy this temple, and I will raise it again in three days."[s]

20The Jews replied, "It has taken forty-six years to build this temple, and you are going to raise it in three days?" 21But the temple he had spoken of was his body.[t] 22After he was raised from the dead, his disciples recalled what he had said.[u] Then they believed the Scripture and the words that Jesus had spoken.

23Now while he was in Jerusalem at the Passover Feast,[v] many people saw the miraculous signs he was doing and believed in his name.[c] 24But Jesus would not entrust himself to them, for he knew all men. 25He did not need man's testimony about man, for he knew what was in a man.[w]

Jesus Teaches Nicodemus

3 Now there was a man of the Pharisees named Nicodemus,[a] a member of the Jewish ruling council.[b] 2He came to Jesus at night and said, "Rabbi, we know you are a teacher who has come from God. For no-one could perform the miraculous signs[c] you

2:1 *a* Jn 4:46; Jn 21:2 *b* Mt 12:46
2:4 *c* Jn 19:26 *d* Mt 8:29 *e* Mt 26:18; Jn 7:6
2:5 *f* Ge 41:55
2:6 *g* Mk 7:3,4; Jn 3:25
2:9 *h* Jn 4:46
2:11 *i* ver 23; Jn 3:2; Jn 4:48; Jn 6:2,14,26,30; Jn 12:37; Jn 20:30 *j* Jn 1:14 *k* Ex 14:31
2:12 *l* Mt 4:13 *m* Mt 12:46
2:13 *n* Jn 11:55 *o* Dt 16:1-6; Lk 2:41
2:16 *p* Lk 2:49
2:17 *q* Ps 69:9
2:18 *r* Mt 12:38
2:19 *s* Mt 26:61; Mt 27:40; Mk 14:58; Mk 15:29
2:21 *t* 1Co 6:19
2:22 *u* Lk 24:5-8; Jn 12:16; Jn 14:26
2:23 *v* ver 13
2:25 *w* Mt 9:4; Jn 6:61,64; Jn 13:11
3:1 *a* Jn 7:50; Jn 19:39 *b* Lk 23:13
3:2 *c* Jn 9:16,33

[a]6 Greek *two to three metretes* (probably about 75 to 115 litres) [b]17 Psalm 69:9 [c]23 Or *and believed in him*

are doing if God were not with him."[d]

3 In reply Jesus declared, "I tell you the truth, no-one can see the kingdom of God unless he is born again."[a][e]

4 "How can a man be born when he is old?" Nicodemus asked. "Surely he cannot enter a second time into his mother's womb to be born!"

5 Jesus answered, "I tell you the truth, no-one can enter the kingdom of God unless he is born of water and the Spirit.[f] 6 Flesh gives birth to flesh, but the Spirit[b] gives birth to spirit.[g] 7 You should not be surprised at my saying, 'You[c] must be born again.' 8 The wind blows wherever it pleases. You hear its sound, but you cannot tell where it comes from or where it is going. So it is with everyone born of the Spirit."

9 "How can this be?"[h] Nicodemus asked.

10 "You are Israel's teacher,"[i] said Jesus, "and do you not understand these things? 11 I tell you the truth, we speak of what we know,[j] and we testify to what we have seen, but still you people do not accept our testimony.[k] 12 I have spoken to you of earthly things and you do not believe; how then will you believe if I speak of heavenly things? 13 No-one has ever gone into heaven[l] except the one who came from heaven[m]—the Son of Man.[d] 14 Just as Moses lifted up the snake in the desert,[n] so the Son of Man must be lifted up,[o] 15 that everyone who believes[p] in him may have eternal life.[e]

16 "For God so loved[q] the world that he gave his one and only Son,[f] that whoever believes in him shall not perish but have eternal life.[r] 17 For God did not send his Son into the world[s] to condemn the world, but to save the world through him.[t] 18 Whoever believes in him is not condemned,[u] but whoever does not believe stands condemned already because he has not believed in the name of God's one and only Son.[g][v] 19 This is the verdict: Light[w] has come into the world, but men loved darkness instead of light because their deeds were evil. 20 Everyone who does evil hates the light, and will not come into the light for fear that his deeds will be exposed.[x] 21 But whoever lives by the truth comes into the light, so that it may be seen plainly that what he has done has been done through God."[h]

John the Baptist's Testimony About Jesus

22 After this, Jesus and his disciples went out into the Judean countryside, where he spent some time with them, and baptised.[y] 23 Now John also was baptising at Aenon near Salim, because there was plenty of water, and people were constantly coming to be baptised. 24 (This was before John was put in prison.)[z] 25 An argument developed between some of John's disciples and a certain Jew[i] over the matter of ceremonial washing.[a] 26 They came to John and said to him, "Rabbi,[b] that man who was with you on the other side of the Jordan—the one you testified[c] about—well, he is baptising, and everyone is going to him."

27 To this John replied, "A man can receive only what is given him from heaven. 28 You yourselves can testify that I said, 'I am not the Christ[j] but am sent ahead of him.'[d] 29 The bride belongs to the bridegroom.[e] The friend who attends the bridegroom waits and listens for him, and is full of joy when he hears the bridegroom's voice.

3:2 d Ac 2:22; Ac 10:38
3:3 e Jn 1:13; 1Pe 1:23
3:5 f Tit 3:5
3:6 g Jn 1:13; 1Co 15:50
3:9 h Jn 6:52,60
3:10 i Lk 2:46
3:11 j Jn 1:18; Jn 7:16,17; k ver 32
3:13 l Pr 30:4; Ac 2:34; Eph 4:8-10; m Jn 6:38,42
3:14 n Nu 21:8,9; o Jn 8:28; Jn 12:32
3:15 p ver 16,36
3:16 q Ro 5:8; Eph 2:4; 1Jn 4:9,10; r ver 36; Jn 6:29,40; Jn 11:25,26
3:17 s Jn 6:29,57; Jn 10:36; Jn 11:42; Jn 17:8,21; Jn 20:21; t Jn 12:47; 1Jn 4:14
3:18 u Jn 5:24; v 1Jn 4:9
3:19 w Jn 1:4; Jn 8:12
3:20 x Eph 5:11,13
3:22 y Jn 4:2
3:24 z Mt 4:12; Mt 14:3
3:25 a Jn 2:6
3:26 b Mt 23:7; c Jn 1:7
3:28 d Jn 1:20,23
3:29 e Mt 9:15

[a] *3* Or *born from above*; also in verse 7
[b] *6* Or *but spirit*
[c] *7* The Greek is plural.
[d] *13* Some manuscripts *Man, who is in heaven*
[e] *15* Or *believes may have eternal life in him*
[f] *16* Or *his only begotten Son*
[g] *18* Or *God's only begotten Son*
[h] *21* Some interpreters end the quotation after verse 15.
[i] *25* Some manuscripts *and certain Jews*
[j] *28* Or *Messiah*

That joy is mine, and it is now complete.[f] 30He must become greater;
I must become less.
31"The one who comes from
above[g] is above all; the one who is
from the earth belongs to the earth,
and speaks as one from the earth.[h]
The one who comes from heaven is
above all. 32He testifies to what he
has seen and heard,[i] but no-one accepts his testimony.[j] 33The man
who has accepted it has certified
that God is truthful. 34For the one
whom God has sent[k] speaks the
words of God, for God[k] gives the
Spirit[l] without limit. 35The Father
loves the Son and has placed everything in his hands.[m] 36Whoever believes in the Son has eternal life,[n]
but whoever rejects the Son will
not see life, for God's wrath remains on him."[l]

Jesus Talks With a Samaritan Woman

4 The Pharisees heard that
Jesus was gaining and baptising more disciples than John,[a] 2al-
though in fact it was not Jesus who
baptised, but his disciples. 3When
the Lord learned of this, he left Judea[b] and went back once more to
Galilee.
4Now he had to go through Samaria. 5So he came to a town in
Samaria called Sychar, near the plot
of ground Jacob had given to his
son Joseph.[c] 6Jacob's well was
there, and Jesus, tired as he was
from the journey, sat down by the
well. It was about the sixth hour.
7When a Samaritan woman came
to draw water, Jesus said to her,
"Will you give me a drink?" 8(His
disciples had gone into the town[d]
to buy food.)
9The Samaritan woman said to
him, "You are a Jew and I am a Samaritan[e] woman. How can you ask
me for a drink?" (For Jews do not
associate with Samaritans.[a])
10Jesus answered her, "If you
knew the gift of God and who it is
that asks you for a drink, you would
have asked him and he would have
given you living water."[f]
11"Sir," the woman said, "you
have nothing to draw with and the
well is deep. Where can you get this
living water? 12Are you greater
than our father Jacob, who gave us
the well[g] and drank from it himself, as did also his sons and his
flocks and herds?"
13Jesus answered, "Everyone
who drinks this water will be
thirsty again, 14but whoever drinks
the water I give him will never
thirst.[h] Indeed, the water I give
him will become in him a spring
of water[i] welling up to eternal
life."[j]
15The woman said to him, "Sir,
give me this water so that I won't
get thirsty[k] and have to keep coming here to draw water."
16He told her, "Go, call your husband and come back."
17"I have no husband," she replied.
Jesus said to her, "You are right
when you say you have no husband.
18The fact is, you have had five husbands, and the man you now have is
not your husband. What you have
just said is quite true."
19"Sir," the woman said, "I can
see that you are a prophet.[l] 20Our
fathers worshipped on this mountain,[m] but you Jews claim that the
place where we must worship is in
Jerusalem."[n]
21Jesus declared, "Believe me,
woman, a time is coming[o] when
you will worship the Father neither
on this mountain nor in Jerusalem.[p] 22You Samaritans worship
what you do not know;[q] we worship what we do know, for salvation
is from the Jews.[r] 23Yet a time is
coming and has now come[s] when
the true worshippers will worship
the Father in spirit[t] and truth, for

3:29 f Jn 16:24; Jn 17:13; Php 2:2; 1Jn 1:4; 2Jn 12
3:31 g ver 13; h Jn 8:23; 1Jn 4:5
3:32 i Jn 8:26; Jn 15:15; j ver 11
3:34 k ver 17; l Mt 12:18; Lk 4:18; Ac 10:38
3:35 m Mt 28:18; Jn 5:20,22; Jn 17:2
3:36 n ver 15; Jn 5:24; Jn 6:47
4:1 a Jn 3:22,26
4:3 b Jn 3:22
4:5 c Ge 33:19; Ge 48:22; Jos 24:32
4:8 d ver 5,39
4:9 e Mt 10:5; Lk 9:52,53
4:10 f Isa 44:3; Jer 2:13; Zec 14:8; Jn 7:37,38; Rev 21:6; Rev 22:1,17
4:12 g ver 6
4:14 h Jn 6:35; i Jn 7:38; j Mt 25:46
4:15 k Jn 6:34
4:19 l Mt 21:11
4:20 m Dt 11:29; Jos 8:33; n Lk 9:53
4:21 o Jn 5:28; Jn 16:2; p Mal 1:11; 1Ti 2:8
4:22 q 2Ki 17:28-41; r Isa 2:3; Ro 3:1,2; Ro 9:4,5
4:23 s Jn 5:25; Jn 16:32; t Php 3:3

[k]34 Greek *he* [l]36 Some interpreters end the quotation after verse 30. [a]9 Or *do not use dishes Samaritans have used*

they are the kind of worshippers the Father seeks. 24God is spirit,[u] and his worshippers must worship in spirit and in truth."

25The woman said, "I know that Messiah" (called Christ)[v] "is coming. When he comes, he will explain everything to us."

26Then Jesus declared, "I who speak to you am he."[w]

The Disciples Rejoin Jesus

27Just then his disciples returned[x] and were surprised to find him talking with a woman. But no one asked, "What do you want?" or "Why are you talking with her?"

28Then, leaving her water jar, the woman went back to the town and said to the people, 29"Come, see a man who told me everything I ever did.[y] Could this be the Christ?"[b][z] 30They came out of the town and made their way towards him.

31Meanwhile his disciples urged him, "Rabbi,[a] eat something."

32But he said to them, "I have food to eat[b] that you know nothing about."

33Then his disciples said to each other, "Could someone have brought him food?"

34"My food," said Jesus, "is to do the will[c] of him who sent me and to finish his work.[d] 35Do you not say, 'Four months more and then the harvest'? I tell you, open your eyes and look at the fields! They are ripe for harvest.[e] 36Even now the reaper draws his wages, even now he harvests[f] the crop for eternal life,[g] so that the sower and the reaper may be glad together. 37Thus the saying 'One sows and another reaps'[h] is true. 38I sent you to reap what you have not worked for. Others have done the hard work, and you have reaped the benefits of their labour."

Many Samaritans Believe

39Many of the Samaritans from that town[i] believed in him because of the woman's testimony, "He told me everything I ever did."[j] 40So when the Samaritans came to him, they urged him to stay with them, and he stayed two days. 41And because of his words many more became believers.

42They said to the woman, "We no longer believe just because of what you said; now we have heard for ourselves, and we know that this man really is the Saviour of the world."[k]

Jesus Heals the Official's Son

43After the two days[l] he left for Galilee. 44(Now Jesus himself had pointed out that a prophet has no honour in his own country.)[m] 45When he arrived in Galilee, the Galileans welcomed him. They had seen all that he had done in Jerusalem at the Passover Feast,[n] for they also had been there.

46Once more he visited Cana in Galilee, where he had turned the water into wine.[o] And there was a certain royal official whose son lay sick at Capernaum. 47When this man heard that Jesus had arrived in Galilee from Judea,[p] he went to him and begged him to come and heal his son, who was close to death.

48"Unless you people see miraculous signs and wonders,"[q] Jesus told him, "you will never believe."

49The royal official said, "Sir, come down before my child dies."

50Jesus replied, "You may go. Your son will live."

The man took Jesus at his word and departed. 51While he was still on the way, his servants met him with the news that his boy was living. 52When he enquired as to the time when his son got better, they said to him, "The fever left him yesterday at the seventh hour."

53Then the father realised that this was the exact time at which

4:24 u Php 3:3
4:25 v Mt 1:16
4:26 w Jn 8:24; Jn 9:35-37
4:27 x ver 8
4:29 y ver 17,18; z Mt 12:23; Jn 7:26,31
4:31 a Mt 23:7
4:32 b Job 23:12; Mt 4:4; Jn 6:27
4:34 c Mt 26:39; Jn 6:38; Jn 17:4; Jn 19:30; d Jn 19:30
4:35 e Mt 9:37; Lk 10:2
4:36 f Ro 1:13; g Mt 25:46
4:37 h Job 31:8; Mic 6:15
4:39 i ver 5; j ver 29
4:42 k Lk 2:11; 1Jn 4:14
4:43 l ver 40
4:44 m Mt 13:57; Lk 4:24
4:45 n Jn 2:23
4:46 o Jn 2:1-11
4:47 p ver 3,54
4:48 q Da 4:2,3; Jn 2:11; Ac 2:43; Ac 14:3; Ro 15:19; 2Co 12:12; Heb 2:4

b29 Or *Messiah*

Jesus had said to him, "Your son will live." So he and all his household[r] believed.

54This was the second miraculous sign[s] that Jesus performed, having come from Judea to Galilee.

The Healing at the Pool

5 Some time later, Jesus went up to Jerusalem for a feast of the Jews. 2Now there is in Jerusalem near the Sheep Gate[a] a pool, which in Aramaic[b] is called Bethesda[a] and which is surrounded by five covered colonnades. 3Here a great number of disabled people used to lie—the blind, the lame, the paralysed.[b] 5One who was there had been an invalid for thirty-eight years. 6When Jesus saw him lying there and learned that he had been in this condition for a long time, he asked him, "Do you want to get well?"

7"Sir," the invalid replied, "I have no-one to help me into the pool when the water is stirred. While I am trying to get in, someone else goes down ahead of me."

8Then Jesus said to him, "Get up! Pick up your mat and walk."[c] 9At once the man was cured; he picked up his mat and walked.

The day on which this took place was a Sabbath,[d] 10and so the Jews[e] said to the man who had been healed, "It is the Sabbath; the law forbids you to carry your mat."[f]

11But he replied, "The man who made me well said to me, 'Pick up your mat and walk.' "

12So they asked him, "Who is this fellow who told you to pick it up and walk?"

13The man who was healed had no idea who it was, for Jesus had slipped away into the crowd that was there.

14Later Jesus found him at the temple and said to him, "See, you are well again. Stop sinning[g] or something worse may happen to you." 15The man went away and told the Jews[h] that it was Jesus who had made him well.

Life Through the Son

16So, because Jesus was doing these things on the Sabbath, the Jews persecuted him. 17Jesus said to them, "My Father is always at his work[i] to this very day, and I, too, am working." 18For this reason the Jews tried all the harder to kill him;[j] not only was he breaking the Sabbath, but he was even calling God his own Father, making himself equal with God.[k]

19Jesus gave them this answer: "I tell you the truth, the Son can do nothing by himself;[l] he can do only what he sees his Father doing, because whatever the Father does the Son also does. 20For the Father loves the Son[m] and shows him all he does. Yes, to your amazement he will show him even greater things than these.[n] 21For just as the Father raises the dead and gives them life,[o] even so the Son gives life[p] to whom he is pleased to give it. 22Moreover, the Father judges no-one, but has entrusted all judgment to the Son,[q] 23that all may honour the Son just as they honour the Father. He who does not honour the Son does not honour the Father, who sent him.[r]

24"I tell you the truth, whoever hears my word and believes him who sent me has eternal life and will not be condemned;[s] he has crossed over from death to life.[t] 25I tell you the truth, a time is coming and has now come[u] when the dead will hear[v] the voice of the Son of God and those who hear will live. 26For as the Father has life in himself, so he has granted the Son to

4:53 *r* Ac 11:14
4:54 *s* ver 48; Jn 2:11
5:2 *a* Ne 3:1; Ne 12:39 *b* Jn 19:13,17,20; Jn 20:16; Ac 21:40; Ac 22:2; Ac 26:14
5:8 *c* Mt 9:5,6; Mk 2:11; Lk 5:24
5:9 *d* Jn 9:14
5:10 *e* ver 16 *f* Ne 13:15-22; Jer 17:21; Mt 12:2
5:14 *g* Mk 2:5; Jn 8:11
5:15 *h* Jn 1:19
5:17 *i* Jn 9:4; Jn 14:10
5:18 *j* Jn 7:1 *k* Jn 10:30,33; Jn 19:7
5:19 *l* ver 30; Jn 8:28
5:20 *m* Jn 3:35 *n* Jn 14:12
5:21 *o* Ro 4:17; Ro 8:11 *p* Jn 11:25
5:22 *q* ver 27; Jn 9:39; Ac 10:42; Ac 17:31
5:23 *r* Lk 10:16; 1Jn 2:23
5:24 *s* Jn 3:18 *t* 1Jn 3:14
5:25 *u* Jn 4:23 *v* Jn 8:43,47

a2 Some manuscripts *Bethzatha*; other manuscripts *Bethsaida* b3 Some less important manuscripts *paralysed—and they waited for the moving of the waters. 4From time to time an angel of the Lord would come down and stir up the waters. The first one into the pool after each such disturbance would be cured of whatever disease he had.*

have life in himself. 27And he has
given him authority to judge[w] because he is the Son of Man.
28"Do not be amazed at this, for a
time is coming[x] when all who are
in their graves will hear his voice
29and come out—those who have
done good will rise to live, and
those who have done evil will rise
to be condemned.[y] 30By myself I
can do nothing;[z] I judge only as I
hear, and my judgment is just,[a] for
I seek not to please myself but him
who sent me.[b]

Testimonies About Jesus

31"If I testify about myself, my
testimony is not valid.[c] 32There is
another who testifies in my favour,[d] and I know that his testimony about me is valid.
33"You have sent to John and he
has testified[e] to the truth. 34Not
that I accept human testimony;[f]
but I mention it that you may be
saved. 35John was a lamp that
burned and gave light,[g] and you
chose for a time to enjoy his light.
36"I have testimony weightier
than that of John.[h] For the very
work that the Father has given me
to finish, and which I am doing,[i]
testifies that the Father has sent
me.[j] 37And the Father who sent me
has himself testified concerning
me.[k] You have never heard his
voice nor seen his form,[l] 38nor
does his word dwell in you,[m] for
you do not believe the one he sent.[n]
39You diligently study[c] the Scriptures[o] because you think that by
them you possess eternal life.
These are the Scriptures that testify about me,[p] 40yet you refuse to
come to me to have life.
41"I do not accept praise from
men,[q] 42but I know you. I know that
you do not have the love of God in
your hearts. 43I have come in my
Father's name, and you do not accept me; but if someone else comes
in his own name, you will accept
him. 44How can you believe if you
accept praise from one another, yet
make no effort to obtain the praise
that comes from the only God?[d][r]
45"But do not think I will accuse
you before the Father. Your accuser is Moses,[s] on whom your
hopes are set.[t] 46If you believed
Moses, you would believe me, for
he wrote about me.[u] 47But since
you do not believe what he wrote,
how are you going to believe what
I say?"[v]

Jesus Feeds the Five Thousand

6:1–13pp Mt 14:13–21; Mk 6:32–44; Lk 9:10–17

6 Some time after this, Jesus
crossed to the far shore of the
Sea of Galilee (that is, the Sea of Tiberias), 2and a great crowd of people followed him because they saw
the miraculous signs[a] he had performed on the sick. 3Then Jesus
went up on a mountainside[b] and
sat down with his disciples. 4The
Jewish Passover Feast[c] was near.
5When Jesus looked up and saw a
great crowd coming towards him,
he said to Philip,[d] "Where shall we
buy bread for these people to eat?"
6He asked this only to test him, for
he already had in mind what he was
going to do.
7Philip answered him, "Eight
months' wages[a] would not buy
enough bread for each one to have
a bite!"
8Another of his disciples, Andrew, Simon Peter's brother,[e]
spoke up, 9"Here is a boy with five
small barley loaves and two small
fish, but how far will they go
among so many?"[f]
10Jesus said, "Make the people sit
down." There was plenty of grass
in that place, and the men sat down,
about five thousand of them.
11Jesus then took the loaves, gave
thanks,[g] and distributed to those
who were seated as much as they

5:27 w ver 22; Ac 10:42; Ac 17:31 **5:28** x Jn 4:21 **5:29** y Da 12:2; Mt 25:46 **5:30** z ver 19; a Jn 8:16; b Mt 26:39; Jn 4:34; Jn 6:38 **5:31** c Jn 8:14 **5:32** d ver 37; Jn 8:18 **5:33** e Jn 1:7 **5:34** f 1Jn 5:9 **5:35** g 2Pe 1:19 **5:36** h 1Jn 5:9; i Jn 14:11; Jn 15:24; j Jn 3:17; Jn 10:25 **5:37** k Jn 8:18; l Dt 4:12; 1Ti 1:17; Jn 1:18 **5:38** m 1Jn 2:14; n Jn 3:17 **5:39** o Ro 2:17,18; p Lk 24:27,44; Ac 13:27 **5:41** q ver 44 **5:44** r Ro 2:29 **5:45** s Jn 9:28; t Ro 2:17 **5:46** u Ge 3:15; Lk 24:27,44; Ac 26:22 **5:47** v Lk 16:29,31 **6:2** a Jn 2:11 **6:3** b ver 15 **6:4** c Jn 2:13; Jn 11:55 **6:5** d Jn 1:43 **6:8** e Jn 1:40 **6:9** f 2Ki 4:43 **6:11** g ver 23; Mt 14:19

c39 Or *Study diligently* (the imperative)
d44 Some early manuscripts *the Only One*
a7 Greek *two hundred denarii*

wanted. He did the same with the fish.

12When they had all had enough to eat, he said to his disciples, "Gather the pieces that are left over. Let nothing be wasted." 13So they gathered them and filled twelve baskets with the pieces of the five barley loaves left over by those who had eaten.

14After the people saw the miraculous sign[h] that Jesus did, they began to say, "Surely this is the Prophet who is to come into the world."[i] 15Jesus, knowing that they intended to come and make him king[j] by force, withdrew again to a mountain by himself.[k]

Jesus Walks on the Water

6:16–21pp Mt 14:22–33; Mk 6:47–51

16When evening came, his disciples went down to the lake, 17where they got into a boat and set off across the lake for Capernaum. By now it was dark, and Jesus had not yet joined them. 18A strong wind was blowing and the waters grew rough. 19When they had rowed three or three and a half miles,[b] they saw Jesus approaching the boat, walking on the water;[l] and they were terrified. 20But he said to them, "It is I; don't be afraid."[m] 21Then they were willing to take him into the boat, and immediately the boat reached the shore where they were heading.

22The next day the crowd that had stayed on the opposite shore of the lake[n] realised that only one boat had been there, and that Jesus had not entered it with his disciples, but that they had gone away alone.[o] 23Then some boats from Tiberias[p] landed near the place where the people had eaten the bread after the Lord had given thanks.[q] 24Once the crowd realised that neither Jesus nor his disciples were there, they got into the boats and went to Capernaum in search of Jesus.

Jesus the Bread of Life

25When they found him on the other side of the lake, they asked him, "Rabbi,[r] when did you get here?"

26Jesus answered, "I tell you the truth, you are looking for me,[s] not because you saw miraculous signs[t] but because you ate the loaves and had your fill. 27Do not work for food that spoils, but for food that endures[u] to eternal life,[v] which the Son of Man[w] will give you. On him God the Father has placed his seal[x] of approval."

28Then they asked him, "What must we do to do the works God requires?"

29Jesus answered, "The work of God is this: to believe[y] in the one he has sent."[z]

30So they asked him, "What miraculous sign[a] then will you give that we may see it and believe you?[b] What will you do? 31Our forefathers ate the manna[c] in the desert; as it is written: 'He gave them bread from heaven to eat.'[c]"[d]

32Jesus said to them, "I tell you the truth, it is not Moses who has given you the bread from heaven, but it is my Father who gives you the true bread from heaven. 33For the bread of God is he who comes down from heaven[e] and gives life to the world."

34"Sir," they said, "from now on give us this bread."[f]

35Then Jesus declared, "I am the bread of life.[g] He who comes to me will never go hungry, and he who believes in me will never be thirsty.[h] 36But as I told you, you have seen me and still you do not believe. 37All that the Father gives me[i] will come to me, and whoever comes to me I will never drive away. 38For I have come down from heaven not to do my will but to do

6:14 h Jn 2:11 i Dt 18:15,18 Mt 11:3 Mt 21:11
6:15 j Jn 18:36 k Mt 14:23 Mk 6:46
6:19 l Job 9:8
6:20 m Mt 14:27
6:22 n ver 2 o ver 15-21
6:23 p ver 1 q ver 11
6:25 r Mt 23:7
6:26 s ver 24 t ver 30 Jn 2:11
6:27 u Isa 55:2 v ver 54 Mt 25:46 Jn 4:14 w Mt 8:20 x Ro 4:11 1Co 9:2 2Co 1:22 Eph 1:13 Eph 4:30 2Ti 2:19 Rev 7:3
6:29 y 1Jn 3:23 z Jn 3:17
6:30 a Jn 2:11 b Mt 12:38
6:31 c Nu 11:7-9 d Ex 16:4,15 Ne 9:15 Ps 78:24 Ps 105:40
6:33 e ver 50
6:34 f Jn 4:15
6:35 g ver 48,51 h Jn 4:14
6:37 i ver 39 Jn 17:2,6,9, 24

b19 Greek *rowed twenty-five or thirty stadia* (about 5 or 6 kilometres) c31 Exodus 16:4; Neh. 9:15; Psalm 78:24,25

the will of him who sent me.[j] 39And
this is the will of him who sent me,
that I shall lose none of all that he
has given me,[k] but raise them up at
the last day.[l] 40For my Father's
will is that everyone who looks to
the Son and believes in him shall
have eternal life,[m] and I will raise
him up at the last day."
41At this the Jews began to grumble about him because he said, "I
am the bread that came down from
heaven." 42They said, "Is this not
Jesus, the son of Joseph,[n] whose
father and mother we know?[o] How
can he now say, 'I came down from
heaven'?"[p]
43"Stop grumbling among yourselves," Jesus answered. 44"No-one
can come to me unless the Father
who sent me draws him,[q] and I will
raise him up at the last day. 45It is
written in the Prophets: 'They will
all be taught by God.'[d][r] Everyone
who listens to the Father and learns
from him comes to me. 46No-one
has seen the Father except the one
who is from God;[s] only he has seen
the Father. 47I tell you the truth, he
who believes has everlasting life.
48I am the bread of life.[t] 49Your
forefathers ate the manna in the
desert, yet they died.[u] 50But here
is the bread that comes down from
heaven,[v] which a man may eat and
not die. 51I am the living bread that
came down from heaven. If anyone
eats of this bread, he will live for
ever. This bread is my flesh, which
I will give for the life of the
world."[w]
52Then the Jews began to argue
sharply among themselves,[x] "How
can this man give us his flesh to
eat?"
53Jesus said to them, "I tell you
the truth, unless you eat the flesh
of the Son of Man[y] and drink his
blood, you have no life in you.
54Whoever eats my flesh and
drinks my blood has eternal life,
and I will raise him up at the last
day.[z] 55For my flesh is real food
and my blood is real drink. 56Who-
ever eats my flesh and drinks my
blood remains in me, and I in him.[a]
57Just as the living Father sent
me[b] and I live because of the
Father, so the one who feeds on me
will live because of me. 58This is
the bread that came down from
heaven. Your forefathers ate
manna and died, but he who feeds
on this bread will live for ever."[c]
59He said this while teaching in the
synagogue in Capernaum.

Many Disciples Desert Jesus

60On hearing it, many of his disciples[d] said, "This is a hard teaching. Who can accept it?"
61Aware that his disciples were
grumbling about this, Jesus said to
them, "Does this offend you?[e]
62What if you see the Son of Man
ascend to where he was before![f]
63The Spirit gives life;[g] the flesh
counts for nothing. The words I
have spoken to you are spirit[e] and
they are life. 64Yet there are some
of you who do not believe." For
Jesus had known[h] from the beginning which of them did not believe
and who would betray him. 65He
went on to say, "This is why I told
you that no-one can come to me unless the Father has enabled him."[i]
66From this time many of his disciples[j] turned back and no longer
followed him.
67"You do not want to leave too,
do you?" Jesus asked the Twelve.[k]
68Simon Peter answered him,[l]
"Lord, to whom shall we go? You
have the words of eternal life. 69We
believe and know that you are the
Holy One of God."[m]
70Then Jesus replied, "Have I not
chosen you,[n] the Twelve? Yet one
of you is a devil!"[o] 71(He meant Judas, the son of Simon Iscariot, who,
though one of the Twelve, was later
to betray him.)

6:38 j Jn 4:34; Jn 5:30
6:39 k Jn 10:28; Jn 17:12; Jn 18:9; l ver 40,44,54
6:40 m Jn 3:15,16
6:42 n Lk 4:22; o Jn 7:27,28; p ver 38,62
6:44 q ver 65; Jer 31:3; Jn 12:32
6:45 r Isa 54:13; Jer 31:33,34; Heb 8:10,11; Heb 10:16
6:46 s Jn 1:18; Jn 5:37; Jn 7:29
6:48 t ver 35,51
6:49 u ver 31,58
6:50 v ver 33
6:51 w Heb 10:10
6:52 x Jn 7:43; Jn 9:16; Jn 10:19
6:53 y Mt 8:20
6:54 z ver 39
6:56 a Jn 15:4-7; 1Jn 3:24; 1Jn 4:15
6:57 b Jn 3:17
6:58 c ver 49-51; Jn 3:36
6:60 d ver 66
6:61 e Mt 11:6
6:62 f Mk 16:19; Jn 3:13; Jn 17:5
6:63 g 2Co 3:6
6:64 h Jn 2:25
6:65 i ver 37,44
6:66 j ver 60
6:67 k Mt 10:2
6:68 l Mt 16:16
6:69 m Mk 8:29; Lk 9:20
6:70 n Jn 15:16,19; o Jn 13:27

d45 Isaiah 54:13   e63 Or *Spirit*

Jesus Goes to the Feast of Tabernacles

7 After this, Jesus went around in Galilee, purposely staying away from Judea because the Jews[a] there were waiting to take his life.[b] 2 But when the Jewish Feast of Tabernacles[c] was near, 3 Jesus' brothers[d] said to him, "You ought to leave here and go to Judea, so that your disciples may see the miracles you do. 4 No-one who wants to become a public figure acts in secret. Since you are doing these things, show yourself to the world." 5 For even his own brothers did not believe in him.[e]

6 Therefore Jesus told them, "The right time[f] for me has not yet come; for you any time is right. 7 The world cannot hate you, but it hates me[g] because I testify that what it does is evil.[h] 8 You go to the Feast. I am not yet**[a]** going up to this Feast, because for me the right time[i] has not yet come." 9 Having said this, he stayed in Galilee.

10 However, after his brothers had left for the Feast, he went also, not publicly, but in secret. 11 Now at the Feast the Jews were watching for him[j] and asking, "Where is that man?"

12 Among the crowds there was widespread whispering about him. Some said, "He is a good man."

Others replied, "No, he deceives the people."[k] 13 But no-one would say anything publicly about him for fear of the Jews.[l]

Jesus Teaches at the Feast

14 Not until halfway through the Feast did Jesus go up to the temple courts and begin to teach.[m] 15 The Jews[n] were amazed and asked, "How did this man get such learning[o] without having studied?"[p]

16 Jesus answered, "My teaching is not my own. It comes from him who sent me.[q] 17 If anyone chooses to do God's will, he will find out[r] whether my teaching comes from God or whether I speak on my own. 18 He who speaks on his own does so to gain honour for himself,[s] but he who works for the honour of the one who sent him is a man of truth; there is nothing false about him. 19 Has not Moses given you the law?[t] Yet not one of you keeps the law. Why are you trying to kill me?"[u]

20 "You are demon-possessed,"[v] the crowd answered. "Who is trying to kill you?"

21 Jesus said to them, "I did one miracle, and you are all astonished. 22 Yet, because Moses gave you circumcision[w] (though actually it did not come from Moses, but from the patriarchs),[x] you circumcise a child on the Sabbath. 23 Now if a child can be circumcised on the Sabbath so that the law of Moses may not be broken, why are you angry with me for healing the whole man on the Sabbath? 24 Stop judging by mere appearances, and make a right judgment."[y]

Is Jesus the Christ?

25 At that point some of the people of Jerusalem began to ask, "Isn't this the man they are trying to kill? 26 Here he is, speaking publicly, and they are not saying a word to him. Have the authorities[z] really concluded that he is the Christ?**[b]** 27 But we know where this man is from;[a] when the Christ comes, no-one will know where he is from."

28 Then Jesus, still teaching in the temple courts,[b] cried out, "Yes, you know me, and you know where I am from.[c] I am not here on my own, but he who sent me is true.[d] You do not know him, 29 but I know him[e] because I am from him and he sent me."

30 At this they tried to seize him, but no-one laid a hand on him,[f]

7:1 a Jn 1:19 b Jn 5:18
7:2 c Lev 23:34 Dt 16:16
7:3 d Mt 12:46
7:5 e Mk 3:21
7:6 f Mt 26:18
7:7 g Jn 15:18,19 h Jn 3:19,20
7:8 i ver 6
7:11 j Jn 11:56
7:12 k ver 40,43
7:13 l Jn 9:22 Jn 12:42 Jn 19:38
7:14 m ver 28 Mt 26:55
7:15 n Jn 1:19 o Ac 26:24 p Mt 13:54
7:16 q Jn 3:11 Jn 14:24
7:17 r Ps 25:14 Jn 8:43
7:18 s Jn 5:41 Jn 8:50,54
7:19 t Jn 1:17 u ver 1 Mt 12:14
7:20 v Jn 8:48 Jn 10:20
7:22 w Lev 12:3 x Ge 17:10-14
7:24 y Isa 11:3,4 Jn 8:15
7:26 z ver 48
7:27 a Mt 13:55 Lk 4:22
7:28 b ver 14 c Jn 8:14 d Jn 8:26,42
7:29 e Mt 11:27
7:30 f ver 32,44 Jn 10:39

a8 Some early manuscripts do not have *yet*.
b26 Or *Messiah*; also in verses 27, 31, 41 and 42

because his time had not yet
come. 31Still, many in the crowd put
their faith in him.[g] They said,
"When the Christ comes, will he do
more miraculous signs[h] than this
man?"
32The Pharisees heard the crowd
whispering such things about him.
Then the chief priests and the
Pharisees sent temple guards to arrest him.
33Jesus said, "I am with you for
only a short time,[i] and then I go to
the one who sent me.[j] 34You will
look for me, but you will not find
me; and where I am, you cannot
come."[k]
35The Jews said to one another,
"Where does this man intend to go
that we cannot find him? Will he go
where our people live scattered[l]
among the Greeks,[m] and teach the
Greeks? 36What did he mean when
he said, 'You will look for me, but
you will not find me,' and 'Where I
am, you cannot come'?"
37On the last and greatest day of
the Feast,[n] Jesus stood and said in
a loud voice, "If anyone is thirsty,
let him come to me and drink.[o]
38Whoever believes in me, as[c] the
Scripture has said,[p] streams of living water[q] will flow from within
him."[r] 39By this he meant the
Spirit,[s] whom those who believed
in him were later to receive.[t] Up to
that time the Spirit had not been
given, since Jesus had not yet been
glorified.[u]
40On hearing his words, some of
the people said, "Surely this man is
the Prophet."[v]
41Others said, "He is the Christ."
Still others asked, "How can the
Christ come from Galilee?[w] 42Does
not the Scripture say that the
Christ will come from David's family[d][x] and from Bethlehem,[y] the
town where David lived?" 43Thus
the people were divided[z] because
of Jesus. 44Some wanted to seize
him, but no-one laid a hand on
him.[a]

7:31
g Jn 8:30
h Jn 2:11
7:33
i Jn 13:33
Jn 16:16
j Jn 16:5,10,17,28
7:34
k Jn 8:21
Jn 13:33
7:35
l Jas 1:1
m Jn 12:20
1Pe 1:1
7:37
n Lev 23:36
o Isa 55:1
Rev 22:17
7:38
p Isa 58:11
q Jn 4:10
r Jn 4:14
7:39
s Joel 2:28
Ac 2:17,33
t Jn 20:22
u Jn 12:23
Jn 13:31,32
7:40
v Mt 21:11
Jn 1:21
7:41
w ver 52
Jn 1:46
7:42
x Mt 1:1
y Mic 5:2
Mt 2:5,6
Lk 2:4
7:43
z Jn 9:16
Jn 10:19
7:44
a ver 30
7:46
b Mt 7:28
7:47
c ver 12
7:48
d Jn 12:42
7:50
e Jn 3:1
Jn 19:39
7:52
f ver 41
8:1
a Mt 21:1
8:2
b ver 20
Mt 26:55
8:5
c Lev 20:10
Dt 22:22
8:6
d Mt 22:15,18

Unbelief of the Jewish Leaders

45Finally the temple guards went
back to the chief priests and Pharisees, who asked them, "Why didn't
you bring him in?"
46"No-one ever spoke the way
this man does,"[b] the guards declared.
47"You mean he has deceived you
also?"[c] the Pharisees retorted.
48"Has any of the rulers or of the
Pharisees believed in him?[d] 49No!
But this mob that knows nothing of
the law—there is a curse on them."
50Nicodemus,[e] who had gone to
Jesus earlier and who was one of
their own number, asked, 51"Does
our law condemn a man without
first hearing him to find out what
he is doing?"
52They replied, "Are you from
Galilee, too? Look into it, and you
will find that a prophet[e] does not
come out of Galilee."[f]

[The earliest and most reliable manuscripts and other ancient witnesses do not have John 7:53–8:11.]

53Then each went to his own
home.
8 But Jesus went to the Mount of
Olives.[a] 2At dawn he appeared again in the temple courts,
where all the people gathered
round him, and he sat down to teach
them.[b] 3The teachers of the law
and the Pharisees brought in a
woman caught in adultery. They
made her stand before the group
4and said to Jesus, "Teacher, this
woman was caught in the act of
adultery. 5In the Law Moses commanded us to stone such women.[c]
Now what do you say?" 6They were
using this question as a trap,[d] in

[c]37, 38 Or *If anyone is thirsty, let him come to me. / And let him drink,* [38]*who believes in me. / As*
[d]42 Greek *seed* [e]52 Two early manuscripts *the Prophet*

order to have a basis for accusing
him.[e]
But Jesus bent down and started
to write on the ground with his
finger. 7When they kept on ques-
tioning him, he straightened up and
said to them, "If any one of you is
without sin, let him be the first to
throw a stone[f] at her."[g] 8Again he
stooped down and wrote on the
ground.
9At this, those who heard began
to go away one at a time, the older
ones first, until only Jesus was left,
with the woman still standing
there. 10Jesus straightened up and
asked her, "Woman, where are
they? Has no-one condemned you?"
11"No-one, sir," she said.
"Then neither do I condemn
you,"[h] Jesus declared. "Go now
and leave your life of sin."[i]

The Validity of Jesus' Testimony

12When Jesus spoke again to the
people, he said, "I am[j] the light of
the world.[k] Whoever follows me
will never walk in darkness, but
will have the light of life."[l]
13The Pharisees challenged him,
"Here you are, appearing as your
own witness; your testimony is not
valid."[m]
14Jesus answered, "Even if I testify on my own behalf, my testimony is valid, for I know where I
came from and where I am going.[n]
But you have no idea where I come
from[o] or where I am going. 15You
judge by human standards;[p] I pass
judgment on no-one.[q] 16But if I do
judge, my decisions are right, because I am not alone. I stand with
the Father, who sent me.[r] 17In your
own Law it is written that the testimony of two men is valid.[s] 18I am
one who testifies for myself; my
other witness is the Father, who
sent me."[t]

8:6 e Mt 12:10
8:7 f Dt 17:7 g Ro 2:1,22
8:11 h Jn 3:17 i Jn 5:14
8:12 j Jn 6:35 k Jn 1:4 Jn 12:35 l Pr 4:18 Mt 5:14
8:13 m Jn 5:31
8:14 n Jn 13:3 Jn 16:28 o Jn 7:28 Jn 9:29
8:15 p Jn 7:24 q Jn 3:17
8:16 r Jn 5:30
8:17 s Dt 17:6 Mt 18:16
8:18 t Jn 5:37
8:19 u Jn 16:3 v Jn 14:7 1Jn 2:23
8:20 w Mt 26:55 x Mk 12:41 y Mt 26:18 Jn 7:30
8:21 z Eze 3:18 a Jn 7:34 Jn 13:33
8:23 b Jn 3:31 Jn 17:14
8:24 c Jn 4:26 Jn 13:19
8:26 d Jn 7:28 e Jn 3:32 Jn 15:15
8:28 f Jn 3:14 Jn 5:19 Jn 12:32
8:29 g ver 16 Jn 16:32 h Jn 4:34 Jn 5:30 Jn 6:38
8:30 i Jn 7:31
8:31 j Jn 15:7 2Jn 9

19Then they asked him, "Where is
your father?"
"You do not know me or my
Father,"[u] Jesus replied. "If you
knew me, you would know my
Father also."[v] 20He spoke these
words while teaching[w] in the temple area near the place where the
offerings were put.[x] Yet no-one
seized him, because his time had
not yet come.[y]
21Once more Jesus said to them,
"I am going away, and you will look
for me, and you will die[z] in your
sin. Where I go, you cannot
come."[a]
22This made the Jews ask, "Will
he kill himself? Is that why he says,
'Where I go, you cannot come'?"
23But he continued, "You are
from below; I am from above. You
are of this world; I am not of this
world.[b] 24I told you that you would
die in your sins; if you do not believe that I am ⌞the one I claim to
be⌟,[a][c] you will indeed die in your
sins."
25"Who are you?" they asked.
"Just what I have been claiming
all along," Jesus replied. 26"I have
much to say in judgment of you.
But he who sent me is reliable,[d]
and what I have heard from him I
tell the world."[e]
27They did not understand that he
was telling them about his Father.
28So Jesus said, "When you have
lifted up the Son of Man,[f] then you
will know that I am ⌞the one I claim
to be⌟ and that I do nothing on my
own but speak just what the Father
has taught me. 29The one who sent
me is with me; he has not left me
alone,[g] for I always do what
pleases him."[h] 30Even as he spoke,
many put their faith in him.[i]

The Children of Abraham

31To the Jews who had believed
him, Jesus said, "If you hold to
my teaching,[j] you are really my

a24 Or *I am he*; also in verse 28

disciples. 32 Then you will know the truth, and the truth will set you free."[k]

33 They answered him, "We are Abraham's descendants[b][l] and have never been slaves of anyone. How can you say that we shall be set free?"

34 Jesus replied, "I tell you the truth, everyone who sins is a slave to sin.[m] 35 Now a slave has no permanent place in the family, but a son belongs to it for ever.[n] 36 So if the Son sets you free, you will be free indeed. 37 I know you are Abraham's descendants. Yet you are ready to kill me,[o] because you have no room for my word. 38 I am telling you what I have seen in the Father's presence,[p] and you do what you have heard from your father."[c]

39 "Abraham is our father," they answered.

"If you were Abraham's children,"[q] said Jesus, "then you would[d] do the things Abraham did. 40 As it is, you are determined to kill me, a man who has told you the truth that I heard from God.[r] Abraham did not do such things. 41 You are doing the things your own father does."[s]

"We are not illegitimate children," they protested. "The only Father we have is God himself."[t]

The Children of the Devil

42 Jesus said to them, "If God were your Father, you would love me,[u] for I came from God[v] and now am here. I have not come on my own;[w] but he sent me.[x] 43 Why is my language not clear to you? Because you are unable to hear what I say. 44 You belong to your father, the devil,[y] and you want to carry out your father's desire.[z] He was a murderer from the beginning, not holding to the truth, for there is no truth in him. When he lies, he speaks his native language, for he is a liar and the father of lies.[a] 45 Yet because I tell the truth,[b] you do not believe me! 46 Can any of you prove me guilty of sin? If I am telling the truth, why don't you believe me? 47 He who belongs to God hears what God says.[c] The reason you do not hear is that you do not belong to God."

The Claims of Jesus About Himself

48 The Jews answered him, "Aren't we right in saying that you are a Samaritan[d] and demon-possessed?"[e]

49 "I am not possessed by a demon," said Jesus, "but I honour my Father and you dishonour me. 50 I am not seeking glory for myself;[f] but there is one who seeks it, and he is the judge. 51 I tell you the truth, if anyone keeps my word, he will never see death."[g]

52 At this the Jews exclaimed, "Now we know that you are demon-possessed! Abraham died and so did the prophets, yet you say that if anyone keeps your word, he will never taste death. 53 Are you greater than our father Abraham?[h] He died, and so did the prophets. Who do you think you are?"

54 Jesus replied, "If I glorify myself,[i] my glory means nothing. My Father, whom you claim as your God, is the one who glorifies me.[j] 55 Though you do not know him,[k] I know him.[l] If I said I did not, I would be a liar like you, but I do know him and keep his word.[m] 56 Your father Abraham[n] rejoiced at the thought of seeing my day; he saw it[o] and was glad."

57 "You are not yet fifty years old," the Jews said to him, "and you have seen Abraham!"

58 "I tell you the truth," Jesus

8:32 k Ro 8:2; Jas 2:12
8:33 l ver 37,39; Mt 3:9
8:34 m Ro 6:16; 2Pe 2:19
8:35 n Gal 4:30
8:37 o ver 39,40
8:38 p Jn 5:19,30; Jn 14:10,24
8:39 q ver 37; Ro 9:7; Gal 3:7
8:40 r ver 26
8:41 s ver 38,44; t Isa 63:16; Isa 64:8
8:42 u 1Jn 5:1; v Jn 16:27; Jn 17:8; w Jn 7:28; x Jn 3:17
8:44 y 1Jn 3:8; z ver 38,41; a Ge 3:4
8:45 b Jn 18:37
8:47 c Jn 18:37; 1Jn 4:6
8:48 d Mt 10:5; e ver 52; Jn 7:20
8:50 f ver 54; Jn 5:41
8:51 g Jn 11:26
8:53 h Jn 4:12
8:54 i ver 50; j Jn 16:14; Jn 17:1,5
8:55 k ver 19; l Jn 7:28,29; m Jn 15:10
8:56 n ver 37,39; o Mt 13:17; Heb 11:13

b33 Greek *seed*; also in verse 37
c38 Or *presence. Therefore do what you have heard from the Father.*
d39 Some early manuscripts *"If you are Abraham's children," said Jesus, "then*

answered, "before Abraham was
born,[p] I am!"[q] 59At this, they
picked up stones to stone him,[r] but
Jesus hid himself,[s] slipping away
from the temple grounds.

Jesus Heals a Man Born Blind

9 As he went along, he saw a
man blind from birth. 2His disciples asked him, "Rabbi,[a] who
sinned,[b] this man[c] or his parents,[d] that he was born blind?"
3"Neither this man nor his parents sinned," said Jesus, "but this
happened so that the work of God
might be displayed in his life.[e] 4As
long as it is day,[f] we must do the
work of him who sent me. Night is
coming, when no-one can work.
5While I am in the world, I am the
light of the world."[g]
6Having said this, he spat[h] on the
ground, made some mud with the
saliva, and put it on the man's eyes.
7"Go," he told him, "wash in the
Pool of Siloam"[i] (this word means
Sent). So the man went and washed,
and came home seeing.[j]
8His neighbours and those who
had formerly seen him begging
asked, "Isn't this the same man who
used to sit and beg?"[k] 9Some
claimed that he was.

Others said, "No, he only looks
like him."

But he himself insisted, "I am the
man."
10"How then were your eyes
opened?" they demanded.
11He replied, "The man they call
Jesus made some mud and put it on
my eyes. He told me to go to Siloam
and wash. So I went and washed,
and then I could see."[l]
12"Where is this man?" they
asked him.

"I don't know," he said.

The Pharisees Investigate the Healing

13They brought to the Pharisees
the man who had been blind. 14Now
the day on which Jesus had made
the mud and opened the man's
eyes was a Sabbath.[m] 15Therefore
the Pharisees also asked him how
he had received his sight.[n] "He
put mud on my eyes," the man
replied, "and I washed, and now I
see."
16Some of the Pharisees said,
"This man is not from God, for he
does not keep the Sabbath."[o]

But others asked, "How can a sinner do such miraculous signs?" So
they were divided.[p]
17Finally they turned again to the
blind man, "What have you to say
about him? It was your eyes he
opened."

The man replied, "He is a
prophet."[q]
18The Jews[r] still did not believe
that he had been blind and had received his sight until they sent for
the man's parents. 19"Is this your
son?" they asked. "Is this the one
you say was born blind? How is it
that now he can see?"
20"We know he is our son," the
parents answered, "and we know
he was born blind. 21But how he can
see now, or who opened his eyes,
we don't know. Ask him. He is of
age; he will speak for himself."
22His parents said this because
they were afraid of the Jews,[s] for
already the Jews had decided that
anyone who acknowledged that
Jesus was the Christ[a] would be put
out[t] of the synagogue.[u] 23That
was why his parents said, "He is of
age; ask him."[v]
24A second time they summoned
the man who had been blind. "Give
glory to God,"[b][w] they said. "We
know this man is a sinner."[x]
25He replied, "Whether he is a
sinner or not, I don't know. One
thing I do know. I was blind but now
I see!"

a22 Or *Messiah* b24 A solemn charge to tell the truth (see Joshua 7:19)

8:58 p Jn 1:2; Jn 17:5,24; q Ex 3:14
8:59 r Lev 24:16; Jn 10:31; Jn 11:8; s Jn 12:36
9:2 a Mt 23:7; b ver 34; Lk 13:2; Ac 28:4; c Eze 18:20; d Ex 20:5; Job 21:19
9:3 e Jn 11:4
9:4 f Jn 11:9; Jn 12:35
9:5 g Jn 1:4; Jn 8:12; Jn 12:46
9:6 h Mk 7:33; Mk 8:23
9:7 i ver 11; 2Ki 5:10; Lk 13:4; j Isa 35:5; Jn 11:37
9:8 k Ac 3:2,10
9:11 l ver 7
9:14 m Jn 5:9
9:15 n ver 10
9:16 o Mt 12:2; p Jn 6:52; Jn 7:43; Jn 10:19
9:17 q Mt 21:11
9:18 r Jn 1:19
9:22 s Jn 7:13; t ver 34; Lk 6:22; u Jn 12:42; Jn 16:2
9:23 v ver 21
9:24 w Jos 7:19; x ver 16

26Then they asked him, "What did
he do to you? How did he open your
eyes?"
27He answered, "I have told you
already[y] and you did not listen.
Why do you want to hear it again?
Do you want to become his disciples, too?"
28Then they hurled insults at him
and said, "You are this fellow's disciple! We are disciples of Moses![z]
29We know that God spoke to
Moses, but as for this fellow, we
don't even know where he comes
from."[a]
30The man answered, "Now that
is remarkable! You don't know
where he comes from, yet he
opened my eyes. 31We know that
God does not listen to sinners. He
listens to the godly man who does
his will.[b] 32Nobody has ever heard
of opening the eyes of a man born
blind. 33If this man were not from
God,[c] he could do nothing."
34To this they replied, "You were
steeped in sin at birth;[d] how dare
you lecture us!" And they threw
him out.[e]

Spiritual Blindness

35Jesus heard that they had
thrown him out, and when he found
him, he said, "Do you believe in the
Son of Man?"
36"Who is he, sir?" the man asked.
"Tell me so that I may believe in
him."[f]
37Jesus said, "You have now seen
him; in fact, he is the one speaking
with you."[g]
38Then the man said, "Lord, I believe," and he worshipped him.[h]
39Jesus said, "For judgment[i] I
have come into this world,[j] so that
the blind will see[k] and those who
see will become blind."[l]
40Some Pharisees who were with
him heard him say this and asked,
"What? Are we blind too?"[m]
41Jesus said, "If you were blind,
you would not be guilty of sin; but
now that you claim you can see,
your guilt remains.[n]

The Shepherd and His Flock

10 "I tell you the truth, the
man who does not enter the
sheep pen by the gate, but climbs in
by some other way, is a thief and a
robber. 2The man who enters by
the gate is the shepherd of his
sheep.[a] 3The watchman opens the
gate for him, and the sheep listen to
his voice.[b] He calls his own sheep
by name and leads them out. 4When
he has brought out all his own, he
goes on ahead of them, and his
sheep follow him because they
know his voice. 5But they will
never follow a stranger; in fact,
they will run away from him because they do not recognise a stranger's voice." 6Jesus used this
figure of speech,[c] but they did not
understand what he was telling
them.
7Therefore Jesus said again, "I
tell you the truth, I am the gate for
the sheep. 8All who ever came before me[d] were thieves and robbers, but the sheep did not listen to
them. 9I am the gate; whoever enters through me will be saved.[a] He
will come in and go out, and find
pasture. 10The thief comes only to
steal and kill and destroy; I have
come that they may have life, and
have it to the full.
11"I am the good shepherd.[e] The
good shepherd lays down his life
for the sheep.[f] 12The hired hand is
not the shepherd who owns the
sheep. So when he sees the wolf
coming, he abandons the sheep and
runs away.[g] Then the wolf attacks
the flock and scatters it. 13The man
runs away because he is a hired
hand and cares nothing for the
sheep.
14"I am the good shepherd;[h] I
know my sheep[i] and my sheep
know me—15just as the Father
knows me and I know the
Father[j]—and I lay down my life
for the sheep. 16I have other

a9 Or *kept safe*

9:27 y ver 15
9:28 z Jn 5:45
9:29 a Jn 8:14
9:31 b Ge 18:23-32; Ps 34:15,16; Ps 66:18; Ps 145:19,20; Pr 15:29; Isa 1:15; Isa 59:1,2; Jn 15:7; Jas 5:16-18; 1Jn 5:14,15
9:33 c ver 16; Jn 3:2
9:34 d ver 2; e ver 22,35; Isa 66:5
9:36 f Ro 10:14
9:37 g Jn 4:26
9:38 h Mt 28:9
9:39 i Jn 5:22; j Jn 3:19; k Lk 4:18; l Mt 13:13
9:40 m Ro 2:19
9:41 n Jn 15:22,24
10:2 a ver 11,14
10:3 b ver 4,5,14,16,27
10:6 c Jn 16:25
10:8 d Jer 23:1,2
10:11 e ver 14; Isa 40:11; Eze 34:11-16,23; Heb 13:20; 1Pe 5:4; Rev 7:17; f Jn 15:13; 1Jn 3:16
10:12 g Zec 11:16,17
10:14 h ver 11; i ver 27
10:15 j Mt 11:27

sheep[k] that are not of this sheep
pen. I must bring them also. They
too will listen to my voice, and
there shall be one flock[l] and one
shepherd.[m] 17The reason my
Father loves me is that I lay down
my life[n]—only to take it up again.
18No-one takes it from me, but I lay
it down of my own accord.[o] I have
authority to lay it down and authority to take it up again. This
command I received from my
Father."[p]
19At these words the Jews were
again divided.[q] 20Many of them
said, "He is demon-possessed[r] and
raving mad.[s] Why listen to him?"
21But others said, "These are not
the sayings of a man possessed by
a demon.[t] Can a demon open the
eyes of the blind?"[u]

The Unbelief of the Jews

22Then came the Feast of Dedication[b] at Jerusalem. It was winter,
23and Jesus was in the temple area
walking in Solomon's Colonnade.[v]
24The Jews[w] gathered round him,
saying, "How long will you keep us
in suspense? If you are the Christ,[c]
tell us plainly."[x]
25Jesus answered, "I did tell
you,[y] but you do not believe. The
miracles I do in my Father's name
speak for me,[z] 26but you do not
believe because you are not my
sheep.[a] 27My sheep listen to my
voice; I know them,[b] and they follow me.[c] 28I give them eternal life,
and they shall never perish; no-one
can snatch them out of my hand.[d]
29My Father, who has given them to
me,[e] is greater than all;[d][f] no-one
can snatch them out of my Father's
hand. 30I and the Father are one."[g]
31Again the Jews picked up
stones to stone him,[h] 32but Jesus
said to them, "I have shown you
many great miracles from the
Father. For which of these do you
stone me?"
33"We are not stoning you for any
of these," replied the Jews, "but for
blasphemy, because you, a mere
man, claim to be God."[i]
34Jesus answered them, "Is it not
written in your Law,[j] 'I have said
you are gods'[e]?[k] 35If he called
them 'gods', to whom the word of
God came—and the Scripture cannot be broken—36what about the
one whom the Father set apart[l] as
his very own[m] and sent into the
world?[n] Why then do you accuse
me of blasphemy because I said, 'I
am God's Son'?[o] 37Do not believe
me unless I do what my Father
does.[p] 38But if I do it, even though
you do not believe me, believe the
miracles, that you may know and
understand that the Father is in me,
and I in the Father."[q] 39Again they
tried to seize him,[r] but he escaped
their grasp.[s]
40Then Jesus went back across
the Jordan[t] to the place where
John had been baptising in the
early days. Here he stayed 41and
many people came to him. They
said, "Though John never performed a miraculous sign,[u] all that
John said about this man was
true."[v] 42And in that place many
believed in Jesus.[w]

The Death of Lazarus

11 Now a man named Lazarus
was sick. He was from
Bethany,[a] the village of Mary and
her sister Martha.[b] 2This Mary,
whose brother Lazarus now lay
sick, was the same one who poured
perfume on the Lord and wiped his
feet with her hair.[c] 3So the sisters
sent word to Jesus, "Lord, the one
you love[d] is sick."
4When he heard this, Jesus said,
"This sickness will not end in
death. No, it is for God's glory[e] so
that God's Son may be glorified
through it." 5Jesus loved Martha

10:16 k Isa 56:8 l Jn 11:52 Eph 2:11-19 m Eze 37:24 1Pe 2:25
10:17 n ver 11,15,18
10:18 o Mt 26:53 p Jn 15:10 Php 2:8 Heb 5:8
10:19 q Jn 7:43 Jn 9:16
10:20 r Jn 7:20 s Mk 3:21
10:21 t Mt 4:24 u Ex 4:11 Jn 9:32,33
10:23 v Ac 3:11 Ac 5:12
10:24 w Jn 1:19 x Jn 16:25,29
10:25 y Jn 8:58 z Jn 5:36
10:26 a Jn 8:47
10:27 b ver 14 c ver 4
10:28 d Jn 6:39
10:29 e Jn 17:2,6,24 f Jn 14:28
10:30 g Jn 17:21-23
10:31 h Jn 8:59
10:33 i Lev 24:16 Jn 5:18
10:34 j Jn 8:17 Ro 3:19 k Ps 82:6
10:36 l Jer 1:5 m Jn 6:69 n Jn 3:17 o Jn 5:17,18
10:37 p ver 25 Jn 15:24
10:38 q Jn 14:10,11,20 Jn 17:21
10:39 r Jn 7:30 s Lk 4:30 Jn 8:59
10:40 t Jn 1:28
10:41 u Jn 2:11 Jn 3:30 v Jn 1:26,27,30,34
10:42 w Jn 7:31

11:1 a Mt 21:17 b Lk 10:38 **11:2** c Mk 14:3 Lk 7:38 Jn 12:3
11:3 d ver 5,36 **11:4** e ver 40 Jn 9:3

b22 That is, Hanukkah c24 Or *Messiah*
d29 Many early manuscripts *What my Father has given me is greater than all* e34 Psalm 82:6

and her sister and Lazarus. 6Yet
when he heard that Lazarus was
sick, he stayed where he was two
more days.
7Then he said to his disciples,
"Let us go back to Judea."[f]
8"But Rabbi,"[g] they said, "a
short while ago the Jews tried to
stone you,[h] and yet you are going
back there?"
9Jesus answered, "Are there not
twelve hours of daylight? A man
who walks by day will not stumble,
for he sees by this world's light.[i]
10It is when he walks by night that
he stumbles, for he has no light."
11After he had said this, he went
on to tell them, "Our friend[j] Lazarus has fallen asleep;[k] but I am going there to wake him up."
12His disciples replied, "Lord, if
he sleeps, he will get better."
13Jesus had been speaking of his
death, but his disciples thought he
meant natural sleep.[l]
14So then he told them plainly,
"Lazarus is dead, 15and for your
sake I am glad I was not there, so
that you may believe. But let us go
to him."
16Then Thomas[m] (called Didymus) said to the rest of the disciples, "Let us also go, that we may
die with him."

Jesus Comforts the Sisters

17On his arrival, Jesus found that
Lazarus had already been in the
tomb for four days.[n] 18Bethany[o]
was less than two miles[a] from
Jerusalem, 19and many Jews had
come to Martha and Mary to comfort them in the loss of their
brother.[p] 20When Martha heard
that Jesus was coming, she went
out to meet him, but Mary stayed at
home.[q]
21"Lord," Martha said to Jesus,
"if you had been here, my brother
would not have died.[r] 22But I know
that even now God will give you
whatever you ask."[s]
23Jesus said to her, "Your brother
will rise again."
24Martha answered, "I know he
will rise again in the resurrection[t]
at the last day."
25Jesus said to her, "I am the resurrection and the life.[u] He who believes in me will live, even though
he dies; 26and whoever lives and believes in me will never die. Do you
believe this?"
27"Yes, Lord," she told him, "I believe that you are the Christ,[b][v] the
Son of God,[w] who was to come into
the world."[x]
28And after she had said this, she
went back and called her sister
Mary aside. "The Teacher[y] is
here," she said, "and is asking for
you." 29When Mary heard this, she
got up quickly and went to him.
30Now Jesus had not yet entered
the village, but was still at the place
where Martha had met him.[z]
31When the Jews who had been with
Mary in the house, comforting
her,[a] noticed how quickly she got
up and went out, they followed her,
supposing she was going to the
tomb to mourn there.
32When Mary reached the place
where Jesus was and saw him, she
fell at his feet and said, "Lord, if
you had been here, my brother
would not have died."[b]
33When Jesus saw her weeping,
and the Jews who had come along
with her also weeping, he was
deeply moved[c] in spirit and troubled.[d] 34"Where have you laid
him?" he asked.
"Come and see, Lord," they replied.
35Jesus wept.[e]
36Then the Jews said, "See how
he loved him!"[f]
37But some of them said, "Could
not he who opened the eyes of the
blind man[g] have kept this man
from dying?"[h]

11:7 *f* Jn 10:40
11:8 *g* Mt 23:7 *h* Jn 8:59 Jn 10:31
11:9 *i* Jn 9:4 Jn 12:35
11:11 *j* ver 3 *k* Ac 7:60
11:13 *l* Mt 9:24
11:16 *m* Mt 10:3 Jn 14:5 Jn 20:24-28 Jn 21:2 Ac 1:13
11:17 *n* ver 6,39
11:18 *o* ver 1
11:19 *p* ver 31 Job 2:11
11:20 *q* Lk 10:38-42
11:21 *r* ver 32,37
11:22 *s* ver 41,42 Jn 9:31
11:24 *t* Da 12:2 Jn 5:28,29 Ac 24:15
11:25 *u* Jn 1:4
11:27 *v* Lk 2:11 *w* Mt 16:16 *x* Jn 6:14
11:28 *y* Mt 26:18 Jn 13:13
11:30 *z* ver 20
11:31 *a* ver 19
11:32 *b* ver 21
11:33 *c* ver 38 *d* Jn 12:27
11:35 *e* Lk 19:41
11:36 *f* ver 3
11:37 *g* Jn 9:6,7 *h* ver 21,32

a18 Greek *fifteen stadia* (about 3 kilometres)
b27 Or *Messiah*

Jesus Raises Lazarus From the Dead

[38]Jesus, once more deeply moved,[i] came to the tomb. It was a cave with a stone laid across the entrance.[j] [39]"Take away the stone," he said.

"But, Lord," said Martha, the sister of the dead man, "by this time there is a bad odour, for he has been there four days."[k]

[40]Then Jesus said, "Did I not tell you that if you believed,[l] you would see the glory of God?"[m]

[41]So they took away the stone. Then Jesus looked up[n] and said, "Father,[o] I thank you that you have heard me. [42]I knew that you always hear me, but I said this for the benefit of the people standing here,[p] that they may believe that you sent me."[q]

[43]When he had said this, Jesus called in a loud voice, "Lazarus, come out!"[r] [44]The dead man came out, his hands and feet wrapped with strips of linen,[s] and a cloth around his face.[t]

Jesus said to them, "Take off the grave clothes and let him go."

The Plot to Kill Jesus

[45]Therefore many of the Jews who had come to visit Mary,[u] and had seen what Jesus did,[v] put their faith in him.[w] [46]But some of them went to the Pharisees and told them what Jesus had done. [47]Then the chief priests and the Pharisees[x] called a meeting[y] of the Sanhedrin.[z]

"What are we accomplishing?" they asked. "Here is this man performing many miraculous signs.[a] [48]If we let him go on like this, everyone will believe in him, and then the Romans will come and take away both our place[c] and our nation."

[49]Then one of them, named Caiaphas,[b] who was high priest that year,[c] spoke up, "You know nothing at all! [50]You do not realise that it is better for you that one man die for the people than that the whole nation perish."[d]

[51]He did not say this on his own, but as high priest that year he prophesied that Jesus would die for the Jewish nation, [52]and not only for that nation but also for the scattered children of God, to bring them together and make them one.[e] [53]So from that day on they plotted to take his life.[f]

[54]Therefore Jesus no longer moved about publicly among the Jews.[g] Instead he withdrew to a region near the desert, to a village called Ephraim, where he stayed with his disciples.

[55]When it was almost time for the Jewish Passover,[h] many went up from the country to Jerusalem for their ceremonial cleansing[i] before the Passover. [56]They kept looking for Jesus,[j] and as they stood in the temple area they asked one another, "What do you think? Isn't he coming to the Feast at all?" [57]But the chief priests and Pharisees had given orders that if anyone found out where Jesus was, he should report it so that they might arrest him.

Jesus Anointed at Bethany

12:1–8Ref Mt 26:6–13; Mk 14:3–9; Lk 7:37–39

12 Six days before the Passover,[a] Jesus arrived at Bethany,[b] where Lazarus lived, whom Jesus had raised from the dead. [2]Here a dinner was given in Jesus' honour. Martha served,[c] while Lazarus was among those reclining at the table with him. [3]Then Mary took about a pint[a] of pure nard, an expensive perfume;[d] she poured it on Jesus' feet and wiped his feet with her hair.[e] And the house was filled with the fragrance of the perfume.

[4]But one of his disciples, Judas Iscariot, who was later to betray

[c]48 Or *temple*

[a]3 Greek *a litra* (probably about 0.5 litre)

11:38 *i* ver 33 *j* Mt 27:60 Lk 24:2 Jn 20:1
11:39 *k* ver 17
11:40 *l* ver 23-25 *m* ver 4
11:41 *n* Jn 17:1 *o* Mt 11:25
11:42 *p* Jn 12:30 *q* Jn 3:17
11:43 *r* Lk 7:14
11:44 *s* Jn 19:40 *t* Jn 20:7
11:45 *u* ver 19 *v* Jn 2:23 *w* Ex 14:31 Jn 7:31
11:47 *x* ver 57 *y* Mt 26:3 *z* Mt 5:22 *a* Jn 2:11
11:49 *b* Mt 26:3 *c* ver 51 Jn 18:13,14
11:50 *d* Jn 18:14
11:52 *e* Isa 49:6 Jn 10:16
11:53 *f* Mt 12:14
11:54 *g* Jn 7:1
11:55 *h* Ex 12:13,23, 27 Mt 26:1,2 Mk 14:1 Jn 13:1 *i* 2Ch 30:17,18
11:56 *j* Jn 7:11
12:1 *a* Jn 11:55 *b* Mt 21:17
12:2 *c* Lk 10:38-42
12:3 *d* Mk 14:3 *e* Jn 11:2

him,[f] objected, 5"Why wasn't this
perfume sold and the money given
to the poor? It was worth a year's
wages."[b] 6He did not say this because he cared about the poor but
because he was a thief; as keeper of
the money bag,[g] he used to help
himself to what was put into it.
7"Leave her alone," Jesus replied. "⌞It was intended⌟ that she
should save this perfume for the
day of my burial.[h] 8You will always have the poor among you,[i]
but you will not always have me."
9Meanwhile a large crowd of
Jews found out that Jesus was
there and came, not only because of
him but also to see Lazarus, whom
he had raised from the dead.[j] 10So
the chief priests made plans to kill
Lazarus as well, 11for on account of
him[k] many of the Jews were going
over to Jesus and putting their
faith in him.[l]

The Triumphal Entry

12:12–15pp Mt 21:4–9; Mk 11:7–10; Lk 19:35–38

12The next day the great crowd
that had come for the Feast heard
that Jesus was on his way to Jerusalem. 13They took palm branches
and went out to meet him, shouting,

"Hosanna!"[c]

"Blessed is he who comes in the
name of the Lord!"[d][m]

"Blessed is the King of Israel!"[n]

14Jesus found a young donkey and
sat upon it, as it is written,

15"Do not be afraid, O Daughter
of Zion;
see, your king is coming,
seated on a donkey's colt."[e][o]

16At first his disciples did not
understand all this.[p] Only after
Jesus was glorified[q] did they realise that these things had been written about him and that they had
done these things to him.
17Now the crowd that was with
him[r] when he called Lazarus from
the tomb and raised him from the
dead continued to spread the word.
18Many people, because they had
heard that he had given this miraculous sign,[s] went out to meet
him. 19So the Pharisees said to one
another, "See, this is getting us nowhere. Look how the whole world
has gone after him!"[t]

Jesus Predicts His Death

20Now there were some Greeks[u]
among those who went up to worship at the Feast. 21They came to
Philip, who was from Bethsaida[v]
in Galilee, with a request. "Sir,"
they said, "we would like to see
Jesus." 22Philip went to tell Andrew; Andrew and Philip in turn
told Jesus.
23Jesus replied, "The hour has
come for the Son of Man to be glorified.[w] 24I tell you the truth, unless
a grain of wheat falls to the ground
and dies,[x] it remains only a single
seed. But if it dies, it produces
many seeds. 25The man who loves
his life will lose it, while the man
who hates his life in this world will
keep it[y] for eternal life. 26Whoever
serves me must follow me; and
where I am, my servant also will
be.[z] My Father will honour the one
who serves me.
27"Now my heart is troubled,[a]
and what shall I say? 'Father,[b]
save me from this hour'?[c] No, it
was for this very reason I came to
this hour. 28Father, glorify your
name!"
Then a voice came from
heaven,[d] "I have glorified it, and
will glorify it again." 29The crowd
that was there and heard it said it
had thundered; others said an
angel had spoken to him.
30Jesus said, "This voice was for
your benefit,[e] not mine. 31Now is

12:4 f Mt 10:4
12:6 g Jn 13:29
12:7 h Jn 19:40
12:8 i Dt 15:11
12:9 j Jn 11:43,44
12:11 k ver 17,18; Jn 11:45; l Jn 7:31
12:13 m Ps 118:25,26; n Jn 1:49
12:15 o Zec 9:9
12:16 p Mk 9:32; q Jn 2:22; Jn 7:39; Jn 14:26
12:17 r Jn 11:42
12:18 s ver 11
12:19 t Jn 11:47,48
12:20 u Jn 7:35; Ac 11:20
12:21 v Mt 11:21; Jn 1:44
12:23 w Jn 13:32; Jn 17:1
12:24 x 1Co 15:36
12:25 y Mt 10:39; Mk 8:35; Lk 14:26
12:26 z Jn 14:3; Jn 17:24; 2Co 5:8; 1Th 4:17
12:27 a Mt 26:38,39; Jn 11:33,38; Jn 13:21; b Mt 11:25; c ver 23
12:28 d Mt 3:17
12:30 e Jn 11:42

b5 Greek *three hundred denarii* c13 A Hebrew expression meaning "Save!" which became an exclamation of praise d13 Psalm 118:25,26 e15 Zech. 9:9

the time for judgment on this
world;[f] now the prince of this
world[g] will be driven out. 32But I,
when I am lifted up from the
earth,[h] will draw all men to myself."[i] 33He said this to show the
kind of death he was going to die.[j]
34The crowd spoke up, "We have
heard from the Law that the
Christ[f] will remain for ever,[k] so
how can you say, 'The Son of Man[l]
must be lifted up'?[m] Who is this
'Son of Man'?"
35Then Jesus told them, "You are
going to have the light[n] just a little
while longer. Walk while you have
the light,[o] before darkness overtakes you.[p] The man who walks in
the dark does not know where he is
going. 36Put your trust in the light
while you have it, so that you may
become sons of light."[q] When he
had finished speaking, Jesus left
and hid himself from them.[r]

The Jews Continue in Their Unbelief

37Even after Jesus had done all
these miraculous signs[s] in their
presence, they still would not believe in him. 38This was to fulfil the
word of Isaiah the prophet:

"Lord, who has believed our
message
and to whom has the arm of
the Lord been
revealed?"[g][t]

39For this reason they could not
believe, because, as Isaiah says
elsewhere:

40"He has blinded their eyes
and deadened their hearts,
so they can neither see with
their eyes,
nor understand with their
hearts,
nor turn—and I would heal
them."[h][u]

41Isaiah said this because he saw
Jesus' glory[v] and spoke about
him.[w]
42Yet at the same time many even
among the leaders believed in
him.[x] But because of the Pharisees[y] they would not confess their
faith for fear they would be put out
of the synagogue;[z] 43for they loved
praise from men more than praise
from God.[a]
44Then Jesus cried out, "When a
man believes in me, he does not believe in me only, but in the one who
sent me.[b] 45When he looks at me,
he sees the one who sent me.[c] 46I
have come into the world as a
light,[d] so that no-one who believes
in me should stay in darkness.
47"As for the person who hears
my words but does not keep them,
I do not judge him. For I did not
come to judge the world, but to
save it.[e] 48There is a judge for the
one who rejects me and does not accept my words; that very word
which I spoke will condemn him[f]
at the last day. 49For I did not speak
of my own accord, but the Father
who sent me commanded me[g]
what to say and how to say it. 50I
know that his command leads to
eternal life. So whatever I say is
just what the Father has told me to
say."

Jesus Washes His Disciples' Feet

13 It was just before the Passover Feast.[a] Jesus knew
that the time had come[b] for him to
leave this world and go to the
Father.[c] Having loved his own
who were in the world, he now
showed them the full extent of his
love.[a]
2The evening meal was being
served, and the devil had already
prompted Judas Iscariot, son of
Simon, to betray Jesus. 3Jesus
knew that the Father had put all
things under his power,[d] and that
he had come from God[e] and was
returning to God; 4so he got up

12:31 f Jn 16:11 g Jn 14:30 Jn 16:11 2Co 4:4 Eph 2:2 1Jn 4:4
12:32 h ver 34 Jn 3:14 Jn 8:28 i Jn 6:44
12:33 j Jn 18:32
12:34 k Ps 110:4 Isa 9:7 Eze 37:25 Da 7:14 l Mt 8:20 m Jn 3:14
12:35 n ver 46 o Eph 5:8 p 1Jn 2:11
12:36 q Lk 16:8 r Jn 8:59
12:37 s Jn 2:11
12:38 t Isa 53:1 Ro 10:16
12:40 u Isa 6:10 Mt 13:13,15
12:41 v Isa 6:1-4 w Lk 24:27
12:42 x ver 11 Jn 7:48 y Jn 7:13 z Jn 9:22
12:43 a Jn 5:44
12:44 b Mt 10:40 Jn 5:24
12:45 c Jn 14:9
12:46 d Jn 1:4 Jn 3:19 Jn 8:12 Jn 9:5
12:47 e Jn 3:17
12:48 f Jn 5:45
12:49 g Jn 14:31
13:1 a Jn 11:55 b Jn 12:23 c Jn 16:28
13:3 d Mt 28:18 e Jn 8:42 Jn 16:27,28, 30

f 34 Or *Messiah* g 38 Isaiah 53:1
h 40 Isaiah 6:10 a 1 Or *he loved them to the last*

from the meal, took off his outer
clothing, and wrapped a towel
round his waist. [5]After that, he
poured water into a basin and began to wash his disciples' feet,[f]
drying them with the towel that
was wrapped round him.
[6]He came to Simon Peter, who
said to him, "Lord, are you going to
wash my feet?"
[7]Jesus replied, "You do not realise now what I am doing, but later
you will understand."[g]
[8]"No," said Peter, "you shall
never wash my feet."
Jesus answered, "Unless I wash
you, you have no part with me."
[9]"Then, Lord," Simon Peter replied, "not just my feet but my
hands and my head as well!"
[10]Jesus answered, "A person who
has had a bath needs only to wash
his feet; his whole body is clean.
And you are clean,[h] though not
every one of you." [11]For he knew
who was going to betray him, and
that was why he said not every one
was clean.
[12]When he had finished washing
their feet, he put on his clothes and
returned to his place. "Do you
understand what I have done for
you?" he asked them. [13]"You call
me 'Teacher'[i] and 'Lord',[j] and
rightly so, for that is what I am.
[14]Now that I, your Lord and
Teacher, have washed your feet,
you also should wash one another's
feet.[k] [15]I have set you an example
that you should do as I have done
for you.[l] [16]I tell you the truth, no
servant is greater than his master,[m] nor is a messenger greater
than the one who sent him. [17]Now
that you know these things, you will
be blessed if you do them.[n]

Jesus Predicts His Betrayal

[18]"I am not referring to all of
you;[o] I know those I have chosen.[p]
But this is to fulfil the scripture:
'He who shares my bread[q] has
lifted up his heel[r] against me.'[b][s]

13:5 f Lk 7:44
13:7 g ver 12
13:10 h Jn 15:3
13:13 i Jn 11:28 j Lk 6:46 1Co 12:3 Php 2:11
13:14 k 1Pe 5:5
13:15 l Mt 11:29
13:16 m Mt 10:24 Lk 6:40 Jn 15:20
13:17 n Mt 7:24,25 Lk 11:28 Jas 1:25
13:18 o ver 10 p Jn 15:16,19 q Mt 26:23 r Jn 6:70 s Ps 41:9
13:19 t Jn 14:29 Jn 16:4 u Jn 8:24
13:20 v Mt 10:40 Lk 10:16
13:21 w Jn 12:27 x Mt 26:21
13:23 y Jn 19:26 Jn 20:2 Jn 21:7,20
13:25 z Jn 21:20
13:27 a Lk 22:3
13:29 b Jn 12:6
13:30 c Lk 22:53
13:31 d Jn 7:39 e Jn 14:13 Jn 17:4 1Pe 4:11
13:32 f Jn 17:1

[19]"I am telling you now before it
happens, so that when it does happen you will believe[t] that I am
He.[u] [20]I tell you the truth, whoever
accepts anyone I send accepts me;
and whoever accepts me accepts
the one who sent me."[v]
[21]After he had said this, Jesus
was troubled in spirit[w] and testified, "I tell you the truth, one of you
is going to betray me."[x]
[22]His disciples stared at one another, at a loss to know which of
them he meant. [23]One of them, the
disciple whom Jesus loved,[y] was
reclining next to him. [24]Simon
Peter motioned to this disciple and
said, "Ask him which one he
means."
[25]Leaning back against Jesus, he
asked him, "Lord, who is it?"[z]
[26]Jesus answered, "It is the one to
whom I will give this piece of bread
when I have dipped it in the dish."
Then, dipping the piece of bread,
he gave it to Judas Iscariot, son of
Simon. [27]As soon as Judas took the
bread, Satan entered into him.[a]
"What you are about to do, do
quickly," Jesus told him, [28]but no-
one at the meal understood why
Jesus said this to him. [29]Since Judas had charge of the money,[b]
some thought Jesus was telling him
to buy what was needed for the
Feast, or to give something to the
poor. [30]As soon as Judas had taken
the bread, he went out. And it was
night.[c]

Jesus Predicts Peter's Denial

13:37,38pp Mt 26:33–35; Mk 14:29–31; Lk 22:33,34

[31]When he was gone, Jesus said,
"Now is the Son of Man glorified[d]
and God is glorified in him.[e] [32]If
God is glorified in him,[c] God will
glorify the Son in himself,[f] and
will glorify him at once.
[33]"My children, I will be with you
only a little longer. You will look
for me, and just as I told the Jews,

[b]18 Psalm 41:9 [c]32 Many early manuscripts do not have *If God is glorified in him.*

so I tell you now: Where I am going, you cannot come.[g]

34"A new command[h] I give you: Love one another.[i] As I have loved you, so you must love one another.[j] 35By this all men will know that you are my disciples, if you love one another."[k]

36Simon Peter asked him, "Lord, where are you going?"

Jesus replied, "Where I am going, you cannot follow now,[l] but you will follow later."[m]

37Peter asked, "Lord, why can't I follow you now? I will lay down my life for you."

38Then Jesus answered, "Will you really lay down your life for me? I tell you the truth, before the cock crows, you will disown me three times![n]

Jesus Comforts His Disciples

14 "Do not let your hearts be troubled.[a] Trust in God;[a] trust also in me. 2In my Father's house are many rooms; if it were not so, I would have told you. I am going there[b] to prepare a place for you. 3And if I go and prepare a place for you, I will come back and take you to be with me that you also may be where I am.[c] 4You know the way to the place where I am going."

Jesus the Way to the Father

5Thomas[d] said to him, "Lord, we don't know where you are going, so how can we know the way?"

6Jesus answered, "I am the way[e] and the truth and the life.[f] No-one comes to the Father except through me. 7If you really knew me, you would know[b] my Father as well.[g] From now on, you do know him and have seen him."

8Philip said, "Lord, show us the Father and that will be enough for us."

9Jesus answered: "Don't you know me, Philip, even after I have been among you such a long time? Anyone who has seen me has seen the Father.[h] How can you say, 'Show us the Father'? 10Don't you believe that I am in the Father, and that the Father is in me?[i] The words I say to you are not just my own.[j] Rather, it is the Father, living in me, who is doing his work. 11Believe me when I say that I am in the Father and the Father is in me; or at least believe on the evidence of the miracles themselves.[k] 12I tell you the truth, anyone who has faith[l] in me will do what I have been doing.[m] He will do even greater things than these, because I am going to the Father. 13And I will do whatever you ask[n] in my name, so that the Son may bring glory to the Father. 14You may ask me for anything in my name, and I will do it.

Jesus Promises the Holy Spirit

15"If you love me, you will obey what I command.[o] 16And I will ask the Father, and he will give you another Counsellor[p] to be with you for ever—17the Spirit of truth.[q] The world cannot accept him,[r] because it neither sees him nor knows him. But you know him, for he lives with you and will be[c] in you. 18I will not leave you as orphans; I will come to you.[s] 19Before long, the world will not see me any more, but you will see me.[t] Because I live, you also will live.[u] 20On that day you will realise that I am in my Father,[v] and you are in me, and I am in you. 21Whoever has my commands and obeys them, he is the one who loves me.[w] He who loves me will be loved by my Father,[x] and I too will love him and show myself to him."

22Then Judas[y] (not Judas Iscariot) said, "But, Lord, why do you intend to show yourself to us and not to the world?"[z]

13:33 g Jn 7:33,34
13:34 h 1Jn 2:7-11; 1Jn 3:11; i Lev 19:18; 1Th 4:9; 1Pe 1:22; j Jn 15:12; Eph 5:2; 1Jn 4:10,11
13:35 k 1Jn 3:14; 1Jn 4:20
13:36 l ver 33; Jn 14:2; m Jn 21:18,19; 2Pe 1:14
13:38 n Jn 18:27
14:1 a ver 27
14:2 b Jn 13:33,36
14:3 c Jn 12:26
14:5 d Jn 11:16
14:6 e Jn 10:9; f Jn 11:25
14:7 g Jn 8:19
14:9 h Jn 12:45; Col 1:15; Heb 1:3
14:10 i Jn 10:38; j Jn 5:19
14:11 k Jn 5:36; Jn 10:38
14:12 l Mt 21:21; m Lk 10:17
14:13 n Mt 7:7
14:15 o ver 21,23; Jn 15:10; 1Jn 5:3
14:16 p Jn 15:26; Jn 16:7
14:17 q Jn 15:26; Jn 16:13; 1Jn 4:6; r 1Co 2:14
14:18 s ver 3,28
14:19 t Jn 7:33,34; Jn 16:16; u Jn 6:57
14:20 v Jn 10:38
14:21 w 1Jn 5:3; x 1Jn 2:5
14:22 y Lk 6:16; Ac 1:13; z Ac 10:41

a1 Or *You trust in God* b7 Some early manuscripts *If you really have known me, you will know* c17 Some early manuscripts *and is*

23 Jesus replied, "If anyone loves
me, he will obey my teaching.[a] My
Father will love him, and we will
come to him and make our home
with him.[b] 24 He who does not love
me will not obey my teaching.
These words you hear are not my
own; they belong to the Father who
sent me.[c]

25 "All this I have spoken while
still with you. 26 But the Counsellor,[d] the Holy Spirit, whom the
Father will send in my name,[e] will
teach you all things[f] and will remind you of everything I have said
to you.[g] 27 Peace I leave with you;
my peace I give you.[h] I do not give
to you as the world gives. Do not let
your hearts be troubled and do not
be afraid.

28 "You heard me say, 'I am going
away and I am coming back to
you.'[i] If you loved me, you would
be glad that I am going to the
Father,[j] for the Father is greater
than I.[k] 29 I have told you now before it happens, so that when it does
happen you will believe.[l] 30 I will
not speak with you much longer,
for the prince of this world[m] is
coming. He has no hold on me, 31 but
the world must learn that I love the
Father and that I do exactly what
my Father has commanded me.[n]

"Come now; let us leave.

The Vine and the Branches

15 "I am the true vine,[a] and
my Father is the gardener.
2 He cuts off every branch in me
that bears no fruit, while every
branch that does bear fruit he
prunes[a] so that it will be even
more fruitful. 3 You are already
clean because of the word I have
spoken to you.[b] 4 Remain in me,
and I will remain in you.[c] No
branch can bear fruit by itself; it
must remain in the vine. Neither
can you bear fruit unless you remain in me.

5 "I am the vine; you are the
branches. If a man remains in me
and I in him, he will bear much
fruit;[d] apart from me you can do
nothing. 6 If anyone does not remain
in me, he is like a branch that is
thrown away and withers; such
branches are picked up, thrown
into the fire and burned.[e] 7 If you
remain in me and my words remain
in you, ask whatever you wish,
and it will be given you.[f] 8 This is to
my Father's glory,[g] that you bear
much fruit, showing yourselves to
be my disciples.[h]

9 "As the Father has loved me,[i]
so have I loved you. Now remain in
my love. 10 If you obey my commands,[j] you will remain in my
love, just as I have obeyed my
Father's commands and remain in
his love. 11 I have told you this so
that my joy may be in you and that
your joy may be complete.[k] 12 My
command is this: Love each other
as I have loved you.[l] 13 Greater
love has no-one than this, that he
lay down his life for his friends.[m]
14 You are my friends[n] if you do
what I command.[o] 15 I no longer
call you servants, because a servant does not know his master's
business. Instead, I have called you
friends, for everything that I
learned from my Father I have
made known to you.[p] 16 You did not
choose me, but I chose you and appointed you[q] to go and bear fruit—
fruit that will last. Then the Father
will give you whatever you ask in
my name. 17 This is my command:
Love each other.[r]

The World Hates the Disciples

18 "If the world hates you,[s] keep
in mind that it hated me first. 19 If
you belonged to the world, it would
love you as its own. As it is, you do
not belong to the world, but I have
chosen you[t] out of the world. That
is why the world hates you.[u] 20 Remember the words I spoke to you:
'No servant is greater than his

14:23 a ver 15 b 1Jn 2:24 Rev 3:20 **14:24** c Jn 7:16 **14:26** d Jn 15:26 Jn 16:7 e Ac 2:33 f Jn 16:13 1Jn 2:20,27 g Jn 2:22 **14:27** h Jn 16:33 Php 4:7 Col 3:15 **14:28** i ver 2-4,18 j Jn 5:18 k Jn 10:29 Php 2:6 **14:29** l Jn 13:19 Jn 16:4 **14:30** m Jn 12:31 **14:31** n Jn 10:18 Jn 12:49 **15:1** a Isa 5:1-7 **15:3** b Jn 13:10 Jn 17:17 Eph 5:26 **15:4** c Jn 6:56 1Jn 2:6 **15:5** d ver 16 **15:6** e ver 2 **15:7** f Mt 7:7 **15:8** g Mt 5:16 h Jn 8:31 **15:9** i Jn 17:23,24, 26 **15:10** j Jn 14:15 **15:11** k Jn 17:13 **15:12** l Jn 13:34 **15:13** m Jn 10:11 Ro 5:7,8 **15:14** n Lk 12:4 o Mt 12:50 **15:15** p Jn 8:26 **15:16** q Jn 6:70 Jn 13:18 **15:17** r ver 12 **15:18** s 1Jn 3:13 **15:19** t ver 16 u Jn 17:14

a2 The Greek for *prunes* also means *cleans*.

master.'[b][v] If they persecuted me,
they will persecute you also.[w] If
they obeyed my teaching, they will
obey yours also. 21They will treat
you this way because of my name,[x]
for they do not know the One who
sent me.[y] 22If I had not come and
spoken to them, they would not be
guilty of sin. Now, however, they
have no excuse for their sin.[z] 23He
who hates me hates my Father as
well. 24If I had not done among
them what no-one else did,[a] they
would not be guilty of sin. But now
they have seen these miracles, and
yet they have hated both me and
my Father. 25But this is to fulfil
what is written in their Law: 'They
hated me without reason.'[c][b]

26"When the Counsellor[c] comes,
whom I will send to you from the
Father,[d] the Spirit of truth[e] who
goes out from the Father, he will
testify about me.[f] 27And you also
must testify,[g] for you have been
with me from the beginning.[h]

16 "All this[a] I have told you
so that you will not go
astray.[b] 2They will put you out of
the synagogue;[c] in fact, a time is
coming when anyone who kills you
will think he is offering a service to
God.[d] 3They will do such things because they have not known the
Father or me.[e] 4I have told you
this, so that when the time comes
you will remember[f] that I warned
you. I did not tell you this at first
because I was with you.

The Work of the Holy Spirit

5"Now I am going to him who sent
me,[g] yet none of you asks me,
'Where are you going?'[h] 6Because
I have said these things, you are
filled with grief. 7But I tell you the
truth: It is for your good that I am
going away. Unless I go away, the
Counsellor[i] will not come to you;
but if I go, I will send him to you.[j]
8When he comes, he will convict
the world of guilt[a] in regard to sin
and righteousness and judgment:
9in regard to sin,[k] because men do
not believe in me; 10in regard to
righteousness,[l] because I am going to the Father, where you can
see me no longer; 11and in regard
to judgment, because the prince
of this world[m] now stands condemned.

12"I have much more to say to
you, more than you can now bear.[n]
13But when he, the Spirit of truth,[o]
comes, he will guide you into all
truth.[p] He will not speak on his
own; he will speak only what he
hears, and he will tell you what is
yet to come. 14He will bring glory to
me by taking from what is mine
and making it known to you. 15All
that belongs to the Father is mine.[q]
That is why I said the Spirit will
take from what is mine and make it
known to you.

16"In a little while[r] you will see
me no more, and then after a little
while you will see me."[s]

The Disciples' Grief Will Turn to Joy

17Some of his disciples said to one
another, "What does he mean by
saying, 'In a little while you will see
me no more, and then after a little
while you will see me,'[t] and 'Because I am going to the Father'?"[u]
18They kept asking, "What does he
mean by 'a little while'? We don't
understand what he is saying."

19Jesus saw that they wanted to
ask him about this, so he said to
them, "Are you asking one another
what I meant when I said, 'In a little
while you will see me no more, and
then after a little while you will see
me'? 20I tell you the truth, you will
weep and mourn[v] while the world
rejoices. You will grieve, but your
grief will turn to joy.[w] 21A woman
giving birth to a child has pain[x] because her time has come; but when
her baby is born she forgets the anguish because of her joy that a

15:20 v Jn 13:16 w 2Ti 3:12
15:21 x Mt 10:22 y Jn 16:3
15:22 z Jn 9:41 Ro 1:20
15:24 a Jn 5:36
15:25 b Ps 35:19 Ps 69:4
15:26 c Jn 14:16 d Jn 14:26 e Jn 14:17 f 1Jn 5:7
15:27 g Lk 24:48 1Jn 1:2 1Jn 4:14 h Lk 1:2
16:1 a Jn 15:18-27 b Mt 11:6
16:2 c Jn 9:22 d Isa 66:5 Ac 26:9,10 Rev 6:9
16:3 e Jn 15:21 Jn 17:25 1Jn 3:1
16:4 f Jn 13:19
16:5 g Jn 7:33 h Jn 13:36 Jn 14:5
16:7 i Jn 14:16,26 Jn 15:26 j Jn 7:39
16:9 k Jn 15:22
16:10 l Ac 3:14 Ac 7:52 1Pe 3:18
16:11 m Jn 12:31
16:12 n Mk 4:33
16:13 o Jn 14:17 p Jn 14:26
16:15 q Jn 17:10
16:16 r Jn 7:33 s Jn 14:18-24
16:17 t ver 16 u ver 5
16:20 v Lk 23:27 w Jn 20:20
16:21 x Isa 26:17 1Th 5:3

[b]20 John 13:16 [c]25 Psalms 35:19; 69:4
[a]8 Or *will expose the guilt of the world*

child is born into the world. 22 So with you: Now is your time of grief,[y] but I will see you again[z] and you will rejoice, and no-one will take away your joy. 23 In that day you will no longer ask me anything. I tell you the truth, my Father will give you whatever you ask in my name.[a] 24 Until now you have not asked for anything in my name. Ask and you will receive, and your joy will be complete.[b]

25 "Though I have been speaking figuratively,[c] a time is coming[d] when I will no longer use this kind of language but will tell you plainly about my Father. 26 In that day you will ask in my name.[e] I am not saying that I will ask the Father on your behalf. 27 No, the Father himself loves you because you have loved me[f] and have believed that I came from God. 28 I came from the Father and entered the world; now I am leaving the world and going back to the Father."[g]

29 Then Jesus' disciples said, "Now you are speaking clearly and without figures of speech.[h] 30 Now we can see that you know all things and that you do not even need to have anyone ask you questions. This makes us believe that you came from God."

31 "You believe at last!"[b] Jesus answered. 32 "But a time is coming,[i] and has come, when you will be scattered,[j] each to his own home. You will leave me all alone. Yet I am not alone, for my Father is with me.[k]

33 "I have told you these things, so that in me you may have peace.[l] In this world you will have trouble.[m] But take heart! I have overcome[n] the world."

Jesus Prays for Himself

17 After Jesus said this, he looked towards heaven[a] and prayed:

"Father, the time has come. Glorify your Son, that your Son may glorify you.[b] 2 For you granted him authority over all people that he might give eternal life to all those you have given him.[c] 3 Now this is eternal life: that they may know you, the only true God, and Jesus Christ, whom you have sent.[d] 4 I have brought you glory[e] on earth by completing the work you gave me to do.[f] 5 And now, Father, glorify me in your presence with the glory I had with you[g] before the world began.[h]

Jesus Prays for His Disciples

6 "I have revealed you[a][i] to those whom you gave me[j] out of the world. They were yours; you gave them to me and they have obeyed your word. 7 Now they know that everything you have given me comes from you. 8 For I gave them the words you gave me[k] and they accepted them. They knew with certainty that I came from you,[l] and they believed that you sent me.[m] 9 I pray for them.[n] I am not praying for the world, but for those you have given me, for they are yours. 10 All I have is yours, and all you have is mine.[o] And glory has come to me through them. 11 I will remain in the world no longer, but they are still in the world,[p] and I am coming to you.[q] Holy Father, protect them by the power of your name—the name you gave me—so that they may be one[r] as we are one.[s] 12 While I was with them, I protected them and kept them safe by that name you gave me. None has been lost[t] except the one doomed to destruction[u] so that Scripture would be fulfilled.

13 "I am coming to you now,

16:22 y ver 6 z ver 16
16:23 a Mt 7:7 Jn 15:16
16:24 b Jn 3:29 Jn 15:11
16:25 c Mt 13:34 Jn 10:6 d ver 2
16:26 e ver 23,24
16:27 f Jn 14:21,23
16:28 g Jn 13:3
16:29 h ver 25
16:32 i ver 2,25 j Mt 26:31 k Jn 8:16,29
16:33 l Jn 14:27 m Jn 15:18-21 n Ro 8:37 1Jn 4:4
17:1 a Jn 11:41 b Jn 12:23 Jn 13:31,32
17:2 c ver 6,9,24 Da 7:14 Jn 6:37,39
17:3 d ver 8,18,21, 23,25 Jn 3:17
17:4 e Jn 13:31 f Jn 4:34
17:5 g Php 2:6 h Jn 1:2
17:6 i ver 26 j ver 2 Jn 6:37,39
17:8 k ver 14,26 l Jn 16:27 m ver 3,18,21, 23,25 Jn 3:17
17:9 n Lk 22:32
17:10 o Jn 16:15
17:11 p Jn 13:1 q Jn 7:33 r ver 21-23 s Jn 10:30
17:12 t Jn 6:39 u Jn 6:70

[b]31 Or *"Do you now believe?"* [a]6 Greek *your name*; also in verse 26

but I say these things while I
am still in the world, so that
they may have the full measure of my joy[v] within them. 14I
have given them your word
and the world has hated
them,[w] for they are not of the
world any more than I am of
the world.[x] 15My prayer is not
that you take them out of the
world but that you protect
them from the evil one.[y]
16They are not of the world,
even as I am not of it.[z] 17Sanc-
tify[b] them by the truth; your
word is truth.[a] 18As you sent
me into the world,[b] I have sent
them into the world.[c] 19For
them I sanctify myself, that
they too may be truly sanctified.

Jesus Prays for All Believers

20"My prayer is not for them
alone. I pray also for those who
will believe in me through
their message, 21that all of
them may be one, Father, just
as you are in me and I am in
you.[d] May they also be in us so
that the world may believe that
you have sent me.[e] 22I have
given them the glory that you
gave me, that they may be one
as we are one:[f] 23I in them and
you in me. May they be brought
to complete unity to let the
world know that you sent me[g]
and have loved them[h] even as
you have loved me.
24"Father, I want those you
have given me to be with me
where I am,[i] and to see my
glory,[j] the glory you have
given me because you loved
me before the creation of the
world.[k]
25"Righteous Father, though
the world does not know you,[l]
I know you, and they know that
you have sent me.[m] 26I have
made you known to them,[n] and
will continue to make you
known in order that the love
you have for me may be in
them[o] and that I myself may
be in them."

Jesus Arrested

18:3–11pp Mt 26:47–56; Mk 14:43–50; Lk 22:47–53

18 When he had finished praying, Jesus left with his disciples and crossed the Kidron
Valley.[a] On the other side there
was an olive grove,[b] and he and his
disciples went into it.[c]
2Now Judas, who betrayed him,
knew the place, because Jesus had
often met there with his disciples.[d] 3So Judas came to the
grove, guiding[e] a detachment of
soldiers and some officials from
the chief priests and Pharisees.[f]
They were carrying torches, lan-
terns and weapons.
4Jesus, knowing all that was going to happen to him,[g] went out and
asked them, "Who is it you want?"[h]
5"Jesus of Nazareth," they replied.
"I am he," Jesus said. (And Judas
the traitor was standing there with
them.) 6When Jesus said, "I am he,"
they drew back and fell to the
ground.
7Again he asked them, "Who is it
you want?"[i]
And they said, "Jesus of Nazareth."
8"I told you that I am he," Jesus
answered. "If you are looking for
me, then let these men go." 9This
happened so that the words he had
spoken would be fulfilled: "I have
not lost one of those you gave
me."[a][j]
10Then Simon Peter, who had a
sword, drew it and struck the high
priest's servant, cutting off his
right ear. (The servant's name was
Malchus.)
11Jesus commanded Peter, "Put
your sword away! Shall I not drink
the cup[k] the Father has given me?"

17:13 *v* Jn 3:29
17:14 *w* Jn 15:19 *x* Jn 8:23
17:15 *y* Mt 5:37
17:16 *z* ver 14
17:17 *a* Jn 15:3
17:18 *b* ver 3,8,21,23, 25 *c* Jn 20:21
17:21 *d* Jn 10:38 *e* ver 3,8,18,23, 25 Jn 3:17
17:22 *f* Jn 14:20
17:23 *g* Jn 3:17 *h* Jn 16:27
17:24 *i* Jn 12:26 *j* Jn 1:14 *k* ver 5 Mt 25:34
17:25 *l* Jn 15:21 Jn 16:3 *m* ver 3,8,18,21, 23 Jn 3:17 Jn 7:29 Jn 16:27
17:26 *n* ver 6 *o* Jn 15:9
18:1 *a* 2Sa 15:23 *b* ver 26 *c* Mt 26:36
18:2 *d* Lk 21:37 Lk 22:39
18:3 *e* Ac 1:16 *f* ver 12
18:4 *g* Jn 6:64 Jn 13:1,11 *h* ver 7
18:7 *i* ver 4
18:9 *j* Jn 17:12
18:11 *k* Mt 20:22

b17 Greek *hagiazo* (*set apart for sacred use* or *make holy*); also in verse 19 a9 John 6:39

Jesus Taken to Annas

18:12,13pp Mt 26:57

12Then the detachment of soldiers with its commander and the
Jewish officials[l] arrested Jesus.
They bound him 13and brought him
first to Annas, who was the father-
in-law of Caiaphas,[m] the high
priest that year. 14Caiaphas was the
one who had advised the Jews that
it would be good if one man died for
the people.[n]

Peter's First Denial

18:16–18pp Mt 26:69,70; Mk 14:66–68; Lk 22:55–57

15Simon Peter and another disciple were following Jesus. Because this disciple was known to
the high priest,[o] he went with
Jesus into the high priest's courtyard,[p] 16but Peter had to wait outside at the door. The other disciple,
who was known to the high priest,
came back, spoke to the girl on
duty there and brought Peter in.
17"You are not one of his disciples, are you?" the girl at the door
asked Peter.

He replied, "I am not."[q]
18It was cold, and the servants
and officials stood round a fire[r]
they had made to keep warm. Peter
also was standing with them,
warming himself.[s]

The High Priest Questions Jesus

18:19–24pp Mt 26:59–68; Mk 14:55–65; Lk 22:63–71

19Meanwhile, the high priest
questioned Jesus about his disciples and his teaching.
20"I have spoken openly to the
world," Jesus replied. "I always
taught in synagogues[t] or at the
temple,[u] where all the Jews come
together. I said nothing in secret.[v]
21Why question me? Ask those who
heard me. Surely they know what I
said."
22When Jesus said this, one of the
officials[w] near by struck him in the
face.[x] "Is this the way you answer
the high priest?" he demanded.
23"If I said something wrong,"
Jesus replied, "testify as to what is
wrong. But if I spoke the truth, why
did you strike me?"[y] 24Then Annas
sent him, still bound, to Caiaphas[z]
the high priest.[b]

Peter's Second and Third Denials

18:25–27pp Mt 26:71–75; Mk 14:69–72; Lk 22:58–62

25As Simon Peter stood warming
himself,[a] he was asked, "You are
not one of his disciples, are you?"
He denied it, saying, "I am not."[b]
26One of the high priest's servants, a relative of the man whose
ear Peter had cut off,[c] challenged
him, "Didn't I see you with him in
the olive grove?"[d] 27Again Peter
denied it, and at that moment a
cock began to crow.[e]

Jesus Before Pilate

18:29–40pp Mt 27:11–18,20–23; Mk 15:2–15; Lk 23:2,3,18–25

28Then the Jews led Jesus from
Caiaphas to the palace of the Roman governor.[f] By now it was
early morning, and to avoid ceremonial uncleanness the Jews did
not enter the palace;[g] they wanted
to be able to eat the Passover.[h] 29So
Pilate came out to them and asked,
"What charges are you bringing
against this man?"
30"If he were not a criminal,"
they replied, "we would not have
handed him over to you."
31Pilate said, "Take him yourselves and judge him by your own
law."

"But we have no right to execute
anyone," the Jews objected. 32This
happened so that the words Jesus
had spoken indicating the kind of
death he was going to die[i] would
be fulfilled.
33Pilate then went back inside
the palace,[j] summoned Jesus and

18:12 l ver 3
18:13 m ver 24; Mt 26:3
18:14 n Jn 11:49-51
18:15 o Mt 26:3 p Mt 26:58; Mk 14:54; Lk 22:54
18:17 q ver 25
18:18 r Jn 21:9 s Mk 14:54,67
18:20 t Mt 4:23 u Mt 26:55 v Jn 7:26
18:22 w ver 3 x Mt 16:21; Jn 19:3
18:23 y Mt 5:39; Ac 23:2-5
18:24 z ver 13; Mt 26:3
18:25 a ver 18 b ver 17
18:26 c ver 10 d ver 1
18:27 e Jn 13:38
18:28 f Mt 27:2; Mk 15:1; Lk 23:1 g ver 33; Jn 19:9 h Jn 11:55
18:32 i Mt 20:19; Mt 26:2; Jn 3:14; Jn 8:28; Jn 12:32,33
18:33 j ver 28,29; Jn 19:9

b24 Or *(Now Annas had sent him, still bound, to Caiaphas the high priest.)*

asked him, "Are you the king of the Jews?"[k]

34"Is that your own idea," Jesus asked, "or did others talk to you about me?"

35"Am I a Jew?" Pilate replied. "It was your people and your chief priests who handed you over to me. What is it you have done?"

36Jesus said, "My kingdom[l] is not of this world. If it were, my servants would fight to prevent my arrest by the Jews.[m] But now my kingdom is from another place."[n]

37"You are a king, then!" said Pilate.

Jesus answered, "You are right in saying I am a king. In fact, for this reason I was born, and for this I came into the world, to testify to the truth.[o] Everyone on the side of truth listens to me."[p]

38"What is truth?" Pilate asked. With this he went out again to the Jews and said, "I find no basis for a charge against him.[q] 39But it is your custom for me to release to you one prisoner at the time of the Passover. Do you want me to release 'the king of the Jews'?"

40They shouted back, "No, not him! Give us Barabbas!" Now Barabbas had taken part in a rebellion.[r]

Jesus Sentenced to be Crucified

19:1–16pp Mt 27:27–31; Mk 15:16–20

19 Then Pilate took Jesus and had him flogged.[a] 2The soldiers twisted together a crown of thorns and put it on his head. They clothed him in a purple robe 3and went up to him again and again, saying, "Hail, king of the Jews!"[b] And they struck him in the face.[c]

4Once more Pilate came out and said to the Jews, "Look, I am bringing him out[d] to you to let you know that I find no basis for a charge against him."[e] 5When Jesus came out wearing the crown of thorns and the purple robe,[f] Pilate said to them, "Here is the man!"

6As soon as the chief priests and their officials saw him, they shouted, "Crucify! Crucify!"

But Pilate answered, "You take him and crucify him.[g] As for me, I find no basis for a charge against him."[h]

7The Jews insisted, "We have a law, and according to that law he must die,[i] because he claimed to be the Son of God."[j]

8When Pilate heard this, he was even more afraid, 9and he went back inside the palace.[k] "Where do you come from?" he asked Jesus, but Jesus gave him no answer.[l] 10"Do you refuse to speak to me?" Pilate said. "Don't you realise I have power either to free you or to crucify you?"

11Jesus answered, "You would have no power over me if it were not given to you from above.[m] Therefore the one who handed me over to you[n] is guilty of a greater sin."

12From then on, Pilate tried to set Jesus free, but the Jews kept shouting, "If you let this man go, you are no friend of Caesar. Anyone who claims to be a king[o] opposes Caesar."

13When Pilate heard this, he brought Jesus out and sat down on the judge's seat[p] at a place known as the Stone Pavement (which in Aramaic[q] is Gabbatha). 14It was the day of Preparation[r] of Passover Week, about the sixth hour.[s]

"Here is your king,"[t] Pilate said to the Jews.

15But they shouted, "Take him away! Take him away! Crucify him!"

"Shall I crucify your king?" Pilate asked.

"We have no king but Caesar," the chief priests answered.

16Finally Pilate handed him over to them to be crucified.[u]

18:33 *k* Lk 23:3; Mt 2:2
18:36 *l* Mt 3:2; *m* Mt 26:53; *n* Lk 17:21; Jn 6:15
18:37 *o* Jn 3:32; *p* Jn 8:47; 1Jn 4:6
18:38 *q* Lk 23:4; Jn 19:4,6
18:40 *r* Ac 3:14
19:1 *a* Dt 25:3; Isa 50:6; Isa 53:5; Mt 27:26
19:3 *b* Mt 27:29; *c* Jn 18:22
19:4 *d* Jn 18:38; *e* ver 6; Lk 23:4
19:5 *f* ver 2
19:6 *g* Ac 3:13; *h* ver 4; Lk 23:4
19:7 *i* Lev 24:16; *j* Mt 26:63-66; Jn 5:18; Jn 10:33
19:9 *k* Jn 18:33; *l* Mk 14:61
19:11 *m* Ro 13:1; *n* Jn 18:28-30; Ac 3:13
19:12 *o* Lk 23:2
19:13 *p* Mt 27:19; *q* Jn 5:2
19:14 *r* Mt 27:62; *s* Mk 15:25; *t* ver 19,21
19:16 *u* Mt 27:26; Mk 15:15; Lk 23:25

The Crucifixion

19:17–24pp Mt 27:33–44; Mk 15:22–32; Lk 23:33–43

So the soldiers took charge of Jesus. [17]Carrying his own cross,[v] he went out to the place of the Skull[w] (which in Aramaic[x] is called Golgotha). [18]Here they crucified him, and with him two others[y]—one on each side and Jesus in the middle.

[19]Pilate had a notice prepared and fastened to the cross. It read: JESUS OF NAZARETH,[z] THE KING OF THE JEWS.[a] [20]Many of the Jews read this sign, for the place where Jesus was crucified was near the city,[b] and the sign was written in Aramaic, Latin and Greek. [21]The chief priests of the Jews protested to Pilate, "Do not write 'The King of the Jews', but that this man claimed to be king of the Jews."[c]

[22]Pilate answered, "What I have written, I have written."

[23]When the soldiers crucified Jesus, they took his clothes, dividing them into four shares, one for each of them, with the undergarment remaining. This garment was seamless, woven in one piece from top to bottom.

[24]"Let's not tear it," they said to one another. "Let's decide by lot who will get it."

This happened that the scripture might be fulfilled[d] which said,

"They divided my garments
among them
and cast lots for my
clothing."[a][e]

So this is what the soldiers did.

[25]Near the cross[f] of Jesus stood his mother,[g] his mother's sister, Mary the wife of Clopas, and Mary Magdalene.[h] [26]When Jesus saw his mother[i] there, and the disciple whom he loved[j] standing near by, he said to his mother, "Dear woman, here is your son," [27]and to the disciple, "Here is your mother." From that time on, this disciple took her into his home.

The Death of Jesus

19:29,30pp Mt 27:48,50; Mk 15:36,37; Lk 23:36

[28]Later, knowing that all was now completed,[k] and so that the Scripture would be fulfilled,[l] Jesus said, "I am thirsty." [29]A jar of wine vinegar[m] was there, so they soaked a sponge in it, put the sponge on a stalk of the hyssop plant, and lifted it to Jesus' lips. [30]When he had received the drink, Jesus said, "It is finished."[n] With that, he bowed his head and gave up his spirit.

[31]Now it was the day of Preparation,[o] and the next day was to be a special Sabbath. Because the Jews did not want the bodies left on the crosses[p] during the Sabbath, they asked Pilate to have the legs broken and the bodies taken down. [32]The soldiers therefore came and broke the legs of the first man who had been crucified with Jesus, and then those of the other.[q] [33]But when they came to Jesus and found that he was already dead, they did not break his legs. [34]Instead, one of the soldiers pierced[r] Jesus' side with a spear, bringing a sudden flow of blood and water.[s] [35]The man who saw it[t] has given testimony, and his testimony is true.[u] He knows that he tells the truth, and he testifies so that you also may believe. [36]These things happened so that the scripture would be fulfilled:[v] "Not one of his bones will be broken,"[b][w] [37]and, as another scripture says, "They will look on the one they have pierced."[c][x]

The Burial of Jesus

19:38–42pp Mt 27:57–61; Mk 15:42–47; Lk 23:50–56

[38]Later, Joseph of Arimathea asked Pilate for the body of Jesus. Now Joseph was a disciple of Jesus, but secretly because he feared the

19:17 v Ge 22:6; Lk 14:27; Lk 23:26 w Lk 23:33 x Jn 5:2
19:18 y Lk 23:32
19:19 z Mk 1:24 a ver 14,21
19:20 b Heb 13:12
19:21 c ver 14
19:24 d ver 28,36,37; Mt 1:22 e Ps 22:18
19:25 f Mt 27:55,56; Mk 15:40,41; Lk 23:49 g Mt 12:46 h Lk 24:18
19:26 i Mt 12:46 j Jn 13:23
19:28 k ver 30; Jn 13:1 l ver 24,36,37
19:29 m Ps 69:21
19:30 n Lk 12:50; Jn 17:4
19:31 o ver 14,42 p Dt 21:23; Jos 8:29; Jos 10:26,27
19:32 q ver 18
19:34 r Zec 12:10 s 1Jn 5:6,8
19:35 t Lk 24:48 u Jn 15:27; Jn 21:24
19:36 v ver 24,28,37; Mt 1:22 w Ex 12:46; Nu 9:12; Ps 34:20
19:37 x Zec 12:10; Rev 1:7

[a]*24* Psalm 22:18 [b]*36* Exodus 12:46; Num. 9:12; Psalm 34:20 [c]*37* Zech. 12:10

Jews. With Pilate's permission, he came and took the body away. 39He was accompanied by Nicodemus,[y] the man who earlier had visited Jesus at night. Nicodemus brought a mixture of myrrh and aloes, about seventy-five pounds.[d] 40Taking Jesus' body, the two of them wrapped it, with the spices, in strips of linen.[z] This was in accordance with Jewish burial customs.[a] 41At the place where Jesus was crucified, there was a garden, and in the garden a new tomb, in which no-one had ever been laid. 42Because it was the Jewish day of Preparation[b] and since the tomb was near by,[c] they laid Jesus there.

The Empty Tomb

20:1–8pp Mt 28:1–8; Mk 16:1–8; Lk 24:1–10

20 Early on the first day of the week, while it was still dark, Mary Magdalene[a] went to the tomb and saw that the stone had been removed from the entrance.[b] 2So she came running to Simon Peter and the other disciple, the one Jesus loved,[c] and said, "They have taken the Lord out of the tomb, and we don't know where they have put him!"[d]

3So Peter and the other disciple started for the tomb.[e] 4Both were running, but the other disciple outran Peter and reached the tomb first. 5He bent over and looked in[f] at the strips of linen[g] lying there but did not go in. 6Then Simon Peter, who was behind him, arrived and went into the tomb. He saw the strips of linen lying there, 7as well as the burial cloth that had been around Jesus' head.[h] The cloth was folded up by itself, separate from the linen. 8Finally the other disciple, who had reached the tomb first,[i] also went inside. He saw and believed. 9(They still did not understand from Scripture[j] that Jesus had to rise from the dead.)[k]

Jesus Appears to Mary Magdalene

10Then the disciples went back to their homes, 11but Mary stood outside the tomb crying. As she wept, she bent over to look into the tomb[l] 12and saw two angels in white,[m] seated where Jesus' body had been, one at the head and the other at the foot.

13They asked her, "Woman, why are you crying?"[n]

"They have taken my Lord away," she said, "and I don't know where they have put him."[o] 14At this, she turned round and saw Jesus standing there,[p] but she did not realise that it was Jesus.[q]

15"Woman," he said, "why are you crying?[r] Who is it you are looking for?"

Thinking he was the gardener, she said, "Sir, if you have carried him away, tell me where you have put him, and I will get him."

16Jesus said to her, "Mary."

She turned towards him and cried out in Aramaic,[s] "Rabboni!"[t] (which means Teacher).

17Jesus said, "Do not hold on to me, for I have not yet returned to the Father. Go instead to my brothers[u] and tell them, 'I am returning to my Father[v] and your Father, to my God and your God.' "

18Mary Magdalene[w] went to the disciples[x] with the news: "I have seen the Lord!" And she told them that he had said these things to her.

Jesus Appears to His Disciples

19On the evening of that first day of the week, when the disciples were together, with the doors locked for fear of the Jews,[y] Jesus came and stood among them and said, "Peace[z] be with you!"[a] 20After he said this, he showed them his hands and side.[b] The disciples were overjoyed[c] when they saw the Lord.

19:39 y Jn 3:1; Jn 7:50
19:40 z Lk 24:12; Jn 11:44; Jn 20:5,7; a Mt 26:12
19:42 b ver 14,31; c ver 20,41
20:1 a ver 18; Jn 19:25; b Mt 27:60,66
20:2 c Jn 13:23; d ver 13
20:3 e Lk 24:12
20:5 f ver 11; g Jn 19:40
20:7 h Jn 11:44
20:8 i ver 4
20:9 j Mt 22:29; Jn 2:22; k Lk 24:26,46
20:11 l ver 5
20:12 m Mt 28:2,3; Mk 16:5; Lk 24:4; Ac 5:19
20:13 n ver 15; o ver 2
20:14 p Mt 28:9; Mk 16:9; q Lk 24:16; Jn 21:4
20:15 r ver 13
20:16 s Jn 5:2; t Mt 23:7
20:17 u Mt 28:10; v Jn 7:33
20:18 w ver 1; x Lk 24:10,22,23
20:19 y Jn 7:13; z Jn 14:27; a ver 21,26; Lk 24:36-39
20:20 b Lk 24:39,40; Jn 19:34; c Jn 16:20,22

d39 Greek *a hundred litrai* (about 34 kilograms)

[21]Again Jesus said, "Peace be with you![d] As the Father has sent me,[e] I am sending you."[f] [22]And with that he breathed on them and said, "Receive the Holy Spirit.[g] [23]If you forgive anyone his sins, they are forgiven; if you do not forgive them, they are not forgiven."[h]

Jesus Appears to Thomas

[24]Now Thomas[i] (called Didymus), one of the Twelve, was not with the disciples when Jesus came. [25]So the other disciples told him, "We have seen the Lord!"[j]

But he said to them, "Unless I see the nail marks in his hands and put my finger where the nails were, and put my hand into his side,[j] I will not believe it."[k]

[26]A week later his disciples were in the house again, and Thomas was with them. Though the doors were locked, Jesus came and stood among them and said, "Peace[l] be with you!"[m] [27]Then he said to Thomas, "Put your finger here; see my hands. Reach out your hand and put it into my side. Stop doubting and believe."[n]

[28]Thomas said to him, "My Lord and my God!"

[29]Then Jesus told him, "Because you have seen me, you have believed;[o] blessed are those who have not seen and yet have believed."[p]

[30]Jesus did many other miraculous signs[q] in the presence of his disciples, which are not recorded in this book.[r] [31]But these are written that you may[a] believe[s] that Jesus is the Christ, the Son of God,[t] and that by believing you may have life in his name.[u]

Jesus and the Miraculous Catch of Fish

21 Afterwards Jesus appeared again to his disciples,[a] by the Sea of Tiberias.[a][b] It happened this way: [2]Simon Peter, Thomas[c] (called Didymus), Nathanael[d] from Cana in Galilee,[e] the sons of Zebedee,[f] and two other disciples were together. [3]"I'm going out to fish," Simon Peter told them, and they said, "We'll go with you." So they went out and got into the boat, but that night they caught nothing.[g]

[4]Early in the morning, Jesus stood on the shore, but the disciples did not realise that it was Jesus.[h]

[5]He called out to them, "Friends, haven't you any fish?"

"No," they answered.

[6]He said, "Throw your net on the right side of the boat and you will find some." When they did, they were unable to haul the net in because of the large number of fish.[i]

[7]Then the disciple whom Jesus loved[j] said to Peter, "It is the Lord!" As soon as Simon Peter heard him say, "It is the Lord," he wrapped his outer garment around him (for he had taken it off) and jumped into the water. [8]The other disciples followed in the boat, towing the net full of fish, for they were not far from shore, about a hundred yards.[b] [9]When they landed, they saw a fire[k] of burning coals there with fish on it,[l] and some bread.

[10]Jesus said to them, "Bring some of the fish you have just caught."

[11]Simon Peter climbed aboard and dragged the net ashore. It was full of large fish, 153, but even with so many the net was not torn. [12]Jesus said to them, "Come and have breakfast." None of the disciples dared ask him, "Who are you?" They knew it was the Lord. [13]Jesus came, took the bread and gave it to them, and did the same with the fish.[m] [14]This was now the third time Jesus appeared to his

20:21 d ver 19; e Jn 3:17; f Mt 28:19; Jn 17:18
20:22 g Jn 7:39; Ac 2:38; Ac 8:15-17; Ac 19:2; Gal 3:2
20:23 h Mt 16:19; Mt 18:18
20:24 i Jn 11:16
20:25 j ver 20; k Mk 16:11
20:26 l Jn 14:27; m ver 21
20:27 n ver 25; Lk 24:40
20:29 o Jn 3:15; p 1Pe 1:8
20:30 q Jn 2:11; r Jn 21:25
20:31 s Jn 3:15; Jn 19:35; t Mt 4:3; u Mt 25:46
21:1 a Jn 20:19,26; b Jn 6:1
21:2 c Jn 11:16; d Jn 1:45; e Jn 2:1; f Mt 4:21
21:3 g Lk 5:5
21:4 h Lk 24:16; Jn 20:14
21:6 i Lk 5:4-7
21:7 j Jn 13:23
21:9 k Jn 18:18; l ver 10,13
21:13 m ver 9

[a]31 Some manuscripts *may continue to*
[a]1 That is, Sea of Galilee [b]8 Greek *about two hundred cubits* (about 90 metres)

disciples[n] after he was raised from the dead.

Jesus Reinstates Peter

15 When they had finished eating, Jesus said to Simon Peter, "Simon son of John, do you truly love me more than these?"

"Yes, Lord," he said, "you know that I love you."[o]

Jesus said, "Feed my lambs."[p]

16 Again Jesus said, "Simon son of John, do you truly love me?"

He answered, "Yes, Lord, you know that I love you."

Jesus said, "Take care of my sheep."[q]

17 The third time he said to him, "Simon son of John, do you love me?"

Peter was hurt because Jesus asked him the third time, "Do you love me?"[r] He said, "Lord, you know all things;[s] you know that I love you."

Jesus said, "Feed my sheep.[t] 18 I tell you the truth, when you were younger you dressed yourself and went where you wanted; but when you are old you will stretch out your hands, and someone else will dress you and lead you where you do not want to go." 19 Jesus said this to indicate the kind of death[u] by which Peter would glorify God.[v] Then he said to him, "Follow me!"

20 Peter turned and saw that the disciple whom Jesus loved[w] was following them. (This was the one who had leaned back against Jesus at the supper and had said, "Lord, who is going to betray you?")[x] 21 When Peter saw him, he asked, "Lord, what about him?"

22 Jesus answered, "If I want him to remain alive until I return,[y] what is that to you? You must follow me."[z] 23 Because of this, the rumour spread among the brothers[a] that this disciple would not die. But Jesus did not say that he would not die; he only said, "If I want him to remain alive until I return, what is that to you?"

24 This is the disciple who testifies to these things[b] and who wrote them down. We know that his testimony is true.[c]

25 Jesus did many other things as well.[d] If every one of them were written down, I suppose that even the whole world would not have room for the books that would be written.

21:14 n Jn 20:19,26
21:15 o Mt 26:33,35 Jn 13:37 p Lk 12:32
21:16 q Mt 2:6 Ac 20:28 1Pe 5:2,3
21:17 r Jn 13:38 s Jn 16:30 t ver 16
21:19 u Jn 12:33 Jn 18:32 v 2Pe 1:14
21:20 w ver 7 Jn 13:23 x Jn 13:25
21:22 y Mt 16:27 1Co 4:5 Rev 2:25 z ver 19
21:23 a Ac 1:16
21:24 b Jn 15:27 c Jn 19:35
21:25 d Jn 20:30

ACTS

Jesus Taken Up Into Heaven

1 In my former book,[a] Theophilus, I wrote about all that Jesus
began to do and to teach[b] [2]until the
day he was taken up to heaven,[c]
after giving instructions[d] through
the Holy Spirit to the apostles[e] he
had chosen.[f] [3]After his suffering,
he showed himself to these men
and gave many convincing proofs
that he was alive. He appeared to
them[g] over a period of forty days
and spoke about the kingdom of
God. [4]On one occasion, while he
was eating with them, he gave them
this command: "Do not leave Jerusalem, but wait for the gift my
Father promised, which you have
heard me speak about.[h] [5]For John
baptised with[a] water, but in a few
days you will be baptised with the
Holy Spirit."
[6]So when they met together, they
asked him, "Lord, are you at this
time going to restore[i] the kingdom to Israel?"
[7]He said to them: "It is not for
you to know the times or dates the
Father has set by his own authority.[j] [8]But you will receive power
when the Holy Spirit comes on
you;[k] and you will be my witnesses[l] in Jerusalem, and in all Judea and Samaria,[m] and to the ends
of the earth."[n]
[9]After he said this, he was taken
up[o] before their very eyes, and a
cloud hid him from their sight.
[10]They were looking intently up
into the sky as he was going, when
suddenly two men dressed in
white[p] stood beside them. [11]"Men
of Galilee,"[q] they said, "why do
you stand here looking into the
sky? This same Jesus, who has
been taken from you into heaven,
will come back[r] in the same
way you have seen him go into
heaven."

Matthias Chosen to Replace Judas

[12]Then they returned to Jerusalem[s] from the hill called the
Mount of Olives,[t] a Sabbath day's
walk[b] from the city. [13]When they
arrived, they went upstairs to the
room[u] where they were staying.
Those present were Peter, John,
James and Andrew; Philip and
Thomas, Bartholomew and Matthew; James son of Alphaeus and
Simon the Zealot, and Judas son
of James.[v] [14]They all joined together constantly in prayer,[w] along
with the women[x] and Mary the
mother of Jesus, and with his
brothers.[y]
[15]In those days Peter stood up
among the believers[c] (a group
numbering about a hundred and
twenty) [16]and said, "Brothers, the
Scripture had to be fulfilled[z]
which the Holy Spirit spoke long
ago through the mouth of David
concerning Judas,[a] who served as
guide for those who arrested
Jesus—[17]he was one of our number[b] and shared in this ministry."[c]
[18](With the reward[d] he got for
his wickedness, Judas bought a
field;[e] there he fell headlong, his
body burst open and all his intestines spilled out. [19]Everyone in
Jerusalem heard about this, so they
called that field in their language
Akeldama, that is, Field of Blood.)
[20]"For," said Peter, "it is written
in the Book of Psalms,

1:1 *a* Lk 1:1-4 *b* Lk 3:23
1:2 *c* ver 9,11 Mk 16:19 *d* Mt 28:19,20 *e* Mk 6:30 *f* Jn 13:18
1:3 *g* Mt 28:17 Lk 24:34,36 Jn 20:19,26 Jn 21:1,14 1Co 15:5-7
1:4 *h* Lk 24:49 Jn 14:16 Ac 2:33
1:6 *i* Mt 17:11
1:7 *j* Mt 24:36
1:8 *k* Ac 2:1-4 *l* Lk 24:48 *m* Ac 8:1-25 *n* Mt 28:19
1:9 *o* ver 2
1:10 *p* Lk 24:4 Jn 20:12
1:11 *q* Ac 2:7 *r* Mt 16:27
1:12 *s* Lk 24:52 *t* Mt 21:1
1:13 *u* Ac 9:37 Ac 20:8 *v* Mt 10:2-4 Mk 3:16-19 Lk 6:14-16
1:14 *w* Ac 2:42 Ac 6:4 *x* Lk 23:49,55 *y* Mt 12:46
1:16 *z* ver 20 *a* Jn 13:18
1:17 *b* Jn 6:70,71 *c* ver 25
1:18 *d* Mt 26:14,15 *e* Mt 27:3-10

a5 Or *in* **b**12 That is, about ¾ of a mile (about 1,100 metres) **c**15 Greek *brothers*

" 'May his place be deserted;
let there be no-one to dwell in
it,'[d][f]

and,

" 'May another take his place of
leadership.'[e][g]

21 Therefore it is necessary to
choose one of the men who have
been with us the whole time the
Lord Jesus went in and out among
us, 22 beginning from John's baptism[h] to the time when Jesus was
taken up from us. For one of these
must become a witness[i] with us of
his resurrection."

23 So they proposed two men: Joseph called Barsabbas (also known
as Justus) and Matthias. 24 Then
they prayed,[j] "Lord, you know
everyone's heart.[k] Show us which
of these two you have chosen 25 to
take over this apostolic ministry,
which Judas left to go where he belongs." 26 Then they cast lots, and
the lot fell to Matthias; so he was
added to the eleven apostles.[l]

The Holy Spirit Comes at Pentecost

2 When the day of Pentecost[a]
came, they were all together[b]
in one place. 2 Suddenly a sound like
the blowing of a violent wind came
from heaven and filled the whole
house where they were sitting.[c]
3 They saw what seemed to be
tongues of fire that separated and
came to rest on each of them. 4 All
of them were filled with the Holy
Spirit and began to speak in other
tongues[a][d] as the Spirit enabled
them.

5 Now there were staying in Jerusalem God-fearing[e] Jews from
every nation under heaven. 6 When
they heard this sound, a crowd
came together in bewilderment,
because each one heard them
speaking in his own language. 7 Utterly amazed,[f] they asked: "Are
not all these men who are speaking
Galileans?[g] 8 Then how is it that
each of us hears them in his own native language? 9 Parthians, Medes
and Elamites; residents of Mesopotamia, Judea and Cappado-
cia,[h] Pontus[i] and Asia,[j] 10 Phrygia[k]
and Pamphylia,[l] Egypt and the
parts of Libya near Cyrene;[m] visi-
tors from Rome 11 (both Jews and
converts to Judaism); Cretans and
Arabs—we hear them declaring
the wonders of God in our own
tongues!" 12 Amazed and perplexed,
they asked one another, "What does
this mean?"

13 Some, however, made fun of
them and said, "They have had too
much wine."[b][n]

Peter Addresses the Crowd

14 Then Peter stood up with the
Eleven, raised his voice and addressed the crowd: "Fellow Jews
and all of you who live in Jerusalem, let me explain this to you;
listen carefully to what I say.
15 These men are not drunk, as you
suppose. It's only nine in the morning![o] 16 No, this is what was spoken
by the prophet Joel:

17 " 'In the last days, God says,
I will pour out my Spirit on all
people.[p]
Your sons and daughters will
prophesy,[q]
your young men will see
visions,
your old men will dream
dreams.
18 Even on my servants, both men
and women,
I will pour out my Spirit in
those days,
and they will prophesy.[r]
19 I will show wonders in the
heaven above
and signs on the earth below,
blood and fire and billows of
smoke.
20 The sun will be turned to
darkness

1:20 f Ps 69:25; g Ps 109:8
1:22 h Mk 1:4; i ver 8
1:24 j Ac 6:6; Ac 14:23; k 1Sa 16:7; Jer 17:10; Ac 15:8; Rev 2:23
1:26 l Ac 2:14
2:1 a Lev 23:15,16; Ac 20:16; b Ac 1:14
2:2 c Ac 4:31
2:4 d Mk 16:17; 1Co 12:10
2:5 e Ac 8:2
2:7 f ver 12; g Ac 1:11
2:9 h 1Pe 1:1; i Ac 18:2; j Ac 16:6; Ro 16:5; 1Co 16:19; 2Co 1:8
2:10 k Ac 16:6; Ac 18:23; l Ac 13:13; Ac 15:38; m Mt 27:32
2:13 n 1Co 14:23
2:15 o 1Th 5:7
2:17 p Isa 44:3; Jn 7:37-39; Ac 10:45; q Ac 21:9
2:18 r Ac 21:9-12

[d]20 Psalm 69:25 [e]20 Psalm 109:8 [a]4 Or *languages*; also in verse 11 [b]13 Or *sweet wine*

and the moon to blood[s]
before the coming of the great
and glorious day of the
Lord.
21 And everyone who calls
on the name of the Lord will
be saved.'[c][t]

22 "Men of Israel, listen to this:
Jesus of Nazareth was a man ac-
credited by God to you by miracles,
wonders and signs,[u] which God
did among you through him,[v] as
you yourselves know. 23 This man
was handed over to you by God's
set purpose and foreknowledge;[w]
and you, with the help of wicked
men,[d] put him to death by nailing
him to the cross.[x] 24 But God raised
him from the dead,[y] freeing him
from the agony of death, because it
was impossible for death to keep its
hold on him.[z] 25 David said about
him:

" 'I saw the Lord always before
me.
Because he is at my right
hand,
I will not be shaken.
26 Therefore my heart is glad and
my tongue rejoices;
my body also will live in hope,
27 because you will not abandon
me to the grave,
nor will you let your Holy One
see decay.[a]
28 You have made known to me
the paths of life;
you will fill me with joy in
your presence.'[e]

29 "Brothers, I can tell you confidently that the patriarch[b] David
died and was buried,[c] and his tomb
is here[d] to this day. 30 But he was a
prophet and knew that God had
promised him on oath that he would
place one of his descendants on his
throne.[e] 31 Seeing what was ahead,
he spoke of the resurrection of the
Christ,[f] that he was not abandoned
to the grave, nor did his body see
decay.[f] 32 God has raised this Jesus
to life,[g] and we are all witnesses[h]
of the fact. 33 Exalted[i] to the right
hand of God,[j] he has received
from the Father[k] the promised
Holy Spirit[l] and has poured out[m]
what you now see and hear. 34 For
David did not ascend to heaven,
and yet he said,

" 'The Lord said to my Lord:
"Sit at my right hand
35 until I make your enemies
a footstool for your feet." '[g][n]

36 "Therefore let all Israel be as-
sured of this: God has made this
Jesus, whom you crucified, both
Lord and Christ."[o]

37 When the people heard this,
they were cut to the heart and said
to Peter and the other apostles,
"Brothers, what shall we do?"[p]

38 Peter replied, "Repent and be
baptised,[q] every one of you, in the
name of Jesus Christ for the forgiveness of your sins.[r] And you
will receive the gift of the Holy
Spirit. 39 The promise is for you and
your children[s] and for all who are
far off[t]—for all whom the Lord
our God will call."

40 With many other words he
warned them; and he pleaded with
them, "Save yourselves from this
corrupt generation."[u] 41 Those who
accepted his message were baptised, and about three thousand
were added to their number that
day.

The Fellowship of the Believers

42 They devoted themselves to the
apostles' teaching and to the fellowship, to the breaking of bread
and to prayer.[v] 43 Everyone was
filled with awe, and many wonders
and miraculous signs were done by
the apostles.[w] 44 All the believers
were together and had everything
in common.[x] 45 Selling their possessions and goods, they gave to

2:20 s Mt 24:29
2:21 t Ro 10:13
2:22 u Jn 4:48; Ac 10:38; v Jn 3:2
2:23 w Lk 22:22; Ac 3:18; Ac 4:28; x Lk 24:20; Ac 3:13
2:24 y ver 32; 1Co 6:14; 2Co 4:14; Eph 1:20; Col 2:12; Heb 13:20; 1Pe 1:21; z Jn 20:9
2:27 a ver 31; Ac 13:35
2:29 b Ac 7:8,9; c Ac 13:36; 1Ki 2:10; d Ne 3:16
2:30 e 2Sa 7:12; Ps 132:11
2:31 f Ps 16:10
2:32 g ver 24; h Ac 1:8
2:33 i Php 2:9; j Mk 16:19; k Ac 1:4; l Jn 7:39; Jn 14:26; m Ac 10:45
2:35 n Ps 110:1; Mt 22:44
2:36 o Lk 2:11
2:37 p Lk 3:10,12,14
2:38 q Ac 8:12,16, 36,38; Ac 22:16; r Lk 24:47; Ac 3:19
2:39 s Isa 44:3; t Ac 10:45; Eph 2:13
2:40 u Dt 32:5
2:42 v Ac 1:14
2:43 w Ac 5:12
2:44 x Ac 4:32

c21 Joel 2:28–32 d23 Or *of those not having the law* (that is, Gentiles) e28 Psalm 16:8–11
f31 Or *Messiah.* "The Christ" (Greek) and "the Messiah" (Hebrew) both mean "the Anointed One"; also in verse 36. g35 Psalm 110:1

anyone as he had need.[y] [46]Every day they continued to meet together in the temple courts.[z] They broke bread[a] in their homes and ate together with glad and sincere hearts, [47]praising God and enjoying the favour of all the people.[b] And the Lord added to their number[c] daily those who were being saved.

Peter Heals the Crippled Beggar

3 One day Peter and John[a] were going up to the temple[b] at the time of prayer—at three in the afternoon.[c] [2]Now a man crippled from birth[d] was being carried to the temple gate[e] called Beautiful, where he was put every day to beg[f] from those going into the temple courts. [3]When he saw Peter and John about to enter, he asked them for money. [4]Peter looked straight at him, as did John. Then Peter said, "Look at us!" [5]So the man gave them his attention, expecting to get something from them.

[6]Then Peter said, "Silver or gold I do not have, but what I have I give you. In the name of Jesus Christ of Nazareth,[g] walk." [7]Taking him by the right hand, he helped him up, and instantly the man's feet and ankles became strong. [8]He jumped to his feet and began to walk. Then he went with them into the temple courts, walking and jumping,[h] and praising God. [9]When all the people[i] saw him walking and praising God, [10]they recognised him as the same man who used to sit begging at the temple gate called Beautiful,[j] and they were filled with wonder and amazement at what had happened to him.

Peter Speaks to the Onlookers

[11]While the beggar held on to Peter and John,[k] all the people were astonished and came running to them in the place called Solomon's Colonnade.[l] [12]When Peter saw this, he said to them: "Men of Israel, why does this surprise you? Why do you stare at us as if by our own power or godliness we had made this man walk? [13]The God of Abraham, Isaac and Jacob, the God of our fathers,[m] has glorified his servant Jesus. You handed him over to be killed, and you disowned him before Pilate,[n] though he had decided to let him go.[o] [14]You disowned the Holy[p] and Righteous One[q] and asked that a murderer be released to you.[r] [15]You killed the author of life, but God raised him from the dead.[s] We are witnesses of this. [16]By faith in the name of Jesus, this man whom you see and know was made strong. It is Jesus' name and the faith that comes through him that has given this complete healing to him, as you can all see.

[17]"Now, brothers, I know that you acted in ignorance,[t] as did your leaders.[u] [18]But this is how God fulfilled what he had foretold[v] through all the prophets,[w] saying that his Christ[a] would suffer.[x] [19]Repent, then, and turn to God, so that your sins may be wiped out,[y] that times of refreshing may come from the Lord, [20]and that he may send the Christ, who has been appointed for you—even Jesus. [21]He must remain in heaven[z] until the time comes for God to restore everything,[a] as he promised long ago through his holy prophets.[b] [22]For Moses said, 'The Lord your God will raise up for you a prophet like me from among your own people; you must listen to everything he tells you.[c] [23]Anyone who does not listen to him will be completely cut off from among his people.'[b][d]

[24]"Indeed, all the prophets[e] from Samuel on, as many as have spoken, have foretold these days.

2:45 y Mt 19:21
2:46 z Lk 24:53; Ac 5:21,42 a Ac 20:7
2:47 b Ro 14:18 c ver 41; Ac 5:14
3:1 a Lk 22:8 b Ac 2:46 c Ps 55:17
3:2 d Ac 14:8 e Lk 16:20 f Jn 9:8
3:6 g ver 16; Ac 4:10
3:8 h Ac 14:10
3:9 i Ac 4:16,21
3:10 j ver 2
3:11 k Lk 22:8 l Jn 10:23; Ac 5:12
3:13 m Ac 5:30 n Mt 27:2 o Lk 23:4
3:14 p Mk 1:24; Ac 4:27 q Ac 7:52 r Mk 15:11; Lk 23:18-25
3:15 s Ac 2:24
3:17 t Lk 23:34 u Ac 13:27
3:18 v Ac 2:23 w Lk 24:27 x Ac 17:2,3; Ac 26:22,23
3:19 y Ac 2:38
3:21 z Ac 1:11 a Mt 17:11 b Lk 1:70
3:22 c Dt 18:15,18; Ac 7:37
3:23 d Dt 18:19
3:24 e Lk 24:27

[a]18 Or *Messiah*; also in verse 20
[b]23 Deut. 18:15,18,19

25 And you are heirs[f] of the prophets and of the covenant[g] God made with your fathers. He said to Abraham, 'Through your offspring all peoples on earth will be blessed.'[c][h] 26 When God raised up[i] his servant, he sent him first[j] to you to bless you by turning each of you from your wicked ways."

Peter and John Before the Sanhedrin

4 The priests and the captain of the temple guard[a] and the Sadducees[b] came up to Peter and John while they were speaking to the people. 2 They were greatly disturbed because the apostles were teaching the people and proclaiming in Jesus the resurrection of the dead.[c] 3 They seized Peter and John, and because it was evening, they put them in jail[d] until the next day. 4 But many who heard the message believed, and the number of men grew[e] to about five thousand.

5 The next day the rulers,[f] elders and teachers of the law met in Jerusalem. 6 Annas the high priest was there, and so were Caiaphas,[g] John, Alexander and the other men of the high priest's family. 7 They had Peter and John brought before them and began to question them: "By what power or what name did you do this?"

8 Then Peter, filled with the Holy Spirit, said to them: "Rulers and elders of the people![h] 9 If we are being called to account today for an act of kindness shown to a cripple[i] and are asked how he was healed, 10 then know this, you and all the people of Israel: It is by the name of Jesus Christ of Nazareth, whom you crucified but whom God raised from the dead,[j] that this man stands before you healed. 11 He is

" 'the stone you builders
 rejected,
which has become the
 capstone.'[a,b][k]

12 Salvation is found in no-one else, for there is no other name under heaven given to men by which we must be saved."[l]

13 When they saw the courage of Peter and John[m] and realised that they were unschooled, ordinary men,[n] they were astonished and they took note that these men had been with Jesus. 14 But since they could see the man who had been healed standing there with them, there was nothing they could say. 15 So they ordered them to withdraw from the Sanhedrin[o] and then conferred together. 16 "What are we going to do with these men?"[p] they asked. "Everybody living in Jerusalem knows they have done an outstanding miracle,[q] and we cannot deny it. 17 But to stop this thing from spreading any further among the people, we must warn these men to speak no longer to anyone in this name."

18 Then they called them in again and commanded them not to speak or teach at all in the name of Jesus.[r] 19 But Peter and John replied, "Judge for yourselves whether it is right in God's sight to obey you rather than God.[s] 20 For we cannot help speaking about what we have seen and heard."

21 After further threats they let them go. They could not decide how to punish them, because all the people[t] were praising God[u] for what had happened. 22 For the man who was miraculously healed was over forty years old.

The Believers' Prayer

23 On their release, Peter and John went back to their own people and reported all that the chief priests and elders had said to them. 24 When they heard this, they raised their voices together in prayer to God. "Sovereign Lord," they said, "you made the heaven and the

3:25 *f* Ac 2:39 *g* Ro 9:4,5 *h* Ge 12:3; Ge 22:18; Ge 26:4; Ge 28:14
3:26 *i* ver 22; Ac 2:24 *j* Ac 13:46; Ro 1:16
4:1 *a* Lk 22:4 *b* Mt 3:7
4:2 *c* Ac 17:18
4:3 *d* Ac 5:18
4:4 *e* Ac 2:41
4:5 *f* Lk 23:13
4:6 *g* Mt 26:3; Lk 3:2
4:8 *h* ver 5; Lk 23:13
4:9 *i* Ac 3:6
4:10 *j* Ac 2:24
4:11 *k* Ps 118:22; Isa 28:16; Mt 21:42
4:12 *l* Mt 1:21; Ac 10:43; 1Ti 2:5
4:13 *m* Lk 22:8 *n* Mt 11:25
4:15 *o* Mt 5:22
4:16 *p* Jn 11:47 *q* Ac 3:6-10
4:18 *r* Ac 5:40
4:19 *s* Ac 5:29
4:21 *t* Ac 5:26 *u* Mt 9:8

c25 Gen. 22:18; 26:4
a11 Or *cornerstone*
b11 Psalm 118:22

earth and the sea, and everything
in them. 25You spoke by the Holy
Spirit through the mouth of your
servant, our father David:[v]

"'Why do the nations rage
and the peoples plot in vain?
26The kings of the earth take
their stand
and the rulers gather together
against the Lord
and against his Anointed
One.'[c,d][w]

27Indeed Herod[x] and Pontius Pilate[y] met together with the Gentiles and the people[e] of Israel in
this city to conspire against your
holy servant Jesus,[z] whom you
anointed. 28They did what your
power and will had decided beforehand should happen.[a] 29Now, Lord,
consider their threats and enable
your servants to speak your word
with great boldness.[b] 30Stretch out
your hand to heal and perform
miraculous signs and wonders[c]
through the name of your holy servant Jesus."[d]
31After they prayed, the place
where they were meeting was
shaken.[e] And they were all filled
with the Holy Spirit and spoke the
word of God boldly.[f]

The Believers Share Their Possessions

32All the believers were one in
heart and mind. No-one claimed
that any of his possessions was his
own, but they shared everything
they had.[g] 33With great power the
apostles continued to testify[h] to
the resurrection[i] of the Lord
Jesus, and much grace was upon
them all. 34There were no needy
persons among them. For from
time to time those who owned lands
or houses sold them,[j] brought the
money from the sales 35and put it
at the apostles' feet,[k] and it was
distributed to anyone as he had
need.[l]
36Joseph, a Levite from Cyprus,
whom the apostles called Barnabas[m] (which means Son of Encouragement), 37sold a field he owned
and brought the money and put it at
the apostles' feet.[n]

Ananias and Sapphira

5 Now a man named Ananias, together with his wife Sapphira,
also sold a piece of property. 2With
his wife's full knowledge he kept
back part of the money for himself,
but brought the rest and put it at
the apostles' feet.[a]
3Then Peter said, "Ananias, how
is it that Satan[b] has so filled your
heart[c] that you have lied to the
Holy Spirit[d] and have kept for
yourself some of the money you received for the land? 4Didn't it belong to you before it was sold? And
after it was sold, wasn't the money
at your disposal? What made you
think of doing such a thing? You
have not lied to men but to God."
5When Ananias heard this, he fell
down and died.[e] And great fear[f]
seized all who heard what had happened. 6Then the young men came
forward, wrapped up his body,[g]
and carried him out and buried him.
7About three hours later his wife
came in, not knowing what had happened. 8Peter asked her, "Tell me,
is this the price you and Ananias
got for the land?"
"Yes," she said, "that is the
price."[h]
9Peter said to her, "How could
you agree to test the Spirit of the
Lord?[i] Look! The feet of the men
who buried your husband are at the
door, and they will carry you out
also."
10At that moment she fell down at
his feet and died.[j] Then the young
men came in and, finding her dead,
carried her out and buried her beside her husband. 11Great fear[k]
seized the whole church and all
who heard about these events.

4:25 v Ac 1:16
4:26 w Ps 2:1,2; Da 9:25; Lk 4:18; Ac 10:38; Heb 1:9
4:27 x Mt 14:1; y Mt 27:2; Lk 23:12; z ver 30
4:28 a Ac 2:23
4:29 b ver 13,31; Ac 9:27; Ac 14:3; Php 1:14
4:30 c Jn 4:48; d ver 27
4:31 e Ac 2:2; f ver 29
4:32 g Ac 2:44
4:33 h Lk 24:48; i Ac 1:22
4:34 j Mt 19:21; Ac 2:45
4:35 k ver 37; Ac 5:2; l Ac 2:45; Ac 6:1
4:36 m Ac 9:27; 1Co 9:6
4:37 n ver 35; Ac 5:2
5:2 a Ac 4:35,37
5:3 b Mt 4:10; c Jn 13:2,27; d ver 9
5:5 e ver 10; f ver 11
5:6 g Jn 19:40
5:8 h ver 2
5:9 i ver 3
5:10 j ver 5
5:11 k ver 5; Ac 19:17

c26 That is, Christ or Messiah d26 Psalm 2:1,2
e27 The Greek is plural.

The Apostles Heal Many

12 The apostles performed many miraculous signs and wonders[l] among the people. And all the believers used to meet together[m] in Solomon's Colonnade.[n] 13 No-one else dared join them, even though they were highly regarded by the people.[o] 14 Nevertheless, more and more men and women believed in the Lord and were added to their number. 15 As a result, people brought the sick into the streets and laid them on beds and mats so that at least Peter's shadow might fall on some of them as he passed by.[p] 16 Crowds gathered also from the towns around Jerusalem, bringing their sick and those tormented by evil[a] spirits, and all of them were healed.[q]

The Apostles Persecuted

17 Then the high priest and all his associates, who were members of the party[r] of the Sadducees,[s] were filled with jealousy. 18 They arrested the apostles and put them in the public jail.[t] 19 But during the night an angel[u] of the Lord opened the doors of the jail[v] and brought them out. 20 "Go, stand in the temple courts," he said, "and tell the people the full message of this new life."[w]

21 At daybreak they entered the temple courts, as they had been told, and began to teach the people.

When the high priest and his associates[x] arrived, they called together the Sanhedrin[y]—the full assembly of the elders of Israel—and sent to the jail for the apostles. 22 But on arriving at the jail, the officers did not find them there. So they went back and reported, 23 "We found the jail securely locked, with the guards standing at the doors; but when we opened them, we found no-one inside." 24 On hearing this report, the captain of the temple guard and the chief priests[z] were puzzled, wondering what would come of this.

25 Then someone came and said, "Look! The men you put in jail are standing in the temple courts teaching the people." 26 At that, the captain went with his officers and brought the apostles. They did not use force, because they feared that the people[a] would stone them.

27 Having brought the apostles, they made them appear before the Sanhedrin[b] to be questioned by the high priest. 28 "We gave you strict orders not to teach in this name,"[c] he said. "Yet you have filled Jerusalem with your teaching and are determined to make us guilty of this man's blood."[d]

29 Peter and the other apostles replied: "We must obey God rather than men![e] 30 The God of our fathers[f] raised Jesus from the dead[g]—whom you had killed by hanging him on a tree.[h] 31 God exalted him to his own right hand[i] as Prince and Saviour[j] that he might give repentance and forgiveness of sins to Israel.[k] 32 We are witnesses of these things,[l] and so is the Holy Spirit,[m] whom God has given to those who obey him."

33 When they heard this, they were furious[n] and wanted to put them to death. 34 But a Pharisee named Gamaliel,[o] a teacher of the law,[p] who was honoured by all the people, stood up in the Sanhedrin and ordered that the men be put outside for a little while. 35 Then he addressed them: "Men of Israel, consider carefully what you intend to do to these men. 36 Some time ago Theudas appeared, claiming to be somebody, and about four hundred men rallied to him. He was killed, all his followers were dispersed, and it all came to nothing. 37 After him, Judas the Galilean appeared in the days of the census[q] and led a band of people in revolt. He too was killed, and all his followers

5:12 *l* Ac 2:43 *m* Ac 4:32 *n* Ac 3:11
5:13 *o* Ac 2:47 Ac 4:21
5:15 *p* Ac 19:12
5:16 *q* Mk 16:17
5:17 *r* Ac 15:5 *s* Ac 4:1
5:18 *t* Ac 4:3
5:19 *u* Mt 1:20 Lk 1:11 Ac 8:26 Ac 27:23 *v* Ac 16:26
5:20 *w* Jn 6:63,68
5:21 *x* Ac 4:5,6 *y* ver 27,34,41 Mt 5:22
5:24 *z* Ac 4:1
5:26 *a* Ac 4:21
5:27 *b* Mt 5:22
5:28 *c* Ac 4:18 *d* Mt 23:35 Mt 27:25 Ac 2:23,36 Ac 3:14,15 Ac 7:52
5:29 *e* Ac 4:19
5:30 *f* Ac 3:13 *g* Ac 2:24 *h* Ac 10:39 Ac 13:29 Gal 3:13 1Pe 2:24
5:31 *i* Ac 2:33 *j* Lk 2:11 *k* Mt 1:21 Lk 24:47 Ac 2:38
5:32 *l* Lk 24:48 *m* Jn 15:26
5:33 *n* Ac 2:37 Ac 7:54
5:34 *o* Ac 22:3 *p* Lk 2:46
5:37 *q* Lk 2:1,2

[a] *16* Greek *unclean*

were scattered. 38Therefore, in the present case I advise you: Leave these men alone! Let them go! For if their purpose or activity is of human origin, it will fail.[r] 39But if it is from God, you will not be able to stop these men; you will only find yourselves fighting against God."[s]

40His speech persuaded them. They called the apostles in and had them flogged.[t] Then they ordered them not to speak in the name of Jesus, and let them go.

41The apostles left the Sanhedrin, rejoicing[u] because they had been counted worthy of suffering disgrace for the Name.[v] 42Day after day, in the temple courts[w] and from house to house, they never stopped teaching and proclaiming the good news that Jesus is the Christ.[b]

The Choosing of the Seven

6 In those days when the number of disciples was increasing,[a] the Grecian Jews[b] among them complained against the Hebraic Jews because their widows[c] were being overlooked in the daily distribution of food.[d] 2So the Twelve gathered all the disciples together and said, "It would not be right for us to neglect the ministry of the word of God in order to wait on tables. 3Brothers,[e] choose seven men from among you who are known to be full of the Spirit and wisdom. We will turn this responsibility over to them 4and will give our attention to prayer[f] and the ministry of the word."

5This proposal pleased the whole group. They chose Stephen,[g] a man full of faith and of the Holy Spirit;[h] also Philip,[i] Procorus, Nicanor, Timon, Parmenas, and Nicolas from Antioch, a convert to Judaism. 6They presented these men to the apostles, who prayed[j] and laid their hands on them.[k]

7So the word of God spread.[l]

5:38 r Mt 15:13
5:39 s Pr 21:30; Ac 7:51; Ac 11:17
5:40 t Mt 10:17
5:41 u Mt 5:12; v Jn 15:21
5:42 w Ac 2:46
6:1 a Ac 2:41; b Ac 9:29; c Ac 9:39,41; d Ac 4:35
6:3 e Ac 1:16
6:4 f Ac 1:14
6:5 g ver 8; Ac 11:19; h Ac 11:24; i Ac 8:5-40; Ac 21:8
6:6 j Ac 1:24; Ac 8:17; Ac 13:3; 2Ti 1:6; k Nu 8:10; Ac 9:17; 1Ti 4:14
6:7 l Ac 12:24; Ac 19:20
6:8 m Jn 4:48
6:9 n Mt 27:32; o Ac 15:23,41; Ac 22:3; Ac 23:34; p Ac 2:9
6:10 q Lk 21:15
6:11 r 1Ki 21:10; s Mt 26:59-61
6:12 t Mt 5:22
6:13 u Ac 21:28
6:14 v Ac 15:1; Ac 21:21; Ac 26:3; Ac 28:17
6:15 w Mt 5:22
7:2 a Ac 22:1; b Ps 29:3; c Ge 11:31; Ge 15:7

The number of disciples in Jerusalem increased rapidly, and a large number of priests became obedient to the faith.

Stephen Seized

8Now Stephen, a man full of God's grace and power, did great wonders and miraculous signs[m] among the people. 9Opposition arose, however, from members of the Synagogue of the Freedmen (as it was called)—Jews of Cyrene[n] and Alexandria as well as the provinces of Cilicia[o] and Asia.[p] These men began to argue with Stephen, 10but they could not stand up against his wisdom or the Spirit by whom he spoke.[q]

11Then they secretly[r] persuaded some men to say, "We have heard Stephen speak words of blasphemy against Moses and against God."[s]

12So they stirred up the people and the elders and the teachers of the law. They seized Stephen and brought him before the Sanhedrin.[t] 13They produced false witnesses, who testified, "This fellow never stops speaking against this holy place[u] and against the law. 14For we have heard him say that this Jesus of Nazareth will destroy this place and change the customs Moses handed down to us."[v]

15All who were sitting in the Sanhedrin[w] looked intently at Stephen, and they saw that his face was like the face of an angel.

Stephen's Speech to the Sanhedrin

7 Then the high priest asked him, "Are these charges true?"

2To this he replied: "Brothers and fathers,[a] listen to me! The God of glory[b] appeared to our father Abraham while he was still in Mesopotamia, before he lived in Haran.[c] 3'Leave your country and

b42 Or *Messiah*

your people,’ God said, ‘and go to
the land I will show you.’[a][d]
4“So he left the land of the Chaldeans and settled in Haran. After
the death of his father, God sent
him to this land where you are now
living.[e] 5He gave him no inheritance here, not even a foot of
ground. But God promised him that
he and his descendants after him
would possess the land,[f] even
though at that time Abraham had
no child. 6God spoke to him in this
way: ‘Your descendants will be
strangers in a country not their
own, and they will be enslaved
and ill-treated for four hundred
years.[g] 7But I will punish the nation they serve as slaves,’ God said,
‘and afterwards they will come out
of that country and worship me in
this place.’[b][h] 8Then he gave Abraham the covenant of circumcision.[i] And Abraham became the
father of Isaac and circumcised
him eight days after his birth.[j]
Later Isaac became the father of
Jacob,[k] and Jacob became the
father of the twelve patriarchs.[l]
9“Because the patriarchs were
jealous of Joseph,[m] they sold him
as a slave into Egypt.[n] But God
was with him[o] 10and rescued him
from all his troubles. He gave Joseph wisdom and enabled him to
gain the goodwill of Pharaoh king
of Egypt; so he made him ruler
over Egypt and all his palace.[p]
11“Then a famine struck all
Egypt and Canaan, bringing great
suffering, and our fathers could
not find food.[q] 12When Jacob heard
that there was grain in Egypt, he
sent our fathers on their first
visit.[r] 13On their second visit, Joseph told his brothers who he
was,[s] and Pharaoh learned about
Joseph’s family. 14After this, Joseph sent for his father Jacob and
his whole family,[t] seventy-five in
all.[u] 15Then Jacob went down to
Egypt, where he and our fathers
died.[v] 16Their bodies were brought
back to Shechem and placed in the
tomb that Abraham had bought
from the sons of Hamor at Shechem for a certain sum of money.[w]
17“As the time drew near for God
to fulfil his promise to Abraham,
the number of our people in Egypt
greatly increased.[x] 18Then another king, who knew nothing
about Joseph, became ruler of
Egypt.[y] 19He dealt treacherously
with our people and oppressed our
forefathers by forcing them to
throw out their newborn babies so
that they would die.[z]
20“At that time Moses was born,
and he was no ordinary child.[c] For
three months he was cared for in
his father’s house.[a] 21When he was
placed outside, Pharaoh’s daughter
took him and brought him up as her
own son.[b] 22Moses was educated in
all the wisdom of the Egyptians[c]
and was powerful in speech and action.
23“When Moses was forty years
old, he decided to visit his fellow Israelites. 24He saw one of
them being ill-treated by an Egyptian, so he went to his defence and
avenged him by killing the Egyptian.
25Moses thought that his own people would realise that God was
using him to rescue them, but they
did not. 26The next day Moses came
upon two Israelites who were fighting. He tried to reconcile them by
saying, ‘Men, you are brothers;
why do you want to hurt each
other?’
27“But the man who was ill-
treating the other pushed Moses
aside and said, ‘Who made you
ruler and judge over us? 28Do you
want to kill me as you killed the
Egyptian yesterday?’[d] 29When Moses
heard this, he fled to Midian,
where he settled as a foreigner and
had two sons.[d]
30“After forty years had passed,
an angel appeared to Moses in the
flames of a burning bush in the

7:3 d Ge 12:1
7:4 e Ge 12:5
7:5 f Ge 12:7; Ge 17:8; Ge 26:3
7:6 g Ex 12:40
7:7 h Ex 3:12
7:8 i Ge 17:9-14; j Ge 21:2-4; k Ge 25:26; l Ge 29:31-35; Ge 30:5-13, 17-24; Ge 35:16-18, 22-26
7:9 m Ge 37:4,11; n Ge 37:28; Ps 105:17; o Ge 39:2,21,23
7:10 p Ge 41:37-43
7:11 q Ge 41:54
7:12 r Ge 42:1,2
7:13 s Ge 45:1-4
7:14 t Ge 45:9,10; u Ge 46:26,27; Ex 1:5; Dt 10:22
7:15 v Ge 46:5-7; Ge 49:33; Ex 1:6
7:16 w Ge 23:16-20; Ge 33:18,19; Ge 50:13; Jos 24:32
7:17 x Ex 1:7; Ps 105:24
7:18 y Ex 1:8
7:19 z Ex 1:10-22
7:20 a Ex 2:2; Heb 11:23
7:21 b Ex 2:3-10
7:22 c 1Ki 4:30; Isa 19:11
7:29 d Ex 2:11-15

a3 Gen. 12:1 b7 Gen. 15:13,14 c20 Or *was fair in the sight of God* d28 Exodus 2:14

desert near Mount Sinai. 31 When he
saw this, he was amazed at the
sight. As he went over to look more
closely, he heard the Lord's
voice:[e] 32 'I am the God of your fathers, the God of Abraham, Isaac
and Jacob.'[e] Moses trembled with
fear and did not dare to look.[f]

33 "Then the Lord said to him,
'Take off your sandals; the place
where you are standing is holy
ground.[g] 34 I have indeed seen the
oppression of my people in Egypt.
I have heard their groaning and
have come down to set them free.
Now come, I will send you back to
Egypt.'[f][h]

35 "This is the same Moses whom
they had rejected with the words,
'Who made you ruler and judge?'[i]
He was sent to be their ruler and
deliverer by God himself, through
the angel who appeared to him in
the bush. 36 He led them out of
Egypt[j] and did wonders and miraculous signs in Egypt, at the Red
Sea[g][k] and for forty years in the
desert.

37 "This is that Moses who told the
Israelites, 'God will send you a
prophet like me from your own
people.'[h][l] 38 He was in the assembly in the desert, with the angel[m]
who spoke to him on Mount Sinai,
and with our fathers;[n] and he received living words[o] to pass on to
us.[p]

39 "But our fathers refused to
obey him. Instead, they rejected
him and in their hearts turned back
to Egypt.[q] 40 They told Aaron,
'Make us gods who will go before
us. As for this fellow Moses who led
us out of Egypt—we don't know
what has happened to him!'[i][r]
41 That was the time they made an
idol in the form of a calf. They
brought sacrifices to it and held a
celebration in honour of what their
hands had made.[s] 42 But God
turned away[t] and gave them over
to the worship of the heavenly
bodies.[u] This agrees with what is
written in the book of the prophets:

" 'Did you bring me sacrifices
and offerings
for forty years in the desert,
O house of Israel?
43 You have lifted up the shrine of
Molech
and the star of your god
Rephan,
the idols you made to worship.
Therefore I will send you into
exile'[j][v] beyond Babylon.

44 "Our forefathers had the tabernacle of the Testimony[w] with them
in the desert. It had been made as
God directed Moses, according to
the pattern he had seen.[x] 45 Having
received the tabernacle, our fathers under Joshua brought it with
them when they took the land from
the nations God drove out before
them.[y] It remained in the land
until the time of David, 46 who enjoyed God's favour and asked that
he might provide a dwelling-place
for the God of Jacob.[k][z] 47 But it
was Solomon who built the house
for him.

48 "However, the Most High does
not live in houses made by men.[a]
As the prophet says:

49 " 'Heaven is my throne,
and the earth is my footstool.[b]
What kind of house will you
build for me?
says the Lord.
Or where will my resting
place be?
50 Has not my hand made all these
things?'[l][c]

51 "You stiff-necked people,[d]
with uncircumcised hearts[e] and
ears! You are just like your fathers: You always resist the Holy
Spirit! 52 Was there ever a prophet your fathers did not persecute?[f] They even killed those who
predicted the coming of the Righteous One. And now you have

7:31 e Ex 3:1-4
7:32 f Ex 3:6
7:33 g Ex 3:5; Jos 5:15
7:34 h Ex 3:7-10
7:35 i ver 27
7:36 j Ex 12:41; Ex 33:1; k Ex 14:21
7:37 l Dt 18:15,18; Ac 3:22
7:38 m ver 53; n Ex 19:17; o Dt 32:45-47; Heb 4:12; p Ro 3:2
7:39 q Nu 14:3,4
7:40 r Ex 32:1,23
7:41 s Ex 32:4-6; Ps 106:19,20; Rev 9:20
7:42 t Jos 24:20; Isa 63:10; u Jer 19:13
7:43 v Am 5:25-27
7:44 w Ex 38:21; x Ex 25:8,9,40
7:45 y Jos 3:14-17; Jos 18:1; Jos 23:9; Jos 24:18; Ps 44:2
7:46 z 2Sa 7:8-16; Ps 132:1-5
7:48 a 1Ki 8:27; 2Ch 2:6
7:49 b Mt 5:34,35
7:50 c Isa 66:1,2
7:51 d Ex 32:9; Ex 33:3,5; e Lev 26:41; Dt 10:16; Jer 4:4; Jer 9:26
7:52 f 2Ch 36:16; Mt 5:12

e 32 Exodus 3:6 f 34 Exodus 3:5,7,8,10
g 36 That is, Sea of Reeds h 37 Deut. 18:15
i 40 Exodus 32:1 j 43 Amos 5:25–27
k 46 Some early manuscripts *the house of Jacob*
l 50 Isaiah 66:1,2

betrayed and murdered him[g]— [53]you who have received the law that was put into effect through angels[h] but have not obeyed it."

The Stoning of Stephen

[54]When they heard this, they were furious[i] and gnashed their teeth at him. [55]But Stephen, full of the Holy Spirit, looked up to heaven and saw the glory of God, and Jesus standing at the right hand of God.[j] [56]"Look," he said, "I see heaven open[k] and the Son of Man[l] standing at the right hand of God."

[57]At this they covered their ears and, yelling at the top of their voices, they all rushed at him, [58]dragged him out of the city[m] and began to stone him.[n] Meanwhile, the witnesses laid their clothes[o] at the feet of a young man named Saul.[p]

[59]While they were stoning him, Stephen prayed, "Lord Jesus, receive my spirit."[q] [60]Then he fell on his knees[r] and cried out, "Lord, do not hold this sin against them."[s] When he had said this, he fell asleep.

8 And Saul[a] was there, giving approval to his death.

The Church Persecuted and Scattered

On that day a great persecution broke out against the church at Jerusalem, and all except the apostles were scattered[b] throughout Judea and Samaria.[c] [2]Godly men buried Stephen and mourned deeply for him. [3]But Saul[d] began to destroy the church.[e] Going from house to house, he dragged off men and women and put them in prison.

Philip in Samaria

[4]Those who had been scattered[f] preached the word wherever they went.[g] [5]Philip[h] went down to a city in Samaria and proclaimed the Christ[a] there. [6]When the crowds heard Philip and saw the miraculous signs he did, they all paid close attention to what he said. [7]With shrieks, evil[b] spirits came out of many,[i] and many paralytics and cripples were healed.[j] [8]So there was great joy in that city.

Simon the Sorcerer

[9]Now for some time a man named Simon had practised sorcery[k] in the city and amazed all the people of Samaria. He boasted that he was someone great,[l] [10]and all the people, both high and low, gave him their attention and exclaimed, "This man is the divine power known as the Great Power."[m] [11]They followed him because he had amazed them for a long time with his magic. [12]But when they believed Philip as he preached the good news of the kingdom of God[n] and the name of Jesus Christ, they were baptised,[o] both men and women. [13]Simon himself believed and was baptised. And he followed Philip everywhere, astonished by the great signs and miracles[p] he saw.

[14]When the apostles in Jerusalem heard that Samaria[q] had accepted the word of God, they sent Peter and John[r] to them. [15]When they arrived, they prayed for them that they might receive the Holy Spirit,[s] [16]because the Holy Spirit had not yet come upon any of them;[t] they had simply been baptised into[c] the name of the Lord Jesus.[u] [17]Then Peter and John placed their hands on them,[v] and they received the Holy Spirit.

[18]When Simon saw that the Spirit was given at the laying on of the apostles' hands, he offered them money [19]and said, "Give me also this ability so that everyone on whom I lay my hands may receive the Holy Spirit."

7:52 g Ac 3:14; 1Th 2:15
7:53 h ver 38; Gal 3:19; Heb 2:2
7:54 i Ac 5:33
7:55 j Mk 16:19
7:56 k Mt 3:16; l Mt 8:20
7:58 m Lk 4:29; n Lev 24:14,16; Dt 13:9; o Ac 22:20; p Ac 8:1
7:59 q Ps 31:5; Lk 23:46
7:60 r Ac 9:40; s Mt 5:44
8:1 a Ac 7:58; b Ac 11:19; c Ac 9:31
8:3 d Ac 7:58; e Ac 22:4,19; Ac 26:10,11; 1Co 15:9; Gal 1:13,23; Php 3:6; 1Ti 1:13
8:4 f ver 1; g Ac 15:35
8:5 h Ac 6:5
8:7 i Mk 16:17; j Mt 4:24
8:9 k Ac 13:6; l Ac 5:36
8:10 m Ac 14:11; Ac 28:6
8:12 n Ac 1:3; o Ac 2:38
8:13 p ver 6; Ac 19:11
8:14 q ver 1; r Lk 22:8
8:15 s Ac 2:38
8:16 t Ac 19:2; u Mt 28:19; Ac 2:38
8:17 v Ac 6:6

[a]5 Or *Messiah* [b]7 Greek *unclean* [c]16 Or *in*

20Peter answered: "May your money perish with you, because you thought you could buy the gift of God with money![w] 21You have no part or share in this ministry, because your heart is not right[x] before God. 22Repent of this wickedness and pray to the Lord. Perhaps he will forgive you for having such a thought in your heart. 23For I see that you are full of bitterness and captive to sin."

24Then Simon answered, "Pray to the Lord for me[y] so that nothing you have said may happen to me."

25When they had testified and proclaimed the word of the Lord, Peter and John returned to Jerusalem, preaching the gospel in many Samaritan villages.[z]

Philip and the Ethiopian

26Now an angel[a] of the Lord said to Philip, "Go south to the road—the desert road—that goes down from Jerusalem to Gaza." 27So he started out, and on his way he met an Ethiopian[d][b] eunuch,[c] an important official in charge of all the treasury of Candace, queen of the Ethiopians. This man had gone to Jerusalem to worship,[d] 28and on his way home was sitting in his chariot reading the book of Isaiah the prophet. 29The Spirit told[e] Philip, "Go to that chariot and stay near it."

30Then Philip ran up to the chariot and heard the man reading Isaiah the prophet. "Do you understand what you are reading?" Philip asked.

31"How can I," he said, "unless someone explains it to me?" So he invited Philip to come up and sit with him.

32The eunuch was reading this passage of Scripture:

"He was led like a sheep to the
  slaughter,
 and as a lamb before the
  shearer is silent,
 so he did not open his mouth.
33In his humiliation he was
  deprived of justice.
 Who can speak of his
  descendants?
 For his life was taken from
  the earth."[e][f]

34The eunuch asked Philip, "Tell me, please, who is the prophet talking about, himself or someone else?" 35Then Philip began[g] with that very passage of Scripture[h] and told him the good news about Jesus.

36As they travelled along the road, they came to some water and the eunuch said, "Look, here is water. Why shouldn't I be baptised?"[f][i] 38And he gave orders to stop the chariot. Then both Philip and the eunuch went down into the water and Philip baptised him. 39When they came up out of the water, the Spirit of the Lord suddenly took Philip away,[j] and the eunuch did not see him again, but went on his way rejoicing. 40Philip, however, appeared at Azotus and travelled about, preaching the gospel in all the towns[k] until he reached Caesarea.[l]

Saul's Conversion

9:1–19pp Ac 22:3–16; 26:9–18

9 Meanwhile, Saul was still breathing out murderous threats against the Lord's disciples.[a] He went to the high priest 2and asked him for letters to the synagogues in Damascus, so that if he found any there who belonged to the Way,[b] whether men or women, he might take them as prisoners to Jerusalem. 3As he neared Damascus on his journey, suddenly a light from heaven flashed around him.[c] 4He fell to the ground and heard a voice say to him, "Saul, Saul, why do you persecute me?"

8:20 w 2Ki 5:16; Da 5:17; Mt 10:8; Ac 2:38
8:21 x Ps 78:37
8:24 y Ex 8:8; Nu 21:7; 1Ki 13:6
8:25 z ver 40
8:26 a Ac 5:19
8:27 b Ps 68:31; Ps 87:4; Zep 3:10 c Isa 56:3-5 d 1Ki 8:41-43; Jn 12:20
8:29 e Ac 10:19; Ac 11:12; Ac 13:2; Ac 20:23; Ac 21:11
8:33 f Isa 53:7,8
8:35 g Mt 5:2 h Lk 24:27; Ac 17:2; Ac 18:28; Ac 28:23
8:36 i Ac 10:47
8:39 j 1Ki 18:12; 2Ki 2:16; Eze 3:12,14; Eze 8:3; Eze 11:1,24; Eze 43:5; 2Co 12:2
8:40 k ver 25 l Ac 10:1,24; Ac 12:19; Ac 21:8,16; Ac 23:23,33; Ac 25:1,4,6,13
9:1 a Ac 8:3
9:2 b Ac 19:9,23; Ac 22:4; Ac 24:14,22
9:3 c 1Co 15:8

d27 That is, from the upper Nile region
e33 Isaiah 53:7,8 f36 Some late manuscripts *baptised?" 37Philip said, "If you believe with all your heart, you may." The eunuch answered, "I believe that Jesus Christ is the Son of God."*

5 “Who are you, Lord?” Saul
asked.
“I am Jesus, whom you are persecuting,” he replied. 6 “Now get up
and go into the city, and you will be
told what you must do.”[d]
7 The men travelling with Saul
stood there speechless; they heard
the sound[e] but did not see anyone.[f] 8 Saul got up from the ground,
but when he opened his eyes he
could see nothing. So they led him
by the hand into Damascus. 9 For
three days he was blind, and did not
eat or drink anything.
10 In Damascus there was a disciple named Ananias. The Lord
called to him in a vision,[g] “Ananias!”
“Yes, Lord,” he answered.
11 The Lord told him, “Go to the
house of Judas on Straight Street
and ask for a man from Tarsus[h]
named Saul, for he is praying. 12 In
a vision he has seen a man named
Ananias come and place his hands
on[i] him to restore his sight.”
13 “Lord,” Ananias answered, “I
have heard many reports about this
man and all the harm he has done to
your saints[j] in Jerusalem.[k] 14 And
he has come here with authority
from the chief priests[l] to arrest all
who call on your name.”
15 But the Lord said to Ananias,
“Go! This man is my chosen instrument[m] to carry my name before
the Gentiles[n] and their kings[o] and
before the people of Israel. 16 I will
show him how much he must suffer
for my name.”[p]
17 Then Ananias went to the house
and entered it. Placing his hands
on[q] Saul, he said, “Brother Saul,
the Lord—Jesus, who appeared to
you on the road as you were coming
here—has sent me so that you may
see again and be filled with the
Holy Spirit.” 18 Immediately, something like scales fell from Saul's
eyes, and he could see again. He got
up and was baptised, 19 and after
taking some food, he regained his
strength.

9:6 d ver 16
9:7 e Jn 12:29 f Da 10:7; Ac 22:9
9:10 g Ac 10:3,17,19
9:11 h ver 30; Ac 21:39; Ac 22:3
9:12 i Mk 5:23
9:13 j ver 32; Ro 1:7; Ro 16:2,15 k Ac 8:3
9:14 l ver 2,21
9:15 m Ac 13:2; Ro 1:1; Gal 1:15 n Ro 11:13; Ro 15:15,16; Gal 2:7,8; Eph 3:7,8 o Ac 25:22,23; Ac 26:1
9:16 p Ac 20:23; Ac 21:11; 2Co 11:23-27
9:17 q Ac 6:6
9:19 r Ac 11:26 s Ac 26:20
9:20 t Ac 13:5,14 u Mt 4:3
9:21 v Ac 8:3 w Gal 1:13,23
9:22 x Ac 18:5,28
9:24 y Ac 20:3,19
9:25 z 1Sa 19:12; 2Co 11:32,33
9:26 a Ac 22:17; Ac 26:20; Gal 1:17,18
9:27 b Ac 4:36 c ver 3-6 d ver 20,22
9:29 e Ac 6:1 f 2Co 11:26
9:30 g Ac 1:16 h Ac 8:40 i ver 11
9:31 j Ac 8:1

Saul in Damascus and Jerusalem

Saul spent several days with
the disciples[r] in Damascus.[s] 20 At
once he began to preach in the
synagogues[t] that Jesus is the Son
of God.[u] 21 All those who heard him
were astonished and asked, “Isn't
he the man who caused havoc in
Jerusalem among those who call on
this name?[v] And hasn't he come
here to take them as prisoners to
the chief priests?”[w] 22 Yet Saul
grew more and more powerful and
baffled the Jews living in Damascus by proving that Jesus is the
Christ.[a][x]
23 After many days had gone by,
the Jews conspired to kill him,
24 but Saul learned of their plan.[y]
Day and night they kept close
watch on the city gates in order to
kill him. 25 But his followers took him
by night and lowered him in a basket through an opening in the wall.[z]
26 When he came to Jerusalem,[a]
he tried to join the disciples, but
they were all afraid of him, not believing that he really was a disciple. 27 But Barnabas[b] took him
and brought him to the apostles. He
told them how Saul on his journey
had seen the Lord and that the Lord
had spoken to him,[c] and how in Damascus he had preached fearlessly
in the name of Jesus.[d] 28 So Saul
stayed with them and moved about
freely in Jerusalem, speaking
boldly in the name of the Lord.
29 He talked and debated with the
Grecian Jews,[e] but they tried to
kill him.[f] 30 When the brothers[g]
learned of this, they took him down
to Caesarea[h] and sent him off to
Tarsus.[i]
31 Then the church throughout Judea, Galilee and Samaria[j] enjoyed
a time of peace. It was strengthened; and encouraged by the Holy
Spirit, it grew in numbers, living in
the fear of the Lord.

a22 Or *Messiah*

Aeneas and Dorcas

32 As Peter travelled about the
country, he went to visit the
saints[k] in Lydda. 33 There he found
a man named Aeneas, a paralytic
who had been bedridden for eight
years. 34 "Aeneas," Peter said to
him, "Jesus Christ heals you.[l] Get
up and tidy up your mat." Immediately Aeneas got up. 35 All those who
lived in Lydda and Sharon[m] saw
him and turned to the Lord.[n]
36 In Joppa[o] there was a disciple
named Tabitha (which, when translated, is Dorcas[b]), who was always
doing good[p] and helping the poor.
37 About that time she became sick
and died, and her body was washed
and placed in an upstairs room.[q]
38 Lydda was near Joppa; so when
the disciples[r] heard that Peter was
in Lydda, they sent two men to him
and urged him, "Please come at
once!"
39 Peter went with them, and
when he arrived he was taken upstairs to the room. All the widows[s]
stood around him, crying and showing him the robes and other clothing that Dorcas had made while she
was still with them.
40 Peter sent them all out of the
room;[t] then he got down on his
knees[u] and prayed. Turning towards the dead woman, he said,
"Tabitha, get up." She opened her
eyes, and seeing Peter she sat up.
41 He took her by the hand and
helped her to her feet. Then he
called the believers and the widows
and presented her to them alive.
42 This became known all over
Joppa, and many people believed in
the Lord. 43 Peter stayed in Joppa
for some time with a tanner named
Simon.[v]

Cornelius Calls for Peter

10 At Caesarea[a] there was a
man named Cornelius, a
centurion in what was known as the
Italian Regiment. 2 He and all his
family were devout and God-
fearing;[b] he gave generously to
those in need and prayed to God
regularly. 3 One day at about three
in the afternoon[c] he had a vision.[d]
He distinctly saw an angel[e] of
God, who came to him and said,
"Cornelius!"
4 Cornelius stared at him in fear.
"What is it, Lord?" he asked.
The angel answered, "Your
prayers and gifts to the poor have
come up as a memorial offering[f]
before God.[g] 5 Now send men to
Joppa[h] to bring back a man named
Simon who is called Peter. 6 He is
staying with Simon the tanner,[i]
whose house is by the sea."
7 When the angel who spoke to
him had gone, Cornelius called two
of his servants and a devout soldier
who was one of his attendants. 8 He
told them everything that had happened and sent them to Joppa.[j]

Peter's Vision

10:9–32Ref Ac 11:5–14

9 About noon the following day as
they were on their journey and approaching the city, Peter went up
on the roof[k] to pray. 10 He became
hungry and wanted something to
eat, and while the meal was being
prepared, he fell into a trance.[l]
11 He saw heaven opened and something like a large sheet being let
down to earth by its four corners.
12 It contained all kinds of four-
footed animals, as well as reptiles
of the earth and birds of the air.
13 Then a voice told him, "Get up,
Peter. Kill and eat."
14 "Surely not, Lord!"[m] Peter replied. "I have never eaten anything
impure or unclean."[n]
15 The voice spoke to him a second
time, "Do not call anything impure
that God has made clean."[o]

9:32 *k* ver 13
9:34 *l* Ac 3:6,16; Ac 4:10
9:35 *m* 1Ch 5:16; 1Ch 27:29; Isa 33:9; Isa 35:2; Isa 65:10 *n* Ac 11:21
9:36 *o* Jos 19:46; 2Ch 2:16; Ezr 3:7; Jnh 1:3; Ac 10:5 *p* 1Ti 2:10; Tit 3:8
9:37 *q* Ac 1:13
9:38 *r* Ac 11:26
9:39 *s* Ac 6:1
9:40 *t* Mt 9:25 *u* Lk 22:41; Ac 7:60
9:43 *v* Ac 10:6
10:1 *a* Ac 8:40
10:2 *b* ver 22,35; Ac 13:16,26
10:3 *c* Ac 3:1 *d* Ac 9:10 *e* Ac 5:19
10:4 *f* Mt 26:13 *g* Rev 8:4
10:5 *h* Ac 9:36
10:6 *i* Ac 9:43
10:8 *j* Ac 9:36
10:9 *k* Mt 24:17
10:10 *l* Ac 22:17
10:14 *m* Ac 9:5 *n* Lev 11:4-8, 13-20; Lev 20:25; Dt 14:3-20; Eze 4:14
10:15 *o* Mt 15:11; Ro 14:14,17, 20; 1Co 10:25; 1Ti 4:3,4; Tit 1:15

b36 Both *Tabitha* (Aramaic) and *Dorcas* (Greek) mean *gazelle*.

16 This happened three times, and immediately the sheet was taken back to heaven.

17 While Peter was wondering about the meaning of the vision, the men sent by Cornelius[p] found out where Simon's house was and stopped at the gate. 18 They called out, asking if Simon who was known as Peter was staying there.

19 While Peter was still thinking about the vision, the Spirit said[q] to him, "Simon, three[a] men are looking for you. 20 So get up and go downstairs. Do not hesitate to go with them, for I have sent them."[r]

21 Peter went down and said to the men, "I'm the one you're looking for. Why have you come?"

22 The men replied, "We have come from Cornelius the centurion. He is a righteous and God-fearing man,[s] who is respected by all the Jewish people. A holy angel told him to have you come to his house so that he could hear what you have to say."[t] 23 Then Peter invited the men into the house to be his guests.

Peter at Cornelius' House

The next day Peter started out with them, and some of the brothers[u] from Joppa went along.[v] 24 The following day he arrived in Caesarea.[w] Cornelius was expecting them and had called together his relatives and close friends. 25 As Peter entered the house, Cornelius met him and fell at his feet in reverence. 26 But Peter made him get up. "Stand up," he said, "I am only a man myself."[x]

27 Talking with him, Peter went inside and found a large gathering of people. 28 He said to them: "You are well aware that it is against our law for a Jew to associate with a Gentile or visit him.[y] But God has shown me that I should not call any man impure or unclean.[z] 29 So when I was sent for, I came without raising any objection. May I ask why you sent for me?"

30 Cornelius answered: "Four days ago I was in my house praying at this hour, at three in the afternoon. Suddenly a man in shining clothes stood before me 31 and said, 'Cornelius, God has heard your prayer and remembered your gifts to the poor. 32 Send to Joppa for Simon who is called Peter. He is a guest in the home of Simon the tanner, who lives by the sea.' 33 So I sent for you immediately, and it was good of you to come. Now we are all here in the presence of God to listen to everything the Lord has commanded you to tell us."

34 Then Peter began to speak: "I now realise how true it is that God does not show favouritism[a] 35 but accepts men from every nation who fear him and do what is right.[b] 36 You know the message God sent to the people of Israel, telling the good news[c] of peace[d] through Jesus Christ, who is Lord of all.[e] 37 You know what has happened throughout Judea, beginning in Galilee after the baptism that John preached—38 how God anointed[f] Jesus of Nazareth with the Holy Spirit and power, and how he went around doing good and healing[g] all who were under the power of the devil, because God was with him.[h]

39 "We are witnesses[i] of everything he did in the country of the Jews and in Jerusalem. They killed him by hanging him on a tree,[j] 40 but God raised him from the dead[k] on the third day and caused him to be seen. 41 He was not seen by all the people,[l] but by witnesses whom God had already chosen—by us who ate[m] and drank with him after he rose from the dead. 42 He commanded us to preach to the people[n] and to testify

10:17 p ver 7,8
10:19 q Ac 8:29
10:20 r Ac 15:7-9
10:22 s ver 2; t Ac 11:14
10:23 u Ac 1:16; v ver 45; Ac 11:12
10:24 w Ac 8:40
10:26 x Ac 14:15; Rev 19:10
10:28 y Jn 4:9; Jn 18:28; Ac 11:3; z Ac 15:8,9
10:34 a Dt 10:17; 2Ch 19:7; Job 34:19; Ro 2:11; Gal 2:6; Eph 6:9; Col 3:25; 1Pe 1:17
10:35 b Ac 15:9
10:36 c Ac 13:32; d Lk 2:14; e Mt 28:18; Ro 10:12
10:38 f Ac 4:26; g Mt 4:23; h Jn 3:2
10:39 i Lk 24:48; j Ac 5:30
10:40 k Ac 2:24
10:41 l Jn 14:17,22; m Lk 24:43; Jn 21:13
10:42 n Mt 28:19,20

a19 One early manuscript *two*; other manuscripts do not have the number.

that he is the one whom God appointed as judge of the living and the dead.[o] 43All the prophets testify about him[p] that everyone[q] who believes in him receives forgiveness of sins through his name."

44While Peter was still speaking these words, the Holy Spirit came on[r] all who heard the message. 45The circumcised believers who had come with Peter[s] were astonished that the gift of the Holy Spirit had been poured out[t] even on the Gentiles.[u] 46For they heard them speaking in tongues[b][v] and praising God.

Then Peter said, 47"Can anyone keep these people from being baptised with water?[w] They have received the Holy Spirit just as we have."[x] 48So he ordered that they be baptised in the name of Jesus Christ.[y] Then they asked Peter to stay with them for a few days.

Peter Explains His Actions

11 The apostles and the brothers[a] throughout Judea heard that the Gentiles also had received the word of God. 2So when Peter went up to Jerusalem, the circumcised believers[b] criticised him 3and said, "You went into the house of uncircumcised men and ate with them."[c]

4Peter began and explained everything to them precisely as it had happened: 5"I was in the city of Joppa praying, and in a trance I saw a vision.[d] I saw something like a large sheet being let down from heaven by its four corners, and it came down to where I was. 6I looked into it and saw four-footed animals of the earth, wild beasts, reptiles, and birds of the air. 7Then I heard a voice telling me, 'Get up, Peter. Kill and eat.'

8"I replied, 'Surely not, Lord! Nothing impure or unclean has ever entered my mouth.'

9"The voice spoke from heaven a second time, 'Do not call anything impure that God has made clean.'[e] 10This happened three times, and then it was pulled up to heaven again.

11"Right then three men who had been sent to me from Caesarea stopped at the house where I was staying. 12The Spirit told[f] me to have no hesitation about going with them.[g] These six brothers also went with me, and we entered the man's house. 13He told us how he had seen an angel appear in his house and say, 'Send to Joppa for Simon who is called Peter. 14He will bring you a message through which you and all your household[h] will be saved.'

15"As I began to speak, the Holy Spirit came on[i] them as he had come on us at the beginning.[j] 16Then I remembered what the Lord had said: 'John baptised with[a] water, but you will be baptised with the Holy Spirit.'[k] 17So if God gave them the same gift as he gave us,[l] who believed in the Lord Jesus Christ, who was I to think that I could oppose God?"

18When they heard this, they had no further objections and praised God, saying, "So then, God has granted even the Gentiles repentance unto life."[m]

The Church in Antioch

19Now those who had been scattered by the persecution in connection with Stephen[n] travelled as far as Phoenicia, Cyprus and Antioch,[o] telling the message only to Jews. 20Some of them, however, men from Cyprus[p] and Cyrene,[q] went to Antioch and began to speak to Greeks also, telling them the good news about the Lord Jesus. 21The Lord's hand was with them,[r] and a great number of people believed and turned to the Lord.[s]

22News of this reached the ears of the church at Jerusalem, and

10:42 o Jn 5:22; Ac 17:31; Ro 14:9; 2Co 5:10; 2Ti 4:1; 1Pe 4:5
10:43 p Isa 53:11; q Ac 15:9
10:44 r Ac 8:15,16; Ac 11:15; Ac 15:8
10:45 s ver 23; t Ac 2:33,38; u Ac 11:18
10:46 v Mk 16:17
10:47 w Ac 8:36; x Ac 11:17
10:48 y Ac 2:38; Ac 8:16
11:1 a Ac 1:16
11:2 b Ac 10:45
11:3 c Ac 10:25,28; Gal 2:12
11:5 d Ac 10:9-32; Ac 9:10
11:9 e Ac 10:15
11:12 f Ac 8:29; g Ac 15:9; Ro 3:22
11:14 h Jn 4:53; Ac 16:15, 31-34; 1Co 1:11,16
11:15 i Ac 10:44; j Ac 2:4
11:16 k Mk 1:8; Ac 1:5
11:17 l Ac 10:45,47
11:18 m Ro 10:12,13; 2Co 7:10
11:19 n Ac 8:1,4; o ver 26,27; Ac 13:1; Ac 18:22; Gal 2:11
11:20 p Ac 4:36; q Mt 27:32
11:21 r Lk 1:66; s Ac 2:47

b46 Or *other languages*   a16 Or *in*

they sent Barnabas[t] to Antioch.
23When he arrived and saw the evidence of the grace of God,[u] he was
glad and encouraged them all to remain true to the Lord with all their
hearts.[v] 24He was a good man, full
of the Holy Spirit and faith, and a
great number of people were
brought to the Lord.[w]

25Then Barnabas went to Tar-
sus[x] to look for Saul, 26and when he
found him, he brought him to Antioch. So for a whole year Barnabas
and Saul met with the church and
taught great numbers of people.
The disciples[y] were called Chris-
tians first[z] at Antioch.

27During this time some prophets[a] came down from Jerusalem to
Antioch. 28One of them, named
Agabus,[b] stood up and through the
Spirit predicted that a severe famine would spread over the entire
Roman world.[c] (This happened
during the reign of Claudius.)[d]
29The disciples,[e] each according to
his ability, decided to provide
help[f] for the brothers[g] living in
Judea. 30This they did, sending
their gift to the elders[h] by Barnabas and Saul.[i]

Peter's Miraculous Escape From Prison

12 It was about this time that
King Herod arrested some
who belonged to the church, intending to persecute them. 2He had
James, the brother of John,[a] put to
death with the sword. 3When he
saw that this pleased the Jews,[b] he
proceeded to seize Peter also. This
happened during the Feast of Unleavened Bread.[c] 4After arresting
him, he put him in prison, handing
him over to be guarded by four
squads of four soldiers each. Herod
intended to bring him out for public
trial after the Passover.

5So Peter was kept in prison, but
the church was earnestly praying
to God for him.[d]

6The night before Herod was to
bring him to trial, Peter was sleeping between two soldiers, bound
with two chains,[e] and sentries
stood guard at the entrance. 7Sud-
denly an angel[f] of the Lord appeared and a light shone in the cell.
He struck Peter on the side and
woke him up. "Quick, get up!" he
said, and the chains fell off Peter's
wrists.[g]

8Then the angel said to him, "Put
on your clothes and sandals." And
Peter did so. "Wrap your cloak
around you and follow me," the
angel told him. 9Peter followed him
out of the prison, but he had no idea
that what the angel was doing was
really happening; he thought
he was seeing a vision.[h] 10They
passed the first and second guards
and came to the iron gate leading to
the city. It opened for them by itself,[i] and they went through it.
When they had walked the length of
one street, suddenly the angel left
him.

11Then Peter came to himself[j]
and said, "Now I know without a
doubt that the Lord sent his angel
and rescued me[k] from Herod's
clutches and from everything the
Jewish people were anticipating."

12When this had dawned on him,
he went to the house of Mary the
mother of John, also called Mark,[l]
where many people had gathered
and were praying.[m] 13Peter
knocked at the outer entrance, and
a servant girl named Rhoda came
to answer the door.[n] 14When she
recognised Peter's voice, she was
so overjoyed[o] she ran back without opening it and exclaimed,
"Peter is at the door!"

15"You're out of your mind," they
told her. When she kept insisting
that it was so, they said, "It must be
his angel."[p]

16But Peter kept on knocking,
and when they opened the door and
saw him, they were astonished.
17Peter motioned with his hand[q]
for them to be quiet and described
how the Lord had brought him out

11:22 t Ac 4:36
11:23 u Ac 13:43; Ac 14:26; Ac 20:24; v Ac 14:22
11:24 w ver 21; Ac 5:14
11:25 x Ac 9:11
11:26 y Ac 6:1,2; Ac 13:52; z Ac 26:28; 1Pe 4:16
11:27 a Ac 13:1; Ac 15:32; 1Co 12:28,29; Eph 4:11
11:28 b Ac 21:10; c Mt 24:14; d Ac 18:2
11:29 e ver 26; f Ro 15:26; 2Co 9:2; g Ac 1:16
11:30 h Ac 14:23; i Ac 12:25
12:2 a Mt 4:21
12:3 b Ac 24:27; c Ex 12:15; Ex 23:15
12:5 d Eph 6:18
12:6 e Ac 21:33
12:7 f Ac 5:19; g Ac 16:26
12:9 h Ac 9:10
12:10 i Ac 5:19; Ac 16:26
12:11 j Lk 15:17; k Ps 34:7; Da 3:28; Da 6:22; 2Co 1:10; 2Pe 2:9
12:12 l ver 25; Ac 15:37,39; Col 4:10; Phm 24; 1Pe 5:13; m ver 5
12:13 n Jn 18:16,17
12:14 o Lk 24:41
12:15 p Mt 18:10
12:17 q Ac 13:16; Ac 19:33; Ac 21:40

of prison. "Tell James[r] and the brothers[s] about this," he said, and then he left for another place.

[18]In the morning, there was no small commotion among the soldiers as to what had become of Peter. [19]After Herod had a thorough search made for him and did not find him, he cross-examined the guards and ordered that they be executed.[t]

Herod's Death

Then Herod went from Judea to Caesarea[u] and stayed there a while. [20]He had been quarrelling with the people of Tyre and Sidon;[v] they now joined together and sought an audience with him. Having secured the support of Blastus, a trusted personal servant of the king, they asked for peace, because they depended on the king's country for their food supply.[w]

[21]On the appointed day Herod, wearing his royal robes, sat on his throne and delivered a public address to the people. [22]They shouted, "This is the voice of a god, not of a man." [23]Immediately, because Herod did not give praise to God, an angel of the Lord struck him down,[x] and he was eaten by worms and died.

[24]But the word of God continued to increase and spread.[y]

[25]When Barnabas[z] and Saul had finished their mission,[a] they returned from[a] Jerusalem, taking with them John, also called Mark.[b]

Barnabas and Saul Sent Off

13 In the church at Antioch[a] there were prophets[b] and teachers: Barnabas,[c] Simeon called Niger, Lucius of Cyrene, Manaen (who had been brought up with Herod[d] the tetrarch) and Saul. [2]While they were worshipping the Lord and fasting, the Holy Spirit said,[e] "Set apart for me Barnabas and Saul for the work[f] to which I have called them."[g] [3]So after they had fasted and prayed, they placed their hands on them[h] and sent them off.[i]

On Cyprus

[4]The two of them, sent on their way by the Holy Spirit,[j] went down to Seleucia and sailed from there to Cyprus.[k] [5]When they arrived at Salamis, they proclaimed the word of God in the Jewish synagogues.[l] John[m] was with them as their helper.

[6]They travelled through the whole island until they came to Paphos. There they met a Jewish sorcerer[n] and false prophet[o] named Bar-Jesus, [7]who was an attendant of the proconsul,[p] Sergius Paulus. The proconsul, an intelligent man, sent for Barnabas and Saul because he wanted to hear the word of God. [8]But Elymas the sorcerer[q] (for that is what his name means) opposed them and tried to turn the proconsul[r] from the faith.[s] [9]Then Saul, who was also called Paul, filled with the Holy Spirit,[t] looked straight at Elymas and said, [10]"You are a child of the devil[u] and an enemy of everything that is right! You are full of all kinds of deceit and trickery. Will you never stop perverting the right ways of the Lord?[v] [11]Now the hand of the Lord is against you.[w] You are going to be blind, and for a time you will be unable to see the light of the sun."

Immediately mist and darkness came over him, and he groped about, seeking someone to lead him by the hand. [12]When the proconsul[x] saw what had happened, he believed, for he was amazed at the teaching about the Lord.

In Pisidian Antioch

[13]From Paphos,[y] Paul and his companions sailed to Perga in Pamphylia, where John[z] left them to

12:17 r Ac 15:13 s Ac 1:16
12:19 t Ac 16:27 u Ac 8:40
12:20 v Mt 11:21 w 1Ki 5:9,11 Eze 27:17
12:23 x 1Sa 25:38 2Sa 24:16,17
12:24 y Ac 6:7 Ac 19:20
12:25 z Ac 4:36 a Ac 11:30 b ver 12
13:1 a Ac 11:19 b Ac 11:27 c Ac 4:36 Ac 11:22-26 d Mt 14:1
13:2 e Ac 8:29 f Ac 14:26 g Ac 22:21
13:3 h Ac 6:6 i Ac 14:26
13:4 j ver 2,3 k Ac 4:36
13:5 l Ac 9:20 m Ac 12:12
13:6 n Ac 8:9 o Mt 7:15
13:7 p ver 8,12 Ac 19:38
13:8 q Ac 8:9 r ver 7 s Ac 6:7
13:9 t Ac 4:8
13:10 u Mt 13:38 Jn 8:44 v Hos 14:9
13:11 w Ex 9:3 1Sa 5:6,7 Ps 32:4
13:12 x ver 7
13:13 y ver 6 z Ac 12:12

[a]25 Some manuscripts *to*

return to Jerusalem. 14From Perga
they went on to Pisidian Antioch.[a]
On the Sabbath[b] they entered the
synagogue[c] and sat down. 15After
the reading from the Law[d] and
the Prophets, the synagogue
rulers sent word to them, saying,
"Brothers, if you have a message of
encouragement for the people,
please speak."
16Standing up, Paul motioned
with his hand[e] and said: "Men of
Israel and you Gentiles who worship God, listen to me! 17The God of
the people of Israel chose our fathers; he made the people prosper
during their stay in Egypt, with
mighty power he led them out of
that country,[f] 18he endured their
conduct[a][g] for about forty years in
the desert,[h] 19he overthrew seven
nations in Canaan[i] and gave their
land to his people[j] as their inheritance. 20All this took about 450
years.
"After this, God gave them
judges[k] until the time of Samuel
the prophet.[l] 21Then the people
asked for a king,[m] and he gave
them Saul[n] son of Kish, of the tribe
of Benjamin,[o] who ruled for forty
years. 22After removing Saul,[p] he
made David their king.[q] He testified concerning him: 'I have found
David son of Jesse a man after my
own heart;[r] he will do everything
I want him to do.'
23"From this man's descendants[s] God has brought to Israel
the Saviour[t] Jesus,[u] as he promised.[v] 24Before the coming of
Jesus, John preached repentance
and baptism to all the people of Israel.[w] 25As John was completing
his work,[x] he said: 'Who do you
think I am? I am not that one.[y] No,
but he is coming after me, whose
sandals I am not worthy to untie.'[z]
26"Brothers, children of Abraham, and you God-fearing Gentiles, it is to us that this message of
salvation[a] has been sent. 27The
people of Jerusalem and their rulers did not recognise Jesus,[b] yet in
condemning him they fulfilled the
words of the prophets[c] that are
read every Sabbath. 28Though they
found no proper ground for a death
sentence, they asked Pilate to have
him executed.[d] 29When they had
carried out all that was written
about him,[e] they took him down
from the tree[f] and laid him in a
tomb.[g] 30But God raised him from
the dead,[h] 31and for many days he
was seen by those who had travelled with him from Galilee to
Jerusalem.[i] They are now his
witnesses[j] to our people.
32"We tell you the good news:[k]
What God promised our fathers[l]
33he has fulfilled for us, their children, by raising up Jesus. As it is
written in the second Psalm:

" 'You are my Son;
today I have become your
Father.'[b,c][m]

34The fact that God raised him
from the dead, never to decay, is
stated in these words:

" 'I will give you the holy and
sure blessings promised to
David.'[d][n]

35So it is stated elsewhere:

" 'You will not let your Holy
One see decay.'[e][o]

36"For when David had served
God's purpose in his own generation, he fell asleep; he was buried
with his fathers[p] and his body decayed. 37But the one whom God
raised from the dead did not see
decay.
38"Therefore, my brothers, I
want you to know that through
Jesus the forgiveness of sins is proclaimed to you.[q] 39Through him
everyone who believes is justified
from everything you could not be
justified from by the law of
Moses.[r] 40Take care that what the

13:14 a Ac 14:19,21 b Ac 16:13 c Ac 9:20
13:15 d Ac 15:21
13:16 e Ac 12:17
13:17 f Ex 6:6,7 Dt 7:6-8
13:18 g Dt 1:31 h Ac 7:36
13:19 i Dt 7:1 j Jos 19:51
13:20 k Jdg 2:16 l 1Sa 3:19,20
13:21 m 1Sa 8:5,19 n 1Sa 10:1 o 1Sa 9:1,2
13:22 p 1Sa 15:23,26 q 1Sa 16:13 Ps 89:20 r 1Sa 13:14
13:23 s Mt 1:1 t Lk 2:11 u Mt 1:21 v ver 32
13:24 w Mk 1:4
13:25 x Ac 20:24 y Jn 1:20 z Mt 3:11 Jn 1:27
13:26 a Ac 4:12
13:27 b Ac 3:17 c Lk 24:27
13:28 d Mt 27:20-25 Ac 3:14
13:29 e Lk 18:31 f Ac 5:30 g Lk 23:53
13:30 h Mt 28:6 Ac 2:24
13:31 i Mt 28:16 j Lk 24:48
13:32 k Ac 5:42 l Ac 26:6 Ro 4:13
13:33 m Ps 2:7
13:34 n Isa 55:3
13:35 o Ps 16:10 Ac 2:27
13:36 p 1Ki 2:10 Ac 2:29
13:38 q Lk 24:47 Ac 2:38
13:39 r Ro 3:28

a18 Some manuscripts *and cared for them*
b33 Or *have begotten you* c33 Psalm 2:7
d34 Isaiah 55:3 e35 Psalm 16:10

prophets have said does not happen
to you:

[41]" 'Look, you scoffers,
wonder and perish,
for I am going to do something
in your days
that you would never believe,
even if someone told you.'[f]"[s]

[42]As Paul and Barnabas were
leaving the synagogue,[t] the people
invited them to speak further about
these things on the next Sabbath.
[43]When the congregation was dismissed, many of the Jews and devout converts to Judaism followed
Paul and Barnabas, who talked
with them and urged them to continue in the grace of God.[u]
[44]On the next Sabbath almost the
whole city gathered to hear the
word of the Lord. [45]When the Jews
saw the crowds, they were filled
with jealousy and talked abusively[v] against what Paul was saying.[w]
[46]Then Paul and Barnabas answered them boldly: "We had to
speak the word of God to you
first.[x] Since you reject it and do
not consider yourselves worthy of
eternal life, we now turn to the
Gentiles.[y] [47]For this is what the
Lord has commanded us:

" 'I have made you[g] a light for
the Gentiles,[z]
that you[g] may bring salvation
to the ends of the
earth.'[h]"[a]

[48]When the Gentiles heard this,
they were glad and honoured the
word of the Lord; and all who were
appointed for eternal life believed.
[49]The word of the Lord spread
through the whole region. [50]But the
Jews incited the God-fearing
women of high standing and the
leading men of the city. They
stirred up persecution against Paul
and Barnabas, and expelled them
from their region.[b] [51]So they shook
the dust from their feet[c] in protest against them and went to

13:41 s Hab 1:5
13:42 t ver 14
13:43 u Ac 11:23; Ac 14:22
13:45 v Ac 18:6; 1Pe 4:4; Jude 10; w 1Th 2:16
13:46 x ver 26; Ac 3:26; y Ac 18:6; Ac 22:21; Ac 28:28
13:47 z Lk 2:32; a Isa 49:6
13:50 b 1Th 2:16
13:51 c Mt 10:14; Ac 18:6; d Ac 14:1,19,21; 2Ti 3:11
14:1 a Ac 13:51
14:3 b Ac 4:29; c Jn 4:48; Heb 2:4
14:4 d Ac 17:4,5
14:5 e ver 19
14:6 f Mt 10:23
14:7 g Ac 16:10; h ver 15,21
14:8 i Ac 3:2
14:9 j Mt 9:28,29
14:10 k Ac 3:8
14:11 l Ac 8:10; Ac 28:6

Iconium.[d] [52]And the disciples were
filled with joy and with the Holy
Spirit.

In Iconium

14 At Iconium[a] Paul and Barnabas went as usual into
the Jewish synagogue. There they
spoke so effectively that a great
number of Jews and Gentiles believed. [2]But the Jews who refused
to believe stirred up the Gentiles
and poisoned their minds against
the brothers. [3]So Paul and Barnabas spent considerable time there,
speaking boldly[b] for the Lord, who
confirmed the message of his
grace by enabling them to do miraculous signs and wonders.[c] [4]The
people of the city were divided;
some sided with the Jews, others
with the apostles.[d] [5]There was a
plot afoot among the Gentiles and
Jews, together with their leaders,
to ill-treat them and stone them.[e]
[6]But they found out about it and
fled[f] to the Lycaonian cities of
Lystra and Derbe and to the surrounding country, [7]where they continued to preach[g] the good news.[h]

In Lystra and Derbe

[8]In Lystra there sat a man crippled in his feet, who was lame from
birth[i] and had never walked. [9]He
listened to Paul as he was speaking.
Paul looked directly at him, saw
that he had faith to be healed[j]
[10]and called out, "Stand up on your
feet!" At that, the man jumped up
and began to walk.[k]
[11]When the crowd saw what Paul
had done, they shouted in the Lycaonian language, "The gods have
come down to us in human form!"[l]
[12]Barnabas they called Zeus, and
Paul they called Hermes because
he was the chief speaker. [13]The
priest of Zeus, whose temple was
just outside the city, brought bulls

[f]41 Hab. 1:5 [g]47 The Greek is singular.
[h]47 Isaiah 49:6

and wreaths to the city gates because he and the crowd wanted to offer sacrifices to them.

14But when the apostles Barnabas and Paul heard of this, they tore their clothes[m] and rushed out into the crowd, shouting: 15"Men, why are you doing this? We too are only men,[n] human like you. We are bringing you good news,[o] telling you to turn from these worthless things[p] to the living God,[q] who made heaven and earth[r] and sea and everything in them.[s] 16In the past, he let[t] all nations go their own way.[u] 17Yet he has not left himself without testimony:[v] He has shown kindness by giving you rain from heaven and crops in their seasons;[w] he provides you with plenty of food and fills your hearts with joy." 18Even with these words, they had difficulty keeping the crowd from sacrificing to them.

19Then some Jews[x] came from Antioch and Iconium[y] and won the crowd over. They stoned Paul[z] and dragged him outside the city, thinking he was dead. 20But after the disciples[a] had gathered round him, he got up and went back into the city. The next day he and Barnabas left for Derbe.

The Return to Antioch in Syria

21They preached the good news in that city and won a large number of disciples. Then they returned to Lystra, Iconium[b] and Antioch, 22strengthening the disciples and encouraging them to remain true to the faith.[c] "We must go through many hardships[d] to enter the kingdom of God," they said. 23Paul and Barnabas appointed elders[a][e] for them in each church and, with prayer and fasting,[f] committed them to the Lord,[g] in whom they had put their trust. 24After going through Pisidia, they came into Pamphylia, 25and when they had preached the word in Perga, they went down to Attalia.

26From Attalia they sailed back to Antioch,[h] where they had been committed to the grace of God[i] for the work they had now completed.[j] 27On arriving there, they gathered the church together and reported all that God had done through them[k] and how he had opened the door[l] of faith to the Gentiles. 28And they stayed there a long time with the disciples.

The Council at Jerusalem

15 Some men[a] came down from Judea to Antioch and were teaching the brothers: "Unless you are circumcised,[b] according to the custom taught by Moses,[c] you cannot be saved." 2This brought Paul and Barnabas into sharp dispute and debate with them. So Paul and Barnabas were appointed, along with some other believers, to go up to Jerusalem[d] to see the apostles and elders[e] about this question. 3The church sent them on their way, and as they travelled through Phoenicia and Samaria, they told how the Gentiles had been converted.[f] This news made all the brothers very glad. 4When they came to Jerusalem, they were welcomed by the church and the apostles and elders, to whom they reported everything God had done through them.[g]

5Then some of the believers who belonged to the party of the Pharisees stood up and said, "The Gentiles must be circumcised and required to obey the law of Moses."

6The apostles and elders met to consider this question. 7After much discussion, Peter got up and addressed them: "Brothers, you know that some time ago God made a choice among you that the Gentiles might hear from my lips the message of the gospel and believe.

14:14 m Mk 14:63
14:15 n Ac 10:26; Jas 5:17 o ver 7,21; Ac 13:32 p 1Sa 12:21; 1Co 8:4; 1Th 1:9 q Mt 16:16 r Ge 1:1; Jer 14:22 s Ps 146:6; Rev 14:7
14:16 t Ac 17:30 u Ps 81:12; Mic 4:5
14:17 v Ac 17:27; Ro 1:20 w Dt 11:14; Job 5:10; Ps 65:10
14:19 x Ac 13:45 y Ac 13:51 z 2Co 11:25; 2Ti 3:11
14:20 a ver 22,28; Ac 11:26
14:21 b Ac 13:51
14:22 c Ac 11:23; Ac 13:43 d Jn 16:33; 1Th 3:3; 2Ti 3:12
14:23 e Ac 11:30; Tit 1:5 f Ac 13:3 g Ac 20:32
14:26 h Ac 11:19 i Ac 15:40 j Ac 13:1,3
14:27 k Ac 15:4,12; Ac 21:19 l 1Co 16:9; 2Co 2:12; Col 4:3; Rev 3:8
15:1 a ver 24; Gal 2:12 b ver 5; Gal 5:2,3 c Ac 6:14
15:2 d Gal 2:2 e Ac 11:30
15:3 f Ac 14:27
15:4 g ver 12; Ac 14:27

a23 Or *Barnabas ordained elders*; or *Barnabas had elders elected*

8God, who knows the heart,[h]
showed that he accepted them by
giving the Holy Spirit to them,[i]
just as he did to us. 9He made no
distinction between us and them,[j]
for he purified their hearts by
faith.[k] 10Now then, why do you try
to test God by putting on the necks
of the disciples a yoke[l] that neither we nor our fathers have been
able to bear? 11No! We believe it is
through the grace[m] of our Lord
Jesus that we are saved, just as
they are."

12The whole assembly became silent as they listened to Barnabas
and Paul telling about the miraculous signs and wonders[n] God had
done among the Gentiles through
them.[o] 13When they finished,
James[p] spoke up: "Brothers, listen
to me. 14Simon[a] has described to
us how God at first showed his concern by taking from the Gentiles a
people for himself. 15The words of
the prophets are in agreement with
this, as it is written:

16" 'After this I will return
and rebuild David's fallen
tent.
Its ruins I will rebuild,
and I will restore it,
17that the remnant of men may
seek the Lord,
and all the Gentiles who bear
my name,
says the Lord, who does these
things'[b][q]
18 that have been known for
ages.[c]

19"It is my judgment, therefore,
that we should not make it difficult
for the Gentiles who are turning to
God. 20Instead we should write to
them, telling them to abstain from
food polluted by idols,[r] from sexual immorality,[s] from the meat of
strangled animals and from
blood.[t] 21For Moses has been
preached in every city from the
earliest times and is read in the
synagogues on every Sabbath."[u]

15:8
h Ac 1:24
i Ac 10:44,47

15:9
j Ac 10:28,34
Ac 11:12
k Ac 10:43

15:10
l Mt 23:4
Gal 5:1

15:11
m Ro 3:24
Eph 2:5-8

15:12
n Jn 4:48
o Ac 14:27

15:13
p Ac 12:17

15:17
q Am 9:11,12

15:20
r 1Co 8:7-13
1Co 10:14-28
Rev 2:14,20
s 1Co 10:7,8
t ver 29
Ge 9:4
Lev 3:17
Dt 12:16,23

15:21
u Ac 13:15
2Co 3:14,15

15:22
v ver 27,32,40

15:23
w ver 1
x ver 41
y Ac 23:25,26
Jas 1:1

15:24
z ver 1
Gal 1:7
Gal 5:10

15:26
a Ac 9:23-25
Ac 14:19

15:28
b Ac 5:32

15:29
c ver 20
Ac 21:25

The Council's Letter to Gentile Believers

22Then the apostles and elders,
with the whole church, decided to
choose some of their own men and
send them to Antioch with Paul
and Barnabas. They chose Judas
(called Barsabbas) and Silas,[v] two
men who were leaders among the
brothers. 23With them they sent the
following letter:

The apostles and elders, your
brothers,

To the Gentile believers in Antioch,[w] Syria and Cilicia:[x]

Greetings.[y]

24We have heard that some
went out from us without our
authorisation and disturbed
you, troubling your minds by
what they said.[z] 25So we all
agreed to choose some men
and send them to you with our
dear friends Barnabas and
Paul—26men who have risked
their lives[a] for the name of
our Lord Jesus Christ. 27There-
fore we are sending Judas and
Silas to confirm by word of
mouth what we are writing.
28It seemed good to the Holy
Spirit[b] and to us not to burden
you with anything beyond the
following requirements: 29You
are to abstain from food sacrificed to idols, from blood, from
the meat of strangled animals
and from sexual immorality.[c]
You will do well to avoid these
things.

Farewell.

30The men were sent off and went
down to Antioch, where they gathered the church together and delivered the letter. 31The people read it

[a]14 Greek *Simeon*, a variant of *Simon*; that is, Peter [b]17 Amos 9:11,12 [c]17,18 Some manuscripts *things'— / 18known to the Lord for ages is his work*

and were glad for its encouraging message. 32 Judas and Silas, who themselves were prophets, said much to encourage and strengthen the brothers. 33 After spending some time there, they were sent off by the brothers with the blessing of peace[d] to return to those who had sent them.**d** 35 But Paul and Barnabas remained in Antioch, where they and many others taught and preached[e] the word of the Lord.

Disagreement Between Paul and Barnabas

36 Some time later Paul said to Barnabas, "Let us go back and visit the brothers in all the towns[f] where we preached the word of the Lord and see how they are doing." 37 Barnabas wanted to take John, also called Mark,[g] with them, 38 but Paul did not think it wise to take him, because he had deserted them[h] in Pamphylia and had not continued with them in the work. 39 They had such a sharp disagreement that they parted company. Barnabas took Mark and sailed for Cyprus, 40 but Paul chose Silas[i] and left, commended by the brothers to the grace of the Lord.[j] 41 He went through Syria[k] and Cilicia,[l] strengthening the churches.[m]

Timothy Joins Paul and Silas

16 He came to Derbe and then to Lystra,[a] where a disciple named Timothy[b] lived, whose mother was a Jewess and a believer, but whose father was a Greek. 2 The brothers[c] at Lystra and Iconium[d] spoke well of him. 3 Paul wanted to take him along on the journey, so he circumcised him because of the Jews who lived in that area, for they all knew that his father was a Greek.[e] 4 As they travelled from town to town, they delivered the decisions reached by the apostles and elders[f] in Jerusalem[g] for the people to obey.[h] 5 So the churches were strengthened[i] in the faith and grew daily in numbers.

Paul's Vision of the Man of Macedonia

6 Paul and his companions travelled throughout the region of Phrygia[j] and Galatia,[k] having been kept by the Holy Spirit from preaching the word in the province of Asia.[l] 7 When they came to the border of Mysia, they tried to enter Bithynia, but the Spirit of Jesus[m] would not allow them to. 8 So they passed by Mysia and went down to Troas.[n] 9 During the night Paul had a vision[o] of a man of Macedonia[p] standing and begging him, "Come over to Macedonia and help us." 10 After Paul had seen the vision, we[q] got ready at once to leave for Macedonia, concluding that God had called us to preach the gospel[r] to them.

Lydia's Conversion in Philippi

11 From Troas[s] we put out to sea and sailed straight for Samothrace, and the next day on to Neapolis. 12 From there we travelled to Philippi,[t] a Roman colony and the leading city of that district of Macedonia.[u] And we stayed there several days.

13 On the Sabbath[v] we went outside the city gate to the river, where we expected to find a place of prayer. We sat down and began to speak to the women who had gathered there. 14 One of those listening was a woman named Lydia, a dealer in purple cloth from the city of Thyatira,[w] who was a worshipper of God. The Lord opened her heart[x] to respond to Paul's message. 15 When she and the members of her household[y] were baptised, she invited us to her home. "If you consider me a believer

15:33 d Mk 5:34; Ac 16:36; 1Co 16:11
15:35 e Ac 8:4
15:36 f Ac 13:4,13, 14,51; Ac 14:1,6,24, 25
15:37 g Ac 12:12
15:38 h Ac 13:13
15:40 i ver 22; j Ac 11:23
15:41 k ver 23; l Ac 6:9; m Ac 16:5
16:1 a Ac 14:6; b Ac 17:14; Ac 18:5; Ac 19:22; Ro 16:21; 1Co 4:17; 2Co 1:1,19; 1Th 3:2,6; 1Ti 1:2,18; 2Ti 1:2,5,6
16:2 c ver 40; d Ac 13:51
16:3 e Gal 2:3
16:4 f Ac 11:30; g Ac 15:2; h Ac 15:28,29
16:5 i Ac 9:31; Ac 15:41
16:6 j Ac 18:23; k Ac 18:23; Gal 1:2; Gal 3:1; l Ac 2:9
16:7 m Ro 8:9; Gal 4:6
16:8 n ver 11; 2Co 2:12; 2Ti 4:13
16:9 o Ac 9:10; p Ac 20:1,3
16:10 q ver 10-17; r Ac 14:7
16:11 s ver 8
16:12 t Ac 20:6; Php 1:1; 1Th 2:2; u ver 9
16:13 v Ac 13:14
16:14 w Rev 1:11; x Lk 24:45
16:15 y Ac 11:14

d33 Some manuscripts *them,* 34*but Silas decided to remain there*

in the Lord," she said, "come and
stay at my house." And she persuaded us.

Paul and Silas in Prison

16 Once when we were going to
the place of prayer,[z] we were met
by a slave girl who had a spirit[a] by
which she predicted the future. She
earned a great deal of money for
her owners by fortune-telling.
17 This girl followed Paul and the
rest of us, shouting, "These men
are servants of the Most High
God,[b] who are telling you the way
to be saved." 18 She kept this up for
many days. Finally Paul became so
troubled that he turned round and
said to the spirit, "In the name of
Jesus Christ I command you to
come out of her!" At that moment
the spirit left her.[c]
19 When the owners of the slave
girl realised that their hope of making money[d] was gone, they seized
Paul and Silas[e] and dragged[f]
them into the market-place to face
the authorities. 20 They brought
them before the magistrates and
said, "These men are Jews, and are
throwing our city into an uproar[g]
21 by advocating customs unlawful
for us Romans[h] to accept or practise."[i]
22 The crowd joined in the attack
against Paul and Silas, and the
magistrates ordered them to be
stripped and beaten.[j] 23 After they
had been severely flogged, they
were thrown into prison, and the
jailer[k] was commanded to guard
them carefully. 24 Upon receiving
such orders, he put them in the inner cell and fastened their feet in
the stocks.[l]
25 About midnight Paul and Silas
were praying and singing hymns[m]
to God, and the other prisoners
were listening to them. 26 Suddenly
there was such a violent earthquake that the foundations of the
prison were shaken.[n] At once all
the prison doors flew open,[o] and
everybody's chains came loose.[p]
27 The jailer woke up, and when he
saw the prison doors open, he drew
his sword and was about to kill himself because he thought the prisoners had escaped.[q] 28 But Paul
shouted, "Don't harm yourself! We
are all here!"
29 The jailer called for lights,
rushed in and fell trembling before
Paul and Silas. 30 He then brought
them out and asked, "Sirs, what
must I do to be saved?"[r]
31 They replied, "Believe in the
Lord Jesus, and you will be saved—
you and your household."[s] 32 Then
they spoke the word of the Lord to
him and to all the others in his
house. 33 At that hour of the night[t]
the jailer took them and washed
their wounds; then immediately he
and all his family were baptised.
34 The jailer brought them into his
house and set a meal before them;
he[u] was filled with joy because he
had come to believe in God—he and
his whole family.
35 When it was daylight, the
magistrates sent their officers to
the jailer with the order: "Release
those men." 36 The jailer[v] told Paul,
"The magistrates have ordered
that you and Silas be released. Now
you can leave. Go in peace."[w]
37 But Paul said to the officers:
"They beat us publicly without a
trial, even though we are Roman
citizens,[x] and threw us into prison.
And now do they want to get rid of
us quietly? No! Let them come
themselves and escort us out."
38 The officers reported this to
the magistrates, and when they
heard that Paul and Silas were Roman citizens, they were alarmed.[y]
39 They came to appease them and
escorted them from the prison, re-
questing them to leave the city.[z]
40 After Paul and Silas came out of
the prison, they went to Lydia's
house,[a] where they met with the
brothers[b] and encouraged them.
Then they left.

16:16 z ver 13; a Dt 18:11; 1Sa 28:3,7
16:17 b Mk 5:7
16:18 c Mk 16:17
16:19 d ver 16; Ac 19:25,26; e Ac 15:22; f Ac 8:3; Ac 17:6; Ac 21:30; Jas 2:6
16:20 g Ac 17:6
16:21 h ver 12; i Est 3:8
16:22 j 2Co 11:25; 1Th 2:2
16:23 k ver 27,36
16:24 l Job 13:27; Job 33:11; Jer 20:2,3; Jer 29:26
16:25 m Eph 5:19
16:26 n Ac 4:31; o Ac 12:10; p Ac 12:7
16:27 q Ac 12:19
16:30 r Ac 2:37
16:31 s Ac 11:14
16:33 t ver 25
16:34 u Ac 11:14
16:36 v ver 23,27; w Ac 15:33
16:37 x Ac 22:25-29
16:38 y Ac 22:29
16:39 z Mt 8:34
16:40 a ver 14; b ver 2; Ac 1:16

In Thessalonica

17 When they had passed through Amphipolis and Apollonia, they came to Thessalonica,[a] where there was a Jewish synagogue. 2 As his custom was, Paul went into the synagogue,[b] and on three Sabbath[c] days he reasoned with them from the Scriptures,[d] 3 explaining and proving that the Christ[a] had to suffer[e] and rise from the dead.[f] "This Jesus I am proclaiming to you is the Christ,"[a][g] he said. 4 Some of the Jews were persuaded and joined Paul and Silas,[h] as did a large number of God-fearing Greeks and not a few prominent women.

5 But the Jews were jealous; so they rounded up some bad characters from the market-place, formed a mob and started a riot in the city.[i] They rushed to Jason's[j] house in search of Paul and Silas in order to bring them out to the crowd.[b] 6 But when they did not find them, they dragged[k] Jason and some other brothers before the city officials, shouting: "These men who have caused trouble all over the world[l] have now come here,[m] 7 and Jason has welcomed them into his house. They are all defying Caesar's decrees, saying that there is another king, one called Jesus."[n] 8 When they heard this, the crowd and the city officials were thrown into turmoil. 9 Then they put Jason[o] and the others on bail and let them go.

In Berea

10 As soon as it was night, the brothers sent Paul and Silas away to Berea.[p] On arriving there, they went to the Jewish synagogue. 11 Now the Bereans were of more noble character than the Thessalonians,[q] for they received the message with great eagerness and examined the Scriptures[r] every day to see if what Paul said was true. 12 Many of the Jews believed, as did also a number of prominent Greek women and many Greek men.

13 When the Jews in Thessalonica learned that Paul was preaching the word of God at Berea, they went there too, agitating the crowds and stirring them up. 14 The brothers immediately sent Paul to the coast, but Silas[s] and Timothy[t] stayed at Berea. 15 The men who escorted Paul brought him to Athens[u] and then left with instructions for Silas and Timothy to join him as soon as possible.[v]

In Athens

16 While Paul was waiting for them in Athens, he was greatly distressed to see that the city was full of idols. 17 So he reasoned in the synagogue[w] with the Jews and the God-fearing Greeks, as well as in the market-place day by day with those who happened to be there. 18 A group of Epicurean and Stoic philosophers began to dispute with him. Some of them asked, "What is this babbler trying to say?" Others remarked, "He seems to be advocating foreign gods." They said this because Paul was preaching the good news about Jesus and the resurrection.[x] 19 Then they took him and brought him to a meeting of the Areopagus,[y] where they said to him, "May we know what this new teaching[z] is that you are presenting? 20 You are bringing some strange ideas to our ears, and we want to know what they mean." 21 (All the Athenians and the foreigners who lived there spent their time doing nothing but talking about and listening to the latest ideas.)

22 Paul then stood up in the meeting of the Areopagus and said: "Men of Athens! I see that in every

17:1 *a* ver 11,13; Php 4:16; 1Th 1:1; 2Th 1:1; 2Ti 4:10
17:2 *b* Ac 9:20; *c* Ac 13:14; *d* Ac 8:35
17:3 *e* Lk 24:26; Ac 3:18; *f* Lk 24:46; *g* Ac 9:22; Ac 18:28
17:4 *h* Ac 15:22
17:5 *i* ver 13; 1Th 2:16; *j* Ro 16:21
17:6 *k* Ac 16:19; *l* Mt 24:14; *m* Ac 16:20
17:7 *n* Lk 23:2; Jn 19:12
17:9 *o* ver 5
17:10 *p* ver 13; Ac 20:4
17:11 *q* ver 1; *r* Lk 16:29; Jn 5:39
17:14 *s* Ac 15:22; *t* Ac 16:1
17:15 *u* ver 16,21,22; Ac 18:1; 1Th 3:1; *v* Ac 18:5
17:17 *w* Ac 9:20
17:18 *x* ver 31,32; Ac 4:2
17:19 *y* ver 22; *z* Mk 1:27

a3 Or *Messiah* **b**5 Or *the assembly of the people*

way you are very religious. 23For as
I walked around and looked carefully at your objects of worship, I
even found an altar with this inscription: TO AN UNKNOWN GOD.
Now what you worship as something unknown[a] I am going to proclaim to you.
24"The God who made the world
and everything in it[b] is the Lord of
heaven and earth[c] and does not
live in temples built by hands.[d]
25And he is not served by human
hands, as if he needed anything, because he himself gives all men life
and breath and everything else.[e]
26From one man he made every nation of men, that they should inhabit the whole earth; and he
determined the times set for them
and the exact places where they
should live.[f] 27God did this so that
men would seek him and perhaps
reach out for him and find him,
though he is not far from each one
of us.[g] 28'For in him we live and
move and have our being.'[h] As
some of your own poets have said,
'We are his offspring.'
29"Therefore since we are God's
offspring, we should not think that
the divine being is like gold or silver or stone—an image made by
man's design and skill.[i] 30In the
past God overlooked[j] such ignorance,[k] but now he commands all
people everywhere to repent.[l]
31For he has set a day when he will
judge[m] the world with justice[n] by
the man he has appointed.[o] He has
given proof of this to all men by
raising him from the dead."[p]
32When they heard about the resurrection of the dead,[q] some of
them sneered, but others said, "We
want to hear you again on this
subject." 33At that, Paul left the
Council. 34A few men became
followers of Paul and believed.
Among them was Dionysius, a
member of the Areopagus,[r] also
a woman named Damaris, and a
number of others.

17:23 a Jn 4:22
17:24 b Isa 42:5; Ac 14:15; c Dt 10:14; Mt 11:25; d Ac 7:48
17:25 e Ps 50:10-12; Isa 42:5
17:26 f Dt 32:8; Job 12:23
17:27 g Dt 4:7; Jer 23:23,24; Ac 14:17
17:28 h Job 12:10; Da 5:23
17:29 i Isa 40:18-20; Ro 1:23
17:30 j Ac 14:16; Ro 3:25; k ver 23; 1Pe 1:14; l Lk 24:47; Tit 2:11,12
17:31 m Mt 10:15; n Ps 9:8; Ps 96:13; Ps 98:9; o Ac 10:42; p Ac 2:24
17:32 q ver 18,31
17:34 r ver 19,22
18:1 a Ac 17:15; b Ac 19:1; 1Co 1:2; 2Co 1:1,23; 2Ti 4:20
18:2 c Ro 16:3; 1Co 16:19; 2Ti 4:19; d Ac 11:28
18:3 e Ac 20:34; 1Co 4:12; 1Th 2:9; 2Th 3:8
18:4 f Ac 13:14
18:5 g Ac 15:22; h Ac 16:1; i Ac 16:9; Ac 17:14,15; j ver 28; Ac 17:3
18:6 k Ac 13:45; l 2Sa 1:16; Eze 18:13; Eze 33:4; m Ac 20:26; n Ac 13:46
18:7 o Ac 16:14

In Corinth

18 After this, Paul left Athens[a] and went to Corinth.[b]
2There he met a Jew named Aquila,
a native of Pontus, who had recently come from Italy with his
wife Priscilla,[c] because Claudius[d]
had ordered all the Jews to leave
Rome. Paul went to see them, 3and
because he was a tentmaker as they
were, he stayed and worked with
them.[e] 4Every Sabbath[f] he reasoned in the synagogue, trying to
persuade Jews and Greeks.
5When Silas[g] and Timothy[h]
came from Macedonia,[i] Paul devoted himself exclusively to
preaching, testifying to the Jews
that Jesus was the Christ.[a][j] 6But
when the Jews opposed Paul and
became abusive,[k] he shook out his
clothes in protest and said to them,
"Your blood be on your own
heads![l] I am clear of my responsibility.[m] From now on I will go to the
Gentiles."[n]
7Then Paul left the synagogue
and went next door to the house of
Titius Justus, a worshipper of
God.[o] 8Crispus,[p] the synagogue
ruler,[q] and his entire household[r]
believed in the Lord; and many of
the Corinthians who heard him believed and were baptised.
9One night the Lord spoke to Paul
in a vision: "Do not be afraid; keep
on speaking, do not be silent. 10For
I am with you,[s] and no-one is going
to attack and harm you, because I
have many people in this city." 11So
Paul stayed for a year and a half,
teaching them the word of God.
12While Gallio was proconsul of
Achaia,[t] the Jews made a united
attack on Paul and brought him into
court. 13"This man," they charged,
"is persuading the people to worship God in ways contrary to the
law."
14Just as Paul was about to speak,

18:8 p 1Co 1:14 q Mk 5:22 r Ac 11:14 **18:10** s Mt 28:20
18:12 t ver 27

[a]5 Or *Messiah*; also in verse 28

Gallio said to the Jews, "If you Jews were making a complaint about some misdemeanour or serious crime, it would be reasonable for me to listen to you. 15But since it involves questions about words and names and your own law[u]—settle the matter yourselves. I will not be a judge of such things." 16So he had them ejected from the court. 17Then they all turned on Sosthenes[v] the synagogue ruler and beat him in front of the court. But Gallio showed no concern whatever.

Priscilla, Aquila and Apollos

18Paul stayed on in Corinth for some time. Then he left the brothers[w] and sailed for Syria, accompanied by Priscilla and Aquila. Before he sailed, he had his hair cut off at Cenchrea[x] because of a vow he had taken.[y] 19They arrived at Ephesus,[z] where Paul left Priscilla and Aquila. He himself went into the synagogue and reasoned with the Jews. 20When they asked him to spend more time with them, he declined. 21But as he left, he promised, "I will come back if it is God's will."[a] Then he set sail from Ephesus. 22When he landed at Caesarea,[b] he went up and greeted the church and then went down to Antioch.[c]

23After spending some time in Antioch, Paul set out from there and travelled from place to place throughout the region of Galatia[d] and Phrygia, strengthening all the disciples.[e]

24Meanwhile a Jew named Apollos,[f] a native of Alexandria, came to Ephesus. He was a learned man, with a thorough knowledge of the Scriptures. 25He had been instructed in the way of the Lord, and he spoke with great fervour[b][g] and taught about Jesus accurately, though he knew only the baptism of John.[h] 26He began to speak boldly in the synagogue. When Priscilla and Aquila heard him, they invited him to their home and explained to him the way of God more adequately.

27When Apollos wanted to go to Achaia,[i] the brothers[j] encouraged him and wrote to the disciples there to welcome him. On arriving, he was a great help to those who by grace had believed. 28For he vigorously refuted the Jews in public debate, proving from the Scriptures[k] that Jesus was the Christ.[l]

Paul in Ephesus

19 While Apollos was at Corinth,[a] Paul took the road through the interior and arrived at Ephesus.[b] There he found some disciples 2and asked them, "Did you receive the Holy Spirit when[a] you believed?"

They answered, "No, we have not even heard that there is a Holy Spirit."

3So Paul asked, "Then what baptism did you receive?"

"John's baptism," they replied.

4Paul said, "John's baptism was a baptism of repentance. He told the people to believe in the one coming after him, that is, in Jesus."[c] 5On hearing this, they were baptised into[b] the name of the Lord Jesus. 6When Paul placed his hands on them,[d] the Holy Spirit came on them,[e] and they spoke in tongues[c][f] and prophesied. 7There were about twelve men in all.

8Paul entered the synagogue[g] and spoke boldly there for three months, arguing persuasively about the kingdom of God.[h] 9But some of them[i] became obstinate; they refused to believe and publicly maligned the Way.[j] So Paul left them. He took the disciples[k] with him and had discussions daily in the lecture hall of Tyrannus. 10This went on for two years,[l] so that all the Jews and Greeks who lived

18:15 *u* Ac 23:29; Ac 25:11,19
18:17 *v* 1Co 1:1
18:18 *w* Ac 1:16 *x* Ro 16:1 *y* Nu 6:2,5,18; Ac 21:24
18:19 *z* ver 21,24; 1Co 15:32
18:21 *a* Ro 1:10; 1Co 4:19; Jas 4:15
18:22 *b* Ac 8:40 *c* Ac 11:19
18:23 *d* Ac 16:6 *e* Ac 14:22; Ac 15:32,41
18:24 *f* Ac 19:1; 1Co 1:12; 1Co 3:5,6,22; 1Co 4:6; 1Co 16:12; Tit 3:13
18:25 *g* Ro 12:11 *h* Ac 19:3
18:27 *i* ver 12 *j* ver 18
18:28 *k* Ac 17:2 *l* ver 5; Ac 9:22
19:1 *a* Ac 18:1 *b* Ac 18:19
19:4 *c* Jn 1:7; Ac 13:24,25
19:6 *d* Ac 6:6; Ac 8:17 *e* Ac 2:4 *f* Mk 16:17; Ac 10:46
19:8 *g* Ac 9:20 *h* Ac 1:3; Ac 28:23
19:9 *i* Ac 14:4 *j* ver 23; Ac 9:2 *k* ver 30; Ac 11:26
19:10 *l* Ac 20:31

[b]25 Or *with fervour in the Spirit* [a]2 Or *after*
[b]5 Or *in* [c]6 Or *other languages*

in the province of Asia[m] heard
the word of the Lord.
11God did extraordinary miracles[n] through Paul, 12so that even
handkerchiefs and aprons that had
touched him were taken to the sick,
and their illnesses were cured[o]
and the evil spirits left them.
13Some Jews who went around
driving out evil spirits[p] tried to invoke the name of the Lord Jesus
over those who were demon-
possessed. They would say, "In
the name of Jesus,[q] whom Paul
preaches, I command you to come
out." 14Seven sons of Sceva, a Jewish chief priest, were doing this.
15⌞One day⌟ the evil spirit answered
them, "Jesus I know, and I know
about Paul, but who are you?"
16Then the man who had the evil
spirit jumped on them and overpowered them all. He gave them
such a beating that they ran out of
the house naked and bleeding.
17When this became known to the
Jews and Greeks living in Ephesus,[r] they were all seized with
fear,[s] and the name of the Lord
Jesus was held in high honour.
18Many of those who believed now
came and openly confessed their
evil deeds. 19A number who had
practised sorcery brought their
scrolls together and burned them
publicly. When they calculated the
value of the scrolls, the total came
to fifty thousand drachmas.[d] 20In
this way the word of the Lord
spread widely and grew in power.[t]
21After all this had happened,
Paul decided to go to Jerusalem,[u]
passing through Macedonia[v] and
Achaia.[w] "After I have been
there," he said, "I must visit Rome
also."[x] 22He sent two of his helpers,[y] Timothy[z] and Erastus,[a] to
Macedonia, while he stayed in the
province of Asia[b] a little longer.

The Riot in Ephesus

23About that time there arose a
great disturbance about the Way.[c]
24A silversmith named Demetrius,
who made silver shrines of Artemis, brought in no little business
for the craftsmen. 25He called them
together, along with the workmen
in related trades, and said: "Men,
you know we receive a good income
from this business.[d] 26And you see
and hear how this fellow Paul has
convinced and led astray large
numbers of people here in Ephesus[e] and in practically the whole
province of Asia. He says that man-
made gods are no gods at all.[f]
27There is danger not only that our
trade will lose its good name, but
also that the temple of the great
goddess Artemis will be discredited, and the goddess herself, who
is worshipped throughout the
province of Asia and the world, will
be robbed of her divine majesty."
28When they heard this, they
were furious and began shouting:
"Great is Artemis of the Ephesians!"[g] 29Soon the whole city was
in an uproar. The people seized
Gaius[h] and Aristarchus,[i] Paul's
travelling companions from Macedonia,[j] and rushed as one man
into the theatre. 30Paul wanted to
appear before the crowd, but the
disciples would not let him. 31Even
some of the officials of the province, friends of Paul, sent him a
message begging him not to venture into the theatre.
32The assembly was in confusion:
Some were shouting one thing,
some another.[k] Most of the people
did not even know why they were
there. 33The Jews pushed Alexander to the front, and some of the
crowd shouted instructions to him.
He motioned[l] for silence in order
to make a defence before the people. 34But when they realised he
was a Jew, they all shouted in unison for about two hours: "Great is
Artemis of the Ephesians!"
35The city clerk quietened the

19:10 m ver 22,26,27
19:11 n Ac 8:13
19:12 o Ac 5:15
19:13 p Mt 12:27 q Mk 9:38
19:17 r Ac 18:19 s Ac 5:5,11
19:20 t Ac 6:7; Ac 12:24
19:21 u Ac 20:16,22; Ro 15:25 v Ac 16:9 w Ac 18:12 x Ro 15:24,28
19:22 y Ac 13:5 z Ac 16:1 a Ro 16:23; 2Ti 4:20 b ver 10,26,27
19:23 c Ac 9:2
19:25 d Ac 16:16,19, 20
19:26 e Ac 18:19 f Dt 4:28; Ps 115:4; Isa 44:10-20; Jer 10:3-5; Ac 17:29; 1Co 8:4; Rev 9:20
19:28 g Ac 18:19
19:29 h Ac 20:4; Ro 16:23; 1Co 1:14 i Ac 20:4; Ac 27:2; Col 4:10; Phm 24 j Ac 16:9
19:32 k Ac 21:34
19:33 l Ac 12:17

[d]19 A drachma was a silver coin worth about a day's wages.

crowd and said: "Men of Ephesus,[m]
doesn't all the world know that the
city of Ephesus is the guardian of
the temple of the great Artemis and
of her image, which fell from
heaven? 36Therefore, since these
facts are undeniable, you ought to
be quiet and not do anything rash.
37You have brought these men
here, though they have neither
robbed temples[n] nor blasphemed
our goddess. 38If, then, Demetrius
and his fellow craftsmen have a
grievance against anybody, the
courts are open and there are pro-
consuls.[o] They can press charges.
39If there is anything further you
want to bring up, it must be settled
in a legal assembly. 40As it is, we
are in danger of being charged with
rioting because of today's events.
In that case we would not be able to
account for this commotion, since
there is no reason for it." 41After he
had said this, he dismissed the assembly.

Through Macedonia and Greece

20 When the uproar had
ended, Paul sent for the
disciples[a] and, after encouraging
them, said good-bye and set out
for Macedonia.[b] 2He travelled
through that area, speaking many
words of encouragement to the
people, and finally arrived in
Greece, 3where he stayed three
months. Because the Jews made a
plot against him[c] just as he was
about to sail for Syria, he decided
to go back through Macedonia.[d]
4He was accompanied by Sopater
son of Pyrrhus from Berea, Aristarchus[e] and Secundus from Thessalonica,[f] Gaius[g] from Derbe,
Timothy[h] also, and Tychicus[i] and
Trophimus[j] from the province of
Asia. 5These men went on ahead
and waited for us[k] at Troas.[l] 6But
we sailed from Philippi[m] after the
Feast of Unleavened Bread, and
five days later joined the others at
Troas,[n] where we stayed seven
days.

Eutychus Raised From the Dead at Troas

7On the first day of the week[o] we
came together to break bread. Paul
spoke to the people and, because he
intended to leave the next day, kept
on talking until midnight. 8There
were many lamps in the upstairs
room[p] where we were meeting.
9Seated in a window was a young
man named Eutychus, who was
sinking into a deep sleep as Paul
talked on and on. When he was
sound asleep, he fell to the ground
from the third storey and was
picked up dead. 10Paul went down,
threw himself on the young man[q]
and put his arms around him.
"Don't be alarmed," he said. "He's
alive!"[r] 11Then he went upstairs
again and broke bread[s] and ate.
After talking until daylight, he left.
12The people took the young man
home alive and were greatly comforted.

Paul's Farewell to the Ephesian Elders

13We went on ahead to the ship
and sailed for Assos, where we
were going to take Paul aboard. He
had made this arrangement because he was going there on foot.
14When he met us at Assos, we took
him aboard and went on to Mity-
lene. 15The next day we set sail
from there and arrived off Kios.
The day after that we crossed over
to Samos, and on the following day
arrived at Miletus.[t] 16Paul had decided to sail past Ephesus[u] to
avoid spending time in the province of Asia, for he was in a hurry
to reach Jerusalem,[v] if possible,
by the day of Pentecost.[w]
17From Miletus, Paul sent to Ephesus for the elders[x] of the church.
18When they arrived, he said to
them: "You know how I lived the

19:35
m Ac 18:19
19:37
n Ro 2:22
19:38
o Ac 13:7,8,12
20:1
a Ac 11:26
b Ac 16:9
20:3
c ver 19
Ac 9:23,24
Ac 23:12,15,30
Ac 25:3
2Co 11:26
d Ac 16:9
20:4
e Ac 19:29
f Ac 17:1
g Ac 19:29
h Ac 16:1
i Eph 6:21
Col 4:7
2Ti 4:12
Tit 3:12
j Ac 21:29
2Ti 4:20
20:5
k Ac 16:10
l Ac 16:8
20:6
m Ac 16:12
n Ac 16:8
20:7
o 1Co 16:2
Rev 1:10
20:8
p Ac 1:13
20:10
q 1Ki 17:21
2Ki 4:34
r Mt 9:23,24
20:11
s ver 7
20:15
t ver 17
2Ti 4:20
20:16
u Ac 18:19
v Ac 19:21
w Ac 2:1
1Co 16:8
20:17
x Ac 11:30

whole time I was with you,[y] from
the first day I came into the province of Asia. 19I served the Lord
with great humility and with tears,
although I was severely tested by
the plots of the Jews.[z] 20You know
that I have not hesitated to preach
anything[a] that would be helpful to
you but have taught you publicly
and from house to house. 21I have
declared to both Jews[b] and Greeks
that they must turn to God in repentance[c] and have faith in our
Lord Jesus.[d]

22"And now, compelled by the
Spirit, I am going to Jerusalem,[e]
not knowing what will happen to
me there. 23I only know that in
every city the Holy Spirit warns
me[f] that prison and hardships are
facing me.[g] 24However, I consider
my life worth nothing to me,[h] if
only I may finish the race and complete the task[i] the Lord Jesus has
given me[j]—the task of testifying
to the gospel of God's grace.

25"Now I know that none of you
among whom I have gone about
preaching the kingdom will ever
see me again.[k] 26Therefore, I declare to you today that I am innocent of the blood of all men.[l] 27For
I have not hesitated to proclaim to
you the whole will of God.[m] 28Keep
watch over yourselves and all the
flock of which the Holy Spirit has
made you overseers.[a][n] Be shepherds of the church of God,[b] which
he bought with his own blood. 29I
know that after I leave, savage
wolves[o] will come in among you
and will not spare the flock.[p]
30Even from your own number men
will arise and distort the truth in
order to draw away disciples[q]
after them. 31So be on your guard!
Remember that for three years[r] I
never stopped warning each of you
night and day with tears.[s]

32"Now I commit you to God[t]
and to the word of his grace, which
can build you up and give you an
inheritance[u] among all those
who are sanctified.[v] 33I have not
coveted anyone's silver or gold or
clothing.[w] 34You yourselves know
that these hands of mine have supplied my own needs and the needs
of my companions.[x] 35In everything I did, I showed you that by
this kind of hard work we must
help the weak, remembering the
words the Lord Jesus himself said:
'It is more blessed to give than to
receive.'"

36When he had said this, he knelt
down with all of them and prayed.[y]
37They all wept as they embraced
him and kissed him.[z] 38What
grieved them most was his statement that they would never see his
face again.[a] Then they accompanied him to the ship.

On to Jerusalem

21 After we[a] had torn ourselves away from them, we
put out to sea and sailed straight to
Cos. The next day we went to
Rhodes and from there to Patara.
2We found a ship crossing over to
Phoenicia,[b] went on board and set
sail. 3After sighting Cyprus and
passing to the south of it, we sailed
on to Syria. We landed at Tyre,
where our ship was to unload its
cargo. 4Finding the disciples[c]
there, we stayed with them seven
days. Through the Spirit[d] they
urged Paul not to go on to Jerusalem. 5But when our time was up,
we left and continued on our way.
All the disciples and their wives
and children accompanied us out of
the city, and there on the beach we
knelt to pray.[e] 6After saying good-
bye to each other, we went aboard
the ship, and they returned home.

7We continued our voyage from
Tyre[f] and landed at Ptolemais,
where we greeted the brothers[g]
and stayed with them for a day.
8Leaving the next day, we reached
Caesarea[h] and stayed at the house

20:18 y Ac 18:19-21; Ac 19:1-41
20:19 z ver 3
20:20 a ver 27
20:21 b Ac 18:5; c Ac 2:38; d Ac 24:24; Ac 26:18; Eph 1:15; Col 2:5; Phm 5
20:22 e ver 16
20:23 f Ac 21:4; g Ac 9:16
20:24 h Ac 21:13; i 2Co 4:1; j Gal 1:1; Tit 1:3
20:25 k ver 38
20:26 l Ac 18:6
20:27 m ver 20
20:28 n 1Pe 5:2
20:29 o Mt 7:15; p ver 28
20:30 q Ac 11:26
20:31 r Ac 19:10; s ver 19
20:32 t Ac 14:23; u Eph 1:14; Col 1:12; Col 3:24; Heb 9:15; 1Pe 1:4; v Ac 26:18
20:33 w 1Sa 12:3; 1Co 9:12; 2Co 7:2; 2Co 11:9; 2Co 12:14-17
20:34 x Ac 18:3
20:36 y Lk 22:41; Ac 21:5
20:37 z Lk 15:20
20:38 a ver 25
21:1 a Ac 16:10
21:2 b Ac 11:19
21:4 c Ac 11:26; d ver 11; Ac 20:23
21:5 e Ac 20:36
21:7 f Ac 12:20; g Ac 1:16
21:8 h Ac 8:40

a28 Traditionally *bishops* b28 Many manuscripts *of the Lord*

of Philip[i] the evangelist,[j] one of
the Seven. 9He had four unmarried
daughters who prophesied.[k]

10After we had been there a number of days, a prophet named
Agabus[l] came down from Judea.
11Coming over to us, he took Paul's
belt, tied his own hands and feet
with it and said, "The Holy Spirit
says, 'In this way the Jews of Jerusalem will bind[m] the owner of this
belt and will hand him over to the
Gentiles.' "[n]

12When we heard this, we and the
people there pleaded with Paul not
to go up to Jerusalem. 13Then Paul
answered, "Why are you weeping
and breaking my heart? I am ready
not only to be bound, but also to
die[o] in Jerusalem for the name of
the Lord Jesus."[p] 14When he would
not be dissuaded, we gave up and
said, "The Lord's will be done."

15After this, we got ready and
went up to Jerusalem. 16Some of
the disciples from Caesarea[q] accompanied us and brought us to the
home of Mnason, where we were to
stay. He was a man from Cyprus[r]
and one of the early disciples.

Paul's Arrival at Jerusalem

17When we arrived at Jerusalem,
the brothers received us warmly.[s]
18The next day Paul and the rest
of us went to see James,[t] and all
the elders[u] were present. 19Paul
greeted them and reported in detail
what God had done among the Gentiles[v] through his ministry.[w]

20When they heard this, they
praised God. Then they said to
Paul: "You see, brother, how many
thousands of Jews have believed,
and all of them are zealous[x] for the
law.[y] 21They have been informed
that you teach all the Jews who live
among the Gentiles to turn away
from Moses,[z] telling them not to
circumcise their children[a] or live
according to our customs.[b] 22What
shall we do? They will certainly
hear that you have come, 23so
do what we tell you. There are four
men with us who have made a
vow.[c] 24Take these men, join in
their purification rites[d] and pay
their expenses, so that they can
have their heads shaved.[e] Then
everybody will know there is no
truth in these reports about you,
but that you yourself are living in
obedience to the law. 25As for the
Gentile believers, we have written
to them our decision that they
should abstain from food sacrificed to idols, from blood, from the
meat of strangled animals and
from sexual immorality."[f]

26The next day Paul took the men
and purified himself along with
them. Then he went to the temple to
give notice of the date when the
days of purification would end and
the offering would be made for
each of them.[g]

Paul Arrested

27When the seven days were
nearly over, some Jews from the
province of Asia saw Paul at the
temple. They stirred up the whole
crowd and seized him,[h] 28shouting,
"Men of Israel, help us! This is the
man who teaches all men everywhere against our people and our
law and this place. And besides, he
has brought Greeks into the temple
area and defiled this holy place."[i]
29(They had previously seen Trophimus[j] the Ephesian[k] in the city
with Paul and assumed that Paul
had brought him into the temple
area.)

30The whole city was aroused,
and the people came running from
all directions. Seizing Paul,[l] they
dragged him[m] from the temple,
and immediately the gates were
shut. 31While they were trying to
kill him, news reached the commander of the Roman troops that
the whole city of Jerusalem was in
an uproar. 32He at once took some
officers and soldiers and ran down
to the crowd. When the rioters saw

21:8 i Ac 6:5; Ac 8:5-40 j Eph 4:11; 2Ti 4:5
21:9 k Lk 2:36; Ac 2:17
21:10 l Ac 11:28
21:11 m ver 33 n 1Ki 22:11
21:13 o Ac 20:24 p Ac 9:16
21:16 q Ac 8:40 r ver 3,4
21:17 s Ac 15:4
21:18 t Ac 15:13 u Ac 11:30
21:19 v Ac 14:27 w Ac 1:17
21:20 x Ac 22:3; Ro 10:2; Gal 1:14 y Ac 15:1,5
21:21 z ver 28 a Ac 15:19-21; 1Co 7:18,19 b Ac 6:14
21:23 c Ac 18:18
21:24 d ver 26; Ac 24:18 e Ac 18:18
21:25 f Ac 15:20,29
21:26 g Nu 6:13-20; Ac 24:18
21:27 h Ac 24:18; Ac 26:21
21:28 i Mt 24:15; Ac 24:5,6
21:29 j Ac 20:4 k Ac 18:19
21:30 l Ac 26:21 m Ac 16:19

the commander and his soldiers, they stopped beating Paul.[n]

33The commander came up and arrested him and ordered him to be bound[o] with two[p] chains.[q] Then he asked who he was and what he had done. 34Some in the crowd shouted one thing and some another,[r] and since the commander could not get at the truth because of the uproar, he ordered that Paul be taken into the barracks.[s] 35When Paul reached the steps,[t] the violence of the mob was so great he had to be carried by the soldiers. 36The crowd that followed kept shouting, "Away with him!"[u]

Paul Speaks to the Crowd

22:3–16pp Ac 9:1–22; 26:9–18

37As the soldiers were about to take Paul into the barracks,[v] he asked the commander, "May I say something to you?"

"Do you speak Greek?" he replied. 38"Aren't you the Egyptian who started a revolt and led four thousand terrorists out into the desert[w] some time ago?"[x]

39Paul answered, "I am a Jew, from Tarsus[y] in Cilicia,[z] a citizen of no ordinary city. Please let me speak to the people."

40Having received the commander's permission, Paul stood on the steps and motioned[a] to the crowd. When they were all silent, he said to them in Aramaic**[a]**:[b]

22 1"Brothers and fathers,[a] listen now to my defence."

2When they heard him speak to them in Aramaic,[b] they became very quiet.

Then Paul said: 3"I am a Jew,[c] born in Tarsus[d] of Cilicia, but brought up in this city. Under[e] Gamaliel[f] I was thoroughly trained in the law of our fathers[g] and was just as zealous[h] for God as any of you are today. 4I persecuted[i] the followers of this Way to their death, arresting both men and women and throwing them into prison,[j] 5as also the high priest and all the Council[k] can testify. I even obtained letters from them to their brothers[l] in Damascus,[m] and went there to bring these people as prisoners to Jerusalem to be punished.

6"About noon as I came near Damascus, suddenly a bright light from heaven flashed around me.[n] 7I fell to the ground and heard a voice say to me, 'Saul! Saul! Why do you persecute me?'

8" 'Who are you, Lord?' I asked.

" 'I am Jesus of Nazareth, whom you are persecuting,' he replied. 9My companions saw the light,[o] but they did not understand the voice[p] of him who was speaking to me.

10" 'What shall I do, Lord?' I asked.

" 'Get up,' the Lord said, 'and go into Damascus. There you will be told all that you have been assigned to do.'[q] 11My companions led me by the hand into Damascus, because the brilliance of the light had blinded me.[r]

12"A man named Ananias came to see me.[s] He was a devout observer of the law and highly respected by all the Jews living there.[t] 13He stood beside me and said, 'Brother Saul, receive your sight!' And at that very moment I was able to see him.

14"Then he said: 'The God of our fathers[u] has chosen you to know his will and to see[v] the Righteous One[w] and to hear words from his mouth. 15You will be his witness[x] to all men of what you have seen and heard. 16And now what are you waiting for? Get up, be baptised[y] and wash your sins away,[z] calling on his name.'[a]

17"When I returned to Jerusalem[b] and was praying at the temple, I fell into a trance[c] 18and saw the Lord speaking. 'Quick!' he said to me. 'Leave Jerusalem

a40 Or possibly *Hebrew*; also in 22:2

21:32 n Ac 23:27
21:33 o ver 11; p Ac 12:6; q Ac 20:23; Eph 6:20; 2Ti 2:9
21:34 r Ac 19:32; s ver 37; Ac 23:10,16, 32
21:35 t ver 40
21:36 u Lk 23:18; Jn 19:15; Ac 22:22
21:37 v ver 34
21:38 w Mt 24:26; x Ac 5:36
21:39 y Ac 9:11; z Ac 22:3
21:40 a Ac 12:17; b Jn 5:2
22:1 a Ac 7:2
22:2 b Ac 21:40
22:3 c Ac 21:39; d Ac 9:11; e Lk 10:39; f Ac 5:34; g Ac 26:5; h Ac 21:20
22:4 i Ac 8:3; j ver 19,20
22:5 k Lk 22:66; l Ac 13:26; m Ac 9:2
22:6 n Ac 9:3
22:9 o Ac 26:13; p Ac 9:7
22:10 q Ac 16:30
22:11 r Ac 9:8
22:12 s Ac 9:17; t Ac 10:22
22:14 u Ac 3:13; v 1Co 9:1; 1Co 15:8; w Ac 7:52
22:15 x Ac 23:11; Ac 26:16
22:16 y Ac 2:38; z Heb 10:22; a Ro 10:13
22:17 b Ac 9:26; c Ac 10:10

immediately, because they will not
accept your testimony about me.'
19" 'Lord,' I replied, 'these men
know that I went from one synagogue to another to imprison[d] and
beat[e] those who believe in you.
20And when the blood of your mar-
tyr[a] Stephen was shed, I stood
there giving my approval and
guarding the clothes of those who
were killing him.'[f]
21"Then the Lord said to me, 'Go;
I will send you far away to the Gentiles.' "[g]

Paul the Roman Citizen

22The crowd listened to Paul until
he said this. Then they raised their
voices and shouted, "Rid the earth
of him![h] He's not fit to live!"[i]
23As they were shouting and
throwing off their cloaks[j] and
flinging dust into the air,[k] 24the
commander ordered Paul to be
taken into the barracks.[l] He directed[m] that he be flogged and
questioned in order to find out why
the people were shouting at him
like this. 25As they stretched him
out to flog him, Paul said to the centurion standing there, "Is it legal
for you to flog a Roman citizen who
hasn't even been found guilty?"[n]
26When the centurion heard this,
he went to the commander and reported it. "What are you going to
do?" he asked. "This man is a Roman citizen."
27The commander went to Paul
and asked, "Tell me, are you a Roman citizen?"
"Yes, I am," he answered.
28Then the commander said, "I
had to pay a big price for my citizenship."
"But I was born a citizen," Paul
replied.
29Those who were about to question him withdrew immediately.
The commander himself was
alarmed when he realised that he
had put Paul, a Roman citizen,[o]
in chains.

22:19 *d* ver 4; Ac 8:3 *e* Mt 10:17
22:20 *f* Ac 7:57-60; Ac 8:1
22:21 *g* Ac 9:15; Ac 13:46
22:22 *h* Ac 21:36 *i* Ac 25:24
22:23 *j* Ac 7:58 *k* 2Sa 16:13
22:24 *l* Ac 21:34 *m* ver 29
22:25 *n* Ac 16:37
22:29 *o* ver 24,25; Ac 16:38
22:30 *p* Ac 23:28 *q* Ac 21:33 *r* Mt 5:22
23:1 *a* Ac 22:30 *b* Ac 22:5 *c* Ac 24:16; 1Co 4:4; 2Co 1:12; 2Ti 1:3; Heb 13:18
23:2 *d* Ac 24:1 *e* Jn 18:22
23:3 *f* Mt 23:27 *g* Lev 19:15; Dt 25:1,2; Jn 7:51
23:5 *h* Ex 22:28
23:6 *i* Ac 22:5 *j* Ac 26:5; Php 3:5 *k* Ac 24:15,21; Ac 26:8
23:8 *l* Mt 22:23
23:9 *m* Mk 2:16 *n* ver 29; Ac 25:25; Ac 26:31 *o* Ac 22:7,17,18

Before the Sanhedrin

30The next day, since the commander wanted to find out exactly
why Paul was being accused by the
Jews,[p] he released him[q] and ordered the chief priests and all the
Sanhedrin[r] to assemble. Then he
brought Paul and had him stand before them.

23 Paul looked straight at the
Sanhedrin[a] and said, "My
brothers,[b] I have fulfilled my duty
to God in all good conscience[c] to
this day." 2At this the high priest
Ananias[d] ordered those standing
near Paul to strike him on the
mouth.[e] 3Then Paul said to him,
"God will strike you, you whitewashed wall![f] You sit there to
judge me according to the law, yet
you yourself violate the law by
commanding that I be struck!"[g]
4Those who were standing near
Paul said, "You dare to insult God's
high priest?"
5Paul replied, "Brothers, I did not
realise that he was the high priest;
for it is written: 'Do not speak evil
about the ruler of your people.'[a]"[h]
6Then Paul, knowing that some of
them were Sadducees and the
others Pharisees, called out in the
Sanhedrin, "My brothers,[i] I am a
Pharisee,[j] the son of a Pharisee. I
stand on trial because of my hope
in the resurrection of the dead."[k]
7When he said this, a dispute broke
out between the Pharisees and the
Sadducees, and the assembly was
divided. 8(The Sadducees say that
there is no resurrection,[l] and that
there are neither angels nor spirits,
but the Pharisees acknowledge
them all.)
9There was a great uproar, and
some of the teachers of the law who
were Pharisees[m] stood up and argued vigorously. "We find nothing
wrong with this man,"[n] they said.
"What if a spirit or an angel has
spoken to him?"[o] 10The dispute

[a]20 Or *witness* [a]5 Exodus 22:28

became so violent that the commander was afraid Paul would be torn to pieces by them. He ordered the troops to go down and take him away from them by force and bring him into the barracks.[p]

11 The following night the Lord stood near Paul and said, "Take courage![q] As you have testified about me in Jerusalem, so you must also testify in Rome."[r]

The Plot to Kill Paul

12 The next morning the Jews formed a conspiracy and bound themselves with an oath not to eat or drink until they had killed Paul.[s] 13 More than forty men were involved in this plot. 14 They went to the chief priests and elders and said, "We have taken a solemn oath not to eat anything until we have killed Paul.[t] 15 Now then, you and the Sanhedrin[u] petition the commander to bring him before you on the pretext of wanting more accurate information about his case. We are ready to kill him before he gets here."

16 But when the son of Paul's sister heard of this plot, he went into the barracks[v] and told Paul.

17 Then Paul called one of the centurions and said, "Take this young man to the commander; he has something to tell him." 18 So he took him to the commander.

The centurion said, "Paul, the prisoner,[w] sent for me and asked me to bring this young man to you because he has something to tell you."

19 The commander took the young man by the hand, drew him aside and asked, "What is it you want to tell me?"

20 He said: "The Jews have agreed to ask you to bring Paul before the Sanhedrin[x] tomorrow on the pretext of wanting more accurate information about him.[y] 21 Don't give in to them, because more than forty[z] of them are waiting in ambush for him. They have taken an oath not to eat or drink until they have killed him.[a] They are ready now, waiting for your consent to their request."

22 The commander dismissed the young man and cautioned him, "Don't tell anyone that you have reported this to me."

Paul Transferred to Caesarea

23 Then he called two of his centurions and ordered them, "Get ready a detachment of two hundred soldiers, seventy horsemen and two hundred spearmen**b** to go to Caesarea[b] at nine tonight.[c] 24 Provide mounts for Paul so that he may be taken safely to Governor Felix."[d]

25 He wrote a letter as follows:

26 Claudius Lysias,

To His Excellency,[e] Governor Felix:

Greetings.[f]

27 This man was seized by the Jews and they were about to kill him,[g] but I came with my troops and rescued him,[h] for I had learned that he is a Roman citizen.[i] 28 I wanted to know why they were accusing him, so I brought him to their Sanhedrin.[j] 29 I found that the accusation had to do with questions about their law,[k] but there was no charge against him[l] that deserved death or imprisonment. 30 When I was informed[m] of a plot[n] to be carried out against the man, I sent him to you at once. I also ordered his accusers[o] to present to you their case against him.

31 So the soldiers, carrying out their orders, took Paul with them during the night and brought him

23:10 p Ac 21:34
23:11 q Ac 18:9; r Ac 19:21; Ac 28:23
23:12 s ver 14,21,30; Ac 25:3
23:14 t ver 12
23:15 u ver 1; Ac 22:30
23:16 v ver 10; Ac 21:34
23:18 w Eph 3:1
23:20 x ver 1; y ver 14,15
23:21 z ver 13; a ver 12,14
23:23 b Ac 8:40; c ver 33
23:24 d ver 26,33; Ac 24:1-3,10; Ac 25:14
23:26 e Lk 1:3; Ac 24:3; Ac 26:25; f Ac 15:23
23:27 g Ac 21:32; h Ac 21:33; i Ac 22:25-29
23:28 j Ac 22:30
23:29 k Ac 18:15; Ac 25:19; l ver 9; Ac 26:31
23:30 m ver 20,21; n Ac 20:3; o ver 35; Ac 24:19; Ac 25:16

b23 The meaning of the Greek for this word is uncertain.

as far as Antipatris. 32The next day
they let the cavalry[p] go on with
him, while they returned to the barracks.[q] 33When the cavalry[r] arrived in Caesarea,[s] they delivered
the letter to the governor[t] and
handed Paul over to him. 34The governor read the letter and asked
what province he was from. Learning that he was from Cilicia,[u] 35he
said, "I will hear your case when
your accusers[v] get here." Then he
ordered that Paul be kept under
guard[w] in Herod's palace.

The Trial Before Felix

24 Five days later the high
priest Ananias[a] went down
to Caesarea with some of the elders
and a lawyer named Tertullus,
and they brought their charges[b]
against Paul before the governor.[c]
2When Paul was called in, Tertullus
presented his case before Felix:
"We have enjoyed a long period of
peace under you, and your fore-
sight has brought about reforms in
this nation. 3Everywhere and in
every way, most excellent[d] Felix,
we acknowledge this with profound gratitude. 4But in order not
to weary you further, I would request that you be kind enough to
hear us briefly.

5"We have found this man to be a
troublemaker, stirring up riots[e]
among the Jews[f] all over the
world. He is a ringleader of the
Nazarene[g] sect[h] 6and even tried
to desecrate the temple;[i] so we
seized him. 8By[a] examining him
yourself you will be able to learn
the truth about all these charges we
are bringing against him."

9The Jews joined in the accusation,[j] asserting that these things
were true.

10When the governor[k] motioned
for him to speak, Paul replied: "I
know that for a number of years
you have been a judge over this nation; so I gladly make my defence.
11You can easily verify that no
more than twelve days[l] ago I went
up to Jerusalem to worship. 12My
accusers did not find me arguing
with anyone at the temple,[m] or stirring up a crowd[n] in the synagogues or anywhere else in the
city. 13And they cannot prove to
you the charges they are now making against me.[o] 14However, I admit that I worship the God of our
fathers[p] as a follower of the Way,[q]
which they call a sect.[r] I believe
everything that agrees with the
Law and that is written in the
Prophets,[s] 15and I have the same
hope in God as these men, that
there will be a resurrection[t] of
both the righteous and the
wicked.[u] 16So I strive always to
keep my conscience clear[v] before
God and man.

17"After an absence of several
years, I came to Jerusalem to bring
my people gifts for the poor[w] and
to present offerings. 18I was ceremonially clean[x] when they found
me in the temple courts doing this.
There was no crowd with me, nor
was I involved in any disturbance.[y] 19But there are some Jews
from the province of Asia, who
ought to be here before you and
bring charges if they have anything against me.[z] 20Or these who
are here should state what crime
they found in me when I stood before the Sanhedrin—21unless it was
this one thing I shouted as I stood in
their presence: 'It is concerning
the resurrection of the dead that I
am on trial before you today.' "[a]

22Then Felix, who was well acquainted with the Way, adjourned
the proceedings. "When Lysias the
commander comes," he said, "I will
decide your case." 23He ordered
the centurion to keep Paul under
guard[b] but to give him some

23:32 p ver 23 q Ac 21:34
23:33 r ver 23,24 s Ac 8:40 t ver 26
23:34 u Ac 6:9 Ac 21:39
23:35 v ver 30 Ac 24:19 Ac 25:16 w Ac 24:27
24:1 a Ac 23:2 b Ac 23:30,35 c Ac 23:24
24:3 d Lk 1:3 Ac 23:26 Ac 26:25
24:5 e Ac 16:20 Ac 17:6 f Ac 21:28 g Mk 1:24 h ver 14 Ac 26:5 Ac 28:22
24:6 i Ac 21:28
24:9 j 1Th 2:16
24:10 k Ac 23:24
24:11 l Ac 21:27 ver 1
24:12 m Ac 25:8 Ac 28:17 n ver 18
24:13 o Ac 25:7
24:14 p Ac 3:13 q Ac 9:2 r ver 5 s Ac 26:6,22 Ac 28:23
24:15 t Ac 23:6 Ac 28:20 u Da 12:2 Jn 5:28,29
24:16 v Ac 23:1
24:17 w Ac 11:29,30 Ro 15:25-28, 31 1Co 16:1-4,15 2Co 8:1-4 Gal 2:10
24:18 x Ac 21:26 y ver 12
24:19 z Ac 23:30
24:21 a Ac 23:6
24:23 b Ac 23:35

[a]6–8 Some manuscripts *him and wanted to judge him according to our law. 7But the commander, Lysias, came and with the use of much force snatched him from our hands 8and ordered his accusers to come before you. By*

freedom[c] and permit his friends to
take care of his needs.[d]
24Several days later Felix came
with his wife Drusilla, who was a
Jewess. He sent for Paul and listened to him as he spoke about faith
in Christ Jesus.[e] 25As Paul dis-
coursed on righteousness, self-
control[f] and the judgment[g] to
come, Felix was afraid and said,
"That's enough for now! You may
leave. When I find it convenient, I
will send for you." 26At the same
time he was hoping that Paul would
offer him a bribe, so he sent for him
frequently and talked with him.
27When two years had passed, Felix was succeeded by Porcius Festus,[h] but because Felix wanted to
grant a favour to the Jews,[i] he left
Paul in prison.[j]

The Trial Before Festus

25 Three days after arriving
in the province, Festus
went up from Caesarea[a] to Jerusalem, 2where the chief priests and
Jewish leaders appeared before
him and presented the charges
against Paul.[b] 3They urgently requested Festus, as a favour to
them, to have Paul transferred to
Jerusalem, for they were preparing an ambush to kill him along the
way. 4Festus answered, "Paul is being held[c] at Caesarea, and I myself
am going there soon. 5Let some of
your leaders come with me and
press charges against the man
there, if he has done anything
wrong."
6After spending eight or ten days
with them, he went down to Caesarea, and the next day he convened
the court[d] and ordered that Paul
be brought before him. 7When
Paul appeared, the Jews who had
come down from Jerusalem stood
around him, bringing many serious charges against him,[e] which
they could not prove.[f]
8Then Paul made his defence: "I
have done nothing wrong against
the law of the Jews or against the
temple[g] or against Caesar."
9Festus, wishing to do the Jews a
favour,[h] said to Paul, "Are you
willing to go up to Jerusalem and
stand trial before me there on these
charges?"[i]
10Paul answered: "I am now
standing before Caesar's court,
where I ought to be tried. I have not
done any wrong to the Jews, as you
yourself know very well. 11If, however, I am guilty of doing anything
deserving death, I do not refuse to
die. But if the charges brought
against me by these Jews are not
true, no-one has the right to hand
me over to them. I appeal to Caesar!"[j]
12After Festus had conferred
with his council, he declared: "You
have appealed to Caesar. To Caesar
you will go!"

Festus Consults King Agrippa

13A few days later King Agrippa
and Bernice arrived at Caesarea[k]
to pay their respects to Festus.
14Since they were spending many
days there, Festus discussed Paul's
case with the king. He said: "There
is a man here whom Felix left as a
prisoner.[l] 15When I went to Jerusalem, the chief priests and elders
of the Jews brought charges
against him[m] and asked that he be
condemned.
16"I told them that it is not the Roman custom to hand over any man
before he has faced his accusers
and has had an opportunity to
defend himself against their
charges.[n] 17When they came here
with me, I did not delay the case,
but convened the court the next
day and ordered the man to be
brought in.[o] 18When his accusers
got up to speak, they did not charge
him with any of the crimes I had expected. 19Instead, they had some
points of dispute[p] with him about
their own religion[q] and about a
dead man named Jesus whom Paul

24:23 c Ac 28:16 d Ac 23:16 Ac 27:3
24:24 e Ac 20:21
24:25 f Gal 5:23 2Pe 1:6 g Ac 10:42
24:27 h Ac 25:1,4,9,14 i Ac 12:3 Ac 25:9 j Ac 23:35 Ac 25:14
25:1 a Ac 8:40
25:2 b ver 15 Ac 24:1
25:4 c Ac 24:23
25:6 d ver 17
25:7 e Mk 15:3 Lk 23:2,10 Ac 24:5,6 f Ac 24:13
25:8 g Ac 6:13 Ac 24:12 Ac 28:17
25:9 h Ac 24:27 i ver 20
25:11 j ver 21,25 Ac 26:32 Ac 28:19
25:13 k Ac 8:40
25:14 l Ac 24:27
25:15 m ver 2 Ac 24:1
25:16 n ver 4,5 Ac 23:30
25:17 o ver 6,10
25:19 p Ac 18:15 Ac 23:29 q Ac 17:22

claimed was alive. 20I was at a loss
how to investigate such matters; so
I asked if he would be willing to go
to Jerusalem and stand trial there
on these charges.[r] 21When Paul
made his appeal to be held over for
the Emperor's decision, I ordered
him to be held until I could send
him to Caesar."[s]

22Then Agrippa said to Festus, "I
would like to hear this man myself."

He replied, "Tomorrow you will
hear him."[t]

Paul Before Agrippa

26:12–18pp Ac 9:3–8; 22:6–11

23The next day Agrippa and Bernice[u] came with great pomp and
entered the audience room with the
high ranking officers and the leading men of the city. At the command of Festus, Paul was brought
in. 24Festus said: "King Agrippa,
and all who are present with us,
you see this man! The whole Jewish community[v] has petitioned me
about him in Jerusalem and here in
Caesarea, shouting that he ought
not to live any longer.[w] 25I found he
had done nothing deserving of
death,[x] but because he made his
appeal to the Emperor[y] I decided
to send him to Rome. 26But I have
nothing definite to write to His
Majesty about him. Therefore I
have brought him before all of you,
and especially before you, King
Agrippa, so that as a result of this
investigation I may have something to write. 27For I think it is un-
reasonable to send on a prisoner
without specifying the charges
against him."

26 Then Agrippa said to Paul,
"You have permission to
speak for yourself."[a]

So Paul motioned with his hand
and began his defence: 2"King
Agrippa, I consider myself fortu-
nate to stand before you today as I
make my defence against all the
accusations of the Jews, 3and
especially so because you are well
acquainted with all the Jewish customs[b] and controversies.[c] Therefore, I beg you to listen to me
patiently.

4"The Jews all know the way I
have lived ever since I was a
child,[d] from the beginning of my
life in my own country, and also in
Jerusalem. 5They have known me
for a long time[e] and can testify, if
they are willing, that according to
the strictest sect of our religion, I
lived as a Pharisee.[f] 6And now it is
because of my hope[g] in what God
has promised our fathers[h] that I
am on trial today. 7This is the promise our twelve tribes[i] are hoping
to see fulfilled as they earnestly
serve God day and night.[j] O King,
it is because of this hope that the
Jews are accusing me.[k] 8Why
should any of you consider it in-
credible that God raises the
dead?[l]

9"I too was convinced[m] that I
ought to do all that was possible to
oppose[n] the name of Jesus of Nazareth.[o] 10And that is just what I did
in Jerusalem. On the authority of
the chief priests I put many of the
saints[p] in prison,[q] and when they
were put to death, I cast my vote
against them.[r] 11Many a time I
went from one synagogue to another to have them punished,[s] and
I tried to force them to blaspheme.
In my obsession against them, I
even went to foreign cities to persecute them.

12"On one of these journeys I was
going to Damascus with the authority and commission of the chief
priests. 13About noon, O King, as I
was on the road, I saw a light from
heaven, brighter than the sun, blazing around me and my companions.
14We all fell to the ground, and I
heard a voice[t] saying to me in Aramaic,[a] 'Saul, Saul, why do you persecute me? It is hard for you to kick
against the goads.'

25:20 r ver 9
25:21 s ver 11,12
25:22 t Ac 9:15
25:23 u ver 13; Ac 26:30
25:24 v ver 2,3,7; w Ac 22:22
25:25 x Ac 23:9; y ver 11
26:1 a Ac 9:15; Ac 25:22
26:3 b ver 7; Ac 6:14; c Ac 25:19
26:4 d Gal 1:13,14; Php 3:5
26:5 e Ac 22:3; f Ac 23:6; Php 3:5
26:6 g Ac 23:6; Ac 24:15; Ac 28:20; h Ac 13:32; Ro 15:8
26:7 i Jas 1:1; j 1Th 3:10; 1Ti 5:5; k ver 2
26:8 l Ac 23:6
26:9 m 1Ti 1:13; n Jn 16:2; o Jn 15:21
26:10 p Ac 9:13; q Ac 8:3; Ac 9:2,14,21; r Ac 22:20
26:11 s Mt 10:17
26:14 t Ac 9:7

a14 Or *Hebrew*

15"Then I asked, 'Who are you,
Lord?'
" 'I am Jesus, whom you are persecuting,' the Lord replied. 16'Now
get up and stand on your feet.[u] I
have appeared to you to appoint
you as a servant and as a witness of
what you have seen of me and what
I will show you.[v] 17I will rescue
you[w] from your own people and
from the Gentiles.[x] I am sending
you to them 18to open their eyes[y]
and turn them from darkness to
light,[z] and from the power of
Satan to God, so that they may receive forgiveness of sins[a] and a
place among those who are sanctified by faith in me.'[b]
19"So then, King Agrippa, I was
not disobedient to the vision from
heaven. 20First to those in Damascus,[c] then to those in Jerusalem[d]
and in all Judea, and to the Gentiles[e] also, I preached that they
should repent[f] and turn to God and
prove their repentance by their
deeds.[g] 21That is why the Jews
seized me[h] in the temple courts
and tried to kill me.[i] 22But I have
had God's help to this very day, and
so I stand here and testify to small
and great alike. I am saying nothing beyond what the prophets and
Moses said would happen[j]—23that
the Christ[b] would suffer and, as
the first to rise from the dead,[k]
would proclaim light to his own
people and to the Gentiles."[l]
24At this point Festus interrupted
Paul's defence. "You are out of
your mind,[m] Paul!" he shouted.
"Your great learning[n] is driving
you insane."
25"I am not insane, most excellent[o] Festus," Paul replied. "What
I am saying is true and reasonable.
26The king is familiar with these
things,[p] and I can speak freely to
him. I am convinced that none of
this has escaped his notice, because it was not done in a corner.
27King Agrippa, do you believe the
prophets? I know you do."
28Then Agrippa said to Paul, "Do
you think that in such a short time
you can persuade me to be a Christian?"[q]
29Paul replied, "Short time or
long—I pray God that not only you
but all who are listening to me today may become what I am, except
for these chains."[r]
30The king rose, and with him the
governor and Bernice[s] and those
sitting with them. 31They left the
room, and while talking with one
another, they said, "This man is not
doing anything that deserves death
or imprisonment."[t]
32Agrippa said to Festus, "This
man could have been set free[u] if he
had not appealed to Caesar."[v]

Paul Sails for Rome

27 When it was decided that
we[a] would sail for Italy,[b]
Paul and some other prisoners
were handed over to a centurion
named Julius, who belonged to the
Imperial Regiment.[c] 2We boarded
a ship from Adramyttium about to
sail for ports along the coast of
the province of Asia,[d] and we put
out to sea. Aristarchus,[e] a Ma-
cedonian[f] from Thessalonica,[g] was
with us.
3The next day we landed at Sidon;[h] and Julius, in kindness to
Paul,[i] allowed him to go to his
friends so they might provide for
his needs.[j] 4From there we put out
to sea again and passed to the lee of
Cyprus because the winds were
against us.[k] 5When we had sailed
across the open sea off the coast of
Cilicia[l] and Pamphylia, we landed
at Myra in Lycia. 6There the centurion found an Alexandrian ship[m]
sailing for Italy[n] and put us on
board. 7We made slow headway for
many days and had difficulty arriving off Cnidus. When the wind did
not allow us to hold our course,[o]

26:16 u Eze 2:1; Da 10:11 v Ac 22:14,15
26:17 w Jer 1:8,19 x Ac 9:15
26:18 y Isa 35:5 z Isa 42:7,16; Eph 5:8; Col 1:13; 1Pe 2:9 a Lk 24:47; Ac 2:38 b Ac 20:21,32
26:20 c Ac 9:19-25 d Ac 9:26-29; Ac 22:17-20 e Ac 9:15; Ac 13:46 f Ac 3:19 g Mt 3:8; Lk 3:8
26:21 h Ac 21:27,30 i Ac 21:31
26:22 j Lk 24:27,44; Ac 10:43; Ac 24:14
26:23 k 1Co 15:20,23; Col 1:18; Rev 1:5 l Lk 2:32
26:24 m Jn 10:20; 1Co 4:10 n Jn 7:15
26:25 o Ac 23:26
26:26 p ver 3
26:28 q Ac 11:26
26:29 r Ac 21:33
26:30 s Ac 25:23
26:31 t Ac 23:9
26:32 u Ac 28:18 v Ac 25:11
27:1 a Ac 16:10 b Ac 18:2; Ac 25:12,25 c Ac 10:1
27:2 d Ac 2:9 e Ac 19:29 f Ac 16:9 g Ac 17:1
27:3 h Mt 11:21 i ver 43 j Ac 24:23; Ac 28:16
27:4 k ver 7
27:5 l Ac 6:9
27:6 m Ac 28:11 n ver 1
27:7 o ver 4

b23 Or *Messiah*

we sailed to the lee of Crete,[p] opposite Salmone. [8]We moved along the coast with difficulty and came to a place called Fair Havens, near the town of Lasea.

[9]Much time had been lost, and sailing had already become dangerous because by now it was after the Fast.[a][q] So Paul warned them, [10]"Men, I can see that our voyage is going to be disastrous and bring great loss to ship and cargo, and to our own lives also."[r] [11]But the centurion, instead of listening to what Paul said, followed the advice of the pilot and of the owner of the ship. [12]Since the harbour was unsuitable to winter in, the majority decided that we should sail on, hoping to reach Phoenix and winter there. This was a harbour in Crete, facing both south-west and north-west.

The Storm

[13]When a gentle south wind began to blow, they thought they had obtained what they wanted; so they weighed anchor and sailed along the shore of Crete. [14]Before very long, a wind of hurricane force,[s] called the "north-easter", swept down from the island. [15]The ship was caught by the storm and could not head into the wind; so we gave way to it and were driven along. [16]As we passed to the lee of a small island called Cauda, we were hardly able to make the lifeboat secure. [17]When the men had hoisted it aboard, they passed ropes under the ship itself to hold it together. Fearing that they would run aground[t] on the sand-bars of Syrtis, they lowered the sea anchor and let the ship be driven along. [18]We took such a violent battering from the storm that the next day they began to throw the cargo overboard.[u] [19]On the third day, they threw the ship's tackle overboard with their own hands. [20]When neither sun nor stars appeared for many days and the storm continued raging, we finally gave up all hope of being saved.

[21]After the men had gone a long time without food, Paul stood up before them and said: "Men, you should have taken my advice[v] not to sail from Crete;[w] then you would have spared yourselves this damage and loss. [22]But now I urge you to keep up your courage,[x] because not one of you will be lost; only the ship will be destroyed. [23]Last night an angel[y] of the God whose I am and whom I serve[z] stood beside me[a] [24]and said, 'Do not be afraid, Paul. You must stand trial before Caesar;[b] and God has graciously given you the lives of all who sail with you.'[c] [25]So keep up your courage,[d] men, for I have faith in God that it will happen just as he told me.[e] [26]Nevertheless, we must run aground[f] on some island."[g]

The Shipwreck

[27]On the fourteenth night we were still being driven across the Adriatic[b] Sea, when about midnight the sailors sensed they were approaching land. [28]They took soundings and found that the water was one hundred and twenty feet[c] deep. A short time later they took soundings again and found it was ninety feet[d] deep. [29]Fearing that we would be dashed against the rocks, they dropped four anchors from the stern and prayed for daylight. [30]In an attempt to escape from the ship, the sailors let the lifeboat[h] down into the sea, pretending they were going to lower some anchors from the bow. [31]Then Paul said to the centurion and the soldiers, "Unless these men stay with the ship, you cannot be saved."[i] [32]So the soldiers cut the

27:7 p ver 12,13,21
27:9 q Lev 16:29-31; Lev 23:27-29; Nu 29:7
27:10 r ver 21
27:14 s Mk 4:37
27:17 t ver 26,39
27:18 u ver 19,38; Jnh 1:5
27:21 v ver 10; w ver 7
27:22 x ver 25,36
27:23 y Ac 5:19; z Ro 1:9; a Ac 18:9; Ac 23:11; 2Ti 4:17
27:24 b Ac 23:11; c ver 44
27:25 d ver 22,36; e Ro 4:20,21
27:26 f ver 17,39; g Ac 28:1
27:30 h ver 16
27:31 i ver 24

a9 That is, the Day of Atonement (Yom Kippur)
b27 In ancient times the name referred to an area extending well south of Italy.
c28 Greek *twenty orguias* (about 37 metres)
d28 Greek *fifteen orguias* (about 27 metres)

ropes that held the lifeboat and let
it fall away.
33Just before dawn Paul urged
them all to eat. "For the last fourteen days," he said, "you have been
in constant suspense and have gone
without food—you haven't eaten
anything. 34Now I urge you to take
some food. You need it to survive.
Not one of you will lose a single
hair from his head."[j] 35After he
said this, he took some bread and
gave thanks to God in front of them
all. Then he broke it[k] and began to
eat. 36They were all encouraged[l]
and ate some food themselves. 37Al-
together there were 276 of us on
board. 38When they had eaten as
much as they wanted, they light-
ened the ship by throwing the grain
into the sea.[m]
39When daylight came, they did
not recognise the land, but they
saw a bay with a sandy beach,[n]
where they decided to run the ship
aground if they could. 40Cutting
loose the anchors,[o] they left them
in the sea and at the same time untied the ropes that held the rud-
ders. Then they hoisted the foresail
to the wind and made for the beach.
41But the ship struck a sand-bar
and ran aground. The bow stuck
fast and would not move, and the
stern was broken to pieces by the
pounding of the surf.[p]
42The soldiers planned to kill the
prisoners to prevent any of them
from swimming away and escaping. 43But the centurion wanted to
spare Paul's life[q] and kept them
from carrying out their plan. He ordered those who could swim to
jump overboard first and get to
land. 44The rest were to get there
on planks or on pieces of the ship.
In this way everyone reached land
in safety.[r]

Ashore on Malta

28 Once safely on shore, we[a]
found out that the island[b]
was called Malta. 2The islanders
showed us unusual kindness. They
built a fire and welcomed us all because it was raining and cold. 3Paul
gathered a pile of brushwood and,
as he put it on the fire, a viper,
driven out by the heat, fastened itself on his hand. 4When the islanders saw the snake hanging from his
hand,[c] they said to each other,
"This man must be a murderer; for
though he escaped from the sea,
Justice has not allowed him to
live."[d] 5But Paul shook the snake
off into the fire and suffered no ill
effects.[e] 6The people expected
him to swell up or suddenly fall
dead, but after waiting a long time
and seeing nothing unusual happen
to him, they changed their minds
and said he was a god.[f]
7There was an estate near by that
belonged to Publius, the chief official of the island. He welcomed us
to his home and for three days entertained us hospitably. 8His father
was sick in bed, suffering from fever and dysentery. Paul went in to
see him and, after prayer,[g] placed
his hands on him and healed him.[h]
9When this had happened, the rest
of the sick on the island came and
were cured. 10They honoured us in
many ways and when we were
ready to sail, they furnished us
with the supplies we needed.

Arrival at Rome

11After three months we put out
to sea in a ship that had wintered in
the island. It was an Alexandrian
ship[i] with the figurehead of the
twin gods Castor and Pollux. 12We
put in at Syracuse and stayed there
three days. 13From there we set sail
and arrived at Rhegium. The next
day the south wind came up, and on
the following day we reached Pu-
teoli. 14There we found some
brothers[j] who invited us to spend
a week with them. And so we came
to Rome. 15The brothers[k] there
had heard that we were coming,
and they travelled as far as the

27:34 j Mt 10:30
27:35 k Mt 14:19
27:36 l ver 22,25
27:38 m ver 18; Jnh 1:5
27:39 n Ac 28:1
27:40 o ver 29
27:41 p 2Co 11:25
27:43 q ver 3
27:44 r ver 22,31
28:1 a Ac 16:10; b Ac 27:26,39
28:4 c Mk 16:18; d Lk 13:2,4
28:5 e Lk 10:19
28:6 f Ac 14:11
28:8 g Jas 5:14,15; h Ac 9:40
28:11 i Ac 27:6
28:14 j Ac 1:16
28:15 k Ac 1:16

Forum of Appius and the Three Taverns to meet us. At the sight of these men Paul thanked God and was encouraged. 16When we got to Rome, Paul was allowed to live by himself, with a soldier to guard him.[l]

Paul Preaches at Rome Under Guard

17Three days later he called together the leaders of the Jews.[m] When they had assembled, Paul said to them: "My brothers,[n] although I have done nothing against our people[o] or against the customs of our ancestors,[p] I was arrested in Jerusalem and handed over to the Romans. 18They examined me[q] and wanted to release me,[r] because I was not guilty of any crime deserving death.[s] 19But when the Jews objected, I was compelled to appeal to Caesar[t]—not that I had any charge to bring against my own people. 20For this reason I have asked to see you and talk with you. It is because of the hope of Israel[u] that I am bound with this chain."[v]

21They replied, "We have not received any letters from Judea concerning you, and none of the brothers[w] who have come from there has reported or said anything bad about you. 22But we want to hear what your views are, for we know that people everywhere are talking against this sect."[x]

23They arranged to meet Paul on a certain day, and came in even larger numbers to the place where he was staying. From morning till evening he explained and declared to them the kingdom of God[y] and tried to convince them about Jesus[z] from the Law of Moses and from the Prophets.[a] 24Some were convinced by what he said, but others would not believe.[b] 25They disagreed among themselves and began to leave after Paul had made this final statement: "The Holy Spirit spoke the truth to your forefathers when he said through Isaiah the prophet:

26" 'Go to this people and say,
"You will be ever hearing but
never understanding;
you will be ever seeing but
never perceiving."
27For this people's heart has
become calloused;[c]
they hardly hear with their
ears,
and they have closed their
eyes.
Otherwise they might see with
their eyes,
hear with their ears,
understand with their hearts
and turn, and I would heal
them.'[a][d]

28"Therefore I want you to know that God's salvation[e] has been sent to the Gentiles,[f] and they will listen!"[b]

30For two whole years Paul stayed there in his own rented house and welcomed all who came to see him. 31Boldly and without hindrance he preached the kingdom of God[g] and taught about the Lord Jesus Christ.

[a]27 Isaiah 6:9,10 [b]28 Some manuscripts *listen!" 29After he said this, the Jews left, arguing vigorously among themselves.*

28:16 l Ac 24:23; Ac 27:3
28:17 m Ac 25:2; n Ac 22:5; o Ac 25:8; p Ac 6:14
28:18 q Ac 22:24; r Ac 26:31,32; s Ac 23:9
28:19 t Ac 25:11
28:20 u Ac 26:6,7; v Ac 21:33
28:21 w Ac 22:5
28:22 x Ac 24:5,14
28:23 y Ac 19:8; z Ac 17:3; a Ac 8:35
28:24 b Ac 14:4
28:27 c Ps 119:70; d Isa 6:9,10
28:28 e Lk 2:30; f Ac 13:46
28:31 g ver 23; Mt 4:23

ROMANS

1 Paul, a servant of Christ Jesus,
called to be an apostle[a] and
set apart[b] for the gospel of
God[c]—2the gospel he promised
beforehand through his prophets
in the Holy Scriptures[d] 3regard-
ing his Son, who as to his human nature[e] was a descendant
of David, 4and who through the
Spirit[a] of holiness was declared
with power to be the Son of God,[b]
by his resurrection from the dead:
Jesus Christ our Lord. 5Through
him and for his name's sake, we received grace and apostleship to call
people from among all the Gentiles[f] to the obedience that comes
from faith.[g] 6And you also are
among those who are called to belong to Jesus Christ.[h]

7To all in Rome who are loved by
God[i] and called to be saints:

Grace and peace to you from God
our Father and from the Lord Jesus
Christ.[j]

Paul's Longing to Visit Rome

8First, I thank my God through
Jesus Christ for all of you,[k] because your faith is being reported
all over the world.[l] 9God, whom I
serve[m] with my whole heart in
preaching the gospel of his Son, is
my witness[n] how constantly I remember you 10in my prayers at all
times; and I pray that now at last by
God's will the way may be opened
for me to come to you.[o]

11I long to see you[p] so that I may
impart to you some spiritual gift to
make you strong—12that is, that
you and I may be mutually encouraged by each other's faith. 13I do
not want you to be unaware,
brothers, that I planned many
times to come to you (but have been
prevented from doing so until
now)[q] in order that I might have a
harvest among you, just as I have
had among the other Gentiles.

14I am bound[r] both to Greeks
and non-Greeks, both to the wise
and the foolish. 15That is why I am
so eager to preach the gospel also
to you who are at Rome.[s]

16I am not ashamed of the gospel,[t] because it is the power of
God[u] for the salvation of everyone
who believes: first for the Jew,[v]
then for the Gentile.[w] 17For in the
gospel a righteousness from God is
revealed,[x] a righteousness that is
by faith from first to last,[c] just as
it is written: "The righteous will
live by faith."[d][y]

God's Wrath Against Mankind

18The wrath of God[z] is being revealed from heaven against all the
godlessness and wickedness of
men who suppress the truth by
their wickedness, 19since what may
be known about God is plain to
them, because God has made it
plain to them.[a] 20For since the creation of the world God's invisible
qualities—his eternal power and
divine nature—have been clearly
seen, being understood from what
has been made,[b] so that men are
without excuse.

21For although they knew God,
they neither glorified him as God
nor gave thanks to him, but their
thinking became futile and their
foolish hearts were darkened.[c]
22Although they claimed to be wise,
they became fools[d] 23and exchanged the glory of the immortal
God for images[e] made to look like

1:1 a 1Co 1:1 b Ac 9:15 c 2Co 11:7
1:2 d Gal 3:8
1:3 e Jn 1:14
1:5 f Ac 9:15 g Ac 6:7
1:6 h Rev 17:14
1:7 i Ro 8:39 j 1Co 1:3
1:8 k 1Co 1:4 l Ro 16:19
1:9 m 2Ti 1:3 n Php 1:8
1:10 o Ro 15:32
1:11 p Ro 15:23
1:13 q Ro 15:22,23
1:14 r 1Co 9:16
1:15 s Ro 15:20
1:16 t 2Ti 1:8 u 1Co 1:18 v Ac 3:26 w Ro 2:9,10
1:17 x Ro 3:21 y Hab 2:4 Gal 3:11 Heb 10:38
1:18 z Eph 5:6 Col 3:6
1:19 a Ac 14:17
1:20 b Ps 19:1-6
1:21 c Jer 2:5 Eph 4:17,18
1:22 d 1Co 1:20,27
1:23 e Ps 106:20 Jer 2:11 Ac 17:29

a4 Or *who as to his spirit* b4 Or *was appointed to be the Son of God with power* c17 Or *is from faith to faith* d17 Hab. 2:4

mortal man and birds and animals and reptiles.

24 Therefore God gave them over[f] in the sinful desires of their hearts to sexual impurity for the degrading of their bodies with one another.[g] 25 They exchanged the truth of God for a lie,[h] and worshipped and served created things[i] rather than the Creator—who is for ever praised.[j] Amen.

26 Because of this, God gave them over[k] to shameful lusts.[l] Even their women exchanged natural relations for unnatural ones.[m] 27 In the same way the men also abandoned natural relations with women and were inflamed with lust for one another. Men committed indecent acts with other men, and received in themselves the due penalty for their perversion.[n]

28 Furthermore, since they did not think it worth while to retain the knowledge of God, he gave them over[o] to a depraved mind, to do what ought not to be done. 29 They have become filled with every kind of wickedness, evil, greed and depravity. They are full of envy, murder, strife, deceit and malice. They are gossips,[p] 30 slanderers, God-haters, insolent, arrogant and boastful; they invent ways of doing evil; they disobey their parents;[q] 31 they are senseless, faithless, heartless,[r] ruthless. 32 Although they know God's righteous decree that those who do such things deserve death,[s] they not only continue to do these very things but also approve[t] of those who practise them.

God's Righteous Judgment

2 You, therefore, have no excuse,[a] you who pass judgment on someone else, for at whatever point you judge the other, you are condemning yourself, because you who pass judgment do the same things.[b] 2 Now we know that God's judgment against those who do such things is based on truth. 3 So when you, a mere man, pass judgment on them and yet do the same things, do you think you will escape God's judgment? 4 Or do you show contempt for the riches[c] of his kindness,[d] tolerance[e] and patience,[f] not realising that God's kindness leads you towards repentance?[g]

5 But because of your stubbornness and your unrepentant heart, you are storing up wrath against yourself for the day of God's wrath, when his righteous judgment[h] will be revealed. 6 God "will give to each person according to what he has done".[a][i] 7 To those who by persistence in doing good seek glory, honour[j] and immortality,[k] he will give eternal life. 8 But for those who are self-seeking and who reject the truth and follow evil,[l] there will be wrath and anger. 9 There will be trouble and distress for every human being who does evil: first for the Jew, then for the Gentile;[m] 10 but glory, honour and peace for everyone who does good: first for the Jew, then for the Gentile.[n] 11 For God does not show favouritism.[o]

12 All who sin apart from the law will also perish apart from the law, and all who sin under the law[p] will be judged by the law. 13 For it is not those who hear the law who are righteous in God's sight, but it is those who obey[q] the law who will be declared righteous. 14 (Indeed, when Gentiles, who do not have the law, do by nature things required by the law,[r] they are a law for themselves, even though they do not have the law, 15 since they show that the requirements of the law are written on their hearts, their consciences also bearing witness, and their thoughts now accusing, now even defending them.) 16 This

1:24 f Eph 4:19 g 1Pe 4:3
1:25 h Isa 44:20 i Jer 10:14 j Ro 9:5
1:26 k ver 24,28 l 1Th 4:5 m Lev 18:22,23
1:27 n Lev 18:22 Lev 20:13
1:28 o ver 24,26
1:29 p 2Co 12:20
1:30 q 2Ti 3:2
1:31 r 2Ti 3:3
1:32 s Ro 6:23 t Ps 50:18 Lk 11:48 Ac 8:1 Ac 22:20
2:1 a Ro 1:20 b 2Sa 12:5-7 Mt 7:1,2
2:4 c Ro 9:23 Eph 1:7,18 Eph 2:7 d Ro 11:22 e Ro 3:25 f Ex 34:6 g 2Pe 3:9
2:5 h Jude 6
2:6 i Ps 62:12 Mt 16:27
2:7 j ver 10 k 1Co 15:53,54
2:8 l 2Th 2:12
2:9 m 1Pe 4:17
2:10 n ver 9
2:11 o Ac 10:34
2:12 p Ro 3:19 1Co 9:20,21
2:13 q Jas 1:22,23, 25
2:14 r Ac 10:35

a6 Psalm 62:12; Prov. 24:12

will take place on the day when God will judge men's secrets[s] through Jesus Christ,[t] as my gospel[u] declares.

The Jews and the Law

17Now you, if you call yourself a Jew; if you rely on the law and brag about your relationship to God;[v] 18if you know his will and approve of what is superior because you are instructed by the law; 19if you are convinced that you are a guide for the blind, a light for those who are in the dark, 20an instructor of the foolish, a teacher of infants, because you have in the law the embodiment of knowledge and truth—21you, then, who teach others, do you not teach yourself? You who preach against stealing, do you steal?[w] 22You who say that people should not commit adultery, do you commit adultery? You who abhor idols, do you rob temples?[x] 23You who brag about the law,[y] do you dishonour God by breaking the law? 24As it is written: "God's name is blasphemed among the Gentiles because of you."[b][z]

25Circumcision has value if you observe the law,[a] but if you break the law, you have become as though you had not been circumcised.[b] 26If those who are not circumcised keep the law's requirements,[c] will they not be regarded as though they were circumcised?[d] 27The one who is not circumcised physically and yet obeys the law will condemn you[e] who, even though you have the[c] written code and circumcision, are a law-breaker.

28A man is not a Jew if he is only one outwardly,[f] nor is circumcision merely outward and physical.[g] 29No, a man is a Jew if he is one inwardly; and circumcision is circumcision of the heart, by the Spirit,[h] not by the written code.[i] Such a man's praise is not from men, but from God.[j]

2:16 *s* Ecc 12:14 *t* Ac 10:42 *u* Ro 16:25
2:17 *v* ver 23 Mic 3:11 Ro 9:4
2:21 *w* Mt 23:3,4
2:22 *x* Ac 19:37
2:23 *y* ver 17
2:24 *z* Isa 52:5 Eze 36:22
2:25 *a* Gal 5:3 *b* Jer 4:4
2:26 *c* Ro 8:4 *d* 1Co 7:19
2:27 *e* Mt 12:41,42
2:28 *f* Mt 3:9 Jn 8:39 Ro 9:6,7 *g* Gal 6:15
2:29 *h* Php 3:3 Col 2:11 *i* Ro 7:6 *j* Jn 5:44 1Co 4:5 2Co 10:18 1Th 2:4 1Pe 3:4
3:2 *a* Dt 4:8 Ps 147:19
3:3 *b* Heb 4:2 *c* 2Ti 2:13
3:4 *d* Jn 3:33 *e* Ps 116:11 *f* Ps 51:4
3:5 *g* Ro 6:19 Gal 3:15
3:6 *h* Ge 18:25
3:7 *i* ver 4
3:8 *j* Ro 6:1
3:9 *k* ver 19,23 Gal 3:22

God's Faithfulness

3 What advantage, then, is there in being a Jew, or what value is there in circumcision? 2Much in every way! First of all, they have been entrusted with the very words of God.[a]

3What if some did not have faith?[b] Will their lack of faith nullify God's faithfulness?[c] 4Not at all! Let God be true,[d] and every man a liar.[e] As it is written:

"So that you may be proved
right when you speak
and prevail when you
judge."[a][f]

5But if our unrighteousness brings out God's righteousness more clearly, what shall we say? That God is unjust in bringing his wrath on us? (I am using a human argument.)[g] 6Certainly not! If that were so, how could God judge the world?[h] 7Someone might argue, "If my falsehood enhances God's truthfulness and so increases his glory,[i] why am I still condemned as a sinner?" 8Why not say—as we are being slanderously reported as saying and as some claim that we say—"Let us do evil that good may result"?[j] Their condemnation is deserved.

No-one Is Righteous

9What shall we conclude then? Are we any better?[b] Not at all! We have already made the charge that Jews and Gentiles alike are all under sin.[k] 10As it is written:

"There is no-one righteous, not
even one;
11 there is no-one who
understands,
no-one who seeks God.
12All have turned away,
they have together become
worthless;

[b]24 Isaiah 52:5; Ezek. 36:22 [c]27 Or *who, by means of a* [a]4 Psalm 51:4 [b]9 Or *worse*

there is no-one who does good,
not even one."[c][l]
13"Their throats are open graves;
their tongues practise
deceit."[d][m]
"The poison of vipers is on their
lips."[e][n]
14 "Their mouths are full of
cursing and bitterness."[f][o]
15"Their feet are swift to shed
blood;
16 ruin and misery mark their
ways,
17and the way of peace they do
not know."[g]
18 "There is no fear of God
before their eyes."[h][p]

19Now we know that whatever
the law says,[q] it says to those who
are under the law,[r] so that every
mouth may be silenced and the
whole world held accountable to
God. 20Therefore no-one will be declared righteous in his sight by observing the law;[s] rather, through the
law we become conscious of sin.[t]

Righteousness Through Faith

21But now a righteousness from
God,[u] apart from law, has been
made known, to which the Law and
the Prophets testify.[v] 22This righteousness from God comes through
faith[w] in Jesus Christ to all who believe. There is no difference,[x]
23for all have sinned and fall short
of the glory of God, 24and are justified freely by his grace[y] through
the redemption[z] that came by
Christ Jesus. 25God presented him
as a sacrifice of atonement,[i][a]
through faith in his blood.[b] He did
this to demonstrate his justice, because in his forbearance he had left
the sins committed beforehand unpunished[c] 26—he did it to demonstrate his justice at the present
time, so as to be just and the one
who justifies those who have faith
in Jesus.

27Where, then, is boasting?[d] It is
excluded. On what principle? On
that of observing the law? No, but
on that of faith. 28For we maintain
that a man is justified by faith
apart from observing the law.[e] 29Is
God the God of Jews only? Is he not
the God of Gentiles too? Yes, of
Gentiles too,[f] 30since there is only
one God, who will justify the circumcised by faith and the uncircumcised through that same
faith.[g] 31Do we, then, nullify the
law by this faith? Not at all! Rather,
we uphold the law.

Abraham Justified by Faith

4 What then shall we say that
Abraham, our forefather, discovered in this matter? 2If, in fact,
Abraham was justified by works,
he had something to boast about—
but not before God.[a] 3What does
the Scripture say? "Abraham believed God, and it was credited to
him as righteousness."[a][b]

4Now when a man works, his
wages are not credited to him as a
gift,[c] but as an obligation. 5How-
ever, to the man who does not work
but trusts God who justifies the
wicked, his faith is credited as
righteousness. 6David says the
same thing when he speaks of the
blessedness of the man to whom
God credits righteousness apart
from works:

7"Blessed are they
whose transgressions are
forgiven,
whose sins are covered.
8Blessed is the man
whose sin the Lord will never
count against him."[b][d]

9Is this blessedness only for
the circumcised, or also for the
uncircumcised?[e] We have been
saying that Abraham's faith was
credited to him as righteousness.[f]
10Under what circumstances was it

3:12 *l* Ps 14:1-3
3:13 *m* Ps 5:9 *n* Ps 140:3
3:14 *o* Ps 10:7
3:18 *p* Ps 36:1
3:19 *q* Jn 10:34 *r* Ro 2:12
3:20 *s* Ac 13:39 Gal 2:16 *t* Ro 7:7
3:21 *u* Ro 1:17 Ro 9:30 *v* Ac 10:43
3:22 *w* Ro 9:30 *x* Ro 10:12 Gal 3:28 Col 3:11
3:24 *y* Ro 4:16 Eph 2:8 *z* Eph 1:7,14 Col 1:14 Heb 9:12
3:25 *a* 1Jn 4:10 *b* Heb 9:12,14 *c* Ac 17:30
3:27 *d* Ro 2:17,23 Ro 4:2 1Co 1:29-31 Eph 2:9
3:28 *e* ver 20,21 Ac 13:39 Eph 2:9
3:29 *f* Ro 9:24
3:30 *g* Gal 3:8
4:2 *a* 1Co 1:31
4:3 *b* ver 5,9,22 Ge 15:6 Gal 3:6 Jas 2:23
4:4 *c* Ro 11:6
4:8 *d* Ps 32:1,2 2Co 5:19
4:9 *e* Ro 3:30 *f* ver 3

[c]12 Psalms 14:1–3; 53:1–3; Eccles. 7:20
[d]13 Psalm 5:9 [e]13 Psalm 140:3
[f]14 Psalm 10:7 [g]17 Isaiah 59:7,8
[h]18 Psalm 36:1 [i]25 Or *as the one who would turn aside his wrath, taking away sin*
[a]3 Gen. 15:6; also in verse 22 [b]8 Psalm 32:1,2

credited? Was it after he was circumcised, or before? It was not after, but before! 11And he received the sign of circumcision, a seal of the righteousness that he had by faith while he was still uncircumcised.[g] So then, he is the father[h] of all who believe[i] but have not been circumcised, in order that righteousness might be credited to them. 12And he is also the father of the circumcised who not only are circumcised but who also walk in the footsteps of the faith that our father Abraham had before he was circumcised.

13It was not through law that Abraham and his offspring received the promise[j] that he would be heir of the world,[k] but through the righteousness that comes by faith. 14For if those who live by law are heirs, faith has no value and the promise is worthless,[l] 15because law brings wrath.[m] And where there is no law there is no transgression.[n]

16Therefore, the promise comes by faith, so that it may be by grace[o] and may be guaranteed[p] to all Abraham's offspring—not only to those who are of the law but also to those who are of the faith of Abraham. He is the father of us all. 17As it is written: "I have made you a father of many nations."[c][q] He is our father in the sight of God, in whom he believed—the God who gives life[r] to the dead and calls[s] things that are not[t] as though they were.

18Against all hope, Abraham in hope believed and so became the father of many nations,[u] just as it had been said to him, "So shall your offspring be."[d][v] 19Without weakening in his faith, he faced the fact that his body was as good as dead[w]—since he was about a hundred years old[x]—and that Sarah's womb was also dead.[y] 20Yet he did not waver through unbelief regarding the promise of God, but was strengthened in his faith and gave glory to God,[z] 21being fully persuaded that God had power to do what he had promised.[a] 22This is why "it was credited to him as righteousness."[b] 23The words "it was credited to him" were written not for him alone, 24but also for us,[c] to whom God will credit righteousness—for us who believe in him[d] who raised Jesus our Lord from the dead.[e] 25He was delivered over to death for our sins[f] and was raised to life for our justification.

Peace and Joy

5 Therefore, since we have been justified through faith,[a] we[a] have peace with God through our Lord Jesus Christ, 2through whom we have gained access[b] by faith into this grace in which we now stand.[c] And we[a] rejoice in the hope[d] of the glory of God. 3Not only so, but we[a] also rejoice in our sufferings,[e] because we know that suffering produces perseverance;[f] 4perseverance, character; and character, hope. 5And hope[g] does not disappoint us, because God has poured out his love into our hearts by the Holy Spirit,[h] whom he has given us.

6You see, at just the right time,[i] when we were still powerless, Christ died for the ungodly.[j] 7Very rarely will anyone die for a righteous man, though for a good man someone might possibly dare to die. 8But God demonstrates his own love for us in this: While we were still sinners, Christ died for us.[k]

9Since we have now been justified by his blood,[l] how much more shall we be saved from God's wrath[m] through him! 10For if, when we were God's enemies,[n] we were reconciled[o] to him through the death of his Son, how much more, having been reconciled, shall we be

4:11 g Ge 17:10,11 h ver 16,17 Lk 19:9 i Ro 3:22
4:13 j Gal 3:16,29 k Ge 17:4-6
4:14 l Gal 3:18
4:15 m Ro 7:7-25 1Co 15:56 2Co 3:7 Gal 3:10 Ro 7:12 n Ro 3:20 Ro 7:7
4:16 o Ro 3:24 p Ro 15:8
4:17 q Ge 17:5 r Jn 5:21 s Isa 48:13 t 1Co 1:28
4:18 u ver 17 v Ge 15:5
4:19 w Heb 11:11,12 x Ge 17:17 y Ge 18:11
4:20 z Mt 9:8
4:21 a Ge 18:14 Heb 11:19
4:22 b ver 3
4:24 c Ro 15:4 1Co 9:10 1Co 10:11 d Ro 10:9 e Ac 2:24
4:25 f Isa 53:5,6 Ro 5:6,8
5:1 a Ro 3:28
5:2 b Eph 2:18 c 1Co 15:1 d Heb 3:6
5:3 e Mt 5:12 f Jas 1:2,3
5:5 g Php 1:20 h Ac 2:33
5:6 i Gal 4:4 j Ro 4:25
5:8 k Jn 15:13 1Pe 3:18
5:9 l Ro 3:25 m Ro 1:18
5:10 n Ro 11:28 Col 1:21 o 2Co 5:18,19 Col 1:20,22

c17 Gen. 17:5 d18 Gen. 15:5 a1, 2, 3 Or *let us*

saved through his life![p] 11Not only
is this so, but we also rejoice in God
through our Lord Jesus Christ,
through whom we have now received reconciliation.

Death Through Adam, Life Through Christ

12Therefore, just as sin entered
the world through one man,[q] and
death through sin,[r] and in this way
death came to all men, because all
sinned—13for before the law was
given, sin was in the world. But sin
is not taken into account when
there is no law.[s] 14Nevertheless,
death reigned from the time of
Adam to the time of Moses, even
over those who did not sin by
breaking a command, as did Adam,
who was a pattern of the one to
come.[t]
15But the gift is not like the trespass. For if the many died by the
trespass of the one man,[u] how
much more did God's grace and the
gift that came by the grace of the
one man, Jesus Christ,[v] overflow
to the many! 16Again, the gift of
God is not like the result of the one
man's sin: The judgment followed
one sin and brought condemnation,
but the gift followed many tres-
passes and brought justification.
17For if, by the trespass of the one
man, death[w] reigned through that
one man, how much more will those
who receive God's abundant provision of grace and of the gift of
righteousness reign in life through
the one man, Jesus Christ.
18Consequently, just as the result
of one trespass was condemnation
for all men,[x] so also the result of
one act of righteousness was justification[y] that brings life for all
men. 19For just as through the disobedience of the one man[z] the
many were made sinners, so also
through the obedience[a] of the one
man the many will be made righteous.
20The law was added so that the
trespass might increase.[b] But
where sin increased, grace increased all the more,[c] 21so that,
just as sin reigned in death,[d] so
also grace might reign through
righteousness to bring eternal life
through Jesus Christ our Lord.

Dead to Sin, Alive in Christ

6 What shall we say, then? Shall
we go on sinning, so that grace
may increase?[a] 2By no means! We
died to sin;[b] how can we live in it
any longer? 3Or don't you know
that all of us who were baptised[c]
into Christ Jesus were baptised
into his death? 4We were therefore
buried with him through baptism
into death in order that, just as
Christ was raised from the dead[d]
through the glory of the Father, we
too may live a new life.[e]
5If we have been united with him
like this in his death, we will certainly also be united with him in his
resurrection.[f] 6For we know that
our old self[g] was crucified with
him[h] so that the body of sin[i]
might be done away with,[a] that we
should no longer be slaves to sin—
7because anyone who has died has
been freed from sin.
8Now if we died with Christ, we
believe that we will also live with
him. 9For we know that since Christ
was raised from the dead,[j] he cannot die again; death no longer has
mastery over him.[k] 10The death he
died, he died to sin[l] once for all;
but the life he lives, he lives to God.
11In the same way, count yourselves dead to sin[m] but alive to God
in Christ Jesus. 12Therefore do not
let sin reign in your mortal body so
that you obey its evil desires. 13Do
not offer the parts of your body to
sin, as instruments of wickedness,[n] but rather offer yourselves
to God, as those who have been
brought from death to life; and offer the parts of your body to him

[a]6 Or *be rendered powerless*

5:10
p Ro 8:34
5:12
q ver 15,16,17; 1Co 15:21,22
r Ge 2:17; Ge 3:19; Ro 6:23
5:13
s Ro 4:15
5:14
t 1Co 15:22,45
5:15
u ver 12,18,19
v Ac 15:11
5:17
w ver 12
5:18
x ver 12
y Ro 4:25
5:19
z ver 12
a Php 2:8
5:20
b Ro 7:7,8; Gal 3:19
c 1Ti 1:13,14
5:21
d ver 12,14
6:1
a ver 15; Ro 3:5,8
6:2
b Col 3:3,5; 1Pe 2:24
6:3
c Mt 28:19
6:4
d Col 2:12
e Ro 7:6; Gal 6:15; Eph 4:22-24; Col 3:10
6:5
f 2Co 4:10; Php 3:10,11
6:6
g Eph 4:22; Col 3:9
h Gal 2:20; Col 2:12,20
i Ro 7:24
6:9
j Ac 2:24
k Rev 1:18
6:10
l ver 2
6:11
m ver 2
6:13
n ver 16,19; Ro 7:5

as instruments of righteousness.[o] 14For sin shall not be your master, because you are not under law,[p] but under grace.[q]

Slaves to Righteousness

15What then? Shall we sin because we are not under law but under grace? By no means! 16Don't you know that when you offer yourselves to someone to obey him as slaves, you are slaves to the one whom you obey—whether you are slaves to sin,[r] which leads to death,[s] or to obedience, which leads to righteousness? 17But thanks be to God[t] that, though you used to be slaves to sin, you wholeheartedly obeyed the form of teaching[u] to which you were entrusted. 18You have been set free from sin[v] and have become slaves to righteousness.

19I put this in human terms[w] because you are weak in your natural selves. Just as you used to offer the parts of your body in slavery to impurity and to ever-increasing wickedness, so now offer them in slavery to righteousness[x] leading to holiness. 20When you were slaves to sin,[y] you were free from the control of righteousness. 21What benefit did you reap at that time from the things you are now ashamed of? Those things result in death![z] 22But now that you have been set free from sin[a] and have become slaves to God,[b] the benefit you reap leads to holiness, and the result is eternal life. 23For the wages of sin is death,[c] but the gift of God is eternal life[d] in[b] Christ Jesus our Lord.

An Illustration From Marriage

7 Do you not know, brothers[a]—for I am speaking to men who know the law—that the law has authority over a man only as long as he lives? 2For example, by law a married woman is bound to her husband as long as he is alive, but if her husband dies, she is released from the law of marriage.[b] 3So then, if she marries another man while her husband is still alive, she is called an adulteress. But if her husband dies, she is released from that law and is not an adulteress, even though she marries another man.

4So, my brothers, you also died to the law[c] through the body of Christ,[d] that you might belong to another, to him who was raised from the dead, in order that we might bear fruit to God. 5For when we were controlled by the sinful nature,[a] the sinful passions aroused by the law[e] were at work in our bodies,[f] so that we bore fruit for death. 6But now, by dying to what once bound us, we have been released from the law so that we serve in the new way of the Spirit, and not in the old way of the written code.[g]

Struggling With Sin

7What shall we say, then? Is the law sin? Certainly not! Indeed I would not have known what sin was except through the law.[h] For I would not have known what coveting really was if the law had not said, "Do not covet."[b][i] 8But sin, seizing the opportunity afforded by the commandment,[j] produced in me every kind of covetous desire. For apart from law, sin is dead.[k] 9Once I was alive apart from law; but when the commandment came, sin sprang to life and I died. 10I found that the very commandment that was intended to bring life[l] actually brought death. 11For sin, seizing the opportunity afforded by the commandment, deceived me,[m] and through the commandment put me to death. 12So then, the law is holy, and the commandment is holy, righteous and good.[n]

6:13 o Ro 12:1; 1Pe 2:24
6:14 p Gal 5:18; q Ro 3:24
6:16 r Jn 8:34; 2Pe 2:19; s ver 23
6:17 t Ro 1:8; 2Co 2:14; u 2Ti 1:13
6:18 v ver 7,22; Ro 8:2
6:19 w Ro 3:5; x ver 13
6:20 y ver 16
6:21 z ver 23
6:22 a ver 18; b 1Co 7:22; 1Pe 2:16
6:23 c Ge 2:17; Ro 5:12; Gal 6:7,8; Jas 1:15; d Mt 25:46
7:1 a Ro 1:13
7:2 b 1Co 7:39
7:4 c Ro 8:2; Gal 2:19; d Col 1:22
7:5 e Ro 7:7-11; f Ro 6:13
7:6 g Ro 2:29; 2Co 3:6
7:7 h Ro 3:20; Ro 4:15; i Ex 20:17; Dt 5:21
7:8 j ver 11; k Ro 4:15; 1Co 15:56
7:10 l Lev 18:5; Lk 10:26-28; Ro 10:5; Gal 3:12
7:11 m Ge 3:13
7:12 n 1Ti 1:8

b23 Or *through*
a5 Or *the flesh*; also in verse 25
b7 Exodus 20:17; Deut. 5:21

13 Did that which is good, then, become death to me? By no means!
But in order that sin might be recognised as sin, it produced death in
me through what was good, so that
through the commandment sin
might become utterly sinful.
14 We know that the law is spiritual; but I am unspiritual,[o] sold[p]
as a slave to sin. 15 I do not understand what I do. For what I want to
do I do not do, but what I hate I do.[q]
16 And if I do what I do not want to
do, I agree that the law is good.[r]
17 As it is, it is no longer I myself
who do it, but it is sin living in me.[s]
18 I know that nothing good lives in
me, that is, in my sinful nature.[c][t]
For I have the desire to do what is
good, but I cannot carry it out.
19 For what I do is not the good I
want to do; no, the evil I do not want
to do—this I keep on doing.[u] 20 Now
if I do what I do not want to do, it is
no longer I who do it, but it is sin
living in me that does it.[v]
21 So I find this law at work:[w]
When I want to do good, evil is right
there with me. 22 For in my inner being[x] I delight in God's law;[y] 23 but
I see another law at work in the
members of my body, waging
war[z] against the law of my mind
and making me a prisoner of the
law of sin at work within my members. 24 What a wretched man I am!
Who will rescue me from this body
of death?[a] 25 Thanks be to God—
through Jesus Christ our Lord!
So then, I myself in my mind am
a slave to God's law, but in the sinful nature a slave to the law of sin.

Life Through the Spirit

8 Therefore, there is now no
condemnation[a] for those who
are in Christ Jesus,[a][b] 2 because
through Christ Jesus the law of the
Spirit of life[c] set me free[d] from
the law of sin[e] and death. 3 For
what the law was powerless[f] to do
in that it was weakened by the sinful nature,[b] God did by sending his
own Son in the likeness of sinful
man[g] to be a sin offering.[c][h] And
so he condemned sin in sinful
man,[d] 4 in order that the righteous
requirements of the law might be
fully met in us, who do not live according to the sinful nature but
according to the Spirit.[i]
5 Those who live according to the
sinful nature have their minds set
on what that nature desires;[j] but
those who live in accordance with
the Spirit have their minds set on
what the Spirit desires.[k] 6 The
mind of sinful man[e] is death, but
the mind controlled by the Spirit is
life[l] and peace; 7 the sinful mind[f]
is hostile to God.[m] It does not submit to God's law, nor can it do so.
8 Those controlled by the sinful
nature cannot please God.
9 You, however, are controlled
not by the sinful nature but by the
Spirit, if the Spirit of God lives in
you.[n] And if anyone does not have
the Spirit of Christ,[o] he does not
belong to Christ. 10 But if Christ is
in you,[p] your body is dead because
of sin, yet your spirit is alive because of righteousness. 11 And if the
Spirit of him who raised Jesus from
the dead[q] is living in you, he who
raised Christ from the dead will
also give life to your mortal
bodies[r] through his Spirit, who
lives in you.
12 Therefore, brothers, we have
an obligation—but it is not to the
sinful nature, to live according to
it. 13 For if you live according to the
sinful nature, you will die; but if by
the Spirit you put to death the misdeeds of the body, you will live,[s]
14 because those who are led by the
Spirit of God[t] are sons of God.[u]
15 For you did not receive a spirit
that makes you a slave again to

7:14 *o* 1Co 3:1 *p* 1Ki 21:20,25; 2Ki 17:17
7:15 *q* ver 19; Gal 5:17
7:16 *r* ver 12
7:17 *s* ver 20
7:18 *t* ver 25
7:19 *u* ver 15
7:20 *v* ver 17
7:21 *w* ver 23,25
7:22 *x* Eph 3:16 *y* Ps 1:2
7:23 *z* Gal 5:17; Jas 4:1; 1Pe 2:11
7:24 *a* Ro 6:6; Ro 8:2
8:1 *a* ver 34 *b* ver 39; Ro 16:3
8:2 *c* 1Co 15:45 *d* Ro 6:18 *e* Ro 7:4
8:3 *f* Ac 13:39; Heb 7:18 *g* Php 2:7 *h* Heb 2:14,17
8:4 *i* Gal 5:16
8:5 *j* Gal 5:19-21 *k* Gal 5:22-25
8:6 *l* Gal 6:8
8:7 *m* Jas 4:4
8:9 *n* 1Co 6:19; Gal 4:6 *o* Jn 14:17; 1Jn 4:13
8:10 *p* Gal 2:20; Eph 3:17; Col 1:27
8:11 *q* Ac 2:24 *r* Jn 5:21
8:13 *s* Gal 6:8
8:14 *t* Gal 5:18 *u* Jn 1:12; Rev 21:7

c18 Or *my flesh* a1 Some later manuscripts *Jesus, who do not live according to the sinful nature but according to the Spirit,* b3 Or *the flesh*; also in verses 4, 5, 8, 9, 12 and 13 c3 Or *man, for sin* d3 Or *in the flesh* e6 Or *mind set on the flesh* f7 Or *the mind set on the flesh*

fear,[v] but you received the Spirit of sonship.[g] And by him we cry, "*Abba*,[h] Father."[w] [16]The Spirit himself testifies with our spirit[x] that we are God's children. [17]Now if we are children, then we are heirs[y]—heirs of God and co-heirs with Christ, if indeed we share in his sufferings in order that we may also share in his glory.[z]

Future Glory

[18]I consider that our present sufferings are not worth comparing with the glory that will be revealed in us.[a] [19]The creation waits in eager expectation for the sons of God to be revealed. [20]For the creation was subjected to frustration, not by its own choice, but by the will of the one who subjected it,[b] in hope [21]that[i] the creation itself will be liberated from its bondage to decay[c] and brought into the glorious freedom of the children of God.

[22]We know that the whole creation has been groaning[d] as in the pains of childbirth right up to the present time. [23]Not only so, but we ourselves, who have the firstfruits of the Spirit,[e] groan[f] inwardly as we wait eagerly[g] for our adoption as sons, the redemption of our bodies. [24]For in this hope we were saved.[h] But hope that is seen is no hope at all. Who hopes for what he already has? [25]But if we hope for what we do not yet have, we wait for it patiently.

[26]In the same way, the Spirit helps us in our weakness. We do not know what we ought to pray for, but the Spirit himself intercedes for us[i] with groans that words cannot express. [27]And he who searches our hearts[j] knows the mind of the Spirit, because the Spirit intercedes for the saints in accordance with God's will.

More Than Conquerors

[28]And we know that in all things God works for the good of those who love him,[j] who[k] have been called[k] according to his purpose. [29]For those God foreknew[l] he also predestined[m] to be conformed to the likeness of his Son,[n] that he might be the firstborn among many brothers. [30]And those he predestined,[o] he also called; those he called, he also justified;[p] those he justified, he also glorified.[q]

[31]What, then, shall we say in response to this?[r] If God is for us, who can be against us?[s] [32]He who did not spare his own Son,[t] but gave him up for us all—how will he not also, along with him, graciously give us all things? [33]Who will bring any charge[u] against those whom God has chosen? It is God who justifies. [34]Who is he that condemns? Christ Jesus, who died[v]—more than that, who was raised to life—is at the right hand of God[w] and is also interceding for us.[x] [35]Who shall separate us from the love of Christ? Shall trouble or hardship or persecution or famine or nakedness or danger or sword?[y] [36]As it is written:

> "For your sake we face death
> all day long;
> we are considered as sheep to
> be slaughtered."[l][z]

[37]No, in all these things we are more than conquerors[a] through him who loved us.[b] [38]For I am convinced that neither death nor life, neither angels nor demons,[m] neither the present nor the future, nor any powers,[c] [39]neither height nor depth, nor anything else in all creation, will be able to separate us from the love of God[d] that is in Christ Jesus our Lord.

8:15 *v* 2Ti 1:7 Heb 2:15 *w* Mk 14:36 Gal 4:5,6
8:16 *x* Eph 1:13
8:17 *y* Ac 20:32 Gal 4:7 *z* 1Pe 4:13
8:18 *a* 2Co 4:17 1Pe 4:13
8:20 *b* Ge 3:17-19
8:21 *c* Ac 3:21 2Pe 3:13 Rev 21:1
8:22 *d* Jer 12:4
8:23 *e* 2Co 5:5 *f* 2Co 5:2,4 *g* Gal 5:5
8:24 *h* 1Th 5:8
8:26 *i* Eph 6:18
8:27 *j* Rev 2:23
8:28 *k* 1Co 1:9 2Ti 1:9
8:29 *l* Ro 11:2 *m* Eph 1:5,11 *n* 1Co 15:49 2Co 3:18 Php 3:21 1Jn 3:2
8:30 *o* Eph 1:5,11 *p* 1Co 6:11 *q* Ro 9:23
8:31 *r* Ro 4:1 *s* Ps 118:6
8:32 *t* Jn 3:16 Ro 4:25 Ro 5:8
8:33 *u* Isa 50:8,9
8:34 *v* Ro 5:6-8 *w* Mk 16:19 *x* Heb 7:25 Heb 9:24 1Jn 2:1
8:35 *y* 1Co 4:11
8:36 *z* Ps 44:22 2Co 4:11
8:37 *a* 1Co 15:57 *b* Gal 2:20 Rev 1:5 Rev 3:9
8:38 *c* Eph 1:21 1Pe 3:22 **8:39** *d* Ro 5:8

[g]15 Or *adoption* [h]15 Aramaic for *Father* [i]20,21 Or *subjected it in hope.* [21]*For* [j]28 Some manuscripts *And we know that all things work together for good to those who love God* [k]28 Or *works together with those who love him to bring about what is good—with those who* [l]36 Psalm 44:22 [m]38 Or *not heavenly rulers*

God's Sovereign Choice

9 I speak the truth in Christ—I
am not lying,[a] my conscience
confirms[b] it in the Holy Spirit—2I
have great sorrow and unceasing
anguish in my heart. 3For I could
wish that I myself[c] were cursed[d]
and cut off from Christ for the sake
of my brothers, those of my own
race,[e] 4the people of Israel. Theirs
is the adoption as sons;[f] theirs
the divine glory, the covenants,[g]
the receiving of the law,[h] the temple worship[i] and the promises.[j]
5Theirs are the patriarchs, and
from them is traced the human ancestry of Christ,[k] who is God over
all,[l] for ever praised![a][m] Amen.

6It is not as though God's word
had failed. For not all who are
descended from Israel are Israel.[n]
7Nor because they are his descendants are they all Abraham's children. On the contrary, "It is
through Isaac that your offspring
will be reckoned."[b][o] 8In other
words, it is not the natural children
who are God's children,[p] but it is
the children of the promise who are
regarded as Abraham's offspring.
9For this was how the promise was
stated: "At the appointed time I will
return, and Sarah will have a
son."[c][q]

10Not only that, but Rebekah's
children had one and the same
father, our father Isaac.[r] 11Yet, before the twins were born or had
done anything good or bad—in order that God's purpose[s] in election
might stand: 12not by works but by
him who calls—she was told, "The
older will serve the younger."[d][t]
13Just as it is written: "Jacob I
loved, but Esau I hated."[e][u]

14What then shall we say? Is God
unjust? Not at all![v] 15For he says to
Moses,

"I will have mercy on whom I
have mercy,
and I will have compassion on
whom I have
compassion."[f][w]

16It does not, therefore, depend on
man's desire or effort, but on God's
mercy.[x] 17For the Scripture says to
Pharaoh: "I raised you up for this
very purpose, that I might display
my power in you and that my name
might be proclaimed in all the
earth."[g][y] 18Therefore God has
mercy on whom he wants to have
mercy, and he hardens whom he
wants to harden.[z]

19One of you will say to me:[a]
"Then why does God still blame us?
For who resists his will?"[b] 20But
who are you, O man, to talk back to
God? "Shall what is formed say to
him who formed it,[c] 'Why did you
make me like this?' "[h][d] 21Does not
the potter have the right to make
out of the same lump of clay some
pottery for noble purposes and
some for common use?[e]

22What if God, choosing to show
his wrath and make his power
known, bore with great patience[f]
the objects of his wrath—prepared
for destruction? 23What if he did
this to make the riches of his
glory[g] known to the objects of his
mercy, whom he prepared in advance for glory[h]—24even us,
whom he also called,[i] not only
from the Jews but also from the
Gentiles?[j] 25As he says in Hosea:

"I will call them 'my people'
who are not my people;
and I will call her 'my loved
one' who is not my loved
one,"[i][k]

26and,

"It will happen that in the very
place where it was said to
them,
'You are not my people,'
they will be called 'sons of the
living God'."[j][l]

9:1 *a* 2Co 11:10; Gal 1:20; 1Ti 2:7 *b* Ro 1:9
9:3 *c* Ex 32:32 *d* 1Co 12:3; 1Co 16:22 *e* Ro 11:14
9:4 *f* Ex 4:22 *g* Ge 17:2; Ac 3:25; Eph 2:12 *h* Ps 147:19 *i* Heb 9:1 *j* Ac 13:32
9:5 *k* Mt 1:1-16 *l* Jn 1:1 *m* Ro 1:25
9:6 *n* Ro 2:28,29; Gal 6:16
9:7 *o* Ge 21:12; Heb 11:18
9:8 *p* Ro 8:14
9:9 *q* Ge 18:10,14
9:10 *r* Ge 25:21
9:11 *s* Ro 8:28
9:12 *t* Ge 25:23
9:13 *u* Mal 1:2,3
9:14 *v* 2Ch 19:7
9:15 *w* Ex 33:19
9:16 *x* Eph 2:8
9:17 *y* Ex 9:16
9:18 *z* Ex 4:21
9:19 *a* Ro 11:19 *b* 2Ch 20:6; Da 4:35
9:20 *c* Isa 64:8 *d* Isa 29:16
9:21 *e* 2Ti 2:20
9:22 *f* Ro 2:4
9:23 *g* Ro 2:4 *h* Ro 8:30
9:24 *i* Ro 8:28 *j* Ro 3:29
9:25 *k* Hos 2:23; 1Pe 2:10
9:26 *l* Hos 1:10

a5 Or *Christ, who is over all. God be for ever praised!* Or *Christ. God who is over all be for ever praised!* b7 Gen. 21:12 c9 Gen. 18:10,14
d12 Gen. 25:23 e13 Mal. 1:2,3
f15 Exodus 33:19 g17 Exodus 9:16
h20 Isaiah 29:16; 45:9 i25 Hosea 2:23
j26 Hosea 1:10

27 Isaiah cries out concerning Israel:

"Though the number of the
  Israelites be like the sand
  by the sea,[m]
only the remnant will be
  saved.[n]
28 For the Lord will carry out
  his sentence on earth with
  speed and finality."[k][o]

29 It is just as Isaiah said previously:

"Unless the Lord Almighty[p]
  had left us descendants,
we would have become like
  Sodom,
we would have been like
  Gomorrah."[l][q]

Israel's Unbelief

30 What then shall we say? That the Gentiles, who did not pursue righteousness, have obtained it, a righteousness that is by faith;[r] 31 but Israel, who pursued a law of righteousness,[s] has not attained it.[t] 32 Why not? Because they pursued it not by faith but as if it were by works. They stumbled over the "stumbling-stone".[u] 33 As it is written:

"See, I lay in Zion a stone that
  causes men to stumble
and a rock that makes them
  fall,
and the one who trusts in him
  will never be put to
  shame."[m][v]

10 Brothers, my heart's desire and prayer to God for the Israelites is that they may be saved. 2 For I can testify about them that they are zealous[a] for God, but their zeal is not based on knowledge. 3 Since they did not know the righteousness that comes from God and sought to establish their own, they did not submit to God's righteousness.[b] 4 Christ is the end of the law[c] so that there may be righteousness for everyone who believes.[d]

5 Moses describes in this way the righteousness that is by the law: "The man who does these things will live by them."[a][e] 6 But the righteousness that is by faith[f] says: "Do not say in your heart, 'Who will ascend into heaven?'[b]"[g] (that is, to bring Christ down) 7 "or 'Who will descend into the deep?'[c]" (that is, to bring Christ up from the dead). 8 But what does it say? "The word is near you; it is in your mouth and in your heart,"[d][h] that is, the word of faith we are proclaiming: 9 That if you confess[i] with your mouth, "Jesus is Lord," and believe in your heart that God raised him from the dead,[j] you will be saved. 10 For it is with your heart that you believe and are justified, and it is with your mouth that you confess and are saved. 11 As the Scripture says, "Anyone who trusts in him will never be put to shame."[e][k] 12 For there is no difference between Jew and Gentile[l]—the same Lord is Lord of all[m] and richly blesses all who call on him, 13 for, "Everyone who calls on the name of the Lord[n] will be saved."[f][o]

14 How, then, can they call on the one they have not believed in? And how can they believe in the one of whom they have not heard? And how can they hear without someone preaching to them? 15 And how can they preach unless they are sent? As it is written, "How beautiful are the feet of those who bring good news!"[g][p]

16 But not all the Israelites accepted the good news. For Isaiah says, "Lord, who has believed our message?"[h][q] 17 Consequently, faith comes from hearing the message,[r] and the message is heard

9:27 m Ge 22:17; Hos 1:10 n Ro 11:5
9:28 o Isa 10:22,23
9:29 p Jas 5:4 q Isa 1:9; Dt 29:23; Isa 13:19; Jer 50:40
9:30 r Ro 1:17; Ro 10:6; Gal 2:16; Php 3:9; Heb 11:7
9:31 s Isa 51:1; Ro 10:2,3 t Gal 5:4
9:32 u 1Pe 2:8
9:33 v Isa 28:16; Ro 10:11
10:2 a Ac 21:20
10:3 b Ro 1:17
10:4 c Gal 3:24; Ro 7:1-4 d Ro 3:22
10:5 e Lev 18:5; Ne 9:29; Eze 20:11,13, 21; Ro 7:10
10:6 f Ro 9:30 g Dt 30:12
10:8 h Dt 30:14
10:9 i Mt 10:32; Lk 12:8 j Ac 2:24
10:11 k Isa 28:16; Ro 9:33
10:12 l Ro 3:22,29 m Ac 10:36
10:13 n Ac 2:21 o Joel 2:32
10:15 p Isa 52:7; Na 1:15
10:16 q Isa 53:1; Jn 12:38
10:17 r Gal 3:2,5

k 28 Isaiah 10:22,23 l 29 Isaiah 1:9
m 33 Isaiah 8:14; 28:16 a 5 Lev. 18:5
b 6 Deut. 30:12 c 7 Deut. 30:13 d 8 Deut. 30:14
e 11 Isaiah 28:16 f 13 Joel 2:32
g 15 Isaiah 52:7 h 16 Isaiah 53:1

through the word of Christ.[s] 18 But
I ask: Did they not hear? Of course
they did:

"Their voice has gone out into
all the earth,
their words to the ends of the
world."[i][t]

19 Again I ask: Did Israel not understand? First, Moses says,

"I will make you envious[u] by
those who are not a nation;
I will make you angry by a
nation that has no
understanding."[j][v]

20 And Isaiah boldly says,

"I was found by those who did
not seek me;
I revealed myself to those who
did not ask for me."[k][w]

21 But concerning Israel he says,

"All day long I have held out
my hands
to a disobedient and obstinate
people."[l][x]

The Remnant of Israel

11 I ask then: Did God reject
his people? By no means![a]
I am an Israelite myself, a descendant of Abraham,[b] from the tribe of
Benjamin.[c] 2 God did not reject his
people, whom he foreknew.[d] Don't
you know what the Scripture says
in the passage about Elijah—how
he appealed to God against Israel:
3 "Lord, they have killed your
prophets and torn down your altars; I am the only one left, and
they are trying to kill me"[a]?[e]
4 And what was God's answer to
him? "I have reserved for myself
seven thousand who have not
bowed the knee to Baal."[b][f] 5 So
too, at the present time there is a
remnant[g] chosen by grace. 6 And if
by grace, then it is no longer by
works;[h] if it were, grace would no
longer be grace.[c]
7 What then? What Israel sought
so earnestly it did not obtain,[i] but
the elect did. The others were hardened,[j] 8 as it is written:

"God gave them a spirit of
stupor,
eyes so that they could not see
and ears so that they could not
hear,[k]
to this very day."[d][l]

9 And David says:

"May their table become a
snare and a trap,
a stumbling-block and a
retribution for them.
10 May their eyes be darkened so
they cannot see,
and their backs be bent for
ever."[e][m]

Ingrafted Branches

11 Again I ask: Did they stumble
so as to fall beyond recovery? Not
at all![n] Rather, because of their
transgression, salvation has come
to the Gentiles[o] to make Israel envious.[p] 12 But if their transgression
means riches for the world, and
their loss means riches for the Gentiles,[q] how much greater riches
will their fulness bring!
13 I am talking to you Gentiles. In-
asmuch as I am the apostle to the
Gentiles,[r] I make much of my ministry 14 in the hope that I may somehow arouse my own people to
envy[s] and save[t] some of them.
15 For if their rejection is the reconciliation[u] of the world, what will
their acceptance be but life from
the dead?[v] 16 If the part of the
dough offered as firstfruits[w] is
holy, then the whole batch is holy;
if the root is holy, so are the
branches.
17 If some of the branches have
been broken off,[x] and you, though
a wild olive shoot, have been

10:17 s Col 3:16
10:18 t Ps 19:4; Mt 24:14; Col 1:6,23; 1Th 1:8
10:19 u Ro 11:11,14 v Dt 32:21
10:20 w Isa 65:1; Ro 9:30
10:21 x Isa 65:2
11:1 a 1Sa 12:22; Jer 31:37 b 2Co 11:22 c Php 3:5
11:2 d Ro 8:29
11:3 e 1Ki 19:10,14
11:4 f 1Ki 19:18
11:5 g Ro 9:27
11:6 h Ro 4:4
11:7 i Ro 9:31 j ver 25; Ro 9:18
11:8 k Mt 13:13-15 l Dt 29:4; Isa 29:10
11:10 m Ps 69:22,23
11:11 n ver 1 o Ac 13:46 p Ro 10:19
11:12 q ver 25
11:13 r Ac 9:15
11:14 s ver 11; Ro 10:19 t 1Co 1:21; 1Ti 2:4; Tit 3:5
11:15 u Ro 5:10 v Lk 15:24,32
11:16 w Lev 23:10,17; Nu 15:18-21
11:17 x Jer 11:16; Jn 15:2

i 18 Psalm 19:4 j 19 Deut. 32:21
k 20 Isaiah 65:1 l 21 Isaiah 65:2
a 3 1 Kings 19:10,14 b 4 1 Kings 19:18
c 6 Some manuscripts *by grace. But if by works, then it is no longer grace; if it were, work would no longer be work.* d 8 Deut. 29:4; Isaiah 29:10
e 10 Psalm 69:22,23

grafted in among the others[y] and now share in the nourishing sap from the olive root, 18do not boast over those branches. If you do, consider this: You do not support the root, but the root supports you.[z] 19You will say then, "Branches were broken off so that I could be grafted in." 20Granted. But they were broken off because of unbelief, and you stand by faith.[a] Do not be arrogant,[b] but be afraid.[c] 21For if God did not spare the natural branches, he will not spare you either.

22Consider therefore the kindness[d] and sternness of God: sternness to those who fell, but kindness to you, provided that you continue[e] in his kindness. Otherwise, you also will be cut off.[f] 23And if they do not persist in unbelief, they will be grafted in, for God is able to graft them in again.[g] 24After all, if you were cut out of an olive tree that is wild by nature, and contrary to nature were grafted into a cultivated olive tree, how much more readily will these, the natural branches, be grafted into their own olive tree!

All Israel Will Be Saved

25I do not want you to be ignorant[h] of this mystery,[i] brothers, so that you may not be conceited:[j] Israel has experienced a hardening[k] in part until the full number of the Gentiles has come in.[l] 26And so all Israel will be saved, as it is written:

"The deliverer will come from
Zion;
he will turn godlessness away
from Jacob.
27And this is[f] my covenant with
them
when I take away their
sins."[g][m]

28As far as the gospel is concerned, they are enemies[n] on your account; but as far as election is concerned, they are loved on account of the patriarchs,[o] 29for God's gifts and his call[p] are irrevocable.[q] 30Just as you who were at one time disobedient[r] to God have now received mercy as a result of their disobedience, 31so they too have now become disobedient in order that they too may now[h] receive mercy as a result of God's mercy to you. 32For God has bound all men over to disobedience[s] so that he may have mercy on them all.

Doxology

33Oh, the depth of the riches[t] of
the wisdom and[i]
knowledge of God![u]
How unsearchable his
judgments,
and his paths beyond tracing
out![v]
34"Who has known the mind of
the Lord?
Or who has been his
counsellor?"[j][w]
35"Who has ever given to God,
that God should repay
him?"[k][x]
36For from him and through him
and to him are all things.[y]
To him be the glory for ever!
Amen.[z]

Living Sacrifices

12 Therefore, I urge you,[a] brothers, in view of God's mercy, to offer your bodies as living sacrifices,[b] holy and pleasing to God—this is your spiritual[a] act of worship. 2Do not conform[c] any longer to the pattern of this world,[d] but be transformed by the renewing of your mind.[e] Then you will be able to test and approve what God's will is[f]—his good, pleasing and perfect will.

3For by the grace given me[g] I

11:17 y Ac 2:39; Eph 2:11-13
11:18 z Jn 4:22
11:20 a 1Co 10:12; 2Co 1:24 b Ro 12:16; 1Ti 6:17 c 1Pe 1:17
11:22 d Ro 2:4 e 1Co 15:2; Heb 3:6 f Jn 15:2
11:23 g 2Co 3:16
11:25 h Ro 1:13 i Ro 16:25 j Ro 12:16 k ver 7; Ro 9:18 l Lk 21:24
11:27 m Isa 27:9; Heb 8:10,12
11:28 n Ro 5:10 o Dt 7:8; Dt 10:15; Ro 9:5
11:29 p Ro 8:28 q Heb 7:21
11:30 r Eph 2:2
11:32 s Ro 3:9
11:33 t Ro 2:4 u Ps 92:5 v Job 11:7
11:34 w Isa 40:13,14; Job 15:8; Job 36:22; 1Co 2:16
11:35 x Job 35:7
11:36 y 1Co 8:6; Col 1:16; Heb 2:10 z Ro 16:27
12:1 a Eph 4:1 b Ro 6:13,16,19; 1Pe 2:5
12:2 c 1Pe 1:14 d 1Jn 2:15 e Eph 4:23 f Eph 5:17
12:3 g Ro 15:15; Gal 2:9; Eph 4:7

f27 Or *will be* g27 Isaiah 59:20,21; 27:9; Jer. 31:33,34 h31 Some manuscripts do not have *now.* i33 Or *riches and the wisdom and the* j34 Isaiah 40:13 k35 Job 41:11
a1 Or *reasonable*

say to every one of you: Do not think of yourself more highly than you ought, but rather think of yourself with sober judgment, in accordance with the measure of faith God has given you. 4Just as each of us has one body with many members, and these members do not all have the same function,[h] 5so in Christ we who are many form one body,[i] and each member belongs to all the others. 6We have different gifts,[j] according to the grace given us. If a man's gift is prophesying, let him use it in proportion to his[b] faith.[k] 7If it is serving, let him serve; if it is teaching, let him teach;[l] 8if it is encouraging, let him encourage;[m] if it is contributing to the needs of others, let him give generously;[n] if it is leadership, let him govern diligently; if it is showing mercy, let him do it cheerfully.

Love

9Love must be sincere.[o] Hate what is evil; cling to what is good. 10Be devoted to one another in brotherly love.[p] Honour one another above yourselves.[q] 11Never be lacking in zeal, but keep your spiritual fervour,[r] serving the Lord. 12Be joyful in hope,[s] patient in affliction,[t] faithful in prayer. 13Share with God's people who are in need. Practise hospitality.[u]

14Bless those who persecute you;[v] bless and do not curse. 15Rejoice with those who rejoice; mourn with those who mourn.[w] 16Live in harmony with one another.[x] Do not be proud, but be willing to associate with people of low position.[c] Do not be conceited.[y]

17Do not repay anyone evil for evil.[z] Be careful to do what is right in the eyes of everybody.[a] 18If it is possible, as far as it depends on you, live at peace with everyone.[b] 19Do not take revenge,[c] my friends, but leave room for God's wrath, for it is written: "It is mine to avenge; I will repay,"[d][d] says the Lord. 20On the contrary:

> "If your enemy is hungry, feed
> him;
> if he is thirsty, give him
> something to drink.
> In doing this, you will heap
> burning coals on his
> head."[e][e]

21Do not be overcome by evil, but overcome evil with good.

Submission to the Authorities

13 Everyone must submit himself to the governing authorities,[a] for there is no authority except that which God has established.[b] The authorities that exist have been established by God. 2Consequently, he who rebels against the authority is rebelling against what God has instituted, and those who do so will bring judgment on themselves. 3For rulers hold no terror for those who do right, but for those who do wrong. Do you want to be free from fear of the one in authority? Then do what is right and he will commend you.[c] 4For he is God's servant to do you good. But if you do wrong, be afraid, for he does not bear the sword for nothing. He is God's servant, an agent of wrath to bring punishment on the wrongdoer.[d] 5Therefore, it is necessary to submit to the authorities, not only because of possible punishment but also because of conscience.

6This is also why you pay taxes, for the authorities are God's servants, who give their full time to governing. 7Give everyone what you owe him: If you owe taxes, pay taxes;[e] if revenue, then revenue; if respect, then respect; if honour, then honour.

12:4 h 1Co 12:12-14; Eph 4:16
12:5 i 1Co 10:17
12:6 j 1Co 7:7; 1Co 12:4,8-10; k 1Pe 4:10,11
12:7 l Eph 4:11
12:8 m Ac 15:32; n 2Co 9:5-13
12:9 o 1Ti 1:5
12:10 p Heb 13:1; q Php 2:3
12:11 r Ac 18:25
12:12 s Ro 5:2; t Heb 10:32,36
12:13 u 1Ti 3:2
12:14 v Mt 5:44
12:15 w Job 30:25
12:16 x Ro 15:5; y Jer 45:5; Ro 11:25
12:17 z Pr 20:22; a 2Co 8:21
12:18 b Mk 9:50; Ro 14:19
12:19 c Lev 19:18; Pr 20:22; Pr 24:29; d Dt 32:35
12:20 e Pr 25:21,22; Mt 5:44; Lk 6:27
13:1 a Tit 3:1; 1Pe 2:13,14; b Da 2:21; Jn 19:11
13:3 c 1Pe 2:14
13:4 d 1Th 4:6
13:7 e Mt 17:25; Mt 22:17,21; Lk 23:2

[b]6 Or *in agreement with the* [c]16 Or *willing to do menial work* [d]19 Deut. 32:35
[e]20 Prov. 25:21,22

Love, for the Day Is Near

8 Let no debt remain outstanding,
except the continuing debt to love
one another, for he who loves his
fellow-man has fulfilled the law.[f]
9 The commandments, "Do not commit adultery," "Do not murder,"
"Do not steal," "Do not covet,"[a][g]
and whatever other commandment
there may be, are summed up in
this one rule: "Love your neighbour
as yourself."[b][h] 10 Love does no
harm to its neighbour. Therefore
love is the fulfilment of the law.[i]
11 And do this, understanding the
present time. The hour has come[j]
for you to wake up from your slumber,[k] because our salvation is
nearer now than when we first believed. 12 The night is nearly over;
the day is almost here.[l] So let us
put aside the deeds of darkness[m]
and put on the armour[n] of light.
13 Let us behave decently, as in the
daytime, not in orgies and drunkenness, not in sexual immorality and
debauchery, not in dissension and
jealousy.[o] 14 Rather, clothe yourselves with the Lord Jesus Christ,[p]
and do not think about how to gratify the desires of the sinful
nature.[c]

The Weak and the Strong

14 Accept him whose faith is
weak,[a] without passing
judgment on disputable matters.
2 One man's faith allows him to eat
everything, but another man,
whose faith is weak, eats only vegetables. 3 The man who eats everything must not look down on[b] him
who does not, and the man who
does not eat everything must not
condemn[c] the man who does, for
God has accepted him. 4 Who are
you to judge someone else's servant?[d] To his own master he
stands or falls. And he will stand,
for the Lord is able to make him
stand.
5 One man considers one day
more sacred than another;[e] another man considers every day
alike. Each one should be fully convinced in his own mind. 6 He who regards one day as special, does so to
the Lord. He who eats meat, eats
to the Lord, for he gives thanks to
God;[f] and he who abstains, does
so to the Lord and gives thanks
to God. 7 For none of us lives to himself alone[g] and none of us dies to
himself alone. 8 If we live, we live
to the Lord; and if we die, we die to
the Lord. So, whether we live or die,
we belong to the Lord.[h]
9 For this very reason, Christ died
and returned to life[i] so that he
might be the Lord of both the dead
and the living.[j] 10 You, then, why
do you judge your brother? Or why
do you look down on your brother?
For we will all stand before God's
judgment seat.[k] 11 It is written:

"'As surely as I live,' says the
Lord,
'Every knee will bow before
me;
every tongue will confess to
God.'"[a][l]

12 So then, each of us will give an account of himself to God.[m]
13 Therefore let us stop passing
judgment[n] on one another. Instead, make up your mind not to put
any stumbling-block or obstacle in
your brother's way. 14 As one who is
in the Lord Jesus, I am fully convinced that no food[b] is unclean in
itself.[o] But if anyone regards
something as unclean, then for him
it is unclean.[p] 15 If your brother is
distressed because of what you eat,
you are no longer acting in love.[q]
Do not by your eating destroy your
brother for whom Christ died.[r]
16 Do not allow what you consider
good to be spoken of as evil.[s] 17 For
the kingdom of God is not a matter
of eating and drinking,[t] but of

[a]9 Exodus 20:13–15,17; Deut. 5:17–19,21
[b]9 Lev. 19:18 [c]14 Or *the flesh*
[a]11 Isaiah 45:23 [b]14 Or *that nothing*

13:8
f ver 10; Jn 13:34; Gal 5:14; Col 3:14
13:9
g Ex 20:13-15, 17; Dt 5:17-19,21
h Lev 19:18; Mt 19:19
13:10
i ver 8; Mt 22:39,40
13:11
j 1Co 7:29-31; 1Co 10:11
k Eph 5:14; 1Th 5:5,6
13:12
l 1Jn 2:8
m Eph 5:11
n Eph 6:11,13
13:13
o Gal 5:20,21
13:14
p Gal 3:27; Gal 5:16; Eph 4:24
14:1
a Ro 15:1; 1Co 8:9-12
14:3
b Lk 18:9
c Col 2:16
14:4
d Jas 4:12
14:5
e Gal 4:10
14:6
f Mt 14:19; 1Co 10:30,31; 1Ti 4:3,4
14:7
g 2Co 5:15; Gal 2:20
14:8
h Php 1:20
14:9
i Rev 1:18
j 2Co 5:15
14:10
k 2Co 5:10
14:11
l Isa 45:23; Php 2:10,11
14:12
m Mt 12:36; 1Pe 4:5
14:13
n Mt 7:1
14:14
o Ac 10:15
p 1Co 8:7
14:15
q Eph 5:2
r 1Co 8:11
14:16
s 1Co 10:30
14:17
t 1Co 8:8

righteousness, peace and joy in the Holy Spirit,[u] 18because anyone who serves Christ in this way is pleasing to God and approved by men.[v]

19Let us therefore make every effort to do what leads to peace[w] and to mutual edification.[x] 20Do not destroy the work of God for the sake of food.[y] All food is clean, but it is wrong for a man to eat anything that causes someone else to stumble.[z] 21It is better not to eat meat or drink wine or to do anything else that will cause your brother to fall.[a]

22So whatever you believe about these things keep between yourself and God. Blessed is the man who does not condemn[b] himself by what he approves. 23But the man who has doubts[c] is condemned if he eats, because his eating is not from faith; and everything that does not come from faith is sin.

15 We who are strong ought to bear with the failings of the weak[a] and not to please ourselves. 2Each of us should please his neighbour for his good,[b] to build him up.[c] 3For even Christ did not please himself[d] but, as it is written: "The insults of those who insult you have fallen on me."[a][e] 4For everything that was written in the past was written to teach us,[f] so that through endurance and the encouragement of the Scriptures we might have hope.

5May the God who gives endurance and encouragement give you a spirit of unity[g] among yourselves as you follow Christ Jesus, 6so that with one heart and mouth you may glorify the God and Father[h] of our Lord Jesus Christ.

7Accept one another,[i] then, just as Christ accepted you, in order to bring praise to God. 8For I tell you that Christ has become a servant of the Jews[b][j] on behalf of God's truth, to confirm the promises[k] made to the patriarchs 9so that the Gentiles[l] may glorify God[m] for his mercy, as it is written:

"Therefore I will praise you
among the Gentiles;
I will sing hymns to your
name."[c][n]

10Again, it says,

"Rejoice, O Gentiles, with his
people."[d][o]

11And again,

"Praise the Lord, all you
Gentiles,
and sing praises to him, all
you peoples."[e][p]

12And again, Isaiah says,

"The Root of Jesse[q] will spring
up,
one who will arise to rule over
the nations;
the Gentiles will hope in
him."[f][r]

13May the God of hope fill you with all joy and peace[s] as you trust in him, so that you may overflow with hope by the power of the Holy Spirit.[t]

Paul the Minister to the Gentiles

14I myself am convinced, my brothers, that you yourselves are full of goodness,[u] complete in knowledge[v] and competent to instruct one another. 15I have written to you quite boldly on some points, as if to remind you of them again, because of the grace God gave me[w] 16to be a minister of Christ Jesus to the Gentiles[x] with the priestly duty of proclaiming the gospel of God,[y] so that the Gentiles might become an offering[z] acceptable to God, sanctified by the Holy Spirit.

17Therefore I glory in Christ Jesus[a] in my service to God.[b] 18I

14:17 u Ro 15:13
14:18 v 2Co 8:21
14:19 w Ps 34:14; Ro 12:18; Heb 12:14 x Ro 15:2; 2Co 12:19
14:20 y ver 15 z 1Co 8:9-12
14:21 a 1Co 8:13
14:22 b 1Jn 3:21
14:23 c ver 5
15:1 a Ro 14:1; Gal 6:1,2; 1Th 5:14
15:2 b 1Co 10:33 c Ro 14:19
15:3 d 2Co 8:9 e Ps 69:9
15:4 f Ro 4:23,24
15:5 g Ro 12:16; 1Co 1:10
15:6 h Rev 1:6
15:7 i Ro 14:1
15:8 j Mt 15:24; Ac 3:25,26 k 2Co 1:20
15:9 l Ro 3:29 m Mt 9:8 n 2Sa 22:50; Ps 18:49
15:10 o Dt 32:43
15:11 p Ps 117:1
15:12 q Rev 5:5 r Isa 11:10; Mt 12:21
15:13 s Ro 14:17 t ver 19; 1Co 2:4; 1Th 1:5
15:14 u Eph 5:9 v 2Pe 1:12
15:15 w Ro 12:3
15:16 x Ac 9:15; Ro 11:13 y Ro 1:1 z Isa 66:20
15:17 a Php 3:3 b Heb 2:17

a3 Psalm 69:9 b8 Greek *circumcision*
c9 2 Samuel 22:50; Psalm 18:49 d10 Deut. 32:43
e11 Psalm 117:1 f12 Isaiah 11:10

will not venture to speak of anything except what Christ has accomplished through me in leading
the Gentiles[c] to obey God[d] by
what I have said and done—19by the
power of signs and miracles,[e]
through the power of the Spirit.[f]
So from Jerusalem[g] all the way
around to Illyricum, I have fully
proclaimed the gospel of Christ.
20It has always been my ambition to
preach the gospel where Christ
was not known, so that I would not
be building on someone else's foundation.[h] 21Rather, as it is written:

> "Those who were not told about
> him will see,
> and those who have not heard
> will understand."[g][i]

22This is why I have often been hindered from coming to you.[j]

Paul's Plan to Visit Rome

23But now that there is no more
place for me to work in these regions, and since I have been longing for many years to see you,[k] 24I
plan to do so when I go to Spain.[l]
I hope to visit you while passing
through and to have you assist me
on my journey there, after I have
enjoyed your company for a while.
25Now, however, I am on my way to
Jerusalem[m] in the service[n] of the
saints there. 26For Macedonia[o] and
Achaia[p] were pleased to make a
contribution for the poor among
the saints in Jerusalem. 27They
were pleased to do it, and indeed
they owe it to them. For if the Gentiles have shared in the Jews' spiritual blessings, they owe it to the
Jews to share with them their material blessings.[q] 28So after I have
completed this task and have made
sure that they have received this
fruit, I will go to Spain and visit you
on the way. 29I know that when I
come to you,[r] I will come in the
full measure of the blessing of
Christ.
30I urge you, brothers, by our
Lord Jesus Christ and by the love
of the Spirit,[s] to join me in my
struggle by praying to God for
me.[t] 31Pray that I may be rescued[u] from the unbelievers in Judea and that my service in
Jerusalem may be acceptable to
the saints there, 32so that by God's
will[v] I may come to you[w] with joy
and together with you be refreshed.[x] 33The God of peace[y] be
with you all. Amen.

Personal Greetings

16 I commend[a] to you our sister Phoebe, a servant[a] of
the church in Cenchrea.[b] 2I ask
you to receive her in the Lord[c] in
a way worthy of the saints and to
give her any help she may need
from you, for she has been a great
help to many people, including me.

3Greet Priscilla[b] and Aquila,[d]
my fellow-workers in Christ
Jesus.[e] 4They risked their lives
for me. Not only I but all the
churches of the Gentiles are
grateful to them.
5Greet also the church that meets
at their house.[f]
Greet my dear friend Epenetus,
who was the first convert[g] to
Christ in the province of Asia.
6Greet Mary, who worked very
hard for you.
7Greet Andronicus and Junias, my
relatives[h] who have been in
prison with me. They are outstanding among the apostles,
and they were in Christ before I
was.
8Greet Ampliatus, whom I love in
the Lord.
9Greet Urbanus, our fellow-
worker in Christ,[i] and my dear
friend Stachys.
10Greet Apelles, tested and approved in Christ.
Greet those who belong to the
household of Aristobulus.

[g]21 Isaiah 52:15 [a]1 Or *deaconess* [b]3 Greek *Prisca*, a variant of *Priscilla*

15:18 c Ac 15:12; Ac 21:19; Ro 1:5 d Ro 16:26
15:19 e Jn 4:48; Ac 19:11 f ver 13 g Ac 22:17-21
15:20 h 2Co 10:15,16
15:21 i Isa 52:15
15:22 j Ro 1:13
15:23 k Ac 19:21; Ro 1:10,11
15:24 l ver 28
15:25 m Ac 19:21 n Ac 24:17
15:26 o Ac 16:9; 2Co 8:1 p Ac 18:12
15:27 q 1Co 9:11
15:29 r Ro 1:10,11
15:30 s Gal 5:22 t 2Co 1:11; Col 4:12
15:31 u 2Th 3:2
15:32 v Ac 18:21 w Ro 1:10,13 x 1Co 16:18
15:33 y Ro 16:20; 2Co 13:11; Php 4:9; 1Th 5:23; Heb 13:20
16:1 a 2Co 3:1 b Ac 18:18
16:2 c Php 2:29
16:3 d Ac 18:2 e ver 7,9,10
16:5 f 1Co 16:19; Col 4:15; Phm 2 g 1Co 16:15
16:7 h ver 11,21
16:9 i ver 3

11 Greet Herodion, my relative.[j]
Greet those in the household of
Narcissus who are in the Lord.
12 Greet Tryphena and Tryphosa,
those women who work hard in
the Lord.
Greet my dear friend Persis, another woman who has worked
very hard in the Lord.
13 Greet Rufus, chosen in the Lord,
and his mother, who has been a
mother to me, too.
14 Greet Asyncritus, Phlegon, Hermes, Patrobas, Hermas and the
brothers with them.
15 Greet Philologus, Julia, Nereus
and his sister, and Olympas and
all the saints[k] with them.[l]
16 Greet one another with a holy
kiss.[m]
All the churches of Christ send
greetings.

17 I urge you, brothers, to watch
out for those who cause divisions
and put obstacles in your way that
are contrary to the teaching you
have learned.[n] Keep away from
them.[o] 18 For such people are not
serving our Lord Christ, but their
own appetites.[p] By smooth talk
and flattery they deceive[q] the
minds of naïve people. 19 Everyone
has heard[r] about your obedience,
so I am full of joy over you; but I
want you to be wise about what is
good, and innocent about what is
evil.[s]
20 The God of peace[t] will soon
crush[u] Satan under your feet.
The grace of our Lord Jesus be
with you.[v]
21 Timothy,[w] my fellow-worker,
sends his greetings to you, as do
Lucius,[x] Jason[y] and Sosipater, my
relatives.[z]
22 I, Tertius, who wrote down this
letter, greet you in the Lord.
23 Gaius, whose hospitality I and
the whole church here enjoy, sends
you his greetings.
Erastus,[a] who is the city's director of public works, and our
brother Quartus send you their
greetings.[c]
25 Now to him who is able[b] to establish you by my gospel[c] and the
proclamation of Jesus Christ, according to the revelation of the
mystery[d] hidden for long ages
past, 26 but now revealed and made
known through the prophetic writings by the command of the eternal
God, so that all nations might believe and obey him — 27 to the only
wise God be glory for ever through
Jesus Christ! Amen.[e]

c23 Some manuscripts *their greetings.* 24 *May the grace of our Lord Jesus Christ be with all of you. Amen.*

16:11 *j* ver 7,21
16:15 *k* ver 2 *l* ver 14
16:16 *m* 1Co 16:20; 2Co 13:12; 1Th 5:26
16:17 *n* Gal 1:8,9; 1Ti 1:3; 1Ti 6:3 *o* 2Th 3:6,14; 2Jn 10
16:18 *p* Php 3:19 *q* Col 2:4
16:19 *r* Ro 1:8 *s* Mt 10:16; 1Co 14:20
16:20 *t* Ro 15:33 *u* Ge 3:15 *v* 1Th 5:28
16:21 *w* Ac 16:1 *x* Ac 13:1 *y* Ac 17:5 *z* ver 7,11
16:23 *a* Ac 19:22
16:25 *b* Eph 3:20 *c* Ro 2:16 *d* Eph 1:9; Col 1:26,27
16:27 *e* Ro 11:36

1 CORINTHIANS

1 Paul, called to be an apostle[a] of Christ Jesus by the will of God,[b] and our brother Sosthenes,[c]

2To the church of God in Corinth,[d] to those sanctified in Christ Jesus and called[e] to be holy, together with all those everywhere who call on the name of our Lord Jesus Christ—their Lord and ours:

3Grace and peace to you from God our Father and the Lord Jesus Christ.[f]

Thanksgiving

4I always thank God for you[g] because of his grace given you in Christ Jesus. 5For in him you have been enriched[h] in every way—in all your speaking and in all your knowledge[i]—6because our testimony[j] about Christ was confirmed in you. 7Therefore you do not lack any spiritual gift as you eagerly wait for our Lord Jesus Christ to be revealed.[k] 8He will keep you strong to the end, so that you will be blameless[l] on the day of our Lord Jesus Christ. 9God, who has called you into fellowship with his Son Jesus Christ our Lord,[m] is faithful.[n]

Divisions in the Church

10I appeal to you, brothers, in the name of our Lord Jesus Christ, that all of you agree with one another so that there may be no divisions among you and that you may be perfectly united in mind and thought. 11My brothers, some from Chloe's household have informed me that there are quarrels among you. 12What I mean is this: One of you says, "I follow Paul";[o] another, "I follow Apollos";[p] another, "I follow Cephas";[a][q] still another, "I follow Christ."

13Is Christ divided? Was Paul crucified for you? Were you baptised into[b] the name of Paul?[r] 14I am thankful that I did not baptise any of you except Crispus[s] and Gaius,[t] 15so no-one can say that you were baptised into my name. (16Yes, I also baptised the household of Stephanas;[u] beyond that, I don't remember if I baptised anyone else.) 17For Christ did not send me to baptise,[v] but to preach the gospel—not with words of human wisdom,[w] lest the cross of Christ be emptied of its power.

Christ the Wisdom and Power of God

18For the message of the cross is foolishness to those who are perishing,[x] but to us who are being saved it is the power of God.[y] 19For it is written:

"I will destroy the wisdom of
the wise;
the intelligence of the
intelligent I will
frustrate."[c][z]

20Where is the wise man?[a] Where is the scholar? Where is the philosopher of this age? Has not God made foolish[b] the wisdom of the world? 21For since in the wisdom of God the world through its wisdom did not know him, God was pleased through the foolishness of what was preached to save those who believe. 22Jews demand miraculous signs[c] and Greeks look for wisdom, 23but we preach Christ crucified: a stumbling-block[d] to Jews and foolishness[e] to Gentiles,

1:1 a Ro 1:1; Eph 1:1 b 2Co 1:1 c Ac 18:17
1:2 d Ac 18:1 e Ro 1:7
1:3 f Ro 1:7
1:4 g Ro 1:8
1:5 h 2Co 9:11 i 2Co 8:7
1:6 j Rev 1:2
1:7 k Php 3:20; Tit 2:13; 2Pe 3:12
1:8 l 1Th 3:13
1:9 m 1Jn 1:3 n Isa 49:7; 1Th 5:24
1:12 o 1Co 3:4,22 p Ac 18:24 q Jn 1:42
1:13 r Mt 28:19
1:14 s Ac 18:8; Ro 16:23 t Ac 19:29
1:16 u 1Co 16:15
1:17 v Jn 4:2 w 1Co 2:1,4,13
1:18 x 2Co 2:15 y Ro 1:16
1:19 z Isa 29:14
1:20 a Isa 19:11,12 b Job 12:17; Ro 1:22
1:22 c Mt 12:38
1:23 d Lk 2:34; Gal 5:11 e 1Co 2:14

a12 That is, Peter
b13 Or *in*; also in verse 15
c19 Isaiah 29:14

24 but to those whom God has
called,[f] both Jews and Greeks,
Christ the power of God and the
wisdom of God.[g] 25 For the foolishness[h] of God is wiser than man's
wisdom, and the weakness[i] of God
is stronger than man's strength.
26 Brothers, think of what you
were when you were called. Not
many of you were wise by human
standards; not many were influen-
tial; not many were of noble birth.
27 But God chose[j] the foolish[k]
things of the world to shame the
wise; God chose the weak things of
the world to shame the strong. 28 He
chose the lowly things of this world
and the despised things—and the
things that are not[l]—to nullify the
things that are, 29 so that no-one
may boast before him.[m] 30 It is because of him that you are in Christ
Jesus, who has become for us
wisdom from God—that is, our
righteousness,[n] holiness and
redemption.[o] 31 Therefore, as it is
written: "Let him who boasts boast
in the Lord."[d][p]

2 When I came to you, brothers,
I did not come with eloquence
or superior wisdom[a] as I proclaimed to you the testimony about
God.[a] 2 For I resolved to know
nothing while I was with you except Jesus Christ and him crucified.[b] 3 I came to you[c] in weakness
and fear, and with much trembling.
4 My message and my preaching
were not with wise and persuasive
words, but with a demonstration of
the Spirit's power,[d] 5 so that your
faith might not rest on men's wisdom, but on God's power.[e]

Wisdom From the Spirit

6 We do, however, speak a message of wisdom among the mature,[f] but not the wisdom of this
age[g] or of the rulers of this age,
who are coming to nothing. 7 No, we
speak of God's secret wisdom, a
wisdom that has been hidden and
that God destined for our glory
before time began. 8 None of the rulers of this age understood it, for if
they had, they would not have crucified the Lord of glory.[h] 9 However, as it is written:

"No eye has seen,
no ear has heard,
no mind has conceived
what God has prepared for
those who love him"[b][i]—

10 but God has revealed[j] it to us by
his Spirit.[k]
The Spirit searches all things,
even the deep things of God. 11 For
who among men knows the
thoughts of a man[l] except the
man's spirit[m] within him? In
the same way no-one knows the
thoughts of God except the Spirit of
God.
12 We have not received the
spirit[n] of the world[o] but the Spirit
who is from God, that we may
understand what God has freely
given us. 13 This is what we speak,
not in words taught us by human
wisdom[p] but in words taught by
the Spirit, expressing spiritual
truths in spiritual words.[c] 14 The
man without the Spirit does not accept the things that come from the
Spirit of God, for they are foolishness[q] to him, and he cannot understand them, because they are
spiritually discerned. 15 The spiritual man makes judgments about
all things, but he himself is not subject to any man's judgment:
16 "For who has known the mind
of the Lord
that he may instruct him?"[d][r]
But we have the mind of Christ.[s]

On Divisions in the Church

3 Brothers, I could not address
you as spiritual[a] but as
worldly[b]—mere infants[c] in Christ
2 I gave you milk, not solid food,[d]

1:24 f Ro 8:28 g ver 30; Col 2:3
1:25 h ver 18 i 2Co 13:4
1:27 j Jas 2:5 k ver 20
1:28 l Ro 4:17
1:29 m Eph 2:9
1:30 n Jer 23:5,6; 2Co 5:21 o Ro 3:24; Eph 1:7,14
1:31 p Jer 9:23,24; 2Co 10:17
2:1 a 1Co 1:17
2:2 b Gal 6:14; 1Co 1:23
2:3 c Ac 18:1-18
2:4 d Ro 15:19
2:5 e 2Co 4:7; 2Co 6:7
2:6 f Eph 4:13; Php 3:15; Heb 5:14 g 1Co 1:20
2:8 h Ac 7:2; Jas 2:1
2:9 i Isa 64:4; Isa 65:17
2:10 j Mt 13:11; Eph 3:3,5 k Jn 14:26
2:11 l Jer 17:9 m Pr 20:27
2:12 n Ro 8:15 o 1Co 1:20,27
2:13 p 1Co 1:17
2:14 q 1Co 1:18
2:16 r Isa 40:13 s Jn 15:15
3:1 a 1Co 2:15 b Ro 7:14; 1Co 2:14 c Heb 5:13
3:2 d Heb 5:12-14; 1Pe 2:2

d31 Jer. 9:24 a1 Some manuscripts *as I proclaimed to you God's mystery* b9 Isaiah 64:4
c13 Or *Spirit, interpreting spiritual truths to spiritual men* d16 Isaiah 40:13

for you were not yet ready for
it.[e] Indeed, you are still not
ready. 3You are still worldly. For
since there is jealousy and quarrelling[f] among you, are you not
worldly? Are you not acting like
mere men? 4For when one says,
"I follow Paul," and another, "I follow Apollos,"[g] are you not mere
men?

5What, after all, is Apollos? And
what is Paul? Only servants,
through whom you came to believe—as the Lord has assigned to
each his task. 6I planted the seed,[h]
Apollos watered it, but God made it
grow. 7So neither he who plants nor
he who waters is anything, but only
God, who makes things grow. 8The
man who plants and the man who
waters have one purpose, and each
will be rewarded according to his
own labour.[i] 9For we are God's
fellow-workers;[j] you are God's
field,[k] God's building.[l]

10By the grace God has given
me,[m] I laid a foundation[n] as an expert builder, and someone else is
building on it. But each one should
be careful how he builds. 11For no-
one can lay any foundation other
than the one already laid, which is
Jesus Christ.[o] 12If any man builds
on this foundation using gold, silver, costly stones, wood, hay or
straw, 13his work will be shown for
what it is,[p] because the Day[q] will
bring it to light. It will be revealed
with fire, and the fire will test the
quality of each man's work. 14If
what he has built survives, he will
receive his reward. 15If it is burned
up, he will suffer loss; he himself
will be saved, but only as one escaping through the flames.[r]

16Don't you know that you yourselves are God's temple[s] and that
God's Spirit lives in you? 17If anyone destroys God's temple, God
will destroy him; for God's temple
is sacred, and you are that temple.

18Do not deceive yourselves. If
any one of you thinks he is wise[t]
by the standards of this age, he
should become a "fool" so that he
may become wise. 19For the wisdom of this world is foolishness[u] in
God's sight. As it is written: "He
catches the wise in their craftiness";[a][v] 20and again, "The Lord
knows that the thoughts of the wise
are futile."[b][w] 21So then, no more
boasting about men![x] All things
are yours,[y] 22whether Paul or
Apollos or Cephas[c][z] or the world
or life or death or the present or the
future[a]—all are yours, 23and you
are of Christ,[b] and Christ is of God.

Apostles of Christ

4 So then, men ought to regard
us as servants of Christ and as
those entrusted[a] with the secret
things[b] of God. 2Now it is required
that those who have been given a
trust must prove faithful. 3I care
very little if I am judged by you or
by any human court; indeed, I do
not even judge myself. 4My conscience is clear, but that does not
make me innocent.[c] It is the Lord
who judges me. 5Therefore judge
nothing[d] before the appointed
time; wait till the Lord comes. He
will bring to light what is hidden in
darkness and will expose the motives of men's hearts. At that time
each will receive his praise from
God.[e]

6Now, brothers, I have applied
these things to myself and Apollos
for your benefit, so that you may
learn from us the meaning of the
saying, "Do not go beyond what is
written."[f] Then you will not take
pride in one man over against another.[g] 7For who makes you different from anyone else? What do you
have that you did not receive?[h]
And if you did receive it, why do
you boast as though you did
not?

8Already you have all you want!

3:2 e Jn 16:12
3:3 f 1Co 1:11; Gal 5:20
3:4 g 1Co 1:12
3:6 h Ac 18:4-11
3:8 i Ps 62:12
3:9 j 2Co 6:1; k Isa 61:3; l Eph 2:20-22; 1Pe 2:5
3:10 m Ro 12:3; n Ro 15:20
3:11 o Isa 28:16; Eph 2:20
3:13 p 1Co 4:5; q 2Th 1:7-10
3:15 r Jude 23
3:16 s 1Co 6:19; 2Co 6:16
3:18 t Isa 5:21; 1Co 8:2
3:19 u 1Co 1:20,27; v Job 5:13
3:20 w Ps 94:11
3:21 x 1Co 4:6; y Ro 8:32
3:22 z 1Co 1:12; a Ro 8:38
3:23 b 1Co 15:23; 2Co 10:7; Gal 3:29
4:1 a 1Co 9:17; Tit 1:7; b Ro 16:25
4:4 c Ro 2:13
4:5 d Mt 7:1,2; Ro 2:1; e Ro 2:29
4:6 f 1Co 1:19,31; 1Co 3:19,20; g 1Co 1:12
4:7 h Jn 3:27; Ro 12:3,6

[a] *19* Job 5:13 [b] *20* Psalm 94:11 [c] *22* That is, Peter

Already you have become rich![i] You have become kings—and that without us! How I wish that you really had become kings so that we might be kings with you! 9For it seems to me that God has put us apostles on display at the end of the procession, like men condemned to die[j] in the arena. We have been made a spectacle[k] to the whole universe, to angels as well as to men. 10We are fools for Christ,[l] but you are so wise in Christ![m] We are weak, but you are strong![n] You are honoured, we are dishonoured! 11To this very hour we go hungry and thirsty, we are in rags, we are brutally treated, we are homeless.[o] 12We work hard with our own hands.[p] When we are cursed, we bless;[q] when we are persecuted, we endure it; 13when we are slandered, we answer kindly. Up to this moment we have become the scum of the earth, the refuse[r] of the world.

14I am not writing this to shame you, but to warn you, as my dear children.[s] 15Even though you have ten thousand guardians in Christ, you do not have many fathers, for in Christ Jesus I became your father through the gospel.[t] 16Therefore I urge you to imitate me.[u] 17For this reason I am sending to you Timothy, my son[v] whom I love, who is faithful in the Lord. He will remind you of my way of life in Christ Jesus, which agrees with what I teach everywhere in every church.[w]

18Some of you have become arrogant, as if I were not coming to you. 19But I will come to you very soon,[x] if the Lord is willing,[y] and then I will find out not only how these arrogant people are talking, but what power they have. 20For the kingdom of God is not a matter of talk but of power. 21What do you prefer? Shall I come to you with a whip,[z] or in love and with a gentle spirit?

4:8 i Rev 3:17,18
4:9 j Ro 8:36 k Heb 10:33
4:10 l 1Co 1:18; Ac 17:18 m 1Co 3:18 n 1Co 2:3
4:11 o Ro 8:35; 2Co 11:23-27
4:12 p Ac 18:3 q 1Pe 3:9
4:13 r La 3:45
4:14 s 1Th 2:11
4:15 t 1Co 9:12,14,18,23
4:16 u 1Co 11:1; Php 3:17; 1Th 1:6; 2Th 3:7,9
4:17 v 1Ti 1:2 w 1Co 7:17
4:19 x 2Co 1:15,16 y Ac 18:21
4:21 z 2Co 1:23; 2Co 13:2,10
5:1 a Lev 18:8; Dt 22:30
5:2 b 2Co 7:7-11
5:3 c Col 2:5
5:4 d 2Th 3:6
5:5 e 1Ti 1:20
5:6 f Jas 4:16 g Mt 16:6,12 h Gal 5:9
5:7 i Mk 14:12; 1Pe 1:19
5:8 j Ex 12:14,15; Dt 16:3
5:9 k Eph 5:11; 2Th 3:6,14
5:10 l 1Co 10:27
5:11 m 1Co 10:7,14

Expel the Immoral Brother!

5 It is actually reported that there is sexual immorality among you, and of a kind that does not occur even among pagans: A man has his father's wife.[a] 2And you are proud! Shouldn't you rather have been filled with grief[b] and have put out of your fellowship the man who did this? 3Even though I am not physically present, I am with you in spirit.[c] And I have already passed judgment on the one who did this, just as if I were present. 4When you are assembled in the name of our Lord Jesus[d] and I am with you in spirit, and the power of our Lord Jesus is present, 5hand this man over[e] to Satan, so that the sinful nature[a] may be destroyed and his spirit saved on the day of the Lord.

6Your boasting is not good.[f] Don't you know that a little yeast[g] works through the whole batch of dough?[h] 7Get rid of the old yeast that you may be a new batch without yeast—as you really are. For Christ, our Passover lamb, has been sacrificed.[i] 8Therefore let us keep the Festival, not with the old yeast, the yeast of malice and wickedness, but with bread without yeast,[j] the bread of sincerity and truth.

9I have written to you in my letter not to associate[k] with sexually immoral people—10not at all meaning the people of this world[l] who are immoral, or the greedy and swindlers, or idolaters. In that case you would have to leave this world. 11But now I am writing to you that you must not associate with anyone who calls himself a brother but is sexually immoral or greedy, an idolater[m] or a slanderer, a drunkard or a swindler. With such a man do not even eat.

a5 *Or that his body; or that the flesh*

[12]What business is it of mine to judge those outside[n] the church? Are you not to judge those inside?[o] [13]God will judge those outside. "Expel the wicked man from among you."[b][p]

Lawsuits Among Believers

6 If any of you has a dispute with another, dare he take it before the ungodly for judgment instead of before the saints?[a] [2]Do you not know that the saints will judge the world?[b] And if you are to judge the world, are you not competent to judge trivial cases? [3]Do you not know that we will judge angels? How much more the things of this life! [4]Therefore, if you have disputes about such matters, appoint as judges even men of little account in the church![a] [5]I say this to shame you.[c] Is it possible that there is nobody among you wise enough to judge a dispute between believers?[d] [6]But instead, one brother goes to law against another—and this in front of unbelievers![e]

[7]The very fact that you have lawsuits among you means you have been completely defeated already. Why not rather be wronged? Why not rather be cheated?[f] [8]Instead, you yourselves cheat and do wrong, and you do this to your brothers.[g]

[9]Do you not know that the wicked will not inherit the kingdom of God?[h] Do not be deceived:[i] Neither the sexually immoral nor idolaters nor adulterers nor male prostitutes nor homosexual offenders [10]nor thieves nor the greedy nor drunkards nor slanderers nor swindlers will inherit the kingdom of God. [11]And that is what some of you were.[j] But you were washed,[k] you were sanctified,[l] you were justified in the name of the Lord Jesus Christ and by the Spirit of our God.

5:12 n Mk 4:11 o ver 3-5 1Co 6:1-4
5:13 p Dt 13:5
6:1 a Mt 18:17
6:2 b Mt 19:28 Lk 22:30
6:5 c 1Co 4:14 d Ac 1:15
6:6 e 2Co 6:14,15
6:7 f Mt 5:39,40
6:8 g 1Th 4:6
6:9 h Gal 5:21 i 1Co 15:33 Jas 1:16
6:11 j Eph 2:2 k Ac 22:16 l 1Co 1:2
6:12 m 1Co 10:23
6:13 n Col 2:22
6:14 o Ro 6:5 Eph 1:19,20
6:15 p Ro 12:5
6:16 q Ge 2:24 Mt 19:5 Eph 5:31
6:17 r Jn 17:21-23 Gal 2:20
6:18 s 2Co 12:21 1Th 4:3,4 Heb 13:4 t Ro 6:12
6:19 u Jn 2:21 v Ro 14:7,8
6:20 w Ac 20:28 1Co 7:23 1Pe 1:18,19 Rev 5:9
7:1 a ver 8,26
7:3 b Ex 21:10 1Pe 3:7

Sexual Immorality

[12]"Everything is permissible for me"—but not everything is beneficial.[m] "Everything is permissible for me"—but I will not be mastered by anything. [13]"Food for the stomach and the stomach for food"—but God will destroy them both.[n] The body is not meant for sexual immorality, but for the Lord, and the Lord for the body. [14]By his power God raised the Lord from the dead, and he will raise us also.[o] [15]Do you not know that your bodies are members of Christ himself?[p] Shall I then take the members of Christ and unite them with a prostitute? Never! [16]Do you not know that he who unites himself with a prostitute is one with her in body? For it is said, "The two will become one flesh."[b][q] [17]But he who unites himself with the Lord is one with him in spirit.[r]

[18]Flee from sexual immorality.[s] All other sins a man commits are outside his body, but he who sins sexually sins against his own body.[t] [19]Do you not know that your body is a temple[u] of the Holy Spirit, who is in you, whom you have received from God? You are not your own;[v] [20]you were bought at a price.[w] Therefore honour God with your body.

Marriage

7 Now for the matters you wrote about: It is good for a man not to marry.[a][a] [2]But since there is so much immorality, each man should have his own wife, and each woman her own husband. [3]The husband should fulfil his marital duty to his wife,[b] and likewise the wife to her husband. [4]The wife's body does not belong to her alone but also to her husband. In the same way, the

[b]13 Deut. 17:7; 19:19; 21:21; 22:21,24; 24:7
[a]4 Or *matters, do you appoint as judges men of little account in the church?* [b]16 Gen. 2:24
[a]1 Or *"It is good for a man not to have sexual relations with a woman."*

husband's body does not belong to
him alone but also to his wife. 5Do
not deprive each other except by
mutual consent and for a time,[c] so
that you may devote yourselves to
prayer. Then come together again
so that Satan[d] will not tempt you[e]
because of your lack of self-
control. 6I say this as a concession,
not as a command.[f] 7I wish that all
men were as I am.[g] But each man
has his own gift from God; one has
this gift, another has that.[h]

8Now to the unmarried and the
widows I say: It is good for them to
stay unmarried, as I am.[i] 9But if
they cannot control themselves,
they should marry,[j] for it is better
to marry than to burn with passion.

10To the married I give this command (not I, but the Lord): A wife
must not separate from her husband.[k] 11But if she does, she must
remain unmarried or else be reconciled to her husband. And a husband must not divorce his wife.

12To the rest I say this (I, not the
Lord):[l] If any brother has a wife
who is not a believer and she is willing to live with him, he must not
divorce her. 13And if a woman has
a husband who is not a believer and
he is willing to live with her, she
must not divorce him. 14For the unbelieving husband has been sanctified through his wife, and the
unbelieving wife has been sanctified through her believing husband. Otherwise your children
would be unclean, but as it is, they
are holy.[m]

15But if the unbeliever leaves, let
him do so. A believing man or
woman is not bound in such circumstances; God has called us to
live in peace.[n] 16How do you know,
wife, whether you will save[o] your
husband?[p] Or, how do you know,
husband, whether you will save
your wife?

17Nevertheless, each one should
retain the place in life that the Lord
assigned to him and to which God
has called him.[q] This is the rule I
lay down in all the churches.[r]
18Was a man already circumcised
when he was called? He should not
become uncircumcised. Was a
man uncircumcised when he was
called? He should not be circumcised.[s] 19Circumcision is nothing
and uncircumcision is nothing.[t]
Keeping God's commands is what
counts. 20Each one should remain
in the situation which he was in
when God called him.[u] 21Were you
a slave when you were called?
Don't let it trouble you—although
if you can gain your freedom, do so.
22For he who was a slave when he
was called by the Lord is the Lord's
freedman;[v] similarly, he who was
a free man when he was called is
Christ's slave.[w] 23You were bought
at a price;[x] do not become slaves
of men. 24Brothers, each man, as
responsible to God, should remain
in the situation God called him to.[y]

25Now about virgins: I have no
command from the Lord,[z] but I
give a judgment as one who by the
Lord's mercy[a] is trustworthy.
26Because of the present crisis, I
think that it is good for you to remain as you are.[b] 27Are you married? Do not seek a divorce. Are
you unmarried? Do not look for a
wife. 28But if you do marry, you
have not sinned; and if a virgin
marries, she has not sinned. But
those who marry will face many
troubles in this life, and I want to
spare you this.

29What I mean, brothers, is that
the time is short.[c] From now on
those who have wives should live as
if they had none; 30those who
mourn, as if they did not; those who
are happy, as if they were not;
those who buy something, as if it
were not theirs to keep; 31those who
use the things of the world, as if not
engrossed in them. For this world in
its present form is passing away.[d]

32I would like you to be free from
concern. An unmarried man is concerned about the Lord's affairs[e]—
how he can please the Lord. 33But a

7:5 c Ex 19:15; 1Sa 21:4,5 d Mt 4:10 e 1Th 3:5
7:6 f 2Co 8:8
7:7 g ver 8; 1Co 9:5 h Mt 19:11,12; Ro 12:6; 1Co 12:4,11
7:8 i ver 1,26
7:9 j 1Ti 5:14
7:10 k Mal 2:14-16; Mt 5:32; Mt 19:3-9; Mk 10:11; Lk 16:18
7:12 l ver 6,10; 2Co 11:17
7:14 m Mal 2:15
7:15 n Ro 14:19; 1Co 14:33
7:16 o Ro 11:14 p 1Pe 3:1
7:17 q Ro 12:3 r 1Co 4:17; 1Co 14:33; 2Co 8:18; 2Co 11:28
7:18 s Ac 15:1,2
7:19 t Ro 2:25-27; Gal 5:6; Gal 6:15; Col 3:11
7:20 u ver 24
7:22 v Jn 8:32,36; Phm 16 w Eph 6:6
7:23 x 1Co 6:20
7:24 y ver 20
7:25 z ver 6; 2Co 8:8 a 2Co 4:1; 1Ti 1:13,16
7:26 b ver 1,8
7:29 c ver 31; Ro 13:11,12
7:31 d 1Jn 2:17
7:32 e 1Ti 5:5

married man is concerned about the affairs of this world—how he can please his wife—34and his interests are divided. An unmarried woman or virgin is concerned about the Lord's affairs: Her aim is to be devoted to the Lord in both body and spirit.[f] But a married woman is concerned about the affairs of this world—how she can please her husband. 35I am saying this for your own good, not to restrict you, but that you may live in a right way in undivided[g] devotion to the Lord.

36If anyone thinks he is acting improperly towards the virgin he is engaged to, and if she is getting on in years and he feels he ought to marry, he should do as he wants. He is not sinning.[h] They should get married. 37But the man who has settled the matter in his own mind, who is under no compulsion but has control over his own will, and who has made up his mind not to marry the virgin—this man also does the right thing. 38So then, he who marries the virgin does right,[i] but he who does not marry her does even better.[b]

39A woman is bound to her husband as long as he lives.[j] But if her husband dies, she is free to marry anyone she wishes, but he must belong to the Lord.[k] 40In my judgment,[l] she is happier if she stays as she is—and I think that I too have the Spirit of God.

Food Sacrificed to Idols

8 Now about food sacrificed to idols:[a] We know that we all possess knowledge.[a][b] Knowledge puffs up, but love builds up. 2The man who thinks he knows something[c] does not yet know as he ought to know.[d] 3But the man who loves God is known by God.[e]

4So then, about eating food sacrificed to idols:[f] We know that an idol is nothing at all in the world[g] and that there is no God but one.[h] 5For even if there are so-called gods,[i] whether in heaven or on earth (as indeed there are many "gods" and many "lords"), 6yet for us there is but one God, the Father,[j] from whom all things came[k] and for whom we live; and there is but one Lord,[l] Jesus Christ, through whom all things came[m] and through whom we live.

7But not everyone knows this. Some people are still so accustomed to idols that when they eat such food they think of it as having been sacrificed to an idol, and since their conscience is weak,[n] it is defiled. 8But food does not bring us near to God;[o] we are no worse if we do not eat, and no better if we do.

9Be careful, however, that the exercise of your freedom does not become a stumbling-block[p] to the weak.[q] 10For if anyone with a weak conscience sees you who have this knowledge eating in an idol's temple, won't he be emboldened to eat what has been sacrificed to idols? 11So this weak brother, for whom Christ died, is destroyed[r] by your knowledge. 12When you sin against your brothers[s] in this way and wound their weak conscience, you sin against Christ. 13Therefore, if what I eat causes my brother to fall into sin, I will never eat meat again, so that I will not cause him to fall.[t]

The Rights of an Apostle

9 Am I not free? Am I not an apostle?[a] Have I not seen Jesus our Lord?[b] Are you not the result of my work in the Lord?[c]

7:34 f Lk 2:37
7:35 g Ps 86:11
7:36 h ver 28
7:38 i Heb 13:4
7:39 j Ro 7:2,3 k 2Co 6:14
7:40 l ver 25
8:1 a Ac 15:20 b Ro 15:14
8:2 c 1Co 3:18 d 1Co 13:8,9,12 1Ti 6:4
8:3 e Ro 8:29 Gal 4:9
8:4 f ver 1,7,10 g 1Co 10:19 h Dt 6:4 Eph 4:6
8:5 i 2Th 2:4
8:6 j Mal 2:10 k Ro 11:36 l Eph 4:5 m Jn 1:3
8:7 n Ro 14:14 1Co 10:28
8:8 o Ro 14:17
8:9 p Gal 5:13 q Ro 14:1
8:11 r Ro 14:15,20
8:12 s Mt 18:6
8:13 t Ro 14:21
9:1 a 2Co 12:12 b 1Co 15:8 c 1Co 3:6 1Co 4:15

b36–38 Or *36If anyone thinks he is not treating his daughter properly, and if she is getting on in years, and he feels she ought to marry, he should do as he wants. He is not sinning. He should let her get married. 37But the man who has settled the matter in his own mind, who is under no compulsion but has control over his own will, and who has made up his mind to keep the virgin unmarried—this man also does the right thing. 38So then, he who gives his virgin in marriage does right, but he who does not give her in marriage does even better.*

a1 Or "We all possess knowledge," *as you say*

2 Even though I may not be an apostle to others, surely I am to you! For you are the seal[d] of my apostleship in the Lord.

3 This is my defence to those who sit in judgment on me. 4 Don't we have the right to food and drink?[e] 5 Don't we have the right to take a believing wife[f] along with us, as do the other apostles and the Lord's brothers[g] and Cephas?[a] 6 Or is it only I and Barnabas[h] who must work for a living?

7 Who serves as a soldier at his own expense? Who plants a vineyard[i] and does not eat of its grapes? Who tends a flock and does not drink of the milk? 8 Do I say this merely from a human point of view? Doesn't the Law say the same thing? 9 For it is written in the Law of Moses: "Do not muzzle an ox while it is treading out the grain."[b][j] Is it about oxen that God is concerned?[k] 10 Surely he says this for us, doesn't he? Yes, this was written for us,[l] because when the ploughman ploughs and the thresher threshes, they ought to do so in the hope of sharing in the harvest.[m] 11 If we have sown spiritual seed among you, is it too much if we reap a material harvest from you?[n] 12 If others have this right of support from you, shouldn't we have it all the more?

But we did not use this right.[o] On the contrary, we put up with anything rather than hinder[p] the gospel of Christ. 13 Don't you know that those who work in the temple get their food from the temple, and those who serve at the altar share in what is offered on the altar?[q] 14 In the same way, the Lord has commanded that those who preach the gospel should receive their living from the gospel.[r]

15 But I have not used any of these rights.[s] And I am not writing this in the hope that you will do such things for me. I would rather die than have anyone deprive me of this boast.[t] 16 Yet when I preach the gospel, I cannot boast, for I am compelled to preach.[u] Woe to me if I do not preach the gospel! 17 If I preach voluntarily, I have a reward;[v] if not voluntarily, I am simply discharging the trust committed to me.[w] 18 What then is my reward? Just this: that in preaching the gospel I may offer it free of charge,[x] and so not make use of my rights in preaching it.

19 Though I am free[y] and belong to no man, I make myself a slave to everyone,[z] to win as many as possible.[a] 20 To the Jews I became like a Jew, to win the Jews.[b] To those under the law I became like one under the law (though I myself am not under the law), so as to win those under the law. 21 To those not having the law I became like one not having the law[c] (though I am not free from God's law but am under Christ's law), so as to win those not having the law. 22 To the weak I became weak, to win the weak. I have become all things to all men[d] so that by all possible means I might save some.[e] 23 I do all this for the sake of the gospel, that I may share in its blessings.

24 Do you not know that in a race all the runners run, but only one gets the prize? Run[f] in such a way as to get the prize. 25 Everyone who competes in the games goes into strict training. They do it to get a crown that will not last; but we do it to get a crown that will last for ever.[g] 26 Therefore I do not run like a man running aimlessly; I do not fight like a man beating the air. 27 No, I beat my body[h] and make it my slave so that after I have preached to others, I myself will not be disqualified for the prize.

Warnings From Israel's History

10 For I do not want you to be ignorant of the fact, brothers, that our forefathers were all under the cloud[a] and that they

9:2 d 2Co 3:2,3
9:4 e 1Th 2:6
9:5 f 1Co 7:7,8; g Mt 12:46
9:6 h Ac 4:36
9:7 i Dt 20:6; Pr 27:18
9:9 j Dt 25:4; 1Ti 5:18; k Dt 22:1-4
9:10 l Ro 4:23,24; m 2Ti 2:6
9:11 n Ro 15:27
9:12 o Ac 18:3; p 2Co 11:7-12
9:13 q Lev 6:16,26; Dt 18:1
9:14 r Mt 10:10; 1Ti 5:18
9:15 s Ac 18:3; t 2Co 11:9,10
9:16 u Ro 1:14; Ac 9:15
9:17 v 1Co 3:8,14; w Gal 2:7; Col 1:25
9:18 x 2Co 11:7; 2Co 12:13
9:19 y ver 1; z Gal 5:13; a Mt 18:15; 1Pe 3:1
9:20 b Ac 16:3; Ac 21:20-26; Ro 11:14
9:21 c Ro 2:12,14
9:22 d 1Co 10:33; e Ro 11:14
9:24 f Gal 2:2; 2Ti 4:7; Heb 12:1
9:25 g Jas 1:12; Rev 2:10
9:27 h Ro 8:13
10:1 a Ex 13:21

a5 That is, Peter b9 Deut. 25:4

all passed through the sea.[b] 2They
were all baptised into Moses in the
cloud and in the sea. 3They all ate
the same spiritual food 4and drank
the same spiritual drink; for they
drank from the spiritual rock[c] that
accompanied them, and that rock
was Christ. 5Nevertheless, God
was not pleased with most of them;
their bodies were scattered over
the desert.[d]

6Now these things occurred as
examples[a] to keep us from setting
our hearts on evil things as they
did. 7Do not be idolaters,[e] as some
of them were; as it is written: "The
people sat down to eat and drink
and got up to indulge in pagan revelry."[b][f] 8We should not commit
sexual immorality, as some of them
did—and in one day twenty-three
thousand of them died.[g] 9We
should not test the Lord, as some
of them did—and were killed
by snakes.[h] 10And do not grumble, as some of them did[i]—and
were killed[j] by the destroying
angel.[k]

11These things happened to them
as examples and were written
down as warnings for us, on whom
the fulfilment of the ages has
come.[l] 12So, if you think you are
standing firm,[m] be careful that you
don't fall! 13No temptation has
seized you except what is common
to man. And God is faithful;[n] he
will not let you be tempted beyond
what you can bear.[o] But when you
are tempted, he will also provide a
way out so that you can stand up under it.

Idol Feasts and the Lord's Supper

14Therefore, my dear friends,
flee from idolatry. 15I speak to sensible people; judge for yourselves
what I say. 16Is not the cup of
thanksgiving for which we give
thanks a participation in the blood
of Christ? And is not the bread that
we break a participation in the
body of Christ?[p] 17Because there is
one loaf, we, who are many, are one
body,[q] for we all partake of the one
loaf.

18Consider the people of Israel:
Do not those who eat the sacrifices[r] participate in the altar? 19Do
I mean then that a sacrifice offered
to an idol is anything, or that an idol
is anything?[s] 20No, but the sacrifices of pagans are offered to demons,[t] not to God, and I do not
want you to be participants with demons. 21You cannot drink the cup of
the Lord and the cup of demons too;
you cannot have a part in both the
Lord's table and the table of demons.[u] 22Are we trying to arouse
the Lord's jealousy?[v] Are we
stronger than he?[w]

The Believer's Freedom

23"Everything is permissible"—
but not everything is beneficial.[x]
"Everything is permissible"—but
not everything is constructive.
24Nobody should seek his own good,
but the good of others.[y]

25Eat anything sold in the meat
market without raising questions
of conscience,[z] 26for, "The earth is
the Lord's, and everything in
it."[c][a]

27If some unbeliever invites you
to a meal and you want to go, eat
whatever is put before you[b] without raising questions of conscience. 28But if anyone says to
you, "This has been offered in sacrifice," then do not eat it, both for
the sake of the man who told you
and for conscience' sake[d][c]—29the
other man's conscience, I mean,
not yours. For why should my
freedom[d] be judged by another's
conscience? 30If I take part in the
meal with thankfulness, why am

10:1 b Ex 14:22,29
10:4 c Ex 17:6; Nu 20:11; Ps 78:15
10:5 d Nu 14:29; Heb 3:17
10:7 e ver 14; f Ex 32:4,6,19
10:8 g Nu 25:1-9
10:9 h Nu 21:5,6
10:10 i Nu 16:41; j Nu 16:49; k Ex 12:23
10:11 l Ro 13:11
10:12 m Ro 11:20
10:13 n 1Co 1:9; o 2Pe 2:9
10:16 p Mt 26:26-28
10:17 q Ro 12:5; 1Co 12:27
10:18 r Lev 7:6,14,15
10:19 s 1Co 8:4
10:20 t Dt 32:17; Ps 106:37; Rev 9:20
10:21 u 2Co 6:15,16
10:22 v Dt 32:16,21; w Ecc 6:10; Isa 45:9
10:23 x 1Co 6:12
10:24 y ver 33; Ro 15:1,2; 1Co 13:5; Php 2:4,21
10:25 z Ac 10:15; 1Co 8:7
10:26 a Ps 24:1
10:27 b Lk 10:7
10:28 c 1Co 8:7,10-12
10:29 d Ro 14:16; 1Co 9:1,19

a6 Or *types*; also in verse 11 b7 Exodus 32:6
c26 Psalm 24:1 d28 Some manuscripts
conscience' sake, for "the earth is the Lord's and everything in it"

I denounced because of something I thank God for?[e]
31So whether you eat or drink or
whatever you do, do it all for the
glory of God.[f] 32Do not cause anyone to stumble,[g] whether Jews,
Greeks or the church of God[h]—
33even as I try to please everybody
in every way.[i] For I am not seeking my own good but the good of
many, so that they may be saved.[j]

11 1Follow my example,[a] as I
follow the example of
Christ.

Propriety in Worship

2I praise you[b] for remembering
me in everything[c] and for holding
to the teachings,[a] just as I passed
them on to you.[d]
3Now I want you to realise that
the head of every man is Christ,[e]
and the head of the woman is
man,[f] and the head of Christ is
God.[g] 4Every man who prays or
prophesies with his head covered
dishonours his head. 5And every
woman who prays or prophesies[h]
with her head uncovered dishonours her head—it is just as though
her head were shaved.[i] 6If a
woman does not cover her head,
she should have her hair cut off;
and if it is a disgrace for a woman
to have her hair cut or shaved off,
she should cover her head. 7A man
ought not to cover his head,[b] since
he is the image[j] and glory of God;
but the woman is the glory of man.
8For man did not come from
woman, but woman from man;[k]
9neither was man created for
woman, but woman for man.[l] 10For
this reason, and because of the
angels, the woman ought to have a
sign of authority on her head.
11In the Lord, however, woman is
not independent of man, nor is man
independent of woman. 12For as
woman came from man, so also
man is born of woman. But everything comes from God.[m] 13Judge
for yourselves: Is it proper for a
woman to pray to God with her
head uncovered? 14Does not the
very nature of things teach you
that if a man has long hair, it is a
disgrace to him, 15but that if a
woman has long hair, it is her
glory? For long hair is given to her
as a covering. 16If anyone wants to
be contentious about this, we have
no other practice—nor do the
churches of God.[n]

The Lord's Supper

11:23–25pp Mt 26:26–28; Mk 14:22–24; Lk 22:17–20

17In the following directives I
have no praise for you,[o] for your
meetings do more harm than good.
18In the first place, I hear that when
you come together as a church,
there are divisions[p] among you,
and to some extent I believe it. 19No
doubt there have to be differences
among you to show which of you
have God's approval.[q] 20When you
come together, it is not the Lord's
Supper you eat, 21for as you eat,
each of you goes ahead without
waiting for anybody else.[r] One remains hungry, another gets drunk.
22Don't you have homes to eat and
drink in? Or do you despise the
church of God[s] and humiliate
those who have nothing?[t] What
shall I say to you? Shall I praise
you[u] for this? Certainly not!
23For I received from the Lord[v]
what I also passed on to you:[w] The
Lord Jesus, on the night he was betrayed, took bread, 24and when he
had given thanks, he broke it and
said, "This is my body, which is for
you; do this in remembrance of
me." 25In the same way, after supper he took the cup, saying, "This

10:30 *e* Ro 14:6
10:31 *f* Col 3:17; 1Pe 4:11
10:32 *g* Ac 24:16 *h* Ac 20:28
10:33 *i* Ro 15:2; 1Co 9:22 *j* Ro 11:14
11:1 *a* 1Co 4:16
11:2 *b* ver 17,22 *c* 1Co 4:17 *d* 1Co 15:2,3; 2Th 2:15
11:3 *e* Eph 1:22 *f* Ge 3:16; Eph 5:23 *g* 1Co 3:23
11:5 *h* Ac 21:9 *i* Dt 21:12
11:7 *j* Ge 1:26; Jas 3:9
11:8 *k* Ge 2:21-23; 1Ti 2:13
11:9 *l* Ge 2:18
11:12 *m* Ro 11:36
11:16 *n* 1Co 7:17
11:17 *o* ver 2,22
11:18 *p* 1Co 1:10-12; 1Co 3:3
11:19 *q* 1Jn 2:19
11:21 *r* 2Pe 2:13; Jude 12
11:22 *s* 1Co 10:32 *t* Jas 2:6 *u* ver 2,17
11:23 *v* Gal 1:12 *w* 1Co 15:3

a2 Or *traditions* b4–7 Or *4Every man who prays or prophesies with long hair dishonours his head. 5And every woman who prays or prophesies with no covering ⌊of hair⌋ on her head dishonours her head—she is just like one of the "shorn women". 6If a woman has no covering, let her be for now with short hair, but since it is a disgrace for a woman to have her hair shorn or shaved, she should grow it again. 7A man ought not to have long hair*

cup is the new covenant[x] in my
blood;[y] do this, whenever you
drink it, in remembrance of me."
26For whenever you eat this bread
and drink this cup, you proclaim
the Lord's death until he comes.
27Therefore, whoever eats the
bread or drinks the cup of the Lord
in an unworthy manner will be
guilty of sinning against the body
and blood of the Lord.[z] 28A man
ought to examine himself[a] before
he eats of the bread and drinks of
the cup. 29For anyone who eats and
drinks without recognising the
body of the Lord eats and drinks
judgment on himself. 30That is why
many among you are weak and
sick, and a number of you have
fallen asleep. 31But if we judged
ourselves, we would not come under judgment.[b] 32When we are
judged by the Lord, we are being
disciplined[c] so that we will not be
condemned with the world.
33So then, my brothers, when you
come together to eat, wait for each
other. 34If anyone is hungry,[d] he
should eat at home,[e] so that when
you meet together it may not result
in judgment.
And when I come[f] I will give
further directions.

Spiritual Gifts

12 Now about spiritual gifts,[a]
brothers, I do not want you
to be ignorant. 2You know that
when you were pagans,[b] somehow
or other you were influenced and
led astray to mute idols.[c] 3There-
fore I tell you that no-one who is
speaking by the Spirit of God says,
"Jesus be cursed,"[d] and no-one can
say, "Jesus is Lord,"[e] except by
the Holy Spirit.[f]
4There are different kinds of
gifts, but the same Spirit.[g] 5There
are different kinds of service, but
the same Lord. 6There are different kinds of working, but the same
God[h] works all of them in all men.
7Now to each one the manifesta-
tion of the Spirit is given for the
common good.[i] 8To one there is
given through the Spirit the message of wisdom,[j] to another the
message of knowledge[k] by means
of the same Spirit, 9to another
faith[l] by the same Spirit, to another gifts of healing[m] by that one
Spirit, 10to another miraculous
powers,[n] to another prophecy, to
another distinguishing between
spirits,[o] to another speaking in different kinds of tongues,[a][p] and to
still another the interpretation of
tongues.[a] 11All these are the work
of one and the same Spirit,[q] and he
gives them to each one, just as he
determines.

One Body, Many Parts

12The body is a unit, though it is
made up of many parts; and though
all its parts are many, they form
one body.[r] So it is with Christ.[s]
13For we were all baptised by[b] one
Spirit[t] into one body—whether
Jews or Greeks, slave or free[u]—
and we were all given the one Spirit
to drink.[v]
14Now the body is not made up of
one part but of many. 15If the foot
should say, "Because I am not a
hand, I do not belong to the body,"
it would not for that reason cease to
be part of the body. 16And if the ear
should say, "Because I am not an
eye, I do not belong to the body," it
would not for that reason cease to
be part of the body. 17If the whole
body were an eye, where would the
sense of hearing be? If the whole
body were an ear, where would the
sense of smell be? 18But in fact God
has arranged[w] the parts in the
body, every one of them, just as he
wanted them to be.[x] 19If they were
all one part, where would the body
be? 20As it is, there are many parts,
but one body.[y]
21The eye cannot say to the hand,

11:25 x Lk 22:20 y 1Co 10:16
11:27 z Heb 10:29
11:28 a 2Co 13:5
11:31 b Ps 32:5; 1Jn 1:9
11:32 c Ps 94:12; Heb 12:7-10; Rev 3:19
11:34 d ver 21 e ver 22 f 1Co 4:19
12:1 a Ro 1:11; 1Co 14:1,37
12:2 b Eph 2:11,12; 1Pe 4:3 c Ps 115:5; Jer 10:5; Hab 2:18,19; 1Th 1:9
12:3 d Ro 9:3 e Jn 13:13 f 1Jn 4:2,3
12:4 g Ro 12:4-8; Eph 4:11; Heb 2:4
12:6 h Eph 4:6
12:7 i Eph 4:12
12:8 j 1Co 2:6 k 2Co 8:7
12:9 l Mt 17:19,20; 2Co 4:13 m ver 28,30
12:10 n Gal 3:5 o 1Jn 4:1 p Mk 16:17
12:11 q ver 4
12:12 r Ro 12:5 s ver 27
12:13 t Eph 2:18 u Gal 3:28; Col 3:11 v Jn 7:37-39
12:18 w ver 28 x ver 11
12:20 y ver 12,14

[a]10 Or *languages*; also in verse 28 [b]13 Or *with*; or *in*

"I don't need *you!*" And the head cannot say to the feet, "I don't need you!" 22On the contrary, those parts of the body that seem to be weaker are indispensable, 23and the parts that we think are less honourable we treat with special honour. And the parts that are unpresentable are treated with special modesty, 24while our presentable parts need no special treatment. But God has combined the members of the body and has given greater honour to the parts that lacked it, 25so that there should be no division in the body, but that its parts should have equal concern for each other. 26If one part suffers, every part suffers with it; if one part is honoured, every part rejoices with it.

27Now you are the body of Christ,[z] and each one of you is a part of it.[a] 28And in the church[b] God has appointed first of all apostles,[c] second prophets, third teachers, then workers of miracles, also those having gifts of healing,[d] those able to help others, those with gifts of administration,[e] and those speaking in different kinds of tongues.[f] 29Are all apostles? Are all prophets? Are all teachers? Do all work miracles? 30Do all have gifts of healing? Do all speak in tongues?[c][g] Do all interpret? 31But eagerly desire[d][h] the greater gifts.

Love

And now I will show you the most excellent way.

13 If I speak in the tongues[a][a] of men and of angels, but have not love, I am only a resounding gong or a clanging cymbal. 2If I have the gift of prophecy and can fathom all mysteries[b] and all knowledge, and if I have a faith[c] that can move mountains,[d] but have not love, I am nothing. 3If I give all I possess to the poor[e] and surrender my body to the flames,[b][f] but have not love, I gain nothing.

4Love is patient,[g] love is kind. It does not envy, it does not boast, it is not proud. 5It is not rude, it is not self-seeking,[h] it is not easily angered, it keeps no record of wrongs. 6Love does not delight in evil[i] but rejoices with the truth.[j] 7It always protects, always trusts, always hopes, always perseveres.

8Love never fails. But where there are prophecies,[k] they will cease; where there are tongues,[l] they will be stilled; where there is knowledge, it will pass away. 9For we know in part[m] and we prophesy in part, 10but when perfection comes,[n] the imperfect disappears. 11When I was a child, I talked like a child, I thought like a child, I reasoned like a child. When I became a man, I put childish ways behind me. 12Now we see but a poor reflection as in a mirror; then we shall see face to face.[o] Now I know in part; then I shall know fully, even as I am fully known.[p]

13And now these three remain: faith, hope and love.[q] But the greatest of these is love.[r]

Gifts of Prophecy and Tongues

14 Follow the way of love[a] and eagerly desire[b] spiritual gifts,[c] especially the gift of prophecy. 2For anyone who speaks in a tongue[a][d] does not speak to men but to God. Indeed, no-one understands him; he utters mysteries[e] with his spirit.[b] 3But everyone who prophesies speaks to men for their strengthening,[f] encouragement and comfort. 4He who speaks in a tongue[g] edifies himself, but he who prophesies[h] edifies the church. 5I would like every one of you to speak in tongues,[c]

12:27 *z* Eph 1:23; Eph 4:12; Col 1:18,24 *a* Ro 12:5
12:28 *b* 1Co 10:32 *c* Eph 4:11 *d* ver 9 *e* Ro 12:6-8 *f* ver 10
12:30 *g* ver 10
12:31 *h* 1Co 14:1,39
13:1 *a* ver 8
13:2 *b* 1Co 14:2 *c* 1Co 12:9 *d* Mt 17:20; Mt 21:21
13:3 *e* Mt 6:2 *f* Da 3:28
13:4 *g* 1Th 5:14
13:5 *h* 1Co 10:24
13:6 *i* 2Th 2:12 *j* 2Jn 4; 3Jn 3,4
13:8 *k* ver 2 *l* ver 1
13:9 *m* ver 12; 1Co 8:2
13:10 *n* Php 3:12
13:12 *o* Ge 32:30; 2Co 5:7; 1Jn 3:2 *p* 1Co 8:3
13:13 *q* Gal 5:5,6 *r* 1Co 16:14
14:1 *a* 1Co 16:14 *b* ver 39; 1Co 12:31 *c* 1Co 12:1
14:2 *d* Mk 16:17 *e* 1Co 13:2
14:3 *f* ver 4,5,12,17, 26; Ro 14:19
14:4 *g* Mk 16:17 *h* 1Co 13:2

c30 Or *other languages* d31 Or *But you are eagerly desiring* a1 Or *languages* b3 Some early manuscripts *body that I may boast*
a2 Or *another language*; also in verses 4, 13, 14, 19, 26 and 27 b2 Or *by the Spirit* c5 Or *other languages*; also in verses 6, 18, 22, 23 and 39

but I would rather have you prophesy.[i] He who prophesies is greater than one who speaks in tongues,[c] unless he interprets, so that the church may be edified.

6 Now, brothers, if I come to you and speak in tongues, what good will I be to you, unless I bring you some revelation[j] or knowledge or prophecy or word of instruction?[k] 7 Even in the case of lifeless things that make sounds, such as the flute or harp, how will anyone know what tune is being played unless there is a distinction in the notes? 8 Again, if the trumpet does not sound a clear call, who will get ready for battle?[l] 9 So it is with you. Unless you speak intelligible words with your tongue, how will anyone know what you are saying? You will just be speaking into the air. 10 Undoubtedly there are all sorts of languages in the world, yet none of them is without meaning. 11 If then I do not grasp the meaning of what someone is saying, I am a foreigner to the speaker, and he is a foreigner to me. 12 So it is with you. Since you are eager to have spiritual gifts, try to excel in gifts that build up the church.

13 For this reason anyone who speaks in a tongue should pray that he may interpret what he says. 14 For if I pray in a tongue, my spirit prays, but my mind is unfruitful. 15 So what shall I do? I will pray with my spirit, but I will also pray with my mind; I will sing[m] with my spirit, but I will also sing with my mind. 16 If you are praising God with your spirit, how can one who finds himself among those who do not understand[d] say "Amen"[n] to your thanksgiving,[o] since he does not know what you are saying? 17 You may be giving thanks well enough, but the other man is not edified.

18 I thank God that I speak in tongues more than all of you. 19 But in the church I would rather speak five intelligible words to instruct others than ten thousand words in a tongue.

20 Brothers, stop thinking like children.[p] In regard to evil be infants,[q] but in your thinking be adults. 21 In the Law[r] it is written:

"Through men of strange
  tongues
 and through the lips of
  foreigners
I will speak to this people,
 but even then they will not
  listen to me,"[e][s]
says the Lord.

22 Tongues, then, are a sign, not for believers but for unbelievers; prophecy,[t] however, is for believers, not for unbelievers. 23 So if the whole church comes together and everyone speaks in tongues, and some who do not understand[f] or some unbelievers come in, will they not say that you are out of your mind?[u] 24 But if an unbeliever or someone who does not understand[g] comes in while everybody is prophesying, he will be convinced by all that he is a sinner and will be judged by all, 25 and the secrets of his heart will be laid bare. So he will fall down and worship God, exclaiming, "God is really among you!"[v]

Orderly Worship

26 What then shall we say, brothers? When you come together, everyone[w] has a hymn,[x] or a word of instruction,[y] a revelation, a tongue or an interpretation. All of these must be done for the strengthening[z] of the church. 27 If anyone speaks in a tongue, two—or at the most three—should speak, one at a time, and someone must interpret. 28 If there is no interpreter, the speaker should keep quiet in

14:5 i Nu 11:29
14:6 j ver 26; Eph 1:17; k Ro 6:17
14:8 l Nu 10:9; Jer 4:19
14:15 m Eph 5:19; Col 3:16
14:16 n Dt 27:15-26; 1Ch 16:36; Ne 8:6; Ps 106:48; Rev 5:14; Rev 7:12; o 1Co 11:24
14:20 p Eph 4:14; Heb 5:12,13; 1Pe 2:2; q Ro 16:19
14:21 r Jn 10:34; s Isa 28:11,12
14:22 t ver 1
14:23 u Ac 2:13
14:25 v Isa 45:14; Zec 8:23
14:26 w 1Co 12:7-10; x Eph 5:19; y ver 6; z Ro 14:19

c5 Or *other languages*; also in verses 6, 18, 22, 23 and 39 d16 Or *among the enquirers*
e21 Isaiah 28:11,12 f23 Or *some enquirers*
g24 Or *or some enquirer*

the church and speak to himself and God.

[29]Two or three prophets should speak, and the others should weigh carefully what is said.[a] [30]And if a revelation comes to someone who is sitting down, the first speaker should stop. [31]For you can all prophesy in turn so that everyone may be instructed and encouraged. [32]The spirits of prophets are subject to the control of prophets.[b] [33]For God is not a God of disorder[c] but of peace.

As in all the congregations of the saints,[d] [34]women should remain silent in the churches. They are not allowed to speak, but must be in submission,[e] as the Law[f] says. [35]If they want to enquire about something, they should ask their own husbands at home; for it is disgraceful for a woman to speak in the church.

[36]Did the word of God originate with you? Or are you the only people it has reached? [37]If anybody thinks he is a prophet[g] or spiritually gifted, let him acknowledge that what I am writing to you is the Lord's command.[h] [38]If he ignores this, he himself will be ignored.**[h]**

[39]Therefore, my brothers, be eager[i] to prophesy, and do not forbid speaking in tongues. [40]But everything should be done in a fitting and orderly[j] way.

The Resurrection of Christ

15 Now, brothers, I want to remind you of the gospel[a] I preached to you, which you received and on which you have taken your stand. [2]By this gospel you are saved,[b] if you hold firmly[c] to the word I preached to you. Otherwise, you have believed in vain.

[3]For what I received[d] I passed on to you[e] as of first importance:**[a]** that Christ died for our sins[f] according to the Scriptures,[g] [4]that he was buried, that he was raised[h] on the third day[i] according to the Scriptures,[j] [5]and that he appeared to Peter,**[b]**[k] and then to the Twelve.[l] [6]After that, he appeared to more than five hundred of the brothers at the same time, most of whom are still living, though some have fallen asleep. [7]Then he appeared to James, then to all the apostles,[m] [8]and last of all he appeared to me also,[n] as to one abnormally born.

[9]For I am the least of the apostles[o] and do not even deserve to be called an apostle, because I persecuted[p] the church of God. [10]But by the grace of God I am what I am, and his grace to me[q] was not without effect. No, I worked harder than all of them[r]—yet not I, but the grace of God that was with me.[s] [11]Whether, then, it was I or they, this is what we preach, and this is what you believed.

The Resurrection of the Dead

[12]But if it is preached that Christ has been raised from the dead, how can some of you say that there is no resurrection of the dead?[t] [13]If there is no resurrection of the dead, then not even Christ has been raised. [14]And if Christ has not been raised,[u] our preaching is useless and so is your faith. [15]More than that, we are then found to be false witnesses about God, for we have testified about God that he raised Christ from the dead.[v] But he did not raise him if in fact the dead are not raised. [16]For if the dead are not raised, then Christ has not been raised either. [17]And if Christ has not been raised, your faith is futile; you are still in your sins.[w] [18]Then those also who have fallen asleep in Christ are lost. [19]If only for this life

14:29 *a* 1Co 12:10
14:32 *b* 1Jn 4:1
14:33 *c* ver 40 *d* Ac 9:13
14:34 *e* 1Ti 2:11,12 *f* Ge 3:16
14:37 *g* 2Co 10:7 *h* 1Jn 4:6
14:39 *i* 1Co 12:31
14:40 *j* ver 33
15:1 *a* Ro 2:16
15:2 *b* Ro 1:16 *c* Ro 11:22
15:3 *d* Gal 1:12 *e* 1Co 11:23 *f* Isa 53:5 1Pe 2:24 *g* Lk 24:27 Ac 26:22,23
15:4 *h* Ac 2:24 *i* Mt 16:21 *j* Ac 2:25,30,31
15:5 *k* Lk 24:34 *l* Mk 16:14
15:7 *m* Lk 24:33,36,37 Ac 1:3,4
15:8 *n* Ac 9:3-6,17 1Co 9:1
15:9 *o* Eph 3:8 1Ti 1:15 *p* Ac 8:3
15:10 *q* Ro 12:3 *r* 2Co 11:23 *s* Php 2:13
15:12 *t* Ac 17:32 Ac 23:8 2Ti 2:18
15:14 *u* 1Th 4:14
15:15 *v* Ac 2:24
15:17 *w* Ro 4:25

h38 Some manuscripts *If he is ignorant of this, let him be ignorant* **a**3 Or *you at the first*
b5 Greek *Cephas*

we have hope in Christ, we are to be
pitied more than all men.[x]
20But Christ has indeed been
raised from the dead,[y] the firstfruits[z] of those who have fallen
asleep.[a] 21For since death came
through a man,[b] the resurrection
of the dead comes also through a
man. 22For as in Adam all die, so in
Christ all will be made alive.[c]
23But each in his own turn: Christ,
the firstfruits;[d] then, when he
comes,[e] those who belong to him.
24Then the end will come, when he
hands over the kingdom[f] to God
the Father after he has destroyed
all dominion, authority and
power.[g] 25For he must reign until
he has put all his enemies under his
feet.[h] 26The last enemy to be destroyed is death.[i] 27For he "has
put everything under his feet".**[c]**[j]
Now when it says that "everything"
has been put under him, it is clear
that this does not include God himself, who put everything under
Christ.[k] 28When he has done this,
then the Son himself will be made
subject to him who put everything
under him,[l] so that God may be all
in all.[m]
29Now if there is no resurrection,
what will those do who are baptised
for the dead? If the dead are not
raised at all, why are people baptised for them? 30And as for us, why
do we endanger ourselves every
hour?[n] 31I die every day[o]—I mean
that, brothers—just as surely as I
glory over you in Christ Jesus our
Lord. 32If I fought wild beasts[p] in
Ephesus[q] for merely human reasons, what have I gained? If the
dead are not raised,

> "Let us eat and drink,
> for tomorrow we die."**[d]**[r]

33Do not be misled: "Bad company
corrupts good character." 34Come
back to your senses as you ought,
and stop sinning; for there are
some who are ignorant of God—I
say this to your shame.

The Resurrection Body

35But someone may ask,[s] "How
are the dead raised? With what
kind of body will they come?"[t]
36How foolish![u] What you sow does
not come to life unless it dies.[v]
37When you sow, you do not plant
the body that will be, but just a
seed, perhaps of wheat or of something else. 38But God gives it a body
as he has determined, and to each
kind of seed he gives its own
body.[w] 39All flesh is not the same:
Men have one kind of flesh, animals have another, birds another
and fish another. 40There are also
heavenly bodies and there are
earthly bodies; but the splendour
of the heavenly bodies is one kind,
and the splendour of the earthly
bodies is another. 41The sun has one
kind of splendour, the moon another and the stars another; and
star differs from star in splendour.
42So will it be[x] with the resurrection of the dead. The body that is
sown is perishable, it is raised imperishable; 43it is sown in dishonour, it is raised in glory;[y] it is sown
in weakness, it is raised in power;
44it is sown a natural body, it is
raised a spiritual body.[z]
If there is a natural body, there is
also a spiritual body. 45So it is written: "The first man Adam became a
living being";**[e]**[a] the last Adam,[b] a
life-giving spirit.[c] 46The spiritual
did not come first, but the natural,
and after that the spiritual. 47The
first man was of the dust of the
earth,[d] the second man from
heaven.[e] 48As was the earthly man,
so are those who are of the earth;
and as is the man from heaven, so
also are those who are of heaven.[f]
49And just as we have borne the
likeness of the earthly man,[g] so
shall we**[f]** bear the likeness of the
man from heaven.[h]

15:19 x 1Co 4:9
15:20 y 1Pe 1:3; z ver 23; Ac 26:23; Rev 1:5; a ver 6,18
15:21 b Ro 5:12
15:22 c Ro 5:14-18
15:23 d ver 20; e ver 52
15:24 f Da 7:14,27; g Ro 8:38
15:25 h Ps 110:1; Mt 22:44
15:26 i 2Ti 1:10; Rev 20:14; Rev 21:4
15:27 j Ps 8:6; k Mt 28:18
15:28 l Php 3:21; m 1Co 3:23
15:30 n 2Co 11:26
15:31 o Ro 8:36
15:32 p 2Co 1:8; q Ac 18:19; r Isa 22:13; Lk 12:19
15:35 s Ro 9:19; t Eze 37:3
15:36 u Lk 11:40; v Jn 12:24
15:38 w Ge 1:11
15:42 x Da 12:3; Mt 13:43
15:43 y Php 3:21; Col 3:4
15:44 z ver 50
15:45 a Ge 2:7; b Ro 5:14; c Jn 5:21; Ro 8:2
15:47 d Ge 2:7; Ge 3:19; e Jn 3:13,31
15:48 f Php 3:20,21
15:49 g Ge 5:3; h Ro 8:29

c27 Psalm 8:6 **d**32 Isaiah 22:13 **e**45 Gen. 2:7
f49 Some early manuscripts *so let us*

50 I declare to you, brothers, that
flesh and blood[i] cannot inherit the
kingdom of God, nor does the perishable inherit the imperishable.
51 Listen, I tell you a mystery:[j] We
will not all sleep, but we will all be
changed[k]—52 in a flash, in the
twinkling of an eye, at the last
trumpet. For the trumpet will
sound,[l] the dead[m] will be raised
imperishable, and we will be
changed. 53 For the perishable must
clothe itself with the imperishable,[n] and the mortal with immortality. 54 When the perishable has
been clothed with the imperishable, and the mortal with immortality, then the saying that is written will come true: "Death has
been swallowed up in victory."[g][o]

55 "Where, O death, is your
victory?
Where, O death, is your
sting?"[h][p]

56 The sting of death is sin,[q] and the
power of sin is the law.[r] 57 But
thanks be to God![s] He gives us the
victory through our Lord Jesus
Christ.[t]
58 Therefore, my dear brothers,
stand firm. Let nothing move you.
Always give yourselves fully to the
work of the Lord,[u] because you
know that your labour in the Lord is
not in vain.

The Collection for God's People

16 Now about the collection[a]
for God's people:[b] Do what
I told the Galatian[c] churches to do.
2 On the first day of every week,[d]
each one of you should set aside a
sum of money in keeping with his
income, saving it up, so that when I
come no collections will have to be
made.[e] 3 Then, when I arrive, I will
give letters of introduction to the
men you approve[f] and send them
with your gift to Jerusalem. 4 If it
seems advisable for me to go also,
they will accompany me.

Personal Requests

5 After I go through Macedonia, I
will come to you[g]—for I will be going through Macedonia.[h] 6 Perhaps
I will stay with you awhile, or even
spend the winter, so that you can
help me on my journey,[i] wherever
I go. 7 I do not want to see you now
and make only a passing visit; I
hope to spend some time with you,
if the Lord permits.[j] 8 But I will
stay on at Ephesus[k] until Pentecost,[l] 9 because a great door for ef-
fective work has opened to me,[m]
and there are many who oppose me.
10 If Timothy[n] comes, see to it
that he has nothing to fear while he
is with you, for he is carrying on
the work of the Lord,[o] just as I am.
11 No-one, then, should refuse to accept him.[p] Send him on his way in
peace[q] so that he may return to
me. I am expecting him along with
the brothers.
12 Now about our brother Apollos:[r] I strongly urged him to go to
you with the brothers. He was quite
unwilling to go now, but he will go
when he has the opportunity.
13 Be on your guard; stand firm[s]
in the faith; be men of courage;
be strong.[t] 14 Do everything in
love.[u]
15 You know that the household of
Stephanas[v] were the first converts[w] in Achaia,[x] and they have
devoted themselves to the service
of the saints. I urge you, brothers,
16 to submit[y] to such as these and to
everyone who joins in the work,
and labours at it. 17 I was glad when
Stephanas, Fortunatus and Achai-
cus arrived, because they have
supplied what was lacking from
you.[z] 18 For they refreshed[a] my
spirit and yours also. Such men deserve recognition.[b]

15:50 i Jn 3:3,5
15:51 j 1Co 13:2 k Php 3:21
15:52 l Mt 24:31 m Jn 5:25
15:53 n 2Co 5:2,4
15:54 o Isa 25:8 Rev 20:14
15:55 p Hos 13:14
15:56 q Ro 5:12 r Ro 4:15
15:57 s 2Co 2:14 t Ro 8:37
15:58 u 1Co 16:10
16:1 a Ac 24:17 b Ac 9:13 c Ac 16:6
16:2 d Ac 20:7 e 2Co 9:4,5
16:3 f 2Co 8:18,19
16:5 g 1Co 4:19 h Ac 19:21
16:6 i Ro 15:24
16:7 j Ac 18:21
16:8 k Ac 18:19 l Ac 2:1
16:9 m Ac 14:27
16:10 n Ac 16:1 o 1Co 15:58
16:11 p 1Ti 4:12 q Ac 15:33
16:12 r Ac 18:24 1Co 1:12
16:13 s Gal 5:1 Php 1:27 1Th 3:8 2Th 2:15 t Eph 6:10
16:14 u 1Co 14:1
16:15 v 1Co 1:16 w Ro 16:5 x Ac 18:12
16:16 y Heb 13:17
16:17 z 2Co 11:9 Php 2:30 **16:18** a Phm 7 b Php 2:29

g 54 Isaiah 25:8 h 55 Hosea 13:14

Final Greetings

[19]The churches in the province of
Asia send you greetings. Aquila
and Priscilla[a][c] greet you warmly
in the Lord, and so does the church
that meets at their house.[d] [20]All
the brothers here send you greetings. Greet one another with a holy
kiss.[e]
[21]I, Paul, write this greeting in
my own hand.[f]
[22]If anyone does not love the
Lord[g]—a curse[h] be on him. Come,
O Lord![b][i]
[23]The grace of the Lord Jesus be
with you.[j]
[24]My love to all of you in Christ
Jesus. Amen.[c]

16:19 c Ac 18:2 d Ro 16:5
16:20 e Ro 16:16
16:21 f Gal 6:11 Col 4:18
16:22 g Eph 6:24 h Ro 9:3 i Rev 22:20
16:23 j Ro 16:20

[a]19 Greek *Prisca*, a variant of *Priscilla* [b]22 In Aramaic the expression *Come, O Lord* is *Marana tha.* [c]24 Some manuscripts do not have *Amen.*

2 CORINTHIANS

1 Paul, an apostle of Christ Jesus by the will of God,[a] and Timothy our brother,

To the church of God[b] in Corinth, together with all the saints throughout Achaia:[c]

2Grace and peace to you from God our Father and the Lord Jesus Christ.[d]

The God of All Comfort

3Praise be to the God and Father of our Lord Jesus Christ,[e] the Father of compassion and the God of all comfort, 4who comforts us[f] in all our troubles, so that we can comfort those in any trouble with the comfort we ourselves have received from God. 5For just as the sufferings of Christ flow over into our lives,[g] so also through Christ our comfort overflows. 6If we are distressed, it is for your comfort and salvation;[h] if we are comforted, it is for your comfort, which produces in you patient endurance of the same sufferings we suffer. 7And our hope for you is firm, because we know that just as you share in our sufferings,[i] so also you share in our comfort.

8We do not want you to be uninformed, brothers, about the hardships we suffered[j] in the province of Asia. We were under great pressure, far beyond our ability to endure, so that we despaired even of life. 9Indeed, in our hearts we felt the sentence of death. But this happened that we might not rely on ourselves but on God,[k] who raises the dead. 10He has delivered us from such a deadly peril,[l] and he will deliver us. On him we have set our hope that he will continue to deliver us, 11as you help us by your prayers.[m] Then many will give thanks[n] on our[a] behalf for the gracious favour granted us in answer to the prayers of many.

Paul's Change of Plans

12Now this is our boast: Our conscience[o] testifies that we have conducted ourselves in the world, and especially in our relations with you, in the holiness and sincerity[p] that are from God. We have done so not according to worldly wisdom[q] but according to God's grace. 13For we do not write to you anything you cannot read or understand. And I hope that, 14as you have understood us in part, you will come to understand fully that you can boast of us just as we will boast of you in the day of the Lord Jesus.[r]

15Because I was confident of this, I planned to visit you[s] first so that you might benefit twice.[t] 16I planned to visit you on my way[u] to Macedonia and to come back to you from Macedonia, and then to have you send me on my way to Judea. 17When I planned this, did I do it lightly? Or do I make my plans in a worldly manner[v] so that in the same breath I say, "Yes, yes" and "No, no"?

18But as surely as God is faithful,[w] our message to you is not "Yes" and "No". 19For the Son of God, Jesus Christ, who was preached among you by me and Silas[b] and Timothy, was not "Yes" and "No", but in him it has always[x] been "Yes." 20For no matter how many promises[y] God has made, they are "Yes" in Christ. And so through him the "Amen"[z] is spoken

1:1 a 1Co 1:1; Eph 1:1; Col 1:1; 2Ti 1:1; b 1Co 10:32; c Ac 18:12
1:2 d Ro 1:7
1:3 e Eph 1:3; 1Pe 1:3
1:4 f 2Co 7:6,7,13
1:5 g 2Co 4:10; Col 1:24
1:6 h 2Co 4:15
1:7 i Ro 8:17
1:8 j 1Co 15:32
1:9 k Jer 17:5,7
1:10 l Ro 15:31
1:11 m Ro 15:30; Php 1:19; n 2Co 4:15
1:12 o Ac 23:1; p 2Co 2:17; q 1Co 2:1,4,13
1:14 r 1Co 1:8
1:15 s 1Co 4:19; t Ro 1:11,13; Ro 15:29
1:16 u 1Co 16:5-7
1:17 v 2Co 10:2,3
1:18 w 1Co 1:9
1:19 x Heb 13:8
1:20 y Ro 15:8; z 1Co 14:16

a11 Many manuscripts *your*
b19 Greek *Silvanus*, a variant of *Silas*

by us to the glory of God. 21 Now it is God who makes both us and you stand firm in Christ. He anointed[a] us, 22 set his seal of ownership on us, and put his Spirit in our hearts as a deposit, guaranteeing what is to come.[b]

23 I call God as my witness[c] that it was in order to spare you[d] that I did not return to Corinth. 24 Not that we lord it over[e] your faith, but we work with you for your joy, because it is by faith you stand firm.[f]

2 1 So I made up my mind that I would not make another painful visit to you.[a] 2 For if I grieve you,[b] who is left to make me glad but you whom I have grieved? 3 I wrote as I did[c] so that when I came I should not be distressed[d] by those who ought to make me rejoice. I had confidence[e] in all of you, that you would all share my joy. 4 For I wrote to you[f] out of great distress and anguish of heart and with many tears, not to grieve you but to let you know the depth of my love for you.

Forgiveness for the Sinner

5 If anyone has caused grief,[g] he has not so much grieved me as he has grieved all of you, to some extent—not to put it too severely. 6 The punishment[h] inflicted on him by the majority is sufficient for him. 7 Now instead, you ought to forgive and comfort him,[i] so that he will not be overwhelmed by excessive sorrow. 8 I urge you, therefore, to reaffirm your love for him. 9 The reason I wrote to you was to see if you would stand the test and be obedient in everything.[j] 10 If you forgive anyone, I also forgive him. And what I have forgiven—if there was anything to forgive—I have forgiven in the sight of Christ for your sake, 11 in order that Satan[k] might not outwit us. For we are not unaware of his schemes.[l]

Ministers of the New Covenant

12 Now when I went to Troas[m] to preach the gospel of Christ[n] and found that the Lord had opened a door[o] for me, 13 I still had no peace of mind,[p] because I did not find my brother Titus[q] there. So I said good-bye to them and went on to Macedonia.

14 But thanks be to God,[r] who always leads us in triumphal procession in Christ and through us spreads everywhere the fragrance[s] of the knowledge of him. 15 For we are to God the aroma of Christ among those who are being saved and those who are perishing.[t] 16 To the one we are the smell of death;[u] to the other, the fragrance of life. And who is equal to such a task?[v] 17 Unlike so many, we do not peddle the word of God for profit.[w] On the contrary, in Christ we speak before God with sincerity,[x] like men sent from God.[y]

3 Are we beginning to commend ourselves[a] again? Or do we need, like some people, letters of recommendation[b] to you or from you? 2 You yourselves are our letter, written on our hearts, known and read by everybody.[c] 3 You show that you are a letter from Christ, the result of our ministry, written not with ink but with the Spirit of the living God, not on tablets of stone[d] but on tablets of human hearts.[e]

4 Such confidence[f] as this is ours through Christ before God. 5 Not that we are competent in ourselves to claim anything for ourselves, but our competence comes from God.[g] 6 He has made us competent as ministers of a new covenant[h]—not of the letter but of the Spirit; for the letter kills, but the Spirit gives life.[i]

The Glory of the New Covenant

7 Now if the ministry that brought death, which was engraved in letters on stone, came with glory, so

1:21 a 1Jn 2:20,27
1:22 b 2Co 5:5
1:23 c Ro 1:9; Gal 1:20; d 1Co 4:21; 2Co 2:1,3; 2Co 13:2,10
1:24 e 1Pe 5:3; f Ro 11:20; 1Co 15:1
2:1 a 2Co 1:23
2:2 b 2Co 7:8
2:3 c 2Co 7:8,12; d 2Co 12:21; e 2Co 8:22; Gal 5:10
2:4 f 2Co 7:8,12
2:5 g 1Co 5:1,2
2:6 h 1Co 5:4,5
2:7 i Gal 6:1; Eph 4:32
2:9 j 2Co 10:6
2:11 k Mt 4:10; l Lk 22:31; 2Co 4:4; 1Pe 5:8,9
2:12 m Ac 16:8; n Ro 1:1; o Ac 14:27
2:13 p 2Co 7:5; q 2Co 7:6,13; 2Co 12:18
2:14 r Ro 6:17; s Eph 5:2; Php 4:18
2:15 t 1Co 1:18
2:16 u Lk 2:34; v 2Co 3:5,6
2:17 w 2Co 4:2; x 1Co 5:8; y 2Co 1:12
3:1 a 2Co 5:12; 2Co 12:11; b Ac 18:27
3:2 c 1Co 9:2
3:3 d Ex 24:12; e Pr 3:3; Jer 31:33; Eze 11:19
3:4 f Eph 3:12
3:5 g 1Co 15:10
3:6 h Lk 22:20; i Jn 6:63

that the Israelites could not look steadily at the face of Moses because of its glory,[j] fading though it was, 8 will not the ministry of the Spirit be even more glorious? 9 If the ministry that condemns men[k] is glorious, how much more glorious is the ministry that brings righteousness![l] 10 For what was glorious has no glory now in comparison with the surpassing glory. 11 And if what was fading away came with glory, how much greater is the glory of that which lasts!

12 Therefore, since we have such a hope, we are very bold.[m] 13 We are not like Moses, who would put a veil over his face[n] to keep the Israelites from gazing at it while the radiance was fading away. 14 But their minds were made dull,[o] for to this day the same veil remains when the old covenant[p] is read.[q] It has not been removed, because only in Christ is it taken away. 15 Even to this day when Moses is read, a veil covers their hearts. 16 But whenever anyone turns to the Lord,[r] the veil is taken away.[s] 17 Now the Lord is the Spirit,[t] and where the Spirit of the Lord is, there is freedom.[u] 18 And we, who with unveiled faces all reflect[a][v] the Lord's glory,[w] are being transformed into his likeness[x] with ever-increasing glory, which comes from the Lord, who is the Spirit.

Treasures in Jars of Clay

4 Therefore, since through God's mercy[a] we have this ministry, we do not lose heart. 2 Rather, we have renounced secret and shameful ways;[b] we do not use deception, nor do we distort the word of God.[c] On the contrary, by setting forth the truth plainly we commend ourselves to every man's conscience[d] in the sight of God. 3 And even if our gospel[e] is veiled,[f] it is veiled to those who are perishing.[g] 4 The god[h] of this age has blinded[i] the minds of unbelievers, so that they cannot see the light of the gospel of the glory of Christ, who is the image of God. 5 For we do not preach ourselves,[j] but Jesus Christ as Lord, and ourselves as your servants[k] for Jesus' sake. 6 For God, who said, "Let light shine out of darkness,"[a][l] made his light shine in our hearts[m] to give us the light of the knowledge of the glory of God in the face of Christ.

7 But we have this treasure in jars of clay[n] to show that this all-surpassing power is from God[o] and not from us. 8 We are hard pressed on every side,[p] but not crushed; perplexed, but not in despair; 9 persecuted,[q] but not abandoned;[r] struck down, but not destroyed.[s] 10 We always carry around in our body the death of Jesus, so that the life of Jesus may also be revealed in our body.[t] 11 For we who are alive are always being given over to death for Jesus' sake,[u] so that his life may be revealed in our mortal body. 12 So then, death is at work in us, but life is at work in you.[v]

13 It is written: "I believed; therefore I have spoken."[b][w] With that same spirit of faith we also believe and therefore speak, 14 because we know that the one who raised the Lord Jesus from the dead will also raise us with Jesus[x] and present us with you in his presence.[y] 15 All this is for your benefit, so that the grace that is reaching more and more people may cause thanksgiving[z] to overflow to the glory of God.

16 Therefore we do not lose heart. Though outwardly we are wasting away, yet inwardly[a] we are being renewed[b] day by day. 17 For our light and momentary troubles are achieving for us an eternal glory that far outweighs them all.[c] 18 So

3:7 *j* Ex 34:29-35
3:9 *k* ver 7 *l* Ro 1:17; Ro 3:21,22
3:12 *m* Eph 6:19
3:13 *n* ver 7; Ex 34:33
3:14 *o* Ro 11:7,8 *p* Ac 13:15 *q* ver 6
3:16 *r* Ro 11:23 *s* Ex 34:34
3:17 *t* Isa 61:1,2 *u* Jn 8:32
3:18 *v* 1Co 13:12 *w* 2Co 4:4,6 *x* Ro 8:29
4:1 *a* 1Co 7:25
4:2 *b* 1Co 4:5 *c* 2Co 2:17 *d* 2Co 5:11
4:3 *e* 2Co 2:12 *f* 2Co 3:14 *g* 1Co 1:18
4:4 *h* Jn 12:31 *i* 2Co 3:14
4:5 *j* 1Co 1:13 *k* 1Co 9:19
4:6 *l* Ge 1:3 *m* 2Pe 1:19
4:7 *n* Job 4:19; 2Co 5:1 *o* 1Co 2:5
4:8 *p* 2Co 7:5
4:9 *q* Jn 15:20 *r* Heb 13:5 *s* Ps 37:24
4:10 *t* Ro 6:5
4:11 *u* Ro 8:36
4:12 *v* 2Co 13:9
4:13 *w* Ps 116:10
4:14 *x* 1Th 4:14 *y* Eph 5:27
4:15 *z* 2Co 1:11
4:16 *a* Ro 7:22 *b* Col 3:10
4:17 *c* Ro 8:18; 1Pe 1:6,7

a 18 Or *contemplate* — a 6 Gen. 1:3
b 13 Psalm 116:10

we fix our eyes not on what is seen, but on what is unseen.[d] For what is seen is temporary, but what is unseen is eternal.

Our Heavenly Dwelling

5 Now we know that if the earthly[a] tent[b] we live in is destroyed, we have a building from God, an eternal house in heaven, not built by human hands. 2Meanwhile we groan,[c] longing to be clothed with our heavenly dwelling,[d] 3because when we are clothed, we will not be found naked. 4For while we are in this tent, we groan and are burdened, because we do not wish to be unclothed but to be clothed with our heavenly dwelling,[e] so that what is mortal may be swallowed up by life. 5Now it is God who has made us for this very purpose and has given us the Spirit as a deposit, guaranteeing what is to come.[f]

6Therefore we are always confident and know that as long as we are at home in the body we are away from the Lord. 7We live by faith, not by sight.[g] 8We are confident, I say, and would prefer to be away from the body and at home with the Lord.[h] 9So we make it our goal to please him,[i] whether we are at home in the body or away from it. 10For we must all appear before the judgment seat of Christ, that each one may receive what is due to him[j] for the things done while in the body, whether good or bad.

The Ministry of Reconciliation

11Since, then, we know what it is to fear the Lord,[k] we try to persuade men. What we are is plain to God, and I hope it is also plain to your conscience.[l] 12We are not trying to commend ourselves to you again,[m] but are giving you an opportunity to take pride in us,[n] so that you can answer those who take pride in what is seen rather than in what is in the heart. 13If we are out of our mind,[o] it is for the sake of God; if we are in our right mind, it is for you. 14For Christ's love compels us, because we are convinced that one died for all, and therefore all died.[p] 15And he died for all, that those who live should no longer live for themselves[q] but for him who died for them and was raised again.

16So from now on we regard no-one from a worldly[r] point of view. Though we once regarded Christ in this way, we do so no longer. 17Therefore, if anyone is in Christ, he is a new creation;[s] the old has gone, the new has come![t] 18All this is from God, who reconciled us to himself through Christ[u] and gave us the ministry of reconciliation: 19that God was reconciling the world to himself in Christ, not counting men's sins against them.[v] And he has committed to us the message of reconciliation. 20We are therefore Christ's ambassadors,[w] as though God were making his appeal through us. We implore you on Christ's behalf: Be reconciled to God. 21God made him who had no sin[x] to be sin[a] for us, so that in him we might become the righteousness of God.[y]

6 As God's fellow-workers[a] we urge you not to receive God's grace in vain. 2For he says,

> "In the time of my favour I
> heard you,
> and in the day of salvation I
> helped you."[a][b]

I tell you, now is the time of God's favour, now is the day of salvation.

Paul's Hardships

3We put no stumbling-block in anyone's path,[c] so that our ministry will not be discredited. 4Rather, as servants of God we commend ourselves in every way: in great endurance; in troubles, hardships and

4:18 d Ro 8:24; Heb 11:1
5:1 a 1Co 15:47; b 2Pe 1:13,14
5:2 c ver 4; Ro 8:23; d 1Co 15:53,54
5:4 e 1Co 15:53,54
5:5 f Ro 8:23; 2Co 1:22
5:7 g 1Co 13:12
5:8 h Php 1:23
5:9 i Ro 14:18
5:10 j Mt 16:27; Ro 14:10; Eph 6:8
5:11 k Heb 10:31; Jude 23; l 2Co 4:2
5:12 m 2Co 3:1; n 2Co 1:14
5:13 o 2Co 11:1,16,17
5:14 p Gal 2:20
5:15 q Ro 14:7-9
5:16 r 2Co 11:18
5:17 s Gal 6:15; t Isa 65:17; Rev 21:4,5
5:18 u Ro 5:10; Col 1:20
5:19 v Ro 4:8
5:20 w 2Co 6:1; Eph 6:20
5:21 x Heb 4:15; 1Pe 2:22,24; 1Jn 3:5; y Ro 1:17
6:1 a 1Co 3:9; 2Co 5:20
6:2 b Isa 49:8
6:3 c Ro 14:13,20; 1Co 9:12; 1Co 10:32

a21 Or *be a sin offering* a2 Isaiah 49:8

distresses; **5**in beatings, imprisonments[d] and riots; in hard work, sleepless nights and hunger;[e] **6**in purity, understanding, patience and kindness; in the Holy Spirit[f] and in sincere love; **7**in truthful speech[g] and in the power of God; with weapons of righteousness[h] in the right hand and in the left; **8**through glory and dishonour,[i] bad report and good report; genuine, yet regarded as impostors;[j] **9**known, yet regarded as unknown; dying,[k] and yet we live on;[l] beaten, and yet not killed; **10**sorrowful, yet always rejoicing;[m] poor, yet making many rich;[n] having nothing, and yet possessing everything.[o]

11We have spoken freely to you, Corinthians, and opened wide our hearts to you.[p] **12**We are not withholding our affection from you, but you are withholding yours from us. **13**As a fair exchange—I speak as to my children[q]—open wide your hearts also.

Do Not Be Yoked With Unbelievers

14Do not be yoked together[r] with unbelievers. For what do righteousness and wickedness have in common? Or what fellowship can light have with darkness?[s] **15**What harmony is there between Christ and Belial?[b] What does a believer[t] have in common with an unbeliever? **16**What agreement is there between the temple of God and idols? For we are the temple[u] of the living God. As God has said: "I will live with them and walk among them, and I will be their God, and they will be my people."[c][v]

17"Therefore come out from
them[w]
and be separate,
says the Lord.
Touch no unclean thing,
and I will receive you."[d][x]
18"I will be a Father to you,
and you will be my sons and
daughters,[y]
says the Lord Almighty."[e]

7 Since we have these promises,[a] dear friends, let us purify ourselves from everything that contaminates body and spirit, perfecting holiness out of reverence for God.

Paul's Joy

2Make room for us in your hearts.[b] We have wronged no-one, we have corrupted no-one, we have exploited no-one. **3**I do not say this to condemn you; I have said before that you have such a place in our hearts[c] that we would live or die with you. **4**I have great confidence in you; I take great pride in you. I am greatly encouraged; in all our troubles my joy knows no bounds.[d]

5For when we came into Macedonia,[e] this body of ours had no rest, but we were harassed at every turn[f]—conflicts on the outside, fears within.[g] **6**But God, who comforts the downcast,[h] comforted us by the coming of Titus,[i] **7**and not only by his coming but also by the comfort you had given him. He told us about your longing for me, your deep sorrow, your ardent concern for me, so that my joy was greater than ever.

8Even if I caused you sorrow by my letter,[j] I do not regret it. Though I did regret it—I see that my letter hurt you, but only for a little while—**9**yet now I am happy, not because you were made sorry, but because your sorrow led you to repentance. For you became sorrowful as God intended and so were not harmed in any way by us. **10**Godly sorrow brings repentance that leads to salvation[k] and leaves no regret, but worldly sorrow brings death. **11**See what this godly

6:5 d 2Co 11:23-25; e 1Co 4:11
6:6 f 1Th 1:5
6:7 g 2Co 4:2; h 2Co 10:4; Eph 6:10-18
6:8 i 1Co 4:10; j Mt 27:63
6:9 k Ro 8:36; l 2Co 1:8-10; 2Co 4:10,11
6:10 m 2Co 7:4; n 2Co 8:9; o Ro 8:32; 1Co 3:21
6:11 p 2Co 7:3
6:13 q 1Co 4:14
6:14 r 1Co 5:9,10; s Eph 5:7,11; 1Jn 1:6
6:15 t Ac 5:14
6:16 u 1Co 3:16; v Lev 26:12; Jer 32:38; Eze 37:27
6:17 w Rev 18:4; x Isa 52:11
6:18 y Isa 43:6
7:1 a 2Co 6:17,18
7:2 b 2Co 6:12,13
7:3 c 2Co 6:11,12
7:4 d 2Co 6:10
7:5 e 2Co 2:13; f 2Co 4:8; g Dt 32:25
7:6 h 2Co 1:3,4; i ver 13; 2Co 2:13
7:8 j 2Co 2:2,4
7:10 k Ac 11:18

[b] *15* Greek *Beliar*, a variant of *Belial*
[c] *16* Lev. 26:12; Jer. 32:38; Ezek. 37:27
[d] *17* Isaiah 52:11; Ezek. 20:34,41
[e] *18* 2 Samuel 7:14; 7:8

sorrow has produced in you: what
earnestness, what eagerness to
clear yourselves, what indignation,
what alarm, what longing, what
concern,[l] what readiness to see
justice done. At every point you
have proved yourselves to be innocent in this matter. 12 So even
though I wrote to you,[m] it was not
on account of the one who did the
wrong[n] or of the injured party, but
rather that before God you could
see for yourselves how devoted to
us you are. 13 By all this we are encouraged.

In addition to our own encouragement, we were especially delighted to see how happy Titus[o]
was, because his spirit has been refreshed by all of you. 14 I had
boasted to him about you,[p] and you
have not embarrassed me. But just
as everything we said to you was
true, so our boasting about you to
Titus[q] has proved to be true as
well. 15 And his affection for you is
all the greater when he remembers
that you were all obedient,[r] receiving him with fear and trembling.[s] 16 I am glad I can have
complete confidence in you.[t]

Generosity Encouraged

8 And now, brothers, we want
you to know about the grace
that God has given the Macedo-
nian[a] churches. 2 Out of the most
severe trial, their overflowing joy
and their extreme poverty welled
up in rich generosity. 3 For I testify
that they gave as much as they
were able,[b] and even beyond their
ability. Entirely on their own, 4 they
urgently pleaded with us for the
privilege of sharing in this service[c] to the saints.[d] 5 And they did
not do as we expected, but they
gave themselves first to the Lord
and then to us in keeping with
God's will. 6 So we urged[e] Titus,[f]
since he had earlier made a beginning, to bring also to completion[g]
this act of grace on your part. 7 But
just as you excel in everything[h]—
in faith, in speech, in knowledge,[i]
in complete earnestness and in
your love for us[a]—see that you
also excel in this grace of giving.

8 I am not commanding you,[j] but
I want to test the sincerity of your
love by comparing it with the earnestness of others. 9 For you know
the grace of our Lord Jesus
Christ,[k] that though he was rich,
yet for your sakes he became
poor,[l] so that you through his poverty might become rich.

10 And here is my advice[m] about
what is best for you in this matter:
Last year you were the first not
only to give but also to have the desire to do so.[n] 11 Now finish the
work, so that your eager willing-
ness[o] to do it may be matched by
your completion of it, according to
your means. 12 For if the willing-
ness is there, the gift is acceptable
according to what one has,[p] not according to what he does not have.

13 Our desire is not that others
might be relieved while you are
hard pressed, but that there might
be equality. 14 At the present time
your plenty will supply what they
need,[q] so that in turn their plenty
will supply what you need. Then
there will be equality, 15 as it is written: "He who gathered much did
not have too much, and he who
gathered little did not have too
little."[b][r]

Titus Sent to Corinth

16 I thank God,[s] who put into the
heart[t] of Titus[u] the same concern
I have for you. 17 For Titus not only
welcomed our appeal, but he is
coming to you with much enthusiasm and on his own initiative.[v]
18 And we are sending along with
him the brother[w] who is praised by
all the churches[x] for his service to
the gospel.[y] 19 What is more, he
was chosen by the churches to

[a]7 Some manuscripts *in our love for you*
[b]15 Exodus 16:18

7:11 *l* ver 7
7:12 *m* ver 8; 2Co 2:3,9 *n* 1Co 5:1,2
7:13 *o* ver 6; 2Co 2:13
7:14 *p* ver 4 *q* ver 6
7:15 *r* 2Co 2:9 *s* Php 2:12
7:16 *t* 2Co 2:3
8:1 *a* Ac 16:9
8:3 *b* 1Co 16:2
8:4 *c* Ac 24:17 *d* Ro 15:25; 2Co 9:1
8:6 *e* ver 17; 2Co 12:18 *f* ver 16,23 *g* ver 10,11
8:7 *h* 2Co 9:8 *i* 1Co 1:5
8:8 *j* 1Co 7:6
8:9 *k* 2Co 13:14 *l* Mt 20:28; Php 2:6-8
8:10 *m* 1Co 7:25,40 *n* 1Co 16:2,3; 2Co 9:2
8:11 *o* 2Co 9:2
8:12 *p* Mk 12:43,44; Lk 21:3
8:14 *q* 2Co 9:12
8:15 *r* Ex 16:18
8:16 *s* 2Co 2:14 *t* Rev 17:17 *u* 2Co 2:13
8:17 *v* ver 6
8:18 *w* 2Co 12:18 *x* 1Co 7:17 *y* 2Co 2:12

accompany us[z] as we carry the offering, which we administer in order to honour the Lord himself and to show our eagerness to help.[a] 20We want to avoid any criticism of the way we administer this liberal gift. 21For we are taking pains to do what is right, not only in the eyes of the Lord but also in the eyes of men.[b]

22In addition, we are sending with them our brother who has often proved to us in many ways that he is zealous, and now even more so because of his great confidence in you. 23As for Titus, he is my partner[c] and fellow-worker[d] among you; as for our brothers,[e] they are representatives of the churches and an honour to Christ. 24Therefore show these men the proof of your love and the reason for our pride in you,[f] so that the churches can see it.

9 There is no need[a] for me to write to you about this service to the saints.[b] 2For I know your eagerness to help, and I have been boasting[c] about it to the Macedonians, telling them that since last year[d] you in Achaia[e] were ready to give; and your enthusiasm has stirred most of them to action. 3But I am sending the brothers in order that our boasting about you in this matter should not prove hollow, but that you may be ready, as I said you would be.[f] 4For if any Macedonians[g] come with me and find you unprepared, we—not to say anything about you—would be ashamed of having been so confident. 5So I thought it necessary to urge the brothers to visit you in advance and finish the arrangements for the generous gift you had promised. Then it will be ready as a generous gift,[h] not as one grudgingly given.[i]

Sowing Generously

6Remember this: Whoever sows sparingly will also reap sparingly, and whoever sows generously will also reap generously.[j] 7Each man should give what he has decided in his heart to give,[k] not reluctantly or under compulsion,[l] for God loves a cheerful giver.[m] 8And God is able[n] to make all grace abound to you, so that in all things at all times, having all that you need,[o] you will abound in every good work. 9As it is written:

> "He has scattered abroad his
> gifts to the poor;
> his righteousness endures for
> ever."[a][p]

10Now he who supplies seed to the sower and bread for food[q] will also supply and increase your store of seed and will enlarge the harvest of your righteousness.[r] 11You will be made rich[s] in every way so that you can be generous on every occasion, and through us your generosity will result in thanksgiving to God.[t]

12This service that you perform is not only supplying the needs[u] of God's people but is also overflowing in many expressions of thanks to God.[v] 13Because of the service[w] by which you have proved yourselves, men will praise God[x] for the obedience that accompanies your confession of the gospel of Christ,[y] and for your generosity in sharing with them and with everyone else. 14And in their prayers for you their hearts will go out to you, because of the surpassing grace God has given you. 15Thanks be to God[z] for his indescribable gift![a]

Paul's Defence of His Ministry

10 By the meekness and gentleness[a] of Christ, I appeal to you—I, Paul,[b] who am "timid" when face to face with you, but "bold" when away! 2I beg you that when I come I may not have to be as bold[c] as I expect to be towards

8:19 z 1Co 16:3,4 a ver 11,12
8:21 b Ro 12:17 Ro 14:18
8:23 c Phm 17 d Php 2:25 e ver 18,22
8:24 f 2Co 7:4,14 2Co 9:2
9:1 a 1Th 4:9 b 2Co 8:4
9:2 c 2Co 7:4,14 d 2Co 8:10 e Ac 18:12
9:3 f 1Co 16:2
9:4 g Ro 15:26
9:5 h Php 4:17 i 2Co 12:17,18
9:6 j Pr 11:24,25 Pr 22:9 Gal 6:7,9
9:7 k Ex 25:2 2Co 8:12 l Dt 15:10 m Ro 12:8
9:8 n Eph 3:20 o Php 4:19
9:9 p Ps 112:9
9:10 q Isa 55:10 r Hos 10:12
9:11 s 1Co 1:5 t 2Co 1:11
9:12 u 2Co 8:14 v 2Co 1:11
9:13 w 2Co 8:4 x Mt 9:8 y 2Co 2:12
9:15 z 2Co 2:14 a Ro 5:15,16
10:1 a Mt 11:29 b Gal 5:2
10:2 c 1Co 4:21 2Co 13:2,10

a9 Psalm 112:9

some people who think that we live by the standards of this world. 3 For though we live in the world, we do not wage war as the world does. 4 The weapons we fight with[d] are not the weapons of the world. On the contrary, they have divine power[e] to demolish strongholds.[f] 5 We demolish arguments and every pretension that sets itself up against the knowledge of God,[g] and we take captive every thought to make it obedient[h] to Christ. 6 And we will be ready to punish every act of disobedience, once your obedience is complete.[i]

7 You are looking only on the surface of things.[a][j] If anyone is confident that he belongs to Christ,[k] he should consider again that we belong to Christ just as much as he.[l] 8 For even if I boast somewhat freely about the authority the Lord gave us for building you up rather than pulling you down,[m] I will not be ashamed of it. 9 I do not want to seem to be trying to frighten you with my letters. 10 For some say, "His letters are weighty and forceful, but in person he is unimpressive[n] and his speaking amounts to nothing."[o] 11 Such people should realise that what we are in our letters when we are absent, we will be in our actions when we are present.

12 We do not dare to classify or compare ourselves with some who commend themselves.[p] When they measure themselves by themselves and compare themselves with themselves, they are not wise. 13 We, however, will not boast beyond proper limits, but will confine our boasting to the field God has assigned to us,[q] a field that reaches even to you. 14 We are not going too far in our boasting, as would be the case if we had not come to you, for we did get as far as you[r] with the gospel of Christ.[s] 15 Neither do we go beyond our limits by boasting of work done by others.[b][t] Our hope is that, as your faith continues to grow,[u] our area of activity among you will greatly expand, 16 so that we can preach the gospel in the regions beyond you.[v] For we do not want to boast about work already done in another man's territory. 17 But, "Let him who boasts boast in the Lord."[c][w] 18 For it is not the one who commends himself[x] who is approved, but the one whom the Lord commends.[y]

Paul and the False Apostles

11 I hope you will put up with[a] a little of my foolishness;[b] but you are already doing that. 2 I am jealous for you with a godly jealousy. I promised you to one husband,[c] to Christ, so that I might present you[d] as a pure virgin to him. 3 But I am afraid that just as Eve was deceived by the serpent's cunning,[e] your minds may somehow be led astray from your sincere and pure devotion to Christ. 4 For if someone comes to you and preaches a Jesus other than the Jesus we preached,[f] or if you receive a different spirit[g] from the one you received, or a different gospel[h] from the one you accepted, you put up with it easily enough. 5 But I do not think I am in the least inferior to those "super-apostles".[i] 6 I may not be a trained speaker,[j] but I do have knowledge.[k] We have made this perfectly clear to you in every way.

7 Was it a sin[l] for me to lower myself in order to elevate you by preaching the gospel of God to you free of charge?[m] 8 I robbed other churches by receiving support from them[n] so as to serve you. 9 And when I was with you and needed something, I was not a burden to anyone, for the brothers who

10:4 d 2Co 6:7 e 1Co 2:5 f Jer 1:10 2Co 13:10
10:5 g Isa 2:11,12 1Co 1:19 h 2Co 9:13
10:6 i 2Co 2:9 2Co 7:15
10:7 j Jn 7:24 k 1Co 1:12 1Co 3:23 1Co 14:37 l 2Co 11:23
10:8 m 2Co 13:10
10:10 n 1Co 2:3 Gal 4:13,14 o 1Co 1:17
10:12 p 2Co 3:1
10:13 q ver 15,16
10:14 r 1Co 3:6 s 2Co 2:12
10:15 t Ro 15:20 u 2Th 1:3
10:16 v Ac 19:21
10:17 w Jer 9:24 1Co 1:31
10:18 x ver 12 y Ro 2:29 1Co 4:5
11:1 a ver 4,19,20 Mt 17:17 b ver 16,17,21 2Co 5:13
11:2 c Hos 2:19 Eph 5:26,27 d 2Co 4:14
11:3 e Ge 3:1-6,13 Jn 8:44 1Ti 2:14 Rev 12:9
11:4 f 1Co 3:11 g Ro 8:15 h Gal 1:6-9
11:5 i 2Co 12:11 Gal 2:6
11:6 j 1Co 1:17 k Eph 3:4
11:7 l 2Co 12:13 m 1Co 9:18
11:8 n Php 4:15,18

a7 Or *Look at the obvious facts*
b13–15 Or 13*We, however, will not boast about things that cannot be measured, but we will boast according to the standard of measurement that the God of measure has assigned us—a measurement that relates even to you.* 14*. . . ,* 15*Neither do we boast about things that cannot be measured in regard to the work done by others.*
c17 Jer. 9:24

came from Macedonia supplied
what I needed. I have kept myself
from being a burden to you[o] in any
way, and will continue to do so. [10]As
surely as the truth of Christ is in
me,[p] nobody in the regions of
Achaia[q] will stop this boasting[r] of
mine. [11]Why? Because I do not love
you? God knows I do![s] [12]And I will
keep on doing what I am doing in
order to cut the ground from under
those who want an opportunity to
be considered equal with us in the
things they boast about.
[13]For such men are false
apostles,[t] deceitful[u] workmen, mas-
querading as apostles of Christ.[v]
[14]And no wonder, for Satan
himself masquerades as an angel
of light. [15]It is not surprising, then,
if his servants masquerade as servants of righteousness. Their
end will be what their actions deserve.[w]

Paul Boasts About His Sufferings

[16]I repeat: Let no-one take me for
a fool.[x] But if you do, then receive
me just as you would a fool, so that
I may do a little boasting. [17]In this
self-confident boasting I am not
talking as the Lord would,[y] but as
a fool. [18]Since many are boasting in
the way the world does, I too will
boast.[z] [19]You gladly put up with
fools since you are so wise![a] [20]In
fact, you even put up with anyone
who enslaves you[b] or exploits you
or takes advantage of you or
pushes himself forward or slaps
you in the face. [21]To my shame I admit that we were too weak[c] for
that!
What anyone else dares to boast
about—I am speaking as a fool—I
also dare to boast about.[d] [22]Are
they Hebrews? So am I.[e] Are they
Israelites? So am I.[f] Are they
Abraham's descendants? So am I.
[23]Are they servants of Christ? (I am
out of my mind to talk like this.) I
am more. I have worked much
harder,[g] been in prison more frequently,[h] been flogged more severely, and been exposed to death
again and again. [24]Five times I received from the Jews the forty
lashes[i] minus one. [25]Three times I
was beaten with rods,[j] once I was
stoned,[k] three times I was shipwrecked, I spent a night and a day
in the open sea, [26]I have been constantly on the move. I have been in
danger from rivers, in danger from
bandits, in danger from my own
countrymen,[l] in danger from Gentiles; in danger in the city,[m] in
danger in the country, in danger at
sea; and in danger from false
brothers.[n] [27]I have laboured and
toiled and have often gone without
sleep; I have known hunger and
thirst and have often gone without
food;[o] I have been cold and naked.
[28]Besides everything else, I face
daily the pressure of my concern
for all the churches. [29]Who is weak,
and I do not feel weak? Who is led
into sin, and I do not inwardly
burn?
[30]If I must boast, I will boast of
the things that show my weakness.[p] [31]The God and Father of the
Lord Jesus, who is to be praised for
ever,[q] knows that I am not lying.
[32]In Damascus the governor under
King Aretas had the city of the
Damascenes guarded in order to
arrest me.[r] [33]But I was lowered in
a basket from a window in the wall
and slipped through his hands.[s]

Paul's Vision and His Thorn

12 I must go on boasting.[a] Although there is nothing to
be gained, I will go on to visions and
revelations[b] from the Lord. [2]I
know a man in Christ who fourteen
years ago was caught up[c] to the
third heaven.[d] Whether it was in
the body or out of the body I do not
know—God knows.[e] [3]And I know
that this man—whether in the body
or apart from the body I do not
know, but God knows—[4]was

11:9 o 2Co 12:13,14,16
11:10 p Ro 9:1 q Ac 18:12 r 1Co 9:15
11:11 s 2Co 12:15
11:13 t 2Pe 2:1 u Tit 1:10 v Rev 2:2
11:15 w Php 3:19
11:16 x ver 1
11:17 y 1Co 7:12,25
11:18 z Php 3:3,4
11:19 a 1Co 4:10
11:20 b Gal 2:4
11:21 c 2Co 10:1,10 d Php 3:4
11:22 e Php 3:5 f Ro 9:4
11:23 g 1Co 15:10 h Ac 16:23 2Co 6:4,5
11:24 i Dt 25:3
11:25 j Ac 16:22 k Ac 14:19
11:26 l Ac 9:23 Ac 14:5 m Ac 21:31 n Gal 2:4
11:27 o 1Co 4:11,12 2Co 6:5
11:30 p 1Co 2:3
11:31 q Ro 9:5
11:32 r Ac 9:24
11:33 s Ac 9:25
12:1 a 2Co 11:16,30 b ver 7
12:2 c Ac 8:39 d Eph 4:10 e 2Co 11:11

caught up to paradise.[f] He heard inexpressible things, things that man is not permitted to tell. 5 I will boast about a man like that, but I will not boast about myself, except about my weaknesses. 6 Even if I should choose to boast, I would not be a fool,[g] because I would be speaking the truth. But I refrain, so no-one will think more of me than is warranted by what I do or say.

7 To keep me from becoming conceited because of these surpassingly great revelations, there was given me a thorn in my flesh,[h] a messenger of Satan, to torment me. 8 Three times I pleaded with the Lord to take it away from me.[i] 9 But he said to me, "My grace is sufficient for you, for my power[j] is made perfect in weakness." Therefore I will boast all the more gladly about my weaknesses, so that Christ's power may rest on me. 10 That is why, for Christ's sake, I delight in weaknesses, in insults, in hardships,[k] in persecutions,[l] in difficulties. For when I am weak, then I am strong.[m]

Paul's Concern for the Corinthians

11 I have made a fool of myself,[n] but you drove me to it. I ought to have been commended by you, for I am not in the least inferior to the "super-apostles",[o] even though I am nothing.[p] 12 The things that mark an apostle—signs, wonders and miracles[q]—were done among you with great perseverance. 13 How were you inferior to the other churches, except that I was never a burden to you?[r] Forgive me this wrong![s]

14 Now I am ready to visit you for the third time,[t] and I will not be a burden to you, because what I want is not your possessions but you. After all, children should not have to save up for their parents,[u] but parents for their children.[v] 15 So I will very gladly spend for you everything I have and expend myself as well.[w] If I love you more, will you love me less? 16 Be that as it may, I have not been a burden to you.[x] Yet, crafty fellow that I am, I caught you by trickery! 17 Did I exploit you through any of the men I sent you? 18 I urged[y] Titus to go to you and I sent our brother[z] with him. Titus did not exploit you, did he? Did we not act in the same spirit and follow the same course?

19 Have you been thinking all along that we have been defending ourselves to you? We have been speaking in the sight of God[a] as those in Christ; and everything we do, dear friends, is for your strengthening.[b] 20 For I am afraid that when I come[c] I may not find you as I want you to be, and you may not find me as you want me to be.[d] I fear that there may be quarrelling,[e] jealousy, outbursts of anger, factions,[f] slander, gossip,[g] arrogance and disorder.[h] 21 I am afraid that when I come again my God will humble me before you, and I will be grieved[i] over many who have sinned earlier[j] and have not repented of the impurity, sexual sin and debauchery in which they have indulged.

Final Warnings

13 This will be my third visit to you.[a] "Every matter must be established by the testimony of two or three witnesses."[a][b] 2 I already gave you a warning when I was with you the second time. I now repeat it while absent: On my return I will not spare[c] those who sinned earlier[d] or any of the others, 3 since you are demanding proof that Christ is speaking through me.[e] He is not weak in dealing with you, but is powerful among you. 4 For to be sure, he was crucified in weakness,[f] yet he lives by God's

12:4 f Lk 23:43; Rev 2:7
12:6 g 2Co 11:16
12:7 h Nu 33:55
12:8 i Mt 26:39,44
12:9 j Php 4:13
12:10 k 2Co 6:4; l Ro 5:3; 2Th 1:4; m 2Co 13:4
12:11 n 2Co 11:1; o 2Co 11:5; p 1Co 15:9,10
12:12 q Jn 4:48
12:13 r 1Co 9:12,18; s 2Co 11:7
12:14 t 2Co 13:1; u 1Co 4:14,15; v Pr 19:14
12:15 w Php 2:17; 1Th 2:8
12:16 x 2Co 11:9
12:18 y 2Co 8:6,16; z 2Co 8:18
12:19 a Ro 9:1; b 2Co 10:8
12:20 c 2Co 2:1-4; d 1Co 4:21; e 1Co 1:11; 1Co 3:3; f Gal 5:20; g Ro 1:29; h 1Co 14:33
12:21 i 2Co 2:1,4; j 2Co 13:2
13:1 a 2Co 12:14; b Dt 19:15; Mt 18:16
13:2 c 2Co 1:23; d 2Co 12:21
13:3 e Mt 10:20; 1Co 5:4
13:4 f Php 2:7,8; 1Pe 3:18

a1 Deut. 19:15

power.[g] Likewise, we are weak[h]
in him, yet by God's power we will
live with him to serve you.
5Examine yourselves[i] to see
whether you are in the faith; test
yourselves.[j] Do you not realise
that Christ Jesus is in you[k]—unless, of course, you fail the test?
6And I trust that you will discover
that we have not failed the test.
7Now we pray to God that you will
not do anything wrong. Not that
people will see that we have stood
the test but that you will do what is
right even though we may seem to
have failed. 8For we cannot do anything against the truth, but only for
the truth. 9We are glad whenever
we are weak but you are strong;
and our prayer is for your perfection.[l] 10This is why I write these
things when I am absent, that when
I come I may not have to be harsh
in my use of authority—the
authority the Lord gave me for
building you up, not for tearing
you down.[m]

Final Greetings

11Finally, brothers,[n] good-bye.
Aim for perfection, listen to my appeal, be of one mind, live in peace.[o]
And the God of love and peace[p]
will be with you.
12Greet one another with a holy
kiss.[q] 13All the saints send their
greetings.[r]
14May the grace of the Lord Jesus
Christ,[s] and the love of God,[t] and
the fellowship of the Holy Spirit[u]
be with you all.

13:4
g Ro 1:4; Ro 6:4
h ver 9
13:5
i 1Co 11:28
j Jn 6:6
k Ro 8:10
13:9
l ver 11
13:10
m 2Co 10:8
13:11
n 1Th 4:1; 2Th 3:1
o Mk 9:50
p Ro 15:33; Eph 6:23
13:12
q Ro 16:16
13:13
r Php 4:22
13:14
s Ro 16:20; 2Co 8:9
t Ro 5:5; Jude 21
u Php 2:1

GALATIANS

1 Paul, an apostle—sent not
from men nor by man, but by
Jesus Christ[a] and God the Father,
who raised him from the dead[b]—
2and all the brothers with me,[c]

To the churches in Galatia:[d]

3Grace and peace to you from
God our Father and the Lord Jesus
Christ,[e] 4who gave himself for our
sins[f] to rescue us from the present
evil age, according to the will of
our God and Father,[g] 5to whom be
glory for ever and ever. Amen.[h]

No Other Gospel

6I am astonished that you are so
quickly deserting the one who
called[i] you by the grace of Christ
and are turning to a different gospel[j]—7which is really no gospel at
all. Evidently some people are
throwing you into confusion[k] and
are trying to pervert the gospel of
Christ. 8But even if we or an angel
from heaven should preach a gospel other than the one we preached
to you,[l] let him be eternally condemned![m] 9As we have already
said, so now I say again: If anybody
is preaching to you a gospel other
than what you accepted,[n] let him
be eternally condemned!

10Am I now trying to win the approval of men, or of God? Or am I
trying to please men?[o] If I were
still trying to please men, I would
not be a servant of Christ.

Paul Called by God

11I want you to know, brothers,[p]
that the gospel I preached is not
something that man made up. 12I
did not receive it from any man,[q]
nor was I taught it; rather, I received it by revelation[r] from
Jesus Christ.

1:1 [a] Ac 9:15 [b] Ac 2:24
1:2 [c] Php 4:21 [d] Ac 16:6; 1Co 16:1
1:3 [e] Ro 1:7
1:4 [f] Mt 20:28; Ro 4:25; Gal 2:20 [g] Php 4:20
1:5 [h] Ro 11:36
1:6 [i] Gal 5:8 [j] 2Co 11:4
1:7 [k] Ac 15:24; Gal 5:10
1:8 [l] 2Co 11:4 [m] Ro 9:3
1:9 [n] Ro 16:17
1:10 [o] Ro 2:29; 1Th 2:4
1:11 [p] 1Co 15:1
1:12 [q] ver 1 [r] ver 16
1:13 [s] Ac 26:4,5 [t] Ac 8:3
1:14 [u] Mt 15:2
1:15 [v] Isa 49:1,5; Jer 1:5 [w] Ac 9:15
1:16 [x] Gal 2:9 [y] Mt 16:17
1:18 [z] Ac 9:22,23 [a] Ac 9:26,27
1:19 [b] Mt 13:55
1:20 [c] Ro 9:1
1:21 [d] Ac 6:9
1:22 [e] 1Th 2:14
1:23 [f] Ac 6:7
1:24 [g] Mt 9:8
2:1 [a] Ac 15:2
2:2 [b] Ac 15:4,12

13For you have heard of my previous way of life in Judaism,[s] how
intensely I persecuted the church
of God and tried to destroy it.[t] 14I
was advancing in Judaism beyond
many Jews of my own age and was
extremely zealous for the traditions of my fathers.[u] 15But when
God, who set me apart from
birth[a][v] and called me[w] by his
grace, was pleased 16to reveal his
Son in me so that I might preach
him among the Gentiles,[x] I did not
consult any man,[y] 17nor did I go up
to Jerusalem to see those who were
apostles before I was, but I went
immediately into Arabia and later
returned to Damascus.

18Then after three years,[z] I went
up to Jerusalem[a] to get acquainted
with Peter[b] and stayed with him
fifteen days. 19I saw none of the
other apostles—only James,[b] the
Lord's brother. 20I assure you before God that what I am writing to
you is no lie.[c] 21Later I went to
Syria and Cilicia.[d] 22I was personally unknown to the churches of Judea[e] that are in Christ. 23They only
heard the report: "The man who
formerly persecuted us is now
preaching the faith[f] he once tried
to destroy." 24And they praised
God[g] because of me.

Paul Accepted by the Apostles

2 Fourteen years later I went up
again to Jerusalem,[a] this time
with Barnabas. I took Titus along
also. 2I went in response to a revelation and set before them the gospel that I preach among the
Gentiles.[b] But I did this privately
to those who seemed to be leaders,
for fear that I was running or had

[a]15 Or *from my mother's womb* [b]18 Greek *Cephas*

run my race[c] in vain. 3 Yet not even Titus,[d] who was with me, was compelled to be circumcised, even though he was a Greek.[e] 4 ⌞This matter arose⌟ because some false brothers[f] had infiltrated our ranks to spy on[g] the freedom[h] we have in Christ Jesus and to make us slaves. 5 We did not give in to them for a moment, so that the truth of the gospel[i] might remain with you.

6 As for those who seemed to be important[j]—whatever they were makes no difference to me; God does not judge by external appearance[k]—those men added nothing to my message. 7 On the contrary, they saw that I had been entrusted with the task[l] of preaching the gospel to the Gentiles,[a][m] just as Peter[n] had been to the Jews.[b] 8 For God, who was at work in the ministry of Peter as an apostle[o] to the Jews, was also at work in my ministry as an apostle to the Gentiles. 9 James, Peter[c][p] and John, those reputed to be pillars,[q] gave me and Barnabas[r] the right hand of fellowship when they recognised the grace given to me.[s] They agreed that we should go to the Gentiles, and they to the Jews. 10 All they asked was that we should continue to remember the poor,[t] the very thing I was eager to do.

Paul Opposes Peter

11 When Peter[u] came to Antioch,[v] I opposed him to his face, because he was clearly in the wrong. 12 Before certain men came from James, he used to eat with the Gentiles.[w] But when they arrived, he began to draw back and separate himself from the Gentiles because he was afraid of those who belonged to the circumcision group.[x] 13 The other Jews joined him in his hypocrisy, so that by their hypocrisy even Barnabas[y] was led astray.

14 When I saw that they were not acting in line with the truth of the gospel,[z] I said to Peter[a] in front of them all, "You are a Jew, yet you live like a Gentile and not like a Jew.[b] How is it, then, that you force Gentiles to follow Jewish customs?

15 "We who are Jews by birth[c] and not 'Gentile sinners'[d] 16 know that a man is not justified by observing the law, but by faith in Jesus Christ.[e] So we, too, have put our faith in Christ Jesus that we may be justified by faith in Christ and not by observing the law, because by observing the law no-one will be justified.

17 "If, while we seek to be justified in Christ, it becomes evident that we ourselves are sinners,[f] does that mean that Christ promotes sin? Absolutely not![g] 18 If I rebuild what I destroyed, I prove that I am a law-breaker. 19 For through the law I died to the law[h] so that I might live for God.[i] 20 I have been crucified with Christ[j] and I no longer live, but Christ lives in me.[k] The life I live in the body, I live by faith in the Son of God,[l] who loved me[m] and gave himself for me.[n] 21 I do not set aside the grace of God, for if righteousness could be gained through the law,[o] Christ died for nothing!"[d]

Faith or Observance of the Law

3 You foolish Galatians! Who has bewitched you?[a] Before your very eyes Jesus Christ was clearly portrayed as crucified.[b] 2 I would like to learn just one thing from you: Did you receive the Spirit by observing the law, or by believing what you heard?[c] 3 Are you so foolish? After beginning with the Spirit, are you now trying to attain your goal by human effort? 4 Have you suffered so much

2:2 c 1Co 9:24; Php 2:16
2:3 d 2Co 2:13; e Ac 16:3; 1Co 9:21
2:4 f 2Co 11:26; g Jude 4; h Ac 15:1; Gal 5:1,13
2:5 i ver 14
2:6 j Gal 6:3; k Ac 10:34
2:7 l 1Th 2:4; 1Ti 1:11; m Ac 9:15; n ver 9,11,14
2:8 o Ac 1:25
2:9 p ver 7,11,14; q 1Ti 3:15; r Ac 4:36; s Ro 12:3
2:10 t Ac 24:17
2:11 u ver 7,9,14; v Ac 11:19
2:12 w Ac 11:3; x Ac 11:2
2:13 y ver 1; Ac 4:36
2:14 z ver 5; a ver 7,9,11; b Ac 10:28
2:15 c Php 3:4,5; d 1Sa 15:18
2:16 e Ac 13:39; Ro 9:30
2:17 f ver 15; g Gal 3:21
2:19 h Ro 7:4; i Ro 6:10,11,14; 2Co 5:15
2:20 j Ro 6:6; k 1Pe 4:2; l Mt 4:3; m Ro 8:37; n Gal 1:4
2:21 o Gal 3:21
3:1 a Gal 5:7; b 1Co 1:23
3:2 c Ro 10:17

a7 Greek *uncircumcised* b7 Greek *circumcised*; also in verses 8 and 9 c9 Greek *Cephas*; also in verses 11 and 14 d21 Some interpreters end the quotation after verse 14.

for nothing—if it really was for nothing? 5 Does God give you his Spirit and work miracles[d] among you because you observe the law, or because you believe what you heard?

6 Consider Abraham: "He believed God, and it was credited to him as righteousness."[a][e] 7 Understand, then, that those who believe[f] are children of Abraham. 8 The Scripture foresaw that God would justify the Gentiles by faith, and announced the gospel in advance to Abraham: "All nations will be blessed through you."[b][g] 9 So those who have faith[h] are blessed along with Abraham, the man of faith.

10 All who rely on observing the law are under a curse, for it is written: "Cursed is everyone who does not continue to do everything written in the Book of the Law."[c][i] 11 Clearly no-one is justified before God by the law, because, "The righteous will live by faith."[d][j] 12 The law is not based on faith; on the contrary, "The man who does these things will live by them."[e][k] 13 Christ redeemed us from the curse of the law[l] by becoming a curse for us, for it is written: "Cursed is everyone who is hung on a tree."[f][m] 14 He redeemed us in order that the blessing given to Abraham might come to the Gentiles through Christ Jesus,[n] so that by faith we might receive the promise of the Spirit.[o]

The Law and the Promise

15 Brothers, let me take an example from everyday life. Just as no-one can set aside or add to a human covenant that has been duly established, so it is in this case. 16 The promises were spoken to Abraham and to his seed.[p] The Scripture does not say "and to seeds", meaning many people, but "and to your seed",[g] meaning one person, who is Christ. 17 What I mean is this: The law, introduced 430 years[q] later, does not set aside the covenant previously established by God and thus do away with the promise. 18 For if the inheritance depends on the law, then it no longer depends on a promise;[r] but God in his grace gave it to Abraham through a promise.

19 What, then, was the purpose of the law? It was added because of transgressions[s] until the Seed[t] to whom the promise referred had come. The law was put into effect through angels[u] by a mediator.[v] 20 A mediator,[w] however, does not represent just one party; but God is one.

21 Is the law, therefore, opposed to the promises of God? Absolutely not![x] For if a law had been given that could impart life, then righteousness would certainly have come by the law.[y] 22 But the Scripture declares that the whole world is a prisoner of sin,[z] so that what was promised, being given through faith in Jesus Christ, might be given to those who believe.

23 Before this faith came, we were held prisoners[a] by the law, locked up until faith should be revealed. 24 So the law was put in charge to lead us to Christ[h][b] that we might be justified by faith.[c] 25 Now that faith has come, we are no longer under the supervision of the law.

Sons of God

26 You are all sons of God[d] through faith in Christ Jesus, 27 for all of you who were baptised into Christ[e] have clothed yourselves with Christ.[f] 28 There is neither Jew nor Greek, slave nor free,[g] male nor female, for you are all one in Christ Jesus.[h] 29 If you belong to Christ,[i] then you are Abraham's

3:5 d 1Co 12:10
3:6 e Ge 15:6; Ro 4:3
3:7 f ver 9
3:8 g Ge 12:3; Ac 3:25
3:9 h ver 7; Ro 4:16
3:10 i Dt 27:26; Jer 11:3
3:11 j Hab 2:4; Gal 2:16; Heb 10:38
3:12 k Lev 18:5; Ro 10:5
3:13 l Gal 4:5; m Dt 21:23; Ac 5:30
3:14 n Ro 4:9,16; o ver 2; Joel 2:28; Ac 2:33
3:16 p Lk 1:55; Ro 4:13,16
3:17 q Ge 15:13,14; Ex 12:40
3:18 r Ro 4:14
3:19 s Ro 5:20; t ver 16; u Ac 7:53; v Ex 20:19
3:20 w Heb 8:6; Heb 9:15; Heb 12:24
3:21 x Gal 2:17; y Gal 2:21
3:22 z Ro 3:9-19; Ro 11:32
3:23 a Ro 11:32
3:24 b Ro 10:4; c Gal 2:16
3:26 d Ro 8:14
3:27 e Mt 28:19; Ro 6:3; f Ro 13:14
3:28 g Col 3:11; h Jn 10:16; Jn 17:11; Eph 2:14,15
3:29 i 1Co 3:23

a *6* Gen. 15:6 b *8* Gen. 12:3; 18:18; 22:18
c *10* Deut. 27:26 d *11* Hab. 2:4 e *12* Lev. 18:5
f *13* Deut. 21:23 g *16* Gen. 12:7; 13:15; 24:7
h *24* Or *charge until Christ came*

seed, and heirs according to the promise.[j]

4 What I am saying is that as long as the heir is a child, he is no different from a slave, although he owns the whole estate. 2He is subject to guardians and trustees until the time set by his father. 3So also, when we were children, we were in slavery[a] under the basic principles of the world.[b] 4But when the time had fully come,[c] God sent his Son, born of a woman,[d] born under law,[e] 5to redeem those under law, that we might receive the full rights[f] of sons. 6Because you are sons, God sent the Spirit of his Son into our hearts,[g] the Spirit who calls out, *"Abba*,[a] Father."[h] 7So you are no longer a slave, but a son; and since you are a son, God has made you also an heir.[i]

Paul's Concern for the Galatians

8Formerly, when you did not know God,[j] you were slaves to those who by nature are not gods.[k] 9But now that you know God—or rather are known by God[l]—how is it that you are turning back to those weak and miserable principles? Do you wish to be enslaved[m] by them all over again?[n] 10You are observing special days and months and seasons and years![o] 11I fear for you, that somehow I have wasted my efforts on you.[p]

12I plead with you, brothers,[q] become like me, for I became like you. You have done me no wrong. 13As you know, it was because of an illness[r] that I first preached the gospel to you. 14Even though my illness was a trial to you, you did not treat me with contempt or scorn. Instead, you welcomed me as if I were an angel of God, as if I were Christ Jesus himself.[s] 15What has happened to all your joy? I can testify that, if you could have done so, you would have torn out your eyes and given them to me. 16Have I now become your enemy by telling you the truth?[t]

17Those people are zealous to win you over, but for no good. What they want is to alienate you ⌊from us⌋, so that you may be zealous for them. 18It is fine to be zealous, provided the purpose is good, and to be so always and not just when I am with you.[u] 19My dear children,[v] for whom I am again in the pains of childbirth until Christ is formed in you,[w] 20how I wish I could be with you now and change my tone, because I am perplexed about you!

Hagar and Sarah

21Tell me, you who want to be under the law, are you not aware of what the law says? 22For it is written that Abraham had two sons, one by the slave woman[x] and the other by the free woman.[y] 23His son by the slave woman was born in the ordinary way;[z] but his son by the free woman was born as the result of a promise.[a]

24These things may be taken figuratively, for the women represent two covenants. One covenant is from Mount Sinai and bears children who are to be slaves: This is Hagar. 25Now Hagar stands for Mount Sinai in Arabia and corresponds to the present city of Jerusalem, because she is in slavery with her children. 26But the Jerusalem that is above[b] is free, and she is our mother. 27For it is written:

"Be glad, O barren woman,
  who bears no children;
break forth and cry aloud,
  you who have no labour pains;
because more are the children
    of the desolate woman
  than of her who has a
    husband."[b][c]

3:29 j ver 16
4:3 a Gal 2:4 b Col 2:8,20
4:4 c Mk 1:15 Eph 1:10 d Jn 1:14 e Lk 2:27
4:5 f Jn 1:12
4:6 g Ro 5:5 h Ro 8:15,16
4:7 i Ro 8:17
4:8 j 1Co 1:21 Eph 2:12 1Th 4:5 k 2Ch 13:9 Isa 37:19
4:9 l 1Co 8:3 m ver 3 n Col 2:20
4:10 o Ro 14:5
4:11 p 1Th 3:5
4:12 q Gal 6:18
4:13 r 1Co 2:3
4:14 s Mt 10:40
4:16 t Am 5:10
4:18 u ver 13,14
4:19 v 1Co 4:15 w Eph 4:13
4:22 x Ge 16:15 y Ge 21:2
4:23 z Ro 9:7,8 a Ge 18:10-14 Heb 11:11
4:26 b Heb 12:22 Rev 3:12
4:27 c Isa 54:1

a6 Aramaic for *Father* b27 Isaiah 54:1

[28]Now you, brothers, like Isaac, are children of promise. [29]At that time the son born in the ordinary way[d] persecuted the son born by the power of the Spirit.[e] It is the same now. [30]But what does the Scripture say? "Get rid of the slave woman and her son, for the slave woman's son will never share in the inheritance with the free woman's son."[c][f] [31]Therefore, brothers, we are not children of the slave woman, but of the free woman.

Freedom in Christ

5 It is for freedom that Christ has set us free.[a] Stand firm,[b] then, and do not let yourselves be burdened again by a yoke of slavery.[c]

[2]Mark my words! I, Paul, tell you that if you let yourselves be circumcised,[d] Christ will be of no value to you at all. [3]Again I declare to every man who lets himself be circumcised that he is required to obey the whole law.[e] [4]You who are trying to be justified by law have been alienated from Christ; you have fallen away from grace.[f] [5]But by faith we eagerly await through the Spirit the righteousness for which we hope.[g] [6]For in Christ Jesus neither circumcision nor uncircumcision has any value.[h] The only thing that counts is faith expressing itself through love.[i]

[7]You were running a good race.[j] Who cut in on you[k] and kept you from obeying the truth? [8]That kind of persuasion does not come from the one who calls you.[l] [9]"A little yeast works through the whole batch of dough."[m] [10]I am confident[n] in the Lord that you will take no other view.[o] The one who is throwing you into confusion[p] will pay the penalty, whoever he may be. [11]Brothers, if I am still preaching circumcision, why am I still being persecuted?[q] In that case the offence[r] of the cross has been abolished. [12]As for those agitators,[s] I wish they would go the whole way and emasculate themselves!

[13]You, my brothers, were called to be free. But do not use your freedom to indulge the sinful nature;[a][t] rather, serve one another[u] in love. [14]The entire law is summed up in a single command: "Love your neighbour as yourself."[b][v] [15]If you keep on biting and devouring each other, watch out or you will be destroyed by each other.

Life by the Spirit

[16]So I say, live by the Spirit,[w] and you will not gratify the desires of the sinful nature.[x] [17]For the sinful nature desires what is contrary to the Spirit, and the Spirit what is contrary to the sinful nature.[y] They are in conflict with each other, so that you do not do what you want.[z] [18]But if you are led by the Spirit, you are not under law.[a]

[19]The acts of the sinful nature are obvious: sexual immorality,[b] impurity and debauchery; [20]idolatry and witchcraft; hatred, discord, jealousy, fits of rage, selfish ambition, dissensions, factions [21]and envy; drunkenness, orgies, and the like.[c] I warn you, as I did before, that those who live like this will not inherit the kingdom of God.

[22]But the fruit[d] of the Spirit is love,[e] joy, peace, patience, kindness, goodness, faithfulness, [23]gentleness and self-control.[f] Against such things there is no law. [24]Those who belong to Christ Jesus have crucified the sinful nature[g] with its passions and desires.[h] [25]Since we live by the Spirit, let us keep in step with the Spirit. [26]Let us not become conceited,[i] provoking and envying each other.

4:29 d ver 23; e Ge 21:9
4:30 f Ge 21:10
5:1 a Jn 8:32; b 1Co 16:13; c Ac 15:10; Gal 2:4
5:2 d Ac 15:1
5:3 e Gal 3:10
5:4 f Heb 12:15; 2Pe 3:17
5:5 g Ro 8:23,24
5:6 h 1Co 7:19; i 1Th 1:3
5:7 j 1Co 9:24; k Gal 3:1
5:8 l Ro 8:28; Gal 1:6
5:9 m 1Co 5:6
5:10 n 2Co 2:3; o Php 3:15; p Gal 1:7
5:11 q Gal 4:29; Gal 6:12; r 1Co 1:23
5:12 s ver 10
5:13 t 1Co 8:9; 1Pe 2:16; u 1Co 9:19; Eph 5:21
5:14 v Lev 19:18; Mt 22:39
5:16 w Ro 8:2,4-6,9,14; x ver 24
5:17 y Ro 8:5-8; z Ro 7:15-23
5:18 a Ro 6:14; 1Ti 1:9
5:19 b 1Co 6:18
5:21 c Ro 13:13
5:22 d Mt 7:16-20; Eph 5:9; e Col 3:12-15
5:23 f Ac 24:25
5:24 g Ro 6:6; h ver 16,17
5:26 i Php 2:3

c*30* Gen. 21:10 a*13* Or *the flesh*; also in verses 16, 17, 19 and 24 b*14* Lev. 19:18

Doing Good to All

6 Brothers, if someone is caught in a sin, you who are spiritual[a] should restore him gently. But watch yourself, or you also may be tempted. 2Carry each other's burdens, and in this way you will fulfil the law of Christ.[b] 3If anyone thinks he is something[c] when he is nothing, he deceives himself. 4Each one should test his own actions. Then he can take pride in himself, without comparing himself to somebody else, 5for each one should carry his own load.

6Anyone who receives instruction in the word must share all good things with his instructor.[d]

7Do not be deceived:[e] God cannot be mocked. A man reaps what he sows.[f] 8The one who sows to please his sinful nature, from that nature[a] will reap destruction;[g] the one who sows to please the Spirit, from the Spirit will reap eternal life.[h] 9Let us not become weary in doing good,[i] for at the proper time we will reap a harvest if we do not give up.[j] 10Therefore, as we have opportunity, let us do good[k] to all people, especially to those who belong to the family[l] of believers.

6:1 *a* 1Co 2:15
6:2 *b* Ro 15:1; Jas 2:8
6:3 *c* Ro 12:3; 1Co 8:2
6:6 *d* 1Co 9:11,14
6:7 *e* 1Co 6:9; *f* 2Co 9:6
6:8 *g* Job 4:8; Hos 8:7; *h* Jas 3:18
6:9 *i* 1Co 15:58; *j* Rev 2:10
6:10 *k* Pr 3:27; *l* Eph 2:19
6:11 *m* 1Co 16:21
6:12 *n* Ac 15:1; *o* Gal 5:11
6:13 *p* Ro 2:25; *q* Php 3:3
6:14 *r* Ro 6:2,6
6:15 *s* 1Co 7:19; *t* 2Co 5:17
6:17 *u* Isa 44:5; 2Co 1:5
6:18 *v* Ro 16:20; *w* 2Ti 4:22

Not Circumcision but a New Creation

11See what large letters I use as I write to you with my own hand![m]

12Those who want to make a good impression outwardly are trying to compel you to be circumcised.[n] The only reason they do this is to avoid being persecuted[o] for the cross of Christ. 13Not even those who are circumcised obey the law,[p] yet they want you to be circumcised that they may boast about your flesh.[q] 14May I never boast except in the cross of our Lord Jesus Christ, through which[b] the world has been crucified to me, and I to the world.[r] 15Neither circumcision nor uncircumcision means anything;[s] what counts is a new creation.[t] 16Peace and mercy to all who follow this rule, even to the Israel of God.

17Finally, let no-one cause me trouble, for I bear on my body the marks[u] of Jesus.

18The grace of our Lord Jesus Christ[v] be with your spirit,[w] brothers. Amen.

[a]8 Or *his flesh, from the flesh* [b]14 Or *whom*

EPHESIANS

1 Paul, an apostle[a] of Christ Jesus by the will of God,[b]

To the saints in Ephesus,[a] the faithful[b][c] in Christ Jesus:

2 Grace and peace to you from God our Father and the Lord Jesus Christ.[d]

Spiritual Blessings in Christ

3 Praise be to the God and Father of our Lord Jesus Christ,[e] who has blessed us in the heavenly realms[f] with every spiritual blessing in Christ. 4 For he chose us in him before the creation of the world to be holy and blameless[g] in his sight. In love[h] 5 he[c] predestined[i] us to be adopted as his sons through Jesus Christ, in accordance with his pleasure[j] and will— 6 to the praise of his glorious grace, which he has freely given us in the One he loves.[k] 7 In him we have redemption[l] through his blood, the forgiveness of sins, in accordance with the riches of God's grace 8 that he lavished on us with all wisdom and understanding. 9 And he[d] made known to us the mystery[m] of his will according to his good pleasure, which he purposed in Christ, 10 to be put into effect when the times will have reached their fulfilment[n]—to bring all things in heaven and on earth together under one head, even Christ.[o]

11 In him we were also chosen,[e] having been predestined according to the plan of him who works out everything in conformity with the purpose[p] of his will, 12 in order that we, who were the first to hope in Christ, might be for the praise of his glory.[q] 13 And you also were included in Christ when you heard the word of truth,[r] the gospel of your salvation. Having believed, you were marked in him with a seal,[s] the promised Holy Spirit, 14 who is a deposit guaranteeing our inheritance[t] until the redemption of those who are God's possession—to the praise of his glory.

Thanksgiving and Prayer

15 For this reason, ever since I heard about your faith in the Lord Jesus and your love for all the saints,[u] 16 I have not stopped giving thanks for you,[v] remembering you in my prayers. 17 I keep asking that the God of our Lord Jesus Christ, the glorious Father,[w] may give you the Spirit[f] of wisdom[x] and revelation, so that you may know him better. 18 I pray also that the eyes of your heart may be enlightened[y] in order that you may know the hope to which he has called you, the riches of his glorious inheritance in the saints, 19 and his incomparably great power for us who believe. That power[z] is like the working of his mighty strength,[a] 20 which he exerted in Christ when he raised him from the dead[b] and seated him at his right hand in the heavenly realms, 21 far above all rule and authority, power and dominion, and every title[c] that can be given, not only in the present age but also in the one to come. 22 And God placed all things under his feet[d] and appointed him to be head[e] over everything for the church, 23 which is his body, the fulness of him who fills everything in every way.

1:1 a 1Co 1:1; b 2Co 1:1; c Col 1:2
1:2 d Ro 1:7
1:3 e 2Co 1:3; f Eph 2:6; Eph 3:10; Eph 6:12
1:4 g Eph 5:27; Col 1:22; h Eph 4:2,15,16
1:5 i Ro 8:29,30; j 1Co 1:21
1:6 k Mt 3:17
1:7 l Ro 3:24
1:9 m Ro 16:25
1:10 n Gal 4:4; o Col 1:20
1:11 p Eph 3:11; Heb 6:17
1:12 q ver 6,14
1:13 r Col 1:5; s Eph 4:30
1:14 t Ac 20:32
1:15 u Col 1:4
1:16 v Ro 1:8
1:17 w Jn 20:17; x Col 1:9
1:18 y Ac 26:18; 2Co 4:6
1:19 z Col 1:29; a Eph 6:10
1:20 b Ac 2:24
1:21 c Php 2:9,10
1:22 d Mt 28:18; e Eph 4:15; Eph 5:23

a *1* Some early manuscripts do not have *in Ephesus.* b *1* Or *believers who are* c *4,5* Or *sight in love.* *5He* d *8, 9* Or *us. With all wisdom and understanding,* *9he* e *11* Or *were made heirs* f *17* Or *a spirit*

Made Alive in Christ

2 As for you, you were dead in your transgressions and sins,[a] 2 in which you used to live[b] when you followed the ways of this world and of the ruler of the kingdom of the air,[c] the spirit who is now at work in those who are disobedient.[d] 3 All of us also lived among them at one time, gratifying the cravings of our sinful nature[a][e] and following its desires and thoughts. Like the rest, we were by nature objects of wrath. 4 But because of his great love for us, God, who is rich in mercy, 5 made us alive with Christ even when we were dead in transgressions[f]—it is by grace you have been saved.[g] 6 And God raised us up with Christ and seated us with him[h] in the heavenly realms[i] in Christ Jesus, 7 in order that in the coming ages he might show the incomparable riches of his grace, expressed in his kindness[j] to us in Christ Jesus. 8 For it is by grace you have been saved,[k] through faith—and this not from yourselves, it is the gift of God—9 not by works,[l] so that no-one can boast.[m] 10 For we are God's workmanship, created[n] in Christ Jesus to do good works,[o] which God prepared in advance for us to do.

One in Christ

11 Therefore, remember that formerly you who are Gentiles by birth and called "uncircumcised" by those who call themselves "the circumcision" (that done in the body by the hands of men)[p]—12 remember that at that time you were separate from Christ, excluded from citizenship in Israel and foreigners to the covenants of the promise,[q] without hope[r] and without God in the world. 13 But now in Christ Jesus you who once were far away have been brought near[s] through the blood of Christ.[t]

14 For he himself is our peace, who has made the two one[u] and has destroyed the barrier, the dividing wall of hostility, 15 by abolishing in his flesh[v] the law with its commandments and regulations.[w] His purpose was to create in himself one[x] new man out of the two, thus making peace, 16 and in this one body to reconcile both of them to God through the cross,[y] by which he put to death their hostility. 17 He came and preached peace to you who were far away and peace to those who were near.[z] 18 For through him we both have access[a] to the Father[b] by one Spirit.[c]

19 Consequently, you are no longer foreigners and aliens,[d] but fellow-citizens[e] with God's people and members of God's household,[f] 20 built on the foundation[g] of the apostles and prophets, with Christ Jesus himself as the chief cornerstone.[h] 21 In him the whole building is joined together and rises to become a holy temple[i] in the Lord. 22 And in him you too are being built together to become a dwelling in which God lives by his Spirit.

Paul the Preacher to the Gentiles

3 For this reason I, Paul, the prisoner[a] of Christ Jesus for the sake of you Gentiles—

2 Surely you have heard about the administration of God's grace that was given to me[b] for you, 3 that is, the mystery[c] made known to me by revelation,[d] as I have already written briefly. 4 In reading this, then, you will be able to understand my insight[e] into the mystery of Christ, 5 which was not made known to men in other generations as it has now been revealed by the Spirit to God's holy apostles and prophets.[f] 6 This mystery is that through the gospel the Gentiles are heirs[g] together with Israel, members together of one body,[h] and sharers

2:1 a ver 5; Col 2:13
2:2 b Col 3:7; c Jn 12:31; Eph 6:12; d Eph 5:6
2:3 e Gal 5:16
2:5 f ver 1; g ver 8; Ac 15:11
2:6 h Eph 1:20; i Eph 1:3
2:7 j Tit 3:4
2:8 k ver 5
2:9 l 2Ti 1:9; m 1Co 1:29
2:10 n Eph 4:24; o Tit 2:14
2:11 p Col 2:11
2:12 q Gal 3:17; r 1Th 4:13
2:13 s ver 17; Ac 2:39; t Col 1:20
2:14 u 1Co 12:13
2:15 v Col 1:21,22; w Col 2:14; x Gal 3:28
2:16 y Col 1:20,22
2:17 z Ps 148:14; Isa 57:19
2:18 a Eph 3:12; b Col 1:12; c 1Co 12:13
2:19 d ver 12; e Php 3:20; f Gal 6:10
2:20 g Mt 16:18; Rev 21:14; h 1Pe 2:4-8
2:21 i 1Co 3:16,17
3:1 a Ac 23:18; Eph 4:1
3:2 b Col 1:25
3:3 c Ro 16:25; d 1Co 2:10
3:4 e 2Co 11:6
3:5 f Ro 16:26
3:6 g Gal 3:29; h Eph 2:15,16

a3 Or *our flesh*

together in the promise in Christ
Jesus.
7I became a servant of this gospel[i] by the gift of God's grace
given me through the working of
his power.[j] 8Although I am less
than the least of all God's people,[k]
this grace was given me: to preach
to the Gentiles the unsearchable
riches of Christ, 9and to make plain
to everyone the administration of
this mystery,[l] which for ages past
was kept hidden in God, who created all things. 10His intent was that
now, through the church, the mani-
fold wisdom of God[m] should be
made known[n] to the rulers and
authorities[o] in the heavenly
realms, 11according to his eternal
purpose which he accomplished in
Christ Jesus our Lord. 12In him and
through faith in him we may approach God[p] with freedom and
confidence.[q] 13I ask you, therefore, not to be discouraged because
of my sufferings for you, which are
your glory.

A Prayer for the Ephesians

14For this reason I kneel[r] before
the Father, 15from whom his whole
family[a] in heaven and on earth de-
rives its name. 16I pray that out of
his glorious riches he may
strengthen you with power[s]
through his Spirit in your inner being,[t] 17so that Christ may dwell in
your hearts[u] through faith. And I
pray that you, being rooted[v] and
established in love, 18may have
power, together with all the saints,
to grasp how wide and long and
high and deep[w] is the love of
Christ, 19and to know this love that
surpasses knowledge—that you
may be filled[x] to the measure of all
the fulness of God.[y]
20Now to him who is able[z] to do
immeasurably more than all we ask
or imagine, according to his power
that is at work within us, 21to him be
glory in the church and in Christ
Jesus throughout all generations,
for ever and ever! Amen.[a]

Unity in the Body of Christ

4 As a prisoner[a] for the Lord,
then, I urge you to live a life
worthy[b] of the calling you have received. 2Be completely humble and
gentle; be patient, bearing with one
another[c] in love.[d] 3Make every effort to keep the unity[e] of the Spirit
through the bond of peace. 4There
is one body and one Spirit[f]—just
as you were called to one hope
when you were called—5one Lord,
one faith, one baptism; 6one God
and Father of all, who is over all
and through all and in all.[g]
7But to each one of us[h] grace has
been given[i] as Christ apportioned
it. 8This is why it[a] says:

> "When he ascended on high,
> he led captives[j] in his train
> and gave gifts to men."[b][k]

9(What does "he ascended" mean
except that he also descended to
the lower, earthly regions?[c] 10He
who descended is the very one who
ascended higher than all the heavens, in order to fill the whole universe.) 11It was he who gave some
to be apostles,[l] some to be prophets, some to be evangelists,[m] and
some to be pastors and teachers,
12to prepare God's people for
works of service, so that the body
of Christ[n] may be built up 13until
we all reach unity[o] in the faith and
in the knowledge of the Son of God
and become mature,[p] attaining to
the whole measure of the fulness of
Christ.
14Then we will no longer be infants,[q] tossed back and forth by
the waves,[r] and blown here and
there by every wind of teaching
and by the cunning and craftiness
of men in their deceitful scheming.[s] 15Instead, speaking the truth
in love, we will in all things grow up

3:7 i 1Co 3:5 j Eph 1:19
3:8 k 1Co 15:9
3:9 l Ro 16:25
3:10 m 1Co 2:7 n 1Pe 1:12 o Eph 1:21
3:12 p Eph 2:18 q Heb 4:16
3:14 r Php 2:10
3:16 s Col 1:11 t Ro 7:22
3:17 u Jn 14:23 v Col 1:23
3:18 w Job 11:8,9
3:19 x Col 2:10 y Eph 1:23
3:20 z Ro 16:25
3:21 a Ro 11:36
4:1 a Eph 3:1 b Php 1:27 Col 1:10
4:2 c Col 3:12,13 d Eph 1:4
4:3 e Col 3:14
4:4 f 1Co 12:13
4:6 g Ro 11:36
4:7 h 1Co 12:7,11 i Ro 12:3
4:8 j Col 2:15 k Ps 68:18
4:11 l 1Co 12:28 m Ac 21:8
4:12 n 1Co 12:27
4:13 o ver 3,5 p Col 1:28
4:14 q 1Co 14:20 r Jas 1:6 s Eph 6:11

[a] 15 Or *whom all fatherhood* [a] 8 Or *God*
[b] 8 Psalm 68:18 [c] 9 Or *the depths of the earth*

into him who is the Head,[t] that is,
Christ. 16From him the whole body,
joined and held together by every
supporting ligament, grows[u] and
builds itself up in love, as each part
does its work.

Living as Children of Light

17So I tell you this, and insist on it
in the Lord, that you must no longer
live as the Gentiles do, in the futility of their thinking.[v] 18They are
darkened in their understanding[w]
and separated from the life of
God[x] because of the ignorance
that is in them due to the hardening of their hearts.[y] 19Having lost
all sensitivity,[z] they have given
themselves over[a] to sensuality[b]
so as to indulge in every kind of impurity, with a continual lust for
more.
20You, however, did not come to
know Christ that way. 21Surely you
heard of him and were taught in
him in accordance with the truth
that is in Jesus. 22You were taught,
with regard to your former way of
life, to put off[c] your old self,[d]
which is being corrupted by its deceitful desires; 23to be made new in
the attitude of your minds;[e] 24and
to put on the new self,[f] created to
be like God in true righteousness
and holiness.[g]
25Therefore each of you must put
off falsehood and speak truth-
fully[h] to his neighbour, for we are
all members of one body.[i] 26"In
your anger do not sin"[d]: Do not let
the sun go down while you are still
angry, 27and do not give the devil a
foothold. 28He who has been stealing must steal no longer, but must
work,[j] doing something useful
with his own hands,[k] that he may
have something to share with those
in need.[l]
29Do not let any unwholesome
talk come out of your mouths,[m] but
only what is helpful for building
others up according to their needs,
that it may benefit those who listen.
30And do not grieve the Holy Spirit
of God,[n] with whom you were
sealed for the day of redemption.[o]
31Get rid of all bitterness, rage and
anger, brawling and slander, along
with every form of malice.[p] 32Be
kind and compassionate to one another, forgiving each other, just as
in Christ God forgave you.[q]

5 Be imitators of God,[a] therefore, as dearly loved children
2and live a life of love, just as
Christ loved us and gave himself up
for us[b] as a fragrant offering and
sacrifice to God.[c]
3But among you there must not
be even a hint of sexual immorality, or of any kind of impurity, or of
greed,[d] because these are im-
proper for God's holy people. 4Nor
should there be obscenity, foolish
talk or coarse joking, which are out
of place, but rather thanksgiving.[e]
5For of this you can be sure: No immoral, impure or greedy person—
such a man is an idolater[f]—has
any inheritance in the kingdom of
Christ and of God.[a][g] 6Let no-one
deceive you with empty words, for
because of such things God's
wrath[h] comes on those who are
disobedient. 7Therefore do not be
partners with them.
8For you were once[i] darkness,
but now you are light in the Lord.
Live as children of light[j] 9(for the
fruit[k] of the light consists in all
goodness, righteousness and truth)
10and find out what pleases the
Lord. 11Have nothing to do with the
fruitless deeds of darkness, but
rather expose them. 12For it is
shameful even to mention what the
disobedient do in secret. 13But
everything exposed by the light[l]
becomes visible, 14for it is light that
makes everything visible. This is
why it is said:

"Wake up, O sleeper,[m]
rise from the dead,[n]
and Christ will shine on you."[o]

4:15 t Eph 1:22
4:16 u Col 2:19
4:17 v Ro 1:21
4:18 w Ro 1:21 x Eph 2:12 y 2Co 3:14
4:19 z 1Ti 4:2 a Ro 1:24 b Col 3:5
4:22 c 1Pe 2:1 d Ro 6:6
4:23 e Col 3:10
4:24 f Ro 6:4 g Eph 2:10
4:25 h Zec 8:16 i Ro 12:5
4:28 j Ac 20:35 k 1Th 4:11 l Lk 3:11
4:29 m Col 3:8
4:30 n 1Th 5:19 o Ro 8:23
4:31 p Col 3:8
4:32 q Mt 6:14,15
5:1 a Lk 6:36
5:2 b Gal 1:4 c 2Co 2:15 Heb 7:27
5:3 d Col 3:5
5:4 e ver 20
5:5 f Col 3:5 g 1Co 6:9
5:6 h Ro 1:18
5:8 i Eph 2:2 j Lk 16:8
5:9 k Gal 5:22
5:13 l Jn 3:20,21
5:14 m Ro 13:11 n Jn 5:25 o Isa 60:1

[d]26 Psalm 4:4 [a]5 Or *kingdom of the Christ and God*

[15]Be very careful, then, how you
live—not as unwise but as wise,
[16]making the most of every opportunity,[p] because the days are
evil.[q] [17]Therefore do not be foolish, but understand what the Lord's
will is.[r] [18]Do not get drunk on
wine,[s] which leads to debauchery.
Instead, be filled with the Spirit.[t]
[19]Speak to one another with psalms,
hymns and spiritual songs.[u] Sing
and make music in your heart to
the Lord, [20]always giving thanks[v]
to God the Father for everything, in
the name of our Lord Jesus Christ.
[21]Submit to one another[w] out of
reverence for Christ.

Wives and Husbands

5:22–6:9pp Col 3:18–4:1

[22]Wives, submit to your husbands[x] as to the Lord.[y] [23]For the
husband is the head of the wife as
Christ is the head of the church,[z]
his body, of which he is the Saviour.
[24]Now as the church submits to
Christ, so also wives should submit
to their husbands in everything.
[25]Husbands, love your wives,[a]
just as Christ loved the church and
gave himself up for her[b] [26]to make
her holy, cleansing[b] her by the
washing[c] with water through the
word, [27]and to present her to himself as a radiant church, without
stain or wrinkle or any other blemish, but holy and blameless.[d] [28]In
this same way, husbands ought to
love their wives[e] as their own
bodies. He who loves his wife loves
himself. [29]After all, no-one ever
hated his own body, but he feeds
and cares for it, just as Christ does
the church—[30]for we are members
of his body.[f] [31]"For this reason a
man will leave his father and
mother and be united to his wife,
and the two will become one
flesh."[c][g] [32]This is a profound mystery—but I am talking about Christ
and the church. [33]However, each
one of you also must love his wife[h]
as he loves himself, and the wife
must respect her husband.

Children and Parents

6 Children, obey your parents in
the Lord, for this is right.[a]
[2]"Honour your father and
mother"—which is the first commandment with a promise—[3]"that
it may go well with you and that you
may enjoy long life on the
earth."[a][b]
[4]Fathers, do not exasperate your
children;[c] instead, bring them up
in the training and instruction of
the Lord.[d]

Slaves and Masters

[5]Slaves, obey your earthly masters with respect[e] and fear, and
with sincerity of heart,[f] just as
you would obey Christ.[g] [6]Obey
them not only to win their favour
when their eye is on you, but like
slaves of Christ, doing the will of
God from your heart. [7]Serve wholeheartedly, as if you were serving
the Lord, not men,[h] [8]because you
know that the Lord will reward
everyone for whatever good he
does,[i] whether he is slave or free.
[9]And masters, treat your slaves
in the same way. Do not threaten
them, since you know that he who is
both their Master and yours[j] is in
heaven, and there is no favouritism
with him.

The Armour of God

[10]Finally, be strong in the Lord[k]
and in his mighty power.[l] [11]Put on
the full armour of God[m] so that you
can take your stand against the
devil's schemes. [12]For our struggle
is not against flesh and blood,
but against the rulers, against the
authorities,[n] against the powers[o]
of this dark world and against
the spiritual forces of evil in the

5:16 *p* Col 4:5 *q* Eph 6:13
5:17 *r* Ro 12:2; 1Th 4:3
5:18 *s* Pr 20:1 *t* Lk 1:15
5:19 *u* Ac 16:25; Col 3:16
5:20 *v* Ps 34:1
5:21 *w* Gal 5:13
5:22 *x* Ge 3:16; 1Pe 3:1,5,6 *y* Eph 6:5
5:23 *z* 1Co 11:3; Eph 1:22
5:25 *a* Col 3:19 *b* ver 2
5:26 *c* Ac 22:16
5:27 *d* Eph 1:4; Col 1:22
5:28 *e* ver 25
5:30 *f* 1Co 12:27
5:31 *g* Ge 2:24; Mt 19:5; 1Co 6:16
5:33 *h* ver 25
6:1 *a* Col 3:20
6:3 *b* Ex 20:12
6:4 *c* Col 3:21 *d* Ge 18:19; Dt 6:7
6:5 *e* 1Ti 6:1 *f* Col 3:22 *g* Eph 5:22
6:7 *h* Col 3:23
6:8 *i* Col 3:24
6:9 *j* Job 31:13,14
6:10 *k* 1Co 16:13 *l* Eph 1:19
6:11 *m* Ro 13:12
6:12 *n* Eph 1:21 *o* Ro 8:38

[b]*26* Or *having cleansed* [c]*31* Gen. 2:24
[a]*3* Deut. 5:16

heavenly realms.[p] 13Therefore put
on the full armour of God, so that
when the day of evil comes, you
may be able to stand your ground,
and after you have done everything, to stand. 14Stand firm then,
with the belt of truth buckled round
your waist,[q] with the breastplate
of righteousness in place,[r] 15and
with your feet fitted with the readiness that comes from the gospel of
peace.[s] 16In addition to all this,
take up the shield of faith,[t] with
which you can extinguish all the
flaming arrows of the evil one.
17Take the helmet of salvation[u]
and the sword of the Spirit, which
is the word of God.[v] 18And pray in
the Spirit on all occasions[w] with all
kinds of prayers and requests.[x]
With this in mind, be alert and always keep on praying for all the
saints.

6:12 p Eph 1:3
6:14 q Isa 11:5 r Isa 59:17
6:15 s Isa 52:7
6:16 t 1Jn 5:4
6:17 u Isa 59:17 v Heb 4:12
6:18 w Lk 18:1 x Mt 26:41 Php 1:4
6:19 y 1Th 5:25 z Ac 4:29 2Co 3:12
6:20 a 2Co 5:20 b Ac 21:33
6:21 c Ac 20:4
6:22 d Col 4:7-9
6:23 e Gal 6:16 1Pe 5:14

19Pray also for me,[y] that whenever I open my mouth, words may
be given me so that I will fearlessly[z] make known the mystery
of the gospel, 20for which I am an
ambassador[a] in chains.[b] Pray that
I may declare it fearlessly, as I
should.

Final Greetings

21Tychicus,[c] the dear brother
and faithful servant in the Lord,
will tell you everything, so that you
also may know how I am and what
I am doing. 22I am sending him to
you for this very purpose, that you
may know how we are,[d] and that he
may encourage you.

23Peace[e] to the brothers, and
love with faith from God the Father
and the Lord Jesus Christ. 24Grace
to all who love our Lord Jesus
Christ with an undying love.

PHILIPPIANS

1 Paul and Timothy,[a] servants of Christ Jesus,

To all the saints[b] in Christ Jesus at Philippi,[c] together with the overseers[a][d] and deacons:[e]

[2]Grace and peace to you from God our Father and the Lord Jesus Christ.[f]

Thanksgiving and Prayer

[3]I thank my God every time I remember you.[g] [4]In all my prayers for all of you, I always pray[h] with joy [5]because of your partnership[i] in the gospel from the first day[j] until now, [6]being confident of this, that he who began a good work in you will carry it on to completion until the day of Christ Jesus.[k]

[7]It is right[l] for me to feel this way about all of you, since I have you in my heart;[m] for whether I am in chains[n] or defending[o] and confirming the gospel, all of you share in God's grace with me. [8]God can testify[p] how I long for all of you with the affection of Christ Jesus.

[9]And this is my prayer: that your love[q] may abound more and more in knowledge and depth of insight, [10]so that you may be able to discern what is best and may be pure and blameless until the day of Christ,[r] [11]filled with the fruit of righteousness[s] that comes through Jesus Christ—to the glory and praise of God.

Paul's Chains Advance the Gospel

[12]Now I want you to know, brothers, that what has happened to me has really served to advance the gospel. [13]As a result, it has become clear throughout the whole palace guard[b] and to everyone else that I am in chains[t] for Christ. [14]Because of my chains,[u] most of the brothers in the Lord have been encouraged to speak the word of God more courageously and fearlessly.

[15]It is true that some preach Christ out of envy and rivalry, but others out of goodwill. [16]The latter do so in love, knowing that I am put here for the defence of the gospel.[v] [17]The former preach Christ out of selfish ambition,[w] not sincerely, supposing that they can stir up trouble for me while I am in chains.[c][x] [18]But what does it matter? The important thing is that in every way, whether from false motives or true, Christ is preached. And because of this I rejoice.

Yes, and I will continue to rejoice, [19]for I know that through your prayers[y] and the help given by the Spirit of Jesus Christ,[z] what has happened to me will turn out for my deliverance.[d] [20]I eagerly expect[a] and hope that I will in no way be ashamed, but will have sufficient courage[b] so that now as always Christ will be exalted in my body,[c] whether by life or by death.[d] [21]For to me, to live is Christ[e] and to die is gain. [22]If I am to go on living in the body, this will mean fruitful labour for me. Yet what shall I choose? I do not know! [23]I am torn between the two: I desire to depart[f] and be with Christ,[g] which is better by far; [24]but it is more necessary for you that I remain in the body. [25]Convinced of this, I know that I will remain, and I will continue with all of you for your progress and joy in

1:1 a Ac 16:1; 2Co 1:1; b Ac 9:13; c Ac 16:12; d 1Ti 3:1; e 1Ti 3:8
1:2 f Ro 1:7
1:3 g Ro 1:8
1:4 h Ro 1:10
1:5 i Ac 2:42; Php 4:15; j Ac 16:12-40
1:6 k ver 10; 1Co 1:8
1:7 l 2Pe 1:13; m 2Co 7:3; n ver 13,14,17; Ac 21:33; o ver 16
1:8 p Ro 1:9
1:9 q 1Th 3:12
1:10 r ver 6; 1Co 1:8
1:11 s Jas 3:18
1:13 t ver 7,14,17
1:14 u ver 7,13,17
1:16 v ver 7,12
1:17 w Php 2:3; x ver 7,13,14
1:19 y 2Co 1:11; z Ac 16:7
1:20 a Ro 8:19; b ver 14; c 1Co 6:20; d Ro 14:8
1:21 e Gal 2:20
1:23 f 2Ti 4:6; g Jn 12:26; 2Co 5:8

a1 Traditionally *bishops* b13 Or *whole palace* c16,17 Some late manuscripts have verses 16 and 17 in reverse order. d19 Or *salvation*

the faith, 26 so that through my being with you again your joy in Christ Jesus will overflow on account of me.

27 Whatever happens, conduct yourselves in a manner worthy[h] of the gospel of Christ. Then, whether I come and see you or only hear about you in my absence, I will know that you stand firm[i] in one spirit, contending[j] as one man for the faith of the gospel 28 without being frightened in any way by those who oppose you. This is a sign to them that they will be destroyed, but that you will be saved—and that by God. 29 For it has been granted to you[k] on behalf of Christ not only to believe on him, but also to suffer[l] for him, 30 since you are going through the same struggle[m] you saw[n] I had, and now hear[o] that I still have.

Imitating Christ's Humility

2 If you have any encouragement from being united with Christ, if any comfort from his love, if any fellowship with the Spirit,[a] if any tenderness and compassion,[b] 2 then make my joy complete[c] by being like-minded,[d] having the same love, being one[e] in spirit and purpose. 3 Do nothing out of selfish ambition or vain conceit,[f] but in humility consider others better than yourselves.[g] 4 Each of you should look not only to your own interests, but also to the interests of others.

5 Your attitude should be the same as that of Christ Jesus:[h]

6 Who, being in very nature[a]
God,[i]
did not consider equality with
God[j] something to be
grasped,
7 but made himself nothing,
taking the very nature[b] of a
servant,[k]
being made in human
likeness.[l]
8 And being found in appearance
as a man,
he humbled himself
and became obedient to
death[m]—even death on
a cross!
9 Therefore God exalted him[n] to
the highest place
and gave him the name that is
above every name,[o]
10 that at the name of Jesus every
knee should bow,[p]
in heaven and on earth and
under the earth,[q]
11 and every tongue confess that
Jesus Christ is Lord,[r]
to the glory of God the Father.

Shining as Stars

12 Therefore, my dear friends, as you have always obeyed—not only in my presence, but now much more in my absence—continue to work out your salvation with fear and trembling,[s] 13 for it is God who works in you[t] to will and to act according to his good purpose.

14 Do everything without complaining[u] or arguing, 15 so that you may become blameless and pure, children of God[v] without fault in a crooked and depraved generation,[w] in which you shine like stars in the universe 16 as you hold out[c] the word of life—in order that I may boast on the day of Christ that I did not run or labour for nothing.[x] 17 But even if I am being poured out like a drink offering[y] on the sacrifice[z] and service coming from your faith, I am glad and rejoice with all of you. 18 So you too should be glad and rejoice with me.

Timothy and Epaphroditus

19 I hope in the Lord Jesus to send Timothy to you soon,[a] that I also may be cheered when I receive news about you. 20 I have no-one else like him,[b] who takes a genuine

[a] 6 Or *in the form of* [b] 7 Or *the form*
[c] 16 Or *hold on to*

1:27 h Eph 4:1 i 1Co 16:13 j Jude 3
1:29 k Mt 5:11,12 l Ac 14:22
1:30 m Col 2:1; 1Th 2:2 n Ac 16:19-40 o ver 13
2:1 a 2Co 13:14 b Col 3:12
2:2 c Jn 3:29 d Php 4:2 e Ro 12:16
2:3 f Gal 5:26 g Ro 12:10; 1Pe 5:5
2:5 h Mt 11:29
2:6 i Jn 1:1 j Jn 5:18
2:7 k Mt 20:28 l Jn 1:14; Heb 2:17
2:8 m Mt 26:39; Jn 10:18; Heb 5:8
2:9 n Ac 2:33; Heb 2:9 o Eph 1:20,21
2:10 p Ro 14:11 q Mt 28:18
2:11 r Jn 13:13
2:12 s 2Co 7:15
2:13 t Ezr 1:5
2:14 u 1Co 10:10; 1Pe 4:9
2:15 v Mt 5:45,48; Eph 5:1 w Ac 2:40
2:16 x 1Th 2:19
2:17 y 2Ti 4:6 z Ro 15:16
2:19 a ver 23
2:20 b 1Co 16:10

interest in your welfare. 21For everyone looks out for his own interests,[c] not those of Jesus Christ. 22But you know that Timothy has proved himself, because as a son with his father[d] he has served with me in the work of the gospel. 23I hope, therefore, to send him as soon as I see how things go with me.[e] 24And I am confident[f] in the Lord that I myself will come soon.

25But I think it is necessary to send back to you Epaphroditus, my brother, fellow-worker[g] and fellow-soldier,[h] who is also your messenger, whom you sent to take care of my needs.[i] 26For he longs for all of you[j] and is distressed because you heard he was ill. 27Indeed he was ill, and almost died. But God had mercy on him, and not on him only but also on me, to spare me sorrow upon sorrow. 28Therefore I am all the more eager to send him, so that when you see him again you may be glad and I may have less anxiety. 29Welcome him in the Lord with great joy, and honour men like him,[k] 30because he almost died for the work of Christ, risking his life to make up for the help you could not give me.[l]

No Confidence in the Flesh

3 Finally, my brothers, rejoice in the Lord! It is no trouble for me to write the same things to you again, and it is a safeguard for you.

2Watch out for those dogs,[a] those men who do evil, those mutilators of the flesh. 3For it is we who are the circumcision,[b] we who worship by the Spirit of God, who glory in Christ Jesus, and who put no confidence in the flesh— 4though I myself have reasons for such confidence.

If anyone else thinks he has reasons to put confidence in the flesh, I have more: 5circumcised[c] on the eighth day, of the people of Israel,[d] of the tribe of Benjamin,[e] a Hebrew of Hebrews; in regard to the law, a Pharisee;[f] 6as for zeal, persecuting the church;[g] as for legalistic righteousness,[h] faultless.

7But whatever was to my profit I now consider loss[i] for the sake of Christ. 8What is more, I consider everything a loss compared to the surpassing greatness of knowing[j] Christ Jesus my Lord, for whose sake I have lost all things. I consider them rubbish, that I may gain Christ 9and be found in him, not having a righteousness of my own that comes from the law,[k] but that which is through faith in Christ—the righteousness that comes from God and is by faith.[l] 10I want to know Christ and the power of his resurrection and the fellowship of sharing in his sufferings,[m] becoming like him in his death,[n] 11and so, somehow, to attain to the resurrection[o] from the dead.

Pressing on Towards the Goal

12Not that I have already obtained all this, or have already been made perfect,[p] but I press on to take hold[q] of that for which Christ Jesus took hold of me.[r] 13Brothers, I do not consider myself yet to have taken hold of it. But one thing I do: Forgetting what is behind[s] and straining towards what is ahead, 14I press on[t] towards the goal to win the prize for which God has called[u] me heavenwards in Christ Jesus.

15All of us who are mature[v] should take such a view of things.[w] And if on some point you think differently, that too God will make clear to you. 16Only let us live up to what we have already attained.

17Join with others in following my example,[x] brothers, and take note of those who live according to the pattern we gave you. 18For, as I have often told you before and now say again even with tears,[y] many live as enemies of the cross of Christ.[z] 19Their destiny is destruction, their god is their stomach,[a]

2:21 c 1Co 10:24; 1Co 13:5
2:22 d 1Co 4:17; 1Ti 1:2
2:23 e ver 19
2:24 f Php 1:25
2:25 g Php 4:3; h Phm 2; i Php 4:18
2:26 j Php 1:8
2:29 k 1Co 16:18; 1Ti 5:17
2:30 l 1Co 16:17
3:2 a Ps 22:16,20
3:3 b Ro 2:28,29; Gal 6:15; Col 2:11
3:5 c Lk 1:59; d 2Co 11:22; e Ro 11:1; f Ac 23:6
3:6 g Ac 8:3; h Ro 10:5
3:7 i Mt 13:44; Lk 14:33
3:8 j Eph 4:13; 2Pe 1:2
3:9 k Ro 10:5; l Ro 9:30
3:10 m Ro 8:17; n Ro 6:3-5
3:11 o Rev 20:5,6
3:12 p 1Co 13:10; q 1Ti 6:12; r Ac 9:5,6
3:13 s Lk 9:62
3:14 t Heb 6:1; u Ro 8:28
3:15 v 1Co 2:6; w Gal 5:10
3:17 x 1Co 4:16; 1Pe 5:3
3:18 y Ac 20:31; z Gal 6:12
3:19 a Ro 16:18

and their glory is in their shame.[b]
Their mind is on earthly things.[c]
20But our citizenship[d] is in
heaven.[e] And we eagerly await a
Saviour from there, the Lord Jesus
Christ,[f] 21who, by the power[g] that
enables him to bring everything
under his control, will transform
our lowly bodies[h] so that they will
be like his glorious body.[i]

4 Therefore, my brothers, you
whom I love and long for,[a] my
joy and crown, that is how you
should stand firm[b] in the Lord,
dear friends!

Exhortations

2I plead with Euodia and I plead
with Syntyche to agree with each
other[c] in the Lord. 3Yes, and I ask
you, loyal yokefellow,[a] help these
women who have contended at my
side in the cause of the gospel,
along with Clement and the rest of
my fellow-workers, whose names
are in the book of life.
4Rejoice in the Lord always. I
will say it again: Rejoice![d] 5Let
your gentleness be evident to all.
The Lord is near.[e] 6Do not be anxious about anything,[f] but in everything, by prayer and petition, with
thanksgiving, present your requests to God.[g] 7And the peace of
God,[h] which transcends all understanding, will guard your hearts
and your minds in Christ Jesus.
8Finally, brothers, whatever is
true, whatever is noble, whatever
is right, whatever is pure, whatever is lovely, whatever is admir-
able—if anything is excellent or
praiseworthy—think about such
things. 9Whatever you have
learned or received or heard from
me, or seen in me—put it into practice.[i] And the God of peace[j] will
be with you.

Thanks for Their Gifts

10I rejoice greatly in the Lord
that at last you have renewed your
concern for me.[k] Indeed, you have
been concerned, but you had no opportunity to show it. 11I am not saying this because I am in need, for I
have learned to be content[l] whatever the circumstances. 12I know
what it is to be in need, and I know
what it is to have plenty. I have
learned the secret of being content
in any and every situation, whether
well fed or hungry,[m] whether living in plenty or in want.[n] 13I can do
everything through him who gives
me strength.[o]
14Yet it was good of you to share[p]
in my troubles. 15Moreover, as you
Philippians know, in the early
days[q] of your acquaintance with
the gospel, when I set out from
Macedonia, not one church shared
with me in the matter of giving and
receiving, except you only;[r] 16for
even when I was in Thessalonica,[s]
you sent me aid again and again
when I was in need.[t] 17Not that I
am looking for a gift, but I am looking for what may be credited to
your account.[u] 18I have received
full payment and even more; I am
amply supplied, now that I have received from Epaphroditus[v] the
gifts you sent. They are a fragrant[w] offering, an acceptable sacrifice, pleasing to God. 19And my
God will meet all your needs[x] according to his glorious riches[y] in
Christ Jesus.
20To our God and Father[z] be
glory for ever and ever. Amen.[a]

Final Greetings

21Greet all the saints in Christ
Jesus. The brothers who are with
me[b] send greetings. 22All the
saints[c] send you greetings, especially those who belong to Caesar's
household.
23The grace of the Lord Jesus
Christ[d] be with your spirit.
Amen.[b]

3:19 b Ro 6:21 c Ro 8:5,6
3:20 d Eph 2:19 e Col 3:1 f 1Co 1:7
3:21 g Eph 1:19 h 1Co 15:43-53 i Col 3:4
4:1 a Php 1:8 b 1Co 16:13 Php 1:27
4:2 c Php 2:2
4:4 d Ro 12:12 Php 3:1
4:5 e Heb 10:37 Jas 5:8,9
4:6 f Mt 6:25-34 g Eph 6:18
4:7 h Isa 26:3 Jn 14:27 Col 3:15
4:9 i Php 3:17 j Ro 15:33
4:10 k 2Co 11:9
4:11 l 1Ti 6:6,8
4:12 m 1Co 4:11 n 2Co 11:9
4:13 o 2Co 12:9
4:14 p Php 1:7
4:15 q Php 1:5 r 2Co 11:8,9
4:16 s Ac 17:1 t 1Th 2:9
4:17 u 1Co 9:11,12
4:18 v Php 2:25 w 2Co 2:14
4:19 x Ps 23:1 2Co 9:8 y Ro 2:4
4:20 z Gal 1:4 a Ro 11:36
4:21 b Gal 1:2
4:22 c Ac 9:13
4:23 d Ro 16:20

a*3* Or *loyal Syzygus* b*23* Some manuscripts do not have *Amen.*

COLOSSIANS

1 Paul, an apostle[a] of Christ
Jesus by the will of God,[b] and
Timothy our brother,

2 To the holy and faithful[a]
brothers in Christ at Colosse:

Grace[c] and peace to you from
God our Father.[b][d]

Thanksgiving and Prayer

3 We always thank God,[e] the
Father of our Lord Jesus Christ,
when we pray for you, 4 because we
have heard of your faith in Christ
Jesus and of the love[f] you have for
all the saints[g]—5 the faith and love
that spring from the hope[h] that is
stored up for you in heaven[i] and
that you have already heard about
in the word of truth, the gospel
6 that has come to you. All over the
world[j] this gospel is bearing
fruit[k] and growing, just as it has
been doing among you since the
day you heard it and understood
God's grace in all its truth. 7 You
learned it from Epaphras,[l] our
dear fellow-servant, who is a faithful minister[m] of Christ on our[c] behalf, 8 and who also told us of your
love in the Spirit.[n]

9 For this reason, since the day we
heard about you,[o] we have not
stopped praying for you and asking
God to fill you with the knowledge
of his will[p] through all spiritual wisdom and understanding.[q]
10 And we pray this in order that you
may live a life worthy[r] of the Lord
and may please him in every way:
bearing fruit in every good work,
growing in the knowledge of God,
11 being strengthened with all
power[s] according to his glorious
might so that you may have great
endurance and patience,[t] and
joyfully 12 giving thanks to the
Father,[u] who has qualified you[d] to
share in the inheritance[v] of the
saints in the kingdom of light. 13 For
he has rescued us from the dominion of darkness[w] and brought us
into the kingdom[x] of the Son he
loves,[y] 14 in whom we have redemption,[e][z] the forgiveness of
sins.[a]

The Supremacy of Christ

15 He is the image[b] of the invisible God,[c] the firstborn over all
creation. 16 For by him all things
were created:[d] things in heaven
and on earth, visible and invisible,
whether thrones or powers or rulers or authorities;[e] all things were
created by him and for him.[f] 17 He
is before all things,[g] and in him all
things hold together. 18 And he is
the head[h] of the body, the church;
he is the beginning and the firstborn from among the dead,[i] so
that in everything he might have
the supremacy. 19 For God was
pleased[j] to have all his fulness[k]
dwell in him, 20 and through him to
reconcile[l] to himself all things,
whether things on earth or things
in heaven,[m] by making peace
through his blood,[n] shed on the
cross.

21 Once you were alienated from
God and were enemies[o] in your
minds[p] because of[f] your evil behaviour. 22 But now he has reconciled you by Christ's physical
body[q] through death to present
you holy in his sight, without blemish and free from accusation[r]—

1:1 *a* 1Co 1:1 *b* 2Co 1:1
1:2 *c* Col 4:18 *d* Ro 1:7
1:3 *e* Ro 1:8
1:4 *f* Gal 5:6 *g* Eph 1:15
1:5 *h* 1Th 5:8 Tit 1:2 *i* 1Pe 1:4
1:6 *j* Ro 10:18 *k* Jn 15:16
1:7 *l* Phm 23 *m* Col 4:7
1:8 *n* Ro 15:30
1:9 *o* Eph 1:15 *p* Eph 5:17 *q* Eph 1:17
1:10 *r* Eph 4:1
1:11 *s* Eph 3:16 *t* Eph 4:2
1:12 *u* Eph 5:20 *v* Ac 20:32
1:13 *w* Ac 26:18 *x* Eph 6:12 2Pe 1:11 *y* Mt 3:17
1:14 *z* Ro 3:24 *a* Eph 1:7
1:15 *b* 2Co 4:4 *c* Jn 1:18
1:16 *d* Jn 1:3 *e* Eph 1:20,21 *f* Ro 11:36
1:17 *g* Jn 1:2
1:18 *h* Eph 1:22 *i* Ac 26:23 Rev 1:5
1:19 *j* Eph 1:5 *k* Jn 1:16
1:20 *l* 2Co 5:18 *m* Eph 1:10 *n* Eph 2:13
1:21 *o* Ro 5:10 *p* Eph 2:3
1:22 *q* Ro 7:4 *r* Eph 5:27

a2 Or *believing* **b**2 Some manuscripts *Father and the Lord Jesus Christ* **c**7 Some manuscripts *your* **d**12 Some manuscripts *us* **e**14 A few late manuscripts *redemption through his blood* **f**21 Or *minds, as shown by*

23 if you continue in your faith, established[s] and firm, not moved from the hope[t] held out in the gospel. This is the gospel that you heard and that has been proclaimed to every creature under heaven,[u] and of which I, Paul, have become a servant.[v]

Paul's Labour for the Church

24 Now I rejoice in what was suffered for you, and I fill up in my flesh what is still lacking in regard to Christ's afflictions,[w] for the sake of his body, which is the church. 25 I have become its servant[x] by the commission God gave me[y] to present to you the word of God in its fulness—26 the mystery[z] that has been kept hidden for ages and generations, but is now disclosed to the saints. 27 To them God has chosen to make known[a] among the Gentiles the glorious riches of this mystery, which is Christ in you, the hope of glory.

28 We proclaim him, admonishing[b] and teaching everyone with all wisdom,[c] so that we may present everyone perfect[d] in Christ. 29 To this end I labour,[e] struggling[f] with all his energy, which so powerfully works in me.[g]

2 I want you to know how much I am struggling[a] for you and for those at Laodicea,[b] and for all who have not met me personally. 2 My purpose is that they may be encouraged in heart[c] and united in love, so that they may have the full riches of complete understanding, in order that they may know the mystery of God, namely, Christ, 3 in whom are hidden all the treasures of wisdom and knowledge.[d] 4 I tell you this so that no-one may deceive you by fine-sounding arguments.[e] 5 For though I am absent from you in body, I am present with you in spirit[f] and delight to see how orderly[g] you are and how firm[h] your faith in Christ is.

Freedom From Human Regulations Through Life With Christ

6 So then, just as you received Christ Jesus as Lord,[i] continue to live in him, 7 rooted[j] and built up in him, strengthened in the faith as you were taught, and overflowing with thankfulness.

8 See to it that no-one takes you captive through hollow and deceptive philosophy,[k] which depends on human tradition and the basic principles of this world[l] rather than on Christ.

9 For in Christ all the fulness of the Deity lives in bodily form, 10 and you have been given fulness in Christ, who is the Head[m] over every power and authority. 11 In him you were also circumcised,[n] in the putting off of the sinful nature,[a][o] not with a circumcision done by the hands of men but with the circumcision done by Christ, 12 having been buried with him in baptism and raised with him[p] through your faith in the power of God, who raised him from the dead.[q]

13 When you were dead in your sins[r] and in the uncircumcision of your sinful nature,[b] God made you[c] alive with Christ. He forgave us all our sins, 14 having cancelled the written code, with its regulations,[s] that was against us and that stood opposed to us; he took it away, nailing it to the cross.[t] 15 And having disarmed the powers and authorities,[u] he made a public spectacle of them, triumphing over them[v] by the cross.[d]

16 Therefore do not let anyone judge you[w] by what you eat or drink,[x] or with regard to a religious festival,[y] a New Moon celebration[z] or a Sabbath day.[a] 17 These are a shadow of the things that were to come;[b] the reality, however, is found in Christ. 18 Do

1:23 s Eph 3:17; t ver 5; u Ro 10:18; v ver 25, 1Co 3:5
1:24 w 2Co 1:5
1:25 x ver 23; y Eph 3:2
1:26 z Ro 16:25
1:27 a Mt 13:11
1:28 b Col 3:16; c 1Co 2:6,7; d Eph 5:27
1:29 e 1Co 15:10; f Col 2:1; g Eph 1:19
2:1 a Col 1:29, Col 4:12; b Rev 1:11
2:2 c Col 4:8
2:3 d Ro 11:33, 1Co 1:24,30
2:4 e Ro 16:18
2:5 f 1Th 2:17; g 1Co 14:40; h 1Pe 5:9
2:6 i Col 1:10
2:7 j Eph 3:17
2:8 k 1Ti 6:20; l Gal 4:3
2:10 m Eph 1:22
2:11 n Ro 2:29, Php 3:3; o Gal 5:24
2:12 p Ro 6:5; q Ac 2:24
2:13 r Eph 2:1,5
2:14 s Eph 2:15; t 1Pe 2:24
2:15 u Eph 6:12; v Lk 10:18
2:16 w Ro 14:3,4; x Ro 14:17; y Ro 14:5; z 1Ch 23:31; a Gal 4:10
2:17 b Heb 8:5

a 11 Or *the flesh* b 13 Or *your flesh* c 13 Some manuscripts *us* d 15 Or *them in him*

not let anyone who delights in false
humility[c] and the worship of
angels disqualify you for the
prize.[d] Such a person goes into
great detail about what he has seen,
and his unspiritual mind puffs him
up with idle notions. 19 He has lost
connection with the Head,[e] from
whom the whole body, supported
and held together by its ligaments
and sinews, grows as God causes it
to grow.[f]
20 Since you died with Christ to
the basic principles of this world,[g]
why, as though you still belonged to
it, do you submit to its rules:[h]
21 "Do not handle! Do not taste! Do
not touch!"? 22 These are all destined to perish[i] with use, because
they are based on human commands and teachings.[j] 23 Such
regulations indeed have an appearance of wisdom, with their self-
imposed worship, their false
humility and their harsh treatment
of the body, but they lack any value
in restraining sensual indulgence.

Rules for Holy Living

3 Since, then, you have been
raised with Christ, set your
hearts on things above, where
Christ is seated at the right hand of
God. 2 Set your minds on things
above, not on earthly things.[a] 3 For
you died,[b] and your life is now hidden with Christ in God. 4 When
Christ, who is your[a] life, appears,[c] then you also will appear
with him in glory.[d]
5 Put to death, therefore, whatever belongs to your earthly
nature: sexual immorality, impurity, lust, evil desires and greed,[e]
which is idolatry.[f] 6 Because of
these, the wrath of God[g] is coming.[b] 7 You used to walk in these
ways, in the life you once lived.[h]
8 But now you must rid yourselves[i]
of all such things as these: anger,
rage, malice, slander[j] and filthy
language from your lips.[k] 9 Do not
lie to each other,[l] since you have
taken off your old self with its
practices 10 and have put on the new
self, which is being renewed[m] in
knowledge in the image of its Creator.[n] 11 Here there is no Greek or
Jew,[o] circumcised or uncircumcised,[p] barbarian, Scythian, slave
or free,[q] but Christ is all,[r] and is
in all.
12 Therefore, as God's chosen
people, holy and dearly loved,
clothe yourselves with compassion, kindness, humility,[s] gentleness and patience.[t] 13 Bear with
each other[u] and forgive whatever
grievances you may have against
one another. Forgive as the Lord
forgave you.[v] 14 And over all these
virtues put on love,[w] which binds
them all together in perfect
unity.[x]
15 Let the peace of Christ[y] rule in
your hearts, since as members of
one body you were called to peace.
And be thankful. 16 Let the word of
Christ[z] dwell in you richly as you
teach and admonish one another
with all wisdom,[a] and as you sing
psalms, hymns and spiritual songs
with gratitude in your hearts to
God.[b] 17 And whatever you do,[c]
whether in word or deed, do it all in
the name of the Lord Jesus, giving
thanks[d] to God the Father through
him.

Rules for Christian Households

3:18–4:1pp Eph 5:22–6:9

18 Wives, submit to your husbands,[e] as is fitting in the Lord.
19 Husbands, love your wives and
do not be harsh with them.
20 Children, obey your parents in
everything, for this pleases the
Lord.
21 Fathers, do not embitter your
children, or they will become discouraged.
22 Slaves, obey your earthly masters in everything; and do it, not
only when their eye is on you and to

2:18 *c* ver 23 *d* Php 3:14
2:19 *e* Eph 1:22 *f* Eph 4:16
2:20 *g* Gal 4:3,9 *h* ver 14,16
2:22 *i* 1Co 6:13 *j* Isa 29:13; Mt 15:9; Tit 1:14
3:2 *a* Php 3:19,20
3:3 *b* Ro 6:2; 2Co 5:14
3:4 *c* 1Co 1:7 *d* 1Pe 1:13; 1Jn 3:2
3:5 *e* Eph 5:3 *f* Eph 5:5
3:6 *g* Ro 1:18
3:7 *h* Eph 2:2
3:8 *i* Eph 4:22 *j* Eph 4:31 *k* Eph 4:29
3:9 *l* Eph 4:22,25
3:10 *m* Ro 12:2; Eph 4:23 *n* Eph 2:10
3:11 *o* Ro 10:12 *p* 1Co 7:19 *q* Gal 3:28 *r* Eph 1:23
3:12 *s* Php 2:3 *t* 2Co 6:6; Gal 5:22,23
3:13 *u* Eph 4:2 *v* Eph 4:32
3:14 *w* 1Co 13:1-13 *x* Eph 4:3
3:15 *y* Jn 14:27
3:16 *z* Ro 10:17 *a* Col 1:28 *b* Eph 5:19
3:17 *c* 1Co 10:31 *d* Eph 5:20
3:18 *e* Eph 5:22

[a]4 Some manuscripts *our* [b]6 Some early manuscripts *coming on those who are disobedient*

win their favour, but with sincerity
of heart and reverence for the
Lord. 23Whatever you do, work at it
with all your heart, as working for
the Lord, not for men, 24since you
know that you will receive an inheritance[f] from the Lord as a reward. It is the Lord Christ you are
serving. 25Anyone who does wrong
will be repaid for his wrong, and
there is no favouritism.[g]

4 Masters, provide your slaves
with what is right and fair, because you know that you also have
a Master in heaven.

Further Instructions

2Devote yourselves to prayer,[a]
being watchful and thankful. 3And
pray for us, too, that God may open
a door[b] for our message, so that we
may proclaim the mystery of
Christ, for which I am in chains.[c]
4Pray that I may proclaim it
clearly, as I should. 5Be wise[d] in
the way you act towards outsiders;[e] make the most of every opportunity.[f] 6Let your conversation
be always full of grace,[g] seasoned
with salt,[h] so that you may know
how to answer everyone.[i]

Final Greetings

7Tychicus[j] will tell you all the
news about me. He is a dear
brother, a faithful minister and
fellow-servant[k] in the Lord. 8I am
sending him to you for the express
purpose that you may know about
our[a] circumstances and that he
may encourage your hearts.[l] 9He
is coming with Onesimus,[m] our
faithful and dear brother, who is
one of you. They will tell you everything that is happening here.

10My fellow-prisoner Aristarchus[n] sends you his greetings, as
does Mark, the cousin of Barnabas.[o] (You have received instructions about him; if he comes to you,
welcome him.) 11Jesus, who is
called Justus, also sends greetings.
These are the only Jews among my
fellow-workers for the kingdom of
God, and they have proved a comfort to me. 12Epaphras,[p] who is one
of you and a servant of Christ
Jesus, sends greetings. He is always wrestling in prayer for you,[q]
that you may stand firm in all the
will of God, mature[r] and fully assured. 13I vouch for him that he is
working hard for you and for those
at Laodicea[s] and Hierapolis. 14Our
dear friend Luke,[t] the doctor, and
Demas[u] send greetings. 15Give my
greetings to the brothers at Laodicea, and to Nympha and the church
in her house.[v]

16After this letter has been read
to you, see that it is also read[w] in
the church of the Laodiceans and
that you in turn read the letter
from Laodicea.

17Tell Archippus:[x] "See to it that
you complete the work you have received in the Lord."[y]

18I, Paul, write this greeting in
my own hand.[z] Remember[a] my
chains. Grace be with you.[b]

3:24 f Ac 20:32
3:25 g Ac 10:34
4:2 a Lk 18:1
4:3 b Ac 14:27 c Eph 6:19,20
4:5 d Eph 5:15 e Mk 4:11 f Eph 5:16
4:6 g Eph 4:29 h Mk 9:50 i 1Pe 3:15
4:7 j Ac 20:4 k Eph 6:21,22
4:8 l Eph 6:21,22
4:9 m Phm 10
4:10 n Ac 19:29 o Ac 4:36
4:12 p Col 1:7 Phm 23 q Ro 15:30 r 1Co 2:6
4:13 s Col 2:1
4:14 t 2Ti 4:11 Phm 24 u 2Ti 4:10
4:15 v Ro 16:5
4:16 w 2Th 3:14
4:17 x Phm 2 y 2Ti 4:5
4:18 z 1Co 16:21 a Heb 13:3 b 1Ti 6:21 2Ti 4:22 Tit 3:15 Heb 13:25

a8 Some manuscripts *that he may know about your*

1 THESSALONIANS

1 Paul, Silas[a] and Timothy,[a]

To the church of the Thessalonians[b] in God the Father and the Lord Jesus Christ:

Grace and peace to you.[b][c]

Thanksgiving for the Thessalonians' Faith

[2]We always thank God for all of you,[d] mentioning you in our prayers. [3]We continually remember before our God and Father your work produced by faith,[e] your labour prompted by love, and your endurance inspired by hope in our Lord Jesus Christ.

[4]For we know, brothers loved by God, that he has chosen you, [5]because our gospel[f] came to you not simply with words, but also with power, with the Holy Spirit and with deep conviction. You know how we lived among you for your sake. [6]You became imitators of us[g] and of the Lord; in spite of severe suffering,[h] you welcomed the message with the joy given by the Holy Spirit.[i] [7]And so you became a model to all the believers in Macedonia and Achaia. [8]The Lord's message rang out from you not only in Macedonia and Achaia—your faith in God has become known everywhere.[j] Therefore we do not need to say anything about it, [9]for they themselves report what kind of reception you gave us. They tell how you turned to God from idols[k] to serve the living and true God, [10]and to wait for his Son from heaven, whom he raised from the dead[l]—Jesus, who rescues us from the coming wrath.[m]

Paul's Ministry in Thessalonica

2 You know, brothers, that our visit to you[a] was not a failure. [2]We had previously suffered[b] and been insulted in Philippi, as you know, but with the help of our God we dared to tell you his gospel in spite of strong opposition. [3]For the appeal we make does not spring from error or impure motives,[c] nor are we trying to trick you. [4]On the contrary, we speak as men approved by God to be entrusted with the gospel.[d] We are not trying to please men[e] but God, who tests our hearts. [5]You know we never used flattery, nor did we put on a mask to cover up greed[f]—God is our witness.[g] [6]We were not looking for praise from men, not from you or anyone else.

As apostles[h] of Christ we could have been a burden to you, [7]but we were gentle among you, like a mother caring for her little children.[i] [8]We loved you so much that we were delighted to share with you not only the gospel of God but our lives as well,[j] because you had become so dear to us. [9]Surely you remember, brothers, our toil and hardship; we worked[k] night and day in order not to be a burden to anyone[l] while we preached the gospel of God to you.

[10]You are witnesses,[m] and so is God, of how holy,[n] righteous and blameless we were among you who believed. [11]For you know that we dealt with each of you as a father deals with his own children,[o] [12]encouraging, comforting and urging you to live lives worthy[p] of God,

1:1 a Ac 16:1; 2Th 1:1; b Ac 17:1; c Ro 1:7
1:2 d Ro 1:8
1:3 e 2Th 1:11
1:5 f 2Th 2:14
1:6 g 1Co 4:16; h Ac 17:5-10; i Ac 13:52
1:8 j Ro 1:8; Ro 10:18
1:9 k 1Co 12:2; Gal 4:8
1:10 l Ac 2:24; m Ro 5:9
2:1 a 1Th 1:5,9
2:2 b Ac 16:22; Php 1:30
2:3 c 2Co 2:17
2:4 d Gal 2:7; e Gal 1:10
2:5 f Ac 20:33; g Ro 1:9
2:6 h 1Co 9:1,2
2:7 i ver 11
2:8 j 2Co 12:15; 1Jn 3:16
2:9 k Ac 18:3; l 2Th 3:8
2:10 m 1Th 1:5; n 2Co 1:12
2:11 o ver 7; 1Co 4:14
2:12 p Eph 4:1

a1 Greek *Silvanus*, a variant of *Silas* b1 Some early manuscripts *you from God our Father and the Lord Jesus Christ* who calls you into his kingdom and glory.

13 And we also thank God continually[q] because, when you received the word of God,[r] which you heard from us, you accepted it not as the word of men, but as it actually is, the word of God, which is at work in you who believe. 14 For you, brothers, became imitators of God's churches in Judea,[s] which are in Christ Jesus: You suffered from your own countrymen[t] the same things those churches suffered from the Jews, 15 who killed the Lord Jesus[u] and the prophets[v] and also drove us out. They displease God and are hostile to all men 16 in their effort to keep us from speaking to the Gentiles[w] so that they may be saved. In this way they always heap up their sins to the limit.[x] The wrath of God has come upon them at last.[a]

Paul's Longing to See the Thessalonians

17 But, brothers, when we were torn away from you for a short time (in person, not in thought),[y] out of our intense longing we made every effort to see you.[z] 18 For we wanted to come to you—certainly I, Paul, did, again and again—but Satan[a] stopped us.[b] 19 For what is our hope, our joy, or the crown[c] in which we will glory[d] in the presence of our Lord Jesus when he comes?[e] Is it not you? 20 Indeed, you are our glory[f] and joy.

3 So when we could stand it no longer,[a] we thought it best to be left by ourselves in Athens.[b] 2 We sent Timothy, who is our brother and God's fellow-worker[a] in spreading the gospel of Christ, to strengthen and encourage you in your faith, 3 so that no-one would be unsettled by these trials. You know quite well that we were destined for them.[c] 4 In fact, when we were with you, we kept telling you that we would be persecuted. And it turned out that way, as you well know.[d] 5 For this reason, when I could stand it no longer,[e] I sent to find out about your faith. I was afraid that in some way the tempter[f] might have tempted you and our efforts might have been useless.[g]

Timothy's Encouraging Report

6 But Timothy has just now come to us from you[h] and has brought good news about your faith and love.[i] He has told us that you always have pleasant memories of us and that you long to see us, just as we also long to see you. 7 Therefore, brothers, in all our distress and persecution we were encouraged about you because of your faith. 8 For now we really live, since you are standing firm[j] in the Lord. 9 How can we thank God enough for you[k] in return for all the joy we have in the presence of our God because of you? 10 Night and day we pray[l] most earnestly that we may see you again[m] and supply what is lacking in your faith.

11 Now may our God and Father himself and our Lord Jesus clear the way for us to come to you. 12 May the Lord make your love increase and overflow for each other[n] and for everyone else, just as ours does for you. 13 May he strengthen your hearts so that you will be blameless[o] and holy in the presence of our God and Father when our Lord Jesus comes[p] with all his holy ones.

Living to Please God

4 Finally, brothers,[a] we instructed you how to live in order to please God,[b] as in fact you are living. Now we ask you and urge you in the Lord Jesus to do this more and more. 2 For you know

2:13 q 1Th 1:2 r Heb 4:12
2:14 s Gal 1:22 t Ac 17:5 2Th 1:4
2:15 u Ac 2:23 v Mt 5:12
2:16 w Ac 13:45,50 x Mt 23:32
2:17 y 1Co 5:3 Col 2:5 z 1Th 3:10
2:18 a Mt 4:10 b Ro 1:13 Ro 15:22
2:19 c Php 4:1 d 2Co 1:14 e Mt 16:27 1Th 3:13
2:20 f 2Co 1:14
3:1 a ver 5 b Ac 17:15
3:3 c Ac 9:16 Ac 14:22
3:4 d 1Th 2:14
3:5 e ver 1 f Mt 4:3 g Gal 2:2 Php 2:16
3:6 h Ac 18:5 i 1Th 1:3
3:8 j 1Co 16:13
3:9 k 1Th 1:2
3:10 l 2Ti 1:3 m 1Th 2:17
3:12 n 1Th 4:9,10
3:13 o 1Co 1:8 p 1Th 2:19
4:1 a 2Co 13:11 b 2Co 5:9

[a]16 Or *them fully* [a]2 Some manuscripts *brother and fellow-worker*; other manuscripts *brother and God's servant*

what instructions we gave you by
the authority of the Lord Jesus.
3 It is God's will that you should
be sanctified: that you should avoid
sexual immorality;[c] 4 that each of
you should learn to control his own
body[a][d] in a way that is holy and
honourable, 5 not in passionate
lust[e] like the heathen,[f] who do not
know God; 6 and that in this matter
no-one should wrong his brother or
take advantage of him.[g] The Lord
will punish men for all such sins,[h]
as we have already told you and
warned you. 7 For God did not call
us to be impure, but to live a holy
life.[i] 8 Therefore, he who rejects
this instruction does not reject man
but God, who gives you his Holy
Spirit.[j]
9 Now about brotherly love[k] we
do not need to write to you,[l] for
you yourselves have been taught
by God to love each other.[m] 10 And
in fact, you do love all the brothers
throughout Macedonia.[n] Yet we
urge you, brothers, to do so more
and more.[o]
11 Make it your ambition to lead a
quiet life, to mind your own business and to work with your hands,[p]
just as we told you, 12 so that your
daily life may win the respect of
outsiders[q] and so that you will not
be dependent on anybody.

The Coming of the Lord

13 Brothers, we do not want you to
be ignorant about those who fall
asleep, or to grieve like the rest of
men, who have no hope.[r] 14 We believe that Jesus died and rose again
and so we believe that God will
bring with Jesus those who have
fallen asleep in him.[s] 15 According
to the Lord's own word, we tell you
that we who are still alive, who are
left till the coming of the Lord, will
certainly not precede those who
have fallen asleep.[t] 16 For the Lord
himself will come down from
heaven, with a loud command, with
the voice of the archangel and with
the trumpet call of God,[u] and the
dead in Christ will rise first.[v]
17 After that, we who are still alive
and are left[w] will be caught up together with them in the clouds[x] to
meet the Lord in the air. And so we
will be with the Lord[y] for ever.
18 Therefore encourage each other
with these words.

5 Now, brothers, about times
and dates[a] we do not need to
write to you,[b] 2 for you know very
well that the day of the Lord[c] will
come like a thief in the night.[d]
3 While people are saying, "Peace
and safety", destruction will come
on them suddenly, as labour pains
on a pregnant woman, and they will
not escape.
4 But you, brothers, are not in
darkness[e] so that this day should
surprise you like a thief. 5 You are
all sons of the light and sons of the
day. We do not belong to the night
or to the darkness. 6 So then, let us
not be like others, who are asleep,[f]
but let us be alert and self-
controlled. 7 For those who sleep,
sleep at night, and those who get
drunk, get drunk at night.[g] 8 But
since we belong to the day, let us be
self-controlled, putting on faith
and love as a breastplate,[h] and the
hope of salvation[i] as a helmet.[j]
9 For God did not appoint us to suffer wrath but to receive salvation
through our Lord Jesus Christ.[k]
10 He died for us so that, whether we
are awake or asleep, we may live
together with him.[l] 11 Therefore
encourage one another and build
each other up, just as in fact you
are doing.

Final Instructions

12 Now we ask you, brothers, to
respect those who work hard
among you, who are over you in the
Lord[m] and who admonish you.
13 Hold them in the highest regard
in love because of their work. Live

4:3 c 1Co 6:18
4:4 d 1Co 7:2,9
4:5 e Ro 1:26; f Eph 4:17
4:6 g 1Co 6:8; h Heb 13:4
4:7 i Lev 11:44; 1Pe 1:15
4:8 j Ro 5:5; Gal 4:6
4:9 k Ro 12:10; l 1Th 5:1; m Jn 13:34
4:10 n 1Th 1:7; o 1Th 3:12
4:11 p Eph 4:28; 2Th 3:10-12
4:12 q Mk 4:11
4:13 r Eph 2:12
4:14 s 1Co 15:18
4:15 t 1Co 15:52
4:16 u Mt 24:31; v 1Co 15:23; 2Th 2:1
4:17 w 1Co 15:52; x Ac 1:9; Rev 11:12; y Jn 12:26
5:1 a Ac 1:7; b 1Th 4:9
5:2 c 1Co 1:8; d 2Pe 3:10
5:4 e Ac 26:18; 1Jn 2:8
5:6 f Ro 13:11
5:7 g Ac 2:15; 2Pe 2:13
5:8 h Eph 6:14; i Ro 8:24; j Eph 6:17
5:9 k 2Th 2:13,14
5:10 l 2Co 5:15
5:12 m 1Ti 5:17; Heb 13:17

[a]4 Or *learn to live with his own wife; or learn to acquire a wife*

in peace with each other.[n] 14And
we urge you, brothers, warn those
who are idle,[o] encourage the timid,
help the weak,[p] be patient with
everyone. 15Make sure that nobody
pays back wrong for wrong,[q]
but always try to be kind to each
other[r] and to everyone else.
16Be joyful always;[s] 17pray continually; 18give thanks in all circumstances, for this is God's will
for you in Christ Jesus.
19Do not put out the Spirit's
fire;[t] 20do not treat prophecies[u] with
contempt. 21Test everything.[v]
Hold on to the good. 22Avoid
every kind of evil.

5:13 n Mk 9:50
5:14 o 2Th 3:6,7,11 p Ro 14:1
5:15 q 1Pe 3:9 r Gal 6:10 Eph 4:32
5:16 s Php 4:4
5:19 t Eph 4:30
5:20 u 1Co 14:1-40
5:21 v 1Co 14:29 1Jn 4:1
5:23 w Ro 15:33
5:24 x 1Co 1:9
5:25 y Eph 6:19

23May God himself, the God of
peace,[w] sanctify you through and
through. May your whole spirit,
soul and body be kept blameless at
the coming of our Lord Jesus
Christ. 24The one who calls you is
faithful[x] and he will do it.

25Brothers, pray for us.[y] 26Greet
all the brothers with a holy kiss.[z]
27I charge you before the Lord to
have this letter read to all the
brothers.[a]
28The grace of our Lord Jesus
Christ be with you.[b]

5:26 z Ro 16:16 **5:27** a Col 4:16 **5:28** b Ro 16:20

2 THESSALONIANS

1 Paul, Silas[a] and Timothy,[a]

To the church of the Thessalonians in God our Father and the
Lord Jesus Christ:

2Grace and peace to you from
God the Father and the Lord Jesus
Christ.[b]

Thanksgiving and Prayer

3We ought always to thank God
for you, brothers, and rightly so,
because your faith is growing more
and more, and the love every one of
you has for each other is increasing.[c] 4Therefore, among God's
churches we boast[d] about your
perseverance and faith[e] in all the
persecutions and trials you are enduring.[f]

5All this is evidence[g] that God's
judgment is right, and as a result
you will be counted worthy of the
kingdom of God, for which you are
suffering. 6God is just: He will pay
back trouble to those who trouble
you[h] 7and give relief to you who
are troubled, and to us as well. This
will happen when the Lord Jesus is
revealed from heaven in blazing
fire with his powerful angels.[i] 8He
will punish those who do not know
God[j] and do not obey the gospel of
our Lord Jesus.[k] 9They will be punished with everlasting destruction[l] and shut out from the presence of the Lord and from the majesty of his power[m] 10on the day[n]
he comes to be glorified[o] in his
holy people and to be marvelled
at among all those who have believed. This includes you, because
you believed our testimony to
you.[p]

11With this in mind, we constantly pray for you, that our God
may count you worthy[q] of his
calling, and that by his power he
may fulfil every good purpose of
yours and every act prompted by
your faith.[r] 12We pray this so that
the name of our Lord Jesus may be
glorified in you,[s] and you in him,
according to the grace of our God
and the Lord Jesus Christ.[b]

The Man of Lawlessness

2 Concerning the coming of our
Lord Jesus Christ and our being gathered to him,[a] we ask you,
brothers, 2not to become easily unsettled or alarmed by some prophecy, report or letter[b] supposed to
have come from us, saying that the
day of the Lord[c] has already come.
3Don't let anyone deceive you[d] in
any way, for ⌞that day will not come⌟
until the rebellion occurs and the
man of lawlessness[a] is revealed,[e]
the man doomed to destruction.
4He will oppose and will exalt himself over everything that is called
God[f] or is worshipped, so that he
sets himself up in God's temple,
proclaiming himself to be God.[g]

5Don't you remember that when I
was with you I used to tell you these
things? 6And now you know what is
holding him back, so that he may be
revealed at the proper time. 7For
the secret power of lawlessness is
already at work; but the one who
now holds it back will continue to
do so till he is taken out of the way.
8And then the lawless one will be
revealed, whom the Lord Jesus will
overthrow with the breath of his
mouth[h] and destroy by the splendour of his coming. 9The coming of
the lawless one will be in accordance with the work of Satan

1:1 *a* Ac 16:1; 1Th 1:1
1:2 *b* Ro 1:7
1:3 *c* 1Th 3:12
1:4 *d* 2Co 7:14 *e* 1Th 1:3 *f* 1Th 2:14
1:5 *g* Php 1:28
1:6 *h* Col 3:25; Rev 6:10
1:7 *i* 1Th 4:16; Jude 14
1:8 *j* Gal 4:8 *k* Ro 2:8
1:9 *l* Php 3:19; 2Pe 3:7 *m* 2Th 2:8
1:10 *n* 1Co 3:13 *o* Jn 17:10 *p* 1Co 1:6
1:11 *q* ver 5 *r* 1Th 1:3
1:12 *s* Php 2:9-11
2:1 *a* Mk 13:27; 1Th 4:15-17
2:2 *b* 2Th 3:17 *c* 1Co 1:8
2:3 *d* Eph 5:6-8 *e* Da 7:25; Da 8:25; Da 11:36; Rev 13:5,6
2:4 *f* 1Co 8:5 *g* Isa 14:13,14; Eze 28:2
2:8 *h* Isa 11:4; Rev 19:15

a *1* Greek *Silvanus*, a variant of *Silas*
b *12* Or *God and Lord, Jesus Christ*
a *3* Some manuscripts *sin*

displayed in all kinds of counterfeit miracles, signs and wonders,[i]
10and in every sort of evil that deceives those who are perishing.[j]
They perish because they refused
to love the truth and so be saved.
11For this reason God sends them[k]
a powerful delusion so that they
will believe the lie 12and so that all
will be condemned who have not
believed the truth but have delighted in wickedness.[l]

Stand Firm

13But we ought always to thank
God for you, brothers loved by the
Lord, because from the beginning
God chose you[b][m] to be saved[n]
through the sanctifying work of the
Spirit[o] and through belief in the
truth. 14He called you to this
through our gospel, that you might
share in the glory of our Lord Jesus
Christ. 15So then, brothers, stand
firm[p] and hold to the teachings[c]
we passed on to you,[q] whether by
word of mouth or by letter.

16May our Lord Jesus Christ himself and God our Father, who loved
us[r] and by his grace gave us eternal encouragement and good hope,
17encourage[s] your hearts and
strengthen[t] you in every good
deed and word.

Request for Prayer

3 Finally, brothers,[a] pray for
us[b] that the message of the
Lord[c] may spread rapidly and be
honoured, just as it was with you.
2And pray that we may be delivered from wicked and evil men,[d]
for not everyone has faith. 3But the
Lord is faithful,[e] and he will
strengthen and protect you from
the evil one.[f] 4We have confidence[g] in the Lord that you are doing and will continue to do the
things we command. 5May the Lord
direct your hearts[h] into God's love
and Christ's perseverance.

Warning Against Idleness

6In the name of the Lord Jesus
Christ,[i] we command you,
brothers, to keep away from[j]
every brother who is idle[k] and
does not live according to the
teaching[a] you received from us.[l]
7For you yourselves know how you
ought to follow our example.[m] We
were not idle when we were with
you, 8nor did we eat anyone's food
without paying for it. On the contrary, we worked[n] night and day,
labouring and toiling so that we
would not be a burden to any of you.
9We did this, not because we do not
have the right to such help,[o] but in
order to make ourselves a model
for you to follow.[p] 10For even when
we were with you,[q] we gave you
this rule: "If a man will not work,[r]
he shall not eat."

11We hear that some among you
are idle. They are not busy; they
are busybodies.[s] 12Such people we
command and urge in the Lord
Jesus Christ[t] to settle down and
earn the bread they eat.[u] 13And as
for you, brothers, never tire of doing what is right.[v]

14If anyone does not obey our instruction in this letter, take special
note of him. Do not associate with
him,[w] in order that he may feel
ashamed. 15Yet do not regard him
as an enemy, but warn him as a
brother.[x]

Final Greetings

16Now may the Lord of peace[y]
himself give you peace at all times
and in every way. The Lord be with
all of you.[z]

17I, Paul, write this greeting in
my own hand,[a] which is the distinguishing mark in all my letters.
This is how I write.

18The grace of our Lord Jesus
Christ be with you all.[b]

2:9 i Mt 24:24; Jn 4:48
2:10 j 1Co 1:18
2:11 k Ro 1:28
2:12 l Ro 1:32
2:13 m Eph 1:4; n 1Th 5:9; o 1Pe 1:2
2:15 p 1Co 16:13; q 1Co 11:2
2:16 r Jn 3:16
2:17 s 1Th 3:2; t 2Th 3:3
3:1 a 1Th 4:1; b 1Th 5:25; c 1Th 1:8
3:2 d Ro 15:31
3:3 e 1Co 1:9; f Mt 5:37
3:4 g 2Co 2:3
3:5 h 1Ch 29:18
3:6 i 1Co 5:4; j Ro 16:17; k ver 7,11; l 1Co 11:2
3:7 m 1Co 4:16
3:8 n Ac 18:3; Eph 4:28
3:9 o 1Co 9:4-14; p ver 7
3:10 q 1Th 3:4; r 1Th 4:11
3:11 s ver 6,7; 1Ti 5:13
3:12 t 1Th 4:1; u 1Th 4:11; Eph 4:28
3:13 v Gal 6:9
3:14 w ver 6
3:15 x Gal 6:1; 1Th 5:14
3:16 y Ro 15:33; z Ru 2:4
3:17 a 1Co 16:21
3:18 b Ro 16:20

b13 Some manuscripts *because God chose you as his firstfruits* c15 Or *traditions*
a6 Or *tradition*

1 TIMOTHY

1 Paul, an apostle of Christ
Jesus by the command of
God[a] our Saviour and of Christ
Jesus our hope,[b]

2 To Timothy[c] my true son[d] in
the faith:

Grace, mercy and peace from
God the Father and Christ Jesus
our Lord.

*Warning Against False
Teachers of the Law*

3 As I urged you when I went into
Macedonia, stay there in Ephesus[e]
so that you may command certain
men not to teach false doctrines[f]
any longer 4 nor to devote themselves to myths[g] and endless
genealogies. These promote controversies[h] rather than God's
work—which is by faith. 5 The goal
of this command is love, which
comes from a pure heart[i] and a
good conscience and a sincere
faith.[j] 6 Some have wandered away
from these and turned to meaningless talk. 7 They want to be teachers
of the law, but they do not know
what they are talking about or what
they so confidently affirm.

8 We know that the law is good[k] if
one uses it properly. 9 We also know
that law[a] is made not for the righteous but for lawbreakers and
rebels,[l] the ungodly and sinful,
the unholy and irreligious; for
those who kill their fathers or
mothers, for murderers, 10 for adulterers and perverts, for slave traders and liars and perjurers—and
for whatever else is contrary to the
sound doctrine[m] 11 that conforms
to the glorious gospel of the
blessed God, which he entrusted
to me.[n]

The Lord's Grace to Paul

12 I thank Christ Jesus our Lord,
who has given me strength,[o] that
he considered me faithful, appointing me to his service. 13 Even
though I was once a blasphemer
and a persecutor[p] and a violent
man, I was shown mercy because I
acted in ignorance and unbelief.[q]
14 The grace of our Lord was poured
out on me abundantly,[r] along with
the faith and love that are in Christ
Jesus.[s]

15 Here is a trustworthy saying[t]
that deserves full acceptance:
Christ Jesus came into the world to
save sinners—of whom I am the
worst. 16 But for that very reason I
was shown mercy[u] so that in me,
the worst of sinners, Christ Jesus
might display his unlimited patience as an example for those who
would believe on him and receive
eternal life. 17 Now to the King[v]
eternal, immortal, invisible,[w] the
only God, be honour and glory for
ever and ever. Amen.[x]

18 Timothy, my son, I give you this
instruction in keeping with the
prophecies once made about you,[y]
so that by following them you may
fight the good fight,[z] 19 holding on
to faith and a good conscience.
Some have rejected these and so
have shipwrecked their faith.[a]
20 Among them are Hymenaeus[b]
and Alexander,[c] whom I have
handed over to Satan[d] to be taught
not to blaspheme.

Instructions on Worship

2 I urge, then, first of all, that requests, prayers, intercession
and thanksgiving be made for
everyone—2 for kings and all those

1:1 a Tit 1:3; b Col 1:27
1:2 c Ac 16:1; d 2Ti 1:2; Tit 1:4
1:3 e Ac 18:19; f Gal 1:6,7
1:4 g 1Ti 4:7; Tit 1:14; h 1Ti 6:4
1:5 i 2Ti 2:22; j 2Ti 1:5
1:8 k Ro 7:12
1:9 l Gal 3:19
1:10 m 2Ti 4:3; Tit 1:9
1:11 n Gal 2:7
1:12 o Php 4:13
1:13 p Ac 8:3; q Ac 26:9
1:14 r Ro 5:20; s 2Ti 1:13
1:15 t 1Ti 3:1; 2Ti 2:11; Tit 3:8
1:16 u ver 13
1:17 v Rev 15:3; w Col 1:15; x Ro 11:36
1:18 y 1Ti 4:14; z 2Ti 2:3
1:19 a 1Ti 6:21
1:20 b 2Ti 2:17; c 2Ti 4:14; d 1Co 5:5

a9 Or *that the law*

in authority,[a] that we may live peaceful and quiet lives in all godliness and holiness. 3 This is good, and pleases God our Saviour, 4 who wants[b] all men[c] to be saved and to come to a knowledge of the truth.[d] 5 For there is one God[e] and one mediator[f] between God and men, the man Christ Jesus, 6 who gave himself as a ransom for all men—the testimony[g] given in its proper time.[h] 7 And for this purpose I was appointed a herald and an apostle—I am telling the truth, I am not lying—and a teacher[i] of the true faith to the Gentiles.[j]

8 I want men everywhere to lift up holy hands[k] in prayer, without anger or disputing.

9 I also want women to dress modestly, with decency and propriety, not with braided hair or gold or pearls or expensive clothes,[l] 10 but with good deeds, appropriate for women who profess to worship God.

11 A woman should learn in quietness and full submission.[m] 12 I do not permit a woman to teach or to have authority over a man; she must be silent. 13 For Adam was formed first, then Eve.[n] 14 And Adam was not the one deceived; it was the woman who was deceived and became a sinner.[o] 15 But women[a] will be saved[b] through childbearing—if they continue in faith, love[p] and holiness with propriety.

Overseers and Deacons

3 Here is a trustworthy saying:[a] If anyone sets his heart on being an overseer,[a][b] he desires a noble task. 2 Now the overseer must be above reproach,[c] the husband of but one wife, temperate, self-controlled, respectable, hospitable,[d] able to teach,[e] 3 not given to drunkenness, not violent but gentle, not quarrelsome,[f] not a lover of money.[g] 4 He must manage his own family well and see that his children obey him with proper respect.[h] 5 (If anyone does not know how to manage his own family, how can he take care of God's church?)[i] 6 He must not be a recent convert, or he may become conceited[j] and fall under the same judgment as the devil. 7 He must also have a good reputation with outsiders, so that he will not fall into disgrace and into the devil's trap.[k]

8 Deacons,[l] likewise, are to be men worthy of respect, sincere, not indulging in much wine,[m] and not pursuing dishonest gain. 9 They must keep hold of the deep truths of the faith with a clear conscience.[n] 10 They must first be tested; and then if there is nothing against them, let them serve as deacons.

11 In the same way, their wives[b] are to be women worthy of respect, not malicious talkers[o] but temperate and trustworthy in everything. 12 A deacon must be the husband of but one wife and must manage his children and his household well.[p] 13 Those who have served well gain an excellent standing and great assurance in their faith in Christ Jesus.

14 Although I hope to come to you soon, I am writing you these instructions so that, 15 if I am delayed, you will know how people ought to conduct themselves in God's household, which is the church[q] of the living God, the pillar and foundation of the truth. 16 Beyond all question, the mystery[r] of godliness is great:

He[c] appeared in a body,[d][s]
  was vindicated by the Spirit,
was seen by angels,
  was preached among the
    nations,[t]

[a] *15* Greek *she* [b] *15* Or *restored*
[a] *1* Traditionally *bishop*; also in verse 2
[b] *11* Or *way, deaconesses* [c] *16* Some manuscripts *God* [d] *16* Or *in the flesh*

2:2 a Ezr 6:10; Ro 13:1
2:4 b Eze 18:23,32; c Tit 2:11; d 2Ti 2:25
2:5 e Ro 3:29,30; f Gal 3:20
2:6 g 1Co 1:6; h 1Ti 6:15
2:7 i 2Ti 1:11; j Ac 9:15; Eph 3:7,8
2:8 k Ps 134:2; Lk 24:50
2:9 l 1Pe 3:3
2:11 m 1Co 14:34
2:13 n Ge 2:7,22; 1Co 11:8
2:14 o Ge 3:1-6,13; 2Co 11:3
2:15 p 1Ti 1:14
3:1 a 1Ti 1:15; b Ac 20:28
3:2 c Tit 1:6-8; d Ro 12:13; e 2Ti 2:24
3:3 f 2Ti 2:24; g Heb 13:5; 1Pe 5:2
3:4 h Tit 1:6
3:5 i 1Co 10:32
3:6 j 1Ti 6:4
3:7 k 2Ti 2:26
3:8 l Php 1:1; m Tit 2:3
3:9 n 1Ti 1:19
3:11 o 2Ti 3:3; Tit 2:3
3:12 p ver 4
3:15 q ver 5; Eph 2:21
3:16 r Ro 16:25; s Jn 1:14; t Col 1:23

was believed on in the world,
was taken up in glory.[u]

Instructions to Timothy

4 The Spirit[a] clearly says that in later times[b] some will abandon the faith and follow deceiving spirits[c] and things taught by demons. 2 Such teachings come through hypocritical liars, whose consciences have been seared as with a hot iron.[d] 3 They forbid people to marry[e] and order them to abstain from certain foods,[f] which God created[g] to be received with thanksgiving[h] by those who believe and who know the truth. 4 For everything God created is good,[i] and nothing is to be rejected if it is received with thanksgiving, 5 because it is consecrated by the word of God and prayer.

6 If you point these things out to the brothers, you will be a good minister of Christ Jesus, brought up in the truths of the faith[j] and of the good teaching that you have followed. 7 Have nothing to do with godless myths and old wives' tales;[k] rather, train yourself to be godly. 8 For physical training is of some value, but godliness has value for all things,[l] holding promise for both the present life[m] and the life to come.

9 This is a trustworthy saying[n] that deserves full acceptance 10 (and for this we labour and strive), that we have put our hope in the living God, who is the Saviour of all men, and especially of those who believe.

11 Command and teach these things.[o] 12 Don't let anyone look down on you because you are young, but set an example[p] for the believers in speech, in life, in love, in faith[q] and in purity. 13 Until I come, devote yourself to the public reading of Scripture, to preaching and to teaching. 14 Do not neglect your gift, which was given you through a prophetic message[r] when the body of elders laid their hands on you.[s]

15 Be diligent in these matters; give yourself wholly to them, so that everyone may see your progress. 16 Watch your life and doctrine closely. Persevere in them, because if you do, you will save both yourself and your hearers.

Advice About Widows, Elders and Slaves

5 Do not rebuke an older man[a] harshly,[b] but exhort him as if he were your father. Treat younger men[c] as brothers, 2 older women as mothers, and younger women as sisters, with absolute purity.

3 Give proper recognition to those widows who are really in need.[d] 4 But if a widow has children or grandchildren, these should learn first of all to put their religion into practice by caring for their own family and so repaying their parents and grandparents,[e] for this is pleasing to God.[f] 5 The widow who is really in need[g] and left all alone puts her hope in God[h] and continues night and day to pray[i] and to ask God for help. 6 But the widow who lives for pleasure is dead even while she lives.[j] 7 Give the people these instructions,[k] too, so that no-one may be open to blame. 8 If anyone does not provide for his relatives, and especially for his immediate family, he has denied[l] the faith and is worse than an unbeliever.

9 No widow may be put on the list of widows unless she is over sixty, has been faithful to her husband,[a] 10 and is well known for her good deeds,[m] such as bringing up children, showing hospitality, washing the feet[n] of the saints, helping those in trouble[o] and devoting herself to all kinds of good deeds.

[a]9 *Or has had but one husband*

3:16 u Mk 16:19
4:1 a Jn 16:13; b 2Ti 3:1; c 2Th 2:3
4:2 d Eph 4:19
4:3 e Heb 13:4; f Col 2:16; g Ge 1:29; h Ro 14:6
4:4 i Ro 14:14-18
4:6 j 1Ti 1:10
4:7 k 2Ti 2:16
4:8 l 1Ti 6:6; m Ps 37:9,11; Mk 10:29,30
4:9 n 1Ti 1:15
4:11 o 1Ti 5:7; 1Ti 6:2
4:12 p Tit 2:7; 1Pe 5:3; q 1Ti 1:14
4:14 r 1Ti 1:18; s Ac 6:6; 2Ti 1:6
5:1 a Tit 2:2; b Lev 19:32; c Tit 2:6
5:3 d ver 5,16
5:4 e Eph 6:1,2; f 1Ti 2:3
5:5 g ver 3,16; h 1Co 7:34; 1Pe 3:5; i Lk 2:37
5:6 j Lk 15:24
5:7 k 1Ti 4:11
5:8 l 2Pe 2:1; Jude 4; Tit 1:16
5:10 m Ac 9:36; 1Ti 6:18; 1Pe 2:12; n Lk 7:44; o ver 16

11 As for younger widows, do not
put them on such a list. For when
their sensual desires overcome
their dedication to Christ, they
want to marry. 12 Thus they bring
judgment on themselves, because
they have broken their first pledge.
13 Besides, they get into the habit of
being idle and going about from
house to house. And not only do
they become idlers, but also gossips and busybodies,[p] saying
things they ought not to. 14 So
I counsel younger widows to
marry,[q] to have children, to manage their homes and to give the enemy no opportunity for slander.[r]
15 Some have in fact already turned
away to follow Satan.[s]

16 If any woman who is a believer
has widows in her family, she
should help them and not let the
church be burdened with them, so
that the church can help those widows who are really in need.[t]

17 The elders[u] who direct the affairs of the church well are worthy
of double honour,[v] especially
those whose work is preaching and
teaching. 18 For the Scripture says,
"Do not muzzle the ox while it
is treading out the grain,"[b][w]
and "The worker deserves his
wages."[c][x] 19 Do not entertain an
accusation against an elder[y] unless it is brought by two or three
witnesses.[z] 20 Those who sin are to
be rebuked[a] publicly, so that the
others may take warning.[b]

21 I charge you, in the sight of God
and Christ Jesus[c] and the elect
angels, to keep these instructions
without partiality, and to do nothing out of favouritism.

22 Do not be hasty in the laying on
of hands,[d] and do not share in the
sins of others.[e] Keep yourself
pure.

23 Stop drinking only water, and
use a little wine[f] because of your
stomach and your frequent illnesses.

24 The sins of some men are
obvious, reaching the place of
judgment ahead of them; the sins
of others trail behind them. 25 In
the same way, good deeds are obvious, and even those that are not
cannot be hidden.

6 All who are under the yoke of
slavery should consider their
masters worthy of full respect,[a] so
that God's name and our teaching
may not be slandered.[b] 2 Those
who have believing masters are not
to show less respect for them because they are brothers.[c] Instead,
they are to serve them even better,
because those who benefit from
their service are believers, and
dear to them. These are the things
you are to teach and urge on
them.[d]

Love of Money

3 If anyone teaches false doctrines[e] and does not agree to the
sound instruction[f] of our Lord
Jesus Christ and to godly teaching,
4 he is conceited and understands
nothing. He has an unhealthy interest in controversies and quarrels
about words[g] that result in envy,
strife, malicious talk, evil suspi-
cions 5 and constant friction between men of corrupt mind, who
have been robbed of the truth[h] and
who think that godliness is a means
to financial gain.

6 But godliness with contentment[i] is great gain.[j] 7 For we
brought nothing into the world, and
we can take nothing out of it.[k] 8 But
if we have food and clothing, we
will be content with that.[l] 9 People
who want to get rich[m] fall into
temptation and a trap[n] and into
many foolish and harmful desires
that plunge men into ruin and destruction. 10 For the love of money[o]
is a root of all kinds of evil. Some
people, eager for money, have wandered from the faith[p] and pierced
themselves with many griefs.

5:13 p 2Th 3:11
5:14 q 1Co 7:9; r 1Ti 6:1
5:15 s Mt 4:10
5:16 t ver 3-5
5:17 u Ac 11:30; v Php 2:29; 1Th 5:12
5:18 w Dt 25:4; 1Co 9:7-9; x Lk 10:7; Lev 19:13; Dt 24:14,15; Mt 10:10; 1Co 9:14
5:19 y Ac 11:30; z Mt 18:16
5:20 a 2Ti 4:2; Tit 1:13; b Dt 13:11
5:21 c 1Ti 6:13; 2Ti 4:1
5:22 d Ac 6:6; e Eph 5:11
5:23 f 1Ti 3:8
6:1 a Eph 6:5; Tit 2:9; 1Pe 2:18; b Tit 2:5,8
6:2 c Phm 16; d 1Ti 4:11
6:3 e 1Ti 1:3; f 1Ti 1:10
6:4 g 2Ti 2:14
6:5 h Tit 1:15
6:6 i Php 4:11; Heb 13:5; j 1Ti 4:8
6:7 k Job 1:21; Ecc 5:15
6:8 l Heb 13:5
6:9 m Pr 15:27; n 1Ti 3:7
6:10 o 1Ti 3:3; p Jas 5:19

b *18* Deut. 25:4 c *18* Luke 10:7

Paul's Charge to Timothy

11But you, man of God,[q] flee from all this, and pursue righteousness, godliness, faith, love,[r] endurance and gentleness. 12Fight the good fight[s] of the faith. Take hold of[t] the eternal life to which you were called when you made your good confession in the presence of many witnesses. 13In the sight of God, who gives life to everything, and of Christ Jesus, who while testifying before Pontius Pilate[u] made the good confession, I charge you[v] 14to keep this command without spot or blame until the appearing of our Lord Jesus Christ, 15which God will bring about in his own time—God, the blessed[w] and only Ruler,[x] the King of kings and Lord of lords,[y] 16who alone is immortal[z] and who lives in unapproachable light, whom no-one has seen or can see.[a] To him be honour and might for ever. Amen.

6:11 *q* 2Ti 3:17 *r* 2Ti 2:22
6:12 *s* 1Co 9:25,26 1Ti 1:18 *t* Php 3:12
6:13 *u* Jn 18:33-37 *v* 1Ti 5:21
6:15 *w* 1Ti 1:11 *x* 1Ti 1:17 *y* Rev 17:14 Rev 19:16
6:16 *z* 1Ti 1:17 *a* Jn 1:18
6:17 *b* Lk 12:20,21 *c* 1Ti 4:10 *d* Ac 14:17
6:18 *e* 1Ti 5:10 *f* Ro 12:8,13
6:19 *g* Mt 6:20
6:20 *h* 2Ti 1:12,14 *i* 2Ti 2:16

17Command those who are rich in this present world not to be arrogant nor to put their hope in wealth,[b] which is so uncertain, but to put their hope in God,[c] who richly provides us with everything for our enjoyment.[d] 18Command them to do good, to be rich in good deeds,[e] and to be generous and willing to share.[f] 19In this way they will lay up treasure for themselves[g] as a firm foundation for the coming age, so that they may take hold of the life that is truly life.

20Timothy, guard what has been entrusted[h] to your care. Turn away from godless chatter[i] and the opposing ideas of what is falsely called knowledge, 21which some have professed and in so doing have wandered from the faith.[j]

Grace be with you.[k]

6:21 *j* 2Ti 2:18 *k* Col 4:18

2 TIMOTHY

1 Paul, an apostle of Christ Jesus by the will of God,[a] according to the promise of life that is in Christ Jesus,[b]

2To Timothy,[c] my dear son:[d]

Grace, mercy and peace from God the Father and Christ Jesus our Lord.

Encouragement to Be Faithful

3I thank God,[e] whom I serve, as my forefathers did, with a clear conscience, as night and day I constantly remember you in my prayers.[f] 4Recalling your tears,[g] I long to see you,[h] so that I may be filled with joy. 5I have been reminded of your sincere faith,[i] which first lived in your grandmother Lois and in your mother Eunice[j] and, I am persuaded, now lives in you also. 6For this reason I remind you to fan into flame the gift of God, which is in you through the laying on of my hands.[k] 7For God did not give us a spirit of timidity,[l] but a spirit of power, of love and of self-discipline.

8So do not be ashamed[m] to testify about our Lord, or ashamed of me his prisoner.[n] But join with me in suffering for the gospel,[o] by the power of God, 9who has saved us and called[p] us to a holy life—not because of anything we have done but because of his own purpose and grace. This grace was given us in Christ Jesus before the beginning of time, 10but it has now been revealed[q] through the appearing of our Saviour, Christ Jesus, who has destroyed death[r] and has brought life and immortality to light through the gospel. 11And of this gospel I was appointed a herald and an apostle and a teacher.[s] 12That is why I am suffering as I am. Yet I am not ashamed, because I know whom I have believed, and am convinced that he is able to guard[t] what I have entrusted to him for that day.[u]

13What you heard from me, keep[v] as the pattern of sound teaching, with faith and love in Christ Jesus.[w] 14Guard the good deposit that was entrusted to you—guard it with the help of the Holy Spirit who lives in us.[x]

15You know that everyone in the province of Asia has deserted me,[y] including Phygelus and Hermogenes.

16May the Lord show mercy to the household of Onesiphorus,[z] because he often refreshed me and was not ashamed of my chains. 17On the contrary, when he was in Rome, he searched hard for me until he found me. 18May the Lord grant that he will find mercy from the Lord on that day! You know very well in how many ways he helped me[a] in Ephesus.

2 You then, my son, be strong[a] in the grace that is in Christ Jesus. 2And the things you have heard me say[b] in the presence of many witnesses[c] entrust to reliable men who will also be qualified to teach others. 3Endure hardship with us like a good soldier[d] of Christ Jesus. 4No-one serving as a soldier gets involved in civilian affairs—he wants to please his commanding officer. 5Similarly, if anyone competes as an athlete, he does not receive the victor's crown[e] unless he competes according to the rules. 6The hardworking farmer should be the first to receive a share of the crops. 7Reflect on what I am saying, for the

1:1 a 2Co 1:1 b Eph 3:6 1Ti 6:19
1:2 c Ac 16:1 d 1Ti 1:2
1:3 e Ro 1:8 f Ro 1:10
1:4 g Ac 20:37 h 2Ti 4:9
1:5 i 1Ti 1:5 j Ac 16:1
1:6 k 1Ti 4:14
1:7 l Ro 8:15
1:8 m Mk 8:38 Ro 1:16 n Eph 3:1 o 2Ti 2:3,9 2Ti 4:5
1:9 p Ro 8:28
1:10 q Eph 1:9 r 1Co 15:26,54
1:11 s 1Ti 2:7
1:12 t 1Ti 6:20 u ver 18
1:13 v Tit 1:9 w 1Ti 1:14
1:14 x Ro 8:9
1:15 y 2Ti 4:10,11, 16
1:16 z 2Ti 4:19
1:18 a Heb 6:10
2:1 a Eph 6:10
2:2 b 2Ti 1:13 c 1Ti 6:12
2:3 d 1Ti 1:18
2:5 e 1Co 9:25

Lord will give you insight into all
this.
8Remember Jesus Christ, raised
from the dead,[f] descended from
David.[g] This is my gospel,[h] 9for
which I am suffering[i] even to the
point of being chained like a criminal. But God's word is not chained.
10Therefore I endure everything[j]
for the sake of the elect, that they
too may obtain the salvation that
is in Christ Jesus, with eternal
glory.[k]
11Here is a trustworthy saying:

If we died with him,
we will also live with him;[l]
12if we endure,
we will also reign with him.[m]
If we disown him,
he will also disown us;[n]
13if we are faithless,
he will remain faithful,[o]
for he cannot disown himself.

A Workman Approved by God

14Keep reminding them of these
things. Warn them before God
against quarrelling about words;[p]
it is of no value, and only ruins
those who listen. 15Do your best to
present yourself to God as one approved, a workman who does not
need to be ashamed and who correctly handles the word of truth.[q]
16Avoid godless chatter,[r] because
those who indulge in it will become
more and more ungodly. 17Their
teaching will spread like gangrene.
Among them are Hymenaeus[s] and
Philetus, 18who have wandered
away from the truth. They say that
the resurrection has already taken
place, and they destroy the faith of
some.[t] 19Nevertheless, God's solid
foundation stands firm,[u] sealed
with this inscription: "The Lord
knows those who are his,"[a][v] and,
"Everyone who confesses the name
of the Lord[w] must turn away from
wickedness."
20In a large house there are articles not only of gold and silver,
but also of wood and clay; some are
for noble purposes and some for ig-
noble.[x] 21If a man cleanses himself
from the latter, he will be an instrument for noble purposes, made
holy, useful to the Master and prepared to do any good work.[y]
22Flee the evil desires of youth,
and pursue righteousness, faith,
love[z] and peace, along with those
who call on the Lord out of a pure
heart.[a] 23Don't have anything to do
with foolish and stupid arguments,
because you know they produce
quarrels. 24And the Lord's servant
must not quarrel; instead, he must
be kind to everyone, able to teach,
not resentful.[b] 25Those who oppose
him he must gently instruct, in the
hope that God will grant them repentance leading them to a knowledge of the truth,[c] 26and that they
will come to their senses and escape from the trap of the devil,[d]
who has taken them captive to do
his will.

Godlessness in the Last Days

3 But mark this: There will be
terrible times in the last
days.[a] 2People will be lovers of
themselves, lovers of money,[b]
boastful, proud,[c] abusive, disobedient to their parents,[d] ungrateful, unholy, 3without love, unfor-
giving, slanderous, without self-
control, brutal, not lovers of
the good, 4treacherous, rash, conceited,[e] lovers of pleasure rather
than lovers of God—5having a form
of godliness but denying its power.
Have nothing to do with them.
6They are the kind who worm
their way[f] into homes and gain
control over weak-willed women,
who are loaded down with sins
and are swayed by all kinds of evil
desires, 7always learning but
never able to acknowledge the
truth. 8Just as Jannes and Jambres
opposed Moses,[g] so also these
men oppose[h] the truth—men of

2:8 f Ac 2:24 g Mt 1:1 h Ro 2:16
2:9 i Ac 9:16
2:10 j Col 1:24 k 2Co 4:17
2:11 l Ro 6:2-11
2:12 m Ro 8:17 1Pe 4:13 n Mt 10:33
2:13 o Nu 23:19 Ro 3:3
2:14 p 1Ti 6:4
2:15 q Eph 1:13 Jas 1:18
2:16 r Tit 3:9
2:17 s 1Ti 1:20
2:18 t 1Ti 1:19
2:19 u Isa 28:16 v Jn 10:14 w 1Co 1:2
2:20 x Ro 9:21
2:21 y 2Ti 3:17
2:22 z 1Ti 1:14 1Ti 6:11 a 1Ti 1:5
2:24 b 1Ti 3:2,3
2:25 c 1Ti 2:4
2:26 d 1Ti 3:7
3:1 a 1Ti 4:1
3:2 b 1Ti 3:3 c Ro 1:30 d Ro 1:30
3:4 e 1Ti 3:6
3:6 f Jude 4
3:8 g Ex 7:11 h Ac 13:8

a19 Num. 16:5 (see Septuagint)

depraved minds,[i] who, as far as the
faith is concerned, are rejected.
9 But they will not get very far because, as in the case of those men,[j]
their folly will be clear to everyone.

Paul's Charge to Timothy

10 You, however, know all about
my teaching,[k] my way of life, my
purpose, faith, patience, love, endurance, 11 persecutions, sufferings—what kinds of things
happened to me in Antioch,[l] Iconium and Lystra, the persecutions
I endured.[m] Yet the Lord rescued
me from all of them.[n] 12 In fact,
everyone who wants to live a godly
life in Christ Jesus will be persecuted,[o] 13 while evil men and impostors will go from bad to worse,[p]
deceiving and being deceived.
14 But as for you, continue in what
you have learned and have become
convinced of, because you know
those from whom you learned it,[q]
15 and how from infancy[r] you have
known the holy Scriptures,[s] which
are able to make you wise[t] for
salvation through faith in Christ
Jesus. 16 All Scripture is God-
breathed[u] and is useful for teaching,[v] rebuking, correcting and
training in righteousness, 17 so that
the man of God[w] may be thoroughly equipped for every good
work.[x]

4 In the presence of God and of
Christ Jesus, who will judge
the living and the dead,[a] and in
view of his appearing and his kingdom, I give you this charge:[b]
2 Preach[c] the Word;[d] be prepared
in season and out of season; correct, rebuke[e] and encourage—
with great patience and careful
instruction. 3 For the time will come
when men will not put up with
sound doctrine.[f] Instead, to suit
their own desires, they will gather
around them a great number of
teachers to say what their itching
ears want to hear. 4 They will turn
their ears away from the truth and
turn aside to myths.[g] 5 But you,
keep your head in all situations,
endure hardship,[h] do the work of
an evangelist,[i] discharge all the
duties of your ministry.

6 For I am already being poured
out like a drink offering,[j] and the
time has come for my departure.[k]
7 I have fought the good fight,[l] I
have finished the race,[m] I have
kept the faith. 8 Now there is in
store for me[n] the crown of righteousness, which the Lord, the
righteous Judge, will award to me
on that day[o]—and not only to me,
but also to all who have longed for
his appearing.

Personal Remarks

9 Do your best to come to me
quickly, 10 for Demas,[p] because he
loved this world,[q] has deserted me
and has gone to Thessalonica. Cres-
cens has gone to Galatia,[r] and Titus to Dalmatia. 11 Only Luke[s] is
with me.[t] Get Mark[u] and bring
him with you, because he is helpful
to me in my ministry. 12 I sent
Tychicus[v] to Ephesus. 13 When you
come, bring the cloak that I left
with Carpus at Troas, and my
scrolls, especially the parchments.

14 Alexander[w] the metalworker
did me a great deal of harm. The
Lord will repay him for what he has
done.[x] 15 You too should be on your
guard against him, because he
strongly opposed our message.

16 At my first defence, no-one
came to my support, but everyone
deserted me. May it not be held
against them.[y] 17 But the Lord
stood at my side[z] and gave me
strength, so that through me the
message might be fully proclaimed
and all the Gentiles might hear it.[a]
And I was delivered from the lion's
mouth. 18 The Lord will rescue me
from every evil attack[b] and will
bring me safely to his heavenly
kingdom. To him be glory for ever
and ever. Amen.[c]

3:8 i 1Ti 6:5
3:9 j Ex 7:12
3:10 k 1Ti 4:6
3:11 l Ac 13:14,50 m 2Co 11:23-27 n Ps 34:19
3:12 o Ac 14:22
3:13 p 2Ti 2:16
3:14 q 2Ti 1:13
3:15 r 2Ti 1:5 s Jn 5:39 t Ps 119:98,99
3:16 u 2Pe 1:20,21 v Ro 4:23,24
3:17 w 1Ti 6:11 x 2Ti 2:21
4:1 a Ac 10:42 b 1Ti 5:21
4:2 c 1Ti 4:13 d Gal 6:6 e 1Ti 5:20 Tit 1:13 Tit 2:15
4:3 f 1Ti 1:10
4:4 g 1Ti 1:4
4:5 h 2Ti 1:8 i Ac 21:8
4:6 j Php 2:17 k Php 1:23
4:7 l 1Ti 1:18 m 1Co 9:24
4:8 n Col 1:5 o 2Ti 1:12
4:10 p Col 4:14 q 1Jn 2:15 r Ac 16:6
4:11 s Col 4:14 t 2Ti 1:15 u Ac 12:12
4:12 v Ac 20:4
4:14 w Ac 19:33 x Ro 12:19
4:16 y Ac 7:60
4:17 z Ac 23:11 a Ac 9:15
4:18 b Ps 121:7 c Ro 11:36

Final Greetings

[19]Greet Priscilla[a] and Aquila[d]
and the household of Onesiphorus.
[20]Erastus[e] stayed in Corinth, and I
left Trophimus[f] sick in Miletus.
[21]Do your best to get here before
winter.[g] Eubulus greets you, and
so do Pudens, Linus, Claudia and all
the brothers.
[22]The Lord be with your spirit.[h]
Grace be with you.[i]

4:19 *d* Ac 18:2
4:20 *e* Ac 19:22 *f* Ac 20:4
4:21 *g* ver 9
4:22 *h* Gal 6:18 Phm 25 *i* Col 4:18

[a]*19* Greek *Prisca*, a variant of *Priscilla*

TITUS

1 Paul, a servant of God[a] and an apostle of Jesus Christ for the faith of God's elect and the knowledge of the truth[b] that leads to godliness— 2 a faith and knowledge resting on the hope of eternal life,[c] which God, who does not lie, promised before the beginning of time,[d] 3 and at his appointed season[e] he brought his word to light[f] through the preaching entrusted to me[g] by the command of God our Saviour,[h]

4 To Titus,[i] my true son in our common faith:

Grace and peace from God the Father and Christ Jesus our Saviour.

Titus' Task on Crete

1:6–8Ref 1Ti 3:2–4

5 The reason I left you in Crete[j] was that you might straighten out what was left unfinished and appoint[a] elders[k] in every town, as I directed you. 6 An elder must be blameless,[l] the husband of but one wife, a man whose children believe and are not open to the charge of being wild and disobedient. 7 Since an overseer[b][m] is entrusted with God's work,[n] he must be blameless—not overbearing, not quick-tempered, not given to drunkenness, not violent, not pursuing dishonest gain.[o] 8 Rather he must be hospitable,[p] one who loves what is good,[q] who is self-controlled, upright, holy and disciplined. 9 He must hold firmly[r] to the trustworthy message as it has been taught, so that he can encourage others by sound doctrine[s] and refute those who oppose it.

10 For there are many rebellious people, mere talkers[t] and deceivers, especially those of the circumcision group.[u] 11 They must be silenced, because they are ruining whole households[v] by teaching things they ought not to teach—and that for the sake of dishonest gain. 12 Even one of their own prophets[w] has said, "Cretans[x] are always liars, evil brutes, lazy gluttons." 13 This testimony is true. Therefore, rebuke[y] them sharply, so that they will be sound in the faith[z] 14 and will pay no attention to Jewish myths[a] or to the commands[b] of those who reject the truth. 15 To the pure, all things are pure, but to those who are corrupted and do not believe, nothing is pure.[c] In fact, both their minds and consciences are corrupted. 16 They claim to know God, but by their actions they deny him.[d] They are detestable, disobedient and unfit for doing anything good.

What Must Be Taught to Various Groups

2 You must teach what is in accord with sound doctrine.[a] 2 Teach the older men to be temperate, worthy of respect, self-controlled, and sound in faith,[b] in love and in endurance.

3 Likewise, teach the older women to be reverent in the way they live, not to be slanderers or addicted to much wine,[c] but to teach what is good. 4 Then they can train the younger women to love their husbands and children, 5 to be self-controlled and pure, to be busy at home, to be kind, and to be subject to their husbands,[d] so that no-one will malign the word of God.[e]

6 Similarly, encourage the young men[f] to be self-controlled. 7 In

1:1 a Ro 1:1 b 1Ti 2:4
1:2 c 2Ti 1:1 d 2Ti 1:9
1:3 e 1Ti 2:6 f 2Ti 1:10 g 1Ti 1:11 h Lk 1:47
1:4 i 2Co 2:13
1:5 j Ac 27:7 k Ac 11:30
1:6 l 1Ti 3:2
1:7 m 1Ti 3:1 n 1Co 4:1 o 1Ti 3:3,8
1:8 p 1Ti 3:2 q 2Ti 3:3
1:9 r 1Ti 1:19 s 1Ti 1:10
1:10 t 1Ti 1:6 u 11:2
1:11 v 2Ti 3:6
1:12 w Ac 17:28 x Ac 2:11
1:13 y 2Co 13:10 z Tit 2:2
1:14 a 1Ti 1:4 b Col 2:22
1:15 c Ro 14:14,23
1:16 d 1Jn 2:4
2:1 a 1Ti 1:10
2:2 b Tit 1:13
2:3 c 1Ti 3:8
2:5 d Eph 5:22 e 1Ti 6:1
2:6 f 1Ti 5:1

a5 Or *ordain*   b7 Traditionally *bishop*

everything set them an example[g]
by doing what is good. In your
teaching show integrity, serious-
ness 8 and soundness of speech that
cannot be condemned, so that those
who oppose you may be ashamed
because they have nothing bad to
say about us.[h]
9 Teach slaves to be subject to
their masters in everything,[i] to
try to please them, not to talk back
to them, 10 and not to steal from
them, but to show that they can be
fully trusted, so that in every way
they will make the teaching about
God our Saviour attractive.[j]
11 For the grace of God that
brings salvation has appeared to all
men.[k] 12 It teaches us to say "No"
to ungodliness and worldly passions,[l] and to live self-controlled,
upright and godly lives[m] in this
present age, 13 while we wait for the
blessed hope—the glorious appearing of our great God and Saviour,
Jesus Christ,[n] 14 who gave himself
for us to redeem us from all wickedness and to purify for himself a
people that are his very own,[o]
eager to do what is good.[p]
15 These, then, are the things you
should teach. Encourage and rebuke with all authority. Do not let
anyone despise you.

Doing What Is Good

3 Remind the people to be subject to rulers and authorities,[a]
to be obedient, to be ready to do
whatever is good,[b] 2 to slander no-
one,[c] to be peaceable and considerate, and to show true humility
towards all men.
3 At one time we too were foolish,
disobedient, deceived and enslaved
by all kinds of passions and pleasures. We lived in malice and envy,
being hated and hating one another. 4 But when the kindness[d]
and love of God our Saviour appeared,[e] 5 he saved us, not because
of righteous things we had done,[f]
but because of his mercy. He saved
us through the washing of rebirth
and renewal[g] by the Holy Spirit,
6 whom he poured out on us[h] generously through Jesus Christ our
Saviour, 7 so that, having been justified by his grace,[i] we might become heirs[j] having the hope[k] of
eternal life.[l] 8 This is a trustworthy saying.[m] And I want you to
stress these things, so that those
who have trusted in God may be
careful to devote themselves to doing what is good.[n] These things are
excellent and profitable for everyone.
9 But avoid foolish controversies
and genealogies and arguments
and quarrels[o] about the law, because these are unprofitable and
useless. 10 Warn a divisive person
once, and then warn him a second
time. After that, have nothing to do
with him.[p] 11 You may be sure that
such a man is warped and sinful; he
is self-condemned.

Final Remarks

12 As soon as I send Artemas or
Tychicus[q] to you, do your best to
come to me at Nicopolis, because I
have decided to winter there.[r]
13 Do everything you can to help
Zenas the lawyer and Apollos[s] on
their way and see that they have
everything they need. 14 Our people
must learn to devote themselves to
doing what is good,[t] in order that
they may provide for daily neces-
sities and not live unproductive
lives.
15 Everyone with me sends you
greetings. Greet those who love us
in the faith.[u]
Grace be with you all.[v]

2:7 g 1Ti 4:12
2:8 h 1Pe 2:12
2:9 i Eph 6:5
2:10 j Mt 5:16
2:11 k 1Ti 2:4
2:12 l Tit 3:3; m 2Ti 3:12
2:13 n 2Pe 1:1
2:14 o Ex 19:5; p Eph 2:10
3:1 a Ro 13:1; b 2Ti 2:21
3:2 c Eph 4:31; 2Ti 2:24
3:4 d Eph 2:7; e Tit 2:11
3:5 f Eph 2:9; g Ro 12:2
3:6 h Ro 5:5
3:7 i Ro 3:24; j Ro 8:17; k Ro 8:24; l Tit 1:2
3:8 m 1Ti 1:15; n Tit 2:14
3:9 o 1Ti 1:4; 2Ti 2:14
3:10 p Ro 16:17
3:12 q Ac 20:4; r 2Ti 4:9,21
3:13 s Ac 18:24
3:14 t ver 8
3:15 u 1Ti 1:2; v Col 4:18

PHILEMON

1 Paul, a prisoner[a] of Christ Jesus, and Timothy our brother,[b]

To Philemon our dear friend and fellow-worker,[c] 2 to Apphia our sister, to Archippus[d] our fellow-soldier[e] and to the church that meets in your home:[f]

3 Grace to you and peace from God our Father and the Lord Jesus Christ.

Thanksgiving and Prayer

4 I always thank my God[g] as I remember you in my prayers, 5 because I hear about your faith in the Lord Jesus and your love for all the saints.[h] 6 I pray that you may be active in sharing your faith, so that you will have a full understanding of every good thing we have in Christ. 7 Your love has given me great joy and encouragement,[i] because you, brother, have refreshed[j] the hearts of the saints.

Paul's Plea for Onesimus

8 Therefore, although in Christ I could be bold and order you to do what you ought to do, 9 yet I appeal to you on the basis of love. I then, as Paul—an old man and now also a prisoner[k] of Christ Jesus—10 I appeal to you for my son[l] Onesimus,[a][m] who became my son while I was in chains. 11 Formerly he was useless to you, but now he has become useful both to you and to me.

12 I am sending him—who is my very heart—back to you. 13 I would have liked to keep him with me so that he could take your place in helping me while I am in chains for the gospel. 14 But I did not want to do anything without your consent, so that any favour you do will be spontaneous and not forced.[n] 15 Perhaps the reason he was separated from you for a little while was that you might have him back for good—16 no longer as a slave, but better than a slave, as a dear brother.[o] He is very dear to me but even dearer to you, both as a man and as a brother in the Lord.

17 So if you consider me a partner,[p] welcome him as you would welcome me. 18 If he has done you any wrong or owes you anything, charge it to me. 19 I, Paul, am writing this with my own hand. I will pay it back—not to mention that you owe me your very self. 20 I do wish, brother, that I may have some benefit from you in the Lord; refresh[q] my heart in Christ. 21 Confident[r] of your obedience, I write to you, knowing that you will do even more than I ask.

22 And one thing more: Prepare a guest room for me, because I hope to be[s] restored to you in answer to your prayers.[t]

23 Epaphras,[u] my fellow-prisoner in Christ Jesus, sends you greetings. 24 And so do Mark,[v] Aristarchus,[w] Demas[x] and Luke, my fellow-workers.

25 The grace of the Lord Jesus Christ be with your spirit.[y]

[a] *10 Onesimus* means *useful.*

1 a ver 9,23; Eph 3:1 b 2Co 1:1 c Php 2:25
2 d Col 4:17 e Php 2:25 f Ro 16:5
4 g Ro 1:8
5 h Eph 1:15; Col 1:4
7 i 2Co 7:4,13 j ver 20
9 k ver 1,23
10 l 1Co 4:15 m Col 4:9
14 n 2Co 9:7; 1Pe 5:2
16 o Mt 23:8; 1Ti 6:2
17 p 2Co 8:23
20 q ver 7
21 r 2Co 2:3
22 s Php 1:25; Php 2:24 t 2Co 1:11
23 u Col 1:7
24 v Ac 12:12 w Ac 19:29 x Col 4:14
25 y 2Ti 4:22

HEBREWS

The Son Superior to Angels

1 In the past God spoke[a] to
our forefathers through the
prophets[b] at many times and in
various ways,[c] 2but in these last
days he has spoken to us by his Son,
whom he appointed heir[d] of all
things, and through whom[e] he
made the universe. 3The Son is the
radiance of God's glory[f] and the
exact representation of his being,
sustaining all things[g] by his powerful word. After he had provided
purification for sins,[h] he sat down
at the right hand of the Majesty in
heaven.[i] 4So he became as much
superior to the angels as the name
he has inherited is superior to
theirs.[j]

5For to which of the angels did
God ever say,

"You are my Son;
today I have become your
Father"[a,b]?[k]

Or again,

"I will be his Father,
and he will be my Son"[c]?[l]

6And again, when God brings his
firstborn into the world,[m] he says,

"Let all God's angels worship
him."[d][n]

7In speaking of the angels he says,

"He makes his angels winds,
his servants flames of
fire."[e][o]

8But about the Son he says,

"Your throne, O God, will last
for ever and ever,
and righteousness will be the
sceptre of your kingdom.
9You have loved righteousness
and hated wickedness;
therefore God, your God, has
set you above your
companions[p]
by anointing you with the oil[q]
of joy."[f]

10He also says,

"In the beginning, O Lord, you
laid the foundations of the
earth,
and the heavens are the work
of your hands.
11They will perish, but you
remain;
they will all wear out like a
garment.[r]
12You will roll them up like a
robe;
like a garment they will be
changed.
But you remain the same,[s]
and your years will never
end."[g][t]

13To which of the angels did God
ever say,

"Sit at my right hand
until I make your enemies
a footstool[u] for your feet"[h]?[v]

14Are not all angels ministering
spirits[w] sent to serve those who
will inherit salvation?[x]

Warning to Pay Attention

2 We must pay more careful attention, therefore, to what we
have heard, so that we do not drift
away. 2For if the message spoken[a]
by angels[b] was binding, and every
violation and disobedience received its just punishment,[c] 3how
shall we escape if we ignore such a

1:1 *a* Jn 9:29; Heb 2:2,3 *b* Ac 2:30 *c* Nu 12:6,8
1:2 *d* Ps 2:8 *e* Jn 1:3
1:3 *f* Jn 1:14 *g* Col 1:17 *h* Heb 7:27 *i* Mk 16:19
1:4 *j* Eph 1:21; Php 2:9,10
1:5 *k* Ps 2:7 *l* 2Sa 7:14
1:6 *m* Heb 10:5 *n* Dt 32:43 (LXX and DSS) Ps 97:7
1:7 *o* Ps 104:4
1:9 *p* Php 2:9 *q* Isa 61:1,3
1:11 *r* Isa 34:4
1:12 *s* Heb 13:8 *t* Ps 102:25-27
1:13 *u* Jos 10:24; Heb 10:13 *v* Ps 110:1
1:14 *w* Ps 103:20 *x* Heb 5:9
2:2 *a* Heb 1:1 *b* Dt 33:2; Ac 7:53 *c* Heb 10:28

a5 Or *have begotten you* b5 Psalm 2:7
c5 2 Samuel 7:14; 1 Chron. 17:13 d6 Deut. 32:43
(see Dead Sea Scrolls and Septuagint)
e7 Psalm 104:4 f9 Psalm 45:6,7
g12 Psalm 102:25–27 h13 Psalm 110:1

great salvation?[d] This salvation, which was first announced by the Lord,[e] was confirmed to us by those who heard him.[f] 4God also testified to it by signs, wonders and various miracles,[g] and gifts of the Holy Spirit[h] distributed according to his will.[i]

Jesus Made Like His Brothers

5It is not to angels that he has subjected the world to come, about which we are speaking. 6But there is a place where someone has testified:

"What is man that you are
mindful of him,
the son of man that you care
for him?[j]
7You made him a little[a] lower
than the angels;
you crowned him with glory
and honour
8 and put everything under his
feet."[b][k]

In putting everything under him, God left nothing that is not subject to him. Yet at present we do not see everything subject to him. 9But we see Jesus, who was made a little lower than the angels, now crowned with glory and honour[l] because he suffered death,[m] so that by the grace of God he might taste death for everyone.[n]

10In bringing many sons to glory, it was fitting that God, for whom and through whom everything exists,[o] should make the author of their salvation perfect through suffering.[p] 11Both the one who makes men holy and those who are made holy[q] are of the same family. So Jesus is not ashamed to call them brothers.[r] 12He says,

"I will declare your name to my
brothers;
in the presence of the
congregation I will sing
your praises."[c][s]

13And again,

"I will put my trust in him."[d][t]

And again he says,

"Here am I, and the children
God has given me."[e][u]

14Since the children have flesh and blood, he too shared in their humanity[v] so that by his death he might destroy[w] him who holds the power of death—that is, the devil[x]—15and free those who all their lives were held in slavery by their fear[y] of death. 16For surely it is not angels he helps, but Abraham's descendants. 17For this reason he had to be made like his brothers[z] in every way, in order that he might become a merciful[a] and faithful high priest[b] in service to God,[c] and that he might make atonement for[f] the sins of the people. 18Because he himself suffered when he was tempted, he is able to help those who are being tempted.[d]

Jesus Greater Than Moses

3 Therefore, holy brothers,[a] who share in the heavenly calling, fix your thoughts on Jesus, the apostle and high priest[b] whom we confess.[c] 2He was faithful to the one who appointed him, just as Moses was faithful in all God's house.[d] 3Jesus has been found worthy of greater honour than Moses, just as the builder of a house has greater honour than the house itself. 4For every house is built by someone, but God is the builder of everything. 5Moses was faithful as a servant[e] in all God's house,[f] testifying to what would be said in the future. 6But Christ is faithful as a son[g] over God's house. And we are his house,[h] if we

2:3 d Heb 10:29 e Heb 1:2 f Lk 1:2
2:4 g Jn 4:48 h 1Co 12:4 i Eph 1:5
2:6 j Job 7:17
2:8 k Ps 8:4-6; 1Co 15:25
2:9 l Ac 2:33; Ac 3:13; Php 2:9 m Php 2:7-9 n Jn 3:16; 2Co 5:15
2:10 o Ro 11:36 p Lk 24:26; Heb 7:28
2:11 q Heb 10:10 r Mt 28:10; Jn 20:17
2:12 s Ps 22:22
2:13 t Isa 8:17 u Isa 8:18; Jn 10:29
2:14 v Jn 1:14 w 1Co 15:54-57; 2Ti 1:10 x 1Jn 3:8
2:15 y 2Ti 1:7
2:17 z Php 2:7 a Heb 5:2 b Heb 4:14,15; Heb 7:26,28 c Heb 5:1
2:18 d Heb 4:15
3:1 a Heb 2:11 b Heb 2:17 c Heb 4:14
3:2 d Nu 12:7
3:5 e Ex 14:31 f ver 2; Nu 12:7
3:6 g Heb 1:2 h 1Co 3:16

a7 Or *him for a little while*; also in verse 9
b8 Psalm 8:4–6
c12 Psalm 22:22
d13 Isaiah 8:17
e13 Isaiah 8:18
f17 Or *and that he might turn aside God's wrath, taking away*

hold on[i] to our courage and the hope[j] of which we boast.

Warning Against Unbelief

7 So, as the Holy Spirit says:[k]

"Today, if you hear his voice,
8 do not harden your hearts
as you did in the rebellion,
during the time of testing in the desert,
9 where your fathers tested and tried me
and for forty years saw what I did.[l]
10 That is why I was angry with that generation,
and I said, 'Their hearts are always going astray,
and they have not known my ways.'
11 So I declared on oath in my anger,
'They shall never enter my rest.'[m]"[a][n]

12 See to it, brothers, that none of you has a sinful, unbelieving heart that turns away from the living God. 13 But encourage one another daily,[o] as long as it is called Today, so that none of you may be hardened by sin's deceitfulness.[p] 14 We have come to share in Christ if we hold firmly[q] till the end the confidence we had at first. 15 As has just been said:

"Today, if you hear his voice,
do not harden your hearts
as you did in the rebellion."[b][r]

16 Who were they who heard and rebelled? Were they not all those Moses led out of Egypt?[s] 17 And with whom was he angry for forty years? Was it not with those who sinned, whose bodies fell in the desert?[t] 18 And to whom did God swear that they would never enter his rest[u] if not to those who disobeyed?[c][v] 19 So we see that they were not able to enter, because of their unbelief.[w]

A Sabbath-rest for the People of God

4 Therefore, since the promise of entering his rest still stands, let us be careful that none of you be found to have fallen short of it.[a] 2 For we also have had the gospel preached to us, just as they did; but the message they heard was of no value to them, because those who heard did not combine it with faith.[a][b] 3 Now we who have believed enter that rest, just as God has said,

"So I declared on oath in my anger,
'They shall never enter my rest.'"[b][c]

And yet his work has been finished since the creation of the world. 4 For somewhere he has spoken about the seventh day in these words: "And on the seventh day God rested from all his work."[c][d] 5 And again in the passage above he says, "They shall never enter my rest."[e]

6 It still remains that some will enter that rest, and those who formerly had the gospel preached to them did not go in, because of their disobedience.[f] 7 Therefore God again set a certain day, calling it Today, when a long time later he spoke through David, as was said before:

"Today, if you hear his voice,
do not harden your hearts."[d][g]

8 For if Joshua had given them rest,[h] God would not have spoken[i] later about another day. 9 There remains, then, a Sabbath-rest for the people of God; 10 for anyone who enters God's rest also rests from his own work, just as God did from his.[j] 11 Let us, therefore, make every effort to enter

3:6 *i* Ro 11:22 *j* Ro 5:2
3:7 *k* Heb 9:8
3:9 *l* Ac 7:36
3:11 *m* Heb 4:3,5 *n* Ps 95:7-11
3:13 *o* Heb 10:24,25 *p* Eph 4:22
3:14 *q* ver 6
3:15 *r* ver 7,8 Ps 95:7,8
3:16 *s* Nu 14:2
3:17 *t* Nu 14:29 Ps 106:26
3:18 *u* Nu 14:20-23 *v* Heb 4:6
3:19 *w* Jn 3:36
4:1 *a* Heb 12:15
4:2 *b* 1Th 2:13
4:3 *c* Ps 95:11 Heb 3:11
4:4 *d* Ge 2:2,3 Ex 20:11
4:5 *e* Ps 95:11
4:6 *f* Heb 3:18
4:7 *g* Ps 95:7,8 Heb 3:7,8,15
4:8 *h* Jos 22:4 *i* Heb 1:1
4:10 *j* ver 4

a11 Psalm 95:7–11 b15 Psalm 95:7,8
c18 Or *disbelieved* a2 Many manuscripts *because they did not share in the faith of those who obeyed* b3 Psalm 95:11; also in verse 5
c4 Gen. 2:2 d7 Psalm 95:7,8

that rest, so that no-one will fall by following their example of disobedience.[k]

12 For the word of God[l] is living and active.[m] Sharper than any double-edged sword,[n] it penetrates even to dividing soul and spirit, joints and marrow; it judges the thoughts and attitudes of the heart.[o] 13 Nothing in all creation is hidden from God's sight.[p] Everything is uncovered and laid bare before the eyes of him to whom we must give account.

Jesus the Great High Priest

14 Therefore, since we have a great high priest who has gone through the heavens,[e][q] Jesus the Son of God, let us hold firmly to the faith we profess.[r] 15 For we do not have a high priest who is unable to sympathise with our weaknesses, but we have one who has been tempted in every way, just as we are[s]—yet was without sin.[t] 16 Let us then approach the throne of grace with confidence, so that we may receive mercy and find grace to help us in our time of need.

5 Every high priest is selected from among men and is appointed to represent them in matters related to God, to offer gifts and sacrifices[a] for sins.[b] 2 He is able to deal gently with those who are ignorant and are going astray,[c] since he himself is subject to weakness.[d] 3 This is why he has to offer sacrifices for his own sins, as well as for the sins of the people.[e]

4 No-one takes this honour upon himself; he must be called by God, just as Aaron was.[f] 5 So Christ also did not take upon himself the glory[g] of becoming a high priest. But God said[h] to him,

> "You are my Son;
> today I have become your
> Father."[a,b][i]

6 And he says in another place,

> "You are a priest for ever,
> in the order of
> Melchizedek."[c][j]

7 During the days of Jesus' life on earth, he offered up prayers and petitions with loud cries and tears[k] to the one who could save him from death, and he was heard because of his reverent submission.[l] 8 Although he was a son, he learned obedience from what he suffered[m] 9 and, once made perfect,[n] he became the source of eternal salvation for all who obey him 10 and was designated by God to be high priest[o] in the order of Melchizedek.[p]

Warning Against Falling Away

6:4–6Ref Heb 10:26–31

11 We have much to say about this, but it is hard to explain because you are slow to learn. 12 In fact, though by this time you ought to be teachers, you need someone to teach you the elementary truths[q] of God's word all over again. You need milk, not solid food![r] 13 Anyone who lives on milk, being still an infant,[s] is not acquainted with the teaching about righteousness. 14 But solid food is for the mature,[t] who by constant use have trained themselves to distinguish good from evil.[u]

6 Therefore let us leave[a] the elementary teachings[b] about Christ and go on to maturity, not laying again the foundation of repentance from acts that lead to death,[a][c] and of faith in God, 2 instruction about baptisms,[d] the laying on of hands,[e] the resurrection of the dead,[f] and eternal judgment. 3 And God permitting,[g] we will do so.

4 It is impossible for those who have once been enlightened,[h] who have tasted the heavenly gift,[i]

4:11 *k* Heb 3:18
4:12 *l* 1Pe 1:23 *m* Jer 23:29 *n* Eph 6:17; Rev 1:16 *o* 1Co 14:24,25
4:13 *p* Ps 33:13-15
4:14 *q* Heb 6:20 *r* Heb 3:1
4:15 *s* Heb 2:18 *t* 2Co 5:21
5:1 *a* Heb 8:3 *b* Heb 7:27
5:2 *c* Heb 2:18 *d* Heb 7:28
5:3 *e* Heb 7:27; Heb 9:7
5:4 *f* Ex 28:1
5:5 *g* Jn 8:54 *h* Heb 1:1 *i* Ps 2:7
5:6 *j* Ps 110:4; Heb 7:17,21
5:7 *k* Mt 27:46,50 *l* Mk 14:36
5:8 *m* Php 2:8
5:9 *n* Heb 2:10
5:10 *o* ver 5 *p* ver 6
5:12 *q* Heb 6:1 *r* 1Co 3:2; 1Pe 2:2
5:13 *s* 1Co 14:20
5:14 *t* 1Co 2:6 *u* Isa 7:15
6:1 *a* Php 3:12-14 *b* Heb 5:12 *c* Heb 9:14
6:2 *d* Jn 3:25 *e* Ac 6:6 *f* Ac 17:18,32
6:3 *g* Ac 18:21
6:4 *h* Heb 10:32 *i* Eph 2:8

e14 Or *gone into heaven* a5 Or *have begotten you* b5 Psalm 2:7 c6 Psalm 110:4
a1 Or *from useless rituals*

who have shared in the Holy
Spirit,[j] 5who have tasted the goodness of the word of God and the
powers of the coming age, 6if they
fall away, to be brought back to repentance,[k] because[b] to their loss
they are crucifying the Son of God
all over again and subjecting him to
public disgrace.
7Land that drinks in the rain
often falling on it and that produces
a crop useful to those for whom
it is farmed receives the blessing
of God. 8But land that produces
thorns and thistles is worthless and
is in danger of being cursed.[l] In
the end it will be burned.
9Even though we speak like this,
dear friends,[m] we are confident of
better things in your case—things
that accompany salvation. 10God is
not unjust; he will not forget your
work and the love you have shown
him as you have helped his people
and continue to help them.[n] 11We
want each of you to show this same
diligence to the very end, in order
to make your hope[o] sure. 12We do
not want you to become lazy, but to
imitate[p] those who through faith
and patience[q] inherit what has
been promised.[r]

The Certainty of God's Promise

13When God made his promise to
Abraham, since there was no-one
greater for him to swear by, he
swore by himself,[s] 14saying, "I will
surely bless you and give you many
descendants."[c][t] 15And so after waiting patiently, Abraham received
what was promised.[u]
16Men swear by someone greater
than themselves, and the oath confirms what is said and puts an end
to all argument.[v] 17Because God
wanted to make the unchanging[w]
nature of his purpose very clear to
the heirs of what was promised,[x]
he confirmed it with an oath. 18God
did this so that, by two unchange-
able things in which it is impossible
for God to lie,[y] we who have fled to
take hold of the hope[z] offered to us
may be greatly encouraged. 19We
have this hope as an anchor for
the soul, firm and secure. It enters
the inner sanctuary behind the
curtain,[a] 20where Jesus, who went
before us, has entered on our
behalf.[b] He has become a high
priest[c] for ever, in the order of
Melchizedek.[d]

Melchizedek the Priest

7 This Melchizedek was king of
Salem and priest of God Most
High.[a] He met Abraham returning
from the defeat of the kings and
blessed him,[b] 2and Abraham gave
him a tenth of everything. First, his
name means "king of righteousness"; then also, "king of Salem"
means "king of peace". 3Without
father or mother, without genealogy,[c] without beginning of days or
end of life, like the Son of God[d] he
remains a priest for ever.
4Just think how great he was:
Even the patriarch[e] Abraham
gave him a tenth of the plunder![f]
5Now the law requires the descendants of Levi who become priests to
collect a tenth from the people[g]—
that is, their brothers—even
though their brothers are descended from Abraham. 6This man,
however, did not trace his descent
from Levi, yet he collected a tenth
from Abraham and blessed[h] him
who had the promises.[i] 7And without doubt the lesser person is
blessed by the greater. 8In the one
case, the tenth is collected by men
who die; but in the other case, by
him who is declared to be living.[j]
9One might even say that Levi,
who collects the tenth, paid the
tenth through Abraham, 10because
when Melchizedek met Abraham,
Levi was still in the body of his
ancestor.

6:4 j Gal 3:2
6:6 k 2Pe 2:21; 1Jn 5:16
6:8 l Ge 3:17,18; Isa 5:6
6:9 m 1Co 10:14
6:10 n Mt 10:40,42; Mt 25:40; 1Th 1:3
6:11 o Heb 3:6
6:12 p Heb 13:7; q 2Th 1:4; Jas 1:3; Rev 13:10; r Heb 10:36
6:13 s Ge 22:16; Lk 1:73
6:14 t Ge 22:17
6:15 u Ge 21:5
6:16 v Ex 22:11
6:17 w Ps 110:4; x Heb 11:9
6:18 y Nu 23:19; Tit 1:2; z Heb 3:6
6:19 a Lev 16:2; Heb 9:2,3,7
6:20 b Heb 4:14; c Heb 2:17; d Heb 5:6
7:1 a Mk 5:7; b Ge 14:18-20
7:3 c ver 6; d Mt 4:3
7:4 e Ac 2:29; f Ge 14:20
7:5 g Nu 18:21,26
7:6 h Ge 14:19,20; i Ro 4:13
7:8 j Heb 5:6; Heb 6:20

b6 Or *repentance while*   c14 Gen. 22:17

Jesus Like Melchizedek

11If perfection could have been
attained through the Levitical
priesthood (for on the basis of it the
law was given to the people),[k] why
was there still need for another
priest to come[l]—one in the order
of Melchizedek,[m] not in the order
of Aaron? 12For when there is a
change of the priesthood, there
must also be a change of the law.
13He of whom these things are said
belonged to a different tribe,[n] and
no-one from that tribe has ever
served at the altar.[o] 14For it is
clear that our Lord descended from
Judah,[p] and in regard to that tribe
Moses said nothing about priests.
15And what we have said is even
more clear if another priest like
Melchizedek appears, 16one who
has become a priest not on the basis
of a regulation as to his ancestry
but on the basis of the power of an
indestructible life. 17For it is declared:

"You are a priest for ever,
in the order of
Melchizedek."[a][q]

18The former regulation is set
aside because it was weak and useless[r] 19(for the law made nothing
perfect),[s] and a better hope is introduced, by which we draw near to
God.[t]
20And it was not without an oath!
Others became priests without any
oath, 21but he became a priest with
an oath when God said to him:

"The Lord has sworn
and will not change his
mind:[u]
'You are a priest for ever.' "[b][v]

22Because of this oath, Jesus has
become the guarantee of a better
covenant.[w]
23Now there have been many of
those priests, since death prevented them from continuing in
office; 24but because Jesus lives
for ever, he has a permanent
priesthood.[x] 25Therefore he is able
to save completely[c] those who
come to God[y] through him, because he always lives to intercede
for them.[z]
26Such a high priest meets our
need—one who is holy, blameless,
pure, set apart from sinners,[a]
exalted above the heavens.[b] 27Un-
like the other high priests, he does
not need to offer sacrifices[c] day
after day, first for his own sins,[d]
and then for the sins of the people.
He sacrificed for their sins once
for all[e] when he offered himself.[f]
28For the law appoints as high
priests men who are weak;[g] but
the oath, which came after the law,
appointed the Son,[h] who has been
made perfect[i] for ever.

The High Priest of a New Covenant

8 The point of what we are saying is this: We do have such a
high priest,[a] who sat down at the
right hand of the throne of the Majesty in heaven, 2and who serves in
the sanctuary, the true tabernacle[b] set up by the Lord, not by man.
3Every high priest is appointed to
offer both gifts and sacrifices,[c]
and so it was necessary for this one
also to have something to offer.[d]
4If he were on earth, he would not
be a priest, for there are already
men who offer the gifts prescribed
by the law.[e] 5They serve at a sanctuary that is a copy[f] and shadow[g]
of what is in heaven. This is why
Moses was warned[h] when he was
about to build the tabernacle: "See
to it that you make everything according to the pattern shown you
on the mountain."[a][i] 6But the ministry Jesus has received is as superior to theirs as the covenant[j] of
which he is mediator[k] is superior
to the old one, and it is founded on
better promises.
7For if there had been nothing

7:11 k ver 18,19; Heb 8:7 l Heb 10:1 m ver 17
7:13 n ver 11 o ver 14
7:14 p Isa 11:1; Mt 1:3; Lk 3:33
7:17 q Ps 110:4; ver 21; Heb 5:6
7:18 r Ro 8:3
7:19 s Ac 13:39; Ro 3:20; Heb 9:9 t Heb 4:16
7:21 u 1Sa 15:29 v Ps 110:4
7:22 w Heb 8:6
7:24 x ver 28
7:25 y ver 19 z Ro 8:34
7:26 a 2Co 5:21 b Heb 4:14
7:27 c Heb 5:1 d Heb 5:3 e Heb 9:12,26, 28 f Eph 5:2; Heb 9:14,28
7:28 g Heb 5:2 h Heb 1:2 i Heb 2:10
8:1 a Heb 2:17
8:2 b Heb 9:11,24
8:3 c Heb 5:1 d Heb 9:14
8:4 e Heb 5:1
8:5 f Heb 9:23 g Col 2:17; Heb 10:1 h Heb 11:7; Heb 12:25 i Ex 25:40
8:6 j Lk 22:20 k Heb 7:22

a17 Psalm 110:4
b21 Psalm 110:4
c25 Or *for ever*
a5 Exodus 25:40

wrong with that first covenant, no
place would have been sought for
another.[l] 8But God found fault
with the people and said:[b]

"The time is coming, declares
 the Lord,
 when I will make a new
 covenant[m]
with the house of Israel
 and with the house of Judah.
9It will not be like the covenant
 I made with their
 forefathers[n]
when I took them by the hand
 to lead them out of Egypt,
because they did not remain
 faithful to my covenant,
 and I turned away from them,
 declares the Lord.
10This is the covenant I will make
 with the house of Israel
 after that time, declares the
 Lord.
I will put my laws in their
 minds
 and write them on their
 hearts.[o]
I will be their God,
 and they will be my people.[p]
11No longer will a man teach his
 neighbour,
 or a man his brother, saying,
 'Know the Lord,'
because they will all know me,[q]
 from the least of them to the
 greatest.
12For I will forgive their
 wickedness
 and will remember their sins
 no more.[r]"[c][s]

13By calling this covenant "new",
he has made the first one obsolete;[t] and what is obsolete and age-
ing will soon disappear.

Worship in the Earthly Tabernacle

9 Now the first covenant had
regulations for worship and
also an earthly sanctuary.[a] 2A tabernacle[b] was set up. In its first
room were the lampstand,[c] the
table[d] and the consecrated
bread;[e] this was called the Holy
Place. 3Behind the second curtain
was a room called the Most Holy
Place,[f] 4which had the golden altar
of incense[g] and the gold-covered
ark of the covenant.[h] This ark contained the gold jar of manna,[i]
Aaron's staff that had budded,[j]
and the stone tablets of the covenant. 5Above the ark were the
cherubim of the Glory,[k] overshadowing the atonement cover.[a]
But we cannot discuss these things
in detail now.

6When everything had been arranged like this, the priests entered regularly[l] into the outer
room to carry on their ministry.
7But only the high priest entered[m]
the inner room, and that only once
a year,[n] and never without blood,
which he offered for himself[o] and
for the sins the people had committed in ignorance. 8The Holy Spirit
was showing[p] by this that the
way[q] into the Most Holy Place had
not yet been disclosed as long as
the first tabernacle was still standing. 9This is an illustration for the
present time, indicating that the
gifts and sacrifices being offered[r]
were not able to clear the conscience of the worshipper. 10They
are only a matter of food[s] and
drink[t] and various ceremonial
washings—external regulations[u]
applying until the time of the new
order.

The Blood of Christ

11When Christ came as high
priest[v] of the good things that are
already here,[b][w] he went through
the greater and more perfect tabernacle[x] that is not man-made,
that is to say, not a part of this creation. 12He did not enter by means
of the blood of goats and calves;[y]

8:7 *l* Heb 7:11,18
8:8 *m* Jer 31:31
8:9 *n* Ex 19:5,6
8:10 *o* 2Co 3:3; Heb 10:16 *p* Zec 8:8
8:11 *q* Isa 54:13; Jn 6:45
8:12 *r* Heb 10:17 *s* Jer 31:31-34
8:13 *t* 2Co 5:17
9:1 *a* Ex 25:8
9:2 *b* Ex 25:8,9 *c* Ex 25:31-39 *d* Ex 25:23-29 *e* Lev 24:5-8
9:3 *f* Ex 26:31-33
9:4 *g* Ex 30:1-5 *h* Ex 25:10-22 *i* Ex 16:32,33 *j* Nu 17:10
9:5 *k* Ex 25:17-19
9:6 *l* Nu 28:3
9:7 *m* Lev 16:11-19 *n* Lev 16:34 *o* Heb 5:2,3
9:8 *p* Heb 3:7 *q* Jn 14:6; Heb 10:19,20
9:9 *r* Heb 5:1
9:10 *s* Lev 11:2-23 *t* Col 2:16 *u* Heb 7:16
9:11 *v* Heb 2:17 *w* Heb 10:1 *x* Heb 8:2
9:12 *y* Heb 10:4

[b]*8* Some manuscripts may be translated *fault and said to the people.* [c]*12* Jer. 31:31–34
[a]*5* Traditionally *the mercy seat*
[b]*11* Some early manuscripts *are to come*

but he entered the Most Holy
Place[z] once for all[a] by his own
blood, having obtained eternal redemption. 13The blood of goats and
bulls and the ashes of a heifer[b]
sprinkled on those who are ceremonially unclean sanctify them so
that they are outwardly clean.
14How much more, then, will the
blood of Christ, who through the
eternal Spirit[c] offered himself un-
blemished to God, cleanse our consciences[d] from acts that lead to
death,[c][e] so that we may serve the
living God!

15For this reason Christ is the
mediator[f] of a new covenant, that
those who are called may receive
the promised eternal inheritance—
now that he has died as a ransom to
set them free from the sins committed under the first covenant.[g]

16In the case of a will,[d] it is necessary to prove the death of the one
who made it, 17because a will is in
force only when somebody has
died; it never takes effect while the
one who made it is living. 18This is
why even the first covenant was
not put into effect without blood.[h]
19When Moses had proclaimed
every commandment of the law to
all the people, he took the blood of
calves, together with water, scarlet
wool and branches of hyssop, and
sprinkled the scroll and all the people.[i] 20He said, "This is the blood
of the covenant, which God has
commanded you to keep."[e][j] 21In
the same way, he sprinkled with
the blood both the tabernacle and
everything used in its ceremonies.
22In fact, the law requires that
nearly everything be cleansed with
blood,[k] and without the shedding
of blood there is no forgiveness.[l]

23It was necessary, then, for the
copies[m] of the heavenly things to
be purified with these sacrifices,
but the heavenly things themselves
with better sacrifices than these.
24For Christ did not enter a man-
made sanctuary that was only a
copy of the true one;[n] he entered
heaven itself, now to appear for us
in God's presence. 25Nor did he enter heaven to offer himself again
and again, the way the high priest
enters the Most Holy Place[o] every
year with blood that is not his
own.[p] 26Then Christ would have
had to suffer many times since the
creation of the world.[q] But now he
has appeared once for all[r] at the
end of the ages to do away with sin
by the sacrifice of himself. 27Just
as man is destined to die once,[s]
and after that to face judgment,[t]
28so Christ was sacrificed once to
take away the sins of many people;
and he will appear a second time,[u]
not to bear sin,[v] but to bring salvation to those who are waiting for
him.[w]

Christ's Sacrifice Once for All

10 The law is only a shadow[a]
of the good things[b] that
are coming—not the realities
themselves.[c] For this reason it can
never, by the same sacrifices repeated endlessly year after year,
make perfect[d] those who draw
near to worship. 2If it could, would
they not have stopped being offered? For the worshippers would
have been cleansed once for all,
and would no longer have felt
guilty for their sins. 3But those sacrifices are an annual reminder of
sins,[e] 4because it is impossible for
the blood of bulls and goats[f] to
take away sins.

5Therefore, when Christ came
into the world,[g] he said:

"Sacrifice and offering you did
not desire,
but a body you prepared for
me;[h]
6with burnt offerings and sin
offerings
you were not pleased.

9:12 z ver 24 a Heb 7:27
9:13 b Nu 19:9,17,18
9:14 c 1Pe 3:18 d Tit 2:14 Heb 10:2,22 e Heb 6:1
9:15 f 1Ti 2:5 g Heb 7:22
9:18 h Ex 24:6-8
9:19 i Ex 24:6-8
9:20 j Ex 24:8 Mt 26:28
9:22 k Lev 8:15 l Lev 17:11
9:23 m Heb 8:5
9:24 n Heb 8:2
9:25 o Heb 10:19 p ver 7,8
9:26 q Heb 4:3 r Heb 7:27
9:27 s Ge 3:19 t 2Co 5:10
9:28 u Tit 2:13 v 1Pe 2:24 w 1Co 1:7
10:1 a Heb 8:5 b Heb 9:11 c Heb 9:23 d Heb 7:19
10:3 e Heb 9:7
10:4 f Heb 9:12,13
10:5 g Heb 1:6 h 1Pe 2:24

c14 Or *from useless rituals* d16 Same Greek word as *covenant*; also in verse 17
e20 Exodus 24:8

7Then I said, 'Here I am—it is
written about me in the
scroll[i]—
I have come to do your will,
O God.' "[a][j]

8First he said, "Sacrifices and offerings, burnt offerings and sin offerings you did not desire, nor were you pleased with them"[k] (although the law required them to be made). 9Then he said, "Here I am, I have come to do your will."[l] He sets aside the first to establish the second. 10And by that will, we have been made holy[m] through the sacrifice of the body[n] of Jesus Christ once for all.[o]

11Day after day every priest stands and performs his religious duties; again and again he offers the same sacrifices,[p] which can never take away sins.[q] 12But when this priest had offered for all time one sacrifice for sins, he sat down at the right hand of God. 13Since that time he waits for his enemies to be made his footstool,[r] 14because by one sacrifice he has made perfect[s] for ever those who are being made holy.

15The Holy Spirit also testifies[t] to us about this. First he says:

16"This is the covenant I will
make with them
after that time, says the Lord.
I will put my laws in their
hearts,
and I will write them on their
minds."[b][u]

17Then he adds:

"Their sins and lawless acts
I will remember no more."[c][v]

18And where these have been forgiven, there is no longer any sacrifice for sin.

A Call to Persevere

19Therefore, brothers, since we have confidence to enter the Most Holy Place[w] by the blood of Jesus, 20by a new and living way[x] opened for us through the curtain,[y] that is, his body, 21and since we have a great priest[z] over the house of God, 22let us draw near to God[a] with a sincere heart in full assurance of faith, having our hearts sprinkled to cleanse us from a guilty conscience[b] and having our bodies washed with pure water. 23Let us hold unswervingly to the hope[c] we profess, for he who promised is faithful.[d] 24And let us consider how we may spur one another on towards love and good deeds. 25Let us not give up meeting together,[e] as some are in the habit of doing, but let us encourage one another[f]—and all the more as you see the Day approaching.

26If we deliberately keep on sinning[g] after we have received the knowledge of the truth, no sacrifice for sins is left, 27but only a fearful expectation of judgment and of raging fire[h] that will consume the enemies of God. 28Anyone who rejected the law of Moses died without mercy on the testimony of two or three witnesses.[i] 29How much more severely do you think a man deserves to be punished who has trampled the Son of God under foot,[j] who has treated as an unholy thing the blood of the covenant[k] that sanctified him, and who has insulted the Spirit[l] of grace?[m] 30For we know him who said, "It is mine to avenge; I will repay,"[d][n] and again, "The Lord will judge his people."[e][o] 31It is a dreadful thing to fall into the hands of the living God.[p]

32Remember those earlier days after you had received the light,[q] when you stood your ground in a great contest in the face of suffering.[r] 33Sometimes you were publicly exposed to insult and persecution;[s] at other times you stood side by side with those who

10:7 *i* Jer 36:2 *j* Ps 40:6-8
10:8 *k* ver 5,6 Mk 12:33
10:9 *l* ver 7
10:10 *m* Jn 17:19 *n* Heb 2:14 1Pe 2:24 *o* Heb 7:27
10:11 *p* Heb 5:1 *q* ver 1,4
10:13 *r* Heb 1:13
10:14 *s* ver 1
10:15 *t* Heb 3:7
10:16 *u* Jer 31:33 Heb 8:10
10:17 *v* Heb 8:12
10:19 *w* Eph 2:18 Heb 9:8,12,25
10:20 *x* Heb 9:8 *y* Heb 9:3
10:21 *z* Heb 2:17
10:22 *a* Heb 7:19 *b* Eze 36:25 Heb 9:14
10:23 *c* Heb 3:6 *d* 1Co 1:9
10:25 *e* Ac 2:42 *f* Heb 3:13
10:26 *g* Nu 15:30 2Pe 2:20
10:27 *h* Isa 26:11 2Th 1:7 Heb 9:27
10:28 *i* Dt 17:6,7 Heb 2:2
10:29 *j* Heb 6:6 *k* Mt 26:28 *l* Eph 4:30 Heb 6:4 *m* Heb 2:3
10:30 *n* Dt 32:35 Ro 12:19 *o* Dt 32:36
10:31 *p* Mt 16:16
10:32 *q* Heb 6:4 *r* Php 1:29,30
10:33 *s* 1Co 4:9

a*7* Psalm 40:6–8 (see Septuagint) b*16* Jer. 31:33 c*17* Jer. 31:34 d*30* Deut. 32:35 e*30* Deut. 32:36; Psalm 135:14

were so treated.[t] 34 You sympathised with those in prison[u] and joyfully accepted the confiscation of your property, because you knew that you yourselves had better and lasting possessions.[v]

35 So do not throw away your confidence; it will be richly rewarded. 36 You need to persevere[w] so that when you have done the will of God, you will receive what he has promised. 37 For in just a very little while,

"He who is coming[x] will come
and will not delay.[y]
38 But my righteous one[f] will
live by faith.[z]
And if he shrinks back,
I will not be pleased with
him."[g]

39 But we are not of those who shrink back and are destroyed, but of those who believe and are saved.

By Faith

11 Now faith is being sure of what we hope for and certain of what we do not see.[a] 2 This is what the ancients were commended for.[b]

3 By faith we understand that the universe was formed at God's command,[c] so that what is seen was not made out of what was visible.

4 By faith Abel offered God a better sacrifice than Cain did. By faith he was commended as a righteous man, when God spoke well of his offerings.[d] And by faith he still speaks, even though he is dead.[e]

5 By faith Enoch was taken from this life, so that he did not experience death; he could not be found, because God had taken him away.[f] For before he was taken, he was commended as one who pleased God. 6 And without faith it is impossible to please God, because anyone who comes to him[g] must believe that he exists and that he rewards those who earnestly seek him.

7 By faith Noah, when warned about things not yet seen, in holy fear built an ark[h] to save his family.[i] By his faith he condemned the world and became heir of the righteousness that comes by faith.

8 By faith Abraham, when called to go to a place he would later receive as his inheritance,[j] obeyed and went,[k] even though he did not know where he was going. 9 By faith he made his home in the promised land[l] like a stranger in a foreign country; he lived in tents,[m] as did Isaac and Jacob, who were heirs with him of the same promise.[n] 10 For he was looking forward to the city[o] with foundations,[p] whose architect and builder is God.

11 By faith Abraham, even though he was past age—and Sarah herself was barren[q]—was enabled to become a father[r] because he[a] considered him faithful who had made the promise. 12 And so from this one man, and he as good as dead,[s] came descendants as numerous as the stars in the sky and as countless as the sand on the seashore.[t]

13 All these people were still living by faith when they died. They did not receive the things promised;[u] they only saw them and welcomed them from a distance.[v] And they admitted that they were aliens and strangers on earth.[w] 14 People who say such things show that they are looking for a country of their own. 15 If they had been thinking of the country they had left, they would have had opportunity to return.[x] 16 Instead, they were longing for a better country—a heavenly one.[y] Therefore God is not ashamed[z] to be called their God,[a] for he has prepared a city[b] for them.

17 By faith Abraham, when God tested him, offered Isaac as a sacrifice.[c] He who had received the

10:33 t Php 4:14; 1Th 2:14
10:34 u Heb 13:3; v Heb 11:16
10:36 w Lk 21:19; Heb 12:1
10:37 x Mt 11:3; y Rev 22:20
10:38 z Ro 1:17; Gal 3:11
11:1 a Ro 8:24; 2Co 4:18
11:2 b ver 4,39
11:3 c Ge 1; Jn 1:3; 2Pe 3:5
11:4 d Ge 4:4; 1Jn 3:12; e Heb 12:24
11:5 f Ge 5:21-24
11:6 g Heb 7:19
11:7 h Ge 6:13-22; i 1Pe 3:20
11:8 j Ge 12:7; k Ge 12:1-4; Ac 7:2-4
11:9 l Ac 7:5; m Ge 12:8; Ge 18:1,9; n Heb 6:17
11:10 o Heb 12:22; Heb 13:14; p Rev 21:2,14
11:11 q Ge 17:17-19; Ge 18:11-14; r Ge 21:2
11:12 s Ro 4:19; t Ge 22:17
11:13 u ver 39; v Mt 13:17; w Ge 23:4; Ps 39:12; 1Pe 1:17
11:15 x Ge 24:6-8
11:16 y 2Ti 4:18; z Mk 8:38; a Ex 3:6,15; b Heb 13:14
11:17 c Ge 22:1-10; Jas 2:21

f38 One early manuscript *But the righteous*
g38 Hab. 2:3,4 a11 Or *By faith even Sarah, who was past age, was enabled to bear children because she*

promises was about to sacrifice his
one and only son, 18 even though
God had said to him, "It is through
Isaac that your offspring[b] will
be reckoned."[c][d] 19 Abraham reasoned that God could raise the
dead,[e] and figuratively speaking,
he did receive Isaac back from
death.

20 By faith Isaac blessed Jacob
and Esau in regard to their future.[f]

21 By faith Jacob, when he was
dying, blessed each of Joseph's
sons,[g] and worshipped as he
leaned on the top of his staff.

22 By faith Joseph, when his end
was near, spoke about the exodus
of the Israelites from Egypt and
gave instructions about his
bones.[h]

23 By faith Moses' parents hid him
for three months after he was
born,[i] because they saw he was no
ordinary child, and they were not
afraid of the king's edict.[j]

24 By faith Moses, when he had
grown up, refused to be known as
the son of Pharaoh's daughter.[k]
25 He chose to be ill-treated[l] along
with the people of God rather than
to enjoy the pleasures of sin for a
short time. 26 He regarded disgrace[m] for the sake of Christ as of
greater value than the treasures
of Egypt, because he was looking
ahead to his reward.[n] 27 By faith he
left Egypt,[o] not fearing the king's
anger; he persevered because he
saw him who is invisible. 28 By faith
he kept the Passover and the
sprinkling of blood, so that the destroyer of the firstborn would not
touch the firstborn of Israel.[p]

29 By faith the people passed
through the Red Sea[d] as on dry
land; but when the Egyptians tried
to do so, they were drowned.[q]

30 By faith the walls of Jericho
fell, after the people had marched
around them for seven days.[r]

31 By faith the prostitute Rahab,
because she welcomed the spies,
was not killed with those who were
disobedient.[e][s]

32 And what more shall I say? I
do not have time to tell about Gideon, Barak,[t] Samson, Jephthah,
David,[u] Samuel[v] and the prophets, 33 who through faith conquered
kingdoms,[w] administered justice,
and gained what was promised;
who shut the mouths of lions,[x]
34 quenched the fury of the flames,
and escaped the edge of the sword;
whose weakness was turned to
strength;[y] and who became powerful in battle and routed foreign
armies.[z] 35 Women received back
their dead, raised to life again.[a]
Others were tortured and refused
to be released, so that they might
gain a better resurrection. 36 Some
faced jeers and flogging,[b] while
still others were chained and put
in prison.[c] 37 They were stoned;[f][d]
they were sawn in two; they were
put to death by the sword.[e] They
went about in sheepskins and goatskins,[f] destitute, persecuted and
ill-treated—38 the world was not
worthy of them. They wandered in
deserts and mountains, and in
caves[g] and holes in the ground.

39 These were all commended[h]
for their faith, yet none of them received what had been promised.[i]
40 God had planned something better for us so that only together with
us would they be made perfect.

God Disciplines His Sons

12 Therefore, since we are
surrounded by such a great
cloud of witnesses, let us throw off
everything that hinders and the sin
that so easily entangles, and let us
run[a] with perseverance[b] the race
marked out for us. 2 Let us fix our
eyes on Jesus, the author and per-
fecter of our faith, who for the joy
set before him endured the cross,[c]

11:18 d Ge 21:12; Ro 9:7
11:19 e Ro 4:21
11:20 f Ge 27:27-29, 39,40
11:21 g Ge 48:1,8-22
11:22 h Ge 50:24,25; Ex 13:19
11:23 i Ex 2:2; j Ex 1:16,22
11:24 k Ex 2:10,11
11:25 l ver 37
11:26 m Heb 13:13; n Heb 10:35
11:27 o Ex 12:50,51
11:28 p Ex 12:21-23
11:29 q Ex 14:21-31
11:30 r Jos 6:12-20
11:31 s Jos 2:1,9-14; Jos 6:22-25; Jas 2:25
11:32 t Jdg 4-5; u 1Sa 16:1,13; v 1Sa 1:20
11:33 w 2Sa 7:11; 2Sa 8:1-3; x Da 6:22
11:34 y 2Ki 20:7; z Jdg 15:8
11:35 a 1Ki 17:22,23
11:36 b Jer 20:2; c Ge 39:20
11:37 d 2Ch 24:21; e 1Ki 19:10; f 2Ki 1:8
11:38 g 1Ki 18:4
11:39 h ver 2,4; i ver 13
12:1 a 1Co 9:24; b Heb 10:36
12:2 c Php 2:8,9

b 18 Greek *seed* c 18 Gen. 21:12
d 29 That is, Sea of Reeds e 31 Or *unbelieving*
f 37 Some early manuscripts *stoned; they were put to the test;*

scorning its shame,[d] and sat down at the right hand of the throne of God. 3Consider him who endured such opposition from sinful men, so that you will not grow weary[e] and lose heart.

4In your struggle against sin, you have not yet resisted to the point of shedding your blood.[f] 5And you have forgotten that word of encouragement that addresses you as sons:

> "My son, do not make light of
> the Lord's discipline,
> and do not lose heart when he
> rebukes you,
> 6because the Lord disciplines
> those he loves,[g]
> and he punishes everyone he
> accepts as a son."[a][h]

7Endure hardship as discipline; God is treating you as sons.[i] For what son is not disciplined by his father? 8If you are not disciplined (and everyone undergoes discipline),[j] then you are illegitimate children and not true sons. 9Moreover, we have all had human fathers who disciplined us and we respected them for it. How much more should we submit to the Father of our spirits[k] and live![l] 10Our fathers disciplined us for a little while as they thought best; but God disciplines us for our good, that we may share in his holiness.[m] 11No discipline seems pleasant at the time, but painful. Later on, however, it produces a harvest of righteousness and peace[n] for those who have been trained by it.

12Therefore, strengthen your feeble arms and weak knees![o] 13"Make level paths for your feet,"[b][p] so that the lame may not be disabled, but rather healed.[q]

Warning Against Refusing God

14Make every effort to live in peace with all men[r] and to be holy;[s] without holiness no-one will see the Lord.[t] 15See to it that no-one misses the grace of God[u] and that no bitter root grows up to cause trouble and defile many. 16See that no-one is sexually immoral, or is godless like Esau, who for a single meal sold his inheritance rights as the oldest son.[v] 17Afterwards, as you know, when he wanted to inherit this blessing, he was rejected. He could bring about no change of mind, though he sought the blessing with tears.[w]

18You have not come to a mountain that can be touched and that is burning with fire; to darkness, gloom and storm;[x] 19to a trumpet blast[y] or to such a voice speaking words that those who heard it begged that no further word be spoken to them,[z] 20because they could not bear what was commanded: "If even an animal touches the mountain, it must be stoned."[c][a] 21The sight was so terrifying that Moses said, "I am trembling with fear."[d]

22But you have come to Mount Zion, to the heavenly Jerusalem,[b] the city[c] of the living God. You have come to thousands upon thousands of angels in joyful assembly, 23to the church of the firstborn, whose names are written in heaven.[d] You have come to God, the judge of all men,[e] to the spirits of righteous men made perfect,[f] 24to Jesus the mediator of a new covenant, and to the sprinkled blood that speaks a better word than the blood of Abel.[g]

25See to it that you do not refuse him who speaks. If they did not escape when they refused him who warned[h] them on earth, how much less will we, if we turn away from him who warns us from heaven?[i] 26At that time his voice shook the earth,[j] but now he has promised, "Once more I will shake not only the earth but also the heavens."[e][k]

12:2 d Heb 13:13
12:3 e Gal 6:9
12:4 f Heb 10:32-34
12:6 g Ps 94:12; Rev 3:19; h Pr 3:11,12
12:7 i Dt 8:5
12:8 j 1Pe 5:9
12:9 k Nu 16:22; l Isa 38:16
12:10 m 2Pe 1:4
12:11 n Isa 32:17; Jas 3:17,18
12:12 o Isa 35:3
12:13 p Pr 4:26; q Gal 6:1
12:14 r Ro 14:19; s Ro 6:22; t Mt 5:8
12:15 u Gal 5:4; Heb 3:12
12:16 v Ge 25:29-34
12:17 w Ge 27:30-40
12:18 x Ex 19:12-22; Dt 4:11
12:19 y Ex 20:18; z Ex 20:19; Dt 5:5,25
12:20 a Ex 19:12,13
12:22 b Gal 4:26; c Heb 11:10
12:23 d Lk 10:20; e Ps 94:2; f Php 3:12
12:24 g Ge 4:10; Heb 11:4
12:25 h Heb 8:5; Heb 11:7; i Heb 2:2,3
12:26 j Ex 19:18; k Hag 2:6

a6 Prov. 3:11,12 b13 Prov. 4:26
c20 Exodus 19:12,13 d21 Deut. 9:19
e26 Haggai 2:6

27 The words "once more" indicate the removing of what can be shaken[l]—that is, created things—so that what cannot be shaken may remain.

28 Therefore, since we are receiving a kingdom that cannot be shaken,[m] let us be thankful, and so worship God acceptably with reverence and awe,[n] 29 for our "God is a consuming fire."[f][o]

Concluding Exhortations

13

Keep on loving each other as brothers.[a] 2 Do not forget to entertain strangers,[b] for by so doing some people have entertained angels without knowing it.[c] 3 Remember those in prison[d] as if you were their fellow-prisoners, and those who are ill-treated as if you yourselves were suffering.

4 Marriage should be honoured by all, and the marriage bed kept pure, for God will judge the adulterer and all the sexually immoral.[e] 5 Keep your lives free from the love of money and be content with what you have,[f] because God has said,

> "Never will I leave you;
> never will I forsake you."[a][g]

6 So we say with confidence,

> "The Lord is my helper; I will
> not be afraid.
> What can man do to me?"[b]

7 Remember your leaders,[h] who spoke the word of God to you. Consider the outcome of their way of life and imitate[i] their faith. 8 Jesus Christ is the same yesterday and today and for ever.[j]

9 Do not be carried away by all kinds of strange teachings.[k] It is good for our hearts to be strengthened[l] by grace, not by ceremonial foods,[m] which are of no value to those who eat them. 10 We have an altar from which those who minister at the tabernacle have no right to eat.[n]

11 The high priest carries the blood of animals into the Most Holy Place as a sin offering, but the bodies are burned outside the camp.[o] 12 And so Jesus also suffered outside the city gate[p] to make the people holy through his own blood. 13 Let us, then, go to him outside the camp, bearing the disgrace he bore.[q] 14 For here we do not have an enduring city, but we are looking for the city that is to come.[r]

15 Through Jesus, therefore, let us continually offer to God a sacrifice[s] of praise—the fruit of lips[t] that confess his name. 16 And do not forget to do good and to share with others,[u] for with such sacrifices[v] God is pleased.

17 Obey your leaders and submit to their authority. They keep watch over you[w] as men who must give an account. Obey them so that their work will be a joy, not a burden, for that would be of no advantage to you.

18 Pray for us.[x] We are sure that we have a clear conscience[y] and desire to live honourably in every way. 19 I particularly urge you to pray so that I may be restored to you soon.[z]

20 May the God of peace,[a] who through the blood of the eternal covenant[b] brought back from the dead[c] our Lord Jesus, that great Shepherd of the sheep,[d] 21 equip you with everything good for doing his will, and may he work in us[e] what is pleasing to him,[f] through Jesus Christ, to whom be glory for ever and ever. Amen.[g]

22 Brothers, I urge you to bear with my word of exhortation, for I have written you only a short letter.[h]

12:27 l 1Co 7:31; 2Pe 3:10
12:28 m Da 2:44; n Heb 13:15
12:29 o Dt 4:24
13:1 a Ro 12:10; 1Pe 1:22
13:2 b Mt 25:35; c Ge 18:1-33
13:3 d Mt 25:36; Col 4:18
13:4 e 1Co 6:9
13:5 f Php 4:11; g Dt 31:6,8; Jos 1:5
13:7 h ver 17,24; i Heb 6:12
13:8 j Heb 1:12
13:9 k Eph 4:14; l Col 2:7; m Col 2:16
13:10 n 1Co 9:13; 1Co 10:18
13:11 o Ex 29:14; Lev 16:27
13:12 p Jn 19:17
13:13 q Heb 11:26
13:14 r Php 3:20; Heb 12:22
13:15 s 1Pe 2:5; t Hos 14:2
13:16 u Ro 12:13; v Php 4:18
13:17 w Isa 62:6; Ac 20:28
13:18 x 1Th 5:25; y Ac 23:1
13:19 z Phm 22
13:20 a Ro 15:33; b Isa 55:3; Eze 37:26; Zec 9:11; c Ac 2:24; d Jn 10:11
13:21 e Php 2:13; f 1Jn 3:22; g Ro 11:36
13:22 h 1Pe 5:12

f29 Deut. 4:24 a5 Deut. 31:6
b6 Psalm 118:6,7

23I want you to know that our
brother Timothy[i] has been released. If he arrives soon, I will
come with him to see you.
24Greet all your leaders[j] and all
God's people. Those from Italy[k]
send you their greetings.
25Grace be with you all.[l]

13:23 *i* Ac 16:1
13:24 *j* ver 7,17 *k* Ac 18:2
13:25 *l* Col 4:18

JAMES

1 James,[a] a servant of God[b]
and of the Lord Jesus Christ,

To the twelve tribes[c] scattered[d]
among the nations:

Greetings.

Trials and Temptations

2Consider it pure joy, my
brothers, whenever you face trials
of many kinds,[e] 3because you
know that the testing of your faith
develops perseverance. 4Persever-
ance must finish its work so that
you may be mature and complete,
not lacking anything. 5If any of you
lacks wisdom, he should ask God,[f]
who gives generously to all without
finding fault, and it will be given to
him.[g] 6But when he asks, he must
believe and not doubt,[h] because he
who doubts is like a wave of the sea,
blown and tossed by the wind.
7That man should not think he will
receive anything from the Lord;
8he is a double-minded man,[i] unstable in all he does.
9The brother in humble circumstances ought to take pride in his
high position. 10But the one who is
rich should take pride in his low position, because he will pass away
like a wild flower.[j] 11For the sun
rises with scorching heat and withers[k] the plant; its blossom falls
and its beauty is destroyed.[l] In the
same way, the rich man will fade
away even while he goes about his
business.
12Blessed is the man who perseveres under trial, because when
he has stood the test, he will receive the crown of life[m] that God
has promised to those who love
him.[n]
13When tempted, no-one should
say, "God is tempting me." For God
cannot be tempted by evil, nor does
he tempt anyone; 14but each one
is tempted when, by his own evil
desire, he is dragged away and
enticed. 15Then, after desire has
conceived, it gives birth to sin;[o]
and sin, when it is full-grown, gives
birth to death.[p]
16Don't be deceived,[q] my dear
brothers.[r] 17Every good and perfect gift is from above,[s] coming
down from the Father of the heavenly lights, who does not change[t]
like shifting shadows. 18He chose to
give us birth[u] through the word of
truth, that we might be a kind of
firstfruits[v] of all he created.

Listening and Doing

19My dear brothers, take note of
this: Everyone should be quick to
listen, slow to speak[w] and slow to
become angry, 20for man's anger
does not bring about the righteous
life that God desires. 21Therefore,
get rid of[x] all moral filth and the
evil that is so prevalent, and humbly accept the word planted in
you,[y] which can save you.
22Do not merely listen to the
word, and so deceive yourselves.
Do what it says. 23Anyone who listens to the word but does not do
what it says is like a man who looks
at his face in a mirror 24and, after
looking at himself, goes away and
immediately forgets what he looks
like. 25But the man who looks intently into the perfect law that
gives freedom,[z] and continues to
do this, not forgetting what he has
heard, but doing it—he will be
blessed in what he does.[a]
26If anyone considers himself
religious and yet does not keep
a tight rein on his tongue,[b] he
deceives himself and his religion

1:1 a Ac 15:13 b Tit 1:1 c Ac 26:7 d Dt 32:26 Jn 7:35 1Pe 1:1
1:2 e Mt 5:12 1Pe 1:6
1:5 f 1Ki 3:9,10 Pr 2:3-6 g Mt 7:7
1:6 h Mk 11:24
1:8 i Jas 4:8
1:10 j 1Co 7:31 1Pe 1:24
1:11 k Ps 102:4,11 l Isa 40:6-8
1:12 m 1Co 9:25 n Jas 2:5
1:15 o Job 15:35 Ps 7:14 p Ro 6:23
1:16 q 1Co 6:9 r ver 19
1:17 s Jn 3:27 t Nu 23:19 Mal 3:6
1:18 u Jn 1:13 v Eph 1:12 Rev 14:4
1:19 w Pr 10:19
1:21 x Eph 4:22 y Eph 1:13
1:25 z Jas 2:12 a Jn 13:17
1:26 b Ps 34:13 1Pe 3:10

is worthless. 27Religion that God our Father accepts as pure and faultless is this: to look after[c] orphans and widows[d] in their distress and to keep oneself from being polluted by the world.[e]

Favouritism Forbidden

2 My brothers, as believers in our glorious[a] Lord Jesus Christ, don't show favouritism.[b] 2Suppose a man comes into your meeting wearing a gold ring and fine clothes, and a poor man in shabby clothes also comes in. 3If you show special attention to the man wearing fine clothes and say, "Here's a good seat for you," but say to the poor man, "You stand there" or "Sit on the floor by my feet," 4have you not discriminated among yourselves and become judges[c] with evil thoughts?

5Listen, my dear brothers:[d] Has not God chosen those who are poor in the eyes of the world[e] to be rich in faith[f] and to inherit the kingdom he promised those who love him?[g] 6But you have insulted the poor.[h] Is it not the rich who are exploiting you? Are they not the ones who are dragging you into court?[i] 7Are they not the ones who are slandering the noble name of him to whom you belong?

8If you really keep the royal law found in Scripture, "Love your neighbour as yourself,"[a][j] you are doing right. 9But if you show favouritism,[k] you sin and are convicted by the law as lawbreakers.[l] 10For whoever keeps the whole law and yet stumbles at just one point is guilty of breaking all of it.[m] 11For he who said, "Do not commit adultery,"[b][n] also said, "Do not murder."[c][o] If you do not commit adultery but do commit murder, you have become a lawbreaker.

12Speak and act as those who are going to be judged by the law that gives freedom,[p] 13because judgment without mercy will be shown to anyone who has not been merciful.[q] Mercy triumphs over judgment!

Faith and Deeds

14What good is it, my brothers, if a man claims to have faith but has no deeds?[r] Can such faith save him? 15Suppose a brother or sister is without clothes and daily food.[s] 16If one of you says to him, "Go, I wish you well; keep warm and well fed," but does nothing about his physical needs, what good is it?[t] 17In the same way, faith by itself, if it is not accompanied by action, is dead.

18But someone will say, "You have faith; I have deeds."

Show me your faith without deeds,[u] and I will show you my faith by what I do.[v] 19You believe that there is one God.[w] Good! Even the demons believe that[x]—and shudder.

20You foolish man, do you want evidence that faith without deeds is useless?[d][y] 21Was not our ancestor Abraham considered righteous for what he did when he offered his son Isaac on the altar?[z] 22You see that his faith and his actions were working together,[a] and his faith was made complete by what he did.[b] 23And the scripture was fulfilled that says, "Abraham believed God, and it was credited to him as righteousness,"[e][c] and he was called God's friend.[d] 24You see that a person is justified by what he does and not by faith alone.

25In the same way, was not even Rahab the prostitute considered righteous for what she did when she gave lodging to the spies and sent them off in a different direction?[e] 26As the body without the spirit is dead, so faith without deeds is dead.[f]

[a]*8* Lev. 19:18 [b]*11* Exodus 20:14; Deut. 5:18 [c]*11* Exodus 20:13; Deut. 5:17 [d]*20* Some early manuscripts *dead* [e]*23* Gen. 15:6

1:27 c Mt 25:36 d Isa 1:17,23 e Ro 12:2
2:1 a 1Co 2:8 b Lev 19:15
2:4 c Jn 7:24
2:5 d Jas 1:16,19 e 1Co 1:26-28 f Lk 12:21 g Jas 1:12
2:6 h 1Co 11:22 i Ac 8:3
2:8 j Lev 19:18
2:9 k ver 1 l Dt 1:17
2:10 m Mt 5:19 Gal 3:10
2:11 n Ex 20:14 Dt 5:18 o Ex 20:13 Dt 5:17
2:12 p Jas 1:25
2:13 q Mt 5:7 Mt 18:32-35
2:14 r Mt 7:26 Jas 1:22-25
2:15 s Mt 25:35,36
2:16 t 1Jn 3:17,18
2:18 u Ro 3:28 v Jas 3:13
2:19 w Dt 6:4 x Mt 8:29 Lk 4:34
2:20 y ver 17,26
2:21 z Ge 22:9,12
2:22 a Heb 11:17 b 1Th 1:3
2:23 c Ge 15:6 Ro 4:3 d 2Ch 20:7 Isa 41:8
2:25 e Heb 11:31
2:26 f ver 17,20

Taming the Tongue

3 Not many of you should presume to be teachers, my brothers, because you know that we who teach will be judged more strictly. 2 We all stumble[a] in many ways. If anyone is never at fault in what he says,[b] he is a perfect man,[c] able to keep his whole body in check.[d]

3 When we put bits into the mouths of horses to make them obey us, we can turn the whole animal.[e] 4 Or take ships as an example. Although they are so large and are driven by strong winds, they are steered by a very small rudder wherever the pilot wants to go. 5 Likewise the tongue is a small part of the body, but it makes great boasts.[f] Consider what a great forest is set on fire by a small spark. 6 The tongue also is a fire,[g] a world of evil among the parts of the body. It corrupts the whole person,[h] sets the whole course of his life on fire, and is itself set on fire by hell.

7 All kinds of animals, birds, reptiles and creatures of the sea are being tamed and have been tamed by man, 8 but no man can tame the tongue. It is a restless evil, full of deadly poison.[i]

9 With the tongue we praise our Lord and Father, and with it we curse men, who have been made in God's likeness.[j] 10 Out of the same mouth come praise and cursing. My brothers, this should not be. 11 Can both fresh water and salt[a] water flow from the same spring? 12 My brothers, can a fig-tree bear olives, or a grapevine bear figs?[k] Neither can a salt spring produce fresh water.

Two Kinds of Wisdom

13 Who is wise and understanding among you? Let him show it[l] by his good life, by deeds done in the humility that comes from wisdom. 14 But if you harbour bitter envy and selfish ambition[m] in your hearts, do not boast about it or deny the truth.[n] 15 Such "wisdom" does not come down from heaven[o] but is earthly, unspiritual, of the devil.[p] 16 For where you have envy and selfish ambition, there you find disorder and every evil practice.

17 But the wisdom that comes from heaven[q] is first of all pure; then peace-loving, considerate, submissive, full of mercy[r] and good fruit, impartial and sincere.[s] 18 Peacemakers who sow in peace raise a harvest of righteousness.[t]

Submit Yourselves to God

4 What causes fights and quarrels[a] among you? Don't they come from your desires that battle[b] within you? 2 You want something but don't get it. You kill and covet, but you cannot have what you want. You quarrel and fight. You do not have, because you do not ask God. 3 When you ask, you do not receive,[c] because you ask with wrong motives,[d] that you may spend what you get on your pleasures.

4 You adulterous people, don't you know that friendship with the world[e] is hatred towards God?[f] Anyone who chooses to be a friend of the world becomes an enemy of God.[g] 5 Or do you think Scripture says without reason that the spirit he caused to live in us envies intensely?[a] 6 But he gives us more grace. That is why Scripture says:

"God opposes the proud
but gives grace to the
humble."[b][h]

7 Submit yourselves, then, to God. Resist the devil,[i] and he will flee from you. 8 Come near to God and he will come near to you.[j] Wash your hands,[k] you sinners, and purify your hearts, you

3:2 a 1Ki 8:46; Jas 2:10 b 1Pe 3:10 c Mt 12:37 d Jas 1:26
3:3 e Ps 32:9
3:5 f Ps 12:3,4
3:6 g Pr 16:27 h Mt 15:11,18,19
3:8 i Ps 140:3; Ro 3:13
3:9 j Ge 1:26,27; 1Co 11:7
3:12 k Mt 7:16
3:13 l Jas 2:18
3:14 m ver 16 n Jas 5:19
3:15 o Jas 1:17 p 1Ti 4:1
3:17 q 1Co 2:6 r Lk 6:36 s Ro 12:9
3:18 t Pr 11:18; Isa 32:17
4:1 a Tit 3:9 b Ro 7:23
4:3 c Ps 18:41 d 1Jn 3:22; 1Jn 5:14
4:4 e Jas 1:27 f 1Jn 2:15 g Jn 15:19
4:6 h Ps 138:6; Pr 3:34; Mt 23:12
4:7 i Eph 4:27; 1Pe 5:6-9
4:8 j 2Ch 15:2 k Isa 1:16

a *11* Greek *bitter* (see also verse 14) a *5* Or *that God jealously longs for the spirit that he made to live in us*; or *that the Spirit he caused to live in us longs jealously* b *6* Prov. 3:34

double-minded.[l] 9Grieve, mourn
and wail. Change your laughter to
mourning and your joy to gloom.[m]
10Humble yourselves before the
Lord, and he will lift you up.
11Brothers, do not slander one
another.[n] Anyone who speaks
against his brother or judges him[o]
speaks against the law and judges
it. When you judge the law, you are
not keeping it,[p] but sitting in judgment on it. 12There is only one Lawgiver and Judge, the one who is
able to save and destroy.[q] But
you—who are you to judge your
neighbour?[r]

Boasting About Tomorrow

13Now listen, you who say, "Today or tomorrow we will go to this
or that city, spend a year there,
carry on business and make
money."[s] 14Why, you do not even
know what will happen tomorrow.
What is your life? You are a mist
that appears for a little while and
then vanishes.[t] 15Instead, you
ought to say, "If it is the Lord's
will,[u] we will live and do this or
that." 16As it is, you boast and brag.
All such boasting is evil.[v] 17Any-
one, then, who knows the good he
ought to do and doesn't do it, sins.[w]

Warning to Rich Oppressors

5 Now listen, you rich people,[a]
weep and wail because of the
misery that is coming upon you.
2Your wealth has rotted, and moths
have eaten your clothes.[b] 3Your
gold and silver are corroded. Their
corrosion will testify against you
and eat your flesh like fire. You
have hoarded wealth in the last
days.[c] 4Look! The wages you
failed to pay the workmen[d] who
mowed your fields are crying out
against you. The cries[e] of the harvesters have reached the ears of
the Lord Almighty.[f] 5You have
lived on earth in luxury and self-
indulgence. You have fattened
yourselves[g] in the day of slaughter.[a][h] 6You have condemned and
murdered innocent men,[i] who
were not opposing you.

Patience in Suffering

7Be patient, then, brothers, until
the Lord's coming. See how the
farmer waits for the land to yield
its valuable crop and how patient
he is for the autumn and spring
rains.[j] 8You too, be patient and
stand firm, because the Lord's
coming is near.[k] 9Don't grumble
against each other, brothers,[l] or
you will be judged. The Judge[m] is
standing at the door![n]
10Brothers, as an example of patience in the face of suffering, take
the prophets[o] who spoke in the
name of the Lord. 11As you know,
we consider blessed[p] those who
have persevered. You have heard
of Job's perseverance[q] and have
seen what the Lord finally brought
about.[r] The Lord is full of compassion and mercy.[s]
12Above all, my brothers, do not
swear—not by heaven or by earth
or by anything else. Let your "Yes"
be yes, and your "No", no, or you
will be condemned.[t]

The Prayer of Faith

13Is any one of you in trouble? He
should pray.[u] Is anyone happy?
Let him sing songs of praise.[v] 14Is
any one of you sick? He should call
the elders of the church to pray
over him and anoint him with oil[w]
in the name of the Lord. 15And the
prayer offered in faith will make
the sick person well; the Lord will
raise him up. If he has sinned, he
will be forgiven. 16Therefore confess your sins[x] to each other and
pray for each other so that you may
be healed.[y] The prayer of a righteous man is powerful and effec-
tive.[z]
17Elijah was a man just like us.[a]
He prayed earnestly that it would

4:8 l Jas 1:8
4:9 m Lk 6:25
4:11 n 1Pe 2:1 o Mt 7:1 p Jas 1:22
4:12 q Mt 10:28 r Ro 14:4
4:13 s Pr 27:1
4:14 t Job 7:7 Ps 102:3
4:15 u Ac 18:21
4:16 v 1Co 5:6
4:17 w Lk 12:47 Jn 9:41
5:1 a Lk 6:24
5:2 b Job 13:28 Mt 6:19,20
5:3 c ver 7,8
5:4 d Lev 19:13 e Dt 24:15 f Ro 9:29
5:5 g Am 6:1 h Jer 12:3 Jer 25:34
5:6 i Heb 10:38
5:7 j Dt 11:14 Jer 5:24
5:8 k Ro 13:11 1Pe 4:7
5:9 l Jas 4:11 m 1Co 4:5 1Pe 4:5 n Mt 24:33
5:10 o Mt 5:12
5:11 p Mt 5:10 q Job 1:21,22 Job 2:10 r Job 42:10, 12-17 s Nu 14:18
5:12 t Mt 5:34-37
5:13 u Ps 50:15 v Col 3:16
5:14 w Mk 6:13
5:16 x Mt 3:6 y 1Pe 2:24 z Jn 9:31
5:17 a Ac 14:15

[a]5 Or *yourselves as in a day of feasting*

not rain, and it did not rain on the
land for three and a half years.[b]
18 Again he prayed, and the heavens
gave rain, and the earth produced
its crops.[c]
19 My brothers, if one of you
should wander from the truth[d] and
someone should bring him back,[e]
20 remember this: Whoever turns a
sinner from the error of his way
will save[f] him from death and
cover over a multitude of sins.[g]

5:17 *b* 1Ki 17:1 Lk 4:25
5:18 *c* 1Ki 18:41-45
5:19 *d* Jas 3:14 *e* Mt 18:15
5:20 *f* Ro 11:14 *g* 1Pe 4:8

1 PETER

1 Peter, an apostle of Jesus
Christ,[a]

To God's elect,[b] strangers in
the world, scattered throughout
Pontus, Galatia, Cappadocia, Asia
and Bithynia,[c] 2who have been
chosen according to the foreknowledge[d] of God the Father, through
the sanctifying work of the Spirit,[e]
for obedience to Jesus Christ and
sprinkling by his blood:[f]

Grace and peace be yours in
abundance.

Praise to God for a Living Hope

3Praise be to the God and Father
of our Lord Jesus Christ![g] In his
great mercy[h] he has given us new
birth into a living hope through the
resurrection of Jesus Christ from
the dead,[i] 4and into an inheritance
that can never perish, spoil or
fade—kept in heaven for you,[j]
5who through faith are shielded by
God's power[k] until the coming of
the salvation that is ready to be revealed in the last time. 6In this you
greatly rejoice,[l] though now for a
little while[m] you may have had to
suffer grief in all kinds of trials.[n]
7These have come so that your
faith—of greater worth than gold,
which perishes even though refined by fire[o]—may be proved
genuine[p] and may result in praise,
glory and honour when Jesus
Christ is revealed.[q] 8Though you
have not seen him, you love him;
and even though you do not see him
now, you believe in him[r] and are
filled with an inexpressible and
glorious joy, 9for you are receiving
the goal of your faith, the salvation
of your souls.[s]

10Concerning this salvation, the
prophets, who spoke[t] of the grace
that was to come to you, searched
intently and with the greatest
care,[u] 11trying to find out the time
and circumstances to which the
Spirit of Christ[v] in them was pointing when he predicted the sufferings of Christ and the glories that
would follow. 12It was revealed to
them that they were not serving
themselves but you, when they
spoke of the things that have now
been told you by those who have
preached the gospel to you[w] by the
Holy Spirit sent from heaven. Even
angels long to look into these
things.

Be Holy

13Therefore, prepare your minds
for action; be self-controlled; set
your hope fully on the grace to be
given you when Jesus Christ is revealed. 14As obedient children, do
not conform[x] to the evil desires
you had when you lived in ignorance.[y] 15But just as he who called
you is holy, so be holy in all you
do;[z] 16for it is written: "Be holy,
because I am holy."[a][a]

17Since you call on a Father who
judges each man's work impartially,[b] live your lives as strangers
here in reverent fear.[c] 18For you
know that it was not with perishable things such as silver or gold
that you were redeemed[d] from the
empty way of life handed down to
you from your forefathers, 19but
with the precious blood of Christ, a
lamb[e] without blemish or defect.[f]
20He was chosen before the creation of the world,[g] but was revealed in these last times[h] for your
sake. 21Through him you believe in
God,[i] who raised him from the

[a]16 Lev. 11:44,45; 19:2; 20:7

1:1 a 2Pe 1:1 b Mt 24:22 c Ac 16:7
1:2 d Ro 8:29 e 2Th 2:13 f Heb 10:22 Heb 12:24
1:3 g 2Co 1:3 Eph 1:3 h Tit 3:5 Jas 1:18 i 1Co 15:20
1:4 j Col 1:5
1:5 k Jn 10:28
1:6 l Ro 5:2 m 1Pe 5:10 n Jas 1:2
1:7 o Job 23:10 Ps 66:10 Pr 17:3 p Jas 1:3 q Ro 2:7
1:8 r Jn 20:29
1:9 s Ro 6:22
1:10 t Mt 26:24 u Mt 13:17
1:11 v 2Pe 1:21
1:12 w ver 25
1:14 x Ro 12:2 y Eph 4:18
1:15 z 2Co 7:1 1Th 4:7
1:16 a Lev 11:44,45
1:17 b Ac 10:34 c Heb 12:28
1:18 d Mt 20:28 1Co 6:20
1:19 e Jn 1:29 f Ex 12:5
1:20 g Eph 1:4 h Heb 9:26
1:21 i Ro 4:24

dead and glorified him, and so your
faith and hope are in God.
22 Now that you have purified[j]
yourselves by obeying the truth
so that you have sincere love for
your brothers, love one another
deeply,[k] from the heart.[b] 23 For
you have been born again,[l] not of
perishable seed, but of imperishable, through the living and enduring word of God.[m] 24 For,

"All men are like grass,
and all their glory is like the
flowers of the field;
the grass withers and the
flowers fall,
25 but the word of the Lord
stands for ever."[c][n]

And this is the word that was
preached to you.

2 Therefore, rid yourselves[a] of
all malice and all deceit,
hypocrisy, envy, and slander[b] of
every kind. 2 Like newborn babies,
crave pure spiritual milk,[c] so that
by it you may grow up[d] in your salvation, 3 now that you have tasted
that the Lord is good.[e]

The Living Stone and a Chosen People

4 As you come to him, the living
Stone[f]—rejected by men but chosen by God and precious to him—
5 you also, like living stones, are
being built[g] into a spiritual house[h]
to be a holy priesthood,[i] offering
spiritual sacrifices acceptable to
God through Jesus Christ.[j] 6 For in
Scripture it says:

"See, I lay a stone in Zion,
a chosen and precious
cornerstone,[k]
and the one who trusts in him
will never be put to
shame."[a][l]

7 Now to you who believe, this stone
is precious. But to those who do not
believe,[m]

1:22 [j] Jas 4:8 [k] Jn 13:34 Heb 13:1
1:23 [l] Jn 1:13 [m] Heb 4:12
1:25 [n] Isa 40:6-8
2:1 [a] Eph 4:22 [b] Jas 4:11
2:2 [c] 1Co 3:2 [d] Eph 4:15,16
2:3 [e] Heb 6:5
2:4 [f] ver 7
2:5 [g] 1Co 3:9 [h] 1Ti 3:15 [i] Isa 61:6 [j] Php 4:18 Heb 13:15
2:6 [k] Eph 2:20 [l] Isa 28:16
2:7 [m] 2Co 2:16 [n] Ps 118:22
2:8 [o] Isa 8:14 1Co 1:23 [p] Ro 9:22
2:9 [q] Dt 10:15 [r] Isa 62:12 [s] Ac 26:18
2:10 [t] Hos 1:9,10
2:11 [u] Gal 5:16 [v] Jas 4:1
2:12 [w] Php 2:15 1Pe 3:16 [x] Mt 5:16 Mt 9:8
2:13 [y] Ro 13:1
2:14 [z] Ro 13:4 [a] Ro 13:3
2:15 [b] 1Pe 3:17 [c] ver 12
2:16 [d] Jn 8:32 [e] Ro 6:22
2:17 [f] Ro 12:10 [g] Ro 13:7

"The stone the builders rejected
has become the
capstone,"[b,c][n]

8 and,

"A stone that causes men to
stumble
and a rock that makes them
fall."[d][o]

They stumble because they disobey the message—which is also
what they were destined for.[p]
9 But you are a chosen people,[q] a
royal priesthood, a holy nation,[r] a
people belonging to God, that you
may declare the praises of him who
called you out of darkness into his
wonderful light.[s] 10 Once you were
not a people, but now you are the
people of God;[t] once you had not
received mercy, but now you have
received mercy.
11 Dear friends, I urge you, as
aliens and strangers in the world,
to abstain from sinful desires,[u]
which war against your soul.[v]
12 Live such good lives among the
pagans that, though they accuse
you of doing wrong, they may see
your good deeds[w] and glorify
God[x] on the day he visits us.

Submission to Rulers and Masters

13 Submit yourselves for the
Lord's sake to every authority[y] instituted among men: whether to the
king, as the supreme authority,
14 or to governors, who are sent by
him to punish those who do wrong[z]
and to commend those who do right.[a]
15 For it is God's will[b] that by doing
good you should silence the ignorant talk of foolish men.[c] 16 Live as
free men,[d] but do not use your
freedom as a cover-up for evil; live
as servants of God.[e] 17 Show proper
respect to everyone: Love the
brotherhood of believers,[f] fear
God, honour the king.[g]

b22 Some early manuscripts *from a pure heart*
c25 Isaiah 40:6–8 a6 Isaiah 28:16 b7 Or *cornerstone* c7 Psalm 118:22 d8 Isaiah 8:14

18Slaves, submit yourselves to
your masters with all respect,[h] not
only to those who are good and considerate,[i] but also to those who are
harsh. 19For it is commendable if a
man bears up under the pain of unjust suffering because he is conscious of God.[j] 20But how is it to
your credit if you receive a beating
for doing wrong and endure it? But
if you suffer for doing good and
you endure it, this is commendable
before God.[k] 21To this[l] you were
called, because Christ suffered for
you, leaving you an example,[m] that
you should follow in his steps.

22"He committed no sin,
and no deceit was found in his
mouth."[e][n]

23When they hurled their insults at
him, he did not retaliate; when he
suffered, he made no threats.[o] Instead, he entrusted himself[p] to
him who judges justly. 24He himself bore our sins[q] in his body on
the tree, so that we might die to
sins[r] and live for righteousness;
by his wounds you have been
healed.[s] 25For you were like sheep
going astray,[t] but now you have
returned to the Shepherd[u] and
Overseer of your souls.

Wives and Husbands

3 Wives, in the same way be submissive[a] to your husbands[b]
so that, if any of them do not believe the word, they may be won
over[c] without words by the behaviour of their wives, 2when they see
the purity and reverence of your
lives. 3Your beauty should not
come from outward adornment,
such as braided hair and the wearing of gold jewellery and fine
clothes.[d] 4Instead, it should be that
of your inner self,[e] the unfading
beauty of a gentle and quiet spirit,
which is of great worth in God's
sight. 5For this is the way the
holy women of the past who put
their hope in God[f] used to make
themselves beautiful. They were
submissive to their own husbands,
6like Sarah, who obeyed Abraham
and called him her master.[g] You
are her daughters if you do what
is right and do not give way to
fear.

7Husbands,[h] in the same way be
considerate as you live with your
wives, and treat them with respect
as the weaker partner and as heirs
with you of the gracious gift of life,
so that nothing will hinder your
prayers.

Suffering for Doing Good

8Finally, all of you, live in harmony with one another; be sym-
pathetic, love as brothers,[i] be
compassionate and humble.[j] 9Do
not repay evil with evil[k] or insult
with insult,[l] but with blessing, because to this[m] you were called so
that you may inherit a blessing.[n]
10For,

"Whoever would love life
and see good days
must keep his tongue from evil
and his lips from deceitful
speech.
11He must turn from evil and do
good;
he must seek peace and
pursue it.
12For the eyes of the Lord are on
the righteous
and his ears are attentive to
their prayer,
but the face of the Lord is
against those who do
evil."[a][o]

13Who is going to harm you if
you are eager to do good?[p] 14But
even if you should suffer for what
is right, you are blessed.[q] "Do
not fear what they fear;[b] do not
be frightened."[c][r] 15But in your
hearts set apart Christ as Lord. Always be prepared to give an answer[s] to everyone who asks you to

2:18 h Eph 6:5 i Jas 3:17
2:19 j 1Pe 3:14,17
2:20 k 1Pe 3:17
2:21 l Ac 14:22 m Mt 16:24
2:22 n Isa 53:9
2:23 o Isa 53:7 p Lk 23:46
2:24 q Heb 9:28 r Ro 6:2 s Isa 53:5; Heb 12:13; Jas 5:16
2:25 t Isa 53:6 u Jn 10:11
3:1 a 1Pe 2:18 b Eph 5:22 c 1Co 7:16; 1Co 9:19
3:3 d Isa 3:18-23; 1Ti 2:9
3:4 e Ro 7:22
3:5 f 1Ti 5:5
3:6 g Ge 18:12
3:7 h Eph 5:25-33
3:8 i Ro 12:10 j 1Pe 5:5
3:9 k Ro 12:17 l 1Pe 2:23 m 1Pe 2:21 n Heb 6:14
3:12 o Ps 34:12-16
3:13 p Pr 16:7
3:14 q 1Pe 2:19,20; 1Pe 4:15,16 r Isa 8:12,13
3:15 s Col 4:6

e22 Isaiah 53:9 a12 Psalm 34:12–16
b14 Or *not fear their threats* c14 Isaiah 8:12

give the reason for the hope that you have. But do this with gentleness and respect, 16keeping a clear conscience,[t] so that those who speak maliciously against your good behaviour in Christ may be ashamed of their slander.[u] 17It is better, if it is God's will,[v] to suffer for doing good[w] than for doing evil. 18For Christ died for sins[x] once for all, the righteous for the unrighteous, to bring you to God. He was put to death in the body[y] but made alive by the Spirit,[z] 19through whom[d] also he went and preached to the spirits in prison[a] 20who disobeyed long ago when God waited patiently in the days of Noah while the ark was being built.[b] In it only a few people, eight in all, were saved[c] through water, 21and this water symbolises baptism that now saves you[d] also—not the removal of dirt from the body but the pledge[e] of a good conscience towards God. It saves you by the resurrection of Jesus Christ,[e] 22who has gone into heaven and is at God's right hand[f]—with angels, authorities and powers in submission to him.[g]

Living for God

4 Therefore, since Christ suffered in his body, arm yourselves also with the same attitude, because he who has suffered in his body is done with sin. 2As a result, he does not live the rest of his earthly life for evil human desires,[a] but rather for the will of God. 3For you have spent enough time in the past[b] doing what pagans choose to do—living in debauchery, lust, drunkenness, orgies, carousing and detestable idolatry. 4They think it strange that you do not plunge with them into the same flood of dissipation, and they heap abuse on you.[c] 5But they will have to give account to him who is ready to judge the living and the dead.[d] 6For this is the reason the gospel was preached even to those who are now dead,[e] so that they might be judged according to men in regard to the body, but live according to God in regard to the spirit.

7The end of all things is near.[f] Therefore be clear minded and self-controlled so that you can pray. 8Above all, love each other deeply,[g] because love covers over a multitude of sins.[h] 9Offer hospitality to one another without grumbling.[i] 10Each one should use whatever gift he has received to serve others,[j] faithfully[k] administering God's grace in its various forms. 11If anyone speaks, he should do it as one speaking the very words of God. If anyone serves, he should do it with the strength God provides,[l] so that in all things God may be praised[m] through Jesus Christ. To him be the glory and the power for ever and ever. Amen.

Suffering for Being a Christian

12Dear friends, do not be surprised at the painful trial you are suffering,[n] as though something strange were happening to you. 13But rejoice that you participate in the sufferings of Christ, so that you may be overjoyed when his glory is revealed.[o] 14If you are insulted because of the name of Christ, you are blessed,[p] for the Spirit of glory and of God rests on you. 15If you suffer, it should not be as a murderer or thief or any other kind of criminal, or even as a meddler. 16However, if you suffer as a Christian, do not be ashamed, but praise God that you bear that name.[q] 17For it is time for judgment to begin with the family of God;[r] and if it begins with us, what will the outcome be for those who do not obey the gospel of God?[s] 18And,

[d] 18,19 Or *alive in the spirit,* 19*through which*
[e] 21 Or *response*

3:16 t Heb 13:18; u 1Pe 2:12,15
3:17 v 1Pe 2:15; w 1Pe 2:20
3:18 x 1Pe 2:21; y Col 1:22; 1Pe 4:1; z 1Pe 4:6
3:19 a 1Pe 4:6
3:20 b Ge 6:3,5,13,14; c Heb 11:7
3:21 d Tit 3:5; e 1Pe 1:3
3:22 f Mk 16:19; g Ro 8:38
4:2 a Ro 6:2
4:3 b Eph 2:2
4:4 c 1Pe 3:16
4:5 d Ac 10:42; 2Ti 4:1
4:6 e 1Pe 3:19
4:7 f Ro 13:11
4:8 g 1Pe 1:22; h Pr 10:12
4:9 i Php 2:14
4:10 j Ro 12:6,7; k 1Co 4:2
4:11 l Eph 6:10; m 1Co 10:31
4:12 n 1Pe 1:6,7
4:13 o Ro 8:17
4:14 p Mt 5:11
4:16 q Ac 5:41
4:17 r Jer 25:29; s 2Th 1:8

"If it is hard for the righteous
to be saved,
what will become of the
ungodly and the
sinner?"[a][t]

19 So then, those who suffer according to God's will should commit themselves to their faithful Creator and continue to do good.

To Elders and Young Men

5 To the elders among you, I appeal as a fellow-elder,[a] a witness[b] of Christ's sufferings and one who also will share in the glory to be revealed:[c] 2 Be shepherds of God's flock[d] that is under your care, serving as overseers—not because you must, but because you are willing, as God wants you to be; not greedy for money,[e] but eager to serve; 3 not lording it over[f] those entrusted to you, but being examples[g] to the flock. 4 And when the Chief Shepherd appears, you will receive the crown of glory[h] that will never fade away.

5 Young men, in the same way be submissive[i] to those who are older. All of you, clothe yourselves with humility towards one another, because,

"God opposes the proud
but gives grace to the
humble."[a][j]

6 Humble yourselves, therefore, under God's mighty hand, that he may lift you up in due time.[k] 7 Cast all your anxiety on him[l] because he cares for you.[m]

8 Be self-controlled and alert. Your enemy the devil prowls around[n] like a roaring lion looking for someone to devour. 9 Resist him,[o] standing firm in the faith,[p] because you know that your brothers throughout the world are undergoing the same kind of sufferings.[q]

10 And the God of all grace, who called you to his eternal glory[r] in Christ, after you have suffered a little while, will himself restore you and make you strong,[s] firm and steadfast. 11 To him be the power for ever and ever. Amen.[t]

Final Greetings

12 With the help of Silas,[b][u] whom I regard as a faithful brother, I have written to you briefly,[v] encouraging you and testifying that this is the true grace of God. Stand fast in it.

13 She who is in Babylon, chosen together with you, sends you her greetings, and so does my son Mark.[w] 14 Greet one another with a kiss of love.[x]

Peace[y] to all of you who are in Christ.

4:18
t Pr 11:31
Lk 23:31

5:1
a Ac 11:30
b Lk 24:48
c 1Pe 1:5,7
Rev 1:9

5:2
d Jn 21:16
e 1Ti 3:3

5:3
f Eze 34:4
g Php 3:17

5:4
h 1Co 9:25

5:5
i Eph 5:21
j Pr 3:34
Jas 4:6

5:6
k Jas 4:10

5:7
l Ps 37:5
Mt 6:25
m Heb 13:5

5:8
n Job 1:7

5:9
o Jas 4:7
p Col 2:5
q Ac 14:22

5:10
r 2Co 4:17
s 2Th 2:17

5:11
t Ro 11:36

5:12
u 2Co 1:19
v Heb 13:22

5:13
w Ac 12:12

5:14
x Ro 16:16
y Eph 6:23

a *18* Prov. 11:31 a *5* Prov. 3:34 b *12* Greek *Silvanus*, a variant of *Silas*

2 PETER

1 Simon Peter, a servant[a] and
apostle of Jesus Christ,[b]
To those who through the righteousness[c] of our God and Saviour
Jesus Christ[d] have received a
faith as precious as ours:

2 Grace and peace be yours in
abundance through the knowledge
of God and of Jesus our Lord.[e]

Making One's Calling and Election Sure

3 His divine power[f] has given us
everything we need for life and
godliness through our knowledge
of him who called us[g] by his own
glory and goodness. 4 Through
these he has given us his very great
and precious promises,[h] so that
through them you may participate
in the divine nature[i] and escape
the corruption in the world caused
by evil desires.[j]
5 For this very reason, make
every effort to add to your faith
goodness; and to goodness, knowledge;[k] 6 and to knowledge, self-
control;[l] and to self-control, perseverance; and to perseverance,
godliness;[m] 7 and to godliness,
brotherly kindness; and to brotherly kindness, love.[n] 8 For if you
possess these qualities in increasing measure, they will keep you
from being ineffective and unproductive[o] in your knowledge of
our Lord Jesus Christ. 9 But if
anyone does not have them, he is
short-sighted and blind,[p] and has
forgotten that he has been cleansed
from his past sins.[q]
10 Therefore, my brothers, be all
the more eager to make your calling and election sure. For if you do
these things, you will never fall,[r]
11 and you will receive a rich

1:1 a Ro 1:1 b 1Pe 1:1 c Ro 3:21-26 d Tit 2:13
1:2 e Php 3:8
1:3 f 1Pe 1:5 g 1Th 2:12
1:4 h 2Co 7:1 i Eph 4:24 Heb 12:10 1Jn 3:2 j 2Pe 2:18-20
1:5 k Col 2:3
1:6 l Ac 24:25 m ver 3
1:7 n 1Th 3:12
1:8 o Jn 15:2 Tit 3:14
1:9 p 1Jn 2:11 q Eph 5:26
1:10 r 2Pe 3:17
1:12 s Php 3:1 1Jn 2:21
1:13 t 2Co 5:1,4
1:14 u 2Ti 4:6 v Jn 21:18,19
1:15 w Lk 9:31
1:16 x Mt 17:1-8
1:17 y Mt 3:17
1:18 z Mt 17:6
1:19 a Ps 119:105 b Rev 22:16
1:21 c 2Ti 3:16 d 2Sa 23:2 Ac 1:16 1Pe 1:11

welcome into the eternal kingdom
of our Lord and Saviour Jesus
Christ.

Prophecy of Scripture

12 So I will always remind you of
these things,[s] even though you
know them and are firmly established in the truth you now have. 13 I
think it is right to refresh your
memory as long as I live in the tent
of this body,[t] 14 because I know
that I will soon put it aside,[u] as our
Lord Jesus Christ has made clear
to me.[v] 15 And I will make every
effort to see that after my departure[w] you will always be able
to remember these things.
16 We did not follow cleverly in-
vented stories when we told you
about the power and coming of our
Lord Jesus Christ, but we were
eye-witnesses of his majesty.[x]
17 For he received honour and glory
from God the Father when the
voice came to him from the Majestic Glory, saying, "This is my Son,
whom I love; with him I am well
pleased."[a][y] 18 We ourselves heard
this voice that came from heaven
when we were with him on the
sacred mountain.[z]
19 And we have the word of the
prophets made more certain, and
you will do well to pay attention to
it, as to a light[a] shining in a dark
place, until the day dawns and the
morning star[b] rises in your hearts.
20 Above all, you must understand
that no prophecy of Scripture came
about by the prophet's own interpretation. 21 For prophecy never
had its origin in the will of man, but
men spoke from God[c] as they were
carried along by the Holy Spirit.[d]

[a] *17* Matt. 17:5; Mark 9:7; Luke 9:35

False Teachers and Their Destruction

2 But there were also false prophets[a] among the people, just as there will be false teachers among you.[b] They will secretly introduce destructive heresies, even denying the sovereign Lord[c] who bought them[d]—bringing swift destruction on themselves. 2 Many will follow their shameful ways and will bring the way of truth into disrepute. 3 In their greed these teachers will exploit you[e] with stories they have made up. Their condemnation has long been hanging over them, and their destruction has not been sleeping.

4 For if God did not spare angels when they sinned, but sent them to hell,[a] putting them into gloomy dungeons[b] to be held for judgment;[f] 5 if he did not spare the ancient world[g] when he brought the flood on its ungodly people, but protected Noah, a preacher of righteousness, and seven others;[h] 6 if he condemned the cities of Sodom and Gomorrah by burning them to ashes,[i] and made them an example[j] of what is going to happen to the ungodly; 7 and if he rescued Lot,[k] a righteous man, who was distressed by the filthy lives of lawless men[l] 8 (for that righteous man, living among them day after day, was tormented in his righteous soul by the lawless deeds he saw and heard)—9 if this is so, then the Lord knows how to rescue godly men from trials[m] and to hold the unrighteous for the day of judgment, while continuing their punishment.[c] 10 This is especially true of those who follow the corrupt desire[n] of the sinful nature[d] and despise authority.

Bold and arrogant, these men are not afraid to slander celestial beings;[o] 11 yet even angels, although they are stronger and more powerful, do not bring slanderous accusations against such beings in the presence of the Lord.[p] 12 But these men blaspheme in matters they do not understand. They are like brute beasts, creatures of instinct, born only to be caught and destroyed, and like beasts they too will perish.[q]

13 They will be paid back with harm for the harm they have done. Their idea of pleasure is to carouse in broad daylight.[r] They are blots and blemishes, revelling in their pleasures while they feast with you.[e][s] 14 With eyes full of adultery, they never stop sinning; they seduce[t] the unstable; they are experts in greed[u]—an accursed brood![v] 15 They have left the straight way and wandered off to follow the way of Balaam[w] son of Beor, who loved the wages of wickedness. 16 But he was rebuked for his wrongdoing by a donkey—a beast without speech—who spoke with a man's voice and restrained the prophet's madness.[x]

17 These men are springs without water[y] and mists driven by a storm. Blackest darkness is reserved for them.[z] 18 For they mouth empty, boastful words[a] and, by appealing to the lustful desires of sinful human nature, they entice people who are just escaping from those who live in error. 19 They promise them freedom, while they themselves are slaves of depravity—for a man is a slave to whatever has mastered him.[b] 20 If they have escaped the corruption of the world by knowing[c] our Lord and Saviour Jesus Christ and are again entangled in it and overcome, they are worse off at the end than they were at the beginning.[d] 21 It would have been better for them not to have known the way of righteousness, than to have known it and then to turn their backs on the

2:1 *a* Dt 13:1-3 *b* 1Ti 4:1 *c* Jude 4 *d* 1Co 6:20
2:3 *e* 2Co 2:17; 1Th 2:5
2:4 *f* Jude 6; Rev 20:1,2
2:5 *g* 2Pe 3:6 *h* Heb 11:7; 1Pe 3:20
2:6 *i* Ge 19:24,25 *j* Nu 26:10; Jude 7
2:7 *k* Ge 19:16 *l* 2Pe 3:17
2:9 *m* 1Co 10:13
2:10 *n* 2Pe 3:3 *o* Jude 8
2:11 *p* Jude 9
2:12 *q* Jude 10
2:13 *r* Ro 13:13 *s* 1Co 11:20,21; Jude 12
2:14 *t* ver 18 *u* ver 3 *v* Eph 2:3
2:15 *w* Nu 22:4-20; Jude 11
2:16 *x* Nu 22:21-30
2:17 *y* Jude 12 *z* Jude 13
2:18 *a* Jude 16
2:19 *b* Jn 8:34; Ro 6:16
2:20 *c* 2Pe 1:2 *d* Mt 12:45

[a]4 Greek *Tartarus* [b]4 Some manuscripts *into chains of darkness* [c]9 Or *unrighteous for punishment until the day of judgment* [d]10 Or *the flesh* [e]13 Some manuscripts *in their love feasts*

sacred command that was passed on to them.[e] 22 Of them the proverbs are true: "A dog returns to its vomit,"[f][f] and, "A sow that is washed goes back to her wallowing in the mud."

The Day of the Lord

3

Dear friends, this is now my second letter to you. I have written both of them as reminders[a] to stimulate you to wholesome thinking. 2 I want you to recall the words spoken in the past by the holy prophets and the command given by our Lord and Saviour through your apostles.

3 First of all, you must understand that in the last days[b] scoffers will come, scoffing and following their own evil desires.[c] 4 They will say, "Where is this 'coming' he promised?[d] Ever since our fathers died, everything goes on as it has since the beginning of creation."[e] 5 But they deliberately forget that long ago by God's word[f] the heavens existed and the earth was formed out of water and by water.[g] 6 By these waters also the world of that time was deluged and destroyed.[h] 7 By the same word the present heavens and earth are reserved for fire,[i] being kept for the day of judgment and destruction of ungodly men.

8 But do not forget this one thing, dear friends: With the Lord a day is like a thousand years, and a thousand years are like a day.[j] 9 The Lord is not slow in keeping his promise,[k] as some understand slowness. He is patient[l] with you, not wanting anyone to perish, but everyone to come to repentance.[m]

10 But the day of the Lord will come like a thief.[n] The heavens will disappear with a roar; the elements will be destroyed by fire, and the earth and everything in it will be laid bare.[a][o]

11 Since everything will be destroyed in this way, what kind of people ought you to be? You ought to live holy and godly lives 12 as you look forward[p] to the day of God and speed its coming.[b][q] That day will bring about the destruction of the heavens by fire, and the elements will melt in the heat.[r] 13 But in keeping with his promise we are looking forward to a new heaven and a new earth,[s] the home of righteousness.

14 So then, dear friends, since you are looking forward to this, make every effort to be found spotless, blameless[t] and at peace with him. 15 Bear in mind that our Lord's patience[u] means salvation,[v] just as our dear brother Paul also wrote to you with the wisdom that God gave him.[w] 16 He writes the same way in all his letters, speaking in them of these matters. His letters contain some things that are hard to understand, which ignorant and unstable[x] people distort, as they do the other Scriptures,[y] to their own destruction.

17 Therefore, dear friends, since you already know this, be on your guard[z] so that you may not be carried away by the error[a] of lawless men and fall from your secure position.[b] 18 But grow in the grace and knowledge of our Lord and Saviour Jesus Christ.[c] To him be glory both now and for ever! Amen.

f22 Prov. 26:11 a10 Some manuscripts *be burned up* b12 Or *as you wait eagerly for the day of God to come*

2:21 e Heb 6:4-6
2:22 f Pr 26:11
3:1 a 2Pe 1:13
3:3 b 1Ti 4:1; c 2Pe 2:10; Jude 18
3:4 d Isa 5:19; Eze 12:22; Mt 24:48; e Mk 10:6
3:5 f Ge 1:6,9; Heb 11:3; g Ps 24:2
3:6 h Ge 7:21,22
3:7 i ver 10,12; 2Th 1:7
3:8 j Ps 90:4
3:9 k Hab 2:3; Heb 10:37; l Ro 2:4; m 1Ti 2:4
3:10 n Lk 12:39; 1Th 5:2; o Mt 24:35; Rev 21:1
3:12 p 1Co 1:7; q Ps 50:3; r ver 10
3:13 s Isa 65:17; Isa 66:22; Rev 21:1
3:14 t 1Th 3:13
3:15 u Ro 2:4; v ver 9; w Eph 3:3
3:16 x 2Pe 2:14; y ver 2
3:17 z 1Co 10:12; a 2Pe 2:18; b Rev 2:5
3:18 c 2Pe 1:11

1 JOHN

The Word of Life

1 That which was from the
beginning,[a] which we have
heard, which we have seen with our
eyes,[b] which we have looked at
and our hands have touched[c]—this
we proclaim concerning the Word
of life. 2The life appeared;[d] we
have seen it and testify to it, and we
proclaim to you the eternal life,
which was with the Father and has
appeared to us. 3We proclaim to
you what we have seen and heard,
so that you also may have fellowship with us. And our fellowship is
with the Father and with his Son,
Jesus Christ.[e] 4We write this[f] to
make our[a] joy complete.[g]

Walking in the Light

5This is the message we have
heard[h] from him and declare to
you: God is light; in him there is no
darkness at all. 6If we claim to have
fellowship with him yet walk in the
darkness,[i] we lie and do not live by
the truth.[j] 7But if we walk in the
light, as he is in the light, we have
fellowship with one another, and
the blood of Jesus, his Son, purifies
us from all[b] sin.[k]
8If we claim to be without sin,[l]
we deceive ourselves and the truth
is not in us.[m] 9If we confess our
sins, he is faithful and just and will
forgive us our sins[n] and purify us
from all unrighteousness. 10If we
claim we have not sinned, we make
him out to be a liar[o] and his word
has no place in our lives.[p]

2 My dear children,[a] I write
this to you so that you will not
sin. But if anybody does sin, we
have one who speaks to the Father
in our defence[b]—Jesus Christ, the
Righteous One. 2He is the atoning
sacrifice for our sins,[c] and not
only for ours but also for[a] the sins
of the whole world.
3We know that we have come to
know him if we obey his commands.[d] 4The man who says, "I
know him," but does not do what he
commands is a liar, and the truth is
not in him.[e] 5But if anyone obeys
his word,[f] God's love[b] is truly
made complete in him.[g] This is
how we know we are in him: 6Who-
ever claims to live in him must
walk as Jesus did.[h]
7Dear friends, I am not writing
you a new command but an old one,
which you have had since the beginning.[i] This old command is the
message you have heard. 8Yet I am
writing you a new command;[j] its
truth is seen in him and you, because the darkness is passing[k] and
the true light[l] is already shining.[m]
9Anyone who claims to be in the
light but hates his brother is still in
the darkness. 10Whoever loves his
brother lives in the light,[n] and
there is nothing in him[c] to make
him stumble. 11But whoever hates
his brother is in the darkness and
walks around in the darkness; he
does not know where he is going,
because the darkness has blinded
him.[o]

12I write to you, dear children,
because your sins have been
forgiven on account of his
name.
13I write to you, fathers,
because you have known him
who is from the beginning.
I write to you, young men,
because you have overcome
the evil one.[p]

1:1 a Jn 1:2 b Jn 1:14; 2Pe 1:16 c Jn 20:27
1:2 d Jn 1:1-4; 1Ti 3:16
1:3 e 1Co 1:9
1:4 f 1Jn 2:1 g Jn 3:29
1:5 h 1Jn 3:11
1:6 i 2Co 6:14 j Jn 3:19-21
1:7 k Heb 9:14; Rev 1:5
1:8 l Pr 20:9; Jas 3:2 m 1Jn 2:4
1:9 n Ps 32:5; Ps 51:2
1:10 o 1Jn 5:10 p 1Jn 2:14
2:1 a ver 12,13,28 b Ro 8:34; Heb 7:25
2:2 c Ro 3:25
2:3 d Jn 14:15
2:4 e 1Jn 1:6,8
2:5 f Jn 14:21,23 g 1Jn 4:12
2:6 h Mt 11:29; 1Pe 2:21
2:7 i 1Jn 3:11,23; 2Jn 5,6
2:8 j Jn 13:34 k Ro 13:12 l Jn 1:9 m Eph 5:8; 1Th 5:5
2:10 n 1Jn 3:14
2:11 o Jn 12:35
2:13 p ver 14

a4 Some manuscripts *your* b7 Or *every*
a2 Or *He is the one who turns aside God's wrath, taking away our sins, and not only ours but also*
b5 Or *word, love for God* c10 Or *it*

I write to you, dear children,
  because you have known the
    Father.
14 I write to you, fathers,
  because you have known him
    who is from the beginning.
I write to you, young men,
  because you are strong,[q]
  and the word of God lives in
    you,[r]
  and you have overcome the
    evil one.[s]

Do Not Love the World

15 Do not love the world or anything in the world.[t] If anyone loves the world, the love of the Father is not in him.[u] 16 For everything in the world—the cravings of sinful man,[v] the lust of his eyes[w] and the boasting of what he has and does—comes not from the Father but from the world. 17 The world and its desires pass away,[x] but the man who does the will of God lives for ever.

Warning Against Antichrists

18 Dear children, this is the last hour; and as you have heard that the antichrist is coming,[y] even now many antichrists have come.[z] This is how we know it is the last hour. 19 They went out from us,[a] but they did not really belong to us. For if they had belonged to us, they would have remained with us; but their going showed that none of them belonged to us.[b]

20 But you have an anointing[c] from the Holy One,[d] and all of you know the truth.[d][e] 21 I do not write to you because you do not know the truth, but because you do know it[f] and because no lie comes from the truth. 22 Who is the liar? It is the man who denies that Jesus is the Christ. Such a man is the antichrist—he denies the Father and the Son.[g] 23 No-one who denies the Son has the Father; whoever acknowledges the Son has the Father also.[h]

24 See that what you have heard from the beginning remains in you. If it does, you also will remain in the Son and in the Father.[i] 25 And this is what he promised us—even eternal life.

26 I am writing these things to you about those who are trying to lead you astray.[j] 27 As for you, the anointing[k] you received from him remains in you, and you do not need anyone to teach you. But as his anointing teaches you about all things and as that anointing is real, not counterfeit—just as it has taught you, remain in him.

Children of God

28 And now, dear children,[l] continue in him, so that when he appears[m] we may be confident[n] and unashamed before him at his coming.[o]

29 If you know that he is righteous,[p] you know that everyone who does what is right has been born of him.

3 How great is the love[a] the Father has lavished on us, that we should be called children of God![b] And that is what we are! The reason the world does not know us is that it did not know him.[c] 2 Dear friends, now we are children of God, and what we will be has not yet been made known. But we know that when he appears,[a] we shall be like him,[d] for we shall see him as he is.[e] 3 Everyone who has this hope in him purifies himself,[f] just as he is pure.

4 Everyone who sins breaks the law; in fact, sin is lawlessness.[g] 5 But you know that he appeared so that he might take away our sins. And in him is no sin.[h] 6 No-one who lives in him keeps on sinning.[i] No-one who continues to sin has either seen him[j] or known him.[k]

7 Dear children,[l] do not let anyone lead you astray.[m] He who does

2:14 q Eph 6:10; r Jn 5:38; 1Jn 1:10; s ver 13
2:15 t Ro 12:2; u Jas 4:4
2:16 v Ro 13:14; w Pr 27:20
2:17 x 1Co 7:31
2:18 y ver 22; 1Jn 4:3; 2Jn 7; z 1Jn 4:1
2:19 a Ac 20:30; b 1Co 11:19
2:20 c 2Co 1:21; d Mk 1:24; e Jn 14:26
2:21 f 2Pe 1:12; Jude 5
2:22 g 2Jn 7
2:23 h Jn 8:19; 1Jn 4:15
2:24 i Jn 14:23
2:26 j 2Jn 7
2:27 k ver 20
2:28 l ver 1; m 1Jn 3:2; n 1Jn 4:17; o 1Th 2:19
2:29 p 1Jn 3:7
3:1 a Jn 3:16; b Jn 1:12; c Jn 16:3
3:2 d Ro 8:29; 2Pe 1:4; e 2Co 3:18
3:3 f 2Co 7:1; 2Pe 3:13,14
3:4 g 1Jn 5:17
3:5 h 2Co 5:21
3:6 i ver 9; j 3Jn 11; k 1Jn 2:4
3:7 l 1Jn 2:1; m 1Jn 2:26

d 20 Some manuscripts *and you know all things*
a 2 Or *when it is made known*

what is right is righteous, just as he is righteous.[n] 8He who does what is sinful is of the devil,[o] because the devil has been sinning from the beginning. The reason the Son of God appeared was to destroy the devil's work. 9No-one who is born of God[p] will continue to sin,[q] because God's seed[r] remains in him; he cannot go on sinning, because he has been born of God. 10This is how we know who the children of God are and who the children of the devil are: Anyone who does not do what is right is not a child of God; nor is anyone who does not love[s] his brother.

Love One Another

11This is the message you heard[t] from the beginning: We should love one another.[u] 12Do not be like Cain, who belonged to the evil one and murdered his brother.[v] And why did he murder him? Because his own actions were evil and his brother's were righteous. 13Do not be surprised, my brothers, if the world hates you.[w] 14We know that we have passed from death to life,[x] because we love our brothers. Anyone who does not love remains in death.[y] 15Anyone who hates his brother is a murderer,[z] and you know that no murderer has eternal life in him.[a]

16This is how we know what love is: Jesus Christ laid down his life for us. And we ought to lay down our lives for our brothers.[b] 17If anyone has material possessions and sees his brother in need but has no pity on him,[c] how can the love of God be in him?[d] 18Dear children,[e] let us not love with words or tongue but with actions and in truth.[f] 19This then is how we know that we belong to the truth, and how we set our hearts at rest in his presence 20whenever our hearts condemn us. For God is greater than our hearts, and he knows everything.

21Dear friends, if our hearts do not condemn us, we have confidence before God[g] 22and receive from him anything we ask,[h] because we obey his commands and do what pleases him.[i] 23And this is his command: to believe[j] in the name of his Son, Jesus Christ, and to love one another as he commanded us.[k] 24Those who obey his commands live in him,[l] and he in them. And this is how we know that he lives in us: We know it by the Spirit he gave us.[m]

Test the Spirits

4 Dear friends, do not believe every spirit, but test the spirits to see whether they are from God, because many false prophets have gone out into the world.[a] 2This is how you can recognise the Spirit of God: Every spirit that acknowledges that Jesus Christ has come in the flesh[b] is from God,[c] 3but every spirit that does not acknowledge Jesus is not from God. This is the spirit of the antichrist,[d] which you have heard is coming and even now is already in the world.

4You, dear children, are from God and have overcome them, because the one who is in you[e] is greater than the one who is in the world.[f] 5They are from the world[g] and therefore speak from the viewpoint of the world, and the world listens to them. 6We are from God, and whoever knows God listens to us; but whoever is not from God does not listen to us.[h] This is how we recognise the Spirit[a] of truth[i] and the spirit of falsehood.

God's Love and Ours

7Dear friends, let us love one another,[j] for love comes from God. Everyone who loves has been born of God and knows God.[k] 8Whoever does not love does not know God,

[a]6 Or *spirit*

3:7 n 1Jn 2:29
3:8 o Jn 8:44
3:9 p Jn 1:13 q 1Jn 5:18 r 1Pe 1:23
3:10 s 1Jn 4:8
3:11 t 1Jn 1:5 u Jn 13:34,35 2Jn 5
3:12 v Ge 4:8
3:13 w Jn 15:18,19 Jn 17:14
3:14 x Jn 5:24 y 1Jn 2:9
3:15 z Mt 5:21,22 Jn 8:44 a Gal 5:20,21
3:16 b Jn 15:13
3:17 c Dt 15:7,8 d 1Jn 4:20
3:18 e 1Jn 2:1 f Eze 33:31 Ro 12:9
3:21 g 1Jn 5:14
3:22 h Mt 7:7 i Jn 8:29
3:23 j Jn 6:29 k Jn 13:34
3:24 l 1Jn 2:6 m 1Jn 4:13
4:1 a 2Pe 2:1 1Jn 2:18
4:2 b Jn 1:14 1Jn 2:23 c 1Co 12:3
4:3 d 1Jn 2:22 2Jn 7
4:4 e Ro 8:31 f Jn 12:31
4:5 g Jn 15:19
4:6 h Jn 8:47 i Jn 14:17
4:7 j 1Jn 3:11 k 1Jn 2:4

because God is love.[l] [9]This is how God showed his love among us: He sent his one and only Son[b] into the world that we might live through him.[m] [10]This is love: not that we loved God, but that he loved us[n] and sent his Son as an atoning sacrifice for[c] our sins.[o] [11]Dear friends, since God so loved us,[p] we also ought to love one another. [12]No-one has ever seen God;[q] but if we love one another, God lives in us and his love is made complete in us.[r]

[13]We know that we live in him and he in us, because he has given us of his Spirit.[s] [14]And we have seen and testify[t] that the Father has sent his Son to be the Saviour of the world.[u] [15]If anyone acknowledges that Jesus is the Son of God,[v] God lives in him and he in God. [16]And so we know and rely on the love God has for us.

God is love.[w] Whoever lives in love lives in God, and God in him.[x] [17]In this way, love is made complete[y] among us so that we will have confidence on the day of judgment, because in this world we are like him. [18]There is no fear in love. But perfect love drives out fear,[z] because fear has to do with punishment. The one who fears is not made perfect in love.

[19]We love because he first loved us.[a] [20]If anyone says, "I love God," yet hates his brother,[b] he is a liar.[c] For anyone who does not love his brother, whom he has seen,[d] cannot love God, whom he has not seen.[e] [21]And he has given us this command: Whoever loves God must also love his brother.[f]

Faith in the Son of God

5 Everyone who believes that Jesus is the Christ[a] is born of God,[b] and everyone who loves the father loves his child as well.[c] [2]This is how we know that we love the children of God: by loving God and carrying out his commands. [3]This is love for God: to obey his commands.[d] And his commands are not burdensome,[e] [4]for everyone born of God overcomes[f] the world. This is the victory that has overcome the world, even our faith. [5]Who is it that overcomes the world? Only he who believes that Jesus is the Son of God.

[6]This is the one who came by water and blood[g]—Jesus Christ. He did not come by water only, but by water and blood. And it is the Spirit who testifies, because the Spirit is the truth.[h] [7]For there are three[i] that testify: [8]the[a] Spirit, the water and the blood; and the three are in agreement. [9]We accept man's testimony,[j] but God's testimony is greater because it is the testimony of God,[k] which he has given about his Son. [10]Anyone who believes in the Son of God has this testimony in his heart.[l] Anyone who does not believe God has made him out to be a liar,[m] because he has not believed the testimony God has given about his Son. [11]And this is the testimony: God has given us eternal life, and this life is in his Son.[n] [12]He who has the Son has life; he who does not have the Son of God does not have life.[o]

Concluding Remarks

[13]I write these things to you who believe in the name of the Son of God[p] so that you may know that you have eternal life.[q] [14]This is the confidence[r] we have in approaching God: that if we ask anything according to his will, he hears us.[s] [15]And if we know that he hears us—whatever we ask—we know[t] that we have what we asked of him.

[16]If anyone sees his brother commit a sin that does not lead to death,

4:8 l ver 7,16
4:9 m Jn 3:16,17; 1Jn 5:11
4:10 n Ro 5:8,10; o 1Jn 2:2
4:11 p Jn 3:16
4:12 q Jn 1:18; 1Ti 6:16; r 1Jn 2:5
4:13 s 1Jn 3:24
4:14 t Jn 15:27; u Jn 3:17
4:15 v Ro 10:9
4:16 w ver 8; x 1Jn 3:24
4:17 y 1Jn 2:5
4:18 z Ro 8:15
4:19 a ver 10
4:20 b 1Jn 2:9; c 1Jn 2:4; d 1Jn 3:17; e ver 12
4:21 f Mt 5:43
5:1 a 1Jn 2:22; b Jn 1:13; 1Jn 2:23; c Jn 8:42
5:3 d Jn 14:15; 2Jn 6; e Mt 11:30
5:4 f Jn 16:33
5:6 g Jn 19:34; h Jn 14:17
5:7 i Mt 18:16
5:9 j Jn 5:34; k Mt 3:16,17; Jn 8:17,18
5:10 l Ro 8:16; Gal 4:6; m Jn 3:33
5:11 n Jn 1:4; 1Jn 2:25
5:12 o Jn 3:15,16,36
5:13 p 1Jn 3:23; q Jn 20:31; 1Jn 1:1,2
5:14 r 1Jn 3:21; s Mt 7:7
5:15 t ver 18,19,20

b9 Or *his only begotten Son* **c**10 Or *as the one who would turn aside his wrath, taking away*
a7,8 Late manuscripts of the Vulgate *testify in heaven: the Father, the Word and the Holy Spirit, and these three are one.* [8]*And there are three that testify on earth: the* (not found in any Greek manuscript before the sixteenth century)

he should pray and God will give him life.[u] I refer to those whose sin does not lead to death. There is a sin that leads to death.[v] I am not saying that he should pray about that.[w] [17]All wrongdoing is sin,[x] and there is sin that does not lead to death.[y]

[18]We know that anyone born of God does not continue to sin; the one who was born of God keeps him safe, and the evil one cannot harm him.[z] [19]We know that we are children of God,[a] and that the whole world is under the control of the evil one.[b] [20]We know also that the Son of God has come and has given us understanding,[c] so that we may know him who is true.[d] And we are in him who is true—even in his Son Jesus Christ. He is the true God and eternal life.[e]

[21]Dear children, keep yourselves from idols.[f]

5:16
u Jas 5:15
v Heb 6:4-6
Heb 10:26
w Jer 7:16

5:17
x 1Jn 3:4
y 1Jn 2:1

5:18
z Jn 14:30

5:19
a 1Jn 4:6
b Gal 1:4

5:20
c Lk 24:45
d Jn 17:3
e ver 11

5:21 *f* 1Co 10:14 1Th 1:9

2 JOHN

1 The elder,[a]

To the chosen[b] lady and her children, whom I love in the truth—and
not I only, but also all who know
the truth[c]—2 because of the truth,[d]
which lives in us[e] and will be with
us for ever:

3 Grace, mercy and peace from
God the Father and from Jesus
Christ,[f] the Father's Son, will be
with us in truth and love.

4 It has given me great joy to find
some of your children walking in
the truth,[g] just as the Father commanded us. 5 And now, dear lady, I
am not writing you a new command
but one we have had from the
beginning.[h] I ask that we love one
another. 6 And this is love:[i] that
we walk in obedience to his commands. As you have heard from the
beginning, his command is that you
walk in love.
7 Many deceivers, who do not
acknowledge Jesus Christ[j] as coming in the flesh, have gone out into the world.[k] Any such person is
the deceiver and the antichrist.[l]
8 Watch out that you do not lose
what you have worked for, but that
you may be rewarded fully.[m] 9 Anyone who runs ahead and does not
continue in the teaching of Christ
does not have God; whoever continues in the teaching has both the
Father and the Son.[n] 10 If anyone comes to you and does not
bring this teaching, do not take him
into your house or welcome
him.[o] 11 Anyone who welcomes him
shares[p] in his wicked work.
12 I have much to write to you, but
I do not want to use paper and ink.
Instead, I hope to visit you and talk
with you face to face,[q] so that our
joy may be complete.

13 The children of your chosen[r]
sister send their greetings.

1 a 3Jn 1 b Ro 16:13 c Jn 8:32
2 d 2Pe 1:12 e 1Jn 1:8
3 f Ro 1:7
4 g 3Jn 3,4
5 h 1Jn 2:7; 1Jn 3:11
6 i 1Jn 2:5
7 j 1Jn 2:22; 1Jn 4:2,3 k 1Jn 4:1 l 1Jn 2:18
8 m 1Co 3:8
9 n 1Jn 2:23
10 o Ro 16:17
11 p 1Ti 5:22
12 q 3Jn 13,14
13 r ver 1

3 JOHN

1 The elder,[a]

To my dear friend Gaius, whom I love in the truth.

2 Dear friend, I pray that you may enjoy good health and that all may go well with you, even as your soul is getting along well. 3 It gave me great joy to have some brothers[b] come and tell about your faithfulness to the truth and how you continue to walk in the truth.[c] 4 I have no greater joy than to hear that my children[d] are walking in the truth.

5 Dear friend, you are faithful in what you are doing for the brothers, even though they are strangers to you.[e] 6 They have told the church about your love. You will do well to send them on their way in a manner worthy of God. 7 It was for the sake of the Name[f] that they went out, receiving no help from the pagans.[g] 8 We ought therefore to show hospitality to such men so that we may work together for the truth.

1
a 2Jn 1

3
b ver 5,10
c 2Jn 4

4
d 1Co 4:15
1Jn 2:1

5
e Ro 12:13
Heb 13:2

7
f Jn 15:21
g Ac 20:33,35

10
h 2Jn 12
i ver 5
j Jn 9:22,34

11
k Ps 37:27
l 1Jn 2:29
m 1Jn 3:6,9,10

12
n 1Ti 3:7
o Jn 21:24

14
p 2Jn 12
q Jn 10:3

9 I wrote to the church, but Diotrephes, who loves to be first, will have nothing to do with us. 10 So if I come,[h] I will call attention to what he is doing, gossiping maliciously about us. Not satisfied with that, he refuses to welcome the brothers.[i] He also stops those who want to do so and puts them out of the church.[j]

11 Dear friend, do not imitate what is evil but what is good.[k] Anyone who does what is good is from God.[l] Anyone who does what is evil has not seen God.[m] 12 Demetrius is well spoken of by everyone[n]—and even by the truth itself. We also speak well of him, and you know that our testimony is true.[o]

13 I have much to write to you, but I do not want to do so with pen and ink. 14 I hope to see you soon, and we will talk face to face.[p]

Peace to you. The friends here send their greetings. Greet the friends there by name.[q]

JUDE

1 Jude,[a] a servant of Jesus Christ
and a brother of James,

To those who have been called,[b]
who are loved by God the Father
and kept by[a] Jesus Christ:[c]

2 Mercy, peace and love be yours
in abundance.[d]

The Sin and Doom of Godless Men

3 Dear friends, although I was
very eager to write to you about the
salvation we share,[e] I felt I had to
write and urge you to contend[f] for
the faith that was once for all entrusted to the saints. 4 For certain
men whose condemnation was
written about[b] long ago have
secretly slipped in among you.[g]
They are godless men, who change
the grace of our God into a licence
for immorality and deny Jesus
Christ our only Sovereign and
Lord.[h]

5 Though you already know all
this, I want to remind you that the
Lord[c] delivered his people out of
Egypt, but later destroyed those
who did not believe.[i] 6 And the
angels who did not keep their positions of authority but abandoned
their own home—these he has kept
in darkness, bound with everlasting chains for judgment on the
great Day.[j] 7 In a similar way,
Sodom and Gomorrah and the surrounding towns[k] gave themselves
up to sexual immorality and perversion. They serve as an example
of those who suffer the punishment
of eternal fire.[l]

8 In the very same way, these
dreamers pollute their own bodies,
reject authority and slander celestial beings.[m] 9 But even the archangel Michael,[n] when he was
disputing with the devil about the
body of Moses, did not dare to
bring a slanderous accusation
against him, but said, "The Lord rebuke you!"[o] 10 Yet these men speak
abusively against whatever they do
not understand; and what things
they do understand by instinct, like
unreasoning animals—these are
the very things that destroy
them.[p]

11 Woe to them! They have taken
the way of Cain;[q] they have rushed
for profit into Balaam's error;[r]
they have been destroyed in Korah's rebellion.[s]

12 These men are blemishes at
your love feasts,[t] eating with you
without the slightest qualm—shepherds who feed only themselves.
They are clouds without rain,[u]
blown along by the wind;[v] autumn
trees, without fruit and uprooted[w]—twice dead. 13 They are
wild waves of the sea,[x] foaming up
their shame;[y] wandering stars, for
whom blackest darkness has been
reserved for ever.[z]

14 Enoch,[a] the seventh from
Adam, prophesied about these
men: "See, the Lord is coming with
thousands upon thousands of his
holy ones[b] 15 to judge[c] everyone,
and to convict all the ungodly of all
the ungodly acts they have done in
the ungodly way, and of all the
harsh words ungodly sinners have
spoken against him."[d] 16 These
men are grumblers and fault-
finders; they follow their own evil
desires; they boast[e] about themselves and flatter others for their
own advantage.

1 *a* Mt 13:55 Ac 1:13 *b* Ro 1:6,7 *c* Jn 17:12
2 *d* 2Pe 1:2
3 *e* Tit 1:4 *f* 1Ti 6:12
4 *g* Gal 2:4 *h* Tit 1:16 2Pe 2:1
5 *i* Nu 14:29 Ps 106:26
6 *j* 2Pe 2:4,9
7 *k* Dt 29:23 *l* 2Pe 2:6
8 *m* 2Pe 2:10
9 *n* Da 10:13,21 *o* Zec 3:2
10 *p* 2Pe 2:12
11 *q* Ge 4:3-8 1Jn 3:12 *r* 2Pe 2:15 *s* Nu 16:1-3, 31-35
12 *t* 2Pe 2:13 1Co 1:120-22 *u* Pr 25:14 2Pe 2:17 *v* Eph 4:14 *w* Mt 15:13
13 *x* Isa 57:20 *y* Php 3:19 *z* 2Pe 2:17
14 *a* Ge 5:18, 21-24 *b* Dt 33:2 Da 7:10
15 *c* 2Pe 2:6-9 *d* 1Ti 1:9
16 *e* 2Pe 2:18

[a] *1* Or *for*; or *in* [b] *4* Or *men who were marked out for condemnation* [c] *5* Some early manuscripts *Jesus*

A Call to Persevere

[17]But, dear friends, remember
what the apostles of our Lord
Jesus Christ foretold.[f] [18]They said
to you, "In the last times[g] there
will be scoffers who will follow their own ungodly desires."[h]
[19]These are the men who divide
you, who follow mere natural
instincts and do not have the
Spirit.[i]

[20]But you, dear friends, build
yourselves up[j] in your most holy
faith and pray in the Holy Spirit.[k]
[21]Keep yourselves in God's love as
you wait[l] for the mercy of our
Lord Jesus Christ to bring you to
eternal life.

[22]Be merciful to those who doubt;
[23]snatch others from the fire and
save them;[m] to others show mercy,
mixed with fear—hating even the
clothing stained by corrupted
flesh.[n]

Doxology

[24]To him who is able[o] to keep you
from falling and to present you before his glorious presence[p] without fault[q] and with great joy—[25]to
the only God[r] our Saviour be
glory, majesty, power and authority, through Jesus Christ our
Lord, before all ages, now and for
evermore![s] Amen.[t]

17 f 2Pe 3:2
18 g 1Ti 4:1; h 2Pe 2:1
19 i 1Co 2:14,15
20 j Col 2:7; k Eph 6:18
21 l Tit 2:13; 2Pe 3:12
23 m Am 4:11; Zec 3:2-5; n Rev 3:4
24 o Ro 16:25; p 2Co 4:14; q Col 1:22
25 r Jn 5:44; 1Ti 1:17; s Heb 13:8; t Ro 11:36

REVELATION

Prologue

1 The revelation of Jesus Christ, which God gave him to show his servants what must soon take place. He made it known by sending his angel[a] to his servant John, 2 who testifies to everything he saw—that is, the word of God and the testimony of Jesus Christ.[b] 3 Blessed is the one who reads the words of this prophecy, and blessed are those who hear it and take to heart what is written in it,[c] because the time is near.

Greetings and Doxology

4 John,

To the seven churches in the province of Asia:

Grace and peace to you from him who is, and who was, and who is to come, and from the seven spirits**a**[d] before his throne, 5 and from Jesus Christ, who is the faithful witness,[e] the firstborn from the dead,[f] and the ruler of the kings of the earth.[g]

To him who loves us and has freed us from our sins by his blood, 6 and has made us to be a kingdom and priests[h] to serve his God and Father—to him be glory and power for ever and ever! Amen.[i]

7 Look, he is coming with the
clouds,[j]
and every eye will see him,
even those who pierced him;
and all the peoples of the
earth will mourn[k] because
of him.
So shall it be! Amen.

8 "I am the Alpha and the Omega,"[l] says the Lord God, "who is, and who was, and who is to come, the Almighty."[m]

One Like a Son of Man

9 I, John, your brother and companion in the suffering[n] and kingdom and patient endurance[o] that are ours in Jesus, was on the island of Patmos because of the word of God and the testimony of Jesus. 10 On the Lord's Day I was in the Spirit,[p] and I heard behind me a loud voice like a trumpet,[q] 11 which said: "Write on a scroll what you see and send it to the seven churches:[r] to Ephesus, Smyrna, Pergamum, Thyatira, Sardis,[s] Philadelphia and Laodicea."

12 I turned round to see the voice that was speaking to me. And when I turned I saw seven golden lampstands,[t] 13 and among the lampstands was someone "like a son of man",**b**[u] dressed in a robe reaching down to his feet and with a golden sash round his chest.[v] 14 His head and hair were white like wool, as white as snow, and his eyes were like blazing fire.[w] 15 His feet were like bronze glowing in a furnace,[x] and his voice was like the sound of rushing waters.[y] 16 In his right hand he held seven stars,[z] and out of his mouth came a sharp double-edged sword.[a] His face was like the sun shining in all its brilliance.

17 When I saw him, I fell at his feet[b] as though dead. Then he placed his right hand on me and said: "Do not be afraid. I am the First and the Last.[c] 18 I am the Living One; I was dead,[d] and behold I am alive for ever and ever![e] And I hold the keys of death and Hades.[f]

1:1 *a* Rev 22:16
1:2 *b* 1Co 1:6; Rev 12:17
1:3 *c* Lk 11:28
1:4 *d* Rev 3:1; Rev 4:5
1:5 *e* Rev 3:14 *f* Col 1:18 *g* Rev 17:14
1:6 *h* 1Pe 2:5 *i* Ro 11:36
1:7 *j* Da 7:13 *k* Zec 12:10
1:8 *l* Rev 21:6 *m* Rev 4:8
1:9 *n* Php 4:14 *o* 2Ti 2:12
1:10 *p* Rev 4:2 *q* Rev 4:1
1:11 *r* ver 4,20 *s* Rev 3:1
1:12 *t* Ex 25:31-40; Zec 4:2
1:13 *u* Eze 1:26; Da 7:13; Da 10:16 *v* Da 10:5; Rev 15:6
1:14 *w* Da 7:9; Da 10:6; Rev 19:12
1:15 *x* Da 10:6 *y* Eze 43:2; Rev 14:2
1:16 *z* Rev 2:1; Rev 3:1 *a* Isa 49:2; Heb 4:12; Rev 2:12,16
1:17 *b* Eze 1:28; Da 8:17,18 *c* Isa 41:4; Isa 44:6; Isa 48:12; Rev 22:13
1:18 *d* Ro 6:9 *e* Rev 4:9,10 *f* Rev 20:1

a*4* Or *the sevenfold Spirit* **b***13* Daniel 7:13

19“Write, therefore, what you
have seen, what is now and what
will take place later. 20The mystery
of the seven stars that you saw
in my right hand and of the seven golden lampstands[g] is this:
The seven stars are the angels[c]
of the seven churches,[h] and the
seven lampstands are the seven
churches.[i]

To the Church in Ephesus

2 “To the angel[a] of the church
in Ephesus write:

These are the words of him
who holds the seven stars in his
right hand[a] and walks among
the seven golden lampstands:[b]
2I know your deeds,[c] your
hard work and your perseverance. I know that you cannot
tolerate wicked men, that you
have tested[d] those who claim
to be apostles but are not, and
have found them false.[e] 3You
have persevered and have
endured hardships for my
name,[f] and have not grown
weary.
4Yet I hold this against you:
You have forsaken your first
love.[g] 5Remember the height
from which you have fallen!
Repent[h] and do the things you
did at first. If you do not repent, I will come to you and
remove your lampstand[i] from
its place. 6But you have this
in your favour: You hate the
practices of the Nicolaitans,[j]
which I also hate.
7He who has an ear, let him
hear[k] what the Spirit says to
the churches. To him who overcomes, I will give the right to
eat from the tree of life,[l]
which is in the paradise[m] of
God.

To the Church in Smyrna

8“To the angel of the church in
Smyrna[n] write:

These are the words of him
who is the First and the Last,[o]
who died and came to life
again.[p] 9I know your afflictions and your poverty—yet
you are rich![q] I know the slander of those who say they are
Jews and are not,[r] but are a
synagogue of Satan.[s] 10Do not
be afraid of what you are about
to suffer. I tell you, the devil
will put some of you in prison
to test you,[t] and you will suffer persecution for ten days.[u]
Be faithful,[v] even to the point
of death, and I will give you the
crown of life.
11He who has an ear, let him
hear what the Spirit says to the
churches. He who overcomes
will not be hurt at all by the
second death.[w]

To the Church in Pergamum

12“To the angel of the church in
Pergamum[x] write:

These are the words of him
who has the sharp, double-
edged sword.[y] 13I know where
you live—where Satan has his
throne. Yet you remain true to
my name. You did not re-
nounce your faith in me,[z] even
in the days of Antipas, my
faithful witness, who was put
to death in your city—where
Satan lives.[a]
14Nevertheless, I have a few
things against you:[b] You have
people there who hold to the
teaching of Balaam,[c] who
taught Balak to entice the Israelites to sin by eating food
sacrificed to idols and by committing sexual immorality.[d]
15Likewise you also have those
who hold to the teaching of the
Nicolaitans.[e] 16Repent therefore! Otherwise, I will soon

1:20 g Zec 4:2; h ver 4,11; i Mt 5:14,15
2:1 a Rev 1:16; b Rev 1:12,13
2:2 c Rev 3:1,8,15; d 1Jn 4:1; e 2Co 11:13
2:3 f Jn 15:21
2:4 g Mt 24:12
2:5 h ver 16,22; i Rev 1:20
2:6 j ver 15
2:7 k Mt 11:15; Rev 3:6,13,22; l Ge 2:9; Rev 22:2,14,19; m Lk 23:43
2:8 n Rev 1:11; o Rev 1:17; p Rev 1:18
2:9 q Jas 2:5; r Rev 3:9; s Mt 4:10
2:10 t Rev 3:10; u Da 1:12,14; v ver 13
2:11 w Rev 20:6,14; Rev 21:8
2:12 x Rev 1:11; y Rev 1:16
2:13 z Rev 14:12; a ver 9,24
2:14 b ver 20; c 2Pe 2:15; d 1Co 6:13
2:15 e ver 6

c20 Or *messengers* a1 Or *messenger*; also in verses 8, 12 and 18

come to you and will fight against them with the sword of my mouth.[f]

17He who has an ear, let him hear what the Spirit says to the churches. To him who overcomes, I will give some of the hidden manna.[g] I will also give him a white stone with a new name[h] written on it, known only to him who receives it.[i]

To the Church in Thyatira

18"To the angel of the church in Thyatira[j] write:

These are the words of the Son of God, whose eyes are like blazing fire and whose feet are like burnished bronze.[k] 19I know your deeds,[l] your love and faith, your service and perseverance, and that you are now doing more than you did at first.

20Nevertheless, I have this against you: You tolerate that woman Jezebel,[m] who calls herself a prophetess. By her teaching she misleads my servants into sexual immorality and the eating of food sacrificed to idols. 21I have given her time[n] to repent of her immorality, but she is unwilling.[o] 22So I will cast her on a bed of suffering, and I will make those who commit adultery[p] with her suffer intensely, unless they repent of her ways. 23I will strike her children dead. Then all the churches will know that I am he who searches hearts and minds,[q] and I will repay each of you according to your deeds. 24Now I say to the rest of you in Thyatira, to you who do not hold to her teaching and have not learned Satan's so-called deep secrets (I will not impose any other burden on you):[r] 25Only hold on to what you have[s] until I come.

26To him who overcomes and does my will to the end, I will give authority over the nations[t]—

27'He will rule them with an
iron sceptre;[u]
he will dash them to
pieces like
pottery'[b][v]—

just as I have received authority from my Father. 28I will also give him the morning star.[w] 29He who has an ear, let him hear[x] what the Spirit says to the churches.

To the Church in Sardis

3 "To the angel[a] of the church in Sardis write:

These are the words of him who holds the seven spirits[b][a] of God and the seven stars.[b] I know your deeds;[c] you have a reputation of being alive, but you are dead.[d] 2Wake up! Strengthen what remains and is about to die, for I have not found your deeds complete in the sight of my God. 3Remember, therefore, what you have received and heard; obey it, and repent.[e] But if you do not wake up, I will come like a thief,[f] and you will not know at what time I will come to you.

4Yet you have a few people in Sardis who have not soiled their clothes.[g] They will walk with me, dressed in white,[h] for they are worthy. 5He who overcomes will, like them, be dressed in white. I will never blot out his name from the book of life,[i] but will acknowledge his name before my Father[j] and his angels. 6He who has an ear, let him hear[k] what the Spirit says to the churches.

2:16 f 2Th 2:8; Rev 1:16
2:17 g Jn 6:49,50; h Isa 62:2; i Rev 19:12
2:18 j Rev 1:11; k Rev 1:14,15
2:19 l ver 2
2:20 m 1Ki 16:31; 1Ki 21:25; 2Ki 9:7
2:21 n Ro 2:4; o Rev 9:20
2:22 p Rev 17:2; Rev 18:9
2:23 q 1Sa 16:7; Jer 11:20; Ac 1:24; Ro 8:27
2:24 r Ac 15:28
2:25 s Rev 3:11
2:26 t Ps 2:8; Rev 3:21
2:27 u Rev 12:5; v Isa 30:14; Jer 19:11
2:28 w Rev 22:16
2:29 x ver 7
3:1 a Rev 1:4; b Rev 1:16; c Rev 2:2; d 1Ti 5:6
3:3 e Rev 2:5; f 2Pe 3:10
3:4 g Jude 23; h Rev 4:4; Rev 6:11; Rev 7:9,13,14
3:5 i Rev 20:12; j Mt 10:32
3:6 k Rev 2:7

[b]27 Psalm 2:9
[a]1 Or *messenger*; also in verses 7 and 14
[b]1 Or *the sevenfold Spirit*

To the Church in Philadelphia

7“To the angel of the church in Philadelphia[l] write:
These are the words of him
who is holy and true,[m] who
holds the key of David.[n] What
he opens no-one can shut, and
what he shuts no-one can open.
8I know your deeds. See, I have
placed before you an open
door[o] that no-one can shut. I
know that you have little
strength, yet you have kept
my word and have not denied
my name.[p] 9I will make those
who are of the synagogue of
Satan,[q] who claim to be Jews
though they are not, but are
liars—I will make them come
and fall down at your feet[r] and
acknowledge that I have loved
you.[s] 10Since you have kept
my command to endure pa-
tiently, I will also keep you[t]
from the hour of trial that is going to come upon the whole
world to test[u] those who live
on the earth.[v]
11I am coming soon. Hold on
to what you have,[w] so that no-
one will take your crown.[x]
12Him who overcomes I will
make a pillar[y] in the temple of
my God. Never again will he
leave it. I will write on him the
name of my God[z] and the
name of the city of my God, the
new Jerusalem,[a] which is
coming down out of heaven
from my God; and I will also
write on him my new name.
13He who has an ear, let him
hear what the Spirit says to the
churches.

To the Church in Laodicea

14“To the angel of the church in
Laodicea write:
These are the words of the
Amen, the faithful and true
witness, the ruler of God's creation.[b] 15I know your deeds,
that you are neither cold nor
hot.[c] I wish you were either
one or the other! 16So, because
you are lukewarm—neither
hot nor cold—I am about to spit
you out of my mouth. 17You
say, ‘I am rich; I have acquired
wealth and do not need a
thing.’[d] But you do not realise
that you are wretched, pitiful,
poor, blind and naked. 18I counsel you to buy from me gold refined in the fire, so that you can
become rich; and white clothes
to wear, so that you can cover
your shameful nakedness;[e]
and salve to put on your eyes,
so that you can see.
19Those whom I love I rebuke
and discipline.[f] So be earnest,
and repent.[g] 20Here I am! I
stand at the door[h] and knock.
If anyone hears my voice and
opens the door,[i] I will come
in[j] and eat with him, and he
with me.
21To him who overcomes, I
will give the right to sit with
me on my throne,[k] just as I
overcame[l] and sat down with
my Father on his throne. 22He
who has an ear, let him hear[m]
what the Spirit says to the
churches.”

The Throne in Heaven

4 After this I looked, and there
before me was a door standing
open in heaven. And the voice I had
first heard speaking to me like a
trumpet[a] said, “Come up here,[b]
and I will show you what must take
place after this.”[c] 2At once I was in
the Spirit,[d] and there before me
was a throne in heaven[e] with
someone sitting on it. 3And the one
who sat there had the appearance
of jasper and carnelian. A rainbow,[f] resembling an emerald, encircled the throne. 4Surrounding
the throne were twenty-four other
thrones, and seated on them were
twenty-four elders.[g] They were

3:7 l Rev 1:11; m 1Jn 5:20; n Isa 22:22; Mt 16:19
3:8 o Ac 14:27; p Rev 2:13
3:9 q Rev 2:9; r Isa 49:23; s Isa 43:4
3:10 t 2Pe 2:9; u Rev 2:10; v Rev 6:10; Rev 17:8
3:11 w Rev 2:25; x Rev 2:10
3:12 y Gal 2:9; z Rev 14:1; Rev 22:4; a Rev 21:2,10
3:14 b Col 1:16,18
3:15 c Ro 12:11
3:17 d Hos 12:8; 1Co 4:8
3:18 e Rev 16:15
3:19 f Pr 3:12; Heb 12:5,6; g Rev 2:5
3:20 h Mt 24:33; i Lk 12:36; j Jn 14:23
3:21 k Mt 19:28; l Rev 5:5
3:22 m Rev 2:7
4:1 a Rev 1:10; b Rev 11:12; c Rev 1:19
4:2 d Rev 1:10; e Isa 6:1; Eze 1:26-28; Da 7:9
4:3 f Eze 1:28
4:4 g Rev 11:16

dressed in white[h] and had crowns
of gold on their heads. 5From the
throne came flashes of lightning,
rumblings and peals of thunder.[i]
Before the throne, seven lamps[j]
were blazing. These are the seven
spirits[a][k] of God. 6Also before the
throne there was what looked like a
sea of glass,[l] clear as crystal.

In the centre, around the throne,
were four living creatures,[m] and
they were covered with eyes, in
front and behind. 7The first living
creature was like a lion, the second
was like an ox, the third had a face
like a man, the fourth was like a flying eagle.[n] 8Each of the four living
creatures had six wings[o] and was
covered with eyes all around, even
under his wings. Day and night
they never stop saying:

> "Holy, holy, holy
> is the Lord God Almighty,[p]
> who was, and is, and is to
> come."[q]

9Whenever the living creatures
give glory, honour and thanks to
him who sits on the throne[r] and
who lives for ever and ever, 10the
twenty-four elders[s] fall down before him[t] who sits on the throne,[u]
and worship him who lives for ever
and ever. They lay their crowns before the throne and say:

> 11"You are worthy, our Lord and
> God,
> to receive glory and honour
> and power,[v]
> for you created all things,
> and by your will they were
> created
> and have their being."[w]

The Scroll and the Lamb

5 Then I saw in the right hand of
him who sat on the throne[a] a
scroll with writing on both sides[b]
and sealed[c] with seven seals. 2And
I saw a mighty angel proclaiming
in a loud voice, "Who is worthy to
break the seals and open the
scroll?" 3But no-one in heaven or on
earth or under the earth could open
the scroll or even look inside it. 4I
wept and wept because no-one was
found who was worthy to open the
scroll or look inside. 5Then one of
the elders said to me, "Do not
weep! See, the Lion[d] of the tribe
of Judah, the Root of David,[e] has
triumphed. He is able to open
the scroll and its seven seals."

6Then I saw a Lamb,[f] looking as
if it had been slain, standing in the
centre of the throne, encircled by
the four living creatures and the
elders. He had seven horns and
seven eyes,[g] which are the seven
spirits[a] of God sent out into all the
earth. 7He came and took the scroll
from the right hand of him who sat
on the throne.[h] 8And when he had
taken it, the four living creatures
and the twenty-four elders fell
down before the Lamb. Each one
had a harp[i] and they were holding
golden bowls full of incense, which
are the prayers[j] of the saints.
9And they sang a new song:[k]

> "You are worthy[l] to take the
> scroll
> and to open its seals,
> because you were slain,
> and with your blood[m] you
> purchased[n] men for God
> from every tribe and language
> and people and nation.
> 10You have made them to be a
> kingdom and priests[o] to
> serve our God,
> and they will reign on the
> earth."

11Then I looked and heard the
voice of many angels, numbering
thousands upon thousands, and ten
thousand times ten thousand.[p]
They encircled the throne and the
living creatures and the elders. 12In
a loud voice they sang:

> "Worthy is the Lamb, who was
> slain,

4:4 h Rev 3:4,5
4:5 i Rev 8:5; Rev 16:18 j Zec 4:2 k Rev 1:4
4:6 l Rev 15:2 m Eze 1:5
4:7 n Eze 1:10; Eze 10:14
4:8 o Isa 6:2 p Isa 6:3; Rev 1:8 q Rev 1:4
4:9 r Ps 47:8
4:10 s ver 4 t Rev 5:8,14 u ver 2
4:11 v Rev 5:12 w Rev 10:6
5:1 a ver 7,13 b Eze 2:9,10 c Isa 29:11; Da 12:4
5:5 d Ge 49:9 e Isa 11:1,10; Ro 15:12; Rev 22:16
5:6 f Jn 1:29 g Zec 4:10
5:7 h ver 1
5:8 i Rev 14:2 j Ps 141:2
5:9 k Ps 40:3 l Rev 4:11 m Heb 9:12 n 1Co 6:20
5:10 o 1Pe 2:5
5:11 p Da 7:10; Heb 12:22

a5 Or *the sevenfold Spirit* a6 Or *the sevenfold Spirit*

to receive power and wealth
and wisdom and strength
and honour and glory and
praise!"[q]

13Then I heard every creature in
heaven and on earth and under the
earth[r] and on the sea, and all that
is in them, singing:

"To him who sits on the throne
and to the Lamb[s]
be praise and honour and glory
and power,
for ever and ever!"[t]

14The four living creatures said,
"Amen",[u] and the elders fell down
and worshipped.[v]

The Seals

6 I watched as the Lamb[a]
opened the first of the seven
seals.[b] Then I heard one of the four
living creatures[c] say in a voice
like thunder,[d] "Come!" 2I looked, and
there before me was a white horse![e]
Its rider held a bow, and he was
given a crown,[f] and he rode out as
a conqueror bent on conquest.[g]
3When the Lamb opened the
second seal, I heard the second living creature[h] say, "Come!" 4Then
another horse came out, a fiery red
one.[i] Its rider was given power to
take peace from the earth[j] and to
make men slay each other. To him
was given a large sword.
5When the Lamb opened the
third seal, I heard the third living
creature[k] say, "Come!" I looked,
and there before me was a black
horse![l] Its rider was holding a pair
of scales in his hand. 6Then I heard
what sounded like a voice among
the four living creatures,[m] saying,
"A quart[a] of wheat for a day's
wages,[b] and three quarts of barley
for a day's wages,[b] and do not
damage[n] the oil and the wine!"
7When the Lamb opened the
fourth seal, I heard the voice of
the fourth living creature[o] say,
"Come!" 8I looked, and there before me was a pale horse![p] Its
rider was named Death, and Hades[q] was following close behind
him. They were given power over a
fourth of the earth to kill by sword,
famine and plague, and by the wild
beasts of the earth.[r]
9When he opened the fifth seal, I
saw under the altar[s] the souls of
those who had been slain[t] because
of the word of God and the testimony they had maintained. 10They
called out in a loud voice, "How
long,[u] Sovereign Lord, holy and
true,[v] until you judge the inhabitants of the earth and avenge our
blood?"[w] 11Then each of them was
given a white robe,[x] and they were
told to wait a little longer, until the
number of their fellow-servants
and brothers who were to be killed
as they had been was completed.[y]
12I watched as he opened the
sixth seal. There was a great earthquake.[z] The sun turned black[a]
like sackcloth made of goat hair,
the whole moon turned blood red,
13and the stars in the sky fell to
earth,[b] as late figs drop from a fig-
tree[c] when shaken by a strong wind.
14The sky receded like a scroll,
rolling up, and every mountain and
island was removed from its place.[d]
15Then the kings of the earth, the
princes, the generals, the rich, the
mighty, and every slave and every
free man hid in caves and among
the rocks of the mountains.[e]
16They called to the mountains and
the rocks, "Fall on us[f] and hide us
from the face of him who sits on the
throne and from the wrath of the
Lamb! 17For the great day[g] of their
wrath has come, and who can
stand?"[h]

144,000 Sealed

7 After this I saw four angels
standing at the four corners of
the earth, holding back the four
winds[a] of the earth to prevent any

5:12 q Rev 4:11
5:13 r ver 3; Php 2:10 s Rev 6:16 t 1Ch 29:11
5:14 u Rev 4:9 v Rev 4:10; Rev 19:4
6:1 a Rev 5:6 b Rev 5:1 c Rev 4:6,7 d Rev 14:2; Rev 19:6
6:2 e Zec 6:3; Rev 19:11 f Zec 6:11; Rev 14:14 g Ps 45:4
6:3 h Rev 4:7
6:4 i Zec 6:2 j Mt 10:34
6:5 k Rev 4:7 l Zec 6:2
6:6 m Rev 4:6,7 n Rev 9:4
6:7 o Rev 4:7
6:8 p Zec 6:3 q Hos 13:14 r Jer 15:2,3; Eze 5:12,17
6:9 s Rev 14:18; Rev 16:7 t Rev 20:4
6:10 u Zec 1:12 v Rev 3:7 w Rev 19:2
6:11 x Rev 3:4 y Heb 11:40
6:12 z Rev 16:18 a Mt 24:29
6:13 b Mt 24:29; Rev 8:10; Rev 9:1 c Isa 34:4
6:14 d Jer 4:24; Rev 16:20
6:15 e Isa 2:10,19,21
6:16 f Hos 10:8; Lk 23:30
6:17 g Zep 1:14,15; Rev 16:14 h Ps 76:7

7:1 a Da 7:2

[a]6 Greek *a choinix* (probably about a litre)
[b]6 Greek *a denarius*

wind from blowing on the land or on the sea or on any tree. 2 Then I saw another angel coming up from the east, having the seal of the living God. He called out in a loud voice to the four angels who had been given power to harm the land and the sea: 3 "Do not harm[b] the land or the sea or the trees until we put a seal on the foreheads[c] of the servants of our God." 4 Then I heard the number[d] of those who were sealed: 144,000[e] from all the tribes of Israel.

5 From the tribe of Judah 12,000
were sealed,
from the tribe of Reuben
12,000,
from the tribe of Gad 12,000,
6 from the tribe of Asher 12,000,
from the tribe of Naphtali
12,000,
from the tribe of Manasseh
12,000,
7 from the tribe of Simeon
12,000,
from the tribe of Levi 12,000,
from the tribe of Issachar
12,000,
8 from the tribe of Zebulun
12,000,
from the tribe of Joseph
12,000,
from the tribe of Benjamin
12,000.

The Great Multitude in White Robes

9 After this I looked and there before me was a great multitude that no-one could count, from every nation, tribe, people and language,[f] standing before the throne[g] and in front of the Lamb. They were wearing white robes and were holding palm branches in their hands. 10 And they cried out in a loud voice:

"Salvation belongs to our God,[h]
who sits on the throne,
and to the Lamb."

11 All the angels were standing round the throne and around the elders[i] and the four living creatures.[j] They fell down on their faces[k] before the throne and worshipped God, 12 saying:

"Amen!
Praise and glory
and wisdom and thanks and
honour
and power and strength
be to our God for ever and
ever.
Amen!"[l]

13 Then one of the elders asked me, "These in white robes—who are they, and where did they come from?"

14 I answered, "Sir, you know."

And he said, "These are they who have come out of the great tribulation; they have washed their robes[m] and made them white in the blood of the Lamb.[n] 15 Therefore,

"they are before the throne of
God[o]
and serve him[p] day and night
in his temple;[q]
and he who sits on the throne
will spread his tent over
them.[r]
16 Never again will they hunger;
never again will they thirst.
The sun will not beat upon
them,
nor any scorching heat.[s]
17 For the Lamb at the centre of
the throne will be their
shepherd;[t]
he will lead them to springs of
living water.
And God will wipe away every
tear from their eyes."[u]

The Seventh Seal and the Golden Censer

8 When he opened the seventh seal,[a] there was silence in heaven for about half an hour.

2 And I saw the seven angels[b] who stand before God, and to them were given seven trumpets.

3 Another angel,[c] who had a

7:3 [b] Rev 6:6 [c] Eze 9:4; Rev 22:4
7:4 [d] Rev 9:16 [e] Rev 14:1,3
7:9 [f] Rev 5:9 [g] ver 15
7:10 [h] Ps 3:8; Rev 12:10; Rev 19:1
7:11 [i] Rev 4:4 [j] Rev 4:6 [k] Rev 4:10
7:12 [l] Rev 5:12-14
7:14 [m] Rev 22:14 [n] Heb 9:14; 1Jn 1:7
7:15 [o] ver 9 [p] Rev 22:3 [q] Rev 11:19 [r] Isa 4:5,6; Rev 21:3
7:16 [s] Isa 49:10
7:17 [t] Ps 23:1; Jn 10:11 [u] Isa 25:8; Rev 21:4
8:1 [a] Rev 6:1
8:2 [b] ver 6-13; Rev 9:1,13; Rev 11:15
8:3 [c] Rev 7:2

golden censer, came and stood at
the altar. He was given much incense to offer, with the prayers of
all the saints,[d] on the golden altar[e]
before the throne. 4 The smoke of
the incense, together with the
prayers of the saints, went up before God[f] from the angel's hand.
5 Then the angel took the censer,
filled it with fire from the altar,[g]
and hurled it on the earth; and
there came peals of thunder,[h]
rumblings, flashes of lightning and
an earthquake.[i]

The Trumpets

6 Then the seven angels who had
the seven trumpets[j] prepared to
sound them.
7 The first angel sounded his
trumpet, and there came hail and
fire[k] mixed with blood, and it was
hurled down upon the earth. A
third[l] of the earth was burned up,
a third of the trees were burned up,
and all the green grass was burned
up.[m]
8 The second angel sounded his
trumpet, and something like a huge
mountain,[n] all ablaze, was thrown
into the sea. A third[o] of the sea
turned into blood,[p] 9 a third[q] of the
living creatures in the sea died, and
a third of the ships were destroyed.
10 The third angel sounded his
trumpet, and a great star, blazing
like a torch, fell from the sky[r] on
a third of the rivers and on the
springs of water[s]—11 the name of
the star is Wormwood.[a] A third[t]
of the waters turned bitter, and
many people died from the waters
that had become bitter.[u]
12 The fourth angel sounded his
trumpet, and a third of the sun was
struck, a third of the moon, and a
third of the stars, so that a third[v]
of them turned dark.[w] A third of
the day was without light, and also
a third of the night.
13 As I watched, I heard an eagle
that was flying in mid-air[x] call out
in a loud voice: "Woe! Woe! Woe[y]
to the inhabitants of the earth, because of the trumpet blasts about to
be sounded by the other three
angels!"

9

The fifth angel sounded his
trumpet, and I saw a star that
had fallen from the sky to the
earth.[a] The star was given the key
to the shaft of the Abyss.[b] 2 When
he opened the Abyss, smoke rose
from it like the smoke from a gi-
gantic furnace.[c] The sun and sky
were darkened[d] by the smoke
from the Abyss. 3 And out of the
smoke locusts[e] came down upon
the earth and were given power
like that of scorpions[f] of the earth.
4 They were told not to harm[g] the
grass of the earth or any plant or
tree,[h] but only those people who
did not have the seal of God on their
foreheads.[i] 5 They were not given
power to kill them, but only to torture them for five months.[j] And
the agony they suffered was like
that of the sting of a scorpion[k]
when it strikes a man. 6 During
those days men will seek death, but
will not find it; they will long to die,
but death will elude them.[l]
7 The locusts looked like horses
prepared for battle.[m] On their
heads they wore something like
crowns of gold, and their faces resembled human faces.[n] 8 Their hair
was like women's hair, and their
teeth were like lions' teeth.[o] 9 They
had breastplates like breastplates
of iron, and the sound of their
wings was like the thundering of
many horses and chariots rushing
into battle.[p] 10 They had tails and
stings like scorpions, and in their
tails they had power to torment
people for five months.[q] 11 They
had as king over them the angel
of the Abyss,[r] whose name in
Hebrew is Abaddon, and in Greek,
Apollyon.[a]
12 The first woe is past; two other
woes are yet to come.[s]

8:3 d Rev 5:8 e Ex 30:1-6; Heb 9:4; Rev 9:13
8:4 f Ps 141:2
8:5 g Lev 16:12,13 h Rev 4:5 i Rev 6:12
8:6 j ver 2
8:7 k Eze 38:22 l ver 7-12; Rev 9:15,18; Rev 12:4 m Rev 9:4
8:8 n Jer 51:25 o ver 7 p Rev 16:3
8:9 q ver 7
8:10 r Isa 14:12; Rev 6:13; Rev 9:1 s Rev 14:7; Rev 16:4
8:11 t ver 7 u Jer 9:15; Jer 23:15
8:12 v ver 7 w Ex 10:21-23; Rev 6:12,13
8:13 x Rev 14:6; Rev 19:17 y Rev 9:12; Rev 11:14
9:1 a Rev 8:10 b ver 2,11; Lk 8:31
9:2 c Ge 19:28; Ex 19:18 d Joel 2:2,10
9:3 e Ex 10:12-15 f ver 5,10
9:4 g Rev 6:6 h Rev 8:7 i Rev 7:2,3
9:5 j ver 10 k ver 3
9:6 l Job 3:21; Jer 8:3; Rev 6:16
9:7 m Joel 2:4 n Da 7:8
9:8 o Joel 1:6
9:9 p Joel 2:5
9:10 q ver 3,5,19
9:11 r ver 1,2
9:12 s Rev 8:13

a*11* That is, Bitterness a*11* *Abaddon* and *Apollyon* mean *Destroyer.*

13The sixth angel sounded his trumpet, and I heard a voice coming from the horns[b][t] of the golden altar that is before God.[u] 14It said to the sixth angel who had the trumpet, "Release the four angels who are bound at the great river Euphrates."[v] 15And the four angels who had been kept ready for this very hour and day and month and year were released to kill a third of mankind.[w] 16The number of the mounted troops was two hundred million. I heard their number.[x]

17The horses and riders I saw in my vision looked like this: Their breastplates were fiery red, dark blue, and yellow as sulphur. The heads of the horses resembled the heads of lions, and out of their mouths[y] came fire, smoke and sulphur.[z] 18A third of mankind was killed[a] by the three plagues of fire, smoke and sulphur[b] that came out of their mouths. 19The power of the horses was in their mouths and in their tails; for their tails were like snakes, having heads with which they inflict injury.

20The rest of mankind that were not killed by these plagues still did not repent of the work of their hands;[c] they did not stop worshipping demons,[d] and idols of gold, silver, bronze, stone and wood—idols that cannot see or hear or walk.[e] 21Nor did they repent[f] of their murders, their magic arts,[g] their sexual immorality[h] or their thefts.

The Angel and the Little Scroll

10 Then I saw another mighty angel[a] coming down from heaven. He was robed in a cloud, with a rainbow above his head; his face was like the sun,[b] and his legs were like fiery pillars.[c] 2He was holding a little scroll, which lay open in his hand. He planted his right foot on the sea and his left foot on the land, 3and he gave a loud shout like the roar of a lion. When he shouted, the voices of the seven thunders[d] spoke. 4And when the seven thunders spoke, I was about to write; but I heard a voice from heaven say, "Seal up what the seven thunders have said and do not write it down."[e]

5Then the angel I had seen standing on the sea and on the land raised his right hand to heaven.[f] 6And he swore by him who lives for ever and ever, who created the heavens and all that is in them, the earth and all that is in it, and the sea and all that is in it,[g] and said, "There will be no more delay![h] 7But in the days when the seventh angel is about to sound his trumpet, the mystery[i] of God will be accomplished, just as he announced to his servants the prophets."

8Then the voice that I had heard from heaven[j] spoke to me once more: "Go, take the scroll that lies open in the hand of the angel who is standing on the sea and on the land."

9So I went to the angel and asked him to give me the little scroll. He said to me, "Take it and eat it. It will turn your stomach sour, but in your mouth it will be as sweet as honey."[k] 10I took the little scroll from the angel's hand and ate it. It tasted as sweet as honey in my mouth, but when I had eaten it, my stomach turned sour. 11Then I was told, "You must prophesy[l] again about many peoples, nations, languages and kings."

The Two Witnesses

11 I was given a reed like a measuring rod[a] and was told, "Go and measure the temple of God and the altar, and count the worshippers there. 2But exclude the outer court;[b] do not measure it, because it has been given to the Gentiles.[c] They will trample on the holy city[d] for 42 months.[e]

9:13 t Ex 30:1-3 u Rev 8:3
9:14 v Rev 16:12
9:15 w ver 18
9:16 x Rev 5:11 Rev 7:4
9:17 y Rev 11:5 z ver 18
9:18 a ver 15 b ver 17
9:20 c Dt 31:29 d 1Co 10:20 e Ps 115:4-7 Ps 135:15-17 Da 5:23
9:21 f Rev 2:21 g Rev 18:23 h Rev 17:2,5
10:1 a Rev 5:2 b Mt 17:2 Rev 1:16 c Rev 1:15
10:3 d Rev 4:5
10:4 e Da 8:26 Da 12:4,9 Rev 22:10
10:5 f Da 12:7
10:6 g Rev 4:11 Rev 14:7 h Rev 16:17
10:7 i Ro 16:25
10:8 j ver 4
10:9 k Jer 15:16 Eze 2:8-3:3
10:11 l Eze 37:4,9
11:1 a Eze 40:3 Rev 21:15
11:2 b Eze 40:17,20 c Lk 21:24 d Rev 21:2 e Da 7:25 Rev 13:5

b13 That is, projections

3And I will give power to my two
witnesses,[f] and they will prophesy
for 1,260 days, clothed in sackcloth."[g] 4These are the two olive
trees[h] and the two lampstands that
stand before the Lord of the
earth.[i] 5If anyone tries to harm
them, fire comes from their
mouths and devours their enemies.[j] This is how anyone who wants
to harm them must die.[k] 6These
men have power to shut up the sky
so that it will not rain during the
time they are prophesying; and
they have power to turn the waters
into blood[l] and to strike the earth
with every kind of plague as often
as they want.

7Now when they have finished
their testimony, the beast[m] that
comes up from the Abyss will attack them,[n] and overpower and
kill them. 8Their bodies will lie in
the street of the great city, which
is figuratively called Sodom[o] and
Egypt, where also their Lord was
crucified.[p] 9For three and a half
days men from every people, tribe,
language and nation will gaze on
their bodies and refuse them
burial.[q] 10The inhabitants of the
earth[r] will gloat over them and
will celebrate by sending each
other gifts,[s] because these two
prophets had tormented those who
live on earth.

11But after the three and a half
days a breath of life from God entered them,[t] and they stood on
their feet, and terror struck those
who saw them. 12Then they heard a
loud voice from heaven saying to
them, "Come up here."[u] And they
went up to heaven in a cloud,[v]
while their enemies looked on.

13At that very hour there was a
severe earthquake[w] and a tenth of
the city collapsed. Seven thousand
people were killed in the earthquake, and the survivors were terrified and gave glory[x] to the God
of heaven.[y]

14The second woe has passed; the
third woe is coming soon.[z]

The Seventh Trumpet

15The seventh angel sounded his
trumpet,[a] and there were loud
voices[b] in heaven, which said:

"The kingdom of the world has
become the kingdom of our
Lord and of his Christ,[c]
and he will reign for ever and
ever."[d]

16And the twenty-four elders,[e]
who were seated on their thrones
before God, fell on their faces and
worshipped God, 17saying:

"We give thanks to you, Lord
God Almighty,[f]
the One who is and who was,
because you have taken your
great power
and have begun to reign.[g]
18The nations were angry;[h]
and your wrath has come.
The time has come for judging
the dead,
and for rewarding your
servants the prophets[i]
and your saints and those who
reverence your name,
both small and great[j]—
and for destroying those who
destroy the earth."

19Then God's temple[k] in heaven
was opened, and within his temple
was seen the ark of his covenant.
And there came flashes of lightning, rumblings, peals of thunder,
an earthquake and a great hailstorm.[l]

The Woman and the Dragon

12 A great and wondrous sign
appeared in heaven: a
woman clothed with the sun, with
the moon under her feet and a
crown of twelve stars on her head.
2She was pregnant and cried out in
pain[a] as she was about to give
birth. 3Then another sign appeared
in heaven: an enormous red dragon
with seven heads and ten horns[b]
and seven crowns[c] on his heads.
4His tail swept a third[d] of the stars

11:3 f Rev 1:5 g Ge 37:34
11:4 h Ps 52:8 Jer 11:16 Zec 4:3,11 i Zec 4:14
11:5 j 2Ki 1:10 Jer 5:14 k Nu 16:29,35
11:6 l Ex 7:17,19
11:7 m Rev 13:1-4 n Da 7:21
11:8 o Isa 1:9 p Heb 13:12
11:9 q Ps 79:2,3
11:10 r Rev 3:10 s Est 9:19,22
11:11 t Eze 37:5,9,10, 14
11:12 u Rev 4:1 v 2Ki 2:11 Ac 1:9
11:13 w Rev 6:12 x Rev 14:7 y Rev 16:11
11:14 z Rev 8:13
11:15 a Rev 10:7 b Rev 16:17 Rev 19:1 c Rev 12:10 d Da 2:44 Da 7:14,27
11:16 e Rev 4:4
11:17 f Rev 1:8 g Rev 19:6
11:18 h Ps 2:1 i Rev 10:7 j Rev 19:5
11:19 k Rev 15:5,8 l Rev 16:21
12:2 a Gal 4:19
12:3 b Da 7:7,20 Rev 13:1 c Rev 19:12
12:4 d Rev 8:7

out of the sky and flung them to the
earth.[e] The dragon stood in front
of the woman who was about to
give birth, so that he might devour
her child[f] the moment it was born.
5She gave birth to a son, a male
child, who will rule all the nations
with an iron sceptre.[g] And her
child was snatched up to God and to
his throne. 6The woman fled into
the desert to a place prepared for
her by God, where she might be
taken care of for 1,260 days.[h]

7And there was war in heaven.
Michael and his angels fought
against the dragon,[i] and the
dragon and his angels fought back.
8But he was not strong enough,
and they lost their place in heav-
en. 9The great dragon was hurled down—that ancient serpent[j]
called the devil,[k] or Satan, who
leads the whole world astray.[l] He
was hurled to the earth,[m] and his
angels with him.

10Then I heard a loud voice in
heaven[n] say:

"Now have come the salvation
 and the power and the
 kingdom of our God,
and the authority of his Christ.
For the accuser of our
 brothers,[o]
who accuses them before our
 God day and night,
has been hurled down.
11They overcame him
by the blood of the Lamb[p]
and by the word of their
 testimony;[q]
they did not love their lives so
 much
as to shrink from death.[r]
12Therefore rejoice, you
 heavens[s]
and you who dwell in them!
But woe[t] to the earth and the
 sea,[u]
because the devil has gone
 down to you!
He is filled with fury,
because he knows that his
 time is short."

12:4
e Da 8:10
f Mt 2:16
12:5
g Ps 2:9
Rev 2:27
12:6
h Rev 11:2
12:7
i ver 3
12:9
j Ge 3:1-7
k Mt 25:41
l Rev 20:3,8,10
m Lk 10:18
Jn 12:31
12:10
n Rev 11:15
o Job 1:9-11
Zec 3:1
12:11
p Rev 7:14
q Rev 6:9
r Lk 14:26
12:12
s Ps 96:11
Isa 49:13
Rev 18:20
t Rev 8:13
u Rev 10:6
12:13
v ver 3
w ver 5
12:14
x Ex 19:4
y Da 7:25
12:17
z Rev 11:7
a Ge 3:15
b Rev 14:12
c Rev 1:2
13:1
a Da 7:1-6
Rev 15:2
b Rev 12:3
c Da 11:36
Rev 17:3
13:2
d Da 7:6
e Da 7:5
f Da 7:4
g Rev 16:10
13:3
h ver 12,14
i Rev 17:8
13:4
j Ex 15:11
13:5
k Da 7:8,11,20,25
Da 11:36
2Th 2:4
l Rev 11:2

13When the dragon[v] saw that he
had been hurled to the earth, he
pursued the woman who had given
birth to the male child.[w] 14The
woman was given the two wings of
a great eagle,[x] so that she might
fly to the place prepared for her in
the desert, where she would be
taken care of for a time, times and
half a time,[y] out of the serpent's
reach. 15Then from his mouth the
serpent spewed water like a river,
to overtake the woman and sweep
her away with the torrent. 16But the
earth helped the woman by opening
its mouth and swallowing the river
that the dragon had spewed out of
his mouth. 17Then the dragon was
enraged at the woman and went off
to make war[z] against the rest of
her offspring[a]—those who obey
God's commandments[b] and hold to
the testimony of Jesus.[c]

13
1And the dragon[a] stood on
the shore of the sea.

The Beast out of the Sea

And I saw a beast coming out of
the sea.[a] He had ten horns and
seven heads,[b] with ten crowns on
his horns, and on each head a blasphemous name.[c] 2The beast I saw
resembled a leopard,[d] but had feet
like those of a bear[e] and a mouth
like that of a lion.[f] The dragon
gave the beast his power and his
throne and great authority.[g] 3One
of the heads of the beast seemed to
have had a fatal wound, but the
fatal wound had been healed.[h] The
whole world was astonished[i] and
followed the beast. 4Men worshipped the dragon because he had
given authority to the beast, and
they also worshipped the beast and
asked, "Who is like[j] the beast?
Who can make war against him?"

5The beast was given a mouth to
utter proud words and blasphemies[k] and to exercise his authority
for forty-two months.[l] 6He opened

a1 Some late manuscripts *And I*

his mouth to blaspheme God, and to slander his name and his dwelling-place and those who live in heaven.[m] 7He was given power to make war[n] against the saints and to conquer them. And he was given authority over every tribe, people, language and nation.[o] 8All inhabitants of the earth[p] will worship the beast—all whose names have not been written in the book of life[q] belonging to the Lamb that was slain from the creation of the world.[b][r]

9He who has an ear, let him hear.[s]

10If anyone is to go into captivity,
 into captivity he will go.
If anyone is to be killed[c] with
 the sword,
 with the sword he will be
 killed.[t]

This calls for patient endurance and faithfulness[u] on the part of the saints.[v]

The Beast out of the Earth

11Then I saw another beast, coming out of the earth. He had two horns like a lamb, but he spoke like a dragon. 12He exercised all the authority[w] of the first beast on his behalf,[x] and made the earth and its inhabitants worship the first beast,[y] whose fatal wound had been healed.[z] 13And he performed great and miraculous signs,[a] even causing fire to come down from heaven[b] to earth in full view of men. 14Because of the signs[c] he was given power to do on behalf of the first beast, he deceived[d] the inhabitants of the earth. He ordered them to set up an image in honour of the beast who was wounded by the sword and yet lived. 15He was given power to give breath to the image of the first beast, so that it could speak and cause all who refused to worship the image to be killed.[e] 16He also forced everyone, small and great,[f] rich and poor, free and slave, to receive a mark on his right hand or on his forehead,[g] 17so that no-one could buy or sell unless he had the mark,[h] which is the name of the beast or the number of his name.[i]

18This calls for wisdom.[j] If anyone has insight, let him calculate the number of the beast, for it is man's number.[k] His number is 666.

The Lamb and the 144,000

14 Then I looked, and there before me was the Lamb,[a] standing on Mount Zion,[b] and with him 144,000[c] who had his name and his Father's name[d] written on their foreheads. 2And I heard a sound from heaven like the roar of rushing waters[e] and like a loud peal of thunder. The sound I heard was like that of harpists playing their harps.[f] 3And they sang a new song[g] before the throne and before the four living creatures and the elders. No-one could learn the song except the 144,000[h] who had been redeemed from the earth. 4These are those who did not defile themselves with women, for they kept themselves pure.[i] They follow the Lamb wherever he goes. They were purchased from among men[j] and offered as firstfruits[k] to God and the Lamb. 5No lie was found in their mouths;[l] they are blameless.[m]

The Three Angels

6Then I saw another angel flying in mid-air,[n] and he had the eternal gospel to proclaim to those who live on the earth[o]—to every nation, tribe, language and people.[p] 7He said in a loud voice, "Fear God[q] and give him glory,[r] because the hour of his judgment has come. Worship him who made the

13:6 m Rev 12:12
13:7 n Da 7:21; Rev 11:7; o Rev 5:9
13:8 p Rev 3:10; q Rev 3:5; Rev 20:12; r Mt 25:34
13:9 s Rev 2:7
13:10 t Jer 15:2; Jer 43:11; u Heb 6:12; v Rev 14:12
13:12 w ver 4; x ver 14; y Rev 14:9,11; z ver 3
13:13 a Mt 24:24; b 1Ki 18:38; Rev 20:9
13:14 c 2Th 2:9,10; d Rev 12:9
13:15 e Da 3:3-6
13:16 f Rev 19:5; g Rev 14:9
13:17 h Rev 14:9; i Rev 14:11; Rev 15:2
13:18 j Rev 17:9; k Rev 15:2; Rev 21:17
14:1 a Rev 5:6; b Ps 2:6; c Rev 7:4; d Rev 3:12
14:2 e Rev 1:15; f Rev 5:8
14:3 g Rev 5:9; h ver 1
14:4 i 2Co 11:2; Rev 3:4; j Rev 5:9; k Jas 1:18
14:5 l Ps 32:2; Zep 3:13; m Eph 5:27
14:6 n Rev 8:13; o Rev 3:10; p Rev 13:7
14:7 q Rev 15:4; r Rev 11:13

b8 Or *written from the creation of the world in the book of life belonging to the Lamb that was slain*
c10 Some manuscripts *anyone kills*

heavens, the earth, the sea and the
springs of water."[s]
8A second angel followed and
said, "Fallen! Fallen is Babylon the
Great,[t] which made all the nations
drink the maddening wine of her
adulteries."[u]
9A third angel followed them and
said in a loud voice: "If anyone worships the beast and his image[v] and
receives his mark on the forehead
or on the hand, 10he, too, will drink
of the wine of God's fury,[w] which
has been poured full strength into
the cup of his wrath.[x] He will be
tormented with burning sulphur in
the presence of the holy angels and
of the Lamb. 11And the smoke of
their torment rises for ever and
ever.[y] There is no rest day or night
for those who worship the beast
and his image, or for anyone who
receives the mark of his name."
12This calls for patient endurance
on the part of the saints[z] who obey
God's commandments and remain
faithful to Jesus.
13Then I heard a voice from
heaven say, "Write: Blessed are the
dead who die in the Lord[a] from
now on."
"Yes," says the Spirit, "they will
rest from their labour, for their
deeds will follow them."

The Harvest of the Earth

14I looked, and there before me
was a white cloud, and seated on
the cloud was one "like a son of
man"[a][b] with a crown[c] of gold on
his head and a sharp sickle in his
hand. 15Then another angel came
out of the temple and called in a
loud voice to him who was sitting
on the cloud, "Take your sickle[d]
and reap, because the time to reap
has come, for the harvest[e] of the
earth is ripe." 16So he who was
seated on the cloud swung his
sickle over the earth, and the earth
was harvested.
17Another angel came out of the
temple in heaven, and he too had a
sharp sickle. 18Still another angel,
who had charge of the fire, came
from the altar and called in a loud
voice to him who had the sharp
sickle, "Take your sharp sickle and
gather the clusters of grapes from
the earth's vine, because its grapes
are ripe." 19The angel swung his
sickle on the earth, gathered its
grapes and threw them into the
great winepress of God's wrath.[f]
20They were trampled in the winepress[g] outside the city,[h] and blood
flowed out of the press, rising as
high as the horses' bridles for a distance of 1,600 stadia.[b]

Seven Angels With Seven Plagues

15 I saw in heaven another
great and marvellous sign:[a]
seven angels[b] with the seven
last plagues[c]—last, because with
them God's wrath is completed.
2And I saw what looked like a sea
of glass[d] mixed with fire and, standing beside the sea, those who had
been victorious over the beast and
his image[e] and over the number
of his name. They held harps giv-
en them by God 3and sang the
song of Moses[f] the servant of God
and the song of the Lamb:

"Great and marvellous are your
  deeds,[g]
 Lord God Almighty.
Just and true are your ways,[h]
 King of the ages.
4Who will not fear you, O Lord,[i]
 and bring glory to your name?
For you alone are holy.
All nations will come
 and worship before you,[j]
for your righteous acts have
 been revealed."

5After this I looked and in heaven
the temple,[k] that is, the tabernacle
of the Testimony,[l] was opened.
6Out of the temple[m] came the
seven angels with the seven

14:7 s Rev 8:10
14:8 t Isa 21:9; Jer 51:8 u Rev 17:2,4; Rev 18:3,9
14:9 v Rev 13:14
14:10 w Isa 51:17; Jer 25:15 x Rev 18:6
14:11 y Isa 34:10; Rev 19:3
14:12 z Rev 13:10
14:13 a 1Co 15:18; 1Th 4:16
14:14 b Da 7:13; Rev 1:13 c Rev 6:2
14:15 d Joel 3:13 e Jer 51:33
14:19 f Rev 19:15
14:20 g Isa 63:3 h Heb 13:12; Rev 11:8
15:1 a Rev 12:1,3 b Rev 16:1 c Lev 26:21
15:2 d Rev 4:6 e Rev 13:14
15:3 f Ex 15:1; Dt 32:4 g Ps 111:2 h Ps 145:17
15:4 i Jer 10:7 j Isa 66:23
15:5 k Rev 11:19 l Nu 1:50
15:6 m Rev 14:15

a 14 Daniel 7:13 b 20 That is, about 180 miles (about 300 kilometres)

plagues.[n] They were dressed in clean, shining linen and wore golden sashes round their chests.[o] 7Then one of the four living creatures[p] gave to the seven angels seven golden bowls filled with the wrath of God, who lives for ever and ever. 8And the temple was filled with smoke[q] from the glory of God and from his power, and no-one could enter the temple[r] until the seven plagues of the seven angels were completed.

The Seven Bowls of God's Wrath

16 Then I heard a loud voice from the temple saying to the seven angels,[a] "Go, pour out the seven bowls of God's wrath on the earth."

2The first angel went and poured out his bowl on the land,[b] and ugly and painful sores[c] broke out on the people who had the mark of the beast and worshipped his image.[d]

3The second angel poured out his bowl on the sea, and it turned into blood like that of a dead man, and every living thing in the sea died.[e]

4The third angel poured out his bowl on the rivers and springs of water,[f] and they became blood.[g] 5Then I heard the angel in charge of the waters say:

"You are just in these
  judgments,[h]
 you who are and who were,[i]
  the Holy One,[j]
 because you have so judged;
6for they have shed the blood of
  your saints and prophets,
 and you have given them
  blood to drink[k] as they
  deserve."

7And I heard the altar[l] respond:

"Yes, Lord God Almighty,
 true and just are your
  judgments."[m]

8The fourth angel[n] poured out his bowl on the sun, and the sun was given power to scorch people with fire.[o] 9They were seared by the intense heat and they cursed the name of God,[p] who had control over these plagues, but they refused to repent[q] and glorify him.[r]

10The fifth angel poured out his bowl on the throne of the beast,[s] and his kingdom was plunged into darkness.[t] Men gnawed their tongues in agony 11and cursed[u] the God of heaven[v] because of their pains and their sores,[w] but they refused to repent of what they had done.[x]

12The sixth angel poured out his bowl on the great river Euphrates,[y] and its water was dried up to prepare the way for the kings from the East.[z] 13Then I saw three evil[a] spirits that looked like frogs; they came out of the mouth of the dragon,[a] out of the mouth of the beast[b] and out of the mouth of the false prophet.[c] 14They are spirits of demons[d] performing miraculous signs, and they go out to the kings of the whole world, to gather them for the battle[e] on the great day of God Almighty.

15"Behold, I come like a thief! Blessed is he who stays awake[f] and keeps his clothes with him, so that he may not go naked and be shamefully exposed."

16Then they gathered the kings together to the place that in Hebrew[g] is called Armageddon.[h]

17The seventh angel poured out his bowl into the air,[i] and out of the temple[j] came a loud voice[k] from the throne, saying, "It is done!"[l] 18Then there came flashes of lightning, rumblings, peals of thunder[m] and a severe earthquake.[n] No earthquake like it has ever occurred since man has been on earth,[o] so tremendous was the quake. 19The great city[p] split into three parts, and the cities of the nations collapsed. God remembered[q] Babylon the Great[r] and gave her

15:6 *n* ver 1 *o* Rev 1:13
15:7 *p* Rev 4:6
15:8 *q* Isa 6:4 *r* Ex 40:34,35 1Ki 8:10,11 2Ch 5:13,14
16:1 *a* Rev 15:1
16:2 *b* Rev 8:7 *c* Ex 9:9-11 *d* Rev 13:15-17
16:3 *e* Ex 7:17-21 Rev 8:8,9
16:4 *f* Rev 8:10 *g* Ex 7:17-21
16:5 *h* Rev 15:3 *i* Rev 1:4 *j* Rev 15:4
16:6 *k* Isa 49:26 Rev 17:6
16:7 *l* Rev 6:9 *m* Rev 15:3 Rev 19:2
16:8 *n* Rev 8:12 *o* Rev 14:18
16:9 *p* ver 11,21 *q* Rev 2:21 *r* Rev 11:13
16:10 *s* Rev 13:2 *t* Rev 9:2
16:11 *u* ver 9,21 *v* Rev 11:13 *w* ver 2 *x* Rev 2:21
16:12 *y* Rev 9:14 *z* Isa 41:2
16:13 *a* Rev 12:3 *b* Rev 13:1 *c* Rev 19:20
16:14 *d* 1Ti 4:1 *e* Rev 17:14
16:15 *f* Lk 12:37
16:16 *g* Rev 9:11 *h* 2Ki 23:29,30
16:17 *i* Eph 2:2 *j* Rev 14:15 *k* Rev 11:15 *l* Rev 21:6
16:18 *m* Rev 4:5 *n* Rev 6:12 *o* Da 12:1

16:19 *p* Rev 17:18 *q* Rev 18:5 *r* Rev 14:8

[a]13 Greek *unclean*

the cup filled with the wine of the fury of his wrath.[s] 20Every island fled away and the mountains could not be found.[t] 21From the sky huge hailstones[u] of about a hundred pounds each fell upon men. And they cursed God on account of the plague of hail,[v] because the plague was so terrible.

The Woman on the Beast

17 One of the seven angels[a] who had the seven bowls[b] came and said to me, "Come, I will show you the punishment[c] of the great prostitute,[d] who sits on many waters.[e] 2With her the kings of the earth committed adultery and the inhabitants of the earth were intoxicated with the wine of her adulteries."[f]

3Then the angel carried me away in the Spirit into a desert.[g] There I saw a woman sitting on a scarlet beast that was covered with blasphemous names[h] and had seven heads and ten horns.[i] 4The woman was dressed in purple and scarlet, and was glittering with gold, precious stones and pearls.[j] She held a golden cup[k] in her hand, filled with abominable things and the filth of her adulteries. 5This title was written on her forehead:

MYSTERY
BABYLON THE GREAT[l]
THE MOTHER OF PROSTITUTES
AND OF THE ABOMINATIONS OF THE
EARTH.

6I saw that the woman was drunk with the blood of the saints,[m] the blood of those who bore testimony to Jesus.

When I saw her, I was greatly astonished. 7Then the angel said to me: "Why are you astonished? I will explain to you the mystery[n] of the woman and of the beast she rides, which has the seven heads and ten horns.[o] 8The beast, which you saw, once was, now is not, and will come up out of the Abyss and go to his destruction.[p] The inhabitants of the earth[q] whose names have not been written in the book of life[r] from the creation of the world will be astonished[s] when they see the beast, because he once was, now is not, and yet will come.

9"This calls for a mind with wisdom.[t] The seven heads are seven hills on which the woman sits. 10They are also seven kings. Five have fallen, one is, the other has not yet come; but when he does come, he must remain for a little while. 11The beast who once was, and now is not,[u] is an eighth king. He belongs to the seven and is going to his destruction.

12"The ten horns[v] you saw are ten kings who have not yet received a kingdom, but who for one hour[w] will receive authority as kings along with the beast. 13They have one purpose and will give their power and authority to the beast.[x] 14They will make war[y] against the Lamb, but the Lamb will overcome them because he is Lord of lords and King of kings[z]—and with him will be his called, chosen[a] and faithful followers."

15Then the angel said to me, "The waters[b] you saw, where the prostitute sits, are peoples, multitudes, nations and languages.[c] 16The beast and the ten horns you saw will hate the prostitute. They will bring her to ruin[d] and leave her naked;[e] they will eat her flesh[f] and burn her with fire.[g] 17For God has put it into their hearts to accomplish his purpose by agreeing to give the beast their power to rule, until God's words are fulfilled.[h] 18The woman you saw is the great city[i] that rules over the kings of the earth."

The Fall of Babylon

18 After this I saw another angel[a] coming down from heaven.[b] He had great authority, and the earth was illuminated by

16:19 s Rev 14:10
16:20 t Rev 6:14
16:21 u Rev 11:19 v Ex 9:23-25
17:1 a Rev 15:1 b Rev 21:9 c Rev 16:19 d Rev 19:2 e Jer 51:13
17:2 f Rev 14:8 Rev 18:3
17:3 g Rev 12:6,14 h Rev 13:1 i Rev 12:3
17:4 j Rev 18:16 k Jer 51:7 Rev 18:6
17:5 l Rev 14:8
17:6 m Rev 18:24
17:7 n ver 5 o ver 3
17:8 p Rev 13:10 q Rev 3:10 r Rev 13:8 s Rev 13:3
17:9 t Rev 13:18
17:11 u ver 8
17:12 v Rev 12:3 w Rev 18:10,17,19
17:13 x ver 17
17:14 y Rev 16:14 z 1Ti 6:15 Rev 19:16 a Mt 22:14
17:15 b Isa 8:7 c Rev 13:7
17:16 d Rev 18:17,19 e Eze 16:37,39 f Rev 19:18 g Rev 18:8
17:17 h Rev 10:7
17:18 i Rev 16:19
18:1 a Rev 17:1 b Rev 10:1

his splendour.[c] 2With a mighty
voice he shouted:

"Fallen! Fallen is Babylon the
Great![d]
She has become a home for
demons
and a haunt for every evil[a]
spirit,
a haunt for every unclean and
detestable bird.[e]
3For all the nations have drunk
the maddening wine of her
adulteries.[f]
The kings of the earth
committed adultery with
her,[g]
and the merchants of the
earth grew rich[h] from her
excessive luxuries."[i]

4Then I heard another voice from
heaven say:

"Come out of her, my people,[j]
so that you will not share in
her sins,
so that you will not receive
any of her plagues;
5for her sins are piled up to
heaven,[k]
and God has remembered[l]
her crimes.
6Give back to her as she has
given;
pay her back[m] double for
what she has done.
Mix her a double portion from
her own cup.[n]
7Give her as much torture and
grief
as the glory and luxury she
gave herself.[o]
In her heart she boasts,
'I sit as queen; I am not a
widow,
and I will never mourn.'[p]
8Therefore in one day[q] her
plagues will overtake her:
death, mourning and famine.
She will be consumed by
fire,[r]
for mighty is the Lord God
who judges her.

9"When the kings of the earth
who committed adultery with her[s]
and shared her luxury see the
smoke of her burning,[t] they will
weep and mourn over her.[u] 10Ter-
rified at her torment, they will
stand far off[v] and cry:

" 'Woe! Woe, O great city,[w]
O Babylon, city of power!
In one hour[x] your doom has
come!'

11"The merchants[y] of the earth
will weep and mourn over her because no-one buys their cargoes
any more[z]—12cargoes of gold, silver, precious stones and pearls;
fine linen, purple, silk and scarlet
cloth; every sort of citron wood,
and articles of every kind made of
ivory, costly wood, bronze, iron and
marble;[a] 13cargoes of cinnamon
and spice, of incense, myrrh and
frankincense, of wine and olive oil,
of fine flour and wheat; cattle and
sheep; horses and carriages; and
bodies and souls of men.[b]
14"They will say, 'The fruit you
longed for is gone from you. All
your riches and splendour have
vanished, never to be recovered.'
15The merchants who sold these
things and gained their wealth
from her[c] will stand far off, terrified at her torment. They will weep
and mourn[d] 16and cry out:

" 'Woe! Woe, O great city,
dressed in fine linen, purple
and scarlet,
and glittering with gold,
precious stones and
pearls![e]
17In one hour[f] such great wealth
has been brought to ruin!'[g]

"Every sea captain, and all who
travel by ship, the sailors, and all
who earn their living from the
sea,[h] will stand far off. 18When
they see the smoke of her burning,

18:1 c Eze 43:2
18:2 d Rev 14:8 e Isa 13:21,22 Jer 50:39
18:3 f Rev 14:8 g Rev 17:2 h Eze 27:9-25 i ver 7,9
18:4 j Isa 48:20 Jer 50:8 2Co 6:17
18:5 k Jer 51:9 l Rev 16:19
18:6 m Ps 137:8 Jer 50:15,29 n Rev 14:10 Rev 16:19
18:7 o Eze 28:2-8 p Isa 47:7,8 Zep 2:15
18:8 q ver 10 Isa 47:9 Jer 50:31,32 r Rev 17:16
18:9 s Rev 17:2,4 t ver 18 Rev 19:3 u Eze 26:17,18
18:10 v ver 15,17 w ver 16,19 x Rev 17:12
18:11 y Eze 27:27 z ver 3
18:12 a Rev 17:4
18:13 b Eze 27:13 1Ti 1:10
18:15 c ver 3 d Eze 27:31
18:16 e Rev 17:4
18:17 f ver 10 g Rev 17:16 h Eze 27:28-30

a2 Greek *unclean*

they will exclaim, 'Was there ever
a city like this great city?'[i] 19They
will throw dust on their heads,[j]
and with weeping and mourning
cry out:

" 'Woe! Woe, O great city,
where all who had ships on the sea
became rich through her wealth!
In one hour she has been brought to ruin![k]
20Rejoice over her, O heaven![l]
Rejoice, saints and apostles and prophets!
God has judged her for the way she treated you.' "[m]

21Then a mighty angel[n] picked
up a boulder the size of a large millstone and threw it into the sea,[o]
and said:

"With such violence
the great city of Babylon will be thrown down,
never to be found again.
22The music of harpists and musicians, flute players and trumpeters,
will never be heard in you again.[p]
No workman of any trade
will ever be found in you again.
The sound of a millstone
will never be heard in you again.[q]
23The light of a lamp
will never shine in you again.
The voice of bridegroom and bride
will never be heard in you again.[r]
Your merchants were the world's great men.[s]
By your magic spell[t] all the nations were led astray.
24In her was found the blood of prophets and of the saints,[u]
and of all who have been killed on the earth."[v]

Hallelujah!

19 After this I heard what
sounded like the roar of a
great multitude[a] in heaven shouting:

"Hallelujah!
Salvation[b] and glory and power[c] belong to our God,
2 for true and just are his judgments.
He has condemned the great prostitute
who corrupted the earth by her adulteries.
He has avenged on her the blood of his servants."[d]

3And again they shouted:

"Hallelujah!
The smoke from her goes up for ever and ever."[e]

4The twenty-four elders[f] and
the four living creatures[g] fell
down[h] and worshipped God, who
was seated on the throne. And they
cried:

"Amen, Hallelujah!"

5Then a voice came from the
throne, saying:

"Praise our God,
all you his servants,[i]
you who fear him,
both small and great!"[j]

6Then I heard what sounded like
a great multitude,[k] like the roar of
rushing waters and like loud peals
of thunder, shouting:

"Hallelujah!
For our Lord God Almighty reigns.
7Let us rejoice and be glad
and give him glory!
For the wedding of the Lamb[l] has come,
and his bride[m] has made herself ready.
8Fine linen, bright and clean,
was given her to wear."

(Fine linen stands for the righteous
acts[n] of the saints.)

18:18 i Eze 27:32; Rev 13:4
18:19 j Jos 7:6; Eze 27:30; k Rev 17:16
18:20 l Jer 51:48; Rev 12:12; m Rev 19:2
18:21 n Rev 5:2; o Jer 51:63
18:22 p Isa 24:8; Eze 26:13; q Jer 25:10
18:23 r Jer 7:34; Jer 16:9; Jer 25:10; s Isa 23:8; t Na 3:4
18:24 u Rev 16:6; Rev 17:6; v Jer 51:49
19:1 a Rev 11:15; b Rev 7:10; c Rev 4:11
19:2 d Dt 32:43; Rev 6:10
19:3 e Isa 34:10; Rev 14:11
19:4 f Rev 4:4; g Rev 4:6; h Rev 5:14
19:5 i Ps 134:1; j Rev 11:18; Rev 20:12
19:6 k Rev 11:15
19:7 l Mt 22:2; Mt 25:10; Eph 5:32; m Rev 21:2,9
19:8 n Rev 15:4

9Then the angel said to me,[o]
"Write:[p] 'Blessed are those who
are invited to the wedding supper
of the Lamb!' "[q] And he added,
"These are the true words of
God."[r]
10At this I fell at his feet to worship him.[s] But he said to me, "Do
not do it! I am a fellow-servant with
you and with your brothers who
hold to the testimony of Jesus. Worship God![t] For the testimony of
Jesus[u] is the spirit of prophecy."

The Rider on the White Horse

11I saw heaven standing open and
there before me was a white horse,
whose rider[v] is called Faithful and
True.[w] With justice he judges and
makes war.[x] 12His eyes are like
blazing fire,[y] and on his head are
many crowns.[z] He has a name
written on him that no-one knows
but he himself.[a] 13He is dressed in
a robe dipped in blood,[b] and his
name is the Word of God.[c] 14The
armies of heaven were following
him, riding on white horses and
dressed in fine linen,[d] white and
clean. 15Out of his mouth comes a
sharp sword[e] with which to strike
down[f] the nations. "He will rule
them with an iron sceptre."[a][g] He
treads the winepress[h] of the fury
of the wrath of God Almighty. 16On
his robe and on his thigh he has this
name written:[i]

KING OF KINGS AND LORD OF
LORDS.[j]

17And I saw an angel standing in
the sun, who cried in a loud voice to
all the birds[k] flying in mid-air,[l]
"Come,[m] gather together for the
great supper of God, 18so that you
may eat the flesh of kings, generals, and mighty men, of horses and
their riders, and the flesh of all
people,[n] free and slave, small and
great."
19Then I saw the beast and the
kings of the earth[o] and their armies gathered together to make
war against the rider on the horse
and his army. 20But the beast was
captured, and with him the false
prophet[p] who had performed the
miraculous signs on his behalf.[q]
With these signs he had deluded
those who had received the mark of
the beast and worshipped his image. The two of them were thrown
alive into the fiery lake[r] of burning sulphur.[s] 21The rest of them
were killed with the sword[t] that
came out of the mouth of the rider
on the horse,[u] and all the birds[v]
gorged themselves on their flesh.

The Thousand Years

20 And I saw an angel coming
down out of heaven,[a] hav-
ing the key[b] to the Abyss and holding in his hand a great chain. 2He
seized the dragon, that ancient serpent, who is the devil, or Satan,[c]
and bound him for a thousand
years.[d] 3He threw him into the
Abyss, and locked and sealed[e] it
over him, to keep him from deceiving the nations[f] any more until the
thousand years were ended. After
that, he must be set free for a short
time.
4I saw thrones[g] on which were
seated those who had been given
authority to judge. And I saw the
souls of those who had been beheaded[h] because of their testimony for Jesus and because of the
word of God. They had not worshipped the beast[i] or his image
and had not received his mark on
their foreheads or their hands.[j]
They came to life and reigned with
Christ for a thousand years. 5(The
rest of the dead did not come to life
until the thousand years were
ended.) This is the first resurrection.[k] 6Blessed[l] and holy are
those who have part in the first resurrection. The second death[m] has
no power over them, but they will
be priests[n] of God and of Christ

[a]15 Psalm 2:9

19:9 o ver 10; p Rev 1:19; q Lk 14:15; r Rev 21:5; Rev 22:6
19:10 s Rev 22:8; t Ac 10:25,26; Rev 22:9; u Rev 12:17
19:11 v Rev 6:2; w Rev 3:14; x Isa 11:4
19:12 y Rev 1:14; z Rev 6:2; a Rev 2:17
19:13 b Isa 63:2,3; c Jn 1:1
19:14 d ver 8
19:15 e Rev 1:16; f Isa 11:4; 2Th 2:8; g Ps 2:9; Rev 2:27; h Rev 14:20
19:16 i ver 12; j Rev 17:14
19:17 k ver 21; l Rev 8:13; m Eze 39:17
19:18 n Eze 39:18-20
19:19 o Rev 16:14,16
19:20 p Rev 16:13; q Rev 13:12; r Da 7:11; Rev 20:10,14,15; Rev 21:8; s Rev 14:10
19:21 t ver 15; u ver 11,19; v ver 17
20:1 a Rev 10:1; b Rev 1:18
20:2 c Rev 12:9; d 2Pe 2:4
20:3 e Da 6:17; f Rev 12:9
20:4 g Da 7:9; h Rev 6:9; i Rev 13:12; j Rev 13:16
20:5 k Lk 14:14; Php 3:11
20:6 l Rev 14:13; m Rev 2:11; n Rev 1:6

and will reign with him[o] for a thousand years.

Satan's Doom

7 When the thousand years are over,[p] Satan will be released from his prison 8 and will go out to deceive the nations[q] in the four corners of the earth—Gog and Magog[r]—to gather them for battle.[s] In number they are like the sand on the seashore.[t] 9 They marched across the breadth of the earth and surrounded[u] the camp of God's people, the city he loves. But fire came down from heaven[v] and devoured them. 10 And the devil, who deceived them,[w] was thrown into the lake of burning sulphur, where the beast and the false prophet had been thrown. They will be tormented day and night for ever and ever.[x]

The Dead Are Judged

11 Then I saw a great white throne[y] and him who was seated on it. Earth and sky fled from his presence, and there was no place for them. 12 And I saw the dead, great and small, standing before the throne, and books were opened.[z] Another book was opened, which is the book of life.[a] The dead were judged according to what they had done[b] as recorded in the books. 13 The sea gave up the dead that were in it, and death and Hades[c] gave up the dead[d] that were in them, and each person was judged according to what he had done. 14 Then death[e] and Hades were thrown into the lake of fire. The lake of fire is the second death. 15 If anyone's name was not found written in the book of life,[f] he was thrown into the lake of fire.

The New Jerusalem

21 Then I saw a new heaven and a new earth,[a] for the first heaven and the first earth had passed away, and there was no longer any sea. 2 I saw the Holy City, the new Jerusalem, coming down out of heaven from God,[b] prepared as a bride beautifully dressed for her husband. 3 And I heard a loud voice from the throne saying, "Now the dwelling of God is with men, and he will live with them. They will be his people, and God himself will be with them and be their God.[c] 4 He will wipe every tear from their eyes.[d] There will be no more death[e] or mourning or crying or pain,[f] for the old order of things has passed away."

5 He who was seated on the throne[g] said, "I am making everything new!" Then he said, "Write this down, for these words are trustworthy and true."[h]

6 He said to me: "It is done.[i] I am the Alpha and the Omega,[j] the Beginning and the End. To him who is thirsty I will give to drink without cost from the spring of the water of life.[k] 7 He who overcomes will inherit all this, and I will be his God and he will be my son. 8 But the cowardly, the unbelieving, the vile, the murderers, the sexually immoral, those who practise magic arts, the idolaters and all liars[l]—their place will be in the fiery lake of burning sulphur. This is the second death."[m]

9 One of the seven angels who had the seven bowls full of the seven last plagues[n] came and said to me, "Come, I will show you the bride,[o] the wife of the Lamb." 10 And he carried me away[p] in the Spirit[q] to a mountain great and high, and showed me the Holy City, Jerusalem, coming down out of heaven from God. 11 It shone with the glory of God,[r] and its brilliance was like that of a very precious jewel, like a jasper, clear as crystal.[s] 12 It had a great, high wall with twelve gates, and with twelve angels at the gates. On the gates were written the names of the twelve tribes of Israel.[t] 13 There were three gates on

20:6 o ver 4
20:7 p ver 2
20:8 q ver 3,10; r Eze 38:2; Eze 39:1; s Rev 16:14; t Heb 11:12
20:9 u Eze 38:9,16; v Eze 38:22; Eze 39:6
20:10 w Rev 19:20; x Rev 14:10,11
20:11 y Rev 4:2
20:12 z Da 7:10; a Rev 3:5; b Jer 17:10; Mt 16:27; Rev 2:23
20:13 c Rev 6:8; d Isa 26:19
20:14 e 1Co 15:26
20:15 f ver 12
21:1 a Isa 65:17; 2Pe 3:13
21:2 b Heb 11:10; Heb 12:22; Rev 3:12
21:3 c 2Co 6:16
21:4 d Rev 7:17; e 1Co 15:26; Rev 20:14; f Isa 35:10; Isa 65:19
21:5 g Rev 4:9; Rev 20:11; h Rev 19:9
21:6 i Rev 16:17; j Rev 1:8; Rev 22:13; k Jn 4:10
21:8 l 1Co 6:9; m Rev 2:11
21:9 n Rev 15:1,6,7; o Rev 19:7
21:10 p Rev 17:3; q Rev 1:10
21:11 r Rev 15:8; Rev 22:5; s Rev 4:6
21:12 t Eze 48:30-34

the east, three on the north, three on the south and three on the west. 14 The wall of the city had twelve foundations, and on them were the names of the twelve apostles of the Lamb.

15 The angel who talked with me had a measuring rod[u] of gold to measure the city, its gates and its walls. 16 The city was laid out like a square, as long as it was wide. He measured the city with the rod and found it to be 12,000 stadia[a] in length, and as wide and high as it is long. 17 He measured its wall and it was 144 cubits[b] thick,[c] by man's measurement, which the angel was using. 18 The wall was made of jasper,[v] and the city of pure gold, as pure as glass.[w] 19 The foundations of the city walls were decorated with every kind of precious stone.[x] The first foundation was jasper, the second sapphire, the third chalcedony, the fourth emerald, 20 the fifth sardonyx, the sixth carnelian,[y] the seventh chrysolite, the eighth beryl, the ninth topaz, the tenth chrysoprase, the eleventh jacinth, and the twelfth amethyst.[d] 21 The twelve gates were twelve pearls, each gate made of a single pearl. The great street of the city was of pure gold, like transparent glass.[z]

22 I did not see a temple[a] in the city, because the Lord God Almighty[b] and the Lamb[c] are its temple. 23 The city does not need the sun or the moon to shine on it, for the glory of God gives it light,[d] and the Lamb is its lamp. 24 The nations will walk by its light, and the kings of the earth will bring their splendour into it.[e] 25 On no day will its gates ever be shut,[f] for there will be no night there.[g] 26 The glory and honour of the nations will be brought into it. 27 Nothing impure will ever enter it, nor will anyone who does what is shameful or deceitful,[h] but only those whose names are written in the Lamb's book of life.

21:15
u Rev 11:1

21:18
v ver 11
w ver 21

21:19
x Isa 54:11,12

21:20
y Rev 4:3

21:21
z ver 18

21:22
a Jn 4:21,23
b Rev 1:8
c Rev 5:6

21:23
d Isa 24:23
Isa 60:19,20
Rev 22:5

21:24
e Isa 60:3,5

21:25
f Isa 60:11
g Zec 14:7
Rev 22:5

21:27
h Isa 52:1
Joel 3:17
Rev 22:14,15

22:1
a Rev 4:6
b Eze 47:1
Zec 14:8

22:2
c Rev 2:7
d Eze 47:12

22:3
e Zec 14:11
f Rev 7:15

22:4
g Mt 5:8
h Rev 14:1

22:5
i Rev 21:25
j Rev 21:23
k Da 7:27
Rev 20:4

22:6
l Rev 1:1
m Rev 19:9
Rev 21:5
n Heb 12:9
o ver 16

22:7
p Rev 3:11
q Rev 1:3

22:8
r Rev 1:1
s Rev 19:10

22:9
t ver 10,18,19
u Rev 19:10

22:10
v Da 8:26
Rev 10:4

The River of Life

22 Then the angel showed me the river of the water of life, as clear as crystal,[a] flowing[b] from the throne of God and of the Lamb 2 down the middle of the great street of the city. On each side of the river stood the tree of life,[c] bearing twelve crops of fruit, yielding its fruit every month. And the leaves of the tree are for the healing of the nations.[d] 3 No longer will there be any curse.[e] The throne of God and of the Lamb will be in the city, and his servants will serve him.[f] 4 They will see his face,[g] and his name will be on their foreheads.[h] 5 There will be no more night.[i] They will not need the light of a lamp or the light of the sun, for the Lord God will give them light.[j] And they will reign for ever and ever.[k]

6 The angel said to me,[l] "These words are trustworthy and true.[m] The Lord, the God of the spirits of the prophets,[n] sent his angel[o] to show his servants the things that must soon take place."

Jesus Is Coming

7 "Behold, I am coming soon![p] Blessed[q] is he who keeps the words of the prophecy in this book."

8 I, John, am the one who heard and saw these things.[r] And when I had heard and seen them, I fell down to worship at the feet[s] of the angel who had been showing them to me. 9 But he said to me, "Do not do it! I am a fellow-servant with you and with your brothers the prophets and of all who keep the words of this book.[t] Worship God!"[u]

10 Then he told me, "Do not seal up[v] the words of the prophecy of

[a] *16* That is, about 1,400 miles (about 2,200 kilometres) [b] *17* That is, about 200 feet (about 65 metres) [c] *17* Or *high* [d] *20* The precise identification of some of these precious stones is uncertain.

this book, because the time is near.[w] 11Let him who does wrong continue to do wrong; let him who is vile continue to be vile; let him who does right continue to do right; and let him who is holy continue to be holy."[x]

12"Behold, I am coming soon![y] My reward is with me,[z] and I will give to everyone according to what he has done. 13I am the Alpha and the Omega,[a] the First and the Last,[b] the Beginning and the End.[c]

14"Blessed are those who wash their robes, that they may have the right to the tree of life[d] and may go through the gates[e] into the city.[f] 15Outside[g] are the dogs,[h] those who practise magic arts, the sexually immoral, the murderers, the idolaters and everyone who loves and practises falsehood.

16"I, Jesus,[i] have sent my angel to give you[a] this testimony for the churches.[j] I am the Root[k] and the Offspring of David, and the bright Morning Star."[l]

17The Spirit[m] and the bride say, "Come!" And let him who hears say, "Come!" Whoever is thirsty, let him come; and whoever wishes, let him take the free gift of the water of life.

18I warn everyone who hears the words of the prophecy of this book: If anyone adds anything to them,[n] God will add to him the plagues described in this book.[o] 19And if anyone takes words away[p] from this book of prophecy, God will take away from him his share in the tree of life and in the holy city, which are described in this book.

20He who testifies to these things[q] says, "Yes, I am coming soon."

Amen. Come, Lord Jesus.[r]

21The grace of the Lord Jesus be with God's people.[s] Amen.

22:10 w Rev 1:3
22:11 x Eze 3:27; Da 12:10
22:12 y ver 7,20; z Isa 40:10
22:13 a Rev 1:8; b Rev 1:17; c Rev 21:6
22:14 d Rev 2:7; e Rev 21:12; f Rev 21:27
22:15 g 1Co 6:9,10; Gal 5:19-21; Col 3:5,6; h Php 3:2
22:16 i Rev 1:1; j Rev 1:4; k Rev 5:5; l 2Pe 1:19; Rev 2:28
22:17 m Rev 2:7
22:18 n Dt 4:2; Pr 30:6; o Rev 15:6-16:21
22:19 p Dt 4:2
22:20 q Rev 1:2 r 1Co 16:22 **22:21** s Ro 16:20

a16 The Greek is plural.

TABLE OF WEIGHTS AND MEASURES

	Approximate Biblical Unit	*Approximate Imperial Unit*	*Metric Equivalent*
Weights			
talent	60 minas	75 pounds	34 kilograms
mina	50 shekels	1¼ pounds	0.6 kilogram
shekel	2 bekas	⅖ ounce	11.5 grams
pim	⅔ shekel	¼ ounce	7.7 grams
beka	10 gerahs	⅕ ounce	5.8 grams
gerah		1/50 ounce	0.6 gram
Length			
cubit		18 inches	0.5 metre
span		9 inches	23 centimetres
handbreadth		3 inches	8 centimetres
Capacity: Dry Measure			
cor [homer]	10 ephahs	6 bushels	220 litres
lethek	5 ephahs	3 bushels	110 litres
ephah	10 omers	⅗ bushel	22 litres
seah	⅓ ephah	13 pints	7.3 litres
omer	1/10 ephah	4 pints	2 litres
cab	1/18 ephah	2 pints	1 litre
Capacity: Liquid Measure			
bath	1 ephah	5 gallons	22 litres
hin	⅙ bath	7 pints	4 litres
log	1/72 bath	½ pint	0.3 litre

The figures of the table are calculated on the basis of a shekel equalling 11.5 grams, a cubit equalling 18 inches and an ephah equalling 22 litres. It is based upon the best available information, but it is not intended to be mathematically precise; like the measurement equivalents in the footnotes, it merely gives approximate amounts and distances. Weights and measures differed somewhat at various times and places in the ancient world. There is uncertainty particularly about the ephah and the bath; further discoveries may give more light on these units of capacity.

INDEX TO MAPS

Many places in the Bible were known by different names at different times or in different languages. Alternative names are given in brackets after the main entries. Place names for which the geographical locations are uncertain are followed by a question mark.

Each place name in the index is followed by a map number and a letter. On the map referred to, the letter can be found at the top of the map frame. The place can be found vertically below the letter.

Map 1 The World of the Bible

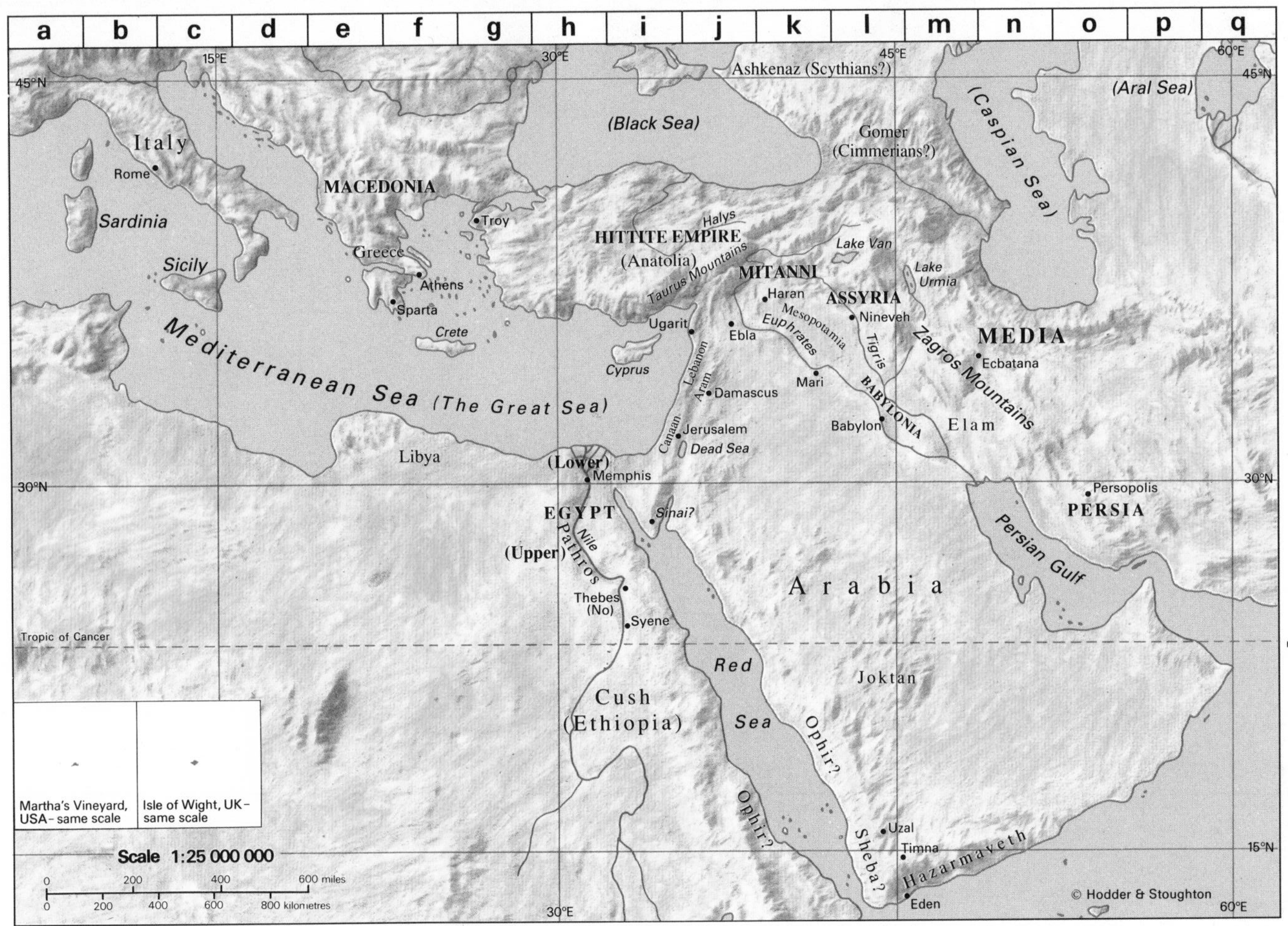

Map 2 The World of the Old Testament

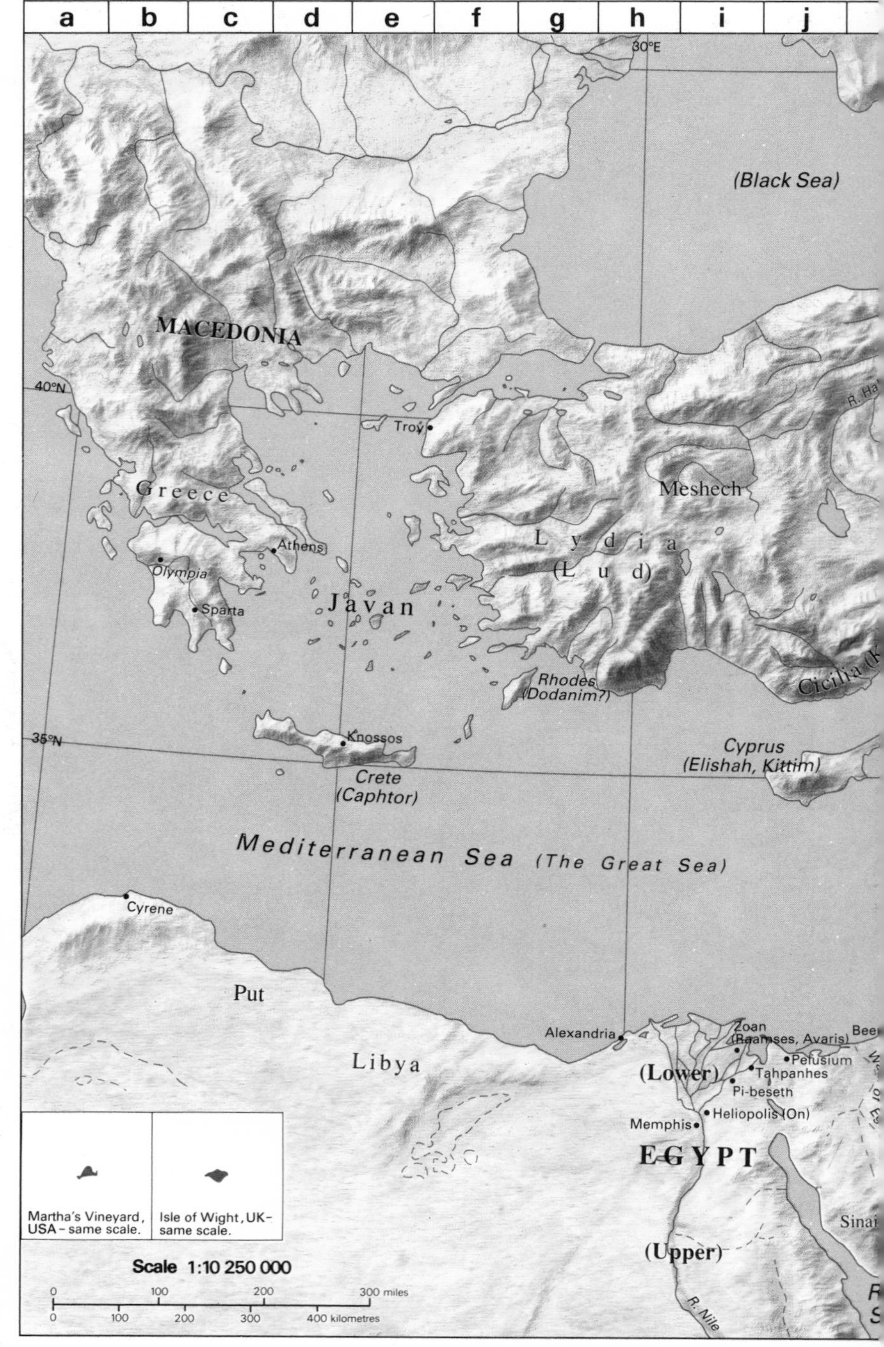

a
b
c
d
e
f
g
h
i
j
30°E
(Black Sea)
MACEDONIA
40°N
Troy
Greece
Meshech
Athens
Olympia
Lydia
(Lud)
Sparta
Javan
Rhodes
(Dodanim?)
Cilicia
35°N
Knossos
Cyprus
(Elishah, Kittim)
Crete
(Caphtor)
Mediterranean Sea (The Great Sea)
Cyrene
Put
Alexandria
Zoan
(Raamses, Avaris)
Pelusium
Tahpanhes
Libya
(Lower)
Pi-beseth
Heliopolis (On)
Memphis
EGYPT
Martha's Vineyard, USA – same scale.
Isle of Wight, UK – same scale.
Sinai
(Upper)
Scale 1:10 250 000
0
100
200
300 miles
0
100
200
300
400 kilometres
R. Nile

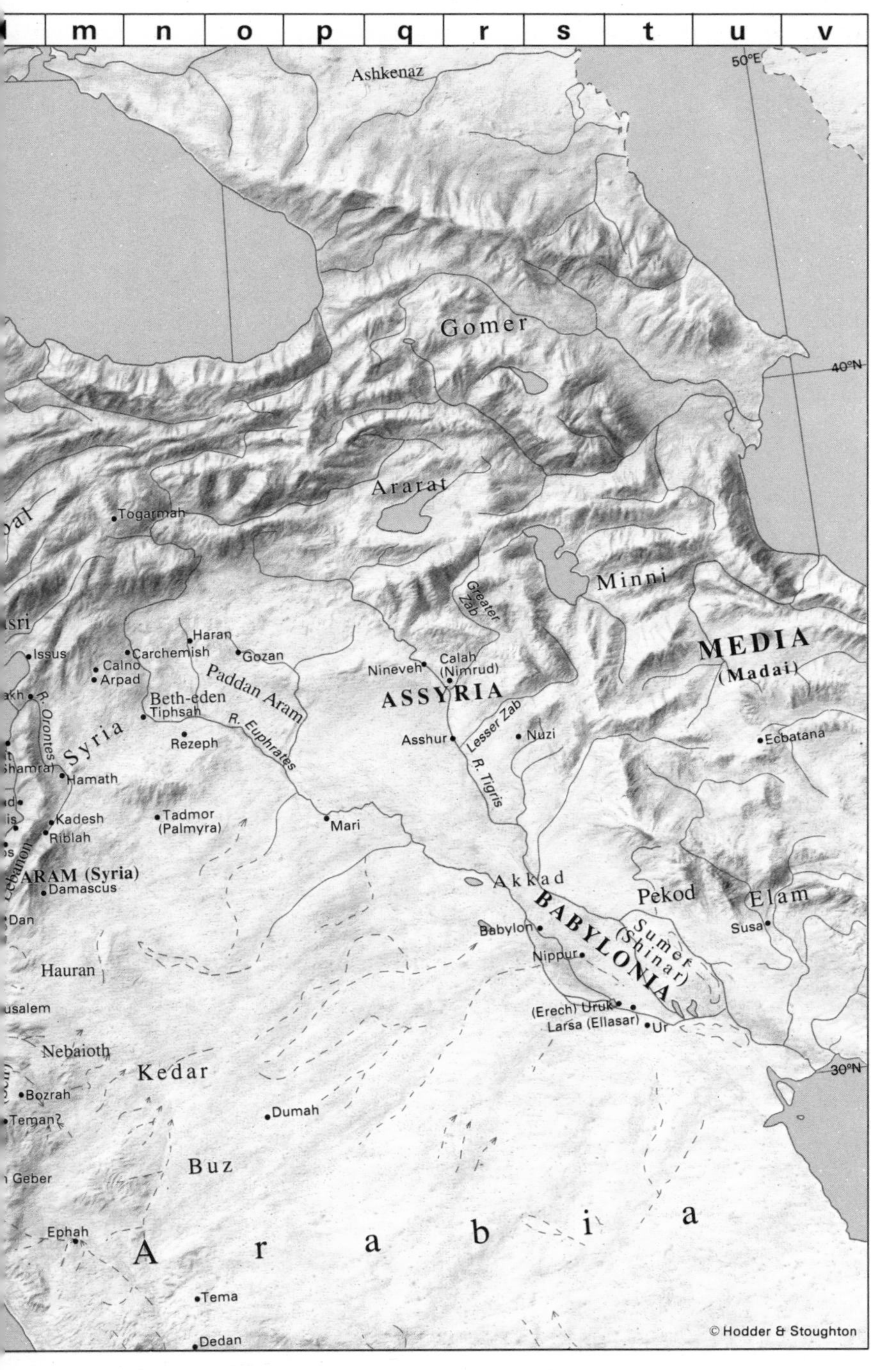
m
n
o
p
q
r
s
t
u
v
Ashkenaz
50°E
Gomer
40°N
Ararat
Togarmah
Minni
Greater Zab
Haran
Issus
Calno
Carchemish
Gozan
Arpad
Nineveh
Calah (Nimrud)
MEDIA (Madai)
Paddan Aram
Beth-eden
Tiphsah
ASSYRIA
R. Orontes
R. Euphrates
Lesser Zab
Syria
Rezeph
Asshur
Nuzi
Ecbatana
Hamath
R. Tigris
Tadmor (Palmyra)
Kadesh
Riblah
Mari
ARAM (Syria)
Damascus
Akkad
Pekod
Elam
BABYLONIA
Dan
Babylon
Sumer (Shinar)
Susa
Nippur
Hauran
(Erech) Uruk
Larsa (Ellasar)
Ur
Nebaioth
Kedar
30°N
Bozrah
Teman?
Dumah
Buz
Arabia
Ephah
Tema
Dedan
© Hodder & Stoughton

Map 3 Abraham to Joseph

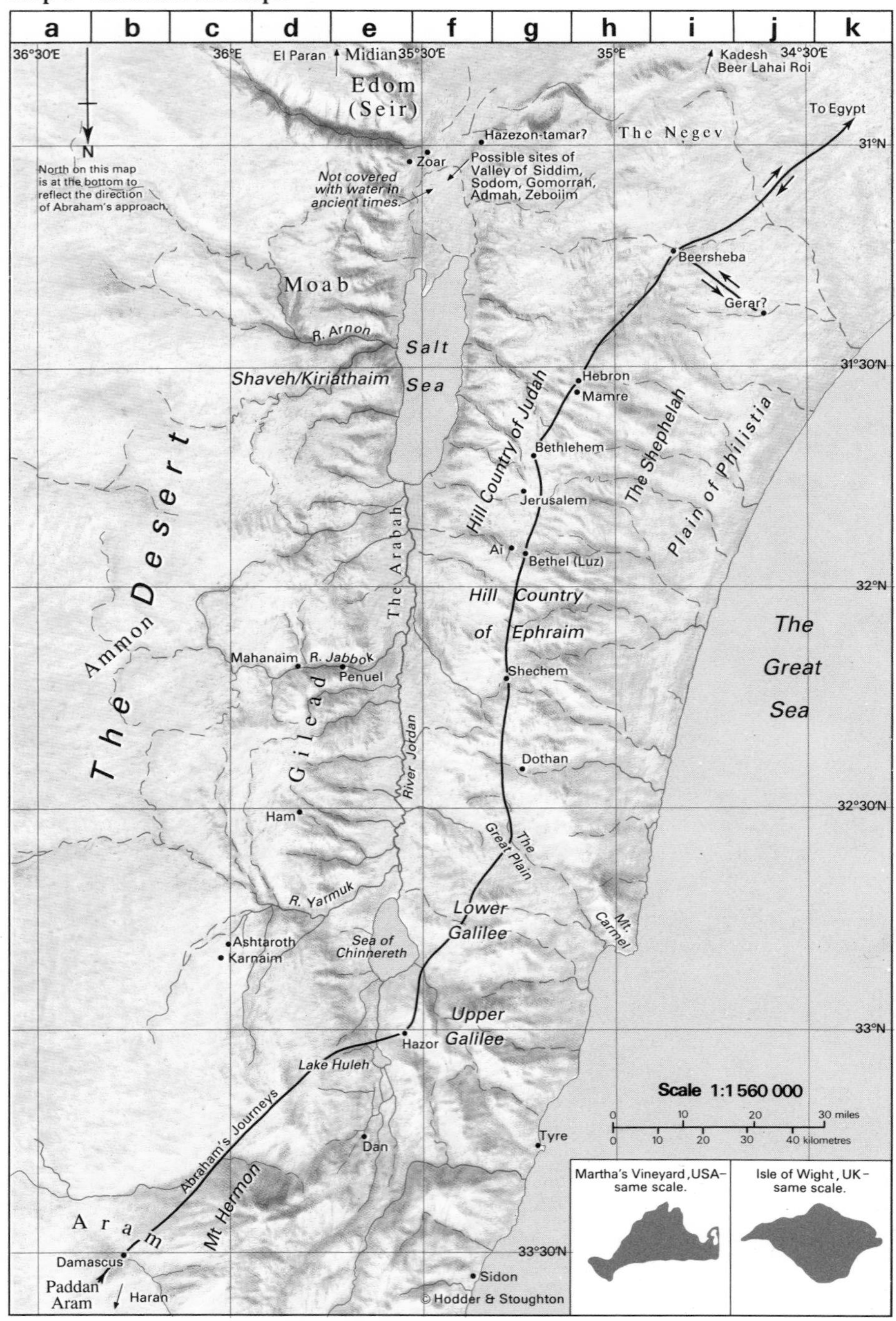

a
b
c
d
e
f
g
h
i
j
k
36°30'E
36°E
El Paran
Midian
35°30'E
35°E
Kadesh
Beer Lahai Roi
34°30'E
Edom
(Seir)
To Egypt
Hazezon-tamar?
The Negev
31°N
N
North on this map is at the bottom to reflect the direction of Abraham's approach.
Zoar
Not covered with water in ancient times.
Possible sites of Valley of Siddim, Sodom, Gomorrah, Admah, Zeboiim
Beersheba
Moab
Gerar?
R. Arnon
Salt Sea
31°30'N
Shaveh/Kiriathaim
Hebron
Mamre
Hill Country of Judah
The Shephelah
Plain of Philistia
Bethlehem
The Desert
Jerusalem
The Arabah
Ai
Bethel (Luz)
32°N
Hill Country of Ephraim
The Great Sea
Ammon
Mahanaim
R. Jabbok
Penuel
Shechem
Gilead
River Jordan
Dothan
Ham
32°30'N
The Great Plain
R. Yarmuk
Lower Galilee
Mt. Carmel
Ashtaroth
Karnaim
Sea of Chinnereth
Upper Galilee
33°N
Hazor
Lake Huleh
Scale 1:1 560 000
0
10
20
30 miles
0
10
20
30
40 kilometres
Abraham's Journeys
Dan
Tyre
Mt Hermon
Martha's Vineyard, USA–same scale.
Isle of Wight, UK–same scale.
Aram
33°30'N
Damascus
Sidon
Paddan Aram
Haran
© Hodder & Stoughton

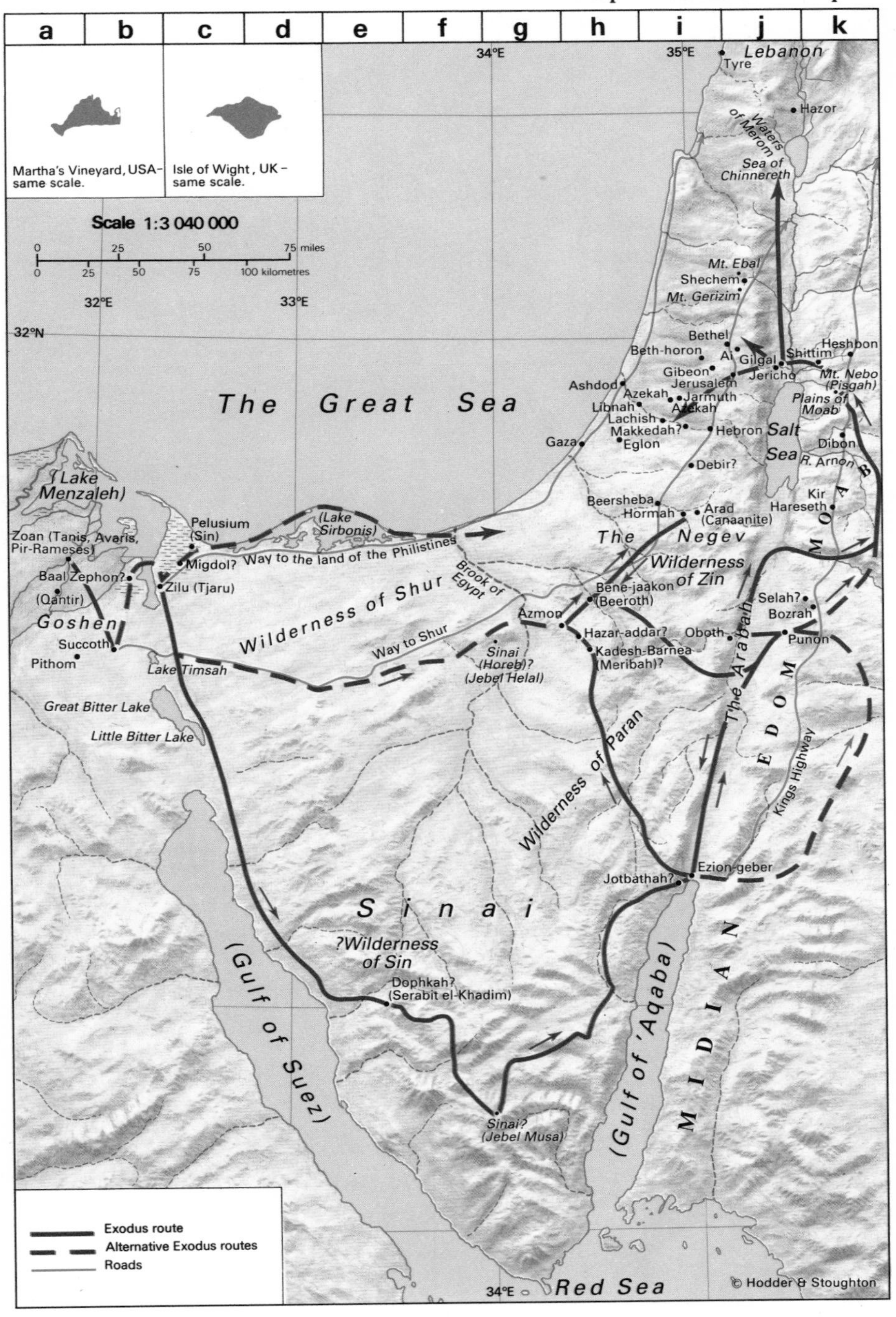

a b c d e f g h i j k
34°E
35°E
Lebanon
Tyre
Hazor
Waters of Merom
Sea of Chinnereth
Martha's Vineyard, USA – same scale.
Isle of Wight, UK – same scale.
Scale 1:3 040 000
0 25 50 75 miles
0 25 50 75 100 kilometres
32°E
33°E
32°N
Mt. Ebal
Shechem
Mt. Gerizim
Bethel
Beth-horon
Ai
Gilgal
Shittim
Heshbon
Gibeon
Jericho
Mt. Nebo (Pisgah)
Jerusalem
Ashdod
Azekah
Jarmuth
Plains of Moab
The Great Sea
Libnah
Azekah
Lachish
Makkedah?
Hebron
Salt Sea
Gaza
Eglon
Dibon
Debir?
R. Arnon
(Lake Menzaleh)
Kir Hareseth
Beersheba
Hormah
Arad (Canaanite)
Pelusium (Sin)
(Lake Sirbonis)
MOAB
Zoan (Tanis, Avaris, Pir-Rameses)
The Negev
Migdol?
Way to the land of the Philistines
Wilderness of Zin
Baal Zephon?
Brook of Egypt
Zilu (Tjaru)
Bene-jaakon (Beeroth)
(Qantir)
Wilderness of Shur
Selah?
Goshen
Azmon
Bozrah
Hazar-addar?
Oboth
Punon
Succoth
Way to Shur
Kadesh-Barnea (Meribah)?
Pithom
Sinai (Horeb)? (Jebel Helal)
Lake Timsah
The Arabah
Great Bitter Lake
EDOM
Little Bitter Lake
Wilderness of Paran
Kings Highway
Ezion-geber
Jotbathah?
Sinai
?Wilderness of Sin
MIDIAN
(Gulf of Suez)
Dophkah? (Serabit el-Khadim)
(Gulf of 'Aqaba)
Sinai? (Jebel Musa)
Exodus route
Alternative Exodus routes
Roads
34°E
Red Sea
© Hodder & Stoughton

Map 5 Palestine before the Monarchy

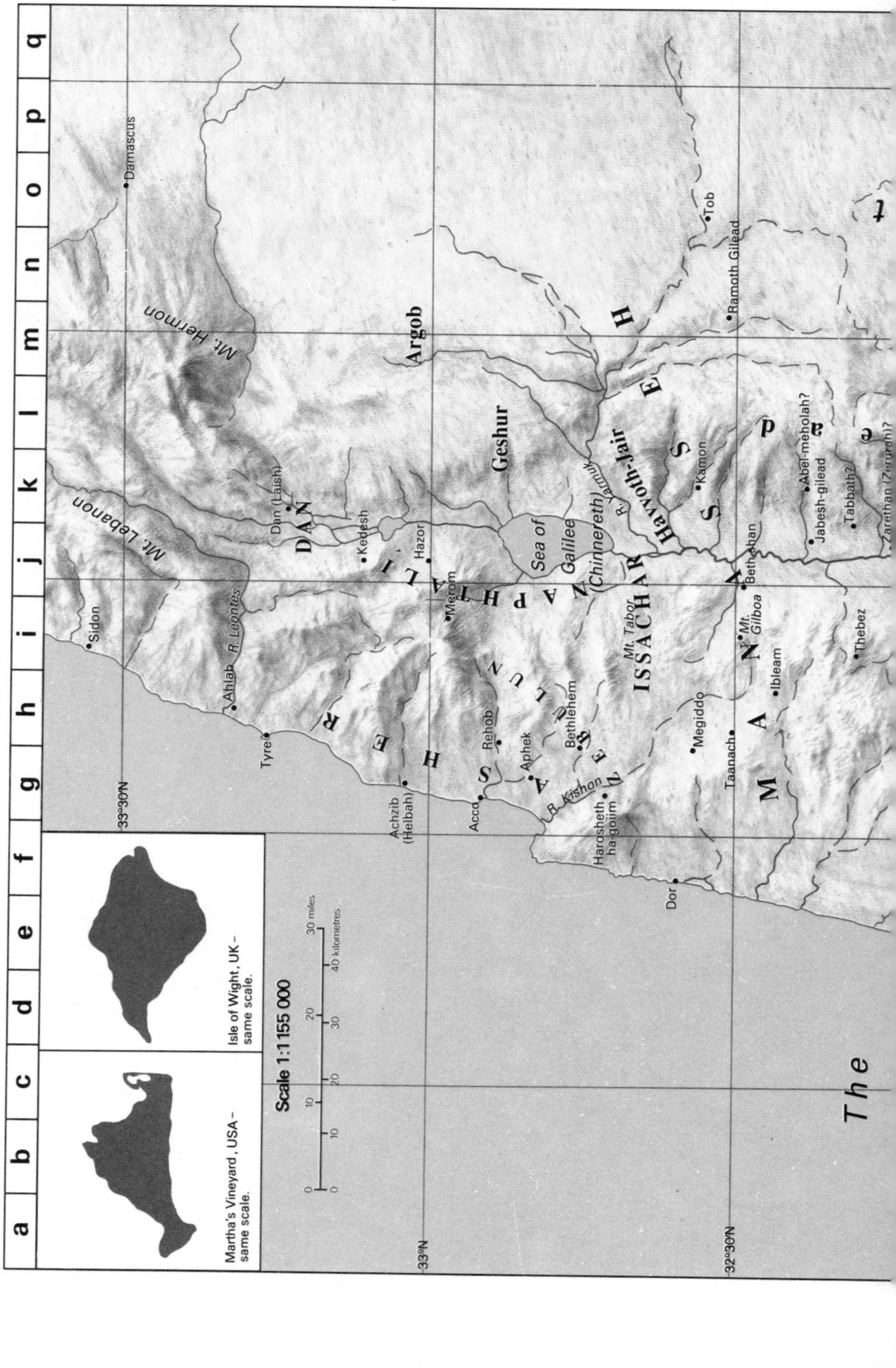

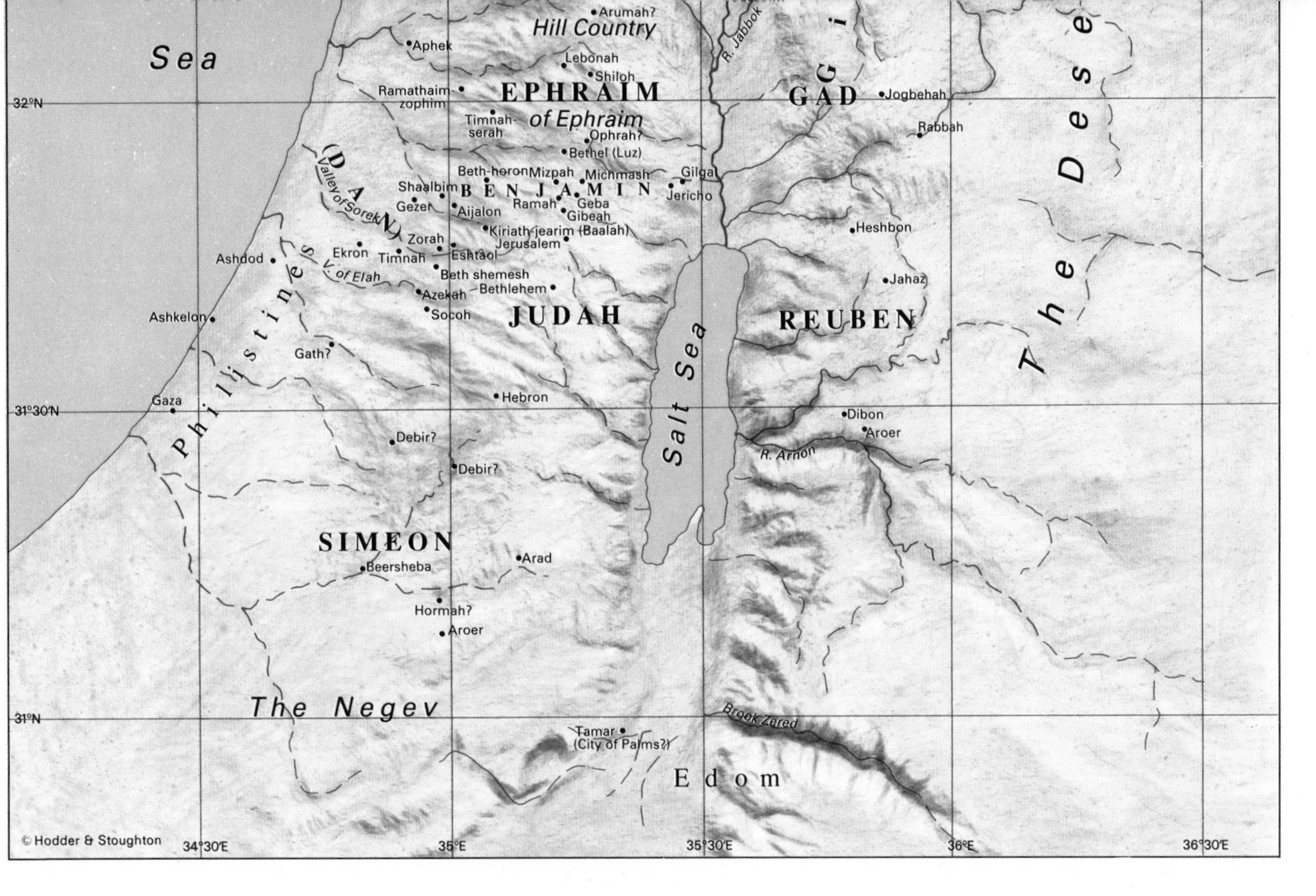

Sea
Arumah?
Hill Country
Aphek
Lebonah
Shiloh
Ramathaim-zophim
EPHRAIM
Timnah-serah
of Ephraim
Ophrah?
Bethel (Luz)
Beth-horon
Mizpah
Michmash
Gilgal
Jericho
Shaalbim
BENJAMIN
Gezer
Aijalon
Ramah
Geba
Gibeah
(DAN)
Valley of Sorek
Kiriath-jearim (Baalah)
Jerusalem
Zorah
Eshtaol
Ekron
Timnah
Ashdod
V. of Elah
Beth shemesh
Bethlehem
Azekah
JUDAH
Socoh
Ashkelon
Philistines
Gath?
Hebron
Gaza
Debir?
Debir?
SIMEON
Arad
Beersheba
Hormah?
Aroer
The Negev
Tamar (City of Palms?)
Edom
Salt Sea
R. Jabbok
GAD
Gi
Jogbehah
Rabbah
Heshbon
Jahaz
REUBEN
Dibon
Aroer
R. Arnon
Brook Zered
The Dese
32°N
31°30'N
31°N
34°30'E
35°E
35°30'E
36°E
36°30'E

Map 6 The Kingdoms of Israel and Judah

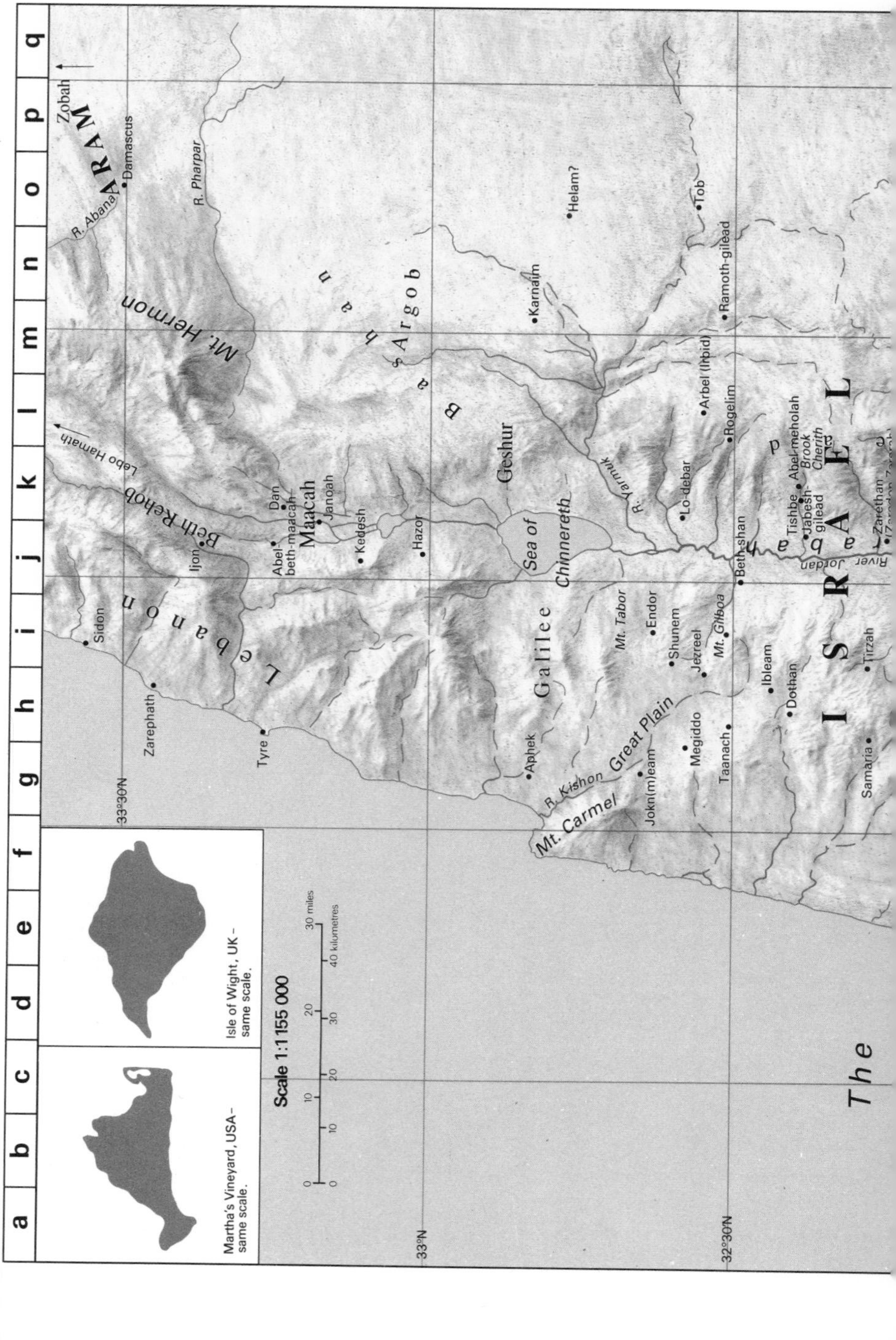

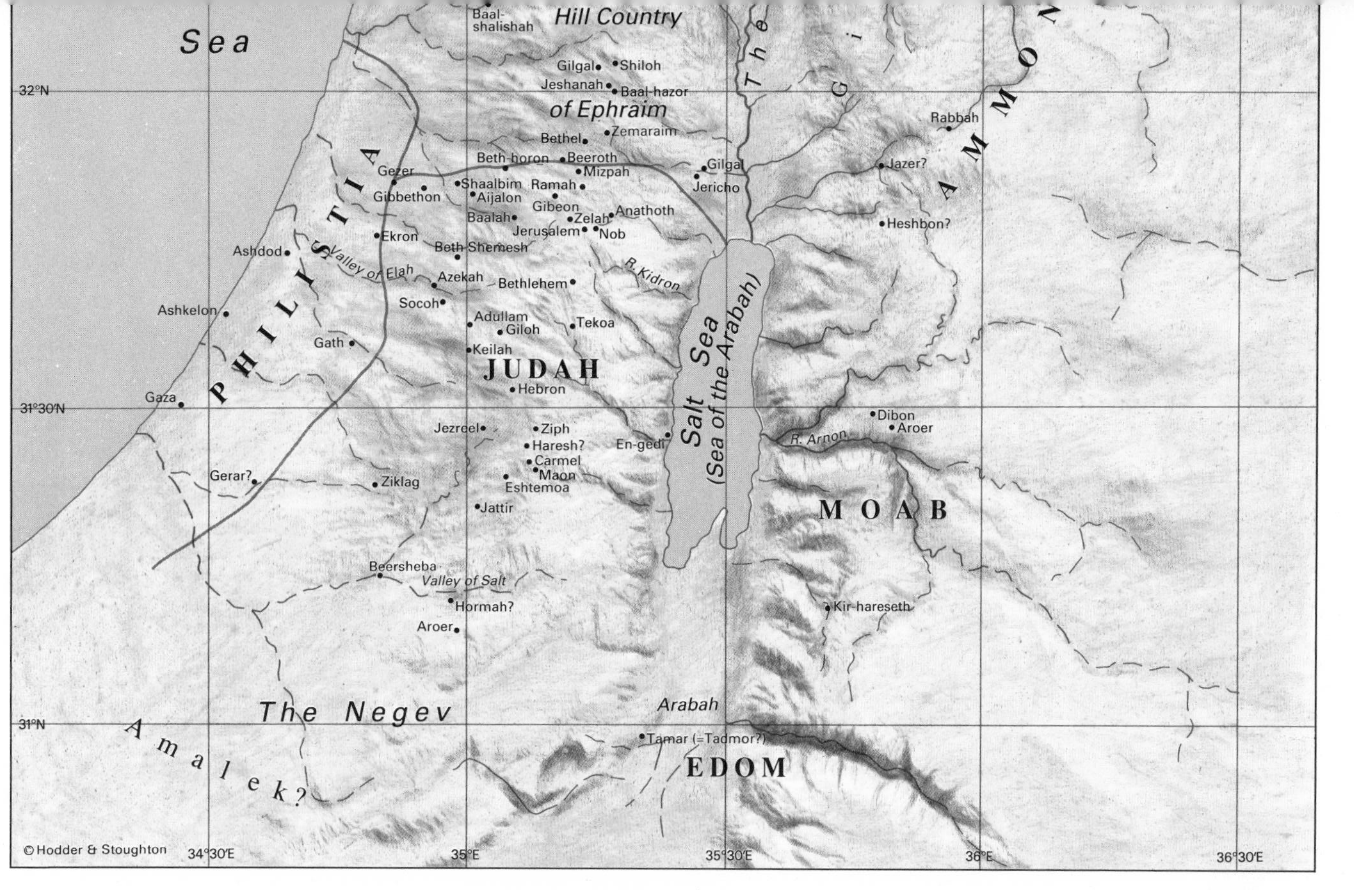

Sea
Baal-shalishah
Hill Country
of Ephraim
Gilgal
Shiloh
Jeshanah
Baal-hazor
Bethel
Zemaraim
Beth-horon
Beeroth
Mizpah
Gilgal
Jericho
Gezer
Gibbethon
Shaalbim
Aijalon
Ramah
Gibeon
Baalah
Zelah
Anathoth
Jerusalem
Nob
Ekron
Beth Shemesh
Ashdod
Valley of Elah
Azekah
Bethlehem
R. Kidron
Ashkelon
Socoh
Adullam
Giloh
Tekoa
Gath
Keilah
PHILISTIA
JUDAH
Hebron
Gaza
Salt Sea
(Sea of the Arabah)
Jezreel
Ziph
Haresh?
Carmel
Maon
Eshtemoa
En-gedi
Gerar?
Ziklag
Jattir
Beersheba
Valley of Salt
Hormah?
Aroer
The Negev
Arabah
Amalek?
Tamar (=Tadmor?)
EDOM
The Gi
AMMON
Rabbah
Jazer?
Heshbon?
Dibon
Aroer
R. Arnon
MOAB
Kir-hareseth
32°N
31°30′N
31°N
34°30′E
35°E
35°30′E
36°E
36°30′E
©Hodder & Stoughton

Map 7 Judah before and after the Exile

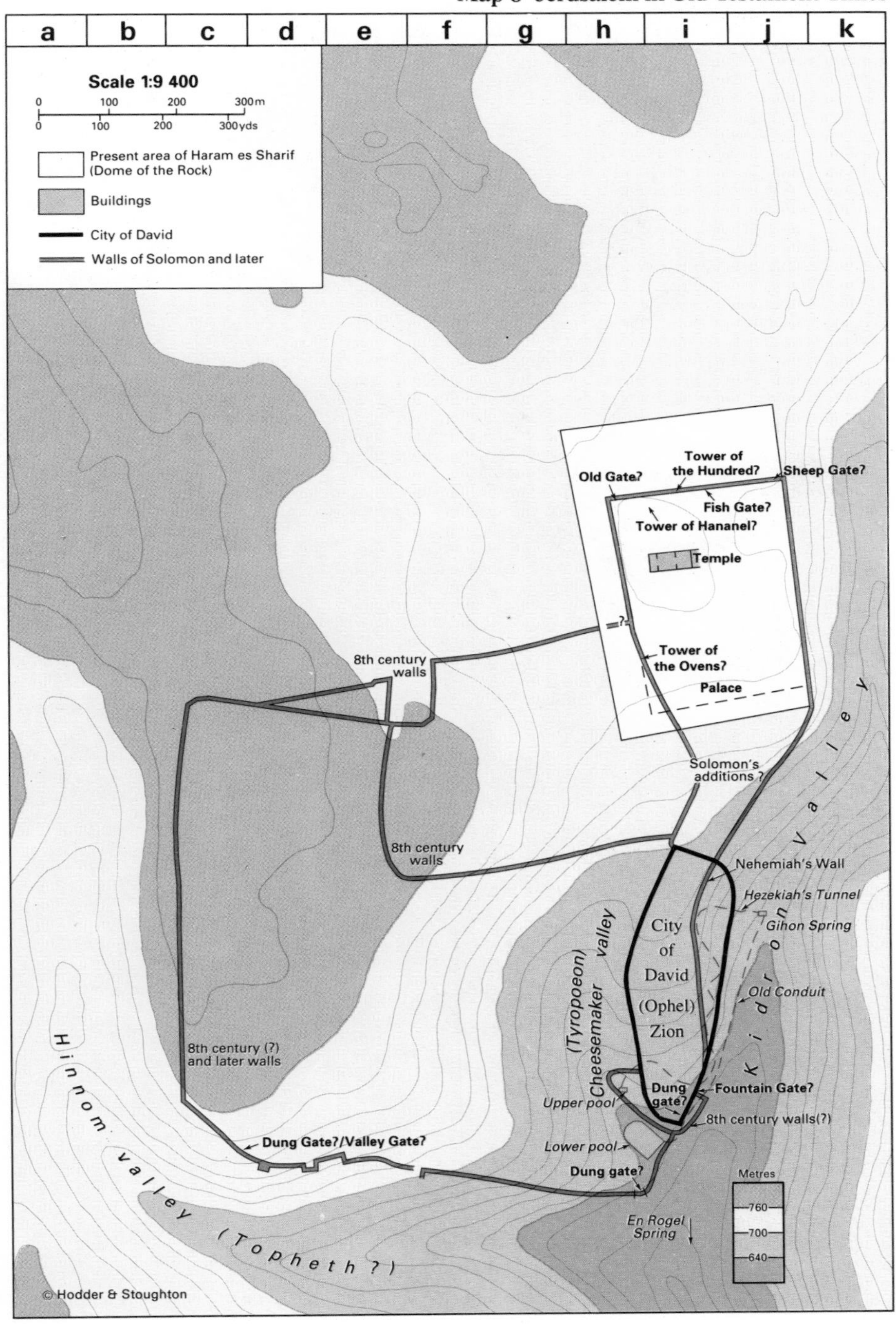
a
b
c
d
e
f
g
h
i
j
k
Scale 1:9 400
0
100
200
300m
0
100
200
300yds
Present area of Haram es Sharif (Dome of the Rock)
Buildings
City of David
Walls of Solomon and later
Tower of the Hundred?
Old Gate?
Sheep Gate?
Fish Gate?
Tower of Hananel?
Temple
Tower of the Ovens?
Palace
8th century walls
Solomon's additions ?
8th century walls
Nehemiah's Wall
Hezekiah's Tunnel
Gihon Spring
City of David (Ophel) Zion
(Tyropoeon) Cheesemaker valley
Kidron Valley
Old Conduit
8th century (?) and later walls
Hinnom valley (Topheth ?)
Dung gate?
Fountain Gate?
Upper pool
8th century walls(?)
Dung Gate?/Valley Gate?
Lower pool
Dung gate?
En Rogel Spring
Metres
760
700
640
© Hodder & Stoughton

Map 9 The World of the New Testament

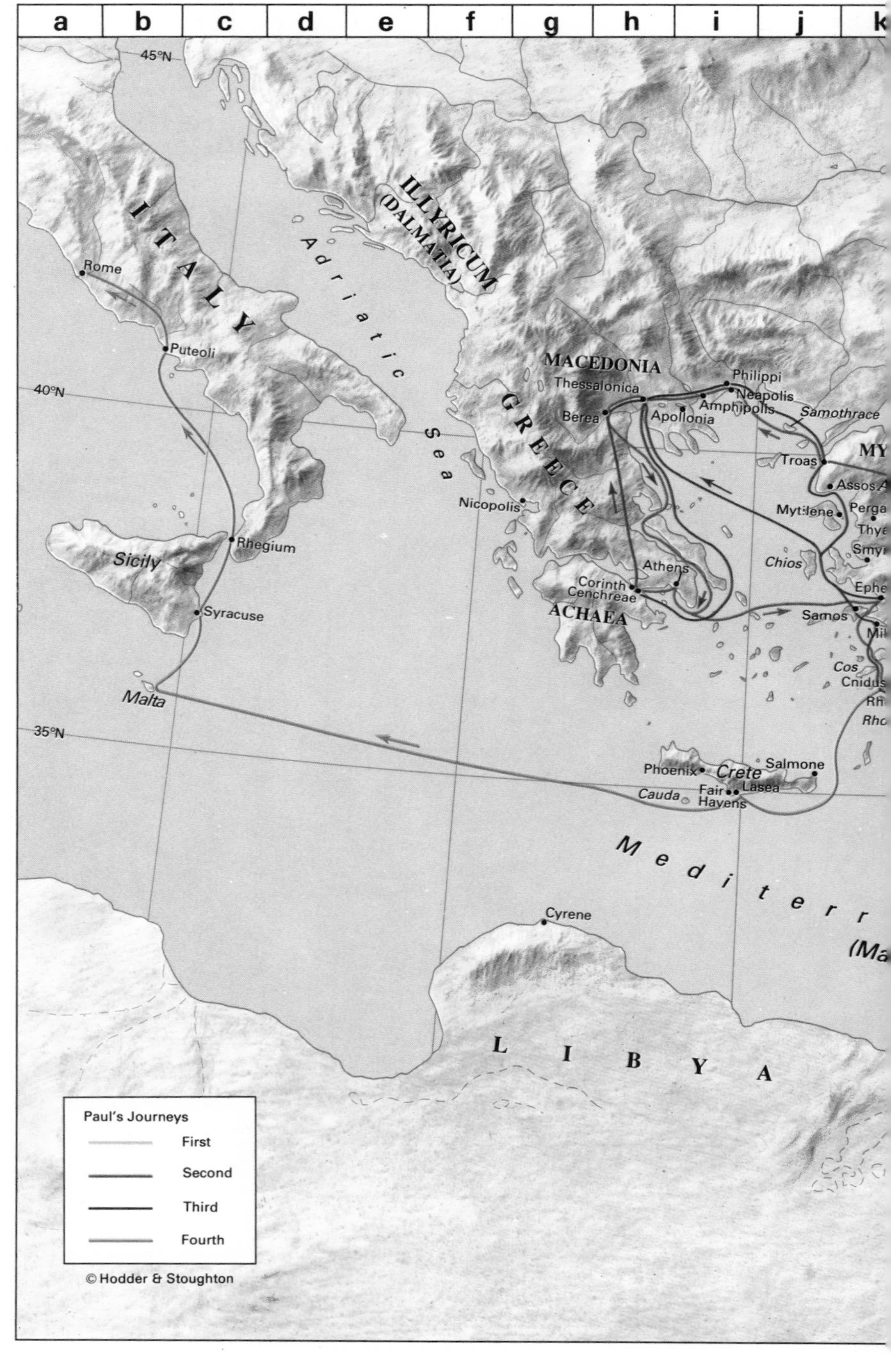

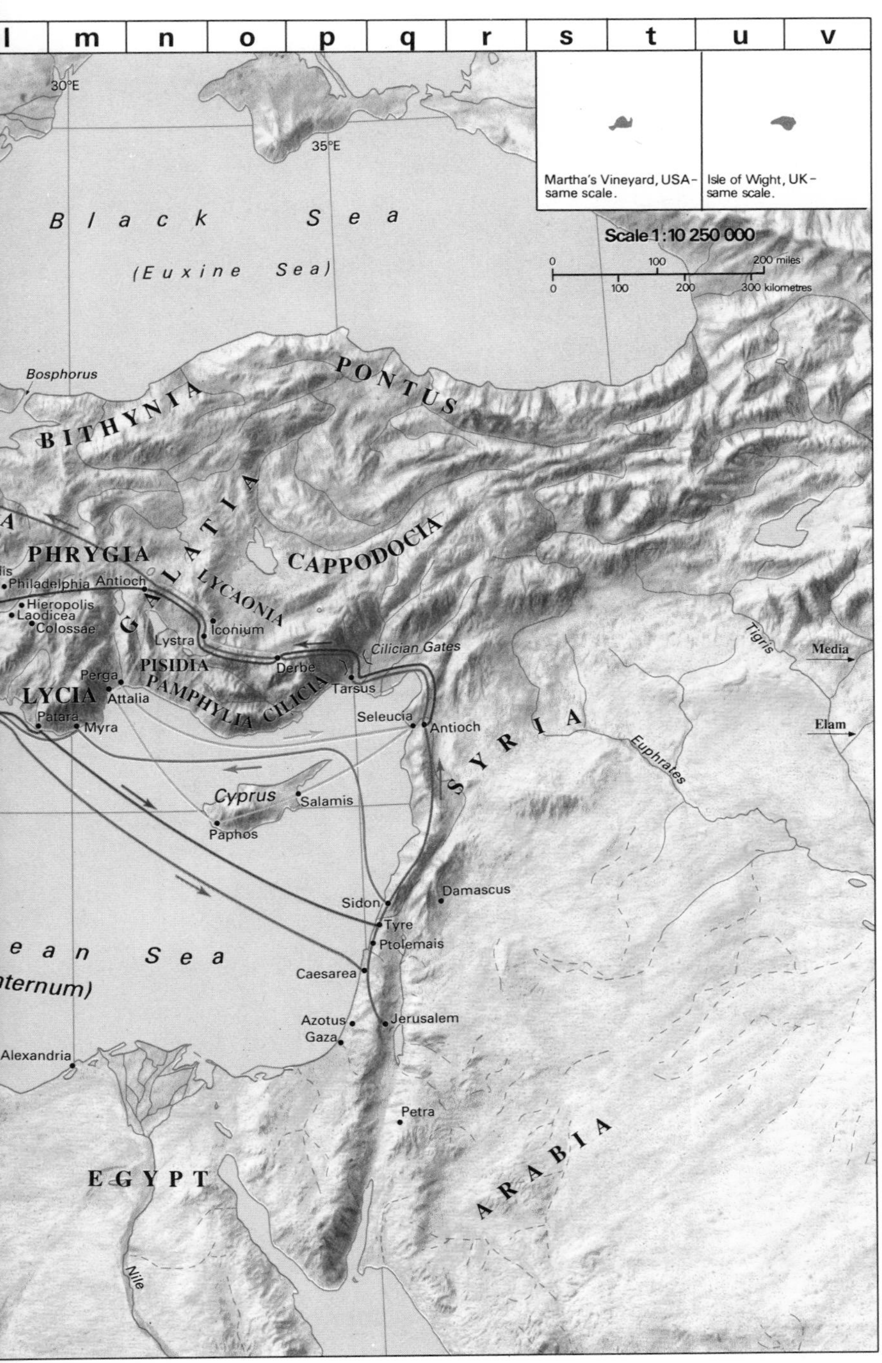

l
m
n
o
p
q
r
s
t
u
v
30°E
35°E
Martha's Vineyard, USA – same scale.
Isle of Wight, UK – same scale.
Black Sea
(Euxine Sea)
Scale 1 : 10 250 000
0
100
200 miles
0
100
200
300 kilometres
Bosphorus
PONTUS
BITHYNIA
GALATIA
PHRYGIA
CAPPODOCIA
Philadelphia
Antioch
Hieropolis
Laodicea
Colossae
LYCAONIA
Iconium
Lystra
Cilician Gates
Tigris
Media
PISIDIA
Derbe
Perga
Tarsus
LYCIA
Attalia
PAMPHYLIA
CILICIA
Patara
Myra
Seleucia
Antioch
SYRIA
Elam
Euphrates
Cyprus
Salamis
Paphos
Damascus
Sidon
Tyre
Ptolemais
ean Sea
nternum)
Caesarea
Azotus
Jerusalem
Gaza
Alexandria
Petra
ARABIA
EGYPT
Nile

Map 10 Palestine in New Testament Times

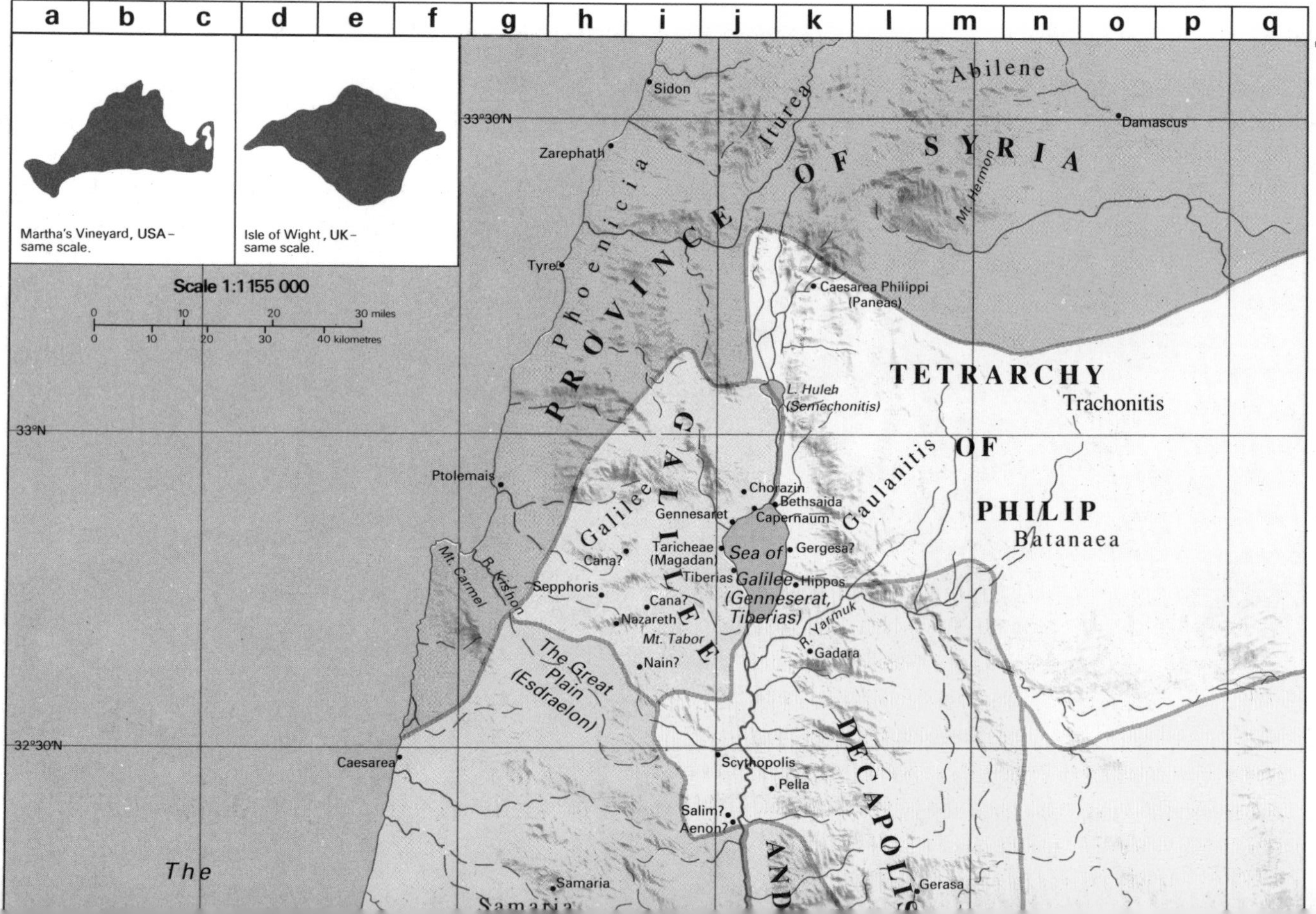

a
b
c
d
e
f
g
h
i
j
k
l
m
n
o
p
q
Martha's Vineyard, USA – same scale.
Isle of Wight, UK – same scale.
Scale 1:1 155 000
0
10
20
30 miles
0
10
20
30
40 kilometres
33°30'N
33°N
32°30'N
Sidon
Abilene
Damascus
Iturea
Zarephath
PROVINCE OF SYRIA
Mt. Hermon
Phoenicia
Tyre
Caesarea Philippi (Paneas)
TETRARCHY OF PHILIP
Trachonitis
Batanaea
L. Huleh (Semechonitis)
Gaulanitis
Ptolemais
GALILEE
Galilee
Chorazin
Bethsaida
Gennesaret
Capernaum
Taricheae (Magadan)
Sea of Galilee (Genneserat, Tiberias)
Gergesa?
Tiberias
Hippos
Cana?
Sepphoris
Cana?
Nazareth
Mt. Tabor
Nain?
R. Yarmuk
Gadara
Mt. Carmel
R. Kishon
The Great Plain (Esdraelon)
Caesarea
Scythopolis
Pella
DECAPOLIS
Salim?
Aenon?
AND
The
Samaria
Gerasa

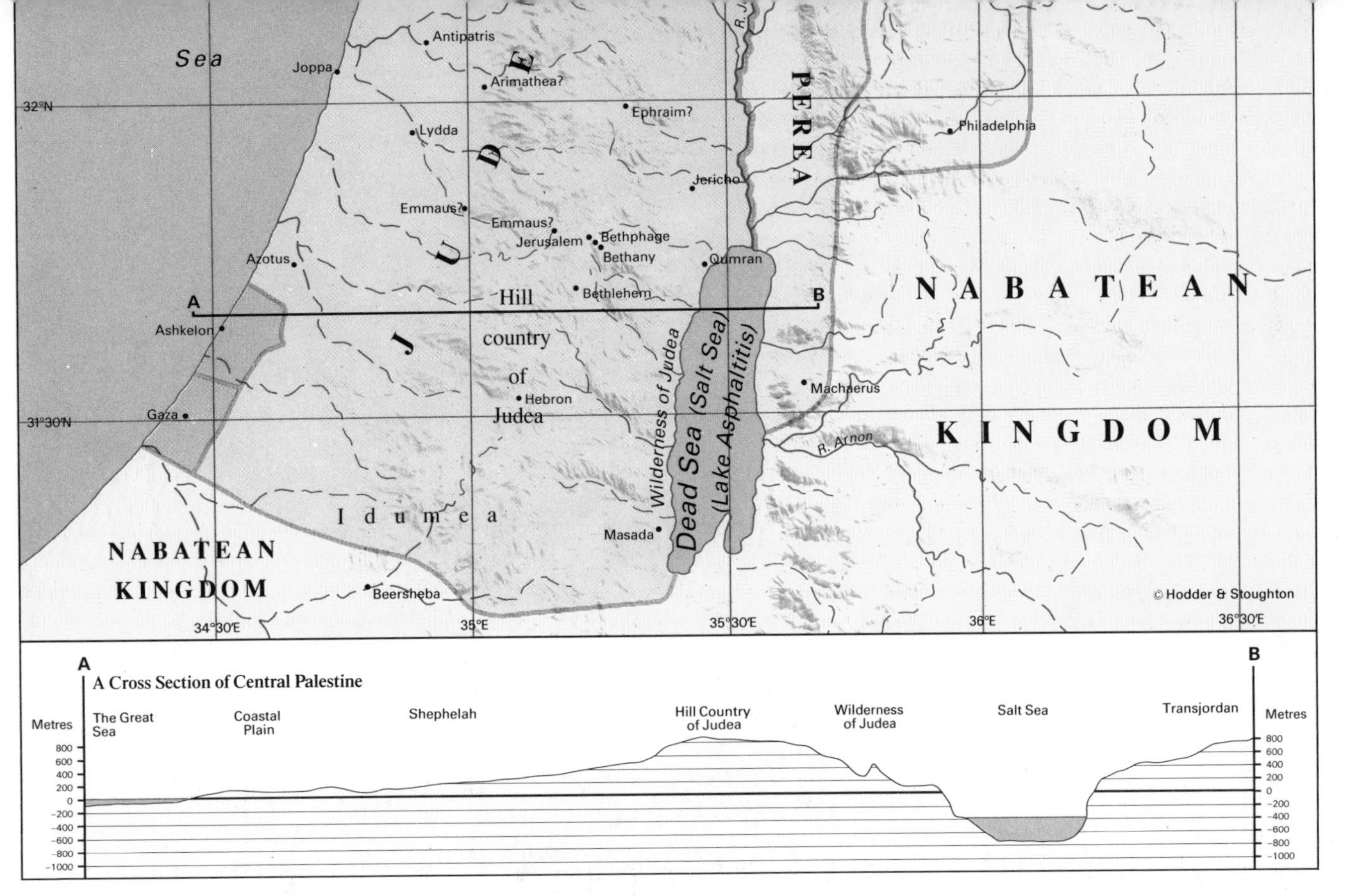

Sea
Joppa
Antipatris
Arimathea?
Ephraim?
Lydda
Philadelphia
J U D E
PEREA
R. J.
Jericho
Emmaus?
Emmaus?
Jerusalem
Bethphage
Bethany
Qumran
Azotus
Bethlehem
A
B
Hill country of Judea
NABATEAN KINGDOM
Ashkelon
Machaerus
Hebron
Gaza
Wilderness of Judea
Dead Sea (Salt Sea)
(Lake Asphaltitis)
R. Arnon
Idumea
Masada
NABATEAN KINGDOM
Beersheba
32°N
31°30'N
34°30'E
35°E
35°30'E
36°E
36°30'E
A Cross Section of Central Palestine
The Great Sea
Coastal Plain
Shephelah
Hill Country of Judea
Wilderness of Judea
Salt Sea
Transjordan
Metres
800
600
400
200
0
−200
−400
−600
−800
−1000

Map 11 Jerusalem in New Testament Times

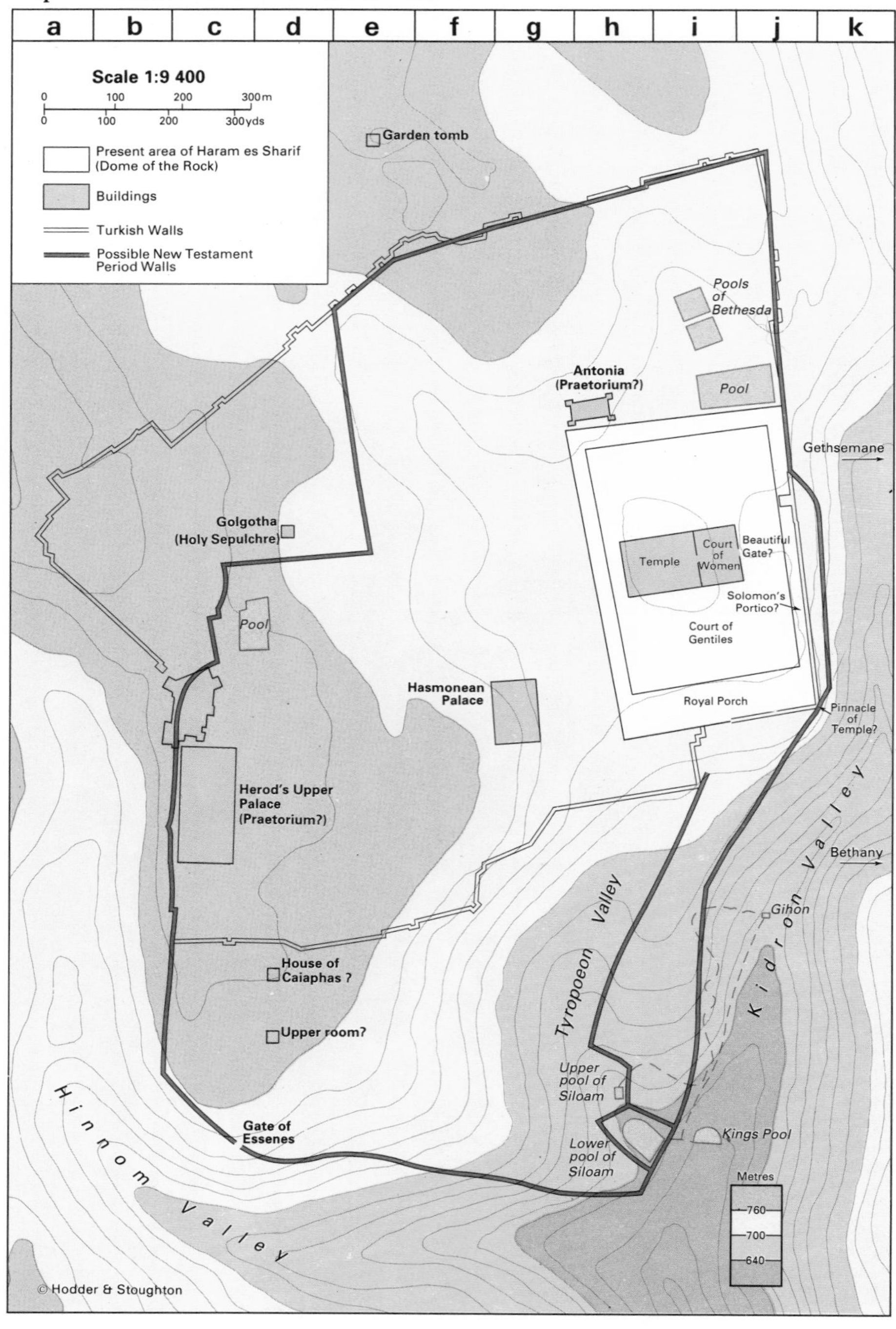

a
b
c
d
e
f
g
h
i
j
k
Scale 1:9 400
0 100 200 300m
0 100 200 300yds
Present area of Haram es Sharif (Dome of the Rock)
Buildings
Turkish Walls
Possible New Testament Period Walls
Garden tomb
Pools of Bethesda
Antonia (Praetorium?)
Pool
Gethsemane
Golgotha (Holy Sepulchre)
Temple
Court of Women
Beautiful Gate?
Solomon's Portico?
Court of Gentiles
Pool
Hasmonean Palace
Royal Porch
Pinnacle of Temple?
Herod's Upper Palace (Praetorium?)
Kidron Valley
Bethany
Tyropoeon Valley
Gihon
House of Caiaphas ?
Upper room?
Upper pool of Siloam
Hinnom Valley
Gate of Essenes
Kings Pool
Lower pool of Siloam
Metres
760
700
640